ROBERTSON DAVIES

The Deptford Trilogy

Fifth Business
The Manticore
World of Wonders

PENGUIN BOOKS

PENGUIN BOOKS

Published by the Penguin Group
Penguin Books Ltd, 80 Strand, London WC2R 0RL, England
Penguin Group (USA) Inc., 375 Hudson Street, New York, New York 10014, USA
Penguin Group (Canada), 90 Eglinton Avenue East, Suite 700, Toronto, Ontario, Canada M4P 2Y3
(a division of Pearson Penguin Canada Inc.)
Penguin Ireland, 25 St Stephen's Green, Dublin 2, Ireland (a division of Penguin Books Ltd)
Penguin Group (Australia), 250 Camberwell Road,
Camberwell, Victoria 3124, Australia (a division of Pearson Australia Group Pty Ltd)
Penguin Books India Pvt Ltd, 11 Community Centre,
Panchsheel Park, New Delhi – 110 017, India
Penguin Group (NZ), 67 Apollo Drive, Rosedale, Auckland 0632, New Zealand
(a division of Pearson New Zealand Ltd)
Penguin Books (South Africa) (Pty) Ltd, 24 Sturdee Avenue,
Rosebank, Johannesburg 2196, South Africa

Penguin Books Ltd, Registered Offices: 80 Strand, London WC2R 0RL, England

www.penguin.com

Fifth Business first published in Canada by The Macmillan Company of Canada Limited 1970
First published in the United States of America by The Viking Press 1970
Published in Penguin Books 1977

The Manticore first published in the United States of America by The Viking Press 1972
Published in Canada by The Macmillan Company of Canada Limited 1972
Published in Penguin Books 1976

World of Wonders first published in Canada by The Macmillan Company of Canada Limited 1975
First published in the United States of America by The Viking Press 1976
Published in Penguin Books 1977

Published in one volume in Penguin Books as *The Deptford Trilogy* 1983
Reissued in this edition 2011
006

Printed in England by Clays Ltd, St Ives plc

ISBN: 978–0–241–95262–7

www.greenpenguin.co.uk

Penguin Books is committed to a sustainable future for our business, our readers and our planet. This book is made from Forest Stewardship Council™ certified paper.

Contents

Fifth Business 1
The Manticore 259
World of Wonders 517

FIFTH BUSINESS

Fifth Business . . . Definition

Those roles which, being neither those of Hero nor Heroine, Confidante nor Villain, but which were nonetheless essential to bring about the Recognition or the dénouement, were called the Fifth Business in drama and opera companies organized according to the old style; the player who acted these parts was often referred to as Fifth Business.

—Tho. Overskou, *Den Danske Skueplads*

Contents

I *Mrs. Dempster* 7

II *I Am Born Again* 64

III *My Fool-Saint* 104

IV *Gyges and King Candaules* 143

V *Liesl* 184

VI *The Soirée of Illusions* 220

·I·

Mrs. Dempster

1

My lifelong involvement with Mrs. Dempster began at 5:58 o'clock p.m. on the 27th of December, 1908, at which time I was ten years and seven months old.

I am able to date the occasion with complete certainty because that afternoon I had been sledding with my lifelong friend and enemy Percy Boyd Staunton, and we had quarrelled, because his fine new Christmas sled would not go as fast as my old one. Snow was never heavy in our part of the world, but this Christmas it had been plentiful enough almost to cover the tallest spears of dried grass in the fields; in such snow his sled with its tall runners and foolish steering apparatus was clumsy and apt to stick, whereas my low-slung old affair would almost have slid on grass without snow.

The afternoon had been humiliating for him, and when Percy was humiliated he was vindictive. His parents were rich, his clothes were fine, and his mittens were of skin and came from a store in the city, whereas mine were knitted by my mother; it was manifestly wrong, therefore, that his splendid sled should not go faster than mine, and when such injustice showed itself Percy became cranky. He slighted my sled, scoffed at my mittens, and at last came right out and said that his father was better than my father. Instead of hitting him, which might have started a fight that could have ended in a draw or even a defeat for me, I said, all right, then, I would go home and he could have the field to himself. This was crafty of me, for I knew it was getting on for suppertime, and one of our home rules was that nobody, under any circumstances, was to be late for a meal. So I was keeping the home rule, while at the same time leaving Percy to himself.

As I walked back to the village he followed me, shouting fresh insults. When I walked, he taunted, I staggered like an old cow; my woollen cap was absurd beyond all belief; my backside was immense and wobbled when I walked; and more of the same sort, for his invention was not lively. I said nothing, because I knew that this spited him more than any retort, and that every time he shouted at me he lost face.

Our village was so small that you came on it at once; it lacked the dignity of outskirts. I darted up our street, putting on speed, for I had looked ostentatiously at my new Christmas dollar watch (Percy had a watch but was not let wear it because it was too good) and saw that it was 5:57; just time to get indoors, wash my hands in the noisy, splashy way my parents seemed to like, and be in my place at six, my head bent for grace. Percy was by this time hopping mad, and I knew I had spoiled his supper and probably his whole evening. Then the unforeseen took over.

Walking up the street ahead of me were the Reverend Amasa Dempster and his wife; he had her arm tucked in his and was leaning toward her in the protective way he had. I was familiar with this sight, for they always took a walk at this time, after dark and when most people were at supper, because Mrs. Dempster was going to have a baby, and it was not the custom in our village for pregnant women to show themselves boldly in the streets—not if they had any position to keep up, and of course the Baptist minister's wife had a position. Percy had been throwing snowballs at me, from time to time, and I had ducked them all; I had a boy's sense of when a snowball was coming, and I knew Percy. I was sure that he would try to land one last, insulting snowball between my shoulders before I ducked into our house. I stepped briskly—not running, but not dawdling—in front of the Dempsters just as Percy threw, and the snowball hit Mrs. Dempster on the back of the head. She gave a cry and, clinging to her husband, slipped to the ground; he might have caught her if he had not turned at once to see who had thrown the snowball.

I had meant to dart into our house, but I was unnerved by hearing Mrs. Dempster; I had never heard an adult cry in pain before and the sound was terrible to me. Falling, she burst into nervous tears, and suddenly there she was, on the ground, with her husband kneeling beside her, holding her in his arms and speaking to her in terms of endearment that were strange and embarrassing to me; I had never heard married people—or any people—speak in unashamedly loving words before. I knew that I was watching a "scene," and my parents had always warned against scenes as very serious breaches of propriety. I stood gaping, and then Mr. Dempster became conscious of me.

"Dunny," he said—I did not know he knew my name—"lend us your sleigh to get my wife home."

I was contrite and guilty, for I knew that the snowball had been meant for me, but the Dempsters did not seem to think of that. He lifted his wife on my sled, which was not hard because she was a small, girlish woman, and as I pulled it toward their house he walked beside it, very awkwardly bent over her, supporting her and uttering soft endearment and encouragement, for she went on crying, like a child.

Their house was not far away—just around the corner, really—but by the time I had been there, and seen Mr. Dempster take his wife inside, and found myself unwanted outside, it was a few minutes after six, and I was late for supper. But I pelted home (pausing only for a moment at the scene of the accident), washed my hands, slipped into my place at table, and made my excuse, looking straight into my mother's sternly interrogative eyes. I gave my story a slight historical bias, leaning firmly but not absurdly on my own role as the Good Samaritan. I suppressed any information or guesswork about where the snowball had come from, and to my relief my mother did not pursue that aspect of it. She was much more interested in Mrs. Dempster, and when supper was over and the dishes washed she told my father she thought she would just step over to the Dempsters' and see if there was anything she could do.

On the face of it this was a curious decision of my mother's, for of course we were Presbyterians, and Mrs. Dempster was the wife of the Baptist parson. Not that there was any ill-will among the denominations in our village, but it was understood that each looked after its own, unless a situation got too big, when outside help might be called in. But my mother was, in a modest way, a specialist in matters relating to pregnancy and childbirth; Dr. McCausland had once paid her the great compliment of saying that "Mrs. Ramsay had her head screwed on straight"; she was ready to put this levelness of head at the service of almost anybody who needed it. And she had a tenderness, never obviously displayed, for poor, silly Mrs. Dempster, who was not twenty-one yet and utterly unfit to be a preacher's wife.

So off she went, and I read my Christmas annual of the *Boy's Own Paper,* and my father read something that looked hard and had small print, and my older brother Willie read *The Cruise of the "Cachalot,"* all of us sitting round the base-burner with our feet on the nickel guard, till half-past eight, and then we boys were sent to bed. I have never been quick to go to sleep, and I lay awake until the clock downstairs struck half-past nine, and shortly after that I heard my mother return. There was a stovepipe in our house that came from the general living-room into the upstairs hall, and it was a fine conductor of sound. I crept out into the hall—Willie slept like a bear—put my ear as near to it as the heat permitted and heard my mother say:

"I've just come back for a few things. I'll probably be all night. Get me all the baby blankets out of the trunk, and then go right down to Ruckle's and make him get you a big roll of cotton wool from the store—the finest he has—and bring it to the Dempsters'. The doctor says if it isn't a big roll to get two."

"You don't mean it's coming now?"

"Yes. Away early. Don't wait up for me."

But of course he did wait up for her, and it was four in the morning when she came home, self-possessed and grim, as I could tell from her voice as I heard them talking before she returned to the Dempsters'—why, I did not know. And I lay awake too, feeling guilty and strange.

That was how Paul Dempster, whose reputation is doubtless familiar to you (though that was not the name under which he gained it), came to be born early on the morning of December 28 in 1908.

2

In making this report to you, my dear Headmaster, I have purposely begun with the birth of Paul Dempster, because this is the cause of so much that is to follow. But why, you will ask, am I writing to you at all? Why, after a professional association of so many years, during which I have been reticent about my personal affairs, am I impelled now to offer you such a statement as this?

It is because I was deeply offended by the idiotic piece that appeared in the *College Chronicle* in the issue of midsummer 1969. It is not merely its illiteracy of tone that disgusts me (though I think the quarterly publication of a famous Canadian school ought to do better), but its presentation to the public of a portrait of myself as a typical old schoolmaster doddering into retirement with tears in his eyes and a drop hanging from his nose. But it speaks for itself, and here it is, in all its inanity:

FAREWELL TO THE CORK

A feature of "break-up" last June was the dinner given in honour of Dunstan ("Corky") Ramsay, who was retiring after forty-five years at the school, and Assistant Head and Senior History Master for the last twenty-two. More than 168 Old Boys, including several MPs and two Cabinet Ministers, were present, and our able dietician Mrs. Pierce surpassed herself in providing a truly fine spread for the occasion. "Corky" himself was in fine form despite his years and the coronary that laid him up following the death of his lifelong friend, the late Boy Staunton, D.S.O., C.B.E., known to us all as an Old Boy and Chairman of the Board of Governors of this school. He spoke of his long years as a teacher and friend to innumerable boys, many of whom now occupy positions of influence and prominence, in firm tones that many a younger man might envy.

"Corky's" career may serve both as an example and a warning to young masters for, as he said, he came to the school in 1924 intending to stay only a few years and now he has completed his forty-fifth. During that time he has taught history, as he sees it, to countless boys, many of whom have gone on to a more scientific study of the subject in the universities of Canada, the U.S., and the U.K. Four heads of history departments in Canadian universities, former pupils of "Corky's," were head-table guests at the dinner, and one of them, Dr. E. S. Warren of the University of Toronto, paid a generous, non-critical tribute to "The Cork," praising his unfailing enthusiasm and referring humorously to his explorations of the borderland between history and myth.

This last subject was again slyly hinted at in the gift presented to "Corky" at the close of the evening, which was a fine tape recorder, by means of which it is hoped he may make available some of his reminiscences of an earlier and undoubtedly less complicated era of the school's history. Tapes recording the Headmaster's fine tribute to "Corky" were included and also one of the School Choir singing what must be "The Cork's" favourite hymn—never more appropriate than on this occasion!—"For all the saints, Who from their labours rest." And so the school says, "Good-bye and good luck, Corky! You served the school well according to your lights in your day and generation! Well done, thou good and faithful servant!"

There you have it, Headmaster, as it came from the pen of that ineffable jackass Lorne Packer, M.A. and aspirant to a Ph.D. Need I anatomize my indignation? Does it not reduce me to what Packer unquestionably believes me to be—a senile, former worthy who has stumbled through forty-five years of teaching armed only with a shallow, *Boy's Book of Battles* concept of history, and a bee in his bonnet about myth—whatever the dullard Packer imagines myth to be?

I do not complain that no reference was made to my V.C.; enough was said about that at the school in the days when such decorations were thought to add to the prestige of a teacher. However, I think something might have been said about my ten books, of which at least one has circulated in six languages and has sold over three-quarters of a million copies, and another exerts a widening influence in the realm of mythic history about which Packer attempts to be jocose. The fact that I am the only Protestant contributor to *Analecta Bollandiana,* and have been so for thirty-six years, is ignored, though Hippolyte Delehaye himself thought well of my work and said so in print. But what most galls me is the patronizing, dismissive tone of the piece—as if I had never had a life outside the classroom, had never risen to the full stature of a man, had never rejoiced or sorrowed or known love or hate, had never, in short, been anything except what lies within the comprehension of the donkey Packer, who has known me slightly for four years. Packer, who pushes me toward oblivion with tags of Biblical quotation, the gross impertinence of which he is unable to appreciate, religious illiterate that he is! Packer and his scientific view of history! Oh God! Packer, who cannot know and could not conceive that I have been cast by Fate and my own character for the vital though never glorious role of Fifth Business! Who could not, indeed, comprehend what Fifth Business is, even if he should meet the player of that part in his own trivial life-drama!

So, as I feel my strength returning in this house among the mountains—a house that itself holds the truths behind many illusions—I am driven to explain myself to you, Headmaster, because you stand at the top of that queer school world in which I seem to have cut such a meagre figure. But what a job it is!

Look at what I wrote at the beginning of this memoir. Have I caught anything at all of that extraordinary night when Paul Dempster was born? I am pretty sure that my little sketch of Percy Boyd Staunton is accurate, but what about myself? I have always sneered at autobiographies and memoirs in which the writer appears at the beginning as a charming, knowing little fellow, possessed of insights and perceptions beyond his years, yet offering these with a false naïveté to the reader, as though to say, "What a little wonder I was, but All Boy." Have the writers any notion or true recollection of what a boy is?

I have, and I have reinforced it by forty-five years of teaching boys. A boy is a man in miniature, and though he may sometimes exhibit notable virtue, as well as characteristics that seem to be charming because they are childlike, he is also schemer, self-seeker, traitor, Judas, crook, and villain—in short, a man. Oh, these autobiographies in which the writer postures and simpers as a David Copperfield or a Huck Finn! False, false as harlots' oaths!

Can I write truly of my boyhood? Or will that disgusting self-love which so often attaches itself to a man's idea of his youth creep in and falsify the story? I can but try. And to begin I must give you some notion of the village in which Percy Boyd Staunton and Paul Dempster and I were born.

3

Village life has been so extensively explored by movies and television during recent years that you may shrink from hearing more about it. I shall be as brief as I can, for it is not by piling up detail that I hope to achieve my picture, but by putting the emphasis where I think it belongs.

Once it was the fashion to represent villages as places inhabited by laughable, lovable simpletons, unspotted by the worldliness of city life, though occasionally shrewd in rural concerns. Later it was the popular thing to show villages as rotten with vice, and especially such sexual vice as Krafft-Ebing might have been surprised to uncover in Vienna; incest, sodomy, bestiality, sadism, and masochism were supposed to rage behind the lace curtains and in the haylofts, while a rigid piety was professed in the streets. Our village never seemed to me to be like that. It was more varied in what it offered to the observer than people from bigger and more sophisticated places generally think, and if it had sins and follies and roughnesses, it also had much to show of virtue, dignity, and even of nobility.

It was called Deptford and lay on the Thames River about fifteen miles east of Pittstown, our county town and nearest big place. We had an official population of about five hundred, and the surrounding farms probably brought the district up to eight hundred souls. We had five churches: the Anglican, poor but believed to have some mysterious social supremacy; the Presbyterian, solvent and thought—chiefly by itself—to be intellectual; the Methodist, insolvent and fervent; the Baptist, insolvent and saved; the Roman Catholic, mysterious to most of us but clearly solvent, as it was frequently and, so we thought, quite needlessly repainted. We supported one lawyer, who was also the magistrate, and one banker in a private bank, as such things still existed at that time. We had two doctors: Dr. McCausland who was reputed to be clever, and Dr. Staunton, who was Percy's father and who was also clever, but in the realm of real estate—he was a great holder of mortgages and owned several farms. We had a dentist, a wretch without manual skill, whose wife underfed him, and who had positively the dirtiest professional premises I have ever seen; and a veterinarian who drank but could rise to an occasion. We had a canning factory, which operated noisily and feverishly when there was anything to can; also a sawmill and a few shops.

The village was dominated by a family called Athelstan, who had done well out of lumber early in the nineteenth century; they owned Deptford's only three-storey house, which stood by itself on the way to the cemetery; most of our houses were of wood, and some of them stood on piles, for the Thames had a trick of flooding. One of the remaining Athelstans lived across the street from us, a poor demented old woman who used from time to time to escape from her nurse-housekeeper and rush into the road, where she threw herself down, raising a cloud of dust like a hen having a dirt-bath, shouting loudly, "Christian men, come and help me!" It usually took the housekeeper and at least one other person to pacify her; my mother often assisted in this way, but I could not do so for the old lady disliked me—I seemed to remind her of some false friend in the past. But I was interested in her madness and longed to talk with her, so I always rushed to the rescue when she made one of her breaks for liberty.

My family enjoyed a position of modest privilege, for my father was the owner and editor of the local weekly paper, *The Deptford Banner*. It was not a very prosperous enterprise, but with the job-printing plant it sustained us and we never wanted for anything. My father, as I learned later, never did a gross business of $5000 in any year that he owned it. He was not only publisher and editor, but chief mechanic and printer as well, helped by a melancholy youth called Jumper Saul and a girl called Nell Bullock. It was a good little paper, respected and hated as a proper local newspaper should be; the editorial comment, which my father composed directly on the typesetting machine, was read carefully every week.

So we were, in a sense, the literary leaders of the community, and my father had a seat on the Library Board along with the magistrate.

Our household, then, was representative of the better sort of life in the village, and we thought well of ourselves. Some of this good opinion arose from being Scots; my father had come from Dumfries as a young man, but my mother's family had been three generations in Canada without having become a whit less Scots than when her grandparents left Inverness. The Scots, I believed until I was aged at least twenty-five, were the salt of the earth, for although this was never said in our household it was one of those accepted truths which do not need to be laboured. By far the majority of the Deptford people had come to Western Ontario from the south of England, so we were not surprised that they looked to us, the Ramsays, for common sense, prudence, and right opinions on virtually everything.

Cleanliness, for example. My mother was clean—oh, but she was clean! Our privy set the sanitary tone of the village. We depended on wells in Deptford, and water for all purposes was heated in a tank called a "cistern" on the side of the kitchen range. Every house had a privy, and these ranked from dilapidated, noisome shacks to quite smart edifices, of which our own was clearly among the best. There has been much hilarity about privies in the years since they became rarities, but they were not funny buildings, and if they were not to become disgraceful they needed a lot of care.

As well as this temple of hygiene we had a "chemical closet" in the house, for use when someone was unwell; it was so capricious and smelly, however, that it merely added a new misery to illness and was rarely set going.

That is all that seems necessary to say about Deptford at present; any necessary additional matter will present itself as part of my narrative. We were serious people, missing nothing in our community and feeling ourselves in no way inferior to larger places. We did, however, look with pitying amusement on Bowles Corners, four miles distant and with a population of one hundred and fifty. To live in Bowles Corners, we felt, was to be rustic beyond redemption.

4

The first six months of Paul Dempster's life were perhaps the most exciting and pleasurable period of my mother's life, and unquestionably the most miserable of mine. Premature babies had a much poorer chance of surviving in 1908 than they have now, but Paul was the first challenge of this sort in my mother's experience of childbirth, and she met it with all her determination and ingenuity. She was not, I must make clear, in any sense a midwife or a trained person—simply a woman of good sense and kindness of heart who enjoyed the authority of nursing and the mystery which at that time still hung about the peculiarly feminine functions. She spent a great part of each day and not a few nights at the Dempsters' during that six months; other women helped when they could, but my mother was the acknowledged high priestess, and Dr. McCausland was good enough to say that without her he could never have pulled little Paul safely up onto the shores of this world.

I learned all the gynaecological and obstetrical details as they were imparted piecemeal to my father; the difference was that he sat comfortably beside the living-room stove, opposite my mother, while I stood barefoot and in my nightshirt beside the stovepipe upstairs, guilt-ridden and sometimes nauseated as I heard things that were new and terrible to my ears.

Paul was premature by some eighty days, as well as Dr. McCausland could determine. The shock of being struck by the snowball had brought Mrs. Dempster to a series of hysterical crying fits, with which her husband was clumsily trying to cope when my mother arrived on the scene. Not long afterward it had become clear that she was about to bear her child, and Dr. McCausland was sent for, but as he was elsewhere making a call he did not arrive until a quarter of an hour before the birth. Because the child was so small it came quickly, as the time for first children goes, and looked so wretched that the doctor and my mother were frightened, though they did not admit this to each other until some weeks afterward. It was characteristic of the time and the place that nobody thought to weigh the child, though the Reverend Amasa Dempster christened it immediately, after a brief wrangle with Dr.

McCausland. This was by no means in accord with the belief of his faith, but he was not himself and may have been acting in response to promptings stronger than seminary training. My mother said Dempster wanted to dip the child in water, but Dr. McCausland brusquely forbade it, and the distracted father had to be content with sprinkling. During the ceremony my mother held the child—now named Paul, as it was the first name that came into Dempster's head—as near the stove as she could, in the hottest towels she could provide. But Paul must have weighed something in the neighbourhood of three pounds, for that was what he still weighed ten weeks later, having gained little, so far as the eye could judge, in all that time.

My mother was not one to dwell on unsightly or macabre things, but she spoke of Paul's ugliness to my father with what was almost fascination. He was red, of course; all babies are red. But he was wrinkled like a tiny old man, and his head and his back and much of his face were covered with weedy long black hair. His proportions were a shock to my mother, for his limbs were tiny and he seemed to be all head and belly. His fingers and toes were almost without nails. His cry was like the mewing of a sick kitten. But he was alive, and something had to be done about him, quickly.

Dr. McCausland had never met with a baby so dismayingly premature as this, but he had read of such things, and while my mother held Paul as near the fire as was safe, he and the badly shaken father set to work to build a nest that would be as much as possible like what the infant was used to. It underwent several changes, but in the end it was an affair of jeweller's cotton and hot-water bottles—assisted at the beginning by a few hot bricks—with a tent over it into which the steam from a kettle was directed; the kettle had to be watched carefully so that it might neither boil dry nor yet boil the baby. The doctor did not know what to do about feeding the child, but he and my mother worked out a combination of a glass fountain-pen filler and a scrap of soft cotton, through which they pumped diluted, sweetened milk into Paul, and Paul feebly pumped it right back out again. It was not for two days that he kept any perceptible portion of the food, but his vomiting gained a very little in strength; it was then that my mother decided that he was a fighter and determined to fight with him.

Immediately after the birth the doctor and my mother were busy with the baby. Mrs. Dempster was left to the care of her husband, and he did the best he knew how for her, which was to kneel and pray out loud by her bedside. Poor Amasa Dempster was the most serious of men, and his background and training had not provided him with tact; he besought God, if He must take the soul of Mary Dempster to Him, to do so with gentleness and mercy. He reminded God that little Paul had been baptized, and that therefore the soul of the infant was secure and would be best able to journey to Heaven in the company of its mother. He laboured these themes with as much eloquence as he could summon, until Dr. McCausland was compelled to read the Riot Act to him, in such terms as a tight-lipped Presbyterian uses when reading the Riot Act to an emotional Baptist. This term—"reading the Riot Act"—was my mother's; she had thoroughly approved of the doctor's performance, for she had the real Scots satisfaction in hearing somebody justifiably scolded and set to rights. "Carrying on like that, right over that girl's bed, while she was fighting for her life," she said to my father, and I could imagine the sharp shake of the head that accompanied her speech.

I wonder now if Mrs. Dempster was really fighting for her life; subsequent circumstances proved that she was stronger than anybody knew. But it was an accepted belief at that time that no woman bore a child without walking very close to the brink of death, and, for anything I know to the contrary, it may have been true at that stage of medical science. But certainly it must have seemed to poor Dempster that his wife was dying. He had hung about all through the birth; he had seen his hideous, misshapen child; he had been pushed about and bustled by the doctor and the good neighbour. He was a parson, of course, but at root he was a frightened farmer lad, and if he lost his head I cannot now blame him. He was one of those people who seem fated to be hurt and thrown aside in life, but doubtless as he knelt by Mary's bed he thought himself as important an actor in the drama as any of the others. This is one of the cruelties of the theatre of life; we all think of ourselves as stars and rarely recognize it when we are indeed mere supporting characters or even supernumeraries.

What the following months cost in disorganization of our household you can imagine. My father never complained of it, for he was devoted to my mother, considered her to be a wonderful woman, and would not have done anything to prevent her from manifesting her wonderfulness. We ate many a scratch meal so that little Paul might not miss his chance with the fountain-pen filler, and when the great day came at last when the infant retained a perceptible part of what it was given, I think my father was even more pleased than my mother.

The weeks passed, and Paul's wrinkled skin became less transparent and angry, his wide-set eyes opened and roamed about, unseeing but certainly not blind, and he kicked his feet just a little, like a real baby. Would he ever be strong? Dr. McCausland could not say; he was the epitome of Scots caution. But my mother's lionlike spirit was already determined that Paul should have his chance.

It was during these weeks that I endured agony of mind that seems to me, looking back over more than sixty years, to have been extraordinary. I have had hard times since then, and have endured them with all the capability for suffering of a grown man, so I do not want to make foolish and sentimental claims for the suffering of a child. But even now I hesitate to recall some of the nights when I feared to go to sleep and prayed till I sweated that God would forgive me for my mountainous crime.

I was perfectly sure, you see, that the birth of Paul Dempster, so small, so feeble and troublesome, was my fault. If I had not been so clever, so sly, so spiteful in hopping in front of the Dempsters just as Percy Boyd Staunton threw that snowball at me from behind, Mrs. Dempster would not have been struck. Did I never think that Percy was guilty? Indeed I did. But a psychological difficulty arose here. When next I met him, after that bad afternoon, we approached each other warily, as boys do after a quarrel, and he seemed disposed to talk. I did not at once speak of the birth of Paul, but I crept up on the subject and was astonished to hear him say, "Yes, my Pa says McCausland has his hands full with that one."

"The baby came too soon," said I, testing him.

"Did it?" said he, looking me straight in the eyes.

"And you know why," I said.

"No I don't."

"Yes you do. You threw that snowball."

"I threw a snowball at you," he replied, "and a good smack."

I could tell by the frank boldness of his tone that he wa "Do you mean to say that's what you think?" I said.

"You bet it's what I think," said he. "And it's what you'd better think too, if you know what's good for you."

We looked into each other's eyes and I knew that he was afraid, and I knew also that he would fight, lie, do anything rather than admit what I knew. And I didn't know what in the world I could do about it.

So I was alone with my guilt, and it tortured me. I was a Presbyterian child and I knew a good deal about damnation. We had a Dante's *Inferno* among my father's books, with the illustrations by Doré, such books were common in rural districts at that time, and probably none of us was really aware that Dante was an R.C.; it had once been a shivery pleasure to look at those pictures. Now I knew that they showed the reality of my situation, and what lay beyond this life for such a boy as I. I was of the damned. Such a phrase seems to mean nothing to people nowadays, but to me it was utterly real. I pined and wasted to some extent, and my mother was not so taken up with the Dempsters that she failed to dose me regularly with cod-liver oil. But though I did not really suffer much physically I suffered greatly in my mind, for a reason connected with my time of life. I was just upon eleven, and I matured early, so that some of the earliest changes of puberty were beginning in me.

How healthy-minded children seem to be nowadays! Or is it just the cant of our time to believe so? I cannot tell. But certainly in my childhood the common attitude toward matters of sex was enough to make a hell of adolescence for any boy who was, like myself, deeply serious and mistrustful of whatever seemed pleasurable in life. So here I was, subject not only to the smutty, whispering speculations of the other boys I knew, and tormented by the suspicion that my parents were somehow involved in this hog-wallow of sex that had begun to bulk so large in my thoughts, but I was directly responsible for a grossly sexual act—the birth of a ild. And what a child! Hideous, stricken, a caricature of a living creature! In the hot craziness of my thinking, I began to believe that I was more responsible for the birth of Paul Dempster than were his parents, and that if this were ever discovered some dreadful fate would overtake me. Part of the dreadful fate would undoubtedly be rejection by my mother. I could not bear the thought, but neither could I let it alone.

My troubles became no less when, at least four months after Paul's birth, I heard this coming up the stovepipe—cooler now, for spring was well advanced:

"I think little Paul is going to pull through. He'll be slow, the doctor says, but he'll be all right."

"You must be pleased. It's mostly your doing."

"Oh no! I only did what I could. But the doctor says he hopes somebody will keep an eye on Paul. His mother certainly can't."

"She isn't coming around?"

"Doesn't appear so. It was a terrible shock for the poor little thing. And Amasa Dempster just won't believe that there's a time to talk about God and a time to trust God and keep your mouth shut. Luckily she doesn't seem to understand a lot of what he says."

"Do you mean she's gone simple?"

"She's as quiet and friendly and sweet-natured as she ever was, poor little soul, but she just isn't all there. That snowball certainly did a terrible thing to her. Who do you suppose threw it?"

"Dempster couldn't see. I don't suppose anybody will ever know."

"I've wondered more than once if Dunstable knows more about that than he's letting on."

"Oh no, he knows how serious it is. If he knew anything he'd have spoken up by now."

"Whoever it was, the Devil guided his hand."

Yes, and the Devil shifted his mark. Mrs. Dempster had gone simple! I crept to bed wondering if I would live through the night, and at the same time desperately afraid to die.

5

Ah, if dying were all there was to it! Hell and torment at once; but at least you know where you stand. It is living with these guilty secrets that exacts the price. Yet the more time that passed, the less I was able to accuse Percy Boyd Staunton of having thrown the snowball that sent Mrs. Dempster simple. His brazen-faced refusal to accept responsibility seemed to deepen my own guilt, which had now become the guilt of concealment as well as action. However, as time passed, Mrs. Dempster's simplicity did not seem to be as terrible as I had at first feared.

My mother, with her unfailing good sense, hit the nail on the head when she said that Mrs. Dempster was really no different from what she had been before, except that she was more so. When Amasa Dempster had brought his little bride to our village the spring before the Christmas of Paul's untimely birth, the opinion had been strong among the women that nothing would ever make a preacher's wife out of that one.

I have already said that while our village contained much of what humanity has to show, it did not contain everything, and one of the things it conspicuously lacked was an aesthetic sense; we were all too much the descendants of hard-bitten pioneers to wish for or encourage any such thing, and we gave hard names to qualities that, in a more sophisticated society, might have had value. Mrs. Dempster was not pretty—we understood prettiness and guardedly admitted it as a pleasant, if needless, thing in a woman—but she had a gentleness of expression and a delicacy of colour that was uncommon. My mother, who had strong features and stood for no nonsense from her hair, said that Mrs. Dempster had a face like a pan of milk. Mrs. Dempster was small and slight, and even the clothes approved for a preacher's wife did not conceal the fact that she had a girlish figure and a light step. When she was pregnant there was a bloom about her that seemed out of keeping with the seriousness of her state; it was not at all the proper thing for a pregnant woman to smile so much, and the least she could have done was to take a stronger line with those waving tendrils of hair that seemed so often to be escaping from a properly severe arrangement. She was a nice little thing, but was that soft voice ever going to dominate a difficult meeting of the Ladies' Aid? And why did she laugh so much when nobody else could see anything to laugh at?

Amasa Dempster, who had always seemed a level-headed man, for a preacher, was plain silly about his wife. His eyes were always on her, and he could be seen drawing pails of water from their outside well, for the washing, when this was fully understood to be woman's work, right up to the last month or so of a pregnancy. The way he looked at her would make you wonder if the man was soft in the head. You would think they were still courting, instead of being expected to get down to the Lord's work and earn his $550 *per annum;* this was what the Baptists paid their preacher, as well as allowing him a house, not quite enough fuel, and a ten-per-cent discount on everything bought in a Baptist-owned store—and a few other stores that "honoured the cloth," as the saying went. (Of course he was expected to give back an exact tenth of it to the church, to set an example.) The hope was widely expressed that Mr. Dempster was not going to make a fool of his wife.

In our village hard talk was not always accompanied by hard action. My mother, who could certainly never have been accused of softness with her family or the world, went out of her way to help Mrs. Dempster—I will not say, to befriend her, because friendship between such unequal characters could never have been; but she tried to "show her the ropes," and whatever these mysterious feminine ropes were, they certainly included many good things that my mother cooked and just happened to leave when she dropped in on the young bride, and not merely the loan, but the practical demonstration of such devices as carpet-stretchers, racks for drying lace curtains, and the art of shining windows with newspaper.

Why had Mrs. Dempster's mother never prepared her for these aspects of marriage? It came out she had been brought up by an aunt, who had money and kept a hired girl, and how were you to forge a preacher's wife from such weak metal as that? When my father teased my mother about the amount of food she took the Dempsters, she became huffy and asked if she was to allow them to starve under her nose while that girl was learning the ropes? But the girl was slow, and my mother's answer to that was that in her condition she couldn't be expected to be quick.

Now it did not seem that she would ever learn the craft of housekeeping. Her recovery from Paul's birth was tardy, and while she grew strong again her husband looked after the domestic affairs, helped by neighbour women and a Baptist widow for whose occasional services he was able to eke out a very little money. As spring came Mrs. Dempster was perfectly able-bodied but showed no signs of getting down to work. She did a little cleaning and some inept cooking, and laughed like a girl at her failures. She hovered over the baby, and as he changed from a raw monster to a small but recognizably Christian-looking infant she was as delighted as a little girl with a doll. She now breast-fed him—my mother and all the neighbours had to admit that she did it well—but she lacked the solemnity they expected of a nursing mother; she enjoyed the process, and sometimes when they went into the house there she was, with everything showing, even though her husband was present, just as if she hadn't the sense to pull up her clothes. I happened upon her once or twice in this condition and gaped with the greedy eyes of an adolescent boy, but she did not seem to notice. And thus the opinion grew that Mrs. Dempster was simple.

There was only one thing to be done, and that was to help the Dempsters as much as possible, without approving or encouraging any tendencies that might run contrary to the right way of doing things. My mother ordered me over to the Dempsters' to chop and pile wood, sweep away snow, cut the grass, weed the vegetable patch, and generally make myself handy two or three times a week and on Saturdays if necessary. I was also to keep an eye on the baby, for my mother could not rid herself of a dread that Mrs. Dempster would allow it to choke or fall out of its basket or otherwise come to grief. There was no chance of such a thing happening, as I soon found, but obeying my instructions brought me much into the company of Mrs. Dempster, who laughed at my concern for the baby. She did not seem to think that it could come to any harm in her keeping, and I know now that she was right, and that my watchfulness must have been intrusive and clumsy.

Caring for a baby is one thing, and the many obligations of a parson's wife are another, and for this work Mrs. Dempster showed no aptitude at all. By the time a year had passed since Paul's birth her husband had become "poor Reverend Dempster" to everybody, a man burdened with a simple-minded wife and a delicate child, and it was a general source of amazement that he could make ends meet. Certainly a man with $550 a year needed a thrifty wife, and Mrs. Dempster gave away everything. There was a showdown once when she gave an ornamental vase to a woman who had taken her a few bakings of bread; the vase was part of the furnishings of the parsonage, not the personal property of the Dempsters, and the ladies of the church were up in arms at this act of feckless generosity and demanded of Amasa Dempster that he send his wife to the neighbour's house to ask for the vase back, and if this meant eating crow she would have to eat crow. But he would not humiliate his wife and went on the distasteful errand himself, which everybody agreed was weakness in him and would lead to worse things. One of my jobs, under instruction from my mother, was to watch for chalk marks on the Dempsters' verandah posts, and rub them out when I saw them; these chalk marks were put there by tramps as signals to one another that the house was good for a generous handout, and perhaps even money.

After a year or so most of the women in our village grew tired of pitying the Baptist parson and his wife and began to think that he was as simple as she. Like many ostracized people, they became more marked in their oddity. But my mother never wavered; her compassion was not of the short-term variety. Consequently, as they became, in a sense, charges of my family, my jobs for the Dempsters grew. My brother Willie did very little about them. He was two years older than I and his schoolwork was more demanding; further, after school hours he now went to the *Banner* printing plant to make himself useful and pick up the trade. But my mother was as watchful as ever, and my father, in whose eyes she could do nothing wrong, approved completely of all that was done.

6

Being unofficial watchdog to the Dempster family was often a nuisance to me and did nothing for my popularity. But at this time

I was growing rapidly and was strong for my age, so not many of the people with whom I went to school liked to say too much to my face; but I knew that they said enough behind my back. Percy Boyd Staunton was one of these.

He had a special place in our school world. There are people who, even as boys, assume superior airs and are taken as grandees by those around them. He was as big as I, and rather fleshy; without being a fat boy he was plump. His clothes were better than ours, and he had an interesting pocket-knife, with a chain on it to fasten to his knickerbockers, and an ink-bottle you could knock over without spilling a drop; on Sundays he wore a suit with a fashionable half-belt at the back. He had once been to Toronto to the Exhibition, and altogether breathed a larger air than the rest of us.

He and I were rivals, for though I had none of his graces of person or wealth I had a sharp tongue. I was raw-boned and wore clothes that had often made an earlier appearance on Willie, but I had a turn for sarcastic remarks, which were known to our group as "good ones." If I was pushed too far I might "get off a good one," and as our community had a long memory such dour witticisms would be remembered and quoted for years.

I had a good one all ready for Percy, if ever he gave me any trouble. I had heard his mother tell my mother that when he was a dear little fellow, just learning to talk, his best version of his name, Percy Boyd, was Pidgy Boy-Boy, and she still called him that in moments of unbuttoned affection. I knew that I had but once to call him Pidgy Boy-Boy in the schoolyard and his goose would be cooked; probably suicide would be his only way out. This knowledge gave me a sense of power in reserve.

I needed it. Some of the oddity and loneliness of the Dempsters was beginning to rub off on me. Having double chores to do kept me out of many a game I would have liked to join; dodging back and forth between their house and ours with this, that, and the other thing, I was sure to meet some of my friends; Mrs. Dempster often stood in the door when I was running home, waving and thanking me in a voice that seemed to me eerie and likely to bring mockery down on my head, not hers, if anybody overheard her, as they often did. I had become especially sensitive to the mockery of girls and knew that some of them had nicknamed me Nursie. They did not call me that to my face, however.

My position here was worst of all. I wanted to be on good terms with the girls I knew; I suppose I wanted them to admire me and think me wonderful in some unspecified way. Enough of them were silly about Percy and sent him mash Valentines on February 14, without any names on them but with handwriting that betrayed the sender. No girl ever sent me a Valentine except Elsie Webb, known to us all as Spider Webb because of her gawky, straddling walk. I did not want Spider Webb, I wanted Leola Cruikshank, who had cork-screw curls and a great way of never meeting your eyes. But my feeling about Leola was put askew by my feeling about Mrs. Dempster. Leola I wanted as a trophy of success, but Mrs. Dempster was beginning to fill my whole life, and the stranger her conduct became, and the more the village pitied and dismissed her, the worse my obsession grew.

I thought I was in love with Leola, by which I meant that if I could have found her in a quiet corner, and if I had been certain that no one would ever find out, and if I could have summoned up the courage at the right moment, I would have kissed her. But, looking back on it now, I know I was in love with Mrs. Dempster. Not as some boys are in love with grown-up women, adoring them from afar and enjoying a fantasy life in which the older woman figures in an idealized form, but in a painful and immediate fashion; I saw her every day, I did menial tasks in her house, and I was charged to watch her and keep her from doing foolish things. Furthermore, I felt myself tied to her by the certainty that I was responsible for her straying wits, the disorder of her marriage, and the frail body of the child who was her great delight in life. I had made her what she was, and in such circumstances I must hate her or love her. In a mode that was far too demanding for my age or experience, I loved her.

Loving her, I had to defend her, and when people said she was crazy I had to force myself to tell them that they were crazy themselves and I would knock their blocks off if they said it again. Fortunately one of the first people with whom I had such an encounter was Milo Papple, and he was not hard to deal with.

Milo was our school buffoon, the son of Myron Papple, the

village barber. Barbers in more sophisticated communities are sometimes men with rich heads of hair, or men who have given a special elegance to a bald head, but Myron Papple had no such outward grace. He was a short, fat, pear-shaped man with the complexion and hair of a pig of the Chester White breed. He had but one distinction; he put five sticks of gum into his mouth every morning and chewed the wad until he closed his shop in the evening, breathing peppermint on each customer as he shaved, clipped, and talked.

Milo was his father in miniature, and admitted by us all to be a card. His repertoire of jokes was small but of timeless durability. He could belch at will, and did. He could also break wind at will, with a prolonged, whining note of complaint, and when he did so in class and then looked around with an angry face, whispering, "Who done that?" our mirth was Chaucerian, and the teacher was reduced to making a refined face, as if she were too good for a world in which such things were possible. Even the girls—even Leola Cruikshank—thought Milo was a card.

One day I was asked if I would play ball after school. I said I had to do some work.

"Sure," said Milo, "Dunny's got to get right over to the bughouse and cut the grass."

"The bughouse?" asked a few who were slow of wit.

"Yep. The Dempsters'. That's the bughouse now."

It was now or never for me. "Milo," I said, "if you ever say that again I'll get a great big cork and stick it up you, and then nobody'll ever laugh at you again." As I said this I walked menacingly toward him, and as soon as Milo backed away I knew I was the victor, for the moment. The joke about Milo and the cork was frugally husbanded by our collectors of funny sayings, and he was not allowed to forget it. "If you stuck a cork in Milo nobody would ever laugh at him again," these unashamed gleaners of the fields of repartee would say and shout with laughter. Nobody said "bughouse" to me for a long time, but sometimes I could see that they wanted to say it, and I knew they said it behind my back. This increased my sense of isolation—of being forced out of the world I belonged to into the strange and unchancy world of the Dempsters.

7

The passing of time brought other isolations. At thirteen I should have been learning the printing business; my father was neat-handed and swift, and Willie was following in his steps. But I was all thumbs in the shop, slow to learn the layout of the frames in which the fonts of type were distributed, clumsy at locking up a forme, messy with ink, a great spoiler of paper, and really not much good at anything but cutting reglet or reading proof, which my father never trusted to anyone but himself in any case. I never mastered the printer's trick of reading things upside down and backward, and I never properly learned how to fold a sheet. Altogether I was a nuisance in the shop, and as this humiliated me, and my father was a kindly man, he sought some other honourable work to keep me from under his feet. It had been suggested that our village library should be open a few afternoons a week so that the more responsible schoolchildren might use it, and somebody was needed to serve as under-librarian, the real librarian being busy as a teacher during the daytime and not relishing the loss of so much of her free time. I was appointed to this job, at a salary of nothing at all, the honour being deemed sufficient reward.

This suited me admirably. Three afternoons a week I opened our one-room library in the upstairs of the Town Hall and lorded it over any schoolchildren who appeared. Once I had the dizzy pleasure of finding something in the encyclopaedia for Leola Cruikshank, who had to write an essay about the equator and didn't know whether it went over the top or round the middle. More afternoons than not, nobody appeared, or else those who came went away as soon as they found what they wanted, and I had the library to myself.

It was not much of a collection—perhaps fifteen hundred books in all, of which roughly a tenth part were for children. The annual budget was twenty-five dollars, and much of that went on subscriptions to magazines that the magistrate, who was chairman of the board, wanted to read. Acquisitions, therefore, were usually gifts from the estates of people who had died, and our local auctioneer gave us any books that he could not sell; we kept what we wanted and sent the rest to the Grenfell Mission, on the principle that savages would read anything.

The consequence was that we had some odd things, of which the oddest were kept in a locked closet off the main room. There was a medical book, with a frightful engraving of a fallen womb, and another of a varicocele, and a portrait of a man with lavish hair and whiskers but no nose, which made me a lifelong enemy of syphilis. My special treasures were *The Secrets of Stage Conjuring* by Robert-Houdin and *Modern Magic* and *Later Magic* by Professor Hoffmann; they had been banished as uninteresting—uninteresting!—and as soon as I saw them I knew that fate meant them for me. By studying them I should become a conjurer, astonish everybody, win the breathless admiration of Leola Cruikshank, and become a great power. I immediately hid them in a place where they could not fall into the hands of unworthy persons, including our librarian, and devoted myself to the study of magic.

I still look back upon those hours when I acquainted myself with the means by which a French conjurer had astonished the subjects of Louis-Napoleon as an era of Arcadian pleasure. It did not matter that everything about the book was hopelessly old-fashioned; great as the gap between me and Robert-Houdin was, I could accept his world as the real world, so far as the wonderful art of deception was concerned. When he insisted on the necessity of things that were unknown to Deptford, I assumed that it was because Deptford was a village and Paris was a great and sophisticated capital, where everybody who was anybody was mad for conjuring and wanted nothing more than to be delightfully bamboozled by an elegant, slightly sinister, but wholly charming master of the art. It did not surprise me in the least that Robert-Houdin's Emperor had sent him on a special diplomatic mission to Algiers, to destroy the power of the marabouts by showing that his magic was greater than theirs. When I read of his feat on the Shah of Turkey's yacht, when he hammered the Shah's jewelled watch to ruins in a mortar, then threw the rubbish overboard, cast a line into the sea, pulled up a fish, asked the Shah's chef to clean it, and stood by while the chef discovered the watch, quite unharmed, enclosed in a silk bag in the entrails of the fish, I felt that this was life as it ought to be lived. Conjurers were obviously fellows of the first importance and kept distinguished company. I would be one of them.

The Scottish practicality that I had imitated from my parents was not really in grain with me; I cared too little for difficulties. I admitted to myself that Deptford was unlikely to yield a conjurer's table—a gilded *guéridon,* with a cunning *servante* on the back of it for storing things one did not wish to have seen, and a *gibecière* into which coins and watches could noiselessly be dropped; I had no tailcoat, and if I had I doubt if my mother would have sewn a proper conjurer's *profonde* in the tails, for disappearing things. When Professor Hoffmann instructed me to fold back my cuffs, I knew that I had no cuffs, but did not care. I would devote myself to illusions that did not require such things. These illusions, I discovered, called for special apparatus, always described by the Professor as "simple," which the conjurer was advised to make himself. For me, a boy who always tied his shoelaces backward and whose Sunday tie looked like a hangman's noose, such apparatus presented a problem that I had to admit, after a few tries, was insuperable. Nor could I do anything about the tricks that required "a few substances, easily obtainable from any chemist," because Ruckle's drugstore had never heard of any of them. But I was not defeated. I would excel in the realm which Robert-Houdin said was the truest, most classical form of conjuring: I would be a master of sleight-of-hand, a matchless *prestidigitateur.*

It was like me to begin with eggs—or, to be precise, one egg. It never occurred to me that a clay egg, of the kind used to deceive hens, would do just as well. I hooked an egg from my mother's kitchen and when the library was empty began to practise producing it from my mouth, elbow, and back of the knee; also putting it into my right ear and, after a little henlike clucking, removing it from my left. I seemed to be getting on splendidly, and when the magistrate made a sudden appearance to get the latest *Scribner's* I had a mad moment when I thought of amazing him by taking an egg out of his beard. Of course I did not dare to go so far, but the delightful thought that I could if I wanted to put me into such a fit of giggles that he looked at me speculatively. When he was gone I handled the egg with greater boldness until, disappearing it into my hip pocket, I put my thumb through it.

Ha ha. Every boy has experiences of this kind, and they are usually thought to be funny and childlike. But that egg led to a dreadful row with my mother. She had missed the egg—it never occurred to me that anybody counted eggs—and accused me of taking it. I lied. Then she caught me trying to wash out my pocket, because, in a house with no running water, washing cannot be a really private business. She exposed my lie and demanded to know what I wanted with an egg. Now, how can a boy of thirteen tell a Scotswoman widely admired for her practicality that he intends to become the world's foremost *prestidigitateur?* I took refuge in mute insolence. She stormed. She demanded to know if I thought she was made of eggs. Visited unhappily by a good one, I said that that was something she would have to decide for herself. My mother had little sense of humour. She told me that if I thought I had grown too old to be beaten she would show me I was mistaken, and from the kitchen cupboard she produced the pony whip.

It was not for ponies. In my boyhood such pretty little whips were sold at country fairs, where children bought them, and flourished them, and occasionally beat trees with them. But a few years earlier my mother had impounded such a whip that Willie had brought home, and it had been used for beatings ever since. It had been at least two years since I had had a beating, but now my mother flourished the whip, and when I laughed she struck me over the left shoulder with it.

"Don't you dare touch me," I shouted, and that put her into such a fury as I had never known. It must have been a strange scene, for she pursued me around the kitchen, slashing me with the whip until she broke me down and I cried. She cried too, hysterically, and beat me harder, storming about my impudence, my want of respect for her, of my increasing oddity and intellectual arrogance—not that she used these words, but I do not intend to put down what she actually said—until at last her fury was spent, and she ran upstairs in tears and banged the door of her bedroom. I crept off to the woodshed, a criminal, and wondered what I should do. Become a tramp, perhaps, like the shabby, sinister fellows who came so often to our back door for a handout? Hang myself? I have been very miserable since—miserable not for an hour but for months on end—but I can still feel that hour's misery in its perfect desolation, if I am fool enough to call it up in my mind.

My father and Willie came home, and there was no supper. Naturally he sided with her, and Willie was very officious and knowing about how intolerable I had become of late, and how thrashing was too good for me. Finally it was settled that my mother would come downstairs if I would beg pardon. This I had to do on my knees, repeating a formula improvised by my father, which included a pledge that I would always love my mother, to whom I owed the great gift of life, and that I begged her—and secondarily God—to forgive me, knowing full well that I was unworthy of such clemency.

I rose from my knees cleansed and purged, and ate very little supper, as became a criminal. When it came time for me to go to bed my mother beckoned me to her, and kissed me, and whispered, "I know I'll never have another anxious moment with my own dear laddie."

I pondered these words before I went to sleep. How could I reconcile this motherliness with the screeching fury who had pursued me around the kitchen with a whip, flogging me until she was gorged with—what? Vengeance? What was it? Once, when I was in my thirties and reading Freud for the first time, I thought I knew. I am not so sure I know now. But what I knew then was that nobody—not even my mother—was to be trusted in a strange world that showed very little of itself on the surface.

8

Instead of sickening me of magic, this incident increased my appetite for it. It was necessary for me to gain power in some realm into which my parents—my mother particularly—could not follow me. Of course, I did not think about the matter logically; sometimes I yearned for my mother's love and hated myself for having grieved her, but quite as often I recognized that her love had a high price on it and that her idea of a good son was a pretty small potato. So I drudged away secretly at the magic.

It was card tricks now. I had no trouble getting a pack of cards, for my parents were great players of euchre, and of the several packs in the house I could spirit away the oldest for a couple of hours any afternoon, if I replaced it at the back of the drawer where it was kept, as being too good to throw away but too slick and supple to use. Having only the one pack, I could not attempt any tricks that needed two cards of the same suit and value, but I mastered a few of those chestnuts in which somebody chooses a card and the conjurer finds it after much shuffling; I even had a beauty, involving a silk thread, in which the chosen card hopped from the deck as the conjurer stood nonchalantly at a distance.

I needed an audience, to judge how well I was doing, and I found one readily in Paul Dempster. He was four, and I was fourteen, so on the pretext of looking after him for an hour or two I would take him to the library and entertain him with my tricks. He was not a bad audience, for he sat solemn and mute when he was bidden, chose cards at my command, and if I presented the deck to him with one card slightly protruding, while I held the deck tight, that was the card he invariably chose. He had his faults; he could neither read nor count, and so he did not relish the full wonder of it when I produced his card triumphantly after tremendous shufflings, but I knew that I had deceived him and told him so. In fact, my abilities as a teacher had their first airing in that little library, and as I was fond of lecturing I taught Paul more than I suspected.

Of course he wanted to play too, and it was not easy to explain that I was not playing but demonstrating a fascinating and involved science. I had to work out a system of rewards, and as he liked stories I read to him after he had watched me do my tricks.

Luckily we both liked the same book. It was a pretty volume I found in the cupboard of banished books, called *A Child's Book of Saints*. It was the work of one William Canton, and it began with a conversation between a little girl and her father, which I thought a model of elegant writing. I can quote passages from it still, for I used to read and reread them to Paul, and he, with the memory of a non-reader, could repeat them by heart. Here is one, and I am sure that though I have not read it for fifty years, I have it right:

Occasionally these legends brought us to the awful brink of religious controversies and insoluble mysteries, but, like those gentle savages who honour the water-spirits by hanging garlands from tree to tree across the river, W.V.—[W.V. was the little girl]—could always fling a bridge of flowers over our abysses. "Our sense," she would declare, "is nothing to God's; and though big people have more sense than children, the sense of all the big people in the world put together would be no sense to His." "We are only little babies to Him; we do not understand Him at all." Nothing seemed clearer to her than the reasonableness of one legend which taught that though God always answers our prayers, He does not always answer in the way we would like, but in some better way than we know. "Yes," she observed, "He is just a dear old Father." Anything about our Lord engrossed her imagination; and it was a frequent wish of hers that He would come again. "Then,"—poor perplexed little mortal! whose difficulties one could not even guess at—"we should be quite sure of things. Miss Catherine tells us from books: He would tell us from His memory. People would not be so cruel to Him now. Queen Victoria would not allow any one to crucify Him."

There was a picture of Queen Victoria hanging in the library, and one look at her would tell you that anybody under her protection was in luck.

Thus for some months I used Paul as a model audience, and paid him off in stories about St. Dorothea and St. Francis, and let him look at the pretty pictures, which were by Heath Robinson.

I progressed from cards to coins, which were vastly more difficult. For one thing, I had very few coins, and when my books of instruction said, "Secure and palm six half-crowns," I was stopped dead, for I had no half-crowns or anything that looked like them. I had one handsome piece—it was a brass medal that the linotype company had prepared to advertise its machines, which my father did not want—and as it was about the size of a silver dollar I practised with that. But oh, what clumsy hands I had!

I cannot guess now how many weeks I worked on the sleight-of-hand pass called The Spider. To perform this useful bit of trickery, you nip a coin between your index and little fingers, and then revolve it by drawing the two middle fingers back and forth, in front or behind it; by this means it is possible to show both sides of the hand without revealing the coin. But just try to do it! Try it with red, knuckly Scots hands, stiffened by grass-cutting and snow-shovelling, and see what skill you develop! Of course Paul wanted to know what I was doing, and, being a teacher at heart, I told him.

"Like this?" he asked, taking the coin from me and performing the pass perfectly.

I was stunned and humiliated, but, looking back on it now, I think I behaved pretty well.

"Yes, like that," I said, and though it took me a few days to realize it, that was the moment I became Paul's instructor. He could do anything with his hands. He could shuffle cards without dropping them, which was something I could never be sure of, and he could do marvels with my big brass medal. His hands were small, so that the coin was usually visible, but it was seen to be doing something interesting; he could make it walk over the back of his hand, nipping it between the fingers with a dexterity that left me gasping.

There was no sense in envying him; he had the hands and I had not, and although there were times when I considered killing him, just to rid the world of a precocious nuisance, I could not overlook that fact. The astonishing thing was that he regarded me as his teacher because I could read and tell him what to do; the fact that he could do it did not impress him. He was grateful, and I was in a part of my life where gratitude and admiration, even from such a thing as Paul, were very welcome.

If it seems cruel to write "such a thing as Paul," let me explain myself. He was an odd-looking little mortal, with an unusually big head for his frail body. His clothes never seemed to fit him; many of them were reach-me-downs from Baptist families, and because his mother was so unhandy they always had holes in them and were ravelled at the edges and ill-buttoned. He had a lot of curly brown hair, because his mother kept begging Amasa Dempster to put off the terrible day when Paul would go to Myron Papple for the usual boy's scalping. His eyes seemed big in his little face, and certainly they were unusually wide apart, and looked dark because his thin skin was so white. My mother worried about that pallor and occasionally took charge of Paul and wormed him—a humiliation children do not seem to need any more. Paul was not a village favourite, and the dislike so many people felt for his mother—dislike for the queer and persistently unfortunate—they attached to the unoffending son.

9

My own dislike was kept for Amasa Dempster. A few of his flock said that he walked very closely with God, and it made him spooky. We had family prayers at home, a respectful salute to Providence before breakfast, enough for anybody. But he was likely to drop on his knees at any time and pray with a fervour that seemed indecent. Because I was often around their house I sometimes stumbled on one of these occasions, and he would motion me to kneel with them until he was finished—which could be as much as ten or fifteen minutes later. Sometimes he mentioned me; I was the stranger within their gates, and I knew he was telling God what a good job I did on the grass and the woodpile; but he usually got in a dig at the end, when he asked God to preserve me from walking with a froward mouth, by which he meant my little jokes to coax a laugh or a smile from his wife. And he never finished without asking God for strength to bear his heavy cross, by which I knew that he meant Mrs. Dempster; she knew it too.

This was the only unkindness he ever offered her. In everything else he was patient and, so far as his spirit permitted, loving. But before Paul's birth he had loved her because she was the blood of his heart; now he seemed to love her on principle. I do not think he knew that he was hinting to God to notice the meek spirit in which he bore his ill luck, but that was the impression his prayers left on my mind. He was no skilled rhetorician, and the poor man had nothing much in the way of brains, so very often what he felt came out more clearly than what he meant to say.

His quality of feeling was weighty. I suppose this is what made him acceptable to the Baptists, who valued feeling very highly—much more highly than we Presbyterians, who were scared of it and tried to swap it for intellect. I got the strength of his feeling one awful day when he said to me:

"Dunny, come with me to my study in the church. I want a word with you."

Wondering what on earth all this solemnity was about, I tagged along with him to the Baptist church, where we went to the tiny parson's room beside the baptismal tank. The first thing he did was to drop to his knees and ask God to assist him to be just but not unkind, and then he went to work on me.

I had brought corruption into the innocent world of childhood. I had offended against one of God's little ones. I had been the agent—unknowingly, he hoped—by means of which the Evil One had trailed his black slime across a pure life.

Of course I was frightened. There were boys and girls known to me who made occasional twilight visits to the groves of trees in the old gravel pit that lay to the west of our village and gave themselves up to exploratory pawing. One of these, a Mabel Heighington, was rumoured to have gone the limit with more than one boy. But I was not of this group; I was too scared of being found out, and also, I must say in justice to my young self, too fastidious, to want the pimply Heighington slut; I preferred my intense, solitary adoration of Leola Cruikshank to such frowzy rough-and-tumble. But all boys used to be open to accusation on matters of sex; their thoughts alone, to say nothing of half-willing, half-disgusted action, incriminated them before themselves. I thought someone must have given him my name to divert attention from the others.

I was wrong. After the preliminary mysterious talk it came out that he was accusing me of putting playing-cards—he called them the Devil's picture-book—into the hands of his son Paul. But worse—much worse than that—I had taught the boy to cheat with the cards, to handle them like a smoking-car gambler, and also to play deceptive tricks with money. That very morning there had been three cents' change from the baker's visit, and Paul had picked them up from the table and caused them to vanish! Of course he had restored them—utter corruption had not yet set in—and after a beating and much prayer it had all come out about the cards and what I had taught him.

This was bad enough, but worse was to follow. Papistry! I had been telling Paul stories about saints, and if I did not know that the veneration of saints was one of the vilest superstitions of the Scarlet Woman of Rome, he was going to have a word with the Presbyterian minister, the Reverend Andrew Bowyer, to make sure I found out. Under conviction of his wickedness Paul had come out with blasphemous stuff about somebody who had spent his life praying on a pillar forty feet high, and St. Francis who saw a living Christ on a crucifix, and St. Mary of the Angels, and more of the same kind, that had made his blood freeze to hear. Now—what was it to be? Would I take the beating I deserved from him, or was he to tell my parents and leave it to them to do their duty?

I was a boy of fifteen at this time, and I did not propose to take a beating from him, and if my parents beat me I would run away and become a tramp. So I told him he had better tell my parents.

This disconcerted him, for he had been a parson long enough to know that complaints to parents about their children were not always gratefully received. I was bold enough to say that maybe he had better do as he threatened and speak to Mr. Bowyer. This was good argument, for our minister was not a man to like advice from Amasa Dempster, and though he would have given me the rough side of his tongue, he would first have eaten the evangelistic Baptist parson without salt. Poor Dempster! He had lost the fight, so he took refuge in banishing me. I was never to set foot in his house again, he said, nor speak to any of his family, nor dare to come near his son. He would pray for me, he concluded.

I left the church in a strange state of mind, for a Deptford boy, though I learned later in life that it was common enough. I did not feel I had done wrong, though I had been a fool to forget how dead set Baptists were against cards. As for the stories about saints, they were tales of wonders, like *Arabian Nights,* and when the Reverend Andrew Bowyer bade all us Presbyterians to prepare ourselves for the Marriage Feast of the Lamb, it seemed to me that *Arabian Nights* and the *Bible* were getting pretty close—and I did not mean this in any scoffing sense. I was most hurt that Dempster had dragged down my conjuring to mere cheating and gambling; it had seemed to me to be a splendid extension of life, a creation of a world of wonder, that hurt nobody. All that dim but glittering vision I had formed of Paris, with Robert-Houdin doing marvels to delight grand people, had been dragged down by this Deptford parson, who knew nothing of such things and just hated whatever did not belong to life at the $550-a-year level. I wanted a better life than that. But I had been worsted by moral bullying, by Dempster's conviction that he was right and I was wrong, and that this gave him an authority over me based on feeling rather than reason: it was my first encounter with the emotional power of popular morality.

In my bitterness I ill-wished Amasa Dempster. This was a terrible thing to do, and I knew it. In my parents' view of life, superstition was trash for ignorant people, but they had a few reservations, and one was that it was very unlucky to ill-wish anybody. The evil wish would surely rebound upon the wisher. But I ill-wished Dempster; I begged Somebody—some God who understood me—that he should be made very sorry for the way he had talked to me.

He said nothing to my parents, nor yet to Mr. Bowyer. I interpreted his silence as weakness, and probably that was an important element in it. I saw him now, a few times each week, at a distance, and it seemed to me that the burdens of his life were bearing him down. He did not stoop, but he looked gaunter and crazier. Paul I saw only once, and he turned away from me and ran toward his home, crying; I was terribly sorry for him. But Mrs. Dempster I saw often, for she had intensified her roaming and would spend a whole morning wandering from house to house—"traipsing" was the word many of the women now used—offering bunches of wilted rhubarb, or some rank lettuce, or other stuff from their garden, which was so ill tended without me that nothing did well in it. But she wanted to give things away and was hurt when neighbours refused these profferings. Her face wore a sweet but woefully un-Deptford expression; it was too clear that she did not know where she was going next, and sometimes she would visit one house three times in a morning, to the annoyance of a busy woman who was washing or getting a meal for a husband and sons.

When I think of my mother now, I try to remember her as she

was in her dealings with Mrs. Dempster. A poor actress, she nevertheless feigned pleasure over the things that were given and always insisted that something be taken in return, usually something big and lasting. She always remembered what Mrs. Dempster had brought and told her how good it had been, though usually it was only fit to be thrown away.

"The poor soul dearly loves to give," she said to my father, "and it would be wicked to deny her. The pity is that more people with more to give don't feel the same way."

I avoided direct meetings with Mrs. Dempster, for she would say, "Dunstable Ramsay, you've almost grown to be a man. Why don't you come to see us any more? Paul misses you; he tells me so."

She had forgotten, or perhaps she never knew, that her husband had warned me away. I never saw her without a pang of guilt and concern about her. But for her husband I had no pity.

10

Mrs. Dempster's wanderings came to an end on Friday, the 24th of October, 1913. It was almost ten o'clock at night and I was reading by the stove, as was my father; my mother sewed—something for the Mission Circle bazaar—and Willie was at a practice of a Youth Band a local enthusiast had organized; Willie played the cornet and had his eye on the first flute, one Ada Blake. When the knock came at the door my father went, and after some quiet muttering asked the callers to come in while he put on his boots. They were Jim Warren, who was our part-time village policeman, and George and Garnet Harper, a couple of practical jokers who on this occasion looked unwontedly solemn.

"Mary Dempster's disappeared," my father explained. "Jim's organizing a hunt."

"Yep, been gone since after supper," said the policeman. "Reverend come home at nine and she was gone. Nowheres round the town, and now we're goin' to search the pit. If she's not there we'll have to drag the river."

"You'd better go along with your father," said my mother to

me. "I'll get right over to Dempsters' and keep an eye on Paul, and be ready when you bring her home."

Much was implied in that speech. In the instant my mother had acknowledged me as a man, fit to go on serious business. She had shown also that she knew that I was as concerned about the Dempsters, perhaps, as herself; there had been no questions about why I had not been going there to do the chores for the past few months. I am sure my parents knew Amasa Dempster had warned me away and had assumed that it was part of the crazy pride and self-sufficiency that had been growing on him. But if Mrs. Dempster was lost at night, all daylight considerations must be set aside. There was a good deal of the pioneer left in people in those days, and they knew what was serious.

I darted off to get the flashlight; my father had recently bought a car—rather a daring thing in Deptford at that time—and a large flashlight was kept in the tool-kit on the runningboard, in case we should be benighted with a flat tire.

We made for the pit, where ten or twelve men were already assembled. I was surprised to see Mr. Mahaffey, our magistrate, among them. He and the policeman were our law, and his presence meant grave public concern.

This gravel pit was of unusual importance to our village because it completely blocked any normal extension of streets or houses on our western side; thus it was a source of indignation to our village council. However, it belonged to the railway company, which valued it as a source of the gravel they needed for keeping their roadbed in order, and which they excavated and hauled considerable distances up and down the track. How big it was I do not accurately know, but it was big, and prejudice made it seem bigger. It was not worked consistently and so was often undisturbed for a year or more at a time; in it there were pools, caused by seepage from the river, which it bordered, and a lot of scrub growth, sumac, sallow, Manitoba maple, and such unprofitable things, as well as goldenrod and kindred trashy weeds.

Mothers hated it because sometimes little children strayed into it and were hurt, and big children sneaked into it and met the like of Mabel Heighington. But most of all it was disliked because it was a refuge for the tramps who rode the rods of the railway. Some of these were husky young fellows; others were old men, or men who seemed old, in ragged greatcoats belted with a piece of rope or a strap, wearing hats of terrible dilapidation, and giving off a stench of feet, sweat, faeces, and urine that would have staggered a goat. They were mighty drinkers of flavouring extracts and liniments that had a heavy alcohol base. All of them were likely to appear at a back door and ask for food. In their eyes was the dazed, stunned look of people who live too much in the open air without eating properly. They were generally given food and generally feared as lawless men.

In later life I have been sometimes praised, sometimes mocked, for my way of pointing out the mythical elements that seem to me to underlie our apparently ordinary lives. Certainly that cast of mind had some of its origin in our pit, which had much the character of a Protestant Hell. I was probably the most entranced listener to a sermon the Reverend Andrew Bowyer preached about Gehenna, the hateful valley outside the walls of Jerusalem, where outcasts lived, and where their flickering fires, seen from the city walls, may have given rise to the idea of a hell of perpetual burning. He liked to make his hearers jump, now and then, and he said that our gravel pit was much the same sort of place as Gehenna. My elders thought this far-fetched, but I saw no reason then why hell should not have, so to speak, visible branch establishments throughout the earth, and I have visited quite a few of them since.

Under the direction of Jim Warren and Mr. Mahaffey it was agreed that fifteen of us would scramble down into the pit and form a line, leaving twenty or thirty feet between each man, and advance from end to end. Anybody who found a clue was to give a shout. As we searched there was quite a lot of sound, for I think most of the men wanted any tramps to know we were coming and get out of the way; nobody liked the idea of coming on a tramps' bivouac—they were called "jungles," which made them seem more terrible—unexpectedly. We had seen only two fires, at the far end of the pit, but there could be quite a group of tramps without a fire.

My father was thirty feet on my left, and a big fellow named Ed Hainey on my right, as I walked through the pit. In spite of the nearness of the men it was lonely work, and though there was a moon it was waning and the light was poor. I was afraid and did not know what I feared, which is the worst kind of fear. We might have gone a quarter of a mile when I came to a clump of sallow. I was about to skirt it when I heard a stirring inside it. I made a sound—I am sure it was not a yell—that brought my father beside me in an instant. He shot the beam of his flashlight into the scrub, and in that bleak, flat light we saw a tramp and a woman in the act of copulation. The tramp rolled over and gaped at us in terror; the woman was Mrs. Dempster.

It was Hainey who gave a shout, and in no time all the men were with us, and Jim Warren was pointing a pistol at the tramp, ordering him to put his hands up. He repeated the words two or three times, and then Mrs. Dempster spoke.

"You'll have to speak very loudly to him, Mr. Warren," she said, "he's hard of hearing."

I don't think any of us knew where to look when she spoke, pulling her skirts down but remaining on the ground. It was at that moment that the Reverend Amasa Dempster joined us; I had not noticed him when the hunt began, though he must have been there. He behaved with great dignity, leaning forward to help his wife rise with the same sort of protective love I had seen in him the night Paul was born. But he was not able to keep back his question.

"Mary, what made you do it?"

She looked him honestly in the face and gave the answer that became famous in Deptford: "He was very civil, 'Masa. And he wanted it so badly."

He put her arm under his and set out for home, just as if they were going for a walk. Under Mr. Mahaffey's direction, Jim Warren took the tramp off to the lock-up. The rest of us dispersed without a word.

11

Dempster visited Mr. Mahaffey early on Saturday and said that he would lay no charge and take part in no trial, so the magistrate took council with my father and a few other wise heads and told

Jim Warren to get the tramp off the village bounds, with a warning never to be seen there again.

The real trial would come on Sunday, and everybody knew it. The buzzing and humming were intense all day Saturday, and at church on Sunday everybody who was not a Baptist was aching to know what would happen at the Baptist service. The Reverend Andrew Bowyer prayed for "all who were distressed in spirit, and especially for a family known to us all who were in sore travail," and something of a similar intention was said in the Anglican and Methodist churches. Only Father Regan at the Catholic church came out flat-footed and said from his pulpit that the gravel pit was a disgrace and a danger and that the railway had its nerve not to clean it up or close it up. But when we heard about that, everybody knew it was beside the point. Mrs. Dempster had given her consent. That was the point. Supposing she was a little off her head, how insane had a woman to be before it came to that? Dr. McCausland, appealed to on the steps of our church by some seekers after truth, said that such conduct indicated a degeneration of the brain, which was probably progressive.

We soon knew what the Baptist parson said that morning: he went into his pulpit, prayed silently for a short time, and then told his congregation that the time had come for him to resign his charge, as he had other duties that were incapable of being combined with it. He asked for their prayers, and went into his study. A prominent member of the congregation, a baker, took charge and turned the service into a meeting; the baker and a few other men were for asking the parson to wait a while, but the majority was against them, especially the women. Not that any of the women spoke; they had done their speaking before church, and their husbands knew the price of peace. So at last the baker and one or two others had to go into the study and tell Amasa Dempster that his resignation was accepted. He left the church without any prospects, a crazy and disgraced wife, a delicate child, and six dollars in cash. There were several men who wanted to do something for him, but the opinion of their wives made it impossible.

There was a terrible quarrel in our household—the more terrible because I had never heard my parents disagree when they knew that Willie and I could hear them; what I heard by way of the stovepipe sometimes amounted to disagreement but never to a quarrel. My father accused my mother of wanting charity; she replied that as the mother of two boys she had standards of decency to defend. That was the meat of the quarrel, but before it had gone very far it reached a point where she said that if he was going to stand up for filthy behaviour and adultery he was a long way from the man she had married, and he was saying that he had never known she had a cruel streak. (I could have told him something about that.) This battle went on at Sunday dinner and drove Willie, who was the least demonstrative of fellows, to throw down his napkin and exclaim, "Oh, for the love of the crows!" and leave the table. I dared not follow, and as my parents' wrath grew I was numbed with misery.

Of course my mother won. If my father had not given in he would have had to live with outraged female virtue for—perhaps the rest of his life. As things were, I do not believe that she ever gave up a suspicion that he was not as firm in his moral integrity as she had once believed. Mrs. Dempster had transgressed in a realm where there could be no shades of right and wrong. And the reason she had offered for doing so—!

That was what stuck in the craws of all the good women of Deptford: Mrs. Dempster had not been raped, as a decent woman would have been—no, she had yielded because a man wanted her. The subject was not one that could be freely discussed even among intimates, but it was understood without saying that if women began to yield for such reasons as that, marriage and society would not last long. Any man who spoke up for Mary Dempster probably believed in Free Love. Certainly he associated sex with pleasure, and that put him in a class with filthy thinkers like Cece Athelstan.

Cecil Athelstan—always known as Cece—was the black sheep of our ruling family. He was a fat, swag-bellied boozer who sat in a chair on the sidewalk outside the Tecumseh House bar when the weather was fine, and on the same chair inside the bar when it was not. Once a month, when he got his cheque, he went for a night or two to Detroit, across the border, and, according to his own account, he was the life and soul of the bawdy houses there. Foul-mouthed bum though he was, he had enough superiority of experience and native wit to hold a small group of loafers in awe, and his remarks, sometimes amusing, were widely quoted, even by people who disapproved of him.

Mrs. Dempster's answer was a gift to a man like Cece. "Hey!" he would shout across the street to one of his cronies, "you feeling civil today? I feel so God-damned civil I got to get to Detroit right away—or maybe just up to You Know Who's!" Or as some respectable woman passed on the other side of the street from the hotel he would sing out, just loud enough to be heard, "I wa-a-ant it! Hey, Cora, I want it so-o-o!" The strange thing was that the behaviour of this licensed fool made the enormity of Mrs. Dempster's words greater, but did not lower the town's esteem of Cece Athelstan—probably because it could go no lower.

At school there were several boys who pestered me for descriptions, with anatomical detail, of what I had seen in the pit. I had no trouble silencing them, but of course Cece and his gang lay beyond my power. It was Cece, with some of his crowd, and the Harper boys (who ought to have known better) who organized the shivaree when the Dempsters moved. Amasa Dempster got out of the Baptist parsonage on the Tuesday after his resignation and took his wife and son to a cottage on the road to the school. The parsonage had been furnished, so they had little enough to move, but a few people who could not bear to think of them in destitution mustered furniture for the new place, without letting it be too clearly known who had done it. (I know my father put up some of the money for this project, very much on the quiet.)

At midnight a gang with blackened faces beat pans and tooted horns outside the cottage for half an hour, and somebody threw a lighted broom on the roof, but it was a damp night and no harm was done. Cece's voice was heard half over the town, shouting, "Come on out, Mary! We want it!" I wish I could record that Amasa Dempster came out and faced them, but he did not.

I never saw a man change so much in so short a time. He was gaunt and lonely before, but there had been fire in his eyes; in two weeks he was like a scarecrow. He had a job; George Alcott, who owned the sawmill, offered Dempster a place as a bookkeeper and timekeeper at twelve dollars a week, which was not a bad wage for the work and in fact made the Dempsters slightly better off than they had been, for there was no church tithe expected out of it. But it was the comedown, the disgrace, that broke Dempster. He had been a parson, which was the work dearest to his heart; now he was nothing in his own eyes, and clearly he feared the worst for his wife.

What passed between them nobody knew, but she was not seen in the village and very rarely in the little yard outside the cottage. There was a rumour that he kept her tied to a long rope inside the house, so that she could move freely through it but not get out. On Sunday mornings, her arm in his, she went to the Baptist church, and they sat in a back pew, never speaking to anyone as they came and went. She began to look very strange indeed, and if she was not mad before, people said, she was mad now.

I knew better. After a few weeks during which I was miserable because of the village talk, I sneaked over there one day and peeped in a window. She was sitting on a chair by a table, staring at nothing, but when I tapped on the pane she looked at me and smiled in recognition. In an instant I was inside, and after a few minutes of uneasiness we were talking eagerly. She was a little strange because she had been so lonely, but she made good sense, and I had enough gumption to keep on general topics. I soon found out that she knew nothing of what was going on in the world because the Dempsters took no newspaper.

After that I went there two or three times a week, with a daily paper, or a copy of our own *Banner,* and I read things to her that I knew would interest her, and kept her up on the gossip of the town. Often Paul was with us, because he never played with other children, and I did what I could for him. It was well understood that these visits were not to be mentioned to Dempster, for I was sure he still thought me a bad influence.

I began this deceitful line of conduct—for my mother would have been furious, and I thought anybody who had seen me going there would have spread the word—hoping I could do something for Mrs. Dempster, but it was not long before I found that she was doing much for me. I do not know how to express it, but she was a wise woman, and though she was only ten years older than myself, and thus about twenty-six at this time, she seemed to me to have a breadth of outlook and a clarity of vision that were strange and wonderful; I cannot remember examples that satisfactorily explain what I mean, and at the time I did not know in what her special quality lay, but I recognize now that it was her lack of fear, of apprehension, of assumption that whatever happened was inevitably going to lead to some worse state of affairs, that astonished and enriched me. She had not been like this when first I knew her, after Paul's birth, but I see now that she had been tending in this direction. When she had seemed to be laughing at things her husband took very seriously, she had been laughing at the disproportion of his seriousness, and of course in Deptford it was very easy to understand such laughter as the uncomprehending gigglings of a fool.

It would be false to suggest that there was anything philosophical in her attitude. Rather, it was religious, and it was impossible to talk to her for long without being aware that she was wholly religious. I do not say "deeply religious" because that was what people said about her husband, and apparently they meant that he imposed religion as he understood it on everything he knew or encountered. But she, tied up in a rotten little house without a friend except me, seemed to live in a world of trust that had nothing of the stricken, lifeless, unreal quality of religion about it. She knew she was in disgrace with the world, but did not feel disgraced; she knew she was jeered at, but felt no humiliation. She lived by a light that arose from within; I could not comprehend it, except that it seemed to be somewhat akin to the splendours I found in books, though not in any way bookish. It was as though she were an exile from a world that saw things her way, and though she was sorry Deptford did not understand her she was not resentful. When you got past her shyness she had quite positive opinions, but the queerest thing about her was that she had no fear.

This was the best of Mary Dempster. Of the disorder and discomfort of that cottage I shall not speak, and though little Paul was loved and cherished by his mother he was in his appearance a pitifully neglected child. So perhaps she was crazy, in part, but it was only in part; the best side of her brought comfort and assurance into my life, which badly needed it. I got so that I did not notice the rope she wore (it was actually a harness that went around her waist and shoulders, with the horse-smelling hemp rope knotted to a ring on one side, so that she could lie down if she wanted to), or the raggedness of her clothes, or the occasional spells when she was not wholly rational. I regarded her as my greatest friend, and the secret league between us as the tap-root that fed my life.

Close as we grew, however, there was never any moment when I could have asked her about the tramp. I was trying to forget the spectacle, so horrible in my visions, of what I had seen when first I happened on them—those bare buttocks and four legs so strangely opposed. But I could never forget. It was my first encounter with a particular kind of reality, which my religion, my upbringing, and the callowly romantic cast of my mind had declared obscene. Therefore there was an aspect of Mary Dempster which was outside my ken; and, being young and unwilling to recognize that there was anything I did not, or could not know, I decided that this unknown aspect must be called madness.

12

The year that followed was a busy one for me, and, except for my visits to Mrs. Dempster, lonely. My school friends accused me of being a know-all, and with characteristic perversity I liked the description. By searching the dictionary I discovered that a know-all was called, among people who appreciated knowledge and culture, a polymath, and I set to work to become a polymath with the same enthusiasm that I had once laboured to be a conjurer. It was much easier work; I simply read the encyclopaedia in our village library. It was a *Chambers'*, the 1888 edition, and I was not such a fool as to think I could read it through; I read the articles that appealed to me, and when I found something particularly juicy I read everything around it that I could find. I beavered away at that encyclopaedia with a tenacity that I wish I possessed now, and if I did not become a complete polymath I certainly gained enough information to be a nuisance to everybody who knew me.

I also came to know my father much better, for after the search for Mrs. Dempster in the pit he put himself out to make a friend of me. He was an intelligent man and well educated in an old-fashioned way; he had gone to Dumfries Academy as a boy, and what he knew he could marshal with a precision I have often envied; it was he and he alone who made the study of Latin anything but a penance to me, for he insisted that without Latin nobody could write clear English.

Sometimes on our Sunday walks along the railroad track we were joined by Sam West, an electrician with a mind above the limitations of his work; as a boy he had been kept hard at the *Bible,* and not only could he quote it freely, but there was not a contradiction or an absurdity in it that he did not know and relish. His detestation of religion and churches was absolute, and he scolded about them in language that owed all its bite to the *Old Testament*. He was unfailingly upright in all his dealings, to show the slaves of priestcraft and superstition that morality has nothing to do with religion, and he was an occasional attendant at all our local churches, in order to wrestle mentally with the sermon and confute it. His imitations of the parsons were finely observed, and he was very good as the Reverend Andrew Bowyer: "O Lord, take Thou a live coal from off Thine altar and touch our lips," he would shout, in a caricature of our minister's fine Edinburgh accent; then, with a howl of laughter, "Wouldn't he be surprised if his prayer was answered!"

If he hoped to make an atheist of me, this was where he went wrong; I knew a metaphor when I heard one, and I liked metaphor better than reason. I have known many atheists since Sam, and they all fall down on metaphor.

At school I was a nuisance, for my father was now Chairman of our Continuation School Board, and I affected airs of near-equality with the teacher that must have galled her; I wanted to argue about everything, expand everything, and generally turn every class into a Socratic powwow instead of getting on with the curriculum. Probably I made her nervous, as a pupil full of green, fermenting information is so well able to do. I have dealt with innumerable variations of my young self in classrooms since then, and I have mentally apologized for my tiresomeness.

My contemporaries were growing up too. Leola Cruikshank was now a village beauty, and well understood to be Percy Boyd Staunton's girl. Spider Webb still thought me wonderful, and I graciously permitted her to worship me from a distance. Milo Papple had found that a gift for breaking wind was not in itself enough for social success, and he learned a few things from the travelling salesmen who were shaved by his father that gave him quite a new status. It was an era when parodies of popular songs were thought very funny, and when conversation flagged he would burst into:

> I had a dewlap,
> A big flabby dewlap,
> And you had
> A red, red nose.

Or perhaps:

> I dream of Jeannie
> With the light brown hair,
> Drunk in the privy
> In her underwear.

These fragments were always very brief, and he counted on his hearers bursting into uncontrollable laughter before they were finished. Nuisance that I was, I used to urge him to continue, for which he very properly hated me. He also had a few pleasantries about smelly feet, which went well at parties. I refused to laugh at them, for I was jealous of anybody who was funnier than I. The trouble was that my jokes tended to be so complicated that nobody laughed but Spider Webb, who obviously did not understand them.

The great event of the spring was the revelation that Percy Boyd Staunton and Mabel Heighington had been surprised in the sexual act by Mabel's mother, who had tracked them to Dr. Staunton's barn and pounced. Mrs. Heighington was a small, dirty, hysterical woman whose own chastity was seriously flawed; she had been a grass-widow for several years. What she said to Percy's father, whom she insisted on seeing just as he got nicely off into his after-dinner nap one day, was so often repeated by herself on the streets that I heard it more than once. If he thought because she was a poor widow her only daughter could be trampled under foot by a rich man's son and then flung aside, by Jesus she would show him different. She had her feelings, like anybody else. Was she to go to

Mr. Mahaffey right then and get the law to work, or was he going to ask her to sit down and talk turkey?

What turkey amounted to remained a mystery. Some said fifty dollars, and others said a hundred. Mrs. Heighington never revealed the precise sum. There were those who said that twenty-five cents would have been a sufficient price for Mabel's virtue, such as it was; she consistently met the brakeman of a freight train that lay on a siding near the gravel pit for half an hour every Friday, and he enjoyed her favours on some sacks in a freight car; she had also had to do with a couple of farmhands who worked over near the Indian Reservation. But Dr. Staunton had money—reputedly lots of money—for he had built up substantial land holdings over the years and was doing very well growing tobacco and sugar-beet, which was just coming into its own as an important crop. The doctoring was a second string with him, and he kept it up chiefly for the prestige it carried. Still, he was a doctor, and when Mrs. Heighington told him that if there was a baby she would expect him to do something about it, she struck a telling blow.

For our village, this amounted to scandal in high society. Mrs. Staunton was elaborately pitied by some of the women; others blamed her for letting Percy have his own way too much. Some of the men thought Percy a young rip, but the Cece Athelstan crowd acclaimed him as one of themselves. Ben Cruikshank, a tough little carpenter, stopped Percy on the street and told him if he ever came near Leola again he would cripple him; Leola wore a stricken face for days, and it was known that she was pining for Percy and forgave him in spite of everything, which made me cynical about women. Some of our more profound moralists harked back to the incident of Mrs. Dempster and said that if a parson's wife behaved like that, it was no wonder young ones picked up notions. Dr. Staunton kept his own counsel, but it became known that he had decided to send Percy away to school, where he would not have his mother to baby him. And that, Headmaster, is how Percy came to be at Colborne College, of which in time he became a distinguished Old Boy, and Chairman of the Board of Governors.

13

The autumn of 1914 was remarkable in most places for the outbreak of the war, but in Deptford my brother Willie's illness ran it close as a subject of interest.

Willie had been ill at intervals for four years. His trouble began with an accident in the *Banner* plant when he had attempted to take some rollers from the big press—the one used for printing the newspaper—without help. Jumper Saul was absent, pitching for the local baseball team. The rollers were not extremely heavy but they were awkward, and one of them fell on Willie and knocked him down. At first it seemed that nothing would come of it except a large bruise on his back, but as time wore on Willie began to have spells of illness marked by severe internal pain. Dr. McCausland could not do much for him; X-ray was unheard of in our part of the world, and the kind of exploratory operations that are so common now were virtually unknown. My parents took Willie to Pittstown a few times to see a chiropractor, but the treatments hurt Willie so much that the chiropractor refused to continue them. Until the autumn of 1914, however, Willie had come round after a few days in bed, with a light diet and a quantity of Sexton Blake stories to help him along.

This time he was really very ill—so ill that he had periods of delirium. His most dramatic symptom, however, spoken of around the village in hushed tones, was a stubborn retention of urine that added greatly to his distress. Dr. McCausland sent to Toronto for a specialist—an alarming move in our village—and the specialist had very little to suggest except that immersions in warm water at four-hour intervals might help; he did not advise an operation yet, for at that time the removal of a kidney was an extremely grave matter.

As soon as the news of what the specialist had said got around we had a group of volunteers to assist with the immersions. These were bound to be troublesome, for we had no bathtub except a portable one, which could be put by the bed, and to which all the warm water had to be carried in pails. I have already said that our village had a kind heart, and practical help of this kind was what it understood best; six immersions a day were nothing, in the light of their desire to lend a hand. Even the new Presbyterian minister, the Reverend Donald Phelps (come to replace the Reverend Andrew Bowyer, retired in the spring of 1914), was a volunteer, comparative stranger though he was; more astonishing, Cece Athelstan was one of the group, and was cold sober every time he turned up. Getting Willie through this bad time became a public cause.

The baths certainly seemed to make Willie a little easier, though the swelling caused by the retention of urine grew worse. He had been in bed for more than two weeks when the Saturday of our Fall Fair came and brought special problems with it. My father had to attend; not only had he to write it up for the *Banner*, but as Chairman of our Continuation School Board he had to judge two or three contests. My mother was expected to attend, and wanted to attend, because the Ladies' Aid of our church was offering a Fowl Supper, and she was a noted organizer and pusher of fancy victuals. The men who would give Willie his six-o'clock plunge bath would arrive in plenty of time, but who was to stay with him during the afternoon? I was happy to do so; I would go to the Fair after supper, because it always seemed particularly gay and romantic as darkness fell.

From two until three I sat in Willie's room, reading, and between three and half-past I did what I could for Willie while he died. What I could do was little enough. He became restless and hot, so I put a cold towel on his head. He began to twist and moan, so I held his hands and said what I could think of that might encourage him. He ceased to hear me, and his twisting became jerking and convulsion. He cried out five or six times—not screaming, but spasmodic cries—and in a very few minutes became extremely cold. I wanted to call the doctor, but I dared not leave Willie. I put my ear to his heart: nothing. I tried to find his pulse: nothing. Certainly he was not breathing, for I hurried to fetch my mother's hand mirror and hold it over his mouth: it did not cloud. I opened one eye: it was rolled upward in his head. It came upon me that he was dead.

It is very easy to say now what I should have done. I can only record what I did do. From the catastrophe of realizing that Willie was dead—it was the psychological equivalent of a house falling inward upon itself, and I can still recall the feeling—I passed quickly into strong revolt. Willie could not be dead. It must not be. I would not have it. And, without giving a thought to calling the doctor (whom I had never really liked, though it was the family custom to respect him), I set out on the run to fetch Mrs. Dempster.

Why? I don't know why. It was not a matter of reason—not a decision at all. But I can remember running through the hot autumn afternoon, and I can remember hearing the faint music of the merry-go-round as I ran. Nothing was very far away in our village, and I was at the Dempsters' cottage in not much more than three minutes. Locked. Of course. Paul's father would have taken him to the Fair. I was through the living-room window, cutting Mrs. Dempster's rope, telling her what I wanted, and dragging her back through the window with me, in a muddle of action that I cannot clearly remember at all. I suppose we would have looked an odd pair, if there had been anyone to see us, running through the streets hand in hand, and I do remember that she hoisted up her skirts to run, which was a girlish thing no grown woman would ever have done if she had not caught the infection of my emotion.

What I do remember was getting back to Willie's room, which was my parents' room, given up to the sick boy because it was the most comfortable, and finding him just as I had left him, white and cold and stiff. Mrs. Dempster looked at him solemnly but not sadly, then she knelt by the bed and took his hands in hers and prayed. I had no way of knowing how long she prayed, but it was less than ten minutes. I could not pray and did not kneel. I gaped—and hoped.

After a while she raised her head and called him. "Willie," said she in a low, infinitely kind, and indeed almost in a cheerful tone. Again, "Willie." I hoped till I ached. She shook his hands gently, as if rousing a sleeper. "Willie."

Willie sighed and moved his legs a little. I fainted.

When I came round, Mrs. Dempster was sitting on Willie's bed, talking quietly and cheerfully to him, and he was replying, weakly but eagerly. I dashed around, fetched a towel to bathe his face, the orange and albumen drink he was allowed in very small quantities, a fan to create a better current of air—everything there was that might help and give expression to my terrible joy. Quite soon Willie fell asleep, and Mrs. Dempster and I talked in whispers. She was deeply pleased but, as I now remember it, did not seem particularly surprised by what had happened. I know I babbled like a fool.

The passing of time that afternoon was all awry, for it did not seem long to me before the men came to get Willie's six-o'clock plunge ready, so it must have been half-past five. They were astonished to find her there, but sometimes extraordinary situations impose their own tactful good manners, and nobody said anything to emphasize their first amazement. Willie insisted that she stand by him while he was being plunged, and she helped in the difficult business of drying him off, for he was tender all around his body. Therefore I suppose it must have been close to half-past six when my mother and father arrived home, and with them Amasa Dempster. I don't know what sort of scene I expected; something on Biblical lines would have appeared appropriate to me. But instead Dempster took his wife's arm in his, as I had seen him do it so often, and led her away. As she went she paused for an instant to blow a kiss to Willie. It was the first time I had ever seen anybody do such a thing, and I thought it a gesture of great beauty; to Willie's everlasting credit, he blew a kiss back again, and I have never seen my mother's face blacker than at that moment.

When the Dempsters were gone, and the men had been thanked, and offered food, which they refused (this was ritual, for only the night plungers, at two and six in the morning, thought it right to accept coffee and sandwiches), there was a scene downstairs which was as bad, though not as prolonged, as anything I later experienced in the war.

What did I mean by failing to send for Dr. McCausland and my parents at the first sign of danger? What under Heaven had possessed me to turn to that woman, who was an insane degenerate, and bring her, not only into our house but to the very bedside of a boy who was dangerously ill? Did all this cynical nonsense I had been talking, and the superior airs I had been assuming, mean that I too was going off my head? How did I come to be so thick with Mary Dempster in her present condition? If this was what all my reading led to, it was high time I was put to a job that would straighten the kinks out of me.

Most of this was my mother, and she performed variations on

these themes until I was heartsick with hearing them. I know now that a lot of her anger arose from self-reproach because she had been absent, making a great figure of herself in the Ladies' Aid, when duty should have kept her at Willie's bedside. But she certainly took it out of me, and so, to a lesser degree, did my father, who felt himself bound to back her up but who plainly did not like it.

This would have gone on until we all dropped with exhaustion, I suppose, if Dr. McCausland had not arrived; he had been in the country and had just returned. He brought his own sort of atmosphere, which was cold and chilly and smelled of disinfectant, and took a good look at Willie. Then he questioned me. He catechized me thoroughly about what symptoms Willie had shown, and how he had behaved before he died. Because I insisted that Willie had indeed died. No pulse; no breathing.

"But clenched hands?" said Dr. McCausland. Yes, said I, but did that mean that Willie could not have been dead? "Obviously he was not dead," said the doctor; "if he had been dead I would not have been talking to him a few minutes ago. I think you may safely leave it to me to say when people are dead, Dunny," he continued, with what I am sure he meant as a kindly smile. It had been a strong convulsion, he told my parents; the tight clenching of the hands was a part of it, and an unskilled person could not be expected to detect very faint breathing, or heartbeat either. He was all reason, all reassurance, and the next day he came early and did an operation on Willie called "tapping"; he dug a hollow needle into his side and drew off an astonishing quantity of bloody urine. In a week Willie was up and about; in four months he had somehow lied his way into the Canadian Army; in 1916 he was one of those who disappeared forever in the mud at St. Eloi.

I wonder if his hands were clenched after death? Later on I saw more men than I could count die, myself, and a surprising number of the corpses I stumbled over, or cleared out of the way, had clenched hands, though I never took the trouble to write to Dr. McCausland and tell him so.

For me, Willie's recall from death is, and will always be, Mrs. Dempster's second miracle.

14

The weeks following were painful and disillusioning. Among my friends I dropped from the position of polymath to that of a credulous ass who thought that a dangerous lunatic could raise the dead. I should explain that Mrs. Dempster was now thought to be dangerous, not because of any violence on her part, but because fearful people were frightened that if she were to wander away again some new sexual scandal would come of it; I think they really believed that she would corrupt some innocent youth or bewitch some faithful husband by the unreason of her lust. It was widely accepted that, even if she could not help it, she was in the grip of unappeasable and indiscriminate desire. Inevitably it came out that I had been visiting her on the sly, and there was a lot of dirty joking about that, but the best joke of all was that I thought she had brought my brother back to life.

The older people took the matter more seriously. Some thought that my known habit of reading a great deal had unseated my reason, and perhaps that dreaded disease "brain fever," supposed to attack students, was not far off. One or two friends suggested to my father that immediate removal from school, and a year or two of hard work on a farm, might cure me. Dr. McCausland found a chance to have what he called "a word" with me, the gist of which was that I might become queer if I did not attempt to balance my theoretical knowledge with the kind of common sense that could be learned from—well, for instance, from himself. He hinted that I might become like Elbert Hubbard if I continued in my present course. Elbert Hubbard was a notoriously queer American who thought that work could be a pleasure.

Our new minister, the Reverend Donald Phelps, took me on and advised me that it was blasphemous to think that anyone—even someone of unimpeachable character—could restore the dead to life. The age of miracles was past, said he, and I got the impression that he was heartily glad of it. I liked him; he meant it kindly, which McCausland certainly did not.

My father talked to me several times in a way that gave me some insight into his own character, for though he was a man of unusual courage as an editor, he was a peace-at-any-pricer at home. I would do best, he thought, to keep my own counsel and not insist on things my mother could not tolerate.

I might even have done so—if she had been content to let the subject drop. But she was so anxious to root out of my mind any fragment of belief in what I had seen, and to exact from me promises that I would never see Mrs. Dempster again and furthermore would accept the village's opinion of her, that she kept alluding to it darkly, or bringing it out for full discussion, usually at meals. It was clear that she now regarded a hint of tenderness toward Mrs. Dempster as disloyalty to herself, and as loyalty was the only kind of love she could bring herself to ask for, she was most passionate when she thought she was being most reasonable. I said very little during these scenes, and she quite rightly interpreted my silence as a refusal to change my mind.

She did not know how much I loved her, and how miserable it made me to defy her, but what was I to do? Deep inside myself I knew that to yield, and promise what she wanted, would be the end of anything that was any good in me; I was not her husband, who could keep his peace in the face of her furious rectitude; I was her son, with a full share of her own Highland temper and granite determination.

One day, after a particularly wretched supper, she concluded by demanding that I make a choice between her and "that woman." I made a third choice. I had enough money for a railway ticket, and the next day I skipped school, went to the county town, and enlisted.

This changed matters considerably. I was nearly two years under age, but I was tall and strong and a good liar, and I had no difficulty in being accepted. She wanted to go to the authorities and get me out, but my father put his foot down there. He said he would not permit me to be disgraced by having my mother drag me out of the Army. So now she was torn between a fear that I would certainly be shot dead the day after I began training, and a conviction that there was something even darker between Mrs. Dempster and me than she had permitted herself to think.

As for my father, he was disgusted with me. He had a poor opinion of soldiers, and as he had run some risks by being pro-Boer in 1901 he had serious doubts about the justice of any war.

Feeling about the war in our village was romantic, because it touched us so little, but my father and Mr. Mahaffey were better aware of what went into the making of that war and could not share the popular feeling. He urged me to reveal my true age and withdraw, but I was pig-headed and spread the news of what I had done as fast as I could.

What my elders thought I did not know or care, but I regained some of the position I had lost among my contemporaries. I loafed at school, as became a man waiting his call to more serious things. My friends seemed to think I might disappear at any hour, and whenever I met Milo Papple, which was at least once a day, he would seize my hand and declaim passionately:

Say cuspidor,
But not spittoon—

which was the barbershop version of a song of the day that began:

Say *au revoir,*
But not good-bye.

Girls took a new view of me, and to my delighted surprise Leola Cruikshank made it clear that she was mine on loan, so to speak. She still pined for Percy Boyd Staunton, but he was away at school and was a bad and irregular letter-writer, so Leola thought that a modest romance with a hero in embryo could do no harm—might even be a patriotic duty.

She was a delightful girl, pretty, full of sentimental nonsense, and clean about her person—she always smelled of fresh ironing. I saw a great deal of her, persuaded her that a few kisses did not really mean disloyalty to Percy, and paraded her up and down our main street on Saturday nights, wearing my best suit.

I had kept away from Mrs. Dempster, partly from obedience and fear, and partly because I could not bear to face her when so many hateful opinions about her were ringing in my ears. I knew, however, that I could not go off to war without saying good-bye, and one afternoon, with great stealth, I reached her cottage and climbed through the window for the last time. She spoke to me as if I had visited her as often as usual, and did not seem greatly surprised by the news that I had joined the Army. We had talked a great deal about the war when first it broke out, and she had laughed heartily at the news that two Deptford women who liked to dabble in spiritualism went several times a week to the cemetery to read the latest news from France to their dead mother, sitting on her grave, picnic-style. When I had to leave she kissed me on both cheeks—a thing she had never done before—and said, "There's just one thing to remember; whatever happens, it does no good to be afraid." So I promised not to be afraid, and may even have been fool enough to think I could keep my promise.

In time my call came. I climbed on the train, proud of my pass to the camp, and waved from the window to my almost weeping mother, and my father, whose expression I could not interpret. Leola was in school, for we had agreed that it would not do for her to come to the station—too much like a formal engagement. But the night before I left she had confided that in spite of her best efforts to keep the image of Percy bright in her heart she had discovered that she really loved me, and would love me forever, and wait until I returned from the battlefields of Europe.

·II·
I Am Born Again

1

I SHALL SAY little about the war, because though I was in it from early 1915 until late 1917 I never found out much about it until later. Commanders and historians are the people to discuss wars; I was in the infantry, and most of the time I did not know where I was or what I was doing, except that I was obeying orders and trying not to be killed in any of the variety of horrible ways open to me. Since then I have read enough to know a little of the actions in which I took a part, but what the historians say throws no great light on what I remember. Because I do not want to posture in this account of myself as anything other than what I was at the time of my narrative, I shall write here only of what I knew when it happened.

When I left Deptford for the training camp I had never been away from home alone before. I found myself among men more experienced in the world than I, and I tried not to attract attention by any kind of singular behaviour. Some of them knew I was desperately homesick and were kindly; others jeered at me and the other very young fellows. They were anxious to make men of us, by which they meant making us like themselves. Some of them were men indeed—grave, slow young farmers and artisans with apparently boundless resources of strength and courage; others were just riffraff of the kind you get in any chance collection of men. None of them had much education; none had any clear idea what the war was about, though many felt that England had been menaced and had to be defended; perhaps the most astonishing thing was that none of us had much notion of geography and thought that going to fight in France might involve almost any kind of climate, from the Pole to the Equator. Of course some of us had had some geography in school and had studied maps, but a school map is a terribly uncommunicative thing.

I was a member of the Second Canadian Division, and later we were part of the Canadian Corps, but such descriptions meant little to me; I was aware of the men directly around me and rarely had a chance to meet any others. I might as well say at once that although I was on pretty good terms with everybody I made no lasting friends. There were men who formed strong friendships, which sometimes led to acts of bravery, and there were men who were great on what they called "pals" and talked and sang loudly about it. Those now living are still at it. But I was a lonely creature, and although I would have been very happy to have a friend I just never happened to meet one.

Probably my boredom was to blame. For I was bored as I have never been since—bored till every bone in my body was heavy with it. This was not the boredom of inactivity; an infantry trainee is kept on the hop from morning till night, and his sleep is sound. It was the boredom that comes of being cut off from everything that could make life sweet, or arouse curiosity, or enlarge the range of the senses. It was the boredom that comes of having to perform endless tasks that have no savour and acquire skills one would gladly be without. I learned to march and drill and shoot and keep myself clean according to Army standards; to make my bed and polish my boots and my buttons and to wrap lengths of dung-coloured rag around my legs in the approved way. None of it had any great reality for me, but I learned to do it all, and even to do it well.

Thus, when I went home for my leave before going abroad, I was an object of some wonderment. I was a man, in appearance. My mother was almost silenced, so far as her customary criticism went; she made a few attempts to reduce me to the status of her own dear laddie, but I was not willing to play that game. Leola Cruikshank was proud to be seen with me, and we got a little beyond the kissing stage in our last encounter. I desperately wanted to see Mrs. Dempster, but it was impossible, for in my uniform I was unable to go anywhere without being noticed, and though I would have died rather than admit it, I was still too much afraid of my mother to defy her openly. Paul I saw once, but I do not think he knew me, for he stared and passed by.

So off I went on a troopship, lectured by officers who were anxious to harden us with tales of German atrocities. These Germans, I gathered, were absolute devils; not winning campaigns, but maiming children, ravishing women (never less than ten to a single victim), and insulting religion were the things they had gone to war to accomplish; they took their tone from their Kaiser, who was a comic, mad monster; they had to be shown that decency still ruled the world, and we were decency incarnate. I had by that time seen enough of Army life to think that if we were decency the Germans must be rough indeed, for a more foul-mouthed, thieving, whoring lot of toughs than some of the soldiers I met it would be hard to imagine. But I was not discontented with soldiering; I was discontented with myself, with my loneliness and boredom.

In France, though my boredom was unabated, loneliness was replaced by fear. I was, in a mute, controlled, desperate fashion, frightened for the next three years. I saw plenty of men whose fear found vent; they went mad, or they shot themselves (dead or badly enough to get out of service), or they were such nuisances to the rest of us that they were got rid of in one way or another. But I think there were many in my own case; frightened of death, of wounds, of being captured, but most frightened of admitting to fear and losing face before the others. This kind of fear is not acute, of course; it is a constant, depleting companion whose presence makes everything gray. Sometimes fear could be forgotten, but never for long.

I saw a good deal of service, for I was strong, did not break down, and miraculously suffered no wounds. I had leaves, when it was possible to grant them, but for months on end I was at what was called the Front. What it was the Front of I never really knew, for there were always men who were ready to tell—God knows how accurately—where the Allied troops were disposed, and where we were in relation to the British and the French, and from what they said it seemed the Front was everywhere. But certainly we were often only a few hundred yards from the German lines and could see the enemy, in their cooking-pot helmets, quite clearly. If you were such a fool as to show your head they might put a bullet through it, and we had men detailed for the same ugly work.

It seems now to have been a very odd war, for we have had another since then, which has set the standard for modernity of fighting. I saw things that now make my pupils regard me as comparable to one of Wellington's men, or perhaps Marlborough's. My war was greatly complicated by horses, for motor vehicles were useless in Flanders mud; if one was among the horses during a bombardment, as I once chanced to be, the animals were just as dangerous as the German shells. I even saw cavalry, for there were still generals who thought that if they could once get at the enemy with cavalry the machine guns would quickly be silenced. These cavalrymen were as wondrous to me as Crusaders, but I would not have been on one of their horses for the earth. And of course I saw corpses, and grew used to their unimportant look, for a dead man without any of the panoply of death is a desperately insignificant object. Worse, I saw men who were not corpses but who would be soon and who longed for death.

It was the indignity, the ignominy, the squalor, to which war reduced a wounded man that most ate into me. Men in agony, smashed so that they will never be whole again even if they live, ought not to be something one ignores; but we learned to ignore them, and I have put my foot on many a wretched fellow and pushed him even deeper into the mud, because I had to get over him and onto some spot that we had been ordered to achieve or die in trying.

This was fighting, when at least we were doing something. But for days and weeks there was not much fighting, during which we lived in trenches, in dung-coloured mud into which dung and every filthiness had been trodden, in our dung-coloured uniforms; we were cold, badly fed, and lousy. We had no privacy whatever and began to doubt our individuality, for we seemed to melt into a mass; this was what the sergeants feared, and they did astonishing work in keeping that danger at bay, most of the time; occasionally the horrible loss of personality, the listlessness of degradation, got beyond them, and then we had to be sent to the rear to what were called rest camps; we never rested in them, but at least we could draw a full breath without the lime-and-dung stench of the latrines in it.

In spite of the terribly public quality of a soldier's life, in which I ate, slept, stood, sat, thought, voided my bowels, and felt the dread of death upon me, always among others, I found a little time for reading. But I had only one book, a *New Testament* some well-meaning body had distributed in thousands to the troops. It would never have been my choice; if it had to be the *Bible* I would have taken the *Old Testament* any day, but I would rather have had some big, meaty novels. But where could a private soldier keep such things? I have read often since those days of men who went through the war with books of all sorts, but they were officers. Once or twice on leaves I got hold of a book or two in English but lost them as soon as we had to fight. Only my *Testament* could be kept in my pocket without making a big bulge, and I read it to the bone, over and over.

This gained me a disagreeable reputation as a religious fellow, a Holy Joe, and even the chaplain avoided that kind, for they were sure trouble, one way or another. My nickname was Deacon, because of my *Testament* reading. It was useless to explain that I read it not from zeal but curiosity and that long passages of it confirmed my early impression that religion and *Arabian Nights* were true in the same way. (Later I was able to say that they were both psychologically rather than literally true, and that psychological truth was really as important in its own way as historical verification; but while I was a young soldier I had no vocabulary for such argument, though I sensed the truth of it.) I think *Revelation* was my favourite book; the Gospels seemed less relevant to me then than John's visions of the beasts and the struggle of the Crowned Woman, who had the moon beneath her feet, with the great Red Dragon.

The nickname Deacon stuck to me until, in one of the rest camps, word went out that an impromptu show was being organized, and men were called on to volunteer if they would do something to amuse the troops. With a gall that now staggers me, I forced myself to offer an imitation of Charlie Chaplin, whom I had seen exactly twice in film shows for the troops behind the lines. I managed to get the right kind of hat from a Frenchman in the nearby village,

I cut myself a little cane from a bush, and when the night came I put on a burnt-cork moustache and shuffled onto the platform; for twelve minutes I told the dirtiest jokes I knew, attaching them to all the officers—including the chaplain—and all the men who had some sort of public character. I now blush at what I remember of what I said, but I drew heavily on the repertoire of Milo Papple and was astonished to find myself a great hit. Even the former vaudevillian (who could sing *If You Were the Only Girl in the World and I Were the Only Boy* in a baritone-and-falsetto duet with himself) was less admired. And from that time forth I was called, not "Deacon," but "Charlie."

What really astonished me was the surprise of the men that I could do such a thing. "Jesus, the old Deacon, eh—getting off that hot one about the Major, eh? Jesus, and that riddle about Cookie, eh? Jesus!" They could hardly conceive that anybody who read the *Testament* could be other than a Holy Joe—could have another, seemingly completely opposite side to his character. I cannot remember a time when I did not take it as understood that everybody has at least two, if not twenty-two, sides to him. Their astonishment was what astonished *me*. Jesus, eh? People don't look very closely at other people, eh? Jesus!

I did not philosophize in the trenches; I endured. I even tried to make a good job of what I had to do. If I had not been so young and handicapped by lack of education—measured in school terms, for the Army did not know that I was a polymath and would not have cared—I might have been sent off for training as an officer. As it was, I eventually became a sergeant; casualties were heavy—which is the Army way of saying that men I had known and liked were exploded like bombs of guts almost under my nose—and my success in hiding my fear was enough to get me a reputation for having a cool head; so a sergeant I became, as well as a veteran of Sanctuary Wood and Vimy Ridge, before I was twenty. But I think my most surprising achievement was becoming Charlie.

2

My fighting days came to an end somewhere in the week of November 5, 1917, at that point in the Third Battle of Ypres where the Canadians were brought in to attempt to take Passchendaele. It was a Thursday or Friday; I cannot be more accurate because many of the details of that time are clouded in my mind. The battle was the most terrible of my experience; we were trying to take a village that was already a ruin, and we counted our advances in feet; the Front was a confused mess because it had rained every day for weeks and the mud was so dangerous that we dared not make a forward move without a laborious business of putting down duckboards, lifting them as we advanced, and putting them down again ahead of us; understandably this was so slow and exposed that we could not do much of it. I learned from later reading that our total advance was a little less than two miles; it might have been two hundred. The great terror was the mud. The German bombardment churned it up so that it was horribly treacherous, and if a man sank in much over his knees his chances of getting out were poor; a shell exploding nearby could cause an upheaval that overwhelmed him, and the likelihood even of recovering his body was small. I write of this now as briefly as I may, for the terror of it was so great that I would not for anything arouse it again.

One of the principal impediments to our advance was a series of German machine-gun emplacements. I suppose they were set out according to some plan, but we were not in a position to observe any plan; in the tiny area I knew about there was one of these things, and it was clear that we would get no farther forward until it was silenced. Two attempts were made at this dangerous job, with terrible loss to us. I could see how things were going, and how the list of men who might be expected to get to that machine-gun nest was dwindling, and I knew it would come to me next. I do not remember if we were asked to volunteer; such a request would have been merely formal anyhow; things had reached a point where pretence of choice had disappeared. Anyhow, I was one of six who were detailed to make a night raid, in one of the intervals of bombardment, to see if we could get to the machine guns and knock them out. We were issued the small arms and other things we needed, and when the bombardment had stopped for five minutes we set out, not in a knot, of course, but spaced a few yards apart.

The men in the nest were expecting us, for we were doing exactly what their side would have done in the same situation. But we crawled forward, spread-eagled in the mud so as to spread our total weight over as wide an area as possible. It was like swimming in molasses, with the additional misery that it was molasses that stank and had dead men in it.

I was making pretty good progress when suddenly everything went wrong. Somebody—it could have been someone on our side at a distance or it could have been one of the Germans in the nest—sent up a flare; you do not see where these flares come from, because they explode in the air and light up the landscape for a considerable area. When such a thing happens and you are crawling toward an objective, as I was, the proper thing to do is to lie low, with your face down, and hope not to be seen. As I was mud from head to foot and had blackened my face before setting out, I would have been hard to see, and if seen I would have looked like a dead man. After the flare had died out I crept forward again and made a fair amount of distance, so far as I could judge; I did not know where the others were, but I assumed that like me they were making for the gun nest and waiting for a signal from our leader, a second lieutenant, to do whatever we could about it. But now three flares exploded, and immediately there began a rattle of machine-gun fire. Again I laid low. But it is the nature of flares, when they are over the arc of their trajectory, to come down with a rush and a characteristic loud hiss; if you are hit by one it is a serious burn, for the last of the flare is still a large gob of fire, and between burning to death or drowning in mud the choice is trivial. Two of these spent flares were hissing in the air above me, and I had to get out of where I was as fast as I could. So I got to my feet and ran.

Now, at a time when we had counted on at least a half-an-hour's lull in the bombardment, it suddenly set up again, and to my bleak horror our own guns, from a considerable distance to the left, began to answer. This sort of thing was always a risk when we were out on small raids, but it was a risk I had never met before. As the shells began to drop I ran wildly, and how long I wallowed around in the dark I do not know, but it could have been anything between three minutes and ten. I became aware of a deafening rattle, with the rhythm of an angry, scolding voice, on my right. I looked for some sort of cover, and suddenly, in a burst of light, there it was right in front of me—an entry concealed by some trash, but unmistakably a door over which hung a curtain of muddy sacking. I pushed through it and found myself in the German machine-gun nest, with three Germans ahead of me firing busily.

I had a revolver, and I shot all three at point-blank range. They did not even see me. There is no use saying any more about it. I am not proud of it now and I did not glory in it then. War puts men in situations where these things happen.

What I wanted to do most of all was to stay where I was and get my breath and my wits before starting back to our line. But the bombardment was increasing, and I knew that if I stopped there one of our shells might drop on the position and blow me up, or the Germans, whose field telephone was already signalling right under my nose, would send some men to see what had happened, and that would be the end of me. I had to get out.

So out I crawled, into mud below and shells above, and tried to get my bearings. As both sides were now at the peak of a bombardment, it was not easy to tell which source of death I should crawl toward, and by bad luck I set out toward the German lines.

How long I crawled I do not know, for I was by this time more frightened, muddled, and desperate than ever before or since. "Disorientation" is the word now fashionable for my condition. Quite soon I was worse than that; I was wounded, and so far as I could tell, seriously. It was shrapnel, a fragment of an exploding shell, and it hit me in the left leg, though where I cannot say; I have been in a car accident in later life, and the effect was rather like that—a sudden shock like a blow from a club; and it was a little time before I knew that my left leg was in trouble, though I could not tell how bad it was.

Earlier I said that I had not been wounded; there were a surprising number of men who escaped the war without a wound. I had not been gassed either, though I had been twice in areas where gas was used nearby. I had dreaded a wound, for I had seen so many. What is a wounded man to do? Crawl to shelter and hope he may be found by his own people. I crawled.

Some men found that their senses were quickened by a wound; their ingenuity rose to exceptional heights under stress of danger. But I was one of the other kind. I was not so much afraid as utterly disheartened. There I was, a mud man in a confusion of noise, flashing lights, and the stink of gelignite. I wanted to quit; I had no more heart for the game. But I crawled, with the increasing realization that my left leg was no good for anything and had to be dragged, and the awful awareness that I did not know where I was going. After a few minutes I saw some jagged masonry on my right and dragged toward it. When at last I reached it I propped myself up with my back to a stone wall and gave myself up to a full, rich recognition of the danger and hopelessness of my position. For three years I had kept my nerve by stifling my intelligence, but now I let the intelligence rip and the nerve dissolve. I am sure there has been worse wretchedness, fright, and despair in the world's history, but I set up a personal record that I have never since approached.

My leg began to declare itself in a way that I can only describe in terms of sound; from a mute condition it began to murmur, then to moan and whine, then to scream. I could not see much of what was wrong because of the mud in which I was covered, but my exploring hand found a great stickiness that I knew was blood, and I could make out that my leg lay on the ground in an unnatural way. You will get tetanus, I told myself, and you will die of lockjaw. It was a Deptford belief that in this disease you bent backward until at last your head touched your heels and you had to be buried in a round coffin. I had seen some tetanus in the trenches, and nobody had needed a round coffin even if one had been available; still, in my condition, the belief was stronger than experience.

I thought of Deptford, and I thought of Mrs. Dempster. Particularly I thought of her parting words to me: "There's just one thing to remember; whatever happens, it does no good to be afraid." Mrs. Dempster, I said aloud, was a fool. I was afraid, and I was not in a situation where doing good, or doing evil, had any relevance at all.

It was then that one of the things happened that make my life strange—one of the experiences that other people have not had or do not admit to—one of the things that makes me so resentful of Packer's estimate of me as a dim man to whom nothing important has ever happened.

I became conscious that the bombardment had ceased, and only an occasional gun was heard. But flares appeared in the sky at intervals, and one of these began to drop toward me. By its light I could see that the remnant of standing masonry in which I was lying was all that was left of a church, or perhaps a school—anyhow a building of some size—and that I lay at the foot of a ruined tower. As the hissing flame dropped I saw there about ten or twelve feet above me on an opposite wall, in a niche, a statue of the Virgin and Child. I did not know it then but I know now that it was the assembly of elements that represent the Immaculate Conception, for the little Virgin was crowned, stood on a crescent moon, which in its turn rested on a globe, and in the hand that did not hold the Child she carried a sceptre from which lilies sprang. Not knowing what it was meant to be, I thought in a flash it must be the Crowned Woman in *Revelation*—she who had the moon beneath her feet and was menaced by the Red Dragon. But what hit me worse than the blow of the shrapnel was that the face was Mrs. Dempster's face.

I had lost all nerve long before. Now, as the last of the flare hissed toward me, I lost consciousness.

3

"May I have a drink of water?"

"Did you speak?"

"Yes. May I have a drink, Sister?"

"You may have a glass of champagne, if there is any. Who are you?"

"Ramsay, D., Sergeant, Second Canadian Division."

"Well, Ramsay-Dee, it's marvellous to have you with us."

"Where is this?"

"You'll find out. Where have *you* been?"

Ah, where *had* I been? I didn't know then and I don't know yet, but it was such a place as I had never known before. Years later, when for the first time I read Coleridge's *Kubla Khan* and came on—

> Weave a circle round him thrice,
> And close your eyes with holy dread,
> For he on honey-dew hath fed,
> And drunk the milk of Paradise

—I almost jumped out of my skin, for the words so perfectly described my state before I woke up in hospital. I had been wonderfully at ease and healingly at peace; though from time to time voices spoke to me I was under no obligation to hear what they said or to make a reply; I felt that everything was good, that my spirit was wholly my own, and that though all was strange nothing was evil. From time to time the little Madonna appeared and looked at me with friendly concern before removing herself; once or twice she spoke, but I did not know what she said and did not need to know.

But here I was, apparently in bed, and a very pretty girl in a nurse's uniform was asking me where I had been. Clearly she meant it as a joke. She thought she knew where I had been. That meant that the joke was on her, for no one, not I myself, knew that.

"Is this a base hospital?"

"Goodness, no. How do you feel, Ramsay-Dee?"

"Fine. What day is this?"

"This is the twelfth of May. I'll get you a drink."

She disappeared, and I took a few soundings. It was not easy work. The last time I had been conscious of was November; if this was May I had been in that splendid, carefree world for quite a while. I wasn't in such a bad place now; I couldn't move my head very much, but I could see a marvellously decorated plaster ceiling, and such walls as lay in my vision were panelled in wood; there was an open window somewhere, and sweet air—no stink of mud or explosive or corpses or latrines—was blowing through it. I was clean. I wriggled appreciatively—and wished I hadn't, for several parts of me protested. But here was the girl again, and with her a red-faced man in a long white coat.

He seemed greatly elated, especially when I was able to remember my Army number, and though I did not learn why at once I found out over a few days that I was by way of being a medical pet, and my recovery proved something; being merely the patient, I was never given the full details, but I believe I was written up in at least two medical papers as a psychiatric curiosity, but as I was referred to only as "the patient" I could never identify myself for sure. The red-faced man was some sort of specialist in shell-shock cases, and I was one of his successes, though I rather think I cured myself, or the little Madonna cured me, or some agencies other than good nursing and medical observation.

Oh, I was a lucky man! Apparently the flare did hit me, and before it expired it burned off a good part of my clothes and consumed the string of my identification disks, so that when I was picked up they were lost in the mud. There had been some doubt as to whether I was dead or merely on the way to it, but I was taken back to our base, and as I stubbornly did not die I was removed eventually to a hospital in France, and as I still refused either to die or live I was shipped to England; by this time I was a fairly interesting instance of survival against all probabilities, and the red-faced doctor had claimed me for his own; I was brought to this special hospital in a fine old house in Buckinghamshire, and had lain unconscious, and likely to remain so, though the red-faced doctor stubbornly insisted that some day I would wake up and tell him something of value. So, here it was May, and I was awake, and the hospital staff were delighted, and made a great pet of me.

They had other news for me, not so good. My burns had been severe, and in those days they were not so clever with burns as they are now, so that quite a lot of the skin on my chest and left side was an angry-looking mess, rather like lumpy sealing wax, and is so still, though it is a little browner now. In the bed, on the left side, was an arrangement of wire, like a bee-skip, to keep the sheets from touching the stump where my left leg had been. While my wits were off on that paradisal holiday I had been fed liquids, and so I was very thin and weak. What is more, I had a full beard, and the pretty nurse and I had a rare old time getting it off.

Let me stop calling her the pretty nurse. Her name was Diana Marfleet, and she was one of those volunteers who got a proper nursing training but never acquired the full calm of a professional nursing sister. She was the first English girl I ever saw at close range, and a fine specimen of her type, which was the fair-skinned, dark-haired, brown-eyed type. Not only was she pretty, she had charm and an easy manner and talked amusingly, for she came of that class of English person who thinks it bad manners to be factual and serious. She was twenty-four, which gave her an edge of four years over me, and it was not long before she confided to me that her fiancé, a Navy lieutenant, had been lost when the *Aboukir* was torpedoed in the very early days of the war. We were on tremendous terms in no time, for she had been nursing me since I had come to the hospital in January, and such nourishment as I had taken had been spooned and poured into me by her; she had also washed me and attended to the bedpan and the urinal, and continued to do so; a girl who can do that without being facetious or making a man feel self-conscious is no ordinary creature. Diana was a wonderful girl, and I am sure I gained strength and made physical progress at an unusual rate, to please her.

One day she appeared at my bedside with a look of great seriousness and saluted me smartly.

"What's that for?"

"Tribute of humble nursing sister to hero of Passchendaele."

"Get away!" (This was a great expression of my father's, and I have never wholly abandoned it.)

"Fact. What do you think you've got?"

"I rather think I've got you."

"No cheek. We've been tracing you, Sergeant Ramsay. Did you know that you were officially dead?"

"Dead! Me?"

"You. That's why your V.C. was awarded posthumously."

"Get away!"

"Fact. You have the V.C. for, with the uttermost gallantry and disregard of all but duty, clearing out a machine-gun nest and thereby ensuring an advance of—I don't know how far but quite a bit. You were the only one of the six who didn't get back to the line, and one of the men saw you—your unmistakable size anyhow—running right toward the machine-gun nest; so it was clear enough, even though they couldn't find your body afterward. Anyway you've got it, and Dr. Houneen is making sure you do get it and it isn't sent home to depress your mother."

The other three men in the room gave a cheer—an ironic cheer. We all pretended we didn't care about decorations, but I never heard of anybody turning one down.

Diana was very sorry in a few days that she had said what she did about the medal going home to my mother, for a letter arrived from the Reverend Donald Phelps, in reply to one Dr. Houneen had sent to my parents, saying that Alexander Ramsay and his wife, Fiona Dunstable Ramsay, had both died in the influenza epidemic of early 1918, though not before they had received news of my presumed death at Passchendaele.

Diana was ashamed because she thought she might have hurt my feelings. I was ashamed because I felt the loss so little.

4

It was years before I thought of the death of my parents as anything other than a relief; in my thirties I was able to see them as real people, who had done the best they could in the lives fate had given them. But as I lay in that hospital I was glad that I did not have to be my mother's own dear laddie any longer, or ever attempt to explain to her what war was, or warp my nature to suit her confident demands. I knew she had eaten my father, and I was glad I did not have to fight any longer to keep her from eating me. Oh, these good, ignorant, confident women! How one grows to hate them! I was mean-spiritedly pleased that my mother had not lived to hear of my V.C.; how she would have paraded in mock-modesty as the mother of a hero, the very womb and matrix of bravery, in consequence of my three years of degradation in the Flanders mud!

I confided none of this to Diana, of course. She was intensely curious about my war experience, and I had no trouble at all in talking to her about it. But as I gave her my confidence and she gave me her sympathy, I was well aware that we were growing very close and that some day this would have to be reckoned with.

I did not care. I was happy to be living at all, and lived only for the sweetness of the moment.

She was a romantic, and as I had never met a female romantic before it was a delight to me to explore her emotions. She wanted to know all about me, and I told her as honestly as I could; but as I was barely twenty, and a romantic myself, I know now that I lied in every word I uttered—lied not in fact but in emphasis, in colour, and in intention. She was entranced by the idea of life in Canada, and I made it entrancing. I even told her about Mrs. Dempster (though not that I was the cause of her distracted state) and felt let down that she did not respond very warmly. But when I told her about the little Madonna at Passchendaele and later as a visitor to my long coma, she was delighted and immediately gave it a conventionally religious significance, which, quite honestly, had never occurred to me. She returned to this theme again and again, and often I was reminded of the introduction to *A Child's Book of Saints* and little W.V., for whom those stories had been told. Personally I had come to think of little W.V. as rather a little pill, but I now reserved my judgement, for Diana was little W.V. to the life, and I was all for Diana.

Gradually it broke in upon me that Diana had marked me for her own, and I was too much flattered to see what that might mean. A lot of the nurses in that hospital were girls of good family, and though they worked very hard and did full nursing duty they had some privileges that cannot have been common. Most of them lived nearby, and they were able to go home in their time off.

When Diana returned from these off-duty jaunts she spoke about her home and her parents, and they seemed to be people unlike parents as I knew them. Her father, Canon Marfleet, was a domestic chaplain at Windsor as well as a parish clergyman; I had little notion what a domestic chaplain might be, but I assumed he jawed the Royal Family about morals, just as the parsons jawed us at home. Her mother was an Honourable, though the Canon was not, which surprised me, and she had been born a De Blaquiere, which, as Diana pronounced it D'Blackyer, I did not get straight for some time. Because of the war the Marfleets were living very simply—only two servants and a gardener three times a week—and the Canon had followed royal example and forbidden alcoholic liquors in his household for the duration, except for a glass or two of port when he felt peaky. They restricted their daily bath-water to three inches, to save fuel for Our Cause; I had never in my life known anyone who bathed every day and assumed that the hospital daily bath was some sort of curative measure that would eventually cease.

Diana was a very educative experience. As she gradually took me over she began to correct me about some of my usages, which she thought quaint—not wrong, just quaint. Fortunately, because I had a good measure of Scots in my speech, we did not have the usual haggle of Old and New World couples about pronunciations, though she was hilarious about me calling a reel of cotton a spool of thread and assured me that pants were things one wore under trousers. But she made it clear that one tore bread, instead of cutting it neatly, and buttered it only in bites, which I thought a time-wasting affectation; she also stopped me from eating like a man who might not live until his next mouthful, a childhood habit that had been exaggerated in the trenches and that still overcomes me when I am nervous. I liked it. I was grateful. Besides, she did it with humour and charm; there was not a nagging breath in her.

Of course this did not happen all at once. It was some time after I woke from my coma before I could get out of bed, and quite a while after that before I could begin experimenting with the succession of artificial legs that came before my final one. I had to learn to walk with crutches, and because so many of my muscles, especially in the left arm, were scarred or reduced to very little, this took time and hurt. Diana saw me through it all. Literally, I leaned on her, and now and then I fell on her. She was a wonderful nurse.

When it was at last possible to do so she took me home, and I met the Canon and the Honourable. The best I can say about them is that they were worthy to be Diana's parents. The Canon was a charming man, quite unlike any clergyman I had ever known, and even at the Sunday midday meal he never talked about religion. Like a good Presbyterian, I tried once or twice to pass him a compliment on his discourse at morning service and pursue its theme, but he wanted none of that. He wanted to talk about the war, and as he was well informed and a Lloyd George supporter it was not the usual hate session in which he invited me to engage;

there must have been a lot like him in England, though you would never have known it from the peace we finally made. The Honourable was a wonder, not like a mother at all. She was a witty, frivolous woman of a beauty congruous with her age—about forty-seven, I suppose—and talked as if she hadn't a brain in her head. But I was not deceived; she was what Diana would be at that age, and I liked every bit of it.

How my spirit expanded in the home of the Marfleets! To a man who had been where I had been it was glorious. I only hope I behaved myself and did not talk like a fool. But when I remember those days I remember the Canon and the Honourable and Diana and what I felt about them, but little of what I did or said.

5

The patchy quality of my recollection of this period is owing, I suppose, to the exhaustion of three years of war. I was out of it at last, and I was happy to take pleasure in security and cleanliness, without paying too close attention to what went on. Now and then it was possible to hear the guns in France; food was short but better than I had had in the trenches; the news came in ominous newspaper dispatches. Nevertheless I was happy and knew that for me, at least, the war was over. My plans were simple—to learn to walk with a crutch, and later with an artificial leg and a cane. Without being positively in love with Diana, I was beglamoured by her and flattered by her attention. I had fought my war and was resting.

We did win it at last, and there was a great hullabaloo in the hospital, and on the day after November 11, Dr. Houneen got a car and drove me and another man who was fit for it, and Diana and another nurse, to London to see the fun. The rejoicing was a little too much like an infantry attack for my taste; I had not been in a crowd since I was wounded, and the noise and crush were very alarming to me. Indeed, I have never been much good at enduring noise and crush since late 1917. But I saw some of the excitement and a few things that shocked me; people, having been delivered from destruction, became horribly destructive themselves; people, having been delivered from license and riot, pawed and mauled and shouted dirty phrases in the streets. Nor am I in any position to talk; it was on the night of November 12, in a house in Eaton Square belonging to one of her De Blaquiere aunts, that I first slept with Diana, the aunt giving her assent by silence and discreet absence; to me at least there seemed something unseemly about the union of my scarred and maimed body with her unblemished beauty. Unseemly or not, it was my first experience of anything of the kind, for I had never been able to bring myself to make use of soldiers' brothels or any of the casual company that was available to men in uniform. Diana was not a novice—the fiancé who went down on the *Aboukir,* I suppose—and she initiated me most tenderly, for which I shall always be grateful. Thus we became lovers in the fullest sense, and for me the experience was an important step toward the completion of that manhood which had been thrust upon me so one-sidedly in the trenches.

The next night, because Diana had luck as well as influence, we had tickets for *Chu-Chin-Chow* at His Majesty's, and this was a great experience too, in quite a different way, for I had never seen any theatre more elaborate than a troop show. On one of my two very brief leaves in Paris I had sought out the site of Robert-Houdin's theatre, but it was no longer there. I must have been an odd young man to have supposed that it might still be in existence. But my historical sense developed later.

I see that I have been so muddle-headed as to put my sexual initiation in direct conjunction with a visit to a musical show, which suggests some lack of balance perhaps. But, looking back from my present age, the two, though very different, are not so unlike in psychological weight as you might suppose. Both were wonders, strange lands revealed to me in circumstances of great excitement. I suppose I was still in rather delicate health, mentally as well as physically.

The next great moment in my life was the reception of my Victoria Cross, from the King himself. Dr. Houneen had established that I was really alive, and so the award that had been published as posthumous was repeated on one of the lists, and in due course I went to Buckingham Palace in a taxi, on a December morning, and got it. Diana was with me, for I was allowed to invite one guest, and she was the obvious choice. We were looked at with sentimental friendliness by the other people in the room, and I suppose an obviously wounded soldier, accompanied by a very pretty nurse, was about as popular a sight as the time afforded.

Most of the details are vague, but a few remain. A military band, in an adjoining room, played Gems from *The Maid of the Mountains* (it was Diana who told me), and we all stood around the walls until the King and some aides entered and took a place in the centre. When my turn came I stumped forward on my latest metal leg, making rather a noisy progress, and got myself into the right position, directly in front of the King. Somebody handed him the medal, and he pinned it on my tunic, then shook my hand and said, "I am glad you were able to get here after all."

I can still remember what a deep and rather gruff voice he had, and also the splendid neatness of his Navy beard. He was a good deal shorter than I, so I was looking down into his very blue, rather glittering eyes, and I thought I had better smile at the royal joke, so I did, and retreated in good order.

There was a moment, however, when the King and I were looking directly into each other's eyes, and in that instant I had a revelation that takes much longer to explain than to experience. Here am I, I reflected, being decorated as a hero, and in the eyes of everybody here I am indeed a hero; but I know that my heroic act was rather a dirty job I did when I was dreadfully frightened; I could just as easily have muddled it and been ingloriously killed. But it doesn't much matter, because people seem to need heroes; so long as I don't lose sight of the truth, it might as well be me as anyone else. And here before me stands a marvellously groomed little man who is pinning a hero's medal on me because some of his forbears were Alfred the Great, and Charles the First, and even King Arthur, for anything I know to the contrary. But I shouldn't be surprised if inside he feels as puzzled about the fate that brings him here as I. We are public icons, we two: he an icon of kingship, and I an icon of heroism, unreal yet very necessary; we have obligations above what is merely personal, and to let personal feelings obscure the obligations would be failing in one's duty.

This was clearer still afterward, at lunch at the Savoy, when the Canon and the Honourable gave us a gay time, with champagne; they all seemed to accept me as a genuine hero, and I did my best to behave decently, neither believing in it too obviously, nor yet protesting that I was just a simple chap who had done his duty when he saw it—a pose that has always disgusted me. Ever since, I have tried to think charitably of people in prominent positions of one kind or another; we cast them in roles, and it is only right to consider them as players, without trying to discredit them with knowledge of their offstage life—unless they drag it into the middle of the stage themselves.

6

The business of getting used to myself as a hero was only part of the work I had on hand during my long stay in the hospital. When first I returned to this world—I will not say to consciousness because it seemed to me that I had been conscious on a different level during what they called my coma—I had to get used to being a man with one leg and a decidedly weakened left arm. I was not so clever at managing these handicaps as were some of the men in that hospital who had lost limbs; I have always been clumsy, and though Diana and the doctor assured me that I would soon walk as well as if I had a real leg I had no belief in it, and indeed I have never managed to walk without a limp and feel much happier with a cane. I was very weak physically, to begin with, and although I was perfectly sane I was a little light-headed for several months, and all my recollections of that period are confused by this quality of light-headedness. But I had to get used to being a hero—that is, not to believe it myself but not to be insulting to those who did so—and I also had to make up my mind about Diana.

There was an unreality about our relationship that had its roots in something more lasting than my light-headedness. I will say nothing against her, and I shall always be grateful to her for teaching me what the physical side of love was; after the squalor of the trenches her beauty and high spirits were the best medicine I got. But I could not be blind to the fact that she regarded me as her own creation. And why not? Hadn't she fed me and washed me and lured me back into this world when I was far away? Didn't she teach me to walk, showing the greatest patience when I was most clumsy? Was she not anxious to retrain me about habits of eating and behaviour? But even as I write it down I know how clear it is that what was wrong between Diana and me was that she was too much a mother to me, and as I had had one mother, and lost her, I was not in a hurry to acquire another—not even a young and beautiful one with whom I could play Oedipus to both our hearts' content. If I could manage it, I had no intention of being anybody's own dear laddie, ever again.

That decision, made at that time, has shaped my life and doubtless in some ways it has warped it, but I still think I knew what was best for me. In the long periods of rest in the hospital I thought as carefully as I could about my situation, and what emerged was this: I had made a substantial payment to society for anything society had given me or would give me in future; a leg and much of one arm are hard coin. Society had decided to regard me as a hero, and though I knew that I was no more a hero than many other men I had fought with, and less than some who had been killed doing what I could not have done, I determined to let society regard me as it pleased; I would not trade on it, but I would not put it aside either. I would get a pension in due time, and my Victoria Cross carried a resounding fifty dollars a year with it; I would take these rewards and be grateful. But I wanted my life to be my own; I would live henceforth for my own satisfaction.

That did not include Diana. She seemed to assume that it did, and perhaps I was unfair to her in not checking her assumptions as soon as I became aware of them. But, to be frank, I liked having her in love with me; it fed my spirit, which was at a low ebb. I liked going to bed with her, and as she liked it too I thought this a fair exchange. But a life with Diana was simply not for me. As girls do, she assumed that we were drifting toward an engagement and marriage; though she never said so in plain words it was clear she thought that when I was strong enough we would go to Canada, and if I did not mistake her utterly, she had in her mind's eye a fine big wheat farm in the West, for she had the English delusion that farming was a great way to live. I knew enough about farming to be sure it was not a life for amateurs or wounded men.

Every two weeks Diana would appear, looking remote and beautiful, and hand me a letter from Leola Cruikshank. These were always difficult occasions because the letters embarrassed me; they were so barren of content, so ill-expressed, so utterly unlike the Leola, all curls and soft lips and whispers, that I remembered. How, I wondered, had I been so stupid as to get myself mixed up with such a pinhead? Diana knew the letters were from a girl, for Leola's guileless writing could not have belonged to any other section of humanity, and intuition told her that, as they were almost the only letters I received, the girl was a special one. I could not have told her how special, for I could no longer remember precisely what pledges I had made to Leola; was I engaged to her or was I not? The letters I wrote in reply, and painstakingly smuggled into the post so Diana should not see them, were as noncommittal as I had the heart to make them; I tried to write in such a way as to evoke from Leola some indication of what she believed our relationship to be, without committing myself. This meant subtlety of a kind that was far outside Leola's scope; she was no hand with the pen, and her flat little letters gave Deptford gossip (with all the spice left out) and usually ended, "Everybody looks forward to your coming home and it will be lovely to see you again, Love, Leola." Was this coolness or maidenly reserve? Sometimes I broke out in a sweat, wondering.

One of Leola's letters came just before Christmas, which I had leave to spend with Diana's family. The Canon had celebrated the Armistice by abandoning the no-alcohol vow and it looked like being a jolly occasion. I had learned to drink neat rum in the Army and was ready for anything. But, on Christmas Eve, Diana contrived a private talk between us and asked me straight out who the girl was who wrote to me from Canada and was I involved with her. *Involved* was her word. I had been dreading this question but had no answer ready, and I havered and floundered and became aware that Leola's name had an uncouth sound when spoken in such circumstances, and hated myself for thinking so. My whole trouble, jackass that I was, sprang from the fact that I tried to be decently loyal to Leola without hurting Diana, and the more I talked the worse mess I made of things. In no time Diana was crying, and I was doing my best to comfort her. But I managed to keep uppermost in my mind the determination I had formed not to get engaged to her, and this led me into verbal acrobatics that quickly brought on a blazing row.

Canadian soldiers had an ambiguous reputation in England at that time; we were supposed to be loyal, furious, hairy fellows who spat bullets at the enemy but ate women raw. Diana accused me of being one of these ogres, who had led her on to reveal feelings I did not reciprocate. Like a fool, I said I thought she was old enough to know what she thought. Aha, she said, that was it, was it? Because she was older than I, she was a tough old rounder who could look out for herself, was she? Not a bit tough, I countered, frank with a flat-footedness that now makes me blush, but after all she had been engaged, hadn't she? There it was again, she countered; I thought she was damaged goods; I was throwing it in her face that she had given herself to a man who had died a hero's death in the very first weeks of the war. I looked on her simply as an amusement, a pastime; she had loved me in my weakness, without knowing how essentially coarse-fibred I was. And much more to the same effect.

Of course this gave way in time to much gentler exchanges, and we savoured the sweet pleasures of making up after a fight, but it was not long before Diana wanted to know, just as someone who wished me well, how far I was committed to Leola. I didn't dare tell her that I wanted to know precisely the same thing; I was too young to be truthful about such a matter. Well then, she continued, was I in love with Leola? I was able to say with a good conscience that I was not. Then I was in love with herself after all, said Diana, making one of those feminine leaps in logic that leave men breathless. I made a long speech about never knowing what people meant when they said they were in love with someone. I loved Diana, I said; I really did. But as for "being in love"—I babbled a good deal of nonsense that I cannot now recall and would not put down if I did.

Diana changed her tactics. I was too intellectual, she said, and analyzed matters on which feeling was the only true guide. If I loved her, she asked no more. What did the future hold for us?

I do not want to make Diana seem crafty in my record of this conversation, but I must say that she had a great gift for getting her own way. *She* had strong ideas on what the future held for us, and I had none, and I am certain she knew it. Therefore she was putting forward this question not to hear from me but to inform me. But I had my little store of craft too. I said that the war had been such a shake-up for me that I had no clear ideas about the future, and certainly had not considered asking her to marry anybody as badly crippled as I.

This proved to be a terrible mistake. Diana was so vehement about what a decent woman felt for a man who had been wounded and handicapped in the war—not to speak of a man who had been given the highest award for bravery—that I nearly lost my head and begged her to be my wife. I cannot look back on my young self in this situation without considerable shame and disgust. So far I had been able to reject this girl's love, but I was nearly captured by her flattery. Not that she meant it insincerely; there was nothing insincere about Diana. But she had been raised on a mental diet of heroism, Empire, decency, and the emotional superiority of womanhood, and she could talk about these things without a blush, as parsons talk about God. And I was only twenty.

What a night that was! We talked till three o'clock, complicating our situation with endless scruple, as young people are apt to do, and trying not to hurt each other's feelings, despite the fact that Diana wanted to get engaged to me and I was fighting desperately to prevent any such thing. But I have said before, and I repeat, Diana was really an exceptional girl, and when she saw she was not going to get her way she gave in with grace.

"All right," she said, sitting up on the sofa and tidying her hair (for we had been very much entangled during parts of our argument, and my latest artificial leg had been giving some ominous croaks); "if we aren't going to be married, that's that. But what *are* you going to do, Dunny? Surely you aren't going to marry that girl with a name like a hair tonic and go on editing your father's potty little paper, are you? There's more to you than that."

I agreed that I was sure there was more to me than that, but I didn't know what it was and I needed time to find out. Furthermore, I knew that the finding out must be done alone. I did not tell Diana that there was the whole question of the little Madonna to be gone into, because I knew that with her conventional Christian background and her generous sentimentality she would begin then and there to explain it for me, and every scrap of intuition I possessed told me that her explanation would be the wrong one. But I did tell her that I was strongly conscious that my lack of formal education was the greatest handicap I had and that I felt that somehow I must get to a university; if I went back to Canada and explored all the possibilities I could probably manage it. It is not easy to put down what one says to a girl in such circumstances, but I managed to make it clear that what I most wanted was time to grow up. The war had not matured me; I was like a piece of meat that is burned on one side and raw on the other, and it was on the raw side I needed to work. I thanked her, as well as I could, for what she had done for me.

"Let me do one thing more for you," she said. "Let me rename you. How on earth did you ever get yourself called Dunstable?"

"My mother's maiden name," said I. "Lots of people in Canada get landed with their mother's maiden name as a Christian name. But what's wrong with it?"

"It's hard to say, for one thing," said she, "and it sounds like a cart rumbling over cobblestones for another. You'll never get anywhere in the world named Dumbledum Ramsay. Why don't you change it to Dunstan? St. Dunstan was a marvellous person and very much like you—mad about learning, terribly stiff and stern and scowly, and an absolute wizard at withstanding temptation. Do you know that the Devil once came to tempt him in the form of a fascinating woman, and he caught her nose in his goldsmith's tongs and gave it a terrible twist?"

I took her nose between my fingers and gave it a twist. This was very nearly the undoing of all that I had gained, but after a while we were talking again. I liked the idea of a new name; it suggested new freedom and a new personality. So Diana got some of her father's port and poured it on my head and renamed me. She was an Anglican, of course, and her light-minded attitude toward some sacred things still astonished the deep Presbyterian in me; but I had not waded through the mud-and-blood soup of Passchendaele to worry about foolish things; blasphemy in a good cause (which usually means one's own cause) is not hard to stomach. When at last we went to bed two splendid things had happened: Diana and

I were friends instead of lovers, and I had an excellent new name.

Christmas Day was even better than I had foreseen. I am sure Diana's parents knew what was in the wind and were game enough not to stand in the way if we had really wanted to marry. But they were much relieved that we had decided against it. How they knew I cannot say, but parents are often less stupid than their children suppose, and I suspect the Honourable smelled it in the morning air. After all, what satisfaction would it have been to them to have their daughter marry a man in my physical state, of very different background, and four years younger than herself, in order to go off to seek a fortune in a country of which they knew nothing? So they were happy, and I was happy, and I suspect that Diana was a good deal happier than she would ever have admitted.

She had fallen in love with me because she felt she had made whatever I was out of a smashed-up and insensible hospital case; but I don't think it was long before she was just as sure as I that our marriage would never have worked. So I lost a possible wife and gained three very good friends that Christmas.

7

Getting back to Canada took some time because of the complication of Army necessities and my supposedly fragile state, but early in the following May I got off the train at Deptford, was greeted by the reeve, Orville Cave, and ceremonially driven around the village as the chief spectacle in a procession.

This grandeur had been carefully planned beforehand, by letter, but it was nonetheless astonishing for that. I had little idea of what four years of war had done in creating a new atmosphere in Deptford, for it had shown little interest in world affairs in my schooldays. But here was our village shoe-repair man, Moses Langirand, in what was meant to be a French uniform, personating Marshal Foch; he had secured this position on the best possible grounds, being the only French-speaking Canadian for miles around, and having an immense grey moustache. Here was a tall youth I did not know, in an outfit that approximated that of Uncle Sam. There were two John Bulls, owing to some misunderstanding that could not be resolved without hurt feelings. There were Red Cross nurses in plenty—six or seven of them. A girl celebrated in my day for having big feet, named Katie Orchard, was swathed in bunting and had a bandage over one eye; she was Gallant Little Belgium. These, and other people dressed in patriotic but vague outfits, formed a procession highly allegorical in its nature, which advanced down our main street, led by a band of seven brass instruments and a thunderous drum. I rode after them in an open Gray-Dort with the reeve, and following us was what was then called a Calithumpian parade, of gaily dressed children tormenting and insulting Myron Papple, who was identifiable as the German Emperor by his immense, upturned false moustache. Myron hopped about and feigned madness and deprivation very amusingly, but with such vigour that we wondered how a fat man could keep it up for long. As ours was a small village we toured through all the streets, and went up and down the main street no less than three times. Even at that we had done our uttermost by 2:45, and I had clumped down off the train at 1:30. It was the strangest procession I have ever seen, but it was in my honour and I will not laugh at it. It was Deptford's version of a Roman Triumph, and I tried to be worthy of it, looked solemn, saluted every flag I saw that was 12-by-8 inches or over, and gave special heed to elderly citizens.

The procession completed, I was hidden in the Tecumseh House until 5:30, when I was to have a state supper at the reeve's house. When I write "hidden" I mean it literally. My fellow townsmen felt that it would be unseemly for me to stroll about the streets, like an ordinary human being, before my apotheosis that night, so I was put in the best bedroom in our hotel, upon the door of which a Canadian Red Ensign had been tacked, and the barman, Joe Gallagher, was given strict orders to keep everyone away from me. So there I sat by my window, looking across a livery-stable yard toward St. James' Presbyterian Church, occasionally reading *War and Peace* (for I was now well embarked on the big, meaty novels I had longed for at the Front), but mostly too excited to do anything but marvel at myself and wonder when I would be free to do as I pleased.

Freedom was certainly not to be mine that day. At six I supped ceremonially at the reeve's; there were so many guests that we ate on the lawn from trestle tables, consuming cold chicken and ham, potato salad and pickles in bewildering variety, and quantities of ice cream, pie, and cake. We then set the whole banquet well awash inside ourselves with hot, strong coffee. Our progress to the Athelstan Opera House was stately, as befitted the grandees of the occasion, and we arrived ten minutes before the scheduled proceedings at 7:30.

If you are surprised that so small a place should have an Opera House, I should explain that it was our principal hall of assembly, upstairs in the Athelstan Block, which was the chief business premises of our village, and built of brick instead of the more usual wood. It was a theatre, right enough, with a stage that had a surprising roller curtain, on which was handsomely painted a sort of composite view, or evocation, of all that was most romantic in Europe; it is many years since I saw it, but I clearly remember a castle on the shores of a lagoon, where gondolas appeared amid larger shipping, which seemed to be plying in and out of Naples, accommodated at the foot of snowtopped Alps. The floor of the Opera House was flat, as being more convenient for dancing, but this was compensated for by the fact that the stage sloped forward toward the footlights, at an angle which made sitting on chairs a tricky and even perilous feat. I do not know how many people it seated, but it was full on this occasion, and people stood or sat in the aisles on extra chairs, borrowed from an undertaker.

The reeve and I and the other notables climbed a back stairs and pushed our way through the scenery to the chairs that had been set for us on the stage. Beyond the curtain we heard the hum of the crowd above the orchestra of piano, violin, and trombone. A little after the appointed time—to allow for latecomers, said the reeve, but no latecomer could have squeezed in—the curtain rose (swaying menacingly inward toward us as it did so), and we were revealed, set off against a set of scenery that portrayed a dense and poisonously green forest. Our chairs were arranged in straight rows behind a table supporting two jugs of water and fully a dozen glasses, to succour the speakers in their thirst. We were a fine group: three clergymen, the magistrate, the Member of Parliament and the Member of the Legislature, the Chairman of the Continuation School Board, and seven members of the township council sat on the stage, as well as the reeve and myself. I expect we looked rather like a minstrel show. I was the only man in uniform on the stage itself, but in the front row were six others, and on the right-hand end of this group sat Percy Boyd Staunton, in a major's uniform, and at his side was Leola Cruikshank.

On the fourth finger of Leola's left hand was a large diamond ring. Diana had taught me something of these refinements and I got the message at once, as that ring flashed its signals to me during the applause that greeted our appearance. Was I stricken to the heart? Did I blench and feel that all my glory was as dross? No; I was rather pleased. There was one of my home-coming problems solved already, I reflected. Nevertheless I was a little put out and thought that Leola was a sneak not to have informed me of this development in one of her letters.

The purpose of the gathering was plainly signalled by the Union Jack that swathed the speaker's table and a painted streamer that hung above our heads in the toxic forest. "Welcome To Our Brave Boys Back From The Front," it shouted, in red and blue letters on a white ground. We stood solemnly at attention while the piano, violin, and trombone worked their way through *God Save the King, O Canada,* and, for good measure, *The Maple Leaf Forever*. But we did not then rush greedily upon the noblest splendours of the evening. We began with a patriotic concert, to hone our fervour to a finer edge.

Muriel Parkinson sang about the *Rose that Blows in No-Man's Land,* and when she shrieked (for her voice was powerful rather than sweet) that "midst the war's great curse stood the Red Cross Nurse," many people mopped their eyes. She then sang a song about Joan of Arc, which was a popular war number of the day, and thus a delicate compliment was paid to France, our great ally. Muriel was followed by a female child, unknown to me, who recited Pauline Johnson's poem *Canadian Born,* wearing Indian dress; it was at this point that I became aware that one of our Brave Boys, namely George Muskrat the Indian sniper, who had picked off Germans just as he used to pick off squirrels, was not present. George was not a very respectable fellow (he drank vanilla extract, which was mostly alcohol, to excess, and shouted in the streets when on a toot), and he had not been given any medals.

The female child reciter had an encore and was well into it before the applause for her first piece had quite subsided. Then, for no perceptible reason, another girl played two pieces on the piano, not very well; one was called *Chanson des Fleurs* and the other *La Jeunesse,* so perhaps they were further compliments to the French. Then a fellow with a local reputation as a wit, named Murray Tiffin, "entertained"; he was often asked to "entertain" at church evenings, but this was his greatest opportunity so far, and he toiled like a cart horse to divert us with riddles, jokes, and imitations, all of some local application.

"What's the bravest thing a man can do?" he demanded. "Is it go right out to Africa and shoot a lion? No! *That's* not the bravest thing a man can do! Is it capture a German machine-gun nest single-handed?" (Great applause, during which I, the worst actor in the world, tried to feign a combination of modesty and mirth.) "No! The bravest thing a man can do is go to the Deptford Post Office at one minute past six on a Saturday night and ask Jerry Williams for a one-cent stamp!" (Uncontrollable mirth, and much nudging and waving at the postmaster, who tried to look like a man who dearly loved a joke against his cranky self.)

Then Murray got off several other good ones, about how much cheaper it was to buy groceries in Bowles Corners than it was even to steal them from the merchants of Deptford, and similar local wit of the sort that age cannot wither nor custom stale; I warmed to Murray, for although his jokes were clean they had much of the quality that had assured my own rest-camp success as Charlie Chaplin.

When Murray had offended individually at least half the people present and delighted us all collectively, the reeve rose and began, "But to strike a more serious note—" and went on to strike that note for at least ten minutes. We were gathered, he said, to honour those of our community who had risked their lives in defence of liberty. When he had finished, the Methodist parson told us, at some length, how meritorious it was to risk one's life in defence of liberty. Then Father Regan solemnly read out the eleven names of the men from our little part of the world who had been killed in service; Willie's was among them, and I think it was in that moment that I really understood that I would never see Willie again.

The Reverend Donald Phelps prayed that we might never forget them, at some length; if God had not been attending to the war, He knew a good deal more about it, from our point of view, by the time Phelps had finished. The Member of the Legislature told us he would not detain us long and talked for forty minutes about the future and what we were going to do with it, building on the sacrifices of the past four years, particularly in the matter of improving the provincial road system. Then the Member of Parliament was let loose upon us, and he talked for three minutes more than one hour, combining patriotism with a good partisan political speech, hinting pretty strongly that although Lloyd George, Clemenceau, and Wilson were unquestionably good men, Sir Robert Borden had really pushed the war to a successful conclusion.

It was by now ten o'clock and even the thirst of a Canadian audience for oratory was almost slaked. Only the great moments that were to follow could have held them. But here it was that the reeve took his second bite at us; in order that Deptford might never forget those who had fought and returned, he said, and in order that our heroes should never lose sight of Deptford's gratitude, every one of us was to receive an engraved watch. Nor was this all. These were no ordinary watches but railway watches, warranted to tell time accurately under the most trying conditions, and probably for all eternity. We understood the merit of these watches because, as we all knew, his son Jack was a railwayman, a brakeman on the Grand Trunk, and Jack swore that these were the best watches to be had anywhere. Whereupon the watches were presented, three by the reeve himself and three by the Member of the Legislature.

As his name and glory were proclaimed, each man in the front row climbed up the steps that led to a pass-door at the side of the stage, squeezed through the green scenery, and made his way to the centre of the platform, while his relatives and townsmen cheered, stamped, and whistled. Percy Boyd Staunton was the sixth, the only officer in the group and the only man who accepted his watch with an air; he had put on his cap before coming to the stage, and he saluted the Member of the Legislature smartly, then turned and saluted the audience; it was a fine effect, and as I grinned and clapped, my stomach burned with jealousy.

I should have been generous, for I was number seven, a V.C., the only man to be given a seat on the stage, and the only man to receive his watch from the hands of our Member of Parliament. He made a speech. "Sergeant Dunstable Ramsay," said he, "I acclaim you as a hero tonight—" and went on for quite a while, though I could not judge how long, because I stood before him feeling a fool and a fake as I had not done when I stood before my King. But at last he handed me the railway watch, and as I had left my hat outside I could not salute, so I had to bob my head, and then bob it at the audience, who cheered and stamped, rather longer than they had done for Percy, I believe. But my feelings were so confused that I could not enjoy it; I heartily wished to get away.

We concluded by singing *God Save the King* again in a classy version in which Muriel Parkinson was supposed to sing some parts alone and the rest of us to join in when she gave a signal; but there were a few people who droned along with her all the way, somewhat spoiling the effect. But when it was done we were free. Nobody seemed inclined to hurry away, and when I had made my way through the green scenery and down the steps by the pass-door I was surrounded by old friends and acquaintances who wanted to talk and shake my hand. I hurried through them as quickly as I could without being rude or overlooking anyone, but I had a little task to perform—a notion I had thought of during the long hour of the Member's speech, and I wanted to be sure I had a good audience. At last I reached Percy and Leola; I seized his hand and shook it vigorously, and then seized Leola in a bear-hug and kissed her resoundingly and at what Deptford would certainly have regarded as a very familiar length.

Leola had always been the kind of girl who closed her eyes when you kissed her, but I kept mine well open and I could see that her eyeballs were rolling wildly beneath her lids; Diana had taught me a thing or two about kisses, and I gave her a pretty good example of that art.

"Darling," I shouted, not letting her go, "you don't know how good it is to see you!"

Percy was grinning nervously. Public kissing was not so common then as it is now, and certainly not in our village. "Dunny, Leola and I have a secret to tell you—not that it will be secret long, of course—but we want you to be the first to hear—outside our families, of course—but we're engaged." And he sprayed his manly grin from side to side, for we were in the middle of a crowd and everybody could hear. There was a happy murmur, and a few people clapped.

I counted three, just to make sure that there was the right sort of pause, then I shook his hand again and roared, "Well, well, the best man has won!"—and kissed Leola again, not so long or so proprietorially, but to show that there had been a contest and that I had been a near winner myself, and had shown some speed in the preliminary heats.

It was a good moment and I enjoyed it thoroughly. Percy was wearing a few medals, the admirable D.S.O. but otherwise minor things, mostly for having been at particular engagements. I have already said that I am not much of an actor, but I gave a powerful, if crude impersonation of the hero who is tremendous on the field of Mars but slighted in the courts of Venus. I am sure that there are people in Deptford to this day who remember it.

I suppose it was mean. But Percy, in his officer's smart uniform, got under my skin just as he had always done, and as for Leola, I didn't particularly want her but resented anybody else having her. I promised that this would be a frank record, so far as I can write one, and God forbid that I should pretend that there is not a generous measure of spite in my nature.

This encounter put us in one of those uneasy situations that are forced on people by fate, for to the crowd—and at that moment Deptford was the whole world—we were the masterspirits of the evening: two men, one of whom was a hero without a left leg and the other a handsome and rich young fellow, only somewhat less a hero, who had aspired to the hand of the prettiest girl in the village, and the winner had been acclaimed; we were a splendidly sentimental story made flesh, and it would have been maladroit in the extreme—a real flying in the face of Providence—if we had not stayed together so people could marvel at us and wonder about us. That was why we went to the bonfire as a threesome.

The bonfire was arranged to take place outside the combination village hall, public library, courthouse, and fire hall; it was to be a gay conclusion, an anti-masque, to the high proceedings in the Opera House. There we had been solemn, acclaiming the heroic young and listening to the wise old: here the crowd was lively and expectant; children dodged to and fro, and there was a lot of laughter about nothing in particular. But not for long. In the distance we heard a great beating on pots and pans and blowing of tin horns, and down our main street came a procession, lit by the flame of brooms dipped in oil—a ruddy, smoky light—accompanying Marshal Foch, the two John Bulls, Uncle Sam, Gallant Little Belgium, the whole gang, dragging at a rope's end Deptford's own conception of the German Emperor, fat Myron Papple, whose writhings and caperings outdid his afternoon efforts as the death aria of an opera tenor outdoes his wooing in Act One.

"Hang him!" we heard the representatives of the Allies shouting as they drew near, and the crowd around the village hall took it up. "Hang him!" they yelled. "Hang the Kaiser!"

Hang him they did. A rope was ready on the flagpole, and during some scrambling preparations a sharp eye would have seen Myron slip away into the darkness as an effigy was tied to the rope by the neck and hauled slowly up the pole. As it rose, one of the Red Cross nurses set fire to it with a broom torch, and by the time it reached the top the figure was burning merrily.

Then the cheers were loud, and the children hopped and scampered round the foot of the flagpole, shouting, "Hang the Kaiser!" with growing hysteria; some of them were much too small to know what hanging was, or what a Kaiser might be, but I cannot call them innocent, for they were being as vicious as their age and experience allowed. And the people in the crowd, as I looked at them, were hardly recognizable as the earnest citizens who, not half an hour ago, had been so biddable under the spell of patriotic oratory, so responsive to *Canadian Born*, so touched by the romantic triangle of Leola, and Percy, and myself. Here they were, in this murky, fiery light, happily acquiescent in a symbolic act of cruelty and hatred. As the only person there, I suppose, who had any idea of what a really bad burn was like, I watched them with dismay that mounted toward horror, for these were my own people.

Leola's face looked very pretty as she turned it upward toward the fire, and Percy was laughing and looking about him for admiration as he shouted in his strong, manly voice, "Hang the Kaiser!"

Myron Papple, an artist to his fingertips, had climbed into the tower of the village hall, so that his screams and entreaties might proceed as near as possible from the height of the burning figure. I could hear him long after I had crept away to my bed in the Tecumseh House. I had not wanted to stay till the end.

8

The next day was a Saturday, and I had plenty to do. Though still an object of wonder, I was now free to move about as I pleased, and my first move was to get the keys of my old home from the magistrate and make a melancholy tour through its six rooms. Everything was where I knew it should be, but all the objects looked small and dull—my mother's clock, my father's desk, with the stone on it he had brought from Dumfries and always used as a paperweight; it was now an unloved house, and want of love had withered it. I picked up a few things I wanted—particularly something that I had long kept hidden—and got out as fast as I could.

Then I went to see Ada Blake, the girl Willie had been sweet on, and had a talk with her; Ada was a fine girl, and I liked her very much, but of course the Willie she remembered was not the brother I knew. I judge they had been lovers, briefly, and that was what Willie meant to her: to me his chief significance now was that he had died twice, and that the first time Mrs. Dempster had brought him back to life. I certainly had no intention of visiting Dr. McCausland, to see if he had changed his opinion on that subject, though I did chat with two or three of our village elders before getting my midday dinner at the hotel.

As soon as I had gobbled my greasy stew and apple pie I crossed the street to get a haircut at Papple's. I had already observed that Milo was on the job alone; his father was presumably at home, resting up after his patriotic exertions of the day before, and it was a chance to catch up on the village news. Milo gave me a hero's welcome and settled me in one of the two chairs, under a striped sheet that smelled, in equal portions, of barber's perfumes and the essence of Deptford manhood.

"Jeez, Dunny, this is the first time I ever give you a haircut—you know that? Trimmed your Pa a coupla times after you went to the Front, but never you. Comes of being the same age, I guess, eh? But now I'm taking over more and more from the old man. His heart's not so good now; he says it's breathing up little bits of hair all his life; he says it forms a kind of a hairball in barbers, and a lot of 'em go that way. I don't believe it; unscientific. He never got past third grade—you know that? But jeez, he certainly had 'em laughing yesterday, eh? And last night! But it told on him. Says he can feel the hairball today, just like it was one of his organs.

"You got a double crown. Did you know that? Makes it hard to give you a good cut. What you going to do with the old place? Live there, eh? Nice place to settle down if you was to get married. Your folks always kept it nice. Cece Athelstan always used to say, 'The Ramsays sure are buggers for paint.' But I guess you won't be marrying Leola, eh? Mind you, for them that had eyes to see, there was never an instant's doubt she was Percy's girl—never an instant's. Oh, I know you and her had some pretty close moments before you went to the war; everybody seen that and they kinda laughed. I had to laugh myself. It was just what we called war-fever—you in uniform, you see. But you got to admit she played fair. Wrote to you right up to the end. Jerry Williams used to tell us the letters come through the Post Office every second Monday like clockwork. Because she wrote you every second Sunday, you know that? But when Percy finished up at that school in Toronto in the summer of 'seventeen, he didn't hesitate for a minute—not for a minute. Into training right away, and went over as an officer, and come back a major. And a D.S.O. But you're the V.C., eh, boy? I guess you had a stroke of luck. I never got enlisted: flat feet. But you and Perse had the luck, I guess. He used to come down here as often as he could, and it was easy seen where Leola had give her heart. That's what her old lady used to say. 'Leola's give her heart,' she'd say. Ben Cruikshank wasn't strong on Perse to begin with, but the old lady shut him up. He's pleased now, all right. See him last night? Of course he thinks the sun rises and sets in Leola. It's hard for a father, I guess. But you were the main attraction last night, eh? Yep, you were the Kandy Kid with Gum Feet and Taffy Legs. One Taffy Leg, anyhow. But not with Leola. She's give her heart.

"Jeez the war's made a difference in this little old burg. Unsettled. You know what I mean? Lots of changes. Two fires—bad ones—and Harry Henderson sold his store. But I guess I mean changes in people. Young kids in trouble a lot. And Jerry Cullen—you remember him?—sent to the penitentiary. His daughter squealed on him. Said he was always at her. She was just a kid, mind you. But the cream of it was, I don't think Jerry ever really knew what he done wrong. I think he thought everybody was like that. He was always kinda stupid. About that kinda thing, though, I guess the worst was young Grace Izzard—maybe you don't remember—she's always called Harelip because she's got this funny-looking lip. Well, she got to fourteen and got to guessing, I suppose, but who'd want her with a face like that? So she promises her kid brother Bobby, who's about twelve, a quarter if he'll do it to her, and he does but only if he gets ten cents first, and then, jeez, when he's finished she only gives him another nickel because she says that's all it's worth! Isn't that a corker, eh? These kids today, eh? And then—"

And then two bastards, a juicy self-induced abortion, several jiltings, an old maid gone foolish in menopause, and a goitre of such proportions as to make all previous local goitres seem like warts, which Dr. McCausland was treating in Bowles Corners. The prurient, the humiliating, and the macabre were Milo's principal areas of enthusiasm, and we explored them all.

"The flu beat everything though. Spanish Influenza, they called it, but I always figured it was worked up by the Huns some ways. Jeez, this burg was like the Valley of the Shadda for weeks. Of course we felt it more than most in here; a barber always has everybody breathing on him, you see. The old man and me, we hung bags of assafoetida around our necks to give the germs a fight. But oh, people just dropped like flies. Like flies. McCausland worked twenty-four hours a day, I guess. Doc Staunton moved out to one of his farms to live and sort of gave up practice. But he'd been mostly a farmer in a big way for years. Rich man now. You remember Roy Janes and his wife, the Anglican minister? They never rested, going around to sick houses, and then both of 'em died themselves within forty-eight hours. The reeve put the town flag at half-mast that day, and everybody said he done right. And your Ma, Dunny—God, she was a wonderful woman! Never let up on nursing and taking soup and stuff around till your Dad went. You know he wouldn't go to bed? Struggled on when he was sick. Of course you could tell. Blue lips. Yeah, just as blue as huckleberries. That was the sign. We give 'em forty-eight hours after that. Your Dad kept on with his lips as blue as a Sunday suit for a day, then he just fell beside the makeup stone, and Jumper Saul got him home on a dray. Your Ma lost heart and she was gone herself before the week was out. Fine folks. Next issue of the *Banner,* Jumper Saul and Nell turned the column rules, and the front page just looked like a big death notice. God, when I saw it I just started bawling like a kid. Couldn't help myself. Do you know, in this little town of five hundred, and the district around, we lost ninety-eight, all told? But the worst was when Jumper turned the column rules. Everybody said he done right.

"You know 'Masa Dempster went? 'Course, he'd been no good for years. Not since his trouble, you remember? Sure you do! We used to see you skin over there after school and climb through the window to see her and Paul. Nobody ever thought there was any wrong going on, of course. We knew your Ma must have sent you. She couldn't do anything for the Dempsters publicly, of course, but she sent you to look after them. Everybody knew it an' honoured her for it. Do you remember how you said Mary Dempster raised Willie from the dead? God, you used to be a crazy kid, Dunny, but I guess the war knocked all that out of you . . .

"Miz' Dempster? Oh no, she didn't get the flu. That kind is always spared when better folks have to go. But after 'Masa went she was a problem. No money, you see. So the reeve and Magistrate Mahaffey found out she had an aunt somewheres near Toronto. Weston, I believe it was. The aunt come and took her. The aunt had money. Husband made it in stoves, I heard.

"No, Paul didn't go with her. Funny about him. Not ten yet, but he run away. He had a kind of a tough time at school, I guess. Couldn't fight much, because he was so undersized, but kids used to get around him at recess and yell, 'Hey, Paul, does your Ma wear any pants?' and stuff like that. Just fun, you know. The way kids are. But he'd get mad and fight and get hurt, and they just tormented him more to see him do it. They'd yell across the street, 'Hoor yuh today, Paul?' Sly, you see, because he knew damn well they didn't mean 'How are you today, Paul?' but 'Your Ma's a hoor.' Kind of a pun, I guess you'd call it. So when the circus was here, autumn of 'eighteen, he run away with one of the shows. Mahaffey tried to catch up with the circus, but he could never get nowheres with them. Tricky people. Funny, it was the best thing Paul ever done, in a way, because every kid wants to run away with a circus, and it made him kind of a hero after he'd gone. But Mary Dempster took it very bad and went clean off her head. Used to yell out the window at kids going to school, 'Have you seen my son Paul?' It would of been sad if we hadn't of known she was crazy. And it was only two or three weeks after that 'Masa got the flu and died. He certainly had a hard row to hoe. And inside a week the aunt come, and we haven't seen hide nor hair of them since."

By this time the haircut was finished, and Milo insisted on anointing me with every scent and tonic he had in the shop, and stifling me with talcum, as a personal tribute to my war record.

The next day was Sunday, and I made a much appreciated appearance in St. James' Presbyterian Church. On Monday, after a short talk with the bank manager and the auctioneer, and a much longer and pleasanter talk with Jumper Saul and Nell, I boarded the train—there was no crowd at the station this time—and left Deptford in the flesh. It was not for a long time that I recognized that I never wholly left it in the spirit.

· III ·
My Fool-Saint

1

In the autumn of 1919 I entered University College, in the University of Toronto, as an Honours student in history. I was not properly qualified, but five professors talked to me for an hour and decided to admit me under some special ruling invoked on behalf of a number of men who had been abroad fighting. This was the first time my boyhood stab at being a polymath did me any good; there was also the fact that it has been my luck to appear more literate than I really am, owing to a cadaverous and scowling cast of countenance and a rather pedantic Scots voice; and certainly my V.C. and general appearance of having bled for liberty did no harm. So there I was, and very pleased about it too.

I had sold the family house for $1200, and its contents, by auction, for an unexpected $600. I had even sold the *Banner*, to a job printer who thought he would like to publish a newspaper, for $750 down and a further $2750 on notes extending over four years; I was an innocent in business, and he was a deadbeat, so I never got all of it. Nevertheless, the hope of money to come was encouraging. I had quite a good pension for my disabilities, and the promise of wooden legs as I needed them, and of course my annual $50 that went with the V.C. I seemed to myself to be the lord of great means, and in a way it proved so, for when I got my B.A. after four years I was able to run to another year's work for an M.A. I had always meant to get a Ph.D. at some later time, but I became interested in a branch of scholarship in which it was not relevant.

During my long summer vacations I worked at undemanding jobs—timekeeper on roadwork and the like—which enabled me to do a lot of reading and keep body and soul together without touching my education money, which was the way I looked on my capital.

I took very kindly to history. I chose it as my special study because during my fighting days I had become conscious that I was being used by powers over which I had no control for purposes of which I had no understanding. History, I hoped, would teach me how the world's affairs worked. It never really did so, but I became interested in it for its own sake, and at last found a branch of it that gripped whatever intelligence I had, and never relaxed its hold. At Varsity I never fell below fifth in my year in anything, and graduated first; my M.A. won me some compliments, though I thought my thesis dull. I gobbled up all the incidentals that were required to give a "rounded" education; even zoology (an introductory course) agreed with me, and I achieved something like proficiency in French. German I learned later, in a hurry, for some special work, and with a Berlitz teacher. I was also one of the handful of really interested students in Religious Knowledge, though it was not much of a course, relying too heavily on St. Paul's journeys for my taste, and avoiding any discussion of what St. Paul was really journeying in aid of. But it was a pleasure to be inside and warm, instead of wallowing in mud, and I worked, I suppose rather hard, though I was not conscious of it at the time. I made no close friends and never sought popularity or office in any of the student committees, but I got on pretty well with everybody. A dull fellow, I suppose; youth was not my time to flower.

Percy Boyd Staunton, however, flowered brilliantly, and I met him fairly often; brilliant young men seem to need a dull listener, just as pretty girls need a plain friend, to set them off. Like me, he had a new name. I had enrolled in the university as Dunstan Ramsay: Percy, somewhere in his Army experience, had thrown aside that name (which had become rather a joke, like Algernon) and had lopped the "d" off the name that remained. He was now Boy Staunton, and it suited him admirably. Just as Childe Rowland and Childe Harold were so called because they epitomized romance and gentle birth, he was Boy Staunton because he summed up in himself so much of the glory of youth in the postwar period. He gleamed, he glowed; his hair was glossier, his teeth whiter than those of common young men. He laughed a great deal, and his voice was musical. He danced often and spectacularly; he always knew the latest steps, and in those days there were new steps every month. Where his looks and style came from I never knew; certainly not from cantankerous old Doc Staunton, with his walrus moustache and sagging paunch, or from his mother, who was a charmless woman. Boy seemed to have made himself out of nothing, and he was a marvel.

He was a perfectionist, however, and not content. I remember him telling me during his first year as a law student that a girl had told him he reminded her of Richard Barthelmess, the screen star; he would rather have reminded her of John Barrymore, and he was displeased. I was quite a moviegoer myself and foolishly said I thought he was more like Wallace Reid in *The Dancin' Fool,* and was surprised by his indignation, for Reid was a handsome man. It was not until later that I discovered that he coveted a suggestion of aristocracy in his appearance and bearing, and Reid lacked it. He was at that time still casting around for an ideal upon whom he could model himself. It was not until his second year in law that he found it.

This ideal, this mould for his outward man, was no one less than Edward Albert Christian George Andrew Patrick David, the Prince of Wales. The papers were full of the Prince at that time. He was the great ambassador of the Commonwealth, but he had also the common touch; he spoke with what horrified old ladies thought a common accent, but he could charm a bird from a branch; he danced and was reputed to be a devil with the girls; he was said to quarrel with his father (my King, the man with the Navy torpedo beard) about matters of dress; he was photographed smoking a pipe with a distinctive apple-shaped bowl. He had romance and mystery, for over his puzzled brow hung the shadow of the Crown; how would such a dashing youth ever settle himself to the duties of kingship? He was gloated over by old women who wondered what princess he would marry, and gloated over by young women because he thought more of looks and charm than of royal blood. There were rumours of high old times with jolly girls when he had visited Canada in 1919. Flaming Youth, and yet, withal, a Prince, remote and fated for great things. Just the very model for Boy Staunton, who saw himself in similar terms.

In those days you could not become a lawyer by going to the university—not in our part of Canada. You must go to Osgoode Hall, where the Law Society of Upper Canada would steer you through until at last you were called to the Bar. This worried Boy, but not very much. The university, he admitted to me—I had not asked for any such admission—put a stamp on a man; but if you got that stamp first and studied law later, you would be old, a positive greybeard, before getting into the full tide of life. So far as I could see, the full tide of life had a lot to do with sugar.

Sugar was what old Doc Staunton was chiefly interested in. He had grabbed up a lot of land in the Deptford district and put it all into sugar-beets. The black, deep alluvial soil of the river flats around Deptford was good for anything, and wonderful for beets. Doc was not yet a Sugar-Beet King, but he was well on his way to it—a sort of Sticky Duke. Boy, who had more vision than his father, managed to get the old man to buy into the secondary process, the refining of the sugar from the beets, and this was proving profitable in such a surprising degree that Doc Staunton was rich in a sense far beyond Deptford's comprehension; so rich, indeed, that they forgot that he had skipped town when the flu epidemic struck. As for the present, a very rich man has something better to do than listen to old women's coughs and patch up farmers who have fallen into the chaff-cutter. Doc Staunton never formally dropped practice, and accepted the sanctity that came with wealth in the way he had accepted his prestige as a doctor—with a sour face and a combination of pomposity and grievance that was all his own. He did not move away from Deptford. He did not know of anywhere else to go, I suppose, and the life of a village Rich Man—far outstripping the Athelstans—suited him very well.

The Athelstans did not like it, and Cece got off a "good one" that the village cherished for years. "If Jesus died to redeem Doc Staunton," he said, "He made a damn poor job of it."

So Boy Staunton knew that he too had a crown awaiting him. He did not mean to practise law, but it was a good training for business and, eventually, politics. He was going to be a very rich man—richer than his father by far—and he was getting ready.

He, like his ideal, was not on the best of terms with his father. Doc Staunton gave Boy what he regarded as a good allowance; it was not bad, but it was not ample either, and Boy needed more. So he made some shrewd short-term investments in the stock market and was thus able to live at a rate that puzzled and annoyed the old man, who waited angrily for him to get into debt. But Boy did not get into debt. Debt was for boobs, he said, and he flaunted such toys as gold cigarette cases and hand-made shoes under the old man's nose, without explaining anything.

Where Boy lived high, I lived—well, not low, but in the way congenial to myself. I thought twenty-four dollars was plenty for a ready-made suit, and four dollars a criminal price for a pair of shoes. I changed my shirt twice a week and my underwear once. I had not yet developed any expensive tastes and saw nothing wrong with a good boarding-house; it was years before I decided that there is really no such thing as a good boarding-house. Once, temporarily envious of Boy, I bought a silk shirt and paid nine dollars for it. It burned me like the shirt of Nessus, but I wore it to rags, to get my money out of it, garment of guilty luxury that it was.

Here we come to a point where I have to make an admission that will put me in a bad light, considering the story I have to tell. Boy was very good about passing on information to me about investment, and now and then I ventured two or three hundred from my small store, always with heartening results. Indeed, during my university days I laid the foundation for the modest but pleasant fortune I have now. What Boy did in thousands I did in hundreds, and without his guidance I would have been powerless, for investment was not in my line; I knew just enough to follow his advice—when to buy and when to sell, and especially when to hang on. Why he did this for me I can only explain on the grounds that he must have liked me. But it was a kind of liking, as I hope will be clear before we have finished, that was not easy to bear.

We were both young, neither yet fully come to himself, and whatever he may have felt about me, I knew that in several ways I was jealous of him. He had something to give—his advice about how to turn my few hundreds into a few thousands—and I make no apology for benefiting from the advice of a man I sneered at in my mind; I was too much a Scot to let a dollar get away from me if it came within my clutch. I am not seeking to posture as a hero in this memoir. Later, when I had something to give and could have helped him, he did not want it. You see how it was: to him the reality of life lay in external things, whereas for me the only reality was of the spirit—of the mind, as I then thought, not having understood yet what a cruel joker and mean master the intellect can be. So if you choose to see me as a false friend, exploiting a frank and talented youth, go ahead. I can but hope that before my story is all told you will see things otherwise.

We met about once every two weeks, by appointment, for our social lives never intersected. Why would they, especially after Boy bought his car, a very smart affair coloured a rich shade of auburn. He helled around to all the dancing places with men of his own stamp and the girls they liked, drinking a good deal out of flasks and making lots of noise.

I remember seeing him at a rugby game in the autumn of 1923; it was not a year since the Earl of Carnarvon had discovered the tomb of Tutankhamen, and already the gentlemen's outfitters had worked up a line of Egyptian fashions. Boy wore a gorgeous pull-over of brownish-red, around which marched processions of little Egyptians, copied from the tomb pictures; he had on the baggiest of Oxford bags, smoked the apple-bowl pipe with casual style, and his demeanour was that of one of the lords of creation. A pretty girl with shingled hair and rolled stockings that allowed you to see delightful flashes of her bare knees was with him, and they were taking alternate pulls at a very large flask that contained, I am sure, something intoxicating but not positively toxic from the stock of the best bootlegger in town. He was the quintessence of the Jazz Age, a Scott Fitzgerald character. It was characteristic of Boy throughout his life that he was always the quintessence of something that somebody else had recognized and defined.

I was filled with a sour scorn that I now know was nothing but envy, but then I mistook it for philosophy. I didn't really want the clothes, I didn't really want the girl or the booze, but it scalded me to see him enjoying them, and I hobbled away grumbling to myself like Diogenes. I recognize now that my limp was always worse when I envied Boy; I suppose that without knowing it I exaggerated my disability so that people would notice and say, "That must be a returned man." God, youth is a terrible time! So much feeling and so little notion of how to handle it!

When we met we usually ended up talking about Leola. It had been agreed by Boy's parents and the Cruikshanks that she should wait until Boy had qualified as a lawyer before they married. There had been some suggestion from Leola that she might train as a nurse in the meanwhile, but it came to nothing because her parents thought the training would coarsen their darling—bedpans and urinals and washing naked men and all that sort of thing. So she hung around Deptford, surrounded by the haze of sanctity that was supposed to envelop an engaged girl, waiting for Boy's occasional weekend visits in the auburn car. I knew from his confidences that they went in for what the euphemism of the day called "heavy petting"—mutual masturbation would be the bleak term for it—but that Leola had principles and they never went farther, so that in a technical, physical sense—though certainly not in spirit—she remained a virgin.

Boy, however, had acquired tastes in the Army that could not be satisfied by agonizingly prolonged and inadequately requited puffings and snortings in a parked car, but he had no clarity of mind that would ease him of guilt when he deceived Leola—as he did, with variety and regularity among the free-spirited girls he met in Toronto. He built up a gimcrack metaphysical structure to help him out of his difficulty and appealed to me to set the seal of university wisdom on it.

These gay girls, he explained, "knew what they were doing," and thus he had no moral responsibility toward them. Some of them were experts in what were then called French kisses or soul kisses, which the irreverent called "swapping spits." Though he might "fall" for one of them for a few weeks—even go so far as to have a "pash" for her—he was not "in love" with her, as he was with Leola. I had made this fine philosophical distinction myself in my dealings with Diana, and it startled me to hear it from Boy's lips; noodle that I was, I had supposed this sophistry was my own invention. So long as he truly and abidingly loved none but Leola, these "pashes" did not count, did they? Or did I think they did? Above all things he wanted to be perfectly fair to Leola, who was so sweet that she had never once asked him if he was tempted to fall for any of the girls he went dancing with in the city.

I would have given much for the strength of mind to tell him I had no opinions on such matters, but I could not resist the bittersweet, prurient pleasure of listening. I knew it gave him a pleasure that he probably did not yet acknowledge to himself, to confront me with his possession of Leola. He had wormed it out of her that she had once thought she loved me, and he assured me that all three of us now regarded this as a passing aberration—mere war-fever. I did not deny it, but neither did I like it.

I did not want her, but it annoyed me that Boy had her. I had not only learned about physical love in splendid guise from Diana; I had also acquired from her an idea of a woman as a delightful creature that walked and talked and laughed and joked and thought and understood, which quite outsoared anything in Leola's modest repertoire of charms. Nevertheless—egotistical dog in the manger that I was—I keenly resented the fact that she had thrown me over for Boy and had not had the courage to write and tell me so. I see now that it was beyond Leola's abilities to put anything really important on paper; however much she may have wanted to do so, she could not have found words for what she ought to have said. But at that time, with her parents holding her, as it were, in erotic escrow for Boy Staunton, I was sour about the whole business.

Why did I not find some other girl? Diana, Headmaster, Diana. I often yearned for her, but never to the point where I wrote to ask if we might not reconsider. I knew that Diana would stand in the way of the kind of life I wanted to live and that she would not be content with anything less than a full and, if possible, a controlling share in the life of any man she married. But that did not stop me, often and painfully, from wanting her.

A selfish, envious, cankered wretch, wasn't I?

2

The kind of life I wanted to live—yes, but I was not at all sure what it was. I had flashes of insight and promptings, but nothing definite. So when I was finished at the university, duly ticketed as an M.A. in history, I still wanted time to find my way, and like many a man in my case I took to schoolmastering.

Was it a dead end? Did I thereby join the ranks of those university men of promise whose promise is never fulfilled? You can answer that question as readily as I, Headmaster, and certainly the answer must be no. I took to teaching like a duck to water, and like a duck I never paid exaggerated attention to the medium in which I moved. I applied for a job at Colborne College principally because, being a private school, it did not demand that I have a provincial teacher's training certificate; I didn't want to waste another year getting that, and I didn't really think I would stay in teaching. I also liked the fact that Colborne was a boys' school; I never wanted to teach girls—don't, in fact, think they are best served by the kind of education devised by men for men.

I have been a good teacher because I have never thought much about teaching; I just worked through the curriculum and insisted on high standards. I never played favourites, never tried to be popular, never set my heart on the success of any clever boy, and took good care that I knew my stuff. I was not easily approachable, but if approached I was civil and serious to the boy who approached me. I have coached scores of boys privately for scholarships, and I have never taken a fee for it. Of course I have enjoyed all of this, and I suppose my enjoyment had its influence on the boys. As I have grown older my bias—the oddly recurrent themes of history, which are also the themes of myth—has asserted itself, and why not? But when I first stepped into a Colborne classroom, wearing the gown that we were all expected to wear then, I never thought that it would be more than forty years before I left it for good.

Simply from the school's point of view, I suppose my life has seemed odd and dry, though admittedly useful. As the years wore on I was finally acquitted of the suspicion that hangs over every bachelor schoolmaster—that he is a homosexual, either overt or frying in some smoky flame of his own devising. I have never been attracted to boys. Indeed, I have never much liked boys. To me a boy is a green apple whom I expect to expose to the sun of history until he becomes a red apple, a man. I know too much about boys to sentimentalize over them. I have been a boy myself, and I know what a boy is, which is to say, either a fool or an imprisoned man striving to get out.

No, teaching was my professional life, to which I gave whatever was its due. The sources from which my larger life was nourished were elsewhere, and it is to write of them that I address this memoir to you, Headmaster, hoping thereby that when I am dead at least one man will know the truth about me and do me justice.

Did I live chastely—I who have been so critical of Boy Staunton's rough-and-tumble sexual affairs? No memoir of our day is thought complete without some comment on the sex life of its subject, and therefore let me say that during my early years as a schoolmaster I found a number of women who were interesting, and sufficiently interested in me, to give me a sex life of a sort. They were the women who usually get into affairs with men who are not the marrying kind. There was Agnes Day, who yearned to take upon herself the sins of the whole world, and sacrifice her body and mind to some deserving male's cause. She soon became melancholy company. Then there was Gloria Mundy, the good-time girl, who had to be stoked with costly food, theatre tickets, and joyrides of all kinds. She cost more than her admittedly good company was worth, and she was kind enough to break up the affair herself. And of course Libby Doe, who thought sex was the one great, true, and apostolic key and cure and could not get enough of it, which I could. I played fair with all of them, I hope; the fact that I did not love them did not prevent me from liking them very much, and I never used a woman simply as an object in my life.

They all had enough of me quite quickly because my sense of humour, controlled in the classroom, was never in check in the bedroom. I was a talking lover, which most women hate. And my physical disabilities were bothersome. The women were quick to assure me that these did not matter at all; Agnes positively regarded my ravaged body as her martyr's stake. But I could not forget my brownish-red nubbin where one leg should have been, and a left side that looked like the crackling of a roast. As well as these offences against my sense of erotic propriety, there were other, and to me sometimes hilarious, problems. What, for instance, is etiquette for the one-legged philanderer? Should he remove his prosthesis before putting on his prophylactic, or *vice versa?* I suggested to my partners that we should write to Dorothy Dix about it. They did not think that funny.

It was many years before I rediscovered love, and then it was not Love's Old Sweet Song, recalling Diana: no, I drank the reviving drop from the Cauldron of Ceridwen. Very well worth waiting for, too.

3

At the age of twenty-six I had become an M.A., and the five thousand dollars or so I had begun with had grown, under Boy's counselling, to a resounding eight, and I had lived as well as I wanted to do in the meanwhile on my pension. What Boy had I do not know, for he spoke of it mysteriously as "a plum" (an expression out of his Prince of Wales repertoire), but he looked glossy and knew no care. When he married Leola in St. James' Presbyterian Church, Deptford, I was his best man, in a hired morning suit and a top hat in which I looked like an ass. It was the most fashionable wedding in Deptford history, marred only by the conduct of some of the groom's legal friends, who whooped it up in the Tecumseh House when the dry party at Doc Staunton's was mercifully over. Leola's parents were minor figures at the wedding; very properly so, in everybody's opinion, for of course "they were not in a position to entertain." Neither were the Stauntons senior, if they had but known it; they were overwhelmed by the worldliness of Boy's friends, and had to comfort themselves with the knowledge that they could buy and sell all of them, and their parents too, and never feel it. It was clear to my eye that by now Boy had far surpassed his father in ambition and scope. All he needed was time.

Everybody agreed that Leola was a radiant bride; even in the awful wedding rig-out of 1924 she looked good enough to eat with a silver spoon. Her parents (no hired finery for Ben Cruikshank, but his boots had a silvery gleam produced by the kind of blacklead more commonly applied to stoves) wept with joy in the church. Up at the front, and without much to do, I could see who wept and who grinned.

The honeymoon was to be a trip to Europe, not nearly so common then as now. I was going to Europe myself, to blow a thousand out of my eight on a reward to myself for being a good boy. I had booked my passage second class—not then called Tourist—on the C.P.R. ship *Melita;* when I read the passenger list in my first hour aboard I was not pleased to find "Mr. and Mrs. Boy Staunton" among the First Class. Like so many people, I regarded a wedding as a dead end and had expected to be rid of Boy and Leola for a while after it. But here they were, literally on top of me.

Well, let them find me. I did not care about distinction of classes, I told myself, but it would be interesting to find out if they did. As so often, I underestimated Boy. A note and a bottle of wine—half-bottle, to be precise—awaited me at my table at dinner, and he came down to see me three or four times during the voyage, explaining very kindly that ship's rules did not allow him to ask me to join them in First Class. Leola did not come but waved to me at the Ship's Concert, at which gifted passengers sang *Roses of Picardy,* told jokes, and watched a midshipman—they still had them to blow bugles for meals and so forth—dance a pretty good hornpipe.

Boy met everybody in First Class, of course, including the knighted passenger—a shoe manufacturer from Nottingham—but the one who most enlarged his world was the Reverend George Maldon Leadbeater, a great prophet from a fashionable New York church, who sailed from Montreal because he liked the longer North Atlantic sea voyage.

"He isn't like any other preacher you've ever met," said Boy. "Honestly, you'd wonder how old dugouts like Andy Bowyer and Phelps ever have the nerve to stand up in a pulpit when there are men like Leadbeater in the business. He makes Christianity make sense for the first time, so far as I'm concerned. I mean, Christ was really a very distinguished person, a Prince of the House of David, a poet and an intellectual. Of course He was a carpenter; all those Jews in Bible days could do something with their hands. But what kind of a carpenter was He? Not making cowsheds, I'll bet. Undoubtedly a designer and a manufacturer, in terms of those days. Otherwise, how did He make his connections? You know, when He was travelling around, staying with all kinds of rich and influential people as an honoured guest—obviously He wasn't just bumming his way through Palestine; He was staying with people who knew Him as a man of substance who also had a great philosophy. You know, the way those Orientals make their pile before they go in for philosophy. And look how He appreciated beauty! When that woman poured the ointment on His feet, He knew good ointment from bad, you can bet. And the Marriage at Cana—a party, and He helped the host out of a tight place when the drinks gave out, because He had probably been in the same fix Himself in His days in business and knew what social embarrassment was. And an economist! Driving the money-changers out of the Temple—why? Because they were soaking the pilgrims extortionate rates, that's why, and endangering a very necessary tourist attraction and rocking the economic boat. It was a kind of market discipline, if you want to look at it that way, and He was the only one with the brains to see it and the guts to do something about it. Leadbeater thinks that may have been at the back of the Crucifixion; the priests got their squeeze out of the Temple exchange, you can bet, and they decided they would have to get rid of this fellow who was possessed of a wider economic vision—as well as great intellectual powers in many other fields, of course.

"Leadbeater—he wants me to call him George, and somehow I've got to get rid of this English trick I've got of calling people by their surnames—George simply loves beauty. That's what gets Leola, you know. Frankly, Dunny, as an old friend, I can tell you that Leola hasn't had much chance to grow in that home of hers. Fine people, the Cruikshanks, of course, but narrow. But she's growing fast. George has insisted on lending her this wonderful novel, *If Winter Comes* by A. S. M. Hutchinson. She's just gulping it down. But the thing that really impresses me is that George is such a good dresser. And not just for a preacher—for anybody. He's going to introduce me to his tailor in London. You have to be introduced to the good ones. He says God made beautiful and seemly things, and not to take advantage of them is to miss what God meant. Did you ever hear any preacher say anything like that?

Of course he's no six-hundred-dollar-a-year Bible-buster, but a man who pulls down eighty-five hundred from his pulpit alone, and doubles it with lectures and books! If Christ wasn't poor—and He certainly wasn't—George doesn't intend to be. Would you believe he carries a handful of gemstones—semi-precious but gorgeous—in his right-hand coat pocket, *just to feel!* He'll pull them out two or three times a day, and strew them on the madder silk handkerchief he always has in his breast pocket, and let the light play on them, and you should see his face then! 'Poverty and sin are not all that God hath wrought,' he says with a kind of poetic smile. 'Lo, these are beautiful even as His raindrops, and no less His work than the leper, the flower, or woman's smile.' I wish you could get up to First Class to meet him, but it's out of the question, and I wouldn't want to ask him to come down here."

So I never met the Reverend George Maldon Leadbeater, though I wondered if he had read the *New Testament* as often as I had. Furthermore, I had read *If Winter Comes* when it first came out; it had been the theme of an extravagant encomium from the Right Honourable William Lyon Mackenzie King, Prime Minister of Canada; he had said it was unquestionably the finest novel of our time, and the booksellers had played it up. It seemed to me that Mr. King's taste in literature, like Leadbeater's in religion, was evidence of a sweet tooth, and nothing more.

4

Boy and Leola left the ship at Southampton. I went on to Antwerp, because the first object of my journey was a tour of the battlefields. Unrecognizable, of course. Neat and trim in the manner of the Low Countries; trenches known to me as stinking mudholes were lined with cement, so that ladies would not dirty their shoes. Even the vast cemeteries woke no feeling in me; because they were so big I lost all sense that they contained men who, had they lived, would have been about my age. I got out as soon as I had scoured Passchendaele for some sign of the place where I had been wounded, and where I had encountered the little Madonna. Nobody I could find was of any use in suggesting where I might have been; the new town had probably buried it under streets and houses. Figures of Our Lady—yes, there were plenty of those, in churches and on buildings, but most of them were new, hideous and unrevealing. None was anything like mine. I would have known her anywhere, as of course I did, many years later.

It was thus my interest in medieval and Renaissance art—especially religious art—came about. The little Madonna was a bee in my bonnet; I wanted to see her again, and quite unreasonably (like a man I knew who lost a treasured walking stick in the London Blitz and still looks hopefully in every curiosity shop in case it may turn up) I kept hoping to find her. The result was that I saw a great many Madonnas of every period and material and quickly came to know a fair amount about them. Indeed, I learned enough to be able to describe the one I sought as a Virgin of the Immaculate Conception, of polychromed wood, about twenty-four inches high, and most probably of Flemish or North German workmanship of the period between 1675 and 1725. If you think I put this together after I had found her, I can only assure you that you are wrong.

First my search, then a mounting enthusiasm for what I saw, led me to scores of churches through the Low Countries, France, Austria, and Italy. I had only afforded myself a few weeks, but I sent for more money and stayed until the latest possible date in August. What are you doing here, Dunstan Ramsay? I sometimes asked myself, and when I had got past telling myself that I was feeding a splendid new enthusiasm for religious art and architecture I knew that I was rediscovering religion as well. Do not suppose I was becoming "religious"; the Presbyterianism of my childhood effectively insulated me against any enthusiastic abandonment to faith. But I became aware that in matters of religion I was an illiterate, and illiteracy was my abhorrence. I was not such a fool or an aesthete as to suppose that all this art was for art's sake alone. It was about something, and I wanted to know what that something was.

As an historian by training, I suppose I should have begun at the beginning, wherever that was, but I hadn't time. Scenes from the Bible gave me no difficulty; I could spot Jael spiking Sisera, or Judith with the head of Holofernes, readily enough. It was the saints who baffled me. So I got to work on them as best I could, and pretty soon knew that the old fellow with the bell was Anthony Abbot, and the same old fellow with hobgoblins plaguing him was Anthony being tempted in the desert. Sebastian, that sanctified porcupine, was easy, and so was St. Roche, with the dog and a bad leg. I was innocently delighted to meet St. Martin, dividing his cloak, on a Swiss coin. The zest for detail that had first made me want to be a polymath stood me in good stead now, for I could remember the particular attributes and symbols of scores of saints without any trouble, and I found their legends delightful reading. I became disgustingly proud and began to whore after rare and difficult saints, not known to the Catholic faithful generally. I could read and speak French (though never without a betraying accent) and was pretty handy in Latin, so that Italian could be picked up on the run—badly, but enough. German was what I needed, and I determined to acquire it during the coming winter. I had no fear; whatever interested me I could learn, and learn quickly.

At this time it never occurred to me that the legends I picked up were quite probably about people who had once lived and had done something or other that made them popular and dear after death. What I learned merely revived and confirmed my childhood notion that religion was much nearer in spirit to the *Arabian Nights* than it was to anything encouraged by St. James' Presbyterian Church. I wondered how they would regard it in Deptford if I offered to replace the captive Dove that sat on the topmost organ pipe with St. James' own cockleshell. I was foolish and conceited, I know, but I was also a happy goat who had wandered into the wondrous enclosed garden of hagiology, and I grazed greedily and contentedly. When the time came at last for me to go home, I knew I had found a happiness that would endure.

5

Schoolmastering kept me busy by day and part of each night. I was an assistant housemaster, with a fine big room under the eaves of the main building, and a wretched kennel of a bedroom, and rights in a bathroom used by two or three other resident masters. I taught all day, but my wooden leg mercifully spared me from the nuisance of having to supervise sports after school. There were exercises to mark every night, but I soon gained a professional attitude toward these woeful explorations of the caves of ignorance and did not let them depress me. I liked the company of most of my colleagues, who were about equally divided among good men who were good teachers, awful men who were awful teachers, and the grotesques and misfits who drift into teaching and are so often the most educative influences a boy meets in school. If a boy can't have a good teacher, give him a psychological cripple or an exotic failure to cope with; don't just give him a bad, dull teacher. This is where the private schools score over state-run schools; they can accommodate a few cultured madmen on the staff without having to offer explanations.

The boys liked me for my wooden leg, whose thuds in the corridor gave ample warning of my approach and allowed smokers, loafers, and dreamers (these last two groups are not the same) to do whatever was necessary before I arrived. I had now taken to using a cane except when I was very much on parade, and a swipe with my heavy stick over the behind was preferred by all sensible boys to a tedious imposition. I may have been the despair of educational psychologists, but I knew boys and I knew my stuff, and it quickly began to show up in examination results.

Boy Staunton was also distinguishing himself as an educator. He was educating Leola, and as I saw them pretty regularly I was able to estimate his success. He wanted to make her into the perfect wife for a rising young entrepreneur in sugar, for he was working hard and fast, and now had a foot in the world of soft drinks, candy, and confectionery.

He had managed brilliantly on a principle so simple that it deserves to be recorded: he set up a little company of his own by borrowing $5000 for four months; as he already had $5000 it was no trouble to repay the loan. Then he borrowed $10,000, and repaid with promptitude. On this principle he quickly established an excellent reputation, always paying promptly, though never prematurely, thereby robbing his creditor of expected interest. Bank managers grew to love Boy, but he soon gave up dealing with branches, and borrowed only at Head Office. He was now a favoured cherub in the heaven of finance, and he needed a wife who could help him to graduate from a cherub to a full-fledged angel, and as soon as possible to an archangel. So Leola had lessons in tennis and bridge, learned not to call her maid "the girl" even to herself, and had no children as the time was not yet at hand. She was prettier than ever, had acquired a sufficient command of cliché to be able to talk smartly about anything Boy's friends were likely to know, and adored Boy, while fearing him a little. He was so swift, so brilliant, so handsome! I think she was always a little puzzled to find that she was really his wife.

It was in 1927 that Boy's first instance of startling good fortune arrived—one of those coincidences that it may be wiser to call synchronicities, which aid the ambitious—something that heaved him, at a stroke, into a higher sphere and maintained him there. He had kept up with his regiment and soldiered regularly; he had thoughts of politics, he told me, and a militia connection would earn a lot of votes. So when the Prince of Wales made his tour of Canada that year, who was more personable, youthful, cheerful, and in every way suited to be one of His Highness's aides-de-camp than Boy Staunton? And not simply for the royal appearance in Toronto, but for the duration of the tour, from sea to sea?

I saw little of this grandeur, except when the Prince paid a visit to the school, for as it has royal patronage he was obliged to do so. We masters all turned out in our gowns and hoods, and sweating members of the Rifle Corps strutted, and yelled, and swooned from the heat, and the slight descendant of King Arthur and King Alfred and Charles the Second did the gracious. I was presented, with my V.C. pinned to the silk of my gown, but my recollection is not of the youthful Prince, but of Boy, who was quite the most gorgeous figure there that day. An Old Boy of the school, and an *aide* to the Prince—it was a great day for him, and the Headmaster of that day doted upon him to a degree that might have seemed a little overdone to a critical eye.

Leola was there too, for though of course she did not go with Boy on the tour, she was expected to turn up now and then at various points across Canada, just as though she happened to be there by chance. She had learned to curtsy very prettily—not easy in the skirts of the period—and eat without seeming to chew, and do other courtier-like things required by Boy. I am sure that for her the Prince was nothing more than an excuse for Boy's brilliant appearances. Never have I seen a woman so absorbed in her love for a man, and I was happy for her and heartily wished her well.

After the Prince had gone home the Stauntons settled down again to be, in a modest manner befitting their youth, social leaders. Boy had a lot of new social usages and took to wearing spats to business. For him and for Leola their Jazz Age period was over; now they were serious, responsible Young Marrieds.

Within a year their first child was born and was conservatively, but significantly, christened Edward David. In due time—how *could* H.R.H. have known?—a christening mug came from Mappin and Webb, with the three feathers and *Ich dien* on it. David used it until he graduated to a cup and saucer, after which it stood on the drawing-room table, with matches in it, quite casually.

6

Doc Staunton and his wife never visited Boy and Leola, on what I suppose must be called religious grounds. When they came to Toronto, which was rarely, they asked the young Stauntons to their hotel—the cheap and conservative Carls-Rite—for a meal, but declined to set foot in a house where drink was consumed, contrary to the law of the land and against God's manifest will. Another stone that stuck in their crop was that Boy and Leola had left the Presbyterian church and become Anglicans.

In a movement that reached its climax in 1924, the Presbyterians and Methodists had consummated a *mysterium coniunctionis* that resulted in the United Church of Canada, with a doctrine (smoother than the creamy curd) in which the harshness of Presbyterianism and the hick piety of Methodism had little part. A few brass-bowelled Presbyterians and some truly zealous Methodists held out, but a majority regarded this union as a great victory for Christ's Kingdom on earth. Unfortunately it also involved some haggling between the rich Presbyterians and the poor Methodists, which roused the mocking spirit of the rest of the country; the Catholics in particular had some Irish jokes about the biggest land-and-property-grab in Canadian history.

During this uproar a few sensitive souls fled to the embrace of Anglicanism; the envious and disaffected said they did it because the Anglican Church was in some way more high-toned than the evangelical faiths, and thus they were improving their social standing. At that time every Canadian had to adhere, nominally, to some church; the officials of the Census utterly refused to accept such terms as "agnostic" or "none" for inclusion in the column marked "Religion," and flattering statistics were compiled on the basis of Census reports that gave a false idea of the forces all the principal faiths could command. Boy and Leola had moved quietly into a fashionable Anglican Church where the rector, Canon Arthur Woodiwiss, was so broad-minded he did not even insist that they be confirmed. David was confirmed, though, when his time came, and so was Caroline, who appeared a well-planned two years after him.

My preoccupation with saints was such that I could not keep it out of my conversation, and Boy was concerned for me. "Watch that you don't get queer, Dunny," he would say, sometimes; and, "Arthur Woodiwiss says that saints are all right for Catholics, who have so many ignorant people to deal with, but we've evolved far beyond all that."

As a result I sneaked even more saints into my conversation, to irritate him. He had begun to irritate rather easily, and be pompous. He urged me to get out of schoolmastering (while praising it as a fine profession) and make something of myself. "If you don't hurry up and let life know what you want, life will damned soon show you what you'll get," he said one day. But I was not sure I wanted to issue orders to life; I rather liked the Greek notion of allowing Chance to take a formative hand in my affairs. It was in the autumn of 1928 that Chance did so, and lured me from a broad highway to a narrower path.

Our Headmaster of that day—your predecessor but one—was enthusiastic for what he called "bringing the world to the school and the school to the world," and every Wednesday morning we had a special speaker at Prayers, who told us about what he did in the world. Sir Archibald Flower told us about rebuilding the Shakespeare Memorial Theatre at Stratford-on-Avon and got a dollar from nearly every boy to help do it; Father Jellicoe talked about clearing London slums, and that cost most of us a dollar too. But ordinarily our speakers were Canadians, and one morning the Headmaster swept in—he wore a silk gown, well suited to sweeping—with Mr. Joel Surgeoner in tow.

Surgeoner was already pretty well known, though I had not seen him before. He was the head of the Lifeline Mission in Toronto, where he laboured to do something for destitute and defeated people, and for the sailors on the boats that plied the Great Lakes—at that time a very tough and neglected group. He spoke to the school briefly and well, for though it was plain that he was a man of little education he had a compelling quality of sincerity about him, even though I suspected him of being a pious liar.

He told us, quietly and in the simplest language, that he had to run his Mission by begging, and that sometimes begging yielded nothing; when this happened he prayed for help, and had never been refused what he needed; the blankets, or more often the food, would appear somehow, often late in the day, and more often than not, left on the steps of the Mission by anonymous donors. Now, pompous young ass that I was, I was quite prepared to believe that St. John Bosco could pull off this trick when he appealed to Heaven on behalf of his boys; I was even persuaded that it might have happened a few times to Dr. Barnardo, of whom the story was also told. But I was far too much a Canadian, deeply if unconsciously convinced of the inferiority of my own country and its people, to think it could happen in Toronto, to a man I could see. I suppose I had a sneer on my face.

Surgeoner's back was to me, but suddenly he turned and addressed me. "I can see that you do not believe me, sir," he said, "but I am speaking the truth, and if you will come down to the Lifeline some night I will show you clothes and blankets and food that God has inspired charitable men and women to give us to do His work among His forgotten children." This had an electrical effect; a few boys laughed, the Headmaster gave me a glance that singed my eyebrows, and Surgeoner's concluding remarks were greeted with a roar of applause. But I had no time to waste in being humiliated, for when Surgeoner looked me in the face I knew him at once for the tramp I had last seen in the pit at Deptford.

I lost no time; I was at the Lifeline Mission that very night. It was on the ground floor of a warehouse down by the lakefront. Everything about it was poor; the lower parts of the windows were painted over with green paint, and the lettering on them—"Lifeline Mission, Come In"—was an amateur job. Inside, the electric light was scanty and eked out by a couple of coal-oil lamps on the table at the front; on benches made of reclaimed wood sat eight or ten people, of whom four or five were bums, and the rest poor but respectable supporters of Surgeoner. A service was in progress.

Surgeoner was praying; he needed a variety of things, the only one of which I can remember was a new kettle for soup, and he suggested to God that the woodpile was getting low. When he had, so to speak, put in his order, he began to speak to us, gently and unassumingly as he had done at the school that morning, and I was able to observe now that he had a hearing-aid in his left ear—one of the clumsy affairs then in use—and that a cord ran down into his collar and appeared to join a bulge in the front of his shirt, obviously a receiving apparatus. But his voice was pleasant and well controlled; nothing like the ungoverned quack of many deaf people.

He saw me, of course, and nodded gravely. I expected that he would try to involve me in his service, probably to score off me as an educated infidel and mocker, but he did not. Instead he told, very simply, of his experience with a lake sailor who was a notable blasphemer, a man whose every remark carried an insult to God's Name. Surgeoner had been powerless to change him and had left him in defeat. One day Surgeoner had talked with an old woman, desperately poor but rich in the Spirit of Christ, who had at parting pressed into his hand a cent, the only coin she had to give. Surgeoner bought a tract with the cent and carried it absent-mindedly in his pocket for several weeks, until by chance he met the blasphemer again. On impulse he pressed the tract upon the blasphemer, who of course received it with an oath. Surgeoner thought no more of the matter until, two months later, he met the blasphemer again, this time a man transfigured. He had read the tract, he had accepted Christ, and he had begun life anew.

I fully expected that it would prove that the old woman was the blasphemer's aged mother and that the two had been reunited in love, but Surgeoner did not go so far. Was this the self-denying chastity of the literary artist, I wondered, or had he not thought of such a dénouement yet? When the meeting had concluded with a dismal rendition of the revival hymn—

Throw out the Life Line,
Throw out the Life Line,
Someone is drifting away.
Throw out the Life Line,
Throw out the Life Line,
Someone is sinking today

—sung with the dispirited drag of the unaccompanied, untalented religious, the little group drifted away—the bums to the sleeping quarters next door and the respectable to their homes—and I was alone with Joel Surgeoner.

"Well, sir, I knew you would come, but I didn't expect you so soon," said he and gestured me into a kitchen chair by the table. He frugally turned off the electricity, and we sat in the light of the lamps.

"You promised to show me what prayer had brought," I said.

"You see it around you," he replied, and then, seeing surprise on my face at the wretchedness of the Mission, he led me to a door into the next room—it was in fact a double door running on a track, of the kind you see in old warehouses—and slid it back. In the gloom leaking down through an overhead skylight I saw a poor dormitory in which about fifty men were lying on cots. "Prayer brings me these, and prayer and hard work and steady begging provide for them, Mr. Ramsay." I suppose he had learned my name at the school.

"I spoke to our Bursar tonight," I said, "and your talk this morning will bring you a cheque for five hundred and forty-three dollars; from six hundred boys and a staff of about thirty, that's not bad. What will you do with it?"

"Winter is coming; it will buy a lot of warm underclothes." He closed the sliding door, and we sat down again in what seemed to be the chapel, common room, and business office of the Mission. "That cheque will probably be a week getting here, and our needs are daily—hourly. Here is the collection from our little meeting tonight." He showed me thirteen cents on a cracked saucer.

I decided it was time to go at him. "Thirteen cents for a thirteen-cent talk," I said. "Did you expect them to believe that cock-and-bull story about the cursing sailor and the widow's mite? Don't you underestimate them?"

He was not disconcerted. "I expect them to believe the spirit of the story," he said, "and I know from experience what kind of story they like. You educated people, you have a craze for what you call truth, by which you mean police-court facts. These people get their noses rubbed in such facts all day and every day, and they don't want to hear them from me."

"So you provide romance," I said.

"I provide something that strengthens faith, Mr. Ramsay, as well as I can. I am not a gifted speaker or a man of education, and often my stories come out thin and old, and I suppose unbelievable to a man like you. These people don't hold me on oath, and they aren't stupid either. They know my poor try at a parable from hard fact. And I won't deceive you: there is something about this kind of work and the kind of lives these people live that knocks the hard edge off fact. If you think I'm a liar—and you do—you should hear some of the confessions that come out in this place on a big night. Awful whoppers, that just pop into the heads of people who have found joy in faith but haven't got past wanting to be important in the world. So they blow up their sins like balloons. Better people than them want to seem worse than they are. We come to God in little steps, not in a leap, and that love of police-court truth you think so much of comes very late on the way, if it comes at all. What is truth? as Pilate asked; I've never pretended that I could have told him. I'm just glad when a boozer sobers up, or a man stops beating his woman, or a crooked lad tries to go straight. If it makes him boast a bit, that's not the worst harm it can do. You unbelieving people apply cruel, hard standards to us who believe."

"What makes you think I'm an unbeliever?" I said. "And what made you turn on me this morning, in front of the whole school?"

"I admit it was a trick," he said. "When you are talking like that, it's always a good job near the end to turn on somebody and accuse them of disbelieving. Sometimes you see somebody laughing, but that isn't needful. Best of all is to turn on somebody behind you, if you can. Makes it look as if you had eyes in the back of your head, see? There's a certain amount of artfulness about it, of course, but a greater end has been served, and nobody has been really hurt."

"That's a thoroughly crooked-minded attitude," said I.

"Perhaps it is. But you're not the first man I've used like that, and I promise you won't be the last. God has to be served, and I must use the means I know. If I'm not false to God—and I try very hard not to be—I don't worry too much about the occasional stranger."

"I am not quite so much a stranger as you think," said I. Then I told him that I had recognized him. I don't know what I expected him to do—deny it, I suppose. But he was perfectly cool.

"I don't remember you, of course," he said. "I don't remember anybody from that night except the woman herself. It was her that turned me to God."

"When you raped her?"

"I didn't rape her, Mr. Ramsay; you heard her say so herself. Not that I wouldn't have done, the state of mind I was in. I was at the end of my rope. I was a tramp, you see. Any idea what it means to be a tramp? They're lost men; not many people understand them. Do you know, I've heard and read such nonsense about how they just can't stand the chains of civilization, and have to breathe the air of freedom, and a lot of them are educated men with a wonderful philosophy, and they laugh at the hard workers and farmers they beg off of—well, it's all a lot of cock, as they'd put it. They're madmen and criminals and degenerates mostly, and tramping makes them worse. It's the open-air life does it to them. Oh, I know the open air is a great thing, when you have food and shelter to go back to, but when you haven't it drives you mad; starvation and oxygen is a crazy mixture for anybody that isn't born to it, like a savage. These fellows aren't savages. Weaklings, mostly, but vicious.

"I got among them a very common way. Know-it-all lad; quarrelled with my old dad, who was hard and mean-religious; ran away, picked up odd jobs, then began to pinch stuff, and got on the drink. Know what a tramp drinks? Shoe-blacking sometimes, strained through a hunk of bread; drives you crazy. Or he gets a few prunes and lets them stand in the sun in a can till they ferment; that's the stuff gives you the black pukes, taken on a stomach with nothing in it but maybe some raw vegetables you've pulled in a field. Like those sugar-beets around Deptford; fermented for a while, they'd eat a hole in a copper pot.

"And sex too. Funny how fierce it gets when the body is ill fed and ill used. Tramps are sodomites mostly. I was a young fellow, and it's the young ones and the real old ones that get used, because they can't fight as well. It's not kid-glove stuff, like that Englishman went to prison for; it's enough to kill you, you'd think, when a gang of tramps set on a young fellow. But it doesn't, you know. That's how I lost my hearing, most of it; I resisted a gang, and they beat me over the ears with my own boots till I couldn't resist any more. Do you know what they say? 'Lots o' booze and buggery,' they say. That's their life. Mine too, till the great mercy of that woman. I know now that God is just as near them as He is to you and me at this instant, but they defy Him, poor souls.

"That night we last met, I was crazy. I'd tumbled off the freight in that jungle by Deptford, and found a fire and seven fellows around it, and they had a stew—somebody'd got a rabbit and it was in a pail over a fire with some carrots. Ever eat that? It's awful, but I wanted some, and after a lot of nastiness they said I could have some after they'd had what they wanted of me. My manhood just couldn't stand it, and I left them. They laughed and said I'd be back when I got good and hungry.

"Then I met this woman, wandering by herself. I knew she was a town woman. Women tramps are very rare; too much sense, I guess. She was clean and looked like an angel to me, but I threatened her and asked her for money. She hadn't any; then I grabbed her. She wasn't much afraid and asked what I wanted. I told her, in tramp's language, and I could see she didn't understand, but when I started to push her down and grab at her clothes she said, 'Why are you so rough?' and then I started to cry. She held my head to her breast and talked nicely to me, and I cried worse, but the strange thing is I still wanted her. As if only that would put me right, you see? That's what I said to her. And do you know what she said? She said, 'You may if you promise not to be rough.' So I did, and that was when you people came hunting her.

"When I look back now I wonder that it wasn't all over with me that moment. But it wasn't. No, it was glory come into my life. It was as if I had gone right down into Hell and through the worst of the fire, and come on a clear, pure pool where I could wash and be clean. I was locked in by my deafness, so I didn't know much of what was said, but I could see it was a terrible situation for her, and there was nothing I could do.

"They turned me loose next morning, and I ran out of that town laughing and shouting like the man who was delivered from devils by Our Lord. As I had been, you see. He worked through that woman, and she is a blessed saint, for what she did for me—I mean it as I say it—was a miracle. Where is she now?"

How did I know? Mrs. Dempster was often in my mind, but whenever I thought of her I put the thought aside with a sick heart, as part of a past that was utterly done. I had tried to get Deptford out of my head, just as Boy had done, and for the same reason; I wanted a new life. What Surgeoner told me made it clear that any new life must include Deptford. There was to be no release by muffling up the past.

We talked for some time, and I liked him more and more. When at last I left I laid a ten-dollar bill on the table.

"Thank you, Mr. Ramsay," said he. "This will get us the soup kettle we need, and a load of wood as well. Do you see now how prayers are answered?"

7

Back to Deptford, therefore, at the first chance, pretending I wanted to consult Mr. Mahaffey about the deadbeat who had bought the *Banner* from me and was still in debt for more than half of the price. The magistrate counselled patience. But I got what I wanted, which was the address of the aunt who had taken Mrs. Dempster after the death of her husband. She was not, as Milo Papple thought, a widow, but an old maid, a Miss Bertha Shanklin, and she lived in Weston. He gave me the address, without asking why I wanted it.

"A bad business, that was," he said. "She seemed a nice little person. Then—a madwoman! Struck by a snowball. I don't suppose you have any idea who threw it, have you? No, I didn't imagine you did, or you would have said so earlier. There was guilt, you know; undoubtedly there was guilt. I don't know quite what could have been done about it, but look at the consequences! McCausland says definitely she became a moral idiot—no sense at all of right and wrong—and the result was that terrible business in the pit. I remember that you were there. And the ruin of her husband's life. Then the lad running away when he was really no more than a baby. I've never seen such grief as hers when she finally realized he had gone. McCausland had to give her very heavy morphia before Miss Shanklin could remove her. Yes, there was guilt, whether any kind of charge could have been laid or not. Guilt, and somebody bears it to this day!"

The old man's vehemence, and the way he kept looking at me over and under and around his small, very dirty spectacles, left no doubt that he thought I knew more than I admitted, and might very well be the guilty party myself. But I saw no sense in telling him anything; I still had a grudge against Boy for what he had done, but I remembered too that if I had not been so sly Mrs. Dempster would not have been hit. I was anxious to regard the whole thing as an accident, past care and past grief.

Nevertheless this conversation reheated my strong sense of guilt and responsibility about Paul; the war and my adult life had banked down that fire but not quenched it. The consequence was that I did something very foolish. I paid a visit to Father Regan, who was still the Catholic priest in Deptford.

I had never spoken to him, but I wanted somebody I could talk to confidentially, and I had the Protestant notion that priests are very close-mouthed and see more than they say. Later in life I got over that idea, but at this moment I wanted somebody who was in Deptford but not wholly of it, and he seemed to be my man. So within fifteen minutes of leaving the magistrate I was in the priest's house, snuffing up the smell of soap, and sitting in one of those particularly uncomfortable chairs that find refuge in priest's parlours all over the globe.

He thought, quite rightly, that I had come fishing for something, and was very suspicious, but when he found out what it was he laughed aloud, with the creaky, short laugh of a man whose life does not afford many jokes.

"A saint, do you say? Well now, that's a pretty tall order. I couldn't help you at all. Finding saints isn't any part of my job. Nor can I say what's a miracle and what isn't. But I don't imagine the bishop would have much to say to your grounds; it'd be his job to think of such things, if anybody did. A tramp reformed. I've reformed a tramp or two myself; they get spells of repentance, like most people. This fella you tell me of, now, seems to be as extreme in his zeal as he was in his sin. I never like that. And this business of raising your brother from his deathbed, as you describe it, was pretty widely talked about when it happened. Dr. McCausland says he never died at all, and I suppose he'd know. A few minutes with no signs of life. Well, that's hardly Lazarus, now, is it? And your own experience when you were wounded—man, you were out of your head. I have to say it plainly. You'd better put this whole foolish notion away and forget it.

"You were always an imaginative young fella. It was said of you when you were a lad, and it seems you haven't changed. You have to watch that kinda thing, you know. Now, you tell me you're very interested in saints. Awright, I'm not fishing for converts, but if that's the way it is you'd better take a good look at the religion saints come from. And when you've looked, I'll betcha a dollar you'll draw back like a man from a flame. You clever, imaginative fellas often want to flirt with Mother Church, but she's no flirty lady, I'm telling you. You like the romance, but you can't bear the yoke.

"You're hypnotized by this idea that three miracles makes a saint, and you think you've got three miracles for a poor woman who is far astray in her wits and don't know right from wrong. Aw, go on!

"Look, Mr. Ramsay, I'll tell it to you as plain as it comes: there's a lot of very good people in the world, and a lot of queer things happen that we don't see the explanation of, but there's only one Church that undertakes to cut right down to the bone and say what's a miracle and what isn't and who's a saint and who isn't, and you, and this poor soul you speak of, are outside it. You can't set up some kind of a bootleg saint, so take my advice and cut it out. Be content with the facts you have, or think you have, and don't push anything too far—or you might get a little bit strange yourself.

"I'm trying to be kind, you know, for I admired your parents. Fine people, and your father was a fair-minded man to every faith. But there are spiritual dangers you Protestants don't even seem to know exist, and this monkeying with difficult, sacred things is a sure way to get yourself into a real old mess. Well I recall, when I was a seminarian, how we were warned one day about a creature called a fool-saint.

"Ever hear of a fool-saint? I thought not. As a matter of fact, it's a Jewish idea, and the Jews are no fools, y'know. A fool-saint is somebody who seems to be full of holiness and loves everybody and does every good act he can, but because he's a fool it all comes to nothing—to worse than nothing, because it is virtue tainted with madness, and you can't tell where it'll end up. Did you know that Prudence was named as one of the Virtues? There's the trouble with your fool-saint, y'see—no Prudence. Nothing but a lotta bad luck'll rub off on you from one of them. Did you know bad luck could be catching? There's a theological name for it, but I misremember it right now.

"Yes, I know a lot of the saints have done strange things, but I don't recall any of 'em traipsing through the streets with a basketful o' wilted lettuce and wormy spuds, or bringing scandal on their town by shameless goings-on. No, no; the poor soul is a fool-saint if she's anything, and I'd strongly advise you to keep clear of her."

So, back to Toronto with a flea in my ear, and advice from Father Regan so obviously good and kind that I had either to take it or else hate Regan for giving it. Knowing by now what a high-stomached fellow I was, you can guess which I did. Within a week I was at Weston, talking with my fool-saint once again.

8

She was now forty but looked younger. An unremarkable woman really, except for great sweetness of expression; her dress was simple, and I suppose the aunt chose it, for it was a good deal longer than the fashion of the time and had a homemade air. She had no recollection of me, to begin with, but when I spoke of Paul I roused painful associations, and the aunt had to intervene, and take her away.

The aunt had not wanted to let me in the house, and as I thought this might be so I presented myself at the door without warning. Miss Bertha Shanklin was very small, of an unguessable age, and had gentle, countrified manners. Her house was pretty and suggested an old-fashioned sort of cultivation; much was ugly in the style of fifty years before, but nothing was trashy; there were a few mosaic boxes, and a couple of muddy oil paintings of the Italian Campagna with classical ruins and picturesque peasants, which suggested that somebody had been to Italy. Miss Shanklin let me talk with Mrs. Dempster for ten minutes or so, before she took her away. I stayed where I was, though decency suggested that it was time for me to go.

"I am sure you mean this visit kindly, Mr. Ramsay," she said when she returned, "but you can see for yourself that my niece is not up to receiving callers. There's not a particle of sense in reminding her of the days past—it frets her and does no good. So I'll say good-afternoon, and thank you for calling."

I talked as well as I could about why I had come, and of my concern for her niece, to whom I owed a great debt. I said nothing of saints; that was not Miss Shanklin's line. But I talked about childhood kindness, and my mother's concern for Mary Dempster, and my sense of guilt that I had not sought her before. This brought about a certain melting.

"That's real kind of you. I know some terrible things went on in Deptford, and it's good to know not everybody has forgotten poor Mary. I suppose I can say to you that I always thought the whole affair was a mistake. Amasa Dempster was a good man, I suppose, but Mary had been used to an easier life—not silly-easy, you understand me, but at least some of the good things. I won't pretend I was friendly toward the match, and I guess I have to bear some of the blame. They didn't exactly run away, but it hurt me the way they managed things, as if there wasn't a soul in the world but themselves. I could have made it easier for her, but Amasa was so proud and even a little mite hateful about Mary having any money of her own that I just said, All right, they can paddle their own canoe. It cost me a good deal to do that. I never saw Paul, you know, and I'd certainly have done anything in the world for him if I could have got things straight with his father. But I guess a little bit of money made me proud, and religion made him proud, and then it was too late. I love her so much, you see. She's all the family I've got. Love can make you do some mean actions when you think it has been snubbed. I was mean, I grant you. But I'm trying to do what I can now, when I guess it's too late."

Miss Shanklin wept, not aloud or passionately, but to the point of having to wipe her eyes and depart for the kitchen to ask for some tea. By the time this tea was brought—by the "hired girl," whose softening influence on Mary Dempster had been so deplored by the matrons of Amasa Dempster's congregation—Miss Shanklin and I were on quite good terms.

"I love to hear you say that Mary was so good and sweet, even after that terrible accident—it was an accident, wasn't it? A blow on the head? From a fall or something?—and that you thought of her even when you were away at the war. I always had such hopes for her. Not just to keep her with me, of course, but—well, I know she loved Amasa Dempster, and love is supposed to excuse anything. But I am sure there would have been other men, and she could hardly have been worse off with one of them, now could she? Life with Amasa seems to have been so dark and wintry and hopeless. Mary used to be so full of hope—before she married.

"Now she remembers so little, and it's better so, because when she does remember she thinks of Paul. I don't even let myself speculate on what would happen to a little fellow like that, running away with show folks. As like as not he's dead long since, and better so, I suppose. But of course she thinks of him as a little boy still. She has no idea of time, you see. When she thinks of him, it's awful to hear her cry and carry on. And I can't get rid of the feeling that if I had just had a little more real sand and horse sense, things would have been very different.

"I'd meant to tell you not to come again, ever, but I won't. Come and see Mary, but promise you'll get to know her again, as a new friend. She hasn't any idea of the past, except for horrible mixed-up memories of being tied up, and Paul disappearing, and Amasa—she always remembers him with a blue mouth, like a rotten hole in his face—telling God he forgave her for ruining his life. Amasa died praying, did you know?"

9

It was the following May, in the fated year 1929, that I had a call from Boy—in itself an unusual thing, but even more unusual in its message.

"Dunny, don't be in too much of a rush, but you oughtn't to lose more than a couple of weeks in getting rid of some of your things." And he named half-a-dozen stocks he knew I had, because he had himself advised me to buy them.

"But they're mounting every week," I said.

"That's right," said he; "now sell 'em, and get hold of some good hard stuff. I'll see that you get another good block of Alpha."

So that is what I did, and it is to Boy's advice I owe a reputation I acquired in the school as a very shrewd businessman. Just about every master, like some millions of other people on this continent, had money in the market, and most of them had invested on margin and were cleaned out before Christmas. But I found myself pleasantly well off when the worst of the crash came, because Boy Staunton regarded me as in certain respects a responsibility.

My mind was not on money at the time, however, for I was waiting impatiently for the end of term so that I could take ship and set out on a great hunt, starting in England and making my way across France, Portugal, Switzerland, Austria, and at last to Czechoslovakia. This was the first of my annual journeys, broken only by the 1939–45 war, saint-hunting, saint-identifying, and saint-describing; journeys that led to my book *A Hundred Saints for Travellers,* still in print in six languages and a lively seller, to say nothing of my nine other books, and my occasional articles. This time I was after big game, a saint never satisfactorily described and occurring in a variety of forms, whose secret I hoped to discover.

There is a saint for just about every human situation, and I was on the track of a curious specimen whose intercession was sought by girls who wanted to get rid of disagreeable suitors. Her home ground, so to speak, was Portugal, and she was reputed to have been the daughter of a Portuguese king, himself a pagan, who had betrothed her to the King of Sicily; but she was a Christian and had made a vow of virginity, and when she prayed for assistance in keeping it, she miraculously grew a heavy beard; the Sicilian king refused to have her, and her angry father caused her to be crucified.

It was my purpose to visit every shrine of this odd saint, compare all versions of the legend, establish or demolish the authenticity of a prayer reputedly addressed to her and authorized by a Bishop of Rouen in the sixteenth century, and generally to poke my nose into anything that would shed light on her mystery. Her case abounded with the difficulties that people of my temperament love. She was commonly called Wilgefortis, supposed to be derived from Virgo-Fortis, but she was also honoured under the names of Liberata, Kummernis, Ontkommena, Livrade, and in England—she once had a shrine in St. Paul's—as Uncumber. The usual fate for Wilgefortis, among the more conservative hagiologists, was dismissal as an ignorant peasant misunderstanding of one of the many paintings of the Holy Face of Lucca, in which a long-haired and bearded figure in a long robe hangs from a cross; it is, of course, Christ, reputedly painted by St. Luke himself; but many copies of it might well be pictures of a bearded lady.

I, however, had one or two new ideas about Uncumber, which I wanted to test. The first was that her legend might be a persistence of the hermaphrodite figure of the Great Mother, which was long worshipped in Cyprus and Carthage. Many a useful and popular wonder-working figure had been pinched from the pagans by Christians in early days, and some not so early. My other bit of information came from two physicians at the State University of New

York, Dr. Moses and Dr. Lloyd, who had published some findings about abnormal growth of hair in unusually emotional women; they instanced a number of cases of rapid beard-growing in girls who had been crossed in love; furthermore, two English doctors attested to a thick beard grown by a girl whose engagement had been brutally terminated. Anything here for Uncumber? I was on my way to Europe to find out.

So I jaunted cheerfully about the Continent on my apparently mad mission, hunting up Uncumber in remote villages as well as in such easy and pleasant places as Beauvais and Wissant, and once positively identifying an image that was said to be Uncumber (Wilgeforte, she was locally called, and the priest was rather ashamed of her) as Galla, the patroness of widows, who is also sometimes represented with a beard. It was not until August that I arrived in the Tyrol, searching for a shrine that was in a village about thirty-five miles northwest of Innsbruck.

It was about the size of Deptford, and its three inns did not expect many visitors from North America; this was still before the winter sports enthusiasm opened up every Tyrolean village and forced something like modern sanitation on every inn and guest-house. I settled in at the inevitable Red Horse and looked about me.

I was not the only stranger in the village.

A tent and some faded banners in the market-place announced the presence of *Le grand Cirque forain de St Vite*. I was certainly not the man to neglect a circus dedicated to St. Vitus, patron of travelling showmen, and still invoked in country places against chorea and palsy and indeed anything that made the body shake. The banners showed neither the cock nor the dog that the name of St. Vitus would have suggested, but they promised a Human Frog, *Le plus grand des Tyroliens*, *Le Solitaire des forêts* and—luck for me—*La Femme à barbe*. I determined to see this bearded lady, and if possible to find out if she had been violently crossed in love.

As a circus it was a pitiable affair. Everything about it stank of defeat and misery. There was no planned performance; now and then, when a sufficient crowd had assembled, a pair of gloomy acrobats did some tumbling and walked a slack wire. The Human

Frog sat down on his own head, but with the air of one who took no pleasure in it. The Wild Man roared and chewed perfunctorily on a piece of raw meat to which a little fur still clung; the lecturer hinted darkly that we ought to keep our dogs indoors that night, but nobody seemed afraid. When not on view the Wild Man sat quietly, and from the motion of his jaws I judged that he was solacing himself with a quid of chewing tobacco.

There was an achondroplasic dwarf who danced on broken bottles; his bare feet were dirty, and from repeated dancing the glass had lost its sharpness. Their great turn was a wretched fellow—*Rinaldo the Heteradelphian*—who removed his robe and showed us that below his breast grew a pitiful wobbling lump that the eye of faith, assisted by the lecturer's description, might accept as a pair of small buttocks and what could have been two little legs without feet—an imperfect twin. The bearded lady sat and knitted; her low-cut gown, revealing the foothills of enormous breasts, dispelled any idea that she was a fake. It was upon her that I fixed my attention, for the Heteradelphian and the frowst of Tyrolean *lederhosen* were trying, even for one used to a roomful of schoolboys.

I had had enough of *Le grand Cirque forain de St Vite* and was about to leave when a young man leapt up on the platform beside *Le Solitaire des forêts* and began, rapidly and elegantly, to do tricks with cards. It was Paul Dempster.

I had acquiesced for some time in the opinion put forward by Mr. Mahaffey and Miss Shanklin that Paul must be dead, or certainly lost forever. Seeing him now, however, I felt no disbelief and no uncertainty. I had last seen Paul in 1915, when he was seven; fourteen years later many men would have been unrecognizably changed, from child to man, but I knew him in an instant. After all, he had been my pupil in the art of manipulating cards and coins, and I had watched him very closely as he demonstrated his superiority to my clumsy self. His face had changed from child to man, but his hands and his style of using them were not to be mistaken.

He gave his patter in French, dropping occasionally into German with an Austrian accent. He was very good—excellent, indeed, but too good for his audience. Those among them who were card-players plainly belonged to the class who play very slow games at the inns they frequent, laying down each card as if it weighed a pound and shuffling with deliberation. His rapid passes and brilliant manipulations dazzled without enlightening them. So it was when he began to work with coins. "Secure and palm six half-crowns"—the daunting phrase came to my mind again as Paul did precisely that with the big Austrian pieces, plucking them from the beards of grown men, or seeming to milk them from the noses of children, or nipping them up with long fingers from the bodices of giggling girls. It was the simplest but also the most difficult kind of conjuring because it depended on the most delicate manual skill; he brought an elegance to it that was as good as anything I had ever seen, for my old enthusiasm had led me to see a conjurer whenever I could.

When he wanted a watch to smash I offered mine, to get his eye, but he ignored it in favour of a large silver turnip handed up by a Tyrolean of some substance. Do what I could, he would not look at me, though I was a conspicuous figure as the only man in the audience not in local dress. When he had beaten the watch to pieces, made the pieces disappear, and invited a large countrywoman to return the watch from her knitting-bag, the performance was over, and the Tyroleans moved heavily toward the door of the tent.

I lingered, and addressed him in English. He replied in French, and when I changed to French he turned at once to German. I was not to be beaten. What passed between us took quite a long time and was slow and uneasy, but in the end he admitted that he was Paul Dempster—or had been so many years before. He had been Faustus Legrand for more years than the ten during which he answered to his earlier name. I spoke of his mother; told him that I had seen her not long before I came abroad. He did not answer.

Little by little, however, I got on better terms with him, principally because the other members of the troupe were curious to know what such a stranger as I wanted with one of them, and crowded around with frank curiosity. I let them know that I was from the village of Paul's birth, and with some of the cunning I had learned when trying to get priests and sacristans to talk about local shrines and the doings of saints, I let it be known that I would consider it an honour to provide the friends of Faustus Legrand with a drink—probably more than one drink.

This eased up the atmosphere at once, and the Bearded Lady, who seemed to be the social leader of *Le grand Cirque forain de St Vite,* organized a party in a very few minutes and closed the tent to business. They all, except *Le Solitaire des forêts* (who had the eyes of a dope-taker), were very fond of drink, and soon we were accommodated with a couple of bottles of that potato spirit sophisticated with brown sugar that goes by the name of Rhum in Austria, but which is not to be confused with rum. I set to work, on this foundation, to make myself popular.

It is not hard to be popular with any group, whether composed of the most conventional Canadians or of Central European freaks, if one is prepared to talk to people about themselves. In an hour I had heard about the Heteradelphian's daughter, who sang in a light opera chorus in Vienna, and about his wife, who had unaccountably wearied of his multiple attractions. The dwarf, who was shy and not very bright, took to me because I saw that he had his fair share of the Rhum. The Human Frog was a German and very cranky about war reparations, and I assured him that everybody in Canada thought they were a crying shame. I was not playing false with these poor people; they were off duty and wanted to be regarded as human beings, and I was quite ready to oblige. I became personal only with the Bearded Lady, to whom I spoke of my search for the truth about Uncumber; she was entranced by the story of the saint and insisted that I repeat it for all to hear; she took it as a tribute to Bearded Ladies in general, and began seriously to discuss having a new banner painted, in which she would advertise herself as Mme. Wilgeforte, and be depicted crucified, gazing sternly at the departing figure of a pagan fiancé. Indeed, this was my best card, for the strangeness of my quest seemed to qualify me as a freak myself and make me more than ever one of the family.

When we needed more Rhum I contrived that Paul should go for it; I judged that the time had come when his colleagues would talk to me about him. And so it was.

"He stays with us only because of Le Solitaire," said the Bearded

Lady. "I will not conceal from you, Monsieur, that Le Solitaire is not a well man, nor could he travel alone. Faustus very properly acknowledges a debt of gratitude, for before Le Solitaire became so incapable that he was forced to adopt the undemanding role of *un solitaire,* he had his own show of which Faustus was a part, and Faustus regards Le Solitaire as his father in art, if you understand the professional expression. I think it was Le Solitaire who brought him home from America."

It was a very merry evening, and before it was over I had danced with the Bearded Lady to music provided by the dwarf, who whistled a polka and drummed with his feet; the sight of a wooden-legged man dancing seemed hilariously funny to the artistes of the one-eyed little circus as the Rhum got to them. When we broke up I had a short private conversation with Paul.

"May I tell your mother that I have seen you?"

"I cannot prevent it, Monsieur Ramsay, but I see no point in it."

"Grief at losing you has made her very unwell."

"As I mean to remain lost I do not see what good it would do to tell her about me."

"I am sorry you have so little feeling for her."

"She is part of a past that cannot be recovered or changed by anything I can do now. My father always told me it was my birth that robbed her of her sanity. So as a child I had to carry the weight of my mother's madness as something that was my own doing. And I had to bear the cruelty of people who thought her kind of madness was funny—a dirty joke. So far as I am concerned, it is over, and if she dies mad, who will not say that she is better dead?"

So next morning I went on my journey in search of the truth about Uncumber, after I had made the necessary arrangements for more money. Because somebody at *Le grand Cirque forain de St Vite* had stolen my pocket-book, and everything pointed to Paul.

·IV·

Gyges and King Candaules

1

BOY STAUNTON MADE a great deal of money during the Depression because he dealt extensively in solaces. When a man is down on his luck he seems to consume all he can get of coffee and doughnuts. The sugar in the coffee was Boy's sugar, and the doughnuts were his doughnuts. When an overdriven woman without the money to give her children a decent meal must give them something bulky, sweet, and interesting to stop their crying, she probably gives them a soft drink; it was Boy's soft drink. When a welfare agency wants to take the harsh look of bare necessity off a handout basket, it puts in a bag of candies for the children; they were Boy's candies. Behind tons of cheap confectionery, sweets, snacks, nibbles, biscuits, and simple cooking sugar, and the accompanying oceans of fizzy, sweet water, disguised with chemical versions of every known fruit flavour, stood Boy Staunton, though not many people knew it. He was the president and managing director of Alpha Corporation, a much-respected company that made nothing itself but controlled all the other companies that did.

He was busy and he was adventurous. When he first went into the bread business, because a large company was in difficulties and could be bought at a rock-bottom price, I asked him why he did not try beer as well.

"I may do that when the economy is steadier," he said, "but at present I feel I should do everything I can to see that people have necessities." And we both took reflective pulls at the excellent whiskies-and-soda he had provided.

Boy's new bread company made quite a public stir with their advertisements declaring that they would hold the price of bread steady. And they did so, though the loaves seemed to be a bit puffier and gassier than they had been before. We ate them at the school, so I was able to judge.

There was filial piety, as well as altruism, in Boy's decision. Old Doc Staunton's annoyance at being outsmarted by his son had given way to his cupidity, and the old man was a large holder in Alpha. To have associated him with beer would have made trouble, and Boy never looked for trouble.

"Alpha concentrates on necessities," Boy liked to say. "In times like these, people need cheap, nourishing food. If a family can't buy meat, our vitaminized biscuits are still within their reach." So much so, indeed, that Boy was fast becoming one of the truly rich, by which I mean one of those men whose personal income, though large, is a trifling part of the huge, mystical body of wealth that stands behind them and cannot be counted, only estimated.

A few cranky politicians of the most radical party tried to estimate it in order to show that, in some way, the very existence of Boy was intolerable in a country where people were in want. But, like so many idealists, they did not understand money, and after a meeting where they had lambasted Boy and others like him and threatened to confiscate their wealth at the first opportunity, they would adjourn to cheap restaurants, where they drank his sugar, and ate his sugar, and smoked cigarettes which, had they known it, benefited some other monster they sought to destroy.

I used to hear him abused by some of the junior masters at the school. They were Englishmen or Canadians who had studied in England, and they were full of the wisdom of the London School of Economics and the doctrines of *The New Statesman,* copies of which used to limp into the Common Room about a month after publication. I have never been sure of my own political opinions (historical studies and my fondness for myth and legend have always blunted my political partisanship), but it amused me to hear these poor fellows, working for terrible salaries, denouncing Boy and a handful of others as "ca-*pittle*-ists"; they always stressed the middle syllables, this being a fashionable pronunciation of the period, and one that seemed to make rich men especially contemptible. I never raised my voice in protest, and none of my colleagues ever knew that I was personally acquainted with the ca-pittle-ist whose good looks, elegant style of life, and somewhat gross success made their own hard fortune and their leather-elbowed jackets and world-weary flannel trousers seem pitiful. This was not disloyalty; rather, it seemed to me that the Boy they hated and did not know was unrelated to the Boy I saw about once a fortnight and often more frequently.

I owed this position to the fact that I was the only person to whom he could talk frankly about Leola. She was trying hard, but she could not keep pace with Boy's social advancement. He was a genius—that is to say, a man who does superlatively and without obvious effort something that most people cannot do by the uttermost exertion of their abilities. He was a genius at making money, and that is as uncommon as great achievement in the arts. The simplicity of his concepts and the masterly way in which they were carried through made jealous people say he was lucky and people like my schoolmaster colleagues say he was a crook: but he made his own luck, and no breath of financial scandal ever came near him.

His ambitions did not rest in finance alone; he had built firmly on his association with the Prince of Wales, and though in hard fact it did not amount to more than the reception of a monogrammed Christmas card once a year it bulked substantially, though never quite to the point of absurdity, in his conversation. "He isn't joining them at Sandringham this year," he would say as Christmas drew near; "pretty stuffy, I suppose." And somehow this suggested that he had some inside information—perhaps a personal letter—though everybody who read the newspapers knew as much. All Boy's friends had to be pretty spry at knowing who "he" was, or they ceased to be friends. In a less glossily successful young man this would have been laughable, but the people Boy knew were not the kind of people who laughed at several million dollars. It was after David's birth it became clear that Leola was lagging in the upward climb.

A woman can go just so far on the capital of being a pretty girl. Leola, like Boy and myself, was now past youth; he was two months younger than I, though I looked older than thirty-two and he somewhat less. Leola was not a full year younger than we, and her girlishness was not well suited to her age or her position. She had toiled at the lessons in bridge, mah-jongg, golf, and tennis; she had plodded through the Books-of-the-Month, breaking down badly in *Kristin Lavransdatter*; she had listened with mystification to gramophone records of *Le Sacre du Printemps* and with the wrong kind of enjoyment to Ravel's *Bolero;* but nothing made any impression on her, and bewilderment and a sense of failure had begun to possess her. She had lost heart in the fight to become the sort of sophisticated, cultivated, fashionably alert woman Boy wanted for a wife. She loved shopping, but her clothes were wrong; she had a passion for pretty things and leaned toward the frilly at a time when fashion demanded clean lines and a general air of knowingness in women's clothes. If Boy let her shop alone she always came back with what he called "another god-damned Mary Pickford rig-out," and if he took her shopping in Paris the sessions often ended in tears, because he sided with the clever shopwomen against his indecisive wife, who always forgot her painfully acquired French as soon as she was confronted with a living French creature. Nor did she speak English as became the wife of one who had once hob-nobbed with a Prince and might do so again. If she positively *had* to use hick expressions, I once heard Boy tell her, she might at least say "For Heaven's sake," and not "For Heaven sakes." And "supper" was a meal one ate after the theatre, *not* the meal they ate every night at half-past seven. Nor could she learn when to refer to herself as "one," or remember not to say "between you and I."

In the early years of their marriage Leola sometimes resented this sort of talk and made spirited replies; she did not see why she should become stuck-up, and talk as she had never talked before, and behave in ways that were unnatural to her. When this happened Boy would give her what he called "the silent treatment"; he said nothing, but Leola's inner ear was so tuned to the silence that she was aware of the answers to all her impertinences and blasphemies: it was *not* stuck-up to behave in a way that accorded with your position in the world, and the speech of Deptford was *not* the speech of the world to which they now belonged; as for unnatural behaviour, natural behaviour was the sort of thing they hired a nurse to root out of young David—eating with both hands and peeing on the floor; let us have no silly talk about being natural. Of course Boy was right, and of course Leola gave in and tried to be the woman he wanted.

It was so easy for him! He never forgot anything that was of use to him, and his own manners and speech became more polished all the time. Not that he lost a hint of his virility or youthfulness, but they sat on him as if he were one of those marvellous English actors—Clive Brook, for instance—who was manly and gentlemanly at once, in a way Canadians as a whole could never manage.

This situation did not come about suddenly; it was a growth of six years of their marriage, during which Boy had changed a great deal and Leola hardly at all. Even being a mother did nothing for her; she seemed to relax when she had performed her biological trick instead of taking a firmer hold on life.

I never intervened when Leola was having a rough time; rows between them seemed to be single affairs, and it was only when I looked backward that I could see that they were sharp outbreaks in a continuous campaign. To be honest, I must say also that I did not want to shoulder the burdens of a peacemaker; Boy never let it be forgotten that he had, as he supposed, taken Leola from me; he was very jocose about it, and sometimes allowed himself a tiny, roguish hint that it might have been better for us all if things had gone the other way. The fact was that I no longer had any feeling for Leola save pity. If I spoke up for her I might find myself her champion, and a man who champions any woman against her husband had better be sure he means business.

I did not mean business, or anything at all. I went to the Stauntons' often, because they asked me and because Boy's brilliant operations fascinated me. I enjoyed my role as Friend of the Family, though I was unlike the smart, rich, determinedly youthful people who were their "set." It was some time before I tumbled to the fact that Boy needed me as someone in whose presence he could think aloud, and that a lot of his thinking was about the inadequacy of the wife he had chosen to share his high destiny.

Personally I never thought Leola did badly; she offset some of the too glossy perfection of Boy. But his idea of a wife for himself would have had the beauty and demeanour of Lady Diana Manners coupled with the wit of Margot Asquith. He let me know that he had been led into his marriage by love, and love alone; though he did not say so it was clear he owed Cupid a grudge.

Only twice did I get into any sort of wrangle with them about their own affairs. The first was early in their marriage, about 1926 I think, when Boy discovered Dr. Emile Coué; the doctor had been very much in the public eye since 1920, but Canada caught up with him just about the time his vogue was expiring.

You remember Dr. Coué and his great success with autosuggestion? It had the simplicity and answer-to-everything quality that Boy, for all his shrewdness, could never resist. If you fell asleep murmuring, "Every day in every way, I am getting better and better," wondrous things came of it. The plugged colon ceased to trouble, the fretful womb to ache; indigestion yielded to inner peace; twitches and trembles disappeared; skin irritations vanished overnight; stutterers became fluent; the failing memory improved; stinking breath became as the zephyr of May; and dandruff but a hateful memory. Best of all it provided "moral energy," and Boy Staunton was a great believer in energy of all kinds.

He wanted Leola to acquire moral energy, after which social grace, wit, and an air of easy breeding would surely follow. She obediently repeated the formula as often as she could, every night for six weeks, but nothing much seemed to be happening.

"You're just not trying, Leo," he said one night when I was dining with them. "You've simply got to try harder."

"Perhaps she's trying too hard," I said.

"Don't be absurd, Dunny. There's no such thing as trying too hard, whatever you're doing."

"Yes there is. Have you never heard of the Law of Reversed Effort? The harder you try, the more likely you are to miss the mark."

"I never heard such nonsense. Who says that?"

"A lot of wise people have said it, and the latest is your Dr. Coué. Don't clench your teeth and push for success, he says, or everything will work against you. Psychological fact."

"Bunk! He doesn't say it in my book."

"But, Boy, you never study anything properly. That miserable little pamphlet you have just gives you a farcical smattering of

Couéism. You should read Baudouin's *Suggestion and Auto-Suggestion* and get things right."

"How many pages?"

"I don't count pages. It's a good-sized book."

"I haven't got time for big books. I have to have the nub of things. If effort is all wrong, why does Coué work for me? I put lots of effort into it."

"I don't suppose it does work for you. You don't need it. Every day in every way you do get better and better, in whatever sense you understand the word 'better,' because that's the kind of person you are. You've got ingrained success."

"Well, bring your book over and explain it to Leo. Make her read it, and you help her to understand it."

Which I did, but it was of no use. Poor Leola did not get better and better because she had no idea of what betterness was. She couldn't conceive what Boy wanted her to be. I don't think I have ever met such a stupid, nice woman. So Dr. Coué failed for her, as he did for many others, for which I lay no blame on him. His system was really a form of secularized, self-seeking prayer, without the human dignity that even the most modest prayer evokes. And like all attempts to command success for the chronically unsuccessful, it petered out.

The second time I came between Boy and Leola was much more serious. It happened late in 1927, after the famous Royal Tour. Boy gave me a number of reels of film and asked me to develop them for him. This was reasonable enough, because in my saint-hunting expeditions I used a camera often and had gained some skill; at the school, as I could not supervise sports, I was in charge of the Camera Club and taught boys how to use the dark room. I was always ready to do a favour for Boy, to whose advice I owed my solvency, and when he said that he did not want to confide these films to a commercial developer I assumed they were pictures of the Tour and probably some of them were of the Prince.

So it was, except for two reels that were amateurish but pretentious "art studies" of Leola, lying on cushions, peeping through veils, sitting at her make-up table, kneeling in front of an open fire, wagging her finger at a Teddy Bear, choosing a chocolate from a large ribboned box—every sentimental posture approved by the taste of the day for "cutie" photographs, and in every one of them she was stark naked. If she had been an experienced model and Boy a clever photographer, they would have been the kind of thing that appeared in the more daring magazines. But their combined inexperience had produced embarrassing snapshots of the sort hundreds of couples take but have the sense to keep to themselves.

I do not know why this made me so angry. Was I so inconsiderable, so much the palace eunuch, that I did not matter? Or was this a way of letting me know what I had missed when Boy won Leola? Or was it a signal that if I wanted to take Leola off his hands Boy would make no objection? He had let me know that Leola had conventional ideas and that his own adventurous appetite was growing tired of her meat-and-potatoes approach to sex. Whatever it was, I was very angry and considered destroying the film. But—I must be honest—I examined the pictures with care, and I suppose with some measure of gloating, and this made me angrier still.

My solution was typical of me. I developed all the pictures as carefully as I could, enlarged the best ones (all those of Leola), returned them without a word, and waited to see what would happen.

Next time I dined with them all the pictures were brought out, and Boy went through them slowly, telling me exactly what H.R.H. had said as each one was taken. At last we came to the ones of Leola.

"Oh, don't show those!"

"Why not?"

"Because."

"Dunny's seen them before, you know. He developed them, I expect he kept a set for himself."

"No," I said, "as a matter of fact I didn't."

"The more fool you. You'll never see pictures of a prettier girl."

"Boy, please put them away or I'll have to go upstairs. I don't want Dunny to see them while I'm here."

"Leo, I never thought you were such a little prude."

"Boy, it isn't nice."

"Nice, nice, nice! Of course it isn't *nice!* Only fools worry about what's *nice*. Now sit here by me, and Dunny on the other side, and be proud of what a stunner you are."

So Leola, sensing a row from the edge in his voice, sat between us while Boy showed the pictures, telling me what lens apertures he had used, and how he had arranged the lights, and how he had achieved certain "values" which, in fact, made Leola's rose-leaf bottom look like sharkskin and her nipples glare when they should have blushed. He seemed to enjoy Leola's discomfiture thoroughly; it was educational for her to learn that her beauty had public as well as private significance. He recalled Margot Asquith's account of receiving callers in her bath though—he was always a careless reader—he did not remember the circumstances correctly.

As we drew near the end of the show he turned to me and said with a grin, "I hope you don't find it too hot in here, old man?"

As a matter of fact I did find it hot. All the anger I had felt when developing the pictures had returned. But I said I was quite comfortable.

"Oh. I just thought you might find the situation a bit unusual, as Leo does."

"Unusual but not unprecedented. Call it historical—even mythological."

"How's that?"

"It's happened before, you know. Do you remember the story of Gyges and King Candaules?"

"Never heard of them."

"I thought not. Well, Candaules was a king of Lydia a long time ago, and he was so proud of his wife's beauty that he insisted his friend Gyges should see her naked."

"Generous chap. What happened?"

"There are two versions. One is that the Queen took a fancy to Gyges and together they pushed Candaules off his throne."

"Really? Not much chance of that here, is there, Leo? You'd find my throne a bit too big, Dunny."

"The other is that Gyges killed Candaules."

"I don't suppose you'll do that, Dunny."

I didn't suppose so myself. But I think I stirred some uxorious fire in Boy, for nine months later I did some careful counting, and

I am virtually certain that it was on that night little David was begotten. Boy was certainly a complex creature, and I am sure he loved Leola. What he thought of me I still do not know. That Leola loved him with all her unreflecting heart there could be no possible doubt. Nothing he could do would change that.

2

Every fortnight during the school term I made the journey to Weston on Saturday morning and had lunch with Miss Bertha Shanklin and Mrs. Dempster. It took less than half an hour on a local train, so I could leave after the Saturday morning study period for boarders, which I supervised, and be back in town by three o'clock. To have stayed longer, Miss Shanklin let me know, would have been fatiguing for poor Mary. She really meant, for herself; like many people who have charge of an invalid, she projected her own feelings on her patient, speaking for Mrs. Dempster as a priest might interpret a dull-witted god. But she was gentle and kind, and I particularly liked the way she provided her niece with pretty, fresh dresses and kept her hair clean and neat; in the Deptford days I had become used to seeing her in dirty disorder as she paced her room on the restraining rope.

At these meals Mrs. Dempster rarely spoke, and although it was clear that she recognized me as a regular visitor, nothing to suggest any memory of Deptford ever passed between us. I played fair with Miss Shanklin and appeared in the guise of a new friend; a welcome one, for they saw few men, and most women, even the most determined spinsters, like a little masculine society.

The only other man to visit that house at any time when I was there was Miss Shanklin's lawyer, Orpheus Wettenhall. I never discovered anything about him that would explain why his parents gave him such a pretentious Christian name; perhaps it ran in the family. He invited me to call him Orph, which was what everybody called him, he said. He was an undersized, laughing man with a big walrus moustache and silver-rimmed glasses.

Orph was quite the most dedicated sportsman I have ever known. During every portion of the year when it was legal to shoot or hook any living creature, he was at it; in off-seasons he shot groundhogs and vermin beneath the notice of the law. When the trout season began, his line was in the water one minute after midnight; when deer might be shot, he lived as did Robin Hood. Like all dedicated hunters, he had to get rid of the stuff he killed; his wife "kicked over the traces" at game more than four or five times a week. He used to turn up at Miss Shanklin's now and then, opening the front door without ceremony and shouting, "Bert! I've brought you a pretty!"; then he would appear an instant later with something wet or bloody, which the hired girl bore away, while Miss Shanklin gave a nicely judged performance of delight at his goodness and horror at the sight of something the intrepid Orph had slain with his own hands.

He was a gallant little particle, and I liked him because he was so cheerful and considerate toward Miss Shanklin and Mrs. Dempster. He often urged me to join him in slaughter, but I pled my wooden leg as an excuse for keeping out of the woods. I had had all the shooting I wanted in the war.

I began my visits in the autumn of 1928 and was faithful in them till February 1932, when Miss Shanklin took pneumonia and died. I did not know of it until I received a letter from Wettenhall, bidding me to the funeral and adding that we must have a talk afterward.

It was one of those wretched February funerals, and I was glad to get away from the graveyard into Wettenhall's hot little office. He was in a black suit, the only time I ever saw him in other than sporting clothes.

"Let's cut the cackle, Ramsay," he said, pouring us each a hearty drink of rye, in glasses with other people's lipmarks on the rims. "It's as simple as this: you're named as Bert's executor. Everything goes to Mary Dempster except some small legacies—one to me, the old sweetheart, for taking good care of her affairs—and a handful of others. You are to have five thousand a year, on a condition. That condition is that you get yourself appointed Mary Dempster's guardian and undertake to look after her and administer her money for her as long as she lives. I'm to see that the Public Guardian is satisfied. After Mary's death everything goes to you. When all debts and taxes are paid, Bert ought to cut up at—certainly not less than a quarter of a million, maybe three hundred thousand. You're allowed to reject the responsibility, and the legacy as well, if you don't want to be bothered. You'll want a couple of days to think it over."

I agreed, though I knew already that I would accept. I said some conventional but perfectly sincere things about how much I had liked Miss Shanklin and how I would miss her.

"You and me both," said Orph. "I loved Bert—in a perfectly decent way, of course—and damned if I know how things will be without her."

He handed me a copy of the will, and I went back to town. I did not go to see Mrs. Dempster, who had not, of course, been at the funeral. I would attend to that when I had made some other arrangements.

The next day I made inquiries as to how I could be appointed the guardian of Mary Dempster and found that it was not a very complicated process but would take time. I experienced a remarkable rising of my spirits, which I can only attribute to the relief of guilt. As a child I had felt oppressively responsible for her, but I had thought all that was dissipated in the war. Was not a leg full and fair payment for an evil action? This was primitive thinking, and I had no trouble dismissing it—so it seemed. But the guilt had only been thrust away, or thrust down out of sight, for here it was again, in full strength, clamouring to be atoned for, now that the opportunity offered itself.

Another element insisted on attention though I tried to put it from me: if Mrs. Dempster was a saint, henceforth she would be *my* saint. Was she a saint? Rome, which alone of human agencies undertook to say who was a saint and who was not, insisted on three well-attested miracles. Hers were the reclamation of Surgeoner by an act of charity that was certainly heroic in terms of the *mores* of Deptford; the raising of Willie from the dead; and her miraculous appearance to me when I was at the uttermost end of my endurance at Passchendaele.

Now I should be able to see what a saint was really like and perhaps make a study of one without all the apparatus of Rome, which I had no power to invoke. The idea possessed me that it might lie in my power to make a serious contribution to the psychology of religion, and perhaps to carry the work of William James a step further. I don't think I was a very good teacher on the day when all of this was racing through my head.

I was a worse teacher two days later, when the police called me to say that Orpheus Wettenhall had shot himself and that they wanted to talk to me.

It was a very hush-hush affair. People talk boldly about suicide, and man's right to choose his own time of death, when it is not near them. For most of us, when it draws close, suicide is a word of fear, and never more so than in small, closely knit communities. The police and the coroner and everybody else implicated took every precaution that the truth about Orph should not leak out. And so, of course, the truth did leak out, and it was a very simple and old story.

Orph was a family lawyer of the old school; he looked after a number of estates for farmers and people like Miss Shanklin, who had not learned about new ways of doing business. Orph's word was as good as his bond, so it would have been unfriendly to ask for his bond. He had been paying his clients a good, unadventurous return on their money for years, but he had been investing that same money in the stock market for big returns, which he kept. When the crash came he was unprepared, and since 1929 he had been paying out quite a lot of his own money (if it may be called that) to keep his affairs on an even keel. The death of Bertha Shanklin had made it impossible to go on.

So the story given to the public was that Orph, who had handled guns all his life, had been cleaning a cocked and loaded shotgun and had unaccountably got the end of the barrel into his mouth, which had so much astonished him that he inadvertently trod on the trigger and blew the top of his head off. Accidental death, as clearly as any coroner ever saw it.

Perhaps a few people believed it, until a day or two later when it was known what a mess his affairs were in, and a handful of old men and women were to be met wandering in the streets, unable to believe their ill-fortune.

Nobody had time or pity for these minor characters in the drama; all public compassion was for Orph Wettenhall. What agonies of mind must he not have endured before taking his life! Was it not significant that he had launched himself into the hereafter apparently gazing upward at the large stuffed head of a moose he had shot a good forty years before! Who would have the heart to take his place on the deerhunt next autumn? When had there been his like for deftness and speed in skinning a buck? But of his ability in skinning a client little was said, except that he had obviously meant to restore the missing funds as soon as he could.

It was not positively so stated, but the consensus seemed to be that Bertha Shanklin had shown poor taste in dying so soon and thus embarrassing the local Nimrod. "There, but for the grace of God, go I," said several citizens; like most people who quote this ambiguous saying, they had never given a moment's thought to its implications. As for Mary Dempster, I never heard her name mentioned. Thus I learned two lessons: that popularity and good character are not related, and that compassion dulls the mind faster than brandy.

All the cash I could find in Miss Shanklin's house amounted to twenty-one dollars; of her bank account, into which Wettenhall had made quarterly payments, everything but about two hundred dollars had been spent on her final illness and burial. So I began then and there to maintain Mrs. Dempster, and never ceased to do so until her death in 1959. What else could I do?

As executor I was able to sell the house and the furniture, but they realized less than four thousand dollars; the Depression was no time for auctions. In the course of time I was duly appointed the guardian of Mary Dempster. But what was I to do with her? I investigated the matter of private hospitals and found that to keep her in one would beggar me. All masters at Colborne had been invited to take a cut in salary to help in keeping the school afloat, and we did so; there were many boys whose parents either could not pay their fees or did not pay them till much later, and it was not in the school's character to throw them out. My investments were better than those of a great many people, but even Alpha was not paying much; Boy said it would not look well at such a time, and so there were stock splits instead, and a good deal of money was "ploughed back" for future advantage. I was not too badly off for a single man, but I had no funds to maintain an expensive invalid. So much against my will I got Mrs. Dempster into a public hospital for the insane, in Toronto, where I could keep an eye on her.

It was a dark day for both of us when I took her there. The staff were good and kind but they were far too few, and the building was an old horror. It was about eighty years old and had been designed for the era when the first thing that was done with an insane patient was to put him to bed, with a view to keeping him there, safe and out of the way, till he recovered or died. Consequently the hospital had few and inadequate common rooms, and the patients sat in the corridors, or wandered up and down the corridors, or lay on their beds. The architecture was of the sort that looks better on the outside than on the inside; the building had a dome and a great number of barred windows and looked like a run-down palace.

Inside the ceilings were high, the light was bad, and in spite of the windows the ventilation was capricious. The place reeked of disinfectant, but the predominating smell was that unmistakable stench of despair that is so often to be found in jails, courtrooms, and madhouses.

She had a bed in one of the long wards, and I left her standing beside it, with a kindly nurse who was explaining what she should do with the contents of her suitcase. But already her face looked as I remembered it in her worst days in Deptford. I dared not look back, and I felt meaner than I have ever felt in my life. But what was I to do?

3

Aside from my teaching, my observation of Boy's unwitting destruction of Leola, and my new and complete responsibility for Mrs. Dempster, this was the most demanding period of my life, for it was during this time I became involved with the Bollandists and found my way into the mainstream of the work that has given me endless delight and a limited, specialized reputation.

I have spent a good deal of time in my life explaining who the Bollandists are, and although you, Headmaster, are assumed by the school to know everything, perhaps I had better remind you that they are a group of Jesuits whose special task is to record all available information about saints in their great *Acta Sanctorum,* upon which they have been at work (with breaks for civil or religious uproar) since John van Bolland began in 1643; they have been pegging away with comparatively few interruptions since 1837; proceeding from the festal days of the Saints beginning in January, they have now filled sixty-nine volumes and reached the month of November.

In addition to this immense and necessarily slow task, they have published since 1882 a yearly collection of material of interest to their work but not within the scope of the *Acta,* called *Analecta Bollandiana;* it is scholarly modesty of a high order to call this "Bollandist Gleanings," for it is of the greatest importance and interest, historically as well as hagiographically.

As a student of history myself, I have always found it revealing to see who gets to be a saint in any period; some ages like wonder-workers, and some prefer gifted organizers whose attention to business produces apparent miracles. In the last few years good old saints whom even Protestants love have been losing ground to lesser figures whose fortune it was to be black or yellow or red-skinned—a kind of saintly representation by population. My Bollandist friends are the first to admit that there is more politics to the making of a saint than the innocently devout might think likely.

It was quite beyond my income to own a set of the *Acta,* but I consulted it frequently—sometimes two or three times a week—at the University Library. However, I did, by luck, get a chance to buy a run of the *Analecta,* and though it cost me a fortune by Depression reckoning, I could not let it go, and its bulk and foreign-looking binding has surprised many visitors to my study in the school.

Boys grow bug-eyed when they find that I actually read in French, German, and Latin, but it is good for them to find that these languages have an existence outside the classroom; some of my colleagues look at my books with amusement, and a few solemn asses have spread the rumour that I am "going over to Rome"; old Eagles (long before your time) thought it his duty to warn me against the Scarlet Woman and demanded rhetorically how I could possibly "swallow the Pope." Since then millions have swallowed Hitler and Mussolini, Stalin and Mao, and we have swallowed some democratic leaders who had to be gagged down without relish. Swallowing the Pope seems a trifle in comparison. But to return to 1932, there I was, a subscriber and greedy reader of the *Analecta,* and busy learning Greek (not the Greek of Homer but the queer Greek of medieval monkish recorders) so as to miss nothing.

It was then that the bold idea struck me of sending my notes on Uncumber to the editor of *Acta,* the great Hippolyte Delehaye; at worst he would ignore them or return them with formal thanks. I had the Protestant idea that Catholics always spat in your eye if they could, and of course Jesuits—crafty and trained to duplicity as they were—might pinch my stuff and arrange to have me blown up with a bomb, to conceal their guilt. Anyhow I would try.

It was little more than a month before this came in the mail:

Cher Monsieur Ramsay,

Your notes on the Wilgefortis-Kummernis figure have been read with interest by some of us here, and although the information is not wholly new, the interpretation and synthesis is of such a quality that we seek your consent to its publication in the next *Analecta.* Will you be so good as to write to me at your earliest convenience, as time presses. If you ever visit Bruxelles, will you give us the pleasure of making your acquaintance? It is always a great satisfaction to meet a serious hagiographer, and particularly one who, like yourself, engages in the work not professionally but as a labour of love.

Avec mes souhaits sincères,
Hippolyte Delehaye S.J.

Société des Bollandistes
24 Boulevard Saint-Michel
Bruxelles

Few things in my life have given me so much delight as this letter; I have it still. I had schooled myself since the war-days never to speak of my enthusiasms; when other people did not share them, which was usual, I was hurt and my pleasure diminished; why was I always excited about things other people did not care about? But I could not hold in. I boasted a little in the Common Room that I had received an acceptance from *Analecta;* my colleagues looked uncomprehendingly, like cows at a passing train, and went on talking about Brebner's extraordinary hole-in-one the day before.

I spoke of it to Boy when next I saw him; all he could get through his head was that I had written my contribution in French. To be fair, I did not tell him the story of Uncumber and her miraculous beard; he was no audience for such psychological-mythological gossip, which appealed only to the simple or the truly sophisticated. Boy was neither, but he had an eye for quality, and it was after this I began to be asked to dinner more often with the Stauntons' smart friends and not as a lone guest. Sometimes I heard Boy speaking of me to the bankers and brokers as "very able chap—speaks several languages fluently and writes for a lot of European publications—a bit of an eccentric, of course, but an old friend."

I think his friends thought I wrote about "current affairs," and quite often they asked me how I thought the Depression was going to pan out. On these occasions I looked wise and said I thought it was moving toward its conclusion but we might not have seen the worst of it—an answer that contained just the mixture of hope and gloom financial people find reassuring. I thought they were a terrible pack of fatheads, but I was also aware that they must be good at something because they were so rich. I would not have had their cast of mind in order to get their money, however, much as I liked money.

They were a strange lot, these moneyed, influential friends of Boy's, but they were obviously interesting to each other. They talked a lot of what they called "politics," though there was not much plan or policy in it, and they were worried about the average man, or as they usually called him "the ordinary fellow." This ordinary fellow had two great faults: he could not think straight and he wanted to reap where he had not sown. I never saw much evidence of straight thinking among these ca-pittle-ists, but I came to the conclusion that they were reaping where they had sown, and that what they had sown was not, as they believed, hard work and great personal sacrifice but talent—a rather rare talent, a talent that nobody, even its possessors, likes to recognize as a talent and therefore not available to everybody who cares to sweat for it—the talent for manipulating money.

How happy they might have been if they had recognized and gloried in their talent, confronting the world as gifted egotists, comparable to painters, musicians, or sculptors! But that was not their style. They insisted on degrading their talent to the level of mere acquired knowledge and industry. They wanted to be thought of as wise in the ways of the world and astute in politics; they wanted to demonstrate in themselves what the ordinary fellow might be if he would learn to think straight and be content to reap only where he had sown. They and their wives (women who looked like parrots or bulldogs, most of them) were so humourless and, except when they were drunk, so cross that I thought the ordinary fellow was lucky not to be like them.

It seemed to me they knew less about the ordinary fellow than I did, for I had fought in the war as an ordinary fellow myself, and most of these men had been officers. I had seen the ordinary fellow's heroism and also his villainy, his tenderness and also his unthinking cruelty, but I had never seen in him much capacity to devise or carry out a coherent, thoughtful, long-range plan; he was just as much the victim of his emotions as were these rich wiseacres. Where shall wisdom be found, and where is the place of understanding? Not among Boy Staunton's ca-pittle-ists, nor among the penniless scheme-spinners in the school Common Room, nor yet at the Socialist-Communist meetings in the city, which were sometimes broken up by the police. I seemed to be the only person I knew without a plan that would put the world on its feet and wipe the tear from every eye. No wonder I felt like a stranger in my own land.

No wonder I sought some place where I could be at home, and until my first visit to the Collège de Saint-Michel, in Brussels, I was so innocent as to think it might be among the Bollandists. I passed several weeks there very happily, for they at once made me free of the hall for foreign students, and as I grew to know some of the Jesuits who directed the place I was taken even more into their good graces and had the run of their magnificent library. More than one hundred and fifty thousand books about saints! It seemed a paradise.

Yet often, usually at about three o'clock in the afternoon when the air grew heavy, and scholars at nearby desks were dozing over their notes, I would think: Dunstan Ramsay, what on earth are you doing here, and where do you think this is leading? You are now thirty-four, without wife or child, and no better plan than your own whim; you teach boys who, very properly, regard you as a signpost on the road they are to follow, and like a signpost they pass you by without a thought; your one human responsibility is a madwoman about whom you cherish a maggoty-headed delusion; and here you are, puzzling over records of lives as strange as fairy tales, written by people with no sense of history, and yet you cannot rid yourself of the notion that you are well occupied. Why don't you go to Harvard and get yourself a Ph.D., and try for a job in a university, and be intellectually respectable? Wake up, man! You are dreaming your life away!

Then I would go on trying to discover how Mary Magdalene had been accepted as the same Mary who was the sister of Martha and Lazarus, and if this pair of sisters, one representing the housewifely woman and the other the sensual woman, had any real counterparts in pagan belief, and sometimes—O, idler and jackass!—if their rich father was anywhere described as being like the rich men I met at Boy Staunton's dinner parties. If he were, who would be surprised if his daughter went to the bad?

Despite these afternoon misgivings and self-reproaches I clung to my notion, ill defined though it was, that a serious study of any important body of human knowledge, or theory, or belief, if undertaken with a critical but not a cruel mind, would in the end yield some secret, some valuable permanent insight, into the nature of life and the true end of man. My path was certainly an odd one for a Deptford lad, raised as a Protestant, but fate had pushed me in this direction so firmly that to resist would be a dangerous defiance. For I was, as you have already guessed, a collaborator with Destiny, not one who put a pistol to its head and demanded particular treasures. The only thing for me to do was to keep on keeping on, to have faith in my whim, and remember that for me, as for the saints, illumination when it came would probably come from some unexpected source.

The Jesuits of the Société des Bollandistes were not so numerous that I did not, in time, get on speaking terms with most of them, and a very agreeable, courteous group they were. I now realize that, although I thought I had purged my mind of nonsense about Jesuits, some dregs of mistrust remained. I thought, for instance, that they were going to be preternaturally subtle and that in conversation I would have to be very careful—about what, I did not know. Certainly if they possessed any extraordinary gifts of subtlety they did not waste them on me. I suspected too that they would smell the black Protestant blood in my veins, and I would never gain their trust. On the contrary, my Protestantism made me a curiosity and something of a pet. It was still a time when the use of index cards for making notes was not universal, and they were curious about mine; most of them made notes on scraps of paper, which they kept in order with a virtuosity that astonished me. But though they used me well in every way, I knew that I would always be a guest in this courteous, out-of-the-world domain, and I quickly discovered that the Society of Jesus discouraged its members from being on terms of intimacy with anyone, including other Jesuits. I was used to living without intimate friends, but I had a sneaking hope that here, among men whose preoccupation I shared, things might be different.

All the more reason to be flattered, therefore, when, at the conclusion of one of the two or three conversations I had with Père Delehaye, the principal editor of the *Analecta,* he said, "Our journal, as you will have observed, publishes material provided by the Bollandists and their friends; I hope you will correspond with us often, and come here when you can, for certainly we think of you now as one of our friends."

This was by way of leave-taking, for I was setting off the next day for Vienna, and I was travelling with an elderly Bollandist, Padre Ignacio Blazon.

Padre Blazon was the only oddity I had met at the Collège de Saint-Michel. He more than made up for the placidly unremarkable appearance and behaviour of the others, and I think they may have been a little ashamed of him. He was so obviously, indeed theatrically, a priest, which is contrary to Jesuit custom. He wore his soutane all the time indoors, and sometimes even in the streets, which was not regarded with favour. His battered black hat suggested that it might have begun long ago as part of Don Basilio's costume in *The Barber of Seville,* and had lost caste and shape since then. He wore a velvet skullcap, now green with whitened seams, indoors, and under his hat when outdoors. Most of the priests smoked, moderately, but he took snuff immoderately, from a large horn box. His spectacles were mended with dirty string. His hair needed, not cutting, but mowing. His nose was large, red, and bulbous. He had few teeth, so that his chaps were caved in. He was, indeed, so farcical in appearance that no theatre director with a scrap of taste would have permitted him on the stage in such a makeup. Yet here he was, a reality, shuffling about the Bollandist library, humming to himself, snuffing noisily, and peeping over people's shoulders to see what they were doing.

He was tolerated, I soon found out, for his great learning and for what was believed to be his great age. He spoke English eloquently, with little trace of foreign accent, and he jumped from language to language with a virtuosity that astonished everybody and obviously delighted himself. When I first noticed him he was chattering happily to an Irish monk in Erse, heedless of discreet shushings and murmurs of "*Tacete*" from the librarian on duty. When he first noticed me he tried to flummox me by addressing me in Latin, but I was equal to that dodge, and after a few commonplaces we changed to English. It was not long before I discovered that one of his enthusiasms was food, and after that we dined together often.

"I am one of Nature's guests," he said, "and if you will take care of the bill I shall be happy to recompense you with information about the saints you will certainly not find in our library. If, on the contrary, you insist that I should take my turn as host, I shall expect you to divert me—and I am not an easy man to amuse, Monsieur Ramezay. As a host I am exigent, rebarbative, unaccommodating. As a guest—ah, quite another set of false teeth, I assure you."

So I was always host, and we visited several of the good restaurants in Brussels. Padre Blazon was more than true to his word.

"You Protestants, if you think of saints at all, regard them with quite the wrong sort of veneration," he said to me at our first dinner. "I think you must be deceived by our cheap religious statuary. All those pink and blue dolls, you know, are for people who think them beautiful. St. Dominic, so pretty and pink-cheeked, with his lily, is a peasant woman's idea of a good man—the precise contrary of the man she is married to, who stinks of sweat and punches her in the breast and puts his cold feet on her backside in the winter nights. But St. Dominic himself—and this is a Jesuit speaking, Ramezay—was no confectionery doll. Do you know that before he was born his mother dreamed she would give birth to a dog with a lighted torch in its mouth? And that was what he was—fierce and persistent in carrying the flame of faith. But show the peasant woman a dog with a torch and she will not care for it; she wants a St. Dominic who can see the beautiful soul in her, and that would be a man without passions or desires—a sort of high-minded eunuch.

"But she is too much herself to want that all the time. She would not take it in exchange for her smelly man. She gives her saints another life, and some very strange concerns, that we Bollandists have to know about but do not advertise. St. Joseph, now—what is his sphere of patronage, Ramezay?"

"Carpenters, the dying, the family, married couples, and people looking for houses."

"Yes, and in Naples, of confectioners; don't ask me why. But what else? Come now, put your mind to it. What made Joseph famous?"

"The earthly father of Christ?"

"Oho, you nice Protestant boy! Joseph is history's most celebrated cuckold. Did not God usurp Joseph's function, reputedly by impregnating his wife through her ear? Do not nasty little seminarians still refer to a woman's *sine qua non* as *auricula*—the ear? And is not Joseph known throughout Italy as Tio Pepe—Uncle Joe—and invoked by husbands who are getting worried? St. Joseph hears more prayers about cuckoldry than he does about house-hunting or confectionery, I can assure you. Indeed, in the underworld hagiology of which I promised to tell you, it is whispered that the Virgin herself, who was born to Joachim and Anna through

God's personal intervention, was a divine daughter as well as a divine mate; the Greeks could hardly improve on that, could they? And popular legend has it that Mary's parents were very rich, which makes an oddity of the Church's respect for poverty but is quite in keeping with the general respect for money. And do you know the scandal that makes it necessary to keep apart the statues of Mary and those of St. John—"

Padre Blazon was almost shouting by this time, and I had to hush him. People in the restaurant were staring, and one or two ladies of devout appearance were heaving their bosoms indignantly. He swept the room with the wild eyes of a conspirator in a melodrama and dropped his voice to a hiss. Fragments of food, ejected from his mouth by this jet, flew about the table.

"But all this terrible talk about the saints is not disrespect, Ramezay. Far from it! It is faith! It is love! It takes the saint to the heart by supplying the other side of his character that history or legend has suppressed—that he may very well have suppressed himself in his struggle toward sainthood. The saint triumphs over sin. Yes, but most of us cannot do that, and because we love the saint and want him to be more like ourselves, we attribute some imperfection to him. Not always sexual, of course. Thomas Aquinas was monstrously fat; St. Jerome had a terrible temper. This gives comfort to fat men and cross men. Mankind cannot endure perfection; it stifles him. He demands that even the saints should cast a shadow. If they, these holy ones who have lived so greatly but who still carry their shadows with them, can approach God, well then, there is hope for the worst of us.

"Sometimes I wonder why so few saints were also wise. Some were, of course, but more were down-right pig-headed. Often I wonder if God does not value wisdom as much as heroic virtue. But wisdom is rather unspectacular; it does not flash in the sky. Most people like spectacle. One cannot blame them. But for oneself—ah, no thank you."

It was with this learned chatterbox that I set out to travel from Brussels to Vienna. I was early at the station, as he had commanded, and found him already in sole possession of a carriage. He beckoned me inside and went on with his task, which was to read aloud from his breviary, keeping the window open the while, so that passers-by would hear him.

"Give me a hand with a Paternoster," he said and began to roar the Lord's Prayer in Latin as loud as he could. I joined in, equally loud, and we followed with a few rousing Aves and Agnus Deis. By dint of this pious uproar we kept the carriage for ourselves. People would come to the door, decide that they could not stand such company, and pass on, muttering.

"Strange how reluctant travellers are to join in devotions that might—who can say?—avert some terrible accident," said Blazon, winking solemnly at me as the guard's whistle blew, the engine peeped, and we drew out of the station. He spread a large handkerchief over his lap and put the big snuffbox in the middle of it, skimmed his dreadful hat into the luggage rack to join a bundle held together by a shawl strap, and composed himself for conversation.

"You have brought the refreshment basket?" said he. I had, and I had not stinted. "It might be provident to take some of that brandy immediately," he said. "I know this journey, and sometimes the motion of the train can be very distressing." So at half-past nine in the morning we began on the brandy, and soon Padre Blazon was launched into one of those monologues, delivered at the top of his voice, which he preferred to more even-handed conversation. I shall boil it down.

"I have not forgotten your questions about the woman you keep in the madhouse, Ramezay. I have said nothing on that subject during our last few dinners, but it has not been absent from my mind, you may be assured. Invariably I come back to the same answer: why do you worry? What good would it do you if I told you she is indeed a saint? I cannot make saints, nor can the Pope. We can only recognize saints when the plainest evidence shows them to be saintly. If you think her a saint, she is a saint to you. What more do you ask? That is what we call the reality of the soul; you are foolish to demand the agreement of the world as well. She is a Protestant. What does it matter? To be a Protestant is halfway to being an atheist, of course, and your innumerable sects have not recognized any saints of their own since the Reformation, so-called. But it would be less than Christian to suppose that heroic virtue may not assert itself among Protestants. Trust your own judgement. That is what you Protestants made such a dreadful fuss to assert your right to do."

"But it is the miracles that concern me. What you say takes no account of the miracles."

"Oh, miracles! They happen everywhere. They are conditional. If I take a photograph of you, it is a compliment and perhaps rather a bore. If I go into the South American jungle and take a photograph of a primitive, he probably thinks it a miracle and he may be afraid I have stolen a part of his soul. If I take a picture of a dog and show it to him, he does not even know what he looks like, so he is not impressed; he is lost in a collective of dogginess. Miracles are things people cannot explain. Your artificial leg would have been a miracle in the Middle Ages—probably a Devil's miracle. Miracles depend much on time, and place, and what we know and do not know. I am going to Vienna now to work on the Catalogue of Greek Manuscripts in what used to be the Emperor's Library. I shall be drowned in miracles, for those simple Greek monks liked nothing better and saw them everywhere. I tell you frankly, I shall be sick of miracles before I am taken off that job. Life itself is too great a miracle for us to make so much fuss about potty little reversals of what we pompously assume to be the natural order.

"Look at me, Ramezay. I am something of a miracle myself. My parents were simple Spanish people living a few leagues from Pamplona. They had seven daughters—think of it, Ramezay, seven! My poor mother was beside herself at the disgrace. So she vowed solemnly, in church, that if she might bear a son, she would give him to the service of God. She made her vow in a Jesuit church, so it was natural enough that she should add that she would make him a Jesuit. Within a year—behold, little Ignacio, so named after the saintly founder of the Society of Jesus. To a geneticist, I suppose it is not breathtaking that after seven daughters a woman should have a son, but to my mother it was a miracle. The neighbours said—you know how the neighbours always say—'Wait, the trouble is to come; he will be a wild one, this Ignacio; the jail gapes for these sanctified children.' Was it so? Not a bit! I seemed to be a Jesuit from the womb—studious, obedient, intelligent, and chaste.

Behold me, Ramezay, a virgin at the age of seventy-six! Of how many can that be said? Girls laid themselves out to tempt me; they were incited to seduce me by my sisters, who had only ordinary chastity and thought mine distasteful. I will not say I was not flattered by these temptations. But always I would say, 'God did not give us this jewel of chastity to be trampled in the dirt, my dear Dolores (or Maria or whoever it was); pray for an honourable and loving marriage, and put me from your mind.' Oh, how they hated that! One girl hit me with a big stone; you see the mark here still, just where my hair used to begin. This was a real miracle, for every morning I had unmistakable assurance that I could have been a great lover—you understand me?—but I loved my vocation more.

"I loved it so much that when the time came for me to enter the Jesuits my examiners were mistrustful. I was too good to be true. My mother's vow, my own abstentions—it worried them. They raked around, trying to discover some streak of unredeemed nature in me—some shadow, as we were saying a while ago—but I had none. Do you know, Ramezay, it stood in my way as much as if I had been a stiff-necked recalcitrant and troublemaker? Yes, my novitiate was very rough, and when I had got through that and was a formed scholastic, every dirty job was put in my way, to see if I would break. It was a full seventeen years before I was allowed to take my four final vows and become a professed member of the Society. And then—well, you see what I am now. I am a pretty useful person, I think, and I have done good work for the Bollandists, but nobody would say I was the flower of the Jesuits. If ever I was a miracle, it is done with now. My shadow manifested itself quite late in life.

"You know that Jesuit training is based on a rigorous reform of the self and achievement of self-knowledge. By the time a man comes to the final vows, anything emotional or fanciful in his piety is supposed to have been rooted out. I think I achieved that, so far as my superiors could discover, but after I was forty I began to have notions and ask questions that should not have come to me. Men have this climacteric, you know, like women. Doctors deny it, but I have met some very menopausal persons in their profession. But my ideas—about Christ, for instance. He will come again, will He? Frankly I doubt if He has ever been very far away. But suppose

He comes again, presumably everybody expects He will come to pull the chestnuts out of the fire for them. What will they say if he comes blighting the vine, flogging the money-changers out of the temple one day and hobnobbing with the rich the next, just as He did before? He had a terrible temper, you know, undoubtedly inherited from His Father. Will He come as a Westerner—let us say, as an Irishman or a Texan—because the stronghold of Christianity is in the West? He certainly won't be a Jew again, or the fat will be in the fire. The Arabs would laugh their heads off if Israel produced an embarrassing Pretender. Will He settle the disagreement between Catholic and Protestant? All these questions seem frivolous, like the questions of a child. But did He not say we are to be as children?

"My own idea is that when He comes again it will be to continue His ministry as an old man. I am an old man and my life has been spent as a soldier of Christ, and I tell you that the older I grow the less Christ's teaching says to me. I am sometimes very conscious that I am following the path of a leader who died when He was less than half as old as I am now. I see and feel things He never saw or felt. I know things He seems never to have known. Everybody wants a Christ for himself and those who think like him. Very well, am I at fault for wanting a Christ who will show me how to be an old man? All Christ's teaching is put forward with the dogmatism, the certainty, and the strength of youth: I need something that takes account of the accretion of experience, the sense of paradox and ambiguity that comes with years! I think after forty we should recognize Christ politely but turn for our comfort and guidance to God the Father, who knows the good and evil of life, and to the Holy Ghost, who possesses a wisdom beyond that of the incarnated Christ. After all, we worship a Trinity, of which Christ is but one Person. I think when He comes again it will be to declare the unity of the life of the flesh and the life of the spirit. And then perhaps we shall make some sense of this life of marvels, cruel circumstances, obscenities, and commonplaces. Who can tell?—we might even make it bearable for everybody!

"I have not forgotten your crazy saint. I think you are a fool to fret that she was knocked on the head because of an act of yours.

Perhaps that was what she was for, Ramezay. She saved you on the battlefield, you say. But did she not also save you when she took the blow that was meant for you?

"I do not suggest that you should fail in your duty toward her; if she has no friend but you, care for her by all means. But stop trying to be God, making it up to her that you are sane and she is mad. Turn your mind to the real problem: who is she? Oh, I don't mean her police identification or what her name was before she was married. I mean, who is she in your personal world? What figure is she in your personal mythology? If she appeared to save you on the battlefield, as you say, it has just as much to do with you as it has with her—much more probably. Lots of men have visions of their mothers in time of danger. Why not you? Why was it this woman?

"Who is she? That is what you must discover, Ramezay, and you must find your answer in psychological truth, not in objective truth. You will not find out quickly, I am sure. And while you are searching, get on with your own life and accept the possibility that it may be purchased at the price of hers and that this may be God's plan for you and her.

"You think that dreadful? For her, poor sacrifice, and for you who must accept the sacrifice? Listen, Ramezay, have you heard what Einstein says?—Einstein, the great scientist, not some Jesuit like old Blazon. He says, 'God is subtle, but He is not cruel.' There is some sound Jewish wisdom for your muddled Protestant mind. Try to understand the subtlety, and stop whimpering about the cruelty. Maybe God wants you for something special. Maybe so much that you are worth a woman's sanity.

"I can see what is in your sour Scotch eye. You think I speak thus because of this excellent picnic you have provided. 'Old Blazon is talking from the inspiration of roast chicken and salad, and plums and confectioneries, and a whole bottle of Beaune, ignited by a few brandies,' I hear you thinking. 'Therefore he urges me to think well of myself instead of despising myself like a good Protestant.' Nonsense, Ramezay. I am quite a wise old bird, but I am no desert hermit who can only prophesy when his guts are knotted with hunger. I am deep in the old man's puzzle, trying to link the wisdom of the body with the wisdom of the spirit until the two are one. At my age you cannot divide spirit from body without anguish and destruction, from which you will speak nothing but crazy lies!

"You are still young enough to think that torment of the spirit is a splendid thing, a sign of a superior nature. But you are no longer a young man; you are a youngish middle-aged man, and it is time you found out that these spiritual athletics do not lead to wisdom. Forgive yourself for being a human creature, Ramezay. That is the beginning of wisdom; that is part of what is meant by the fear of God; and for you it is the only way to save your sanity. Begin now, or you will end up with your saint in the madhouse."

Saying which, Padre Blazon spread his handkerchief over his face and went to sleep, leaving me to think.

4

It was all very well for Blazon to give me advice, and to follow it up during the years that followed with occasional postcards (usually of the rowdier Renaissance masters—he liked fat nudes) on which would be written in purple ink some such message as, "How do you fare in the Great Battle? Who is she? I pray for you. I.B., S.J." These caused great curiosity in the school, where one rarely got a postcard before two or three other people had read it. But even if I had been better at taking advice than I am, my path would have been strewn with difficulties.

My visits to Mrs. Dempster weighed on me. She was not a troublesome patient at the hospital, but she became very dull; the occasional lightening of the spirit that had shown itself when she lived with Bertha Shanklin never came now. My weekly visits were the high spots of her life; she was always waiting for me on Saturday afternoon with her hat on. I knew what the hat meant; she hoped that this time I would take her away. This was the hope of many of the patients, and when the presiding physician made his appearance there were scenes in which women clutched at his sleeves and even—I could not have believed it if I had not seen it—fell on their knees and tried to kiss his hands, for all those who had some freedom of movement knew that the power to dismiss them lay with him. A few of the younger ones tried to make a sexual association of it, and their cries were, "Aw, Doc, you know I'm your girl, Doc; you're gonna let me go this time, aren't you, Doc? You know you like me best." I couldn't have stood it, but he did. The sexual fetor in the place was hateful to me. Of course, I was known as "Mary's fella," and they assured her that every visit was sure to bring deliverance. I took her chocolates because they were something she could give the others, most of whom did not have regular visitors.

Let me say again that I was not bitter against the hospital; it was a big place in a big city, obliged to take all who were brought to it. But an hour among these friendless, distracted people was all I could bear. Many of them became known to me, and I got into the custom of telling them stories; as the stories of the saints were the bulk of my store, I told many of those, avoiding anything too miraculous or disquieting, and especially—after one bad experience—anything about wonderful deliverances from prison or bondage of any sort. They liked to be talked to, and when I was talking to a group I was at least not struggling to make conversation with Mrs. Dempster alone, and seeing the unvoiced expectancy in her eyes.

Those visits rubbed deep into me the knowledge that though reason may be injured, feeling lives intensely in the insane. I know my visits gave her pleasure, in spite of the weekly disappointment about not being taken elsewhere; after all, I was her special visitor, looked on by the others as an amusing fellow with a fund of tales to tell, and I gave her a certain status. I am ashamed to say how much it cost me in resolution; some Saturdays I had to flog myself to the hospital, cursing what seemed to be a life sentence.

I should have been objective. I should have regarded it as my "good work." But my association with Mrs. Dempster made that impossible. It was as though I were visiting a part of my own soul that was condemned to live in hell.

Are you wondering: Why didn't he go to Boy Staunton and ask for money to put Mrs. Dempster in a better place, on the grounds that she was a Deptford woman in need, if not because of Staunton's part in making her what she was? There is no simple reply. Staunton did not like to be reminded of Deptford except as a joke.

Also, Boy had a way of dominating anything with which he was associated; if I got help from him—which was not certain, for he always insisted that one of the first requirements for success was the ability to say "no"—he would have established himself as Mrs. Dempster's patron and saviour, and I would have been demoted to his agent. My own motives were not clear or pure: I was determined that if I could not take care of Mrs. Dempster, nobody else should do it. She was mine.

Do you ask: If he couldn't afford to put the woman in a private hospital, or get her into a private patients' section of a government hospital, how did he pay for those jaunts abroad every summer? He seems not to have stinted himself there. True, but in my servitude to Mrs. Dempster I was not wholly lost to my own needs and concerns. I was absorbed in my enthusiasm for the world of the saints, and ambitious to distinguish myself in explaining them to other people. And I had to have some rest, some refreshment of the spirit.

My diary tells me that I visited Mrs. Dempster forty Saturdays every year and at Easter, Christmas, and on her birthday in addition. If that does not seem much to you, try it, and judge then. She was always downcast when I announced that I was off on my summer travels, but I hardened myself and promised her plenty of postcards, for she liked the pictures, and the receipt of mail gave her status among the patients. Did I do all that I could? It seemed so to me, and certainly it was not my intention to join my saint in the madhouse, as Blazon had threatened, by making myself a mere appendage to her sickness.

My life was absorbing as well. I was now a senior master in the school, and a very busy man. I had completed my first book *A Hundred Saints for Travellers,* and it was selling nicely in five languages, though mostly in English, for Europeans do not travel as Britishers and Americans do. It was written simply and objectively, telling readers how to identify the most common saints they saw in pictures and statuary, and why these saints were popular. I avoided the Catholic gush and the Protestant smirk. I was collecting material for my next book, a much bigger piece of work, to be called *The Saints: A Study in History and Popular Mythology,* in which I wanted to explore first of all why people needed saints, and then how much their need had to do with the saintly attainments of a wide range of extraordinary and gifted people. This was biting off a very large chunk indeed, and I was not sure I could chew it, but I meant to try. I was keeping up my association with the Bollandists too, and writing for *Analecta* and also for the Royal Historical Society whenever I had anything to say.

I had become even more caught up in the life of the Stauntons. Boy liked to have me around much as he liked to have valuable pictures and handsome rugs; I gave the right tone to the place. By that I mean that it put him in a position of advantage with his friends to have someone often in his house who was from a different world, and when he introduced me as a Writer I could hear the capital letter. Of course he had other writers, and painters, musicians, and actors as well, but I was the fixture in the collection, and the least troublesome.

If this sounds like a sneering requital for the hundred-weights of excellent food and the pailfuls of good drink I consumed under his roof, let me say that I paid my way: I was the man who could be called at the last minute to come to dinner when somebody else failed, and I was the man who would talk to the dullest woman in the room, and I was the man who disseminated an air of culture at the most Philistine assemblage of sugar-boilers and wholesale bakers without making the other guests feel cheap. Having me in the dining-room was almost the equivalent of having a Raeburn on the walls; I was classy, I was heavily varnished, and I offended nobody.

Why did I accept a place that I now describe in such terms? Because I was tirelessly curious to see how Boy was getting on, to begin with. Because I really liked him, in spite of his affectations and pomposities. Because if I did not go there, where else would I meet such a variety of people? Because I was always grateful to Boy for his financial advice, which was carrying me nicely through the Depression, and which would in time make it possible for me to do better for Mrs. Dempster and to arrange a broader life for myself. My motives, like those of most people, were mingled.

If his social life interested me, his private life fascinated me. I have never known anyone in whose life sex played such a dominating part. He didn't think so. He once told me that he thought this fellow Freud must be a madman, bringing everything down to sex the way he did. I attempted no defence of Freud; by this time I was myself much concerned with that old fantastical duke of dark corners, C. G. Jung, but I had read a great deal of Freud and remembered his injunction against arguing in favour of psychoanalysis with those who clearly hated it.

Sex was so much of the very grain of Boy's life that he noticed it no more than the air he breathed. Little David must be manly in all things; I remember a noisy row he had with Leola when she allowed the child to have a Highlander doll; did she want to make his son a sissy? The doll was put in the garbage pail before the weeping eyes of David, who liked to take it to bed (he was six at the time), and then he was rewarded with a fine practical steam-engine, which drove a circular saw that would really cut a matchstick in two. At eight he was given boxing gloves and had to try to punch his father on the nose as Boy knelt before him.

With little Caroline, Boy was humorously gallant. "How's my little sweetheart tonight?" he would say as he kissed her small hand. When she had been brought in by the nurse, to be shown off to a roomful of guests, Boy always followed them into the hall, to tell Caroline that she had been by far the prettiest girl in the room. Not surprisingly, David was a confused lad, pitifully anxious to please, and Caroline was spoiled rotten.

Leola was never told that she was the prettiest woman in the room. Boy's usual attitude toward her was one of chivalrous patience, with a discernible undertone of exasperation. She loved him abjectly, but she was the one person on whom he spent none of his sexual force—except in the negative form of bullying. I tried to stand up for Leola as much as I could, but as she was utterly unable to stand up for herself I had to be careful. If I was angry with Boy, as sometimes happened, she took his side. She lived her life solely in relation to him; if he thought poorly of her, it did not matter what I might say to defend her. He must be right.

Of course it was not always as black-and-white as this. I remember very well when first she discovered that he was having affairs with other women. She did so by the classic mishap of finding a revealing note in his pocket—the Stauntons rarely escaped cliché in any of the essential matters of life.

I knew of his philandering, of course, for Boy could not keep anything to himself and used to justify his conduct to me late at night, when we had both had plenty of his whisky. "A man with my physical needs can't be tied down to one woman—especially not a woman who doesn't see sex as a partnership—who doesn't give anything, who just lies there like a damned sandbag," he would say, making agonized faces so that I would know how tortured he was.

He was explicit about his sexual needs; he had to have intercourse often, and it had to be all sorts of things—intense, passionate, cruel, witty, challenging—and he had to have it with a Real Woman. It all sounded very exhausting and strangely like a sharp workout with the punching bag; I was glad I was not so demandingly endowed. So there were two or three women in Montreal—not whores, mind you, but women of sophistication and spirit, who demanded their independence even though they were married—whom he visited as often as he could. He had business associations in Montreal and it was easy.

The mention of business reminds me of another phase of Boy's sexuality of which he was certainly unconscious, but which I saw at work on several occasions. It was what I thought of as Corporation Homosexuality. He was always on the lookout for promising young men who could be advanced in his service. They must be keen apostles of sugar, or doughnuts, or pop, or whatever it might be, but they must also be "clean-cut." Whenever he discovered one of these, Boy would "take him up"—ask him to luncheon at his club, to dinner at his home, and to private chats in his office. He would explain the mystique of business to the young man and push him ahead as fast as possible in the corporation, sometimes to the chagrin of older men who were not clean-cut but merely capable and efficient.

After a few months of such an association disillusion would come. The clean-cut young man, being ambitious and no more given to gratitude than ambitious people usually are, would assume that all of this was no more than his due and would cease to be as eagerly receptive and admiring as he had been at the beginning of the affair, and might even display a mind of his own. Boy was dismayed to find that these protégés thought him lucky to have such gifted associates as themselves.

Some went so far as to marry on the strength of their new-found hopes, and Boy always asked them to bring their brides to dinner at his house. Afterward he would demand of me why a clean-cut young fellow with everything in his favour would wreck his chances by marrying a girl who was obviously a dumb cluck and would simply hold him back from real success in the corporation? One way or another, Boy was disappointed in most of these clean-cut young men; of those who survived this peril he wearied in the natural course of things, and they became well placed but not influential in his empire.

I do not suggest that Boy ever recognized these young men as anything but business associates; but they were business associates with an overtone of Jove's cup-bearer that I, at least, could not ignore. Corporation Ganymedes, they did not know their role and thus were disappointments.

Leola's awakening came at the fated Christmas of 1936. It had been an emotionally exhausting year for Boy. The old King, George V, had died in January, and in memory of that glance that had once passed between us I wore a black tie for a week. But Boy was in high feather, for "he" would at last mount the Throne; they had not met for nine years, but Boy was as faithful to his hero as ever. He reported every bit of gossip that came his way; there would be great changes, a Throne more meaningful than ever before, a wholesale ousting of stupid old men, a glorious upsurge of youth around the new King, and of course a gayer Court—the gayest, probably, since that of Charles the Second. And a gay Court, to Boy, meant an exaltation of the punching-bag attitude to sex. If he had ever read any of those psychologists who assert that a crowned and anointed King is the symbolic phallus of his people, Boy would have agreed whole-heartedly.

As everyone knows, it was not long before the news took a contrary turn. On the North American continent we got it sooner than the people of England, for our papers did not have to be so tactful. The young King—he was forty-two, but to people like Boy he seemed very young—was having trouble with the old men, and the old men with him. Stanley Baldwin, who had been with him on that visit to Canada in 1927 and whom Boy had revered as a statesman with a strong literary bent, became a personal enemy of Boy's, and he spoke of the Archbishop of Canterbury in terms that even Woodiwiss—now an archdeacon—found it hard to overlook.

When the crisis came, there was some extravagant talk of forming a group of "King's Men" who would, in an unspecified way, rally to the side of their hero and put his chosen lady beside him on the Throne. Boy was determined to be a King's Man; everybody who considered himself a gentleman, and a man who understood the demanding nature of love, must necessarily feel as he did. He lectured me about it every time we met; as a historian I was very sorry for the King but could see no clear or good way out of the mess. I believe Boy even sent a few telegrams of encouragement, but I never heard of any answers. When the black month of November came I began to fear for his reason; he read everything, heard every radio report, and snatched at every scrap of gossip. I was not with him when he heard the sad broadcast of Abdication on December 11, but I looked in at his house that evening and found him, for the only time in his life, to my knowledge, very drunk and alternating between tears and dreadful tirades against all the repressive forces that worked against true love and the expression of a man's real self.

Christmas was a dark day at the Stauntons'. Leola had had to buy all the presents for the children, and Boy found fault with most of them. The fat janitor from the Alpha offices appeared in a hired suit to play Santa Claus, and Boy told him, in front of the children, not to make a jackass of himself but to get on with his job and get out. He would not open his own gifts from Leola and the children. By the time I had made my visit to Mrs. Dempster at the hospital, and turned up for midday Christmas dinner, Leola was in tears, David was huddled up in a corner with a book he was not reading, and Caroline was rampaging through the house demanding attention for a doll she had broken. I joked with David, mended the doll so that it was crippled but in one piece, and tried to be decent to Leola. Boy told me that if I had to behave like one of the bloody saints I was always yapping about, he wished I would do it somewhere else. I unwisely told him to take his Abdication like a man, and he became silently hateful and soured the food in our stomachs.

He announced that he was going for a walk, and he was going alone.

Leola, grieved for him, went to fetch his overcoat and happened on the note from one of the great-spirited women in Montreal while looking for his gloves in a pocket. She was crouching on the stairs, sobbing dreadfully, when he went out into the hall, and he took in the meaning of her desolation at a glance.

"There's no reason to carry on like that," he said, picking up the fallen coat and putting it on. "Your situation is perfectly secure. But if you think I intend to be tied down to this sort of thing"—and he gestured toward the drawing-room, which was, I must say, a dismal, toy-littered waste of wealthy, frumpish domesticity—"you can think again." And off he went, leaving Leola howling.

I wish I did not have to say howling, but Leola was not beautiful in her grief. The nurse was off duty for the day, but I managed to shoo the children upstairs to their own quarters and spent a hard hour quieting her. I wish I could say I comforted her, but only one man could have done that, and he was trudging through the snow, deep in some egotistical hell of his own. At last I persuaded her to sleep, or at least to lie down, and wait to see what would happen. Nothing was ever quite so bad as it looked, I assured her. I did not really believe it, but I intended to have a word with Boy.

She went to her room, and when I thought a sufficient time had passed I went up to see how things were getting on. She had washed her face and tidied her hair and was in bed in one of the expensive nightdresses Boy liked.

"Will you be all right if I go now?"

"Kiss me, Dunny. No, not like that. That's just a peck. You used to like to kiss me."

Whether she knew it or not, this was an invitation that might lead to much more. Was the story of Gyges and Candaules to have the ending in which Gyges takes his friend's wife? No; upon the whole I thought not. But I leaned over and kissed her a little less formally.

"That's no good. Kiss me *really*."

So I did, and if my artificial leg had not given an ominous croak as I knelt on the bed I might have gone on, doubtless to cuckold Boy Staunton, which he certainly deserved. But I recovered myself and stood up and said, "You must sleep now. I'll look in later tonight and we'll talk with Boy."

"You don't love me!" she wailed.

I hurried out the door as she burst into tears again.

Of course I didn't love her. Why would I? It had been at least ten years since I had thought of her with anything but pity. I had made my bed and I intended to lie on it, and there was no room for Leola in it. On my last few visits abroad I had spent a weekend with Diana and her husband at their delightful country house near Canterbury and had enjoyed myself greatly. I had survived my boyish love for Diana, and I certainly had survived anything I ever felt for Leola. I was not to be a victim of her self-pity. The emotional upheaval caused by her disappointment about Boy's unfaithfulness had sharpened her sexual appetite; that was all. I do not suppose Boy had slept with her since the beginning of the trouble that led to the Abdication. I was not going to be the victim of somebody else's faulty chronology. I went for a walk myself, had another Christmas dinner—it was impossible to avoid heavy food on that day—and arrived back at the school at about nine o'clock, intending to do some reading.

Instead I was greeted by a message from the furnace man, who was the only person left on duty that day. I was to call the Stauntons' number at once. It was an emergency.

I called, and the children's nurse spoke. She had come back from her holiday, found the housemaid and the cook and butler still out, and had looked in on Mrs. Staunton to say goodnight. Had found her in a very bad way. Did not like to explain over the phone. Yes, had called the doctor but it was Christmas night and an hour had gone by and he still had not come. Would I come at once? Yes, it was *very* serious.

The nurse was becoming a little hysterical, and I hurried to obey. But on Christmas night it is not simple to get taxis, and altogether it was half an hour before I ran upstairs to Leola's bedroom and found her in bed, white as the sheets, with her wrists bound up in gauze, and the nurse near to fits.

"Look at this," she said, gasping, and pushed me toward the bathroom.

The bath seemed to be full of blood. Apparently Leola had cut her wrists and laid herself down to die in the high Roman fashion, in a warm bath. But she was not a good anatomist and had made a gory but not a fatal job of it.

The doctor came not long after, rather drunk but fairly capable. The nurse had done all that was immediately necessary, so he redressed the wrists, gave Leola an injection of something, and said he would call again on Boxing Day.

"I sent for you at once because of this," said the nurse as soon as the doctor had gone. She handed me a letter with my name on the envelope. It read:

Dearest Dunny:

This is the end. Boy does not love me and you don't either so it is best for me to go. Think of me sometimes. I always loved you.

Love,
Leola

Fool, fool, fool! Thinking only of herself and putting me in an intolerable position with such a note. If she had died, how would it have sounded at an inquest? As it was, I am sure the nurse read it, for it was not sealed. I was furious with Leola, poor idiot. No note for Boy. No, just a note for me, which would have made me look like a monster if she had not made a mess of this, as of so much else.

However, as she began to pull around I could not reproach her, though I was very careful not to mention the note. Nor did she. It was never spoken of between us.

Boy could not be found. His business address in Montreal knew nothing of him, and he did not return until after New Year's Day, by which time Leola was on the mend, though feeble. What passed between them I do not know and was never told, but from that time onward they seemed to rub along without open disagreement, though Leola faded rapidly and looked more than her years. Indeed, the pretty face that had once ensnared both Boy and me became pudgy and empty. Leola had joined the great company of the walking wounded in the battle of life.

The people who seemed to suffer most from this incident were the children. The nurse, controlled and efficient in emergency, had broken down in the nursery and hinted broadly that Mummy had almost died. This, taken with the quarrel earlier in the day, was enough to put them on edge for a long time; David was increasingly quiet and mousy, but Caroline became a screamer and thrower of tantrums.

David told me many years later that he hated Christmas more than any other day in the calendar.

·V·
Liesl

1

LET ME PASS as quickly as possible over the years of the Second World War—or World War Too, as the name my pupils give it always sounds in my ears; it is as if they were asserting firmly that the World War I remember so vividly was not the only, or the biggest, outburst of mass lunacy in our century. But I cannot leave it out altogether, if only because of the increase in stature it brought to Boy Staunton. His growth as an industrialist with, figuratively speaking, his finger in hundreds of millions of pies, not to speak of other popular goodies, made him a man of might in the national economy, and when the war demanded that the ablest men in the country be pressed into the national service, who but he was the obvious candidate for the post of Minister of Food in a coalition Cabinet?

He was very good in the job. He knew how to get things done, and he certainly knew what the great mass of people like to eat. He put the full resources of his Alpha Corporation, and all the subsidiary companies it controlled, to the job of feeding Canada, feeding its armed services, and feeding Britain so far as the submarine war would permit. He was tireless in promoting research that would produce new concentrates—chiefly from fruits—that would keep fighting men, and the children in a bombed country, going when bulkier eatables were not to be had. If the average height of the people of the British Isles is rather greater today than it was in 1939, much of the credit must go to Boy Staunton. He was one of the few men not a professional scientist who really knew what a vitamin was and where it could be found and put to work cheaply.

Of course he had to spend most of his time in Ottawa. He saw little of Leola or his children during the war years, except on flying visits during which lost intimacies could not be recaptured, not even with his adored Caroline.

I saw him from time to time because he was by now a member of our Board of Governors, and also because David was a boarder in the school. David could have lived at home, but Boy wanted him to have the experience of a community life and of being disciplined by men. So the boy spent the years from his tenth to his eighteenth birthday at Colborne, and when he got into the Upper School, at about twelve, he came under my eye almost every day.

Indeed it was my duty in 1942 to tell this unhappy boy that his mother had died. Poor Leola had become more and more listless since the outbreak of war; as Boy grew in importance and his remarkable abilities became increasingly manifest, she faded. She was not one of those politicians' wives who lets it be known that her husband's competence is kept up to the mark by the support and understanding she gives him. Nor was she of the other strain, who tell the newspapers and the women's clubs that though their husbands may be men of mark to the world, they are sorry wretches at home. Leola had no public life and wanted none.

She had completely given up any pretence at golf or bridge or any of the other pastimes in which she had attained to mediocrity in her younger days; she no longer read fashionable books or anything at all. Whenever I went to see her she was knitting things for the Red Cross—vast inner stockings for seaboots and the like—which she seemed to do automatically while her mind was elsewhere. I asked her to dinner a few times, and it was heavy work, though not so heavy as having dinner at the Stauntons' house. With Boy away and both the children in school, that richly furnished barrack became more and more lifeless, and the servants were demoralized, looking after one undemanding woman who was afraid of them.

When Leola fell ill of pneumonia I informed Boy and did all the obvious things and did not worry. But that was before the drugs for dealing with pneumonia were as effective as they now are, and after the worst of it was over a considerable period of convalescence was needed. As it was difficult to travel to any warmer climate, and as there was nobody to go with Leola, she had to spend it at home. Although I cannot vouch for this, I have always thought it suspicious that Leola opened her windows one afternoon, when the nurse had closed them, and took a chill, and was dead in less than a week.

Boy was in England, arranging something or other connected with his Ministry, and duty and the difficulty of transatlantic flights in wartime kept him there. He asked me, by cable, to do what had to be done, so I arranged the funeral, which was easy, and told the people who had to be told, which was not. Caroline made a loud fuss, and I left her with some capable schoolmistresses who bore the weight of that. But David astonished me.

"Poor Mum," he said, "I guess she's better off, really."

Now what was I to make of that, from a boy of fourteen? And what was I to do with him? I could not send him home, and I had no home of my own except my study and bedroom in the school, so I put him there and made sure one of the matrons looked in every hour or so to see that he was not utterly desolate and had anything it was in the school's power to give him. Fortunately he slept a lot, and at night I sent him to the infirmary, where he could have a room of his own.

I kept him by me at the funeral, for both the older Stauntons were now dead, and the Cruikshanks were so desolated themselves that they could only hold hands and weep. Association with the Cruikshanks had not been encouraged by Boy, so David was not really well known to them.

It was one of those wretched late autumn funerals, and though it did not actually rain everything was wet and miserable. There were not a great many present, for all the Stauntons' friends were important people, and it seemed that all the important people were so busy fighting the war in one way or another that they could not come. But there were mountains of costly flowers, looking particularly foolish under a November sky.

One unexpected figure was at the graveside. Older, fatter, and unwontedly quiet though he was, I knew Milo Papple in an instant. As Woodiwiss read the committal, I found myself thinking that his own father had died at least twelve years before, and I had written to Milo at that time. But the Kaiser (whom Myron Papple had impersonated so uproariously at the hanging-in-effigy after the Great War) had lived, presumably untroubled by the hatred of Deptford and places like it, until 1941; had lived at Doorn, sawing wood and wondering what world madness had dethroned him, for twenty-three years after his fall. I pondered on the longevity of dethroned monarchs when I should have been taking farewell of Leola. But I well knew that I had taken leave of her, so far as any real feeling went, that Christmas afternoon when she had appealed to me for comfort and I had run away. Everything since had been a matter of duty.

Milo and I shook hands as we left the cemetery. "Poor Leola," he said in a choked voice. "It's the end of a great romance. You know we always thought her and Perse was the handsomest pair that ever got married in Deptford. And I know why you never got married. It must be tough on you to see her go, Dunny."

My shame was that it was not tough at all. What was tough was to go with David back to that awful, empty house and talk to him until the servants gave us a poor dinner; then take him back to school and tell him I thought it better that he should go to his own room, as he must some time resume his ordinary life, and the sooner the better.

Boy was always fussing that David would not be a real man. He seemed a very real man to me through all this bad time. I could not have seen as much of him as I did if I had not been temporary Headmaster. When the war began our Head had rushed off to throw himself upon the foe from the midst of the Army's education program; he stepped in front of a truck one night in the blackout, and the school mourned him as a hero. When he left, the Governors had to get a Headmaster in a hurry, but the war made good men so scarce that they appointed me, *pro tem,* without any increase in salary, as we must all shoulder our burdens without thought of self. It was taxing, thankless work, and I hated all the administrative side of it. But I bent to the task and did what I could until 1947, when I had a difficult conversation with Boy, who was now a C.B.E. (for his war work) and the Chairman of our Board of Governors.

"Dunny, you've done a superb job during the whole of the war, and long beyond. But it was fun, wasn't it?"

"No, not fun. Damned hard slogging. Endless trouble getting

and keeping staff. Managing with our old men and some young ones who weren't fit for service—or for teaching, if it comes to that. Problems with 'war-guest' boys who were homesick, or hated Canada, or thought they could slack because they weren't in England. Problems with the inevitable hysteria of the school when the news was bad, and the worse hysteria when it was good. The fag of keeping up nearly all my own teaching and doing the administration as well. Not fun, Boy."

"None of us had an easy war, Dunny. And I must say you look well on it. The question is, what are we to do now?"

"You're the Chairman of the Board. You tell me."

"You don't want to go on being Head, do you?"

"That depends on the conditions. It might be much pleasanter now. I've been able to get a pretty good staff during the last eighteen months, and I suppose money will be more plentiful now that the Board can think about it again."

"But you've just said you hated being Head."

"In wartime—who wouldn't? But, as I say, things are improving. I might get to like it very much."

"Look, old man, let's not make a long business of this. The Board appreciates everything you've done. They want to give you a testimonial dinner. They want to tell you in front of the whole school how greatly indebted they are to you. But they want a younger Headmaster."

"How young? You know my age. I'm not quite fifty, like yourself. How young does a Headmaster have to be nowadays?"

"It isn't entirely that. You're making this awfully tough for me. You're unmarried. A Headmaster needs a wife."

"When I needed a wife, I found that you needed her even more."

"That's hitting below the belt. Anyhow, Leo wouldn't have—never mind. You have no wife."

"Perhaps I could find one in a hurry. Miss Gostling, at our sister school, Bishop Cairncross's, has been giving me the glad eye in an academic way for two or three years."

"Be serious. It's not just the wife. Dunny, we have to face it. You're queer."

"The Sin of Sodom, you mean? If you knew boys as I do, you would not suggest anything so grotesque. If Oscar Wilde had pleaded insanity, he would have walked out of court a free man."

"No, no, no! I don't mean kid-simple, I mean *queer*—strange, funny, not like other people."

"Ah, that's very interesting. How am I queer? Do you remember poor old Iremonger who had a silver plate in his head and used to climb the waterpipes in his room and address his class from the ceiling? Now he was queer. Or that unfortunate alcoholic Bateson who used to throw a wet boxing glove at inattentive boys and then retrieve it on a string? I always thought they added something to the school—gave boys a knowledge of the great world that the state schools dare not imitate. Surely you do not think I am queer in any comparable way?"

"You are a fine teacher. Everybody knows it. You are a great scholarship-getter, which is quite another thing. You have a reputation as an author. But there it is."

"There is what?"

"It's this saint business of yours. Of course your books are splendid. But if you were a father, would you want to send your son to a school headed by a man who was an authority on saints? Even more, would you do it if you were a mother? Women hate anything that's uncanny about a man if they think of entrusting a son to him. Religion in the school is one thing; there is a well-understood place for religion in education. But not this misty world of wonder-workers and holy wizards and juiceless women. Saints aren't in the picture at all. Now I'm an old friend, but I am also Chairman of the Board, and I tell you it won't do."

"Are you kicking me out?"

"Certainly not. Don't be extreme. You surely understand that you are a tremendous addition to the school as a master—well-known writer on a difficult subject, translated into foreign languages, amusingly eccentric, and all that—but you would be a disaster as a peacetime Headmaster."

"Eccentric? Me!"

"Yes, you. Good God, don't you think the way you rootle in your ear with your little finger delights the boys? And the way you waggle your eyebrows—great wild things like moustaches, I don't know why you don't trim them—and those terrible Harris tweed suits you wear and never have pressed. And that disgusting trick of blowing your nose and looking into your handkerchief as if you expected to prophesy something from the mess. You look ten years older than your age. The day of comic eccentrics as Heads has gone. Parents nowadays want somebody more like themselves."

"A Headmaster created in their own image, eh? Well, you obviously have somebody virtually hired or you wouldn't be in such a rush to get rid of me. Who is it?"

(Boy named you, Headmaster. I had never heard of you then, so there can be no malice in reporting this conversation.)

We haggled a little more, and I made Boy squirm a bit, for I felt I had been shabbily used. But at last I said, "Very well, I'll stay on as chief of history and Assistant Head. I don't want your testimonial dinner, but I should like you, as Chairman, to address the school and make it very clear that I have not been demoted as soon as you could get somebody their parents like better. It will be a lie, but I want my face saved. Say the demands of my writing made me suggest this decision and I pledge my full support to the new man. And I want six months' leave of absence, on full pay, before I return to work."

"Agreed. You're a good sport, Dunny. Where will you go for your six months?"

"I have long wanted to visit the great shrines of Latin America. I shall begin in Mexico, with the Shrine of the Virgin of Guadalupe."

"There you go, you see! You go right on with the one thing that really stood between you and a Headmaster's job."

"Certainly. You don't expect me to pay attention to the opinion of numskulls like you and your Board and the parents of a few hundred cretinous boys, do you?"

2

So there I was, a few months later, sitting in a corner of the huge, nineteenth-century Byzantine basilica at Guadalupe, watching the seemingly endless crowd of men and women, old and young, as it shuffled forward on its knees to get as near as possible to the miraculous picture of the Virgin.

The picture was a surprise to me. Whether it was because I had some ignorant preconception about the tawdriness of everything Mexican, or the extravagantly Latin nature of the legend, I had expected something artistically offensive. I was by now in a modest way a connoisseur in holy pictures, ranging from catacombs and the blackened and glaring Holy Face at Lucca to the softest Raphaels and Murillos. But here was a picture reputedly from no mortal hand—not even that of St. Luke—that had appeared miraculously on the inside of a peasant's cloak.

In 1531 the Virgin had appeared several times on this spot to Juan Diego and bidden him to tell Bishop Zumárraga that a shrine in her honour should be built here; when Zumárraga very naturally asked for some further evidence of Juan Diego's authority, the Virgin filled the peasant's cloak with roses, though it was December; and when he opened his cloak before the Bishop, not only were the roses there, but also, on the inner side of it, this painting, before which the Bishop fell on his knees in wonderment.

As unobtrusively as possible (for I try hard not to be objectionable when visiting shrines) I examined the picture through a powerful little pocket telescope. Certainly it was painted on cloth of a very coarse weave, with a seam up the middle of it that deviated from the straight just enough to avoid the Virgin's face. The picture was in the mode of the Immaculate Conception; the Virgin, a peasant girl of about fifteen, stood on a crescent moon. The painting was skilled, and the face beautiful, if you dismiss from your mind the whorish mask that modern cosmetics have substituted for beauty and think of the human face. Why was the right eye almost closed, as though swollen? Very odd in a holy picture. But the colours were fine, and the gold, though lavish, was not barbarically splashed on. Spain might be proud of such a picture. And the proportions—the width would go about three and a half times into the length—were those of a *tilma* such as I had seen peasants wearing outside the city. A very remarkable picture indeed.

The picture was not my chief concern, however. My eyes were on the kneeling petitioners, whose faces had the beauty virtually every face reveals in the presence of the goddess of mercy, the Holy Mother, the figure of divine compassion. Very different, these, from the squinnying, lip-biting, calculating faces of the art lovers one sees looking at Madonnas in galleries. These petitioners had no conception of art; to them a picture was a symbol of something else, and very readily the symbol became the reality. They were untouched by modern education, but their government was striving with might and main to procure this inestimable benefit for them; anticlericalism and American bustle would soon free them from belief in miracles and holy likenesses. But where, I ask myself, will mercy and divine compassion come from then? Or are such things necessary to people who are well fed and know the wonders that lie concealed in an atom? I don't regret economic and educational advance; I just wonder how much we shall have to pay for it, and in what coin.

Day after day I sat in the basilica for a few hours and wondered. The sacristans and nuns who gave out little prints of the miraculous picture grew accustomed to me; they thought I must be a member of that tiny and eccentric group, the devout rich, or perhaps I was writing an article for a tourist magazine. I put something in every out-thrust box and was left alone. But I am neither rich nor conventionally devout, and what I was writing, slowly, painstakingly, and with so many revisions that the final version was not even in sight, was a sort of prologue to a discussion of the nature of faith. Why do people all over the world, and at all times, want marvels that defy all verifiable fact? And are the marvels brought into being by their desire, or is their desire an assurance rising from some deep knowledge, not to be directly experienced and questioned, that the marvellous is indeed an aspect of the real?

Philosophers have tackled this question, of course, and answered it in ways highly satisfactory to themselves; but I never knew a philosopher's answer to make much difference to anyone not in the trade. I was trying to get at the subject without wearing either the pink spectacles of faith or the green spectacles of science. All I had managed by the time I found myself sitting in the basilica of Guadalupe was a certainty that faith was a psychological reality, and that where it was not invited to fasten itself on things unseen, it invaded and raised bloody hell with things seen. Or in other words, the irrational will have its say, perhaps because "irrational" is the wrong word for it.

Such speculation cannot fill the whole of one's day. I used to rise early and go to the shrine in the morning. After luncheon I followed the local custom and slept. I explored the city until dinner. After dinner, what? I could not sit in the public rooms in my hotel for they were uncomfortable after the Spanish fashion. The writing-room was dominated by a large painting of the Last Supper, a more than usually gloomy depiction of that gloomiest of parties; apparently nobody had been able to touch a bite, and a whole lamb, looking uncomfortably alive though flayed, lay on a platter in the middle of the table with its eyes fixed reproachfully on Judas.

I tried the theatre and found myself sitting through a drama that I identified as Sardou's *Frou Frou,* heavily Hispanicized and given a further Mexican flavour. It was slow going. I went to one or two films, American pieces with Spanish sound tracks. With relief I discovered from a morning paper that a magician might be seen at the Teatro Chueca, and I booked a seat through my hotel.

Enthusiasm for magic had never wholly died in me, and I had seen the best illusionists of my time—Thurston, Goldin, Blackstone, the remarkable German who called himself Kalanag, and Harry Houdini, not long before his death. But the name of the man who was to perform in Mexico was unknown to me; the advertisement announced that Magnus Eisengrim would astonish Mexico City after having triumphantly toured South America. I assumed that he was a German who thought it impolitic to appear in the States at present.

Very soon after the curtain rose I knew that this was a magic entertainment unlike any I had ever seen. In the twentieth century stage magicians have always been great jokers; even Houdini grinned like a film star through most of his show. They kept up a run of patter designed to assure the audience that they were not to be taken seriously as wonder-workers; they were entertainers and mighty clever fellows, but their magic was all in fun. Even when they included a little hypnotism—as Blackstone did so deftly—nobody was given any cause for alarm.

Not so Magnus Eisengrim. He did not wear ordinary evening clothes, but a beautiful dress coat with a velvet collar, and silk knee breeches. He began his show by appearing in the middle of the stage out of nowhere; he plucked a wand from the air and, wrapping himself in a black cloak, suddenly became transparent;

members of his company—girls dressed in fanciful costumes—seemed to walk through him; then, after another flourish of the cloak, he was present in the flesh again, and four of the girls were sufficiently ghostly for him to pass his wand through them. I began to enjoy myself; this was the old Pepper's Ghost illusion, familiar enough in principle but newly worked up into an excellent mystery. And nobody on the stage cracked a smile.

Eisengrim now introduced himself to us. He spoke in elegant Spanish, and it was clear at once that he did not present himself as a funny-man but as one who offered an entertainment of mystery and beauty, with perhaps a hint of terror as well. Certainly his appearance and surroundings were not those of the usual stage magician; he was not tall, but his bearing was so impressive that his smallness was unimportant. He had beautiful eyes and an expression of dignity, but the most impressive thing about him was his voice; it was much bigger than one would expect from a small man, and of unusual range and beauty of tone. He received us as honoured guests and promised us an evening of such visions and illusions as had nourished the imagination of mankind for two thousand years—and a few trifles for amusement as well.

This was a novelty—a poetic magician who took himself seriously. It was certainly not the role in which I had expected to re-encounter Paul Dempster. But this was Paul, without a doubt, so self-assured, so polished, so utterly unlike the circus conjurer with the moustache and beard and shabby clothes whom I had met in *Le grand Cirque forain de St Vite* more than fifteen years before, that it was some time before I could be sure it was he. How had he come by this new self, and where had he acquired this tasteful, beautiful entertainment?

It was so elegantly presented that I doubt if anyone in the Teatro Chueca but myself realized how old it was in essence. Paul did not do a single new trick; they were all classics from the past, well known to people who were interested in the history of this curious minor art and craft.

He invited members of the audience to have a drink with him before he began his serious work, and poured red and white wine, brandy, tequila, whisky, milk, and water from a single bottle; a very old trick, but the air of graceful hospitality with which he did it was enough to make it new. He borrowed a dozen handkerchiefs—mine among them—and burned them in a glass vessel; then from the ashes he produced eleven handkerchiefs, washed and ironed; when the twelfth donor showed some uneasiness, Eisengrim directed him to look toward the ceiling, from which his handkerchief fluttered down into his hands. He borrowed a lady's handbag, and from it produced a package that swelled and grew until he revealed a girl under the covering; he caused this girl to rise in the air, float out over the orchestra pit, return to the table, and, when covered, to dwindle once again to a package, which, when returned to the lady's purse, proved to be a box of bon-bons. All old tricks. All beautifully done. And all offered without any of the facetiousness that usually makes magic shows so restless and tawdry.

The second part of his entertainment began with hypnotism. From perhaps fifty people who volunteered to be subjects he chose twenty and seated them in a half-circle on the stage. Then, one by one, he induced them to do the things all hypnotists rely on—row boats, eat invisible meals, behave as guests at a party, listen to music, and all the rest of it—but he had one idea that was new to me; he told a serious-looking man of middle age that he had just been awarded the Nobel Prize and asked him to make a speech of acceptance. The man did so, with such dignity and eloquence that the audience applauded vigorously. I have seen displays of hypnotism in which people were made to look foolish, to show the dominance of the hypnotist; there was nothing of that here, and all of the twenty left the stage with dignity unimpaired, and indeed with a heightened sense of importance.

Then Eisengrim showed us some escapes, from ropes and straps bound on him by men from the audience who fancied themselves as artists in bondage. He was tied up and put into a trunk, which was pulled on a rope up into the ceiling of the theatre; after thirty seconds Eisengrim walked down the centre aisle to the stage, brought the trunk to ground, and revealed that it contained an absurd effigy of himself.

His culminating escape was a variation of one Houdini originated and made famous. Eisengrim, wearing only a pair of bathing trunks, was handcuffed and pushed upside down into a metal container like a milk can, and the top of the milk can was fastened shut with padlocks, some of which members of the audience had brought with them; the milk can was lowered into a tank of water, with glass windows in it so that the audience could see the interior clearly; curtains were drawn around the tank and its contents, and the audience sat in silence to await events. Two men were asked to time the escape; and if more than three minutes elapsed, they were to order the theatre fireman who was in attendance to break open the milk can without delay.

The three minutes passed. The fireman was given the word and made a very clumsy business of getting the can out of the tank and opening the padlocks. But when he had done so the milk can was empty, and the fireman was Eisengrim. It was the nearest thing to comedy the evening provided.

The third and last part of the entertainment was serious almost to the point of solemnity, but it had an erotic savour that was unlike anything I had ever seen in a magic show, where children make up a considerable part of the audience. *The Dream of Midas* was a prolonged illusion in which Eisengrim, assisted by a pretty girl, produced extraordinary sums of money in silver dollars from the air, from the pockets, ears, noses, and hats of people in the audience, and threw them all into a large copper pot; the chink of the coins seemed never to stop. Possessed by unappeasable greed, he turned the girl into gold, and was horrified by what he had done. He tapped her with a hammer; he chipped off a hand and passed it through the audience; he struck the image in the face. Then, in an ecstasy of renunciation, he broke his magician's wand. Immediately the copper pot was empty, and when we turned our attention to the girl she was flesh again, but one hand was missing and blood was running from her lip. This spice of cruelty seemed to please the audience very much.

His last illusion was called *The Vision of Dr. Faustus,* and the program assured us that in this scene, and this alone, the beautiful Faustina would appear before us. Reduced to its fundamentals, it was the familiar illusion in which the magician makes a girl appear in two widely separated cabinets without seeming to pass between them. But as Eisengrim did it, the conflict was between Sacred and Profane Love for the soul of Faust: on one side of the stage would appear the beautiful Faustina as Gretchen, working at her spinning wheel and modestly clothed; as Faust approached her she disappeared, and on the other side of the stage in an arbour of flowers appeared Venus, wearing as near to nothing at all as the Mexican sense of modesty would permit. It was plain enough that Gretchen and Venus were the same girl, but she had gifts as an actress and conveyed unmistakably the message that beauty of spirit and lively sensuality might inhabit one body, an idea that was received with delight by the audience. At last Faust, driven to distraction by the difficulties of choice, killed himself, and Mephistopheles appeared in flames to drag him down to Hell. As he vanished, in the middle of the stage but about eight feet above the floor and supported apparently on nothing at all, appeared the beautiful Faustina once more, as, one presumes, the Eternal Feminine, radiating compassion while showing a satisfactory amount of leg. The culminating moment came when Mephistopheles threw aside his robe and showed that, whoever may have been thrust down into Hell, this was certainly Eisengrim the Great.

The audience took very kindly to the show, and the applause for the finale was long and enthusiastic. An usher prevented me from going through the pass-door to the stage, so I went to the stage door and asked to see Señor Eisengrim. He was not to be seen, said the doorman. Orders were strict that no one was to be admitted. I offered a visiting card, for although these things have almost gone out of use in North America they still possess a certain amount of authority in Europe, and I always carry a few. But it was no use.

I was not pleased and was about to go away in a huff when a voice said, "Are you Mr. Dunstan Ramsay?"

The person who was speaking to me from the last step of the stairs that led up into the theatre was probably a woman but she wore man's dress, had short hair, and was certainly the ugliest human creature I had ever seen. Not that she was misshapen; she was tall, straight, and obviously very strong, but she had big hands and feet, a huge, jutting jaw, and a heaviness of bone over the eyes that seemed to confine them to small, very deep caverns. However, her voice was beautiful and her utterance was an educated speech of some foreign flavour.

"Eisengrim will be very pleased to see you. He noticed you in the audience. Follow me, if you please."

The backstage arrangements were not extensive, and the corridor into which she led me was noisy with the sound of a quarrel in a language unfamiliar to me—probably Portuguese. My guide knocked and entered at once with me behind her, and we were upon the quarrellers. They were Eisengrim, stripped to the waist, rubbing paint off his face with a dirty towel, and the beautiful Faustina, who was naked as the dawn, and lovely as the breeze, and madder than a wet hen; she also was removing her stage paint, which seemed to cover most of her body; she snatched up a wrapper and pulled it around her, and extruded whatever part she happened to be cleaning as we talked.

"She says she must have more pink light in the last tableau," said Eisengrim to my guide in German. "I've told her it will kill my red Mephisto spot, but you know how pig-headed she is."

"Not now," said the ugly woman. "Mr. Dunstan Ramsay, your old friend Magnus Eisengrim, and the beautiful Faustina."

The beautiful Faustina gave me an unnervingly brilliant smile and extended a very greasy hand that had just been wiping paint off her upper thigh. I may be a Canadian of Scots descent, and I may have first seen the light in Deptford, but I am not to be disconcerted by Latin American showgirls, so I kissed it with what I think was a good deal of elegance. Then I shook hands with Eisengrim, who was smiling in a fashion that was not really friendly.

"It has been a long time, Mr. Dunstable Ramsay," he said in Spanish. I think he meant to put me at a disadvantage, but I am pretty handy in Spanish, and we continued the conversation in that language.

"It has been over thirty years, unless you count our meeting in *Le grand Cirque forain de St Vite,*" said I. "How are *Le Solitaire des forêts* and my friend the Bearded Lady?"

"Le Solitaire died very shortly after we met," said he. "I have not seen the others since before the war."

We made a little more conversation, so stilted and uneasy that I decided to leave; obviously Eisengrim did not want me there. But when I took my leave the ugly woman said, "We hope very much that you can lunch with us tomorrow?"

"Liesl, are you sure you know what you are doing?" said Eisengrim in German, and very rapidly.

But I am pretty handy in German, too. So when the ugly woman replied, "Yes, I am perfectly sure and so are you, so say no more about it," I got it all and said in German, "It would be a very great pleasure, if I am not an intruder."

"How can a so old friend possibly be an intruder?" said Eisengrim in English, and thenceforth he never spoke any other language to me, though his idiom was creaky. "You know, Liesl, that Mr. Ramsay was my very first teacher in magic?" He was all honey now. And as I was leaving he leaned forward and whispered, "That temporary loan, you remember—nothing would have induced me to accept it if *Le Solitaire* had not been in very great need—you must permit me to repay it at once." And he tapped me lightly on the spot where, in an inside pocket, I carry my cash.

That night when I was making my usual prudent Canadian-Scots count, I found that several bills had found their way into my wallet, slightly but not embarrassingly exceeding the sum that had disappeared from it when last I met Paul. I began to think better of Eisengrim. I appreciate scrupulosity in money matters.

3

Thus I became a member of Magnus Eisengrim's entourage, and never made my tour of the shrines of South America. It was all settled at the luncheon after our first meeting. Eisengrim was there, and the hideous Liesl, but the beautiful Faustina did not come. When I asked after her Eisengrim said, "She is not yet ready to be seen in public places." Well, thought I, if he can appear in a good restaurant with a monster, why not with the most beautiful woman I have ever seen? Before we had finished a long luncheon, I knew why.

Liesl became less ugly after an hour or two. Her clothes were like a man's in that she wore a jacket and trousers, but her shirt was soft and her beautiful scarf was drawn through a ring. If I had been in her place I should not have worn men's patent-leather dancing shoes—size eleven at least—but otherwise she was discreet. Her short hair was smartly arranged, and she even wore a little colour on her lips. Nothing could mitigate the extreme, the deformed ugliness of her face, but she was graceful, she had a charming voice, and gave evidence of a keen intelligence held in check, so that Eisengrim might dominate the conversation.

"You see what we are doing," he said. "We are building up a magic show of unique quality, and we want it to be in the best possible condition before we set out on a world tour. It is rough still—oh, very kind of you to say so, but it is rough in comparison with what we want to make it. We want the uttermost accomplishment, combined with the sort of charm and romantic flourish that usually goes with ballet—European ballet, not the athletic American stuff. You know that nowadays the theatre has almost abandoned charm; actors want to be sweaty and real, playwrights want to scratch their scabs in public. Very well; it is in the mood of the times. But there is always another mood, one precisely contrary to what seems to be the fashion. Nowadays this concealed longing is for romance and marvels. Well, that is what we think we can offer, but it is not done with the back bent and a cringing smile; it must be offered with authority. We are working very hard for authority. You remarked that we did not smile much in the performance; no jokes, really. A smile in such a show is half a cringe. Look at the magicians who appear in night clubs; they are so anxious to be loved, to have everybody think 'What a funny fellow,' instead of 'What a brilliant fellow, what a mysterious fellow.' That is the disease of all entertainment: love me, pet me, pat my head. That is not what we want."

"What do you want? To be feared?"

"To be wondered at. This is not egotism. People want to marvel at something, and the whole spirit of our time is not to let them do it. They will pay to do it, if you make it good and marvellous for them. Didn't anybody learn anything from the war? Hitler said, 'Marvel at me, wonder at me, I can do what others can't,'—and they fell over themselves to do it. What we offer is innocent—just an entertainment in which a hungry part of the spirit is fed. But it won't work if we let ourselves be pawed and patronized and petted by the people who have marvelled. Hence our plan."

"What is your plan?"

"That the show must keep its character all the time. I must not be seen off the stage except under circumstances that carry some *cachet;* I must never do tricks outside the theatre. When people meet me I must be always the distinguished gentleman conferring a distinction; not a nice fellow, just like the rest of the boys. The girls must have it in their contract that they do not accept invitations unless we approve, appear anywhere except in clothes we approve, get into any messes with boy friends, or seem to be anything but ladies. Not easy, you see. Faustina herself is a problem; she has not yet learned about clothes, and she eats like a lioness."

"You'll have to pay heavily to make people live like that."

"Of course. So the company must be pretty small and the pay tempting. We shall find the people."

"Excuse me, but you keep saying *we* will do this and *we* will do that. Is this a royal *we?* If so, you may be getting into psychological trouble."

"No, no. When I speak of *we* I mean Liesl and myself. I am the magician. She is the autocrat of the company, as you shall discover."

"And why is Liesl the autocrat of the company?"

"That also you shall discover."

"I'm not at all sure of that. What do you want me for? My abilities as a magician are even less than when you were my audience in the Deptford Free Library."

"Never mind. Liesl wants you."

I looked at Liesl, who was smiling as charmingly as her dreadfully enlarged jaw would permit, and said, "She cannot possibly know anything about me."

"You underestimate yourself, Ramsay," she said. "Are you not the writer of *A Hundred Saints for Travellers*? And *Forgotten Saints of the Tyrol*? And *Celtic Saints of Britain and Europe*? When Eisengrim mentioned last night that he had seen you in the audience and that you had insisted on lending your handkerchief, I wanted to meet you at once. I am obliged to you for much information, but far more for many happy hours reading your delightful prose. A distinguished hagiographer does not often come our way."

There is more than one kind of magic. This speech had the effect of revealing to me that Liesl was not nearly so ugly as I had thought, and was indeed a woman of captivating intellect and charm, cruelly imprisoned in a deformed body. I know flattery when I hear it; but I do not often hear it. Furthermore, there is good flattery and bad; this was from the best cask. And what sort of woman was this who knew so odd a word as "hagiographer" in a language not her own? Nobody who was not a Bollandist had ever called me that before, yet it was a title I would not have exchanged to be called Lord of the Isles. Delightful prose! I must know more of this.

Many people when they are flattered seek immediately to show themselves very hard-headed, to conceal the fact that they have taken the bait. I am one of them.

"Your plan sounds woefully uneconomic to me," I said. "Travelling shows in our time are money-losers unless they play to capacity audiences and have strong backing. You are planning an entertainment of rare quality. What makes you think it can survive? Certainly I have no advice to give you that can be of help there."

"That is not what we ask of you," said Liesl. "We shall look for advice about finance from financiers. From you we want the benefit of your taste, and a particular kind of unusual assistance. For which, of course, we expect to pay."

In other words, no amateurish interference or inquisitiveness about the money. But what could this unusual assistance be?

"Every magician has an autobiography, which is sold in the theatre and elsewhere," she continued. "Most of them are dreadful things, and all of them are the work of another hand—do you say ghost-written? We want one that will be congruous with the entertainment we offer. It must be very good, yet popular, persuasive, and written with style. And that is where you come in, dear Ramsay."

With an air that in another woman would have been flatteringly coquettish, she laid a huge hand over one of mine and engulfed it.

"If you want me to write it over my own name it is out of the question!"

"Not at all. It is important that it appear to be an autobiography. We ask you to be the ghost. And in case such a proposal is insulting to such a very good writer, we offer a substantial fee. Three thousand five hundred dollars is not bad; I have made inquiries."

"Not good either. Give me that and a half-share in the royalties and I might consider it."

"That's the old, grasping Ramsay blood!" said Eisengrim and laughed the first real laugh I had heard from him.

"Well, consider what you ask. The book would have to be fiction. I presume you don't think the world will swallow a courtier of polished manner if he is shown to be the son of a Baptist parson in rural Canada—"

"You never told me your father was a parson," said Liesl. "What a lot we have in common! Several of my father's family are parsons."

"The autobiography, like the personality, will have to be handmade," said I, "and as you have been telling me all through lunch, distinguished works of imagination are not simply thrown together."

"But you will not be hard on us," said Liesl. "You see, not any writer will do. But you, who have written so persuasively about the saints—slipping under the guard of the sceptic with a candour that is brilliantly disingenuous, treating marvels with the seriousness of fact—you are just the man for us. We can pay, and we will pay, though we cannot pay a foolish price. But I think that you are too much an old friend of magic to say no."

In spite of her marred face her smile was so winning that I could not say no. This looked like an adventure, and, at fifty, adventures do not come every day.

4

At fifty, should adventures come at all? Certainly that was what I was asking myself a month later. I was heartily sick of Magnus Eisengrim and his troupe, and I hated Liselotte Vitzlipützli, which was the absurd name of his monstrous business partner. But I could not break the grip that their vitality, their single-mindedness, and the beautiful mystery of their work had fastened on my loneliness.

For the first few days it was flattering to my spirit to sit in the stalls in the empty theatre with Liesl while Eisengrim rehearsed. Not a day passed that he did not go through a searching examination of several of his illusions, touching up one moment, or subduing another, and always refining that subtle technique of misdirecting the attention of his audience, which is the beginning and end of the conjurer's art.

To me it was deeply satisfying to watch him, for he was a master of all those sleights that had seemed so splendid, and so impossible, in my boyhood. "Secure and palm six half-crowns." He could do it with either hand. His professional dress coat almost brought tears to my eyes, such a marvel was it of loading-pockets, *pochettes* and *profondes;* when it was filled and ready for his appearance in *The Dream of Midas* it weighed twelve pounds, but it fitted him without a bulge.

My opinion was sought, and given, about the program. It was on my advice that the second part of his entertainment was reshaped. I suggested that he cut out the escape act entirely; it was not suitable to an illusionist, for it was essentially a physical trick and not a feat of magic. There was no romance about being stuck in a milk can and getting out again. This gave Liesl a chance to press for the inclusion of *The Brazen Head of Friar Bacon* and I supported her strongly; it was right for the character of the show they were building. But Eisengrim the Great had never heard of Friar Bacon, and like so many people who have not heard of something, he could not believe that anybody but a few eccentrics would have done so.

"It is unmistakably your thing," I said. "You can tell them about the great priest-magician and his Brazen Head that foretold the future and knew the past; I'll write the speech for you. It doesn't matter whether people have heard of Bacon or not. Many of them haven't heard of Dr. Faustus, but they like your conclusion."

"Oh, every educated person has heard of Faust," said Eisengrim with something like pomposity. "He's in a very famous opera." He had no notion that Faust was also in one of the world's greatest plays.

He had virtually no education, though he could speak several languages, and one of the things Liesl had to teach him, as tactfully as possible, was not to talk out of his depth. I thought that much of his extraordinarily impressive personality arose from his ignorance—or, rather, from his lack of a headful of shallow information that would have enabled him to hold his own in a commonplace way among commonplace people. As a schoolmaster of twenty years' experience I had no use for smatterers. What he knew, he knew as well as anybody on earth; it gave him confidence, and sometimes a naïve egotism that was hard to believe.

We worked very hard on the Brazen Head, which was no more than a very good thought-reading act dressed in a new guise. The Brazen Head was "levitated" by Eisengrim and floated in the middle of the stage, apparently without wires or supports; then the girls moved through the audience, collecting objects that were sealed in envelopes by their lenders. Eisengrim received these envelopes on a tray on the stage and asked the Head to describe the objects and identify their owners; the Head did so, giving the row and seat number for each; only then did Eisengrim touch them. Next, the Head gave messages to three members of the audience, chosen apparently at random, relating to their personal affairs. It was a first-rate illusion, and I think the script I wrote for it, which was plain and literate and free of any of the pompous rhetoric so dear to conjurers, had a substantial part in creating its air of mystery.

Rehearsal was difficult because much depended on the girls who collected the objects; they had to use their heads, and their heads were not the best-developed part of them. The random messages were simple but dangerous, for they relied on the work of the company manager, a pickpocket of rare gifts; but he had an air of transparent honesty and geniality, and as he mingled with the audience when it entered the theatre, shaking hands and pressing through the crowd as if on his way somewhere else to do something very important, nobody suspected him. Sometimes he found invaluable letters in the coats of distinguished visitors when he took these to his office to spare such grandees the nuisance of lining up at the *garderobe*. But in the case of ladies or men of no special importance it was straight "dipping," and potentially dangerous. He enjoyed it; it put him in mind of the good old days before he got into trouble and left London for Rio.

Because of a message the Brazen Head gave a beautiful lady in the very first audience before which it was shown, a duel was fought the next day between a well-known Mexican lawyer and a dentist who fancied himself as a Don Juan. Nothing could have been better publicity, and all sorts of people offered large sums to be permitted to consult the Brazen Head privately. Eisengrim, who had a perfectionist's capacity for worry, was fearful that such revelations would keep people out of the theatre, but Liesl was confident and exultant; she said they would come to hear what was said about other people, and they did.

Liesl's job was to speak for the Brazen Head, because she was the only member of the company capable of rapidly interpreting a letter or an engagement book, and composing a message that was spicy without being positively libellous. She was a woman of formidable intelligence and intuition: she had a turn for improvising and phrasing ambiguous but startling messages that would have done credit to the Oracle at Delphi.

The Brazen Head was such a success that there was some thought of putting it at the end of the show, as the "topper," but I opposed this; the foundation of the show was romance, and *The Vision of Dr. Faustus* had it. But the Head was our best effort in sheer mystery.

I cannot refrain from boasting that it was I who provided the idea for one of the illusions that made Eisengrim the most celebrated magician in the world. Variety theatres everywhere abounded with magicians who could saw a woman in two; it was my suggestion that Eisengrim should offer to saw a member of the audience in two.

His skill as a hypnotist made it possible. When we had worked out the details and put the illusion on the stage, he would first perform the commonplace illusion, sawing one of his showgirls into two sections with a circular saw and displaying her with her head smiling from one end of a box while her feet kicked from the other—but with a hiatus of three feet between the two parts of the box. Then he would offer to do the same thing with a volunteer from the audience. The volunteer would be "lightly anaesthetized" by hypnosis, ostensibly so that he would not wriggle and perhaps injure himself, after which he would be put in a new box, and Eisengrim would saw him in two with a large and fearsome lumberman's saw. The volunteer was shown to be divided but able to kick his feet and answer questions about the delightfully airy feeling in his middle. Rejoined, the volunteer would leave the stage decidedly dazed, but marvelling at himself and pleased with the applause. The high point of this illusion was when two assistants held a large mirror so that the volunteer could see for himself that he had been sawn in two. We substituted this illusion for the rather ordinary hypnotic stuff that had been in the show when first I saw it.

Working on these illusions was delightful but destructive of my character. I was aware that I was recapturing the best of my childhood; my imagination had never known such glorious freedom; but as well as liberty and wonder I was regaining the untruthfulness, the lack of scruple, and the absorbing egotism of a child. I heard myself talking boastfully, lying shamelessly. I blushed but could not control myself. I had never, so far as I can tell, been absorbed completely into the character of a Headmaster—a figure of authority, of scholarship, of probity—but I was an historian, a hagiographer, a bachelor of unstained character, a winner of the Victoria Cross, the author of several admired books, a man whose course of life was set and the bounds of whose success were defined. Yet here I was, in Mexico City, not simply attached to but subsumed in a magic show. The day I found myself slapping one of the showgirls on the bottom and winking when she made her ritual protest, I knew that something was terribly wrong with Dunstan Ramsay.

Two things that were wrong I could easily identify: I had become a dangerously indiscreet talker, and I was in love with the beautiful Faustina.

I cannot say which dismayed me the more. Almost from the earliest days of my childhood I had been close-mouthed; I never passed on gossip if I could help it, though I had no objection to hearing it; I never betrayed a confidence, preferring the costive pleasure of being a repository of secrets. Much of my intimacy with Boy Staunton rested on the fact that he could be sure I would never repeat anything I was told in confidence, and extremely little that was not so regarded. My pleasure depended on what I knew, not on what I could tell. Yet here I was, chattering like a magpie, telling things that had never before passed my lips, and to Liesl, who did not look to me like a respecter of confidences.

We talked in the afternoons, while she was working on the properties and machinery of the illusions in the tiny theatre workshop under the stage. I soon found out why Liesl dominated the company. First, she was the backer, and the finance of the whole thing rested either on her money or money she had guaranteed. She was a Swiss, and the company buzz was that she came of a family that owned one of the big watch firms. Second, she was a brilliant mechanic; her huge hands did wonders with involved springs, releases and displacements, escapements and levers, however tiny they might be. She was a good artificer too; she made the Brazen Head out of some light plastic so that it was an arresting object; nothing in Eisengrim's show was tawdry or untouched by her exacting taste. But unlike many good craftsmen, she could see beyond what she was making to its effect when in use.

Sometimes she lectured me on the beauty of mechanics. "There are about a dozen basic principles," she would say, "and if they cannot be made to do everything, they can be made to create magic—if you know what you want. Some magicians try to use what they call modern techniques—rays and radar and whatnot. But every boy understands those things. Not many people really understand clockwork because they carry it on their wrists in full sight and never think about it."

She insisted on talking to me about the autobiography of Eisengrim I was preparing. I had never been used to talking to anyone about a work in progress—had indeed a superstitious feeling that such talk harmed the book by robbing it of energy that should go into the writing. But Liesl always wanted to know how it was getting on, and what line I meant to take, and what splendid lies I was concocting to turn Paul Dempster into a northern wizard.

We had agreed in general terms that he was to be a child of the Baltic vastnesses, reared perhaps by gnomelike Lapps after the death of his explorer parents, who were probably Russians of high birth. No, better not Russians; probably Swedes or Danes who had lived long in Finland; Russians caused too much trouble at borders, and Paul still kept his Canadian passport. Or should his parents perish in the Canadian vastnesses? Anyhow, he had to be a child of the steppes, who had assumed his wolf-name in tribute to the savage animals whose midnight howls had been his earliest lullaby, and to avoid revealing his distinguished family name. I had worked on the lives of several northern saints, and I had a store of this highly coloured material at my fingers' ends.

As we discussed these fictions, it was not surprising that Liesl should want to know the facts. In spite of her appearance, and the mistrust of her I felt deep within me, she was a woman who could draw out confidences, and I heard myself rattling on about Deptford, and the Dempsters, and Paul's premature birth, though I did not tell all I knew of that; I even told her about the sad business in the pit, and what came of it, and how Paul ran away; to my dismay I found that I had told her about Willie, about Surgeoner, and even about the Little Madonna. I lay awake the whole night after this last piece of blethering, and got her alone as soon as I could the next day, and begged her not to tell anyone.

"No, Ramsay, I won't promise anything of the sort," said she. "You are too old a man to believe in secrets. There is really no such thing as a secret; everybody likes to tell, and everybody does tell. Oh, there are men like priests and lawyers and doctors who are supposed not to tell what they know, but they do—usually they do. If they don't they grow very queer indeed; they pay a high price for their secrecy. You have paid such a price, and you look like a man full of secrets—grim-mouthed and buttoned-up and hard-eyed and cruel, because you are cruel to yourself. It has done you good to tell what you know; you look much more human already. A little shaky this morning because you are so unused to being without the pressure of all your secrets, but you will feel better quite soon."

I renewed my appeal again that afternoon, but she would give no promise, and I don't think I would have believed her if she had done so; I was irrationally obsessed with an ideal of secrecy that I had carried for fifty years, only to betray it now.

"If a temperamental secret-keeper like you cannot hold in what he knows about Eisengrim, how can you expect it of anyone you despise as you despise me?" she said. "Oh yes, you do despise me. You despise almost everybody except Paul's mother. No wonder she seems like a saint to you; you have made her carry the affection you should have spread among fifty people. Do not look at me with that tragic face. You should thank me. At fifty years old you should be glad to know something of yourself. That horrid village and your hateful Scots family made you a moral monster. Well, it is not too late for you to enjoy a few years of almost normal humanity.

"Do not try to work on me by making sad faces, Ramsay. You are a dear fellow, but a fool. Now, tell me how you are going to get the infant Magnus Eisengrim out of that dreadful Canada and into a country where big spiritual adventures are possible?"

If the breakdown of character that made me a chatterbox was hard to bear, it was a triviality beside the tortures of my love for the beautiful Faustina.

It was a disease, and I knew it was a disease. I could see plainly everything that made her an impossible person for me to love. She was at least thirty years younger than I, to begin, and she had nothing that I would have recognized as a brain in her head. She was a monster of vanity, venomously jealous of the other girls in the show, and sulky whenever she was not being admired. She rebelled against the company rule that she might not accept invitations from men who had seen her on the stage, but she delighted in having them surge forward when she left the stage door, to press flowers, sweets, and gifts of all kinds on her as she stepped into a hired limousine with Eisengrim. There was one wild-eyed student boy who thrust a poem into her hand, which, as it was writing, I suppose she took for a bill and handed back to him. My heart bled for the poor simpleton. She was an animal.

But I loved her! I hung about the theatre to see her come and go. I lurked in the wings—to which I had been given the entrée, for large screens were set up to protect the illusions from stage hands who were not members of the company—to watch her very rapid changes from Gretchen to Venus and back again, because there was an instant when, in spite of the skilled work of two dressers, she was almost naked. She knew it, and some nights she threw me a smile of complicity and on others she looked offended. She could not resist admiration from anyone, and although I was something of a mystery to most of the company, she knew that I had a voice that was listened to in high places.

There were whole nights when I lay awake from one o'clock till morning, calling up her image before my imagination. On such nights I would suffer, again and again, the worst horror of the lover: I would find myself unable to summon up the adored one's face and—I write it hardly expecting to be believed except by someone who has suffered this abjection of adoration—I would shake at the blasphemy of having thus mislaid her likeness. I plagued myself with fruitless questions: would the promise of a life's servitude be enough to make her stoop to me? And then—for common sense never wholly left me—I would think of the beautiful Faustina talking to curious, gaping boys at Colborne College, or meeting the other masters' wives at one of their stupefying tea parties, and something like a laugh would shake me. For I was so bound to my life in Canada, you see, that I always thought of Faustina in terms of marriage and the continuance of my work.

My work! As if she could have understood what education was, or why anyone would give a life to it! When I wrestled with the problem of how it could be explained to her I was further shaken because, for the first time in my life, I began to wonder if education could be quite the splendid vocation I had, as a professional, come to think it. How could I lay my accomplishments at her beautiful feet when she was incapable of knowing what they were? Somebody—I suppose it was Liesl—told her I knew a lot about saints, and this made a kind of sense to her.

One happy day, meeting me in the corridor of the theatre after I had been watching her transformations in *The Vision of Dr. Faustus,* she said, "Good evening, St. Ramsay."

"St. Dunstan," said I.

"I do not know St. Dunstan. Was he a bad old saint who peeps, eh? O-o-h, shame on you, St. Dunstan!" She made a very lewd motion with her hips and darted into the dressing-room she shared with Eisengrim.

I was in a melting ecstasy of delight and despair. She had spoken to me! She knew I watched her and probably guessed that I loved her and longed for her. That bump, or grind, or whatever they called it, made it very clear that—yes, but to call me St. Dunstan! What about that? And "bad old saint"—she thought me old. So I was. I was fifty, and in the chronology of a Peruvian girl who was probably more than half Indian, that was very old. But she had spoken, and she had shown awareness of my passion for her, and—

I muddled on and on, most of that night, attributing subtleties to Faustina that were certainly absurd but that I could not fight down.

Officially she was Eisengrim's mistress, but they were always quarrelling, for he was exquisitely neat and she made a devastation of their dressing-room. Further, it was clear enough to me that his compelling love affair was with himself; his mind was always on his public personality, and on the illusions over which he fussed psychologically quite as much as Liesl did mechanically. I had seen a good deal of egotism in my life, and I knew that it starved love for anyone else and sometimes burned it out completely. Had it not been so with Boy and Leola? Still, Eisengrim and the beautiful Faustina shared quarters at the hotel. I knew it, because I had left my own place and moved into the even more Spanish establishment that housed the superior members of the company. They shared a room, but did it mean anything?

I found out the day after she called me St. Dunstan. I was in the theatre about five o'clock in the afternoon and chanced to go down the corridor on which the star's dressing-room lay. The door was open, and I saw Faustina naked—she was always changing her clothes—in the arms of Liesl, who held her close and kissed her passionately; she had her left arm around Faustina, and her right hand was concealed from me, but the movement of Faustina's hips and her dreamy murmurs made it clear, even to my unaccustomed eyes, what their embrace was.

I have never known such a collapse of the spirit even in the worst of the war. And this time there was no Little Madonna to offer me courage or ease me into oblivion.

5

"Well, dear Ramsay, you are looking a little pale."

It was Liesl who spoke. I had answered a tap on my door at about one o'clock in the morning, and there she stood in pyjamas and dressing-gown, smiling her ugly smile.

"What do you want?"

"To talk. I love to talk with you, and you are a man who needs talk. Neither of us is sleeping; therefore we shall talk."

In she came, and as the little room offered only one uncompromising straight-backed chair, she sat down on the bed.

"Come and sit by me. If I were an English lady, or somebody's mother, I suppose I should begin by saying, 'Now what is the matter?'—but that is just rhetoric. The matter is that you saw me and Faustina this afternoon. Oh yes, I saw you in the looking-glass. So?"

I said nothing.

"You are just like a little boy, Ramsay. Or no, I am forgetting that only silly men like to be told they are like little boys. Very well, you are like a man of fifty whose bottled-up feelings have burst their bottle and splashed glass and acid everywhere. That is why I called you a little boy, for which I apologize; but you have no art of dealing with such a situation as a man of fifty, so you are thrown back to being like a little boy. Well, I am sorry for you. Not very much, but some."

"Don't patronize me, Liesl."

"That is an English word I have never really understood."

"Don't bully me, then. Don't know best. Don't be the sophisticated European, the magic-show gypsy, the wonderfully intuitive woman, belittling the feelings of a poor brute who doesn't know any better than to think in terms of decency and honour and not taking advantage of people who may not know what they're doing."

"You mean Faustina? Ramsay, she is a wonderful creature, but in a way you don't begin to grasp. She isn't one of your North American girls, half B.A. and half B.F. and half good decent spud—that's three halves, but never mind. She is of the earth, and her body is her shop and her temple, and whatever her body tells her is all of the law and the prophets. You can't understand such a person, but there are more of them in the world than of the women who are tangled up in honour and decency and the other very masculine things you admire so much. Faustina is a great work of the Creator. She has nothing of what you call brains; she doesn't need them for her destiny. Don't glare at me because I speak of her destiny. It is to be glorious for a few years; not to outlive some dull husband and live on his money till she is eighty, going to lectures and comparing the attractions of winter tours that offer the romance of the Caribbean."

"You talk as if you thought you were God."

"I beg your pardon. That is your privilege, you pseudo-cynical old pussy-cat, watching life from the sidelines and knowing where all the players go wrong. Life is a spectator sport to you. Now you have taken a tumble and found yourself in the middle of the fight, and you are whimpering because it is rough."

"Liesl, I am too tired and sick to wrangle. But let me tell you this, and you may laugh as loud and as long as you please, and babble it to everybody you know because that is your professed way of dealing with confidences: I loved Faustina."

"But you don't love her now because of what you saw this afternoon! Oh, knight! Oh, saint! You loved her but you never gave her a gift, or paid her a compliment, or asked her to eat with you, or tried to give her what Faustina understands as love—a sweet physical convulsion shared with an interesting partner."

"Liesl, I am fifty, and I have a wooden leg and only part of one arm. Is that interesting for Faustina?"

"Yes, anything is for Faustina. You don't know her, but far worse you don't know yourself. You are not so very bad, Ramsay."

"Thank you."

"Oooh, what dignity! Is that a way to accept a compliment from a lady? I tell him he is not so very bad, and he ruffles up like an old maid and makes a sour face. I must do better; you are a fascinating old fellow. How's that?"

"If you have said what you came to say, I should like to go to bed now."

"Yes, I see you have taken off your wooden leg and stood it in the corner. Well, I should like to go to bed now too. Shall we go to bed together?"

I looked at her with astonishment. She seemed to mean it.

"Well, do not look as if it were out of the question. You are fifty and not all there: I am as grotesque a woman as you are likely to meet. Wouldn't it have an unusual savour?"

I rose and began to hop to the door. Over the years I have become a good hopper. But Liesl caught me by the tail of my pyjama coat and pulled me back on the bed.

"Oh, you want it to be like Venus and Adonis! I am to drag you into my arms and crush out your boyish modesty. Good!"

She was much stronger than I would have supposed, and she had no silly notions about fighting fair. I was dragged back to the bed, hopping, and pulled into her arms. I can only describe her body as rubbery, so supple yet muscular was it. Her huge, laughing face with its terrible jaw was close to my own, and her monkeylike mouth was thrust out for a kiss. I had not fought for years—not since my war, in fact—but I had to fight now for—well, for what? In my genteel encounters with Agnes Day, and Gloria Mundy, and Libby Doe, now so far in the past, I had always been the aggressor, insofar as there was any aggression in those slack-twisted amours. I certainly was not going to be ravished by a Swiss gargoyle. I gave a mighty heave and got a handful of her pyjama coat and a good grip on her hair and threw her on the floor.

She landed with a crash that almost brought down plaster. Up she bounced like a ball, and with a grab she caught up my wooden leg and hit me such a crack over my single shin that I roared and cursed. But when next she brought it down—I had never considered it as a weapon, and it was terrible with springs and rivets—I had a pillow ready and wrenched it from her.

By this time someone downstairs was pounding on his ceiling and protesting in Spanish, but I was not to be quieted. I hopped toward Liesl, waggling the leg with such angry menace that she made the mistake of retreating, and I had her in a corner. I dropped the leg and punched her with a ferocity that I should be ashamed to recall; still, as she was punching back and had enormous fists, it was a fair enough fight. But she began to be afraid, for I had a good Highland temper and it was higher than I have ever known. Tears of pain or fright were running from her deep-set eyes, and blood was dribbling from a cut lip. After a few more smart cuffs, keeping my legless side propped against the wall, I began to edge her toward the door. She grasped the handle behind her, but as she turned it I got a good hold on the bedhead with one hand, and seized her nose between the fingers of the other, and gave it such a twist that I thought I heard something crack. She shrieked, managed to tug the door open, and thundered down the passage.

I sank back on the bed. I was worn out, I was puffing, but I felt fine. I felt better than I had done for three weeks. I thought of Faustina. Good old Faustina! Had I trounced Liesl to avenge her? No, I decided that I had not. A great cloud seemed to have lifted from my spirit, and though it was too soon to be sure, I thought that perhaps my reason, such as it was, had begun to climb back into the saddle and that with care I might soon be myself again.

I had eaten no dinner in my misery, and I discovered I was hungry. I had no food, but I had a flask of whisky in my briefcase. I found it and lay back on the bed, taking a generous swig. The room was a battlefield, but I would tidy it in the morning. Liesl's dressing-gown and a few rags from her pyjamas lay about, and I left them where they were. Honourable trophies.

There came a tap on the door.

"What is it?" I called out in English.

"Señor," hissed a protesting voice, "zis honeymoon—oh, very well, very well for you, señor, but please to remember there are zose below who are not so young, if you please, señor!"

I apologized elaborately in Spanish, and the owner of the voice shuffled back down the passage. Honeymoon! How strangely people interpret sound!

In a few minutes there was another tap, even gentler. I called out, "Who is it?"—in Spanish this time.

The voice was Liesl's voice. "You will be so kind as to allow me to recover my key," it said thickly and very formally.

I opened the door, and there she stood, barefooted and holding what was left of her pyjama coat over her bosom.

"Of course, señora," said I, bowing as gracefully as a one-legged man can do and gesturing to her to come in. Why I closed the door after her I do not know. We glared at each other.

"You are much stronger than you look," said she.

"So are you," said I. Then I smiled a little. A victor's smile, I suppose; the kind of smile I smile at boys whom I have frightened out of their wits. She picked up the dressing-gown, taking care not to turn her back on me.

"May I offer you a drink," said I, holding out the flask. She took it and raised it to her lips, but the whisky stung a cut in her mouth and she winced sharply. That took all the lingering spite out of me. "Sit down," I said, "and I'll put something on those bruises."

She sat down on the bed, and not to make a long tale of it, I washed her cuts and put a cold-water compress on her nose, which had swollen astonishingly, and in about five minutes we were sitting up in the bed with the pillows behind us, taking turn and turn about at the flask.

"How do you feel now?" said I.

"Much better. And you? How is your shin?"

"I feel better than I have felt in a very long time."

"Good. That is what I came to make you feel."

"Indeed? I thought you came to seduce me. That seems to be your hobby. Anybody and anything. Do you often get beaten up?"

"What a fool you are! It was only a way of trying to tell you something."

"Not that you love me, I hope. I have believed some strange things in my time, but that would test me pretty severely."

"No. I wanted to tell you that you are human, like other people."

"Have I denied it?"

"Listen, Ramsay, for the past three weeks you have been telling me the story of your life, with great emotional detail, and certainly it sounds as if you did not think you were human. You make yourself responsible for other people's troubles. It is your hobby. You take on the care of a poor madwoman you knew as a boy. You put up with subtle insult and being taken for granted by a boyhood friend—this big sugar-man who is such a power in your part of the world. You are a friend to this woman—Leola, what a name!—who gave you your *congé* when she wanted to marry Mr. Sugar. And you are secret and stiff-rumped about it all, and never admit it is damned good of you. That is not very human. You are a decent chap to everybody, except one special somebody, and that is Dunstan Ramsay. How can you be really good to anybody if you are not good to yourself?"

"I wasn't brought up to blow a trumpet if I happened to do something for somebody."

"Upbringing, so? Calvinism? I am a Swiss, Ramsay, and I know

Calvinism as well as you do. It is a cruel way of life, even if you forget the religion and call it ethics or decent behaviour or something else that pushes God out of it.

"But even Calvinism can be endured, if you will make some compromise with yourself. But you—there is a whole great piece of your life that is unlived, denied, set aside. That is why at fifty you can't bear it any longer and fly all to pieces and pour out your heart to the first really intelligent woman you have met—me, that's to say—and get into a schoolboy yearning for a girl who is as far from you as if she lived on the moon. This is the revenge of the unlived life, Ramsay. Suddenly it makes a fool of you.

"You should take a look at this side of your life you have not lived. Now don't wriggle and snuffle and try to protest. I don't mean you should have secret drunken weeks and a widow in a lacy flat who expects you every Thursday, like some suburban ruffian. You are a lot more than that. But every man has a devil, and a man of unusual quality, like yourself, Ramsay, has an unusual devil. You must get to know your personal devil. You must even get to know his father, the Old Devil. Oh, this Christianity! Even when people swear they don't believe in it, the fifteen hundred years of Christianity that has made our world is in their bones, and they want to show they can be Christians without Christ. Those are the worst; they have the cruelty of doctrine without the poetic grace of myth.

"Why don't you shake hands with your devil, Ramsay, and change this foolish life of yours? Why don't you, just for once, do something inexplicable, irrational, at the devil's bidding, and just for the hell of it? You would be a different man.

"What I am saying is not for everybody, of course. Only for the twice-born. One always knows the twice-born. They often go so far as to take new names. Did you not say that English girl renamed you? And who was Magnus Eisengrim? And me—do you know what my name really means, Liselotte Vitzliputzli? It sounds so funny, but one day you will stumble on its real meaning. Here you are, twice-born, and nearer your death than your birth, and you have still to make a real life.

"Who are you? Where do you fit into poetry and myth? Do you know who I think you are, Ramsay? I think you are Fifth Business.

"You don't know what that is? Well, in opera in a permanent company of the kind we keep up in Europe you must have a prima donna—always a soprano, always the heroine, often a fool; and a tenor who always plays the lover to her; and then you must have a contralto, who is a rival to the soprano, or a sorceress or something; and a basso, who is the villain or the rival or whatever threatens the tenor.

"So far, so good. But you cannot make a plot work without another man, and he is usually a baritone, and he is called in the profession Fifth Business, because he is the odd man out, the person who has no opposite of the other sex. And you must have Fifth Business because he is the one who knows the secret of the hero's birth, or comes to the assistance of the heroine when she thinks all is lost, or keeps the hermitess in her cell, or may even be the cause of somebody's death if that is part of the plot. The prima donna and the tenor, the contralto and the basso, get all the best music and do all the spectacular things, but you cannot manage the plot without Fifth Business! It is not spectacular, but it is a good line of work, I can tell you, and those who play it sometimes have a career that outlasts the golden voices. Are you Fifth Business? You had better find out."

This is not a verbatim report, Headmaster; I said a good deal myself, and I have tidied Liesl's English, and boiled down what she said. But we talked till a clock somewhere struck four, and then fell happily asleep, but not without having achieved the purpose for which Liesl had first of all invaded my room.

With such a gargoyle! And yet never have I known such deep delight or such an aftermath of healing tenderness!

Next morning, tied to my door handle, was a bunch of flowers and a message in elegant Spanish:

> Forgive my ill manners of last night. Love conquers all and youth must be served. May you know a hundred years of happy nights. Your Neighbour in the Chamber Below.

·VI·
The Soirée of Illusions

1

THE AUTOBIOGRAPHY OF Magnus Eisengrim was a great pleasure to write, for I was under no obligation to be historically correct or to weigh evidence. I let myself go and invented just such a book about a magician as I would have wanted to read if I had been a member of his public; it was full of romance and marvels, with a quiet but sufficient undertone of eroticism and sadism, and it sold like hot-cakes.

Liesl and I had imagined it would sell reasonably well in the lobbies of theatres where the show was appearing, but it did well in book stores and, in a paper-back edition that soon followed, it was a steady seller in cigar stores and other places where they offer lively, sensational reading. People who had never done an hour's concentrated work in their lives loved to read how the young Magnus would rehearse his card and coin sleights for fourteen hours at a stretch, until his body was drenched in nervous sweat, and he could take no nourishment but a huge glass of cream laced with brandy. People whose own love-lives were pitched entirely in the key of C were enchanted to know that at the time when he was devoting himself entirely to the study of hypnotism, his every glance was so supercharged that lovely women forced themselves upon him, poor moths driven to immolate themselves in his flame.

I wrote about the hidden workshop in a Tyrolean castle where he devised his illusions, and dropped hints that girls had sometimes been terribly injured in some device that was not quite perfect; of course Eisengrim paid to have them put right again; I made him something of a monster but not too much of a monster. I also made his age a matter of conjecture. It was a lively piece of work, and all I regretted was that I had not made a harder bargain for my share of the profit. As it was, it brought me a pleasant annual addition to my income and does so still.

I wrote it in a quiet place in the Adirondacks to which I went a few days after my nocturnal encounter with Liesl. Eisengrim's engagement at the Teatro Chueca was drawing to an end, and the show was to visit a few Central American cities before going to Europe, where a long tour was hoped for. I gave the beautiful Faustina a handsome and fairly expensive necklace as a parting present, and she gave me a kiss, which she and I both regarded as a fair exchange. I gave Eisengrim a really expensive set of studs and links for his evening dress, which staggered him, for he was a miser and could not conceive of anybody giving anything away. But I had talked earnestly with him and wrung from him a promise to contribute to the maintenance of Mrs. Dempster; he did not want to do it, swore that he owed her nothing and had indeed been driven from home by her bad reputation. I pointed out to him, however, that if this had not been the case, he would not have become the Great Eisengrim but would probably be a Baptist parson in rural Canada. This was false argument and hurt his vanity, but it helped me gain my point. Liesl helped too. She insisted that Eisengrim sign a banker's order for a sum to be paid to me monthly; she knew that if he had to send me cheques he would forget very soon. The studs and links were something to soothe his wounded avarice. I gave nothing to Liesl; by this time she and I were strong friends and took from each other something that could find no requital in presents.

That money from Eisengrim was not entirely necessary, but I was glad to get it. Within a month of the end of the war I had been able to transfer Mrs. Dempster from the public wards of that hateful city asylum to a much better hospital near a small town, where she could have the status of a private patient, enjoying company if she wanted it and gaining the advantages of better air and extensive grounds. I was able to work this through a friend who had some influence; the asylum doctors agreed that she would be better in such a place, and that she was unfit for liberty even if there had been anywhere for her to go. It meant a substantial monthly cost, and though my fortunes had increased to the point where I could afford it, my personal expenditures had to be curtailed, and I was wondering how often in future I would be able to travel in Europe. I would have thought myself false to her, and to the memory of Bertha Shanklin, if I had not made this change in her circumstances, but it meant a pinch, considering that I was trying to build up a fund for my retirement as well. My position was a common one; I wanted to do the right thing but could not help regretting the damnable expense.

So, as I say, I was glad to get a regular sum from Eisengrim, which amounted to about a third of what was needed, and my sense of relief led me into a stupid error of judgement. When first I visited Mrs. Dempster after returning from my six months' absence I told her I had found Paul.

Her condition at this time was much improved, and the forlorn and bemused look she had worn for so many years had given place to something that was almost like the sweet and sometimes humorously perceptive expression I remembered from the days when she lived at the end of a rope in Deptford. Her hair was white, but her face was not lined and her figure was slight. I was very pleased by the improvement. But she was still in a condition to which the psychiatrists gave a variety of scientific names but which had been called "simple" in Deptford. She could look after herself, talked helpfully and amusingly to other patients, and was of use in taking some of the people who were more confused than herself for walks. But she had no ordered notion of the world about her, and in particular she had no sense of time. Amasa Dempster she sometimes recalled as if he were somebody in a book she had once read inattentively; she knew me as the only constant factor in her life, but I came and went, and now if I were absent for six months it was not greatly different in her mind from the space between my weekly visits. The compulsion to visit her regularly was all my own and sprang from a sense of duty rather than from any feeling that she missed me. Paul, however, held a very different place in her confused world, as I soon discovered.

Paul, to her, was still a child, a lost boy—lost a distance of time ago that was both great and small—and to be recovered just as he had run away. Not that she really thought he had run away; surely he had been enticed, by evil people who knew what a great treasure he was; they had stolen him to be cruel, to rob a mother of her child and a child of his mother. Of such malignity she could form no clear picture, but sometimes she spoke of gypsies; gypsies have carried the burden of the irrational dreads of stay-at-homes for many hundreds of years. I had written a passage in my life of Eisengrim in which he spent some of his youth among gypsies, and as I listened to Mrs. Dempster now I was ashamed of it.

If I knew where Paul was, why had I not brought him? What had I done to recover him? Had he been ill used? How could I tell her that I had news of Paul if I havered and temporized and would neither bring her child to her or take her to him?

In vain I told her that Paul was now over forty, that he travelled much, that he had a demanding career in which he was not his own master, that he would surely visit Canada at some time not now very far in the future. I said that he sent his love—which was a lie, for he had never said anything of the kind—and that he wanted to provide her with comfort and security. She was so excited, and so unlike herself, that I was shaken and even said that Paul was maintaining her in the hospital, which God knows was untrue, and proved to be another mistake.

To say that a child was keeping her in a hospital was the most ridiculous thing she had ever heard. So that was it? The hospital was an elaborately disguised prison where she was held to keep her from her son! She knew well enough who was her jailer. I was the man. Dunstan Ramsay, who pretended to be a friend, was a snake-in-the-grass, an enemy, an undoubted agent of those dark forces who had torn Paul from her.

She rushed at me and tried to scratch my eyes. I was at a great disadvantage, for I was alarmed and unnerved by the storm I had caused, and also my reverence for Mrs. Dempster was so great that I could not bear to be rough with her. Fortunately—though it scared the wits out of me at the moment—she began to scream, and a nurse came on the run, and between us we soon had her powerless. But what followed was a half-hour of confusion, during which I explained to a doctor what the trouble was, and Mrs. Dempster was put to bed under what they called light restraint—straps—with an injection of something to quiet her.

When I called the hospital the next day the report was a bad one. It grew worse during the week, and in time I had to face the fact that I seemed to have turned Mrs. Dempster from a woman who was simple and nothing worse, into a woman who knew there was a plot to deprive her of her little son, and that I was its agent. She was under restraint now, and it was inadvisable that I should visit her. But I did go once, driven by guilt, and though I did not see her, her window was pointed out to me, and it was in the wing where the windows are barred.

2

Thus I lost, for a time, one of the fixed stars in my universe, and as I had brought about this great change in Mrs. Dempster's condition by my own stupidity I felt much depressed by it. But I suffered another loss—or at least a marked change—when Boy Staunton married for the second time, and I did not meet with the approval of his wife.

During the war Boy acquired a taste for what he believed to be politics. He had been elected in easy circumstances, for he was a Conservative, and in their plan for a coalition Cabinet the Liberals had not nominated anybody to oppose him. But in the years when he had great power he forgot that he had been elected by acclamation and came somehow to think of himself as a politician—no, a statesman—with a formidable following among the voters. He had all the delusions of the political amateur, and after the war was over he insisted that he detected an undertone, which grew in some parts of the country to a positive clamour, that he should become leader of the Conservative party as fast as possible and deliver the people of Canada from their ignominious thralldom to the Liberals. He had another delusion of the political novice: he was going to apply "sound business principles" to government and thereby give it a fine new gloss.

So he attempted to become Conservative leader, but as he was a newcomer he had no chance of doing so. It seemed to me that everything about Boy was wrong for politics: he was very rich and could not understand that very rich men are not loved by the majority; he was handsome, and handsome men are not popular in politics, even with women; he had no political friends and could not understand why they were necessary.

In spite of his handicaps he was elected once, when a by-election opened a Parliamentary seat traditionally Conservative. The voters remembered his services during the war and gave him a majority of less than a thousand. But he made a number of silly speeches in the Commons, which caused a few newspapers to say that he was an authoritarian; then he abused the newspapers in the Commons, and they made him smart for it. Boy had no idea what a mark he presented to jealous or temperamentally derisive people. However, he gained some supporters, and among them was Denyse Hornick.

She was a power in the world of women. She had been in the W.R.N.S. during the war and had risen from the ranks to be a lieutenant commander and a very capable one. After the war she had established a small travel agency and made it a big one. She liked what Boy stood for in politics, and after a few meetings she liked Boy personally. I must not read into her actions motives of which I can have no knowledge, but it looked to me as if she decided that she would marry him and make him think it was his own idea.

Boy had always been fond of the sexual pleasure women could give him, but I doubt if he ever knew much about women as people, and certainly a determined and clever woman like Denyse was something outside his experience. He was drawn to her at first because she was prominent in two or three groups that worked for a larger feminine influence in public affairs, and thus could influence a large number of votes. Soon he discovered that she understood his political ideas better than anybody else, and he paid her a compliment typical of himself by assuring everybody that she had a masculine mind.

The by-election gave him a couple of years in Parliament before a general election came along to test his real strength. By that time any public gratitude for what he had done as a war organizer had been forgotten, the Conservative party found him an embarrassment because he was apt to criticize the party leader in public, the Liberals naturally wanted to defeat him, and the newspapers were out to get him. It was a dreadful campaign on his part, for he lost his head, bullied his electors when he should have wooed them, and got into a wrangle with a large newspaper, which he threatened to sue for libel. He was defeated on election day so decisively that it was obviously a personal rather than a political rejection.

He made an unforgettable appearance on television as soon as his defeat had been conceded. "How do you feel about the result in your riding, Mr. Staunton?" asked the interviewer, expecting something crisp, but not what he got. "I feel exactly like Lazarus," said Boy, "licked by the dogs!"

The whole country laughed about it, and the newspaper he thought had libelled him read him a pompous little editorial lecture about the nature of democracy. But there were those who were faithful, and Denyse was at the top of that list.

In the course of time the press tired of baiting him, and there were a few editorials regretting that so much obvious ability was not being used for the public good. But it was no use. Boy was through with politics and turned back to sugar, and everything sugar could be made to do, with new resolve.

Denyse had other ambitions for him, and she was a wilier politician than he. She thought he would make a very fine Lieutenant-Governor of the Province of Ontario and set to work to see that he got it.

Necessarily it was a long campaign. The Lieutenant-Governorship was in the gift of the Crown, which meant in effect that the holder of the office was named by the Dominion Cabinet. A Lieutenant-Governor had only recently been appointed, and as he was in excellent health it would be five years and possibly longer before Boy would have a chance. On his side was one strong point; it cost a lot of money to be Lieutenant-Governor, for the duties were ample and the stipend was not, so candidates for the post were never many. But a Liberal Government at Ottawa would not be likely to appoint a former Conservative parliamentarian to such a post, so there would have to be a change of government if Boy were to have a chance. It was a plan full of risks and contingencies, and if it were to succeed it would be through careful diplomacy and a substantial amount of luck. It was characteristic of Denyse that she decided to get busy with the diplomacy at once, so as to be ready for the luck if it came.

Boy thought the idea a brilliant one. He had never lost his taste for matters connected with the Crown; he had no doubt of his ability to fill a ceremonial post with distinction, and even to give it larger dimensions. He had everything the office needed with one exception. A Lieutenant-Governor must have a wife.

It was here that Denyse's masculinity of mind showed itself with the greatest clarity. Boy told me exactly what she said when first the matter came up between them. "I can't help you there," she said; "you're on your own so far as that goes." And then she went straight on to discuss the rationale of the Lieutenant-Governor's office—those privileges which made it a safeguard against any tyrannous act on the part of a packed legislature. It was by no means a purely ceremonial post, she said, but an agency through which the Crown exercised its traditional function of safeguarding the Constitution against politicians who forgot that they had been elected to serve the people and not to exploit them. She had informed herself thoroughly on the subject and knew the powers and limitations of a Lieutenant-Governor as well as any constitutional lawyer.

Boy had been aware for some time that Denyse was attractive; now he saw that she was lovable. Her intelligent, cool, unswerving devotion to his interests had impressed him from very early in their association, but her masculinity of mind had kept him at a distance. Now he became aware that this poor girl had sacrificed so much of her feminine self in order to gain success in the business world, and to advance the cause of women who lacked her clarity of vision and common sense, that she had almost forgotten that she was a woman, and a damned attractive one.

When love strikes the successful middle-aged they bring a weight of personality and a resolution to it that makes the romances of the young seem timid and bungling. They are not troubled by doubt; they know what they want and they go after it. Boy decided he wanted Denyse.

Denyse was not so easily achieved. Boy told me all about his wooing. Matters between us were still as they had been for thirty years, and the only difference was that Liesl had taught me that his confidences were not wrung from him against his will but gushed like oil from a well, and that I as Fifth Business was his logical confidant. Denyse at first refused to hear his professions of love. Her reasons were two: her business was her creation and demanded the best of her, and as a friend of Boy's she did not want him to imperil a fine career by an attachment that contained dangers.

What dangers? he demanded. Well, she confided, rather unwillingly, there had been Hornick. She had married him very early in the war, when she was twenty; it had been a brief and disagreeable marriage, which she had terminated by a divorce. Could a representative of the Crown have a wife who was a divorcee?

Boy swept this aside. Queen Victoria was dead. Even King George was dead. Everybody recognized the necessity and humanity of divorce nowadays, and Denyse's splendid campaigns for liberalizing the divorce laws had put her in a special category. But Denyse had more to confess.

There had been other men. She was a woman of normal physical needs—she admitted it without shame—and there had been one or two other attachments.

Poor kid, said Boy, she was still a victim of the ridiculous Double Standard. He told Denyse about his dreadful mistake with Leola, and how it had driven him—positively driven him—to seek outside marriage qualities of understanding and physical response that were not to be found at home. She understood this perfectly, but he had to argue for a long time to get her to see that the same commonsense view applied to herself. It was in such things as this, Boy told me with a fatuous smile, that Denyse's masculinity of mind failed her. He had to be pretty stern with her to make her understand that what was sauce for the gander was certainly sauce for the goose. Indeed, he called her Little Goose for a few days but gave it up because of the ribald connotation of the word.

Then—he smiled sadly when he explained the absurdity of this to me—there was her final objection, which was that people might imagine she married him for his money and the position he could give her. She was a small-town girl, and though she had gained a certain degree of know-how through her experience of life (I am not positive but I think she even went so far as to say that she was a graduate of the School of Hard Knocks), she doubted if she was up to being Mrs. Boy Staunton, and just possibly the Lieutenant-

Governor's lady. Suppose—just suppose for a moment—that she were called upon to entertain Royalty! No, Denyse Hornick knew her strengths and her weaknesses and she loved Boy far too well ever to expose him to embarrassment on her account.

Yes, she loved him. Had always done so. Understood the fiery and impatient spirit that could not endure the popularity-contest side of modern politics. Thought of him—didn't want to seem highbrow, but she did do a little serious reading—as a Canadian Coriolanus. "You common cry of curs, whose breath I hate." She could imagine him saying it to those sons-of-bitches who had turned on him at the last election. Yearned toward him in her heart as a really great man who was too proud to shake hands and kiss babies to persuade a lot of riff-raff to let him do what he was so obviously born to do.

Thus the masculinity of mind that had made Denyse Hornick a success in her world was swept aside, and the tender, loving woman beneath was discovered and awakened by Boy Staunton. They were married after appropriate preparations.

As a wedding it was neither a religious ceremony nor a merry-making. It is best described as A Function. Everybody of importance in Boy's world was there, and by clever work on Denyse's part quite a few Cabinet Ministers from Ottawa were present and the Prime Minister sent a telegram composed by the most eloquent of his secretaries. Bishop Woodiwiss married them, being assured that Denyse had not been the offending party in her divorce; he demurred even then, but Boy persuaded him, saying to me afterward that diocesan cares and rumours of the death of God were eroding the Bishop's intellect. The bride wore a ring of unusual size; the best man was a bank president; the very best champagne flowed like the very best champagne under the care of a very good caterer (which is to say, not more than three glasses to a guest unless they made a fuss). There was little jollity but no bitterness except from David.

"Do we kiss the bride?" a middle-aged guest asked him.

"Why not?" said he. "She's been kissed oftener than a police-court Bible and by much the same class of people."

The guest hurried away and told somebody that David was thinking of his mother.

I do not think this was so. Neither David nor Caroline liked Denyse, and they hated and resented her daughter, Lorene.

Not much attention had been paid to Lorene during the courtship, but she was an element to be reckoned with. She was the fruit of the unsatisfactory marriage with Hornick, who may, perhaps, have had the pox, and at this time she was thirteen. Adolescence was well advanced in Lorene, and she had large, hard breasts that popped out so close under her chin that she seemed to have no neck. Her body was heavy and short, and her physical coordination was so poor that she tended to knock things off tables that were quite a distance from her. She had bad vision and wore thick spectacles. She already gave rich promise of superfluous hair and sweated under the least stress. Her laugh was loud and frequent, and when she let it loose, spittle ran down her chin, which she sucked back with a blush. Unkind people said she was a half-wit, but that was untrue; she went to a special boarding-school where her teachers had put her in the Opportunity Class, as being more suited to her powers than the undemanding academic curriculum, and she was learning to cook and sew quite nicely.

At her mother's wedding Lorene was in tearing high spirits. Champagne dissolved her few inhibitions, and she banged and thumped her way among the guests, wet-chinned and elated. "I'm just the luckiest kid in the world today," she whooped. "I've got a wonderful new Daddy, my Daddy-Boy—he says I can call him Daddy-Boy. Look at the bracelet he gave me!"

In the goodness of her innocent heart Lorene tried to be friendly with David and Caroline. After all, were they not one family now? Poor Lorene did not know how many strange gradations of relationship the word "family" can imply. Caroline, who had never had a pleasant disposition, was extremely rude to her. David got drunk and laughed and made disrespectful remarks in an undertone when Boy made his speech in response to the toast to the bride.

Rarely is there a wedding without its clown. Lorene was the clown at Boy's second marriage, but it was not until she fell down—champagne or unaccustomed high heels, or both—that I took her into an anteroom and let her tell me all about her dog, who was marvellously clever. In time she fell asleep, and two waiters carried her out to the car.

3

Denyse had the normal dislike of a woman for the friends her husband has made before he married her, but I felt she was more than usually severe in my case. She possessed intelligence, conventional good looks, and unusual quality as an intriguer and politician, but she was a woman whose life and interests were entirely external. It was not that she was indifferent to the things of the spirit; she sensed their existence and declared herself their enemy. She had made it clear that she consented to a church wedding only because it was expected of a man in Boy's position; she condemned the church rite because it put women at a disadvantage. All her moral and ethical energy, which was abundant, was directed toward social reform. Easier divorce, equal pay for equal work as between men and women, no discrimination between the sexes in employment—these were her causes, and in promoting them she was no comic-strip feminist termagant, but reasonable, logical, and untiring.

Boy often assured me that underneath this public personality of hers there was a shy, lovable kid, pitifully anxious for affection and the tenderness of sex, but Denyse did not choose to show this aspect of herself to me. She had a fair measure of intuition, and she sensed that I regarded women as something other than fellow-citizens who had been given an economic raw deal because of a few unimportant biological differences. She may even have guessed that I held women in high esteem for qualities she had chosen to discourage in herself. But certainly she did not want me around the Staunton house, and if I dropped in, as had been my habit for thirty years, she picked a delicate quarrel with me, usually about religion. Like many people who are ignorant of religious matters, she attributed absurd beliefs to those who were concerned with them. She had found out about my interest in saints; after all, my books were not easy to overlook if one was in the travel business. The whole notion of saints was repugnant to her, and in her eyes I was on a level with people who believed in teacup reading or Social Credit. So, although I was asked to dinner now and then, when the other guests were people who had to be worked off for some tiresome reason, I was no longer an intimate of the household.

Boy tried to smooth things over by occasionally asking me to lunch at his club. He was more important than ever, for as well as his financial interests, which were now huge, he was a public figure, prominent in many philanthropic causes, and even a few artistic ones, as these became fashionable.

I sensed that this was wearing on him. He hated committees, but they were unavoidable even when he bossed them. He hated inefficiency, but a certain amount of democratic inefficiency had to be endured. He hated unfortunate people, but, after all, these are one's raw material if one sets up shop as a philanthropist. He was still handsome and magnetic, but I sensed grimness and disillusion when he was at his ease, as he was with me. He had embraced Denyse's rationalism—that was what she called it—fervently, and one day at the York Club, following the publication and varied reviews of my big book on the psychology of myth and legend, he denounced me petulantly for what he called my triviality of mind and my encouragement of superstition.

He had not read the book and I was sharp with him. He pulled in his horns a little and said, as the best he could do in the way of apology, that he could not stand such stuff because he was an atheist.

"I'm not surprised," said I. "You created a God in your own image, and when you found out he was no good you abolished him. It's a quite common form of psychological suicide."

I had only meant to give him blow for blow, but to my surprise he crumpled up.

"Don't nag me, Dunny," he said. "I feel rotten. I've done just about everything I've ever planned to do, and everybody thinks I'm a success. And of course I have Denyse now to keep me up to the mark, which is lucky—damned lucky, and don't imagine I don't feel it. But sometimes I wish I could get into a car and drive away from the whole damned thing."

"A truly mythological wish," I said. "I'll save you the trouble of reading my book to find out what it means: you want to pass into oblivion with your armour on, like King Arthur, but modern medical science is too clever to allow it. You must grow old, Boy; you'll have to find out what age means, and how to be old. A dear old friend of mine once told me he wanted a God who would teach him how to grow old. I expect he found what he wanted. You must do the same, or be wretched. Whom the gods hate they keep forever young."

He looked at me almost with hatred. "That's the most lunatic defeatist nonsense I've ever heard in my life," he said. But before we drank our coffee he was quite genial again.

Although I had been rather rough I was worried about him. As a boy he had been something of a bully, a boaster, and certainly a bad loser. As he grew up he had learned to dissemble these characteristics, and to anyone who knew him less well than I it might have appeared that he had conquered them. But I have never thought that traits that are strong in childhood disappear; they may go underground or they may be transmuted into something else, but they do not vanish; very often they make a vigorous appearance after the meridian of life has been passed. It is this, and not senility, that is the real second childhood. I could see this pattern in myself; my boyhood trick of getting off "good ones" that went far beyond any necessary self-defence and were likely to wound, had come back to me in my fifties. I was going to be a sharp-tongued old man as I had been a sharp-tongued boy. And Boy Staunton had reached a point in life where he no longer tried to conceal his naked wish to dominate everybody and was angry and ugly when things went against him.

As we neared our sixties the cloaks we had wrapped about our essential selves were wearing thin.

4

Mrs. Dempster died the year after Boy's second marriage. It came as a surprise to me, for I had a notion that the insane lived long and had made preparations in my will for her maintenance if I should die before her. Her health had been unimpaired by the long and wretched stay in the city asylum, and she had been more robust and cheerful after her move to the country, but I think my foolish talk about Paul broke her. After that well-meant piece of stupidity she was never "simple" again. There were drugs to keep her artificially passive, but I mistrusted them (perhaps ignorantly) and asked that so far as possible she be spared the ignominy of being stunned into good conduct. This made her harder to care for and cost more money. So she spent some of her time in fits of rage against me as the evil genius of her life, but much more in a state of grief and desolation.

It wore her out. I could not talk to her, but sometimes I looked at her through a little spy-hole in her door, and she grew frailer and less like herself as the months passed. She developed physical ailments—slight diabetes, a kidney weakening, and some malfunctioning of the heart—which were not thought to be very serious and were controlled in various ways; the doctors assured me, with the professional cheeriness of their kind, that she was good for another ten years. But I did not think so, for I was born in Deptford, where we were very acute in detecting when someone was "breaking up," and I knew that was what was happening to her.

Nevertheless it was a surprise when I was called by the hospital authorities to say she had had a serious heart seizure and might have another within a few hours. I had known very little of life without Mrs. Dempster, and despite my folk wisdom about "breaking up" I had not really faced the fact that I might lose her. It gave me a clutching around my own heart that scared me, but I made my way to the hospital as quickly as I could, though it was some hours after the telephone call when I arrived.

She was in the infirmary now, and unconscious. The outlook was bad, and I sat down to wait—presumably for her death. But after perhaps two hours a nurse appeared and said she was asking for me. As it was now some years since she had seen me without great distress of mind I was doubtful about answering the call, but I was assured it would be all right, and I went to her bedside.

She looked very pale and drawn, but when I took her hand she opened her eyes and looked at me for quite a long time. When she spoke her speech was slack and hardly audible.

"Are you Dunstable Ramsay?" she said.

I assured her. Another long silence.

"I thought he was a boy," said she and closed her eyes again.

I sat by her bed for quite a long time but she did not speak. I thought she might say something about Paul. I sat for perhaps an hour, and then to my astonishment the hand I held gave a little tug, the least possible squeeze. It was the last message I had from Mrs. Dempster. Soon afterward her breathing became noisy and the nurses beckoned me away. In half an hour they came to tell me she was dead.

It was a very bad night for me. I kept up a kind of dismal stoicism until I went to bed, and then I wept. I had not done such a thing since my mother had beaten me so many years before—no, not even in the worst of the war—and it frightened and hurt me. When at last I fell asleep I dreamed frightening dreams, in some of which my mother figured in terrible forms. They became so intolerable that I sat up and tried to read but could not keep my mind on the page; instead I was plagued by fantasies of desolation and wretchedness so awful that I might as well not have been sixty years old, a terror to boys, and a scholar of modest repute, for they crushed me as if I were the feeblest of children. It was a terrible invasion of the spirit, and when at last the rising bell rang in the school I was so shaken I cut myself shaving, vomited my breakfast half an hour after I had eaten it, and in my first class spoke so disgracefully to a stupid boy that I called him back afterward and apologized. I must have looked stricken, for my colleagues were unusually considerate toward me, and my classes were uneasy. I think they thought I was very ill, and I suppose I was, but not of anything I knew how to cure.

I had arranged for Mrs. Dempster's body to be sent to Toronto, as I wanted it to be cremated. An undertaker had it in his care, and the day after her death I went to see him.

"Dempster," he said. "Yes, just step into Room C."

There she was, not looking very much like herself, for the embalmer had been generous with the rouge. Nor can I say that she looked younger, or at peace, which are the two conventional comments. She just looked like a small, elderly woman, ready for burial. I knelt, and the undertaker left the room. I prayed for the repose of the soul of Mary Dempster, somewhere and somehow unspecified; under the benevolence of some power unidentified but deeply felt. It was the sort of prayer that supported all the arguments of Denyse Staunton against religion, but I was in the grip of an impulsion that it would have been spiritual suicide to deny. And then I begged forgiveness for myself because, though I had done wha.

I imagined was my best, I had not been loving enough, or wise enough, or generous enough in my dealings with her.

Then I did an odd thing that I almost fear to record, Headmaster, for it may lead you to dismiss me as a fool or a madman or both. I had once been fully persuaded that Mary Dempster was a saint, and even of late years I had not really changed my mind. There were the three miracles, after all; miracles to me, if to no one else. Saints, according to tradition, give off a sweet odour when they are dead; in many instances it has been likened to the scent of violets. So I bent over the head of Mary Dempster and sniffed for this true odour of sanctity. But all I could smell was a perfume, good enough in itself, that had obviously come out of a bottle.

The undertaker returned, bringing a cross with him; seeing me kneel, he had assumed that the funeral would be of the sort that required one. He came upon me sniffing.

"Chanel Number Five," he whispered, "we always use it when nothing is supplied by the relatives. And perhaps you have noticed that we have padded your mother's bosom just a little; she had lost something there, during the last illness, and when the figure is reclining it gives a rather wasted effect."

He was a decent man, working at a much-abused but necessary job, so I made no comment except to say that she was not my mother.

"I'm so sorry. Your aunt?" said he, desperate to please and be comforting but not intimate.

"No, neither mother nor aunt," I said, and as I could not use so bleak and inadequate a word as "friend" to name what Mary Dempster had been to me, I left him guessing.

The following day I sat quite alone in the crematory chapel as Mary Dempster's body went through the doors into the flames. After all, who else remembered her?

5

She died in March. The following summer I went to Europe and visited the Bollandists, hoping they would pay me a few compliments on my big book. I am not ashamed of this; who knew better than they if I had done well or ill, and whose esteem is sweeter than that of an expert in one's own line? I was not disappointed; they were generous and welcoming as always. And I picked up one piece of information that pleased me greatly: Padre Blazon was still alive, though very old, in a hospital in Vienna.

I had not meant to go to Vienna, though I was going to Salzburg for the Festival, but I had not heard from Blazon for years and could not resist him. There he was, in a hospital directed by the Blue Nuns, propped up on pillows, looking older but not greatly changed except that his few teeth were gone; he even wore the deplorable velvet skullcap rakishly askew over his wild white hair.

He knew me at once. "Ramezay!" he crowed as I approached. "I thought you must be dead! How old you look! Why, you must be all kinds of ages! What years? Come now, don't be coy! What years?"

"Just over the threshold of sixty-one," I said.

"Aha, a patriarch! You look even more though. Do you know how old I am? No, you don't, and I am not going to tell. If the Sisters find out they think I am senile. They wash me too much now; if they knew how old I am they would flay me with their terrible brushes—flay me like St. Bartholomew. But I will tell you this much—I shall not see one hundred again! How much over that I tell nobody, but it will be discovered when I am dead. I may die any time. I may die as we are talking. Then I shall be sure to have the last word, eh? Sit down. You look tired!

"You have written a fine book! Not that I have read it all, but one of the nuns read some of it to me. I made her stop because her English accent was so vile she desecrated your elegant prose, and she mispronounced all the names. A real murderer! How ignorant these women are! Assassins of the spoken word! For a punishment I made her read a lot of *Le Juif errant* to me. Her French is very chaste, but the book nearly burned her tongue—so very anticlerical, you know. And what it says about the Jesuits! What evil magicians, what serpents! If we were one scruple as clever as Eugène Sue thought we should be masters of the world today. Poor soul, she could not understand why I wanted to hear it or why I laughed so much. Then I told her it was on the Index, and now she thinks I am an ogre disguised as an old Jesuit. Well, well, it passes the time. How is your fool-saint?"

"My what?"

"Don't shout; my hearing is perfectly good. Your fool-saint, your madwoman who dominates your life. I thought we might get something about her in your book but not a word. I know. I read the index first; I always do. All kinds of saints, heroes, and legends but no fool-saint. Why?"

"I was surprised to hear you call her that because I haven't heard that particular expression for thirty years. The last man to use it about Mary Dempster was an Irishman." And I told him of my conversation with Father Regan so long ago.

"Ah, Ramezay, you are a rash man. Imagine asking a village priest a question like that! But he must have been a fellow of some quality. Not all the Irish are idiots; they have a lot of Spanish blood, you know. That he should know about fool-saints is very odd. But do you know that one is to be canonized quite soon? Bertilla Boscardin, who did wonders—truly wonders—during the First World War with hospital patients; many miracles of healing and heroic courage during air-raids. Still, she was not quite a classic fool-saint; she was active and they are more usually passive—great lovers of God, with that special perception that St. Bonaventura spoke of as beyond the power of even the wisest scholar."

"Father Regan assured me that fool-saints are dangerous. The Jews warn against them particularly because they are holy meddlers and bring ill-luck."

"Well, so they do, sometimes, when they are more fool than saint; we all bring ill-luck to others, you know, often without in the least recognizing it. But when I talk of a fool-saint I do not mean just some lolloping idiot who babbles of God instead of talking filth as they usually do. Remind me about this Mary Dempster."

So I did remind him, and when I had finished he said he would think about the matter. He was growing weary, and a nun signalled to me that it was time to leave.

"He is a very dear and good old man," she told me, "but he does so love to tease us. If you want to give him a treat, bring him some of that very special Viennese chocolate; he finds the hospital diet a great trial. His stomach is a marvel. Oh, that I might have such a stomach, and I am not even half his massive age!"

So next day I appeared with a lot of chocolate, most of which I gave to the nun to be rationed to him; I did not want him to gorge himself to death before my eyes. But the box I gave him was one of those pretty affairs with a little pair of tongs for picking out the piece one wants.

"Aha, St. Dunstan and his tongs!" he whispered. "Keep your voice down, St. Dunstan, or all these others will want some of my chocolate, and it probably would not be wholesome for them. Oh, you saintly man! I suppose a bottle of really good wine could not be got past the nuns? They dole out a thimbleful of some terrible belly-vengeance they buy very cheap, on their infrequent feast days.

"Well, I have been thinking about your fool-saint, and what I conclude is this: she would never have got past the Bollandists, but she must have been an extraordinary person, a great lover of God, and trusting greatly in His love for her. As for the miracles, you and I have looked too deeply into miracles to dogmatize; you believe in them, and your belief has coloured your life with beauty and goodness; too much scientizing will not help you. It seems far more important to me that her life was lived heroically; she endured a hard fate, did the best she could, and kept it up until at last her madness was too powerful for her. Heroism in God's cause is the mark of the saint, Ramezay, not conjuring tricks. So on All Saints' Day I do not think you will do anything but good by honouring the name of Mary Dempster in your prayers. By your own admission you have enjoyed many of the good things of life because she suffered a fate that might have been yours. Though a boy's head is hard, Ramezay, hard—as you, being a schoolmaster, must surely know. You might just have had a nasty knock. Nobody can say for sure. But your life has been illuminated by your fool-saint, and how many can say so much?"

We talked a little further of friends we shared in Brussels, and then suddenly he said, "Have you met the Devil yet?"

"Yes," I replied, "I met Him in Mexico City. He was disguised as a woman—an extremely ugly woman but unquestionably a woman."

"Unquestionably?"

"Not a shadow of a doubt possible."

"Really, Ramezay, you astonish me. You are a much more remarkable fellow than one might suppose, if you will forgive me for saying so. The Devil certainly changed His sex to tempt St. Anthony the Great, but for a Canadian schoolmaster! Well, well, one must not be a snob in spiritual things. From your certainty I gather the Devil tempted you with success?"

"The Devil proved to be a very good fellow. He suggested that a little compromise would not hurt me. He even suggested that an acquaintance with Him might improve my character."

"I find no fault with that. The Devil knows corners of us all of which Christ Himself is ignorant. Indeed, I am sure Christ learned a great deal that was salutary about Himself when He met the Devil in the wilderness. Of course, that was a meeting of brothers; people forget too readily that Satan is Christ's elder brother and has certain advantages in argument that pertain to a senior. On the whole, we treat the Devil shamefully, and the worse we treat Him the more He laughs at us. But tell me about your encounter."

I did so, and he listened with a great show of prudery at the dirty bits; he sniggered behind his hand, rolling his eyes up until only the whites could be seen; he snorted with laughter; when I described Liesl and the beautiful Faustina in the dressing-room he covered his face with his hands but peeped wickedly between his fingers. It was a virtuoso display of clerical-Spanish modesty. But when I described how I had wrung Liesl's nose until the bone cracked he kicked his counterpane and guffawed until a nun hurried to his bedside, only to be repelled with full-arm gestures and hissing.

"Oho, Ramezay, no wonder you write so well of myth and legend! It was St. Dunstan seizing the Devil's snout in his tongs, a thousand years after his time. Well done, well done! You met the Devil as an equal, not cringing or frightened or begging for a trashy favour. That is the heroic life, Ramezay. You are fit to be the Devil's friend, without any fear of losing yourself to Him!"

On the third day I took farewell of him. I had managed to arrange for some chocolate to be procured when he needed more, and as a great favour the nuns took six bottles of a good wine into their care to be rationed to him as seemed best.

"Good-bye," he cried cheerfully. "We shall probably not meet again, Ramezay. You are beginning to look a little shaky."

"I have not yet found a God to teach me how to be old," I said. "Have you?"

"Shhh, not so loud. The nuns must not know in what a spiritual state I am. Yes, yes, I have found Him, and He is the very best of company. Very calm, very quiet, but gloriously alive: we *do*, but He *is*. Not in the least a proselytizer or a careerist, like His sons." And he went off into a fit of giggles.

I left him soon after this, and as I looked back from the door for a last wave, he was laughing and pinching his big copper nose with the tiny chocolate tongs. "God go with you, St. Dunstan," he called.

He was much in my mind as I tasted the pleasures of Salzburg, and particularly so after my first visit to the special display called *Schöne Madonnen*, in the exhibition rooms in the Cathedral. For here, at last, and after having abandoned hope and forgotten my search, I found the Little Madonna I had seen during my bad night at Passchendaele. There she was, among these images of the Holy Mother in all her aspects, collected as examples of the wood and stone carver's art, and drawn from churches, museums, and private collections all over Europe.

There she was, quite unmistakable, from the charming crown that she wore with such an air to her foot set on the crescent moon. Beneath this moon was what I had not seen in the harsh light of the flare—the globe of the earth itself, with a serpent encircling it, and an apple in the mouth of the serpent. She had lost her sceptre, but not the Divine Child, a fat, reserved little person who looked out at the world from beneath half-closed eyelids. But the face of the Madonna—was it truly the face of Mary Dempster? No, it was not, though the hair was very like; Mary Dempster, whose face my mother had described as being like a pan of milk, had never been so beautiful in feature, but the expression was undeniably hers—an expression of mercy and love, tempered with perception and penetration.

I visited her every day during my week in Salzburg. She belonged, so the catalogue told me, to a famous private collection and was considered a good, though late, example of the Immaculate Conception aspect of the Madonna figure. It had not been considered worthy of an illustration in the catalogue, so when my week was up I never saw it again. Photography in the exhibition was forbidden. But I needed no picture. She was mine forever.

6

The mysterious death of Boy Staunton was a nine days' wonder, and people who delight in unsolved crimes—for they were certain it must have been a crime—still talk of it. You recall most of the details, Headmaster, I am sure: at about four o'clock on the morning of Monday, November 4, 1968, his Cadillac convertible was recovered from the waters of Toronto harbour, into which it had been driven at a speed great enough to carry it, as it sank, about twenty feet from the concrete pier. His body was in the driver's seat, the hands gripping the wheel so tightly that it was very difficult for the police to remove him from the car. The windows and the roof were closed, so that some time must have elapsed between driving over the edge and the filling of the car with water. But the most curious fact of all was that in Boy's mouth the police found a stone—an ordinary piece of pinkish granite about the size of a small egg—which could not possibly have been where it was unless he himself, or someone unknown, had put it there.

The newspapers published columns about it, as was reasonable, for it was local news of the first order. Was it murder? But who would murder a well-known philanthropist, a man whose great gifts as an organizer had been of incalculable value to the nation during the war years? Now that Boy was dead, he was a hero to the press. Was it suicide? Why would the President of the Alpha Corporation, a man notably youthful in appearance and outlook, and one of the two or three richest men in Canada, want to kill himself? His home-life was of model character; he and his wife (the former Denyse Hornick, a figure of note in her own right as an advocate of economic and legal reform on behalf of women) had worked very closely in a score of philanthropic and cultural projects. Besides, the newspapers thought it now proper to reveal, his appointment by the Crown to the office of Lieutenant-Governor of Ontario was to have been announced within a few days. Was a man with Boy Staunton's high concept of service likely to have killed himself under such circumstances?

Tributes from distinguished citizens were many. There was a heartfelt one from Joel Surgeoner, within a few hundred yards of whose Lifeline Mission the death occurred—a Mission that the dead man had supported most generously. You wrote one yourself, Headmaster, in which you said that he had finely exemplified the school's unremitting insistence that much is demanded of those to whom much has been given.

His wife was glowingly described, though there was little mention of "a former marriage, which ended with the death of the first Mrs. Staunton, née Leola Crookshanks, in 1942." In the list of the bereaved, Lorene took precedence over David (now forty, a barrister and a drunk) and Caroline (now Mrs. Beeston Bastable and mother of one daughter, also Caroline).

The funeral was not quite a state funeral, though Denyse tried to manage one; she wanted a flag on the coffin and she wanted soldiers, but it was not to be. However, many flags were at half-staff, and she did achieve a very fine turnout of important people, and others who were important because they represented somebody too important to come personally. It was agreed by everyone that Bishop Woodiwiss paid a noble tribute to Boy, whom he had known from youth, though it was a pity poor Woodiwiss mumbled so now.

The reception after the funeral was in the great tradition of such affairs, and the new house Denyse had made Boy build in the most desirable of the suburbs was filled even to its great capacity. Denyse was wonderfully self-possessed and ran everything perfectly. Or almost perfectly; there was one thing in which she did not succeed.

She approached me after she had finished receiving the mourners—if that is the right way to describe the group who were now getting down so merrily to the Scotch and rye—and, "Of course you'll write the official life," said she.

"What official life?" I asked, startled and clumsy.

"What official life do you suppose?" she said, giving me a look that told me very plainly to brace up and not be a fool.

"Oh, is there to be one?" I asked. I was not trying to be troublesome; I was genuinely unnerved, and with good cause.

"Yes, there is to be one," she said, and icicles hung from every word. "As you knew Boy from childhood, there will be a good deal for you to fill in before we come to the part where I can direct you."

"But how is it official?" I asked, wallowing in wonderment. "I mean, what makes it official? Does the government want it or something?"

"The government has had no time to think about it," she said, "but I want it, and I shall do whatever needs to be done about the government. What I want to know now is whether you are going to write it or not." She spoke like a mother who is saying "Are you going to do what I tell you or not?" to a bad child. It was not so much an inquiry as a flick of the whip.

"Well, I'll want to think it over," I said.

"Do that. Frankly, my first choice was Eric Roop—I thought it wanted a poet's touch—but he can't do it, though considering how many grants Boy wangled for him I don't know why. But Boy did even more for you. You'll find it a change from those saints you're so fond of." She left me angrily.

Of course I did not write it. The heart attack I had a few days later gave me an excellent excuse for keeping free of anything I didn't want to do. And how could I have written a life of Boy that would have satisfied me and yet saved me from murder at the hands of Denyse? And how could I, trained as a historian to suppress nothing, and with the Bollandist tradition of looking firmly at the shadow as well as the light, have written a life of Boy without telling all that I have told you, Headmaster, and all I know about the way he died? And even then, would it have been the truth? I learned something about the variability of truth as quite rational people see it from Boy himself, within an hour of his death.

You will not see this memoir until after my own death, and you will surely keep what you know to yourself. After all, you cannot prove anything against anyone. Nor was Boy's manner of death really surprising to anyone who knows what you now know about his life.

It was like this.

7

Magnus Eisengrim did not bring his famous display of illusions to Canada until 1968. His fame was now so great that he had once had his picture on the cover of *Time* as the greatest magician in history. The *Autobiography* sold quite well here, though nobody knew that its subject (or its author) was a native. It was at the end of October he came to Toronto for two weeks.

Naturally I saw a good deal of him and his company. The beautiful Faustina had been replaced by another girl, no less beautiful, who bore the same name. Liesl, now in early middle age and possessed of a simian distinction of appearance, was as near to me as before, and I spent all the time I could spare with her. She and Blazon were the only people I have ever met with whom one resumed a conversation exactly where it had been discontinued, whether yesterday or six years earlier. It was through her intercession—perhaps it would be more truthful to call it a command—that I was able to get Eisengrim to come to the school on the Sunday night in the middle of his fortnight's engagement, to talk to the boarders about hypnotism; schoolmasters are without conscience in exacting such favours.

He was a huge success, of course, for though he had not wanted to come he was not a man to scamp anything he had undertaken. He paid the boys the compliment of treating them seriously, explaining what hypnotism really was and what its limitations were. He emphasized the fact that nobody can be made to do anything under hypnotism that is contrary to his wishes, though of course people have wishes that they are unwilling to acknowledge, even to themselves. I remember that this concept gave trouble to several of the boys, and Eisengrim explained it in terms, and with a clarity, that suggested to me that he was a much better-informed man than I had supposed. The idea of the hypnotist as an all-powerful demon, like Svengali, who could make anybody do anything, he pooh-poohed; but he did tell some amusing stories about odd and embarrassing facets of people's personalities that had made their appearance under hypnotism.

Of course the boys clamoured for a demonstration, but he refused to break his rule of never hypnotizing anyone under twenty-one without written consent from their parents. (He did not add that young people and children are difficult hypnotic subjects because of the variability of their power of concentration.) However, he did hypnotize me, and made me do enough strange things to delight the boys without robbing me of my professional dignity. He made me compose an extemporary poem, which is something I had never done before in my life, but apparently it was not bad.

His talk lasted for about an hour, and as we were walking down the main corridor of the classroom building Boy Staunton came out of the side door of your study, Headmaster. I introduced them, and Boy was delighted.

"I saw your show last Thursday," he said. "It was my stepdaughter's birthday, and we were celebrating. As a matter of fact, you gave her a box of sweets."

"I remember perfectly," said Eisengrim. "Your party was sitting in C21-25. Your stepdaughter wears strong spectacles and has a characteristic laugh."

"Yes, poor Lorene. I'm afraid she became a bit hysterical; we had to leave after you sawed a man in two. But, may I ask you a very special favour?—how did your Brazen Head know what was implied in the message it gave to Ruth Tillman? That has caused some extraordinary gossip."

"No, Mr. Staunton, I cannot tell you that. But perhaps you will tell me how you know what was said to Mrs. Tillman, who sat in F32 on Friday night, if your party came to the theatre on Thursday?"

"Mightn't I have heard it from friends?"

"You might, but you did not. You came back to see my exhibition on Friday night because you had missed some of it by reason of your daughter's over-excitement. I can only assume my exhibition offered something you wanted. A great compliment. I appreciated it, I assure you. Indeed, I appreciated it so much that the Head decided not to name you and tell the audience that your appointment as Lieutenant-Governor would be announced on Monday. I am sure you understand how much renunciation there is in refusing such a scoop. It would have brought me wonderful publicity, but it would have embarrassed you, and the Head and I decided not to do that."

"But you can't possibly have known! I hadn't had the letter myself more than a couple of hours before going to the theatre. I had it with me as a matter of fact."

"Very true, and you have it now; inside right-hand breast pocket. Don't worry, I haven't picked your pocket. But when you lean forward, however slightly, the tip of a long envelope made of thick creamy paper can just be seen; only governments use such ostentatious envelopes, and when a man so elegantly dressed as you are bulges his jacket with one of them, it is probably—you see? There is an elementary lesson in magic for you. Work on it for twenty years and you may comprehend the Brazen Head."

This took Boy down a peg; the good-humoured, youthful chuckle he gave was his first step to get himself on top of the conversation again. "As a matter of fact," he said, "I've just been showing it to the Headmaster; because, of course, I'll have to resign as Chairman of the Board of Governors. And I was just coming to talk to you about it, Dunny."

"Come along then," I said. "We were going to have a drink."

I was conscious already that Boy was up to one of his special displays of charm. He had put his foot wrong with Eisengrim by asking him to reveal the secret of an illusion; it was unlike him to be so gauche, but I suppose the excitement about his new appointment blew up his ego a little beyond what he could manage. It seemed to me that I could already see the plumed, cocked hat of a Lieutenant-Governor on his head.

Eisengrim had been sharp enough with him to arouse hostility, and Boy loved to defeat hostility by turning the other cheek—which is by no means a purely Christian ploy, as Boy had shown me countless times. Eisengrim further topped him by the little bit of observation about the letter, which had made Boy look like a child who is so besotted by a new toy that it cannot let the toy out of its grasp. Boy wanted a chance to right the balance, which of course meant making him master of the situation.

It was clear to me that one of those sympathies, or antipathies, or at any rate unusual states of feeling, had arisen between these two which sometimes lead to falling in love, or to sudden warm friendships, or to lasting and rancorous enmities, but which are always extraordinary. I wanted to see what would happen, and my appetite was given the special zest of knowing who Eisengrim really was, which Boy did not, and perhaps would never learn.

It was like Boy to seek to ingratiate himself with the new friend by treating the old friend with genial contempt. When the three of us had made our way to my room at the end of the top-floor corridor—my old room, which I have always refused to leave for more comfortable quarters in the newer buildings—he kicked the door open and entered first, turning on the lights and touring the room as he said, "Still the same old rat's nest. What are you going to do when you have to move? How will you ever find room anywhere else for all this junk? Look at those books! I'll bet you don't use some of them once a year."

It was true that several of the big volumes were spread about, and I had to take some of them out of an armchair for Eisengrim, so I was a little humbled.

But Eisengrim spoke. "I like it very much," said he. "I so seldom get to my home, and I have to live in hotel rooms for weeks and months on end. Next spring I go on a world tour; that will mean something like five years of hotels. This room speaks of peace and a mind at work. I wish it were mine."

"I wouldn't say old Dunny's mind was at work," said Boy. "I wish all I had to do was teach the same lessons every year for forty years."

"You are forgetting his many and excellent books, are you not?" said Eisengrim.

Boy understood that he was not going to get what he wanted, which cannot have been anything more than a complicity with an interesting stranger, by running me down, so he took another tack. "You mustn't misunderstand if I am disrespectful toward the great scholar. We're very old friends. We come from the same little village. In fact I think we might say that all the brains of Deptford—past, present, and doubtless to come—are in this room right now."

For the first time in Boy's company, Eisengrim laughed. "Might I be included in such a distinguished group?" he asked.

Boy was pleased to have gained a laugh. "Sorry, birth in Deptford is an absolute requirement."

"Oh, I have that already. It was about my achievements in the world that I had doubt."

"I've looked through your *Autobiography*—Lorene asked me to buy a copy for her. I thought you were born somewhere in the far north of Sweden."

"That was Magnus Eisengrim; my earlier self was born in Deptford. If the *Autobiography* seems to be a little high in colour you must blame Ramsay. He wrote it."

"Dunny! You never told me that!"

"It never seemed relevant," said I. I was amazed that Paul would tell him such a thing, but I could see that he, like Boy, was prepared to play some high cards in this game of topping each other.

"I don't remember anybody in the least like you in Deptford. What did you say your real name was?"

"My real name is Magnus Eisengrim; that is who I am and that is how the world knows me. But before I found out who I was, I was called Paul Dempster, and I remember you very well. I always thought of you as the Rich Young Ruler."

"And are you and Dunny old friends?"

"Yes, very old friends. He was my first teacher of magic. He also taught me a little about saints, but it was the magic that lingered. His specialty as a conjurer was eggs—the Swami of the Omelette. He was my only teacher till I ran away with a circus."

"Did you? You know I wanted to do that. I suppose it is part of every boy's dream."

"Then boys are lucky that it remains a dream. I should not have said a circus; it was a very humble carnival show. I was entranced by Willard the Wizard; he was so much more skilful than Ramsay. He was quite clever with cards and a very neat pickpocket. I begged him to take me, and was such an ignorant little boy—perhaps I might even call myself innocent, though it is a word I don't like—that I was in ecstasy when he consented. But I soon found out that Willard had two weaknesses—boys and morphia. The morphia had already made him careless or he would never have run the terrible risk of stealing a boy. But when I had well and truly found out what travelling with Willard meant, he had me in slavery; he told me that if anybody ever found out what we did together I would certainly be hanged, but he would get off because he knew all the judges everywhere. So I was chained to Willard by fear; I was his thing and his creature, and I learned conjuring as a reward.

One always learns one's mystery at the price of one's innocence, though my case was spectacular. But the astonishing thing is that I grew to like Willard, especially as morphia incapacitated him for his hobby and ruined him as a conjurer. It was then he became a Wild Man."

"Then he was *Le Solitaire des forêts?*" I asked.

"That was even later. His first decline was from conjurer to Wild Man—essentially a geek."

"Geek?" said Boy.

"That is what carnival people call them. They are not an advertised attraction, but word that a geek is in a back tent is passed around quietly, and money is taken without any sale of tickets. Otherwise the Humane Societies make themselves a nuisance. The geek is represented as somebody who simply has to have raw flesh, and especially blood. After the spieler has lectured terrifyingly on the psychology and physiology of the geek, the geek is given a live chicken; he growls and rolls his eyes, then he gnaws through its neck until the head is off, and he drinks the spouting blood. Not a nice life, and very hard on the teeth, but if it is the only way to keep yourself in morphia, you'd rather geek than have the horrors. But geeking costs money; you need a live chicken every time, and even the oldest, toughest birds cost something. Before Willard got too sick even to geek, he was geeking with worms and gartersnakes when I could catch them for him. The rubes loved it; Willard was something even the most disgusting brute could despise.

"There was trouble with the police, at last, and I thought we would do better abroad. We had been over there quite a time, Ramsay, before you and I met in the Tyrol, and by then Willard was in very poor health, and *Le Solitaire des forêts* was all he could manage. I doubt if he even knew where he was. So that is what running away with a circus was like, Mr. Staunton."

"Why didn't you leave him when he was down to geeking?"

"Shall I answer you honestly? Very well, then; it was loyalty. Yes, loyalty to Willard, though not to his geeking or his nasty ways with boys. I suppose it was loyalty to his dreadful, inescapable human need. Many people feel these irrational responsibilities and cannot crush them. Like Ramsay's loyalty to my mother, for instance. I am sure it was an impediment to him, and certainly it must have been a heavy expense, but he did not fail her. I suppose he loved her. I might have done so if I had ever known her. But, you see, the person I knew was a woman unlike anybody else's mother, who was called 'hoor' by people like you, Mr. Staunton."

"I really don't remember," said Boy. "Are you sure?"

"Quite sure. I have never been able to forget what she was or what people called her. Because, you see, it was my birth that made her like that. My father thought it his duty to tell me, so that I could do whatever was possible to make it up to her. My birth was what robbed her of her sanity; that sometimes happened, you know, and I suppose it happens still. I was too young for the kind of guilt my father wanted me to feel; he had an extraordinary belief in guilt as an educative force. I couldn't stand it. I cannot feel guilt now. But I can call up in an instant what it felt like to be the child of a woman everybody jeered at and thought a dirty joke—including you, the Rich Young Ruler. But I am sure your accent is much more elegant now. A Lieutenant-Governor who said 'hoor' would not reflect credit on the Crown, would he?"

Boy had plenty of experience in being baited by hostile people, and he did not show by a quiver how strange this was to him. He prepared to get the attack into his own hands.

"I forget what you said your name was."

Eisengrim continued to smile, so I said, "He's Paul Dempster."

This time it was my turn for surprise. "Who may Paul Dempster be?" asked Boy.

"Do you mean to say you don't remember the Dempsters? In Deptford? The Reverend Amasa Dempster?"

"No. I don't remember what is of no use to me, and I haven't been in Deptford since my father died. That's twenty-six years."

"You have no recollection of Mrs. Dempster?"

"None at all. Why should I?"

I could hardly believe he spoke the truth, but as we talked on I had to accept it as a fact that he had so far edited his memory of his early days that the incident of the snowball had quite vanished from his mind. But had not Paul edited his memories so that only pain and cruelty remained? I began to wonder what I had erased from my own recollection.

We had drinks and were sitting as much at ease as men can amid so many strong currents of feeling. Boy made another attempt to turn the conversation into a realm where he could dominate.

"How did you come to choose your professional name? I know magicians like to have extraordinary names, but yours sounds a little alarming. Don't you find that a disadvantage?"

"No. And I did not choose it. My patron gave it to me." He turned his head toward me, and I knew that the patron was Liesl. "It comes from one of the great northern beast fables, and it means Wolf. Far from being a disadvantage, people like it. People like to be in awe of something, you know. And my magic show is not ordinary. It provokes awe, which is why it is a success. It has something of the quality of Ramsay's saints, though my miracles have a spice of the Devil about them—again my patron's idea. That is where you make your mistake. You have always wanted to be loved; nobody responds quite as we would wish, and people are suspicious of a public figure who wants to be loved. I have been wiser than you. I chose a Wolf's name. You have chosen forever to be a Boy. Was it because your mother used to call you Pidgy Boy-Boy, even when you were old enough to call my mother 'hoor'?"

"How in God's name did you know that? Nobody in the world now living knows that!"

"Oh yes, two people know it—myself and Ramsay. He told me, many years ago, under an oath of secrecy."

"I never did any such thing!" I shouted, outraged. Yet, even as I shouted, a doubt assailed me.

"But you did, or how would I know? You told me that to comfort me once, when the Rich Young Ruler and some of his gang had been shouting at my mother. We all forget many of the things we do, especially when they do not fit into the character we have chosen for ourselves. You see yourself as the man of many confidences, Ramsay. It would not do for you to remember a time when you told a secret. Dunstan Ramsay—when did you cease to be Dunstable?"

"A girl renamed me when I had at last broken with my mother. Liesl said it made me one of the twice-born. Had you thought that we are all three of the company of the twice-born? We have all rejected our beginnings and become something our parents could not have foreseen."

"I can't imagine your parents foreseeing that you would become a theorizer about myth and legend," said Eisengrim. "Hard people—I remember them clearly. Hard people—especially your mother."

"Wrong," said I. And I told him how my mother had worked and schemed and devised a nest to keep him alive, and exulted when he decided to live. "She said you were a fighter, and she liked that."

Now it was his turn to be disconcerted. "Do you mind if I have one of your cigars?" he said.

I do not smoke cigars, but the box he took from a shelf on the other side of the room might easily be mistaken for a humidor—rather a fine one. But as he took it down and rather superciliously blew dust from it his face changed.

He brought it over and laid it on the low table around which our chairs were grouped. "What's this?" he asked.

"It is what it says it is," said I.

The engraving on the silver plaque on the lid of the box was beautiful and clear, for I had chosen the script with care:

Requiescat in pace
MARY DEMPSTER
1888–1959
Here is the patience
and faith of the saints.

We looked at it for some time. Boy was first to speak.

"Why would you keep a thing like that with you?"

"A form of piety. A sense of guilt unexpiated. Indolence. I have always been meaning to put them in some proper place, but I haven't found it yet."

"Guilt?" said Eisengrim.

Here it was. Either I spoke now or I kept silence forever. Dunstan Ramsay counselled against revelation, but Fifth Business would not hear.

"Yes, guilt. Staunton and I robbed your mother of her sanity." And I told them the story of the snowball.

"Too bad," said Boy. "But if I may say so, Dunny, I think you've let the thing build up into something it never was. You unmarried men are terrible fretters. I threw the snowball—at least you say so, and for argument's sake let that go—and you dodged it. It precipitated something which was probably going to happen anyhow. The difference between us is that you've brooded over it and I've forgotten it. We've both done far more important things since. I'm sorry if I was offensive to your mother, Dempster. But you know what boys are. Brutes, because they don't know any better. But they grow up to be men."

"Very important men. Men whom the Crown delighteth to honour," said Eisengrim with an unpleasant laugh.

"Yes. If you expect me to be diffident about that, you're wrong."

"Men who retain something of the brutish boy, even," said I.

"I don't think I understand you."

Fifth Business insisted on being heard again. "Would this jog your memory?" I asked, handing him my old paperweight.

"Why should it? An ordinary bit of stone. You've used it to hold down some of the stuff on your desk for years. I've seen it a hundred times. It doesn't remind me of anything but you."

"It is the stone you put in the snowball you threw at Mrs. Dempster," I said. "I've kept it because I couldn't part with it. I swear I never meant to tell you what it was. But, Boy, for God's sake, get to know something about yourself. The stone-in-the-snowball has been characteristic of too much you've done for you to forget it forever!"

"What I've done! Listen, Dunny, one thing I've done is to make you pretty well-off for a man in your position. I've treated you like a brother. Given you tips nobody else got, let me tell you. And that's where your nice little nest-egg came from. Your retirement fund you used to whine about."

I hadn't thought I whined, but perhaps I did. "Need we go on with this moral bookkeeping?" I said. "I'm simply trying to recover something of the totality of your life. Don't you want to possess it as a whole—the bad with the good? I told you once you'd made a God of yourself, and the insufficiency of it forced you to become an atheist. It's time you tried to be a human being. Then maybe something bigger than yourself will come up on your horizon."

"You're trying to get me. You want to humiliate me in front of this man here; you seem to have been in cahoots with him for years, though you never mentioned him or his miserable mother to me—your best friend, and your patron and protector against your own incompetence! Well, let him hear this, as we're dealing in ugly truths: you've always hated me because I took Leola from you. And I did! It wasn't because you lost a leg and were ugly. It was because she loved me better."

This got me on the raw, and Dunstable Ramsay's old inability to resist a cruel speech when one occurred to him came uppermost. "My observation has been that we get the women we deserve, King Candaules," I said, "and those who eat jam before breakfast are cloyed before bedtime."

"Gentlemen," said Eisengrim, "deeply interesting though this is, Sunday nights are the only nights when I can get to bed before midnight. So I shall leave you."

Boy was all courtesy at once. "I'm going too. Let me give you a lift," said he. Of course; he wanted to blackguard me to Eisengrim in the car.

"Thank you, Mr. Staunton," said Eisengrim. "What Ramsay has told us puts you in my debt—for eighty days in Paradise, if for nothing in this life. We shall call it quits if you will drive me to my hotel."

I lifted the casket that contained Mary Dempster's ashes. "Do you want to take this with you, Paul?"

"No thanks, Ramsay. I have everything I need."

It seemed an odd remark, but in the emotional stress of the situation I paid no heed to it. Indeed, it was not until after the news of Boy's death reached me next morning that I noticed my paperweight was gone.

8

Because of the way he died, the consequent police investigations, and the delays brought about by Denyse's determination to make the most of the nearly official funeral, Boy was not buried until Thursday. The Saturday evening following I went to see Eisengrim's *Soirée of Illusions,* as he now called it, at its last performance, and though I spent much of the evening behind the scenes with Liesl, I went into the front of the house during *The Brazen Head of Friar Bacon.* Or rather, I hid myself behind the curtains of an upper box so that I could look down into the auditorium of our beautiful old Royal Alexandra Theatre and watch the audience.

Everything went smoothly during the collecting and restoration of borrowed objects, and the faces I saw below me were the usual studies in pleasure, astonishment, and—always the most interesting—the eagerness to be deceived mingled with resentment of deception. But when the Head was about to utter its three messages to people in the audience and Eisengrim had said what was to come, somebody in the top balcony shouted out, "Who killed Boy Staunton?"

There was murmuring in the audience and a hiss or two, but silence fell as the Head glowed from within, its lips parted, and its voice—Liesl's voice, slightly foreign and impossible to identify as man's or woman's—spoke.

"He was killed by the usual cabal: by himself, first of all; by the woman he knew; by the woman he did not know; by the man who granted his inmost wish; and by the inevitable fifth, who was keeper of his conscience and keeper of the stone."

I believe there was an uproar. Certainly Denyse made a great to-do when she heard of it. Of course she thought "the woman he knew" must be herself. The police were hounded by her and some of her influential friends, but that was after Eisengrim and his *Soirée of Illusions* had removed by air to Copenhagen, and the police had to make it clear that they really could not investigate impalpable offences, however annoying they might be. But I knew nothing about it, because it was there, in that box, that I had my seizure and was rushed to the hospital, as I was afterward told, by a foreign lady.

When I was well enough to read letters I found one—a postcard, to my horror—that read:

> Deeply sorry about your illness which was my fault as much as most such things are anybody's fault. But I could not resist my temptation as I beg you not to resist this one: come to Switzerland and join the Basso and the Brazen Head. We shall have some high old times before The Five make an end of us all.
>
> Love,
>
> L.V.

And that, Headmaster, is all I have to tell you.

Sankt Gallen
1970

THE MANTICORE

Contents

I *Why I Went to Zürich* 263

II *David Against the Trolls* 322

III *My Sorgenfrei Diary* 479

·I·
Why I Went to Zürich

1

WHEN DID YOU decide you should come to Zürich, Mr. Staunton?

"When I heard myself shouting in the theatre."

"You decided at that moment?"

"I think so. Of course I put myself through the usual examination afterward to be quite sure. But I could say that the decision was made as soon as I heard my own voice shouting."

"The usual examination? Could you tell me a little more about that, please."

"Certainly. I mean the sort of examination one always makes to determine the nature of anyone's conduct, his degree of responsibility, and all that. It was perfectly clear. I was no longer in command of my actions. Something had to be done, and I must do it before others had to do it on my behalf."

"Please tell me again about this incident when you shouted. With a little more detail, please."

"It was the day before yesterday, that is to say November ninth, at about ten forty-five p.m. in the Royal Alexandra Theatre in Toronto, which is my home. I was sitting in a bad seat in the top gallery. That in itself was unusual. The performance was something rather grandiosely called *The Soirée of Illusions*—a magic show, given by a conjuror called Magnus Eisengrim. He is well known, I understand, to people who like that kind of thing. He had an act which he called *The Brazen Head of Friar Bacon.* A large head that looked like brass, but was made of some almost transparent material, seemed to float in the middle of the stage; you couldn't see how it was done—wires of some sort, I suppose. The Head gave what purported to be advice to people in the audience. That was what infuriated me. It was imprudent, silly stuff hinting at scandal—adulteries, little bits of gossip, silly, spicy rubbish—and I felt irritation growing in me that people should be concerned about such trash. It was an unwarranted invasion of privacy, you understand, by this conjuror fellow whose confident assumption of superiority—just a charlatan, you know, seeming to patronize serious people! I knew I was fidgeting in my seat, but it wasn't until I heard my own voice that I realized I was standing up, shouting at the stage."

"And you shouted—?"

"Well, what would you expect me to shout? I shouted, as loud as I could—and that's very loud, because I have some experience of shouting—I shouted, 'Who killed Boy Staunton?' And then all hell broke loose!"

"There was a furore in the theatre?"

"Yes. A man standing in a box gave a cry and fell down. A lot of people were murmuring and some stood up to see who had shouted. But they quieted down immediately the Brazen Head began to speak."

"What did it say?"

"There are several opinions. The broadcast news reported that the Head suggested he had been killed by a gang. All I heard was something about 'the woman he knew—the woman he did not know,' which, of course, could only mean my stepmother. But I was getting away as fast as I could. It is a very steep climb up to the doors in that balcony, and I was in a state of excitement and shame at what I had done, so I didn't really hear well. I wanted to get out before I was recognized."

"Because you are Boy Staunton?"

"No, no, no; Boy Staunton was my father."

"And was he killed?"

"Of course he was killed! Didn't you read about it? It wasn't just some local murder where a miser in a slum is killed for a few hundred dollars. My father was a very important man. It's no exaggeration to say it was international news."

"I see. I am very sorry not to have known. Now, shall we go over some of your story again?"

And we did. It was long, and often painful for me, but he was an intelligent examiner, and at times I was conscious of being an unsatisfactory witness, assuming he knew things I hadn't told him, or that he couldn't know. I was ashamed of saying "of course" so often, as if I were offering direct evidence instead of stuff that was at best presumptive—something I would never tolerate in a witness myself. I was embarrassed to be such a fool in a situation that I had told myself and other people countless times I would never submit to—talking to a psychiatrist, ostensibly seeking help, but without any confidence that he could give it. I have never believed these people can do anything for an intelligent man he can't do for himself. I have known many people who leaned on psychiatrists, and every one of them was a leaner by nature, who would have leaned on a priest if he had lived in an age of faith, or leaned on a teacup-reader or an astrologer if he had not had enough money to afford the higher hokum. But here I was, and there was nothing to do now but go through with it.

It had its amusing side. I had not known what to expect, but I rather thought I would be put on a couch and asked about sex, which would have been a waste of time, as I have no sex to tell about. But here, in the office of the Director of the Jung Institute, 27 Gemeindestrasse, Zürich, there was no couch—nothing but a desk and two chairs and a lamp or two and some pictures of a generally Oriental appearance. And Dr. Tschudi. And Dr. Tschudi's big Alsatian, whose stare of polite, watchful curiosity was uncannily like the doctor's own.

"Your bodyguard?" I had said when I entered the room.

"Ha ha," laughed Dr. Tschudi in a manner I came to be well acquainted with in Switzerland; it is the manner which acknowledges politely that a joke has been made, without in any way encouraging further jokiness. But I received the impression—I am rather good at receiving impressions—that the doctor met some queer customers in that very Swiss little room, and the dog might be useful as more than a companion.

The atmosphere of the whole Jung Institute, so far as I saw it, puzzled me. It was one of those tall Zürich houses with a look that is neither domestic nor professional, but has a smack of both. I had had to ring the bell several times to be admitted through the door, the leaded glass of which made it impossible to see if anyone was coming; the secretary who let me in looked like a doctor herself, and had no eager public-relations grin; to reach Dr. Tschudi I had to climb a tall flight of stairs, which echoed and suggested my sister's old school. I was not prepared for any of this; I think I expected something that would combine the feeling of a clinic with the spookiness of a madhouse in a bad film. But this was—well, it was Swiss. Very Swiss, for though there was nothing of the cuckoo-clock, or the bank, or milk chocolate about it, it had a sort of domesticity shorn of coziness, a matter-of-factness within which one could not be quite sure of its facts, that put me at a disadvantage. And though when visiting a psychiatrist I had expected to lose something of my professional privilege of always being at an advantage, I could not be expected to like it when I encountered it.

I was an hour with the Director, and a few important things emerged. First, that he thought I might benefit by some exploratory sessions with an analyst. Second, that the analyst would not be himself, but someone he would recommend who was free to accept another patient at this time and to whom he would send a report; third, that before that I must undergo a thorough physical examination to make sure that analysis, rather than some physical treatment, was appropriate for me. Dr. Tschudi rose and shook me by the hand. I offered also to shake the paw of the Alsatian, but it scorned my jocosity, and the Director's smile was wintry.

I found myself once again in Gemeindestrasse, feeling a fool. Next morning, at my hotel, I received a note giving directions as to where my medical examination would take place. I was also instructed to call at ten o'clock in the morning, three days hence, on Dr. J. von Haller, who would be expecting me.

2

The clinic was thorough beyond anything I had ever experienced. As well as the familiar humiliations—hanging about half-naked in the company of half-naked strangers, urinating in bottles and handing them warm and steamy to very young nurses, coughing at the behest of a physician who was prodding at the back of my scrotum, answering intimate questions while the same physician thrust a long finger up my rectum and tried to catch my prostate in some irregularity, trudging up and down a set of steps while the physician counted; gasping, puffing, gagging, sticking out my tongue, rolling my eyes, and doing all the other silly tricks which reveal so much to the doctor while making the patient feel a fool—I underwent a few things that were new to me. Quite a lot of blood was taken from me at various points—much more than the usual tiny bit removed from the ear lobe. I drank a glass of a chocolate-flavoured mixture and was then, every hour for six hours, stood on my head on a movable X-ray table to which I had been strapped, as pictures were taken to see how the mess was getting through my tripes. A variety of wires was attached to me whose purpose I could only guess, but as my chair was whirled and tilted I suppose it had something to do with my nervous system, sense of balance, hearing, and all that. Countless questions, too, about how long my grandparents and parents had lived, and of what they had died. When I gave the cause of my father's death as "Murder" the clinician blinked slightly, and I was glad to have disturbed his Swiss phlegm, even for an instant. I had not been feeling well when I came to Zürich, and after two days of medical rough-house I was tired and dispirited and in a mood to go—not home, most certainly not—somewhere else. But I thought I ought to see Dr. J. von Haller at least once, if only for the pleasure of a good row with him.

Why was I so hostile toward a course of action I had undertaken of my own will? There was no single answer to that. As I told the Director, I made the decision on a basis of reason, and I would stick with it. Netty had always told me that when something unpleasant must be done—medicine taken, an apology made for bad behaviour, owning up to something that would bring a beating from my father—I had to be "a little soldier." Little soldiers, I understood, never hesitated; they did what was right without question. So I must be a little soldier and visit Dr. J. von Haller at least once.

Ah, but did little soldiers ever have to go to the psychiatrist?

They visited the dentist often, and many a time I had shouldered my little invisible musket and marched off in that direction. Was this so very different? Yes, it was.

I could understand the use of a dentist. He could grind and dig and refill, and now and then he could yank. But what could psychiatrists do? Those I had seen in court contradicted each other, threw up clouds of dust, talked a jargon which, in cross-examination, I could usually discredit. I never used them as witnesses if I could avoid it. Still, there was a widespread belief in their usefulness in cases like mine. I had to do whatever seemed best, whether I personally approved or not. To stay in Toronto and go mad simply would not do.

Why had I come to Zürich? The Director accepted it as perfectly in order for me to do so, but what did he know about my situation? Nothing would have got me to a psychiatrist in Toronto; such treatment is always supposed to be confidential, but everybody seems to know who is going regularly to certain doctors, and everybody is ready to give a guess at the reason. It is generally assumed to be homosexuality. I could have gone to New York, but everyone who did so seemed to be with a Freudian, and I was not impressed by what happened to them. Of course, it need not have been the Freudians' fault, for as I said, these people were leaners, and I don't suppose Freud himself could have done much with them. Nothing will make an empty bag stand up, as my grandfather often said. Of the Jungians I knew nothing, except that the Freudians disliked them, and one of my acquaintances who was in a Freudian analysis had once said something snide about people who went to Zürich to—

hear sermons
From mystical Germans
Who preach from ten till four.

But with a perversity that often overtakes me when I have a personal decision to make, I had decided to give it a try. The Jungians had two negative recommendations: the Freudians hated them, and Zürich was a long way from Toronto.

3

It was a sharp jolt to find that Dr. J. von Haller was a woman. I have nothing against women; it had simply never occurred to me that I might talk about the very intimate things that had brought me to Zürich with one of them. During the physical examination two of the physicians I encountered were women and I felt no qualm. They were as welcome to peep into my inside as any man that ever lived. My mind, however, was a different matter. Would a woman—could a woman—understand what was wrong? There used to be a widespread idea that women are very sensitive. My experience of them as clients, witnesses, and professional opponents had dispelled any illusions I might have had of that kind. Some women are sensitive, doubtless, but I have met with nothing to persuade me that they are, on the whole, more likely to be sensitive than men. I thought I needed delicate handling. Was Dr. J. von Haller up to the work? I had never heard of a woman psychiatrist except as someone dealing with children. My troubles were decidedly not those of a child.

Here I was, however, and there was she in a situation that seemed more social than professional. I was in what appeared to be her sitting-room, and the arrangement of chairs was so unprofessional that it was I who sat in the shadow, while the full light from the window fell on her face. There was no couch.

Dr. von Haller looked younger than I; about thirty-eight, I judged, for though her expression was youthful there was a little gray in her hair. Fine face; rather big features but not coarse. Excellent nose, aquiline if one wished to be complimentary but verging on the hooky if not. Large mouth and nice teeth, white but not American-white. Beautiful eyes, brown to go with her hair. Pleasant, low voice and a not quite perfect command of colloquial English. Slight accent. Clothes unremarkable, neither fashionable nor dowdy, in the manner Caroline calls "classic." Altogether a person to inspire confidence. But then, so am I, and I know all the professional tricks of how that is done. Keep quiet and let the client do all the talking; don't make suggestions—let the client unburden himself; watch him for revealing fidgets. She was doing all these things, but so was I. The result was a very stilted conversation, for a while.

"And it was the murder of your father that decided you to come here for treatment?"

"Doesn't it seem enough?"

"The death of his father is always a critical moment in a man's life, but usually he has time to make psychological preparation for it. The father grows old, relinquishes his claims on life, is manifestly preparing for death. A violent death is certainly a severe shock. But then, you knew your father must die sometime, didn't you?"

"I suppose so. I don't remember ever thinking about it."

"How old was he?"

"Seventy."

"Hardly a premature death. The psalmist's span."

"But this was murder."

"Who murdered him?"

"I don't know. Nobody knows. He was driven, or drove himself, off a dock in Toronto harbour. When his car was raised he was found clutching the steering-wheel so tightly that they had to pry his hands from it. His eyes were wide open, and there was a stone in his mouth."

"A stone?"

"Yes. This stone."

I held it out to her, lying on the silk handkerchief in which I carried it. Exhibit A in the case of the murder of Boy Staunton: a piece of Canadian pink granite about the size and shape of a hen's egg.

She examined it carefully. Then, slowly, she pushed it into her own mouth, and looked solemnly at me. Or was it solemnly? Was there a glint in her eye? I don't know. I was far too startled by what she had done to tell. Then she took it out, wiped it very carefully on her handkerchief, and gave it back.

"Yes; it could be done," she said.

"You're a cool customer," said I.

"Yes. This is a very cool profession, Mr. Staunton. Tell me, did no one suggest that your father might have committed suicide?"

"Certainly not. Utterly unlike him. Anyhow, why does your mind turn immediately to that? I told you he was murdered."

"But no evidence of murder was found."

"How do you know?"

"I had Dr. Tschudi's report about you, and I asked the librarian at our *Neue Zürcher Zeitung* to check their archive. They did report your father's death, you know; he had connections with several Swiss banks. The report was necessarily discreet and brief, but it seemed that suicide was the generally accepted explanation."

"He was murdered."

"Tschudi's report suggests you think your stepmother had something to do with it."

"Yes, yes; but not directly. She destroyed him. She made him unhappy and unlike himself. I never suggested she drove him off the dock. She murdered him psychologically—"

"Really? I had the impression you didn't think much of psychology, Mr. Staunton."

"Psychology plays a great part in my profession. I am rather a well-known criminal lawyer—or have you checked that, too? I have to know something about the way people function. Without a pretty shrewd psychological sense I couldn't do what I do, which is to worm things out of people they don't want to tell. That's your job, too, isn't it?"

"No. My job is to listen to people say things they very badly want to tell but are afraid nobody else will understand. You use psychology as an offensive weapon in the interest of justice. I use it as a cure. So keen a lawyer as yourself will appreciate the difference. You have shown you do. You think your stepmother murdered your father psychologically, but you don't think that would be enough to drive him to suicide. Well—I have known of such things. But if she was not the real murderer, who do you think it might have been?"

"Whoever put the stone in his mouth."

"Oh, come, Mr. Staunton, nobody could put that stone in a man's mouth against his will without breaking his teeth and creating great evidence of violence. I have tried it. Have you? No, I thought you hadn't. Your father must have put it there himself."

"Why?"

"Perhaps somebody told him to do it. Somebody he could not or did not wish to disobey."

"Ridiculous. Nobody could make Father do anything he didn't want to do."

"Perhaps he wanted to do this. Perhaps he wanted to die. People do, you know."

"He loved life. He was the most vital person I have ever known."

"Even after your stepmother had murdered him psychologically?"

I was losing ground. This was humiliating. I am a fine cross-examiner and yet here I was, caught off balance time and again by this woman doctor. Well, the remedy lay in my own hands.

"I don't think this line of discussion profitable, or likely to lead to anything that could help me," I said. "If you will be good enough to tell me your fee for the consultation, we shall close it now."

"As you wish," said Dr. von Haller. "But I should tell you that many people do not like the first consultation and want to run away. But they come back. You are a man of more than ordinary intelligence. Wouldn't it simplify things if you skipped the preliminary flight and continued? I am sure you are much too reasonable to have expected this kind of treatment to be painless. It is always difficult in the beginning for everyone, and especially people of your general type."

"So you have typed me already?"

"I beg your pardon; it would be impertinent to pretend anything of the kind. I meant only that intelligent people of wealth, who are used to having their own way, are often hostile and prickly at the beginning of analytical treatment."

"So you suggest that I bite the bullet and go on."

"Go on, certainly. But let us have no bullet-biting. I think you have bitten too many bullets recently. Suppose we proceed a little more gently."

"Do you consider it gentle to imply that my father killed himself when I tell you he was murdered?"

"I was telling you only what was most discreetly implied in the news report. I am sure you have heard the implication before. And I know how unwelcome such an implication usually is. But let us change our ground. Do you dream much?"

"Ah, so we have reached dreams already? No, I don't dream

much. Or perhaps I should say that I don't pay much attention to the dreams I have."

"Have you had any dreams lately? Since you decided to come to Zürich? Since you arrived?"

Should I tell her? Well, this was costing me money. I might as well have the full show, whatever it might be.

"Yes. I had a dream last night."

"So?"

"Quite a vivid dream, for me. Usually my dreams are just scraps—fragmentary things that don't linger. This was of quite a different order."

"Was it in colour?"

"Yes. As a matter of fact, it was full of colour."

"And what was the general tone of the dream? I mean, did you enjoy it? Was it pleasant?"

"Pleasant. Yes, I would say it was pleasant."

"Tell me what you dreamed."

"I was in a building that was familiar, though it was nowhere known to me. But it was somehow associated with me, and I was somebody of importance there. Perhaps I should say I was surrounded by a building, because it was like a college—like some of the colleges at Oxford—and I was hurrying through the quadrangle because I was leaving by the back gate. As I went under the arch of the gate two men on duty there—porters, or policemen, functionaries and guardians of some kind—saluted me and smiled as if they knew me, and I waved to them. Then I was in a street. Not a Canadian street. Much more like a street in some pretty town in England or in Europe; you know, with trees on either side and very pleasant buildings like houses, though there seemed to be one or two shops, and a bus with people on it passed by me. But I was hurrying because I was going somewhere, and I turned quickly to the left and walked out into the country. I was on a road, with the town behind me, and I seemed to be walking beside a field in which I could see excavations going on, and I knew that some ruins were being turned up. I went through the field to the little makeshift hut that was the centre of the archaeological work—because I knew that was what it was—and went in the door. The hut was very different inside from what I had expected, because as I said it looked like a temporary shelter for tools and plans and things of that kind, but inside it was Gothic; the ceiling was low, but beautifully groined in stone, and the whole affair was a stone structure. There were a couple of young men in there, commonplace-looking fellows in their twenties, I would say, who were talking at the top of what I knew was a circular staircase that led down into the earth. I wanted to go down, and I asked these fellows to let me pass, but they wouldn't listen, and though they didn't speak to me and kept on talking to one another, I could tell that they thought I was simply a nosey intruder, and had no right to go down, and probably didn't want to go down in any serious way. So I left the hut, and walked to the road, and turned back toward the town, when I met a woman. She was a strange person, like a gypsy, but not a dressed-up showy gypsy; she wore old-fashioned, ragged clothes that seemed to have been faded by sun and rain, and she had on a wide-brimmed, battered black velvet hat with some gaudy feathers in it. She seemed to have something important to say to me, and kept pestering me, but I couldn't understand anything she said. She spoke in a foreign language; Romany, I presumed. She wasn't begging, but she wanted something, all the same. I thought, 'Well, well; every country gets the foreigners it deserves'—which is a stupid remark, when you analyse it. But I had a sense that time was running short, so I hurried back to town, turned sharp to the right, this time, and almost ran into the college gate. One of the guardians called to me, 'You can just make it, sir. You won't be fined this time.' And next thing I knew I was sitting at the head of a table in my barrister's robes, presiding over a meeting. And that was it."

"A very good dream. Perhaps you are a better dreamer than you think."

"Are you going to tell me that it means something?"

"All dreams mean something."

"For Joseph and Pharaoh, or Pilate's wife, perhaps. You will have to work very hard to convince me that they mean anything here and now."

"I am sure I shall have to work hard. But just for the moment, tell me without thinking too carefully about it if you recognized any of the people in your dream."

"Nobody."

"Do you think they might be people you have not yet seen? Or had not seen yesterday?"

"Doctor von Haller, you are the only person I have seen whom I did not know yesterday."

"I thought that might be so. Could I have been anybody in your dream?"

"You are going too fast for me. Are you suggesting that I could have dreamed of you before I knew you?"

"That would certainly seem absurd, wouldn't it? Still—I asked if I could have been anybody in your dream?"

"There was nobody in the dream who could possibly have been you. Unless you are hinting that you were the incomprehensible gypsy. And you won't get me to swallow that."

"I am sure nobody could get a very able lawyer like you to swallow anything that was ridiculous, Mr. Staunton. But it is odd, don't you think, that you should dream of meeting a female figure of a sort quite outside your experience, who was trying to tell you something important that you couldn't understand, and didn't want to understand, because you were so eager to get back to your enclosed, pleasant surroundings, and your barrister's robes, and presiding over something?"

"Doctor von Haller, I have no wish to be rude, but I think you are spinning an ingenious interpretation out of nothing. You must know that until I came here today I had no idea that J. von Haller was a woman. So even if I had dreamed of coming to an analyst in this very fanciful way, I couldn't have got that fact right, could I?"

"It is not a fact, except insofar as all coincidences are facts. You met a woman in your dream, and I am a woman. But not necessarily that woman. I assure you it is nothing uncommon for a new patient to have an important and revealing dream before treatment begins—before he has met his doctor. We always ask, just in case. But an anticipatory dream containing an unknown fact is a rarity. Still, we need not pursue it now. There will be time for that later."

"Will there be any later? If I understand the dream, I cannot make head or tail of the gypsy woman with the incomprehensible conversation, and go back to my familiar world. What do you deduce from that?"

"Dreams do not foretell the future. They reveal states of mind in which the future may be implicit. Your state of mind at present is very much that of a man who wants no conversation with incomprehensible women. But your state of mind may change. Don't you think so?"

"I really don't know. Frankly, it seems to me that this meeting has been a dogfight, a grappling for advantage. Would the treatment go on like this?"

"For a time, perhaps. But it could not achieve anything on that level. Now—our hour is nearly over, so I must cut some corners and speak frankly. If I am to help you, you will have to speak to me from your best self, honestly and with trust; if you continue to speak always from your inferior, suspicious self, trying to catch me out in some charlatanism, I shall not be able to do anything for you, and in a few sessions you will break off your treatment. Perhaps that is what you want to do now. We have one minute, Mr. Staunton. Shall I see you at our next appointment, or not? Please do not think I shall be offended if you decide not to continue, for there are many patients who wish to see me, and if you knew them they would assure you that I am no charlatan, but a serious, experienced doctor. Which is it to be?"

I have always hated being put on the spot. I was very angry. But as I reached for my hat, I saw that my hand was shaking, and she saw it, too. Something had to be done about that tremor.

"I shall come at the appointed time," I said.

"Good. Five minutes before your hour, if you please. I keep a very close schedule."

And there I was, out in the street, furious with myself, and Dr. von Haller. But in a quiet corner of my mind I was not displeased that I should be seeing her again.

4

Two days passed before my next appointment, during which I changed my mind several times, but when the hour came, I was there. I had chewed over everything that had been said and had thought of a number of good things that I would have said myself if I had thought of them at the proper time. The fact that the doctor was a woman had put me out more than I cared to admit. I have my own reasons for not liking to be instructed by a woman, and by no means all of them are associated with that intolerable old afreet Netty Quelch, who has ridden me with whip and spur for as long as I can remember. Nor did I like the dream-interpretation game, which contradicted every rule of evidence known to me; the discovery of truth is one of the principal functions of the law, to which I have given the best that is in me; is truth to be found in the vapours of dreams? Nor had I liked the doctor's brusque manner of telling me to make up my mind, not to waste her time, and to be punctual. I had been made to feel like a stupid witness, which is as ridiculous an estimate of my character as anybody could contrive. But I would not retreat before Dr. Johanna von Haller without at least one return engagement, and perhaps more than that.

A directory had told me her name was Johanna. Beyond that, and that she was a Prof. Dr. med. und spezialarzt für Psychiatrie, I could find out nothing about her.

Ah well, there was the tremor of my hand. No sense in making a lot of that. Nerves, and no wonder. But was it not because of my nerves I had come to Zürich?

This time we did not meet in the sitting-room but in Dr. von Haller's study, which was rather dark and filled with books, and a few pieces of modern statuary that looked pretty good, though I could not examine them closely. Also, there was a piece of old stained glass suspended in the window, which was fine in itself, but displeased me because it seemed affected. Prominent on the desk was a signed photograph of Dr. Jung himself. Dr. von Haller did not sit behind the desk, but in a chair near my own; I knew this trick, which is supposed to inspire confidence because it sets aside the natural barrier—the desk of the professional person. I had my eye on the doctor this time, and did not mean to let her get away with anything.

She was all smiles.

"No dogfight this time, I hope, Mr. Staunton?"

"I hope not. But it is entirely up to you."

"Entirely? Very well. Before we go further, the report has come from the clinic. You seem to be in depleted general health and a little—nervous, shall we say? What used to be called neurasthenic. And some neuritic pain. Rather underweight. Occasional marked tremor of the hands."

"Recently, yes. I have been under great stress."

"Never before?"

"Now and then, when my professional work was heavy."

"How much have you had to drink this morning?"

"A good sharp snort for breakfast, and another before coming here."

"Is that usual?"

"It is what I usually take on a day when I am to appear in court."

"Do you regard this as appearing in court?"

"Certainly not. But as I have already told you several times, I have been under heavy stress, and that is my way of coping with stress. Doubtless you think it a bad way. I think otherwise."

"I am sure you know all the objections to excessive use of alcohol?"

"I could give you an excellent temperance lecture right now. Indeed, I am a firm believer in temperance for the kind of people who benefit from temperance. I am not one of them. Temperance is a middle-class virtue, and it is not my fate, or good fortune if you like that better, to be middle-class. On the contrary, I am rich and in our time wealth takes a man out of the middle class, unless he made all the money himself. I am the third generation of money in my family. To be rich is to be a special kind of person. Are you rich?"

"By no means."

"Quick to deny it, I observe. Yet you seem to live in a good professional style, which would be riches to most people in the world. Well—I *am* rich, though not so rich as people imagine. If you are rich you have to discover your own truths and make a great many of your own rules. The middle-class ethic will not serve you, and if you devote yourself to it, it will trip you up and make a fool of you."

"What do you mean by rich?"

"I mean good hard coin, Doctor. I don't mean the riches of the mind or the wealth of the spirit, or any of that pompous crap. I mean money. Specifically, I count a man rich if he has an annual income of over a hundred thousand dollars *before* taxes. If he has that he has plenty of other evidences of wealth, as well. I have considerably more than a hundred thousand a year, and I make much of it by being at the top of my profession, which is the law. I am what used to be called 'an eminent advocate.' And if being rich and being an eminent advocate also requires a drink before breakfast, I am prepared to pay the price. But to assure you that I am not wholly unmindful of my grandparents, who hated liquor as the prime work of the Devil, I always have my first drink of the day with a raw egg in it. That is my breakfast."

"How much in a day?"

"Call it a bottle, more or less. More at present, because as I keep telling you, I have been under stress."

"What made you think you needed an analyst, instead of a cure for alcoholics?"

"Because I do not think of myself as an alcoholic. To be an alcoholic is a middle-class predicament. My reputation in the country where I live is such that I would cut an absurd figure in Alcoholics Anonymous; if a couple of the brethren came to minister to me, they would be afraid of me; anyhow I don't go on the rampage or pass out or make a notable jackass of myself—I just drink a good deal and talk rather frankly. If I were to go out with another A.A. to cope with some fellow who was on the bottle, the sight of me would terrify him; he would think he had done something dreadful in his cups, and that I was his lawyer and the police were coming with the wagon. Nor would I be any good in group therapy; I took a look at that, once; I am not an intellectual snob, Doctor—at least, that is my story at present—but group therapy is too chummy for me. I lack the confessional spirit; I prefer to encourage it in others, preferably when they are in the witness-box. No, I am not an alcoholic, for alcoholism is not my disease, but my symptom."

"Then what do you call your disease?"

"If I knew, I would tell you. Instead, I hope you can tell me."

"Such a definition might not help us much at present. Let us call it stress following your father's death. Shall we begin talking about that?"

"Don't we start with childhood? Don't you want to hear about my toilet-training?"

"I want to hear about your trouble now. Suppose we begin with the moment you heard of your father's death."

"It was about three o'clock in the morning on November 4 last. I was wakened by my housekeeper, who said the police wanted to talk to me on the telephone. It was an inspector I knew who said I should come to the dock area at once as there had been an accident involving my father's car. He didn't want to say much, and I didn't want to say anything that would arouse the interest of my housekeeper, who was hovering to hear whatever she could, so I called a taxi and went to the docks. Everything there seemed to be in confusion, but in fact it was all as orderly as the situation permitted. There was a diver in a frog-man outfit, who had been down to the car first; the Fire Department had brought a crane mounted on a truck, which was raising the car; there were police cars and a truck with floodlights. I found the inspector, and he said it was my father's car for a certainty and there was a body at the wheel. So far as they could determine, the car had been driven off the end of a pier at a speed of about forty miles an hour; it had carried on some distance after getting into the water. A watchman put in an alarm as soon as he heard the splash, but by the time the police arrived it was difficult to find exactly where it was, and then all the diving, and getting the crane, and putting a chain on the front part of the frame, had taken over two hours, so that they had seen the licence plate only a matter of minutes before I was called; it was a car the police knew well. My father had a low, distinctive licence number.

"It was one of those wretched situations when you hope that something isn't true which common sense tells you is a certainty.

Nobody else drove that car except my father. At last they got it on the pier, filthy and dripping. A couple of firemen opened the doors as slowly as the weight of water inside would allow, because the police didn't want anything to be washed out that might be of evidence. But it was quickly emptied, and there he sat, at the wheel.

"I think what shocked me most was the terrible dishevelment of his body. He was always such an elegant man. He was covered with mud and oil and harbour filth, but his eyes were wide open, and he was gripping the wheel. The firemen tried to get him out, and it was then we found that his grip was so tight nothing ordinary would dislodge it. Probably you know what emergencies are like; things are done that nobody would think of under ordinary circumstances; finally they got him free of the wheel, but his hands had been terribly distorted and afterward we found that most of the fingers had been broken in doing it. I didn't blame the firemen; they did what had to be done. They laid him on a tarpaulin and then everybody held back, and I knew they were waiting for me to do something. I knelt beside him and wiped his face with a handkerchief, and it was then we saw that there was something amiss about his mouth. The police surgeon came to help me, and when my father's jaws were pried open we found the stone I showed you. The stone you tried yourself because you doubted what I told you."

"I am sorry if I shocked you. But patients come with such strange stories. Go on, please."

"I know police procedure. They were as kind as possible, but they had to take the body to the morgue, make reports, and do all the routine things that follow the most bizarre accidents. They strained a point by letting me get away with the stone, though it was material evidence; they knew I would not withhold it if it should be necessary, I suppose. Even as it was, some reporter saw me do it, or tricked the doctor into an admission, and the stone played a big part in the news. But they all had work to do, and so had I, but I had nobody to help me with my work.

"So I did what had to be done. I went at once to my father's house and wakened Denyse (that's my stepmother) and told what had happened. I don't know what I expected. Hysterics, I suppose. But she took it with an icy self-control for which I was grateful, because if she had broken down I think I would have had some sort of collapse myself. But she was extremely wilful. 'I must go to him,' she said. I knew the police would be making their examination and tried to persuade her to wait till morning. Not a chance. Go she would, and at once. I didn't want her to drive, and it is years since I have driven a car myself, so that meant rousing the chauffeur and giving some sort of partial explanation to him. Oh, for the good old days—if there ever were such days—when you could tell servants to do something without offering a lot of reasons and explanations! But at last we were at the central police station, and in the morgue, and then we had another hold-up because the police, out of sheer decency, wouldn't let her see the body until the doctor had finished and some not very efficient cleaning-up had been done. As a result, when she saw him he looked like a drunk who has been dragged in out of the rain. Then she did break down, and that was appalling for me, because you might as well know now that I heartily dislike the woman, and having to hold her and soothe her and speak comfort to her was torture, and it was then I began to taste the full horror of what had happened. The police doctor and everybody else who might have given me a hand were too respectful to intrude; wealth again, Dr. von Haller—even your grief takes on a special quality, and nobody quite likes to dry your golden tears. After a while I took her home, and called Netty to come and look after her.

"Netty is my housekeeper. My old nurse, really, and she has kept my apartment for me since my father's second marriage. Netty doesn't like my stepmother either, but she seemed the logical person to call, because she has unshakable character and authority.

"Or rather, that is what I thought. But when Netty got over to my father's house and I told her what had happened, she flew right off the handle. That is her own expression for being utterly unstrung, 'flying right off the handle.' She whooped and bellowed and made awful feminine roaring noises until I was extremely frightened. But I had to hold her and comfort her. I still don't know what ailed her. Of course my father was a very big figure in her life—as he was in the life of anybody who knew him well—but she was no kin, you know. The upshot of it was that very soon my stepmother was attending to Netty, instead of the other way round, and as the chauffeur had roused all the other servants there was a spooky gathering of half-clad people in the drawing-room, staring and wondering as Netty made a holy show of herself. I got somebody to call my sister, Caroline, and quite soon afterward she and Beesty Bastable appeared, and I have never been so glad to see them in my life.

"Caroline was terribly shocked, but she behaved well. Rather a cold woman, but not a fool. And Beesty Bastable—her husband—is one of those puffing, goggle-eyed, fattish fellows who don't seem worth their keep, but who have sometimes a surprising touch with people. It was he, really, who got the servants busy making hot drinks—and got Netty to stop moaning, and kept Caroline and my stepmother from having a fight about nothing at all, or really because Caroline started in much too soon assuming that proprietorial attitude people take toward the recently bereaved, and my stepmother didn't like being told to go and lie down in her own house.

"I was grateful to Beesty because when things were sorted out he said, 'Now for one good drink, and then nothing until we've had some sleep, what?' Beesty says 'what?' a great deal, as a lot of Old Ontario people with money tend to do. I think it's an Edwardian affectation and they haven't found out yet that it's out of fashion. But Beesty kept me from drinking too much then, and he stuck to me like a burr for hours afterward, I suppose for the same reason. Anyhow, I went home at last to my apartment, which was blessedly free of Netty, and though I didn't sleep and Beesty very tactfully kept me away from the decanters, I did get a bath, and had two hours of quiet before Beesty stuck his head into my room at eight o'clock and said he'd fried some eggs. I didn't think I wanted fried eggs; I wanted an egg whipped up in brandy, but it was astonishing how good the fried eggs tasted. Don't you think it's rather humbling how hungry calamity makes one?

"As we ate, Beesty told me what had to be done. Odd, perhaps, because he's only a stockbroker and my father and I had always tended to write him off as a fool, though decent enough. But his family is prominent, and he'd managed quite a few funerals and knew the ropes. He even knew of a good undertaker. I wouldn't have known where to look for one. I mean, who's ever met an undertaker? It's like what people say about dead donkeys: who's ever seen one? He got on the telephone and arranged with his favourite undertaker to collect the body whenever the police were ready to release it. Then he said we must talk with Denyse to arrange details of the burial. He seemed to think she wouldn't want to see us until late in the morning, but when he called she was on the line at once and said she would see us at nine o'clock and not to be late because she had a lot to do.

"That was exactly like Denyse, whom as I told you I have never liked because of this very spirit she showed when Beesty called. Denyse is all business, and nobody can help her or do anything for her without being made a subordinate: she must always be the boss. Certainly she bossed my father far more than he knew, and he was not a man to subject himself to anybody. But women are like that. Aren't they?"

"Some women, certainly."

"In my experience, women are either bosses or leaners."

"Isn't that your experience of men, too?"

"Perhaps. But I can talk to men. I can't talk to my stepmother. From nine o'clock till ten, Denyse talked to us, and would probably have talked longer if the hairdresser had not been coming. She knew she would have to see a lot of people, and it was necessary for her hair to be dressed as she would have no opportunity later.

"And what she said! My hair almost stood on end. Denyse hadn't slept either: she had been planning. And I think this is the point, Doctor, when you will admit that I have cause to be nervous. I've told you my father was a very important man. Not just rich. Not just a philanthropist. He had been in politics, and during the greater part of the Second World War he had been our Minister of Food, and an extraordinarily able one. Then he had left active politics. It was the old story, not unlike Churchill's; the public hate a really capable man except when they can't get along without him. The decisive, red-tape-cutting qualities that made my father necessary in war got him into trouble with the little men as soon as the war was over, and they hounded him out of public life. But he was too big to be ignored and his public service entitled him to recognition, and he was to be the next Lieutenant-Governor of our Province. Do you know what a Lieutenant-Governor is?"

"Some sort of ceremonial personage, I suppose."

"Yes: a representative of the Crown in a Canadian province."

"A high honour?"

"Yes, but there are ten of them. My father might suitably have been Governor-General, which is top of the heap."

"Ah yes; very grand, I see."

"Silly people smile at these ceremonial offices because they don't understand them. You can't have a parliamentary system without these official figures who represent the state, the Crown, the whole body of government, as well as the elected fellows who represent their voters.

"He had not taken office. But he had received the official notice of his appointment from the Secretary of State, and the Queen's charge would have come at the proper time, which would have been in about a month. But Denyse wanted him to be given a state funeral, as if he were already in office.

"Well! As a lawyer, I knew that was absurd. There was a perfectly valid Lieutenant-Governor at the time we were discussing this crazy scheme. There was no way in the world my father could be given an official funeral. But that was what she wanted—soldiers in dress uniform, a cushion with his D.S.O. and his C.B.E. on it, a firing-party, a flag on the coffin, as many officials and politicians as could be mustered. I was flabbergasted. But whatever I said, she simply replied, 'I know what was owing to Boy even if you don't.'

"We had a blazing row. Things were said that had poor Beesty white with misery, and he kept mumbling, 'Oh come on, Denyse, come on, Davey; let's try to get along'—which was idiotic, but poor Beesty has no vocabulary suitable to large situations. Denyse dropped any pretence of liking me and let it rip. I was a cheap mouthpiece for crooks of the worst kind, I was a known drunk, I had always resented my father's superiority and tried to thwart him whenever I could, I had said inexcusable things about her and spied on her, but on this one occasion, by the living God, I would toe the line or she would expose me to unimaginable humiliations and disgraces. I said she had made a fool of my father since first she met him, reduced his stature before the public with her ridiculous, ignorant pretensions and stupidities, and wanted to turn his funeral into a circus in which she would ride the biggest elephant.

It was plain speaking for a while, I can tell you. It was only when Beesty was near to tears—and I don't mean that metaphorically; he was sucking air noisily and mopping his eyes—and when Caroline turned up that we became a little quieter. Caroline has a scornful manner that exacts good behaviour from the humbler creation, even Denyse.

"So in the end Beesty and I were given our orders to go to the undertaker and choose a splendid coffin. Bronze would be the thing, she thought, because it would be possible to engrave directly upon it.

" 'Engrave what?' I asked. I will say for her that she had the grace to colour a little under her skilful make-up. 'The Staunton arms,' she said. 'But there aren't any—' I began, when Beesty pulled me away. 'Let her have it,' he whispered. 'But it's crooked,' I shouted. 'It's pretentious and absurd and crooked.' Caroline helped him to bustle me out of the room. 'Davey, you do it and shut up,' she said, and when I protested, 'Carol, you know as well as I do that it's illegal,' she said, 'Oh, *legal!*' with terrible feminine scorn."

5

At my next appointment, feeling rather like Scheherazade unfolding one of her never-ending, telescopic tales to King Schahriar, I took up where I had left off. Dr. von Haller had said nothing during my account of my father's death and what followed, except to check a point here and there, and she made no notes, which surprised me. Did she truly hold all the varied stories told by her patients in her head, and change from one to another every hour? Well, I did no less with the tales my clients told me.

We exchanged a few words of greeting, and I continued.

"After we had finished with the undertaker, Beesty and I had a great many details to attend to, some of them legal and some arising from the arrangement of funeral detail. I had to get in touch with Bishop Woodiwiss, who had known my father for over forty years, and listen to his well-meant condolences and go over the whole funeral routine. I went to the Diocesan House, and was a little surprised, I can't really say why, that it was so businesslike, with secretaries drinking coffee, and air-conditioning and all the atmosphere of business premises. I think I had expected crucifixes on the walls and heavy carpets. There was one door that said 'Diocesan Chancellery: Mortgages' that really astonished me. But the Bishop knew how to do funerals, and there wasn't really much to it. There were technicalities: our parish church was St. Simon's, but Denyse wanted a cathedral ceremony, as more in keeping with her notions of grandeur, and as well as the Bishop's, the Dean's consent had to be sought. Woodiwiss said he would take care of that. I still don't know why I was so touchy about the good man's words of comfort; after all, he had known my father before I was born, and had christened and confirmed me, and he had his rights both as a friend and a priest. But I felt very personally about the whole matter—"

"Possessively, would you say?"

"I suppose so. Certainly I was angry that Denyse was determined to take over and have everything her own way, especially when it was such a foolish, showy way. I was still furious about that matter of engraving the coffin with heraldic doodads that weren't ours, and couldn't ever be so, and which my father had rejected himself, after a lot of heart-searching. I want that to be perfectly clear to you; I have no quarrel with heraldry, and people who legitimately possess it can use it as they like, but the Staunton arms weren't ours. Do you want to know why?"

"Later, I think. We'll come to it. Go on now about the funeral."

"Very well. Beesty took over the job of seeing the people from the papers, but it was snatched from him by Denyse, who had prepared a handout with biographical details. Silly, of course, because the papers had that already. But she achieved one thing by it that made me furious: the only mention of my mother in the whole obituary was a reference to 'an earlier marriage to Leola Crookshanks, who died in 1942.' Her name was Cruikshank, *not* Crookshanks, and she had been my father's wife since 1924 and the mother of his children, and a dear, sad, unhappy woman. Denyse knew that perfectly well, and nothing will convince me that the mistake wasn't the result of spite. And of course she dragged in a reference to her own wretched daughter, Lorene, who has nothing to do with the Staunton family—nothing at all.

"When was the funeral to be? That was the great question. I was for getting it over as quickly as possible, but the police did not release the body until late on Monday—and *that* took some arranging, I can assure you. Denyse wanted as much time as possible to arrange her semi-state funeral and assemble all the grandees she could bully, so it was decided to have it on Thursday.

"Where was he to be buried? Certainly not in Deptford, where he was born, though his parents had providently bought a six-holer in the cemetery there years ago, and were themselves the only occupants. But Deptford wouldn't do for Denyse, so a grave had to be bought in Toronto.

"Have you ever bought a grave? It's not unlike buying a house. First of all they show you the poor part of the cemetery, and you look at all the foreign tombstones with photographs imbedded in them under plastic covers, and the inscriptions in strange languages and queer alphabets, and burnt-out candles lying on the grass, and your heart sinks. You wonder, can this be death? How sordid! Because you aren't your best self, you know; you're a stinking snob; funerals bring out that sort of thing dreadfully. You've told yourself for years that it doesn't matter what happens to a corpse, and when cocktail parties became drunken-serious you've said that the Jews have the right idea, and the quickest, cheapest funeral is the best and philosophically the most decent. But when you get into the cemetery, it's quite different. And the cemetery people know it. So you move out of the working-class and ethnic district into the area of suburban comfiness, but the gravestones are really rather close together and the inscriptions are in bad prose, and you almost expect to see jocular inscriptions like 'Take-It-Aisy' and 'Dunroamin' on the stones along with 'Till the Day Breaks' and 'In the Everlasting Arms.' Then things begin to brighten; bigger plots, no crowding, an altogether classier type of headstone and—best of all—the names of families you know. On the Resurrection Morn, after all, one doesn't want to jostle up to the Throne with a pack of strangers. And that's where the deal is settled.

"Did you know, by the way, that somebody has to own a grave? Somebody, that is, other than the occupant. I own my father's grave. A strange thought."

"Who owns your mother's grave? And why was your father not buried near her?"

"I own her grave, because I inherited it as part of my father's estate. The only bit of real estate he left me, as a matter of fact. And because she died during the war, when my father was abroad, the funeral had to be arranged by a family friend, and he just bought one grave. A good one, but single. She lies in the same desirable area as my father, but not near. As in life.

"By Tuesday night the undertakers had finished their work, and the coffin was back in his house, at the end of the drawing-room, and we were all invited in to take a look. Difficult business, of course, because an undertaker—or at any rate his embalmer—is an artist of a kind, and when someone has died by violence it's a challenge to see how well they can make him look. I must say in justice they had done well by Father, for though it would be stupid to say he looked like himself, he didn't look as though he had been drowned. But you know how it is; an extremely vital, mercurial man, who has always had a play of expression and even of colour, doesn't look like himself with a mat complexion and that inflexible calm they produce for these occasions. I have had to see a lot of people in their coffins, and they always look to me as if they were under a malign enchantment and could hear what was said and would speak if the enchantment could be broken. But there it was, and somebody had to say a kind word or two to the undertakers, and it was Beesty who did it. I was always being amazed at the things he could do in this situation, because my father and I had never thought he could do anything except manage his damned bond business. The rest of us looked with formal solemnity, just as a few years before we had gathered to look at Caroline's wedding cake with formal pleasure; on both occasions we were doing it chiefly to give satisfaction to the people who had created the exhibit.

"That night people began to call. Paying their respects is the old-fashioned phrase for it. Beesty and Caroline and I hung around in the drawing-room and chatted with the visitors in subdued voices. 'So good of you to come. . . . Yes, a very great shock. . . . It's extremely kind of you to say so. . . .' Lots of that sort of thing.

Top people from my father's business, the Alpha Corporation, doing the polite. Lesser people from the Alpha Corporation, seeing that everybody who came signed a book; a secretary specially detailed to keep track of telegrams and cables, and another to keep a list of the flowers.

"Oh, the flowers! Or, as just about everybody insisted on calling them, the 'floral tributes.' Being November, the florists were pretty well down to chrysanthemums, and there were forests of them. But of course the really rich had to express their regret with roses because they were particularly expensive at the time. The rich are always up against it, you see; they have to send the best, however much they may hate the costly flower of the moment, or somebody is sure to say they've been cheap. Denyse had heard somewhere of a coffin being covered with a blanket of roses, and she wanted one as her own special offering. It was Caroline who persuaded her to hold herself down to a decent bunch of white flowers. Or really, persuaded isn't the word; Caroline told me she was finally driven to saying, 'Are you trying to make us look like the Medici?' and that did it, because Denyse had never heard any good spoken of the Medici.

"This grisly business went on all day Wednesday. I was on duty in the morning, and received and made myself pleasant to the Mayor, the Chief of Police, the Fire Chief, a man from the Hydro-Electric Power Commission, and quite a crowd of dignitaries of one sort and another. There was a representative of the Bar Association, which called to mind the almost forgotten fact that my father's professional training had been as a lawyer; I knew this man quite well because he was a frequent associate of my own, but the others were people I knew only by name or from their pictures in the newspapers. There were bank presidents, naturally.

"Denyse, of course, did none of the receiving. It wouldn't have suited the role for which she had cast herself. Officially, she was too desolated to be on view, and only special people were taken to an upstairs room where she held state. I don't quarrel with that. Funerals are among the few ceremonial occasions left to us, and we assume our roles almost without thinking. I was the Only Son, who was bearing up splendidly, but who was also known not to be, and to have no expectation of ever being, the man his father was. Beesty was That Decent Fellow Bastable, who was doing everything he could under difficult circumstances. Caroline was the Only Daughter, stricken with grief, but of course not so catastrophically stricken as Denyse, who was the Widow and assumed to be prostrate under her affliction. Well—all right. That's the pattern, and we break patterns at our peril. After all, they became patterns because they conform to realities. I have been in favour of ceremonial and patterns all my life, and I have no desire to break the funeral pattern. But there was too much real feeling behind the pattern for me to be anything other than wretchedly overwrought, and the edicts Denyse issued from her chamber of affliction were the worst things I had to bear.

"Her edict that at all costs I was to be kept sober, for instance. Beesty was very good about that. Not hatefully tactful, you know, but he said plainly that I had to do a great many things that needed a level head and I'd better not drink much. He knew that for me not drinking much meant drinking what would be a good deal for him, but he gave me credit for some common sense. And Caroline was the same. 'Denyse is determined that you're going to get your paws in the sauce and disgrace us all. So for God's sake spite her and don't,' was the way she put it. Even Netty, after her first frightful outburst, behaved very well and didn't try to watch over me for my own good, though she lurked a good deal. Consequently, though I drank pretty steadily, I kept well within my own appointed bounds. But I hated Denyse for her edict.

"Nor was that her only edict. On Wednesday, before lunch, she called Beesty to her and told him to get me to look over my father's will that afternoon, and see her after I had done so. This was unwarrantable interference. I knew I was my father's principal executor, and I knew, being a lawyer, what had to be done. But it isn't considered quite the thing to get down to business with the will before the funeral is over. There's nothing against it, particularly if there is suspicion of anything that might prove troublesome in the will, but in my father's case that was out of the question. I didn't know what was in the will, but I was certain it was all in perfect order. I thought Denyse was rushing things in an unseemly way.

"I suppose if you are to do anything for me, Doctor, I must be as frank as possible. I didn't want to look at the will until it became absolutely necessary. There have been difficulties about wills in our family. My father had a shock when he read his own father's will, and he had spoken to me about it more than once. And relations between my father and myself had been strained since his marriage to Denyse. I thought there might be a nasty surprise for me in the will. So I put my foot down and said nothing could be done until Thursday afternoon.

"I don't know why I went to my father's house so early on Thursday, except that I woke with an itching feeling that there was a great deal to be settled, and I would find out what it was when I was on the spot. And I wanted to take farewell of my father. You understand? During the last forty-eight hours it had been impossible to be alone in the room with his body, and I thought if I were early I could certainly manage it. So I went to the drawing-room as softly as possible, not to attract attention, and found the doors shut. It was half-past seven, so there was nothing unusual about that.

"But from inside there were sounds of a man's voice and a woman's voice, apparently quarrelling, and I heard scuffling and thudding. I opened the door, and there was Denyse at the coffin, holding up my father's body by the shoulders, while a strange man appeared to be punching and slapping its face. You know what people say in books—'I was thunderstruck . . . my senses reeled.' "

"Yes. It is a perfectly accurate description of the sensation. It is caused by a temporary failure of circulation to the head. Go on."

"I shouted something. Denyse dropped the body, and the man jumped backward as if he thought I might kill him. I knew him then. He was a friend of Denyse's, a dentist; I had met him once or twice and thought him a fool.

"The body had no face. It was entirely covered in some shiny pinkish material, so thickly that it was egglike in its featurelessness. It was this covering they were trying to remove.

"I didn't have to ask for an explanation. They were unnerved and altogether too anxious to talk. It was a story of unexampled idiocy.

"This dentist, like so many of Denyse's friends, was a dabbler in the arts. He had a tight, ill-developed little talent as a sculptor, and he had done a few heads of Chairmen of the Faculty of Dentistry at the University, and that sort of thing. Denyse had been visited by one of her dreadful inspirations, that this fellow should take a death-mask of my father, which could later be used as the basis for a bust or perhaps kept for itself. But he had never done a corpse before, and it is quite a different business from doing a living man. So, instead of using plaster, which is the proper thing if you know how to work it, he had the lunatic idea of trying some plastic mess used in his profession for taking moulds, because he thought he could get a greater amount of detail, and quicker. But the plastic wasn't for this sort of work, and he couldn't get it off!

"They were panic-stricken, as they had every right to be. The room was full of feeling. Do you know what I mean? The atmosphere was so alive with unusual currents that I swear I could feel them pressing on me, making my ears ring. Don't say it was all the whisky I had been drinking. I was far the most self-possessed of us three. I swear that all the tension seemed to emanate from the corpse, which was in an unseemly state of dishevelment, with coat and shirt off, hair awry, and half-tumbled out of that great expensive coffin.

"What should I have done? I have gone over that moment a thousand times since. Should I have seized the poker and killed the dentist, and forced Denyse's face down on that dreadful plastic head and throttled her, and then screamed for the world to come and look at the last scene of some sub-Shakespearean tragedy? What in fact I did was to order them both out of the room, lock it, telephone the undertakers to come at once, and then go into the downstairs men's room and vomit and gag and retch until I was on the floor with my head hanging into the toilet bowl, in a classic Skid Row mess.

"The undertakers came. They were angry, as they had every right to be, but they were fairly civil. If a mask was wanted, they asked, why had they not been told? They knew how to do it. But what did I expect of them now? I had pulled myself together, though I knew I looked like a drunken wreck, and I had to do whatever talking was done. Denyse was upstairs, having divorced herself in that wonderful feminine way from the consequences of her actions, and I am told the dentist left town for a week.

"It was a very bad situation. I heard one of the undertakers ask the butler if he could borrow a hammer, and I knew the worst. After a while I had my brief time beside my father's coffin; the undertakers did not spare me that. The face was very bad, some teeth had been broken; no eyebrows or lashes, and a good deal of the front hair was gone. Much worse than when he lay on the dock, covered in oil and filth, with that stone in his mouth.

"So of course we had what is called a closed-coffin funeral. I know they are common here, but in North America it is still usual to have the corpse on display until just before the burial service begins. I sometimes wonder if it is a hold-over from pioneer days, to assure everybody that there has been no foul play. That was certainly not the case this time. We had had fool play. I didn't explain to Caroline and Beesty; simply said Denyse had decided she wanted it that way. I know Caroline smelled a rat, but I told her nothing because she might have done something dreadful to Denyse.

"There we all were, in the cathedral, with Denyse in the seat of the chief mourner, of course, and looking so smooth a louse would have slipped off her, as Grandfather Staunton used to say. And he would certainly have said I looked like the Wreck of the Hesperus; it was one of his few literary allusions.

"There was the coffin, so rich, so bronzey, so obviously the sarcophagus of somebody of the first rank. Right above where that pitifully misused face lay hidden was the engraving of the Staunton arms: Argent two chevrons sable within a bordure engrailed of the same. Crest, a fox statant proper. Motto, *En Dieu ma foy.*

"Bishop Woodiwiss might have been in on the imposture, so richly did he embroider the *En Dieu ma foy* theme. I have to give it to the old boy; he can't have seen that engraving until the body arrived at the cathedral door, but he seized on the motto and squeezed it like a bartender squeezing a lemon. It was the measure of our dear brother gone, he said, that the motto of his ancient family should have been this simple assertion of faith in Divine Power and Divine Grace, and that never, in all the years he had known Boy Staunton, had he heard him mention it. No: deeds, not words, was Boy Staunton's mode of life. A man of action; a man of great affairs; a man loving and tender in his personal life, open-handed and perceptive in his multitudinous public benefactions, and the author of countless unknown acts of simple generosity. But no jewel of great price could be concealed forever, and here we saw, at last, the mainspring of Boy Staunton's great and—yes, he would say it, he would use the word, knowing that we would understand it in its true sense—his beautiful life. *En Dieu ma foy.* Let us all carry that last word from a great man away with us, and feel that truly, in this hour of mourning and desolation, we had found an imperishable truth. *En Dieu ma foy.*

"Without too much wriggling, I was able to look about me. The congregation was taking it with that stuporous receptivity which is common to Canadians awash in oratory. The man from the Prime Minister's department, sitting beside the almost identical man from the Secretary of State's department; the people from the provincial government; the civic officials; the Headmaster of Colborne School; the phalanx of rich business associates: not one of them looked as if he were about to leap up and shout, 'It's a God-damned lie; his lifelong motto wasn't *En Dieu ma foy* but *En moi-même ma foy* and that was his tragedy.' I don't suppose they knew. I don't suppose that even if they knew, they cared. Few of them could have explained the difference between the two faiths.

"My eye fell on one man who could have done it. Old Dunstan Ramsay, my father's lifelong friend and my old schoolmaster, was there, not in one of the best seats—Denyse can't stand him—but near a stained-glass window through which a patch of ruby light fell on his handsome ravaged old mug, and he looked like a devil hot from hell. He didn't know I was looking, and at one point, when Woodiwiss was saying *En Dieu ma foy* for the sixth or seventh time, he grinned and made that snapping motion with his mouth that some people have who wear ill-fitting false teeth.

"Is this hour nearly finished, by the way? I feel wretched."

"I am sure you do. Have you told anyone else about the death-mask?"

"Nobody."

"That was very good of you."

"Did I hear you correctly? I thought you analysts never expressed opinions."

"You will hear me express many opinions as we get deeper in.

It is the Freudians who are so reserved. You have your schedule of appointments? No doubts about coming next time?"

"None."

6

Back again, after two days' respite. No: respite is not the word. I did not dread my appointment with Dr. von Haller, as one might dread a painful or depleting treatment of the physical kind. But my nature is a retentive, secretive one, and all this revelation went against the grain. At the same time, it was an enormous relief. But after all, what was there in it? Was it anything more than Confession, as Father Knopwood had explained it when I was confirmed? Penitence, Pardon, and Peace? Was I paying Dr. von Haller thirty dollars an hour for something the Church gave away, with Salvation thrown in for good measure? I had tried Confession in my very young days. Father Knopwood had not insisted that I kneel in a little box, while he listened behind a screen; he had modern ways, and he sat behind me, just out of sight, while I strove to describe my boyish sins. Of course I knelt while he gave me Absolution. But I had always left the two or three sessions when I tried that feeling a fool. Nevertheless, despite our eventual quarrel, I wouldn't knock Knopwood now, even to myself; he had been a good friend to me at a difficult time in my life—one of the succession of difficult times in my life—and if I had not been able to continue in his way, others had. Dr. von Haller now—had it something to do with her being a woman? Whatever it was, I looked forward to my next hour with her in a state of mind I could not clarify, but which was not wholly disagreeable.

"Let me see; we had finished your father's funeral. Or had we finished? Does anything else occur to you that you think significant?"

"No. After the Bishop's sermon, or eulogy or whatever it was, everything seemed to be much what one might have expected. He had so irrevocably transposed the whole thing into a key of fantasy, with his rhapsodizing on that irrelevant motto, that I went through the business at the cemetery without any real feeling, except wonderment. Then perhaps of the funeral people a hundred and seventy trooped back to the house for a final drink—a lot of drinking seems to go on at funerals—and stayed for a fork lunch, and when that was over I knew that all my time of grace had run out and I must get on with the job of the will.

"Beesty would have been glad to help me, I know, and Denyse was aching to see it, but she wasn't in a position to bargain with me after the horrors of the morning. So I picked up copies for everybody concerned from my father's solicitors, who were well known to me, and took them to my own office for a careful inspection. I knew I would be cross-examined by several people, and I wanted to have all the facts at my finger-tips before any family discussion.

"It was almost an anticlimax. There was nothing in the will I had not foreseen, in outline if not in detail. There was a great deal about his business interests, which were extensive, but as they boiled down to shares in a single controlling firm called Alpha Corporation it was easy, and his lawyers and the Alpha lawyers would navigate their way through all of that. There were no extensive personal or charity bequests, because he left the greatest part of his Alpha holdings to the Castor Foundation.

"That's a family affair, a charitable foundation that makes grants to a variety of good, or apparently good, causes. Such things are extremely popular with rich families in North America. Ours had a peculiar history, but it isn't important just now. Briefly, Grandfather Staunton set it up as a fund to assist temperance movements. But he left some loose ends, and he couldn't resist some fancy wording about 'assisting the public weal,' so when father took it over he gently eased all the preachers off the board and put a lot more money into it. Consequence: we now support the arts and the social sciences, in all their lunatic profusion. The name is odd. Means 'beaver' of course, and so it has Canadian relevance; but it also means a special type of sugar—do you know the expression castor-sugar, the kind that goes in shakers?—and my father's money was made in part from sugar. He began in sugar. The name was suggested years ago as a joke by my father's friend Dunstan

Ramsay; but Father liked it, and used it when he created the Foundation. Or, rather, when he changed it from the peculiar thing it was when Grandfather Staunton left it.

"This large bequest to Castor ensured the continuance of all his charities and patronages. I was pleased, but not surprised, that he had given a strong hint in the will that he expected me to succeed him as Chairman of Castor. I already had a place on its Board. It's a very small Board—as small as the law will permit. So by this single act he had made me a man of importance in the world of benefactions, which is one of the very few remaining worlds where the rich are allowed to say what shall be done with the bulk of their money.

"But there was a flick of the whip for me in the latter part of the will, where the personal bequests were detailed.

"I told you that I am a rich man. I should say that I have a good deal of money, caused, if not intended, by a bequest from my grandfather, and I make a large income as a lawyer. But compared with my father I am inconsiderable—just 'well-to-do,' which was the phrase he used to dismiss people who were well above the poverty line but cut no figure in the important world of money. First-class surgeons and top lawyers and some architects were well-to-do, but they manipulated nothing and generated nothing in the world where my father trod like a king.

"So I wasn't looking for my bequest as something that would greatly change my way of life or deliver me from care. No, I wanted to know what my father had done about me in his will because I knew it would be the measure of what he thought of me as a man, and as his son. He obviously thought I could handle money, or he wouldn't have tipped me for the chairmanship of Castor. But what part of his money—and you must understand money meant his esteem and his love—did he think I was worth?

"Denyse was left very well off, but she got no capital—just a walloping good income for life or—this was Father speaking again—so long as she remained his widow. I am sure he thought he was protecting her against fortune-hunters; but he was also keeping fortune-hunters from getting their hands on anything that was, or had been, his.

"Then there was a bundle for 'my dear daughter, Caroline' which was to be hers outright and without conditions—because Beesty could have choked on a fishbone at his club any day and Caroline remarried at once and Father wouldn't have batted an eye.

"Then there was a really large capital sum in trust 'for my dear grandchildren, Caroline Elizabeth and Boyd Staunton Bastable, portions to be allotted *per stirpes* to any legitimate children of my son Edward David Staunton from the day of their birth.' There it was, you see."

"Your father was disappointed that you had no children?"

"Certainly that is how he would have expected it to be interpreted. But didn't you notice that I was simply his son, when all the others were his dear this and dear that? Very significant, in something carefully prepared by Father. It would be nearer the truth to say he was angry because I wouldn't marry—wouldn't have anything to do with women at all."

"I see. And why is that?"

"It's a very long and complicated story."

"Yes. It usually is."

"I'm not a homosexual, if that's what you are suggesting."

"I am not suggesting that. If there were easy and quick answers, psychiatry would not be very hard work."

"My father was extremely fond of women."

"Are you fond of women?"

"I have a very high regard for women."

"That is not what I asked."

"I like them well enough."

"Well enough for what?"

"To get along pleasantly with them. I know a lot of women."

"Have you any women friends?"

"Well—in a way. They aren't usually interested in the things I like to talk about."

"I see. Have you ever been in love?"

"In love? Oh, certainly."

"Deeply in love?"

"Yes."

"Have you had sexual intercourse with women?"

"With a woman."

"When last?"

"It would be—let me think for a moment—December 26, 1945."

"A very lawyer-like answer. But—nearly twenty-three years ago. How old were you?"

"Seventeen."

"Was it with the person with whom you were deeply in love?"

"No, no; certainly not!"

"With a prostitute?"

"Certainly not."

"We seem to be approaching a painful area. Your answers are very brief, and not up to your usual standard of phrasing."

"I am answering all your questions, I think."

"Yes, but your very full flow of explanation and detail has dried up. And our hour is drying up, as well. So there is just time to tell you that next day we should take another course. Until now we have been clearing the ground, so to speak. I have been trying to discover what kind of man you are, and I hope you have been discovering something of what I am, as well. We are not really launched on analysis, because I have said little and really have not helped you at all. If we are to go on—and the time is very close when you must make that decision—we shall have to go deeper, and if that works, we shall then go deeper still, but we shall not continue in this extemporaneous way. Just before you go, do you think that by leaving you nothing in his will except this possibility of money for your children, your father was punishing you—that in his own terms he was telling you he didn't love you?"

"Yes."

"And you care whether he loved you or not?"

"Must it be called love?"

"It was your own word."

"It's a very emotional term. I cared whether he thought I was a worthy person—a man—a proper person to be his son."

"Isn't that love?"

"Love between father and son isn't something that comes into society nowadays. I mean, the estimate a man makes of his son is in masculine terms. This business of love between father and son sounds like something in the Bible."

"The patterns of human feeling do not change as much as many people suppose. King David's estimate of his rebellious son Absalom was certainly in masculine terms. But I suppose you recall David's lament when Absalom was slain?"

"I have been called Absalom before, and it isn't a comparison I like."

"Very well. There is no point in straining an historical comparison. But do you think your father might have meant something more than scoring a final blow in the contest between you when he arranged his will as he did?"

"He was an extremely direct man in most things, but in personal relationships he was subtle. He knew the will would be studied by many people and that they would know he had left me obligations suitable to a lawyer but nothing that recognized me as his child. Many of these people would know also that he had had great hopes of me at one time, and had named me after his hero, who had been Prince of Wales when I was born, and that therefore something had gone wrong and I had been a disappointment. It was a way of driving a wedge between me and Caroline, and it was a way of giving Denyse a stick to beat me with. We had had some scenes about this marriage and woman business, and I would never give in and I would never say why. But he knew why. And this was his last word on the subject: spite me if you dare; live a barren man and a eunuch; but don't think of yourself as my son. That's what it meant."

"How much does it mean to you to think of yourself as his son?"

"The alternative doesn't greatly attract me."

"What alternative is that?"

"To think that I am Dunstan Ramsay's son."

"The friend? The man who was grinning at the funeral?"

"Yes. It has been hinted. By Netty. And Netty might just have known what she was talking about."

"I see. Well, we shall certainly have much to talk about when next we meet. But now I must ask you to give way to my next patient."

I never saw these next patients or the ones who had been with the doctor before me because her room had two doors, one from the waiting-room but the other giving directly into the corridor. I was glad of this arrangement, for as I left I must have looked very queer. What had I been saying?

7

"Let me see; we had reached Friday in your bad week, had we not? Tell me about Friday."

"At ten o'clock, the beginning of the banking day, George Inglebright and I had to meet two men from the Treasury Department in the vault of the bank to go through my father's safety-deposit box. When somebody dies, you know, all his accounts are frozen and all his money goes into a kind of limbo until the tax people have had a full accounting of it. It's a queer situation because all of a sudden what has been secret becomes public business, and people you've never seen before outrank you in places where you have thought yourself important. Inglebright had warned me to be very quiet with the tax men. He's a senior man in my father's firm of lawyers, and of course he knows the ropes, but it was new to me.

"The tax men were unremarkable fellows, but I found it embarrassing to be locked up in one of the bank's little cubbyholes with them while we counted what was in the safety-deposit box. Not that I counted; I watched. They warned me not to touch anything, which annoyed me because it suggested I might snatch a bundle of brightly coloured stock certificates and make a run for it. What was in the box was purely personal, not related to Alpha or any of the companies my father controlled. It wasn't as personal as I feared, however; I've heard stories of safety-deposit boxes with locks of hair, and baby shoes, and women's garters, and God knows what in them. But there was nothing of that sort. Only shares and bonds amounting to a very large amount, which the tax men counted and inventoried carefully.

"One of the things that bothered me was that these men, obviously not paid much, were cataloguing what was in itself a considerable fortune: what did they think? Were they envious? Did they hate me? Were they glorying in their authority? Were they conscious of putting down the mighty from their seat and exalting the humble and meek? They looked crusty and non-committal, but what was going on in their heads?

"It took most of the morning and I had nothing whatever to do but watch, which I found exhausting because of the reflections it provoked. It was the kind of situation that leads one to trite philosophizing: here is what remains of a very large part of a life's effort—that kind of thing. Now and then I thought about the chairmanship of Castor, and a phrase I hadn't heard since my law-student days came into my head and wouldn't be driven out. *Damnosa hereditas;* a ruinous inheritance. It's a phrase from Roman Law; comes in Gaius's *Institutes,* and means exactly what it says. Castor could very well be that to me because it is big already, and with what will come into it from my father's estate it will be a very large charitable foundation even by American standards, and being the head of it will devour time and energy and could very well be the end of the kind of career I have tried to make for myself. *Damnosa hereditas.* Did he mean it that way? Probably not. One must assume the best. Still—

"I gave George lunch, then marched off like a little soldier to talk to Denyse and Caroline about the will. They had had a chance to go over their own copies, and Beesty had explained most of it, but he isn't a lawyer and they had a lot of points they wanted clarified. And of course there was a row, because I think Denyse had expected some capital, and in fairness I must say that she was within her rights to do so. What really burned her, I think, was that there was nothing for her daughter Lorene, though what she had been left for herself would have been more than enough to take care of all that. Lorene is soft in the head, you see, though Denyse pretends otherwise, and she will have to be looked after all her life. Although Lorene's name was never mentioned, I could sense her presence; she had called my father Daddy-Boy, and Daddy-Boy hadn't lived up to expectation.

"Caroline is above fussing about inheritances. She is really a very fine person, in her frosty way. But naturally she was pleased to have been taken care of so handsomely, and Beesty was openly delighted. After all, with the trust money and Caroline's personal fortune and what would come from himself and his side of the family, his kids were in the way of being rich even by my father's demanding standards. Both Caroline and Beesty saw how I had been dealt with, but they were too tactful to say anything about it in front of Denyse.

"Not so Denyse herself. 'This was Boy's last chance to get you back on the rails, David,' said she, 'and for his sake I hope it works.'

" 'What particular rails are you talking about?' I said. I knew well enough, but I wanted to hear what she would say. And I will admit I led her on to put her foot in it because I wanted a chance to dislike her even more than I did already.

" 'To be utterly frank, dear, he wanted you to be married, and to have a family, and to cut down on your drinking. He knew what a balancing effect a wife and children have on a man of great talents. And of course everybody knows that you have great talents—potentially.' Denyse was not one to shrink from a challenge.

" 'So he has left me the toughest job in the family bundle, and some money for children I haven't got,' I said. 'Do you happen to know if he had anybody in mind that he wanted me to marry? I'd like to be sure of everything that is expected of me.'

"Beesty was wearing his toad-under-the-harrow expression, and Caroline's eyes were fierce. 'If you two are going to fight, I'm going home,' she said.

" 'There will be no fighting,' said Denyse. 'This is not the time or the place. David asked a straight question and I gave him a straight answer—as I have always done. And straight answers are something David doesn't like except in court, where he can ask the questions that will give him the answers he wants. Boy was very proud of David's success, so far as it went. But he wanted something from his only son that goes beyond a somewhat notorious reputation in the criminal courts. He wanted the continuance of the Staunton name. He would have thought it pretentious to talk of such a thing, but you know as well as I do that he wanted to establish a line.'

"Ah, that line. My father had not been nearly so reticent about mentioning it as Denyse pretended. She has never understood what real reticence is. But I was sick of the fight already. I quickly tire of quarrelling with Denyse. Perhaps, as she says, I only like quarrelling in court. In court there are rules. Denyse makes up her rules as she goes along. As I must say women tend to do. So the talk shifted, not very easily, to other things.

"Denyse had two fine new bees in her bonnet. The death-mask idea had failed, and she knew I would not tell the others, so as far as she was concerned it had perished as though it had never been. She does not dwell on her failures.

"What she wanted now was a monument for my father, and she had decided that a large piece of sculpture by Henry Moore would be just the thing. Not to be given to the Art Gallery or the City, of course. To be put up in the cemetery. I hope that gives you the measure of Denyse. No sense of congruity; no sense of humour; no modesty. Just ostentation and gall working under the governance of a fashionable, belligerent, unappeasable ambition.

"Her second great plan was for a monument of another kind; she announced with satisfaction that my father's biography was to be written by Dunstan Ramsay. She had wanted Eric Roop to do it—Roop was one of her protégés and as a poet he was comparable to her dentist friend as a sculptor—but Roop had promised himself a fallow year if he could get a grant to see him through it. I knew this already, because Roop's fallow years were as familiar to Castor as Pharaoh's seven lean kine, and his demand that we stake him to another had been circulated to the Board, and I had seen it. The Ramsay plan had merit. Dunstan Ramsay was not only a schoolmaster but an author who had enjoyed a substantial success in a queer field: he wrote about saints—popular books for tourists, and at least one heavy-weight work that had brought him a reputation in the places where such things count.

"Furthermore, he wrote well. I knew because he had been my history master at school; he insisted on essays in what he called the Plain Style; it was, he said, much harder to get away with nonsense in the Plain Style than in a looser manner. In my legal work I had found this to be true and useful. But—what would we look like if a life of Boy Staunton appeared over the name of a man notable as a student of the lives of saints? There would be jokes, and one or two of them occurred to me immediately.

"On the other hand, Ramsay had known my father from boyhood. Had he agreed? Denyse said he had wavered a little when she put it to him, but she would see that he made up his mind. After all, his own little estate—which was supposed to be far beyond what a teacher and author could aspire to—was built on the advice my father had given him over the years. Ramsay had a nice little block of Alpha. The time had come for him to pay up in his own coin. And Denyse would work with him and see that the job was properly done and Ramsay's ironies kept under control.

"Neither Caroline nor I was very fond of Ramsay, who had been a sharp-tongued nuisance in our lives, and we were amused to think of a collaboration between him and our stepmother. So we made no demur, but determined to spike the Henry Moore plan.

"Caroline and Beesty got away as soon as they could, but I had to wait and hear Denyse talk about the letters of condolence she had been receiving in bulk. She graded them; some were Official, from public figures, and subdivided into Warm and Formal; some were from personal friends, and these she classified as Moving and Just Ordinary; and there were many from Admirers, and the best of these were graded Touching. Denyse has an orderly mind.

"We did not talk about a dozen or so hateful letters of abuse that had come unsigned. Nor did we say much about the newspaper pieces, some of which had been grudging and covertly offensive. We were both habituated to the Canadian spirit, to which generous appreciation is so alien.

"It had been a wearing afternoon, and I had completed all my immediate tasks, so I thought I would permit myself a few drinks after dinner. I dined at my club and had the few drinks, but to my surprise they did nothing to dull my wretchedness. I am not a man who is cheered by drink. I don't sing or make jokes or chase girls, nor do I stagger and speak thickly; I become remote—possibly somewhat glassy-eyed. But I do manage to blunt the edge of that heavy axe that seems always to be chopping away at the roots of my being. That night it was not so. I went home and began to drink seriously. Still the axe went right on with its destructive work. At last I went to bed and slept wretchedly.

"It is foolish to call it sleep. It was a long, miserable reverie, relieved by short spells of unconsciousness. I had a weeping fit, which frightened me because I haven't cried for thirty years; Netty and my father had no use for boys who cried. It was frightening because it was part of the destruction of my mind that was going on; I was being broken down to a very primitive level, and absurd kinds of feeling and crude, inexplicable emotions had taken charge of me.

"Imagine a man of forty crying because his father hadn't loved him! Particularly when it wasn't true, because he obviously had loved me, and I know I worried him dreadfully. I even sank so low that I wanted my mother, though I knew that if that poor woman could have come to me at that very time, she wouldn't have known what to say or do. She never really knew what was going on, poor soul. But I wanted something, and my mother was the nearest identification I could find for it. And this blubbering booby was Mr. David Staunton, Q.C., who had a dark reputation because the criminal world thought so highly of him, and who played up to the role, and who secretly fancied himself as a magician of the courtroom. But in the interest of justice, mind you; always in the constant and perpetual wish that everyone shall have his due.

"Next morning the axe was making great headway, and I began with the bottle at breakfast, to Netty's indignation and dismay. She didn't say anything, because once before when she had interfered I had given her a few sharp cuffs, which she afterward exaggerated into 'beating her up.' Netty hasn't seen some of the beatings-up I have observed in court or she wouldn't talk so loosely. She has never mastered the Plain Style. Of course I had been regretful for having struck her, and apologized in the Plain Style, but she understood afterward that she was not to interfere.

"So she locked herself in her room that Saturday morning, taking care to do it when I was near enough to hear what she was doing; she even pushed the bed against the door. I knew what she was up to; she wanted to be able to say to Caroline, 'When he's like that I just have to barricade myself in, because if he flew off the handle like he did that time, the Dear knows what could happen to me.' Netty liked to tell Caroline and Beesty that nobody knew what she went through. They had a pretty shrewd notion that most of what she went through was in her own hot imagination.

"I went back to my club for luncheon on Saturday, and although the barman was as slow as he could be when I wanted him, and absent from the bar as much as he could manage, I got through quite a lot of Scotch before I settled down to having a few drinks before dinner. A member I knew called Femister came in and I heard the barman mutter something to him about 'tying on a bun' and I knew he meant me.

"A bun! These people know nothing. When I bend to the work it is no trivial bun, but a whole baking of double loaves I tie on. Only this time nothing much seemed to be happening, except for a generalized remoteness of things, and the axe was chopping away as resolutely as ever. Femister is a good fellow, and he sat down by me and chatted. I chatted right back, clearly and coherently, though perhaps a little fancifully. He suggested we have dinner together, and I agreed. He ate a substantial club dinner, and I messed my food around on my plate and tried to take my mind off its smell, which I found oppressive. Femister was kindly, but my courteous *non sequiturs* were just as discouraging as I meant them to be, and after dinner it was clear that he had had all the Good Samaritan business he could stand.

" 'I've got an appointment now,' he said. 'What are you going to do? You certainly don't want to spend the evening all alone here, do you? Why don't you go to the theatre? Have you seen this chap at the Royal Alec? Marvellous! Magnus Eisengrim his name is, though it sounds unlikely, doesn't it? The show is terrific! I've never seen such a conjuror. And all the fortune-telling and answering questions and all that. Terrific! It would take you right out of yourself.'

" 'I can't imagine anywhere I'd rather be,' I said, slowly and deliberately. 'I'll go. Thank you very much for suggesting it. Now you run along, or you'll miss your appointment.'

"Off he went, grateful to have done something for me and to have escaped without trouble. He wasn't telling me anything I didn't already know. I had been to Eisengrim's *Soirée of Illusions* the week before, with my father and Denyse and Lorene, whose birthday it was. I was sucked into it at the last minute, and had not liked the show at all, though I could see that it was skilful. But I detested Magnus Eisengrim.

"Shall I tell you why? Because he was making fools of us all, and so cleverly that most of us liked it; he was a con man of a special kind, exploiting just that element in human credulity that most arouses me—I mean the *desire* to be deceived. You know that maddening situation that lies behind so many criminal cases, where somebody is so besotted by somebody else that he lays himself open to all kinds of cheating and ill-usage, and sometimes to murder?

It isn't love, usually; it's a kind of abject surrender, an abdication of common sense. I am a victim of it, now and then, when feeble clients decide that I am a wonder-worker and can do miracles in court. I imagine you get it, as an analyst, when people think you can unweave the folly of a lifetime. It's a powerful force in life, yet so far as I know it hasn't even a name—"

"Excuse me—yes, it has a name. We call it projection."

"Oh. I've never heard that. Well, whatever it is, it was going full steam ahead in that theatre, where Eisengrim was fooling about twelve hundred people, and they were delighted to be fooled and begging for more. I was disgusted, and most of all with the nonsense of the Brazen Head.

"It was second to the last illusion on his program. I never saw the show to the end. I believe it was some sexy piece of nonsense vaguely involving Dr. Faustus. But *The Brazen Head of Friar Bacon* was what had caused the most talk. It began in darkness, and slowly the light came up inside a big human head that floated in the middle of the stage, so that it glowed. It spoke, in a rather foreign voice. 'Time is,' it said, and there was a tremble of violins; 'Time was,' it said, and there was a chord of horns; 'Time's past,' it said, and there was a very quiet ruffle of drums, and the lights came up just enough for us to see Eisengrim—he wore evening clothes, but with knee-breeches, as if he were at Court—who told us the legend of the Head that could tell all things.

"He invited the audience to lend him objects, which his assistants sealed in envelopes and carried to the stage, where he mixed them up in a big glass bowl. He held up each envelope as he chose it by chance, and the Head identified the owner of the hidden object by the number of the seat in which he was sitting. Very clever, but it made me sick, because people were so delighted with what was, after all, just a very clever piece of co-operation by the magician's troupe.

"Then came the part the audience had been waiting for and that caused so much sensation through the city. Eisengrim said the Head would give personal advice to three people in the audience. This had always been sensational, and the night I was there with my father's theatre party the Head had said something that brought the house down, to a woman who was involved in a difficult legal case; it enraged me because it was virtually contempt of court—a naked interference in something that was private and under the most serious consideration our society provides. I had talked a great deal about it afterward, and Denyse had told me not to be a spoil-sport, and my father had suggested that I was ruining Lorene's party—because of course this sort of nonsense was just the kind of thing a fool like Lorene would think marvellous.

"So you see I wasn't in the best mood for the *Soirée of Illusions,* but some perversity compelled me to go, and I bought a seat in the top gallery, where I assumed nobody would know me. A lot of people had been going to this show two and even three times, and I didn't want anybody to say I had been among their number.

"The program was the same, but the flatness I had expected in a show I had seen before was notably missing, and that annoyed me. I didn't want Eisengrim to be as good as he was. I thought him dangerous and I grudged him the admiration the audience plainly felt for him. The show was very clever; I must admit that. It had real mystery, and beautiful girls very cleverly and tastefully displayed, and there was a quality of fantasy about it that I have never seen in any other magician's performance, and very rarely in the theatre.

"Have you ever seen the Habima Players do *The Dybbuk?* I did, long ago, and this had something of that quality about it, as if you were looking into a stranger and more splendid world than the one you know—almost a solemn joy. But I had not lost my grievance, and the better *The Soirée of Illusions* was, the more I wanted to wreck it.

"I suppose the drink was getting to me more than I knew, and I muttered two or three times until people shushed me. When *The Brazen Head of Friar Bacon* came, and the borrowed objects had been identified, and Eisengrim was promising his answers to secret questions, I suddenly heard myself shouting, 'Who killed Boy Staunton?' and I found I was on my feet, and there was a sensation in the theatre. People were staring at me. There was a crash in one of the boxes, and I had the impression that someone had fallen and knocked over some chairs. The Head began to glow, and I heard the foreign voice saying something that seemed to begin, 'He was killed by a gang . . .' then something about 'the woman he knew . . . the woman he did not know,' but really I can't be sure what I heard because I was dashing up the steps of the balcony as hard as I could go—they are very steep—and then pelting down two flights of stairs, though I don't think anybody was chasing me. I rushed into the street, jumped into one of the taxis that had begun to collect at the door, and got back to my apartment, very much shaken.

"But it was as I was leaving the theatre in such a sweat that the absolute certainty came over me that I had to do something about myself. That is why I am here."

"Yes, I see. I don't think there can be any doubt that it was a wise decision. But in the letter from Dr. Tschudi he said something about your having put yourself through what you called 'the usual examination.' What did you mean?"

"Ah—well. I'm a lawyer, as you know."

"Yes. Was it some sort of legal examination, then?"

"I am a thorough man. I think you might say a whole-hearted man. I believe in the law."

"And so—?"

"You know what the law is, I suppose? The procedures of law are much discussed, and people know about lawyers and courts and prisons and punishment and all that sort of thing, but that is just the apparatus through which the law works. And it works in the cause of justice. Now, justice is the constant and perpetual wish to render to everyone his due. Every law student has to learn that. A surprising number of them seem to forget it, but I have not forgotten it."

"Yes, I see. But what is 'the usual examination'?"

"Oh, it's just a rather personal thing."

"Of course, but clearly it is an important personal thing. I should like to hear about it."

"It is hard to describe."

"Is it so complex, then?"

"I wouldn't say it was complex, but I find it rather embarrassing."

"Why?"

"To someone else it would probably seem to be a kind of game."

"A game you play by yourself?"

"You might call it that, but it misrepresents what I do and the consequences of what I do."

"Then you must be sure I do not misunderstand. Is this game a kind of fantasy?"

"No, no; it is very serious."

"All real fantasy is serious. Only faked fantasy is not serious. That is why it is so wrong to impose faked fantasy on children. I shall not laugh at your fantasy. I promise. Now—please tell me what 'the usual examination' is."

"Very well, then. It's a way I have of looking at what I have done, or might do, to see what it is worth. I imagine a court, you see, all perfectly real and correct in every detail. I am the Judge, on the Bench. And I am the prosecuting lawyer, who presents whatever it is in the worst possible light—but within the rules of pleading. That means I may not express a purely personal opinion about the rights or wrongs of the case. But I am also the defence lawyer, and I put the best case I can for whatever is under examination—but again I mayn't be personal and load the pleading. I can even call myself into the witness-box and examine and cross-examine myself. And in the end Mr. Justice Staunton must make up his mind and give a decision. And there is no appeal from that decision."

"I see. A very complete fantasy."

"I suppose you must call it that. But I assure you it is extremely serious to me. This case I am telling you about took several hours. I was charged with creating a disturbance in a public place while under the influence of liquor, and there were grave special circumstances—creating a scandal that could seriously embarrass the Staunton family, for one."

"Surely that is a moral rather than a legal matter?"

"Not entirely. And anyhow, the law is, among other things, a codification of a very large part of public morality. It expresses the moral opinion of society on a great number of subjects. And in Mr. Justice Staunton's court, morality carries great weight. It's obvious."

"Truly? What makes it obvious?"

"Oh, just a difference in the Royal Arms."

"The Royal Arms?"

"Yes. Over the judge's head, where they are always displayed."

"And what is the difference? . . . Another of your pauses, Mr. Staunton. This must mean a great deal to you. Please describe the difference."

"It's nothing very much. Only that the animals are complete."

"The animals?"

"The supporters, they are called. The Lion and the Unicorn."

"And are they sometimes incomplete?"

"Almost always in Canada. They are shown without their privy parts. To be heraldically correct they should have distinct, rather saucy pizzles. But in Canada we geld everything, if we can, and dozens of times I have sat in court and looked at those pitifully deprived animals and thought how they exemplified our attitude toward justice. Everything that spoke of passion—and when you talk of passion you talk of morality in one way or another—was ruled out of order or disguised as something else. Only Reason was welcome. But in Mr. Justice Staunton's court the Lion and the Unicorn are complete, because morality and passion get their due there."

"I see. Well, how did the case go?"

"It hung, in the end, on the McNaghton Rule."

"You must tell me what that is."

"It is a formula for determining responsibility. It takes its name from a nineteenth-century murderer called McNaghton whose defence was insanity. He said he did it when he was not himself. This was the defence put forward for Staunton. The prosecution kept hammering away at Staunton to find out whether, when he shouted in the theatre, he fully understood the nature and quality of his act, and if he did, did he know it was wrong? The defence lawyer—Mr. David Staunton, a very eminent Q.C.—urged every possible extenuating circumstance: that the prisoner Staunton had been under severe stress for several days; that he had lost his father in a most grievous fashion, and that he had undergone severe psychological harassment because of that loss; that unusual responsibilities and burdens had been placed upon him; that his last hope of regaining the trust and approval of his late father had been crushed. But the prosecutor—Mr. David Staunton, Q.C., on behalf of the Crown—would not recognize any of that as exculpatory, and in the end he put the question that defence had been dreading all along. 'If a policeman had been standing at your elbow, would you have acted as you did? If a policeman had been in the seat next to you, would you have shouted your scandalous question at the stage?' And of course the prisoner Staunton broke down and wept and had to say, 'No,' and then, to all intents, the case was over. The Judge—Mr. Justice Staunton, known for his fairness but also for his sternness—didn't even leave the Bench. He found the prisoner Staunton guilty, and the sentence was that he should seek psychiatric help at once."

"Then what did you do?"

"It was seven o'clock on Sunday morning. I called the airport, booked a passage to Zürich, and twenty-four hours later I was here. Three hours after arrival I was sitting in Dr. Tschudi's office."

"Was the prisoner Staunton very much depressed by the outcome of the case?"

"It could hardly have been worse for him, because he has a very poor opinion of psychiatry."

"But he yielded?"

"Doctor von Haller, if a wounded soldier in the eighteenth century had been told he must have a battlefield amputation, he would know that his chances of recovery were slim, but he would have no choice. It would be: die of gangrene or die of the surgeon's knife. My choice in this instance was to go mad unattended or to go mad under the best obtainable auspices."

"Very frank. We are getting on much better already. You have begun to insult me. I think I may be able to do something for you, Prisoner Staunton."

"Do you thrive on insult?"

"No. I mean only that you have begun to feel enough about me to want to strike some fire out of me. That is not bad, that comparison between eighteenth-century battlefield surgery and modern psychiatry; this sort of curative work is still fairly young and in the way it is sometimes practised it can be brutal. But there were recoveries, even from eighteenth-century surgery, and as you point out, the alternative was an ugly one.

"Now let us get down to work. The decisions must be entirely yours. What do you expect of me? A cure for your drunkenness?

You have told me that it is not your disease, but your symptom; symptoms cannot be cured—only alleviated. Illnesses can be cured when we know what they are and if circumstances are favourable. Then the symptoms abate. You have an illness. You have talked of nothing else. It seems very complicated, but all descriptions of symptoms are complicated. What did you expect when you came to Zürich?"

"I expected nothing at all. I have told you that I have seen many psychiatrists in court, and they are not impressive."

"That's nonsense. You wouldn't have come if you hadn't had some hope, however reluctant you were to admit it. If we are to achieve anything you must give up the luxury of easy despair. You are too old for that, though in certain ways you seem young for your age. You are forty. That is a critical age. Between thirty-five and forty-five everybody has to turn a corner in his life, or smash into a brick wall. If you are ever going to gain a measure of maturity, now is the time. And I must ask you not to judge psychiatrists on what you see in court. Legal evidence and psychological evidence are quite different things, and when you are on your native ground in court, with your gown on and everything going your way, you can make anybody look stupid, and you do—"

"And I suppose the converse is that when you have a lawyer in your consulting-room, and you are the doctor, you can make him look stupid and you do?"

"It is not my profession to make anyone look stupid. If we are to do any good here, we must be on terms that are much better than that; our relationship must go far beyond merely professional wrangling for trivial advantages."

"Do you mean that we must be friends?"

"Not at all. We must be on doctor-and-patient terms, with respect on both sides. You are free to dispute and argue anything I say if you must, but we shall not go far if you play the defence lawyer every minute of our time. If we go on, we shall be all kinds of things to each other, and I shall probably be your stepmother and your sister and your housekeeper and all sorts of people in the attitude you take toward me before we are through. But if your chief concern is to maintain your image of yourself as the brilliant, drunken counsel with a well-founded grudge against life, we shall take twice as long to do our work because that will have to be changed before anything else can be done. It will cost you much more money, and I don't think you like wasting money."

"True. But how did you know?"

"Call it a trade secret. No, that won't do. We must not deal with one another in that vein. Just recognize that I have had rich patients before, and some of them are great counters of their pennies. . . . Would you like a few days to consider what you are going to do?"

"No. I've already decided. I want to go ahead with the treatment."

"Why?"

"But surely you know why."

"Yes, but I must find out if you know why."

"You agree with me that the drinking business is a symptom, and not my disease?"

"Let us not speak of disease. A disease in your case would be a psychosis, which is what you fear and what of course is always possible. Though the rich are rarely mad. Did you know that? They may be neurotic and frequently they are. Psychotic, rarely. Let us say that you are in an unsatisfactory state of mind and you want to get out of it. Will that do?"

"It seems a little mild, for what has been happening to me."

"You mean, like your Netty, nobody knows what you are going through? I assure you that very large numbers of people go through much worse things."

"Aha, I see where we are going. This is to destroy my sense of uniqueness. I've had lots of that in life, I assure you."

"No, no. We do not work on the reductive plan, we of the Zürich School. Nobody wants to bring your life's troubles down to having been slapped because you did not do your business on the pot. Even though that might be quite important, it is not the mainspring of a life. You are certainly unique. Everyone is unique. Nobody has ever suffered quite like you before because nobody has ever been you before. But we are members of the human race, as well, and our unique quality has limits. Now—about treatment. There are a few simple things to begin with. You had better leave your hotel and take rooms somewhere. There are quite good pensions where you can be quiet, and that is important. You must have quiet and retirement, because you will have to do a good deal of work yourself between appointments with me, and you will find that tiring."

"I hate pensions. The food is usually awful."

"Yes, but they have no bars, and they are not pleased if guests drink very much in their rooms. It would be best if it were inconvenient, but not impossible, for you to drink very much. I think you should try to ration yourself. Don't stop. Just take it gently. Our Swiss wines are very nice."

"Oh God! Don't talk about *nice* wine."

"As you please. But be prudent. Much of your present attitude toward things comes from the exacerbations of heavy drinking. You say it doesn't affect you, but of course it does."

"I know people who drink just as much as I do and are none the worse."

"Yes. Everybody knows such people. But you are not one of them. After all, you would not be in that chair if you were."

"If we are not going to talk about my toilet-training, what is the process of your treatment? Bullying and lectures?"

"If necessary. But it isn't usually necessary, and when it is, that is only a small part of the treatment."

"Then what are you going to do?"

"I am not going to *do* anything to you. I am going to try to help you in the process of becoming yourself."

"My best self, I expected you to say. A good little boy."

"Your real self may not be a good little boy. It would be very unfortunate if that were so. Your real self may be something very disagreeable and unpleasant. This is not a game we are playing, Mr. Staunton. It can be dangerous. Part of my work is to see the dangers as they come and help you to get through them. But if the dangers are inescapable and possibly destructive, don't think I can help you to fly over them. There will be lions in the way. I cannot pull their teeth or tell them to make paddy-paws; I can only give you some useful tips about lion-taming."

"Now you're trying to scare me."

"I am warning you."

"What do we do to get to the lions?"

"We can start almost anywhere. But from what you have told

me I think we would be best to stick to the usual course and begin at the beginning."

"Childhood recollections?"

"Yes, and recollections of your life up to now. Important things. Formative experiences. People who have meant much to you, whether good or bad."

"That sounds like the Freudians."

"We have no quarrel with the Freudians, but we do not put the same stress on sexual matters as they do. Sex is very important, but if it were the single most important thing in life it would all be much simpler, and I doubt if mankind would have worked so hard to live far beyond the age when sex is the greatest joy. It is a popular delusion, you know, that people who live very close to nature are great ones for sex. Not a bit. You live with primitives—I did it for three years, when I was younger and very interested in anthropology—and you find out the truth. People wander around naked and nobody cares—not even an erection or a wiggle of the hips. That is because their society does not give them the brandy of Romance, which is the great drug of our world. When sex is on the program they sometimes have to work themselves up with dances and ceremonies to get into the mood for it, and then of course they are very active. But their important daily concern is with food. You know, you can go for a lifetime without sex and come to no special harm. Hundreds of people do so. But you go for a day without food and the matter becomes imperative. In our society food is just a start for our craving. We want all kinds of things—money, a big place in the world, objects of beauty, learning, sainthood, oh, a very long list. So here in Zürich we try to give proper attention to these other things, as well.

"We generally begin with what we call *anamnesis*. Are you a classicist? Do you know any Greek? We look at your history, and meet some people there whom you may know or perhaps you don't, but who are portions of yourself. We take a look at what you remember, and at some things you thought you had forgotten. As that goes on we find we are going much deeper. And when that is satisfactorily explored, we decide whether to go deeper still, to that part of you which is beyond the unique, to the common heritage of mankind."

"How long does it take?"

"It varies. Sometimes long, sometimes surprisingly short, especially if you decide not to go beyond the personal realm. And though of course I give advice about that, the decision, like all the decisions in this sort of work, must be your own."

"So I should begin getting a few recollections together? I don't want to be North American about this, but I haven't unlimited time. I mean, three years or anything of that sort is out of the question. I'm the executor of my father's will. I can do quite a lot from here by telephone or by post but I can't be away forever. And there is the problem of Castor to be faced."

"I have always understood that it takes about three years to settle an estate. In civilized countries, that is; there are countries here in Europe where it can go on for ten if there is enough money to pay the costs. Does it impress you as interesting that to settle a dead man's affairs takes about the same length of time as settling a life's complications in a man of forty? Still, I see your difficulty. And that makes me wonder if a scheme I have been considering for you might not be worth a trial."

"What are you thinking of?"

"We do many things to start the stream of recollection flowing in a patient, and to bring forth and give clues to what is important for him. Some patients draw pictures, or paint, or model things in clay. There have even been patients who have danced and devised ceremonies that seemed relevant to their situation. It must be whatever is most congenial to the nature of the analysand."

"Analysand? Am I an analysand?"

"Horrid word, isn't it? I promise I shall never call you that. We shall stick to the Plain Style, shall we, in what we say to one another?"

"Ramsay always insisted that there was nothing that could not be expressed in the Plain Style if you knew what you were talking about. Everything else was Baroque Style, which he said was not for most people, or Jargon, which was the Devil's work."

"Very good. Though you must be patient, because English is not my cradle-tongue, and my work creates a lot of Jargon. But about you, and what you may do; I think you might create something, but not pictures or models. You are a lawyer, and you seem to be a great man for words: what would you say to writing a brief of your case?"

"I've digested hundreds of briefs in my time."

"Yes, and some of them were for cases pleaded before Mr. Justice Staunton."

"This would be for the case pleaded in the court of Mr. Justice von Haller."

"No, no; Mr. Justice Staunton still. You cannot get away from him, you know."

"I haven't often pleaded very successfully for the defendant Staunton in that court. The victories have usually gone to the prosecution. Are you sure we need to do it this way?"

"I think there is good reason to try. It is the heroic way, and you have found it without help from anyone else. That suggests that heroic measures appeal to you, and that you are not really afraid of them."

"But that was just a game."

"You played it with great seriousness. And it is not such an uncommon game. Do you know Ibsen's poem—

> To live is to battle with trolls
> in the vaults of heart and brain.
> To write: that is to sit
> in judgement over one's self.

I suggest that you make a beginning. Let it be a brief for the defence; you will inevitably prepare a brief for the prosecution as you do so, for that is the kind of court you are to appear in—the court of self-judgement. And Mr. Justice Staunton will hear all, and render judgement, perhaps more often than is usual."

"I see. And what are you in all this?"

"Oh, I am several things; an interested spectator, for one, and for another, I shall be a figure that appears only in military courts, called Prisoner's Friend. And I shall be an authority on precedents, and germane judgements, and I shall keep both the prosecutor and the defence counsel in check. I shall be custodian of that constant and perpetual wish to render to everyone his due. And if Mr. Justice Staunton should doze, as judges sometimes do—"

"Not Mr. Justice Staunton. He slumbers not, nor sleeps."

"We shall see if he is as implacable as you suppose. Even Mr. Justice Staunton might learn something. A judge is not supposed to be an enemy of the prisoner, and I think Mr. Justice Staunton sounds a little too eighteenth century in his outlook to be really good at his work. Perhaps we can lure him into modern times, and get him to see the law in a modern light. . . . And now—until Monday, isn't it?"

· II ·
David Against the Trolls

(This is my Zürich Notebook, containing notes and summaries used by me in presenting my case to Dr. von Haller; also memoranda of her opinions and interpretations as I made them after my hours with her. Without being a verbatim report, this is the essence of what passed between us.)

1

IT IS NOT EASY to be the son of a very rich man.

This could stand as an epigraph for the whole case, for and against myself, as I shall offer it. Living in the midst of great wealth without being in any direct sense the possessor of it has coloured every aspect of my life and determined the form of all my experience.

Since I entered school at the age of seven I have been aware that one of the inescapable needs of civilized man—the need for money—showed itself in my life in a way that was different from the experience of all but a very few of my acquaintances. I knew the need for money. Simple people seem to think that if a family has money, every member dips what he wants out of some ever-replenished bag that hangs, perhaps, by the front door. Not so. I knew the need for money, as I shall demonstrate, with special acuteness because although as a boy I was known to be the son of a very rich man, I had in fact a smaller allowance than was usual in my school. I knew that my carefulness about buying snacks or a ticket to the movies was a source of amusement and some contempt among the other boys. They thought I was mean. But I knew that I was supposed to be learning to manage money wisely, and that this was a part of the great campaign to make a man of me. The other boys could usually get an extra dollar or two from their fathers, and were virtually certain to be able to raise as much again from their mothers; to them their allowance was a basic rather than an aggregate income. Their parents were good-natured and didn't seem to care whether, at the age of nine or ten, they could manage money or not. But with my dollar a week, of which ten cents was earmarked for Sunday-morning church, and much of which might be gobbled up by a sudden need for a pair of leather skate-laces or something of that sort, I had to be prudent.

My father had read somewhere that the Rockefeller family preserved and refined the financial genius of the Primal Rockefeller by giving their children tiny allowances with which they had learned, through stark necessity, to do financial miracles. It may have been fine for the Rockefellers, but it was no good for me. My sister Caroline usually had lots of money because she was under no necessity to become a man and had to have money always about her for unexplained reasons connected with protecting her virtue. Consequently I was always in debt to Caroline, and because she domineered over me about it I was always caught up in some new method of scrimping or cheese-paring. When I was no more than eight a boy at school told my friends that Staunton was so mean he would skin a louse for the hide and tallow. I was ashamed and hurt; I was not a mini-miser: I was simply, in terms of my situation, poor. I knew it; I hated it; I could not escape from it.

I am not asking for pity. That would be absurd. I lived among the trappings of wealth. Our chauffeur dropped me at school every morning from a limousine that was an object of wonder to car-minded little boys. I was not one of them; to me a car was, and still is, anything that—mysteriously and rather alarmingly—goes. In the evening, after games, he picked me up again, and as Netty was usually with him, ready to engulf me, it was impossible for me to offer car-fanciers a ride. At home we lived in what I now realize was luxury, and certainly in most ways it was less troublesome than real poverty, which I have since had some opportunities to examine. I was enviable, and if I had the power to cast curses, I should rank the curse of being enviable very high. It has extensive ramifications and subtle refinements. As people assured me from time to time, I had everything. If there was anything I wanted, I could get it by asking my father for it and convincing him that I really needed it and was not merely yielding to a childish whim. This was said to be a very simple matter, but in my experience it might have been simple for Cicero on one of his great days. My father would listen carefully, concealing his amusement as well as he could, and in the end he would knuckle my head affectionately and say: "Davey, I'll give you a piece of advice that will last you all your life: never buy anything unless you really need it; things you just *want* are usually junk."

I am sure he was right, and I have always wished I could live according to his advice. I have never managed it. Nor did he, as I gradually became aware, but somehow that was different. I needed to be made into a man, and he was fully and splendidly and obviously a man. Everybody knew it.

Lapped as I was in every comfort, and fortunate above other boys, how could I have thought I needed money?

What I did need, and very badly, was character. Manhood. The ability to stand on my own feet. My father left me in no doubt about these things, and as my father loved me very much there could be no question that he was right. Love, in a parent, carries with it extraordinary privileges and unquestionable insight. This was one of the things which was taken for granted in our family, and so it did not need to be said.

Was I then a poor little rich boy, wistful for the pleasures available to my humble friends, the sons of doctors and lawyers and architects, most of whom could not have passed even the hundred-thousand-a-year test? Not at all. Children do not question their destiny. Indeed, children do not live their lives; their lives, on the contrary, live them. I did not imagine myself to be the happiest of mortals because no such concept as happiness ever entered my head, though sometimes I was happy almost to the point of bursting. I was told I was fortunate. Indeed, Netty insisted that I thank God for it every night, on my knees. I believed it, but I wondered why I was thanking God when it was so obviously my father who was the giver of all good things. I considered myself and my family to be the norm of human existence, by which all other lives were to be measured. I knew I had troubles because I was short of pocket-money, but this was trivial compared with the greater trouble of not being sure I would ever be a man, and able to stand on my own two feet, and be worthy of my father's love and trust. I was told that everything that happened to me was for my good, and by what possible standard of judgement would I have reached a dissenting opinion?

So you must not imagine I have come here to whine and look for revenge on the dead; this retrospective spiting and birching of parents is one of the things that gets psychoanalysis a bad name. As a lawyer I know there is a statute of limitations on personal and spiritual wrongs as well as on legal ones, and that there is no court in the world that can provide a rescript on past griefs. But if some thoughtful consideration of my past can throw useful light on my present, I have the past neatly tucked away and can produce it on demand.

DR. VON HALLER: Yes, I think that would be best. You have got into your swing, and done all the proper lawyer-like things. So now let us get on.

MYSELF: What do you mean, exactly, by "the proper lawyer-like things"?

DR. VON HALLER: Expressing the highest regard for the person you are going to destroy. Declaring that you have no real feeling in the matter and are quite objective. Suggesting that something is cool and dry which by its nature is hot and steamy. Very good. Continue, please.

MYSELF: If you don't believe what I say, what is the point of continuing? I have said I am not here to blacken my father; I don't know what else I can do to convince you that I speak sincerely.

DR. VON HALLER: Very plainly you must go on, and convince me that way. But I am not here to help you preserve the *status quo*, and leave all your personal relationships exactly as you believe them to be now. Remember, among other things, I am Prisoner's Friend. You know what a friend is, I suppose?

MYSELF: Frankly, I'm not sure that I do.

DR. VON HALLER: Well—let us hope you will find out. About your early childhood—?

I was born on September 2, 1928, and christened Edward David because my father had been an aide-de-camp—and a friend, really—of the Prince of Wales during his 1927 tour of Canada. My father sometimes jokingly spoke of the Prince as my godfather, though he was nothing of the kind. My real godfathers were a club friend of Father's named Dorris and a stockbroker named Taylor, who moved out of our part of the world not long after my christening; I have no recollection of either of them. I think they had just been roped in to fill a gap, and Father had dropped them both by the time I was ready to take notice. But the Prince sent me a mug with his cipher on it, and I used to drink my milk from it; I still have it, and Netty keeps it polished.

I had a number of childhood diseases during my first two years, and became what is called "delicate." This made it hard to keep nurses, because I needed a lot of attention, and children's nurses are scarce in Canada and consequently don't have to stay in demanding places. I had English and Scots nurses to begin with, I believe, and later I used to hear stories of the splendid outfits they wore, which were the wonder of the part of Toronto where we lived. But none of them stuck, and it was my Grandmother Staunton who said that what I needed was not one of those stuck-up Dolly Vardens but a good sensible girl with her head screwed on straight who would do what she was told. That was how Netty Quelch turned up. Netty has been with us ever since.

Because I was delicate, life in the country was thought good for me, and for all of my early years I spent long summers with my grandparents in Deptford, the little village where they lived. My upbringing was a good deal dominated by my grandparents at that time because neither of my parents could stand Deptford, though they had both been born there, and referred to it between themselves as "that hole." So every May I was shipped off to Deptford, and stayed till the end of September, and my memories of it are happy. I suppose unless you are unlucky, anywhere you spend your summers as a child is an Arcadia forever. My grandmother couldn't

coddling. He looked, in fact, not unlike J. P. Morgan, and like Morgan he had a big strawberry nose. I know he liked me, but it was not his way to show affection, though on a few occasions he called me "boykin," an endearment nobody else used. He had great resources of dissatisfaction and disapproval, but he never vented them on me. However, so much of his conversation with my grandmother was rancorous about the government, or Deptford, or his employees, or his handful of remaining patients, that I felt him to be dangerous and never took liberties.

Netty held him in great awe because he was rich, and a doctor, and looked on life as a serious, desperate struggle. As I grew older, I found out more about him by snooping in his office. He had qualified as a physician in 1887, but before that he had done some work, under the old Upper Canada medical-apprentice system, with a Dr. Gamsby, who had been the first doctor in Deptford. He had retained all Doc Gamsby's professional equipment, for he was never a man to get rid of anything, and it lay in neglect and disorder in a couple of glass-fronted cases in his office, a fearful museum of rusty knives, hooks, probes, speculums, and even a wooden stethoscope like a little flageolet. And Doc Gamsby's books! When I could give Netty the slip—and she never thought of looking for me in Grandfather's consulting-room, which was holy ground to her—I would very quietly lift one out of the shelves and gloat over engravings of people swathed in elaborate bandages, or hiked up in slings for "luxations," or being cauterized, or—this was an eye-popper—being reamed out for fistula. There were pictures of amputations of all kinds, with large things like pincers for cutting off breasts, diggers for getting at polyps in the nose, and fierce saws for bone. Grandfather did not know I looked at his books, but once, when he met me in the hall outside his room, he beckoned me in and took something out of Doc Gamsby's cabinet.

"Look at this, David," he said. "Any idea what that might be?"

It was a flat metal plate about six inches by three, and perhaps three-quarters of an inch thick, and at one end of it was a round button.

"That's for rheumatism," he said. "People with rheumatism always tell the doctor they can't move. Seized right up so they can't budge. Now this thing here, Davey, is called a scarifier. Suppose a man has a bad back. Nothing helps him. Well, in the old days, they'd hold this thing here right tight up against where he was stiff, and then they'd press this button—"

Here he pressed the button, and from the surface of the metal plate leapt twelve tiny knife-points, perhaps an eighth of an inch long.

"Then he'd budge," said Grandfather, and laughed.

His laugh was one I have never heard in anyone else; he did not blow laughter out, he sucked it in, with a noise that sounded like snuk-snuk, snuk-snuk, snuk.

He put the scarifier away and took out a cigar and hooked the spittoon toward him with his foot, and I knew I was dismissed, having had my first practical lesson in medicine.

What he taught Netty was the craft of dealing with constipation. He had been trained in an era when this was a great and widespread evil, and in rural districts it was, as he himself said with unconscious humour, a corker. Farm people understandably dreaded their draughty privies in winter and cultivated their powers of retention to a point where, in my grandfather's opinion, they were inviting every human ill. During his more active days as a doctor he had warred against constipation, and he kept up the campaign at home. Was I delicate? Obviously I was full of poisons, and he knew what to do. On Friday nights I was given cascara sagrada, which rounded up the poisons as I slept, and on Saturday morning, before breakfast, I was given a glass of Epsom salts to drive them forth. On Sunday morning, therefore, I was ready for church as pure as the man from whom Paul drove forth the evil spirits. But I suppose I became habituated to these terrible weekly aids, and nothing happened in between. Was Doc Staunton beaten? He was not. I was a candidate for Dr. Tyrrell's Domestic Internal Bath.

This nasty device had been invented by some field-marshal in the war against auto-intoxication, and it was supposed to bring all the healing miracle of Spa or Aix-les-Bains to its possessor. It was a rubber bag of a disagreeable gray colour, on the upper side of which was fixed a hollow spike of some hard, black composition. It was filled with warm water until it was fat and ugly; I was impaled on the spike, which had been greased with Vaseline; a control stopcock was turned, and my bodily weight was supposed to force the water up inside me to seek out the offending substances. I was not quite heavy enough, so Netty helped by pushing downward on my shoulders. As I was dismayingly invaded below, her breath, like scorching beef, blew in my face. Oh, Calvary!

Grandfather had made a refinement of his own on the great invention of Dr. Tyrrell; he added slippery elm bark to the warm water, as he had a high opinion of its healing and purgative properties.

I hated all of this, and most of all the critical moment when I was lifted off the greasy spike and carried as fast as Netty could go to the seat of ease. I felt like an overfilled leather bottle, and was in dread lest I should spill. But I was a child, and my wise elders, led by all-knowing Grandfather Staunton, who was a doctor and could see right through you, had decreed this misery as necessary. Did Grandfather Staunton ever resort to the Domestic Internal Bath himself? I once asked timidly. He looked me in the eye and said solemnly that there had been a time when, he was convinced, he owed his life to its efficacy. There was no answer to that except the humblest acquiescence.

Was I therefore a spiritless child? I don't think so. But I seem to have been born with an unusual regard for authority and the power of reason, and I was too small to know how readily these qualities can be brought to the service of the wildest nonsense and cruelty. Any comment?

DR. VON HALLER: Are you constipated now?

MYSELF: No. Not when I eat.

DR. VON HALLER: All of this is still only part of the childhood scene. We usually remember painful and humiliating things. But are they all of what we remember? What pleasant recollections of childhood have you? Would you say that on the whole you were happy?

MYSELF: I don't know about "on the whole." Sensations in childhood are so intense I can't pretend to recall their duration. When I was happy I was warmly, brimmingly happy, and when I was unhappy I was in hell.

DR. VON HALLER: What is the earliest recollection you can honestly vouch for?

MYSELF: Oh, that's easy. I was standing in my grandmother's garden, in warm sunlight, looking into a deep red peony. As I recall it, I wasn't much taller than the peony. It was a moment of very great—perhaps I shouldn't say happiness, because it was really an intense absorption. The whole world, the whole of life, and I myself, became a warm, rich peony-red.

DR. VON HALLER: Have you ever tried to recapture that feeling?

MYSELF: Never.

DR. VON HALLER: Well, shall we go on with your childhood?

MYSELF: Aren't you even interested in Netty and the Domestic Internal Bath? Nothing about homosexuality yet?

DR. VON HALLER: Have you ever subsequently felt drawn toward the passive role in sodomy?

MYSELF: Good God, no!

DR. VON HALLER: We shall keep everything in mind. But we need more material. Onward, please. What other happy recollections?

Church-going. It meant dressing up, which I liked. I was an observant child, so the difference between Toronto church and Deptford church kept me happy every Sunday. My parents were Anglicans, and I knew this was a sore touch with my grandparents, who belonged to the United Church of Canada, which was a sort of amalgam of Presbyterians and Methodists, and Congregationalists, too, wherever there happened to be any. Its spirit was evangelical and my grandmother, who was the child of the late Reverend Ira Boyd, a hell-fire Methodist, was evangelical; she had family prayers every morning, and Netty and I and the hired girl all had to be there; Grandfather wasn't able to make it very often, but the general feeling was that he didn't need it because of being a doctor. She read a chapter of the Bible every day of her life. And this was the 'thirties, mind you, not the reign of Queen Victoria. So I was put in the way of thinking a lot about God, and wondering what God thought about me. As with the Prince of Wales, I suspected that He thought rather well of me.

As for church, I liked to compare the two rituals to which I was exposed. The Uniteds didn't think they were ritualists, but that was not how it looked to me. I acquired some virtuosity in ritual. In the Anglican church I walked in smiling, bent my right knee just the proper amount—my father's amount—before going into the pew, and then knelt on the hassock, gazing with unnaturally wide-open eyes at the Cross on the altar. In the United Church, I put on a meek face, sat forward in my pew, and leaned downward, with my hand shielding my eyes, and inhaled the queer smell of the hymn-books in the rack in front of me. In the Anglican church I nodded my head, as if to say "Quite so," or (in the slang of the day) "Hot spit!" whenever Jesus was named in a hymn. But in the United Church if Jesus turned up I sang the name very low, and in the secret voice I used when talking to my grandmother about what my bowels were doing. And of course I was aware that the United minister wore a black robe, a great contrast to Canon Woodiwiss's splendid and various vestments, and that Communion at Deptford meant that everybody got a little dose of something in his pew, and there was no walking about and traffic control by the sidesmen, as at St. Simon Zelotes. It was a constant, delightful study, and I appreciated all its refinements. This won me a reputation outside the family as a pious child, and I think I was held up to lesser boys as an example. Imagine it—rich *and* pious! I suppose I bodied forth some ideal for a lot of people, as the plaster statues of the Infant Samuel at Prayer used to do in the nineteenth century.

Sunday was always a great day. Dressing up, my hobby of ritual study, and a full week to go before another assault on my uncooperative colon! But there were wonderful weekdays, too.

Sometimes my grandfather took me and Netty to what was called "the farm" but was really his huge sugar-beet plantation and the big mill at the centre of it. The country around Deptford is very flat, alluvial soil. So flat, indeed, that often Netty took me to the railway station, which she elegantly called "the deepo" just before noon, so that I could have the thrill of seeing a plume of smoke rising far down the track as the approaching train left Darnley, seven miles away. As we drove along the road Grandfather would sometimes say, "Davey, I own everything on both sides of this road for as far as you can see. Did you know that?" And I always pretended I didn't know it and was amazed, because that was what he wanted. A mile or more before we reached the mill its sweet smell was apparent, and when we drew nearer we could hear its queer noise. It was an oddly inefficient noise—a rattly, clattering noise—because the machinery used for chopping the beets and pressing them and boiling down their sweetness was all huge and powerful, rather than subtle. Grandfather would take me through the mill, and explain all the processes, and get the important man who managed the gauge on the boiler to show me how that worked and how he tested the boiling every few minutes to see that its texture was right.

Best of all was a tiny railway, like a toy, that pulled little carloads of beets from distant fields, puffing and occasionally tooting in a deeply satisfying way as it bustled along. My grandfather owned a railway! And—oh, joy beyond all telling!—he would sometimes tell the engine-driver, whose name was Elmo Pickard, to take me on one of his jaunts into the fields, riding in the little engine! Whether Grandfather wanted to give me a rest, or whether he simply thought women had no place near engines, I don't know, but he never allowed Netty to go with me, and she sat at the mill, fretting that I would get dirty, for the two hours it took to make a round trip. The little engine burned wood, and the wood was covered in a fine layer of atomized sugar syrup, like everything else near the mill, so its combustion was dirty and deliciously smelly.

Elmo and I chuffed and rattled through the fields, flat as Holland, which seemed to be filled with dwarves, for most of the workers were Belgian immigrants who worked on their knees with sawed-off hoes. Elmo scorned them and had only a vague notion where they came from. "Not a bad fella, fer an Eye-talian!" was the best he would say of the big hulking Flemings, who talked (Elmo said they "jabbered") in a language that was in itself like the fibrous crunching of chopped beets. But there were English-speaking foremen here and there on the line, and from their conversation with Elmo I learned much that would not have done for Netty's ears. When we had filled all the trucks, we hurtled back to the mill, doing ten miles an hour at the very least, and I was allowed to pull the whistle to tell the mill, and the frantic Netty, that we were approaching.

There were other expeditions. Once or twice every summer

Grandmother would say, "Do you want to go see the people down by the crick today?" I knew from her tone that no great enthusiasm would be welcome. The people down by the crick were my other grandparents, my mother's people, the Cruikshanks.

The Cruikshanks were poor. That was really all that was wrong with them. Ben Cruikshank was a self-employed carpenter, a small dour Scot, whose conversation was full of references to himself as "independent" and "self-respecting" and "owing nothing to no man." I realize now that he was talking at me, justifying himself for daring to be a grandfather without any money. I think the Cruikshanks were frightened of me because I was such a glossy little article and full of politeness which had a strong edge of sauce. Netty held them cheap; mere orphan though she was herself, she carried a commission from the great Doc Staunton. Well do I remember the day when my Cruikshank grandmother, who was making jam, offered me some of the frothy barm to eat as she skimmed it from the pot. "Davey isn't let eat off of an iron spoon," said Netty, and I saw tears in the inferior grandmother's eyes as she meekly found a spoon of some whiter metal (certainly not silver) for her pernickety grandson. She must have mentioned it to Ben, because later in the day he took me into his workshop and showed me his tools and all the things they could do, while talking in a strain I did not understand, and often in a kind of English I could not easily follow. I know now that he was quoting Burns.

The rank is but the guinea stamp;
The man's the gowd for a' that—

he said, and in strange words I could not follow I nevertheless knew he was getting at Grandfather Staunton—

Ye see yon birkie, ca'd a lord
Wha struts and stares, and a' that:
Tho' thousands worship at his word,
He's but a coof for a' that,
For a' that, and a' that,
His riband, star and a' that,

The man of independent mind
He looks and laughs at a' that.

But I was a child, and I suppose I was a hateful child, for I snickered at the repetitions of "for a' that" and the Lowland speech because I was on Grandfather Staunton's side. And in justice I suppose it must be said that poor Ben overdid it; he was as self-assertive in his humility as the Stauntons were in their pride, and both came to the same thing; nobody had any real charity or desire to understand himself or me. He just wanted to be on top, to be best, and I was a prize to be won rather than a fellow-creature to be respected.

God, I've seen the gross self-assertion of the rich in its most sickening forms, but I swear the orgulous self-esteem of the deserving poor is every bit as bad! Still, I wish I could apologize to Ben and his wife now. I behaved very, very badly, and it's no good saying that I was only a child. So far as I understood, and with the weapons I had at hand, I hurt them and behaved badly toward them. The people down by the crick . . .

(Here I found I was weeping and could not go on.)

It was at this point Dr. von Haller moved into a realm that was new in our relationship. She talked quite a long time about the Shadow, that side of oneself to which so many real but rarely admitted parts of one's personality must be assigned. My bad behaviour toward the Cruikshanks was certainly a reality, however much my Staunton grandparents might have allowed it to grow. If I had been a more loving child, I would not have behaved so. Lovingness had not been greatly encouraged in me; but had it shown itself as present for encouragement? Slowly, as we talked, a new concept of Staunton-as-Son-of-a-Bitch emerged, and for a few days he gave me the shivers. But there he was. He had to be faced, not only in this, but in a thousand instances, for if he were not understood, none of his good qualities could be redeemed.

Had he good qualities? Certainly. Was he not unusually observant, for a child, of social differences and other people's moods? At a time when so many children move through life without much awareness of anything but themselves and their wants, did he not see beyond, to what other people were and wanted? This was not just infant Machiavellianism; it was sensitivity.

I had never thought of myself as sensitive. Touchy, certainly, and resentful of slights. But were all the slights unreal? And were my antennae always used for negative purposes? Well, perhaps not. Sensitivity worked both in sunlight and shadow.

MYSELF: And I presume the notion is to make the sensitivity always work in a positive way.

DR. VON HALLER: If you manage that, you will be a very uncommon person. We are not working to banish your Shadow, you see, but only to understand it, and thereby to work a little more closely with it. To banish your Shadow would be of no psychological service to you. Can you imagine a man without a Shadow? Do you know Chamisso's story of Peter Schlemihl? No? He sold his shadow to the Devil, and he was miserable ever after. No, no; your Shadow is one of the things that keeps you in balance. But you must recognize him, you know, your Shadow. He is not such a terrible fellow if you know him. He is not lovable; he is quite ugly. But accepting this ugly creature is needful if you are really looking for psychological wholeness. When we were talking earlier I said I thought you saw yourself to some extent in the role of Sydney Carton, the gifted, misunderstood, drunken lawyer. These literary figures, you know, provide us with an excellent shorthand for talking about aspects of ourselves, and we all encompass several of them. You are aware of Sydney; now we are getting to know Mr. Hyde. Only he isn't Dr. Jekyll's gaudy monster, who trampled a child; he is just a proud little boy who hurt some humble people, and knew it and enjoyed it. You are the successor to that little boy. Shall we have some more about him?

Very well. I could pity the boy, but that would be a falsification because the boy never pitied himself. I was a little princeling in Deptford, and I liked it very much. Netty stood between me and everyone else. I didn't play with the other boys in the village because they weren't clean. Probably they did not wash often enough under their foreskins. Netty was very strong on that. I was bathed every day, and I dreaded Netty's assault, the culmination of the bath, when I stood up and she stripped back my foreskin and washed under it with soap. It tickled and it stang and I somehow felt it to be ignominious, but she never tired of saying, "If you're not clean under there, you're not clean anyplace; you let yourself get dirty under there, and you'll get an awful disease. I've seen it thousands of times." Not being clean in this special sense was as bad as spitting. I was not allowed to spit, which was a great deprivation in a village filled with accomplished spitters. But it was possible, Netty warned, to spit your brains out. Indeed, I remember seeing an old man in the village named Cece Athelstan, who was quite a well-known character; he had the staggering, high-stepping gait of a man well advanced in syphilis, but Netty assured me that he was certainly a victim of unchecked spitting.

My greatest moment as the young princeling of Deptford was certainly when I appeared as the Groom in a Tom Thumb Wedding at the United Church.

It was in late August, when I was eight years old, and it was an adjunct of the Fall Fair. This was a great Deptford occasion, and in addition to all the agricultural exhibits, the Indians from the nearby reservation offered handiwork for sale—fans, bead-work, sweet-grass boxes, carved walking-canes, and so forth—and there was a little collection of carnival games, including one called Hit the Nigger in the Eye! where, for twenty-five cents, you could throw three baseballs at a black man who stuck his head through a canvas and defied you to hit him. My grandfather bought three balls for me, and I threw one short, one wide, and one right over the canvas, to the noisy derision of some low boys who were watching and at whom the black man—obviously a subversive type—kept winking as I made a fool of myself. But I pitied their ignorance and despised them, because I knew that when night fell I would be the star of the Fair.

A Tom Thumb Wedding is a mock nuptial ceremony in which all the participants are children, and the delight of it is its miniature quality. The Ladies' Aid of the United Church had arranged one of these things to take place in the tent where, during the day, they had served meals to the fair-goers, and it was intended to offer a refined alternative to the coarse pleasures of the carnival shows. At half-past seven everything was ready. Quite a large audience was assembled, consisting chiefly of ladies who were congratulating themselves on having minds above sword-swallowing and the pickled foetuses of two-headed babies. The tent was hot, and the light from the red, white, and blue bulbs was wavering and rather sickly. At the appropriate moment the boy who played the part of the minister and my best man and I stepped forward to await the Bride.

This was a little girl who had been given the part for her virtue in Sunday School rather than for outward attractions, and although her name was Myrtle she was known to her contemporaries as Toad Wilson. A melodeon played the Wedding Chorus from *Lohengrin* and Toad, supported by six other little girls, walked toward us as slowly as she could, producing an effect rather of reluctance than ceremony.

Toad was dressed fit to kill in a wedding outfit over which her mother and nobody knows how many others had laboured for weeks; her figure was bunchy, but she lacked nothing in satin and lace, and was oppressed by her wreath and veil. She should have been the centre of attention, but my grandmother and Netty had taken care of that.

I was a figure of extraordinary elegance, for my grandmother had kept old Mrs. Clements, the local dressmaker, busy for a month. I wore black satin trousers, a tail-coat made of velvet, and a sash, or cummerbund, of red silk. With a satin shirt and a large flowing red bow tie I was a rich, if rather droopy, sight. Everybody agreed that a silk hat was what was wanted to crown my finery, but of course there was none of the right size; however, in one of the local stores, my grandmother had unearthed a bowler hat of a type fashionable perhaps in 1900, for it had a narrow flat brim and a very high crown, as if it might have been made for a man with a pointed skull. It fitted, when plenty of cotton wool had been pressed under the inner band. I wore this until the Bride approached, at which moment I swept it off and held it over my heart. This was my own idea, and I think it shows some histrionic flair, because it kept Toad from unfairly monopolizing everybody's attention.

The ceremony was intended to be funny, and the parson was

the clown of the evening. He had many things to say that were in a script some member of the Ladies' Aid must have kept since the heyday of Josh Billings—because these Tom Thumb Weddings were already old-fashioned in the 'thirties. "Do you, Myrtle, promise to get up early and serve a hot breakfast every day in the week?" was one of his great lines, and Toad piped up solemnly, "I do." And I recall that I had to promise not to chew tobacco in the house, or use my wife's best scissors to cut stovepipe wire.

All, however, led up to the culminating moment when I kissed the Bride. This had been carefully rehearsed, and it was meant to bring down the house, for I was to be so pressing, and kiss the Bride so often, that the parson, after feigning horror, had to part us. Sure-fire comedy, for it had just that spice of sanctified lewdness that the Ladies' Aid loved, the innocence of children giving it a special savour. But here again I had an improvement; I disliked being laughed at as a child, and I felt that being kissed by me was a serious matter and far too good for such a pie-face as Toad Wilson. I had been to the movies a few times, as a great treat, and had seen kissers of international renown at work. So I went along with the foolish ideas of the Ladies' Aid at rehearsals, but when the great moment arrived at the performance, I threw my hat to one side, knelt gracefully, and lifted Toad's unready paw to my lips. Then I rose, seized her around her nail-keg waist, and pressed a long and burning kiss upon her mouth, bending her backward at the same time as much as her thicky-thumpy body would allow. This, I thought, would show Deptford what romance could be in the hands of a master.

The effect was all I could have hoped. There were oohs and ahs, some of delight, some of disapproval. As Toad and I walked down the aisle to wheezy Mendelssohn it was I, and not the Bride, who held all eyes. Best of all, I heard one woman murmur, with implications that I did not then understand, "That young one is Boy Staunton's son, all right." Toad showed a tendency to shine up to me afterward, when we were having ice-cream and cake at the Ladies' Aid expense, but I was cold. When I have squeezed my orange, I throw it away; that was my attitude at the time.

Netty was not pleased. "I suppose you thought you were pretty smart, carrying on like that," was her comment as I was going to bed, and this led to high words and tears. My grandmother thought I was overwrought by public performance, but my chief sensation was disappointment because nobody seemed to understand how remarkable I truly was.

(It was not easy work, this dredging up what could be recovered of my childish past and displaying it before another person. Quite a different thing from realizing, as everybody does, that at some far-off time they have not behaved well. It was at this period that I had a dream, or a vision between waking and sleeping one night, that I was once again on that pier, and was wiping filth and oil from the face of a drowned figure; but as I worked I saw that it was not my father, but a child who lay there, and that the child was myself.)

2

Dreaming had become a common experience for me, though I had never been a great dreamer. Dr. von Haller asked me to recover some dreams from childhood, and although I was doubtful, I found that I could do so. There was my dream from my sixth year that I saw Jesus in the sky, floating upward as in pictures of the Ascension; within His mantle, and it seemed to me part of His very figure, was a globe of the world, which He engulfed as though protecting it and displaying it to me, as I stood in the middle of the road down below. Had this been a dream, or a day-time vision? I could never satisfactorily decide, but it was brilliantly clear. And of course there was my recurrent dream, so often experienced, always in a somewhat different form but always the same in the quality of dread and terror that it brought. In this dream I was in a castle or fortress, closed against the outer world, and I was the keeper of a treasure—or sometimes it seemed to be a god or idol—the nature of which I never knew though its value was great in my mind. An Enemy was threatening it from without; this Enemy would run from window to window, looking for a way in, and I would pant from room to room to thwart it and keep it at bay. This dream had been attributed by Netty to my reading of a book called *The Little Lame Prince,* in which a lonely boy lived in a tower, and the book was arbitrarily forbidden; Netty liked to forbid books and always mistrusted them. But I knew perfectly well that I had had the dream long before I read the book and continued to have it long after the book had lost colour in my mind. The intensity of the dream and its sense of threat were of quite a different order from any book I knew.

Dr. von Haller and I worked for some time on this dream, trying to recover associations that would throw light on it. Although it seems plain enough to me now, it took several days for me to recognize that the tower was my life, and the treasure was what made it precious and worth defending against the Enemy. But who was this Enemy? Here we had quite a struggle because I insisted that the Enemy was external, whereas Dr. von Haller kept leading me back to some point at which I had to admit that the Enemy might be some portion of myself—some inadmissible entity in David which did not accept every circumstance of his life at face value, and which, if it beheld the treasure or the idol, might not agree about its superlative value. But at last, when I had swallowed that and admitted with some reluctance that it might be true, I was anxious to consider what the treasure might be, and it was here that the doctor showed reluctance. Better to wait, she said, and perhaps the answer would emerge of itself.

DR. VON HALLER: We do not want to use your grandfather's severe methods for getting at harmful things, do we? We must not press you down upon the hateful, invading spike. Let it alone, allow Nature to have her curative way, and all will be well.

MYSELF: I'm not afraid, you know. I'm willing to go straight ahead and get it over.

DR. VON HALLER: You have had quite enough of being a little soldier for the moment. Please accept my assurance that patience will bring better results here than force.

MYSELF: I don't want to go on stressing this, but I am not a stupid person. Haven't I been quick to accept—as an hypothesis anyhow—your ideas about dream interpretation?

DR. VON HALLER: Indeed, yes. But accepting an hypothesis

is not facing psychological truth. We are not building up an intellectual system; we are attempting to recapture some forgotten things and arousing almost forgotten feelings in the hope that we may throw new light on them, but even more new light on the present. Remember what I have said so many times; this is not simply rummaging in the trash-heap of the past for its own sake. It is your present situation and your future that concern us. All of what we are talking about is gone and unchangeable; if it had no importance we could dismiss it. But it has importance, if we are to heal the present and ensure the future.

MYSELF: But you are holding me back. I am ready to accept all of what you say; I am ready and anxious to go ahead. I learn quickly. I am not stupid.

DR. VON HALLER: Excuse me, please. You *are* stupid. You can think and you can learn. You do these things like an educated modern man. But you cannot feel, except like a primitive. Your plight is quite a common one, especially in our day when thinking and learning have been given such absurd prominence, and we have thought and learned our way into world-wide messes. We must educate your feeling and persuade you to experience it like a man and not like a maimed, dull child. So you are not to gobble up your analysis greedily, and then say, "Aha, I understand that!" because understanding is not the point. Feeling is the point. Understanding and experiencing are not interchangeable. Any theologian understands martyrdom, but only the martyr experiences the fire.

I was not prepared to accept this, and we set off on a long discussion which it would be useless to record in detail, but it hung on the Platonic notion that man apprehends the world about him in four main ways. Here I thought I was at a considerable advantage, because I had studied *The Republic* pretty thoroughly in my Oxford days and had the Oxford man's idea that Plato had been an Oxford man before his time. Yes, I recalled Plato's theory of our fourfold means of apprehension, and could name them: Reason, Understanding, Opinion, and Conjecture. But Dr. von Haller, who had not been to Oxford, wanted to call them Thinking, Feeling, Sensation, and Intuition, and seemed to have some conviction that it was not possible for a rational man to make his choice or establish his priorities among these four, plumping naturally for Reason. We were born with a predisposition toward one of the four, and had to work from what we were given.

She did say—and I was pleased about this—that Thinking (which I preferred to call Reason) was the leading function in my character. She also thought I was not badly endowed with Sensation, which made me an accurate observer and not to be confused about matters of physical detail. She thought I might be visited from time to time by Intuition, and I knew better than she how true that was, for I have always had a certain ability to see through a brick wall at need and have treasured Jowett's rendering of Plato's word for that; he called it "perception of shadows." But Dr. von Haller gave me low marks for Feeling, because whenever I was confronted with a situation that demanded a careful weighing of values, rather than an accurate formulation of relevant ideas, I flew off the handle, as Netty would put it. "After all, it was because your feelings became unbearable that you decided to come to Zürich," said she.

MYSELF: But I told you; that was a rational decision, arrived at somewhat fancifully but nevertheless on the basis of a strict examination of the evidence, in Mr. Justice Staunton's court. I did everything in my power to keep Feeling out of the matter.

DR. VON HALLER: Precisely. But have you never heard that if you drive Nature out of the door with a pitchfork, she will creep around and climb in at the window? Feeling does that with you.

MYSELF: But wasn't the decision a right one? Am I not here? What more could Feeling have achieved than was brought about by Reason?

DR. VON HALLER: I cannot say, because we are talking about you, and not about some hypothetical person. So we must stick to what you are and what you have done. Feeling types have their own problems; they often think very badly, and it gets them into special messes of their own. But you should recognize this, Mr. Justice Staunton: your decision to come here was a cry for help, however carefully you may have disguised it as a decision based on reason or a sentence imposed on yourself by your intellect.

MYSELF: So I am to dethrone my Intellect and set Emotion in its place. Is that it?

DR. VON HALLER: There it is, you see! When your unsophisticated Feeling is aroused you talk like that. I wonder what woman inside you talks that way? Your mother, perhaps? Netty? We shall find out. No, you are not asked to set your Intellect aside, but to find out where it can serve you and where it betrays you. And to offer a little nourishment and polish to that poor Caliban who governs your Feeling at present.

(Of course it took much longer and demanded far more talk than what I have put down in these notes, and there were moments when I was angry enough to abandon the whole thing, pay off Dr. von Haller, and go out on a monumental toot. I have never been fond of swallowing myself, and one of my faults in the courtroom is that I cannot hide my chagrin and sense of humiliation when a judge decides against me. However, my hatred of losing has played a big part in making me win. So at last we went on.)

If Deptford was my Arcadia, Toronto was a place of no such comfort. We lived in an old, fashionable part of the city, in a big house in which the servants outnumbered the family. There were four Stauntons, but the houseman (who was now and then sufficiently good at his job to be called a butler), the cook, the parlourmaid, the laundry maid, the chauffeur, and of course Netty were the majority and dominated. Not that anybody wanted it that way, but my poor mother had no gift of dealing with them that could prevent it.

People who have no servants often have a quaint notion that it would be delightful to have people always around to do one's bidding. Perhaps so, though I have never known a house where that happened, and certainly our household was not a characteristic one. Servants came and went, sometimes bewilderingly. Housemen drank or seduced the women-servants; cooks stole or had terrible tempers; laundry maids ruined expensive clothes or put crooked creases in the front of my father's trousers; housemaids would do no upstairs work and hadn't enough to do downstairs; the chauffeur was absent when he was wanted or borrowed the cars for joyriding. The only fixed and abiding star in our household firmament was Netty, and she tattled on all the others and grew in course of time to want the absolute control of a housekeeper, and so was always in a complicated war with the butler. Some servants were foreign and talked among themselves in languages that Netty assumed must conceal dishonest intentions; some were English and Netty knew they were patronizing her. Children always live closer to the servants than their elders, and Caroline and I never knew where we stood with anybody, and sometimes found ourselves hostages in dark, below-stairs intrigues.

The reason, of course, was that my poor mother, who had never had a servant in her life before her marriage (unless you count Grandmother Cruikshank, who seemed to fear her daughter and defer to her and I suppose had always done so) had no notion how to manage such a household. She was naturally kind, and somewhat fearful, and haunted by dread that she would not come up to the standards the servants expected. She courted their favour, asked their opinions, and I suppose it must be said that she was more familiar with them than was prudent. If the housemaid were near her own age she would invite her views on dress; my father knew this, and disapproved, and sometimes said Mother dressed like a housemaid on her day out. Mother knew nothing about the kind of food professional cooks prepare, and let them have their head, so that Father complained that the same few dishes appeared in a pattern. Mother did not like being driven by a chauffeur, so she had a car of her own which she drove, and the chauffeur had not enough to do. She did not insist that the servants speak of my sister and myself as Miss Caroline and Mr. David, which was what my father wanted. I suppose there must have been good servants somewhere—other people seemed to find them, and keep them—but we never found any except Netty, and Netty was a nuisance.

There were two major things wrong with Netty. She was in love with my father, and she had known my mother before her marriage and subsequent wealth. It was not until my mother's death that I recognized this, but Caroline was quick to spot it, and it was she who opened my eyes. Netty loved Father abjectly and wordlessly. I doubt if it ever entered her head that her love might be requited in any lasting way—certainly not in any physical way. All she wanted was an occasional good word, or one of his wonderful smiles. As for my mother, I think if Netty had ever clarified her thoughts she would have recognized my mother as a beautiful toy, but without real substance or importance as a wife, and it was not in Netty's nature to recognize any justice in the position my mother had achieved because of her beauty. She had been aware of Mother as the most beautiful girl in Deptford—no, better than that, for Mother was the most beautiful woman I have ever seen—but she had known Mother as the daughter of the people down by the crick. And beauty excepted, what set somebody from down by the crick above Netty herself?

My mother could not have known anything of the spirit that drove my father on and sometimes made him behave in a way that very few people—perhaps nobody but myself—understood. People saw only his present success; they knew nothing of his great dreams and his discontentment with things as they were. He was rich, certainly, and he had made his money by his own efforts. Grandfather Staunton was quite content to be the local rich man in Deptford, and his ventures in beet sugar had been shrewd. But it was my father who saw that the trifling million and a half pounds of beet sugar produced every year in Canada was nothing compared to what might be done by a man who moved boldly but intelligently into the importation and refining of cane sugar. People eat about a hundred pounds of sugar a year in one form or another. Father supplied eighty-five pounds of it. And certainly it was Father who saw that much of what had been thought of as waste from the refining process could be used as mineral supplement to poultry and stock foods. So it was not very long before Father was heavily involved in all kinds of bakeries and candy-making and soft drinks and scientifically prepared animal foods, which were managed from a single central agency called the Alpha Corporation. But to look on that as the guiding element in his life was to misunderstand him completely.

His deepest ambition was to be somebody remarkable, to live a fully realized life, to leave nothing undone that came within the range of his desires. He hated people who slouched and slummocked through life, getting nowhere and being nothing. He used to quote a line from a Browning poem he had studied at school about "the unlit lamp and the ungirt loin." His lamp was always blazing and his loins were girded as tight as they could be. I suppose that according to the rigmarole about types to which Dr. von Haller was introducing me (and which I was inclined to take with a pinch of salt) he would be called a Sensation man, because his sense of the real, the actual and tangible, was so strong. But he was sometimes mistaken about people, and I am much afraid he was mistaken about my mother.

She was a great beauty, but not in the classical style. Hers was the sort of beauty people admired so much in the 'twenties, when girls were supposed to have boyish figures and marvellous big eyes and pretty pouting mouths and above all a great air of vitality. Mother could have been a success in the movies. Or perhaps not, because although she had the looks she was not in the least a performer. I think Father saw in her something that wasn't really there. He thought that a girl with such stunning looks couldn't be just a Deptford girl; I think he supposed that her association with the people down by the crick was not one of parents-and-child, but a fairy-tale arrangement where a princess has been confided to the care of simple cottage folk. It was just a matter of lots of fine clothes and lots of dancing and travelling abroad and unlimited lessons at tennis and bridge, and the princess would stand revealed as what she truly was.

Poor Mother! I always feel guilty about her because I should have loved her more and supported her more than I did, but I was under my father's spell, and I understand now that I sensed his disappointment, and anyone who disappointed him could not have my love. I took all his ambitions and desires for my own and had as much as I could do to endure the fact which became so plain as I grew older, that I was a disappointment myself.

During my work with Dr. von Haller I was astonished when one night Felix came to me in a dream. Felix had been my great comfort and solace when I was about four years old, but I had forgotten him.

Felix was a large stuffed bear. He had come to me at a very bitter time, when I had disappointed my father by playing with a doll. Not a girl doll, but a doll dressed like a Highlander that somebody had given me—I cannot recall who it was because I tore all details of the affair out of my mind. It made no difference to Father that it was a soldier doll; what he saw was that I had wrapped it up in a doll's blanket belonging to Caroline and taken it to bed. He smashed the doll against the wall and demanded of Netty in a terrible voice if she was bringing his son up to be a sissy, and if that were so, what further plans had she? Dresses, perhaps? Was she encouraging me to urinate sitting down, so that I could use the ladies' room in hotels when I grew up? I was desolate, and Netty was stricken but tearless, and it was a dreadful bedtime which took unlimited cocoa to alleviate. Only my mother stood up for me, but all she could say was, "Boy, don't be so *silly!*" and this merely succeeded in drawing his anger on herself.

However, she must have made some compromise with him, for next day she brought Felix to me and said he was a very strong, brave bear for a very strong, brave boy, and we would have lots of daring adventures together. Felix was large, as nursery bears go, and a rich golden-brown, to begin with, and he had an expression of thoughtful determination. He had been made in France, and that was how he came to be named Felix; my mother thought of all the French names for boys that she knew, which were Jules and Felix, and Jules was rejected as not being so fully masculine as we desired and not fitting the character of this brave bear. So Felix he was, and he was the first of a large brotherhood of bears which I took to bed every night. There was a time when there were nine bears of various sizes in my bed, and not much room left for me.

My father knew about the bears, or at least about Felix, but he raised no objection, and from one or two remarks he let drop I know why. He had been impressed by what he had heard of Winnie-the-Pooh, and he felt that a bear was a proper toy for an upper-class little English boy; he had a great admiration for whatever was English and upper class. So Felix and I led an untroubled life together even after I had begun to go to school.

My father's admiration for whatever was English was one aspect of the ambiguous relationship between Canada and England. I suppose unkind people would say it was evidence of a colonial quality of mind, but I think it was the form taken by his romanticism. There was something terribly stuffy about Canada in my boyhood—a want of daring and great dimension, a second-handedness in cultural matters, a frowsy old-woman quality—that got on his nerves. You could make money, certainly, and he was doing that as fast as he could. But living the kind of life he wanted was very difficult and in many respects impossible. Father knew what was wrong. It was the Prime Minister.

The Right Honourable William Lyon Mackenzie King was undoubtedly an odd man, but subsequent study has led me to the conclusion that he was a political genius of an extraordinary order. To Father, however, he was the embodiment of several hateful qualities; Mr. King's mistrust of England and his desire for greater autonomy for Canada seemed to my father simply a perverse preferring of a lesser to a greater thing; Mr. King's conjuror-like ability to do something distracting with his right hand while preparing the denouement of his trick unobtrusively with his left hand had not the dash and flair my father thought he saw in British statesmanship; but the astonishing disparity between Mr. King's public and his personal character was what really made my father boil.

"He talks about reason and necessity on the platform, while all the time he is living by superstition and the worst kind of voodoo," he would roar. "Do you realize that man never calls an election without getting a fortune-teller in Kingston to name a lucky day? Do you realize that he goes in for automatic writing? And decides important things—nationally important things—by opening his Bible and stabbing at a verse with a paper-knife, while his eyes are shut? And that he sits with the portrait of his mother and communes—*communes* for God's sake!—with her spirit and gets her advice? Am I being taxed almost out of business because of something that has been said by Mackenzie King's mother's ghost? And this is the man who postures as a national leader!"

He was talking to his old friend Dunstan Ramsay, and I was not supposed to be listening. But I remember Ramsay saying, "You'd better face it, Boy; Mackenzie King rules Canada because he himself is the embodiment of Canada—cold and cautious on the outside, dowdy and pussy in every overt action, but inside a mass of intuition and dark intimations. King is Destiny's child. He will probably always do the right thing for the wrong reasons."

That was certainly not the way to reconcile Father to Mackenzie King.

Especially was this so when, around 1936, things began to go wrong in England in a way that touched my father nearly.

3

I never really understood Father's relationship with the Prince of Wales, because I had included the Prince as a very special and powerful character in my childish daydreams, and the truth and the fantasy were impossible to disentangle. But children hear far more than people think, and understand much, if not everything. So it began to be clear to me in the autumn of 1936 that the Prince was being harassed by some evil men, whose general character was like that of Mackenzie King. It had to do with a lady the Prince loved, and these bad men—a Prime Minister and an Archbishop—wanted to thwart them both. Father talked a great deal—not to me, but within my hearing—about what every decent man ought to do to show who was boss, and what principles were to prevail. He lectured my mother on this theme with an intensity I could not understand but which seemed to oppress her. It was as if he could think of nothing else. And when the actual Abdication came about he ordered the flag on the Alpha building to fly at half-staff, and was utterly miserable. Of course we were miserable with him, because it seemed to Caroline and me that terrible misfortune had overtaken our household and the world, and that nothing could ever be right again.

Christmas of that year brought one of the great upheavals that influenced my life. My father and mother had some sort of dreadful quarrel, and he left the house; as it proved, he did not come back for several days. Dunstan Ramsay, the family friend I have mentioned so often, was there, and he was as kind to Caroline and me as he knew how to be—but he had no touch with children and when our father was angry and in pain we wanted nothing to do with any other man—and he seemed to be very kind and affectionate toward Mother. Netty was out for the day, but Ramsay sent us children up to our own quarters, saying he would look in later; we went, but kept in close touch with what was going on downstairs. Ramsay talked for a long time to our weeping mother; we could hear his deep voice and her sobs. At last she went to her bedroom, and after some rather confused discussion, Carol and I thought we would go along and see her; we didn't know what we would do when we were with her, but we desperately wanted to be with somebody loving and comforting, and we had always counted on her for that. But if she were crying? This was terrible, and we were not sure we could face it. On the other hand we couldn't possibly stay away. We were lonely and frightened. So we crept silently into the passage, and were tiptoeing toward her door when it opened and Ramsay came out, and his face was as we had never seen it before, because he was grinning, but he was also quite clearly angry. He had an alarming face for children, all eyebrows and big nose and lantern jaws, and although he was genial toward us we were always a little frightened by him.

But far worse than this we heard Mother's voice, strange with grief, crying, "You don't love me!" It was in no tone we had ever heard from her before, and we were terribly alarmed. Ramsay did not see us, because we were some distance away, and when he had thumped downstairs—he has a wooden leg from the First Great War—we scuttled back to our nursery in misery.

What was wrong? Caroline was only six and all she could think of was that Ramsay was hateful not to love Mother and make her cry. But I was eight—a thinking eight—and I had all kinds of emotions I could not understand. Why should Ramsay love Mother? That was what Father did. What was Ramsay doing in Mother's room? I had seen movies and knew that men did not go to bedrooms just to make conversation; something special went on there, though I had no clear idea what it was. And Mother so wretched when Father had inexplicably gone away! Bad things were going on in the world; wicked men were interfering between people who loved each other; what mischief might Ramsay be making between my parents? Did this in some way connect with the misfortunes of the Prince? I thought about it till I had a headache, and I was cross with Caroline, who was not inclined to put up with that from me and made a terrible fuss.

At last Netty came home. She had been spending Christmas with her brother Maitland and his fiancée's family, and she was loaded down with things they had given her. But when she wanted to show them to us we would have none of it. Mother was crying and had gone to bed, and Mr. Ramsay had been in her room, and she had called those strange words after him in that strange voice. Netty became very grave and went to Mother's room, Caroline and I close on her heels. Mother was not in her bed. The bathroom door was slightly ajar, and Netty tapped on it. No answer. Netty peeped around the door. And shrieked. Then she turned at once and drove us from the room with instructions to go to the nursery and not dare to budge out of it till she came.

She came at last, and though she was not inclined to yield to our demands to see our mother she must have seen that it was the only way to keep us from further hysteria, so we were allowed to go to her room and very quietly creep up to the bed and kiss her. Mother was apparently asleep, pale as we had never seen her, and her arms lay stiffly on the counterpane, wrapped in bandages. She roused herself enough to smile faintly at us, but Netty forbade any talk and quickly led us away.

But out of the corner of my eye, in an instant as I passed, I saw the horror in the bathroom, and what seemed to be a tub filled with blood. I did not cry out, but cold terror seized me, and it was quite a long time before I could tell Caroline. Not, indeed, until Mother was dying.

Children do not give way to emotional stresses as adults do; they do not sit and mope or go to bed. We went back to the nursery and Caroline played with a doll, wrapping and unwrapping its wrists with a handkerchief and murmuring comfort; I held a book I was not able to read. We were trying to cling to normality; we were even trying to get some advantage out of being up much later than was proper. So we knew that Dunstan Ramsay came back and thumped up the stairs to the room he had left four hours ago, and a doctor came, and Netty did a great deal of running about. Then the doctor came to see us and suggested that we each have some warm milk with a few drops of rum in it to make us sleep.

Netty was horrified by the suggestion of rum, so we had crushed aspirin, and at last we slept.

And that was the Christmas of the Abdication for us.

After that, home was never really a secure place. Mother was not the same, and we supposed it was because of whatever happened on Christmas night. The vitality of the 'twenties girl never returned, and her looks changed. I shall never say that she was anything but beautiful, but she had always seemed to have even more energy than her children, which is one of the great fascinations in adults, and after that terrible night she had it no longer, and Netty kept telling us not to tire her.

I see now that this milestone in our family history meant a great advance in power for Netty, because she was the only person who knew what had happened. She had a secret, and a secret is an invaluable adjunct of power.

Her power was not exercised for her own direct advantage. I am sure that all of Netty's world and range of ambition was confined to what went on in our house. Later, when I was studying history, I saw a great deal of the feudal age in terms of Netty. She was loyal to the household and never betrayed it to any outside power. But within the household she was not to be thought of as a paid servant who could be discharged with two weeks' notice, nor do I think it ever crossed her mind that she was free to leave on the same terms. She was somebody. She was Netty. And because of who she was and what she felt, she was free to express opinions and take independent lines that lay far outside the compass of a servant in the ordinary sense. My father once told me that in all the years of their association Netty never asked him for a raise in pay; she assumed that he would give her what was fair and that in emergency she could call upon him with complete certainty of her right to do so. I recall years later some friend of Caroline's questioning the strange relationship between Don Giovanni and Leporello in the opera; if Leporello didn't like the way the Don lived, why didn't he leave him? "Because he was a Netty," said Caroline, and although the friend, who was very much of this age, didn't understand, it seemed to me to be an entirely satisfactory answer. "Though he slay me, yet will I trust in him," expressed half of Netty's attitude toward the Staunton family; the remainder was to be found in the rest of that verse—"but I will maintain mine own ways before him." Netty knew about Deptford; she knew about the people down by the crick; she knew what happened on Abdication Christmas. But it was not for lesser folk to know these things.

Did all of this make Netty dear to us? No, it made her a holy terror. People who prate about loyal old servants rarely know the hard-won coin of the spirit in which their real wages are paid. Netty's terrible silences about things that were foremost in our minds oppressed Caroline and me and were a great part of what seemed to us to be the darkness that was falling over our home.

Dr. von Haller: Did you never ask Netty what happened on Christmas night?

Myself: I cannot recall whether I did, but Caroline asked the next day and got Netty's maddening answer, "Ask no questions and you'll be told no lies." When Caroline insisted, "But I want to know," there came another predictable answer, "Then Want will have to be your master."

Dr. von Haller: And you never asked your mother?

Myself: How could we? You know how it is with children; they know there are forbidden areas, charged with intense feeling. They don't know that most of them are concerned with sex, but they suspect something in the world that would open up terrifying things and threaten their ideas about their parents; half of them wants to know, and half dreads to know.

Dr. von Haller: Did you know nothing of sex, then?

Myself: Odds and ends. There was Netty's insistence about washing "under there," which conveyed something special. And in Grandfather Staunton's office I had found a curious students' aid called Philips' Popular Manikin, which was a cardboard man who opened up to show his insides, and who had very discreet privy parts like my own. There was also a Popular Manikin (Female) who was partly flayed so that her breasts could only be guessed at, but who had a kind of imperforate bald triangle where the gentleman had ornaments. From some neat spy-work when Caroline was being dressed I knew that Philips had not told the whole story, and as soon as I went to school I was deluged with fanciful and disgusting information, none of which threw much light on anything and which I never dreamed of associating with my mother. I don't think I was as curious about sex as most boys. I wanted to keep things—meaning the state of my own knowledge—pretty much as it was. I suppose I had an intuition that more knowledge would mean greater complications.

Dr. von Haller: Were you happy at school?

It was a good school, and on the whole I liked it there. Happiness was not associated with it because my real life was with my home and family. I was not bad at lessons and managed well enough at games not to be in trouble, though I never excelled. Until I was twelve I went to the preparatory part of the school by the day, but when I was twelve Father decided I should be a boarder and come home only at weekends. That was in 1940, and the war was getting into its stride, and he had to be away a great deal and thought I ought to have masculine influences in my life that Netty certainly could not have provided and my fading mother didn't know about.

Father became very important during the war because one of our jobs in Canada was to provide as much food as we could for Britain. Getting it there was a Navy job, but providing as much as possible of the right things was a big task of organization and expert management, and that was Father's great line. Quite soon he was asked to take on the Ministry of Food, and after warm assurances from the hated Prime Minister that he could have things his own way, Father decided that Mr. King had great executive abilities and that anyhow personal differences had to be set aside in an emergency. So he was away for months at a time, in Ottawa and often abroad, and home became a very feminine place.

I see now that one of the effects of this was to make Dunstan Ramsay a much bigger figure in my life. He was the chief history master at my school, Colborne College, and because he was a bachelor and lived a queer kind of inward life, he was one of the masters who was resident in the school and supervised the boarders. Indeed he was Acting Headmaster for most of the war years, because the real Headmaster had gone into the Army Education Service. But he still taught a good many classes, and he always taught history to the boys who were fresh from the Prep, because he wanted them to get a good grounding in what history was; he caught up with them afterward when they were in the top classes and gave them a final polishing and pushed them for university scholarships. So I saw Ramsay nearly every day.

Like so many good schoolmasters, he was an oddity, and the boys liked him and dreaded him and jeered at him. His nickname was Old Buggerlugs, because he had a trick of jabbing his little finger into his ear and rooting with it, as if he were scratching his brain. The other masters called him Corky because of his artificial leg, and they thought we did so too, but it was Buggerlugs when the boys were by themselves.

The bee in his bonnet was that history and myth are two aspects of a kind of grand pattern in human destiny: history is the mass of observable or recorded fact, but myth is the abstract or essence of it. He used to dredge up extraordinary myths that none of us had ever heard of and demonstrate—in a fascinating way, I must admit—how they contained some truth that was applicable to widely divergent historical situations.

He had another bee, too, and it was this one that made him a somewhat suspect figure to a lot of parents and consequently to their sons—for the school always had a substantial anti-Ramsay party among the boys. This was his interest in saints. The study of history, he said, was in part a study of the myths and legends that mankind has woven around extraordinary figures like Alexander the Great or Julius Caesar or Charlemagne or Napoleon; they were mortal men, and when the fact could be checked against the legend it was wonderful to see what hero-worshippers had attributed to them. He used to show us a popular nineteenth-century picture of Napoleon during the retreat from Moscow, slumped tragically in his sleigh, defeat and a sense of romantic doom written on his face and on those of the officers about him: then he would read us Stendhal's account of the retreat, recording how chirpy Napoleon was and how he would look out of the windows of his travelling carriage—no open sleigh for him, you can bet—saying, "Wouldn't those people be amazed if they knew who was so near to them!" Napoleon was one of Ramsay's star turns. He would show us the famous picture of Napoleon on Elba, in full uniform, sitting on a rock and brooding on past greatness. Then he would read us reports of daily life on Elba, when the chief concern was the condition of the great exile's pylorus, and the best possible news was a bulletin posted by his doctors, saying, "This morning, at 11.22 a.m., the Emperor passed a well-formed stool."

But why, Ramsay would ask, do we confine our study to great political and military figures to whom the generality of mankind has attributed extraordinary, almost superhuman qualities, and leave out the whole world of saints, to whom mankind has attributed phenomenal virtue? It is trivial to say that power, or even vice, are more interesting than virtue, and people say so only when they have not troubled to take a look at virtue and see how amazing, and sometimes inhuman and unlikable, it really is. The saints also belong among the heroes, and the spirit of Ignatius Loyola is not so far from the spirit of Napoleon as uninformed people suppose.

Ramsay was by way of being an authority on saints, and had written some books about them, though I have not seen them. You can imagine what an uncomfortable figure he could be in a school that admitted boys of every creed and kind but which was essentially devoted to a modernized version of a nineteenth-century Protestant attitude toward life. And of course our parents were embarrassed by real concern about spiritual things and suspicious of anybody who treated the spirit as an ever-present reality, as Ramsay did. He loved to make us uncomfortable intellectually and goad us on to find contradictions or illogicalities in what he said. "But logic is like cricket," he would warn, "it is admirable so long as you are playing according to the rules. But what happens to your game of cricket when somebody suddenly decides to bowl with a football or bat with a hockey-stick? Because that is what is continually happening in life."

The war was a field-day for Ramsay as an historian. The legends that clustered around Hitler and Mussolini were victuals and drink to him. "The Führer is inspired by voices—as was St. Joan: Il Duce feels no pain in the dentist's chair—neither did St. Appollonia of Tyana when her teeth were wrenched out by infidels. These are the attributes of the great; and I say attributes advisedly, because it is we who attribute these supernormal qualities to them. Only after his death did it leak out that Napoleon was afraid of cats."

I liked Ramsay, then. He worked us hard, but he was endlessly diverting and made some pretty good jokes in class. They were repeated around the school as Buggerlugs' Nifties.

My feelings about him underwent a wretched change when my mother died.

4

That was in the late autumn of 1942, when I was in my fifteenth year. She had had pneumonia, and was recovering, but I don't think she had much will to live. Whatever it was, she was convalescent and was supposed to rest every afternoon. The doctor had given instructions that she was on no account to take a chill, but she hated heavy coverings and always lay on her bed under a light rug. One day there was a driving storm, turning toward snow, and her bedroom windows were open, although they certainly should have been shut. We assumed that she had opened them herself. A chill, and in a few days she was dead.

Ramsay called me to his room at school and told me. He was kind in the right way. Didn't commiserate too much, or say anything that would break me down. But he kept me close to him during the next two or three days, and arranged the funeral because Father had to be in London and had cabled to ask him to do it. The funeral was terrible. Caroline didn't come because it was still thought by Netty and the Headmistress of her school that girls didn't go to funerals, so I went with Ramsay. There was a small group, but the people from down by the crick were there, and I tried to talk to them; of course they hardly knew me and what could anybody say? Both my Staunton grandparents were dead, so I suppose if there was a Chief Mourner—the undertakers asked who it was and Ramsay dealt with that tactfully—I was the one. My only feeling was a kind of desolated relief, because without ever quite forming the thought in my mind, I knew my mother had not been happy for some years, and I supposed it was because she felt she had failed Father in some way.

I recall saying to Ramsay that I thought perhaps Mother was better off, because she had been so miserable of late; I meant it as an attempt at grown-up conversation, but he looked queer when he heard it.

Much more significant to me than my mother's actual death and funeral—for, as I have said, she seemed to be taking farewell of us for quite a long time—was the family dinner on the Saturday night following. Caroline had been at home all week, under Netty's care, and I went home from school for the weekend. There was a perceptible lightening of spirits, and an odd atmosphere, for Father was away and Caroline and I were free of the house as we had never been. What I would have done about this I don't know; I suppose I should have swanked about a little and perhaps drunk a glass of beer to show my emancipation. But Caroline had different ideas.

She was always the daring one. When she was eight and I was ten she had cut one of Father's cigars in two and dared me to a smoke-down; we were to light up and puff away while soaring and descending rhythmically on the see-saw in the garden. She won. She had a reputation at her school, Bishop Cairncross's, as a practical joker, and had once captured a beetle and painted it gaily before offering it to the nature mistress for identification. The nature mistress, who was up to that one, got off the traditional remark in such circumstances. "This is known as the *nonsensicus impudens,* or Impudent Humbug, Caroline," she had said, and gained great face among her pupils as a wit. But when Mother died, Caroline was twelve, and in that queer time between childhood and nubile girlhood, when some girls seem to be wise without experience, and perhaps more clear-headed than they will be again until after their menopause. She took a high line with me on this particular Saturday and said I was to make myself especially tidy for dinner.

Sherry beforehand! We had never been allowed that before, but Caroline had it set out in the drawing-room, and Netty was taken unaware and did not get her objection in until we had glasses. Netty took none herself; she was fiercely T.T. But Caroline had asked her to dine with us, and Netty must have been shaken by that, because it had never occurred to her that she would do otherwise. She had put on some ceremonial garments instead of her nurse's uniform, and Caroline was in her best and had even put on a dab of lipstick. But this was merely a soft prelude to what was to follow.

There were three places at table and it was clear enough that I was to have Father's chair, but when Netty was guided by Caroline to the other chair of state—my mother's—I wondered what was up. Netty demurred, but Caroline insisted that she take this seat of honour, while she herself sat at my right. It did not occur to me that Caroline was pulling Netty's teeth; she was exalting her as a guest, only to cast her down as a figure of authority. Netty was confused, and missed her cue when the houseman brought in wine and poured a drop for me to approve; she barely recovered in time to turn her own glass upside down. We had had wine before; on great occasions my father gave us wine diluted with water, which he said was the right way to introduce children to one of the great pleasures of life; but undiluted wine, and me giving the nod of approval to the houseman, and glasses refilled under Netty's popping eyes—this was a new and heady experience.

Heady indeed, because the wine, following the sherry, was strong within me, and I knew my voice was becoming loud and assertive and that I was nodding agreement to things that needed no assent.

Not Caroline. She hardly touched her wine—the sneak!—but she was very busy guiding the conversation. We all missed Mother dreadfully, but we had to bear up and go on with life. That was what Mother would have wanted. She had been such a gay person; the last thing she would wish would be prolonged mourning. That is, she had been gay until five or six years ago. What had happened? Did Netty know? Mother had trusted Netty so, and of course she knew things that we were not thought old enough to know—certainly not when we had been quite small children, really. But that was long ago. We were older now.

Netty was not to be drawn.

Daddy was away so much. He couldn't avoid it, really, and the country needed him. Mummy must have felt the loneliness. Odd that she seemed to see so little of her friends during the last two or three years. The house had been gloomy. Netty must have felt it. Nobody came, really, except Dunstan Ramsay. But he was a very old friend, wasn't he? Hadn't Daddy and Mummy known him since before they were married?

Netty was a little more forthcoming. Yes, Mr. Ramsay had been a Deptford boy. Much older than Netty, of course, but she heard a few things about him as she grew up. Always a queer one.

Oh? Queer in what way? We had always remembered him coming to the house, so perhaps we didn't notice the queerness. Daddy always said he was deep and clever.

I felt that as host I should get into this conversation—which was really more like a monologue by Caroline, punctuated with occasional grunts from Netty. So I told a few stories about Ramsay as a schoolmaster, and confided that his nickname was Buggerlugs. Netty said I should be ashamed to use a word like that in front of my sister.

Caroline put on a face of modesty, and then said she thought Mr. Ramsay was handsome in a kind of scary way, like Mr. Rochester in *Jane Eyre,* and she had always wondered why he never married.

Maybe he couldn't get the girl he wanted, said Netty.

Really? Caroline had never thought of that. Did Netty know any more? It sounded romantic.

Netty said it had seemed romantic to some people who had nothing better to do than fret about it.

Oh, Netty, don't tease! Who was it?

Netty underwent some sort of struggle, and then said if anybody had wanted to know they had only to use their eyes.

Caroline thought it must all have been terribly romantic when Daddy was young and just back from the war, and Mummy so lovely, and Daddy so handsome—as he still was, didn't Netty think so?

The handsomest man she had ever seen, said Netty, with vehemence.

Had Netty ever seen him in those days?

Well, said Netty, she had been too young to pay much heed to such things when the war ended. After all, she wasn't exactly Methuselah. But when Boy Staunton married Leola Cruikshank in 1924 she had been ten, and everybody knew it was a great love-match, and they were the handsomest pair Deptford had ever seen or was ever likely to see. Nobody had eyes for anyone but the bride, and she guessed Ramsay was like all the rest. After all, he had been Father's best man.

Here Caroline pounced. Did Netty mean Mr. Ramsay had been in love with Mother?

Netty was torn between her natural discretion and the equally natural desire to tell what she knew. Well, there had been those that said as much.

So that was why he was always around our house! And why he had taken so much care of Mother when Father had to be away on war business. He was heart-broken but faithful. Caroline had never heard of anything so romantic. She thought Mr. Ramsay was sweet.

This word affected Netty and me in different ways. Old Buggerlugs sweet! I laughed much louder and longer than I would have done if I had not had two glasses of Burgundy. But Netty snorted with disdain, and there was that in her burning eyes that showed what she thought of such sweetness.

"Oh, but you'd never admit any man was attractive except Daddy," said Caroline. She even leaned over and put her hand on Netty's wrist.

What did Caroline mean by that, she demanded.

"It sticks out a mile. You adore him."

Netty said she hoped she knew her place. It was a simple remark, but extremely old-fashioned for 1942, and if ever I have seen a woman ruffled and shaken, it was Netty as she said it.

Caroline let things simmer down. Of course everybody adored Daddy. It was inescapable. He was so handsome, and attractive, and clever, and wonderful in every way that no woman could resist him. Didn't Netty think so?

Netty guessed that was about the size of it.

Later Caroline brought up another theme. Wasn't it extraordinary that Mother had taken that chill, when everybody knew it was the worst possible thing for her? How could those windows have been open on such a miserable day?

Netty thought nobody would ever know.

Did Netty mean Mother had opened them herself, asked Caroline, all innocence. But—she laid down her knife and fork—that would be suicide! And suicide was a mortal sin! Everybody at Bishop Cairncross's—yes, and at St. Simon Zelotes, where we went to church—was certain of that. If Mother had committed a mortal sin, were we to think that now—? That would be horrible! I swear that Caroline's eyes filled with tears.

Netty was rattled. No, of course she meant nothing of the kind. Anyway that about mortal sins was just Anglican guff and she had never held with it. Never.

But then, how did Mother's windows come to be open?

Somebody must have opened them by mistake, said Netty. We'd never know. There was no sense going on about it. But her baby girl wasn't to think about awful things like suicide.

Caroline said she couldn't bear it, because it wasn't just Anglican guff, and everybody knew suicides went straight to Hell. And to think of Mummy—!

Netty never wept, that I know of. But there was, on very rare occasions, a look of distress on her face which in another woman would have been accompanied by tears. This was such a time.

Caroline leapt up and ran to Netty and buried her face in her shoulder. Netty took her out of the room and I was left amid the ruins of the feast. I thought another glass of Burgundy would be just the thing at that moment, but the butler had removed it, and I had not quite the brass to ring the bell, so I took another apple from the dessert plate and ate it reflectively all by myself. I could not make head or tail of what had been going on. When the apple was finished, I went to the drawing-room and sat down to listen to a hockey-game on the radio. But I soon fell asleep on the sofa.

When I woke, the game was over and some dreary war news was being broadcast. I had a headache. As I went upstairs I saw a light under Caroline's door, and went in. She was in pyjamas, carefully painting her toe-nails red.

"You'd better not let Netty catch you at that."

"Thank you for your invaluable, unsought advice. Netty is no longer a problem in my life."

"What have you two been hatching up?"

"We have been reaching an understanding. Netty doesn't fully comprehend it yet, but I do."

"What about?"

"Dope! Weren't you listening at dinner? No, you weren't, of course. You were too busy stuffing your face and guzzling booze to know what was happening."

"I saw everything that happened. What didn't I see? Don't pretend to be so smart."

"Netty opened up and made a few damaging admissions. That's what happened."

"I didn't hear any damaging admissions. What are you talking about?"

"If you didn't hear it was because you were drinking too much. Booze will be your downfall. Many a good man has gone to hell by the booze route, as Grandfather used to say. Didn't you hear Netty admit that she loves Father?"

"What? She never said that!"

"Not in so many words. But it was plain enough."

"Well! She certainly has a crust!"

"For loving Father? How refreshingly innocent you are! One of these days, if you remind me, I'll give you my little talk about the relation of the sexes. It's a lot more complicated than your low schoolboy mind can comprehend."

"Oh, shut up! I'm older than you are. I know things you've never even heard of."

"You probably mean about fairies. Old stuff, my poor boy!"

"Carol, I'm going to have to swat you."

"Putting me to silence by brute strength? Okay, Tarzan. Then you'll never hear the rest—which is also the best."

"What?"

"Do you acknowledge me as the superior mind?"

"No. What do you know that makes you so superior?"

"Just the shameful secret of your birth, that's all."

"What!"

"I have every reason to believe that you are the son of Dunstan Ramsay."

"Me!"

"You. Now I take a good look, in the light of my new information, you are quite a bit like him."

"I am not! Listen, Carol, you just explain what you've said or I'll kill you!"

"Lay a finger on me, dear brother, and I'll clam up and leave you forever in torturing doubt."

"Is that what Netty said?"

"Not in so many words. But you know my methods, Watson. Apply them. Now, attend very carefully. Daddy took Mummy away from Dunstan Ramsay and married her. Dunstan Ramsay went right on visiting this house as Trusted Friend. If you read more widely and intelligently you would know the role that Trusted Friend plays in all these affairs. Cast your mind back six years, to that awful Christmas. A quarrel. Daddy sweeps out in a rage. Ramsay remains. We are sent upstairs. Later we see Ramsay leave Mummy's bedroom, where she is in her nightie. We hear her call out, 'You don't love me.' A few hours later, Mummy tries to kill herself. You remember all that blood, that you couldn't keep your mouth shut about. Daddy isn't around home nearly so much after that, but Ramsay keeps coming. The obvious—the only—conclusion is that Daddy discovered Ramsay was Mummy's lover and couldn't bear it."

"Carol, you turd! You utter, vile, maggoty, stinking turd! How can you say that about Mother?"

"I don't enjoy saying it, fathead. But Mummy was a very beautiful, attractive woman. Being rather in that line myself I understand the situation, and her feelings, as you never will. I know how passion drives people on. And I accept it. To know all is to forgive all."

"You'll never get me to believe it."

"Don't, then. I can't help what you believe. But if you don't believe that you certainly won't believe what came of it."

"What?"

"What's the good of my telling you, if you don't want to hear?"

"You've got to tell me. You can't just tell me part. I'm a member of this family too, you know. Come on. If you don't I'll get hold of Father next time he's home and tell him what you just said."

"No you won't. That is one thing you will never do. Admit yourself to be Ramsay's son! Daddy would probably disinherit you. You'd have to go and live with Ramsay. You'd be branded as a bastard, a love-child, a merry-begot—"

"Stop milking the dictionary, and tell me."

"Okay. I am in a kindly mood, and I won't torture you. Netty killed Mummy."

I must have looked very queer, for Caroline dropped her Torquemada manner and went on.

"This is deduction, you understand, but deduction of a very superior kind. Consider: the orders were strict against Mummy getting a chill, so we must accept either that Mummy opened those windows herself or somebody else opened them, and the only person around who could have done it was Netty. If Mummy did it, she killed herself knowingly, and that would be suicide, and forgetting all that Netty so rightly calls Anglican guff are you ready to believe Mummy killed herself?"

"But why would Netty do it?"

"Love, dumb-bell. That tempest of passion of which you still know nothing. Netty loves Daddy. Netty has a very fierce, loyal nature. Mummy had deceived Daddy. Listen, do you know what she said to me, after we had left you hogging the wine? We talked a long time about Mummy, and she said, 'Everything considered, I think your mother's better out of it.' "

"But that isn't admitting she killed anybody."

"I am not simple. I put the question directly—or as directly as seemed possible in the rather emotional situation. I said, 'Netty, tell me truly, who opened the windows? Netty, darling, I'll never breathe it to a soul—did you do it, out of loyalty to Daddy?' She gave me the very queerest look she's ever given me—and there have been some dillies—and said, 'Caroline don't you ever breathe or hint any such terrible thing again!' "

"Well, then, there you have it. She said she didn't."

"She said no such thing! If she didn't, who did? Things make sense, Davey. There is nothing without an explanation. And that is the only explanation possible. She didn't say she hadn't done it. She chose her words carefully."

"God! What a mess."

"But fascinating, don't you think? We are children of a fated house."

"Oh, bullshit! But look—you've jumped to a lot of conclusions. I mean, about us being Ramsay's children—"

"About you being Ramsay's child. I don't come into that part."

"Why me?"

"Well, look at me; I am unmistakably Boy Staunton's daughter. Everybody says so. I look very much like him. Do you?"

"That doesn't prove anything."

"I can quite understand you don't want to think so."

"I think this is all something you've made up to amuse yourself. And I think it's damn nasty—throwing dirt on Mother and making me out to be a bastard. And all this crap about love. What do you know about love? You're just a kid! You haven't even got your monthlies yet!"

"So what, Havelock Ellis? I've got my full quota of intelligence and that's more than you can say."

"Intelligence! You're just a nasty-minded, mischief-making kid!"

"Oh, go and pee up a tree!" said my sister, who picked up a lot of coarse language at Bishop Cairncross's.

I took my headache, which was now much worse, to my own room. I looked in the mirror. Caroline was crazy. There was nothing in my face to suggest Dunstan Ramsay. Or was there? If you put my beautiful mother and old Buggerlugs together, would you produce anything like me? Caroline had such certainty. Of course she was a greedy novel-reader and romancer, but she was no fool. I didn't look in the least like my father, or the Stauntons, or the Cruikshanks. But—?

I went to bed disheartened but could not sleep. I wanted something, and it took me a long time to admit to myself what I wanted. It was Felix. This was terrible. At my age, wanting a toy bear! It must be the drink. I would never touch a drop of that awful stuff again.

Next day, with elaborate casualness, I asked Netty what had happened to Felix.

"I threw him out years ago," she said. "What would you want with an old thing like that? He'd only breed moths."

Dr. von Haller: Your sister sounds very interesting. Is she still like that?

Myself: In an adult way, yes, she is. A great manager. And quite a mischief-maker.

Dr. von Haller: She sounds like a very advanced Feeling Type.

Myself: Was it Feeling to sow a doubt in my mind that I have never completely settled since?

Dr. von Haller: Oh, certainly. The Feeling Type understands feeling; that does not mean that such people always share feeling or use it tenderly. They are very good at evoking and managing feeling in others. As your sister did with you.

Myself: She caught me off balance.

Dr. von Haller: At fourteen, you were no match for a girl of twelve who was an advanced Feeling Type. You were trying to think your way out of an extremely emotional situation. She was just interested in stirring things up and getting Netty under her thumb. Probably it never occurred to her that you would take seriously what she said about your parentage, and would have laughed at you for being foolish if she knew that you did so.

Myself: She planted terrible doubts in my mind.

Dr. von Haller: Yes, but she woke you up. You must be grateful to her for that. She made you think of who you were. And she put your beautiful mother in a different perspective, as somebody over whom men might quarrel, and whom another woman might think it worth-while to murder.

Myself: I don't see the good of that.

Dr. von Haller: Very few sons ever do. But it is hard on women to be looked on as mothers only. You North American men are especially guilty of casting your mothers in a cramping, minor role. It is bad for men to look back toward their mothers without recognizing that they were also people—people who might be loved, or possibly murdered.

Myself: My mother knew great unhappiness.

Dr. von Haller: You have said that many times. You have even said it about periods when you were too young to have known anything of the sort. It is a kind of refrain in your story. These refrains are always significant. Suppose you tell me what genuine reasons you have for thinking of your mother as an unhappy woman. Reasons that Mr. Justice Staunton would admit as evidence in his strict court.

MYSELF: Direct evidence? Does a woman ever tell her children she is unhappy? A neurotic woman, perhaps, who is trying to get some special response out of them by saying so. My mother was not neurotic. She was a very simple person, really.

DR. VON HALLER: What indirect evidence, then?

MYSELF: The way she faded after that terrible Abdication Christmas. She seemed to be more confused than before. She was losing her hold on life.

DR. VON HALLER: She had been confused before, then?

MYSELF: She had problems. My father's high expectations. He wanted a brilliant wife, and she tried to be one, but she wasn't cut out for it.

DR. VON HALLER: You observed this before her death? Or did you think of it afterward? Or did somebody tell you it was so?

MYSELF: You're worse than Caroline! My father told me so. He gave me some advice one time: Never marry your childhood sweetheart, he said; the reasons that make you choose her will all turn into reasons why you should have rejected her.

DR. VON HALLER: He was talking of your mother?

MYSELF: He was really talking about a girl I was in love with. But he mentioned Mother. He said she hadn't grown.

DR. VON HALLER: And did you think she had grown?

MYSELF: Why would I care whether she had grown or not? She was my mother.

DR. VON HALLER: Until you were fourteen. At that age one is not intellectually demanding. If she were alive now, do you think that you and she would have much to say to one another?

MYSELF: That is not the kind of question that is admitted in Mr. Justice Staunton's court.

DR. VON HALLER: Was she a woman of any education? Had she any mind?

MYSELF: Does it matter? I suppose not, really.

DR. VON HALLER: Were you angry with your father because of what he said?

MYSELF: I thought it was a hell of a thing to say to a boy

about his mother, and I thought it was an unforgivable thing to say about the woman who had been his wife.

Dr. von Haller: I see. Suppose we take a short cut. I wish you would take some time during the next few days to sort out why you think your father must always be impeccable in conduct and opinion, but that very much must be forgiven your mother.

Myself: She did try to commit suicide, remember. Doesn't that speak of unhappiness? Doesn't that call for pity?

Dr. von Haller: So far we do not know why she made that attempt. Your sister could be right, don't you see? It could have been because of Ramsay.

Myself: That's nonsense! You've never seen Ramsay.

Dr. von Haller: Only through your eyes. As I have seen your parents. But I have seen many women with lovers, and it is not always Venus and Adonis, I assure you. But let us leave this theme until we have done more work, and you have had time to do some private investigation of your feelings about your mother. See what you can do to form an opinion of her as a woman—as a person you might meet. . . . But now I should like to talk for a moment about Felix. You tell me he has been appearing in your dreams? What does he do there?

Myself: He doesn't do anything. He's just there.

Dr. von Haller: Alive?

Myself: Alive as he was when I knew him. He seemed to have a personality, you know. Rather puzzled and considering, and I did all the talking. And he usually agreed. Sometimes he was doubtful and said no. But his attention seemed to lend something to whatever I had talked about or decided. Do I make any sense?

Dr. von Haller: Oh, yes; excellent sense. These figures we have in our deep selves, you know, have a way of being both external and internal. That one we talked of—the Shadow—he was inward, wasn't he? And yet as we talked, it appeared that so many of the things you disliked so strongly about him were also to be found in people you knew. You were particularly vehement about Netty's brother, Maitland Quelch—

MYSELF: Yes, but I should have made it clear that I very rarely met him. I just heard about him from Netty. He was so deserving and he had his way to make in the world single-handed, and he would have been so glad of some of the chances I hardly seemed to notice, and all that sort of thing. Matey's struggle to qualify as a Chartered Accountant pretty much paralleled my own studies for the Bar, but of course in Netty's eyes everything had been made easy for me, whereas he did it the hard way. Meritorious Matey! But when I met him, which was as seldom as decency allowed, I always thought he was a loathsome little squirt—

DR. VON HALLER: I know. We went into that quite extensively. But in the end we agreed, I think, that you simply read into Matey's character things you disliked, and these proved after some more investigation to be things which were not wholly absent from your own character. Isn't that so?

MYSELF: It's difficult for me to be objective about Matey. When I talk about him I feel myself becoming waspish, and I can't help describing him as if he were some sort of Dickensian freak. But is it my fault he has damp hands and a bad breath and shows his gums when he smiles and calls me Ted, which nobody else on God's green earth does, and exudes democratic forgiveness of my wealth and success—

DR. VON HALLER: Yes, yes: we were through all that, and at last you admitted that Matey was your scapegoat—a type of all you disliked and feared might come to the surface in yourself—please, one moment—not in these physical characteristics but in the character of the Deserving Person, ill rewarded and ill understood by a careless world. The Orphan of the Storm: the Battered Baby. You don't have to blush for harbouring something of this in your most secret image of yourself. The important thing is to know what you are doing. That tends to defuse it, you understand. I was not trying during those difficult hours to make you like Matey. I was trying to persuade you to examine a dark corner of yourself.

MYSELF: It was humiliating, but I suppose it must be true.

DR. VON HALLER: The truth will grow as we work. That is what we are looking for. The truth, or some part of it.

Myself: But although I admit I projected some of the least admirable things in my own character on Matey—you notice how I am picking up words like "projected" from you—I have a hunch that there is something fishy about him. He's too good to be true.

Dr. von Haller: I am not surprised. Unless one is very naïve, one does not project one's own evil on people who are especially good. As I have said, if psychiatry worked by rules, every policeman would be a psychiatrist. But let us get back to Felix.

Myself: Does his appearance now mean some sort of reversion to childhood?

Dr. von Haller: Only to an emotion you felt in childhood, and which does not seem to have been very common with you since. Felix was a friend. He was a loving friend, but because of your own disposition, he was very much a thinking, considering friend. Now just as the Shadow makes his appearance in this sort of personal investigation, so does a figure we call the Friend. And because you have worked well and diligently for the last few weeks, when the going cannot have been very pleasant, I am glad to be able to give you good news. The appearance of the Friend in your inner life and in your dreams is a favourable sign. It means that your analysis is going well.

Myself: You're quite right. This probing and recollecting hasn't been pleasant. There have been times when I have been annoyed and disgusted with you. There were moments when I wondered if I were really out of my mind to put myself in the hands of anyone who tormented me and thwarted me as you have done.

Dr. von Haller: Quite so. I was aware of it, of course. But as we go on you will find that I seem to be many things to you. If you understand me, part of my professional task is to be the bearer of your projections. When the Shadow was under investigation, and so much of your inferior self was coming to light, you found the Shadow in me. Now we seem to have awakened the image of the Friend in your mind, your spirit, your soul—these are not scientific terms but I promised not to deluge you with jargon—and perhaps I shall not now be so intolerable.

MYSELF: I'm delighted. I would truly like to know you better.

DR. VON HALLER: It is yourself you must truly know better. And I should warn you that I shall appear as the Friend only for a limited time. Yes; I have many other parts to play before we are done. And even the Friend is not always benevolent: sometimes friends are truest when they seem unfriendly. It's funny that your Friend is a bear; I mean, the Friend often appears as an animal, but rarely as a savage animal. . . . Now, let me see; we have reached your mother's death, and the moment when Caroline, mischievously but perhaps not untruly, made some suggestions that made you see yourself in a new light. It sounds almost like the end of childhood.

5

It was. I was adolescent now. Of course I knew a good deal about what people stupidly call the facts of life, but I had not had much physical experience of what sex meant. Now it began to be very troublesome. I find it odd, now, to read some of the popular books that glorify masturbation; I never thought it would kill me, or anything stupid like that, but I did my best to control it because—well, it seemed such a shabby thing. I suppose I didn't bring much imagination to it.

As I look back now I see that, although I knew a good deal about sex, I had retained an unusual innocence for my age, and I suppose it was my father's money, and the sense of isolation it brought, that made my innocence possible.

I told you what Netty had said about "Anglican guff." She was scornful of what she called "Pancake Christianity" because we ate pancakes at Shrove; she used to snort when my parents had lobster salad on Fridays in Lent and always demanded that meat be sent up to the nursery for herself. She never, I think, quite forgave my parents for leaving the wholesome bosom of evangelistic Protestantism. Church matters—I won't call it religion—played a big part in my growing up. We were attached to St. Simon Zelotes, which had the reputation of being a rich people's church. It wasn't the most fashionable Anglican church in the city, but it had a special cachet. The fashionable one, I suppose, was St. Paul's, but it was Broad Church. I suppose you are familiar with these distinctions? And the High Church was St. Mary Magdalene, but it was poor. St. Simon Zelotes was neither so High as Mary Mag, nor so rich as Paul's. The vicar was Canon Woodiwiss—he later became an Archdeacon and finally Bishop—and he was a gifted apostle to the well-to-do. I don't say that sneeringly. There always seems to be a notion that the rich can't be devout and that God doesn't like them as much as He likes the poor. There are lots of Christians who are all pity and charity for the miserable and the outcast, but who think it a spiritual duty to give the rich a good snubbing whenever they can. So Woodiwiss was a real find for a church like Simon Zelotes.

He soaked the rich for money, which was fair enough. At least once a year he preached his famous sermon about "it is easier for a camel to go through the eye of a needle than for a rich man to enter into the kingdom of God." He would explain that the Needle's Eye was the name of a gate to Jerusalem which was so narrow that a heavily laden camel had to be relieved of some of its burden to get through, and that custom demanded that whatever was taken from the camel became the property of the Temple. So the obvious course for a rich man was to divest himself of some of his wealth for the church and thereby take a step toward salvation. I believe that in terms of history and theology this is all moonshine and Woodiwiss may even have invented it himself, but it worked like a charm. Because, as he said, following on from his text, "with God all things are possible." So he persuaded his rich camels to strip off a few bales of this world's goods and leave the negotiation of the needle's eye in his capable hands.

I didn't see much of the Canon, though I heard many of his wonder-working sermons. He had the gift of the gab as few parsons do. But I came much under the influence of one of his curates, who was named Gervase Knopwood.

Father Knopwood, as he liked us to call him, had an extraordinary way with boys, though on the face of it this seemed unlikely.

He was an Englishman with an almost farcically upper-class accent and long front teeth and an appearance of being an elderly schoolboy. He wasn't old; probably he was in his early forties, but his hair was almost white and he had deep furrows in his face. He wasn't a joker or a jolly good fellow, and he played no games, though he was tough enough to have been a missionary in the Canadian West in some very difficult territory. But everybody respected him, and everybody feared him in a special way, for his standards were high, he expected the best from boys, and he had some ideas that to me were original.

For one thing, he didn't pay the usual lip-service to Art, which enjoyed more than sacred status in the kind of society in which we lived. I discovered this one day when I was talking to him in one of the rooms at the back of the church where we met for the Servers' Guild and Confirmation classes and that sort of thing. There was a picture on the wall, a perfectly hideous thing in vivid colours, of a Boy Scout looking the very picture of boyish virtue, and behind him stood the figure of Christ with His hand on the Scout's shoulder. I was making great game of it for the benefit of some other boys when I became aware that Father Knopwood was standing at a little distance, listening carefully.

"You don't think much of it, Davey?"

"Well, Father, could anybody think much of it? I mean, look at the way it's drawn, and the raw colours. And the sentimentality!"

"Tell us about the sentimentality."

"Well—it's obvious. I mean, Our Lord standing with His hand on the fellow's shoulder, and everything."

"I seem to have missed something you have seen. Why is it sentimental to suggest that Christ stands near to anyone, whether it is a boy, or a girl, or an old man, or anyone at all?"

"That's not sentimental, of course. But it's the way it's done. I mean, the concept is so crude."

"Must a concept be sophisticated to be a good one?"

"Well—surely?"

"Must the workmanship always be superior? If something is to be said, must it always be said with eloquence and taste?"

"That's what they teach us in the Art Club. I mean, if it's not well done it's no good, is it?"

"I don't know. I've never been able to make up my mind. A lot of modern artists are impatient of technical skill. It's one of the great puzzles. Why don't you come and see me after the meeting, and we'll talk about it and see what we can find out."

This led to seeing a lot of Father Knopwood. He used to ask me to meals in his rooms, as he called a bed-sitter with a gasring in a cupboard that he had not far from the church. He wasn't poison-poor, but he didn't believe in spending money on himself. He taught me a lot and put some questions I have never been able to answer.

The art thing was one of his pet subjects. He loved art and knew a lot about it, but he was always rather afraid of it as a substitute religion. He was especially down on the idea that art was a thing in itself—that a picture was simply a flat composition of line and pigment, and the fact that it seemed also to be Mona Lisa or The Marriage at Cana was an irrelevance. Every picture, he insisted, was "of" something or "about" something. He was interesting about very modern pictures, and once he took me to a good show of some of the best, and talked about them as manifestations of questing, chaos, and sometimes of despair that artists sensed in the world about them and could not express adequately in any other way. "A real artist never does anything gratuitously or simply to be puzzling," he would say, "and if we don't understand it now, we shall understand it later."

This was not what Mr. Pugliesi said in the Art Club at school. We had a lot of clubs, and the Art Club had rather a cachet, as attracting the more intellectual boys; you were elected to it, you didn't simply join. Mr. Pugliesi was always warning us not to look for messages and meanings but to take heed of the primary thing—the picture as an object—so many square feet of painted canvas. Messages and meanings were what Father Knopwood chiefly sought, so I had to balance my ideas pretty carefully. That was why he got after me for laughing at the Boy Scout picture. He agreed that it was an awful picture, but he thought the meaning redeemed it. Thousands of boys would understand it who would never notice a Raphael reproduction if we put one in its place.

I have never been convinced that he was right, and was shocked by his idea that not everybody needed art to be educated. He saved me from becoming an art snob, and he could be terribly funny about changes in art taste; the sort of fashionable enthusiasm that admires Tissot for thirty years, kicks him out of the door for forty, and then drags him back through the window as an artist of hitherto unappreciated quality. "It's simply the immature business of assuming that one's grandfather must necessarily be a fool, and then getting enough sense to realize that the old gentleman was almost as intelligent as oneself," he said.

This was important to me because another kind of art was coming to the fore at home. Caroline, who had always had lessons on the piano, was beginning to show some talent as a musician. We had both had some musical training and used to go to Mrs. Tattersall's Saturday morning classes, where we sang and played rhythm instruments and learned some basic stuff very pleasantly. But I had no special ability, and Caroline had. By the time she was twelve she had fought through a lot of the donkey-work of learning that extraordinarily difficult instrument that all unmusical parents seem to think their children should play, and she was pretty good. She has never become a first-rate pianist, but she is a much better than average amateur.

When she was twelve, though, she was sure that she was going to be another Myra Hess and worked very hard. She played musically, which is really quite rare, even among people who get paid big fees to do it. Like Father Knopwood, she was interested in content as well as technique, and it was always a puzzle to me how she got to be that way, for nothing at home encouraged it. She played the things young pianists play—Schumann's *The Prophet Bird* and his *Scenes from Childhood*, and of course lots of Bach and Scarlatti and Beethoven. She could wallop out Schumann's *Carnaval* with immense authority for a girl of twelve or thirteen. The mischievous little snip she was in her personal life seemed to disappear, and somebody much more important took her place. I think I liked it best when she played some of the easier things she had learned in earlier years and fully commanded. There is one trifle—I don't suppose it has much musical value—by Stephen Heller, called in English *Curious Story*, which is a very misleading translation of *Kuriose Geschichte;* she really succeeded in making it eerie, not by playing in a false, spooky way, but by a refined, Hans Andersen treatment. I loved listening to her, and though she tormented me horribly at other times, we seemed to be able to reach one another when she was playing and I was listening, and Netty was somewhere else.

Caroline was glad to see me at weekends, because the house was even gloomier than before our mother died. It wasn't neglected; there were still servants, though the staff had been cut down, and they polished and tidied things that never grew dim or untidy because nobody ever touched them; but the life had gone out of the house, and even though its former life had been unhappy, it had been life of a kind. Caroline lived there, supposedly under the care of Netty, and once a week Father's secretary, an extremely efficient woman from Alpha Corporation, called to see that everything was in good order. But this secretary didn't want to be involved personally, and I don't blame her. Caroline was a day-girl at Bishop Cairncross's, so she had friends and a social life there, as I did at Colborne College.

We rarely asked anybody home, and our first attempt to take over the house as our own soon spent itself. Father wrote letters now and then, and I know he asked Dunstan Ramsay to keep an eye on us, but Ramsay had his hands full at the school during those war years, and he didn't trouble us often. I rather think he disliked Carol, so he confined his supervision to questioning me now and then at school.

You might suppose my sister and I were to be pitied, but we rather liked our weekend solitude. We could lighten it whenever we pleased by going out with friends, and people were kind about inviting us both to parties and such things, though during the war they were on a very modest scale. But I didn't want to go out much because I had no money and could get into embarrassing positions; I borrowed all I could from Carol but didn't want to be wholly in her clutch.

What we both liked best were the Saturday evenings when we were together, because it had become the custom for Netty to devote that time to her pestilent brother Maitland and his deserving young family. Carol played the piano, and I looked through books about art which I was able to borrow from the school library. I was determined about this because I didn't want her to think that I had no independent artistic interest of my own, but as I looked at pictures and read about them, I was really listening to her. It was the only time the drawing-room showed any hint of life, but the big empty fireplace—the secretary from Alpha and Netty agreed that it was foolish to light it during wartime, when presumably even cord-wood was involved in our total war effort—was a reminder that the room was merely enduring us, and that as soon as we went to bed a weight of inanition would settle on it again.

I remember one night when Ramsay did drop in, and laughed to see us.

"Music and painting," said he; "the traditional diversions of the third generation of wealthy families. Let us hope you will both become discriminating patrons. God knows they are rare."

We didn't like this, and Carol was particularly offended by his assumption that she would never do anything directly as a musician. But time has proved him right, as it does with so many disagreeable people. Carol and Beesty are now generous patrons of music, and I collect pictures. With both of us, as Father Knopwood feared, it has become the only spiritual life we have, and not a very satisfactory one when life is hard.

Knopwood prepared me for Confirmation, and it was a much more important experience than I believe is usually the case. Most curates, you know, take you through the Catechism and bid you to ask them about anything you don't understand. Of course most people don't understand any of it, but they are content to let sleeping dogs lie. Most curates give you a vaguely worded talk about keeping yourself pure, without any real hope that you will.

Knopwood was very different. He expounded the Creed in tough terms, very much in the C. S. Lewis manner. Christianity was serious and demanding, but worth any amount of trouble. God is here, and Christ is now. That was his line. And when it came to the talk about purity, he got down to brass tacks better than anybody I have ever known.

He didn't expect you to chalk up a hundred per cent score, but he expected you to try, and if you sinned, he expected you to know what you had done and why it was sin. If you knew that, you were better armed next time. This appealed to me. I liked dogma, for the same reason that I grew to like law. It made sense, it told you where you stood, and it had been tested by long precedent.

He was very good about sex. It was pleasure: yes. It could be a duty: yes. But it wasn't divorced from the rest of life, and what you did sexually was of a piece with what you did in your friendships and in your duty to other people in your public life. An adulterer and a burglar were bad men for similar reasons. A seducer and a sneak-thief were the same kind of man. Sex was not a toy. The great sin—quite possibly the Sin against the Holy Ghost—was to use yourself or someone else contemptuously, as an object of convenience. I saw the logic of that and agreed.

There were problems. Not everybody fitted all rules. If you found yourself in that situation you had to do the best you could, but you had to bear in mind that the Sin against the Holy Ghost would not be forgiven you, and the retribution would be in this world.

The brighter members of Knoppy's Confirmation classes knew what he was talking about at this point. It was clear enough that he was himself a homosexual and knew it, and that his work with boys was his way of coping with it. But he never played favourites, he was a dear and thoroughly masculine friend, and there was never any monkey-business when he asked you to his rooms. I suppose there are hundreds like me who remember him with lasting affection and count having known him as a great experience. He stood by me during my early love-affair in a way I can never forget and which nothing I could do would possibly repay.

I wish we could have remained friends.

6

People jeer at first love, and in ridiculous people it is certainly ridiculous. But I have seen how hot its flame can be in people of passionate nature, and how selfless it is in people who are inclined to be idealistic. It does not demand to be requited, and it can be a force where it is obviously hopeless. The worst fight I saw in my schooldays was caused when a boy said something derogatory about Loretta Young; another boy, who cherished a passion for the actress, whom he had seen only in films, hit this fellow in the mouth, and in an instant they were on the ground, the lover trying to murder the loudmouth. Our gym master parted them and insisted that they fight it out in the ring, but it was hopeless: the lover ignored all rules, kicked and bit and seemed like a madman. Of course nobody could explain to the master what the trouble was, but all of us supposed it was a fight about love. What I know now was that it was really a fight about honour and idealism—what Dr. von Haller calls a projection—and that it was a necessary part of the spiritual development of the lover. It may also have done something for the fellow who was so free with the name of Miss Young.

I fell in love, with a crash and at first sight, on a Friday night in early December of 1944. I had been in love before, but trivially. Many boys, I think, are in love from the time they are able to walk, and I had cherished my hidden fancies and had had my conquests, of whom Toad Wilson was by no means the best example. Those were childish affairs, with shallow roots in Vanity. But now I was sixteen, serious and lonely, and in three hours Judith Wolff became the central, absorbing element in my life.

Caroline's school, named for a Bishop Cairncross who had been a dominant figure in the nineteenth-century life of our Canadian province, had a reputation for its plays and its music. Every school needs to be known for something other than good teaching, and its Christmas play was its speciality. In the year when I was sixteen the school decided to combine music and drama and get up a piece by Walter de la Mare called *Crossings*. I heard a good deal about it because it had a lot of music and four songs in it, and Caroline was to play the piano offstage. She practised at home and talked about the play as if it were the biggest musical show since Verdi wrote *Aida* for the Khedive of Egypt.

I read the playbook she had to work from, and I did not think much of it. It was certainly not in the Plain Style, and I was now much under the influence of Ramsay's enthusiasm for unadorned prose. It was not a Broadway kind of play, and I am not certain it is even a good play, but it is unmistakably a poet's play, and I was the most deeply enchanted of an audience that seemed, in a variety of ways suitable to their age and state of mind and relationship to the players or the school, to be delighted by it.

It is about some children who are left to their own devices because of a legacy. They have an aunt who has strict educational theories and expects them to get into hopeless messes without her guidance; instead they have some fine adventures with strange people, including fairy people. The oldest child is a girl called Sally, and that was Judith Wolff.

Sally is very much a de la Mare girl, and I don't think I ever saw Judith except through de la Mare eyes. The curtain went up (or rather, was drawn apart with a wiry hiss) and there she sat, at a piano, precisely as the poet describes her in the stage directions—slim, dark, of mobile face, speaking in a low clear voice as if out of her thoughts. She had a song almost at once. The illusion that she was playing the piano was not successful, because the sound was plainly coming from Caroline backstage, and her pretence to be playing was no better than it usually is. But her voice made shortcomings of that sort irrelevant. I suppose it was just a charming girl's voice, but I shall never know. It was a voice that seemed to be for me only in all the world. I was engulfed in love, and I suppose I have been in love with Judith ever since. Not as she is now. I see her from time to time, by chance; a woman of my own age, still gravely beautiful. But she is a Mrs. Julius Meyer, whose husband is an admired professor of chemistry, and I know that she has three clever children and is an important figure on the committee of the Jewish hospital. Mrs. Julius Meyer is not Judith Wolff to me, but her ghost, and when I see her I get away as fast as possible. The David Staunton who fell in love still lives in me, but Judith Wolff—the girl of the de la Mare play—lives only in my memories.

Judith had two songs in *Crossings*. She acted as she sang, with a grave natural charm, and was much, much, much the best of the girls in the play.

There were people who thought differently. As always at these affairs, there were people who thought the girls who played masculine parts were wildly funny, and I suppose that when they turned their whiskered, carefully made-up faces away, and we saw their girl-shaped bottoms, it was funny if that is where you find your fun. There was much applause for a small blonde who played the Queen of the Fairies; she acted with a sweetness which I thought painfully overdone. There was a ballet of fairies, very pretty as they danced through a snow-scene, holding little lanterns; there were plenty of parents with eyes only for a special fairy. But I saw nothing clearly but Judith, and in justice to the audience generally I must say that they thought that she was—always excepting their own child—the best. For the curtain call the stage was filled with the whole cast, and also the inevitable clown assembly of mistresses in sensible shoes who had helped in some way, looking as such helpers always do, too big and too clumsy to have had anything to do with creating an illusion. Judith stood in the centre of the first line, and it seemed to me that she was aware of her popularity and was blushing at it.

I applauded uproariously, and I noticed some parents looking approvingly at me. I suppose they thought I was clapping for Caroline and was a loyal brother. Caroline was on the stage, certainly, holding the score of the music so people would know what she had done, but I had no eyes for her. After the party for the cast and friends—school coffee and school cookies—I took Caroline home and tried to find out something about Judith Wolff. She had been surrounded by some foreign-looking people whom I supposed to be her parents and their friends, and I had not been able to get a good look at her. But Caroline was full of herself, as always, and demanded again and again that I reassure her that the music had been suitably audible, yet not too loud, and had supported the weaker singers without seeming to dominate them, and had really carried the ballet, who were just little girls and had no more sense of rhythm than so many donkeys, and had indeed been fully orchestral in effect. This was egotistical nonsense, but I had to put up with it in order to bring the conversation around to what I wanted to know.

Weren't they lucky to get such a good girl for the part of Sally? Who was she?

Oh—Judy Wolff. Nice voice, but dark. Brought it too much from the back of her throat. Needed some lessons in production.

Perhaps. Good for that part, though.

Possibly. A bit of a cow at rehearsal. Hard to stir her up.

I considered killing Caroline and leaving her battered body on the lawn of one of the houses we were passing.

Caroline knew I wouldn't have noticed, because it was a fine point not many people would get, but in Sally's *Lullaby* in Act

Two, at "Leap fox, hoot owl, wail warbler sweet," Judy was all over the place, and as Caroline had a very tricky succession of chromatic chords to play there was nothing she could do to drag Judy back, and she just hoped it would be better tomorrow night.

You cannot have a sister like Caroline without picking up a few tricks. I asked if there was any chance that I could see the play again on Saturday night?

"So you can go and moon at Judy again?" she said. In another age Caroline would have been burnt as a witch; she could smell what you were thinking, especially when you wanted to conceal it. I set aside plans for burning her then and there.

"Judy who? Oh, the Sally girl. Don't be silly. No, I just thought it was good, and I'd like to see it again. And I was thinking you didn't really get the recognition you deserved tonight. If I came tomorrow night, I could send you a bouquet, and it could be handed up over the footlights at the end, and people would know what you were worth."

"Not a bad idea, but where would you get any money to send a bouquet? You're broke."

"I'd wondered if you could possibly see your way to making me a small loan. As it's really for you, anyhow."

"What's the need? Why can't I just send myself a bouquet? That would cut out the middleman."

"Because it's ridiculous and undignified and cheap and generally two-bit and no-account, and if Netty heard of it, as she would from me, she would make your life a burden. Whereas if the bouquet comes from me, nobody need know, and if they find out they'll think what a sweet brother I am. But I'll put a big ticket on it with 'Homage to those eloquent fingers, from Arturo Toscanini' if you like."

It worked. I thought it would be a cheap dollar bouquet, but I had underrated Caroline's vanity, and she handed over a nice, resounding five bucks as a tribute to herself. This was splendid because I had craftily decided to sequester some portion of whatever I got from Caroline, and use it to send another bouquet to Judy Wolff. With five dollars I could do the thing in style.

Florists were more grasping than I had supposed, but after shopping around on Saturday I managed quite a showy tribute for

Caroline, of chrysanthemums with plenty of fern to eke them out, for a dollar seventy-five. With the remaining three twenty-five, to which I added fifty cents I ground out of Netty by pretending I had to get a couple of special pencils for making maps, I bought roses for Judy. Not the best roses; I had no money for those; but indubitable roses.

I was playing a dangerous game. I knew it, yet I could not help myself. Caroline would find out about the two bouquets and would take it out of me in some dreadful way, for she was a terrible skinflint. But I was ready to risk anything, so long as Judy Wolff received the tribute that was her due. The thought of the evening sustained me through a nervous, worrisome Saturday.

It worked out quite differently from anything I could have foreseen. In the first place, Netty wanted to go to *Crossings,* and it was assumed that I should take her. There is a special sort of enraged misery that overcomes a young man who is absorbed in his love for an ideal girl and who is thrust into the company of a distasteful, commonplace older woman. Dr. von Haller talks about the concept of the Shadow; how much of my Shadow—of my impatience, my snobbery, my ingratitude—was visited on poor Netty that night! To have to sit beside her, and answer her tomfool questions and listen to her crass assertions, and breathe up her smell of fevered flesh and laundry starch, and be conscious of her garment of state, her sheared mouton coat, among all the minky mothers, was torture to me. Had I been Romeo and she the Nurse, I could have risen above her with aristocratic ease, and everybody would have known she was my retainer; but I was Davey and she was Netty who had washed under my foreskin and threatened to cut my heart out with a whip when I was naughty, and my dread was that the rest of the audience would think she was my mother! But Netty was not sensitive; she was on a spree; she was to witness the triumph of her adored Caroline. I was merely her escort, and she felt kindly toward me and sought to divert me with her Gothic vivacity. How was I to insinuate myself into the moonlight world of Judith Wolff after the play, with this goblin in tow?

Consequently I did not enjoy the play as I had expected to do. I was conscious of faults Caroline had been niggling about all day, and although my worship of Judy was more agonizing than before, it heaved on a sea of irritability and discontentment. And always there was the dread of the moment when the bouquets would be presented.

Here again I had reckoned without Fate, which was disposed to spare me from the consequences of my folly. When the curtain call came, some of the girls who had been serving as ushers rushed to the footlights like Birnam Wood moving to Dunsinane, loaded with bouquets. Judy got my roses and another much finer bunch from another usher. Caroline was handed the measly bundle of chrysanthemums, but also a very grand bunch of yellow roses, which were her favourites; she pretended extreme astonishment, read the card, and gave a little jump of joy! When the applause was over and almost every girl on the stage had been given flowers of some sort, I stumbled out of the hall like one who has, at the last minute, been snatched from in front of the firing-squad.

The party in the school's dining-room was larger and gayer than the night before, though the food was the same. There were so many people that they stood in groups, and not in a single mass. Netty made a bee-line for Caroline, demanding to know who had sent her flowers. Caroline was busy displaying the roses and the card that was with them, on which was printed, in bold script, "From a devoted admirer, who wishes to remain unknown." The chrysanthemums and their rotten little card, on which I had printed "Congratulations and Good Luck," she gave to Netty to hold. She was in tearing high spirits and loved all mankind; she seized me by the arm and rushed me over to Judy Wolff and shrieked, "Judy, I want you to meet my baby brother; he thinks you're the tops," and left me gangling. But she immediately showed her roses to Judy, and made a great affair of wondering who could have sent them; Judy, like every girl when confronted with an obvious admirer, ignored me and chattered away to Caroline and tried to talk about the mystery of her own roses. My roses. Hopeless. Caroline was not to be distracted. But in time she did go away, and I was left with Judy, and had opened my mouth to say my carefully prepared speech—"You sang awfully well; you must have a marvellous teacher." (Oh, was it too daring? Would she think I was a pushy nuisance? Would she think it was just a line I used with all the dozens of girls I knew who sang? Would she think I was trying to move in on her like some football tough who—Knopwood, stand by me now!—wanted to use her as an object of convenience?) But near her were the same smiling, dark-skinned, big-nosed people I had seen last night, and they took me over as Judy (what manners, what aplomb, she must be foreign) introduced me as Caroline's brother. My father, Dr. Louis Wolff. My mother. My Aunt Esther. My uncle, Professor Bruno Schwarz.

They were very kind to me, but they all had X-ray eyes, or extrasensory perception, because they assumed without asking that it was I who had sent Judy the other bouquet of roses. And this flummoxed me. There I stood, a declared lover, a role for which I had no preparation whatever, and which I had entered on a level of roses, which I was utterly unable to sustain. But what was most remarkable was that they took it for granted that I should admire Judy and send her flowers as an entirely suitable way of getting to know her. I gathered that being Caroline's brother was, to them, a sufficient introduction. How little they knew Caroline! They understood. They sympathized. Of course they said nothing directly, but their attitude toward me and their conversation made it plain that they supposed I wanted to be accepted as a friend, and were willing that it should be so. I didn't know what to do. The course of true love was, contrary to everything that was right and proper, running smooth, and I was not ready for it.

Friends of mine at school were in love with girls. The parents of these girls were always hilarious nuisances, eager to tar and feather Cupid and make a clown of him; or, if not that, they were unpleasantly ironic and seemed to have forgotten all about love except as something that ailed puppies and calves. The Wolffs took me seriously as a human being. I had hoped for a furtive romance, unknown to anyone else in the world. But here was Mrs. Wolff saying that they were always at home on Sunday afternoons between four and six, and if I liked to look in, they would be delighted to see me. I asked if tomorrow would be too soon. No, tomorrow would do beautifully. They were delighted to meet me. They hoped we would meet often.

During all of this, Judy said very little, and when I shook hands with her at parting—an awful struggle; was this the thing to do, or not; did one shake the hands of girls?—she cast down her eyes.

This was something I had never seen a girl do. Caroline's friends always looked you straight in the eye, especially if they had something disagreeable to say. This dropping of the gaze almost disembowelled me with its modest beauty.

But the publicity of it all! Can I have been so obvious? On the way home even Netty remarked that I certainly seemed to be taken with that dark girl, and when I asked her haughtily what she meant she said she had eyes in her head like anybody else, and I had been lallygagging so nobody could miss it.

Netty was in high good humour. Dunstan Ramsay had been at *Crossings,* invited, I suppose as Headmaster of a neighbouring school. He had paid Netty a good deal of attention. That was like Buggerlugs; he never overlooked anybody, and he seemed to put himself out to be gallant to women nobody else could stand. He had introduced Netty to Miss Gostling, the Headmistress of Bishop Cairncross's, and had said she was the mainstay of the Staunton household while Father had to be away on war business. Miss Gostling had been quite the lady; hadn't put on any airs. But it was a good thing that place was a school and not a hotel, because their coffee would choke a dog.

As we were going to bed, Caroline came to my room to thank me for the flowers. "I must say you did it in style," said she, "and you must have shopped around for quite a while to get yellow roses like that for five dollars. I know what these things cost; this is identical with the bunch Buggerlugs sent Ghastly Gostling, and I'll bet it didn't cost him a cent less than eight."

I was in a mood to dare much. "Who sent you the other flowers?" I asked.

"Scotland Yard suspects Tiger McGregor," she replied. "He's been lurking for a couple of months. Cheap creep! It looks like about a dollar seventy-five"—this with a glint of her pawnbroker's eye—"and he'll probably expect me to go to the Colborne dance with him on the strength of it. Maybe I will, at that. . . . By the way, you and I are invited to tea at Judy Wolff's tomorrow. I worked that for you, so clean yourself up and do me credit."

So Buggerlugs had sent the roses and saved me from God knows what humiliation and servitude to Carol! Could he have known anything? Not possibly. He was just doing right by an old friend's daughter and having a little joke on his card. But he was a friend, whether he knew it or not. Was he more than a friend? . . . Damn Carol!

We went to tea with the Wolffs next day. It was not a social occasion I knew anything about, and I was in a frenzy of nerves. But the Wolff apartment was full of people, and Tiger McGregor was there and kept Caroline out of my way. I had a few words with Judy, and once she gave me a plate of sandwiches to hand around, so obviously she thought I was a trustworthy person and not just somebody who regarded her as an object of convenience. Her parents were charming and kind, and although I had experienced kindness, I was a stranger to charm, so I fell in love with all the Wolffs and Schwarzes in properly respectful degrees, and felt that I had suddenly moved into a new sort of world.

Thus began a love which fed my life and expanded my spirit for a year, before it was destroyed by an act of kindness which was in effect an act of shattering cruelty.

Need we go into details about what I said to Judy? I am no poet, and I suppose what I said was very much what everybody always says, and although I remember her as speaking golden words, I cannot recall precisely anything she said. If love is to be watched and listened to without embarrassment, it must be transmuted into art, and I don't know how to do that, and it is not what I have come to Zürich to learn.

DR. VON HALLER: We must go into it a little, I think. You told her you loved her?

MYSELF: On New Year's Day. I said I would love her always, and I meant it. She said she couldn't be sure about loving me; she would not say it unless she was sure she meant it, and forever. But she would not withhold it, if ever she were sure, and meanwhile the greatest kindness I could show was not to press her.

DR. VON HALLER: And did you?

MYSELF: Yes, quite often. She was always gentle and always said the same thing.

DR. VON HALLER: What was she like? Physically, I mean.

Was her appearance characteristically feminine? A well-developed bosom? Was she a clean person?

MYSELF: She was dark. Complexion what is called olive, but with wonderful deep red colour in her cheeks when she blushed. Hair dark brown. Not tall, but not short. She laughed at herself about being fat, but of course she wasn't. Curvy. Those uniforms that schools like Bishop Cairncross's insisted on at that time were extraordinarily revealing. If a girl had breasts, they showed up under those middies, and some girls had positive shelves almost under their chins. And those absurd short blue skirts, showing seemingly miles of leg from ankle to thigh. It was supposed to be a modest outfit, to make them look like children, but a pretty girl dressed like that is a quaint, touching miracle. The sloppy ones and the fatties were pretty spooky, but not a girl like Judy.

DR. VON HALLER: You felt physical desire for her, then?

MYSELF: I most certainly did! There were times when I nearly fried! But I was heedful of what Knopwood said. Of course I talked to Knopwood about it, and he was wonderful. He said it was a very great experience, but I was the man, and the greater responsibility was mine. So—nothing that would harm Judy. He also gave me a hint about Jewish girls; said they were brought up to be modest and that her parents, being Viennese, were probably pretty strict. So—no casual Canadian ways, and never get the parents against me.

DR. VON HALLER: Did you have erotic dreams about her?

MYSELF: Not about her. But wild dreams about women I couldn't recognize, and sometimes frightful hags, who ravished me. Netty began to look askew and hint about my pyjamas. And of course she had some awful piece of lore from Deptford to bring out. It seems there had been some woman there when she was a little girl who had always been "at it" and had eventually been discovered in a gravel pit, "at it" with a tramp; of course this woman had gone stark, staring mad and had had to be kept in her house, tied up. But I think this tale of lust rebuked was really for Caroline's benefit, because Tiger McGregor was lurking more and more, and Carol was getting silly. I spoke to her about it myself, and she replied with some quotation about showing her the steep and thorny way to heaven, while I was making an ass of myself over Judy Wolff. But I kept my eye on her, just the same.

DR. VON HALLER: Yes? A little more, please.

MYSELF: It's not a part of my life I take pride in. Now and then I would gum-shoe around the house when Tiger was there, just to see that everything was on the level.

DR. VON HALLER: And was it?

MYSELF: No. There was a lot of prolonged kissing, and once I caught them on the sofa, and Carol's skirt was practically over her head, and Tiger was snorting and puffing, and it was what Netty would call a scene.

DR. VON HALLER: Did you intervene?

MYSELF: No. I didn't quite do that, but I was as mad as hell, and went upstairs and walked around over their heads and then took another peep, and they had straightened up.

DR. VON HALLER: Were you jealous of your sister?

MYSELF: She was just a kid. She oughtn't to have known about that kind of thing. And I couldn't trust Tiger to understand that the greater responsibility was his. And Carol was as hot as a Quebec heater anyhow.

DR. VON HALLER: What did you say to Tiger?

MYSELF: That's where the shame of the thing comes in. I didn't say anything to him. I was pretty strong; I got over all that nonsense about being frail by the time I was twelve; but Tiger was a football tough, and he could have killed me.

DR. VON HALLER: Should you not have been prepared to fight for Father Knopwood's principles?

MYSELF: Knopwood prepared Carol for Confirmation; she knew what his principles were as well as I did. But she laughed at him and referred to him as my "ghostly father." And Tiger had no principles, and still hasn't. He's ended up as a public-relations man in one of Father's companies.

DR. VON HALLER: So what was perfectly all right for you and Judy was not all right for Tiger and Carol?

MYSELF: I loved Judy.

DR. VON HALLER: And you had no sofa-scenes?

MYSELF: Yes—but not often. The Wolffs lived in an apartment, you see, and though it was a big one there was always somebody going or coming.

DR. VON HALLER: In fact, they kept their daughter on a short string?

MYSELF: Yes, but you wouldn't think of it that way. They were such charming people. A kind of person I'd never met before. Dr. Wolff was a surgeon, but you'd never know it from his conversation. Art and music and the theatre were his great interests. And politics. He was the first man I ever met who was interested in politics without being a partisan of some kind. He was even cool about Zionism. He actually had good words for Mackenzie King; he admired King's political astuteness. He weighed the war news as nobody else did, that I knew, and even when the Allies were having setbacks near the end, he was perfectly certain the end was near. He and Professor Schwarz, who was his brother-in-law, had seen things clearly enough to leave Austria in 1932. There was a sophistication in that house that was a continual refreshment to me. Not painted on, you know, but rising from within.

DR. VON HALLER: And they kept their daughter on a short string?

MYSELF: I suppose so. But I was never aware of the string.

DR. VON HALLER: And there were some tempestuous scenes between you?

MYSELF: Whenever it was possible, I suppose.

DR. VON HALLER: To which she consented without being sure that she loved you?

MYSELF: But I loved her. She was being kind to me because I loved her.

DR. VON HALLER: Wasn't Carol being kind to Tiger?

MYSELF: Carol was being kind to herself.

DR. VON HALLER: But Judy wasn't being kind to herself?

MYSELF: You won't persuade me that the two things were the same.

DR. VON HALLER: But what would Mr. Justice Staunton say if these two young couples were brought before him? Would he make a distinction? If Father Knopwood were to appear as a special witness, would he make a distinction?

MYSELF: Knopwood was the soul of charity.

DR. VON HALLER: Which you are not? Well, don't answer now. Charity is the last lesson we learn. That is why so much of the charity we show people is retrospective. Think it over and we shall talk about it later. Tell me more about your wonderful year.

It was wonderful because the war was ending. Wonderful because Father was able to get home for a weekend now and then. Wonderful because I found my profession. Wonderful because he raised my allowance, because of Judy.

That began badly. One day he told Caroline he wanted to see her in his office. She thought it was about Tiger, and was in a sweat for fear Netty had squealed. Only Supreme Court cases took place in Father's office. But he just wanted to know why she had been spending so much money. Miss Macmanaway, the secretary, advanced Caroline money as she needed it, without question, but of course she kept an account for Father. Caroline had been advancing me the money I needed to take Judy to films and concerts and plays, and to lunch now and then. I think Caroline thought it kept me quiet about Tiger, and I suppose she was right. But when Father wanted to know how she had been getting through about twenty-five dollars a week, apart from her accounts for clothes and oddments, she lost her nerve and said she had been giving money to me. Why? He takes this girl out, and you know what he's like when he can't have his own way. Carol warned me to look out for storms.

There was no storm. Father was amused, after he had scared me for a few minutes. He liked the idea that I had a girl. Raised my allowance to seven dollars and fifty cents a week, which was a fortune after my miserable weekly dollar for so long. Said he had forgotten I was growing up and had particular needs.

I was so relieved and grateful and charmed by him—because he was really the most charming man I have ever known, in a sunny, open way which was quite different from the Wolffs' complex, baroque charm—that I told him a lot about Judy. Oddly enough, like Knopwood, he warned me about Jewish girls; very strictly guarded on the level of people like the Wolffs. Why didn't I look a little lower down? I didn't understand that. Why would I want a girl who was less than Judy, when not only she, but all her family, had such distinction? I knew Father liked distinguished people. But he didn't make any reply to that.

So things were very much easier, and I was out of Carol's financial clutch.

7

Summer came, and the war had ended, in Europe, on May 7.

I went to camp for the last time. Every year Caroline and I were sent to excellent camps, and I liked mine. It was not huge, it had a sensible program instead of one of those fake-Indian nightmares, and we had a fair amount of freedom. I had grown to know a lot of the boys there, and met them from year to year, though not otherwise because few of them were from Colborne College.

There was one fellow who particularly interested me because he was in so many ways unlike myself. He seemed to have extraordinary dash. He never looked ahead and never counted the cost. His name was Bill Unsworth.

I went to camp willingly enough because Judy's parents were taking her to California. Professor Schwarz was going there to give some special lectures at Cal Tech. and other places, and the Wolffs went along to see what was to be seen. Mrs. Wolff said it was time Judy saw something of the world, before she went to Europe to school. I did not grasp the full significance of that, but thought the end of the war must have something to do with it.

Camp was all very well, but I was growing too old for it, and Bill Unsworth was already too old, though he was a little younger than I. When the camp season finished, about the middle of August, he asked me and two other boys to go with him to a summer place his parents owned which was in the same district, for a few days before we returned to Toronto. It was pleasant enough, but we had had all the boating and swimming we wanted for one summer, and we were bored. Bill suggested that we look for some fun.

None of us had any idea what he had in mind, but he was certain we would like it, and enjoyed being mysterious. We drove some distance—twenty miles or so—down country roads, and then he stopped the car and said we would walk the rest of the way.

We struck into some pretty rough country, for this was Muskoka and it is rocky and covered with scrub which is hard to break through. After about half an hour we came to a pretty summer house on a small lake; it was a fussy place, with a little rock garden around it—gardens come hard in Muskoka—and a lot of verandah furniture that looked as if it had been kept in good condition by fussy people.

"Who lives here?" asked Jerry Wood.

"I don't know their names," said Bill. "But I do know they aren't here. Trip to the Maritimes. I heard it at the store."

"Well—did they say we could use the place?"

"No. They didn't say we could use the place."

"It's locked," said Don McQuilly, who was the fourth of our group.

"The kind of locks you open by spitting on them," said Bill Unsworth.

"Are you going to break a lock?"

"Yes, Donny, I am going to break a lock."

"But what for?"

"To get inside. What else?"

"But wait a minute. What do you want to get inside for?"

"To see what they've got in there, and smash it to buggery," said Bill.

"But why?"

"Because that's the way I feel. Haven't you ever wanted to wreck a house?"

"My grandfather's a judge," said McQuilly. "I have to watch my step."

"I don't see your grandfather anywhere around," said Bill, sweeping the landscape with eyes shaded by his hand like a pirate in a movie.

We had an argument about it. McQuilly was against going ahead, but Jerry Wood thought it might be fun to get in and turn a few things upside down. I was divided in my opinion, as usual. I was sick of camp discipline; but I was by nature law-abiding. I had often wondered what it would be like to wreck something; but on the other hand I had a strong conviction that if I did anything wrong I would certainly be caught. But no boy likes to lose face in the eyes of a leader, and Bill Unsworth was a leader, of a sort. His sardonic smile as we haggled was worth pages of wordy argument. In the end we decided to go ahead, I for one feeling that I could put on the brakes any time I liked.

The lock needed rather more than spitting on, but Bill had brought some tools, which surprised and rather shocked us. We got in after a few minutes. The house was even more fussy inside than the outside had promised. It was a holiday place, but everything about it suggested elderly people.

"The first move in a job like this," Bill said, "is to see if they've got any booze."

They had none, and this made them enemies, in Bill's eyes. They must have hidden it, which was sneaky and deserved punishment. He began to turn out cupboards and storage places, pulling everything onto the floor. We others didn't want to seem poor-spirited, so we kicked it around a little. Our lack of zeal angered the leader.

"You make me puke!" he shouted and grabbed a mirror from the wall. It was round, and had a frame made of that plaster stuff twisted into flowers that used to be called barbola. He lifted it high above his head, and smashed it down on the back of a chair. Shattered glass flew everywhere.

"Hey, look out!" shouted Jerry. "You'll kill somebody."

"I'll kill you all," yelled Bill, and swore for three or four minutes, calling us every dirty name he could think of for being so chicken-hearted. When people talk about "leadership quality" I often think of Bill Unsworth; he had it. And like many people who have it, he could make you do things you didn't want to do by a kind of cunning urgency. We were ashamed before him. Here he was, a bold adventurer, who had put himself out to include us—lily-livered wretches—in a daring, dangerous, highly illegal exploit, and all we could do was worry about being hurt! We plucked up our spirits and swore and shouted filthy words, and set to work to wreck the house.

Our appetite for destruction grew with feeding. I started gingerly, pulling some books out of a case, but soon I was tearing out pages by handfuls and throwing them around. Jerry got a knife and ripped the stuffing out of the mattresses. He threw feathers from sofa cushions. McQuilly, driven by some dark Scottish urge, found a crowbar and reduced wooden things to splinters. And Bill was like a fury, smashing, overturning, and tearing. But I noticed that he kept back some things and put them in a neat heap on the dining-room table, which he forbade us to break. They were photographs.

The old people must have had a large family, and there were pictures of young people and wedding groups and what were clearly grandchildren everywhere. When at last we had done as much damage as we could, the pile on the table was a large one.

"Now for the finishing touch," said Bill. "And this is going to be all mine."

He jumped up on the table, stripped down his trousers, and squatted over the photographs. Clearly he meant to defecate on them, but such things cannot always be commanded, and so for several minutes we stood and stared at him as he grunted and swore and strained and at last managed what he wanted, right on the family photographs.

How long it took I cannot tell, but they were critical moments in my life. For as he struggled, red-faced and pop-eyed, and as he appeared at last with a great stool dangling from his apelike rump, I regained my senses and said to myself, not "What am I doing here?" but "Why is he doing that? The destruction was simply a prelude to this. It is a dirty, animal act of defiance and protest against—well, against what? He doesn't even know who these people are. There is no spite in him against individuals who have injured him. Is he protesting against order, against property, against privacy? No; there is nothing intellectual, nothing rooted in principle—even the principle of anarchy—in what he is doing. So far as I can judge—and I must remember that I am his accomplice in all but this, his final outrage—he is simply being as evil as his strong will and deficient imagination will permit. He is possessed, and what possesses him is Evil."

I was startled out of my reflection by Bill shouting for something with which to wipe himself.

"Wipe on your shirt-tail, you dirty pig," said McQuilly. "It'd be like you."

The room stank, and we left at once, Bill Unsworth last, looking smaller, meaner, and depleted, but certainly not repentant.

We went back to the car in extremely bad temper. Nobody spoke on the way to the Unsworths' place, and the next day Wood, McQuilly, and I took the only train home to Toronto. We did not speak of what we had done, and have never done so since.

On the long journey from Muskoka back to Toronto I had plenty of time to think, and I made my resolve then to be a lawyer. I was against people like Bill Unsworth, or who were possessed as he was. I was against whatever it was that possessed him, and I thought the law was the best way of making my opposition effective.

8

It was a surprise that brought no pleasure when I discovered that I was in love with Dr. von Haller.

For many weeks I had been seeing her on Mondays, Wednesdays, and Fridays and was always aware of changes in my attitude toward her. In the beginning, indifference; she was my physician, and though I was not such a fool as to think she could help me without my co-operation I assumed that there would be limits to that; I would answer questions and provide information to the best of my ability, but I assumed without thinking that some reticences would be left me. Her request for regular reports on my dreams I did not take very seriously, though I did my best to comply and even reached a point where I was likely to wake after a dream and make notes on it before sleeping again. But the idea of dreams as a key to anything very serious in my case or any other was still strange and, I suppose, unwelcome. Netty had set no store by dreams, and the training of a Netty is not quickly set aside.

In time, however, quite a big dossier of dreams accumulated, which the doctor filed, and of which I kept copies. I had taken rooms in Zürich; a small service flat, looking out on a courtyard, did me very well; meals with wine could be taken at the *table d'hôte,* and I found after a time that the wine was enough, with a nightcap of whisky, just so that I should not forget what it tasted like. I was fully occupied, for the doctor gave me plenty of homework. Making up my notes for my next appointment took far more time than I had expected—quite as much as preparing a case for court—because my problem was to get the tone right; with Johanna von Haller I was arguing not for victory, but for truth. It was hard work, and I took to napping after lunch, a thing I had never done before. I walked, and came to know Zürich fairly well—certainly well enough to understand that my knowledge was still that of a visitor and a stranger. I took to the museums; even more, I took to the churches, and sometimes sat for long spells in the Grossmünster, looking at the splendid modern windows. And all the time I was thinking, remembering, reliving; what I was engaged on with Dr. von Haller (which I suppose must be called an analysis, though it was nothing like what I had ever imagined an analysis to be) possessed me utterly.

To what extent should I surrender myself, I asked, and as I asked I was aware that the time for turning back had passed and I no longer had any choice in the matter. I even lost my embarrassment about dreams, and would take a good dream to my appointment as happily as a boy who has prepared a good lesson.

(The dream dossier I kept in another notebook, and only a few references to its contents appear here. This is not wilful concealment. The dreams of someone undergoing such treatment as mine are numbered in tens and hundreds, and extracting meaning from the mass is slow work, for dreams say their say in series, and only rarely is a single dream revelatory. Reading such a record of dreams is comparable to reading the whole of a business correspondence when preparing a case—dull panning for gold, with a hundredweight of gravel discarded for every nugget.)

Indifference gave way to distaste. The doctor seemed to me to be a commonplace person, not as careful about her appearance as I had at first thought, and sometimes I suspected her of a covert antipathy toward me. She said things that seemed mild enough until they were pondered, and then a barb would appear. I began to wonder if she were not like so many people I have met who can never forgive me for being a rich and privileged person. Envy of the rich is understandable enough in people whose lives are lived under a sky always darkened by changing clouds of financial worry and need. They see people like me as free from the one great circumstance that conditions their lives, their loves, and the fate of their families—want of cash. They say, glibly enough, that they do not envy the rich, who must certainly have many cares; the reality is something very different. How can they escape envy? They must be especially envious when they see the rich making fools of themselves, squandering big sums on trivialities. What that fellow has spent on his yacht, they think, would set me up for life. What they do not understand is that folly is to a great extent a question of opportunity, and that fools, rich or poor, are always as foolish as they can manage. But does money change the essential man? I have been much envied, and I know that many people who envy me my money are, if they only knew it, envying me my brains, my character, my appetite for work, and a quality of toughness that the wealth of an emperor cannot buy.

Did Dr. von Haller, sitting all day in her study listening to other people's troubles, envy me? And perhaps dislike me? I felt that it was not impossible.

Our relationship improved after some time. It seemed to me that the doctor was friendlier, less apt to say things that needed careful inspection for hidden criticism. I have always liked women, in spite of my somewhat unusual history with them; I have women friends, and have had a substantial number of women clients whose point of view I pride myself on understanding and setting forward successfully in court.

In this new atmosphere of friendship, I opened up as I had not done before. I lost much of my caution. I felt that I could tell her things that showed me in a poor light without dreading any reprisal. For the first time in my life since I lost Knopwood, I felt the urge to confide. I know what a heavy burden everybody carries of the unconfessed, which sometimes appears to be the unspeakable. Very often such stuff is not disgraceful or criminal; it is merely a sense of not having behaved well or having done something one knew to be contrary to someone else's good; of having snatched when one should have waited decently; of having turned a sharp corner when someone else was thereby left in a difficult situation; of having talked of the first-rate when one was planning to do the second-rate; of having fallen below whatever standards one had set oneself. As a lawyer I heard masses of such confession; a fair amount of what looks like crime has its beginning in some such failure. But I had not myself confided in anybody. For in whom could I confide? And, as a criminal lawyer—comic expression, but the usual one for a man who, like myself, spends much of his time defending people who are, or possibly may be, criminals—I knew how dangerous confession was. The priest, the physician, the lawyer—we all know that their lips are sealed by an oath no torture could compel them to break. Strange, then, how many people's secrets become quite well known. Tell nobody anything, and be close-mouthed even about that, had been my watchword for more than twenty of my forty years. Yet was it not urgent need for confession that brought me to Zürich? Here I was, confident that I could confide in this Swiss doctor, and thinking it a luxury to do so.

What happened to my confidences when I had made them? What did I know about Johanna von Haller? Where was she when she was not in her chair in that room which I now knew very well? Whence came the information about the world that often arose in our talks? I took to reading *Die Neue Zürcher Zeitung* to keep abreast of her, and although at first I thought I had never read such an extraordinary paper in my life, my understanding and my German improved, and I decided that I had indeed never read such an extraordinary paper, meaning that in its most complimentary sense.

Did she go to concerts? Did she go to the theatre? Or to films? I went to all of these entertainments, because I had to do something at night. I had made no friends, and wanted none, for my work on my analysis discouraged it, but I enjoyed my solitary entertainments. I took to arriving early at the theatre and staring about at the audience to see if I could find her. My walks began to lead me near her house, in case I should meet her going or coming. Had she any family? Who were her friends? Did she know any men? Was there a husband somewhere? Was she perhaps a Lesbian? These intellectual women—but no, something told me that was unlikely. I had seen a good many collar-and-tie teams in my professional work, and she was neither a collar nor a tie.

Gradually I realized that I was lurking. This is not precisely spying; it is a kind of meaningful loitering, in hopes. Lurking could only mean one thing, but I couldn't believe it of myself. In love with my analyst? Absurd. But why absurd? Was I too old for love? No, I was going on forty-one, and knew the world. She was mature. Youthful, really, for her probable age. I took her to be about thirty-eight, but I had no way of finding out. Except for the relationship in which we stood to one another, there was nothing in the world against it. And what was that, after all, but doctor and patient? Didn't doctors and patients fall in love? I have been involved in more than one case that made it clear they did.

Everything in me that had kept its reason was dismayed. What could come of such a love? I didn't want to marry; I didn't want an affair. No, but I wanted to tell Johanna von Haller that I loved her. It had to be said. Love and a cough cannot be hid, as Netty told me when I was seventeen.

I dressed with special care for my next appointment, and told Johanna that before we began, I had something of importance to say. I said it. She did not seem to be as dumbfounded as I had expected, but after all, she was not a girl.

"So what is to be done?" I said.

"I think we should continue as before," said she. But she smiled quite beautifully as she said it. "I am not ungrateful, or indifferent, you know; I am complimented. But you must trust me to be honest with you, so I must say at once that I am not surprised. No, no; you must not imagine you have been showing your feelings and I have been noticing. Better be completely frank: it is part of the course of the analysis, you understand. A very pleasant part. But still well within professional limits."

"You mean I can't even ask you to dinner?"

"You may certainly ask me, but I shall have to say no."

"Do you sit there and tell me it is part of my treatment that I should fall in love with you?"

"It is one of those things that happens now and then, because I am a woman. But suppose I were a wise old doctor, like our great

Dr. Jung; you would hardly fall in love with me then, would you? Something quite other would happen; a strong sense of discipleship. But always there comes this period of special union with the doctor. This feeling you have—which I understand and respect, believe me—is because we have been talking a great deal about Judy Wolff."

"You are not in the least like Judy Wolff."

"Certainly not—in one way. In another way—let us see. Have you had any dreams since last time?"

"Last night I dreamed of you."

"Tell."

"It was a dream in colour. I found myself in an underground passage, but some light was entering it, because I could see that it was decorated with wall-paintings, in the late Roman manner. The whole atmosphere of the dream was Roman, but the Rome of the decadence; I don't know how I knew that, but I felt it. I was in modern clothes. I was about to walk down the passage when my attention was taken by the first picture on the left-hand side. These pictures, you understand, were large, almost life-size, and in the warm but not reflective colours of Roman frescoes. The first picture—I couldn't see any others—was of you, dressed as a sibyl in a white robe with a blue mantle; you were smiling. On a chain you held a lion, which was staring out of the picture. The lion had a man's face. My face."

"Any other details?"

"The lion's tail ended in a kind of spike, or barb."

"Ah, a manticore!"

"A what?"

"A manticore is a fabulous creature with a lion's body, a man's face, and a sting in his tail."

"I never heard of it."

"No, they are not common, even in myths."

"How can I dream about something I've never heard of?"

"That is a very involved matter, which really belongs to the second part of your analysis. But it is a good sign that this sort of material is making its way into your dreams already. People very often dream of things they don't know. They dream of minotaurs without ever having heard of a minotaur. Thoroughly respectable women who have never heard of Pasiphaë dream that they are a queen who is enjoying sexual congress with a bull. It is because great myths are not invented stories but objectivizations of images and situations that lie very deep in the human spirit; a poet may make a great embodiment of a myth, but it is the mass of humanity that knows the myth to be a spiritual truth, and that is why they cherish his poem. These myths, you know, are very widespread; we may hear them as children, dressed in pretty Greek guises, but they are African, Oriental, Red Indian—all sorts of things."

"I should like to argue that point."

"Yes, I know, but let us take a short cut. What do you suppose this dream means?"

"That I am your creature, under your subjection, kept on a short string."

"Why are you so sure that I am the woman in the sibyl's robe?"

"How can it be anyone else? It looked like you. You are a sibyl. I love you. You have me under your control."

"You must believe me when I tell you that the only person you can be certain of recognizing in a dream is yourself. The woman might be me. Because of what you feel about me—please excuse me if I say what you at present suppose you feel about me—the woman could be me, but if so why do I not appear as myself, in this modern coat and skirt with which I am sure you are becoming wearily familiar."

"Because dreams are fanciful. They go in for fancy dress."

"I assure you that dreams are not fanciful. They always mean exactly what they say, but they do not speak the language of every day. So they need interpretation, and we cannot always be sure we have interpreted all, or interpreted correctly. But we can try. You appear in this dream; you are in two forms, yourself and this creature with your face. What do you make of that?"

"I suppose I am observing my situation. You see, I have learned something about dream interpretation from you. And my situation is that I am under your dominance; willingly so."

"Women have not appeared in your dreams very prominently, or in a flattering light, until recently. But this sibyl has the face of someone you love. Did you think it was the face of someone who loved you?"

"Yes. Or at any rate someone who cared about me. Who was guiding me, obviously. The smile had extraordinary calm beauty. So who could it be but you?"

"But why are you a manticore?"

"I haven't any idea. And as I never heard of a manticore till now, I have no associations with it."

"But we have met a few animals in your dreams before now. What was Felix?"

"We agreed that Felix was a figure who meant some rather kind impulses and some bewilderment that I was not quite willing to accept as my own. We called him the Friend."

"Yes. The Animal-Friend, and because an animal, related to the rather undeveloped instinctual side of your nature. He was one of the characters in your inner life. Like the Shadow. Now, as your sister Caroline used to say, you know my methods, Watson. You know that when the Shadow and the Friend appeared, they had a special vividness. I felt the vividness and I bore the character of Shadow and Friend. That was quite usual; part of my professional task. I told you I should play many roles. This latest dream of yours is vivid, and apparently simple, and clearly important. What about the manticore?"

"Well, as he is an animal, I suppose he is some baser aspect of me. But as he is a lion, he can't be wholly base. And he has a human face, my face, so he can't be wholly animal. Though I must say the expression on the face was fierce and untrustworthy. And there I run out of ideas."

"What side of your nature have we considered as not being so fully developed as it could be?"

"Oh, my feeling. Though I must say once more that I have plenty of feeling, even if I don't understand and use it well."

"So might not your undeveloped feeling turn up in a dream as a noble creature, but possibly dangerous and only human in part?"

"This is the fanciful side of this work that always rouses my resistance."

"We have agreed, have we not, that everything that makes man a great, as opposed to a merely sentient creature, is fanciful when tested by what people call common sense? That common sense often means no more than yesterday's opinions? That every great advance began in the realm of the fanciful? That fantasy is the mother not merely of art, but of science as well? I am sure that when the very first primitives began to think that they were individuals and not creatures of a herd and wholly bound by the ways of the herd, they seemed fanciful to their hairy, low-browed brothers—even though those hairy lowbrows had no concept of fantasy."

"I know. You think the law has eaten me up. But I have lived by reason, and this is unreason."

"I think nothing of the kind. I think you do not understand the law. So far as we can discover, anything like a man that has inhabited this earth lived by some kind of law, however crude. Primitives have law of extraordinary complexity. How did they get it? If they worked it out as a way of living tribally, it must once have been fantasy. If they simply knew what to do from the beginning, it must have been instinct, like the nest-building instinct of birds."

"Very well; if I accept that the lion represents my somewhat undeveloped feeling, what about it?"

"Not a lion; a manticore. Do not forget that stinging tail. The undeveloped feelings are touchy—very defensive. The manticore can be extremely dangerous. Sometimes he is even described as hurling darts from his tail, as people once thought the porcupine did. Not a bad picture of you in court, would you say? Head of a man, brave and dangerous as a lion, capable of wounding with barbs? But not a whole man, or a whole lion, or a merely barbed opponent. A manticore. The Unconscious chooses its symbolism with breath-taking artistic virtuosity."

"All right. Suppose I am the manticore. Why shouldn't you be the sibyl?"

"Because we have come to a part of our work together where a woman, or a variety of women, are very likely to appear in your dreams in just some such special relationship to you as this. Did you notice the chain?"

"I noticed everything, and I can call it up now. It was a handsome gold chain."

"Good. That is much better than if it had been an iron chain, or a chain with spikes. Now, what have we: an image that appears on the left-hand side, which means that it comes from the Unconscious—"

"I haven't completely swallowed the idea of the Unconscious, you know."

"Indeed I do know. 'Fanciful . . . fancy dress . . .' all these scornful words come up whenever we discuss it. But we are at a point where you are going to have to face it, because that is where that blue-mantled sibyl resides. She has emerged from the Unconscious and can be of great help to you, but if you banish her you might as well stop this work now and go home."

"I have never heard you so threatening before."

"There comes a time when one must be strong with rationalists, for they can reduce anything whatever to dust, if they happen not to like the look of it, or if it threatens their deep-buried negativism. I mean of course rationalists like you, who take some little provincial world of their own as the whole of the universe and the seat of all knowledge."

"Little, provincial world . . . I see. Well, what is the name of this lady I am compelled to meet?"

"Oho—irony! How well that must sound in court! The lady's name is Anima."

"Latin for Soul. I gave up the idea of a soul many years ago. Well?"

"She is one of the figures in your psychological make-up, like the Shadow and the Friend, whom you have met and about whom you entertain few doubts. She is not a soul as Christianity conceives it. She is the feminine part of your nature: she is all that you are able to see, and experience, in woman: she is not your mother, or any single one of the women you have loved, but you have seen all of them—at least in part—in terms of her. If you love a woman you project this image upon her, at least at the beginning, and if you hate a woman it is again the Anima at work, because she has a very disagreeable side which is not at all like the smiling sibyl in the blue mantle. She has given rise to some of the world's greatest art and poetry. She is Cleopatra, the enchantress, and she is Faithful Griselda, the patient, enduring woman; she is Beatrice, who glorifies the life of Dante, and she is Nimue, who imprisons Merlin in a thorn-bush. She is the Maiden who is wooed, the Wife who bears the sons, and she is the Hag who lays out her man for his last rest. She is an angel, and she may also be a witch. She is Woman as she appears to every man, and to every man she appears somewhat differently, though essentially the same."

"Quite a nicely practised speech. But what do women do about this fabulous creature?"

"Oh, women have their own deep-lying image of Man, the Lover, the Warrior, the Wizard, and the Child—which may be either the child of a few months who is utterly dependent, or the child of ninety years who is utterly dependent. Men often find it very hard to carry the projection of the Warrior or the Wizard that is put upon them by some woman they may not greatly like. And of course women have to bear the projection of the Anima, and although all women like it to some degree, only rather immature women like that and nothing else."

"Very well. If the Anima is my essential image, or pattern of woman, why does she look like you? Isn't this proof that I love you?"

"No indeed; the Anima must look like somebody. You spoke of dreadful hags who assailed you in sexual dreams when you were a boy. They were the Anima, too. Because your sister and Netty could see you were in love, which I expect was pretty obvious, you projected witchlike aspects of the Anima on their perfectly ordinary heads. But you can never see the Anima pure and simple, because she has no such existence; you will always see her in terms of something or somebody else. Just at present, you see her as me."

"I am not convinced."

"Then think about it. You are good at thinking. Didn't you dislike me when the Shadow was being slowly brought to your notice; do you suppose I didn't see your considering looks as you eyed my rather perfunctory attempts at fashionable dress; do you suppose I was unaware of the criticism and often the contempt in your voice? Don't look alarmed or ashamed. It is part of my professional duty to assume these roles; the treatment would be ineffective without these projections, and I am the one who is nearest and best equipped to carry them. And then when we changed to the Friend, I know very well that my features began to have a look, in your eyes, of Felix's charming bear-expression of puzzled goodwill. And now we have reached the Anima, and I am she; I am as satisfactory casting for the role as I was for the Shadow or the

Friend. But I must assure you that there is nothing personal about it.

"And now our hour is finished. We shall go on next day talking more about Judy Wolff. I trust it will be delightful."

"Well, Dr. von Haller, I am sorry to inform you, sibyl though you seem to be, that you are about to be disappointed."

9

The autumn that followed the war was wonderful. The world seemed to breathe again, and all sorts of things that had been taut were unfolding. Women's clothes, which had been so skimped during the war, changed to an altogether more pleasing style. When Judy was not in the Bishop Cairncross uniform she was marvellous in pretty blouses and flaring skirts; it was almost the last time that women were allowed by their epicene masters of fashion to wear anything that was unashamedly flattering. I was happy, for I was on top of my world: I had Judy, I was in my last year at Colborne College, and I was a prefect.

How can I describe my relationship with Judy without looking a fool or a child? Things have changed so startlingly in recent years that the idealism with which I surrounded everything about her would seem absurd to a boy and girl of seventeen now. Or would it? I can't tell. But now, when I see girls who have not yet attained their full growth storming the legislatures for abortion on demand, and adolescents pressing their right to freedom to have intercourse whenever and however they please, and read books advising women that anal intercourse is a jolly lark (provided both partners are "squeaky clean"), I wonder what has happened to the Davids and Judys, and if the type is extinct? I think not; it is merely waiting for another age, different from our supernal autumn but also different from this one. And, as I look back, I do not really wish we had greater freedom than was ours; greater freedom is only another kind of servitude. Physical fulfilment satisfies appetite, but does it sharpen perception? What we had of sex was limited; what we had of love seems, in my recollection, to have been illimitable. Judy was certainly kept on a short string, but the free-ranging creature is not always the best of the breed.

That autumn Bishop Cairncross's was shaken by unreasonable ambition; the success of *Crossings* had been so great that the music staff and all the musical girls like Caroline and Judy were mad to do a real opera. Miss Gostling, after the usual Headmistress's doubts about the effect on schoolwork, gave her consent, and it was rumoured that unheard-of sums of money had been set aside for the project—something in the neighbourhood of five hundred dollars, which was a Metropolitan budget for the school.

What opera? Some of the girls were shrieking for Mozart; a rival band, hateful to Caroline, thought Puccini would be more like it, and with five hundred dollars they could not see why *Turandot* would not be the obvious choice. Of course the mistresses made the decision, and the music mistress resurrected, from somewhere, Mendelssohn's *Son and Stranger*. It was not the greatest opera ever written; it contained dialogue, which to purists made it no opera at all; nevertheless, it was just within the range of what schoolgirls could manage. So *Son and Stranger* it was to be, and quite hard enough, when they got down to it.

I heard all about it. Judy told me of its charms because its gemütlich, nineteenth-century naïveté appealed strongly to her; either she was innocent in her tastes or else sophisticated in seeing in this humble little work delights and possibilities the other girls missed; I rather think her feeling was a combination of both these elements. Caroline was a bore about its difficulties. She and another girl were to play the overture and accompaniments at two pianos, which is trickier than it seems. In full view, too; no hiding behind the scenes this time. Of course, as always with Caroline, nobody but herself knew just how it ought to be done, and the music mistress, and the mistress who directed the production, and the art mistress who arranged the setting, were all idiots, without a notion of how to manage anything. I even had my own area of agitation and knowing-best; if Miss Gostling were not such a lunatic, insisting that everything about the production be kept within the school, I could have mustered a crew of carpenters and scene-shifters and painters and electricians among the boys at Colborne who would have done all the technical work at lightning speed, with masculin·

thoroughness and craftsmanship, and guaranteed wondrous result. Both Judy and Carol and most of their friends agreed that this was undoubtedly so, but none of them quite saw her way to suggesting it to Miss Gostling, who was, as we all agreed, the last surviving dinosaur.

Not many people know *Son and Stranger*. Mendelssohn wrote it for private performance, indeed for the twenty-fifth wedding anniversary of his parents, and it is deeply, lumberingly domestic in the nineteenth-century German style. "A nice old bit of Biedermeier," said Dr. Wolff, and lent some useful books to the art mistress for her designs.

The plot is modest; the people of a German village are expecting a recruiting-sergeant who will take their sons away to fight in the Napoleonic wars; a peddler, a handsome charlatan, turns up and pretends to be the sergeant, hoping to win the favours of the Mayor's ward Lisbeth; but he is unmasked by the real sergeant, who proves to be Herrmann, the Mayor's long-lost soldier son, and Lisbeth's true love. The best part is the peddler, and there was the usual wrangle as to whether it should be played by a girl who could act but couldn't sing, or whether a girl who could sing but couldn't act should have it. The acting girl was finally banished to the comic role of the Mayor, who must have been no singer in the original production, for Mendelssohn had given him a part which stayed firmly on one note. Judy was Lisbeth, of course, and had some pretty songs and a bit of acting for which her quiet charm was, or seemed to me, to be exactly right.

At last early December came, *Son and Stranger* was performed for two nights, and of course it was a triumph. What school performance of anything is ever less than a triumph? Judy sang splendidly; Caroline covered herself with honour; even the embarrassing dialogue—rendered from flat-footed German into murderous English, Dr. Wolff assured me—was somehow bathed in the romantic light that enveloped the whole affair.

This year my father was in the audience, and cut a figure because everybody knew him from newspaper pictures and admired the great work he had done during the war years. I took Netty on the Friday and went again with Father on Saturday. He asked me if I really wanted to go twice or was I going just to keep him company;

not long after Judy appeared on the stage I felt him looking at me with curiosity, so I suppose I was as bad at concealing my adoration as I had always been. Afterward, at the coffee and school-cake debauch in the dining-room, I introduced him to the Wolffs and the Schwarzes, and to my astonishment Judy curtsied to him—one of those almost imperceptible little bobs that girls used to do long ago in Europe and which some girls of Bishop Cairncross's kept for the Bishop, who was the patron of the school. I knew Father was important, but I had never dreamed of him as the kind of person anybody curtsied to. He liked it; he didn't say anything, but I knew he liked it.

If any greater glory could be added to my love for Judy, Father's approval supplied it. I had been going through hell at intervals ever since Mother's death because of Carol's declaration that I was Dunstan Ramsay's son. I had come to the conclusion that whether or not I was Ramsay's son in the flesh, I was Father's son in the spirit. He had not been at home during the period of my life when boys usually are possessed with admiration for their fathers, and I was having, at seventeen, a belated bout of hero-worship. Sometimes I had found Ramsay's saturnine and ironic eye on me at school, and I had wondered if he were reflecting that I was his child. That seemed less significant now because Father's return had diminished Ramsay's importance; after all, Ramsay was the Acting Headmaster of Colborne, filling in for the war years, but Father was the Chairman of the school's Board of Governors and in a sense Ramsay's boss, as he seemed to be the boss of so many other people. He was a natural boss, a natural leader. I know I tried to copy some of his mannerisms, but they fitted me no better than his hats, which I also tried.

Father's return to Toronto caused a lot of chatter, and some of it came to my ears because the boys with whom I was at school were the sons of the chatterers. He had been remarkable as a Minister of Food, a Cabinet position that had made him even more significant in the countries we were supplying during the war than at home. He had been extraordinary in his ability to get along with Mackenzie King without wrangling and without any obvious sacrifice of his own opinions, which were not often those of the P.M. But there was another reputation that came home with him, a reputation spoken of less freely, with an ambiguity I did not understand or even notice for a time. This was a reputation as something called "a swordsman."

It is a measure of my innocence that I took this word at its face value. It was new then in the connotation it has since acquired, and I was proud of my father being a swordsman. I assumed it meant a gallant, cavalier-like person, a sort of Prince Rupert of the Rhine as opposed to the Cromwellian austerity of Mackenzie King.

When boys at school talked to me about Father, as they did because he was increasingly a public figure, I sometimes said, "You can sum him up pretty much in a word—a swordsman." I now remember with terrible humiliation that I said this to the Wolffs, who received it calmly, though I thought I saw Mrs. Wolff's nostrils pinch and if I had been more sensitive I would surely have noticed a drop in the social temperature. But the word had such a fine savour in my mouth that I think I repeated it; I knew the Wolffs and Schwarzes liked me, but how much better they would like me if they understood that I was the son of a man who was recognized for aristocratic behaviour and a temperament far above that of the upper-bourgeois world in which we lived and which, in Canada, was generally supposed to be the best world there was. Swordsmen were people of a natural distinction, and I was the son of one of them. Would I ever be a swordsman myself? Oh, speed the day!

The Wolffs, like many Jewish people, were going to a resort for Christmas, so I was not dismayed by the thought of any loss of time with Judy when my father asked me to go with him to Montreal on Boxing Day. He had some business to do there and thought I might like to see the city. So we went, and I greatly enjoyed the day-long journey on the train and putting up at the Ritz when we arrived. Father was a good traveller; everybody heeded him and our progress was princely.

"We're having dinner with Myrrha Martindale," he said; "she's an old friend of mine, and I think you'll like her very much."

She was, it appeared, a singer, and had formerly lived in New York and had been seen—though not in leading roles—in several Broadway musical comedies. A wonderful person. Witty. Belonged to a bigger world. Would have had a remarkable career if she had not sacrificed everything to marriage.

"Was it worth it?" I asked. I was at the age when sacrifice and renunciation were great, terrifying, romantic concepts.

"No, it blew up," said Father. "Jack Martindale simply had no idea what a woman like that is, or needs. He wanted to turn her into a Westmount housewife. Talk about Pegasus chained to the plough!"

Oh, indeed I was anxious to talk about Pegasus chained to the plough. That was just the kind of swordsman thing Father could say; he could see the poetry in daily life. But he didn't want to talk about Myrrha Martindale; he wanted me to meet her and form my own opinion. That was like him, too: not dictating or managing, as so many of my friends' fathers seemed to do.

Mrs. Martindale had an apartment on Côte des Neiges Road with a splendid view over Montreal; I guessed it was costing the banished Jack Martindale plenty, and I thought it was quite right that it should do so, for Mrs. Martindale was indeed a wonderful person. She was beautiful in a mature way, and had a delightful voice, with an actress's way of making things seem much more amusing than they really were. Not that she strove to shine as a wit. She let Father do that, very properly, but her responses to his jokes were witty in themselves—not topping him, but supporting him and setting him off.

"You mustn't expect a real dinner," she said to me. "I thought it would be more fun if we were just by ourselves, the three of us, so I sent my maid out. I hope you won't be disappointed."

Disappointed! It was the most grown-up affair I had ever known. Wonderful food that Myrrha—she insisted I call her Myrrha, because all her friends did—produced herself from under covers and off hot-trays, and splendid wines that were better than anything I had ever tasted. I knew they must be good because they had that real musty aftertaste, like dusty red ink instead of fresh red ink.

"This is terribly good of you, Myrrha," said Father. "It's time Davey learned something about wines. About vintage wines, instead of very new stuff." He raised his glass to Mrs. Martindale, and she blushed and looked down as I had so often seen Judy do, only Mrs. Martindale seemed more in command of herself. I raised my glass to her, too, and she was delighted and gave me her hand, obviously meaning that I should kiss it. I had kissed Judy often enough, though never while eating and seldom on the hand, but I took it as gallantly as I could—surely I was getting to be a swordsman—and kissed it on the tips of the fingers. Father and Mrs. Martindale looked pleased but didn't say anything, and I felt I had done well.

It was a wonderful dinner. It wasn't necessary to be excited, as if I were with people my own age; calmness was the keynote, and I told myself that it was educational in the very best sense and I ought to keep alert and not miss anything. And not drink too much wine. Father talked a lot about wines, and Mrs. Martindale and I were fascinated. When we had coffee he produced a huge bottle of brandy, which was very hard to get at that time.

"Your Christmas gift, Myrrha dear," he said. "Winston gave it to me last time I saw him, so you can be sure it's good."

It was. I had tasted whisky, but this was a very different thing. Father showed me how to roll it around in the mouth and get it on the sides of the tongue where the tastebuds are, and I rolled and tasted in adoring imitation of him.

How wonderfully good food and drink lull the spirit and bring out one's hidden qualities! I thought something better than just warm agreement with everything that was said was expected of me, and I raked around in my mind for a comment worthy of the occasion. I found it.

"And much as Wine has played the Infidel,
And robbed me of my Robe of Honour—Well,
I wonder often what the Vintners buy
One half so precious as the stuff they sell,"

said I, looking reflectively at the candles through my glass of brandy, as I felt a swordsman should. Father seemed nonplussed, though I knew that was an absurd idea. Father? Nonplussed? Never!

"Is that your own, Davey?" he said.

I roared with laughter. What a wit Father was! I said I wished it was and then reflected that perhaps a swordsman ought to have said Would that it were, but by then it was too late to change. Myrrha looked at me with the most marvellous combination of amusement and admiration, and I felt that in a modest way I was making a hit.

At half-past nine Father said he must keep another appointment. But I was not to stir. Myrrha too begged me not to think of going. She had known all along that Father would have to leave early, but then she was so grateful that he had been able to spare her a few hours from a busy life. She would love it if I would stay and talk further. She knew Omar Khayyam too, and would match verses with me. Father kissed her and said to me that we would meet at breakfast.

So Father went, and Myrrha talked about Omar, whom she knew a great deal better than I did, and it seemed to me that she brought a weight of understanding to the poem that was far outside my reach. All that disappointment with Martindale, I supposed. She was absolutely splendid about the fleetingness of life and pleasure and the rose that blows where buried Caesar bled, and it seemed to me she was piercing into a world of experience utterly strange to me but which, of course, I respected profoundly.

> "Yet Ah, that Spring should vanish with the Rose!
> That Youth's sweet-scented manuscript should close!
>   The Nightingale that in the branches sang,
> Ah, whence, and whither flown again, who knows!"

she recited, thrillingly, and talked about what a glorious thing youth was, and how swift its passing, and the terrible sadness of life which pressed on and on, without anybody being able to halt it, and how wise Omar was to urge us to get on with enjoyment when we could. This was all wonderful to me, for I was new to poetry and had just begun reading some because Professor Schwarz said it was his great alternative to chemistry. If a professor of chemistry thought well of poetry, it must be something better than the stuff we worked through so patiently in Eng. Lit. at school. I had just begun to see that poetry was about life, and not ordinary life but the essence and miraculous underside of life. What a leap my understanding took when I heard Myrrha reciting in her beautiful voice; she was near to tears, and so was I. She mastered herself, and with obvious effort not to break down she continued—

"Ah Love! could you and I with Him conspire
To grasp this sorry Scheme of Things entire,
Would not we shatter it to bits—and then
Remold it nearer to the Heart's Desire!"

I could not speak, nor could Myrrha. She rose and left me to myself, and I was full of surging thoughts, recognition of the evanescence of life, and wonder that this glorious understanding woman should have stirred my mind and spirit so profoundly.

I do not know how much time passed until I heard her voice from another room, calling me. She has been crying, I thought, and wants me to comfort her. And so I should. I must try to tell her how tremendous she is, and how she has opened up a new world to me, and perhaps hint that I know something about the disappointment with Martindale. I went through a little passage into what proved to be her bedroom, very pretty and full of nice things and filled with the smell of really good perfume.

Myrrha came in from the bathroom, wearing what it is a joke to call a diaphanous garment, but I don't know how else to name it. I mean, as she stood against the light, you could see she had nothing under it, and its fullness and the way it swished around only made it seem thinner. I suppose I gaped, for she really was beautiful.

"Come here, angel," she said, "and give me a very big kiss."

I did, without an instant of hesitation. I knew a good deal about kissing, and I took her in my arms and kissed her tenderly and long. But I had never kissed a woman in a diaphanous garment before, and it was like Winston Churchill's brandy. I savoured it in the same way.

"Wouldn't you like to take off all those stupid clothes?" she said, and gave me a start by loosening my tie. It is at this point I cease to understand my own actions. I really didn't know where this was going to lead and had no time for thought, because life seemed to be moving so fast, and taking me with it. But I was delighted to be, so to speak, under this life-enlarging authority. I got out of my clothes quickly, dropping them to the floor and kicking them out of the way.

There is a point in a man's undressing when he looks stupid, and nothing in the world can make him into a romantic figure. It is at the moment when he stands in his underwear and socks. I suppose a very calculating man would keep his shirt on to the last, getting rid of his socks and shorts as fast as possible, and then cast off the shirt, revealing himself as an Adonis. But I was a schoolboy undresser, and had never stripped to enchant. When I was in the socks-shorts moment, Myrrha laughed. I whipped off the socks, hurling them toward the dressing-table, and trampled the shorts beneath my feet. I seized her, held her firmly, and kissed her again.

"Darling," said she, breaking away, "not like a cannibal. Come and lie down with me. Now, there's no hurry whatever. So let us just do nice things for a while, shall we, and see what comes of it."

So we did that. But I was a virgin, bursting with partly gratified desire for Judy Wolff, and had no notion of preliminaries; nor, in spite of her words, did Myrrha seem greatly interested in them. I was full of poetry and power.

> Now is she in the very lists of love,
> Her champion mounted for the hot encounter—

thought I when, after some discreet stage-management by Myrrha, I was properly placed and out of danger of committing an unnatural act. It was male vanity. I was seventeen, and it was the first time I had done this; it would have been clear to anyone but me that I was not leading the band. Very quickly it was over, and I was lying by Myrrha, pleased as Punch.

So we did more nice things, and after a while I was conscious that Myrrha was nudging and manœuvring me back into the position of advantage. Good God! I thought; do people do it twice at a time? Well, I was ready to learn, and well prepared for my lesson. Myrrha rather firmly gave the time for this movement of the symphony, and it was a finely rhythmic *andante,* as opposed to the lively *vivace* I had set before. She seemed to like it better, and I began to understand that there was more to this business than I had supposed. It seemed to improve her looks, though it had not occurred to me that they needed improvement. She looked younger, dewier, gentler. I had done that. I was pleased with myself in quite a new way.

More nice things. Quite a lot of talk, this time, and some scraps of Omar from Myrrha, who must have had him by heart. Then again the astonishing act, which took much longer, and this time it was Myrrha who decided that the third movement should be a *scherzo.* When it was over, I was ready for more talk. I liked the talking almost as much as the doing, and I was surprised when Myrrha showed a tendency to fall asleep. I don't know how long she slept, but I may have dozed a little myself. Anyhow, I was in a deep reverie about the strangeness of life in general, when I felt her hand on my thigh. Again? I felt like Casanova, but as I had never read Casanova, and haven't to this day, I suppose I should say I felt as a schoolboy might suppose Casanova to feel. But I was perfectly willing to oblige and soon ready. I have read since that the male creature is at the pinnacle of his sexual power at seventeen, and I was a well-set-up lad in excellent health.

If I am to keep up the similitude of the symphony, this movement was an *allegro con spirito.* Myrrha was a little rough, and I wondered who was the cannibal now? I was even slightly alarmed, because she seemed unaware of my presence just when I was most poignantly aware of being myself, and made noises that I thought out of character. She puffed. She grunted. Once or twice I swear she roared. We brought the symphony to a fine Beethovenian finish with a series of crashing chords. Then Myrrha went to sleep again.

So did I. But not before she did, and I was lost in wonderment.

I do not know how long it was until Myrrha woke, snapped on her bedside light, and said, "Good God, sweetie, it's time you went home." It was in that instant of sudden light that I saw her differently. I had not observed that her skin did not fit quite so tightly as it once had done, and there were some little puckers at the armpits and between the breasts. When she lay on her side her stomach hung down, slightly but perceptibly. And under the light of the lamp, which was so close, her hair had a metallic sheen. As she turned to kiss me, she drew one of her legs across mine, and it was like a rasp. I knew women shaved their legs, for I had seen Carol do it, but I did not know that this sandpaper effect was the result. I kissed her, but without making a big thing of it, dressed myself, and prepared to leave. What was I to say?

"Thanks for a wonderful evening, and everything," I said.

"Bless you, darling," said she, laughing. "Will you turn out the lights in the sitting-room as you go?" and with that she turned over, dragging most of the bed-clothes with her, and prepared to sleep again.

It was not a great distance back to the Ritz, and I walked through the snowy night, thinking deeply. So that was what sex was! I dropped into a little all-night place and had two bacon-and-egg sandwiches, two slices of their hot mince pie, and two cups of chocolate with whipped cream, for I found I was very hungry.

DR. VON HALLER: When did you realize that this ceremony of initiation was arranged between your father and Mrs. Martindale?

MYSELF: Father told me as we went back to Toronto in the train; but I didn't realize it until I had a terrible row with Knopwood. What I mean is, Father didn't say in so many words that it was an arranged thing, but I suppose he was proud of what he had done for me, and he gave some broad hints that I was too stupid to take. He said what a wonderful woman she was and what an accomplished amorist—that was a new word to me—and that if there were such a thing as a female swordsman, certainly Myrrha Martindale was one.

DR. VON HALLER: How did he bring up the subject?

MYSELF: He remarked that I was looking very pleased with myself, and that I must have enjoyed my evening with Myrrha. Well, I knew that you aren't supposed to blab about these things, and anyhow she was Father's friend and perhaps he felt tenderly toward her and might be hurt if he discovered she had fallen for me so quickly. So I simply said I had, and he said she could teach me a great deal, and I said yes, she was very well read, and he laughed and said that she could teach me a good deal that wasn't to be found in books. Things that would be very helpful to me with my little Jewish piece. I was shocked to hear Judy called a "piece" because it isn't a word you use about anybody you love or respect, and I tried to set him right about Judy and how marvellous she was and what very nice people her family were. It was then he became serious about never marrying a girl you met when you were very young. "If you want fruit, take all you want, but don't buy the tree," he said. It hurt me to hear him talk that way when Judy was obviously in his mind, and then when he went on to talk about swordsmen I began to wonder for the first time if I knew everything there was to know about that word.

DR. VON HALLER: But did he say outright that he had arranged your adventure?

MYSELF: Never flatly. Never in so many words. But he talked about the wounding experiences young men often had learning about sex from prostitutes or getting mixed up with virgins, and said that the only good way was with an experienced older woman, and that I would bless Myrrha as long as I lived, and be grateful it had been managed so intelligently and pleasantly. That's the way the French do it, he said.

DR. VON HALLER: Was Myrrha Martindale his mistress?

MYSELF: Oh, I don't imagine so for a minute. Though he did leave some money for her in his will, and I know from things that came out later that he helped her with money from time to time. But if he ever had an affair with her, I'm sure it was because he loved her. It couldn't have been a money thing.

DR. VON HALLER: Why not?

MYSELF: It would be sordid, and Father always had such style.

DR. VON HALLER: Have you ever read Voltaire's *Candide?*

MYSELF: That was what Knopwood asked me. I hadn't, and he explained that Candide was a simpleton who believed everything he was told. Knopwood was furious with Father. But he didn't know Father, you see.

DR. VON HALLER: And you did?

MYSELF: I sometimes think I knew him better than anyone. Do you suggest I didn't?

DR. VON HALLER: That is one of the things we are working to find out. Tell me about your row with Father Knopwood.

I suppose I brought it on because I went to see Knopwood a few days after returning to Toronto. I was in a confused state of mind. I didn't regret anything about Myrrha; I was grateful to her, just as Father had said, though I thought I had noticed one or two things about her that had escaped him, or that he didn't care about. Really they only meant that she wasn't as young as Judy. But I was worried about my feelings toward Judy. I had gone to see her as soon as I could after returning from Montreal; she was ill—bad headache or something—and her father asked me to chat for a while. He was kind, but he was direct. Said he thought Judy and I should stop seeing each other so much, because we weren't children any longer, and we might become involved in a way we would regret. I knew he meant he was afraid I might seduce her, so I told him I loved her, and would never do anything to hurt her, and respected her too much to get her into any kind of mess. Yes, he said, but there are times when good resolutions weaken, and there are also hurts that are not hurts of the flesh. Then he said something I could hardly believe; he said that he was not sure Judy might not weaken at some time when I was also weak, and then what would our compounded weakness lead to? I had assumed the man always led in these things, and when I said that to Dr. Wolff he smiled in what I can only describe as a Viennese way.

"You and Judy have something that is charming and beautiful," he said, "and I advise you to cherish it as it is, for then it will always be a delight to you. But if you go on, we shall all change our roles; I shall have to be unpleasant to you, which I have no wish to do, and you will begin to hate me, which would be a pity, and perhaps you and Judy will decide that in order to preserve your self-respect you must deceive me and Judy's mother. That would be painful to us, and I assure you it would also be dangerous to you."

Then he did an extraordinary thing. He quoted Burns to me! Nobody had ever done that except my Cruikshank grandfather, down by the crick in Deptford, and I had always assumed that Burns was a sort of crick person's poet. But here was this Viennese Jew, saying,

"The sacred lowe of well-placed love,
Luxuriously indulge it;
But never tempt th' illicit rove
Tho' naething should divulge it;
I waive the quantum of the sin
The hazard of concealing;
But, och! it hardens a' within,
And petrifies the feeling.

"You are a particularly gentle boy," he said (and I was startled and resented it); "it would not take many bad experiences to scar your feelings over and make you much less than the man you may otherwise become. If you seduced my daughter, I should be very angry and might hate you; the physical injury is really not very much, if indeed it is anything at all, but the psychological injury—you see I am too much caught up in the modern way of speaking to be quite able to say the spiritual injury—could be serious if we all parted bad friends. There are people, of course, to whom such things are not important, and I fear you have had a bad example, but you and Judy are not such people. So be warned, David, and be our friend always; but you will never be my daughter's husband, and you must understand that now."

"Why are you so determined I should never be Judy's husband?" I asked.

"I am not determined alone," said he. "There are many hundreds of determining factors on both sides. They are called ancestors, and there are some things in which we are wise not to defy them."

"You mean, I'm not a Jew," I said.

"I had begun to wonder if you would get to it," said Dr. Wolff.

"But does that matter in this day and age?" I said.

"You were born in 1928, when it began to matter terribly, and not for the first time in history," said Dr. Wolff. "But set that aside. There is another way it matters which I do not like to mention because I do not want to hurt you and I like you very much. It is a question of pride."

We talked further, but I knew the conversation was over. They were planning to send Judy to school abroad in the spring. They would be happy to see me from time to time until then. But I must understand that the Wolffs had talked to Judy, and though Judy felt very badly, she had seen the point. And that was that.

It was that night I went to Knopwood. I was working up a rage against the Wolffs. A question of pride! Did that mean I wasn't good enough for Judy? And what did all this stuff about being Jews mean from people who gave no obvious external evidence of their Jewishness? If they were such great Jews, where were their side-curls and their funny underwear and their queer food? I had heard of these things as belonging to the bearded Jews in velours hats who lived down behind the Art Gallery. I had assumed the Wolffs and the Schwarzes were trying to be like us; instead I had been told I wasn't good enough for them! Affronted Christianity roiled up inside me. Christ had died for me, I was certain, but I wouldn't take any bets on His having died for the Wolffs and the Schwarzes! Off to Knopwood! He would know.

I was with him all evening, and in the course of an involved conversation everything came out. To my astonishment he sided with Louis Wolff. But worst of all, he attacked Father in terms I had never heard from him, and he was amused, and contemptuous and angry about Myrrha.

"You triple-turned jackass!" he said, "couldn't you see it was an arranged thing? And you thought it was your own attraction that got you into bed with such a scarred old veteran! I don't blame you for going to bed with her; show an ass a peck of oats and he'll eat it, even if the oats is musty. But it is the provincial vulgarity of the whole thing that turns my stomach—the winesmanship and the tatty gallantries and the candlelit frumpery of it! The 'good talk,' the imitations of Churchill by your father, the quotations from *The Rubaiyat*. If I could have my way I'd call in every copy of that twenty-fourth-rate rhymed gospel of hedonism and burn it! How it goes to the hearts of trashy people! So Myrrha matched verses with you, did she? Well, did the literary strumpet quote this—

" 'Well,' murmured one, 'Let whoso make or buy,
My Clay with long Oblivion is gone dry:
  But fill me with the old familiar Juice
Methinks I might recover by and by.'

Did she whisper that in your ear as Absalom went in unto his father's concubine?"

"You don't understand," I said; "this is a thing French families do to see that their sons learn about sex in the right way."

"Yes, I have heard that, but I didn't know they put their cast mistresses to the work, the way you put a child rider on your safe old mare."

"That's enough, Knoppy," I said; "you know a lot about the Church and religion, but I don't think that qualifies you to talk about what it is to be a swordsman."

That made him really furious. He became cold and courteous. "Help me then," he said. "Tell me what a swordsman is and what lies behind the mystique of the swordsman."

I talked as well as I could about living with style, and not sticking to dowdy people's ways. I managed to work in the word amorist because I thought he might not know it. I talked about the Cavaliers as opposed to the Roundheads, and I dragged in Mackenzie King as a sort of two-bit Cromwell, who had to be resisted. Mr. King had made himself unpopular early in the war by urging the Canadian people to "buckle on the whole armour of God," which when it was interpreted meant watering and rationing whisky without reducing the price. I said that if that was the armour of God, I would back the skill and panache of the swordsman against it any day. As I talked he seemed to be less angry, and when I had finished he was almost laughing.

"My poor Davey," he said, "I have always known you were an innocent boy, but I have hoped your innocence was not just the charming side of a crippling stupidity. And now I am going to try to do something that I had never expected to do, and of which I disapprove, but which I think is necessary if between us we are going to save your soul. I am going to disillusion you about your father."

He didn't, of course. Not wholly. He talked a lot about Father as a great man of business, but that cut no ice with me. I don't mean he suggested Father was anything but honest, because there were never any grounds for that. But he talked about the corrupting power of great wealth and the illusion it created in its possessor that he could manipulate people, and the dreadful truth that there were a great many people whom he undoubtedly could manipulate, so that the illusion was never seriously challenged. He talked about the illusion wealth creates that its possessor is of a different clay from that of common men. He talked about the adulation great wealth attracts from people to whom worldly success is the only measure of worth. Wealth bred and fostered illusion and illusion brought corruption. That was his theme.

I was ready for all of this because Father had talked a great deal to me since he began to be more at home. Father said that a man you could manipulate had to be watched because other people could manipulate him as well. Father had also said that the rich man differed from the ordinary man only in that he had a wider choice, and that one of his dangerous choices was a lightly disguised slavery to the source of his wealth. I even told Knoppy something he had never guessed. It was about what Father called the Pathological Compassion of Big Business, which seems to demand that above a certain executive level a man's incompetence or loss of quality had to be kept from him so that he would not be destroyed in the eyes of his family, his friends, and himself. Father estimated that Corporation Compassion cost him a few hundred thousand every year, and this was charity of a kind St. Paul had never foreseen. Like a lot of people who have no money, Knoppy had some half-baked ideas about people who had it, and the foremost of these was that wealth was achieved, and held, only by people who were essentially base. I accused him of lack of charity, which I knew was a very great matter to him. I accused him of a covert, Christian jealousy, that blinded him to Father's real worth because he could not see beyond his wealth. People strong enough to get wealth are sometimes strong enough to resist illusion. Father was such a man.

"You should do well at the Bar, Davey," he said. "You are already an expert at making the worser seem the better cause. To be cynical is not the same as avoiding illusion, for cynicism is just another kind of illusion. All formulas for meeting life—even many philosophies—are illusion. Cynicism is a trashy illusion. But a swordsman—shall I tell you what a swordsman is? It is just what the word implies: a swordsman is an expert at sticking something long and thin, or thick and curved, into other people; and always with intent to wound. You've read a lot lately. You've read some D. H. Lawrence. Do you remember what he says about heartless, cold-blooded fucking? That's what a swordsman is good at, as the word is used nowadays by the kind of people who use it of your father. A swordsman is what the Puritans you despise so romantically would call a whoremaster. Didn't you know that? Of course swordsmen don't use the word that way; they use other terms, like amorist, though that usually means somebody like your Myrrha, who is a great proficient at sex without love. Is that what you want? You've told me a great deal about what you feel for Judy Wolff. Now you have had some skilful instruction in the swordsman-and-amorist game. What is it? Nothing but the cheerful trumpet-and-drum of the act of kind. Simple music for simple souls. Is that what you want with Judy? Because that is what her father fears. He doesn't want his daughter's life to be blighted by a whoremaster's son and, as he very shrewdly suspects, a whoremaster's pupil."

This was hitting hard, and though I tried to answer him I knew I was squirming. Because—believe it or not, but I swear it is the truth—I had never understood that was what people meant when they talked about a swordsman, and it suddenly accounted for some of the queer responses I had met with when I applied the word so proudly to Father. I remembered with a chill that I had even used this word about him to the Wolffs, and I was sure they were up to every nuance of speech in three languages. I had made a fool of myself, and of course the realization made me both weak and angry. I lashed out at Knoppy.

"All very well for you to be so pernickety about people's sexual tastes," I said. "But what cap do you wear? Everybody knows what you are. You're a fairy. You're a fairy who's afraid to do anything about it. So what makes you such an authority about real men and women, who have passions you can't begin to share or understand?"

I had hit home. Or so I thought. He seemed to become smaller in his chair, and all the anger had gone out of him.

"Davey, I want you to listen very carefully," he said. "I suppose I am a homosexual, really. Indeed, I know it. I'm a priest, too. By efforts that have not been trivial I have worked for over twenty years to keep myself always in full realization of both facts and to put what I am and the direction in which my nature leads me at the service of my faith and its founder. People wounded much worse than I have been good fighters in that cause. I have not done too badly. I should be stupid and falsely humble if I said otherwise. I have done it gladly, and I shall only say that it has not been easy. But it was my personal sacrifice of what I was to what I loved.

"Now I want you to remember something because I don't think we shall meet again very soon. It is this; however fashionable despair about the world and about people may be at present, and however powerful despair may become in the future, not everybody, or even most people, think and live fashionably; virtue and honour will not be banished from the world, however many popular moralists and panicky journalists say so. Sacrifice will not cease to be because psychiatrists have popularized the idea that there is often some concealed, self-serving element in it; theologians always knew that. Nor do I think love as a high condition of honour will be lost; it is a pattern in the spirit, and people long to make the pattern a reality in their own lives, whatever means they take to do so. In short, Davey, God is not dead. And I can assure you God is not mocked."

10

I never saw Knopwood after that. What he meant when he said we would not meet again was soon explained; he had been ordered off to some more missionary work, and he died a few years ago in the West, of tuberculosis, working almost till the end among his Indians. I have never forgiven him for trying to blacken Father. If that is what his Christianity added up to, it wasn't much.

Dr. von Haller: As you report what Father Knopwood said about Mrs. Martindale, he was abusive and contemptuous; did he know her, by any chance?

Myself: No, he just hated her because she was very much a woman, and I have told you what he was. He made up his mind she was a harlot, and that was that.

DR. VON HALLER: You don't think any of it was indignation on your behalf—because she had, so to speak, abused your innocence?

MYSELF: How had she done that? I think that's silly.

DR. VON HALLER: She had been party to a plan to manipulate you in a certain direction. I don't mean your virginity, which is simply physical and technical, but the scheme to introduce you to what Knopwood called the cheerful trumpet-and-drum, the simple music.

MYSELF: One has to meet it somehow, I suppose? Better in such circumstances than many we can imagine. I had forgotten the Swiss were so Puritanical.

DR. VON HALLER: Ah, now you are talking to me as if I were Father Knopwood. True, everybody has to encounter sex, but usually the choice is left to themselves. They find it; it is not offered to them like a tonic when somebody else thinks it would be good for them. May not the individual know the right time better than someone else? Is it not rather patronizing to arrange a first sexual encounter for one's son?

MYSELF: No more patronizing than to send him to any other school, so far as I can see.

DR. VON HALLER: So you are in complete agreement with what was arranged for you. Let me see—did you not say that the last time you had sexual intercourse was on December 26, 1945?—Was Mrs. Martindale the first and the last, then?—Why did you hesitate to put this valuable instruction to further use?—Take all the time you please, Mr. Staunton. If you would like a glass of water there is a carafe beside you.

MYSELF: It was Judy, I suppose.

DR. VON HALLER: Yes. About Judy—do you realize that in what you have been telling me Judy remains very dim? I am getting to know your father, and I have a good idea of Father Knopwood, and you implied much about Mrs. Martindale in a very few words. But I see very little of Judy. A well-bred girl, somewhat foreign to your world, Jewish, who sings. Otherwise you say only that she was kind and delightful and vague words like that which give her no individuality at all. Your sister suggested that she was cowlike; I attach quite a lot of significance to that.

MYSELF: Don't. Carol is very sharp.

DR. VON HALLER: Indeed she is. You have given a sharp picture of her. She is very perceptive. And she said Judy was cowlike. Do you know why?

MYSELF: Spite, obviously. She sensed I loved Judy.

DR. VON HALLER: She sensed Judy was an Anima-figure to you. Now we must be technical for a little while. We talked about the Anima as a general term for a man's idea of all a woman is or may be. Women are very much aware of this figure when it is aroused in men. Carol sensed that Judy had suddenly embodied the Anima for you, and she was irritated. You know how women are always saying, "What does he see in her?" Of course what he sees is the Anima. Furthermore, he is usually only able to describe it in general terms, not in detail. He is in the grip of something that might as well be called an enchantment; the old word is as good as any new one. It is notorious that when one is enchanted, one does not see clearly.

MYSELF: Judy was certainly clear to me.

DR. VON HALLER: Even though you do not seem to remember one thing she said that is not a commonplace? Oh, Mr. Staunton—a pretty, modest girl, whom you saw for the first time in enchanting circumstances, singing—an Anima, if ever I heard of one.

MYSELF: I thought you people weren't supposed to lead your witnesses?

DR. VON HALLER: Not in Mr. Justice Staunton's court, perhaps, but this is my court. Now tell me; after your talk with your father, in which he referred to Judy as "your little Jewish piece," and your talk with her father, when he said you must not think of Judy as a possible partner in your life, and after your talk with that third father, the priest, how did matters stand between you and Judy?

MYSELF: It went sour. Or it lost its gloss. Or anything you like to express a drop in intensity, a loss of power. Of course we met and talked and kissed. But I knew she was an obedient daughter, and when we kissed I knew Louis Wolff was near, though invisible. And try as I would, when we kissed I could hear a voice—it wasn't my father's, so don't think it was—saying "your Jewish piece." And hateful Knopwood seemed always to be near, like Christ in his sentimental picture, with His hand on the Boy Scout's shoulder. I don't know how it would have worked out because I had rather a miserable illness. It would probably be called mononucleosis now, but they didn't know what it was then, and I was out of school for a long time and confined to the house with Netty as my nurse. When Easter came I was still very weak, and Judy went to Lausanne to a school. She sent me a letter, and I meant to keep it, of course, but I'll bet any money Netty took it and burned it.

Dr. von Haller: But you remember what it said?

Myself: I remember some of it. She wrote, "My father is the wisest and best man I know, and I shall do what he says." It seemed extraordinary, for a girl of seventeen.

Dr. von Haller: How, extraordinary?

Myself: Immature. Wouldn't you say so? Oughtn't she to have had more mind of her own?

Dr. von Haller: But wasn't that precisely your attitude toward your own father?

Myself: Not after my illness. Nevertheless, there was a difference. Because my father really was a great man. Dunstan Ramsay once said he was a genius of an unusual, unrecognized kind. Whereas Louis Wolff, though very good of his kind, was just a clever doctor.

Dr. von Haller: A very sophisticated man; sophisticated in a way your father was not, it appears. And what about Knopwood? You seem to have dismissed him because he was a homosexual.

Myself: I see a good many of his kind in court. You can't take them seriously.

Dr. von Haller: But you take very few people seriously when you have them in court. There are homosexuals we do well to take seriously and you are not likely to meet them in court. You spoke, I recall, of Christian charity?

MYSELF: I am no longer a Christian, and too often I have uncovered pitiable weakness masquerading as charity. Those who talk about charity and forgiveness usually lack the guts to push anything to a logical conclusion. I've never seen charity bring any unquestionable good in its train.

DR. VON HALLER: I see. Very well, let us go on. During your illness I suppose you did a lot of thinking about your situation. That is what these illnesses are for, you know—these mysterious ailments that take us out of life but do not kill us. They are signals that our life is going the wrong way, and intervals for reflection. You were lucky to be able to keep out of a hospital, even if it did return you to the domination of Netty. Now, what answers did you find? For instance, did you think about why you were so ready to believe your mother had been the lover of your father's best friend, whereas you doubted that Mrs. Martindale had been your father's mistress?

MYSELF: I suppose children favour one parent more than the other. I have told you about Mother. And Father used to talk about her sometimes when he visited me when I was ill. Several times he warned me against marrying a boyhood sweetheart.

DR. VON HALLER: Yes, I suppose he knew what was wrong with you. People often do, you know, though nothing would persuade them to bring such knowledge to the surface of their thoughts or admit what they so deeply know. He sensed you were sick for Judy. And he gave you very good advice, really.

MYSELF: But I loved Judy. I really did.

DR. VON HALLER: You loved a projection of your own Anima. You really did. But did you ever know Judy Wolff? You have told me that when you see her now, as a grown woman with a husband and family, you never speak to her. Why? Because you are protecting your boyhood dream. You don't want to meet this woman who is somebody else. When you go home you had better make an opportunity to meet Mrs. Professor Whoever-It-Is, and lay that ghost forever. It will be quite easy, I assure you. You will see her as she is now, and she will see the famous criminal lawyer. It will all be smooth as silk, and you will be delivered forever. So far as possible, lay your ghosts. . . . But you have not answered my question: why adultery for mother but not for father?

MYSELF: Mother was weak.

DR. VON HALLER: Mother was your father's Anima-figure, whom he had been so unfortunate, or so unwise, as to marry. No wonder she seemed weak, poor woman, with such a load to carry for such a man. And no wonder he turned against her, as you would probably have turned against poor Judy if she had been so unfortunate as to fall into the clutch of such a clever thinker and such a primitive feeler as you are. Oh, men revenge themselves very thoroughly on women they think have enchanted them, when really these poor devils of women are merely destined to be pretty or sing nicely or laugh at the right time.

MYSELF: Don't you think there is any element of enchantment in love, then?

DR. VON HALLER: I know perfectly well that there is, but has anybody ever said that enchantment was a basis for marriage? It will be there at the beginning, probably, but the table must be laid with more solid fare than that if starvation is to be kept at bay for sixty years.

MYSELF: You are unusually dogmatic today.

DR. VON HALLER: You have told me you like dogma. . . . But let us get back to an unanswered question: why did you believe your mother capable of adultery but not your father?

MYSELF: Well—adultery in a woman may be a slip, a peccadillo, but in a man, you see—you see, it's an offense against property. I know it doesn't sound very pretty, but the law makes it plain and public opinion makes it plainer. A deceived husband is merely a cuckold, a figure of fun, whereas a deceived wife is someone who has sustained an injury. Don't ask me why; I simply state the fact as society and the courts see it.

DR. VON HALLER: But this Mrs. Martindale, if I understood

you, had left her husband, or he had left her. So what injury could there be?

MYSELF: I am thinking of my mother: Father knew her long before Mother's death. He may have drifted away from Mother, but I can't believe he would do anything that would injure her—that might have played some part in her death. I mean, a swordsman is one thing—a sort of chivalrous concept, which may be romantic but is certainly not squalid. But an adulterer—I've seen a lot of them in court, and none of them was anything but squalid.

DR. VON HALLER: And you could not associate your father with anything you considered squalid? So: you emerged from this illness without your beloved, and without your priest, but with your father still firmly in the saddle?

MYSELF: Not even that. I still adored him, but my adoration was flawed with doubts. That was why I determined not to try to be like him, not to permit myself any thought of rivalling him but to try to find some realm where I could show that I was worthy of him.

DR. VON HALLER: My God, what a fanatic!

MYSELF: That seems a rather unprofessional outburst.

DR. VON HALLER: Not a bit. You are a fanatic. Don't you know what fanaticism is? It is overcompensation for doubt. Well: go on.

Yes, I went on, and what my life lacked in incident it made up for in intensity. I finished school, pretty well but not as well as if I had not had such a long illness, and I was ready for university. Father had always assumed I would go to the University of Toronto, but I wanted to go to Oxford, and he jumped at that. He had never been to a university himself because he was in the First World War—got the D.S.O., too—during what would have been his college years; he had wanted to get on with life and had qualified as a lawyer without taking a degree. You could still do that, then. But he had romantic ideas about universities, and Oxford appealed to him. So I went there, and because Father wanted me to be in a big college, I got into Christ Church.

People are always writing in their memoirs about what Oxford meant to them. I can't pretend the place itself meant extraordinary things to me. Of course it was pleasant, and I liked the interesting buildings; architectural critics are always knocking them, but after Toronto they made my eyes pop. They spoke of an idea of education strange to me; discomfort there was, but no meanness, no hint of edification on the cheap. And I liked the feel of a city of youth, which is what Oxford seems to be, though anybody with eyes in his head can see that it is run by old men. But my Oxford was a post-war Oxford, crammed to the walls and rapidly growing into a big industrial city. And there was much criticism of the privilege it implied, mostly from people who were sitting bang in the middle of the privilege and getting all they could out of it. Oxford was part of my plan to become a special sort of man, and I bent everything that came my way to my single purpose.

I read law, and did well at it. I was very lucky in being assigned Pargetter of Balliol as my tutor. He was a great law don, a blind man who nevertheless managed to be a famous chess-player and such a teacher as I had never known. He was relentless and exacting, which was precisely what I wanted because I was determined to be a first-class lawyer. You see, when I told Father I wanted to be a lawyer, he assumed at once that I wanted law as a preparation for business, which was what he himself had made of it. He was sure I would follow him in Alpha; indeed I don't think any other future for me seemed possible to him. I was perhaps a little bit devious because I did not tell him at once that I had other ideas. I wanted the law because I wanted to master something in which I would know where I stood and which would not be open to the whims and preconceptions of people like Louis Wolff, or Knopwood—or Father. I wanted to be a master of my own craft and I wanted a great craft. Also, I wanted to know a great deal about people, and I wanted a body of knowledge that would go as far as possible to explain people. I wanted to work in a realm that would give me some insight into the spirit that I had seen at work in Bill Unsworth.

I had no notions of being a crusader. One of the things I had arrived at during that wearisome, depleting illness was a determination to be done forever with everything that Father Knopwood stood for. Knoppy, I saw, wanted to manipulate people; he wanted to make them good, and he was sure he knew what was good. For him, God was here and Christ was now. He was prepared to accept himself and impose on others a lot of irrational notions in the interests of his special idea of goodness. He thought God was not mocked. I seemed to see God being mocked, and rewarding the mocker with splendid success, every day of my life.

I wanted to get away from the world of Louis Wolff, who now appeared to me as an extremely shrewd man whose culture was never allowed for an instant to interfere with some age-old ideas that governed him and must also govern his family.

I wanted to get away from Father and save my soul, insofar as I believed in such a thing. I suppose what I meant by my soul was my self-respect or my manhood. I loved him and feared him, but I had spied tiny chinks in his armour. He too was a manipulator and, remembering his own dictum, I did not mean to be a man who could be manipulated. I knew I would always be known as his son and that I would in some ways have to carry the weight of wealth that I had not gained myself in a society where inherited wealth always implies a stigma. But somehow, in some part of the great world, I would be David Staunton, unreachable by Knopwood or Louis Wolff, or Father, because I had outstripped them.

The idea of putting sex aside never entered my head. It just happened, and I was not aware that it had become part of my way of living until it was thoroughly established. Pargetter may have had something to do with it. He was unmarried, and being blind he was insulated against a great part of the charm of women. He seized on me, as he did on all his students, with an eagle's talons, but I think he knew by the end of my first year that I was his in a way that the others, however admiring, were not. If you hope to master the law, he would say, you are a fool, for it has no single masters; but if you hope to master some part of it, you had better put your emotions in cold storage at least until you are thirty. I decided to do that, and did it, and by the time I was thirty I liked the chill. It helped to make people afraid of me, and I liked that, too.

Pargetter must have taken to me, though he was not a man to hint at any such thing. He taught me chess, and although I was never up to his standard I grew to play well. His room never had enough light, because he didn't need it and I think he was a little cranky about making people who had their eyesight use it to the full. We would sit by his insufficient fire in a twilight that could have been dismal, but which he contrived somehow to give a legal quality, and play game after game; he sat fatly in his arm-chair, and I sat by the board and made all the moves; he would call his move, I would place the piece as he directed, and then I would tell him my counter-move. When he had beaten me he would go back over the game and tell me precisely the point at which I had gone wrong. I was awed by such a memory and such a spatial sense in a man who lived in darkness; he was contemptuous of me when I could not remember what I had done six or eight moves back, and of sheer necessity I had to develop the memory-trick myself.

He really was alarming: he had three or four boards set up around his room, on which he played chess by post with friends far away. If I arrived for an early tutorial he would say, "There's a postcard on the table; I expect it's from Johannesburg; read it." I would read a chess move from it and make the move on a board which he had not touched for perhaps a month. When my tutorial was finished he would dictate a counter-move to me, and I would rearrange the board accordingly. He won a surprising number of these long-distance, tortoise-paced games.

He had never learned Braille. He wrote in longhand on paper he fitted into a frame which had guide-wires to keep him on the lines, and he never seemed to forget anything he had written. He had a prodigious knowledge of law books he had never seen, and when he sent me, with exact directions, to his shelves to hunt up a reference, I often found a slip of paper in the book with a note in his careful, printlike hand. He kept up with books and journals by having them read to him, and I felt myself favoured when he began to ask me to read; he would make invaluable comment as he listened, and it was always a master-lesson in how to absorb, weigh, select, and reject.

This was precisely what I wanted and I came almost to worship Pargetter. Exactitude, calm appraisal, close reasoning applied to problems which so often had their beginning in other people's untidy emotions acted like balm on my hurt mind. It was not ordinary legal instruction and it did not result in ordinary legal practice. Many lawyers are beetle-witted ignoramuses, prey to their own emotions and those of their clients; some of them work up big practices because they can fling themselves fiercely into other people's fights. Their indignation is for sale. But Pargetter had honed his mind to a shrewd edge, and I wanted to be like Pargetter. I wanted to know, to see, to sift, and not to be moved. I wanted to get as far as possible from that silly boy who had not realized what a swordsman was when everybody else knew, and who mooned over Judy Wolff and was sent away by her father to play with other toys. I wanted to be melted down, purged of dross, and remoulded in a new and better form; Pargetter was just the man to do it. I had other instructors, of course, and some of them were very good, but Pargetter continues to be my ideal, my father in art.

11

I wrote to Father every week and grew aware that my letters were less and less communicative, for I was entering a world where he could not follow. I visited Canada once a year, for as short a time as I could manage, and it was when I was about to enter my third year at Oxford that he took me to dinner one night, and after some havering which I realize now was shyness about what he was going to say, he made what seemed to me to be an odd request.

"I've been wondering about the Stauntons," he said. "Who do you suppose they could have been? I can't find out anything about Father, though I've wormed out a few facts. He graduated from the medical school here in Toronto in 1887, and the records say he was twenty then, so he must have been born in 1867. They really just gave doctors a lick and a promise then, and I don't suppose he knew much medicine. He was a queer old devil, and as you probably know, we never hit it off. All I know about his background is that he wasn't born in Canada. Mother was, and I've traced her family, and it was easy and dull; farmers culminating in a preacher. But who was Dr. Henry Staunton? I want to know. You see, Davey, though it sounds vain, I have a strong hunch that there must be some good blood somewhere in our background.

Your grandfather had a lot of ability as a businessman; more than I could ever persuade him to put to work. His plunge into sugar, when nobody else could see its possibilities, took imagination. I mean, when he was a young man, a lot of people were still rasping their sugar off a loaf with a file, and it all came from the Islands. He had drive and foresight. Of course lots of quite ordinary people have done very well for themselves, but I wonder if he was quite ordinary? When I was in England during the war I wanted to look around and find out anything I could, but the time was wrong and I was very busy with immediate things. But I met two people over there at different times who asked me if I were one of the Warwickshire Stauntons. Well, you know how Englishmen like it when Canadians play simple and rough-hewn, so I always answered that so far as I knew I was one of the Pitt County Stauntons. But I tucked it away in the back of my mind, and it might just be so. Who the Warwickshire Stauntons are I haven't the slightest idea, but they appear to be well known to people who are interested in old families. So, when you go back to Oxford, I'd like you to make some enquiries and let me know what you find. We're probably bastards, or something, but I'd like to know for certain."

I had long known Father was a romantic, and I had once been a romantic myself—two or three years ago—so I said I would do what I could.

How? And what? Go to Warwickshire and find the Stauntons, and ask if they had any knowledge of a physician who had been Pitt County's foremost expert on constipation, and to the end of his days a firm believer in *lignum vitae* sap as a treatment for rheumatism? Not for me, thank you. But one day in the Common Room I was looking through the *Times Literary Supplement,* and my eye fell on a modest advertisement. I can see it now:

> GENEALOGIES erected and pedigrees searched by an Oxonian curiously qualified. Strict confidence exacted and extended.

This was what I wanted. I made a note of the box number, and that night I wrote my letter. I wanted a pedigree searched, I said, and if it proved possible to erect a genealogy on it I should like that, too.

I don't know what I expected, but the advertisement suggested a pedant well past youth and of a sharp temper. I was utterly unprepared for the curiously qualified Oxonian when he arrived in my study two days later. He seemed not to be much older than myself, and had a shy, girlish manner and the softest voice that was compatible with being heard at all. The only elderly or pedantic thing about him was a pair of spectacles of a kind nobody wore then—gold-rimmed and with small oval lenses.

"I thought I'd come round instead of writing, because we are near neighbours," he said, and handed me a cheap visiting-card on which was printed—

> ADRIAN PLEDGER-BROWN
>
> CORPUS CHRISTI

So this was the curiously qualified Oxonian!

"Sit down," I said. "You erect genealogies?"

"Oh, indeed," he breathed. "That is to say, I know precisely how it is done. That is to say, I have examined many scores of pedigrees which have already been erected, and I am sure I could do it myself if I were to be entrusted with such a task. It involves research, you see, of a kind I understand quite well and could undertake with a very fair likelihood of success. I know, you see, where to look, and that is everything. Almost everything."

He smiled such a girlish smile and his eyes swam so unassumingly behind the comic specs that I was tempted to be easy with him. But that was not the Pargetter way. Beware of a witness who appeals to you, he said. Repress any personal response, and if it seems to be gaining the upper hand, go to the other extreme and be severe with the witness. If Ogilvie had remembered that in-

Cripps-Armstrong *vs.* Clatterbos & Dudley in 1884 he would have won the case, but he let Clatterbos's difficulty with English arouse his compassion; it's a famous instance. So I sprang upon Pledger-Brown, and rent him.

"Am I right in deducing that you have never erected a genealogy independently before?"

"That would be—well, to put it baldly—yes, you might say that."

"Never mind what I might say or might not say. I asked a plain question, and I want a plain answer. Is this your first job?"

"My first professional engagement? Working as an independent investigator? If you wish to put it that way, I suppose the answer must be that it is."

"Aha! You are in a word, a greenhorn."

"Oh, dear, no. I mean, I have studied the subject, and the method, extensively."

"But you have never done a job of this kind before, for a fee. Yes or no?"

"To be completely frank, yes; or rather, no."

"But your advertisement said 'curiously qualified.' Tell me, Mr.—(business of consulting card)—ah, Pledger-Brown, in precisely what direction does your curious qualification lie?"

"I am the godson of Garter."

"Godson of—?"

"Garter."

"I do not understand."

"Quite possibly not. But that is why you need me, you see. I mean, people who want genealogies erected and pedigrees searched don't usually know these things. Americans in particular. I mean that my godfather is the Garter King of Arms."

"What's that?"

"He is the principal officer of the College of Heralds. I hope that one day, with luck, I may be a member of the College myself. But I must make a beginning somewhere, you see."

"Somewhere? What do you imply by somewhere? You regard me as a starting-point, is that it? I would be rough material for your prentice-hand; is that what you mean?"

"Oh, dear me, no. But I must do some independent work before I can hope to get an official appointment, mustn't I?"

"How should I know what you must do? What I want to know is whether there is any chance that you can undertake the job I want done and do it properly."

"Well, Mr. Staunton, I don't think anybody will do it for you if you go on like this."

"Like this? Like this? I don't understand you. What fault have you to find with the way I have been going on, as you express it?"

Pledger-Brown was all mildness, and his smile was like a Victorian picture of a village maiden.

"Well, I mean playing Serjeant Buzfuz and treating me really quite rudely when I've only come in answer to your letter. You're a law student, of course. I've looked you up, you see. And your father is a prominent Canadian industrialist. I suppose you want some ancestors. Well, perhaps I can find some for you. And I want the work, but not badly enough to be bullied about it. I mean, I am a beginner at genealogy, but I've studied it: you're a beginner at the law, but you've studied it. So why are you being so horrid when we are on an even footing?"

So I stopped being horrid, and in quite a short time he had accepted a glass of sherry and was calling me Staunton and I was calling him Pledger-Brown, and we were discussing what might be done.

He was in his third year at Corpus, which I could almost have hit with a stone from my windows, because I was in Canterbury Quad at the rear of Christ Church. He was mad for genealogy and couldn't wait to get at it, so he had advertised while he was still an undergraduate, and his anxiety for strict confidence was because his college would have been unsympathetic if they thought he was conducting any sort of business within their walls. He was obviously poor, but he had an air of breeding, and there was a strain of toughness in him that lay well below his wispy, maidenly ways. I took to him because he was as keen about his profession as I was about mine, and for anything I knew his diffidence may have been the professional manner of his kind. Soon he was cross-examining me.

"This Dr. Henry Staunton who has no known place of birth is a very common figure in genealogical work for people from the New World. But we can usually find the origin of such people, if we sift the parish records, wills, records of Chancery and Exchequer, and Manor Court Rolls. That takes a long time and runs into money. So we start with the obvious, hoping for a lucky hit. Of course, as your father thinks, he may be a Staunton of Longbridge in Warwickshire, but there are also Stauntons of Nottingham, Leicester, Lincolnshire, and Somerset, all of a quality that would please your father. But sometimes we can take a short cut. Was your grandfather an educated man?"

"He was a doctor. I wouldn't call him a man of wide cultivation."

"Good. That's often a help. I mean, such people often retain some individuality under the professional veneer. Perhaps he said some things that stuck in your mind? Used unusual words that might be county dialect words? Do you recall anything like that?"

I pondered. "Once he told my sister, Caroline, she had a tongue sharp enough to shave an urchin. I've repeated it to her often."

"Oh, that's quite helpful. He did use some dialect words then. But urchin as a word for the common hedgehog is very widespread in country districts. Can you think of anything more unusual?"

I was beginning to respect Pledger-Brown. I had always thought an urchin was a boy you didn't like, and could never figure out why Grandfather would want to shave one. I thought further.

"I do just remember that he called some of his old patients who stuck with him, and were valetudinarians, 'my old wallowcrops.' Is that of any use? Could he have made the word up?"

"Few simple people make up words. 'Wallowcrop'; I'll make a note of that and see what I can discover. Meanwhile keep thinking about him, will you? And I'll come again when I have a better idea what to do."

Think about Grandfather Staunton, powerful but dim in my past. A man, it seemed to me now, with a mind like a morgue in which a variety of defunct ideas lay on slabs, kept cold to defer decay. A man who knew nothing about health, but could identify a number of diseases. A man whose medical knowledge belonged to a time when people talked about The System and had spasms and believed in the efficacy of strong, clean smells, such as oil of peppermint, as charms against infection. A man who never doubted that spankings were good for children, and once soundly walloped both Caroline and me because we had put Eno's Fruit Salts in the bottom of Granny's chamber-pot, hoping she would have a fantod when it foamed. A furious teetotaller, malignantly contemptuous of what he called "booze-artists" and never fully reconciled to my father when he discovered that Father drank wines and spirits but had contumaciously failed thereby to become a booze-artist. A man whom I could only recall as gloomy, heavy, and dull, but pleased with his wealth and unaffectedly scornful of those who had not the wit or craft to equal it; preachers were excepted as being a class apart, and sacred, but needing frequent guidance from practical men in the conduct of their churches. In short, a nasty old village moneybags.

A strange conduit through which to convey the good blood Father thought we Stauntons must have. But then, Father had never troubled to pretend that he had much regard for Doc Staunton. Which was strange in itself, in a way, for Father was very strong on the regard children should have for parents. Not that he ever said so directly, or urged Caroline and me to honour our father and mother. But I recall that he was down on H. G. Wells, because in his *Experiment in Autobiography* Wells had said frankly that his parents weren't up to much and that escape from them was his first step toward a good life. Father was not consistent. But Doc Staunton had been consistent, and what had consistency made of him?

The hunt was up, and Doc Staunton was the fox.

Notes from Pledger-Brown punctuated the year that followed. He wrote an elegant Italic hand, as became a genealogist, and scraps of intelligence would arrive by the college messenger service: "*Wallowcrop* Cumberland dialect word. Am following up this clue. A.P-B." And, "Sorry to say nothing comes of enquiries in Cumberland. Am casting about in Lincoln." Or, "Tally-ho! A Henry Staunton born 1866 in Somerset!" followed a week later by, "False scent; Somerset Henry died aged 3 mos." Clearly he was having a wonderful adventure, but I had little time to think about it. I was up to my eyes in Jurisprudence, that formal science of positive law, and in addition to formal studies Pargetter was making me read Kelly's *Famous Advocates and Their Speeches* and *British Forensic Eloquence* aloud to him, dissecting the rhetoric of notable counsel and trying to make some progress in that line myself. Pargetter was determined that I should not be what he called an ignorant pettifogger, and he made it clear that as a Canadian I started well behind scratch in the journey toward professional literacy and elegance.

" 'The law, besides being a profession, is one of the humanities,' " he said to me one day, and I knew from the way he spoke he was quoting. "Who said that?" I didn't know. "Then never forget that it was one of your countrymen, your present Prime Minister, Louis St. Laurent," he said, punching me sharply in the side, as he often did when he wanted to make a point. "It's been said before, but it's never been said better. Be proud it was a Canadian who said it." And he went on to belabour me, as he had often done before, with Sir Walter Scott's low opinion of lawyers who knew nothing of history or literature; from these studies, said he, I would learn what people were and how they might be expected to behave. "But wouldn't I learn that from clients?" I asked, to try him. "Clients!" he said, and I would not have believed anyone could make a two-syllable word stretch out so long; "you'll learn precious little from clients except folly and duplicity and greed. You've got to stand above that."

Working as I was under the English system I had to be a member of one of the Inns of Court and go to London at intervals to eat dinners in its Hall; I was enrolled in the Middle Temple, and reverently chewed through the thirty-six obligatory meals. I liked it. I liked the ceremony and solemnity of the law, not only as safeguards against trivializing of the law but as pleasant observances in themselves. I visited the courts, studied the conduct and courtesy of their workings, and venerated judges who seemed able to carry a mass of detail in their heads and boil it down and serve it up in a kind of strong judicial consommé for the jury when all the pleading and testimony were over. I liked the romance of it, the star personalities of the great advocates, the swishing of gowns and flourishing of impractical but traditional blue bags full of papers. I was delighted that although most people seemed to use more modern instruments, everybody had access to quill pens, and could doubtless have called for sand to do their blotting, with full confidence that sand would have been forthcoming. I loved wigs, which established a hierarchy that was palpable and turned unremarkable faces into the faces of priests serving a great purpose. What if all this silk and bombazine and horsehair awed and even frightened the simple people who came to court for justice? It would do them no harm to be a little frightened. Everybody in court, except the occasional accused creature in the dock, seemed calmed, reft from the concerns of everyday; those who were speaking on oath seemed to me, very often, to be revealing an aspect of their best selves. The juries took their duties seriously, like good citizens. It was an arena in which gladiators struggled, but the end for which they struggled was that right, so far as right could be determined, should be done.

I was not naïve. That is how I think of courts still. I am one of the very few lawyers I know who keeps his gown beautifully clean, whose collar and bands and cuffs are almost foppishly starched, whose striped trousers are properly pressed, whose shoes gleam. I am proud that the newspapers often say I cut an elegant figure in court. The law deserves that. The law is elegant. Pargetter took good care that I should not be foolishly romantic about the law, but he knew that there was a measure of romance in my attitude toward it, and if he had thought it should be rooted out, he would have done so. One day he paid me a walloping great compliment.

"I think you'll make an advocate," said he. "You have the two necessities, ability and imagination. A good advocate is his client's *alter ego;* his task is to say what his client would say for himself if he had the knowledge and the power. Ability goes hand in hand with the knowledge: the power is dependent on imagination. But when I say imagination I mean capacity to see all sides of a subject and weigh all possibilities; I don't mean fantasy and poetry and moonshine; imagination is a good horse to carry you over the ground, not a flying carpet to set you free from probability."

I think I grew a foot, spiritually, that day.

DR. VON HALLER: So you might. And how lucky you were. Not everybody encounters a Pargetter. He is a very important addition to your cast of characters.

MYSELF: I don't think I follow you. What I am telling you is history, not invention.

DR. VON HALLER: Oh, quite. But even history has characters, and a personal history like yours must include a few people whom it would be stupid to call stock characters, even though they appear in almost all complete personal histories. Or let us put it differently. You remember the little poem by Ibsen that I quoted to you during one of our early meetings?

MYSELF: Only vaguely. Something about self-judgement.

DR. VON HALLER: No, no; self-judgement comes later. Now pay attention, please:

> To *live* is to battle with trolls
> in the vaults of heart and brain.
> To *write:* that is to sit
> in judgement over one's self.

MYSELF: But I have been writing constantly; everything I have told you has been based on careful notes; I have tried to be as clear as possible, to follow Ramsay's Plain Style. I have raked up some stuff I have never told to another living soul. Isn't this self-judgement?

DR. VON HALLER: Not at all. This has been the history of your battle with the trolls.

MYSELF: Another of your elaborate metaphors?

DR. VON HALLER: If you like. I use metaphor to spare you jargon. Now consider: what figures have we met so far in our exploration of your life? Your Shadow; there was no difficulty about that, I believe, and we shall certainly meet him again. The Friend: Felix was the first to play that part, and you may yet come to recognize Knopwood as a very special friend, though I know you are still bitter against him. The Anima; you are very rich there, for of course there were your mother and Caroline and Netty, who all demonstrate various aspects of the feminine side of life, and finally Judy. This figure has been in eclipse for some years, at least in its positive aspect; I think we must count your stepmother as an Anima-figure, but not a friendly one; we may still find that she is not so black as you paint her. But there are happy signs that the eclipse is almost over, because of your dream—let us be romantic and call it The Maiden and the Manticore—in which you were sure you recognized me. Perfectly in order. I have played all of these roles at various stages of our talks. Necessarily so: an analysis like this is certainly not emotion recollected in tranquillity. You may call these figures many things. You might call them the Comedy Company of the Psyche, but that would be flippant and not do justice to the cruel blows you have had from some of them. In my profession we call them archetypes, which means that they represent and body forth patterns toward which human behaviour seems to be disposed; patterns which repeat themselves endlessly, but never in precisely the same way. And you have just been telling me about one of the most powerful of all, which we may call the Magus, or the Wizard, or the Guru, or anything that signifies a powerful formative influence toward the development of the total personality. Pargetter appears to have been a very fine Magus indeed: a blind genius who accepts you as an apprentice in his art! But he has just turned up, which is unusual though not seriously so. I had expected him earlier. Knopwood looked rather like a Magus for a time, but we shall have to see if any of his influence lasted. But the other man, the possible father, the man you call Old Buggerlugs—I had expected rather more from him. Have you been keeping anything back?

MYSELF: No. And yet . . . there was always something about him that held the imagination. He was an oddity, as I've said. But a man who never seemed to come to anything. He wrote some books, and Father said some of them sold well, but they were queer stuff, about the nature of faith and the necessity of faith—not Christian faith, but some kind of faith, and now and then in classes he would point at us and say, "Be sure you choose what you believe and know why you believe it, because if you don't choose your beliefs, you may be certain that some belief, and probably not a very creditable one, will choose you." Then he would go on about people whose belief was in Youth, or Money, or Power, or something like that, and who had found that these things were false gods. We liked to hear him rave, and some of his demonstrations from history were very amusing, but we didn't take it seriously. I have always looked on him as a man who missed his way in life. Father liked him. They came from the same village.

DR. VON HALLER: But you never felt any urge to learn from him?

MYSELF: What could he have taught me, except history and the Plain Style?

DR. VON HALLER: Yes, I see. It seemed to me for a time that he had something of the quality of a Magus.

MYSELF: In your Comedy Company, or Cabinet of Archetypes, you don't seem to have any figure that might correspond to my father.

DR. VON HALLER: Oh, do not be impatient. These are the common figures. You may depend on it that your father will not be forgotten. Indeed, it seems to me that he has been very much present ever since we began. We talk of him all the time. He may prove to be your Great Troll. . . .

MYSELF: Why do you talk of trolls? It seems to me that you Jungians sometimes go out of your way to make yourselves absurd.

DR. VON HALLER: Trolls are not Jungian; they are just part of my promise not to annoy you with jargon. What is a troll?

MYSELF: A kind of Scandinavian spook, isn't it?

DR. VON HALLER: Yes, spook is a very good word for it—another Scandinavian word. Sometimes a troublesome goblin, sometimes a huge, embracing lubberfiend, sometimes an ugly animal creature, sometimes a helper and server, even a lovely enchantress, a true Princess from Far Away: but never a full or complete human being. And the battle with trolls that Ibsen wrote about is a good metaphor to describe the wrestling and wrangling we go through when the archetypes we carry in ourselves seem to be embodied in people we have to deal with in daily life.

MYSELF: But people are people, not trolls or archetypes.

DR. VON HALLER: Yes, and our great task is to see people as people and not clouded by archetypes we carry about with us, looking for a peg to hang them on.

MYSELF: Is that the task we are working at here?

DR. VON HALLER: Part of it. We take a good look at your life, and we try to lift the archetypes off the pegs and see the people who have been obscured by them.

MYSELF: And what do I get out of that?

DR. VON HALLER: That depends on you. For one thing, you will probably learn to recognize a spook when you see one, and keep trolls in good order. And you will recover all these projections which you have visited on other people like a magic lantern projecting a slide on a screen. When you stop doing that you are stronger, more independent. You have more mental energy. Think about it. And now go on about the genealogist.

12

I didn't pay much attention to him, because as I told Dr. von Haller, I was greatly taken up with my final year of law studies. Pargetter expected me to get a First, and I wanted it even more than he. The notes kept arriving with reports of nothing achieved in spite of impressive activity. I had written to Father that I had a good man on the job, and had his permission to advance money as it was needed. Pledger-Brown's accounts were a source of great delight to me; I felt like Diogenes, humbled in the presence of an honest man. Sometimes in the vacations he went off hunting Stauntons and sent me bills detailing third-class tickets, sixpenny rides on buses, shillings spent on beer for old men who might know something, and cups of tea and buns for himself. There was never any charge for his time or his knowledge, and when I asked about that he replied that we would agree on a fee when he produced his results. I foresaw that he would starve on that principle, but I cherished him as an innocent. Indeed, I grew to be very fond of him, and we were Adrian and Davey when we talked. His besotted enthusiasm for the practise of heraldry refreshed me; I knew nothing about it, and couldn't see the use of it, and wondered why anybody bothered with it, but in time he brought me to see that it had once been necessary and was still a pleasant personal indulgence, and—this was important—that using somebody else's armorial bearings was no different in spirit from using his name; it was impersonation. It was, in legal terms, no different from imitating a trade-mark, and I knew what that meant. Undoubtedly Pledger-Brown was the best friend I made at Oxford, and I keep up with him still. He got into the College of Heralds, by the way, and is now Clarencieux King of Arms and looks exceedingly peculiar on ceremonial occasions in a tabard and a hat with a feather.

What finally bound us into the kind of friendship that does not fade was complicity in a secret.

Early in the spring term of my third year, when I was deep in work for my Final Schools, a message arrived: "I have found Henry Staunton. A.P-B." I had a mountain of reading to do and had planned to spend all afternoon at the Codrington, but this called for something special, so I got hold of Adrian and took him to lunch. He was as nearly triumphant as his diffident nature would allow.

"I was just about to offer you a non-grandfather," said he; "there was a connection of the Stauntons of Warwickshire—not a Longbridge Staunton but a cousin—who cannot be accounted for and might perhaps have gone to Canada at the age of eighteen or so. By a very long shot he might have been your grandfather; without better evidence it would be guesswork to say he was. But then during the Easter vacation I had a flash. You otiose ass, Pledger-Brown, I said to myself, you've never thought of Staunton as a place-name. It is an elementary rule in this work, you know, to check place-names. There is Staunton Harold in Leicestershire and two or three Stauntons, and of course I had quite overlooked Staunton in Gloucestershire. So off I went and checked parish records. And there he was in Gloucestershire: Albert Henry Staunton, born April 4, 1866, son of Maria Ann Dymock, and if you can find a better West Country name than Dymock, I'd be glad to hear it."

"What kind of Staunton is he?" I asked.

"He's an extraordinarily rum Staunton," said Pledger-Brown, "but that's the best of it. You get not only a grandfather but a good story as well. You know, so many of these forbears that people ferret out are nothing at all; I mean, perfectly good and reputable, but no personal history of any interest. But Albert Henry is a conversation-piece. Now listen.

"Staunton is a hamlet about ten miles north-west of Gloucester, bearing over toward Herefordshire. In the middle of the last century it had only one public house, called the Angel, and by rights it ought to have been near a church named for the Annunciation, but it isn't. That doesn't matter. What is important is that in the 1860s there was an attractive girl working at the Angel who was called Maria Ann Dymock, and she must have been a local Helen, because she was known as Mary Dymock the Angel."

"A barmaid?" I asked, wondering how Father was going to take to the idea of a barmaid.

"No, no," said Adrian; "barmaids are a bee in the American bonnet. A country pub of that time would be servéd by its landlord. Maria Ann Dymock was undoubtedly a domestic servant. But she became pregnant, and she said the child's father was George Applesquire, who was the landlord of the Angel. He denied it and said it could have been several other men. Indeed, he said that all Staunton could claim to be the child's father, and he would have nothing to do with it. He or his wife turned Maria Ann out of the Angel.

"Now, the cream of the story is this. Maria Ann Dymock must have been a girl of some character, for she bore the child in the local workhouse and in due time marched off to church to have it christened. 'What shall I name the child?' said parson. 'Albert Henry,' said Maria Ann. So it was done. 'And the father's name?' said parson; 'shall I say Dymock?' 'No,' said Maria Ann, 'say Staunton, because it's said by landlord the whole place could be his father, and I want him to carry his father's name.' I get all this out of the county archaeological society's records, which include quite an interesting diary of the clergyman in question, whose name was the Reverend Theophilus Mynors, by the way. Mynors must have been a sport, and probably he thought the girl had been badly used by Applesquire, because he put down the name as Albert Henry Staunton in the parish record.

"It caused a scandal, of course. But Maria Ann stuck it out, and when Applesquire's cronies threatened to make things too hot for her to stay in the parish, she walked the village street with a collecting bag, saying, 'If you want me out of Staunton, give me something for my journey.' She must have been a Tartar. She didn't get much, but the Rev. Theophilus admits that he gave her five pounds on the quiet, and there were one or two other contributors who admired her pluck, and soon she had enough to go abroad. You could still get a passage to Quebec for under five pounds in those days if you supplied your own food, and infants travelled free. So off went Maria Ann in late May of 1866, and undoubtedly she was your great-grandmother."

We were eating in one of those Oxford restaurants that spring up and sink down again because they are run by amateurs, and we had arrived at the stage of eating a charlotte russe made of stale cake, tired jelly, and chemicals; I can still remember its taste because it is associated with my bleak wonder as to what I was going to report to Father. I explained to Pledger-Brown.

"But my dear Davey, you're missing the marvel of it," he said; "what a story! Think of Maria Ann's resource and courage! Did she slink away and hide herself in London with her bastard child, gradually sinking to the basest forms of prostitution while little Albert Henry became a thief and a pimp? No! She was of the stuff of which the great New World has been forged! She stood up on her feet and demanded to be recognized as an individual, with inalienable rights! She braved the vicar, and George Applesquire, and all of public opinion. And then she went off to carve out a glorious life in what were then, my dear chap, still the colonies and not the great self-governing sisterhood of the Commonwealth! She was there when Canada became a Dominion! She may have been among the cheering crowds who hailed that moment in Montreal or Ottawa or wherever it was! You're not grasping the thing at all."

I was grasping it. I was thinking of Father.

"I confess that I've been meddling," said Adrian, turning very red; "Garter would be as mad as hops if he knew I'd been playing with my paint-box like this. But after all, this is my first shot at tracing a forbear independently, and I can't help it. So I beg you, as a friend, to accept this trifle of *anitergium* from me."

He handed me a cardboard roll, and when I had pried the metal cap off one end, I found a scroll inside it. I folded it out on the table where the medical charlotte russe had given place to some coffee—a Borgia speciality of the place—and it was a coat-of-arms.

"Just a very rough shot at something the College of Heralds would laugh at, but I couldn't help myself," he said. "The description in our lingo would be 'Gules within a bordure wavy or, the Angel of the Annunciation bearing in her dexter hand a sailing-ship of three masts and in her sinister an apple.' In other words, there's Mary the Angel with the ship she went to Canada on, and a good old Gloucester cider apple, on a red background with a wiggly golden border around the shield. Sorry about the wavy border; it means bastardy, but you don't have to tell everybody. Then here's the crest: 'a fox statant guardant within his jaws a sugar cane, all proper.' It's the Staunton crest, but slightly changed for your purposes, and the sugar cane says where you got your lolly from, which good heraldry often does. The motto, you see is *De forte egressa est dulcedo*—'Out of the strong came forth sweetness'—from the Book of Judges, and couldn't be neater, really. And look here—you see I've given the fox rather a saucy privy member, just as a hint at your father's prowess in that direction. How do you like it?"

"You called it something," said I; "a trifle of something?"

"Oh, *anitergium,*" said Adrian. "It's just one of those Middle Latin terms I like to use for fun. It means a trifle, a sketch, something disposable. Well, actually the monks used it for the throw-outs from the scriptorium which they used for bum-wipe."

I hated to hurt his feelings, but Pargetter always said that hard things should be said as briefly as possible.

"It's bum-wipe, all right," I said. "Father won't have that."

"Oh, most certainly not. I never meant that he should. The College of Heralds would have to prepare you legitimate arms, and I don't suppose it would be anything like this."

"I don't mean the *anitergium,*" I said. "I mean the whole story."

"But Davey! You told me yourself your father said you were probably bastards. He must have a sturdy sense of humour."

"He has," I said, "but I doubt if it extends to this. However, I'll try it."

I did. And I was right. His letter in reply was cold and brief. "People talk jokingly about being bastards, but the reality is something different. Remember that I am in politics now and you can imagine the fun my opponents would have. Let us drop the whole thing. Pay off Pledger-Brown and tell him to keep his trap shut."

And that, for a while, was that.

13

I suppose nobody nowadays gets through a university without some flirtation with politics, and quite a few lasting marriages result. I had my spell of socialism, but it was measles rather than scarlet fever, and I soon recovered; as a student of law, I was aware that in our time whatever a man's political convictions may be he lives under a socialist system. Furthermore, I knew that my concern for mankind disposed me toward individuals rather than masses, and as Pargetter was pushing me toward work in the courts, and especially toward criminal law, I was increasingly interested in a class of society for which no political party has any use. There was, Pargetter said, somewhat less than five per cent of society which could fittingly be called the criminal class. That five per cent were my constituents.

I got my First Class in law at Oxford, and was in time called to the Bar in London, but I had always intended to practise in Canada, and this involved me in three more years of work. Canadian law, though rooted in English law, is not precisely the same, and the differences, and a certain amount of professional protectionism, made it necessary for me to qualify all over again. It was not hard. I was already pretty good and was able to do the Canadian work with time to spare for other reading. Like many well-qualified professional men I knew very little but my job, and Pargetter was very severe on that kind of ignorance. " 'If practice be the whole that he is taught, practice must also be the whole that he will ever know,' " he would quote from Blackstone. So I read a lot of history, as my schoolwork with Ramsay had given me a turn in that direction, and quite a few great classical works which have formed the minds of men for generations, and of which I retain nothing but a vague sense of how long they were and how clever people must be who liked them. What I really liked was poetry, and I read a lot of it.

It was during this time, too, that I became financially independent of my father. He had been making a man of me, so far as a tight check on my expenditures would do it; his training was effective, too, for I am a close man with money to this day, and have never come near to spending my income, or that part of it taxation allows me to keep. My personal fortune began quite unexpectedly when I was twenty-one.

Grandfather Staunton had not approved of Father, who had become what the old man called a "high-flyer," and although he left him a part of his estate, he left half of it to Caroline, in trust. To me he left what Father regarded as a joke legacy, in the form of five hundred acres of land in Northern Ontario, which he had bought as a speculation when it was rumoured that there was coal up there. Coal there may have been, but as there was no economically sane way of getting it down to places where it could be sold, the land lay idle. Nobody had ever seen it, and it was assumed that it was a wilderness of rock and scrub trees. Grandfather's executor, which was a large trust company, did nothing about this land until my majority, and then suggested that I sell it to a company which had offered to buy it for a hundred dollars an acre; there was fifty thousand dollars to be picked up for nothing, so to speak, and they advised me to take it.

I was stubborn. If the land was worthless, why did anyone want to pay a hundred dollars an acre for it? I had a hunch that I might as well see it before parting with it, so I set off to look at my inheritance. I am no woodsman, and it was a miserable journey from the nearest train-stop to my property, but I did it by canoe, in the company of a morose guide, and was frightened out of my wits by the desolation, the dangers of canoeing in some very rough water, and the apparent untrustworthiness of my companion. But after a couple of days we were on my land, and as I tramped around it I found that there were other people on it, too, and that they were unmistakably drilling for minerals. They were embarrassed, and I became thoughtful, for they had no authority to be doing what they were doing. Back in Toronto I made a fuss with the trust company, who knew nothing about the drillers, and I made something more than a fuss to the mining company. So after some legal huffing and puffing, and giving them the Pargetter treatment, I disposed of my northern land at a thousand dollars an acre, which would have been dirt cheap if there had been a mine. But there was nothing there, or not enough. I emerged from this adventure with half a million dollars. A nice, round sum, surely never foreseen by Grandfather Staunton.

Father was not pleased, because the trust company who had been so casual about my affairs was one of which he was a director, and at one point I had threatened to sue them for mismanagement, which he considered unfilial. But I stuck to my guns, and when it was all over asked him if he would like me to move out of the family house. But he urged me to stay. It was large, and he was lonely when his political career allowed him to be there, and so I stayed where I was and thus came once again under the eye of Netty.

Netty was the survivor of an endless train of servants. She had never been given the title of housekeeper, but she was the Black Pope of the domestic staff, never frankly tattling but always hinting or wearing the unmistakable air of someone who could say a great deal if asked. With no children to look after, she had become almost a valet to Father, cleaning his clothes and washing and ironing his shirts, which she declared nobody else could do to his complete satisfaction.

When I had finished my Canadian legal studies I gave offence to Father once again, for he had always assumed that I would be content to have him find a place for me in the Alpha Corporation. But that was not at all my plan; I wanted to practise as a criminal lawyer. Pargetter, with whom I kept in constant touch (though he never raised me to the level of one of his long-distance chess opponents) urged me to get some general practice first, and preferably in a small place. "You will see more of human nature, and get a greater variety of experience, in three years in a country town than you will get in five years with a big firm in a city," he wrote. So once again I returned, not to Deptford, but to the nearby county town, a place of about sixty thousand people, called Pittstown. I easily got a place in the law office of Diarmuid Mahaffey, whose father had once been the lawyer in Deptford and with whom there was a family connection.

Diarmuid was very good to me and saw that I got a little work of every kind, including a few of those mad clients all lawyers seem to have if their practice extends into the country. I don't suggest that city lawyers have no madmen on their books, but I honestly believe the countryside breeds finer examples of the *paranoia querulans,* the connoisseurs of litigation. He bore in mind that I wanted to work in the courts and put me in the way of getting some of those cases on which most young lawyers cut their teeth; some indigent or incompetent accused person needs a lawyer, and the court appoints a lawyer, usually a young man, to act for him.

I learned a valuable lesson from my first case of this kind. A Maltese labourer was charged with indecent assault; it was not a very serious matter, because the aspiring rapist had trouble with his buttons, and the woman, who was considerably bigger than he, hit him with her handbag and ran away. "You must tell me honestly," said I, "did you do it? I'll do my best to get you off, but I must know the truth." "Meester Stown," said he, with tears in his eyes, "I swear to you on the grave of my dead mother, I never did no such dirty thing. Spit in my mouth if I even touch this woman!" So I gave the court a fine harangue, and the judge gave my client two years. My client was delighted. "That judge, he's very clever man," he said to me afterward; "he knew all the time I done it." Then he shook my hand and trotted off with the warder, pleased to have been punished by such an expert in human nature. I decided then that the kind of people with whom I had chosen to associate myself were not to be trusted, or at least not taken literally.

My next serious case was a far bigger thing, nothing less than a murderess. Poor woman, she had shot her husband. He was a farmer, known far and wide to be no good and brutal to her and his livestock, but he was decisively dead; she had poked a shotgun through the back window of the privy while he was perched on the seat and blown his head off. She made no denial, and was indeed silent and resigned through all the preliminaries. But they still hanged women in those days, and it was my job to save her from the gallows if I could.

I spent a good deal of time with her and thought so much about the case that Diarmuid began to call me Sir Edward, in reference to Marshall Hall. But one night I had a bright idea, and the next day I put a question to my client and got the answer I expected.

When at last the case came to trial I spoke of extenuating circumstances, and at the right moment said that the murdered man had repeatedly beaten his wife in order to make her perform *fellatio*.

"Know your judge" was one of Diarmuid's favourite maxims; of course no barrister knows a judge overtly, but most of the Bar know him before he is elevated to the Bench and have some estimate of his temperament. Obviously you don't take a particularly messy divorce before a Catholic judge, or a drunk who has caused an accident before a teetotal judge, if you can help it. I was lucky in this case because our assize judge that season was Orley Mickley, known to be a first-rate man of the law, but in his private life a pillar of rectitude and a great deplorer of sexual sin. As judges often are, he was innocent of things that lesser people know, and the word *fellatio* had not come his way.

"I assume that is a medical term, Mr. Staunton," said he; "will you be good enough to explain it to the court."

"May I ask your lordship to order the court cleared?" said I; "or if your lordship would call a recess I should be glad to explain the term in your chambers. It is not something that any of us would take pleasure in hearing."

I was playing it up for all it would stand, and I had an intimation—Dr. von Haller says I have a good measure of intuition—that I was riding the crest of a wave.

The judge cleared the court and asked me to explain to him and the jury what *fellatio* was. I dragged it out. Oral and lingual caress of the erect male organ until ejaculation is brought about was the way I put it. The jury knew simpler terms for this business, and my delicacy struck them solemn. I did not need to labour the fact that the dead man had been notably dirty: the jury had all seen him. Usually performed by the woman on her knees, I added, and two women jurors straightened up in their chairs. A gross indignity exacted by force; a perversion for which some American states exacted severe penalties; a grim servitude no woman with a spark of self-respect could be expected to endure without cracking.

It worked like a charm. The judge's charge to the jury was a marvel of controlled indignation; they must find the woman guilty but unless they added a recommendation of clemency his faith in mankind would be shattered. And of course they did so, and the judge gave her a sentence which, with good conduct, would not be more than two or three years. I suppose the poor soul ate better and slept better in the penitentiary than she had ever done in her life.

"That was a smart bit of business," said Diarmuid to me afterward, "and I don't know how you guessed what the trouble was. But you did, and that's what matters. B'God, I think old Mickley would have hung the corpse, if it'd had a scrap of neck left to put in a rope."

This case gained me a disproportionate reputation as a brilliant young advocate filled with compassion for the wretched. The result was that a terrible band of scoundrels who thought themselves misunderstood or ill used shouted for my services when they got into well-deserved trouble. And thus I gained my first client to go to the gallows.

Up to this time I had delighted unashamedly in the law. Many lawyers do, and Diarmuid was one of them. "If lawyers allowed their sense of humour free play, b'God they wouldn't be able to work for laughing," he once said to me. But the trial and hanging of Jimmy Veale showed me another aspect of the law. What I suppose Dr. von Haller would call its Shadow.

Not that Jimmy didn't have a fair trial. Not that I didn't exert myself to the full on his behalf. But his guilt was clear, and all I could do was try to find explanations for what he had done, and try to arouse pity for a man who had no pity for anyone else.

Jimmy had a bad reputation and had twice been in jail for petty thievery. He was only twenty-two, but he was a thoroughgoing crook of an unsophisticated kind. When I met him the provincial police had run him down, hiding in the woods about thirty miles north of Pittstown, with sixty-five dollars in his pocket. He had entered the house of an old woman who lived alone in a rural area, demanded her money, and when she would not yield he sat her on her own stove to make her talk. Which she did, of course, but when Jimmy found the money and left, she appeared to be dead. However, she was not quite dead, and when a neighbour found her in the morning she lived long enough to describe Jimmy and assure the neighbour that he had repeatedly sworn that he would kill her if she didn't speak up. In this evidence the neighbour was not to be shaken.

Jimmy's mother, who thought him wild but not bad, engaged me to defend him, and I did what I could by pleading insanity. It is a widespread idea that people who are unusually cruel must be insane, though the corollary of that would be that anybody who is unusually compassionate must be insane. But the Crown Attorney applied the McNaghton Rule to Jimmy, and I well recall the moment when he said to the jury, "Would the prisoner have acted as he did if a policeman had been standing at his elbow?" Jimmy, lounging in the prisoner's dock, laughed and cried out, "Jeeze, d'you think I'm crazy?" After which it did not take the court long to send him to the gallows.

I decided that I had better be present when Jimmy was hanged. It is a common complaint against the courts that they condemn people to punishments of which the legal profession have no direct knowledge. It is a justifiable reproach when it is true, but it is true less often than tender-hearted people think. There are people who shrink from the whole idea of a court, and there are the There-But-for-the-Grace-of-Godders who seem to think it is only by a narrow squeak that they have kept out of the prisoner's dock themselves; they are bird-brains to whom God's grace and good luck mean the same thing. There are the democrats of justice, who seem to believe that every judge should begin his career as a prisoner at the bar and work his way up to the Bench. Tender-minded people, all of them, but they don't know criminals. I wanted to know criminals, and I made my serious start with Jimmy.

I was sorry for his mother, who was a fool but punished for it with unusual severity; she had not spoiled Jimmy more than countless mothers spoil boys who turn out to be sources of pride. Jimmy had been exposed to all the supposed benefits of a democratic state; he had the best schooling that could be managed for as long as he cared to take it—which was no longer than the law demanded; his childhood had been embowered in a complexity of protective laws, and his needs had been guaranteed by Mackenzie King's Baby Bonus. But Jimmy was a foul-mouthed crook who had burned an old woman to death, and never, in all the months I knew him, expressed one single word of regret.

He was proud of being a condemned man. While awaiting trial he acquired from somewhere a jail vocabulary. Within a day of his imprisonment he would greet the trusty who brought him his food with "Hiya, shit-heel!" that being the term the hardened prisoners used for those who co-operated with the warden. After his trial, when the chaplain tried to talk to him he was derisive, shouting, "Listen, I'm gonna piss when I can't whistle, and that's all there is to it, so don't give me none of your shit." He regarded me with some favour, for I qualified as a supporting player in his personal drama; I was his "mouthpiece." He wanted me to arrange for him to sell his story to a newspaper, but I would have nothing to do with that. I saw Jimmy at least twice a week while he was waiting for execution, and I never heard a word from him that did not make me think the world would be better off without him. None of his former friends tried to see him, and when his mother visited him he was sullen and abusive.

When the time for his hanging came, I spent a dismal night with the sheriff and the chaplain in the office of the warden of the jail. None of them had ever managed a hanging, and they were nervous and haggled about details, such as whether a flag should be flown to show that justice had been done upon Jimmy; it was a foolish question, for a flag would have to be flown at seven o'clock anyway, and that was the official hour for Jimmy's execution; in fact he was to be hanged at six, before the other prisoners were awakened. Whether they were sleeping or not I do not know, but certainly there was none of that outcry or beating on cell-bars which is such a feature of romantic drama on this subject. The hangman was busy about concerns of his own. I had seen him; a short, stout, unremarkable man who looked like a carpenter dressed for a funeral, which I suppose is what he was. The chaplain went to Jimmy and soon returned. The doctor came at five, and with him two or three newspaper reporters. In all, there were about a dozen of us at last, of whom only the hangman had ever been present at such an affair before.

As we waited, the misery which had been palpable in the small office became almost stifling, and I went out with one of the reporters to walk in the corridor. As six o'clock drew near we moved into the execution chamber, a room like an elevator shaft, though larger, and stuffy from long disuse. There was a platform about nine feet high of unpainted new wood, and under it hung some curtains of unbleached cotton that were crumpled and looked as if they had been used before and travelled far; above the platform, from the roof, was suspended a heavily braced steel beam, painted the usual dirty red, and from this hung the rope, with its foot-long knot which would, if all was well, dislocate Jimmy's cervical vertebrae and break his spinal cord. To my surprise, it was almost white; I do not know what I expected, but certainly not a white rope. The hangman in his tight black suit was bustling about trying the lever that worked the trap. Nobody spoke. When everything was to his liking, the hangman nodded, and two warders brought Jimmy in.

He had been given something by the doctor beforehand, and needed help as he walked. I had seen him the day before, in his cell where the lights always burned and where he had spent so many days without a belt, or braces, or even laces in his shoes—deprivations which seemed to rob him of full humanity, so that he appeared to be ill or insane. Now his surly look was gone, and he had to be pushed up the ladder that led to the platform. The hangman, whom he never saw, manœuvred Jimmy gently to the right spot, then put the noose over his head and adjusted it with great care—in other circumstances one might say with loving care. Then he slid down the ladder—literally, for he put his feet on the outsides of the supports and slipped down it like a fireman—and immediately pulled the lever. Jimmy dropped out of sight behind the curtains, with a loud thump, as the cord stretched tight.

The silence, which had been so thick before, was now broken as Jimmy swung to and fro and the rope banged against the sides of the trap. Worse than that, we heard gurgling and gagging, and the curtains bulged and stirred as Jimmy swung within them. The hanging, as is sometimes the case, had not gone well, and Jimmy was fighting for life.

The doctor had told us that unconsciousness was immediate, but that the cessation of Jimmy's heartbeat might take from three to five minutes. If Jimmy were unconscious, why am I sure that I heard him cry out—curses, of course, for these had always been Jimmy's eloquence? But I did hear him, and so did the others, and one of the reporters was violently sick. We looked at one another in terror. What was to be done? The hangman knew. He darted inside the curtains, and beneath them we saw a great shuffling of feet, and soon the violent swinging stopped, and the sighs and murmurings were still. The hangman came out again, flustered and angry, and mopped his brow. None of us met his eye. When five minutes had passed the doctor, not liking his work, went inside the curtains with his stethoscope ready, came out again almost at once, and nodded to the sheriff. And so it was over.

Not quite over for me. I had promised Jimmy's mother that I would see him before he was buried, and I did. He was laid on a table in a neighbouring room, and I looked him right in the face, which took some resolution in the doing. But I noticed also a damp stain on the front of his prison trousers, and looked enquiringly at the doctor.

"An emission of semen," he said; "they say it always happens. I don't know."

So that was what Jimmy meant when he said he'd piss when he couldn't whistle. Where could he have picked up such a jaunty, ugly, grotesque idea of death by hanging? But that was Jimmy; he had a flair for whatever was brutal and macabre and such knowledge sought him out because he was eager for it.

I had seen a hanging. Worse things happen in wars and in great catastrophes, but they are not directly planned and ordered. This had been the will of Jimmy's fellow-countrymen, as expressed through the legal machinery devised to deal with such people as he. But it was unquestionably a squalid business, an evil deed, and we had all of us, from the hangman down to the reporters, been drawn into it and fouled by it. If Jimmy had to be got rid of—and I fully believe that was all that could have been done with such a man, unless he were to be kept as a caged, expensive nuisance for another fifty years—why did it have to be like this? I do not speak of hanging alone; the executioner's sword, the guillotine, the electric chair are all dreadful and involve the public through its legal surrogates in a revolting act. The Greeks seem to have known a better way than these.

Jimmy's evil had infected us all—had indeed spread far beyond his prison until something of it touched everybody in his country. The law had been tainted by evil, though its great import was for good, or at least for order and just dealing. But it would be absurd to attribute so much power to Jimmy, who was no more than a fool whose folly had become the conduit by which evil had poured into so many lives. When I visited Jimmy in prison I had sometimes seen on his face a look I knew, the look I had seen on the face of Bill Unsworth as he squatted obscenely over a pile of photographs. It was the look of one who has laid himself open to a force that is inimical to man, and whose power to loose that force upon the world is limited only by his imagination, his opportunities, and his daring. And it seemed to me then that it was with such people I had cast my lot, for I was devoting my best abilities to their defence.

I changed my mind about that later. The law gives every accused man his chance, and there must be those who do for him what he cannot do for himself; I was one of these. But I was always aware that I stood very near to the power of evil when I undertook the cases that brought me the greatest part of my reputation. I was a highly skilled, highly paid, and cunning mercenary in a fight which was as old as man and greater than man. I have consciously played the Devil's Advocate and I must say I have enjoyed it. I like the struggle, and I had better admit that I like the moral danger. I am like a man who has built his house on the lip of a volcano. Until the volcano claims me I live, in a sense, heroically.

DR. VON HALLER: Good. I was wondering when he would make his appearance.

MYSELF: Whom are we talking about now?

DR. VON HALLER: The hero who lives on the lip of the volcano. We have talked of many aspects of your inner life, and we have identified them by such names as Shadow, Anima, and so on. But one has been seen only in a negative aspect, and he is the man you show to the outer world, the man in whose character you appear in court and before your acquaintances. He has a name, too. We call him the Persona, which means, as you know, the actor's mask. This man on the edge of the volcano, this saturnine lawyer-wizard who snatches people out of the jaws of destruction, is your Persona. You must enjoy playing the role very much.

MYSELF: I do.

DR. VON HALLER: Good. You would not have admitted that a few months ago, when you first sat in that chair. Then you were all for imposing him on me as your truest self.

MYSELF: I'm not sure that he isn't.

DR. VON HALLER: Oh, come. We all create an outward self with which to face the world, and some people come to believe that is what they truly are. So they people the world with doctors who are nothing outside the consulting-room, and judges who are nothing when they are not in court, and businessmen who wither with boredom when they have to retire from business, and teachers who are forever teaching. That is why they are such poor specimens when they are caught without their masks on. They have lived chiefly through the Persona. But you are not such a fool, or you would not be here. Everybody needs his mask, and the only intentional impostors are those whose mask is one of a man with nothing to conceal. We all have much to conceal, and we must conceal it for our soul's good. Even your Wizard, your mighty Pargetter, was not all Wizard. Did you ever find some chink in his armour?

MYSELF: Yes, and it was a shock. He died without a will. A lawyer who dies without a will is one of the jokes of the profession.

DR. VON HALLER: Ah, but making a will is not part of a Persona; it is, for most of us, an hour when we look our mortality directly in the face. If he did not want to do that, it is sad, but do you really think it diminishes Pargetter? It lessens him as the perfect lawyer, certainly, but he must have been something more than that, and a portion of that something else had a natural, pathetic fear of death. He had built his Persona so carefully and so handsomely that you took it for the whole man; and it must be said that you might not have learned so much from him if you had seen him more fully;

young people love such absolutes. But your own Persona seems to be a very fine one. Surely it was built as a work of art?

MYSELF: Of art, and of necessity. The pressures under which I came to live were such that I needed something to keep people at bay. And so I built what I must say I have always thought of as my public character, my professional manner, but which you want me to call a Persona. I needed armour. You see—this is not an easy thing for me to say, even to someone who listens professionally to what is usually unspeakable—women began to throw out their lures for me. I would have been a good catch. I came of a well-known family; I had money; I was at the start of a career of a kind that some women find as attractive as that of a film actor.

DR. VON HALLER: And why were you so unresponsive? Anything to do with Myrrha Martindale?

MYSELF: That wore off, after a time. I had come to hate the fact that I had been initiated into the world of physical sex in something Father had stage-managed. It wasn't sex itself, but Father's proprietorial way with it, and with me. I was young and neither physically cold nor morally austere, but even when the urge and the opportunity were greatest I wanted no more of it. It seemed like following in the swordsman's footsteps, and I wanted none of that. But I might have married if Father had not gone before me, even there.

DR. VON HALLER: This was the second marriage, to Denyse?

MYSELF: Yes, when I was twenty-nine. I had passed my third year in Pittstown with Diarmuid, and was thinking it was time to be moving, for one does not become a first-rank criminal lawyer in a town where criminals are few and of modest ambition. One day a letter came from Father; would I meet Caroline for dinner at the family house in Toronto, as he had something of great importance to tell us? Since getting into politics Father had not dwindled in self-esteem, I can assure you, and this was in what painters call his later manner. So up to Toronto I went on the appointed day, and the other guests at dinner were Caroline and Beesty. Caroline had married Beeston Bastable the year before, and it had done her a lot of good; he was no Adonis, running rather to fat, but he was a fellow of what I can only call a sweet disposition, and after Caroline had tormented and jeered at him long enough she discovered she loved him, and that was that. But Father was not there. Only a letter, to be read while we were having coffee. I wondered what it could be, and so did Beesty, but Caroline jumped to it at once, and of course she was right. The letter was rather a floundering and pompous piece of work, but it boiled down to the fact that he was going to marry again and hoped we would approve and love the lady as much as he did, and as much as she deserved. There was a tribute in it to Mother, rather stiffly worded. Stuff about how he could never be happy in this new marriage unless we approved. And, finally, the name of the lady herself. It was Denyse Hornick. Of course we knew who she was. She ran a good-sized travel agency of her own, and was prominent in politics, on the women's side.

Dr. von Haller: A women's liberationist?

Myself: Not in any extreme way. An intelligent, moderate, but determined and successful advocate of equality for women under the law, and in business and professional life. We knew she had attached herself to Father's personal group of supporters during his not very fortunate post-war political career. None of us had ever met her. But we met her that night because Father brought her home at about half-past nine to introduce her. It wasn't an easy situation.

Dr. von Haller: He seems to have managed it rather heavy-handedly.

Myself: Yes, and I suppose it was immature of me, but it galled me to see him so youthful and gallant toward her when they came in, like a boy bringing his girl home to run the gauntlet of the family. After all, he was sixty. And she was modest and sweet and deferential like a girl of seventeen, though she was in fact a hefty forty-one. I don't mean fat-hefty, but a psychological heavy-weight, a woman of obvious self-confidence and importance in her sphere, so that these milkmaid airs were a grotesque fancy dress. Of course we did the decent thing, and Beesty bustled around and prepared drinks with the modesty proper to an in-law at a somewhat tense family affair, and eventually everybody had kissed Denyse and the farce of seeking our approval had been played out. An hour later Denyse had so far thrown aside her role as milkmaid that when I showed some signs of getting drunk she said, "Now only one more tiny one, baa-lamb, or you'll hate yourself in the morning." I knew at that moment I couldn't stand Denyse, and that one more very serious thing had come between me and Father.

Dr. von Haller: You were never reconciled to her?

Myself: You doubtless have some family, Doctor. You must know of the currents that run through families? I'll tell you of one that astonished me. It was Caroline who told Netty about the approaching marriage, and Netty broke into a fit of sobs—she had no tears, apparently—and said, "And after what I've done for him!" Caroline dropped on that at once, for it could have been proof of her favourite theory that Netty killed Mother, or at least put her in the way of dying. Surely those words couldn't have simply referred to those shirts she'd ironed so beautifully? But with her notion of "her place" it wouldn't be like Netty to think that years of service gave her a romantic claim on Father. Caroline couldn't get Netty to admit, in so many words, that she had put Mother out of the way because she was an embarrassment to Father. Nevertheless, there was something fishy there. If I could have Netty in the witness-box for half an hour, I bet I could break her down! What do you think of that? This isn't some family in the mythic drama of Greece I'm telling you about; it is a family of the twentieth century, and a Canadian family at that, supposedly the quintessence of everything that is emotionally dowdy and unaware.

Dr. von Haller: Mythic pattern is common enough in contemporary life. But of course few people know the myths, and fewer still can see a pattern under a mass of detail. What was your response to this woman who was so soon proprietorial in her manner toward you?

Myself: Derision tending toward hatred; with Caroline it was just derision. Every family knows how to make the newcomer feel uncomfortable, and we did what we dared. And I did more than spar with her when we met. I found out everything I could about her through enquiries from credit agencies and by public records; I also had some enquiries made through underworld characters who had reason to want to please me—

Dr. von Haller: You spied on her?

Myself: Yes.

Dr. von Haller: You have no doubts about the propriety of that?

Myself: None. After all, she was marrying considerably over a hundred million dollars. I wanted to know who she was.

Dr. von Haller: And who was she?

Myself: There was nothing against her. She had married a serviceman when she was in the W.R.N.S. and divorced him as soon as the war was over. That was where Lorene came from.

Dr. von Haller: The retarded daughter?

Myself: An embarrassing nuisance, Denyse's problem. But Denyse liked problems and wanted to add me to her list.

Dr. von Haller: Because of your drinking. When did that begin?

Myself: In Pittstown it began to be serious. It is very lonely living in a small town where you are anxious to seem quite ordinary but everybody knows that there is a great fortune, as they put it, "behind you." How far behind, or whether you really have anything more than a romantic claim on it, nobody knows or cares. More than once I would hear some Pittstown worthy whisper of me, "He doesn't have to work, you know; his father's Boy Staunton." But I did work; I tried to command my profession. I lived in the best hotel in town, which, God knows, was a dismal hole with wretched food; I confined my living to a hundred and twenty-five dollars a week, which was about what a rising young lawyer might be expected to have. I wanted no favours and if it had been practical to take another name I would have done it. Nobody understood, except Diarmuid, and I didn't care whether they understood or not. But it was lonely, and while I was hammering out the character of David Staunton the rising criminal lawyer, I also created the character of David Staunton who drank too much. The two went well together in the eyes of many romantic people, who like a brilliant man to have some large, obvious flaw in his character.

DR. VON HALLER: This was the character you took with you to Toronto, where I suppose you embroidered it.

MYSELF: Embroidered it richly. I achieved a certain courtroom notoriety; in a lively case I drew a good many spectators because they wanted to see me win. They also had the occasional thrill of seeing me stagger. There were rumours, too, that I had extensive connections in the underworld, though that was nonsense. Still, it provided a whiff of sulphur for the mob.

DR. VON HALLER: In fact, you created a romantic Persona that successfully rivalled that of the rich, sexually adventurous Boy Staunton without ever challenging him on his own ground?

MYSELF: You might equally well say that I established myself as a man of significance in my own right without in any way wearing my father's cut-down clothes.

DR. VON HALLER: And when did the clash come?

MYSELF: The—?

DR. VON HALLER: The inevitable clash between your father and yourself. The clash that gave so much edge to the guilt and remorse you felt when he died, or was killed, or whichever it was.

MYSELF: I suppose it really came into the light when Denyse made it clear that her ambition was to see Father appointed Lieutenant-Governor of Ontario. She made it very clear to me that what she insisted on calling my "image"—she had a walletful of smart terms for everything—would not fit very well with my position as son of a man who was the Queen's representative.

DR. VON HALLER: In effect she wanted to reclaim you and make you into your father's son again.

MYSELF: Yes, and what a father! She is a great maker of images, is Denyse! It disgusted and grieved me to see Father being filed and pumiced down to meet that inordinate woman's idea of a fit candidate for ceremonial office. Before, he had style—his personal style: she made him into what she would have been if she had been born a man. He became an unimaginative woman's creation. Delilah had shorn his locks and assured him he looked much neater and cooler without them. He gave her his soul, and she transformed it into a cabbage. She reopened the whole business of the Staunton arms because he would need something of the sort in an official position and it looked better to take the position with all the necessary trappings than to cobble them up during his first months in office. Father had never told her about Maria Ann Dymock, and she wrote boldly to the College of Arms, and I gather she pretty much demanded that the arms of the Warwickshire Stauntons, with some appropriate differences, be officially granted to Father.

Dr. von Haller: What did your father think about it?

Myself: Oh, he laughed it off. Said Denyse would manage it if anyone could. Didn't want to talk about it. But it never happened. The College took a long time answering letters and asked for information that was hard to provide. I knew all about it because by this time my old friend Pledger-Brown was one of the pursuivants, and we had always written to each other at least once a year. One of his letters said, as I remember it, "This can never be, you know; not even your stepdame's New World determination can make you Stauntons of Longbridge. My colleague in charge of the matter is trying to persuade her to apply for new arms, which your father might legitimately have, for after all bags of gold are a very fair earnest of gentility, and always have been. But she is resolute, and nothing will do but a long and very respectable descent. It is one of the touching aspects of our work here in the College that so many of you New World people, up to the eyebrows in all the delights of republicanism, hanker after a link with what is ancient and rubbed by time to a fine sheen. It's more than snobbery; more than romanticism; it's a desire for an ancestry that somehow postulates a posterity and for an existence in the past that is a covert guarantee of immortality in the future. You talk about individualism; what you truly want is to be links in a long unbroken chain. But you, with our secret about Maria Ann and the child whose father might have been all Staunton, know of a truth which is every bit as good in its way, even though you use it only as food for your sullen absalonism."

DR. VON HALLER: Absalonism; I do not know that word. Explain it, please.

MYSELF: It was one of Adrian's revivals of old words. It refers to Absalom, the son of King David, who resisted and revolted against his father.

DR. VON HALLER: A good word. I shall remember it.

14

The time was drawing near to Christmas, when I knew that Dr. von Haller would make some break in my series of appointments. But I was not prepared for what she said when next we met.

"Well, Mr. Staunton, we seem to have come to the end of your *anamnesis*. Now it is necessary to make a decision about what you are going to do next."

"The end? But I have a sheaf of notes still! I have all sorts of questions to ask."

"Doubtless. It is possible to go on as we have been doing for several years. But you have been at this work for a little more than one year, and although we could haggle over fine points and probe sore places for at least another year, I think that for you that is unnecessary. Ask your questions of yourself. You are now in a position to answer them."

"But if I give wrong answers?"

"You will soon know that they are wrong. We have canvassed the main points in the story of your life; you are equipped to attend to details."

"I don't feel it. I'm not nearly through with what I have to say."

"Have you anything to say that seems to you extraordinary?"

"But surely I have been having the most remarkable spiritual—well, anyhow, psychological—adventures?"

"By no means, Mr. Staunton. Remarkable in your personal experience, which is what counts, but—forgive me—not at all remarkable in mine."

"Then you mean this is the end of my work with you?"

"Not if you decide otherwise. But it is the end of this work—this reassessment of some personal, profound experience. But what is most personal is not what is most profound. If you want to continue—and you must not be in a hurry to say you will—we shall proceed quite differently. We shall examine the archetypes with which you are already superficially familiar, and we shall go beyond what is personal about them. I assure you that is very close and psychologically demanding work. It cannot be undertaken if you are always craving to be back in Toronto, putting Alpha and Castor and all those things into good order. But you are drinking quite moderately now, aren't you? The symptom you complained of has been corrected. Wasn't that what you wanted?"

"Yes, though I had almost forgotten that was what I came for."

"Your general health is much improved? You sleep better?"

"Yes."

"And you will not be surprised or angry when I say you are a much pleasanter, easier person?"

"But if I go on—what then?"

"I cannot tell you, because I don't know, and in this sort of work we give no promises."

"Yes, but you have experience of other people. What happens to them?"

"They finish their work, or that part of it that can be done here, with a markedly improved understanding of themselves, and that means of much that goes beyond self. They are in better command of their abilities. They are more fully themselves."

"Happier, in fact."

"I do not promise happiness, and I don't know what it is. You New World people are, what is the word, hipped on the idea of happiness, as if it were a constant and measurable thing, and settled and excused everything. If it is anything at all it is a by-product of other conditions of life, and some people whose lives do not appear to be at all enviable, or indeed admirable, are happy. Forget about happiness."

"Then you can't or won't, tell me what I would be working for?"

"No, because the answer lies in you, not in me. I can help, of course. I can put the questions in such a way as to draw forth your answer, but I do not know what your answer will be. Let me put it this way: the work you have been doing here during the past year has told you *who* you are; further work would aim at showing you *what* you are."

"More mystification. I thought we had got past all that. For weeks it seems to me that we have been talking nothing but common sense."

"Oh, my dear Mr. Staunton, that is unworthy of you! Are you still scampering back to that primitive state of mind where you suppose psychology must be divorced from common sense? Well—let me see what I can do. Your dreams—We have worked through some dozens of your dreams, and I think you are now convinced that they are not just incomprehensible gases that get into your head during sleep. Recall your dream of the night before you first came to me. What was that enclosed, private place where you commanded such respect, from which you walked out into strange country? Who was the woman you met, who talked in an unknown language? Now don't say it was me, because you had never met me then, and though dreams may reflect deep concerns and thus may hint at the future, they are not second sight. After some exploration, you came to the top of a staircase that led downward, and some commonplace people discouraged you from going down, though you sensed there was treasure there. Your decision now is whether or not you are going to descend the staircase and find the treasure."

"How do I know it will be a treasure?"

"Because your other recurrent dream, where you are the little prince in the tower, shows you as the guardian of a treasure. And you manage to keep your treasure. But who are all those frightening figures who menace it? We should certainly encounter them. And why are you a prince, and a child?—Tell me, did you dream last night?"

"Yes. A very odd dream. It reminded me of Knopwood because it was Biblical in style. I dreamed I was standing on a plain, talking with my father. I was aware it was Father, though his face was turned away. He was very affectionate and simple in his manner, as I don't think I ever knew him to be in his life. The odd thing was that I couldn't really see his face. He wore an ordinary business suit. Then suddenly he turned from me and flew up into the air, and the astonishing thing was that as he rose, his trousers came down, and I saw his naked backside."

"And what are your associations?"

"Well, obviously it's the passage in Exodus where God promises Moses that he shall see Him, but must not see His face; and what Moses sees is God's back parts. As a child I always thought it funny for God to show His rump. Funny, but also terribly real and true. Like those extraordinary people in the Bible who swore a solemn oath clutching one another's testicles. But does it mean that I have seen the weakness, the shameful part of my father's nature because he gave so much of himself into the keeping of Denyse and because Denyse was so unworthy to treat him properly? I've done what I can with it, but nothing rings true."

"Of course not, because you have neglected one of the chief principles of what I have been able to tell you about the significance of dreams. That again is understandable, for when the dream is important and has something new to tell us, we often forget temporarily what we know to be true. But we have always agreed, haven't we, that figures in dreams, whoever or whatever they may look like, are aspects of the dreamer? So who is this father with the obscured face and the naked buttocks?"

"I suppose he is my idea of a father—of my own father?"

"He is something we would have to talk about if you decided to go on to a deeper stage in the investigation of yourself. Because your real father, your historical father, the man whom you last saw lying so pitiably on the dock with his face obscured in filth, and then so dishevelled in his coffin with his face destroyed by your stepmother's ambitious meddling, is by no means the same thing as the archetype of fatherhood you carry in the depths of your being, and which comes from—well, for the present we won't attempt to say where. Now tell me, have you had any of those demanding, humiliating sessions in Mr. Justice Staunton's court during the past few weeks? You haven't mentioned them."

"No. They don't seem to have been necessary recently."

"I thought that might be so. Well, my friend, you know now

how very peculiar dreams are, and you know that they are not liars. But I don't believe you have found out yet that they sometimes like a little joke. And this is one. I believe that you have, in a literal sense, seen the end of Mr. Justice Staunton. The old Troll King has lost his trappings. No court, no robes, a sense of kindliness and concern, a revelation of that part of his anatomy he keeps nearest to the honoured Bench, and which nobody has ever attempted to invest with awe or dignity, and then—gone! If he should come again, as he well may, at least you have advanced so far that you have seen him with his trousers down. . . . Our hour is finished. If you wish to arrange further appointments, will you let me know sometime in the week between Christmas and the New Year? I wish you a very happy holiday."

·III·

My Sorgenfrei Diary

»»»» ««««

DEC. 17, Wed.: Wretched letter from Netty this morn. Was feeling particularly well because of Dr. Johanna's saying on Monday that I had finished my *anamnesis* so far as she thought it necessary to go; extraordinary flood of energy and cheerfulness. Now this.

Seven pages of her big script, like tangled barbed wire, the upshot of which is that Meritorious Matey has at last done what I always expected him to do—revealed himself as a two-bit crook and opportunist. Has fiddled trust funds which somehow lay in his clutch; she doesn't say how and probably doesn't know. But she is certain he has been wronged. Of course he is her brother and the apple of her eye and Netty is nothing if not loyal, as the Staunton family knows to its cost—and also, I suppose, to its extraordinary benefit. One must be fair.

But how can I be fair to Matey? He has always been the deserving, hard-working fellow with his own way to make, while I have hardly been able to swallow for the weight of the silver spoon in my mouth. Certainly this is how Netty has put it to me, and when Father refused to take Matey into Alpha and wouldn't let Matey's firm handle the audit of Castor, she thought we were bowelless ingrates and oppressors. But Father smelled Matey as no good, and so did I, because of the way he sponged on Netty when he had no need. And now Netty begs me to return to Canada as soon as possible and undertake Matey's defence. "You have spent your talents on many a scoundrel, and you ought to be ready to see that a wronged honest boy is righted before the world"; that is how she puts it. And: "I've never asked you or the family for a thing and God knows what I've done for the Stauntons through thick and thin, and some things will never be known, but now I'm begging you on my bended knees."

There is a simple way of handling this, and I have done the simple thing already. Cabled Huddleston to look into it and let me know; he can do whatever can be done fully as well as I. Do I now write Netty and say I am unwell, and the doctor forbids, etc., and Frederick Huddleston, Q.C., will take over? But Netty doesn't believe there is anything wrong with me. She has let Caroline know that she is sure I am in some fancy European home for booze-artists, having a good time and reading books, which I was always too ready to do anyhow. She will think I am dodging. And in part she will be right.

Dr. Johanna has freed me from many a bogey, but she has also sharpened my already razorlike ethical sense. In her terms I have always projected the Shadow onto Matey; I have seen in him the worst of myself. I have been a heel in too many ways to count. Spying on Carol; spying on Denyse; making wisecracks to poor slobbering Lorene that she wasn't able to understand and which would have hurt her if she had understood; being miserable to Knopwood; miserable to Louis Wolff; worst of all, miserable to Father about things where he was vulnerable and I was strong. The account is long and disgusting.

I have accepted all that; it is part of what I am and unless I know it, grasp it, and acknowledge it as my own, there can be no freedom for me and no hope of being less a miserable stinker in future.

Before I came to my present very modest condition of self-recognition I was a clever lad at projecting my own faults onto other people, and I could see them all and many more in Maitland Quelch, C.A. Of course he had his own quiverful of perfectly real faults; one does not project one's Shadow on a man of gleaming virtue. But I detested Matey more than was admissible, for he never put a stone in my way, and in his damp-handed, grinning fashion he tried to be my friend. He was not a very nice fellow, and now I know that it was my covert spiritual kinship with him that made me hate him.

So when I refuse to go back to Canada and try to get Matey off, what is my ethical position? The legal position is perfectly clear; if Matey is in trouble with the Securities Commission there is good reason for it, and the most I could do would be to try to hoodwink the court into thinking he didn't know what he was doing, which would make him look like a fool if slightly less a crook. But if I refuse to budge and hand him over even to such a good man as Huddleston, am I still following a course that I am trying, in the middle of my life, to change?

Oh Matey, you bastard, why couldn't you have kept your nose clean and spared me this problem at a time when I am what I suppose must be called a psychic convalescent?

»»»» ««««

DEC. 18, Thurs.: Must get away. Might have stayed in Zürich over Xmas if it were not for this Matey thing, but Netty will try to get me on the telephone, and if I talk with her I will be lost. . . . What did she mean by "some things will never be known"? Could it possibly be that Carol was right? That Netty put Mother in the way of dying (much too steep to say she killed her) because she thought Mother had been unfaithful to Father and Father would be happier without her? If Netty is like that, why hasn't she put rat-poison in Denyse's martinis? She hates Denyse, and it would be just like Netty to think that her opinion in such a matter was completely objective and beyond dispute.

Thinking of Netty puts me in mind of Pargetter's warning about the witnesses, or clients, whose creed is *esse in re;* to such people the world is absolutely clear because they cannot understand that our personal point of view colours what we perceive; they think everything seems exactly the same to everyone as it does to themselves. After all, they say, the world is utterly objective; it is plain before our eyes; therefore what the ordinary intelligent man (this is always themselves) sees is all there is to be seen, and anyone who sees differently is mad, or malign, or just plain stupid. An astonishing number of judges seem to belong in this category. . . .

Netty was certainly one of those, and I never really knew why I was always at odds with her (while really loving the old girl, I must confess) till Pargetter rebuked me for being an equally wrong-headed, though more complex and amusing creature, whose creed is *esse in intellectu solo*. "You think the world is your idea," he said one November day at a tutorial when I had been offering him some fancy theorizing, "and if you don't understand that and check it now it will make your whole life a gigantic hallucination." Which, in spite of my success, is pretty much what happened, and my extended experiments as a booze-artist were chiefly directed to checking any incursions of unwelcome truth into my illusion.

But what am I headed for? Where has Dr. Johanna been taking me? I suspect toward a new ground of belief that wouldn't have occurred to Pargetter, which might be called *esse in anima:* I am beginning to recognize the objectivity of the world, while knowing also that because I am who and what I am, I both perceive the world in terms of who and what I am and project onto the world a great deal of who and what I am. If I know this, I ought to be able to escape the stupider kinds of illusion. The absolute nature of things is independent of my senses (which are all I have to perceive with), and what I perceive is an image in my own psyche.

All very fine. Not too hard to formulate and accept intellectually. But to *know* it; to bring it into daily life—that's the problem. And it would be real humility, not just the mock-modesty that generally passes for humility. Doubtless that is what Dr. Johanna has up her sleeve for me when we begin our sessions after Christmas.

Meanwhile I must go away for Christmas. Netty will get at me somehow if I stay here. . . . Think I shall go to St. Gall. Not far off and I could hire ski stuff if I wanted it. It is said to have lots to see besides the scenery.

»»»» ««««

DEC. 19, Fri.: Arrive St. Gall early p.m. Larger than I expected; about 70,000, which was the size of Pittstown, but this place has an unmistakable atmosphere of consequence. Reputedly the highest city in Europe, and the air is thin and clean. Settle into a good hotel (Walhalla—why?) and walk out to get my bearings. Not much snow, but everything is decorated for Christmas very prettily; not in our N. American whorehouse style. Find the Klosterhof square, and admire it, but leave the Cathedral till tomorrow. Dinner at a very good restaurant (Metropole) and to the Stadtheater. It has been rebuilt in the Brutalist-Modern manner, and everything is rough cement and skew-whiff instead of right-angled or curved, so it is an odd setting for Lehar's *Paganini,* which is tonight's piece. Music prettily Viennese. How simple, loud, and potent love always is in these operettas! If I understood the thing, Napoleon would not permit Pag to have his countess because he was not noble: once I could not have the girl I loved because I was not a Jew. But Pag made a lot of eloquent noise about it, whereas I merely went sour. . . . Did I love Judy? Or just something of myself in her as Dr. Johanna implies? Does it matter, now? Yes, it matters to me.

»»»» ««««

DEC. 20, Sat.: Always the methodical sight-seer, I am off to the Cathedral by 9:30. Knew it was Baroque, but had not been prepared for something *so* Baroque; breath-taking enormities of spiritual excess everywhere, but no effect of clutter or gimcrackery. Purposely took no guide-book; wanted to get a first impression before fussing about detail.

Then to the Abbey library, which is next door, and gape at some very odd old paintings and the wonders of their Baroque room. Keep my coat on as there is no heating in any serious sense; the woman who sells tickets directs me to put on huge felt overshoes to protect the parquet. Superb library to look at, and there are two or three men of priestly appearance actually reading and writing in a neighbouring room, so it must also be more than a spectacle. I gape reverently at some splendid MSS, including a venerable *Nibelungenlied* and a *Parsifal,* and wonder what a frowsy old mummy, with what appear to be its own teeth, is doing there. I suppose in an earlier and less specialized time libraries were also repositories for curiosities. Hovered over a drawing of Christ's head, done entirely in calligraphy; dated "nach 1650." Some painstaking penman had found a way of writing the Scripture account of the Passion with such a multitude of eloquent squiggles and crinkum-crankum that he had produced a monument of pious ingenuity, if not a work of art.

At last the cold becomes too much, and I scuttle out into the sunshine, and look for a bookshop where I can buy a guide, and turn myself thereby into a serious tourist. Find a fine shop, get what I want, and am poking about among the shelves when my eye is taken by two figures; a man in an engulfing fur coat over what was obviously one of those thick Harris-tweed suits is talking loudly to a woman who is very smartly and expensively dressed, but who is the nearest thing to an ogress I have ever beheld.

Her skull was immense, and the bones must have been monstrously enlarged, for she had a gigantic jaw, and her eyes peered out of positive caverns. She had made no modest concessions to her ugliness, for her iron-gray hair was fashionably dressed, and she wore a lot of make-up. They spoke in German, but there was something decidedly un-German and un-Swiss about the man and the more I stared (over the top of a book) the more familiar his back appeared. Then he moved, with a limp that could only belong to one man in the world. It was Dunstan Ramsay. Old Buggerlugs, as I live and breathe! But why in St. Gall, and who could his dreadful companion be? Someone of consequence, unquestionably, for the manageress of the shop was very attentive. . . . Now: was I to claim acquaintance, or sneak away and preserve the quiet of my holiday? As so often in these cases, the decision was not with me. Buggerlugs had spotted me.

—Davey! How nice to see you.

—Good-morning, sir. A pleasant surprise.

—The last person I would have expected. I haven't seen you since poor Boy's funeral. What brings you here?

—Just a holiday.

—Have you been here long?

—Since yesterday.

—How is everyone at home? Carol well? Denyse is well, undoubtedly. What about Netty? Still your dragon?

—All well, so far as I know.

—Liesl, this is my lifelong friend—his life long, that's to say—David Staunton. David, this is Fraulein Doktor Liselotte Naegeli, whose guest I am.

The ogress gave me a smile which was extraordinarily charming, considering what it had to work against. When she spoke her voice was low and positively beautiful. It seemed to have a faintly familiar ring, but that is impossible. Amazing what distinguished femininity the monster had. More chat, and they asked me to lunch.

The upshot of that was that my St. Gall holiday took an entirely new turn. I had counted on being solitary, but like many people who seek solitude I am not quite so fond of it as I imagine, and when Liesl—in no time I was asked to call her Liesl—asked me to join them at her country home for Christmas, I had said yes before I knew what I was doing. The woman is a spellbinder, without seeming to exert much effort, and Buggerlugs has changed amazingly. I have never fully liked him, as I told Dr. Johanna, but age and a heart attack he said he had had shortly after Father's death seem to have improved him out of all recognition. He was just as inquisitorial and ironic as ever, but there was a new geniality about him. I gather he has been convalescing with the ogress, whom I suppose to be a medico. She took an odd line with him.

—Wasn't I lucky, Davey, to persuade Ramsay to come to live with me? Such an amusing companion. Was he an amusing schoolmaster? I don't suppose so. But he is a dear man.

—Liesl, you will make Davey think we are lovers. I am here for Liesl's company, certainly, but almost as much because this climate suits my health.

—Let us hope it suits Davey's health, too. You can see he has been seriously unwell. But is your cure coming along nicely, Davey? Don't pretend you aren't working toward a cure.

—How can you tell that, Liesl? He looks better than when I last saw him, and no wonder. But what makes you think he is taking a cure?

—Well, look at him, Ramsay. Do you think I've lived near Zürich so long and can't recognize the "analysand look"? He is obviously working with one of the Jungians, probing his soul and remaking himself. Which doctor do you go to, Davey? I know several of them.

—I can't guess how you know, but there's no use pretending, I suppose. I've been a little more than a year with Fraulein Doktor Johanna von Haller.

—Jo von Haller! I have known her since she was a child. Not friends, really, but we know each other. Well, have you fallen in love with her yet? All her male patients do. It's supposed to be part of the cure. But she is very ethical and never encourages them. I suppose with her successful lawyer husband and her two almost grown-up sons it mightn't do. Oh, yes; she is Frau Doktor, you know. But I suppose you spoke in English and it never came up.

Well, after a year with Jo, you need something more lively. I wish we could promise you a really gay Christmas at Sorgenfrei, but it is certain to be dull.

—Don't believe it, Davey. Sorgenfrei is an enchanted castle.

—Nothing of the sort, but it should at least be a little more friendly than a hotel in St. Gall. Can you come back with us now?

And so it was. An hour after finishing lunch I had picked up my things and was sitting beside Liesl in a beautiful sports car, with Ramsay and his wooden leg crammed into the back with the luggage, dashing eastward from St. Gall on the road to Konstanz, and Sorgenfrei—whatever it might be. One of those private clinics, perhaps, that are so frequent in Switzerland? We were mounting all the time, and at last, after half a mile or so through pine woods we emerged onto a shelf on a mountainside, with a breath-taking view—really breath-taking, for the air was very cold and thinner than at St. Gall—and Sorgenfrei commanding it.

Sorgenfrei is like Liesl, a fascinating monstrosity. In England it would be called Gothic Revival; I don't know the European equivalent. Turrets, mullioned windows, a squat tower for an entrance and somewhere at the back a much taller, thinner tower like a lead-pencil rising very high. But bearing everywhere the unmistakable double signature of the nineteenth century and a great deal of money. Inside, it is filled with bearskin rugs, gigantic pieces of furniture on which every surface has been carved within an inch of its life with fruits, flowers, birds, hares, and even, on one thing which seems to be an altar to greed but is more probably a sideboard, full-sized hounds; six of them with real bronze chains on their collars. This is the dream castle of some magnate of 150 years ago, conceived in terms of the civilization which has given the world, among a host of better things, the music box and the cuckoo clock.

We arrived at about five p.m., and I was taken to this room, which is as big as the board-room of Castor, and where I am seizing my chance to bring my diary up to the minute. This is exhilarating. Is it the air, or Liesl's company? I am glad I came.

Later: Am I still glad I came? It is after midnight and I have had the most demanding evening since I left Canada.

This house troubles me and I can't yet say why. Magnificent houses, palaces, beautiful country houses, comfortable houses—I know all these either as a guest or a tourist. But this house, which seems at first appearances to be rather a joke, is positively the damnedest house I have ever entered. One might think the architect had gained all his previous experience illustrating Grimm's fairy stories, for the place is full of fantasy—but spooky, early-nineteenth-century fantasy, not the feeble Disney stuff. Yet, on second glance, it seems all to be meant seriously, and the architect was obviously a man of gifts, for though the house is big, it is still a house for people to live in and not a folly. Nor is it a clinic. It is Liesl's home, I gather.

Sorgenfrei. Free of care. Sans Souci. The sort of name someone of limited imagination might give to a country retreat. But there is something here that utterly contradicts the suggestion of the rich bourgeoisie resting from their money-making.

When I went down to dinner I found Ramsay in the library. That is to say, in an English country-house it would have been the library, comfortable and pleasant, but at Sorgenfrei it is too oppressively literary; bookshelves rise to a high, painted ceiling, on which is written in decorative Gothic script what I can just make out to be the Ten Commandments. There is a huge terrestrial globe, balanced by an equally huge celestial one. A big telescope, not much less than a century old, I judged, is mounted at one of the windows that look out on the mountains. On a low table sits a very modern object, which I discovered was five chess-boards mounted one above another in a brass frame; there are chessmen on each board, arranged as for five different games in progress; the boards are made of transparent lucite or some such material, so that it is possible to look down through them from above and see the position of every man. There was a good fire, and Ramsay was warming his legs, one flesh and one artificial, in front of it. He caught my mood at once.

—Extraordinary house, isn't it?

—Very. Is this where you live now?

—I'm a sort of permanent guest. My position is rather in the eighteenth-century mode. You know—people of intellectual tastes kept a philosopher or a scholar around the place. Liesl likes my conversation. I like hers. Funny way for a Canadian schoolmaster to end up, don't you think?

—You were never an ordinary schoolmaster, sir.

—Don't call me sir, Davey. We're old friends. Your father was my oldest friend; if friends is what we were, which I sometimes doubted. But you're not a lad now. You're a notable criminal lawyer; what used to be called "an eminent silk." Of course the problem is that I haven't any name by which all my friends call me. What did you call me at school? Was it Corky? Corky Ramsay? Stupid name, really. Artificial legs haven't been made of cork in a very long time.

—If you really want to know, we called you Buggerlugs. Because of your habit of digging in your ear with your little finger, you know.

—Really? Well, I don't think I like that much. You'd better call me Ramsay, like Liesl.

—I notice she generally calls you "dear Ramsay."

—Yes; we're rather close friends. More than that, for a while. Does that surprise you?

—You've just said I'm an experienced criminal lawyer; nothing surprises me.

—Never say that, Davey. Never, never say that. Especially not at Sorgenfrei.

—You yourself just said it was an extraordinary house.

—Oh, quite so. Rather a marvel, in its peculiar style. But that wasn't precisely what I meant.

We were interrupted by Liesl, who appeared through a door which I had not noticed because it is one of those nineteenth-century affairs, fitted close into the bookshelves and covered with false book-backs, so that it can hardly be seen. She was wearing something very like a man's evening suit, made in dark velvet, and looked remarkably elegant. I was beginning not to notice her Gorgon face. Ramsay turned to her rather anxiously, I thought.

—Is himself joining us at dinner tonight?

—I think so. Why do you ask?

—I just wondered when Davey would meet him.

—Don't fuss, dear Ramsay. It's a sign of age, and you are not old. Look, Davey, have you ever seen a chess-board like this?

Liesl began to explain the rules of playing what is, in effect, a single game of chess, but on five boards at once and with five sets of men. The first necessity, it appears, is to dismiss all ideas of the normal game, and to school oneself to think both horizontally and laterally at the same time. I, who could play chess pretty well but had never beaten Pargetter, was baffled—so much so that I did not notice anyone else entering the room, and I started when a voice behind me said:

—When am I to be introduced to Mr. Staunton?

The man who spoke was surprising enough in himself, for he was a most elegant little man with a magnificent head of curling silver hair, and the evening dress he wore ended not in trousers, but in satin knee-breeches and silk stockings. But I knew him at once as Eisengrim, the conjuror, the illusionist, whom I had twice seen in Toronto at the Royal Alexandra Theatre, the last time when I was drunk and distraught, and shouted at the Brazen Head, "Who killed Boy Staunton?" Social custom is ground into our bones, and I put out my hand to shake his. He spoke:

—I see you recognize me. Well, are the police still trying to involve me in the murder of your father? They were very persistent. They even traced me to Copenhagen. But they had nothing to go on. Except that I seemed to know rather more about it than they did, and they put all sorts of fanciful interpretations on some improvised words of Liesl's. How pleasant to meet you. We must talk the whole thing over.

No point in reporting in detail what followed. How right Ramsay was! Never say you can't be surprised. But what was I to do? I was confronted by a man whom I had despised and even hated when last I saw him, and his opening remarks to me were designed to be disconcerting if not downright quarrel-picking. But I was not the same man who shouted his question in the theatre; after a year with Dr. Johanna I was a very different fellow. If Eisingrim was cool, I would be cooler. I have delicately slain and devoured many an impudent witness in the courts, and I am not to be bamboozled by a mountebank. I think my behaviour was a credit to Dr. Johanna, and to Pargetter; I saw admiration in Ramsay's face, and Liesl made no attempt to conceal her pleasure at a situation that seemed to be entirely to her taste.

We went in to dinner, which was an excellent meal and not at all in the excessive style of the house. There was plenty of good wine, and cognac afterward, but I knew myself well enough to be sparing with it, and once again I could see that Ramsay and Liesl were watching me closely and pleased by what I did. There was none of that English pretence that serious things should not be discussed while eating, and we talked of nothing but my father's murder and what followed it, his will and what sprang from that, and what Denyse, and Carol, and Netty and the world in general—so far as the world in general paid any attention—had thought and said about it.

It was a trial and a triumph for me, because since I came to Zürich I have spoken to nobody of these things except Dr. Johanna, and then in the most subjective terms possible. But tonight I found myself able to be comparatively objective, even when Liesl snorted with rude laughter at Denyse's antics with the death-mask. Ramsay was sympathetic, but he laughed when I said that Father had left some money for my nonexistent children. His comment was:

—I don't believe you ever knew what a sore touch it was with Boy that you were such a Joseph about women. He felt it put him in the wrong. He always felt that the best possible favour you could do a woman was to push her into bed. He simply could not understand that there are men for whom sex is not the greatest of indoor and outdoor sports, hobbies, arts, sciences, and food for reverie. I always felt that his preoccupation with women was an extension of his miraculous touch with sugar and sweetstuffs. Women were the most delightful confectioneries he knew, and he couldn't understand anybody who hadn't a sweet tooth.

—I wonder what your father would have made of a woman like Jo von Haller?

—Women of that kind never came into Boy's ken, Liesl. Or women like you, for that matter. His notion of an intelligent woman was Denyse.

I found it still pained me to hear Father talked of in this objective strain, so I tried to turn the conversation.

—I suppose all but a tiny part of life lies outside anybody's ken, and we all get shocks and starts, now and then. For instance, who would have supposed that after such a long diversion through Dr. von Haller's consulting-room I should meet you three by chance? There's a coincidence, if you like.

But Ramsay wouldn't allow that to pass.

—As an historian, I simply don't believe in coincidence. Only very rigid minds do. Rationalists talk about a pattern they can see and approve as logical; any pattern they can't see and wouldn't approve they dismiss as coincidental. I suppose you had to meet us, for some reason. A good one, I hope.

Eisengrim was interested but supercilious; after dinner he and Liesl played the complex chess game. I watched for a while, but I could make nothing of what they were doing, so I sat by the fire and talked with Ramsay. Of course I was dying to know how he came to be part of this queer household, but Dr. von Haller has made me more discreet than I used to be about cross-examining in private life. That suggestion that he and Liesl had once been lovers—could it be? I probed, very, very gently. But I had once been Buggerlugs' pupil, and I still feel he can see right through me. Obviously he did, but he was in a mood to reveal, and like a man throwing crumbs to a bird he let me know:

1. That he had known Eisengrim from childhood.
2. That Eisengrim came from the same village as Father and himself, and Mother—my Deptford.
3. That Eisengrim's mother had been a dominant figure in his own life. He spoke of her as "saintly," which puzzles me. Wouldn't Netty have mentioned somebody like that?
4. That he met Liesl travelling with Eisengrim in Mexico and that they had discovered an "affinity" (his funny, old-fashioned word) which existed still.
5. When we veered back to the coincidence of my meeting them in St. Gall, he laughed and quoted G. K. Chesterton: "Coincidences are a spiritual sort of puns."

He has, it appears, come to Switzerland to recuperate himself after his heart attack, and seems likely to stay here. He is working on another book—something about faith as it relates to myth, which is his old subject—and appears perfectly content. This is not a bad haul, and gives me encouragement for further fishing.

Eisengrim affects royal airs. Everything suggests that this is Liesl's house, but he seems to regard himself as the regulator of manners in it. After they adjourned their game (I gather it takes days to complete), he rose, and I was astonished to see that Liesl and Ramsay rose as well, so I followed suit. He shook us all by the hand, and bade us good-night with the style of a crowned head taking leave of courtiers. He had an air of You-people-are-welcome-to-sit-up-as-long-as-you-please-but-We-are-retiring, and it was pretty obvious he thought the tone of the gathering would drop when he left the room.

Not so. We all seemed much easier. The huge library, where the curtains had now been drawn to shut out the night sky and the mountaintops and the few lights that shone far below us, was made almost cosy by his going. Liesl produced whisky, and I thought I might allow myself one good drink. It was she who brought up what was foremost in my mind.

—I assure you, Davey, there is nothing premeditated about this. Of course when we met in the bookshop I knew you must be the son of the man who died so spectacularly when Eisengrim was last in Toronto, but I had no notion of the circumstances.

—Were you in Toronto with him?

—Certainly. We have been business partners and artistic associates for a long time. I am his manager or impresario or whatever you want to call it. On the programs I use another name, but I assure you I am very much present. I am the voice of the Brazen Head.

—Then it was you who gave that extraordinary answer to my question?

—What question are you talking about?

—Don't you recall that Saturday night in the theatre when somebody called out, "Who killed Boy Staunton?"

—I remember it very clearly. It was a challenge, you may suppose, coming suddenly like that. We usually had warning of the questions the Head might have to answer. But was it you who asked the question?

—Yes, but I didn't hear all of your answer.

—No; there was confusion. Poor Ramsay here was standing at the back of an upstairs box, and that was when he had his heart attack. And I think a great many people were startled when he fell forward into sight. Of course there were others who thought it was part of the show. It was a memorable night.

—But do you remember what you said?

—Perfectly. I said: "He was killed by the usual cabal: by himself, first of all; by the woman he knew; by the woman he did not know; by the man who granted his inmost wish; and by the inevitable fifth, who was keeper of his conscience and keeper of the stone."

—I don't suppose it is unreasonable of me to ask for an explanation of that rigmarole?

—Not unreasonable at all, and I hope you get an answer that satisfies you. But not tonight. Dear Ramsay is looking a little pale, and I think I should see him to bed. But there is plenty of time. I know you will take care that we talk of this again.

And with that I have to be contented at least until tomorrow.

»»»» ««««

DEC. 21, Sun.: This morn. Liesl took me on a tour of the house, which was apparently built in 1824 by some forbear who had made money in the watch-and-clock business. The entrance hall is dominated by what I suppose was his masterpiece, for it has dials to show seconds, days of the week, days of the months, the months, the seasons, the signs of the zodiac, the time at Sorgenfrei and the time at Greenwich, and the phases of the moon. It has a chime of thirty-seven bells, which play a variety of tunes, and is ornamented with figures of Day and Night, the Seasons, two heads of Time, and God knows what else, all in fine *verd-antique*. Monstrous but fascinating, like Liesl, and she seems to love it. As we wandered through the house and climbed unexpected staircases and looked at the bewildering views from cunningly placed windows, I did my best to bring the conversation to the strange words of the Brazen Head about Father's death, but Liesl knows every trick of evasion, and in her own house I could not nail her down as I might in court. But she did say one or two things:

—You must not interpret too closely. Remember that I, speaking for the Head, had no time—not even ten seconds—to reflect. So I gave a perfectly ordinary answer, like any experienced fortune-teller. You know there are always things that fit almost any enquirer: you say those things and they will do the interpreting. "The woman he knew—the woman he did not know." . . . From what I know now, which is only what Ramsay has told me at one time or another, I would have said the woman he knew was your mother, and the woman he did not know was your stepmother. He felt guilty about your mother, and the second time he married a woman who was far stronger than he had understood. But I gather from the terrible fuss your stepmother made that she thought she must be the woman he knew, and was very angry at the idea that she had any part in bringing about his death. . . . I really can't tell you any more than that about why I spoke as I did. I have a tiny gift in this sort of thing; that was why Eisengrim trusted me to speak for the Head; maybe I sensed something—because one does, you know, if one permits it. But don't brood on it and try to make too much of it. Let it go.

—My training has not been to let things go.

—But Davey, your training and the way you have used yourself have brought you at last to Zürich for an analysis. I'm sure Jo von Haller, who is really excellent, though not at all my style, has made you see that. Are you going to do more work with her?

—That's a decision I must make.

—Well, don't be in a hurry to say you will.

Went for a long walk alone this afternoon, and thought about Liesl's advice.

This eve. after dinner Eisengrim showed us some home-movies of himself doing things with coins and cards. New illusions, it seems, for a tour they begin early in January. He is superb, and knows it. What an egotist! And only a conjuror, after all. Who gives a damn? Who needs conjurors? Yet I am unpleasantly conscious of a link between Eisengrim and myself. He wants people to be in awe of him, and at a distance; so do I.

»»»» ««««

DEC. 22, Mon.: I suppose Eisengrim sensed my boredom and disgust last night, because he hunted me up after breakfast and took me to see his workrooms, which are the old stables of Sorgenfrei; full of the paraphernalia of his illusions, and with very fine workbenches, at one of which Liesl was busy with a jeweller's magnifying-glass stuck in her eye. . . . "You didn't know I had the family knack of clockwork, did you?" she said. But Eisengrim wanted to talk himself:

—You don't think much of me, Staunton? Don't deny it; it is part of my profession to sniff people's thoughts. Well, fair enough. But I like you, and I should like you to like me. I am an egotist, of course. Indeed, I am a great egotist and a very unusual one, because I know what I am and I like it. Why not? If you knew my history, you would understand, I think. But you see that is just what I don't want, or ask for. So many people twitter through life crying, "Understand me! Oh, please understand me! To know all is to forgive all!" But you see I don't care about being understood, and I don't ask to be forgiven. Have you read the book about me?

(I have read it, because it is the only book in my bedroom, and so obviously laid out on the bedside table that it seems an obligation of the household to read the thing. I had seen it before; Father bought a copy for Lorene the first time we went to see Eisengrim, on her birthday. *Phantasmata: the Life and Adventures of Magnus Eisengrim*. Shortish; about 120 pages. But what a fairy-tale! Strange birth to distinguished Lithuanian parents, political exiles from Poland; infancy in the Arctic, where father was working on a secret scientific project (for Russia, it was implied, but because of his high lineage the Russians did not want to acknowledge the association); recognition of little Magnus by an Eskimo shaman as a child of strange gifts; little Magnus, between the ages of four and eight, learns arts of divination and hypnosis from the shaman and his colleagues. Father's Arctic work completed and he goes off to do something similar in the dead centre of Australia (because it is implied that father, the Lithuanian genius, is some sort of extremely advanced meteorological expert) and there little Magnus is taught by a tutor who is a great savant, who has to keep away from civilization for a while because he has done something dreadfully naughty. Little Magnus, after puberty, is irresistible to women, but he is obliged to be careful about this as the shaman had warned him women would disagree with his delicately balanced nerves.

Nevertheless, great romances are hinted at; a generous gobbet of sadism spiced with pornography here. Having sipped, and rejected with contumely the learning of several great universities, Magnus Eisengrim determines to devote his life to the noble, misunderstood science which he first encountered in the Arctic, and which claimed him for its own. . . . And this is supposed to explain why he is travelling around with a magic show. A very good magic show, but still—a travelling showman.)

—Is one expected to take it seriously?

—I think it deserves to be taken more seriously than most biographies and autobiographies. You know what they are. The polished surface of a life. What the Zürich analysts call the Persona—the mask. Now, *Phantasmata* says what it is quite frankly in its title; it is an illusion, a vision. Which is what I am, and because I am such a thoroughly satisfactory illusion, and because I satisfy a hunger that almost everybody has for marvels, the book is a far truer account of me than ordinary biographies, which do not admit that their intent is to deceive and are woefully lacking in poetry. The book is extremely well written, don't you think?

—Yes. I was surprised. Did you write it?

—Ramsay wrote it. He has written so much about saints and marvels, Liesl and I thought he was the ideal man to provide the right sort of life for me.

—But you admit it is a pack of lies?

—It is not a police-court record. But as I have already said, it is truer to the essence of my life than the dowdy facts could ever be. Do you understand? I am what I have made myself—the greatest illusionist since Moses and Aaron. Do the facts suggest or explain what I am? No: but Ramsay's book does. I am truly Magnus Eisengrim. The illusion, the lie, is a Canadian called Paul Dempster. If you want to know his story, ask Ramsay. He knows, and he might tell. Or he might not.

—Thank you for being frank. Are you any more ready than Liesl to throw some light on the answer of the Brazen Head?

—Let me see. Yes, I am certainly "the man who granted his inmost wish." You would never guess what it was. But he told me. People do tell me things. When I met him, which was on the night of his death, he offered me a lift back to my hotel in his car. As we drove he said—and as you know this was at one of the peaks of his career, when he was about to realize a dream which he, or your stepmother, had long cherished—he said, "You know, sometimes I wish I could step on the gas and drive right away from all of this, all the obligations, the jealousies, the nuisances, and the relentlessly demanding people." I said, "Do you mean that? I could arrange it." He said, "Could you?" I replied, "Nothing easier." His face became very soft, like a child's, and he said, "Very well. I'd be greatly obliged to you." So I arranged it. You may be sure he knew no pain. Only the realization of his wish.

—But the stone? The stone in his mouth?

—Ah, well, that is not my story. You must ask the keeper of the stone. But I will tell you something Liesl doesn't know, unless Ramsay has told her: "the woman he did not know" was my mother. Yes, she had some part in it.

With that I had to be contented because Liesl and a workman wanted to talk with him. But somehow I found myself liking him. Even more strange, I found myself believing him. But he was a hypnotist of great powers; I had seen him demonstrate that on the stage. Had he hypnotized Father and sent him to his death? And if so, why?

Later: That was how I put the question to Ramsay when I cornered him this afternoon in the room he uses for his writing. Pargetter's advice: always go to a man in *his* room, for then he has no place to escape to, whereas you may leave when you please. What did he say?

—Davey, you are behaving like the amateur sleuth in a detective story. The reality of your father's death is much more complex than anything you can uncover that way. First, you must understand that nobody—not Eisengrim or anyone—can make a man do something under hypnotism that he has not some genuine inclination to do. So: Who killed Boy Staunton? Didn't the Head say, "Himself, first of all?" We all do it, you know, unless we are taken off by some unaccountable accident. We determine the time of our death, and perhaps the means. As for the "usual cabal" I myself think "the woman he knew and the woman he did not know" were the same person—your mother. He never had any serious appraisal of her weakness or her strength. She had strength, you know, that he never wanted or called on. She was Ben Cruikshank's daughter, and don't suppose that was nothing just because Ben wasn't a village grandee like Doc Staunton. Boy never had any use for your mother as a grown-up woman, and she kept herself childish in the hope of pleasing him. When we have linked our destiny with somebody, we neglect them at our peril. But Boy never knew that. He was so well graced, so gifted, such a genius in his money-spinning way, that he never sensed the reality of other people. Her weakness galled him, but her occasional shows of strength shamed him.

—You loved Mother, didn't you?

—I thought I did when I was a boy. But the women we really love are the women who complete us, who have the qualities we can borrow and so become something nearer to whole men. Just as we complete them, of course; it's not a one-way thing. Leola and I, when romance was stripped away, were too much alike; our strengths and weaknesses were too nearly the same. Together we would have doubled our gains and our losses, but that isn't what love is.

—Did you sleep with her?

—I know times have changed, Davey, but isn't that rather a rum question to put to an old friend about your mother?

—Carol used to insist that you were my father.

—Then Carol is a mischief-making bitch. I'll tell you this, however: your mother once asked me to make love to her, and I refused. In spite of one very great example I had in my life I couldn't rise to love as an act of charity. The failure was mine, and a bitter one. Now I'm not going to say the conventional thing and tell you I wish you were my son. I have plenty of sons—good men I've taught, who will carry something of me into places I would never reach. Listen, Davey, you great clamorous baby-detective, there is something you ought to know at your age: every man who amounts to a damn has several fathers, and the man who begat him in lust or drink or for a bet or even in the sweetness of honest love may not be the most important father. The fathers you choose for yourself are the significant ones. But you didn't choose Boy, and you never knew him. No; no man knows his father. If Hamlet had known his father he would never have made such an almighty fuss about a man who was fool enough to marry Gertrude. Don't you be a two-bit Hamlet, clinging to your father's ghost until you are destroyed. Boy is dead; dead of his own will, if not wholly of his own doing. Take my advice and get on with your own concerns.

—My concerns are my father's concerns and I can't escape that. Alpha is waiting for me. And Castor.

—Not your father's concerns. Your kingdoms. Go and reign, even if he has done a typical Boy trick by leaving you a gavel where he used a golden sceptre.

—I see you won't talk honestly with me. But I must ask one more question; who was "the inevitable fifth, who was keeper of his conscience and keeper of the stone?"

—I was. And as keeper of his conscience, and as one who has a high regard for you, I will say nothing about it.

—But the stone? The stone that was found in his mouth when they rescued his body from the water? Look, Ramsay, I have it here. Can you look at it and say nothing?

—It was my paperweight for over fifty years. Your father gave it to me, very much in his own way. He threw it at me, wrapped up in a snowball. The rock-in-the-snowball man was part of the father you never knew, or never recognized.

—But why was it in his mouth?

—I suppose he put it there himself. Look at it; a piece of that pink granite we see everywhere in Canada. A geologist who saw it on my desk told me that they now reckon that type of stone to be something like a thousand million years old. Where has it been, before there were any men to throw it, and where will it be when you and I are not even a pinch of dust? Don't cling to it as if you owned it. I did that. I harboured it for sixty years, and perhaps my hope was for revenge. But at last I lost it, and Boy got it back, and he lost it, and certainly you will lose it. None of us counts for much in the long, voiceless, inert history of the stone. . . . Now I am going to claim the privilege of an invalid and ask you to leave me.

—There's nothing more to be said?

—Oh, volumes more, but what does all this saying amount to? Boy is dead. What lives is a notion, a fantasy, a whimwham in your head that you call Father, but which never had anything seriously to do with the man you attached it to.

—Before I go: who was Eisengrim's mother?

—I spent decades trying to answer that. But I never fully knew. *Later:* Found out a little more about the super-chess game this eve. Each player plays both black and white. If the player who draws white at the beginning plays white on boards one, three, and five, he must play black on boards two and four. I said to Liesl that this must make the game impossibly complicated, as it is not five games played consecutively, but one game.

—Not half so complicated as the game we all play for seventy or eighty years. Didn't Jo von Haller show you that you can't play the white pieces on all the boards? Only people who play on one, flat board can do that, and then they are in agonies trying to figure out what black's next move will be. Far better to know what you are doing, and play from both sides.

»»»» ««««

DEC. 23, Tues.: Liesl has the ability to an extraordinary extent to worm things out of me. My temperament and professional training make me a man to whom things are told; somehow she makes me into a teller. I ran into her—better be honest, I sought her out—this morning in her workshop, where she sat with a jeweller's magnifying glass in her eye and tinkered with a tiny bit of mechanism, and in five minutes had me caught in a conversation of a kind I don't like but can't resist when Liesl creates it.

—So you must give Jo a decision about more analysis? What is it to be?

—I'm torn about it. I'm seriously needed at home. But the work with Dr. von Haller holds out the promise of a kind of satisfaction I've never known before. I suppose I want to have it both ways.

—Well, why not? Jo has set you on your path; do you need her to take you on a tour of your inner labyrinth? Why not go by yourself?

—I've never thought of it—I wouldn't know how.

—Then find out. Finding out is half the value. Jo is very good. I say nothing against her. But these analyses, Davey—they are duets between the analyst and the analysand, and you will never be able to sing louder or higher than your analyst.

—She has certainly done great things for me in the past year.

—Undoubtedly. And she never pushed you too far, or frightened you, did she? Jo is like a boiled egg—a wonder, a miracle, very easy to take—but even with a good sprinkling of salt she is invalid food, don't you find?

—I understand she is one of the best in Zürich.

—Oh, certainly. Analysis with a great analyst is an adventure in self-exploration. But how many analysts are great? Did I ever tell you I knew Freud slightly? A giant, and it would be apocalyptic to talk to such a giant about oneself. I never met Adler, whom everybody forgets, but he was certainly another giant. I once went to a seminar Jung gave in Zürich, and it was unforgettable. But one must remember that they were all men with systems. Freud, monumentally hipped on sex (for which he personally had little use) and almost ignorant of Nature: Adler, reducing almost everything to the will to power: and Jung, certainly the most humane and gentlest of them, and possibly the greatest, but nevertheless the descendant of parsons and professors, and himself a super-parson and a super-professor. All men of extraordinary character, and they devised systems that are forever stamped with that character. . . . Davey, did you ever think that these three men who were so splendid at understanding others had first to understand themselves? It was from their self-knowledge they spoke. They did not go trustingly to some doctor and follow his lead because they were too lazy or too scared to make the inward journey alone. They dared heroically. And it should never be forgotten that they made the inward journey while they were working like galley-slaves at their daily tasks, considering other people's troubles, raising families, living full lives. They were heroes, in a sense that no space-explorer can be a hero, because they went into the unknown absolutely alone. Was their heroism simply meant to raise a whole new crop of invalids? Why don't you go home and shoulder your yoke, and be a hero too?

—I'm no hero, Liesl.

—Oh, how modest and rueful that sounds! And you expect me to think, isn't he splendid to accept his limitations so manfully. But I don't think that. All that personal modesty is part of the cop-out personality of our time. You don't know whether or not you are a hero, and you're bloody well determined not to find out, because you're scared of the burden if you are and scared of the certainty if you're not.

—Just a minute. Dr. von Haller, of whom you think so little, once suggested that I was rather inclined toward heroic measures in dealing with myself.

—Good for Jo! But she didn't encourage you in it, did she? Ramsay says you are very much the hero in court—voice of the mute, hope of the hopeless, last resort of those society has condemned. But of course that's a public personality. Why do you put yourself on this footing with a lot of riff-raff, by the way?

—I told Dr. von Haller that I liked living on the lip of a volcano.

—A good, romantic answer. But do you know the name of the volcano? That's what you have to find out.

—What are you suggesting? That I go home and take up my practice and Alpha and Castor and see what I can do to wriggle crooks like Matey Quelch off the hooks on which they have been caught? And at night, sit down quietly and try to think my way out of all my problems, and try to make some sort of sense of my life?

—Think your way out. . . . Davey, what did Jo say was wrong with you? Obviously you have a screw loose somewhere; everybody has. What did she find at the root of most of your trouble?

—Why should I tell you?

—Because I've asked, and I truly want to know. I'm not just a gossip or a chatterer, and I like you very much. So tell me.

—It's nothing dreadful. She just kept coming back to the point that I am rather strongly developed in Thinking, and seem to be a bit weak in Feeling.

—I guessed that was it.

—But honestly I don't know what's wrong with thinking. Surely it's what everybody is trying to do?

—Oh yes; very fine work, thinking. But it is also the greatest bolt-hole and escape-hatch of our time. It's supposed to excuse everything. . . . "I think this . . . I thought that. . . . You haven't really thought about it. . . . Think, for God's sake. . . . The thinking of the meeting (or the committee, or God help us, the symposium) was that. . . ." But so much of this thinking is just mental masturbation, not intended to beget anything. . . . So you are weak in feeling, eh? I wonder why?

—Because of Dr. von Haller, I can tell you. In my life feeling has not been very handsomely rewarded. It has hurt like hell.

—Nothing unusual in that. It always does. But you could try. Do you remember the fairy-tale about the boy who couldn't shudder and was so proud of it? Nobody much likes shuddering, but it's better than existing without it, I can assure you.

—I seem to have a natural disposition to think rather than feel, and Dr. von Haller has helped me a good deal there. But I am not ambitious to be a great feeler. Wouldn't suit my style of life at all, Liesl.

—If you don't feel, how are you going to discover whether or not you are a hero?

—I don't want to be a hero.

—So? It isn't everybody who is triumphantly the hero of his own romance, and when we meet one he is likely to be a fascinating monster, like my dear Eisengrim. But just because you are not a roaring egotist, you needn't fall for the fashionable modern twaddle of the anti-hero and the mini-soul. That is what we might call the Shadow of democracy; it makes it so laudable, so cosy and right and easy to be a spiritual runt and lean on all the other runts for support and applause in a splendid apotheosis of runtdom. Thinking runts, of course—oh, yes, thinking away as hard as a runt can without getting into danger. But there are heroes, still. The modern hero is the man who conquers in the inner struggle. How do you know you aren't that kind of hero?

—You are as uncomfortable company as an old friend of mine who asked for spiritual heroism in another way. "God is here and Christ is now," he would say, and ask you to live as if it were true.

—It is true. But it's equally true to say "Odin is here and Loki is now." The heroic world is all around us, waiting to be known.

—But we don't live like that, now.

—Who says so? A few do. Be the hero of your own epic. If others will not, are you to blame? One of the great follies of our time is this belief in some levelling of Destiny, some democracy of *Wyrd*.

—And you think I should go it alone?

—I don't think: I feel that you ought at least to consider the possibility, and not cling to Jo like a sailor clinging to a lifebelt.

—I wouldn't know how to start.

—Perhaps if you felt something powerfully enough it would set you on the path.

—But what?

—Awe is a very unfashionable, powerful feeling. When did you last feel awe in the presence of anything?

—God, I can't remember ever feeling what I suppose you mean by awe.

—Poor Davey! How you have starved! A real little workhouse boy, an Oliver Twist of the spirit! Well, you're rather old to begin.

—Dr. von Haller says not. I can begin the second part of this exploration with her, if I choose. But what is it? Do you know, Liesl?

—Yes, but it isn't easily explained. It's a thing one experiences—feels, if you like. It's learning to know oneself as fully human. A kind of rebirth.

—I was told a lot about that in my boyhood days, when I thought I was a Christian. I never understood it.

—Christians seem to have got it mixed up, somehow. It's certainly not crawling back into your mother's womb; it's more a re-entry and return from the womb of mankind. A fuller comprehension of one's humanity.

—That doesn't convey much to me.

—I suppose not. It's not a thinker's thing.

—Yet you suggest I go it alone?

—I don't know. I'm not as sure as I was. You might manage it. Perhaps some large experience, or even a good, sharp shock, might put you on the track. Perhaps you are wrong even to listen to me.

—Then why do you talk so much, and throw out so many dangerous suggestions?

—It's my métier. You thinkers drive me to shake you up.

Maddening woman!

»»»» ««««

DEC. 24, Wed. and Christmas Eve: Was this the worst day of my life, or the best? Both.

Liesl insisted this morning that I go on an expedition with her. You will see the mountains at their best, she said; it is too cold for the tourists with their sandwiches, and there is not enough snow for skiers. So we drove for about half an hour, uphill all the way, and at last came to one of those cable-car affairs and swayed and joggled dizzily through the air toward the far-off shoulder of a mountain. When we got out of it at last, I found I was panting.

—We are about seven thousand feet up now. Does it bother you? You'll soon get used to it. Come on. I want to show you something.

—Surely the view elsewhere is the same as it is here?

—Lazy! What I want to show you isn't a view.

It was a cave; large, extremely cold as soon as we penetrated a few yards out of the range of the sun, but not damp. I couldn't see much of it, and although it is the first cave I have ever visited it convinced me that I don't like caves. But Liesl was enthusiastic, because it is apparently quite famous since somebody, whose name I did not catch, proved conclusively in the 'nineties that primitive men had lived here. All the sharpened flints, bits of carbon, and other evidence had been removed, but there were a few scratches on the walls which appear to be very significant, though they looked like nothing more than scratches to me.

—Can't you imagine them, crouching here in the cold as the sun sank, with nothing to warm them but a small fire and a few skins? But enduring, enduring, enduring! They were heroes, Davey.

—I don't suppose they conceived of anything better. They can't have been much more than animals.

—They were our ancestors. They were more like us than they were like any animal.

—Physically, perhaps. But what kind of brains had they? What sort of mind?

—A herd-mind, probably. But they may have known a few things we have lost on the long journey from the cave to—well, to the law-courts.

—I don't see any good in romanticizing savages. They knew how to get a wretched living and hang on to life for twenty-five or thirty years. But surely anything human, any sort of culture or civilized feeling or whatever you want to call it, came ages later?

—No, no; not at all. I can prove it to you now. It's a little bit dangerous, so follow me, and be careful.

She went to the very back of the cave, which may have been two hundred feet deep, and I was not happy to follow her, because it grew darker at every step, and though she had a big electric torch it seemed feeble in that blackness. But when we had gone as far as seemed possible, she turned to me and said, "This is where it begins to be difficult, so follow me very closely, close enough to touch me at all times, and don't lose your nerve." Then she stepped behind an outcropping of rock which looked like solid cave wall and scrambled up into a hole about four feet above the cave floor.

I followed, very much alarmed, but too craven to beg off. In the hole, through which it was just possible to move on hands and knees, I crept after the torch, which flickered intermittently because every time Liesl lifted her back she obscured its light. And then, after perhaps a dozen yards of this creeping progress over rough stone, we began what was to me a horrible descent.

Liesl never spoke or called to me. As the hole grew smaller she dropped from her knees and crawled on her belly, and there was nothing for me but to do the same. I was as frightened as I have ever been in my life, but there was nothing for me to do but follow, because I had no idea of how I could retreat. Nor did I speak to her; her silence kept me quiet. I would have loved to hear her speak, and say something in reply, but all I heard was the shuffling as she crawled and wriggled, and now and then one of her boots kicked against my head. I have heard of people whose sport it is to crawl into these mountain holes, and read about some of them who had stuck and died. I was in terror, but somehow I kept on wriggling forward. I have not wriggled on my belly since I was a child, and it hurt; my shoulders and neck began to ache torturingly, and at every hunch forward my chest, privates, and knees were scraped unpleasantly on the stone floor. Liesl had outfitted me in some winter clothes she had borrowed from one of the workmen at Sorgenfrei, and though they were thick, they were certainly not much protection from the bruises of this sort of work.

How far we wriggled I had no idea. Later Liesl, who had made the journey several times, said it was just under a quarter of a mile, but to me it might have been ten miles. At last I heard her say,

Here we are, and as I crawled out of the hole and stood up—very gingerly because for some reason she did not use her electric torch and the darkness was complete and I had no idea how high the roof might be—there was the flash of a match, and soon a larger flame that came from a torch she had lit.

—This is a pine-torch; I think it the most appropriate light for this place. Electricity is a blasphemy here. The first time I came, which was about three years ago, there were remains of pine-torches still by the entry, so that was how they must have lit this place.

—Who are you talking about?

—The people of the caves. Our ancestors. Here, hold this torch while I light another. It takes some time for the torches to give much light. Stand where you are and let it unfold before you.

I thought she must mean that we had entered one of those caves, of which I have vaguely heard, which are magnificently decorated with primitive paintings. I asked her if that were it, but all she would say was, "Very much earlier than that," and stood with her torch held high.

Slowly, in the flickering light, the cave revealed itself. It was about the size of a modest chapel; I suppose it might have held fifty people; and it was high, for the roof was above the reach of the light from our torches. It was bitter cold but there was no ice on the walls; there must have been lumps of quartz, because they twinkled eerily. Liesl was in a mood that I had never seen in her before; all her irony and amusement were gone and her eyes were wide with awe.

—I discovered this about three years ago. The outer cave is quite famous, but nobody had noticed the entrance to this one. When I found it I truly believe I was the first person to enter it in—how long would you guess, Davey?

—I can't possibly say. How can you tell?

—By what is here. Haven't you noticed it yet?

—It just seems to be a cave. And brutally cold. Do you suppose somebody used it for something?

—Those people. The ancestors. Look here.

She led me toward the farthest wall from where we had entered, and we came to a little enclosure, formed by a barrier made of heaped up stones; in the cave wall, above the barrier, were seven niches, and I could just make out something of bone in each of these little cupboards; old, dark brown bone, which I gradually made out to be skulls of animals.

—They are bears. The ancestors worshipped bears. Look, in this one bones have been pushed into the eyeholes. And here, you see, the leg-bones have been carefully piled under the chin of the skull.

—Do you suppose the bears lived in here?

—No cave-bear could come through the passage. No; they brought the bones here, and the skins, and set up this place of worship. Perhaps someone pulled on the bear skin, and there was a ceremony of killing.

—That was their culture, was it? Playing bears in here?

—Flippant fool! Yes, that was their culture.

—Well, don't snap at me. I can't pretend it means much to me.

—You don't know enough for it to mean anything to you. Worse for you, you don't feel enough for it to mean anything to you.

—Liesl, are we going to go over all that again in the depths of this mountain? I want to get out. If you want to know, I'm scared. Now look: I'm sorry I haven't been respectful enough about your discovery. I'm sure it means a lot in the world of archaeology, or ethnology, or whatever it may be. The men around here worshipped bears. Good. Now let's go.

—Not just the men around here. The men of a great part of the world. There are such caves as this all over Europe and Asia, and they have found some in America. How far is Hudson Bay from where you live?

—A thousand miles, more or less.

—They worshipped the bear there, between the great ice ages.

—Does it matter, now?

—Yes, I think it matters now. What do we worship today?

—Is this the place or the time to go into that?

—Where better? We share the great mysteries with these people. We stand where men once came to terms with the facts of death and mortality and continuance. How long ago, do you suppose?

—I haven't any idea.

—It was certainly not less than seventy-five thousand years ago;

possibly much, much more. They worshipped the bear and felt themselves better and greater because they had done so. Compared with this place the Sistine Chapel is of yesterday. But the purpose of both places is the same. Men sacrificed and ate of the noblest thing they could conceive, hoping to share in its virtue.

—Yes, yes: I read *The Golden Bough* when I was young.

—Yes, yes; and you misunderstood what you read because you accepted its rationalist tone instead of understanding its facts. Does this place give you no sense of the greatness and indomitability and spiritual splendour of man? Man is a noble animal, Davey. Not a good animal; a noble animal.

—You distinguish between the two?

—Yes, you—you lawyer, I do.

—Liesl, we mustn't quarrel. Not here. Let's get out and I'll argue all you please. If you want to split morality—some sort of accepted code—off from the highest values we have, I'll promise you a long wrangle. I am, as you say, a lawyer. But for the love of God let's get back to the light.

—For the love of God? Is not God to be found in the darkness? Well, you mighty lover of the light and the law, away we go.

But then, to my astonishment, Liesl flung herself on the ground, face down before the skulls of the bears, and for perhaps three minutes I stood in the discomfort we always feel when somebody nearby is praying and we are not. But what form could her prayers be taking? This was worse—much worse—than Dr. Johanna's Comedy Company of the Psyche. What sort of people had I fallen among on this Swiss journey?

When she rose she was grinning and the charm I had learned to see in her terrible face was quite gone.

—Back to the light, my child of light. You must be reborn into the sun you love so much, so let us lose no time. Leave your torch, here, by the way out.

She dowsed her own torch by stubbing it on the ground and I did so too. As the light diminished to a few sparks I heard a mechanical clicking, and I knew she was snapping the switch of her electric torch, but no light came.

—Something is wrong. The batteries or the bulb. It won't light.

—But how are we to get back without light?

—You can't miss the path. Just keep crawling. You'd better go first.

—Liesl, am I to go into that tunnel without a glimmer of light?

—Yes, unless you wish to stay here in the dark. I'm going, certainly. If you are wise you will go first. And don't change your mind on the way, because if anything happens to you, Davey, I can't turn back, or wriggle backward. It's up and out for both of us, or death for both of us. . . . Don't think about it any longer. Go on!

She gave me a shove toward the hole of the tunnel, and I hit my head hard against the upper side of it. But I was cowed by the danger and afraid of Liesl, who had become such a demon in the cave, and I felt my way into the entrance and began to wriggle.

What had been horrible coming in, because it was done head downward, was more difficult than anything I have ever attempted until I began the outward journey; but now I had to wriggle upward at an angle that seemed never less than forty-five degrees. It was like climbing a chimney, a matter of knees and elbows, and frequent cracks on the skull. I know I kicked Liesl in the face more than once, but she made no sound except for the grunting and panting without which no progress was possible. I had worn myself out going in; going out I had to find strength from new and unguessed-at sources. I did not think; I endured, and endurance took on a new character, not of passive suffering but of anguished, fearful striving. Was it only yesterday I had been called the boy who could not shudder?

Suddenly, out of the darkness just before me, came a roar so loud, so immediate, so fearful in suggestion that I knew in that instant the sharpness of death. I did not lose consciousness. Instead I knew with a shame that came back in full force from childhood that my bowels had turned to water and gushed out into my pants, and the terrible stench that filled the tunnel was my own. I was at the lowest ebb, frightened, filthy, seemingly powerless, because when I heard Liesl's voice—"Go on, you dirty brute, go on"—I couldn't go on, dragging with me that mess which, from being hot as porridge, was cooling quickly in the chill of the tunnel.

—It's only a trick of the wind. Did you think it was the bear-god coming to claim you? Go on. You have another two hundred yards at least. Do you think I want to hang about here with your stink? Go on!

—I can't, Liesl. I'm done.

—You must.

—How?

—What gives you strength? Have you no God? No, I suppose not. Your kind have neither God nor Devil. Have you no ancestors?

Ancestors? Why, in this terrible need, would I want such ornaments? Then I thought of Maria Dymock, staunch in the street of Staunton, demanding money from the passers-by to get herself and her bastard to Canada. Maria Dymock, whom Doc Staunton had suppressed, and about whom my father would hear nothing after that first, unhappy letter. (What had Pledger-Brown said? "Too bad, Davey; he wanted blood and all we could offer was guts.") Would Maria Dymock see me through? In my weakened, terrified, humiliated condition I suppose I must have called upon Maria Dymock and something—but it's absurd to think it could have been she!—gave me the power I needed to wriggle that last two hundred yards, until an air that was sweeter but no less cold told me that the outer cave was near.

Out of the darkness into the gloom. Out of the gloom into sunshine, and the extraordinary realization that it was about three o'clock on a fine Christmas Eve, and that I was seven thousand feet above the sea on a Swiss mountain. An uncomfortable, messy walk back to the cable-railway and the discovery—God bless the Swiss!—that the little station had a good men's toilet with lots of paper towels. A dizzy, light-headed journey downward on one of the swaying cars, during which Liesl said nothing but sulked like some offended shaman from the days of her bear-civilization. We drove home in silence; even when she indicated that she wished me to sit on a copy of the *Neue Zürcher Zeitung* that was in the car, so as not to soil her upholstery, she said nothing. But when we drove into the stable-yard which led to the garages at Sorgenfrei, I spoke.

—Liesl, I am very, very sorry. Not for being afraid, or messing my pants, or any of that. But for falling short of what you expected. You thought me worthy to see the shrine of the bears, and I was too small a person to know what you meant. But I think I have a glimmering of something better, and I beg you not to shut me out of your friendship.

Another woman might have smiled, or taken my hand, or kissed me, but not Liesl. She glared into my eyes.

—Apology is the cheapest coin on earth, and I don't value it. But I think you have learned something, and if that is so, I'll do more than be your friend. I'll love you, Davey. I'll take you into my heart, and you shall take me into yours. I don't mean bed-love, though that might happen, if it seemed the right thing. I mean the love that gives all and takes all and knows no bargains.

I was bathed and in bed by five o'clock, dead beat. But so miraculous is the human spirit, I was up and about and able to eat a good dinner and watch a Christmas broadcast from Lausanne with Ramsay and Eisengrim and Liesl, renewed—yes, and it seemed to me reborn, by the terror of the cave and the great promise she had made to me a few hours before.

»»»» ««««

DEC. 25, Thurs. and Christmas Day: Woke feeling better than I have done in years. To breakfast very hungry (why does happiness make us hungry?) and found Ramsay alone at the table.

—Merry Christmas, Davey. Do you recall once telling me you hated Christmas more than any day in the year?

—That was long ago. Merry Christmas, Dunny. That was what Father used to call you, wasn't it?

—Yes, and I always hated it. I think I'd almost rather be called Buggerlugs.

Eisengrim came in and put a small pouch beside my plate. Obviously he meant me to open it, so I did, and out fell a fine pair of ivory dice. I rolled them a few times, without much luck. Then he took them.

—What would you like to come up?

—Double sixes, surely?

He cast the dice, and sure enough, there they were.

—Loaded?

—Nothing so coarse. They are quite innocent, but inside they have a little secret. I'll show you how it works later.

Ramsay laughed.

—You don't suppose an eminent silk would use such things, Magnus? He'd be thrown out of all his clubs.

—I don't know what an eminent silk might do with dice but I know very well what he does in court. Are you a lucky man? To be lucky is always to play with—well, with dice like these. You might like to keep them in your pocket, Davey, just as a reminder of—well, of what our friend Ramsay calls the variability and mutability and general rumness of things.

Liesl had come in, and now she handed me a watch.

—From the Brazen Head.

It was a handsome piece, and on the back was engraved, "Time is . . . Time was . . . Time is past," which is perfectly reasonable if you like inscribed watches, and of course these were the words she and Eisengrim used to introduce their Brazen Head illusion. I knew that, between us, it meant the mystery and immemorial age of the cave. I was embarrassed.

—I had no idea there was to be an exchange of gifts. I'm terribly sorry, but I haven't anything for anyone.

—Don't think of it. It is just as one feels. You see, dear Ramsay has not worried about gifts either.

—But I have. I have my gifts here. I wanted to wait till everyone was present before giving mine.

Ramsay produced a paper bag from under the table and solemnly handed us each a large gingerbread bear. They were handsome bears, standing on their hindlegs and each holding a log of wood.

—These are the real St. Gall bears; the shops are full of them at this time of year.

Eisengrim nibbled at his bear experimentally.

—Yes, they are made like the bear which is the city crest, or totem, aren't they?

—Indeed, they are images of the veritable bear of St. Gall himself. You know the legend. Early in the seventh century an Irish monk, Gallus, came to this part of the world to convert the wild mountaineers. They were bear-worshippers, I believe. He made his hermitage in a cave near where the present city stands, and preached and prayed. But he was so very much a holy man, and so far above merely creatural considerations, that he needed a servant or a friend to help him. Where would he find one? Now it so happened that Gallus's cave had another inhabitant, a large bear. And Gallus, who was extremely long-headed, made a deal with the bear. If the bear would bring him wood for his fire, he would give the bear bread to eat. And so it was. And this excellent gingerbread—I hope I may say it is excellent without seeming to praise my own gift—reminds us even today that if we are really wise, we will make a working arrangement with the bear that lives with us, because otherwise we shall starve or perhaps be eaten by the bear. You see, like every tale of a saint it has a moral, and the moral is my Christmas gift to you, Davey, you poor Canadian bear-choker, and to you, Magnus, you enchanting fraud, and to you, my dearest Liesl, though you don't need it: cherish your bear, and your bear will feed your fire.

Later: For a walk with Ramsay. It was not long after three o'clock, but already in the mountains sunset was well advanced. He cannot walk far with his game leg, but we went a few hundred yards, toward a precipice; a low stone wall warned us not to go too near, for the drop was steep toward a valley and some little farmsteads. Talked to him about the decision Liesl wants me to make and asked his advice.

—Liesl likes pushing people to extremes. Are you a man for extremes, Davey? I don't think I can help you. Or can I? You still have that stone. . . . You know, the one that was found in Boy's mouth?

I took it out of my pocket and handed it to him.

—I can do this for you, anyhow, Davey.

He raised his arm high, and with a snap of the wrist threw it far down into the valley. In that instant it was possible to see that he had once been a boy. We both watched until the little speck could no longer be seen against the valley dusk.

—There. At least that's that. Pray God it didn't hit anybody.

We turned back toward Sorgenfrei, walking in companionable silence. My thoughts were on the dream I dreamed the night before I first confronted Dr. von Haller. It was splendidly clear in my recollection. I had left my enclosed, ordered, respected life. Yes. And I had ventured into unknown country, where archaeological digging was in progress. Yes. I had attempted to go down the circular staircase inside the strange, deceptive hut—so wretched on the outside and so rich within—and my desire had been thwarted by trivial fellows who behaved as if I had no right there. Yes. But as I thought about it, the dream changed; the two young men were no longer at the stairhead, and I was free to go down if I pleased. And I did please, for I sensed that there was treasure down there. I was filled with happiness, and I knew this was what I wanted most.

I was walking with Ramsay, I was fully aware of everything about me, and yet it was the dream that was most real to me. The strange woman, the gypsy who spoke so compellingly, yet incomprehensibly—where was she? In my waking dream I looked out of the door of the hut, and there she was, walking toward me; to join me, I knew. Who was she? "Every country gets the foreigners it deserves." The words which I had thought so foolish still lingered in my mind. They meant something more important than I could yet understand, and I struggled for an explanation. Was I going down the staircase to a strange land? Was I, then, to be a stranger there? But how could I be foreign in the place where my treasure lay? Surely I was native there, however long I had been absent?

Across the uneven ground the woman came, with a light step. Nearer and nearer, but still I could not see whether her face was that of Liesl or Johanna.

Then Ramsay spoke, and the dream, or vision or whatever it was, lost its compelling quality. But I know that not later than tomorrow I must know what face the woman wore, and which woman is to be my guide to the treasure that is mine.

WORLD OF WONDERS

Contents

I *A Bottle in the Smoke* 521
II *Merlin's Laugh* 655
III *Le Lit de Justice* 805

· I ·

A Bottle in the Smoke

1

"OF COURSE HE was a charming man. A delightful person. Who has ever questioned it? But not a great magician."

"By what standard do you judge?"

"Myself. Who else?"

"You consider yourself a greater magician than Robert-Houdin?"

"Certainly. He was a fine illusionist. But what is that? A man who depends on a lot of contraptions—mechanical devices, clockwork, mirrors, and such things. Haven't we been working with that sort of rubbish for almost a week? Who made it? Who reproduced that *Pâtissier du Palais-Royal* we've been fiddling about with all day? I did. I'm the only man in the world who could do it. The more I see of it the more I despise it."

"But it is delightful! When the little baker brings out his bonbons, his patisseries, his croissants, his glasses of port and Marsala, all at the word of command, I almost weep with pleasure! It is the most moving reminiscence of the spirit of the age of Louis Philippe! And you admit that you have reproduced it precisely as it was first made by Robert-Houdin. If he was not a great magician, what do you call a great magician?"

"A man who can stand stark naked in the midst of a crowd and keep it gaping for an hour while he manipulates a few coins, or cards, or billiard balls. I can do that, and I can do it better than anybody today or anybody who has ever lived. That's why I'm tired of Robert-Houdin and his Wonderful Bakery and his Inexhaustible Punch Bowl and his Miraculous Orange Tree and all the rest of his wheels and cogs and levers and fancy junk."

"But you're going to complete the film?"

"Of course. I've signed a contract. I've never broken a contract in my life. I'm a professional. But I'm bored with it. What you're asking me to do is like asking Rubinstein to perform on a player-piano. Given the apparatus anybody could do it."

"You know of course that we asked you to make this film simply because you are the greatest magician in the world—the greatest magician of all time, if you like—and that gives tremendous added attraction to our film—"

"It's been many years since I was called an added attraction."

"Let me finish, please. We are presenting a great magician of today doing honour to a great magician of the past. People will love it."

"It shows me at a disadvantage."

"Oh, surely not. Consider the audience. After we have shown this on the B.B.C. it will appear on a great American network—the arrangements are almost complete—and then it will go all over the world. Think how it will be received in France alone, where there is still a great cult of Robert-Houdin. The eventual audience will be counted in millions. Can you be indifferent to that?"

"That just shows what you think about magic, and how much you know about it. I've already been seen all over the world. And I mean *I've been seen*, and the unique personal quality of my performance has been felt by audiences with whom I've created a unique relationship. You can't do that on television."

"That is precisely what I expect to do. I don't want to speak boastfully. Perhaps we have had enough boasting here tonight. But I am not unknown as a film-maker. I can say without immodesty that I'm just as famous in my line as you are in yours. I am a magician too, and not a trivial one—"

"If my work is trivial, why do you want my help? Film—yes, of course it's a commonplace nowadays that it is an art, just as people used to say that Robert-Houdin's complicated automatic toys were art. People are always charmed by clever mechanisms that give an effect of life. But don't you remember what the little actor in Noel Coward's play called film? 'A cheesy photograph'."

"Please—"

"Very well, let's not insist on 'cheesy'. But we can't escape 'photograph'. Something is missing, and you know what it is: the inexplicable but beautifully controlled sympathy between the artist and his audience. Film isn't even as good as the player-piano; at least you could add something personal to that, make it go fast or slow, loud or soft as you pleased."

"Film is like painting, which is also unchanging. But each viewer brings his personal sensibility, his unique response to the completed canvas as he does to the film."

"Who are your television viewers? Ragtag and bobtail; drunk and sober; attentive or in a nose-picking stupor. With the flabby concentration of people who are getting something for nothing. I am used to audiences who come because they want to see *me,* and have paid to do it. In the first five minutes I have made them attentive as they have never been before in their lives. I can't guarantee to do that on TV. I can't see my audience, and what I can't see I can't dominate. And what I can't dominate I can't enchant, and humour, and make partners in their own deception."

"You must understand that that is where my art comes in. I am your audience, and I contain in myself all these millions of whom we speak. You satisfy me and you satisfy them, as well. Because I credit them with my intelligence and sensitivity and raise them to my level. Have I not shown it in more than a dozen acknowledged film masterpieces? This is my gift and my art. Trust me. That is what I am asking you to do. Trust me."

2

This was the first serious quarrel since we had begun filming. Should I say "we"? As I was living in the house, and extremely curious about everything connected with the film, they let me hang around while they worked, and even gave me a job; as an historian I kept an eye on detail and did not allow the film-makers to stray too far from the period of Louis Philippe and his Paris, or at least no farther than artistic licence and necessity allowed. I had foreseen a quarrel. I was not seventy-two years old for nothing, and I knew Magnus Eisengrim very well. I thought I was beginning to know a little about the great director Jurgen Lind, too.

The project was to make an hour-long film for television about the great French illusionist, Jean-Eugène Robert-Houdin, who died in 1871. It was not simply to mark this centenary; as Lind had said, it would doubtless make the rounds of world television for years. The title was *Un Hommage à Robert-Houdin*—easily translatable—and its form was simple; the first twelve minutes were taken up with the story of his early life, as he told it in his *Confidences d'un prestidigitateur,* and for this actors had been employed; the remainder of the hour was to be an historical reproduction of one of Robert-Houdin's *Soirées Fantastiques* as he gave it in his own theatre in the Palais-Royal. And to play the part of the great conjuror the film-makers and the British Broadcasting Corporation had engaged, at a substantial fee, the greatest of living conjurors, my old friend Magnus Eisengrim.

If they had filmed it in a studio, I do not suppose I should have been involved at all, but the reproduction of Robert-Houdin's performance demanded so much magical apparatus, including several splendid automata which Eisengrim had made particularly for it, that it was decided to shoot this part of the picture in Switzerland, at Sorgenfrei, where Eisengrim's stage equipment was stored in a large disused riding-school on the estate. It was not a difficult matter for the scene designers and artificers to fit Robert-Houdin's tiny theatre, which had never seated more than two hundred spectators, into the space that was available.

This may have been a bad idea, for it mixed professional and domestic matters in a way that could certainly cause trouble. Eisengrim lived at Sorgenfrei, as permanent guest and—in a special sense—the lover of its owner and mistress, Dr. Liselotte Naegeli. I also had retired to Sorgenfrei after I had my heart attack, and dwelt there very happily as the permanent guest and—in a special sense—the lover of the same Dr. Liselotte, known to us both as Liesl. When I use the word "lover" to describe our relationship, I do not mean that we were a farcical *ménage à trois,* leaping in and out of bed at all hours and shrieking comic recriminations at one another. We did occasionally share a bed (usually at breakfast, when it was convenient and friendly for us all three to tuck up together and sample things from one another's trays), but the athleticism of love was a thing of the past for me, and I suspect it was becoming an infrequent adventure for Eisengrim. We loved Liesl none the less—indeed rather more, and differently—than in our hot days, and what with loving and arguing and laughing and talking, we fleeted the time carelessly, as they did in the Golden World.

Even the Golden World may have welcomed a change, now and then, and we had been pleased when Magnus received his offer from the B.B.C. Liesl and I, who knew more about the world, or at least the artistic part of it, than Eisengrim, were excited that the film was to be directed by the great Jurgen Lind, the Swedish film-maker whose work we both admired. We wanted to meet him, for though we were neither of us naive people we had not wholly lost our belief that it is delightful to meet artists who have given us pleasure. That was why Liesl proposed that, although the film crew were living at an inn not far down the mountain from Sorgenfrei, Lind and one or two of his immediate entourage should dine with us as often as they pleased, ostensibly so that we could continue discussion of the film as it progressed, but really so that we could become acquainted with Lind.

We should have known better. Had we learned nothing from our experience with Magnus Eisengrim, who had a full share, a share pressed down and overflowing, of the egotism of the theatre artist? Who could not bear the least slight; who expected, as of right, to be served first at table, and to go through all doors first; who made the most unholy rows and fusses if he were not treated virtually as royalty? Lind had not been on the spot a day before we knew that he was just such another as our dear old friend Magnus, and that they were not going to hit it off together.

Not that Lind was like him in external things. He was modest, reticent, dressed like a workman, and soft of speech. He always hung back at doors, cared nothing for the little ceremonials of daily life in a rich woman's house, and conferred with his chief colleagues about every detail. But it was clear that he expected and got his own way, once he had determined what it was.

Moreover, he seemed to me to be formidably intelligent. His long, sad, unsmiling face, with its hanging underlip that showed long, yellow teeth, the tragedy line of his eyelids, which began high on the bridge of his nose and swept miserably downward toward his cheeks, and the soft, bereaved tone of his voice, suggested a man who had seen too much to be amused by life; his great height—he was a little over six feet eight inches—gave him the air of a giant mingling with lesser creatures about whom he knew some unhappy secret which was concealed from themselves; he spoke slowly in an elegant English only slightly marked by that upper-class Swedish accent which suggests a man delicately sucking a lemon. He had been extensively educated—his junior assistants all were careful to speak of him as Dr. Lind—and he had as well that theatre artist's quality of seeming to know a great deal, without visible study or effort, about whatever was necessary for his immediate work. He did not know as much about the politics and economics of the reign of Louis Philippe as I did, for after all I had given my life to the study of history; but he seemed to know a great deal about its music, the way its clothes ought to be worn, the demeanour of its people, and its quality of life and spirit, which belonged to a sensibility far beyond mine. When historians meet with this kind of informed, imaginative sympathy with a past era in a non-historian, they are awed. How on earth does he know that, they are forced to ask themselves, and why did I never tumble to that? It takes a while to discover that the knowledge, though impressive and useful, has its limitations, and when the glow of imaginative creation no longer suffuses it, it is not really deeply grounded. But Lind was at work on the era of Louis Philippe, and specifically on the tiny part of it that applied to Robert-Houdin the illusionist, and for the present I was strongly under his spell.

That was the trouble. To put it gaudily but truly, that was where the canker gnawed. Liesl and I were both under Lind's spell, and Eisengrim's nose was out of joint.

That was why he was picking a quarrel with Lind, and Lind, who had been taught to argue logically, though unfairly, was at a disadvantage with a man who simply argued—pouted, rather—to get his own way and be cock of the walk again.

I thought I should do something about it, but I was forestalled by Roland Ingestree.

He was the man from the B.B.C., the executive producer of the film, or whatever the proper term is. He managed all the business, but was not simply a man of business, because he brooded, in a well-bred, don't-think-I'm-interfering-but manner, over the whole venture, including its artistic side. He was a sixtyish, fattish, bald Englishman who always wore gold-rimmed half-glasses, which gave him something of the air of Mr. Pickwick. But he was a shrewd fellow, and he had taken in the situation.

"We mustn't delude ourselves, Jurgen," he said. "Without Eisengrim this film would be nothing—nothing at all. He is the only man in the world who can reproduce the superlatively complex Robert-Houdin automata. It is quite understandable that he looks down on achievements that baffle lesser beings like ourselves. After all, as he points out, he is a magnificent classical conjuror, and he hasn't much use for mechanical toys. That's understood, of course. But what I think we've missed is that he's an actor of the rarest sort; he can really give us the outward form of Robert-Houdin, with all that refinement of manner and perfection of grace that made Robert-Houdin great. How he can do it, God alone knows, but he can. When I watch him in rehearsal I am utterly convinced that a man of the first half of the nineteenth century stands before me. Where could we have found anyone else who can act as he is acting? John? Too tall, too subjective. Larry? Too flamboyant, too corporeal. Guinness? Too dry. There's nobody else, you see. I hope I'm not being offensive, but I think it's as an actor we must think of Eisengrim. The conjuring might have been faked. But the acting—tell me, frankly, who else is there that could touch him?"

He was not being offensive, and well he knew it. Eisengrim glowed, and all might have been well if Kinghovn had not pushed the thing a little farther. Kinghovn was Lind's cameraman, and I gathered he was a great artist in his own right. But he was a man whose whole world was dominated by what he could see, and make other people see, and words were not his medium.

"Roly is right, Jurgen. This man is just right for looks. He compels belief. He can't go wrong. It is God's good luck, and we mustn't quarrel with it."

Now Lind's nose was out of joint. He had been trying to placate a prima donna, and his associates seemed to be accusing him of underestimating the situation. He was sure that he never underestimated anything about one of his films. He was accused of flying in the face of good luck, when he was certain that the best possible luck that could happen to any film was that he should be asked to direct it. The heavy lip fell a little lower, the eyes became a little sadder, and the emotional temperature of the room dropped perceptibly.

Ingestree put his considerable talents to the work of restoring Lind's self-esteem, without losing Eisengrim's goodwill.

"I think I sense what troubles Eisengrim about this whole Robert-Houdin business. It's the book. It's that wretched *Confidences d'un prestidigitateur*. We've been using it as a source for the biographical part of the film, and it's certainly a classic of its kind. But did anybody ever read such a book? Vanity is perfectly acceptable in an artist. Personally, I wouldn't give you sixpence for an artist who lacked vanity. But it's honest vanity I respect. The false modesty, the exaggerated humility, the greasy bourgeois assertions of respectability, of good-husband-and-father, of debt-paying worthiness are what make the *Confidences* so hard to swallow. Robert-Houdin was an oddity; he was an artist who wanted to pass as a bourgeois. I'm sure that's what irritates both you men, and sets you against each other. You feel that you are putting your very great, fully realized artistic personalities to the work of exalting a man whose attitude toward life you despise. I don't blame you for being irritable—because you have been, you know; you've been terribly irritable tonight—but that's what art is, as you very well know, much of the time: the transformation and glorification of the commonplace."

"The revelation of the glory in the commonplace," said Lind, who had no objection to being told that his vanity was an admirable and honest trait, and was coming around.

"Precisely. The revelation of the glory in the commonplace. And you two very great artists—the great film director and (may I say it) the great actor—are revealing the glory in Robert-Houdin, who perversely sought to conceal his own artistry behind that terrible good-citizen mask. It hampered him, of course, because it was against the grain of his talent. But you two are able to do an extraordinary, a metaphysical thing. You are able to show the world, a century after his death, what Robert-Houdin would have been if he had truly understood himself."

Eisengrim and Lind were liking this. Magnus positively beamed, and Lind's sad eyes rolled toward him with a glance from which the frost was slowly disappearing. Ingestree was well in the saddle now, and was riding on to victory.

"You are both men of immeasurably larger spirit than he. What was he, after all? The good citizen, the perfection of the bourgeoisie under Louis Philippe that he pretended? Who can believe it? There is in every artist something black, something savouring of the crook, which he may not even understand himself, and which he certainly keeps well out of the eye of his public. What was it in Robert-Houdin?

"He gives us a sniff of it in the very first chapter of his other book, which I have read, and which is certainly familiar to you, Mr. Ramsay"—this with a nod to me—"called *Les Secrets de la prestidigitation et de la magie*—"

"My God, I read it as a boy!" I said.

"Very well. Then you recall the story of his beginnings as a magician? How he was befriended by the Count de l'Escalopier? How this nobleman gave a private show in his house, where Robert-Houdin amused the guests? How his best trick was burning a piece of paper on which the Archbishop of Paris had written a splendid compliment to Robert-Houdin, and the discovery of the piece of paper afterward in the smallest of twelve envelopes which were all sealed, one inside the other? It was a trick he learned from his master, de Grisy. But how did he try to make it up to l'Escalopier for putting him on his feet?"

"The trap for the robber," I said.

"Exactly. A thief was robbing l'Escalopier blind, and nothing he tried would catch him. So Robert-Houdin offered to help, and what did he do? He worked out a mechanism to be concealed in the Count's desk, so that when the robber opened it a pistol would be discharged, and a claw made of sharp needles would seize the thief's hand and crunch the world 'Voleur' on the back of it. The needles were impregnated with silver nitrate, so that it was in effect tattooing—branding the man for life. A nice fellow, eh? And do you remember what he says? That this nasty thing was a refinement of a little gubbins he had made as a boy, to catch and mark another boy who was pinching things from his school locker. That was the way Robert-Houdin's mind worked; he fancied himself as a thief-catcher. Now, in a man who makes such a parade of his integrity, what does that suggest? Over-compensation, shall we say? A deep, unresting doubt of his own honesty?

"If we had time, and the gift, we could learn a lot about the inner life of Robert-Houdin by analysing his tricks. Why are so many of the best of them concerned with giving things away? He gave away pastries, sweets, ribbons, fans, all sorts of stuff at every performance; yet we know how careful he was with money. What was all that generosity meant to conceal? Because he was concealing something, take my word for it. The whole of the *Confidences* is a gigantic whitewash job, a concealment. Analyse the tricks and you will get a subtext for the autobiography, which seems so delightfully bland and cosy.

"And that's what we need for our film. A subtext. A reality running like a subterranean river under the surface; an enriching, but not necessarily edifying, background to what is seen.

"Where are we to get it? Not from Robert-Houdin. Too much trouble and perhaps not worth the trouble when we got it. No. It must come from the working together of you two great artists: Lind the genius-director and Eisengrim the genius-actor. And you must fish it up out of your own guts."

"But that is what I always do," said Lind.

"Of course. But Eisengrim must do it, as well. Now tell me, sir: you can't always have been the greatest conjuror in the world. You learned your art somewhere. If we asked you—invited you—begged you—to make your own experience the subtext for this film about a man, certainly lesser than yourself, but of great and lasting fame in his special line, what would it be?"

I was surprised to see Eisengrim look as if he were considering this question very seriously. He never revealed anything about his past life, or his innermost thoughts, and it was only because I had known him—with very long intervals of losing him—since we had been boys together, that I knew anything about him at all. I had fished—fished cunningly with the subtlest lures I could devise—for more information about him than I had, but he was too clever for me. But here he was, swimming in the flattery of this clever Englishman Ingestree, and he looked as if he might be about to spill the beans. Well, anyhow I would be present when, and if, he did so. After some consideration, he spoke.

"The first thing I would tell you would be that my earliest instructor was the man you see in that chair yonder: Dunstan Ramsay. God knows he was the worst conjuror the world has ever seen, but he introduced me to conjuring, and by a coincidence his textbook was *The Secrets of Stage Conjuring*, by the man we are all talking about and, if you are right in what you say, Mr. Ingestree, serving! Robert-Houdin."

This caused some sensation, as Eisengrim knew it would. Ingestree, having forced the oyster to yield a little, pressed the knife in. "Wonderful! We would never have taken Ramsay for a conjuror. But there must have been somebody else. If Ramsay was your first master, who was your second?"

"I'm not sure I'm going to tell you," said Eisengrim. "I'll have to think about it very carefully. Your idea of a subtext—the term and the idea are both new to me—is interesting. I'll tell you this much. I began to learn conjuring seriously on August 30, 1918. That was the day I descended into hell, and did not rise again for seven years. I'll consider whether I'm going to go farther than that. Now I'm going to bed."

3

Liesl had said little during the quarrel—or rivalry of egotisms, or whatever you choose to call it—but she caught me the following morning before the film crew arrived, and seemed to be in high spirits.

"So Magnus has come to the confessional moment in his life," she said. "It's been impending for several months. Didn't you notice? You didn't! Oh, Ramsay, you are such a dunce about some things. If Magnus were the kind of man who could write an autobiography, this is when he would do it."

"Magnus has an autobiography already. I should know. I wrote it."

"A lovely book. *Phantasmata: the Life and Adventures of Mag-*

nus Eisengrim. But that was for sale at his performances; a kind of super-publicity. A splendid Gothic invention from your splendid Gothic imagination."

"That's not the way he regards it. When people ask he tells them that it is a poetic autobiography, far more true to the man he has become than any merely factual account of his experience could be."

"I know. I told him to say that. You don't suppose he thought it out himself, do you? You know him. He's marvelously intelligent in his own way—sensitive, aware, and intuitive—but it's not a literary or learned intelligence. Magnus is a truly original creature. They are of the greatest rarity. And as I say, he's reached the confessional time of life. I expect we shall hear some strange things."

"Not as strange as I could tell about him."

"I know, I know. You are obsessed with the idea that his mother was a saint. Ramsay, in all your rummaging among the lives of the saints, did you ever encounter one who had a child? What was that child like? Perhaps we shall hear."

"I'm a little miffed that he considers telling these strangers things he's never told to you and me."

"Ass! It's always strangers who turn the tap that lets out the truth. Didn't you yourself babble out all the secrets of your life to me within a couple of weeks of our first meeting? Magnus is going to tell."

"But why, now?"

"Because he wants to impress Lind. He's terribly taken with Lind, and he has his little fancies, like the rest of us. Once he wanted to impress me, but it wasn't the right time in his life to spill the whole bottle."

"But Ingestree suggested that Lind might do some telling, too. Are we to have a great mutual soul-scrape?"

"Ingestree is very foxy, behind all that fat and twinkling bonhomie. He knows Lind won't tell anything. For one thing, it's not his time; he's only forty-three. And he is inhibited by his education; it makes people cagey. What he tells us he tells through his films, just as Ingestree suggested that Robert-Houdin revealed himself through his tricks. But Magnus is retired—or almost. Also he is not inhibited by education, which is the great modern destroyer of truth and originality. Magnus knows no history. Have you ever seen him read a book? He really thinks that whatever has happened to him is unique. It is an enviable characteristic."

"Well, every life is unique."

"To a point. But there are only a limited number of things a human creature can do."

"So you think he is going to tell all?"

"Not all. Nobody tells that. Indeed, nobody knows everything about themselves. But I'll bet you anything you like he tells a great deal."

I argued no further. Liesl is very shrewd about such things. The morning was spent in arrangements about lighting. A mobile generator from Zürich had to be put in place, and all the lamps connected and hung; the riding-school was a jungle of pipe-scaffolding and cable. Kinghovn fussed over differences which seemed to me imperceptible, and as a script-girl stood in for Eisengrim while the lighting was being completed, he had time to wander about the riding-school, and as lunchtime approached he steered me off into a corner.

"Tell me about subtext," he said.

"It's a term modern theatre people are very fond of. It's what a character thinks and knows, as opposed to what the playwright makes him say. Very psychological."

"Give me an example."

"Do you know Ibsen's *Hedda Gabler*?"

He didn't, and it was a foolish question. He didn't know anything about any literature whatever. I waded in.

"It's about a beautiful and attractive woman who has married, as a last resort, a man she thinks very dull. They have returned from a honeymoon during which she has become greatly disillusioned with him, but she knows she is already pregnant. In the first act she is talking to her husband's adoring aunt, trying to be civil as the old woman prattles on about the joys of domesticity and the achievements of her nephew. But all the time she has, in her mind, the knowledge that he is dull, timid, a tiresome lover, that she is going to have a child by him, and that she fears childbirth. That's the subtext. The awareness of it thickens up the actress's performance, and emphasizes the irony of the situation."

"I understand. It seems obvious."

"First-rate actors have always been aware of it, but dramatists like Shakespeare usually brought the subtext up to the surface and gave it to the audience directly. Like Hamlet's soliloquies."

"I've never seen *Hamlet.*"

"Well—that's subtext."

"Do you think the circumstances of my own life really form a subtext for this film?"

"God only knows. One thing is certain: unless you choose to tell Lind and his friends about your life, it can't do so."

"You're quite wrong. I would know, and I suppose whatever I do is rooted in what I am, and have been."

It was never wise to underestimate Magnus, but I was always doing so. The pomposity of the learned. Because he didn't know *Hamlet* and *Hedda* I tended to think him simpler than he was.

"I'm thinking of telling them a few things, Dunny. I might surprise them. They're all so highly educated, you know. Education is a great shield against experience. It offers so much, ready-made and all from the best shops, that there's a temptation to miss your own life in pursuing the lives of your betters. It makes you wise in some ways, but it can make you a blindfolded fool in others. I think I'll surprise them. They talk so much about art, but really, education is just as much a barrier between a man and real art as it is in other parts of life. They don't know what a mean old bitch art can be. I think I'll surprise them."

So Liesl had been right! He was ready to spill.

Well, I was ready to hear. Indeed, I was eager to hear. My reason was deep and professional. As an historian I had all my life been aware of the extraordinary importance of documents. I had handled hundreds of them: letters, reports, memoranda, sometimes diaries; I had always treated them with respect, and had come in time to have an affection for them. They summed up something that was becoming increasingly important to me, and that was an earthly form of immortality. Historians come and go, but the document remains, and it has the importance of a thing that cannot be changed or gainsaid. Whoever wrote it continues to speak through it. It might be honest and it might be complete: on the other hand it could be thoroughly crooked or omit something of importance. But there it was, and it was all succeeding ages possessed.

I deeply wanted to create, or record, and leave behind me a document, so that whenever its subject was dealt with in future, the notation "Ramsay says . . ." would have to appear. Thus, so far as this world is concerned, I should not wholly die. Well, here was my chance.

Would anyone care? Indeed they would. I had written an imaginative account of the life of Magnus Eisengrim, the great conjuror and illusionist, at his own request and that of Liesl, who had been the manager and in a very high degree the brains of his great show, the *Soirée of Illusions*. The book was sold in the foyers of any theatre in which he appeared, but it had also had a flattering success on its own account; it sold astonishingly in the places where the really big sales of books are achieved—cigar stores, airports, and bus stops. It had extravagantly outsold all my other books, even my *Hundred Saints for Travellers* and my very popular *Celtic Saints of Britain and Europe*. Why? Because it was a wonderfully good book of its kind. Readable by the educated, but not rebuffing to somebody who simply wanted a lively, spicy tale.

Its authorship was still a secret, for although I received a half-share of the royalties it was ostensibly the work of Magnus Eisengrim. It had done great things for him. People who believed what they read came to see the man who had lived the richly adventurous and macabre life described in it; sophisticates came to see the man who had written such gorgeous, gaudy lies about himself. As Liesl said, it was Gothic, full of enormities bathed in the delusive lights of nineteenth-century romance. But it was modern enough, as well; it touched the sexy, rowdy string so many readers want to hear.

Some day it would be known that I had written it. We had already received at Sorgenfrei a serious film offer and a number of inquiries from earnest Ph.D. students who explained apologetically that they were making investigations, of one kind or another, of what they called "popular literature". And when it became known that I had written it, which would probably not be until Eisengrim and I were both dead, then—Aha! then my document would come into its own. For then the carefully tailored life of Magnus Eisengrim, which had given pleasure to so many millions in English, French, German, Danish, Italian, Spanish, and Portuguese, and had been accorded the distinction of a pirated version in Japanese, would be compared with the version I would prepare from Eisengrim's own confessions, and "Ramsay says . . ." would certainly be heard loud and clear.

Was this a base ambition for an historian and a hagiologist? What had Ingestree said? In every artist there is something black, something savouring of the crook. Was I, in a modest way, an artist? I was beginning to wonder. No, no; unless I falsified the record what could be dishonest, or artistic, about making a few notes?

4

"I have spent a good deal of time since last night wondering whether I should tell you anything about my life," said Eisengrim, after dinner that evening, "and I think I shall, on the condition that you regard it as a secret among ourselves. After all, the audience doesn't have to know the subtext, does it? Your film isn't Shakespeare, where everything is revealed; it is Ibsen, where much is implied."

How quickly he learns, I thought. And how well he knows the power of pretending something is secret which he has every intention of revealing. I turned up my mental, wholly psychological historian's hearing-aid, determined to miss nothing, and to get at least the skeleton of it on paper before I went to sleep.

"Begin with going to hell," said Ingestree. "You've given us a date: August 30, 1918. You told us you knew Ramsay when you were a boy, so I suppose you must be a Canadian. If I were going to hell, I don't think I'd start from Canada. What happened?"

"I went to the village fair. Our village, which was called Deptford, had a proud local reputation for its fair. Schoolchildren were admitted free. That helped to swell the attendance, and the Fair Board liked to run up the biggest possible annual figure. You wouldn't imagine there was anything wrong in what I did, but judged by the lights of my home it was sin. We were an unusually religious household, and my father mistrusted the fair. He had promised me that he might, if I could repeat the whole of Psalm 79 without an error, at suppertime, take me to the fair in the evening, to see the animals. This task of memorizing was part of a great undertaking that he had set his heart on: I was to get the whole of the Book of Psalms by heart. He assured me that it would be a bulwark and a stay to me through the whole of my life. He wasn't rushing the job; I was supposed to learn ten verses each day, but as I was working for a treat, he thought I might run to the thirteen verses of Psalm 79 to get to the fair. But the treat was conditional; if I stumbled, the promise about the fair was off."

"It sounds very much like rural Sweden, when I was a boy," said Kinghovn. "How do the children of such people grow up?"

"Ah, but you mustn't misunderstand. My father wasn't a tyrant; he truly wanted to protect me against evil."

"A fatal desire in a parent," said Lind, who was known throughout the world—to film-goers at least—as an expert on evil.

"There was a special reason. My mother was an unusual person. If you want to know the best about her, you must apply to Ramsay. I don't suppose I can tell you my own story without giving you something of the other side of her nature. She was supposed to have some very bad instincts, and our family suffered for it. She had to be kept under confinement. My father, with what I suppose must be described as compassion, wanted to make sure I wouldn't follow in her ways. So, from the age of eight, I was set to work to acquire the bulwark and the stay of the Psalms, and in a year and a half—something like that—I had gnawed my way through them up to Psalm 79."

"How old were you?" said Ingestree.

"Getting on for ten. I wanted fiercely to go to the fair, so I set to work on the Psalm. Do you know the Psalms? I have never been able to make head or tail of a lot of them, but others strike with a terrible truth on your heart, if you meet them at the right time. I plugged on till I came to *We are become a reproach to our neighbours, a scorn and derision to them that are round about us.* Yes! Yes, there we were! The Dempsters, a reproach to our neighbours, a scorn and derision to the whole village of Deptford. And particularly to the children of Deptford, with whom I had to go to school. School was to begin on the day after Labour Day, less than a week from the day when I sat puzzling over Psalm 79. Tell me, Lind, you know so much about evil, and have explored it in your films, Liesl tells me, like a man with an ordnance map in his hand; have you ever explored the evil of children?"

"Even I have never dared to do that," said Lind, with the tragic grin which was the nearest he ever came to a laugh.

"If you ever decide to do so, call me in as a special adviser. It's a primal evil, a pure malignance. They really enjoy giving pain. This is described by sentimentalists as innocence. I was tormented by the children of our village from the earliest days I can remember. My mother had done something—I never found out what it was—that made most of the village hate her, and the children knew that, so it was all right to hate me and torture me. They said my mother was a hoor—that was the local pronunciation of whore—and they tormented me with a virtuosity they never showed in anything else they did. When I cried, somebody might say, 'Aw, let the kid alone; he can't help it his mother's a hoor.' I suppose the philosopher-kings who struggled up to that level have since become the rulers of the place. But I soon determined not to cry.

"Not that I became hard. I simply accepted the wretchedness of my station. Not that I hated them—not then; I learned to hate them later in life. At that time I simply assumed that children must be as they were. I was a misfit in the world, and didn't know why.

"Onward I went with Psalm 79. *O remember not against us former iniquities: let thy tender mercies speedily prevent us: for we are brought very low.* But as soon as I put my nose into the schoolyard they would remember former iniquities against me. God's tender mercies had never reached the Deptford schoolyard. And I was unquestionably brought very low, for all that desolation would begin again next Tuesday.

"Having got that far with me, Satan had me well on the path to hell. I knew where some money was kept; it was small change for the baker and the milkman when they called; under my mother's very nose—she was sitting in a chair, staring into space, tied by a rope to a ringbolt my father had set in the wall—I pinched fifteen cents; I held it up so that she could see it, so that she would think I was going to pay one of the deliverymen. Then I ran off to the fair, and my heart was full of terrible joy. I was wicked, but O what a delicious release it was!

"I pieced out the enjoyment of the fair like a gourmet savouring a feast. Begin at the bottom, with what was least amusing. That would be the Women's Institute display of bottled pickles, embalmed fruit, doilies, home-cooking, and 'fancy-work'. Then the animals, the huge draught-horses, the cows with enormous udders, the prize bull (though I did not go very near to him, for some of my schoolmates were lingering there, to snigger and work themselves up into a horny stew, gaping at his enormous testicles), the pigs so unwontedly clean, and the foolish poultry, White Wyandottes, Buff Orpingtons, and Mrs. Forrester's gorgeous Cochin Chinas, and in a corner a man from the Department of Agriculture giving an educational display of egg-candling.

"Pleasure now began to be really intense. I looked with awe and some fear at the display from the nearby Indian Reservation. Men with wrinkled, tobacco-coloured faces sat behind a stand, not really offering slim walking-canes, with ornate whittled handles into which patterns of colour had been worked; their women, as silent and unmoving as they, displayed all sorts of fancy boxes made of sweet-grass, ornamented with beads and dyed porcupine quill. But these goods, which had some merit as craftwork, were not so gorgeous in my eyes as the trash offered by a booth which was not of local origin, in which a man sold whirligigs of gaudy celluloid, kewpie dolls with tinsel skirts riding high over their gross stomachs, alarm-clocks with *two* bells for determined sleepers, and beautiful red or blue ponywhips. I yearned toward those whips, but they cost a whole quarter apiece, and were thus out of my reach.

"But I was not cut off from all the carnal pleasures of the fair. After a great deal of deliberation I spent five of my ill-gotten cents on a large paper cornet of pink candy floss, a delicacy I had never seen before. It had little substance, and made my mouth sticky and dry, but it was a luxury, and my life had known nothing of luxuries.

"Then, after a full ten minutes of deliberation, I laid out another five cents on a ride on the merry-go-round. I chose my mount with care, a splendid dapple-grey with flaring nostrils, ramping wonderfully up and down on his brass pole; he seemed to me like the horse in Job that saith among the trumpets, Ha, ha; for a hundred and eighty seconds I rode him in ecstasy, and dismounted only when I was chased away by the man who took care of such things and was on the look-out for enchanted riders like myself.

"But even this was only leading up to what I knew to be the crown of the fair. That was Wanless's World of Wonders, the one pleasure which my father would certainly never have permitted me. Shows of all kinds were utterly evil in his sight, and this was a show that turned my bowels to water, even from the outside.

"The tent seemed vast to me, and on a scaffold on its outside were big painted pictures of the wonders within. A Fat Woman, immense and pink, beside whom even the biggest pigs in the agricultural tents were starvelings. A man who ate fire. A Strong Man, who would wrestle with anybody who dared to try it. A Human Marvel, half man and half woman. A Missing Link, in itself worth more than the price of admission, because it was powerfully educational, illustrating what Man had been before he decided to settle in such places as Deptford. On a raised platform outside the tent a man in fine clothes was shouting to the crowd about everything that was to be seen; it was before the days of microphones, and he roared hoarsely through a megaphone. Beside him stood the Fire Eater, holding a flaming torch in front of his mouth. 'See Molza, the man who can always be sure of a hot meal,' bellowed the man in the fine clothes, and a few Deptfordians laughed shyly. 'See Professor Spencer, born without arms, but he can write a finer hand with his feet than any of your schoolteachers. And within the tent the greatest physiological marvel of the age, Andro, the Italian nobleman so evenly divided between the sexes that you may see him shave the whiskers offa the one side of his face, while the other displays the peachy smoothness of a lovely woman. A human miracle, attested to by doctors and men of science at Yale, Harvard, and Columbia. Any local doctor wishing to examine this greatest of marvels may make an appointment to do so, in the presence of myself, after the show tonight.'

"But I was not very attentive to the man in the fine clothes, because my eyes were all for another figure on the platform, who was doing wonders with decks of cards; he whirled them out from his hands in what appeared to be ribbons, and then drew them—magically it seemed to me—back into his hands again. He spread them in fans. He made them loop-the-loop from one hand to another. The man in the fine clothes introduced him as Willard the Wizard, positively the greatest artist in sleight-of-hand in the world today, briefly on loan from the Palace Theatre in New York.

"Willard was a tall man, and looked even taller because he wore what was then called a garter-snake suit, which had wriggling lines of light and dark fabric running perpendicularly through it. He was crowned by a pearl-grey hard hat—what we called a Derby, and known in Deptford only as part of the Sunday dress of doctors and other grandees. He was the most elegant thing I had ever seen in my life, and his thin, unsmiling face spoke to me of breathtaking secrets. I could not take my eyes off him, nor did I try to still my ravening desire to know those secrets. I too was a conjuror, you see; I had continued, on the sly, to practise the few elementary sleights and passes I had learned from Ramsay, before my father put a stop to it. I longed with my whole soul to know what Willard knew. As the hart pants after the water brooks, even so my blasphemous soul panted after the Wizard. And the unbelievable thing was that, of the fifteen or twenty people gathered in front of the platform, he seemed to look most often at me, and once I could swear I saw him wink!

"I paid my five cents—a special price for schoolchildren until six o'clock—and entered in the full splendour of Wanless's World of Wonders. It is impossible for me to describe the impression it made on me then, because I came to know it so well later on. It was just a fair-sized tent, capable of holding ten or twelve exhibits and the spectators. It was of that discouraged whitey-grey colour that such tents used to be before somebody had the good idea of colouring canvas brown. A few strings of lights hung between the three main poles, but they were not on, because it was assumed that we could see well enough by the light that leaked in from outdoors. The exhibits were on stands the height of a table; indeed, they were like collapsible tables, and each exhibit had his own necessities. Professor Spencer had the blackboard on which he wrote so elegantly with his feet; Molza had his jet of flaming gas, and a rack to hold the swords he swallowed; it was really, I suppose, very tacky and ordinary. But I was under the spell of Willard, and I didn't, at that time, take much heed of anything else, not even of the clamorous Fat Woman, who seemed never to be wholly quiet, even when the other exhibits were having their turn.

"The loud-voiced man had followed us inside, and bellowed about each wonder as we toured round the circle. Even to such an innocent as I, it was plain that the wonders were shown in an ascending order of importance, beginning with the Knife Thrower and Molza, and working upward through Zovene the Midget Juggler and Sonny the Strong Man to Professor Spencer and Zitta the Serpent Woman. She seemed to mark a divide, and after her came Rango the Missing Link, then the Fat Woman, called Happy Hannah, then Willard, and finally Andro the Half-Man Half-Woman.

"Even though my eyes constantly wandered toward Willard, who seemed now and then to meet them with a dark and enchantingly wizard-like gaze, I was too prudent to ignore the lesser attractions. After all, I had invested five ill-gotten cents in this adventure, and I was in no position to throw money away. But we came to Willard at last, and the loud-voiced man did not need to introduce him, because even before Happy Hannah had finished her noisy harangue and had begun to sell pictures of herself, he threw away his cigarette, sprang to his feet, and began to pluck coins out of the air. He snatched them from everywhere—from the backs of his knees, from his elbows, from above his head—and threw them into a metal basin on his little tripod table. You could hear them clink as they fell, and as the number increased the sound from the basin changed. Then, without speaking a word, he seized the basin and hurled its contents into the crowd. People ducked and shielded their faces. But the basin was empty! Willard laughed a mocking laugh. Oh, very Mephistophelian! It sounded like a trumpet call to me, because I had never heard anybody laugh like that before. He was laughing at us, for having been deceived. What power! What glorious command over lesser humanity! Silly people often say that they are enraptured by something which has merely pleased them, but I was truly enraptured. I was utterly unaware of myself, whirled into a new sort of comprehension of life by what I saw.

"You must understand that I had never seen a conjuror before. I knew what conjuring was, and I could do some tricks. But I had never seen anybody else do sleight-of-hand except Ramsay here, who made very heavy weather of getting one poor coin from one of his great red hands to the other, and if he had not explained that the pass was supposed to be invisible you would never have known it was a trick at all. Please don't be hurt, Ramsay. You are a dear fellow and rather a famous writer in your own line, but as a conjuror you were abject. But Willard! For me the Book of Revelation came alive: here was an angel come down from heaven, having great power, and the earth was lightened with his glory; if only I could be like him, surely there would be no more sorrow, nor crying, nor any more pain, and all former things—my dark home, my mad, disgraceful mother, the torment of school—would pass away."

"So you ran away with the show," said Kinghovn, who had no tact.

"Ramsay tells me they say in Deptford that I ran away with the show," said Eisengrim, smiling what I would myself have called a Mephistophelian smile, beneath which he looked like any other man whose story has been interrupted by somebody who doesn't understand the form and art of stories. "I don't think Deptford would ever comprehend that it was not a matter of choice. But if you have understood what I have said about the way Deptford regarded me, you will realize that I had no choice. I did not run away with the show; the show ran away with me."

"Because you were so utterly entranced by Willard?" said Ingestree.

"No, I think our friend means something more than that," said Lind. "These possessions of the soul are very powerful, but there must have been something else. I smell it. The Bible obsession must somehow have supported the obsession with the conjuror. Not even a great revelation wipes out a childhood's indoctrination; the two must have come together in some way."

"You are right," said Eisengrim. "And I begin to see why people call you a great artist. Your education and sophistication haven't gobbled up your understanding of the realities of life. Let me go on.

"Willard's show had to be short, because there were ten exhibits in the tent, and a full show was not supposed to run over forty-five minutes. As one of the best attractions he was allowed something like five minutes, and after the trick with the coins he did some splendid things with ribbons, pulling them out of his mouth and throwing them into the bowl, from which he produced them neatly braided. Then he did some very flashy things with cards, causing any card chosen by a member of the audience to pop out of a pack that was stuck in a wineglass as far away from himself as his platform allowed. He finished by eating a spool of thread and a packet of needles, and then producing the thread from his mouth, with all the needles threaded on it at intervals of six inches. During the Oohs and Aahs, he nonchalantly produced the wooden spool from his ear, and threw it into the audience—threw it so that I caught it. I remember being amazed that it wasn't even wet, which shows how very green I was.

"I didn't want to see Andro, whose neatly compartmentalized sexuality meant nothing to me. As the crowd moved on to hear the loud-mouthed man bellow about the medical miracle called hermaphroditism—*only one in four hundred million births, ladies and gentlemen, only six thoroughly proven hermaphrodites in the whole long history of mankind, and one of them stands before you in Deptford today!*—I hung around Willard's table. He leapt down from it and lighted another cigarette. Even the way he did that was magical, for he flicked the pack toward his mouth, and the cigarette leaped between his lips, waiting for the match he was striking with the thumbnail of his other hand. There I was, near enough to the Wizard to touch him. But it was he who touched me. He reached toward my left ear and produced a quarter from it, and flicked it toward me. I snatched it out of the air, and handed it back to him. 'No, it's for you, kid,' he said. His voice was low and hoarse, and not in keeping with the rest of his elegant presentation, but I didn't care. A quarter! For me! I had never known such riches in my life. My infrequent stealings had never, before this day, aspired beyond a nickel. The man was not only a Wizard; he was princely.

"I was inspired. Inspired by you, Ramsay, you may be surprised to hear. You remember your trick in which you pretended to eat money, though one could always see it in your hand as you took it away from your mouth? I did that. I popped the quarter into my mouth, chewed it up, showed Willard that it was gone, and that I had nothing in my hands. I could do a little magic, too, and I was eager to claim some kinship with this god.

"He did not smile. He put his hand on my shoulder and said, 'Come with me, kid. I got sumpn to show ya,' and steered me toward a back entry of the tent which I had not noticed.

"We walked perhaps halfway around the fairground, which was not really very far, and we kept behind tents and buildings. I would have been proud to be seen by the crowd with such a hero, but we met very few people, and they were busy with their own affairs in the agricultural tents, so I do not suppose anybody noticed us. We came to the back of the barn where the horses were stabled when they were not being shown; it was one of the two or three permanent buildings of the fair. Behind it was a lean-to with a wall which did not quite reach to the roof, nor fully to the ground. It was the men's urinal, old, dilapidated, and smelly. Willard peeped in, found it empty, and pushed me in ahead of him. I had never been in such a place before, because it was part of my training that one never 'went' anywhere except at home, and all arrangements had to be made to accommodate this rule. It was a queer place, as I remember it; just a tin trough nailed to the wall, sloping slightly downward so that it drained into a hole in the ground. A pile of earth was ready to fill in the hole, once the fair was over.

"At the end of this shanty was a door which hung partly open, and it was through this that Willard guided me. We were in an earth closet, as old as Deptford fair, I should judge, for a heavy, sweetish, old smell hung over it. Hornets buzzed under the sloping roof. The two holes in the seat were covered by rounds of wood, with crude handles. I think I would know them if I saw them now.

"Willard took a clean white handkerchief out of his pocket, twisted it quickly into a roll, and forced it between my teeth. No: I should not say 'forced'. I thought this was the beginning of some splendid illusion, and opened my mouth willingly. Then he whirled me round, lifted me up on the seat in a kneeling position, pulled down my pants and sodomized me.

"Quickly said: an eternity in the doing. I struggled and resisted: he struck me such a blow over the ear that I slackened my grip with the pain, and he had gained an entry. It was rough: it was painful, and I suppose it was soon over. But as I say, it seemed an eternity, for it was a kind of feeling I had never guessed at.

"I am anxious you should not misunderstand me. I was no Greek lad, discovering the supposed pleasures of pederastic love in a society that knew it and condoned it. I was a boy not yet quite ten years old, who did not know what sex was in any form. I thought I was being killed, and in a shameful way.

"The innocence of children is very widely misunderstood. Few of them—I suppose only children brought up in wealthy families that desire and can contrive a conspiracy of ignorance—are unknowing about sex. No child brought up so near the country as I was, and among schoolchildren whose ages might reach as high as fifteen or sixteen, can be utterly ignorant of sex. It had touched me, but not intimately. For one thing, I had heard the whole of the Bible read through several times by my father; he had a plan of readings which, pursued morning and evening, worked through the whole of the book in a year. I had heard the sound as an infant, and as a little child, long before I could understand anything of the sense. So I knew about men going in unto women, and people raising up seed of their loins, and I knew that my father's voice took on a special tone of shame and detestation when he read about Lot and his daughters, though I had never followed what it was they did in that cave, and thought their sin was to make their father drunk. I knew these things because I had heard them, but they had no reality for me.

"As for my mother, who was called hoor by my schoolmates, I knew only that hoors—my father used the local pronunciation, and I don't think he knew any other—were always turning up in the Bible, and always in a bad sense which meant nothing to me as a reality. Ezekiel, sixteen, was a riot of whoredoms and abominations, and I shivered to think how terrible they must be: but I did not know what they were, even in the plainest sense of the words. I only knew that there was something filthy and disgraceful that pertained to my mother, and that we all, my father and I, were spattered by her shame, or abomination, or whatever it might be.

"I was aware that there was some difference between boys and girls, but I didn't know, or want to know, what it was, because I connected it somehow with the shame of my mother. You couldn't be a hoor unless you were a woman, and they had something special that made it possible. What I had, as a male, I had most strictly been warned against as an evil and shameful part of my body

'Don't you ever monkey with yourself, down there,' was the full extent of the sexual instruction I had from my father. I knew that the boys who were gloating over the bull's testicles were doing something dirty, and my training was such that I was both disgusted and terrified by their sly nastiness. But I didn't know why, and it never would have occurred to me to relate the bull's showy apparatus with those things I possessed, in so slight a degree, and which I wasn't to monkey with. So you can see that without being utterly ignorant, I was innocent, in my way. If I had not been innocent, how could I have lived my life, and even have felt some meagre joy, from time to time?

"Sometimes I felt that joy when I was with you, Ramsay, because you were kind to me, and kindness was a great rarity in my life. You were the only person in my childhood who had treated me as if I were a human creature. I don't say, who loved me, you notice. My father loved me, but his love was a greater burden, almost, than hate might have been. But you treated me as a fellow-being, because I don't suppose it ever occurred to you to do anything else. You never ran with the crowd.

"The rape itself was horrible, because it was painful physically, but worse because it was an outrage on another part of my body which I had been told to fear and be ashamed of. Liesl tells me that Freud has had a great deal to say about the importance of the functions of excretion in deciding and moulding character. I don't know anything about that; don't want to know it, because all that sort of thinking lies outside what I really understand. I have my own notions about psychology, and they have served me well. But this rape—it was something filthy going in where I knew only that filthy things should come out, as secretly as could be managed. In our house there was no word for excretion, only two or three prim locutions, and the word used in the schoolyard seemed to me a horrifying indecency. It's very popular nowadays in literature, I'm told by Liesl. She reads a great deal. I don't know how writers can put it down, though there was a time when I used it often enough in my daily speech. But as I have grown older I have returned to that early primness. We don't get over some things. But what Willard did to me was, in a sense I could understand, a reversal of the order of nature, and I was terrified that it would kill me.

"It didn't, of course. But that, and Willard's heavy breathing, and the flood of filthy language that he whispered as a kind of ecstatic accompaniment to what he was doing, were more horrible to me than anything I have met with since.

"When it was over he pulled my head around so that he could see my face and said, 'You O.K., kid?' I can remember the tone now. He had no idea at all of what I was, or what I might feel. He was obviously happy, and the Mephistophelian smile had given place to an expression that was almost boyish. 'Go on now,' he said. 'Pull up your pants and beat it. And if you blat to anybody, by the living Jesus I'll cut your nuts off with a rusty knife.'

"Then I fainted, but for how long, or what I looked like when I did it, I of course can't tell you. Perhaps I was out for a few minutes, because when I became aware again Willard was looking anxious, and patting my cheeks lightly. He had taken the gag out of my mouth. I was crying, but making no noise. I had learned very early in life not to make a noise when I cried. I was still crumpled up on the horrible seat, and now its stench was too much for me and I vomited. Willard sprang back, anxious for his fine trousers and the high polish on his shoes. But he dared not leave me. Of course I had no idea how frightened he was. He felt he could trust in my shame and his threats up to a point, but I might be one of those terrible children who go beyond the point set for them by adults. He tried to placate me.

" 'Hey,' he whispered, 'you're a pretty smart kid. Where'd you learn that trick with the quarter, eh? Come on now, show it to me again. I never seen a better trick than that, even at the Palace, New York. You're the kid that eats money; that's who you are. A real show-business kid. Now look, I'll give you this, if you'll eat it.' He offered me a silver dollar. But I turned my face away, and sobbed, without sound.

" 'Aw now, look, it wasn't as bad as that,' he said. 'Just some fun between us two. Just playing paw and maw, eh? You want to grow up to be smart, don't you? Want to have fun? Take it from me, kid, you can't start too young. The day'll come, you'll thank me. Yes sir, you'll thank me. Now look here. I show you I've got nothing in my hands, see? Now watch.' He spread his fingers one by one, and magically quarters appeared between them until he held four quarters in each hand. 'Magic money, see? All for you; two whole dollars if you'll shut up and get the hell outa here, and never say anything to anybody.'

"I fainted again, and this time when I came round Willard was looking deeply worried. 'What you need is rest,' he said. 'Rest, and time to think about all that money. I've gotta get back for the next show, but you stay here, and don't let anybody in. Nobody, see? I'll come back as soon as I can and I'll bring you something. Something nice. But don't let anybody in, don't holler, and keep quiet like a mouse.'

"He went, and I heard him pause for a moment outside the door. Then I was alone, and I sobbed myself to sleep.

"I did not wake until he came back, I suppose an hour later. He brought me a hot dog, and urged me to eat it. I took one bite—it was my first hot dog—and vomited again. Willard was now very worried indeed. He swore fiercely, but not at me. All he said to me was, 'My God you're a crazy kid. Stay here. Now *stay* here, I tell ya. I'll come back as soon as I can.'

"That was not very soon. Perhaps two hours. But when he came he had an air of desperation about him, which I picked up at once. Terrible things had happened, and terrible remedies must be found. He had brought a large blanket, and he wrapped me in it, so that not even my head was showing, and lugged me bodily—I was not very heavy—out of the privy; I felt myself dumped into what I suppose was the back of a buggy or a carry-all, or something, and other wraps were thrown over me. Off I went, bumping along in the back of the cart, and it was some time later that I felt myself lifted out again, carried over rough ground, and humped painfully up onto what seemed to be a platform. Then another painful business of being lugged over a floor, some sounds of objects being moved, and at last the blanket was taken off. I was in a dark place, and only vaguely conscious that some distance away a door, like the door of a shed, was open, and I could see the light of dusk through it.

"Willard lost no time. 'Get in here,' he commanded, and pushed me into a place that was entirely dark, and confined. I had to climb upward, boosted by him, until I came to what seemed to be a shelf, or seat, and on this he pushed me. 'Now you'll be all right,' he said, in a voice that carried no confidence at all that I would be all right. It was a desperate voice. 'Here's something for you to eat.' A box was pushed in beside me. Then a door below me was closed, and snapped from the outside, and I was in utter darkness.

"After a while I felt around me. Irregular walls, seeming to be curved everywhere; there was even a small dome over my head. A smell, not clean, but not as disgusting as the privy at the fair. A little fresh air from a point above my head. I fell asleep again.

"When I woke, it was because I heard the whistle of a train, and a train-like thundering near by. But I was not moving. I was wretchedly hungry, and in the darkness I explored Willard's box. Something lumpy and sticky inside it, which I tried to eat, and then greedily ate it all. Sleep again. Terrible fatigue all through my body, and the worst pain of all in my bottom. But I could not move very much in any direction, and I had to sit on my misery. At last, a space of time that seemed like a geological age later, I felt movement. Banging and thumping which went on for some time. A sound of voices. The sound of another whistle, and then trundling, lumbering movement, which increased to a good speed. For the first time in my life I was on a train, but of course I didn't know that.

"And that, my friends, is the first instalment of my subtext to the memoirs of Robert-Houdin, whose childhood, you recall, was such an idyll of family love and care, and whose introduction to magic was so charmingly brought about. Enough, I think, for one evening. Good-night."

5

When I made my way to bed, some time later, I tapped at Eisengrim's door. As I had expected, he was awake, and lay, looking very fine, against his pillows, wearing a handsome dressing-robe.

"Kind of you to come in and say good-night, Dunny."

"I expected you'd be waiting up to see what your notices were."

"A disgusting way of putting it. Well, what were they?"

"About what you'd expect. Kinghovn had a fine sense of the

appearance of everything. I'll bet that as you talked he had that fair all cut up into long shots, close-ups, and atmosphere shots. And of course he's a devil for detail. For one thing, he wondered why nobody wanted to use the privy while you were left in it for so long."

"Simple enough. Willard wrote a note which said 'INFECTION: Closed by Doctor's Order', and pinned it to the door."

"Also he was anxious to know what it was you ate when you found yourself in the curious prison with the rounded walls."

"It was a box of Cracker-Jack. I didn't know what it was at the time, and had never eaten it before. Why should I have included those details in my story? I didn't know them then. It would have been a violation of narrative art to tell things I didn't know. Kinghovn ought to have more sense of artistic congruity."

"He's a cameraman. He wants to get a shot of everything, and edit later."

"I edit as I go along. What did the others say?"

"Ingestree talked for quite a while about the nature of puritanism. He doesn't know anything about it. It's just a theological whimwham to him. He's talked about puritanism at Oxford to Ronny Knox and Monsignor D'Arcy, but that stuff means nothing in terms of the daily, bred-in-the-bone puritanism we lived in Deptford. North American puritanism and the puritanism the English know are worlds apart. I could have told him a thing or two about that, but my time for instructing people is over. Let 'em wallow in whatever nonsense pleases 'em, say I."

"Did Lind have anything to say?"

"Not much. But he did say that nothing you told us was incomprehensible to him, or even very strange. 'We know of such things in Sweden,' he said."

"I suppose people know of such things everywhere. But every rape is unique for the aggressor and the victim. He talks as if he knew everything."

"I don't think he means it quite that way. When he talks about Sweden, I think it is a mystical rather than a geographical concept. When he talks of Sweden he means himself, whether he knows it or not. He really does understand a great deal. You remember what

Goethe said? No, of course you don't. He said he'd never heard of a crime of which he could not believe himself capable. Same with Lind, I suppose. That's his strength as an artist."

"He's a great man to work with. I think between us we'll do something extraordinary with this film."

"I hope so. And by the way, Magnus, I must thank you for the very kind things you said about me tonight. But I assure you I didn't especially mean to be kind to you, when we were boys. I mean, it wasn't anything conscious."

"I'm sure it wasn't. But that's the point, don't you see? If you'd done it out of duty, or for religious reasons, it would have been different. But it was just decency. You're a very decent man, Dunny."

"Really? Well—it's nice of you to think so. I've heard dissenting opinions."

"It's true. That's why I think you ought to know something I didn't see fit to tell them tonight."

"You suggested you had been editing. What did you leave out?"

"One gets carried away, telling a story. I may have leaned a little too heavily on my character as the wronged child. But would they have understood the whole truth? I don't, after fifty years, when I have thought of it over and over. You believe in the Devil, don't you?"

"In an extremely sophisticated way, which would take several hours to explain, I do."

"Yes. Well, when the Devil is walking beside you, as he was walking beside me at that fair, it doesn't take a lot of argument to make him seem real."

"I won't insult you by saying you're a simple man, but you're certainly a man of strong feeling, and your feelings take concrete shapes. What did the Devil do to you that you withheld when you were talking downstairs?"

"The whole nub of the story. When Willard gave me that quarter in the tent, we were standing behind the crowd, which was gaping at Andro who was showing his big right bicep while twitching his sumptuous left breast. Nobody was looking. Willard slipped his hand down the back of my pants and gently stroked my left buttock.

Gave it a meaning squeeze. I remember very well how warm his hand felt."

"Yes?"

"I smiled up into his face."

"Yes?"

"Is that all you have to say? Don't you see what I'm getting at? I had never had any knowledge of sex, had never known a sexual caress before, even of the kind parents quite innocently give their children. But at this first sexual approach I yielded. I cosied up to Willard. How could I, without any true understanding of what I was doing, respond in such a way to such a strange act?"

"You were mad to learn his magic. It doesn't seem very strange to me."

"But it made me an accomplice in what followed."

"You think that? And you still blame yourself?"

"What did I know of such things? I can only think it was the Devil prompting me, and pushing me on to what looked then, and for years after, like my own destruction."

"The Devil isn't a popular figure nowadays. The people who take him seriously are few."

"I know. How he must laugh. I don't suppose God laughs at the people who think He doesn't exist. He's above jokes. But the Devil isn't. That's one of his most endearing qualities. But I still remember that smile. I had never smiled like that before. It was a smile of complicity. Now where would such a child as I was learn such a smile as that?"

"From that other old joker, Nature, do you suppose?"

"I don't take much stock in Nature. . . . Thanks for coming in. Good-night, decent man."

"Magnus, are you becoming sentimental in your old age?"

"I'm fully ten years younger than you, you sour Scot. Good-night, kind man."

I went to my room, and to my bed, but it was a long time before I slept. I lay awake, thinking about the Devil. Many people would have considered my bedroom at Sorgenfrei a first-class place for such reflection, because so many people associate the Devil with a high standard of old-fashioned luxury. Mine was a handsome room in a corner tower, with an area of floor as big as that of a modest modern North American house. Sorgenfrei was an early-nineteenth-century construction, built by a forebear of Liesl's who seemed to have something in common, at least in his architectural taste, with the mad King of Bavaria; it was a powerfully romantic Gothic Revival house, built and furnished with Teutonic thoroughness. Everything was heavy, everything was the best of its kind, everything was carved, and polished, and gilded, and painted to the highest possible degree, and everything would drive a modern interior decorator out of his tasteful mind. But it suited me splendidly.

Not, however, when I wanted to think about the Devil. It was too romantic, too Germanic altogether. As I lay in my big bed, looking out of the windows at the mountains on which moonlight was falling, what could be easier than to accept an operatic Devil, up to every sort of high-class deception, and always defeated at the end of the story by the power of sheer, simple-minded goodness? All my life I have been a keen operagoer and playgoer, and in the theatre I am willing to accept the notion that although the Devil is a very clever fellow, he is no match for some ninny who is merely good. And what is this goodness? A squalid, know-nothing acceptance of things as they are, an operatic version of the dream which, in North America, means Mom and apple pie. My whole life had been a protest against this world, or the smudged, grey version of it into which I had been born in my rural Canada.

No, no; that Devil would never do. But what else is there? Theologians have not been so successful in their definitions of the Devil as they have been in their definitions of God. The words of the Westminster Confession, painstakingly learned by heart as a necessity of Presbyterian boyhood, still seemed, after many wanderings, to have the ring of indisputable authority. God was *infinite in being and perfection, a most pure spirit, invisible, without body, parts or passions, immutable, immense, eternal, incomprehensible, almighty, most wise, most holy, most free, most absolute, working all things according to the counsel of his own immutable and most righteous will, for his own glory.* Excellent, even if one is somewhat seduced by the high quality of the prose of 1648. What else? *Most loving, most gracious, merciful, longsuffering, abundant in good-*

ness and truth, forgiving iniquity, transgression and sin; the rewarder of those that diligently seek him. Aha, but where does one seek God? In Deptford, where Eisengrim and I were born, and might still be living if, in my case, I had not gone off to the First World War, and in his case, if he had not been abducted by a mountebank in a travelling show? I had sought God in my lifelong, unlikely (for a Canadian schoolmaster) preoccupation with that fantastic collection of wise men, virtuous women, thinkers, doers, organizers, contemplatives, crack-brained simpletons, and mad mullahs that are all called Saints. But all I had found in that lifelong study was a complexity that brought God no nearer. Had Eisengrim sought God at all? How could I know? How can anybody know what another man does in this most secret part of his life? What else had I been taught in that profound and knotty definition? That God was *most just and terrible in his judgements, hating all sin, one who will by no means clear the guilty*. Noble words, and (only slightly cloaked by their nobility) a terrifying concept. And why should it not be terrifying? A little terror, in my view, is good for the soul, when it is terror in the face of a noble object.

The Devil, however, seems never to have been so splendidly mapped and defined. Nor can you spy him simply by turning a fine definition of God inside out; he is something decidedly more subtle than just God's opposite.

Is the Devil, then, sin? No, though sin is very useful to him; anything we may reasonably call sin involves some personal choice. It is flattering to be asked to make important choices. The Devil loves the time of indecision.

What about evil, then? Is the Devil the origin and ruler of that great realm of manifestly dreadful and appalling things which are not, so far as we can determine, anybody's fault or the consequence of any sin? Of the cancer wards, and the wards for children born mis-shapen and mindless? I have had reason to visit such places—asylums for the insane in particular—and I do not think I am fanciful or absurdly sensitive in saying that I have felt evil to be palpable there, in spite of whatever could be done to lessen it.

These are evil things within my knowledge: I am certain there are worse things I have never encountered. And how constant this evil is! Let mankind laboriously suppress leprosy, and tuberculosis rages: when tuberculosis is chained, cancer rushes to take its place. One might almost conclude that such evils were necessities of our collective life. If the Devil is the inspirer and ruler of evil, he is a serious adversary indeed, and I cannot understand why so many people become joky and facetious at the mention of his name.

Where is the Devil? Was Eisengrim, whose intuitions and directness of observation in all things concerning himself I had come to respect, right in saying the Devil stood beside him when Willard the Wizard solicited him to an action which, under the circumstances, I should certainly have to call evil? Both God and the Devil wish to intervene in the world, and the Devil chooses his moments shrewdly.

What had Eisengrim told us? That on August 30, 1918, he had descended into hell, and did not rise again for seven years? Allowing for his wish to startle us, and his taste for what a severe critic might call flashy rhetoric, could what he said be discounted?

It was always a mistake, in my experience, to discount Magnus Eisengrim. The only thing to do was to wait for the remainder of his narrative, and hope that it would make it possible for me to reach a conclusion. And that would be my much-desired document.

6

I knew nothing about filming, but Lind's subordinates told me that his methods were not ordinary. He was extremely deliberate, and because he liked careful rehearsal and would not work at night he seemed to take a lot of time. But as he wasted none of this time, his films were not as devastatingly expensive as impatient people feared they might be. He was a master of his craft. I did not presume to question him about it, but I sensed that he attached more importance to Eisengrim's story than ordinary curiosity would explain, and that the dinners and discussions at Sorgenfrei fed the fire of his creation. Certainly he and Kinghovn and Ingestree were anxious for more as we settled down in the library on the third night. Liesl had seen to it that there was plenty of brandy, for although Eisengrim drank very little, and I was too keen on my document to drink much, Lind loved to tipple as he listened and had a real Scandinavian head; brandy never changed him in the least. Kinghovn was a heavy drinker, and Ingestree, a fatty, could not resist anything that could be put into his mouth, be it food, drink, or cigar.

Magnus knew they were waiting, and after he had toyed with them for a few minutes, and appeared to be leading them into general conversation, he yielded to Lind's strong urging that he go on with his story or—as Ingestree now quite seriously called it—"the subtext."

"I told you I was on a train, but didn't know it. I think that is true, but I must have had some notion of what was happening to me, because I had heard the whistle, and felt the motion, and of course I had seen trains. But I was so wretched that I couldn't reason, or be sure of anything, except that I was in close quarters in pitchy darkness. My mind was on a different unhappiness. I knew that when I was in trouble I should pray, and God would surely help me. But I couldn't pray, for two reasons. First, I couldn't kneel, and to me prayer without kneeling was unknown. Second, if I had been able to kneel I could not have dared to do it, because I was horribly aware that what Willard had done to me in that disgusting privy had been done while I was in a kneeling posture. I assure you, however strange it may seem, that I didn't know what he had done, but I felt strongly that it was a blasphemy against kneeling, and if I knew nothing of sex I certainly knew a lot about blasphemy. I guessed I might be on a train, but I knew for a certainty that I had angered God. I had been involved in what was very likely the Sin against the Holy Ghost. Can you imagine what that meant to me? I had never known such desolation. I had wept in the privy and now I could weep no more. Weeping meant sound, and I had a confused idea that although God certainly knew about me, and undoubtedly had terrible plans for me, He might be waiting for me to betray myself by sound before He went to work on me. So I kept painfully still.

"I suppose I was in a state of what would now be called shock. How long it went on I could not then tell. But I know now that it was from Friday night until the following Sunday morning that I sat in my close prison, without food or water or light. The train had not been travelling all that time. All day Saturday Wanless's

World of Wonders had a day's work at a village not many miles from Deptford, and I was conscious of the noises of unloading the train in the morning, and of loading it again very late at night, though I could not interpret them. But Sunday morning brought a kind of release.

"There were more men's voices, and more sounds of heavy things being methodically moved near where I was. Then after a period of silence I heard Willard's voice. 'He's in there,' it said. Then sounds somewhat below me, and a hand reached up and touched my leg. I made no sound—could not make a sound, I suppose—and was rather roughly hauled out into a dim light, and laid on the floor. Then a strange voice. 'Jesus, Willard,' it said, 'you've killed him. Now we're all up the well-known creek.' But then I moved a little. 'Christ, he's alive,' said the strange voice; 'thank God for that.' Then Willard's voice: 'I'd rather he was dead,' it said; 'what are we going to do with him now?'

" 'We got to get Gus,' said the strange voice. 'Gus is the one who'll know what to do. Don't talk about him being dead. Haven't you got any sense? We got to get Gus right now.' Then Willard spoke. 'Yeah, Gus, Gus, Gus; it's always Gus with you. Gus hates me. I'll be outa the show.' 'Leave Gus to me about you and the show,' said the other voice; 'but only Gus can deal with this right now. You wait here.'

"The other man went away, and as he went I heard the heavy door of the freight-car—for I was in a freight-car in which the World of Wonders took its trappings from town to town—and I was for a second time alone with Willard. Through my eyelashes I could see him sitting on a box beside me. His Mephistophelian air of command was gone; he looked diminished, shabby, and afraid.

"After a time the other man returned with Gus, who proved to be a woman—a real horse's godmother of a woman, a little, hard-faced, tough woman who looked like a jockey. But she inspired confidence, and while it would be false to say that my spirits lightened, I felt a little less desolate. I have always had a quick response to people, and though it is sometimes wrong it is more often right. If I like them on sight they are lucky people for me, and that's really all I care about. Gus was in a furious temper.

" 'Willard, you son-of-a-bitch, what the hell have you got us into now? Lemme look at this kid.' Gus knelt and hauled me round so that she could see me. Then she sent the other man to open the doors further, to give her a better light.

"Gus had a rough touch, and she hurt me so that I whimpered. 'What's your name, kid?' she said. 'Paul Dempster.' 'Who's your Dad?' 'Reverend Amasa Dempster.' This pushed Gus's rage up a few notches. 'A reverend's kid,' she shouted; 'you had to go and kidnap a reverend's kid. Well, I wash my hands of you, Willard. I hope they hang you, and if they do, by God I'll come and swing on your feet!'

"I can't pretend to remember all their talk, because Gus sent the unknown man, whom she called Charlie, to get water and milk and food for me, and while they wrangled she fed me, first, sugared water from a spoon, and then, when I had plucked up a little, some milk, and finally a few biscuits. I can still remember the pain as my body began to return to its normal state, and the pins-and-needles in my arms and legs. She put me on my feet and walked me up and down but I was wobbly, and couldn't stand much of that.

"Nor can I pretend that I understood much of what was said at that time, though later, from knowledge I picked up over a period of years, I know what it must have been. I was not Gus's chief problem; I was a complication of a problem that was already filling the foreground of her mind. Wanless's World of Wonders belonged to Gus, and her brothers Charlie and Jerry; they were Americans, although their show toured chiefly in Canada, and Charlie ought to have been in the American Army, for the 1917 draft had included him and he had had his call-up. But Charlie had no mind for fighting, and Gus was doing her best to keep him out of harm's way, in hopes that the War would end before his situation became desperate. Charlie was very much her darling, and I judge he must have been at least ten years younger than she; Jerry was the oldest. Therefore, involvements with the law were not to Gus's taste, even though they might bring about the downfall of Willard. She detested him because he was Charlie's best friend, and a bad influence. Willard, in his panic, had abducted me, and it was up to Gus to get me out of the way without calling attention to the Wanless family.

"It is easy now to think of several things they might have done, but none of those three were thinkers. Their obsession was that I must be kept from running to the police and telling my tale of seduction, abduction, and hard usage; it never occurred to them to ask me, or they would have found out that I had no clear idea of who or what the police were, and had no belief in any rights of mine that might have gone contrary to the will of any adult. They assumed that I was aching to return to my loving family, whereas I was frightened of what my father would do when he found out what had happened in the privy, and what the retribution would be for having stolen fifteen cents, a crime of the uttermost seriousness in my father's eyes.

"My father was no brute, and I think he hated beating me, but he knew his duty. 'He that spareth his rod hateth his son; but he that loveth him chasteneth him betimes'; this was part of the prayer that always preceded a beating and he laid the rod on hard, while my mother wept or—this was very much worse, and indeed quite horrible—laughed sadly as if at something my father and I did not and could not know. But Gus Wanless was a sentimentalist, American-style, and it never entered her head that a boy in my situation would be prepared to do anything rather than go home.

"There was another thing which seems extraordinary to me now, but which was perfectly in keeping with that period in history and the kind of people into whose hands I had fallen. There was never, at any time, any reference to what had happened in the privy. Gus and Charlie certainly knew that Willard had not stolen a boy, or thought it necessary to conceal a boy, simply as a matter of caprice. As I grew to know these carnival people I discovered that their deepest morality was precisely that of the kind of people they amused; whatever freedom their travelling way of life might give them, it did not cut far into the rock of North American accepted custom and morality. If Willard had despoiled a girl, I think Gus would have known better what to do, but she was unwilling to strike out into the deep and dirty waters that Willard's crime had revealed in the always troubled landscape of Wanless's World of Wonders.

"I think she was right: if Willard had fallen into the hands of the law as we knew it in Deptford, and in the county of which it was a part, the scandal would have wrecked the World of Wonders and Charlie would have been shipped back to the States to face the music. A showman, a magician at that, a stranger, an American, who had ravaged a local child in a fashion of which I am certain half the village had never heard except as something forbidden in the Bible—we didn't go in for lynchings in our part of the world, but I think Willard might have been killed by the other prisoners when he went to jail; jails have their own morality, and Willard would have found himself outside it. So nothing was said about that, then or afterward. This was all the worse for me, as I found out in the years to come. I was part of something shameful and dangerous everybody knew about, but which nobody would have dreamed of bringing into the light.

"What were they to do with me? I am sure Willard had spoken truly when he wished me dead, but he hadn't the courage to kill me when he had his chance. Now that Gus, who was the whole of the law and the prophets in the World of Wonders, knew about me, that moment had passed. As I have said, none of them had any capacity for thought or reasoning, and as they talked on and on Gus's mood turned from rage to fear. Willard was more at home in the air of fear than in that of anger.

" 'Honest to God, Gus, nothing would ever have happened, if the kid hadn't shown some talent.'

"This was a lucky string to touch. Gus was sure she knew everything there was to know about Talent—a word she always pronounced with the air of one giving it a capital letter. And so it came out that when Willard had given me a quarter, out of pure open-heartedness, I had immediately done a trick with it. As neat a palm-and-pass as Willard had ever seen. Good enough for the Palace Theatre in New York.

" 'You mean the kid can do tricks?' It was Charlie who spoke. 'Then why can't we fix him up a little with some hair-dye and maybe colour his skin, and use him as a Boy-Conjuror—Bonzo the Boy Wonder, or like that?'

"But this did not sit well with Willard. He wanted no rival conjurors in the show.

" 'Jeeze, Willard, I only meant as a kind of assistant to you. Hand you things and like that. Maybe do a funny trick or two when you're not looking. You could plan something.'

"Now it was Gus who objected. 'Charlie, you ought to know by now that you can't never disguise anybody from somebody that knows him well. The law's going to follow the show; just keep that in mind. The kid's Dad, this reverend, comes into the show, sees a kid this size, and no hair-dye and blackface is going to hide him. Anyway, the kid sees his Dad, this reverend, and he gives him the high-sign. Use whatever head you got, Charlie.'

"Now it was Willard's turn to have a bright idea. 'Abdullah!' he said.

"Even though I was busy with the biscuits I stopped eating to look at them. They were like people from whose minds a cloud had lifted.

" 'But can he handle Abdullah?' said Gus.

" 'I betcha he can. I tell you, this kid's Talent. A natural. He's made for Abdullah. Don't you see, Gus? This is the silver lining. I made a little slip, I grant ya. But if Abdullah's back in the show, what does it matter? Abdullah's the big draw. Now look; we put Abdullah back, and I go to the top of the show, and let's not hear any more about Happy Hannah or that gaffed morphodite Andro.'

" 'Just hold your horses, Willard. I'll believe a kid can handle Abdullah when I've seen it. You got to show me.'

" 'And I'll show you. Gimme time, just a very little time, and I'll show you. Kid, can you handle a pack of cards?' Nothing could make me admit that I could handle a pack of cards. Ramsay had taught me a few card tricks, but when my father found it out he gave me such a beating as only a thoroughgoing Baptist can give a son who has been handling the Devil's Picture Book. It had been thoroughly slashed into my backside that cards were not for me. I denied all knowledge of cards before I had thought for an instant. Yet, immediately I had spoken, the four suits and the ways in which they could be made to dance began to rise in my memory.

"Willard was not troubled by my lack of knowledge. He had the real showman's enthusiasm for a new scheme. But Gus was dubious.

" 'Just give me today, Gus,' said Willard. 'Only just this one

Sunday, to show you what can be done. I'll work him in. You'll see. We can do it right here.'

"That was how I became the soul of Abdullah, and entered into a long servitude to the craft and art of magic.

"We began at once. Gus bustled away on some of the endless business she always had in hand, but Charlie remained, and he and Willard began to uncover something at the very back of the car—the only object in it which the handlers had not unloaded for Monday's fair—which was under several tarpaulins. Whatever it was, this was the prison in which I had spent my wretched, starving hours.

"When it was pulled forward and the wraps thrown aside, it was revealed as, I think still, the most hideous and offensive object I have ever seen in my life. You gentlemen know how particular I have always been about the accoutrements of my show. I have spent a great deal of money, which foolish people have thought unnecessary, on the beauty and workmanship of everything I have exhibited. In this I have been like Robert-Houdin, who also thought that the best was none too good for himself and his audiences. Perhaps some of my fastidiousness began with my hatred of the beastly figure that was called Abdullah.

"It was a crude effigy of a Chinese, sitting on top of a chest, with his legs crossed. To begin with, the name was crassly wrong. Why call a Chinese figure Abdullah? But everything about it was equally inartistic and inept. Its robes were of frowsy sateen; its head was vulgarly moulded in papier mâché with an ugly face, sharply slanted eyes, dangling moustaches, and yellow fangs which hung down over the lower lip. The thing was, in itself, reason for a sharp protest from the Chinese Ambassador, if there had been one. It summed up in itself all that spirit combined of jocosity and hatred with which ignorant people approach whatever is foreign and strange.

"The chest on which this monster sat was in the same mode of workmanship. It was lacquered with somebody's stupid notion of a dragon, half hideous and half cute, in gaudy red on a black background. A lot of cheap gold paint had been splashed about.

"Neither Willard nor Charlie explained to me what this thing was, or what relationship I was expected to bear to it However,

I was used to being ignored and rather liked it; being noticed had, in my experience, usually meant trouble. All they told me was that I was to sit in this thing and make it work, and my lesson began as soon as Abdullah was unveiled.

"Once again, but this time in daylight and with some knowledge of what I was doing, I crawled into the chest at the back of the figure, and thence upward, rather like an old-fashioned chimney-sweep climbing a chimney, into the body, where there was a tiny ledge on which I could sit and allow my feet to hang down. But that was not the whole of my duty. When I was in place, Willard opened various doors in the front of the chest, then turned the whole figure around on the wheels which supported the chest, and opened a door in the back. These doors revealed to the spectators an impressive array of wheels, cogs, springs, and other mechanical devices, and when Willard touched a lever they moved convincingly. But the secret of these mechanisms was that they were shams, displayed in front of polished steel mirrors, so that they seemed to fill the whole of the chest under the figure of Abdullah, but really left room for a small person to conceal himself when necessary. And that time came after Willard had closed the doors in the chest, and pulled aside Abdullah's robes to show some mechanism, and nothing else, in the figure itself. When that was happening, I had to let myself down into the secret open space in the chest and keep out of the way. Once Abdullah's mechanical innards had been displayed I crept back up into the figure, thrust aside the fake mechanism, which folded out of the way, and prepared to make Abdullah do his work.

"Willard and Charlie both treated me as if I were very stupid, which God knows I was not. However, I thought it best not to be too clever in the beginning. This was intuition; I did not figure it out consciously. They showed me a pack of cards, and painstakingly taught me the suits and the values. What Abdullah had to do was to play cards, on a very simple principle, with anybody who would volunteer from an audience to try their luck with him. This spectator—the Rube, as Willard called him—shuffled and cut a deck which lay on a little tray across Abdullah's knees. Then the Rube drew a card and laid it face down on the tray. At this point Willard pulled a lever on the side of Abdullah's chest, which set up a mechanical sound in the depths of the figure, which in fact I, the concealed boy, set going by pumping a pedal with my left foot. While this was going on it was my job to discover what card the Rube had drawn—which was easy, because he had put it face downward on a ground-glass screen, and I could fairly easily make it out—and to select a higher card from a rack concealed inside Abdullah ready to my hand. Having chosen my card, I set Abdullah's left arm in motion, slipping my own arm into the light framework in its sleeve; at the far end of this framework was a device into which I inserted the card that was to confound the Rube. I then made Abdullah's right arm move slowly to the deck of cards on the tray, and cut them; this was possible because the fingers had a pincers device in them which could be worked from inside the arm by squeezing a handle. When Abdullah had cut the cards his left hand moved to the deck and took a card from the top. But in fact he did nothing of the sort, because his sleeve fell forward for a moment and concealed what was really happening; it was at this instant I pushed the little slide which shot the card I had chosen from the rack into Abdullah's fingers, and it seemed to the spectators that this was the card he picked up from the deck. The Rube was then invited to turn up his card—a five, let us say; then a spectator was asked to turn up Abdullah's card. A seven in the same suit! Consternation of the Rube! Applause of the audience! Great acclaim for Willard, who had never touched a card at any time and had merely pulled the lever which set in motion Abdullah, the Card-Playing Automaton, and Scientific Marvel of the Age!

"We slaved away all of that Sunday. I lost my fright because Willard and Charlie were so pleased with what I could do, and although they still talked about me as though I had no ears to hear them, and no understanding, the atmosphere became cheerful and excited and I was the reason for it. I must not pretend that I mastered the mechanisms of Abdullah in an instant, and even when I had done so I had to be taught not to be too quick; I thought the essence of the work was to do it as fast as possible. Willard and Charlie knew, though they never bothered to tell me, that a very deliberate, and even slow, pace created a far better effect on the spectators. And I had much to learn. When I sat inside Abdullah my head was at the level of his neck, and here his robes parted a little to allow me to see through a piece of wire mesh that was painted the colour of his gown. It was by observing the actions of the Rube that I timed my own work. I had to learn to pump the little treadle that made the mechanical noise which simulated the finely scientific machinery of the automaton, and it was easy to forget, or to pump too fast and make Abdullah too noisy. The hardest part was ducking my head just enough to see what card the Rube had chosen and laid on the tray; as I said, this was ground glass, and there was a mirror underneath it so that I could see the suit and value of his card, but it was not as easy or as convenient as you might suppose, because the light was dim. And I had to be quick and accurate in choosing a card of greater value. A deck identical with the one used by the Rube was set up in a rack concealed by Abdullah's folded legs; it had eight pigeon-holes, in which each suit was divided into the cards from two to ten, and the Jack, Queen, King, and Ace by themselves. It was dark in Abdullah, and there was not much time for choosing, so I had to develop a good deal of dexterity.

"It was thrilling, and I worked feverishly to make myself perfect. How many times we went through the routine, when once I had mastered the general principle of it, I cannot guess, but I remember well that it was the management of the arms that gave me the most trouble, and any mistiming there made a mess of the whole deception. But we toiled as only people toil who are busy at the delicious work of putting something over on the public. There was a short noonday pause for a picnic, of which my share was milk and a lot of sticky buns; Gus had left instructions that I was not to be starved or overworked, because I was still weak, and I certainly was not starved.

"It was a hot day, and hotter still inside Abdullah. Also, Abdullah had a heavy smell, because of all the papier mâché and glue and size with which he was made. During my thirty-six hours or so of imprisonment I had been compelled to urinate, in spite of my awful thirst, and this had done nothing to freshen the atmosphere of that close confinement. Moreover, although I did not know it then, I learned later that the former operator of Abdullah had been a dwarf who cannot have been fastidious about his person, and there was a strong whiff of hot dwarf as I grew hotter myself. I suppose I became rather feverish, but although I would not describe my emotion as happiness I was possessed by an intensity of interest and ambition that was better than anything I had ever known in my life. When you were teaching me magic, Ramsay, I felt something like it, but not to the same degree, because—please don't be hurt—you were so tooth-achingly rotten at all your simple tricks. But this was the real thing. I didn't know quite what this reality was, but it was wonderful, and I was an important part of it.

"Charlie, who was as good-hearted as he was soft-headed, did all he could to make a game of it. He played the part of the Rube, and he did his best to include every kind of Rube he could think of. He was a terrible ham, but he was funny. He approached Abdullah as Uncle Zeke, the euchre champion of Pumpkin Centre, and as Swifty Dealer, the village tinhorn sport, and as Aunt Samantha, who didn't believe she could be bested by any Chinaman that ever lived, and as a whole gallery of such caricatures. I had to beg him not to be so funny, because I couldn't concentrate on my work when I was laughing so much. But Willard never laughed. He was the taskmaster, demanding the greatest skill I could achieve in the management of the mechanism. Charlie was a hearty praiser; he would gladly tell me that I was a wonderful kid and a gift to the carnival business and the possessor of a golden future. But Willard never praised a good piece of management; he was sharp about mistakes, and demanded more and more refinement of success. I didn't care. I felt that inside Abdullah I had entered into my kingdom.

"Come five o'clock Willard and Charlie thought we were ready to show our work to Gus. I had never been associated with any kind of show folk, and I thought it quite wonderful the way Gus climbed into the freight-car and behaved as if she had never seen any of us before; Willard and Charlie too behaved as if it were a real show and Gus a stranger. Willard gave a speech that I had not heard before, about the wonders of Abdullah, and the countless hours and boundless ingenuity that had gone into his construction; during all of it I kept as still as a mouse, and fully convinced myself that Gus did not know I was anywhere near; perhaps she thought I had run away. Then Gus, at the right time, came forward reluctantly and suspiciously, like a real Rube and not one of Charlie's comic turns, and cut the deck and chose a card: either Gus knew some sleight-of-hand herself or Willard had prepared a sharp test for me, because it was the Ace of Spades; there was no card to top it. And then I had one of those flashes which, I think I may say without boasting, have lifted my work above that of even a very good illusionist. At the bottom of the tray that held the court-cards in spades, there was a Joker, and that was what I caused Abdullah to put down on the tray to top Gus's Ace. Of course it would not do so, but it showed that I was able to meet an unexpected situation, and Charlie gave a whoop that would have drawn a crowd if there had been anybody hanging around the railway siding on a late Sunday afternoon.

"Gus was impressed, but the expression of her jockey's face did not change. 'O.K. I guess it'll do,' was what she said, and immediately the three began haggling again about some of the questions that had come up in the morning. I did not understand them then, but they concerned Abdullah's place in the show, which Willard insisted should be next to last, the place of honour reserved for the top attraction. It was now held by Andro, against whom Willard harboured a complicated grudge. Gus did not want to be rushed, and insisted that Abdullah should not be shown for a while, until we were far from Deptford.

"Charlie begged very hard that Abdullah should go into the show at once. Business wasn't good; they needed a strong attraction, especially now Hannah was getting out of hand and would have to be sat on; nobody would know the kid was in Abdullah because they would all be convinced Abdullah was a mechanical marvel. Yes, countered Gus, but how was she going to explain to the Talent a kid who turned up without warning and whom they would certainly know was the secret of Abdullah's card-playing genius? Would they just tell her that? A kid out of nowheres! Especially if there was any inquiry by Nosey Parkers and policemen. Could Hannah be trusted not to spill the beans? She was a religious old bitch and would love to do a mean thing for a holy reason. Ah, said Charlie, Gus surely knew how to handle Hannah; if Hannah had to go for as much as eight hours without the assistance of Elephant Gus, where would she be? And here Willard struck in to say that he knew a thing or two about Hannah that would keep her in order. And so on, at length, because they all argued in a circle, enjoying the contention rather than wishing to reach a conclusion. I had had a hard day, and the inside of Abdullah was like a Turkish bath; they had quite forgotten the living reality of the thing they were discussing. So I fell into an exhausted sleep. I did not understand it at the time, but I came to understand it very well later: when I was in Abdullah, I was Nobody. I was an extension and a magnification of Willard; I was an opponent and a baffling mystery to the Rube; I was something to be gawped at, but quickly forgotten, by the spectators. But as Paul Dempster I did not exist. I had found my place in life, and it was as Nobody."

The film-makers sipped their brandy for a time before Lind spoke. "It would be interesting to do a film about Nobody," he said. "I know I mustn't hurry you, so I won't ask you if you were Nobody for long. But you are going to continue, aren't you?"

"You must," said Ingestree. "Now we are getting a true story. Not like Robert-Houdin's faked-up reminiscences. He was never Nobody. He was always triumphantly and self-assuredly Somebody. He was charming, lively little Eugene Robert, the delight of his family and his friends; or he was that deserving young watch- and clock-maker; or he was the interesting young traveller who extracted the most amazing confidences from everybody; or he was the successful Parisian entertainer, drawing the cream of society to his little theatre, but always respectful, always conscious of his place, always the perfect bourgeois, always Somebody. Do you suppose many people are Nobody?"

Eisengrim looked at him with a not very agreeable smile. "Have you any recollection of being Nobody?" he said.

"Not really. No, I can't say I have."

"Have you ever met anyone who was Nobody?"

"I don't believe so. No, I'm sure I haven't. But then, if one met Nobody, I don't suppose Nobody would make much of an impression on one."

"Obviously not," said Eisengrim.

It was I who saw the film-makers to their car and watched them begin the descent from Sorgenfrei to the village where their inn was. Then I went back to the house as fast as my artificial leg would carry me and caught Eisengrim as he was getting into bed.

"About the Devil," I said; "I've been thinking more about what we said."

"Have you pinned him down, then?"

"Nothing like it. I am simply trying to get a better hold on his attributes. The attributes of God have been very carefully explored. But the Devil's attributes have been left vague. I think I've found one of them. It is he who puts the prices on things."

"Doesn't God put a price on things?"

"No. One of his attributes is magnanimity. But the Devil is a setter of prices, and a usurer, as well. You buy from him at an agreed price, but the payments are all on time, and the interest is charged on the whole of the principal, right up to the last payment, however much of the principal you think you have paid off in the meantime. Do you suppose the Devil invented numbers? I shouldn't be surprised if the Devil didn't invent Time, with all the subtle terrors that Time comprises. I think you said you spent seven years in hell?"

"I may have underestimated my sentence."

"That's what I mean."

"You're developing into a theologian, Dunny."

"A diabologian, rather. It's a fairly clear field, these days."

"Do you think you can study evil without living it? How are you going to discover the attributes of the Devil without getting close to him? Are you the man for that? Don't bother your old grey head, Dunny."

That was Magnus all over. He simply had to be the damnedest man around. What an egotist!

7

We were eating sandwiches and drinking beer at a lunch-break the following day. Magnus was not with us, because he had gone off to make some repairs and alterations in his make-up, about which he was extremely particular. Robert-Houdin had been a handsome man, in a French style, with strong features, a large, mobile mouth, and particularly fine eyes: Magnus would make no concession to a likeness, and insisted on playing the role of the great illusionist as his handsome self, and he darted away to touch up his face whenever he could. As soon as he was out of the way, Kinghovn turned the conversation to what we had heard the night before.

"Our friend puzzles me," he said. "You remember that he said the image of Abdullah was the ugliest thing he had ever seen? Then he described it, and it sounded like the sort of trash one would expect in such a poor little travelling show, and just what would seem marvellous to a small boy. How much is he colouring his story with opinions he formed later?"

"But inevitably it's all coloured by later opinions," said Ingestree. "What can you expect? It's the classic problem of autobiography; it's inevitably life seen and understood backwards. However honest we try to be in our recollections we cannot help falsifying them in terms of later knowledge, and especially in terms of what we have become. Eisengrim is unquestionably the greatest magician of our day, and to hear him tell it, of any day. How is he to make himself into a photographic record of something that happened fifty years ago?"

"Then how can we reconstruct the past?" said Kinghovn. "Look at it from my point of view—really my point of view, which is through the camera. Suppose I had to make a film of what Eisengrim has told us, how could I be sure of what Abdullah looked like?"

"You couldn't," said Lind. "And you know it. But you and I and a good designer would work together, and we would produce an Abdullah that would give the right effect, though it might be far, far away from the real Abdullah of 1918. What would the real Abdullah be? Perhaps not as ugly as Eisengrim says, but certainly a piece of cheap junk. You and I, Harry, would show the world not simply what little Paul Dempster saw, but what he felt. We would even get that whiff of hot dwarf across to the public somehow. That's what we do. That's why we are necessary people."

"Then the truth of the past can never be recovered?"

"Harry, you should never talk. Your talk is the least useful part of you. You should just stick to your cameras, with which you are a man of genius. The truth of the past is to be seen in museums, and what is it? Dead things, sometimes noble and beautiful, but dead. And cases and cases of coins, and snuffboxes, and combs, and mirrors that won't reflect any more, and clothes that look as if the wearers had all been midgets, and masses of frowsy tat that tells us nothing at all. Once a man showed me a great treasure of his family; it was a handkerchief which somebody, on January 30, 1649, had dipped in the blood of the executed English King Charles I. It was a disgusting, rusty rag. But if you and I and Roly here had the money and the right people, we could fake up an execution of King Charles that would make people weep. Which is nearer to the truth? The rag, or our picture?"

I thought it was time for me to intervene. "I wouldn't call either the rag or your picture truth," I said; "I am an historian by training and temperament, and I would go to the documents, and there are plenty of them, about the execution of Charles, and when I had read and tested and reflected on them, I would back my truth against yours, and win."

"Ah, but you see, my dear Ramsay, we would not dream of making our picture until we had consulted you or somebody like you, and given the fullest importance to your opinion."

"Well, would you be content to film the execution on a grey day? Wouldn't you want a shot of the sun rising behind Whitehall as the sun of English monarchy was setting on the scaffold?"

Lind looked at me sadly. "How you scholars underestimate us artists," he said, with wintry Scandinavian melancholy. "You think we are children, always beguiled by toys and vulgarities. When have you ever known me to stoop to a sunrise?"

"Besides, you don't understand what we could do with all those wonderful pearly greys," said Kinghovn.

"You will never persuade me to believe that truth is no more than what some artist, however gifted he may be, thinks is truth," I said. "Give me a document, every time."

"I suppose somebody has to write the document?" said Lind. "Has he no feeling? Of course he has. But because he is not used to giving full weight to his feelings, he is all the more likely to be deluded into thinking that what he puts into his document is objective truth."

Ingestree broke in. "Eisengrim is coming back from tarting himself up for the next few shots," he said. "And so far as his story is concerned, we might as well make up our minds that all we are going to get is his feeling. As a literary man, I am just pleased that he has some feelings. So few autobiographers have any feeling except a resolute self-protectiveness."

"Feeling! Truth! Balls! Let's get a few hundred good feet in the can before our star decides he is tired," said Kinghovn. And that is what we did.

A good day's filming put Magnus in an expansive mood. Ingestree's flattery about the quality of his acting had also had its effect on him, and that night he gave us a gallery of impersonations.

"Charlie had his way, and I was soon on the show. Charlie was right; Abdullah pulled them in because people cannot resist automata. There is something in humanity that is repelled and entranced by a machine that seems to have more than human powers. People love to frighten themselves. Look at the fuss nowadays about computers; however deft they may be they can't do anything that a man isn't doing, through them; but you hear people giving themselves delicious shivers about a computer-dominated world. I've often thought of working up an illusion, using a computer, but it would be prohibitively expensive, and I can do anything the public would find amusing better and cheaper with clockwork and bits of string. But if I invented a computer-illusion I would take care to dress the computer up to look like a living creature of some sort—a Moon Man or a Venusian—because the public cannot resist clever dollies. Abdullah was a clever dolly of a simple kind, and the Rubes couldn't get enough of him.

"That was where Gus had to use her showman's discretion. Charlie and Willard would have put Abdullah in a separate tent to milk him for twenty shows a day, but Gus knew that would exhaust his appeal. Used sparingly, Abdullah was good for years, and Gus took the long view. It appeared, too, that I was an improvement on the dwarf, who had become unreliable through some personal defect—booze, I would guess—and was apt to make a mess of the illusion, or give way to a fit of temperament and deal a low card when he should have dealt a high one. Willard had had no luck with Abdullah; he had bought the thing, and hired the dwarf, but the dwarf was so unreliable it was risky to put the automaton on the show, and then the dwarf had disappeared. It had been months since Abdullah was in commission, and so far as the show was concerned it was a new attraction.

"I was anxious to succeed as Abdullah, though I had no particular expectation of gaining anything thereby. I had no notion of the world, and for quite a long time I did not understand how powerful I was, or that I might profit by it. Nor did anyone in the World of Wonders seek to enlighten me. So far as I can recall my feelings during those first few months, they were restricted to a desire to do the best I could, lest I should be sent back to my father and inevitable punishment. To begin with, I liked being the hidden agent who helped in the great game of hoodwinking Rubes, and I was happiest when I was out of sight, in the smelly bowels of Abdullah.

"When I was in the open air I was Cass Fletcher. I always hated the name, but Willard liked it because he had invented it in one of his very few flights of fancy. Willard had no imagination, to speak of. I learned as time went on that he had learned his conjuring skill from an old performer, and had never expanded it or altered it by a jot. He had as little curiosity as any man I have ever known. But when we were riding on the train, in my very first week, he found that I must have a name, because the other performers, riding in the car reserved for the World of Wonders, were surprised to see a small boy in their midst, for whom no credentials were offered. Who was I?

"When the question was put directly to him by the wife of Joe Dark the Knife Thrower, Willard hesitated a moment, looked out of the window, and said: 'Oh, this is young Cass, a kind of relative of mine; Cass Fletcher.' Then he went off into one of his very rare fits of laughter.

"As soon as he could catch Charlie, who wandered up and down the car as it travelled through the flatlands of Western Ontario, and gossiped with everybody, Willard told him his great joke. 'Em Dark wanted to know the kid's name, see, and I was thinking who the hell is he, when I looked outa the window at one of these barns with a big sign saying FLETCHER'S CASTORIA, CHILDREN CRY FOR IT; and quick as a wink I says Cass Fletcher, that's his name. Pretty smart way to name a kid, eh?' I was offended at being named from a sign on a barn, but I was not consulted, and a general impression spread that I was Willard's nephew.

"At least, that was the story that was agreed on. As time went on I heard whispers between Molza the Fire Eater and Sonny Sonnenfels the Strong Man that Willard was something they called an arse-bandit—an expression I did not understand—and that the kid was probably more to him than just a nephew and the gaff for Abdullah.

"Gaff. That was a word I had to learn at once, in all its refinements. The gaff was the element of deception in an exhibition, and though all the Talent would have admitted you couldn't manage without it, there was a moral stigma attaching to it. Sonnenfels was not gaffed at all; he really was a strong man who picked up big bar-bells and tore up telephone books with his hands and lifted anybody who would volunteer to sit in a chair, which Sonny then heaved aloft with one hand. There are tricks to being a strong man, but no gaff; anybody was welcome to heft the bar-bells if they wanted to. Frank Molza the Fire Eater and Sword Swallower was partly gaffed, because his swords weren't as sharp as he pretended, and eating fire is a complicated chemical trick which usually proves bad for the health. But Professor Spencer, who had been born without arms—really he had two pathetic little flippers but he did not show them—was wholly free of gaff; he wrote with his feet, on a blackboard and, if you wanted to pay twenty-five cents, in an elegant script on twelve visiting cards, where your name would be handsomely displayed. Joe Dark and his wife Emily were not gaffed at all; Joe threw knives at Emily with such accuracy that he outlined her form on the soft board against which she stood; it was skill, and the only skill poor Joe possessed, for he was certainly the dullest man in the World of Wonders. Nor could you say that there was any gaff about Heinie Bayer and his educated monkey Rango; it was an honest monkey, as monkeys go, and its tricks were on the level. The Midget Juggler, Piccino Zovene, was honest as a juggler, but as crooked as a corkscrew in any human dealings; he wasn't much of a juggler, and might have been improved by a little gaff.

"Gaff may have been said to begin with Zitta the Jungle Queen, whose snakes were kept quiet by various means, especially her sluggish old cobra who was over-fed and drugged. Snakes don't live long in the sort of life Zitta gave them; they can't stand constant mauling and dragging about; she was always wiring a supplier in Texas for new rattlers. I judged that a snake lived about a month to six weeks when once Zitta had got hold of it; they were nasty things, and I never felt much sympathy for them. Zitta was a nasty thing, too, but she was too stupid to give her nastiness serious play. Andro the Hermaphrodite was all gaff. He was a man, of a kind, and besottedly in love with himself. The left side of his body was supposed to be the female half, and he spent a lot of time on it with depilatories and skin creams; when he attached a pretty good left breast to it, and combed out the long, curly hair he allowed to grow on one side of his head, he was an interesting sight. His right side he exercised strenuously, so that he had big leg and arm muscles which he touched up with some fancy shadowing. I never became used to finding him using the men's bucket in the donniker—which was the word used on the show for the primitive sanitary conveniences in the small back dressing tent. He was a show-off; in show business you get used to vanity, but Andro was a very special case.

"Of course Abdullah was one hundred per cent gaff. I don't think anybody would have cared greatly, if they had not been stirred up to it by the one very remarkable Talent I haven't yet mentioned. She was Happy Hannah the Fat Lady.

"A Fat Lady, or a Fat Man, is almost a necessity for a show like Wanless's. Just as the public is fascinated by automata, it is unappeasable in its demand for fat people. A Human Skeleton is hardly worth having if he can't do something else—grow hair to his feet, or eat glass or otherwise distinguish himself. But a Fat Lady merely has to be fat. Happy Hannah weighed 487 pounds; all she needed to do was to show herself sitting in a large chair, and her living was assured. But that wasn't her style at all; she was an interferer, a tireless asserter of opinions, and—worst of all—a determined Moral Influence. It was this quality in her which made it a matter of interest whether she was gaffed or not.

"Willard was her enemy, and Willard said she was gaffed. For one thing, she wore a wig, a very youthful chestnut affair, curly and flirtatious; a kiss-curl coiled like a watchspring in front of each rosy ear. The rosy effect was gaffed, too, for Hannah was thickly made up. But these things were simple showmanship. Willard's insistence that the Fat Lady was gaffed rose from an occupational disability of Fat Ladies; this is copious sweating, which results, in a person whose bodily creases may be twelve inches deep, in troublesome chafing. Three or four times a day Hannah had to retire to the women's part of the dressing tent, and there Gus stripped her down and powdered her in these difficult areas with cornstarch. Very early in my experience on the show I peeped through a gap in the lacing of the canvas partition that divided the men's dressing-room from the women's, and was much amazed by what I saw; Hannah, who looked fairly jolly sitting on her platform, in a suit of pink cotton rompers, was a sorry mass of blubber when she was bent forward, her hands on the back of a chair; she had collops of fat on her flanks, like the wicked man in the Book of Job; her monstrous abdomen hung almost to her knees, the smart wig concealed an iron-grey crewcut, and her breasts hung like great half-filled wallets of suet far down on her belly. I have seen nothing like her since, except for an effigy of Smet Smet, the Hippopotamus Goddess, in an exhibition of African art Liesl made me attend a few years ago. The gaffing consisted of two large bath-towels, which were rolled and tucked under her breasts, giving them what was, in comparison with the reality, a buxom contour. These towels were great matters of contention between Hannah and Willard, for she insisted that they were sanitary necessities, and he said they were gross impostures on the public. He cared nothing about gaffing; it was Hannah who made it a moral issue and drew a sharp line between gaffed Talent, like Abdullah, and honest Talent, like Fat Ladies.

"They wrangled about it a good deal. Hannah was voluble and she had a quality of shrewishness that came strangely from one whose professional personality depended on an impression of sunny good nature. She would nag about it for half an hour at a stretch, as we travelled on the train, until at last the usually taciturn Willard would say, in a low, ugly voice: 'Listen, Miz Hannah, you shut your goddam trap or next time we got a big crowd I'm gonna tell 'em about those gaffed tits of yours. See? Now shut up, I tell ya!'

"He would never have done it, of course. It would have been unforgivable professional conduct, and even Charlie would not have been able to keep Gus from throwing him off the show. But the menace in his voice would silence Hannah for a few hours.

"I was entranced by the World of Wonders during those early weeks and I had plenty of time to study it, for it was part of the agreement under which I lived that I must never be seen during working hours, except when real necessity demanded a quick journey to the donniker, between tricks. I often ate in the seclusion of Abdullah. The hours of the show were from eleven in the morning until eleven at night, and so I ate as big a breakfast as I could get, and depended on a hot dog or something of the sort being brought to me at noon and toward evening. Willard was supposed to attend to it, but he often forgot, and it was good-hearted Emily Dark who saw that I did not starve. Willard never ate much, and like so many people he could not believe that anyone wanted more than himself. There was an agreement of some sort between Willard and Gus as to what my status was; I know he got extra money for me, but I never saw any of it; I know Gus made him promise he would look after me and treat me well, but I don't think he had any idea what such words meant, and from time to time Gus would give him a dressing down about the condition I was in; for years I never had any clothes except those Gus bought me, stopping the money out of Willard's pay, but Gus had no idea of how to dress a child, and always bought everything too big, so that I would have lots of room to grow into it. Not that I needed many clothes; inside Abdullah I wore nothing but cotton shorts. I see now that it was a miserable life, and it is a wonder it didn't kill me; but at the time I accepted it as children must accept the world made for them by their guardians.

"At the beginning I was beglamoured by the show, and peeped at it out of Abdullah's bosom with unresting excitement. There was one full show an hour, and the whole of it was known as a trick. The trick began outside the tent on a platform beside the ticket-seller's box, and this part of it was called the bally. Not ballyhoo, which was an expression I never heard in the carnival world in my time. Gus usually sold the tickets, though there was someone to spell her when she had other business to attend to.

Charlie was the outside talker, not a barker, which is another expression I did not hear until a movie or a play made it popular. He roared through a megaphone to tell the crowd about what was to be seen inside the tent. Charlie was a flashy dresser and handsome in a flashy way, and he did his job well, most of the time.

"High outside the tent hung the banners, which were the big painted signs advertising the Talent; each performer had to pay for his own banner, though Gus ordered them from the artist and assured that there would be a pleasing similarity of style. As well as the banners, some of the Talent had to appear on the bally, and this boring job usually fell to the lesser artists; Molza ate a little fire, Sonny heaved a few weights, the Professor would lie on his back and write 'Pumpkin Centre, Agricultural Capital of Pumpkin County' on a huge piece of paper with his feet, and this piece of paper was thrown into the crowd, for whoever could grab it; Zovene the Midget Juggler did a few stunts, and now and then if business was slow Zitta would take out a few snakes, and the Darks would have to show themselves. But the essence of the bally was to create an appetite for what was inside the tent, not to give away entertainment, and Charlie pushed the purchase of tickets as hard as he could.

"After Abdullah was put on the show, which was as soon as we could get a fine banner sent up from New York, Willard did not have to take a turn on the bally.

"The bally and the sale of tickets took about twenty minutes, after which a lesser outside talker than Charlie did what he could to collect a crowd, and Charlie hurried inside, carrying a little cane he used as a pointer. Once in the tent he took on another role, which was called the lecturer, because everything in the World of Wonders was supposed to be improving and educational; Charlie's style underwent a change, too, for outside he was a great joker, whereas inside he was professorial, as he understood the word.

"I was much impressed by the fact that almost all the Talent spoke two versions of English—whatever was most comfortable when they were off duty, and a gaudy, begemmed, and gilded rhetoric when they were before the public. Charlie was a master of the impressive introduction when he presented the Talent to an audience.

"As spectators bought their tickets they were permitted into the tent, where they walked around and stared until the show began. Sometimes they asked questions, especially of Happy Hannah. 'You will assuredly hear everything in due season,' she would reply. The show was not supposed to begin without Charlie. When he pranced into the tent—he had an exaggeratedly youthful, high-stepping gait—he would summon the crowd around him and begin by introducing Sonny, *the Strongest Man you have ever seen, ladies and gentlemen, and the best-natured giant in the known world.* Poor old Sonny wasn't allowed to speak, because he had a strong German accent, and Germans were not popular characters in rural Canada in the late summer of 1918. Sonny was not allowed to linger over his demonstration, either, because Charlie was hustling the crowd toward Molza the Human Salamander, who thrust a lighted torch into his mouth, and then blew out a jet of flame which ignited a piece of newspaper Charlie held in his hand; Molza then swallowed swords until he had four of them stuck in his gullet. When I came to know him I got him to show me how to do it, and I can still swallow a paper-knife, or anything not too sharp. But swallowing swords and eating fire are hard ways to get a living, and dangerous after a few years. Then Professor Spencer wrote with his feet, having first demonstrated with some soap and a safety-razor with no blade in it how he shaved himself every day; the Professor would write the name of anybody who wished it; with his right foot he would write from left to right, and at the same time, underneath it and with his left foot, he would write the name from right to left. He wrote with great speed in a beautiful hand—or foot, I should say. It was quite a showy act, but the Professor never had his full due, I thought, because people were rather embarrassed by him. Then the Darks did their knife-throwing act.

"It was a very good act, and if only Joe had possessed some instinct of showmanship it would have been much better. But Joe was a very simple soul, a decent, honest fellow who ought to have been a workman of some sort. His talent for throwing knives was one of those freakish things that are sometimes found in people who are otherwise utterly unremarkable. His wife, Emily, was ambitious for him; she wanted him to be a veterinary, and when we were on the train she kept him pegging away at a correspondence course which would, when it was completed, bring him a diploma from some cut-rate college deep in the States. But it was obvious to everybody but Emily that it would never be completed, because Joe couldn't get anything into his head from a printed page. He could throw knives, and that was that. They both wore tacky home-made costumes, which bunched unbecomingly in the wrong places, and Emily stood in front of a pine board while Joe outlined her pleasant figure in knives. Nice people: minor Talent.

"By this time the audience had climbed the ladder of marvels to Rango the Missing Link, exhibited by Heinie Bayer. Rango was an orang-outang, who could walk a tightrope carrying a parasol; at the mid-point, he would suddenly swing downward, clinging to the rope with his toes, and reflectively eat a banana; then he would whirl upright, throw away the skin, and complete his journey. After that he sat at a table, and rang a bell, and Heinie, dressed as a clown waiter, served him a meal, which Rango ate with affected elegance, until he was displeased with a badly prepared dish, and pelted Heinie with food. Rango was surefire. Everybody loved him, and I was of their number until I tried to make friends with him and Rango spat some chewed-up nuts in my face. It was part of Heinie's deal with the management that Rango had to share a berth with him in our Pullman; although he was house-trained he was a nuisance because he was a bad sleeper, and likely to stick his hand into your berth in the night and pinch you—a very mean, twisting pinch. It was uncanny to poke your head out of your berth and see Rango swinging along the car, holding on to the tops of the green curtains, as if they were part of his native jungle.

"After Rango came Zitta the Jungle Queen. Snake acts are all the same. She pulled the snakes around her neck, wound them around her arms, and as a topper she knelt down and charmed her cobra *by no other power than that of the unaided human eye, with which she exerts hypnotic dominance over this most dreaded of jungle monsters,* as Charlie said, and ended by kissing it on its ugly snout.

"This was good showmanship. First the funny side of nature, then the ominous side of nature. The trick, I learned, was that Zitta leaned down to the cobra from above its head; cobras cannot strike upwards. It was a thrill, and Zitta had to know her business. As

I grew older and more cynical I sometimes wondered what it would be like if Zitta exercised her hypnotic powers on Rango, and kissed him, for a change. I don't think Rango was a lady's man.

"This left only Willard, Andro the Hermaphrodite, and Happy Hannah to complete the show; Zovene the Midget Juggler was only useful to get the audience out of the tent. On the basis of public attraction it was acknowledged that Willard must have the place of honour once Abdullah was on display. Charlie was in favour of giving Andro the place just before Abdullah but Happy Hannah would have none of it. She was clamorous. If a natural, educational wonder like herself, without any gaff about her, didn't take precedence over a gaffed monsterosity she was prepared to leave carnival life and despair of the human race. She made herself so unpleasant that she won the argument; Andro became very shrewish when he was under attack, but he lacked Hannah's large, embracing, Biblical flow of condemnation. When he had said that Hannah was a fat, loud-mouthed old bitch his store of abuse was exhausted; but she sailed into him with all guns firing.

" 'Don't think I hold it against you personally, Andro. No, I know you for what you are. I know the rock from whence ye are hewn—that no-good bunch o' Boston Greek fish-peddlers and small-time thieves; and I likewise know the hole of the Pit whence ye are digged—offering yourself to stand bare-naked in front of artists, some of 'em women, at fifty cents an hour. So I know it isn't really you that's speaking against me; it's the spirit of an unclean devil inside of you, crying with a loud voice; and I rebuke it just as our dear Lord did; I'm sitting right here, crying, "Hold thy peace and come out of him!" '

"This was Hannah's strength. All her immense bulk was crammed with Bible knowledge and quotations and it oozed out of her like currant-juice oozing out of a jelly-bag. She offered herself to the public as a Biblical marvel, a sort of she-Leviathan. She would not allow Charlie to speak for her. As soon as he had given her a lead—*And now, ladies and gentlemen, I present Happy Hannah, four hundred and eighty-seven pounds of good humour and chuckles*—she would burst in, 'Yes friends, and I'm the living proof of how fat a person can get and still bear it gladly in the Lord's name. I hope every person here knows his Bible and if they do, they know the comforting message of Proverbs eleven, twenty-five: *The liberal soul shall be made fat.* Yes friends, I am here not as a curiosity and certainly not as a monsterosity but to attest in my daily life and my public career to the Lord's abounding grace. I don't hafta be here; many offers from missionary societies and the biggest evangelists have been turned down in order that I may get around this whole continent and talk to the biggest possible audience of the real people, God's own folks, and attest to the Faith. Portraits of me as you see me now, each one individually autographed by my own hand, may be purchased at twenty-five cents apiece, and for another mere quarter I will include a priceless treasure, this copy of the New Testament which fits in the pocket and in which each and every word uttered by our Lord Jesus Christ during his earthly ministry is printed in RED. No Testament sold except with a portrait. Don't miss this great offer which is made by me at a financial sacrifice in order that the Lord's will may be done more abundantly here in Pumpkin Centre. Don't hang back folks; grab what I'm giving to you; I been made fat and when you possess this portrait of me as you see me now and this New Testament you'll hafta admit that I'm certainly the Liberal Soul. Come on, now, who's gonna be the first?'

"Hannah was able to hawk her pictures and her Testaments because of an arrangement written into every artiste's contract that they should be allowed to sell something at every show. They made their offer, or Charlie made it for them, as the crowd was about to move on to the next Wonder. The price was always twenty-five cents. Sonny had a book on body-building; Molza had only a picture of himself with his throat full of swords—a very slow item in terms of sales; Professor Spencer offered his personally written visiting cards, which were a nuisance because they took quite a while to prepare; Em Dark sold throwing knives Joe made in his spare time out of small files—a throwing knife has no edge, only a point; Heinie sold pictures of Rango; Zitta offered belts and bracelets which she made out of the skins of the snakes she had mauled to death—though Charlie didn't put it quite like that; Andro was another seller of pictures; Willard sold a pamphlet called *Secrets of Gamblers Revealed*, which was offered by Charlie as an infallible protection against dishonest card-players you might meet on trains; a lot of people bought them who didn't look like great travellers, and I judged they wanted to know the secrets of gamblers for some purpose of their own. I read it several times, and it was a stupefyingly uncommunicative little book, written at least thirty years before 1918. The agreement was that each Wonder offered his picture or whatever it might be after he had been exhibited, and that when the show had been completed, except for the Midget Juggler, Charlie would invite the audience once again not to leave without one of *these valuable mementoes of a unique and unforgettable personal experience and educational benefit*.

"From being an extremely innocent little boy it did not take me long to become a very knowing little boy. I picked up a great deal as we travelled from village to village on the train, for our Pullman was an educational benefit and certainly, for me, an unforgettable personal experience. I had an upper berth at the very end of the car, at some distance from Willard, whose importance in the show secured him a lower in the area where the shock of the frequent shuntings and accordion-like contractions of the train were least felt. I came to know who had bottles of liquor, and also who was generous with it and who kept it for his own use. I knew that neither Joe nor Em Dark drank, because it would have been a ruinous indulgence for a knife-thrower. The Darks, however, were young and vigorous, and sometimes the noises from their berth were enough to raise comment from the other Talent. I remember one night when Heinie, who shared his bottle with Rango, put Rango up to opening the curtains of the Darks' upper; Em screamed, and Joe grabbed Rango and threw him down into the aisle so hard that Rango screamed; Heinie offered to fight Joe, and Joe, stark naked and very angry, chased Heinie back to his berth and pummelled him. It took a full hour to soothe Rango; Heinie assured us that Rango was used to love and could not bear rough usage; Rango had to have at least two strong swigs of straight rye before he could sleep. But in the rough-and-tumble I had had a good look at Em Dark naked, and it was very different from Happy Hannah, I can assure you. All sorts of things that I had never heard of began, within a month, to whirl and surge and combine in my mind.

"A weekly event of some significance in our Pullman was Hannah's Saturday-night bath. She lived in continual hope of managing it without attracting attention, but that was ridiculous. First Gus would bustle down the aisle with a large tarpaulin and an armful of towels. Then Hannah, in an orange mobcap and a red dressing-gown, would lurch and stumble down the car; she was too big to fall into anybody's berth, but she sometimes came near to dragging down the green curtains when we were going around a bend. We all knew what happened in the Ladies' Retiring Room; Gus spread the tarpaulin, Hannah stood on it hanging onto the wash-basin, and Gus swabbed her down with a large sponge. It was for this service of Christian charity that she was called Elephant Gus when she was out of earshot. Drying Hannah took a long time, because there were large portions of her that she could not reach herself, and Gus used to towel her down, making a hissing noise between her teeth, like a groom.

"Sometimes Charlie and Heinie and Willard would be sitting up having a game of poker, and while the bath was in progress they would sing a hymn, 'Wash me and I shall be whiter than snow'. If they were high they had another version—

Wash me in the water
  That you washed the baby in,
And I shall be whiter
  Than the whitewash on the wall.

This infuriated Hannah, and on her return trip she would favour them with a few Biblical admonitions; she had a good deal to say about lasciviousness, lusts, excess of wine, revellings, banquetings, games of hazard, and abominable idolatries, out of First Peter. But she hocussed the text. There is no mention of 'games of hazard' or gambling anywhere in the Bible. She put that in for her own particular satisfaction. I knew it, and I soon recognized Hannah as my first hypocrite. A boy's first recognition of hypocrisy is, or ought to be, more significant than the onset of puberty. By the time Gus had stowed her into her special lower, which was supported from beneath with a few fence-posts, she was so refreshed by anger that she fell asleep at once, and snored so that she could be heard above the noise of the train.

"Very soon I became aware that the World of Wonders which had been a revelation to me, and I suppose to countless other country village people, was a weary bore to the Talent. This is the gnawing canker of carnival life: it is monstrously boring.

"Consider. We did ten complete shows a day; we had an hour off for midday food and another hour between six and seven; otherwise it was unremitting. We played an average of five days a week, which means fifty shows. We began our season as early as we could, but nothing much was stirring in the outdoor carnival line till mid-May, and after that we traipsed across country playing anywhere and everywhere—I soon stopped trying to know the name of the towns, and called them all Pumpkin Centre, like Willard—until late October. That makes something over a thousand shows. No wonder the Talent was bored. No wonder Charlie's talks began to sound as if he was thinking about something else.

"The only person who wasn't bored was Professor Spencer. He was a decent man, and couldn't give way to boredom, because his affliction meant perpetual improvisation in the details of his life. For instance, he had to get somebody to help him in the donniker, which most of us were ready to do, but wouldn't have done if he had not always been cheerful and fresh. He offered to teach me some lessons, because he said it was a shame for a boy to leave school as early as I had done. So he taught me writing, and arithmetic, and an astonishing amount of geography. He was the one man on the show who had to know where we were, what the population of the town was, the name of the mayor, and other things that he wrote on his blackboard as part of his show. He was a good friend to me, was Professor Spencer. Indeed, it was he who persuaded Willard to teach me magic.

"Willard had not been interested in doing that, or indeed anything, for me. I was necessary, but I was a nuisance. I have never met anyone in my life who was so bleakly and unconsciously selfish as Willard, and for one whose life has been spent in the theatre and carnival world that is a strong statement. But Professor Spencer nagged him into it—you could not shame or bully or cajole Willard into anything, but he was open to nagging—and he began to show me a few things with cards and coins. As my years with the World of Wonders wore on, I think what he taught me saved my reason. Certainly it is at the root of anything I can do now.

"Whoever taught Willard did it very well. He never gave names to the things he taught me, and I am sure he didn't know them. But since that time I have found that he taught me all there is to know about shuffling, forcing, and passing cards, and palming, ruffling, changing, and bridging, and the wonders of the *biseauté* pack, which is really the only trick pack worth having. With coins he taught me all the basic work of palming and passing, the French drop, *La Pincette, La Coulée,* and all the other really good ones. His ideal among magicians was Nelson Downs, whose great act, The Miser's Dream, he had seen at the Palace Theatre, New York, which was the paradise of his limited imagination. Indeed, it was a very much debased version of The Miser's Dream that he had been doing when I first saw him. He now did little conjuring in the World of Wonders, because of the ease of managing Abdullah.

"Inside Abdullah I was busy for perhaps five minutes in every hour. My movement was greatly restricted; I could not make a noise. What was I to do? I practised my magic, and for hours on end I palmed coins and developed my hands in the dark, and that is how I gained the technique which has earned me the compliment of this film you gentlemen are making. I recommend the method to young magicians; get yourself into a close-fitting prison for ten hours a day, and do nothing but manipulate cards and coins; keep that up for a few years and, unless you are constitutionally incapable, like poor Ramsay here, you should develop some adroitness, and you will at least have no chance to acquire the principal fault of the bad magician, which is looking at your hands as you work. That was how I avoided boredom: constant practice, and entranced observation, through Abdullah's bosom, of the public and the Talent of the World of Wonders.

"Boredom is rich soil for every kind of rancour and ugliness. In my first months on the show this attached almost entirely to the fortunes of the War. I knew nothing about the War, although as a schoolchild I had been urged to bring all my family's peachstones to school, where they were collected for some warlike purpose. Knowing boys said that a terrible poison gas was made from them.

Every morning in prayers our teacher mentioned the Allied Forces, and especially the Canadians. Once again knowing boys said you could always tell where her brother Jim was by the prayer, which was likely to contain a special reference to 'our boys at the Front', and later, 'our boys in the rest camps', and later still, 'our boys in the hospitals'. The War hung over my life like the clouds in the sky, and I heeded it as little. Once I saw Ramsay in the street, in what I later realized was the uniform of a recruit, but at the time I couldn't understand why he was wearing such queer clothes. I saw men in the streets with black bands on their arms, and asked my father why they wore them, but I can't remember what he answered.

"In the World of Wonders the War seemed likely at times to tear the show to pieces. The only music on the fairgrounds where we appeared came from the merry-go-round; tunes were fed into its calliope by the agency of large steel discs, perforated with rectangular holes; they worked on the same principle as the roll of a player-piano, but were much more durable, and rotated instead of uncoiling. Most of the music was of the variety we associate with merry-go-rounds. Who wrote it? Italians, I suspect, for it always had a gentle, quaintly melodious quality, except for one new tune which Steve, who ran the machine, had bought to give the show a modern air. It was the American war song—by that noisy fellow Cohan, was it?—called 'Over There!' It was less than warlike on a calliope, played at merry-go-round tempo, but everybody recognized it, and now and then some Canadian wag would sing loudly, to the final phrase—

And we won't be over
Till it's over
Over there!

If Hannah heard this, she became furious, for she was an inflamed American patriot and the War, for her, had begun when the Americans entered it in 1917. The Darks were Canadians, and not as tactful as Canadians usually are when dealing with their American cousins. I remember Em Dark, who was a most unlikely person to tell a joke, saying one midday, in September of 1918, when the

Talent was in the dressing tent, eating its hasty picnic: 'I heard a good one yesterday. This fellow says, Say, why are the American troops called Doughboys? And the other fellow says, Gee, I dunno; why? And the first fellow says, It's because they were needed in 1914 but they didn't rise till 1917. Do you get it? Needed, you see, like kneading bread, and—' But Em wasn't able to continue with her explanation of the joke because Hannah threw a sandwich at her and told her to knead that, and she was sick and tired of ingratitude from the folks in a little, two-bit backwoods country where they still had to pay taxes to the English King, and hadn't Em heard about the Argonne and the American blood that was being shed there by the bucketful, and how did Em think they would make the Hun say Uncle anyways with a lot of fat-headed Englishmen and Frenchmen messing it all up, and what they needed over there was American efficiency and American spunk?

"Em didn't have a chance to reply, because Hannah was immediately in trouble with Sonnenfels and Heinie Bayer, who smouldered under a conviction that Germany was hideously wronged and that everybody was piling on the Fatherland without any cause at all, and though they were just as good Americans as anybody they were damn well sick of it and hoped the German troops would show Pershing something new about efficiency. Charlie tried to quiet them down by saying that everybody knew the War was a put-up job and nobody was getting anything out of it but the Big Interests. This was a mistake, because Sonny and Heinie turned on him and told him that they knew why he was so glad to be in Canada, and if they were younger men they'd be in the scrap and they weren't going to say which side they'd be on, neither, but if they met anything like Charlie on the battlefield they'd just put a chain on him and show him off beside Rango.

"The battle went on for weeks, during which Joe Dark suffered the humiliation of having Em tell everybody that he wasn't in the Canadian Army because he had flat feet, and Hannah replying that you didn't need feet to fly a plane, but you sure needed brains. The only reasonable voice was that of Professor Spencer, who was a great reader of the papers, and an independent thinker; he was all for an immediate armistice and a peace conference. But as nobody wanted to listen to him, he lectured me, instead, so that I still have a very confused idea of the causes of that War, and the way it was fought. Hannah got a Stars and Stripes from somewhere, and stuck it up on her little platform. She said it made her feel good just to have it there.

"It all came about because of boredom. Boredom and stupidity and patriotism, especially when combined, are three of the greatest evils of the world we live in. But a worse and more lasting source of trouble was the final show in each village, which was called the Last Trick.

"It was agreed that the Last Trick ought to be livelier than the other nine shows of the day. The fair was at its end, the serious matters like the judging of animals and fancy-work had been completed, and most of the old folks had gone home, leaving young men and their girls, and the village cutups on the fairground. It was then that the true, age-old Spirit of Carnival descended on Wanless's World of Wonders, but of course it didn't affect everybody in the same way. Outside, the calliope was playing its favourite tune, 'The Poor Butterfly Waltz'; supposedly unknown to Gus, the man who ran the cat-rack had slipped in the gaff, so that the eager suitor who was trying to win a Kewpie Doll for the girl of his heart by throwing baseballs found that the stuffed pussycats wouldn't be knocked down. It was a sleazier, crookeder fair altogether than the one the local Fair Board had planned, but there was always a young crowd that liked it that way.

"On the bally, Charlie allowed his wit a freer play. As Zovene juggled with his spangled Indian clubs, Charlie would say, in a pretended undertone which carried well beyond his audience: 'Pretty good, eh? He isn't big, but he's good. Anyways, how big would you be if you'd been strained through a silk handkerchief?' The young bloods would guffaw at this, and their girls would clamour to have it explained to them. And when Zitta showed her snakes, she would drag the old cobra suggestively between her legs and up her front, while Charlie whispered, 'Boys-oh-boys, who wouldn't be a snake?'

"Inside the tent Charlie urged the young men to model themselves on Sonnenfels, so that all the girls would be after them, and they'd be up to the job. And when he came to Andro he would ogle his hearers and say, 'He's the only guy in the world who's glad to wake up in the morning and find he's beside himself.' He particularly delighted in tormenting Hannah. She did her own talking, but as she shrieked her devotion to the Lord Jesus, Charlie would lean down low, and say, in a carrying whisper, 'She hasn't seen her ace o' spades in twenty years.' The burst of laughter made Hannah furious, though she never caught what was said. She knew, however, that it was something dirty. However often she complained to Gus, and however often Gus harangued Charlie, the Spirit of Carnival was always too much for him. Nor was Gus whole-hearted in her complaints; what pleased the crowd was what Gus liked.

"Hannah attempted to fight fire with fire. She often made it known, in the Pullman, that in her opinion these modern kids weren't bad kids, and if you gave them a chance they didn't want this Sex and all like that. Sure, they wanted fun, and she knew how to give 'em fun. She was just as fond of fun as anybody, but she didn't see the fun in all this Smut and Filth. So she gave 'em fun.

" 'Lots o' fun in your Bible, boys and girls,' she would shout. 'Didn't you know that? Didya think the Good Book was all serious? You just haven't read it with the Liberal Heart, that's all. Come on now! Come on now, all of you! Who can tell me why you wouldn't dare to take a drink outa the first river in Eden? Come on, I bet ya know. Sure ya know. You're just too shy to say. Why wouldn't ya take a drink outa the first river in Eden?—Because it was Pison, that's why! If you don't believe me, look in Genesis two, eleven.' Then she would go off into a burst of wheezing laughter.

"Or she would point—and with an arm like hers, pointing was no trifling effort—at Zovene, shouting: 'You call him small? Say, he's a regular Goliath compared with the shortest man in the Bible. Who was he? Come on, who was he?—He was Bildad the Shuhite, Job two, eleven. See, the Liberal Heart can even get a laugh outa one of Job's Comforters. I betcha never thought of that, eh?' And again, one of her terrible bursts of laughter.

"Hannah understood nothing of the art of the comedian. It is dangerous to laugh at your own jokes, but if you must, it is a great mistake to laugh first. Fat people, when laughing, are awesome sights, enough to strike gravity into the onlooker. But Hannah was a whole World of Wonders in herself when she laughed. She forced her laughter, for after all, when you have told people for weeks that the only man in the Bible with no parents was Joshua, the son of Nun, the joke loses some of its savour. So she pushed laughter out of herself in wheezing, whooping cries, and her face became unpleasantly marbled with dabs of a darker red under the rouge she wore. Her collops wobbled uncontrollably, her vast belly heaved and trembled as she sucked breath, and sometimes she attempted to slap her thigh, producing a wet splat of sound. Fat Ladies ought not to tell jokes; their mirth is of the flesh, not of the mind. Fat Ladies ought not to laugh; a chuckle is all they can manage without putting a dangerous strain on their breathing and circulatory system. But Hannah would not listen to reason. She was determined to drive Smut back into its loathsome den with assaults of Clean Fun, and if she damaged herself in the battle, her wounds would be honourable.

"Sometimes she had an encouraging measure of success. Quite often there would be in the crowd some young man who was of a serious, religious turn of mind, and usually he was accompanied by a girl who had preacher's daughter written all over her. They had been embarrassed by Charlie's jokes when they understood them. They had been even more embarrassed when Rango, at a secret signal from Heinie, left his pretended restaurant table and urinated in a corner, while Heinie pantomimed a waiter's dismay. But with that camaraderie which exists among religious people just as it does among tinhorns and crooks, they recognized Hannah as a benign influence, and laughed with her, and urged her on to greater flights. She gave them her best. 'What eight fellas in the Bible milked a bear? *You* know! You musta read it a dozen times. D'ya give it up? Well, listen carefully: Huz, Buz, Kemuel, Chesed, Hazo, Pildash, Jidlaph, and Bethuel—*these eight did Milcah bear to Nahor, Abraham's brother*. Didya never think of it that way? Eh? Didn't ya? Well, it's in Genesis twenty-two.'

"When one of these obviously sanctified couples appeared, it was Hannah's pleasure to single them out and hold them up to the rest of the crowd as great cutups. 'Oh, I see ya,' she would shout; 'it's the garden of Eden all over again; the trouble isn't with the apple in the tree, it's with that pair on the ground.' And she would point at them, and they would blush and laugh and be grateful to be given a reputation for wickedness without having to do anything to acquire it.

"All of this cost Hannah dearly. After a big Saturday night, when she had exhausted her store of Bible riddles, she was almost too used up for her ritual bath. But she had worked herself up into a shocking sweat, and sometimes the smell of wet cornstarch from her sopping body spread a smell like a gigantic nursery pudding through the whole of the tent, and bathed she had to be, or there would be trouble with chafing.

"Her performance on these occasions made Willard deeply, cruelly angry. He would stand beside Abdullah and I could hear him swearing, repetitively but with growing menace, as she carried on. The worst of it was, if she secured any sort of success, she was not willing to stop; even when the crowd had passed on to see Abdullah, she would continue, at somewhat lesser pitch, with a few lingerers, who hoped for more Bible fun. In the Last Trick it was Willard's custom to have three people cut the cards for the automaton, instead of the usual one, and he wanted the undivided attention of the crowd. He hated Hannah, and from my advantageous peephole I was not long in coming to the conclusion that Hannah hated him.

"There were plenty of places in southern Ontario at that time where religious young people were numerous, and in these communities Hannah did not scruple to give a short speech in which she looked forward to seeing them next year, and implored them to join her in a parting hymn. 'God be with you till we meet again', she would strike up, in her thin, piercing voice, like a violin string played unskilfully and without a vibrato, and there were always those who, from religious zeal or just because they liked to sing, would join her. Nor was one verse enough. Charlie would strike in, as boldly as he could: *And now, ladies and gentlemen, our Master Marvel of the World of Wonders—Willard the Wizard and his Card-Playing Automaton, Abdullah, as soon to be exhibited on the stage of the Palace Theatre, New York*—but Hannah would simply put on more steam, and slow down, and nearly everybody in the tent would be wailing—

God be with you till we meet again!
Keep love's banner floating o'er you,
Smite death's threatening wave before you:
God be with you till we meet again!

And then the whole dismal chorus. It was a hymn of hate, and Willard met it with such hate as I have rarely seen.

"As for me, I was only a child, and my experience of hatred was slight, but so far as I could, and with what intensity of spirit I could muster, I hated them both. Hate and bitterness were becoming the elements in which I lived."

Eisengrim had a fine feeling for a good exit-line, and at this point he rose to go to bed. We rose, as well, and he went solemnly around the circle, shaking hands with us all in the European manner. Lind and Kinghovn even bowed as they did so, and when Magnus turned at the door to give us a final nod, they bowed again.

"Now why do you suppose we accord these royal courtesies to a man who has declared that he was Nobody for so many years," said Ingestree, when we had sat down again. "Because it is so very plain that he is not Nobody now. He is almost oppressively Somebody. Are we rising, and grinning, and even bowing out of pity? Are we trying to make it up to a man who suffered a dreadful denial of personality by assuring him that now we are quite certain he is a real person, just like us? Decidedly not. We defer to him, and hop around like courtiers because we can't help it. Why? Ramsay, do you know why?"

"No," said I; "I don't, and it doesn't trouble me much. I rather enjoy Magnus's lordly airs. He can come off his perch when he thinks proper. Perhaps we do it because we know he doesn't take it seriously; it's part of a game. If he insisted, we'd rebel."

"And when you rebelled, you would see a very different side of his nature," said Liesl.

"You play the game with him, I observe," said Ingestree. "You stand up when His Supreme Self-Assurance leaves the company. Yet you are mistress here, and we are your guests. Now why is that?"

"Because I am not quite sure who he is," said Liesl.

"You don't believe this story he's telling us?"

"Yes. I think that he has come to the time of his life when he feels the urge to tell. Many people feel it. It is the impulse behind a hundred bad autobiographies every year. I think he is being as honest as he can. I hope that when he finishes his story—if he does finish it—I shall know rather more. But I may not have my answer then."

"I don't follow; you hope to hear his story out, but you don't think it certain that you will know who he is even then, although you think he is being honest. What is this mystery?"

"Who is anybody? For me, he is whatever he is to me. Biographical facts may be of help, but they don't explain that. Are you married, Mr. Ingestree?"

"Well, no, actually, I'm not."

"The way you phrase your reply speaks volumes. But suppose you were married; do you think that your wife would be to you precisely what she was to her women friends, her men friends, her doctor, lawyer, and hairdresser? Of course not. To you she would be something special, and to you that would be the reality of her. I have not yet found out what Magnus is to me, although we have been business associates and friendly intimates for a long time. If I had been the sort of person who is somebody's mistress, I would have been his mistress, but I've never cared for the mistress role. I am too rich for it. Mistresses have incomes, and valuable possessions, but not fortunes. Nor can I say we have been lovers, because that is a messy expression people use when they are having sexual intercourse on fairly regular terms, without getting married. But I have had many a jolly night with Magnus, and many an exciting day with him. I still have to decide what he is to me. If humouring his foible for royal treatment helps me to come to a conclusion, I have no objection."

"Well, what about you, Ramsay? He keeps referring to you as his first teacher of magic. You knew him from childhood, then? You could surely say who he was?"

"I was almost present at his birth. But does that mean anything? An infant is a seed. Is it an oak seed or a cabbage seed? Who knows? All mothers think their children are oaks, but the world never lacks for cabbages. I would be the last man to pretend that knowing somebody as a child gave any real clue to who he is as a man. I can tell you this: he jokes about the lessons I gave him when he was a child, but he didn't think them funny then; he had a great gift for something I couldn't do at all, or could do with absurd effort. He was deadly serious during our lessons, and for a good reason. I could read the books and he couldn't. I think that may throw some light on what we have been hearing about the World of Wonders, which he presents as a kind of joke. I am perfectly certain it wasn't a joke at the time."

"I am sure he wasn't joking when he spoke of hatred," said Lind. "He was funny, or ironic, or whatever you want to call it, about the World of Wonders. We all know why people talk in that way; if we are amusing about our trials in the past, it is as if we say, 'See what I overcame—now I treat it as a joke—see how strong I have been and ask yourself if you could have overcome what I overcame?' But when he spoke of hatred, there was no joking."

"I don't agree," said Ingestree. "I think joking about the past is a way of suggesting that it wasn't really important. A way of veiling its horror, perhaps. We shudder when we hear of yesterday's plane accident, in which seventy people were killed; but we become increasingly philosophical about horrors that are further away. What is the Charge of the Light Brigade now? We remember it as a military blunder and we use it as a stick to beat military commanders, who are all popularly supposed to be blunderers. It has become a poem by Tennyson that embarrasses us by its exaltation of unthinking obedience. We joke about the historical fact and the poetic artifact. But how many people ever think of the young men who charged? Who takes five minutes to summon up in his mind what they felt as they rushed to death? It is the fate of the past to be fuel for humour."

"Have you put your finger on it?" said Lind. "Perhaps you have. Jokes dissemble horrors and make them seem unimportant. And why? Is it in order that more horrors may come? In order that we may never learn anything from experience? I have never been very fond of jokes. I begin to wonder if they are not evil."

"Oh rubbish, Jurgen," said Ingestree. "I was only talking about one aspect of humour. It's absolutely vital to life. It's one of the marks of civilization. Mankind wouldn't be mankind without it."

"I know that the English set a special value on humour," said

Lind. "They have a very fine sense of humour and sometimes they think theirs the best in the world, like their marmalade. Which reminds me that during the First World War some of the English troops used to go over the top shouting, 'Marmalade!' in humorously chivalrous voices, as if it were a heroic battle-cry. The Germans could never get used to it. They puzzled tirelessly to solve the mystery. Because a German cannot conceive that a man in battle would want to be funny, you see. But I think the English were dissembling the horror of their situation so that they would not notice how close they were to Death. Again, humour was essentially evil. If they had thought of the truth of their situation, they might not have gone over the top. And that might have been a good thing."

"Let's not theorize about humour, Jurgen," said Ingestree; "it's utterly fruitless and makes the very dullest kind of conversation."

"Now it's my turn to disagree," I said. "This notion that nobody can explain humour, or even talk sensibly about it, is one of humour's greatest cover-ups. I've been thinking a great deal about the Devil lately, and I have been wondering if humour isn't one of the most brilliant inventions of the Devil. What have you just been saying about it? It diminishes the horrors of the past, and it veils the horrors of the present, and therefore it prevents us from seeing straight, and perhaps from learning things we ought to know. Who profits from that? Not mankind, certainly. Only the Devil could devise such a subtle agency and persuade mankind to value it."

"No, no, no, Ramsay," said Liesl. "You are in one of your theological moods. I've watched you for days, and you have been moping as you do only when you are grinding one of your homemade theological axes. Humour is quite as often the pointer to truth as it is a cloud over truth. Have you never heard the Jewish legend—it's in the Talmud, isn't it?—that at the time of Creation the Creator displayed his masterwork, Man, to the Heavenly Host, and only the Devil was so tactless as to make a joke about it. And that was why he was thrown out of Heaven, with all the angels who had been unable to suppress their laughter. So they set up Hell as a kind of jokers' club, and thereby complicated the universe in a way that must often embarrass God."

"No," I said; "I've never heard that and as legends are my

speciality I don't believe it. Talmud my foot! I suspect you made that legend up here and now."

Liesl laughed loud and long, and pushed the brandy bottle toward me. "You are almost as clever as I am, and I love you, Dunstan Ramsay," she said.

"New or old, it's a very good legend," said Ingestree. "Because that's always one of the puzzles of religion—no humour. Not a scrap. What is the basis of our faith, when we have a faith? The Bible. The Bible contains precisely one joke, and that is a schoolmasterish pun attributed to Christ when he told Peter that he was the rock on which the Church was founded. Very probably a later interpolation by some Church Father who thought it was a real rib-binder. But monotheism leaves no room for jokes, and I've thought for a long time that is what is wrong with it. Monotheism is too po-faced for the sort of world we find ourselves in. What have we heard tonight? A great deal about how Happy Hannah tried to squeeze jokes out of the Bible in the hope of catching a few young people who were brimming with life. Frightful puns; the kind of bricks you make without straw. Whereas the Devil, when he is represented in literature, is full of excellent jokes, and we can't resist him because he and his jokes make so much sense. To twist an old saying, if the Devil had not existed, we should have had to invent him. He is the only explanation of the appalling ambiguities of life. I give you the Devil!"

He raised his glass, but only he and Liesl drank the toast. Kinghovn, who had been getting into the brandy very heavily, was almost asleep. Lind was musing, and no sign of amusement appeared on his long face. I couldn't possibly have drunk such a toast, offered in such a spirit. Ingestree was annoyed.

"You don't drink," said he.

"Perhaps I shall do so later, when I have had time to think it over," said Lind. "Private toasts are out of fashion in the English-speaking world; you only drink them on formal occasions, as part of the decorum of stupidity. But we Scandinavians have still one foot in Odin's realm, and when we drink a toast we mean something quite serious. When I drink to the Devil I shall want to be quite serious."

"I hesitate to say so, Roland," I said, "but I wish you hadn't done that. I quite agree that the Devil is a great joker, but I don't think it is particularly jolly to be the butt of one of his jokes. You have called his attention to you in what I must call a frivolous way—damned silly, to be really frank. I wish you hadn't done that."

"You mean he'll do something to me? You mean that from henceforth I'm a Fated Man? You know, I've always fancied the role of Fated Man. What do you think it'll be? Car accident? Loss of job? Even a nasty death?"

"Who am I to probe the mind of a World Spirit?" I said. "But if I were the Devil—which, God be thanked, I am not—I might throw a joke or two in your direction that would test your sense of humour. I don't suppose you're a Fated Man."

"You mean I'm too small fry for that?" said Ingestree. He was smiling, but he didn't like my serious tone and was inviting me to insult him. Luckily Kinghovn woke up, slightly slurred in speech but full of opinion.

"You're all out of your heads," he shouted. "No humour in the Bible. All right. Scrub out the Bible. Use the script Eisengrim has given us. Film the subtext. Then I'll show you some humour: that Fat Woman—let me give you a peep-shot of her groaning in the donniker, or being swilled down by Gus; let me show her shrieking her bloody-awful jokes while the Last Trick gets dirtier and dirtier. Then you'll hear some laughter. You're all mad for words. Words are just farts from a lot of fools who have swallowed too many books. Give me things! Give me the appearance of a thing, and I'll show you the way to photograph it so the reality comes right out in front of your eyes. The Devil? Balls! God? Balls! Get me that Fat Woman and I'll photograph her one way and you'll know the Devil made her, then I'll photograph her another way and you'll swear you see the work of God! Light! That's the whole secret. Light! And who understands it? I do!"

Lind and Ingestree decided it was time to take him to his bed. As they manhandled him down the long entry-steps of Sorgenfrei he was shouting, "Light! Let there be light! Who said that? I said it!"

8

The film-makers were drawing near the end of their work. All but a few special scenes of *Un Hommage à Robert-Houdin* were "in the can"; what remained was to arrange backstage shots of Eisengrim being put into his "gaffed" conjuror's evening coat by the actor who played the conjuror's son and assistant; of assistants working quietly and deftly while the great magician produced astonishing effects on the stage; of Mme Robert-Houdin putting the special padded covers over the precious and delicate automata; of the son-assistant gently loading a dozen doves, or three rabbits, or even a couple of ducks into a space which seemed incapable of holding them; of all the splendidly efficient organization which was needed to produce the effect of the illogical and incredible. That night, therefore, Eisengrim moved his narrative along a little faster.

"You don't want a chronological account of my seven years as the mechanism of Abdullah," he said, "and indeed it would be impossible for me to give you one. Something was happening all the time, but only two or three matters were of any importance. We were continually travelling and seeing new places, but in fact we saw nothing. We brought excitement and perhaps a whisper of magic into thousands of rural Canadian lives, but our own lives were vast unbroken prairies of boredom. We were continually on the alert, sizing up the Rubes and trying to match what we gave to what they wanted, but no serious level of our minds was ever put to work.

"For Sonnenfels, Molza, and poor old Professor Spencer it was the only life they knew or could expect to have; the first two kept themselves going by nursing some elaborate, inexhaustible, ill-defined personal grievance which they shared; Spencer fed himself on complex, unworkable economic theories, and he would jaw you half to death about bimetallism, or Social Credit, if you gave him a chance. The Fat Woman had her untiring crusade against smut and irreligion; she could not reconcile herself to being simply fat, and I suppose this suggests some kind of mental or spiritual life in her. I saw hope dying in poor Em Dark, as Joe proved his incapacity to learn anything that would get them out of carnival life. Zitta was continually on the lookout for somebody to marry; she couldn't make any money, because she had to spend so much on new, doctored snakes; but how do you get a sucker to the altar if you are always on the move? She would have snatched at Charlie, but Charlie liked something fresher, and anyhow Gus was vigilant to save Charlie from designing women. Zovene was locked in the misery of dwarfdom; he wasn't really a midget, because a midget has to be perfectly formed, and he had a small but unmistakable hump; he was a sour little fellow, and deeply unhappy, I'm sure. Heinie Bayer had lived so long with Rango that he was more like Rango than like a man; they did not bring out the best in each other.

"Like a lot of monkeys Rango was a great masturbator, and when Happy Hannah complained about it Heinie would snicker and say, 'It's natural, ain't it?' and encourage Rango to do it during the Last Trick, where the young people would see him. Then Hannah would shout across the tent, 'Who so shall offend one of these little ones which believe in me, it were better for him that a millstone were hanged about his neck, and that he were drowned in the depth of the sea.' But the youngsters can't have been believers in the sense of the text, for they hung around Rango, some snickering, some ashamedly curious, and some of the girls obviously unable to understand what was happening. Gus tried to put a stop to this, but even Gus had no power over Rango, except to put him off the show, and he was too solid a draw for that. Hannah decided that Rango was a type of natural, unredeemed man, and held forth at length on that theme. She predicted that Rango would go mad, if he had any brains to go mad with. But Rango died unredeemed.

"So far as I was concerned, the whole of Wanless's World of Wonders was unredeemed. Did Christ die for these, I asked myself, hidden in the shell of Abdullah. I decided that He didn't. I now think I was mistaken, but you must remember that I began these reflections when I was ten years old, and deep in misery. I was in a world which seemed to me to be filthy in every way; I had grown up in a world where there was little love, but much concern about goodness. Here I could see no goodness, and felt no goodness."

Lind intervened. "Excuse me if I am prying," he said, "but you have been very frank with us, and my question is one of deep concern, not simple curiosity. You were swept into the carnival because Willard had raped you; was there any more of that?"

"Yes, much more of it. I cannot pretend to explain Willard, and I think such people must be rare. I know very well that homosexuality includes love of all sorts, but in Willard it was just a perverse drive, untouched by affection or any concern at all, except for himself. At least once every week we repeated that first act. Places had to be found, and when it happened it was quick and usually done in silence except for occasional whimpers from me and—this was very strange—something very like whimpers from Willard."

"And you never complained, or told anybody?"

"I was a child. I knew in my bones that what Willard did to me was very wrong, and he was careful to let me know that it was my fault. If I said a word to anybody, he told me, I would at once find myself in the hands of the law. And what would the law do to a boy who did what I did? Terrible things. When I dared to ask what the law would do to him, he said the law couldn't touch him; he knew highly placed people everywhere."

"How can you have continued to believe that?"

"Oh, you people who are so fortunately born, so well placed, so sure the policeman is your friend! Do you remember my home, Ramsay?"

"Very well."

"An abode of love, was it?"

"Your mother loved you very much."

"My mother was a madwoman. Why? Ramsay has very fine theories about her; he had a special touch with her. But to me she was a perpetual reproach because I knew that her madness was my fault. My father told me that she had gone mad at the time of my birth, and because of it. I was born in 1908, when all sorts of extraordinary things were still believed about childbirth, especially in places like Deptford. Those were the sunset days of the great legend of motherhood. When your mother bore you, she went down in her anguish to the very gates of Death, in order that you might have life. Nothing that you could do subsequently would work off your birth-debt to her. No degree of obedience, no unfailing love, could put the account straight. Your guilt toward her was a burden you carried all your life. Christ, I can hear Charlie now, standing on the stage of a thousand rotten little vaude houses, giving out that message in a tremulous voice, while the pianist played 'In a Monastery Garden'—

> M is for the million smiles she gave me;
> O means only that she's growing old;
> T is for the times she prayed to save me;
> H is for her heart, of purest gold;
> E is every wrong that she forgave me;
> R is right—and Right she'll always be!
> Put them all together, they spell MOTHER—
> A word that means the world to me!

That was the accepted attitude toward mothers, at that time, in the world I belonged to. Well? Imagine what it was like to grow up with a mother who had to be tied up every morning before my father could go off to his work as an accountant at the planing-mill; he was a parson no longer because her disgrace had made it impossible for him to continue his ministry. What was her disgrace? Something that made my schoolmates shout 'Hoor!' when they passed our house. Something that made them call out filthy jokes about hoors when they saw me. So there you have it. A disgraced and ruined home, and for what reason? Because I was born into it. That was the reason.

"That wasn't all. I said that when Willard used me he whimpered. Sometimes he spoke in his whimpering, and what he said then was, 'You goddam little hoor!' And when it was over, more than once he slapped me mercilessly around the head, saying, 'Hoor! You're nothing but a hoor!' It wasn't really condemnation; it seemed to be part of his fulfilment, his ecstasy. Don't you understand? 'Hoor' was what my mother was, and what had brought our family down because of my birth. 'Hoor' was what I was. I was the filthiest thing alive. And I was Nobody. Now do you ask me why I didn't complain to someone about ill usage? What rights had I? I hadn't even a conception of what 'rights' were."

"Could this go on without anybody knowing, or at least suspecting?" Lind was pale; he was taking this hard; I had not thought of him as having so much compassionate feeling.

"Of course they knew. But Willard was crafty and they had no proof. They'd have had to be very simple not to know that something was going on, and carnival people weren't ignorant about perversion. They hinted, and sometimes they were nasty, especially Sonnenfels and Molza. Heinie and Zovene thought it was a great joke. Em Dark had spells of being sorry for me, but Joe didn't want her to mix herself up in anything that concerned Willard, because Willard was a power in the World of Wonders. He and Charlie were very thick, and if Charlie turned against any of the Talent, there were all kinds of ways he could reduce their importance in the show, and then Gus might get the idea that some new Talent was wanted.

"Furthermore, I was thought to be bad luck by most of the Talent, and show people are greatly involved with the idea of luck. Early in my time on the show I got into awful trouble with Molza because I inadvertently shifted his trunk a few inches in the dressing tent. It was on a bit of board I wanted to use in my writing-lesson with Professor Spencer. Suddenly Molza was on me, storming incomprehensibly, and Spencer had trouble quieting him down. Then Spencer warned me against ever moving a trunk, which is very bad luck indeed; when the handlers bring it in from the baggage wagon they put it where it ought to go, and there it stays until they take it back to the train. I had to go through quite a complicated ceremony to ward off the bad luck, and Molza fussed all day.

"The idea of the Jonah is strong with show people. A bringer of ill luck can blight a show. Some of the Talent were sure I was a Jonah, which was just a way of focussing their detestation of what I represented, and of Willard, whom they all hated.

"Only the Fat Woman ever spoke to me directly about who and what I was. I forget exactly when it was, but it was fairly early in my experience on the show. It might have been during my second or third year, when I was twelve or thereabouts. One morning before the first trick, and even before the calliope began its toot-up, which was the signal that the World of Wonders and its adjuncts were opening for business, she was sitting on her throne and I was doing something to Abdullah, which I checked carefully every day for possible trouble.

" 'Come here, kid,' she said. 'I wanta talk to you. And I wanta talk mouth to mouth, even apparently, and not in dark speeches. Them words mean anything to you?'

" 'That's from Numbers,' I said.

" 'Numbers is right; Numbers twelve, verse eight. How do you know that?'

" 'I just know it.'

" 'No, you don't just know it. You been taught it. And you been taught it by somebody who cared for your soul's salvation. Was it your Ma?'

" 'My Pa,' I said.

" 'Then did he ever teach you Deuteronomy twenty-three, verse ten?'

" 'Is that about uncleanness in the night?'

" 'That's it. You been well taught. Did he ever teach you Genesis thirteen, verse thirteen? That's one of the unluckiest verses in the Bible.'

" 'I don't remember.'

" 'Not that the men of Sodom were wicked and sinners before the Lord exceedingly?'

" 'I don't remember.'

" 'I bet you remember Leviticus twenty, thirteen.'

" 'I don't remember.'

" 'You do so remember! If a man also lie with mankind as he lieth with a woman, both of them have committed an abomination; they shall surely be put to death; their blood shall be upon them.'

"I said nothing, but I am sure my face gave me away. It was one of Willard's most terrible threats that if I were caught I should certainly be hanged. But I was mute before the Fat Woman.

" 'You know what that means, dontcha?'

"Oh, I knew what it meant. In my time on the show I had already learned a great deal about mankind lying with women, because Charlie talked about little else when he sat on the train with Willard. It was a very dark matter, for all I knew about it was the parody of this act which I was compelled to go through with

Willard, and I assumed that the two must be equally horrible. But I clung to the child's refuge: silence.

" 'You know where that leads, dontcha? Right slap to Hell, where the worm dieth not and the fire is not quenched.'

"From me, nothing but silence.

" 'You're in a place where no kid ought to be. I don't mean the show, naturally. The show contains a lotta what's good. But that Abdullah! That's an idol, and that Willard and Charlie encourage the good folks that come in here for an honest show to bow down and worship almost before it, and they won't be held guiltless. No sirree! Nor you, neither, because you're the works of an idol and just as guilty as they are.'

" 'I just do what I'm told,' I managed to say.

" 'That's what many a sinner's said, right up to the time when it's no good saying it any longer. And those tricks. You're learning tricks, aren't you? What do you want tricks for?'

"I had a happy inspiration. I looked her straight in the eye. 'I count them but dung, that I may win Christ,' I said.

" 'That's the right way to look at it, boy. Put first things first. If that's the way you feel, maybe there's some hope for you still.' She sat a little forward in her chair, which was all she could manage, and put her pudgy hands on her great knees, which were shown off to advantage by her pink rompers. 'I'll tell you what I always say,' she continued; 'there's two things you got to be ready to do in this world, and that's fight for what's right, and read your Bible every day. I'm a fighter. Always have been. A mighty warrior for the Lord. And you've seen me on the train, reading my old Bible that's so worn and thumbed that people say to me, "That's a disgrace; why don't you get yourself a decent copy of the Lord's Word?" And I reply, "I hang onto this old Bible because it's seen me through thick and thin, and what looks like dirt to you is the wear of love and reverence on every page." A clean sword and a dirty Bible! That's my war-cry in my daily crusade for the Lord: a clean sword and a dirty Bible! Now, you remember that. And you ponder on Leviticus twenty, thirteen, and cut out all that fornication and Sodom abomination before it's too late, if it isn't too late already.'

"I got away, and hid myself in Abdullah and thought a lot about what Happy Hannah had said. My thoughts were like those of many a convicted sinner. I was pleased with my cleverness in thinking up that text that had averted her attack. I sniggered that I had even been able to use a forbidden word like 'dung' in a sanctified sense. I was frightened by Leviticus twenty, thirteen, and—you see how much a child of the superstitious carnival I had already become—by the double thirteen verse from Genesis. Double thirteen! What could be more ominous! I knew I ought to repent, and I did, but I knew I could not leave off my sin, or Willard might kill me, and not only was I afraid to die, I quite simply didn't want to die. And such is the resilience of childhood that when the first trick advanced as far as Abdullah, I was pleased to defeat a particularly obnoxious Rube.

"After that I had many a conversation with Hannah in which we matched texts. Was I a hypocrite? I don't think so. I had simply acquired the habit of adapting myself to my audience. Anyhow, my readiness with the Bible seemed to convince her that I was not utterly damned. I had no such assurance, but I was getting used to living with damnation.

"I had a Bible. I stole it from a hotel. It was one of those sturdy copies the Gideons spread about so freely in hotel rooms. I snitched one at the first opportunity, and as Professor Spencer was teaching me to read very capably I spent many an hour with it. I felt no compunction about the theft, because theft was part of the life I lived. Willard was as good a pickpocket as I have ever known, and one of the marks of his professionalism was that he was not greedy or slapdash in his methods.

"He had an agreement with Charlie. At a point about the middle of the bally, during one of the night shows, Charlie would interrupt his description of the World of Wonders to say, very seriously, *Ladies and gentlemen, I think I ought to warn you, on behalf of the management, that pickpockets may be at work at this fair. I give you my assurance that nothing is farther from the spirit of amusement and education represented by our exhibition than the utterly indefensible practice of theft. But as you know, we cannot control everything that may happen in the vicinity of our show. And therefore I urge you, as your friend and as a member of the Wanless organization which holds nothing dearer than its repu-*

tation for unimpeachable honesty, that you should keep a sharp eye, and perhaps also a hand, on your wallets. And if there should be any loss—which the Wanless organization most sincerely hopes may not be the case—we beg you to report it to us, and to your excellent local police force, so that the thief may be apprehended if that should prove to be possible. The gaff here was that when he spoke of thieves, Rubes who had a full wallet were likely to put a hand on it. Willard spotted them from the back of the crowd, and during the rest of Charlie's pious spiel he would gently lift one from a promising Rube. It had to be very quick work. Then, when he had taken the money, he substituted a wad of newspaper of the appropriate size, and either during the bally, or when the Rube came into the tent, he would put the wallet back in place. Rubes generally carried their wallets on the left hip, and as their pants were often a tight fit, a light hand was necessary.

"Willard was never caught. If the Rube came to complain that he had been robbed, Charlie put on a show for him, shook his head sadly, and said that this was one of the problems that confronted honest show folks. Willard never pinched more than one bankroll in a town, and never robbed in the same town two years running. Willard liked best to steal from the local cop, but as cops rarely had much money this was a larcenous foppery which he did not often allow himself.

"Gus never caught on. Gus was a strangely innocent woman in everything that pertained to Charlie and his doings. Of course Charlie got a fifty per cent cut of what Willard stole.

"Willard knew I stole the Bible, and he was angry. Theft, he gave me to understand, was serious business and not for kids. Get caught stealing some piece of junk, and how were you to get back to serious theft again? Never steal anything trivial. This was perhaps the only moral precept Willard ever impressed on me.

"Anyhow, I had a hotel Bible, and I read it constantly, in many another hotel. The carnival business is a fair-weather business, and in winter it could not be pursued and the carnival had to be put to bed.

"That did not mean a cessation of work. The brother who never travelled with the carnival, but who did all our booking, was Jerry Wanless, and he handled the other side of the business, which was vaudeville booking. As soon as the carnival season was over, Willard and Abdullah were booked into countless miserable little vaudeville theatres throughout the American and Canadian Middle West.

"It was an era of vaudeville and there were thousands of acts to fill thousands of spots all over the continent. There was a hierarchy of performance, beginning with the Big Time, which was composed of top acts that played in the big theatres of big cities for a week or more at a stretch. After it came the Small Big Time, which was pretty good and played lesser houses in big and middle-sized cities. Then came the Small Time, which played smaller towns in the sticks and was confined to split weeks. Below that was a rabble of acts that nobody wanted very much, which played for rotten pay in the worst vaude houses. Nobody ever gave it a name, and those who belonged to it always referred to it as Small Time, but it was really Very Small Time. That was where Jerry Wanless booked incompetent dog acts, jugglers who were on the booze, dirty comedians, Single Women without charm or wit, singers with nodes on their vocal chords, conjurors who dropped things, quick-change artistes who looked the same in all their impersonations, and a crowd of carnies like Willard and some of the other Talent from the World of Wonders.

"It was the hardest kind of entertainment work, and we did it in theatres that seemed never to have been swept, for audiences that seemed never to have been washed. We did continuous vaudeville: six acts followed by a 'feature' movie, round and round and round from one o'clock in the afternoon until midnight. The audience was invited to come when it liked and stay as long as it liked. In fact, it changed completely almost every show, because there was always an act called a 'chaser' which was reckoned to be so awful that even the people who came to our theatres couldn't stand it. Quite often during my years in vaudeville Zovene the Midget Juggler filled this ignominious spot. Poor old Zovene wasn't really as awful as he appeared, but he was pretty bad and he was wholly out of fashion. He dressed in a spangled costume that was rather like the outfit worn by Mr. Punch—a doublet and tight knee-breeches, with striped stockings and little pumps. He had only one outfit, and he had shed spangles for so long that he looked very shabby. There was still a wistful prettiness about him as he skipped nimbly to 'Funiculi funicula' and tossed coloured Indian clubs in the air. But it was a prettiness that would appeal only to an antiquarian of the theatre, and we had no such rarities in our audiences.

"There is rank and precedence everywhere, and here, on the bottom shelf of vaudeville, Willard was a headliner. He had the place of honour, just before Zovene came on to empty the house. The 'professor' at the piano would thump out an Oriental theme from *Chu Chin Chow* and the curtain would rise to reveal Abdullah, bathed in whatever passed for an eerie light in that particular house. Behind Abdullah might be a backdrop representing anything—a room in a palace, a rural glade, or one of those improbable Italian gardens, filled with bulbous balustrades and giant urns, which nobody has ever seen except a scene-painter.

"Willard would enter in evening dress, wearing a cape, which he doffed with an air, and held extended briefly at his right side; when he folded it, a shabby little table with his cards and necessaries had appeared behind it. Applause? Never! The audiences we played to rarely applauded and they expected a magician to be magical. If they were not asleep, or drunk, or pawing the woman in the next seat, they received all Willard's tricks with cards and coins stolidly.

"They liked it better when he did a little hypnotism, asking for members of the audience to come to the stage to form a 'committee' which would watch his act at close quarters, and assure the rest of the audience that there was no deception. He did the conventional hypnotist's tricks, making men saw wood that wasn't there, fish in streams that had no existence, and sweat in sunlight that had never penetrated into that dismal theatre. Finally he would cause two of the men to start a fight, which he would stop. The fight always brought applause. Then, when the committee had gone back to their seats, came the topper of his act, Abdullah the Wonder Automaton of the Age. It was the same old business; three members of the audience chose cards, and three times Abdullah chose a higher one. Applause. Real applause, this time. Then the front-drop—the one with advertisements painted on it—came down and poor old Zovene went into his hapless act.

"The only other Talent from the World of Wonders that was booked into the places where we played were Charlie, who did a monologue, and Andro.

"Andro was becoming the worst possible kind of nuisance. He was showing real talent, and to hear Charlie and Willard talk about it you would think he was a traitor to everything that was good and pure in the world of show business. But I was interested in Andro, and watched him rehearse. He never talked to me, and probably regarded me as a company spy. There were such things, and they reported back to Jerry in Chicago what Talent was complaining about money, or slacking on the job, or black-mouthing the management. But Andro was the nearest thing to real Talent I had met with up to that time, and he fascinated me. He was a serious, unrelenting worker and perfectionist.

"Imitators of his act have been common in night-clubs for many years, and I don't suppose he was the first to do it, but certainly he was the best of the lot. He played in the dark, except for a single spotlight, and he waltzed with himself. That is to say, on his female side he wore a red evening gown, cut very low in the back, and showing lots of his female leg in a red stocking; on his masculine side he wore only half a pair of black satin knee-breeches, a black stocking and a pump with a phoney diamond buckle. When he wrapped himself in his own arms, we saw a beautiful woman in the arms of a half-naked muscular man, whirling rhythmically around the stage in a rapturous embrace. He worked up all sorts of illusions, kissing his own hand, pressing closer what looked like two bodies, and finally whirling offstage for what must undoubtedly be further romance. He was a novelty, and even our audiences were roused from their lethargy by him. He improved every week.

"Willard and Charlie couldn't stand it. Charlie wrote to Jerry and I heard what he said, for Charlie liked his own prose and read it aloud to Willard. Charlie deplored 'the unseemly eroticism' of the act, he said. It would get Jerry a bad name to book such an act into houses that catered to a family trade. Jerry wrote back telling Charlie to shut up and leave the booking business to him. He suggested that Charlie clean up his own act, of which he had received bad reports. Obviously some stoolpigeon had it in for Charlie.

"As a monologist, Charlie possessed little but the self-assurance necessary for the job. Such fellows used to appear before the audience, flashily dressed, with the air of a relative who has made good in the big city and come home to amuse the folks. 'Friends, just before the show I went into one of your local restaurants and looked down the menoo for something tasty. I said to the waiter, Say, have you got frogs' legs? No sir, says he, I walk like this because I got corns. You know, one of the troubles today is Prohibition. Any disagreement? No. I didn't think there would be. But the other day I stepped into a blind pig not a thousand miles from this spot, and I said to the waiter, Bring me a couple of glasses of beer. So he did. So I drank one. Then I got up to leave, and the waiter comes running. Hey, you didn't pay for those two glasses of beer, he said. That's all right, I said, I drank one and left the other to settle. Then I went to keep a date with a pretty schoolteacher. She's the kind of schoolteacher I like best—lots of class and no principle. I get on better with schoolteachers now than I did when I was a kid. My education was completed early. One day in school I put up my hand and the teacher said, What is it, and I said, Please may I leave the room? No, she says, you stay here and fill the inkwells. So I did, and she screamed, and the principal expelled me. . . .' And so on, for ten or twelve minutes, and then he would say, 'But seriously folks—' and go into a rhapsody about his Irish mother, and a recitation of that tribute to motherhood. Then he would run off the stage quickly, laughing as if he had been enjoying himself too much to hold it in. Sometimes he got a spatter of applause. Now and then there would be dead silence, and some sighing. Vaudeville audiences in those places could give the loudest sighs I have ever heard. Prisoners in the Bastille couldn't have touched them.

"In the monologues of people like Charlie there were endless jokes about minorities—Jews, Dutch, Squareheads, Negroes, Irish, everybody. I never heard of anybody resenting it. The sharpest jokes about Jews and Negroes were the ones we heard from Jewish and Negro comedians. Nowadays I understand that a comedian doesn't dare to make a joke about anyone but himself, and if he does too much of that he is likely to be tagged as a masochist, playing for sympathy because he is so mean to himself. The old vaude jokes were sometimes cruel, but they were fairly funny and they were lightning-rods for the ill-will of audiences like ours, who had a plentiful supply of ill-will. We played to people who had not been generously used by life, and I suppose we reflected their state of mind.

"I spent my winters from 1918 until 1928 in vaudeville houses of the humblest kind. As I sat inside Abdullah and peeped out through the spy-hole in his bosom I learned to love these dreadful theatres. However wretched they were, they appealed to me powerfully. It was not until much later in my life that I learned what it was that spoke to me of something fine, even when the language was garbled. It was Liesl, indeed, who showed me that all theatres of that sort—the proscenium theatres that are out of favour with modern architects—took their essential form and style from the ball-rooms of great palaces, which were the theatres of the seventeenth and eighteenth centuries. All the gold, and stucco ornamentation, the cartouches of pan-pipes and tambourines, the masks of Comedy, and the upholstery in garnet plush were democratic stabs at palatial luxury; these were the palaces of the people. Unless they were Catholics, and spent some time each week in a gaudy church, this was the finest place our audiences could enter. It was heart-breaking that they should be so tasteless and rundown and smelly, but their ancestry was a noble one. And of course the great movie and vaudeville houses where Charlie and Willard would never play, or enter except as paying customers, were real palaces of the people, built in what their owners and customers believed to be a regal mode.

"There was nothing regal about the accommodation for the Talent. The dressing-rooms were few and seemed never to be cleaned; when there were windows they were filthy, and high in the walls, and were protected on the outside by wire mesh which caught paper, leaves, and filth; as I remember them now most of the rooms had a dado of deep brown to a height of about four feet from the floor, above which the walls were painted a horrible green. There were wash-basins in these rooms, but there was never more than one donniker, usually in a pitiful state of exhaustion, sighing and wheezing the hours away at the end of a corridor. But there was always a star painted on the door of one of these dismal holes, and it was in the star dressing-room that Willard, and Charlie (as a relative of the management) changed their clothes, and where I was tolerated as a dresser and helper.

"It was as a dresser that I travelled, officially. Dresser, and assistant to Willard. It was never admitted that I was the effective part of Abdullah, and we carried a screen which was set up to conceal the back of the automaton, so that the stagehands never saw me climbing into my place. They knew, of course, but they were not supposed to know, and such is the curious loyalty and discipline of even these rotten little theatres that I never heard of anyone telling the secret. Everybody backstage closed ranks against the audience, just as in the carnival we were all in league against the Rubes.

"I spent all day in the theatre, because the only alternative was the room I shared with Willard in some cheap hotel, and he didn't want me there. My way of life could hardly have been more in contradiction of what is thought to be a proper environment for a growing boy. I saw little sunlight, and I breathed an exhausted and dusty air. My food was bad, because Willard kept me on a very small allowance of money, and as there was nobody to make me eat what I should, I ate what I liked, which was cheap pastry, candy, and soft drinks. I was not a fanatical washer, but as I shared a bed with Willard he sometimes insisted that I take a bath. By every rule of hygiene I should have died of several terrible diseases complicated with malnutrition, but I didn't. In a special and thoroughly unsuitable way, I was happy. I even contrived to learn one or two things which were invaluable to me.

"Except for his dexterity as a conjuror, pickpocket, and cardsharp, Willard did nothing with his hands. As I told you, Abdullah had some mechanism in his base, and when Willard moved the handle that set it in motion, it was supposed to enable Abdullah to do clever things with cards. The mechanism was a fake only in so far as it related to Abdullah's skill; otherwise it was genuine enough. But it was always breaking down, and this was embarrassing when we were on show. Early in my time with Willard I explored those wheels and springs and cogs, and very soon discovered how to set them right when they stuck. The secret was very simple; Willard never oiled the wheels, and if somebody else oiled them for him, he allowed the oil to grow thick and dirty so that it clogged the works. Quite soon I took over the care of Abdullah's fake mechanism, and though I still did not really understand it I was capable enough at maintaining it.

"I suppose I was thirteen or so when a property man at one of the theatres where we played saw me cleaning and oiling these gaffs, and we struck up a conversation. He was interested in Abdullah, and I was nervous about letting him probe the works, fearing that he would find out that they were fakes, but I need not have worried. He knew that at a glance. 'Funny that anybody'd take the trouble to put this class of work into an old piece of junk like this,' he said. 'D'you know who made it?' I didn't. 'Well, I'll bet anything you like a clockmaker made it,' said he. 'Lookit; I'll show you.' And he proceeded to give me a lecture that lasted for almost an hour about the essentials of clockwork, which is a wonderful complexity of mechanism that is, at base, quite simple and founded on a handful of principles. I won't pretend that everybody would have understood him as well as I did, but I am not telling you this story to gain a reputation for modesty. I took to it with all the enthusiasm of a curious boy who had nothing else in the world to occupy his mind. I pestered the property man whenever he had a moment of spare time, demanding more explanation and demonstration. He had been trained as a clock- and watch-maker as a boy—I think he was a Dutchman but I never bothered to learn his name except that it was Henry—and he was a kindly fellow. The third day, which was our last stay in that town, he opened his own watch, took out the movement, and showed me how it could be taken to pieces. I felt as if Heaven had opened. My hands were by this time entirely at my command because of my hundreds of hours of practice in the deeps of Abdullah, and I begged him to let me reassemble the watch. He wouldn't do that; he prized his watch, and though I showed some promise he was not ready to take risks. But that night, after the last show, he called me to him and handed me a watch—a big, old-fashioned turnip with a German-silver case—and told me to try my luck with that. 'When you come back this way,' he said, 'let's see how you've got on.'

"I got on wonderfully. During the next year I took that watch apart and reassembled it time after time. I tinkered and cleaned and oiled and fiddled with the old-fashioned regulator until it was as accurate a timepiece as its age and essential character allowed. I longed for greater knowledge, and one day when opportunity served I stole a wrist-watch—they were novelties still at that time—and discovered to my astonishment that it was pretty much the same inside as my old turnip, but not such good workmanship. This was the foundation of my mechanical knowledge. I soon had the gaffed works of Abdullah going like a charm, and even introduced a few improvements and replaced some worn parts. I persuaded Willard that the wheels and springs of Abdullah should be on view at all times, and not merely during his preliminary lecture; I put my own control handle inside where I could reach it and cause Abdullah's wheels to change speed when he was about to do his clever trick. Willard didn't like it. He disapproved of changes, and he didn't want me to get ideas above my station.

"However, that is precisely what I did. I began to understand that Willard had serious limitations, and that perhaps his power over me was not so absolute as he pretended. But I was still much too young and frightened to challenge him in anything serious. Like all great revolutions, mine was a long time preparing. Furthermore, the sexual subjection in which I lived still had more power over me than the occasional moments of happiness I enjoyed, and which even the most miserable slaves enjoy.

"From the example of Willard and Charlie I learned a cynicism about mankind which it would be foolish to call deep, but certainly it was complete. Humanity was divided into two groups, the Wise Guys and the Rubes, the Suckers, the Patsys. The only Wise Guys within my range were Willard and Charlie. It was the law of nature that they should prey on the others.

"Their contempt for everyone else was complete, but whereas Charlie was good-natured and pleased with himself when he got the better of a Sucker, Willard merely hated the Sucker. The sourness of his nature did not display itself in harsh judgements or wisecracks; he possessed no wit at all—not even the borrowed wit with which Charlie decked his act and his private conversation. Willard simply thought that everybody but himself was a fool, and his contempt was absolute.

"Charlie wasted a good deal of time, in Willard's opinion, chasing girls. Charlie fancied himself as a seducer, and waitresses and chambermaids and girls around the theatre were all weighed by him in terms of whether or not he would be able to 'slip it to them'. That was his term. I don't think he was especially successful, but he worked at his hobby and I suppose he had a measure of success. 'Did you notice that kid in the Dancing Hallorans?' he would ask Willard. 'She's got round heels. I can always tell. What do you wanta bet I slip it to her before we get outa here?' Willard never wanted to bet about that; he liked to bet on certainties.

"The Rubes who wanted to play cards with Abdullah in the vaude houses were of a different stamp from those we met in the carnival world. The towns were bigger than the villages which supported country fairs, and in every one there were a few gamblers. They would turn up at an evening show, and it was not hard to spot them; a gambler looks like anyone else when he is not gambling, but when he takes the cards or the dice in his hands he reveals himself. They were piqued by their defeat at the hands of an automaton and wanted revenge. It was Charlie who sought them out and suggested a friendly game after the theatre was closed.

"The friendly game always began with another attempt to defeat Abdullah, and sometimes money was laid on it. After a sufficient number of defeats—three was usually enough—Willard would say, 'You're not going to get anywhere with the Old Boy here, and I don't want to take your money. But how about a hand or two of Red Dog?' He always started with Red Dog, but in the end they played whatever game the Suckers chose. There they would sit, in a corner of the stage, with a table if they could find one, or else playing on top of a box, and it would be three or four in the morning before they rose, and Willard and Charlie were always the winners.

"Willard was an accomplished card-sharp. He never bothered with any of the mechanical aids some crooks use—hold-outs, sleeve pockets, and such things—because he thought them crude and likely to be discovered, as they often are. He always played with his coat off and his sleeves rolled up, which had an honest look; he depended on his ability as a shuffler and dealer, and of course he used marked cards. Sometimes the Rubes brought their own cards, which he would not allow them to use with Abdullah—he explained that Abdullah used a sensitized deck—but which he was perfectly willing to play with in the game. If they were marked he knew it at once, and after a game or two he would say, in a quiet but firm voice, that he thought a change of deck would be pleasant, and produced a new deck fresh from a sealed package, calling attention to the fact that the cards were not marked and could not be.

"They did not remain unmarked for long, however. Willard had a left thumbnail which soon put the little bumps in the tops and sides of the cards that told him all he needed to know. He let the Rubes win for an hour or so, and then their luck changed, and sometimes big money came into Willard's hands at the end of the game. He was the best marker of cards I have ever known except myself. Some gamblers hack their cards so that you could almost see the marks across a room, but Willard had sensitive hands and he nicked them so cleverly that a man with a magnifying glass might have missed it. Nor was he a flashy dealer; he left that to the Rubes who wanted to show off. He dealt rather slowly, but I never saw him deal from the bottom of the deck, although he certainly did so in every game. He and Charlie would sometimes move out of a town with five or six hundred dollars to split between them, Charlie being paid off as the steerer who brought in the Rubes, and Willard as the expert with the cards. Charlie sometimes appeared to be one of the losers in these games, though never so much so that it looked suspicious. The Rubes had a real Rube conviction that show folks and travelling men ought to be better at cards than the opponents they usually met.

"I watched all of this from the interior of Abdullah, because after the initial trials against the automaton it was impossible for me to escape. I was warned against falling asleep, lest I might make some sound that would give away the secret. So, heavy-eyed, but not unaware, I saw everything that was done, saw the greed on the faces of the Rubes, and saw the quiet way in which Willard dealt with the occasional quarrels. And of course I saw how much money changed hands.

"What happened to all that money? Charlie, I knew, was being paid seventy-five dollars a week for his rotten monologues, which would have been good pay if he had not had to spend so much of it on travel; part of Jerry's arrangement was that all Talent paid for its own tickets from town to town, as well as costs of room and board. Very often we had long hops from one stand to another, and travel was a big expense. And of course Charlie spent a good deal on bootleg liquor and the girls he chased.

"Willard was paid a hundred a week, as a headliner, and because the transport of Abdullah, and myself at half-fare, cost him a good deal. But Willard never showed any sign of having much money, and this puzzled me for two or three years. But then I became aware that Willard had an expensive habit. It was morphine. This of course was before heroin became the vogue.

"Sharing a bedroom with him I could not miss the fact that he gave himself injections of something at least once a day, and he told me that it was a medicine that kept him in trim for his demanding work. Taking dope was a much more secret thing in those days than it has become since, and I had never heard of it, so I paid no attention. But I did notice that Willard was much pleasanter after he had taken his medicine than he was at other times, and it was then that he would sometimes give me a brief lesson in sleight-of-hand.

"Occasionally he would give himself a little extra treat, and then, before he fell asleep, he might talk for a while about what the future held. 'It'll be up to Albee,' he might say; 'he'll have to make his decision. I'll tell him—E.F., you want me at the Palace? Okay, you know my figure. And don't tell me I have to arrange it with Martin Beck. You talk to Beck. You paid that French dame, that Bernhardt, $7,000 a week at the Palace. I'm not going to up the ante on you. That figure'll do for me. So any time you want me, you just have to let me know, and I promise you I'll drop everything else to oblige you—' Even in my ignorant ears this sounded unlikely. Once I asked him if he would take Abdullah to the Palace, and he gave one of his rare, snorting laughs. 'When I go to the Palace, I'll go alone,' he said; 'the day I get the high sign from Albee, you're on your own.' But he didn't hear from Albee, or any manager but Jerry Wanless.

"He began to hear fairly often from Jerry, whose stoolpigeons were reporting that Willard was sometimes vague on the stage, mistimed a trick now and then, and even dropped things, which is something a headline magician, even on Jerry's circuit, was not supposed to do. I thought these misadventures came from not eating enough, and used to urge Willard to get himself a square meal, but he had never cared much for food, and as the years wore on he ate less and less. I thought this was why he so rarely needed to go to the donniker, and why he was so angry with me when I was compelled to do so, and it was not until years later that I learned that constipation is a symptom of Willard's indulgence. He was usually better in health and sharper on the job when we were with the carnival, because he was in the open air, even though he worked in a tent, but during the winters he was sometimes so dozy—that was Charlie's word for it—that Charlie was worried.

"Charlie had reason to be worried. He was Willard's source of supply. Charlie was a wonder at discovering a doctor in every town who could be squared, because he was always on the lookout for abortionists. Not that he needed abortionists very often, but he belonged to a class of man who regards such knowledge as one of the hallmarks of the Wise Guy. An abortionist might also provide what Willard wanted, for a price, and if he didn't, he knew someone else who would do so. Thus, without, I think, being malignant or even a very serious drug pusher, Charlie was Willard's supplier, and a large part of Willard's winnings in the night-long card games stuck to Charlie for expenses and recompense for the risks he took. When Willard began to be dozy, Charlie saw danger to his own income, and he tried to keep Willard's habit within reason. But Willard was resistant to Charlie's arguments, and became in time even thinner than he had been when first I saw him, and he was apt to be twitchy if he had not had enough. A twitchy conjuror is useless; his hands tremble, his speech is hard to understand, and he makes disturbing faces. The only way to keep Willard functioning efficiently, both as an entertainer and as a card-sharp, was to see that he had the dose he needed, and if his need increased, that was his business, according to Charlie.

"When Willard felt himself denied, it was I who had to put up with his ill temper and spite. There was only one advantage in the gradual decline of Willard so far as I was concerned, and that was that as morphine became his chief craze, his sexual approaches to me became fewer. Sharing a bed with him when he was restless was nervous work, and I usually preferred to sneak one of his blankets and lie on the floor. If the itching took him, his wriggling and scratching were dreadful, and went on until he was exhausted and fell into a stupor rather than a sleep. Sometimes he had periods of extreme sweating, which were very hard on a man who was already almost a skeleton. More than once I have had to rouse Charlie in the middle of the night, and tell him that Willard had to have some of his medicine, or he might go mad. It was always called 'his medicine' by me and by Charlie when he talked to me. For of course I was included in the all-embracing cynicism of these two. They assumed that I was stupid, and this was only one of their serious mistakes.

"I too became cynical, with the whole-hearted, all-inclusive vigour of the very young. Why not? Was I not shut off from mankind and any chance to gain an understanding of the diversity of human temperament by the life I led and the people who dominated me? Yet I saw people, and I saw them very greatly to their disadvantage. As I sat inside Abdullah, I saw them without being seen, while they gaped at the curiosities of the World of Wonders. What I saw in most of those faces was contempt and patronage for the show folks, who got an easy living by exploiting their oddities, or doing tricks with snakes or fire. They wanted us; they needed us to mix a little leaven in their doughy lives, but they did not like us. We were outsiders, holiday people, untrustworthy, and the money they spent to see us was foolish money. But how much they revealed as they stared! When the Pharisees saw us they marvelled, but it seemed to me that their inward parts were full of ravening and wickedness. Day after day, year after year, they believed that somehow they could get the better of Abdullah, and their greed and stupidity and cunning drove them on to try their hands at it. Day after day, year after year, I defeated them, and scorned them because they could not grasp the very simple fact that if Abdullah could be defeated, Abdullah would cease to be. Those who tried their luck I despised rather less than those who hung back and let somebody else try his. The change in their loyalty was always the same; they were on the side of the daring one until he was defeated, and then they laughed at him, and sided with the idol.

"In those years I formed a very low idea of crowds. And of all those who pressed near me the ones I hated most, and wished the worst luck, were the young, the lovers, who were free and happy. Sex to me meant terrible bouts with Willard and the grubby seductions of Charlie. I did not believe in the happiness or the innocence or the goodwill of the couples who came to the fair for a good time. My reasoning was simple, and of a very common kind: if I were a hoor and a crook, were not whoredom and dishonesty the foundations on which humanity rested? If I were at the outs with God—and God never ceased to trouble my mind—was anyone else near Him? If they were, they must be cheating. I very soon came to forget that it was I who was the prisoner: I was the one who saw clearly and saw the truth because I saw without being seen. Abdullah was the face I presented to the world, and I knew that Abdullah, the undefeated, was worth no more than I.

"Suppose that Abdullah were to make a mistake? Suppose when Uncle Zeke or Swifty Dealer turned up a ten of clubs, Abdullah were to reply with a three of hearts? What would Willard say? How would he get out of his predicament? He was not a man of quick wit and as the years wore on I understood that his place in the world was even shakier than my own. I could destroy Willard.

"Of course I didn't do it. The consequences would have been terrible. I was greatly afraid of Willard, afraid of Charlie, of Gus, and most afraid of the world into which such an insubordinate act would certainly throw me. But do we not all play, in our minds, with terrible thoughts which we would never dare to put into action? Could we live without some hidden instincts of revolt, of some protest against our fate in life, however enviable it may seem to those who do not have to bear it? I have been, for twenty years past, admittedly the greatest magician in the world. I have held my place with such style and flourish that I have raised what is really a very petty achievement to the dignity of art. Do you imagine that in my best moments when I have had very distinguished audiences—crowned heads, as all magicians love to boast—that I have not thought fleetingly of producing a full chamber-pot out of a hat, and throwing it into the royal box, just to show that it can be done? But we all hug our chains. There are no free men.

"As I sat in the belly of Abdullah, I thought often of Jonah in the belly of the great fish. Jonah, it seemed to me, had an easy time of it. 'Out of the belly of hell cried I, and thou heardest my voice'; that was what Jonah said. But I cried out of the belly of hell, and nothing whatever happened. Indeed, the belly of hell grew worse and worse, for the stink of the dwarf gave place to the stink of Cass Fletcher, who was not a clean boy and ate a bad diet; we can all stand a good deal of our own stink, and there are some earthy old sayings which prove it, but after a few years Abdullah was a very nasty coffin, even for me. Jonah was a mere three days in his fish. After three years I was just beginning my sentence. What did Jonah say? 'When my soul fainted within me I remembered the Lord.' So did I. Such was the power of my early training that I never became cynical about the Lord—only about his creation. Sometimes I thought the Lord hated me; sometimes I thought he was punishing me for—for just about everything that had ever happened to me, beginning with my birth; sometimes I thought he had forgotten me, but that thought was blasphemy, and I chased it away as fast as I could. I was an odd boy, I can tell you.

"Odd, but—what is truly remarkable—not consciously unhappy. Unhappiness of the kind that is recognized and examined and brooded over is a spiritual luxury. Certainly it was a luxury beyond my means at that time. The desolation of the spirit in which I lived was in the grain of my life, and to admit its full horror would have destroyed me. Deep in my heart I knew that. Somehow I had to keep from falling into despair. So I seized upon, and treasured, every lightening of the atmosphere, everything that looked like kindness, every joke that interrupted the bleak damnation of the World of Wonders. I was a cynic about the world, but I did not dare to become a cynic about myself. Who does? Certainly not Willard or Charlie. If one becomes a cynic about oneself the next step is the physical suicide which is the other half of that form of self-destruction.

"This was the life I lived, from that ill-fated thirtieth of August in 1918 until ten years had passed. Many things happened, but the pattern was invariable; the World of Wonders from the middle of May until the middle of October, and the rest of the time in the smallest of small-time vaudeville. I ranged over all of central Canada, and just about every town of medium size in the middle of the U.S. west of Chicago. When I say that many things happened

I am not talking about events of world consequence; in the carnival and the vaude houses we were isolated from the world, and this was part of the paradox of our existence. We seemed to bring a breath of something larger into country fairs and third-rate theatres, but we were little touched by the changing world. The automobile was linking the villages with towns, and the towns with cities, but we hardly noticed. In the vaude houses we knew about the League of Nations and the changing procession of American Presidents because these things provided the jokes of people like Charlie. The splendour of motherhood was losing some of its gloss, and something called the Jazz Age was upon us. So Charlie dropped mother, and substituted a recitation that was a parody of 'Gunga Din', which older vaudevillians were still reciting.

Though I've belted you and flayed you
By the Henry Ford that made you
You're a better car than Packard
Hunka Tin!

—he concluded, and quite often the audience laughed. As we traipsed around the middle of the Great Republic we hardly noticed that the movies were getting longer and longer, and that Hollywood was planning something that would put us all out of work. Who were the Rubes? I think we were the Rubes.

"My education continued its haphazard progress. I would do almost anything to fight the boredom of my life and the sense of doom that I had to suppress or be destroyed by it. I hung around the property-shops of theatres that possessed such things, and learned a great deal from the old men there who had been compelled, in their day, to produce anything from a workable elephant to a fake diamond ring, against time. I sometimes haunted watch-repair shops, and pestered busy men to know what they were doing; I even picked up their trick of looking through a jeweller's *loupe* with one eye while surveying the world fishily through the other. I learned some not very choice Italian from Zovene, some Munich German from Sonny, and rather a lot of pretty good French from a little man who came on the show when Molza's mouth finally became so painful that he took the extraordinary step of visiting a doctor, and came back to the World of Wonders with a very grey face, and packed up his traps. This Frenchman, whose name was Duparc, was an India Rubber Wonder, a contortionist and an uncommonly cheerful fellow. He became my teacher, so far as I had one; Professor Spencer was becoming queerer and queerer and gave up selling the visiting cards which he wrote with his feet; instead he tried to persuade the public to buy a book he had written and printed at his own expense, about monetary reform. He was, I believe, one of the last of the Single Tax men. In spite of the appearance of Duparc, and the disappearance of Andro, who had left the very small time and was now a top-liner on the Orpheum Circuit, we had all been together in the World of Wonders for too many years. But Gus was too tender-hearted to throw anybody off the show, and Jerry got us cheap, and such is the professional vanity of performers of all kinds that we didn't notice that the little towns were growing tired of us.

"Duparc taught me French, and I knew I was learning, but I had another teacher from whom I learned without knowing. Almost everything of great value I have learned in life has been taught me by women. The woman who taught me the realities of hypnotism was Mrs. Constantinescu, a strange old girl who travelled around with our show for a few years, running a mitt-camp.

"It was not part of the World of Wonders; it was a concession which Jerry rented, as he rented the right to run a hot-dog stand, a Wheel of Fortune, the cat-rack and, of course, the merry-go-round. The mitt-camp was a fortune-telling tent, with a gaudy banner outside with the signs of the zodiac on it, and an announcement that inside Zingara would reveal the Secrets of Fate. Mrs. Constantinescu was Zingara, and for all I know she may have been a real gypsy, as she claimed; certainly she was a good fortune-teller. Not that she would ever admit such a thing. Fortune-telling is against the law in just about every part of Canada and the U.S. When her customers came in she would sell them a copy of *Zadkiel's Dream Book* for ten cents, and offer a personal interpretation for a further fifteen cents, and a full-scale investigation of your destiny for fifty cents, *Zadkiel* included. Thus it was possible for her to say that she was simply selling a book, if any nosey cop interfered with her. They very rarely did so, because it was the job of our advance man to square the cops with money, bootleg hooch, or whatever their fancy might be. Her customers never complained. Zingara knew how to deliver the goods.

"She liked me, and that was a novelty. She was sorry for me, and except for Professor Spencer, nobody had been sorry for me in a very long time. But what made her really unusual in the World of Wonders was that she was interested in people; the Talent regarded the public as Rubes, to be exploited, and whether it was Willard's kind of exploitation or Happy Hannah's, it came to the same thing. But Zingara never tired of humanity or found it a nuisance. She enjoyed telling fortunes and truly thought that she did good by it.

" 'Most people have nobody to talk to,' she said to me many times. 'Wives and husbands don't talk; friends don't really talk because people don't want to get mixed up in anything that might cost them something in the end. Nobody truly wants to hear anybody else's worries and troubles. But everybody has worries and troubles and they don't cover a big range of subjects. People are much more like one another than they are unlike. Did you ever think of that?

" 'Well? So I am somebody to talk to. I'll talk, and I'll be gone in the morning, and everything I know goes away with me. I don't look like the neighbours. I don't look like the doctor or the preacher, always judging, always tired. I've got mystery, and that's what everybody wants. Maybe they're church-goers, the people in these little dumps, but what does the church give them? Just sermons from some poor sap who doesn't understand life any more than they do; they know him, and his salary, and his wife, and they know he's no great magician. They want to talk, and they want the old mystery, and that's what I give 'em. A good bargain.'

"Clearly they did want it, for though there was never any crowd around Zingara's tent she took in twenty to twenty-five dollars a day, and after fifty a week had been paid to Jerry, that left her with more money than most of the Talent in the World of Wonders.

" 'You have to learn to look at people. Hardly anybody does that. They stare into people's faces, but you have to look at the whole person. Fat or thin? Where is the fat? What about the feet? Do the feet show vanity or trouble? Does she stick out her breast or curl her shoulders to hide it? Does he stick out his chest or his stomach? Does he lean forward and peer, or backward and sneer? Hardly anybody stands straight. Knees bent, or shoved back? The bum tight or drooping? In men, look at the lump in the crotch; big or small? How tall is he when he sits down? Don't miss hands. The face comes last. Happy? Probably not. What kind of unhappy? Worry? Failure? Where are the wrinkles? You have to look good, and quick. And you have to let them see that you're looking. Most people aren't used to being looked at except by the doctor, and he's looking for something special.

" 'You take their hand. Hot or cold? Dry or wet? What rings? Has a woman taken off her wedding-ring before she came in? That's always a sign she's worried about a man, probably not the husband. A man—big Masonic or K. of C. ring? Take your time. Tell them pretty soon that they're worried. Of course they're worried; why else would they come to a mitt-camp at a fair? Feel around, and give them chances to talk; you know as soon as you touch the sore spot. Tell them you have to feel around because you're trying to find the way into their lives, but they're not ordinary and so it takes time.

" 'Who are they? A young woman—it's a boy, or two boys, or no boy at all. If she's a good girl—you know by the hair-do—probably her mother is eating her. Or her father is jealous about boys. An older woman—why isn't my husband as romantic as I thought he was; is he tired of me; why haven't I got a husband; is my best friend sincere; when are we going to have more money; my son or daughter is disobedient, or saucy, or wild; have I had all the best that life is going to give me?

" 'Suppose it's a man; lots of men come, usually after dark. He wants money; he's worried about his girl; his mother is eating him; he's two-timing and can't get rid of his mistress; his sex is wearing out and he thinks it's the end; his business is in trouble; is this all life holds for me?

" 'It's an old person. They're worried about death; will it come soon and will it hurt? Have I got cancer? Did I invest my money right? Are my grandchildren going to make out? Have I had all life holds for me?

" 'Sure you get smart-alecs. Sometimes they tell you most. Flatter them. Laugh at the world with them. Say they can't be deceived. Warn them not to let their cleverness make them hard, because they're really very fine people and will make a big mark in the world. Look to see what they are showing to the world, then tell them they are the exact opposite. That works for almost everybody.

" 'Flatter everybody. Is it crooked? Most people are starved to death for a kind word. Warn everybody against something, usually something they will be let in for because they are too honest, or too good-natured. Warn against enemies; everybody's got an enemy. Say things will take a turn for the better soon, because they will; talking to you will make things better because it takes a load off their minds.

" 'But not everybody can do it. You have to know how to get people to talk. That's the big secret. That Willard! He calls himself a hypnotist, so what does he do? He stands up a half-dozen Rubes and says, I'm going to hypnotize you! Then he bugs his eyes and waves his hands and after a while they're hypnotized. But the real hypnotism is something very different. It's part kindness and part making them feel they're perfectly safe with you. That you're their friend even though they never saw you until a minute ago. You got to lull them, like you'd lull a child. That's the real art. You mustn't overdo it. No saying, you're safe with me, or anything like that. You have to give it out, and they have to take it in, without a lot of direct talk. Of course you look at them hard, but not domineering-hard like vaude hypnotists. You got to look at them as if they was all you had on your mind at the moment, and you couldn't think of anything you'd rather do. You got to look at them as if it was a long time since you met an equal. But don't push; don't shove it. You got to be wide open to them, or else they won't be wide open to you.'

"Of course I wanted to have my fortune told by Mrs. Constantinescu, but it was against the etiquette of carnival. We never dreamed of asking Sonnenfels to lift anything heavy, or treated the Fat Woman as if she was inconvenient company. But of course Zingara knew what I thought, and she teased me about it. 'You want to know your future, but you don't want to ask me? That's right; don't put your faith in sideshow gypsies. Crooks, the whole lot of them. What do they know about the modern world? They belong to the past. They got no place in North America.' But one day, when I suppose I was looking blue, she did tell me a few things.

" 'You got an easy fortune to tell, boy. You'll go far. How do I know? Because life is goosing you so hard you'll never stop climbing. You'll rise very high and you'll make people treat you like a king. How do I know? Because you're dirt right now, and it grinds your gizzard to be dirt. What makes me think you've got the stuff to make the world admire you? Because you couldn't have survived the life you're leading if you hadn't got lots of sand. You don't eat right and you got filthy hair and I'll bet you've been lousy more than once. If it hasn't killed you, nothing will.'

"Mrs. Constantinescu was the only person who had ever talked to me about what Willard was still doing to me. The Fat Woman muttered now and then about 'abominations' and Sonny was sometimes very nasty to me, but nobody came right out and said anything unmistakable. But old Zingara said: 'You're his bumboy, eh? Well, it's not good, but it could be worse. I've known men who liked goats best. It gives you a notion what women got to put up with. The stories I hear! If he calls you "hoor" just think what that means. I've known plenty of hoors who made it a ladder to something very good. But if you don't like it, do something about it. Get your hair cut. Keep yourself clean. Stop wiping your nose on your sleeve. If you got no money, here's five dollars. Now you start out with a good Turkish bath. Build yourself up. If you gotta be a hoor, be a clean hoor. If you don't want to be a hoor, don't look like a lousy bum.'

"At that time, which was the early twenties, a favourite film star was Jackie Coogan; he played charming waifs, often with Charlie Chaplin. But I was a real waif, and sometimes when a Coogan picture was showing in the vaude houses where Willard and I appeared, I was humiliated by how far I fell short of the Coogan ideal.

"I tried a more thorough style of washing, and I got a haircut, a terrible one from a barber who wanted to make everybody look like Rudolph Valentino. I bought some pomade for my hair from him, and the whole World of Wonders laughed at me. But Mrs. Constantinescu encouraged me. Later, when I was with Willard on the vaude circuit, we had three days in a town where there was a Turkish bath, and I spent a dollar and a half on one. The masseur worked on me for half an hour, and then said: 'You know what? I never seen a dirtier guy. Jeeze, there's still grey stuff comin' outa ya! Look at these towels! What you do for a living, kid? Sweep chimneys?' I developed quite a taste for Turkish baths, and stole money regularly from Willard to pay for them. I'm sure he knew I stole, but he preferred that to having me ask him for money. He was growing very careless about money, anyhow.

"I was emboldened to steal enough, over a period of a few weeks, to buy a suit. It was a dreadful suit, God knows, but I had been wearing Willard's cast-offs, cheaply cut down, and it was a royal robe to me. Willard raised his eyebrows when he saw it, but he said nothing. He was losing his grip on the world, and losing his grip on me, and like many people who are losing their grip, he mistook it for the coming of a new wisdom in himself. But when summer came, and Mrs. Constantinescu saw me, she was pleased.

" 'You're doing fine,' she said. 'You got to get yourself ready to make a break. This carnival is running downhill. Gus is getting tired. Charlie is getting too big a boy for her to handle. He's drunk on the show now, and she don't even bawl him out. Bad luck is coming. How do I know? What else could be coming to a stale tent-show like this? Bad luck. You watch out. Their bad luck will be your good luck, if you're smart. Keep your eyes open.'

"I mustn't give the impression that Mrs. Constantinescu was always at my elbow uttering gypsy warnings. I didn't understand much of what she said, and I mistrusted some of what I understood. That business about looking at people as if you were interested in nothing else, for instance; when I tried it, I suppose I looked foolish, and Happy Hannah made a loud fuss in the Pullman one day, declaring that I was trying to learn the Evil Eye, and she knew who was teaching me. Mrs. Constantinescu was very high on her list of abominations. She urged me to search Deuteronomy to learn what happened to people who had the Evil Eye; plagues wonderful, and plagues of my seed, even great plagues of long continuance, and sore sickness; that was what was in store for me unless I stopped bugging my eyes at folks who had put on the whole armour of God, that they might stand against the wiles of the Devil. Like every young person, I was abashed at the apparent power of older people to see through me. I suppose I was pitifully transparent, and Happy Hannah's inveterate malignancy gave her extraordinary penetration. Indeed, I was inclined to think at that time that Mrs. Constantinescu was a nut, but she was an interesting nut, and willing to talk. It wasn't until years later that I realized how much good sense was in what she said.

"Of course she was right about bad luck coming to the show. It happened suddenly.

"Em Dark was a nice woman, and she tried to fight down her growing disappointment with Joe by doing everything she could for him, which included making herself attractive. She was small, and rather plump, and dressed well, making all her clothes herself. Joe was very proud of her appearance, and I think poor Joe was beginning to be aware that the best thing about him was his wife. So he was completely thrown off base one day, as the Pullman was carrying us from one village to another, to see a horrible caricature of Em walk past him and down the aisle toward Heinie and Sonny, who were laughing their heads off in the door of the smoking-room. It was Rango, dressed in Em's latest and best, with a *cloche* hat on his head, and one of Em's purses in his hairy hand. There is no doubt that Heinie and Sonny meant to get Joe's goat, and to spatter the image of Em, because that was the kind of men they were, and that was what they thought funny. Joe looked like a man who has seen a ghost. He was working, as he so often was, on one of the throwing knives he sold as part of his act, and I think before he knew what he had done, he threw it, and got Rango right between the shoulders. Rango turned, with a look of dreadful pathos on his face, and fell in the aisle. The whole thing took less than thirty seconds.

"You can imagine the uproar. Heinie rushed to Rango, coddled him in his arms, wept, swore, screamed, and became hysterical. But Rango was dead. Sonny stormed and accused Joe in German; he was the kind of man who jabs with his forefinger when he is angry. Gus and Professor Spencer tried to restore order, but nobody wanted order; the excitement was the most refreshing thing that had happened to the World of Wonders in years. Everybody had a good deal to say on one side or the other, but mostly against Joe.

The love between Joe and Em concentrated the malignancy of those unhappy people, but this was the first time they had been given a chance to attack it directly. Happy Hannah was seized with a determination to stop the train. What good that would have done nobody knew, but she felt that a big calamity demanded the uttermost in drama.

"I did not at first understand the full enormity of what Joe had done. To kill Rango was certainly a serious injury to Heinie, whose livelihood he was. To buy and train another orang-outang would be months of work. It was Zovene, busily crossing himself, who put the worst of the horror in words: it is a well-known fact in the carnival and circus world that if anybody kills a monkey, three people will die. Heinie wanted Joe to be first on the list, but Gus held him back; luckily for him, because in a fight Joe could have murdered anybody on the show, not excluding Sonny.

"What do you do with a dead monkey? First of all Rango had to be disentangled from Em Dark's best outfit, which Em quite understandably didn't want and threw off the back of the car with Rango's blood on it. (What do you suppose the finder made of that?) Then the body had to be stowed somewhere, and Heinie would have it nowhere except in his berth, which Rango customarily shared with him. You can't make a dead monkey look dignified, and Rango was not an impressive corpse. His eyes wouldn't shut; one stared and the other eyelid drooped, and soon both eyes took on a bluish film; his yellow teeth showed. The Darks felt miserable, because of what Joe had done, and because their love had been held up to mockery in the naked passion and hatred of the hour after Rango's death. Heinie had not scrupled to say that Rango was a lot more use on the show and a lot better person, even though not human, than a little floozie who just stood up and let a dummkopf of a husband throw knives at her; if Joe was so good at hitting Rango, how come he never hit that bitch of a wife of his? This led to more trouble, and it was Em who had to prevent Joe from battering Heinie. I must say that Heinie took the fullest advantage of the old notion that a man is not responsible for what he does in his misery. He got very drunk that night, and wailed and grieved all up and down the car.

"Indeed, the World of Wonders got drunk. Private bottles appeared from everywhere, and were private no more. Professor Spencer accepted a large drink, and it went a very long way with him, for he was not used to it. Indeed, even Happy Hannah took a drink, and quite shortly everyone wished she hadn't. It had been her custom for some years to drink a lot of cider vinegar; she said it kept her blood from thickening, to the great danger of her life, and she got away with so much vinegar that she always smelled of it. Her unhappy inspiration was to spike her evening slug of vinegar with a considerable shot of bootleg hooch which Gus pressed on her, and it was hardly down before it was up again. A nauseated Fat Woman is a calamity on a monumental scale, and poor Gus had a bad night of it with Happy Hannah. Only Willard kept out of the general saturnalia; he crept into his berth, injected himself with his favourite solace, and was out of that world of sorrow, over which the corpse of Rango spread an increasing influence.

"From time to time the Talent would gather around Heinie's berth, and toast the remains. Professor Spencer made a speech, sitting on the edge of the upper berth opposite the one which had become Rango's bier; in this comfortable position he was able to hold his glass with a device he possessed, attached to one foot. He was drunkenly eloquent, and talked touchingly if incoherently about the link between Man and the Lesser Creation, which was nowhere so strong or so truly understood as in circuses and carnivals; had we not, through the years, come to esteem Rango as one of ourselves, a delightful Child of Nature who spoke not with the tongue of man, but through a thousand merry tricks, which now, alas, had been brought to an untimely end? ('Rango'd of been twenty next April,' sobbed Heinie; 'twenty-two, more likely, but I always dated him from when I bought him.') Professor Spencer did not want to say that Rango had been struck down by a murderer's hand. No, that wasn't the way he looked at it. He would speak of it more as a Cream Passional, brought on by the infinite complexity of human relationships. The Professor rambled on until he lost his audience, who took affairs into their own hands, and drank toasts to Rango as long as the booze held out, with simple cries of 'Good luck and good-bye, Rango old pal.'

"At last Rango's wake was over. The Darks had lain unseen in their berth ever since it had been possible to go to bed, but it was half past three when Heinie crawled in beside Rango and wept himself to sleep with the dead monkey in his arms. By now Rango was firmly advanced in *rigor mortis* and his tail stuck from between the curtains of the berth like a poker. But Heinie's devotion was much admired; Gus said it warmed the cuckolds of her heart.

"Next morning, at the fairground, our first business was to bury Rango. 'Let him lay where his life was spent for others,' was what Heinie said. Professor Spencer, badly hung over, asked God to receive Rango. The Darks came, and brought a few flowers, which Heinie ostentatiously spurned from the grave. All Rango's possessions—his cups and plates, the umbrella with which he coquetted on the tightrope—were buried with him.

"Was Zingara tactless, or mischievous, when she said loudly, as we broke up to go about our work: 'Well, how long do we wait to see who's first?' The calliope began the toot-up—it was 'The Poor Butterfly Waltz'—and we got ready for the first trick which, without Rango, put extra work on all of us.

"As the days passed we realized just how much extra work the absence of Rango did mean. There was nothing Heinie could do without him, and five minutes of performance time had somehow to be made up at each trick. Sonnenfels volunteered to add a minute to his act, and so did Duparc; Happy Hannah was always glad to extend the time during which she harassed her audience about religion, and it was simple for Willard to extend the doings of Abdullah for another minute; so it seemed easy. But an additional ten minutes every day was not so easy for Sonnenfels as for the others; as Strong Men go, he was growing old. Less than a fortnight after the death of Rango, at the three o'clock trick, he hoisted his heaviest bar-bell to his knee, then level with his shoulders, then dropped it with a crash and fell forward. There was a doctor on the fairground, and it was less than three minutes before he was with Sonny, but even at that he came too late. Sonny was dead.

"It is much easier to dispose of a Strong Man than it is of a monkey. Sonny had no family, but he had quite a lot of money in a belt he wore at all times, and we were able to bury him in style. He had been a stupid, evil-speaking, bad-tempered man—quite the opposite of the genial giant described by Charlie in his introduction—and no one but Heinie regretted him deeply. But he left another hole in the show, and it was only because Duparc could do a few tricks on the tightrope that the gap could be filled without making the World of Wonders seem skimpy. Heinie mourned Sonny as uproariously as he had mourned Rango, but this time his grief was not so well received by the Talent.

"Sonny's death was proof positive that the curse of a dead monkey was a fact. Zingara was not slow to point out how short a time had been needed to set the bad luck to work. The Talent turned against Heinie with just as much extravagance of sentimentality as they had shown in pitying him. They were inclined to blame him for Sonny's death. He was still hanging around the show, and he was still drawing a salary, because he had a contract which said nothing about the loss of his monkey by murder. He was on the booze. Gus and Charlie resented him because he cost money without bringing anything in. His presence was a perpetual reminder of bad luck, and soon he was suffering the cold shoulder that had been my lot when Happy Hannah first decided I was a Jonah. Heinie was a proven Jonah, and to look at him was to be reminded that somebody was next on the list of the three who must atone for Rango. Heinie had ceased to be Talent; his reason for being was buried with Rango. He was an outsider, and in the carnival world an outsider is very far outside indeed.

"We were near the end of the autumn season, and no more deaths occurred before we broke up for winter, some of us to our vaudeville work, and others, like Happy Hannah, to a quiet time in dime museums and Grand Congresses of Strange People in the holiday grounds of the warm south. Zingara was not the only one to remark that poor Gus was looking very yellow. Happy Hannah thought Gus must be moving into The Change, but Zingara said The Change didn't make you belch a lot, and go off your victuals, like Gus, and whispered a word of fear. When we assembled again the following May, Gus was not with us.

"There the deaths seemed to stop, for those who were less perceptive than Zingara, and myself. But something happened during the winter season that was surely a death of a special kind.

"It was in Dodge City. Willard was fairly reliable during our act, but sometimes during the day he was perceptibly under the influence of morphine, and at other and much worse times he was feeling the want of it. I did not know then how prolonged addiction works on the imagination; I was simply glad that his sexual demands on me had dropped almost to nothing. Therefore I did not know what to make of it when he seized me one afternoon in the wings of the vaude house, and accused me violently of sexual unfaithfulness to him. I was 'at it', he said, with a member of a Japanese acrobatic troupe on the bill, and he wasn't going to stand for that. I was a hoor right enough, but by God I wasn't going to be anybody else's hoor. He cuffed me, and ordered me to get into Abdullah, and stay there, so he would know where I was; and I wasn't to get out of the automaton any more, ever. He hadn't kept me all these years to be cheated by any such scum as I was.

"All of this was said in a low voice, because although he was irrational, he wasn't so far gone that he wanted the stage manager to drop on him, and perhaps fine him, for making a row in the wings during the show. I was seventeen or eighteen, I suppose—I had long ago forgotten my birthday, which had never been a festival in our house anyhow—and although I was still small I had some spirit, and it all rushed to my head when he struck me over the ear. Abdullah was standing in the wings in the place where the image was stored between shows, and I was beside it. I picked up a stage-brace, and lopped off Abdullah's head with one strong swipe; then I took after Willard. The stage manager was soon upon us, and we scampered off to the dressing-room, where Willard and I had such a quarrel as neither of us had ever known before. It was short, but decisive, and when it ended Willard was whining to me to show him the kind of consideration he deserved, as one who had been more than a father to me, and taught me an art that would be a fortune to me; I had declared that I was going to leave him then and there.

"I did nothing of the kind. These sudden transformations of character belong to fiction, not to fact, and certainly not to the world of dependence and subservience that I had known for so many years. I was quite simply scared to leave Willard. What could I do without him? I found out very quickly.

"The stage manager had told the manager about the brief outburst in the wings, and the manager came to set us right as to what he would allow in his house. But with the manager came Charlie, who carried great weight because he was the brother of Jerry, who booked the Talent for that house. It was agreed that—just this once—the matter would be overlooked.

"Willard could not be overlooked a couple of hours later, when he was so far down in whatever world his drug took him to that it was impossible for him to go on the stage. There was all the excitement and loud talk you might expect, and the upshot was that I was ordered to take Willard's place at the next show, and do his act as well as I could, without Abdullah. And that is what I did. I was in a rattle of nerves, because I had never appeared on a stage before, except when I was safely concealed in the body of the automaton. I didn't know how to address an audience, how to time my tricks, or how to arrange an act. The hypnotism was beyond me, and Abdullah was a wreck. I suppose I must have been dreadful, but somehow I filled in the time, and when I had done all I could the spatter of applause was only a little less encouraging than it had been for Willard for several months past.

"When Willard recovered enough to know what had happened he was furious, but his fury simply persuaded him to seek relief from the pain of a rotten world with the needle. This was what precipitated the crisis that delivered me from Abdullah forever; Jerry was on the long-distance telephone, wrangling with Charlie, and the upshot of Charlie's best persuasion was that Willard could finish his season if Charlie would keep him in condition to appear on the stage, and that if Willard didn't appear, I was to do so, and I was to be made to perform a proper, well-planned act. I see now that this was very decent of Jerry, who had all the problems of an agent to trouble him. He must have been fond of Charlie. But it seemed a dreadful sentence at the time. Beginners in the entertainment world are all supposed to be panting for a chance to rush before an audience and prove themselves; I was frightened of Willard, frightened of Jerry, and most frightened of all of failure.

"As is usually the case with understudies I neither failed nor succeeded greatly. In a short time I had worked out a version of The Miser's Dream that was certainly better than Willard's, and on Charlie's strong advice I did it as a mute act. I had very little voice, and what I had was a thin, ugly croak; I had no vocabulary of the kind that a magician needs; my conversation was conducted in illiterate carnival slang, varied now and then with some Biblical turn of speech that had clung to me. So I simply appeared on the stage and did my stuff without sound, while the pianist played whatever he thought appropriate. My greatest difficulty was in learning how to perform slowly enough. In my development of a technique while I was concealed in Abdullah I had become so fast and so slick that my work was incomprehensible; the quickness of the hand should certainly deceive the eye, but not so fast the eye doesn't realize that it is being deceived.

"Abdullah simply dropped out of use. We lugged him around for a few weeks, but his transport was costly, and as I would not get inside him now he was useless baggage. So one morning, on a railway siding, Charlie and I burned him, while Willard moaned and grieved that we were destroying the greatest thing in his life, and an irreplaceable source of income.

"That was the end of Abdullah, and the happiest moment of my life up to then was when I saw the flames engulf that ugliest of images.

"In their strange way Charlie and Willard were friends, and Charlie thought the moment had come for him to reform Willard. He set about it with his usual enthusiasm, conditioned by a very simple mind. Willard must break the morphine habit. He was to cut the stuff out, at a stroke, and with no thought of looking back. Of course this meant that in a very few days Willard was a raving lunatic, rolling on the floor, the sweating, shrieking victim of crawling demons. Charlie was frightened out of his wits, brought in one of his ambiguous doctors, bought Willard a syringe to replace the one he had dramatically thrown away, and loaded him up to keep him quiet. There was no more talk of abstinence. Charlie kept assuring me that 'somehow we've got to see him through it.' But there was no way through it. Willard was a gone goose.

"I speak of this lightly now, but at the time I was just as frightened and puzzled as Charlie. I was alarmed to find how dependent on Willard I had become. I had lived with him in dreadful servitude for almost half my life, and now I didn't know what I should do without him. Furthermore, he had been jolted by his attempt at reform into one of those dramatic changes of character which are so astonishing to people who find themselves responsible for a drug addict. He who had been domineering and ugly became embarrassingly fawning and frightened. His great dread was that Charlie and I would put him in a hospital. All he wanted was to be cared for, and supplied with enough morphine to keep him comfortable. A simple demand, wasn't it? But somehow we managed it, and one consequence was that I became involved in the nuisance of finding suppliers of the drug, making approaches to them, and paying the substantial prices they demanded.

"By the time it was the season for rejoining the World of Wonders, I had taken over completely the job of filling Willard's place in the vaude programs, and Willard was an invalid who had to be dragged from date to date. It was a greatly changed carnival that season. Gus was gone, and the new manager was a tough little carnie who knew how to manage the show, but had none of Gus's pride in it; he took his tone from Charlie, as the real representative of the owners. Charlie had finally wakened up to the fact that the day of such shows was passing, and that fair dates were harder to get. That was when he decided to add a blow-off to the World of Wonders, and as well to set up in a little business of his own, unknown to Jerry.

"A blow-off is an annex to a carnival show. Sometimes it is well-advertised, if it is a speciality that does not quite fit into the show proper, like Australian stock-whip performers, or a man and a girl who do tricks with lariats, in cowboy costume. But it can also be a part of the show that is very quietly introduced, and that is not necessarily seen during every performance. Charlie's blow-off was of this latter kind, and the only attractions in it were Zitta and Willard.

"Zitta was now too fat and too ugly to hold a place in the main tent, but in the blow-off, which occupied a smaller tent entered through the World of Wonders, she could still do a dirty act with some snakes, a logical development from the stunts she had formerly done during the Last Trick. But it was Willard's role that startled me. Charlie had decided to exhibit him as a Wild Man. Willard sat in ragged shirt and pants, his feet bare, in the dust. After he had gone for a few weeks without shaving he looked convincingly wild. His skin had by this time taken on the bluish tinge of the morphine addict, and his eyes, with their habitually contracted pupils, looked terrifying enough to the rural spectators. Charlie's explanation was that Zitta and Willard came from the Deep South, and were sad evidence of what happened when fine old families, reduced from plantation splendour, became inbred. The suggestion was that Willard was the outcome of a variety of incestuous matings. I doubt if many of the people who came to see Willard believed it, but the appetite for marvels and monsters is insatiable, and he was a good eyeful for the curious. The Shame of the Old South, as the blow-off was called, did pretty good business.

"As for Charlie's little enterprise, he had become a morphine-pusher. 'Cut out the middle man,' he said to me by way of explanation; he now bought the stuff from even bigger pushers, and sold it at a substantial price to those who wanted it. The medical profession, he said to me, was intolerably greedy, and he didn't see why he should always be on the paying end of a profitable trade.

"I am sorry to say that I shared Charlie's opinion at that time, and for a while I was his junior in the business. I offer no excuses. I had become fond of the things money can buy, and keeping Willard stoked with what he wanted was very costly. So I became a supplier, rather than a purchaser, and did pretty well by it. But I never put all my eggs in one basket. I was still primarily a conjuror, and the World of Wonders, even in its reduced circumstances, paid me sixty-five dollars a week to do my version of The Miser's Dream for five minutes an hour, twelve hours a day.

"I am going to ask you to excuse me from a detailed account of what followed during the next couple of years. It was inevitable, I suppose, that a simpleton like Charlie, with a greenhorn like myself as his lieutenant, should be caught in one of the periodic crackdowns on drug trafficking. The F.B.I. in the States and the R.C.M.P. in Canada began to pick up some of the small fry like ourselves, as leads to the bigger fish who were more important in the trade. I do not pretend that I behaved particularly well, and the upshot was that Charlie was nabbed and I was not, and that I made my escape by ship with a passport that cost me a great deal of money; I have it still, and it is a beautiful job, but it is not as official as it looks. My problem when the trouble came was what I was going to do with Willard. My solution still surprises me.

When every consideration of good sense and self-preservation said that I should ditch him, and let the police find him, I decided instead to take him with me. Explain it as you will, by saying that my conscience overcame my prudence, or that there had grown up a real affection between us during all those years when I was his slave and the secret source of his professional reputation, but I decided that I must take Willard where I was going. Willard was always reminding me that he had never abandoned me when it would have been convenient to do so. So, one pleasant Friday morning in 1927, Jules LeGrand and his invalid uncle, Aristide LeGrand, sailed from Montreal on a C.P.R. ship bound for Cherbourg, and somewhat later Charlie Wanless stood trial in his native state of New York and received a substantial sentence.

"The passports and the steamship passages just about cleaned me out, but I think Willard saved me from being caught. He made a very convincing invalid in his wheelchair, and although I know the ship was watched we had no trouble. But when we arrived in France, what was to be done? Thanks to Duparc I could speak French pretty well, though I could neither read nor write the language. I was a capable conjuror, but the French theatrical world did not have the kind of third-class variety theatre into which I could make my way. However, there were small circuses, and eventually I got a place in *Le grand Cirque forain de St. Vite* after some rough adventures during which I was compelled to exhibit Willard as a geek.

"You know what a geek is, Ramsay, but perhaps these gentlemen are not so well versed in the humbler forms of carnival performance. You let it be known that you have, concealed perhaps in a stable at the back of a village inn, a man who eats strange food. When the crowd comes—and not too much of a crowd, because the police don't like such shows—you lecture for a while on the yearning of the geek for raw flesh and particularly for blood; you explain that it is something the medical profession knows about, but keeps quiet so that the relatives of people thus afflicted will not be put to shame. Then, if you can get a chicken, you give the geek a chicken, and he growls and gives a display of animal passion, and finally bites the chicken in the neck, and seems to drink some of its blood. If you are reduced to the point where you can't afford even a superannuated chicken, you find a grass snake or two, or perhaps a rabbit. I was the lecturer, and Willard was the geek. It raised enough money to keep us from starvation, and to keep Willard supplied with just enough of his fancy to prevent a total breakdown.

"You discovered us under the banner of St. Vite, Ramsay, when we were travelling in the Tyrol. I suppose it looked very humble to you, but it was a step on an upward path for us. I appeared, you remember as Faustus LeGrand, the conjuror; I thought Faustus sounded well for a magician; poor old Willard was *Le Solitaire des forêts,* which was certainly an improvement on geeking and sounds much more elegant than Wild Man."

"I remember it very well," said I, "and I remember that you were not at all anxious to recognize me."

"I wasn't anxious to see anybody from Canada. I hadn't seen you for—surely it must have been fourteen years. How was I to know that you hadn't enlisted in the R.C.M.P.—possibly become the pride of the Narcotics Squad? But let that go. I was in a confused state of mind at the time. Do you know what I mean? Something is taking all your attention—something inward—and the outer world is not very real, and you deal with it hastily and badly. I was still battling in my conscience about Willard. By this time I thoroughly hated him. He was an expensive nuisance, yet I couldn't make up my mind to get rid of him. Besides, he might just have enough energy, prompted by anger, to betray me to the police, even at the cost of his own destruction. Still, his life lay in my power. A smallish extra injection some day would have disposed of him.

"But I couldn't do it. Or rather—I've said so much, and put myself so thoroughly to the bad, that I might just as well go all the way—I didn't really want to do it because I got a special sort of satisfaction from his presence. This confused old wreck had been my master, my oppressor, the man who let me live hungry and dirty, who used my body shamefully and never let me lift my head above the shame. Now he was utterly mine; he was my thing. That was how it was now between me and Willard. I had the upper hand, and I admit frankly that it gave me a delicious satisfaction to have the upper hand. Willard had just enough sense of reality left to understand without any question of a mistake who was master. Not that I stressed it coarsely. No, no. If thine enemy be hungry, give him bread to eat; and if he be thirsty, give him water to drink; for thou shalt heap coals of fire on his head, and the Lord shall reward thee. Indeed so. The Lord rewarded me richly, and it seemed to me the Lord's face was dark and gleeful as he did so.

"This was Revenge, which we have all been told is a very grave sin, and in our time psychologists and sociologists have made it seem rather lower class, and unevolved, as well. Even the State, which retains so many primitive privileges that are denied to its citizens, shrinks from Revenge. If it catches a criminal the State is eager to make it clear that whatever it chooses to do is for the possible reform of that criminal, or at the very most for his restraint. Who would be so crass as to suggest that the criminal might be used as he has used his fellow man? We don't admit the power of the Golden Rule when it seems to be working in reverse gear. Do unto others as society says they should do unto you, even when they have done something quite different. We're all sweetness and light now, in our professions of belief. We have shut our minds against the Christ who cursed the fig-tree. Revenge—horrors! So there it was: I was revenging myself on Willard, and I'm not going to pretend to you that when he crunched into a grass snake to give a thrill to a stable filled with dull peasants, who despised him for doing it, I didn't have a warm sense of satisfaction. The Lord was rewarding me. Under the banner of St. Vite, the man who had once been Mephistopheles in my life was now just a tremulous, disgusting Wild Man, and if anybody was playing Mephistopheles, the role was mine. Blessed be the name of the Lord, who forgettest not his servant.

"Don't ask me if I would do it now. I don't suppose for a moment that I would. But I did it then. Now I am famous and rich and have delightful friends like Liesl and Ramsay; charming people like yourselves come from the B.B.C. to ask me to pretend to be Robert-Houdin. But in those days I was Paul Dempster, who had been made to forget it and take a name from the side of a barn, and be the pathic of a perverted drug-taker. Do you think I have forgotten that even now? I have a lifelong reminder. I am a sufferer from a tiresome little complaint called *proctalgia fugax*. Do you know it? It is a cramping pain in the anus that wakes you out of a sound sleep and gives you five minutes or so of great unease. For years I thought that Willard, by his nasty use of me, had somehow injured me irreparably. It took a little courage to go to a doctor and find out that it was quite harmless, though I suppose it has some psychogenic origin. It is useless to ask Magnus Eisengrim if he would exert himself to torment a worm like Willard the Wizard; he has the magnanimity that comes so easily to the rich and powerful. But if you had put the question to Faustus LeGrand in 1929 his answer would have been the one I have just given you.

"Yes, gentlemen, it was Revenge, and it was sweet. If I am to be damned for a sin, I expect that will be the one. Shall I tell you the cream of it—or the worst of it, according to your point of view? There came a time when Willard could stand no more. Jaunting around southern France, and the Tyrol and parts of Switzerland, even when he had absorbed the minimum dose I allowed him, was a weariness that he could no longer endure. He wanted to die, and begged me for death. 'Just gimme a little too much, kid,' was what he said. He was never eloquent but he managed to put a really heart-breaking yearning into those words. What did I reply? 'I couldn't do it, Willard. Really I couldn't. I'd have your life on my conscience. You know we're forbidden by every moral law to take life. If I do what you ask, not only am I a murderer, but you are a suicide. Can you face the world to come with that against you?' Then he would curse and call me every foul name he could think of. And next day it would be the same. I didn't kill him. Instead I withheld death from him, and it was balm to my spirit to be able to do it.

"Of course it came at last. From various evidence I judge that he was between forty and forty-five, but he looked far worse than men I have seen who were ninety. You know how such people die. He had been blue before, but for a few hours before the end he was a leaden colour, and as his mouth was open it was possible to see that it was almost black inside. His teeth were in very bad condition from geeking, and he looked like one of those terrible drawings by Daumier of a pauper corpse. The pupils of his eyes were barely perceptible. His breath was very faint, but what there was of it stank horribly. Till quite near the end he was begging for a shot of his fancy. The only other person with us was a member of the St. Vite troupe, a bearded lady—you remember her, don't you, Ramsay?—but as Willard spoke no French she didn't know what he was saying, or if she did she gave no sign. Then a surprising thing happened; a short time before he died his pupils dilated extraordinarily, and that, with his wide-stretched mouth and his colour, gave him the look of a man dying of terror. Indeed, perhaps it was so. Was he aware of the lake which burneth with fire and brimstone, where he would join the unbelieving and the abominable, the whoremongers, sorcerers, and idolaters? I had seen Abdullah go into the fire. Was it so also with Willard?

"But he was dead, and I was free. Had I not been free for years? Free since I struck the head off Abdullah? No; freedom does not come suddenly. One has to grow into it. But now that Willard was dead, I felt truly free, and I hoped that I might throw off some of the unpleasant characteristics I had taken upon myself but not, I hoped, forever taken within myself.

"I finished my season with *Le grand Cirque* because I did not want to attract attention by leaving as soon as Willard was out of the way. Without his luxury to pay for I was able to give up occasional pocket-picking, and save a little money. I knew what I wanted to do. I wanted to get to England; I knew there were vaude houses or variety shows of some kind in England, and I thought I could get a job there.

"I remember that I took stock of myself, as cold-bloodedly as I could, but not, I think, unjustly. The Deptford parson's son, the madwoman's son, had become a pretty widely experienced young tough; I could pick pockets, I could push dope. I could fight with a broken bottle and I had picked up the French knack of boxing with my feet. I could now speak and read French, and a little German and Italian, and I could speak a terrible patois of English, in which I sounded like the worst of Willard and Charlie combined.

"What was there on the credit side? I was an expert conjuror, and I was beginning to have some inkling of what Mrs. Constantinescu meant when she talked about real hypnotism as opposed to the sideshow kind. I was a deft mechanic, could mend anybody's watch, and humour an old calliope. Although I had been the passive partner in countless acts of sodomy I was still, so far as my own sexual activity was concerned, a virgin, and likely to remain one, because I knew nothing about women other than Fat Ladies, Bearded Ladies, Snake Women, and mitt-camp gypsies; on the whole I liked women, but I had no wish to do to anybody I liked what Willard had done to me—and although of course I knew that the two acts differed I supposed they were pretty much the same to the recipient. I had none of Charlie's unresting desire to 'slip it' to anybody. As you see, I was a muddle of toughness and innocence.

"Of course I didn't think of myself as innocent. What young man ever does? I thought I was the toughest thing going. A verse from the Book of Psalms kept running through my head that seemed to me to describe my state perfectly. 'I am become like a bottle in the smoke.' It's a verse that puzzles people who think it means a glass bottle, but my father would never have allowed me to be so ignorant as that. It means one of those old wineskins the Hebrews used; it means a goatskin that has been scraped out, and tanned, and blown up, and hung over the fire till it is as hard as a warrior's boot. That was how I saw myself.

"I was twenty-two, so far as I could reckon, and a bottle that had been thoroughly smoked. What was life going to pour into the bottle? I didn't know, but I was off to England to find out.

"And you are off to England in the morning gentlemen. Forgive me for holding you so long. I'll say good-night."

And for the last time at Sorgenfrei we went through that curious little pageant of bidding our ceremonious good-night to Magnus Eisengrim, who said his farewells with unusual geniality.

Of course the film-makers didn't go back to their inn. They poured themselves another round of drinks and made themselves comfortable by the fire.

"What I can't decide," said Ingestree, "is how much of what we have heard we are to take as fact. It's the inescapable problem of the autobiography: how much is left out, how much has been genuinely forgotten, how much has been touched up to throw the subject into striking relief? That stuff about Revenge, for instance. Can he have been as horrible as he makes out? He doesn't seem a cruel man now. We must never forget that he's a conjuror by profession; his lifelong pose has been demonic. I think he'd like us to believe he played the demon in reality, as well."

"I take it seriously," said Lind. "You are English, Roly, and the

English have a temperamental pull toward cheerfulness; they don't really believe in evil. If the Gulf Stream ever deserted their western coast, they'd think differently. Americans are supposed to be the great optimists, but the English are much more truly optimistic. I think he has done all he says he has done. I think he killed his enemy slowly and cruelly. And I think it happens oftener than is supposed by people who habitually avert their minds from evil."

"Oh, I'm not afraid of evil," said Ingestree. "Glad to look on the dark side any time it seems necessary. But I think people dramatize themselves when they have a chance."

"Of course you are afraid of evil," said Lind. "You'd be a fool if you weren't. People talk about evil frivolously, just as Eisengrim says they do; it's a way of diminishing its power, or seeming to do so. To talk about evil as if it were just waywardness or naughtiness is very stupid and trivial. Evil is the reality of at least half the world."

"You're always philosophizing," said Kinghovn; "and that's the dope of the Northern mind. What's evil? You don't know. But when you want an atmosphere of evil in your films you tell me and I arrange lowering skies and funny light and find a good camera angle; if I took the same thing in blazing sunlight, from another place, it'd look like comedy."

"You're always playing the tough guy, the realist," said Lind, "and that's wonderful. I like you for it, Harry. But you're not an artist except in your limited field, so you leave it to me to decide what's evil and what's comedy on the screen. That's something that goes beyond appearances. Right now we're talking about a man's life."

Liesl had said very little at any of these evening sessions, and I think the film-makers had made the mistake of supposing she had nothing to say. She struck in now.

"Which man's life are you talking about?" she said. "That's another of the problems of biography and autobiography, Ingestree, my dear. It can't be managed except by casting one person as the star of the drama, and arranging everybody else as supporting players. Look at what politicians write about themselves! Churchill and Hitler and all the rest of them seem suddenly to be secondary figures surrounding Sir Numskull Poop, who is always in the limelight. Magnus is no stranger to the egotism of the successful performing artist. Time after time he has reminded us that he is the greatest creature of his kind in the world. He does it without shame. He is not held back by any middle-class notion that it would be nicer if we said it instead of himself. He knows we're not going to say it, because nothing so destroys the sense of equality on which all pleasant social life depends as perpetual reminders that one member of the company out-ranks all the rest. When it is so, it is considered good manners for the pre-eminent one to keep quiet about it. Because Magnus has been talking for a couple of hours we have assumed that his emphasis is the only emphasis.

"This business of the death of Willard: if we listen to Magnus we take it for granted that Magnus killed Willard after painfully humiliating him for quite a long time. The tragedy of Willard's death is the spirit in which Faustus LeGrand regarded it. But isn't Willard somebody, too? As Willard lay dying, who did he think was the star of the scene? Not Magnus, I'll bet you. And look at it from God's point of view, or if that strains you uncomfortably, suppose that you have to make a movie of the life and death of Willard. You need Magnus, but he is not the star. He is the necessary agent who brings Willard to the end. Everybody's life is his Passion, you know, and you can't have much of a Passion if you haven't got a good strong Judas. Somebody has to play Judas, and it is generally acknowledged to be a fine, meaty role. There's a pride in being cast for it. You recall the Last Supper? Christ said that he would be betrayed by one of those who sat at the table with him. The disciples called out, Lord, is it I? And when Judas asked, Christ said it was he.

"Has it never occurred to you that there might have been just the tiniest feeling in the bosom of one of the lesser apostles—Lebbaeus, for instance, whom tradition represents as a fat man—that Judas was thrusting himself forward again? Christ died on the Cross, and Judas also had his Passion, but can anybody tell me what became of Lebbaeus? Yet he too was a man, and if he had written an autobiography do you suppose that Christ would have had the central position? There seems to have been a Bearded Lady at the deathbed of Willard, and I would like to know her point of view. Being a woman, she probably had too much intelligence to think that she was the central figure, but would she have awarded that role to Willard or to Magnus?"

"Either would do," said Kinghovn; "but you need a point of focus, you know. Otherwise you get this *cinéma vérité* stuff, which is sometimes interesting but it damn well isn't *vérité* because it fails utterly to convince. It's like those shots of war you see on TV; you can't believe anything serious is happening. If you want your film to look like truth you need somebody like Jurgen to decide what truth is, and somebody like me to shoot it so it never occurs to you that it could appear any other way. Of course what you get is not truth, but it's probably a lot better in more ways than just the cinematic way. If you want the death of Willard shot from the point of view of the Bearded Lady I can certainly do it. And simply because I can do it to order I don't know how you can pretend it has any special superiority as truth."

"I suppose it's part of that human condition silly-clever people are always grizzling about," said Liesl. "If you want truth, I suppose you must shoot the film from God's point of view and with God's point of focus, whatever it may be. And I'll bet the result won't look much like *cinéma vérité*. But I don't think either you or Jurgen are up to that job, Harry."

"There is no God," said Kinghovn; "and I've never felt the least necessity to invent one."

"Probably that is why you have spent your life as a technician; a very fine one, but a technician," said Lind. "It's only by inventing a few gods that we get that uneasy sense that something is laughing at us which is one of the paths to faith."

"Eisengrim talks a lot about God," said Ingestree, "and God seems still to be a tremendous reality to him. But there's no question of God laughing. The bottle in the smoke—that's what he was. I really must read the Bible some time; there are such marvellous goodies in it, just waiting to be picked up. But even these Bibles Designed to be Read as Literature are so bloody thick! I suppose one could browse, but when I browse I never seem to find anything except tiresome stud-book stuff about Aminadab begetting Jonadab and that kind of thing."

"We've only had part of the story," I said. "Magnus has carefully pointed out to us that he is looking backward on his early life as a man who has changed decisively in the last forty years. What's his point of focus?"

"Nobody changes so decisively that they lose all sense of the reality of their youth," Lind said. "The days of childhood are always the most vivid. He has let us think that his childhood made him a villain. So I think we must assume that he is a villain now. A quiescent villain, but not an extinct one."

"I think that's a lot of romantic crap," said Kinghovn. "I'm sick of all the twaddle about childhood. You should have seen me as a child; a flaxen-haired little darling playing in my mother's garden in Aalborg. Where is he now? Here I sit, a very well-smoked bottle like our friend who has gone to bed. If I met that flaxen-haired child now I would probably give him a good clout over the ear. I've never much liked kids. Which was the greater use in the world? That child, so sweet and pure, or me, as I am now, not sweet and damned well not pure?"

"That's a dangerous question for a man who doesn't believe in God," I said, "because there is no answer to it without God. I could answer it for you, if I thought you were open to anything but drink and photography, Harry, but I'm not going to waste precious argument. What I want is to defend Eisengrim against the charge of being a villain, now or at any other time. You must look at his history in the light of myth—"

"Aha, I thought we should get to myth in time," said Liesl.

"Well, myth explains much that is otherwise inexplicable, just because myth is a boiling down of universal experience. Eisengrim's story of his childhood and youth is as new to me as it is to you, although I knew him when he was very young—"

"Yes, and you were an influence in making him what he is," said Liesl.

"Because you taught him conjuring?" said Lind.

"No, no; Ramsay was personally responsible for the premature birth of little Paul Dempster, and responsible also for Paul's mother's madness, which marked him so terribly," said Liesl.

I gaped at her in astonishment. "This is what comes of confiding in women! Not only can they not keep a secret; they re-tell it in an utterly false way! I must put this matter right. It is true that Paul Dempster was born prematurely because his mother was hit on the head by a snowball. It is true that the snowball was meant to hit me, and it hit her instead because I dodged it. It is true that the blow on the head and the birth of the child seemed to precipitate an instability that sometimes amounted to madness. And it is true that I felt some responsibility in the matter. But that was long ago and far away, in a country which you would scarcely recognize as modern Canada. Liesl, I blush for you!"

"What a lovely old-fashioned thing to say, dear Ramsay. Thank you very much for blushing for me, because I long ago lost the trick of blushing for myself. But I didn't spill the beans about you just to make you jump. I wanted to make the point that you are a figure in this story, too. A very strange figure, just as odd as any in your legends. You precipitated, by a single action—and who could think you guilty just because you jumped out of the way of a snowball (who, that is, but a grim Calvinist like yourself, Ramsay)—everything that we have been hearing from Magnus during these nights past. Are you a precipitating figure in Magnus's story, or he in yours? Who could comb it all out? But get on with your myth, dear man. I want to hear what lovely twist you will give to what Magnus has told us."

"It is not a twist, but an explication. Magnus has made it amply clear that he was brought up in a strict, unrelenting form of puritanism. In consequence he still blames himself whenever he can, and because he knows the dramatic quality of the role, he likes to play the villain. But as for his keeping Willard as a sort of hateful pet, in order to jeer at him, I simply don't believe it was like that at all. What is the mythical element in his story? Simply the very old tale of the man who is in search of his soul, and who must struggle with a monster to secure it. All myth and Christianity—which has never been able to avoid the mythical pull of human experience—are full of similar instances, and people all around us are living out this basic human pattern every day. In the study of hagiography—"

"I knew you'd get to saints before long," said Liesl.

"In the study of hagiography we have legends and all those splendid pictures of saints who killed dragons, and it doesn't take much penetration to know that the dragons represent not simply evil in the world but their personal evil, as well. Of course, being saints, they are said to have killed their dragons, but we know that dragons are not killed; at best they are tamed, and kept on the chain. In the pictures we see St. George, and my special favourite, St. Catherine, triumphing over the horrid beast, who lies with his tongue out, looking as if he thoroughly regretted his mistaken course in life. But I am strongly of the opinion that St. George and St. Catherine did not kill those dragons, for then they would have been wholly good, and inhuman, and useless and probably great sources of mischief, as one-sided people always are. No, they kept the dragons as pets. Because they were Christians, and because Christianity enjoins us to seek only the good and to have nothing whatever to do with evil, they doubtless rubbed it into the dragons that it was uncommonly broadminded and decent of them to let the dragons live at all. They may even have given the dragon occasional treats: you may breathe a little fire, they might say, or you may leer desirously at that virgin yonder, but if you make one false move you'll wish you hadn't. You must be a thoroughly submissive dragon, and remember who's boss. That's the Christian way of doing things, and that's what Magnus did with Willard. He didn't kill Willard. The essence of Willard lives with him today. But he got the better of Willard. Didn't you notice how he was laughing as he said good-night?"

"I certainly did," said Ingestree. "I didn't understand it at all. It wasn't just the genial laughter of a man saying farewell to some guests. And certainly he didn't seem to be laughing at us. I thought perhaps it was relief at having got something off his chest."

"The laugh troubled me," said Lind. "I am not good at humour, and I like to be perfectly sure what people are laughing at. Do you know what it was, Ramsay?"

"Yes," I said, "I think I do. That was Merlin's Laugh."

"I don't know about that," said Lind.

"If Liesl will allow it, I must be mythological again. The magician Merlin had a strange laugh, and it was heard when nobody else was laughing. He laughed at the beggar who was bewailing his fate as he lay stretched on a dunghill; he laughed at the foppish young man who was making a great fuss about choosing a pair of shoes. He laughed because he knew that deep in the dunghill was a golden cup that would have made the beggar a rich man; he laughed because he knew that the pernickety young man would be stabbed in a quarrel before the soles of his new shoes were soiled. He laughed because he knew what was coming next."

"And of course our friend knows what is coming next in his own story," said Lind.

"Are we to take it then that there was some striking reversal of fortune awaiting him when he went to England?" said Ingestree.

"I know no more than you," said I. "I do not hear Merlin's Laugh very often, though I think I am more sensitive to its sound than most people. But he spoke of finding out what wine would be poured into the well-smoked bottled that he had become. I don't know what it was."

Ingestree was more excited than the rest. "But are we never to know? How can we find out?"

"Surely that's up to you," said Lind. "Aren't you going to ask Eisengrim to come to London to see the rushes of this film we have been making? Isn't that owing to him? Get him in London and ask him to continue."

Ingestree looked doubtful. "Can it be squeezed out of the budget?" he said. "The corporation doesn't like frivolous expenses. Of course I'd love to ask him, but if we run very much over budget, well, it would be as good as my place is worth, as servants used to say in the day when they knew they were servants."

"Nonsense, you can rig it," said Kinghovn. But Ingestree still looked like a worried, rather withered baby.

"I know what is worrying Roly," said Liesl. "He thinks that he could squeeze Eisengrim's expenses in London out of the B.B.C., but he knows he can't lug in Ramsay and me, and he's too nice a fellow to suggest that Magnus travel without us. Isn't that it, Roly?"

Ingestree looked at her. "Bang on the head," he said.

"Don't worry about it," said Liesl. "I'll pay my own way, and even this grinding old miser Ramsay might unchain a few pennies for himself. Just let us know when to come."

And so, at last, they went. As we came back into the large, gloomy, nineteenth-century Gothic hall of Sorgenfrei, I said to Liesl: "It was nice of you to think of Lebbaeus, tonight. People don't mention him very often. But you're wrong, you know, saying that there is no record of what he did after the Crucifixion. There is a non-canonical Acts of Thaddaeus—Thaddaeus was his surname, you recall—that tells all about him. It didn't get into the Bible, but it exists."

"What's it like?"

"A great tale of marvels. Real Arabian Nights stuff. Puts him dead at the centre of affairs."

"Didn't I say so! Just like a man. I'll bet he wrote it himself."

II
Merlin's Laugh

1

Because of Jurgen Lind's slow methods of work, it took longer to get *Un Hommage à Robert-Houdin* into a final form than we had expected, and it was nearly three months later when Eisengrim, Liesl, and I journeyed to London to see what it looked like. The polite invitation suggested that criticism would be welcome. Eisengrim was the star, and Liesl had put up a good deal of the money for the venture, expecting to get it back over the next two or three years, with substantial gains, but I think we all knew that criticism of Lind would not be gratefully received. A decent pretence was to be kept up, all the same.

We three rarely travelled together; when we did there was always a good deal of haggling about where we should stay. I favoured small, modest hotels; Liesl felt a Swiss nationalist pull toward any hotel, anywhere, that was called the Ritz; Eisengrim wanted to stop at the Savoy.

The suite we occupied at the Savoy was precisely to his taste. It had been decorated in the twenties, and not changed since; the rooms were large, and the walls were in that most dismal of decorators' colours, "off-white"; below the ceiling of the drawing-room was a nine-inch border of looking-glass; there was an Art Moderne fireplace with an electric fire in it which, when in use, gave off a heavy smell of roasted dust and reminiscences of mice; the furniture was big, and clumsy in the twenties mode. The windows looked out on what I called an alley, and what even Liesl called "a mean street", but to our amazement Magnus came up with the comment that nobody who called himself a gentleman ever looked out of the window. (What did he know about the fine points of upper-class behaviour?) There was a master bedroom of astonishing size, and Magnus grabbed it for himself, saying that Liesl might have the other bed in it. My room, not quite so large but still a big room, was nearer the bathroom. That chamber was gorgeous in a style long forgotten, with what seemed to be Roman tiling, a sunken bath, and a giantess's bidet. The daily rate for this grandeur startled me even when I had divided it by three, but I held my peace, and hoped we would not stay long. I am not a stingy man, but I think a decent prudence becoming even in the very rich, like Liesl. Also, I knew enough about the very rich to understand that I should not be let off with a penny less than my full third of whatever was spent.

Magnus was taking his new position as a film star—even though it was only as the star of a television "special"—with a seriousness that seemed to me absurd. The very first night he insisted on having Lind and his gang join us for what he called a snack in our drawing-room. Snack! Solomon and the Queen of Sheba would have been happy with such a snack; when I saw it laid out by the waiters I was so oppressed by the thought of what a third of it would come to that I wondered if I should be able to touch a morsel. But the others ate and drank hugely, and almost as soon as they entered the room began hinting that Magnus should continue the story he had begun at Sorgenfrei. That was what I wanted, too, and as it was plain that I was going to pay dear to hear it, I overcame my scruple and made sure of my share of the feast.

The showing of *Hommage* had been arranged for the following afternoon at three o'clock. "Good," said Magnus; "that will allow me the morning to make a little sentimental pilgrimage I have in mind."

Polite interest from Ingestree, and delicately inquisitive probings as to what this pilgrimage might be.

"Something associated with a turning-point in my life," said Magnus. "I feel that one should not be neglectful of such observances."

Was it anything with which the B.B.C. could be helpful, Ingestree asked.

"No, not at all," said Magnus. "I simply want to lay some flowers at the foot of a monument."

Surely, Ingestree persisted, Magnus would permit somebody from the publicity department, or from a newspaper, to get a picture of this charming moment? It could be so helpful later, when it was necessary to work up enthusiasm for the film.

Magnus was coy. He would prefer not to make public a private act of gratitude and respect. But he was willing to admit, among friends, that what he meant to do was part of the subtext of the film; an act related to his own career; something he did whenever he found himself in London.

He had now gone so far that it was plain he wanted to be coaxed, and Ingestree coaxed him with a mixture of affection and respect that was worthy of admiration. It was plain to be seen how Ingestree had not merely survived, but thriven, in the desperate world of television. It was not long before Magnus yielded, as I suppose he meant to do from the beginning.

"It's nothing in the least extraordinary. I'm going to lay a few yellow roses—I hope I can get yellow ones—at the foot of the monument to Henry Irving behind the National Portrait Gallery. You know it. It's one of the best-known monuments in London. Irving, splendid and gracious, in his academical robes, looking up Charing Cross Road. I promised Milady I'd do that, in her name and my own, if I ever came to the point in life where I could afford such gestures. And I have. And so I shall."

"Now you really mustn't tease us any more," said Ingestree. "We must be told. Who is Milady?"

"Lady Tresize," said Magnus, and there was no hint of banter in his voice any longer. He was solemn. But Ingestree hooted with laughter.

"My God!" he said, "You don't mean Old Mother Tresize? Old Nan? You knew her?"

"Better than you apparently did," said Magnus. "She was a dear friend of mine, and very good to me when I needed a friend. She was one of Irving's protégées, and in her name I do honour to his memory."

"Well—I apologize. I apologize profoundly. I never knew her well, though I saw something of her. You'll admit she was rather a joke as an actress."

"Perhaps. Though I saw her give some remarkable performances. She didn't always get parts that were suited to her."

"I can't imagine what parts could ever have suited her. It's usually admitted she held the old man back. Dragged him down, in fact. He really may have been good, once. If he'd had a decent leading lady he mightn't have ended up as he did."

"I didn't know that he had ended up badly. Indeed I know for a fact that he had quite a happy retirement, and was happier because he shared it with her. Are we talking about the same people?"

"I suppose it depends on how one looks at it. I'd better shut up."

"No, no," said Lind. "This is just the time to keep on. Who are these people called Tresize? Theatre people, I suppose?"

"Sir John Tresize was one of the most popular romantic actors of his day," said Magnus.

"But in an absolutely appalling repertoire," said Ingestree, who seemed unable to hold his tongue. "He went on into the twenties acting stuff that was moth-eaten when Irving died. You should have seen it, Jurgen! *The Lyons Mail*, *The Corsican Brothers*, and that interminable *Master of Ballantrae*; seeing him in repertory was a peep into the dark backward and abysm of time, let me tell you!"

"That's not true," said Magnus, and I knew how hot he was by the coolness with which he spoke. "He did some fine things, if you would take the trouble to find out. Some admired Shakespearean performances; a notable Hamlet. The money he made on *The Master of Ballantrae* he spent on introducing the work of Maeterlinck to England."

"Maeterlinck's frightfully old hat," said Ingestree.

"Now, perhaps. But fashions change. And when Sir John Tresize introduced Maeterlinck to England he was an innovator. Have you no charity toward the past?"

"Not a scrap."

"I think less of you for it."

"Oh, come off it! You're an immensely accomplished actor yourself. You know how the theatre is. Of all the arts it has least patience with bygones."

"You have said several times that I am a good actor, because I can put up a decent show as Robert-Houdin. I'm glad you think so. Have you ever asked yourself where I learned to do that? One of the things that has given my work a special flavour is that I give my audiences something to look at apart from good tricks. They like the way I act the part of a conjuror. They say it has romantic flair. What they really mean is that it is projected with a skilled nineteenth-century technique. And where did I learn that?"

"Well, obviously you're going to tell me you learned it from old Tresize. But it isn't the same, you know. I mean, I remember him. He was lousy."

"Depends on the point of view, I suppose. Perhaps you had some reason not to like him."

"Not at all."

"You said you knew him."

"Oh, very slightly."

"Then you missed a chance to know him better. I had that chance and I took it. Probably I needed it more than you did. I took it, and I paid for it, because knowing Sir John didn't come cheap. And Milady was a great woman. So tomorrow morning—yellow roses."

"You'll let us send a photographer?"

"Not after what you've been saying. I don't pretend to an overwhelming delicacy, but I have some. So keep away, please, and if you disobey me I won't finish the few shots you still have to make on *Hommage*. Is that clear?"

It was clear, and after lingering a few minutes, just to show that they could not be easily dismissed, Ingestree, and Jurgen Lind, and Kinghovn left us.

2

Both Liesl and I went with Magnus the following morning on his sentimental expedition. Liesl wanted to know who Milady was; her curiosity was aroused by the tenderness and reverence with which he spoke of the woman who appeared to Ingestree to be a figure of fun. I was curious about everything concerning him. After all, I had my document to consider. So we both went with him to buy the roses. Liesl protested when he bought an expensive bunch of two dozen. "If you leave them in the street, somebody will steal them," she said; "the gesture is the same whether it's one rose or a bundle. Don't waste your money." Once again I had occasion to be surprised at the way very rich people think about money; a costly apartment at the Savoy, and a haggle about a few roses! But Eisengrim was not to be changed from his purpose. "Nobody will steal them, and you'll find out why," said he. So off we went on foot along the Strand, because Magnus felt that taking a taxi would lessen the solemnity of his pilgrimage.

The Irving monument stands in quite a large piece of open pavement; near by a pavement artist was chalking busily on the flagstones. Beside the monument itself a street performer was unpacking some ropes and chains, and a woman was helping to get ready for his performance. Magnus took off his hat, laid the flowers at the foot of the statue, arranged them to suit himself, stepped back, looked up at the statue, smiled, and said something under his breath. Then he said to the street performer: "Going to do a few escapes, are you?"

"Right you are," said the man.

"Will you be here long?"

"Long as anybody wants to watch me."

"I'd like you to keep an eye on those flowers. They're for the Guvnor, you see. Here's a pound. I'll be back before lunch, and if they're still there, and if you're still here, I'll have another pound for you. I want them to stay where they are for at least three hours; after that anybody who wants them can have them. Now let's see your show."

The busker and the woman went to work. She rattled a tambourine, and he shook the chains and defied the passers-by to tie him up so that he couldn't escape. A few loungers gathered, but none of them seemed anxious to oblige the escape-artist by tying him up. At last Magnus did it himself.

I didn't know what he had in mind, and I wondered if he meant to humiliate the poor fellow by tying him up and leaving him to struggle; after all, Magnus had been a distinguished escape-artist himself in his time, and as he was a man of scornful mind such a trick would not have been outside his range. He made a thorough job of it, and before he had done there was a crowd of fifteen or twenty people gathered to see the fun. It is not every day that one of these shabby street performers has a beautifully dressed and distinguished person as an assistant. I saw a policeman halt at the back of the crowd, and began to worry. My philosophical indifference to human suffering is not as complete as I wish it were. If Magnus tied up the poor wretch and left him, what should I do? Interfere, or run away? Or would I simply hang around and see what happened?

At last Magnus was contented with his work, and stepped away from the busker, who was now a bundle of chains and ropes. The man dropped to the ground, writhed and grovelled for a few seconds, worked himself up on his knees, bent his head and tried to get at one of the ropes with his teeth, and in doing so fell forward and seemed to hurt himself badly. The crowd murmured sympathetically, and pressed a bit nearer. Then, suddenly, the busker gave a triumphant cry, and leapt to his feet, as chains and ropes fell in a tangle on the pavement.

Magnus led the applause. The woman passed the tattered cap that served as a collection bag. Some copper and a few silver coins were dropped in it. Liesl contributed a fifty-penny piece, and I found another. It was a good round for the busker; astonishingly good, I imagine, for the first show of the day.

When the crowd had dispersed, the busker said softly to Magnus: "Pro, ain't yer?"

"Yes, I'm a pro."

"Knew it. You couldn't of done them ties without bein' a pro. You playin' in town?"

"No, but I have done. Years ago, I used to give a show right where we're standing now."

"You did! Christ, you've done well."

"Yes. And I started here under the Guvnor's statue. You'll keep an eye on his flowers, won't you?"

"Too right I will! And thanks!"

We walked away, Magnus smiling and big with mystery. He knew how much we wanted to know what lay behind what we had just seen, and was determined to make us beg. Liesl, who has less pride about such things than I, spoke before we had passed the pornography shops into Leicester Square.

"Come along, Magnus. Enough of this. We want to know and you want to tell. I can feel it. When did you ever perform in the London streets?"

"After I got away from France, and the travelling circus, and the shadow of Willard. I came to London, which was dangerous with the kind of passport I carried, but I managed it. What was I to do? You don't get jobs in variety theatres just by hanging around the stage doors. It's a matter of agents, and having press cuttings, and being known to somebody. And I was down and out. I hadn't a penny. No, that's not quite true; I had forty-two shillings and that was just enough to buy a few old ropes and chains. So I took a look around the West End, and soon found out that the choice position for open-air shows was the place we've just visited. But even that wasn't free; street artists of long standing had first call on the space. I tried to do my little act when they weren't busy, and three of them took me up an alley and convinced me that I had been tactless. Nevertheless, with a black eye I managed to show them a little magic that persuaded one of them to let me add something to his own show, and for that I got a very small daily sum. Still, I was seen, and it wasn't more than a few days before I was taken to Milady, and after that everything was glorious."

"Why should Milady want to see you? Really, Magnus, you are intolerable. You are going to tell us, so why don't you do it without making me corkscrew every word out of you?"

"If I tell you now, in the street, don't you think I am being rather unfair to Lind? He wants to know too, you know."

"Last night you virtually ordered Lind and his friends out of the hotel. Do you mean you are going to change your mind about that?"

"I was annoyed with Ingestree."

"Yes, I know that. But what's so bad about Ingestree? He doesn't agree with you about Milady. Is the man to have no mind of his own? Must everybody agree with you? Ingestree isn't a bad fellow."

"Not a bad fellow. A fool perhaps."

"Since when is it a criminal offence to be a fool? You're rather a fool yourself, especially about women. I insist on knowing whatever there is to know about Milady."

"And so you shall, my dear Liesl. So you shall. You have only to wait until this evening. I guarantee that when we go back to the Savoy we shall find that Lind has called, that Ingestree is ready to apologize, and that we are all three asked to dinner tonight so that I may very graciously go on with my subtext to *Hommage*. Which I am perfectly willing to do. And Ramsay will be pleased, because the free dinner he gets tonight will somewhat offset the cost of the dinner he had to share in giving last night. You see, all things work together for good to them that love God."

"Sometimes I wish I were a professing Christian, so that I would have the right to tell you how much your blasphemous quoting of Scripture annoys me. And you mustn't torment Ramsay. He hasn't had your advantages. He's never been really poor, and that is a terrible drawback to a man.—Will you promise to be decent to Ingestree?"

An unwonted sound: Eisengrim laughed aloud: Merlin's laugh, if ever I heard it.

3

Magnus was having one of his tiresome spells, during which he was right about everything. We were indeed asked to dine as Lind's guests after the showing of *Hommage*. What we saw in the poky little viewing-room was a version of the film that was almost complete; everything that was to be cut out had been removed, but a few shots—close-ups of Magnus—had still to be taken and incorporated. It was a source of astonishment, for I saw nothing that I had not seen while it was being filmed; but the skill of the cutting, and the juxtapositions, and the varieties of pace that had been achieved, were marvels to me. Clearly much of what had been done owed its power to the art of Harry Kinghovn, but the unmistakable impress of Lind's mind was on it, as well. His films possessed a weight of implication—in St. Paul's phrase, "the evidence of things not seen"—that was entirely his own.

The greatest surprise was the way in which Eisengrim emerged. His unique skill as a conjuror was there, of course, but somehow magic is not so impressive on the screen as it is in direct experience, just as he had said himself at Sorgenfrei. No, it was as an actor that he seemed like a new person. I suppose I had grown used to him over the years, and had seen too much of his backstage personality, which was that of the theatre martinet, the watchful, scolding, impatient star of the *Soirée of Illusions*. The distinguished, high-bred, romantic figure I saw on the screen was someone I felt I did not know. The waif I had known when we were boys in Deptford, the carnival charlatan I had seen in Austria as Faustus LeGrand in *Le grand Cirque forain de St. Vite*, the successful stage performer, and the amusing but testy and incalculable permanent guest at Sorgenfrei could not be reconciled with this fascinating creature, and it couldn't all be the art of Lind and Kinghovn. I must know more. My document demanded it.

Liesl, too, was impressed, and I am sure she was as curious as I. So far as I knew, she had at some time met Magnus, admired him, befriended him, and financed him. They had toured the world together with their *Soirée of Illusions,* combining his art as a public performer with her skill as a technician, a contriver of magical apparatus, and her artistic taste, which was far beyond his own. If he was indeed the greatest conjuror of his time, or of any time, she was responsible for at least half of whatever had made him so. Moreover, she had educated him, in so far as he was formally educated, and had transformed him from a tough little carnie into someone who could put up a show of cultivation. Or was that the whole truth? She seemed as surprised by his new persona on the screen as I was.

This was clearly one of Magnus's great days. The film people were delighted with him, as entrepreneurs always are with anybody who looks as if he could draw in money, and at dinner he was clearly the guest of honour.

We went to the Café Royal, where a table had been reserved in the old room with the red plush benches against the wall, and the lush girls with naked breasts holding up the ceiling, and the flattering looking-glasses. We ate and drank like people who were darlings of Fortune. Ingestree was on his best behaviour, and it was not until we had arrived at brandy and cigars that he said—

"I passed the Irving statue this afternoon. Quite by chance. Nothing premeditated. But I saw your flowers. And I want to repeat how sorry I am to have spoken slightingly about your old friend Lady Tresize. May we toast her now?"

"Here's to Milady," said Magnus, and emptied his glass.

"Why was she called that?" said Liesl. "It sounds terribly pretentious if she was simply the wife of a theatrical knight. Or it sounds frowsily romantic, like a Dumas novel. Or it sounds as if you were making fun of her. Or was she a cult figure in the theatre? The Madonna of the Greasepaint? You might tell us, Magnus."

"I suppose it was all of those things. Some people thought her pretentious, and some thought the romance that surrounded her was frowsy, and people always made a certain amount of fun of her, and she was a cult figure as well. In addition she was a wonderfully kind, wise, courageous person who was not easy to understand. I've been thinking a lot about her today. I told you that I was a busker beside the Irving statue when I came to London. It was there Holroyd picked me up and took me to Milady. She decided I should have a job, and made Sir John give me one, which he didn't want to do."

"Magnus, do please, I implore you, stop being mysterious. You know very well you mean to tell us all about it. You want to, and furthermore, you must. Do it to please me." Liesl was laying herself out to be irresistible, and I have never known a woman who was better at the work.

"Do it for the sake of the subtext," said Ingestree, who was also making himself charming, like a naughty boy who has been forgiven.

"All right. So I shall. My show under the shadow of Irving was not extensive. The buskers I was working with wouldn't give me much of a chance, but they allowed me to draw a crowd by making some showy passes with cards. It was stuff I had learned long ago with Willard—shooting a deck into the air and making it slide back into my hand like a beautiful waterfall, and that sort of thing. It can be done with a deck that is mounted on a rubber string, but I could do it with any deck. It's simply a matter of hours of practice, and confidence that you can do it. I don't call it conjuring. More like juggling. But it makes people gape.

"One day, a week or two after I had begun in this underpaid, miserable work, I noticed a man hanging around at the back of the crowd, watching me very closely. He wore a long overcoat, though it wasn't a day for such a coat, and he had a pipe stuck in his mouth as if it had grown there. He worried me because, as you know, my passport wasn't all it should have been. I thought he might be a detective. So as soon as I had done my short trick, I made for a nearby alley. He was right behind me. 'Hi!' he shouted, 'I want a word with you.' There was no getting away, so I faced him. 'Are you interested in a better job than that?' he asked. I said I was. 'Can you do a bit of juggling?' said he. Yes, I could do juggling, though I wouldn't call myself a juggler. 'Any experience walking a tightrope?' Because of the work I had done with Duparc I was able to say I could. 'Then you come to this address tomorrow morning at twelve,' said he, and gave me a card on which was his name—James Holroyd—and he had scribbled a direction on it.

"Of course I was there, next day at noon. The place was a pub called The Crown and Two Chairmen, and when I asked for Mr. Holroyd I was directed upstairs to a big room, in which there were a few people. Holroyd was one of them, and he nodded to me to wait.

"Queer room. Just an empty space, with some chairs piled in a corner, and a few odds and ends of pillars, and obelisks and altar-like boxes, which I knew were Masonic paraphernalia, also stacked against a wall. It was one of those rooms common enough in London, where lodges met, and little clubs had their gatherings, and which theatrical people rented by the day for rehearsal space.

"The people who were there were grouped around a man who was plainly the boss. He was short, but by God he had presence; you would have noticed him anywhere. He wore a hat, but not as I had ever seen a hat worn before. Willard and Charlie were hat men, but somehow their hats always looked sharp and dishonest—you know, too much down on one side? Holroyd wore a hat, a hard hat of the kind that Winston Churchill made famous later; a sort of top hat that had lost courage and hadn't grown the last three inches, or acquired any gloss. As I came to know Holroyd I sometimes wondered if he had been born in that hat and overcoat, because I hardly ever saw him without both. But this little man's hat looked as if it should have had a plume in it. It was a perfectly ordinary, expensive felt hat, but he gave it an air of costume, and when he looked from under the brim you felt he was sizing up your costume, too. And that was what he was doing. He took a look at me and said, in a kind of mumble, 'That's your find, eh? Doesn't look much, does he, mph? Not quite as if he might pass for your humble, what? Eh, Holroyd? Mph?'

" 'That's for you to say, of course,' said Holroyd.

" 'Then I say no. Must look again. Must be something better than that, eh?'

" 'Won't you see him do a few tricks?'

" 'Need I? Surely the appearance is everything, mph?'

" 'Not everything, Guvnor. The tricks are pretty important. At least the way you've laid it out makes the tricks very important. And the tightrope, too. He'd look quite different dressed up.'

" 'Of course. But I don't think he'll do. Look again, eh, like a good chap?'

" 'Whatever you say, Guvnor. But I'd have bet money on this one. Let him flash a trick or two, just to see.'

"The little man wasn't anxious to waste time on me, but I didn't mean to waste time either. I threw a couple of decks in the air, made them do a fancy twirl, and let them slip back into my hands. Then I twirled on my toes, and made the decks do it again, in a spiral, which looks harder than it is. There was clapping from a corner—the kind of soft clapping women produce by clapping in gloves they don't want to split. I bowed toward the corner, and that was the first time I saw Milady.

"It was a time when women's clothes were plain; the line of the silhouette was supposed to be simple. There was nothing plain or simple about Milady's clothes. Drapes and swags and swishes, and scraps of fur everywhere, and the colours and fabrics were more like upholstery than garments. She had a hat, like a witch's, but with more style to it, and some soft stuff wrapped around the crown dangled over the brim to one shoulder. She was heavily made up —really she wore an extraordinary amount of make-up—in colours that were too emphatic for daylight. But neither she nor the little man seemed to be meant for daylight; I didn't realize it at the time, but they always looked as if they were ready to step on the stage. Their clothes, and manner and demeanour all spoke of the stage."

"The Crummles touch," said Ingestree. "They were about the last to have it."

"I don't know who Crummles was," said Magnus. "Ramsay will tell me later. But I must make it clear that these two didn't look in the least funny to me. Odd, certainly, and unlike anything I had ever seen, but not funny. In fact, ten years later I still didn't think them funny, though I know lots of people laughed. But those people didn't know them as I did. And as I've told you I first saw Milady when she was applauding my tricks with the cards, so she looked very good to me.

" 'Let him show what he can do, Jack,' she said. And then to me, with great politeness, 'You do juggling, don't you? Let us see you juggle.'

"I had nothing to juggle with, but I didn't mean to be beaten. And I wanted to prove to the lady that I was worth her kindness. So with speed and I hope a reasonable amount of politeness I took her umbrella, and the little man's wonderful hat, and Holroyd's hat and the soft cap I was wearing myself, and balanced the brolly on my nose and juggled the three hats in an arch over it. Not easy, let me tell you, for all the hats were of different sizes and weights, and Holroyd's hefted like iron. But I did it, and the lady clapped again. Then she whispered to the little man she called Jack.

" 'I see what you mean, Nan,' he said, 'but there must be some sort of resemblance. I hope I'm not vain, but I can't persuade myself we can manage a resemblance. Mphm?'

"I put on a little more steam. I did some clown juggling, pretending every time the circle went round that I was about to drop Holroyd's hat, and recovering it with a swoop, and at last keeping that one in the air with my right foot. That made the little man laugh, and I knew I had had a lucky inspiration. Obviously Holroyd's hat was rather a joke among them. 'Come here, m'boy,' said the boss. 'Stand back to back with me.' So I did, and we were exactly of a height. 'Extraordinary,' said the boss; 'I'd have sworn he was shorter.'

" 'He's a little shorter, Guvnor,' said Holroyd, 'but we can put him in lifts.'

" 'Aha, but what will you do about the face?' said the boss. 'Can you get away with the face?'

" 'I'll show him what to do about the face,' said the lady. 'Give him his chance, Jack. I'm sure he's lucky for us and I'm never wrong. After all, where did Holroyd find him?'

"So I got the job, though I hadn't any idea what the job was, and nobody thought to tell me. But the boss said I was to come to rehearsal the following Monday, which was five days away. In the meantime, he said, I was to give up my present job, and keep out of sight. I would have accepted that, but again the lady interfered.

" 'You can't ask him to do that, Jack,' she said. 'What's he to live on in the meantime?'

" 'Holroyd will attend to it,' said the little man. Then he offered the lady his arm, and put his hat back on his head (after Holroyd had dusted it, quite needlessly) and they swept out of that grubby assembly room in the Crown and Two Chairmen as if it were a palace.

"I said to Holroyd, 'What's this about lifts? I'm as tall as he is; perhaps a bit taller.'

" 'If you want this job, m'boy, you'll be shorter and stay shorter,' said Holroyd. Then he gave me thirty shillings, explaining that it was an advance on salary. He also asked for a pledge in return, just so that I wouldn't make off with the thirty shillings; I gave him my old silver watch. I respected Holroyd for that; he belonged to my world. It was clear that it was time for me to go, but I still didn't know what the job was, or what I was letting myself in for. That was obviously the style around there. Nobody explained anything. You were supposed to know.

"So, not being a fool, I set to work to find out. I discovered downstairs in the bar that Sir John Tresize and his company were rehearsing above, which left me not much wiser, except that it was some sort of theatricals. But when I went back to the buskers and told them I was quitting, and why, they were impressed, but not pleased.

" 'You gone legit on us,' said the boss of the group, who was an escape-man, like the one we saw this morning. 'You and your Sir John-bloody-Tresize. Amlet and Oh Thello and the like of them. If you want my opinion, you've got above yourself, and when they find out, don't come whinin' back to me, that's all. Don't come whinin' bloody back here.' Then he kicked me pretty hard in the backside, and that was the end of my engagement as an open-air entertainer.

"I didn't bother to resent the kick. I had a feeling something important had happened to me, and I celebrated by taking a vacation. Living for five days on thirty shillings was luxury to me at that time. I thought of augmenting my money by doing a bit of pocket-picking, but I rejected the idea for a reason that will show you what had happened to me; I though such behaviour would be unsuitable to one who had been given a job because of the interference of a richly-dressed lady with an eye for talent.

"The image of the woman called Nan by Sir John Tresize dominated my mind. Her umbrella, as I balanced it on my nose, gave forth an expensive smell of perfume, and I could recall it even in the petrol stink of London streets. I was like a boy who is in love for the first time. But I wasn't a boy; it was 1930, so I must have been twenty-two, and I was a thorough young tough—side-show performer, vaudeville rat, pick-pocket, dope-pusher, a forger in a modest way, and for a good many years the despised utensil of an arse-bandit. Women, to me, were members of a race who were either old and tougher than the men who work in carnivals, or the flabby, pallid strumpets I had occasionally seen in Charlie's room when I went to rouse him to come to the aid of Willard. But so far as any sexual association with a woman went, I was a virgin. Yes, ladies and gentlemen, I was a hoor from the back and a virgin from the front, and so far as romance was concerned I was as pure as the lily in the dell. And there I was, over my ears in love with Lady Tresize, professionally known as Miss Annette de la Borderie, who cannot have been far off sixty and was, as Ingestree is eager to tell you, not a beauty. But she had been kind to me and said she would show me what to do about my face—whatever that meant—and I loved her.

"What do I mean? That I was constantly aware of her, and what I believed to be her spirit transfigured everything around me. I held wonderful mental conversations with her, and although they didn't make much sense they gave me a new attitude toward myself. I told you I put aside any notion of picking a pocket in order to refresh my exchequer because of her. What was stranger was that

I felt in quite a different way about the poor slut that helped the escape-artist who kicked me; he was rough with her, I knew, and I pitied her, though I had taken no notice of her before then. It was the dawn of chivalry in me, coming rather late in life. Most men, unless they are assembled on the lowest, turnip-like principle, have a spell of chivalry at some time in their lives. Usually it comes at about sixteen. I understand boys quite often wish they had a chance to die for the one they love, to show that their devotion stops at nothing. Dying wasn't my line; a good religious start in life had given me too much respect for death to permit any extravagance of that sort. But I wanted to live for Lady Tresize, and I was overjoyed by the notion that, if I could do whatever Holroyd and Sir John wanted, I might be able to manage it.

"It wasn't lunacy. She had that effect, in lesser measure, on a lot of people, as I found out when I joined the Tresize Company. Everybody called Sir John 'Guvnor', because that was his style; lots of heads of theatrical companies were called Guvnor. But they called Lady Tresize 'Milady'. It would have been reasonable enough for her maid to do that, but everybody did it, and it was respectful, and affectionately mocking at the same time. She understood both the affection and the mockery, because Milady was no fool.

"Five days is a long time to be cut off from Paradise, and I had nothing to occupy my time. I suppose I walked close to a hundred miles through the London streets. What else was there to do? I bummed around the Victoria and Albert Museum quite a lot, looking at the clocks and watches, but I wasn't dressed for it and I suppose a young tough who hung around for hours made the guards nervous. I looked like a ruffian, and I suppose I was one, and I held no grudge when I was politely warned away. I saw a few free sights—churches and the like—but they meant little to me. I liked the streets best, so I walked and stared, and slept in a Salvation Army hostel for indigents. But I was no indigent; I was rich in feeling, and that was a luxury I had rarely known.

"As the Monday drew near when I was to present myself again I worried a lot about my clothes. All I owned was what I stood up in, and my very poor things were a good protective covering in the streets, where I looked like a thousand others, but they weren't what I needed for a great step upward in the theatrical world.

There was nothing to be done, and with my experience I knew my best plan was to present an appearance of honest poverty, so I spent some money on a bath, and washed the handkerchief I wore around my throat in the bathwater, and got a street shoeshine boy to do what he could with my dreadful shoes, which were almost falling apart.

"When the day came, I was well ahead of time, and had my first taste of a theatrical rehearsal. Milady didn't appear at it, and that was a heavy disappointment, but there was plenty to take in, all the same.

"It was education by observation. Nobody paid any heed to me. Holroyd nodded when I went into the room, and told me to keep out of the way, so I sat on a windowsill and watched. Men and women appeared very promptly to time, and a stage manager set out a few chairs to mark entrances and limits to the stage on the bare floor. Bang on the stroke of ten Sir John came in, and sat down in a chair behind a table, tapped twice with a silver pencil, and they went to work.

"You know what early rehearsals are like. You would never guess they were getting up a play. People wandered on and off the stage area, reading from sheets of paper that were bound up in brown covers; they mumbled and made mistakes as if they had never seen print before. Sir John mumbled worse than anyone. He had a way of talking that I could hardly believe belonged to a human being, because almost everything he said was cast in an interrogative tone, and was muddled up with a lot of 'Eh?' and 'Mphm?' and a queer noise he made high up in the back of his nose that sounded like 'Quonk?' But the actors seemed used to it and amid all the muttering and quonking a good deal of work seemed to be done. Now and then Sir John himself would appear in a scene, and then the muttering sank almost to inaudibility. Very soon I was bored.

"It was not my plan to be bored, so I looked for something to do. I was a handy fellow, and a lot younger than the stage manager, so when the chairs had to be arranged in a different pattern I nipped forward and gave him a hand, which he allowed me to do without comment. Before the rehearsal was finished I was an established chair lifter, and that was how I became an assistant stage manager.

My immediate boss was a man called Macgregor, whose feet hurt; he had those solid feet that seem to be all in one piece, encased in heavy boots; he was glad enough to have somebody who would run around for him. It was from him, during a break in the work, that I found out what we were doing.

" 'It's the new piece,' he explained. '*Scaramouche*. From the novel by Rafael Sabatini. You'll have heard of Rafael Sabatini? You haven't? Well, keep your lugs open and you'll get the drift of it. Verra romantic, of course.'

" 'What am I to do, Mr. Macgregor?' I asked.

" 'Nobody's told me,' he said. 'But from the cut of your jib I'd imagine you were the Double.'

" 'Double what?'

" 'The Double in Two, two,' he said, in a very Scotch way. I learned long ago, from you, Ramsay, that it's no use asking questions of a Scot when he speaks like that—dry as an old soda biscuit. So I held my peace.

"I picked up a little information by listening and asking an occasional question when some of the lesser actors went downstairs to the bar for a modest lunch. After three or four days I knew that *Scaramouche* was laid in the period of the French Revolution, though when that was I did not know. I had never heard that the French had a revolution. I knew the Americans had had one, but so far as detail went it could have been because George Washington shot Lincoln. I was pretty strong on the kings of Israel; later history was closed to me. But the story of the play leaked out in dribbles. Sir John was a young Frenchman who was 'born with a gift of laughter and a sense that the world was mad'; that was what one of the other actors said about him. The astonishing thing was that nobody thought it strange that Sir John was so far into middle age that he was very near to emerging from the far side of it. This young Frenchman got himself into trouble with the nobility because he had advanced notions. To conceal himself he joined a troupe of travelling actors, but his revolutionary zeal was so great that he could not hold his tongue, and denounced the aristocracy from the stage, to the scandal of everyone. When the Revolution came, which it did right on time when it was needed, he became a revolutionary leader, and was about to revenge himself on the nobleman who had vilely slain his best friend and nabbed his girl, when an elderly noblewoman was forced to declare that she was his mother and then, much against her will, further compelled to tell him that his deadly enemy whom he held at the sword's point was—his father!

"Verra romantic, as Macgregor said, but not so foolish as I have perhaps led you to think. I give it to you as it appeared to me on early acquaintance. I was only interested in what I was supposed to do to earn my salary. Because I now had a salary—or half a salary, because that was the pay for the rehearsal period. Holroyd had presented me with a couple of pages of wretchedly typed stuff, which was my contract. I signed it Jules LeGrand, so that it agreed with my passport. Holroyd looked a little askew at the name, and asked me if I spoke French. I was glad that I could say yes, but he gave me a pretty strong hint that I might consider finding some less foreign name for use on the stage. I couldn't imagine why that should be, but I found out when we reached Act Two, scene two.

"We had approached this critical point—critical for me, that's to say—two or three times during the first week of rehearsal, and Sir John had asked the actors to 'walk through' it, without doing more than find their places on the stage. It was a scene in which the young revolutionary lawyer, whose name was André-Louis, was appearing on the stage with the travelling actors. They were a troupe of Italian Comedians, all of whom played strongly marked characters such as Polichinelle the old father, Climene the beautiful leading lady, Rhodomont the braggart, Leandre the lover, Pasquariel, and other figures from the Commedia dell' Arte. I didn't know what that was, but I picked up the general idea, and it wasn't so far away from vaudeville as you might suppose. Indeed, some of it reminded me of poor Zovene, the wretched juggler. André-Louis (that was Sir John) had assumed the role of Scaramouche, a dashing, witty scoundrel.

"In Act Two, scene two, the Italian Comedians were giving a performance, and at the very beginning of it Scaramouche had to do some flashy juggling tricks. Later, he seized his chance to make a revolutionary speech which was not in the play as the Comedians had rehearsed it; when his great enemy and some aristocratic chums stormed the stage to punish him, he escaped by walking across the stage on a tightrope, far above their heads, making jeering gestures as he did so. Very showy. And clearly not for Sir John. So I was to appear in a costume exactly like his, do the tricks, get out of the way so Sir John could make his revolutionary speech, and take over again when it was time to walk the tightrope.

"This would take some neat managing. When Macgregor said, 'Curtain up,' I leapt onto the stage area from the audience's right, and danced toward the left, juggling some plates; when Polichinelle broke the plates with his stick, causing a lot of clatter and uproar, I pretended to dodge behind his cloak, and Sir John popped into sight immediately afterward. Sounds simple, but as we had to pretend to have the plates, and the cloak, and everything else, I found it confusing. The tightrope trick was 'walked' in the same way; Sir John was always talking about 'walking' something when we weren't ready to do it in reality. At the critical moment when the aristocrats rushed the stage, Sir John retreated slowly toward the left side, keeping them off with a stick; then he hopped backward onto a chair—which I must say he did with astonishing spryness—and there was a flurry of cloaks, during which he got out of the way and I emerged above on the tightrope, having stepped out on it from the wings. Easy, you would say, for an old carnival hand? But it wasn't easy at all, and after a few days it looked as if I would lose my job. Even when we were 'walking', I couldn't satisfy Sir John.

"As usual, nobody said anything to me, but I knew what was up one morning when Holroyd appeared with a fellow who was obviously an acrobat and Sir John talked with him. I hung around, officiously helping Macgregor, and heard what was said, or enough of it. The acrobat seemed to be very set on something he wanted, and it wasn't long before he was on his way, and Sir John was in an exceedingly bad temper. All through the rehearsal he bullied everybody. He bullied Miss Adele Chesterton, the pretty girl who played the second romantic interest; she was new to the stage and a natural focus for temper. He bullied old Frank Moore, who played Polichinelle, and was a very old hand and an extraordinarily nice person. He was crusty with Holroyd and chivvied Macgregor. He didn't shout or swear, but he was impatient and exacting, and his annoyance was so thick it cut down the visibility in the room to about half, like dark smoke. When the time came to rehearse

Two, two, he said he would leave it out for that day, and he brought the rehearsal to an early close. Holroyd asked me to wait after the others had gone, but not to hang around. So I kept out of the way near the door while Sir John, Holroyd, and Milady held a summit conference at the farther end of the room.

"I couldn't hear much of what they said, but it was about me, and it was hottish. Holroyd kept saying things like, 'You won't get a real pro to agree to leaving his name off the bills,' and 'It's not as easy to get a fair resemblance as you might suppose—not under the conditions.' Milady had a real stage voice, and when she spoke her lowest it was still as clear as a bell at my end of the room, and her talk was all variations on 'Give the poor fellow a chance, Jack—everybody must have at least one chance.' But of Sir John I could hear nothing. He had a stage voice, too, and knew how far it could be heard, so when he was being confidential he mumbled on purpose and threw in a lot of Eh and Quonk, which seemed to convey meaning to people who knew him.

"After ten minutes Milady said, so loudly that there could be no pretence that I was not to hear, 'Trust me, Jack. He's lucky for us. He has a lucky face. I'm never wrong. And if I can't get him right, we'll say no more about it.' Then she swept down the room to me, using the umbrella, with more style than you'd think possible, as a walking-stick, and said, 'Come with me, my dear boy; we must have a very intimate talk.' Then something struck her, and she turned to the two men; 'I haven't a penny,' she said, and from the way both Sir John and Holroyd jumped forward to press pound notes on her you could tell they were both devoted to her. That made me feel warmly toward them, even though they had been talking about sacking me a minute before.

"Milady led the way, and I tagged behind. We went downstairs, where she poked her head into the Public Bar, which was just opening and said, in a surprisingly genial voice, considering that she was Lady Tresize talking to a barman, 'Do you think I could have Rab Noolas for a private talk, for about half an hour, Joey?', and the barman shouted back, 'Whatever you say, Milady,' and she led me into a gloomy pen, surrounded on three sides by dingy etched glass, with Saloon Bar on the door. When I closed the door behind us this appeared in reverse and I understood that we were now in Rab Noolas. The barman came behind the counter on our fourth side and asked us what it would be. 'A pink gin, Joey,' said Milady, and I said I'd have the same, not knowing what it was. Joey produced them, and we sat down, and from the way Milady did so I knew it was a big moment. Fraught, as they say, with consequence.

" 'Let us be very frank. And I'll be frank first, because I'm the oldest. You simply have no notion of the wonderful opportunity you have in *Scaramouche*. Such a superb little cameo. I say to all beginners: they aren't tiny parts, they're little cameos, and the way you carve them is the sign of what your whole career will be. Show me a young player who can give a superb cameo in a small part, and I'll show you a star of the future. And yours is one of the very finest opportunities I have ever seen in my life in the theatre, because you must be so marvellous that nobody—not the sharpest-eyed critic or the most adoring fan—can distinguish you from my husband. Suddenly, before their very eyes, stands Sir John, juggling marvellously, and of course they adore him. Then, a few minutes later, they see Sir John walking the tightrope, and they see half a dozen of his little special tricks of gesture and turns of the head, and they are thunderstruck because they can't believe that he has learned to walk the tightrope. And the marvel of it, you see, is that it's you, all the time! You must use your imagination, my dear boy. You must see what a stunning effect it is. And what makes it possible? You do!'

" 'Oh I do see all that, Milady,' I said. 'But Sir John isn't pleased. I wish I knew why. I'm honestly doing the very best I can, considering that we haven't anything to juggle with, or any tightrope. How can I do better?'

" 'Ah, but you've put your finger on it, dear boy. I knew from the moment I saw you that you had great, great understanding—not to speak of a lucky face. You have said it yourself. You're doing the best *you* can. But that's not what's wanted, you see. You must do the best Sir John can.'

" 'But—Sir John can't do anything,' I said. 'He can't juggle and he can't walk rope. Otherwise why would he want me?'

" 'No, no; you haven't understood. Sir John can, and will, do something absolutely extraordinary: he will make the public—the great audiences of people who come to see him in everything—believe he is doing those splendid, skilful things. He can make them want to believe he can do anything. They will quite happily accept you as him, if you can get the right rhythm.'

" 'But I still don't understand. People aren't as stupid as that. They'll guess it's a trick.'

" 'A few, perhaps. But most of them will prefer to believe it's a reality. That's what the theatre's about, you see. People want to believe that what they see is true, even if only for the time they're in the playhouse. That's what theatre is, don't you understand? Showing people what they wish were true.'

"Then I began to get the idea. I had seen that look in the faces of the people who watched Abdullah, and who saw Willard swallow needles and thread and pull it out of his mouth with the needles all dangling from the thread. I nervously asked Milady if she would like another pink gin. She said she certainly would, and gave me a pound note to pay for it. When I demurred she said, 'No, no; you must let me pay. I've got more money than you, and I won't presume on your gallantry—though I value it, my dear, don't imagine I don't value it.'

"When the gins came, she continued: 'Let us be very, very frank. Your marvellous cameo must be a great secret. If we tell everybody, we stifle some of their pleasure. You saw that young man who came this morning, and argued so tiresomely? He could juggle and he could walk the rope, quite as well as you, I expect, but he was no use whatever, because he had the spirit of a circus person; he wanted his name on the program, and he wanted featured billing. Wanted his name to come at the bottom of the bills, you see, after all the cast had been listed, "AND Trebelli". An absurd request. Everybody would want to know who Trebelli was and they would see at once that he was the juggler and rope-walker. And Romance would fly right up the chimney. Besides which I could see that he would never deceive anyone for an instant that he was Sir John. He had a brassy, horrid personality. Now you, my dear, have the splendid qualification of having very little personality. One hardly notices you. You are almost a *tabula rasa*.'

" 'Excuse me, Milady, but I don't know what that is.'

" 'No? Well, it's a—it's a common expression. I've never really had to define it. It's a sort of charming nothing; a dear, sweet little zero, in which one can paint any face one chooses. An invaluable possession, don't you see? One says it of children when one's going to teach them something perfectly splendid. They're wide open for teaching.'

" 'I want to be taught. What do you want me to learn?'

" 'I knew you were quite extraordinarily intelligent. More than intelligent, really. Intelligent people are so often thoroughly horrid. You are truly sensitive. I want you to learn to be exactly like Sir John.'

" 'Imitate him, you mean?'

" 'Imitations are no good. There have been people on the music-halls who have imitated him. No: if the thing is to work as we all want it to work, you must quite simply *be* him.'

" 'How, if I don't imitate him?'

" 'It's a very deep thing. Of course you must imitate him, but be careful he doesn't catch you at it, because he doesn't like it. Nobody does, do they? What I mean is—oh, dear, it's so dreadfully difficult to say what one really means—you must catch his walk, and his turn of the head, and his gestures and all of that, but the vital thing is that you must catch his rhythm.'

" 'How would I start to do that?'

" 'Model yourself on him. Make yourself like a marvellously sensitive telegraph wire that takes messages from him. Or perhaps like wireless, that picks up things out of the air. Do what he did with the Guvnor.'

" 'I thought he was the Guvnor.'

" 'He is now, of course. But when we both worked under the dear old Guvnor at the Lyceum Sir John absolutely adored him, and laid himself open to him like Danae to the shower of gold—you know about that, of course?—and became astonishingly like him in a lot of ways. Of course Sir John is not so tall as the Guvnor; but you're not tall either, are you? It was the Guvnor's romantic splendour he caught. Which is what you must do. So that when you dance out before the audience juggling those plates they don't feel as if the electricity had suddenly been cut off. Another pink gin, if you please.'

"I didn't greatly like pink gin. In those days I couldn't afford to drink anything, and pink gin is a bad start. But I would have drunk hot fat to prolong this conversation. So we had another one each, and Milady dealt with hers much better than I did. A pink gin later—call it ten minutes—I was thoroughly confused, except that I wanted to please her, and must find out somehow what she was talking about.

"When she wanted to leave I rushed to call her a taxi, but Holroyd was ahead of me, and in much better condition. He must have been in the Public Bar. We both bowed her into the cab—I seem to remember having one foot in the gutter and the other on the pavement and wondering what had happened to my legs—and when she drove off he took me by the arm and steered me back into the Public Bar, where we tucked into a corner with old Frank Moore.

" 'She's been giving him advice and pink gin,' said Holroyd.

" 'Better give him a good honest pint of half-and-half to straighten him out,' said Frank, and signalled to the barman.

"They seemed to know what Milady had been up to, and were ready to put it in language that I could understand, which was kind of them. They made it seem very simple: I was to imitate Sir John, but I was to do it with more style than I had been showing. I was supposed to be imitating a great actor who was imitating an eighteenth-century gentleman who was imitating a Commedia dell' Arte comedian—that's how simple it was. And I was doing everything too bloody fast, and slick and cheap, so I was to drop that and catch Sir John's rhythm.

" 'But I don't get it about all this rhythm,' I said. 'I guess I know about rhythm in juggling; it's getting everything under control so you don't have to worry about dropping things because the things are behaving properly. But what the hell's all this human rhythm? You mean like dancing?'

" 'Not like any dancing I suppose you know,' said Holroyd. 'But yes—a bit like dancing. Not like this Charleston and all that jerky stuff. More a fine kind of complicated—well, rhythm.'

" 'I don't get it at all,' I said. 'I've got to get Sir John's rhythm. Sir John got his rhythm from somebody called the Guvnor. What Guvnor? Is the whole theatre full of Guvnors?'

" 'Ah, now we're getting to it,' said old Frank. 'Milady talked about the Guvnor, did she? The Guvnor was Irving, you muggins. You've heard of Irving?'

" 'Never,' I said.

"Old Frank looked wonderingly at Holroyd. 'Never heard of Irving. He's quite a case, isn't he?'

" 'Not such a case as you might think, Frank,' said Holroyd. 'These kids today have never heard of anybody. And I suppose we've got to remember that Irving's been dead for twenty-five years. You remember him. You played with him. I just remember him. But what's he got to do with a lad like this?—Well, now just hold on a minute. Milady thinks there's a connection. You know how she goes on. Like a loony, sometimes. But just when you can't stand it any more she proves to be right, and righter than any of us. You remember where I found you?' he said to me.

" 'In the street. I was doing a few passes with the cards.'

" 'Yes, but don't you remember where? I do. I saw you and I came back to rehearsal and said to Sir John, I think I've got what we want. Found him under the Guvnor's statue, picking up a few pennies as a conjuror. And that was when Milady pricked up her ears. Oh Jack, she said, it's a lucky sign! Let's see him at once. And when Sir John wanted to ask perfectly reasonable questions about whether you would do for height, and whether a resemblance could be contrived between you and him, she kept nattering on about how you must be a lucky find because I saw you, as she put it, working the streets under Irving's protection. You know how the Guvnor stood up for all the little people of the theatre, Jack, she said. I'm sure this boy is a lucky find. Do let's have him. And she's stood up for you ever since, though I don't suppose you'll be surprised to hear that Sir John wants to get rid of you.'

"The pint of half-and-half had found its way to the four pink gins, and I was having something like a French Revolution in my innards. I was feeling sorry for myself. 'Why does he hate me so,' I said, snivelling a bit. 'I'm doing everything I know to please him.'

" 'You'd better have it straight,' said Holroyd. 'The resemblance is a bit too good. You look too much like him.'

" 'Just what I said when I first set eyes on you,' said old Frank. 'My God, I said, what a Double! You might have been spit out of his mouth.'

" 'Well, isn't that what they want?' I said.

" 'You have to look at it reasonable,' said Holroyd. 'Put it like this: you're a famous actor, getting maybe just the tiniest bit past your prime—though still a top-notcher, mind you—and for thirty years everybody's said how distinguished you are, and what a beautiful expressive face you have, and how Maeterlinck damn near threw up his lunch when you walked on the stage in one of his plays, and said to the papers that you had stolen his soul, you were so good—meaning spiritual, romantic, poetic, and generally gorgeous. You still get lots of fan letters from people who find some kind of ideal in you. You've had all the devotion—a bit cracked some of it, but mostly very real and touching—that a great actor inspires in people, most of whom have had some kind of short-change experience in life. So: you want a Double. And when the Double comes—and such a Double that you can't deny him—he's a seedy little carnie, with the shifty eyes of a pickpocket and the breath of somebody that eats the cheapest food, and you wouldn't trust him with sixpennorth of copper, and every time you look at him you heave. He looks like everything inside yourself that you've choked off and shut out in order to be what you are now. And he looks at you all the time—you do this, you know—as if he knew something about you you didn't know yourself. Now: fair's fair. Wouldn't you want to get rid of him? Yet here's your wife, who's stood by you through thick and thin, and held you up when you were ready to sink under debts and bad luck, and whom you love so much everybody can see it, and thinks you're marvellous because of it, and what does she say? She says this nasty mess of a Double is lucky, and has to be given his chance. You follow me? Try to be objective. I don't want to say hard things about you, but truth's truth and must be served. You're not anybody's first pick for a Double, but there you are. Sir John's dead spit, as Frank here says.'

"Very soon I was going to have to leave them. My stomach was heaving. But I was still determined to find out whatever I could to keep my job. I wanted it now more desperately than before. 'So what do I do?' I asked.

"Holroyd puffed at his pipe, groping for an answer, and it was old Frank who spoke. He spoke very kindly. 'You just keep on keeping on,' he said. 'Try to find the rhythm. Try to get inside Sir John.'

"These were fatal words. I rushed out into the street, and threw up noisily and copiously in the gutter. Try to get inside Sir John! Was this to be another Abdullah?

"It was, but in a way I could not have foreseen. Experience never repeats itself in quite the same way. I was beginning another servitude, much more dangerous and potentially ruinous, but far removed from the squalor of my experience with Willard. I had entered upon a long apprenticeship to an egoism.

"Please notice that I say egoism, not egotism, and I am prepared to be pernickety about the distinction. An egotist is a self-absorbed creature, delighted with himself and ready to tell the world about his enthralling love affair. But an egoist, like Sir John, is a much more serious being, who makes himself, his instincts, yearnings, and tastes the touchstone of every experience. The world, truly, is his creation. Outwardly he may be courteous, modest, and charming—and certainly when you knew him Sir John was all of these—but beneath the velvet is the steel; if anything comes along that will not yield to the steel, the steel will retreat from it and ignore its existence. The egotist is all surface; underneath is a pulpy mess and a lot of self-doubt. But the egoist may be yielding and even deferential in things he doesn't consider important; in anything that touches his core he is remorseless.

"Many of us have some touch of egoism. We who sit at this table are no strangers to it. You, I should think, Jurgen, are a substantial egoist, and so are you, Harry. About Ingestree I can't say. But Liesl is certainly an egoist and you, Ramsay, are a ferocious egoist battling with your demon because you would like to be a saint. But none of you begins to approach the egoism of Sir John. His egoism was fed by the devotion of his wife, and the applause he could call forth in the theatre. I have never known anyone who came near him in the truly absorbing and damning sin of egoism."

"Damning?" I leapt on the word.

"We were both brought up to believe in damnation, Dunny," said Eisengrim, and he was deeply serious. "What does it mean? Does it mean shut off from the promptings of compassion; untouched by the feelings of others except in so far as they can serve us; blind and deaf to anything that is not grist to our mill? If that is what it means, and if that is a form of damnation, I have used the word rightly.

"Don't misunderstand. Sir John wasn't cruel, or dishonourable or overreaching in common ways; but he was all of these things where his own interest as an artist was concerned; within that broad realm he was without bowels. He didn't make Adele Chesterton cry at every rehearsal because he was a brute. He hadn't brought Holroyd—who was a tough nut in every other way—to a condition of total subjection to his will because he liked to domineer over a fellow-being. He hadn't turned Milady into a kind of human oilcan who went about cooling wheels he had worn red-hot because he didn't know that she was a woman of rare spirit and fine sensitivity. He did these things and a thousand others because he was wholly devoted to an ideal of theatrical art that was contained—so far as he was concerned—within himself. I think he knew perfectly well what he did, and he thought it worth the doing. It served his art, and his art demanded a remorseless egoism.

"He was one of the last of a kind that has now vanished. He was an actor-manager. There was no Arts Council to keep him afloat when he failed, or pick up the bill for an artistic experiment or act of daring. He had to find the money for his ventures, and if the money was lost on one production he had to get it back from another, or he would soon appeal to investors in vain. Part of him was a financier. He asked people to invest in his craft and skill and sense of business. Beyond that, he asked people to invest in his personality and charm, and the formidable technique he had acquired to make personality and charm vivid to hundreds of thousands of people who bought theatre seats. In justice it must be said that he had a particular sort of taste and flair that lifted him above the top level of actors to the very small group of stars with an assured following. He wasn't personally greedy, though he liked to live well. He did what he did for art. His egoism lay in his belief that art, as he embodied it, was worth any sacrifice on his part and on the part of people who worked with him.

"When I became part of his company the fight against time had begun. Not simply the fight against the approach of age, because he was not deluded about that. It was the fight against the change in the times, the fight to maintain a nineteenth-century idea of theatre in the twentieth century. He believed devoutly in what he did; he believed in Romance, and he couldn't understand that the concept of Romance was changing.

"Romance changes all the time. His plays, in which a well-graced hero moved through a succession of splendid adventures and came out on top—even when that meant dying for some noble cause—were becoming old hat. Romance at that time meant *Private Lives*, which was brand-new. It didn't look to its audiences like Romance, but that was what it was. Our notion of Romance, which is so often exploration of squalor and degradation, will become old hat, too. Romance is a mode of feeling that puts enormous emphasis—but not quite a tragic emphasis—on individual experience. Tragedy puts something above humanity; so does Comedy; Romance puts humanity first. The people who liked Sir John's kind of Romance were middle-aged, or old. Oh, lots of young people came to see him, but they weren't the most interesting kind of young people. Perhaps they weren't really young. The interesting young people were going to see a different sort of play. They were flocking to *Private Lives*. You couldn't expect Sir John to understand. His ideal of Romance was far from that, and he had shaped a formidable egoism to serve his ideal."

"It's the peril of the actor," said Ingestree. "Do you remember what Aldous Huxley said? 'Acting inflames the ego in a way which few other professions do. For the sake of enjoying regular emotional self-abuse, our societies condemn a considerable class of men and women to a perpetual inability to achieve non-attachment. It seems a high price to pay for our amusements.' A profound comment. I used to be deeply influenced by Huxley."

"I gather you got over it," said Eisengrim, "or you wouldn't be talking about non-attachment over the ruins of a tremendous meal and a huge cigar you have been sucking like a child at its mother's breast."

"I thought you had forgiven me," said Ingestree, being as winsome as his age and appearance allowed. "I don't pretend to have set aside the delights of this world; I tried that and it was no good. But I have my intellectual fopperies, and they pop out now and then. Do go on about Sir John and his egoism."

"So I shall," said Magnus, "but at another time. The waiters are hovering and I perceive the delicate fluttering of paper in the hands of the chief bandit yonder."

I watched with envy as Ingestree signed the bill without batting an eyelash. I suppose it was company money he was spending. We went out into the London rain and called for cabs.

4

In the days that followed, Magnus was busy filming the last scraps of *Hommage* in a studio near London; these were close-ups, chiefly of his hands, as he did intricate things with cards and coins, but he insisted on wearing full costume and make-up. There was also a time-taking quarrel with a fashionable photographer who was to provide publicity pictures, and who kept assuring Magnus that he wanted to catch "the real you". But Magnus didn't want candid pictures of himself, and he was rather personal in his insistence that the photographer, a bearded fanatic who wore sandals, was not likely to capture with his camera something he had taken pains to conceal for more than thirty years. So we went to a very famous photographer who was celebrated for his pictures of royalty, and he and Magnus plotted some portraits, taken in a splendid old theatre, that satisfied both of them. All of this took time, until there was no longer any reason for us to stay in London. But Lind and Ingestree, and to a lesser degree Kinghovn, were determined to hear the remainder of Magnus's story, and after a good deal of teasing and protesting that there was really nothing to it, and that he was tired of talking about himself, it was agreed that they should spend our last day in London with us, and have their way.

"I'm doing it for Ingestree, really," said Magnus, and I thought it an odd remark, as he and Roly had not been on the best of terms since they first met at Sorgenfrei. Inquisitive, as always, I found a time to mention this to Roly, who was puzzled and flattered. "Can't imagine why he said that," was his comment; "but there's something about him that rouses more than ordinary curiosity in me. He's terribly like someone I've known, but I can't say who it is. And I'm fascinated by his crusty defence of old Tresize and his wife. I know a bit about Sir John that puts him in a very different light from the rosy glow Magnus spreads over his memories. These recollections of old actors, you know—awful old hams, most of them. It's the most perishable of the arts. Have you ever had the experience of seeing a film you saw thirty or even forty years ago and thought wonderful? Avoid it, I urge you. Appallingly disillusioning. One remembers something that never had any reality. No, old actors should be let die."

"What about old conjurors?" I said; "why *Hommage*? Why don't you leave Robert-Houdin in his grave?"

"That's precisely where he is. You don't think this film we're making is really anything like the old boy, do you? With every modern technique at our command, and Jurgen Lind sifting every shot through his own marvellously contemporary concept of magic—no, no, if you could be whisked back in time and see Robert-Houdin you'd see something terribly tacky in comparison with what we're offering. He's just a peg on which Jurgen is hanging a fine modern creation. We need all the research and reconstruction and whatnot to produce something inescapably contemporary; a paradox, but that's how it is."

"Then you believe that there is no time but the present moment, and that everything in the past is diminished by the simple fact that it is irrecoverable? I suppose there's a name for that point of view, but at present I can't put my tongue to it."

"Yes, that's pretty much what I believe. Eisengrim's raptures about Sir John and Milady interest me as a phenomenon of the present; I'm fascinated that he should think as he does at this moment, and put so much feeling into expressing what he feels. I can't be persuaded for an instant that those two old spooks were anything very special."

"You realize, of course, that you condemn yourself to the same treatment? You've done some work that people have admired and admire still. Are you agreed that it should be judged as you judge Magnus's idols?"

"Of course. Let it all go! I'll have my whack and that'll be the end of me. I don't expect any yellow roses on my monument. Nor a monument, as a matter of fact. But I'm keenly interested in other monument-worshippers. Magnus loves the past simply because it feeds his present, and that's all there is to it. It's the piety and ancestor-worship of a chap who, as he's told us, had a nasty family and a horrid childhood and has had to dig up a better one. Before he's finished he'll tell us the Tresizes were his real parents, or his parents in art, or something of that sort. Want to bet?"

I never bet, and I wouldn't have risked money on that, because I thought that Ingestree was probably right.

5

Our last day was a Saturday, and the three film-makers appeared in time for lunch at the Savoy. Liesl had arranged that we should have one of the good tables looking out over the Embankment, and it was a splendid autumn day. The light, as it fell on our table, could not have been improved on by Kinghovn himself. Magnus never ate very much, and today he confined himself to some cold beef and a dish of rice pudding. It gave him a perverse pleasure to order these nursery dishes in restaurants where other people gorged on luxuries, and he insisted that the Savoy served the best rice pudding in London. The others ate heartily, Ingestree with naked and rather touching relish, Kinghovn like a man who has not seen food for a week, and Lind with a curious detachment, as though he were eating to oblige somebody else, and did not mean to disappoint them. Liesl was in one of her ogress moods and ordered steak tartare, which seemed to me no better than raw meat. I had the set lunch; excellent value.

"You spoke of Tresize's egoism when last we dealt with the subtext," said Lind, champing his great jaws on a lamb chop.

"I did, and I may have misled you. Shortly after I had my talk with Milady, we stopped rehearsing at the Crown and Two Chairmen, and moved into the theatre where *Scaramouche* was to appear. It was the Globe. We needed a theatre with plenty of backstage room because it was a pretty elaborate show. Sir John still held to the custom of opening in London with a new piece; no out-of-town tour to get things shaken down. It was an eye-opener to me to walk into a theatre that was better than the decrepit vaudeville houses where I had appeared with Willard; there was a discipline and a formality I had never met with. I was hired as an assistant stage manager (with a proviso that I should act 'as cast' if required) and I had everything to learn about the job. Luckily old Macgregor was a patient and thorough teacher. I had lots to do. That was before the time when the stagehands' union was strict about people who were not members moving and arranging things, and some of my work was heavy. I was on good terms with the stage crew at once, and I quickly found out that this put a barrier between me and the actors, although I had to become a member of Actors' Equity. But I was 'crew', and although everybody was friendly I was not quite on the level of 'company'. What was I? I was necessary, and even important, to the play, but I found out that my name was to appear on the program simply as Macgregor's assistant. I had no place in the list of the cast.

"Yet I was rehearsed carefully, and it seemed to me that I was doing well. I was trying to capture Sir John's rhythm, and now, to my surprise, he was helping me. We spent quite a lot of time on Two, two. I did my juggling with my back to the audience, but as I was to wear a costume identical with Sir John's, the audience would assume that was who I was, if I could bring off another sort of resemblance.

"That was an eye-opener. I was vaudeville trained, and my one idea of stage deportment was to be fast and gaudy. That wasn't Sir John's way at all. 'Deliberately: deliberately,' he would say, over and over again. 'Let them see what you're doing. Don't be flashy and confusing. Do it like this.' And then he would caper across the stage, making motions like a man juggling plates, but at a pace I thought impossibly slow. 'It's not keeping the plates in the air that's important,' he would say. 'Of course you can do that. It's being Scaramouche that's important. It's the character you must get across. Eh? You understand the character, don't you? Eh? Have you looked at the Callots?'

"No, I hadn't looked at the Callots, and didn't know what they were. 'Here m'boy; look here,' he said, showing me some funny little pictures of people dressed as Scaramouche, and Polichinelle and other Commedia characters. 'Get it like that! Make that real! You must be a Callot in motion!'

"It was new and hard work for me to catch the idea of making myself like a picture, but I was falling under Sir John's spell and was ready to give it a try. So I capered and pointed my toes, and struck exaggerated postures like the little pictures, and did my best.

" 'Hands! Hands!' he would shout, warningly, when I had my work cut out to make the plates dance. 'Not like hooks, m'boy, like this! See! Keep 'em like this!' And then he would demonstrate what he wanted, which was a queer trick for a juggler, because he wanted me to hold my hands with the little finger and the forefinger extended, and the two middle fingers held together. It looked fine as he did it, but it wasn't my style at all. And all the time he kept me dancing with my toes stuck out and my heels lifted, and he wanted me to get into positions which even I could see were picturesque, but couldn't copy.

" 'Sorry, Sir John,' I said one day. 'It's just that if feels a bit loony.'

" 'Aha, you're getting it at last!' he shouted, and for the first time he smiled at me. 'That's what I want! I want it a bit loony. Like Scaramouche, you see. Like a charlatan in a travelling show.'

"I could have told him a few things about charlatans in travelling shows, and the way their looniness takes them, but it wouldn't have done. I see now that it was Romance he was after, not realism, but it was all a mystery to me then. I don't think I was a slow learner, and in our second rehearsal in the theatre, where we had the plates, and the cloaks, and the tightrope to walk, I got my first real inkling of what it was all about, and where I was wrong and Sir John—in terms of Romance—was right.

"I told you I had to caper across the tightrope, as Scaramouche escaping from the angry aristocrats. I was high above their heads, and as I had only about thirty feet to go, at the farthest, I had to take quite a while over it while pretending to be quick. Sir John wanted the rope—it was a wire, really—to be slackish, so that it rocked and swayed. Apparently that was the Callot style. For balance I carried a long stick that I was supposed to have snatched from Polichinelle. I was doing it circus-fashion, making it look as hard as possible, but that wouldn't do: I was to rock on the wire, and be very much at ease, and when I was half-way across the stage I was to thumb my nose at the Marquis de la Tour d'Azyr, my chief enemy. I could thumb my nose. Not the least trouble. But the way I did it didn't please Sir John. 'Like this,' he would say, and put an elegant thumb to his long, elegant nose, and twiddle the fingers. I did it several times, and he shook his head. Then an idea seemed to strike him.

" 'M'boy, what does that gesture mean to you?' he asked, fixing me with a lustrous brown eye.

" 'Kiss my arse, Sir John,' said I, bashfully: I wasn't sure he would know such a rude word. He looked grave, and shook his head slowly from side to side three or four times.

" 'You have the essence of it, but only in the sense that the snail on the garden wall is the essence of *Escargots à la Niçoise.* What you convey by that gesture is all too plainly the grossly derisive invitation expressed by your phrase, Kiss my arse; it doesn't even get as far as *Baisez mon cul.* What I want is a Rabelaisian splendour of contempt linked with a Callotesque elegance of grotesquerie. What it boils down to is that you're not thinking it right. You're thinking Kiss my arse with a strong American accent, when what you ought to be thinking is—' and suddenly, though he was standing on the stage, he swayed perilously and confidently as though he were on the wire, and raised one eyebrow and opened his mouth in a grin like a leering wolf, and allowed no more than the tip of a very sharp red tongue to loll out on his lips and there it was! Kiss my arse *with class,* and God knows how many years of actor's technique and a vivid memory of Henry Irving all backing it up.

" 'I think I get it,' I said, and had a try. He was pleased. Again. Better pleased. 'You're getting close,' he said; 'now, tell me what you're thinking when you do that? Mph? Kiss my arse, quonk? But what kind of Kiss my arse? Quonk? Quonk?'

"I didn't know what to tell him, but I couldn't be silent. 'Not Kiss my arse at all,' I said.

" 'What then? What are you thinking? Eh? You must be thinking something, because you're getting what I want. Tell me what it is?'

"Better be truthful, I thought. He sees right into me and he'll spot a lie at once. I took my courage in my hand. 'I was thinking that I must be born again,' I said. 'Quite right, m'boy; born again and born different, as Mrs. Poyser very wisely said,' was Sir John's comment. (Who was Mrs. Poyser? I suppose it's the kind of thing Ramsay knows.)

"Born again! I'd always thought of it, when I thought about it at all, as a spiritual thing; you went through a conversion, or you found Christ, or whatever it was, and from that time you were different and never looked back. But to get inside Sir John I had to be born again physically, and if the spiritual trick is harder than that, Heaven must be thinly populated. I spent hours capering about in quiet places offstage, whenever Macgregor didn't need me, trying to be like Sir John, trying to get style even into Kiss my arse. What was the result? Next time we rehearsed Two, two, I was awful. I nearly dropped a plate, and for a juggler that's a shattering experience. (Don't laugh! I don't mean it as a joke.) But worse was to come. At the right moment I stepped out on the swaying wire, capered toward middle stage, thumbed my nose at Gordon Barnard, who was playing the Marquis, lost my balance, and fell off; Duparc's training stood by me, and I caught the wire with my hands, swung in mid-air for a couple of seconds, and then heaved myself back up and got my footing, and scampered to the opposite side. The actors who were rehearsing that day applauded, but I was destroyed with shame, and Sir John was grinning exactly like Scaramouche, with an inch of red tongue between his lips.

" 'Don't think they'll quite accept you as me if you do that, m'boy,' said he. 'Eh, Holroyd? Eh, Barnard? Quonk? Try it again.'

"I tried it again, and didn't fall, but I knew I was hopeless; I hadn't found Sir John's style and I was losing my own. After another bad try Sir John moved on to another scene, but Milady beckoned me away into a box, from which she was watching the rehearsal. I was full of apologies.

" 'Of course you fell,' she said. 'But it was a good fall. Laudable pus, I call it. You're learning.'

"Laudable pus! What in God's name did she mean! I thought I would never get used to Milady's lingo. But she saw the bewilderment in my face, and explained.

" 'It's a medical expression. Out of fashion now, I expect. But my grandfather was rather a distinguished physician and he used it often. In those days, you know, when someone had a wound, they couldn't heal it as quickly as they do now; they dressed it and probed it every few days to see how it was getting on. If it was healing well, from the bottom, there was a lot of nasty stuff near the surface, and that was evidence of proper healing. They called it laudable pus. I know you're trying your very best to please Sir John, and it means a sharp wound to your own personality. As the wound heals, you will be nearer what we all want. But meanwhile there's laudable pus, and it shows itself in clumsiness and falls. When you get your new style, you'll understand what I mean.'

"Had I time to get a new style before the play opened? I was worried sick, and I suppose it showed, because when he had a chance old Frank Moore had a word with me.

" 'You're trying to catch the Guvnor's manner and you aren't making a bad fist of it, but there are one or two things you haven't noticed. You're an acrobat, good enough to walk the slackwire, but you're tight as a drum. Look at the Guvnor: he hasn't a taut muscle in his body, nor a slack one, either. He's in easy control all the time. Have you noticed him standing still? When he listens to another actor, have you seen how still he is? Look at you now, listening to me; you bob about and twist and turn and nod your head with enough energy to turn a windmill. But it's all waste, y'see. If we were in a scene, you'd be killing half the value of what I say with all that movement. Just try to sit still. Yes, there you go; you're not still at all, you're frozen. Stillness isn't looking as if you were full of coiled springs. It's repose. Intelligent repose. That's what the Guvnor has. What I have, too, as a matter of fact. What Barnard has. What Milady has. I suppose you think repose means asleep, or dead.

" 'Now look, my lad, and try to see how it's done. It's mostly your back. Got to have a good strong back, and let it do ninety per cent of the work. Forget legs. Look at the Guvnor hopping around when he's being Scaramouche. He's nippier on his pins than you are. Look at me. I'm real old, but I bet I can dance a hornpipe better than you can. Look at this! Can you do a double shuffle like that? That's legs, to look at, but it's back in reality. Strong back. Don't pound down into the floor at every step. Forget legs.

" 'How do you get a strong back? Well, it's hard to describe it, but once you get the feel of it you'll see what I'm talking about. The main thing is to trust your back and forget you have a front; don't stick out your chest or your belly; let 'em look after themselves. Trust your back and lead from your back. And just let your head float on top of your neck. You're all made of whipcord and wire. Loosen it up and take it easy. But not slump, mind! Easy.'

"Suddenly the old man grabbed me by the neck and seemed about to throttle me. I jerked away, and he laughed. 'Just as I said, you're all wire. When I touch your neck you tighten up like a spring. Now you try to strangle me.' I seized him by the neck, and I thought his poor old head would come off in my hands; he sank to the floor, moaning, 'Nay, spare m'life!' Then he laughed like an old loony, because I suppose I looked horrified. 'D'you see? I just let myself go and trusted to my back. You work on that for a while and bob's your uncle; you'll be fit to act with the Guvnor.'

" 'How long do you think it will take?' I said. 'Oh, ten or fifteen years should see you right,' said old Frank, and walked away, still chuckling at the trick he had played on me.

"I had no ten or fifteen years. I had a week, and much of that was spent slaving for Macgregor, who kept me busy with lesser jobs while he and Holroyd fussed about the scenery and trappings for *Scaramouche*. I had never seen such scenery as the stage crew began to rig from the theatre grid; the vaudeville junk I was used to didn't belong in the same world with it. The production had all been painted by the Harker Brothers, from designs by a painter who knew exactly what Sir John wanted. It was a revelation to me then, but now I understand that it owed much to prints and paintings of France during the Revolutionary period, and a quality of late-eighteenth-century detail had been used in it, apparently in a careless and half-hidden spirit, but adding up to pictures that supported and explained the play just as did the handsome costumes. People are supposed not to like scenery now, but it could be heart-stirring stuff when it was done with love by real theatre artists.

"The first act setting was in the yard of an inn, and when it was all in place I swear you could smell the horses, and the sweet air from the fields. Nowadays they fuss a lot about light in the theatre, and even stick a lot of lamps in plain sight of the audience, so you won't miss how artistic they are being; but Sir John didn't trouble about light in that way—the subtle effects of light were painted on the scenery, so you knew at once what time of day it was by the way the shadows fell, and what the electricians did was to illuminate the actors, and Sir John in particular.

"During all the years I worked with Sir John there was one standing direction for the electricians that was so well understood Macgregor hardly had to mention it: when the play began all lights were set at two-thirds of their power, and when Sir John was about to make his entrance they were gradually raised to full power, so that as soon as he came on the stage the audience had the sensation of seeing—and therefore understanding—much more clearly than before. Egoism, I suppose, and a little hard on the supporting actors, but Sir John's audiences wanted him to be wonderful and he did whatever was necessary to make sure that he damned well was wonderful.

"Ah, that scenery! In the last act, which was in the salon of a great aristocratic house in Paris, there were large windows at the back, and outside those windows you saw a panorama of Paris at the time of the Revolution that conveyed, by means I don't pretend to understand, the spirit of a great and beautiful city under appalling stress. The Harkers did it with colour; it was mostly in reddish browns highlighted with rose, and shadowed in a grey that was almost black. Busy as I was, I still found time to gape at that scenery as it was assembled.

"Costumes, too. Everybody had been fitted weeks before, but when the clothes were all assembled, and the wig-man had done his work, and the actors began to appear in carefully arranged ensembles in front of that scenery, things became clear that I had missed completely at rehearsals: things like the relation of one character to another, and of one class to another, and the Callot spirit of the travelling actors against the apparently everyday clothes of inn-servants and other minor people, and the superiority and unquestioned rank of the aristocrats. Above all, of the unquestioned supremacy of Sir John, because, though his clothes were not gorgeous, like those of Barnard as the Marquis, they had a quality of style that I did not understand until I had tried them on myself. Because, you see, as his double, I had to have a costume exactly like his when he appeared as the charlatan Scaramouche, and the first time I put it on I thought there must be some mistake, because it didn't seem to fit at all. Sir John showed me what to do about that.

" 'Don't try to drag your sleeves down, m'boy; they're intended to be short, to show your hands to advantage, mphm? Keep 'em up, like this, and if you use your hands the way I showed you, everything will fit, eh? And your hat—it's not meant to keep off the rain, m'boy, but to show your face against the inside of the brim, quonk? Your breeches aren't too tight; they're not to sit down in—I don't pay you to sit down in costume—but to stand up in, and show off your legs. Never shown your legs off before, have you? I thought as much. Well, learn to show 'em off now, and not like a bloody chorus-girl, but like a man. Use 'em in masculine postures, but not like a butcher boy either, and if you aren't proud of your legs they're going to look damned stupid, eh, when you're walking across the stage on that rope.'

"I was green as grass. Naive, though I didn't know the word at that time. It was very good for me to feel green. I had begun to think I knew all there was about the world, and particularly the performing world, because I had won in the struggle to keep alive in Wanless's World of Wonders, and in *Le grand Cirque forain de St. Vite*. I had even dared in my heart to think I knew more about the world of travelling shows than Sir John. Of course I was right, because I knew a scrap of the reality. But he knew something very different, which was what the public wants to think the world of travelling shows is like. I possessed a few hard-won facts, but he had artistic imagination. My job was somehow to find my way into his world, and take a humble, responsible part in it.

"Little by little it dawned on me that I was important to *Scaramouche*; my two short moments, when I juggled the plates, and walked the wire and thumbed my nose at the Marquis, added a cubit to the stature of the character Sir John was creating. I had also to swallow the fact that I was to do that without anybody knowing it. Of course the public would tumble to the fact that Sir John, who was getting on for sixty, had not learned juggling and wire-walking since last they saw him, but they wouldn't understand it until they had been thrilled by the spectacle, apparently, of the great man doing exactly those things. I was anonymous and at the same time conspicuous.

"I had to have a name. Posters with the names of the actors were already in place outside the theatre, but in the program I must appear as Macgregor's assistant, and I must be called something. Holroyd mentioned it now and again. My name at that time, Jules LeGrand, wouldn't do. Too fancy and, said Holroyd, a too obvious fake.

"Here again I was puzzled. Jules LeGrand an obvious fake? What about the names of some of the other members of the company? What about Eugene Fitzwarren, who had false teeth and a wig and, I would bet any money, a name that he had not been born to? What about C. Pengelly Spickernell, a withered, middle-aged fruit, whose eyes sometimes rested warmly on my legs, when Sir John was talking about them? Had any parents, drunk or sober, with such a surname as Spickernell, ever christened a child Cuthbert Pengelly? And if it came to fancy sounds, what about Milady's stage name? Annette de la Borderie? Macgregor assured me that it was indeed her own, and that she came from the Channel Islands, but why was it credible when Jules LeGrand was not?

"Of course I was too green to know that I did not stand on the same footing as the other actors. I was just a trick, a piece of animated scenery, when I was on the stage. Otherwise I was Macgregor's assistant, and none too experienced at the job, and a grand name did not befit my humble station. What was I to be called?

"The question was brought to a head by Holroyd, who approached, not me, but Macgregor, in a break between an afternoon and evening rehearsal during the final week of preparation. I was at hand, but obviously not important to the discussion. 'What are you going to call your assistant, Mac?' said Holroyd. 'Time's up. He's got to have a name.' Macgregor looked solemn. 'I've given it careful thought,' he said, 'and I think I've found the verra word for him. Y'see, what's he to the play? He's Sir John's double. That and no more. A shadow, you might say. But can you call him Shadow? Nunno: absurd! And takes the eye, which is just what we don't want to do. So where do we turn—' Holroyd broke in here, because he was apt to be impatient when Macgregor had one of his explanatory fits. 'Why not call him Double? Dick Double! Now there's a good, simple name that nobody's going to notice.' 'Hut!' said Macgregor; 'that's a foolish name. Dick Double! It sounds like some fella in a pantomime!' But Holroyd was not inclined to give up his flight of fancy. 'Nothing wrong with Double,' he persisted. 'There's a Double in Shakespeare. *Henry IV*, Part Two, don't you remember? Is Old Double dead? So there must have been somebody called Double. The more I think of it the better I like it. I'll put him down as Richard Double.' But Macgregor wouldn't have it. 'Nay, nay, you'll make the lad a figure of fun,' he said. 'Now listen to me, because I've worked it out verra carefully. He's a double. And what's a double? Well, in Scotland, when I was a boy, we had a name for such things. If a man met a creature like himself in a lane, or in town, maybe, in the dark, it was a sure sign of ill luck or even death. Not that I suggest anything of that kind here. Nunno; as I've often said Airt has her own rules, and they're not the rules of common life. Now: such an uncanny creature was called a fetch. And this lad's a fetch, and we can do no better than to name him Fetch.' By this time old Frank Moore joined the group, and he liked the sound of Fetch. 'But what first name will you tack on to it?' he said. 'I suppose he's got to be something Fetch? Can't be just naked, unaccommodated Fetch.' Macgregor closed his eyes and raised a fat hand. 'I've thought of that, also,' he said. 'Fetch being a Scots name, he'd do well to carry a Scots given name, for added authority. Now I've always had a fancy for the name Mungo. In my ear it has a verra firm sound. Mungo Fetch. Can we do better?' He looked around, for applause. But Holroyd was not inclined to agree; I think he was still hankering after Double. 'Sounds barbaric to me. A sort of cannibal-king name, to my way of thinking. If you want a Scotch name why don't you call him Jock?' Macgregor looked disgusted. 'Because Jock is not a name, but a diminutive, as everybody knows well. It is the diminutive of John. And John is not a Scots name. The Scots form of that name is Ian. If you want to call him Ian Fetch, I shall say no more. Though I consider Mungo a much superior solution to the problem.'

"Holroyd nodded at me, as if he and Macgregor and Frank Moore had been generously expending their time to do me a great favour. 'Mungo Fetch it's to be then, is it?' he said, and went about his business before I had time to collect my wits and say anything at all.

"That was my trouble. I was like someone living in a dream. I was active and occupied and heard what was said to me and responded reasonably, but nevertheless I seemed to be in a lowered state of consciousness. Otherwise, how could I have put up with a casual conversation that saddled me with a new name—and a name nobody in his right mind would want to possess? But not since my first days in Wanless's World of Wonders had I been so little in command of myself, so little aware of what fate was doing to me. It was as if I were being thrust toward something I did not know by something I could not see. Part of it was love, for I was beglamoured by Milady and barely had sense enough to understand that my state was as hopeless as it could possibly be, and that my passion was in every way absurd. Part of it must have been physical, because I was getting a pretty good regular wage, and could eat better than I had done for several months. Part of it was just astonishment at the complex business of getting a play on the stage, which presented me with some new marvel every day.

"As Macgregor's assistant I had to be everywhere and consequently I saw everything. Because of my mechanical bent I took pleasure in all the mechanism of a fine theatre, and wanted to know how the flymen and scene-shifters organized their work, how the electrician contrived his magic, and how Macgregor controlled it all with signal-lights from his little cubbyhole on the left-hand side of the stage, just inside the proscenium. I had to make up the call-lists, so that the call-boy—who was no boy but older than myself—could warn the actors when they were wanted on stage five minutes before each entrance. I watched Macgregor prepare his Prompt Book, which was an interleaved copy of the play, with every cue for light, sound, and action entered into it; he was proud of his books, and marked them in a fine round hand, in inks of different colours, and every night the book was carefully locked in a safe in his little office. I helped the property-man prepare his lists of everything that was needed in the play, so that a mass of materials from snuffboxes to hay-forks could be organized on the property-tables in the wings; my capacity to make or mend fiddling little bits of mechanism made me a favourite with him. Indeed the property-man and I worked up a neat little performance as a flock of hens who were heard clucking in the wings when the curtain rose on the inn scene. It was my job to hand C. Pengelly Spickernell the trumpet on which he sounded a fanfare just before the travelling-cart of the Commedia dell' Arte players made its entrance into the inn-yard; to hand it to him and recover it later, and shake C. Pengelly's spit out of it before putting it back on the property-table. There seemed to be no end to my duties.

"I had also to learn to make up my face for my brief appearance. Vaudevillian that I was, I had been accustomed to colour my face a vivid shade of salmon, and touch up my eyebrows; I had never made up my neck or my hands in my life. I quickly learned that something more subtle was expected by Sir John; his make-up was elaborate, to disguise some signs of age but even more to throw his best features into prominence. Eric Foss, a very decent fellow in the company, showed me what to do, and it was from him I learned that Sir John's hands were always coloured an ivory shade, and that his ears were liberally touched up with carmine. Why red ears, I wanted to know. 'The Guvnor thinks it gives an appearance of health,' said Foss, 'and make sure you touch up the insides of your nostrils with the same colour, because it makes your eyes look bright.' I didn't understand it, but I did as I was told.

"Make-up was a subject on which every actor had strong personal opinions. Gordon Barnard took almost an hour to put on his face, transforming himself from a rather ordinary-looking chap into a strikingly handsome man. Reginald Charlton, on the other hand, was of the modern school and used as little make-up as possible, because he said it made the face into a mask, and inexpressive. Grover Paskin, our comedian, put on paint almost with a trowel, and worked like a Royal Academician building up warts and nobbles and tufts of hair on his rubbery old mug. Eugene Fitzwarren strove for youth, and took enormous pains making his eyes big and lustrous, and putting white stuff on his false teeth so that they would flash to his liking.

"Old Frank Moore was the most surprising of the lot, because he had become an actor when water colours were used for make-up instead of the modern greasepaints. He washed his face with care, powdered it dead white, and then applied artist's paints out of a large Reeves' box, with fine brushes, until he had the effect he wanted. In the wings he looked as if his face were made of china, but under the lights the effect was splendid. I particularly marvelled at the way he put shadows where he wanted them by drawing the back of a lead spoon over the hollows of his eyes and cheeks. It wasn't good for his skin, and he had a hide like an alligator in private life, but it was certainly good for the stage, and he was immensely proud of the fact that Irving, who made up in the same way, had once complimented him on his art.

"So, working fourteen hours a day, but nevertheless in a dream, I made my way through the week of the final dress rehearsal, and something happened there that changed my life. I did my stage manager's work in costume, but with a long white coat over it, to keep it clean, and when Two, two came I had to whip it off, pop on my hat, take a final look in the full-length mirror just offstage in the corridor, and dash back to the wings to be ready for my plate-juggling moment. That went as rehearsed, but when it was time for my second appearance, walking the rope, I forgot something. During the scene when André-Louis made his revolutionary speech, he began by taking off his hat, and thrusting his Scaramouche mask up on his forehead. It was a half-mask, coming down to the mouth only; it was coloured a rosy red, and had a very long nose, just as Callot would have drawn it. When Sir John thrust it up on his brow, revealing his handsome, intent revolutionary's face, extremely picturesque, it was a fine accent of colour, and the long nose seemed to add to his height. But when I appeared on the rope I was to have the mask pulled down, and when I made my contemptuous gesture toward the Marquis it was the long red nose of the mask I was to thumb.

"I managed very well till it came to the nose-thumbing bit, when I realized with horror that it was my own nose flesh I was thumbing. I had forgotten the mask! Unforgivable! So as soon as I could get away from Macgregor during the interval for the scene-change, I rushed to find Sir John and make my apologies. He had gone out into the stalls of the theatre, and was surrounded by a group of friends, who were congratulating him in lively tones, and I didn't need to listen for long to find out that it was his performance on the rope they were talking about. So I crept away, and waited till he came backstage again. Then I approached him and said my humble say.

"Milady was with him and she said, 'Jack, you'd be mad to throw it away. It's a gift from God. If it fooled Reynolds and Lucy Bellamy it will fool anyone. They've known you for years, and it deceived them completely. You must let him do it.' But Sir John was not a man to excuse anything, even a happy accident, and he fixed me with a stern eye. 'Do you swear that was by accident? You weren't presuming? Because I won't put up with any presumption from a member of my company.' 'Sir John, I swear on the soul of my mother it was a mistake,' I said. (Odd that I should have said that, but it was a very serious oath of Zovene's, and I needed something serious at that moment; actually, at the time I spoke, my mother was living and whatever Ramsay says to the contrary, her soul was in bad repair.) 'Very well,' said Sir John, 'we'll keep it in. In future, when you walk the rope, wear your mask up on your head, as I do mine. And you'd better come to me for a lesson in make-up. You look like Guy Fawkes. And bear in mind that this is not to be a precedent. Any other clever ideas that come to you you'd be wise to suppress. I don't encourage original thought in my productions.' He looked angry as he walked away. I wanted to thank Milady for intervening on my behalf, but she was off to make a costume change.

"When I went back to Macgregor I thought he looked at me very queerly. 'You're a lucky laddie, Mungo Fetch,' said he, 'but don't press your luck too hard. Many a small talent has come to grief that way.' I asked him what he meant, but he just made his Scotch noise—'Hut'—and went on with his work.

"I don't think I would have dared to carry the matter any further if Holroyd and Frank Moore had not borne down on Macgregor after the last act. 'What do you think of your Mungo now?' said Frank, and once again they began to talk exactly as if I were not standing beside them, busy with a time-sheet. 'I think it would have been better to give him another name,' said Macgregor; 'a fetch is an uncanny thing, and I don't want anything uncanny in any theatre where I am in a place of responsibility.' But Holroyd was as near buoyant as I ever saw him. 'Uncanny, my eye,' he said; 'it's the cherry on the top of the cake. The Guvnor's close friends were deceived. *Coup de théâtre,* they called it; that's French for a bloody good wheeze.' 'You don't need to tell me it's French,' said Macgregor. 'I've no use for last-minute inspirations and unrehearsed effects. Amateurism, that's what that comes to.'

"I couldn't be quiet. 'Mr. Macgregor, I didn't mean to do it,' I said; 'I swear it on the soul of my mother.' 'All right, all right, I believe you without your Papist oaths,' said Macgregor, 'and I'm just telling you not to presume on the resemblance any further, or you'll be getting a word from me.' 'What resemblance?' I said. 'Don't talk to us as if we're fools, m'boy,' said old Frank. 'You know damned well you're the living image of the Guvnor in that outfit. Or the living image of him when I first knew him, I'd better say. Don't you hear what's said to you? Didn't I tell you a fortnight ago? You're as like the Guvnor as if you were spit out of his mouth. You're his fetch, right enough.' 'Dinna say that,' shouted Macgregor, becoming very broad in his Scots; 'haven't I told you it's uncanny?' But I began to understand, and I was as horrified as Macgregor. The impudence of it! Me, looking like the Guvnor! 'What'd I better do?' I said, and Holroyd and old Frank laughed like a couple of loonies. 'Just be tactful, that's all,' said Holroyd. 'It's very useful. You're the best double the Guvnor's ever had, and it'll be a livelihood to you for quite a while, I dare say. But be tactful.'

"Easy to tell me to be tactful. When your soul is blasted by a sudden uprush of pride, it's cruel hard work to be tactful. Within an hour my sense of terrible impertinence in daring to look like the Guvnor had given way to a bloating vanity. Sir John was handsome, right enough, but thousands of men are handsome. He was something far beyond that. He had a glowing splendour that made him unlike anybody else—except me, it appeared, when the circumstances were right. I won't say he had distinction, because the word has been chewed to death to describe all kinds of people who simply look frozen. Take almost any politician and put a special cravat on him and stick a monocle in his eye and he becomes the distinguished Sir Nincome Poop, M.P. Sir John wasn't frozen and his air of splendour had nothing to do with oddity. I suppose living and breathing Romance through a long career had a great deal to do with it, but it can't have been the whole thing. And I was his fetch! I hadn't really understood it when Moore and Holroyd had told me in the Crown and Two Chairmen that I looked like him. I knew I was of the same height, and we were built much the same—shorter than anybody wants to be, but with a length of leg that made the difference between being small and being stumpy. In my terrible clothes and with my flash, carnie's ways—outward evidence of the life I had led and the kind of thinking it begot in me—I never thought the resemblance went beyond a reasonable facsimile. But when Sir John and I were on equal terms—dressed and wigged alike, against the same scenery and under the same lights, and lifted into the high sweet air of Romance—his friends had been deceived by the likeness. That was a stupefying drink for Paul Dempster, alias Cass Fletcher, alias Jules LeGrand—cheap people, every one of them. Ask me to be tactful in the face of that! Ask the Prince of Wales to call you a taxi!

"With the first night at hand my new vanity would not have been noticed, even if I had been free to display it. Our opening was exciting, but orderly. Macgregor, splendid in a dinner jacket, was a perfect field officer and everything happened smartly on cue. Sir John's first entrance brought the expected welcome from the audience, and in my new role as a great gentleman of the theatre I watched carefully while he accepted it. He did it in the old style, though I didn't know that at the time: as he walked swiftly down the steps from the inn, calling for the ostler, he paused as though surprised at the burst of clapping; 'My dear friends, is this generosity truly for me?' he seemed to be saying, and then, as the applause reached its peak, he gave the least perceptible bow, not looking toward the house, but keeping within the character of André-Louis Moreau, and began calling once more, which brought silence. Easy to describe, but no small thing to do, as I learned when my time came to do it myself. Only the most accomplished actors know how to manage applause, and I was lucky to learn it from a great master.

"Milady was welcomed in the same way, but her entrance was showy, as his was not—except, of course, for that little vanity of the lighting, which was a great help. She came on with the troupe of strolling players, and it couldn't have failed. There was C. Pengelly Spickernell on the trumpet, to begin with, and a lot of excited shouting from the inn-servants, and then further shouting from the Italian Comedians, as they strutted onstage with their travelling-wagon; Grover Paskin led on the horse that pulled the cart, and it was heaped high with drums and gaudy trunks, baskets and rolls of flags, and on the top of the heap sat Milady, making more racket than anybody as she waved a banner in the air. It would have brought a round from a Presbyterian General Assembly. The horse alone was a sure card, because an animal on the stage gives an air of opulence to a play no audience can resist, and this stage horse was famous Old Betsy, who did not perhaps remember Garrick but who had been in so many shows that she was an admired veteran. My heart grew big inside me at the wonder of it, as I watched from the wings, and my eyes moistened with love.

"They were not too moist to notice one or two things that followed. The other women in the troupe of players walked on foot. How slim they looked, and I saw that Milady, with every aid of costume, was not slim. How fresh and pretty they looked, and Milady, though extraordinary, was not fresh nor pretty. When Eugene Fitzwarren gave her his arm to descend from the cart I could not help seeing that she came down on the stage heavily, with an audible plop that she tried to cover with laughter, and the ankles she showed were undeniably thick. All right, I thought, in my fierce loyalty, what of it? She could act rings around any of them, and did it. But she was not young, and if I had been driven to the last extreme of honesty I should have had to admit that she was like nothing in the heavens above, nor in the earth beneath, nor in the waters under the earth. I only loved her the more, and yearned for her to show how marvellous she was, though—it had to be faced—too old for Climene. She was supposed to be the daughter of old Frank Moore as Polichinelle, but I fear she looked more like his frivolous sister.

"It was not until I read the book, years later, that I found out what sort of woman Sabatini meant Climene to be. She was a child just on the verge of love whose ambition was to find a rich protector and make the best bargain for her beauty. That wasn't in Milady's range, physically or temperamentally, for there was nothing calculating or cheap about her. So, by patient rewriting of the lines during rehearsals, she became a witty, large-hearted actress, as young as the audience would believe her to be, but certainly no child, and no beauty. Or should I say that? She had a beauty all her own, of that rare kind that only great comic actresses have; she had beauty of voice, boundless charm of manner, and she made you feel that merely pretty women were lesser creatures. She had also I cannot tell how many decades of technique behind her, because she had begun her career when she really was a child, in Irving's Lyceum, and she could make even an ordinary line sound like wit.

"I saw all of that, and felt it through and through me like the conviction of religion, but still, alas, I saw that she was old, and eccentric, and there was a courageous pathos about what she was doing.

"I was bursting with loyalty—a new and disturbing emotion for me—and Two, two went just as Sir John wanted it. My reward was that when I appeared on the tightrope there was an audible gasp from the house, and the curtain came down to great applause and even a few cries of Bravo. They were for Sir John; of course I knew that and wished it to be so. But I was aware that without me that climax would have been a lesser achievement.

"The play went on, it seemed to me, from triumph to triumph, and the last act, in Madame de Plougastel's salon, shook me as it had never done in rehearsal. When André-Louis Moreau, now a leader in the Revolution, was told by the tearful Madame de Plougastel that she was his mother and that his evil genius, the Marquis de la Tour d'Azyr, was his father—this revelation drawn from her only when Moreau had his enemy at the sword's point—it seemed to me drama could go no higher. The look that came over Sir John's face of disillusion and defeat, before he burst into Scaramouche's mocking laugh, I thought the perfection of acting. And so it was. So it was. It wouldn't do now—quite out of fashion—but if you're going to act that kind of thing, that's the way to do it.

"Lots of curtain calls. Flowers for Milady and some for Adele Chesterton, who had not been very good but who was so pretty you wanted to eat her with a silver spoon. Sir John's speech, which I came to know very well, in which he declared himself and Milady to be the audience's 'most obedient, most devoted, and most humble servants'. Then the realities of covering the furniture with dust-sheets, covering the tables of properties, checking the time-sheet with Macgregor, and watching him hobble off to put the prompt-copy to bed in the safe. Then taking off my own paint, with a feeling of exaltation and desolation combined, as if I had never been so happy before, and would certainly never be so happy again.

"It was never the custom in that company to sit up and wait to see what the newspapers said; I think that was always more New York's style than London's. But when I went to the theatre the following afternoon to attend to some duties, all the reports were in but those of the great Sunday thunderers, which were very important indeed. Most of the papers said kind things, but even I sensed something about these criticisms that I could have wished otherwise expressed, or not said at all. 'Unabashed romanticism . . . proof positive that the Old School is still vital . . . dear, familiar situations, resolved in the manner hallowed by romance . . . Sir John's perfect command shows no sign of diminution with the years . . . Lady Tresize brings a wealth of experience to a role which, in younger hands, might have seemed contrived . . . Sabatini is a gift to players who require the full-flavoured melodrama of an earlier day . . . where do we look today for acting of this scope and authority?'

"Among the notices there had been one, in the *News-Chronicle*, where a clever new young man was on the job, which was downright bad. PITCHER GOES TOO OFTEN TO WELL, it was headed, and it said flatly that the Tresizes were old-fashioned and hammy, and should give way to the newer theatre.

"When the Sunday papers came, the *Observer* took the same line as the dailies, as though they had been looking at something very fine, but through the wrong end of the binoculars; it made *Scaramouche* seem small and very far away. James Agate, in the *Sunday Times*, condemned the play, which he likened to clockwork, and used Sir John and Milady as sticks to beat modern actors who did not know how to speak or move, and were ill bred and brittle.

" 'Nothing there to pull 'em in,' I heard Holroyd saying to Macgregor.

"Nevertheless, we did pull 'em in for nearly ten weeks. Business was slack at the beginning of each week, and grew from Wednesday onward; matinees were usually sold out, chiefly to women from the suburbs, in town for a look at the shops and a play. But I knew from the gossip that business like that, in a London theatre, was covering running costs at best, and the expenses of production were still on the Guvnor's overdraft. He seemed cheerful, and I soon found out why. He was going to do the old actor-manager's trick and play *Scaramouche* as long as it would last and then replace it 'by popular request' with a few weeks of his old war-horse, *The Master of Ballantrae*."

"Oh my God!" said Ingestree, and it seemed to me that he turned a little white.

"You remember this play?" said Lind.

"Vividly," said Roly.

"A very bad play?"

"I don't want to hurt the feelings of our friend here, who feels so strong about the Tresizes," said Ingestree. "It's just that *The Master of Ballantrae* coincided with rather a low point in my own career. I was finding my feet in the theatre, and it wasn't really the kind of thing I was looking for."

"Perhaps you would like me to pass over it," said Magnus, and although he was pretending to be solicitous I knew he was enjoying himself.

"Is it vital to your subtext?" said Ingestree, and he too was half joking.

"It is, really. But I don't want to give pain, my dear fellow."

"Don't mind me. Worse things have happened since."

"Perhaps I can be discreet," said Magnus. "You may rely on me to be as tactful as possible."

"For God's sake don't do that," said Ingestree. "In my experience tact is usually worse than the brutalities of truth. Anyhow, my recollections of that play can't be the same as yours. My troubles were mostly private."

"Then I shall go ahead. But please feel free to intervene whenever you feel like it. Put me right on matters of fact. Even on shades of opinion. I make no pretence of being an exact historian."

"Shoot the works," said Ingestree. "I'll be as still as a mouse. I promise."

"As you wish. Well—*The Master of Ballantrae* was another of the Guvnor's romantic specials. It too was from a novel, by somebody-or-other—"

"By Robert Louis Stevenson," said Ingestree, in an undertone, "though you wouldn't have guessed it from what appeared on the stage. These adaptations! Butcheries would be a better word—"

"Shut up, Roly," said Kinghovn. "You said you'd be quiet."

"I'm no judge of what kind of adaptation it was," said Magnus, "because I haven't read the book and I don't suppose I ever will. But it was a good, tight, well-caulked melodrama, and people had been eating it up since the Guvnor first brought it out, which I gathered was something like thirty years before the time I'm talking about. I told you he was an experimenter and an innovator, in his day. Well, whenever he had lost a packet on Maeterlinck, or something new by Stephen Phillips, he would pull *The Master* out of the storehouse and fill up the bank-account again. He could go to Birmingham, and Manchester, and Newcastle, and Glasgow, and Edinburgh or any big provincial town—and those towns had big theatres, not like the little pill-boxes in London—and pack 'em in with the *The Master*. Especially Edinburgh, because they seemed to take the play for their own. Macgregor told me, '*The Master*'s been a mighty get-penny for Sir John.' When you saw him in it you knew why it was so. It was made for him."

"It certainly was," said Ingestree. "Made for him out of the blood and bones of poor old Stevenson. I have no special affection for Stevenson, but he didn't deserve that."

"As you can see, it was a play that called forth strong feeling," said Magnus. "I never read it, myself, because Macgregor always held the prompt-copy and did the prompting himself, if anybody was so absurd as to need prompting. But of course I picked up the story as we rehearsed.

"It had a nice meaty plot. Took place in Scotland around the middle of the eighteenth century. There had been some sort of trouble—I don't know the details—and Scottish noblemen were divided in allegiance between Bonnie Prince Charlie and the King of England. The play was about a family called Durie; the old Lord of Durrisdeer had two sons, the first-born being called the Master of Ballantrae and the younger being simply Mr. Henry Durie.

The old Lord decided on a sneaky compromise when the trouble came, and sent the Master off to fight for Bonny Charlie, while Mr. Henry remained at home to be loyal to King George. On those terms, you see, the family couldn't lose, whichever way the cat jumped.

"The Master was a dashing, adventurous fellow, but essentially a crook, and he became a spy in Prince Charlie's camp, leaking information to the English: Mr. Henry was a scholarly, poetic sort of chap, and he stayed at home and mooned after Miss Alison Graeme; she was the old Lord's ward, and of course she loved the dashing Master. When news came from the wars that the Master had been killed, she consented to marry Mr. Henry as a matter of duty and to provide Durrisdeer with an heir. 'But ye ken she never really likit the fella,' as Macgregor explained it to me; her heart was always with the Master, alive or dead. But the Master wasn't dead; he wasn't the dying kind: he slipped away from the battle and became a pirate—not one of your low-living dirty-faced pirates, but a very classy privateer and spy. And so, when the troubles had died down and Bonnie Charlie was out of the way, the Master came back to claim Miss Alison, and found that she was Mrs. Henry, and the mother of a fine young laird.

"The Master tried to lure Miss Alison away from her husband: Mr. Henry was noble about it, and he nobly kept mum about the Master having turned spy during the war. 'A verra strong situation,' as Macgregor said. Consequence, a lot of taunting talk from the Master, and an equal amount of noble endurance from Mr. Henry, and at last a really good scene, of the kind Roly hates, but our audiences loved.

"The Master had picked up in his travels an Indian servant, called Secundra Dass; he knew a lot of those Eastern secrets that Western people believe in so religiously. When Mr. Henry could bear things no longer, he had a fight with the Master, and seemed to kill him: but as I told you, the Master wasn't the dying kind. So he allowed himself to be buried, having swallowed his tongue (he'd learned that from Secundra Dass) and, as it said in the play, 'so subdued his vital forces that the spark of life, though burning low, was not wholly extinguished.' Mr. Henry, tortured by guilt, confessed his crime to his wife and the old Lord, and led them to the grove of trees where the body was buried. When the servants dug up the corpse, it was no corpse at all, but the Master, in very bad shape; the tongue-trick hadn't worked quite as he expected—something to do with the chill of the Scottish climate, I expect—and he came to life only to cry, 'Murderer, Henry—false, false!' and drop dead, but not before Mr. Henry shot himself. Thereupon the curtain came down to universal satisfaction.

"I haven't described it very respectfully. I feel irreverent vibrations coming to me from Roly, the way mediums do when there is an unbeliever at a seance. But I assure you that as the Guvnor acted it, the play compelled belief and shook you up pretty badly. The beauty of the old piece, from the Guvnor's point of view, was that it provided him with what actors used to call 'a dual role'. He played both the Master and Mr. Henry, to the huge delight of his audiences; his fine discrimination between the two characters gave extraordinary interest to the play.

"It also meant some neat work behind the scenes, because there were times when Mr. Henry had barely left the stage before the Master came swaggering on through another door. Sir John's dresser was an expert at getting him out of one coat, waistcoat, boots, and wig and into another in a matter of seconds, and his characterization of the two men was so sharply differentiated that it was art of a very special kind.

"Twice, a double was needed, simply for a fleeting moment of illusion, and in the brief last scene the double was of uttermost importance, because it was he who stood with his back to the audience, as Mr. Henry, while the Guvnor, as the Master, was being dug up and making his terrible accusation. Then—doubles don't usually get such opportunities—it was the double's job to put the gun to his head, fire it, and fall at the feet of Miss Alison, under the Master's baleful eye. And I say with satisfaction that as I was an unusually successful double—or dead spit, as old Frank Moore insisted on saying—I was allowed to fall so that the audience could see something of my face, instead of dying under suspicion of being somebody else.

"Rehearsals went like silk, because some of the cast were old hands, and simply had to brush up their parts. Frank Moore had played the old Lord of Durrisdeer scores of times, and Eugene

Fitzwarren was a seasoned Secundra Dass; Gordon Barnard had played Burke, the Irishman, and built it up into a very good thing; C. Pengelly Spickernell fancied himself as Fond Barnie, a loony Scot who sang scraps of song, and Grover Paskin had a good funny part as a drunken butler; Emilia Pauncefort, who played Madame de Plougastel in *Scaramouche*, loved herself as a Scots witch who uttered the dire Curse of Durrisdeer—

Twa Duries in Durrisdeer,
  Ane to bide and ane to ride;
An ill day for the groom,
  And a waur day for the bride.

And of course the role of Alison, the unhappy bride of Mr. Henry and the pining adorer of the Master, had been played by Milady since the play was new.

"That was where the difficulty lay. Sir John was still great as the Master, and looked surprisingly like himself in his earliest photographs in that part, taken thirty years before; time had been rougher with Milady. Furthermore, she had developed an emphatic style of acting which was not unacceptable in a part like Climene but which could become a little strong as a highbred Scots lady.

"There were murmurs among the younger members of the company. Why couldn't Milady play Auld Cursin' Jennie instead of Emilia Pauncefort? There was a self-assertive girl in the company named Audrey Sevenhowes who let it be known that she would be ideally cast as Alison. But there were others, Holroyd and Macgregor among them, who would not hear a word against Milady. I would have been one of them too, if anybody had asked my opinion, but nobody did. Indeed, I began to feel that the company thought I was rather more than an actor who doubled for Sir John; I was a double indeed, and a company spy, so that any disloyal conversation stopped as soon as I appeared. Of course there was lots of talk; all theatrical companies chatter incessantly. On the rehearsals went, and as Sir John and Milady didn't bother to rehearse their scenes together, nobody grasped how extreme the problem had become.

"There was another circumstance about those early rehearsals that caused some curiosity and disquiet for a while; a stranger had appeared among us whose purpose nobody seemed to know, but who sat in the stalls making notes busily, and now and then exclaiming audibly in a tone of disapproval. He was sometimes seen talking with Sir John. What could he be up to? He wasn't an actor, certainly. He was young, and had lots of hair, but he wasn't dressed in a way that suggested the stage. His sloppy grey flannels and tweed coat, his dark blue shirt and tie like a piece of old rope—hand-woven, I suppose—and his scuffed suede shoes made him look even younger than he was. 'University man,' whispered Audrey Sevenhowes, who recognized the uniform. 'Cambridge,' she whispered, a day later. Then came the great revelation—'Writing a play!' Of course she didn't confide these things to me, but they leaked from her close friends all through the company.

"Writing a play! Rumour was busily at work. It was to be a grand new piece for Sir John's company, and great opportunities might be secured by buttering up the playwright. Reginald Charlton and Leonard Woulds, who hadn't much to do in *Scaramouche* and rather less in *The Master*, began standing the university genius drinks; Audrey Sevenhowes didn't speak to him, but was frequently quite near him, laughing a silvery laugh and making herself fascinating. Old Emilia Pauncefort passed him frequently, and gave him a stately nod every time. Grover Paskin told him jokes. The genius liked it all, and in a few days was on good terms with everybody of any importance, and the secret was out. Sir John wanted a stage version of *Dr. Jekyll and Mr. Hyde*, and the genius was to write it. But as he had never written a play before, and had never had stage experience except with the Cambridge Marlowe Society, he was attending rehearsals, as he said to 'get the feel of the thing'.

"The genius was free with his opinions. He thought little of *The Master of Ballantrae*. 'Fustian' was the word he used to describe it, and he made it clear that the era of fustian was over. Audiences simply wouldn't stand it any more. A new day had dawned in the theatre, and he was a particularly bright beam from the rising sun.

"He was modest, however. There were brighter beams than he, and the brightest, most blinding beam in the literature of the time was somebody called Aldous Huxley. No, Huxley didn't write plays. It was his outlook—wry, brilliantly witty, rooted in tremendous scholarship, and drenched in the Ironic Spirit—that the genius admired, and was about to transfer to the stage. In no time he had a tiny court, in which Charlton and Woulds and Audrey Sevenhowes were the leaders, and after rehearsals they were always to be seen in the nearest pub, laughing a great deal. With my very long ears it wasn't long before I knew they were laughing at Milady and Frank Moore and Emilia Pauncefort, who were the very warp and woof of fustian, and who couldn't possibly be worked into the kind of play the genius had in mind. No, he hadn't begun writing yet, but he had a Concept, and though he hated the word 'metaphysical' he didn't mind using it to give a rough idea of how the Concept would take shape.

"Sir John didn't know about the Concept as yet, but when it was explained to him he would get a surprise. The genius was hanging around *The Master of Ballantrae* because it was from a novel by the same chap that had written *Jekyll and Hyde*. But this chap—Roly says his name was Stevenson, and I'm sure he knows—had never fully shouldered the burden of his own creative gift. This was something the genius would have to do for him. Stevenson, when he had thought of *Jekyll and Hyde*, had seized upon a theme that was Dostoevskian, but he had worked it out in terms of what some people might call Romance, but the genius regretfully had to use the word fustian. The only thing the genius could do, in order to be true to his Concept, was to re-work the Stevenson material in such a way that its full implications—the ones Stevenson had approached, and run away from in fright—were revealed.

"He thought it could be done with masks. The genius confessed, with a laugh at his own determination, that he would not attempt the thing at all unless he was given a completely free hand to use masks in every possible way. Not only would Jekyll and Hyde wear masks, but the whole company would wear them, and sometimes there would be eight or ten Jekylls on the stage, all wearing masks showing different aspects of that character, and we would see them exchange the masks of Jekyll—because there was to be no nonsense about realism, or pretending to the audience that what they saw had any relationship to what they foolishly thought of as real life—for masks of Hyde. There would be dialogue, of course, but mostly in the form of soliloquies, and a lot of the action would be carried out in mime—a word which the genius liked to pronounce 'meem', to give it the flavour he thought it needed.

"Charlton and Woulds and Audrey Sevenhowes thought this sounded wonderful, though they had some reservations, politely expressed, about the masks. They thought stylized make-up might do just as well. But the genius was rock-like in his insistence that it would be masks or he would throw up the whole project.

"When this news leaked through to the other members of the company they were disgusted. They talked about other versions of *Jekyll and Hyde* they had seen, which did very well without any nonsense about masks. Old Frank Moore had played with Henry Irving's son 'H.B.' in a Jekyll and Hyde play where H.B. had made the transformation from the humane doctor to the villainous Hyde before the eyes of the audience, simply by ruffling up his hair and distorting his body. Old Frank showed us how he did it: first he assumed the air of a man who is about to be wafted off the ground by his own moral grandeur, then he drank the dreadful potion out of his own pot of old-and-mild, and then, with an extraordinary display of snarling and gnawing the air, he crumpled up into a hideous gnome. He did this one day in the pub and some strangers, who weren't used to actors, left hurriedly and the landlord asked Frank, as a personal favour, not to do it again. Frank had an extraordinarily gripping quality as an actor.

"Nevertheless, as I admired his snorting and chomping depiction of evil, I was conscious that I had seen even more convincing evil in the face of Willard the Wizard, and that there it had been as immovable and calm as stone.

"Suddenly, one day at rehearsal, the genius lost stature. Sir John called to him, 'Come along, you may as well fit in here, mphm? Give you practical experience of the stage, quonk?', and before we knew what was happening he had the genius acting the part of one of the menservants in Lord Durrisdeer's household. He wasn't bad at all, and I suppose he had learned a few things in his amateur days at Cambridge. But at a critical moment Sir John said, 'Clear away your master's chair, m'boy; when he comes downstage to Miss Alison you take the chair back to the upstage side of the fireplace.' Which the genius did, but not to Sir John's liking; he put one hand under the front of the seat, and the other on the back of the armchair, and hefted it to where he had been told. Sir John said, 'Not like that, m'boy; lift it by the arms.' But the genius smiled and said, 'Oh no, Sir John, that's not the way to handle a chair; you must always put one hand under its apron, so as not to put a strain on its back.' Sir John went rather cool, as he did when he was displeased, and said, 'That may have been all very well in your father's shop, m'boy, but it won't do on my stage. Lift it as I tell you.' And the genius turned exceedingly red, and began to argue. At which Sir John said to the other extra, 'You do it, and show him how.' And he ignored the genius until the end of the scene.

"Seems a trivial thing, but it rocked the genius to his foundations; after that he never seemed to be able to do anything right. And the people who had been all over him before were much cooler after that slight incident. It was the mention of the word 'shop'. I don't think actors are particularly snobbish, but I suppose Audrey Sevenhowes and the others had seen him as a gilded undergraduate; all of a sudden he was just a clumsy actor who had come from some sort of shop, and he never quite regained his former lustre. When we dress-rehearsed *The Master* it was apparent that he knew nothing about make-up; he appeared with a horrible red face and a huge pair of false red eyebrows. 'Good God, m'boy,' Sir John called from the front of the house, when this spook appeared, 'what have you been doing to your face?' The genius walked to the footlights—inexcusable, he should have spoken from his place on the stage—and began to explain that as he was playing a Scots servant he thought he should have a very fresh complexion to suggest a peasant ancestry, a childhood spent on the moors, and a good deal more along the same lines. Sir John shut him up, and told Darton Flesher, a good, useful actor, to show the boy how to put on a decent, unobtrusive face, suited to chair-lifting.

"The genius was huffy, backstage, and talked about throwing up the whole business of Jekyll and Hyde and leaving Sir John to stew in his own juice. But Audrey Sevenhowes said, 'Oh, don't be so silly; everybody has to learn,' and that cooled him down. Audrey also threw him a kind word about how she couldn't spare him because he was going to write a lovely part for her in the new play, and gave him a smile that would have melted—well, I mustn't be extreme—that would have melted a lad down from Cambridge whose self-esteem had been wounded. It wouldn't have melted me; I had taken Miss Sevenhowes' number long before. But then, I was a hard case.

"Not so hard that I hadn't a little sympathy for Adele Chesterton, whose nose was out of joint. She was still playing in *Scaramouche*, but she had not been cast in *The Master*; an actress called Felicity Larcombe had been brought in for the second leading female role in that. She was one of the most beautiful women I have ever seen anywhere: very dark brown hair, splendid eyes, a superb slim figure, and that air of enduring a secret sorrow bravely which so many men find irresistible. What was more, she could act, which poor Adele Chesterton, who was the Persian-kitten type, could only do by fits and starts. But she was a decent kid, and I was sorry for her, because the company, without meaning it unkindly, neglected her. You know how theatre companies are: if you're working with them, you're real, and if you aren't, you have only a half-life in their estimation. Adele was the waning, and Felicity the waxing, moon.

"As usual, Audrey Sevenhowes had a comment. 'Nobody to blame but herself,' said she; 'made a Horlicks—an utter Horlicks—of her part. I could have shown them, but—' Her shrug showed what she thought of the management's taste. 'Horlicks' was a word she used a lot; it suggested 'ballocks' but avoided a direct indecency. Charlton and Woulds loved to hear her say it; it seemed delightfully daring, and sexy, and knowing. It was my first encounter with this sort of allurement, and I disliked it.

"I mentioned to Macgregor that Miss Larcombe seemed a very good, and probably expensive, actress for her small part in *The Master*. 'Ah, she'll have a great deal to do on the tour,' he replied, and I pricked up my ears. But there was nothing more to be got out of him about the tour.

"It was all clear before we opened *The Master*, however; Sir John was engaging a company to make a longish winter tour in Canada, with a repertoire of some of his most successful old pieces, and *Scaramouche* as a novelty. Holroyd was asking people to drop into his office and talk about contracts.

"Of course the company buzzed about it. For the established actors a decision had to be made: would they absent themselves from London for the best part of a winter season? All actors under a certain age are hoping for some wonderful chance that will carry them into the front rank of their profession, and a tour in Sir John's repertoire wasn't exactly it. On the other hand, a tour of Canada could be a lark, because Sir John was known to be a great favourite there and they would play to big audiences, and see a new country while they did it.

"For the middle-aged actors it was attractive. Jim Hailey and his wife Gwenda Lewis jumped at it, because they had a boy to educate and it was important to them to keep in work. Frank Moore was an enthusiastic sightseer and traveller, and had toured Australia and South Africa but had not been to Canada since 1924. Grover Paskin and C. Pengelly Spickernell were old standbys of Sir John's, and would cheerfully have toured Hell with him. Emilia Pauncefort wasn't likely to get other offers, because stately old women and picturesque hags were not frequent in West End shows that season, and the Old Vic, where she had staked out quite a little claim in cursing queens, had a new director who didn't fancy her.

"But why Gordon Barnard, who was a very good leading man, or Felicity Larcombe, who was certain to go to the top of the profession? Macgregor explained to me that Barnard hadn't the ambition that should have gone with his talent, and Miss Larcombe, wise girl, wanted to get as much varied experience as she could before descending on the West End and making it hers forever. There was no trouble at all in recruiting a good company, and I was glad to sign my own contract, to be assistant to Mac and play doubles without having my name on the program. And to everybody's astonishment, the genius was offered a job on the tour, and took it. So eighteen actors were recruited, not counting Sir John and Milady, and with Holroyd and some necessary technical staff, the final number of the company was to be twenty-eight.

"The work was unrelenting. We opened *The Master of Ballantrae*, and although the other critics were not warm about it Agate gave it a push and we played a successful six weeks in London. God, what audiences! People came out of the woodwork to see it, and it seemed they had all seen it before and couldn't get enough of it. 'It's like peeping into the dark backward and abysm of time,' the genius said, and even I felt that in some way the theatre had been put back thirty years when we appeared in that powerful, thrilling, but strangely antique piece.

"Every day we were called for rehearsal, in order to get the plays ready for the tour. And what plays they were! *The Lyons Mail* and *The Corsican Brothers*, in both of which I doubled for Sir John, and *Rosemary*, a small play with a minimum of scenery, which was needed to round out a repertoire in which all the other plays were big ones, with cartloads of scenery and dozens of costumes. I liked *Rosemary* especially, because I didn't double in it but I had a showy appearance as a stilt walker. How we sweated! It was rough on the younger people, who had to learn several new parts during days when they were working a full eight hours, but Moore and Spickernell and Paskin and Miss Pauncefort seemed to have been playing these melodramas for years, and the lines rolled off their tongues like grave old music. As for Sir John and Milady, they couldn't have been happier, and there is nothing so indestructibly demanding and tireless as a happy actor.

"Did I say we worked eight hours? Holroyd and Macgregor, with me as their slave, worked much longer than that, because the three plays we were adding to *Scaramouche* and *The Master* had to be retrieved from storage and brushed up and made smart for the tour. But it was all done at last, and we closed in London one Saturday night, with everything finished that would make it possible for us to sail for Canada the following Tuesday.

"A small matter must be mentioned. The genius's mother turned up for one of the last performances of *The Master*, and it fell to me to show her to Sir John's dressing-room. She was a nice little woman, but not what one expects of the mother of such a splendid creature, and when I showed her through the great man's door she looked as if she might faint from the marvel of it all. I felt sorry for her; it must be frightening when one mothers such a prodigy, and she had the humble look of somebody who can't believe her luck."

It was here that Roland Ingestree, who had been decidedly out of sorts for the past half-hour, intervened.

"Magnus, I don't much mind you taking the mickey out of me,

if that's how you get your fun, but I think you might leave poor old Mum out of it."

Magnus pretended astonishment. "But my dear fellow, I don't see how I can. I've done my best to afford you the decency of obscurity. I'd hoped to finish my narrative without letting the others in on our secret. I could have gone on calling you 'the genius', though you had other names in the company. There were some who called you 'the Cantab' because of your degree from Cambridge, and there were others who called you 'One' because you had that mock-modest trick of referring to yourself as One when in your heart you were crying, 'Me, me, glorious ME!' But I can't leave you out, and I don't see how I can leave your Mum out, because she threw so much light on you, and therefore lent a special flavour to the whole story of Sir John's touring company."

"All right, Magnus; I was a silly young ass, and I freely admit it. But isn't one permitted to be an ass for a year or two, when one is young, and the whole world appears to be open to one, and waiting for one? Because you had a rotten childhood, don't suppose that everybody else who had better luck was utterly a fool. Have you any idea what *you* looked like in those days?"

"No, I haven't, really, but I see you are dying to tell me. Do please go ahead."

"I shall. You were disliked and distrusted because everybody thought you were a sneak, as you've said yourself. But you haven't told us that you *were* a sneak, and blabbed to Macgregor about every trivial breach of company discipline—who came into the theatre after the half-hour call, and who might happen to have a friend in the dressing-room during the show, and who watched Sir John from the wings when he had said they weren't to, and anything else you could find out by pussy-footing and snooping. Even that might have passed as your job, if you hadn't had such a nasty personality—always smiling like a pantomime demon—always stinking of some sort of cheap hair oil—always running like a rabbit to open doors for Milady—and vain as a peacock about your tuppenny-ha'penny juggling and wirewalking. You were a thoroughly nasty little piece of work, let me tell you."

"I suppose I was. But you make the mistake of thinking I was pleased with myself. Not a bit of it. I was trying to learn the ropes of another mode of life—"

"Indeed you were! You were trying to be Sir John off the stage as well as on. And what a caricature you made of it! Walking like Spring-Heeled Jack because Frank Moore had tried to show you something about deportment, and parting your greasy long hair in the middle because Sir John was the last actor on God's earth to do so, and wearing clothes that would make a cat laugh because Sir John wore eccentric duds that looked as if he'd had 'em since Mafeking Night."

"Do you think I'd have been better off to model myself on you?"

"I was no prize as an actor. Don't think I don't know it. But at least I was living in 1932, and you were aping a man who was still living in 1902, and if there hadn't been a very strong uncanny whiff about you you'd have been a total freak."

"Ah, but there was an uncanny whiff about me. I was Mungo Fetch, don't forget. We fetches can't help being uncanny."

Lind intervened. "Dear friends," he said, being very much the courtly Swede, "let us not have a quarrel about these grievances which are so long dead. You are both different men now. Think, Roly, of your achievements as a novelist and broadcaster; One, and the Genius and the Cantab are surely buried under that? And you, my dear Eisengrim, what reason have you to be bitter toward anyone? What have you desired that life has not given you? Including what I now see is a very great achievement; you modelled yourself on a fine actor of the old school, and you have put all you learned at the service of your own art, where it has flourished wonderfully. Roly, you sought to be a literary man, and you are one; Magnus, you wanted to be Sir John, and it looks very much as if you had succeeded, in so far as anyone can succeed—"

"Just a little more than most people succeed," said Ingestree, who was still hot; "you ate poor old Sir John. You ate him down to the core. We could see it happening, right from the beginning of that tour."

"Did I really?" said Magnus, apparently pleased. "I didn't know it showed so plainly. But now you are being melodramatic, Roly. I simply wanted to be like him. I told you, I apprenticed myself to an egoism, because I saw how invaluable that egoism was. Nobody can steal another man's ego, but he can learn from it, and I learned. You didn't have the wits to learn."

"I'd have been ashamed to toady as you did, whatever it brought me."

"Toady? Now that's an unpleasant word. You didn't learn what there was to be learned in that company, Ingestree. You were at every rehearsal and every performance of *The Master of Ballantrae* that I was. Don't you remember the splendid moment when Sir John, as Mr. Henry, said to his father: 'There are double words for everything: the word that swells and the word that belittles; my brother cannot fight me with a word.' Your word for my relationship to Sir John is toadying, but mine is emulation, and I think mine is the better word."

"Yours is the dishonest word. Your emulation, as you call it, sucked the pith out of that poor old ham, and gobbled it up and made it part of yourself. It was a very nasty process."

"Roly, I idolized him."

"Yes, and to be idolized by you, as you were then, was a terrible, vampire-like feeding on his personality and his spirit—because his personality as an actor was all there was of his spirit. You were a double, right enough, and such a double as Poe and Dostoevski would have understood. When we first met at Sorgenfrei I thought there was something familiar about you, and the minute you began to act I sensed what it was; you were the fetch of Sir John. But I swear it wasn't until today, as we sat at this table, that I realized you really were Mungo Fetch."

"Extraordinary! I recognized you the minute I set eyes on you, in spite of the rather Pickwickian guise you have acquired during the past forty years."

"And you were waiting for a chance to knife me?"

"Knife! Knife! Always these belittling words! Have you no sense of humour, my dear man?"

"Humour is a poisoned dagger in the hands of a man like you. People talk of humour as if it were all jolly, always the lump of sugar in the coffee of life. A man's humour takes its quality from what a man is, and your humour is like the scratch of a rusty nail."

"Oh, balls," said Kinghovn. Ingestree turned on him, very white in the face.

"What the hell do you mean by interfering?" he said.

"I mean what I say. Balls! You people who are so clever with words never allow yourselves or anybody else a moment's peace. What is this all about? You two knew each other when you were young and you didn't hit it off. So now we have all this gaudy abuse about vampires and rusty nails from Roly, and Magnus is leading him on to make a fool of himself and cause a fight. I'm enjoying myself. I like this subtext and I want the rest of it. We had just got to where Roly's Mum was paying a visit to Sir John backstage. I want to know about that. I can see it in my mind's eye. Colour, angle of camera, quality of light—the whole thing. Get on with it and let's forget all this subjective stuff; it has no reality except what somebody like me can provide for it, and at the moment I'm not interested in subjective rubbish. I want the story. Enter Roly's Mum; what next?"

"Since Roly's Mum is such a hot potato, perhaps Roly had better tell you," said Eisengrim.

"So I will. My Mum was a very decent body, though at the time I was silly enough to underrate her; as Magnus has made clear I was a little above myself in those days. University does it, you know. It's such a protected life for a young man, and he so easily loses his frail hold on reality.

"My people weren't grand, at all. My father had an antique shop in Norwich, and he was happy about that because he had risen above his father, who had combined a small furniture shop with an undertaking business. Both my parents had adored Sir John, and ages before the time we are talking about—before the First Great War, in fact—they did rather a queer thing that brought them to his attention. They loved *The Master of Ballantrae*; it was just their meat, full of antiquery and romance; they liked selling antiques because it seemed romantic, I truly believe. They saw *The Master* fully ten times when they were young, and loved it so that they wrote out the whole play from memory—I don't suppose it was very accurate, but they did—and sent it to Sir John with an adoring letter. Sort of tribute from playgoers whose life he had illumined, you know. I could hardly believe it when I was young, but I know better now; fans get up to the queerest things in order to associate themselves with their idols.

"Sir John wrote them a nice letter, and when next he was near Norwich, he came to the shop. He loved antiques, and bought them all over the place, and I honestly think his interest in them was simply romantic, like my parents'. They never tired of telling about how he came into the shop, and enquired about a couple of old chairs, and finally asked if they were the people who had sent him the manuscript. That was a glory-day for them, I can tell you. And afterward, whenever they had anything that was in his line, they wrote to him, and quite often he bought whatever it was. That was why it was so bloody-minded of him to take it out of me about the proper way to handle a chair, and to make that crack about the shop. He knew it would hurt.

"Anyhow, my mother was out of her mind with joy when she wangled me a job with his company; thought he was going to be my great patron, I suppose. My father had died, and the shop could keep her, but certainly not me, and anyhow I was set on being a writer. I admit I was pleased to be asked to do a literary job for him; it wasn't quite as grand as I may have pretended to Audrey Sevenhowes, but who hasn't been a fool in his time? If I'd been shrewd enough to resist a pretty girl I'd have been a sharp little piece of glass like Mungo Fetch, instead of a soft boy who had got a swelled head at Cambridge, and knew nothing about the world.

"When my Mum knew I was going to Canada with the company she came to London to say good-bye—I'm ashamed to say I had told her there was no chance of my going to Norwich, though I suppose I could have made it—and she wanted to see Sir John. She'd brought him a gift, the loveliest little wax portrait relievo of Garrick you ever saw; I don't know where she picked it up, but it was worth eighty pounds if it was worth a ha'penny, and she gave it to him. And she asked him, in terms that made me blush, to take good care of me while I was abroad. I must say the old boy was decent, and said very kindly that he was sure I didn't need supervision, but that he would always be glad to talk with me if anything came up that worried me."

"Audrey Sevenhowes put it about that your Mum had asked Milady to see that you didn't forget your bedsocks in the Arctic wildernesses of Canada," said Eisengrim.

"You don't surprise me. Audrey Sevenhowes was a bitch, and she made a fool of me. But I don't care. I'd rather be a fool than a tough any day. But I assure you there was no mention of bedsocks; my Mum was not a complex woman, but she wasn't stupid, either."

"Ah, there you have the advantage of me," said Magnus, with a smile of great charm. "My mother, I fear, was very much more than stupid, as I have already told you. She was mad. So perhaps we can be friends again, Roly?"

He put out his hand across the table. It was not a gesture an Englishman would have made, and I couldn't quite make up my mind whether he was sincere or not. But Ingestree took his hand, and it was perfectly plain that he meant to make up the quarrel.

The waiters were beginning to look at us meaningly, so we adjourned upstairs to our expensive apartment, where everybody had a chance to use the loo. The film-makers were not to be shaken. They wanted the story to the end. So, after the interval—not unlike an interval at the theatre—we reassembled in our large sitting-room, and it now seemed to be understood, without anybody having said so, that Roly and Magnus were going to continue the story as a duet.

I was pleased, as I was pleased by anything that gave me a new light or a new crumb of information about my old friend, who had become Magnus Eisengrim. I was puzzled, however, by the silence of Liesl, who had sat through the narration at the lunch table without saying a word. Her silence was not of the unobtrusive kind; the less she said the more conscious one became of her presence. I knew her well enough to bide my time. Though she said nothing, she was big with feeling, and I knew that she would have something to say when she felt the right moment had come. After all, Magnus was in a very real sense her property: did he not live in her house, treat it as his own, share her bed, and accept the homage of her extraordinary courtesy, yet always understanding who was the real ruler of Sorgenfrei? What did Liesl think about Magnus undressing himself, inch by inch, in front of the film-makers? Particularly now that it was clear that there was an old, unsettled hostility between him and Roland Ingestree, what did she think?

What did I think, as I carefully wiped my newly scrubbed dentures on one of the Savoy's plentiful linen hand-towels, before slipping them back over my gums? I thought I wanted all I could get of this vicarious life. I wanted to be off to Canada with Sir John Tresize. I knew what Canada meant to me: what had it meant to him?

6

When I returned to our drawing-room Roly was already aboard ship.

"One of my embarrassments—how susceptible the young are to embarrassment—was that my dear Mum had outfitted me with a vast woolly steamer-rug in a gaudy design. The company kept pestering Macgregor to know what tartan it was, and he thought it looked like Hunting Cohen, so The Hunting Cohen it was from that time forth. I didn't need it, God knows, because the C.P.R. ship was fiercely hot inside, and it was too late in the season for anyone to sit on deck in any sort of comfort.

"My Mum was so solicitous in seeing me off that the company pretended to think I needed a lot of looking after, and made a great game of it. Not unkind (except for Charlton and Woulds, who were bullies) but very joky and hard to bear, especially when I wanted to be glorious in the eyes of Audrey Sevenhowes. But my Mum had also provided me with a *Baedeker's Canada*, the edition of 1922, which had somehow found its way into the shop, and although it was certainly out of date a surprising number of people asked for a loan of it, and informed themselves that the Government of Canada issued a four-dollar bill, and that the coloured porters on the sleeping-cars expected a minimum tip of twenty-five cents a day, and that a guard's van was called a caboose on Canadian railways, and similar useful facts.

"The Co. may have thought me funny, but they were a quaint sight themselves when they assembled on deck for a publicity picture before we left Liverpool. There were plenty of these company pictures taken through the whole length of the tour, and in every one of them Emilia Pauncefort's extraordinary travelling coat (called behind her back the Coat of Many Colours) and the fearful man's cap that Gwenda Lewis fastened to her head with a hatpin, so that she would be ready for all New World hardships, and the fur cap C. Pengelly Spickernell wore, assuring everybody that a skin cap with earflaps was absolutely *de rigueur* in the Canadian winter, Grover Paskin's huge pipe, with a bowl about the size of a brandy-glass, and Eugene Fitzwarren's saucy Homburg and coat with velvet collar, in the Edwardian manner—all these strange habiliments figured prominently. Even though the gaudy days of the Victorian mummers had long gone, these actors somehow got themselves up so that they couldn't have been taken for anything else on God's earth but actors.

"It was invariable, too, that when Holroyd had mustered us for one of these obligatory pictures, Sir John and Milady always appeared last, smiling in surprise, as if a picture were the one thing in the world they hadn't expected, and as if they were joining in simply to humour the rest of us. Sir John was an old hand at travelling in Canada, and he wore an overcoat of Raglan cut and reasonable weight, but of an amplitude that spoke of the stage—and, as our friend has told us, the sleeves were always a bit short so that his hands showed to advantage. Milady wore fur, as befitted the consort of an actor-knight; what fur it was nobody knew, but it was very furry indeed, and soft, and smelled like money. She topped herself with one of those *cloche* hats that were fashionable then, in a hairy purple felt; not the happiest choice, because it almost obscured her eyes, and threw her long duck's-bill nose into prominence.

"But never—never, I assure you—in any of these pictures would you find Mungo Fetch. Who can have warned him off? Whose decision was it that a youthful Sir John, in clothes that were always too tight and sharply cut, wouldn't have done in one of these pictures which always appeared in Canadian papers with a caption that read: 'Sir John Tresize and his London company, including Miss Annette de la Borderie (Lady Tresize), who are touring Canada after a triumphant season in the West End.'"

"It was a decision of common sense," said Magnus. "It never worried me. I knew my place, which is more than you did, Roly."

"Quite right. I fully admit it. I didn't know my place. I was under the impression that a university man was acceptable everywhere, and inferior to no one. I hadn't twigged that in a theatrical company—or any artistic organization, for that matter—the hierarchy is decided by talent, and that art is the most rigorously aristocratic thing in our democratic world. So I always pushed in as close to Audrey Sevenhowes as I could, and I even picked up the trick from Charlton of standing a bit sideways, to show my profile, which I realize now would have been better kept a mystery. I was an ass. Oh, indeed I was a very fine and ostentatious ass, and don't think I haven't blushed for it since."

"Stop telling us what an ass you were," said Kinghovn. "Even I recognize that as an English trick to pull the teeth of our contempt. 'Oh, I say, what a jolly good chap: says he's an ass, don't yer know; he couldn't possibly say that if he was really an ass.' But I'm a tough-minded European; I think you really were an ass. If I had a time-machine, I'd whisk myself back into 1932 and give you a good boot in the arse for it. But as I can't, tell me why you were included on the tour. Apparently you were a bad actor and an arguing nuisance as a chair-lifter. Why would anybody pay you money, and take you on a jaunt to Canada?"

"You need a drink, Harry. You are speaking from the deep surliness of the deprived boozer. Don't fuss; it'll be the canonical, appointed cocktail hour quite soon, and then you'll regain your temper. I was taken as Sir John's secretary. The idea was that I'd write letters to fans that he could sign, and do general dog's-body work, and also get on with Jekyll-and-Hyde.

"That was where the canker gnawed, to use an appropriately melodramatic expression. I had thought, you see, that I was to write a dramatization of Stevenson's story, and as Magnus has told you I was full of great ideas about Dostoevski and masks. I used to quote Stevenson at Sir John: 'I hazard the guess that man will be ultimately known for a mere polity of multifarious, incongruous, and independent denizens,' I would say, and entreat him to let me put the incongruous denizens on the stage, in masks. He merely shook his head and said, 'No good, m'boy; my public wouldn't like it.' Then I would have at him with another quotation, in which Jekyll tells of 'those appetites I had long secretly indulged, and had of late begun to pamper'. Once he asked me what I had in mind. I had lots of Freudian capers in mind: masochism, and sadism, and rough-stuff with girls. That rubbed his Victorianism the wrong way. 'Unwholesome rubbish,' was all he would say.

"In the very early days of our association I was even so daring as to ask him to scrap Jekyll-and-Hyde and let me do a version of *Dorian Gray* for him. That really tore it! 'Don't ever mention that man to me again,' he said; 'Oscar Wilde dragged his God-given genius in unspeakable mire, and the greatest kindness we can do is to forget his name. Besides, my public wouldn't hear of it.' So I was stuck with Jekyll-and-Hyde.

"Stuck even worse than I had at first supposed. Ages and ages before, at the beginning of their career together, Sir John and Milady had concocted *The Master of Ballantrae* themselves, with their own innocent pencils. They made the scenario, down to the last detail, then found some hack to supply dialogue. This, I discovered to my horror, was what they had done again. They had made a scheme for Jekyll-and-Hyde, and they expected me to write some words for it, which he had the gall to say they would *polish*. Those two mountebanks *polish* my stuff! I was no hack; hadn't I got a meritorious second in Eng.Lit. at Cambridge? And it would have been a first, if I had been content to crawl and stick to the party line about everything on the syllabus from Beowulf on down! Don't laugh, you people. I was young and I had pride."

"But no stage experience," said Lind.

"Perhaps not, but I wasn't a fool. And you should have seen the scenario Sir John and Milady had cobbled up between them. Stevenson must have turned in his grave. Do you know *The Strange Case of Dr. Jekyll and Mr. Hyde*? It's tremendously a *written* book. Do you know what I mean? Its quality is so much in the narrative manner; extract the mere story from it and it's just a tale of bugaboo. Chap drinking a frothy liquid that changes from clear to purple and then to green—*green* if you can imagine anything so corny—and he shrinks into his wicked *alter ego*. I set myself to work to discover a way of getting the heart of the literary quality into a stage version.

"Masks would have helped enormously. But those two had seized on what was, for them, the principal defect of the original, which was that there was no part for a woman in it. Well, imagine! What would the fans of Miss Annette de la Borderie say to that? So they had fudged up a tale in which Dr. Jekyll had a secret sorrow; it was that a boyhood friend had married the girl he truly loved, who discovered after the marriage that she truly loved Jekyll. So he adored her honourably, while her husband went to the bad through drink. The big Renunciation ploy, you see, which was such a telling card in *The Master*.

"To keep his mind off his thwarted love, Dr. Jekyll took to mucking with chemicals, and discovered the Fateful Potion. Then the husband of the True Love died of booze, and Jekyll and she were free to marry. But by that time he was addicted to the Fateful Potion. Had taken so much of it that he was likely to give a shriek and dwindle into Hyde at any inconvenient moment. So he couldn't marry his True Love and couldn't tell her why. Great final scene, where he is locked in his laboratory, changed into Hyde, and quite unable to change back, because he's run out of the ingredients of the F.P.; True Love, suspecting something's up, storms the door with the aid of a butler and footman who break it in; as the blows on the door send him into the trembles, Jekyll, with one last superhuman clutching at his Better Self, realizes that there is only one honourable way out; he takes poison, and hops the twig just as True Love bursts in; she holds the body of Hyde in her arms, weeping piteously, and the power of her love is so great that he turns slowly back into the beautiful Dr. Jekyll, redeemed at the very moment of death."

"A strong curtain," said I. "I don't know what you're complaining about. I should like to have seen that play. I remember Tresize well; he could have done it magnificently."

"You must be pulling my leg," said Ingestree, looking at me in reproach.

"Not a bit of it. Good, gutsy melodrama. You've described it in larky terms, because you want us to laugh. But I think it would have worked. Didn't you ever try?"

"Oh yes, I tried. I tried all through that Canadian tour. I would slave away whenever I got a chance, and then show my homework to Sir John, and he would mark it up in his own spidery handwriting. Kept saying I had no notion of how to make words effective, and wrote three sentences where one would do.

"I tried everything I knew. I remember saying to myself one night, as I lay in my berth in a stiflingly hot Canadian train, What would Aldous Huxley do, in my position? And it came to me that Aldous would have used what we call a distancing-technique—you know, he would have written it all apparently straight, but with a choice of vocabulary that gave it all an ironic edge, so that the perceptive listener would realize that the whole play was ambiguous, and could be taken as a hilarious send-up. So I tried a scene or two like that, and I don't believe Sir John even twigged; he just sliced out all the telling adjectives, and there it was, melodrama again. I never met a man with such a deficient literary sense."

"Did it never occur to you that perhaps he knew his job?" said Lind. "I've never found that audiences liked ambiguity very much. I've got all my best effects by straight statement."

"Dead right," said Kinghovn. "When Jurgen wants ambiguity he tips me the wink and I film the scene a bit skew-whiff, or occasionally going out of focus, and that does the trick."

"You're telling me this now," said Ingestree, "and I expect you're right, in your unliterary way. But there was nobody to tell me anything then, except Sir John, and I could see him becoming more and more stagily patient with me, and letting whatever invisible audience he acted to in his offstage moments admire the way in which the well-graced actor endured the imbecilities of the dim-witted boy. But I swear there was something to be said on my side, as well. But as I say I was an ass. Am I never to be forgiven for being an ass?"

"That's a very pretty theological point," I said. " 'In the law of God there is no statute of limitations.' "

"My God! Do you remember that one?" said Ingestree.

"Oh yes; I've read Stevenson too, you know, and that chilly remark comes in *Jekyll and Hyde*, so you are certainly familiar with it. Are we ever forgiven for the follies even of our earliest years? That's something that torments me often."

"Bugger theology!" said Kinghovn. "Get on with the story."

"High time Harry had a drink," said Liesl. "I'll call for some things to be sent up. And we might as well have dinner here, don't you think? I'll choose."

When she had gone into the bedroom to use the telephone Magnus looked calculatingly at Ingestree, as if at some curious creature he had not observed before. "You describe the Canadian tour simply as a personal Gethsemane, but it was really quite an elaborate affair," he said. "I suppose one of your big problems was trying to fit a part into Jekyll-and-Hyde for the chaste and lovely Sevenhowes. Couldn't you have made her a confidential maid to the True Love, with stirring lines like, 'Ee, madam, Dr. Jekyll'e do look sadly mazy-like these latter days, madam'? That would have been about her speed. A rotten actress. Do you know what became of her? Neither do I. What becomes of all those pretty girls with a teaspoonful of talent who seem to drift off the stage before they are thirty? But really, my dear Roly, there was a great deal going on. I was working like a galley-slave."

"I'm sure you were," said Ingestree; "toadying to Milady, as I said earlier. I use the word without malice. Your approach was not describable as courtier-like, nor did it quite sink to the level of fawning; therefore I think toadying is the appropriate expression."

"Call it toadying if it suits your keen literary sense. I have said several times that I loved her, but you choose not to attach any importance to that. Loved her not in the sense of desiring her, which would have been grotesque, and never entered my head, but simply in the sense of wishing to serve her and do anything that was in my power to make her happy. Why I felt that way about a woman old enough to be my mother is for you dabblers in psychology to say, but nothing you can think of will give the real quality of my feeling; there is a pitiful want of resonance in so much psychological explanation of what lies behind things. If you had felt more, Roly, and been less remorselessly literary, you might have seen possibilities in the plan for the Jekyll and Hyde play. A man redeemed and purged of evil by a woman's love—now there's a really unfashionable theme for a play in our time! So unfashionable as to be utterly incredible. Yet Sir John and Milady seemed to know what such themes were all about. They were more devoted than any people I have ever known."

"Like a couple of old love-birds," said Ingestree.

"Well, what would you prefer? A couple of old scratching cats? Don't forget that Sir John was a symbol to countless people of romantic love in its most chivalrous expression. You know what Agate wrote about him once—'He touches women as if they were camellias.' Can you name an actor on the stage today who makes love like that? But there was never a word of scandal about them, because off the stage they were inseparables.

"I think I penetrated their secret: undoubtedly they began as lovers but they had long been particularly close friends. Is that common? I haven't seen much of it, if it is. They were sillies, of course. Sir John would never hear a word that suggested that Milady was unsuitably cast as a young woman, though I know he was aware of it. And she was a silly because she played up to him, and clung quite pitiably to some mannerisms of youth. I knew them for years, you know; you only knew them on that tour. But I remember much later, when a newspaper interviewer touched the delicate point, Sir John said with great dignity and simplicity, 'Ah, but you see, we always felt that our audiences were ready to make allowances if the physical aspect of a character was not ideally satisfied, because they knew that so many other fine things in our performances were made possible thereby.'

"He had a good point, you know. Look at some of the leading women in the Comédie Française; crone is not too hard a word when first you see them, but in ten minutes you are delighted with the art, and forget the appearance, which is only a kind of symbol, anyhow. Milady had extraordinary art, but alas, poor dear, she did run to fat. It's better for an actress to become a bag of bones, which can always be equated somehow with elegance. Fat's another thing. But what a gift of comedy she had, and how wonderfully it lit up a play like *Rosemary*, where she insisted on playing a character part instead of the heroine. Charity, Roly, charity."

"You're a queer one to be talking about charity. You ate Sir John. I've said it once and I'll say it again. You ate that poor old ham."

"That's one of your belittling words, like 'toady'. I've said it: I apprenticed myself to an egoism, and if in the course of time, because I was younger and had a career to make, the egoism became more mine than his, what about it? Destiny, m'boy? Inevitable, quonk?"

"Oh, God, don't do that, it's too horribly like him."

"Thank you. I thought so myself. And, as I tell you, I worked to achieve it!

"You had quite a jolly time on the voyage to Canada, as I recall. But don't you remember those rehearsals we held every day, in such holes and corners of the ship as the Purser could make available to us? Macgregor and I were too busy to be seasick, which was a luxury you didn't deny yourself. You were sick the night of the ship's concert. Those concerts are utterly a thing of the past. The Purser's assistant was busy almost before the ship left Liverpool, ferreting out what possible talent there might be on board—ladies who could sing 'The Rosary' or men who imitated Harry Lauder. A theatrical company was a godsend to the poor man. And in the upshot C. Pengelly Spickernell sang 'Melisande in the Wood' and 'The Floral Dance' (nicely contrasted material, was what he called it) and Grover Paskin told funny stories (insecurely cemented together with 'And that reminds me of the time—') and Sir John recited Clarence's Dream from *Richard III*; Milady made the speech hitting up the audience for money for the Seaman's Charities, and did it with so much charm and spirit that they got a record haul.

"But that's by the way. We worked on the voyage and after we'd docked at Montreal the work was even harder. We landed on a Friday, and opened on Monday at Her Majesty's for two weeks, one given wholly to *Scaramouche* and the second to *The Corsican Brothers* and *Rosemary*. We did first-rate business, and it was the beginning of what the old actors loved to call a triumphal tour. You wouldn't believe how we were welcomed, and how the audiences ate up those romantic plays—"

"I remember some fairly cool notices," said Roly.

"But not cool audiences. That's what counts. Provincial critics are always cool; they have to show they're not impressed by what comes from the big centres of culture. The audiences thought we were wonderful."

"Magnus, the audiences thought England was wonderful. The Tresize company came from England, and if the truth is to be told it came from a special England many of the people in those audiences cherished—the England they had left when they were young, or the England they had visited when they were young, and in many cases an England they simply imagined and wished were a reality.

"Even in 1932 all that melodrama was terribly old hat, but every audience had a core of people who were happy just to be listening to English voices repeating noble sentiments. The notion that everybody wants the latest is a delusion of intellectuals; a lot of people want a warm, safe place where Time hardly moves at all, and to a lot of those Canadians that place was England. The theatre was almost the last stronghold of the old colonial Canada. You know very well it was more than twenty years since Sir John had dared to visit New York, because his sort of theatre was dead there. But it did very well in Canada because it wasn't simply theatre there—it was England, and they were sentimental about it.

"Don't you remember the smell of mothballs that used to sweep up onto the stage when the curtain rose, from all the bunny coats and ancient dress suits in the expensive seats? There were still people who dressed for the theatre, though I doubt if they dressed for anything else, except perhaps a regimental ball or something that also reminded them of England. Sir John was exploiting the remnants of colonialism. You liked it because you knew no better."

"I knew Canada," said Magnus. "At least, I knew the part of it that had responded to Wanless's World of Wonders and Happy Hannah's jokes. The Canada that came to see Sir John was different, but not wholly different. We didn't tour the villages; we toured the cities with theatres that could accommodate our productions, but we rushed through many a village I knew as we jaunted all those thousands of miles on the trains. As we travelled, I began to think I knew Canada pretty well. But quite another thing was that I knew what entertains people, what charms the money out of their pockets, and feeds their imagination.

"The theatre to you was a kind of crude extension of Eng.Lit. at Cambridge, but the theatre I knew was the theatre that makes people forget some things and remember others, and refreshes dry places in the spirit. We were both ignorant young men, Roly. You were the kind that is so scared of life that you only know how to despise it, for fear you might be tricked into liking something that wasn't up to the standards of a handful of people you admired. I was the kind that knew very little that wasn't tawdry and tough and ugly, but I hadn't forgotten my Psalms, and I thirsted for something better as the hart pants for the water-brooks. So Sir John's plays, and the decent manners he insisted on in his company, and the regularity and honesty of the Friday treasury, when I got my pay without having to haggle or kick back any part of it to some petty crook, did very well for me."

"You're idealizing your youth, Magnus. Lots of the company just thought the tour was a lark."

"Yes, but even more of the company were honest players and did their best in the work they had at hand. You saw too much of Charlton and Woulds, who were no good and never made any mark in the profession. And you were under the thumb of Audrey Sevenhowes, who was another despiser, like yourself. Of course we had our ridiculous side. What theatrical troupe hasn't? But the effect we produced wasn't ridiculous. We had something people wanted, and we didn't give them short weight. Very different from my carnival days, when short weight was the essence of everything."

"So for you the Canadian tour was a time of spiritual growth," said Lind.

"It was a time when I was able to admit that honesty and some decency of life were luxuries within my grasp," said Magnus. "Can you imagine that? You people all have the flesh and finish of those who grew up feeling reasonably safe in the world. And you grew up as visible people. Don't forget that I had spent most of my serious hours inside Abdullah."

"Melodrama has eaten into your brain," said Roly. "When I knew you, you were inside Sir John, inside his body and inside his manner and voice and everything about him that a clever double could imitate. Was it really different?"

"Immeasurably different."

"I wish you two would stop clawing one another," said Kinghovn. "If it was all so different—and I'm quite ready to believe it was—how was it different? If it's possible to find out, of course. You two sound as if you had been on different tours."

"Not a bit of it. It was the same tour, right enough," said Magnus; "but I probably remember more of its details than Roly. I'm a detail man; it's the secret of being a good illusionist. Roly has the big, broad picture, as it would have appeared to someone of his temperament and education. He saw everything it was proper for the Cantab and One to notice; I saw and tried to understand everything that passed before my eyes.

"Do you remember Morton W. Penfold, Roly? No, I didn't think you would. But he was one of the casters on which that tour rolled. He was our Advance.

"The tour was under the management of a syndicate of rich Canadians who wanted to encourage English theatre companies to visit Canada, partly because they wanted to stem what they felt was a too heavy American influence, partly in the hope that they might make a little money, partly because they felt the attraction of the theatre in the ignorant way rich businessmen sometimes do. When we arrived in Montreal some of them met the ship and bore Sir John and Milady away, and there was a great deal of wining and dining before we opened on Monday. Morton W. Penfold was their representative, and he went ahead of us like a trumpeter all across the country. Arranged about travel and saw that tickets for everybody were forthcoming whenever we mounted a train. Saw that trains were delayed when necessary, or that an improvised special helped us to make a difficult connection. Arranged that trucks and sometimes huge sleighs were ready to lug the scenery to and from the theatres. Arranged that there were enough stagehands for our heavy shows, and a rough approximation of the number of musicians we needed to play our music, and college boys or other creatures of the right height and bulk who were needed for the supers in *The Master* and *Scaramouche*. Saw that a horse of guaranteed good character and continence was hired to pull Climene's cart. Placed the advertisements in the local papers ahead of our appearance, and also tasty bits of publicity about Sir John and Milady; had a little anecdote ready for every paper that made it clear that the name Tresize was Cornish and that the emphasis came on the second syllable; also provided a little packet of favourable reviews from London, Montreal, and Toronto papers for the newspapers in small towns where there was no regular critic, and such material might prime the pump of a local reporter's invention. He also saw that the information was provided for the programs, and warned local theatre managers that Madame de Plougastel's Salon was not a misprint for Madame de Plougastel's Saloon, which some of them were apt to think.

"Morton W. Penfold was a living marvel, and I learned a lot from him on the occasions when he was in the same town with us for a few days. He was more theatrical than all but the most theatrical of the actors; had a big square face with a blue jaw, a hypnotist's eyebrows, and a deceptive appearance of dignity and solemnity, because he was a fellow of infinite wry humour. He wore one of those black Homburg hats that politicians used to affect, but he never dinted the top of it, so that he had something of the air of a Mennonite about the head; wore a stiff choker collar and one of those black satin stocks that used to be called a dirty-shirt necktie, because it covered everything within the V of his waistcoat. Always wore a black suit, and had a dazzling ten-cent shoeshine every day of his life. His business office was contained in the pockets of his black overcoat; he could produce anything from them, including eight-by-ten-inch publicity pictures of the company.

"He was pre-eminently a great fixer. He seemed to know everybody, and have influence everywhere. In every town he had arranged for Sir John to address the Rotarians, or the Kiwanians, or whatever club was meeting on an appropriate day. Sir John always gave the same speech, which was about 'cementing the bonds of the British Commonwealth'; he could have given it in his sleep, but he was too good an actor not to make it seem tailor-made for every new club.

"If we were going to be in a town that had an Anglican Cathedral over a weekend it was Morton W. Penfold who persuaded the Dean that it was a God-given opportunity to have Sir John read the Second Lesson at the eleven o'clock service. His great speciality was getting Indian tribes to invest a visiting English actor as a Chief, and he had convinced the Blackfoot that Sir John should be rechristened Soksi-Poyina many years before the tour I am talking about.

"Furthermore, he knew the idiosyncrasies of the liquor laws in every Canadian province we visited, and made sure the company did not run dry; this was particularly important as Sir John and Milady had a taste for champagne, and liked it iced but not frozen, which was not always a simple requirement in that land of plentiful ice. And in every town we visited, Morton W. Penfold had made sure that our advertising sheets, full-size, half-size, and folio, were well displayed and that our little flyers, with pictures of Sir John in some of his most popular roles, were on the reception desks of all the good hotels.

"And speaking of hotels, it was Morton W. Penfold who took particulars of everybody's taste in accommodation on that first day in Montreal, and saw that wherever we went reservations had been made in the grand railway hotels, which were wonderful, or in the dumps where people like James Hailey and Gwenda Lewis stayed, for the sake of economy.

"Oh, those cheap hotels! I stayed in the cheapest, where one electric bulb hung from a string in the middle of the room, where the sheets were like cheesecloth, and where the mattresses—when they were revealed as they usually were after a night's restless sleep—were like maps of strange worlds, the continents being defined by unpleasing stains, doubtless traceable to the incontinent dreams of travelling salesmen, or the rapturous deflowerings of brides from the backwoods.

"Was he well paid for his innumerable labours? I don't know, but I hope so. He said very little that was personal, but Macgregor told me that Morton W. Penfold was born into show business, and that his wife was the granddaughter of the man whom Blondin the Magnificent had carried across Niagara Gorge on his shoulders in 1859. It was under his splendid and unfailing influence that we travelled thousands of miles across Canada and back again, and played a total of 148 performances in forty-one towns, ranging from places of about twenty thousand souls to big cities. I think I could recite the names of the theatres we played in now, though they showed no great daring in what they called themselves; there were innumerable Grands, and occasional Princesses or Victorias, but most of them were just called Somebody's Opera House."

"Frightful places," said Ingestree, doing a dramatic shudder.

"I've seen worse since," said Magnus. "You should try a tour in Central America, to balance your viewpoint. What was interesting about so many of the Canadian theatres, outside the big cities, is that they seemed to have been built with big ideas, and then abandoned before they were equipped. They had pretty good foyers and auditoriums with plush seats, and invariably eight boxes, four on each side of the stage, from which nobody could see very well. All of them had drop curtains with views of Venice or Rome on them, and a spy-hole through which so many actors had peeped that it was ringed with a black stain from their greasepaint. Quite a few had special curtains on which advertisements were printed for local merchants; Sir John didn't like those, and Holroyd had to do what he could to suppress them.

"Every one had a sunken pen for an orchestra, with a fancy balustrade to cut it off from the stalls, and nobody ever seemed to sweep in there. At performance time a handful of assassins would creep into the pen from a low door beneath the stage, and fiddle and thump and toot the music to which they were accustomed. C. Pengelly Spickernell used to say bitterly that these musicians were all recruited from the local manager's poor relations; it was his job to assemble as many of them as could get away from their regular work on a Monday morning and take them through the music that was to accompany our plays. Sir John was fussy about music, and always had a special overture for each of his productions, and usually an entr'acte as well.

"God knows it was not very distinguished music. When we heard it, it was a puzzle to know why 'Overture to *Scaramouche*' by Hugh Dunning did any more for the play that followed than if the orchestra had played 'Overture to *The Master of Ballantrae*' by Festyn Hughes. But there it was, and to Sir John and Milady these two lengths of mediocre music were as different as daylight and dark, and they used to sigh and raise their eyebrows at one another when they heard the miserable racket coming from the other side of the curtain, as if it were the ravishing of a masterpiece. In addition to this specially written music we carried a substantial body of stuff with such titles as 'Minuet d'Amour', 'Peasant Dance', and 'Gaelic Memories', which did for *Rosemary*; and for *The Corsican Brothers* Sir John insisted on an overture that had been written for Irving's production of *Robespierre* by somebody called

Litolff. Another great standby was 'Suite: At the Play', by York Bowen. But except in the big towns the orchestra couldn't manage anything unfamiliar, so we generally ended up with 'Three Dances from *Henry VIII*', by Edward German, which I suppose is known to every bad orchestra in the world. C. Pengelly Spickernell used to grieve about it whenever anybody would listen, but I honestly think the audiences liked that bad playing, which was familiar and had associations with a good time.

"Backstage there was nothing much to work with. No light, except for a few rows of red, white, and blue bulbs that hardly disturbed the darkness when they were full on. The arrangements for hanging and setting our scenery were primitive, and only in the big towns was there more than one stagehand with anything that could be called experience. The others were jobbed in as they were needed, and during the day they worked in factories or lumber-yards. Consequently we had to carry everything we needed with us, and now and then we had to do some rapid improvising. It wasn't as though these theatres weren't used; most of them were busy for at least a part of each week for seven or eight months every year. It was simply that the local magnate, having put up the shell of a theatre, saw no reason to go further. It made touring adventurous, I can tell you.

"The dressing-rooms were as ill equipped as the stages. I think they were worse than those in the vaude houses I had known, because those at least were in constant use and had a frowsy life to them. In many towns there were only two washbasins backstage for a whole company, one behind a door marked M and the other behind a door marked F. These doors, through years of use, had ceased to close firmly, which at least meant that you didn't need to knock to find out if they were occupied. Sir John and Milady used small metal basins of their own, to which their dressers carried copper jugs of hot water—when there was any hot water.

"One thing that astonished me then, and still surprises me, is that the stage door, in nine towns out of ten, was up an unpaved alley, so that you had to pick your way through mud, or snow in the cold weather, to reach it. You knew where you were heading because the only light in the alley was one naked electric bulb, stuck laterally into a socket above the door, with a wire guard around it. It was not the placing of the stage door that surprised me, but the fact that, for me, that desolate and dirty entry was always cloaked in romance. I would rather go through one of those doors, even now, than walk up a garden path to be greeted by a queen."

"You were stage-struck," said Roly. "You rhapsodize. I remember those stage doors. Ghastly."

"I suppose you're right," said Magnus. "But I was very, very happy. I'd never been so well placed, or had so much fun in my life. How Macgregor and I used to labour to teach those stage-hands their job! Do you remember how, in the last act of *The Corsican Brothers*, when the Forest of Fontainebleau was supposed to be covered in snow, we used to throw down coarse salt over the stage-cloth, so that when the duel took place Sir John could kick some of it aside to get a firm footing? Can you imagine trying to explain how that salt should be placed to some boob who had laboured all day in a planing-mill, and had no flair for romance? The snow was always a problem, though you'd think that Canadians, of all people, would understand snow. At the beginning of that act the forest is supposed to be seen in that dull but magical light that goes with snow-fall. Old Boissec the wood-cutter—Grover Paskin in one of his distinguished cameos—enters singing a little song; he represents the world of everyday, drudging along regardless of the high romance which is shortly to burst upon the scene. Sir John wanted a powdering of snow to be falling as the curtain rose; just a few flakes, falling slowly so that they caught a little of the winter light. Nothing so coarse as bits of paper for us! It had to be fuller's earth, so that it would drift gently, and not be too fiercely white. Do you think we could get one of those stage-hands on the road to grasp the importance of the speed at which that snow fell, and the necessity to get it exactly right? If we left it to them they threw great handfuls of snow bang on the centre of the stage, as if some damned great turkey with diarrhoea were roosting up in a tree. So it was my job to get up on the catwalk, if there was one, and on something that had been improvised and was usually dangerous if there wasn't, and see that the snow was just as Sir John wanted it. I suppose that's being stage-struck, but it was worth every scruple of the effort it took. As I said, I'm a detail man, and without the uttermost organization of detail there is no illusion, and consequently no romance. When I was in charge of the snow the audience was put in the right mood for the duel, and for the Ghost at the end of the play."

"You really can't blame me for despising it," said Roly. "I was one of the New Men; I was committed to a theatre of ideas."

"I don't suppose I've ever had more than half a dozen ideas in my life, and even those wouldn't have much appeal for a philosopher," said Magnus. "Sir John's theatre didn't deal in ideas, but in feelings. Chivalry, and loyalty and selfless love don't rank as ideas, but it was wonderful how they seized on our audiences; they loved such things, even if they had no intention of trying them out in their own lives. No use arguing about it, really. But people used to leave our performances smiling, which isn't always the case with a theatre of ideas."

"Art as soothing syrup, in fact."

"Perhaps. But it was very good soothing syrup. We never made the mistake of thinking it was a universal panacea."

"Soothing syrup in aid of a dying colonialism."

"I expect you're right. I don't care, really. It's true we thumped the good old English drum pretty loudly, but that was one of the things the syndicate wanted. When we visited Ottawa, Sir John and Milady were the Governor General's guests at Rideau Hall."

"Yes, and what a bloody nuisance that was! Actors ought never to stay in private houses or official residences. I had to scamper out there every morning with the letters, and get my orders for the day. Run the gamut of snotty aides who never seemed to know where Lady Tresize was to be found."

"Didn't she ever tell you any stories about that? Probably not. I don't think she liked you much better than you liked her. Certainly she told me that it was like living in a very pretty little court, and that all sorts of interesting people came to call. Don't you remember that the Governor General and his suite came to *Scaramouche* one night when we were playing in the old Russell Theatre? 'God Save the King' was played after they came in, and the audience was so frozen with etiquette that nobody dared to clap until the G.G. had been seen to do so. There were people who sucked in their breath when I thumbed my nose while walking the tightrope; they thought

I was Sir John, you see, and they couldn't imagine a knight committing such an unspeakable rudery in the presence of an Earl. But Milady told me the Earl was away behind the times; he didn't know what it meant in Canadian terms, and thought it still meant something called 'fat bacon', which I suppose was Victorian. He guffawed and thumbed his nose and muttered, 'Fat bacon, what?' at the supper party afterward, at which Mr. Mackenzie King was a guest; Mr. King was so taken aback he could hardly eat his lobster. Apparently he got over it though, and Milady said she had never seen a man set about a lobster with such whole-souled enthusiasm. When he surfaced from the lobster he talked to her very seriously about dogs. Funny business, when you think of it—I mean all those grandees sitting at supper at midnight, after a play. That must have been romantic too, in its way, although there were no young people present—except the aides and one or two ladies-in-waiting, of course. In fact, I thought a lot of Canada was romantic."

"I didn't. I thought it was the rawest, roughest, crudest place I had ever set eyes on, and in the midst of that, all those vice-regal pretensions were ridiculous."

"I wonder if that's what you really thought, Roly? After all, what were you comparing it with? Norwich, and Cambridge, and a brief sniff at London. And you weren't in a condition to see anything except through the spectacles of a thwarted lover and playwright. You were being put through the mincer by the lovely Sevenhowes; you were her toy for the tour, and your agonies were the sport of her chums Charlton and Woulds. Whenever we were on one of those long train hops from city to city, we all saw it in the dining-car.

"Those dining-cars! There was romance for you! Rushing through the landscape; that fierce country north of Lake Superior, and the marvellous steppes of the prairies, in an elegant, rather too hot, curiously shaped dining-room, full of light, glittering with tablecloths and napkins so white they looked blue, shining silver (or something very close), and all those clean, courteous, friendly black waiters—if that wasn't romance you don't know the real thing when you see it! And the food! Nothing hotted up or melted out in those days, but splendid stuff that came on fresh at every big stop; cooked brilliantly in the galley by a real chef; fresh fish, tremendous meat, real fruit—don't you remember what their baked apples were like? With thick cream! Where does one get thick cream now? I remember every detail. The cube sugar was wrapped in pretty white paper with Castor printed on it, and every time we put it in our coffee I suppose we enriched our dear friend Boy Staunton, so clear in the memory of Dunny and myself, because he came from our town, though I didn't know that at the time. . . ." (My ears pricked up: I swear my scalp tingled. Magnus had mentioned Boy Staunton, the Canadian tycoon, and also my lifelong friend, whom I was pretty sure Magnus had murdered. Or, if not murdered, had given a good push on a path that looked like suicide. This was what I wanted for my document. Had Magnus, who withheld death cruelly from Willard, given it almost as a benefaction to Boy Staunton? Would his present headlong confessional mood carry him to the point where he would admit to murder, or at least give a hint that I, who knew so much but not enough, would be able to interpret? . . . But I must miss nothing, and Magnus was still rhapsodizing about C.P.R. food as once it was.) ". . . And the sauces; real sauces, made by the chef—exquisite!

"There were bottled sauces, too. Commercial stuff I learned to hate because at every meal that dreary utility actor Jim Hailey asked for Garton's; then he would wave it about saying, 'Anybody want any of the Handkerchief?' because, as he laboriously pointed out, if you spelled Garton's backward it came out Snotrag; poor Hailey was that depressing creature, a man of one joke. Only his wife laughed and blushed because he was being 'awful', and she never failed to tell him so. But I suppose you didn't see because you always tried to sit at the table with Sevenhowes and Charlton and Woulds; if she was cruel and asked Eric Foss to sit with them instead, you sat as near as you could and hankered and glowered as they laughed at jokes you couldn't hear.

"Oh, the trains, the trains! I gloried in them because with Wanless's I had done so much train travel and it was wretched. I began my train travel, you remember, in darkness and fear, hungry, with my poor little bum aching desperately. But here I was, unmistakably a first-class passenger, in the full blaze of that piercing, enveloping, cleansing Canadian light. I was quite content to sit at a table with some of the technical staff, or sometimes with old Mac and Holroyd, and now and then with that Scheherazade of the railways, Morton W. Penfold, when he was making a hop with us.

"Penfold knew all the railway staff; I think he knew all the waiters. There was one conductor we sometimes encountered on a transcontinental, who was a special delight to him, a gloomy man who carried a real railway watch—one of those gigantic nickel-plated turnips that kept very accurate time. Penfold would hail him: 'Lester, when do you think we'll be in Sault Ste. Marie?' Then Lester would pull up the watch out of the well of his waistcoat, and look sadly at it, and say, 'Six fifty-two, Mort, *if we're spared.*' He was gloomy-religious, and everything was conditional on our being spared; he didn't seem to have much confidence in either God or the C.P.R.

"Penfold knew the men on the locomotives, too, and whenever we came to a long, straight stretch of track, he would say, 'I wonder if Fred is dipping his piles.' This was because one of the oldest and best of the engineers was a martyr to haemorrhoids, and Penfold swore that whenever we came to an easy piece of track, Fred drew off some warm water from the boiler into a basin, and sat in it for a few minutes, to ease himself. Penfold never laughed; he was a man of deep, private humour, and his solemn, hypnotist's face never softened, but the liquid on his lower eyelid glittered and occasionally spilled over, and his head shook; that was his laugh.

"Now and then, on long hauls, the train carried a private car for Sir John and Milady; these luxuries could not be hired—or only by the very rich—but sometimes a magnate who owned one, or a politician who had the use of one, would put it at the disposal of the Tresizes, who had armies of friends in Canada. Sir John, and Milady especially, were not mingy about their private car, and always asked a few of the company in, and now and then, on very long hauls, they asked us all in and we had a picnic meal from the dining-car. Now surely that was romance, Roly? Or didn't you find it so? All of us perched around one of those splendid old relics, most of which had been built not later than the reign of Edward the Seventh, full of marquetry woodwork (there was usually a little plaque somewhere that told you where all the woods came from) and filigree doodads around the ceiling, and armchairs with a fringe made of velvet bobbles everywhere that fringe could be imagined.

In a sort of altar-like affair at one end of the drawing-room area were magazines in thick leather folders—and what magazines! Always *The Sketch* and *The Tatler* and *Punch* and *The Illustrated London News*—it was like a club on wheels. And lashings of drink for everybody—that was Penfold's craft at work—but it wasn't at all the thing for anybody to guzzle and get drunk, because Sir John and Milady didn't like that."

"He was a great one to talk," said Ingestree. "He could drink any amount without showing it, and it was believed everywhere that he drank a bottle of brandy a day just to keep his voice mellow."

"Believed, but simply not true. It's always believed that star actors drink heavily, or beat their wives, or deflower a virgin starlet every day to slake their lust. But Sir John drank pretty moderately. He had to. Gout. He never spoke about it, but he suffered a lot with it. I remember one of those parties when the train lurched and Felicity Larcombe stumbled and stepped on his gouty foot, and he turned dead white, but all he said was, 'Don't speak of it, my dear,' when she apologized."

"Yes, of course you'd have seen that. You saw everything. Obviously, or you couldn't tell us so much about it now. But we saw you seeing everything, you know. You weren't very good at disguising it, even if you tried. Audrey Sevenhowes and Charlton and Woulds had a name for you—the Phantom of the Opera. You were always somewhere with your back against a wall, looking intently at everything and everybody. 'There's the Phantom, at it again,' Audrey used to say. It wasn't a very nice kind of observation. It had what I can only call a wolfish quality about it, as if you were devouring everything. Especially devouring Sir John. I don't suppose he made a move without you following him with your eyes. No wonder you knew about the gout. None of the rest of us did."

"None of the rest of you cared, if you mean the little clique you travelled with. But the older members of the company knew, and certainly Morton W. Penfold knew, because it was one of his jobs to see that the same kind of special bottled water was always available for Sir John on every train and in every hotel. Gout's very serious for an actor. Any suggestion that a man who is playing the Master of Ballantrae is hobbling is bad for publicity. It was clear enough that Sir John wasn't young, but it was of the uttermost importance that on the stage he should seem young. To do that he had to be able to walk slowly; it's not too hard to seem youthful when you're leaping about the stage in a duel, but it's a very different thing to walk as slowly as he had to when he appeared as his own ghost at the end of *The Corsican Brothers*. Detail, my dear Roly; without detail there can be no illusion. And one of the odd things about Sir John's kind of illusion (and my own, when later on I became a master illusionist) is that the showiest things are quite simply arranged, but anything that looks like simplicity is extremely difficult.

"The gout wasn't precisely a secret, but it wasn't shouted from the housetops, either. Everybody knew that Sir John and Milady travelled a few fine things with them—a bronze that he particularly liked, and she always had a valuable little picture of the Virgin that she used for her private devotions, and a handsome case containing miniatures of their children—and that these things were set up in every hotel room they occupied, to give it some appearance of personal taste. But not everybody knew about the foot-bath that had to be carried for Sir John's twice-daily treatment of the gouty foot; a bathtub wouldn't do, because it was necessary that all of his body be at the temperature of the room, while the foot was in a very hot mineral solution.

"I've seen him sitting in his dressing-gown with the foot in that thing at six o'clock, and at half-past eight he was ready to step on the stage with the ease of a young man. I never thought it was the mineral bath that did the trick; I think it was more an apparatus for concentrating his will, and determination that the gout shouldn't get the better of him. If his will ever failed, he was a goner, and he knew it.

"I've often had reason to marvel at the heroism and spiritual valour that people put into causes that seem absurd to many observers. After all, would it have mattered if Sir John had thrown in the towel, admitted he was old, and retired to cherish his gout? Who would have been the loser? Who would have regretted *The Master of Ballantrae*? It's easy to say, No one at all, but I don't think that's true. You never know who is gaining strength as a result of your own bitter struggle; you never know who sees *The*

Master of Ballantrae, and quite improbably draws something from it that changes his life, or gives him a special bias for a lifetime.

"As I watched Sir John fighting against age—watched him wolfishly, I suppose Roly would say—I learned something without knowing it. Put simply it is this: no action is ever lost—nothing we do is without result. It's obvious, of course, but how many people ever really believe it, or act as if it were so?"

"You sound woefully like my dear old Mum," said Ingestree. "No good action is ever wholly lost, she would say."

"Ah, but I extend your Mum's wisdom," said Magnus. "No evil action is ever wholly lost, either."

"So you pick your way through life like a hog on ice, trying to do nothing but good actions? Oh, Magnus! What balls!"

"No, no, my dear Roly, I am not quite such a fool as that. We can't know the quality or the results of our actions except in the most limited way. All we can do is to try to be as sure as we can of what we are doing so far as it relates to ourselves. In fact, not to flail about and be the deluded victims of our passions. If you're going to do something that looks evil, don't smear it with icing and pretend it's good; just bloody well do it and keep your eyes peeled. That's all."

"You ought to publish that. *Reflections While Watching an Elderly Actor Bathing His Gouty Foot.* It might start a new vogue in morality."

"I was watching a little more than Sir John's gouty foot, I assure you. I watched him pumping up courage for Milady, who had special need of it. He wasn't a humorous man; I mean, life didn't appear to him as a succession of splendid jokes, big and small, as it did to Morton W. Penfold. Sir John's mode of perception was romantic, and romance isn't funny except in a gentle, incidental way. But on a tour like that, Sir John had to do things that had their funny side, and one of them was to make that succession of speeches, which Penfold arranged, at service clubs in the towns where we played. It was the heyday of service clubs, and they were hungrily looking for speakers, whose job it was to say something inspirational, in not more than fifteen minutes, at their weekly luncheon meetings. Sir John always cemented the bonds of the Commonwealth for them, and while he was waiting to do it they levied fines on one another for wearing loud neckties, and recited their extraordinary creeds, and sang songs they loved but which were as barbarous to him as the tribal chants of savages. So he would come back to Milady afterward, and teach her the songs, and there they would sit, in the drawing-room of some hotel suite, singing

Rotary Ann, she went out to get some clams,
Rotary Ann, she went out to get some clams,
Rotary Ann, she went out to get some clams,
But she didn't get a— —clam!

—and at the appropriate moments they would clap their hands to substitute for the forbidden words 'God-damn', which good Rotarians knew, but wouldn't utter.

"I tell you it was eerie to see those two, so English, so Victorian, so theatrical, singing those utterly uncharacteristic words in their high-bred English accents, until they were laughing like loonies. Then Sir John would say something like 'Of course one shouldn't laugh at them, Nan, because they're really splendid fellows at heart, and do marvels for crippled children—or is it tuberculosis? I can never remember.' But the important thing was that Milady had been cheered up. She never showed her failing spirits—at least she thought she didn't—but he knew. And I knew.

"It was another of those secrets like Sir John's gout, which Mac and Holroyd and some of the older members of the company were perfectly well aware of but never discussed. Milady had cataracts, and however courageously she disguised it, the visible world was getting away from her. Some of the clumsiness on stage was owing to that, and much of the remarkable lustre of her glance—that bluish lustre I had noticed the first time I saw her—was the slow veiling of her eyes. There were days that were better than others, but as each month passed the account was further on the debit side. I never heard them mention it. Why would I? Certainly I wasn't the kind of person they would have confided in. But I was often present when all three of us knew what was in the air.

"I have you to thank for that, Roly. Ordinarily it would have been the secretary who would have helped Milady when something had to be read, or written, but you were never handily by, and when you were it was so clear that you were far too busy with literary things to be just a useful pair of eyes that it would have been impertinence to interrupt you. So that job fell to me, and Milady and I made a pretence about it that was invaluable to me.

"It was that she was teaching me to speak—to speak for the stage, that's to say. I had several modes of speech; one was the tough-guy language of Willard and Charlie, and another was a half-Cockney lingo I had picked up in London; I could speak French far more correctly than English, but I had a poor voice, with a thin, nasal tone. So Milady had me read to her, and as I read she helped me to place my voice differently, breathe better, and to choose words and expressions that did not immediately mark me as an underling. Like so many people of deficient education, when I wanted to speak classy—that was what Charlie called it—I always used as many big words as I could. Big words, said Milady, were a great mistake in ordinary conversation, and she made me read the Bible to her to rid me of the big-word habit. Of course the Bible was familiar ground to me, and she noticed that when I read it I spoke better than otherwise, but as she pointed out, too fervently. That was a recollection of my father's Bible-reading voice. Milady said that with the Bible and Shakespeare it was better to be a little cool, rather than too hot; the meaning emerged more powerfully. 'Listen to Sir John,' she said, 'and you'll find that he never pushes a line as far as it will go.' That was how I learned about never doing your damnedest; your next-to-damnedest was far better.

"Sir John was her ideal, so I learned to speak like Sir John, and it was quite a long time before I got over it, if indeed I ever did completely get over it. It was a beautiful voice, and perhaps too beautiful for everybody's taste. He produced it in a special way, which I think he learned from Irving. His lower lip moved a lot, but his upper lip was almost motionless, and he never showed his upper teeth; completely loose lower jaw, lots of nasal resonance, and he usually spoke in his upper register, but sometimes he dropped into deep tones, with extraordinary effect. She insisted on careful phrasing, long breaths, and never accentuating possessive pronouns—she said that made almost anything sound petty.

"So I spent many an hour reading the Bible to her, and refreshing my memory of the Psalms. 'Consider and hear me, O Lord my God: lighten mine eyes, lest I sleep the sleep of death. Lest mine enemy say, I have prevailed against him; and those that trouble me rejoice when I am moved.' We had that almost every day. That, and 'Open thou mine eyes, that I may behold wondrous things out of thy law.' It was not long before I understood that Milady was praying, and I was helping her, and after the first surprise—I had been so long away from anybody who prayed, except for Happy Hannah, whose prayers were like curses—I was pleased and honoured to do it. But I didn't intrude upon her privacy; I was content to be a pair of eyes, and to learn to be a friendly voice. May I put in here that this was another side of apprenticeship to Sir John's egoism, and it was not something I had greedily sought. On the contrary it was something to which I seemed to be fated. If I stole something from the old man, the impulse for the theft was not wholly mine; I seemed to be pushed into it.

"One of the things that pushed me was that as Milady's sight grew dimmer, she liked to have somebody near to whom she could speak in French. As I've told you, she came from the Channel Islands, and from her name I judge that French was her cradle-tongue. So, under pretence of correcting my French pronunciation, we had many a long talk, and I read the Bible to her in French, as well as in English. That was a surprise for me! Like so many English-speaking people I could not conceive of the words of Christ in any language but my own, but as we worked through Le Nouveau Testament in her chunky old Geneva Bible, there they were, coloured quite differently. *Je suis le chemin, & la vérité, & la vie: nul ne vient au Père sinon par moi.* Sounded curiously frivolous, but nothing to *Bienheureux sont les débonnaires: car ils hériteront la terre.* I thought I concealed the surprise in my voice at that one, but Milady heard it (she heard everything) and explained that I must think of *débonnaire* as meaning *clément*, or perhaps *les doux*. But of course we all interpret Holy Writ to suit ourselves as much as we dare; I liked *les débonnaires,* because I was striving as hard as I could to be debonair myself, and I had an eye on at least a good-sized chunk of *la terre* for my inheritance. Learning to speak English and French with an upper-class accent—or at least a stage accent, which was a little more precise than merely upper class—was part of my campaign.

"As well as reading aloud, I listened to her as she rehearsed her lines. The old plays, like *The Master of Ballantrae*, were impressed on her memory forever, but she liked to go over her words for *Rosemary* and *Scaramouche* before every performance, and I read her cues for her. I learned a good deal from that, too, because she had a fine sense of comedy (something Sir John had only in a lesser degree), and I studied her manner of pointing up a line so that something more than just the joke—the juice in which the joke floated—was carried to the audience. She had a charming voice, with a laugh in it, and I noticed that clever Felicity Larcombe was learning that from her, as well as I.

"Indeed, I became a friend of Milady's, and rather less of an adorer. Except for old Zingara, who was a very different pair of shoes, she was the only woman I had ever known who seemed to like me, and think I was of any interest or value. She rubbed it into me about how lucky I was to be working with Sir John, and doing marvellous little cameos which enhanced the value of a whole production, but I had enough common sense to see that she was right, even though she exaggerated.

"One thing about me that she could not understand was that I had no knowledge of Shakespeare. None whatever. When I knew the Bible so well, how was it that I was in darkness about the other great classic of English? Had my parents never introduced me to Shakespeare? Of course Milady could have had no idea of the sort of people my parents were. I suppose my father must have heard of Shakespeare, but I am sure he rejected him as a fellow who had frittered away his time in the theatre, that Devil's domain where lies were made attractive to frivolous people.

"I have often been amazed at how well comfortable and even rich people understand the physical deprivations of the poor, without having any notion of their intellectual squalor, which is one of the things that makes them miserable. It's a squalor that is bred in the bone, and rarely can education do much to root it out if education is simply a matter of schooling. Milady had come of quite rich parents, who had daringly allowed her to go on the stage when she was no more than fourteen. In Sir Henry Irving's company, of course, which wasn't like kicking around from one stage door to another, and snatching for little jobs in pantomime. To be one of the Guvnor's people was to be one of the theatrically well-to-do, not simply in wages but in estate. And at the Lyceum she had taken in a lot of Shakespeare at the pores, and had whole plays by heart. How could anyone like that grasp the meagreness of the household in which I had been a child, and the remoteness of intellectual grace from the Deptford life? So I was a pauper in a part of life where she had always been wrapped in plenty.

"I was on friendly terms, with proper allowance for the disparity in our ages and importance to the company, by the time we had journeyed across Canada and played Vancouver over Christmas. We were playing two weeks at the Imperial; the holiday fell on the middle Sunday of our fortnight that year, and Sir John and Milady entertained the whole company to dinner at their hotel. It was the first time I had ever eaten a Christmas dinner, though during the previous twenty-three years I suppose I must have taken some sort of nourishment on the twenty-fifth of December, and it was the first time I had ever been in a private dining-room in a first-class hotel.

"It seemed elegant and splendid to me, and the surprise of the evening was that there was a Christmas gift for everybody. They were vanity things and manicure sets and scarves and whatnot for the girls, and the men had those big boxes of cigarettes that one never sees any more and notecases and all the range of impersonal but pleasant stuff you would expect. But I had a bulky parcel, and it was a complete Shakespeare—one of those copies illustrated with photographs of actors in their best roles; this one had a coloured frontispiece of Sir John as Hamlet, looking extremely like me, and across it he had written, 'A double blessing is a double grace—Christmas Greetings, John Tresize.' Everybody wanted to see it, and the company was about equally divided between those who thought Sir John was a darling to have done that for a humble member of his troupe, and those who thought I must be gaining a power that was above my station; the latter group did not say anything, but their feelings could be deduced from the perfection of their silence.

"I was in doubt about what I should do, because it was the first time in my life that anybody had ever given me anything; I had earned things, and stolen things, but I had never been given anything before and I was embarrassed, suspicious, and clumsy in my new role.

"Milady was behind it, of course, and perhaps she expected me to bury myself in the book that night, and emerge, transformed by poetry and drama, a wholly translated Mungo Fetch. The truth is that I had a nibble at it, and read a few pages of the first play in the book, which was *The Tempest*, and couldn't make head nor tail of it. There was a shipwreck, and then an old chap beefing to his daughter about some incomprehensible grievance in the past, and it was not my line at all, and I gave up.

"Milady was too well bred ever to question me about it, and when we were next alone I managed to say some words of gratitude, and I don't know whether she ever knew that Shakespeare and I had not hit it off. But the gift was very far from being a dead loss: in the first place it was a gift, and the first to come my way; in the second it was a sign of something much akin to love, even if the love went no further than the benevolence of two people with a high sense of obligation to their dependants and colleagues, down to the humblest. So the book became something more than an unreadable volume; it was a talisman, and I cherished it and gave it an importance among my belongings that was quite different from what it was meant to be. If it had been a book of spells, and I a sorcerer's apprentice who was afraid to use it, I could not have held it in greater reverence. It contained something that was of immeasurable value to the Tresizes, and I cherished it for that. I never learned anything about Shakespeare, and on the two or three occasions when I have seen Shakespearean plays in my life they have puzzled and bored me as much as *The Tempest,* but my superstitious veneration of that book has never failed, and I have it still.

"There's evidence, if you need it, that I am not really a theatre person. I am an illusionist, which is a different and probably a lesser creature. I proved it that night. After the dinner and the gifts, we had an impromptu entertainment, a very mixed bag. Audrey Sevenhowes danced the Charleston, and did it very well; C. Pengelly Spickernell sang two or three songs, vaguely related to Christmas, and Home, and England. Grover Paskin sang a comic song about an old man who had a fat sow, and we all joined in making pig-noises on cue. I did a few tricks, and was the success of the evening.

"Combined with the special gift, that put me even more to the bad with the members of the company who were always looking for hidden meanings and covert grabs for power. My top trick was when I borrowed Milady's Spanish shawl and produced from beneath it the large bouquet the company had clubbed together to give her; as I did it standing in the middle of the room, with no apparent place to conceal anything at all, not to speak of a thing the size of a rosebush, it was neatly done, but as sometimes happens with illusions, it won almost as much mistrust as applause. I know why. I had not at that time grasped the essential fact that an illusionist must never seem to be pleased with his own cleverness, and I suppose I strutted a bit. The Cantab and Sevenhowes and Charlton and Woulds sometimes spoke of me as The Outsider, and that is precisely what I was. I don't regret it now. I've lived an Outsider's life, though not in quite the way they meant; I was outside something beyond their comprehension.

"That was an ill-fated evening, as we discovered on the following day. There was champagne, and Morton W. Penfold, who was with us, gained heroic stature for finding it in what the English regarded as a desert. Everybody drank as much as they could get, and there were toasts, and these were Sir John's downfall. The Spartan regime of a gouty man was always a burden to him, and he didn't see why he should drink whisky when everybody else was drinking the wine he loved best. He proposed a toast to The Profession, and told stories about Irving; it called for several glasses, though not really a lot, and before morning he was very ill. A doctor came, and saw that there was more than gout wrong with him. It was an inflamed appendix, and it had to come out at once.

"Not a great calamity for most people, even though such an operation wasn't as simple then as it is now, but it was serious for a star actor, half-way through a long tour. He would be off the stage for not less than three weeks.

"Sir John's illness brought out the best and the worst in his company. All the old hands, and the people with a thoroughly professional attitude, rallied round at once, with all their abilities at top force. Holroyd called a rehearsal for ten o'clock Monday morning, and Gordon Barnard, who was our second lead, sailed through *Scaramouche* brilliantly; he was very different from Sir John, as a six-foot-two actor of the twentieth century must be different from a five-foot-two actor who is still in the nineteenth, but there was no worry whatever about him. Darton Flesher, who had to step into Barnard's part, needed a good deal of help, solid man though he was. But then somebody had to fill in for Flesher, and that was your friend Leonard Woulds, Roly, who proved not to know the lines which, as an understudy, he should have had cold. So it was a busy day.

"Busy for Morton W. Penfold, who had to tell the papers what had happened, and get the news on the Canadian Press wire, and generally turn a misfortune into some semblance of publicity. Busy for Felicity Larcombe, who showed herself a first-rate person as well as a first-rate actress; she undertook to keep an eye on Milady, so far as anyone could, because Milady was in a state. Busy also for Gwenda Lewis, who was a dull actress and silly about her dull husband, Jim Hailey; but Gwenda had been a nurse before she went on the stage, and she helped Felicity to keep Milady in trim to act that evening. Busy for old Frank Moore and Macgregor, who both spread calm and assurance through the company—you know how easily a company can be rattled—and lent courage where it was wanted.

"The consequence was that that night we played *Scaramouche* very well, to a capacity audience, and did excellent business until it was time for us to leave Vancouver. The only hitch, which both the papers mentioned humorously, was that when Scaramouche walked the tightrope, it looked as if Sir John had mischievously broken out of the hospital and taken the stage. But there was nothing anybody could do about that, though I did what I could by wearing my red mask.

"It seemed as though the public were determined to help us through our troubles, because we played to full houses all week. Whenever Milady made her first entrance, there was warm applause, and this was a change indeed, because usually Morton W. Penfold had to arrange for the local theatre manager to be in the house at that time to start the obligatory round when she came on. Indeed, by the end of the week, Penfold was able to circulate a funny story to the papers that Sir John had announced from his hospital bed that it was obvious that the most profitable thing a visiting star could do was to go to bed and send his understudy on in his place. Dangerous publicity, but it worked.

"So everything appeared to be in good order, except that we had to defer polishing up *The Lyons Mail*, which we had intended to put into the repertory instead of *The Corsican Brothers* for our return journey across Canada.

"Not everything was satisfactory, however, because the Sevenhowes, Charlton, and Woulds faction were making mischief. Not very serious mischief in the theatre, because Holroyd would not have put up with that, but personal mischief in the company was much more difficult to check. They tried sucking up to Gordon Barnard, who was now the leading man, telling him how much easier it was to act with him than with Sir John. Barnard wouldn't have any of that, because he was a decent fellow, and he knew his own shortcomings. One of these was that in *The Master* and *Scaramouche* we used a certain number of extras, and these inexperienced people tended to look wooden on the stage unless they were jollied, or harried, into more activity than they could generate by themselves; Sir John was an expert jollier and harrier—as I understand Irving also was—and he had his own ways of hissing remarks and encouragement to these inexperienced people that kept them up to the mark; Barnard couldn't manage it, because when he hissed the extras immediately froze in their places, and looked at him in terror. Just a question of personality, but there it was; he was a good actor, but a poor inspirer. When this happened, Charlton and Woulds laughed, sometimes so that the audience could see them, and Macgregor had to speak to them about it.

"They also made life hard for poor old C. Pengelly Spickernell, in ways that only actors understand; when they were on stage with him, they would contrive to be in his way when he had to make a move, and in a few seconds the whole stage picture was a little askew, and it looked as if it were his fault; also, in *Scaramouche*, where he played one of the Commedia dell' Arte figures, and wore a long, dragging cloak, one or other of them would contrive to be standing on the end of it when he had a move to make, pinning him to the spot; it was only necessary for them to do this two or three times to put him in terror lest it should happen every time, and he was a man with no ability to defend himself against such harassment.

"They were ugly to Gwenda Lewis, overrunning her very few cues, but Jim Hailey settled that by going to their dressing-room and talking it over with them in language he had learned when he had been in the Navy. Trivial things, but enough to make needless trouble, because a theatrical production is a mechanism of exquisitely calculated details. On tour it was useless to threaten them with dismissal, because they could not be replaced, and although there was a tariff of company fines for unprofessional conduct it was hard for Macgregor to catch them red-handed.

"Their great triumph had nothing to do with performance, but with the private life of the company. I fear this will embarrass you, Roly, but I think it has to be told. The great passion the Cantab felt for Audrey Sevenhowes was everybody's business; love and a cough cannot be hid, as the proverb says. I don't think Audrey was really an ill-disposed girl, but her temperament was that of a flirt of a special order; such girls used to be called cock-teasers; she liked to have somebody mad about her, without being obliged to do anything about it. She saw herself, I suppose, as lovely Audrey, who could not be blamed for the consequences of her fatal attraction. I am pretty sure she did not know what was going on, but Charlton and Woulds began a campaign to bring that affair to the boil; they filled the Cantab full of the notion that he must enjoy the favours of Miss Sevenhowes to the fullest—in the expression they used, he must 'tear off a branch' with Audrey—or lose all claim to manhood. This put the Cantab into a sad state of self-doubt, because he had never torn off a branch with anybody, and they assured him that he mustn't try to begin with the Sevenhowes, as he might expose himself as a novice, and become an object of ridicule. Might make a Horlicks of it, in fact. They bustled the poor boob into thinking that he must have a crash course in the arts of love, as a preparation for his great conquest; they would help him in this educational venture.

"It would have been nothing more than rather nasty joking and manipulation of a simpleton if they had kept their mouths shut, but of course that was not their way. I disliked them greatly at that time, but since then I have met many people of their kind, and I know them to be much more conceited and stupid than really cruel. They both fancied themselves as lady-killers, and such people are rarely worse than fools.

"They babbled all they were up to around the company; they chattered to Eric Foss, who was about their own age, but a different sort of chap; they let Eugene Fitzwarren in on their plan, because he looked worldly and villainous, and they were too stupid to know that he was a past president of the Anglican Stage Guild and a great worker on behalf of the Actors' Orphanage, and altogether a highly moral character. So very soon everybody in the company knew about it, and thought it a shame, but didn't know precisely what to do to stop the nonsense.

"It was agreed that there was no use talking to the Cantab, who wasn't inclined to take advice from anybody who could have given him advice worth having. It was also pretty widely felt that interfering with a young man's sexual initiation was rather an Old Aunty sort of thing to do, and that they had better let nature take its course. The Cantab must tear off a branch some time; even C. Pengelly Spickernell agreed to that; and if he was fool enough to be manipulated by a couple of cads, whose job was it to protect him?

"It became clear in the end that Mungo Fetch was elected to protect him, though only in a limited sense. —No, Roly, you can't possibly want to go to the loo again. You'd better sit down and hear this out. —The great worriers about the Cantab were Holroyd and Macgregor, and they were worrying on behalf of Sir John and Milady. Not that the Tresizes knew about the great plot to deprive the Cantab of his virginity; Sir John would have dealt with the matter summarily, but he was in hospital in Vancouver, and Milady was much bereft by his absence and telephoned to the hospital wherever we were. But Macgregor and Holroyd felt that this tasteless practical joke somehow reflected on those two, whom they admired whole-heartedly, and whose devotion to each other established a standard of sexual behaviour for the company that must be respected, if not fully maintained.

"Holroyd kept pointing out to Macgregor that the Cantab was

in a special way a charge delivered over to Sir John by his Mum, and that it was therefore incumbent on the company as a whole—or the sane part of it, he said—to watch over the Cantab while Sir John and Milady were unable to do so. Macgregor agreed, and added Calvinist embroideries to the theme; he was no great friend to sex, and I think he held it against the Creator that the race could not be continued without some recourse to it; but he felt that such recourse should be infrequent, hallowed by church and law, and divorced as far as possible from pleasure. It seems odd, looking back, that nobody felt any concern about Audrey Sevenhowes; some people assumed that she was in on the joke, and the others were confident she could take care of herself.

"Charlton and Woulds laid their plan with gloating attention to detail. Charlton explained to the Cantab, and to any man who happened to be near, that women are particularly open to seduction in the week just preceding the onset of their menstrual period; during this time, he said, they simply ravened for intercourse. Furthermore, they had to be approached in the right way; nothing coarsely direct, no grabbing at the bosom or anything of that sort, but a psychologically determined application of a particular caress; this was a firm, but not rough, placing of the hand on the waist, on the right side, just below the ribs; the hand should be as warm as possible, and this could easily be achieved by keeping it in the trousers pocket for a few moments before the approach. This was supposed to impart special, irresistible warmth to the female liver; Liesl tells me it is a very old belief."

"I think Galen mentions it," said Liesl, "and like so much of Galen, it is just silly."

"Charlton considered himself an expert at detecting the menstrual state of women, and he had had his eye on Miss Sevenhowes; she would be ripe and ready to fall when we were in Moose Jaw, and therefore the last place in which the Cantab could achieve full manhood would be Medicine Hat. He approached Morton W. Penfold for information about the altars to Aphrodite in Medicine Hat, and was informed that, so far as the advance agent knew, they were few and of a Spartan simplicity. Penfold advised against the whole plan; if that was the kind of thing they wanted, they had better put it on ice till they got to Toronto. Anyhow he wanted no part of it. But Charlton and Woulds had no inclination to let their great plan rest until after Sir John had rejoined the company, for though they mocked him, they feared him.

"They played on the only discernible weakness in the strong character of Morton W. Penfold. His whole reputation, Charlton pointed out, rested on his known ability to supply anything, arrange anything, and do anything that a visiting theatrical company might want in Canada; here they were, asking simply for an address, and he couldn't supply it. They weren't asking him to take the Cantab to a bawdy-house, wait, and escort him home again; they just wanted to know where a bawdy-house might be found. Penfold was touched in his vanity. He made some enquiries among the locomotive crew, and returned with the address of a Mrs. Quiller in Medicine Hat, who was known to have obliging nieces.

"We were playing a split week, of which Thursday, Friday, and Saturday were spent in Medicine Hat. On Thursday, with Charlton and Woulds at his elbow, the Cantab telephoned Mrs. Quiller. She had no idea what he was talking about, and anyways she never did business over the phone. Might he drop in on Friday night? It all depended; was he one of them actors? Yes, he was. Well, if he come on Friday night she supposed she'd be t'home but she made no promises. Was he comin' alone? Yes, he would be alone.

"All day Friday the Cantab looked rather green, and Charlton and Woulds stuck to him like a couple of bridesmaids, giving any advice that happened to come into their heads. At half past five Holroyd sent for me in the theatre, and I found him in the tiny stage-manager's office, with Macgregor and Morton W. Penfold. 'I suppose you know what's on tonight?' said he. '*Scaramouche*, surely?' I said. 'Don't be funny with me, boy,' said Holroyd; 'you know what I mean.' 'Yes, I think I do,' said I. 'Then I want you to watch young Ingestree after the play, and follow him, and stay as close to him as you can without being seen, and don't leave him till he's back in his hotel.' 'I don't know how I'm going to do that—' I began, but Holroyd wasn't having it. 'Yes, you do,' he said; 'there's nothing green about you, and I want you to do this for the company; nothing is to happen to that boy, do you understand?' 'But he's going with the full intention of having something happen to him,' I said; 'you don't expect me to hold off the girls with a gun, do you?' 'I just want you to see that he doesn't get robbed, or beaten up, or anything worse than what he's going for,' said Holroyd. 'Oh, Nature, Nature, what an auld bitch ye are!' said Macgregor, who was taking all this very heavily.

"I thought I had better get out before I laughed in their faces; Holroyd and Macgregor were like a couple of old maids. But Morton W. Penfold knew what was what. 'Here's ten dollars,' he said; 'I hear it's the only visiting card Old Ma Quiller understands; tell her you're there to keep an eye on young Ingestree, but you mustn't be seen; in her business I suppose she gets used to queer requests and odd provisos.' I took it, and left them, and went off for a good laugh by myself. This was my first assignment as guardian angel.

"All things considered, everything went smoothly. After the play I left Macgregor to do some of my tidy-up work himself, and followed the Cantab after he had been given a back-slapping send-off by Charlton and Woulds. He didn't walk very fast, though it was a cold January night, and Medicine Hat is a cold town. After a while he turned in to an unremarkable-looking house, and after some enquiries at the door he vanished inside. I chatted for a few minutes with an old fellow in a tuque and mackinaw who was shovelling away an evening snowfall, then I knocked at the door myself.

"Mrs. Quiller answered in person, and though she was not the first madam I had seen—now and then one of the sisterhood would appear in search of Charlie, who had a bad habit of forgetting to settle his bills—she was certainly the least remarkable. I am always amused when madams in plays and films appear as wonderful, salty characters, full of hard-won wisdom and overflowing, compassionate understanding. Damned old twisters, any I've ever seen. Mrs. Quiller might have been any suburban housewife, with a dyed perm and bifocal specs. I asked if I could speak to her privately, and waggled the ten-spot, and followed her into her living-room. I explained what I had come for, and the necessity that I was not to be seen; I was just someone who had been sent by friends of Mr. Ingestree to see that he got home safely. 'I getcha,' said Mrs. Quiller; 'the way that guy carries on, I think he needs a guardeen.'

"I settled down in the kitchen with Mrs. Quiller, and accepted a cup of tea and some soda crackers—her nightly snack, she explained—and we talked very comfortably about the theatre. After a while we were joined by the old snow-shoveller, who said nothing, and devoted himself to a stinking cigar. She was not a theatre-goer herself, Mrs. Quiller said—too busy at night for that; but she liked a good fillum. The last one she seen was *Laugh, Clown, Laugh* with Lon Chaney in it, and this girl Loretta Young. Now there was a sweet fillum, but it give you a terrible idea of the troubles of people in show business, and did I think it was true to life? I said I thought it was as true as anything dared to be, but the trials of people in the theatre were so many and harrowing that the public would never believe them if they were shown as they really were. That touched the spot with Mrs. Quiller, and we had a fine discussion about the surprises and vicissitudes life brought to just about everybody, which lasted some time.

"Then Mrs. Quiller grew restless. 'I wonder what's happened to that friend of yours,' she said; 'he's takin' an awful long time.' I wondered, too, but I thought it better not to make any guesses. It was not long till another woman came into the kitchen; I would have judged her to be in her early hard-living thirties, and she had never been a beauty; she had an unbecoming Japanese kimono clutched around her, and her feet were in slippers to which remnants of maribou still clung. She looked at me with suspicion. 'It's okay,' said Mrs. Quiller, 'this fella's the guardeen. Anything wrong, Lil?' 'Jeez, I never seen such a guy,' said Lil; 'nothin' doin' *yet*. He just lays there with the droops, laughin', and talkin'. I never heard such a guy. He keeps sayin' it's all so ridiculous, and would I believe he'd once been a member of some Marlowe Society or something. What are they, anyways? A bunch o' queers? But anyways I'm sick of it. He's ruining my self-confidence. Is Pauline in yet? Maybe she could do something with him.'

"Mrs. Quiller obviously had great qualities of generalship. She turned to me. 'Unless you got any suggestions, I'm goin' to give him the bum's rush,' she said. 'When he come in I thought, his heart's not in it. What do you say?' I said I thought she had summed up the situation perfectly. 'Then you go back up there, Lil, and tell him to come back when he feels better,' said Mrs. Quiller. 'Don't shame him none, but get rid of him. And no refund, you understand.'

"So that was how it was. Shortly afterward I crept from Mrs. Quiller's back door, and followed the desponding Cantab back to his hotel. I don't know what he told Charlton and Woulds, but they hadn't much to say to him from then on. The odd thing was that Audrey Sevenhowes was quite nice to him for the rest of the tour. Not in a teasing way—or with as little tease as she could manage—but just friendly. A curious story, but not uncommon, would you say, gentlemen?"

"I say it's time we all had a drink, and dinner," said Liesl. She took the arm of the silent Ingestree and sat him at the table beside herself, and we were all especially pleasant to him, except Magnus who, having trampled his old enemy into the dirt, seemed a happier man and, in some strange way, cleansed. It was as if he were a scorpion, which had discharged its venom, and was frisky and playful in consequence. I taxed him with it as we left the dinner table.

"How could you," I said. "Ingestree is a harmless creature, surely? He has done some good work. Many people would call him a distinguished man, and a very nice fellow."

Magnus patted my arm and laughed. It was a low laugh, and a queer one. Merlin's laugh, if ever I heard it.

7

Eisengrim was altogether in high spirits, and showed no fatigue from his afternoon's talking. He pretended to be solicitous about the rest of us, however, and particularly about Lind and Kinghovn. Did they really wish to continue with his narrative? Did they truly think what he had to say offered any helpful subtext to the film about Robert-Houdin? Indeed, as the film was now complete, of what possible use could a subtext be?

"Of the utmost possible use when next I make a film," said Jurgen Lind. "These divergences between the acceptable romance of life and the clumsily fashioned, disproportioned reality are part of my stock-in-trade. Here you have it, in your tale of Sir John's tour of Canada; he took highly burnished romance to a people whose life was lived on a different plateau, and the discomforts of his own life and the lives of his troupe were on other levels. How reconcile the three?"

"Light," said Kinghovn. "You do it with light. The romance of the plays is theatre-light; the different romance of the company is the queer train-light Magnus has described; think what could be done, with that flashing strobe-light effect you get when a train passes another and everything seems to flicker and lose substance. And the light of the Canadians would be that hard, bright light you find in northern lands. Leave it to me to handle all three lights in such a way that they are a variation on the theme of light, instead of just three kinds of light, and I'll do the trick for you, Jurgen."

"I doubt if you can do it simply in terms of appearances," said Lind.

"I didn't say you could. But you certainly can't do it without a careful attention to appearances, or you'll have no romance of any kind. Remember what Magnus says: without attention to detail you will have no illusion, and illusion's what you're aiming at, isn't it?"

"I had rather thought I was aiming at truth, or some tiny corner of it," said Lind.

"Truth!" said Kinghovn. "What kind of talk is that for a sane man? What truth have we been getting all afternoon? I don't suppose Magnus thinks he's been telling us the truth. He's giving us a mass of detail, and I don't doubt that every word he says is true in itself, but to call that truth is ridiculous even for a philosopher of film like you, Jurgen. What's he been doing to poor old Roly? He's cast him as the clown of the show—mother's boy, pompous Varsity ass, snob, and sexual nonstarter—and I'm sure it's all true, but what has it to do with our Roly? The man you and I work with and lean on? The thoroughly capable administrator, literary man, and smoother-of-the-way? Eh?"

"Thank you for these few kind words, Harry," said Ingestree. "You save me the embarrassment of saying them myself. Don't suppose I bear any malice. Indeed, if I may make a claim for my admittedly imperfect character, it is that I have never been a malicious man. I accept what Magnus says. He has described me as I no doubt appeared to him. And I haven't scrupled to let you know that so far as I was concerned he was an obnoxious little squirt and climber. That's how I would describe him if I were writing my autobiography, which I may do, one of these days. But what's an autobiography? Surely it's a romance of which one is oneself the hero. Otherwise why write the thing? Perhaps you give yourself a rather shopworn character, like Rousseau, or H. G. Wells, and it's just another way of making yourself interesting. But Mungo Fetch and the Cantab belong to the drama of the past; it's forty years since they trod the boards. We're two different people now. Magnus is a great illusionist and, as I have said time after time, a great actor: I'm what you so generously described, Harry. So let's not fuss about it."

Magnus was not satisfied. "You don't believe, then," said he, "that a man is the sum and total of all his actions, from birth to death? That's what Dunny believes, and he's our Sorgenfrei expert on metaphysics. I think that's what I believe, too. Squirt and climber; not a bad summing-up of whatever you were able to understand of me when first we met, Roly. I'm prepared to stand by it, and when your autobiography comes out I shall look for myself in the Index under S and C: 'Squirts I have known, Mungo Fetch', and 'Climbers I have encountered, Fetch, M.'. We must all play as cast, as my contract with Sir John put it. As for truth, I suppose we have to be content with the constant revisions of history. Though there is the odd inescapable fact, and I still have one or two of those to impart, if you want me to go on."

They wanted him to go on. The after-dinner cognac was on the table and I made it my job to see that everyone had enough. After all, I was paying my share of the costs, and I might as well cast myself as host, so far as lay in my power. God knows, that piece of casting would be undisputed when the bill was presented.

"As we made the return journey across Canada, a change took place in the spirit of the company," said Magnus; "going West it was all adventure and new experiences, and the country embraced us; as soon as we turned round at Vancouver it was going home, and much that was Canadian was unfavourably compared with the nests in the suburbs of London toward which many of the company were yearning. The Haileys talked even more about their son, and their grave worry that if they didn't get him into a better school he would grow up handicapped by an undesirable accent.

Charlton and Woulds were hankering for restaurants better than the places, most of them run by Chinese, we found in the West. Grover Paskin and Frank Moore talked learnedly of great pubs they knew, and of the foreign fizziness of Canadian beer. Audrey Sevenhowes, having squeezed the Cantab, threw him away and devoted herself seriously to subduing Eric Foss. During our journey West we had seen the dramatic shortening of the days which has such ominous beauty in northern countries, and which I loved; now we saw the daylight lengthen, and it seemed to be part of our homeward journey; we had gone into the darkness and now we were heading back toward the light, and every night, as we went into those queer little stage doors, the naked bulb that shone above them seemed less needful.

"The foreignness of Canada seemed to abate a little at every sunset, but it was not wholly gone. When we played Regina for a week there was one memorable night when five Blackfoot Indian chiefs, asserting their right as tribal brothers of Sir John, sat as his guests in the left-hand stage box: it was rum, I can tell you, playing *Scaramouche* with those motionless figures, all of them in blankets, watching everything with unwinking, jetty black eyes. What did they make of it? God knows. Or perhaps Sir John had some inkling, because Morton W. Penfold arranged that he should meet them in an interval, when there was an exchange of gifts, and pictures were taken. But I doubt if the French Revolution figured largely in their scheme of things. Milady said they loved oratory, and perhaps they were proud of Soksi-Poyina as he harangued the aristocrats so eloquently.

"Sir John had rejoined us by that time, and it was a shock when he appeared in our midst, for his hair had turned almost entirely grey during his time in the hospital. Perhaps he had touched it up before then, and the dye had run its course; he never attempted to return it to its original dark brown, and although the grey became him, he looked much older, and in private life he was slower and wearier. Not so on the stage. There he was as graceful and light-footed as ever, but there was something macabre about his youthfulness, in my eyes, at least. With his return the feeling of the company changed; we had supported Gordon Barnard with all our hearts, but now we felt that the ruler had returned to his kingdom;

the lamp of romance burned with a different flame—a return, perhaps, to gaslight, after some effective but comparatively charmless electricity.

"I had a feeling, too, that the critics changed their attitude toward us on the homeward journey, and it was particularly evident in Toronto. The important four were in their seats, as usual: the man who looked like Edward VII from *Saturday Night*; the stout little man, rumoured to be a Theosophist, from *The Globe*; the smiling little fellow in pince-nez from *The Telegram*; and the ravaged Norseman who wrote incomprehensible rhapsodies for *The Star*. They were friendly (except Edward VII, who was jocose about Milady), but they would persist in remembering Irving (whether they had ever actually seen him, or not), and that bothered the younger actors. Bothered Morton W. Penfold, too, who mumbled to Holroyd that perhaps the old man would be wise to think about retirement.

"The audiences came in sufficient numbers, and were warm in their applause, particularly when we played *The Lyons Mail*. It was another of the dual roles in which Sir John delighted, and so did I, because it gave me a new chance to double. If Roly had been looking for it, he would have found the seed of his Jekyll and Hyde play here, for it was a play in which, as the good Leserques, Sir John was all nobility and candour, and then, seconds later, lurched on the stage as the drunken murderer Dubosc, chewing a straw and playing with a knobbed cudgel. There was one moment in that play that never failed to chill me: it was when Dubosc had killed the driver of the mail coach, and leaned over the body, rifling the pockets; as he did it, Sir John whistled the 'Marseillaise' through his teeth, not loudly, but with such terrible high spirits that it summoned up, in a few seconds, a world of heartless, demonic criminality. But even I, enchanted as I was, could understand that this sort of thing, in this form, could not last long on the stage that Noel Coward had made his own. It was acting of a high order, but it was out of time. It still had magic here in Canada, not because the people were unsophisticated (on the whole they were as acute as English audiences in the provinces) but because, in a way I cannot explain, it was speaking to a core of loneliness and deprivation in these Canadians of which they were only faintly aware. I think it was loneliness, not just for England, because so many of these people on the prairies were not of English origin, but for some faraway and long-lost Europe. The Canadians knew themselves to be strangers in their own land, without being at home anywhere else.

"So, night by night, Canada relinquished its hold on us, and day by day we became weary, not perhaps of one another, but of our colleagues' unvarying heavy overcoats and too familiar pieces of luggage; what had been the romance of long hops going West—striking the set, seeing the trucks loaded at the theatre and unloaded onto the train, climbing aboard dead tired at three o'clock in the morning, and finding berths in the dimmed, heavily curtained sleeping-car—grew to be tedious. Another kind of excitement, the excitement of going home, possessed us, and although we were much too professional a company to get out of hand, we played with a special gloss during our final two weeks in Montreal. Then aboard ship, a farewell telegram to Sir John and Milady from Mr. Mackenzie King (who seemed to be a great friend of the theatre, though outwardly a most untheatrical man), and off to England by the first sailing after the ice was out of the harbour.

"I had changed substantially during the tour. I was learning to dress like Sir John, which was eccentric enough in a young man, but at least not vulgar in style. I was beginning to speak like him, and as is common with beginners, I was overdoing it. I was losing, ever so little, my strong sense that every man's hand was against me, and my hand against every man. I had encountered my native land again, and was reconciled to all of it except Deptford. We passed through Deptford during the latter part of our tour, on a hop between Windsor and London: I found out from the conductor of the train that we would stop to take on water for the engine there, and that the pause would be short, but sufficient for my purpose; as we chugged past the gravel pit beside the railway line I was poised on the steps at the back of the train, and as we pulled in to the station, so small and so familiar, I swung down onto the platform and surveyed all that was to be seen of the village.

"I could look down most of the length of our main street. I recognized a few buildings and saw the spires of the five churches—Baptist, Methodist, Presbyterian, Anglican, and Catholic—among the leafless trees. Solemnly, I spat. Then I went behind the train to the siding where, so many years ago, Willard had imprisoned me in Abdullah, and there I spat again. Spitting is not a ceremonious action, but I crowded it with loathing, and when I climbed back on the train I felt immeasurably better. I had not settled any scores, or altered my feelings, but I had done something of importance. Nobody knew it, but Paul Dempster had visited his childhood home. I have never returned.

"Back to England, and another long period of hand-to-mouth life for me. Sir John wanted a rest, and Milady had the long trial of waiting for her eyes to be ready for an operation—they called it 'ripening' in cases of cataracts then—and the operation itself, which was successful in that it made it possible for her to see with thick, disfiguring lenses that were a humiliation for a woman who still thought of herself as a leading actress. Macgregor decided to retire, which was reasonable but made a gap in the organization on which Sir John depended. Holroyd was a thoroughgoing pro, and could get a good job anywhere, and I think he saw farther than either Sir John or Milady, because he went to Stratford-on-Avon and stayed at the Memorial Theatre until he too retired. Nothing came of the Jekyll and Hyde play, though I know the Tresizes tinkered with the scenario for years, as an amusement. But they were comfortably off for money—rich, by some standards—and they could settle down happily in their suburban home, which had a big garden, and amuse themselves with the antiques that gave them so much delight. I visited them there often, because they kept a kind interest in me, and helped me as much as they were able. But their influence in the theatre was not great; indeed, a recommendation from them took on a queer look in the hands of a young man, because to so many of the important employers of actors in the London theatre in the mid-thirties they belonged to a remote past.

"Indeed, they never appeared at the head of a company again. Sir John had one splendid appearance in a play by a writer who had been a great figure in the theatre before and just after the First World War, but his time, too, had passed; his play suffered greatly from his own illness and some justifiable but prolonged caprice on the part of the star players. Sir John was very special in that play, and he was given fine notices by the press, but nothing could conceal the fact that he was not the undoubted star, but 'distinguished support in a role which could not have been realized with the same certainty of touch and golden splendour of personality by any other actor of our time'—so James Agate said, and everybody agreed.

"There was one very bad day toward the end of his life which, I know, opened the way for his death. In the autumn of 1937, when people were thinking of more immediately pressing things, some theatre people were thinking that the centenary of the birth of Henry Irving should not pass unnoticed. They arranged an all-star matinee, in which tribute to the great actor should be paid, and as many as possible of the great theatre folk of the day should appear in scenes selected from the famous plays of his repertoire. It should be given at his old theatre, the Lyceum, as near as possible to his birthday, which was February 6 in the following year.

"Have you ever had anything to do with such an affair? The idea is so splendid, the sentiment so admirable, that it is disillusioning to discover what a weight of tedious and seemingly unnecessary diplomacy must go into its arrangement. Getting the stars to say with certainty that they will appear is only the beginning of it; marshalling the necessary stage-settings, arranging rehearsals, and publicizing the performance, without ruinously disproportionate expense, is the bulk of the work, and I understand that an excellent committee did it with exemplary patience. But inevitably there were muddles, and in the first enthusiasm many more people were asked to appear than could possibly have been crowded on any stage, even if the matinee had been allowed to go on for six or seven hours.

"Quite reasonably, one of the first people to be asked for his services was Sir John, because he was the last actor of first-rate importance still living who had been trained under Irving. He agreed that he would be present, but then, prompted by God knows what evil spirit of vanity, he began to make conditions: he would appear, and he would speak a tribute to Irving if the Poet Laureate would write one. The committee demurred, and the Poet Laureate was not approached. So Sir John, with the bit between his teeth, approached the Poet Laureate himself, and the Poet Laureate said he would have to think about it. He thought for six weeks, and then, in response to another letter from Sir John, said he didn't see his way clear to doing it.

"Sir John communicated this news to the committee, who had meanwhile gone on with other plans, and they did not reply because, I suppose, they were up to their eyes in complicated arrangements which they had to carry through in the spare time of their busy lives. Sir John, meanwhile, urged an ancient poet of his acquaintance, who had been a very minor figure in the literary world before the First World War, to write the poetic tribute. The ancient poet, whose name was Urban Frawley, thought a villanelle would do nicely. Sir John thought something more stately was called for; his passion for playing the literary Meddlesome Mattie was aroused, and he and the ancient poet had many a happy hour, wrangling about the form the tribute should take. There was also the great question about what Sir John should wear, when delivering it. He finally decided on some robes he had worn not less than twenty-five years earlier, in a play by Maeterlinck; like everything else in his wardrobe it had been carefully stored, and when Holroyd had been summoned from Stratford to find it, it was in good condition, and needed only pressing and some loving care to make it very handsome. This valet work became my job, and in all I made three journeys to Richmond, where the Tresizes lived, to attend to it. Everything seemed to be going splendidly, and only I worried about the fact that nothing had been heard from the committee for a long time.

"There was less than a week to go before the matinee when at last I persuaded Sir John that something must be done to make sure that he had been included in the program. This was tactless, and he gave me a polite dressing-down for supposing that when Irving was being honoured, his colleagues would be so remiss as to forget Irving's unquestioned successor. I was not so confident, because since the tour I had mingled a little with theatre people, and had learned that there were other pretenders to Irving's crown, and that Sir Johnston Forbes-Robertson and Sir Frank Benson had been spoken of in this regard, and Benson was still living. I took my scolding meekly, and went right on urging him not to leave things to chance. So, rather in the spirit of the Master of Ballantrae giving orders to the pirates, he telephoned the secretary of the committee, and talked, not to him, but to his anonymous assistant.

"Sir John told him he was calling simply to say that he would be on hand for the matinee, as he had been invited to do some months before; that he would declaim the tribute to Irving which had been specially written by that favoured child of the Muses, Urban Frawley; that he would not arrive at the theatre until half past four, and he would arrive in costume, as he knew the backstage resources of the theatre would be crowded, and nothing was further from his mind than to create any difficulty by requiring the star dressing-room. All of this was delivered in the jocular but imperative mode that was his rehearsal speciality, with much 'eh' and 'quonk' to make it sound friendly. The secretary's secretary apparently gave satisfactory replies, because when Sir John had finished his call he looked at me slyly, as if I were a silly lad who didn't understand how such things were done.

"It was agreed that I should drive him to the theatre, because he might want assistance in arranging his robes, and although he had an old and trusted chauffeur, the man had no skill as a dresser. So, with lots of time to spare, I helped him into the back seat in his heavy outfit of velvet and fur, climbed into the driver's place, and off we went. It was one of those extremely class-conscious old limousines; Sir John, in the back, sat on fine whipcord, and I, in front, sat on leather that was as cold as death; we were separated by a heavy glass partition, but from time to time he spoke to me through the speaking tube, and his mood was triumphal.

"Dear old man! He was going to pay tribute to Irving, and there was nobody else in the world who could do it with a better right, or more reverent affection. It was a glory-day for him, and I was anxious that nothing should go wrong.

"As it did, of course. We pulled up at the stage door of the Lyceum, and I went in and told the attendant that Sir John had arrived. He wasn't one of your proper old stage doormen, but a young fellow who took himself very seriously, and had a sheaf of papers naming the people he was authorized to admit. No Sir John Tresize was on the list. He showed it to me, in support of his downright refusal. I protested. He stuck his head out of the door and looked at our limousine, and made off through the passage that led to the stage, and I stuck close to him. He approached an elegant figure whom I knew to be one of the most eminent of the younger actor-knights and hissed, 'There's an old geezer outside dressed as Nero who says he's to appear; will you speak to him, sir?' I intervened; 'It's Sir John Tresize,' I said, 'and it was arranged that he was to speak an Epilogue—a tribute to Irving.' The eminent actor-knight went rather pale under his make-up (he was rigged out as Hamlet) and asked for details, which I supplied. The eminent actor-knight cursed with brilliant invention for a few seconds, and beckoned me to the corridor. I went, but not before I was able to identify the sounds that were coming from the stage as a passage from *The Lyons Mail*; the rhythm, the tune of what I heard was all wrong, too colloquial, too matter-of-fact.

"We made our way back to the stage door, and the eminent actor-knight darted across the pavement, leapt into the limousine beside Sir John, and began to talk to him urgently. I would have given a great deal to hear what was said, but I could only catch scraps of it from where I sat in the driver's seat. 'Dreadful state of confusion . . . can't imagine what the organization of such an affair entails . . . would not for the world have slighted so great a man of the theatre and the most eminent successor of Irving . . . but when the proposal to the Poet Laureate fell through all communication had seemed to stop . . . nothing further had been heard . . . no, there had been no message during the past week or something would certainly have been done to alter the program . . . but as things stand . . . greatest reluctance . . . beg indulgence . . . express deepest personal regret but as you know I do not stand alone and cannot act on personal authority so late in the afternoon. . . .'

"A great deal of this; the eminent actor-knight was sweating and I could see in the rear-vision mirror that his distress was real, and his determination to stick to his guns was equally real. They were a notable study. You could do wonders with them, Harry: the young actor so vivid, the old one so silvery in the splendour of his distinction; both giving the quality of art to a common human blunder. Sir John's face was grave, but at last he reached out and patted the knee in the Hamlet tights and said, 'I won't say I understand, because I don't; still, nothing to be done now, eh?

Damned embarrassing for us both, quonk? But I think I may say a little more than just embarrassing for me.' Then Hamlet, delighted to have been let off the hook, smiled the smile of spiritual radiance for which he was famous, and did an inspired thing: he took the hand Sir John extended to him and raised it to his lips. It seemed under the circumstances precisely the right thing to do.

"Then I drove Sir John back to Richmond, and it was a slow journey, I can tell you. I hardly dared to look in the mirror, but I did twice, and both times tears were running down the old man's face. When we arrived I helped him inside and he leaned very heavily on my arm. I couldn't bear to hang around and hear what he said to Milady. Nor would they have wanted me.

"So that was how you knifed him, Roly. Don't protest. When the stage doorman showed me that list of people who were included in the performance, it was signed by you, on behalf of the eminent actor-knight. You simply didn't let that telephone message go any farther. It's a pity you couldn't have been on hand to see the scene in the limousine."

Magnus said no more, and nobody else seemed anxious to break the silence. Ingestree appeared to be thinking, and at last it was he who spoke.

"I don't see any reason now for denying what you've said. I think you have coloured it absurdly, but your facts are right. It's true I devilled for the committee about that Irving matinee; I was just getting myself established in the theatre in a serious way and it was a great opportunity for me. All the stars who formed the committee heaped work on me, and that was as it should be. I don't complain. But if you think Sir John Tresize was the only swollen ego I had to deal with, you'd better think again; I had months of tiresome negotiating to do, and because no money was changing hands I had to treat over a hundred people as if they were all stars.

"Yes, I got the call from Tresize, and it came just at the time when I was hardest pressed. Yes, I did drop it, because by that time I had been given a program for that awful afternoon that we had to stick to or else disturb I can't think how many careful arrangements. You saw one old man disappointed; I saw at least twenty. All my life I've had to arrange things, because I'm that uncommon creature, an artist with a good head for administration. One of the lessons I've learned is to give no ground to compassion, because the minute you do that a dozen people descend upon you who treat compassion as weakness, and drive you off your course without the slightest regard for what happens to you. You've told us that you apprenticed yourself to an egoism, Magnus, and so you did, and you've learned the egoism-game splendidly; but in my life I've had to learn how to deal with people like you without becoming your slave, and that's what I've done. I'm sorry if old Tresize felt badly, but on the basis of what you've told us I think everybody else here will admit that it was nobody's fault but his own."

"I don't think I'm ready to admit that," said Lind. "There is a hole in your excellent story: you didn't tell your superior about the telephone call. Surely he was the man to make final decisions?"

"There were innumerable decisions to be made. If you've ever had any experience of an all-star matinee you can guess how many. During the last week everybody was happy if a decision could be made that would stick. I don't remember the details very clearly. I acted for what seemed the best."

"Without any recollection of being told how to carry a chair, or that unfortunate reference to your father's shop, or the disappointment about Jekyll-and-Hyde in masks and meem?" said Magnus.

"What do you suppose I am? You can't really imagine I would take revenge for petty things of that sort."

"Oh yes; I can imagine it without the least difficulty."

"You're ungenerous."

"Life has made me aware of how far mean minds rely on generosity in others."

"You've always disliked me."

"You didn't like the old man."

"No. I didn't."

"Well, in my judgement at least, you killed him."

"Did I? Something had to kill him, I suppose. Something kills everybody. And when you say something you often mean somebody. Eventually something or somebody will kill us all. You're not going to back me into a corner that way."

"No, I don't think you can quite attribute Sir John's death to

Roly," said Lind. "But a not very widely understood or recognized element in life—I mean the jealousy youth feels for age—played a part in it. Have you been harbouring ill-will toward Roly all these years because of this incident? Because I really think that what Sir John was played a large part in the way he died, as is usually the case."

"Very well," said Magnus; "I'll reconsider the matter. After all, it doesn't really signify whether I think Roly killed him, or not. But Sir John and Milady were the first two people in my life I really loved, and the list isn't a long one. After the matinee Sir John wasn't himself; in a few weeks he had flu, which turned to pneumonia, and he didn't last long. I went to Richmond every day, and there was one dreadful afternoon toward the end when I went into the room where Milady was sitting; when she heard my footstep she said, 'Is that you, Jack?' and I knew she wasn't going to live long, either.

"She was wandering, of course, and as I have told you I had learned so much from Sir John that I even walked like him; it was eerie and desolating to be mistaken for him by the person who knew him best. Roly says I ate him. Rubbish! But I had done something that I don't pretend to explain, and when Milady thought he was well again, and walking as he had not walked for a year, I couldn't speak to her, or say who I was, so I crept away and came back later, making it very clear that it was Mungo Fetch who had come, and would come as long as he was wanted.

"He died, and at that time everybody was deeply concerned about the war that was so near at hand, and there were very few people at the funeral. Not Milady; she wasn't well enough to go. But Agate was there, the only time I ever saw him. And a handful of relatives were there, and I noticed them looking at me with unfriendly, sidelong glances. Then it broke on me that they thought I must be some sort of ghost from the past, and very probably an illegitimate son. I didn't approach them, because I was sure that nothing would ever make it clear to them that I was indeed a ghost, and an illegitimate son, but in a sense they would never understand.

"Milady died a few weeks later, and there were even fewer at her funeral; Macgregor and Holroyd were there, and as I stood with them nobody bothered to look twice at me. Odd: it was not until they died that I learned they were both much older than I had supposed.

"The day after we buried Milady I left England; I had wanted to do so for some time, but I didn't want to go so long as there was a chance that I could do anything for her. There was a war coming, and I had no stomach for war; the circumstances of my life had not inclined me toward patriotism. There was nothing for me to do in England. I had never gained a foothold on the stage because my abilities as an actor were not of the fashionable kind, and I had not been able to do any better with magic. I kept bread in my mouth by taking odd jobs as a magician; at Christmas I gave shows for children in the toy department of one of the big shops, but the work was hateful to me. Children are a miserable audience for magic; everybody thinks they are fond of marvels, but they are generally literal-minded little toughs who want to know how everything is done; they have not yet attained to the sophistication that takes pleasure in being deceived. The very small ones aren't so bad, but they are in a state of life where a rabbit might just as well appear out of a hat as from anywhere else; what really interests them is the rabbit. For a man of my capacities, working for children was degrading; you might just as well confront them with Menuhin playing 'Pop Goes the Weasel'. But I drew streams of half-crowns from tiny noses, and wrapped up turtles that changed into boxes of sweets in order to collect my weekly wage. Now and then I took a private engagement, but the people who employed me weren't serious about magic. It sounds odd, but I can't put it any other way; I was wasted on them and my new egoism was galled by the humiliation of the work.

"I had to live, and I understood clocks. Here again I was at a disadvantage because I had no certificate of qualification, and anyhow ordinary cleaning and regulating of wrist-watches and mediocre mantel clocks bored me. But I hung around the clock exhibition in the Victoria and Albert Museum, and worked my way into the private room of the curator of that gallery in order to ask questions, and it was not long before I had a rather irregular job there. It is never easy to find people who can be trusted with fine old pieces, because it calls for a kind of sympathy that isn't directly hitched to mechanical knowledge.

"With those old clocks you need to know not only how they work, but why they are built as they are. Every piece is individual, and something of the temperament of the maker is built into them, so the real task is to discern whatever you can of the maker's temperament and work within it, if you hope to humour his clock and persuade it to come to life again.

"In the States and Canada they talk about 'fixing' clocks; it's a bad word, because you can't just fix a clock if you hope to bring it to life. I was a reanimator of clocks, and I was particularly good at the *sonnerie*—you know, the bells and striking apparatus—which is especially hard to humour into renewed life. You've all heard old clocks that strike as if they were being managed by very old, arthritic gnomes; the notes tumble along irregularly, without any of the certainty and dignity you want from a true chime. It's a tricky thing to restore dignity to a clock that has been neglected or misused or that simply has grown old. I could do that, because I understood time.

"I mean my own time, as well as the clock's. So many workmen think in terms of their own time, on which they put a value. They will tell you it's no good monkeying with an old timepiece because the cost of the labour would run too close to the value of the clock, even when it was restored. I never cared how long a job took, and I didn't charge for my work by the hour; not because I put no value on my time but because I found that such an attitude led to hurried work, which is fatal to humouring clocks. I don't suppose I was paid as much as I could have demanded if I had charged by the hour, but I made myself invaluable, and in the end that has its price. I had a knack for the work, part of which was the understanding I acquired of old metal (which mustn't be treated as if it were modern metal), and part of which was the boundless patience and the contempt for time I had gained sitting inside Abdullah, when time had no significance.

"I suppose the greatest advantage I have had over other people who have wanted to do what I can do is that I really had no education at all, and am free of the illusions and commonplace values that education brings. I don't speak against education; for most people it is a necessity; but if you're going to be a genius you should try either to avoid education entirely, or else work hard to get rid of any you've been given. Education is for commonplace people and it fortifies their commonplaceness. Makes them useful, of course, in an ordinary sort of way.

"So I became an expert on old clocks, and I know a great many of the finest chamber clocks, and lantern clocks, and astronomical and equation clocks in the finest collections in the world, because I have rebuilt them, and tinkered them, and put infinitesimal new pieces into them (but always fashioned in old metal, or it would be cheating), and brought their chimes back to their original pride, and while I was doing that work I was as anonymous as I had been when I was inside Abdullah. I was a back-room expert who worked on clocks which the Museum undertook, as a special favour, to examine and put in order if it could be done. And when I had become invaluable I had no trouble in getting a very good letter of recommendation, to anybody whom it might concern, from the curator, who was a well-known man in his field.

"With that I set off for Switzerland, because I knew that there ought to be a job for a good clock-man there, and I was certain that when the war came Switzerland would be neutral, though probably not comfortable. I was right; there were shortages, endless problems about spies who wouldn't play their game according to the rules, bombings that were explained as accidental and perhaps were, and the uneasiness rising toward hysteria of being in the middle of a continent at war when other nations use your neutrality on the one hand, and hate you for it on the other. We were lucky to have Henri Guisan to keep us in order.

"I say 'we', though I did not become a Swiss and have never done so; theirs is not an easy club to join. I was Jules LeGrand, and a Canadian, and although that was sometimes complicated I managed to make it work.

"I presented my letter at the biggest watch and clock factories, and although I was pleasantly received I could not get a job, because I was not a Swiss, and at that time there were many foreigners who wanted jobs in important industries, and it was probable that some of them were spies. If I were going to place a spy, I would get a man who could pass for a native, and equip him with unexceptionable papers to show that he was a native; but when people are afraid of spies they do not think rationally. Still, after some patient application I wrangled an interview at the Musée d'Art et d'Histoire in Geneva, and after waiting a while Jules LeGrand found himself once more in the back room of a museum. It was there that one of the great strokes of luck in my life occurred, and most uncharacteristically it came through an act of kindness I had undertaken. There must be a soft side to my nature, and perhaps I should have trusted it more than I have done.

"I was living in a pension, the proprietor of which had a small daughter. The daughter had got herself into deep trouble because she had broken her father's walking-stick, and as the stick had been a possession of her grandfather it had something of the character of an heirloom. It was no ordinary walking-stick, but one of those joke sticks that fashionable young men used to carry—a fine Malacca cane, but with a knob on the top that did a trick. The knob of this particular specimen was of ivory, carved prettily like the head of a monkey; but when you pressed a button in its neck the monkey opened its mouth, stuck out a red tongue, and rolled its blue eyes up to heaven. The child had been warned not to play with grandfather's stick, and had predictably done so, and jammed it so that the monkey was frozen in an expression of idiocy, its tongue half out and its eyes half raised.

"The family made a great to-do, and little Rosalie was lectured and hectored and deprived of her allowance for an indefinite period, and the tragedy of the stick was brought up at every meal; everybody at the pension had ideas about either child-rearing or the mending of the stick and I became thoroughly sick of hearing about it, though not as sick as poor Rosalie, who was a nice kid, and felt like a criminal. So I offered to take it to my workroom at the Musée and do what I could. Mending old toys could not be so very different from mending old clocks, and Rosalie was growing pale, so clearly something must be done. The family had tried a few watch-repair people, but none of them wanted to be bothered with what looked like a troublesome job; it is astonishing that in a place like Geneva, which numbers watch mechanics in the thousands, there should be so few who are prepared to tackle anything old. Something new delights them, but what is old seems to clog their works. I suppose it is a matter of sympathetic approach, which was my chief stock-in-trade as a reanimator of old timepieces.

"The monkey was not really difficult, but he took time. Releasing the silver collar that kept the head in position without destroying it; removing the ivory knob without damage; penetrating the innards of the knob in such a way as to discover its secrets without wrecking them: these were troublesome tasks, but what someone has made, someone else can dismantle and make again. It proved to be a matter of an escapement device that needed replacing, and that meant making a tiny part on one of my tiny lathes from metal that would work well, but not too aggressively, with the old metal in the monkey's works. Simple, when you know how and are prepared to take several hours to do it; not simple if you are in a hurry to finish. So I did it, and restored the stick to its owner with a flowery speech in which I begged forgiveness for Rosalie, and Rosalie thought I was a marvellous man (in which she was quite correct) and a very nice man (in which I fear she was mistaken).

"The significant detail is that one evening after the museum's working day was done I was busy with the walking-stick when the curator of my department walked through the passage outside the small workshop, saw my light, and came in, like a good Swiss, to turn it off. He asked what I was doing, and when I explained he showed some interest. It was a year later that he sent for me and asked if I knew much about mechanical toys; I said I didn't, but that it would be odd if a toy were more complex than a clock. Then he said, 'Have you ever heard of Jeremias Naegeli?' and I hadn't. 'Well,' said he, 'Jeremias Naegeli is very old, very rich, and very much accustomed to having his own way. He has retired, except for retaining the chairmanship of the board of So-and-So'—and he mentioned the name of one of the biggest clock, watch, and optical equipment manufacturers in Switzerland—'and he has collected a great number of mechanical toys, all of them old and some of them unique. He wants a man to put them in order. Would you be interested in a job like that?'

"I said, 'If Jeremias Naegeli commands several thousand expert technicians, why would he want me?' 'Because his people are expected to keep on the job during wartime,' said my boss; 'it would not look well if he took a first-rate man for what might appear to be a frivolous job. He is old and he doesn't want to wait until the war is over. But if he borrows you from the museum, and you are a foreigner not engaged in war production, it's a different thing, do you understand?' I understood, and in a couple of weeks I was on my way to St. Gallen to be looked over by the imperious Jeremias Naegeli.

"It proved that he lived at some distance from St. Gallen on his estate in the mountains, and a driver was sent to take me there. That was my first sight of Sorgenfrei. As you gentlemen know, it is an impressive sight, but try to imagine how impressive it was to me, who had never been in a rich house before, to say nothing of such a gingerbread castle as that. I was frightened out of my wits. As soon as I arrived I was taken by a secretary to the great man's private room, which was called his study, but was really a huge library, dark, hot, stuffy, and smelling of leather furniture, expensive cigars, and rich man's farts. It was this expensive stench that destroyed the last of my confidence, because it was as if I had entered the den of some fearsome old animal, which was precisely what Jeremias Naegeli was. It had been many years—in Willard's time—since I had been afraid of anyone, but I was afraid of him.

"He played the role of great industrialist, contemptuous of ceremony and without an instant to spare on inferior people. 'Have you brought your tools?' was the first thing he said to me; although it was a silly question—why wouldn't I have brought my tools?—he made it sound as if I were just the sort of fellow who would have travelled across the whole of Switzerland without them. He questioned me carefully about clockwork, and that was easy because I knew more about that subject than he did; he understood principles but I don't suppose he could have made a safety-pin. Then he heaved himself out of his chair and gestured to me with his cigar to follow; he was old and very fat, and progress was slow, but we crawled back into the entrance hall, where he showed me the big clock there, which you have all seen; it has dials for everything you can think of—time at Sorgenfrei and at Greenwich, seconds, the day of the week, the date of the month, the seasons, and the signs of the zodiac, the phases of the moon, and a complex *sonnerie*. 'What's that?' he said. So I told him what it was, and how it was integrated and what metals were probably used to balance one another off with enough compensation to keep the thing from needing continual readjustment. He didn't say anything, but I knew he was pleased. 'That clock was made for my grandfather, who designed it,' he said. 'He must have been a very great technician,' I said, and that pleased him as well, as I meant it to do. Most men are much more partial to their grandfathers than to their fathers, just as they admire their grandsons but rarely their sons. Then he beckoned me to follow again, and this time we went on quite a long journey, down a flight of steps, through a long corridor, and up steps again into what I judged was another building; we had been through a tunnel.

"In a tall, sunny room in this building there was the most extraordinary collection of mechanical toys that anyone has ever seen; there can be no doubt about that, because it is now in one of the museums in Zürich, and its reputation is precisely what I have said—the most extensive and extraordinary in the world. But when I first saw it, the room looked as if all the little princes and princesses and serene highnesses in the world had been having a thoroughly destructive afternoon. Legs and arms lay about the floor, springs burst from little animals like metal guts, paint had been gashed with sharp points. It was a breathtaking scene of destruction, and as I wandered here and there looking at the little marvels and the terrible damage, I was filled with awe, because some of those things were of indisputable beauty and they had been despoiled in a fit of crazy fury.

"It was here that the old man showed the first touch of humanity I had seen in him. There were tears in his eyes. 'Can you mend this?' he asked, waving his heavy stick to encompass the room. It was not a time for hesitation. 'I don't know that I can mend it all,' I said, 'but if anybody can do it, I can. But I mustn't be pressed for time.' That fetched him. He positively smiled, and it wasn't a bad smile either. 'Then you must begin at once,' he said, 'and nobody shall ever ask you how you are getting on. But you will tell me sometimes, won't you?' And he smiled the charming smile again.

"That was how I began life at Sorgenfrei. It was odd, and I never became fully accustomed to the routine of the house. There were a good many servants, most of whom were well up in years, as otherwise they would have been called away for war work. There were also two secretaries, both invalidish young men, and the old

Direktor—which was what everybody called him—kept them busy, because he either had, or invented, a lot of business to attend to. There was another curious functionary, also unfit for military service, whose job it was to play the organ at breakfast, and play the piano at night if the old man wanted music after dinner. He was a fine musician, but he can't have been driven by ambition, or perhaps he was too ill to care. Every morning of his life, while the Direktor consumed a large breakfast, this fellow sat in the organ loft and worked his way methodically through Bach's chorales. The old man called them his prayers and he heard three a day; he consumed spiced ham and cheese and extraordinary quantities of rolls and hot breads while he was listening to Bach, and when he had finished he hauled himself up and lumbered off to his study. From that time until evening the musician sat in the secretaries' room and read, or looked out of the window and coughed softly, until it was time for him to put on his dress clothes and eat dinner with the Direktor, who would then decide if he wanted any Chopin that evening.

"We all dined with the Direktor, and with a severe lady who was the manager of his household, but we took our midday meal in another room. It was the housekeeper who told me that I must get a dinner suit, and sent me to St. Gallen to buy one. There were shortages in Switzerland, and they were reflected in the Direktor's meals, but we ate extraordinarily well, all the same.

"The Direktor was as good as his word; he never harried me about time. We had occasional conferences about things I needed, because I required seasoned metal—not new stuff—that his influence could command from the large factories in the complex of which he was the nominal ruler and undoubted financial head; I also had to have some rather odd materials to repair finishes, and as I wanted to use egg tempera I needed a certain number of eggs, which were not the easiest things to get in wartime, even in Switzerland.

"I had never dealt with an industrialist before, and I was bothered by his demand for accurate figures; when he asked me how much spring-metal of a certain width and weight I wanted I was apt to say, 'Oh, a fair-sized coil,' which tried his temper dreadfully. But after he had seen me working with it, and understood that I really knew what I was doing, he regained his calm, and may even have recognized that in the sort of job he had given me accuracy of estimate was not to be achieved in the terms he understood.

"The job was literally a mess. I set to work methodically on the first day to canvass the room, picking up everything and putting the component parts of every toy in a separate box, so far as I could identify them. It took ten days, and when I had done I estimated that of the hundred and fifty toys that had originally been on the shelves, all but twenty-one could be identified and put into some sort of renewed life. What remained looked like what is found after an aircraft disaster; legs, heads, arms, bits of mechanism and unidentifiable rubbish lay there in a jumble that made no sense, sort it how I would.

"It was a queer way to spend the worst years of the war. So far as work and the nurture of my imagination went, I was in the nineteenth century. None of the toys was earlier than 1790, and most of them belonged to the 1830s and '40s, and reflected the outlook on life of that time, and its quality of imagination—the outlook and imagination, that's to say, of the kind of people—French, Russian, Polish, German—who liked mechanical toys and could afford to buy them for themselves or their children. Essentially it was a stuffy, limited imagination.

"If I have been successful in penetrating the character of Robert-Houdin and the sort of performance he gave, it is because my work with those toys gave me the clue to it and his audience. They were people who liked imagination to be circumscribed: you were a wealthy bourgeois papa, and you wanted to give your little Clothilde a surprise on her birthday, so you went to the very best toymaker and spent a lot of money on an effigy of a little bootblack who whistled as he shined the boot he held in his hands. See Clothilde, see! How he nods his head and taps with his foot as he brushes away! How merrily he whistles 'Ach, du lieber Augustin'! Open the back of his case—carefully, my darling, better let papa do it for you—and there is the spring, which pumps the little bellows and works the little barrel-and-pin device that releases the air into the pipes that make the whistle. And these little rods and eccentric wheels make the boy polish the boot and wag his head and tap his toe. Are you not grateful to papa for this lovely surprise?

Of course you are, my darling. And now we shall put the little boy on a high shelf, and perhaps on Saturday evenings papa will make it work for you. Because we mustn't risk breaking it, must we? Not after papa spent so much money to buy it. No, we must preserve it with care, so that a century from now Herr Direktor Jeremias Naegeli will include it in his collection.

"But somebody had gone through Herr Direktor Naegeli's collection and smashed it to hell. Who could it be?

"Who could be so disrespectful of all the careful preservation, painstaking assembly, and huge amounts of money the collection represented? Who can have lost patience with the bourgeois charm of all these little people—the ballerinas who danced so delightfully to the music of the music-boxes, the little bands of Orientals who banged their cymbals and beat their drums and jingled their little hoops of bells, the little trumpeters (ten of them) who could play three different trumpet tunes, the canary that sang so prettily in its decorative cage, the mermaid who swam in what looked like real water, but was really revolving spindles of twisted glass, the little tightrope walkers, and the big cockatoo that could ruffle its feathers and give a lifelike squawk—who can have missed their charm and seen instead their awful rigidity and slavery to mechanical pattern?

"I found out who this monster was quite early in my long task. After I had sorted the debris of the collection, and set to work, I spent from six to eight hours a day sitting in that large room, with a jeweller's glass stuck in my eye, reassembling mechanisms, humouring them till they worked as they ought, and then touching up the paintwork and bits of velvet, silk, spangles, and feathers that had been damaged on the birds, the fishes, monkeys, and tiny people who gave charm to the ingenious clockwork which was the important part of them.

"I am a concentrated worker, and not easily interrupted, but I began to have a feeling that I was not alone, and that I was being watched by no friendly eye. I could not see anything in the room that would conceal a snooper, but one day I felt a watcher so close to me that I turned suddenly and saw that I was being watched through one of the big windows, and that the watcher was a very odd creature indeed—a sort of monkey, I thought, so I waved to it and grinned, as one does at monkeys. In reply the monkey jabbed a fist through the window and cursed fiercely at me in some Swiss patois that was beyond my understanding. Then it unfastened the window by reaching through the hole it had made in the glass, threw up the sash, and leapt inside.

"Its attitude was threatening, and although I saw that it was human, I continued to behave as if it were a monkey. I had known Rango pretty well in my carnival days, and I knew that with monkeys the first rule is never to show surprise or alarm; but neither can you win monkeys by kindness. The only thing to do is to keep still and quiet and be ready for anything. I spoke to it in conventional German—"

"You spoke in a vulgar Austrian lingo," said Liesl. "And you took the patronizing tone of an animal-trainer. Have you any idea what it is like to be spoken to in the way people speak to animals? A fascinating experience. Gives you quite a new feeling about animals. They don't know words, but they understand tones. The tone people usually use to animals is affectionate, but it has an undertone of 'What a fool you are!' I suppose an animal has to make up its mind whether it will put up with that nonsense for the food and shelter that goes with it, or show the speaker who's boss. That's what I did. Really Magnus, if you could have seen yourself at that moment! A pretty, self-assured little manikin, watching to see which way I'd jump. And I did jump. Right on top of you, and rolled you on the floor. I didn't mean to do you any harm, but I couldn't resist rumpling you up a bit."

"You bit me," said Magnus.

"A nip."

"How was I to know it was only meant to be a nip?"

"You weren't. But did you have to hit me on the head with the handle of a screwdriver?"

"Yes, I did. Not that it had much effect."

"You couldn't know that the most ineffective thing you could do to me was to hit me on the head."

"Liesl, you would have frightened St. George *and* his dragon. If you wanted gallantry you shouldn't have hit me and squeezed me and banged my head on the floor as you did. So far as I knew I was fighting for my life. And don't pretend now that you meant it just as a romp. You were out to kill. I could smell it on your breath."

"I could certainly have killed you. Who knew or cared that you were at Sorgenfrei, mending those ridiculous toys? In wartime who would have troubled to trace one insignificant little mechanic, travelling on a crooked passport, who happened to vanish? My grandfather would have been angry, but he would have had to hush the thing up somehow. He couldn't hand his granddaughter over to the police. The old man loved me, you know. If he hadn't, he would probably have killed me or banished me after I smashed up his collection of toys."

"And why did you smash them?" said Lind.

"Pure bloody-mindedness. For which I had good cause. You have heard what Magnus says: I looked like an ape. I still look like an ape, but I have made my apishness serve me and now it doesn't really matter. But it mattered then, more than anything else in the world, to me. It mattered more than the European War, more than anybody's happiness. I was so full of spleen I could have killed Magnus, and enjoyed it, and then told my grandfather to cope with the situation, and enjoyed that. And he would have done it.

"You'd better let me tell you about it, before Magnus rushes on and puts the whole thing in his own particular light. My life was pretty much that of any lucky rich child until I was fourteen. The only thing that was in the least unusual was that my parents—my father was Jeremias Naegeli's only son—were killed in a motor accident when I was eleven. My grandfather took me on, and was as kind to me as he knew how to be. He was like the bourgeois papa that Magnus described giving the mechanical toy to little Clothilde; my grandfather belonged to an era when the attitude toward children was that they were all right as long as they were loved and happy, and their happiness was obviously the same as that of their guardians. It works pretty well when nothing disturbs the pattern, but when I was fourteen something very disturbing happened in my pattern.

"It was the beginning of puberty, and I knew all about that because my grandfather was enlightened and I was given good, if rather Calvinist, instruction by a woman doctor. So when I began to grow rather fast I didn't pay much attention until it seemed that the growth was too much for me and I began to have fainting fits. The woman doctor appeared again and was alarmed. Then began a wretched period of hospitals and tests and consultations and head-shakings and discussions in which I was not included, and after all that a horrible time when I was taken to Zürich three times a week for treatment with a large ray-machine. The treatments were nauseating and depressing, and I was wretched because I supposed I had cancer, and asked the woman doctor about it. No, not cancer. What, then? Some difficulty with the growing process, which the ray treatment was designed to arrest.

"I won't bore you with it all. The disease was a rare one, but not so rare they didn't have some ideas about it, and Grandfather made sure that everything was done that anyone could do. The doctors were delighted. They did indeed control my growth, which made them as happy as could be, because it proved something. They explained to me, as if it were the most wonderful Christmas gift any girl ever had, that if they had not been able to do wonders with their rays and drugs I would have been a giant. Think of it, they said; you might have been eight feet tall, but we have been able to halt you at five foot eleven inches, which is not impossibly tall for a woman. You are a very lucky young lady. Unless, of course, there is a recurrence of the trouble, for which we shall keep the most vigilant watch. You may regard yourself as cured.

"There were, of course, a few side effects. One cannot hope to escape such an experience wholly unscathed. The side effects were that I had huge feet and hands, a disfiguring thickening of the skull and jaw, and surely one of the ugliest faces anyone has ever seen. But wasn't I lucky not to be a giant, as well?

"I was so perverse as not to be grateful for my luck. Not to be a giant, at the cost of looking like an ape, didn't seem to me to be the greatest good luck. Surely Fortune had something in her basket a little better than that? I raved and I raged, and I made everybody as miserable as I could. My grandfather didn't know what to do. Zürich was full of psychiatrists but my grandfather belonged to a pre-psychiatric age. He sent for a bishop, a good Lutheran bishop, who was a very nice man but I demolished him quickly; all his talk about resignation, recognition of the worse fate of scores of poor creatures in the Zürich hospitals, the necessity to humble oneself before the inscrutable mystery of God's will, sounded to me like mockery. There sat the bishop, with his snowy hair smelling of expensive cologne and his lovely white hands moulding invisible loaves of bread in the air before him, and there sat I, hideous and destroyed in mind, listening to him prate about resignation. He suggested that we pray, and knelt with his face in the seat of his chair. I gave him such a kick in the arse that he limped for a week, and rushed off to my own quarters.

"There was worse to come. With the thickening of the bones of my head there had been trouble with my organs of speech, and there seemed to be nothing that could be done about that. My voice became hoarse, and as my tongue thickened I found speech more and more difficult, until I could only utter in a gruff tone that sounded to me like the bark of a dog. That was the worst. To be hideous was humiliating and ruinous to my spirit, but to sound as I did threatened my reason. What was I to do? I was young and very strong, and I could rage and destroy. So that is what I did.

"It had all taken a long time, and when Magnus first saw me at the window of his workroom I was seventeen. I had gone on the rampage one day, and wrecked Grandfather's collection of toys. It was usually kept locked up but I knew how to get to it. Why did I do it? To hurt the old man. Why did I want to hurt the old man? Because he was at hand, and the pity I saw in his eyes when he came to see me—I kept away from the life in the house—made me hate him. Who was he, so old, so near death, so capable of living the life he liked, to pity me? If Fate had a blow, why didn't Fate strike him? He would not have had to endure it long. But I might easily live to be as old as he, trapped in my ugliness for sixty years. So I smashed his toys. Do you know, he never said a word of reproach? In the kind of world the bishop inhabited his forbearance would have melted my heart and brought me to a better frame of mind. But misfortune had scorched all the easy Christianity out of me, and I despised him all the more for his compassion, and wondered where I could attack him next.

"I knew Grandfather had brought someone to Sorgenfrei to mend the toys, and I wanted to see who it was. There was not much fun to be got out of the secretaries, and I had exhausted the possibilities of tormenting Hofstätter, the musician; he was poor game, and wept easily, the feeble schlemiel. I had spied on Magnus for quite a time before he discovered me; looking in the windows of his workroom meant climbing along a narrow ledge some distance above ground and as I looked like an ape I thought I might as well behave like one. So I used to creep along the ledge, and watch the terribly neat, debonair little fellow bent over his workbench, tinkering endlessly with bits of spring and tiny wires, and filing patiently at the cogs of little wheels. He always had his jeweller's glass stuck in one eye, and a beautifully fresh long white coat, and he never sat down without tugging his trousers gently upward to preserve their crease. He was handsome, too, in a romantic, nineteenth-century way that went beautifully with the little automata he was repairing.

"Before my trouble I had loved to go to the opera, and *Contes d'Hoffmann* was one of my favourites; the scene in Magnus's workroom always reminded me of the mechanical doll, Olympia, in *Hoffmann*, though he was not a bit like the grotesque old men who quarrelled over Olympia. So there it was, Hoffmann inside the window and outside, what? The only person in opera I resembled at all was Kundry, the monstrous woman in *Parsifal*, and Kundry always seemed to be striving to do good and be redeemed. I didn't want to do good and had no interest in being redeemed.

"I read a good deal and my favourite book at that time was Spengler's *Der Untergang des Abendlandes*—I was not a stupid girl, you understand—and from it I had drawn a mishmash of notions which tended to support whatever I felt like doing, especially when I wanted to be destructive. Most adolescents are destructive, I suppose, but the worst are certainly those who justify what they do with a half-baked understanding of somebody's philosophy. It was under the banner of Spengler, then, that I decided to surprise Magnus and rough him up a bit. He looked easy. A man who worried so much in private about the crease of his trousers was sure to be a poor fighter.

"The surprise was mine. I was bigger and stronger but I hadn't had his experience in carnival fights and flophouses. He soon found out that hitting me on the head was no good, and hit me a most terrible blow in the diaphragm that knocked out all my breath.

Then he bent one of my legs backward and sat on me. That was when we had our first conversation.

"It was long, and I soon discovered that he spoke my language. I don't mean German; I had to teach him proper German later. I mean that he asked intelligent questions and expected sensible answers. He was also extremely rude. I told you I had a hoarse, thick voice, and he had trouble understanding me in French and English. 'Can't you speak better than that?' he demanded, and when I said I couldn't he simply said, 'You're not trying; you're making the worst of it in order to seem horrible. You're not horrible, you're just stupid. So cut it out.'

"Nobody had ever talked to me like that. I was the Naegeli heiress, and I was extremely unfortunate; I was used to deference, and people putting up with whatever I chose to give them. Here was little Herr Trousers-Crease, who spoke elegant English and nice clean French and barnyard German, cheeking me about the way I spoke. And laying down the law and making conditions! 'If you want to come here and watch me work you must behave yourself. You should be ashamed, smashing up all these pretty things! Have you no respect for the past? Look at this: a monkey orchestra of twenty pieces and a conductor, and you've reduced it to a boxful of scraps. I've got to mend it, and it won't take less than four to six months of patient, extremely skilled work before the monkeys can play their six little tunes again. And all because of you! Your grandfather ought to tie you to the weathervane and leave you on the roof to die!'

"Well, it was a change from the bishop and my grandfather's tears. Of course I knew it was bluff. He may have hoped to shame me, but I think he was cleverer than that. All he was doing was serving notice on me that he would not put up with any nonsense; he knew I was beyond shame. But it was a change. And I began, just a little, to like him. Little Herr Trousers-Crease had quality, and an egoism that was a match for my own.

"Now—am I to go on? If there is to be any more of this I think I should be the one to speak. But is this confessional evening to know no bounds?"

"I think you'd better go ahead, Liesl," said I. "You've always been a great one to urge other people to tell their most intimate secrets. It's hardly fair if you refuse to do so."

"Ah, yes, but dear Ramsay, what follows isn't a tale of scandal, and it isn't really a love-story. Will it be of any interest? We must not forget that this is supposed to provide a subtext for Magnus's film about Robert-Houdin. What is the real story of the making of a great conjuror as opposed to Robert-Houdin's memoirs, which we are pretty much agreed are a bourgeois fake? I don't in the least mind telling my side of the story, if it's of any interest to the film-makers. What's the decision?"

"The decision is that you go on," said Kinghovn. "You have paused simply to make yourself interesting, as women do. No—that's unjust. Eisengrim has been doing the same thing all day. But go on."

"Very well, Harry, I shall go on. But there won't be much for you in what I have to tell, because this part of the story could not be realized in visual terms, even by you. What happened was that I came more and more to the workroom where little Herr Trousers-Crease was mending Grandfather's automata, and I fell under the enchantment of what he was able to do. He has told you that he humoured those little creatures back into life, but you would have to see him at work to get any kind of understanding of what it meant, because only part of it was mechanical. I suppose one of Grandfather's master technicians—one of the men who make those marvellous chronometers that are given to millionaires by their wives, and which never vary from strict time by more than a second every year—could have mended all those little figures so that they worked, but only Magnus could have read, in a cardboard box full of parts, the secret of the tiny performance that the completed figure was meant to give. When he had finished one of his repair jobs, the little bootblack did not simply brisk away at his little boot with his miniature brush, and whistle and tap his foot: he seemed to live, to have a true quality of being as though when you had turned your back he would leap up from his box and dance a jig, or run off for a pot of beer. You know what those automata are like: there is something distasteful about their rattling merriment; but Magnus made them *act*—they gave a little performance. I had seen them before I broke them, and I swear that when Magnus had remade them they were better than they had ever been.

"Was little Herr Trousers-Crease a very great watchmaker's mechanic, then? No, something far beyond that. There must have been in him some special quality that made it worth his while to invest these creatures of metal with so much vitality and charm of action. Roly has talked about his wolfishness; that was part of it, because with that wolfishness went an intensity of imagination and vision. The wolfishness meant only that he never questioned the overmastering importance of what he—whoever and whatever he was—might be doing. But the artistry was of a rare kind, and little by little I began to understand what it was. I found it in Spengler.

"You have read Spengler? No: it is not so fashionable as it once was. But Spengler talks a great deal about what he calls the Magian World View, which he says we have lost, but which was part of the *Weltanschauung*—you know, the world outlook—of the Middle Ages. It was a sense of the unfathomable wonder of the invisible world that existed side by side with a hard recognition of the roughness and cruelty and day-to-day demands of the tangible world. It was a readiness to see demons where nowadays we see neuroses, and to see the hand of a guardian angel in what we are apt to shrug off ungratefully as a stroke of luck. It was religion, but a religion with a thousand gods, none of them all-powerful and most of them ambiguous in their attitude toward man. It was poetry and wonder which might reveal themselves in the dunghill, and it was an understanding of the dunghill that lurks in poetry and wonder. It was a sense of living in what Spengler called a quivering cavern-light which is always in danger of being swallowed up in the surrounding, impenetrable darkness.

"This was what Herr Trousers-Crease seemed to have, and what made him ready to spend his time on work that would have maddened a man of modern education and modern sensibility. We have paid a terrible price for our education, such as it is. The Magian World View, in so far as it exists, has taken flight into science, and only the great scientists have it or understand where it leads; the lesser ones are merely clockmakers of a larger growth, just as so many of our humanist scholars are just cud-chewers or system-grinders. We have educated ourselves into a world from which wonder, and the fear and dread and splendour and freedom of wonder have been banished. Of course wonder is costly. You couldn't incorporate it into a modern state, because it is the antithesis of the anxiously worshipped security which is what a modern state is asked to give. Wonder is marvellous but it is also cruel, cruel, cruel. It is undemocratic, discriminatory, and pitiless.

"Yet here it was, in this most unexpected place, and when I had found it I apprenticed myself to it. Literally, for I begged Herr Trousers-Crease to teach me what he knew, and even with my huge hands I gained skill, because I had a great master. And that means very often an exacting, hot-tempered, and impatient master, because whatever my great countrymen Pestalozzi and Froebel may have said about the education of commonplace people, great things are not taught by blancmange methods. What great thing was I learning? The management of clockwork? No; any great craft tends at last toward the condition of a philosophy, and I was moving through clockwork to the Magian World View.

"Of course it took time. My grandfather was delighted, for what he saw was that his intractable, hideous granddaughter was quietly engaged in helping to repair what she had destroyed. He also saw that I improved physically, because my agony over my sickness had been terribly destructive; physically I had become slouching and simian, and as Magnus saw at once, I made my speech trouble far worse than it was, to spite myself and the world. Magnus helped me with that. Re-taught me, indeed, because he would not tolerate my uncouth mutterings, and gave me some sharp and demanding instruction in the manner of speech he had learned from Lady Tresize. And I learned. It was a case of learn to speak properly or get out of the workroom, and I wanted to stay.

"We were an odd pair, certainly. I knew about the Magian World View, and recognized it in my teacher. He knew nothing of it, because he knew nothing else: it was so much in the grain of the life he had lived, so much a part of him, that he didn't understand that everybody else didn't think—no, not think, feel—as he did. I would not for the world have attempted to explain it to him, because that would have endangered it. His was not the kind of mind that is happy with explanations and theories. In the common sense of the expression, he had no brains at all, and hasn't to this day. What does it matter? I have brains for him.

"As his pupil, is it strange that I should fall in love with him? I was young and healthy, and hideous though I was, I had my yearnings—perhaps exaggerated by the unlikelihood that they could find satisfaction. How was I to make him love me? Well, I began, as all the beginners in love do, with the crazy notion that if I loved him enough he must necessarily respond. How could he ignore the devotion I offered? Pooh! He didn't notice at all. I worked like a slave, but that was no more than he expected. I made little gestures, gave him little gifts, tried to make myself fascinating—and that was uphill work, let me assure you. Not that he showed distaste for me. After all, he was a carnival man, and had grown used to grotesques. He simply didn't think of me as a woman.

"At least, that is how I explained it to myself, and I made myself thoroughly miserable about it. At last, one day, when he spoke to me impatiently and harshly, I wept. I suppose I looked dreadful, and he became even more rough. So I seized him, and demanded that he treat me as a human creature and not simply as a handy assistant, and blubbered out that I loved him. I did all the youthful things: I told him that I knew it was impossible that he should love me, because I was so ugly, but that I wanted some sort of human feeling from him.

"To my delight he took me quite seriously. We sat down at the workbench, and settled to a tedious task that needed some attention, but not too much, and he told me about Willard, and his childhood, and said that he did not think that love in the usual sense was for him, because he had experienced it as a form of suffering and humiliation—a parody of sex—and he could not persuade himself to do to anyone else what had been done to him in a perverse and terrifying mode.

"This was going too fast for me. Of course I wanted sexual experience, but first of all I wanted tenderness. Under my terrible appearance—I read a lot of old legends and I thought of myself as the Loathly Maiden in the Arthurian stories—I was still an upper-class Swiss girl of gentle breeding, and I thought of sexual intercourse as a splendid goal to be achieved, after a lot of pleasant things along the way. And being a sensible girl, under all the outward trouble and psychological muddle, I said so. That led to an even greater surprise.

"He told me that he had once been in love with a woman, who had died, and that he could not feel for anyone else as he had felt for her. Romance! I rose to it like a trout to a fly. But I wanted to know more, and the more I heard the better it was. Titled lady of extraordinary charm, understanding, and gentleness. All this was to the good. But then the story began to slide sidewise into farce, as it seemed to me. The lady was not young; indeed, as I probed, it came out that she had been over sixty when he first met her. There had been no tender passages between them, because he respected her too much, but he had been privileged to read the Bible to her. It was at this point I laughed.

"Magnus was furious. The more he stormed the more I laughed, and I am sorry to say that the more I laughed the more I jeered at him. I was young, and the young can be horribly coarse about love that is not of their kind. From buggery to selfless, knightly adoration at one splendid leap! I made a lot of it, and hooted with mirth.

"I deserved to be slapped, and I was slapped. I hit back, and we fought, and rolled on the floor and slugged each other. But of course everyone knows that you should never fight with women if you want to punish them; the physical contact leads to other matters, and it did. I was not ready for sexual intercourse so soon, and Magnus did not want it, but it happened all the same. It was the first time for both of us, and it is a wonder we managed at all. It is like painting in water-colours, you know; it looks easy but it isn't. Real command only comes with experience. We were both astonished and cross. I thought I had been raped; Magnus thought he had been unfaithful to his real love. It looked like a deadlock.

"It wasn't, however. We did it lots of times after that—I mean, in the weeks that followed—and the habit is addictive, as you all know, and very agreeable, if not really the be-all and end-all and cure-all that stupid people pretend. It was good for me. I became quite smart, in so far as my appearance allowed, and paid attention to my hair, which as you see is very good. My grandfather was transported, because I began to eat at the family table again, and when he had guests I could be so charming that they almost forgot how I looked. The Herr Direktor's granddaughter Fräulein Orang-Outang, so charming and witty, though it is doubtful if even the old man's money will find her a husband.

"I am sure Grandfather knew I was sleeping with Magnus, and it must have given him severe Calvinist twinges, but he did not become a great industrialist by being a fool; he weighed the circumstances and was pleased by the obvious balance on the credit side. I think he would have consented to marriage if Magnus had mentioned it. But of course he didn't.

"Nor would I have urged it. The more intimate we became, the more I knew that we were destined to be very great friends, and probably frequent bed-mates, but certainly not a happy bourgeois married couple. For a time I called Magnus Tiresias, because like that wonderful old creature he had been for seven years a woman, and had gained strange wisdom and insight thereby. I thought of him sometimes as Galahad, because of his knightly obsession with the woman we now know as Milady, but I never called him that to his face, because I had done with mocking at his chivalry. I have never understood chivalry, but I have learned to keep my mouth shut about it."

"It's a man's thing," said I; "and I think we have seen the last of it for a while on this earth. It can't live in a world of liberated women, and perhaps the liberation of women is worth the price it is certain to cost. But chivalry won't die easily or unnoticed; banish chivalry from the world and you snap the mainspring of many lives."

"Good, grey old Ramsay," said Liesl, reaching over to pat my hand; "always gravely regretting, always looking wistfully backward."

"You're both wrong," said Magnus. "I don't think chivalry belongs to the past; it's part of that World View Liesl talks so much about, and that she thinks I possess but don't understand. What captured my faith and loyalty about Milady had just as much to do with Sir John. He was that rare creature, the Man of One Woman. He loved Milady young and he loved her old and much of her greatness was the creation of his love. To hear people talk and to look at the stuff they read and see in the theatre and the films, you'd think the true man was the man of many women, and the more women, the more masculine the man. Don Juan is the ideal. An unattainable ideal for most men, because of the leisure and money it takes to devote yourself to a life of womanizing—not to speak of the relentless energy, the unappeasable lust, and the sheer woodpecker-like vitality of the sexual organ that such a life demands. Unattainable, yes, but thousands of men have a dab at it, and in their old age they count their handful of successes like rosary beads. But the Man of One Woman is very rare. He needs resources of spirit and psychological virtuosity beyond the common, and he needs luck, too, because the Man of One Woman must find a woman of extraordinary quality. The Man of One Woman was the character Sir John played on the stage, and it was the character he played in life, too.

"I envied him, and I cherished the splendour those two had created. If, by any inconceivable chance, Milady had shown any sexual affection for me, I should have been shocked, and I would have rebuked her. But she didn't, of course, and I simply warmed myself at their fire, and by God I needed warmth. I once had a hope that I might have found something of the sort for myself, with you, Liesl, but my luck was not to run in that direction. I would have been very happy to be a Man of One Woman, but that wasn't your way, nor was it mine. I couldn't forget Milady."

"No, no; we went our ways," said Liesl. "And you know you were never much of a lover, Magnus. What does that matter? You were a great magician, and has any great magician ever been a great lover? Look at Merlin: his only false step was when he fell in love and ended up imprisoned in a tree for his pains. Look at poor old Klingsor: he could create gardens full of desirable women, but he had been castrated with a magic spear. You've been happy with your magic. And when I gained enough confidence to go out into the world again, I was happy in a casual, physical way with quite a few people, and some of the best of them were of my own sex."

"Yes, indeed," said Magnus. "Who snatched the Beautiful Faustina from under my very nose?"

"Oh, Faustina, Faustina, you always bring her up when you feel a grievance. You must understand, gentlemen, that when my grandfather died, and I was heir to a large fortune, Magnus and I realized a great ambition we had in common; we set up a magic show, which developed and gained sophistication and gloss until it became the famous *Soirée of Illusions*. It takes money to get one of those things on its feet, as you well know, but when it is established it can be very profitable.

"You can't have a magic show without a few beautiful girls to be sawn in two, or beheaded, or whisked about in space. Sex has its place in magic, even if it is not the foremost place. As ours was the best show in existence, or sought to become the best, we had to have some girls better than the pretty numskulls who are content to take simple jobs in which they are no more than living stage properties.

"I found one in Peru, a great beauty indeed but not far evolved in the European sense; a lovely animal. I bought her, to be frank. You can still buy people, you know, if you understand how to go about it. You don't go to a peasant father and say, 'Sell me your daughter'; you say, 'I can open up a splendid future for your daughter, that will make her a rich lady with many pairs of shoes, and as I realize you need her to work at home, I hope you won't be offended if I offer you five hundred American dollars to recompense you for the loss.' He isn't offended; not in the least. And you make sure he puts his mark on an official-looking piece of paper that apprentices the girl to you, to learn a trade—in this case the trade of sempstress, because actress has a bad sound if there is any trouble. And there you are. You wash the girl, teach her to stand still on stage and do what she is told, and you clout her over the ear if she is troublesome. Quite soon she thinks she is a great deal more important than she really is, but that can be endured.

"Faustina was a thrill on the stage, because she really was stunningly beautiful, and for a while it seemed to be good business to let curious people think she was Magnus's mistress; only a few rather perceptive people know that great magicians, as opposed to ham conjurors, don't have mistresses. In reality, Faustina was my mistress, but we kept that quiet, in case some clamorous moralist should make a fuss about it. In Latin America, in particular, the clergy are pernickety about such things. You remember Faustina, Ramsay? I recall you had a wintry yearning toward her yourself."

"Don't be disagreeable, Liesl," I said. "You know who destroyed that."

"Destroyed it, certainly, and greatly enriched you in the process," said Liesl, and touched me gently with one of her enormous hands. "So there you have it, gentlemen," she continued. "Now you know everything, it seems to me."

"Not everything," said Ingestree. "The name, Magnus Eisengrim—whose inspiration was that?"

"Mine," said Liesl. "Did I tell you I took my degree at the University of Zürich? Yes, in the faculty of philosophy where I leaned toward what used to be called philology—quite a Teutonic speciality. So of course I was acquainted with the great beast-legends of Europe, and in Reynard the Fox, you know, there is the great wolf Eisengrim, whom everyone fears, but who is not such a bad fellow, really. Just the name for a magician, don't you think?"

"And your name," said Lind. "Liselotte Vitzlipützli? You were always named on the programs as Theatre Autocrat—Liselotte Vitzlipützli."

"Ah, yes. Somebody has to be an autocrat in an affair of that kind, and it sounds better and is more frank than simply Manager. Anyhow, I wasn't quite a manager: I was the boss. It was my money, you see. But I knew my place. Manager I might be, but without Magnus Eisengrim I was nothing. Consequently—Vitzlipützli. You understand?"

"No, gnädiges Fräulein, I do not understand," said Lind, "and you know I do not understand. What I am beginning to understand is that you are capable of giving your colleagues Eisengrim and Ramsay a thoroughly difficult time when it is your whim. So again—Vitzlipützli?"

"Dear, dear, how ignorant people are in this supposedly brilliant modern world," said Liesl. "You surely know *Faust*? Not Goethe's *Faust*, of course; every Teuton has that by heart—both parts of it—but the old German play on which he based his poem. Look among the characters there, and you will find that the least of the demons attending on the great magician is Vitzlipützli. So that was the name I chose. A delicate compliment to Magnus. It takes a little of the sting out of the word Autocrat.

"But an autocrat is what I must be now. Gentlemen, we have talked for a long time, and I hope we have given you your subtext. You have seen what a gulf lies between the reality of a magician with the Magian World View and such a pack of lies as Robert-Houdin's bland, bourgeois memoirs. You have seen, too, what a distance there is between the pack of lies Ramsay wrote so artfully as a commercial life of our dear Eisengrim, and the sad little boy from Deptford. And now, we must travel tomorrow, and I must pack my two old gentlemen off to their beds, or they will not be happy for the plane. So it is time to say good night."

Profuse thanks for hospitality, for the conversation, for the pleasure of working together on the film *Un Hommage à Robert-Houdin*, from Lind. A rather curious exchange of friendly words and handshakes between Eisengrim and Roland Ingestree. The business of waking Kinghovn from a drunken stupor, of getting him to understand that he must not have another brandy before going home. And then, at last, we three were by ourselves.

"Strange to spend so many hours answering questions," said Liesl.

"Strange, and disagreeable," said Eisengrim.

"Strange what questions went unasked and unanswered," said I.

"Such as—?" said Liesl.

"Such as 'Who killed Boy Staunton?' " said I.

·III·

Le Lit de Justice

1

"You know the police in Toronto are still not satisfied that you told them all you know about Staunton's death?"

"I told them all I thought proper."

"Which wasn't everything?"

"Certainly not. The police must work with facts, not fancies and suppositions. The facts were simple. I met him, for the first time in my life, when I visited you at your school in Toronto on the night of November 3, 1968; we went to your room and had a talk that lasted less than an hour. I accepted his offer to drive me back to my hotel. We chatted for a time, because we were both Deptford boys. I last saw him as he drove away from the hotel door."

"Yes. And he was found less than three hours later in the harbour, into which he appeared to have driven in his powerful car, and when the police recovered the body they found a stone in his mouth."

"So I understand."

"If that had been all there was to it, would the police still be wondering about you?"

"No indeed."

"It was my fault," said Liesl. "If I had been more discreet, the police would have been satisfied with what Magnus told them. But one has one's pride as an artist, you know, and when I was asked a question I thought I could answer effectively I did so, and then the fat was in the fire."

Would anyone who saw us at this moment have thought we were talking about murder? I was convinced that Magnus had murdered Staunton, and with reason. Was not Staunton the initiator of most of what we had heard in the subtext of the life of Magnus Eisengrim? If, when both he and I were ten years old, Percy Boyd Staunton had not thrown a snowball at me, which had instead hit Mrs. Amasa Dempster, bringing about the premature birth of her son Paul and robbing her of her wits, would I at this moment be in bed with Magnus Eisengrim and Liselotte Vitzlipützli in the Savoy Hotel, discussing Staunton's death?

We had come to this because we were inclined to share a bed when we had anything important to talk about. People who think of beds only in terms of sexual exercise or sleep simply do not understand that a bed is the best of all places for a philosophical discussion, an argument, and if necessary a show-down. It was not by chance that so many kings of old administered justice from their beds, and even today there is something splendidly parliamentary about an assembly of concerned persons in a bed.

Of course it must be a big bed. The Savoy had outfitted Magnus's room with two splendid beds, each of which was easily capable of accommodating three adults without undue snuggling. (The Savoy is above the meanness of "single" beds.) So there we were, at the end of our long day of confession and revelation, lying back against the ample pillows, Liesl in the middle, Magnus on her left, and I on her right. He wore a handsome dressing-gown and a scarf he twisted around his head when he slept, because he had a European fear of draughts. I am a simple man; a man of blue pyjamas. Liesl liked filmy night-robes, and she was a delightful person to be in bed with because she was so warm. As I grow older I fuss about the cold, and for some reason I feel the cold for an hour or so after I have removed my artificial leg, as of course I had done before climbing in with them. My chilly stump was next to Liesl.

There we lay, nicely tucked up. I had my usual glass of hot milk and rum, Liesl had a balloon glass of cognac, and Magnus, always eccentric, had the glass of warm water and lemon juice without which he thought he could not sleep. I am sure we looked charmingly domestic, but my frame of mind was that of the historian on a strong scent and eager for the kill. If ever I was to get the confession that would complete my document—the document which would in future enable researchers to write "Ramsay says . . ." with authority—it would be before we slept. If Magnus would not tell me what I wanted to know, surely I might get it from Liesl?

"Consider the circumstances," she said. "It was the final Saturday night of our two weeks' engagement at the Royal Alexandra Theatre in Toronto; we had never taken the *Soirée of Illusions* there before and we were a huge success. By far our most effective illusion was *The Brazen Head of Friar Bacon,* second to last on the program.

"Consider how it worked, Ramsay: the big pretend-brass Head hung in the middle of the stage, and after it had identified a number of objects of which nobody but the owners could have had knowledge, it gave three pieces of advice. That was always the thing that took most planning; the Head would say, 'I am speaking to Mademoiselle Such-A-One, who is sitting in Row F, number 32.' (We always called members of the audience Madame and Monsieur and so forth because it gave a tiny bit of elegance to the occasion in an English-speaking place.) Then I would give Mademoiselle Such-A-One a few words that would make everybody prick up their ears, and might even make Mademoiselle squeal with surprise. Of course we picked up the gossip around town, through our advance agent, or the company manager might get a hint of it in the foyer, or even by doing a little snooping in handbags and pocket-books—he was a very clever old dip we valued for this talent. I was the Voice of the Head, because I have a talent for making a small piece of information go a long way.

"We had, in the beginning, decided never to ask for questions from the audience. Too dangerous. Too hard to answer effectively. But on that Saturday night somebody shouted from the gallery—we know who it was, it was Staunton's son David, who was drunk as a fiddler's bitch and almost out of his mind about his father's death—'Who killed Boy Staunton?'

"Ramsay, what would you have done? What would you expect me to do? You know me; am I one to shy away from a challenge? And there it was: a very great challenge. In an instant I had what seemed to me an inspiration—just right in terms of the Brazen Head, that's to say; just right in terms of the best magic show in the world. Magnus had been talking to me about the Staunton thing all week; he had told me everything Staunton had said to him. Was I to pass up that chance? Ramsay, use your imagination!

"I signalled to the electrician to bring up the warm lights on the Head, to make it glow, and I spoke into the microphone, giving it everything I could of mystery and oracle, and I said—you remember what I said—*He was killed by the usual cabal: by himself, first of all; by the woman he knew; by the woman he did not know; by the man who granted his inmost wish; and by the inevitable fifth, who was keeper of his conscience and keeper of the stone.* You remember how well it went."

"Went well! Liesl, is that what you call going well?"

"Of course; the audience went wild. There was greater excitement in that theatre than the *Soirée* had ever known. It took a long time to calm them down and finish the evening with *The Vision of Dr. Faustus.* Magnus wanted to bring the curtain down then and there. He had cold feet—"

"And with reason," said Magnus; "I thought the cops would be down on us at once. I was never so relieved in my life as when we got on the plane to Copenhagen the following morning."

"You call yourself a showman! It was a triumph!"

"A triumph for you, perhaps. Do you remember what happened to me?"

"Poor Ramsay, you had your heart attack, there in the theatre. Right-hand upper stage box, where you had been lurking. I saw you fall forward through the curtains and sent someone to take care of you at once. But would you grudge that in the light of the triumph for the *Soirée*? It wasn't much of a heart attack, now was it? Just a wee warning that you should be careful about excitement. And were you the only one? Staunton's son took it very badly. And Staunton's wife! As soon as she heard about it—which she did within an hour—she forgot her role as grieving widow and was after us with all the police support she could muster, which luckily wasn't enthusiastic. After all, what could they charge us with? Not even fortune-telling, which is always the thing one has to keep clear of. But any triumph is bound to bring about a few casualties. Don't be small, Ramsay."

I took a pull at my rum and milk, and reflected on the consuming vanity of performers: Magnus, a monster of vanity, which he said he had learned from Sir John Tresize; and Liesl, not one whit less vain, to whom a possible murder, a near-riot in a theatre, an outraged family, and my heart attack—*mine*—were mere sparks from the anvil on which she had hammered out her great triumph. How does one cope with such people?

One doesn't; one thanks God they exist. Liesl was right; I mustn't be small. But if I was allowed my own egoism, I must have the answers I wanted. This was by no means the first time the matter of the death of Boy Staunton had come up among the three of us. On earlier occasions Magnus had put me aside with jokes and evasions, and when Liesl was present she stood by him in doing so; they both knew that I was deeply convinced that somehow Magnus had sent Staunton to his death, and they loved to keep me in doubt. Liesl said it was good for me not to have an answer to every question I asked, and my burning historian's desire to gather and record facts she pretended to regard as mere nosiness.

It was now or never. Magnus had opened up to the film-makers as he had never done to anyone—Liesl knew a little, I presume, but certainly her knowledge of his past was far from complete—and I wanted my answers while the confessional mood was still strong in him. Press on, Ramsay: even if they hate you for it now, they'll get cool in the same skins they got hot in.

One way of getting right answers is to venture a few wrong answers yourself. "Let me have a try at identifying the group you called 'the usual cabal,' " I said. "He was killed by himself, because it was he who drove his car off the dock; the woman he did not know, I should say, was his first wife, whom I think I knew quite well, and certainly he did not know her nearly so well; the woman he did know was certainly his second wife; he came to know her uncomfortably well, and if ever a man stuck his foot in a bear-trap when he thought he was putting it into a flower-bed, it was Boy Staunton when he married Denyse Hornick; the man who granted his inmost wish I suppose must have been you, Magnus, and I am sure you know what is in my mind—you hypnotized poor Boy, stuck that stone in his mouth, and headed him for death. How's that?"

"I'm surprised by the crudeness of your suspicions, Dunny. 'I am become as a bottle in the smoke: yet do I fear thy statutes.' One of those statutes forbids murder. Why would I kill Staunton?"

"Vengeance, Magnus, vengeance!"

"Vengeance for what?"

"For what? Can you ask that after what you have told us about your life? Vengeance for your premature birth and your mother's madness. For your servitude to Willard and Abdullah and all those wretched years with the World of Wonders. Vengeance for the deprivation that made you the shadow of Sir John Tresize. Vengeance for a wrench of fate that cut you off from ordinary love, and made you an oddity. A notable oddity, I admit, but certainly an oddity."

"Oh, Dunny, what a coarsely melodramatic mind you have! Vengeance! If I had been as big an oddity as you are I would have embraced Boy Staunton and thanked him for what he had done for me. The means may have been a little rough, but the result is entirely to my taste. If he hadn't hit my mother on the head with that snowball—having hidden a rock in it, which was dirty play—I might now be what my father was: a Baptist parson in a small town. I have had my ups and downs, and the downs were very far down indeed, but I am now a celebrity in a limited way, and I am a master of a craft, which is a better thing by far. I am a more complete human being than you are, you old fool. I may not have had a very happy sex-life, but I certainly have love and friendship, and much of the best of that is in bed with me at this moment. I have admiration, which everybody wants and very few people achieve. I get my living by doing what I most enjoy, and that is rare indeed. Who gave me my start? Boy Staunton! Would I murder such a man? It is to his early intervention in my life I owe what Liesl calls the Magian World View.

"Vengeance, you cry. If anybody wanted vengeance, it was you, Dunny. You lived near Staunton all your life, watched him, brooded over him, saw him destroy that silly girl you wanted—or thought you wanted—and ill-wished him a thousand times. You're the man of vengeance. I never wanted vengeance in my life for anything."

"Magnus! Remember how you withheld death from Willard when he begged for it! What did you do today to poor Roly Ingestree? Don't you call that vengeance?"

"I admit I toyed with Roly. He hurt people I loved. But if he hadn't come back into my life by chance I should never have bothered about him. I didn't harbour evidence of his guilt for sixty years, as you harboured that stone Staunton put in the snowball."

"Don't twist, Magnus! When you and Staunton left my room at the College to go back to your hotel you took that stone, and when next it was seen the police had to pry it out of poor Staunton's jaws, where it was clenched so tight they had to break his teeth to get at it!"

"I didn't take the stone, Dunny; Staunton took it himself."

"Did he?"

"Yes. I saw him. You were putting your box back in the bookshelves. The box that contained my mother's ashes. Dunny, what on earth made you keep those ashes? It was ghoulish."

"I couldn't bear to part with them. Your mother was a very special figure in my life. To me she was a saint. Not just a good woman, but a saint, and the influence she had in my life was miraculous."

"So you've often told me, but I knew her only as a madwoman. I had stood at the window of our miserable house trying not to cry while Boy Staunton and his gang shouted 'Hoor!' as they passed on their way to school."

"Yes, and you let the police think you had never met him until the night he died."

"Perfectly true. I knew who he was, when he was fifteen and I was five. He was the Rich Young Ruler in our village, as you well know. But we had never been formally introduced until you brought us together, and I presumed that was what the police were talking about."

"A quibble."

"An evasion, possibly. But I was answering questions, not instructing my questioners. I was working on advice given me long ago by Mrs. Constantinescu: don't blat everything you know, especially to cops."

"You didn't tell them you knew that Boy had been appointed Lieutenant-Governor of the province when nobody else knew it."

"Everybody knew it was in the air. I knew it the second night he came to the theatre, because he had the letter of appointment in the inner pocket of his handsome dinner jacket. Liesl has told you we had a member of our troupe—our company manager—who welcomed important patrons in the foyer. I suppose our man found out that the rumour had become a fact by means which I always thought it better not to investigate too closely. So I knew. And the Brazen Head could have spilled the beans that evening, from the stage, but Liesl and I thought it might be just a teeny bit indiscreet."

"That was another thing you didn't tell the police. Boy Staunton came twice to the *Soirée of Illusions*."

"Lots of people used to come twice. And three and four times. It's a very good show. But you're right; Staunton came to see me. He was interested in me in the way people used to be interested in Sir John. I suppose there was something about my personality, as there was about Sir John's, that had a special attraction for some people. My personality is a valuable part of our bag of tricks, as you very well know."

Indeed I did. And how it had come pressing off the screen in *Un Hommage à Robert-Houdin*! I had always thought personal attributes lost something in the cinema; it seemed reasonable that a photograph of a man should be less striking than the man himself. But not when the art of Lind and that rumpot of genius Kinghovn lay behind the photograph. I had sat in the little viewing-room at the B.B.C. entranced by what I saw of a Magnus more vivid than ever I had seen him on the stage. True, his performance was a tiny bit stagy, considered as cinematic acting, but it was a staginess of such grace, such distinction and accomplishment, that nobody could have wished it otherwise. As I watched I remembered what used to be said of stage favourites when I was a boy: they were *polished*. They had enviable repose. They did nothing quite the way anyone else did it, and they had an attitude toward their audiences which was, quite apart from the role they were playing, splendidly courteous, as if a great man were taking friendly notice of us. I had thought of this when Magnus told us how Sir John accepted applause when he made his first entrance in *Scaramouche*, and later gave those curtain-speeches all across Canada, which seemed to embrace audiences of people who yearned mutely for such attention. Magnus had this polish in the highest and most subtle degree, and I could understand how Boy Staunton, who was a lifelong hero-worshipper and had not got it out of his system even at the age of seventy, would have responded to it.

Polish! How Boy had honed and yearned after polish! What idols he had worshipped! And as a Lieutenant-Governor elect I could imagine how he coveted what Magnus displayed on the stage. A Lieutenant-Governor with that sort of distinction—that would astonish the Rubes!

We were silent for a while. But I was full of questions, mad for certainties even though I understood there were no certainties. I broke the silence.

"If you weren't the man who granted his inmost wish, who was it? I have swallowed the pill that I was 'the inevitable fifth, who was keeper of his conscience and keeper of the stone'—though I accept that only as Liesl's oracular phraseology. But who granted his wish? And what was the wish?"

This time it was Liesl who spoke. "It could very well have been his son, Ramsay. Don't forget David Staunton, who represented continuance to his father. Have you no understanding of how some men crave for continuance? They see it as their immortality. Boy Staunton who had built up the great fortune, from a few fields of sugar-beets to a complex of business that was known all over the world. You must pardon my nationalist bias, but it is significant that when Staunton died—or killed himself, as it was supposed—his death was reported at some length in our *Neue Zürcher Zeitung*. That paper, like the London *Times*, recognizes only the most distinguished achievements of the Angel of Death. Their obituary columns are almost the Court Circular of the Kingdom of God. Well, who inherits an important man's earthly glory? People like Staunton hope it will be a son.

"A son Staunton had, we know. But what a son! Not a disgrace. One might find the spaciousness of tragedy in a disgrace. David Staunton was a success; a notable criminal lawyer, but also a sharp critic of his father's life. A man whose cold eye watched the glorious Boy growing older, and richer, and more powerful, and was not impressed. A man who did not admire or seek to emulate his father's great success with women. A man who understood, by tie of blood and by a child's intuition, the terrible, unappeasable hunger that lies at the bottom of ambition like Boy Staunton's. I don't know whether David ever understood that consciously; but he thwarted his father's terrible craving to be everything, command everything, and possess everything, and he did it in the way that hurt most: he refused to produce a successor to himself. He refused to continue the Staunton line and the Staunton name and the glory that was Staunton. That was pressing the knife into the vital spot. But don't jump to conclusions: the man who granted his inmost wish wasn't David Staunton."

"Aren't you doing a lot of fancy guessing?"

"No. Staunton told Magnus and Magnus told me."

"It was one of those situations Liesl is always talking about," said Eisengrim. "You know: a man reaches the confessional time in his life. Sometimes he writes an autobiography; sometimes he tells his story to a group of listeners, as I have been doing. Sometimes there is only one listener, and that was how it was with Staunton.

"Surely you remember what it was like in your room that night of November 3? Staunton and I had clicked, in the way people sometimes do. He wanted to know me: I was more than commonly interested in him because he was from my past, and not at all what one would have predicted for the fattish, purse-proud kid who had shouted, 'Hoor' at my mother. You understood that we'd clicked, and you didn't like it at all. That was when you decided to spill the beans, and told Staunton who I was, how he had literally brought about my birth, how you knew about the rock in the snowball and had kept it all those years. You even had my mother's ashes in a casket. And through it all Staunton was cool as a cucumber. Denied everything that he had not—quite honestly, I believe—forgotten. Chose to regard the whole affair as something only very remotely connected with himself. Considering the way you went at him, I thought he showed enviable self-possession. But he said some sharp things about you.

"When we were in his car, driving down the long avenue from the school, he expanded on what he'd said. He cursed you very thoroughly, Dunny. Told me that for boyhood friendship he had kept an eye on your money all through the years, and made you secure and even well-off. Befriended you and brought you to the notice of really important people—people in a very big way of business—as a guest in his house. Confided in you when his first marriage was going on the rocks, and was patient when you sided with his wife. Put up with your ironic attitude toward his success, because he knew it had its root in jealousy.

"He was offended that you never mentioned Mary Dempster—he never spoke of her as my mother—and her long years in asylums; he would have been glad to help a Deptford woman who had come to grief. And he was angry and hurt that you kept that damned stone on your desk to remind you of a grudge you had against him. A stone in a snowball! The kind of thing any boy might do, just for devilment. He would never have thought the dark, judgmatical Ramsay blood in you was so bitter with hate—you, who had made money out of saints!

"It was then I began to know him. Oh yes, I came to know him quite well during the next hour. We'd clicked, as I said, but I've always distrusted that kind of thing since I first clicked with Willard. It's unchancy. There was sympathy of character, I suppose. There was a wolfishness in Boy Staunton that he kept very well under, and probably never recognized in himself. But I know that wolfishness. Liesl has told you I have a good measure of it in myself, and that was why she suggested I take the professional name of Eisengrim, the name of the wolf in the old fables; but the name really means the sinister hardness, the cruelty of iron itself. I took the name, and recognized the fact, and thereby got it up out of my depths so that at least I could be aware of it and take a look at it, now and then. I won't say I domesticated the wolf, but I knew where his lair was, and what he might do. Not Boy Staunton. He had lived facing the sun, and he had no real comprehension of the shadow-wolf that loped after him.

"We wolves like to possess things, and especially people. We are unappeasably hungry. There is no reason or meaning in the hunger. It just exists, and possesses you. I saw it once, in myself, and though I didn't know what it was at the time, I knew that it was something that was at the very heart of my being. When we played *Scaramouche* through Canada, I had a little meeting with Sir John, every night, just before Two, two; we had to stand in front of a mirror, to make sure every detail of costume and make-up was identical, so that when I appeared as his double the illusion would be as perfect as possible. I always enjoyed that moment, because I am wolfish about perfection.

"There we stood, the night I speak of; it was in Ottawa, in his dressing-room at the old Russell, and we had a good mirror, a full-length one. He looked, and I looked. I saw that he was good. An egoist, as only a leading actor can be, but in his face, which was old under the make-up, there was gentleness and compassion toward me, because I was young, and had so much to learn, and was so likely to make a fool of myself through my driving greed. Compassion for me, and a silvery relish for himself, too, because he knew he was old, and had the mastery of age. But in my face, which was so like his that my doubling gave the play a special excitement, there was a watchful admiration beneath which my wolfishness could be seen—my hunger not just to be like him but to *be* him, whatever that might cost him. I loved him and served him faithfully right up to the end, but in my inmost self I wanted to eat him, to possess him, to make him mine.

"He saw it, too, and he gave me a little flick with his hand as though to say, 'You might let me live out my life, m'boy. I've earned it, eh? But you look as if you'd devour my very soul. Not really necessary, quonk?' Not a word was spoken, but I blushed under my make-up. And whatever I did for him afterward, I couldn't keep the wolf quiet. If I was a little sharp with Roly, it was because I was angry that he had seen what I truly thought I had kept hidden.

"That was how it was with Boy Staunton. Oh, not on the surface. He had a lovely glaze. But he was a devourer.

"He set to work to devour me. He went at it with the ease of long custom, and I don't suppose he had an instant's real awareness of what he was doing. He laid himself out to be charming, and to get me on his side. When he had finished damning you, Dunny, he began to excuse you, in a way that was supposed to be complimentary to me: you had lived a narrow, schoolmaster's life, and had won a certain scholarly reputation, but he and I were the glittering successes and breathed a finer air than yours.

"He was extremely good at what he was doing. It is not easy to assume an air of youth successfully, but when it is well done it has extraordinary charm, because it seems to rock Age, and probably Death, back on their heels. He had kept his voice youthful, and his vocabulary was neither stupidly up-to-the-minute nor flawed with betraying fossil slang. I had to keep reminding myself that this man must be seventy. I have to present a professional picture of physical well-being, if not actually of youth, and I know how it is done because I learned it from Sir John. But Boy Staunton—an amateur, really—could teach me things about seeming youthful without resorting to absurdities. I knew he was eager to make me his own, to enchant me, to eat me up and take me into himself. He had just discovered a defeat; he thought he had eaten you, Ramsay, but you were like those fairy-tale figures who cut their way out of the giant's belly.

"So, not at all unlike a man who loses one girl and bounces to another, he tried to eat me.

"We really must talk, he said. We were driving down from your school to my hotel, and as we were rounding Queen's Park Circle he pulled off the road into what I suppose was a private entry beside the Legislature; there was a porte-cochère and a long flight of steps. It won't be long before this is my personal entrance to this building, he said.

"I knew what he was talking about: the appointment that would be announced next morning; he was full of it."

"I'll bet he was," I said; "it was just his thing—top dog in a large area—women curtsying to him—all that. And certainly his wife wanted it, and engineered it."

"Yes, but wait: having got it, he wasn't so sure. If you are one of the wolfish brotherhood you sometimes find that you have no sooner achieved what you wanted than you begin to despise it. Boy's excitement was like that of a man who thinks he has walked into a trap."

"Well, the job isn't all fun. What ceremonial appointment is? You drive to the Legislature in a carriage, with soldiers riding before and behind, and there is a lot of bowing, because you represent the Crown, and then you find you are reading a speech written by somebody else, announcing policies you may not like. If he didn't want to be a State figurehead, he should have choked off Denyse when she set to work to get him the job."

"Reason, reason, reason! Dunny, you surely know how limited a part reason plays in some of our most important decisions. He coveted the state landau and the soldiers, and he had somehow managed to preserve the silly notion that as Lieutenant-Governor he would really do some governing. But already he knew he was mistaken. He had looked over the schedule of duties for his first month in office, and been dismayed by the places he would have to go, and the things he would have to do. Presenting flags to Boy Scouts; opening a home for old people; eating a hundredweight of ceremonial dinners to raise money to fight diseases he'd rather not hear about. And he couldn't get out of it; his secretary made it clear that there was no choice in the matter; the office demanded these things and he was expected to deliver the goods. But that wasn't what truly got under his skin.

"Such appointments aren't done in a few days, and he had known it was coming for several weeks. During that time he had some business in London and while he was there he had thought it a good idea to take care of the matter of his ceremonial uniform. That was how he put it, but as a fellow-wolf I knew how eager he must have been to explore the possibilities of state finery. So—off to Ede and Ravenscroft to have the job done in the best possible way and no expense spared. They happened to have a uniform of the right sort which he tried on, just to get the general effect. Even though it was obvious that the uniform was for a smaller man, the effect was catastrophic. 'Suddenly I didn't look like myself at all,' he said; 'I looked old. Not shaky old, or fat old, or grim old, but certainly old.'

"He expected me to sympathize, but wolf should never turn to wolf for sympathy. 'You are old,' I said to him. 'Very handsome and well preserved, but nobody would take you for a young man.' 'Yes,' he said, 'but not old as that uniform suggested; not a figurehead. I tried putting the hat a little on one side, to see if that helped, but the man with the measuring-tape around his neck who was with me said, *Oh no, sir; never like that,* and put it straight again. And I understood that forever after there would always be somebody putting my hat straight, and that I would be no more than the animation of that uniform, or some version of it.'

"As one who had spent seven years as the cunning bowels of Abdullah I didn't see that fate quite as he did. Of course, Abdullah wasn't on the level. He was out to trounce the Rubes. A Lieutenant-Governor can't have any fun of that kind. He is the embodiment of everything that is correct, and on the level, and unsurprising. The Rubes have got him and he must do their will.

" 'I have lost my freedom of choice,' he said, and he seemed to expect me to respond with horror. But I didn't. I was enjoying myself. Boy Staunton was an old story to you, Dunny, but he was new to me, and I was playing the wolf game, too, in my way. I had not forgotten Mrs. Constantinescu, and I knew that he was ready to talk, and I was ready to hear. So I remembered old Zingara's advice. Lull 'em. So I lulled him.

" 'I can see that you're in a situation you never would have chosen with your eyes open. But there's usually some way out. Is there no way out for you?'

" 'Even if I found a way, what would happen if I suddenly bowed out?' he said.

" 'I suppose you'd go on living much as you do now,' I told him. 'There would be criticism of you because you refused an office you had accepted, under the Crown. But I dare say that's been done before.'

"I swear I had nothing in particular in mind when I made that comment. But it galvanized him. He looked at me as if I had said something of extraordinary value. Then he said: 'Of course it was different for him; he was younger.'

" 'What do you mean?' I said.

"He looked at me very queerly. 'The Prince of Wales,' he said; 'he was my friend, you know. Or rather, you don't know. But many years ago, when he toured this country, I was his aide, and he had a profound effect on me. I learned a great deal from him. He was special, you know; he was truly a remarkable man. He showed it at the time of the Abdication. That took guts.'

" 'Called for guts from several of his relatives, too,' I said. 'Do you think he lived happily ever after?'

" 'I hope so,' said he. 'But he was younger.'

" 'I've said you were old,' said I, 'but I didn't mean life had nothing for you. You are in superb condition. You can expect another fifteen years, at least, and think of all the things you can do.'

" 'And think of all the things I can't do,' he said, and in a tone that told me what I had suspected, because with all the fine surface, and bonhomie, and his careful wooing of me I had sensed something like despair in him.

" 'I suppose you mean sex,' I said.

" 'Yes,' he said. 'Not that I'm through, you know; by no means. But it isn't the same. Now it's more reassurance than pleasure. And young women—they have to be younger and younger—they're flattered because of what I am and who I am, but there's always a look you surprise when they don't think you're watching: He's-amazing-for-his-age-I-wonder-what-I'd-do-if-he-had-a-heart-attack-would-I-have-to-drag-him-out-into-the-hall-and-leave-him-by-the-elevator-and-how-would-I-get-his-clothes-on? However well I perform—and I'm still good, you know—there's an element of humiliation about it.'

"Humiliation was much on his mind. The humiliation of age, which you and I mustn't underestimate, Dunny, just because we've grown old and made our age serve us; it's a different matter if you've devoted your best efforts to setting up an image of a wondrous Boy; there comes a time when the pretty girls think of you not as a Boy but as an Old Boy. The humiliation of discovering you've been a mug, and that the gorgeous office you've been given under the Crown is in fact a tyranny of duty, like the Crown itself. And the humiliation of discovering that a man you've thought of as a friend—rather a humble, eccentric friend from your point of view, but nevertheless a friend—has been harbouring evidence of a mean action you did when you were ten, and still sees you, at least in part, as a mean kid.

"That last was a really tough one—disproportionately so—but Boy was the kind of man who truly believes you can wipe out the past simply by forgetting it yourself. I'm sure he'd met humiliations in his life. Who hasn't? But he'd been able to rise above them. These were humiliations nothing could lift from his heart.

" 'What are you going to do with the stone?' I asked him.

" 'You saw me take it?' he said. 'I'll get rid of it. Throw it away.'

" 'I wouldn't throw it a second time,' I said.

" 'What else?' said he.

" 'If it really bothers you, you must come to terms with it,' I said. 'In your place I'd do something symbolic: hold it in your hand, re-live the moment when you threw it at Ramsay and hit my mother, and this time *don't* throw it. Give yourself a good sharp knock on the head with it.'

" 'That's a damned silly game to play,' he said. And would you believe it, he was pouting—the glorious Boy was pouting.

" 'Not at all. Consider it as a ritual. An admission of wrong-doing and penitence.'

" 'Oh, balls to that,' he said.

"I had become uncomfortable company: I wouldn't be eaten, and I made peculiar and humiliating suggestions. Also, I could tell that something was on his mind, and he wanted to be alone with it. He started the car and very shortly we were at my hotel—the Royal York, you know, which is quite near the docks. He shook hands with the warmth that I suppose had marked him all his life. 'Glad to have met you: thanks for the advice,' said he.

" 'It's only what I would do myself, in the circumstances,' I said. 'I'd do my best to swallow that stone.' Now I swear to you that I only meant what I said symbolically—meaning to come to terms with what the stone signified. And he seemed not to notice.

" 'I meant your advice about the Abdication,' he said. 'It was stupid of me not to have thought of that myself.'

"I suddenly realized what he meant. He was going to abdicate, like his hero before him. But unlike his Prince of Wales he didn't mean to live to face the world afterward. There it is, Dunny: Liesl and I are convinced that the man who truly granted his inmost wish, though only by example, was the man who decided not to live as Edward VIII.

"What should I have done? Insisted that he come to my room, and plied him with hot coffee and sweet reasonableness? Not quite my line, eh? Hardly what one expects of a brother wolf, quonk?"

"You let him leave you in that frame of mind?"

"Liesl likes to talk about what she calls my Magian World View. She makes it sound splendid and like the Arabian Nights, and dolls it up with fine phrases from Spengler—"

"Phantasmagoria and dream-grotto," said Liesl, taking a swig of her cognac; "only that's not Spengler—that's Carlyle."

"Phantasmagoria and dream-grotto if you like," said Magnus, "but—and it is a vital *but*—combined with a clear-eyed, undeluded observation of what lies right under your nose. Therefore—no self-deceiving folly and no meddlesome compassion, but a humble awareness of the Great Justice and the Great Mercy whenever they choose to make themselves known. I don't talk about a Magian World View; I've no touch with that sort of thing. In so far as it concerns me, I live it. It's just the way things strike me, after the life I've lived, which looks pretty much like a World of Wonders when I spread it out before me, as I've been doing. Everything has its astonishing, wondrous aspect, if you bring a mind to it that's really your own—a mind that hasn't been smeared and blurred with half-understood muck from schools, or the daily papers, or any other ragbag of reach-me-down notions. I try not to judge people, though when I meet an enemy and he's within arm's length, I'm not above giving him a smart clout, just to larn him. As I did with Roly. But I don't monkey with what I think of as the Great Justice—"

"Poetic justice," said Liesl.

"What you please. Though it doesn't look poetic in action; it's rough and tough and deeply satisfying. And I don't administer it. Something else—something I don't understand, but feel and serve and fear—does that. It's sometimes horrible to watch, as it was when my poor, dear old master, Sir John, was brought down by his own vanity, and Milady went with him, though I think she knew what the truth was. But part of the glory and terror of our life is that somehow, at some time, we get all that's coming to us. Everybody gets their lumps and their bouquets and it goes on for quite a while after death.

"So—here was a situation when it was clear to me that the Great Justice had called the name of Boy Staunton. Was it for me to hold him back?

"And to be frank why would I? You remember what was said in your room that night, Dunny. You're the historian: surely you remember everything important? What did I say to Boy when he offered me a lift in his car?"

I couldn't remember. That night I had been too overwrought myself by the memories of Mary Dempster to take note of social conversation.

"You don't remember? I do: I said—'What Ramsay tells me puts you in my debt for eighty days in Paradise, if for nothing in this life. We shall call it quits if you will drive me to my hotel.' "

"Eighty days in Paradise?"

"I was born eighty days before my time. Poor little Paul. Popular opinion is very rough on foetuses these days. Horrid little nuisances. Rip 'em out and throw them in the trash pail. But who knows what they feel about it? The depth psychologists Liesl is so fond of think they have a very jolly time in the womb. Warm, protected, bouncing gently in their beautiful grotto light. Perhaps it is the best existence we ever know, unless there is something equally splendid for us after death—and why not? That earliest life is what every humanitarian movement and Welfare State seeks to restore, without a hope of success. And Boy Staunton, by a single mean-spirited action, robbed me of eighty days of that princely splendour. Was I the man to fret about the end of his life when he had been so cavalier about the beginning of mine?"

"Oh, Magnus, that's terribly unjust."

"As this world's justice goes, perhaps. But what about the Greater Justice?"

"I see. Yes, I really do see. So you let him dree his weird?"

"You're getting really old, Dunny. You're beginning to dredge up expressions from your Scotch childhood. But it says it all. Yes, I let him dree his weird."

"I can very well understand," I said, "that you wouldn't have got far explaining that to the police."

Liesl laughed, and threw her empty brandy balloon against the farthest wall. It made a fine costly crash.

2

"Ramsay."

"Liesl! How kind of you to come to see me."

"Magnus has been asleep for hours. But I have been worrying about you. I hope you didn't take it too badly—his suggestion that you played rather a crucial part in Staunton's death."

"No, no; I faced that, and swallowed it even before I joined you in Switzerland. While I was recovering from my heart attack, indeed. In an old Calvinist like me the voice of conscience has always spoken long before any mortal accuser."

"I'm glad. Glad that you're not grieving and worrying, that's to say."

"Boy died as he lived: self-determined and daring, but not really imaginative. Always with a well-disguised streak of petulance that sometimes looked like malice. The stone in the snowball: the stone in the corpse's mouth—always a nasty surprise for somebody."

"You think he gobbled the stone to spite you?"

"Unquestionably. Magnus thinks I kept the stone for spite, and I suppose there was something of that in it. But I also kept it to be a continual reminder of the consequences that can follow a single action. It might have come out that it was my paperweight, but even if it didn't, he knew I would know what it was, and Boy reckoned on having the last word in our lifelong argument that way."

"What a detestable man!"

"Not really. But it's always a good idea to keep your eye on the genial, smiling ones, and especially on those who seem to be eternally young."

"Jealousy, Ramsay, you battered antique."

"A little jealousy, perhaps. But the principle holds."

"Is that what you are making notes about, on all that excellent Savoy notepaper?"

"Notes for a work I have in mind. But it's about Magnus; he told me, you know, that the Devil once intervened decisively in his life."

"He likes to talk that way, and I am sure it is true. But life is a succession of decisive interventions. Magnus himself intervened in my life, and illuminated it, at a time when I needed an understanding friend even more than I needed a lover. It wasn't the Devil that sent him."

"Why should it be? God wants to intervene in the world, and how is he to do it except through man? I think the Devil is in the same predicament. It would be queer, wouldn't it, if the Devil had only made use of Magnus that one time? And God, too: yes, certainly God as well. It's the moment of decision—of will—when those Two nab us, and as they both speak so compellingly it's

Contents

Colour section 1–24

Introduction 6
Where to go 8
When to go 10
Things not to miss 14

Basics 25–66

Getting there.......................... 27
Insurance 35
Health 36
Getting around........................ 41
Accommodation 47
Food and drink 49
The media............................... 53
Festivals 54
Travelling with children 56
Women travellers 57
Travel essentials 57

Guide 67–786

1. Rio de Janeiro..................... 69
2. Minas Gerais and Espírito Santo 171
3. Bahia.................................. 257
4. The Northeast 305
5. The Amazon....................... 411
6. Brasília, Goiás and Tocantins 507
7. Mato Grosso 555
8. São Paulo 609
9. The South 677

Contexts 787–852

The historical framework........ 789
Amazon ecology and Indian rights 810
Race in Brazilian society 822
Music.................................... 824
Books 833
Brazilian cinema..................... 849

Language 853–866

Pronunciation......................... 855
Brazilian Portuguese words and phrases 858
A Brazilian menu reader......... 860
A glossary of Brazilian terms and acronyms 864

Travel store 867–872

Small print & Index 873–888

Amazon flora and fauna colour section following p.456

Brazilian food and drink colour section following p.648

◀◀ Morro de São Paulo ◀ Paraty

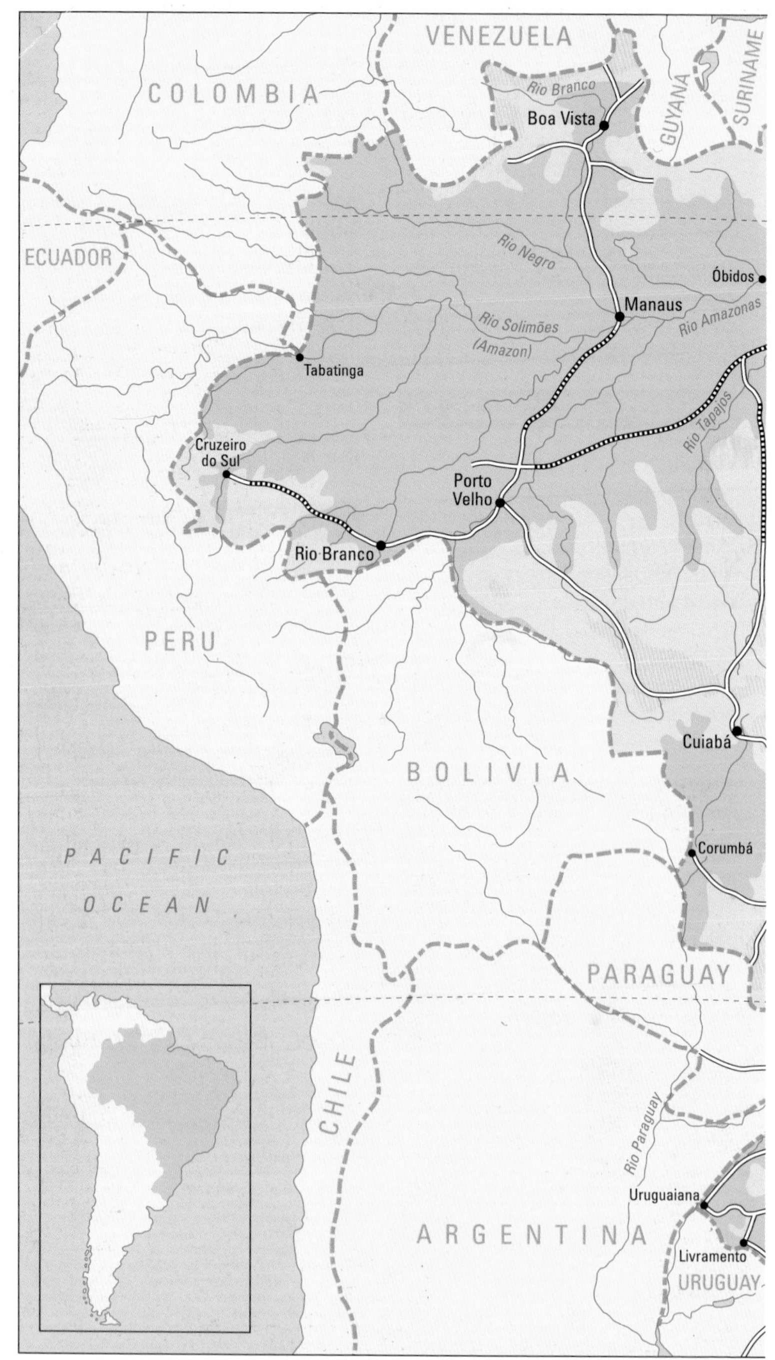
VENEZUELA
COLOMBIA
GUYANA
SURINAME
Rio Branco
Boa Vista
ECUADOR
Rio Negro
Óbidos
Manaus
Rio Solimões
(Amazon)
Rio Amazonas
Tabatinga
Rio Tapajós
Cruzeiro
do Sul
Porto
Velho
Rio Branco
PERU
Cuiabá
BOLIVIA
PACIFIC
OCEAN
Corumbá
PARAGUAY
CHILE
Rio Paraguay
Uruguaiana
ARGENTINA
Livramento
URUGUAY

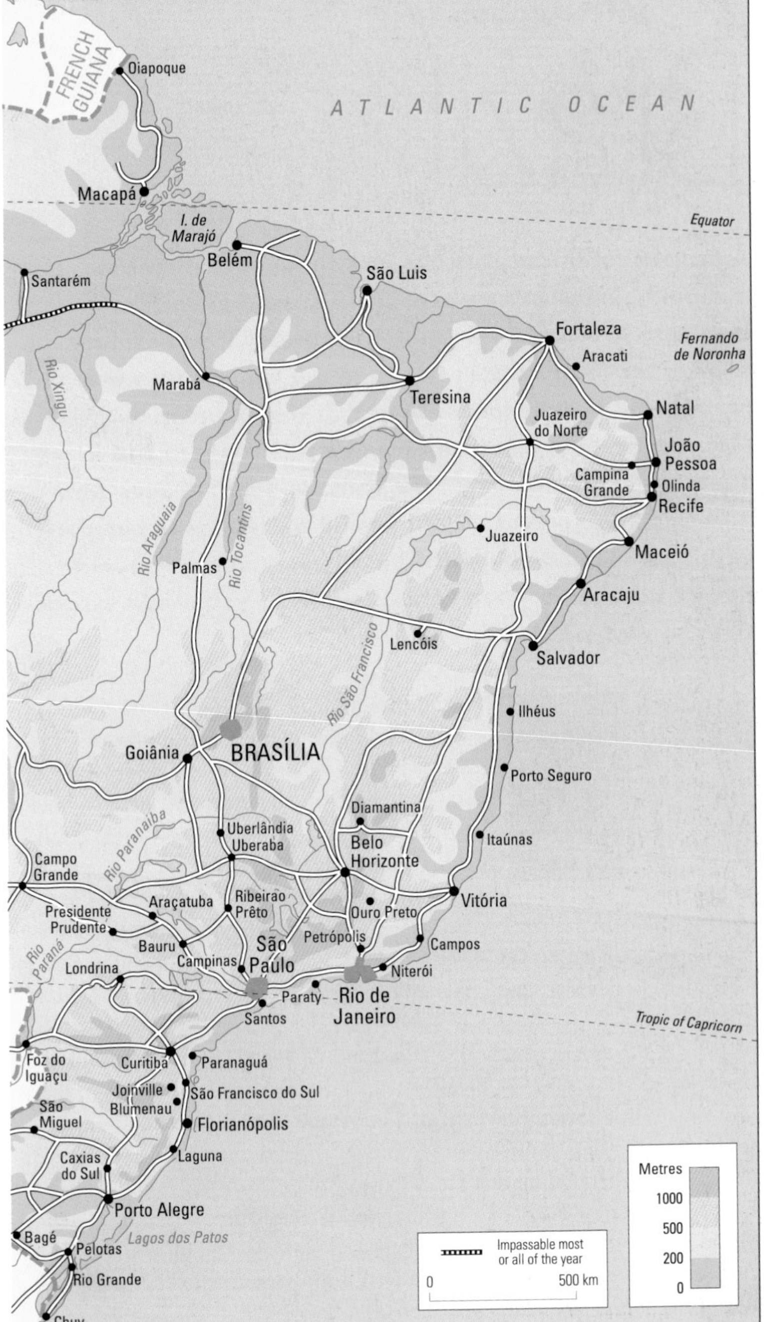
ATLANTIC OCEAN
FRENCH GUIANA
Oiapoque
Macapá
I. de Marajó
Belém
São Luis
Santarém
Equator
Fortaleza
Aracati
Fernando de Noronha
Marabá
Teresina
Rio Xingu
Natal
Juazeiro do Norte
João Pessoa
Campina Grande
Olinda
Recife
Rio Araguaia
Rio Tocantins
Juazeiro
Maceió
Palmas
Aracaju
Lençóis
Rio São Francisco
Salvador
Ilhéus
BRASÍLIA
Goiânia
Porto Seguro
Rio Paranaiba
Diamantina
Uberlândia
Uberaba
Belo Horizonte
Itaúnas
Campo Grande
Araçatuba
Ribeirão Prêto
Presidente Prudente
Ouro Preto
Vitória
Bauru
Petrópolis
Campos
Rio Paraná
Campinas
São Paulo
Londrina
Niterói
Paraty
Rio de Janeiro
Santos
Tropic of Capricorn
Foz do Iguaçu
Curitiba
Paranaguá
Joinville
São Francisco do Sul
Blumenau
São Miguel
Florianópolis
Laguna
Caxias do Sul
Porto Alegre
Bagé
Lagos dos Patos
Pelotas
Rio Grande
Chuy
Impassable most or all of the year
0
500 km
Metres
1000
500
200
0

Introduction to Brazil

Brazilians often say they live in a continent rather than a country, and that's an excusable exaggeration. The landmass is bigger than the United States if you exclude Alaska; the journey from Recife in the east to the western border with Peru is longer than that from London to Moscow, and the distance between the northern and southern borders is about the same as that between New York and Los Angeles. Brazil has no mountains to compare with its Andean neighbours, but in every other respect it has all the scenic – and cultural – variety you would expect from so vast a country.

Despite the immense expanses of the interior, roughly two-thirds of Brazil's **population** live on or near the coast and well over half live in cities – even in the Amazon. In Rio and São Paulo, Brazil has two of the world's great metropolises, and nine other cities have over a million inhabitants. Yet Brazil still thinks of itself as a frontier country, and certainly the deeper into the interior you go, the thinner the population becomes. That said, the frontier communities have expanded relentlessly during the last fifty years, usually hand in hand with the planned expansion of the road network into remote regions.

Other South Americans regard Brazilians as a **race** apart, and language has a lot to do with it – Brazilians understand Spanish, just about, but Spanish-speakers won't understand Portuguese. And Brazilians look different. They're one of the most ethnically diverse peoples in the world: in the extreme south, German and Italian immigration has left distinctive European features; São Paulo has the world's largest Japanese community outside Japan; there's a large black population concentrated in Rio, Salvador and São Luís; while the Indian influence is most visible in the people of Amazônia and the Northeastern interior.

▲ Celebration in Salvador

Brazil is a land of profound **economic** contradictions. Rapid post-war industrialization made Brazil one of the world's ten largest economies and put it among the most developed of Third World countries. But this has not improved the lot of the vast majority of Brazilians. The cities are dotted with *favelas*, shantytowns that crowd around the skyscrapers, and the contrast between rich and poor is one of the most glaring anywhere. There are wide **regional differences**, too: Brazilians talk of a "Switzerland" in the Southeast, centred along the Rio–São Paulo axis, and an "India" above it; and although this is a simplification, it's true that the level of economic development tends to fall the further north you go. This throws up facts that are hard to swallow: Brazil is the industrial powerhouse of South America, but cannot feed and educate its people. In a country almost the size of a continent, the extreme inequalities in land distribution have led to land shortages but not to agrarian reform. Brazil has enormous natural resources but their exploitation so far has benefited just a few. The IMF and the greed of First World banks must bear some of the blame for this situation, but institutionalized corruption and the reluctance of the country's large middle class to do anything that might jeopardize its comfortable lifestyle are also part of the problem.

These difficulties, however, rarely seem to overshadow everyday life in Brazil. It's fair to say that nowhere in the world do people know how to enjoy themselves more – most famously in the annual orgiastic celebrations of **Carnaval**, but reflected, too, in the lively year-round nightlife that you'll find in any decent-sized town. This national hedonism also manifests itself in Brazil's highly developed **beach culture**; the country's superb **music**

Fact file

- By far the largest country in South America, Brazil covers nearly half the continent and is only slightly smaller than the US, with an area of just over 8.5 million square kilometres. It shares common boundaries with every South American country except Chile and Ecuador.
- The population of Brazil is around 180 million, making it the fifth most populous country in the world. Of this, about 55 percent is white (Portuguese, German, Italian, etc), 38 percent is of mixed white and black descent and six percent is black, with "others" (including Amerindian) accounting for a mere one percent.
- Almost ninety percent of Brazil's electricity is generated from hydropower, about six percent from fossil fuels and six percent from nuclear power.
- Paved highways account for a meagre 0.2 million km, while unpaved highways add up to more than 1.8 million km.
- Brazilian exports consist mainly of manufactured products (including automobiles, machinery and footwear), iron ore, soybeans and coffee. Brazil also produces ninety percent of the world's gems.

and dancing; rich regional **cuisines**; and in the most relaxed and tolerant attitude to **sexuality** – gay and straight – that you'll find anywhere in South America. And if you needed more reason to visit, there's a strength and variety of **popular culture**, and a genuine friendliness and humour in the people that is tremendously welcoming and infectious.

Where to go

The most heavily populated and economically advanced part of the country is the Southeast, where the three largest cities – **São Paulo**, **Rio de Janeiro** and **Belo Horizonte** – form a triangle around which the economy pivots. All are worth visiting in their own right, though Rio, one of the world's most stupendously sited cities, stands head and shoulders above

▲ Igreja do Bonfim, Salvador

▲ Carnaval in Olinda

the lot. The **South**, encompassing the states of Paraná, Santa Catarina and Rio Grande do Sul, stretches down to the borders with Uruguay and northern Argentina, and westwards to Paraguay, and includes much of the enormous **Paraná** river system. The spectacular **Iguaçu Falls** (at the northernmost point where Brazil and Argentina meet) are one of the great natural wonders of South America.

The vast hinterland of the South and Southeast is often called the Centre-West and includes an enormous central plateau of savanna and rock escarpments, the **Planalto Central**. In the middle stands **Brasília**, the country's space-age capital, built from nothing in the late 1950s and still developing today. The capital is the gateway to a vast interior, the **Mato Grosso**, only fully charted and settled over the last three decades; it includes the mighty **Pantanal** swampland, the richest wildlife reserve on the continent. North and west, the Mato Grosso shades into the **Amazon**, a mosaic of jungle, rivers, savanna and marshland that also contains two major cities – **Belém**, at the mouth of the Amazon itself, and **Manaus**, some 1600km upstream. The tributaries of the Amazon, rivers like the Tapajós, the Xingú, the Negro, the Araguaia or the Tocantins, are virtually unknown outside Brazil, but each is a huge river system in its own right.

The other major sub-region of Brazil is the **Northeast**, the part of the country that curves out into the Atlantic Ocean. This was the first part of Brazil to be settled by the Portuguese and colonial remains are thicker on the ground here than anywhere else in the country – notably in the cities

River tourism

Though some might imagine it to be quite arduous, travelling by boat on the powerful Rio Amazonas (known as the Rio Solimões above Manaus) can be surprisingly relaxing. Even if you don't have your own cabin, there are few experiences as laid-back as lounging in a hammock for days on end. With a good book and a few pennies to buy the odd beer at the bar in the afternoons, the long river kilometres flow by quickly. If you've selected one of the larger boats, the top deck will probably have a massive sound system for stirring samba nights, along with satellite TV and tables for card and domino games. If you want to get a close-up view of the jungle and its wildlife, you're better off choosing the smaller boats, which travel closer to the shore going upstream and can negotiate the smaller streams; going downstream, however, they tend to cruise in the mid-stream currents, far from shore.

Exploring the rivers, tributaries and rainforest around Manaus by houseboat is probably the most comfortable way to see the South American jungle. The forest scenery is nothing short of breathtaking and the time easily filled with piranha fishing, forest walks and canoe rides through alligator-filled creeks. For details on planning a river trip, see p.418.

of **Salvador** and **São Luís** and the lovely town of **Olinda**. It's a region of dramatic contrasts: a lush, tropical coastline with the best beaches in Brazil, slipping inland into the *sertão*, a semi-arid interior plagued by drought and appallingly unequal land distribution. All the major cities of the Northeast are on the coast; the two most famous are Salvador and **Recife** – both magical blends of Africa, Portugal and the Americas – but **Fortaleza** is also impressive, bristling with skyscrapers and justly proud of its progressive culture.

When to go

Brazil splits into four distinct **climatic** regions. The coldest part – in fact the only part of Brazil that ever gets really cold – is the **South and Southeast**, the region roughly from central Minas Gerais to Rio Grande do Sul that includes Belo Horizonte, São Paulo and Porto Alegre. Here, there's a distinct winter between June and September, with occasional cold, wind and rain. However, although Brazilians complain, it's all fairly mild. Temperatures rarely hit freezing overnight, and when they do it's featured on the TV news. The coldest part is the interior of Rio

Football

Football was introduced into Brazil by Scottish railway engineers in the 1890s, and Brazilians took to it like a duck to water. By the 1920s the **Rio and São Paulo leagues** that dominate Brazilian football had been founded, and Brazil became the first South American country to compete in the **World Cup** (*Copas*) in Europe, sending a squad to France in 1938. Brazil is the only country in the world to have participated in every *Copa*, and it has won more titles than any other country.

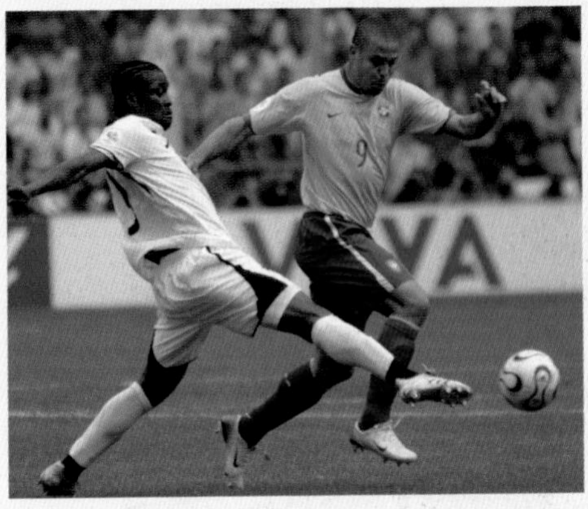

A series of great teams, all with the legendary **Pelé** as playmaker, won the World Cup in Stockholm in 1958 (the only World Cup won by a South American team in Europe), Chile in 1962 and, most memorably, **1970 in Mexico**, where Pelé played alongside such great names as Jairzinho, Rivelino, Carlos Alberto, Gerson and Tostão. It took Brazil until 1994 to reclaim the World Cup, but they won again in 2002, with superstar **Ronaldo** scoring two goals in a fairytale final against Germany. Unfortunately, Brazil's 2006 campaign saw the country's great expectations come crashing to earth, thanks to a combination of complacency, poor management and over-confidence.

Brazil's *favelas* and small towns, to whom football offers a glittering exit route, are a permanent conveyor belt of talent, ensuring that the country will always be a contender at the highest level.

Grande do Sul, in the extreme south of the country, but even here there are many warm, bright days in winter, and the summer (Dec–March) is hot. Only in Santa Catarina's central highlands does it occasionally snow.

The **coastal climate** is exceptionally good. Brazil has been called a "crab civilization" because most of its population lives on or near the coast – with good reason. Seven thousand kilometres of coastline, from Paraná to near the equator, bask under a warm tropical climate. There is a "winter", when there are cloudy days and sometimes the temperature dips below 25°C (77°F), and a rainy season, when it can really pour. In Rio and points south, **the summer rains** last from October through to January, but they come much earlier in the Northeast, lasting about three months from April

◀ Teatro Amazonas, Manaus

in Fortaleza and Salvador, and from May in Recife. Even in winter or the rainy season, the weather will be excellent much of the time.

The **Northeast** is too hot to have a winter. Nowhere is the average monthly temperature below 25°C (77°F) and the interior, semi-arid at the best of times, often soars beyond that – regularly to as much as 40°C (104°F). Rain is sparse and irregular, although violent. **Amazônia** is stereotyped as being steamy jungle with constant rainfall, but much of the region has a distinct dry season – apparently getting longer every year in the most deforested areas of its eastern and western regions. And in the large expanses of savanna in the northern and central Amazon basin, rainfall is far from constant. Belém is closest to the image of a steamy tropical city: it rains there an awful lot from January to May, and merely quite a lot for the rest of the year. Manaus and central Amazônia, in contrast, have a marked dry season from July to October.

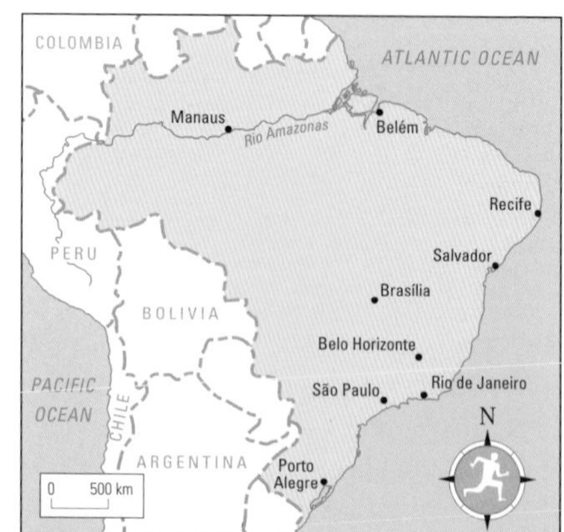

Average temperatures (°C) and rainfall

The first figure is the average maximum temperature; the second the average minimum; and the third the average number of rainy days per month. To convert °C to °F, multiply by 9, then divide by 5 and add 32.

	Jan	Feb	Mar	Apr	May	Jun	Jul	Aug	Sep	Oct	Nov	Dec
Belém												
max. temp.	31	30	30	31	31	32	32	32	32	32	32	32
min. temp.	23	23	23	23	23	23	22	22	22	22	22	22
rainy days	24	26	25	22	24	15	14	15	13	10	11	14
Belo Horizonte												
max. temp.	27	27	27	27	25	24	24	25	27	27	27	26
min. temp.	18	18	17	16	12	10	10	12	14	16	17	18
rainy days	15	13	9	4	4	2	2	1	2	10	12	14
Brasília												
max. temp.	27	28	28	28	27	26	26	28	30	29	27	27
min. temp.	18	18	18	17	15	13	13	14	16	18	18	18
rainy days	19	16	15	9	3	1	0	2	4	11	15	20
Manaus												
max. temp.	30	30	30	30	31	31	32	33	33	33	32	31
min. temp.	23	23	23	23	24	23	23	24	24	24	24	24
rainy days	20	18	21	20	18	12	12	5	7	4	12	16
Porto Alegre												
max. temp.	31	30	29	25	22	20	20	21	22	24	27	29
min. temp.	20	20	19	16	13	11	10	11	13	15	17	18
rainy days	9	10	10	6	6	8	8	8	11	10	8	8
Recife												
max. temp.	30	30	30	30	29	28	27	27	28	29	30	30
min. temp.	25	25	24	23	23	22	21	22	22	23	24	24
rainy days	7	8	10	11	17	16	17	14	7	3	4	4
Rio de Janeiro												
max. temp.	30	30	27	29	26	25	25	25	25	26	28	28
min. temp.	23	23	23	21	20	18	18	18	19	20	20	22
rainy days	13	11	9	9	6	5	5	4	5	11	10	12
Salvador												
max. temp.	29	29	29	28	27	26	26	26	27	28	28	29
min. temp.	23	23	24	23	22	21	21	21	21	22	23	23
rainy days	6	9	17	19	22	23	18	15	10	8	9	11
São Paulo												
max. temp.	28	28	27	25	23	22	21	23	25	25	25	26
min. temp.	18	18	17	15	13	11	10	11	13	14	15	16
rainy days	15	13	12	6	3	4	4	3	5	12	11	14

32 things not to miss

It's not possible to see everything that Brazil has to offer in one trip – and we don't suggest you try. What follows is a selective and subjective taste of the country's highlights: vibrant cities, world-class festivals, natural wonders and stunning architecture. They're arranged in five colour-coded categories to help you find the very best things to see, do and experience. All entries have a page reference to take you straight into the text, where you can find out more.

01 Carnaval Page **54** • For a memorable experience, take in the most important of Brazil's festivals, celebrated in notably grand style in Rio, Salvador and Olinda.

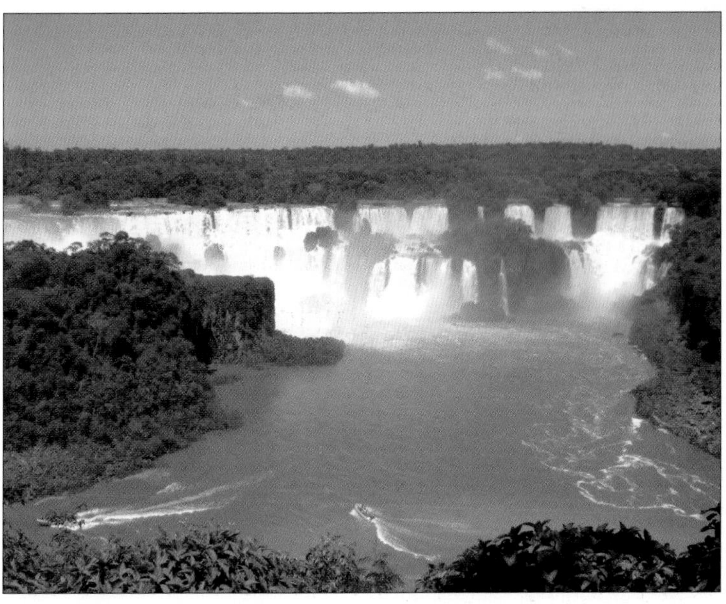

02 Iguaçu Falls Page **708** • The power and beauty of the falls is quite simply astonishing, only rivalled by the tranquillity of the Mata Atlântica behind.

03 Teatro Amazonas Page **465** • If you can't attend one of the regular concerts, be sure to take a guided tour of this remarkable opera house, painstakingly built from materials brought from Europe.

04 Reggae bands Page **399** • Keep your ears open for infectious reggae beats throughout the Northeast, whether in atmospheric bars or on the street.

05 Views from the Corcovado, Rio Page 102 • Ascend the Corcovado mountain – where the image of Christ the Redeemer stands – for breathtaking views taking in the whole of Rio and Guanabara Bay.

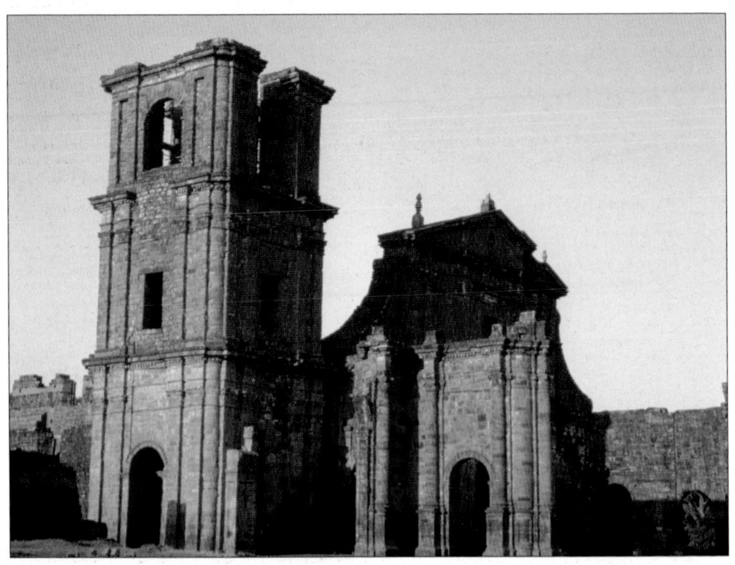

06 The Jesuit missions Page 777 • Admire the striking ruins of São Miguel in Brazil or combine a visit with other Jesuit missions in what is now Argentina and Paraguay.

07 Ouro Preto Page **199** • Some truly remarkable Baroque churches are tucked away in the steep, narrow streets of this charming town.

08 Parque Nacional da Tijuca Page **121** • This impressive expanse of Mata Atlântica is criss-crossed by shaded trails and features refreshing waterfalls and spectacular views across Rio.

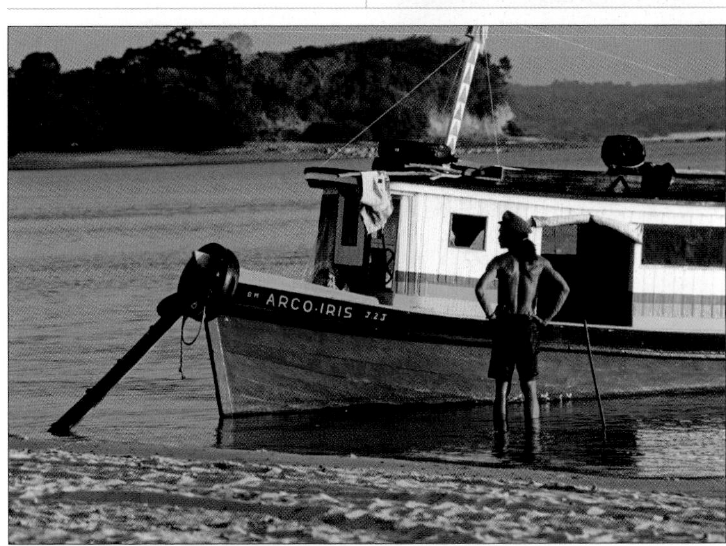

09 River journeys Page **418** • Take a slow boat along the Amazon for close-up views of the mighty river and its wildlife.

10 Visiting Rio's beaches Page **105** • On weekends you can hang with locals who escape to Rio's sands to play sports, catch up on gossip or simply people-watch.

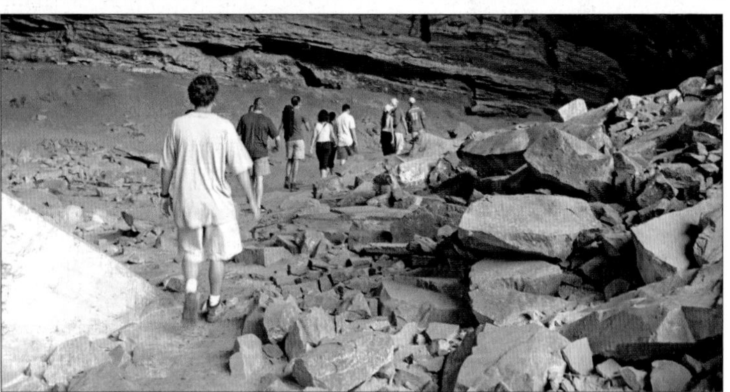

11 Trekking in the Chapada Diamantina Page **294** • Explore the dramatic terrain of this enormous national park, which includes mesas, forest, river beaches, waterfalls and a kilometre-long grotto.

12 Brazilian Baroque art Page **212** • Within this style, Aleijadinho's sculptures are remarkable, none more so than the *Passion* figures in Congonhas.

13 Theatro Municipal, Rio Page **97** • If you can't catch a show inside Rio's sumptuous belle époque theatre, be sure to stop for lunch or a drink in its lavish, Assyrian-inspired café.

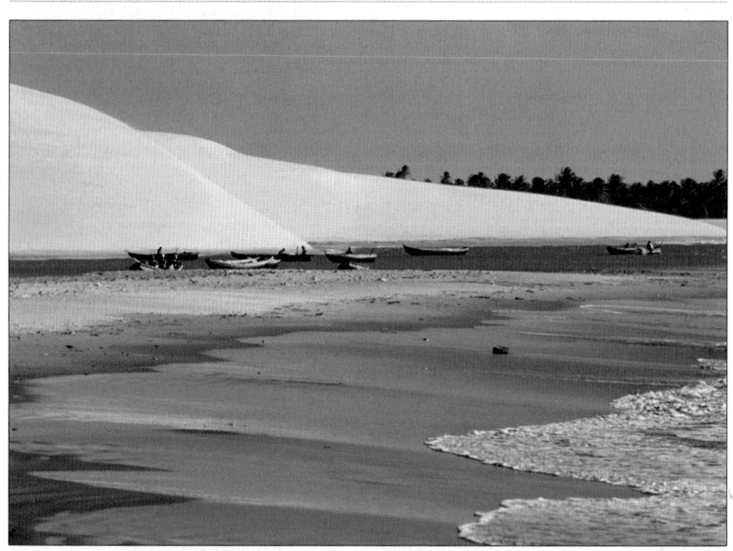

14 Northeast beaches Page **391** • North of Salvador the coastline is stunning, with waters good for surfing or sailing in a traditional *jangada*, as well as fine white sand dunes like the ones at Jericoacoara.

15 Ilhabela Page **668** • A playground for São Paulo's rich, this island boasts some of the area's most beautiful beaches, thanks to strictly enforced environmental protection laws.

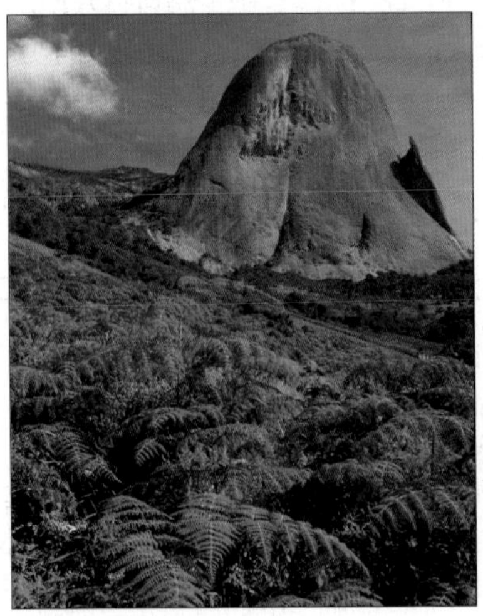

17 Pedra Azul Page **250** • This massive stone mountain is renowned for the shade of blue it seems to turn at dawn and at sunset.

16 The Pantanal Page **583** • You'll be hard-pressed to not spot wildlife in the world's biggest inland swamp.

18 Churrascarias Page **50** • Sample grilled meats of all kinds at these typical *gaúcho* barbecue houses.

19 Capoeira Page **270** • Stop into a *capoeira* school, where you can watch the dance-like sparring of this distinctive martial art for free.

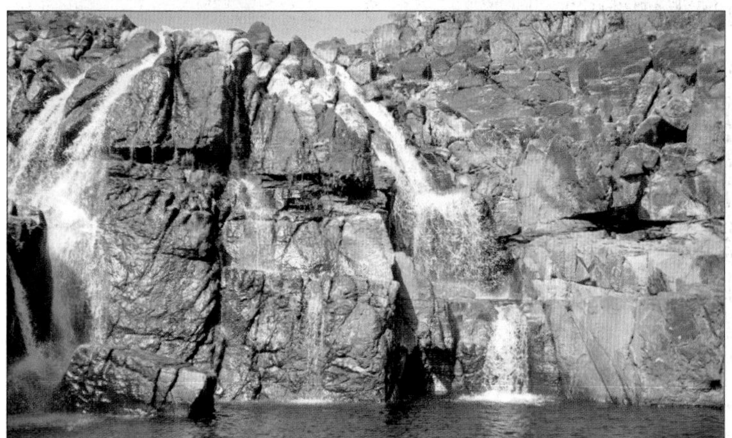

20 Parque Nacional Chapada dos Veadeiros Page **548** • Head just a few hours north of Brasília to take in this spectacular wilderness area, dotted with striking geological formations, caves, waterfalls and hiking trails.

21 Museu de Arte Contemporânea, Niterói Page **142** • Take a short ferry ride from Rio and spend some time at this spaceship-like museum, one of Oscar Niemeyer's architectural masterpieces.

22 Olinda Page **335** • The cobbled streets of the city's historic centre offer up countless examples of beautiful colonial architecture.

23 Rio nightlife Page **129** • A rather seedy inner-city *bairro* by day, Lapa at night pounds to infectious Brazilian rhythms, its nightclubs and bars teeming with locals and tourists alike.

24 Fazendas Page **661** • Visit these impressive rural estates, relics of São Paulo's coffee-producing boom. The *Fazenda Pinhal*, near São Carlos, is among the best preserved.

25 Colonial Rio Page **109** • There are more colonial churches in Rio than anywhere else in Brazil, and the Igreja de Nossa Senhora da Glória do Outeiro is quite simply the prettiest.

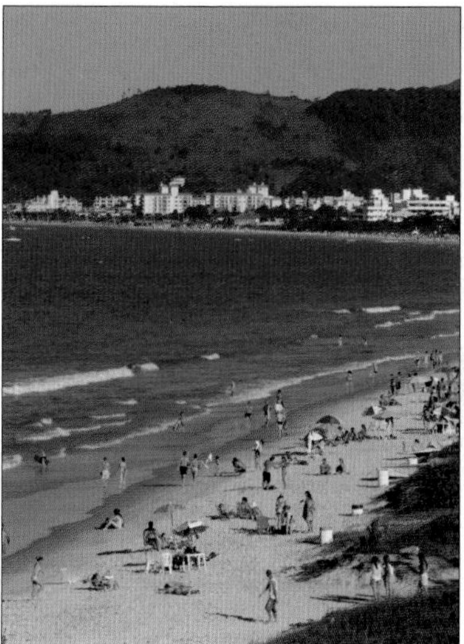

26 Florianópolis beaches Page **722** • Head to the island capital of Santa Catarina state, where kilometres of beaches include treacherous surfing spots and calm waters for safe swimming.

27 Avenida Paulista, São Paulo Page **634** • Get a sense of the city's impressive modern face through its major thoroughfare, lined with skyscrapers as well as opulent mansions.

28 Paraty Page **155** • This picturesque spot remains one of Brazil's best-preserved colonial towns, and it's a great base from which to explore the surrounding Costa Verde.

29 Brazilian architecture Page **525 & 632** • Whether it looks like a futuristic dream or a nightmare, Brazil's modern-day architecture is often otherworldly.

30 Markets Page **629** • Walk through any market in Brazil to get a sense of the country's natural abundance. São Paulo's Mercado Municipal, crammed with produce from all over Brazil, is particularly impressive.

31 Candomblé celebrations Page **279** • Usually identifiable by their white dress, followers of this popular Afro-Brazilian religious cult worship together in exuberant dance ceremonies as well as at fiestas.

32 The Aquário Natural Page **575** • Snorkel among some thirty-odd species of fish in the crystalline waters of this marine sanctuary, or else spy on them from above in a glass-bottomed boat.

Basics

Basics

Getting there 27
Insurance 35
Health 36
Getting around 41
Accommodation 47
Food and drink 49
The media 53
Festivals 54
Travelling with children 56
Women travellers 57
Travel essentials 57

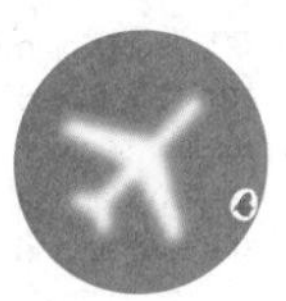

Getting there

Unless you are entering Brazil overland from a neighbouring South American country, you'll almost certainly arrive by air. Airfares always depend on the season: the specific dates vary somewhat between airlines, but high season is generally July and August, then again mid-December to 25 December; low season is any other time. Fares don't normally rise over Carnaval (Feb–March), but getting a seat can be difficult. Airline competition is fierce, however, and special offers are often available.

You can usually cut costs by going through a **specialist flight agent** – either a consolidator, who buys up blocks of tickets from the airlines and sells them at a discount, or a **discount agent**, who in addition to dealing with discounted flights may also offer special student and youth fares and a range of other travel-related services such as travel insurance, car rentals, tours and the like. If you plan on purchasing some kind of air pass or want to book a hotel room for your first few days in Brazil, it is certainly easier to go through a specialist agent.

Apart from discounted tickets, it's worth checking fares **directly with the airlines** that fly to Brazil. Especially during low season, airlines frequently offer competitive fares, although they may carry certain restrictions such as having to spend at least seven days abroad (maximum stay three months).

If you plan to do a fair amount of travelling within Brazil (or to other South American countries), think about buying an **air pass** with your main ticket. Depending on your itinerary, these passes can offer worthwhile savings, but can only be bought outside South America with your international ticket. See p.41 for details of the various options.

Flights from the US and Canada

There are numerous gateways to Brazil in the **US and Canada**; direct flights leave from Atlanta, LA, Chicago, Dallas, Miami, New York, Orlando, Washington and Toronto. Varig and TAM are the only Brazilian carriers. The vast majority of flights go to either Rio or São Paulo, though it is possible to fly into Belo Horizonte, Recife, Salvador, Manaus and Belém. The other carriers serving Brazil are American, Air Canada, Continental, Delta, Japan Airlines and United. If your ultimate destination is somewhere other than these cities, unless you enter the country on one of the relatively few flights into a Brazilian regional airport, it is almost always best to connect in São Paulo, the main hub for internal flights.

From the US

The greatest number of flights and destinations from the US are offered by the Brazilian airlines **Varig** and **TAM**. Varig flies regularly to **Rio** and **São Paulo** from New York, LA and Miami, as well as weekly to **Fortaleza** and **Recife** from Miami. **TAM**, which has the advantage of better service and a newer fleet now carries more passengers to Brazil from the United States than Varig: flights run from Miami, Orlando and New York to Rio and São Paulo. Excursion-fare ticket prices vary depending on your length of stay in Brazil: count on spending at least US$150 more for a ticket valid for up to three months than a ticket for up to one month. Fares to Rio and São Paulo are almost always the same. Varig offers one-month excursion fares from New York to São Paulo for US$759, from Miami to São Paulo for US$626, and from LA to São Paulo for US$756 – all valid year-round. Unrestricted fares are much higher: a three-month ticket from New York to São Paulo, for example, costs US$1345 low season, US$1465 high season.

The **other airlines** serving Brazil fly chiefly out of New York, LA or Miami to Rio and São Paulo. There are also direct flights from Washington-Dulles and Chicago with United,

Dallas with American, Houston with Continental and Atlanta with Delta. An excellent option for those planning to focus mainly on the Amazon is Lloyd Aero Boliviano's thrice-weekly service to Santa Cruz in Bolivia from Miami, which stops at Manaus (US$800 return).

In a country the size of Brazil, **open-jaw tickets** can be very good value, allowing you to fly into one city and out from another. Varig's fares from LA to Rio and São Paulo, for example, are US$1244 low season and US$1356 high season for an open-jaw Apex ticket valid for a minimum of 21 days.

If you plan to include Brazil as a stop on a **round-the-world ticket**, figure on US$1800 for a ticket including New York, Paris, Madrid, São Paulo, and a return to New York. Slightly more than US$4000 will get you from London to Rio, South Africa, North Africa, Southeast Asia, Australia, Japan, the US and back to London.

Flights via other countries

If you're looking for slightly cheaper fares, and can put up with the longer flight times, or you're tempted to break your journey, it's worth checking out what the national airlines of Brazil's South American neighbours have to offer. Aerolíneas Argentinas, for instance, flies to Rio and São Paulo from Miami and New York via Buenos Aires. Others routings worth investigating include travelling via Bogotá with Avianca or Panama with Copa Airlines. TACV flies from Boston to Fortaleza via Cape Verde Islands for US$1100.

If you plan on travelling in other South American countries besides Brazil, the **Mercosur Airpass** or the **TAM South American Airpass** are good-value options (see p.41).

From Canada

Direct flight choices from Canada are limited to Air Canada's daily service from Toronto to São Paulo. Discount travel agents will be able to offer good prices on routes via the US, which tend to be cheaper. Travel Cuts is the most reliable student/youth agency, and also offers some deals for non-students; or check the travel ads in your local newspaper and consult a good travel agent. From Toronto or elsewhere in eastern Canada, expect to pay around C$1800 during high season (July and August and 15 to 25 December) and C$1400 during low season. Fares from Vancouver and western Canada are around C$1900 in the high season and C$1500 in the low season).

Flights from the UK and Ireland

There are plenty of choices of carriers to Brazil **from the UK**, with São Paulo and Rio being the usual points of arrival. If your ultimate destination is neither of these cities, it is almost always best to fly to connect in São Paulo, the main hub for internal flights, unless you enter the country on one of the relatively few flights into a Brazilian regional airport. Since direct flights can be booked up well in advance and can be more expensive, you may want to consider a flight via another country.

Two airlines operate **direct flights** to Brazil from the UK: British Airways and Varig (Brazilian Airlines). Despite British Airways having newer planes and a much higher level of service, the official fares of the two airlines are usually very similar, currently starting at around £700 for a thirty-day return **to Rio or São Paulo** in low season, £860 high season (July and August and 14–25 December). With these tickets, return dates are in theory fixed, but once in Brazil both airlines will allow you to change the date (within the thirty days) for a fee of around £75. These fares are pretty notional and you will usually get the same tickets through travel agencies at reduced prices.

There are almost always good deals available from travel **agencies specializing in Latin America** as well as from general discount travel agencies; fares are sometimes as low as £450 in low season, rising to around £700 for high-season departures. The **cheapest fares**, however, are often offered on **routes via Europe** – with Air France via Paris, TAP via Lisbon or Iberia via Madrid. Other inexpensive options to São Paulo only include Alitalia via Milan, KLM via Amsterdam and Swiss via Zurich. You may be offered an attractive fare to Rio or São Paulo with Lufthansa via Frankfurt, but in reality this is likely to be a code-shared Varig flight. Prices tend to be the same whether you begin your journey in London or at one of the UK's **regional airports**; you may find it better value and more convenient to use one of these airlines rather than flying out of Heathrow with British Airways or Varig.

As Brazil is such a large country, an open-jaw ticket – flying into one city and leaving from another – may, according to your itinerary, make sense. Rio and São Paulo offer most airline possibilities, but flying with TAP broadens your options, including also Fortaleza, Natal, Recife and Salvador.

There are no direct flights **from Ireland** to Brazil. There are, however, connections via London or other European capitals. The best deals are available from budget or student travel agents in Ireland, but it's also worth contacting specialist agents in England for cheap fares, an unusual route or a package.

Flying out of Dublin, the cheapest discount fare is currently with Air France (€800 low season, €1200 high season) via Paris, though other airlines also offer competitive fares.

The Northeast and the Amazon

If you want the **Northeast** to be your point of entry into Brazil, TAP offers by far the best

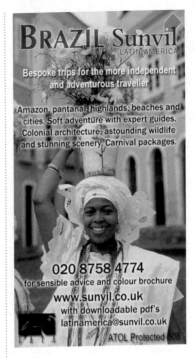

range of destinations, with flights via Lisbon most days to Fortaleza, Natal, Recife and Salvador. Alternatively, once a week the Brazilian airline TAM flies to Recife from Paris. **Fares** are very similar, with £415 typically offered for low season departures, rising to £640 in the high season. Competitive fares to Fortaleza are available with TACV (£520 low season, £600 high season) from Amsterdam, which allow the option of a stopover in the Cape Verde Islands, off the coast of West Africa, at no additional cost.

Flying to the **Amazon** is expensive and time-consuming. The quickest way is to catch a plane to Miami, where you can connect with the twice-weekly Lloyd Aéreo Boliviano service to Manaus (around US$800 return). It is usually much cheaper, however, to fly from Heathrow to Manaus with Varig, changing planes in São Paulo. An unusual but fairly expensive and time-consuming route is with Air France via Paris to Cayenne in French Guiana (£520 low season, £680 high season), and then onwards with Air Caraïbes to Belém (£150). If you want the western Amazon to be your point of arrival, you're best off making your way to Bogotá in Colombia and taking a connecting internal flight to Leticia, just a short taxi ride from the Brazilian town of Tabatinga.

Other ticket options

Several airlines offer **stopovers** to or from Brazil at no extra cost. Apart from the airlines with European (and Cape Verdean) transit points already mentioned, stopover possibilities most commonly involve the **US**. United Airlines via Washington or New York is generally the least expensive option (around £450 low season, £700 high season) with good deals also sometimes available with American Airlines via Miami or New York or with Continental via Newark or Houston.

Combining Brazil with a longer trip in the southern hemisphere, or putting together a **round-the-world ticket**, is possible but expensive. The most popular ticket option is a one-way to Sydney via Brazil and Argentina (around £470 low season, £650 high season) and a separate ticket back to London via Southeast Asia or North America. Another possibility is onward to Johannesburg from São Paulo on South African Airways.

Flights from Australia, New Zealand and South Africa

The best deals and fastest routing to Brazil **from Australasia** are offered by Aerolíneas Argentina and LanChile. There are fewer options flying via the US and fares are more expensive and take much more time. Round-the-world fares that include South America tend to cost more than other RTW options, but can be worthwhile if you have the time to make the most of a few stopovers.

From **Australia**, flights to South America leave from Sydney. The most direct route is with Aerolíneas Argentinas, which flies via Auckland to Buenos Aires, from where there are good connections direct to Florianópolis, Porto Alegre, Rio and São Paulo. LanChile has a weekly direct flight via Auckland to Santiago, with onward connections to Rio or São Paulo. More long-winded, there are twice-weekly connections via Papeete and Easter Island with Air New Zealand and LanChile to Santiago. Travelling through the US, United Airlines, American Airlines or Delta can fly you to São Paulo or Rio via either Los Angeles or San Francisco and Atlanta or Miami. From **New Zealand**, you can pick up one of the United, Aerolíneas Argentinas or Air New Zealand/LanChile flights in Auckland.

In general, fares depend on the **duration of stay**, rather than the season – cut-off points when flying via Chile and Argentina are 35 days, 45 days, 90 days, 6 months and 1 year; flying via the US they are 21 days, 45 days and 180 days – but bear in mind that prices for flights (and everything else) soar during Christmas and Carnaval (Dec–March).

On the **more direct routes** with Aerolíneas Argentina you should be able to get a return fare for A$2400/NZ$2600. Flying via Santiago with LanChile you can expect to pay around A$3100/NZ$3300, while fares via the US will be at least A$3500/NZ$3700.

An **open-jaw ticket** can work out to be a convenient option. Flying into Rio and out of São Paulo (or vice versa) on Aerolíneas Argentinas or LanChile, for example, won't

Fly less – stay longer! Travel and climate change

Climate change is a serious threat to the ecosystems that humans rely upon, and air travel is among the fastest-growing contributors to the problem. Rough Guides regard travel, overall, as a global benefit, and feel strongly that the advantages to developing economies are important, as is the opportunity of greater contact and awareness among peoples. But we all have a responsibility to limit our personal impact on global warming, and that means giving thought to how often we fly, and what we can do to redress the harm that our trips create.

Flying and climate change

Pretty much every form of motorized travel generates CO2 – the main cause of human-induced climate change – but planes also generate climate-warming contrails and cirrus clouds and emit oxides of nitrogen, which create ozone (another greenhouse gas) at flight levels. Furthermore, flying simply allows us to travel much further than we otherwise would do. The figures are frightening: one person taking a return flight between Europe and California produces the equivalent impact of 2.5 tonnes of CO2 – similar to the yearly output of the average UK car.

Fuel-cell and other less harmful types of plane may emerge eventually. But until then, there are really just two options for concerned travellers: to reduce the amount we travel by air (take fewer trips – stay for longer!), and to make the trips we do take "climate neutral" via a carbon offset scheme.

Carbon offset schemes

Offset schemes run by ⓦclimatecare.org, ⓦcarbonneutral.com and others allow you to make up for some or all of the greenhouse gases that you are responsible for releasing. To do this, they provide "carbon calculators" for working out the global-warming contribution of a specific flight (or even your entire existence), and then let you contribute an appropriate amount of money to fund offsetting measures. These include rainforest reforestation and initiatives to reduce future energy demand – often run in conjunction with sustainable development schemes.

Rough Guides, together with Lonely Planet and other concerned partners in the travel industry, are supporting a **carbon offset scheme** run by climatecare.org. Please take the time to view our website and see how you can help to make your trip climate neutral.

ⓦwww.roughguides.com/climatechange

cost you any more than a straight through-fare to Rio.

Flights from South Africa

Brazil can be reached directly by a number of airlines from Johannesburg. South African Airlines fly to Salvador and São Paulo; Varig and TAP Portugal fly to Rio and São Paulo; and British Airways and Malaysian Airlines fly only to São Paulo.

RTW flights

If Brazil is only one stop on a longer journey, you might want to consider buying a **round-the-world (RTW) ticket**. Some travel agents can sell you an "off-the-shelf" RTW ticket that will have you touching down in about half a dozen cities (Rio de Janeiro and São Paulo are on some itineraries); others will have to assemble one for you, which can be tailored to your needs but is apt to be more expensive.

The limited choice, and the fact that most fares are mileage-based, make RTW routes via South America more expensive than other RTW options. Ultimately, your choice of route will depend on where else you want to visit besides Brazil. To include Brazil in a RTW itinerary, expect to pay at least A$4000/ NZ$4300.

Ships

It is still just about possible to get to Brazil from Europe **by ship**, though it's expensive and slow. You'll arrive by cargo boat, most of which have room for around twelve passengers travelling in some luxury – there's usually a swimming pool, for example – though the food tends to be plain. Ships take about two weeks to cross the Atlantic, depending on where they call en route.

The Strand Cruise Centre (Charing Cross Shopping Concourse, The Strand, London WC2; ⓣ020/7836 6363) is the agent for a range of ships departing from Tilbury and Southampton. Most ships dock in Rio and Santos (a few stop first in Recife, Salvador and Vitória), before heading south to Paranaguá, Itajaí and Buenos Aires and, less frequently, on to Rio Grande and Montevideo. The cheapest one-way berth in a shared inside cabin to any east coast port is about £950, with prices rising steeply to over £3000 for a return passage in a single outside cabin.

Airlines, agents and operators

Online booking

ⓦ**www.expedia.co.uk** (in UK), ⓦ**www.expedia.com** (in US), ⓦ**www.expedia.ca** (in Canada), ⓦ**www.lastminute.com** (in UK), ⓦ**www.opodo.co.uk** (in UK), ⓦ**www.orbitz.com** (in US), ⓦ**www.travelocity.co.uk** (in UK), ⓦ**www.travelocity.com** (in US), ⓦ**www.travelocity.ca** (in Canada), ⓦ**www.zuji.com.au** (in Australia), ⓦ**www.zuji.co.nz** (in New Zealand).

Airlines

Aerolíneas Argentinas Australia ⓣ02/9252-5150, New Zealand ⓣ09/379-3675, ⓦwww.aerolineas.com.
Air Canada ⓣ1-888/247-2262, ⓦwww.aircanada.ca.
Air Caraïbes US ⓣ1-877/772-1005, France ⓣ01/4783-8975, ⓦwww.aircaribes.com. ⓦwww.aircaraibes.com.
Air France UK ⓣ0845/084-5111, Republic of Ireland ⓣ01/844-5633, ⓦwww.airfrance.fr.
Air New Zealand Australia ⓣ13 24 76, ⓦwww.airnz.com.au, New Zealand ⓣ0800/737-000, ⓦwww.airnz.co.nz.
Alitalia UK ⓣ0870/544-8259, ⓦwww.alitalia.co.uk, Republic of Ireland ⓣ01/677-5171, ⓦwww.alitalia.ie.
American Airlines UK ⓣ0/7365-0777 or 0845/7789-789, ⓦwww.aa.co.uk, Republic of Ireland ⓣ01/602-0550, ⓦwww.americanairlines.ie.
Avianca ⓣ1-800/284-2622, ⓦwww.avianca.com.
British Airways UK ⓣ0870/850-9850, Republic of Ireland ⓣ1800/626-747, ⓦwww.britishairways.com.
Continental Airlines US and Canada ⓣ1-800/523-3273, UK ⓣ0845/607-6760, Ireland ⓣ1890/925-252, Australia ⓣ2/9244-2242, NZ ⓣ9/308-3350, International ⓣ1-800/231-0856, ⓦwww.continental.com.
Copa Airlines US ⓣ1-800/FLY-COPA, ⓦwww.copaair.com.
Delta US and Canada ⓣ1-800/221-1212, UK ⓣ0845/600-0950, Republic of Ireland ⓣ1850/882-031 or 01/407-3165, Australia ⓣ1-300/302-849, New Zealand ⓣ09/379-3370, ⓦwww.delta.com.
Iberia US ⓣ1-800/772-4642, UK ⓣ020/7830-0011, Republic of Ireland ⓣ01/677-9846, ⓦwww.iberia.com.
JAL (Japan Air Lines) US and Canada ⓣ1-800/525-3663, UK ⓣ0845/774-7700, Ireland ⓣ01/408-3757, Australia ⓣ02/9272-1111, New Zealand ⓣ09/379-9906, ⓦwww.jal.com or ⓦwww.japanair.com.
KLM (Royal Dutch Airlines) See Northwest/KLM. UK ⓣ0870/507-4074, Republic of Ireland ⓣ0870/507-4074, Australia ⓣ1-300/303-747, New Zealand ⓣ09/309-1782; ⓦwww.klm.com.
LanChile US and Canada ⓣ1-866/435-9526, UK ⓣ0800/917-0572, Australia ⓣ1-300/361-400 or 02/9244-2333, New Zealand ⓣ09/977-2233, ⓦwww.lan.com.
Lloyd Aéreo Boliviano UK ⓣ020/7565-9606, ⓦwww.labairlines.com.
Lufthansa US ⓣ1-800/645-3880, Canada ⓣ1-800/563-5954, UK ⓣ0845/773-7747 or 0845/773-7747, Republic of Ireland ⓣ01/844-5544, Australia ⓣ1300/655-727, New Zealand ⓣ09/303-1529, ⓦwww.lufthansa.com.
Swiss ⓣ1-877/FLY-SWIS, UK ⓣ0845/601-0956, Australia ⓣ1300/724-666, New Zealand ⓣ09/977-2238, ⓦwww.swiss.com.
Syrian Airlines UK ⓣ020/7631-3511, ⓦwww.syrianairlines.co.uk.
TAC ⓣ1-866/359-8228, ⓦwww.tacv.cv.
Taca US ⓣ1-800/400-TACA, Canada ⓣ1-800/722-TACA, UK ⓣ0870/2410-340, Australia ⓣ02/824/80020, ⓦwww.taca.com.
TACV (Cape Verde Airlines) UK ⓣ0196/453-6191.
TAM UK ⓣ020/8903-4003, ⓦwww.tam.br.
TAP (Air Portugal) US and Canada ⓣ1-800/221-7370, ⓣ020/8745-7562, Australia ⓣ02/9244-2344, New Zealand ⓣ09/308-3373, ⓦwww.flytap.com.
United Airlines US ⓣ1-800/241-6522, UK ⓣ0845/844-4777, Republic of Ireland

Ⓣ1-800/535-300, Australia Ⓣ13 17 77, Ⓦwww.united.com.
Varig (Brazilian Airlines) US and Canada Ⓣ1-800/GO-VARIG, UK Ⓣ0845/603-7601, Ⓦwww.varig.com.

Agents and operators

Abercrombie & Kent Ⓣ1-800/323-7308 or 630/954-2944, Ⓦwww.abercrombiekent.com. Tours to the Amazon, multi-country tours, and individually customized tours.
Adventure Associates Australia Ⓣ02/9389-7466 or Ⓣ 1800/222-141, Ⓦwww.adventureassociates.com. Offers a wide range of tours, from four-day Pantanal eco-tours and week-long Carnaval packages, to individually tailored adventure and special interest holidays.
Adventure Center Ⓣ 1-800/228-8747 or 510/654-1879, Ⓦwww.adventurecenter.com. Group tours of South America that include Brazil.
Adventure Specialists Australia Ⓣ02/9261-2927, Ⓦsydney.citysearch.com.au. Overland specialist. Agents for Encounter Overland's expeditions, and G.A.P.'s Amazon river cruises.
Adventure World Australia Ⓣ02/8913-0755, Ⓦwww.adventureworld.com.au; New Zealand Ⓣ09/524-5118, Ⓦwww.adventureworld.co.nz. Agents for a vast array of international adventure travel companies – including Explore Worldwide – that offer tours in Brazil.
Anywhere Travel Australia Ⓣ02/9663-0411, Ⓦwww.anywheretravel.com.au.
Brazil Nuts Ⓣ1-800/553-9959, Ⓦwww.brazilnuts.com. Tours that promise to take you off the beaten track to experience Brazil's cities, the Amazon basin and the Pantanal.
Brazil Tours UK Ⓣ0870/442-4241, Ⓦwww.braziltours.co.uk. Flight agents and tour operators to Brazil and elsewhere in South America.
Bridge the World UK Ⓣ0870/444-7474, Ⓦwww.bridgetheworld.com. Specializing in round-the-world tickets, including Brazil, with good deals aimed at the backpacker market.
Club Travel P.O. Box 2055, Cape Town 8000 Ⓣ027/21 487-4200, Ⓔfatimas@clubtravel.co.za, Ⓦwww.clubtravel.co.za.
Conservation International Ⓣ1-800/429-5660, Ⓦwww.conservation.org. Offers the opportunity to work on environmental volunteer projects in Brazil.
Contours Travel Australia Ⓣ03/9670-6900, Ⓦwww.contourstravel.com.au. Specialists in tailored city packages and ecotours, including trips to Rio, Iguassu, the Amazon and the Pantanal.
Earthwatch Institute Ⓣ978/461-0081 or 1-800/776-0188, Ⓦwww.earthwatch.org. Organizes trips for volunteers to work overseas on scientific and cultural projects, with a strong emphasis on protection and preservation of the ecology and environment.
ebookers UK Ⓣ0800/082-3000, Republic of Ireland Ⓣ01/488-3507, Ⓦwww.ebookers.com. Low fares on an extensive selection of scheduled flights and package deals.
EcoAdventures Ⓣ1-800/326-5025, Ⓦwww.ecoadven.com. Individually tailored packages and river cruises.
Encounter Overland UK Ⓣ017/2886-2222 020/7370-6845, Ⓦwww.encounter.co.uk. One of the oldest overland companies going, offering activities such as hiking, climbing and rafting as well as trips off the beaten track in their own converted trucks.
Exodus UK Ⓣ020/8675-5550, Republic of Ireland Ⓣ01/677-1029, Ⓦwww.exodus.co.uk. Adventure tour operator organizing tours for small groups, including walking, biking, overland, adventure and cultural trips.
Explore Worldwide UK Ⓣ01252/760-000, Ⓦwww.explore.co.uk. Small-group tours, treks, expeditions and safaris. Offers 17-day tours of Rio, the Pantanal, the Amazon and Salvador, with accommodation mostly in small local hotels.
Festival Tours Ⓣ1-800/225-0117, Ⓦwww.festivaltours.com. An all-encompassing tour operator to Central and South America focusing on main tourist sights.
Flight Centres Australia Ⓣ13 31 33 or 02/9235-3522, Ⓦwww.flightcentre.com.au; New Zealand Ⓣ0800-243-544 or 09/358-4310, Ⓦwww.flightcentre.co.nz.
Flight Finders International Republic of Ireland Ⓣ01/676-8326. Discounted flights.
Flightbookers UK Ⓣ 0870/010-7000, Ⓦwww.ebookers.com. Low fares on an extensive selection of scheduled flights. Extended opening hours at their branch at Gatwick train station (Ⓣ 01293/568-300).
Focus Tours US Ⓣ01/505/989-7193 Ⓦwww.focustours.com. Ecology-oriented tours, custom-designed to take groups or individuals to destinations such as the Amazon, the Pantanal and the Atlantic forest regions.
Holiday Shoppe New Zealand Ⓣ0800/808-480, Ⓦwww.holidayshoppe.co.nz.
Joe Walsh Tours Republic of Ireland Ⓣ01/676-0991, Ⓦwww.joewalshtours.ie. General budget fares agent.
Journey Latin America Flight agents and tour operators offering 22-day guided tours of Brazil (prices range between about £1500 and £2500) as well as larger-scale overland options, which also take in Paraguay, Bolivia and Peru, or Chile and Argentina.
Last Frontiers UK Ⓣ01296/653-000, Ⓦwww.lastfrontiers.com. Tailor-made itineraries to

Packages and tours

If your trip is short, and if your plan is simply to visit Rio for two weeks, then **package holidays** (flight and accommodation included) can be very good value. A week in a three-star hotel in Copacabana can cost less than £700, and for an extra £400 you can add on a week's tour taking in three or four key places such as Manaus, Salvador and Iguaçu. These packages can be found in brochures at any travel agent, such as Kuoni and Thomas Cook, and through some of the specialists listed here. If you want to go for Carnaval, you'll need to book months in advance and be prepared to pay more.

More varied **tours** are offered by many specialist operators and upmarket package companies. If the ready-packaged tours don't appeal to you, specialist operators can plan itineraries to meet individual requirements, including hotels and transportation within Brazil.

Package tours from Australia and New Zealand are few and far between but, while they may seem a little expensive, can be well worth it, especially if your time is limited, you're unfamiliar with the country's customs and language or you just don't like travelling alone. Specialist travel agents and operators like Adventure World and Adventure Associates offer a range of Brazilian itineraries, from the full package experience to shorter **add-on tours** that give you the flexibility of combining independent travel with, say, an Amazon cruise (three days from Manaus starts at A$/NZ$600 per person, including all meals). Or, if you've got your heart set on Carnaval, pre-booked accommodation costs from A$/NZ$700 per person for four nights.

Adventure tours are worth considering if you want to cover a lot of ground or get to places that could be difficult to reach independently. Encounter Overland's 25-day Argentinian and Brazilian Encounter tour takes you from Tierra del Fuego through Patagonia to Iguaçu Falls and Rio (land only A$/NZ$1600–1800, plus US$275 kitty).

Brazil with a strong wildlife slant. Friendly and knowledgeable staff will point you towards small hotels in destinations throughout Brazil and occasionally organize small groups to attend *rodeios* or to learn to play polo.

Led Tours & Travel P.O. Box 23761, Claremont 7735 ⓣ027/21-531-3493, ⓔledtours@iafrica.com, ⓦwww.ledtours.com.

Lost World Adventures ⓣ1-800/999-0558, ⓦwww.lostworldadventures.com. Customized individual and group tours in Brazil, including Amazon River excursions, and multi-country tours.

Nature Expeditions International ⓣ1-800/869-0639, ⓦwww.naturexp.com. Customized individual and group tours offering ecological adventures and Amazon River cruises.

New Zealand Destinations Unlimited New Zealand ⓣ09/414 1685, ⓦwww.holiday.co.nz.

North South Travel UK ⓣ & ⓕ 01245/608291, ⓦwww.northsouthtravel.co.uk. Friendly, competitive travel agency offering discounted fares worldwide – profits are used to support projects in the developing world, especially the promotion of sustainable tourism.

Skylink ⓣ212/599-0430 or 1-800/633-4488, ⓦwww.skylinkus.com. Consolidator with branches in Chicago, LA, Montréal, Toronto and Washington DC.

Solar Tours ⓣ202/861-5864, ⓦwww.solartours.com. A big operator throughout Latin America, offering cruises, city tours, jungle trips and Carnaval specials.

South American Adventure Travel Australia ⓣ07/3854-1022. Independent and group travel specialists.

South America Travel Centre Australia ⓣ1800/655-051 or 03/9642-5353, ⓦwww.satc.com.au. Specialize in tailor-made trips to Brazil.

Steamond Travel UK ⓣ020/7730-8646, ⓦwww.easyticket.com. Flight agents and tour operators for Brazil and Latin America.

STA Travel UK ⓣ0870/1600-599, ⓦwww.statravel.co.uk. Worldwide specialists in low-cost flights and tours for students and under-26s, though other customers welcome. Also over 200 offices abroad.

Student Uni Travel Australia ⓣ02/9232-8444, ⓦwww.sut.com.au; New Zealand ⓣ09/379-4224, ⓦwww.sut.co.nz

Thompsons Tours South Africa P.O. Box 41032, Craighall 2024 ⓣ027/11-770-7700, ⓔinfo@thompsons.co.za, ⓦwww.thompsons.co.za.
Trailfinders UK ⓣ 020/7628-7628, ⓦwww.trailfinders.co.uk, Republic of Ireland ⓣ01/677-7888, ⓦwww.trailfinders.ie. One of the best-informed and most efficient agents for independent travellers; produces a very useful quarterly magazine worth scrutinizing for round-the-world routes. Offers competitive fares with connections out of all Irish airports.
travel.com.au and travel.co.nz Australia ⓣ1300/130-482 or 02/9249-5444, ⓦwww.travel.com.au; New Zealand ⓣ0800/468 332, ⓦwww.travel.co.nz.
Travel Avenue ⓣ312/876-6866 or 1-800/333-3335, ⓦwww.travelavenue.com. Full-service travel agent that offers discounts in the form of rebates.
Travel Cuts UK ⓣ020/725-2082 or 7255-1944, ⓦwww.travelcuts.co.uk. Canadian company specializing in budget, student and youth travel and round-the-world tickets.
Travel Pak International South Africa P.O. Box 2106, Pinetown 3600 ⓣ 027/31-702-2736, ⓔtravelpak@pixie.co.za.
Travel Vision P.O. Box 4779, Johannesburg 2000 ⓣ027/11-482-5222, ⓔRes@Tvision.co.za, ⓦwww.tvision.co.za.
Veloso Tours UK ⓣ020/8762-0616, ⓦwww.veloso.com. Tailor-made itineraries, especially good beach and family holidays.
Victor Emanuel Nature Tours ⓣ1-800/328-8368, ⓦwww.ventbird.com. Birdwatching tours.
Wild Frontiers South Africa P.O. Box 844, Halfway House 1685 ⓣ027/11-702-2035, ⓔwildfront@icon.co.za, ⓦwww.wildfrontiers.com.
Worldtek Travel ⓣ1-800/243-1723 or 203/772-0470. Discount travel agency

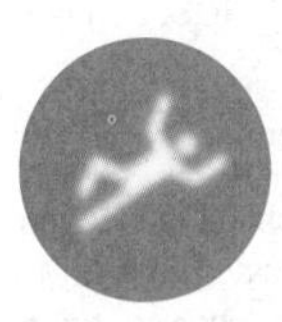

Insurance

Prior to travelling, you should take out an insurance policy to cover against theft, loss and illness or injury. Before paying for a new policy, however, it's worth checking whether you already have some degree of coverage. Credit card companies, home-insurance policies and private medical plans sometimes cover you and your belongings when you're abroad. Most travel agents, tour operators, banks and insurance brokers will be able to help you, or you could consider the travel insurance offered by Rough Guides. Remember that when securing baggage insurance, make sure that the per-article limit – typically under £500 equivalent – will cover your most valuable possession.

After exhausting the possibilities above, you might want to contact a **specialist travel insurance company**. A typical travel insurance policy provides coverage for the loss of baggage, tickets and a certain amount of cash or traveller's cheques, as well as the

Rough Guides Travel Insurance

Rough Guides has teamed up with Columbus Direct to offer you **travel insurance** that can be tailored to suit your needs. Products include a low-cost **backpacker** option for long stays; a **short break** option for city getaways; a typical **holiday package** option; and others. There are also annual **multi-trip** policies for those who travel regularly. Different sports and activities (trekking, skiing, etc) can usually be covered if required.

See our website (ⓦwww.roughguidesinsurance.com) for eligibility and purchasing options. Alternatively, UK residents should call ⓣ0870/033-9988; US citizens should call ⓣ1-800/749-4922; Australians should call ⓣ1-300/669-999. All other nationalities should call ⓣ+44 870/890-2843.

cancellation or curtailment of your trip. Most policies exclude so-called **dangerous sports** (which, in Brazil, can mean scuba diving and trekking, though probably not jeep trips) unless an extra premium is paid. Many policies can be adapted to reflect the coverage you want – for example, sickness and accident benefits can often be excluded or included at will. If you do take medical coverage, verify if benefits will be paid during treatment or only after your return home, and whether there is a 24-hour medical emergency number. If you need to make a claim, keep receipts for medicines and medical treatment. Also, if you have anything stolen from you, you must file an official police report.

Health

Although there are no compulsory vaccinations required to enter the country, certain precautions should be taken, certainly if you're staying for any length of time or visiting the more remote regions. Taking out travel insurance is vital (see p.35), and you should take all possible precautions to guard against AIDS, a major worry in Brazil.

Pharmacies and medical treatment

Most standard drugs are available in **pharmacies**, *farmácias*, which you'll find everywhere – no prescriptions are necessary. A pharmacy will also give injections (you need a tetanus jab if you get bitten by a dog) and free medical advice, and they're a good first line of defence if you fall ill.

If you are unlucky enough to need **medical treatment** in Brazil, forget about the public hospitals – as a foreigner you have virtually no chance of getting a bed unless you have an infectious disease, and the level of health care offered by most is appalling. You can get reasonably good medical and dental care privately: North Americans will think it fairly inexpensive, Europeans used to state-subsidized health care will not. A doctor's visit will cost on average US$25–45; drugs are relatively cheap. Local tourist offices and smart hotels in big cities will have lists of English-, French- and German-speaking **doctors**; ask for a *médico*. Outside the larger centres, you will probably have to try out your Portuguese. If a medical emergency occurs in an out-of-the-way location, there's an excellent **air ambulance** service (Ⓣ011/5506-0606, Ⓕ846-8689) that guarantees collection anywhere in the country within 24 hours of calling. If considering this option (and if you have time), be sure to contact your travel insurance company before phoning for a plane and check that you're fully covered.

Food and water

Many diseases are directly or indirectly related to impure **water** (see "Water purification" box, opposite) and contaminated **food**, and care should be taken in choosing what to eat and drink.

You should, of course, take particular care with seafood, especially **shellfish** – don't eat anything that's at all suspicious. Fruit and salad ingredients should be washed in bottled or purified water or, preferably, peeled. Ultimately you are going to run some risks with food, so if you're going to enjoy your stay to the full, there's no sense in being too paranoid.

Even in the most remote towns and villages **mineral water** (*água mineral*), either sparkling (*com gás*) or still (*sem gás*), is easily available and cheap. To avoid dehydration be sure to drink plenty of non-alcoholic liquids, always carry a bottle of water on long trips and check that the seal on any bottled water you use is intact.

As with food, it's difficult to be on guard all the time while drinking; fruit juices are more often than not diluted, at best with only filtered water, and while it is wise to avoid ice in general, this is well-nigh impossible.

Yellow fever

Getting a **yellow fever vaccination**, which offers protection for ten years, is highly recommended if you're going to **Amazônia, Goiás or Mato Grosso**. Additionally, countries neighbouring Brazil often require a yellow fever vaccination card. This viral disease is transmitted by mosquitoes and can be fatal. Symptoms include headache, fever, abdominal pain and vomiting, and though victims may appear to recover, without medical help they may suffer from bleeding, shock, and kidney and liver failure. While you're waiting for help, it is important to keep the fever as low as possible and prevent dehydration.

Malaria

Malaria is endemic in **northern Brazil**, and anyone intending to travel anywhere in Amazônia should take precautions very seriously. In recent years, rates have climbed as mosquitoes have become more resistant to insecticides, and a few unwary tourists die avoidably every year. With simple precautions you can minimize the chances of getting it even in highly malarial areas, and, properly treated, a dose of malaria should be no worse than a severe bout of flu. But make no mistake – unless you follow the **precautions** outlined here, and take malaria prophylaxis before, during and after you pass through Amazônia, malaria can kill.

There are two kinds of malaria in Brazil: **falciparum**, which is more serious but less common, and **vivax**. Both are transmitted by anopheles mosquitoes, which are most active at sunrise and for an hour or so before sunset. Even in very malarial areas, only around five percent of anopheles are infected with malarial parasites, so the more you minimize mosquito bites, the less likely you are to catch it. Use **insect repellent**: the most commonly used in Brazil is **Autan**, often in combination with Johnson's Baby Oil to minimize skin irritation. The most

Water purification

Contaminated water is a major cause of sickness due to the presence of bacteria, viruses and cysts. These micro-organisms cause diseases such as diarrhoea, gastroenteritis, typhoid, cholera, dysentery, poliomyelitis, hepatitis A, giardiasis and bilharziasis and can be present even when water looks clean and safe to drink.

Bottled water is widely available in Brazil, but, if you are considering trekking in remote regions or want to take all possible precautions, there are various methods of **treating water** whilst you are travelling. **Boiling** is the time-honoured method, which will be effective in sterilizing water, although it will not remove unpleasant tastes. A minimum boiling time of five minutes (longer at higher altitudes) is sufficient to kill micro-organisms.

Chemical sterilization can be carried out using either chlorine or iodine tablets or a tincture of iodine liquid. When using tablets it is essential to follow the manufacturer's dosage and contact time; with tincture of iodine, you add a couple of drops to one litre of water and leave to stand for twenty minutes. Iodine tablets are preferred to chlorine as the latter leave an especially unpalatable taste in the water and also are not effective in preventing such diseases as amoebic dysentery and giardiasis. If you are using sterilizing tablets, a water filter is useful, not least to improve the taste. **Water filters** alone will remove most bacteria and cysts, but not viruses, which, due to their microscopic size, pass through into the filtered water.

Purification, a two-stage process involving both filtration and sterilization, removes or destroys all waterborne disease-causing micro-organisms. Portable water purifiers range in size from units weighing as little as 60 grams which can be slipped into a pocket, to 800 grams for carrying in a backpack, and are available from specialist outdoor equipment retailers.

effective mosquito repellents – worth looking out for before you leave home – contain **DEET** (diethyl toluamide). DEET is strong stuff, so follow the manufacturers' instructions, particularly with use on children. If you have sensitive skin, a natural alternative is citronella or, in the UK, Mosi-guard Natural, made from a blend of eucalyptus oils (though still use DEET on clothes and nets). Wear long-sleeved shirts and trousers, shoes and socks during the times of day when mosquitoes are most active. Sleep under a sheet and, crucially, use a **mosquito net**. Nets for hammocks (*mosqueteiro para rede*) are reasonable and easily available in Amazonian cities. Mosquito coils also help keep the insects at bay.

When taking **preventive tablets** it's important to keep a routine and cover the period before and after your trip with doses. Doctors can advise on which kind to take. As resistance to chloroquin-based drugs increases, mefloquin, which goes under the brand name of Lariam, has become the recommended prophylactic for most travellers to Brazil. This has very strong side effects, and its use is controversial. The website ⓦwww.cdc.gov/travel/regionalmalaria is a useful resource, giving advice on risk areas in Brazil and the best methods of protection.

Malaria has an incubation period of around two weeks. The first **signs of malaria** are remarkably similar to flu – muscle pains, weakness and pain in the joints, which will last for a day or two before the onset of malaria fever proper – and may take months to appear: if you suspect anything go to a hospital or clinic immediately. You need immediate treatment and a blood test to identify the strain. **Malaria treatment** is the one public health area where Brazil can take some credit. Dotted everywhere around Amazonia are small malaria control posts and **clinics**, run by the anti-malaria agency SUCAM – ask for the *posto da SUCAM*. They may not look like much, but the people who staff them are very experienced and know their local strains better than any city specialist. Treatment in a *posto* is free, and if you do catch malaria you should get yourself taken to one as quickly as possible; don't shiver in your hammock and wait for it to pass. It often does, but it can also kill.

A traveller's first-aid kit

Among items you might want to carry with you – especially if you're planning to go trekking – are:

- a course of Flagyl antibiotics
- antiseptic cream
- diarrhoea treatment
- hypodermic needles and sterilized skin wipes
- Imodium (Lomotil) for emergency
- insect repellent
- knee supports
- lint and sealed bandages
- multi-vitamin and mineral tablets
- paracetamol/aspirin
- plasters/band aids
- rehydration sachets
- water sterilization tablets or water purifier
- wipes

Chagas's disease

Another serious disease you should guard against is **Chagas's disease**, which is endemic in parts of the **Northeast** and **Amazônia** and, although it is difficult to catch, it can be serious, leading to heart and kidney problems that appear up to twenty years after infection. The disease is carried in the faeces of beetles that live in the cracks of adobe walls, so when sleeping in an adobe hut make sure nothing can crawl into your hammock; either use a mosquito net or sling the hammock as far from walls as you can. The beetle bites and then defecates next to the spot: scratching of the bite will rub in the infected faeces, so before scratching a bite that you know wasn't caused by a mosquito, **bathe it in alcohol**. If you are infected, you will have a fever for a few days that will then clear up, and though the disease can be treated in its early stages, it becomes incurable once established. If you travel through a Chagas area and get an undiagnosed fever, have a blood test as soon as possible afterwards.

Dengue fever

Dengue fever, a viral disease transmitted by mosquito bites, is increasingly common in all Brazilian cities save the extreme south of the country. The symptoms are debilitating rather than dangerous: light but persistent fever, tiredness, muscle and joint pains, especially in the fingers, and nausea and vomiting. It is easily treatable, but you will feel pretty grim for a week or so. It is much more widespread than any other disease in urban areas, and is currently the focus of much educational and preventive work by the Brazilian government. The same precautions against mosquito bites outlined in the section on malaria above apply here.

Hepatitis

Wherever you go, protection against **hepatitis A** is a sensible precaution. The disease is transmitted through contaminated water and food, resulting in fever and diarrhoea, and it can also cause liver damage. Gammaglobulin injections, one before you go and boosters every six months, are the standard protection. If you plan to spend much time in Amazônia or the Northeast, or if you know that you will be travelling rough, it's well worth protecting yourself. If you have had jaundice, you may well have immunity and should have a blood test to see if you need the injections. A newer vaccine – Havrix – is very effective and lasts for up to ten years.

Diarrhoea, dysentery and giardia

Diarrhoea is something everybody gets at some stage, and there's little to be done except drink a lot (but not alcohol) and bide your time. You should also replace salts either by taking oral rehydration salts or by mixing a teaspoon of salt and eight of sugar in a litre of purified water. You can minimize the risk by being sensible about what you eat, and by not drinking tap water anywhere. This isn't difficult, given the extreme cheapness and universal availability of soft drinks and *água mineral*, while Brazilians are great believers in herbal teas, which often help alleviate cramps.

If your diarrhoea contains blood or mucus, the cause may be dysentery or giardia. With a fever, it could well be caused by **bacillic dysentery** and may clear up without treatment. If you're sure you need it, a course of antibiotics such as tetracyclin or ampicillin (travel with a supply if you are going off the beaten track for a while) should sort you out, but they also destroy "gut flora" which help protect you. Similar symptoms without fever indicate **amoebic dysentery**, which is much more serious, and can damage your gut if untreated. The usual cure is a course of metronidazole (Flagyl), an antibiotic which may itself make you feel ill, and should not be taken with alcohol. Similar symptoms, plus rotten-egg belches and farts, indicate **giardia**, for which the treatment is again metronidazole. If you suspect you have any of these, seek medical help, and only start on the metronidazole (750mg three times daily for a week for adults) if there is definitely blood in your diarrhoea and it is impossible to see a doctor.

Cholera

Cholera is a waterborne bacterial disease that has become endemic to many parts of Brazil, albeit rare most of the time. It flourishes in a combination of hot climates and unsanitary conditions, and can be found anywhere in Brazil from Rio northwards. The disease is most common in the big cities of the Northeast, especially Fortaleza, and in the western Amazon in the border region with Peru. Rarely fatal for the young and fit if acted on immediately, the illness in most cases is no more severe than a sudden and nasty bout of diarrhoea, which can be treated with standard rehydration methods, antibiotics and a saline drip. Left untreated, it can kill within 24 hours by dehydrating its victims. Provided you take sensible precautions with food (especially shellfish) and drinking water, you shouldn't get it. If you are really concerned, vaccines are available with an effectiveness rate of between sixty and seventy percent.

HIV and AIDS

Brazil has one of the world's highest number of people with **AIDS and HIV**. There are many reasons for this: a scandalous lack of screening of either blood donors or supplies in the 1980s; the level of gay sex between Brazilian men, amongst whom bisexuality is common; the popularity of anal sex, not least amongst heterosexual couples; and the sharing of needles, both amongst drug users in large cities and, in the past, when injections were given for medical purposes, even in hospitals. Although high-profile public education campaigns are visible on TV and billboards, there is still widespread ignorance of how the disease is transmitted, and fear and persecution of its victims. Things have not been helped by the Catholic Church, in Brazil usually so liberal on many issues, which has taken a firmly conservative stance on the use of condoms. Nevertheless, it is not all doom and gloom. Brazil led the world in facing down international drug companies with the threat that they would independently manufacture AIDS drugs, with the result that all HIV-positive Brazilians now receive free anti-retroviral medicines in a programme that has become a global model for developing countries.

A straightforward understanding of the disease and how it is transmitted is the best defence. Firstly, AIDS is not evenly distributed throughout Brazil. A large majority of sufferers and HIV carriers are concentrated in **Rio** and **São Paulo**, where you should take extra care. As anywhere else, sex with a prostitute is a high-risk activity. Wherever you are, make sure that if you have an injection it is with a needle you see being removed from its packaging. (It is now possible to buy travellers' medical packs that contain sterile needles, attachments for intravenous drips and the like: they're available from immunization centres.) **Avoid blood transfusions unless absolutely necessary**. Although the situation with blood and blood products has improved enormously, there are still occasional slip-ups.

Finally, **use a condom**. Only a tiny minority of sexually active Brazilian men carry them as a matter of course. They are widely available in pharmacies, where you should ask for a *camisinha* or a *camiseta de Vênus*. There are often local shortages, however, and Brazilian condoms are not as durable nor as reliable as condoms in the developed world. Take a good supply along with you: you can always give them away if you don't use them.

In the Amazon

Given the remoteness of many parts of the Amazon and the prevalence of insects and snakes, health care takes on a special significance. In rural areas, despite the heat, you should wear long trousers all the time and use repellent to guard against disease-spreading insect bites. If you are trekking through forest or savanna, it is vital to wear good boots that protect your ankles from snake bites, chiggers and scorpions, and you should never trek alone.

Snakes are timid and only attack if you step on them, unless you are unlucky. Many of the most poisonous snakes are tiny, easily able to snuggle inside a shoe or a rucksack pocket. Always shake out your hammock and clothes, keep rucksack pockets tightly closed and take special care when it rains, as snakes, scorpions and other nasty beasties quite sensibly head for shelter in huts. If you do get bitten by a snake, try to catch it for identification. Use a shoelace or a torn piece of shirt wound round the limb with a stick as a tourniquet, which you should repeatedly tighten for twenty seconds and then release for a minute, to slow down the action of the poison. Contrary to popular belief, cutting yourself and sucking out blood will do you more harm than good. It goes without saying that you should get yourself to a doctor as soon as possible. If you are well off the beaten track, health posts in the nearest town may have serum, but you must know the type of snake involved.

Due to the humidity, any **cut** or **wound** gets infected very easily. Always clean cuts or bites with alcohol or purified water before dressing. As a general rule, leave all insects alone and never handle them. Even the smallest ants, caterpillars and bees can give you nasty stings and bites, and scorpions, large soldier ants and some species of bee will give you a fever for a day or two as well.

Getting around

Local travel in Brazil is always easy. Public transport outside of the Amazon is generally by bus or plane, though there are a few passenger trains, too. However you travel, services will be crowded, plentiful and, apart from planes, cheap. Car rental is possible, but driving in Brazil is not for the faint-hearted. Some international car rental companies have local agencies and there are quite a few reliable Brazilian ones as well. Hitchhiking, over any distance, is not recommended.

By air

It's hardly surprising that a country the size of Brazil relies on **air travel** a good deal; in some parts of Amazônia air links are more important than either the roads or rivers. Any town has at least an airstrip, and all cities have airports, usually some distance from the city but not always: Santos Dumont in Rio, Congonhas in São Paulo and Guararapes in Recife are all pretty central.

Air passes

When buying your international ticket, you should consider the possibility of adding an **air pass**. Although travellers used to purchase them almost automatically if flying within Brazil, the emergence of budget airlines in the country means that they now only make sense if you plan a series of long-haul trips – from the South to the Amazon and back via the Northeast, for example. Brazil's two main airlines – Varig (along with its regional subsidiaries RioSul and Nordeste) and TAM – both offer passes. Their route options vary somewhat but their basic conditions are virtually identical: passes can only be bought **outside Brazil** in advance of your trip with a return air ticket to the country.

Varig's **Star Alliance Brazil Airpass** (minimum of four stops from US$499) and their standard **Brazil Airpass** (minimum of five stops from US$692) are easily available and give access to the largest route networks, but the former can only be purchased if you travel into Brazil with Varig (or one of its Star Alliance partners such as United, Air Canada, Mexicana, Pluna and Lufthansa). The air passes are all valid for a maximum period of 21 consecutive days. Coupons (per flight hop) are not valid for the same route in the same direction more than once. Connecting flights count as only one coupon and you can buy a maximum of five additional coupons (for example, eight coupons on the Star Alliance Brazil Airpass would cost US$979, while eight on the standard Brazil Airpass cost US$1052). Routes generally have to be specified at the time of purchase (but check with your agent on this), in which case changes of route are not permitted – though flight times and dates can usually be altered. Bear in mind, however, that flights on some routes can be heavily booked long in advance. Less expensive regional Varig passes providing four coupons valid during a 21-day period are also available covering south and central Brazil (US$350 low season, US$400 high season) or the Northeast and the Amazon (US$290 low season, US$340 high season).

The **TAM Brazil Airpass** is similar to the Varig's, in that it lasts a maximum of 21 days and requires a minimum of four hops (costing US$572 for four, or up to eight for US$1044); flights are limited to the Tam, Varig, RioSul and Nordeste airline coverage.

If Brazil is only one stop on a longer trip, consider buying the **Mercosur Airpass**, which covers eight airlines of Argentina, Brazil, Chile, Paraguay and Uruguay; the **LAN South America Air Pass**, which covers flights from points in Chile to Peru, Argentina and Ecuador (but not Brazil directly); or the **TAM South America Air Pass**, which can be issued with any incoming international carrier flight at the time of purchase. It has a maximum of thirty days validity, is costed according to the air miles covered and includes flights to Argentina, Bolivia, Chile, Paraguay, and Uruguay as well as Brazil. The regulations are fairly complicated but the passes basically allow two stopovers per country (plus point of origin) up to a maximum of eight coupons, although an extra coupon is allowed to give you use of both the Argentine and Brazilian airports at Iguaçu Falls. The route must include at least two countries and the price of a pass is based on the number of miles flown, which always works out costing far less than purchasing regular tickets. Prices may be affected by the time of year that you travel.

Lastly, if you have an air pass and change the time or date of your flight, always remember to **cancel the original flight**. If you don't, the computer flags you as a no-show, and all your other air pass reservations will also be cancelled.

Budget airlines

A recent phenomenon in Brazil is the appearance of budget airlines, of which the biggest is **GOL** (Ⓣ0800/701-2131, Ⓦwww.voegol.com.br). GOL has an extensive network and cheap seats, but also very long check-in lines. (Also, irritatingly, American Express is the only foreign credit card that's accepted on its website.) Varing and TAM have therefore responded with a blizzard of promotional fares. The best of these fares can usually only be booked on the web, but only Varig's site accepts payment with foreign credit cards and fares quoted in US dollars and pounds. Travel agents abroad will usually quote much higher fares to those that are available on an airline's website. If you can book online at least a month in advance there is usually not much difference between the budget airlines and Varig.

Flying to the Northeast or Amazônia from southern Brazil can be tiresome, as many of these long-distance routes are no more than glorified bus runs, stopping everywhere before heading north. In planning your itinerary, it's a good idea to check carefully how many times a plane stops – for example, between São Paulo and Fortaleza a flight may stop as many as four times or as few as one.

There are **safety issues** to consider when flying in the Amazon, where investigations following a recent series of crashes revealed serious problems in a number of regional airlines, notably **Rico.** Stick to Varig and TAM when flying around the Amazon, if at all possible. In many parts of Amazônia air travel in small planes, or **aerotaxis**, is very common – the regional word for these flights is *teco-teco*. Before taking one, you should be aware that the airstrips are often dangerous, the planes routinely fly overloaded and are not reliably maintained, and no checks are made on the qualifications of pilots – some don't have any.

Although flying in Brazil has not yet reached the levels of crowding in the US and some parts of Europe, much of it is catching up fast. Brasília, Congonhas and above all Guarulhos in São Paulo are chronically crowded, with long check-in lines. If flying internationally from Guarulhos, add at least an extra hour to account for the phenomenal queues to get through passport control, and don't be surprised, on arrival, for it to take an hour or more to clear customs and immigration. If travelling with children, go straight to the front of the lines: families, pregnant women and seniors have priority.

Tickets and fares

Flights are rarely booked up in advance outside holiday periods, but it is always a good idea to book a *passagem* as far ahead as you can, if possible from an airline's website. Prices are reasonable in the South and Northeast but climb steeply as soon as the Amazon is involved: Rio–São Paulo costs US$85/£50, Rio–Salvador US$165/£95, Rio–Iguaçu US$170/£100, Rio–Manaus around US$370/£215; return fares are double the one-way fares. Tickets are almost always much cheaper when purchased in Brazil or, with Varig via its website, as you can benefit from special promotions. (For tickets bought inside of Brazil there's a $10 charge if you alter the date.)

By rail

You probably won't be taking many **trains** in Brazil. Although there's an extensive rail network, most of it is for cargo only, and even where there are passenger trains they're almost invariably slower and less convenient than the buses. Exceptions are a few **tourist journeys** worth making for themselves, in the South and Minas Gerais especially.

By bus

The **bus system** in Brazil is excellent and makes travelling around the country easy, comfortable and economical, despite the distances involved. Intercity buses leave from a station called a **rodoviária**, usually built on city outskirts.

Buses are operated by hundreds of private companies, but **prices** are standardized, even when more than one firm plies the same route, and are reasonable: Rio to São Paulo is around R$70, Rio to Belo Horizonte R$52, Rio to Foz do Iguaçu R$170, Rio to Salvador R$200 and São Paulo to Brasília R$120. Long-distance buses are comfortable enough to sleep in, and have on-board toilets (which can get smelly on long journeys): the lower your seat number, the further away from them you'll be. Buses stop every two or three hours at well-supplied *postos*, but as prices are relatively high it's not a bad idea to bring along water and some food to last the journey. Some bus companies will supply meal vouchers for use at the *postos* on long journeys.

There are luxury buses, too, called **leitos**, which do nocturnal runs between the major cities – worth taking once for the experience, with fully reclining seats in curtained partitions, freshly ironed sheets and an attendant plying insomniacs with coffee and conversation. They cost about a third of the price of an air ticket, and between two and three times as much as a normal long-distance bus; they're also less frequent and need to be booked a few days in advance. No matter what kind of bus, it's a good idea to have a light sweater or blanket during night journeys, as the air conditioning is always uncomfortably cold.

Going any distance, it's best to **buy your ticket** at least a day in advance, from the *rodoviária* or, in some cities, from travel agents. An exception is the Rio–São Paulo route, where a shuttle service means you can always turn up without a ticket and never have to wait more than fifteen minutes. Numbered seats are provided on all routes: if you want a window ask for *janela*. If you cross a state line you will get a small form with the ticket, which asks for the number of your seat (*poltrona*), the number of your ticket (*passagem*), the number of your passport (*identidade*) and your destination (*destino*). You have to fill it in and give it to the driver before you'll be let on board. Buses have **luggage** compartments, which are safe: you check pieces at the side of the bus and get a ticket for them. Keep an eye on your hand luggage, and take anything valuable with you when you get off for a halt.

By car

Driving standards in Brazil hover between the abysmal and the appalling. Brazil has one of the highest death tolls from driving-related accidents in the world, and on any journey you can see why, with thundering trucks and drivers treating the road as if it were a Grand Prix racetrack. Fortunately, inter-city bus drivers are the exception to the rule: they are usually very good, and many buses have devices fitted that make it impossible for them to exceed the speed limit. Electronic speed traps are widely in place, and if you get caught by one in a rental car, the fine will simply be added to your credit card.

Timetables

Although plane and bus **timetables** are kept to whenever possible, in the less developed parts of the country – most notably Amazônia but also the interior of the Northeast – delays often happen. Brazilians are very Latin in their attitude to time, and if ever there was a country where patience will stand you in good stead it's Brazil. Turn up at the arranged time, but don't be surprised at all if you're kept waiting. (Waiting times are especially long if you have to deal with any part of the state bureaucracy, like extending a visa.) There is no way out of this; just take a good book.

Road quality varies according to region: the South and Southeast have a good paved network; the Northeast has a good network on the coast but is poor in the interior; and roads in Amazônia are by far the worst, with even major highways closed for weeks or months at a time as they are washed away by the rains. Most cities are fairly well signposted, so getting out of town shouldn't be too difficult; if city traffic is daunting, try to arrange to collect your car on a Sunday when traffic is light. If at all possible, avoid driving at night because potholes (even on main roads) and *lombardas* (speed bumps) may not be obvious, and breaking down after dark in a strange place could be dangerous. Outside the big cities, Brazilian roads are deathtraps at night; poorly lit, in bad condition and lightly policed. Especially worth avoiding at night are the **Via Dutra**, linking Rio and São Paulo, because of the huge numbers of trucks and the treacherous ascent and descent of the Serra do Mar, and the **Belém-Brasília highway**, whose potholes and uneven asphalt make it difficult enough to drive even in daylight. Where possible, avoid driving after dark in the Mato Grosso and Amazon regions as well; though rare, armed roadside robberies have been known to happen there.

An **international driving licence** is useful: although foreign licences are accepted for visits of up to six months, you may have a hard time convincing a police officer of this (the old-style paper UK licenses are not accepted by road police). It's more than likely that you'll be stopped by police at some point during your travels, but they usually leave foreigners alone, unless there is something obviously amiss with your car. Occasionally they can be quite intimidating as they point to trumped up contraventions (for example, that your driving licence isn't valid, that the car's licence plates are somehow irregular). What the police are probably angling for is a bribe and an on-the-spot *multa*, or fine, may be suggested. It's a personal judgment whether to stand one's ground (which may take up a long time) or just pay up. Whatever you do, no matter how certain you are of the righteousness of your position, try and stay calm and bend over backwards to appear polite. If your passport is confiscated, demand to be permitted to phone your consulate – there should always be a duty officer available. Outside of the towns and cities, service stations can be few and far between, so keep a careful eye on the fuel gauge. Service stations sell both *gasolina* and *álcool*, with new cars (including rentals) usually capable of running on either fuel. *Álcool*, though roughly half the price of *gasolina*, isn't as efficient and it performs badly in cool weather – something that is only really a problem in winter in the South. Service stations in rural areas do not always accept international credit cards, so make sure you have sufficient cash on a long trip. In urban areas plastic is almost universally accepted at petrol stations, although a common scam is to charge around 20% more per litre when payment is made by credit card rather than cash: always check in advance whether there is a price difference if you intend to pay by credit card.

Parking, especially in the cities, can be tricky due to security and finding a space, and it's worth paying extra for a hotel with some kind of lock-up garage. A universal feature of city driving in Brazil is the *flanelinha*, named for the flannel informal parking attendants wave at approaching cars; these attendants will help you into and out of parking spaces and guard your car, in return for 50 centavos or so. Brazilians will go to almost any lengths to avoid paying them, but they're making a living and providing a service, so do the decent thing. In any event, never leave anything valuable inside the car if you don't want to lose it.

Regarding **safety issues**, driving in Brazil is very different from Europe or the US. Do not expect Brazilians to pay much attention to lane markings, use indicators or worry about cutting you off or overtaking you on the inside. Use your rear and wing mirrors constantly when city driving. At night you should cautiously roll through red lights in city centres or deserted-looking streets, to avoid *assaltantes*. And a crucial thing to know is that **flashing lights** from an oncoming car mean "I'm coming through – get out of the way" and NOT "please go ahead", as in the UK and US. It sounds intimidating, and it is for the first couple of days, but it is surprising how quickly you get used to it.

Renting a car

Renting a car in Brazil is relatively straightforward. Of the big-name international companies, Hertz and Avis are the most widely represented, with Budget just beginning to make inroads. There are also plenty of reliable Brazilian alternatives, such as Interlocadora, Nobre and Localiza. Unidas are also represented throughout the country and are highly recommended, as their cars are always in excellent condition, service is efficient and – if you take out their comprehensive insurance policy – there is no excess payable if your car is stolen or damaged. Often, though, you'll find the lowest rates are offered by smaller, local companies, but this can be a risky proposition as their cars may be old and in poor condition and there won't be such a good breakdown service. Car rental offices (*locadoras*) can be found at every airport and in most towns regardless of size. Try to avoid renting an alcohol-powered car: they always take two or three tries before they start, they accelerate more slowly and have a maddening tendency to cut out in lower gear if you make the slightest mistake with the clutch.

Rates start from around R$100 a day for a Group A car (Fiat Punto or similar) including unlimited mileage; a basic air-conditioned model will start at around R$140, also including unlimited mileage. Four-wheel-drive vehicles, such as Toyota Land Cruisers, are sometimes available, but are extremely expensive. Only luxury vehicles are available with automatic transmission. Prices don't always include **insurance** – a comprehensive policy will be an additional R$20 or so with a deductable of R$500. If you have a US or Canadian credit card, you may find that it can be used to cover the additional liability – check before leaving home. In any case, a credit card is essential for making a deposit when renting a car. It's not a bad idea to reserve a car before you arrive in Brazil, as you can be sure to get the best available rate.

As you would anywhere, carefully check the condition of the car before accepting it and pay special attention to the state of the tyres (including the spare), and make sure there's a jack, warning triangle and fire extinguisher. All cars have front and back seatbelts; their use is compulsory, and stiff on-the-spot fines are imposed on drivers and front-seat passengers found not to be wearing them.

Car rental agencies

Avis US ⓣ1-800/331-1084, Canada ⓣ1-800/272-5871, UK ⓣ0870/606-0100, Northern Ireland ⓣ028/9024-0404, Republic of Ireland ⓣ01/605-7500, Australia ⓣ13 63 33 or 02/9353-9000, New Zealand ⓣ09/526-2847 or 0800/655-111, ⓦwww.avis.com.

Budget US ⓣ1-800/527-0700, Canada ⓣ1-800/268-8900, UK ⓣ0800/181-181, Australia ⓣ1300/362-848, New Zealand ⓣ09/976-2222, ⓦwww.budget.com.

Hertz US ⓣ1-800/654-3001, Canada ⓣ1-800/263-0600, ⓦwww.hertz.com UK, ⓣ0870/844-8844, Republic of Ireland ⓣ01/676-7476, Australia ⓣ13 30 39 or 03/9698-2555, New Zealand ⓣ0800/654-321, ⓦwww.hertz.com.

Interlocadora Brazil ⓣ0800/138-000, ⓦwww.interlocadora.com.br.

Addresses

Trying to find an address can be confusing: streets often have two names, numbers don't always follow a logical sequence, and parts of the address are often abbreviated (Brasília is a special case – see p.518). The street name and number will often have a floor, apartment or room number tacked on: thus R. Afonso Pena 111-3° s.234 means third floor, room 234. "R" is short for Rua, "s" for *sala*, and you may also come across *andar* (floor), *Ed.* (*edifício*, or building) or *s/n* (*sem número*, no number), very common in rural areas and small towns. All addresses in Brazil also have an eight-digit postcode, or *CEP*, often followed by two capital letters for the state; leaving it out causes delay in delivery. So a full address might read:

Rua do Sol 132-3° andar, s.12
65000-100 São Luís – MA

Amazon riverboats

In Amazônia, rivers have been the main highways for centuries, and the Amazon itself is navigable to ocean-going ships as far west as Iquitos in Peru, nearly 3000km upstream from Belém.

In all the large riverside cities of the Amazon – notably Belém, Manaus and Santarém – there are *hidroviárias*, ferry terminals for waterborne bus services. **Amazon river travel** is slow and can be tough going, but it's a fascinating experience. On longer journeys there are a number of classes; in general it's better to avoid *cabine*, where you swelter in a cabin, and choose *primeiro* (first class) instead, sleeping in a hammock on deck. *Segundo* (second class) is usually hammock space in the lower deck or engine room. Take plenty of provisions, and expect to practise your Portuguese.

The **range of boat transport** in the Amazon runs from luxury tourist boats and large three-level riverboats to smaller one- or two-level boats (the latter normally confining their routes to main tributaries and local runs) and covered launches operated by tour companies. The most popular route is the **Belém–Manaus trip**, which takes four to six days.

Localiza Brazil ⓣ0800/992-000, ⓦwww.localiza.com.br.
Nobre Brazil ⓣ0800/125-888, ⓦwww.nobrerentacar.com.br.
Unidas Brazil ⓣ 0800/121 121, ⓦwww.unidas.com.br.

Taxis

There are enormous numbers of **taxis** in Brazilian cities, and they're very cheap, especially if there are two or more passengers. City cabs are metered, and have two rates; 1 is cheaper, 2 more expensive. Which rate the taxi is using is indicated on the taximeter, after the fare. Rate 2 is automatic on trips to and from airports and bus stations in big cities, after 8 at night, and all day Sunday and public holidays. Many cities give taxi drivers a Christmas bonus by allowing them to charge Rate 2 for the whole of December. Occasionally drivers will refer to a sheet and revise the fare slightly upwards – they are not necessarily ripping you off, but referring to price updating tables which will fill the gap until taximeters can be readjusted to reflect the official annual increases.

Taxis in small towns and rural areas do not often have meters, so it's best to agree on the fare in advance – they'll be more expensive than in the cities. Most airports and some bus stations are covered by taxi cooperatives, which operate under a slightly different system: attendants give you a coupon with fares to various destinations printed on it – you pay either at a kiosk in advance, or the driver. These are more expensive than regular taxis, but they're reliable and often more comfortable. Tipping is not obligatory, but appreciated.

By ferries and boats

Water travel and ferries are also important forms of transport in parts of Brazil. Specific details are included in the relevant parts of the Guide, but look out for the ferry to Niterói, without which no journey to **Rio** would be complete; **Salvador**, where there are regular services to islands and towns in the huge bay on which the city is built; in the **South** between the islands of the Bay of Paranaguá; and most of all in **Amazônia**.

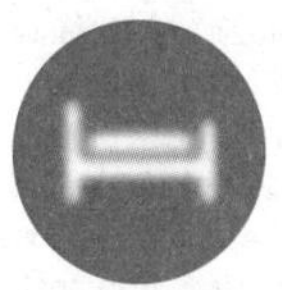

Accommodation

Accommodation in Brazil covers the full range, from hostels and basic lodging clustered around bus stations to luxury resort hotels. You can sometimes succeed in finding places to sleep for as little as R$15 a night, but, more realistically, a clean double room in a one-star hotel will set you back upwards of R$25–40. As is so often the case, single travellers get a bad deal, usually paying almost as much as the cost of a double room. In whatever category of place you stay, in tourist spots – both large and small – over New Year and Carnaval, you'll be expected to book a room for a minimum of four or five days.

Hotels

Hotels proper run from dives to luxury apartments. There is a Brazilian **classification system**, from one to five stars, but the absence of stars doesn't necessarily mean a bad hotel: they depend on bureaucratic requirements like the width of lift shafts and kitchen floor space as much as on the standard of accommodation – many perfectly good hotels don't have stars.

Hotels offer a range of different rooms, with significant price differences: a **quarto** is a room without a bathroom, an **apartamento** is a room with a shower (Brazilians don't use baths); an *apartamento de luxo* is normally just an *apartamento* with a fridge full of (marked-up) drinks; a **casal** is a double room; and a **solteiro** a single. In a starred hotel, an *apartamento* upwards would normally come with telephone, air conditioning (*ar condicionado*) and a TV; a *ventilador* is a fan.

Rates for rooms vary tremendously between different parts of Brazil, but start at around R$20 in a one-star hotel, around R$50 in a two-star hotel, and around R$70 in a three-star place. Generally speaking, for R$50–70 a night you could expect to stay in a reasonable mid-range hotel, with bathroom and air conditioning. Many hotels in this range in Brazil are excellent value for the standard of accommodation they offer. During the off-season most hotels in tourist areas offer hefty **discounts**, usually around 25–35 percent.

Most hotels – although not all – will add a ten percent **service charge** to your bill, the *taxa de serviço*: those that don't will have a sign at the desk saying "*Nos não cobramos taxa de serviço*", and it's very bad form to leave the hotel without tipping the receptionist. The price will almost invariably include breakfast – gargantuan helpings of fruit, cheese, bread and coffee – but no other meals, although there will often be a restaurant on-site. Hotels usually have a **safe deposit box**, a *caixa*, which is worth asking about when you check in; they are free for you to use and, although they're not invulnerable, anything left in a *caixa* is safer

Accommodation price codes

In this guide, accommodation has been categorized according to the price codes outlined below. These categories represent the minimum you can expect to pay for a **double room in high season** – though note that many of the budget places will also have more expensive rooms. Rates for hostels and basic hotels where guests are charged **per person** are given in R$, instead of being indicated by price code.

- ❶ Under R$25
- ❷ R$25–50
- ❸ R$50–80
- ❹ R$80–120
- ❺ R$120–180
- ❻ R$180–240
- ❼ R$240–350
- ❽ R$350–500
- ❾ R$500 and over

than on your person or unguarded in your room. Many hotels also offer a safe deposit box in your room, which is the safest option of all.

Finally, a **motel**, as you'll gather from the various names and decor, is strictly for couples. This is not to say that it's not possible to stay in one if you can't find anything else – since they're used by locals they're rarely too expensive – but you should be aware that most of the other rooms will be rented by the hour.

Pensões, postos and pousadas

In a slightly higher price range are the small, family-run hotels, called either a **pensão** (*pensões* in the plural) or a *hotel familiar*. These vary a great deal: some are no more appealing than a *dormitório*, while others are friendlier and better value than many hotels and can be places of considerable character and luxury. *Pensões* tend to be better in small towns than in large cities, but are also usefully thick on the ground in some of the main tourist towns, where conventional hotels are pretty well non-existent. In southern Brazil, many of the **postos**, highway service stations on town outskirts, have cheap rooms and showers, and are usually well kept and clean.

You will also come across the **pousada**, which can just be another name for a *pensão*, but can also be a small hotel, running up to luxury class but usually less expensive than a hotel proper. In some small towns – such as Ouro Preto and Paraty – *pousadas* form the bulk of mid- and upper-level accommodation options. In the Amazon and Mato Grosso in particular, *pousadas* tend to be purpose-built *fazenda* lodges geared towards the growing ecotourist markets and are not aimed at budget travellers.

Camping

There are a fair number of **campsites** in Brazil and almost all of them are on the coast near the bigger beaches – mostly they're near cities rather than in out-of-the-way places. They will usually have basic facilities – running water and toilets, perhaps a simple restaurant – and are popular with young Argentines and Brazilians. A few fancier sites are designed for people with camper vans or big tents in the back of their cars. Having your own tent, or hiring one, is also particularly useful in ecotourist regions such as the Amazon and the Pantanal, where it can really open up the wilderness to you. In all cases, however, the problem is **security**, partly of your person, but more significantly of your possessions, which can never really be made safe. Great caution should be exercised before camping off-site – only do so if you're part of a group and you've received assurances locally as to safety.

Dormitories and hostels

At the bottom end of the scale, in terms of both quality and price, are **dormitórios**, small and very basic (to put it mildly) hotels, situated close to bus stations and in the poorer parts of town. They are extremely cheap (just a few dollars a night), but usually unsavoury and sometimes positively dangerous.

You could stay for not much more, in far better conditions, in a **youth hostel**, an *albergue de juventude*, also sometimes called a *casa de estudante*, where the cost per person is between US$5 and US$10 a night. There's an extensive network of these hostels, with at least one in every state capital, and they are very well maintained, often in restored buildings. It helps to have an IYHF card (available from the youth hostel associations listed below) with a recent photograph – you're not usually asked for one, but every so often you'll find an *albergue* which refuses entry unless it's produced. The Federação Brasileira dos Albergues de Juventude in Rio publishes an excellent illustrated guide to Brazil's official hostels, and there's a growing number of hostels that aren't affiliated with the IYHF – many of which are very good.

Demand for places far outstrips supply at certain times of year – December to Carnaval, and July – but if you travel with a **hammock** you can often hook it up in a corridor or patio. A major advantage that hostels have is to throw you together with young Brazilians, the main users of the network.

Youth hostel associations

US and Canada

Hostelling International-American Youth Hostels ⓣ202/783-6161, ⓦwww.hiayh.org. Annual membership for adults (18–55) is US$25, for seniors (55 or over) US$15, and for under-18s and groups of ten or more, free. Lifetime memberships are US$250.

Hostelling International Canada ⓣ1-800/663-5777 or 613/237-7884, ⓦwww.hostellingintl.ca. Rather than sell the traditional 1- or 2-year memberships, the association now sells one Individual Adult membership with a 28- to 16-month term. The length of the term depends on when the membership is sold, but a member can receive up to 28 months of membership for just US$35. Membership is free for under-18s and you can become a lifetime member for US$175.

UK and Ireland

Northern Ireland Hostelling International Northern Ireland ⓣ028/9032-4733, ⓦwww.hini.org.uk. Adult membership £10; under-18s £6; family £20; lifetime £75.

Republic of Ireland ⓣ01/830-4555, ⓦwww.irelandyha.org. Annual membership €10.50.

Scottish Youth Hostel Association ⓣ0870/155-3255, ⓦwww.syha.org.uk. Annual membership £6, for under-18s £2.50.

Youth Hostel Association (YHA) ⓣ0870/770-8868, ⓦwww.yha.org.uk. Annual membership £13; under-18s £6.50; lifetime £190 (or five annual payments of £40).

Australia, New Zealand and South Africa

Australia Youth Hostels Association ⓣ02/9261-1111, ⓦwww.yha.com.au. Adult membership rate A$52 (under-18s, A$16) for the first twelve months and then A$32 each year after.

Youth Hostelling Association New Zealand ⓣ0800/278 299 or 03/379 9970, ⓦwww.yha.co.nz. Adult membership NZ$40 for one year, NZ$60 for two and NZ$80 for three; under-18s free; lifetime NZ$300.

In Brazil

Federação Brasileira dos Albergues de Juventude Rua da Assembléia 10, sala 1211, Centro, Rio de Janeiro (ⓣ021/252-4829, ⓦwww.alberguesp.com.br). Annual membership US$15.

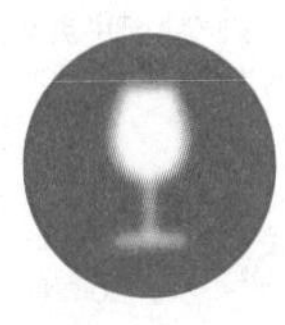

Food and drink

It's hard to generalize about Brazilian food, largely because there is no single national cuisine but numerous very distinct regional ones. Nature dealt Brazil a full hand for these varying cuisines: there's an abundant variety of fruit, vegetables and spices, as you can see for yourself walking through any food market.

There are five main **regional cuisines**: *comida mineira* from Minas Gerais, based on pork, vegetables (especially *couve*, a relative of spinach) and *tutu*, a kind of refried bean cooked with manioc flour and used as a thick sauce; *comida baiana* from the Salvador coast, the most exotic to gringo palates, using superb fresh fish and shellfish, hot peppers, palm oil, coconut milk and fresh coriander; *comida do sertão* from the interior of the Northeast, which relies on rehydrated dried or salted meat and the fruit, beans and tubers of the region; *comida gaúcha* from Rio Grande do Sul, the most carnivorous diet in the world, revolving around every imaginable kind of meat grilled over charcoal, and *comida amazônica,* based on river fish, manioc sauces and the many fruits and palm products of northern Brazil. *Comida do sertão* is rarely served outside its homeland, but you'll find restaurants serving the others throughout Brazil, although – naturally – they're at their best in their region of origin.

Alongside the regional restaurants, there is a **standard fare** available everywhere that can soon get dull unless you cast around:

steak (*bife*) or chicken (*frango*), served with *arroz e feijão*, rice and beans, and often with salad, fries and *farinha*, dried manioc (cassava) flour that you sprinkle over everything. *Farofa* is toasted *farinha*, and usually comes with onions and bits of bacon mixed in. In cheaper restaurants all this would come on a single large plate: look for the words *prato feito*, *prato comercial* or *refeição completa* if you want to fill up without spending too much.

Feijoada is the closest Brazil comes to a national dish: a stew of pork, sausage and smoked meat cooked with black beans and garlic, garnished with slices of orange. Eating it is a national ritual at weekends, when restaurants serve *feijoada* all day.

Some of the **fruit** is familiar – *manga*, mango, *maracujá*, passion fruit, *limão*, lime – but most of it has only Brazilian names: *jaboticaba*, *fruta do conde*, *sapoti* and *jaca*. The most exotic fruits are Amazonian: try *bacuri*, *açaí* and the extraordinary *cupuaçú*, the most delicious of all. These all serve as the basis for juices and **ice cream**, *sorvete*, which can be excellent; keep an eye out for *sorvetarias*, ice cream parlours.

For a list of common **menu** terms, see p.860.

Snacks and street food

On every street corner in Brazil you will find a **lanchonete**, a mixture of café and bar that sells beer and rum, snacks, cigarettes, soft drinks, coffee and sometimes small meals. **Bakeries** – *padarias* – often have a *lanchonete* attached, and they're good places for cheap snacks: an *empada* or *empadinha* is a small pie, which has various fillings (*carne*, meat, *palmito*, palm heart and *camarão*, shrimp, the best); a *pastel* is a fried, filled pasty; an *esfiha* is a savoury pastry stuffed with spiced meat; and a *coxinha* is spiced chicken rolled in manioc dough and then fried. In central Brazil try *pão de queijo*, a savoury cheese snack that goes perfectly with coffee. All these savoury snacks fall under the generic heading *salgados*.

If you haven't had **breakfast** (*café da manha*) at your hotel, then a bakery/*lanchonete* is a good place to head for; and for a more substantial meal *lanchonetes* will generally serve a *prato comercial*, too. In both *lanchonetes* and *padarias* you usually pay first at the till, and then take your ticket to the counter to get what you want.

You'll find a growing number of **fast food** outlets in cities. Menus in them are easy to understand because they are in mangled but recognizable English, albeit with Brazilian pronunciation. A hamburger is a *X-burger* (pronounced "*sheezboorga*"), a hot dog a *cachorro quente*; a *baurú* is a club sandwich with steak and egg; a *mixto quente* a toasted cheese and ham sandwich.

Food sold by **street vendors** in Brazil should be treated with caution, but not dismissed out of hand. You can practically see the hepatitis bugs and amoebas crawling over some of the food you see on sale in the streets, but plenty of vendors have proper stalls and can be very professional, with a loyal clientele of office workers and locals. Some of the food they sell has the advantage of being cooked a long time, which reduces the chance of picking anything up, and in some places – Salvador and Belém especially – you can get good food cheaply in the street; just choose your vendor sensibly. In Salvador try *acarajé*, only available from street vendors – a delicious fried bean mix with shrimp and hot pepper; and in Belém go for *maniçoba*, spiced sausage with chicory leaves, or *pato no tucupi*, duck stewed in manioc sauce.

Restaurants

Restaurants – *restaurantes* – are ubiquitous, portions are very large and prices are extremely reasonable. A *prato comercial* is around R$8, while a good full meal can usually be had for about R$30, even in expensive-looking restaurants. Cheaper restaurants, though, tend only to be open for lunch. One of the best options offered by many restaurants, typically at lunchtime only, is self-service *comida por kilo*, where a wide choice of food is priced according to the weight of the food on your plate. Specialist restaurants to look out for include a *rodizio*, where you pay a fixed charge and eat as much as you want; most *churrascarias* – restaurants specializing in charcoal-grilled meat of all kinds, especially beef – operate this system, too, bringing a constant supply of meat on huge spits to the tables.

Many restaurants will present unsolicited food the moment you sit down – the **couvert**, which can consist of anything from a couple of bits of raw carrot and an olive to quite an elaborate and substantial plate. Although the price is generally modest, it still has to be paid for. If you don't want it, ask the waiter to take it away.

Brazil also has a large variety of **ethnic restaurants**, thanks to the generations of Portuguese, Arabs, Italians, Japanese and other immigrants who have made the country their home. The widest selection is in São Paulo, with the best Italian, Lebanese and Japanese food in Brazil, but anywhere of any size will have good ethnic restaurants, often in surprising places: Belém, for example, has several excellent Japanese restaurants, thanks to a Japanese colony founded fifty years ago in the interior. Ethnic food may be marginally more expensive than Brazilian, but it's never exorbitant.

While the bill normally comes with a ten percent service charge, you should still tip, as waiters rely more on tips than on their very low wages.

Vegetarian foods

Being a **vegetarian** – or at least a strict one – is no easy matter in Brazil. Many Brazilians are unwilling vegetarians, of course, surviving on the staple diet of rice, beans and *farinha* – and there's wonderful fruit everywhere – but this is not food that you'll find in restaurants, except as side dishes.

If you eat fish there's no problem, especially in the Northeast and Amazônia where seafood forms the basis of many meals. You can usually get a fair choice of vegetarian food at a *comida por kilo* restaurant, which offers a range of salads and vegetables, as well as rice, manioc and potatoes. However, they are often only open during the day, as are the occasional vegetarian restaurants (usually described as *Restaurante Natural*) that can be found in the larger cities. But otherwise you're up against one of the world's most carnivorous cultures. In the South and centre-west, *churrasco* rules – served at restaurants where you eat as many different cuts of meat as you can manage, and where requests for meals without meat are greeted with astonishment. At most restaurants – even *churrascarias* – huge salads are available but, if you're a vegan, always enquire whether eggs or cheese are included. If you get fed up with rice, beans and salad, there are always pizzerias around.

Hot drinks and soft drinks

Coffee is the great national drink, served strong, hot and sweet in small cups and drunk quickly. However, coffee is often a great disappointment in Brazil: most of the good stuff is exported, and what's available often comes so stiff with sugar that it's almost undrinkable. By far the best coffee is found in São Paulo and points south. You are never far from a *cafézinho* (as these small cups of coffee are known; *café* refers to coffee in its raw state). Coffee is sold from flasks in the street, in *lanchonetes* and bars, and in restaurants, where it comes free after the meal. The best way to start your day is with *café com leite*, hot milk with coffee added to taste. Decaffeinated coffee is almost impossible to find in restaurants, and difficult even in delicatessens.

Tea (*chá*) is surprisingly good. Try **chá mate**, a strong green tea with a noticeable caffeine hit, or one of the wide variety of herbal teas, most notably that made from *guaraná* (see p.52). One highly recommended way to take tea is using the *chimarrão*, very common in Rio Grande do Sul: a gourd filled with *chá mate* and boiling water, sucked through a silver straw. You will need some practice to avoid burning your lips, but once you get used to it, it is a wonderfully refreshing way to take tea.

The great variety of fruit in Brazil is put to excellent use in **sucos**: fruit is popped into a liquidizer with sugar and crushed ice to make a deliciously refreshing drink. Made with milk rather than water it becomes a *vitamina*. Most *lanchonetes* and bars sell *sucos* and *vitaminas*, but for the full variety you should visit a specialist *casa de sucos*, which are found in most town centres. Widely available, and the best option to quench a thirst, are *suco de maracujá*, passion fruit, and *suco de limão*, lime. In the North and Northeast, try *graviola*, *bacuri* and *cupuaçu*. Sugar will always be added to a *suco* unless you ask for it *sem açúcar* or *natural*; some, notably *maracujá* and *limão*, are undrinkable without it.

Soft drinks are the regular products of corporate capitalism and all the usual brands are available. Outshining them all, though, is a local variety, *guaraná*, a fizzy and very sweet drink made out of Amazonian berries. An energy-loaded powder is made from the same berries and sold in health stores in the developed world – basically, the effect is like a smooth release of caffeine without the jitters.

Alcoholic drinks

Beer is mainly of the lager type. Brazilians drink it ice-cold and it comes mostly in 600ml bottles: ask for a *cerveja*. Many places only serve beer on draught – called *chopp*. Generally acknowledged as the best brands are the regional beers of Pará and Maranhão, Cerma and Cerpa, but the best nationally available beers are Skol and Brahma. Antártica is similar and more widely available, Kaiser is a little watery.

Wine, *vinho*, is mostly mediocre and sweet, though some of the wines produced in the South are pretty good. In the Italian areas of Rio Grande do Sul, try the small farmers' own wines – very different from European and US wines but excellent in their own right. Among the better commercial ones are Almaden, Château Chandon, Baron de Lantier and Côtes de Blancs (white – *branco*) and Forestier, Conde de Foucaud, Château Duvalier and Baron de Lantier (red – *tinto*). The most reliable widely available Brazilian label is Miolo, a smallish producer whose wines are found in good supermarkets throughout Brazil. Best of all, though, are the wines of the Casa Valduga, sometimes available in Rio's and São Paulo's best hotels and restaurants and gourmet food stores or, better still, but rarely available even in Rio Grande do Sul, Don Laurindo. Just about drinkable wine is also produced in Santa Catarina and in Paraná, while the wine from Espírito Santo and São Paulo is pretty dreadful, produced purely for regional consumption. Commercial wine production has recently started in Bahia's São Francisco valley, with some surprisingly good results: the Miolo shiraz can be found in many supermarkets. Despite the undoubted improvement in the quality of Brazilian wines in recent years, imported wines from Chile and Argentina (or Europe) remain more reliable and can be cheaper than the best that Brazil produces.

As for **spirits**, you can buy **Scotch** (*uisque*), either *nacional*, made up from imported whisky essence and not worth drinking, or *internacional*, imported and extremely expensive. Far better to stick to what Brazilians drink, *cachaça* (also called *pinga* or in Rio, *paraty*), which is sugar-cane rum. The best *cachaça* is produced in stills on country farms; it is called *cachaça da terra* and, when produced with care, has a smoothness and taste the larger commercially produced brands lack. Apart from in the area where it's produced, you won't find it in stores. Alternatively, there are scores of brands of commercially produced rum: some of the better ones are Velho Barreiro, Pitu and 51. The best *cachaças* are produced in Minas Gerais, but those from elsewhere, particularly São Paulo, can also be good. Note that while *cachaça* produced and sold in Paraty comes in the most attractive bottles, generally it's pretty rough stuff.

Brazilians drink *cachaça* either neat or mixed with fruit juice. Taken neat, it's very fiery, but in a cocktail it can be delicious. By far the best way to drink it is in a **caipirinha**, along with football and music one of Brazil's great gifts to world civilization – rum mixed with fresh lime, sugar and crushed ice: it may not sound like much, but it is the best cocktail you're ever likely to drink. Be sure to stir it regularly while drinking, and treat it with healthy respect – it is much more powerful than it tastes. Variants are the *caipirosca* or *caipiríssima*, the same made with vodka. Waiters will often assume foreigners want vodka, so make sure you say *caipirinha de cachaça*. You can also get *batidas*, rum mixed with fruit juice and ice, which flow like water during Carnaval: they also pack quite a punch, despite tasting like a soft drink. For a rum and Coke, ask for a *cuba libre*.

There are no **licensing laws** in Brazil, so you can get a drink at any time of day or night.

The media

As in the US, Brazil has a regional press rather than a national one. Even the best of Rio and São Paulo is a little parochial; elsewhere newspapers are at best mediocre but are always valuable for listings of local events. Brazil also boasts a lurid but enjoyable yellow press, specializing in gruesome murders, political scandals and football.

Newspapers and magazines

The top **newspapers** are the slightly left-of-centre *Folha de São Paulo* and the Rio-based right-of-centre *Jornal do Brasil*, usually available, a day late, in large cities throughout the country. Both are independent and have extensive international news, cultural coverage and entertainment listings, but are respectable rather than exciting. Even stodgier but reasonable is the right-wing *Estado de São Paulo*, while the *Gazeta Mercantil* is a high-quality equivalent of the *Financial Times* or *Wall Street Journal*. Also widely available is *O Globo*, the mouthpiece of Roberto Marinho's Globo empire (see opposite), right of centre, but with the advantage of Caruso, the best of Brazil's political cartoonists. In Brazil, as in Argentina and Chile, the political cartoon is a widely respected art form and often screamingly funny. The most enjoyable of the yellow press is *Última Hora*, especially good for beginners in Portuguese, with a limited vocabulary and lots of pictures.

There are also two good weekly current affairs **magazines**, *Veja* and *Isto É*. For most Brazilians, however, they are expensive, around US$2, since their readership is exclusively middle class. You will find Brazilian editions of most major fashion and women's magazines. The weekly *Placar* is essential for anyone wanting to get to serious grips with Brazilian football. *Vogue Brasil*, edited in São Paulo and published by Condé Nast, is a quality magazine offering great insight into the style of the Brazilian elite, while *Plástica* is a glossy monthly magazine that offers insights into Brazil's apparent obsession with plastic surgery.

Apart from in airports, five-star hotels, Rio and São Paulo, where you can find the *International Herald Tribune* and the *Economist*, **English-language newspapers** and magazines are very difficult to find in Brazil.

Radio

Radio is always worth listening to if only for the music, so a cheap transistor radio is a good thing to take with you. FM stations abound everywhere and you should always be able to find a station that plays local music. Shortwave reception for the BBC World Service is good in Brazil.

Television

Brazilian **TV** is ghastly, the worst you are ever likely to see, and therefore compulsive viewing even if you don't understand a word of Portuguese. There are several national channels, of which the most dominant is TV Globo, the centrepiece of the Globo empire, Latin America's largest media conglomerate. The empire was built up by Brazil's answer to Rupert Murdoch, Roberto Marinho, who died in 2003. One of the most powerful men in Brazil, Marinho was very cosy with the military regime and prone to use his papers and TV channels as platforms for his ultra-conservative views. The other major national channels are Manchete, TV Bandeirantes, SBT and Record.

The channels are dominated by **telenovelas**, glossy soap operas that have massive audiences in the evenings. **Football coverage** is also worth paying attention to, a gabbling and incomprehensible stream of commentary, punctuated by remarkably elongated shouts of "Gooooool" whenever anyone scores – which is often, Brazilian defenses being what they are. However, there are a few genuine highlights, notably **Jô Soares**, the funniest and cleverest of Brazilian comedians, who hosts a very civilized late-night chat show on Globo every weekday.

Festivals

Carnaval is the most important festival in Brazil, but there are other parties, too, from saints' days to celebrations based around elections or the World Cup.

Carnaval

When **Carnaval** comes, the country gets down to some of the most serious partying in the world. A Caribbean carnival might prepare you a little, but what happens in Brazil goes on longer, is more spectacular and on a far larger scale. Every place in Brazil, large or small, has some form of Carnaval, and in three places especially – Rio, Salvador and Olinda – Carnaval has become a mass event, involving seemingly the entire populations of the cities and drawing visitors from all over the world.

When exactly Carnaval begins depends on the ecclesiastical calendar: it starts at midnight of the Friday before Ash Wednesday and ends on the Wednesday night, though effectively people start partying on Friday afternoon – over four days of continuous, determined celebration. It usually happens in the middle of February, although very occasionally it can be early March. But in effect the entire period from Christmas is a kind of run-up to Carnaval. People start working on costumes, songs are composed and rehearsals staged in school playgrounds and back yards, so that Carnaval comes as a culmination rather than a sudden burst of excitement and colour.

During the couple of weekends immediately before Carnaval proper there are carnival balls, *bailes carnavalescos*, which get pretty wild. Don't expect to find many things open or to get much done in the week before Carnaval, or the week after it, when the country takes a few days off to shake off its enormous collective hangover. During Carnaval itself, stores open briefly on Monday and Tuesday mornings, but banks and offices stay closed. Domestic airlines, local and inter-city buses run a Sunday service during the period.

Three Brazilian Carnavals in particular have become famous, each with a very distinctive feel. The most familiar and most spectacular is in **Rio**, dominated by samba and the parade of samba schools down the enormous concrete expanse of the gloriously named Sambódromo. One of the world's great sights, and televised live to the whole country, Rio's Carnaval has its critics. It is certainly less participatory than Olinda or Salvador, with people crammed into grandstands watching, rather than down following the schools.

Salvador is, in many ways, the antithesis of Rio, with several focuses around the old city centre: the parade is only one of a number of things going on, and people follow parading schools and the *trio elétrico*, groups playing on top of trucks wired for sound. Samba is only one of several types of

A Carnaval warning

Wherever you go at Carnaval, take care of your possessions: it is high season for **pickpockets and thefts**. Warnings about specific places are given in the text, but the basic advice is – if you don't need it, don't take it with you.

Carnaval dates

2007 Feb 17–20
2008 Feb 2–5
2009 Feb 21-24
2010 Feb 13-16
2011 March 5-8

music being played, and, if it's music you're interested in, Salvador is the best place to hear and see it.

Olinda, in a magical colonial setting just outside Recife, has a character all its own, less frantic than Rio and Salvador; musically it's dominated by *frevo*, the fast, whirling beat of Pernambuco.

Some places you would expect to be large enough to have an impressive Carnaval are in fact notoriously bad at it: cities in this category are São Paulo, Brasília and Belo Horizonte. On the other hand, there are also places that have much better Carnavals than you would expect: the one in **Belém** is very distinctive, with the Amazonian food and rhythms of the *carimbó*, and **Fortaleza** also has a good reputation. The South, usually written off by most people as far as Carnaval is concerned, has major events in Florianópolis primarily aimed at attracting Argentine and São Paulo tourists, and the smaller but more distinctive Carnaval in Laguna. For full details of the events, music and happenings at each of the main Carnavals, see under the relevant sections of the Guide.

Other festivals

The third week in June sees the **festas juninas**, geared mainly towards children, who dress up in straw hats and checked shirts and release paper balloons with candles attached (to provide the hot air), causing anything from a fright to a major conflagration when they land.

Elections and the World Cup are usually excuses for impromptu celebrations, too, while official celebrations, with military parades and patriotic speeches, take place on September 7 (Independence Day) and November 15, the anniversary of the declaration of the Republic.

In towns and rural areas you may well stumble across a **dia de festa**, the day of the local patron saint, a very simple event in which the image of the saint is paraded through the town, with a band and firecrackers, a thanksgiving mass is celebrated, and then everyone turns to the secular pleasures of the fair, the market and the bottle. In **Belém** this tradition reaches its fullest expression in the annual Cirio on the second Sunday of October (see p.430), when crowds of over a million follow the procession of the image of Nossa Senhora de Nazaré, but most *festas* are small-scale, small-town events.

In recent years many towns have created new festivals, usually glorified **industrial fairs** or **agricultural shows**. Often these events are named after the local area's most important product such as the Festa Nacional do Frango e do Peru (chickens and turkeys) in Chapecó (see p.750). Occasionally these local government creations can be worth attending as some promote local popular culture as well as industry. One of the best is Pomerode's annual **Festa Pomerana** (see p.740), which takes place in the first half of January and has done much to encourage the promotion of local German traditions.

Travelling with children

Travelling with children is relatively easy in Brazil and, because South Americans hold the family unit in high regard, they're made to feel welcome in hotels and restaurants in a way that's not always so in Europe or North America.

Travelling around Brazil takes time, so try not to be too ambitious in terms of how much you aim to cover. Because of frequent scheduled stops and unscheduled delays it can take all day to fly from one part of the country to another. Long bus journeys are scheduled overnight and can be exhausting. Children pay full **fare** on buses if they take up a seat, ten percent on planes if under two years old, half-fare between two and twelve, and full fare thereafter. Newer **airports** have a **nursery** (*berçário*) where you can change or nurse your baby and where an attendant will run your baby a bath, great on a hot day or if your plane's delayed. If you plan on **renting a car**, bring your own child or **baby seat** as rental companies never supply them and they are very expensive in Brazil. Cars are fitted with three-point shoulder seatbelts in the front, but many only have lap seatbelts in the back.

In **hotels**, kids are generally free up to the age of five and rooms often include both a double and a single bed; a baby's cot may be available, but don't count on it. It's rare that a room will sleep more than three, but larger hotels sometimes have rooms with an interlinking door. Hotels will sometimes offer discounts, especially if children share rooms and even beds with siblings or parents; the lower- to mid-range hotels are probably the most flexible in this regard. If you're planning on staying more than a few days in a city you may find it cheaper and more convenient to stay in an **apartment-hotel**, which will sleep several people and comes with basic cooking facilities. Baths are rare in Brazil, so get your kids used to **showers** before leaving home. Occasionally a hotel will provide a plastic baby bath, but bring along a travel plug as shower pans are often just about deep enough to create a bath.

Many of the mid- and upper-range hotels have TV lounges, TVs in rooms, swimming pools, gardens and even games rooms, which are often useful in **entertaining** kids. Most large towns also have cinemas, the best often being the new multiplexes found in shopping centres.

Food shouldn't be a problem as, even if your kids aren't adventurous eaters, familiar dishes are always available and there's also the ubiquitous *comida por kilo* option. Portions tend to be huge, often sufficient for two large appetites, and it's perfectly acceptable to request additional plates and cutlery. Most hotels and restaurants provide high chairs (*cadeira alta*) as well. Commercial **baby food** is sold in Brazilian supermarkets. Remember to avoid tap water and use only mineral water when preparing formula and washing out bottles. Medium-category hotels and upwards have a **minibar** (*frigobar*) in the rooms where you can store bottles and baby food, but where there isn't one you will be able to store things in the hotel's refrigerator. A small cooler box or insulated bag is a good idea and, while ice compartments of *frigobars* are useless, you can always place your freezer blocks in the hotel's freezer (*congelador*).

In general, Brazilian infants don't use disposable **nappies/diapers** (*fraldas*), due to the cost, around R$12 for twenty – very expensive for most Brazilians. As brands such as Pampers are sold in pharmacies and supermarkets, it's worth only bringing a minimum with you until you can make it to a shop.

Health shouldn't be a problem, but before planning your itinerary, make enquiries as to whether the **vaccines** recommended or required in some parts of Brazil (in particular the Amazon) are likely to have any unpleasant side effects for babies or young children. For most of Brazil, the only likely problem will be the strength of the tropical sun and the viciousness of the mosquitoes: bring plenty of **sunscreen** (at least factor 20 for babies and factor 15 for young children) and an easy-to-apply **non-toxic insect repellent**.

Women travellers

Despite the nation's ingrained *machismo*, sexual harassment is not the problem you might expect in Brazil. Wolf-whistles and horn-tooting are less common than they would be in Spain or Italy, and, while you do see a lot of men cruising, more than you might think aren't looking for women, which spreads what hassle there is more evenly between the sexes for a change. The further north you go, blondes (men as well as women) bring out the stares, but attention which can seem threatening is often no more than curiosity combined with a language barrier.

Chances of trouble depend, to an extent, on where you are: the stereotype of free-and-easy cities and of small towns and rural areas that are formal to the point of prudishness often holds good – but not always. Many interior Amazon towns have a frontier feel and a bad, *machista* atmosphere. Also bear in mind that in any town of any size the area around the *rodoviária* or train station is likely to be a red-light district at night – not somewhere to hang around. The transport terminals themselves, though, are usually policed and fairly safe at all hours.

Women travelling alone will arouse curiosity, especially outside the cities, but the fact that you're a crazy foreigner explains why you do it in most Brazilian eyes; it shouldn't make you a target.

There is no national **women's movement** in Brazil, but there are loosely linked organizations in big cities and some university campuses, and a growing awareness of the issues. *Mulherio* is a national feminist paper.

Travel essentials

Costs

The **cost of living** in Brazil is low. Particularly reasonable are hotels (except in Rio), foodstuffs (including eating out in most restaurants), clothing and bus travel. Plane tickets work out around the same as a US or European budget airline, in dollar terms. Other things are more expensive: film, sun cream and anything having to do with computers. All the same, Brazil is very much a viable destination for the budget traveller. The cheapness of food and budget hotels – and the fact that the best attractions, like the beaches, are free – still makes it possible to have a very enjoyable time for under R$125 a day. Staying in good hotels, travelling by comfortable buses or planes and not stinting on the extras will cost you around R$500 a day.

Crime and personal safety

Brazil has a reputation as a rather dangerous place, and while it's not entirely undeserved, it is often overblown. If you take the precautions outlined below, you are extremely unlikely to come to any harm – although you might still have something stolen somewhere along the way.

Robberies, hold-ups and thefts

Criminals know that any injury to a foreign tourist is going to mean a heavy clampdown, which in turn means no pickings for a while. So unless you resist during an incident, nothing is likely to happen to you. That said, having a knife or a gun held on you is something of a shock: it's very difficult to think rationally. But if you are unlucky enough to be the victim of an **assalto** (a hold-up), try to remember that it's your possessions rather than you that's the target. Your money and anything you're carrying will be snatched, your watch will get pulled off your wrist, but within a couple of seconds it will be over. On no account resist: it isn't worth the risk.

Taking precautions

As a rule, **assaltos** are most common in the larger cities, and are rare in the countryside and towns. Most *assaltos* take place at night, in back streets with few people around, so stick to busy, well-lit streets; in a city, it's always a lot safer to take a taxi than walk. Also, prepare for the worst by locking your money and passport in the hotel safe – if you must carry them, make sure they're in a **moneybelt** or a **concealed internal pocket**. Do not carry your valuables in a pouch hanging from your neck. Only take along as much money as you'll need for the day, but do take at least some money, as the average *assaltante* won't believe a *gringo* could be out of money, and might get rough. Don't wear an expensive watch or jewellery: if you need a watch you can always buy a cheap plastic digital one on a street corner for a couple of dollars. And keep wallets and purses out of sight – pockets with buttons or zips are best.

You need to take special care when carrying a laptop – around business-oriented airports, like Congonhas in São Paulo and Santos Dumont in Rio, laptop stealing has become epidemic. Scouts wait at exits and phone ahead to thieves on motorbikes, who pull alongside your taxi when it is stuck in traffic and tap on the window with a revolver. Conceal laptops inside bags that do not look like computer bags, and try to avoid looking like a business person even if you are one.

More common than an *assalto* is a simple theft, a **furto**. Brand new, designer-label bags are an obvious target, so go for the downmarket look. You're at your most vulnerable when travelling and though the luggage compartments of buses are pretty safe – remember to get a baggage check from the person putting them in and don't throw it away – the overhead racks inside are less safe; keep an eye on things you stash there, especially on night journeys. On a city beach, never leave things unattended while you take a dip: any beachside bar will stow things for you. Most hotels (even the cheaper ones) will have a safe, a *caixa*, and unless you have serious doubts about the place you should lock away your most valuable things: the better the hotel, the more

Surviving an assalto

Every year, a number of tourists are killed unnecessarily through no fault of their own, simply because they did not know how to react to an armed hold-up or *assalto*. The simplest *assalto* happens on the street; just hand over your wallet and you're done. If in a car, and someone taps on the window with a gun, they probably want your wallet – hand it out through the window. If they want the car they will signal you out of it; get out immediately and do not delay to pick up anything. If you try to drive off at speed, there is a better than even chance they will shoot. If in a restaurant or sitting down, make no sudden movements and do not stand up, even if only to get your wallet out – wriggle instead.

secure it's likely to be. In cheaper hotels, where rooms are shared, the risks are obviously greater – some people take along a small padlock for extra security and many wardrobes in cheaper hotels have latches fitted for this very purpose. Finally, take care at Carnaval as it's a notorious time for pickpockets and thieves.

At international **airports**, particularly Rio and São Paulo, certain scams operate; for instance, well-dressed and official-looking men target tourists arriving off international flights in the arrivals lounge, identify themselves as policemen, often flashing a card, and tell the tourists to go with them. The tourists are then pushed into a car outside and robbed. If anyone, no matter how polite or well dressed they are, or how good their English is, identifies themselves as a policeman to you, be instantly on your guard – real policemen generally leave foreigners well alone. They won't try anything actually inside a terminal building, so go to any airline desk or grab one of the security guards, and on no account leave the terminal building with them or leave any luggage in their hands.

The police

If you are robbed or held up, it's not necessarily a good idea to go to the **police**. Except with something like a theft from a hotel room, they're very unlikely to be able to do anything, and reporting something can take hours even without the language barrier. You may have to do it for insurance purposes, when you'll need a local police report: this could take an entire, and very frustrating, day to get, so think first about how badly you want to be reimbursed. If your passport is stolen, go to your consulate and they'll smooth the path. Stolen traveller's cheques are the least hassle if they're American Express: in Rio and São Paulo they take your word they've been stolen, and don't make you go to the police.

If you have to deal with the police, there are various kinds. The best are usually the **Polícia de Turismo**, or tourist police, who are used to tourists and their problems and often speak some English or French, but they're thin on the ground outside Rio. In a city, their number should be displayed on or near the desk of reasonable hotels. The most efficient police by far are the **Polícia Federal**, the Brazilian equivalent of the American FBI, who deal with visas and their extension; they have offices at frontier posts, airports and ports and in state capitals. The ones you see on every street corner are the **Polícia Militar**, with green uniforms and caps. They look mean – and very often are – but, apart from at highway road blocks, they generally leave gringos alone. There is also a plain-clothes **Polícia Civil**, to whom thefts are reported if there is no tourist police post around – they are overworked, underpaid and extremely slow. If you decide to go to the police in a city where there is a consulate, get in touch with the consulate first and do as they tell you.

Drugs

You should be extremely careful about **drugs**. **Marijuana** – *maconha* – is common, but you are in serious trouble if the police find any on you. You'll be able to bribe your way out of it, but it will be an expensive business. Foreigners sometimes get targeted for a shakedown and have drugs planted on them – the area around the Bolivian border has a bad reputation for this. The idea isn't to lock you up but to get a bribe out of you, so play it by ear. If the bite isn't too outrageous it might be worth paying to save the hassle, but the best way to put a stop to it would be to deny everything, refuse to pay and insist on seeing a superior officer and telephoning the nearest consulate – this approach is only for the patient.

Cocaine is not as common as you might think, as most of it simply passes through Brazil from Bolivia or Colombia bound for Europe. Nevertheless, the home market has grown in recent years, most worryingly for crack cocaine, which is generally controlled by young and vicious gang leaders from the *favelas* of the major cities.

Be careful about taking anything illegal on buses: they are sometimes stopped and searched at state lines. The most stupid thing you could do would be to take anything illegal anywhere near Bolivia, as buses heading to or from that direction get taken apart by the *federais*. Much the same can be said of smuggling along the rivers into Peru and Colombia: don't even think about it.

Disabled travellers

Travelling in Brazil for people with disabilities is likely to be difficult if special facilities are required. For example, access even to recently constructed buildings may be impossible, as lifts are often too narrow to accept wheelchairs or there may be no lift at all. In general, though, you'll find that hotel and restaurant staff are helpful and will bend over backwards to be of assistance to try to make up for the deficiencies in access and facilities.

Buses in cities are really only suitable for the agile and for those who don't mind being thrown about. **Taxis**, however, are plentiful. Long-distance buses are generally quite comfortable, with the special *leito* services offering fully reclining seats. Internal **airlines** are helpful, and wheelchairs are available at all the main airports.

Contacts for travellers with disabilities

In Brazil

Centro de Vida Independente Rua Marques de São Vicente 225, Gavea, Est. da PUC, Rio de Janeiro ⓣ021/257-0019. Campaigning organization for disabled rights and advice on travel in Brazil.

In New Zealand

Disabled Persons Assembly 4/173–175 Victoria St, Wellington, New Zealand ⓣ04/801-9100 (also TTY), ⓦwww.dpa.org.nz. Provides lists of travel agencies and tour operators for people with disabilities.

In the UK

Access Travel 6 The Hillock, Astley, Lancashire M29 7GW ⓣ01942/888-844, ⓕ891-811, ⓦwww.access-travel.co.uk. Tour operator that can arrange flights, transfers and accommodation.

RADAR (Royal Association for Disability and Rehabilitation) 12 City Forum, 250 City Rd, London EC1V 8AF ⓣ020/7250-3222, minicom ⓣ020/7250-4119, ⓦwww.radar.org.uk. A good source of advice on holidays and travel abroad.

Tripscope Alexandra House, Albany Rd, Brentford, Middlesex TW8 0NE ⓣ0845/758-5641, ⓦwww.tripscope.org.uk. This registered charity provides a national telephone information service offering free advice on UK and international transport for those with a mobility problem.

In the US

Directions Unlimited 123 Green Lane, Bedford Hills, NY 10507 ⓣ1-800/533-5343 or 914/241-1700. Travel agency specializing in custom tours for people with disabilities.

Mobility International USA 451 Broadway, Eugene, OR 97401 ⓣ541/343-1284, ⓦwww.miusa.org. Information and referral services, access guides, tours and exchange programmes. Annual membership US$35 (includes quarterly newsletter).

Society for the Advancement of Travel for the Handicapped (SATH) 347 5th Ave, New York, NY 10016 ⓣ212/447-7284, ⓦwww.sath.org. Non-profit travel-industry referral service that passes queries on to its members as appropriate; allow plenty of time for a response.

Electricity

Electricity supplies vary – sometimes 110V and sometimes 220V – so check before plugging anything in. It's a fair bet that you'll blow the fuses anyway. Plugs have two round pins, as in continental Europe.

Entry requirements

Citizens of most European countries and also New Zealand and South Africa only need a valid passport and either a return or onward ticket, or evidence of funds to pay for one, to enter Brazil. You fill in an entry form on arrival and get a tourist visa allowing you to stay for ninety days. Australian, US and Canadian citizens need visas in advance, available from Brazilian consulates abroad; a return or onward ticket is usually a requirement. You'll also need to submit a passport photo with your visa application and pay a processing fee (consulates in the US only accept postal money orders, while consulates in other countries may accept bank or personal cheques). Fees vary according to nationality, with US citizens paying US$100, Canadians CDN$108 and Australians AUS$90.

Try not to lose the **carbon copy of the entry form** the police hand you back at passport control; you are meant to return it when you leave Brazil, but you are no longer fined if you don't. If you lose your passport, report to the **Polícia Federal** (every state capital has a federal police station with a visa section: ask for the *delegacia da Polícia Federal*; see p.59) and obtain a replacement travel document from your nearest consulate. You'll then have to return to the Polícia Federal, who will put an endorsement in your passport. EU citizens can extend a tourist permit for an additional ninety days if you apply at least fifteen days before your initial one expires, but it will only be extended once; if you want to stay longer you'll have to leave the country and re-enter. There's nothing in the rule book to stop you re-entering immediately, but it's advisable to wait at least a day. You'll be fined if you overstay your tourist permit or visa. A $10 charge, payable in local currency, is made on tourist permit and visa extensions.

Consulates

Foreign countries are represented at **embassy level** in Brasília, and most also maintain **consulates** in Rio and São Paulo. Elsewhere in this vast country, consulates, vice-consulates or honorary consulates are found in many major cities, from Manaus to Porto Alegre. Levels of service will vary depending on the nature of the particular post, but at the very least you can count on some immediate advice. Addresses and telephone numbers of embassies and consulates can be found in the "Listings" section of the cities in the Guide. Where their country doesn't have a representative, in an emergency a Commonwealth national can seek help at a British mission, and a European Union citizen at another EU mission.

Brazilian embassies and consulates abroad

Australia Embassy: 19 Forster Crescent, Yarralumla, Canberra, ACT 2600 ⓣ02/6273-2372 ⓦwww.brazil.org.au; Consulate: 31 Market St, Sydney ⓣ02/9267-4414.
Canada 450 Wilbroad St, Sandyhill, Ottawa, ON K1V 6M8 ⓣ613/237-1090 ⓦwww.brasembottawa.org; consulates also in Montréal ⓣ514/499-0968; and Toronto ⓣ416/922-2503.
Ireland HSBC House, 41-54 Harcourt Centre, Harcourt St, Dublin 2 ⓣ01/475-6000 ⓦwww.brazil.ie.
New Zealand 10 Brandon Street – Level 9, P.O. Box 5032, Wellington ⓣ04/473-3516, ⓦwww.brazil.org.nz.
South Africa Block C, 1st Floor, Hatfield Office Park, 1267 Pretorius St, Hatfield, Pretoria ⓣ012/426-9400, ⓦwww.brazilianembassy.org.za; also consulate in Cape Town ⓣ021/421-4040.
UK Embassy: 32 Green St, London W1Y 4AT ⓣ020/7499-0877, ⓦwww.brazil.org.uk; Consulate: 6 St Alban's St, London SW1Y 4SQ ⓣ020/7930-9055).
US 3006 Massachusetts Ave NW, Washington DC 20008 ⓣ202/238-2700, ⓦwww.brasilemb.org; consulates also in Boston ⓣ617/542-4000; Chicago ⓣ312/464-0244; Houston ⓣ713/961-3063; LA ⓣ323/651-2664; Miami ⓣ305/285-6200; New York ⓣ917/777-7777; San Francisco ⓣ415/981-8170; and Washington ⓣ202/238-2818.

Longer stays: academic visits

Academic visitors and researchers making a short trip or attending a conference are best advised to enter on a tourist visa, which cuts down on the bureaucracy. If you're staying for a longer period, or intend to do research, you need to get a special visa, known as a **"Temporario"** before you leave home. The requirements change constantly, so check first at your nearest Brazilian consulate, and plan ahead, because the process can easily take six months or longer. As a minimum, you'll need to present a letter from a Brazilian institution of higher education saying it knows about, and approves, your research, and where you will have a formal affiliation during the period of your stay in Brazil. Visas are issued for six months, a year or two years; if in any doubt about exactly how long you're going to stay, apply for the two-year visa. One-year visas can be extended for a further year inside Brazil, but only after months of chasing up the police, and often involving a trip to the Ministry of Justice in Brasília.

On arrival on a Temporario you must **register** within thirty days at the *seção dos estrangeiros* office in the federal police station nearest to where you are based. You'll need to fill out forms, supply an authenticated photocopy of your passport, pay a registration fee and provide some passport photographs. Several weeks later you'll be issued with an identity card; you can expect registering and getting the card to take at least a day of mindless drudgery and sitting in lines, but it has to be done. If your work involves taking samples out of Brazil, a whole new bureaucratic ball game begins; you will need to get in touch well in advance with the Brazilian embassy in your home country and with your sponsoring Brazilian institution. New rules meant to deter bio-piracy mean that exporting plant materials from Brazil is now almost impossible.

If you are moving to Brazil, to work or because you have a Brazilian spouse, take the trouble to get a Temporario visa before entering the country, as it's very difficult to arrange one after you arrive: Brazilian bureaucracy is not flexible. Brazilian consulates will advise you on what documentation you need. Work visas will allow you to stay up to two years as a foreign taxpayer; from then on you pay Brazilian taxes. This is not usually an issue for Europeans, but US citizens have to deal with the double taxation issue and should invest in an accountant if possible.

Gay and lesbian travellers

Gay life in Brazil still thrives in the large cities, despite the long shadow cast by AIDS (see p.39). In general, the scene has benefited from relatively relaxed attitudes towards sexuality – certainly when compared to the rest of Latin America – and the divide between gay and straight nightlife is very blurred.

Attitudes, however, vary from region to region. Rural areas and small towns, especially in Minas Gerais, the Northeast and the South, are deeply conservative; the medium-sized and larger cities less so. The two most popular gay destinations are Rio and Salvador, though even here the scene is remarkably discreet when compared to many northern European, North American and Australian cities.

And even in Brazil's big cities, there's an ugly undercurrent of homophobia present and gay visitors are advised to be cautious. Each year scores of gay men and lesbians are murdered in Brazil as a direct consequence of their sexuality, and there have been widely publicized murders in gay cruising areas.

A useful resource to consult before your trip is ⓦwww.guiagaybrasil.com.br; although the text is in Portuguese, there are enough English indicators to allow non-Portuguese speakers to navigate easily through it and benefit from the listings and tips.

Tipping

Bills usually come with ten percent *taxa de serviço* included, in which case you don't have to tip – ten percent is about right if it is not included. Waiters and some hotel employees depend on tips, so don't be too mean. You don't have to tip taxi drivers (though they won't say no), but you are expected to tip barbers, hairdressers, shoeshine kids, self-appointed guides and porters. It's useful to keep change handy for them and for beggars.

Football

Football is far and away the biggest sport in Brazil, as the country boasts the most wins (five) in World Cup history. **Going to a football match** is something that even those bored by the game will enjoy purely as spectacle: a big match is watched behind a screen of ticker-tape and waving flags to the accompaniment of massed drums and thousands of roaring voices. The best grounds are the temples of Brazilian football, Maracanã in Rio and the Art Deco Pacaembú in São Paulo, one of the most beautiful football stadiums in the world. Even the small cities have international-class stadiums – in essence, symbols of municipal virility.

Tickets are cheap – less than a couple of dollars to stand on the terraces (*geral*), around US$5 for stand seats (*arquibancada*); championship and international matches cost a little more. Except for important matches, you can usually turn up and pay at the turnstile rather than having to get a ticket in advance.

The number of regional championships and national play-offs means there is football virtually all the year round in Brazil – the **national championship** is a complicated mix of state leagues and national sudden-death play-offs.

Good teams are thickest on the ground in Rio and São Paulo. In Rio, **Flamengo** and **Fluminense** have historically had the most intense rivalry in Brazilian club football, though the latter are currently in steep decline and their place has been taken by **Vasco**; together with **Botafogo** they dominate *carioca* football. In São Paulo there is similar rivalry between **São Paulo** and **Coríntians**, whose pre-eminence is challenged by **Guaraní**, **Palmeiras**, **Portuguesa** and **Santos**, the last of these now a shadow of the team that Pelé led to glory in the

1960s. The only clubs elsewhere that come up to the standards of the best of Rio and São Paulo are **Internacional** and **Grêmio** in Porto Alegre, **Atlético Mineiro** in Belo Horizonte, **Vitória** and **Bahia** in Bahia, and **Sport** in Recife.

Internet

Like most rapidly developing nations, Brazil has latched on to the Internet, with a majority of hotels and businesses now on-line. Public access has exploded, with cybercafés in all regions of the country and hotels and hostels offering Internet access too. The general **hourly rate** for Internet access in Brazil is between R$4 and R$7.

Laundry

Even the humblest hotel has a *lavadeira*, who will wash and iron your clothes. Agree on a price beforehand, but don't be too hard – livelihoods are at stake. Larger hotels have set prices for laundry services – usually surprisingly expensive. Laundries outside of hotels are not generally geared to the needs of travellers.

Living in Brazil

Study and work programmes

AFS Intercultural Programs US ⓣ1-800/AFS-INFO, Canada ⓣ1-800/361-7248 or 514/288-3282, UK ⓣ0113/242-6136, Australia ⓣ1300/131-736 or ⓣ02/9215-0077, NZ ⓣ0800/600-300 or 04/494-6020, international enquiries ⓣ+1-212/807-8686, ⓦwww.afs.org. Global UN-recognized organization running summer programmes to foster international understanding.

From the US and Canada

American Institute for Foreign Study ⓣ1-866/906-2437, ⓦwww.aifs.com. Language study and cultural immersion, as well as au pair and Camp America programmes.

BUNAC USA (British Universities North America Club) ⓣ1-800/GO-BUNAC, ⓦwww.bunac.org. Offers students the chance to work in Australia, New Zealand, Ireland or Britain.

Council on International Educational Exchange (CIEE) ⓣ1-800/40-STUDY or ⓣ1/207-533-7600, ⓦwww.ciee.org. Leading NGO offering study programmes and volunteer projects around the world.

Earthwatch Institute ⓣ1-800/776-0188 or 978/461-0081, ⓦwww.earthwatch.org. International non-profit organization that does research projects in countries all over the world.

From the UK and Ireland

BTCV (British Trust for Conservation Volunteers) ⓣ01302/572-244, ⓦwww.btcv.org.uk. One of the largest environmental charities in Britain, with a programme of national and international working holidays (as a paying volunteer).

BUNAC (British Universities North America Club) ⓣ020/7251-3472, ⓦwww.bunac.co.uk. Organizes working holidays in the US and other destinations for students.

Camp America Camp America ⓣ020/7581-7373, ⓦwww.campamerica.co.uk.

Council Exchange ⓣ020/8939-9057, ⓦwww.councilexchanges.org.uk. International study and work programmes for students and recent graduates.

Earthwatch Institute ⓣ01865/318-838, ⓦwww.uk.earthwatch.org. Long-established international charity with environmental and archeological research projects worldwide.

From Australia and New Zealand

AFS Intercultural Programs Australia ⓣ1300/131-736 or ⓣ02/9215-0088, NZ ⓣ0800/600-300 or 04/494-6020, ⓦwww.afs.org.au, ⓦwww.afsnzl.org.nz. Runs summer experiential programmes aimed at fostering international understanding for teenagers and adults.

From South Africa

AFS Intercultural Programs ⓣ27/11-339-2741. Non-profit, self-funded and volunteer-based NGO organization. ⓦwww.afs.org/southafrica.

Mail

A **post office** is called a *correio*, identifiable by their bright yellow postboxes and signs. An imposing *Correios e Telégrafos* building will always be found in the centre of a city of any size, and from here you can send telegrams as well; but there are also small offices and kiosks scattered around which only deal with mail. Because post offices in Brazil deal with other things besides post, queues are often a problem. Save time by using one of their franking machines for stamps; the lines move much more quickly. **Stamps** (*selos*) are most commonly available in two varieties – either for mailing within Brazil or abroad. A foreign postage stamp costs around R$1.30 for either a postcard or a letter up to 10 grammes. It is expensive to send parcels abroad.

Mail within Brazil takes three or four days, longer in the North and Northeast, while **airmail** letters to Europe and North America usually take about a week or sometimes even less. **Surface mail** takes about a month to North America, and three to Europe. Although the postal system is generally very reliable, it is not advisable to send valuables through the mail.

Maps

We've provided **maps** of all the major towns and cities and various other regions. More detailed maps are surprisingly hard to get hold of outside Brazil and are rarely very good: there are plenty of maps of South America, but the only widely available one that is specifically of Brazil is the *Bartholomew Brazil & Bolivia* (1:5,000,000) which is not very easy to read. Much better are the six regional maps in the *Mapa Rodoviário Touring* series (1:2,500,000), which clearly mark all the major routes, although these, even in Brazil, are difficult to find.

A useful compendium of **city maps** and **main road networks** is published by Guias Quatro Rodas, a Brazilian motoring organization, which also has maps to Rio, São Paulo and other cities, states and regions. These are easy to find in bookstores, newsagents and magazine stalls. Very clear 1:960,000 maps of individual states are published by On Line Editora, and are usually available in Brazilian bookstores and newspaper kiosks; topographical and hiking maps are difficult to find, though very occasionally they are available from municipal tourist offices or national parks in Brazil, or from local trekking equipment shops or tour operators

Money

The Brazilian currency is the *real* (pronounced "hey-al"); its plural is *reais* (pronounced "hey-ice"). The *real* is made up of one hundred *centavos*, written ¢. Notes, all the same size but different colours, are for 1, 2, 5, 10, 20, 50 and 100 *reais*; coins are 1, 5, 10, 25, 50 *centavos* and 1 *real*. Coins look irritatingly similar, and to tell them apart you'll have to scrutinize them closely. Throughout the Guide, all prices are given in Brazilian *reaís* (R$) unless otherwise noted. However, US dollars are easy enough to change in banks and exchange offices anywhere, and are also readily accepted by luxury hotels, tour companies and souvenir shops in the big cities.

Changing money in Brazil is simple; just take your bank or credit card with PIN (Personal Identification Number, which you must set up with your bank before your trip), and use **ATMs** – they are now ubiquitous in Brazil, to be found in most supermarkets, many pharmacies and all airports, as well as banks. Only Visa cards can be used to withdraw cash advances at the ATMs of Banco do Brasil and Banco Bradesco; only Mastercard at HSBC, Itaú and Banco Mercantil. Increasing numbers of Brazilian banks are linking their cash dispensers to the Cirrus and Maestro networks; the most reliable and widespread is the Banco 24 Horas network. For security reasons, between 10pm and 6am ATMs only allow the withdrawal of R$60.

The main **credit cards** are widely accepted by shops, hotels and restaurants throughout Brazil, even in rural areas. Mastercard and Visa are the most prevalent, with Diners Club and American Express also widespread. It's a good idea to inform your credit card issuer about your trip before you leave so that the card isn't stopped for uncharacteristic use.

Given the ease of using plastic, **traveller's cheques** are not recommended, unless you want a small emergency reserve. Only the head offices of major **banks** (Banco do Brasil, HSBC, Banco Itaú, Banespa) will have an exchange department (ask for *câmbio*); whether changing cash or traveller's cheques you'll need your passport. You can also change cash and traveller's cheques in smart hotels and in some large travel agencies. Exchange departments of banks often close early, sometimes at 1pm, although more often at 2pm or 3pm, and it can take up to two hours to complete all the necessary paperwork. Some banks will only change a minimum of $100 per transaction. Airport banks are open seven days a week, others only Monday to Friday. You'll find life much easier if you bring only **US dollar bank notes and plastic**. Euro notes are

Exchange rates

You will see two rates being quoted for cash: the *oficial*, which is what a bank will pay you, and the *turismo*, which is what you will get in a hotel or travel agency; traveller's cheques have slightly lower rates, even in banks. The *turismo* is usually only two or three points less than the *oficial* and, unless you're changing large amounts of money, it's often worth living with this lower rate to avoid the inconvenience of changing your money in a bank.

You can check current exchange rates and convert figures on Ⓦwww.xe.net/currency. At the time of writing, the Brazilian *real* was worth R$2.50 to US$1 or R$4 to £1

slowly being recognized, but at poor rates of exchange.

Opening hours and public holidays

Basic hours for most stores and businesses are from 9am to 6pm, with an extended lunch hour from around noon to 2pm. Banks don't open until 10am, and stay open all day, but usually stop changing money at either 2pm or 3pm; except for those at major airports, they're closed at weekends and on public holidays. Museums and monuments more or less follow office hours but many are closed on Monday.

Brazilian public holidays

There are plenty of local and state holidays, but on the following **national holidays** just about everything in the country will be closed:

January 1 New Year's Day
Carnaval The four days leading up to Ash Wednesday
Good Friday
April 21 Remembrance of Tiradentes
May 1 Labour Day
Corpus Christi
September 7 Independence Day
October 12 Nossa Senhora Aparecida
November 2 Dia dos Finados (the Day of the Dead)
November 15 Proclamation of the Republic
December 25 Christmas Day

Phones

Phones are operated by **phonecards** (*cartão telefônico*), which are on sale everywhere – from newspaper stands, street sellers' trays and most cafés. For local calls a 5-*real* card will last for several conversations; for long-distance or international calls, higher-value phonecards come in 10, 20, 50 or 100 *real* denominations. Calls to the US or Europe cost about US$1.50 per minute. Before dialling direct, lift the phone from the hook, insert the phonecard and listen for a dialling tone. Note that long-distance calls are cheaper after 8pm.

The **dialling tone** is a single continuous note, **engaged** is rapid pips, and the **ringing tone** is regular peals, as in the US. The phone system in Brazil is continually overloaded. If you get an engaged tone, keep trying – nine times out of ten, the phone is not actually engaged and you get through after seven or eight attempts. The smaller the place, the more often you need to try: be patient.

Long-distance and international calls can also be made from a *posto telefônico*, which all operate in the same way: you ask at the counter for a *chave* and are given a numbered key. You go to the booth, insert the key and turn it to the right, and can then make up to three completed calls. You are billed when you return the key. To make a call between cities, you need to dial the trunk code, the *código* DDD (pronounced "daydayday"), listed at the front of phone directories. For international calls, ask for *chamada internacional*; a reverse-charge call is a *chamada a cobrar*. Reversing the charges costs about twice as much as paying locally, and it is much cheaper to use a telephone charge card from home. Except in the most remote parts of Amazônia and the Northeast, everything from a small town upwards has a *posto*, though note that outside large cities they shut at 10pm.

Long-distance telephone access codes

The privatization of Brazil's telephone system has led to a proliferation of new telephone companies and increased competition. Before making a national or international call

Calling home from abroad

Note that the initial zero is omitted from the area code when dialing the UK, Ireland, Australia and New Zealand from abroad.
US and Canada international access code + 1 + area code.
Australia international access code + 61 + city code.
New Zealand international access code + 64 + city code.
UK international access code + 44 + city code.
Republic of Ireland international access code + 353 + city code.
South Africa international access code + 27 + city code.

you must now select the telephone company you wish to use by inserting a **two-digit code** between the zero and the area code or country code of the number you are calling. To call Rio, for example, from anywhere else in the country, you would dial 0xx21 (zero + phone company code + city code) followed by the seven-digit number. For local calls you simply dial the seven- or eight-digit number.

As different phone companies are responsible for different areas of the country, pay phones will display which company code should be used from that particular phone, or the hotel receptionist will let you know the correct code to be used if calling from your hotel. Only two companies (Embratel – code 21; and Intelig – code 23) allow you to make **international calls** from Brazil – one of these numbers will be an option from most phones.

Time

Brazil is large enough to have different time zones. Most of the country is three hours behind GMT, but the states of Amazonas, Acre, Rondônia, Mato Grosso and Mato Grosso do Sul are four hours behind – that includes the cities of Manaus, Corumbá, Rio Branco, Porto Velho, Cuiabá and Campo Grande.

Tourist information

You'll find tourist information fairly easy to come by once in Brazil, and there are some sources to be tapped before you leave home. Brazil's embassies or larger consulates (see p.61) have tourist sections, where you can pick up brochure information and advice.

Popular destinations like Rio, Salvador, the Northeast beach resorts and towns throughout the South have efficient and helpful **tourist offices**, but anywhere off the beaten track has nothing at all – only Manaus, Belém and Porto Velho have offices in the Amazon region, for example.

Most **state capitals** have tourist information offices, which are announced by signs saying **"Informações Turísticas"**. Many of these provide free city maps and booklets, but they are usually all in Portuguese, although you occasionally see atrociously mangled English. As a rule, only the airport tourist offices have **hotel booking services**, and none of them is very good on advising about budget accommodation. Tourist offices are run by the different state and municipal governments, so you have to learn a new acronym every time you cross a state line. In Rio, for example, you'll findTurisRio, which advises on the state, and Riotur, which provides information on the city. There's also **EMBRATUR,** the national tourist organization, but it doesn't have direct dealings with the general public apart from its excellent website, Ⓦwww.embratur.gov.br.

Tourist offices and government sites

Australian Department of Foreign Affairs Ⓦwww.dfat.gov.au, Ⓦww.smartraveller.gov.au.
Brazilian Tourist Office Ⓦwww.braziltourism.org
British Foreign & Commonwealth Office Ⓦwww.fco.gov.uk.
Canadian Department of Foreign Affairs Ⓦwww.dfait-maeci.gc.ca.
EMBRATUR Ⓦwww.embratur.gov.br
Irish Department of Foreign Affairs Ⓦwww.foreignaffairs.gov.ie.
New Zealand Ministry of Foreign Affairs Ⓦwww.mft.govt.nz.
US State Department Ⓦwww.travel.state.gov.

Guide

Guide

1 Rio ... 69–170

2 Minas Gerais and Espírito Santo ... 171–256

3 Bahia ... 257–304

4 The Northeast ... 305–410

5 The Amazon ... 411–506

6 Brasília, Goiás and Tocantins ... 507–554

7 Mato Grosso ... 555–608

8 São Paulo ... 609–676

9 The South ... 677–786

Rio de Janeiro

VENEZUELA
GUYANA
SURINAME
FRENCH GUIANA
COLOMBIA
N
5
4
3
PERU
7
6
BOLIVIA
2
8
1
PARAGUAY
CHILE
9
ARGENTINA
0
1000 km
URUGUAY

CHAPTER 1 Highlights

✱ **The Corcovado** Its giant statue of Christ with outstretched arms is Rio's most famous image, and it has the best views across the beautiful city. See p.102

✱ **Igreja de Nossa Senhora da Glória do Outeiro** One of the smallest of Rio's colonial churches, but certainly the most beautiful. See p.109

✱ **Ipanema beach** Definitely the beach for people watching. See p.115

✱ **Instituto Moreira Salles** This splendid modernist house hosts noteworthy exhibits of nineteenth-century Brazilian art and photography. See p.118

✱ **Parque Nacional de Tijuca** With trails and a wealth of flora and fauna, this fine city park offers spectacular views of Rio. See p.121

✱ **Lapa nightlife** Samba, *forró* and other Brazilian rhythms pound out of the bars and nightclubs of this Bohemian district in central Rio. See p.131

✱ **Museu de Arte Contemporânea** One of Oscar Niemeyer's most beautiful creations; on a fine day its views across the bay to Rio are dazzling. See p.142

✱ **Paraty** Among the prettiest and best-preserved colonial towns in Brazil, Paraty is also a great base to explore the Costa Verde's islands and beaches. See p.155

△ The Corcovado

1

Rio de Janeiro

The citizens of the ten-million-strong city of **Rio de Janeiro** call it the Cidade Marvilhosa – and there can't be much argument about that. Although riven by inequality, Rio de Janeiro has great style. Its international renown is bolstered by a series of symbols that rank as some of the greatest landmarks in the world: the **Corcovado** ("hunchback") mountain supporting the great statue of Christ the Redeemer; the rounded incline of the **Sugar Loaf** mountain, standing at the entrance to the bay; and the famous sweeps of **Copacabana** and **Ipanema** beaches, probably the most notable lengths of sand on the planet. It's a setting enhanced annually by the frenetic sensuality of **Carnaval**, an explosive celebration which – for many people – sums up Rio and her citizens, the **cariocas**. The major downside in a city given over to conspicuous consumption is the rapacious development that is engulfing Rio de Janeiro. As the rural poor, escaping drought and poverty in other regions of Brazil, flock to swell Rio's population, the city is being squeezed like a toothpaste tube between mountains and sea, pushing its human contents ever further out along the coast in either direction. The city's rich architectural heritage is being whittled away and, if the present form of economic development is sustained, the natural environment will eventually be destroyed, too. It's a process unwittingly hastened by Rio's citizens who optimistically look towards the future – most with the hope of relief from poverty, but some with an eye on the chance of greater wealth.

The **state of Rio de Janeiro**, surrounding the city, is a fairly recent phenomenon, established in 1975 as a result of the amalgamation of Guanabara state and Rio city, the former federal capital. Fairly small by Brazilian standards, the state is both beautiful and accessible, with easy trips either east along the **Costa do Sol** or west along the **Costa Verde**, taking in unspoilt beaches, washed by a relatively unpolluted ocean. **Inland** routes make a welcome change from the sands, especially the trip to **Petrópolis**, a nineteenth-century mountain retreat for Rio's rich.

The **best time to visit** both city and state, at least as far as the **climate** goes, is between May and August, when the region is cooled by trade winds, the temperature remains at around 22–32°C and the sky tends to be clear. Between December and March (the rainy season), it's more humid, with the temperature around 40°C; but even then it's rarely as oppressive as it is in northern Brazil, and there's a chance of blue sky for at least part of the day.

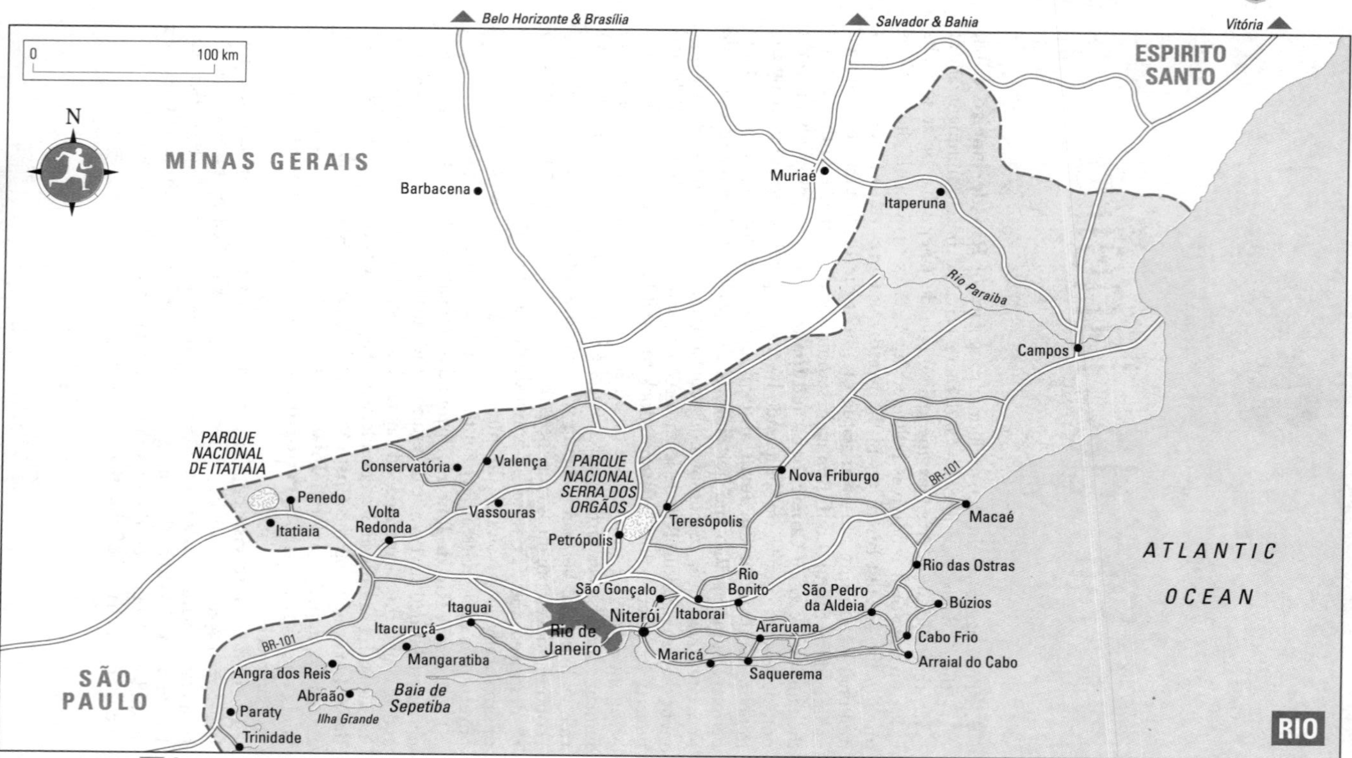
Belo Horizonte & Brasília
Salvador & Bahia
Vitória
0
100 km
N
MINAS GERAIS
ESPIRITO SANTO
Barbacena
Muriaé
Itaperuna
Rio Paraiba
Campos
PARQUE NACIONAL DE ITATIAIA
Conservatória
Valença
PARQUE NACIONAL SERRA DOS ORGÃOS
Nova Friburgo
BR-101
Penedo
Volta Redonda
Vassouras
Teresópolis
Macaé
Itatiaia
Petrópolis
ATLANTIC
OCEAN
Rio das Ostras
Rio Bonito
São Gonçalo
São Pedro da Aldeia
Búzios
Itaguai
Niterói
Itaboraí
Itacuruçá
Rio de Janeiro
Araruama
Cabo Frio
BR-101
Maricá
Mangaratiba
Arraial do Cabo
Saquerema
SÃO PAULO
Angra dos Reis
Abraão
Baia de Sepetiba
Paraty
Ilha Grande
Trinidade
RIO
São Paulo
Santos

Rio de Janeiro city

Without a shadow of a doubt, **Rio de Janeiro** is one of the world's greatest cities. Rio sits on the southern shore of a landlocked harbour within the magnificent natural setting of Guanabara Bay. Extending for 20km along an alluvial strip, between an azure sea and jungle-clad mountains, the city's streets and buildings have been moulded around the foothills of the mountain range that provides its backdrop, while out in the bay there are innumerable rocky islands fringed with white sand. The aerial views over Rio are breathtaking, and even the concrete skyscrapers that dominate the city's skyline add to the attraction. Although to many visitors Rio is synonymous with beaches, the city holds many other attractions besides. As the former capital of Brazil and its second largest city, Rio has a remarkable architectural heritage, some of the country's best museums and galleries, superb restaurants and a vibrant nightlife. With so much to see and do, Rio can easily occupy a week and you may well find it difficult to drag yourself away from the city.

Some history

Over five hundred years have seen **RIO DE JANEIRO** transformed from a fortified outpost on the rim of an unknown continent into one of the world's great cities. Its recorded past is tied exclusively to the legacy of the colonialism on which it was founded. No lasting vestige survives of the civilization of the **Tamoios** people, who inhabited the land before the Europeans arrived, and the city's history effectively begins on January 1, 1502, when a **Portuguese** captain, André Gonçalves, steered his craft into Guanabara Bay, thinking he was heading into the mouth of a great river. (The city takes its name from this event – Rio de Janeiro means the "River of January".) In 1555, the French, keen to stake a claim on the New World, established a garrison near the Sugar Loaf mountain, and the governor general of Brazil, Mem de Sá, made an unsuccessful attempt to oust them. It was left to his son, Estácio de Sá, finally to defeat them in 1567, though he fell – mortally wounded – during the battle. The city then acquired its official name, São Sebastião de Rio de Janeiro, after the infant king of Portugal, and Rio began to develop on and around the Morro do Castelo – in front of where Santos Dumont airport now stands.

With Bahia the centre of the new Portuguese colony, initial progress in Rio was slow, and only in the 1690s, when **gold** was discovered in the neighbouring state of Minas Gerais, did the city's fortunes look up, as it became the control and taxation centre for the gold trade. During the seventeenth century the **sugar cane** economy brought new wealth to Rio, but despite being a prosperous entrepôt, the city remained poorly developed. For the most part it comprised a collection of narrow streets and alleys, cramped and dirty, bordered by habitations built from lath and mud. However, Rio's strategic importance grew as a result of the struggle with the Spanish over territories to the south (which would become Uruguay), and in 1763 the city replaced Bahia (Salvador) as Brazil's capital city.

By the eighteenth century, the majority of Rio's inhabitants were **African** slaves. Unlike most other foreign colonies, in Brazil miscegenation became the rule rather than the exception: even the Catholic Church tolerated procreation between the races, on the grounds that it supplied more souls to be saved. As a result, virtually nothing in Rio remained untouched by African customs, beliefs and behaviour – a state of affairs that clearly influences today's city, too, with its mixture of Afro-Brazilian music, spiritualist cults and cuisine.

In March 1808, having fled before the advance of Napoleon Bonaparte's forces during the Peninsular War, **Dom João VI** of Portugal arrived in Rio, bringing with him an astounding ten thousand nobles, ministers, priests and servants of the royal court. So enamoured of Brazil was he that after Napoleon's defeat in 1815 he declined to return to Portugal and instead proclaimed it "the United Kingdom of Portugal, Brazil and the Algarves, of this side and the far side of the sea, and the Guinea Coast of Africa" – the greatest **colonial empire** of the age, with Rio de Janeiro as its capital. During Dom João's reign the Enlightenment came to Rio, the city's streets were paved and lit, and Rio acquired a new prosperity centred on **coffee production**.

Royal patronage allowed the arts and sciences to flourish, and Rio was visited by many of the illustrious European names of the day. In their literary and artistic work they left a vivid account of contemporary Rio society – colonial, patriarchal and slave-based. Yet while conveying images of Rio's street life, fashions and natural beauty, they don't give any hint of the heat, stench and squalor of living in a tropical city with over 100,000 inhabitants and no sewerage system. Behind the imperial gloss, Rio was still mostly a slum of dark, airless habitations, intermittently scourged by outbreaks of yellow fever, its economy completely reliant upon human **slavery**.

However, by the late nineteenth century, Rio had lost much of its mercantilist colonial flavour and started to develop as a modern city: trams and trains replaced sedans, the first sewerage system was inaugurated in 1864, a telegraph link was established between Rio and London and a tunnel was excavated that opened the way to Copacabana, as people left the crowded centre and looked for new living space. Under the administration of the engineer **Francisco Pereira Passos**,

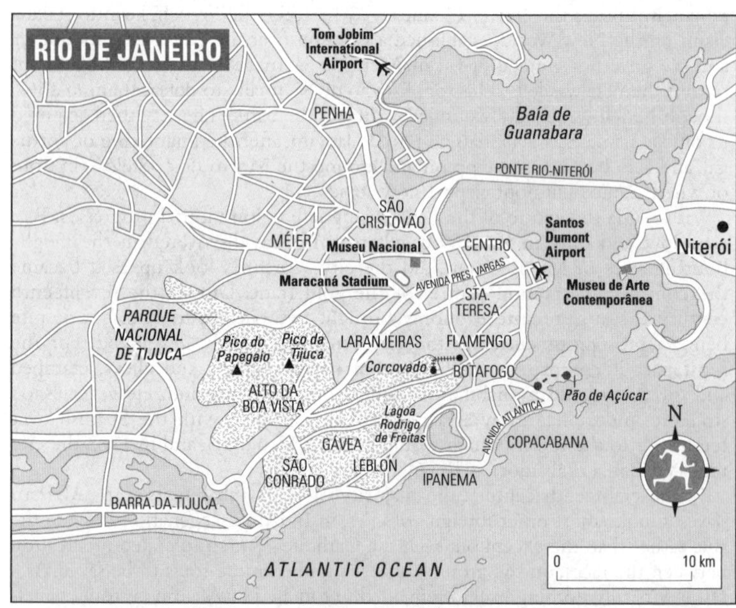

Rio went through a period of urban reconstruction that all but destroyed the last vestiges of its colonial design. The city was torn apart by a period of frenzied building between 1900 and 1910, its monumental splendour modelled on the *belle époque* of Paris of the Second Empire. Public buildings, grand avenues, libraries and parks were all built to embellish the city, lending it the dignity perceived as characteristic of the great capital cities of the Old World.

During the 1930s and 1940s Rio enjoyed international renown, buttressed by Hollywood images presented by the likes of **Carmen Miranda** and the patronage of the first-generation jet set. Rio became the nation's commercial centre, too, and a new wave of modernization swept the city, leaving little more than the Catholic churches as monuments to the past. Even the removal of the country's political administration to the new federal capital of Brasília in 1960 did nothing to discourage the developers. Today, with the centre rebuilt many times since colonial times, the interest of most visitors lies not in Rio's architectural heritage but firmly in the **beaches** to the south of the city centre, in an area called the Zona Sul. For more than seventy years these beaches have been Rio's heart and soul, providing a constant source of recreation and income for *cariocas*. In stark contrast, Rio's **favelas** (see box, p.118), clinging precariously to the hillsides of the Zona Sul and across large expanses of the Zona Norte, show another side to the city, saying much about the divisions within it. Although not exclusive to the capital, these slums seem all the more harsh in Rio because of the abundance and beauty that lie right next to them.

Orientation

Arriving in a big city can be a daunting experience, and many people come to Rio de Janeiro, scramble their way to Copacabana or Ipanema and go no further, except on an occasional foray by guided tour. The beaches, though, are only one facet of Rio. The city is divided into three parts – centre, north and south – and the various *bairros* (neighbourhoods) have retained their individuality and characteristic atmosphere. So, while you'll certainly want to get a good dose of the beaches, you may prefer to put up in a quieter quarter and explore the rich history of the centre as well. Rio's layout is straightforward and the transport system makes it easy to get around – but given the city's vast size, it's worth carrying a good map; they're available from any city kiosk.

Centro

Centro is the commercial and historic centre of Rio, and, though the elegance of its colonial and Neoclassical architecture has become overshadowed by the towering office buildings, it has by no means yet been swamped. The area is laid out in an effective grid, cut by two main arteries at right angles to each other: **Avenida Presidente Vargas** and **Avenida Rio Branco**. Presidente Vargas runs west from the waterfront and the Candelária church to Dom Pedro II **train station** and on to the **Sambódromo**, where the Carnaval procession takes place. Rio Branco crosses it in front of the Candelária church, running from **Praça Mauá** in the dockland area, south through **Praça Mahatma Gandhi** to the **Avenida Beira Mar**. On the west side of Avenida Rio Branco, **Largo da Carioca** provides access to the hilly suburb of **Santa Teresa**, whose leafy streets wind their way upwards and westwards towards the Corcovado. Just south of Centro, at the foot of the slope on which Santa Teresa is built, lies **Lapa**, an inner-city residential and red-light district, its past grandeur reflected in the faded elegance of the **Passeio Público** park.

Staying safe

Although it sometimes seems that one half of Rio is constantly being robbed by the other, don't let paranoia ruin your stay. It's true that there is a lot of petty theft in Rio: pockets are picked and bags and cameras swiped. But use a little common sense and you'll encounter few problems. Most of the real violence affecting Rio is drug related and concentrated in the *favelas*. In addition, there are certain areas that should be avoided.

In **Centro**, contrary to popular belief, Sunday is not the best time to stroll around – the streets are empty, which means you can be more easily identified, stalked and robbed. And with nobody about, there is little hope of immediate assistance. The area around **Praça Mauá**, just to the north of Centro, should be avoided after nightfall, and even during the day care should be taken. **Lapa**, one of Rio's key nightlife districts, is another place that requires caution. Although **Copacabana**'s record has improved since the authorities started to floodlight the beach at night, it's still not a good idea to remain on the sand after sunset; along Avenida Atlântica, the biggest trouble you're likely to encounter is being hassled by prostitutes who congregate in front of the *Help Discoteque* and the *Othon Palace Hotel*. Around the **Praça do Lido** in Leme, a red-light district, gringos are fair game, and in the Zona Sul's **Parque do Flamengo** it's inadvisable to wander unaccompanied after nightfall.Similarly, tourists who choose to walk between **Cosme Velho** and the **Corcovado** have been subject to robbery and assault – both of which can be best avoided by taking the train.

Apart from these clearly identifiable pockets of Rio, caution should be used in general throughout the city. Drug lords have effectively been able to shut down huge swaths of town as a demonstration of their power, ordering shops and businesses to close under threat of violence; hijackings, burning of buses and even some bomb blasts have been known to occur in the wake of these closings. If such an event should take place during your stay – you'll notice shops' shutters being pulled down and the streets emptying in a hurry – you should immediately return to your hotel and wait until you're told that the threat has passed.

On the east side of Rio Branco, **Rua da Assembléia** runs into **Praça XV de Novembro** – the square near the water where you'll find the station for **ferries** and hydrofoils to **Niterói** (across the bay) and **Ilha de Paquetá** (to the north).

Both Avenida Rio Branco and Praça XV de Novembro are good places to catch a **bus to the southern beaches** of the Zona Sul – any bus with the name of a distant beach, like Leblon, passes along the coastline, or parallel to it.

Zona Norte

The northernmost part of Rio, the **Zona Norte**, contains the city's industrial areas – large expanses of *favelas* and other working-class residential *bairros* with little in the way of historic interest or natural beauty. However, the **Museu Nacional** in the Quinta da Boa Vista park is a splendid collection well worth making time for. This apart, you're not likely to go much further north than Praça Mauá, exceptions being trips to and from the international airport, the inter-city bus terminal, the **Feira Nordestina** and the **Maracanã Stadium**, Brazil's football Mecca.

Zona Sul

The **Zona Sul**, the name used to cover everything south of the city centre, though generally taken to mean just the *bairros* shouldering the coastline, has much more to attract you than the Zona Norte.

Following the Avenida Beira Mar south from Centro, the zone is heralded by the **Parque do Flamengo**, an extensive area of reclaimed land transformed into a public recreation area and beach. First up is the *bairro* of **Glória**, where the whitewashed church of Nossa Senhora da Glória do Outeiro, high on a wooded hill, makes an unmistakeable landmark. Beyond, Beira Mar becomes Avenida Praia do Flamengo, which leads into the *bairros* of **Catete** and **Flamengo** – together with Glória, areas where you'll find innumerable cheap hotels. On the other side of Flamengo is the **Largo do Machado**, whose central position, between the centre and the beach areas, makes it a good place to use as a base. From the square you can reach the *bairros* of **Laranjeiras** and **Cosme Velho**, to the west. The latter is the site of the **Corcovado** and the famous hilltop statue of Christ the Redeemer.

Further south, the bay of **Botafogo** is overshadowed by the **Sugar Loaf** mountain, looming above the *bairro* of **Urca**. From Botafogo, the **Pasmado Tunnel** leads to **Leme**, a small *bairro* whose 3km of beach, bordered by **Avenida Atlântica**, sweep around to **Copacabana**. Now one of the world's most densely populated areas, Copacabana is less classy than it once was, losing ground to its western neighbours, **Ipanema** and **Leblon**, which provide another 4km of sand and surf. These areas are the most chic of the residential *bairros*, with clubs and restaurants sitting amidst the stylish homes of Rio's more prosperous citizens.

Ipanema and Leblon are situated on a thin strip of land, only a few hundred metres wide, between the Atlantic Ocean and the **Lagoa Rodrigo de Freitas**, a lake tucked beneath the green hills of the **Tijuca National Park**. The **Jardim Botânico** and **Jockey Club** racecourse are on the north side of the lake, and the *bairro* of **Gávea** lies just to the west. Further south, through Gávea, the Auto-Estrada Lagoa-Barra leads into **São Conrado** and its southern neighbour, **Barra de Tijuca**, the new ghetto of Rio's middle classes. São Conrado, in particular, shows up the great contradictions in Brazilian society: overlooking the elegant Gávea Golf Club and the prosperous residences that surround it is the **Favela Roçinha**, a shantytown clinging to the mountainside and home to over 200,000 people.

Arrival and information

You're most likely to fly in to Rio or arrive by bus, as the city's train station is now only used for commuter services. Be warned that opportunistic thieves are active at all points of arrival, so don't leave baggage unattended or valuables exposed; be especially careful of dangling cameras and wallets stuffed into back pockets.

By air

Rio de Janeiro is served by two airports. The Tom Jobim **international airport** (Ⓣ21/3398-4526) – usually referred to by its old name, **Galeão** – which also serves most Brazilian destinations, lies on the Ilha do Governador in Guanabara Bay, 20km north of the city. Apart from international flights, this airport also serves destinations throughout Brazil. On arrival, make sure that your passport is stamped and that you retain your immigration form, as failure to do so can cause problems come departure. In the arrivals hall, consult one of the official **tourist information** desks – Riotur or TurisRio. (Avoid those that represent private concerns, trying to pass themselves off as official agencies.) Here staff will check hotels for vacancies for you, though not at the very cheapest places. **Changing money** is not a problem as there's a branch of the Banco do Brasil as well as several ATMs on the third floor of the airport. After 10pm you can only withdraw up to R$60 from the machines.

To reach your hotel, catch one of the air-conditioned **executivo buses** (R$5), which run every half-hour between 5.20am and 11pm, either via Centro to Santos Dumont, or along the coast, via Centro, to Copacabana and on to São Conrado. Outside these hours, a **taxi** ride is the only alternative. Buy a ticket at the taxi desks, near the arrivals gate, and give it to the driver at the taxi rank; a ticket to Flamengo costs about R$50, Copacabana R$60 and Ipanema R$70. It's best not to take the ordinary taxis – you're likely to end up being overcharged – and don't risk accepting a lift from one of the unofficial drivers hanging about in the airport. The ride takes about fifteen minutes into the centre or approximately half an hour to Zona Sul, unless you hit rush hour.

Heading out to the international airport, ask your hotel to arrange for a fixed-fare taxi to pick you up, or take the air-conditioned bus that follows the Zona Sul coastline and can be caught on Avenida Delfim Moreira (Leblon), Avenida Vieira Souto (Ipanema), Avenida Atlântica (Copacabana), Avenida Beira Mar (Flamengo), or on the Avenida Rio Branco in Centro – allow at least an hour from the beaches.

Inside Galeão, departure desks are split into three sections: internal Brazilian flights from Sector A; Sectors B and C for international flights. Duty-free shops only accept US currency or credit cards – not Brazilian *reaís*. There's a pretty good range of shops in the departure lounge where you can buy T-shirts, fine (and expensive) jewellery and *cachaça*.

Santos Dumont airport (Ⓣ21/3814-7070) at the north end of the Parque de Flamengo in the city centre mainly handles the shuttle services to and from São Paulo. From here, every 40 minutes an air-conditioned **executivo bus** (R$5) will take you through the Zona Sul, stopping wherever passengers want to get off along the beaches of Copacabana, Ipanema, Leblon and São Conrado. Ordinary **taxis** (yellow with a blue stripe) are readily available from outside the terminal but you're likely to be overcharged by drivers not willing to activate the meter if you're obviously new to town – the fare should cost around R$30 to Copacabana. A less stressful option is to purchase a voucher from one of the radio-taxi stands within the terminal. You'll be directed to your cab and will be charged a flat rate of R$35 to Copacabana or R$45 to Ipanema. Alternatively, cross the road and catch an ordinary bus from Avenida Marechal Câmara, which you can reach by taking the pedestrian walkway in front of the airport terminal: #438 to Ipanema and Leblon via Botafogo; #442 to Urca; #472 to Leme. For Copacabana, #484 goes from Avenida General Justo, over which the walkway also crosses.

By bus

All major inter-city bus services arrive at the **Rodoviária Novo Rio** (Ⓣ21/3213-1800), 3km north of Centro in the São Cristovão *bairro*, close to the city's dockside at the corner of Avenida Rodrigues Alves and Avenida Francisco Bicalho. International buses from Santiago, Buenos Aires, Montevideo and Asunción, among others, use this terminus, too. The *rodoviária* has two sides, one for departures, the other for arrivals: once through the gate at arrivals, either purchase a voucher for a taxi (about R$15 to Centro, R$30 to Copacabana or R$35 to Ipanema), catch an *executivo* air-conditioned bus along the coast towards Copacabana, Ipanema and Leblon (R$4; every half-hour from directly outside the arrivals side of the station), or cross the road to the ordinary bus terminal in Praça Hermes. Alternatively, go to platform 60 where you can catch the *Integração Expressa* bus (number 406A; R$2.60) to Largo do Machado *metrô* station; from there trains will take you towards Copacabana. The **tourist office** desk (daily 8am–8pm) is located at the bottom of the stairs, in front of the main exit – they'll help with hotels, and advise which buses to catch. There are spotlessly clean showers at the *rodoviária* that you can use for around R$7 (with towel included).

Leaving Rio by bus and travelling out of the state, it's best to book two days in advance. The same goes for services to popular in-state destinations, like Búzios or Paraty, whose buses fill up at weekends; or for travelling anywhere immediately before or after Carnaval. Most **tickets** can be bought from travel agents all over the city, while inside the main *rodoviária*, on both sides, upstairs and down, you'll find the ticket offices of the various bus companies. You can reach the *rodoviária* on bus #104 from Centro, #127 or #128 from Copacabana, and #456, #171 or #172 from Flamengo.

Information

There are two official **tourist agencies** in the city, neither of them particularly efficient. Information about Rio itself is from **Riotur** (ⓦwww.riotur.com.br), which distributes maps and brochures and has a helpful English-speaking telephone information service, Alô Rio (daily 9am–6pm; ⓣ0800/707-1808). Riotur's main office is in Centro at Rua da Assembléia 10, ninth floor (Mon–Fri 9am–6pm; ⓣ21/2217-7552), and it also has a branch in Copacabana at Av. Princesa Isabel 183 (daily 8am–8pm; ⓣ21/2541-7522). Most of Riotur's information can also be picked up at their booths at Rodoviária Novo Rio (daily 8am–8pm) and Galeão international airport (daily 6am–midnight). Limited information about other parts of the state of Rio is available from **TurisRio** (ⓦwww.turisrio.rj.gov.br), located at Rua da Ajuda 5 in Centro (Mon–Fri 9am–6pm, ⓣ0800/282-2007) and on the ground floor of Rio Sul shopping centre in Botafogo (Mon–Sun 10am–10pm & Sun 3–9pm).

Getting around

Rio's **public transport** system is inexpensive and effective: most places can be easily reached by *metrô*, bus or taxi, or a combination of these. Bus services for getting about the state are also excellent but you might want to rent a car – though driving in the city itself is not recommended unless you have nerves of steel.

The metrô

The safest and most comfortable way to travel is by using Rio's **metrô** system, in operation since 1979. It's limited to just two lines, which run from Monday to Saturday, 5am to 12pm and Sunday and holidays 7am to 11pm: **Linha 1** runs from central Copacabana (Siqueira Campos station), north through Centro and then out to the Sãens Pena station in the *bairro* of Maracanã; **Linha 2** comes in from Maria de Graça, to the north of the city, via the Maracanã stadium, and meets Linha 1 at Estação Central, by Dom Pedro II train station. The system is well designed and efficient, the stations bright, cool, clean and secure, and the trains gently air-conditioned, which is a relief if you've just descended from the scorching world above.

Tickets are bought as singles (*unitário*; R$2.25) or returns (*duplo*; R$4.50), or are valid for ten journeys (*múltiplo*; R$22.50). Ten-journey tickets can save time (but not money) and can't be shared, as the electronic turnstiles only allow entrance at eight-minute intervals. You can also buy a combined bus/*metrô* ticket (*integrado*;

Organized tours

Organized tours highlighting different aspects of Rio are well worth considering. Carlos Roquette (☎21/3322-4872, ⓦwww.culturalrio.com.br; around R$80 per person), has been leading historical and cultural tours of the city for years, and while his mainstays are "Colonial Rio", "Imperial Rio", "Belle Époque Rio" and "Art Deco Rio", he also designs tours to meet the particular interests of individuals or groups – not the least of which are explorations of homosexual life, past and present, in the city's varied *bairros*. Also highly recommended are Marcel Armstrong's "Favela Tour" (R$65 per person; see p.118), as well as "Rio Hiking" (see p.122), which concentrates on Rio's green spaces (from R$100 per person) but also take visitors to Lapas' bars.

R$2.20 or R$2.60, depending on the destination), the air-conditioned Itegração Expressa buses useful for making the link from Rodoviária Novo Rio and Copacabana or Santa Teresa (via Largo do Machado *metrô* station; R$2.60) between the *metrô* station at Botafogo and Urca (R$2.60). Currently, Linha 1 is being extended to Ipanema but completion of the much-delayed project is still a few years off. In the meantime Itegração Expressa buses connect Copacabana's Siqueira Campos station, the line's terminus, with Praça General Osório in Ipanema (R$2.25).

Buses

While some people avoid using the **city buses** because they're badly driven and prone to much petty theft, it's well worth mastering the system: with over three hundred routes and six thousand buses, you never have to wait more than a few moments for a bus, they run till midnight and it's not that easy to get lost.

Numbers and **destinations** are clearly marked on the front of buses, and there are also plaques at the front and by the entrance detailing the route. You get on at the back, pay the seated conductor (the price is on a card behind his head) and then push through the turnstile and find yourself a seat. Buses are jam-packed at **rush hour** (around 7–9am and 5–7pm), so if your journey is short, start working your way to the front of the bus as soon as you're through the turnstile; you alight at the front. If the bus reaches the stop before you reach the front, haul on the bell and the driver will wait. In the beach areas of the Zona Sul, especially along the coast, **bus stops** are not always marked. Stick your arm out to flag the bus down, or look for groups of people by the roadside facing the oncoming traffic, as this indicates a bus stop.

As a precaution against **being robbed** on the bus, don't leave wallets or money in easily accessible pockets and don't flash cameras around. If there's a crush, carry any bags close to your chest. Have your fare ready so that you can pass through the turnstile immediately – pickpockets operate at the rear of the bus, by the entrance, so that they can make a quick escape – and make sure that you carry any items in front of you as you pass through the turnstile. Special care should be taken on buses known to carry mostly tourists (such as those to the Sugar Loaf mountain) and that are consequently considered easy targets by thieves.

Taxis

Taxis in Rio come in two varieties: **yellow** ones with a blue stripe that cruise the streets and the larger, newer, air-conditioned **radio cabs**, which are white with a red-and-yellow stripe and are ordered by phone. Both have meters and, unless you have pre-paid at the airport, you should insist that it is activated (check, too, that it has been cleared after the last fare). The flag, or *bandeira*, over the meter denotes the tariff. Normally this will read "1", but after 10pm, and on

Sundays, holidays and throughout December, you have to pay twenty percent more; then the *bandeira* will read "2".

Generally speaking, Rio's taxi service is reasonably priced (Centro to Ipanema costs around R$20, Botafogo to Copacabana around R$15) and it is not in the cabbies' interest to alienate tourists by ripping them off; the only time to avoid ordinary (yellow and blue) taxis is when you're coming into town from an airport. However, late at night, drivers often quote a fixed price that can be up to three times the normal fare. Radio cabs are thirty percent more expensive than the regular taxis, but they are reliable; companies include Coopertramo (Ⓣ21/2560-2022) and Transcoopass (Ⓣ21/2560-6891).

Ferries and hydrofoils

From Praça XV de Novembro **ferries** transport passengers across Guanabara Bay to the city of Niterói and to Paquetá Island, a popular day-trip destination to the north of Guanabara Bay. The ferries are extremely cheap and the view of Rio they afford, especially at sunset, is well worth the effort. The twenty-minute crossings to **Niterói** are very frequent and cost R$2; just turn up and buy a ticket. Barcas Transportes Maritímos (Ⓣ21/4004-3113) run Monday to Saturday, roughly every fifteen minutes from 6am to 10pm with less frequent services throughout the night; Sunday and public holidays, every thirty minutes from 6am to 11pm and then hourly. Barcas also operate **hydrofoil** service to Niterói roughly every twenty minutes from 7am to 8.30pm; the journey takes ten minutes and costs about R$5.

Barcas operate nine departures a day from Praça XV de Novembro to the island of **Paquetá**, between 5.15am and 11pm. Tickets cost R$3.30 (or R$4.50 on weekends) and crossings take seventy minutes.

Rio: some useful bus routes

From Avenida Rio Branco: #119, #121, #123, #127, #173 and #177 to Copacabana; #128 (via Copacabana), #132 (via Flamengo) and #172 (via "Jóquei Clube") to Leblon.

From Praça XV do Novembro: #119, #154, #413, #415 to Copacabana; #154 and #474 to Ipanema.

From Avenida Beira Mar, in Lapa, near the Praça Deodoro: #158 (via "Jóquei Clube"), #170, #172 (via Jardim Botânico), #174 (via Praia do Botafogo), #438, #464, #571 and #572 to Leblon; #472 to Leme; #104 to Jardim Botânico.

From Copacabana: #455 to Centro; #464 to Maracanã.

From Urca: #511 (via "Jóquei Clube") and #512 (via Copacabana) to Leblon.

From the Menezes Cortes terminal, adjacent to Praça XV de Novembro: air-conditioned buses along the coast to Barra de Guaratiba, south of Rio; on the return journey, these buses are marked "Castelo", the name of the area near Praça XV.

From Rodoviária Novo Rio: #104 from Centro, #127 or #128 to Copacabana, and #456, #171 or #172 to Flamengo.

To the train station: any bus marked "E. Ferro".

Parque do Flamengo: any bus marked "via Aterro" passes along the length of the Parque do Flamengo without stopping.

Between Centro and the Zona Sul, most buses run along the coast as far as Botafogo; those for Copacabana continue around the bay, past the Rio Sul shopping centre, and through the Pasmado Tunnel; those for Leblon, via the "Jóquei Clube", turn right at Botafogo and travel along Avenida São Clemente.

Trams

Rio's last remaining electric **trams**, the *bondes* (pronounced "bonjis"), climb from near Largo Carioca, across the eighteenth-century Aqueduto da Carioca, to the inner suburb of Santa Teresa and on to Dois Irmãos. Two lines run every fifteen minutes between 5am and midnight: the one for Dois Irmãos permits you to see more of Santa Teresa; the other line terminates at Largo do Guimarães. The trams still serve their original purpose of transporting locals, and haven't yet become a tourist service. The views of Rio from them are excellent, but beware of the young men who jump aboard and attempt to relieve you of your possessions. The best times of day to ride the tram are mid-morning and mid-afternoon when it's less crowded and, consequently, less chaotic. For added safety, hop on a tram that's carrying a police officer assigned to watch over tourists. The tram station is downtown, behind the monumentally ugly Petrobrás building and adjacent to the Nova Catedral. Waiting passengers stand in eight lines, one for every row of seats on the tram; the fare is just 60¢, which you pay at the station turnstile going up to Santa Teresa and on board going down.

On Saturdays at 10am, a special tram service – the Bonde Turístico Especial – runs for tourists (R$4). This goes way beyond the normal Dois Irmãos terminal, leaving the built-up area of Santa Teresa and entering the edge of the Tijuca forest, which is a good starting point for a stroll.

Driving in Rio

If you're renting a **car** then you must understand what you're letting yourself in for. Rio's road system is characterized by a confusion of one-way streets, tunnels, access roads and flyovers, and **parking** is not easy (it's all but impossible downtown). **Lane markings**, apart from lending a little colouring to the asphalt, serve no apparent practical purpose, **overtaking** on the right appears to be mandatory and, between 10pm and 6am, to avoid an armed holdup, you merely have to slow down as you approach a red **traffic light**. If you do rent a car in Rio, you're well advised to only use it to venture out of the city. Car rental agencies are listed on p.45.

Accommodation

Although there's usually no shortage of **accommodation** in Rio, there are considerable seasonal variations in terms of demand and prices. **High season** is from December to February, so if you arrive then without an advance booking, either make one through a tourist office or leave your luggage in the *guarda volumes* (baggage offices) at the *rodoviária* or at Santos Dumont airport while you look; there's no point lugging heavy bags around Rio's hot thoroughfares, and it makes you vulnerable to theft as well. During **Carnaval**, prices soar, accommodation becomes that much harder to find and most hotels and hostels accept bookings for a minimum of four nights' stay. During the low season, hotels usually decrease their prices by between thirty and fifty percent but, when a discount is given, you may not be allowed to pay with a credit card – indeed, most of the cheapest hotels never accept cards and require advance payment.

For much of the year there's keen competition for guests and you should be able to find a reasonable double room, usually with air-conditioning, for around R$120. The highest concentrations of budget places are in Glória, Catete and Flamengo, but reasonably priced accommodation can be found just about anywhere. With just a few exceptions, only luxury-class hotels have pools, which is especially frustrating during periods when the beaches are unsafe due to pollution or strong waves.

There are several very good **hostels** in Urca, Botafogo, Copacabana and Ipanema. These usually charge around R$45 per person but during Carnaval their rates triple. In the Bohemian neighbourhood of Santa Teresa, there's an excellent bed and breakfast network (see p.84) – a contrast to Rio's strangely uninteresting hotel options. For **apartments**, try Rio Star Imóveis Ltda (Ⓣ21/3275-8393) or Rio Flat Service (Ⓣ21/3512-9922), which has buildings in Copacabana, Leblon and Lagoa; prices range from R$150 a day for a studio or one-bedroom unit with a swimming pool. If you want to be in Ipanema, call Ipanema Sweet (Ⓣ21/3239-1819), who have one- and two-bedroom apartments near the beach beginning at R$170 per day. Pathenon Flats (Ⓦwww.accorhoteis.com.br) have very good properties in Botafogo, Arpoador, Ipanema and Leblon; one- and two-bedroom apartments with a pool start around R$140 per day, depending on the location.

The city centre: Centro and Lapa

Most of the cheap *pensões* are in the north of the city, or near Dom Pedro II train station, but they're mostly inhabited by full-time residents, usually single men, who are working in Rio. It's hard to find a vacancy, and you will be looking in areas that are not particularly safe. Lapa, in the southern corner of the city centre, is a far better bet. There are countless small hotels in this down-at-heel red-light area, and – surprisingly – most of them are clean and respectable enough. Though somewhat noisy at times, Cinelândia is also worth considering: it's an easy walk from the heart of the city centre, it's well connected by bus and *metrô* to the Zona Sul and it has a handful of good bars.

Ambassador Rua Senador Dantas 25, Centro Ⓣ21/2531-1633, Ⓦwww.ambassadorhotel.com. Although this hotel, popular with Brazilian business executives, has seen better days, it offers high standards of comfort and weekend discounts. Located in the heart of Cinelândia, it's ideal for visiting the Biblioteca Nacional. ❹

Arcos Rio Palace Av. Mem de Sá 117, Lapa Ⓣ21/2242-8116, Ⓦwww.arcosriopalacehotel.com.br. Rooms at this busy, comfortable, well-equipped hotel are both secure and inexpensive. Ideally situated for enjoying Lapa's nightlife. ❸

Belas Artes Av. Visconde do Rio Branco 52, Centro Ⓣ21/2252-6336, Ⓦwww.hotelbelasartes.com.br. This small and highly respectable city-centre hotel has simply furnished but impeccably clean rooms. ❸

Guanabara Palace Av. Presidente Vargas 392, Centro Ⓣ21/2195-6000, Ⓦwww.windsorhoteis.com. Expense-account visitors stay at this lone luxury hotel in the city centre. Although utterly soulless, it's good value with spacious guest rooms, a comfortable lounge, a business centre and the added bonus of a pool. ❹

Marajó Rua São Joaquim da Silva 99 Ⓣ21/2224-4134. Comfortable beds and efficient showers make this most likely the best choice in the area. Also has some singles for around R$25. ❷

Nelba Rua Senador Dantas 46 Ⓣ21/2210-3235. Although the street noise from surrounding Cinelândia can be considerable, the simple rooms are clean. ❸

Glória and Santa Teresa

Glória is not entirely without its share of prostitution, but the *bairro* is not a dangerous area and has a slightly faded grandeur that's worth getting to know. Additionally, it's conveniently located between Centro and the beaches and restaurants of Zona Sul. Behind Glória is Santa Teresa, which, despite its leafy aspect and spirited nightlife, has only one hotel – although its numerous bed-and-breakfasts (see box, p.84) offer some of the most pleasant accommodation in Rio. Santa Teresa is best reached from Centro, and, while it is possible to walk between Glória and Santa Teresa, stay alert if doing so.

Glória Rua do Russel 632, Glória Ⓣ21/2555-7272, Ⓦwww.hotelgloriario.com.br. Built in the 1920s and set amidst the cobbled roads of the Morro da Glória, this is one of Rio's most traditional hotels – strong on style and atmosphere. Most rooms are spacious and offer fantastic views, and there are two excellent pools and a fine restaurant. This is by far the best hotel within easy reach of Downtown, and it's also a 15min taxi ride from Ipanema. Rates vary enormously, with heavy discounts often available outside of high season if you book directly with the hotel. ❻

Golden Park Hotel Rua do Russel 374, Glória ⓣ21/2556-8150, ⓦwww.hotelgoldenparkrio.com.br. This medium-sized hotel has modern facilities and a small rooftop pool. Rooms are basic but comfortable and all are a/c – be sure to request one in the front, where you'll get more light and have a park view. ❹

Rio Hostel Rua Joaquim Murtinho 361, Santa Teresa ⓣ21/3852-0827, ⓦwww.riohostel.com. This small and friendly hostel has attractive communal areas and even a small pool. Though its location is a bit isolated, it's near Lapa and an easy stroll to Santa Teresa's many bars and restaurants. R$37 per person in a dorm room or ❸ for a double room with private bathroom.

Santa Teresa Rua Almirante Alexandrino 660, Santa Teresa ⓣ21/2508-9088. Santa Teresa's only hotel is this no-frills, slightly shabby *pousada* located in a late nineteenth-century house. ❸

Turístico Ladeira da Glória 30, Glória ⓣ21/2557-7698, ⓕ2558-9388. Though this friendly spot is a bit overpriced, rooms are clean, spacious and a/c, and they come with baths and balconies. Formerly a popular spot for backpackers, this is now favoured by budget travellers who prefer not to stay at hostels. To reach the hotel from the Glória *metrô* station, climb up to the right of the Igreja da Glória and through the Largo da Glória. ❸

Catete, Flamengo, Botafogo and Urca

Catete and Flamengo, centred on the Largo do Machado and once the chic residential *bairros* of the middle classes, are well served by hotels – all a good bit cheaper than the ones at Copacabana and conveniently located between the centre and the beach zone, with buses, taxis and the *metrô* providing easy access. For some reason, Botafogo offers few hotel possibilities, but if you want to stay in what is one of Rio's best eating-out districts there are a couple of options. Finally, the only accommodation in Urca is a youth hostel, but this upscale area is a peaceful yet easy-to-reach neighbourhood.

Carioca Easy Hostel Rua Marechal Cantuaria 168, Urca ⓣ21/2295-7805, ⓦwww.cariocahostel.com.br. This attractive hostel near Sugar Loaf is located in one of Rio's quietest neighbourhoods and is just a 10min bus ride from Copacabana. Facilities include a tiny pool and Internet access. R$40 per person in a dorm, R$110 for a double room.

Chave do Rio Hostel Rua General Dionísio 63, Botafogo ⓣ21/2286-0303, ⓦwww.riohostel.com.br. Comfortable and friendly HI-associated accommodation in a beautiful renovated house just off Voluntaríos da Patria in Botafogo. The 70 beds, in dorms sleeping 2 to 12 people, go for R$40 (including breakfast) per person, and some rooms are a/c. Book ahead during Brazilian university vacations (July & Dec–March).

Bed and breakfast in Santa Teresa

Given Rio's long association with glamour and international tourism, the city's hotels and hostels are in general extremely disappointing. One refreshing development has been the emergence of a **bed-and-breakfast** network in Santa Teresa, offering considerable comfort and opportunities to meet local residents.

The members of *Cama e Café* group are a fascinating cross section of the Santa Teresa community. **Hosts** tend to be either artists or professionals and include economists, sculptors, university professors and even circus-arts trainers. Almost all speak English and they're tremendous sources of local knowledge and advice. The hundred or so hosts and their **properties** have been carefully vetted and graded by *Cama e Café* staff according to style and levels of comfort. Double rooms range in price from R$100 to R$180 per night, and every effort is made to match guests to suitable hosts. For information, contact: *Cama e Café*, Rua Progresso 67, Santa Teresa (ⓣ21/2221-7635, ⓦwww.camaecafe.com).

Flórida Rua Ferreira Viana 81, Flamengo ⓣ21/2195-6800, ⓦwww.windsorhoteis.com. A highly recommended and long-established hotel that retains a traditional atmosphere and offers spacious rooms, the nicest of which overlook the gardens of neighbouring Palácio do Catete. Amenities include a rooftop pool, a good restaurant and a business centre with free Internet usage. ❹

Imperial Rua do Catete 186, Catete ⓣ21/2556-5212, ⓦwww.imperialhotel.com.br. Spacious and comfortable rooms are housed in an attractive, renovated 1880s building well located near the *metrô* station and the park. Parking is available and there's also a decent pool, which is unusual for a hotel in this price category. ❸

Inglês, Rua Silveira Martins 20, Catete ⓣ21/2558-3052, ⓦwww.hotelingles.com.br. A recent refurbishment has made this small, long-established hotel one of the best places to stay in Catete. The spacious rooms, all with bathrooms, have a/c, TV and *frigobar.* ❹

Monte Blanco Rua do Catete 160, Catete ⓣ21/2225-0121. A spotless and welcoming place, though with no a/c and a fair amount of street noise. ❷

Monterrey Rua Artur Bernardes 39, Catete ⓣ21/2265-9899. At this safe and quiet budget option, rooms have a/c from 8pm to 8am and breakfast is brought to you in the morning. ❷

Paysandú Rua Paissandu 23, Catete ⓣ21/2558-7270, ⓦwww.paysanduhotel.com.br. Clean but plain rooms have TVs and large bathrooms, and there's a decent restaurant on the ground floor. ❹

Real Rua Real Grandeza 122, Botafogo ⓣ21/2286-3093. This inexpensive, no-frills hotel is a bit of a trek from the *metrô* but convenient for catching buses heading downtown and to the beaches. Rooms are clean if rather dilapidated, and all have a/c and private bathrooms. ❸

Regina Rua Ferreira Viana 29, Flamengo ⓣ21/3289-9999, ⓦwww.hotelregina.com.br. Rooms are on the small side but they are well looked after and feature all the basics: comfortable beds, minibars and a/c. With pleasant public areas, a friendly staff and an excellent location one block from the beach, this is a highly recommended spot. ❸

Copacabana and Leme

Copacabana's street life and general raucousness help to make it the kind of place you either love or hate. And while the area has certainly seen better days, it has by far the greatest concentration of places to stay in the city, ranging from hostels to luxury hotels. Leme – really a continuation of Copacabana – is less frenetic due to its location at the far end of the stretch of beach in the opposite direction of Ipanema.

Acapulco Copacabana Rua Gustavo Sampaio 854, Leme ⓣ21/2275-0022, ⓦwww.acapulcopacabanahotel.com.br. This comfortable, highly recommended hotel is in a quiet location behind *Le Meridien,* a couple of minutes' walk from the Cardeal Arcoverde *metrô* station. Rooms are modern, reasonably spacious and well decorated; some of the balconies just about offer a beach view and the staff are very helpful. ❺

Apa Hotel Rua República do Peru 305, Copacabana ⓣ21/2548-8112, ⓦwww.apahotel.com.br. A dreary-looking but perfectly respectable hotel with simple, clean rooms (all with a/c and balconies) in a central area of Copacabana. The rooms that sleep four people are excellent value. ❺

Atlantis Copacabana Rua Bulhões de Carvalho 61, Copacabana, ⓣ21/2521-1142. In a quiet location just one block from Ipanema, this hotel offers compact but clean rooms and an extremely helpful staff. The small rooftop pool (not a typical feature of similar budget hotels in Rio) has great views. ❺

Biarritz Rua Aires Saldanha 54, Copacabana ⓣ21/2522-0542, ⓕ2287-7640. Just one block from Av. Atlântica and the beach, this basic but clean and friendly place is located in a quiet back street. ❸

Canadá Av. N.S. de Copacabana 687, Copacabana ⓣ21/2257-1864, ⓔhotel.canada@uol.com.br. Though a popular choice with foreign visitors, it's difficult to understand why, as the dark guest rooms are in need of major refurbishment. At least the noisy a/c and fridges drown out the street noise. ❹

Che Lagarto Hostel Rua Santa Clara 304, ⓦwww.chelagarto.com. Located in central Copacabana some five blocks from the beach, this relaxed but friendly hostel is the cheapest and most basic of *Che Largarto*'s three Rio hostels. R$35 per person in a dorm sleeping four to eight or ❹ for a double room with private facilities.

Copa Linda Av. N.S. de Copacabana 956, Copacabana ⓣ21/2267-3399. This hotel, above a row of shops, provides good, no-frills accommodation, although many rooms are small. ❸

Copacabana Chalet Hostel Rua Pompeu Loureiro 99, Copacabana ⓣ21/2236-0047, ⓦwww.geocities.com/thetropics/cabana/7617. Just a short walk from the beach, this small and friendly hostel is always popular. Advance booking at peak holiday periods is essential. R$40 per person in 6-bed dorms.

Copacabana Palace Av. Atlântica 1702, Copacabana ⓣ21/2548-7070, ⓦwww.copacabanapalace.com.br. Anyone who's anyone has stayed in this glorious Art Deco landmark, which, despite Copacabana's general decline, remains *the* place to stay in Rio. Although every possible facility is on offer, there's a curious lack of communal areas, apart from the large pool in a central courtyard. All in all, this is a great place to relax if you can afford to do so. ❾

Copacabana Praia Hostel Rua Tenente Marones de Gusmão 85, Copacabana ⓣ21/2547-5422, ⓦwww.wcenter.com.br/copapraia. This efficiently run but rather institutional hostel – set several blocks back from the beach, off Rua Figueiredo Magalhães – is by far the largest in Rio. It charges R$35 per head in a six-bed dorm, but studios sleeping two to four people (including a private bathroom and basic cooking facilities) are also available. ❸

Debret Av. Atlântica 3564, Copacabana ⓣ21/2522-0132, ⓦwww.debret.com.br. A firm favourite among European independent travellers, though the overpriced rooms are small and long overdue for refurbishing. Despite the address, few rooms have ocean views. ❻

Excelsior Copacabana Av. Atlântica 1800, Copacabana ⓣ21/3259-5323, ⓦwww.windsorhoteis.com. A reasonable upper-end choice in the middle of Copacabana's beachfront. Rooms are well equipped, and the rooftop pool has spectacular views. One of the oldest hotels on the *avenida* (opened in 1950), it tries to maintain the atmosphere of a bygone age. ❽

Grandarrell Ouro Verde Av. Atlântica 1456, Copacabana ⓣ21/2543-4123, ⓦwww.dayrell.com.br. Viewed from the outside, this 1950s hotel looks like nothing special; inside, however, it's discreetly elegant, with spacious and well-kept rooms (go for the more expensive ones with sea views) and excellent service and value. Its regular guests consider it the only place to stay in Rio. ❻

Le Meridien Av. Atlântica 1020, Leme ⓣ21/3873-8888, ⓦwww.lemeridien.com. This huge hotel has all the conveniences you'd expect for the price. There's a large pool and the beach in front of the hotel is carefully watched by security patrols. With its cafés, restaurants and boutiques, *Le Meridien* is for many guests their only experience of Rio. ❽

Martinique Rua Sá Ferreira 30, Copacabana ⓣ21/2195-5200, ⓦwww.windsorhoteis.com. Popular hotel located near the quiet, western end of Copacabana, close to the Forte de Copacabana. Modern rooms have large, exceptionally comfortable beds and there's a small rooftop pool. ❺

Portinari Design Rua Francisco Sá 17, Copacabana ⓣ21/3222-8800, ⓦwww.hotelportinari.com.br. One of the few hotels in Rio that dares to be a bit different. Each floor has been conceived by a different Brazilian designer, with some much more successful than others. Decor differs in terms of colour, tone and texture, but all the rooms are exceptionally well equipped, if on the small side. Located less than a block from the beach. ❺

Praia Leme Av. Atlântica 866, Leme ⓣ21/2275-3322. This cosy two-storey hotel offers the best value for a beachfront location. Due to its popularity, an advance reservation is highly recommended. ❹

Rio Othon Palace Av. Atlântica 3264, Copacabana ⓣ21/2525-1500, ⓦwww.othon.com.br. With almost 600 guest rooms, this is a favourite of large tour groups. The hotel has all the facilities that you'd expect of a place this size and price, including several bars and restaurants, a rooftop pool and a business centre. The spacious rooms are in need of renovation, but they're perfectly comfortable; those facing the front have marvellous ocean views. ❾

Santa Clara Rua Décio Vilares 316, Copacabana ⓣ21/2256-2650, ⓦwww.hotelsantaclara.com.br. This small, simple but well-maintained hotel offers attentive service and good value. Located in a tranquil spot five blocks from the beach and close to the Túnel Velho leading to Botafogo's restaurants and museums. ❺

Toledo Rua Domingos Ferreira 71, Copacabana ⓣ21/2257-1995, ⓦwww.hoteisgandara.com.br. Small but adequate rooms (including singles and some that sleep three people) halfway down Copacabana, just one block from the beach. ❺

Ipanema and Leblon

Ipanema's safe streets and fashionable beach, along with its good shopping and dining options, make the *bairro* an attractive place to stay and, despite being one of Rio's more upscale areas, it has a pretty good range of accommodation. Just beyond Ipanema lies Leblon, an exclusive residential neighbourhood with fewer places to stay, but some excellent eating and nightlife possibilities.

Arpoador Inn Rua Francisco Otaviano 177, Arpoador ⓣ21/2523-0060, ⓔarpoador@unisys.com.br. In a peaceful location on the edge of Ipanema (bordering Copacabana), this popular hotel is reasonably priced for the area; because room rates don't change much during the year, however, in low season the basic accommodations may seem overpriced. Beachfront rooms cost double. ❻

Caesar Park Av. Vieira Souto 460, Ipanema ⓣ21/2525-2525, ⓦwww.caesarpark-rio.com.br. Thought of by some as Rio's finest hotel, the *Cesar Park* is certainly the city's most expensive and features every modern luxury that its celebrity guests would expect. Even the most basic of rooms (all of which are completely soundproof) are vast with elegant furniture and huge beds. The rooftop restaurant and pool have superb views, and the hotel provides security and lifeguards on the beach fronting the property. ❾

Carlton Rua João Lira 68, Leblon ⓣ21/2259-1932. Small, tatty hotel in one of Rio's most classy areas, with friendly staff but somewhat gloomy rooms. ❹

Che Lagarto Hostel Rua Paul Redfern 48, Ipanema ⓣ21/2512-8076, ⓦwww.chelagarto.com. The newest and best of Rio's *Che Lagarto* hostels is in a good location just a couple of blocks from the beach and a short walk to the bars and nightlife of both Ipanema and Leblon. Excellent facilities include laundry, a kitchen and Internet access, plus the staff are helpful and there's a bar offering occasional live music. R$45 per person in a dorm that sleeps four or ❺ for an a/c double room with private bathroom.

Hostel Harmonia Rua Barão da Torre 177, Casa 18, Ipanema ⓣ21/2523-4904, ⓦwww.hostelharmonia.com. With a great location near excellent bars, restaurants and the beach, this is one of Rio's most popular hostels – despite the dorms (sleeping two to six people) being extremely cramped, the atmosphere impersonal and the facilities standard. R$45 per person.

Hostel Ipanema Rua Barão da Torre 177, Casa 14, Ipanema ⓣ21/2247-7269, ⓦwww.hostelipanema.com. A welcoming and relaxed spot three blocks from the beach, in the same very safe courtyard in which the *Hostel Harmonia* is located. Internet access and laundry facilities are offered and there are bikes for rent. The hostel's owner also runs Rio's most reliable hang-gliding operation and gives discounts to hostel guests. R$45 per person in dorms sleeping three to six people. Airport pick-up can be arranged.

Ipanema Inn Rua Maria Quitéria 29, Ipanema ⓣ21/2523-6092, ⓕ2511-5094. This excellent-value and very popular hotel is just a block from the beach and in one of the best parts of Ipanema. Comfortable rooms, while small, can squeeze in an extra (fold-out) bed. ❻

Ipanema Plaza Rua Farme de Amoedo 34, Ipanema ⓣ21/3687-2000, ⓦwww.ipanemaplazahotel.com. The luxurious *Ipanema Plaza* (part of the Dutch-owned Golden Tulip chain) is small enough that it provides individual attention. Rooms and suites are all tastefully furnished with natural wood and beige tones and there's a small rooftop pool with wonderful beach views. Popular with gay visitors due to its location near the beach's gay strip. ❽

Marina Palace Rua Delfim Moreira 630, Leblon ⓣ21/2172-1000, ⓦwww.hotelmarina.com.br. Beachside *Marina Palace* is the largest of Leblon's hotels and offers amenities you might expect, such as a business centre and both a restaurant and a (curiously small) pool with great views. The rooms are on the small side, but suites are also available. ❼

São Marco Rua Visconde de Pirajá 524, Ipanema ⓣ21/2540-5032, ⓦwww.sanmarcohotel.net. A good deal for its location, on the main shopping street just a few minutes from the beach. The small rooms (and tiny bathrooms) were recently refurbished, but there's rather a lot of street noise. ❺

Vermont Rua Visconde de Pirajá 254, Ipanema ⓣ21/2522-0057, ⓕ2267-7046. Simple though perfectly adequate rooms in a central location. The "special" rooms (some of which sleep three people) are much larger and lighter and well-worth the modest additional cost. All rooms are a/c but not likely to suit those bothered by street noise. ❺

The city centre

Much of historical Rio is concentrated in **Centro**, with pockets of interest, too, in the neighbouring **Saúde** and **Lapa** quarters of the city. You'll find you can tour the centre fairly easily on foot, but bear in mind that the real interests of Rio lie elsewhere – at the beaches of the Zona Sul, and the heights of Urca and Corcovado – and it's not the most exciting city in Brazil to explore. Lots of the old historical squares, streets and buildings disappeared in the twentieth

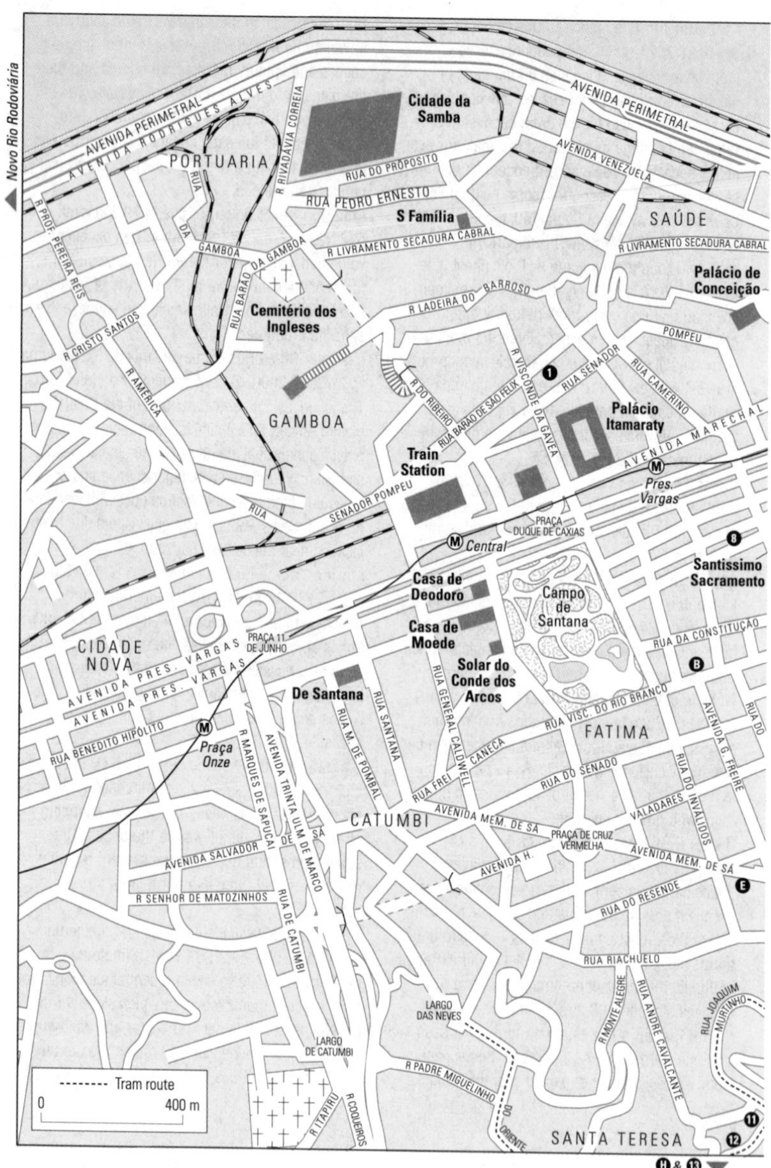

century under a torrent of redevelopment, and fighting your way through the traffic – the reason many of the streets were widened in the first place – can be quite a daunting prospect.

However, while much of what remains is decidedly low-key, there are enough churches and interesting museums to keep anybody happy for a day or two. The cultural influences that shaped the city through its five centuries of existence – the austere Catholicism of the city's European founders, the squalor of

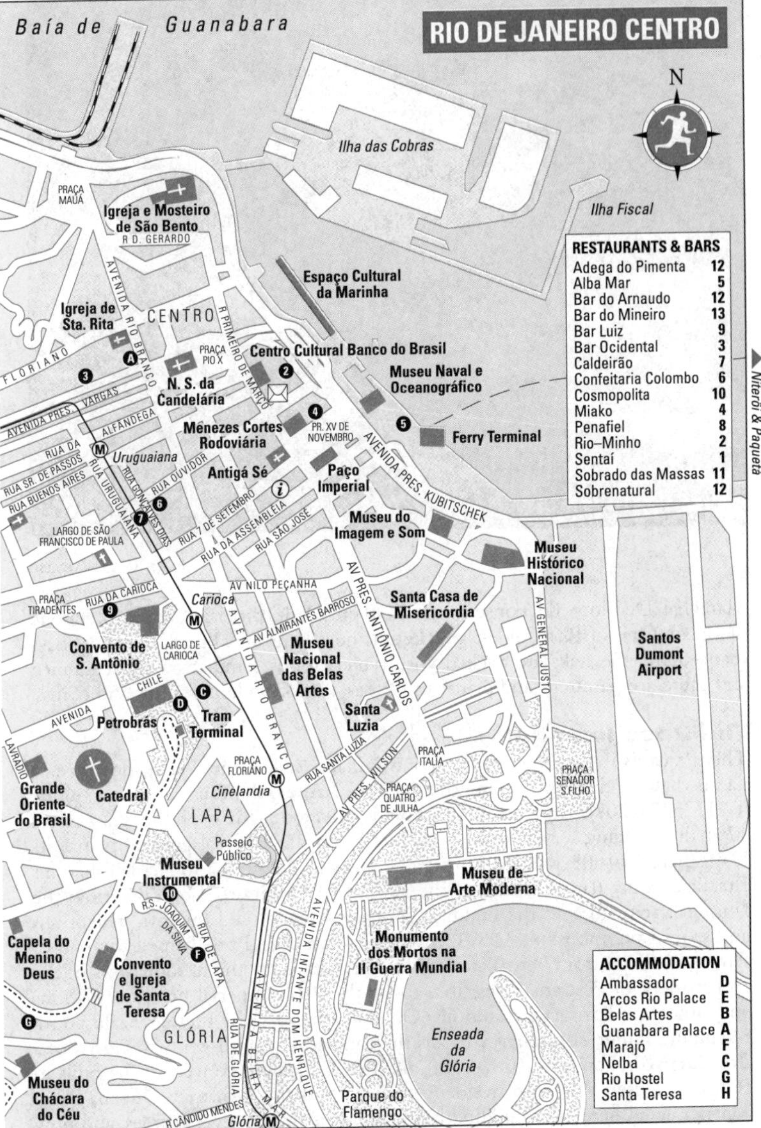

colonialism and the grandiose design of the Enlightenment – are all reflected in the surviving churches, streets and squares.

Praça XV de Novembro and around

Praça XV de Novembro is the obvious place to start. Once the hub of Rio's social and political life, it takes its name from the day (Nov 15) in 1899 when

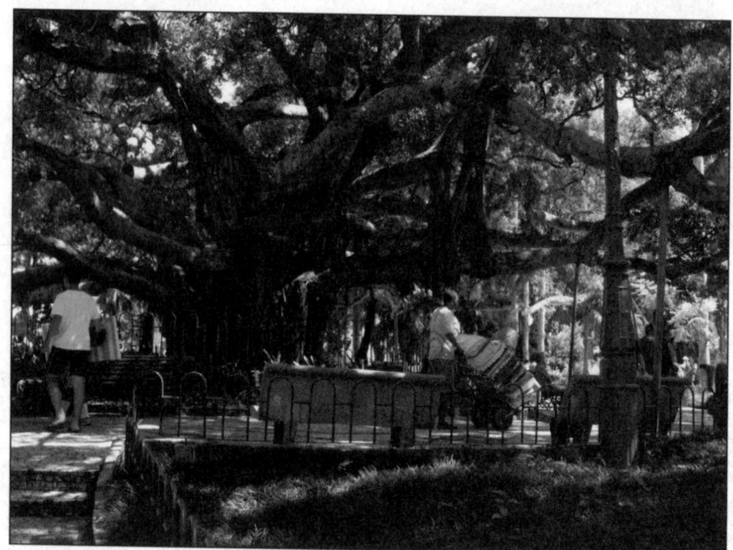

△ Praça XV de Novembro

Marechal Deodoro de Fonseca, the first president, proclaimed the Republic of Brazil. One of Rio's oldest **markets** is held here on Thursdays and Fridays (8am–6pm): the stalls are packed with typical foods, handicrafts and ceramics, and there are paintings and prints, as well as a brisk trade in stamps and coins.

The Paço Imperial

The Praça XV de Novembro was originally called the Largo do Paço, a name that survives in the imposing **Paço Imperial** (Tues–Sun noon–6pm, ⓣ21/2533-4207). Built in 1743, though tinkered with over the years, until 1791 the building served as the palace of Portugal's colonial governors in Rio. It was here, in 1808, that the Portuguese monarch, Dom João VI, established his Brazilian court (later shifting to the Palácio da Quinta da Boa Vista, now the Museu Nacional), and the building continued to be used for royal receptions and special occasions: on May 13, 1888, Princess Isabel proclaimed the end of slavery in Brazil from here. Later the building served as the headquarters of the Department of Post and Telegraph. Today, the Paço Imperial hosts installations and other modern art exhibitions. On the ground floor there's a café and a restaurant. Right on the *praça*, too, is the early seventeenth-century **Convento do Carmo** (Mon–Fri 10am–5pm), the first Carmelite convent to be built in Rio. Later used as a royal residence (after 1808 the Dowager Queen, Dona Maria I, lived here), the building has since been altered several times, and now houses part of the Universidade Cândido Mendes.

The Arco de Teles

On the northern side of the square, the **Arco de Teles** was named after the judge and landowner Francisco Teles de Meneza, who ordered its construction upon the site of the old *pelourinho* (pillory) around 1755. Though more of an arcade than an arch, the *arco* links the Travessa do Comércio to the Rua Ouvidor and originally contained three houses; one of these was home to the

Menezes family, but all were severely damaged by fire in 1790. More engaging than the building itself is the social history of the Arco de Teles and its immediate vicinity. Families belonging to Rio's wealthy classes lived in the luxurious apartments above street level, while the street below was traditionally a refuge for "beggars and rogues of the worst type; lepers, thieves, murderers, prostitutes and hoodlums" – according to Brasil Gerson in his 1954 book *História das ruas do Rio de Janeiro*. In the late eighteenth and early nineteenth centuries, one of the leprous local inhabitants – **Bárbara dos Prazeres** – achieved notoriety as a folk devil: it was a common belief that the blood of a dead dog or cat applied to the body provided a cure for leprosy, and Bárbara is supposed to have earned her reputation around the Arco de Teles by attempting to enhance the efficacy of this cure by stealing newborn babies and sucking their blood. Behind the Arco de Teles is the **Beco de Teles**, a narrow cobblestone alley with some charming nineteenth-century buildings.

Igreja de Nossa Senhora do Carmo da Antigá Sé

At the back of Praça XV de Novembro, on the corner where Rua VII de Setembro meets Rua I de Março, you'll find the **Igreja de Nossa Senhora do Carmo da Antigá Sé** (Mon–Fri 9am–5pm), which served, until 1980, as Rio's cathedral. Construction started in 1749 and, to all intents and purposes, continued right into the twentieth century as structural collapse and financial difficulties necessitated several restorations and delays: the present tower, for example, was built as late as 1905 by the Italian architect Rebecchi. Inside, the high altar is detailed in silver and boasts a beautiful work by the painter Antônio Parreires, representing Nossa Senhora do Carmo seated amongst the clouds and surrounded by the sainted founders of the Carmelite Order. Below, in the **crypt**, are the supposed mortal remains of Pedro Alvares Cabral, Portuguese discoverer of Brazil. In actual fact, he was almost certainly laid to rest in Santarém in Portugal.

Museu Naval e Oceanográfico and around

Close to Praça XV de Novembro, at Rua Dom Manuel 15, the **Museu Naval e Oceanográfico** (daily noon–4.30pm) is housed in what was originally the naval headquarters. The museum's excellent collection shows Brazil's naval history and includes pieces such as sixteenth-century nautical charts, scale replicas of European galleons, paintings depicting scenes from the Brazil–Paraguay War and exhibits of twentieth-century naval hardware. Above all, the collections provide an insight into the colonial nature of Brazilian history: the exhibits demonstrate that Brazilian naval engagements were determined by the interests of the Portuguese Empire until the nineteenth century; as a primarily slave-based plantation economy until 1888, Brazil's military hardware came from the foundries of industrialized Europe. The most impressive items on display are the handcrafted replicas of sixteenth-century galleons – the *São Felipe* complete with its 98 cannons – and the first map of the New World, drawn by Pedro Alvares Cabral between 1492 and 1500.

If you have a serious interest in naval history, follow the bayside Avenida Alfredo Agache north a couple blocks to the **Espaço Cultural da Marinha** (Tues–Sun noon–5pm). This long dockside building was once used as the port's main customs point, but today houses exhibition halls aimed purely at the naval enthusiast. From the docks by the Espaço Cultural da Marinha you can reach the small **Ilha Fiscal** (Thurs–Sun noon–5.30pm), where, in the 1880s, a customs collection centre was built. It was here also that the last grand Imperial ball was held, just days before the collapse of the monarchy in November 1889.

Connected by a series of lengthy causeways that lead from the mainland and the Ilha das Cobras, the Ilha Fiscal is most easily – and most enjoyably – reached by boat. Crossings (R$5; 15min) are on Thursdays through Sundays at 1pm, 2.30pm and 4pm; to ensure a place, arrive at the departure point at least an hour in advance. Standing alone on the tiny island, surrounded by swaying palm trees, is a wonderful fort-like structure, built in an ornately hybrid Gothic-Moorish style, which is now an unremarkable naval museum.

Along Rua I de Março to Praça Pio X

Heading up **Rua I de Março** from the *praça* you'll pass the late eighteenth-century **Igreja da Ordem Terceira do Monte do Carmo** (Mon–Fri 8am–4pm, Sat 8am–noon), whose seven altars each bear an image symbolizing a moment from the Passion of Christ, from Calvary to the Crucifixion, sculpted by Pedro Luiz da Cunha. The high altar itself is beautifully worked in silver. The church and adjacent convent are linked by a small public chapel, dedicated to Our Lady of the Cape of Good Hope, and decorated in *azulejos* tiling.

A little further along Rua I de Março is the museum and church of **Santa Cruz dos Militares** (Mon–Fri 9am–3pm), its name giving a hint of its curious history. In 1628, a number of army officers organized the construction of the first church here, on the site of an early fort. It was used for the funerals of serving officers until, in 1703, the Catholic Church attempted to take over control of the building. The proposal met stiff resistance, and it was only in 1716 that the Fathers of the Church of São Sebastião, which had become severely dilapidated, succeeded in installing themselves in Santa Cruz. Sadly, they were no more successful in the maintenance of this church either, and by 1760 it had been reduced to a state of ruin – only reversed when army officers again took control of the reconstruction work in 1780, completing the granite and marble building that survives today. Inside, the nave, with its stuccoed ceiling, has been skilfully decorated with plaster relief images from Portugal's imperial past. The two owners long since reconciled, there's a **museum** on the ground floor with a collection of military and religious relics.

Across Rua I de Março from these churches is the **Centro Cultural Banco do Brasil** (Tues–Sun noon–10pm), a former bank headquarters now housing one of Rio's foremost arts centres (see p.133).

The Igreja de Nossa Senhora da Candelária

At the end of Rua I de Março you emerge onto **Praça Pio X**, dominated by the **Igreja de Nossa Senhora da Candelária** (Mon–Fri 7.30am–4pm, Sat 8am–noon & Sun 9am–1pm), an interesting combination of Baroque and Renaissance features resulting from the financial difficulties that delayed the completion of the building for more than a century after its foundation in 1775. Inside, the altars, walls and supporting columns are sculpted from variously coloured marble, while high above, the eight pictures in the dome represent the three theological virtues (Faith, Hope and Charity), the cardinal virtues (Prudence, Justice, Strength and Temperance) and the Virgin Mary – all of them late nineteenth-century work of the Brazilian artist João Zeferino da Costa. There's more grand decoration in the two pulpits, luxuriously worked in bronze and supported by large white angels sculpted in marble.

The Avenida Presidente Vargas

Until 1943 the Igreja da Candelária was hemmed in by other buildings, but it was appointed its own space when the **Avenida Presidente Vargas** was constructed, opening up new vistas. When work started on it in 1941 there was considerable opposition from the owners of houses and businesses that were demolished in its path – not to mention clerical dissent at the destruction of a number of churches. The avenue was inaugurated with a military parade in 1944, watched by Vargas himself in the year before he was deposed by a quiet coup. Today it's Rio's widest avenue, running west for almost 3km and comprising fourteen lanes of traffic.

Back towards the waterfront, turn into Rua Visconde de Itaborai and you will pass the **Alfândega Antiga**, the old Customs House, which was constructed in 1820 in Neoclassical style by the French architect Grandjean de Montigny. Although now empty apart from a small, rather ordinary restaurant occupying part of the rear of the building, it's been home to a bizarre array of organizations in its time, from the English merchants who arrived after the opening of the port to free trade in 1808 to the Mauá Gas Company and the Brazilian Society for the Protection of Animals, to the Socialist organizers of Rio's 1918 general strike.

From São Bento to the Largo da Carioca

Heading north, on the continuation of Rua I de Março, the Ladeira de São Bento leads to the **Igreja e Mosteiro de São Bento** (daily 7–11am & 2–6pm; open also for Mass with Gregorian chant Sun 10am), in the *bairro* of **Saúde** overlooking the Ilha das Cobras. The monastery was founded by Benedictine monks who arrived in Rio in 1586 by way of Bahia; building started in 1633, finishing nine years later. The facade displays a pleasing architectural simplicity, its twin towers culminating in pyramid-shaped spires, while the interior is richly adorned. Images of saints cover the altars, and there are statues representing various popes and bishops, work executed by the deft hand of Mestre Valentim. Panels and paintings from the late seventeenth-century are particularly valuable examples of colonial art.

There is not much else to grab your attention in the area: the monastery is next to **Praça Mauá** and the docklands – a seedy and rundown part of the city that you'd do best to avoid, especially at night. There are vague plans for major redevelopment of this zone as a cultural centre, but for the time being some of the huge dockside warehouses are used as spaces for theatre productions and exhibitions.

Largo Santa Rita

Heading along Rua Dom Gerardo from the monastery leads you to the north end of Avenida Rio Branco, on the west side of which (off Visconde de Inhaúma) is **Largo Santa Rita** and its church, the **Igreja da Santa Rita** (Mon–Sun 8–11.30am & 2.30–5pm). Built on land previously used as a burial ground for slaves, the structure dates from 1721, its bell tower tucked to one side giving it a lopsided look. It's not one of Rio's more attractive churches, but the interior stonework is a fine example of Rococo style; additionally, it's magnificently decorated with a series of panels, three on the high altar and eight on the ceiling, painted by Ananias Correia do Amaral and depicting scenes from the life of Santa Rita.

Rua Uruguaiana: Saara and Largo de São Francisco de Paula

To return south, to the Largo da Carioca in Centro, cross Avenida Presidente Vargas and continue down **Rua Uruguaiana**. In the streets to your left (between Uruguaiana and I de Março) lies the most interesting concentration of stores in Rio, in the area known as **Saara**. Traditionally the cheapest place to shop, it was originally peopled by Jewish and Arab merchants, who moved into the area after a ban prohibiting their residence within the city limits was lifted in the eighteenth century; in recent years, a new wave of Jewish and Arab business owners – along with, most recently, Chinese and Koreans – has moved here. The maze of narrow streets is lined with stalls selling trinkets and stores offering everything from basic beachware and handicraft items to expensive jewellery; additionally, the throngs of street traders and folk musicians make it an always lively place to visit. Particularly good buys here include sports equipment, musical instruments, CDs and tapes.

Halfway down Rua Uruguaiana is **Largo de São Francisco de Paula**, whose church, the **Igreja de São Francisco de Paula** (Mon–Fri 9am–1pm), has hosted some significant moments in Brazil's history. Behind the monumental carved wooden entrance door the Te Deum was sung in 1816 to celebrate Brazil's promotion from colony to kingdom; in 1831, the Mass celebrating the "swearing-in" of the Brazilian Constitution was performed here. More tangibly, the chapel of Nossa Senhora da Vitória, on the right as you enter, was dedicated by Pope Pius X to the victory of the Christian forces over the Turkish in the naval battle of Lepanto in 1571. The meticulous decoration is attributed to Mestre Valentim, who spent thirty years working on the chapel, while the paintings on the walls were created by a slave who called himself Manoel da Cunha. With the consent of his owner, Manoel travelled to Europe as the assistant of the artist João de Souza, and on his return bought his own freedom with money earned from the sale of his artwork.

Across from the church, the **Real Gabinete Português de Leitura** (Ⓣ21/2221-3138, Ⓦwww.realgabinete.com.br; Mon–Fri 9am–6pm) is a library dedicated to Portugal and Portuguese literature. The building was completed in 1887 and is immediately identifiable by its magnificently ornate facade, styled after fifteenth-century Portuguese architecture. The reading room is lit by a red, white and blue stained-glass skylight and contains many of the library's 350,000 volumes. Amongst the rarest is the 1572 first edition of *Os Lusíados*, the Portuguese national epic poem by Luis de Camões, based on Vasco da Gama's voyage of exploration, that is occasionally on view.

Largo da Carioca

From Largo de São Francisco de Paula, Rua Ramalho Ortigão leads the short distance to **Rua Carioca**. On the way, you can stop for a well-earned beer in Rio's oldest *cervejaria*, the *Bar Luiz* at no. 39. It's been here since 1887, changing its original name – the *Bar Adolfo* – following World War II, for obvious reasons. The place was once a favourite watering hole for Rio's Bohemian and intellectual groups and, though it's a little faded these days, it's still a bustling, enjoyable spot. The wonderful Art Nouveau *Confeitaria Colombo* is just one block from here at Rua Gonçalves Dias 32 (see p.123).

The **Largo da Carioca** itself has undergone considerable transformation since the turn of the nineteenth century, many of its buildings demolished to allow widening of the square and the improving of nearby roads. Today street traders selling leather goods dominate the centre of the square, while a couple of things of interest remain, most notably the **Igreja e Convento de Santo Antônio** (Mon–Fri 8am–7pm, Sat 8–11am & 4–6pm, Sun 9–11am), standing above the *largo*, and known as St Anthony of the Rich (to differentiate it from St Anthony of the Poor, which is located elsewhere in the city). A tranquil, cloistered refuge, built between 1608 and 1620, this is the oldest church in Rio and was founded by Franciscan monks who arrived in Brazil in 1592. A popular saint in Brazil, St Anthony's help was sought during the French invasion of 1710: he was made a captain in the Brazilian army and in a startling lack of progress through the ranks it was 1814 before he was promoted to lieutenant-colonel, retiring from service in 1914. Also curious is the tomb of **Wild Jock of Skelater** that lies in the crypt. A Scottish mercenary who entered the service of the Portuguese Crown during the Napoleonic Wars, he was later appointed commander-in-chief of the Portuguese army in Brazil.

This aside, the interior of the church boasts a beautiful sacristy, constructed from Portuguese marble and decorated in *azulejos* depicting the miracles performed by St Anthony. There is rich wooden ornamentation throughout, carved from *jacaranda*, including the great chest in the sacristy. The image of Christ, adorned with a crown of thorns, came from Portugal in 1678 – a remarkable work of great skill.

West from Praça Tiradentes

Leave Largo da Carioca by turning left along Rua Carioca, and you're soon in **Praça Tiradentes**, named after the leader of the so-called Minas Conspiracy of 1789, a plot hatched in the state of Minas Gerais to overthrow the Portuguese regime (see p.204). In the square stands the **Teatro João Caetano**, named after João Caetano dos Santos, who based his drama company in the theatre from 1840. He also notches up a bust that stands in the square, a reward for producing shows starring such theatrical luminaries as Sarah Bernhardt. In the second-floor hall of the theatre hang two large panels painted in 1930 by Emiliano di Cavalcanti (one of Brazil's great modernist artists), which, with strong tropical colours typical of di Cavalcanti, explore the themes of Carnaval and popular religion. The original theatre on this site, the Teatro Real, erected in 1813, had a much more political history: it was here in 1821 that Dom João VI swore obedience to the Constitution promulgated in Lisbon after the Porto Revolution. Three years later, at the end of the ceremony proclaiming Dom Pedro I Emperor of Brazil, a fire razed the building to the ground.

Campo de Santana and around

Three blocks west of Praça Tiradentes, along Rua Visconde do Rio Branco, the **Praça da República** lies in the **Campo de Santana**. Until the beginning of the seventeenth century this area was outside the city limits, which extended only as far as Rua Uruguaiana. Its sandy and swampy soils made it unsuitable for cultivation and the only building here was the chapel of St Domingo, sited in the area now covered by the asphalt of Avenida Presidente Vargas and used by the Fraternity of St Anne to celebrate the festivals of their patron saint – hence the name, Campo de Santana (field of St Anne).

By the end of the eighteenth century the city had spread to surround the Campo de Santana, and in 1811 a barracks was built to house the Second Regiment of the Line, who used the square as a parade ground. It was here that Dom Pedro I proclaimed Brazil's independence from the Portuguese Crown in 1822, and after 1889 the lower half of the square became known as Praça da República. The first president of the new republic, Deodoro de Fonseca, lived at no. 197 Praça da República. At the start of the twentieth century, the square was landscaped, and today it's a pleasant place for a walk, with lots of trees and small lakes ruled by swans. The **Parque João Furtado** lies in the centre and is worth visiting in the evening, when small, furry shapes can be seen scuttling about in the gloom – agoutis, happily, not rats.

Directly across Avenida Presidente Vargas is the Praça Duque de Caxias and the **Panteão Nacional**, on top of which stands the equestrian statue of the

Duque de Caxias, military patron and general in the Paraguayan War – his remains lie below in the Pantheon. Nearby, the **Dom Pedro II train station** – known more commonly as the Central do Brasil and made famous by Walter Salles' 1997 film *Central Station* – is an unmistakeable landmark, its tower rising 110m into the sky and supporting clock faces measuring 7.5m by 5.5m, all linked to a central winding mechanism. Just beyond the station, at Av. Marechal Floriano 196, the **Palácio do Itamaraty** is one of Rio's best examples of Neoclassical architecture. Completed in 1853 as the pied-à-terre of the great landowner Baron of Itamaraty, it was bought by the government and became home to a number of the republic's presidents. The *palácio* now houses the **Museu Histórico e Diplomático do Itamaraty** (Mon, Wed & Fri guided visits 2pm, 3pm & 4pm), a repository of documents, books and maps relating to Brazil's diplomatic history, its collections primarily of interest to serious researchers (archives open for consultation only by appointment Mon–Fri 1–5pm; ⓣ21/2253-2828). Of perhaps wider interest is the section of the building that has been painstakingly restored with period furnishings to show how the upper classes lived in the nineteenth century.

North of Itamaraty is Gamboa, an extremely seedy port area that's also one of the oldest parts of Rio and home to its first *favela*. Right alongside is the strangely beautiful **Cemitério dos Ingleses**, or English Cemetery (Rua da Gamboa 181, Mon–Fri 8am–4pm, Sat & Sun 8am–12.30pm), the oldest Protestant burial site in the country. In 1809 the British community was given permission to establish a cemetery and Anglican church in Rio – essential if English merchants were to be attracted to the newly independent Brazil. Still in use today, the cemetery is set in a dramatic hillside location looking down to Guanabara Bay. The inscriptions on many of the stones make poignant reading, recalling the days when early death was almost expected.

There's long been talk about developing the dockside area in front of the cemetery, but until recently little has been done apart from turning some of the warehouses into temporary centres for performing arts events. One important project has been the **Cidade da Samba**, a vast complex where Rio's fourteen top samba schools will practice and make their floats for Carnaval. Although the main pavilion was officially opened in 2006, at the time of writing the opening hours and programme have yet to be announced.

Located in an area with a reputation for being dangerous, you'd be wise to go to either the cemetery or Cidade da Samba by taxi – under no circumstances walk alone along the approach road passing through the tunnel from the nearby central train station. When visiting the cemetery, ask your driver to wait for you as taxis rarely pass by the gates.

From the Nova Catedral to Cinelândia and Praça Floriano

South of the Largo da Carioca, the unmistakeable shape of the **Nova Catedral Metropolitana** (daily 7.30am–6pm) rises up like some futuristic teepee. Built between 1964 and 1976, it's an impressive piece of modern architecture and a considerable engineering feat, whatever you think of the style: the Morro de Santo Antônio was levelled to make way for the cathedral's construction, and the thousands of tons of resulting soil were used for the land reclamation project that gave rise to the Parque de Flamengo (see p.111). The cathedral is 83m high with a diameter of 104m and a capacity of 20,000 people. Inside, it feels vast, a remarkable sense of space enhanced by the absence of supporting columns. Filtering the sunlight, four huge stained-glass windows dominate, each measuring 20m by 60m and corresponding to a symbolic colour scheme – ecclesiastical green, saintly red, Catholic blue and apostolic yellow. From outside, you'll be able to see the mid-eighteenth-century **Aqueduto da Carioca** (often called the Arcos da Lapa), which since 1896 has carried trams up to Santa Teresa, the beautiful *bairro* on the hill opposite (see p.101); the tram terminal is between the cathedral and the Largo da Carioca, behind what is certainly the ugliest building in Rio, the glass, steel and concrete hulk that is the headquarters of Petrobrás, the state oil company.

△ Nova Catedral Metropolitana

Along Avenida República de Chile, and right down **Avenida Rio Branco**, you'll come to Praça Marechal Floriano and the area known as **Cinelândia**, named after long-gone movie houses built in the 1930s. Rio Branco, originally named Avenida Central, must once have been Latin America's most impressive urban thoroughfare. Old photos of Avenida Rio Branco show its entire length bordered by Neoclassical-style buildings of no more than three storeys high, its pavements lined with trees, and with a promenade that ran right down the centre. Nowadays, however, the once-graceful avenue has been marred by ugly office buildings and traffic pollution.

Praça Floriano

The **Praça Floriano** is the one section of Avenida Rio Branco that still impresses. Several sidewalk cafés on the western side of the square serve as popular central meeting points in the evening, when the surrounding buildings are illuminated and at their most elegant. In the centre of the *praça* is a bust of **Getúlio Vargas**, still anonymously decorated with flowers on the anniversary of the ex-dictator's birthday, March 19. At the north end, the **Theatro Municipal** (Ⓦwww.theatromunicipal.rj.gov.br), opened in 1909 and a dramatic example of Neoclassical architecture, was modelled on the Paris Opéra – all granite, marble and bronze, with a foyer decorated in the white and gold characteristic of Louis XV style. Since opening, the theatre has been Brazil's most prestigious artistic venue, hosting visiting Brazilian and foreign orchestras, opera and theatre companies and singers. Tours are available round the building; enquire at the box office at the back of the building. The theatre has a decent restaurant and bar, the *Café do Teatro* (Mon–Fri 11am–4pm), which is richly adorned with elaborate Assyrian-inspired mosaics.

On the opposite side of the road, the **Museu Nacional das Belas Artes** (Tues–Fri 10am–6pm, Sat, Sun & public holidays 2–6pm; R$4, Sun free; Ⓣ21/2240-0068, Ⓦwww.mnba.gov.br) is a grandiose Neoclassical pile built in 1908 as the Escola Nacional das Belas Artes, with the museum created in 1937. The modest European collection includes works by Boudin, Tournay and Franz Post amongst many others, but it's the **Brazilian collection** that's of most interest. Organized in chronological order, each room shows the various stages in the development of Brazilian painting as well as the influences imported from Europe: the years of diversification (1919–28); the movement into modernism (1921–49); and the consolidation of modern forms between 1928 and 1967, especially in the works of Cândido Portinari, Djanira and Francisco Rebolo.

The last building of note on the Praça Floriano is the **Biblioteca Nacional** (Mon–Fri 9am–10pm, Sat 9am–5pm; ⓣ21/2220-9433, ⓦwww.bn.br), whose stairway was decoratively painted by some of the most important artists of the nineteenth century, including Modesto Brocas, Eliseu Visconti, Rodolfo Amoedo and Henrique Bernadelli. If you speak Portuguese and want to use the library, the staff are very obliging.

Lapa

Continuing south from Cinelândia, Avenida Rio Branco passes Praça Mahatma Gandhi, which borders the **Passeio Público** park (daily 7.30am–9pm), well into the Lapa *bairro*. Beautifully renovated and maintained, the park is a green oasis away from the hustle and bustle of the city. Opened in 1783, it was designed in part by Mestre Valentim da Fonseca e Silva, Brazil's most important late eighteenth-century sculptor, its trees providing shade for busts commemorating famous figures from the city's history, including Mestre Valentim himself. A recent bust to be placed in the park is that of Chiquinho Gonzaga, who wrote the first recorded samba for Carnaval – *Pelo Telefone*.

The rest of **Lapa** has much the same faded charm as the park – attractive enough to merit exploring, though it would be wise not to wander the streets unaccompanied at night. Lapa is an old *bairro*; Brasil Gerson, writing in his *História das ruas do Rio de Janeiro*, noted that it was traditionally known as an "area of 'cabarets' and bawdy houses, the haunt of scoundrels, of gamblers, swashbucklers and inverteds and the 'trottoir' of poor, fallen women" – evidently a place to rush to, or avoid, depending upon your taste in entertainment. Until the mid-seventeenth century, Lapa was a beach, known as the "Spanish Sands", but development and land reclamation assisted its slide into shabby grandeur. More recently, things have been looking up for Lapa, and the area has blossomed into one of Rio's liveliest spots for nightlife (see p.131).

From Lapa you can walk down to the Avenida Beira Mar, where the **Monumento aos Mortos na Segunda Guerra Mundial** (Monument to the Dead of World War II; Tues–Sun 10am–4pm) is a clearly visible landmark. Next to the monument, at the north end of the Parque do Flamengo (see p.111), is the glass and concrete **Museu de Arte Moderna** (Tues–Fri noon–5.30pm, Sat & Sun noon–6.30pm; R$5; ⓣ21/2240-4944, ⓦwww.mamrio.com.br), designed by the Brazilian architect and urbanist Affonso Reidy and inaugurated in 1958. The museum's collection was devastated by a fire in 1978 and only reopened in 1990 following the building's restoration. The permanent collection is still small and, despite boasting some of the great names of twentieth-century Brazilian art, extremely weak. Even so, the museum hosts visiting exhibitions that are occasionally worth checking out.

Northeast to the Museu Histórico Nacional

Heading northeast from the Passeio Público, along Rua Santa Luzia, you pass the **Igreja de Santa Luzia** in the Praça da Academia, an attractive eighteenth-century church whose predecessor stood on the seashore – hard to believe today, as it's overwhelmed by surrounding office buildings. On December 13 each year, devotees enter the "room of miracles" at the back of the church and bathe their eyes in water from the white marble font – reputedly a miraculous cure for eye defects.

Rua Santa Luzia intersects with the busy Avenida Presidente Antônio Carlos, on which you'll find the imposing **Fazenda Federal**, the Federal Treasury building. Directly across the road from here, the **Santa Casa de Misericórdia**, a large colonial structure dating from 1582, was built by the Sisterhood of Misericordia, a nursing order dedicated to caring for the sick and providing asylum to orphans and invalids. It was here in 1849 that, for the first time in Rio, a case of yellow fever was diagnosed, and from 1856 to 1916 the building was used as Rio's Faculty of Medicine. The Santa Casa is not open to the public, but you can visit its **Museu da Farmácia** (Mon–Fri 8am–noon & 1–5pm) for its collection of pharmacological implements. Also attached to the Santa Casa is the **Igreja de Nossa Senhora de Bonsucesso** (Mon–Fri 9am–5pm), which contains finely detailed altars, a collection of Bohemian crystal and an eighteenth-century organ.

Close by, in Praça Rui Barbosa, the **Museu do Imagem e Som** (Ⓦwww.mis.rj.gov.br, Ⓣ21/2220-3481; Mon–Fri 1–6pm) explains Rio's social history using records, tape recordings, books and film. There's also a fascinating photographic collection (numbering some 10,000 prints, though inevitably only a fraction are displayed) documenting the city's cultural life from the turn of the nineteenth century until the 1940s.

Museu Histórico Nacional

The nearby **Museu Histórico Nacional** (Tues–Fri 10am–5.30pm, Sat, Sun & public holidays 2–6pm; R$6; Ⓣ21/2550-9255, Ⓦwww.museuhistoriconacional.com.br) is uncomfortably located in the shadow of the Presidente Kubitschek flyover that runs into the Parque do Flamengo. Built in 1762 as an arsenal, it later served as a military prison where escaped slaves were detained. In 1922 the building was converted into an exhibition centre for the centenary celebrations of Brazil's independence from Portugal and has remained a museum ever since.

The large **collection** contains some pieces of great value – from furniture to nineteenth-century firearms and locomotives – and after decades of neglect, the museum has been successfully reorganized. The displays on the second floor, a documentation of Brazilian history since 1500, make this museum a must. Artefacts, charts and written explanations trace the country's development from the moment of discovery to the proclamation of the Republic in 1889 – a fascinating insight into the nature of imperial conquest and subsequent colonial culture. Clearly demonstrated, for example, is the structure of sixteenth-century Brazilian society, including the system of *sesmarias*, or royal land grants of enormous dimensions, which provided the basis for the highly unequal system of land tenure that endures today. Through the use of scale models and imaginatively arranged displays, the agrarian and cyclical nature of Brazil's economic history is explained, too, organized around a slave-labour plantation system that produced – at different times – sugar cane, cattle, cotton, rubber and coffee. The story continues into the eighteenth and nineteenth centuries, following the impact of England's Industrial Revolution, the spread of new ideas following the French Revolution and the transition from slavery to free labour and the importance of immigration. More recent twentieth-century developments are taken up by the Museu da República (see p.110).

△ Tram in Santa Teresa

Santa Teresa and the Corcovado

Before you hit the beaches of the Zona Sul, two of the most pleasant city excursions are to *bairros* to the southwest of Centro. **Santa Teresa** offers an excellent respite from the steamy hubbub of Rio's main thoroughfares, while visiting Rio without making the tourist pilgrimage up the **Corcovado** is unthinkable.

Santa Teresa

Santa Teresa, a leafy *bairro* of labyrinthine, cobbled streets and steps (*ladeiras*), and with stupendous vistas of the city and bay below, makes a refreshing contrast to the city centre. Although it clings to the side of a hill, Santa Teresa is no *favela*: it's a slightly dishevelled residential area dominated by the early nineteenth-century mansions and walled gardens of a prosperous community that still enjoys something of a Bohemian reputation. The attractions are enhanced by an absence of the kind of development that is turning the rest of Rio into a cracked, concrete nightmare.

In recent years, the *bairro* has become an important artistic centre, with many artists choosing to live and work here. Twice a year (the last weekend in May and November), about a hundred artists open their studios, offering the public an opportunity to buy or simply look at their work. For details of the participating artists, consult the organizer's website: Ⓦwww.vivasanta.com.br. At other times, the best place to see the efforts of local artists is at La Vereda, an excellent arts and crafts shop in the centre of Santa Teresa at Largo dos Guimarães.

There is not a great deal of traffic on the roads in Santa Teresa, which are dominated instead by ageing **trams** (*bondes*) hauling their human load up and down the hill – a bone-rattling trip that's highly recommended. Trams run up here from Centro, from the terminal behind the massive Petrobrás building, instantly recognizable for being one of the most hideous buildings in Rio. The trams take you across the mid-eighteenth-century **Arcos da Lapa**, a monumental Roman-style aqueduct, high over Lapa, and past the **Carmelite Convento de Santa Teresa**, which marks the spot where a French force was defeated by the city's inhabitants in 1710. As you climb, the panoramic view of Guanabara Bay drifts in and out of view between the trees that line the streets. On your right, you'll pass the **Bar do Arnaudo**, a traditional meeting place of artists and intellectuals (see p.124); when the tram reaches the terminus at the top, you can stay on (and pay again) to descend to the bar for something to eat. Moments from here, at Largo dos Guimarães, is the **Museu do Bonde** (daily 9am–4.30pm), which is worth a visit even if you're not especially interested in transport. The small and attractively displayed collection includes an old tram, photo displays and memorabilia documenting the history of trams in Rio from their nineteenth-century introduction; it's curious to see how this means of public transport enabled the city to expand so rapidly along the coast. Also at Largo dos Guimarães is the Livraría e Café Largo das Letras (Wed–Sat 2–10pm & Sun 2–8pm), a delightful community bookshop housed in an attractive mansion and a pleasant place for a coffee or cold drink.

From the museum, it's an easy and enjoyable ten-minute walk downhill to the **Museu Chácara do Céu** (Rua Murtinho Nobre 93; daily, except Tues, noon–5pm; R$2, free Wed; Ⓣ21/2507-1932, Ⓦwww.museuscastromaya.com.br), located in a modernist stone building erected in 1957. The museum made headline news during the 2006 Carnaval when it was raided in broad daylight. Armed thieves took four paintings by Matisse, Monet, Picasso and Dali valued at US$50 million before melting into the crowd outside. Despite these important losses (at time of writing the pieces have yet to be recovered), it certainly remains one of Rio's better museums, holding a good, eclectic European collection as well as works by Cândido Portinari and Emiliano Di Cavalcanti. In the upper hall, two screens depict the life of Krishna and there are twin seventh-century iron-sculptured horses from the Imperial Palace in Beijing as well; on the second floor look for artwork by Brazilian painters Heitor dos Prazeres and Djanira.

A pathway links the museum to the **Parque das Ruínas** (Wed–Fri & Sat 10am–10pm, Sun 10am–5pm), an attractive public garden containing the ruins of a mansion that was once home to Laurinda Santos Lobo, a Brazilian heiress around whom artists and intellectuals gathered in the first half of the twentieth century. After her death in 1946, the mansion was allowed to fall into disrepair, but in the 1990s it was partially renovated as a cultural centre and today houses art exhibitions. A pleasant café and a small stage where jazz concerts are held most Thursday evenings are on-site as well.

The Corcovado

The most famous of all images of Rio de Janeiro is that of the vast statue of Christ the Redeemer (Cristo Redentor) gazing across the bay from the **Corcovado** (hunchback) hill, arms outstretched in welcome, or as if preparing for a dive into the waters below. The Art Deco **statue** (daily 9am–7pm), 30m high and weighing over 1000 metric tons, was scheduled to be completed in 1922 as part of Brazil's centenary independence celebrations, but this symbol of Rio wasn't, in fact, finished until 1931. The French sculptor Paul Landowski was responsible for the head and hands, while the engineers Heitor Silva Costa and Pedro Viana constructed the rest.

In clear weather, fear no anticlimax: climbing to the statue is a stunning experience by day, and nothing short of miraculous in the early evening. In daylight the whole of Rio and Guanabara Bay is laid out before you; after dark the floodlit statue can be seen from everywhere in the Zona Sul, seemingly suspended in the darkness that surrounds it and often shrouded in eerie cloud. Up on the platform at the base of the statue, the effect of the clouds, driven by warm air currents, and the thousands of tiny winged insects clustering round the spotlights, help give the impression that the statue is careering through space out into the blackness that lies beyond the arc of the lights – dramatic, and not a little hypnotic.

The **view** from the statue can be very helpful for **orientation** if you've just arrived in Rio. On a clear day, you can see as far as the outlying districts of the Zona Norte, while on the south side of the viewing platform you're directly over the Lagoa Rodrigo de Freitas, with Ipanema on the left and Leblon on the right. On the near side of the lake, Rua São Clemente is visible, curving its way through Botafogo, towards the Jardim Botânico and the racecourse, and on your left, the small *bairro* of Lagoa can be seen tucked in beneath the Morro dos Cabritos, on the other side of which is Copacabana.

Getting to the Corcovado

All major hotels organize **excursions** to the Corcovado. Alternatively, the easiest way to get there by yourself is to take a **taxi** – about R$30 from the Zona Sul, a little more from Centro. **Buses** run to the *bairro* of Cosme Velho – take the #422 or #497 from Largo do Machado, the #583 from Leblon or the #584 from Copacabana – and stop at the **Estação Cosme Velho**, at Rua Cosme Velho 513. From there you take a cog-train (every 30min between 8.30am & 6pm; R$36 return, which also entitles you to half-price admission at the Museu Internacional de Arte Naïf; ⓦwww.corcovado.com.br), a twenty-minute ride to the top from where there's an escalator leading to the viewing platform. You can also **drive** up to a car park near the top if you wish, but if you want to **walk** go in a group, as reports of assaults and robberies are frequent. However you choose to get there, keep an eye on the weather before setting out: what ought to be one of Rio's highlights can turn into a great disappointment if the Corcovado is shrouded in clouds.

Visiting the statue is, of course, a thoroughly exploited tourist experience. There are the usual facilities for eating, drinking and buying souvenirs. On the way, someone will probably take your photograph clandestinely and, when you descend, a saucer, complete with your photograph superimposed on it, will be thrust before you – if you don't want the saucer, just say so, however.

Back down at the bottom of the statue, if you have the time and inclination, a five-minute walk uphill from the cog-train station on Rua Cosme Velho will take you to the **Museu Internacional de Arte Naïf** (Tues–Fri 10am–6pm, Sat & Sun, public holidays noon–6pm; R$5; ⓣ21/2205-8612, ⓦwww.museunaif.com.br), which boasts the world's largest naive art collection. Although most of the work displayed is by Brazilian artists, the museum features paintings from throughout the world, with work from Haiti, the former Yugoslavia, France and Italy especially well presented. Across the road, a short distance further uphill, you'll reach the much-photographed **Largo do Boticário**, named after the nineteenth-century apothecary to the royal family (Joaquim Luiz da Silva Santo) who lived here. With its pebbled streets and fountain set in the small courtyard, this is a particularly picturesque little corner of Rio. However, as old as the Largo might appear to be, the original mid-nineteenth-century houses were demolished in the 1920s and replaced by colourful neocolonial-style homes, some with fronts decorated with *azulejos*.

Zona Norte

The parts of the **Zona Norte** you'll have seen on the way in from the transport terminals aren't very enticing, and they're a fair reflection of the general tenor of northern Rio. Most of the area between the international airport and the city centre is given over to vast *favelas* and other low-income housing. A few buildings do stand out, however, in particular the Igreja de Nossa Senhora da Penha. Perched dramatically on a cliff top, the late nineteenth-century, colonial-style church is an important place of pilgrimage, attracting many thousands of worshippers during the month-long Festa da Penha in October. Close-up, however, the church is thoroughly unremarkable and does not warrant visiting, especially as the area around it is not at all safe. But there are a few places in the Zona Norte that are nearer to the centre and well worth making the effort to visit – especially the **Museu Nacional** in the Quinta da Boa Vista, west of the city centre, which you reach by *metrô* (get off at Estação São Cristovão) or by buses #472, #474 or #475 from Copacabana or Flamengo or #262 from Praça Mauá.

The Quinta da Boa Vista

The area covered by the **Quinta da Boa Vista** (daily 9am–6pm) was once incorporated in a *sesmaria* held by the Society of Jesus in the sixteenth and seventeenth centuries. The Jesuits used the area as a sugar plantation, though it later became the *chácara* (country seat) of the royal family when the Portuguese merchant Elias Antônio Lopes presented the Palácio de São Cristovão (today the Museu Nacional) and surrounding lands to Dom João VI in 1808. The park, with its wide-open expanses of greenery, tree-lined avenues, lakes, sports areas and games tables, is an excellent place for a stroll, though the weekends can get very crowded. You may as well make a day of it and see all the sights once you're here.

The Museu Nacional

In the centre of the park, on a small hill, stands the imposing Neoclassical structure of the **Museu Nacional** (Tues–Sun 10am–4pm; ⓣ21/2568-8262, ⓦacd.ufrj.br/museu; R$3), the oldest scientific institution in Brazil and certainly one of the most important, containing extensive archeological, zoological and botanic collections, an excellent ethnological section and a good display of artefacts dating from classical antiquity – altogether, an estimated one million pieces are exhibited in 22 rooms.

The **archeological** section deals with the human history of Latin America, displaying Peruvian ceramics, the craftsmanship of the ancient Aztec, Mayan and Toltec civilizations of Mexico and mummies excavated in the Chiu-Chiu region of Chile. In the Brazilian room, exhibits of Tupi-Guaraní and Marajó ceramics lead on to the indigenous **ethnographical** section, uniting pieces collected from the numerous tribes that once populated Brazil. The genocidal policies of Brazil's European settlers, together with the ravages of disease, reduced the indigenous population from an estimated six million in 1500 to the present-day total of less than two hundred thousand. The **ethnology** section has a room dedicated to Brazilian folklore, centred on an exhibition of the ancient Afro- and Indo-Brazilian cults – such as *macumba*, *candomblé* and *umbanda* – that still play an important role in modern Brazilian society.

On a different tack, the mineral collection's star exhibit is the **Bendigo Meteorite**, which fell to earth in 1888 (for sign-seekers, the year slavery was abolished) in the state of Bahia. Its original weight of 5360kg makes it the heaviest metallic mass known to have fallen through the Earth's atmosphere. And beyond the rich native finds you'll also come across Etruscan pottery, Greco-Roman ceramics, Egyptian sarcophagi and prehistoric remains – all in all, a good half-day's worth of exploring.

Museu da Fauna, Jardim Zoólogico and the Feira Nordestina

The **Museu da Fauna** (Tues–Sun 9am–4.30pm), also in the Quinta da Boa Vista, has organized a collection of stuffed birds, mammals and reptiles from throughout Brazil that is worth a passing look on the way to the nearby **Jardim Zoólogico** (daily 9am–4.30pm; R$5). Founded in 1888, the zoo was a run-down and dirty place for decades; in recent years, however, it has been transformed – the animals look happier and the grounds are now kept scrupulously clean by zealous functionaries – but it's still basically an old-fashioned site where animals are kept in small cages. That said, the zoo serves an important scientific role in Brazil, managing some prominent breeding programmes for endangered native fauna.

The **Feira Nordestina**, held daily (Mon–Thurs 10am–4pm & nonstop Fri 10am to Sun 10pm; ⓦwww.feiradesaocristovao.com.br) in the Campo de São Cristovão, close to the Quinta da Boa Vista, is the best of Rio's regular **markets**. Its roots extend back to the late nineteenth century and the first large-scale migration of impoverished Northeasterners to Rio, but since 2003 it has been held in a vast, purpose-built stadium. A replica of the great Northeastern markets, it comprises **seven hundred stalls** (many of which are run by people in traditional costume) selling typical handicrafts, caged birds, food and drink, while music from the parched Northeastern backlands fills the air. Best buys are beautifully worked hammocks, leather bags and hats, *literatura de cordel* (illustrated folk literature pamphlets), herbal medicines and spices. Weekends are the best days to go along with migrants enjoying their day off and listening to live music in the evenings. To get there, take any bus marked "São Cristovão" – #469 from Leblon, #461 from Ipanema, #462 or #463 from Copacabana.

Maracanã Stadium

To the west of Quinta da Boa Vista, a short walk across the rail line, over the Viaduto São Cristovão, stands the **Maracanã Stadium** or, more formally, the Estádio Jornalista Mário Filho. Built in 1950 for the World Cup, it's the biggest stadium of its kind in the world, holding nearly 200,000 people – in the final match of the tournament, 199,854 spectators turned up here to watch Brazil lose to Uruguay. Well over 100,000 fans attend local derbies, like the Flamengo v Fluminense fixture, and during November and December games are played here three times a week, as many of Rio's teams have followings that exceed the capacity of their own stadiums; kick-off is at 5pm.

Attending a **game** is one of the most extraordinary experiences Rio has to offer, even if you don't like football, and it's worth going just for the theatrical spectacle. The stadium looks like a futuristic colosseum, its upper stand (the *arquibancadas*) rising almost vertically from the playing surface. Great silken banners wave across the stand, shrouded by the smoke from fireworks, while support for each team is proclaimed by the insistent rhythm of massed samba drums that drive the game along. *Carioca* supporters are animated to say the least, often near-hysterical, but their love of the game is infectious.

The Maracanã is open for **guided tours**, too (daily 9am–5pm, match days 8–11am; ⓣ21/2299-2941; R$14). You'll be shown through the interesting **Museu dos Esportes**, with its extensive collection of Brazilian sporting memorabilia, and get to see the view from the presidential box (reached by lift), wander through the changing rooms and have a chance to tread on the hallowed turf itself.

Getting there and seeing a game

The Maracanã is an easy and inexpensive destination to reach by **taxi**, but if you come by **metrô** (line 2) get off at the Maracanã station and walk southeast, along Avenida Osvaldo Aranha. By **bus**, catch the #464 from Leblon (Ataúlfo Paiva) via Ipanema (on Visconde de Pirajá), Copacabana (Av. N.S. de Copacabana) and Flamengo (Praia do Flamengo).

The stadium's **entrance** is on Rua Prof Eurico Rabelo, Gate 18. Arrive in plenty of time (at least a couple of hours before kick-off for big games) and buy your entrance card at any of the **ticket offices** set in the perimeter wall – a ticket for the *gerais* (lower terracing) costs about $4, the *arquibancadas* (all-seated upper terracing) about $6; then go round to the entrance and pass your card through a machine at the turnstile. Things get frantic around the ticket offices before big games and if you're not there early enough you may get stranded outside, as the kiosk attendants leave their positions as soon as the starting whistle blows so as not to miss an early goal. After the game, it's a bit tedious getting back into town, as transport is packed. Be sure to watch your belongings in the thick crowds.

Zona Sul

From Rio's Bay of Guanabara to the Bay of Sepetiba, to the west, there are approximately 90km of sandy **beaches**, including one of the world's most famous – Copacabana. Uniquely, Rio's identity is closely linked to its beaches, which shape the social life of all the city's inhabitants, who use them as a source of recreation and inspiration. For many, the beach provides a source of livelihood and a sizeable service industry has developed around it, providing for the needs of those who regard the beach as a social environment – as significant, say, as the pub is in England.

Rio de Janeiro's sophisticated **beach culture** is entirely a product of the twentieth century. The 1930s saw Rio's international reputation emerge, as Hollywood started to incorporate images of the city in its productions, and film stars began to grace the Copacabana. Rio was one of the first destinations for

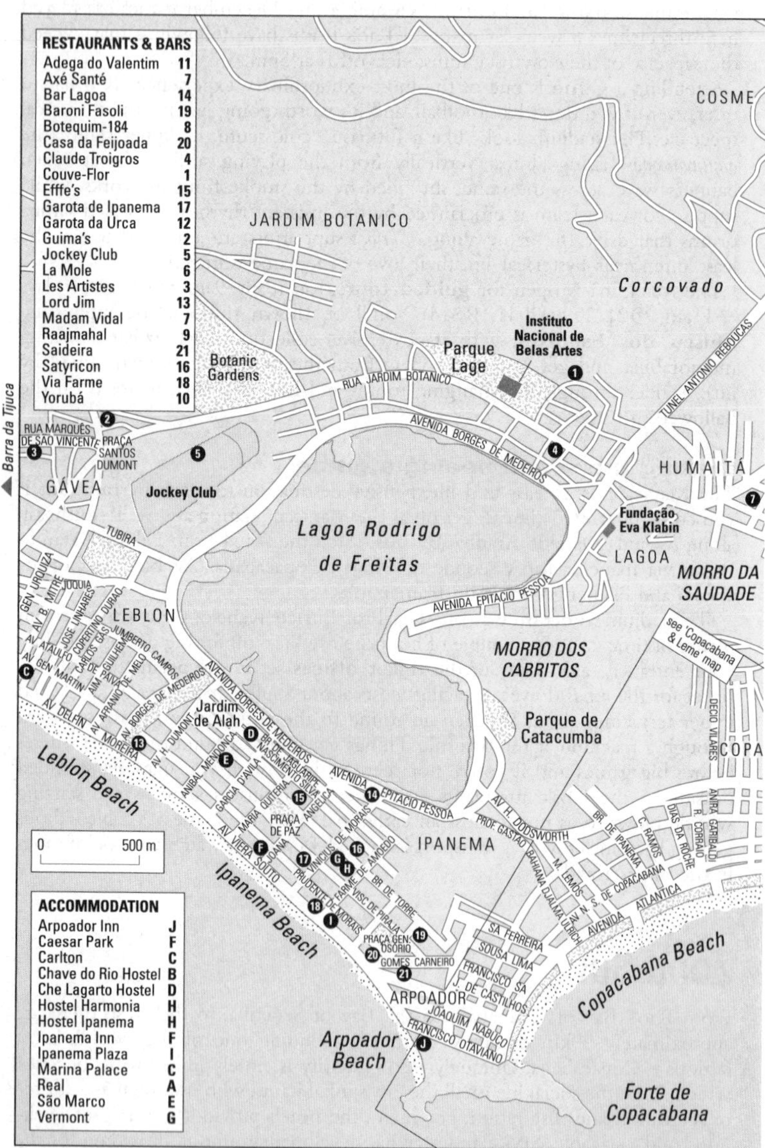

the newly established jet set: "flying down to Rio" became an enduring cliché, celebrated in music, film and literature for the last seventy-odd years.

The most renowned of the beaches, **Copacabana**, was originally an isolated area, cut off from the city by mountains until 1892 when the Túnel Velho link with Botafogo was inaugurated. The open sea and strong waves soon attracted beachgoers, though Copacabana remained a quiet, sparsely populated *bairro*

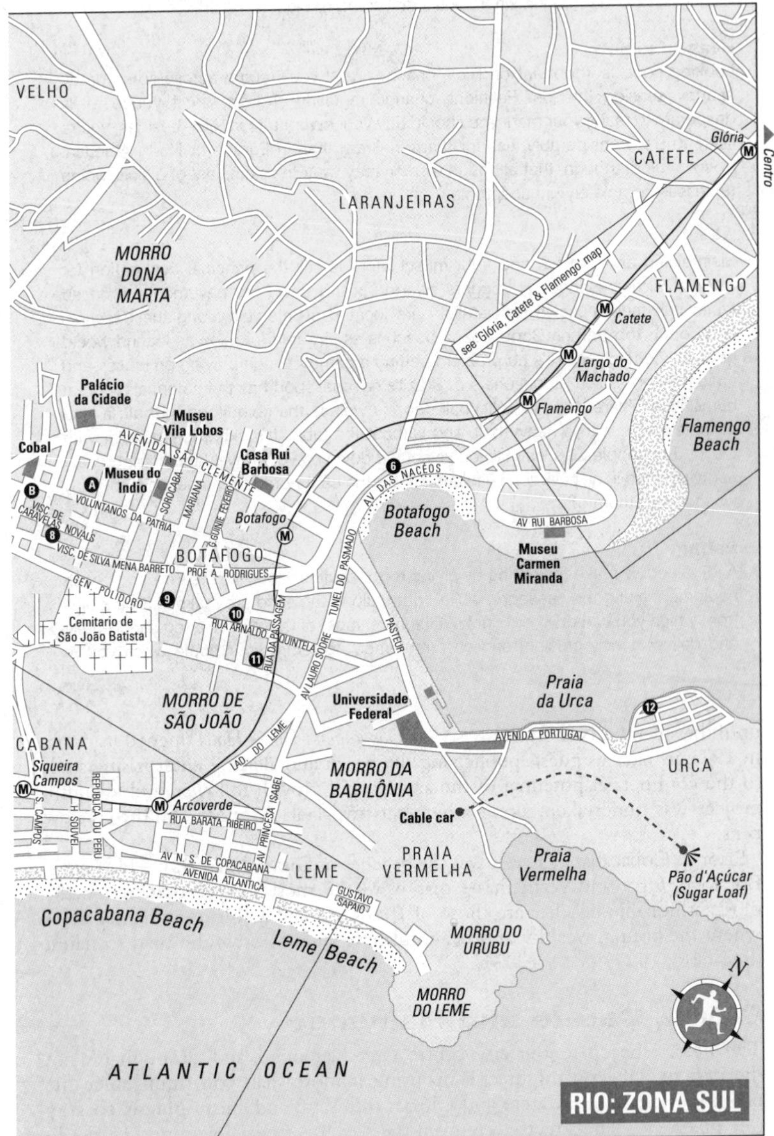

On the beach

Rio's beaches may attract hordes of tourists but they're first and foremost the preserve of *cariocas*. Rich or poor, old or young, everybody descends on the beaches throughout the week, treating them simply as city parks. The beaches are divided into informal segments, each identified by *postos* (marker posts) assigned a number. In Copacabana and Ipanema in particular, gay men, families, beach-sport aficionados and even intellectuals claim specific segments, and it won't take you long to identify a stretch of beach where you'll feel comfortable.

Beach fashion

Looking good is important on Rio's beaches, and you'll come across some pretty snappy seaside threads. Fashions change regularly, though, so if you're really desperate to make your mark you should buy your **swimsuits** in Rio – besides, you're likely to pay considerably less for them in Brazil than in Europe or North America. Keep in mind, though, that although women may wear the skimpiest of bikinis, going topless is completely unacceptable.

Beach sports

Maintaining an even tan and tight musculature is still the principal occupation for most of Rio's beachgoers. Joggers swarm up and down the pavements, bronzed types flex their muscles on parallel bars located at intervals along the beaches, and **beach football** on Copacabana beach is as strong a tradition as legend would have it – certainly, there's no problem getting a game, though playing on loose sand amidst highly skilled practitioners of Brazil's national sport has the potential for great humiliation. There's lots of volleyball, too, as well as the ubiquitous **batball**, a kind of table tennis with a heavy ball, and without the table. It's extremely popular with the kind of people who wait till you've settled down on your towel, and then run past spraying sand in all directions – taking an electric cattle-prod to the beach is the only way to keep them off.

Eating

A lot of people make their living by plying **food** – fruit, sweets, ice cream – and beach equipment along the seashore, while dotted along the sand are makeshift canopies from which you can buy cold drinks. Like bars, most of these have a regular clientele and deliver a very efficient service – remember to return your bottle when you've

until the splendid Neoclassically styled *Copacabana Palace Hotel* opened its doors in 1923, its famous guests publicizing the beach and alerting enterprising souls to the commercial potential of the area. Rapid growth followed and a landfill project was undertaken, along which the two-lane **Avenida Atlântica** now runs.

Prior to Copacabana's rise, it was the beaches of **Guanabara Bay** – Flamengo, Botafogo, Urca and Vermelha – that were the most sought after. Today, the most fashionable beaches are those of **Ipanema** and **Leblon**, residential areas where the young, wealthy and beautiful have only to cross the road to flaunt their tans.

Glória, Catete and Flamengo

The nearest beach to the city centre is at Flamengo, and although it's not the best in Rio you might end up using it more than you think, since the neighbouring *bairros*, Catete and Glória, are useful and cheap **places to stay** (see pp.83–84). The streets away from the beach – especially around Largo do finished. Coconut milk, *côco verde*, is sold everywhere, and is a brilliant hangover cure. You don't need to be wary of the edibles either: if the traders were to start poisoning their customers, they'd soon lose their hard-won trading space on the beach and their livelihood.

Staying safe

Many of the beaches are **dangerous**. The seabed falls sharply away, the waves are strong, and currents can pull you down the beach. Mark your spot well before entering the water, or you'll find youself emerging from a paddle twenty or thirty metres from where you started – which, when the beaches are packed at weekends, can cause considerable problems when it comes to relocating your towel. Copacabana is particularly dangerous, even for strong swimmers. However, the beaches are well served by **lifeguards**, whose posts are marked by a white flag with a red cross; a **red flag** indicates that bathing is prohibited. Constant surveillance of the beachfronts from helicopters and support boats means that, if you do get into trouble, help should arrive quickly.

Pollution is another problem to bear in mind. Although much has been done in recent years to clean up Guanabara Bay, it is still not safe to swim in the water from Flamengo or Botafogo beaches. While the water beyond the bay at Copacabana and Ipanema is usually clean, there are times when it and the beaches themselves aren't, especially following a prolonged period of heavy summer rain and the city's strained drainage system overflows and deposits raw sewage on the streets, which often later ends up on the beaches. Unfortunately, these periods are increasingly common – if you've chosen Rio essentially as a beach vacation, you may well be in for a major disappointment.

Natural dangers aside, the beaches hold other unwelcome surprises. Giving your passport, money and **valuables** the chance of a suntan, rather than leaving them in the hotel safe, is madness. Take only the clothes and money that you'll need – it's quite acceptable to use public transport while dressed for the beach. Don't be caught out either by the young lad who approaches you from one side, distracting your attention with some request, while his mate approaches from the other side and whips your bag: it's the most common and efficient method of relieving you of things you shouldn't have brought with you in the first place.

Machado and along Rua do Catete – are full of inexpensive hotels, and there's a pleasant atmosphere to this part of town. Until the 1950s, Flamengo and Catete were the principal residential zones of Rio's wealthier middle classes, and, although the mantle has now passed to Ipanema and Leblon, the *bairros* still have a relaxed appeal. Busy during the day, the tree-lined streets come alive at night with residents eating in the local restaurants; and though the nightlife is nothing special, it's tranquil enough to encourage sitting out on the pavement at the bars, beneath the palm trees and apartment buildings.

Glória

Across from the **Glória** *metrô* station, on top of the Morro da Glória, stands the early eighteenth-century **Igreja da Nossa Senhora da Glória do Outeiro** (Mon–Fri 9am–5pm, Sat & Sun 9am–1pm), notable for its innovative octagonal ground plan and domed roof, the latter decked with excellent seventeenth-century blue-and-white *azulejos* tiles and nineteenth-century marble masonry. Painstakingly renovated, the church, quite simply the prettiest in Rio, is an absolute gem, easily worth a quick detour. Behind it you'll find the **Museu da Imperial**

△ Igreja da Nossa Senhora da Glória do Outeiro

Irmandade de Nossa Senhora da Glória (Mon–Fri 9am–5pm, Sat & Sun 9am–1pm), which has a small collection of religious relics, *ex votos* and the personal possessions of Empress Tereza Cristina.

Catete

On the Rua do Catete, adjacent to the **Catete** *metrô* station, the Palácio do Catete is home to the **Museu da República** (Tues noon–5pm, Wed 2–5pm, Thurs & Fri noon–5pm, Sat & Sun 2–6pm; ⓣ21/2558-6350, ⓦwww.museudarepublica.org.br; R$6, free Wed & Sun). The palace was used as the presidential residence from 1897 until 1960, and it was here, in 1954, that Getúlio Vargas turned his gun on himself and took his own life, believing he had been betrayed. The building was erected in the 1860s as the Rio home of the Barão de Nova Friburgo, a wealthy coffee *fazenda* owner. As a historical museum, the *palácio* continues where the Museu Histórico Nacional (see p.99) leaves off, with the establishment of the first Republic in 1888. The collection features both period furnishings and presidential memorabilia – including Vargas's bloodied pyjamas – though it's the opulent marble and stained glass of the building itself that make a visit so worthwhile. The grounds include a new exhibition space, theatre and art gallery, which means there is often something happening here at night, while the floodlit gardens make it a beautiful venue. The restaurant, in a glassed-in, turn-of-the-twentieth-century terrace overlooking the gardens, is only open at lunchtime and boasts one of the best salad buffets in Rio.

Divided between two buildings, one inside the palace grounds and the other in an adjacent house, the **Museu de Folclore Edison Cruz** (Tues–Fri 11am–6pm, Sat & Sun 3–6pm) is a fascinating folkloric collection that unites pieces from all over Brazil – leatherwork, musical instruments, ceramics, toys, Afro-Brazilian cult paraphernalia, photographs and *ex votos*. Behind the palace lies the **Parque do Catete** (daily 9am–6pm), whose birdlife, towering palms and quiet walking trails are good for a quick break. This is a nice place to take small children as it has a pond with ducks and other waterfowl, a playground and tricycles and other toys.

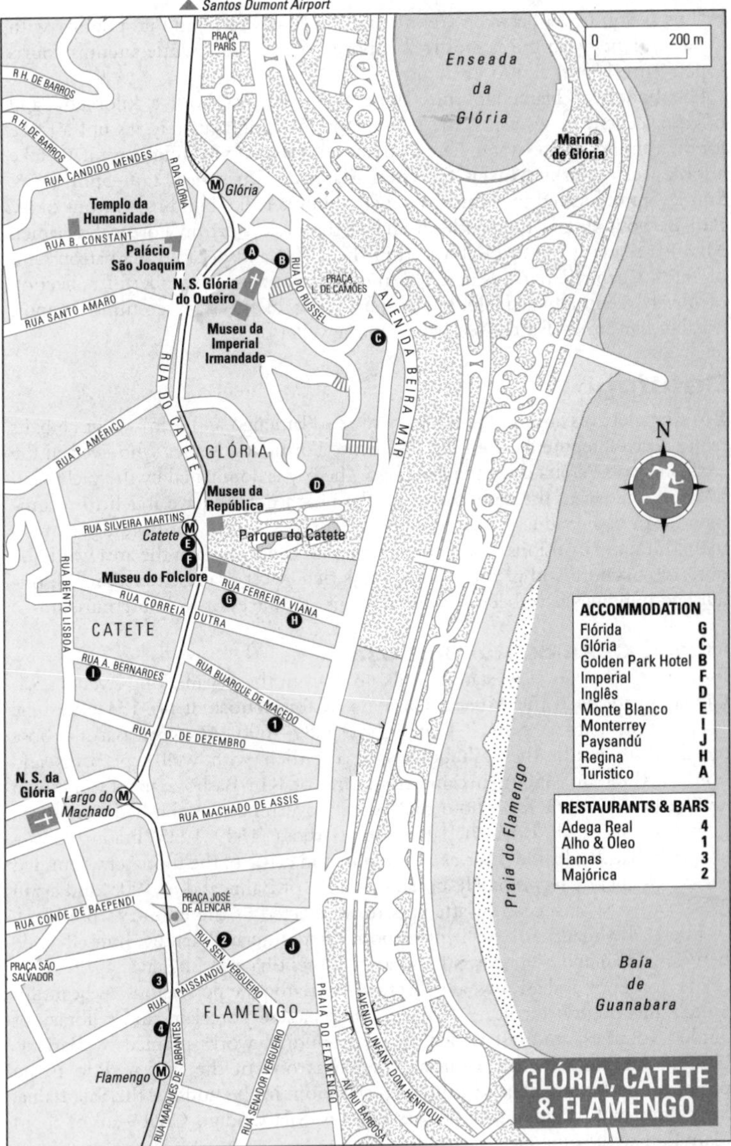

Flamengo

If you follow Avenida Beira Mar away from Centro you enter the **Parque do Flamengo**, the biggest land reclamation project in Brazil, designed by the great Brazilian landscape architect and gardener Roberto Burle Marx, and completed in 1960. Sweeping round as far as Botafogo Bay, it comprises 1.2 square kilometres of prime seafront. You'll pass through the park many times by bus as you travel between Centro and the beach zone, and it's popular with local residents who use it mostly for sports – there are countless tennis courts (open 9am–11pm) and football pitches.

The **beach** at Flamengo runs along the park for about a kilometre and offers excellent views across the bay to Niterói. Unfortunately, it's not a place for swimming as the water here is polluted. Instead, you might want to take a look at the quirky **Museu Carmen Miranda** (Tues–Fri 11am–5pm, Sat & Sun 2–5pm), located in a curious concrete bunker-like building in front of Av. Rui Barbosa 560, at the southern end of the park. Born in Portugal, Carmen Miranda made it big in Hollywood in the 1940s and became the patron saint of Rio's Carnaval transvestites. The museum contains a wonderful collection of kitsch memorabilia including posters, some of the star's costumes – most notably her famed fruit-laden hats – and jewellery.

Botafogo

Botafogo curves around the 800m between Flamengo and Rio's yacht club. Its name derives, reputedly, from the first white Portuguese settler who lived in the area, one João Pereira de Souza Botafogo. The bay is dominated by the yachts and boats moored near the club, and again the beach doesn't have much to recommend it to bathers due to the pollution of the bay. In many of Botofogo's streets there still stand mansions built in the nineteenth century when the area was Rio's outermost suburb and preserve of the city's rich. Most of these remaining distinguished buildings have been converted for use as offices or to house museums.

Museu Casa de Rui Barbosa

From the Botafogo *metrô* station, walk away from the ocean along Avenida São Clemente to reach the **Museu Casa de Rui Barbosa** at no. 134 (Tues–Fri 10am–5pm, Sat & Sun 2–6pm; ⓣ21/3289-4600, ⓦwww.casaruibarbosa.gov.br), set amidst the lush bowers of a garden with well-kept paths and borders. Built in 1850, it became the home of Rui Barbosa, jurist, statesman and author, in 1893, for whom the federal government established a museum here after his death. Born in Bahia state, Barbosa (1849–1923) graduated as a lawyer in São Paulo and, later, as a journalist and critic of the monarchy, founded the newspaper *A Imprensa*. He became senator of Bahia and in 1905, and again in 1909, made unsuccessful attempts to be elected as the country's president. A liberal, he made an excellent opposition politician, earning himself exile between 1893 and 1895, years he spent in Argentina and England.

The museum is basically a collection of Barbosa's possessions – beautiful Dutch and English furniture, Chinese and Japanese porcelain, and a library of 35,000 volumes, amongst which are two hundred works penned by Barbosa himself. Additionally, the bathroom here was one of the first in Rio to be plumbed. Barbosa conferred a title on each room in the house – the Sala Bahia, Sala Questão Religiosa, Sala Habeas Corpus, Sala Código Civil – all of them identified with some part of his life.

Museu Villa-Lobos and Museu do Índio

On Rua Sorocaba, a turning off Avenida São Clemente, is the **Museu Villa-Lobos** at no. 200 (Mon–Fri 10am–5.30pm; ⓣ21/2266-3894, ⓦwww.museuvillalobos.org.br). Established in 1960 to celebrate the work of the great Brazilian composer, Heitor Villa-Lobos (1887–1959), it's largely a display of his personal possessions and original music scores, but you can also buy CDs of his music here.

Botafogo's other museum, the **Museu do Índio** (Tues–Fri 9am–5.30pm, Sat & Sun 1–5pm; ⓣ21/2286-8899, ⓦwww.museudoindio.org.br), lies on the next street along, at Rua das Palmeiras 55. Housed in a mansion dating from 1880, the museum was inaugurated on April 19, 1953, the commemoration of Brazil's "Day of the Indian" – not that there were many around by then to celebrate. It's a broad and interesting collection, including utensils, musical instruments, tribal costumes and ritual devices from many of Brazil's dwindling indigenous peoples. Perhaps most interesting of all are the full-size shelters of the Guaraní (from Angra dos Reis), Wajãpi (from Amapá) and Kuikuro (from Mato Grosso's Xingú) peoples that have been erected on the museum's grounds. There's a good photographic exhibition, too, and an accessible anthropological explanation of the rituals and institutions of some of the tribes. The attached shop is excellent, selling a quality range of carefully sourced original artefacts at reasonable prices. The ethnographical section of the Museu Histórico Nacional (see p.99) probably provides you with more information, but this museum offers much of interest.

Urca and the Sugar Loaf

The best bet for swimming this close to the centre is around **Urca**. There are small beaches on each side of the promontory on which this small, wealthy *bairro* stands, its name an acronym of the company that undertook its construction – Urbanizador Construção. Facing Botafogo, the **Praia da Urca**, only 100m long, is frequented almost exclusively by local inhabitants, while in front of the cable car station, beneath the Sugar Loaf mountain, **Praia Vermelha** is a cove sheltered from the South Atlantic, whose relatively gentle waters are popular with swimmers.

You should come to Urca at least once during your stay to visit the **Pão de Açúcar**, which rises where Guanabara Bay meets the Atlantic Ocean. In Portuguese the name means "**Sugar Loaf**", referring to the ceramic or metal mould used during the refining of sugar cane. Liquid sugar cane juice was poured into the mould and removed when the sugar had set, producing a shape reminiscent of the mountain. The name may also come from the native Tamoyan Indian word *Pau-nh-Açuquá*, meaning "high, pointed or isolated hill" – a more apt description. The first recorded non-indigenous ascent to the summit was made in 1817 by an English nanny, Henrietta Carstairs. Today, mountaineers scaling the smooth, precipitous slopes are a common sight, but there is a cable car ride to the summit for the less adventurous.

The **cable car** system has been in place since 1912; sixty years later the present Italian system, which can carry 1360 passengers every hour, was installed (daily 8am–10pm, every 30min; R$35; ⓦwww.bondinho.com.br). The base station is in Praça General Tibúrcio, which can be reached by buses marked "Urca" or "Praia Vermelha" from Centro, #107 from Centro, Catete and Flamengo, or #511 and #512 from Zona Sul (returning to Copacabana takes 1hr 30min, as the bus first passes through Botafogo, Leblon and Ipanema). The 1400-metre journey is made in two stages, first to the summit of **Morro da Urca** (220m), where there is a theatre, restaurant and shops, and then on to the top of Pão de Açúcar itself (396m). The cable cars have glass walls and the view from the top is as glorious as you could wish. Facing inland, you can see right over the city, from Centro and the Santos Dumont airport all the way through Flamengo and Botafogo; face Praia Vermelha and the cable car terminal, and to the left you'll see the sweep of Copacabana and on into Ipanema, while back from the coast the mountains around which Rio was built rise to the Tijuca National Park. Try and avoid the busy times between 10am and 3pm: the ride is best at sunset on a clear day, when the lights of the city are starting to twinkle. Leading down from the summit are a series of wooded trails along which you'll encounter curious small marmosets, and it's easy – and safe – to get away from the crowds.

On the Morro da Urca, the Beija Flor **samba school** performs every Monday at 10pm (see p.130). This hill is also the location of the expensive Carnaval ball (see p.137).

Leme and Copacabana

Leme and **Copacabana** are different stretches of the same four-kilometre beach. Avoid walking through the Túnel Novo that links Botafogo with Leme, as it's a favourite place for tourists to be relieved of their wallets. The **Praia do**

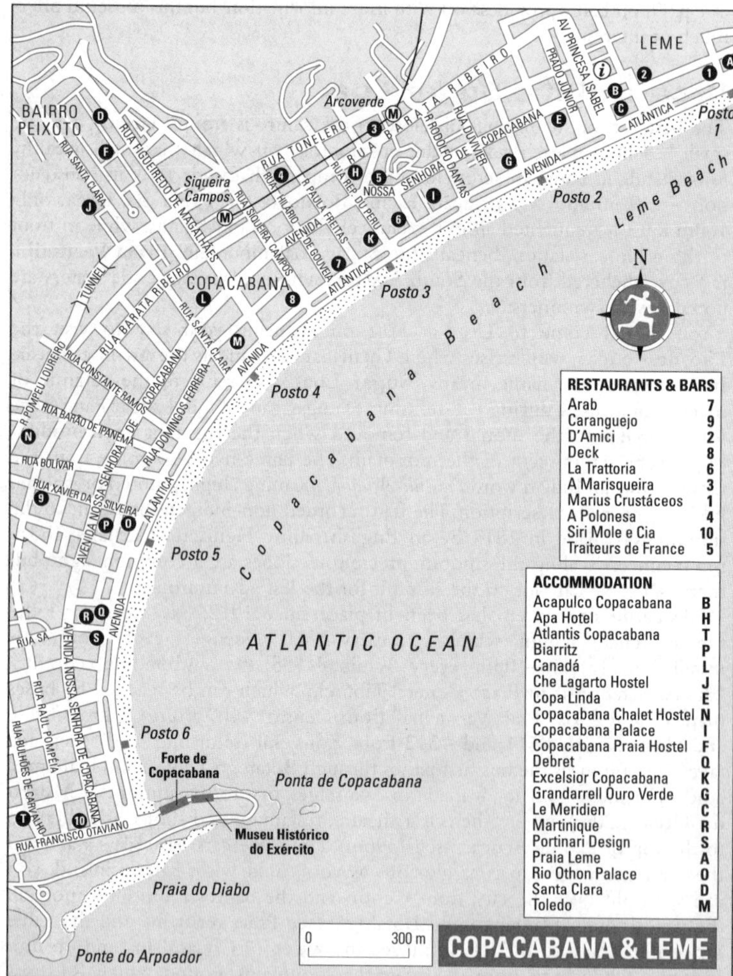

Leme extends for a kilometre, between the Morro do Leme and Avenida Princesa Isabel, by the luxury hotel *Le Meridien*. From there, the **Praia de Copacabana** runs for a further 3km to the Forte de Copacabana. The fort (Tues–Sun 10am–5pm; R$4), built to protect the entrance to Guanabara Bay, is open to the public and well worth visiting for the impressive views towards Copacabana beach, rather than for the military hardware on display in the **Museu Histórico do Exército**; there's an outdoor café here, too, popular with tourists and elderly wives of officers, which serves light meals, cakes and cold drinks.

Leme beach is slightly less packed than Copacabana and tends to attract families. Bear in mind that the *Meridien* maintains a hawkish security watch on the part of the beach nearest the hotel, so it's a good place to park your towel.

Copacabana is amazing, the over-the-top atmosphere apparent even in the mosaic pavements, designed by Burle Marx to represent images of rolling waves. The seafront is backed by a line of prestigious, high-rise hotels and luxury apartments that have sprung up since the 1940s, while a steady stream of noisy traffic patrols the two-lane **Avenida Atlântica**. Some fine examples of Art Deco architecture are scattered around the *bairro*, none more impressive than the *Copacabana Palace Hotel* on Avenida Atlântica, built in 1923 and considered one of Rio's best hotels. Families, friends and couples cover the palm-fringed sand – at weekends it's no easy matter to find space – the bars and restaurants along the avenue pulsate and the busy **Avenida Nossa Senhora de Copacabana** is lined with assorted stores, which – like the *bairro* in general – are in a state of decline, being pushed aside by the boutiques of trendy Ipanema and the shopping malls of the Zona Sul.

Copacabana is dominated to the east by the Pão de Açúcar and circled by a line of hills that stretch out into the bay. A popular residential area, the *bairro*'s expansion has been restricted by the Morro de São João, which separates it from Botafogo, and the Morro dos Cabritos, which forms a natural barrier to the west. Consequently, it's one of the world's most densely populated areas as well as a frenzy of sensual activity, most of which takes place in a thoroughly impressive setting. Some say that Copacabana is past its prime and certainly it's not as exclusive as it once was. You'll be frequently accosted by a stream of the dispossessed (young and old) who want money or the scraps off your plate, while the street traders work into the night selling T-shirts, lace tablecloths and plastic Rio car numberplates. It's still an enjoyable place to sit and watch the world go by, though, and at night on the floodlit beach football is played into the early hours.

Of course Copacabana hasn't always been as it is today. Traces remain of the former fishing community that dominated the area until the first decades of the twentieth century. Each morning before dawn the boats of the *colônia de pescadores* (the descendents of the fishermen) set sail from the Forte de Copacabana, returning to the beach by 8am to sell their fish across from the *Sofitel* hotel.

Arpoador, Ipanema and Leblon

On the other side of the point from Forte de Copacabana, the lively waters off the **Praia do Arpoador** are popular with families and the elderly as the ocean here is slightly calmer than at **Ipanema**, which is a couple of kilometres away (**Leblon** lies thereafter). There are few apartment buildings in either Ipanema and Leblon that don't have their own guards, with eyes alert to anyone who looks out of place in these rich persons' hangouts. Much calmer than Copacabana, the beaches in these areas are stupendous, while the only bar/restaurant on the beachfront is *Caneco*, at the far end of Leblon – a good spot to aim for anyway as you'll enjoy a fine view towards Ipanema from here. As with Copacabana, Ipanema's beach is unofficially divided according to the supposed interest of the beach users. Thus the stretch of sand east from Rua Farme de Amoedo to Rua Teixeira de Melo around *posto 8* is where gay men are concentrated, while the nearby *posto 9* is where artists and intellectuals ponder life. On Sunday, the seafront roads – Avenida Vieira Souto in Ipanema and Avenida Delfim Moreira in Leblon – are closed to traffic, given over to strollers, skateboarders and rollerbladers.

Since the 1960s, Ipanema has developed a reputation as a fashion centre second to none in Latin America. Although many in São Paulo and Buenos Aires would dispute this, certainly the *bairro* is packed with *bijou*, little boutiques flogging the very best Brazilian names in fine threads. If you do go shopping here, go on Friday and take in the large **food and flower market** on the Praça de Paz. Prices compare very well to their European or North American equivalents, but visitors are more likely to be able to afford something at the so-called **Feira Hippie**, held between 9am and 6pm on Sunday in Praça General Osório. The variety and quality of the goods here – leather, jewellery, cushion covers, hammocks and crocheted tablecloths – is very poor, and you're much more likely to find something interesting that's worth buying at the Babilônia Feira Hype at the Jockey Club in Gávea (see opposite).

Lagoa

Back from Ipanema's plush beaches is the Lagoa Rodrigo de Freitas, always referred to simply as Lagoa. A lagoon linked to the ocean by a narrow canal that passes through Ipanema's Jardim de Allah, Lagoa is fringed by apartment buildings where some of Rio's most seriously rich and status-conscious have chosen to live since the 1920s. One of the few remaining original homes now contains the **Fundação Eva Klabin** (guided visits Wed–Sun 2.30pm & 4pm; ⓣ21/2523-3471, ⓦwww.evaklabin.org.br), a cultural centre at Avenida Epitácio Pessoa 2480. Built in 1931, the house is typical of the resort-style Norman architecture popular at the time and became the family residence of Eva Klabin, a wealthy art collector of Lithuanian origin. The wide-ranging collection of Egyptian, classical Greek and Roman, Italian, French and Flemish works of art is beautifully displayed in elegant, wood-panelled rooms and classical music recitals are regularly held here. All this seems utterly at odds with the lifestyle of the Zona Sul but serves as a reminder of the Brazilian elite's traditional cultural affinity with all things European.

Until recently, the lagoon's water was badly polluted, but a programme to clean it up has been remarkably successful and its mangrove swamps are now steadily recovering. The shore surrounding the lagoon forms the Parque Tom Jobim (named in memory of Rio's famed bossa nova composer who died in 1994), and the area comes alive each Sunday as people walk, rollerblade, jog or cycle along the 7.5km perimeter pathway, play or watch baseball or just gaze at the passers-by. Summer evenings are especially popular when, on the west side of the lagoon in the area known as the Parque dos Patins (Skaters' Park), there are food stalls, live music and *forró* dancing.

The steep hill slopes behind the area's apartment buildings are still well forested, and in 1979 a *favela* was cleared away and the **Parque da Catacumba** (daily 8am–7pm) developed in its place on one of the more accessible hills, by the southeast corner of the lagoon on Avenida Epitácio Pessoa. It's a wonderful, shaded place to relax, and the dense tropical vegetation forms an excellent backdrop for one of Brazil's few **sculpture parks**.

Jardim Botânico and Gávea

To the northwest of the Lagoa lies the *bairro* of **Jardim Botânico**, whose **Parque Lage** (daily 8am–5pm), designed by the English landscape gardener John Tyndale in the early 1840s, consists of 137 hectares of foliage, including pristine Atlantic forest on the slopes of the Corcovado, with a labyrinthine path network and seven small lakes. A little further along the Rua Jardim Botânico, at no. 1008, is the **Jardim Botânico** itself (daily 8am–5pm; R$4; Ⓦwww.jbrj.gov.br). Over half of it is natural forest, while the rest is laid out in impressive avenues lined with immense imperial palms that date from the garden's inauguration in 1808. Dom João used the gardens to introduce foreign plants into Brazil – tea, cloves, cinnamon and pineapples among them – and they were opened to the public in 1890. One of the world's finest botanic gardens, there are now five thousand plant species, amongst which live monkeys, parrots and other assorted wildlife. There are also a number of sculptures to be seen throughout the garden, notably the *Ninfa do Eco* and *Caçador Narciso* (1783) by Mestre Valentim, the first two metal sculptures cast in Brazil.

Gávea and the Jockey Club

On the **Gávea** side of Lagoa, the **Jockey Club**, also known as the Hipódromo da Gávea, can be reached on any bus marked "via Jóquei" – get off at Praça Santos Dumont at the end of Rua Jardim Botânico. Racing in Rio was introduced by the British and dates back to 1825, though the Hipódromo wasn't built until 1926. Today, **races** take place four times a week, every week of the year (Mon 6.30–11.30pm, Fri 4–9.30pm, Sat & Sun 2–8pm), with the international Grande Prêmio Brazil taking place on the first Sunday of August. A night at the races is great fun and foreigner visitors can get into the palatial members' stand for just a few *reais*, but remember, no one in shorts is admitted. The club is an entertaining place, especially during the floodlit evening races, when the air is balmy and you can eat or sip a drink as you watch the action. You don't have to bet to enjoy the experience – it's not very easy to understand the betting system they use anyway. On alternate weekends throughout the year, part of the club is taken over by the **Babilônia Feira Hype** (2–11pm; R$5). You'll find a good selection of handicrafts

Hang-gliding above Rio

For a bird's-eye view of Rio's beaches and forest, take off with an experienced pilot on a tandem hang-glider flight from the Pedra Bonita ramp on the western edge of the Parque Nacional de Tijuca (see p.121), 520m above the beach at São Conrado. Depending on conditions, flights last between ten and thirty minutes, flying alongside the mountains and over the forest and ocean before landing on the beach at São Conrado.

The most experienced and reliable operator, Just Fly (Ⓣ21/2268-0565 or 9985-7540, Ⓦwww.justfly.com.br), offers flights daily (usually 10am–3pm) when weather permits, which includes pick-up and drop-off from your hotel. Flights are cancelled if the chief pilot, Paulo Celani, has the slightest doubt about conditions, whether on safety grounds or because poor visibility or overly strong winds generally make for a short, uncomfortable flight.

If you make your reservation by phone in person, mention the Rough Guide and you'll receive a ten percent discount on the standard price of R$240 – by leaving arrangements to your hotel you may well end up with a less reliable operator. If you're an experienced pilot and want to fly alone, you'll have to bring your own equipment to Rio, as hang-gliders are not available to rent locally.

as well as clothes and jewellery by young designers hoping to get noticed, and if you stay into the evening you can watch the horses race.

About 3km northwest of the Jockey Club, at Rua Marquês de São Vicente 476, the **Instituto Moreira Salles** (Tues–Sun 1–8pm; ⓣ21/3284-7400, ⓦwww.ims.com.br) is one of Rio's most beautiful private cultural centres. Located in the former home of the Moreira Salles family (the owners of Unibanco, one of the country's most important banks), the centre is worth a visit just to get a glimpse into the lives of the wealthy. Designed by the Brazilian architect Olavo Redig de Campos and completed in 1951, the house is stunningly beautiful – one of the most refined examples of modernist residential architecture in Brazil – with gardens landscaped by Roberto Burle Marx, who also contributed a tile mural alongside the terrace. Unibanco is a major collector of Brazilian art, and, since the cultural centre opened to the public in 1999, it has hosted important exhibitions of nineteenth- and twentieth-century painting and photography. In the house a tearoom serves light lunches, cakes and ice creams and, at R$40 per person, a good, but expensive, high tea. It's a good half-hour walk to the Instituto Moreira Salles from the Jockey Club; alternatively, you can take bus #170 from Centro (Av. Rio Branco), Botafogo, Humaitá or Jardim Botânico, or #174 from Copacabana, Ipanema or Leblon.

Also in Gávea is the **Parque da Cidade** (daily 8am–5pm) and **Museu Histórico da Cidade** (Tues–Sun 11–5pm), at the end of Estrada de Santa Marinha: buses #591, #593 or #594 from Copacabana; #179 or #178 from Centro. The museum is housed within a two-storey nineteenth-century mansion once owned by the Marquês de São Vicente, and the entire collection is related

Rio's favelas

In a low-wage economy, and without even half-decent social services, life is extremely difficult for the majority of Brazilians. During the last thirty years the rural poor have descended upon urban centres in search of a livelihood. Unable to find accommodation, or pay rent, they have established shantytowns, or *favelas*, on any available empty space, which in Rio usually means the slopes of the hills around which the city has grown.

Favelas start off as huddles of cardboard boxes and plastic sheeting, and slowly expand and transform: metal sheeting and bricks provide more solid shelters of often two or more storeys. Clinging to the sides of Rio's hills, and glistening in the sun, they can from a distance appear not unlike a medieval Spanish hamlet, perched secure atop a mountain. It is, however, a spurious beauty. The *favelas* are creations of need, and their inhabitants are engaged in an immense daily struggle for survival, worsened by the prospect of landslides caused by heavy rains, which could tear their dwellings from their tenuous hold on precipitous inclines.

Life for Rio's *favela* dwellers is beginning to change for the better, however. Bound together by their shared poverty and exclusion from effective citizenship, the *favelados* display a great resourcefulness and cooperative strength. Self-help initiatives – some of which are based around the *escolas de samba* (see p.135) that are mainly *favela*-based – have emerged, and the authorities are finally recognizing the legitimacy of *favelas* by promoting "*favela-bairro*" projects aimed at fully integrating them into city life. Private enterprise, too, is taking an interest as it becomes alert to the fact that the quarter of the city's population living in *favelas* represent a vast, untapped market.

Favela tours

Wandering into a *favela* does not, as many middle-class *cariocas* would have you believe, guarantee being robbed or murdered. Law and order is essentially in the to the history of Rio from its founding until the end of the Old Republic in 1930. The exhibits – paintings, weapons, porcelain, medals and the like – are arranged in chronological order; the first salon deals with the city's foundation, the rest with the colonial period.

The coast west of Leblon

Back on the coast, to the west of Leblon, lies kilometre after kilometre of white sand. **Praia do Vidigal**, tucked under the Morro Dois Irmãos, is only about 500m long, and used to be the preserve of the inhabitants of the **Favela do Vidigal** – one of the biggest shantytowns in Rio – until they lost their beach with the construction of the *Rio Sheraton Hotel*.

West again, the beautiful beach at **São Conrado**, dominated by apartment buildings and high-rise hotels, is becoming ever trendier: frequented by the famous and packed with hang-gliders and surfers at weekends, it's an area where the upper classes flaunt their wealth without shame, though some are uncomfortable with the encroachment of nearby *favelas*. Above São Conrado, on the slopes between the Tijuca mountains and the peak of Pedra dos Dois Irmãos, sits **Favela Roçinha** (see box, below) – misleadingly picturesque and glistening in the tropical sun. Over 200,000 Brazilians live here, where a salary of around R$100 a month is about as much as an entire family can expect. **Bus** #500 from Urca will take you to São Conrado via Avenida Atlântica (Copacabana), Avenida Vieira Souto (Ipanema) and Avenida Delfim Moreira (Leblon).

hands of highly organized drugs gangs, but it's simply not in their interest to create trouble for visitors, as this would only attract the attention of the police who normally stay clear of *favelas*. Alone, you're liable to get lost and, as in any isolated spot, may run into opportunistic thieves, but if accompanied by a *favela* resident you'll be perfectly safe and received with friendly curiosity. For the majority of people, however, the best option is to take a tour, with the most insightful and longest-established run by Marcelo Armstrong. Marcelo, who speaks excellent English, is widely known and respected in the *favelas* that are visited and has made a point of getting community approval. It is strongly advised to make your own arrangements with Marcelo rather than through a travel agent or hotel front desk, where you may end up with an inferior tour and be charged too much – some operators treat the *favelas* rather as they might an African game park, ferrying groups in open-topped camouflaged jeeps. But if you're worried about voyeurism, you shouldn't be: residents want outsiders to understand that *favelas* are not in fact terrifying and lawless ghettos, but inhabited by people as decent as anywhere else, eager to improve the local quality of life.

Marcelo's highly responsible tours usually take in two *favelas*: Roçinha, Rio's largest, with over 200,000 inhabitants, and Vila Canoas, much smaller, with around 3000 residents. Twice a day (9am and 2pm; R$65, part of which is donated to community projects in the *favelas*), tourists are picked up from their hotels or pre-arranged spots in the Zona Sul for the two-hour tour, which stops at look-out points, a day-care centre, a bar and other places of interest. Marcelo offers a fascinating commentary, pointing out the achievements of *favelas* and their inhabitants without romanticizing their lives. To reserve a place on a tour, call Marcelo on ⓣ21/3322-2727, mobiles 9989-0074 or 9772-1133 or for more information check out ⓦwww.favelatour.com.br.

The last area within the city limits is **Barra de Tijuca**, where property developers have been building massive apartment buildings and shopping malls at breakneck speed. But the clean waters and white sands that run for over 16km remain popular at weekends with the beach party and barbecue set. You can reach Barra de Tijuca by **bus** from Copacabana (#553), or from Botafogo *metrô* station (#524).

Sítio Roberto Burle Marx

Some 25km along the coast from Barra de Tijuca is the quiet and unremarkable village of Guaratiba. The countryside around the village is popular amongst *cariocas* seeking a discreet retreat, and it was here in 1949 that the influential landscape gardener **Roberto Burle Marx** bought a forty-hectare former coffee plantation, the Sítio, and converted it into a nursery for the plants that he collected on his travels around the country. In 1973 Burle Marx moved permanently to the Sítio, living there until his death in 1994.

Today the Sítio is used as a botany research and teaching centre, and **tours** (daily 9.30am and 1.30pm; R$5; ⓣ21/2410-1412) of the property and grounds are given to the public, though only in Portuguese. Tours last around ninety minutes and it's essential to book in advance. Burle Marx was not only a collector of plants, but also of Brazilian folk art and Peruvian ceramics – his vast collection is on display along with his own paintings and textiles inside the house. A small Benedictine chapel, dating from 1610, and the Sítio's original colonial-era farmhouse are also on the grounds. Just across the road from the Sítio's front gates, the *Restaurante do Cesar* (daily 11.30am–6.30pm; weekend reservations essential; ⓣ21/2410-1202) serves excellent local seafood and is owned by Burle Marx's favourite cook; a full meal for two will cost around R$60.

To get to the Sítio, take **bus** #387 ("Marambaia–Passeio") from the Passeio Público in Centro, which passes through Copacabana, Ipanema and Barra de Tijuca, and will leave you right outside the Sítio's entrance gate – allow ninety minutes from Centro. Alternatively, the air-conditioned "Santa Cruz–Via Barra"

△ Parque Nacional da Tijuca

or "Campo Grande–Via Barra" buses follow the same route, but will leave you at the Ipiranga petrol station in Guaratiba from where you should ask for directions; the Sítio is a fifteen-minute walk away.

Parque Nacional da Tijuca and Alta da Boa Vista

When the Portuguese arrived, the area that is now the city of Rio was covered by dense green tropical forest. As the city grew, the trees were felled and the timber used in construction or for charcoal. However, if you look up from the streets of Zona Sul today, the mountains running southwest from the Corcovado are still covered with exuberant forest, the periphery of the **Parque Nacional da Tijuca** (daily 8am–5pm), which covers an area of approximately 120 square kilometres and is maintained by Brazil's State Institute of Forestry (IBDF).

In the seventeenth century the forests of Tijuca were cut down for their valuable hardwood and the trees replaced by sugar cane and, later, coffee plantations and small-scale agriculture. In the early nineteenth century the city authorities became alarmed by a shortage of pure water and by landslides from the Tijuca slopes. Eventually it was decided that a concerted effort was needed to restore Rio's watershed and, in 1857, a **reafforestation project** was initiated: by 1870 over 100,000 trees had been planted and the forest was reborn. Most of the seeds and cuttings that were planted were native to the region, and today the park serves as a remarkable example of the potential for the regeneration of the Mata Atlântica.

Following on from the success of the forest, the IBDF has gradually been reintroducing fauna to the extent that the forest is once again the home of insects and reptiles, ocelots, howler monkeys, agoutis, three-toed sloths and other animals. Most successful of all has been the return of **birdlife**, making Tijuca a paradise for birdwatchers. At the same time, overstretched park rangers have been struggling in recent years to keep residents of the eight neighbouring *favelas* from hunting wildlife for food or for trade.

Routes into the park

The park offers lots of walks and some excellent views of Rio, and though areas of it have been burnt by forest fires it remains an appealing place to get away from the city for a few hours. Buses don't enter the park, so a **car** is useful if you plan to do an extensive tour: you can go in via Cosme Velho *bairro*, near the **Entrada dos Caboclos**, and follow Estrada Heitor da Silva Costa. (Areas of the park are used as *terrenos*, places where *candomblé* and *umbanda* ritual ceremonies are performed: *caboclos* is the collective name for the spirits involved in these cults.) An alternative entrance is at Rua Leão Pacheco, which runs up the side of the Jardim Botânico (off Rua Jardim Botânico) and leads to the **Entrada dos Macacos** and on to the **Vista Chinesa**, above the Museu Histórico da Cidade in Gávea. From here there's a marvellous view of Guanabara Bay and the Zona Sul. Both of these entrances lead to different roads that run through the park, but they converge eventually in the *bairro* of **Alta da Boa Vista**. If you're intent upon **walking**, you should be warned that even the shorter trip from the Entrada dos Macacos will mean a hot, dehydrating climb for more than 20km.

If you don't have your own transport, it's much easier to aim for the area to the north of the park known as the **Floresta de Tijuca**. Take a bus to Alto da Boa Vista (#221 from Praça XV de Novembro; #233 or #234 from the *rodoviária*; #133 from Rua Jardim Botânico) and get off at Praça Alfonso

Viseu near the **Entrada da Floresta**, with its distinctive stone columns. A few hundred metres after the entrance (where you can buy a **map**, though the main paths are well signposted) is a 35-metre-high waterfall and, further on, the **Capela do Mairynk**, built in 1860, but virtually entirely rebuilt in the 1940s. The chapel's most interesting feature is the three altar panels painted by Cândido Portinari, one of Brazil's greatest twentieth-century artists. In fact, the originals now form part of the much-depleted collection of the Museu de Arte Moderna (see p.98) and those in the chapel are reproductions. If you have the energy for an all-day climb, you can go all the way to the **Pico do Papagaio** (975m) or **Pico da Tijuca** (1021m) – peaks in the far north of the forest, above the popular picnic spot known as **Bom Retiro**. The whole park is a good place for a picnic, in fact; come well supplied with drinks and snacks as vendors are few and far between.

Alternatively, you can join an **organized tour** of the park. Most of those offered by hotels and travel agents involve nothing more strenuous than a short walk along a paved road, but more personal – and infinitely more rewarding – are the tours run by Rio Hiking (T21/2552-9204 or mobile 9721-0594, W www.riohiking.com.br), which take small groups of people on half- or full-day hikes along the park's many trails. Operating at weekends and on some weekdays too, the tours are led by Denise Werneck and her son Gabriel, both of whom speak excellent English and are extremely knowledgeable about the park's biodiversity. Rio Hiking also run occasional three-day walking trips to Ilha Grande (see p.153) and Parque Nacional do Itatiaia (see p.163), and Denise takes groups to sample the nightlife of Bohemian Lapa (see p.98) as well.

Eating and drinking

As one of the world's most exotic tourist resorts and with (for Brazil) a relatively large middle-class population, Rio is well served by restaurants offering a wide variety of cuisines – from traditional Brazilian to French and Japanese. In general, eating out in Rio is not cheap – and can, in fact, be very expensive – but there's no shortage of low-priced places to grab a lunchtime meal, or just a snack and a drink: at a *galeto*, where you eat, diner-style, at the counter; or at a *lanchonete*, the ubiquitous Brazilian café, which serves very cheap combined plates of meat, beans and rice, as well as other snacks. *Cariocas* dine late, and restaurants don't start to fill up until after 9pm. Generally, last orders will be taken around midnight in most places, but there are others where you can get a meal well after 2am.

A note on drinking

The lists given below are for both eating and drinking. Pretty well all bars serve *pestiscos* (snacks) or even full meals, while lots of restaurants allow a night's drinking, too, so you should be able to find somewhere that suits you. In most regions of Brazil, beer comes to your table in a bottle, but in Rio draught beer – or *chopp*, pronounced "shopee" – predominates. A good place to sample Brazil's national drink, *cachaça*, is at the *Academia da Cachaça*, Rua Cde. Bernadotte 26, Leblon, a small and always crowded bar where there are three hundred available brands to sample – treat the spirit with respect at all times. Also well worth considering are the bars and clubs in Lapa (see p.131), a Bohemian neighbourhood known for some prime drinking spots; additionally, you can eat, listen to music and dance there, too.

Fast food, snacks, cakes and ice cream

There are numerous **hamburger** joints in Rio, though it's worth bearing in mind that there's a good chance that the ground beef used comes from the Amazon, where immense ranches are displacing Indians, peasants and trees at a criminal rate. You'll get better, more authentic and cheaper food at any *galeto* or *lanchonete* – there are plenty in Centro or at Copacabana, though most are closed at night. You won't really need any guidance to find these; the places given below deal in more specialized fare.

If you're just peckish, then it's nice to take **tea and cakes** at ✱ *Confeitaria Colombo* at Rua Gonçalves Dias 32, Centro (closed Sat at 1pm and all day Sun). Founded in 1894, the *Colombo* recalls Rio's *belle époque*, with its ornate interior and air of tradition; there's also a rather plain-looking branch in Copacabana at Av. N.S. de Copacabana 890. A traditional venue for Rio society ladies to meet for afternoon tea is the *Hotel Glória* (Thurs 3.30–6pm), seemingly attracting many of the same guests since opening in the 1920s. More modern surroundings, but as lavish (and expensive) a tea are offered at the Instituto Moreira Salles in Gávea. In Leblon, *Garcia & Rodriques*, at Av. Ataulfo de Paiva 1251, has a wonderful bakery providing excellent sandwiches and cakes, while you'll get a fresh, crisp **salad** at *Gulla Gulla* in the *Hotel Marina Palace*, Av. Delfim Moreira 630 – a bit pricier than usual, but recommended.

For **ice cream**, there are plenty of choices: *Chaika* at Rua Visconde de Pirajá 32 or the excellent *Felice Caffé* at Rua Gomes Carneiro 30 – both in Ipanema; La Basque at Rua Rainha Guilhermina 90 in Leblon; or, best of all (but relatively expensive), *Sorvete Mil Frutas*, at Rua Garcia D'Ávila 134 in Ipanema, which boasts dozens of flavours – including exotic Brazilian fruit such as *pitanga* and *jabuticaba* – that vary according to the season; there's also a branch near the Jardim Botânico on Rua Seabra.

Centro and Lapa

The restaurants in the city centre cater largely for people working in the area, and at lunchtime the service is rushed. There are lots of cheap eating places, bakeries and bars around the Praça Tiradentes, while after work, Downtown office workers flock to the Arco de Teles area (see p.90), the pedestrian zone centred on Travessa do Comércio and Rua Ouvidor, for early-evening drinks and *petiscos* in the many unassuming bars. Later on, the action shifts to burgeoning Lapa, one of the most important nightlife spots in Rio (see p.131).

Alba Mar Praça Marechal Âncora 186, a short walk from Praça XV de Novembro. Founded in 1933 and housed in the remaining tower of the old municipal market, this cool, green, octagonal building provides a superb view of Guanabara Bay. Stick with the moderately priced seafood, served by stern waiters in white uniforms. Lunch only, closed Sun.

Bar Luiz Rua Carioca 39. Near Largo da Carioca, this manic but essentially run-of-the-mill restaurant and bar, serving German-style food and ice-cold *chopp*, is considered quite an institution and has long been a popular meeting place for journalists and intellectuals. Closed Sun.

Bar Ocidental Rua Miguel Couto 124. One of several bars on a small pedestrianized road near the Largo de São Francisco de Paulo. Sit at a table outside and enjoy an early evening *chopp* and a plate of fresh sardines.

Caldeirão Rua do Ouvidor 26. Open at lunchtime for good, cheap seafood, with a pleasant atmosphere – try *badejo* (a type of fish) or *capixaba* (seafood stew).

Cosmopolita Travessa do Mosqueira 4, Lapa. An excellent Portuguese restaurant established in 1926 with a loyal, rather Bohemian, clientele. Fish dishes – cod-based, in particular – are the firm favourites here. Closed Sun.

Miako Rua do Ouvidor 45, north side of Praça XV de Novembro. One of the first Japanese restaurants in Rio, serving reliable sushi, sashimi, *teppan-yaki*

Vegetarian food

Vegetarians won't have any serious problems in Rio. While beans and rice are always available for basic sustenance, don't be shy of asking the waiter in any restaurant to have the kitchen prepare something a little more tasty: if nothing else, you'll get a plate of fresh vegetables.

Celeiro Rua Dias Ferreira 199, Leblon. Rio's best *por kilo* restaurant, with an extremely varied salad bar, excellent bread and delicious desserts. Well worth the sometimes long wait for a table and the price, over twice the amount you'd normally expect to pay at a *por kilo* restaurant. Mon–Sat 10am–5.30pm.

Empório Natural Rua Barrão da Torre 167, Ipanema. A great vegetarian *por kilo* restaurant with a wide range of hot and cold choices; a decent health-food store is adjacent.

Macro Nature Travessa Cristiano Lacorte, Copacabana. An excellent health-food shop and restaurant (though the menu is limited to a narrow range of salads and bean stews). Closed Sat & Sun evening.

Natural Rua 19 de Fevereiro 118 (Botafogo) and Rua Barão de Torre 171 (Ipanema). Not strictly a vegetarian restaurant, as fish can be had, too, but the food is tasty and cheap. Lunch only.

Sabor Saúde Rua da Quitanda 21, Centro. An inexpensive, above-average restaurant and health-food store serving only organically grown produce, slipping in the occasional fish-based dish as well. Mon–Fri 11.30am–4pm.

and *filé na chapa*, as well as a few Chinese dishes for good measure. Mon–Sat lunch only.

Penafiel Rua Senhor dos Passos 121. Superb – and amazingly inexpensive – Portuguese dishes have been served here since 1912. Fish dishes and stews (such as those based on yellow wax bean, ox tongue and tripe) are specialities. Lunch only, closed Sat & Sun.

Rio–Minho Rua do Ouvidor 10. The *Rio-Minho* has been going strong for over 120 years, serving tasty Brazilian food at fair prices. The kitchen concentrates on seafood – try *badejo* fish, lobster in butter, prawn in coconut milk or the fried fish with red peppers, rice and broccoli. Lunch only, closed Sat & Sun.

Sentaí (O Rei da Lagosta) Rua Barão de São Felix 75. A wonderful daytime-only Portuguese seafood restaurant full of local colour. Despite being in a rundown part of Downtown, it's a strangely fashionable restaurant. Lunch only, Mon–Fri.

Santa Teresa

If at all possible, make time for a visit up into the airy hills of Santa Teresa. There are several good restaurants here and the *bairro* is an enjoyable ten-minute tram ride from Centro. On Friday and Saturday evenings, young people congregate in the bars and restaurants around Largo dos Guimarães.

Adega do Pimenta Rua Almirante Alexandrino 296. Most people go to this moderately priced German spot for the sausage and sauerkraut, but the duck with red cabbage is excellent.

Aprazível Rua Aprazível 62 ⓣ21/2508-9174. Excellent and fairly expensive Franco-Mineira dishes are offered, plus there's an attractive terrace with wonderful views across Rio. The quail, served with a *jabuticaba* chutney, is a remarkable creation, while the goat is roasted to perfection. Advance booking is advised. Thurs–Fri 8pm–midnight, Sat noon–midnight, Sun and holidays 1–6pm.

Bar do Arnaudo Rua Almirante Alexandrino 316. Just up from the *Adega do Pimenta*, this is an excellent mid-priced place to sample traditional food from Brazil's Northeast, such as *carne do sol* (sun-dried meat), *macaxeira* (sweet cassava) and *pirão de bode* (goat-meat soup). Sat & Sun closed from 8pm & closed Mon.

Bar do Mineiro Rua Paschoal Carlos Magno 99. Authentic country-style food in an old bar that could be in any small town in Minas Gerais. Also has good beers and an excellent range of *cachaças*.

Sobrado das Massas Largo dos Guimarães. Most of the week this restaurant serves up heavy pasta dishes, but on Saturday it lays out the best *feijoada* in Santa Teresa – a portion for two to three people costs just R$10.

Sobrenatural Rua Almirante Alexandrino 432. Basically a fish restaurant, where the highlights are the *moquecas* and the catch of the day. Deliberately rustic looking, this is an inviting place for a leisurely meal. Closed Mon.

Flamengo

In addition to the places listed below, there are numerous restaurants, *galetos* and *lanchonetes* around the Largo do Machado.

Adega Real Rua Marquês de Abrantes. No haughty *nouvelle cuisine* here, just piles of good basics – if you like decent-quality food in large quantities, this place is recommended, as the friendly staff serve portions sufficient for at least two people. The restaurant opens onto the street, and on Fridays you can sit at the bar and swallow draught beer until 4am; the *bolinhas de bacalhau* (cod balls) are well worth trying.

Alho & Óleo Rua Barque de Macedo 13, down at the foot near Praia do Flamengo. Tasty and reasonably priced home-made pasta and other good Italian fare (try the salami flavoured with pepper and lemon) is served in an upmarket atmosphere.

Lamas Rua Marquês de Abrantes 18. This ever-popular and highly recommended restaurant has been serving well-prepared Brazilian food since 1874 (the Oswaldo Aranha steak – pan-fried with lots of garlic – is a staple). Always busy, with a vibrant atmosphere and clientele of artist and journalist types, *Lamas* is a good example of *carioca* middle-class tradition. Open until 4am.

Majórica Rua Senador Vergueiro 11–15, Flamengo. A long-established, better-than-average place to tuck into some meat – the *picanha especial* (special rump steak) is the favourite. If you're not in the mood for beef, try the excellent grilled trout from the mountains near Petrópolis.

Porcão Rio's Av. Infante Dom Henrique s/n, Aterro do Flamengo. A vast *churrascaria* offering, for R$60 per person, a vast abundance of red meat served *rodizio*-style, along with chicken, fish and a varied choice from the salad buffet. Although part of a chain (there's a branch in Ipanema, the food is top quality and service is always efficient. This spot is located alongside the ocean and features glorious views of Guanabara Bay and Sugar Loaf mountain.

Botafogo, Humaitá and Urca

Botafogo and Humaitá undoubtedly host some of Rio's most interesting restaurants, often overlooked by tourists because they lie a bit off the beaten track, hidden away in back streets. At the Humaitá's impressive indoor market, **Cobal**, Rua Voluntários da Pátria 446, you can take your pick of the moderately priced but excellent *lanchonetes* serving Brazilian Northeastern, Italian and Japanese food; this is a very popular lunch and meeting point for local residents. Although there are few places to eat in Urca, one of Rio's quietest *bairros*, it's a pleasant place for a relaxing meal.

Adega do Valentim Rua da Passagem 178, Botafogo ☎21/295-2748. A comfortable restaurant (especially the front salon) serving up authentic Portuguese food. Expect to pay around R$25 per person for one of the fifteen cod dishes, roast suckling pig or goat. The smoked meats are especially good (though expensive) and there's a nice wine list, too.

A Mineira Rua Duque de Caxias, Humaitá. A perfect introduction to the food of Minas Gerais, with all the standard dishes on offer as part of the excellent-value (R$15 per person) all-you-can-eat buffet.

Axé Santé Rua Capitão Solomão 55, Botafogo. An extravagantly decorated French-Bahian restaurant with live music. The food is well presented and tasty – try the salad with mango and nuts, or the *carne do sol* with banana purée.

Botequim-184 Rua Visconde de Caravelas 184, Humaitá. Good, varied and inexpensive food in a lively environment; next door, the *Overnight Bar* is a friendly place for a few drinks afterwards.

Garota da Urca Av. João Luiz Alves, Urca. Though hardly stylish, *Garotada Urca* boasts one of the best views of any Rio restaurant, looking back towards Botafogo and the Corcovado. The food – Brazilian with Italian twists – is good enough, but you can also stop by for just a drink. Try the *peixe a garota* – a delicious fish risotto that serves two for around R$25.

La Mole Praia de Botafogo 228, Botafogo. Inexpensive, decent Italian food is served at *La Mole*, long a popular venue for families. Nearby and similar are *Bella Blu*, Rua da Passagem 44, and *Bella Roma*, Rua General Gois Monteiro 18.

Madam Vidal Rua Capitão Solomão 69, Botafogo. This gay-friendly music club and restaurant serves tasty dishes that incorporate Brazilian, European and Japanese influences. The jazz nights with acclaimed singer Leila Maria are a treat. Mon–Sat until 3am; closed Sun.

Raajmahal Rua General Polidoro 29, Botafogo. This English-owned Indian restaurant extends itself well beyond the basic curry. Let the waiter know how well seasoned you want your dish, as the restaurant tends to cater for the local preference for mild curries. Closed Sun.

Yorubá Rua Arnaldo Quintela 94, Botafogo. Friendly restaurant serving up moderately priced Afro-Bahian cooking. The beautifully presented meals always take a long time to appear, but the *bobó* (a dish based on mandioca purée), *moquecas* and other Bahian specialities are well worth the wait. Closed Mon & Tues; lunch only Sun.

Copacabana and Leme

It comes as no surprise that Copacabana and adjoining Leme are riddled with restaurants, but that doesn't mean that the choice is particularly good – unless you enjoy sitting in a restaurant swamped with holiday-makers being shuttled about by tour companies. Although eating here is generally disappointing, there are a number of places that are in fact well worth trying.

Arab Av. Atlântica 1936. At this reasonably priced Lebanese restaurant you can enjoy a cold beer and a snack on the terrace or have a full meal inside (the *por kilo* lunch is excellent value). Though the menu is rather heavy on meat choices, vegetarians certainly won't go hungry. One of the very few good restaurants on Av. Atlântica.

Caranguejo Rua Barata Ribeiro 771, corner of Rua Xavier da Silveira. Excellent, inexpensive seafood – especially the *caranguejos* (crabs) – served in an utterly unpretentious environment packed with locals and tourists alike. Closed Mon.

D'Amici Rua Antonio Vieira 18, Leme ⓣ21/2541-4477. One of Rio's best – and most expensive – Italian restaurants where people go as much to see and be seen as they do for the food. The meals, though, are excellent; besides the pastas and risottos, the roast lamb is particularly good.

Deck Av. Atlântica 2316, corner of Rua Siqueira Campos. This always-busy restaurant serves an all-you-can-eat Brazilian buffet for just R$15 per person until 5pm, after which the offerings include *rodizio de galeto* (mouthwatering thyme-and-garlic chicken with polenta fried in palm oil) and all-you-can-eat pasta for R$10.

La Trattoria Rua Fernando Mendes 7. Cheap and cheerful place serving the best Italian food in Copacabana. Amongst the excellent range of pasta dishes, the fettuccine doused in a mixed seafood sauce is especially recommended.

A Marisqueira Rua Barata Ribeiro 232. For over fifty years this restaurant has been serving well-prepared Portuguese-style food, if perhaps a little unimaginative and a touch on the pricey side. Still, it's a good spot for seafood dishes or the Sunday special of calf's foot and white bean stew.

Marius Crustáceos Av. Atlântica 290, Leme ⓣ21/2543-6363. Rio's best-known place to come for oysters, crabs, crayfish, prawns and other seafood choices. The expensive menu is varied, though Italian–Brazilian styles dominate and the waiters have a tendency towards the brusque.

A Polonesa Rua Hilário de Gouveia 116 ⓣ21/2547-7378. A tiny restaurant where the menu features mostly reasonably priced, traditional (and rather heavy) Polish dishes, such as beetroot soup and fish in a horseradish sauce suitable for a chilly winter's evening. For dessert, the soufflés and apple cake are a treat. Closed Tues–Fri lunchtime & Mon.

Siri Mole e Cia Rua Francisco Otaviano 50 ⓣ21/2267-0894. A rarity in Rio – an excellent Bahian restaurant serving beautifully presented dishes (many of them spicy) in an upmarket, yet comfortable, setting. Inside, the restaurant is quite formal, but there are also a few tables outside where you can munch on *acarajé* and other Bahian snacks. There's another branch located in Centro at Av. Rio Branco 1 (ⓣ21/2233-0107).

Traiteurs de France Av. Nossa Senhora de Copacabana 386 ⓣ21/2548-6440. Simple cooking from one of the very few affordable and good French restaurants in Rio. Try the duck magret with spicy pears or one of the tasty fish dishes. Mon–Thurs lunch only; Fri–Sat lunch and dinner; closed Sun.

Lagoa

Most of the restaurants in Lagoa are on the Avenida Epitácio Pessoa, which runs along the east side of the lake: generally serving uninspiring "international" food, they're plush, pricey, air-conditioned and boastful of their views over the lake – which are usually obscured by trees.

Bar Lagoa Av. Epitácio Pessoa 1674, tucked into the southern shores of the lake by Ipanema. The cheapest and oldest (dating back to 1934) of the lakeside restaurants, *Bar Lagoa* is usually full of families from the adjacent neighbourhoods, attended to by white-coated waiters delivering beer, German sausage and smoked pork chops the size of football boots to their tables. Arrive by 9pm and grab a seat on the patio, from where there's a good view of the lake. Inexpensive and definitely recommended.

The Queen's Legs Av. Epitácio Pessoa 5030. A facsimile of a Victorian pub, good for a beer and a game of darts downstairs – but don't bother with the upstairs restaurant, which is overpriced and over-regarded.

Ipanema

There's a fair selection of good (and expensive) restaurants in Ipanema. For budget eating, however, you'll generally do rather better in Copacabana while more interesting restaurants tend to be in Leblon.

Baroni Fasoli Rua Jangadeiras 14, near Praça General Osório. Reasonably priced Italian spot in an area otherwise brimming with expensive choices. The pasta dishes are especially good.

Casa da Feijoada Rua Prudente de Morais 10. Usually served only on Saturdays, *feijoada* is offered seven days a week here, along with other traditional, moderately priced and extremely filling Brazilian dishes.

Efffe's Rua Barão da Torre 422 ☎21/2286-2176. Expensive, modern Brazilian cuisine is prepared with strong French and Italian undertones (such as chicken in a tarragon sauce, *carpaccios* and pastas). Downstairs, the restaurant serves excellent-value lunch specials, while its more formal upstairs dining room offers beautiful views of Ipanema.

Garota de Ipanema Rua Vinícius de Morais 49. Always busy, this bar entered the folk annals of Rio de Janeiro when the song *The Girl from Ipanema* was written here one night by Tom Jobim, the song's composer. While certainly touristy (with unexceptional and overpriced food), there are few better places in Rio for a beer.

Gula Gula Rua Aníbal de Mendonça 132. A good choice of reasonably priced and very tasty salads, grilled dishes and desserts makes this a firm local favourite. The set menu is R$25.

Livraria da Travessa Rua Visconde de Pirajá 572. An informal restaurant in Rio's best bookshop serving breakfast, sandwiches and cakes as well as full meals. The food is excellent – modern Brazilian with Italian and other foreign touches – and the atmosphere unhurried. Mon–Sat 9am–11pm, Sun noon–9pm.

Lord Jim Rua Paul Redfern 63. An English pub serving steak and kidney pie, fish and chips and high tea. Downstairs, there's a dart board amongst the horse brasses and fake half-timbering.

Porcão Ipanema Rua Barão da Torre 218. Part of a reliable chain of *churrascarias* (there's a branch by Flamengo beach), this huge restaurant serves a *rodizio* of high-quality cuts of meat (R$55 or R$35 Mon–Fri lunch), including choices from the buffet *mediterrâneo*, a salad bar featuring Middle Eastern dishes.

Saideira Rua Gomes Carneiro, near Praça General Osório. Eating and drinking through the night, until 8am. The term *saideira* means "one for the road" and it's a place that the night-people stop off at after strenuous entertainment in the clubs round about. Worth considering for a late – or early – snack.

Satyricon Rua Barão de Torre 192 ☎21/2521-0955. Though excessively formal (and very expensive), the Italian food served here is understandably rated as the best in Rio. Seafood is the restaurant's speciality, with a sushi bar giving the place something of a cosmopolitan atmosphere. There are also plenty of meat dishes, and there's an excellent range of pasta choices, too.

Via Farme Rua Farme de Amoedo 47. Good Italian food is served here, with the pizzas and seafood especially worth trying. Choose from an air-conditioned room upstairs or open-air dining downstairs. While it's not cheap, *Via Farme* is reasonable for the area.

Leblon

Many of Leblon's restaurants are situated along the Avenida Ataúlfo de Paiva, where you'll also find many of the late-opening bars. Another popular destination for food and drink is Baixo Leblon, the area around Rua Dias Ferreira three or four blocks back from the beach, which boasts some of Rio's most chic restaurants and turns very lively on weekends. One quite modest-looking but superb lunchtime choice here is **Celeiro**, Rio's most imaginative vegetarian *por kilo* restaurant. Locals of all ages also flock to Leblon's excellent **Cobal** market, at Rua Gilberto Cardoso, where the abundant and affordable *lanchonetes* serve everything from pizza and sushi to Brazilian regional fare until late at night.

Antiquarius Rua Aristides Espínola 19 ⓣ21/2294-1049. Rio has many fine Portuguese restaurants, and this is arguably its best. Especially good for seafood (and not just cod), but goat and wild boar are other fine choices here, as are the rich desserts. Very expensive, and definitely no shorts allowed.

Carlota Rua Dias Ferreira 64 ⓣ21/2540-6821. Imaginative, expensive pan-Asian cooking with a few North African influences is served in a very pleasant atmosphere. The seven kinds of spring rolls are especially noteworthy. Mon–Thurs dinner only, Fri & Sat lunch & dinner, Sun lunch only.

Garcia & Rodriques Av. Ataulfo de Paiva 1251. A foodie's paradise: while the French restaurant is unimaginative and stuffy, there's an excellent bistro, wine shop, ice-cream parlour, bakery and deli. In addition, this is one of the few places in Rio where you can buy genuinely good bread (and croissants) and there's an excellent choice of take-out salads and other prepared meals. Sun–Fri 8am–midnight; Sat 8am–1am.

Nam Thai Rua Rainha Guilhermina 95 ⓣ21/2259-2962. Rio's top pan-Asian restaurant, although the menu is predominantly Thai-influenced. The cauliflower-coriander soup is not to be missed. Tues–Fri dinner only, Sat & Sun lunch and dinner, closed Mon.

Plataforma Rua Adalberto Ferreira 32. Upstairs, tourists are entertained by a samba show, while *cariocas* mingle at the steakhouse restaurant downstairs. After your meal, you can stagger to the *Academia de Cachaça* round the corner (see box, p.122) and sample a few with the benefit of a good lining in the stomach.

Sushi Leblon Rua Dias Ferreira 256. Superb (but expensive) sushi, along with other Japanese-inspired dishes such as grilled squid stuffed with shiitake, are offered at this stylish restaurant – a well-known meeting point of actors, models and artists. Mon–Sat evenings only; Sun 1.30pm–midnight.

Zuka Rua Dias Ferreira 233 ⓣ21/3205-7154. Food is grilled in front of your eyes, then doused in amazing sauces by a chef capable of creating unforgettable fusion cuisine: one of his specialities is seared tuna in a cashew crust, served with a potato-horseradish sauce. Around R$70 per person.

Jardim Botânico and Gávea

Set slightly apart from Rio's main hotel and residential neighbourhoods, these are not obvious areas for restaurants; there are, however, a few enjoyable options following a morning strolling around the botanical gardens or after a night at the races.

Claude Troigros Rua Custódio Serrão 62, Jardim Botânico ⓣ21/2537-8582. An early creator of Franco-Brazilian fusion food, chef/owner Claude Troigros makes regular expeditions to the Amazon and other remote regions in search of new ingredients. Expect unusual combinations, such as quails stuffed with *farofa* and coriander and served with an *aça* sauce, and sole cooked with banana.

Couve-Flor Rua Pacheco Leão 724, Jardim Botânico. The range and quality of the inexpensive to moderately priced salads and hot meals make *Couve-Flor* one of Rio's most popular *por kilo* restaurants. Brazilian dishes predominate but there's much more besides, such as roast beef, duck, pasta and sushi. Don't forget to leave room for dessert: the guava cheesecake is remarkable. Located a short walk from the side entrance of the botanic gardens.

Guima's Rua José Roberto Macedo Soares 5, on the opposite side of Praça Santos Dumont from the Jockey Club. A small, intimate restaurant with a happy atmosphere, catering for an arty and intellectual crowd. The food is delicious, and, unusually,

Gay Rio

If you're expecting Rio's **gay nightlife** to rival San Francisco's or Sydney's, you may well be disappointed. In general nightlife is pretty integrated, with gay men, lesbians and heterosexuals tending to share the same venues; apart from transvestites who hang out on street corners and are visible during Carnaval, the scene is unexpectedly discreet.

A good starting point for an evening out is Rua Visconde Silva in Botafogo, which is lined with gay and lesbian cafés, bars and restaurants that are liveliest on Friday and Saturday nights. The classic introduction to Rio's more traditional male gay society is *Le Ball*, a bar in the Travessa Cristiano Lacorte, just off Rua Miguel Lemos, at the Ipanema end of Copacabana. Opposite this, the *Teatro Brigitte Blair* hosts a gay transvestite show from around 10pm. Also in Copacabana, the bar and nightclub *Inc* (formerly called *Encontros*), at Praça Serzedelo Correia 15, next to Rua Siquera Campos, is open nightly and very popular, although mainly with tourists.

In Lapa, at Rua Mem de Sá 25, behind a pink facade under the Aqueduto da Carioca, the *Casanova* is Rio's oldest and most interesting gay bar. In business since 1929, the *Casanova* features drag shows, lambada and samba music, with large ceiling fans to cool down the frenetic dancers. Very different, but also wild, are the gay nights on Saturdays at the *Cine Ideal* at Rua da Carioca 62, Centro, an informal club that always draws huge crowds. The most popular gay nightclub at the moment is undoubtedly *Le Boy* (☎21/2513-4993) at Rua Raul Pompéia 102 (in Copacabana, towards Ipanema). Based in a former cinema, this huge club is open nightly apart from Mondays and features dance floors, drag shows and much more besides.

The strip of beach between Rua Farme de Amoedo and Rua Teixeira do Melo in Ipanema is the best-known daytime gay meeting point. For Ipanema's post-beach gay crowd, there's *Boofetada*, a bar and café at Rua Farme de Amoedo 87. The beach area in front of the *Copacabana Palace Hotel* is also frequented by gay bathers, and the café next door, *Maxims*, is a fun gay place to hang out. Nearby on Avenida Atlântica at the junction with Rua Siqueira Campos, is the Gay Kiosk Rainbow, a summertime **information point** for gay visitors – ask about circuit parties, usually held in Centro.

For information about Rio's gay balls, see the "Carnaval section", p.137. If it's tours highlighting Rio's gay history you're after, Carlos Roquette, a rather dapper former federal judge turned tour guide, can help you to explore (see p.80).

the *couvert* (wholemeal bread and pâté) is worth the price. Try steak in a mustard and pear sauce and leave space for the delectable chocolate and cream pudding. Though this is one of Rio's best restaurants, it's not too expensive.

Jockey Club Praça Santos Dumont. Palatial surroundings of a bygone era and good, reasonably priced food in this restaurant overlooking the racetrack.

Les Artistes Rua de São Vicente 75 (☎21/2239-4242). This decent, reasonably priced French restaurant is an unexpected find in Brazil. On Wed and Sat good *cassoulet* is served.

Nightlife and entertainment

The best way to find out what's on and where in Rio is to consult *Caderno B*, a separate section of the *Jornal do Brasil*, which lists cinema, arts events and concerts; *O Globo*, too, details sporting and cultural goings-on in the city. *Veja*, Brazil's answer to *Newsweek*, includes an excellent weekly Rio supplement with news of concerts, exhibitions and other events; the magazine reaches the newsstands on Sunday. Regardless, you should never find yourself stuck: there's no end of things to do come nightfall in the city whose name is synonymous with Carnaval (see p.134), samba and jazz.

Samba

Samba shows are inevitably tourist affairs, where members of Rio's more successful samba schools perform glitzy music and dance routines. Still, some are worth catching. Every Monday night at 10pm, the Beija Flor (☎21/791-1353) school performs at the Morro da Urca, halfway up Pão d'Açúcar; the R$90 entrance fee includes dinner (from 8pm), a well-executed show and spectacular city views. On Thursday and Friday live music shows start at 10pm, and you can eat and drink till 2am. For a less touristy experience of a samba school, you can easily arrange to watch rehearsals held from August to February (see box, p.135), mainly at various points in the Zona Norte. For cheap early-evening entertainment, there are the *Seis e Meia* samba shows (at 6.30pm, as the name suggests): in Centro try the Teatro João Caetano on Praça Tiradentes, or the Paço Imperial on Praça XV de Novembro.

Of the **clubs**, it's worth making the trek out to Barra de Tijuca as the *Clube do Samba*, Estrada de Barra 65 in Barra de Tijuca, is great for dancing and has a nice open-air bar. Dedicated just to samba, Saturday here often sees shows by big names like Beth Carvalho, Alcione, João and Giza Nogeuiral (check in the *Jornal do Brasil*); entrance costs about R$25, which is typical for this type of set-up. Otherwise, make for the bars and clubs of Lapa, where samba and other local rhythms play to an enthusiastic and overwhelmingly local crowd. Especially recommended there is *Carioca da Gama* (Mon–Sat from 6pm) at Av. Mem de Sá 79: look out for Teresa Cristina, who brings the house down with her steamy sounds. Excellent samba artists also perform on Friday and Saturday at *Bar Semente* at Rua Joaquim Silva 138.

Discos

Although Rio's discos attempt sophistication, the end result is generally bland and unpalatable. Too often they pump out a steady stream of British and American hits, interspersed with examples from Brazil's own dreadful pop industry. Soft options for the wealthy and unadventurous are *Hippopotamus*, Rua Barão de Torre 354, Ipanema, and *Studio C*, Rua Xavier da Silveira 7, under the *Othon Palace* in Copacabana. If you want to avoid fellow tourists, a good first stop is the Arco de Teles area in Centro, while fashionable nightclubs that attract both *cariocas* and tourists are all found in the Zona Sul.

00 Av. Padre Leonel Franca 240, Gávea ☎21/2540-8041. The nightclub of the moment, frequented by a rich and trendy crowd, where some of Brazil's top DJs play an eclectic mix of music. Like most places it doesn't really get going until after 11pm, though on Sun the best time to go is 7pm, immediately after returning from the beach.

Arco Imperial Travessa do Comércio 13, Lapa ☎21/2242-2695. This dance club is always packed from the comparatively early hour of 10pm. The music is a mix of European and Brazilian disco sounds.

Biblos Av. Epitácio Pessoa 1484, Lagoa. A laid-back atmosphere, with popular home-grown music and jazz on Tues.

Bunker Rua Raul Pompéia 94, Copacabana. Located near Ipanema, this spot is a favourite of students, young locals and tourists alike. Music varies with nights dedicated to drum 'n' bass, techno and alternative beats; entrance is around R$15.

Casa da Matriz Rua Henrique Novaes 107, Botafogo ☎21/2266-1014. An extremely stylish, aggressively modern club that features more Brazilian music than is typical of discos – though this varies throughout the week.

Dito e Feito Rua do Mercardo 21, Centro. The action starts early – from 8pm – with mainstream disco sounds. Open Mon through Sat, but Fri is the busiest night when local office workers stream into the club.

Help Av. Atlântica 3432, Copacabana. A massive disco that gets mobbed – overwhelmingly by foreign men and prostitutes – at weekends; entrance is about R$25.

Melt Rua Rita Ludolf 47, Leblon (☎21/2249-9309). A stylish, hipster haven, with a pretty good range of music, such as samba-rock on Wed and drum 'n' bass on Fri.

△ Lapa nightlife

Mess Club Rua Francisco Otaviano 20, Copacabana ⓣ21/2227-0419, ⓦwww.messclu.com.br. Very hip, but without a trace of snobbishness, this spot is mainly popular with twenty-somethings, though the crowd is pretty mixed. Music changes nightly, with Tuesday's "Afro Rio" especially recommended, when DJs play hip-hop, soul, reggae and other black music styles accompanied by live percussion.

Peoples Av. Bartolomeu Mitre 370, Leblon ⓣ21/512-8824. Long one of the trendiest spots in Rio, though with a R$30 cover charge it's not the cheapest night out. Eclectic music is offered most nights, ranging from 1970s disco beats to techno-house.

Six Electro Rua das Marrecas 38, Lapa ⓣ21/2510-3230. With three dance floors featuring hip-hop and soul, trance and drum 'n' bass, this is a good place to end up after some Lapa bar-hopping. Located in an old house that has been renovated to convey a rustic-chic air.

Jazz

Rio de Janeiro has a tradition of **jazz music** that extends well beyond *The Girl from Ipanema*. Amongst the clubs that specialize in **live jazz** and tend to have consistently good programmes are *Jazzmania*, Rua Rainha Elizabeth 769 (ⓣ21/2287-0085) in Ipanema, near Copacabana; *Mistura Fina*, Av. Borges de Madeiros 3207, Lagoa (ⓣ21/2537-2844; ⓦwww.misturafina.com.br); and *Peoples*, Av. Bartolomeu Mitre 370, Leblon (see above); all have cover charges of at least R$20. In each case, it's a good idea to call to find out who's playing; be prepared to be turned away if it's especially crowded and you're not dressed stylishly enough. Also worth checking out is *Cais do Oriente* in a sprawling late nineteenth-century mansion in Centro, at Rua Visconde de Itaboraí 8 (ⓣ21/2203-0178; Tues–Sat noon to midnight); it's both a spectacularly stylish (though not very good) restaurant and a jazz club (R$25 cover) with a beautiful open patio.

Music in Lapa

Live music options abound in **Lapa**, an atmospheric district that in the early decades of the twentieth century was synonymous with music, and since the 1990s has made a comeback as one of the city's best spots for *forró*, *choro*, samba, *axé* – and other kinds of fusion and Brazilian sounds. Although tourists are attracted to Lapa in increasing numbers, the clubs and bars still mainly attract locals of all ages.

A good first place to make for is Rua Joaquim da Silva, where the packed bars attract a mix of *bairro* residents and college students – if walking, take care not to veer onto the badly lit side streets and be alert even when walking from just one block to the next. If you feel uncomfortable going alone – or simply want company – contact Rio Hiking (see p.122), which regularly takes small groups bar-hopping in Lapa (R$100 per person, excluding drinks).

In addition to places mentioned under "Samba" (see p.130), the following bars and clubs in Lapa are well worth checking out.

Arcos de Velha Av. Mem de Sá 21, Lapa. Bands play *fundo do quintal* style – around a table rather than on the stage.

Assa Branca Av. Mem da Sá, Lapa. A very informal dance hall that's been immensely popular for decades, always attracting big-name samba, *choro* and, especially, *forró* bands. Tues–Sat from 10pm and also Sat 2–9pm.

Bar Semente at Rua Joaquim Silva 138, Lapa. Fri and Sat nights are basically reserved for samba at this easy-going bar. From Mon through Thurs other traditional styles of Brazilian music, in particular *choro*, are performed. Daily from 8.30pm.

Café Cultural Sacrilégio Rua do 81, Lapa ⓣ21/3970-1461. A small old townhouse with a great atmosphere and killer *batidas* (*cachaça*-based drinks). The place attracts some great *choro* singers who perform classical works as well as samba and fusion rock-samba artists. Tues–Sat from 6pm until early morning.

Carioca da Gema Av. Mem de Sá 79, Lapa ⓣ21/2221-0043, ⓦwww.barcariocadagema.com.br. Stop in for very reliable *choro* and samba: look out for Teresa Cristina, one of Rio's greatest female samba voices, and her regular Fri-night appearance.

Circo Voador Rua dos Arcos s/n, Lapa ⓣ21/2533-5873, ⓦwww.circovoador.com.br. Whereas other Lapa clubs have a very mixed-age clientele, with its programme of rap, funk and fusion samba-punk-rock, *Circo Voador*, set in a large circus tent, is dominated by young people who come to dance and discover new bands.

Estrela da Lapa Av. Mem de Sá 130, Lapa ⓣ21/2509-9626, ⓦwww.estreladalapa.com.br. Located in a beautifully restored late nineteenth-century house, this rather upmarket and somewhat expensive spot offers *choro*, samba and MPB.

Rio Scenarium Rua do Lavradio 20, Lapa ⓣ21/2233-3239, ⓦwww.riodcenarium.com.br. Located in an old baronial townhouse filled with antiques, this is nonetheless one of the liveliest places in Lapa. More popular for its music than for its dancing, visitors can sit on one of the several landings and watch the daily shows on the stage below. While specializing in *choro*, samba and local fusions are also performed. Reservations recommended on weekends.

Other live music

The largest music venue in Rio is *Claro Hall* in Barra da Tijuca, attracting **Brazilian and international stars**; programmes and tickets are available at ⓦwww.ticketmaster.com.br – expect to pay up to R$100. Top Brazilan artists (such as Caetano Veloso) also perform at *Canecão* (ⓣ21/2105-2000; ⓦwww.canecao.com.br; up to R$60), a venue next to the Rio Sul shopping centre in Botafogo. Despite the often superb shows, the venue feels overly formal, with up to 2000 people seated at tables being serviced by suited waiters offering food and drinks.

Brazilian dancing

Brazilians can dance, no question about that. The various regionally rooted traditions in folk music remain alive and popular, and, if you'd like to get into a bit of Brazilian swing, go in search of the more traditional dance halls.

Gafieiras

Gafieiras originally sprang up in the 1920s as ballrooms for the poorer classes, and today they remain popular because they are places where *cariocas* can be assured of traditional dance music. The oldest surviving of them is ✱ *Estudantina*,

Praça Tiradentes 79, Centro (Thurs 8pm–1am, Fri & Sat 10pm–4am), with decor recalling its roots dating back to 1928. Attracting locals and visitors of all ages, the live bands on the stage keep up to 1500 dancers moving. Also in Centro, but smaller and more traditional in style (with less modern music and dancers wearing formal attire) is the *Elite*, hidden away behind the arches of a pretty pink nineteenth-century building at Rua Frei Caneca 4 (Fri & Sat 11pm–4am, Sun 9pm–3am). If you're looking for a traditional *gafiera* in Lapa, check out *Assa Branca*; for the most beautiful of surroundings and lively Brazilian music, try *Botanic Dancing Brazil*, in the Jardim Botânico, from Thursdays to Sundays after 10pm. All these *gafieiras* charge around R$10 entrance.

Forró

For some accordion-driven swing from Brazil's Northeast, look for a **forró** club. The term *forró* (pronounced "fawhaw") originates from the English "for all", a reference to the dances financed by English engineering companies for their manual labour forces, as opposed to the balls organized for the elite. As drought and poverty have forced *nordestinos* to migrate south in search of employment in Brazil's large urban centres, so the culture has followed. In recent years *forró* has gained a following across the class divide and can often be heard in *gafieras* and even in the glitzy Zona Sul discos. Nevertheless, there are still some venues dedicated to *forró*. At Rua Catete 235, in the *bairro* of Catete, *Forró Forrado* (Fri–Sun 10pm–late), has an excellent band and a mixed clientele that spans Rio's social scale. On Saturday nights, there's also the *Forró da Praia*, on Avenida Nações Unidas near the Botafogo recreation ground, *Forró do Leblon* at Rua Bartolomeu Mitre 630 in Leblon, and *Forró do Copacabana* at Av. Nossa Senhora de Copacabana 435, in Copacabana.

Film, classical music and exhibitions

Rio is the home of the **Orquestra Sinfônica Brasileira** – the orchestra of the Theatro Municipal (see p.97), which is also home to the city's **ballet** troupe and **opera** company. The theatre serves as the venue for almost everything that happens in terms of "high culture", offering four or five major productions a year. All kinds of events attract famous names, and prices are reasonable. For musical, photographic and fine art **exhibitions**, keep an eye on the listings in the *Jornal do Brasil* or *Veja*.

The **Centro Cultural Banco do Brasil**, Rua Primeiro de Março 66, Centro (Tues–Sun 10am–9pm; ⓣ21/3808-2020, ⓦwww.bb.com.br/cultura), puts on an especially varied programme of exhibitions, as well as films, music and plays, often free. Situated in the grand former headquarters of the Banco do Brasil, the building has several exhibition halls, a cinema, two theatres, a tearoom and a restaurant. Also particularly worth checking out are the temporary exhibitions at the Instituto Moreira Salles (see p.118), Museu Chácara do Céu (see p.101) and the Museu Nacional Belas Artes (see p.97).

Film

Brazil is one of the world's largest film markets. Most European and American films are quickly released in Brazil and play to large audiences on big screens with their original soundtracks. **Cinemas** are quite inexpensive (R$10–17) and among the best are the Odeon in Praça Floriana, Cinelândia; Largo do Machado I & II and the São Luiz I & II, both in Largo do Machado; the Ricamar and the Roxy, along Avenida N.S. de Copacabana; and Condor Copacabana in Rua Figueiredo Magalhães. *Jornal do Brasil* lists what's on and where. There's an excellent chain of art-house cinemas, called Estação (ⓦwww.estacaovirtual.com), showing the latest

Brazilian and foreign films. Check out the Estação Paço, Praça XV de Novembro, Centro; Estação Paissandu, near the corner of Rua Senador Vergueiro 35, Flamengo; the Estação Botafogo, Rua Voluntários da Pátria 35 and also across the road at no. 88; and the Estação Ipanema at Rua Visconde de Pirajá 605.

Rio de Janeiro hosts one of Latin America's most important international film festivals, the **Festival do Rio**. The festival, which takes place over two weeks in late September and early October, is based in the *Copacabana Palace Hotel* (see p.86) and screens over four hundred films from dozens of countries in cinemas all over the city. For more information, contact the organizers at Rua Arnaldo Quintela 62, Botafogo (Ⓣ21/2543-4968; Ⓦwww.festivaldorui.com.br), in Flamengo.

Carnaval

Carnaval is celebrated in all of Brazil's cities, but Rio's party is the biggest and most flashy. From the Friday before Ash Wednesday to the following Thursday, the city shuts up shop and throws itself into the world's most famous manifestation of unbridled hedonism. Carnaval's greatest quality is that it has never become stale, thanks to its status as the most important celebration on the Brazilian calendar, easily outstripping either Christmas or Easter. In a city riven by poverty, Carnaval represents a moment of freedom and release, when the aspirations of *cariocas* can be expressed in music and song. And at the end of the very intense long weekend there's a brief collective hangover before attention turns to preparing for the following year's event.

The background

The origins of Carnaval in Rio can be traced back to a fifteenth-century tradition of Easter revelry in the Azores that caught on in Portugal and was exported to Brazil. Anarchy reigned in the streets for four days and nights, the festivities often so riotous that they were formally abolished in 1843 – this edict was ignored, however, allowing street celebrations to stand out as the most accessible and widely enjoyed feature of Carnaval ever since. In the mid-nineteenth century, **masquerade balls** – *bailes* – were first held by members of the social elite, while processions, with carriages decorated in allegorical themes, also made an appearance, thus marking the ascendancy of the procession over the general street melee. Rio's masses, who were denied admission to the balls, had their own music – *jongo* – and they reinforced the tradition of street celebration by organizing in *Zé Pereira* bands, named after the Portuguese tambor that provided the basic musical beat. The organizational structure behind today's samba schools (*escolas da samba*) was partly a legacy of those bands sponsored by migrant Bahian port workers in the 1870s. Theirs was a more disciplined approach to the Carnaval procession: marching to stringed and wind instruments, using costumes and appointing people to coordinate different aspects of the parade.

Music written specifically for Carnaval emerged in the early twentieth century, by composers like Chiquinho Gonzaga, who wrote the first recorded samba piece in 1917 (*Pelo Telefone*), and Mauro de Almeida e Donga. In the 1930s, recordings began to spread the music of Rio's Carnaval, and competition between different samba schools became institutionalized: in 1932 the Estação Primeira Mangueira school won the first prize for its performance in the Carnaval parade. The format has remained virtually unchanged since then, except for the emergence in the mid-1960s of the **blocos** or **bandas**: street processions by the residents of various *bairros*, who eschew style, discipline and prizes and give themselves up to the most traditional element of Carnaval – street revelry, of which even the principal Carnaval procession in the Sambódromo is technically a part.

The action

Rio's street celebrations centre on the **evening processions** that fill **Avenida Rio Branco** (*metrô* to Largo do Carioca or Cinelândia). Be prepared for the crowds and beware of pickpockets: even though the revellers are generally high-spirited and good-hearted, you should keep any cash you take with you in hard-to-reach places (like your shoes), wear only light clothes and leave your valuables locked up at the hotel.

Most of what's good takes place down the Avenida Rio Branco. The processions include samba schools (though not the best), *Clubes de Frevo*, whose loudspeaker-laden floats blast out the frenetic dance music typical of the Recife Carnaval, and the *Blocos de Empolgacão*, including the Bafo da Onça and Cacique de Ramos clubs, between which exists a tremendous rivalry. There are also *rancho* bands playing a traditional *carioca* carnival music that predates samba. See Ⓦwww.rio-carnival.net for a complete schedule of events.

Samba schools

The **samba schools**, each representing a different neighbourhood or social club, are divided into three leagues that vie for top ranking following the annual Carnaval parades. Division 1 (the top league) schools play in the Sambódromo,

Carnaval rehearsals

If you can't make Carnaval, give the shows put on for tourists in the Zona Sul a miss and get a taste of the samba schools at the *ensaios* (rehearsals) below. They take place at weekends from August to February: phone to confirm times and days. After New Year, Saturday nights are packed solid with tourists and prices triple. Instead, go to one on a mid-week evening or, better still, on Sunday afternoon when there's no entrance fee and locals predominate.

Most of the schools are in distant *bairros*, often in, or on the edge of, a *favela*, but there's no need to go accompanied by a guide. It's easy, safe and not too expensive to take a taxi there and back (there are always plenty waiting to take people home). Of the schools, Mangueira is certainly the most famous; it has a devoted following, a great atmosphere and includes children and old people amongst its dancers. The gay-friendly Salgueiro has a more white middle-class following.

The new Cidade da Samba (see p.96), a purpose-built arena and studio complex in Centro, is an even easier way of observing Carnaval preparations and watching rehearsals. All the Division 1 schools are represented here and their daily musical and dance demonstrations are mounted for the public.

Beija-Flor Rua Pracinha Wallace Paes Leme 1652, Nilopolis Ⓣ21/2253-2860, Ⓦwww.beija-flor.com.br. Founded 1948; blue and white. **Mangueira** Rua Visconde de Niterói 1072, Mangueira Ⓣ21/2567-4637, Ⓦwww.mangueira.com.br. Founded 1928; green and pink.

Moçidade Independente de Padre Miguel Rua Cel. Tamarindo 38, Padre Miguel Ⓣ21/3332-5823. Founded 1952; green and white.

Portela Rua Clara Nunes 81, Madureira Ⓣ21/3390-0471. Founded 1923; blue and white.

Salgueiro Rua Silva Telles 104, Tijuca Ⓣ21/2238-5564, Ⓦwww.salgueiro.com.br. Founded 1953; red and white.

Division 2 on Avenida Rio Branco and Division 3 on Avenida 28 de Setembro, near the Maracanã Stadium.

Preparations start in the year preceding Carnaval, as each samba school mobilizes thousands of supporters to create the various parts of the school's display. A theme is chosen, music written and costumes created, while the dances are choreographed by the **carnavelesco**, the school's director. By December, rehearsals have begun and, in time for Christmas, the sambas are recorded and released to record stores.

The main procession of Division 1 schools – the **Desfile** – takes place on the Sunday and Monday nights of Carnaval week in the purpose-built **Sambódromo**, further along the avenue beyond the train station; the concrete structure is 1700m long and can accommodate 90,000 spectators. The various samba schools – involving some 50,000 people – take part in a spectacular piece of theatre: no simple parade, but a competition between schools attempting to gain points from their presentation, which is a mix of song, story, dress, dance and rhythm. The schools pass through the Passarela da Samba, the Sambódromo's parade ground, and the judges allocate points according to a number of criteria. Each school must parade for between 85 and 95 minutes, no more and no less.

Regardless of the theme adopted by an individual samba school, all include certain basic elements within their performances. The **bateria**, the percussion section, has to sustain the cadence that drives the school's song and dance; the *samba enredo* is the music, the *enredo* the accompanying story or lyric. The **harmonia** refers to the degree of synchronicity between the *bateria* and the dance by the thousands of **passistas** (samba dancers); the dancers are conducted by the **pastoras**, who lead by example. The **evolução** refers to the quality of the dance, and the choreography is judged on its spontaneity, the skill of the *pastoras* and the excitement that the display generates. The costumes, too, are judged on their originality; their colours are always the traditional ones adopted by each school. The **carros alegóricos** (no more than ten metres high and eight wide) are the gigantic, richly decorated floats, which carry some of the **Figuras de Destaque** ("prominent figures"), amongst them the **Porta-Bandeira** ("flag bearer") – a woman who carries the school's symbol, a potentially big point scorer. The **Mestre-Sala** is the dance master, also an important symbolic figure, whose ability to sustain the rhythm of his dancers is of paramount importance. The **Comissão da Frente**, traditionally a school's "board of directors", marches at the head of the procession, a role often filled these days by invited TV stars or sports teams. The bulk of the procession behind is formed by the **alas**, the wings or blocks consisting of hundreds of costumed individuals each linked to a part of the school's theme.

In addition to a parade, every school has an **Ala das Baianas** – a procession of hundreds of women dressed in the flowing white costumes and African-style headdresses typical of Salvador – in remembrance of the debt owed to the Bahian emigrants, who introduced many of the traditions of the Rio Carnaval procession.

The **parade** of schools starts at 7.30pm, with eight Division 1 schools performing on each of the two nights, and goes on till noon the following day.

Carnaval dates

The four days of Carnaval for the next few years are as follows:

2007 Feb 17–20
2008 Feb 2–5
2009 Feb 21-24
2010 Feb 13-16
2011 March 5-8

Two stands (7 & 9) in the Sambódromo are reserved for foreign visitors and **seats** cost over R$150 per night. Though much more expensive than other areas, the seats here are more comfortable and have good catering facilities. Other sections of the Sambódromo cost from R$15 to R$60 and there are three seating options: the high stands (*arquibancadas*), lower stands (*geral*) and the ringside seats (*cadeiras de pista*) – the last being the best, consisting of a table, four chairs and full bar service.

Unless you have a very tough backside you will find sitting through a ten-hour show to be an intolerable test of endurance. Most people don't turn up until 11pm, by which time the show is well under way and hotting up considerably. **Tickets** are available from the organizers online (Ⓦwww.rio-carnival.net) or at premium prices from travel agents in Rio. Book well in advance if you can, or try local travel agents who often have tickets available for a modest commission.

Blocos

In whatever *bairro* you're staying there will probably be a **bloco** or **bandas** – a small samba school that doesn't enter an official parade – organized by the local residents; ask about them in your hotel. These schools offer a hint of what Carnaval was like before it became regulated and commercialized. Starting in mid-afternoon, they'll continue well into the small hours, the popular ones accumulating thousands of followers as they wend their way through the neighbourhood. They all have a regular starting point, some have set routes, others wander freely; but they're easy to follow – there's always time to have a beer and catch up later.

Some of the best *blocos* are: the Banda da Glória, which sets off from near the Estação Glória *metrô* station; the Banda da Ipanema (the first to be formed, in 1965), which gathers behind Praça General Osório in Ipanema; the Banda da Vergonha do Posto 6, starting in Rua Francisco Sá in Copacabana; and the Carmelitas de Santa Teresa, which gathers in the *bairro* of the same name. There are dozens of others, including several in each *bairro* of the Zona Sul, each providing a mix of music, movement and none-too-serious cross-dressing – a tradition during Carnaval that even the most macho of men indulge in.

Carnaval balls

It's the **Carnaval balls** that really signal the start of the celebrations – warm-up sessions in clubs and hotels for rusty revellers, which are quite likely to get out of hand as inhibitions give way to a rampant eroticism. The balls start late, normally after 10pm, and the continual samba beat supplied by live bands drives the festivities into the new day. At most of the balls, *fantasia* (fancy dress) is the order of the day, with elaborate costumes brightening the already hectic proceedings; don't worry if you haven't got one, though – just dress reasonably smartly.

You'll often have to pay an awful lot to get into these affairs, as some of the more fashionable ones attract the rich and famous. There's none more grand than the Magic Ball held at the *Copacabana Palace Hotel* (Ⓣ21/2545-8790; see p.86) attracting the elite from throughout the world. For the privilege of joining in, expect to pay well over R$1000 – black tie or an extravagant costume is obligatory. If you've got the silly costume but a little less money, other lavish balls worth checking out include the Pão de Açúcar, on the Friday before Carnaval, halfway up the famous landmark – spectacular views, exotic company, but well over R$200 a head and very snobby (Ⓣ21/3541-3737 for details). The Hawaiian Ball, hosted by the Rio Yacht Club, opens the season on the Friday of the week before Carnaval: it takes place around the club's swimming pool, amid lavish decorations, and is popular and expensive (about R$150); tickets are available from the Yacht Club, on Avenida Pasteur, a few hundred metres before the Sugar Loaf cable car terminus. On the same Friday other big parties take place, with the Baile de Champagne and the Baile Vermelho e Preto being amongst the most important. The latter (the "Red and Black Ball") has developed a particular reputation as a no-holds-barred affair. Named after the colours of Rio's favourite football team, Flamengo, it's a media event with TV cameras scanning the crowds for famous faces – exhibitionism is an inadequate term for the immodest goings-on at the Red and Black celebrations. In Leblon the Monte Libano (Ⓣ21/3239-0032 for details) hosts a number of "last days of Rome" festivities – the Baile das Gatas, Baile Fio Dental, even Bum Bum Night – sexually charged exercises all, though safe to attend and reasonable at around R$40 a ticket. In recent years, the *Rio Scala* club at Av. Afrânio de Melo Franco 292, Leblon has become an important centre for balls, each night of Carnaval hosting a different school of samba. To reserve a table (R$300) go to the box office (Ⓣ21/2239-4448) at least five days before the event. To stand, you can simply show up on the night – tickets cost R$40.

There are a number of **gay balls**, too, which attract an international attendance. The Grande Gala G is an institution, usually held in the *Help* disco on Copacabana's Avenida Atlântica. Another is the Baile dos Enxutos, hosted by the *Hotel Itália* on Praça Tiradentes, Centro.

Shopping

It's not hard to find things to buy in Rio, but it's surprisingly difficult to find much that's distinctively Brazilian. Throughout the city are shops geared to tourists (most of which sell a similar line in semi-precious stones, mounted piranha fish and T-shirts), but the best shopping area is undoubtedly Ipanema, with a wealth of boutiques lining Rua Visconde de Pirajá and its side streets. Books and CDs, however, make good purchases – sales assistants in music stores are usually delighted to offer recommendations and you'll be able to listen before you buy. Of Rio's **markets**, the so-called Hippie Market (see p.116) at Ipanema has nowadays become rather touristy; much better is the Babilônia Feira Hype (see p.117) in Gávea, or the Feira de Antigüidades at Praça Santos (Sun 9am–5pm), good for antiques (or, more accurately, bric-a-brac). For arts, crafts and food from Brazil's Northeast, there's nowhere better than the Feira de São Crisavão in the Zona Norte.

Shopping centres

Purpose-built, air-conditioned **shopping centres** – *shoppings* – have mushroomed in Rio during the last few decades. The largest, best known and most central is Rio Sul (Mon–Sat 10am–10pm, Sun 3–9pm), before the Pasmado Tunnel at the end of Botafogo. Inside there are department stores, a supermarket, and hundreds of fashion boutiques, record stores and places to grab a snack or meal. Other *shoppings* include the smaller Shopping Gávea, Rua Marquês de São Vicente (Mon–Sat 10am–10pm), and the upmarket São Conrado Fashion Mall, Estrada da Gávea 899 (Mon–Thurs 10am–9pm, Fri & Sat 10am–11pm, Sun 3–9pm). Definitely worth seeking out is Originallis, which has branches at all of Rio's *shoppings*. Brazil's answer to the Body Shop or Lush, the chain sells natural soaps infused with essential oils – the colours and smells are fantastic.

Crafts

Handicraft shops are scattered all over Rio but, in general, are disappointing. That said, some good places do exist – though bear in mind that the items on sale are more likely than not to be from other parts of the country. The places listed here all have excellent stocks and reasonable prices.

Brasil & Cia Rua Maria Quitéria 27, Ipanema. A range of carefully chosen ceramic, paper, textile and other crafts sourced from throughout the country.

Casa de Artesanato do Estado do Rio Rua Real Grandeza 293, Botafogo. Crafts from around the state of Rio, but the quality is unlikely to impress. Looks for occasional interesting items of basketry and embroidery.

Feira Nordestina (see p.104) in the Zona Norte. Stalls selling all kinds of handicrafts, hand-made household items, food and drink from Brazil's Northeast.

Loja Artíndia, Museu do Índio, Botafogo (see p.113). The best place in the city for Amerindian crafts – an excellent selection of basketry, necklaces, feather items and ceramics with the tribes and places of origin all clearly identified.

Raiz Forte Produtos da Terra Av. Ataulfo de Paiva 1160, Leblon. Specializing in crafts and popular art, including lithographs from Pernambuco.

O Sol, Rua Corcovado 213, Jardim Botânico. A non-profit outlet selling folk art including basketware, ceramics and wood carvings.

La Vereda Rua Almirante Alexandrino 428, Largo dos Guimarães, Santa Teresa. One of the best handicraft shops, with a varied collection from all over Brazil (including work by local artists).

Although not a shopping centre, Ipanema's Rua Visconde de Pirajá has similar stores to those found in the likes of Rio Sul, as well as some more unusual boutiques. Brightly coloured and interesting designs of bags and other accessories are the hallmark of the Brazilian designer Gilson Martins; his shop is located at Rua Visconde de Pirajá 462.

Music and books

CDs are much cheaper in Rio than in either Europe or North America and make great souvenirs. Many stores still have old recordings available on vinyl at bargain prices. The largest music stores in Rio include Modern Sound at Rua Barata Ribeiro 502 (near the corner of Rua Santa Clara), Copacabana, and the Saraiva Megastore, Rua do Ouvidor 98, Centro (with a branch in the Rio Sul shopping centre). For secondhand records, go to Top Discos, located at Rua Uruguaiana 18 and Rua 7 Setembro 139, with both branches in Centro.

Ipanema's Rua Visconde de Pirajá is home to several of Rio's better bookshops, with the largest and best being the Livraria da Travessa, at no. 572. The English-language section is small, but the shop has an excellent stock of art and other coffee-table books on Brazilian subjects. It also has a good selection of CDs, including many by Brazilian artists, as well as an excellent restaurant (see p.127). A smaller branch is located at no. 462 on the same street. The Saraiva Megastore (see above) also happens to be the largest bookshop in Centro, though its English-language section is limited. A great place to browse is the Café com Letras at Av. Bartolomeu Mitre 297, Leblon, where, apart from a good selection of titles, there's a café with excellent light meals and cakes and regular live music and Internet access. Smaller, but just as pleasant, is the Livraría e Café Largo das Letras (Weds–Sat 2–10pm & Sun 2–8pm), a community bookshop and café housed in an early twentieth-century mansion at Largo dos Guimarães in the heart of Santa Teresa.

Listings

Airlines Aerolíneas Argentinas ⓣ21/2242-7272 or 3398-3737; Air Canada ⓣ21/2220-5343; Air France ⓣ21/3212-1845 or 3398-3490; Alitalia ⓣ21/2292-4424 or 3398-3663; American Airlines ⓣ0800/789-7778; Avianca ⓣ21/2240-4413 or 3398-3145; British Airways ⓣ0300/789-6140 or 3398-3990; Continental Airlines ⓣ21/2531-1850 or 3398-3023; Delta Airlines ⓣ21/4003-2121; Gol ⓣ0800/701-2131; Iberia ⓣ21/2282-1336 or 3398-3164; Lan Chile ⓣ21/2240-9388 or 3398-3601; Lloyd Aéreo Boliviano ⓣ21/2220-9548 or 3398-4709; Lufthansa ⓣ21/2217-6111 or 3398-3855; Pluna ⓣ21/2240-8217 or 3398-2000; TAM ⓣ20/3212-9300 or 3398-2179; TAP–Air Portugal ⓣ0800/707-7787; United Airlines ⓣ0800/162-323 or 3398-2450; Varig ⓣ21/4003-7000.

Airports Galeão airport ⓣ21/3398-4526 or 3398-4527; Santos Dumont ⓣ21/3814-7070.

Banks and exchange Main bank branches are concentrated in Av. Rio Branco in Centro and Av. N.S. de Copacabana in Copacabana. Note that although most banks remain open until 4.30pm, you can usually exchange money only until 3pm or 3.30pm. There are ATMs located throughout the city.

Car rental Avis, Av. Princesa Isabel 150, Copacabana ⓣ21/2542-3392; Hertz, Av. Princesa Isabel 334, Copacabana ⓣ21/2275-3245 & 0800-701-7300; Interlocadora, Av. Princesa Isabel 186, Copacabana ⓣ21/2275-7440; Localiza-National, Av. Princesa Isabel 214, Copacabana ⓣ0800-99-2000; Unidas, Av. Princesa Isabel 350, Copacabana ⓣ21/2275-8496. Prices start at about R$100 per day and you'll need a credit card to rent the vehicle. It's often cheaper to reserve in advance from abroad.

Consulates Argentina, Praia de Botafogo 228, Botafogo ⓣ21/2553-1646; Australia, Av. Presidente Wilson 231, 23rd floor, Centro ⓣ21/3824-4624; Canada, Av. Atlântica 1130, 5th floor, Copacabana ⓣ21/2543-3004; Ireland, Rua 24 de Maio 347, Riachuelo ⓣ21/2501-4975; Peru, Av. Rui Barbosa 314, 2nd floor, Flamengo ⓣ21/2551-9596; UK, Praia do Flamengo 284, 2nd floor, Flamengo ⓣ21/2555-9600; US, Av. Presidente Wilson 147, Centro ⓣ21/3823-2000; Uruguay, Praia de Botafogo 242, Botafogo ⓣ21/2552-6699; Venezuela, Praia de Botafogo 242, Botafogo ⓣ21/2551-5398.

Dentists Dentário Rollin, Rua Cupertinho Durão 81, Leblon ⓣ21/2259-2647; Clínica de Urgência, Rua Marquês de Abrantes 27, Botafogo ⓣ21/2226-0083; Sorriclin, Rua Visconde de Pirajá 207, Ipanema ⓣ21/2522-1220.

Health matters For medical emergencies, English-speakers should try a private clinic such as Sorocaba Clinic, Rua Sorocaba 464, Botafogo (ⓣ21/2286-0022) or Centro Médico Ipanema, Rua Anibal Mendonça 135, Ipanema (ⓣ21/2239-4647). For general medical treatment, try Medtur, Av. N.S. de Copacabana 647, Copacabana (ⓣ21/2235-3339). Your best bet for any non-emergencies is the Rio Health Collective, Banco Nacional building (room 303), Av. das Américas 4430, Barra de Tijuca; a non-profit organization, its phone-in service (ⓣ21/3325-9300, ext 44) is free and provides names of qualified professionals who speak foreign languages. Alternatively, your consulate should have a list of professionals who speak your language.

Internet Available in all hostels and most hotels. Try also Comprio, Rua da Assembléia 10, basement loja 114, Centro (Mon–Fri 9am–6.30pm); Telerede Internet Café, Rua N.S. de Copacabana 209, Copacabana (8am–midnight); Letras e Expressões, Rua Visconde de Pirajá 276, Ipanema (8am–midnight).

Laundry All hotels have a laundry service, but these are always very expensive, while most hostels have laundry facilities. Good prices for service washes and dry cleaning are offered by Lavanderia Ipanema, Rua Farme de Amoedo 55, Ipanema (Mon–Sat 7.30am–9pm) and Lavakilo, Rua Almirante Gonçalves 50, Copacabana (Mon–Fri 7.30am–7.30pm & Sat 8am–5pm).

Newspapers and magazines Foreign-language newspapers and magazines are available in kiosks at junctions along Av. N.S. de Copacabana, Copacabana, on Rua Visconde de Pirajá in Ipanema, and along Av. Rio Branco in Centro as well as in the bookstore Letras e Expressões, Rua Visconde de Pirajá 276, Ipanema. The *Herald Tribune* and the *Financial Times* are the most commonly available English-language newspapers in Rio, and *Time*, *Newsweek* and the *Economist* are also easy to find. The *Jornal do Brasil* and *O Globo* are Rio's two main newspapers, while the weekly news magazine *Veja* features a useful insert (*Veja Rio*) that lists and reviews cultural events in the city.

Pharmacies 24-hour service from Farmácia do Leme, Av. Prado Junior 237, Leme; Drogaria Pacheco, Av. N.S. de Copacabana 115, Copacabana; City Farma, Rua Gomes Carneiro 144, Ipanema; Farmácia Piauí, Av. Ataúlfo de Paiva 1283, Ipanema.

Police Emergency number ⓣ190. The beach areas have police posts located at regular intervals. The special Tourist Police are located at Av. Afrânio de Melo Franco (opposite the Teatro Casa Grande),

Leblon (☎21/3399-7170); they are helpful, speak English and efficiently process reports of theft or other incidents. Open 24 hours a day, 7 days a week.

Post offices *Correios* are open Mon–Fri 8am–6pm, Sat 8am–noon. Main post offices are at Rua Primeiro do Março (corner of Rosario) in Centro; Av. N.S. de Copacabana 540 in Copacabana; Rua Visconde de Pirajá 452, Ipanema; Av. Ataúlfo de Paiva 822, Leblon.

Public holidays In addition to the normal Brazilian public holidays (see p.65), most things close in Rio on January 20 (Dia de São Sebastião) and March 1 (Founding of the City).

Visa and tourist card renewal If you're going to stay in Brazil for over six months and need to extend your visa or tourist card, apply in person at the Polícia Federal's Registro de Estrangeiros, Av. Venezuela 2, Centro – just behind Praça Mauá (Mon–Fri 10am–4pm; ☎21/3263-3747).

Rio de Janeiro state

It's easy to get out of Rio city, something you'll probably want to do at some stage during your stay. There are good **bus** services to all the places mentioned below, while the easiest trips are by ferry just over the bay to the **Ilha de Paquetá** – a car-free zone popular with locals – or to **Niterói**, whose Museu de Arte Contemporânea has become an essential sight for visitors to Rio. After that, the choice is a simple one: either head east along the **Costa do Sol** to Cabo Frio and Búzios, or west along the **Costa Verde** to Ilha Grande and Paraty; both coasts offer endless good beaches and little holiday towns, developed to varying degrees. Or strike off **inland** to Petrópolis and Teresópolis, where the mountainous interior provides a welcome, cool relief from the frenetic goings-on back in Rio.

Inter-urban buses fanning out to all points in the state make getting out of the city easy. If you plan on **renting a car** (see opposite for addresses in Rio), this is as good a state as any to brave the traffic: the coasts are an easy drive from the city and stopping off at more remote beaches is simple; additionally, having your own wheels would let you get to grips with the extraordinary scenery up in the mountains. If you've never driven in Brazil before, it's a good idea to collect your car on a Sunday when traffic in Rio is fairly light and there are few trucks on the highways outside of the city.

Ilha de Paquetá

The **ILHA DE PAQUETÁ** is an island of one square kilometre in the north of Guanabara Bay, an easy day-trip that is very popular with *cariocas* at weekends. It was first occupied by the Portuguese in 1565 and later was a favourite resort of Dom João VI, who had the São Roque chapel built here in 1810. During the naval revolt of 1893 against the government of Floriano Peixoto, the island was the insurgents' principal base: their HQ, the Chácara dos Coqueiros, still stands, though it's not open to the public. Nowadays the island is almost entirely given over to tourism. About 2000 people live here, but at weekends that number is multiplied several times by visitors from the city. They come for the tranquillity – the only motor vehicle allowed is an ambulance – and for the beaches, which, sadly, are now heavily polluted. Still, the island makes a pleasant day's excursion – with colonial-style buildings that retain a certain shabby charm – and the trip is an attraction in itself: if possible, time your return to catch the sunset over the city as you sail back. Weekdays are best if you want to avoid the crowds, or come in August for the wildly celebrated **Festival de São Roque**.

The best way to get around Ilha de Paquetá is by **bike**, thousands of which are available to rent very cheaply from alongside the ferry terminal; you can also take a ride in a small horse-drawn cart (*charrete*) or rent one by the hour if you want to take your time and stop off along the way – not that there's a great deal to see. When you disembark, head along the road past the Yacht Club and you'll soon reach the first **beaches**: Praia da Ribeira and Praia dos Frades. **Praia da Guarda**, a few hundred metres on, has the added attraction of the *Lido* restaurant and the **Parque Duque de Mattos**, with its exuberant vegetation and panoramic views from the top of the Morro da Cruz, a hill riddled with tunnels dug to extract china clay.

Practicalities

Ferries (see p.81) for Paquetá leave from near Rio's Praça XV de Novembro, Centro; the seventy-minute ride costs R$3.30 on weekdays and R$4.50 at weekends.

If you want to stay over, there are a few pleasant small **hotels**, the cheapest being the *Paquetá* at Praça Bom Jesus 15 (Ⓣ21/3397-0052; ❷). More expensive, but with air conditioning, are the *Lido*, Praia José Bonifácio 59 (Ⓣ21/3397-0377; ❸), and the *Flamboyant* at Praia Grossa 58 (Ⓣ21/397-0028; ❸), the largest hotel on the island. There's a **tourist office** on Praia José Bonifácio, near the intersection with Rua Manuel de Macedo, on the opposite side of the island from the ferry landing.

East: Niterói and the Costa do Sol

Across the strait at the mouth of Guanabara Bay lies **Niterói**, founded in 1573 and until 1975 the capital of the old state of Guanabara. Though lacking the splendour of the city of Rio, Niterói, with a population of half a million, has a busy commercial centre, an important museum and lively nightlife – well worth a visit, certainly, as it's also the gateway to the **Costa do Sol** to the east.

Buses out of Niterói head east along the Costa do Sol, which is dominated by three large **lakes** – Maricá, Saquerema and Araruama, separated from the ocean by long, narrow stretches of white sandy beach – and flecked with small towns bearing the same names as the lakes. Approximately 10km directly south of Niterói are a number of smaller lakes, too, collectively known as the **Lagos Fluminenses**, though these aren't really worth the effort to get to as the water is polluted. However, the evil-smelling sludge that surrounds them is purported to have medicinal properties. The main lakes are also muddy, but at least the water here is clean and much used for water sports of all kinds. The brush around the lakes is full of wildlife (none of it particularly ferocious), while the fresh, salty air makes a pleasing change from the city streets.

Niterói

Cariocas have a tendency to sneer at **NITERÓI**, typically commenting that the only good thing about the city is its views back across Guanabara Bay to Rio. While it's certainly true that the vistas are absolutely gorgeous on a clear day, Niterói has plenty more to offer, not least of which is the stunning Oscar Niemeyer–designed **Museu de Arte Contemporânea** (Tues–Fri 10am–6pm; R$4; Wed free), or MAC as it is more commonly called. Opened in 1996, and located just south of the centre on a promontory by the Praia da Boa Viagem, the flying saucer–shaped building offers a 360-degree perspective of Niterói and across the bay to Rio. The museum boasts a worthy, though hardly exciting,

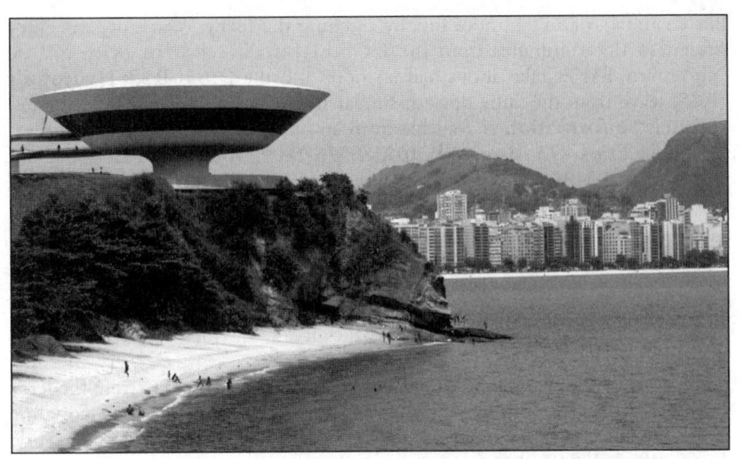

△ Museu de Arte Contemporânea

permanent display of Brazilian art of the second half of the twentieth century and also hosts temporary exhibitions, although these are rarely of much interest. Instead, the real work of art is the building itself, which even hardened critics of Niemeyer find difficult to dismiss out of hand. The curved lines of the building are simply beautiful, and the views of the headland, nearby beaches and Guanabara Bay as you walk around inside it breathtaking.

The Museu de Arte Contemporânea aside, Niterói has a few other sights worth seeing, but they are in isolated spots throughout the city. A short distance southwest of the ferry terminal, the **Ilha da Boa Viagem** (April–Dec, 4th Sun of each month, 1–5pm), connected to the mainland by a causeway leading from Vermelha and Boa Viagem beaches, offers yet more excellent views across the bay to Rio. On the island, guarding the entrance to the bay, are the ruins of a fort, built in 1663, and opposite there's a small chapel dating from the seventeenth century.

Niteroí's beaches are every bit as good as those of Rio's Zona Sul. **Praia de Jurujuba**, long and often crowded, is reached from the centre along the beautiful bayside road by bus #33 ("via Fróes"). On the way, it's worth taking a look at the church of **São Francisco Xavier**, a pretty colonial structure said to have been built in 1572. The church is open rather irregularly, but the priest lives next door and will open it up on request.

A short distance southeast along the coast, through Jurujuba, is the **Fortaleza de Santa Cruz**, dating from the sixteenth century. The largest fort guarding the bay, it's still in use as a military establishment, but you can visit daily between 9am and 4pm (except Mon). As the nearest point across the bay to Rio's Sugar Loaf mountain, the views are particularly good from here. If you have time, also check out the **Museu de Arqueologia de Itaipu** (Wed–Sun 1–5pm), in the ruined eighteenth-century Santa Teresa convent near Itaipu beach, for its collection of ceramics and other artefacts excavated from ancient burial mounds. Around here, to the east of Niterói, beyond the bay, there are numerous **restaurants**, **bars and hotels**, all of which fill up with *cariocas* at weekends.

Practicalities

You can reach Niterói either by car or **bus** across the 14km of the Ponte Costa e Silva, the Rio–Niterói bridge (bus #999 from the Menezes Cortes bus terminal), or, much more fun, by catching the **ferry**, which departs every fifteen to thirty minutes from the CONERJ docks, close to Praça XV de Novembro; ferries take about half an hour and the fare is R$2. **Hydrofoils** (R$5) leave from the same dock at similar intervals and take just ten minutes.

Tourist information is available from an office in São Francisco at Estrada Leopoldo Fróes 773 (9am–6pm, ⓣ21/3376-1809), some distance from both the ferry and MAC. Although there are some good **places to eat** in Niterói, none is outstanding. Worth considering, however, are *Coelho á Caçarola* at Av. Central 20, in Itaipu (closed Mon–Wed), which has on its menu some 25 rabbit dishes; *Churrascaria Vacaria do Sul* at Rua do Rosário 147, the best place in town to satisfy a meat craving; *Dona Henriqueta* at Rua Francisco Dutra 147, which is a fine Portuguese restaurant; and the excellent *Marius,* 7km from the centre at Praia de Charitas, at Av. Prefeito Sílvio Picanço 479, which specializes in crab dishes.

Finally, a word of warning: although MAC is located just 1.5km from the ferry terminal, do not attempt to walk there, as tourists have been robbed along the route. A taxi won't cost much, and it's also possible to take a bus to Praia de Icaraí and walk from there.

Maricá and Saquerema

MARICÁ, 40km from Niterói, is the first stop on the Costa do Sol. A sprawling fishing centre standing on the north bank of the lagoon, its peaceful waters are only narrowly separated from the ocean surf by the **Barra de Maricá** and **Ponta Negra** beaches, which are more laid-back than Rio's Zona Sul. From Ponta Negra the view of the coast is breathtaking. Nearby, in **UBATIBA**, the colonial farm of Rio Fundo has been turned into a museum exhibiting relics from the centuries of slavery.

SAQUEREMA, 100km east of Rio, is a smaller town in a beautiful natural setting, squeezed between the sea and its sixteen-kilometre-long lagoon, retaining vestiges of its origins as a fishing village. Local anti-pollution legislation means that the environment still sustains much wildlife, including the *microleão* monkey, which you may be able to glimpse on a walk into the nearby forests. Saquerema has a healthy agricultural sector, too, based on fruit cultivation, and orchards surround the town. The main business nowadays, though, is holiday-making: you'll find holiday homes, arts and crafts shops and young surfers here in abundance. Saquerema is widely rated as second only to Florianópolis (see p.722) as Brazil's surfing capital, and the **Praia de Itaúna**, 3km from town, is a favourite with the surfers, who gather every year for the National Championship in mid-May. A strong undertow makes its waters potentially dangerous for the casual swimmer, so if you want to swim without struggling against the currents head instead for the **Praia da Vila**, where the seventeenth-century church, Nossa Senhora de Nazaré (daily 8am–5pm), stands on the rocky promontory. For fishing, the **Praia de Jaconé** is a popular haunt, stretching 4km west of Saquerema.

All in all, if you're looking for a place to stop awhile, there's a lot to recommend Saquerema: a relaxed atmosphere, plenty of bars and restaurants, and lots of action at the weekend. **Places to stay** near the centre of town include the *Costa do Sol*, Av. Salgado Filho 5720 (ⓣ22/2651-1233; ❸) an inexpensive but tidy option, and the *Lagoa Azul*, Av. Saquerema 1580 (ⓣ22/2651-1142; ❹), which has a pool and more comfortable rooms. Further out, on the Praia de Itaúna, is the small and attractive *Pousada do Suiço*, Rua das Pitangas 580 (ⓣ22/2651-2203; ❸), also with a pool.

Araruama and around

Fourteen kilometres further along the coast, **ARARUAMA** stands on the edge of one of the largest lakes in Brazil. The lake – of the same name as the town – covers an area of 192 square kilometres, its saline water fringed with sand that is said to be effective in treating rheumatic and dermatological conditions.

The town itself has sprawled considerably over recent years as holiday homes, campsites and hotels have sprung up to accommodate the growing numbers of *cariocas* who come here at the weekend. There's no shortage of unpolluted **beaches** within walking distance, though the most popular ones are located some distance away – **Praia Seca**, the nearest of these, with its impressive dunes, is about 16km away, part of the much larger **Maçambaba** beach, which continues all the way to Arraial do Cabo (see p.146). The road between Araruama and Cabo Frio passes alongside these beaches; there's an occasional bus, or you can take a taxi, though either way it can be hard to get transport back.

Several moderately priced **places to stay** line the road out towards Praia Seca. Two good *pousadas*, both with pools, are the *Suba Pra Ver* at Km 11 (Ⓣ22/2661-2171; ❸), with pleasant rooms on attractive grounds, and the *Praia dos Amores* at Km 3.5 (Ⓣ22/2665-6005, Ⓦwww.praiadosamores.com.br; ❸), where the simple but well-decorated rooms are slightly more comfortable and afford wonderful views across the lake.

São Pedro da Aldeia

The countryside around Araruama is one of Brazil's most important salt-producing regions, and the windmills that pull the saline solution up to the surface dominate the skyline. The saltpans into which the solution emerges are of various sizes but are always square and arranged juxtaposed like a great patchwork quilt, speckled with small piles of salt brushed into heaps from the surface of the pans. At the north end of the Lagoa de Araruama, the small town of **SÃO PEDRO DA ALDEIA**, a 22-kilometre bus ride east of Araruama on the way to Cabo Frio, is built around a Jesuit church and mission house (Mon–Fri 8am–noon & 2–5pm, Sat & Sun 8am–noon), which date back to 1617. Perched on a hill above the shores of the lake, the town provides a marvellous view over the saltpans and surrounding area.

The cheapest **pousada** in town, located beside an attractive lagoon, is the *Aldeia dos Ventos*, Rua João Martins 160 (Ⓣ22/2621-2919; ❸), with very basic rooms. It's worth paying more, however, for the colonial-style *Pousada Ponta da Peça* (Ⓣ22/2621-1181, Ⓦwww.pontadapeca.com.br; ❹), 5km from town on the Praia do Sudoeste, for its well-appointed rooms, pretty garden with a pool and stunning views across the lagoon and surrounding countryside. Excellent fish dishes can be had at the *Restaurante Vovó Chica* at Av. Getúlio Vargas 32.

Cabo Frio

During the summer months, and especially at weekends, **CABO FRIO** is at a pitch of holiday excitement, generated by the out-of-towners who come here to relax in the fresh sea breezes. The town was founded in the late sixteenth century, but it was only really in the twentieth century that it developed, thanks to the salt and tourist industries. Built around sand dunes, there are **beaches** everywhere in Cabo Frio – indeed, this is the only attraction, since the town is both extremely ugly and poorly planned, but it's a relaxed place and the bars are full of happy holiday-makers at night.

The closest beaches to town are the small **Praia do Forte**, near the centre, with its fort of **São Mateus** (daily 8am–6pm) built by the French in 1616 for protection against pirates, and the larger, more popular **Praia da Barra**. The best beaches, though, all lie outside Cabo Frio, a taxi ride or decent walk away on the route to Arraial do Cabo, another small town a few kilometres to the south. Six kilometres north in the direction of Búzios, near Ogivas, lies **Praia do Peró**, a good surfing spot, peaceful and deserted on weekdays, and further on is the small **Praia das Conchas**, with its sand dunes and clear, calm, blue waters.

On arrival, it's a three-kilometre walk in from the **bus station** to the centre, along Avenida Júlia Kubitschek. There are excellent bus connections to and from Rio, São Paulo, Belo Horizonte and Petrópolis as well as up and down the coast. Praça Porto Rocha, the location of the telephone office and a branch of Banco do Brasil, marks the centre of town. Alongside the square is one of the town's very few buildings of note, the church of **Nossa Senhora da Assunção**, built in 1615 by the Jesuits, which has been perfectly preserved. One block west of here, at Largo de Santo Antônio 55, is the post office.

Practicalities

There are plenty of **hotels** and **pousadas** in and around Cabo Frio, though during summer weekends it can be impossible to find a room. The **tourist office** (Mon–Fri 8am–6pm, Sat & Sun 9am–6pm; ⓣ22/2647-6227) at Praça Cristóvão Colombo near to the Praia do Forte can help find you a room. The lowest-priced *pousadas*, all offering pretty basic accommodation, are in the town centre on Rua Jorge Lóssio and Rua José Bonifácio; the best ones include *Porto Fino* on the former at no. 160 (ⓣ22/2643-6230; ④) and *Cochicho do Xandico* at no. 224 (ⓣ22/2643-2525; ④), and on the latter, *Atlântico* at no. 302 (ⓣ22/2643-0996; ③). Most hotels and *pousadas*, and those with better facilities, however, are concentrated along the beaches. Praia do Peró boasts Cabo Frio's most expensive hotel, the well-appointed *La Plage* (ⓣ22/2643-1746, ⓦwww.redebela.com.br; ⑥), along with the more attractive *Quintais das Dunas* (ⓣ22/2643-3894; ⑤), which also has a pool. The *Porto Peró* (ⓣ22/2644-5568, ⓦwww.pousadaportopero.com.br; ④), a new, rather characterless *pousada*, has the advantage of being on a particularly attractive stretch of beach. There's also a very popular **youth hostel** at Rua Goiás 266 (ⓣ22/2644-3123, ⓦwww.perohostel.com.br; R$40 per person), with rooms sleeping two to six people.

Cabo Frio has no shortage of **restaurants** in either the town centre or on the beaches. In the centre, the *Picolino* at Rua Marechal Floriano 319 is noted for serving the town's best fish dishes, while at Praia do Forte, *La Carreta*, Av. Nilo Peçanha 443, is an excellent *churrascaria*.

Arraial do Cabo

Six kilometres south of Cabo Frio, **ARRAIAL DO CABO** nestles amongst more sand dunes, surrounded by hills. It's home to the Institute of Marine Research, based on Cabo Frio island 4km east of the village, whose object is to increase the level of marine life in the region. The aim is a laudable one, though it's uncertain whether the real purpose has more to do with replenishing stocks for next season's marine sports than preserving the area's ecology. The **beaches** around Arraial do Cabo are some of the most beautiful in the state and are usually packed in high season. Praia dos Anjos is perfectly fine considering the area behind is so built up, though you'd do much better by walking (15mins) along a path over a steep promontory to the unspoilt Praia do Forno. A boat ride is required to reach the absolutely stunning Praia do Pontal and the **Ilha de Cabo Frio**, a small, pristine island with powdery white beaches, sand dunes and superb views from its 390-metre peak. Boats leave from Praia dos Anjo and charge around R$30 per person for a four-hour excursion. Another attractive beach is Prainha, which has the advantage of shade but can get crowded as it's easily reached by car. Even so, the water is beautiful and it's easy to ignore the people around you. At all beaches – even the most isolated – you can get drinks and snacks.

Arraial do Cabo is a much more attractive place to stay than overdeveloped Cabo Frio, but has little in the way of budget **accommodation**. Your best bet is to make for the Praia dos Anjos: the *Estalagem do Porto* (Ⓣ22/2622-2892, Ⓦwww.estalagemdoporto.com.br; ❺) is a comfy place with rooms sleeping up to six people; *Capitão n'Areia* (Ⓣ22/2622-2720, Ⓦwww.capitaopousada.com.br; ❹) is a similar but rather prettier *pousada*, with the added attraction of a pool. Also at Praia dos Anjos, there's an excellent IYHF **youth hostel** at Rua Bernardo Lens 145 (Ⓣ22/2622-4060, Ⓦwww.marinadosanjos.com.br; R$40 per person), with dorms as well as private rooms that sleep two people (members ❸, non-members ❹). Guests can rent canoes, diving equipment and bicycles, and the staff are extremely knowledgeable about the local area.

Búzios

Keep time free for **ARMAÇÃO DOS BÚZIOS**, or Búzios as it's more commonly known; direct buses run to this peninsula from Rio at least seven times a day, or every fifteen minutes from Cabo Frio, a bumpy fifty-minute ride along a cobbled road. A place of great natural beauty and with less than 35 days of rain a year, mostly falling in September and October, it's a bit like taking a step out of Brazil and into an upscale Mediterranean resort: Armação, the main settlement, is built in a vaguely Portuguese colonial style, its narrow cobbled streets are lined with restaurants, bars and chic boutiques, and even the surrounding landscape appears more Mediterranean than Brazilian. Búzios has been nicknamed "Brazil's St Tropez", and it comes as little surprise to find that it was "discovered" by none other than Brigitte Bardot, who stumbled upon it by accident while touring the area in 1964. Despite being transformed overnight from humble fishing village to playground of the rich, Búzios didn't change much until some serious property development took hold in the 1980s. Now, during the high season (Dec to Feb), the population swells from 22,000 to well over 150,000, the fishing boats that once ferried the catch back to shore take pleasure-seekers beach-hopping and scuba diving, and the roads connecting the town with the outlying beaches have been paved. This is the kind of place one either loves or hates: if a crowded resort full of high-spending beautiful people is your thing, then you're sure to fall for Búzios; if not, give it a miss. Outside of the peak summer high season it's hard not to be taken in by the peninsula's sheer beauty, with March and April the perfect time to visit as tourists are relatively few, prices low and the weather generally perfect.

Accommodation

Accommodation in Búzios is expensive and in the high season reservations are essential, although the tourist offices will do their best to help you find a room in one of the resort's more than 150 hotels and *pousadas*. If nothing's available in Búzios, you might consider staying in Cabo Frio, where rooms are always cheaper and easier to come by. The lower-priced *pousadas* can be found in or near Armação or Ossos; they are generally the nicest, too, as well as very friendly and mainly owned and run by Argentines, who have been an important presence in Búzios since the 1960s – even today making up two-thirds of the tourists. The price codes below are based on high-season prices; at other times you can expect hefty discounts.

Búzios Central Hostel Av. José Bento Ribeiro Dantas 1475, Armação ⓣ22/2623-9232; ⓦwww.buzioscentral.com.br. While the double rooms are small (❻) and the dorms are equally cramped (R$33 per person), the pleasant common areas and general atmosphere makes this one of the best HI-affiliated youth hostels in Brazil.

Hibiscus Beach Rua 1, Praia de João Fernandes ⓣ22/2623-6221, ⓦwww.hibiscusbeach.com.br. Spacious bungalows, each with a small terrace and wonderful sea views, make up this welcoming British-owned and -run *pousada*. There's a good-sized pool and the area's best snorkelling beach is very close, while Armaçao's nightlife is a five-minute taxi ride (or half-hour walk) away. ❻

Meu Sonho Av. José Bento Ribeiro Dantas 1289, Ossos ⓣ22/2623-0902; ⓦwww.meusonho-buzios.8k.com. Located one block from the beach, this *pousada* has clean, basic rooms and a plunge pool, with the only Internet café in Búzios next door. ❼

Morombo Av. José Bento Ribeiro Dantas 1242, Armação ⓣ22/2623-1532. An extremely hospitable Argentine owner, good rooms and an attractive terrace make this an appealing place to stay. Located on the waterfront road leading to Ossos. ❹

Recanto do Mar Praça Santos Dumont 304, Armação ⓣ22/2623-4413. Room are simple and small and the staff is rather unfriendly, but the lounge is attractive and it's right in the centre of Armação. ❹

Santa Fé Praça Santos Dumont 300, Armação ⓣ22/2623-6404, ⓦwww.pousadasantafe.com. Similar in just about every respect to the *Recanto do Mar*, including the staff's distant attitude. Even so, it's good value and very popular thanks to its proximity to Búzios's nightlife. ❺

Seria Dourada Praia dos Ossos ⓣ22/2623-1131. One of the cheapest places to stay in Búzios. Rooms are basic but comfortable, with a quiet beach-side location. ❸

Solar do Peixe Vivo Rua José Bento Ribeiro Dantas 999, Armação ⓣ22/2623-1850, ⓦwww.solardopeixevivo.com.br. At this friendly, relaxed place, the guest rooms, in cabins in the garden, are simple but spacious; there's a pool in the garden and the beach is directly across the road. The main reception building is notable for being one of the oldest structures in Búzios. ❺

Vila do Mar Travessa dos Pescadores 88, Armação ⓣ22/2623-1466. A very attractive rustic-chic *pousada*, with comfortable rooms – some with sea views – and a small pool. ❻

The town and its beaches

Búzios consists of three main settlements, each with its own distinct character. **Manguinos**, on the isthmus, is the main service centre with a tourist office (24hr; ⓣ0800/24-9999), a medical centre, banks and petrol stations. Midway along the peninsula, linked to Manguinos by a road lined with brash hotels, is **Armação**, an attractive village where cars are usually banned from the cobbled roads. Most of Búzio's best restaurants and boutiques are concentrated here, along with some of the resort's nicest *pousadas*, and there's also a helpful tourist office on the main square, Praça Santos Dumont (daily 9am–8pm; ⓣ22/2623-2099). A fifteen-minute walk along the coast from Armação, passing the lovely seventeenth-century Igreja Nossa Senhora de Sant'Ana on the way, brings you to **Ossos**, the oldest settlement, comprised of a pretty harbour, a quiet beach and a few bars, restaurants and *pousadas*.

Within walking distance of all the settlements are beautiful white-sand **beaches**, 27 in total, cradled between rocky cliffs and promontories, and bathed by crystal blue waters. A good way to get oriented is to hop on the **Búzios Trolley** (9am, noon, 3pm; 2 hrs; R$40 including drinks and snacks) at Praça Santos Dumont, which goes to twelve beaches and two look-out points and offers an English-language commentary on the peninsula's vegetation, micro-climate and history. The beaches are varied, with the north-facing ones having the calmest and warmest seas, while those facing the south and east have the most surf. Though the beaches at Búzios' urban centre of Armação – the **Praia do Canto** and **Praia da Armação** and, to a lesser extent, the **Praia dos Ossos** – look good, the water is polluted and swimming should be avoided; a short distance to the northeast of Armação, however, are the very clean waters of the small, rather isolated and extremely picturesque beaches of **Azeda** and **Azedinha** as well as the rather larger **João Fernandes**, the best place around here for snorkelling. Further east is **Praia Brava**, which is rarely over-crowded as there are few hotels close by. On the north of the peninsula, to the west of Armação, is the **Praia da Tartaruga**, where the water is pristine and, apart from some bars, there are few buildings. South of Armação the lovely bay of **Praia da Ferradura** is quite built up (and consequently crowded), but not nearly as bad as **Praia de Geribá**, which is solidly backed by condominium developments. Further out, the appealing **Praia de Tucuns** is a long stretch of sand that attracts surprisingly few people. Apart from walking, you can get from beach to beach by minivan ($R1.50), taxi (rarely more than R$10) or by hitching lifts, a fairly common way of getting around though, as usual, caution should be taken. Once at the beaches, you can rent kayaks or *pedalos*, or indulge in a little windsurfing. Several dive operators, based in Armação, lead scuba trips to the Ilha Âncoa (R$180 for two dives) – try Casamar, based at Rua das Pedras 241 (Ⓣ22/2623-2441, Ⓦwww.casamar.com.br). Alternatively, the dive operators rent snorkelling equipment (R$15 a day) for use at Praia João Fernandes.

Eating

With few exceptions, **restaurants** are, predictably, expensive. The best places to eat, including those listed below, are concentrated in Armação, especially along Rua das Pedras and its extension, Avenida José Bento Ribeiro Dantas. Cheaper options include some excellent *por kilo* restaurants in the town centre or the beachside *barracas* selling grilled fish.

Acquarello Rua das Pedras 130. An elegant (and expensive) Italian restaurant with a menu that includes some unusual dishes, such as shrimp flambéed in cognac with a tomato curry cream sauce.

Bananaland Rua Manoel Turíbio de Farias 50, on a parallel street to Rua das Pedras. One of the best *por kilo* restaurant in Búzios, and one of the cheapest for a solid meal; the choice amongst the buffet of salads and hot dishes is outstanding.

Buzin Rua Manoel Turibio de Farias 273, on the road immediately parallel to Rua das Pedras. The extensive and sophisticated range of dishes at this pleasant and moderately priced *por kilo* restaurant includes unusual salads, seafood and excellent Argentine beef. Similar *por kilo* fare is offered at *Boom* on the same road at no. 110.

Chez Michou Crêperie Rua das Pedras 90. Thanks to its open-air bar, cheap drinks and authentic crêpes, this has long been Armação's most popular hangout. Open until dawn, when it serves breakfast to the patrons pouring out of the *Fashion Café*.

Cigalon Rua das Pedras 265. Excellent, authentic French cooking, with the occasional uniquely Brazilian ingredient thrown in. The house specialities are duck breast in a honey, ginger and pear sauce, and prawns flambéed with cognac served with almond rice. Formal and expensive, but remarkable value for a top restaurant.

Estância Don Juan Rua das Pedras 178. An airy Argentine restaurant serving first-rate meat to a demanding (mainly Argentine) clientele. If cuts of beef mean little to you, opt for the *bife de chorizo*, the Argentine standard cut. Moderate–expensive.

Mil Frutas Rua das Pedras 24. Of the numerous ice-cream places, this is by far the best in Búzios, offering flavours both familiar and exotic – from *jabuticaba* to "Romeu e Julieta" (guava and cream).

Pizzaria Capricciosa Av. José Bento Ribeiro Dantas 500. The place for pizza in Búzios, with wood-burning ovens and dozens of varieties of moderately priced pizza to choose from.

Samsara Rua Santana Maia 684, just off Rua das Pedras. This inexpensive vegetarian restaurant offers an excellent lunch buffet of hot and cold dishes and à la carte dining in the evening, featuring interesting pasta offerings from the Italian chef that make use of fresh, organic produce.

Satyricon Rua das Pedras 500. Seafood is the speciality at this extremely expensive Italian restaurant (with a branch in Rio). Red snapper baked encrusted in sea salt is a signature, but all the shellfish dishes are outstandingly good as well. Though overly formal for laid-back Búzios, those with money to burn are in for a treat.

Sawasdee Av. José Bento Ribeiro Dantas 422. Excellent, spicy Thai food is based around vegetables and seafood. One of the best creations is "Khao Tom", a delicious spicy shellfish risotto; the steamed filet of sole in a tamarind sauce is also excellent. Although quite expensive, most of the dishes are suitable for two people.

Nightlife

Nightlife – which gets going at around 11pm and continues until dawn – is largely limited to eating, drinking and people watching along Rua das Pedras. It's impossible to exaggerate how crowded Armação gets in January and February, but even in the off-season Rua das Pedras is quite lively at weekends at night. The *Pátio Havana*, a rather upscale restaurant and bar at Rua das Pedras 101, is well worth checking out for the first-rate **jazz** artists from Rio, São Paulo and abroad who are hosted there. Strangely, nightclubs haven't taken off here as they have at other similar resorts, but if you want to **dance** (or just watch with a drink), *the* place to head for is the *Fashion Café*, on Rua das Pedras, across the road from the *Chez Michou Crêperie*. Always packed with a mainly youthful crowd, the club has DJs playing a safe mix of Europop and other disco sounds, and there's usually live music by Brazilian or Argentine performers.

Northeast to Campos

If you're not yet tired of **beaches**, you'll find more beautiful examples around the pretty colonial village of Barra de São João and Rio das Ostras, an hour or so up the coast. Near the latter, the iodized waters of the **Lagoa da Coca-Cola** (yes, really) boast more medicinal qualities – everyone must be very healthy in this neck of the woods. If you want to stay round here, you'll find *pousadas* in both these places, though there's been much uncontrolled development along this stretch of coast, leading to pretty hideous results.

The next town of any size is **MACAÉ**, on the edge of a large sugar-cane-producing region. The beaches here are utterly unremarkable, the city is extremely ugly and much more industrial than what has gone before and the arrival of offshore oil drilling has done nothing to increase its attractions. From here the main road heads northeast, inland through very attractive rolling countryside to **CAMPOS**, on the River Paraíba some 50km before it flows into the sea. Again it's predominantly a sugar-cane-processing town, and its primarily agro-industrial nature makes it a less than attractive target, given the local alternatives. If you're travelling from Cabo Frio or Búzios north to Espírito Santos or Bahia, your best best is to take a bus to Campos where you'll be able to pick up a connection without much delay.

West: the Costa Verde

The mountainous littoral and calm green waters of the aptly named **Costa Verde** ("Green Coast") provide a marked contrast to the sand and surf of the coastline east of Rio. One of Brazil's truly beautiful landscapes, the Costa Verde has been made much more accessible by the **Rio–Santos BR-101 Highway** – something, however, that has led to an increase in commercial penetration of this region. The fate of this 280-kilometre stretch of lush vegetation, rolling hills and tropical beaches hangs in the balance between rational development and ecological destruction, and so far the signs augur badly. Ecologists warn that fish stocks in the Bay of Sepetiba, which covers almost half the length of the Costa Verde, are in constant danger of destruction because of pollution. Enjoy your trip; you may be amongst the last to have the privilege.

There are two ways to reach the Costa Verde from Rio. By **car**, drive through the Zona Sul by way of Barra de Tijuca, to Barra de Guaratiba; alternatively, from Rio's *rodoviária*, take one of the **buses** that leave the city by way of the Zona Norte and follow the BR-101 to Itacuruçá and beyond.

Time bombs in paradise

There's no doubt that the Costa Verde is one of Brazil's most beautiful stretches of coast, so it's not surprising that so many hotel and holiday home complexes are appearing on the hillsides and in the picturesque coves. What is incredible, however, is that the coast was chosen as the location of two complexes with the potential to cause the most environmental destruction – an oil terminal and a nuclear power plant.

The Petrobrás **oil terminal** is, at least, out of sight, located 25km east of Angra, so you only need contemplate the damage that an oil spill could wreak on this ecologically fragile stretch of coast when you pass the barrack-like housing complexes for the Petrobrás workers on the BR-101, the main coastal road towards Angra.

Perhaps more worrying are the **nuclear power plants**, Angra-1 and Angra-2, some 40km west of Angra. The project was directly managed by the Brazilian military, and it's difficult to imagine a more insane place to put a nuclear reactor. Not only would there be enormous difficulties should an emergency evacuation be necessary, as the mountains here plunge directly into the sea, but in addition the plant is in an earthquake fault zone, in a cove that local Indians call *Itaorna*, the moving rock.

The Angra-1's safety record is already in doubt, and since 1985 the plant has been shut down for unspecified repairs over twenty times. Officials insist that there has been no leak of radiation beyond the plant, but environmentalists, who say there may be cracks in the reactor's primary container system, want the plant shut down for good. Its future, however, looks secure: it would be humiliating for the military to abandon the project – it's claimed Angra-1 supplies twenty percent of the state of Rio's electricity needs while Angra-2, in operation since 1999, has similar output – and there would be huge problems in decommissioning the plant. There remain plans on the drawing board to build a third reactor, but work will not begin for some time, if ever.

Should you want to stop by the plant, the **visitors' centre** offers a predictably professional public relations show (Mon–Fri 8.30am–4.30pm, Sat & Sun 8.30am–3pm).

Itacuruçá and Mangaratiba

ITACURUÇÁ, around 90km from Rio, is a tranquil hamlet that draws wealthy yachting types. The attraction here is obvious: the village nestles between rolling hills and a malachite-coloured sea, its offshore **islands** – Jaguanum and Itacaruçú, with their pleasant walks and beaches – easily reached by boat. Tours of the islands can be arranged with the **tourist office** at Praça da Igreja 130, in Itacuruçá. Both islands have luxury **hotels**: *Hotel Pierre* (Ⓣ21/2688-1560, Ⓦwww.hotelpierre.com.br; ❻), set against a glorious Mata Atlântica backdrop on Itacuruçú, is the best, with comfortable rooms, private beaches, a good restaurant and a pool. Almost as good, but slightly cheaper and less exclusive, is *Hotel Elias C* (Ⓣ21/2680-7089; ❺). On the neighbouring island of Jaguanum, *Hotel Jaguanum* (Ⓣ21/2235-2893; ❻) offers similar accommodation but costs slightly more.

Muddy beaches and the incongruous industrial presence of the nearby Terminal de Sepetiba put off many people stopping at **MANGARATIBA**, which lies 25km west of Itacuruçá along the BR-101. Even so, the town's immediate setting is attractive, with a mountain backdrop, a beautiful bay in front with fishing boats at anchor and a late eighteenth-century church dominating the main square. On the whole, however, the initial impression is the correct one; there are better spots to stay further along the coast. Five **buses** a day run from Rio to Mangaratiba – at 5.30am, 9am, 12.30pm, 3pm and 6.45pm – and if you catch the earliest bus you'll make the daily ferry that sails from Mangaratiba to Ilha Grande (see p.153). Nevertheless, if you do need to stay, Mangaratiba is by no means an unpleasant place to spend a night. There are a couple of **hotels** in town, such as the very basic *Rio Branco* (❸) on the main square and the air-conditioned *Pensão do Almir* (❹) on the road leading to the hospital. If you head from the main square along the seashore, you'll find several good fish restaurants.

Angra dos Reis

From Mangaratiba, the road continues to hug the coast as it wends its way westwards, rising and falling between towering green-clad mountains and the ocean. Roughly 60km west of Mangaratiba lies the shabby and rather unprepossessing little town of **ANGRA DOS REIS**. The lands around here were "discovered" by the navigator André Gonçalves in 1502, though it wasn't until 1556 that a colonial settlement was established. The port first developed as an entrepôt for the exportation of agricultural produce from São Paulo and Minas Gerais in the seventeeth century. Fifteen slave-worked sugar refineries dominated the local economy, which, with the abolition of slavery at the end of the nineteenth century, suffered a dramatic collapse. The 1930s saw the economy regenerated, with the construction of a new port, and shipbuilding remains an important local trade – although the latest venture is Brazil's first nuclear power station, located nearby.

The main reason to come here is to get out to the thirty or so local islands in the bay. Numerous leisurely **boat and fishing trips** are on offer, and most yachts have a bar at which you can fill the time between stops for swimming at beaches penned in between clear waters and tropical forest. Visiting **Gipóia** by boat, for instance, allows you a couple of hours to splash about and get something to eat in the *Luiz Rosa* bar – all together a very relaxing excursion. Various companies offer excursions, so it's best to ask at the **tourist information office** (daily 8am–6pm; ⓣ24/3367-7855) in Largo do Lapa, right across from the bus station and next to the **Cais de Santa Luzia**, from where the boats depart. Trips can also be arranged on the quay with independent operators, but check on the noticeboard for those boat owners who have been authorized to carry tourists. Most trips leave around 10am and return in the late afternoon; on average you'll pay around R$30 a head.

Beaches in the town are nothing special. Better ones are found by following the Estrada do Contorno (by car), or catching a **bus** from the bus station (hourly) to the beaches of Bonfim, Gordas, Grande, Tanguá, Tanguazinho, Ribeira or Retiro. There are other beaches within reach, too: along the main BR-101 highway, in the direction of Rio, good spots for bathing and free camping are Garatucaia and Monsuaba.

Practicalities

The bus station, the tourist information office and the passenger ferry for Ilha Grande (see opposite) are all located within a few steps of each other in Angra dos Reis. There's no shortage of **hotels** if you're planning to stay around for the beaches and islands, but most are on the pricey side. Try the modest but comfortable *Hotel Londres*, Av. Raul Pompéia 75 (ⓣ24/3365-0044; ❸); for only slightly more you'll get a pool at the *Acrópolis Marina* on Av. das Caravelas 89 (ⓣ24/3365-2225; ❹). The town's modern **youth hostel** (ⓣ24/3364-4759, ⓦwww.riobracui.com.br; $R40 per person or ❹ for a double room) is conveniently located right in the centre at Praça da Matriz 152.

You'll have no trouble finding places for eating and drinking either, with lots of restaurants and bars to choose from: try *Cheiro Verde*, Rua Pereira Peixoto 53, which serves satisfying Lebanese cuisine, or *Taberna 33* at Av. Raul Pompéia 110 for decent pizzas.

Inland from Angra

If you want to take a break from beaches, the forested **Serra do Mar** lies inland immediately behind Angra. By far the easiest and most enjoyable way to penetrate the forest is by **train**, on the line constructed a hundred years ago to export coffee from the once rich coffee region of Rio Claro. Today the line is mainly used to take coal to the Volta Redonda steel mills, but on weekends and holidays a train takes tourists 40km inland as far as Lídice; it stops from time to time, allowing passengers to take pictures of the coast below, several waterfalls and forest. The train leaves Angra at 10.30am, arriving back at 4.30pm; tickets ($10 including lunch on the train) should be purchased at least a day in advance from Montmar Turismo, Rua do Comércio 11, Angra (Ⓣ24/3365-1705).

An excellent **youth hostel**, the *Hospedagem Rio Bracuí* (Ⓣ21/3531-2234; R$30 per person), is some 22km beyond Angra, a little way inland on the bank of the Rio Bracuí. This is a great spot from which to take walks into the Serra do Mar, following one of the numerous forest trails. To get here, take any bus going along the coast and get off just after the bridge that crosses the Rio Bracuí. Turn right and head inland along the Estrada do Surubim, and the hostel is located 200m on your left.

Ilha Grande

ILHA GRANDE comprises 193 square kilometres of mountainous jungle, historic ruins and beautiful beaches, excellent for some scenic tropical rambling. The entire island is a state park and the authorities have been successful at limiting development and in maintaining a ban on motor vehicles, whether owned by visitors or locals. The main drawback is the ferocity of the insects, especially during the summer, so come equipped with repellent.

Islands like this deserve a good pirate story, and Ilha Grande is no exception. According to legend, the pirate **Jorge Grego** was heading for the Straits of Magellan when his ship was sunk by a British fleet. He managed to escape with his two daughters to Ilha Grande, where he became a successful farmer and merchant. In a fit of rage he murdered the lover of one of his daughters and, shortly afterwards, a terrible storm destroyed all his farms and houses. From then on, Jorge Grego passed his time roaming the island, distraught, pausing only long enough to bury his treasure before his final demise. If there is any treasure today, though, it's in the island's **wildlife**: parrots, exotic hummingbirds, butterflies and monkeys abound in the thick vegetation.

Ilha Grande offers lots of beautiful **walks** along well-maintained and fairly well-signposted trails, but it's sensible to take some basic precautions. Be sure to set out as early as possible and always inform people at your *pousada* where you are going – in writing if possible. Carry plenty of water with you and remember to apply sunscreen and insect repellent at regular intervals. Darkness comes suddenly, and even on a night with a full moon the trails are likely to be pitch-black due to the canopy formed by the overhanging foliage; it's best to carry a flashlight with you, and most *pousadas* will be happy to lend you one. Whatever you do, avoid straying from the trail: not only could you easily get hopelessly lost, but there are also rumours of booby traps primed to fire bullets, left over from the days when the island hosted a high-security prison.

Around the island

As you approach the low-lying, whitewashed colonial port of **VILA DO ABRAÃO**, the mountains rise dramatically from the sea, and in the distance there's the curiously shaped summit of Bico do Papagaio ("Parrot's Beak"), which rises to a height of 980m and can be reached in about three hours.

There's really very little to see in Abraão itself, but it's a pleasant enough base from which to explore the rest of the island. The ruins of the **Antigo Presídio** lie a half-hour walk along the coast west from Abraão. Originally built as a hospital, it was converted to a prison for political prisoners in 1910 and was finally dynamited in the early 1960s. Among the ruins, you'll find the *cafofo*, the containment centre where prisoners who had failed in escape attempts were immersed in freezing water. Just fifteen minutes inland from Abraão, and overgrown with vegetation, stands the **Antigo Aqueduto** that used to channel the island's water supply. There's a fine view of the aqueduct from the **Pedra Mirante**, a hill near the centre of the island, and, close by, a waterfall provides the opportunity for a cool bathe on a hot day.

For the most part the **beaches** – Aventureiro, Lopes Mendes, Canto, Júlia and Morcegoare to name a few – are still wild and unspoilt. They can be most easily reached by **boat**; a typical day-long excursion costs R$25–35 per person, and departure time from Abraão's jetty is at 10.30am, with stops for snorkelling (equipment provided) before continuing on to a beach where you'll be picked up later in the day to arrive back in Abraão at around 4.30pm. Most beaches can also be reached on **foot**, and there are some lovely quiet beaches within an hour's walk of Abraão. The hike from Abraão across the island to **Praia da Parnaioca** will take about five hours, so it's no jaunt. By the coconut-fringed *praia* is an old fishing village that was abandoned by its inhabitants because of their fear of escaped prisoners from a second prison that was built on the island. This prison closed in April 1994, though not before earning the island something of a dangerous reputation, as escapes were not infrequent. Today the only dangers come from *borachudos*, almost invisible but vicious gnats that bite without your hearing them or, until later, feeling them. A tiny fishing community has slowly been established here, and if you need to stay over you should have little trouble finding a room to rent and something to eat. Many of the other beaches have a *barraca* or two selling snacks and cold drinks, but you should bring supplies with you.

Practicalities

There are **boats** from both Mangaratiba and Angra dos Reis to Vila do Abraão on Ilha Grande, each taking an hour or so. From **Mangaratiba** to Abraão, the boat leaves daily at 8am (with an extra boat on Friday at 10pm) and returns at 5.30pm. From **Angra dos Reis**, boats leave at 3.30pm Monday through Friday and at 1.30pm Saturday and Sunday, returning at 10am daily. Tickets cost R$5 during the week or R$12 Saturday, Sunday and holidays from both Mangaratiba and Angra; if you miss the ferry you can usually count on finding a small launch to do the crossing, charging around R$20 per person and taking around 90 minutes. During the summer there's a constant flow of these launches from both mainland towns, but at other times Angra is the best bet. If you have a car, you'll have to leave it behind on the mainland, though you can get advice at the ferry terminals on where to find a secure, lock-up parking spot. Be sure to come with plenty of **cash**: changing dollars or travellers' cheques is impossible on the island, there's no ATM and few *pousadas* and restaurants accept credit cards.

Accommodation is mostly around Vila do Abraão, and when you arrive you'll probably be approached by youths intent on taking you to a room in a private house (around R$25 per person) – a good option if you're on a tight budget. There are quite a few *pousadas* in Abraão, most of which are quite simple but fairly expensive. Reservations in the high season, especially at weekends, are absolutely essential; try to come in the off-season when prices are halved. One of the nicest *pousadas* is the cosy and friendly *Pousada Oásis* (Ⓣ24/3361-5116; ❹), peacefully located on the far end of the beach, a ten-minute walk from the jetty. Almost next door is the similarly sized *Pousada Porto Girassol* (ⓣ24/331-5277; ❹) and the larger, though by no means impersonal, *Pousada do Canto* (ⓣ21/3361-5115; ❺). More hotel-like is the *Pousada Água Viva* (ⓣ21/3361-5166; ❺), located amidst a busy strip of shops and restaurants. The always popular *Pousada do Holandês* (ⓣ24/3361-5034; ❷), an extremely friendly **youth hostel**, is behind the beach, next to the Assembléia de Deus.

A few more *pousadas* can be found outside of Abraão. One of the most attractive is the *Pousada Sankay* (ⓣ21/3365-4065, ⓦwww.pousadasankay.com.br; ❼), one hour by boat west of Abraão on the Praia de Bananal. Further west along the coast, in the quiet fishing hamlet at Praia Grande de Araçatiba, there are two more charming options: the *Cantinho de Ará* (ⓣ24/3365-1184; ❸) and the *Refúgio do Capitão* (ⓣ19/3273-9401; ❷). If you can cope with the bugs, **camping** is a possibility, as there are several good, secure sites in Abraão; you can also camp at beaches around the island, and you can arrange for fishermen to take you from beach to beach if hiking through the forests with your gear doesn't appeal.

Summertime **nightlife** in Abraão is always lively, with the *Bar Verdinho da Ilha* bashing out some eminently danceable *forró* music. Restaurants, predictably, concentrate on seafood (try the *Rei dos Caldos*, which specializes in fish soups), but there are also a couple of pizzerias. **Carnaval** is well celebrated here – much more relaxed than the Rio experience – and watch, too, for the festival of São João (Jan 20) and the Pirate Regatta, which takes place in February.

Tarituba

Back on the mainland, the road west rises amidst the most exhilarating scenery that the whole coast has to offer. About 60km from Angra, **TARITUBA**, a charming little fishing village just off the coast road, is still relatively untouched by tourism. Any bus going along the coast will let you off at the side road that leads to the village, or there are buses several times a day from Paraty, 35km further west.

There's not much to the village – a pier along which fishing boats land their catches, a pretty church and a few *barracas* on the beach serving fried fish and cold drinks – it's simply a place to relax in, away from the often brash commercialism of Angra and Paraty. There are a couple of decent **pousadas**, but it can be difficult to get a room in high season or even to make telephone reservations. The most comfortable place is the *Tarituba* (ⓣ24/3371-6619; ❹), where large rooms with private verandahs and hammocks overlook the pool and beach beyond. The *Pousada de Carminha* (ⓣ24/3371-1120; ❸), simple but very friendly, is right on the beach and offers either private or shared bathrooms. Bear in mind that here, as right along the coast, the *borachudos* and mosquitoes are murder, so bring plenty of insect repellent and mosquito coils with you.

Paraty

About 300km from Rio on the BR-101 is the Costa Verde's main attraction, the town of **PARATY**. Inhabited since 1650, Paraty (or, officially, Vila de Nossa Senhora dos Remédios de Paraty) has remained fundamentally unaltered since its heyday as a staging post for the eighteenth-century trade in Brazilian gold, passing from Minas Gerais to Portugal. Before white settlement, the land had been occupied by the **Guaianá Indians**, and the gold routes followed the old Indian trails down to Paraty and its sheltered harbour. Inland raids and pirate attacks necessitated the establishment of a new route linking Minas Gerais directly with Rio de Janeiro, and, as trade was diverted to Rio, Paraty's fortunes declined. Apart from a short-lived coffee-shipping boom in the nineteenth century, Paraty remained hidden away off the beaten track, intact but quietly stagnating. Nowadays, however, Paraty is very much alive; UNESCO considers it one of the world's most important examples of Portuguese colonial architecture, and the entire city has been elevated to the status of a national monument. Paraty and the surrounding area's population of 30,000 is actively involved in fishing, farming and tourism.

The town centre was one of Brazil's first planned urban projects, and its narrow cobbled streets, out of bounds to motorized transport, are bordered by houses built around courtyards adorned with brightly coloured flowers and teeming with hummingbirds. The cobbles of the streets are arranged in channels to drain off storm water and allow the sea to enter and wash the streets at high tides and full moon. Although businesses in Paraty's historic centre are overwhelmingly geared to tourists, the wider community has not been totally engulfed by wealthy outsiders and by and large provides a more satisfying experience than Búzios, its chic counterpart on the Costa do Sol.

Arrival, information and accommodation

The **rodoviária** is about half a kilometre from the old town; turn right out of the bus station and walk straight ahead. The **tourist office** (daily 8am–7pm; ⓣ24/3371-1897) is near the entrance of the historic centre, on the corner of

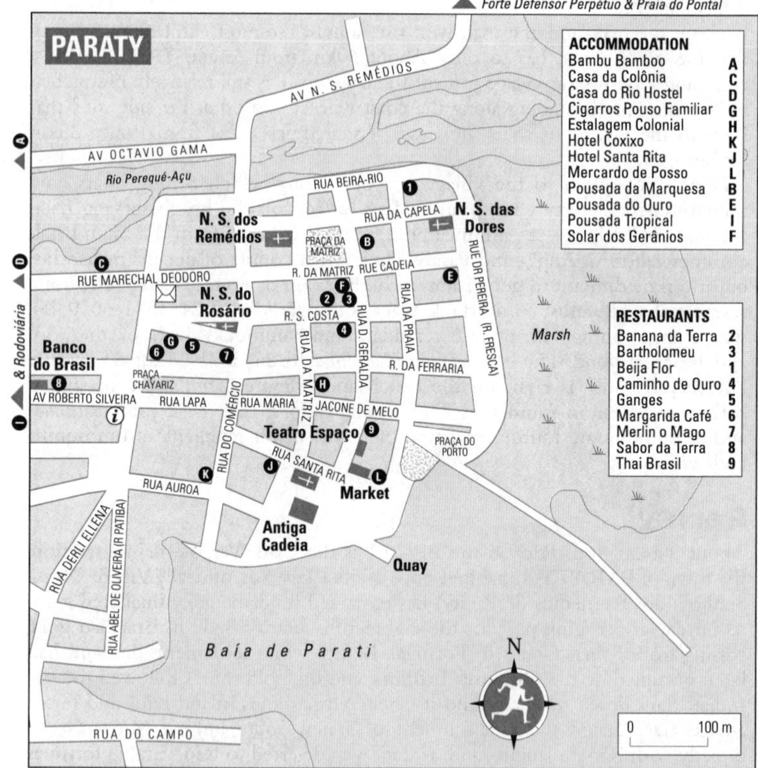

Avenida Roberto Silveira and Praça Macedo Soares, and can supply a map of the town, local bus times and a list of hotels and restaurants.

You might well be offered **accommodation** by people waiting at the bus station, but it's usually easy to track it down yourself; the standard is high, and rooms are often amazing value for money. Most of the best **pousadas** are in the colonial centre, a few minutes' walk from the bus station. From late December to after Carnaval and when special events are held, however, this entire area is packed and hotel space becomes hard to find: if you are without a reservation try to arrive by noon, when you might get a room from people leaving Paraty earlier than planned. Your best hope will be to find a room outside of the historic centre, in a hotel used by tour groups – ask the tourist office for advice. At other times, expect discounts of up to fifty percent from the high-season prices given below.

Bambu Bamboo Rua Glauber Rocha 9 ⓣ24/3371-8629, ⓦwww.bambubamboo.com. In a peaceful location by the river and a ten-minute walk from the historic centre, this is one of Paraty's most pleasant *pousadas*. Rooms are much more spacious than those found in the centre and there is a good-sized pool in the attractive garden. Breakfasts are a real treat and the British and Brazilian owners are always helpful. ❺

Casa da Colônia Rua Marechal Deodoro 50 ⓣ24/3371-2343. Located just outside the historic centre, this is a no-frills but attractive old *pousada*. Rooms are well equipped, and some sleep four people. ❸

Casa do Rio Hostel Rua Antônio Vidal 120 ⓣ24/3371-2223, ⓦwww.paratyhostel.com. Somewhat cramped, but otherwise excellent, this official youth hostel is located alongside the river, just a few minutes not, but, walk from Paraty's historic centre. Helpful staff and a range of beach and inland tours are organized by the hostel. R$25 per person in a dorm or ❸ for a double or family room with private bathroom.

Cigarros Pouso Familiar Largo do Rosário 7 ⓣ24/3371-1497. A lovely old house with just four simply furnished rooms. All have private bathrooms and one has a kitchenette. The atmosphere is relaxed and there are attractive views from the shared terrace. ❸

Estalagem Colonial Rua da Matriz 9 ⓣ24/3371-1626. All rooms at this basic but delightful *pousada* are attractively furnished and have lovely views; it's worth spending a little more for one of the larger rooms. ❸

Hotel Coxixo Rua do Comércio 362 ⓣ24/3371-1460, ⓦwww.hotelcoxixo.com.br. Rooms are comfortable and there's an attractive garden and a good-size pool. Since this is one of the larger hotels in the historic centre, you'll have a chance of securing last-minute accommodation here. Apart from babies under 12 months, only children over the age of 15 are accepted. ❻

Hotel Santa Rita Rua Santa Rita 335 ⓣ24/3371-1206. This friendly but unpretentious hotel has just six rooms, three of which have wonderful views of the sea. Situated alongside one of the prettiest churches in Paraty. ❹

Mercardo de Posso Largo de Santa Rita ⓣ24/3371-1114, ⓦwww.mercadodepouso.com.br. A very comfortable *pousada* in an imaginatively restored old market building. Rooms and suites (some sleeping four) are spacious and feature rustic but comfortable furniture; the courtyard garden is cool and relaxing. Rates are low because there's no pool. ❺

Pousada da Marquesa Rua Dona Geralda 69 ⓣ24/3371-2163, ⓦwww.pousadamarquesa.com.br. The least expensive luxury *pousada* in Paraty, boasting an attractive pool and wonderful views of the town from the bedrooms. Avoid the rooms in the annex, as they're on the small side. ❺

Pousada do Ouro Rua Dr Pereira 145 ⓣ24/3371-2033, ⓦwww.pousadaouro.com.br. Discreet luxury *pousada* offering a range of tastefully furnished rooms – spacious and light in the main building, but rather small and dark in the annex. There's a pretty walled garden and a good-size pool, too. ❻–❼

Pousada Tropical Rua Waldemar Mathias 38 ⓣ24/3371-2020. Set in a residential area next to the *rodoviária*. Rooms are plain, but ask for one on the upper floor, as they're quieter and have better ventilation. ❸

Solar dos Gerânios Praça da Matriz ⓣ24/3371-1550. This beautiful and long-established *pousada* is filled with rustic furniture and curios. The rooms (including some singles) are small and spartan but impeccably kept; most have a balcony and all have a private bathroom. The *pousada* is superb value (prices remain much the same throughout the year) and the multilingual owner and her cats are extremely welcoming. Because it's popular, reservations are usually essential – request a room overlooking the *praça*. ❸

The town

Paraty is a perfect place simply to wander aimlessly, each turn of the corner bringing another picturesque view. The town's small enough that there's no danger of getting lost and, no matter what time of day or night, you can feel pretty confident that you won't be a victim of an assault. Additionally, there are several buildings worth seeking out if you don't happen to come across them.

As with most small colonial towns in Brazil, each of Paraty's churches traditionally served a different sector of the population. Dating back to 1646, **Nossa Senhora dos Remédios** (daily 9am–5pm), on the Praça da Matriz, is Paraty's main church and the town's largest building. During the late eighteenth century, the church – built for local bourgeoisie – underwent major structural reforms and the exterior, at least, has remained unchanged since then. In 1800 Paraty's aristocracy had their own church built: the particularly graceful **Igreja das Dores** (daily 1–5pm), which has a small cemetery, is located three blocks from the main church, by the sea. Along Rua do Comércio is the smallest church, the **Igreja do Rosário** (Wed–Sun 9am–noon & 1.30–5pm), constructed in 1725 and used by slaves. Finally, at the southern edge of the town, the **Igreja de Santa Rita dos Pardos Libertos** (Wed–Sun 9am–noon & 2–5pm) is the oldest and architecturally most significant of Paraty's churches. Built in 1722 for the freed mulatto population, the structure is notable for its elaborate facade, done in Portuguese Baroque style; the small Museu de Arte Sacra, a repository of religious artefacts from Paraty's churches, is attached. Next to Santa Rita you'll find the late eighteenth-century jail, the **Antiga Cadeia**, now the main tourist information office and a handicraft centre, while opposite to it is the lively **fish market**. On the corner of Rua Dona Geralda and Rua Samuel Costa, the beautifully maintained **Casa da Cultura** (Sun, Mon, Wed, Thurs 10am–6.30pm & Fri, Sat 1–9.30pm; R$5) is worth stopping by at for the sometimes excellent locally inspired art and photography exhibitions.

To the north of the old town, across the Rio Perequé-Açu on the Morro de Vilha Velha, is the **Forte Defensor Perpétuo**, constructed in 1703 to defend Paraty from pirates seeking to plunder gold ships leaving the port. The fort underwent restoration in 1822 and today the rudimentary structure houses the Museu de Artes e Tradições Populares (Wed–Sun 9am–noon & 2–5pm), which has a permanent display of fishing tools and basket ware as well as handicrafts for sale.

Beaches and islands

Keeping yourself amused while visiting Paraty should be no problem, even if you quickly exhaust the possibilities of the town itself. From the **Praia do Pontal** on the other side of the Perequé-Açu River from town, and from the **port quay**, schooners leave for the beaches of Paraty-Mirim, Jurumirim, Lula and Picinguaba. In fact, there are 65 islands and about 200 beaches to choose from, and anyone can tell you which are the current favourites. Tickets for trips out to the islands, typically costing R$20 per person, leave Paraty at noon, stop at three or four islands for swimming opportunities and return at 6pm. These trips can be pretty rowdy affairs, with the larger boats capable of carrying several dozen people and usually blaring out loud music. Alternatively, for around R$200 (or R$100 in the low season) you can easily charter a small fishing boat suitable for three or four passengers. Boats also leave from the quay for the **Boa Vista distillery**, or *alambique*. Home of the famous Quero Esse brand of *cachaça*, the old colonial house here was once the residence of Thomas Mann's grandfather, Johan Ludwig Brown, before he returned to Germany around 1850. The caretaker, and master distiller, will give guided tours of the *alambique* (R$30) before plying you with a liquor that has distinctly invigorating properties.

△ Paraty

You can reach some of the mainland beaches by road – ask at the tourist office for details of bus times. If you're really feeling energetic, you can hire a **mountain bike** for R$35 a day from Paraty Tours at Av. Roberto Silveira 11, who also supply maps marked with suggested itineraries covering beaches, mountains or forests. They can also arrange **car rental** for around R$120 a day.

To the north, the fishing village of **Tarituba** (see p.155) makes a pleasant excursion, with several delightful beaches (such as Praia Grande and Prainha) to stop off at on the way.

Seventeen kilometres southwest of Paraty, including 8km along an unpaved road (which should be avoided following heavy rains), is **Paraty-Mirim**, an attractive bay with calm water ideal for swimming. Although there are a couple of bars serving food, there's nowhere to stay at the beach. Roughly halfway between the beach and the main road, however, is the *Vila Volta* (Ⓣ24/9815-7689, Ⓦwww.vilavolta.com.br; ❹), a rustic but comfortable *pousada* run by a Dutch and Brazilian couple. Here you'll find a friendly reception, peaceful setting, excellent food, trails and natural swimming pools.

Some of the best beaches are near the village of **Trindade**, 21km southwest of Paraty and reached by a steep, but good, winding road (7 buses daily; 45min). Sandwiched between the ocean and Serra do Mar, Trindade has reached the physical limits of growth, the dozens of inexpensive *pousadas*, holiday homes, camping sites, bars and restaurants crammed with tourists in the peak summer season. The main beach is nice enough, but you're better off walking away from the village across the rocky outcrops to Praia Brava or Praia do Meio, where the only signs of development on what are some of the most perfect mainland beaches on this stretch of coast are simply a few bars. If you plan to stay over at New Year or Carnaval, without a reservation your best bet for securing accommodation is to arrive several days early and ask around for vacant rooms. The best place (though hardly luxurious) is the *Pousada do Pelé* (Ⓣ24/3371-5125; ❹), which is situated right on the beach and has rooms that sleep two to four people. There are numerous modest *pousadas* slightly back from the beach, all with private bathrooms: try the *Agua do Mar* (Ⓣ24/3371-5210; ❸); the *Pouso Trindade* (Ⓣ24/3371-5121; ❸); or the *Ponta da Trindade* (Ⓣ24/3371-5113; ❷), which also has space to pitch a tent.

Academy of Cooking and Other Pleasures

For an unusual dining experience, drop by the **Academy of Cooking and Other Pleasures** at Rua Dona Geralda 211 (ⓣ24/3371-6468, ⓦwww.chefbrazil.com) to find out about events hosted by Yara Castro Roberts, a professional cook who lived in Massachusetts for many years doing much to encourage interest in Brazilian food through cookery classes and television segments. Several evenings a week, Yara gives demonstrations in her home, alternating between menus drawn from Rio, Bahia, the Amazon and Minas Gerais, her home state. The high point of the evening comes when Yara and her guests sit around her dining room table to enjoy food and wine and sample some fine *cachaças*, of which she is a connoisseur. The evening, which usually lasts from 7.30 to 10.30pm, costs R$130 per person, with groups limited to eight or so people.

Eating

The town has a good choice of **restaurants** in all price brackets, though often the expensive-looking ones can be surprisingly reasonable, thanks to portions big enough for two people. The cheapest places to eat are outside of the historic centre – while none of these are remarkable, you won't have any difficulty finding a filling meal of fish, meat, beans, rice and salad for under ten *reais*. Predictably, fish is the local speciality, but there are many other options, with the restaurants listed here being the more noteworthy.

Banana da Terra Rua Dr Samuel Costa 198. Arguably Paraty's most interesting restaurant, the *Banana da Terra* emphasizes local ingredients (such as bananas and plantains) and regional cooking. The grilled fish with garlic-herb butter and served with banana is delicious, as are the wonderful banana desserts. At well over R$100 per person, this restaurant is expensive. Evenings only except Sat & Sun, when lunch is also served; closed Wed.

Bartholomeu Rua Dr Samuel Costa 176. A relatively simple but excellent and moderately priced menu that gives pride of place to Argentine beef filled with roquefort and seafood *moquecas*. The ceviche is an absolutely divine starter.

Caminho de Ouro Rua Dr Samuel Costa 81. Contemporary Brazilian cooking that draws heavily on traditional recipes of both Rio and Minas Gerais. Prices are moderate.

Ganges Largo do Rosário. Indian flavours rather than truly Indian food permeate the imaginative, mainly vegetarian menu. Inexpensive–moderate.

Le Gite d'Indaiatiba BR-101, km 562, Graúna (ⓣ24/3371-7174 or 9999-9923, ⓦwww.legitedindaiatiba.com.br). At this outstanding restaurant, the French chef serves a few classic dishes as well as his own creations based on local ingredients. Main courses are around R$80. Set inland from Paraty, the mountainside location is stunning and it's a wonderful place to spend an afternoon – or longer, as it's also a *pousada* (double rooms ❺–❻). If you don't have your own transport, phone ahead for a possible lift.

Margarida Café Praça Chafariz. Imaginative, well-prepared modern Brazilian cooking is the speciality here; the desserts are a special treat, none more than bananas flambéed in *cachaça*. There's a nice bar, plus remarkably good live music on most nights. Expect to pay at least R$60 per person for a full meal.

Merlin o Mago Rua do Comércio 376. Though overly formal for laid-back Paraty, the French-influenced fish dishes are excellent, if expensive. Evenings only, closed Wed.

Sabor da Terra Av. Roberto Silveira 180. This is Paraty's best *por kilo* restaurant, offering a wide variety of inexpensive hot and cold dishes that include excellent seafood. Located outside of the historic centre, next to the Banco do Brasil.

Thai Brasil Rua Dona Geralda 345. Well-presented, moderately priced Thai food is served in a bright and attractive setting. The German owner has created remarkably authentic dishes, with the fish being especially good.

Drinking and entertainment

Paraty has plenty of watering holes to keep you amused into the evening, though out of season when the town is extremely quiet you may well find yourself drinking alone. Amongst the bars with **live music** to try are *Paraty 33*, on Rua da Lapa alongside the cathedral, and *Margarida Café* (see p.160). Many of the buildings in the historic centre have been converted into shops, where you can pick up clothes, artworks, *cachaça* (gevnerally not as good as the rustic-looking bottle might suggest) and souvenirs until late at night. Otherwise, you might try the **cinema** on Avenda no. Roberto Silveira, which usually shows English-language films; a more novel alternative is the **puppet troupe** Grupo Contadores de Estórias, internationally renowned for their wordless performances that nimbly leap between comedy and tragedy, exploring such adult themes as death, sex and betrayal (you must be 14 years or over to attend). Performances are every Wednesday and Saturday at their Teatro Espaço at Rua Dona Geralda 327 (Ⓣ24/3371-1575, Ⓦwww.paraty.com.br/teatro.htm; R$35), which occasionally hosts other theatre, dance or music events, too.

May, June and July see frequent **festivals** celebrating local holidays, and Paraty's square comes alive during this time with folk dances – *cerandis*, *congadas* and *xibas* – showcasing the European and African influences on Brazilian culture. While such goings-on certainly demonstrate that local traditions can survive against the onslaught of tourism, they are small in scale compared with newly established events. Taking place since 2002 over the course of a week in either July or early August, the **Festa Literária Internacional de Parati** (FLIP) immediately established itself as Brazil's single most influential literary gathering, with panels featuring some of the most important writers from throughout the world. If you plan on attending, bear in mind that accommodation must be reserved long in advance. For the FLIP programme, see Ⓦwww.flip.org.br.

Inland from Paraty

Another good way to see a bit of the landscape is to drive, cycle or catch a bus from the *rodoviária*, following the Cunha road up into the Serra do Mar. The easiest place to head for is at Km 4, where there's a well-signposted side road leading 900m to the **Fazenda Murycana** (daily 10am–6pm; R$5), a farm complex that dates back to the seventeenth century. As well as a farm, Murycana originally served as an inn for travellers on the Caminho do Ouro (see below) and also as a toll post where the royal tax of twenty percent on goods was levied. The restored buildings can be visited, the most interesting being the slightly ramshackle, yet still attractive, **casa grande**, now a museum. There's a restaurant serving typical country food (R$20 per person) and one can taste and purchase the *fazenda's* famous, but poor quality, *cachaça* and liquors. Horse riding is offered, as are a number of adventure sports such as canopy walking in the surrounding forest. Be sure to note, however, that this is one of the most popular excursions and the *fazenda* can get unpleasantly crowded, especially at lunchtime, with the arrival of tour groups.

Continuing up the Cunha road to Km 6, you'll spot signs pointing to the **Cachoeira das Penhas**, a waterfall up in the mountains that offers a chance to bake on the sun-scorched rocks of the river gully and then cool off in the river. From here you can descend from rock to rock for a few hundred metres before scrambling up to a road above you. About 2km along the road, just across a small bridge, you'll enter **PONTE BRANCA** where, at the far end of the village, overlooking the river, is the *Ponte Branca* restaurant, where you can take a break and enjoy a cold drink. The easy walk from the waterfall takes you through the hills and valleys, and past tropical fruit plantations, all very pleasant. If you don't have your own transport, you'll probably manage to get a lift back to Paraty from the restaurant or you can wait by the Cunha road for a bus.

For a more rugged experience, consider hiking along a restored segment of the **Caminho do Ouro** – the seventeenth-century mule trail that connected the port of Paraty with the gold mines of Minas Gerais. If you have your own transport, you can reach the trail's access point by continuing along the Cunha road to the visitors' centre. Here you can buy a combined map and entrance ticket (R$10 per person – also available at the Teatro Espaço in Paraty, see p.161) to the trail, which starts alongside the building. Otherwise you're better off joining a group tour organized through the Teatro Espaço – it costs R$35 per person and includes transport by minibus, a bilingual guide, admission and lunch (Wed–Sun departing 10am). The partially cobbled trail is very slippery after the rain, and even in dry conditions you'll need good footwear to tackle the steep uneven trail. The landscape, which appears pleasantly pastoral at first, grows increasingly impressive, and you'll have spectacular views of the forested mountains all around, as well as Paraty and the ocean. After about an hour you'll reach a gated area where display panels explain (in English and Portuguese) the region's history and ecology; there's also a waterfall to shower under and a source of fresh drinking water.

From here you can either continue along a more forested segment of the trail for a few more kilometres or follow a separate path to a **restaurant** that serves an excellent full lunch of simple local dishes from Thursday to Sunday in high season (excluding Fri in low season) and light meals the rest of the week – if no one's on duty at the gate leading to the restaurant just ring the bell and someone will eventually come out. There's also a modest **pousada** here, called the *Sítio Históric* (☎24/3371-1575; ❹ full board), where the four tastefully furnished rooms have amazing views down towards the coast. Reservations are essential, not least to arrange for a mule to carry your luggage.

Inland: north to the mountains

Excellent bus services from Rio de Janeiro make the **interior** of the state easily accessible, and its mountainous wooded landscape and relatively cool climate are a pleasant contrast to the coastal heat. There's not a great deal in the way of historical interest, but the scenic beauty of the countryside, studded with small towns still bearing their colonial heritage, is an attraction in itself.

Volta Redonda

From Rio, the Cidade do Aço bus company runs a service along the BR-116 to **VOLTA REDONDA** and the heartland of Brazil's steel industry. Situated on the banks of the **River Paraíba**, the city is dominated by steel mills, and though it may once have been a picturesque little village it's now an expanding industrial monster.

If you feel inclined to visit the **steel mill**, you need to arrange for a guided tour about a week in advance, either with the headquarters of the Companhia Siderúrgica Nacional on Avenida XIII de Maio, Rio de Janeiro, or locally at the *Hotel Bela Vista* (☎24/3348-2022; ❺). Tour buses organized by the Companhia Siderúrgica leave from Rio and travel direct to the mills; the journey takes about three hours and the price is negligible. If you want to **stay** in the town centre, apart from the *Bela Vista*, there's the *Sider Palace Hotel* at Av. Alberto Pasqualini 10 (☎24/3348-1032; ❹), and the *Embaixador* at Travessa Luís Augusto Félix 36 (☎24/3348-3665; ❸).

Volta Redonda serves as a textbook example of the (often disastrous) way in which Brazil is developing, economically and socially. To all intents and purposes, the city has been a company town since 1941, and the urban structure represents the priorities of the company – slums for the poor and nice neighbourhoods for the management sprawl sit on opposite sides of the river. The river itself is so polluted by industrial and domestic effluence that its plant and animal life have been almost completely destroyed. Apart from industrial conflict and pollution, according to a report in the *Jornal do Brazil* the citizens of Volta Redonda also have the highest incidence of hypertension and deaths caused by cardiovascular disease in the entire country. All this in what four decades ago must have been one of the healthiest climates in Brazil.

Parque Nacional do Itatiaia

Nestling in the northwest corner of the state, 165km from Rio, between the borders of São Paulo and Minas Gerais, the **Parque Nacional do Itatiaia** (R$3 entrance) is the oldest national park in Brazil, founded in 1937 and covering 120 square kilometres of the Mantigueira mountain range. People come here to climb – favourites are the **Pico das Agulhas Negras** (2787m) and the **Pico de Prateleira** (2540m) – and the park is also an important nature reserve.

The park comprises waterfalls, primary forest, wildlife and orchids – but tragically a fire in 1988 ravaged some twenty percent of the park's area. In the sections affected by the fire, forest and pasture land were devastated, rare orchids and native conifers (*Podocarpus lamperti* and *Araucaria angustifolia*) destroyed; the fire reached areas of the Serra da Mantigueira, 2500m above sea level, wiping out forty kilometres of mountain pathways. In the areas most favoured by biologists, who come to study the rich fauna and flora, the once-beautiful alpine scenery now resembles a lunar landscape. Also severely affected were the many natural springs and streams that combine to form the Bonito, Preto, Pirapitinga and Palmital rivers; these supply the massive hydrographic basin of the Paraíba plate, giving much-needed oxygenation to the Paraíba watercourse in one of its most polluted stretches. The situation is gradually improving, but ecologists reckon that it will still take many more years to repair this environmental disaster. For the casual walker, however, there's still plenty of unaffected park to be seen.

Itatiaia

The town of **ITATIAIA**, situated on the BR-116, is surrounded by beautiful scenery and makes a good base: it has plenty of **hotels**, mainly found along Via Dutra, the two-kilometre-long road that links the town and park – take the minibus marked "Hotel Simon" from Praça São José. The *Hotel Simon* itself (Ⓣ24/3352-1122, Ⓦwww.hotelsimon.com.br; ❺ full board) is extremely comfortable and in a gorgeous setting, with a wonderful orchid garden attached (daily 9–11am). Nearby and also set amidst lovely grounds is the more intimate *Pousada Aldeia dos Pássaros* (Ⓣ24/3352-1152, Ⓦwww.paldeiadospassaros.com.br; ❸). In town, there's a **youth hostel** at Rua João Mauricio de Macedo Costa 352 (Ⓣ24/2352-1232; R$20 per person). There's accommodation in **cabins** in the park, but they should normally be booked about two weeks in advance at the Administração do Parque Nacional de Itatiaia (Ⓣ24/2352-1461) in Itatiaia town. You can get **information** and maps at the visitors' centre (daily 8am–5pm) and at the Museu Regional de Fauna and Flora (Tues–Sun 10am–4pm). Tourist information on Itatiaia and the park is also available from the Secretaría de Turismo in Itatiaia, at Rua São José 210 (Ⓣ24/2352-1660, ext 305).

Penedo

The other possible base for visting the park is the small town of **PENEDO**, 14km away and connected to Itatiaia by regular buses. Penedo was settled in 1929 by immigrants from Finland, one of numerous Finnish utopian communities established in Latin America at about the same time. With vegetarianism and agricultural self-sufficiency being amongst the settlement's founding tenets, the Finnish community struggled to survive as they discovered that the land they occupied was unsuitable for cultivation. Those Finns who opted to remain in Penedo turned to tourism and the area gradually became popular with weekenders from São Paulo and Rio, who come for the horse riding and to buy the chocolates, jams, preserves and local liquors that are produced here. Much is made of this Nordic heritage, despite the fact that today only a very small minority of the population are of Finnish origin. Nevertheless, Finnish tango, polka and other dances are performed every Saturday night (9pm–1am) at the *Clube Finlândia*, and the **Museu Finlandês da Dona Eva** at Av. das Mangueiras 2601 (Wed–Sat 10am–5pm, Sun 9am–3pm) has displays of documents, photos, handicrafts and furniture relating to Finnish immigration in the region. Penedo is also a good place to visit if you like saunas, since most hotels have one. It's usually easy to find a **place to stay** – there are dozens of hotels in and near the town, though few real budget places. *Pequena Suécia* at Rua Toivo Suni 33 (Ⓣ24/3351-1275, Ⓦwww.pequenasuecia.com.br; ❺) is an excellent choice, and also features a fine Swedish restaurant; alternatively the *Pousada A Trilha* at Estrada das Três Cachoeiras 3951 (Ⓣ24/3351-1349, Ⓦwww.penedo.com/trilha; ❹) is comfortably rustic. A more basic option is the *Rio das Pedras* at Rua Resende 39 (Ⓣ24/3351-1019; ❸). Most people eat at their hotels, but there are also a good number of decent Scandinavian- and Finnish-style restaurants in town. Especially worth trying are the delicious open sandwiches at the *Restaurante Skandinávia*, Av. das Mangueiras 2631 (daily, 6–11pm) and the smorgasbord and fresh trout at *Koskenkorva*, one of the county's only Finnish restaurants, at Estrada das Três Cachoeiras 3955 (daily, noon–midnight).

Vassouras and Valença

Northeast of Volta Redonda, the university towns of **Vassouras** and **Valença** make good targets if you have a car and a few spare days. Both are considered national historical monuments, key centres of Brazil's nineteenth-century coffee-based economy. Today, dairy farming has almost totally replaced coffee production, but relics from the days when the "coffee barons" reigned supreme are still visible.

Vassouras, on the main BR-393, is the smaller and more appealing of the two towns, with many late nineteenth-century buildings in the centre of town around the Campo Belo. However, it's the old **coffee fazenda houses** nearby that are the main attraction, but without your own car you won't be able to see much. The tourist information office is at Rua Barão de Capivari 20 (Mon–Fri 9am–6pm) and will give details of which of the privately owned houses are open for visits. The most impressive ones are located off the RJ-115 highway north of town, with **Santa Mônica** being the oldest, best preserved and generally the most interesting of the houses. Another beautifully preserved house that's often open to visitors is **São Fernando**, about 1km from Massambará, an outlying district in the *municipio* of Vassouras. If you want to **stay** overnight, the *Gramado da Serra* at Rua Aldo Cavalli 7 (Ⓣ24/2471-2314; ❷), the *Mara Palace* at Rua Chanceler Raul Fernandes 121 (Ⓣ24/2471-2524; ❸) and the *Santa Amelia*, Av. Rui Barbosa 526 (Ⓣ24/2471-1897; ❹), are all central. While Valença is less attractive than Vassouras, the *fazenda* houses off RJ-145 and RJ-151 to the east merit a look: ask at the tourist office at Praça XV de Novembre 676 (Mon–Fri 9am–6pm). The easiest to visit is the *Fazenda São Polycarpo* (10am–5pm) at Km 18 on the road leading to the village of Rio das Flores. Built in 1834 for the

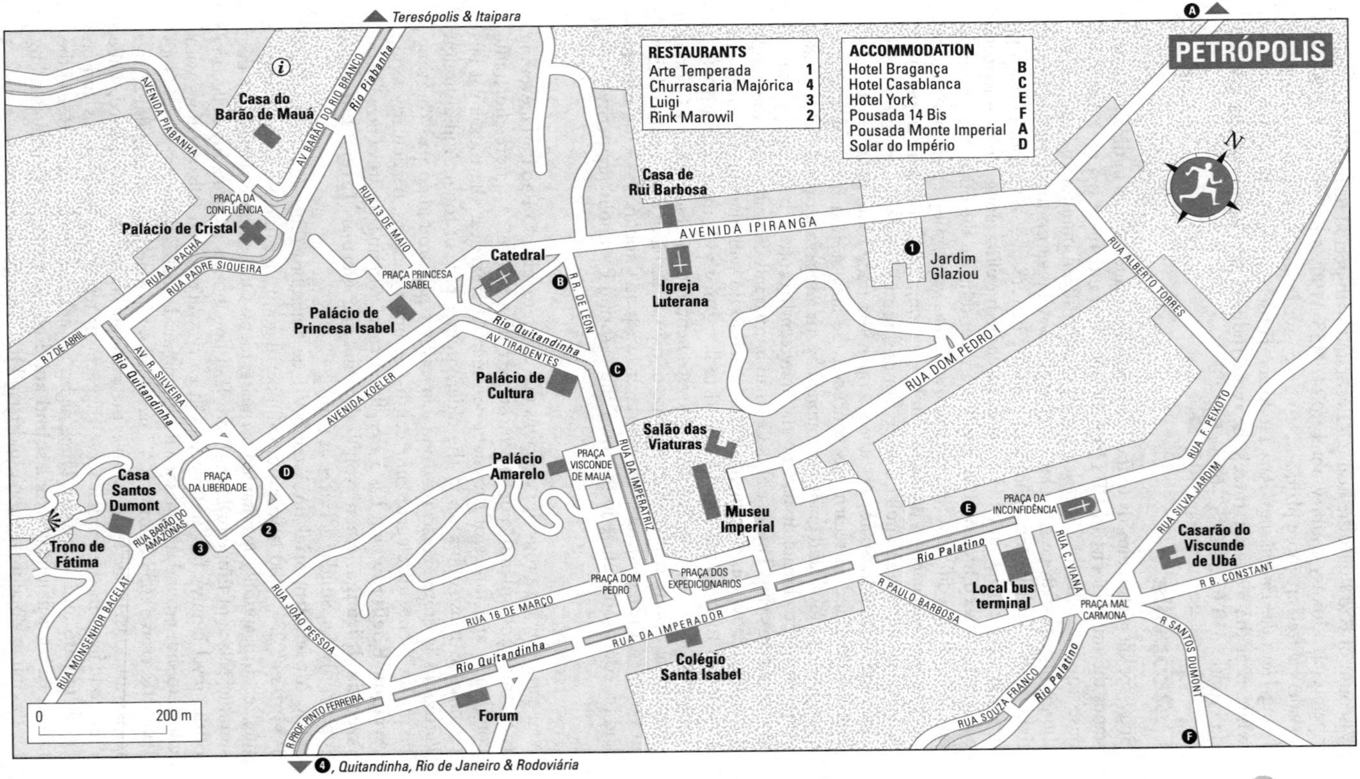

PETRÓPOLIS

RESTAURANTS

Arte Temperada	1
Churrascaria Majórica	4
Luigi	3
Rink Marowil	2

ACCOMMODATION

Hotel Bragança	B
Hotel Casablanca	C
Hotel York	E
Pousada 14 Bis	F
Pousada Monte Imperial	A
Solar do Império	D

Teresópolis & Itaipara
A
4, Quitandinha, Rio de Janeiro & Rodoviária

Casa do Barão de Mauá
Palácio de Cristal
Praça da Confluência
Catedral
Casa de Rui Barbosa
Igreja Luterana
Jardim Glaziou
Palácio de Princesa Isabel
Praça Princesa Isabel
Palácio de Cultura
Palácio Amarelo
Praça Visconde de Maua
Salão das Viaturas
Museu Imperial
Praça dos Expedicionarios
Praça Dom Pedro
Praça da Liberdade
Casa Santos Dumont
Trono de Fátima
Colégio Santa Isabel
Forum
Praça da Inconfidência
Local bus terminal
Praça Mal Carmona
Casarão do Viscunde de Ubá

Avenida Piabanha
Av Barão do Rio Branco
Rio Piabanha
Rua 13 de Maio
Rua A. Pacha
Rua Padre Siqueira
R 7 de Abril
Av R. Silveira
Rio Quitandinha
Avenida Koeler
Av Tiradentes
R R. de Leon
Avenida Ipiranga
Rua Alberto Torres
Rua Dom Pedro I
Rua F. Peixoto
Rua Silva Jardim
R B. Constant
R Santos Dumont
Rua Souza Franco
Rio Palatino
Rua C. Viana
R Paulo Barbosa
Rua da Imperatriz
Rua da Imperador
Rua 16 de Março
Rua João Pessoa
Rua Barão do Amazonas
Rua Monsenhor Bacelat
R Prof. Pinto Ferreira

0 200 m

Viscount of Rio Preto, the house is decorated with period furnishings and now operates as a luxury country hotel (ⓣ24/2458-1190; ❺ full board). The **hotels** in Valença itself are more plain and less expensive than in Vassouras, with the best being *Hotel dos Engenheiros*, Rua Teodorico Fonseca 525 (ⓣ24/2453-4530; ❷), while, near the *rodoviária*, there's the more rudimentary *Valenciano*, Praça Paulo de Frontin 360 (ⓣ24/2452-0890; ❷).

Petrópolis

Sixty-six kilometres directly to the north of Rio de Janeiro, high in the mountains, stands the imperial city of **PETRÓPOLIS**. The route there is a busy one, with buses run by Fácil and Única leaving Rio every fifteen minutes. In fine weather, the journey to Petrópolis is glorious. On the way up, sit on the left-hand side of the bus and don't be too concerned with the driver's obsession with overtaking heavy goods vehicles on blind corners. You'll be traveling along a one-way road, bordered by naked rock on one side and a sheer drop on the other; the return to Rio is made by a different route that also snakes its way through terrifying mountain passes. The scenery is dramatic, climbing among forested slopes that give way suddenly to ravines and gullies, while clouds shroud the surrounding mountains.

In 1720, Bernardo Soares de Proença opened a trade route between Rio and Minas Gerais, and in return was conceded the area around the present site of Petrópolis as a royal land grant. Surrounded by stunning scenery, and with a gentle, alpine summer climate, it had by the nineteenth century become a favourite retreat of Rio's elite. The arrival of German immigrants contributed to the development of Petrópolis as a town, and has much to do with the curious European Gothic feel to the place. Dom Pedro II took a fancy to Petrópolis and in 1843 designated it the summer seat of his government. He also established a German agricultural colony, which failed because of the unsuitability of the soil, and then in 1849 – with an epidemic of yellow fever sweeping through Rio – the emperor and his court took refuge in the town, thus assuring Petrópolis' prosperity.

The town

You can easily do a tour of Petrópolis in a day, returning to Rio in the evening (or continuing inland). For the most part it's possible to ignore the traffic congestion and fumes of the main commercial area, near the municipal bus terminal as most sights are in the older, quieter part of town. And although Petrópolis is quite spread out, one can easily stroll around to pass the time, taking in plenty of elegant nineteenth-century mansions, particularly along **Avenida Koeller**, which has a tree-lined canal running up its centre, or on **Avenida Ipiranga**, where you'll also find the German **Igreja Luterana** (open only for Sunday services at 9am).

The **Museu Imperial** on Avenida VII de Setembro (Tues–Sun 11am–6pm; R$4; ⓣ24/2237-8000, ⓦwww.museuimperial.gov.br) is a fine Neoclassical structure set in beautifully maintained formal gardens. Once the remarkably modest summer palace of Emperor Dom Pedro II, it now houses a fascinating collection of the royal family's bits and pieces. On entry, you're given felt overshoes with which to slide around the polished floors, and inside there's everything from Dom Pedro II's crown (639 diamonds, 77 pearls, all set in finely wrought gold) to the regal commode. In the former stables the royal railway carriage is displayed, while other buildings in the garden serve as space for temporary exhibitions and an excellent **café and tearoom**. Three nights a week (Thurs–Sat 8pm; R$28) the former palace is illuminated for a **sound and light show** – well worth attending for the music alone if you don't understand the Portuguese narration.

The **Catedral São Pedro de Alcântara** (8am–6pm) blends with the rest of the architecture around, but is much more recent than its rather overbearing neo-Gothic style suggests – while work began in 1884, it was only finished in 1939. Inside, on the walls, are ten relief sculptures depicting scenes from the Crucifixion; in the mausoleum lie the tombs of Dom Pedro himself, Princess Regent Dona Isabel and several other royal personages. Other historic buildings worth tracking down are the **Palácio de Cristal**, Rua Alfredo Pacha (Tues–Sun 9am–6.30pm); **Casa Santos Dumont** at Rua do Encanto 22 (Tues–Sun 9.30am–5pm), an alpine chalet built in 1918 and the home of the Brazilian aviator of that name, containing personal memorabilia; the **Casa do Barão de Maurá** at Praça da Confluência 3 (Mon–Sat 9am–6.30pm, Sun 9am–5pm), featuring displays devoted to the baron, best known for his role in constructing Brazil's first railway; and the rather grand, half-timbered Norman-style **Palácio Quitandinha** on the Estrada de Quitandinha, just outside of town. Once the Quitandinha Casino, this last building stopped receiving the rich and famous when the Brazilian government prohibited gambling in 1946, and it was eventually converted into a luxury apartment building. Nearby, at Rua Cristóvão Colombo 1034, the **Museu Casa do Colono** (Tues–Sun 9.30am–5pm) is a simple house dating back to 1847 that has a small collection relating to the German immigrants who settled in and around Petrópolis in the early nineteenth century. German-speaking visitors in particular may also be interested in visiting the tomb of the Austrian-born writer **Stefan Zweig**, one of the greatest European writers of the twentieth century, who in 1942 committed suicide in Petrópolis together with his wife. You can take a look at the outside of his house at Rua Gonçalves Dias 34 in the suburb of Valparaiso, near the municipal cemetery.

Practicalities

Buses from Rio, São Paulo, Belo Horizonte and Teresópolis arrive and depart from the new **rodoviária**, some 10km from town approaching from Rio. From there you can take a bus to the municipal bus terminal, a short walk to most of the sights in Petrópolis.

There's an extremely helpful **tourist office** (☎0800-241-516) at the entrance to town at Quitandinha (Mon–Thurs & Sun 8am–7pm; Fri & Sat 8am–8pm), with a branch at the Casa do Barão de Maurá, Praça da Confluência 3 (Mon–Sat 9am–6.30pm; Sun and holidays 9am–5pm). Town attractions aside, Petrópolis has easy access to some lovely climbing country, and if you're planning to do any **hiking** contact the Centro Alpinista, Rua Irmãos d'Angelo 28 – it's an amateur association, so go after 8pm.

Restaurants are surprisingly lacklustre in Petrópolis, most of the best being some distance from town. However, there's a good and moderately priced Portuguese restaurant in the *Hotel Bragança*, and an excellent *por kilo* choice, *Rink Marowil*, at Praça Rui Barbosa 27. Much more atmospheric is the *Arte Temperada* (Thurs–Mon lunch, Fri & Sat also dinner), in a converted stable of a beautiful nineteenth-century mansion at Rua Ipiranga 716; the modern Brazilian offerings include local trout and salads. Rather similar in style is the restaurant at *Solar do Império*'s (see p.168), housed within the main building of an elegant mansion. For Italian food, decent pasta and pizza are offered by *Luigi* at Praça da Liberdade 185. If you feel like venturing out from the centre, the place to head for either lunch or dinner is the *Pousada Alcobaça* at Rua Dr Agostinho Goulão 298 (☎24/2221-1240) in the northern suburb of Corrêas. Using fresh ingredients such as local dairy produce, freshwater fish and vegetables and herbs from the *pousada*'s kitchen garden, the moderately priced food is both unpretentious and excellent. Be sure to allow time after lunch for a gentle walk in the beautiful gardens.

Accommodation

There are some reasonable **hotels** in town, but most people prefer staying outside of the centre where there are dozens of attractive *pousadas*, usually with beautiful gardens. These, however, are only practical if you have a car.

Albergue da Quitandinha Rua Uruguai 570, Quitandinha ⓣ 24/2247-9165, ⓦ www.alberguequitandinha.com.br. Located in a pleasant residential suburb near the *rodoviária*, this secure and comfortable youth hostel offers both double rooms (❸) and beds in dorms (R$35 per person).

Atelier Molinaro Rua Dr Hermogênio Silva 606, Retiro ⓣ 24/2242-2436, ⓦ www.pousadamolinaro.com. Located 5km north of the city centre, this is one of Petrópolis's most accessible country hotels and, by local standards, unpretentious. Rooms are comfortable and the grounds a delight. ❼

Hotel Casablanca Rua da Imperatriz 286 ⓣ 24/2242-6662, ⓦ www.casablancahotel.com.br. This once stylish hotel next to the *Palácio Imperial* is somewhat institutional in character. Nevertheless, the pool, central location and clean, well-appointed rooms make this a popular city-centre choice. ❺

Hotel York Rua do Imperador 78 ⓣ 24/2243-2662, ⓦ www.hotelyork.com.br. Though lacking atmosphere, the perfectly comfortable *York* is a decent budget choice that's an easy walk to the town's museums and handy for the municipal bus station. ❹

Pousada 14 Bis Rua Santos Dumont 162 ⓣ 24/2231-0946, ⓦ www.pousada14bis.com.br. A lovely centrally located pousada with tastefully furnished bedrooms, a cosy lounge full of Santos Dumont (the Brazilian aviator) memorabilia and relaxing gardens. ❹–❺

Pousada Monte Imperial Rua José Alencar 27 ⓣ 24/2237-1664, ⓦ www.pousadamonteimperial.com.br. Located on a hilltop, this *pousada* has the air of a country inn and is a stiff walk from the town's attractions. Rooms are quite small but appealing, and there's a nice garden with a pool, too; the English-speaking owner is extremely friendly. ❻

Solar do Império Av. Koeler 376 ⓣ 24/2103-3000, ⓦ www.solardoimperio.com.br. Located in one of the quietest corners of the city centre, this Neoclassical mansion dating from 1875 is now a discreetly luxurious hotel. All the rooms have recently been restored to their period splendour, while every modern convenience and comfort is also offered. The grounds include a small indoor pool and there's a fine restaurant as well. ❼

Teresópolis

While **TERESÓPOLIS** can be reached directly from Rio by bus, the best route is from Petrópolis. It's not a long journey, no more than 40km from Petrópolis, but the road to the highest town in the state (872m) passes through the **Serra dos Órgãos**, much of which is a national park – dramatic rock formations here resemble rows of organ pipes (hence the range's name), dominated by the towering **Dedo de Deus** ("God's Finger") peak. Teresópolis, like Petrópolis, owed its initial development to the opening of a road between Minas Gerais and Rio during the eighteenth century. It, too, was a favoured summer retreat (for Empress Teresa Cristina, for whom the town was named) and though smaller than Petrópolis it also shares some of its Germanic characteristics, including a benevolent alpine climate. The town itself is extremely dull, centred on one main street that changes its name every couple of blocks, and the interest lies entirely in the surrounding countryside. There are, however, magnificent views from almost anywhere in town – especially from **Soberbo**, where the Rio highway enters Teresópolis, with its panoramic view of Rio and the Baixada Fluminense.

Around Teresópolis

There's plenty to do in the surrounding countryside, within a few kilometres of town. Lakes and waterfalls – the **Cascata dos Amores** and the **Cascata do Imbuí** – make for good swimming; there's the **Mulher de Pedra** rock formation with its series of peaks rising to 2040m; and birdwatching opportunities are found amongst the lakes of the **Granja Comary** plateau (on the BR-495).

The main attraction, though, is the **Parque Nacional da Serra dos Órgãos**, where favourite peaks for those with mountain-goat tendencies are the Agulha do Diablo (2050m) and the Pedra do Sino (2263m); the latter has a path leading to the summit, a relatively easy three-hour trip (take refreshments). It costs R$3 per person, and an additional R$5 per car, to enter the park, and basic **accommodation** for climbers and hikers is available at the *Pousada Refúgio do Parque* (Ⓣ21/9687-4539; ❷; reservations essential). There are some campsites, too, but no equipment for rent, so you'll need to come prepared.

For more information, visit Teresópolis' **tourist office** (Mon–Fri 8am–5pm; Ⓣ21/2642-1737) at Praça Olimpica. **Guidebooks and trail maps** can be purchased in front of the Igreja Matriz at the Cupelo Banco de Jornais – maps are a must, as walks are not signposted. In the national park, you'll also be able to hire guides inexpensively.

Practicalities

Most of the numerous **hotels** in Teresópolis are located in the picturesque hills, far from the town centre. The best of them, set in a large park with several swimming pools and an extensive network of trails, is the *Rosa dos Ventos* (Ⓣ21/2644-8833, Ⓦwww.hotelrosadosventos.com.br; ❽) on the Nova Friburgo road, some 22km from town; however, the hotel does not accept children under the age of 14. Cheaper alternatives are the *Philipp*, Rua Duval Fonseca 1333 (Ⓣ21/2742-2970; ❸) and the *Center*, Rua Sebastião Teixeira 245 (Ⓣ21/2742-5870; ❸), functional hotels that seem more geared for business travellers than tourists. A far better option near the town centre and set in attractive grounds is the very pretty *Pousada das Mansardas*, Rua Wilhelm Christian Klene 230 (Ⓣ21/3641-5102, Ⓦwww.mansardas.com.br; ❹). Also fine is the *Várzea Palace Hotel*, Rua Sebastião Teixeira 41 (Ⓣ21/2742-0878; ❸), a beautiful white building that was once the most elegant place to stay. Only faint traces of its former luxury remain, but the hotel is clean, welcoming and very inexpensive. There is also a well-equipped **youth hostel**, the *Recanto do Lord*, near the centre of town at Rua Luiza Pereira Soares 109 (Ⓣ21/2742-5586, Ⓦwww.teresopolishostel.com.br; R$35 per person), which has private rooms as well (❸). Of the dozens of **restaurants** in and around town, only two stand out, but both are expensive: *Dona Irene*, Rua Tenente Luís Meireles 1800, Bom Retiro (Ⓣ21/2742-2901; closed Sun evening and all Mon & Tues), serves marvellous Russian food and reservations are essential; *Margô* at Rua Heitor de Moura Estevão 259 (closed Mon) serves up satisfying German cuisine.

Nova Friburgo

NOVA FRIBURGO, an attractive city of 180,000 people, lies in a valley surrounded by mountains to the northeast of Teresópolis. It was founded by a hundred Swiss immigrant families from the canton of Fribourg, transferred to the region by royal decree in 1818. The Germanic influence remains, principally in the architecture of the *bairro* of **Conego**. During the summer, the many hotels and *pousadas* outside Nova Friburgo's centre are brimming with city folk who come to enjoy the waterfalls and wooded trails or take on the local peaks – like **Caledonia**, a favourite with hang-gliders. Less of a hike, the dramatic rock formations of the **Furnos da Catete** forestry reserve on the road to Bom Jardim (23km north on the BR-492) offer an excellent walk; and for an easy view of the world a cable car (9am–5.30pm) from Praça dos Suspiros in town takes you to the summit of **Morro da Cruz**, some 1800m up.

You could easily stay awhile in this peaceful area, and there are some good **hotels** to choose from. Some, like the very pretty *Pousada do Riacho* (Ⓣ22/2522-2823,

Ⓦwww.pousadadoriacho.com.br; ❻) at Km 60 of the Teresópolis–Nova Friburgo road lie a short distance outside of town and feature park-like grounds and every comfort; nearer the centre is the faded, though still comfortable, *Hotel São Paulo*, Rua Monsenhor Miranda 41 (Ⓣ24/2522-9135, Ⓦwww.hotelsaopaulo.com.br; ❸). Other budget options include *Hotel Montanus*, Rua Fernando Bizzotto 26 (Ⓣ24/2522-1235; ❸), or the *Hotel Fabris* (Ⓣ24/2522-2852; ❸), at Av. Alberto Braune 148, the same street as the bus station. There's also the excellent *Alêfriburgo* **youth hostel** at Rua Ernesto Bizoto Filho 2 (Ⓣ24/2522-0540, Ⓦwww.ajfriburgo.cjb.net; R$23 per person or ❸ for a double room) with clean accommodation, a small pool and stunning mountain views.

For **food**, try the *Oberland* delicatessen on Rua Fernando Bizzotto, which doubles as a restaurant with cheap, tasty Swiss and German food – veal sausage, sauerkraut and the like. The *Churrascaria Majórica*, Praça Getúlio Vargas 74, is good, too, and in the same square you can buy home-made preserves and liqueurs. For a major splurge, head out to the district of Amparo, 14km east of town on the RJ-150, and try the excellent French–Swiss restaurant the *Auberge Suisse*, located in a small and rather exclusive hotel of the same name.

To reach Nova Friburgo from Rio takes about three hours by **bus** (departures from Rodoviária Novo Rio every 30min). You'll head across the Rio–Niterói bridge, and out on Highways 101, 104 and 116. It's also possible to get a bus from Teresópolis.

Travel details

Buses

International departures daily from Rio to Asunción (30hr), Buenos Aires (46hr), Montevideo (37hr) and Santiago de Chile (72hr).

Paraty to: Angra dos Reis (every 30min; 2hr); Rio (8 daily; 4hr 30min); São Paulo (4 daily; 5hr); Trindade (7 daily; 45min); Ubatuba (3 daily; 2hr).

Petrópolis to: Belo Horizonte (5 daily; 5hr); Rio (every 30min; 90min); São Paulo (2 daily; 6hr 30min); Teresópolis (4 daily; 1hr 30min).

Rio to: Angra dos Reis (hourly; 3hr); Belém (1 daily; 50hr); Belo Horizonte (20 daily; 6hr 30min); Brasília (8 daily; 17hr); Búzios (7 daily; 3hr); Cabo Frio (6 daily; 2hr 30min); Campo Grande (5 daily; 21hr); Florianópolis (3 daily; 18hr); Fortaleza (1 daily; 44hr); Foz do Iguaçu (6 daily; 22hr); Ouro Preto (1 daily; 7hr); Paraty (9 daily; 4hr 30min); Petrópolis (every 30min; 90min); Porto Seguro (3 daily; 19hr); Recife (4 daily; 38hr); Salvador (6 daily; 24hr); São Luis (1 daily; 51hr); São Paulo (every 15min; 6hr); Teresópolis (every hour; 2hr); Vitória (hourly; 7hr 30min).

Planes

Frequent **domestic** flights from Sector A of Galeão airport on Ilha do Governador to most state capitals and many other internal destinations.

Rio–São Paulo shuttle and flights within the state of Rio from Santos Dumont, downtown, every 30min from 6.30am to 10.30pm (55min).

2

Minas Gerais and Espírito Santo

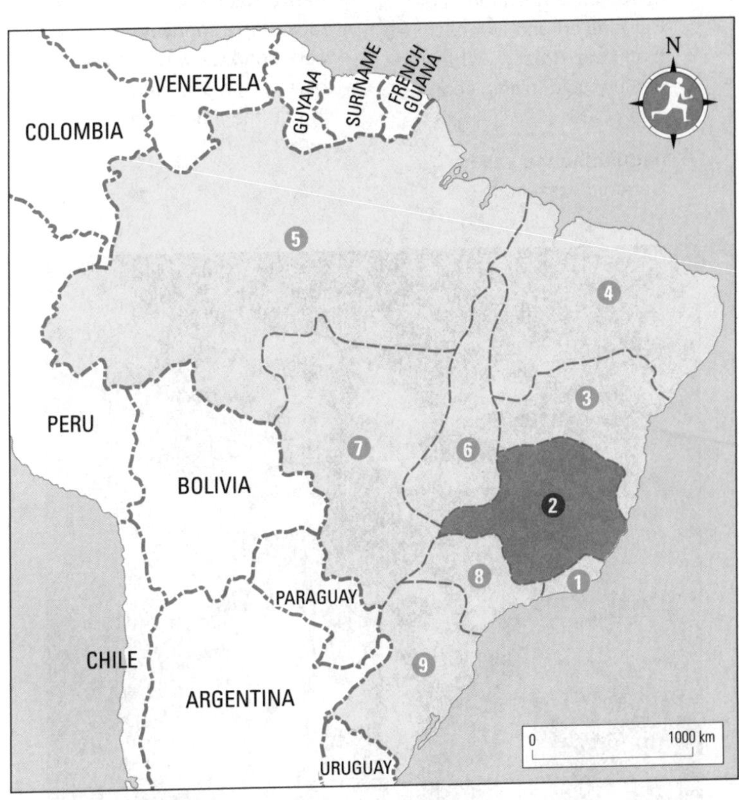

CHAPTER 2

Highlights

* **Sculptures by Aleijadinho** Amazingly, the master sculptor of Brazilian Baroque produced his best work after his hands were deformed by leprosy. See p.196

* **Historic Ouro Preto** Nowhere in Brazil is there a more rich concentration of Baroque art and architecture than here, Brazil's eighteenth-century gold mining centre. See p.199

* **Jequitinhonha Valley** Ceramic vessels, in human- and animal-inspired shapes of pre-colonial heritage, are still produced in remote areas of northern Minas Gerais and sold in places like the excellent Centro de Artesanato in Araçuaí. See p.226

* **Pedra Azul** This vast granite rock in the eponymous state park sparkles with tints of blues or greens, depending on the time of day. See p.250

△ Igreja São Francisco de Assis

2

Minas Gerais and Espírito Santo

The French geologist Gorceix summed up **Minas Gerais** 150 years ago, when he wrote that the state had "a breast of iron and a heart of gold". Its hills and mountains contain the richest mineral deposits in Brazil, and led to the area being christened "General Mines" when gold and diamonds were found at the end of the seventeenth century. The gold strikes sparked a wave of migration from Rio and São Paulo, which lasted a century and shifted the centre of gravity of Brazil's economy and population from the Northeast decisively to the South, where it has remained ever since. In the nineteenth century new metals, especially iron, steel and manganese, replaced gold in importance, while the uplands in the west and east proved ideal for coffee production. Land too steep for coffee bushes was converted to cattle pasture, and the luxuriant forests of southern Minas were destroyed and turned into charcoal for smelting. The bare hills are a foretaste of what parts of Amazônia might look like a century from now, and only their strange beauty – sea-like, as waves of them recede into the distance – saves them from seeming desolate.

While mineral wealth still flows from Minas' hills, the area's eighteenth-century mining settlements are now quiet, beautiful colonial towns, with a fraction of the population they had two hundred years ago. Called *as cidades históricas*, "the historic cities", they are the only colonial remnants in southern Brazil that stand comparison with the Northeast. Most importantly, they're the repository of a great flowering of Baroque **religious art** that took place here in the eighteenth century: *arte sacra mineira* was the finest work of its time in the Americas, and Minas Gerais can lay claim to undisputably the greatest figure in Brazilian cultural history – the mulatto leper sculptor, **Aleijadinho**, whose magnificent work is scattered throughout the historic cities. The most important of the *cidades históricas* are **Ouro Preto**, **Mariana** and **Sabará**, all within easy striking distance of Belo Horizonte, and **Congonhas**, **São João del Rei**, **Tiradentes** and **Diamantina**, a little further afield.

In more recent times, Minas Gerais has also been at the centre of Brazilian history. *Mineiros*, who own a well-deserved reputation for political cunning, have produced the two greatest postwar Brazilian presidents: **Juscelino Kubitschek**, the builder of Brasília, and **Tancredo Neves**, midwife to the rebirth of Brazilian democracy in 1985. It was troops from Minas who put down the São Paulo revolt against Getúlio Vargas' populist regime in the brief civil war of 1932 and, less creditably, it was the army division in Minas that moved against Rio in 1964 and ensured the success of the military coup.

In keeping with this economic and political force, the capital of Minas, **Belo Horizonte**, is a thriving, modern metropolis – one of the largest cities in Brazil and second only to São Paulo as an industrial centre, which, with its forest of skyscrapers and miles of industrial suburbs, it rather resembles. It lies in the centre of the rich mining and agricultural hinterland that has made the state one of the economic powerhouses of Brazil, running from the coffee estates of western Minas to the mines and cattle pastures of the valley of the **Rio Doce**, in the east of the state. You can read the area's history in its landscape, the jagged horizons a direct result of decades of mining. The largest cities of the region apart from Belo Horizonte are Juiz de Fora in the south, Governador Valadares to the east, and Uberaba and Uberlândia in the west – all modern and unprepossessing; only Belo Horizonte can honestly be recommended as worth visiting.

All *mineiros* would agree that the soul of the state lies in the rural areas, in the hill and mountain villages of its vast **interior**. North of Belo Horizonte, the grassy slopes and occasional patches of forest are swiftly replaced by the stubby trees and savanna of the Planalto Central (leading to Brasília and central Brazil proper) and, in northeastern Minas, by the cactus, rock and perennial drought of the *sertão* – as desperately poor and economically backward as anywhere in the Northeast proper. The northern part of the state is physically dominated by the hills and highlands of the **Serra do Espinhaço**, a range that runs north–south through the state like a massive dorsal fin before petering out south of Belo Horizonte. To its east, the **Rio Jequitinhonha** sustains life in the parched landscapes of the *sertão mineiro*; to the west is the flat river valley of the **Rio São Francisco**, which rises here before winding through the interior of the Northeast. The extreme west of Minas Gerais state is taken over by the agricultural **Triângulo Mineiro**, a wealthy region centred on the city of Uberlândia, with far closer economic ties with São Paulo than with the rest of Minas Gerais. Many people in the Triângulo Mineiro believe that the region would benefit from being a separate state – a cause that some local politicians have adopted.

In the southwest of Minas, in fine mountainous scenery near the border with São Paulo, are a number of **spa towns** built around mineral water springs: **São Lourenço** and **Caxambu** are small and quiet, but **Poços de Caldas** is a large and very lively resort. Perhaps the most scenically attractive part of Minas Gerais – though also the least visited – is the **eastern** border with Espírito Santo. There's some spectacular walking country in the **Caparaó** national park, where the third highest mountain in Brazil, the 2890-metre **Pico da Bandeira**, is more easily climbed than its height suggests.

Espírito Santo, the small state that separates eastern Minas from the Atlantic, is the kind of place that you rarely hear about, even within Brazil. With the exception of its coastal resorts, it's almost completely off the tourist map. This is hard to understand, as the interior of the state has some claim to being one of the most beautiful parts of Brazil. Settled mostly by Italians and Germans, it has a disconcertingly European feel – cows graze in front of German-looking farm houses, and, if it weren't for the heat, palm trees, coffee bushes and humming-birds darting around, you might imagine yourself somewhere in Switzerland. Vast numbers of *mineiros* head for Espírito Santo for their holidays, but are only interested in the beaches, the one thing landlocked Minas lacks. This has the fortunate effect of cramming all the crowds into an easily avoidable coastal strip, leaving the interior free for you to explore.

The only places of any size in Espírito Santo are **Vitória**, a rather grimy city saved by a fine location (on an island surrounded by hills and granite outcrops) and **Vila Velha**, its equally uninspiring twin city. These were amongst the few spots on the coast that could be easily defended, and the **Botocudo Indians** were able to restrict the Portuguese to scattered coastal settlements until the last century. This is one of the reasons the interior is relatively thinly settled; the other is the sheer difficulty of communications in the steep, thickly forested hills that rear up into mountains along the border with Minas. The semi-deciduous tropical forest that once carpeted much of the southern coast of Brazil still survives relatively unscathed here – and is what southern Minas would have looked like before the gold rushes. To a degree, the forest resembles Amazonian jungle, but if you look closely during autumn and winter (April to Sept) you'll see that many of the trees have shed their leaves. The best way to view the region is to make the round of the towns that began as German and Italian colonies: **Santa Teresa**, **Santa Leopoldina**, **Santa Maria**, **Domingos Martins** and **Venda Nova** – the last near the remarkable sheer granite face of **Pedra Azul**, one of the least-known but most spectacular sights in the country.

Belo Horizonte

The best way to approach **BELO HORIZONTE** is from the south, over the magnificent hills of the Serra do Espinhaço, on a road that winds back and forth before finally cresting a ridge where the entire city is set out before you. It's a spectacular sight, as Belo Horizonte sprawls in an enormous bowl surrounded by hills, a sea of skyscrapers, *favelas* and industrial suburbs. From the centre, the jagged, rust-coloured skyline of the Serra do Espinhaço, which gave the city its name, is always visible on the horizon – still being transformed by the mines gnawing away at the "breast of iron".

Despite its size and importance, Belo Horizonte is little more than a century old, laid out in the early 1890s on the site of the poor village of Curral del Rey – of which nothing remains – and shaped by the novel ideas of "progress" that emerged with the new Republic. Belo Horizonte was the first of Brazil's planned cities and is arguably the most successful. As late as 1945 it had only 100,000 inhabitants; now it has well over twenty times that number (forty times if one includes the city's metropolitan hinterland), an explosive rate of growth even by Latin American standards. It rapidly became the most important pole of economic development in the country, after São Paulo, and, while it may not be as historic as the rest of the state, it's difficult not to be impressed by the city's scale and energy. Moreover, Belo Horizonte's central location and proximity to some of the most important *cidades históricas* (Sabará is just outside the city, Ouro Preto and Mariana only two hours away by road) make it a good base for exploring Minas Gerais.

The **central zone** of Belo Horizonte is contained within the inner ring road, the **Avenida do Contorno**; the centre is laid out in a grid pattern, crossed by diagonal *avenidas*, which makes it easy to find your way around on foot, though difficult by car because of a complex system of one-way traffic. The spine of the city is the broad **Avenida Afonso Pena**, with the *rodoviária* at its northern end, in the heart of the downtown area. Just down from the *rodoviária* along Avenida Afonso Pena is the obelisk in the **Praça Sete**, the middle of the hotel and financial district and the city's busiest part; a few blocks further down Afonso Pena are the trees and shade of the **Parque Municipal**. A short distance south of the centre, the **Praça da Liberdade**, Belo Horizonte's main square, is dominated by a double row of imperial palms and important public buildings; the chic residential area of **Savassi**, with its restaurants, nightlife and boutiques, lies southeast.

The only places **beyond the Contorno** you're likely to visit are the artificial lake and Niemeyer buildings of **Pampulha**, to the north, the **Museu Histórico Abílio Barreto** to the southwest and the rambling nature reserve of **Mangabeiras**, on the southern boundary of the city.

Arrival, information and city transport

The nearer of Belo Horizonte's two **airports** is Pampulha (Ⓣ31/3689-2700), 9km from the centre and connected by bus #1202. All flights from other parts of Minas Gerais arrive here, as do a few flights from Brasília, Rio and São Paulo. The much newer Aeroporto Internacional Tancredo Neves (Ⓣ31/3490-2001), usually refered to as Confins, the name of the nearby town, handles most domestic flights as well as the city's few international flights. The airport is well over 30km from Belo Horizonte and, as the connecting road is so bad,

△ Belo Horizonte's train station

the journey can take an hour. Confins is linked to the centre by **airport buses** that leave you either at the *rodoviária* (the *ônibus convencional*; R$1.30) or at the tourist centre, Terminal Turístico JK, west along Avenida Amazonas (the faster, air-conditioned *ônibus executivo*; R$13.50). Both buses have rather erratic timetables (every 20min at best, every 2hr at worst); if you're leaving by plane, phone in advance to check departure times (*convencional* ⓣ31/3271-1335, *executivo* ⓣ31/3271-4522). **Taxis** to the city centre cost around R$20 from Pampulha or R$60 from Confins; there are desks in the arrivals areas from where you can purchase vouchers at rates fixed according to your destination.

The **rodoviária** is on Praça Rio Branco, an easy walk from the commercial centre of the city, and offers direct bus services throughout Minas Gerais and to

Airports & Pampulha
RESTAURANTS
Amigo do Rei 15
Badejo 7
Bem Natural 3
Bonomi Panificadora 9
Buona Tavola 12
Cervejaria Brasil 4
Dona Derna 11
Dona Lucinha 16
Dona Lucinha II 14
Dragon Center 1
Haus München 5
Minas Tênis Clube 10
Quibelanches 2
Sushi Naka 8
Vecchio Sogno 6
Vila Árabe 13
AV OIAPOQUE
Rodoviária
RUA DOS CAETÉS
CENTRO
RUA DOS TUPINAMBAS
RUA DOS CARIJOS
AV. PARANÁ
AVENIDA DO CONTORNO
RUA DOS TAMOIOS
PRAÇA SETE
RUA SÃO PAULO
Igreja São José
RUA CURITIBA
RUA DOS TUPIS
BARRO PRETO
RUA DOS GOITACAZES
PRAÇA RAUL SOARES
Mercado Central
RUA DOS GUAJAJARAS
AV AUGUSTO DE LIMA
Terminal Turístico JK
AVENIDA AMAZONAS
RUA DOS GUAJAJARAS
AVENIDA BIAS FORTES
RUA DOS TIMBIRAS
RUA JUIZ DE FORA
AVENIDA BARBACENA
AVENIDA OLEGARIO MACIEL
CABRAL
RUA DOS AIMORÉS
Brasília & São Paulo
AVENIDA DO CONTORNO
RUA SANTA CATARINA
AVENIDA ALVARES
RUA BERNARDO GUIMARÃES
RUA GONÇALVES DIAS
STO. AGOSTINHO
AVENIDA BIAS FORTES
RUA ALVARENGA PEIXOTO
Museu de Mineralogia
RUA TOMÁS GONZAGA
RUA PROF. ANTONIO ALEIXO
Museu Histórico
Teatro Izabel Hendrix
RUA ANTÔNIO ALBUQUERQUE
LOURDES
RUA RIO DE JANEIRO
ACCOMMODATION
Brasil Palace E
Continental A
HI Chalé Mineiro O
Ibis K
Liberty Palace Q
Majestic BH Centro B
Max Savassi Suite P
Mercure N
Metrópole J
Othon Palace H
Pousadinha Mineira D
Praça da Liberdade L
Savassi M
Sol Belo Horizonte I
Sorrento G
O Sorriso do Largarto R
Sun América Palace C
Wimbledon F
N
RUA FERNANDES TOURINHO
AVENIDA DO CONTORNO
0
500 m

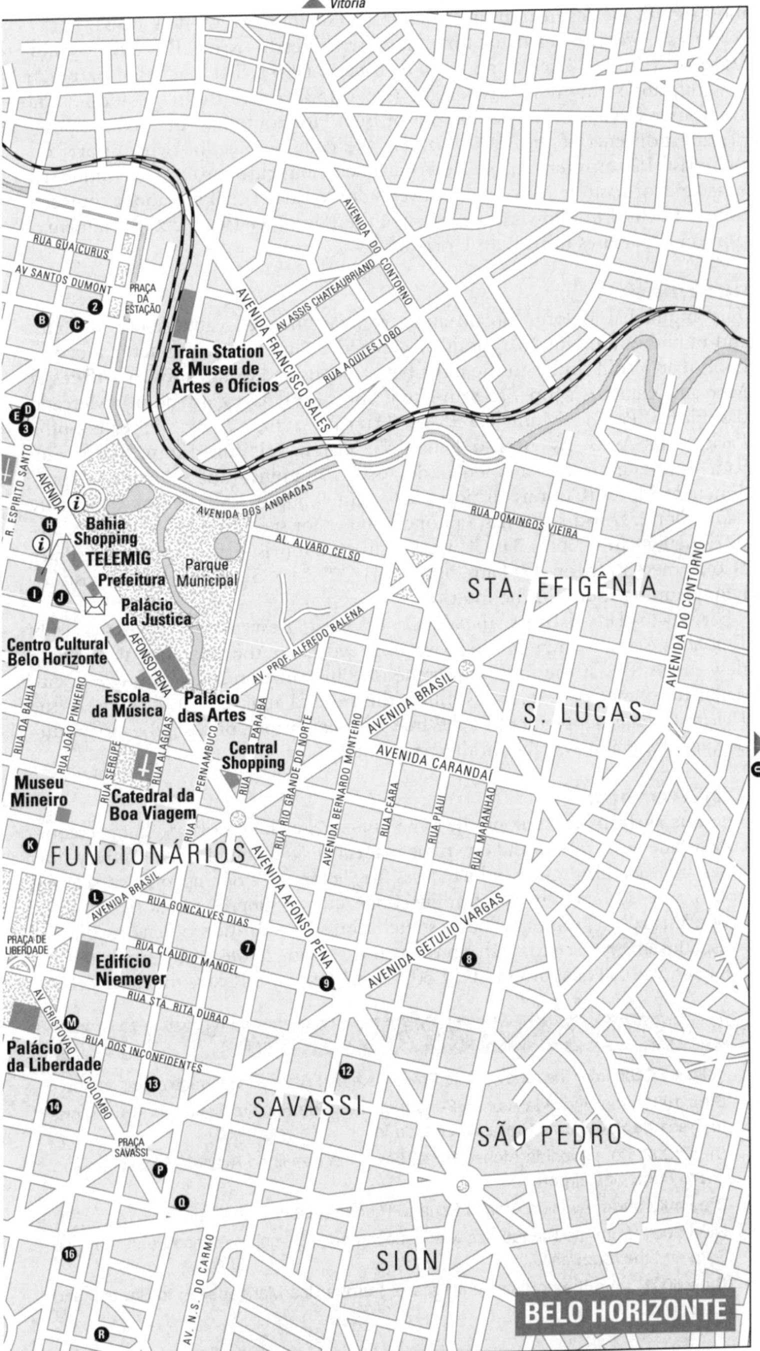
Vitória
RUA GUAICURUS
AV SANTOS DUMONT
PRAÇA DA ESTAÇÃO
Train Station & Museu de Artes e Ofícios
AVENIDA DO CONTORNO
AV ASSIS CHATEAUBRIAND
AVENIDA FRANCISCO SALES
RUA AQUILES LOBO
AVENIDA DOS ANDRADAS
R. ESPIRITO SANTO
AVENIDA
Bahia Shopping
TELEMIG
Prefeitura
Parque Municipal
Palácio da Justica
Centro Cultural Belo Horizonte
AFONSO PENA
RUA DOMINGOS VIEIRA
AL. ALVARO CELSO
STA. EFIGÊNIA
AV. PROF. ALFREDO BALENA
AVENIDA DO CONTORNO
AVENIDA BRASIL
S. LUCAS
RUA DA BAHIA
RUA JOÃO PINHEIRO
Escola da Música
Palácio das Artes
RUA SERGIPE
RUA ALAGOAS
RUA PERNAMBUCO
RUA PARAÍBA
Central Shopping
RUA RIO GRANDE DO NORTE
AVENIDA BERNARDO MONTEIRO
AVENIDA CARANDAÍ
RUA CEARA
RUA PIAUI
RUA MARANHAO
Museu Mineiro
Catedral da Boa Viagem
FUNCIONÁRIOS
AVENIDA AFONSO PENA
AVENIDA BRASIL
RUA GONCALVES DIAS
AVENIDA GETULIO VARGAS
PRAÇA DE LIBERDADE
RUA CLAUDIO MANOEL
Edifício Niemeyer
RUA STA. RITA DURAO
AV. CRISTOVÃO COLOMBO
RUA DOS INCONFIDENTES
Palácio da Liberdade
SAVASSI
SÃO PEDRO
PRAÇA SAVASSI
AV. N.S. DO CARMO
SION
BELO HORIZONTE
Rio de Janeiro & Ouro Preto
Mangabeiras

most significant destinations in the country. The information desk (☎31/3271-3000) can provide details of times and fares. Nearby is the Edwardian **train station** (☎31/3273-5976) on Praça da Estação (also called Praça Rui Barbosa), a significant sight in its own right (see p.182). Apart from the local *metrô* commuter service, only one line out of Belo Horizonte has survived the post-privatization cuts of the 1990s, namely the daily connection with Vitória on the coast. It's an interminably slow but fascinating ride through the industrial heartland of eastern Minas (via Governador Valadares), taking about fourteen hours, much of it following the valley of the Rio Doce (see p.255 for information on departures from Belo Horizonte).

Information

The municipal Belotur organization is very knowledgeable about the city and publishes a useful, free monthly guide, the *Guia Turística*, which contains a good map. You'll find it in the city's better hotels and in the **tourist offices** at Mercado Central (Mon–Sat 8am–6pm, Sun & holidays 8am–noon); Mercado das Flores, Parque Municipal (Mon–Fri 8am–7pm, Sat & Sun 8am–3pm); Palácio das Artes, Av. Afonso Pena 1537 (Mon–Fri 9am–10pm, Sat & Sun 9am–4pm); Igreja São Francisco de Assis, Pampulha (Tues–Sun 9am–7pm); Tancredo Neves (Confins) airport (daily 8am–9.30pm); and the *rodoviária* (daily 8am–10pm). Belotur also has a phone number for specific queries: ☎31/3277-9777 (daily 8am–10pm). The Minas Gerais state tourist office, Sectur, is at Praça Rio Branco 56 (Mon–Fri 9am–6pm; ☎31/3272-8585), and is worth a visit for help planning routes in the interior.

For up-to-date **listings**, the *Estado de Minas* **newspaper** features a daily *Espetáculo* section, highlighting ongoing events in the city and previewing new shows. By far the most comprehensive information source, however, with detailed reviews of restaurants, films, theatre and nightlife of all sorts, is the *Roteiro Cultural* supplement of the free *Pampulha* paper, published every Saturday and generally available in the city's hotels.

City transport

The **bus system** works along the same lines as elsewhere in Brazil but is colour-coded: blue buses run up and down the main *avenidas* within the city centre, yellow buses have circular routes, white buses are "express", stopping only at selected points, and red buses are radial, connecting outlying suburbs and *favelas* with the centre. Virtually all routes include a stretch along Avenida Afonso Pena, usually the most convenient place to catch a bus if you are staying in the centre. Buses are very frequent, with all fares around R$1.30; see the box on this page for route details.

Useful bus routes

Yellow SCO2: from the *rodoviária* to Praça Sete and Savassi, via Praça da Liberdade.

Blue 1001: from Avenida Afonso Pena (between Rua Espírito Santo and Rua Tupis) to Praça da Savassi via Praça da Liberdade.

Blue 1202: from Avenida Afonso Pena, down the tree-lined Avenida Amazonas and out to Pampulha airport.

Blue 4001: from Avenida Afonso Pena to Praça da Liberdade.

Blue 2001: from the Parque das Mangabeiras down Avenida Afonso Pena to Praça Sete and the *rodoviária*.

Blue 6001: from the northern entrance of Parque das Mangabeiras to Savassi and the centre.

Otherwise, with distances being short between most points of interest in the city, **taxis** (BH Táxi ⓣ31/3215-8081; Coopertramo ⓣ3454-5757) are not very expensive. There is a city **metrô system** as well, but this was built with workers rather than tourists in mind and serves only to link the industrial suburbs with the centre. It runs daily between 5.45am and 11pm (R$1.85).

Accommodation

You don't need to stray far from the centre for **accommodation**, as there are scores of hotels, most extremely reasonable, within easy reach of the *rodoviária*. There are also some good options in the pleasant Savassi area, an easy taxi or bus ride (or a half-hour walk) from the centre, and a few in Funcionários, midway between the two. For those on a tight budget, you can choose from three decent **youth hostels**.

As in most other business-oriented cities, mid- and upper-range hotels will usually offer substantial **discounts** to the official rates indicated below: you can often expect up to thirty percent off during the week and up to fifty percent at weekends, except when there's a major congress or other event taking place in the city.

Brasil Palace Rua Carijós 269, Centro ⓣ & ⓕ31/3273-3811. A fine 1940s building that overlooks the Praça Sete and still resembles the cinema it once was. The rooms are excellent value, with baths as well as showers, TV, *frigobar* and a/c. ❷

Continental Av. Paraná 241, Centro ⓣ31/3201-7944, ⓕ3201-7336. A respectable, inexpensive hotel near the *rodoviária*. The rooms (both double and single) are small but clean, very quiet and newly furnished. ❷

HI Albergue de Juventude Chalé Mineiro Rua Santa Luzia 288 ⓣ31/3467-1576, ⓦwww.chalemineirohostel.com.br. A short, 3km taxi ride away (or bus #2701) from the centre in the *bairro* of Santa Efigênia, where the city's main hospitals are concentrated. The hostel has its own garden and pool and is always very popular, so phone ahead to check availability. R$20 per person.

Ibis Av. João Pinheiro, Centro ⓣ31/3224-9494, ⓦwww.accorhotels.com.br. This efficient hotel on the edge of Funcionários is typical of the French-owned chain. Located in a renovated old house with a modern extension behind, the no-frills rooms are small, but each has a shower and all are a/c. ❹

Liberty Palace Rua Paraíba 1465, Savassi ⓣ31/3282-0900, ⓦwww.libertypalace.com.br. The most expensive place to stay in Savassi, with all the facilities you would expect of one of the city's top hotels (pool, business centre, decent restaurant, etc). Many of the rooms on the sixth floor and above have panoramic views and all feature plush furnishings. ❻

Majestic BH Centro Rua Espírito Santo 284, Centro ⓣ31/3222-3390, ⓕ3222-3146. Though hardly majestic, this hotel has a wide range of large, clean, basic rooms – nothing special but well priced, and *quartos* are considerably cheaper. ❷

Max Savassi Suite Rua Antônio de Albuquerque 335, Savassi ⓣ31/3225-6466, ⓦwww.maxsavassi.com.br. All of the units at this excellent-value apartment hotel, located on a pleasant tree-lined street, have a bedroom, a living room and a small kitchen; the whole building shares a pool. ❹

Mercure Av. do Contorno 7315, Santo Antônio ⓣ31/3298-4100, ⓦwww.accor.com.br. Situated on the edge of Savassi, this is the largest, newest luxury hotel in the city. Service couldn't be more efficient, the facilities – including a pool and a fitness centre – are excellent and most of the rooms have wonderful views across the city. ❼

Metrópole Rua da Bahia 1023, Centro ⓣ & ⓕ31/3273-1544. This splendid Art Deco edifice wouldn't appear out of place in Miami's fashionable South Beach district. While its central location is convenient, the most attractive rooms (at the front of the hotel, with balconies) are very noisy during the day. The rooms have seen better days, but they're clean and well equipped, with a/c, cable TV and *frigobar*. ❸

Othon Palace Av. Afonso Pena 1050, Centro ⓣ31/3247-0000, ⓦwww.othon.com.br. A huge and recently refurbished 1970s skyscraper with friendly and highly professional staff, well-equipped rooms and a fine rooftop pool. Be sure to request a room on one of the upper floors facing the front of the building: the views across the Parque Municipal and onwards to the Serra do Curral are absolutely spectacular. ❻

Pousadinha Mineira Rua Espírito Santo 604 ⓣ31/3273-8156. With two hundred beds this is by far the largest youth hostel in the city. As a former hotel, it has a decidedly institutional feel, but its very central location is a plus. R$20 per person.

Praça da Liberdade Av. Brasil 1912, Funcionários ⓣ31/3261-1711, ⓦwww.pracadaliberdade.com.br. Located in a pleasant area filled with government offices, this mini high-rise hotel is within easy walking distance of the city centre and Savassi. The 29 rooms, while small, are well appointed. ❹

Savassi Rua Sergipe 939, Savassi ⓣ31/3261-3266, ⓕ3261-4328. A mid-range hotel with rather dark but perfectly comfortable rooms and a tiny rooftop pool with fantastic views towards the Serra do Curral. Savassi's restaurants and bars are just a short walk away. ❹

Sol Belo Horizonte Rua Bahia 1040, Centro ⓣ31/3274-1344, ⓦwww.solmeliabh.com.br. This four-star downtown hotel (part of the Spanish-owned Meliá chain) has pleasant rooms, efficient though somewhat impersonal service, a pool and a sauna. Popular with business executives, the place empties at weekends. ❻

O Sorriso do Lagarto Rua Padre Severino 285, Savassi ⓣ31/3283-9325, ⓦwww.osorrisodolagarto.com.br. A friendly and fairly small youth hostel on the edge of one of the city's most fashionable neighbourhoods. R$22

Sorrento Praça Raul Soares 354, Centro ⓣ31/3272-1100, ⓕ3271-2805. Clean, comfortable and efficiently run budget hotel in a pleasant downtown location on the edge of Barro Preto and its nightlife zone. The nicest rooms overlook the *praça*, but can be a little noisy. ❸

Sun América Palace Av. Amazonas 50, Centro ⓣ31/3201-1722, ⓕ3212-7117. A once grand – and still quite striking at first glance – 1930s hotel that offers very basic rooms at good value. ❸

Wimbledon Av. Afonso Pena 772, Centro ⓣ31/3222-6160, ⓦwww.wimbledon.com.br. Good mid-range hotel in the heart of Downtown. The rooms are fairly small and simply furnished, but all have cable TV, a/c and a rather ageing *frigobar*, plus there's a very small pool. Ask for one of the rooms overlooking Av. Afonso Pena, as these are much brighter. ❺

The city

Even the most patriotic *mineiro* would make few claims for the architecture of Belo Horizonte, dominated as it is by non-descript 1960s and 1970s high-rises. Nonetheless, there are some notable exceptions, chiefly on and around **Praça da Liberdade**. And if you stand in the heart of the city, in **Praça Sete**, and look down the broad Avenida Afonso Pena towards the Parque Municipal, or along the graceful palm-lined Avenida Amazonas, you'll notice that the city has a number of attractive features.

The Praça da Estação and the Praça Sete

A good place to begin one's wanderings through downtown Belo Horizonte is the beautifully renovated **train station** on Praça da Estação, one of the city's most elegant buildings. The Neoclassical yellow-coloured edifice, which replaced Belo Horizonte's original main station in 1922, is among Brazil's finest examples of tropical Edwardiana, although these days the station's platforms are used only by passengers on the once-daily Vitória-bound service or commuters riding the city's *metrô*. Housed inside the station is the **Museu de Artes e Ofícios** (Tues & Thurs–Fri noon–7pm, Wed noon–9pm, Sat & Sun 11am–5pm; ⓣ31/3248-8600, ⓦwww.mao.com.br; R$4), which traces the history of arts and crafts in Minas Gerais. Though impressively displayed, the museum's extensive collection of handicrafts and tools provides little in the way of social or economic context, making a visit here seem somewhat pointless. You can, however, admire the craftsmanship of the hardwood staircases, stained-glass windows and iron and plaster work inside the building, all of which are well worth a look.

Graced on both sides by imperial palms, Avenida Amazonas, one of the city's main arteries, leads up from Praça da Estação into the **Praça Sete**. Humming with activity, Praça Sete is full of office workers (the area immediately around is the city's main financial district) and is also the main venue of street draughts tournaments, when rows of hustlers set up boards on the pavement and play all comers for money. Surrounding the square are bars and *lanchonetes*, which stay open until midnight (even later at weekends); when the rest of the city has gone home to sleep the square is taken over by scores of homeless people, huddling around fires on deserted pavements.

A ten-minute stroll beyond Praça Sete, at the intersection of Rua Goitacazes and Rua Santa Catarina, is the **Mercado Central** (Mon–Sat 7am–6pm, Sun 7am–1pm), a sprawling indoor market of almost four hundred stalls. There's an incredible variety of goods on offer, ranging from the usual fruit, vegetables, cheeses and meats to animals, *cachaças*, spices, medicinal herbs, kitchen equipment, rustic handicrafts, and *umbanda* and *candomblé* accessories.

Avenida Afonso Pena and the Parque Municipal

Running southeast from Praça Sete, the broad Avenida Afonso Pena bisects Belo Horizonte and is home to some of the city's showcase buildings, as well as the **Instituto Moreira Salles**, near Praça Sete, at no. 737 (Tues–Fri 1–7pm, Sat & Sun 1–6pm; ⓣ31/3213-7900, ⓦwww.ims.com.br), a cultural centre that hosts major exhibitions of nineteenth- and twentieth-century Brazilian art collections (often photographic) of its sponsor, Unibanco.

Further along the avenue, midway between Rua Tamoios and Rua Espírito Santo at the top of a flight of steps, is the **Igreja São José** (Mon–Sat 7–11am & 3–8pm and Sun 7am–noon & 3–8pm), which dates back to 1906 and was the first church in the new capital; its eclectic manueline and gothic style is characteristically Brazilian, and it is set in an attractive tree-filled garden. Further south along the avenue between Rua da Bahia and Avenida Álvares Cabral, the Art Deco–influenced **Prefeitura** (town hall) was built in the 1930s as an early boast of civic pride; just a short distance on are the imposing **Palácio da Justiça** and the **Escola da Música,** each supported by Corinthian columns. On the other side of the avenue is one of the very few large-scale areas of relief from the traffic and noise of downtown: the green and shade of the **Parque Municipal** (Tues–Sun 6am–6pm). Beautifully laid out by the French landscape artist Paul Villon, the park encompasses a boating lake, two thousand species of tree, shaded walks much patronized by courting couples, aviaries, a permanent fairground and exercise yards where Brazilian men make their sweaty sacrifices to the national cult of the body beautiful. It also contains the main arts complex in the city, the Palácio das Artes.

The Palácio das Artes

The **Palácio das Artes** (entrance on Av. Afonso Pena 1537 ⓣ31/3237-7399, ⓦwww.palaciodasartes.com.br) is one of the finest modern buildings in the city, a complex of which the citizens of Belo Horizonte are justifiably proud. So much so, in fact, that when parts of the *palácio* burned down in March 1997, reconstruction began barely a week later, and a mammoth benefit show was organized in the *mineirão* football stadium to fund the repairs. Now fully restored, the *palácio* is divided into a number of well laid-out **galleries** (daily 9am–9pm; free), with exhibitions concentrating on modern Brazilian art, a couple of small **theatres** and one big one, the **Grande Teatro**, which suffered most in the fire.

Though it's hard to believe in such a large city, the *palácio* is one of the very few places in Belo Horizonte where you'll come across a good display of the distinctive *artesanato* of the state, in the **Centro de Artesanato Mineiro** (Mon 1–6pm, Tues–Fri 9am–9pm, Sat 9am–1pm, Sun 10am–2pm). A large shop rather than a gallery proper, it's nevertheless a place you can wander around and look without being pressured to buy. Although there's a lot of dross here, there is also some excellent pottery – stubby figurines and realistic clay tableaux, the most distinctive of which comes from the valley of the Rio Jequitinhonha. Hammocks, clothes, wall hangings and rugs, roughly woven from the cotton that grows in northern Minas, are also of a high quality. Despite the sleek surroundings, the prices here are reasonable – not more than twice what you'd pay where the work comes from.

Feira de Arte e Artesanato

It's worth making an effort to be in Belo Horizonte on a Sunday morning for the **Feira de Arte e Artesanato**. One of the best of its kind anywhere in the country, with buyers and sellers coming from all over Brazil, this massive market takes over the Avenida Afonso Pena bordering the Parque Municipal. It's always packed, and by mid-morning, moving through the narrow avenues between rows of stalls gets difficult; by 2pm, stallholders are packing up and leaving, and by 4pm the city's efficient street cleaners will have removed all trace of the market. An excellent place for bargains, the market is split into sections, with related stalls grouped together – jewellery, leather goods, lace, ceramics, cane furniture, clothes, food, paintings and drinks, to name but a few. Prices of more expensive items and clothes are fixed, with many things on view being labelled, but otherwise there is some scope for bargaining.

As always with Brazilian markets, what's going on around you is just as interesting as what's for sale. If you can find a seat, set up camp at one of the **bars** at the corner with Rua da Bahia and watch the stallholders hustling, buyers negotiating and people doing the same as you; it's exciting to simply enjoy the action or listen to the buskers and serious musicians who play at the fringes of the crowds and sell tapes of their work.

Funcionários and Praça da Liberdade

Southwest of Avenida Afonso Pena, behind the grand public buildings, are the hilly tree-lined roads of **Funcionários**, a neighbourhood – as the name suggests – dominated by government offices of all sorts. The district also contains the **Catedral da Boa Viagem**, Rua Alagoas (Mon & Sat 11am–10pm, Tues–Fri & Sun 6am–10pm), inaugurated in 1922 to mark the centenary of Brazilian independence. For a cathedral of a major city, the neo-Gothic structure is surprisingly small and plain, but the grounds are beautiful.

A short walk southeast of the cathedral, the impressive, Neoclassical **Museu Mineiro**, Av. João Pinheiro 342 (Tues–Fri 11.30am–6.30pm, Sat, Sun & holidays 10am–4pm), was one of the first buildings in Belo Horizonte, dating from 1897. The building served as the state Senate from 1905 to 1930, only being converted for use as a museum much later, and today houses an unremarkable sample of the tradition of religious art in Minas. One block east from Avenida João Pinheiro is the steep Rua da Bahia where, at no. 1149, you'll find the **Centro de Cultura Belo Horizonte** (Mon–Fri 9am–9pm, Sat & holidays 9am–6pm, Sun 2–6pm), a curious neo-Gothic structure that was constructed in 1914 as the city's legislative assembly. The inside of the building, with its wood panelling and sweeping staircase, is worth a look, and there are often small exhibitions or concerts going on. One block down the road, the shocking-pink and blue *Hotel Metrópole* is one of the purest examples of Art Deco in the city.

The park-like **Praça da Liberdade** lies to the south of Funcionários. With its beautiful trees, Edwardian bandstand and fountains, the square is a wonderful

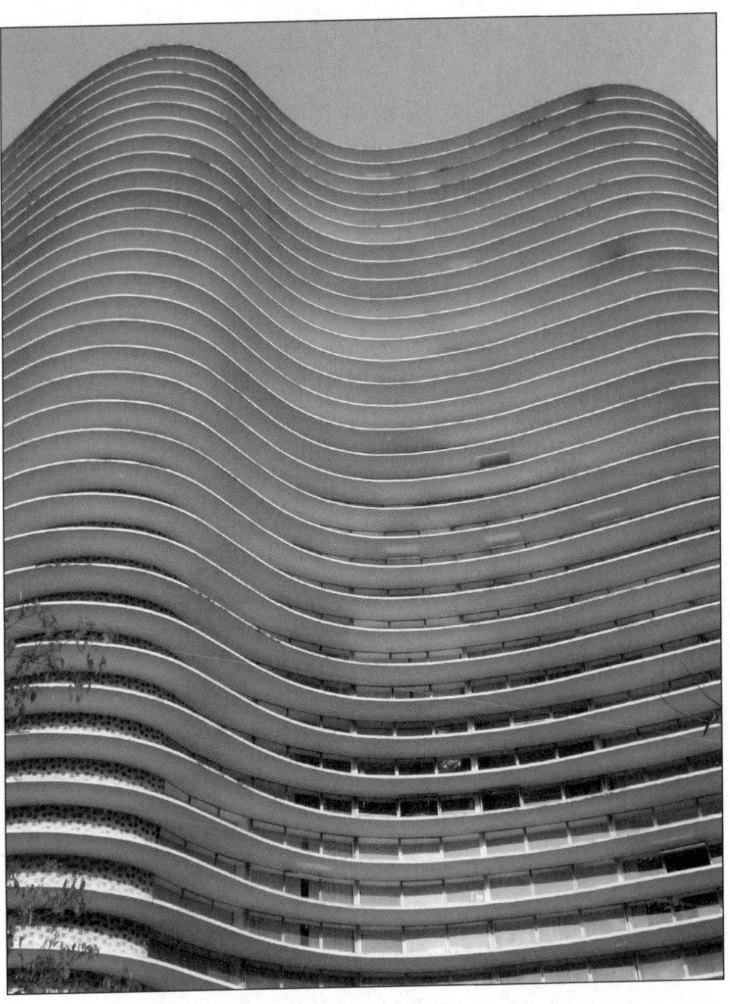

△ Edifício Niemeyer

place to sit and while away the time; it's especially popular on weekends when residents of neighbouring apartment buildings come out to rollerblade or sit and read in the sun. The square is dominated by the elegant French Art-Nouveau-style **Palácio da Liberdade** (last Sun of the month 9am–5pm), built between 1895 and 1898 as the residence of the president of Minas Gerais. Today, the *palácio* remains the administrative centre of the state government and the official residence of the governor, primarily used for state functions. Another building to look out for on the square is the **Edifício Niemeyer** apartment building, whose flowing lines were designed by architect Oscar Niemeyer in the 1950s; it's still one of Belo Horizonte's most prestigious residential city-centre addresses today. Directly across the *praça* from the apartment building, at Av. Bias Fortes 50, sits the ugly glass-and-steel **Museu de Mineralogia** (Tues–Sun 9am–5pm), whose extensive collection of minerals and local fossils is likely to be of interest only to geologists.

Museu Histórico Abílio Barreto

One of the very few museums in the city really worth a visit is the **Museu Histórico Abílio Barreto** (Tues–Sun 10am–5pm) at Rua Bernardo Mascarenhas in Cidade Jardim. To get there, take the #5901 bus (marked "Nova Floresta/ Santa Lúcia"); the most convenient stop to catch it is along Avenida Amazonas between Rua Espírito Santo and Rua dos Caetés. If you ask the conductor for the Museu Histórico, you'll be dropped on Avenida do Contorno, a block away, from where there are signs to the museum on Rua Bernardo Mascarenhas. The surrounding area of Cidade Jardim is rapidly becoming one of the most fashionable, upper-class parts of the city, with new skyscrapers sprouting like weeds. It's an ironic location for the oldest building in the city, the only one that predates 1893, when construction of the new capital began.

The museum was once a *fazenda*, built in 1883, comfortable but not luxurious, and typical of the ranches of rural Minas. Though now swamped by the burgeoning city, it once stood on its own, a few kilometres away from the church and hovels of the hamlet of Curral del Rey, which straggled along what is now the stretch of Avenida Afonso Pena opposite the Parque Municipal. The *fazenda* has been perfectly preserved and now houses the usual collection of old furniture and mediocre paintings, upstairs, and in the garden an old tram and turn-of-the-twentieth-century train used in the construction of Belo Horizonte. Far better is the rustic wooden veranda at the front, where you can sit with your feet up and imagine yourself back in the 1880s.

By far the most interesting part of the museum is the **galeria de fotografias**, juxtaposing images from the sleepy village before it was obliterated – mules, mud huts and ox carts – with views of the modern city through the decades; there are a couple of well-designed maps to help you get your bearings. The last remnant of Curral del Rey, the eighteenth-century Igreja Matriz, was flattened in 1932: a few photographs, and carved bits of the church piled in a shed in the garden, are all that remain of the vanished community.

Equally remarkable is the series of photographs that record the construction of Belo Horizonte and its early years: a trashed building site becomes the Parque Municipal; the train station stands in glorious isolation (it's now dwarfed by the surrounding buildings); and the Praça Sete is shown as it was in the 1930s, ringed by trees and fine Art Deco buildings, of which only the Cine Brasil (now the *Brasil Palace Hotel*) is still standing. Like Rio, urban architecture in Belo Horizonte was at its peak in the 1930s and 1940s, when the city was an elegant political capital, rather than an economic centre, and it has suffered since at the hands of the developers. A classic demonstration of this is the wonderful Art Deco market building, the Feira de Amostras Permanentes, which you can now only appreciate here in the museum. It was demolished in 1970 and replaced by the *rodoviária*.

Parque das Mangabeiras

Unlikely as it may seem amid the skyscrapers of Avenida Afonso Pena, the city limits are only a short bus ride away to the south. Here, the urban sprawl is abruptly cut off by the steep hills of the **Serra do Curral**, a natural barrier that forces the city to expand in other directions. The slopes are the site of a huge nature reserve, the 600-hectare **Parque das Mangabeiras** (Tues–Sun 8am–6pm), where you can walk along forest paths that open out now and again to reveal spectacular views of the city below. To get there, catch the blue #2001-C bus, marked "Aparecida", from Avenida Afonso Pena between Avenida Amazonas and Rua Tamóios: it's a fifteen-minute steep drive to the terminus above the park entrance. When returning to the city, you can avoid having to climb back up to the main entrance by leaving the park through the small northern gate, much lower down, and catching the #6001 bus just outside.

The park is so big it has its own **internal bus service**; buses leave every thirty minutes from the left of the entrance, and end up there again twenty minutes later after making a circuit of the park. Near the entrance is a well-kept leisure area, with fountains, rows of *lanchonetes* and an open-air amphitheatre, the **Teatro de Arena**, where there's often something showing on Sundays. There's an excellent view of the city from the **Mirante da Mata** viewing platform, a twenty-minute amble from the entrance; the finest walks are along the nature trails and streams of the **Parque Florestal**, a little further along. **Maps** of the park are available from the office near the main entrance.

Mirante da Cidade

The single most spectacular view of the city is from the **Mirante da Cidade**, outside the park and largely hidden by trees behind the governor's palatial residence. Take the #2001-C bus for Mangabeiras (or the #2001-A), but get off just before at Praça do Papa and walk east up the steep Rua Bady Salum for a short kilometre. The view is splendid: too high up for the grime and *favelas* to register (although pollution can obscure things on a bad day), it makes Belo Horizonte seem like Los Angeles, an impression reinforced if you go by night, when the carpet of lights below really is magnificent.

Pampulha

Some 10km north of the centre (an hour or so by bus), the luxurious district of **Pampulha** is built around an artificial lake that is overlooked by some of the finest modern buildings in the city – the Museu de Arte, the modernist Igreja de São Francisco and the Casa do Baile. They are instantly recognizable as the work of architect **Oscar Niemeyer**, creator of Brasília, and landscape designer **Roberto Burle Marx** – both of whom, with their socialist ideals, were presumably horrified by the subsequent development of the area as a rich residential district.

The Igreja de São Francisco de Assis

The construction of the **Igreja de São Francisco de Assis** (Mon–Sun 8–6pm), with its striking curves, *azulejo* frontage and elegant bell tower, provides a roll call of the greatest names of Brazilian modernism: Burle Marx laid out its grounds, Niemeyer designed the church, Cândido Portinari did the tiles and murals depicting the fourteen stations of the cross and João Ceschiatti (best known for his gravity-defying angels in Brasília's cathedral) contributed the bronze baptismal font. The church's design was decades ahead of its time and it's astonishing to realize that it dates from the early 1940s. So shocked was the intensely conservative local Catholic hierarchy by the building's daring that the archbishop refused to consecrate it and almost twenty years passed before Mass could be held there. Nowadays Sunday Mass is held at 10.30am and 6pm. To get there, take bus #2004 (marked "Bandeirantes/Olhos d'Água") from Avenida Afonso Pena, between Avenida Amazonas and Rua Tupinambás.

The Museu de Arte (MAP) and Casa do Baile

The **Museu de Arte da Pampulha** (Tues–Sun & holidays 9am–7pm; R$4) – or MAP as it is usually called – is more difficult to reach: take the #2215 bus from Rua dos Caetés and get off when you see a sign for the *museu* to the left – you then have to walk down to the lakeside Avenida Otacílio Negrão de Lima, turn right, and the museum is on a small peninsula jutting out into the lake. It's worth the trip, although the small collection of modern art it holds isn't at all compelling in itself. The structure, however, is a product of two geniuses at the height of their powers: Niemeyer created a virtuoso building, all straight lines and right angles at the front but melting into rippling curves at the back, with a marvellous use of glass; Burle Marx set the whole thing off beautifully, with a sculpture garden out back and an exquisite garden framing the building in front. It was built as a casino in 1942, but the Brazilian government abolished gambling soon after and not until 1957 was the building inaugurated as an art museum.

Directly opposite, on the other side of the lake, the **Casa do Baile** (Tues–Sun 9am–7pm), a former dance hall, is by the same duo. The building is now used as a space for temporary exhibitions of art and design that are sometimes worth a brief visit, with a very nice café also on site. Get there on the #1202 bus from Rua São Paulo between Avenida Amazonas and Rua Carijós.

Football in Pampulha

Belo Horizonte's main football stadium, the **Mineirão** (Ⓣ31/3499-1100) is also situated in prestigious Pampulha. (The #2004 bus passes by the stadium.) With a capacity of 90,000, the Mineirão is a world-class stadium, but it's rarely full. One of Brazil's better teams, Atlético Mineiro, play here, and they're worth catching if you're in Belo Horizonte on a Sunday during a home game. Local derbies, especially against Cruzeiro, are torrid and very entertaining affairs, but they often end with supporters of the rival teams destroying a large number of the city's buses. Entrance costs are around R$8 for the *arquibancada* (stands), rising to R$30 for better seats.

Eating, drinking and nightlife

You can eat well in Belo Horizonte and prices are generally quite reasonable, though outside the immediate downtown area, **restaurants** and **bars** tend to be more upmarket. Savassi has a particularly good range of options. The monthly *Guia Turístico* and the weekly paper *Pampulha* both contain up-to-date listings of the city's better restaurants.

Belo Horizonte's chic **nightlife** is also concentrated in Savassi, but you'll find lively pockets of bars and clubs throughout the central area, as well as in the *bairros* of Barro Preto and Pampulha.

Snacks, street food and restaurants

The best area for moderately priced meals is **Downtown**, around Praça Sete and towards the train station, where many of the *lanchonetes* serve good, simple and cheap *comida mineira*. Also downtown, there's a good range of upmarket *comida por kilo* restaurants – both *mineiro* and international – in the Bahia Shopping centre, one block west from Avenida Afonso Pena on Rua da Bahia. Rua Pernambuco in **Funcionários** is also a fine place for reasonable *comida mineira por kilo* restaurants, especially popular at lunchtime with workers from nearby government offices.

Street food is worth trying as well. On Saturdays between 10am and 4pm, food stalls go up at the Feira Tom Jobim (a street market where antiques and bric-a-brac are sold) along Avenida Bernardo Monteiro on the corner with Avenida Brasil; the stands serve foreign and Brazilian regional food (including, of course, *mineiro*), which is often extremely good and is always cheap. Similar stalls crowd the busy Sunday market on Avenida Afonso Pena. For your own supplies, head for the modern and colourful **Mercado Central** (see p.183).

Restaurants

Oddly enough, exceptionally good **comida mineira restaurants** are not easy to find in Belo Horizonte, as the state's regional specialities (see box, p.191) are more associated with small town and country life than city sophistication. There are, however, a good range of restaurants serving up **international cuisine**, ranging from inexpensive Lebanese to pricey French, Italian or Japanese.

Amigo do Rei Rua Quintiliano 118, Santo Antônio ☎31/3296-3881. Probably the only Iranian restaurant in Brazil, serving simple but very tasty moderately priced food in a casually elegant setting; the meat dishes (both stewed, typically with a pomegranate sauce, and grilled) are a highlight.

Badejo Rua Rio Grande do Norte 836, Funcionários ☎31/3261-2023. Lots of fish and other seafood choices are available at this restaurant, which specializes in the food of Espírito Santo. If you won't be visiting that state, at least try one of the distincive *mocquecas* – a tomato-based stew, unlike the Bahian dish of the same name which uses coconut milk. Closed Mon and also Sun evening.

Bem Natural Av. Afonso Pena 941, Edifício Sulacap, 2 blocks east of Praça Sete. This restaurant, which combines with a health-food shop and alternative bookstore, serves excellent vegetarian food as well as chicken and fish dishes. Inexpensive and highly recommended. Open Mon–Fri; full menu at lunchtime, soup only 5–8pm.

Bonomi Panificadora Rua Cláudio Manoel 460, Funcionários ☎31/3261-3460. Located in a burgundy-coloured building without a sign near Av. Afonso Pena, this "bakery" serves excellent light meals (salads, pasta, soups and sandwiches), wonderful cakes and what is certainly the best bread anywhere in the state.

Buona Tavola Rua Santa Rita Durão 309, Funcionários ☎31/3227-6155. Near the intersection with Av. Afonso Pena, this is a relatively simple and quite authentic Italian restaurant. Expect to pay around R$40 per person.

Cervejaria Brasil Rua dos Aimorés 90, Funcionários ☎31/3287-3299. One of the best centrally located *churrascarias* with a selection of meat likely to bewilder the most dedicated of carnivores. Pleasant surroundings and moderate prices.

Churrascaria Porcão Rua Raja Gabaglia 2985, São Bento ☎31/3293-8787. Although especially good for meat, the buffet also has a vast array of seafood dishes, pasta and salads for R$50 per person. Located a short taxi ride a little southwest of the Contorno, the breathtaking views of the Serra do Corral and of the city are every bit as good as the food.

Dona Derna Rua Tomee de Sousa 1380, Funcionários ☎31/3223-6954. Very good (if rather heavy) traditional northern Italian cooking with a strong emphasis on meat dishes. Moderate.

Dona Lucinha II Rua Sergipe 811, Funcionários ☎31/3261-5930. This and its sister restaurant (*Dona Lucinha*, Rua Padre Odorico 38, São Pedro; ☎31/3227-0562) offer a very authentic *comida mineira* buffet for just R$20 per person. The vast range of meat and vegetables dishes, and the wonderful desserts, are all helpfully labelled in English, and excellent home-made *cachaça*-based liqueurs are available to sample. If you have time for just one meal in Belo Horizonte, this is the place to go. Closed Sun evening.

Dragon Center Av. Afonso Pena 549, near the *rodoviária*. This Chinese restaurant is the nearest available option for decent food if you have a couple of hours to kill while changing buses.

Emporium Armazém Mineiro Av. Afonso Pena 4034, Mangabeiras ☎31/3281-1277. Decent *comida mineira* is served amidst an attractive rustic-chic ambience. For a main dish, such as *tutu a mineira* (see p.191), suitable for two people, expect to pay about R$35. Aside from the main dining room, there's a *cachaçeria*, modelled on a typical village bar, where you can sample *cachaças* and tasty snacks. Take bus #5508 from Rua dos Caetés or #2001 from Av. Afonso Pena in the centre. Closed Sun evening.

Haus München Rua Juiz de Fora 1257, Santo Agostinho ☎31/3291-6900. The decent and inexpensive traditional German food here is along the lines of pork, sauerkraut and good beer. Closed Sun evening.

Minas Tênis Clube Rua da Bahia 2244, Lourdes ☎31/3516-1310. The tennis club's excellent value (R$15 per person) lunch-time buffet is one of the city centre's best-kept secrets. Choose a table on the terrace overlooking the tennis courts, gardens and pool and marvel at the club's Art Deco splendour. The food's good too – a varied selection of salads and hot dishes.

Quibelanches corner of Rua dos Caetés and Av. Amazonas. One of the cheapest Lebanese restaurants in the city – simple but with a wide range of authentic dishes, both *por kilo* (at lunch time) and à la carte.

Sushi Naka Rua Gonçalves Dias 92, Funcionários ⓣ31/3227-2676. Because Belo Horizonte is a long way from the nearest fishing port, the fish served at *Sushi Naka* – despite being the city's cheapest Japanese restaurant – is still fairly expensive (though reliable). Closed Mon.

Vecchio Sogno Rua Martim de Carvalho 75, Santo Agostinho ⓣ31/3292-5231. Widely considered to be one of the best restaurants in the city (and one of the most expensive; expect to pay around R$100 per person), *Vecchio Sogno* has made a name for itself with an imaginative mix – and sometimes fusion – of Italian, French and Brazilian recipes. Try the duck lasagna with wild mushrooms or the herb gnocchi with a prawn sauce, and don't miss the banana *tarte tatine* served with *queijo-de-minas* ice cream. Closed Sat lunch & Sun evening.

Vila Árabe Rua Pernambuco 781, Savassi ⓣ31/3362-1600. Moderately priced and very tasty Lebanese food is served in attractive surroundings. The buffet is good value at R$20, or you can opt for the vegetarian or mixed *mezze* at R$25 for two. The *cordeiro* (lamb) dishes are especially good.

Xapuri Rua Mandacaru 260, Pampulha ⓣ31/3496-6198. The superb *comida mineira* includes dishes you're unlikely to find elsewhere. The veal *osso buco* with banana is cooked to perfection and the buffet of thirty different desserts rounds off an excellent meal. *Xapuri* has a nice atmosphere too – that of a country house, the kitchen's wood-fired stoves and ovens clearly visible – and it's a good place to purchase *artesanato* as well as *doces* made on the premises.

Nightlife and entertainment

Compared to Rio and São Paulo, Belo Horizonte's nightlife is extremely measured and discreet, but there are several areas in the central part of the city where the **bars** spring to life once it gets dark. Most days of the week, the bottom end of **Rua da Bahia** between Avenida Afonso Pena and Praça da Estação is lively: the bars put out tables under the palm trees and the action goes on until the late hours. The area around the intersection of **Rua Rio de Janeiro and Avenida Augusto de Lima** is also good, but more student-like. There are a couple of small theatres and cinemas close by, and a group of bars and restaurants: a good one is *Mateus*, serving a range of light snacks and pizzas on the corner. It's also worth checking out the bars along **Rua Guajajaras** between Rua Espírito Santo and Rua da Bahia. Much further out, with outlandish performance art "happenings" at 8.30pm and the rare knack of peacefully blending in the oddest of people, is the 24-hour *Bar do Lulu*, Rua Leopoldina 415, Bairro Santo Antônio – take a taxi.

The more sophisticated spots are in **Savassi** and neighbouring **Funcionários**, both pleasant places in which to spend an evening. Drinks are only marginally more expensive here than anywhere else, and the bars get very crowded at weekends. *Chopperia Margherita Ville* and *Sausalito Point*, at the intersection of *ruas* Tomé de Souza and Pernambuco, are always busy, and most people end up drinking their beer on the street outside (both are open till 4am).

Cachaça

If you want to be initiated into the wonderful world of **cachaça** (sugar-cane rum), a trip out to the *Alambique Cachaçaria*, Av. Raja Gabáglia 3200, Chalé 1, Estoril, is a must, and also offers beautiful night views of Belo Horizonte from the top of the hill. Besides the live music, the main attraction here is the *cachaça Germana*, their own brew which is available plain or infused with herbs and honey. They also serve the traditional *caipirinhas* – *cachaça* with ice, lemon and sugar – as well as straight shots. A single shot costs R$2.50 and a bottle begins at R$25. The easiest way to get here is to take a taxi from the centre: a ten- to fifteen-minute ride for about R$15. While few people in Brazil would dispute a *mineiro*'s claim that their *cachaça* is generally the best in the country, owing to the combination of

Comida mineira

Minas Gerais' tasty (if heavy) **regional food**, *comida mineira*, is one of Brazil's most distinctive – based mainly on pork, the imaginative use of vegetables, *couve* (a green vegetable somewhat like kale), and the famous *tutu*, a thick bean sauce made by grinding uncooked beans with manioc flour and cooking the mixture. Many of the dishes originate from the early mule trains and *bandeirante* expeditions of the eighteenth century, when food had to keep for long periods (hence the use of salted pork, now usually replaced by fresh) and be easily prepared without elaborate ingredients.

Comida mineira is not difficult to find: outside Belo Horizonte it is rare to come across restaurants that serve anything else, and the capital itself has plenty of authentic establishments, provided you know where to look. There are also small stores everywhere serving Minas Gerais' *doces* (cakes and sweetmeats), local melt-in-the-mouth cheeses, made both from goats' and cows' milk, and, of course, *cachaça*, usually drunk neat here before a meal "to prepare the stomach". **Typical dishes** include:

Brigadeiro The ultimate in truffle-like chocolate snacks, so rich it should come with a health warning.

Carne picadinha A straightforward, rich stew of either beef or pork, cooked for hours until tender.

Costelinha Stewed ribs of ham.

Dobradinha Tripe stew cooked with sweet potatoes. Stews (including the two above) often include the excellent Minas sausages, smoked and peppery.

Doce de leite A rich caramel sludge.

Feijão tropeiro ("Mule driver's beans") A close relative to *tutu a mineira* (see below), with a name that betrays its eighteenth-century origins; it features everything that is in a *tutu* but also has beans fried with *farinha* (manioc flour), egg and onion thrown into the mix.

Frango ao molho pardo Definitely one for hardened carnivores only: essentially chicken cooked in its own blood. It's better than it sounds, but rather bitter in taste.

Frango com quiabo Chicken roasted with okra and served sizzling with a side plate of *anju*, a corn porridge that *mineiros* eat with almost anything.

Tutu a mineira Most common of all dishes, found on every menu; roasted pork served with lashings of *tutu*, garnished with steamed *couve* and *torresmo* (an excellent salted pork crackling).

the soil and altitude where the sugar cane is grown, bottles of *Germana* or other good quality non-industrial *cachaça* from Minas Gerais are remarkably difficult to find outside the state, even in Rio or São Paulo. If you want to take some quality *cachaça* home, it's a good idea to stock up before leaving Minas Gerais – Belo Horizonte's stalls in the Mercado Central (see p.183) have a very good selection.

Discos and live music

Although Minas Gerais is considered to be one of Brazil's more conservative states, Belo Horizonte stands out for having quite a mix of nightclubs and places simply to hear live music. Big names play at *Minascentro*, Av. Augusto de Lima 785 (Ⓣ31/3201-0122); at the *Palácio das Artes* (Ⓣ31/3237-7333) and at the *Teatro Izabela Hendrix*, Rua da Bahia 2020 (Ⓣ31/3292-4405). Check the local papers to see who is playing; expect to pay around R$15 for a ticket for a lesser-known act or over R$50 for a star performer. In addition to the places listed below, there's an ever changing clubbing scene in **Barro Preto**, where Avenida

Raja Gabáglia is stuffed with gritty live music venues, simple *mineiro* restaurants and small bars good for listenting to *setaneja* (Brazilian country music) or dancing to more mainstream sounds.

Café Cancun Rua Sergipe 1208. With its Latin and Brazilian rhythms and Mexican drinks and nibbles, this theme-bar attracts a predominantly young and wealthy crowd.

Café com Letras Rua Antônio de Albuquerque 781 ⓣ31/3225-9973. Small and inexpensive and usually featuring good jazz. Popular with people of all ages and artist and intellectual types.

Café Concerto Av. Bandeirantes 1299, Mangabeiras. A downbeat bar that hosts some interesting up-and-coming local bands.

Centro Cultural Casa África Rua Leopoldinha 48, Santo Antônio. For African dance music, this is the place to go on Fri and Sat nights.

Circuito Rua Conquista 308 ⓣ31/3271-3211. A relaxed and very mixed club that's strong on Bahian sounds.

Mamãe já sabia Av. do Contorno 2317, Santa Tereza ⓣ31/3213-9063. A bar and nightclub in the Bohemian neighbourhood of Santa Tereza attracting a largely gay and lesbian crowd. DJs offer disco sounds interspersed with local bands performing an eclectic mix of Brazilian music.

Máscaras Rua Santa Rita Durão 667, Savassi ⓣ31/3261-6050. With two dance floors, separate bars and video rooms, all kitted out in chic, modern style, this nightclub (open until 6am at weekends) is extremely popular. It operates a system similar to many of Brazil's more swish clubs, where you pay for seats at a table.

Paco Pigalle Rua Ouro Preto 301 (ⓣ31/3291-0747). Plays a mix of hip-hop, reggae, salsa and disco to a young and trendy crowd.

Parte Non Rua Rio Grande do Norte 1470, Savassi (ⓣ31/3221-9856). A glitzy club that's favoured by scotch-drinking twenty-somethings who don't want to stray beyond their upmarket neighbourhood.

Terra Brasilis Rua Tomé de Souza 987. This bar has excellent live samba.

Cinema and theatre

There are several **art cinemas** in Belo Horizonte with imaginative and non-dubbed programming: check out the Cine Humberto Mauro (ⓣ31/3237-7234) in the Palácio das Artes (see p.183) and the Cineclube Unibanco Savassi (ⓣ31/3227-6648) at Rua Levindo Lopes in Savassi. Also well worth checking out are the films shown at the *Centro Cultural Casa África* at Rua Leopoldinha 48, Santo Antônio; other African and Afro-Brazilian themed events are also held here such as dance performances and plays and there's a nice bar. For **theatre**, there are numerous venues around town, though all productions are in Portuguese: the Palácio das Artes (ⓣ31/3201-8900) and the Teatro Izabela Hendrix (see p.191) both host top Brazilian companies that are visiting the city. The Palácio das Artes also occasionally shows opera and dance – try to catch a performance of the Grupo Corpo, an internationally renowned dance company that emerged in Belo Horizonte in the 1970s, or watch out for the amazing puppetry of the Grupo Giramundo, also based in the city.

Listings

Airlines Aerolíneas Argentinas ⓣ31/3224-7466; Air Canada ⓣ31/3344-8355; American Airlines ⓣ31/3274-3166; British Airways ⓣ31/3274-6211; Continental Airlines ⓣ31/3274-3177; Delta Airlines ⓣ31/3287-0001; Gol ⓣ31/3490-2073; Pluna ⓣ31/3291-9292; TAM ⓣ31/3689-2233; TAP ⓣ31/3213-1611; United Airlines ⓣ31/3269-3939; Varig/Nordeste/Rio-Sul ⓣ31/3339-6000.

Airports Pampulha ⓣ31/3490-2010; Tancredo Neves (Confins) ⓣ31/3689-2700.

Banks and exchange Banks are concentrated downtown on Av. João Pinheiro, between Rua dos Timbiras and Av. Afonso Pena. There are branches throughout the city and ATMs are common.

Bookshops For a city the size of Belo Horizonte, bookshops are extremely disappointing and none has more than a few books in English. The following are reasonable for Brazilian art, history and literature: Livraria da Travessa, Av. Getúlio Vargas 1427, near Praça Savassi; the *Café com Letras*,

Rua Antônio de Albuquerque 781, also near Praça Savassi; Livraria Van Damme, Rua Guarajaras 505, Centro; and Livraria UFMG (the university bookshop), Av. Afonso Pena 1534, Centro.

Car rental Hertz, at the airports and Av. João Pinheiro 341 ⓣ31/3224-5166 or 224-1279; Interlocadora, at the airports and Rua dos Timbiras 2229 ⓣ31/3275-4090; Localiza, at the airports and Av. Bernardo Monteiro 1567 ⓣ0800-312-121; Unidas, at the airports and Av. Santa Rosa 100 ⓣ0800-121-121.

Consulates Argentina, Rua Ceará 1566, 3rd floor, Funcionários ⓣ31/3281-5288; Paraguay, Rua Guandaus 60, apto. 102, Santa Lúcia ⓣ31/3344-6349; UK, Rua dos Inconfidentes 1075, sala 1302, Savassi ⓣ31/3261-2072.

Health matters For an ambulance, phone ⓣ192. Hospital das Clínicas da UFMG is attached to the university, Av. Alfredo Badalena 190, Santa Efigênia ⓣ31/3239-7100.

Laundry Laundromat, Rua dos Timbiras 1264, beside the Igreja Boa Viagem (Mon–Sat 8am–8pm).

Police ⓣ190. For visa or tourist permit extension, go to the Polícia Federal at Rua Nascimento Gurgel 30, Guiterrez (ⓣ31/3330-5200).

Post office The main post office is at Av. Afonso Pena 1270 (Mon–Fri 9am–6pm, Sat 9am–1pm). Smaller offices are scattered around the city, including at Rua Pernambuco 1322, Savassi and at the *rodoviária*.

Shopping The main centres for *artesanato* in the city are the Centro de Artesanato Mineiro in the Palácio das Artes (see p.183), and the Sunday market in the Parque Municipal (see p.183). Also excellent is the range of carefully selected items at Mãos de Minas at Rua Grão Mogol 678, Sion (Mon–Fri 9am–7pm and Sat 9am–1pm). Food, medicinal plants, *umbanda* and *candomblé* (voodoo) accessories and wickerwork can be found in the Mercado Central (see p.183). Interesting Afro-Brazilian items are sold at the Centro Cultural Casa África, Rua Leopoldina 48, Santo Antônio (Mon–Thurs 8am–noon & 2–6pm, Fri–Sat 8am–midnight).

In Savassi, there's a good range of elegant boutiques to be found in BHZ Fashion Mall, Rua Paraíba 1132 (daily 9am–7pm), as well as on the streets extending off Praça da Savassi.

Travel and tour companies There are a number of specialist ecotourism agencies dealing with trekking, hiking, caving, canoeing, rafting and cycling trips in Minas. Contact Terra Nossa, Rua Domingos Vieira 348, sala 1309, Santa Efigênia (ⓣ31/3241-6161); Trilhas d'Água, Rua Presidente Arthur Bernardes 409, Boa Esperança, Santa Luzia (ⓣ31/3641-3185); or Primotur, Rua Piumí 364, loja 4, Cruzeiro (ⓣ31/3221-3118). Trilhar, Rua Osmário Soares 310, Dom Bosco (ⓣ31/3417-6746) organize day-trips.

Around Belo Horizonte

The most popular trips out from the capital are to the *cidades históricas* (see p.195), but there are a couple of other less-frequented sites that also warrant a visit: to the north, the **Gruta Rei do Mato** is a convenient stop if you are heading for Brasília or Diamantina; to the east, lying beyond the nearest of the *cidades históricas*, Sabará, is the beautiful **Parque do Caraça**.

Gruta Rei do Mato

One of the most astonishing underground attractions of Minas Gerais lies 60km northwest of Belo Horizonte on BR-040, opposite the junction for Sete Lagoas, and makes for either an excellent day-trip from the capital or a good place to stop on the way to Diamantina. Legend has it that a mysterious fugitive originally discovered this enormous cave and used it as a home. He became known as "Rei do Mato" (King of the Bush) and the name has stuck to the cave itself.

The series of caverns (8am–4.30pm; ⓣ31/3773-0888; R$8) extends for over 2000m, is 300m deep in some parts and includes some prehistoric cave art. The third room is particularly impressive, with two parallel columns formed by interlocking stalactites and stalagmites, and is regarded as the only equal in the world to the formations in the famous caves at Altamira in Spain. **Buses** from Belo Horizonte to Sete Lagoas (every 30min from 6.30am to 1pm), Diamantina or Brasília pass the cave; the journey takes about an hour. There is a **bar** that sells refreshments at the site.

Parque Natural do Caraça

The striking **Parque Natural do Caraça** (daily 7am–5pm), named after the impression of a gigantic face in the surrounding mountains, lies 130km east of Belo Horizonte. The park is situated at 2400m above sea level; temperatures drop sharply on summer evenings and it can get very cold in winter. There are plenty of signed walks of varying difficulty on the tracks through the mountains – information is available from the hotel at the park entrance. The park's imposing lake provides a good opportunity for swimming from its small beaches, and there are also several natural pools by the waterfalls within the park. **Buses** from Belo Horizonte to Santa Bárbara (about 4 daily) will drop you at the entrance to the park, and a trip here makes an excellent weekend break from the city.

Santuário do Caraça

Situated at the only entrance to the park is the **Santuário do Caraça**, a former seminary and school. The **school**, famous in Brazil, was founded on the site of a hermitage and seminary in 1774, and for 150 years educated the upper classes of Minas Gerais, including generations of Brazilian politicians. In 1965 a fire destroyed much of the building, the theatre was burnt to the ground and the library lost two-thirds of its thirty thousand books.

Fazenda hotels

In recent years, with farming in Brazil increasingly dominated by large-scale agribusiness, small and medium-sized farms in Minas Gerais have had to look for new opportunities, and many of those set in particularly attractive countryside, or retaining a grand old *fazenda* house, have turned to tourism to generate income. Within just an hour or so of Belo Horizonte there are several superb **country hotels**, full of character and offering great facilities. If you don't have your own transport, arrangements can usually be made to be picked up locally or even from Belo Horizonte – phone ahead. Reservations are essential, particularly during summer and holiday weekends, and rates always include full board.

Fazenda Boa Esperança Florestal ⓣ31/3536-2344, ⓦwww.fazendaboaesperanca.com.br. Set in a working 450-hectare dairy farm 45km from Belo Horizonte, the buildings are colonial-style and the guestrooms are simply but comfortably furnished. There's a large pool in the gardens that surround the main building and the property includes some 40 hectares of natural forest with trails that you can explore on foot or on horseback. You certainly won't go hungry, as the meals are local cooking at its best. ❼

Fazenda das Minhocas Jaboticatubas ⓣ31/3681-1161, ⓦwww.fazendadasminhocas.com.br. A historic site in its own right, the *casa grande* dates from 1712 and there's an old Baroque chapel in the grounds as well as a sugar-mill and a comfortable, if rustic, *pousada*. There are pleasant trails on the property and facilities for swimming and horse riding. ❾

Fazenda Recanto dos Fonda Distrito de Ravena, Sabará ⓣ31/3672-3399, ⓦwww.recantodosfonda.com.br. This modern *fazenda* complex includes a swimming pool and horse-riding facilities, and serves good country food. Set amidst 200 hectares of lakes and woodland in pleasant walking country, 40km from Belo Horizonte. ❺

Pousada Altos de Minas Município de Nova Minas ⓣ31/9981-1930, ⓦwww.agendabh.com.br/altosdeminas. A modern but colonial-style country hotel 25km from Belo Horizonte, set in attractive gardens with a pool. The restaurant offers *mineiro* food as well as international fare. ❺

The building was restored in 1991 and transformed into a **hotel**, the *Hospedaria do Caraça* (☎31/3837-2698, reservations essential; ❸), managed by the remaining members of the order. It's a comfortable, low-key place to spend a few relaxing days. Some parts still remain from the original building, including rooms for private prayer, a few bedrooms and the cellar. The neo-Gothic church of Nossa Senhora Mãe Dos Homens, added in 1883, was also spared by the fire, and has beautiful French stained-glass windows, marble and soapstone carvings and a seven-hundred-pipe organ built in the seminary itself.

A small **museum** is attached to the church and displays items rescued from the fire, including English and Chinese porcelain, furniture and a sundial. One of the greatest attractions, however, is the **wolves** (*lobo-guará*) that live in the surrounding woods – there's a longstanding tradition of monks leaving food for them near the church.

The cidades históricas

The **cidades históricas** of Minas Gerais – small enough really to be towns rather than cities – were founded within a couple of decades of each other in the early eighteenth century. Rough and violent mining camps in their early days, they were soon transformed by mineral wealth into treasure houses, not merely of gold, but also of Baroque art and architecture. Well preserved and carefully maintained, together the towns form one of the most impressive sets of colonial remains in the Americas, comparable only to the silver-mining towns that flourished in Mexico at roughly the same time. In Brazil, they are equalled only by the remnants of the plantation culture of the Northeast, to which they contributed much of the gold you see in the gilded churches of Olinda and Salvador.

Although some have acquired a modern urban fringe, all the historic cities have centres untouched by modern developers; a couple, like **Tiradentes**, look very much as they did two centuries ago. All have colonial churches (**Ouro Preto** has thirteen), at least one good museum, steep cobbled streets, ornate mansions and the particular atmosphere of a place soaked in history. It was in these cities that the **Inconfidência Mineira**, Brazil's first bungling attempt to throw off the Portuguese yoke, was played out in 1789. And here the great sculptor Antônio Francisco Lisboa – **Aleijadinho** or the "little cripple" – spent all his life, leaving behind him a collection unmatched by any other figure working in the contemporary Baroque tradition.

Practicalities

The nearest *cidade histórica* to Belo Horizonte is **Sabará**, only a local bus ride away; the furthest is **Diamantina**, six hours north by bus from the capital in the wild scenery of the Serra do Espinhaço. Two hours southeast from Belo Horizonte, **Ouro Preto** is the ex-capital of the state and the largest of the historic cities, with **Mariana** a short distance away. And two hours to the south of Belo Horizonte is **Congonhas**, where Aleijadinho's masterpiece, the church of Bom Jesus de Matosinhos, is located. A two-hour bus ride further south are **São João del Rei** and **Tiradentes**.

Only in Sabará is **accommodation** difficult to find. All the other cities are well supplied with places to stay and worth more than a quick day-trip. If you only have a little time to spare, the best option from Belo Horizonte is Ouro Preto: you can easily get there and back in a day, and – though everyone has their own favourites – it is the most classically beautiful of all.

Sabará

SABARÁ lies strung out over a series of hills, wound around the Rio das Velhas. Many of its cobbled streets are so steep they have to be taken slowly,

Aleijadinho (Antônio Francisco Lisboa)

Although little is known of his life, we do know roughly what the renowned sculptor **Aleijadinho** looked like. In the Museu de Aleijadinho in Ouro Preto, a crude but vivid portrait shows an intense, aquiline man who is clearly what Brazilians call *pardo* – of mixed race. His hands are under his jacket, which seems a trivial detail unless you know what makes his achievements truly astonishing: the great sculptor of the *barroco mineiro* was presumably a leper, and produced much of his best work after he had lost the use of his hands.

Antônio Francisco Lisboa was born in Ouro Preto in 1738, the son of a Portuguese craftsman; his mother was probably a slave. For the first half of his exceptionally long life he was perfectly healthy: a womanizer and *bon viveur* despite his exclusively religious output. His prodigious talent – equally on display in wood or stone, human figures or abstract decoration – allowed him to set up a workshop with apprentices while still young, and he was much in demand. Although he always based himself in Ouro Preto, he spent long periods in all the major historic towns except Diamantina, working on commissions; but he never travelled beyond the state. Self-taught, he was an obsessive reader of the Bible and medical textbooks (the only two obvious influences in his work), one supplying its imagery, the other underlying the anatomical detail of his human figures.

In the late 1770s, Aleijadinho's life changed utterly. He began to suffer from a progressively debilitating disease that is thought to have been leprosy. As it got worse he became a recluse, only venturing outdoors in the dark, and increasingly obsessed with his work. His physical disabilities were terrible: he lost his fingers, toes and the use of his lower legs. Sometimes the pain was so bad his apprentices had to stop him hacking away at the offending part of his body with a chisel.

Yet despite all this Aleijadinho actually increased his output, working with hammer and chisel strapped to his wrists by his apprentices, who moved him about on a wooden trolley. It was under these conditions that he sculpted his masterpiece, the 12 massive figures of the prophets and the 64 lifesize Passion figures for the **Basílica do Senhor Bom Jesus de Matosinhos** (see p.212) in Congonhas, between 1796 and 1805. These figures were his swansong: failing eyesight finally forced him to stop work and he ended his life as a hermit in a hovel on the outskirts of Ouro Preto. The death he longed for finally came on November 18, 1814: he is buried in a simple grave in the church he attended all his life, Nossa Senhora da Conceição in Ouro Preto.

Aleijadinho's prolific output would have been remarkable under any circumstances: given his condition it was nothing short of miraculous – a triumph of the creative spirit. The bulk of his work is to be found in Ouro Preto, but there are significant items in Sabará, São João del Rei, Mariana and Congonhas. His achievement was to stay within the Baroque tradition, yet bring to its ornate conventions a raw physicality and unmatched technical skill that makes his work unique.

but ascents are rewarded with gorgeous churches that are austere on the outside and choked with ornamentation inside. Sabará's proximity to Belo Horizonte would make it the ideal base for seeing the metropolis, but for its lack of accommodation. Fortunately, the frequency of the **bus** link (every 15min from 4am to midnight) makes it an easy day-trip from Belo Horizonte: catch the red #5509 bus on Rua dos Caetés one block up from Avenida Afonso Pena. Start early and avoid visiting on Monday when most sights are closed.

The Town

Standing in **Praça Santa Rita**, you're in the centre not just of the oldest part of Sabará, but of the oldest inhabited streets in southern Brazil. Founded in 1674, Sabará was the first major centre of gold mining in the state, although attention shifted southwards to Ouro Preto and Mariana by the end of the seventeenth century. The city was established by Borba Gato, a typical *paulista* cut-throat who combined Catholic fervour – Sabará's original name was Vila Real de Nossa Senhora da Conceição de Sabarabuçú – with ruthlessness: his determined extermination of the local Indians made gold mining possible here.

Not until forty years after its foundation were the mud huts and stockades of the early adventurers replaced by stone buildings, and it wasn't until the second quarter of the eighteenth century, when gold production was at its peak, that serious church building began and the village acquired an air of permanence. A fair proportion of the local gold ended up gilding the interiors of the town's churches, but by the turn of the nineteenth century all the alluvial gold had been exhausted and the town entered a steep decline. Sophisticated deep-mining techniques, introduced by Europeans in the nineteenth century, failed to stop the decline and Sabará became a small and grindingly poor place; today, the colonial zone is fringed by *favelas*.

Igreja de Nossa Senhora de Ó

The very early days of Sabará are represented by the tiny **Igreja de Nossa Senhora de Ó** (Mon–Fri 8am–5pm and Sat & Sun 9am–noon & 2–5pm), one of the most unusual colonial churches in Brazil. It's a couple of kilometres from Praça Santa Rita, either via a signposted walk or a local bus marked "Esplanada", which leaves from the square. The church doesn't look in the least Portuguese: its austere, irregularly shaped exterior is topped off by an unmistakeably Chinese tower, complete with pagoda-like upturns at the corners. The cramped interior, dominated by a gilded arch over the altar, also shows distinct oriental influences, but the church is so old (it was started in 1698) that nobody knows who was responsible for its design. The most likely explanation is that the Portuguese, despairing of the local talent, imported a group of Chinese craftsmen from Macau.

Matriz Nossa Senhora da Conceição

Sabará's main church, **Matriz Nossa Senhora da Conceição** (Mon–Fri 9am–5pm and Sat & Sun 9am–noon & 2–5pm) is on Praça Getúlio Vargas, signposted from Praça Santa Rita. Started by the Jesuits in 1720, it's a fine example of the so-called first and second phases *of barroco mineiro*. Succeeding generations added features to the original layout and inside it's extremely impressive, with a double row of heavily carved and gilded arches, a beautifully decorated ceiling and, once again, Chinese influence in the gildings and painted panels of the door leading to the sacristy.

Minas Baroque

There are three distinct phases of **Baroque church architecture** in Minas. The **first**, from the beginning of the eighteenth century to about 1730, was very ornate and often involved extravagant carving and gilding, but left exteriors plain; sculpture was formal, with stiff, rather crude statues. The **second phase** dominated the middle decades of the eighteenth century, with equally extravagant decorations inside, especially around the altar, and the wholesale plastering of everything with gold; the exteriors were now embellished with curlicues and panels in fine Minas soapstone, ceilings were painted and sculpture noticeably more natural, although still highly stylized. The peak was the period from 1760 to 1810, and this **third phase** of *barroco mineiro* produced stunning work: the exterior decoration was more elaborate, with fine carving in both wood and stone, but the interiors were less cluttered, with walls often left plain. By now, too, the religious sculpture, with its flowing realism, had broken the stylistic bounds that confine most Baroque art.

Nossa Senhora do Carmo

The church of **Nossa Senhora do Carmo** (Tues–Sun 9–11.30am & 1–5.30pm; R$2) on Rua do Carmo, a third-phase church, demonstrates the remarkable talents of Aleijadinho, who oversaw its construction and contributed much of the decoration between 1770 and 1783. The interior manages to be elaborate and uncluttered at the same time, with graceful curves in the gallery, largely plain walls, comparatively little gilding and a beautifully painted ceiling. Aleijadinho left his mark everywhere: the imposing soapstone and painted wood pulpits, the banister in the nave, the flowing lines of the choir, and above all in the two statues of São João da Cruz and São Simão Stock. You can tell an Aleijadinho from the faces: the remarkably lifelike one of São Simão is complete with wrinkles and transfixed by religious ecstacy.

Nossa Senhora do Rosário dos Pretos da Barra

Despite being unfinished and open to the elements, the church of **Nossa Senhora do Rosário dos Pretos da Barra** (always open), fifteen minutes' signposted walk from Praça Santa Rita on Praça Melo Viana, is just as fascinating as the more ornate buildings. Slaves who worked in the gold mines built it in typical Portuguese colonial style. Organized into lay societies called *irmandades*, the slaves paid for and built churches, but this one was begun late, in 1767, and with the decline of the mines the money ran out. Although sporadic restarts were made during the nineteenth century, it was never more than half-built, and when slavery was abolished in 1888 it was left as a memorial.

The Museu do Ouro

The **Museu do Ouro** (Tues–Sun noon–5.30pm) is a short but steep signposted walk up from Praça Santa Rita on Rua da Intendência and well worth the effort. Built in 1732, this is the only royal foundry house remaining in Brazil. When gold was discovered in Minas Gerais, the Portuguese Crown was entitled to a fifth of the output but had to collect it first. To do so, it put a military cordon around the gold mines and then built several royal foundries, where gold from the surrounding area was melted down, franked and then given accordingly to the king. The functional building that now houses the museum easily reveals its origins: it is built around an interior courtyard, overlooked by a balcony on three sides, from where the officials could keep an eagle eye on gold being melted into bars and weighed. Along with the other royal foundry in Ouro Preto, it was Brazil's most heavily guarded building.

Most of the museum is devoted to gold-mining history. **Downstairs** are rooms full of scales, weights, pans and other mining instruments, and a strong-room containing plaster cast replicas of eighteenth-century gold bars. **Upstairs** you'll find a collection of colonial furniture and *arte sacra* as well as a very fine painted ceiling, representing the four continents known at the time it was built. In a room off the courtyard is a model of the **Morro Velho** mine in nearby Nova Lima, the deepest gold mine in the world outside South Africa. There's a commemorative photograph of the 44 Cornish mining engineers and single Brazilian lawyer who began it, all working for the wonderfully named St John d'El Rey Gold Mining Company.

The rest of the town

If you tire of colonial sightseeing, just wandering around the bars and cobbled streets near the Praça Santa Rita is very pleasant, too. There are a number of impressive buildings, notably the **Prefeitura** on Rua Dom Pedro II, and the **Teatro Municipal** (daily 8am–noon & 1–5pm), on the same street, which was designed as an opera house and opened in 1819 just as the gold ran out. Before you leave the town, have some water from the mid-eighteenth century **Chafariz do Rosário** on Praça Melo Viana, as it's believed that all those who drink from the fountain will one day come back to Sabará.

Practicalities

The nineteen-kilometre journey from Belo Horizonte takes roughly thirty minutes, though the bus station is at the far eastern end of town; ask the driver to show you the best stop for the colonial centre, from where you should easily find Praça Santa Rita. There is a rudimentary **tourist office** (Ⓣ31/3672-7690) around the corner, but it doesn't stock maps. If in doubt, any road going uphill will invariably lead you to a church, from where it's easy to get your bearings. **Buses back to Belo Horizonte** are best caught on the main road leading out of town at the bottom of the colonial zone by the river.

There are several **bars and restaurants**, which really only get busy on weekends: *Cê Qui Sabe* at Rua Mestre Caetano 56 and *Bar-ôco* at Rua Mestre Ritinha 115 both serve a reliable *comida mineira*. Cheaper places are clustered around Praça Santa Rita and dotted throughout the old centre, often in people's front rooms. If you want to **stay**, a lovely place to try is the *Solar dos Sepúlvedas*, Rua Intendência 371 (Ⓣ31/3671-2705, Ⓦwww.solardosepulvedas.com.br; ❸), a restored eighteenth-century house with just seven rooms, well-tended gardens and a pool. An equally intimate *pousada* is the *Vila Real*, Rua Serafim Mota Barro 76 (Ⓣ31/3671-2121; ❷).

Ouro Preto

The drive to **OURO PRETO**, 100km southeast of Belo Horizonte, begins unpromisingly with endless industrial complexes and *favelas* spread over the hills, but in its later stretches becomes spectacular as it winds around hill country 1000m above sea level and passes several valleys where patches of forest survive; imagine the entire landscape covered with it and you have an idea of what greeted the gold-seekers in the 1690s. On arrival, the first thing that strikes you is how small the town is, considering that until 1897 it was the capital of Minas (its

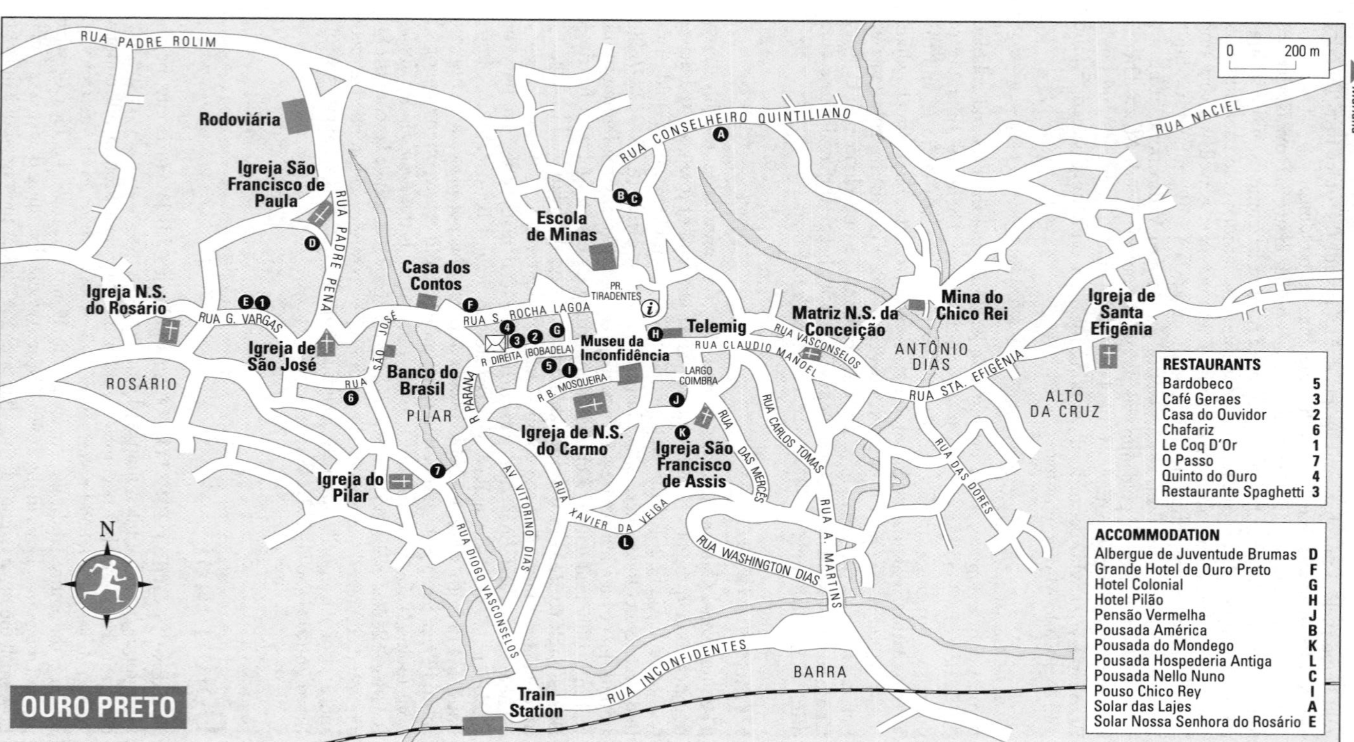
OURO PRETO
Mariana
Buses for Belo Horizonte
Buses for Belo Horizonte
0 200 m
N
RUA PADRE ROLIM
RUA CONSELHEIRO QUINTILIANO
RUA NACIEL
RUA PADRE PENA
RUA G. VARGAS
RUA SÃO JOSÉ
RUA S. ROCHA LAGOA
PR. TIRADENTES
R DIREITA (BOBADELA)
R. B. MOSQUEIRA
R. PARANÁ
RUA CLAUDIO MANOEL
RUA VASCONSELOS
LARGO COIMBRA
RUA CARLOS TOMAS
RUA DAS MERCÊS
RUA STA. EFIGÊNIA
RUA DAS DORES
RUA A. MARTINS
RUA WASHINGTON DIAS
RUA XAVIER DA VEIGA
AV VITORINO DIAS
RUA DIOGO VASCONSELOS
RUA INCONFIDENTES
ROSÁRIO
PILAR
ANTÔNIO DIAS
ALTO DA CRUZ
BARRA
Rodoviária
Igreja São Francisco de Paula
Igreja N.S. do Rosário
Igreja de São José
Casa dos Contos
Banco do Brasil
Igreja do Pilar
Escola de Minas
Museu da Inconfidência
Igreja de N.S. do Carmo
Igreja São Francisco de Assis
Telemig
Matriz N.S. da Conceição
Mina do Chico Rei
Igreja de Santa Efigênia
Train Station
RESTAURANTS
Bardobeco 5
Café Geraes 3
Casa do Ouvidor 2
Chafariz 6
Le Coq D'Or 1
O Passo 7
Quinto do Ouro 4
Restaurante Spaghetti 3
ACCOMMODATION
Albergue de Juventude Brumas D
Grande Hotel de Ouro Preto F
Hotel Colonial G
Hotel Pilão H
Pensão Vermelha J
Pousada América B
Pousada do Mondego K
Pousada Hospederia Antiga L
Pousada Nello Nuno C
Pouso Chico Rey I
Solar das Lajes A
Solar Nossa Senhora do Rosário E

population is still only 68,000). That said, you can see at a glance why the capital had to be shifted to Belo Horizonte: the steep hills the town is built around, straddling a network of creeks, severely limit space for expansion. Today, the hills and vertiginous streets (some so steep they have steps rather than pavements) of Ouro Preto's historic centre are vital ingredients in what is architecturally one of the loveliest towns in Brazil, albeit one that can no longer in all honesty lay claim to being the unspoilt eighteenth-century jewel that it was just a few years back.

Avoid coming on Monday if you want to see the sights, as all the churches and most of the museums close for the day. Also, buy your onward ticket as soon as you arrive, as buses fill up quickly. Some people complain about Ouro Preto being touristy but they miss the point: it's precisely because there really is something to savour here that the visitors come. If you have the time, aim to spend at least a night or two so that you can enjoy the city after all the day-trippers have departed.

Ouro Preto has an extremely popular street **Carnaval** that attracts visitors from far afield: be sure to reserve accommodation long in advance. Likewise, at **Easter** time, the town becomes the focus of a spectacular series of plays and processions lasting for about a month before Easter Sunday; the last days of the life of Christ are played out in open-air theatres throughout the town.

Some history

Less than a decade after gold was struck at Sabará, a *paulista* adventurer called **Antônio Dias** pitched camp underneath a mountain the Indians called Itacolomi, with an unmistakeable thumb-shaped rock on its summit. Panning the streams nearby, he found "black gold" – alluvial gold mixed with iron ore – and named his camp after it. It attracted a flood of people as it became clear the deposits were the richest yet found in Minas, and so many came that they outstripped the food supply. In 1700 there was a famine and legend has it that people died of hunger with gold nuggets in their hands.

The early years were hard, made worse by a war started in 1707 between the Portuguese and *paulista bandeirantes*, who resisted the Crown's attempts to take over the area. The war, the **Guerra das Emboabas**, lasted for two years and was brutal, with ambushes and massacres the preferred tactics of both sides. Ouro Preto was the Portuguese base, and troops from here drove the *paulistas* from their headquarters at Sabará and finally annihilated them near São João del Rei. From then on, Ouro Preto was the effective **capital** of the gold-producing area of Minas, although it wasn't officially named as such until 1823. Indeed, compared to places like nearby Mariana, Ouro Preto was a late developer; all but two of its churches date from the second half of the eighteenth century, and several of its finest buildings, like the school of mining and the town hall on Praça Tiradentes, were not finished until well into the nineteenth century.

The gold gave out about the time that Brazil finally became independent in 1822, but for decades the town survived as an administrative centre and university town; a school of mining was founded in 1876. After the capital moved to Belo Horizonte, steady decline set in, though the populist government of Getúlio Vargas brought back the bodies of the Inconfidêntes (see box and Museu da Inconfidência on p.204) to a proper shrine, and sensitively restored the crumbling monuments.

Since the 1980s, **tourism** has become increasingly important for the town, as has the aluminium industry, which has attracted job-hungry migrants from throughout the state, many of whom end up living in the *favelas* of the surrounding hillsides. Indeed, for many locals Ouro Preto's architectural heritage and tourism are getting in the way of economic expansion; meanwhile hasty construction is threatening the city's coveted status as a UNESCO World Heritage Site, a potential embarrassment for Brazil, not least for the revenue

△ Ouro Preto

it helps generate from tourism. Although heavy vehicle traffic has been re-routed to avoid the historic centre and there's talk of re-housing *favela* dwellers, tensions between various interest groups are proving difficult to resolve.

Arrival, information and accommodation

All buses arrive at the **rodoviária**, some ten minutes' walk westwards from the centre on Rua Padre Rolim. Minibuses or taxis will take you to the Praça Tiradentes, the main square. There's also a **train service** linking Ouro Preto with Mariana (see p.211), 12km to the east, which makes for a very pleasant day-trip. The train station is located south of the city centre.

Praça Tiradentes is dominated by a statue of the martyr to Brazilian independence and lined with beautiful colonial buildings. On the east side at no. 41 is the **municipal tourist office** (Mon–Fri 8am–6pm; ⓣ31/3559-3269), which sells an excellent city map for R$4; it also provides details of some spectacular walks in the surrounding countryside. The town gets crowded at weekends and holiday periods, so it's a good idea to reserve a room in advance, but even during Carnaval the tourist office can usually help you find somewhere to stay.

There are ATMs at Bradesco on Praça Tiradentes, HSBC at Rua São José 105 and the Banco do Brasil at Rua São José 189.

Accommodation

The price codes below are based on weekend (Fri–Sun) and high-season prices; midweek and in low season, Ouro Preto's hotels offer discounts of around 20–30 percent.

Albergue de Juventude Brumas Ladeira de São Francisco de Paula 68 ⓣ31/3551-2944, ⓦwww.brumasonline.hpg.ig.com.br. Part of the Hostelling International network, this place offers extremely basic dorms, kitchen and laundry facilities. Reached by a steep 5-minute trek, the hostel offers commanding views of Ouro Preto's historic centre. R$30 per person.

Grande Hotel de Ouro Preto Rua Senador Rocha Lagoa 164 ⓣ31/3551-1488, ⓦwww.hotelouropreto.com.br. Opened in 1940, this is one of Oscar Niemeyer's earliest creations – though not one of his best. The "standard" rooms at this three-star hotel are on the small side and overlook the garden but the suites have tremendous views. Offers good service and there's a nice pool in the Burle Marx–designed gardens. ❺–❻

Hotel Colonial Travessa Padre Camilo Veloso 26 ⓣ31/3551-3133, ⓦwww.hotelcolonial.com.br. A rather drab but convenient place located one street back from Praça Tiradentes (it's signposted), with a range of *apartamentos* sleeping up to three people, all with *frigobar*, TV, a/c and telephones. The better rooms are in the wing to the right of the entrance; some of them are on two levels. ❹

Hotel Pilão Praça Tiradentes 51, next to the tourist office ⓣ31/3551-3066, ⓕ3551-3275. Extremely simple rooms overlook the square (which can be noisy at night); some sleep up to six people. Not the friendliest of places. ❷

Pensão Vermelha Largo de Coimbra, at the corner with Rua Antônio Pereira ⓣ31/3551-1138. Quiet, family-run place with clean, simple rooms; some overlook the magnificent facade of the São Francisco church. ❷

Pousada América Rua Camilo de Brito 15 ⓣ31/3551-2525. Popular with international travellers, this family-run spot offers good *apartamentos* and *quartos* (both same price), though they're slightly expensive for being pretty basic. About 100m off Praça Tiradentes along Rua Barão de Camargos (the bus from Mariana passes it). ❸

Pousada do Mondego Largo de Coimbra 38 ⓣ31/3551-2040, ⓕ3551-3094. Excellent accommodation in a beautiful restored mid-eighteenth-century building across from the Igreja de São Francisco de Assis. Period furniture is in all rooms – ask for one with a balcony. ❻

Pousada Hospederia Antiga Rua Xavier da Veiga 1 ⓣ31/3551-2203, ⓦwww.antiga.com.br. A charming old house with simple but spacious and spotlessly clean rooms, all with private facilities. The quiet location involves a tiring, five-minute, uphill walk to reach the centre. Excellent value. ❸

Pousada Nello Nuno Rua Camilo de Brito 59 ⓣ31/3551-3375. A very pretty small *pousada* built around a courtyard. The rooms are attractively furnished in natural woods and the artwork is mostly by the proprietor who works in her printing atelier in the same building. ❷

Pouso Chico Rey Rua Brigador Mosqueira 90 ⓣ31/3551-1274. A small eighteenth-century house converted into a pleasant *pensão*, filled with a collection of eighteenth-century antiques that would do credit to a museum. There's a wonderful view from the reading room on the first floor, plus excellent breakfasts are served. There are only six rooms, so book in advance. ❹

Solar das Lajes Rua Conselheiro Quintilhiano 604 ⓣ31/3551-3388, ⓦwww.solardaslajes.com.br. Simple but comfortable rooms offer tremendous views across town or of the tree-filled garden. In a quiet location five minutes' walk from the city centre, the English-speaking owner – a sculptor of some renown – is very hospitable. The best budget *pousada* in Ouro Preto. ❸–❹

Solar Nossa Senhora do Rosário Rua Getúlio Vargas 270 ⓣ31/3551-5200, ⓦwww.hotelsolardorosario.com.br. Built in 1840, this hotel remains the most luxurious in Ouro Preto. Rooms have a pleasant mix of period and modern furnishings, plus there is a pool and comfortable lounges. The restaurant, one of the best in the city, serves fine Franco-*mineiro* dishes. ❻

The Town

Praça Tiradentes, with roads leading off it to most of Ouro Preto's sights, is the best place to start a tour of the town. Given the thirteen colonial churches, seven chapels, six museums and several other places of interest, you could easily spend two or three days here.

The Escola de Minas

Right on the Praça Tiradentes is the **Escola de Minas**, now housed in the old governor's palace. Established in 1876, it's the best mining school in the country, and its students lend a slightly Bohemian air to the town. The white turrets make the building look rather like a fortress: the exterior, with a fine marble entrance, dates from the 1740s, but the inside was gutted during the nineteenth century and not improved by it. Attached to the school is the **Museu de Ciência e Técnica** (ⓦwww.museu.em.ufop.br; Tues–Sun noon–5pm; R$4), founded in 1877 as the Museu de Mineralogia thanks to the collection of the French geologist Henri Gorceix. Although most of the exhibits are of interest only to geologists, there is one fascinating room where gold and precious stones are beautifully displayed, in contrast to the chaos in the rest of the museum.

The Paço Municipal and Museu da Inconfidência

Also in the *praça* are the old city chambers, the **Paço Municipal** (Tues–Sun noon–5.30pm), a glorious eighteenth-century building that provides a perfect example of the classical grace of Minas colonial architecture; its beautifully restored interior lives up to expectations. Like many colonial town halls, the building was also a jail, and many of the huge rooms, so well suited to the display of *arte sacra*, were once dungeons.

The Paço Municipal contains the **Museu da Inconfidência** (Ⓦwww.museuinconfidencia.com.br; Tues–Sun noon–5.30pm; R$4), which is interesting enough since the surrounding towns have been stripped of a great deal of their wealth to stock its halls. There are relics of eighteenth-century daily life, from sedan chairs and kitchen utensils (including the seal the bishop used to stamp his coat of arms on his cakes) to swords and pistols. A ground-floor room contains the museum's highlight: four exquisite, small Aleijadinho statues that are a fitting introduction to the flowing detail of his best work.

Upstairs there's colonial furniture and more art, but the spiritual heart of the place is found at the rear of the ground floor, where the cell in which **Tiradentes** spent the last night of his life is now the **shrine to the Inconfidêntes** (see box, p.204). An antechamber holds documents, like the execution order and birth and death registrations of Tiradentes, and leads into a room containing his remains and those of his fellow conspirators – all in the vaguely Fascist style the Vargas era usually chose for its public monuments. Most of the conspirators died in Africa, some in Portugal; all but Tiradentes were exiled for the rest of their lives and never returned to Brazil.

The Igreja de Nossa Senhora do Carmo

Next door to the Paço Municipal on Praça Tiradentes, the **Igreja de Nossa Senhora do Carmo** (Tues–Sun 1–4.45pm) is one of the finest churches in Ouro Preto. It was designed by Manoel Francisco Lisboa, Aleijadinho's father, and

The Inconfidência Mineira

Ouro Preto is most famous in Brazil as the birthplace of the **Inconfidência Mineira**, the first attempt to free Brazil from the Portuguese. Inspired by the French Revolution, and heartily sick of the heavy taxes levied by a bankrupt Portugal, a group of twelve prominent town citizens led by **Joaquim José da Silva Xavier** began in 1789 to discuss organizing a rebellion. Xavier was a dentist, known to everyone as Tiradentes, "teeth-puller". Another of the conspirators was **Tomas Gonzaga**, whose hopeless love poems to the beautiful **Marília Dirceu**, promised by her family to another, made the couple into the Brazilian equivalent of Romeo and Juliet: "When you appear at dawn, all rumpled/like a badly wrapped parcel, no ribbons or flowers/how Nature shines, how much lovelier you seem."

The conspiracy proved a fiasco and all were betrayed and arrested before any uprising was organized. The leaders were condemned to hang, but the Portuguese, realizing that they could ill afford to offend the inhabitants of a state whose taxes kept them afloat, arranged a royal reprieve, commuting the sentence to exile in Angola and Mozambique. Unfortunately the messenger arrived two days too late to save Tiradentes, marked as the first to die. He was hanged where the column now stands in the square that bears his name, his head stuck on a post and his limbs despatched to the other mining towns to serve as a warning.

construction began just before his death in 1766. Aleijadinho himself then took over the building of the church and finished it six years later. He contributed the carving of the exterior and worked on the interior, on and off, for four decades. The baptismal font in the sacristy is a masterpiece, as are the carved doors leading to the pulpits. Two of the side chapels in the main church (São João and Nossa Senhora da Piedade) were among the last commissions he was able to complete, in 1809; the accounts book for the time has Aleijadinho complaining he was paid with "false gold". Of the major churches in Ouro Preto, the Igreja de Nossa Senhora do Carmo is distinctive as the only one to have *azulejo*-tiled panels, placed to make the Portuguese who patronized it feel at home.

To the side of the church is the **Museu do Oratório** (Ⓦwww.oratorio.com.br; Tues–Sun 9.30am–5.30pm; R$2), housed in an excellently restored mansion that was once the meeting house for the lay society attached to Nossa Senhora do Carmo. On view is a very well displayed and high-quality collection of oratories from throughout Brazil. Although there are some glittering shrines featuring gold and silver, the most touching examples are the portable oratories carried by muleteers and other travellers to protect themselves from danger. Also fascinating are the Afro-Brazilian oratories where African gods are depicted to look like Catholic saints.

The Igreja do Pilar

It's a lovely walk from Praça Tiradentes to Ouro Preto's oldest church. **Rua Brigador Mosqueira**, which runs downhill from the square, is one of the quietest and most beautiful streets in town, with almost every building on it worth savouring. Wander down, bear left at the bottom, and you come out onto the incredibly steep Rua do Pilar, from where you can glimpse the towers of the Igreja do Pilar well before the plunging, cobbled path deposits you in front it.

With an exterior ornate even by Baroque standards, the **Igreja do Pilar** (Tues–Sun 9–10.45am & noon–4.45pm; R$3) is the finest example anywhere of early Minas Baroque architecture. It was begun in 1711 and the interior is the opposite of the Carmo's restraint: a wild explosion of glinting Rococo, liberally plastered with gold. The best carving was done by Francisco Xavier de Brito, who worked in Minas from 1741 until his early death ten years later – and about whom nothing is known except that he was Portuguese and influenced Aleijadinho. He was responsible for the astonishing arch over the altar, where the angels supporting the Rococo pillars seem to swarm out of the wall on either side.

The Casa dos Contos

From the Igreja do Pilar, turn right up Rua Rondolfo Bretos and round into **Rua São José** (also, confusingly, called Rua Tiradentes), whose many bars and restaurants make it a good place to take a breather. Crossing the small stone bridge, you come to the perfectly proportioned **Casa dos Contos**, the old treasury building that's now a museum (Mon 2–6pm, Tues–Sat 10–6pm, Sun 10am–4pm). Finished in 1787, it was built as a bank-cum-mansion by Ouro Preto's richest family, and in 1803 became the Fazenda Real, a foundry where the Crown extracted its fifth of the gold and assembled armed convoys to escort it down to Rio for shipment to Portugal. The collection is no more than moderately interesting – the usual mixture of *arte sacra* and furniture – but the building is terrific: a magnificent colonial mansion built when Ouro Preto was at its peak. An imposing staircase that climbs four storeys high dominates the entrance hall, and the mansion is constructed around a beautiful courtyard large enough for a dozen cavalry troopers. The most interesting places radiate off the courtyard: the huge furnace for melting the gold and shaping it into bars, the slave quarters, the stables (horses were better accommodated than slaves) and even an eighteenth-century privy. And don't forget to go right up to the *mirante* on the top floor of the Casa for one of the best views of Ouro Preto.

The Igreja de São Francisco de Assis

From Praça Tiradentes, Rua Cláudio Manoel winds downhill, lined with stores selling rather expensive precious stones and jewellery that don't in fact come from Ouro Preto but from eastern Minas. Ahead, on the right, is arguably the most beautiful church in Ouro Preto, the **Igreja de São Francisco de Assis** (Tues–Sun 8.30–11.45am & 1.30–5pm; R$3). The small square that sets it off – Largo do Coimbra – plays host to a mediocre arts and crafts market in the afternoon.

The church was begun in 1765, and no other in Ouro Preto contains more works by Aleijadinho. The magnificent exterior soapstone panels are his, as is virtually all the virtuoso carving, in both wood and stone, inside; to top it off, Aleijadinho also designed the church and supervised its construction. Further, in 1801 the church commissioners contracted the best painter of the *barroco mineiro*, **Manoel da Costa Athayde**, to decorate the ceilings. It took him nine years, using natural dyes made from plant juices and powdered iron ore, and his work has stood the test of time far better than other church paintings of the period. The squirming mass of cherubs and saints are framed within a cunning trompe l'oeil effect, which extends the real Baroque pillars on the sides of the nave into painted ones on the ceiling, making it seem like an open-air canopy through which you can glimpse clouds. There are also painted *azulejos* that look remarkably like the real thing.

The Matriz de Nossa Senhora da Conceição and Museu do Aleijadinho

Returning to Rua Cláudio Manoel, follow the winding Rua Bernardo de Vasconcelos, to the left – this is the back way down to the last of the major churches in Ouro Preto, **Matriz de Nossa Senhora da Conceição** (Tues–Sun 8–11.45am & 1.30–4.45pm), and it's a steep descent. Coming this way, you're leaving the main tourist area and everything looks just as it did the day Aleijadinho died: the Matriz is famous as the church he belonged to and where he is buried. The one-time cut-throat Antônio Dias, who founded Ouro Preto and died old and rich in 1727, left his fortune to build this church on the spot of his first camp – so this is where it all began, and, with the death of Aleijadinho, where it can also be said to have ended.

Despite Aleijadinho's connection with the church, he never worked on it. All the same, it is an impressive example of mid-period Minas Baroque, and the painting and carving are very fine, especially the figures of saints in the side altars – note the pained expression and movement of St Sebastian, on the left of the nave. Aleijadinho is buried in a simple **tomb** on the right of the nave, marked "Antônio Francisco Lisboa" and covered by nothing more elaborate than a plain wooden plank.

A side door by the main altar of the church leads to the sacristy and the fascinating **Museu do Aleijadinho** (Tues–Sun 8.30–noon & 1.30–5pm; R$3), which is worth lingering over – not so much a museum of Aleijadinho's work as of his life and times. The ground floor is taken up by an excellent collection of religious art, but the highlight is upstairs, in a room dedicated not just to Aleijadinho but to all the legendary figures of Ouro Preto's golden age. What work there is by Aleijadinho is in the basement, and is quite remarkable: don't miss the four magnificent lions that once served as supports for the plinth on which coffins were laid. Aleijadinho, never having seen a lion, drew from imagination and produced medieval monsters with the faces of monkeys.

The museum contains reproductions of the birth and death entries in the parish register for Aleijadinho, Marília Dirceu and Manoel Athayde. But even better are the eighteenth-century *ex votos* on the wall, a riveting insight into the tribulations of bygone daily life. One shows a black slave on her sickbed, with the inscription "Ana, slave of António Dias, had me made after finding herself gravely ill, without hope of life, but praying to Our Lord of the Slaves miraculously recovered". Opposite is a gruesome one from 1778 giving thanks for the successful setting of a broken leg, shown in graphic detail. Also on the wall is a small **portrait**, crude but priceless, of Aleijadinho in middle age. It doesn't flatter so is probably a good likeness: slightly hunched, with sharp features.

Igreja de Santa Efigênia

Further out from the centre is the less important but no less fascinating **Igreja de Santa Efigênia** (Tues–Sun; R$3), the church for slaves, located on the east hill some 3km from Praça Tiradentes. To get there, continue along Rua Cláudio Manoel down to the river, cross over and climb up Rua Santa Efigênia. Although plain in comparison to what you'll see in Ouro Preto's other churches, the artwork here is well worth the steep climb and the views towards town are outstanding. The altar was carved by Javier do Briton, the mentor of Aleijadinho; the interior panels are by Manoel Rabelo de Souza; and the exterior image of Nossa Senhora do Rosário is by Aleijadinho himself. Slaves contributed to its construction by smuggling gold in their teeth cavities and under their fingernails.

Mina do Chico Rei

If you don't have time to visit the Mina da Passagem **gold mine** near Mariana (see p.208), much closer, and cheaper too, is the **Mina do Chico Rei** (guided tours daily 8am–5pm; R$5), at Rua Dom Silvério 108 in the eastern *bairro* of Antônio Dias. Founded in 1702, barely seven years after gold was first struck in Sabará, the mine continued in operation until 1888. Though visually not as striking as the Mina da Passagem, it nonetheless boasts some impressive statistics, which give an idea of just how rich Ouro Preto must once have been: the mine, constructed on five levels, contains an astonishing eighty square kilometres of tunnels, vaults and passages.

Eating and drinking

One of the nice things about Ouro Preto is the number of places where you can eat, drink or just hang out; when the students are out in force on weekend nights, it has none of the quiet atmosphere of a small interior town that you might expect. During term-time, at the weekend, the steep Rua Conde de Bobadela (also called Rua Direita), leading up to Praça Tiradentes, is packed with students spilling out of the **bars** and cafés; more congregate in the square itself, though most of the bars there have been turned into expensive restaurants. The modern wing of the mining school on the square has a bar and a **live music** venue (see the posters in its lobby), while the *Booze Café Concerto*, a large basement area at Rua Direita 42, attracts jazz and rock bands from as far away as Belo Horizonte. If you prefer a quiet drink without the crowds, try *Bar Sena*, a local dive on the corner outside the Igreja do Pilar.

There is no shortage of **restaurants**, either; the better-value ones are clustered at the bottom of the hill on Rua São José, of which the best is unquestionably *Restaurante Chafariz* at no. 167; its superb *mineiro* buffet costs about R$25. Established in 1929, the restaurant has become something of a local institution, with pleasantly rustic décor and smooth service – altogether highly recommended.

More expensive places are clustered at the top of Rua Direita (Rua Conde de Bobadela), where you'll get good regional food in uniformly attractive surroundings for R$25–35 per person: a particularly appealing choice is the rather elegant *Restaurante Casa do Ouvidor*, Rua Direita 42. For a splurge, try *Le Coq D'Or* (☎31/3551-1032), a Franco-*mineiro* restaurant in the *Hotel Solar do Rosário*, Rua Vargas 270, where you can expect to pay around R$60 per person.

If you've had your fill of *mineira* cooking, one of the few alternatives is the pizza (and wine) served at *O Passo*, Rua São José 56. Open daily from 4.30pm, there's a terrace with delightful views onto a small park and the river. Expect to pay about R$25 per person. Alternatively, the excellent *Café Geraes* at Rua Direita 122 offers sandwiches and soups (R$15), delicious cakes (R$7) and wine; next door, reasonable pasta is served in the *Restaurante Spaghetti*.

Thankfully, for those on a tight budget, there are also several **cheap places to eat**, namely the basic *lanchonetes* on Rua Senador Rocha Lagoa (also called Rua das Flôres) just off the square (the *Vide Gula* here is good) and several on Rua Conde de Bobadela of which, at no. 76, the *Quinto do Ouro* has an excellent *por kilo* buffet for less than R$10 for a full meal.

There are plenty of bars, attracting tourists, students and locals alike. For a vast selection of *cachaças* as well as tasty snacks, try the cave-like *Bardobeco* at Travessa do Areira 15 (an alley just off Rua Direita).

Mariana

MARIANA is one of the major colonial towns, and in the first half of the eighteenth century was grander by far than its younger rival 12km to the west, Ouro Preto. Despite regular riots and the war between *paulistas* and the Portuguese, Mariana was the administrative centre of the gold mines of central Minas until the 1750s. The first governors of Minas had their residence here and the first bishops their palace, and the town proudly celebrated its tercentenary in 1996. Yet today Mariana's churches are far less grand than its illustrious neighbour's, and it's really no more than a large village, albeit one that is steadily expanding. It does, however, have a fine museum and a perfectly preserved colonial centre, mercifully free of steep climbs, that is less crowded and commercialized than Ouro Preto. As Mariana's only a twenty-minute bus ride away, if you can't stand the crowds in Ouro Preto you might stay here instead. There are also at least seven daily buses direct from Belo Horizonte as well as direct services from São Paulo (3 daily; 12hr).

The Town

Orientation in Mariana is fairly straightforward. The colonial area begins at Praça Cláudio Manoel, in front of the large Catedral Basílica; from here, Rua Frei Durão, lined with several of the noblest eighteenth-century public buildings, leads to the exquisite Praça Gomes Freire, with its bandstand, trees and pond, lined on all sides by colonial *sobrados*, two-storey mansions. Nearby are the two finest churches in Mariana and a lovely Prefeitura building in Praça João Pinheiro, complete with *pelourinho*, the old stone whipping post to which slaves and miscreants were tied and beaten.

The Museu Arquidiocesano

Although it has been overshadowed by its neighbour for over two centuries, you can still get a good idea of Mariana's early flourishing in one of the best

The Garimpeiros of Mariana

If you have spare time, an interesting place to stroll to is the town *garimpo*, a small **mining camp**. Stand on the last of the bridges over the Carmo creek and you can see figures digging and panning upstream: these *garimpeiros* (gold-miners) are using methods almost unchanged since gold was first found here in 1696 – the only difference now is that the pans are metal rather than wood. They dig channels into the stream bed, divert the flow and sift through the gravel with pans. To take a closer look, you can get there easily from Rua Rosário Velho. The *garimpeiros* are friendly, if a little bemused that gringos should find what they are doing interesting.

museums in Minas Gerais, the **Museu Arquidiocesano** in the old bishop's palace on Rua Frei Durão (Tues–Sun 8.30am–noon & 1.30–5pm).

The **building** itself is magnificent, with parts dating from the first decade of the eighteenth century, when it began life, bizarrely, as a prison for erring churchmen. The Franciscans were deeply involved in the *paulista* expeditions and were notorious for being the worst cut-throats of all. Between 1720 and 1756 the building was extended and became the bishop's palace: the door and window frames are massive, built in beautifully worked local soapstone. Inside, the **collection** is predictable – *arte sacra* and colonial furniture – but distinguished by its quality and age, often predating the earliest material in Ouro Preto by two or three decades. It gives a vivid idea of how Mariana was thriving, with stone buildings and all the trappings of the early eighteenth-century good life, when Ouro Preto was still a collection of hovels.

On the ground floor there's a sobering collection of chains and manacles draped along the walls, and also the "treasure room", containing the ecclesiastical gold and silver, but the bulk of things to see are upstairs. The stairwell is dominated by a powerful painting of *Christ's Passion* by Athayde, his best-known work. The stairs lead up to a number of graceful colonial rooms, including the luxurious private quarters of the bishops, which contain an excellent collection of religious art, notably the largest number of Aleijadinho figures anywhere outside a church. They are instantly recognizable: São João Nepomuceno, the bearded São Joaquim in religious ecstacy and a marvellous São Miguel in the corner by the window.

The colonial furniture section, usually the dullest part of Minas museums, is actually worth seeing here: lovely writing desks and chests of drawers, all early eighteenth century and most made of jacaranda wood (there was a glut on the market at the time, as the forests were felled to get at the gold). The most unusual exhibit is a false bookcase, with wooden "books" painted to resemble leather. You can also wander around the bishop's audience room – the throne is also by Aleijadinho, who was nothing if not versatile – and there's a separate gallery of the bishops' portraits, amongst which are three rather good, incongruously included, local landscapes by the German artist Nobauer.

The churches

Mariana's colonial churches are smaller and less extravagant than Ouro Preto's, though most are decorated with paintings by **Athayde**, who came from here and is buried in the Igreja de São Francisco (see p.216).

The oldest church is the **Catedral de Nossa Senhora da Assunção** on Praça Cláudio Manoel (Tues–Sun 7am–6pm), begun in 1709 and choked with gilded Rococo detail. This is very much an Aleijadinho family venture: his father, Manoel Francisco Lisboa, designed and built it, while Aleijadinho contributed the carvings in the sacristy and a font. The interior is dominated by a massive German organ dating from 1701 and donated by the king of Portugal in 1751. Look closely and you can see Chinese-style decorations carved by slaves, who also worked the bellows. You can hear the organ in action, in recitals given at 11am on Fridays and at 12.15pm on Sundays.

The two churches on Praça João Pinheiro, around the corner, show how tastes had changed by the end of the century. Their ornate facades and comparatively restrained interiors are typical of the third phase of *barroco mineiro*. The **Igreja de São Francisco de Assis** (daily 9am–5pm), finished in 1794, has the finest paintings of any Mariana church, as befits the place where Athayde is buried. The numbers on the church floor are where members of the lay Franciscan brotherhood are buried; Athayde is no. 94. Inside you'll see a fine sacristy as well as an altar and pews by Aleijadinho, who, in addition, put his signature on the church in his usual way, by sculpting the sumptuous soapstone "medal" over the door. On the other side of the square, the **Igreja de Nossa Senhora do Carmo** (daily 8am–noon & 2–5pm), with its less elaborate exterior, is disappointing in comparison. But the combination of the two churches with the equally graceful **Prefeitura** makes the bare grass square an attractive place to take a break.

From here, it's a short uphill walk via the unspoilt Rua Dom Silvério to the mid-eighteenth-century **Basílica Menor de São Pedro dos Clérigos** (Tues–Sun 8am–noon & 1–4pm) that overlooks the town, framed by groves of towering palms; you pass the strange, geometric **Igreja da Arquiconfraria** on the way. The object is not so much to check out the Basílica, but to enjoy the view of the town stretched out before you. If you follow the path along the top the views are even better.

Mina da Passagem

Four kilometres from Mariana, amongst steep hills bearing clear traces of centuries of mining, the ancient gold mine of **Mina da Passagem** (or Mina de Ouro) is one of the area's more unusual sights. If you don't have your own transport, take an Ouro Preto-bound bus from Mariana and get off at the stop opposite the mine.

Gold was first extracted here in 1719, making Mina da Passagem one of the oldest deep-shaft gold mines in Minas, although most of the seventeen kilometres of galleries date from the nineteenth century. The mine's nine faces have long since closed and the site exists today as a tourist attraction. Delightfully ramshackle but engaging **tours** operate every day from 9am until 5pm (R$17) and last about an hour.

Among the series of repair yards is probably the oldest functioning machine in Brazil – a vintage 1825 **British steam engine**, now adapted to run on compressed air. It powers a drum cable that drives railcars into and out of the mine – safer than it looks, though you do need to be careful of bumping your head once you trundle 315m into the galleries. There are other bits of nineteenth-century mining equipment knocking around, and the dripping gallery opens out into a small, crystalline floodlit lake, 120m underground. Back up on the surface, the visit is rounded off with a demonstration of gold panning, complete with real gold.

The history of the mine is a roll call of economic imperialism. It was sold by the Portuguese to a German enterprise in 1819, who sold it to British owners in 1854 who happily worked it with slaves at the same time as the Royal Navy was intercepting slavers in the Atlantic. It was then offloaded onto the French in 1883, nationalized by Vargas in 1937, sold to a South African company in 1970, and finally ceased operations in 1985.

Practicalities

The local **buses from Ouro Preto** leave you right in the centre at Praça Tancredo Neves, opposite an excellent **tourist information post**, the Terminal Turístico (daily 8am–5pm; ⓣ31/3557-1158), which sells a good map and supplies accredited guides for tours in the region (around R$50 a day). If you're coming from Belo Horizonte, you'll arrive at the **rodoviária** (ⓣ31/3557-1122), on the main road a couple of kilometres from the centre; if you don't wish to walk into the centre, catch one of the buses from Ouro Preto, which pass through the *rodoviária* every twenty minutes or so. A much nicer way of travelling between Ouro Preto and Mariana is by **train**, with the steam engines operating Thurrsday to Sunday, leaving Mariana at 9am and 2.30pm and returning from Ouro Preto at 11am and 4.30pm (R$18 one way, R$30 return). After several decades of being idle, the service was reactivated in 2006; there's a long-term aim for trains to also eventually link Belo Horizonte with Ouro Preto and Mariana.

All the **places to stay** are within easy walking distance of Praça Tancredo Neves. One of the nicest is the *Solar dos Corrêa*, Rua Josafá Macedo 70 (ⓣ31/3557-2080, ⓦwww.pousadasolardoscorrea.com.br; 4), midway between the Terminal Turístico and the two churches on Praça João Pinheiro. The hotel is full of character, with fifteen very different rooms done up with mock-colonial furniture, ranging from the rather gloomy loft conversions to a gorgeous first-floor room (no. 8) with wonderful views. It pays to come mid-week to secure the room of your choice, as at weekends you'd be lucky to get one at all. Similar in style and price is the *Pousada da Typographia* at Praça Gomes Freire 220 (ⓣ31/3557-1577; ④), an eighteenth-century mansion restored in period detail. The rooms are spacious and comfortable and the location especially attractive. Cheaper options include the basic *Hotel Central* (ⓣ & ⓕ31/3557-1630; ③), a beautiful but run-down colonial building at Rua Frei Durão 8, overlooking the Praça Gomes Freire; and excellent value is the clean and tidy *Hotel Providência*, Rua Dom Silvério 233 (ⓣ31/3577-1444; ②), along the road that leads up to the Basílica, which has use of the neighbouring school's pool when classes finish at noon.

Mariana has some reasonable **restaurants**, generally cheaper than those in Ouro Preto though none as good as the neighbouring city's best. Those with the nicest views look out onto Praça Gomes Freire (all open daily until midnight): the cosy *Restaurante Pizzeria Senzala* serves good food at lunchtime and turns into a lively and very friendly bar in the evenings; and *Mangiare della Mamma*, three doors up at Rua Dom Viçoso 27, does a top-notch *mineiro comida à kilo*, presented in heavy iron casseroles sizzling on a hot, wood-fired iron stove. Just up from Praça Gomes Freire at Travessa João Pinheiro 26, next to the Igreja São Francisco, is arguably the town's best *mineiro* restaurant, *Tambau*. For bargain lunches, a good place to try is the self-service *Panela de Pedra*, a restaurant attached to the Terminal Turístico.

Congonhas

CONGONHAS, a rather ugly, modern town 72km south of Belo Horizonte, sits ill as one of the historic cities. In truth, there's only one reason for coming here: to see the Basílica do Senhor Bom Jesus de Matosinhos. It's a long way to travel just to see one thing, but this is no ordinary church: if one place represents the flowering of *barroco mineiro*, this is it – the spiritual heart of Minas Gerais.

Getting to Congonhas is relatively easy from both Belo Horizonte (6 buses daily; 1hr) and São João del Rei (5 buses daily; 2hr). There are also two daily buses from Ouro Preto (2hr). It's possible to start out from Belo Horizonte or

Ouro Preto, visit Bom Jesus in Congonhas and still get to São João del Rei in the evening (last bus 8.20pm, 10.20pm on Sun), but only if you begin your trip early. To get from Congonhas's main *rodoviária*, a couple of kilometres out of town, to Bom Jesus, catch the **local bus** marked "Basílica", which takes you all the way up the hill to the church; it's impossible to miss.

Most people visit Congonhas on a day-trip, but if you decide to spend the night, the most comfortable option is the *Colonial Hotel* (Ⓣ31/3731-1834; Ⓦwww.hotelcolonialcongonhas.com.br; ④), alongside the Basílica, with its own small pool. The *Max Mazza Hotel* (Ⓣ31/3731-1970; ③) at Av. Júlia Kubitschek 410, is more modern, but lacks a pool. For food, head to the *Cova do Daniel*, a good regional **restaurant** at Praça da Basílica 76, next to Bom Jesus.

Bom Jesus de Matosinhos

Built on a hill overlooking the town, with a panoramic view of the hills around it, the **Basílica do Senhor Bom Jesus de Matosinhos** (Tues–Sun 6am–6pm) is set in a magnificent sloping **garden** studded with palms and what look like six tiny mosques with oriental domes. These are, in fact, small **chapels** commemorating episodes of the Passion; each is filled with life-size statues dramatizing the scene in a tableau. Looking down on them from the parapets of the extraordinary terrace leading up to the church itself are twelve towering soapstone **statues** of Old Testament prophets. Everything, the figures and the statues, was sculpted by **Aleijadinho**. His presumed leprosy was already advanced, and he could only work with chisels strapped to his wrists. The results are astonishing, a masterpiece made all the more moving by the fact that it seems likely it was a conscious swan song on Aleijadinho's part: there is no other explanation for the way a seriously ill man pushed so hard to finish such a massive undertaking, whose theme was immediately relevant to his own suffering.

The whole complex is modelled on the shrine of Bom Jesus in Braga, in northern Portugal. The idea and money came from a Portuguese adventurer, **Feliciano Mendes**, who, towards the end of his life, planned to recreate the pilgrimage church of his native Braga to house an image of the dead Christ he brought with him from Portugal in 1713. Mendes died in 1756, when work had only just begun, and it was forty years before the local bishop contracted Aleijadinho to produce the figures of the Passion and the prophets. Somehow, with his apprentices filling in fine detail, Aleijadinho managed to complete everything by 1805; it almost defies belief that the finished project was executed by a man who had lost the use of his hands.

The Passion

There are always **guides** hanging around the church who do know their stuff and can fill in a lot of interesting detail for just a few *reais*, but you're not obliged to go around with one. If you'd rather take a self-guided tour, start at the bottom of the garden to better appreciate the deep religious mysticism that lies behind the design. The **slope** symbolizes the ascent towards the Cross and governs the sequence of tableaux, the scenes leading you up from the Garden of Gethsemane through Christ's imprisonment, trial, whipping, wearing of the crown of thorns, and carrying of the Cross to Calvary. On top, guarded by the prophets, is the church, which houses both the wooden image of Christ's body and the real body, in the Communion host: built in the shape of a cross the church represents both the Crucifixion and the Kingdom of Heaven.

Viewing of the **statues** inside the chapels isn't ideal: there are grilles to stop people getting in, and some of the figures are difficult or impossible to see. All are sculpted from cedar and were brightly painted by Athayde, using his preferred

△ Statues at Bom Jesus de Matosinhos

natural paints made from ox blood, egg whites, crushed flowers and vegetable dyes. The statues are marvellously lifelike: you can see Christ's veins and individual muscles, the bulging of a soldier's cheeks as he blows a trumpet and a leering dwarf carrying a nail for Christ's crucifixion. Too savage and realistic to be Baroque art, there is nothing with which to compare it – it's as if Aleijadinho was driven to take his genius for realism to its logical conclusion, and finally shatter the restrictions of the Baroque tradition he had worked in all his life.

Things become even more interesting on the **symbolic** front when you look closely at the figures. Christ is more than once portrayed with a vivid red mark around his neck, which makes many think he also represents Tiradentes (see box, p.204). Support for the theory comes from the Roman soldiers, viciously caricatured, whom Aleijadinho gives two left feet and ankle boots – which only the Portuguese wore. Although nothing is known of Aleijadinho's politics, he was a native Brazilian and lived through the *Inconfidência* in Ouro Preto. He would certainly have known Tiradentes by sight, and it is more than likely that the Congonhas Christ is meant to represent him.

The prophets and the church

If the cedar figures are outside the Baroque tradition, the statues of the **prophets** are its finest expression in all Brazil: carved from blocks of soapstone, they dominate both the garden they look down on and the church they lead to. They are remarkably dramatic, larger than life-size, full of movement and expression; perched on the parapet, you look up at them against the backdrop of either hills or sky.

The **church** is inevitably something of an anti-climax, but still interesting. The effigy of the dead Christ that Mendes brought over from Portugal is in a glass case in the altar, and through the door to the right of the altar is the cross that carried the image. The lampholders are Chinese dragons, yet more of the Macau influence visible in Sabará and Diamantina.

Next to the church is a small building with a fascinating collection of **ex votos**; it keeps irregular hours but the friendly uniformed guards will open it up for you – though they're not around at lunchtime. The display will be familiar to anyone who has been to other pilgrimage centres in Brazil, and the photos, pictures and messages from grateful sufferers elicit a voyeuristic fascination. This collection is remarkable for the number of really old *ex votos*, the earliest from a slave who recovered from fever in 1722. Others record in crude but vivid paintings incidents like being gored by a bull, being seriously burnt or escaping from a bus crash.

The **bus** to take you back to the *rodoviária* leaves from the parking bay behind the church.

São João del Rei and around

SÃO JOÃO DEL REI is the only one of the historic cities to have adjusted successfully to life after the gold rush. It has all the usual trappings of the *cidades históricas* – gilded churches, well-stocked museums, colonial mansions – but it's also a thriving market town, easily the largest of the historic cities, with a population of just over 80,000. This modern prosperity complements the colonial atmosphere rather than compromising it, and, with its wide central thoroughfare enclosing a small stream, its stone bridges, squares and trees, São João is quite attractive. Come evening though, it's a rather dreary place and overshadowed by **Tiradentes**, its much smaller and prettier neighbour, in terms of good places to stay. While most visitors to São João del Rei come on an easy day-trip from Tiradentes, if possible, stay over in São João before a Friday, Saturday or Sunday when you can take a ride on the "Maria Fumaça" ("Smoking Mary"), a lovingly restored nineteenth-century steam train that links the two towns (see p.219).

Founded in 1699 on the São João River, the town had the usual turbulent early years, but distinguished itself by successfully turning to ranching and trade when the gold ran out early in the nineteenth century. São João's carpets were once famous, and there is still a textile factory today. Among the famous names associated with São João are Tiradentes, who was born here, Aleijadinho, who worked here and, in more recent times, native son **Tancredo Neves**, the great *mineiro* politician who shepherded Brazil out of military rule when he was elected president in 1985. Tragically, Neves died before he took office (see

"History" in Contexts) and is buried in the closest thing the town has to a shrine in the cemetery of São Francisco.

Arrival, orientation and accommodation

The centre of town is fifteen minutes' walk southwest from the **rodoviária**, or you can take a local bus in: the stop isn't the obvious one immediately outside the *rodoviária*'s main entrance – instead, turn left and take any bus from the stop on the other side of the road. Local buses enter the old part of town along **Avenida Tancredo Neves**, with its small stream and grassy verges to your left. There's a **tourist office** (daily 8am–5pm; ⓣ32/3372-738), across from the Catedral, where you can pick up a tourist booklet with a helpful map. On Avenida Tancredo Neves you'll find branches of the Banco do Brasil, Banespa and HSBC wth **ATMs**.

São João is divided into two main districts, each with a colonial area, separated by a small stream – the **Córrego do Lenheiro** – which runs between the broad Avenida Tancredo Neves, on the north side, and **Avenida Hermílio Alves**, which turns into **Avenida Eduardo Magalhães**, to the south. Relatively small and easy to find your way around, the districts are linked by a number of small bridges, including two eighteenth-century stone ones and a late nineteenth-century footbridge made of cast iron.

On the south side, the colonial zone is clustered around the beautiful **Igreja de São Francisco de Assis**, at the far western end of town. On the other side is the commercial centre, usually bustling with people, cars and the horse-drawn trailers of rural Minas. This commercial zone sprang up in the nineteenth century and shields the colonial area proper, several blocks of cobbled streets that jumble together Baroque churches, elegant mansions and the pastel fronts of humbler houses. For once you have the luxury of wandering around without losing your breath, as São João is largely flat.

Accommodation

Finding somewhere to stay is rarely a problem as **accommodation** in São João is plentiful and good value, though hotels and *pousadas* here are not nearly as attractive as those in neighbouring Tiradentes (see p.218). Bear in mind, however, that the town is a popular spot to spend Carnaval in, and Easter celebrations also attract huge numbers of visitors; at these times advance reservations are essential. The *Pousada Grande Hotel* (Ⓣ32/3371-7475; ❷–❸) at Rua Manoel Anselmo, right in the centre overlooking the Lenheiro stream, is a favourite budget choice, though its basic rooms are rather noisy and lack air conditioning. Very similar accommodation is offered by the *Pousada Portal del Rey* at Praça Severiano Resende 134 (Ⓣ32/3371-8820; ❷), above a restaurant.

Of the medium-range places, best value is the *Pousada Casarão*, Rua Ribeiro Bastos 94 (Ⓣ32/3371-7447; Ⓦwww.pousadacasarao.com; ❹), a wonderful converted mansion near São Francisco church, with the added attraction of a small swimming pool. At a similar price, the *Quinta do Ouro*, towards the western end of Avenida Tancredo Neves on Praça Severiano de Rezende (Ⓣ32/3371-2565; ❹), has four lovely rooms, three with salons (reservations essential). Top of the range, but excellent value and with a very good pool, is the comfortable *Pousada Villa Magnólia* (Ⓣ32/3373-5065, Ⓦwww.pousadavillamagnolia.com.br; ❹–❺), just outside of the historic centre at Rua Ribeiro Bastos 2.

The Town

São João's colonial sections are complemented by some fine buildings from more recent eras, notably the end of the nineteenth century, when the town's prosperity and self-confidence were high. The 1920s and 1930s were also good times – some of the vaguely Art Deco buildings combine surprisingly well with the colonial ones. The main public buildings line the south bank of the stream, best viewed from Avenida Tancredo Neves on the north side; there's a sumptuous French-style **theatre** (1893), and the graceful blue **Prefeitura** with an imposing Banco do Brasil building facing it. The relaxed atmosphere is reinforced by the number of bars and restaurants.

The Igreja de São Francisco de Assis and the Memorial Tancredo Neves

The most impressive of the town's colonial churches, the **Igreja de São Francisco de Assis** (daily 8am–5pm), is one block off the western end of Avenida Eduardo Magalhães. Overlooking a square with towering palms – some more than a century old – the church, finished in 1774, is exceptionally large, with an ornately carved exterior by a pupil of Aleijadinho. The master himself contributed the intricate decorations of the side chapels, which can be seen in all their glory now that the original paint and gilding has been stripped off. From the plaques, you'll see that the church has been visited by some illustrious guests, including President Mitterand of France. They came to pay homage at the **grave of Tancredo Neves**, in the cemetery behind the church. Sunday at 9.15am is an especially good time to stop in, when eighteenth-century music is played to accompany Mass.

Tancredo was a canny and pragmatic politician in the Minas tradition, but with a touch of greatness; transition to civilian rule 1985 is unlikly to have been so smoothly achieved without his skills. He was born and spent all his life in São João, where he was loved and is still very much admired. Eerily, to some, he died on the same day of the year as Tiradentes, who was also born in São João – their statues face each other in Praça Severiano de Rezende, on the other side of the Córrego do Lenheiro. Tancredo's black marble grave has a rather fine epitaph from one of his speeches: "You shall have my bones, land that I love, the final blending of my being with these blessed hills".

Just around the corner from the Igreja de São Francisco, on Rua José Maria Xavier at the corner with Avenida Eduardo Magalhães, is the **Memorial Tancredo Neves** (Sat, Sun & holidays 9am–5pm). This small nineteenth-century town house shelters a collection of personal artefacts and documents relating to the president's life, and *ex votos* used to decorate his grave, thanking him "for graces granted" – only really of interest to those Brazilians for whom Tancredo was nothing less than a modern saint.

The Museu de Arte Sacra and Rua Getúlio Vargas

Over on the other side of the stream, one block north from Avenida Tancredo Neves, lies the main street of the other colonial area, **Rua Getúlio Vargas**. The western end is formed by the small early eighteenth-century **Igreja da Nossa Senhora do Rosário** (Tues–Sun noon–6pm), built for the town's slave population, which looks onto a cobbled square dominated by two stunning colonial mansions. The one nearest the church is the Solar dos Neves, the family home of the Neves clan for over two centuries, the place where Tancredo was born and lived.

A couple of buildings east along from the Solar dos Neves is an excellent **Museu de Arte Sacra** (Tues–Sun noon–5pm), contained within another sensitively restored house. The collection is small but very good; highlights are a finely painted St George and a remarkable figure of Christ mourned by Mary Magdalene, with rubies representing drops of blood. As you go around, you're accompanied by Baroque church music, which matches the pieces perfectly. The museum also has a small gallery for exhibitions by São João's large artistic colony.

The Catedral Basílica de Nossa Senhora de Pilar and other churches

Almost next door to the Museu de Arte Sacra on Avenida Getúlio Vargas is a magnificent early Baroque church, the **Catedral Basílica de Nossa Senhora de Pilar** (Mon–Fri 8–10.30am & 1–8pm, Sat & Sun 8–10.30am & 5–8pm), completed in 1721. The interior is gorgeous: only Pilar in Ouro Preto and Santo Antônio in Tiradentes are as liberally plastered with gold. The gilding is seen to best effect over the altar, a riot of Rococo pillars, angels and curlicues. The ceiling painting is all done with vegetable dyes, and there's a beautiful tiled floor.

There are further churches to visit in this part of town, if you're enthusiastic, though none of the same standard as either São Francisco or Pilar. The **Igreja de Nossa Senhora das Mercês** (Tues–Sun noon–5pm), behind Pilar, dates from 1750 and is notable for the variety and artistry of the graffiti, some of it dating back to the nineteenth century, etched into its stone steps, while the elegant facade of **Nossa Senhora do Carmo** (Mon–Sat 7am–noon & 4–7pm; Sun 7–11am & 5–7pm) dominates a beautiful triangular *praça* at the eastern end of Avenida Getúlio Vargas.

The Museu Regional

Near the cathedral, just off Avenida Tancredo Neves on Largo Tamandaré, is the excellent **Museu Regional** (Mon–Fri noon–5.30pm, Sat & Sun 8am–1pm), housed in a magnificently restored colonial mansion. Perhaps the most fascinating pieces here are the eighteenth-century *ex votos* on the ground floor, their vivid illustrations detailing the trials that both masters and slaves experienced – José Alves de Carvalho was stabbed in the chest while crossing a bridge on the way home in 1765; a slave called Antônio had his leg broken and was half buried for hours in a mine cave-in. On the first floor are several figures of saints made by ordinary people in the eighteenth century: they have a simplicity and directness that makes them stand out. There's a collection of furniture and relics too, and, on the top floor, is one of the oddest items – a machine used until 1928 to select the draft numbers of unfortunate army conscripts.

Eating, drinking and nightlife

On the **north side** of the Lenheiro stream, on Praça Severiano de Rezende, you'll find two of the town's best **restaurants**: the *Churrascaria Ramon*, which does a good-value *churrasco*, and the *Quinta do Ouro*, whose *mineiro* food is the best in São João, though fairly expensive at around R$40–50 per person. On the same *praça* is the perfectly adequate and cheaper *por kilo Restaurante Rex* (11am–4pm). Alternatively, a very pleasant place for light meals and excellent afternoon teas is the *Sinhazinha* (Mon–Fri 1–6pm, Sat, Sun & holidays 8am–10pm), directly across from the Igreja de São Francisco.

The best places, however, combining good food with lively atmosphere, are on the **south side**, where tourists, young townsfolk and families flock to drink, eat and go to the cinema. Many of the **bars** have live music at weekends and get very crowded later on when people start spilling out onto the pavements. Almost all of the action is concentrated on Avenida Tiradentes, which runs parallel to Eduardo Magalhães, the avenue that runs alongside the stream. The bars are bunched both at Tiradentes' western end near São Francisco – where *Cabana do Zotti* at no. 805 (9pm onwards) is always packed and does good snacks – and halfway along Tiradentes at the junction with Rua Gabriel Passos (the road that runs in from the blue Prefeitura). For a meal, the *Restaurante Villeiros* at Rua Padré Maria Xavier 132 offers very good *comida mineira* – a *por kilo* buffet at lunch and à la carte in the evening.

Tiradentes

Although it was founded as early as 1702, by the 1730s **TIRADENTES** had already been overshadowed by São João and is now no more than a sleepy village with a population of only 5000. The core is much as it was in the eighteenth century, straggling down the side of a hill crowned by the twin towers of the **Igreja Matriz de Santo Antônio** (daily 9am–5pm; R$3). Begun in 1710 and completed around 1730, it's one of the earliest and largest of the major Minas Baroque churches; in 1732 it began to acquire the gilding for which it is famous, becoming in the process one of the richest churches in any of the mining towns. The church was decorated with the special extravagance of the newly rich, using more gold, the locals say, than any other church in Brazil, save the Capela Dourada in Recife. Whether this is true or not – and Pilar in Ouro Preto is probably as rich as either – the glinting and winking of the gold around the altar is certainly impressive. You can tell how early the altar is from the comparative crudeness of the statues and carvings: formal, stiff and with none of the movement of developed Minas Baroque. The beautifully carved soapstone panels on the facade are not by Aleijadinho, as some believe, but by his pupil, Cláudio Pereira Viana, who worked with the master on his last projects.

From the steps of the church you look down an unspoilt colonial street – the old town hall with the veranda has a restored eighteenth-century jail – framed by the crests of the hills. If you had to take one photograph to summarize Minas

Gerais, this would be it. Before walking down the hill, check out the **Museu Padre Toledo** (Tues–Sun 9am–4pm; R$3), to the right of Santo Antônio as you're standing on the steps. Padre Toledo was one of the *Inconfidêntes* and built the mansion that is now the museum. He obviously didn't let being a priest stand in the way of enjoying the pleasures of life: the two-storey *sobrado* must have been very comfortable, and even though the ceiling paintings are dressed up as classical allegories, they're not the sort of thing you would expect a priest to commission, featuring, as they do, so much naked flesh. The museum comprises the usual mixture of furniture and religious art, but the interesting part is the old slave quarters in the yard out back (which are unusual for having not been demolished), now converted into toilets. A more substantial reminder of the slave presence is the **Igreja da Nossa Senhora do Rosário dos Pretos** (Tues–Sun 9am–noon & 2–5pm), down the hill and along the first street to the right. There could be no more eloquent reminder of the harsh divisions between masters and slaves than this small chapel, built by slaves for their own worship. There is gilding even here – some colonial miners were freed blacks working on their own account – and two fine figures of the black St Benedict stand out, but overall the church is moving precisely because it is so simple and dignified.

Practicalities

Tiradentes might have a placid and timeless air during the week, but it gets surprisingly lively at weekends, as the bars and guesthouses fill up with people

The São João del Rei–Tiradentes train

If you're in São João between Friday and Sunday, don't miss the half-hour **train ride** to the colonial village of **Tiradentes**, 12km away. There are frequent buses too (8 daily from São João's *rodoviária*), but they don't compare to the trip on a nineteenth-century steam train, with rolling stock from the 1930s, immaculately maintained and run with great enthusiasm. You may think yourself immune to the romance of steam, and be bored by the collection of old steam engines and rail equipment in São João's nineteenth-century station on Avenida Hermílio Alves – the **Estação Ferroviária** (museum open Tues–Sun 9–11am & 1–5pm; ⓣ32/3371-8485) – but by the time you've bought your ticket you'll be hooked: the booking hall is right out of a 1930s movie, the train hisses and spits out cinders and as you sit down in carriages filled with excited children, it's all you can do not to run up and down the aisle with them.

Built in the 1870s, as the textile industry took off in São João, this was one of the earliest rail lines in Brazil, and the trains were immediately christened Maria-Fumaça, "Smoking Mary". The service runs only on Friday, Saturday, Sunday and holidays, when trains leave São João at 10am and 3pm, returning from Tiradentes at 1pm and 5pm (ⓦwww.city10.com.br/efom; R$22 return). If you want to stay longer, accommodation in Tiradentes is usually easy to find, or you could get one of the many local buses back to São João. Sit on the left leaving São João for the best views, and as far from the engine as you can: steam trains bring tears to your eyes in more ways than one.

The half-hour ride is very scenic, following a winding valley of the Serra de São José, which by the time it gets to Tiradentes has reared up into a series of rocky bluffs. The train travels through one of the oldest areas of gold-mining in Minas Gerais, and from it you'll see clear traces of the eighteenth-century mine workings in the hills. In the foreground, the rafts on the river have pumps that suck up alluvium from the river bed, from which gold is extracted by modern *garimpeiros*, heirs to over two centuries of mining tradition.

attracted by its welcoming atmosphere. The efficient **tourist office** at Largo das Forras 71 (Mon–Fri 9am–12.30pm & 1.30–5.30pm and Sat & Sun 9am–5pm) provides helpful advice with accommodation, excursions and bus schedules. For **Internet access**, go to *Estação Almazen* at Rua Ministro Gabriel Passos 182, next to the *Bradesco* bank and ATM.

Accommodation

Finding a place to stay in Tiradentes is rarely a problem, as a good proportion of the town's population have turned their homes into *pousadas* (there are well over forty), many of them exceptionally beautiful. During Carnaval, over Easter and in July, advanced reservations are essential, and most *pousadas* will only accept bookings of at least four nights.

Pousada Arco Íris Rua Frederico Ozanan 340 ⓣ32/3355-1167. Basic single, double and triple rooms for just R$35 per person. The added bonus of a pool makes this the best budget choice in Tiradentes. ③

Pousada da Bia Rua Frederico Ozanan 330 ⓣ32/3355-1173. One of the cheapest and friendliest places to stay, with clean, simple rooms and a kitchen for guests' use. ③–④)

Pousada do Largo Largo das Forras 48 ⓣ32/3355-1166, ⓦwww.pousadadolargo.com.br. A very pleasant *pousada* with simple but comfortable guest rooms and attractive lounges with a mix of colonial-style and modern furniture. There's a small pool and a rooftop terrace. ④

Pousada do Ó Rua Jogo da Bola 98 ⓣ32/3355-1699. This small, simple *pousada* near the Igreja Matriz has attractive rooms and a pleasant garden. No kids under the age of 12 allowed. ④

Pousada Richard Rothe Rua Padre Toledo 124 ⓣ32/3355-1333, ⓦwww.pousadarichardrothe.com.br. Discreetly luxurious with beautifully furnished colonial-style rooms and an attractive garden and a small pool; kids under 12 aren't allowed. ⑥

Pousada Villa Allegra Travessa Pedro Lourenço da Costa 31 ⓣ32/3355-1597, ⓦwww.villaallegra.com.br. Though this modern *pousada* is a five-minute walk from the town's centre and guest rooms are on the small side, the English-speaking owner could not be more welcoming, there's a nice pool and a good breakfast is served. ⑥

Pousada Villa Paolucci Final da Rua do Chafariz ⓣ32/3355-1350, ⓦwww.villapaolucci.cjb.net. This welcoming mid-eighteenth-century *casa grande* is set amidst a working *fazenda* on the outskirts of town; rooms feature colonial-style furniture and there are several comfortable lounges to relax in. Reservations are essential. ⑦–⑧

Pouso Alforria Rua Custódio Gomes 286 ⓣ32/3355-1536, ⓦwww.pousoalforria.com.br. Unlike most *pousadas* in Tiradentes, this place is unapologetically modern. The guest rooms are spacious, and the lounge areas, garden and pool are larger than usual. The peaceful location and charming English-speaking owners compensate for the five-minute walk from the town centre. No kids under 12. ⑥

Solar da Ponte Praça das Mercês ⓣ32/3355-1255, ⓦwww.solardaponte.com.br. Quite possibly the best *pousada* in Brazil. The gardens (which include a pool), guest rooms and lounges are as relaxing as they are beautiful, and the the service is both friendly and efficient. The price includes an excellent afternoon tea. No kids under 12. ⑦

Eating

Given that eating out is promoted as being one of Tiradentes' great attractions, it's surprising that few of the **restaurants** are particulary good and none are outstanding. *Viradas do Largo,* at Rua do Moinho 11, is considered the best for *comida mineira* but the food and general ambiance are hardly exceptional, although the price, around R$45 for a meal for two, is good. Similarly decent, though not remarkable, *mineiro* dishes are served at the *Estalgem do Sabor* at Rua Ministero Gabriel Passos 280. A brave, and sometimes successful, attempt at modernizing *comida mineira* by producing lighter dishes is made by *Tragaluz* at Rua Direita 52; expect to pay around R$50 per person. For a complete break from *mineiro* food, try *Sapore d'Italia*, Rua São Francisco de Paula 13, a reasonably priced and above-average Italian restaurant, or the *Mandalun*, Rua Padre Toledo 172, an attractive and very good Lebanese place.

Excursions

Tiradentes is surrounded by hills, but as the trails aren't marked and you'll, want to explore the area then you're best off going with a guide. *Caminhos e Trilhas* (Rua dos Inconfidêntes 207 ⓣ32/3355-2477) leads small groups on fairly easy **hikes**, stopping at spots from where there are views of Tiradentes, at natural pools and picnic areas. Hikes last about 4hr 30min and cost R$35 per person including a picnic. The same agency also arranges 2– to 3-hour **horse-riding** trips (R$35–45) and rents out **mountain bikes**.

Diamantina and the Jequitinhonha Valley

DIAMANTINA, home town of Juscelino Kubitschek, the president responsible for the creation of Brasília, is the only historic city to the north of Belo Horizonte and, at six hours by bus, is by some way the furthest from it. Yet the journey itself is one of the reasons for going there, as the road heads into the different landscapes of northern Minas on its way to the *sertão mineiro*. The second half of the 288-kilometre journey is the most spectacular, so to see it in daylight you need to catch a morning bus from Belo Horizonte.

Diamantina has a very different atmosphere to any of the other colonial towns. Still a functioning diamond-mining town, it is also the gateway to the **Jequitinhonha Valley**, the river valley that is the heart of the Minas *sertão*. The green hills that characterize so much of the southern half of Minas are utterly absent in Diamantina, which instead is set in a rocky, windswept and often cold highland zone – be sure to bring a sweater or jacket.

The road to Diamantina

Diamantina itself, scattered down the steep side of a rocky valley, faces escarpments the colour of rust; the setting has a lunar quality you also come across in parts of the Northeast's *sertão*. In fact, at Diamantina you're not quite in the *sertão* – that begins roughly at Araçuaí, some 300km to the north – but in the uplands of the **Serra do Espinhaço**, the highlands that form the spine of the state. Almost as soon as you leave Belo Horizonte, the look of the land changes to the stubby trees and savanna of the Planalto Central, the inland plateau that makes up much of central Brazil. Some 60km from Belo Horizonte you pass the Rei do Mato cave (see p.193), and after another 54km, roughly halfway to Diamantina, the road forks – left to Brasília and the Planalto proper, right to Diamantina and the *sertão*.

You hit the highland foothills soon after the dull modern town of Curvelo, and from then on the route is very scenic. The well-maintained road winds its way up spectacularly forbidding hills, the granite outcrops enlivened by cactus, wild flowers and the bright yellow and purple *ipê* trees, until it reaches the upland plateau, 1300m above sea level. The plateau heralds yet another change: windswept moorland with few trees and strange rock formations. Look carefully on the left and you'll see traces of an old stone road, with flagstones seemingly going nowhere. This is the old slave road, which for over a century was the only communication line between southern Minas and the *sertão*.

The Town

Even if it were not set in such a striking landscape, Diamantina has a distinctive **history** that would still mark it out from the other *cidades históricas*. The Portuguese

Crown had reason to feel bitter about the gold strikes in Minas Gerais: it had been forced to expend blood and treasure in prising the gold from the hands of the *paulistas*, and when diamonds were found here in 1720 the same mistakes were not repeated. **Arraial do Tijuco**, as Diamantina was called at first, was put under strict military control. People could only come and go with royal passes and the town was isolated for almost a century. This may explain Diamantina's very distinctive atmosphere. Although it has few buildings or churches to rival the masterpieces of Ouro Preto or Congonhas, the passage of time has had little effect on the large colonial centre of the town, which is the least spoilt of any of the *cidades históricas*. The narrow stone-flagged streets, with their overhanging Chinese eaves and perfectly preserved colonial houses, are exactly as they have been for generations.

Diamantina takes the *mineiro* penchant for building on slopes to extremes. Although the **rodoviária** (Ⓣ38/3531-1471) is not far from the centre of town, it's on a steep hill, and the only way back to it once in the centre is by taxi (around R$8), unless you have the legs and lungs of a mountain goat. The streets are either too narrow or too steep even for Brazil's intrepid local bus drivers. Fortunately the place is small enough for you to get your bearings very quickly. The central square in the old town is **Praça Conselheiro Mota**, which has the Catedral Metropolitana de Santo Antônio built in the middle of it – everyone calls the cathedral and the square "Sé". Most of the sights and places to stay are within a stone's throw of here.

The Museu do Diamante

The **Museu do Diamante** (Tues–Sat noon–5.30pm, Sun 9am–noon), set in a mid-eighteenth century town house on the cathedral square, is the best place to get an idea of what *garimpagem* has meant to Diamantina. It's one of the best museums in Minas – not so much for the glories of its exhibits but for the effort it makes to give you an idea of daily life in old Diamantina.

The room behind the entrance desk is devoted to the town's mining history and is filled with old mining instruments, maps and prints. Dominating everything is an enormous cast-iron English safe, brought by ox cart all the way from

△ Diamantina

Rio in the eighteenth century (it took eighteen months to get here). Inside the safe is a riveting display of genuine gold, and replicas of diamond jewellery and cut diamonds – the originals are stashed in the Banco do Brasil across the road. On the upper shelf is a genuine pile of uncut diamonds and emeralds, much as they would appear to *garimpeiros* panning; only the occasional dull glint distinguishes them from ordinary gravel. Disturbingly, there is an appalling display of whips, chains and brands used on slaves right up until the late nineteenth century, though the terrifying-looking tongs, underneath the chains, are in fact colonial hair-curlers, and not torture instruments.

The rest of the museum is great to wander through, stuffed with memorabilia that ranges from mouldering top hats to photos of long-dead town bandsmen: Diamantina has strong musical traditions and still supports *serestas*, small bands of accordion, guitar and flute players who stroll through the streets and hold dances around Carnaval, or on the evening of September 12, the *Dia da Seresta*.

The Catedral and other churches

Despite the comparative ugliness of the **Catedral Metropolitana de Santo Antônio**, built in 1940 on the site of an old colonial church, the cathedral square (Praça Correia Rabelo) is worth savouring. It's lined with *sobrados*, many of them with exquisite ornamental bronze- and ironwork, often imported from Portugal – look closely and you'll see iron pineapples on the balconies. Most impressive of all are the serried windows of the massive Prefeitura, and the ornate Banco do Brasil building next to it – possibly unique in Brazil in that it spells the country name the old way, with a "z".

Diamantina's **other churches** are distinctive, simple but very striking, with stubby towers and Chinese eaves: street names, like Rua Macau de Meio and Rua Macau de Cima, recall the days when these streets were home to Chinese artisans imported by the Portuguese during the eighteenth century. With one exception, though, the churches' exteriors are actually more interesting than the interiors.

The church that's most worth entering is the **Igreja de Nossa Senhora do Carmo** (Tues–Sat 8am–noon & 2–6pm, Sun 8am–noon) on Rua do Carmo. Built between 1760 and 1784, legend has it that the heir of Diamantina's richest miner made sure the tower was built at the back of the church rather than the front, as was usual, so the bells didn't disturb his wife's beauty sleep. Inside is an atypically florid interior, whose two main features are a rich, intricately carved altar screen and a gold-sheathed organ, which was actually built in Diamantina.

On the cobbled street leading down the hill from here is a local curiosity. The church at the bottom, **Igreja de Nossa Senhora do Rosário dos Pretos** (Tues–Sat 8am–noon & 2–5.30pm, Sun 8am–noon), has a tree growing in front of it: look closely and you can see a large distorted wooden cross embedded in the trunk and lower branches. The story behind this reads like something from Gabriel García Márquez, but did really happen. The year the old Sé church was knocked down, in 1932, the padre of Rosário planted a wooden cross outside his church to commemorate the chapel that old Diamantina had originally been built around. A fig tree sprouted up around it so that at first the cross seemed to flower – there's a photo of it at this stage in the Museu do Diamante – and eventually, rather than knocking it down, the tree grew up around the cross and ended up absorbing it. As for the church itself, it was built in 1728 to serve Diamantina's slave population and features a marvellous Baroque altar and a simple, yet stunning, painted ceiling.

The Mercado dos Tropeiros

Diamantina's other important economic role, besides diamond mining, is as the market town for the Jequitinhonha Valley. It's here that the products of the remote *sertão* towns of northeastern Minas are shipped and stockpiled before making their way to Belo Horizonte. The old **Mercado dos Tropeiros** on Praça Barão do Guaicuí, just a block downhill from the cathedral square, is the focus of Diamantina's trade, and worth seeing for the building alone – an interesting tiled wooden structure built in 1835 as a trading station by the Brazilian army. Its frontage, a rustic but very elegant series of shallow arches, played a significant role in modern Brazilian architecture. Niemeyer, who lived in Diamantina for a few months in the 1950s to build the *Hotel do Tijuco*, was fascinated by it, and later used the shape for the striking exterior of the presidential palace in Brasília, the Palácio da Alvorada.

The market itself (Sat only) has a very Northeastern feel, with its cheeses, *doces* made from sugar and fruit, blocks of salt and raw sugar, *cachaça* sold by the shot as well as by the bottle and mules and horses tied up alongside the pick-ups. The food at the stalls here is very cheap, but only for the strong-stomached: the rich *mineiro* sausages (*linguiça*) are especially worth trying. The rest of the week the market is used for exhibitions and book stalls, and on most evenings hippies from around Diamantina set up stalls selling jewellery, embroidery and other simple handicrafts. From the market you have a fine vantage point of a square that is, if anything, even richer than the Praça Conselheiro Mota, a cornucopia of colonial window frames and balconies and exquisite ironwork. Most of the ground floors are still ordinary shops, open throughout the week.

The **artesanato** section of the Mercado dos Tropeiros is small and uninspiring, which is unfortunate since the most distinctive products of the Jequitinhonha Valley are its beautiful clay and pottery figures. The Casa da Cultura, however, nearby on Praça Antônio Eulálio, has a very fine collection that makes a good introduction to Jequitinhonha pottery, and has a small selection of items for sale. An excellent collection of ceramic figures are for sale at *Artevale*, a

Juscelino Kubitschek

Juscelino Kubitschek, one of Brazil's great postwar presidents, was born in Diamantina and spent the first seventeen years of his life in the town. His enduring monument is the capital city he built on the Planalto Central, Brasília, which fired Brazil's and the world's imagination and where his remains are interned (he was killed in a road accident in 1976). The house where he was born and his later home, Casa de Juscelino, is preserved as a shrine to his memory (Tues–Sat 9am–6pm, Sun 9am–1pm), on the steep Rua São Francisco, uphill from his statue at the bottom.

Juscelino had a meteoric political career, fuelled by his energy, imagination and uncompromising liberal instincts. You can understand his lifelong concern with the poor from the small, unpretentious house where he spent the first part of his life in poverty (Juscelino was from a poor Czech-gypsy family). Restoration has rather flattered the house, as the photos of how it was when he lived there make plain; no Brazilian president has yet to come from a humbler background. The photos and the simplicity of the house are very moving – a refreshing contrast to the pampered corruption of many of his successors.

Juscelino and his wife, Julia, are still sources of considerable pride for the inhabitants of the town he clearly never left in spirit. September 12, his birthday, is Diamantina's most important *festa*, featuring music of all kinds late into the night performed in the town's *praças*. Many of the bars still display photographs of him, largely dating from before he became president in 1956. And many still don't believe his death was a genuine accident, just as few *mineiros* believe Tancredo really died of natural causes. The massive turnout for Juscelino's funeral in Brasília in 1976 was one of the first times Brazilians dared to show their detestation of the military regime.

very friendly shop situated just across from the market. Also very reliable for items from the Jequitinhonha Valley is *Relíquias do Vale*, on the same street as the *Hotel do Tijuco*, at Rua Macau do Meio 401. Additionally, there are a number of shops on Beca da Tecla. Besides the pottery, they also have a good stock of the rough but very rugged cotton clothes, hammocks, rugs and wall hangings that are the other specialities of the region. You'll find numerous other carpet shops dotted around town.

Diamantina practicalities

You can get free **maps** from the **tourist office**, tucked away at Praça Antônio Eulálio 53 (Mon–Fri 8am–6pm, Sat 9am–5pm, Sun 8am–noon; ⓣ38/3531-9532). You're unlikely to find anyone who speaks English, but the staff will point you towards hotels and offer advice on excursions.

Accommodation

Hotels in Diamantina are plentiful and generally inexpensive. The largest, priciest and most comfortable is the *Pousada do Garimpo*, a five-minute walk from the town centre at Av. da Saudade 265, on the western continuation of Rua Direita (ⓣ38/3531-1044, ⓦwww.pousadadogarimpo.com.br; ❹); the hotel is friendly, has a pool and is well equipped, but there's a somewhat soulless feel to it. Much more interesting, and with similar rates, is the town's 1951 Niemeyer creation, the *Hotel do Tijuco*, Rua Macau do Meio 211 (ⓣ38/3531-1022, ⓦwww.hoteltijuco.com.br; ❹–❺), where it's worth paying for one of the more expensive "luxo" rooms, which are larger and brighter and have balconies offering wonderful views across Diamantina. Just up from the cathedral, at Rua Macau de Baixo 104, the *Pousada Relínquias do Tempo* (ⓣ38/3531-1627; ❸) is located in a wonderfully converted nineteenth-century home filled with period furnishings and decorated with handicrafts from the Jequitinhonha Valley. The excellent-value *Dália Hotel*, Praça JK 25 (ⓣ38/3531-1477, ⓕ3531-3526; ❹), is just down from the cathedral. Housed in a lovely two-storey building with creaking floors and wood panelling, it offers good rooms and fine views over the square. Slightly cheaper, and behind the *Dália*, the *Pousada Ariana* (ⓣ38/3531-3624; ❸) has perfectly acceptable rooms and friendly service. Another very good bet is the *Pousada dos Cristais*, Rua Jogo da Bola 53, west from Rua Direita (ⓣ38/3531-2897; ❸), an appealing family-run place with large, comfortable, rustic rooms. If you want somewhere cheaper still in the old part of town, the *Pousada Gameleira*, Rua do Rosário 209 (ⓣ38/3531-1900) is an attractive choice and charges around R$25 per person; ask for a room facing the Igreja do Rosário. Other inexpensive options, with *quartos* upwards of R$20 per person, are clustered around the *rodoviária* in the upper part of town and are ideal if you can't face the prospect of dragging your luggage uphill when it's time to leave: *Hotel JK*, for example, immediately opposite the bus station at Largo Dom João 62 (ⓣ38/3531-1142; ❷), is a perfectly adequate place to stay.

Eating and drinking

The streets around the cathedral are the heart of the town, and there's no shortage of simple bars and *mineiro* **restaurants** here, though the food on offer is rather monotonous: the area around Diamantina is almost entirely unsuited to agricultural, so traditionally almost all food had to be brought in from afar. Local dishes include little in the way of fresh ingredients, with the staples being beans, rice, salt pork, *carne seca* and *bacalhau* (salted cod). The *Apocalipse Point*, across from the market at Praça Barão do Guaicuí 78, is a popular *por kilo* restaurant (lunch only) with a good selection of typical *mineira* dishes; expect to pay around R$10–15 per person. Quite good and reasonably priced *comida mineira* is also served at the restaurant of the *Pousada do Garimpo* (see p.225). Opposite the cathedral, the *Restaurante Cantina do Marinho*, at Rua Direita 113 and open daily for lunch and dinner, specializes in *bacalhao* dishes but also serves quite reasonable pizza. Along Beco da Tecla (an alleyway off the Praça Barão do Guaicuí), there are a few nice places to eat and drink: at no. 39 there's the *Recanto do Antônio*, which has the appearance of a country tavern and serves beer, wine, sausage and *carne do sol*; at no 31, lighter meals as well as good coffee and cakes are available at the *Livraria Espaço*, a small bookshop and Internet café. This is one of the few places in town that remains open late: until midnight Monday to Thursday and 2am Friday to Sunday.

Diamantina goes to sleep early but, in addition to the *Livraria Espaço*, there are several very popular **bars** on Boca do Mota, an alley off the cathedral square, and others on Rua Direita.

The Jequitinhonha Valley

If you want to get a clearer idea of where the Jequitinhonha *artesanato* comes from, you have to head out into the *sertão* proper, and Diamantina is the obvious place to start your journey. Travelling into the **Jequitinhonha Valley** is not something to be undertaken lightly: it is one of the poorest and remotest parts of Brazil, the roads are bad, there are no hotels except bare flophouse *dormitórios*, and unless you speak good Portuguese you are liable to be looked on with great suspicion. There have been problems in recent years with foreigners buying up mining concessions and kicking out *garimpeiros*, and unless you can explain yourself people will assume you have ulterior motives. As the region is so poor and isolated, it's difficult for people to understand why outsiders, especially foreigners, would want to go there.

If you need reasons, though, you don't have to look much further than the **scenery**, which is spectacularly beautiful, albeit forbidding. The landscapes bear some resemblance to the deserts of the American Southwest: massive granite hills and escarpments, cactus, rock, occasional wiry trees and people tough as nails speaking with the lilting accent of the interior of the Northeast. Here you're a world away from the developed sophistication of southern and central Minas.

Araçuaí and beyond

It seems wrong to say somewhere as off the beaten track as **ARAÇUAÍ** is easy to get to, but it is the most accessible Jequitinhonha destination from Diamantina. Booking the day before is usually essential for one of the two daily buses (2am and 1.30pm) to Araçuaí – and the journey is hard: over five hours of bouncing around on dusty dirt roads, hot as hell during the day and, in winter, cold at night. **Accommodation** is unlikely to present a problem: the cheapest option is the *dormitório* (Ⓣ33/3731-2184;) by the bus station (but take a hammock to avoid having to sleep in one of their lumpy and none-too-clean beds) or, for more comfort, head for the *Pousada das Araras* (Ⓣ33/3731-1707; ❷). Until recently Araçuaí was just a sleepy little village, but with improved agricultural techniques and better roads, it has expanded to become a major processing and distribution centre for mangos. Its attraction for tourists, however, is that it's the best place in the whole region for buying **artesanato**. A good choice of ceramic and other items is available at the producers' cooperative called Centro de Artesanato, open Tuesday to Saturday. Another attraction in town is aquamarine and, especially, **tourmaline**, as the mines around Araçuaí are the sources of some of the best in Brazil. Unless you really know your minerals, however, you'd be foolish to make any purchases here – although you won't have any trouble tracking down dealers at the market.

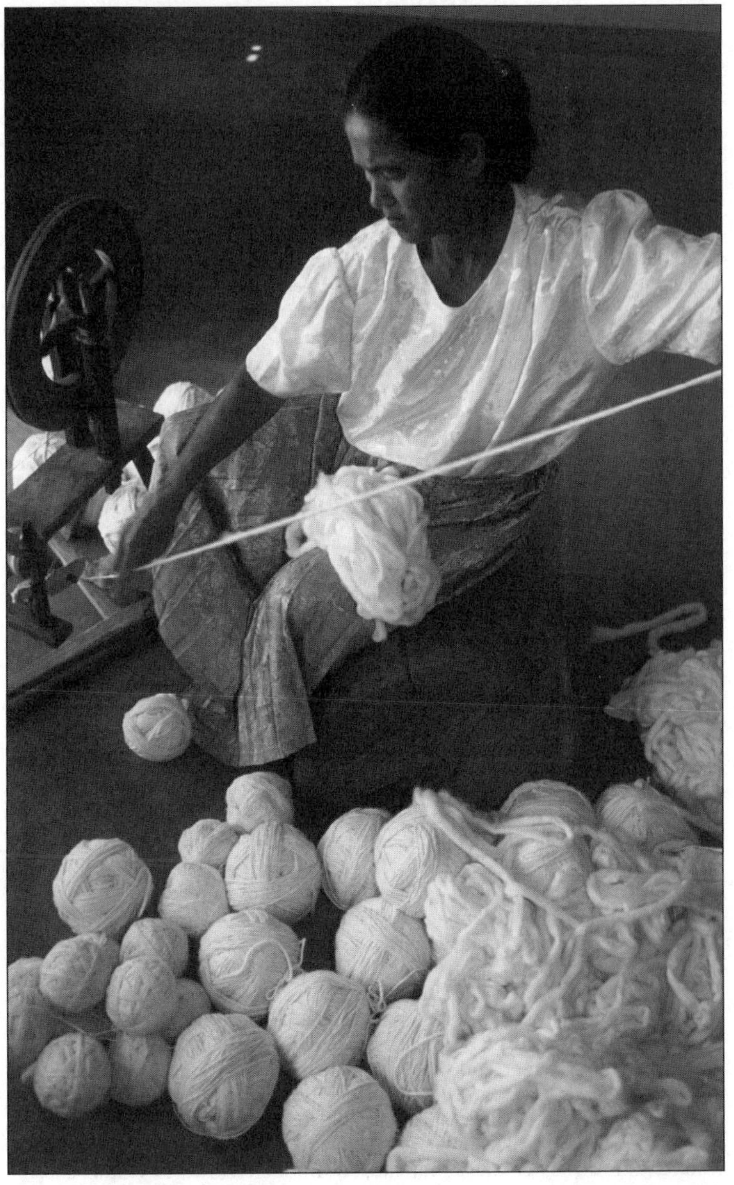

△ Worker in the Jequitinhonha Valley

From Araçuaí, if time were no object, you could hop local buses to **Itinga** and then on 30km to the good-quality BR-116 highway into **Bahia** state. Once you get to Vitória da Conquista there are ready connections to all Bahian cities, but it could well take you a couple of days to get that far. It is often quicker to take the bus that leaves every other day to Belo Horizonte and make your connections there.

South to Serro

South of Diamantina, the main point of interest is the sleepy colonial town of Serro, a two-hour bus ride away. From Diamantina, there are two ways of getting there: on the main, asphalt-covered, road or on the unpaved (but fairly good quality) road. One daily bus runs along the latter, passing through rugged, wide-open spaces with the almost lunar appearance occasionally interrupted by patches of vegetation where a stream flows through. Even in these rugged conditions cattle can somehow graze and land be cultivated. Twenty-three kilometres from Diamantina in a lush valley there's a very simple working *fazenda* where the nineteenth-century *casa grande* has been turned into a *pousada*. The *Pousada Rural Recanto do Vale* (Ⓣ31/3271-0200, Ⓦwww.pousadarecantodovale.com.br ❷) does not offer luxury accommodation of the kind sometimes available in old *fazenda* properties, but instead provides an opportunity to experience everyday life well off the beaten track. Even so, the rooms are perfectly comfortable, while the simple meals (entirely from the *fazenda*'s produce) are delicious as well as great value at R$10. Horse riding can be arranged and there are easy walks to natural swimming spots.

Nine kilometres further along the road is **SÃO GONÇALO DO RIO DAS PEDRAS,** a delightful village in an oasis-like setting of palm trees and intensely green fields. Apart from an eighteenth-century church, and a few houses and bars, there's very little to the place, but São Gonçalo's tranquillity and its natural pools and waterfalls – good for bathing – make for an enjoyable break. There are several simple, but extremely nice, *pousadas* here, the best of which is undoubtedly the *Refúgio dos 5 Amigos* (Ⓣ38/3541-6037, Ⓦwww.pousadarfugio5amigos.com.br; R$40 per person, half-board), located right in the centre of the village. While very simple, the *pousada* is tastefully furnished and impeccably maintained, and the owner, originally from Switzerland, knows every trail hereabouts. If that's full, try the *Pousada do Pequi* (Ⓣ38/3541-6100; ❷), with comfortable rooms and a friendly atmosphere.

The next village, 7km down the road (and 27km from Serro), is **MILHO VERDE**, a place that's becoming popular as a weekend retreat with people from Belo Horizonte. Although not as pretty as São Gonçalo, Milho Verde is more lively and there are several cheap but perfectly acceptable places to stay: try *Pousada André Luiz* (Ⓣ038/3541-1071; ❷) or the slightly larger *Rancho Velho* (Ⓣ038/3541-1062; ❷), or look out for the signs outside people's houses saying "*Aluga-se*".

Situated 90km south of Diamantina, **Serro** is set in beautiful hill country, dominated by the eighteenth-century pilgrimage church of **Santa Rita** (Sat 3–7pm) on a rise above the centre, reached by steps cut into the slope. Little-visited, this is not so much a place to see and do things as it is somewhere peaceful to unwind and appreciate the leisurely pace of life in small-town Minas. There are six colonial churches, but most are closed to visitors and the rest open only for a few hours on either Saturday or Sunday; a spate of thefts has made the keyholders reluctant to let you in. Founded in 1702, when gold was discovered in the stream nearby, Serro was at one time a rather aristocratic place. Across the valley, easily recognizable from the clump of palms, is the **Chácara do Barão do Serro** (Mon–Sat noon–5pm, Sun 9am–noon), which now houses the town's Centro Cultural. The old house is a fascinating example of a nineteenth-century *casa grande*, and you are free to wander through the main building and the former slaves' quarters outside.

Just along the road from here on Praça Cristiano Otoni, the **Museu Regional** (Tues–Sat noon–5.30pm, Sun 9am–noon) has a reasonable collection of period drawings and paintings, kitchen equipment and furniture. From the front of the museum you get a good view of the finest buildings in the village, namely the enormous **Casa do Barão de Diamantina**, clinging to the hillside, beautifully restored and now a school, and the twin Chinese towers of the **Igreja da Matriz de Nossa Senhora da Conceição** (Sun 8am–7.30pm). Dating from 1713, the church forms one end of a main street that is completely unspoilt; at the other end, up an extremely steep incline, at the historic centre's highest point, is the very pretty eighteenth-century Igreja de Santa Rita from where there are fine **views** across the village and towards the surrounding countryside.

The *Pousada Vila do Príncipe*, just down from the Igreja de Santa Rita on the main street, Rua Antônio Honório Pires, at no. 38 (Ⓣ38/3541-1485; ❸), is the best **place to stay**; rooms are small and simple, but the views are fantastic. Also very central are the fairly basic *Pousada Serrano*, Travessa Magalhães 55 (Ⓣ38/3541-1949; ❷), as well as several cheap *pensões*. There are few places to eat: try simple *Restaurante Itacolomi* at Praça João Pinheiro 20, which has a good *por kilo* buffet of regional dishes at lunch and an à la carte menu in the evening. While here, be sure to sample the cheese, considered the best in Minas Gerais, if not Brazil. The *rodoviária* (Ⓣ38/3541-1366) is almost in the centre: ignore the attentions of the taxi drivers, walk uphill for some thirty metres and you're in the heart of the village.

Southern Minas: The spa towns

The drive from Belo Horizonte **south to Rio** turns into one of the most spectacular in Brazil once you cross the state border and encounter the glorious scenery of the Serra dos Órgãos, but there is little to detain you in Minas along the way. The route passes Juiz de Fora, one of the larger interior cities, but it's an ugly industrial centre, best seen from the window of a bus.

The route **southwest towards São Paulo**, however, is altogether different. The hills, rising into mountains near the state border, make this one of the most attractive parts of Minas. Six or seven hours from Belo Horizonte, to the south of the main route, there's a cluster of **spa towns** – the Circuito das Águas, or "Circuit of the Waters", as the spa resorts of Cambuquira, São Lourenço, Caxambu and Lambari are collectively known. They are all small, quiet and popular with older people, who flock there to take the waters and baths. Each is centred on a *parque hidromineral*, a park built around the springs, incorporating bathhouses and fountains. Set in spectacular volcanic mountains to the north of the São Paulo road, the city of Poços de Caldas is also based around mineral springs but is much livelier and a traditional place for couples to spend their honeymoons.

From Belo Horizonte to the Circuito das Águas

It's five hours from Belo Horizonte, or three from São João del Rei, before you hit the gateway to the Circuito das Águas. **TRÊS CORAÇÕES** is a good place for making onward bus connections and, although not a resort town itself, it is more famous, in Brazil at least, than any of the spas. This rather anonymous modern town was the birthplace of Edson Arantes do Nascimento – **Pelé**, the greatest footballer ever – and it's a holy place for any lover of the game. Keep an eye out on the left as the bus winds its way through the centre and you'll see a bronze statue of him holding aloft the World Cup, which Brazil (and Pelé) won in 1958, 1962 and 1970. If you find yourself stuck here overnight while waiting for a bus, the *Cantina Calabresa* hotel, Rua Joaquim Bento de Carvalho 65 (Ⓣ35/3231-1183, Ⓦwww.hotelcalabreza.com.br; ❸), has good rooms and a pool.

After Três Corações the hill country begins, although it's hardly got going before you run into the first and smallest of the spas, **CAMBUQUIRA**, a pleasant enough place but nothing to compare with the other resorts. If you do want to **stay**, a good cheap option, with its own pool, is *Pousada Passe Fique*, 1km out on the BR-267 Lambari road (Ⓣ35/3251-1587; ❸); more central and upmarket, with a sauna as well as a pool, is *Hotel Santos Dumont*, Av. Virgílio de Melo Franco 400 (Ⓣ35/3251-1466; ❹). The thermal baths in the Parque das Águas are open daily between 6am and 7pm.

Caxambu

Just beating São Lourenço for the title of nicest of the smaller spas, **CAXAMBU** was a favourite haunt of the Brazilian royal family in the nineteenth century. The **Parque das Águas** (7am–6pm), in the centre of town, is delightful. Built in the last decades of the nineteenth century and the early years of the twentieth, it's dotted with eleven oriental-style pavilions sheltering the actual springs and houses an ornate Turkish bathhouse that is very reasonably priced – R$12 gets you a Turkish bath in turn-of-the-century opulence, and there are also various kinds of sauna (R$10) and massage (R$30–45) available. The bathhouse, which has separate facilities for men and women, is open Tuesday to Saturday 8.30am–noon and 3–5pm, and on Sunday 8.30am–noon.

Next to the park is a good **market** that specializes in honey and homemade syrupy sweets and leads on to a tree-shaded square, **Praça Dom Pedro**, with yet another oriental pavilion. If you're tired of walking, there's a **chairlift** (R$10) that runs from opposite the bus station up to the Cristo Redentor, which overlooks the centre. At the top there's a tremendous view, not only of the town and the park but also the lovely hill country in which it nestles. There's a restaurant, too, where the views are better than the food. The only drawback is that the chairlift closes down at 4.30pm, which means you can't appreciate what would be a very spectacular sunset.

Practicalities

The *rodoviária* (Ⓣ35/3341-5566), served by direct bus services from Belo Horizonte, Rio and São Paulo, is on the far western edge of town on Praça Castilho Moreira, but Caxambu is so small that it doesn't really matter. A **tourist information post** (Ⓣ35/3341-1298) in the terminal building hands out free town maps, but, again, you don't need them to find your way around. There's just one main street, Rua Wenceslau Braz, much of which is taken up by the Parque das Águas, and around which the town is built. Although walking is easy, it's fun to get one of the **horse-drawn cabs**, or *charretes*, that seem especially appropriate to Caxambu's turn-of-the-century surroundings.

For its size, Caxambu has a surprising range of **hotels**; their rates always include full board and drop by almost half in the off season. The sumptuous *Grande Hotel*, Rua Dr Viotti 438 (ⓣ35/3341-1099, ⓦwww.grandehotelltda.com.br; ❹), and the luxury-class *Hotel Glória*, opposite the park at Av. Camilo Soares 590 (ⓣ35/3341-3000, ⓦwww.hotelgloriacaxambu.com.br; ❺), both have pools and saunas. The best mid-range place in town – especially out of season – is the *Palace Hotel*, Rua Dr Viotti 567 (ⓣ35/3341-3341, ⓦwww.palacehotel.com.br; ❹). Built in 1894, it's crammed with antique furniture; additionally, it has a pool and a sauna, a children's games room, a drawing room, a massive lounge and a ballroom. Cheaper options include the *Santa Cecília* on Rua Dr Enout 162 (ⓣ35/3341-3511; ❸), which offers simple apartments with private kitchens, and the *Jardim Imperial* (ⓣ35/3341-1163; ❸), in a quiet spot near the bus station on Rua Dr Viotti.

The only **restaurant** worth going out of your way for is the Danish *La Forelle*, 5km out of town on the BR-354 towards Itamonte (Fri 7pm–midnight, Sat noon–3pm & 8pm–midnight, Sun noon–3pm; reservations essential on ⓣ35/3343-1900); it's fairly expensive, but does an excellent line in Scandinavian-*mineiro* cooking (a legacy of a small wave of Danish immigrants who settled in the area in the 1920s as dairy farmers) and is especially good for trout and salmon. In town, *Sputinik* at Av. Camilo Soares 648, has a varied, but hardly exciting, *por kilo* buffet.

São Lourenço

If Caxambu is the last word in Edwardian elegance, **SÃO LOURENÇO** rivals it with its displays of Art Deco brilliance. Its Parque das Águas is studded with striking 1940s pavilions and has a stunning bathhouse – the Balneário – which looks more like a film set for a Hollywood high-society comedy. The most upmarket and modern-looking of the small spas, the town is popular with young and old alike.

São Lourenço is built along the shores of a beautiful lake, a large chunk of which has been incorporated into the **Parque das Aguas** (daily 8am–5.20pm; the pavilions with the mineral water fountains are closed 11.30am–2pm), and during the day it's where everything happens. Much larger than the one in Caxambu, and much more modern, the park is kept to the same immaculate standard: again, a lovely place for a stroll, with its brilliant white pavilions, forested hillside, clouds of butterflies and birds – though steer clear of the black swans on the lake, which have a nasty temper. There are **rowing boats** for rent, and an artificial island in the middle of the lake.

The **Balneário** itself offers baths (*duchas*; R$7), saunas (R$8) and massages (R$25–35), and it's worth paying for the elegant surroundings: marbled floors, mirror walls and white-coated attendants. There are separate sections for men and women.

Practicalities

The **tourist information kiosk** is on Praça Duque de Caixas in front of the *parque* (daily 8.30am–noon & 2–6pm; ⓣ35/3349-8459). The **rodoviária** (ⓣ35/3332-5966) served by Belo Horizonte, Rio and São Paulo buses, is just off the main street, Avenida Dom Pedro II, which is lined with bars, hotels and restaurants. There is a very large **youth hostel** at no. 468, the *Albuergue da Juventude Recanto dos Caravalhos* (ⓣ35/3799-4000; R$20 per person), and a good low-price **hotel**, the *Hotel Aliança* (ⓣ & ⓕ035/3332-4300; ❸, full board ❹) at no. 505. Cheaper, but very decent, is the *Pousada Normandy*, Rua Batista Luzardo 164 (ⓣ35/3332-4724; ❸), just 200m from the Parque das Aguas, or try the *Santa Rita* at Av. Getúlio Vargas 31 (ⓣ35/3332-2522; ❸), with basic but clean rooms. For a splurge, the *Hotel Brasil*, Alameda João Lage 87 (Ⓣ35/3332-1313, Ⓦwww.hotelbrasil.com.br; ❺–❻), which dominates the Praça Duque de Caixas, is luxury-class and has the works, including four pools and water-slides.

Buses to Lambari, the next town on the circuit, take about ninety minutes. Buses to Caxambu leave several times a day, or take a taxi from the post in front of the *parque*. There's no direct bus to Poços de Caldas; you need to get the 11.45am to Pouso Alegre and make a connection there – total journey time is around six hours. Schedules change frequently, so be sure to check departure times in advance with the *rodoviária*.

Lambari

LAMBARI is the nearest you get to a downmarket spa town on the Circuito das Águas, though you wouldn't guess it from the prices of its main hotels. It has a beautiful lake and the obligatory spa park, but lacks the prosperous feel of Caxambu and São Lourenço. The **rodoviária**, on Avenida Dr José Nicolau Mileo, is within easy walking distance of the main square, Praça Conselheiro João Lisboa. Housed in the square, the **Parque das Águas** is small and scruffy but has six fountains, each with different types of water, as well as a fizzy *carbogasosa* pool.

There are several budget **hotels** near the *rodoviária*, while mid-range options (all with pools and rates that include full board) can be found either on or near the main square. Of these, the basic but comfortable *Hotel Ideal*, at Rua Afonso Vilhena Paiva 245 (Ⓣ35/3271-1143, Ⓕ3271-1650; ❸), is probably the best value. The *Hotel Itaici* (Ⓣ & Ⓕ035/3271-1366; ❸) at Rua Dr José dos Santos 320 is of a similar standard. The town's best hotel, the *Hotel Parque*, Rua Américo Werneck 46 (Ⓣ35/3271-2000, Ⓦwww.parquehotellambari.com.br; ❹), with its own lake, thermal pools, fishing and other sports facilities, is appealing and excellent value.

Poços de Caldas

Of all the Minas spa resorts, **POÇOS DE CALDAS** is the easiest to get to. Rich Brazilians from the large cities of Southeast Brazil like to take breaks here, and there are daily bus services to and from Rio and São Paulo as well as Belo Horizonte. It's some distance from the smaller spa towns, and it's an altogether different place; with a population of 150,000, Poços de Caldas is definitely a city rather than a town, and is quite the most animated spot in Minas after Belo Horizonte.

If possible, you should make the journey in daylight, because the countryside is something special and shouldn't be missed. After the ugly modern town of Pouso Alegre comes one of the more spectacular climbs into mountains that Brazil has to offer, with superb views of slopes clad in a mixture of pine and eucalyptus, and plains laid out like sheets behind and beneath the road. It is easy to see why the whole region became a resort area.

The city itself, almost on the state line with São Paulo, nestles in the bowl of an extinct volcano – you can trace the rim of what must once have been an enormous crater along the broken horizons. The centre is mostly modern, laid out in a grid pattern with a few skyscrapers, but made very attractive by huge tree-studded squares, an enormous but elegant bathhouse and the closeness of the thickly forested slopes of Alto da Serra, the hill crowned with the obligatory Cristo Redentor overlooking the city.

The City

If first impressions counted on arrival, you'd probably take one look at the dirty and decrepit **rodoviária** and catch the next bus out: its sole redeeming feature is its location – just a short distance from the huge central square, **Praça Pedro Sanchez**, which is recognizable by the large Edwardian-style bathhouse set amid gardens and fountains. Everything goes on around the square and in the blocks to the east of it, and the grid pattern makes it easy to get your bearings.

Unlike Caxambu and São Lourenço, Poços de Caldas doesn't have a single mineral-water park that encompasses all the springs; they are scattered all over the city and somehow don't seem as impressive when not set in a garden. The nearest, within easy walking distance of the centre, is **Fonte Frayha**, on the corner of Rua Amazônas and Rua Pernambuco, but you can take the same waters in style in the opulent bathhouse, the **Termas Antônio Carlos** (Mon–Sat 8–11.30am & 4–7.30pm, Sun 8–11.30am), whose Edwardian bulk looms over the main square. It's less personal than the *balneários* in the smaller resorts, but the increase in scale makes a Turkish bath in such splendid surroundings an experience.

On one side of the *praça*, not far from the bathhouse on Avenida Francisco Salles, is a **cable car** station (July & Dec–Feb daily 8am–6pm; rest of the year Mon & Wed–Fri 2–6pm, Sat & Sun 8am–6pm; R$7 return), from where you're whisked up to the **Alto da Serra** and the Christ statue overlooking the city, at 1678m above sea level. It's a must, as the views from the top are tremendous, there's the usual restaurant with sweeping panoramas and it's the starting point for an exceptionally scenic walk back down.

Although hardly a cultural hot spot, the city has an excellent **Casa da Cultura** (Tues–Fri 1–7pm, Sat & Sun 1–6pm), really a branch of Unibanco's remarkable Instituto Moreira Salles. The wooden building (one of Poços de Caldas's first houses) itself is quite wondeful, constructed in a tropical high Victorian style in 1894, and the exhibitions of historic photographs and art from Unibanco's extensive collection are usually first rate. The Casa da Cultura is at Rua Teresópolis 90, in the suburb of Jardim dos Estados, which can easily be reached by foot from the centre or on the bus marked "Santa Rosália".

Practicalities

The **tourist office** is located in the Palace Casino on Parque José Afonso Junqueira (Mon–Sat 8am–noon & 1.30–6pm, Sun 8am–noon; ⓣ35/3697-2300); they have a good free map of the town and provide information on special events.

Accommodation will be the least of your worries. The entire city is geared to catering for visitors, and even during holiday periods, when people flock from as far afield as Rio and São Paulo, capacity is rarely stretched and prices are generally very keen. Many of the pricier hotels are scattered some way out of town in their own gardens or estates: the recently opened *Monreale Hotel Resort*, Av. Leonor Furlaneto Delgado 3033, 7km out on the Belo Horizonte road (ⓣ35/3712-7777, ⓦwww.monreale.com.br; ❼ half board), is rather typical, offering splendid views, a pool, a sauna and horse riding, but little in the way of character. The most luxurious hotel in the town itself is the *Palace*, at Praça Sanches (ⓣ35/3722-3636; ⓦwww.carltonhoteis.com.br; ❻ half board), opened in 1922 and very much in the European "grand hotel" tradition. Slightly more modest, but similarly old-fashioned is the *Minas Gerais*, Rua Pernambuco 615 (ⓣ35/3722-1686, ⓦwww.hotelminasgerais.com.br; ❻ half board); it's superb value, with two pools, a sauna and a playground. There are plenty of modern and centrally located budget places too: *Príncipe*, Rua Dr Francisco Faria Lobato 84 (ⓣ35/3722-1740, ⓦwww.principehotelpocos.com.br; ❹ full board), which also has a pool, and, very similar in style and facilities, the *Imperador*, at Av Francisco Salles 273 (ⓣ35/3722-2166; ❹ full board). For something even cheaper, try one of the hotels on Rua São Paulo, such as the *Guaranyat* at no. 106 (ⓣ35/3722-2585; ❸).

As you would expect in a place so popular with young couples, the **nightlife** here is very lively, especially at weekends. Busiest of all is the stretch of **Rua São Paulo** leading down to the square. There is a very good upstairs **bar** here, *Verde Amarelo*, which has high-quality live Brazilian music for free on Friday and Saturday nights, and possibly the best **juice bar** in Minas Gerais, *Casa de Sucos*, on the corner of São Paulo and Assis Figueiredo. It has an amazing variety of freshly made *sucos* and an excellent range of sandwiches and desserts. By and large, **restaurants** are unexciting, as most visitors eat at their hotels. However, *L'Itália* at Av. Francisco Salles 86 (daily to 8.30pm), offers a good Italian-based *por kilo* lunch buffet and excellent *café colonial* (high tea); if you're in the mood for meat, try the *Pampa* (closed all Mon and Sun evening), a *churrascaria* located a couple of kilometres from the centre of town in the suburb of Santana at Av. José Remígio Prézi 683.

Eastern Minas

Eastern Minas Gerais is the least-visited part of the state and, travelling along the BR-262 highway leading to Espírito Santo state and the Atlantic, it seems very clear why. Although the *mineiro* hill country is pretty enough, the towns scattered along it are ugly industrial centres, steel mills belching fumes common even in the gaps between the towns. However, if you persevere right to the border with Espírito Santo, you enter an unrivalled part of Minas, where lush hills are covered with coffee bushes in terraced rows, like contour lines on a map. These hills gradually give way to the craggy, spectacular mountains of the **Parque Nacional do Caparaó** and the highest peak in southern Brazil, the **Pico da Bandeira**. The best time to go is from June to August, as at other times of year the mists and rain make it difficult to see the marvellous scenery.

Towards Caparaó

Getting to the Parque Nacional do Caparaó can be complicated, and the fact that Caparaó is the name of both the national park and a village just outside it – which itself is next to another village called Alto do Caparaó – makes things more confusing. You need to head for Alto do Caparaó to get to the park; you can make the journey from either Belo Horizonte or Vitória, the capital of Espírito Santo (Vitória is considerably nearer) but there are no direct buses and you can bank on spending most of the day getting there, and possibly longer, wherever you start from.

Initially, you should head towards the two towns in the vicinity. **Manhuaçu** is served by direct buses from Belo Horizonte, Ouro Preto and also Vitória. From Manhuaçu, local services run the 20km to **Manhumirim**, much closer to the park and a far nicer place to spend the night if necessary. There are also direct buses to Manhumirim from Belo Horizonte, Ouro Preto, and Vitória. Wherever you start from you'll need to book your **ticket** the day before if possible, as these routes fill up quickly, especially on Friday and Sunday.

Once you get to **MANHUMIRIM**, your next destination will be Alto Caparaó, 25km further on. It's an exceptionally scenic ride, so it's worth staying the night if you arrive after dark. Manhumirim is, in any case, a pleasant place, a very typical interior town where foreigners rarely appear and the people are friendly and curious. The bars in the centre get surprisingly lively on weekend evenings, and the best (though still basic) **hotel** is the *São Luis* (Ⓣ33/3341-1178; ❸), a short taxi ride from the *rodoviária*.

The easiest way to reach Alto Caparaó is by **taxi**, which costs about R$25 from Manhumirim. There are seven direct local **buses** a day, too, leaving from the *rodoviária* at regular intervals from 6.30am to 8pm and taking about ninety minutes.

Alto do Caparaó

The pretty village of **ALTO CAPARAÓ** is effectively a single sloping road with the Praça da Matriz marking its centre – buses stop there and the village's few **hotels** are all just a short walk away. Two places to stay are unusually good value, namely the basic *Pousada Vale Verde* at the Praça da Matriz (Ⓣ31/3747-2529; meal and packed lunch provided; ❷), and, on the same *praça*, the simple *Pousada Serra Azul* (Ⓣ31/3747-2674; ❷). Two other hotels lie up the winding signposted road, Rua Vale Verde, which leads from the bus stop. The *Caparaó Parque Hotel* (Ⓣ31/3747-2559, Ⓦwww.caparaoparquehotel.com.br; ❺ half board), 1km along, is a beautiful place with stunning mountain views out back, good food and friendly staff. The national park entrance is only a short walk from the hotel. On the same road, and considerably cheaper, is *Pousada da Bezerra* (Ⓣ31/3747-2628, Ⓦwww.pousadadobezerra.com.br; ❹), which, like the *Caparaó Parque*, has a pool and a sauna – bliss after a long day's walk. Alternative accommodation for serious hikers is camping in the park, where there are two official campsites that you can use as a base for walking.

Opposite the *Caparaó Parque Hotel* you can **hire mules** (Ⓣ31/3747-2659; R$60 for a daytime ride, R$120 in the evening, including a guide) if you feel like exploring the park in a saddle rather than on foot. Here too you'll find a simple, but welcoming, unnamed **bar** in a rustic wooden house with fantastic views back down the valley – a wonderful place from which to watch the sunsets.

Leaving Alto do Caparaó

There are three **buses** a day from Alto do Caparaó to Manhumirim, at 5.30am, 1pm and 6pm, taking about ninety minutes. Otherwise, there are always jeeps outside the entrance of the *Caparaó Parque Hotel* that will take you to Manhumirim for R$30 (you can book them in advance from Transtur Turismo on Ⓣ31/3747-2537). There are also several buses each day from Manhumirim to Belo Horizonte.

Parque Nacional do Caparaó

The official **park entrance** (daily 7am–10pm; R$3), 4km from Alto do Caparaó, is the only way to get into the park. Here you will be handed a useful brochure, also given out free at the reception of the *Caparaó Parque Hotel*, which has a very clear **map** on the back – you'll need it, as the park is huge, covering 250 square kilometres of some of the most spectacular scenery in Brazil. The park comprises two **ecological zones**. The lower half is extremely beautiful: thickly forested valleys, hills and streams giving way, as the hills lead into mountains proper, to treeless alpine uplands strewn with wild flowers, heather and rock formations. Major **trails**, marked on the map, are just about passable by jeep; there is an (unmapped) maze of smaller trails off these, which you can only explore on foot or horseback.

There are two official **campsites** along the trail to the Pico da Bandeira summit, each with piped spring water, a basic shelter and toilets. You need your own equipment and you'll have to **reserve a place** at least a week in advance with the park's office (ⓣ32/3747-2555; only Portuguese spoken).

Some twenty minutes into the park, the **main trail** forks: left to the mountains, and right to **Vale Verde**, an enchanting forested valley where a stream forms a series of small waterfalls and shallow pools. A picnic site here is a good base for exploring several trails leading off into the forest. If you carefully pick your way downstream, after about 100m you come to a natural viewing platform looking back down Caparaó valley, framed by forest trees – a wonderfully peaceful spot.

Pico da Bandeira

Despite being 2890m high, the **Pico da Bandeira** is not difficult to climb and the four-hour (return) hike takes you through some truly spectacular scenery. The winter dry season (May to Aug) is the best time to visit for the clarity of the sky and the views, and the trail is easily walked; in the summer months (Sept to April), you can find relief from the often intense heat by taking refreshing showers beneath the park's many waterfalls. In the winter you will need a thick sweater or jacket to guard against the wind, and at all times you'll need sun block, a packed lunch, a water bottle and a good pair of walking or training shoes – the climb isn't steep enough for boots to be necessary. Be careful, too, not to be caught out after dark. Although well marked, the path is treacherous in places, and you shouldn't attempt it once the light has gone. Let the rangers at the park entrance know you are going and roughly when you expect to return.

To Tronqueira

The first **campsite** on the route to the summit is called **Tronqueira** and is 8km from the park entrance – uphill all the way, the hike there takes about three hours, or two if you're a seasoned walker. You're rewarded by stunning views, as the road winds its way out of the forest into the alpine zone, with panoramas of the Caparaó valley below. The road culminates at *Tronqueira* itself, where a platform has been built to allow you to appreciate one of the finest views in the country, as the hills far below recede to the jagged horizon. Just before you get to *Tronqueira*, a fork to the left takes you to **Cachoeira Bonita**, where the José Pedro stream, which forms the state border between Minas Gerais and Espírito Santo, plunges eighty metres down a rockface into a thickly wooded gorge; another viewing platform allows full appreciation of the spectacle.

The less taxing way to do the Pico, but the only method that allows you to get back to Caparaó the same day if you're not accustomed to long hikes, is to cover the section to *Tronqueira* **by jeep**. There are usually jeeps hanging around the entrance of the *Caparaó Parque Hotel*; if not, the reception will ring for you even if you're not a guest. You need to arrange the jeep the day before, as you have to set out by 8am at the latest to be back the same day. The jeep leaves you at *Tronqueira*, taking about thirty minutes to get there, and returns at 4pm to pick you up – return fare is around R$20. If you're staying at the hotel, let them know the day before and they'll prepare a packed lunch.

The hike to the summit

The path up the mountain from *Tronqueira* starts at the opposite end of the campsite from the viewing platform. The return trip to the summit from here is almost 20km, about six hours' walking time for most people, with another couple of hours for rests and lunch along the way. The very first stretch up from *Tronqueira* is extremely steep, but don't be discouraged: it soon flattens out into a pleasant stroll along a mountain valley, with the path hugging a crystalline mountain stream that forms swimmable pools at a couple of points. There is evidence of a forgotten episode in modern Brazilian history along the way, in the shape of bits of a military transport plane that crashed here in 1965. After the 1964 coup a group of left-wing militants took to these hills hoping to foment a Cuban-style popular rebellion, but were either hunted down or driven away – the plane that crashed was supplying the army patrols combing the area.

Halfway to the summit you come to **Terreirão**, the second official **campsite** and a good spot for lunch. A path to the right leads to a point overlooking a valley dominated by two mountains, the rocky crags of **Pico do Calçado** to the left and **Pico do Cristal** to the right. Both are only a hundred metres shorter than Pico da Bandeira and have trails leading up them if you felt so inclined – though only attempt a hike if you are camping at *Terreirão*, or you will find yourself still on the mountain at nightfall. Also, fill your water bottle at *Terreirão*, as there is no drinking water between here and the summit. The path up to Pico da Bandeira continues from the opposite end of the campsite. After the first stretch it hits rocky, treeless moorland where the exact path is sometimes difficult to see, especially when cloud closes in, but there are painted arrows to help you get your bearings.

The only really steep part of the climb is right at the end, when you need to scramble up a rocky path to get to the **summit** itself. The arrows disappear, but by now you can get a bearing on the tower that marks the peak. Once there, on a clear day you are rewarded with an absolutely superb 360-degree panorama of the mountains and hills of Espírito Santo and Minas Gerais.

Espírito Santo

Espírito Santo, a compact combination of mountains and beaches, is one of the smallest states in Brazil (with a population of only 2.6 million), but as Minas Gerais' main outlet to the sea it is strategically very important. More iron ore is exported through its capital, **Vitória**, than any other port in the world. Not surprisingly the preponderance of docks, rail yards and smelters limits the city's tourist potential, despite a fine natural location. To a *mineiro*, Espírito Santo means only one thing: **beaches**. During weekends and holiday seasons, people flock to take the waters, tending to concentrate on the stretch immediately south of Vitória, especially the large resort town of **Guarapari**. The best beaches, however, lie on the strip of coastline 50km south of Guarapari, and in the north of state, heading towards Bahia.

The hinterland of Vitória, far less visited, is exceptionally beautiful – a spectacular mix of lush forest, river valleys, mountains and granite hills. It's here that the state's real pleasures lie. The soils of this central belt are fertile, and since the latter part of the nineteenth century the area has been colonized by successive waves of Italians, Poles and Germans. Their descendants live in hillside homesteads and in a number of small, very attractive country towns that combine a European look and feel with a thoroughly tropical landscape. All are easy to get to from Vitória, not more than a couple of hours over good roads, linked by frequent buses. Around the towns, the lack of mineral deposits and the sheer logistical difficulties in penetrating such a hilly area have preserved huge chunks of **Mata Atlântica**, the lush semi-deciduous forest that once covered all the coastal parts of southern Brazil. Credit should also go to the local Indians, notably the Botocudo, whose dedicated resistance pinned the Portuguese down throughout the colonial period.

Vitória

As a city, **VITÓRIA** is vaguely reminiscent of Rio, its backdrop a combination of sea, steep hills, granite outcrops and irregularly shaped mountains on the horizon. Founded in 1551, it's one of the oldest cities in Brazil, but few traces of its past remain and nowadays most of the centre is urban sprawl. Vitória is not a tourist town, and few people visit it unless they have a very definite reason. The heart of Vitória is an island connected to the mainland by a series of bridges, but the city has long since broken its natural bounds, spreading onto the mainland north and south: the major beach areas are on these mainland zones, **Canto** and **Camburi** to the north and **Vila Velha** with its beach **Praia da Costa** to the south. While Vitória is renowned as the world capital of marlin fishing, it also has the unfortunate distinction of having the highest murder rate in Brazil. Violence is unlikely to affect the casual visitor, but appropriate care should be taken nonetheless.

Arrival and information

The enormous, modern *rodoviária* (Ⓣ27/3222-3366) is only a kilometre from the centre and, outside, all **local buses** from the stop across the road run into town; returning from the centre, most buses from Avenida Jerônimo Monteiro pass the *rodoviária* and will have it marked as a destination on their route cards. If you're heading straight for the **beaches** on arrival, any bus that says "Aeroporto", "UFES", "Eurico Sales" or "Via Camburi" will take you to Camburi; to the southern beaches you need "P. da Costa", "Vila Velha" or "Itapoan" – all can be caught at the stops outside the *rodoviária* or in the centre. As an alternative to the buses, **taxis** are quite cheap and a good option in this small city, where the distances are relatively short.

Over in the mainland district of Cariacica, the daily **train** from Belo Horizonte pulls into the Estação Ferroviária Pedro Nolasco (Ⓣ27/3226-4169), 1km west of the *rodoviária*; it's connected to the city and *rodoviária* by yellow buses marked "Terminal Itacibá" and by most of the city's orange buses, including those marked "Jardim América" and "Campo Grande".

The **airport** (Aeroporto Eurico Sales; Ⓣ27/3235-6300) is situated a couple of kilometres from Camburi beach, some 10km from the city centre, and is served by frequent green buses that can drop you on Avenida Beira Mar, the westward continuation of Avenida Getúlio Vargas, or at the *rodoviária*.

There are very helpful **tourist information** booths at the *rodoviária* (Mon–Fri 8am–9pm, Sat 9am–4pm) and at the airport (daily 8am–noon & 1–9pm; Ⓣ27/3382-6364), both of which have lists of hotels, brochures and city maps. The central office of the state tourist company, CETUR, is at Av. Princesa

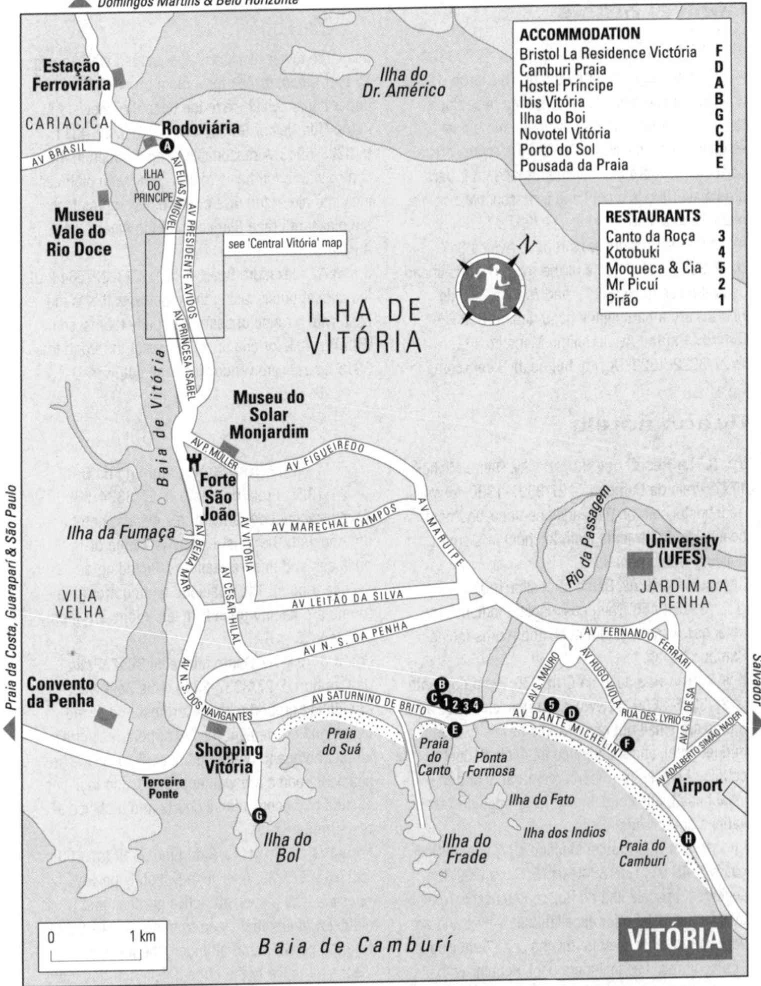

Isabel 54, fourth floor (Mon–Fri 8am–6pm; ⓣ27/3322-8888). Listings for cinema, theatre, music and art exhibitions can be found in *A Gazeta*, the main local daily newspaper.

Accommodation

The choice for **accommodation** is generally between the upmarket establishments in the beach suburbs and the less expensive hotels in the centre. For really **cheap** places, there's a row of rather grim hotels facing the main entrance of the *rodoviária*, but a better budget option is the *Hostel Príncipe*, Av. Dario Lourenço da Souza 120 (ⓣ27/3322-2799), an HI-affiliated **youth hostel**, just 200m from the *rodoviária*.The hostel is very well equiped and charges R$25 per person in a dorm or R$60 for a double room.

Central hotels

Alice Vitória Praça Getúlio Vargas 5 ⓣ27/3322-1144, ⓦwww.gruponeffa.com.br. This large, 1970s hotel was once considered to be the best place to stay in Vitória, but little evidence of its past elegance remains. Nevertheless, the rooms are perfectly comfortable, but the a/c and mini-bars are noisy. There's a pool and a reasonable *por kilo* restaurant, too. ❹

Avenida Av. Presidente Florentino Avidos 347 ⓣ27/3223-4317. Some of the rooms at this cheap central place have a/c, TV and *frigobar*. Single *quartos* are a particularly good deal at R$25. ❷

Cannes Palace Av. Jerônimo Monteiro 111 ⓣ27/3222-1522. Dowdy but neatly kept rooms in this large tower block are all equipped with ageing TV and *frigobars*. Ask for a room on one of the upper floors, which have the benefit of views. ❸

Prata Rua Nestor Gomes 201 ⓣ27/3222-4311, ⓕ3223-0943. A reasonable budget option in the centre where the basic rooms come with high ceilings and either fan or a/c. The better rooms face the pleasant Praça Climaco and the Palácio de Anchieta. ❸

Spala Av. Alexandre Buaiz 495 ⓣ27/3222-5648. Of the budget hotels facing the *rodoviária*, this is the best, with a range of spartan but tidy rooms, some with TVs. Ask for one of the rooms at the front; the R$15 *quartos* are windowless and dingy. ❷

Beach hotels

Bristol La Residence Victória Av. Dante Michelini 1777, Praia de Camburí ⓣ27/3397-1300, ⓦwww.redebristol.com.br. Well-equipped one-bedroom beachside apartments (with kitchen) in a smart building with a pool. ❺

Camburi Praia Av. Dante Michelini 1007 ⓣ27/3325-0455. This reasonable, medium-size hotel has a sauna and a pool, and rooms facing Camburi beach. ❹

Ibis Vitória Rua João da Cruz 385, Praia do Canto ⓣ27/3345-8600, ⓦwww.accorhotels.com.br. a/c rooms are small but comfortable at this excellent budget hotel, and the service is efficient. Just a couple of blocks from bars, restaurants and the local beach, this hotel is extremely popular; reservations are advised. ❹

Ilha do Boi Rua Bráulio Macedo 417, Ilha do Boi ⓣ27/3345-0111, ⓕ3345-0115. Set amidst the secluded, upscale Ilha do Boi, rooms at this relatively small hotel offer excellent sea views and are very comfortable, despite having seen better days. The good facilities include a pool. Popular with small conferences and parties, the place tends to be either totally full or nearly empty. ❻

Novotel Vitória Av. Saturnino de Brito 1327, Praia do Canto ⓣ27/3334-5300, ⓦwww.accor.com.br. Vitória's newest hotel and the one with the most extensive range of business and leisure facilities (including an excellent pool). The spacious and comfortable rooms are keenly priced; reservations are highly advised. ❻

Porto do Sol Av. Dante Michelini 3957, Praia de Camburi ⓣ27/3337-2244. This Best Western–linked property, at the farthest end of the beach and convenient for the airport, is Vitória's largest hotel and one of its most expensive. The spacious rooms are well appointed, and facilities include two pools, tennis courts and a choice of restaurants. ❺

Pousada da Praia Av. Saturnino de Brito 1500 ⓣ27/3225-0233. A secluded, slightly dowdy *pousada* with a pool, attractive gardens and eighteen rooms that sleep from one to five people. Offering personalized attention, the place is an ideal alternative to the large hotels that dominate the beach areas. Situated by the Ponta Formosa, overlooking the Praia do Canto. ❸

The City

Vitória is built into a steep hillside overlooking the **docks** along the narrow Baía de Vitória, but the main streets are all at shore level. The name of the street that hugs the shore changes as you go eastwards from the *rodoviária*; initially called Avenida Elias Miguel, then Avenida Getúlio Vargas, Avenida Mal. de Moraes and finally Avenida Beira Mar, the whole stretch is generally known to locals as **Avenida Beira Mar**. From along here, you can catch buses to the beach districts; the yellow TRANSCOL bus #500 goes over the massive **Terceira Ponte** (third bridge) to the southern district of town, **Vila Velha**, handy for the **Praia da Costa** and site of the **Convento da Penha**, with its spectacular views over the city. From the bridge itself you can also get a good idea of Vitória's layout.

From **Avenida Jerônimo Monteiro**, the main downtown shopping street, a number of stairways (*escadarias*) lead to the Cidade Alta (the upper city), the location of the colonial Palácio de Anchieta, now the state governor's palace. Just down from here the pleasant, tree-shaded **Praça Costa Pereira** is the heart of the downtown area.

At the western end of Avenida Beira Mar, the city's oldest inhabited quarter, the **Ilha do Príncipe**, is a labyrinth of narrow paths and blind alleys. It occupies a small but very steep hill behind the *rodoviária*, and although no trace remains of the original dwellings, the atmosphere is of a bygone age, with houses constructed one on top of another, many of them propped up on stilts, complete with the stench of broken sewers and mounds of garbage. Tourists seldom venture here, but it's well worth an hour's ramble for an alternative insight into daily Vitórian life, and it harbours a few local bars should you wish to hang out a while longer. But do take care, avoid the area at night and leave valuables in your hotel.

The centre

One of the few truly historic buildings in the centre of Vitória is the fine palace of the state governor, the **Palácio de Anchieta**, which dates from the 1650s but is almost entirely closed to visitors. The one part you can see – the **tomb of Padre Anchieta**, accessible by a side entrance (Tues–Sun noon–5pm) – is something of a curiosity. Anchieta, the first of a series of great Jesuit missionaries to Brazil, is most famous for being one of the two founders of São Paulo, building the rough chapel the town formed around in the sixteenth century and giving his name to one of that city's main avenues, the Via Anchieta. He was a stout defender of the rights of Indians, doing all he could to protect them from the ravages of the Portuguese and pleading their case several times to the Portuguese Crown; he was also the first to compile a grammar and dictionary of the Tupi language. Driven out of São Paulo by enraged Portuguese settlers, he retired to Vitória, died in 1597 and was finally canonized. The tomb is simple, set off by a small exhibition devoted to his life.

From the *palácio*, it's a short walk along winding roads to the sixteenth-century **Capela de Santa Luzia** (Mon–Fri 8am–6pm) on Rua José Marcelino, the first building to be erected in Vitória. The simple whitewashed chapel, with its attractive Baroque altar, would not be out of place in a Portuguese village, a vivid reminder that the coast of Espírito Santo was one of the first parts of Brazil settled by Europeans. A block east of the chapel – and on an altogether different scale – is the large and unremarkable early twentieth-century neo-Gothic **Catedral Metropolitana** (Mon–Fri 8–11am & 2–7pm, Sat–Sun 8–11am & 5–7pm). From there walk along Rua Erothildes Rosendo to the shaded Praça Costa Pereira, a busy pedestrian intersection. There are a number of distinguished-looking buildings surrounding the *praça*, the most notable being the **Teatro Carlos Gomes**, a replica of La Scala in Milan, built between 1925 and 1927. Astride a steep hillside just behind the *praça* on Rua do Rosário, and fronted by an impressive pair of towering imperial palms, is the whitewashed **Igreja do Rosário** (Tues–Fri 8am–5pm), which was built in 1765 by and for local slaves. Like the Capela de Santa Luzia, the church is now protected as a national monument, its plain interior housing a similarly impressive Baroque altar. Continuing along Rua do Rosário to the intersection with Avenida Jerônimo Monteiro, turn right and at no. 631 you'll find the **Museu de Arte do Espírito Santo** (Tues–Fri 8am–5pm), home to a sad collection of poorly displayed, mediocre modern art (a remarkable feat considering Vitória is the capital of one of four states that make up Brazil's wealthiest region).

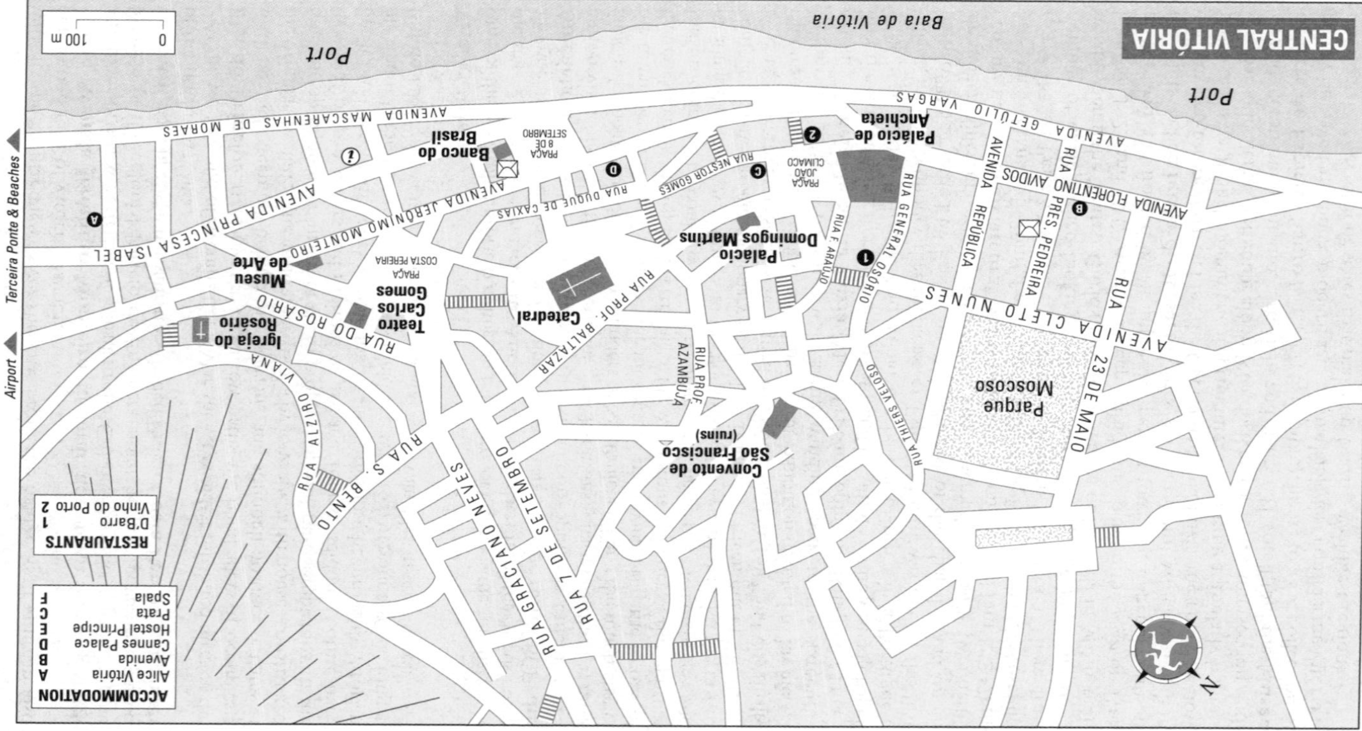
CENTRAL VITÓRIA
ACCOMMODATION
Alice Vitória A
Avenida B
Cannes Palace D
Hostel Príncipe E
Prata C
Spala F
RESTAURANTS
D'Barro 1
Vinho do Porto 2
Airport
Terceira Ponte & Beaches
Rodoviária, E & F
0 100 m
Port
Baia de Vitória
Igreja do Rosário
Museu de Arte
Teatro Carlos Gomes
Praça Costa Pereira
Banco do Brasil
Praça 8 de Setembro
Catedral
Palácio Domingos Martins
Praça João Climaco
Palácio de Anchieta
Convento de São Francisco (ruins)
Parque Moscoso
Avenida Princesa Isabel
Avenida Mascarenhas de Moraes
Avenida Jerônimo Monteiro
Rua do Rosário
Rua Alziro Viana
Rua S. Bento
Rua Graciano Neves
Rua 7 de Setembro
Rua Prof. Baltazar
Rua Duque de Caxias
Rua Nestor Gomes
Rua Prof. Azambuja
Rua F. Araújo
Rua General Osório
Rua Thiers Veloso
Avenida República
Rua Pres. Pedreira
Avenida Florentino Avidos
Avenida Getúlio Vargas
Avenida Cleto Nunes
Rua 23 de Maio

There is, however, one museum in the city that is really worth a look – the **Museu do Solar Monjardim** (Tues–Fri 12–5.30pm, Sat & Sun 1–5pm), on Avenida Paulino Müller, in the *bairro* of Jucutuquara to the southeast of the centre; take the bus marked "Circular Maruipe" or "Joana d'Arc" from Avenida Beira Mar. The museum is a restored nineteenth-century mansion filled with period furniture and household utensils, and it gives a good idea of the layout and domestic routines of a colonial estate. But if you're used to the fine displays of colonial artwork in the museums of Minas Gerais, you're likely to find it disappointing.

Vitória's beach suburbs

Come evening and at weekends, downtown Vitória is pretty well deserted and the action shifts to the middle-class **beach suburbs**, where all of Vitória's best shops, hotels and restaurants are located. Both the main city beaches here look attractive, with palm trees and promenades in the best Brazilian tradition. **Praia de Camburi**, however, is overlooked by the port of Tubarão in the distance, where iron ore and bauxite from Minas are either smelted or loaded onto supertankers, benefiting the economy but ruining the water. More exclusive, but still not recommended for swimming, is the **Praia do Canto,** where the rich flaunt themselves on the sands. To see where the city's truly wealthy live, walk across the bridge linking the Praia do Canto to the **Ilha do Frade**, an elite enclave of large, modern houses with spectacular views up and down the coast; there's also a small park in the centre of the island with the ruins of a Benedictine monastery. A short distance south of here, and joined to the mainland by a short causeway, is the **Ilha do Boi**, once used as a cattle quarantine station but now visited for its two small beaches that are popular with families and good for snorkelling. If you want to take a dip, you're better off crossing the *baía* to Vila Velha (see p.243) or travelling further afield for a perfect coast.

Vila Velha

Three bridges span the narrow Baía de Vitória, linking Espírito Santo's capital with **Vila Velha**, the state's largest city. For practical purposes, the two cities are a single metropolitan area, with people commuting in both directions. Whereas Vitória is the state's administrative centre, commercially Vila Velha is of greater significance. The city is also an important transport hub, as a railway terminus and a modern port, which is highlighted in the **Museu Vale do Rio Doce**, one of Vila Velha's few tourist attractions. Vila Velha is no more attractive than Vitória, but its **beaches**, particularly the **Praia da Costa**, located just south of the **Convento da Penha** (one of the state's oldest buildings), at least allow for safe swimming.

Museu Vale do Rio Doce

Directly across the *baía* from downtown Vitória is the fascinating **Museu Vale do Rio Doce** (Tues–Sun 10am–6pm). The museum was created by the Companhia do Vale do Rio Doce (CVRD) – a giant mining and industrial combine that's hugely important to the economy of Espírito Santo – and is housed in a former train station that was built in 1927. Focusing on the history of the **Vitória to Minas railway**, which was constructed in the early twentieth century to carry iron ore to the coast from the interior, the exhibits include a steam engine and carriages, a model railway and maps, documents, photographs and company memorabilia relating to the 664-kilometre line. The museum is also the only public venue in either Vila Velha or Vitória for the showing of important works of **modern and contemporary art**, noted for excellent exhibitions curated on themes loosely linked with the Brazilian mining industry, metallurgy or railways.

There's also a pleasant **café** (Tues–Thurs & Sat–Sun 10am–6pm, Fri noon–8pm), in a converted railway carriage positioned alongside the *baía*, where both snacks and full meals are served. The easiest way to get to the museum from downtown Vitória is by taxi, crossing the Ponte Florentino Avidos to the Antiga Estação Pedro Nolasco on Rua Vila Isabel. Alternatively, catch a bus marked "Vila Velha – Argolas" for the half-hour journey.

The Convento da Penha

The most memorable reminder of Vitória's colonial past is on the southern mainland in Vila Velha: the chapel and one-time **Convento da Penha**, founded in 1558 (Mon–Sat 5.30am–4.45pm, Sun 4.30am–4.45pm). Perched on a granite outcrop towering over the city, it's worth visiting not so much for the convent itself, interesting though it is, as for the marvellous panoramic views over the entire city. It is a major pilgrimage centre, and in the week after Easter thousands come to pay homage to the image of Nossa Senhora da Penha, the most devout making the climb up to the convent on their knees. It also marks the southernmost point that the Dutch managed to reach in the sugar wars of the seventeenth century; an expedition arrived here in 1649 and sacked the embryonic city, but were held off until a relief force sent from Rio drove them out – you can see how the 154m hill must have been almost impregnable.

There are a choice of **walks** up to the top. The steepest and most direct is the fork off the main road to the left, shortly after the main entrance, where a steep cobbled (and extremely treacherous) path leads up to the convent. Less direct, but considerably safer and with better views, is the winding Rua Luísa Grinalda – a very pleasant thirty-minute walk. Once at the top, the city is stretched out below you, the centre to the north framed by the silhouettes of the mountains inland and, to the south, by the golden arcs of Vila Velha's beaches. The builders of the **chapel** thoughtfully included a viewing platform, which you reach through a door to the left of the altar. More interesting than the chapel itself is the **Sala das Milagres**, next door to the café: a collection of photos, *ex votos*, artificial limbs and artefacts from grateful pilgrims.

To **get to the convent** from the centre, take the #500 bus and ask the driver to let you off at the third stop after the Terceira Ponte, which will leave you within easy walking distance of the convent. From the bus stop there are also plenty of buses to the Praia da Costa.

Praia da Costa

Fringed by apartment buildings and a boardwalk built of granite, the **Praia da Costa** is the most popular beach hereabouts, not because of any great beauty but owing to it being cleaner and less polluted than its counterparts on the north side of the Baía de Vitória, a couple of kilometres away. For a city beach it's not bad, though it gets packed solid on summer weekends. The Praia da Costa is easily reached from Vitória or any part of Vila Velha by buses marked "Praia da Costa".

Eating, drinking and nightlife

Local cuisine, which is pretty good, is based around seafood: crab is a key ingredient for many dishes, and lobster is plentiful, cheap and tastiest *na brasa* (charcoal-grilled). No stay in Vitória is complete without trying the **moqueca capixaba**, the distinctive local seafood stew in which the sauce is less spicy and uses more tomatoes than the better-known Bahian variety. For a taste of local sweets and other delicacies, try the stalls in the Sunday market (8am–noon) on Praça Costa Pereira.

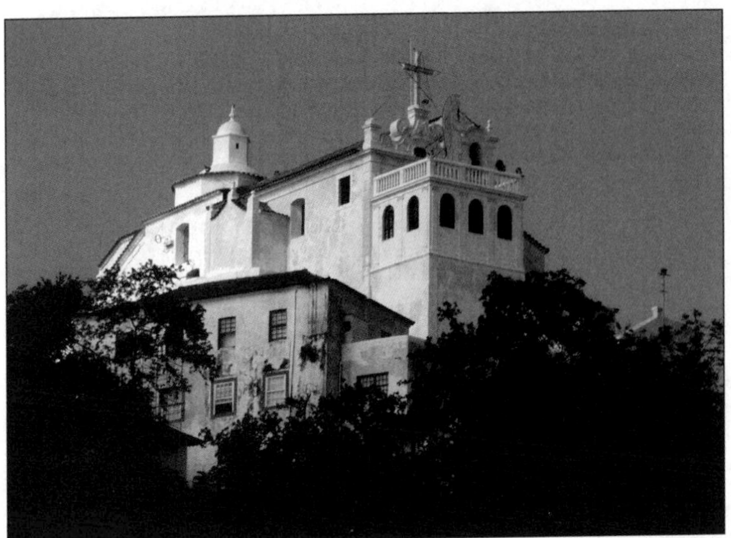

△ Convento da Penha

Restaurants in the **centre of Vitória** are generally lacklustre, though there are a number of cheap *por kilo* places near the Palácio de Anchieta along the Escadaria Maria Ortiz stairway; the best, with a great selection of both *mineiro* and local dishes, is *D'Barro Restaurante* at no. 29. The only classy restaurant in the centre is the *Vinho do Porto* at Rua Nestor Gomes 152, near the Palácio Anchieta. Specializing in Portuguese dishes, and strong on seafood, this cosy spot provides a welcome contrast from the hustle and heat outside. Otherwise, even the most humble *lanchonete* will tend to have one or two local seafood dishes on offer beside the usual *salgados* and hot dogs.

For better eating, however, Vitória's beach suburbs are the places to head for. The **Praia do Canto** is especially good, with numerous restaurants concentrated in the streets around the intersection of Rua Joaquim Lírio and Rua João da Cruz. But while most are fine, few stand out as being exceptional. Many specialize in regional dishes, such as *mocqueca capixaba* and *torta capixaba* (a kind of seafood cake and an Easter speciality), though it's served at restaurants throughout the year. Of these, undoubtedly the best is *Pirão* at Rua Joaquim Lírio 753 (closed Sun evening), but there are many other similar places to choose from. Other good restaurants in this area include: *Quinzinho*, at Rua Aleixo Neto 1370 (closed Sun evening), serving very authentic Portuguese dishes; *Mr Picuí*, at Rua Joaquim Lírio 813, specializing in Northeastern food; *Canto da Roça*, at Rua João da Cruz 280, offering a typical *mineiro* buffet in an attractively rustic, open-air setting; and *Kotobuki*, a good, reasonably priced Japanese restaurant at Rua Afonso Cláudio 60 (evenings only, closed Mon) that takes full advantage of the excellent seafood available here.

Praia de Camburi also has a fair number of restaurants (the green buses to the airport will take you past several), though they're spread out across a wide area. Authentic regional fare is available at many spots, with *Moqueca & Cia*, at Av. Dante Michelini 977, being a good, moderately priced choice.

Vitória's **nightlife** is concentrated in a couple of areas. The **Praia do Canto** (particularly the streets around Rua Joaquim Lírio and Rua João da Cruz) has loads of bars, and the area attracts people from all backgrounds. There are a couple of good **live music** venues here too: *Boca da Noite*, Rua João da Cruz 535, and *Academeia,* a few doors down on the same street, or stop by the *Oil Pub* at Rua Rômulo Samorini 33. The **Jardim da Penha** district, with the Universidade Federal do Espírito Santo (UFES) nearby, is also lively, with bars open into the small hours of the morning. The well-established *Loft Jump Bar*, Avenida Fernando Ferrari (Thurs–Sat from 11pm), opposite the university, is the city's trendiest nightclub; to get there take the airport bus or taxi. Also in Jardim da Penha, there's *forró* music every Friday (from 10pm) and samba and *pagodé* on Sunday (after 9pm) at *Chalana*, Rua Regina Vervloet 30.

Listings

Airlines Gol, at the airport ☎27/3327-5364; Rio Sul/Nordeste, Rua Eugênio Neto 68, Praia do Canto ☎27/3327-1588; TAM, at the airport ☎27/3324-1044; Varig, Av. Jerônimo Monteiro 1000, ground floor, Centro ☎27/3327-0304.

Bookshops Books in English are virtually unavailable here. The best bookshops are Livraria da Ilha, Shopping Vitória (2nd floor) and the university bookshop on the UFES campus, which has a remarkable stock of books published by lesser-known Brazilian university presses.

Car rental All are based at the airport: Avis ☎27/3327-2348; Localiza ☎0800-99-2000; Unidas ☎27/3327-0180.

Health matters 24-hour health care at Pronto Socorro do Coração, Av. Leitão da Silva 2351, Santa Lúcia (☎27/3327-4833).

Police The tourist police station (open 24hr) is at Rua João Carlos de Souza 730, Barro Vermelho.

Post office There are post offices throughout the city, including at Praça 8 de Setembre and Rua Presidente Pedreira in the centre, Rua Sampaio 204 at Praia do Canto and in the Shopping Vitória (see below for address).

Shopping Handicrafts are available at Artesanato Brasil at Praça Costa Pereira 226, Centro (Mon–Fri 8am–6pm), and at Mercado Capixaba de Artesanato at Av. Princesa Isabel 251, Centro (Mon–Fri 8.30am–6.30pm & Sat 8.30am–1pm); there's little distinctive on sale apart from rustic baskets and ceramics items, in particular *panelas de barro* (black cooking pots used for making the *moqueca capixaba*). Shopping Vitória, at Av. Nossa Senhora dos Navegantes 1440, Enseada do Suá, is the largest shopping centre in the state.

Taxis Coopertaxi ☎27/3200-2021; Radiotaxi ☎27/3336-7111; Teletáxi ☎27/3325-4343.

Trains The Estação Ferroviária Pedro Nolasco is just over the bridge from the *rodoviária* in Cariacica (enquiries on ☎27/3226-4169). There are daily services to Belo Horizonte at 7.30am, taking just over 14hr.

The coast

Espírito Santo's **coastline** is basically one long beach, some 400km in length. With the state sandwiched between Rio and Bahia, by rights the beaches should be stunning, but the reality is rather different. There's a wide coastal plain along most of the state, and with few exceptions the beaches' backdrops are hardly dramatic. Even so, if you're travelling between Rio and Bahia there are a few places where you could easily spend a few days enjoying little-visited stetches of sand, such as **Anchieta** to the south ofVitória and **Itaunas** to its north.

South of Vitória

The most beautiful beaches near to Vitória lie around the town of **GUARAPARI**, 54km to the south of the state capital, to which it's linked by buses running every half hour. There are dozens of hotels here, mostly white skyscrapers catering for visitors from Minas Gerais (prices are generally in the ❸–❹ brackets). If you fancy raucous nightlife and holiday-making Brazilian-style, then Guarapari is the place. On the other hand, if you need to escape to somewhere tranquil, a mere 7km to the south of Guarapari along the ES-060 is the **Praia dos Padres**, a protected area lapped by a wonderfully green sea. Just south of here, the fishing village of **Meaípe** has some excellent restaurants: the *Cantinho do Curuca* is especially recommended for its *bolinhos de aipim* and *moqueca capixaba*. Meaípe is also a good place to stay overnight – set on a hillside with views along the coast, the *Pousada Enseada Verde* (Ⓣ27/3272-1376, Ⓦwww.enseadaverde.com.br; ❹) is particularly comfortable and has a pool. For something more basic, try the *Pousada Solar Meaípe* (Ⓣ27/3272-1400; ❸). The beaches around here are amongst the finest in southern Espírito Santo, with a pleasant backdrop of hills covered in tropical vegetation, and as such they're extremely popular in the summer.

Twenty kilometres south of Guarapari, the town of **ANCHIETA** is one of the oldest settlements in the state. Of particular interest here is the imposing **Santuário Nacional Padre Anchieta** (Mon–Fri 9am–noon & 2–5pm, Sat & Sun 9am–5pm; R$3), which dominates the town from a hilltop position. Built sometime around the late sixteenth century as a Jesuit mission, the complex includes a well-kept museum commemorating the evangelical work amongst Indians of the sixteenth century Jesuit priest José de Anchieta. An important fishing port, Anchieta is one of the few places along this stretch of coast where life isn't focused on tourism, and, as such, the hotels here are mainly grim. One exception is the *Anchieta* (Ⓣ27/3536-1258; ❷–❸), a sprawling building dating from 1911 that still offers hints of its days as a "grand hotel". Heading south along the coast you pass a string of small beaches – some of which, like Praia dos Coqueiros, are quite pretty and not overly developed – before reaching **IRIRI**, a busy holiday resort about 10km from Anchieta with a mix of low-budget *pousadas* and holiday homes.

North of Vitória

Considering what there is to look forward to in Bahia and elsewhere in the Northeast, most visitors heading northward from Vitória choose not to linger on Espírito Santo's **northern coast**. Indeed, the BR-101 remains far from the shore, never offering a glimpse of the ocean, and apart from the Serra do Mar far off to the west, this entire area is low-lying with a mix of cattle pasture and immense eucalyptus plantations as well as, nearer to the shore, mangrove swamps, patches of Mata Atlântica and beaches fringed with shrubs or wind-stunted coconut palms. The area does hold a few attractions, however. Coastal villages such as tiny **Regência** and **Itaúnas** remain fundamentally fishing communities, preserving traditions that have been gradually lost elsewhere, while a visit to the **Reserva Natural da Vale do Rio Doce** is a must for amateur naturalists.

Getting around these parts is usually easy, as **buses** link Vitória with Espírito Santo's northern towns along the BR-101 and beyond to southern Bahia. Onward connections to the beaches, however, can be few and far between.

Regência

Some 35km north of Aracruz on the BR-101 is the turn-off to the village of **Regência**, a fishing community of barely 1200 inhabitants. Outside the rainy season between October and December, the unpaved, forty-kilometre road leading to Regência is always passable, but it's slow going, with buses stopping frequently at entrances to local cattle farms. As the road reaches the ocean, look out on your right for the Projeto Tamar **turtle research station** (daily 8am–5pm, Ⓦwww.projetotamar.org.br), which monitors a thirty five-kilometre beach nearby where, between October and January, sea turtles of all kinds come to lay their eggs. If you're lucky, you'll be invited to join the scientists in the early evening as they monitor the nests of giant leatherback turtles and watch the hatchlings as they crawl into the sea between January and March. At the visitors' centre, interns guide you through exhibits explaining the turtles' lifecycle and to tanks where you can view mature turtles.

The village of Regência itself holds little of interest, apart from the small **Museu Histórico de Regência** (Tues–Sun 10am–5pm), which charts local history through old photographs and artefacts. In summer, the village comes alive with young people from Belo Horizonte and Vitória. If you find the need **to stay**, there are several simple **pousadas**, such as the *Pousada Careba* (Ⓣ27/3274-1089; ❷), right on the beach, and a couple of restaurants serving simple fish-based meals. When it's time to move on, you can catch a bus to Linhares (3 daily; 1hr 30min), from where you can connect with buses heading north and south.

Reserva Natural da Vale do Rio Doce

Some 30km north of the industrial town of Linhares is the **Reserva Natural da Vale do Rio Doce** (daily 7.30am–4.30pm; Ⓣ27/3371-9797, Ⓦwww.cvrd.com.br/linhares; R$8), home to forty percent of Espírito Santo's remaining portion of Mata Atlântica. All but a tiny fraction of the 22,000-hectare reserve is open to the public, but you'll need at least a couple of days to begin to appreciate the area, which encompasses five different eco-systems ranging from tablelands forest to mangrove swamps. Although there's a wealth of flora and fauna, it's the four hundred-odd species of birds that are the biggest draw; the best time for **birdwatching** is between September and November, when the forests are most abundant with fruit. Parrots and parakeets are easily spotted, while you may see a rare cherry-throated tanager if you're very lucky.

The reserve is easily accessible: any bus heading north from Linhares will drop you at the entrance, from where you can walk 500m to the **visitors' centre** and get an excellent overview (in English and Portuguese) of the region's history and ecology; there's also a *lanchonete*, souvenir shop and playground here as well. It's best to contact the reserve in advance to arrange for a guide to lead you along the forest trails, but someone's usually available and there's no charge. Without a guide, you're only allowed to wander the lightly forested, rather park-like, trails that skirt the visitors' centre and hotel complex.

The reserve has its own **hotel** (Ⓣ27/3371-9797, Ⓦwww.cvrd.com.br/linhares; ❺ full board), with accommodation ranging from fairly simple rooms to chalets so luxurious that they feel at odds with the forest surroundings. There's also a good restaurant and, reserved for hotel guests, a large pool.

Conceição da Barra and Itaúnas

Some 95km further north, near the border with Bahia, is the resort town of **CONCEIÇÃO DA BARRA**. Its beaches are popular with Mineiros in the summer and there are many reasonable **pousadas** on the attractive Praia da Guaxindiba, including the *Pousada do Sol*, Av. Atlântica 226 (Ⓣ27/3762-1412; ❸), which has a pool, and, at no. 399, the simpler but very pleasant *Companhia do Mar* (Ⓣ27/3762-2020, Ⓦwww.ciamar.tur.br; ❸). A much more enjoyable place to stay, however, is the village of **ITAÚNAS**, some 20km further north on the edge of the Parque Estadual Itaúnas, best known for its thirty-metre-high sand dunes. Beneath these dunes lies a small town that was engulfed and evacuated in the 1970s after the vegetation surrounding it had been cleared for farmland. It is said that occasionally the **dunes** shift in the wind to uncover the spire of the old church. The beaches are long and – with only low-lying vegetation – exposed, but at the height of the summer are extremely popular with students, drawn by the party feel to the place, where *axê* music pounds from the bars until the small hours of the morning. Very different in atmosphere to coastal settlements further south, Itaúnas is said to be where northeastern Brazil begins. Keep your ears open for **forró** music – which may owe its recent popularity in Rio and São Paulo to tourists returning from Itaúnas; dances here typically get going around midnight and continue until 10am.

There are only a few *pousadas* in Itaúnas and it's always worth calling ahead in the summer. No-frills, but friendly and blending in with the environment, is the very pretty *Pousada da Praia* (Ⓣ27/3762-5028, Ⓦwww.casadapraiaitaunas.com.br; ④), or for a bit more comfort (and a pool) the *Pousada das Tartarugas* (Ⓣ27/9988-8155, Ⓦwww.pousadatartarugas.com.br; ④) and the *Pousada dos Corais* (Ⓣ27/3762-5200, Ⓦwww.pousadadoscoraisitaunas.com.br; ④) are both recommended. As for **places to eat**, there are plenty of inexpensive seafood restaurants around, of which *Cipó Cravo* is famous for its desserts. When it's time to move on, catch a bus to the road leading to Conceição from where you'll be able to pick up a bus to Vitória or to Porto Seguro in Bahia.

Inland from Vitória

In the hills and mountains inland from Vitória are several small towns surrounded by superb walking country, great for a day-trip or as a base for a relaxing few days. You can easily spot where the first immigrants came from: the houses and churches of **Santa Teresa** look as Italian as those of **Domingos Martins**, **Santa Leopoldina** or **Santa Maria** look German. The smallest of these towns, **Venda Nova**, is home to the remarkable sight of **Pedra Azul**, a grey granite outcrop almost 1000m high that's one of the unsung natural wonders of Brazil. If you're heading for Minas Gerais, Venda Nova lies on the main Vitória–Belo Horizonte highway, Domingos Martins just off it. The area is a popular destination for residents of Vitória, so if you plan to stay over a weekend – in particular in the winter dry season, when the trails can be approached most comfortably, the sky is blue and there's a chill in the air – pre-booking accommodation is advisable.

Domingos Martins

The closest of the inland towns to Vitória is **DOMINGOS MARTINS**, 42km away on the north side of the Belo Horizonte highway. Confusingly, it has two names: Domingos Martins is the most common, but Campinho is also used. The drive there from Vitória manages to pack a remarkable amount of scenery into a very short distance – sit on the right-hand side of the bus for the best views. Almost as soon as the bus leaves the city limits the road starts to climb into the highlands, and very quickly presents wonderful views of hills and forest. Almost completely surrounded by steep hills, Domingos Martins is high enough to be bracingly fresh by day and distinctly cold at night; it looks like a run-down German mountain village, with its triangular wooden houses modelled after alpine chalets.

Get off the bus at the first stop in the town, rather than continuing to the *rodoviária*. The cheapest **accommodation** is the *Hotel Campinho* near the bus stop (②), but if you continue the few metres to the immaculately manicured main square there's a wonderful hotel, the imposing *Imperador*, Rua Duque de Caxias 275 (Ⓣ27/3268-1115; ③), built in German style. Although the hotel has seen better days, it's superb value with very comfortable rooms and a small pool.

There's not much to Domingos Martins, just a small museum, the **Casa da Cultura** (daily 8am–5pm), almost opposite the bus stop at Av. Presidente Vargas 520, which has some old documents and artefacts dating from the colony's early days after it was founded by Pomeranians in 1847. If you're into flora, it's well worth the hassle getting to the **Reserva Kautsky** (Mon–Fri 7–10am & 2–5pm, phone in advance of visit ⓣ27/3268-1209), some way out of town and accessible only by four-wheel-drive. It has an extensive collection of orchids and camellias – ask at any hotel for details. The main pastime in Domingos Martins in decent weather is **walking** in the surrounding forest and hills; the Casa da Cultura can provide further details and maps of possible itineraries.

In the centre of town, near the Casa da Cultura, is a very good and inexpensive *por kilo* **restaurant**, *Tia Ria*, with a buffet featuring a large variety of German- and Italian-influenced dishes, as well as more familiar Brazilian ones. For the authentic German-Brazilian culinary experience, the *Restaurante Bigosch* (open Wed–Sun), at Ladeira Francisco dos Santos Silva 50 near the Casa da Cultura, is good and reasonably priced, while for enormous and excellent high teas, try the *Café Expresso Koeler* along Rua João Batista Wernersbach. There's a good selection of jams, preserves and biscuits on offer at the town's Prefeitura-run *Casa do Artesanato*, all produced by local *colonos*, or smallholders.

When it's time to **move on**, you can either return to Vitória or take any Belo Horizonte-bound bus and get off in Venda Nova.

Venda Nova and Pedra Azul

VENDA NOVA DO IMIGRANTE, to give it its full name, is an Italian village some 67km further west of Domingo Martins on the Vitória–Belo Horizonte highway (the BR-262). Even by the standards of the state, the landscape in which it is set is extraordinary, a delightful mix of rich Mata Atlântica, valleys and escarpments.

Venda Nova itself is nothing more than a small village strung along the highway, with the centre, such as it is, based on Avenida Domingos Perim, the ES-166. The **Loja do Agroturismo** (Mon–Fri 7.30am–5.30pm, Sat, Sun & holidays 8am–5pm), an association of *colonos* (family farmers) that encourages rural tourism, is near the *Alpes Hotel* at the intersection of ES-166 and BR-262; you can pick up a very good local map there that gives the locations of the various small **farms** in the vicinity that are set up to receive visitors. There are several within a kilometre of the centre, one of the most attractive being that of the Sossai-Altoé family, south of the centre along Avenida Domingos Perim; the farm is clearly signposted and visitors are free to drop by. The ⛹ Sossai-Altoé property is typical of the smallholdings (*roças*) hereabouts: the family, which emigrated to Brazil from the northern Italian province of Veneto in 1880, cultivate just five hectares of land, producing corn, beans, sugar cane and, most important of all commercially, coffee. Tourism has become vitally important for what are typically large families, and the Sossai-Altoés are happy to show their produce to visitors and demonstrate how they make their fruit wines and *cachaça*. All the farms have a small shop selling jams, wines and liquors, and it's only polite to make a purchase before leaving. An especially distinctive fruit is *jabuticaba*, a purplish-black-skinned berry that grows on the trunks of trees and has a flavour rather like that of lychees; it can be eaten fresh or as jam or wine.

Ten kilometres outside the village is the most remarkable sight in Espírito Santo, a towering bare granite mountain shaped like a thumb and almost 1000m high – the **Pedra Azul**, or "blue stone". Its peak is actually 2000m above sea level, the other thousand accounted for by the hill country from which it sprouts, an area popular with mountaineers. It's like an enormous version of the Sugar Loaf in Rio, except that no vegetation grows on its bare surface, which rears up from thick forest and looks so smooth that from a distance it appears more like

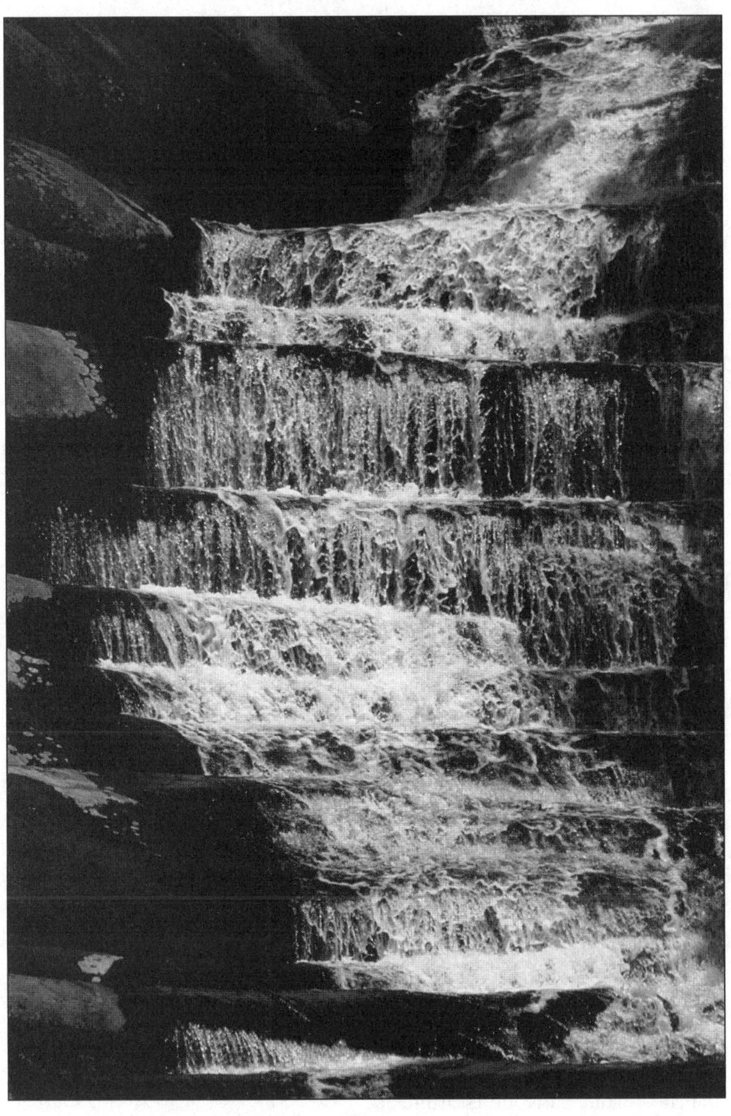

△ Pedra Azul

glass than stone. During the day sunlight does strange things to it – it really does look blue in shadow – but the time to see it is at either dawn or sunset, when it turns all kinds of colours in a spectacular natural show. The Pedra Azul forms the centrepiece of a state park, the **Parque Estadual da Pedra Azul** (Wed–Sun 9am–5.30pm; R$5 to the base or R$10 to the pools); there's a small visitors' centre at the foot of Pedra Azul with exhibits on local fauna and flora, and the park rangers will point you towards the trail leading up the stone – a tiring, but not very difficult, three-hour walk, though the area is closed when there's been heavy rain. Bring food and drink for the trek, and swimwear too if you want to enjoy a refreshing dip on the way up in one of the natural pools. An excellent, very detailed map (R$5) of the Pedra Azul area is available at most local hotels.

Practicalities

There's a good range of **accommodation** in Venda Nova. The *Alpes Hotel*, on the BR-262 near the centre of Venda Nova is rather sterile but comfortable nonetheless, with its own pool and sauna (Ⓣ27/3546-1367, Ⓦwww.alpeshotel.com.br; ④). Cheaper, on the other side of the highway, is the simple *Hotel Canal* (Ⓣ27/3546-1322; ②). Far more distinctive than either of these places, however, is the *Pousada Nonno Beppi* (Ⓣ27/3546-1965; ③), 2km from the centre of Venda Nova on the BR-262 in the direction of Domingo Martins. Owned by a family of Italian descent who've farmed here since 1912, the *pousada*'s main building is a rustic farmhouse. The best (though still not very good) place to eat in town is the *Ristorante Dalla Ninna*, attached to the *Alpes Hotel,* which serves reasonably priced, Italian-inspired food.

There are also several good places to stay **nearer the park**. The *Pousada dos Pinhos* (Ⓣ27/3248-1109; ④ full board), just off Km 90 on the BR-262, is an outstanding complex that would not look out of place in any European Alpine resort. A little cheaper, near the access road for the park at Km 88 of the BR-262 (where it meets ES-164), is the charming *Pousasa Peterle* (Ⓣ27/3248-1243; ④ full board), consisting of several pleasant chalets, all with superb views. On the continuation of the same access road, ES-164, some 6km beyond Pedra Azul, the basic, clean and friendly *Pousada Aargau* (Ⓣ27/3248-2175; ③) is located in some of the most beautiful countryside in the area. Owned and run by the son of Swiss immigrants, the *pousada* also offers an enormous *café colonial* (high tea; R$15), available every day.

There are three direct **buses** a day from Vitória to Pedra Azul, but any bus that goes to Minas Gerais also passes by the peak as it's on the highway to Belo Horizonte. A constant flow of local buses links Venda Nova with the access road to the Parque Estadual da Pedra Azul, from where it's an easy three-kilometre hike to the park entrance.

Santa Teresa

SANTA TERESA is only 90km northwest from Vitória but the hills between them are steep, reducing buses to a crawl for significant stretches and padding the journey out to a good two hours. The initial run up the main highway towards Bahia to the hill town of Fundão is attractive enough, but the winding road that takes you the 13km from here to Santa Teresa is something special, with great views on either side of the bus. The soils are rich, and dense forest is interspersed with coffee bushes and intensively cultivated hill farms, framed by dramatic granite cliffs and escarpments.

The closer you get to Santa Teresa, the more insistent the echoes of Europe become. The tiled hill farms look more Italian and less Brazilian, you see vines (and signs advertising local wines) and when you finally pull into the sturdy village you could be arriving somewhere in the foothills of the Italian Alps. The first colonists, mainly Italians but also several Polish and Russian Jewish families, arrived here in 1875; the last shipload of Italian immigrants docked in Vitória in 1925. Today, only the very oldest of inhabitants living in isolated smallholdings continue to speak the Italian dialects of Lombardy and Trento, although interest in the Italian heritage remains, in the form of musical bands and choirs and with young people taking Italian evening classes.

The town has grown very little in more recent times, and is still laid out along two streets in the shape of a cross. You go right down the main artery to arrive at the **rodoviária** (Ⓣ27/3259-1300) at the far end of the village. There is a beautifully tended square, Praça Domingos Martins, full of flowers, trees and hummingbirds darting around. Along the adjacent street and at the far end, next to the school, is Santa Teresa's main attraction, the Museu de Mello Leitão, a natural history museum and nature reserve covering eighty square kilometres (see below).

From the square, steps that are cut into the hillside lead to a ridge, and five minutes' walk brings you to an unmistakeably Italian **Igreja Matriz**, complete with roundels and cupola; the names of the first colonists are engraved on a plaque on its outside wall. Rua São Lourenço, the street leading uphill from here, is the oldest in the village, now lined with solidly built houses erected in the early twentieth century by the first wave of settlers. Five hundred metres along it, you come to the surviving two-storey wattle-and-daub houses put up by the first Italian and Polish immigrants; oldest of all is the Casa de Virgílio Lambert, a farmhouse opposite the tiny chapel that was built around 1876. Also around here are numerous **cantinas** where the local wines are made and sold; the limited production from grapes is, to say the least, an acquired taste, but in any case most is made from *jabuticaba*, a berry-like fruit that grows locally on tree trunks. To taste something even stronger, carry on a further 4km along the road to Cachaça da Mata, the producer of the best **cachaça** in Espírito Santo. The best time to visit the area is during the September to December harvest, during which you can see every stage of the distilling process, but visitors are welcome to tastings throughout the year.

The Museu de Biologia Professor Mello Leitão

Santa Teresa is full of flowers, and of hummingbirds feeding off them, and early this century they aroused the interest of one of the first generation of Italians to be born here, **Augusto Ruschi**. He turned a childhood fascination into a lifetime of study and became a pioneering natural scientist and ecologist decades before it was fashionable. Specializing in the study of **hummingbirds**, he became the world's leading expert in the field and, in the later years of his life, was almost single-handedly responsible for galvanizing the state government into action to protect the exceptional beauty of the interior of Espírito Santo; that so much forest remains is due in no small measure to him. He died in 1986, at the age of 71, after being poisoned by the secretions of a tree frog he collected on one of his many expeditions into the forest.

The **Museu de Biologia Professor Mello Leitão**, Av. José Ruschi 4 (Tues–Sun 8am–5pm) was named by Ruschi as a tribute to a former teacher. It represents Ruschi's life's work, designed and laid out by him from the early 1930s. The museum contains his library and all his collections of animals, birds and insects, as well as a small zoo, a snake farm, a butterfly garden and the richest park in the state, home to thousands of species of trees, orchids, flowers and cacti – a beautiful place to wander around and a fine memorial to an extraordinary man.

Practicalities

Tourist information is available at the museum or from the Prefeitura at Av. Jerônimo Verloet 145 (Mon–Fri 8am–6pm; Ⓣ27/3259-2268); a branch of the Banco do Brasil with an ATM is opposite the Prefeitura. The most comfortable **hotel**, the *Solar dos Colibris*, lies 3km from the town centre at Av. dos Manacás 400, Jardim da Montanha (Ⓣ27/3259-2200, Ⓦwww.hotelsolardoscolibris.com.br; ❹–❺), and has a sauna, a heated pool and park-like gardens. Slightly nearer to town, along the very pretty Estrada Lombardia, the simple but appealing *Pousada Paradiso* (☎27/3259-3191; ❷) is set in a lovely forested valley. In town itself, the dreary-looking, but extremely welcoming *Pierazzo Hotel*, Av. Getúlio Vargas 115 (☎27/3259-1233; ❷–❸) offers excellent value. Booking ahead is essential during the Festa do Imigrante Italiano de Santa Teresa, an annual celebration of Italian culture and traditions that takes place over a four-day period coinciding with the last weekend of June. Among **restaurants**, *Mazzolin di Fiori* on Praça Domingos Martins serves local specialities (lunchtimes only), as does *Zitu's* on Avenida Getúlio Vargas, near the *Pierazzo Hotel*.

Santa Leopoldina

The drive to **SANTA LEOPOLDINA** (commonly known as just Leopoldina) from Santa Teresa is fabulous, along a country road winding through thickly forested hills and gorges. There are a few hair-raising drops, which the bus drivers – who know every stone and curve – negotiate with aplomb, grinding gears and holding shouted conversations with the passengers, mostly blonde peasants clutching string bags and chickens. Despite the temporary look of the road and the tiny settlements you pass through – clearings in the forest uncannily like Amazon highway settlements – these are long-established communities dating from 1919, when the road was finished.

Ironically, the completion of the road to Santa Teresa meant the end of the line for Santa Leopoldina. Founded in 1857 by 160 Swiss colonists, who were followed over the next forty years by more than a thousand Luxembougers, Saxons, Pomeranians and Austrians, Santa Leopoldina was one of the earliest European colonies in Espírito Santo and also the most successful: coffee grew well on the hills and found a ready market on the coast. Built on the last navigable stretch of the Rio Santa Maria, inland from Vitória, Leopoldina was the main point of entry for the whole region. Once the road was finished, however, Santa Teresa swiftly outgrew it, leaving only a few streets of rather ugly houses and trading posts as a reminder of earlier prosperity. The town's German character has faded almost entirely, but the outlying parts of the *município* are still mainly inhabited by descendants of Germans, many of whom have retained the language or dialect of earlier generations.

The bus drops you at one end of the main street, **Rua do Comércio**. Nearby, on the same road, is the *Prefeitura* (Mon–Fri 8am–5pm), where you can pick up an excellent map of the *município*. Back along the street, the interesting **Museu do Colono** (Tues–Sun 11am–5pm), housed in the mansion of what used to be the leading German family in town, spotlights the early decades of German settlement with photographs – including some fascinating ones of the construction of the road to Santa Teresa in 1919 – along with relics and documents.

Unfortunately, there is nowhere to **stay** in town, but a couple of options can be found nearby: *Gasthof Tirol* (☎27/3330-1042; ❷), about 15km south of Santa Leopoldina in the hamlet of Tirol, offers basic rooms and very good Austrian-Brazilian food; the charming *Pousada Parque Bosque da Prata* (☎27/266-1137; ❸), 6km north of town on the unpaved road leading to Santa Teresa, has a pool. There are two **buses** a day to Santa Maria and three buses covering the 28km to Santa Teresa. At a pinch, it's possible to walk to either town, but allow plenty of time, carry lots to drink and remember that the route is extremely hilly.

Santa Maria

The road leading to **SANTA MARIA DE JETIBÁ** passes through hilly terrain, densely cultivated with coffee bushes, interspersed with pine plantations and, on the steepest of hillsides, patches of Mata Atlântica. As you enter Santa Maria – essentially one long street, the Avenida Frederico Grulke – you are greeted by a "Willkommen" sign. This is an outward expression of Santa Maria's intense pride in its German (or, to be more accurate, Pomeranian) heritage, an ancestry that the village is keen to promote as a tourist attraction. Virtually the entire population is descended from mid-nineteenth-century immigrants from Pomerania (what is now northeast Germany and northern Poland) and today remain bound together by a common heritage based on the continued use of the *Pommersch Platt* dialect and membership in the Lutheran Church.

Santa Maria is a pleasant enough place, most of the time just a sleepy village, but there's intense activity every Monday morning as blonde-haired *colonos* arrive from their smallholdings to purchase supplies and carry out banking and other business. Santa Maria also comes to life during the periodic **festivals** (most notably the Festa do Colono, held annually over the weekend closest to July 25), organized by the local authorities as a means of celebrating Pomeranian culture and boosting the local economy. The history of the area's settlement is well covered by the **Museu da Imigração Pomerana** (Tues–Sun 9–11am & 2.30–5.30pm; R$2) in the centre of the village at Rua Dalmácio Espíndula 260.

The very helpful **Centro de Informações Turísticas** (Mon–Fri 7.30–11am & 12.30–5pm) is housed in a German-style building on the main street. If you want to **stay** over, the excellent-value *Pommer Haus Hotel* (Ⓣ27/3263-1718; ❷), in the centre at Av. Frederico Grulke 455 (above the Banco do Brasil), is comfortable and surprisingly large for a village of Santa Maria's size. If the *Pommer Haus* is full, or you'd like something even cheaper, try the extremely rudimentary *Dormitório Boa Vista* (Ⓣ27/3263-1345; R$15 per person). **Food** is strangely disappointmenting in the village, with the only places to eat being a couple of *lanchonetes* and pizzerias on Av. Frederico Grulke and nothing even remotely German on offer.

Travel details

Buses

Belo Horizonte to: Brasília (5 daily; 14hr); Campo Grande (3 daily; 23hr); Congonhas (hourly; 2hr); Cuiabá (4 daily; 33hr); Curitiba (2 daily; 18hr); Diamantina (6 daily; 6hr); Fortaleza (1 daily; 36hr); Goiânia (5 daily; 16hr); Mariana (hourly; 2hr); Ouro Preto (hourly; 2hr); Poços de Caldas (4 daily; 8hr); Recife (2 daily; 40hr); Rio (20 daily; 6hr 30min); Sabará (every 15min; 30min); Salvador (5 daily; 28hr); São João del Rei (8 daily; 4hr); São Lourenço (2 daily; 6hr); São Paulo (hourly; 10hr); Vitória (4 daily; 8hr).

Diamantina to: Araçuaí (2 daily; 5hr); Belo Horizonte (6 daily; 6hr); São Paulo (1 daily; 16hr); Serro (1 daily; 2hr).

Ouro Preto to: Belo Horizonte (10 daily; 2hr); Brasília (1 daily 11hr); Mariana (every 20min; 30min); Rio (3 daily; 7hr); São João del Rei (2 daily; 5hr); São Paulo (2 daily; 11hr).

São João del Rei to: Belo Horizonte (7 daily; 4hr); Caxambu (4 weekly; 3hr); Ouro Preto (2 daily; 5hr); Rio (4 daily; 4hr); São Paulo (2 daily; 8hr); Tiradentes (hourly; 30min); Três Corações (4 daily; 4hr); Vitória (1 daily; 13hr).

Vitória to: Belo Horizonte (6 daily; 8hr); Brasília (1 daily; 22hr); Domingos Martins (13 daily; 1hr); Fortaleza (5 weekly; 36hr); Guarapari (every 30min; 1hr); Linhares (4 daily; 3hr); Manhuaçu (2 daily; 4hr); Manhumirim (2 daily; 4hr); Rio (hourly; 7hr 30min); Salvador (2 daily; 17hr); Santa Teresa (6 daily Mon–Sat, 3 on Sun; 2hr); São João del Rei (1 daily; 13hr); São Paulo (5 daily; 14hr); Venda Nova (hourly; 3hr).

Trains

Calling at all stations, including Governador Valadares and Itabira:

Belo Horizonte to: Vitória (daily at 7.30am; 14hr).
Vitória to: Belo Horizonte (daily at 7.30am; 14hr).

Tourist steam service:

Mariana to: Ouro Preto (Thurs–Sun at 9am and 2.30pm; 1hr 10min).
Ouro Preto to: Mariana (Thurs–Sun at 11am and 4.30pm; 1hr 10min).
São João del Rei to: Tiradentes (Fri–Sun & holidays at 10am and 3pm; 35min).
Tiradentes to: São João del Rei (Fri–Sun & holidays at 1pm and 5pm; 35min).

Bahia

CHAPTER 3 Highlights

* **Capoeira** Watch nimble displays of this Afro-Brazilian martial art at one of the organized *capoeira* schools. See p.270

* **Salvador's nightlife** The vibrant backstreets of Pelourinho offer the city's best live music, including samba. See p.277

* **Candomblé celebrations** The dance rituals of this religious cult can be memorable, if you're lucky enough to catch one. See p.279

* **Diogo** Relax in a stylish *pousada* cooled by ocean breezes, with vast, empty beaches just a short stroll away. See p.284

* **Parque Nacional da Chapada Diamantina** There's plenty of diverse terrain to keep hikers happy in this huge national park. See p.295

* **Capão** Soak in a steaming hot tub after a day of trekking in this hippy valley. See p.295

△ Igreja da Nossa Senhora dos Pretos

3

Bahia

With over 1000km of coconut-fringed beaches and the most agreeable climate in the Northeast – hot and sunny, but not as blistering as elsewhere – **Bahia** has long been one of the country's most popular destinations for foreign visitors. Constituting over a third of Northeast Brazil, it sits to the south of the area's other states. At its heart are the **Chapada Diamantina Mountains**, offering fabulous trekking and breathtaking climbing opportunities, while, just north of there, the massive **São Francisco Lakes** are quite popular for canoeing and other water sports. The countryside changes to the south of **Salvador** – site of the first Portuguese landings in 1500 – with mangrove swamps and fast-developing island resorts around the town of **Valença**, before reverting to a spectacular coastline. **Ilhéus** is a thriving beach resort, as is **Porto Seguro**, whose early settlement pre-dates even Salvador's. Beyond the coastline, Bahia comprises a vast grain-producing western sector and semi-arid landscape. The Bahian **sertão** is massive, a desert-like land that supports some

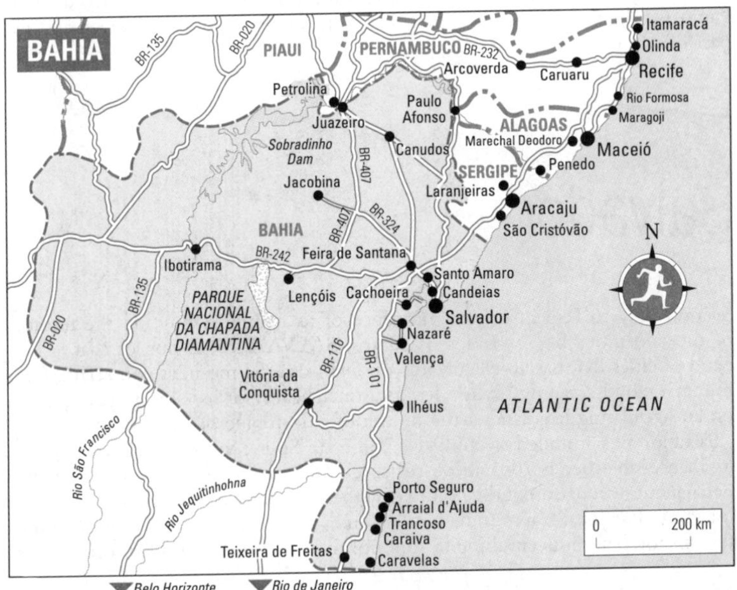

fascinating frontier towns – the mining bases of **Jacobina** and **Lençóis** and the river terminus of **Ibotirama** are just three.

Salvador, the capital of Bahia, sits prominently at the mouth of All Saints Bay, by far the greatest inlet along the coastline here despite the not insignificant estuaries of the Rio Contas as well as the Rios Pardo and Jequitinhonha – all located south of the capital. Exciting and attractive, Salvador is the most historic city in Brazil, possessing the largest collection of colonial architecture in Latin America and perhaps the richest living cultural mix in the country, with plenty of excellent Afro-Brazilian bands and performers. **Carnaval** reaches a frenzied peak in Salvador every February, when the city heaves with two million revellers enjoying traditional tunes, from the popular and loud **Barra** to the more arty **Pelhourinho**. In addition, a string of colonial towns, including **Santo Amaro** and **Cachoeira**, are all within striking distance of the city.

The bay on which Salvador was built afforded its settlers a superb natural anchorage, while the surrounding lands of Bahia state were ideal country for sugar-cane and tobacco plantations. In the seventeeth century, Salvador became the centre of the **Recôncavo**, the richest plantation zone in Brazil before the arrival of coffee the following century. It was the national capital for over two centuries, before relinquishing the title to Rio in 1763. These days, Bahia's two main north–south highways are the BR-116 and BR-101 which, together with the state's extensive network of secondary paved and unpaved roads, link all the main cities and tourist destinations.

Transport

You can reach Bahia from almost any direction, though most people will arrive first at Salvador, either by air, bus or boat. Direct, there are **flights** to Salvador from Europe and North America, and frequent **buses** from all parts of Brazil. **Getting around** Bahia is straightforward thanks to the region's extensive bus network. The main coastal roads are in fairly good shape, but start to deteriorate away from the principal routes. You'll find ferries, a catamaran and air service connecting Salvador with some of the southern resorts, such as Morro de São Paulo. Car hire is easy, but be aware that there are plenty of crazy drivers in this part of Brazil.

Salvador

Second only to Rio in the magnificence of its natural setting, on the mouth of the enormous bay of Todos os Santos, **SALVADOR** is one of that select band of cities that has an electricity you feel from the moment you arrive. The modern cloud-scraping skyline has a distinct beauty of its own, poised as it is on an undulating headland at the mouth of a deep blue ocean bay.

Salvador was founded in 1549 by Tomé de Sousa, who chose the city for its inaccessible perch 70m above sea level. This marked the beginning of the permanent occupation of the country by the **Portuguese**, though it wasn't easy for them. The local Caeté Indians killed and ate both the first governor and the first bishop before succumbing to superior force and steel. Salvador was also the

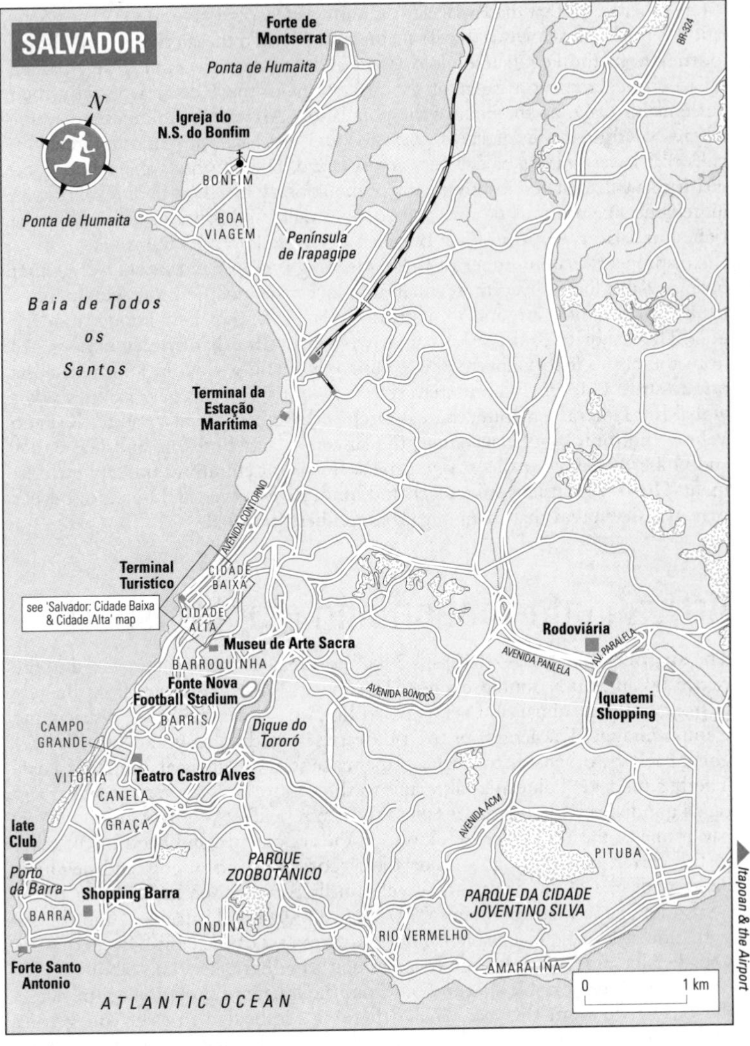

scene of a great battle in 1624, when the Dutch destroyed the Portuguese fleet in the bay and took the town by storm, only to be forced out again within a year by a joint Spanish and Portuguese fleet. For the first 300 years of its existence, Salvador was the most important port and city in the South Atlantic.

Much of the plantation wealth of the **Recôncavo** was used to adorn the city with imposing public buildings, ornate squares and, above all, churches. Today, Salvador is a large, modern city, but significant chunks of it are still recognizably colonial. Taken as a whole it doesn't have the unsullied calm of, say, Olinda but many of its individual churches, monasteries and convents are magnificent, the finest colonial buildings anywhere in Brazil.

The other factor that marks Salvador is immediately obvious – most of the population is black. Salvador was Brazil's main slave port, and the survivors of the brutal journey from the Portuguese Gold Coast and Angola were immediately packed off to city construction gangs or the plantations of the Recôncavo; today, their descendants make up the bulk of the population. **African influences** are everywhere. Salvador is the cradle of *candomblé* and *umbanda*, Afro-Brazilian religious cults that have millions of devotees across Brazil. The city has a marvellous local **cuisine**, much imitated in other parts of the country, based on traditional African ingredients like palm oil, peanuts and coconut milk. And Salvador has possibly the richest **artistic tradition** of any Brazilian city; only Rio can rival it.

A disproportionate number of Brazil's leading **writers** and **poets** were either born in Salvador or lived there, including Jorge Amado, the most widely translated Brazilian novelist, and Vinícius de Morães, Brazil's best-known modern poet. The majority of the great names who made Brazilian **music** famous hail from the city – João Gilberto, the leading exponent, with Tom Jobim, of bossa nova; Astrud Gilberto, whose quavering version of *The Girl from Ipanema* was a global hit; Dorival Caymmi, the patriarch of Brazilian popular music; Caetano Veloso, the founder of *tropicalismo*; the singers Maria Bethânia and Gal Costa; and Gilberto Gil, who was at one time secretary of culture in the city government. The city's music is still as rich and innovative as ever, and bursts out every year in a **Carnaval** that many regard as the best in Brazil.

Arrival, information and city transport

The **airport** (☎71/3204-1010) sits 20km northeast of the city, connected to the centre by an hourly shuttle express bus service (R$5) that leaves from directly in front of the terminal, and takes you to Praça da Sé via the beach districts and Campo Grande. The length of the ride varies according to traffic, but if you're going back the other way to catch a plane make sure you allow an hour and a half. The bus marked "Politeama" also runs to the centre, but gets very crowded and isn't a good idea with luggage. A taxi to the centre will set you back around R$85; pay at one of the Taxi Coometas kiosks in the arrivals area and hand the voucher to the driver; or, simply go outside the airport concourse doors and negotiate direct with one of the drivers (they will usually accept R$65 to R$75).

Salvador's superb **rodoviária** (☎71/3460-8300) – well organized and packed with almost every conceivable facility – is 8km east of the centre. To get to the Cidade Alta and its hotels from here, it's best to either take a taxi (about R$25) or catch the comfortable *executivo* bus from the Iguatemi shopping centre across the busy road from the *rodoviária* – there's a footbridge to stop you getting mowed down by traffic. The bus costs R$5 and makes stately progress through the beach districts of Pituba and Rio Vermelho before dropping you in the Praça da Sé.

Information

Salvador's **tourist information** is better than anywhere else in the state. The state tourist agency, **Bahiatursa**, is used to foreigners; most of its offices have English-speakers; and it provides a variety of maps and handouts on the city: the best two are the *Mapa Turístico de Salvador da Bahia* (R$4) and the free *Guia do Pelourinho*. If you're travelling on to other parts of Bahia, you should also ask for whatever material they have on the rest of the state, as elsewhere the service is nowhere near as good.

Personal safety: a warning

Salvador has more of a problem with **robberies** and **muggings** than anywhere else in Bahia.The main tourist area around Pelourinho is heavily policed until quite late at night and is consequently safe. However, the fact that such a large police presence is needed suggests that some **precautions** are still in order. Don't wander down ill-lit side streets at night unless you are within sight of a policeman and don't use the Lacerda elevator (see p.264) after early evening. You should also avoid walking up and down the winding roads that connect the Cidade Alta and the Cidade Baixa, and you should be careful about using ordinary city buses on Sundays when there are few people around; the *executivo* bus is always a safe option. Give the Avenida do Contorno – the seafront road that runs north from the harbour past the *Solar do Unhão* restaurant – a miss too. It's a shame to put it out of bounds as it's a very scenic walk, but it's dangerous even in daylight as gangs lie in wait for tourists who don't know any better; if you want to go to the restaurant, or the Museu de Arte Moderna near it, take a taxi.

There are **information posts** on arrival at the airport (daily 7.30am–11pm; ⓣ71/204-1244) and the *rodoviária* (daily 8am–11pm; ⓣ71/450-3871). Bahiatursa's **main office** is in Cidade Alta at Rua das Laranjeiras 12 (also sometimes called Rua Francisco Muniz Barreto; daily 8.30am–9pm or until 10pm at weekends; ⓣ71/3321-2463, ⓦwww.bahia.com.br), and there are other offices at the Mercado Modelo (Mon–Sat 9am–6pm, Sun 9am–2pm; ⓣ71/3241-0242); in Barra Shopping, Av. Centenario 2992 (Mon–Sat 10am–10pm; ⓣ71/3264-0242); and in Iguatemi Shopping, Av. Tancredo Neves 148 (Mon–Fri 9am–11pm, Sat 9am–2pm; ⓣ71/3480-5511). An additional source of information is the **tourist hotline**, "Disque Turismo" – just ring ⓣ102 from any telephone and you should find an English-speaker on the other end. Finally, if you need further detail, Bahiatursa's main offices are in the Centro de Convenções da Bahia, Loteamento Jardin Armação in the Avenida Simon Bolivar, first floor, Boca do Rio (ⓣ71/3370-8690 or 3370-8400). For tourist protection matters and to report a robbery go to the **Delegacia de Proteção ao Turista**, Praça Ancieta 14, Cruzeiro do Sao Fancisco, Pelhourinho (Mon–Sat 9am-6pm; ⓣ71/3322-7155). Several useful websites cover Bahia and Salvador including ⓦwww.bahia-online.net, ⓦwww.portalsalvador.net, ⓦwww.carnaval.com.br and ⓦwww.agendasalvador.com.br.

One thing to bear in mind when finding your way around the city is that many **roads** have two **names**: the main seafront road, for example, is sometimes called Avenida Presidente Vargas, but more usually Avenida Oceânica. In general we've gone for the name that actually appears on the street signs.

City transport

Conveniently, many of the museums, churches and historic buildings are concentrated within **walking** distance of each other in Cidade Alta. Failing that, **taxis** are plentiful, although all the beach areas except Barra are a long ride from the centre.

There are three **local bus terminals**, and the bus system is efficient and easy to use. From **Praça da Sé**, local services head to Barra and to **Campo Grande**, another central terminus with connections to the airport, *rodoviária* and Itapoan (also spelt Itapoã). The Praça da Sé bus stop is also the place to catch the *executivo* (R$5) a comfortable express bus service, well worth using instead of the crowded city buses. There are only two routes on this service: buses marked "Iguatemi" run through the city to Barra, head down the coast to Rio Vermelho, and stop at the glossy shopping centre at Iguatemi, from where a short walkway leads to the *rodoviária* – the fastest way to reach it by public transport, though still count on at least 45 minutes in transit; the "Aeroporto" service, meanwhile, follows the same route until Rio Vermelho, before continuing along past Pituba to Itapoan, and on to the airport – cutting journey times to any of the beach areas to at least half that of a regular city bus. The third city bus terminal is **Estação da Lapa**, in Barris, which has connections to everywhere in the city; it's remarkably well laid out, with destinations clearly labelled. To reach the centre, any bus with "Sé", "C. Grande" or "Lapa" on the route card will do.

Salvador also has **ferry** services to islands in the bay and points on the mainland. There are two ferry terminals: the **Terminal Turístico**, behind the Mercado Modelo, clearly visible from Cidade Alta, is for launch services – *lanchas* – and excursion boats to the island of Itaparica, across the bay as well as two-hour passage direct to Morro de São Paulo (Ⓣ71/3326-1977); the **Terminal da Estação Marítima** (or Terminal São Joaquim Ⓣ71/3327-2530), to the north, past the the docks and Polícia Federal offices at Av. Oscar Pontes 1051, handles the full-size car ferries to Itaparica (every 30min during the day; 1hr) and also the less frequent catamaran service (20 minutes).

The quickest way to get to the ferry terminals – and Cidade Baixa in general – is to take the **Lacerda elevator** or the **funicular railway**, both of which connect Cidade Alta with the heart of Cidade Baixa. They run every few minutes from early morning to late at night (though see the box on "Personal Safety", p.263), and cost only a few cents a ride.

Accommodation

Salvador is the second most popular tourist destination in Brazil and correspondingly full of **hotels**. Unless you want be near the beaches, the best area to head for is **Cidade Alta**, not least because of the spectacular view across the island-studded bay. The wealthy suburb of **Barra** has by far the closest of the beaches to the centre; the small but lovely Praia do Porto is especially pleasant and the best for swimming. Barra also has plenty of cafés and nightspots as well as being one of the most reasonably priced beach areas with several quality medium-priced hotels and *pousadas*. The official **campsite**, *Camping Ecológica Stella Maris,* at Alameda da Praia (near the *farol*) in Itapoá (Ⓣ71/3374-3506), has shower and restaurant facilities, and enough space for motorhomes too. For apartments to rent in Salvador, try the reasonable L'Appart d@Artistes in Pelhourino (Ⓣ71/9908-4915, Ⓦwww.bahia-online.net/Gerard.htm, Ⓔgerard.laffuste@ig.com.br). Paradise Properties (Ⓣ71/3264-6649, Ⓔtodd@paradisepropertiesbahia.com) offers more exclusive spaces. The exclusive and very expensive *Renaissance* resort and condominiums (Ⓣ0800/703-1512 Ⓦwww.marriott.com.br) sits less than an hour north of the airport on the beautiful Costa do Sauípe; security and comfort levels are top-notch.

City centre

Albergue das Laranjeiras Rua da Ordem Terceira (previously Inácio Acciole) 13 Ⓣ & Ⓕ71/3321-1366, Ⓔlaranjeiradhostel.com.br, Ⓦwww.laranjeirashostel.com.br. Excellent, lively youth hostel in the heart of the historic centre, with Internet access, inexpensive laundry facilities and a trendy café. R$60 per person without private bathroom and R$70 with.

Albergue do Passo Rua do Passo 3 Ⓣ71/3326-1951, Ⓕ3351-3285 Pleasant Pelourinho hostel in an attractive building featuring rooms with showers, good breakfasts and a communal room with cable TV. Staff speak English, French and Spanish. Room prices go up twenty-fold for Carnaval, but, under normal conditions, dorm beds start at R$35 per person. ❸

Arthemis Hotel Praça da Se 398, Edf. Themis, 7th floor Ⓣ71/3322-0724, Ⓦwww.artemishotel.com.br. At the top of an office block in the middle of the city, with tremendous views, a patio bar and café. Rooms are comfortable enough for the price. ❷–❸

Hotel Granada Av. Sete de Setembro 512 ⓣ71/3243-2301. Good medium-priced option surrounded by the hustle and bustle of Cidade Alta's shopping district. ④

Hotel Maridina Av. Sete de Setembro 6 ⓣ71/3242-7176, ⓕ3452-5269. This family-run hotel just off Praça Castro Alves is mainly frequented by Brazilians and has a friendly, laid-back atmosphere. ③

Hotel Nogueira Rua da Ajuda 12 ⓣ71/3241-4788, ⓕ3322-4395. A small, anonymous-looking hotel squeezed into a tall building behind the *Hotel Palace*; all rooms are small, some dark, but most have TV and private shower. ③

Hotel Palace Rua Chile 20 ⓣ71/3322-1155, ⓕ3243-1109, ⓔpalace@e-net.com.br. If you want a bit more comfort than a no-frills room, this is a good bet; all rooms are cosy but the ones with a/c are easily the best. ④

Hotel Pelourinho Rua Alfredo de Brito 20 ⓣ71/3243-2324. Long one of the most popular hotels in Cidade Alta, though it's no longer cheap and is now rather formal and anonymous. ④

Hotel Redfish Ladeira do Boqueiraõ 1, Santo Antônio ⓣ71/3243-8473 & 3241-0639, ⓦwww.hotelredfish.com, ⓔinfo@hotelredfish.com. Spacious and well-appointed *pousada* run by an English artist and his Brazilian wife; the top two floors have terraces with hammock-swinging space. Located on a large residential street that runs between Pelourinho and Largo do San Antonio. Sound advice given on trips and tours. ④

Hotel Solara Largo do Pelourinho 25 ⓣ71/3326-4583. Cheap, basic hotel in an excellent spot at the bottom end of Largo do Pelourinho; it can be wild around here at weekends, though. ②

Ibiza Hotel Rua do Bispo 6-8, at Praça da Sé ⓣ71/3322-4305 & 3322-6929. Clean, well-run budget hotel with small but pleasant rooms with TV, fans or a/c and bar service. ④–⑤

Pousada da Praça Hotel Rua Rui Barbosa 5, just off Praça Castro Alves ⓣ71/3321-0642, ⓦwww.pousadadapracahotel.com.br. Highly recommended budget hotel offering great service, more than adequate bedrooms and a great breakfast. ③

Pousada do Boqueirão Rua Direita de Santo Antônio 48, Santo Antônio ⓣ71/3241-2262, ⓦwww.pousadadoboquirao.com.br, ⓔboqueirao@terra.com.br. Family-run *pousada* with excellent breakfasts and helpful staff. Pleasant decor with antique period pieces. Many of the higher-level rooms offer excellent sea views. Within walking distance of Largo do Pelhourinho. ④–⑤

Quilombo do Pelo Hotel Rua Portas do Carmo 13, Pelhourinho ⓣ71/3322-4371, ⓦwww.quilombodopelo.hpg.com.br. Excellent hotel in the old centre of Pelhourinho and just half a block from Terreiro de Jesus. Rooms are small but there's a good little Jamaican restaurant attached. ⑤–⑥

The beaches

Albergue do Porto Rua Barão de Sergy 197, Barra ⓣ71/3264-6600, ⓦwww.alberguedoporto.com.br. Just a block from the seafront, this relaxed hostal has dormitories as well as double and family rooms, a snack bar, Internet access, hammocks and a communal kitchen. Rooms have TV and a/c. ④–⑤

Âmbar Pousada Rua Afonso Celso 485, Barra ⓣ71/3264-6956, ⓕ3264-3791, ⓦwww.ambarpousada.com.br. Friendly *pousada* near Praia do Porto da Barra. Simple but neat, cosy rooms on two storeys, with or without baths, set around an attractive courtyard. Excellent value. ④

Bahia Othon Palace Hotel Av. Oceânica 2294, Praia de Ondina ⓣ71/3203-2000, ⓦwww.othon.com.br. Superb luxury hotel on the seafront at the Praia Ondina. The 280 apartments, many with great views, all come with minibar and TV, and there's also a pool, sauna and an excellent restaurant. ⑧

Barra Turismo Hotel Av. Sete de Setembro 3691, Praia do Porto da Barra ⓣ71/3264-7433, ⓕ3264-0038, ⓦwww.barraturismo.com.br. A modern hotel with a cool, spacious lobby overlooking the beach; pretty good service, a restaurant and reasonable rooms for the price. ④

Hotel Caramuru Av. Sete de Setembro 2125, Vitória ⓣ71/3336-9951. Excellent value, unpretentious small hotel with a nice verandah and comfortable rooms. They can help organize *candomblé* visits and tours to Itaparica. The hotel is 35min by car from the airport and 20min from the bus station. ④

Hotel Catharina Paraguaçu Rua João Gomes 128, Rio Vermelho ⓣ71/3334-0089, ⓦwww.hotelcatharinaparaguacu.com.br. One of Brazil's most elegant hotels – beautifully restored and full of character. For some reason, taxi drivers have difficulty finding it even though it's on a main road. ⑤

Hotel Porto da Barra Av. Sete de Setembro 3783, Praia do Porto da Barra ⓣ71/3264-7711, ⓦwww.hotelportodobarra.com.br. Basic but comfortable hotel opposite the beach; all rooms have either a/c or fan. Breakfasts are OK. ④

Hotel Praia Av. Sete de Setembro 3739, Praia do Porto da Barra ⓣ71/3264-7144, ⓦwww.hotelprai.hpg.com.br. Good-value, no-frills, no-nonsense hotel right by the beach; Internet access and all rooms have a/c or fan. ③

Pousada Azul Rua Praguer Froes 102, Porto da Barra ⓣ71/3264-9798, ⓔinfo@pousadaazul.com.br, ⓦwww.pousadaazul.com.br. Immaculately clean and well run with stylish rooms, Internet access, a snack bar and city tours. ❹–❺

Pousada Estrela do Mar Rua Afonso Celso 119, Porto da Barra ⓣ71/3264-4882, ⓦwww.estreladomarsalvador.com, ⓔinfo@estreladomarsalvador.com. A pleasant *pousada*, less than two blocks from the seafront near the Farol, with a small courtyard, nice breakfast room and Internet access. One room has a terrace and those with two windows are airy; TV, a/c or fan available. ❷

Pousada Malu Av. Sete de Setembro 3801, Porto da Barra ⓣ71/3264-4461. A small, exceptionally clean *pousada* on the seafront opposite the Forte de Santa Maria; a friendly place in a safe location. ❷

Verdemar Av. Otávio Mangabeira 513, Pituba ⓣ71/3270-7377, ⓦwww.verdemar.com.br. Comfortable hotel set in one of the cheapest of all the beach areas, Pituba, and handily close to the airport, although a little far from the centre. Internet access and rooms have a/c and TVs. ❺

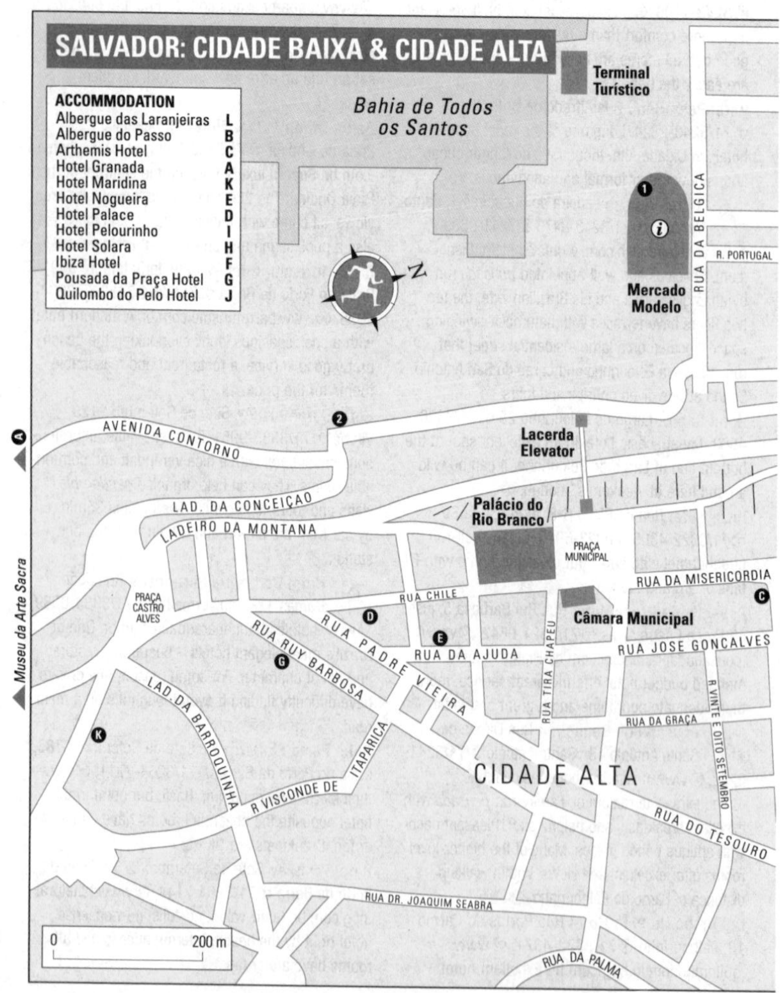

The City

Salvador is built around the craggy, fifty-metre-high bluff that dominates the eastern side of the bay, and splits the central area into upper and lower sections. The heart of the old city, **Cidade Alta** (or simply Centro), is strung along its top, linked to the **Cidade Baixa** by precipitous streets, a funicular railway and the towering Art Deco lift shaft of the Carlos Lacerda elevator, the city's largest landmark. Cidade Alta is the administrative and cultural centre of the city, Cidade Baixa the financial and commercial district.

In the last century the city expanded into the still elegant areas of **Barris** and **Canela**, to the south of Cidade Alta, and up to the exclusive residential suburb of **Barra**, the headland at the mouth of the bay around which the city is built.

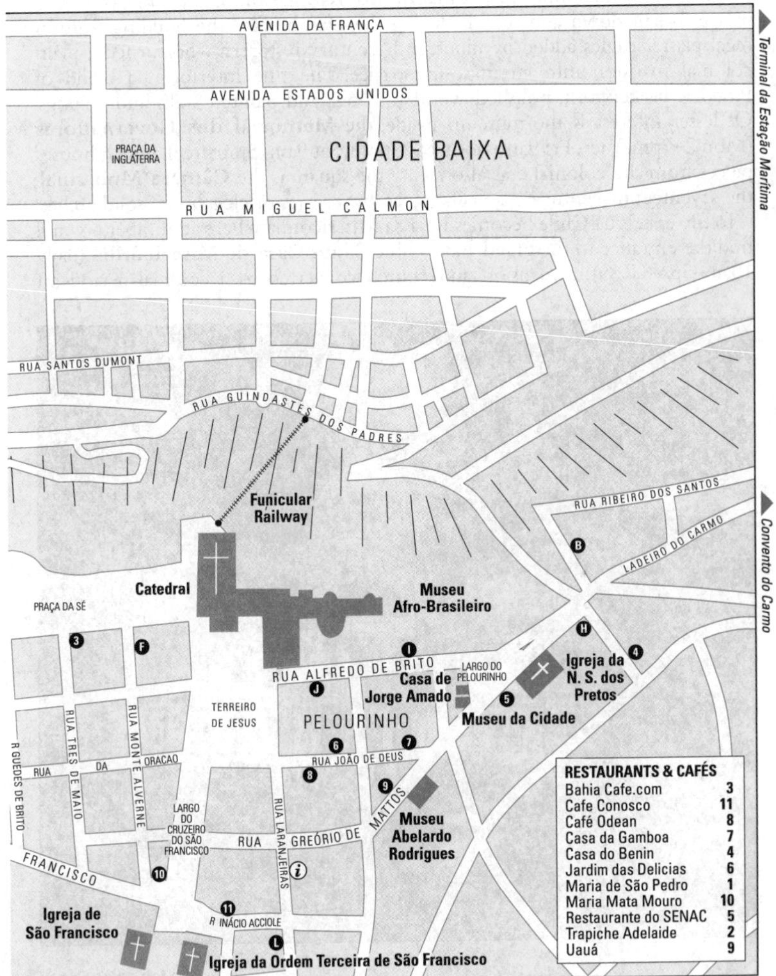

From Barra, a broken coastline of coves and beaches, large and small, is linked by the twisting **Avenida Oceânica** (also known as the Avenida Presidente Vargas), which runs along the shore through **Ondina**, **Rio Vermelho** and **Pituba**, the main beach areas. Further on is the one-time fishing village of **Itapoan**, after which the city peters out.

Most of Salvador's 26 **museums** and 34 **colonial churches** are concentrated within a short distance of each other in Cidade Alta, which makes sightseeing fairly straightforward. A single meandering walk from the Praça da Sé, taking in all the highlights, but not stopping at any of them, would take about an hour; more realistically, you'll need at least two days, and possibly three, if you want to explore the city in depth.

From Praça Municipal to Terreiro de Jesus

The best spot to begin a walking tour is at the **Praça Municipal**, the square dominated by the impressive **Palácio do Rio Branco**, the old governor's palace. Burnt down and rebuilt during the Dutch wars, the building features regal plaster eagles added by nineteenth-century restorers, who turned a plain colonial mansion into an imposing palace. The fine interior is a blend of Rococo plasterwork, polished wooden floors, and painted walls and ceilings. Of lesser interest is the museum inside, the **Memorial dos Governadores** (Mon 2–7pm, Tues–Fri 9am–noon & 2–6pm, Sat 9am–5pm; free), which houses pieces from the colonial era. Also facing the square is the **Câmara Municipal**, the seventeenth-century city hall, graced by a series of elegant yet solid arches.

To the east, Rua Chile becomes Rua da Misericórdia where at number 6 you'll find the entrance to the grand and sombre **Santa Casa de Misericórdia** (daily 10am–5pm; R$5), a mansion and church converted to a colonial-period art

△ Palácio do Rio Branco

museum with an interesting contemporary art annex. Head up to the mansion's upper rooms for breathtaking views across the bay. Originally a hospice and shelter for the sick and hungry (including abandoned children), Misericórdia's assets were built up through donations and income from property rental.

From here, the Rua da Misericórdia leads into **Praça da Sé**, the heart of Cidade Alta, where the *executivo* buses terminate. The **Terreiro de Jesus** lies to the south in front of the plain **Catedral Basílica** (Mon–Sat 8–11.30am & 2–5.30pm, Sun 10.30am–12.30pm), once the chapel of the largest Jesuit seminary outside Rome. Its interior is one of the most beautiful in the city, particularly the stunning panelled ceiling of carved and gilded wood, which gives the church a light, airy feel that's an effective antidote to the overwrought Rococo altar and side chapels. To the left of the altar is the tomb of **Mem de Sá**, third viceroy of Brazil from 1556 to 1570, and the most energetic and effective of all Brazil's colonial governors. It was he who supervised the first phase of building in Salvador, in the process destroying the Caeté Indians. Look in on the restored sacristy, too, while you're here – portraits of Jesuit luminaries, set into the walls and ceiling, gaze down intimidatingly on intruders.

The Museu Afro-Brasileiro

Next to the cathedral stands one of the best museums in the city, the **Museu Afro-Brasileiro** (Mon–Fri 9am–6pm, Sat & Sun 10am–5pm; R$5), contained within a large nineteenth-century building that used to be the university medical faculty; in the shady yard behind is the restored circular lecture theatre. The main building houses three different collections, one on each of the storeys.

Largest and best is on the **ground floor**, recording and celebrating the black contribution to Brazilian culture. Four rooms are dedicated to different aspects of black culture – popular religion, *capoeira*, weaving, music and Carnaval – and everything, for once, is very well laid out. The section on *capoeira*, the balletic martial art the slaves developed (see box, p.270), is fascinating, supported by photos and old newspaper clippings. But there are other highlights, too, like the gallery of large photographs of *candomblé* leaders, some dating from the nineteenth century, most in full regalia and exuding pride and authority; and the famous carved panels by Carybé, in the exhibition room past the photo gallery. Carybé, Bahia's most famous artist, was Argentinian by birth but came to Salvador 35 years ago to find inspiration in the city and its culture. The carved panels in the museum, imaginatively decorated with scrap metal, represent the gods and goddesses of *candomblé*.

The **first floor** houses a rather dull museum of the faculty of medicine, dominated by busts and dusty bookcases. A better idea is to look in the **basement**, at the **Museu Arqueológico e Etnológico**. Largely given over to fossils and artefacts from ancient burial sites, it also incorporates the only surviving part of the old Jesuit college, a section of the cellars, in the arched brickwork at the far end. A diagram at the entrance to the museum shows how enormous the college was, extending all the way from what is now the Praça da Sé to Largo do Pelourinho. It was from here that the conversion of the Brazilian Indians was organized, and one of the many Jesuit priests who passed through its gates was Antônio Vieira, whose impassioned sermons defending Indian rights against the demands of the Portuguese slavers are generally regarded as the finest early prose in the Portuguese language. After the Jesuits were expelled in 1759, most of the college was demolished by the rich for building material for their mansions, part of the site used to found a university, and the rest parcelled out and sold for redevelopment.

Capoeira

Capoeira began in Angola as a ritual fight to gain the nuptial rights of women when they reached puberty, and has evolved into a graceful semi-balletic art form somewhere between fighting and dancing. It evolved in this way because the slaves that were brought over from Africa were denied the right to use their ritual fighting and so it was disguised or changed into the singing and dancing form of fighting that is seen today. You'll find many displays of *capoeira* in Salvador. It's usually accompanied by the characteristic rhythmic twang of the **berimbau**, and takes the form of a pair of dancers/fighters leaping and whirling in stylized "combat" – which, with younger *capoeiristas*, occasionally slips into a genuine fight when blows land by accident and the participants lose their temper.

The *capoeirstas* normally create a **roda** which anyone may join. It involves a circle of spectators including drummers, *berimbaus*, singing and clapping to encourage the two "playing" inside the *roda*. A spectator may take the place of one of the *capoeristas* by exposing the palm of their hand towards the person they would like to "play" with and a new game begins. The basic method of moving around the *roda* is the *ginga*, a standing, stepping motion that includes the *role* and *au*, rolling and cartwheeling movements respectively. These are not set moves, so *capoeristas* can adapt them to their own style. The players then attack and defend themselves using these basic methods along with a range of kicks such as the spinning *armada*. To avoid the kicks, players fall into various stances like the *queda de tres*, a crouching position with one arm raised to defend the head. Only the feet, hands and head of the players should touch the floor during the game.

There are regular displays, largely for the benefit of tourists but interesting nevertheless, on Terreiro de Jesus and near the entrances to the Mercado Modelo in Cidade Baixa, where contributions from onlookers are expected. You'll find the best *capoeira*, however, in the **academias de capoeira**, organized schools with classes that anyone can watch, free of charge. All ages take part, and many of the children are astonishingly nimble; most *capoeiristas* are male, but some girls and women take it up as well. The oldest and most famous school, the Associação de Capoeira Mestre Bimba, named after the man who popularized *capoeira* in Salvador in the 1920s, is still the best and may have classes open to tourists. Other schools are at the other end of Cidade Alta, at the Forte de Santo Antônio Além do Carmo. The Grupo de Capoeira Pelourinho has classes on Tuesday, Thursday and Saturday from 7pm to 10pm; and the Centro Esportivo de Capoeira Angola is open all day until 10.30pm on weekdays, though you have to turn up to find out when the next class is – late afternoon is best, as afternoon and evening sessions are generally better attended. Saturday is the surest day for classes in most schools, but stop by any early evening or late afternoon and just ask.

Capoiera schools:

Capoeira Angola Irmaoes Gemoes e Metre Curio Rua Gregoria de Mattos 9 (upstairs), Pelourinho ⓣ71/3321-0396, ⓔmaestrecurio@yahoo.com.br.

Associacao de Capoiera Mestre Bimba Rua Francisco Muniz Barreto 1, Pelourinho ⓣ71/3322-0639, ⓦwww.capoieramestrebimba.com.br, ⓔacm_bimba@aol.com.br.

Grupo Internacional de Capoiera Topazio Ladeira de Sautano 2, Loja 9, Edificio Marque de Moltavao, ⓣ71/3521-3366, ⓦwww.capoieratopazio.com.br.

Grupo de Capoeira Lei Aurea Rua Sao Jose de Lima ⓣ71/3241-9767, ⓦwww.leiaurea.com.br.

Grupo de Capeira Angola Pelourihno Forte de Sao Antonio, Barra ⓣ71/3208-1662

Escola de Capoeria Mestre Lua Rasta Rua Inacio Acioli, Pelourinho ⓣ71/3321-6334.

The churches of São Francisco

Terreiro de Jesus has more than its fair share of churches; there are two more fine sixteenth-century examples on the square itself. But outshining them both, on nearby **Largo do Cruzeiro de São Francisco** (an extension of Terreiro de Jesus sometimes known as Praça Anchieta), are the superb carved stone facades of two ornate Baroque buildings, set in a single, large complex dedicated to St Francis: the **Igreja de São Francisco** (Mon–Sat 8am–5.30pm, Sun 7am–noon) and the **Igreja da Ordem Terceira de São Francisco** (Mon–Fri 8am–5pm). Of the two the latter has the edge: it's covered with a wild profusion of saints, virgins, angels and abstract patterns. Remarkably, the facade was hidden for 150 years, until in 1936 a painter knocked off a chunk of plaster by mistake and revealed the original frontage, Brazil's only example of high-relief facade carved in ashlar (square cut stones). It took nine years of careful chipping before the facade was returned to its original glory, and today the whole church is a strong contender for the most beautiful single building in the city. Its **reliquary**, or *ossuário*, is extraordinary, the entire room redecorated in the 1940s in Art Deco style, one of the most unusual examples you're ever likely to come across. From here, there's a door onto a pleasant garden at the back.

To get into the complex, you have to go via the Igreja de São Francisco (the entrance is by a door to the right of the main doors). The small cloister in this church is decorated with one of the finest single pieces of *azulejo* work in Brazil. Running the entire length of the cloister, this **tiled wall** tells the story of the marriage of the son of the king of Portugal to an Austrian princess; beginning with the panel to the right of the church entrance, which shows the princess being ferried ashore to the reception committee, it continues with the procession of the happy couple in carriages through Lisbon, passing under a series of commemorative arches set up by the city guilds, whose names you can still just read – "The Royal Company of Bakers", "The Worshipful Company of Sweetmakers". The vigour and realism of the incidental detail in the street scenes is remarkable: beggars and cripples display their wounds, dogs skulk, children play in the gutter; and the panoramic view of Lisbon it displays is an important historical record of how Lisbon looked before the calamitous earthquake of 1755.

Around Largo do Pelourinho

Heading down the narrow Rua Alfredo de Brito, next to the Museu Afro-Brasileiro, brings you to the beautiful, cobbled **Largo do Pelourinho**, still much as it was during the eighteenth century. Lined with solid colonial mansions, it's topped by the oriental-looking towers of the **Igreja da Nossa Senhora dos Pretos** (Mon–Fri 9.30am–6pm, Sat 9.30am-5pm, Sun 10am–noon), built by and for slaves and still with a largely black congregation. Across from here is the **Casa de Jorge Amado** (Mon noon–6pm, Tues–Sat 9am–6pm), a museum given over to the life and work of the hugely popular novelist, who doesn't number modesty among his virtues; you can have fun spotting his rich and famous friends in the collection of photographs.

Next door, on the corner of Rua Gregório de Mattos, is the **Museu da Cidade** (Mon & Wed–Fri 10am–4pm; usually R$1, but free on Thurs), housed in an attractive Pelourinho mansion. The lower levels are given over to paintings and sculpture by young city artists, some startlingly good and some pretty dire, while luxuriously dressed dummies show off Carnaval costumes from years gone by. There are models of *candomblé* deities and, on the first floor, a room containing the personal belongings of the greatest Bahian poet, Castro Alves, with some fascinating photographs from the beginning of the twentieth century. Completing the constellation of museums around Pelourinho is the **Museu Abelardo**

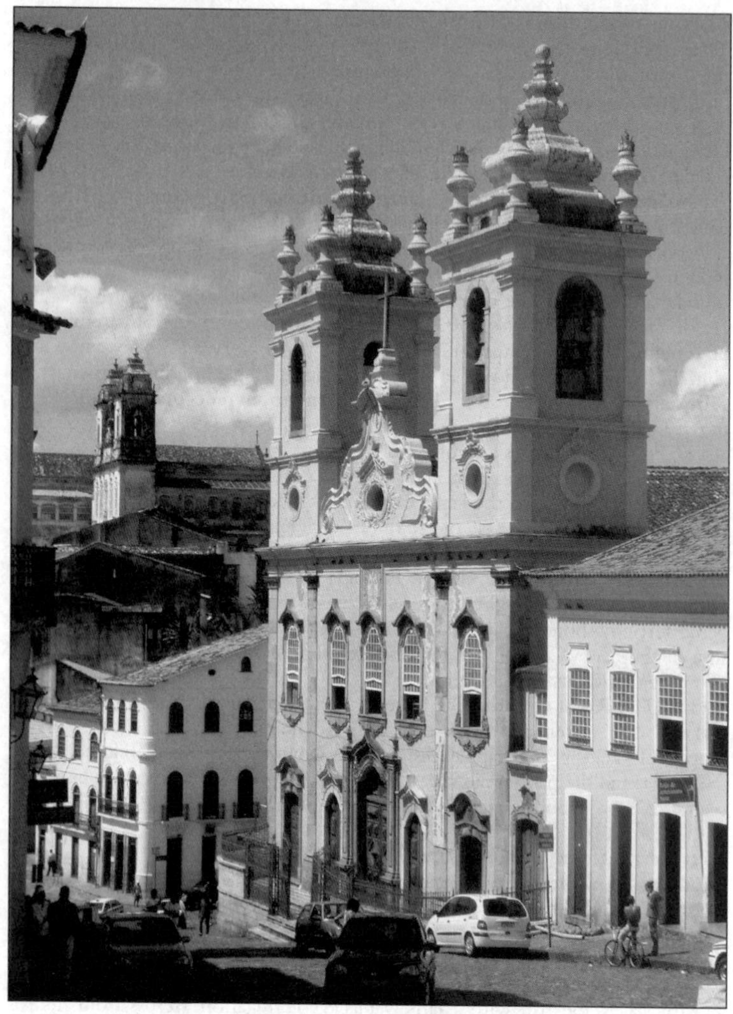

△ Igreja da Nossa Senhora dos Pretos

Rodrigues (daily 1–6pm, closed Mon & Sun; R$1) at Rua Gregório de Mattos 45, which has a good collection of Catholic art from the sixteenth century onwards, well displayed in a restored seventeenth-century mansion.

From Largo do Pelourinho, a steep climb up Ladeira do Carmo rewards you with two more exceptional examples of colonial architecture: on the left is the **Convento da Ordem Primeira do Carmo** (Mon–Sat 9am–noon & 2–6pm), and on the right the **Igreja da Ordem Terceira de Nossa Senhora do Carmo** (Mon–Sat 9am–1pm & 2–6pm; 50¢). Both are built around large and beautiful cloisters, with a fine view across the old city at the back, and have chaotic but interesting museums attached. The convent museum is very eclectic, mostly religious but including collections of coins and furniture, with hundreds

ACM and the restoration of Pelourinho

The Pelourinho district is now an attractive and much visited area, but it wasn't always this way. As recently as 1991 the area was virtually derelict, with many of the colonial buildings falling to pieces and tourism in decline. The neighborhood's makeover is thanks to Bahia's most famous – and controversial – politician, **Antônio Carlos Magalhães**. Widely disliked elsewhere in Brazil as an unreconstructed representative of the country's landed elite, the silver-haired **ACM** (as he's known) is popular in Bahia because of his tireless campaigns on behalf of his home state, and you'll see his picture hanging up in many of the city's bars. Pelourinho's revival, which he undertook as state governor, was certainly impressive. Some of the most important colonial architecture has been restored to its original glory, the pastel pinks and blues creating a wonderfully gaudy effect. Critics point to the fact that many local residents had to be moved out and complain that the area has become dominated by tourism. There is some truth to this, but you'll still see plenty of locals enjoying themselves alongside the tourists, and the economy is clearly thriving; on the whole, it's hard to argue that Pelourinho was better off as a decaying shadow of its former self. Furthermore, you only have to wander fifty metres off the beaten Pelhourinho path to find yourself in dark and sometimes dodgy back streets.

of unlabelled exhibits jumbled together in gloomy rooms. The highlight is a superbly expressive statue of Christ at the whipping post by Salvador's greatest colonial artist, the half-Indian slave **Francisco Manuel das Chagas**, whose powerful religious sculpture broke the formalistic bonds of the period – most of Chagas' work was completed in the 1720s. Unfortunately, Chagas died young of tuberculosis, leaving only a small body of work; this statue is appallingly displayed, jumbled together with much inferior work in a glass case in a corner of the rear gallery. In the church museum next door is another Chagas statue, a life-size body of Christ, this time sensibly displayed alone and, if anything, even more powerful. If you look closely at both statues, you'll find that the drops of blood are small rubies inlaid in the wood.

The rest of Cidade Alta is still largely colonial, and fascinating to wander around – although do it in daylight if you want to get off the main streets, and try to stick to where there are people around. Good streets to try are **Rua Gregório de Mattos** and the road on from the Carmo museums, **Rua Joaquim Távora**, which leads away from the heavier concentrations of tourists to the quiet Largo Cruz Pascoa and eventually ends up at the fort of **Santo Antônio Além do Carmo**, with a spectacular view across the bay. The simple bars on Largo Santo Antônio in front of the fort are a good place to rest your legs, have a drink and watch the stunning sunsets. Other good sundowner viewpoints on the edge of the bluff are the Praça da Sé itself, the bar of the *Hotel Pelourinho* (open to non-residents) and an unnamed bar on the left just after Largo Cruz Pascoa.

The Museu da Arte Sacra

Despite the concentration of riches in Cidade Alta, you have to leave the old city to find one of the finest museums of Catholic art in Brazil, the **Museu da Arte Sacra** at Rua Sodré 276 (Mon–Fri 11.30am–5.30pm; R$4). It's slightly difficult to find: if you're coming into Praça Castro Alves from Rua Chile, go straight ahead and up Rua Carlos Gomes. Then take the first right down the steep Ladeira de Santa Teresa and you'll see the museum in front of you. It's housed in the seventeenth-century Santa Teresa convent, a magnificent building with much of its original furniture and fittings still intact, and with galleries on three floors surrounding a cloister. The chapel on the ground floor is lavishly decorated with elaborate, gilded carvings, and it leads into a maze of small galleries stuffed with a remarkably rich collection of colonial art, dating from the sixteenth century. The hundreds of statues, icons, paintings and religious artefacts are enough to occupy you for hours, the only real flaw in the collection being the absence of anything by Chagas or Aleijadinho. There's still some high-quality work, though: small soapstone carvings on the top floor, marvellous tiling in the sacristy behind the chapel and a display of ornately carved religious accessories in solid gold and silver.

Cidade Baixa

Cidade Baixa, the part of the city at the foot of the bluff, takes in the docks, the old harbour dominated by the circular sixteenth-century **Forte do Mar**, the ferry terminals and the main city markets. For the most part it's ugly modern urban sprawl, but for once the developers can't be blamed: the area was always the most neglected part of the city because its low-lying location deprived it of the sea breezes and cooler air of the higher ground above. Since the sixteenth century, the city's inhabitants have only ventured down into the Cidade Baixa to work, choosing to live in the much pleasanter areas above and around.

All the same, it's not completely without interest. You are likely at least to pass through to get to the **ferry terminals** And there is one essential stop: the **Mercado Modelo** (daily 10am–6pm; free), an old covered market set on its own by the old harbour, across the road from the foot of the Lacerda elevator. It houses a huge and very enjoyable arts and crafts market, always crowded with Bahians as well as tourists, with the best selection of *artesanato* in the city. Not everything is cheap, so it helps to have the confidence to haggle. Some of the nicest souvenirs are the painted statues of *candomblé* deities – look for signs saying *artigos religiosos*. Even if you don't buy anything the building is a joy, a spacious nineteenth-century cathedral to commerce. There is always something going on in and around the market, with displays of *capoeira* common (and donations expected). There is an **information office** to the left of the front entrance, and upstairs you will find a couple of good **restaurants**.

The Igreja do Bonfim

The Igreja do Bonfim, as everyone calls the **Igreja do Nosso Senhor do Bonfim** (Tues–Sun 6.30am–noon & 2–6pm; free), sits on a hill overlooking the bay in the northwestern suburbs. The church is the focal point of colourful religious festivals that attract thousands of devotees from all over Brazil. To get there, take the buses marked "Bonfim" or "Ribeira" from the Estação da Lapa, or the bottom of the Lacerda elevator.

The church is not, by any means, the oldest or most beautiful in the city – completed in 1745 with a plain white exterior and simple interior – but it's easily the most interesting. The force of popular devotion is obvious from the moment you leave the bus. The large square in front of the church is lined with stalls catering to the hundreds of pilgrims who arrive every day, and you'll be besieged by small children selling *fitas*, ribbons in white and blue, the church colours, to tie around your wrist for luck and to hang in the church when you make your requests; it's ungracious to enter the church without a few. It's always at least half-full of people worshipping, often with almost hypnotic fervour: middle-class matrons and uniformed military officers rub shoulders with peasants from the *sertão* and women from the *favelas*.

For a clearer idea of what this place means to the people of Bahia, go to the right of the nave where a wide corridor leads to the **Museu dos Ex-Votos**

do Senhor do Bonfim (Tues–Sat 9am–noon & 2–5pm; R$2). An incredibly crowded antechamber gives you an idea of what to expect: it's lined to the roof with thousands of small photographs of supplicants, with notes pinned to the wall requesting intervention or giving thanks for benefits received. Every spare inch is covered with a forest of ribbons, one for each request, some almost rotted away with age, and many of the written pleas are heart-rending: for the life of a dying child, for news from a husband who emigrated south, for the safe return of sailors and fishermen, for success in an exam, for money to pay for a college education, for a favourite football team to win a championship – in short, a snapshot of everyday worries and hopes. Hanging from the roof are dozens of body parts – limbs, heads, even organs like hearts and lungs – made of wood or plastic for anxious patients asking for protection before an operation, silver for relieved patients giving thanks after successful surgery. Some people blessed by a particularly spectacular escape pay tribute by leaving a pictorial record of the miracle: photos of smashed cars that the driver walked away from, or crude but vivid paintings of fires, sinkings and electrocutions.

Upstairs in the museum proper is the oldest material and recent offerings judged worthy of special display. It's not only the poor who come asking for help: there are several university classbooks deposited here, and military insignia commemorating promotion up to the rank of general. The more valuable *ex votos* are displayed here in ranks of cases, classified according to the part of the body: silver heads and limbs you might expect, even silver hearts, lungs, ears, eyes and noses, but the serried ranks of silver kidneys, spleens, livers and intestines are striking. There are also football shirts – the city's two big teams always make a visit at the start of the season – models of the church, and dozens of paintings, especially of fires and shipwrecks.

Museu Nautico da Bahia

Prominently located on the Avenida Oceânica in the wealthy suburb of Barra, the **Museu Nautico** (open Tues–Sun, 9am–9pm; R$5) sits within the lighthouse in the picturesque white Forte de Santo Antônio on the windy Barra point – the spot where the Atlantic Ocean becomes the bay of Todos os Santos. The museum houses an interesting collection of seafaring instruments, maps, model boats, art and a small amount of written historical information. Built in 1503, this was the first European fort on the Brazilian coast, built to defend the newly founded settlement and access to the bay. There's a good book and gift shop, but most people come here for the views from the internal terrace in the fort, above the museum: this is a very popular place to sit and have a cocktail as the sun sets. Local buses and the *executivo* service to Barra leave from the Praça da Sé.

Eating, drinking and nightlife

Eating out is one of the major pleasures Salvador has to offer, and the local cuisine (*comida baiana*) is deservedly famous. There's a huge range of restaurants and, although Cidade Alta has an increasing number of stylish, expensive places, it's still quite possible to eat well for significantly less than R$25, though easier to spend R$50, including drinks. You should certainly treat yourself to at least one slap-up feed before leaving the city.

Restaurants and cafés

The cheapest places for a sit-down meal are around **Praça Castro Alves** and in **Cidade Baixa**. Restaurants in the **Pelourinho** area and the **beach districts** are classier and tend to be more expensive. Especially at Barra and Rio Vermelho, the

Comida Baiana: dishes and ingredients

The secret of Bahian cooking is twofold: a rich seafood base, and the abundance of traditional West African **ingredients** like palm oil, nuts, coconut and ferociously strong peppers. Many ingredients and dishes have African names: most famous of all is *vatapá*, a bright yellow porridge of palm oil, coconut, shrimp and garlic, which looks vaguely unappetizing but is delicious. Other dishes to look out for are *moqueca*, seafood cooked in the inevitable palm-oil-based sauce; *caruru*, with many of the same ingredients as *vatapá* but with the vital addition of loads of okra; and *acarajé*, deep-fried bean cake stuffed with *vatapá*, salad and (optional) hot pepper. Bahian cuisine also has good **desserts**, less stickily sweet than elsewhere: *quindim* is a delicious small cake of coconut flavoured with vanilla, which often comes with a prune in the middle.

Some of the best food is also the cheapest, and even gourmets could do a lot worse than start with the street-corner *baianas*, women in traditional white dress. Be careful of the *pimenta*, the very hot pepper sauce, which newcomers should treat with respect, taking only a few drops. The *baianas* serve *quindim*, *vatapá*, slabs of maize pudding wrapped in banana leaves, fried bananas dusted with icing sugar, and fried sticks of sweet batter covered with sugar and cinnamon – all absolutely wonderful.

seafront promenade is lined with bars, cafés and restaurants, and the best option is to take a bus and hop off wherever you fancy. The non-Brazilian cuisines tend to be concentrated in **Barra**, where Salvador's upper middle class lives.

Aconchego da Zuzu Rua Quintana Bocaiuva 18, Garcia ☏71/3331-5074. Enjoyably different and highly Bahian, this small family-run restaurant sits in a courtyard on a back street of the Garcia suburb. Choose from a wide range of local cuisine (try the *peixa au molho de camarão*); superb, traditional percussion music is sometimes performed. Open Mon–Sat lunch only.

Aquarela Av. Oceânica, Barra 141 ☏71/3261-3222. Popular restaurant serving up Greek food and fish dishes. Moderate.

Bahia Cafe.com Praça da Sé 20 ☏71/3322-1266. Great little café with excellent coffee, Internet access and windows that open onto the street.

Cafe Conosco Rua da Ordem Terceira 4, Pelhourinho ☏71/3321-0481. Attractive café set in an early eighteenth-century house that doubles as a small museum; good coffee and cake, Internet access and a tranquil escape from the hubbub of the streets.

Café Odean Rua Joao de Deus 01, 1st floor, Pelourinho ☏71/3321-5725. Trendy, modern café with loads of weird organic material and objects woven into the fabric of the furniture. Right in the middle of the action, the place gets especially busy on Fri and Sat nights when there's a R$7 minimum consumption charge.

Casa da Gamboa Rua João de Deus 32, Pelourinho ☏71/3321-3393. One of the district's top restaurants and worth a splurge. Serves mainly Bahian dishes; expect to pay at least R$50 per head. Closed Sun.

Casa do Benin Padre Agustinho Gomes 17, Pelourinho. Excellent, reasonably priced African food at the southern edge of Largo do Pelourinho.

Don Vitellone's Trattoria Rua Dom Marcos Teixeira 25, Barra ☏71/3267-4996. Good Italian food accompanied by slightly fussy service. Notable for its great antipasto buffet plus a wide range of tasty menu choices and some fine wines.

Jardim das Delicias Rua João de Deus 12, Pelourinho ☏71/3321-1449. Fantastic Bahian and international cuisine served both inside and out (in the lovely garden); the salads are especially good. Cover charge for gentle live music most weekend evenings.

Maria de São Pedro Mercado Modelo 1st floor, Cidade Baixa. A good Bahian restaurant, and one of the oldest, with great views across the bay – if you can get a table on the terrace. Next door, the *Camafeu de Oxóssi* offers much the same fare at moderate prices. Open Mon–Sat 11am-7pm, Sun 11am–4pm.

Maria Mata Mouro Rua Inacio Acioly 08, Pelourinho ☏71/3321-3929. One of the finest Bahian restaurants in the district, with prices to match; whatever you choose will be divine and lovingly presented. Very busy at weekends, so it's best to book a table in advance.

Mustafa Rua Alexandre Maia 6, Clube de Bridge da Bahia, Graça ⓣ71/3247-9884. Arabic restaurant, popular with locals and serving excellent food, including a buffet, though it's not cheap. Getting a taxi from the Barra seafront is the easiest way to get there, as the road is a little obscure. Open Mon–Sat 11.30am–3pm, Sun noon–4pm.

Pereira Av. Sete de Setembro 3959, Porto da Barra ⓣ71/3264-6464. Stylish spot with a cool interior and pleasant terrace overlooking the road and beach. The food and drinks are great but expensive; the seafood and salads are fabulous.

Restaurante do SENAC Largo do Pelourinho, opposite the Casa Jorge Amado, Pelourinho ⓣ71/3321-5502. Municipal restaurant-school in a finely restored colonial mansion. It looks very expensive from the outside, but it's good value for what you get. You pay a set charge – about R$40 – and take as much as you want from a quality buffet of around fifty dishes, all helpfully labelled so that you know what you're eating. If you go for dinner, try to finish before 10pm, when there's a rather touristy folklore show.

Sukiyaki Av. Oceânica 3562, near Ondina seafront, Barra ⓣ71/3247-5063. Excellent, trendy Japanese place with fresh, tasty food. There's a branch at the Aeroclube Plaza Show in Boca do Rio (ⓣ71/3461-0365).

Trapiche Adelaide Praça Dos Tupinambas 2, Av. Contorno Comercio ⓣ71/3326-0443, ⓦwww.trapicheadelaide.com.br. One of the flashiest and most exclusive restaurants in Salvador. It's right next to the sea below the Cidade Alta, close to the yachts and private jetties of the wealthy. The food, which ranges from Bahian *novo cuisine* to French, is superb, and there's also a trendy *Bar da Ponta* which serves drinks and less formal meals; the bar extends out into the sea on a glass-housed pier with flood-lit fishes swimming below.

Uauá Rua Gregório de Mattos 36, Pelourinho ⓣ71/3321-3089. Popular restaurant specializing in Northeastern food from both the coast and the interior, with prices on the moderate to expensive side.

Yemanjá Av. Otávio Mangabeira 4655, Pituba ⓣ71/3461-9010. Highly recommended Bahian restaurant– a far better bet than the large, overpriced restaurants at the far end of the district.

Nightlife

You'll find Salvador's most distinctive **nightlife** in **Pelourinho**. The whole area is always very lively, and there are any number of bars where you can sit and while the evening away. The Rua das Laranjeiras, Cruzeiro de São Francisco and Rua Castro Rabelo are all good places to head for, and it's local custom to start off the evening at the *O Gravinho* bar, Largo Terreiro de Jesus 03, for a glass of specially flavoured *cachaça*, the most traditional being made from essence of clove or ginger.

Bars aside, undoubtedly the biggest attraction of the area is the chance to hear **live music**. In that realm, Salvador marches to a different beat from the rest of Brazil. Instead of being connected to a single style, as Rio is to samba and Recife is to *frevo*, Salvador has spawned several, and in recent years it has overtaken Rio to become the most creative centre of Brazilian music. Some of the best music in the city comes from organized cultural groups, who work in the communities that produced them, and have their own clubhouses and an *afoxé* or two – Salvador's Africanized version of a *bloco* – for Carnaval. They are overwhelmingly black and a lot of their music is political. In the weeks leading up to Carnaval, their *afoxés* have public rehearsals around the clubhouses, and the music is superb (see "Carnaval", p.280). For the rest of the year, the clubhouses are used as bars and meeting places, often with music at weekends.

You can always catch live music in Pelourinho and every Sunday night at least one band plays for free at Terreiro de Jesus. Also, **pagode music** is frequently played at the Mercado Modelo from 6pm on Friday evenings. For an up-to-date list of events, ask at the tourist information office in Pelourinho. Many find it a bit claustrophobic in Cidade Alta and head for the **beaches** instead. For **dancing** into the small hours, Amaralina and Pituba are probably the liveliest areas to head for, and Friday and Saturday nights are best. Bars, too, often have **live music**, and listings appear in the local papers at weekends; try the Sunday edition of *A Tarde*. Check out ⓦwww.nightbahia.com.br for up-to-the-minute listings

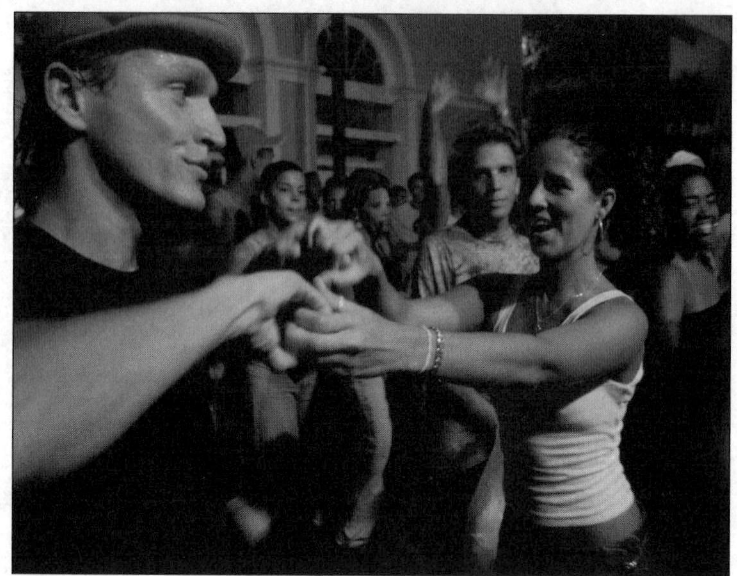

△ Nightlife in Pelourinho

for cultural events and music. As far as specific places go, *Travessia* at Av. Otávio Mangabeira 168 in Pituba (open 24hr Fri–Sun only) gets very busy, playing mostly samba, reggae or *forró*, and there's often good music, too, at *Canteiros*, Rua Minas Gerais in Pituba, starting after 9pm on Friday and Saturday.

There's more live music (mainly popular Brazilian and rock) and the chance to kick up your heels at the *Cachaçaria Alambique* **shows** in Rio Vermelho and at the *Rock in Rio Cafe*, Av. Otávio Mangabeira 6000, Boca do Rio (☎71/3461-0300). You can sample regional cuisine and folk dancing at *Solar de União* (noon–midnight), a popular restaurant and club in the former slave market, north along the seafront from the Mercado Modelo and the new marina.

Big names in Brazilian music play the Teatro Castro Alves on Campo Grande. The SENAC building on Largo do Pelourinho has an outdoor arena and basement theatre, used for plays, concerts and displays. Also scan posters and local papers (under *Lazer*) or ask at the tourist office.

Salvador also has a lively **gay scene**. *Holmes 24th* on Rua Gamboa de Cima, opposite the Rua Banco dos Ingleses, is especially hopping on Fridays (take a taxi). *Caverna*, Rua Carlos Goma 616, Centro (☎71/3358-2410), is a popular underground spot close to Salvador's best nightlife, while *New Look Bar Holme*, Rua Gamboa de Cima 24, in Gamboa (☎71/3336-4949), is a bit more laid-back. The popular *Off Club*, Rua Dias D'Avila 33 (☎71/3267-6215) is near the Farol in Barra; and there's *Beco dos Artistas*, a predominantly gay bar by the Teatro Castro Alves, on Rua Leovigildo Filgueirias (entrance beside the pizzeria).

Salvador's festivals

The two main **popular festivals** of the year, besides Carnaval, take place either in or near the Igreja do Bonfim. On New Year's Day the **Procissão no Mar**, the "Sea Procession", sees statues of the seafarers' protectors, Nosso Senhor dos Navegantes and Nossa Senhora da Conceição, carried in a decorated nineteenth-century

Candomblé

Candomblé, a popular Afro-Brazilian religious cult, permeates the city. Its followers often dress in white and worship together in ecstatic dance rituals accompanied by lots of drumming and singing, or otherwise communicate with and make offerings to the Orixás spirits, personal protectors, guides and go-betweens for people and their creator-god Olorum.

A *candomblé* cult house, or *terreiro*, is headed by a *mãe do santo* (woman) or *pai do santo* (man), who directs the operations of dozens of novices and initiates. The usual object is to persuade the **spirits** to descend into the bodies of worshippers, which is achieved by **sacrifices** (animals are killed outside public view and usually during the day), offerings of food and drink, and above all by drumming, dancing and the invocations of the *mãe* or *pai do santo*. In a central dance area, which may be decorated, devotees dance for hours to induce the trance that allows the spirits to enter them. Witnessing a possession can be quite frightening: sometimes people whoop and shudder, their eyes roll up, and they whirl around the floor, bouncing off the walls while other cult members try to make sure they come to no harm. The *mãe* or *pai do santo* then calms them, blows tobacco smoke over them, identifies the spirit, gives them the insignia of the deity – a pipe or a candle, for example – and lets them dance on. Each deity has its own songs, animals, colours, qualities, powers and holy day; and there are different types of *candomblé*, as well as other related Afro-Brazilian religions like *umbanda*.

Many travel agencies offer tours of the city that include a visit to a *terreiro*, but no self-respecting cult house would allow itself to be used in this way – those which do are to be avoided. The best alternative is to go to the main Bahiatursa office (see p.262), which has a list of less commercialized *terreiros*, all fairly far out in the suburbs and best reached by taxi. Make sure that the *terreiro* is open first: they only have ceremonies on certain days sacred to one of the pantheon of gods and goddesses, and you just have to hope you strike lucky – though fortunately there's no shortage of deities.

If you go to a *terreiro*, there are certain **rules** you must observe. A *terreiro* should be respected and treated for the church it is. Clothes should be smart and modest: long trousers and a clean shirt for men, non-revealing blouse and trousers or long skirt for women. The dancing area is a sacred space and no matter how infectious you find the rhythms you should do no more than stand or sit around its edges. And don't take photographs without asking permission from the *mãe* or *pai do santo* first, or you will give offence. You may find people coming round offering drinks from jars, or items of food: it's impolite to refuse, but watch what everyone else does first – sometimes food is not for eating but for throwing over dancers, and the story of the gringos who ate the popcorn intended as a sacred offering to the spirits is guaranteed to bring a smile to any Brazilian face.

To read more on *candomblé* as practiced in Cachoeira, see box on p.287. To make contact with *candomblé* practicioners and attend a session, either book through C&C Turismo, Rua das Portas do Carmo 28, Largo do Pelourinho (☎71/3326-6969); or, approach a *terreiro* directly. It's important to call and check times, dates and terms of access (or ask the tourist information office in Pelourinho for help in booking). Below are a list of *terreiros*:

Axé Opo Afonja Rua Direita de Sao Goncalo do Retiro 557 ☎71/3384-3321.

Ile Axé Ode Primera Travessa 1, Francisco Rubelo 35, Garcia ☎71/3361-5281.

Terreiro do Oxum Rua Helio Machado 108, Bairro Bocado Rio ☎71/3232-1460.

Tereiro de Oxossi Rua 6 de Janeiro 29 (by entrance to Escolinha Rosa Vermelho), Bairro Sete de Abril ☎71/3393-1168.

boat across the bay from the old harbour to the church of Boa Viagem, on the shore down from Bonfim. The boat leaves at around 9am from Praça Cairú, next to the Mercado Modelo in Cidade Baixa, and hundreds of schooners and fishing boats wait to join the procession as the statues' boat passes: you can buy a place on the phalanx of boats that leaves with the statues, but the crowds are thick and if you want to go by sea you should get there early. On the shores of Boa Viagem, thousands wait to greet the holy images, after which there's a packed Mass in the church, and then Nossa Senhora da Conçeicão is taken back by land in another procession to her church near the foot of the Lacerda elevator. The celebrations around both churches go on for hours, with thousands drinking and dancing the night away. The spectacle, with the bay as an enormous backdrop, is impressive enough: participating in it is exhilarating.

Soon afterwards, on the second Thursday of January, comes the **Lavagem do Bonfim**, "the washing of Bonfim", second only to Carnaval in scale. Hundreds of *baianas*, women in the traditional all-white costume of turban, lace blouse and billowing long skirts, gather in front of the Igreja de Nossa Senhora da Conceição, and a procession follows them the 12km along the seafront to the Igreja do Bonfim, with tens of thousands more lining the route: the pace is slow, and there is no shortage of beer and music while you wait. At the church, everyone sets to scrubbing the square spotless, cleaning the church and decorating the exterior with flowers and strings of coloured lights, and that evening, and every evening until Sunday, raucous celebrations go on into the wee hours, the square crowded with people. If you have the stamina, the focus switches on Monday to Ribeira, the headland beyond Bonfim, for a completely secular preview of Carnaval. Here you can freshen up after dancing in the hot sun by swimming at the excellent beaches.

Carnaval

Having steadfastly resisted commercialization, Carnaval in Salvador has remained a street event of mass participation. The main hubs of activity are **Cidade Alta**, especially the area around Praça Castro Alves – which turns into a seething mass of people that, once joined, is almost impossible to get out of – and, in recent years, **Porto da Barra**, equally crowded and just as enjoyable. The other focal point of Carnaval is the **northern beaches**, especially around the hotels in Rio Vermelho and Ondina, but here it's more touristy and lacks the energy of the centre.

From December onwards Carnaval groups hold **public rehearsals** and dances all over the city. The most famous are Grupo Cultural Oludum: they rehearse on Sunday nights from 6.30pm onwards in the Largo do Pelourinho itself and on Tuesdays from 7.30pm in the Teatro Miguel Santana on Rua Gregório de Mattos. On Friday night, it's the turn of Ara Ketu, who start their show at 7pm in Rua Chile, and Ilê Aiyê rehearse on Saturdays from 8pm near the fort of Santo Antônio Além do Carmo. These rehearsals get very crowded, so be careful with your belongings. One of the oldest and best loved of the *afoxés* is Filhos de Gandhi ("Sons of Gandhi"), founded in the 1940s, who have a clubhouse in Rua Gregório de Mattos, near Largo do Pelourinho, easily recognized by the large papier-mâché white elephant in the hall.

Information about Carnaval is published in special supplements in the local papers on Thursday and Saturday. Bahiatursa and EMTURSA offices also have schedules, route maps, and sometimes sell tickets for the Campo Grande grandstands. One point worth bearing in mind is that all-black *blocos* may be black culture groups who won't appreciate being joined by non-black Brazilians, let alone gringos, so look to see who's dancing before leaping in amongst them.

Listings

Airlines Air France, Rua Portugal 17, Ed. Regente Feijó, Cidade Baixa ⓣ21/3312-1818, ⓦwww.airfrance.com.br; British Airways ⓣ71/0300-789-7778, ⓦwww.british-airways.com; Lufthansa, Av. Tancredo Neves 805, sala 601, Iguatemi ⓣ71/4503-5000, ⓦwww.lufthansa.com.br; TAP Air Portugal, Av. Estados Unidos 137 (4th floor), Ed. Cidade de Ilhéus, Cidade Baixa ⓣ71/3243-6122, ⓦwww.tap-airportugal.com.br; Gol, airport desk ⓣ71/3204-1603; Varig, Rua Carlos Gomes 6, Cidade Alta ⓣ71/3343-3100 or 204-1050, or Rua Miguel Calmon 19, Cidade Baixa ⓣ71/243-9311; TAM, airport desk ⓣ71/3342-0123; United Airlines ⓣ71/0800-162-323, ⓦwww.ual.com.br.

Airport Aeroporto Deputado Luis Eduardo do Magalhães ⓣ71/3204-1010.

Banks and exchange Many shopping centres and banks have ATMs that accept most cards. There are several places where you can change money in the Pelourinho area, including Olímpio Turismo on Largo do Cruzeiro de São Francisco and Vert-Tour on Rua das Laranjeiras. You'll get lower, but still reasonable, rates for dollars (cash and travellers' cheques) at the smarter beach hotels in Ondina and Pituba. On no account change on the street, especially around the Lacerda elevator. Banco do Brasil has branches, all with Visa ATMs, at Av. Sete de Setembro 254 in Cidade Alta; Av. Estados Unidos 561 in Cidade Baixa; and in Shopping Barra, among many others around the city. Bahia Dourada shop at Praça da Sé 04/24, in the historic centre, offers reasonable money exchange rates in a relatively safe environment.

Boat services Bahia Scuba and Brazil Yacht Charter, Av. Do Contorno 1010, Bahia Marina (ⓦwww.byc.com.br), rent equipment and run boat trips, mainly by sail. Passeios de Veleros (ⓣ71/8156-5254) offer short sailboat trips in Baia de Todos Santos and to Itaparica and even Morro de São Paulo.

Bus services Real express for Chapada Diamantina ⓣ71/3450-9310; Aguia Branca for Porto Seguro ⓣ71/3450-5539; Itapemirim for Recife ⓣ71/3450-5644.

Car rental Avis Rentacar, Av. Sete de Setembro 1796 ⓣ71/3377-2276; Europa, Rua Osvaldo Cruz 266, Rio Vermelho ⓣ71/3335-0133; Localiza, based at airport ⓣ71/3332-1999; Nobre Rent a Car, Av. Oceânica 409 ⓣ71/3245-8022.

Consulates Canada, Av. Presidente Vargas 2400, sala 311, Ondina Apart Hotel, Ondina ⓣ71/3331-0064; Finland ⓣ71/3247-3312; Holland ⓣ71/3341-0410; UK, Av. Estados Unidos 4, 18-B 8th floor, Cidade Baixa ⓣ71/3243-7399; US, Rua Pernambuco 51, Pituba ⓣ71/3345-1545.

Diving and scuba Dive Bahia Porta da Barra 3809, on the seafront (ⓣ71/3264-3820, ⓦwww.divebahia.com.br) offers certification-level courses which take a few days for R$600 and they also rent out diving equipment. Bahia Scuba and Brazil Yacht Charter (see above) also rents out equipment.

Football Salvador has a couple of good teams. The most popular, Bahia, have a tradition of playing open, attacking football in the best Brazilian tradition. The biggest matches take place on Sunday afternoons in the Estádio Otávio Mangabeira, close to the centre; take the bus marked "Nazaré" from Campo Grande, or it's a short taxi ride.

Internet *Bahia Africa Internet Café*, Rua Gregorio Matos 32, Pelourinho; *CafeBrasil.com* at Praça da Sé 24, in the heart of the historic centre; *Groovy Dig's Cybercafe*, Av. Sete de Setembro 3713, Barra (daily 8am–midnight); *Internet Café* at Rua João de Deus 2, Pelourinho; and *Ondina Apart Hotel*, Av. Presidente Vargas 2400, Loja 37.

Language schools IDIOMA, Rua Greenfeld 46, 2nd floor, Barra ⓣ71/3267-7012; Adriana Albert ⓣ71/3321-2830, ⓔdrialbert@yahoo.com.br; Silmara Andrade ⓣ71/9934-8795, ⓔsilmara-andrade@bol.com.br.

Laundry Lavanderia Lavalimpo, Rua do Pilar 31, Cidade Baixa; O Casal Lavanderia, Rua Cesar Zama 20, Loja 1, Barra (English spoken); Lav–Lev, Av. Manoel Dias da Silva 2364, Pituba.

Post office At the airport; Marquês de Caravelas 101, Barra; Shopping Barra, 3rd floor; Av. Amaralina 908, Amaralina; Rua J. Seabra 234; the *rodoviária*; Rua Rui Barbosa 19, Cidade Alta; at the Praça da Inglaterra, Cidade Baixa. Post office open hours are Mon–Fri 8am–6pm.

Shopping The main place for *artesanato* is the Mercado Modelo in Cidade Baixa (see p.274). Good, cheap leatherwork is available from the street stalls of Barroquinha, the steep street leading downhill just before Praça Castro Alves; and clothes and shoes can be found in the commercial area further down. For luxury items, clothes, books, CDs and food, head for either Shopping Barra or Iguatemi Shopping. Projecto Axé, Rua das Laranjeiras 22, sells great, colourful clothing – the money from which goes to support street kids. For films and camera equipment, try Fotografa, Rua Chile 10; Fotosystem, Rua Chile 4; or Minilab, on the corner of Rua Chile and Rua do Tiro Chapén. For gem stones, try Agua Marina, Terreiro de Jesus 15, Pelourinho, or Kaufmann Gems at Rua Alfredo de Brito 09, Pelourinho.

Taxis Radio Taxi Cometas ⓣ71/3377-6311; Chame Táxi ⓣ71/3241-2266; Teletáxi ⓣ71/3341-9988.
Telephones You can make international collect calls from a booth on Terreiro de Jesus; other *postos telefônicos* are in the airport, the *rodoviária*, in Campo da Pôlvora in Cidade Alta, and in Iguatemi Shopping. International calls can be made direct with phone cards from almost any phone kiosk in Salvador.
Travel and tour companies Ceu e Mar Turismo, Rua Fonte do Boi 12, Rio Vermelho (ⓣ71/3334-7566, ⓕ3335-1351, ⓔceuemar@e-net.com.br), is a good travel agent and also represents the Student Travel Bureau. LR Turismo, Rua Marques de Leao 172, Barra (ⓣ71/3264-0999, ⓔlrturismo@e-net.com.br) runs several exciting tours, from historic Bahia to boat trips to the tropical islands in the Bahia de Todos os Santos. Tours Bahia, Cruzeiro de Sao Francisco 416, Pelourinho (ⓣ71/3322-4383, ⓦwww.toursbahia.com.br), are expensive but offer a range of good-quality services, covering city tours, airline tickets, transfers and money exchange. Privé Tur, Av. Sete de Setembro 2068, Vitória (ⓣ71/3338-1320, ⓦwww.privetur.com.br) organize city tours, beach trips and schooner cruises.

Around Salvador

Salvador looks onto the **Baía de Todos os Santos**, a bay ringed with beaches and dotted with tropical **islands**. To the **northeast** of the city a string of fishing villages lies along a beautiful coastline – in short, there's no lack of places to explore.

The bay: Ilha de Itaparica

Itaparica is always visible from Salvador, looking as if it forms the other side of the bay, but in reality it's a narrow island, 35km long, that acts as a natural breakwater. After the local Indians were driven out, it was taken over by the Jesuits in 1560, making it one of the earliest places to be settled by the Portuguese. Its main town, also called **ITAPARICA**, was briefly the capital of Bahia before the Portuguese were expelled from Salvador, though little evidence remains here of these times, apart from a couple of small seventeenth-century chapels. The lovely island is now very much seen as an appendage of the city, whose inhabitants flock to its beaches at weekends, building villas by the score as they go. It's quiet enough during the week, though, and big enough to find calmer spots even at the busiest times. Apart from the beaches, Itaparica is famous for its fruit trees, especially its mangoes, which are prized throughout Bahia.

Most **ferries** (see p.264) leave you at the **Bom Despacho** terminal in Itaparica town, although some boats also go to the anchorage at **Mar Grande**, a couple of kilometres away. For **getting around** once you're there, use the Kombis (minibuses) and buses that ply the coastline, or rent **bicycles** (rental places are easily spotted by the bikes piled up on the pavement). If you want to stay on the island, there are some reasonable hotels, but most are on the expensive side thanks to Itaparica's popularity as a resort for Salvador's middle classes, and cheaper ones are often full from December to Carnaval. Good options include *Club Méditerranée*, Estr. Praia da Conceição (ⓣ71/3681-8800, ⓦwww.clubmed.com.br; ❽), a luxury hotel set directly on the beachfront; *Pousada Jardim Tropical*, Estr. da Rodagem, Praia Ponta de Areia 3.5km (ⓣ71/3831-1409; ❹), with a pool and a reasonable restaurant; and the new *Pousada Canto da Praia*, Tr. do Coqueral 20, Praia de Ponta da Areia (ⓣ71/3631-4449, ⓦwww.pousadacantodapraia.com.br; ❸), on the seafront with 23 rooms and a reasonable restaurant.

To see anything of the **other islands** scattered across the bay – 31 of them, most either uninhabited or home to a few simple fishing villages – travel agents in Salvador offer day-long cruises in private schooners; the kiosks in the city's Terminal Turístico are the easiest places to buy tickets. It's less busy during the week, but crowded schooners have their advantages. If you manage to get on one full of Brazilian tourists you're likely to have a very lively time indeed, and drinks are often included in the price.

The Coconut Coast: Arembepe, Itacimirim, Praia do Forte and Imbassai

Buses from Salvador's *rodoviária* run northeast along the coastal road (Estrada do Coco or Coconut Road) to **AREMBEPE**, 50km away, a former hippy hangout now gone up in the world, though still peaceful and very pretty, with a pleasant little beach sheltered by a coral reef. The journey there takes you past some fine beaches and small, friendly villages, and you can get off wherever takes your fancy. A fifteen-minute walk from town brings you to the **Aldeia Hippie**, made famous in the 1960s when Mick Jagger and other stars enjoyed its pleasures. Here there's still a custom of cooling off in the Capivara River in the late afternoons. Arembepe lies on a well-beaten tourist track, but don't be put off by this – it's a beautiful coastline and the beaches are long enough to swallow the crowds. There are plenty of **places to stay** in Arembepe itself or close by: basic options on the seafront include the *Praia de Arembepe Hotel*, Largo São Francisco (Ⓣ71/3624-1415; ❷), and the *Pousada Enseada do Cabral* (Ⓣ71/3624-1231; ❸), the latter with a restaurant. The *Pousada Gispy* (Ⓣ71/3624-3266, Ⓦwww.pousadagipsy.com.br; ❹), Rua Eduardo Pinto (Lot. Volta da Robalo), some 3km from the centre, has a pool and restaurant. More upmarket are the beachfront *Pousada Ondas do Mar* (Ⓣ71/3624-1052; ❺), a comfortable place overlooking the harbour, and the good-value *O Turbarão Hotel*, Rua Manoel Coelho (Ⓣ71/3624-1055; ❹), which has a pool, and rooms and apartments facing the beach. For **food**, the main *praça* has some options, but for cold beer and the best seafood in town head for the *Restaurant Coló*, which features a shaded terrace on the beach; try the *peixes moqueca* or the *lagosta salada* (lobster salad). Close to the harbour, the small seafood **market**, Mercado do Frutas Mar (Mon–Sat mornings), sells delicious-looking *lagosta* and *carangueijo* (crab).

Fifteen kilometres further northeast, the beach resort of **Itacimirim** is not as developed as many, though there are a few hotels and lots of smart weekend residences. Out of high season and during the week, you can have this palm-fringed paradise with several natural pools to swim in, more or less to yourself. If you want **to stay** over, the *Hotel Itacimirim* (Ⓣ71/3626-1304, Ⓕ826-1503; ❸) is right on the beach, while nearby, set back from the sands, there's the modern and less characterful *Hotel Beira Mar* (Ⓣ71/3626-1217; ❸), which has a small pool, a bar and plain but nice rooms, some with ocean views. More comfortable and also with a pool, the *Pousada Mar de Luz*, Rua Praia da Espera 7 (Ⓣ71/3626-1622; ❺), has pleasant, well-appointed apartments.

A little further up the road, the hip little resort of **PRAIA DO FORTE**, 83km north of Salvador, has a couple of exceptionally nice, if small, beaches, lots of arty craft shops and some good restaurants, but is best known for the Projecto Tamar **turtle reserve** (daily 8am–7pm; R$4). Of the seven species of sea turtle in the world, four nest off the coast of Bahia, but over-fishing and the destruction of nesting sites by human activity and urban development have seriously threatened their survival. The work of the Projecto Tamar (Ⓣ71/3676-1403 or 3676-1045, Ⓦwww.projetotamar.org.br; open for visits daily 9am–6pm; R$7) has included identifying the turtles' main nesting areas along a 1000-kilometre stretch of coastline and ensuring their protection. The local community at Praia do Forte was mainly a fishing village until ecotourism and the turtle project arrived in the mid-1990s; today most of the 2000 residents make their income from tourism. The beaches and turtle reserve are at the end of the main drag, beyond all the craft shops and stalls. Inside the reserve, you can see many turtles in large aquariums, most of them injured and unlikely to survive in the wild. The nesting season is from September to March.

You'll find several good options if you want **to stay** in Praia do Forte: the *Pousada do Forte*, Almeda do Sol 4 (ⓣ71/3676-1043; ❹), offers great-value rooms and a small pool, and is on the main sandy drag, while the *Pousada Ogum Marinho* (ⓣ71/3676-1165; ❺), close to the beach at the end of the main street, Avenida ACM, has cosy rooms and a nice hammock verandah. The *Do Souza*, on the first corner of the main street as you come into town, is a popular seafood **restaurant**, its terrace shaded by a massive angelin tree. There's a small sushi bar on one of the side streets, too, and an ice-cream parlour, the *Tutti Frutti*, nearby.

At the entrance to the town itself, you'll spot a **tourist information** kiosk (ⓣ71/3676-1091) standing alone on a small grassy mound. **Buses** leave regularly (4 daily) from the main street for Salvador and for further north up the coast to Imbassai. For general tourist information and photos of the area, check out ⓦwww.praiadoforte.org.br.

Increasingly popular alternatives to Arembepe and Prai do Forte are the beautiful palm-fringed beaches just 16km further north around **IMBASSAÍ**; they tend to be less busy, making it easier to find cheaper accommodation. The *Pousada Canto de Imbassaí* (ⓣ71/3677-1082, ⓦwww.cantodeimbassai.cjb.net; ❹) sits on the beach itself and has a pool and air-conditioning in all rooms. The *Pousada Agua Marina*) is more expensive but also more comfortable with bar, restaurant and pool; they also have horses to hire. Horse riding along the beach or inland towards the *mata* is a good way to explore the area; Jones Vianna (ⓣ71/3677-1111, ⓔjonesvianna@hotmail.com) is passionate about the local flora and fauna and offers an excellent horse-riding service as well as riding lessons. For eating, you'll find good seafood and even French crêpes at the *Ilha do Dende* beside the Praia Imbassaí. The *Micasa Bar* (ⓣ71/3677-1303), on the Rua das Amendoeiras, has drinks, snacks and cool music.

For an even sleepier place to stay, there are camping and *pousada* options at the village of **Diogo**. A relatively new *Pousada Too Cool na Bahia* (ⓣ71/9952-2190, ⓦwww.toocoolnabahia.com, ⓔinfo@toocoolnabahia.com; ❹–❺) offers stylish and comfortable chalet accommodation, hearty breakfasts and the chance to swing in hammocks, relax under the shade of mango trees and canoe along the river. Heading north from Imbassaí along the Linha Verde road towards Aracaju, Diogo is accessed by a right-turn side road that turns into track by the time it reaches the village. From the village, a track crosses the river and leads through some attractive dunes before reaching a massive, usually empty, beach. The nearby fishing village of **Santo Tomas** has a few bars and rustic eating spots, or, better still, head for the *barracas* on the beach, which serve fresh fish and chilled drinks.

The Recôncavo and Valença

The **Recôncavo**, the early Portuguese plantation zone named after the concave shape of the bay, arcs out from Salvador along 150km of coastline, before petering out in the mangrove swamps around the town of **Valença**. It's one of the most lush tropical coastlines in Brazil, with palm-covered hills breaking up the green and fertile coastal plains. And it's still one of the most important agricultural areas in Bahia, supplying the state with much of its fruit and spices. Only the sugar plantations around Recife could match the wealth of the Recôncavo, but, unlike that region, the Recôncavo survived the decline of the sugar trade by diversifying into tobacco and spices – especially peppers and cloves. It was

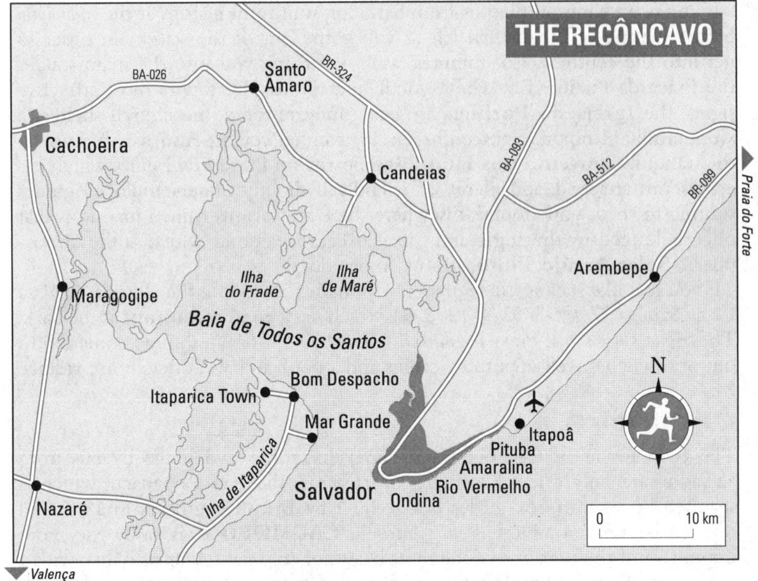

the agricultural wealth of the Recôncavo that paid for most of the fine buildings of Salvador and, until the cocoa boom in southern Bahia in the 1920s, **Cachoeira** was considered the second city of the state. The beauty of the area and the richness of its colonial heritage make it one of the more rewarding parts of the region to explore.

Access is good, with the main highway, the BR-324, approximately following the curve of the bay, and good local roads branching off to the towns in the heart of the Recôncavo. Thirty kilometres out of Salvador, a turn-off leads to Candéias, continuing on to Santo Amaro and the twin towns of Cachoeira and São Félix. Regular buses go to all these places from the *rodoviária* in Salvador.

Candéias and Santo Amaro

CANDÉIAS is nowhere special, a modern market town 30km from Salvador, but 7km outside there's a good introduction to the history of the area in the **Museu do Recôncavo** (Tues, Thurs & Sun 9am–5pm), situated in a restored plantation called the Engenho da Freguesia, where pictures and artefacts from three centuries illustrate the economic and social dimensions of plantation life. The owners' mansion and the slave quarters have been impressively restored, juxtaposing the horrors of slave life – there's a fearsome array of manacles, whips and iron collars – with the elegant period furniture and fittings of the mansion. The only problem is that no bus service passes the museum: if you don't go by car you have to take a taxi from Candéias, around R$35.

SANTO AMARO, a further 20km from Salvador, is a lovely colonial town straddling the banks of a small river. It was the birthplace and is still the home of Caetano Veloso, one of Bahia's most famous singers and poets, who sings Santo Amaro's praises on many of his records. There's no tourist office, and the best thing to do is simply to wander around the quiet streets and squares, absorbing the atmosphere.

If you're arriving on the bus from Salvador, wait until it stops at the *rodoviária* before getting off, then turn left as you come out of the station in order to get into the centre. A few minutes' walk will bring you into the main square, the Praça da Purificação, where you'll find one of the town's most attractive sights, the **Igreja da Purificação**: beautifully restored, the church shelters a wonderfully elaborate eighteenth-century painted ceiling. Also worth a visit is the tranquil **Convento dos Humildes**, nearby on Praça Frei Bento, which has a museum attached, and plenty of friendly if slightly under-employed guides waiting to show you around. Elsewhere there are various ruined mansions that once belonged to the sugar and tobacco barons, among which is the atmospheric **Solar Araújo Pinto**, at Rua Imperador 1.

If you feel like staying, there are a few **pensões**, including the *Amarós*, on Rua Cons. Saraiva 27 (Ⓣ75/3241-1202; ❷), which has a good **restaurant** at the back. The *Agua Viva Praia*, Praia Fazenda (Ⓣ75/3699-1176; ❹), though some 34km out of town, has well-appointed cabins and a pool, and also offers horse riding.

Cachoeira

The twin towns of Cachoeira and São Félix, some two hours by bus from Salvador, are only a few kilometres apart across the Rio Paraguaçu, which is spanned by an iron box-girder bridge built by British engineers in 1885 and opened by Emperor Dom Pedro himself. **CACHOEIRA** is easily the more impressive of the two, one of the most beautiful colonial towns of Bahia, with a profusion of fine old buildings as evidence of its importance in the eighteenth century. Close to the bus station there is a large and colourful open air market (closed on Sunday) selling a wide variety of local produce including some crafts. The rich sugar plantations of the **Paraguaçu Valley** supported a trading centre that rivalled Salvador in size and wealth until the beginning of the nineteenth century. The town was the site of a short but vicious war in 1822 to expel the Portuguese from Bahia, when a docked Portuguese warship was stormed by the inhabitants, the city becoming the first in Brazil to declare allegiance to Dom Pedro I. The Portuguese general, Madeira de Melo, bombarded the town in retaliation, but this only provoked the countryside into general revolt, and troops from Cachoeira led a victorious assault on Salvador. After that began the long decline that turned it into the splendidly preserved small town it is today.

The Town

Get off the bus in Rua Lauro de Freitas at the bus company office; don't wait until it crosses the river into São Félix or you'll have to walk back across the bridge. A couple of blocks back along Rua Lauro de Freitas past the market you'll come to the fine Praça Doutor Milton, with its Baroque public fountain and the early eighteenth-century bulk of the **Santa Casa da Misericórdia**, which has a beautiful small garden. Leaving Praça Doutor Milton in the direction of the river, go up the narrow, cobbled Rua da Ajuda, and after a short climb you'll come to a peaceful little square that contains the **Capela de Nossa Senhora da Ajuda**, the city's oldest church. Begun in 1595 and completed eleven years later, it just about qualifies as sixteenth century, which makes it a rarity. Sadly, the simple but well-proportioned interior is often closed to visitors for fear of thieves, but if you knock on the door there might be someone around to let you in.

If you go straight on down the hill as you come out of the Capela de Nossa Senhora da Ajuda, you'll find yourself in Rua 13 de Maio. On your right is the **Museu da Irmandade da Boa Morte**, which is connected with the August festival known as Nossa Senhora da Boa Morte (see box, opposite). Just a few

Candomblé in Cachoeira

Cachoeira is known for its **candomblé**, with some *terreiros* still conducting rituals in African dialects that nobody now speaks, recognizable as variants of West African and Angolan languages. One of the best-known *candomblé* events is Cachoeira's fiesta of **Nossa Senhora da Boa Morte**, which always begins on the first Friday before August 15. It's staged by a sisterhood, the Irmandade da Boa Morte, founded by freed women slaves in the mid-nineteenth century, partly as a religious group and partly to work for the emancipation of slaves by acting as an early cooperative bank to buy people their liberty. All the local *candomblé* groups turn out with drummers and singers, and although the name of the fiesta is Catholic it's a celebration of *candomblé*, with centre stage held by the dignified matriarchs of the sisterhood. The other great day in the *candomblé* year is the **Festa de Santa Barbara**, on December 4 in São Félix, dedicated to the goddess Iansã. There are several other fiestas worth catching, like the **São João** celebrations, from June 22 to 24, while five saints' days are crammed into the last three months of the year; check with Bahiatursa for exact dates (see p.262).

steps in the other direction sits a renovated building that houses the small **Museu Hansen Bahia**, dedicated to the work of a German engraver who settled in the town. There's a lively tradition of **woodcarving** in Cachoeira and several sculptors have studios open to the public. One of the best is **Louco Junior**, who displays his wonderful elongated carvings in his studio on Rua 13 de Maio. The first turning on your left out of Rua 13 de Maio takes you up to Rua Ana Néri and the impressive **Igreja Matriz de Nossa Senhora do Rosário**. Again, the church has been robbed all too frequently and is sometimes shut, but if you can get in you'll see two huge five-metre-high *azulejo* panels dating from the 1750s.

At the end of Rua Ana Néri, in the opposite direction from Praça Doutor Milton, is the finest and most spacious square in the town, **Praça da Aclamação**. On one side, it's lined with civil buildings from the golden age of Cachoeira in the eighteenth century, including the Prefeitura and the old city chambers. The other side of the square is dominated by the huge bulk of the **Conjunto do Carmo**, built in the eighteenth century and now beautifully restored, in four parts: a church, a museum, a *pousada* and a conference centre. The museum contains rare seventeenth-century furniture and some fine sacred art, including carvings and statues from Macau that bring an unexpectedly Chinese flavour to the collection. The cloister leads to the church, decorated with seventeenth-century tiles and an extravagant Rococo gold-leaf interior.

On the stretch of waterfront nearest the old centre is Praça Teixeira de Freitas, from where you can take a launch out to the Ilha do Farol in the river, and over to **SÃO FÉLIX**. The main reason for going is the great view back across the river, with the colonial facades reflected in the water.

Practicalities

Cachoeira has no *rodoviária*, just an office by the bus stop in Rua Lauro de Freitas. There's a **Bahiatursa** office in Praça da Aclamação (☎75/3425-1214), where you can get a map and some basic information. The nicest **place to stay** is the *Pousada do Convento de Cachoeira* (☎75/3425-1716; ❸), which is part of the Conjunto do Carmo on Praça da Aclamação and has a pool, an attractive patio and a bar. Other options include the simple *Hotel Colombo*, at Rua Sete de Setembro 19 (no phone; ❶); the *Hotel Santo Antônio* on Praça Maciel (☎75/3251-1402; ❶), which is handy for the bus station but noisy at times; and the friendly, no-frills *Pousada do Guerreiro*, at Rua 13 de Maio 14 (☎75/3215-1104; ❷). There's also the excellent-value *Pousada do Pai Thomaz*, at Rua 25 de Junho 12 (☎75/3215-1288; ❹), with spotless rooms. For fantastic regional dishes head for the *Restaurant Gruta Azul*, Praça Manuel Vitorino 2 (daily 11am–6pm).

Valença and around

After Cachoeira, the coast becomes swampy and by the time you get to **VALENÇA** you're in mangrove country. Fortunately, though, instead of alligators, the swamps are dominated by shellfish of all kinds, most of them edible. Valença lies on the banks of the Rio Una, about 10km from the sea, at the point where the river widens into a delta made up of dozens of small islands, most of which support at least a couple of fishing villages. At one time the town was an industrial centre – the first cotton factory in Brazil was built here – but it has long since reverted to fishing and boat building. Today, it's also an increasingly popular destination for tourists from Salvador, mainly as a stop-off point for the nearby island resort of Morro de São Paulo (see opposite), but the town is not yet over-commercialized.

The Town

Valença's **rodoviária** is close to the centre of town, which is just a few blocks' walk away along the riverside towards the market. There are a couple of colonial churches – the most interesting is the Igreja de Nossa Senhora do Amparo, built in 1757 on a hill affording beautiful views over the city and accessed from near the market. Valença is mostly the connection point for **Morro de São Paulo** and **Boipeba** islands (see p.290) or a place for walks, boat trips and lazing on beaches rather than sightseeing. By far the most absorbing thing the town has to offer is its **boatyards**, the *estaleiros*; follow the river 500m downstream from the central Praça Admar Braga Guimarães. They produce a whole series of wooden boats here, largely by hand, ranging from small fishing smacks to large schooners, and local boat builders are renowned throughout the the state for their skill. Provided you don't get in the way – try going around midday, when work stops for a couple of hours – and ask permission, people are pleased to let you take a closer look and often take pride in showing off their work.

Practicalities

Accommodation is easy to find. There are several hotels and *pensões*: the *Hotel Tourist* at Rua Marechal Floriano 167 (❷) and the *Guaibim* on Praça da Independência (☎75/3641-1110; ❸) are welcoming and good value; the *Hotel do Porto* at Av. Maconica 50 (☎75/3641-2383; ❸) offers attractive rooms and spectacular views, while the *Portal Rio Una* on Rua Maestro Barrinha (☎75/3641-2383; ❺) is a more luxurious option. If you're on a tight budget, the rented hammock space at Prainha on the island of Tinharé (see p.290) costs next to nothing.

Many visitors choose to stay out of town at the beach resort of **Guaibim**, just 20 minutes' drive from Valença near the international airport. Of these, the *Aguas do Guaibim*, on Avenida Taquary (☎75/3482-1047, Ⓦwww.aguasdoguaibim.tur.br; ❸) is hard to top, with its attractive apartments, pool and beach access; there's also the *Royal Praia Hotel* on the same road (☎75/3482-1131; ❸), with stylish if slightly down-at-heel rooms and a beachside pool. Slightly cheaper is the *Taquary Hotel*, a pleasant, relatively isolated complex, with a small pool and recreation room, at the very end of Avenida Taquay, block 22 (☎75/3482-1144, Ⓦwww.taquary.com.br; ❸–❹).

The **restaurants** in town are simple and reasonably priced, and serve excellent food; the combination of fresh seafood and palm oil is definitely a treat.

Valença is famous for its *dendê* – indeed, this stretch of coastline is known as the Dende Coast. Try the seafood *rodizio* (where you pay a flat fee and have all you can eat) at the *Akuarius*, on Praça da Independência, or a plate of *moqueca* at the *Bar Kardy*, on Rua Governador Gonçalves, which has the added attraction of live music. On the relaxed Praça da República, the *Skinas Bar* is a good option for drinking or munching and, opposite, there's the very cheap *Casa do Bolo,* fine for set lunch menus. You'll find other good spots on the north side of the river, along a well-lit promenade with plenty of *barracas*, bars and restaurants, and a laid-back atmosphere on most evenings.

Tourist information is available from an office in the old Prefeitura building, Rua Comendador Madureira 10 (ⓣ75/3641-3311), facing the river by the Praça Admar Braga Guimarães. The best place to **change money** is the Banco do Brasil on Calle Calçado, the main pedestrianized street in the old centre. A good way of getting around the town is by **bicycle**. You can rent them cheaply all over the place: look out for signs saying "Aluga-sebicicleta".

From Valença five daily **buses** head back to Salvador, and the trip takes around five hours. Alternatively, you can travel to Salvador via Nazaré and Itaparica, thereby reducing the journey by 150km; Excursões e Turismo, on the Praça da República (ⓣ75/3741-5305), sell combined ferry-Kombi tickets that cut the journey time by a couple of hours.

Morro de São Paulo

The obvious place to head for around Valença is the island of **Tinharé** and its famous beaches at **MORRO DE SÃO PAULO**, where there's always a great atmosphere, with reggae bars, hippy dives and great seafood restaurants. With no roads on the island, it's still relatively peaceful and undeveloped, though at the weekends, especially between December and March, Morro de São Paulo can get unbearably crowded.

Several **boats** a day travel from Valença to Tinharé (more than one an hour generally); they cost about R$7 and take ninety minutes to get there. There's also a quicker and more expensive *lancha rapida*, which takes thirty to forty minutes and costs around R$20. In high season a direct boat leaves from the Terminal Turístico in Salvador (it's also worth enquiring about it in low season, as the boat may operate on certain days then, too). It costs about R$70 for a one-way trip and takes about three hours, but the sea can be rough. There's also the occasional catamaran (R$125; 1hr).

The small settlement of Morro de São Paulo sits on a hill between the port and the first of the beaches, Primeira Praia. If you don't mind being a few minutes' walk from the beach, it's a pleasant place to stay, close to the shops and restaurants. There's little of interest in town, apart from an atmospheric old fort overlooking the harbour, with a rusting canon and a Moorish-looking gun turret still standing on its crumbling battlements. To get here, follow the coastal path (clockwise round the island).

For **accommodation**, the *Pousada Natureza*, at the top of the steps leading to the pier (ⓣ75/3652-1361, ⓕ3652-1044, ⓦwww.hotelnatureza.com; ❹), has lovely rooms with hammock verandahs, some apartments with Jacuzzis, a patio bar set in attractive gardens and a pool. Other good options are the *O Casarão* (ⓣ75/3652-1049, ⓕ3652-1022, ⓦwww.ocasarao.net; ❹) at Praça Aureliano Lima 190, which offers apartments and chalets plus a little pool, and the more modest but excellent-value *Porto da Cima* (❸).

The *Pizzaria Forno a Lenha* on Praça Aureliano is a good **restaurant** and one of the best places to meet people in the evenings and find out where the parties are happening. More restaurants and ice-cream parlours line the track from the square down to Primeira Praia, where *Restaurante Da Dona Elda* (ⓣ75/3652-1041) serves excellent seafood dishes, such as delicious *moqueca de peixe* and *bobó de camarão*, on their airy upstairs patio; there are also several shops and **tour agents** offering **money exchange** and **Internet access** along this stretch; one of the best is Marlins Viagems e Turismo (ⓣ75/3652-1242). The **tourist information office** is on Praça Aureliano Lima (ⓣ75/3652-1104 and 3652-1083, ⓦwww.morrosp.com.br), a short walk from the dock.

The beaches

Four main beaches line the populated corner of the island, all linked by paths. The **Primeira Praia** has the best range of accommodation, but isn't the nicest of the beaches and you'd be better off heading five minutes further south round the island to **Segunda Praia**, which is the most popular with the in-crowd from São Paulo and Salvador and has the best swimming and snorkelling. The *Villa das Pedras Pousada* (ⓣ75/3652-1075, ⓕ3652-1122, ⓦwww.villadaspedras.com.br; ❺) is a good option here, with its own beachside pool. **Terceira Praia** is narrow but pleasant, more laid-back than Segunda Praia, with wooden shack bars along the lapping edge of the ocean when the tide is in. Here you'll find the plush *Villegaignon Resort* (ⓣ75/3652-1010, ⓕ3652-1012; ❻); the reasonable *Pousada Tia Lita* (ⓣ75/3652-1532, ⓦwww.pousadatialita.com.br; ❷), with views in some of the rooms; and the cheapest option, *Camping Natureza*, where you can put up a tent and stay for less than R$7 per person. **Quarta Praia** is the least developed of the beaches, long and quite glorious, and has some of the island's best restaurants. Right on the beach sits the *Pousada Catavento Praia* (ⓣ75/3652-1052, ⓦwww.pousadacatavento.com.br; ❸), with twelve apartments and a bar and restaurant.

On the opposite side of the small island, 15km away, is the hamlet of **Prainha**. Here you'll find the **Casa da Sogra**, home of a local poet and sculptor who has papered the walls with his poems and decorative painted maps of the region. There are no hotels here but, if you want **to stay** for a few days of idyllic tranquillity, the locals – mainly fishing families – rent out hammock space: there is little except grilled fish and shellfish to eat, but it's a lifestyle you could easily get used to. At least one boat from Morro calls every day.

You'll find good **diving** in the clear waters surrounding the island; Companhia do Mergulho, Primeira Praia (ⓣ75/3652-1200, ⓦwww.ciamergulho.terra.com.br) offer scuba trips for certified divers both day and night (R$100 per day) and also a six-day scuba course for beginners (R$500).

Ilha de Boipeba

The beaches on the island of **BOIPEBA**, separated from the Ilha de Tinharé by the Rio do Inferno, are even more beautiful than those at Morro de São Paulo, but much less developed, still possessing the tranquillity that Morro hasn't seen for over fifteen years. The settlement here is small and scattered across the island, with few facilities – just a couple of restaurants and a handful of *pousadas*. The beaches are simply gorgeous, and there's good scuba diving at the coral reefs near the Ponta da Castelhauos at the southernmost point of the island.

For **accommodation**, the excellent ★ *Pousada Luar das Aguas* on the beach (ⓣ75/3653-6015, mobile ⓣ9981-1012, ⓕ3653-3373, ⓔluardasaguas@neth.com.br; ❹) has attractive bungalows with hammock verandahs and a palm-thatched circular beach restaurant that serves some of the best seafood south of Fortaleza. The *Pousada do Outeiro*, Praia Tassimirim (ⓣ & ⓕ75/3653-1535; ❹), is another good place to stay, with ten beachfront apartments. The *Pousada e Restaurante Santa Clara* (ⓣ75/3653-6085, ⓔchasbras@terra.com.br; ❹) is famed for its good Bahian cooking. There's also a **campsite** at the Kioska Ponto do Almendeira, between the port and the beach restaurants.

Boats run to Boipeba from Valença (3hr 30min; R$40), and from Segunda Praia on the Ilha de Tinharé (2hr; R$25). You can save some time by renting a speedboat (for 4–5 people) to take you between Boipeba and Morro de São Paulo for around R$200. On the island it's possible to arrange **outdoor activities** through your *pousada*, including canoeing in the mangrove swamps, spotting wildlife in the coastal woodlands and horse riding on the beach as well as surfing and diving.

Inland: the Bahian sertão

The **Bahian sertão** is immense: an area considerably larger than any European country and constituting most of the land area of Bahia state. Much of it is semi-desert, endless expanses of rock and cactus broiling in the sun. But it can be spectacular, with ranges of hills to the north and broken highlands to the west, rearing up into the tableland of the great **Planalto Central**, the plateau that extends over most of the state of Goiás and parts of Minas Gerais. No part of the Bahian *sertão* is thickly populated, and most of it is positively hostile to human habitation: in some places, no rain falls for years at a stretch. Its inhabitants suffer more from drought than anywhere else in the region and in parts of the *sertão* there's still desperate poverty.

Despite its reputation, not all the *sertão* is desert. Winding through it, like an enormous snake, is the **Rio São Francisco**, sprawling out into the huge hydroelectric reservoir of **Sobradinho**. River and lake support a string of towns, notably Paulo Afonso and Juazeiro. Other possible destinations to the north are **Jacobina**, in the midst of spectacular hill country, where gold and emeralds have been mined for nearly three centuries, and **Canudos**, site of a mini civil war a hundred years ago, and a good place to get a feel for *sertão* life. By far the most popular route into the *sertão,* though, is westwards along the BR-242, which eventually hits the Belém–Brasília highway in Goiás: en route you'll pass the old mining town of **Lençóis**, gateway to the breathtaking natural wonders of the Chapada Diamantina – one of Brazil's best and most accessible trekking areas.

Travelling in the sertão requires some preparation, as the interior is not geared to tourism. Hotels are fewer and dirtier; buses are less frequent, and you often have to rely on country services that leave very early in the morning and seem to stop every few hundred yards. A **hammock** is essential, as it's the coolest and most comfortable way to sleep, much better than the grimy beds in inland hotels, all of which have hammock hooks set into the walls as a standard fitting. The towns are much smaller here than on the coast, and in most places there's little to do in the evening, as the population turns in early to be up for work at dawn. Far more people carry arms than on the coast, but in fact the *sertão* is one of the safest areas of Brazil for travellers – the guns are mainly used on animals, especially small birds, which are massacred on an enormous scale. Avoid tap **water** and stick to bottled: dysentery is common, and although not dangerous these days it's extremely unpleasant.

Don't let these considerations put you off, however. People in the *sertão* are intrigued by gringos and are invariably very friendly. And while few *sertão* towns may have much to offer in terms of excitement or entertainment, the surrounding landscape is spectacular.

Jacobina

It's difficult to miss Feira de Santana – a flat, dull and faceless major market town that mainly deals in automotive parts these days. After Feira de Santana, however, the BR-324 strikes into the interior proper. While the scenery is dull for the first couple of hours, the road then climbs into the highlands of the **Chapada Diamantina**, with rock massifs rising out of the scrub, vaguely reminiscent of the American Southwest. At the small town of Capim Grosso the BR-407 branches off on a 300-kilometre journey north to Juazeiro, but sticking with the BR-324 for another hour brings you to the old mining town of **JACOBINA**. It nestles on the slopes of several hills with panoramic views over the **Serra da Jacobina**, one of the first parts of the *sertão* to be settled in strength by the Portuguese. The clue to what attracted them is the name of one of the two fast-flowing rivers that bisect the town, the Rio de Ouro, "Gold River". **Gold** was first found here in the early seventeenth century, and several *bandeirante* expeditions made the trip north from São Paulo to settle here. Although cattle and farming are now more important, mining still continues: there are emerald mines at nearby Pindobaçu, two large gold mines, and the diamonds that gave the Chapada Diamantina its name. The last big rush was in 1948, but miners still come down from the hills every now and then to sell gold and precious stones to traders in the town – you'll notice that many of them have precision scales on their counters.

The **town** itself is notably friendly – they don't see many tourists and people are curious – while the altitude takes the edge off the temperature most days, which makes it a good place to walk. It's a typical example of an interior town, quiet at night save for the squares and the riverbanks, where the young congregate, especially around the *Zululândia* bar in the centre, while their parents pull chairs into the streets and gossip until the TV soaps start. In all directions, **paths** lead out of town into the surrounding hills, with spectacular views, but it still gets hot during the day and some of the slopes are steep, so it's best to take water along. The *Hotel Serra do Ouro* runs trips (around R$50 per person) out to the **emerald mines** of Pindobaçu, around 60km to the north, and to the **gold mines** of Canavieiras and Itapicuru, though these are a bit disappointing in some respects: to the untrained eye uncut emeralds look like bits of gravel.

Practicalities

It's about a six-hour ride to Jacobina on the two daily **buses** from Salvador. There's no tourist office, although you might be able to get hold of a pamphlet with a street map from Bahiatursa in Salvador (see p.262). Still, it's small enough to get by without one. The bus leaves you near the centre, where there are several cheap **hotels** and *pensões*. The best, the *Hotel Serra do Ouro* (Ⓣ74/3621-3324, Ⓦwww.newnet.com.br/serradoouro; ❸), is on the outskirts, built on a hillside with a magnificent view of the town. A cheaper, though less attractive, option is the *Jacobina Palace Hotel*, Rua Manoel Navares 210 (Ⓣ74/3621-2600; ❷).

Jacobina is a good place for getting acquainted with the **food** of the interior: *carne do sol com pirão de leite* is rehydrated dried meat with a delicious milk-based sauce; *bode assado* is roast goat, surprisingly tender when done well; and *buchada*, a spicy kind of haggis made from intestines, is much nicer than it sounds but not for delicate stomachs. Good **restaurants** are *Carlito's*, on the banks of the Rio Ouro, and the *Cheguei Primeiro*, which only serves *caça* (game): the best dish is *tatu*, armadillo, which has a tender white flesh that tastes vaguely like pork. You should also try *doce de buriti*, a tangy, acidic-tasting paste made from the fruit of the buriti palm; it's sold in neat boxes made from the wood of the palm, which keep it fresh almost indefinitely. The favoured restaurant with locals is the *Rancho Catarinense*, at Av. N.S. da Conceição 1188, which specializes in meat. For **nightlife**, check out *Status*, a *dancetaria* on the slopes of the Serra da Caixa above the town, only accessible by taxi and worth checking out on Friday and Saturday nights.

Canudos

A different route north from Feira de Santana along the bumpy BR-116 takes you to **CANUDOS**, site of Antônio Conselheiro's rebellion in the 1890s (see box, below). The main reason for coming here is to get a taste of these remarkable events, but it's also a chance to sample the atmosphere of a typical small town in the *sertão*, where life is still dominated by the all-important question of rain or the lack of it. Despite the obvious poverty, it's a rewarding place to visit: everything centres on the main square, with weather-beaten *sertanejos* trudging around during the day, and the local youngsters taking over at night. If you've come from a big city, you'll certainly notice the sense of isolation provided by the *caatinga* all around.

You have to leave the town if you want to visit the **site of the Canudos war**. The valley where it all happened was flooded by a dam in the 1960s and the new Canudos is the result of a shift a few miles down the road. There is a bus that will drop you at the battlefield (ask for "Velho Canudos"), but you'll have to wait a long time to be picked up again so it may be better to arrange your own transport if you can find someone to take you. Alternatively, you could walk it in a couple of hours, but it can get very hot and you should take plenty of sun protection. When you get to the edge of the valley you'll see a few houses, a statue of Antônio Conselheiro and a small museum, which is usually closed. More interesting is the valley itself, where the water has sunk to such a low level that you can now see the tops of trees and houses that may have formed part of the original Canudos. It's incredible to think that this valley was once a place that was thought to threaten the future of the Brazilian Republic.

Antônio Conselheiro's rebellion

The Bahian *sertão* provided the backdrop for one of the most remarkable events in Brazilian history, the **rebellion** of the messianic religious leader **Antônio Conselheiro**, who gathered thousands of followers, built a city called Canudos, and declared war on the young republic in 1895 for imposing new taxes on an already starving population. The rebels held out for two years. The forces sent confidently north from Salvador were terribly mauled by the *sertanistas*, who proved to be great guerrilla fighters, with an intimate knowledge of the harsh country which the city troops found as intimidating as their human enemies. Twice military columns were beaten, and then a third force of over a thousand troops commanded by a national hero, a general in the Paraguayan war, was sent against the rebels. In the worst shock the young republic had suffered up to that point, the force was completely annihilated: the next expedition discovered the bleached skulls of the general and his staff laid out in a neat row in front of a thorn tree. Not until 1897, when a fourth expedition was sent, did Canudos fall, and almost all of its defenders were killed; Antônio Conselheiro himself had died of fever a few weeks before the end. One member of the force, **Euclides da Cunha**, immortalized the war in his book *Os Sertões*, generally recognized as the greatest Portuguese prose ever written by a Brazilian – it was translated into English as "Rebellion in the Backlands". It's a good introduction to the Bahian *sertão*, but a more entertaining read is *The War of the End of the World* by the Peruvian novelist Mario Vargas Llosa (see "Books", p.847), which gives a haunting fictionalized account of the incredible events in Canudos.

Back in the new Canudos, there are two or three **places to stay**: *Grapiuna* on Praça Monsenhor Berenguer (Ⓣ75/3275-1157; ❸) is a good bet. **Transport** there and away is also not a problem: there's a daily bus to Salvador and another daily service to Juazeiro, on the border with Pernambuco. The **food** isn't great: the local speciality is *bode assado*, roast goat, which is not particularly popular with outsiders, and there's a distinct lack of fresh fruit and vegetables. But there are plenty of biscuits in the shops, so you won't starve.

The Chapada Diamantina

The route **west** into the *sertão* is along the BR-242, which skirts Feira de Santana and swings south, where a turn-off signposted to Brasília heads inland, into the heart of the *sertão*. The scenery is remarkably similar to that along the Jacobina road 200km to the north: you're still in the tablelands of the Chapada Diamantina, with its rock spurs and mesas forming an enormous chain of foothills to the Planalto Central.

Lençóis

Five hours' ride down the BR-242, **LENÇÓIS** is another mining town and the main tourist centre in the Chapada Diamantina. The name of the town, meaning "sheets", derives from the camp that grew up around a diamond strike in 1844. The miners, too poor to afford tents, made do with sheets draped over branches. Lençóis is a pretty little town, set in the midst of the spectacular Parque Nacional da Chapada Diamantina (see opposite). Most of its fine old buildings date back to the second half of the nineteenth century, when the town was a prosperous mining community, attracting diamond buyers from as far afield as Europe. The **Mercado Municipal**, next to the bridge over the Rio Lençóis that runs through the centre, is where most of the diamonds were sold – it has Italian- and French-style trimmings tacked on to make the buyers feel at home. The centre of the town, between two lovely squares, Praça Otaviano Alves and Praça Horácio de Matos, is made up of cobbled streets, lined with well-proportioned two-storey nineteenth-century houses with high, arched windows. On Praça Horácio, the **Subconsulado Francês**, once the French consulate, was built with the money of the European diamond buyers, who wanted an office to take care of export certificates. **Tourist information** is available from an office in the old market on Praça dos Nagôs (Ⓣ75/3334-1112) beside the river bridge. You'll also find several people offering themselves as guides to the town: at a dollar or two for an extensive tour they're not expensive, and as life is not easy around here it might help someone out.

There are three **buses** a day for the six-hour journey from Salvador to Lençóis, all leaving from the main *rodoviária*. The best, and most expensive, **place to stay** in town is the *Portal de Lençóis*, Rua Altina Alves (Ⓣ & Ⓕ75/3334-1233; ❽). Cheaper, but still expensive and very good, are the beautiful riverside ★ *Pousada Canto das Aguas* (Ⓣ & Ⓕ75/3334-1154, Ⓦwww.lencois.com.br; ❻), with hearty breakfasts, lovely grounds by the river and a pool; at the top end of town, another luxurious spot is *Hotel de Lençóis* (Ⓣ75/3334-1102; ❻) with decent rooms with air conditioning, but it's the lovely *fazenda*-style decor that sets it apart. Budget options include *Colonial*, at Praça Otaviano Alves 750 (Ⓣ75/3334-1114; ❸), and the *Tradição*, Rua José Florêncio (Ⓣ75/3334-1120; ❷). One of the friendliest of the basic options is *Pousada Safira*, Rua do Pires (Ⓣ & Ⓕ75/3334-1443; ❷), with just a few small rooms, all with own bath; it's a little hard to find in the back streets at the heart of town. The simple, central ★ *Pousada Aguas Claras*, Rua P. Benjamin (Ⓣ75/3334-1471 Ⓔgal700@hotmail.com; ❸), is a good bet – and the owner is also married to a reliable **taxi driver** (Ⓣ75/9966-1471). You'll find a

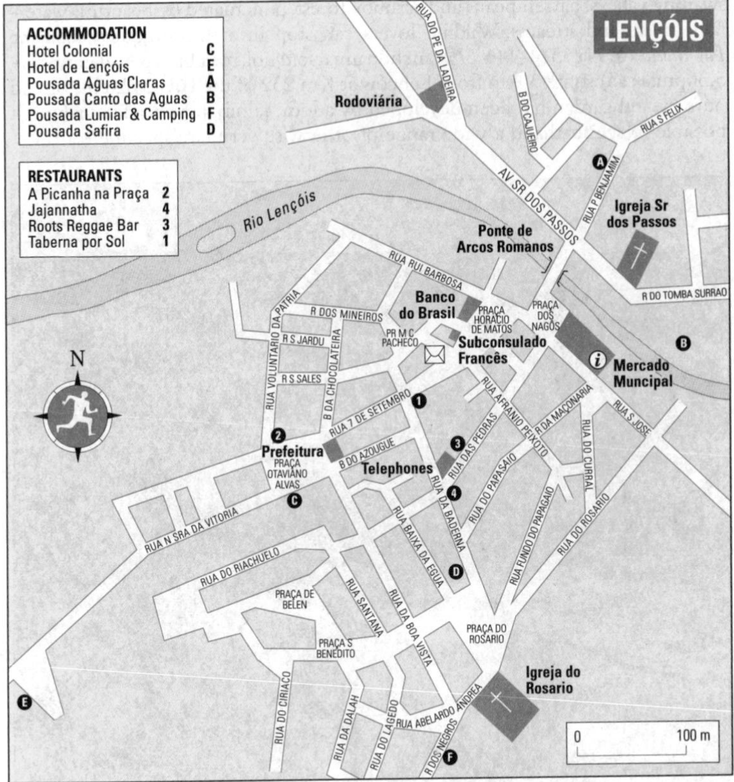

campsite, *Lumiar Camping*, on the grounds of the Pousada Lumiar at Praça do Rosário 70 (ⓣ75/3334-1241, ⓦwww.pousadaecampinglumiar.com.br).

The popular *A Picanha na Praça*, Praça Octaviano Alves 153, serves a meat-based menu and has fast service and an open patio. The vegetarian restaurant *Jajannatha*, Rua das Pedras 133, has outside tables. For *comida por kilo* lunches it's hard to beat the extensive menu at the large, airy *Taberna por Sol* on the corner of Ruas 7 de Setembro and Baderna. In the evenings, the restaurant-bars on Rua das Pedras, such as *Roots Reggae Bar*, and around Praça Horácio de Matos tend to be the focus of **nightlife**.

Local **artesanato** is very good, particularly the bottles filled with coloured sand arranged into intricate patterns; get a guide to take you to the **Salão das Areias** on the outskirts of town, where you can see the sand being gathered and put into bottles by local artisans – even children do it. You can buy the finished product at Gilmar Nunes on Rua Almirante Barroso, or at Manoel Reis, Rua São Félix.

Parque Nacional da Chapada Diamantina and Capão

The **Parque Nacional da Chapada Diamantina** was established in 1985 after much local campaigning and covers over 38,000 square kilometres (or 152 million hectares) – an area larger than the Netherlands – in the mountainous regions to the south and west of Lençóis. Its dramatic landscape incorporates swampy valleys, barren peaks and scrubby forest, punctuated by beautiful waterfalls, rivers and streams. Wildlife lovers can stop in at the unique *Orquidario Pai Inacio* (Ⓣ71/3374-4468, Ⓔranchopaiinacio@uol.com.br; open daily 8am–5.30pm; R$5) some 30km from Lençóis at Km 232 of the BR-242. This orchid nursery and garden has been developed by a local family for decades, making it possible to see firsthand a wide range of otherwise very rare specimens.

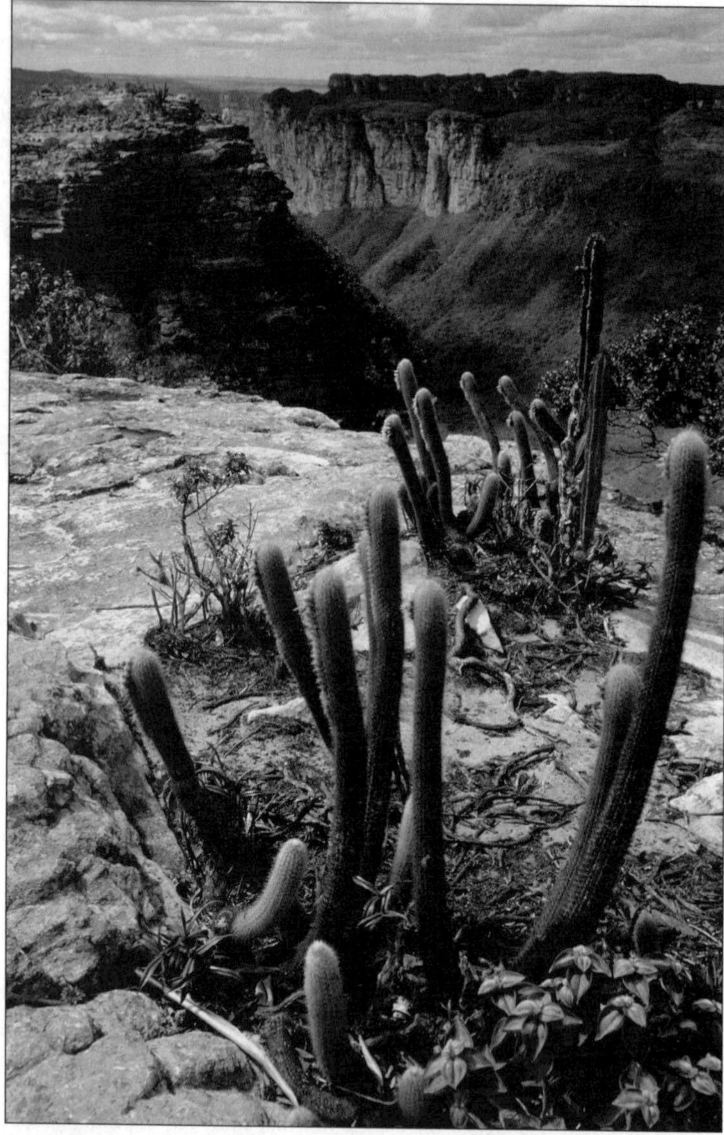

△ Parque Nacional da Chapada Diamantina

The Parque Nacional da Chapada Diamantina is one of Brazil's major trekking destinations, but it also offers plenty of opportunities for canoeing, climbing and even chilling out at the hippy rural community of **Capão**. In recent years Capão has attracted young people from Salvador in search of a bohemian or New Age lifestyle. You'll find retreats and meditation spots here, and many of the *pousadas* offer luxuries such as hot tubs and saunas – though it's hard to beat a dip in the river, as it gets very hot here in January and February. It takes three days to walk to Capão from Lençóis, or you can take a bus as far as the town of Palmeiras, which is about 15km from Capão; a taxi takes two hours. Despite the poor track in from Palmeiras and the lack of general facilities, laid-back Capão, with several stores and restaurants, can make for a relaxing base while visiting Chapada. Most of the *pousadas*, including *Pousada Verde* (Ⓣ75/3334-1109) and *Pousada Galixito* (Ⓣ75/3334-1187), are scattered around Capão's undulating landscape; you should book and get confirmation far in advance and try to get someone from your accommodation to pick you up from Palmeiras or Lençóis. For **guides** from Capão, stop in at the Associação dos Conductores de Visitantes do Vale do Capão (Ⓣ75/3344-1087, Ⓔacv@valedocapao.com), which has an office in the valley, signposted from the main road at a cluster of huts and a shop, before the road dips down to the main settlement. The guides can take groups to most of the usual sites in and around the parks.

Some places in the park you could just about manage without a guide, like the **Gruta do Lapão**, a remarkable grotto over a kilometre long, with a cathedral-like entrance of layered rock and stalactites. It's a short drive or a long walk (a full-day round trip) from the centre, but it's probably better to have someone take you there. The only other place within easy reach is the **Cascatas do Serrano**, a fifteen-minute walk from town, where the river flows over a rock plate forming a series of small waterfalls and pools that are good for swimming – very popular with the local children.

Anywhere more distant and you'll need a proper guide, as the countryside can be difficult to negotiate. Reliable operators in Lençóis include Marimbus Ecoturismo, Praça da Coreto (Ⓣ75/3334-1292, Ⓦwww.marimbus.com), and Lentur, at Av. 7 de Setembro 10 (Ⓣ75/3334-1271, Ⓦwww.lentur.com.br). For more demanding activities like climbing, try Trilhar Turismo, Rua Pirilo Benjamin 37 (Ⓣ75/3334-1045, Ⓦwww.trilhar.com.br), and Extreme, Avenida 7 de Setembro 15 (Ⓣ75/3341-1727, Ⓦwww.extremeecoadventure.com.br). Alternatively, if you'd rather opt for an **independent guide**, contact Roy Funch (through the Fundacao Chapada Diamantina at Rua Pé de Ladeira 212; Ⓣ75/3334-1305), a resident American and author of an excellent guidebook to the region; he may not be able to guide you himself, but can certainly recommend someone and suggest places to head for. Standard rates for independent guides are between R$40 and R$70 a day. Sunglasses, a hat, and sun cream are all essential, as well as taking along water: it can get very hot and several of the walks are strenuous.

Amongst the most popular destinations is **Morro do Pai Inácio**, a 300-metre-high mesa formation 27km from Lençóis (don't be deceived by how near it looks). It is, though, much more easily climbed than seems possible from a distance, and you're rewarded with quite stunning views across the tablelands and the town once you get to the top, which is covered in highland cacti, trees and shrubs. Thirty kilometres away, but with much easier road access, is **Rio Mucugezinho**, another series of small waterfalls and pools that are fun to swim in; a closer river beach is the **Praia do Rio São José**, also called Zaidã. Finally, and most spectacular of all, is the highest waterfall in Brazil, the **Cachoeira Glass**, a small stream that tumbles 400m down over a mesa, becoming little more than a fine mist by the time it reaches the bottom. It's closer to town than most of the other places, and if you only feel up to one day's walking it's the best choice.

South from Salvador

The BR-101 highway is the main route to the **southern Bahian coast**, a region immortalized in the much translated and filmed novels of Jorge Amado. From the bus window you'll see the familiar fields of sugar replaced by huge plantations of *cacau*, cocoa. Southern Bahia produces two-thirds of Brazil's cocoa, almost all of which goes for export, making this part of Bahia the richest agricultural area of the state. The *zona de cacau* seems quiet and respectable enough today, with its pleasant towns and prosperous countryside, but in the last decades of the nineteenth century and the first decades of the twentieth, it was one of the most turbulent parts of Brazil. Entrepreneurs and adventurers from all over the country carved out estates here, often violently – a process chronicled by Amado in his novel *The Violent Lands* (see "Books", p.846).

Ilhéus and around

In literary terms **ILHÉUS**, Amado's birthplace, is the best-known town in Brazil, the setting for his most famous novel, *Gabriela, Cravo e Canela*, translated into English as "Gabriela, Clove and Cinnamon" – by far the most renowned Brazilian novel internationally. If you haven't heard of it before visiting Ilhéus, you soon will; it seems like every other bar, hotel and restaurant is either named after the novel or one of its characters.

The town is on the coast 400km south of Salvador, where the local coastline is broken up by five rivers and a series of lagoons, bays and waterways. Much of it is modern but it's still an attractive place, with the heart of Ilhéus perched on a small hill that overlooks one of the largest and finest-looking beaches in Bahia. Before you head for the sands, however, take time to look around the town. The modern cathedral, built in the 1930s with extravagant Gothic towers and pinnacles, is a useful landmark. Nearby, the oldest church in the city, the **Igreja Matriz de São Jorge**, on Praça Rui Barbosa, finished in 1556, has a religious art museum, while the domed roof and towers of the **Igreja de Nossa Senhora de Lourdes** dominate the shoreline nearest to the centre. Domes are rare in church architecture in Brazil, and this combination of dome and towers is unique. The **Casa da Cultura**, at Rua Jorge Amado 21, is well worth half an hour for a whistle-stop tour of the city's history, including interesting exhibits on the region's chocolate industry and Ilhéus's remarkable literary tradition. The house itself was once the home of Amado himself.

The main leisure options in Ilhéus have changed little from Amado's time: hanging around in the **bars** and squares, and heading for the beaches. The *Vezúvio* on Praça Dom Eduardo, the cathedral square, is the most famous bar in Brazil; in Amado's book it's owned by the hero Nacib, and is a watering hole of the cocoa planters. You pay a little extra for drinks, but it's a good bar, with renowned Arab food. Apart from the centre, you'll find the main concentration of bars along the fine beach promenade of the Avenida Atlântica – the beach itself called simply **Avenida** – though much of it is now polluted and not recommended for bathing. There are other **beaches to the north**, past the port: the first is **Isidro Ramos** (bus from the centre or Avenida), followed by **Praia do Marciano** and **Praia do Norte**.

Most locals prefer the coastline to the south, particularly around the village of **OLIVENÇA**, served by local buses from the centre. Half an hour out of town is the beautiful beach at **Cururupe**, where Governor Mem de Sá trapped the Tupiniquim Indians in 1567 between his troops and the sea. It was called the "Battle of the Swimmers", after the Indians' desperate attempts to escape by water, but it was more of a massacre than a battle, and the tribe was almost wiped out. Today there are a series of bars and some holiday homes, peaceful groves of palm trees and no hint of the place's dark past. In Olivença itself the main attraction is the **Balneário**, public swimming baths built around supposedly healthy mineral water from the Rio Tororomba, which flows through. The healing powers of the water are exaggerated, but the baths complex is very pleasant, with an artificial waterfall, and bar and restaurant attached. The coast between Ilhéus and Olivença is very beautiful: you can **camp** virtually anywhere along the way.

Alternatively, head for the unspoiled beaches north of Ilhéus, among the best that Bahia has to offer. Frequent buses run to the busiest beach town along this stretch, **ITACARÉ**, 70km from Ilhéus, and a fishing port in its own right. The town is a haven for **water-based adventure sports**, including rafting and canoeing, which you can arrange through Papaterra (Ⓣ73/3251-2252, Ⓦwww.papaterra.com.br) and Hawaii Aqui, at Rua Pedro Longo 169 (Ⓣ73/3251-3050, Ⓦwww.hawaiiaqui@bol.com.br), which is also a *pousada* and Internet café. There's no shortage of cafés, restaurants and bars in town, especially at the southern end of the beach.

Practicalities

The **rodoviária** (Ⓣ73/3251-3461) is on Praça Cairu, a little way from the centre of Ilhéus, but buses outside marked "Centro" or "Olivença" take you into town. The **airport** is 4km away (Ⓣ73/3231-7629), connected to town by taxi (R$20) and hourly buses. There's a **tourist information** post at the *rodoviária*, with good town maps, and an Ilhéustur office near the port at Av. Soares Lopes 1741 (Mon–Sat 9am–6pm; Ⓣ73/3251-3461, Ⓦwww.ilheus.com.br).

Your best bet for **accommodation** in Ilhéus is probably on one of the beaches, although there's no shortage of places in town if you prefer. *Pousada Vitória* (❶) is a budget option on Praça Cairu, next to the *rodoviária*. In the centre, *Ilhéus*, Rua Estáquio Bastos 144 (Ⓣ73/3251-4242; ❸), is good value, and the *Britânia*, close to the cathedral at Rua 28 de Junho 16 (Ⓣ73/3251-1722; ❸), is one of the cheapest central hotels. For beachside accommodation, there's the *Pousada Sol e Mar*, 14km from town on the Ilhéus–Olivença road (Ⓣ & Ⓕ73/3251-1148; ❹); frequent buses run into town. If you can afford it, one of the best places to stay is the *Pousada Aldea da Mata* (Ⓣ73/9981-8692, Ⓦwww.aldeiadamata.com.br; ❻), on the edge of the Mata Atlântica roughly halfway between Ilheus and Itacaré; look out for the partially hidden entrance at Km 31.5 on the Ilheus–Serra Grande road. Rooms are in bungalow-style accommodation, and amenities include a terraced bar, natural hot spring shower and even massages; the beach here is empty and fabulous. If you want to stay in Itacaré, try the family-run *Pousada Sol e Mar*, Rua Nova Conquista (Ⓣ73/3251-2795; ❸), which is away from the beach but has well-kept rooms, some with balconies and TV. There's also the lovely *Pousada Sitio Ilha Verde*, Rua A. Setubal 234 (Ⓣ73/3251-2056, Ⓦwww.itacare.com.br; ❹), set in beautiful grounds amid mango trees, with individually decorated rooms and a pool.

Buses to Ilhéus from Salvador take around six hours: catch the one in the morning if you want to see the pleasant countryside en route; you'll have to book at least a day in advance. Otherwise take one of the three night departures. There are direct buses from Ilhéus, once a week, to Rio and São Paulo, but book at least two days ahead for these. For a **taxi**, call ⓣ73/3251-6750. Messias Viagens (ⓣ73/3251-1949) can arrange **city tours**; other reliable tour operators are Agua Branca Receptivo, Rua do Bonfim, Pontal 255 (ⓣ73/3231-1424) and Costa do Sol, Av. Bahia 294, Cidade Nova (ⓣ73/3231-2788). **Money exchange** is available at Emcamtur, Rua Dom Pedro II 116, in downtown Ilheus (ⓣ73/3251-6535, ⓔemcamtur@maxnet.com.br). For **Internet access** try Cybercafe.com, Rua Cel. Camara 38, Centro, or Café Oclus.com.br on Rua Brigadeiro Eduardo Gomes (ⓣ73/3251-6668).

Porto Seguro

The most popular destination in southern Bahia is the resort area around the town of **PORTO SEGURO**, where Cabral "discovered" Brazil in 1500. Founded in 1526, it has some claim to being the oldest town in Brazil, and buildings still survive from that period.

The story goes that in 1500 **Pedro Alvares Cabral** and his men, alerted to the presence of land by the changing colour of the sea and the appearance of land birds, finally saw a mountain on the horizon, which must have been Monte Páscoal, to the south of today's Porto Seguro. First landfall was made on Good Friday, on a beach to the north of Porto Seguro, and the anchorage Cabral used was probably the cove where the village of Santa Cruz de Cabrália now stands. The Indians were friendly at first, though they might have been better advised otherwise, since Cabral claimed the land for the king of Portugal, and thus began over three centuries of Portuguese rule.

These days Porto Seguro is about as far as you can get from pre-colonial tranquillity. It's become one of the biggest holiday resorts in Brazil, and heaves with Brazilian tourists throughout the year, reaching saturation point at New Year and Carnaval. You may actually enjoy yourself here if your main interest is nightlife, but you've got to like crowds, and don't expect much peace and quiet. All the same, Porto Seguro has somehow managed to retain its reputation as a fairly classy destination.

The Town

The colonial area, **Cidade Alta**, is built on a bluff overlooking the town, with fine views out to sea and across the Rio Buranhém. The **Igreja da Misericórdia**, begun in 1526, is one of the two oldest churches in Brazil. The **Igreja de Nossa Senhora da Pena**, nearby, dates from 1535 and has the oldest religious icon in Brazil, a St Francis of Assisi, brought over in the first serious expedition to Brazil, in 1503. There are the ruins of a Jesuit church and chapel (dating from the 1540s) and a small, early fort; the squat and thick-walled style of the churches shows their early function as fortified strongpoints, in the days when Indian attacks were common. Near the ruins of the Jesuit college is the **Marca do Descobrimento**, the two-metre-high column sunk to mark Portuguese sovereignty in 1503; on one side is a crude face of Christ, almost unrecognizable now, and on the other the arms of the Portuguese Crown.

Cidade Baixa, below the colonial area, is where the modern action is. The riverside Avenida 22 de Abril and its continuation, Avenida Portugal, are a mass of bars, restaurants and hotels – so much so that Avenida Portugal changes its name at night to become the Passarela do Álcool, or "Alcohol Street". One stretch of road – where competing stallholders urge you to try their fiendishly strong cocktails – particularly merits this name.

North of town, you'll find a string of superb beaches along the Beira Mar coast road. The nearest, **Praia Curuípe**, is 3km away and has some natural pools and reefs, as well as the usual beachside restaurants. More popular, and just a few kilometres further away, is **Praia Itacimirim**. These beaches, and others further north (notably Mundaí and Taperapuã, both good for scuba diving), are connected to Porto Seguro by regular seafront buses.

Practicalities

The **rodoviária** is a little way out of town, but taxis are cheap and plentiful. Three **buses** a day make the eleven-hour journey from Salvador, but one of these is an extremely expensive *leito* service, and you should book well ahead. There are also direct **flights** from Rio and Salvador. There are **tourist information** offices at the *rodoviária*, the airport, and in the centre of town at the Secretaria de Turismo, Praça Visconde de Porto Seguro, in the Casa da Lenha (Ⓣ73/3288-1390 or 3288-4124). The tour agencies Pataxó Turismo, Av. dos Navegantes 333 (Ⓣ73/3288-1256), and Taípe Viagens e Turismo, Av. 22 de Abril 1077 (Ⓣ73/3288-3127), are also helpful. **Internet access** is available from an office on the second floor of the Avenida Shopping Mall in the town centre (R$12 per hour).

Finding **accommodation** should be the least of your worries as Porto Seguro is jammed with hotels. However, prices vary astonishingly between high and low season: a budget hotel in, say, November, can triple in price by Christmas. Bear this in mind when considering the high-season prices we've quoted. If you want to be right in the thick of the nightlife, try the *Pousada da Orla*, at Av. Portugal 404 (Ⓣ73/3288-2434; ③). A couple of roads back from the riverfront, in a wooden colonial-style building, is the relatively peaceful *Hotel Terra Á Vista*, Av. Getúlio Vargas 124 (Ⓣ73/3288-2035; ④). A hotel with some real old-fashioned character is the friendly *Pousada Oásis do Pacatá*, at Rua Marechal Deodoro 286 (Ⓣ73/3288-2221; ④), which is run by a Frenchwoman, and has a swimming pool. You'll find chalet accommodation at the *Pousada São Luiz*, Av. 22 de Abril 329 (Ⓣ73/3288-2238; ④), and even greater luxury at the *Park Palace Hotel*, Av. 22 de Abril 400 (Ⓣ73/3288-3777; ⑥). The clean but rather noisy **youth hostel** is at Rua Cova da Moça 729 (Ⓣ73/3288-1742; from R$20 per person), while the best-equipped **campsite** is *Camping da Gringa* (Ⓣ73/3288-2076) at the edge of town; there's another on Mundaí beach (Ⓣ73/3679-2287), which starts in front of Cidade Alta.

You'll find a huge number of **places to eat** in Porto Seguro, though the more sophisticated ones, like the *Cruz de Malta*, Av. Getúlio Vargas 358 (11am–midnight), specializing in Bahian seafood, tend to be quite expensive. You can dine more cheaply at *Tché*, on Travessa Augusto Borges, just off the Passarela do Álcool, where a half-portion of *carne do sol* will satisfy even the most ravenous carnivore. Avenida Portugal is generally the liveliest area of town for **nightlife**. The *Sotton Bar* on Praça de Baudeira and the *Porto Prego* club on Rua Pedro Alvares Cabral are both good for live music and dancing.

South of Porto Seguro

South of Porto Seguro are three less developed, more relaxed beach resorts generally preferred by backpacking foreigners, though there are plenty of Brazilian tourists as well. You'll definitely enjoy yourself here if you're looking for beaches and nightlife, and the resorts get quieter the further south you go.

Arraial d'Ajuda

ARRAIAL D'AJUDA is the closest of the three to Porto Seguro and the easiest to get to: catch the ferry from the centre of Porto Seguro for the ten-minute journey across the Rio Buranhém. From the other side there are buses that climb the hill and drop you in the centre of town: don't stay on the bus after this or you'll find yourself making a very boring round trip. In the centre itself and on the roads running down the steep hill to the beach are an incredible number of **places to stay**. The nicest of these is the *Hotel Pousada Marambaia*, at Alameda dos Flamboyants 116 (☎73/3875-1275; ④), which has clean, chalet-style rooms around a peaceful courtyard, complete with swimming pool and gently jangling cowbells. The *Hotel Pousada Buganville*, at Alameda dos Flamboyants 170 (☎73/3875-1007; ④), has a friendly atmosphere, while the *Pousada Vento Sul*, on the Caminho da Praia, the hill that runs down to the beach (☎73/3875-1294; ③), is for those with a taste for loud techno music, thumping out from the bar below.

The **beach** is lively and can become very crowded in places, though the further you get from the bars and the restaurants, the easier it is to find a peaceful spot under the sun. The main problem with Arraial d'Ajuda is that it's become too popular too quickly – whatever rubbish collection there is simply can't cope with the huge amounts of litter left by tourists.

Trancoso and Caraíva

Further south down the coast – more peaceful, but next in the developers' sights – is **TRANCOSO**. You can get there either **by bus** (about five a day from Arraial d'Ajuda, taking fifty minutes) or **on foot**. It's a beautiful walk – 12km down the beach from Arraial – but you have to ford a couple of rivers so be prepared to get wet. Once again, there's no shortage of **accommodation**: *Gulab Mahal* (③), on the main square, the Quadrado, is highly recommended for its hospitality. In the rural area outside of Trancoso, the *Mata Nativa Pousada* (☎73/3668-1830, Ⓦwww.matanativapousada.com.br; ⑥–⑦) offers lovely accommodation in tropical gardens by a river; English, Italian and French are spoken and there are four rooms with air-conditioning and private baths.

If you really want to get away from civilization in this part of Bahia, you have to go even further south, to **CARAÍVA**, which has no electricity apart from that provided by generators, and no cars. It's time-consuming to get to: there are **boats** from Porto Seguro (consult a travel agent) and Trancoso that take four and two hours respectively, and two **buses** a day from Trancoso – a bumpy ride, ending with a boat journey across a river. Once there, you'll find superb beaches, a few rustic places to stay, some good food and plenty of peace and quiet.

Caravelas and around

On the banks of the Rio Caravelas, in the extreme south of Bahia, lies **CARAVELAS**, an attractive, unpretentious colonial town that makes an ideal farewell or introduction to Bahia. Founded in 1503, it became an important trading centre in the seventeenth and eighteenth centuries. Today both the town and its nearby beach are – despite the growth of tourism – extremely relaxing places to hang out. Caravelas is also the jumping-off point for the **Parque Nacional Marinho dos Abrolhos**, one of the best places in Brazil to see exotic marine life, including – at certain times of year – humpback whales.

Apart from organizing your trip to Abrolhos, there isn't a whole lot to do in Caravelas, but it's an extremely agreeable place to wander round. Most of the interest lies in the streets between the river and the *rodoviária*, which is on Praça Teófilo Otoni in the centre of town. One block to your left as you come out of the *rodoviária* is Praça Quinze, the liveliest square in this sleepy town. Another block further on and running parallel to the river is Rua Marcílio Diaz, which becomes Rua Sete de Setembro and eventually leads to the beautiful **Praça**

de Santo Antônio. This is definitely the architectural highlight of Caravelas and contains the eponymous **Igreja de Santo Antônio**, which you may – if you're lucky – find open.

Practicalities

In order to get to Caravelas, you have to go first to **Teixeira de Freitas**, further inland. Águia Branca run five **buses** a day on the four-hour journey between Porto Seguro and Teixeira de Freitas. From Teixeira de Freitas, Expresso Brasileiro operates five buses a day to Caravelas, an agreeable two-hour meander through lush tropical fields. From the south, you can get there from Minas Gerais or Espírito Santo or, if you want to miss out those two states altogether, São Geraldo run a daily *executivo* service from Rio that leaves in mid-afternoon and takes fifteen hours (R$120).

An excellent **place to stay** near the *rodoviária* on Praça Teófilo Otoni is the cosy *Pousada Caravelense* (Ⓣ73/3297-1182; ❷), which has friendly service and a pool table. There are several other hotels, most of them to your left as you come out of the *rodoviária*. The *Pousada da Ponte*, on Rua Anibal Benevolo (❷), is a simple, charming place built right on the riverbank. The *Pousada Caravelas* (❷), on Rua Sete de Setembro, just next to the Banco do Brasil, is modern and clean, while for a real budget option, try the *Hotel Shangri-La* (❶) further down the same road. There's also accommodation **on the beach**, called Praia do Grauçá or Barra de Caravelas – a half-hour journey from the *rodoviária* in Caravelas and well worth a visit even if you don't stay there. The *Pousada das Sereias* (Ⓣ73/3874-1033; ❸) is the obvious choice if you don't want to spend too much money, while the *Hotel Marina Porto Abrolhos* (Ⓣ73/3674-1082, Ⓦwww.marinaportoabrolhos.com.br; ❻) offers beachside luxury.

You'll find a number of good **restaurants** in town. *Carenagem*, just by the petrol station on Praça Quinze, is very good value, as is the *Muroroa Reggae Night*, which sits on the riverbank at the other end of town, near the Praça de

△ Parque Nacional Marinho dos Abrolhos

Santo Antônio – the *carne do sol* here is amazingly good. There's another good place to eat down on the beach at Barra de Caravelas, the *Museu da Baleia*, a seafood restaurant that owes its name to the enormous whale skeleton partially assembled outside – but rest assured that whale meat is not on the menu.

Parque Nacional Marinho dos Abrolhos

For all Caravelas' attractions, there's no doubt that the main reason people come here is to see the extraordinary profusion of marine and bird life in the **Parque Nacional Marinho dos Abrolhos.** The park consists of an archipelago of five islands lying 52km offshore. Among the clear waters and coral reefs you can see all kinds of rare fish, sea turtles and birds, and between July and early November the waters are home to **whales** taking refuge from the Antarctic winter.

There are two main **tour companies** in Caravelas that offer trips to Abrolhos: the well-established Abrolhos Turismo, on Praça Dr Imbassay (Ⓣ73/3297-1149), and the slightly cheaper Abrolhos Embarcações, at Av. das Palmeiras 2, more or less on Praça Quinze (Ⓣ73/3297-1172). Abrolhos Turismo offers a basic day-trip to the national park in a launch, leaving at 7am and returning at 5pm, for about R$280. The same sort of trip costs about US$100 at Abrolhos Embarcações, though the day is shorter, starting at 8am and returning at 4pm. In either case, you can pay extra to rent snorkels, masks and more sophisticated diving equipment. Both companies also offer longer yacht trips to Abrolhos of up to three nights, for which you pay just over R$100 a day at Abrolhos Turismo and about R$75 at Abrolhos Embarcações. Again, hiring diving equipment costs extra.

Travel details

Buses

Salvador to: Belém (4 weekly; 35hr); Brasília (6 daily; 26hr); Cachoeira (hourly; 2hr 30min); Feira de Santana (hourly; 2hr); Ilhéus (6 daily; 6hr 30min); Jacobina (2 daily; 6hr); Lençóis (2 daily; 6hr); Porto Seguro (4 daily; 11hr); Praia do Forte (4 daily; 2hr); Recife (6 daily; 13hr); Rio (2 daily; 30hr); Santo Amaro (every 30min; 2hr); São Paulo (2 daily; 35hr); Valença (6 daily; 5hr).

Ferries

Salvador to: Itaparicá (every 30min; 60min).

Flights

Salvador is connected by at least daily flights to most major Brazilian cities, including Natal.

The Northeast

VENEZUELA
GUYANA
SURINAME
FRENCH GUIANA
COLOMBIA
PERU
BOLIVIA
PARAGUAY
CHILE
ARGENTINA
URUGUAY
N
5
4
3
7
6
2
8
1
9
0 1000 km

CHAPTER 4 Highlights

* **Olinda** Best visited during Carnaval, where colourful parades snake through beautifully preserved colonial streets. See p.335

* **Porto de Galinhas** One of the Northeast's most active hippy beaches, this place really comes to life during high season, when sound systems and DJs from Recife's trendiest clubs move out here. See p.346

* **Fernando de Noronha** A gorgeous archipelago visited by thousands of dolphins early each morning. See p.354

* **Northeast beaches** Quintessential tropical beaches line much of the region's coast, including the idyllic Ponta Negra near Natal. See p.376

* **Jericoacoara** With some of the finest beaches and among the best surf and wind in Brazil, Jericoacoara, near Fortaleza, attracts great crowds of young people. See p.391

* **Reggae bands** You'll hear excellent reggae throughout the region, but especially in São Luís, the reggae capital of Brazil. See p.399

△ A beach in Recife

4

The Northeast

Divided politically into eight separate states, the **Northeastern part of Brazil** is fairly united in being one of the country's poorest areas. Nevertheless, beach life and coastal tourism are thriving, but the area has not yet been spoilt by its own success. There are major cities along the coast: some, like Olinda, Recife, São Luís and Fortaleza, have deep colonial heritage; others, like Maceio and Natal, have developed mostly in recent decades. All have their own city **beaches** plus more idyllic and deserted resorts hidden up or down the coast (though generally accessible by bus or taxi). The semi-arid region inland, with sparse leafy vegetation but abundant cacti, is known as the **sertão**. It suffers periods of intense drought, yet in the wet season it is transformed to a verdant green, if only for a couple of months. Few people traverse the interior of the Northeast, except maybe en route to Belém at the mouth of the Amazon; but if you do visit the region, there are a number of quite isolated and windswept market towns – like Campina Grande in Paraiba state – that are worth stopping off at. Piauí, too, boasts more than one stunningly beautiful national park. The **Ilha de Fernando de Noronha**, hundreds of kilometres off the coast from Natal, is one of the finest oceanic wildlife reserves in the world. And the coast of Maranhão is known, among other things these days, for its reggae.

Some history

By the end of the sixteenth century, sugar plantations were already importing African slaves to the Northeast of Brazil. **Olinda** was a major colonial centre and, like Salvador, developed into a relatively large town, while Rio de Janeiro remained little more than a swampy village. The Northeast quickly became Europe's main supplier of **sugar**. The merchants and plantation owners grew rich and built mansions and churches, but their very success led to their downfall. It drew the attention of the **Dutch**, who were so impressed that they destroyed the Portuguese fleet in Salvador in 1624, burnt down Olinda six years later and occupied much of the coast, paying particular attention to sugar-growing areas. It took more than two decades of vicious guerrilla warfare before the Dutch were expelled, and even then they had the last laugh: they took their new experience of sugar growing to the West Indies, which soon began to edge Brazilian sugar out of the world market.

The Dutch invasion, and the subsequent decline of the sugar trade, proved quite a fillip to the development of the interior. With much of the coast in the hands of the invaders, the **colonization** of the *sertão* and the *agreste* – a narrow, hilly zone between the *sertão* and the coastal Mata Atlântica – was stepped up. The Indians and escaped slaves already there were joined by

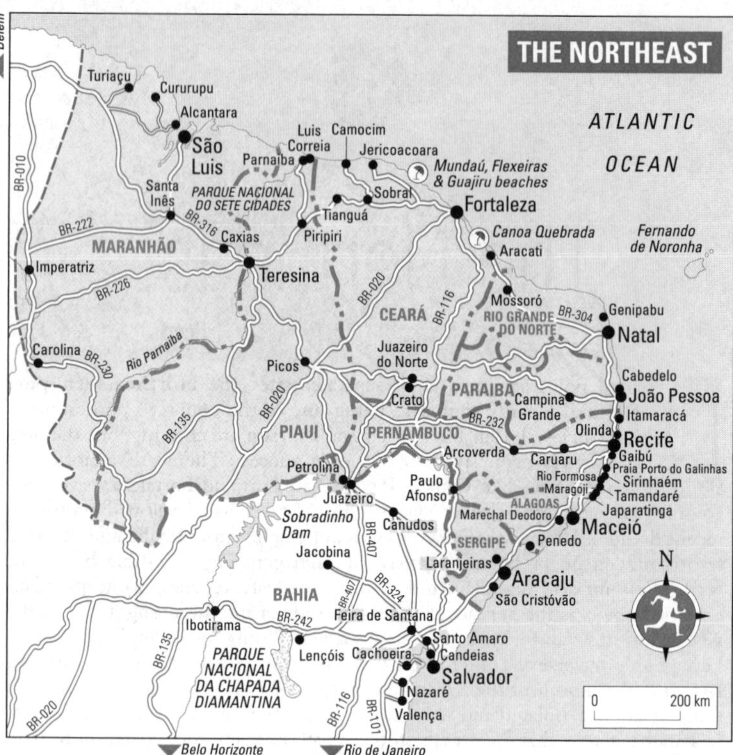

cattlemen (*vaqueiros*), as trails were opened up into the highlands and huge ranches carved out of the interior. Nevertheless, it took over two centuries, roughly from 1600 to 1800, before these regions were fully absorbed into the rest of Brazil. In the *agreste*, where some fruit and vegetables could be grown and cotton did well, market villages developed into towns. However, the *sertão* became, and still remains, cattle country, with an economy and society very different from the coast.

Life in the **interior** has always been hard. The landscape is dominated by cactus and dense scrub – *caatinga* – the heat is fierce, and for most of the year the countryside is parched brown. But it only requires a few drops of rain to fall for an astonishing transformation to take place – within a few hours the *sertão* blooms. Its plant life, adapted to semi-arid conditions, rushes to take advantage of the moisture: trees bud, cacti burst into flower, shoots sprout up from the earth and, literally overnight, the brown is replaced by a carpet of green. Too often, however, the rain never comes, or arrives too late, too early or in the wrong place, and the cattle begin to die. The first recorded **drought** was as early as 1710, and since then droughts have struck the *sertão* at ten- or fifteen-year intervals, sometimes lasting for years. The worst was in the early 1870s, when as many as two million people died of starvation; 1999 was also a particularly bad year. The problems caused by drought were, and still are, aggravated by the inequalities in land ownership. The fertile areas around rivers were taken over in early times by powerful cattle barons, whose descendants still dominate much of the interior. The rest of the people of the interior, pushed into less favoured areas, are regularly forced by drought to seek refuge in the coastal cities until the rains return. For centuries, periodic waves of refugees, known as *os flagelados* (the scourged ones), have poured out of the *sertão* fleeing droughts: modern Brazilian governments have been no more successful in dealing with the special problems of the interior than the Portuguese colonizers before them.

Transport

You can reach the Northeast from almost any direction. Direct, there are **flights** to Recife from Europe and North America, and frequent **buses** to the main Northeastern cities from all parts of Brazil. From **southern and central Brazil**, buses converge upon Salvador, from where you can get to most other destinations. **Brasília to Fortaleza** is another possible, if very long, overland route into the Northeast. From the **Amazon**, buses from Belém run to São Luís, Teresina, Fortaleza and points east, or further south to Salvador.

Getting around the Northeast is straightforward thanks to the region's extensive bus network. However, even the main highways can be a little bumpy at times, and minor roads are often precarious. This is especially true in the rainy season: in Maranhão the rains come in February, in Piauí and Ceará in March, and points east in April, lasting for around three months. These are only general rules, though: Maranhão can be wet even in the dry season, and Salvador's skies are liable to give you a soaking at any time of year.

Alagoas and Sergipe

Alagoas and **Sergipe** are the smallest Brazilian states. Sandwiched between Bahia to the south and Pernambuco to the north, they have traditionally been overshadowed by their neighbours and, to this day, still have a reputation for being something of a backwater – though this isn't entirely fair. While it's true that there's nowhere comparable to the cosmopolitan cities of Recife or Salvador, there are the two state capitals of **Maceió** and **Aracaju**, together with some well-preserved colonial towns, and exceptional **beaches** in Alagoas, which many rate as the best in the Northeast. Also, the harshness of the *sertão* here is much alleviated by the São Francisco river valley, which forms the border between the two states.

Alagoas is very poor, as you immediately discover from the potholes in its roads and its rickety local buses. Thousands of Alagoanos leave every year to look for work as far afield as Rio, São Paulo and Amazônia, giving the state the highest emigration rate of any in Brazil. Don't let this put you off, however; the coast is beautiful, and Maceió is a lively city, probably the best base from which to explore the state and its neighbour, Sergipe. Sergipe was, for most of its history, in a similar position to Alagoas, but since the 1960s a minor offshore oil boom has brought affluence to parts of the coast. Brazil being what it is, this doesn't mean there's less poverty: it's simply that the rich in Aracaju tend to be richer than the rich elsewhere in the Northeast.

Maceió

Originally founded in the seventeenth century, based around a large sugar plantation, **MACEIÓ**, the state capital of Alagoas, fronts the Atlantic Ocean with several attractive beaches; it also faces onto the Lagoa Mundau, an inland lake accessible from the sea that offers a wide natural harbour. Photos of Maceió's centre from the 1930s and 40s show an elegant city of squares and houses nestling under palm trees. Today, while the city is still attractive in places, you can't help wishing the clock could be turned back. Some of the graceful squares and buildings remain, faded yet full of character, but the city as a whole has suffered in recent years from the attentions of planners. Their worst crime was the wrecking of a once-famous waterfront promenade that faced the harbour and around which the city grew. An early nineteenth-century customs house once stood here, framed by offices and the fine houses of traders – all now gone and replaced by grimy concrete boxes.

The city's modern claim to fame – or infamy – is as the place where **Fernando Collor de Melo** cut his political teeth, becoming mayor and then state governor during the 1980s, before being elected Brazil's president in 1990. His term ended in disgrace after he was found to be at the centre of a huge corruption network, and further scandal was to come for Maceió with the violent death of Collor's adviser and chief accomplice in crime, **P.C. Farias**. In 1996 he and his girlfriend were found shot dead in a beachside hotel in Maceió – conspiracy theories abounded and the latest evidence suggests the deaths were an act of political revenge.

Arrival, information and accommodation

By Brazilian standards the **rodoviária** (☎82/3221-4615) is relatively close to the centre, though it's still well beyond walking distance for either the old town or the beach area. Buses marked "Ouro Preto" or "Serraria Mercado" connect

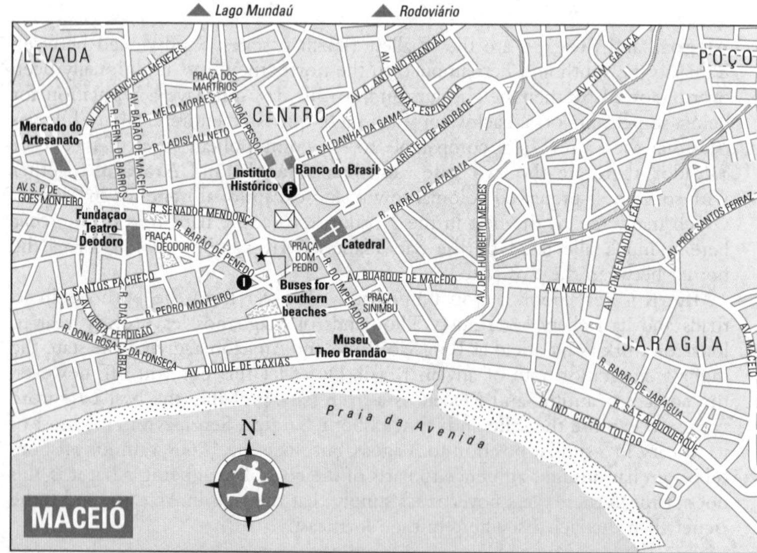

it with the old town, from where, to go on to the beaches you should take the "Ponta Verde", "Jardim Vaticano" or "Jatiúca" bus. Alternatively, a taxi direct to either the old town or the beaches will cost around R$12. The new Zumbi dos Palmares **airport** (ⓣ82/3214-4000) is some way from the city, and a taxi will set you back around R$45. Shoals of local buses make **getting around** very simple. All routes pass through the main squares in the centre, notably Praça Deodoro and Praça Dom Pedro II, names you'll often see on route cards propped in the front windows. The Estação Ferroviária is the place to get buses for local routes south of the city, and you may use it to go to nearby Marechal Deodoro or the glorious beach of Praia do Francês.

There's a **tourist information** booth at Avenida Dr Antônio Gouveia (Mon–Fri 8am–2pm; ⓣ82/3315-5700 and 3315-1600 or 3315-1603), close to the small tourist market on the promenade of the Praia de Pajuçara, easily recognizable by the *jangada* sailboats offering trips a mile out to the reef. SETURMA, the Maceió Tourism Office, can be contacted by phone (ⓣ82/3336-4409) for hotel and information on cultural events. There are other tourist information offices at the *rodoviária* (daily 8am–11pm), the airport (daily 8am–11.30pm), in the centre at Av. Sete de Setembro 1546 (ⓣ82/3633-2850 or 3652-1120) and at Rua Saldanha da Gama 71, Farol (Mon–Fri 8am–noon & 2–6pm; ⓣ82/3223-4016). The staff are friendly and can usually provide details of Maceió's lively **out-of-season Carnaval** (mid-December) as well as maps of the city and its nearby beaches, and information on hotels and tours. You can also check ⓦwww.coisasalagoas.com.br and ⓦwww.visitealagoas.com.br for general information on Maceió, and, if you're into diving, ⓦwww.bahiascuba.com.br.

Accommodation

The area around the **rodoviária** is a good bet for budget but downmarket hotels. Otherwise, it's a largely one-sided choice between **Centro** and the

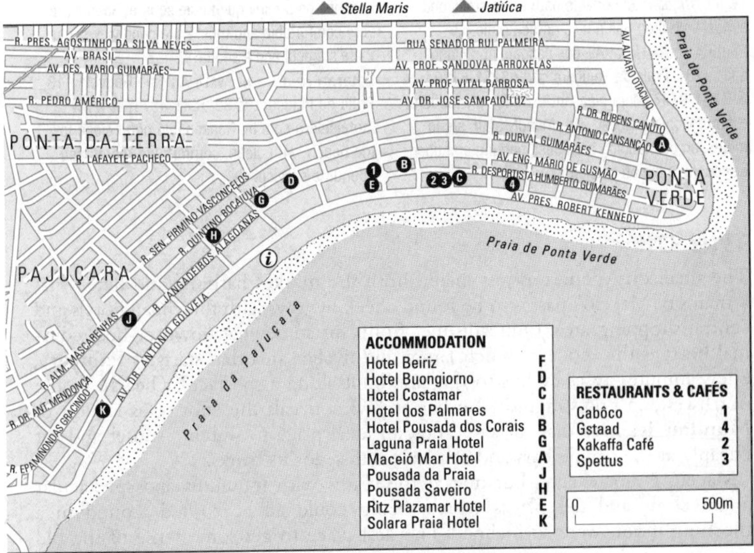

beach districts of **Pajuçara** and **Ponta Verde**: the latter are only a short bus ride away, and accommodation is more plentiful and of better quality than in the centre. Buses there are marked "Ponta Verde", "Pajuçara" or "Ponta da Terra" and run one block in from the beach, along Avenida dos Jangadeiros Alagoanos. Conveniently, this road is strung with a series of small hotels and *pousadas*, with more down the side streets. The beach promenade is where the luxury hotels are, and there are several good medium-priced hotels on Avenida Dr Antônio Gouveia, the first stretch of promenade after the centre.

Hotel Beiriz Rua do Sol 290, Centro Ⓣ82/3336-6200, Ⓕ3336-6282. Clean, mid-priced hotel that's difficult to spot from the road because there's no sign; it's next to a church. ❸

Hotel Buongiorno Av. dos Jangadeiros Alagoanos 1437, Pajuçara Ⓣ82/3327-4442 or 3327-1530. Small, modest but attractive hotel, one block from the heart of the beach and close to most of the best restaurants. ❸

Hotel Costamar Rua Desportista Guimaraes 420, Ponta Verde Ⓣ82/3327-6767 or 3231-8033 for reservations. A tall, thin concrete hotel with large and well-fitted rooms (though few have great views). There's a very small pool and a good self-service breakfast Is served from the top floor, which offers excellent panoramas. ❺

Hotel dos Palmares Praça dos Palmares 253, Centro Ⓣ82/3223-7024. A good budget option in the city centre. Rooms are built around a courtyard, though some are a bit stuffy when it gets warm. ❷

Hotel Pousada Dos Corais Rua Desp. Humberto Guimaraes 80, Ponta Verde Ⓣ82/3231-9096, Ⓦwww.hotelpousadadoscorais.hpg.com.br. Very good value, but rooms – though equipped with TV, a/c, *frigobar* and private bath – are small and almost cell-like. Has a nice garden patio. ❸

Laguna Praia Hotel Av. dos Jangadeiros Alagoanas 1231, Praia da Pajuçara Ⓣ82/3231-6180, Ⓕ3231-9737. More pleasant than its ugly modern exterior would suggest, with friendly staff, a/c in rooms, an outstanding breakfast, parking and good discounts in the off season. ❹

Maceió Mar Hotel Av. Álavaro Octacílio 2991, Praia de Ponta Verde Ⓣ82/2122-8000, Ⓦwww.maceomarhotel.com.br. Quality hotel with very spacious and comfortable rooms, plus a bar and a sauna; located close to the southern end of Praia de Ponta Verde beach. Offers fine views over the ocean, as well as especially good views for December's Carnaval. ❼

Pousada da Praia Av. dos Jangadeiros Alagoanos 545, Praia de Pajuçara Ⓣ82/3231-6843. A good option in the beach area, with reasonably cosy chalet-style rooms. You can arrange price reductions if you're staying for longer than a couple of nights. ❷–❸

Pousada Saveiro Av. dos Jangadeiros Alagoanos 805, Pajuçara Ⓣ82/3231-9831, Ⓦwww.pousadasaveiro.com.br. Very clean and friendly, this small *pousada* is one of the nicest in its range; rooms with ventilators are cheaper than those with a/c. ❸

Ritz Plazamar Hotel Rua Carlos Tenorio 105, Ponta Verde Ⓣ82/2121-4700 Ⓦwww.ritzplazamar.com.br. This big and modern place (just over 10 years old) is set back a block from the beaches on a fairly quiet little square. Rooms are very comfortable and most have good views, plus there's a pool and a sauna. ❹–❺

Solara Praia Hotel Av. Dr Antônio Gouveia 113, Praia de Pajuçara Ⓣ82/3231-4371, Ⓦwww.hotelsolara.com.br. Reasonable hotel close to the beach, with clean, comfortable rooms and adequate service. ❸

The City

The small **city centre** is just inland from the modest harbour, and here what remains of Maceió's past is to be found cheek by jowl with the cheap hotels and central shopping area. Quite distinct from this somewhat down-at-heel colonial heart is the modern, much larger and livelier area that starts at **Pajuçara**, a few minutes away by bus to the east, built along a spectacular beach. To the northwest, an undistinguished urban sprawl conceals the enormous lagoon of **Mundaú**. It's here that the city ends, an ideal place to watch a sunset and eat cheaply at the simple bars and restaurants that dot its banks.

Maceió is not exactly bursting at the seams with museums and spectacular architecture, and the places worth seeing could all be rushed around in a morning if you were so inclined. The best place to get some sense of the old

Lampião

Lampião was born Virgulino Ferreira da Silva in 1897 in the Northeastern state of Pernambuco. As Virgulino grew up, he and his family got involved in local feuding and they ended up of the wrong side of the law. Virgulino's father was killed in a police raid on his home, turning Virgulino, only 25 years old, into a bandit gang leader and deadly threat to the local establishment for the next 15 years. The "Robin Hood of Brazil" image he cultivated belies the reality of a complex, vain and extremely brutal man. It is perhaps his boldness that made him stand out, often fighting battles when his gang was outnumbered more than three to one.

Maceió is **Praça dos Martírios**, the finest square in the city, and an abject lesson to those who destroyed the waterfront. At one end is the eighteenth-century **Igreja Bom Jesus dos Martírios**, whose exterior, covered with well-preserved blue-and-white *azulejo* tiling, overshadows anything inside. At the other end the colonial **Governor's Palace** faces onto the palm-shaded square, brilliantly white during the day, floodlit at night. The **Praça Deodoro** is less splendid; at its heart there's a pleasant and shady rectangular park whose centrepiece is a statue of Marechal Deodoro da Fonseca himself, gallantly astride a horse and waving his hat at an imaginary crowd. The mid-nineteenth-century **Catedral**, on the Praça Dom Pedro II, is nothing special, but it's a useful landmark in a confusing city centre.

The **commercial heart** of the old centre runs along a couple of largely pedestrianized streets, the Rua do Livramento and Avenida Moreira Lima. At the bottom end of the latter, you'll find a massive and grubby weekend **street market**, where you can buy virtually anything – from recycled car parts to fighting cocks.

There are several museums, but the one in nearby Marechal Deodoro (see p.316) outclasses them all. The **Museu Theo Brandão**, at Praça Visconde Sinimbu 206, first floor (also called the Museu do Folclore; Tues–Fri 9am–noon & 2–5pm, Sat & Sun 3–6pm), has the usual bundles of Indian arrows and moth-eaten feather ornaments. On Thursdays at 8pm they present folklore music shows (☎82/3221-2651). Judged strictly on exhibits, the **Instituto Histórico e Geográfico** at Rua do Sol 382 (Mon–Fri 8am–1.30pm & 2–5pm) has the edge, and is worth seeing for the various relics and photographs of the bandit leader Lampião, including the famous "team photo" of his severed head along with those of his wife, Maria Bonita, and his closest lieutenants. All were preserved in alcohol by the police detachment that shot them in 1938, so that they could be shown in market towns in the interior – the only way to convince people he really had been killed. (Even today, the Brazilian media occasionally publish pictures of an old man who died in 1996 and bears a striking resemblance to Lampião.) Two other museums worth a visit if you've time on your hands are the **Fundação Teatro Deodoro** on Praça Deodoro (guided tours Mon & Tues 4–7pm; ☎82/3326-5252), which contains nineteenth-century furniture and fittings, and the **Museu de Arte Sacra Pierre Chalita**, Rua Loriano Peixoto 517 (Mon–Fri 8am–noon & 2–5.30pm; ☎82/3223-4298), which displays a number of religious paintings, statues and baroque altars.

The beaches

The main city beach is at **Pajuçara**, whose curving road and wide mosaic promenade are studded with palm trees. The water is not always the cleanest here and many people hire *jangadas* (around R$15 an hour) and head 2km out to sea to swim in the natural pools that form at low tide.

The bay then curves past the yacht club into the less crowded beach of **Ponta Verde**, an easy walk from Pajuçara, with some good spots to eat – try the *Sol Maior*, which has a large palm-shaded patio and serves excellent fresh fish and crab – and wind-surfing and canoeing equipment for rent. **Diving** lessons or tours can be arranged in Ponta Verde with the Bali Hai Diving School, Av. Robert Kennedy 1473, Loja 5, Galeria 7 Coqueiros (Ⓣ82/3327-3535).

Ponta Verde and the neighbouring beach of Jatiúca are the beginning of a series of fine sands to the north of Maceió. The best way to get to them is to take buses marked "Mirante" or "Fátima" from the centre, which take you along the coast as far as **Pratagi** (also called Mirante da Sereia), 13km north, where there are coral pools in the reef at low tide. You can get off the bus anywhere that takes your fancy; the main beaches, in order of appearance, are **Cruz das Almas**, **Jacarecica**, **Guaxuma**, **Garça Torta** and **Riacho Doce**, all of them less crowded than the city beaches during the week, but very popular at weekends.

Further afield, the large fishing village of **BARRA DE SANTO ANTÔNIO** is a popular day-trip 40km north of Maceió. Barra, which also fills up on the weekends, has a fine beach on a narrow neck of land jutting out from the coast a short canoe ride away, and good, fresh seafood is served in the cluster of small beachside hotels. The village is a stop for some Recife–Maceió interstate buses. North around 140km, just 15km before the border with Pernambuco state, the beautiful but sleepy beachside settlement of **MARAGOGI** has a handful of upmarket accommodation: the superb *Hotel Salinas*, Rodoviária AL101 Km 124 (Ⓣ81/3296-3000 and 3296-1122, Ⓦwww.salinas.com.br; ❾), a luxury hotel with every conceivable facility set on Maragogi beach, and the *Praia dos Sonhos*, Rodoviária AL101, Km 124 (Ⓣ81/3222-4598; ❻), on Peroba beach. If you're passing by on the road between Recife and Maceió, it's well worth stopping off here to try the local shrimps. An even more laid-back fishing and resort settlement, **Japaratinga**, can be found, some 40kms south of Maragogi, back towards Maceió; close to here at São Bento there is accommodation with an excellent beachside restaurant, *Marazul* (Ⓣ82/3296-7228).

Most visitors to Maceió flood north to the beaches, which leaves the coast **to the south** in relative calm, though the crowds are now beginning to make their way here too. Hourly buses marked "Deodoro" leave from the bus stop in front of the old train station in Maceió, near the harbour, passing out of the city over the Trapiche bridge into a flat, swampy coastline. Sixteen kilometres south, the road swings left to a beach called **Praia do Francês**, which even by Alagoan standards is something special. An enormous expanse of white sand, surf and thick palm forest, it even boasts a couple of small hotels; the *Hotel Cumarú* (❸) is the best value.

Eating, drinking and nightlife

Maceió is particularly well known for its excellent shrimp and lobster dishes, but caters for just about everyone. Some of the best places to eat and drink in the city are out of the centre, at Mundaú lagoon and Pajuçara beach. From Praça dos Martírios you can take a taxi, or a local bus marked "Mundaú" or "Ponta da Barra", for the short ride to **Lagoa Mundaú**, where you can have a *caipirinha* at a **waterfront bar** to accompany the routinely spectacular sunset. There are simple but excellent **eating places** here, too, selling fish and shrimp, and the early evening is a good time to watch prawn fishermen at work on punts in the lagoon, their silhouetted figures throwing out nets against the sunset.

At **Pajuçara**, you'll find a series of **bars** built around thatched emplacements – *barracas* – at intervals along the beach. They mix excellent *caipirinhas* and serve cheaper food than you're likely to find in the seafront restaurants on the other side of the road, all much the same. Seafood is, naturally, best: the *sopa de ostra* manages to get more oysters into a single dish than most gringos see in a lifetime; they're so common, you can even get an oyster omelette. There are one or two **cafés** in the old town centre, but more are located on the beach front, which is also lined with *barracas* at regular intervals. The new and very trendy, *Kakaffa* coffee shop has a huge air-conditioning apparatus inside as well as tables out front; their speciality is machiatto and caramel coffee, but they also serve fine snacks. Of the **restaurants**, branches of *Spettus* (daily 11.30am until late; ⓣ82/3327-4714) at Av. Roberto Kennedy 1911 (also known as Av. Carlos Luna Viana) and at Av. Alvaro Otacilio 3309, both in Ponta Verde, are the best places in town for steaks and *rodizios*, but they're not cheap. Slightly more expensive, the sophisticated French restaurant *Gstaad*, on the same street at no. 2167, is well known for its salmon dishes. Good budget options are the Chinese restaurant *Nova China* and *Restaurante Japones*, Rua Senador Rui Palmeira 46 (ⓣ82/3337-0253). If you can afford to spend a bundle, there's the stylish *Sushi Bar New Hakata*, Rua Eng. Paulo Brandao Nogueira 95, in Stella Maris (ⓣ82/3325-6160). More reasonable is the *Creperia Flor das Aguas*, Av. Alvaro Otacilio 3309, Ponta Verde (Mon–Fri noon–11pm, Sat & Sun 4–11pm; ⓣ82/3231-2335), which serves good waffles and, of course, crepes. For simple but tasty Italian dishes, it's hard to beat *Restaurante Carlito* (ⓣ82/3231-4029) at Barraca 32, on the beach at Ponta Verde; they also deliver. Perhaps surprisingly, there's a great little Peruvian restaurant, *Wanchako*, at Rua São Francisco de Assis 93 (ⓣ82/3327-8701) in the Jatiuca suburb; open Monday to Friday for lunch (12–3pm) and dinner (7–11.30pm) but just in the evening on Saturday. For good quality but inexpensive lunchtime self-service meals, try *Cabôco's* on the corner of Rua Eng. Mario de Gusmão with Rua Carlos Tenorio, just behind the *Ritz Plazamar Hotel* in Ponta Verde.

For **nightlife**, the area around Rua Sá de Albuquerque (in the Jaraguá sector), is a newly fashionable part of the city that's especially lively from Thursday through Saturday each week, when the main street is closed off to traffic and the bars and restaurants put their tables outside. The liveliest of Maceió's two main clubs is here, at Rua Sá de Albuquerque 588: the cavernous *Aeroporco's* (Thurs–Sat; ⓣ82/3326-5145) has Brazilian DJs, lots of samba and a sushi bar. The other club, *Aquarela*, at Antônio Gomes de Barros 66, in Jatiúca, also has a large dance floor, as well as reasonably good live bands playing *pagode* and *forró*, and some touristy dance shows. The Fundação Teatro Deodoro on Praça Deodoro sometimes presents spectacular dance performances; check the cultural listings in the *Tribuna de Alagoas* newspaper or call ⓣ82/3327-2727 for information.

There are a number of **gay and lesbian clubs** in Maceió, notably *Blackout* and *Heaven*, both in the Rio Uruguay sector, while *Bar Sensensura* on Rua Sá de Albuquerque has great *pagode* nights on Sundays. Stella Maris is another trendy area of town for nightlife, gay or straight.

Listings

Airlines TAM, Rua Epaminodas Gracindo 92, Pajucara ⓣ82/3327-6400 or at airport ⓣ82/3214-4114 or 3214-4112; Varig ⓣ82/3214-4100; Transbrasil ⓣ82/3221-8286. For information on flights, call the airport on ⓣ82/3214-4000.

Banks and exchange Banco do Brasil and HSBC are both on the first block of Rua do Livramento, close to the corner with Rua Boa Vista. You can change money and traveller's cheques at Aero Turismo, Av. Santos Pacheco 65.

Car rental Sul Car, Rua Tenente Darcy Barbosa 82-a, Poço ⓣ82/9999-2366; Comercial Locadora, Rua Zeferino Rodrigues 100, Pajuçara ⓣ82/3327-9145; and Turisauto ⓣ3033-5748.

Internet At Ponta Verde, there's a small Internet café (without food or drink, however) on the second floor of the artesanato shopping centre, Pavilão do Artesanato; additionally, there's *Cafeconet*, Rua Emp. Carlos da Silva Nogueira 192, Loja C, in Jatiúca (℡82/3235-5334). Emporio Jaragua Cybercafe, Rua Sá de Albuquerque 378, in Jaraguá, has good food and coffee; also at Loja 7a Rua Jangadeiros Alagoanos 1292 (℡82/3337-4718), in a complex by the *Othon Hotel*.

Post office The post office is at Rua João Pessoa 57 in the centre near the Asamblea building, with a branch in Shopping Centro de Artesabato Jaraguá, Rua Sá da Albuquerque 417.

Shopping The Pavilão do Artesanato, just over the road from Ponta Verde's beachside tourist information centre, is stuffed with local crafts such as filigree lace bedspreads, Irish lace tablecloths or other pieces with unusual colours and geometric or floral designs. The city's other main craft centre is the cheaper and more rustic Mercado do Artesanato, with shell ornaments, ceramics and wooden objects and utensils; located at Rua Melo Moraes 617 (℡82/3221-1258).

Taxis SINTAXI ℡82/3336-6786; Tele Taxi ℡82/3320-3232; Liga Taxi ℡82/3326-2121.

Travel and tour companies Marcão Turismo, Rua Firmino de Vasconcelos 685, Pajuçara (℡82/3327-7711, Ⓦwww.maceioturismo.com.br) offer city tours, trips to the Lagoa Mundaú and the southern and northern beaches, and excursions as far afield as Recife and Olinda. Jaragua Turismo, Rua Jangadeiros Alagoanos 999, Pajucara (℡82/3337-2780 Ⓦwww.jaraguaturismo.com.br) run tours to the Praia do Frances, around the city, to nearby islands as well as the São Francisco delta. A range of local beach, city and entertainment tours are available through Status Turismo, Av. Robert Kennedy 1785, Ponta Verde (℡82/3327-7771, Ⓦwww.statusturismo.com.br). Transamerica Turismo, Av. Dr Antonio Gouveia 487 (℡82/3231-7334) operate daily trips to Lagoa Mundaú and other beauty spots. For diving, contact ScuBrasil at Rua Mexihão 12, Corais do Frances, Marechal Deodoro (℡82/3260-1417, Ⓦwww.scubrasil.com.br).

Marechal Deodoro

The beautifully preserved colonial town of **MARECHAL DEODORO** lies 22km south of Maceió. Basically it's no more than a small market town, built on rising ground on the banks of a lagoon, with streets that are either dirt or cobbled. But it's immaculately kept, with not a single building that looks as if it were constructed this century. Nor is it simply preserved for tourists to gawp at: the locals spit in the streets, gossip and hang about in bars as they would anywhere else, and there's a real air of small-town tranquillity.

The bus from Maceió drives right to the end of town before reaching its terminus. You should get off a little earlier, in the manicured **Praça Pedro Paulinho**, which is dominated by the imposing facade of the Igreja de Santa Maria Magdalena, with the older **Convento de São Francisco**, finished in 1684, attached. The convent's plain exterior conceals an austere, yet strikingly beautiful interior, which is now turned over to the excellent **Museu de Arte Sagrada** (Mon & Wed–Sat 9am–5pm; entrance is from the road running down towards the lake from Praça Pedro Paulinho). The convent is built around a cool courtyard, with the main galleries on the first storey. Everything on display is high Catholic religious art, with little concession made to the tropical setting save for the large number of portrayals of São Benedito, the black patron saint of the slaves who manned the *engenhos* all around and built most of Marechal Deodoro itself. The highlight of the collection, extracted from churches all over the state, is the group of seventeenth- to nineteenth-century statues of saints and virgins, in the first gallery to the right. Most are no more than a foot high, made of wood or plaster, and intricately painted. Look, too, for the couple of life-size (and frighteningly lifelike) carved wooden bodies of Christ, with gruesome wounds. In comparison, the **Igreja de Santa Maria Magdalena** is not as impressive, a typical mid-eighteenth-century building, though less cloyingly Rococo than most. In front of a small side chapel, opposite the entrance from the museum, is a concealed entrance to a secret tunnel, a relic from the original chapel that stood on the site during the Dutch wars.

Down the road curving to the right past the museum is the modest house that was the birthplace of **Marechal Deodoro**, proclaimer and first president of the Republic in 1889; it's now preserved as a **museum** (Rua Mal. Deodoro 92; daily 8am–5pm). Deodoro was the son of an army officer who served with distinction in the Paraguayan war, and rose to become head of the armed forces with the sonorous title "Generalissimo of the Forces of Land and Sea". He was the first Brazilian to mount a military coup, unceremoniously dumping the harmless old emperor Dom Pedro II, but he proved an arrogant and inept president, the earliest in a depressingly long line of incompetent military authoritarians. Dissolving Congress and declaring a state of siege in 1891, he did everyone a favour by resigning when he couldn't make it stick. There's no hint, of course, of his disastrous political career in the museum, which is basically a mildly interesting collection of personal effects and period furniture.

In the streets around you'll find several **lacemakers**, with goods displayed in the windows. Marechal Deodoro is famous for its lace, which you see in any sizeable market in the Northeast. It's high-quality stuff, and costs less than half the price you pay elsewhere when bought at source in the town. The Cooperative Artesanal in Rua Dr Ladislam Netto is a good place to look.

If you want to stay, there's a **pensão**, *Deodoré* (❶), on Praça Pedro Paulinho, but there's no sign so you'll have to ask. There's also a **campsite** (Ⓣ82/3263-1378), clean and with good facilities, half an hour's walk beyond the square; the road is marked by a sign near the small bus company office. For **tourist information** call the municipal tourist line on Ⓣ82/221-4615 or check out Ⓦwww.marechaldeodoro.net.com.br.

Paulo Afonso and around

Inland from Maceió, 300km to the west, the most popular destination of all in Alagoas is the **Cachoeira de Paulo Afonso**, once the largest waterfall on the Rio São Francisco and the third largest in Brazil, but now largely emasculated by a hydroelectric scheme that diverted most of the flow – a spectacular piece of ecological vandalism surpassed only by the destruction of the even more impressive Sete Quedas waterfall in Paraná by similar means in the early 1990s. These days the only time a considerable amount of water passes over the falls is during the rains of January and February, but the whole surrounding area – a spectacular deep rocky gorge choked with tropical forest and declared a national park – is very scenic all year round.

You can get there by bus from Salvador, but the journey from Maceió is shorter, with two **buses** daily from the *rodoviária* there. They leave you in the small river town of **PAULO AFONSO**, on the Bahian riverbank, where there is a cluster of reasonable **hotels** near the bus station; the *Belvedere*, Av. Apolônio Sales 457 (Ⓣ75/3281-1814; ❺), is more upmarket than the others, but good value.

The **waterfall** is some way out of town and you can only get there by taxi, which will cost you about R$12 an hour, but the drivers do know the best spots. Alternatively, you may be able to organize something with the tourist office in the centre of town on Rua Apolônio Sales (Mon–Sat 9am–6pm; Ⓣ75/3281-2757), which doubles up as the best place to find local guides.

Penedo

A couple of hours, and some 168km, south of Maceió is the lively colonial town of **PENEDO**. Originally developed to control the illegal exportation of lumber by French merchant ships in the sixteenth century, it was occupied by the Dutch between 1637 and 1645, who built the original fort here. There are several colonial churches in town that are all marked on a useful map, obtainable at the **tourist office** (Mon–Fri 8–11am & 2–5pm) in the main central square, the Praça Barão de Penedo. The most attractive is the early eighteenth-century *azulejo*-decorated **Igreja de Nossa Senhora da Corrente**, which has a stunning gold-leaf altar inside. The **museum** in the Casa do Penedo, Rua João Pessoa 126 (Mon–Sat 9am–noon & 2–4pm; R$2.50), is also worth a visit for its displays of period furniture and historical photographs and documents.

Penedo is strategically placed at the mouth of the Rio São Francisco, and, while the trading prosperity it might have expected as a result never quite materialized, it's still a busy little place, much of whose life revolves around the river and the waterfront. The waterfront park, with its shaded paths and kiosks selling drinks, is a good place to watch the to-ing and fro-ing of the boats. You can negotiate with boat owners to go on **cruises**: the main destinations are **Piassabussu**, a sleepy and little-visited fishing village right on the mouth of the river, and the village of **Neópolis**, opposite Penedo, where there's nothing to do except have a drink and catch the boat back – but it's a nice trip.

Penedo is served by four **buses** daily from Maceió's *rodoviária* and for once they leave you in the centre of the town, which is well supplied with good **places to stay**: try *Pousada Colonial*, Praça 12 de Abril (Ⓣ82/3551-2355, Ⓕ3551-3737; ❷), which has adequate rooms plus excellent views over Penedo, or the more comfortable *São Francisco*, on Avenida Floriano Peixoto (Ⓣ823/3551-2273, Ⓕ3551-2274, Ⓦwww.hotelsaofrancisco-penedo.com.br; ❹), both in the heart of town; nearer the **rodoviária** (Ⓣ82/3551-2602) on Rua Siqueira Campos, are a number of budget hotels with prices starting at around R$30. One of the town's better **restaurants** is *Forte da Rocheira* (Ⓣ82/3551-3273) on Rua da Rocheira, specializing in fish dishes. Out of town, 30km east of Penedo near the town of Piaçabuço, the *Pousada Piaçabuçu* (Ⓣ82/3557-1112, Ⓔroeland@sidtecnet.com.br) offers ecological tours of the surrounding countryside.

Aracaju

From Maceió seven buses a day run to **ARACAJU**, capital of the neighbouring state of **Sergipe** (population 430,000), a little-visited and rather anonymous place. Although the Portuguese founded a colony at Aracaju in 1592, the capital of the infant state was later moved to nearby São Cristóvão. Then, in the mid-nineteenth century, there was a sudden vogue for purpose-built administrative centres (similar to the urge that led to the construction of Brasília a century later), and the core of modern Aracaju was thrown up overnight, with the city becoming the state capital again in 1855. Aracaju is – to put it mildly – something of an architectural desert, built on an American-style grid layout. Oil wealth has stimulated a lot of recent building and given the city council enough money to keep everything clean and tidy, but there is a very un-Brazilian dullness about the place. However, the people are friendly, some of the beaches are good and the small colonial towns of Laranjeiras and São Cristóvão are only a short bus ride away.

The new **rodoviária** (☎79/2359-2848) is quite a way out of town, linked to the centre by frequent local buses; the old *rodoviária* (Terminal Velha, ☎79/3214-2578), which serves mainly local buses, is five blocks north of Praça Olimpia Campos. The **airport** (☎79/3212-8500) is also out of town (12km) but not far from the beach of Atalaia Velha; buses marked "Aeroporto" will get you into the centre. Sergipe's **tourist office** has its headquarters at Tr. Baltazar Gois 86, in the centre (☎79/3179-1940), while the SEBRAE office is at the Centro de Turismo (daily 8am–8pm; ☎79/3214-8848 and 3255-1413), in the shopping centre known as Rua 24 Horas, just next to Praça Olímpio Campos. Rua 24 Horas is actually a very pleasant place, set in a restored nineteenth-century building, with cafés, restaurants and a stage where shows are sometimes put on.

The cheaper **hotels** are as usual in the city centre, several of them near the municipal bus station, the Rodoviária Velha. For a real budget option you could stay at the *Sergipe Hotel*, Rua Geru 205 (☎79/3222-7898; ❶–❷), which is perfectly adequate for the price. Two comfortable mid-range hotels in the same area are the *Oásis*, at Rua São Cristóvão 466 (☎79/3224-1181; ❸), and the *Amado*, at Rua Laranjeiras 532 (☎79/3211-9937; ❸). Right next to the Rodoviária Velha is the plusher and pricier *Grande Hotel*, at Rua Itabaianinha 371 (☎79/3211-1383; ❹), while down at the southern end of the city centre the *Hotel Jangadeiro*, at Rua Santa Luiza 269 (☎79/3211-1350, ⓦwww.jangadeira.com.br; ❸), has a pool and decent rooms with TV and telephone.

The two main **beaches** are Atalaia Velha and Atalaia Nova. **ATALAIA VELHA** lies about 5km south down the road from the city centre and is the more developed of the two. It's easy to get to there by bus, but the whole area is rather soulless and uninspiring. There are, however, a huge number of restaurants and **hotels**, including the *Pousada do Sol*, Rua Atalaia 43 (☎79/3226-5500, ⓦwww.psol.com.br; ❹), the *Nascimento Praia*, Av. Santos Dumont 1813 (☎79/3255-2090; ❹–❺), which has a small pool, and, for total luxury, the *Del Mar Hotel*, Av. Santos Dumont 1500 (☎79/2106-9100, ⓦwww.delmarhotel.com.br; ❻–❼). **ATALAIA NOVA** lies on an island in the Rio Sergipe, accessible by boat from the *hidroviária* in the city centre. The ferry leaves every ten minutes and costs just R$1.50; you can then get a bus to Atalaia Nova from the ferry terminal. Although the beach itself isn't great, the island is quite a pleasant place to stay – hotels are expensive, but there are plenty of rooms for rent.

Laranjeiras and São Cristóvão

Sergipe's main attractions are two attractive colonial towns that come as a welcome relief from Aracaju's anonymity, reminders of the time when sugar made the *sergipano* coast one of the most strategically valuable parts of Brazil. Innumerable skirmishes were fought around them during the Dutch wars, but no trace of their turbulent past survives into their tranquil present, as they slide from important market centres into rural backwaters.

The pleasantly decrepit village of **LARANJEIRAS** is 40 minutes by half-hourly bus from Aracaju's Rodoviária Velha. Dominated by a hill crowned with the ruins of an old *engenho* chapel, Laranjeiras boasts a couple of small museums as well as the inevitable churches. The interesting **Museu Afro-Brasileiro**, Rua José do Prado Franco 70 (Tues–Sun 8am–noon &

2–5.30pm), concentrates on slave life and popular religion, while the **Centro de Cultura João Ribeiro**, Rua João Ribeiro (Mon–Fri 8am–10pm, Sat 8am–1pm, Sun 2–5pm), is mostly given over to *artesanato* and relics of plantation life. But the main attraction is simply wandering around the winding streets, taking in the quiet squares, pastel-painted houses and small bars where locals sit around and watch the world go by. There are a couple of **pensões**, but no hotels as yet.

The other colonial town worth visiting is the old state capital of **SÃO CRISTÓVÃO**, also reached by local bus (hourly) from Aracaju's Rodoviária Velha, a thirty-minute journey. The town was founded in 1590 and much of it hasn't changed since, as the shifting of the capital to Aracaju preserved it from the developers. Packed into its small area is the full panoply of a colonial administrative centre, including an old governor's palace, a parliament building and half a dozen period churches, together with the small **Museu de Arte Sacra e Histórico** in the Convento de São Francisco (Tues–Sun 9am–noon & 2–5.30pm). The convent contains a chapel decorated with paintings by José Teófilo de Jesus, one of the most important sacred painters from the Northeast.

Pernambuco

Recife, capital of the state of **Pernambuco**, shares with São Luis the distinction of not having been founded by the Portuguese: when they arrived in the 1530s, they settled just to the north, building the beautiful colonial town of **Olinda** and turning most of the surrounding land over to sugar. A century later, the Dutch, under Maurice of Nassau, burned Olinda down, choosing to build a new capital, Recife, on swampy land to the south, where there was the fine natural harbour that Olinda had lacked. The Dutch, playing to their strengths, drained and reclaimed the low-lying land, and the main evidence of the Dutch presence today is not so much their few surviving churches and forts dotted up and down the coast, as the reclaimed land on which the core of Recife is built.

Out of Recife, there are good beaches in both directions. The Portuguese first developed the coastline as far **north** as the island of **Itamaracá**, growing sugar cane on every available inch. This erstwhile fishing village still retains its Dutch fort, built to protect the new colonial power's acquisitions, but these days it's a fairly blighted weekenders' resort. Best is the **coastal route south**, where a succession of small towns and villages interrupts a glorious stretch of palm-fringed beach.

Head **inland** and the scenery changes quickly to the hot, dry and rocky landscape of the *sertão*. **Caruaru** is the obvious target, home of the largest market in the Northeast, and close by is **Alto do Moura**, centre of the highly rated Pernambucan pottery industry. If you plan to go any further inland than this you'll need to prepare well for any kind of extended *sertão* journey, though it's straightforward enough to reach the twin river towns of **Petrolina** and **Juazeiro**.

Recife

The Northeast's second-largest city, **RECIFE**, appears rather dull on first impressions, but it's lent a colonial grace and elegance by Olinda, 6km to the north and considered part of the same conurbation. Recife itself has long since burst its original colonial boundaries, and much of the centre is now given over to uninspired modern skyscrapers and office buildings. But there are still a few quiet squares where an inordinate number of impressive churches lie cheek by jowl with the uglier urban sprawl of the past thirty years. North of the centre are some pleasant leafy suburbs, dotted with museums and parks, and to the south there is the modern beachside district of **Boa Viagem**. Other beaches lie within easy reach, both north and south of the city, and there's also all the **nightlife** one would expect from a city of nearly two million Brazilians.

Tourists wandering around Recife should be particularly careful with their possessions and it's best, too, to use taxis to get home after an evening out. Recife is one of Brazil's most violent cities, an unsurprising statistic given the immediately obvious disparity of wealth and stark poverty, and the large number of homeless people on the streets. On Sundays in the old centre of Recife, the streets often seem deserted except for beggars; everyone else seems to be on the beach at Boa Viagem. Tourists tend to hang out in the much more pleasant environment of laid-back Olinda.

Arrival, information and city transport

The **airport** (☎81/3464-4188) is fairly close to the city centre, at the far end of Boa Viagem. A taxi to Boa Viagem itself shouldn't be more than R$20, to the neighbouring island of Santo Antônio about R$30; or take the Aeroporto bus (R$6) from right outside, which will drive through Boa Viagem and drop you in the centre. The **rodoviária** is miles out, though this is not really a problem since the **metrô** (☎81/3252-6100 for information), an overground rail link, whisks you very cheaply and efficiently into the centre, giving you a good introduction to city life as it glides through various *favelas*. It will deposit you at the old train station, called **Estação Central** (or simply "Recife"). To get to your hotel from there, whether in the central hotel district, Boa Viagem or even Olinda, you're best off taking a **taxi** – Recife is a confusing city even when you've been there a few days, and the extra money will be well spent.

Information

The most helpful **tourist information** in Recife is the large office at the airport (daily 8am–6pm; ☎81/3326-9603 and 3462-4960) where you may find English-speaking staff and a few maps and calendars of events. They'll also ring hotels for you, but are no good for the cheapest places. There's another good little office on the corner of Praça at the end of Rua da Guia in the heart of the newly restored **Bairro do Recife** (☎81/3224-2361).

EMPETUR has its headquarters inconveniently located at the **Centro de Convenções** (Mon–Fri 9am–6pm; ☎81/3425-8460), an ugly concrete building more or less en route between Recife and Olinda. In **Boa Viagem**, there is a Delegacia do Turista at Praça do Boa Viagem (8am-8pm; ☎81/3463-3621) that can help with accommodation at the beach. Alternatively, there's the **tourist hotline** (Mon–Fri 8am–6pm; ☎81/3425-8409), on which you should be able to find someone who speaks English.

For up-to-date **listings** of events in and around Recife, try the *Roteiro* section of the daily *Jornal do Comércio*, or the *Viver* section of the *Diário de Pernambuco*, also daily. Alternatively, the *Agenda Cultural do Recife* is a useful guide to museums and theatre, plus dance, music and photography events, and is available from the Casa da Cultura (see p.328) or online at Ⓦwww.recife.pe.gov.br.

City transport

Recife's **bus network** (Ⓣ81/3452-1999) is an appalling mess. Routes change frequently, the destinations marked on the front of the buses are places you've never heard of, and, unlike in Rio or Salvador, there are no helpful signs on the side of the vehicle showing where it stops along the way. To make things worse, the complex layout of the city means that it's hard to get your bearings. What follows is a basic guide to getting around, but you'll probably still have to ask.

Most city buses originate and terminate on the central island of **Santo Antônio**, on Avenida Dantas Barreto, either side of the **Pracinha do Diário** (also known as Praça da Independência). There are more stops nearby on Avenida Guararapes outside the main post office. To get from the city centre **to Boa Viagem**, take buses marked "Aeroporto", "Iguatemi" or "Boa Viagem", or catch the more comfortable *frescão* (an air-conditioned bus) marked "Aeroporto", just outside the offices of the newspaper *Diário de Pernambuco*, on the Pracinha do Diário; it leaves every 20 minutes and costs about R$6. To get to **Olinda** from central Recife, walk south down Avenida Dantas Barreto from the Pracinha do Diário to the last of the series of bus stops, and catch the bus marked "Casa Caiada" – you'll think you're heading in the wrong direction at first, but, after half an hour or so, you will eventually get there. Alternatively, a taxi from central Recife to Olinda will cost a few dollars and take about fifteen minutes.

From Boa Viagem, most buses in either direction can be caught on Avenida Engenheiro Domingos Ferreira, three blocks in from the sea. Buses marked "Dantas Barreto" will get you **to the city centre**, and so should most of those marked "Conde de Boa Vista", though it's probably best to ask. You can get directly from Boa Viagem **to Olinda** on buses marked "Rio Doce".

If you're completely fed up with the buses, there are always **shared taxis**. These small vans tear around the city towards the end of the afternoon, offering lifts to various destinations for between R$2 and R$6. They'll stop almost anywhere and are a pretty good way of getting around as long as you're not too nervous a passenger, though it's clear that many locals don't like to use them.

Accommodation

It's cheapest to stay in the rather run-down centre, and most expensive in the beach district of Boa Viagem. The other obvious area to consider staying in is Olinda (see p.335), where prices fall somewhere between the two and, although there's not much of a beach, it has a lot more to offer culturally. Recife's **youth hostel**, the *Albergue da Juventude Maracatus do Recife*, is in Boa Viagem at Rua Maria Carolina 185 (Ⓣ81/3326-1964). Complete with swimming pool and free breakfast, it's excellent value at R$40 a night.

The centre: Boa Vista and Santo Antônio

Most central hotels are concentrated around Rua do Hospício, near the bridges linking Santo Antônio with the neighbouring island of Boa Vista.

Hotel America Praça Maciel Pinheiro 48, Boa Vista Ⓣ81/3221-1300. Two-star hotel that's not as expensive as it looks; rooms are a bit run down but adequate and safe. ❸

Hotel Central Av. Manoel Borba 209, Boa Vista Ⓣ81/3423-6411. As its name suggests, this hotel is central and is located on one of Recife's quieter and more elegant streets. Does a superb breakfast. ❹

Hotel Nassau Rua Largo do Rosário 253, Santo Antônio ⓣ81/3224-3977. A comfortable hotel in a good location; the spacious rooms come with private baths. ❸

Hotel Quatro de Outubro Rua Floriano Peixoto 141, Santo Antônio ⓣ81/3224-4900. Close to Recife's main *metrô* station, the hotel is rundown but reasonable value; all rooms have a/c and TV. ❹–❺

Hotel São Domingos Praça Maciel Pinheiro 66, Boa Vista ⓣ81/3231-1388. Clean and modern two-star hotel just a few blocks from the beach; quite comfortable, but a little lacking in style. All rooms have private baths. ❸

Recife Plaza Rua da Aurora 225, Boa Vista ⓣ81/3231-1200. Nondescript place close to the central river bridge, the Ponte do Coelho. Rooms are reasonable, with a/c and TV, and there's a restaurant, a sauna and a swimming pool. ❹

Boa Viagem

In Boa Viagem, finding a hotel is the least of your problems – it sometimes seems as if they outnumber apartment buildings. The difficulty is finding a reasonably cheap one, as the majority cater for international tourists and rich Brazilians. Even so, you should be able to find somewhere for between R$40 and R$60 a night, certainly if you're prepared to stay a little way back from the seafront.

Atlante Plaza Av. Boa Viagem 5426 ⓣ81/3302-3333, freephone/toll-free for reservations ⓣ81/3302-3344, ⓦwww.atlanteplaza.com.br. Large, modern and well located in the centre of beach and night life, this upmarket hotel boasts elevators with panoramic views, plus a bar, restaurant, swimming pool, saunas and a fitness suite. ❼

Hotel 54 Rua Prof. José Brandão 54 ⓣ81/3465-2396. A pleasant place to stay with a/c and TV, but no pool. ❸

Hotel 200 Milhas Av. Boa Viagem 864 ⓣ81/3326-5921. Cheap hotel that's incredible value given its seafront location. ❸

Hotel Boa Viagem Av. Boa Viagem 5000 ⓣ81/3341-4144. The least expensive of all the four-star seafront hotels, this modern place has stylish rooms (some with ocean views) plus good showers. ❻

Hotel Park Rua dos Navegantes 9 ⓣ & ⓕ81/3465-4666. Large, modern and upmarket place (but still quite good value) in the centre of the action. Located just a block from the beach, but also has a pool. ❹

Hotel Portal do Sol Av. Cons. Aguiar 3217 ⓣ81/3326-9740. Moderately priced hotel in a good location just two blocks away from the beach and on Recife's principal bus routes. ❹

Hotel Savaroni Av. Boa Viagem 3772 ⓣ81/3465-4299, ⓕ3463-7664. A mid-sized, good-value place with standard rooms and apartments with all the modern conveniences. Has a bar, a pretty good restaurant and a small pool as well. ❼

Park Othon Hotel Rua dos Navegantes 9 ⓣ81/3465-4666. An anonymous high-rise, but just a stone's throw from the beach. Its restaurant serves good seafood dishes. ❼

Pousada Aconchego Rua Felix de Brito 382 ⓣ81/3326-2989, ⓦwww.hotelaconchego.com.br. This small and comfortable hotel has a swimming pool and a good restaurant open 24 hours a day. ❹

Recife Monte Hotel Rua dos Navegantes 363 ⓣ81/3465-7422, ⓦwww.recifemontehotel.com.br. A glorified apartment building with all mod cons, whose claim to fame is that Chico Buarque and Charles Aznavour once stayed here. ❼

Recife Palace Av. Boa Viagem 4070 ⓣ81/3464-2500, ⓕ3465-6767, ⓦwww.lucsimhoteis.com.br. Superb beach views and all comforts; this is the cheapest of the five-star hotels by a long way. ❼

Vila Rica Ideale Hotel Av. Boa Viagem 4308 ⓣ81/3465-8111. A good deal in this price range, boasting every four-star luxury. ❺

The City

Modern Recife sprawls onto the mainland, but the heart of the city is three small **islands** – Santo Antônio, Boa Vista and Recife proper – connected with each other and the mainland by more than two dozen bridges over the rivers Beberibe and Capibaribe. This profusion of waterways has led to the inevitable description of Recife as the "Venice of Brazil" – a totally ludicrous idea. Recife island, now known as old Recife, or the **Bairro do Recife,** is where

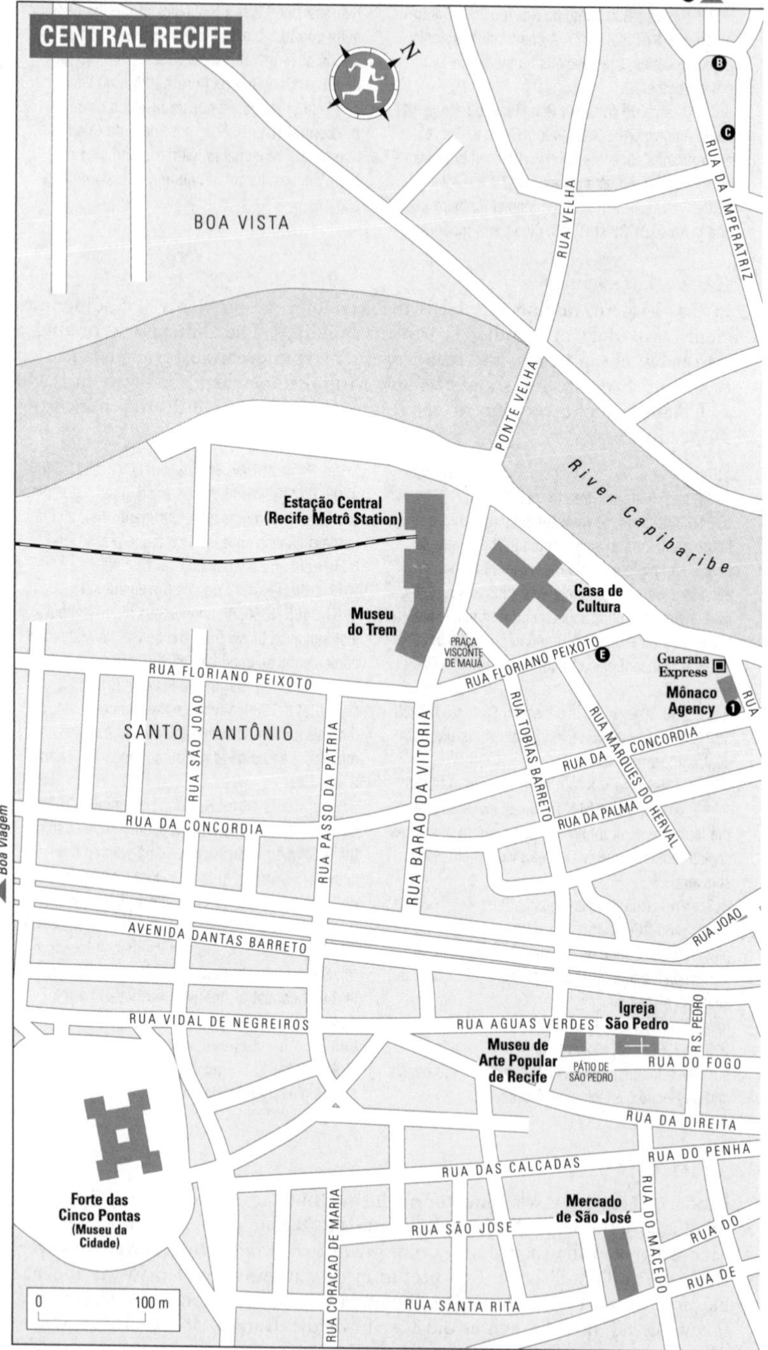
CENTRAL RECIFE
N
BOA VISTA
RUA VELHA
RUA DA IMPERATRIZ
PONTE VELHA
River Capibaribe
Estação Central
(Recife Metrô Station)
Casa de
Cultura
Museu
do Trem
PRAÇA
VISCONTE
DE MAUÁ
RUA FLORIANO PEIXOTO
Guarana
Express
Mônaco
Agency
RUA
SANTO ANTÔNIO
RUA SÃO JOAO
RUA PASSO DA PATRIA
RUA BARAO DA VITORIA
RUA TOBIAS BARRETO
RUA MARQUES DO HERVAL
RUA DA CONCORDIA
RUA DA PALMA
Boa Viagem
AVENIDA DANTAS BARRETO
RUA JOAO
RUA VIDAL DE NEGREIROS
RUA AGUAS VERDES
Igreja
São Pedro
R. S. PEDRO
Museu de
Arte Popular
de Recife
PÁTIO DE
SÃO PEDRO
RUA DO FOGO
RUA DA DIREITA
RUA DO PENHA
RUA DAS CALCADAS
Forte das
Cinco Pontas
(Museu da
Cidade)
Mercado
de São José
RUA DO MACEDO
RUA SÃO JOSE
RUA DO
RUA DE
RUA CORACAO DE MARIA
RUA SANTA RITA
0
100 m

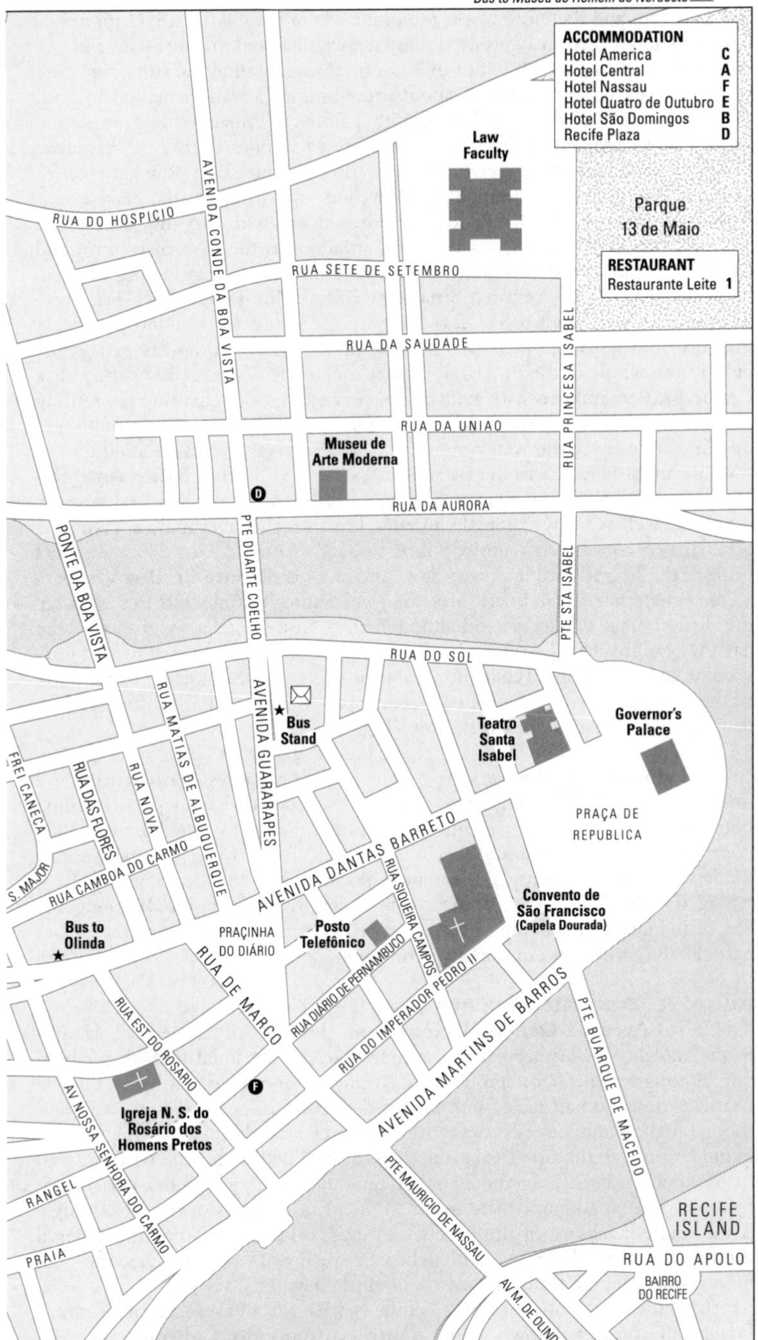
Bus to Museu do Homem do Nordeste
ACCOMMODATION
Hotel America C
Hotel Central A
Hotel Nassau F
Hotel Quatro de Outubro E
Hotel São Domingos B
Recife Plaza D
RESTAURANT
Restaurante Leite 1
Law Faculty
Parque 13 de Maio
RUA DO HOSPICIO
AVENIDA CONDE DA BOA VISTA
RUA SETE DE SETEMBRO
RUA DA SAUDADE
RUA PRINCESA ISABEL
RUA DA UNIAO
Museu de Arte Moderna
RUA DA AURORA
PONTE DA BOA VISTA
PTE DUARTE COELHO
PTE STA ISABEL
RUA DO SOL
Bus Stand
AVENIDA GUARARAPES
RUA MATIAS DE ALBUQUERQUE
RUA NOVA
RUA DAS FLORES
FREI CANECA
Teatro Santa Isabel
Governor's Palace
PRAÇA DE REPUBLICA
AVENIDA DANTAS BARRETO
RUA SIQUEIRA CAMPOS
RUA CAMBOA DO CARMO
S. MAJOR
Convento de São Francisco
(Capela Dourada)
Bus to Olinda
PRAÇINHA DO DIÁRIO
Posto Telefônico
RUA DIÁRIO DE PERNAMBUCO
RUA DO IMPERADOR PEDRO II
RUA DE MARCO
RUA EST DO ROSARIO
AVENIDA MARTINS DE BARROS
PTE BUARQUE DE MACEDO
Igreja N. S. do Rosário dos Homens Pretos
AV NOSSA SENHORA DO CARMO
RANGEL
PRAIA
PTE MAURICIO DE NASSAU
RECIFE ISLAND
RUA DO APOLO
BAIRRO DO RECIFE
AV M. DE OLINDA

the docks are and therefore marks the point where the city began. Until only a few years ago it was a dangerous, rundown area inhabited mainly by drunks and prostitutes, but the investment of millions of dollars by the local authorities and private businesses have brought about something of a transformation in both the look and feel of the area. The brightly painted colonial buildings make the small, easily negotiable island a pleasant place to wander during the day, even though there aren't many specific things to do. And the island now has Recife's best nightlife, its streets jammed with revellers right through the early hours. The streets and *praças* of Bairro do Recife are stocked with bars and cafes, which are very busy at weekends, but the main attraction is the ambience of the old city heart around Rua da Guia and Rua do Bom Jesus. A fascinating visit can be made to the newly restored **Sinagoga Kahal Zur Israel** (Tues–Fri, 9am–4.30pm, Sun 3–6.30pm ⓣ81/3224-2128 or 3225-0068, ⓦrabulpho.com.br) at Rua do Bom Jesus 125 (the old Rua dos Judeus). This was the first synagogue built in the whole of the Americas; it dates back to 1637 and today is the Judaic Centre for Pernambuco state, with permanent exhibitions covering the settling of Jews in the city. The walls display original seventeenth-century moulds and upstairs you can see the well-restored and quite special synagogue itself.

Whilst nighlife is best in the Bairro do Recife, the island of **Santo Antônio**, which is split by Avenida Dantas Barreto, is home to the area's central business district as well as many colonial churches. Just over the river is **Boa Vista**, the other major commercial centre, linked to Santo Antônio by a series of small bridges; the brightly painted criss-cross girders of the **Ponte de Boa Vista** are a convenient central landmark over the river. Santo Antônio and Boa Vista are the dirtiest areas of Recife, and although they bustle with activity during the day they empty at night, when the enormous, largely deserted streets are a little spooky and forbidding. Residential suburbs stretch to the north, but the bulk of the middle-class population is concentrated to the south, in a long ribbon development along the beach at **Boa Viagem**.

There's no excuse for being bored in Recife. There are literally dozens of colonial **churches** in the city, one excellent and several lesser **museums**, and some lovely public buildings. The churches tend not to have regular opening hours, but if the main door is shut you can often get in by knocking on a side door – if there's anyone inside they'll be only too happy to let you in. Even for the less determined sightseer, there are parks, **beaches** and a number of places where the most interesting thing to do is simply drift about, absorbing the feel of the city and watching people get on with their lives – something that's particularly good to do in the city's **markets**.

Avenida Dantas Barreto and São Francisco

The broad **Avenida Dantas Barreto** forms the spine of the central island of Santo Antônio. In southern Brazil, avenues like this are lined with skyscrapers, but, although some have sprouted in Recife's financial district, generally the centre is on a human scale, with crowded, narrow lanes lined with stalls and shops opening out directly onto the streets. Dantas Barreto, the main thoroughfare, ends in the fine **Praça da República**, lined with majestic palms and surrounded by Recife's grandest public buildings – the governor's palace (not open to visitors) and an ornate theatre. One of the charms of the city, though, is the unpredictability of the streets, and even off this main boulevard you'll stumble upon old churches sandwiched between modern buildings, the cool hush inside a refuge from the noise and bustle beyond.

Perhaps the most enticing of the central buildings is the seventeenth-century Franciscan complex known as the **Santo Antônio do Convento de São**

△ Recife

Francisco, on Rua do Imperador – a combination of church, convent and museum. Outside, you'll be besieged by crowds of beggars displaying sores and stumps, but negotiate your way through to the entrance of the museum (Mon–Fri 8–11.30am & 2–5pm, Sat 2–5pm), pay the nominal fee, and you'll find yourself in a cool and quiet haven. Built around a beautiful small cloister, the museum contains some delicately painted statues of saints and other artwork rescued from demolished or crumbling local churches. But the real highlight here is the **Capela Dourada** (Golden Chapel), which has a lot in common with the churches in the old gold towns of Minas Gerais. Like them, it's a rather vulgar demonstration of colonial prosperity. Finished in 1697, the Baroque chapel is the usual wall-to-ceiling ornamentation, except that everything is covered with gold-leaf. If you look closely at the carving under the gilt you'll see that the level of workmanship is actually quite crude, but the overall effect of so much gold is undeniably impressive. What really gilded the chapel, of course, was sugar cane: the sugar trade was at its peak when it was built, and the sugar elite were building monuments to their wealth all over the city.

São Pedro, the Mercado de São José and the Museu da Cicade

The church of **São Pedro** (Mon–Fri 8–11am & 2–4pm, Sat 8–10am) is situated on the Pátio de São Pedro, just off the Avenida Dantas Barreto. The impressive facade is dominated by a statue of St Peter, which was donated to the church in 1980 by a master sculptor from the ceramics centre of Tracunhaém in the interior. Inside the church there's some exquisite woodcarving and a trompe l'oeil ceiling, and on another corner of the Pátio is the **Museu de Arte Popular de Recife** (Mon–Fri 9am–7pm), which has some interesting exhibits, including pottery and wooden sculpture. If you've missed the church's opening hours, content yourself with the exterior views, best seen with a cold beer in hand from one of the several bars that set up tables in the square outside. The whole of the Pátio has in fact been beautifully restored, which lends this part of the city a charm of its own.

Recife is probably the best big Brazilian city in which to find **artesanato**, and the area around São Pedro is the best place to look for it. If you shop around, even tight budgets can stretch to some wonderful bargains. There are stalls all over the city, but they coagulate into a bustling complex of winding streets, lined with beautiful but dilapidated early nineteenth-century tenements, which begins on the Pátio de São Pedro. The streets are choked with people and goods, all of which converge on the market proper, the **Mercado de São José**, an excellent place for *artesanato*.

If you simply can't face the crowds, there's a very good **craft shop**, Penha, on the corner of the Pátio de São Pedro. It's the main city outlet for some of Recife's excellent woodcut artists. In the same shop you'll also find extremely inexpensive prints on both cloth and paper, known as **cordel**. The usual themes are stock Northeastern stories about cowboys, devils, saints and bandits, although there are also *cordel* based on political events, educational ballads about disease and hygiene and even poems about how AIDS is transmitted and the need to use condoms. Even if you don't understand a word of Portuguese, the printed covers are often worth having in their own right, and they're extremely cheap, around R$2.50 each. Outside the shop, you can dig out *cordel* around the *mercado* or in Praça de Sebo, where the secondhand booksellers have stalls.

Determined culture vultures could also make the hop from here to Recife's most central museum, the **Museu da Cidade** (Mon–Sat 9am–6pm, Sun 1–5pm), in the star-shaped fort, the Forte das Cinco Pontas, off the western end of Avenida Dantas Barreto; the best view of it is coming in by bus from Boa Viagem. Built in 1630 by the Dutch, the fort was the last place they surrendered when they were expelled in 1654. The building is actually far more interesting than the museum itself, which is dedicated entirely to the history of the city, shown through old engravings and photographs.

The Casa da Cultura and Estação Central

Right opposite the Estação Central, now known as the Terminal Integrado do Recife (because it combines a bus station with the railway station), in Rua Floriano Peixoto, the forbidding **Casa da Cultura de Pernambuco** (Mon–Sat 9am–7pm, Sun 10am–5pm) was once the city's prison and is now an essential stop for visitors. It's cunningly designed, with three wings radiating out from a central point, so that a single warder could keep an eye on all nine corridors. The whole complex has been turned into an arts and crafts centre, the cells converted into little boutiques and one or two places for refreshment. The quality of the goods on offer here is high, but the prices are a lot higher than elsewhere in the city, so go to look rather than to buy. The Casa da Cultura is also the best place to get **information** on cultural events in the city, providing a monthly *Agenda Cultural* listing plays, films and other entertainments; dancing displays are often laid on too, which are free and not at all bad.

Over in the Estação Central itself, on the busy little Praça Visconde de Mauá, the **Museu do Trem** (Mon–Sat 10am–6pm, Sun 2–6pm) is worth a look, too, tracing the history of the railways that played a vital role in opening up the interior of the Northeast. British visitors can wax nostalgic over the exploits of the Great Western Railway of Brazil Limited, some of whose engines and wagons decorate the forecourt between the museum and the *metrô* terminal. The fine station, lovingly restored in 1997, is a relic of the days when British companies dominated the Brazilian economy.

The Museu de Arte Moderna and the Forte do Brum

The **Museu de Arte Moderna Aloisio Magalhães**, located in Boa Vista just over the river from Santo Antônio at Rua da Aurora 256 (Tues–Sun noon–6pm), has prestigious changing exhibitions of mainly Brazilian modern artists, many amongst Pernambuco's best. Of less general interest is the **Museu Militar** on Praça Comunidade Luso-Brasileira (Tues–Fri 9am–6pm, Sat & Sun 9am–4pm). Housed in the seventeeth-century **Forte do Brum** at the northern end of Recife island, the museum displays weapons, photographs, World War II artefacts and some local ethnographic pieces – only really of interest to military enthusiasts. The fort, a prominent, white-walled four-pointed structure, also puts on occasional modern art exhibitions – check for details in the monthly *Agenda Cultural do Recife*.

The Museu do Homem do Nordeste and Museu do Estado

The **Museu do Homem do Nordeste** (Mon–Fri 9am–5pm, Sat & Sun 1–5pm ⓣ81/3441-5500), assembled by anthropologists, is one of Brazil's great museums and the best introduction there is to the history and culture of the Northeast. It's quite a way out of central Recife, in Casa Forte at Avenida 17 de Agosto 2223. Take the "Dois Irmãos" bus from outside the post office or from Parque 13 de Maio, at the bottom of Rua do Hospício; there are two "Dois Irmãos" services, but the one marked "via Barbosa" is the one to get, a pleasant half-hour drive through leafy northern suburbs. The museum is not very easy to spot (on the left-hand side), so ask the driver or conductor where to get off.

The museum is split into several galleries, each devoted to one of the great themes of Northeastern economy and society: sugar, cattle, fishing, popular religion, festivals, ceramics and so on. The historical material is well displayed and interesting, but the museum's strongest point is its unrivalled collection of **popular art** – there are displays not just of handicrafts, but also of cigarette packets, tobacco pouches and, best of all, a superb collection of postwar bottles of *cachaça* (rum). A look at the designs on the labels, very Brazilian adaptations of Western 1950s and 1960s kitsch, leaves you with nothing but admiration for the imagination of the people who put the display together.

The first floor of the museum is largely devoted to the rich regional tradition of clay sculpture and pottery that still flourishes in the *agreste* and *sertão*, especially around Caruaru. The work of **Mestre Vitalino**, a peasant farmer in the village of Alto do Moura, is a highlight. In the 1920s, he began to make small statues depicting scenes of rural life, filled with an astonishing vitality and power; the feeling and expression in the faces is quite remarkable, for example, in the leering devil appearing to a terrified drunk clutching a bottle of rum. As Vitalino grew older, he began to incorporate the changes happening in the countryside around him into his work. There are statues of migrants, and urban themes appear with a series of portraits of professionals: the lawyer, doctors and dentists (very gruesome), the journalist and the secretary. These themes take over in the work of the next generation of artists, the sons of Vitalino and other pioneers, like the almost equally well-known **Zé Caboclo**, whose work fills the next few cases. In the third generation the style changed, and it's interesting that the best contemporary sculptors are women, notably the granddaughters of Zé Caboclo. The statues remain true to the established themes, but they are miniaturized, and their effect comes from the extreme delicacy of detail and painting, which contrasts with the cruder vigour of their male precursors. You'll see reproductions of many of the statues here on market stalls across Brazil, but Pernambuco is the place to get the real thing: the work of many of the artists displayed in the museum can still be bought fairly cheaply, especially in Alto do Moura itself (see p.350).

The "Dois Irmãos via Barbosa" bus is also the one to take for the **Museu do Estado** (Tues–Fri 10am–5pm, Sat & Sun 2–5pm; ⓣ81/3427-9322), a fine nineteenth-century mansion at Av. Rui Barbosa 660, in Graças. It's on the right-hand side about 20 minutes after leaving the city centre, well before the Museu do Homem do Nordeste, but again difficult to spot, so you might need to ask. Here you'll find some fine engravings of Recife as it was in the early part of the last century, all of them by English artists, and upstairs there are good paintings by Teles Júnior, which give you an idea of what tropical Turners might have looked like. On the last Sunday of the month there's also a busy little antiques fair held at the museum.

If the bus is crowded, or you can't make the driver understand where you want to get off, don't worry: after the museums it runs on to the **Horto Zoobotânico** (Tues–Sun 8am–5pm; R$2), a combined zoo and botanical garden. The gardens are the best part, with outdoor cafés and shady paths to walk along; the zoo, like most in Brazil, is shockingly bad, with the animals confined in concrete boxes far too small for them, where they're constantly taunted by children and adults who ought to know better.

The Olaria de Brennand

If you have time, try and round off your sightseeing with the bizarre **Instituto Ricardo Brennand** (Tues–Sun 10am–5pm; ⓣ81/3271-1544, ⓦwww.institutoricardobrennand.org.br), an industrial estate in the northern suburbs styled after a castle (complete with working drawbridge) – there can't be anywhere more impressively offbeat in the whole of Brazil. One of three brothers who inherited a huge tile, ceramic and brickwork factory, Brennand became a very strange kind of tycoon. Although already rich beyond the dreams of avarice, he was driven to become an internationally famous ceramic artist. His factory estate, far from being an industrial wasteland, nestles in the middle of the only part of the old coastal forest (the Mata Atlântica) still surviving in the metropolitan area. It's a very beautiful piece of land, and it's sobering to think that without it, nothing at all would remain to show what the coast around Recife looked like before the arrival of the Europeans.

Past the rows of workers' cottages and a brickworks, you come to the *oficina*, an enormous personal gallery containing thousands of Brennand's sculptures, decorated tiles, paintings and drawings. A lot of the work is good, and has strong erotic overtones – to say that genitals are a recurring theme is putting it mildly. Nearby, you'll find the most important collection of arms in Brazil inside the **Castle Museum**, which also has beautiful tapestries, sculpture, stained-glass windows and other curiosities from the sixteenth and seventeenth centuries. The estate also has a **library** that holds some 20,000 volumes relating to the Dutch period of Brazilian history.

The estate is a long way from the centre, but is definitely worth the effort. A taxi from Santo Antônio will set you back around R$25 and if you don't want to walk back you'll have to arrange for it to pick you up again, because no taxis pass anywhere near. Alternatively, take the bus marked "CDU–Várzea" from outside the post office to its terminus: once there you can either take a taxi or walk – it's not far (about 10 minutes) but you'll need to ask the way. Make sure you say "a oficina de Brennand" with the stress on the second syllable of "Brennand", or nobody will know what you're talking about. The staff are always pleased to see foreign visitors.

Boa Viagem: the beach

Regular buses make it easy to get down to **Boa Viagem** and the beach, an enormous skyscraper-lined arc of sand that constitutes the longest stretch of urbanized seafront in Brazil. As you'd expect of a city of islands, Recife was once studded with beaches, but they were swallowed up by industrial development, leaving only Boa Viagem within the city's limits – though there are others a short distance away to the north and south. In the seventeenth century, Boa Viagem's name was Ilha Cheiro Dinheiro, or "Smell Money Island" – as if whoever named it knew it would become the most expensive piece of real estate in the Northeast.

Much of Boa Viagem is only three or four blocks deep, so it's easy to find your way around. Take your bearings from one of the three main roads: the seafront **Avenida Boa Viagem**, with its posh hotels and a typically Brazilian promenade of palm trees and mosaic pavements; the broad Avenida Conselheiro Aguiar two blocks up; and Avenida Engenheiro Domingos Ferreira, one block up from the latter.

The **beach** itself is longer and (claim the locals) better even than Copacabana, with warm natural rock pools to wallow in just offshore when the tide is out. It's also rather narrow, however, and more dominated by the concrete culture around it than most in the Northeast. It gets very crowded at the weekends, but weekdays are relatively relaxed. There's a constant flow of people selling fresh coconut milk, iced beers, ready-mixed *batidas* (rum cocktails), pineapples, watermelon, shrimp, crabs, oysters, ice cream, straw hats and suntan lotion.

The heart of the action emanates from Praça Boa Viagem. Close to here are some of the liveliest restaurants and *choparias* (bars with draught beer and serving snacks and full meals). At weekends there's a thriving and colourful food and craft fair in the Praça Boa Viagem, busiest on Sunday evenings.

The usual cautions apply about not taking valuables to the beach or leaving things unattended while you swim. There have also been a small number of shark attacks over the years, but they have almost always involved surfers far from shore.

Eating

Eating out is cheapest in Santo Antônio, more expensive in Recife island and Boa Viagem, with Olinda (see p.335) somewhere in between. *Recifense* cuisine revolves around **fish** and **shellfish**. Try *carangueijo mole* – crabs cooked in a spicy sauce until shells and legs are soft and edible, which solves the problem of digging out the meat; small crabs called *guaiamum*; and *agulhas fritas*, fried needle fish. As befits a sugar city, a favourite local drink is *caldo de cana*, the juice pressed from sugar cane by hypnotic Victorian-looking machines.

Cheapest of all, and surprisingly pleasant, are the **food sellers** and *suco* **stalls** clogging the streets of **Santo Antônio**, with the usual selection of iced fruit juices, kebabs, cakes, sandwiches and sweet and savoury pastries. Here you will also find a **guaraná juice café**, *Guarana Express*, at Rua Frei Caneca 179. There's a row of reasonably priced stalls licensed by the city authorities on the pedestrianized **Rua da Palma**, across the road from the main post office, much patronized by office workers. The area also has many cheap *lanchonetes* and restaurants, although as their clientele is mainly workers they tend to close in the early evening. There's also an inexpensive lunchtime-only **vegetarian** restaurant, *O Vegetal*, which has branches on Avenida Guararapes (no. 210, 2nd floor) and Avenida Dantas Barreto (no. 507). Santo Antônio is pretty dead at night, with the exception of the cobbled square around São Pedro church, the

Pátio de São Pedro, where there are some good regional restaurants, with tables in the square and nice views of the church. Also worth a visit is the classy *Restaurante Leite*, Praça Joaquim Nabuco 147 (☎81/3224-7977), close to the *Hotel Quatro de Outubro*, which serves tasty local dishes in a very stylish nineteenth-century interior.

The Bairro do Recife has plenty of restaurants, and you may want to eat there as a prelude to going on to a bar or a nightclub. But prices are relatively high and the emphasis is on sophistication rather than good old-fashioned hearty Brazilian cooking. *Sabor Antigo*, at Rua Vigario Tenorio 213 (Mon–Fri 11am–2.30pm; ☎81/3224-7321) offers regional dishes at lunchtime, featuring chicken, steaks and seafood. *Buon Gustaio*, on Rua do Bom Jesus, does superb Italian food, and *Gambrinus*, at Rua Marquês de Olinda 263, is one of the places where you can get some satisfying local dishes. There's also a branch of the vegetarian restaurant, *O Vegetal*, on Rua do Brum (lunchtime only).

Down on **the beach** you'll find hundreds of places to eat, with one of the biggest concentrations in the **Pina** district, between the city centre and Boa Viagem. Catch a bus in the direction of Boa Viagem and get off on Avenida Herculano Bandeira, which is just where the bus veers round to run parallel to the sea. Almost the whole of the *avenida* is taken up with restaurants, most of them concentrating on seafood; especially recommended are *Marinho's* and *Pra Vocês*.

In **Boa Viagem** itself the best value is to be found at the seafood places on the promenade near the city-centre end of the beach, and in the dining rooms of the cheaper hotels, all of which are open to non-residents. *Peixada do Lula*, at Av. Boa Viagem 244, is a reasonably priced seafood restaurant known for its shrimp and lobster dishes; *Bargaço*, on the same street at no. 670, does a mixture of traditional seafood and spicier Bahian fare; *Edmilson da Carne de Sol*, at Rua José Trajano 82, is a good place for meat; and *La Pinha*, Praça Boa Viagem, is a pleasant and inexpensive little pizzeria and seafood restaurant. On either side of the main drag Avenida Domingos Ferreira, there are a number of other dining options, such as the *comida por kilo Restaurant Laçador*, or the more expensive *Shanghai Palace*, which serves tasty Chinese dishes with the added touch of fresh tropical ingredients.

Nightlife

As elsewhere in Brazil, **nightlife** in Recife starts late, after 10pm. The variety of music and dance is enormous, and the city has its own frenetic Carnaval music, the **frevo**, as well as **forró**, which you hear all over the Northeast. The dancing to *forró* can be really something, couples swivelling around the dance floors with ball bearings for ankles. In the past couple of years, Recife island has become the most happening place in the city centre, but there's also plenty of action in Boa Viagem as well as in Olinda (see p.335). There are other interesting nightspots in suburbs like Graças and Casa Forte, but they're not well served by public transport, so you'll have to take a taxi.

For a taste of strongly regional music of all types it's worth trying out an **espaço cultural** or two. The *Espaço Nodaloshi*, at Estrada dos Remédios 1891 in Madalena (☎81/3228-3511), frequently brings together large numbers of musicians from all over Pernambuco, generally starting the shows around 10pm or later. The Espaço Cultural Alberto Cunha Melo, at Rua Leila Félix Karan 15 in Bongi (☎81/3228-6846), runs similar live music shows. These and other similar places generally promote their programmes through the *Agenda Cultural* (see p.322).

Bars

In **Santo Antônio**, virtually the only place with any zip to it is the **Pátio de São Pedro**, with its clutch of bars and restaurants. Occasionally something extra happens here, though: music and dance groups often appear at weekends, and it's one of the centres of Recife's Carnaval.

As night falls and the rest of the city centre shuts down, the **Bairro do Recife** comes to life. There are all kinds of bars here, including quiet places where middle-aged professionals sit and discuss the events of the day. But the scene is mainly young and noisy in and around the vicinity of the Praça do Arsenal: **Rua do Apolo** in particular has a string of bars with names like *Armazém da Cerveja* ("Beer Warehouse") and *Arsenal da Praça Chopp* ("Beer Arsenal"), which gives you some idea of the spirit of the place. In the same street, the *Moritzstad* club frequently holds live concerts of the Mangue Beat bands, one of Pernambuco's modern musical movements. You should certainly sample the atmosphere here at least once just to get an idea of how seriously young *recifenses* take enjoying themselves. *A Casa da Rock*, Rua Vigario Tenonrio 105, also in Recife Antigo (the Bairro do Recife), is also popular and busy on weekend evenings; and there's the ritzy *Espaço Antonio Maria* on Bon Jesus 163.

In **Boa Viagem**, bars open and close with bewildering speed, which makes it difficult to keep track of them. The liveliest area, though, is around Praça de Boa Viagem (quite a long way down the beach from the city centre, near the junction of Avenida Boa Viagem and Rua Bavão de Souza Leão); the *Lapinha* bar and restaurant is a popular meeting place, as is the *Caktos* bar, Av. Conselheiro Aguiar 2328.

Quieter and classier is the northern suburb of **Casa Forte**. Be sure to check out *Agua de Beber*, a gem of a bar at Praça de Casa Forte 661: situated in a large house with an expensive restaurant upstairs, it also has a leafy courtyard in which you can sit and drink soothing *caipirinhas*.

Gay nightlife revolves around a handful of bars and clubs. *Banana Republica*, Rua Francisco Pesoa de Melo 260, in Candeias, and *Anjo Solto*, Rua Herculano Bandeira 513, Galeria Joanna, in D'Arc-Pina are the most popular bars, while the best-known clubs are *CATS*, Rua do Brum 85, in old Recife, *Butterfly*, Rua Raul Azedo 165 (Fri–Sun from 9pm; ⓣ81/3465-8073) and *Cyborg 2000*, Av. Real de Torre 1013, Madalena.

Dancing

If you're looking to lay down a few steps, you need to head for a **casa de forró**; the best time to go is around midnight on a Friday or Saturday. In all of them you can drink and eat fairly cheaply, too. They often have rules about only letting in couples, but these are very haphazardly enforced, especially for foreigners. There's a small entry fee, usually around R$10 or R$15 and you may be given a coupon as you go in for the waiters to mark down what you have – don't lose it or you'll have to pay a fine when you leave. Taxis back are rarely a problem, even in the small hours. Two good *casas de forró* are the *Belo Mar* on Avenida Bernardo Vieira de Melo, in Candeias, and the *Casa de Festejo* on Praça do Derby in the *bairro* of Torre. Otherwise, look in local papers or ask at one of the many useful tourist information offices (see p.321) for details, as there are dozens of others. One place that mixes *forró* with samba is the lively *Cavalo Dourado* (Fri & Sat only), at Rua Carlos Gomes 390, in the *bairro* of Prado. More westernized, but still good, is *Over Point Dancing* at Rua das Graças 261 in Graças.

Recife island has a good share of **nightclubs**, though the emphasis is on Western dance music rather than *forró*, at places like *Planeta Maluco* on Rua do

Apolo. But the best nights in the docks district are Thursdays between October and March, when a large area along Avenida Marquês de Olinda is given over to hours of live music and open-air dancing, called – appropriately enough – Dançando na Rua ("Dancing in the Street"). The *Depois Dancing Bar*, at Av. Rio Branco 66 in Recife Antigo (8pm–late), is a nightclub with live Western and *forró* music from Wednesday to Saturday and a reasonable restaurant.

Carnaval in Recife

Carnaval in Recife is overshadowed by the one in Olinda, but the city affair is still worth sampling. The best place for **Carnaval information** is the tourist office, which publishes a free broadsheet with timetables and route details of all the Carnaval groups. You can also get a timetable in a free supplement to the *Diário de Pernambuco* newspaper on the Saturday of Carnaval, but be warned that it's only a very approximate guide.

The *blocos*, or **Carnaval groups**, come in all shapes and sizes: the most famous is called Galo da Madrugada; the most common are the *frevo* groups (trucks called *freviocas*, with an electric *frevo* band aboard, circulate around the centre, whipping up already frantic crowds); but most visually arresting are *caboclinhos*, who wear modern Brazilian interpetations of a traditional Amazon Indian costume – feathers, animal-tooth necklaces – and carry bows and arrows, which they use to beat out the rhythm as they dance. It's also worth trying to see a *maracatu* group, unique to Pernambuco: they're mainly black, and wear bright costumes, the music an interesting (and danceable) hybrid of African percussion and Latin brass.

In Recife the **main events** are concentrated in Santo Antônio and Boa Vista. There are also things going on in Boa Viagem, in the area around the *Recife Palace Lucsim Hotel* on Avenida Boa Viagem, but it's too middle-class for its own good and is far inferior to what's on offer elsewhere. Carnaval in Recife officially begins with a trumpet fanfare welcoming *Rei Momo*, the Carnaval king and queen, on Avenida Guararapes at midnight on Friday, the cue for wild celebrations. At night, activities centre on the grandstands on Avenida Dantas Barreto, where the *blocos* parade under the critical eyes of the judges. The other central area to head for is the Pátio de São Pedro. During the day the *blocos* follow a route of sorts: beginning in the Praça Manuel Pinheiro, and then via Rua do Hospício, Avenida Conde de Boa Vista, Avenida Guararapes, Praça da República and Avenida Dantas Barreto, to Pátio de São Pedro. Good places to hang around are near churches, especially Rosário dos Pretos, on Largo do Rosário, a special target for *maracatu* groups. The balconies of the *Hotel do Parque* are a good perch, too, if you can manage to get up there. Daylight hours is the best time to see the *blocos* – when the crowds are smaller and there are far more children around. At night it's far more intense and the usual safety warnings apply.

Listings

Airlines Aerolíneas Argentinas, Av. Mn. Borba 324 ⓣ81/3423-4188; Air France, Rua Sete de Setembro 42, Boa Vista ⓣ81/3231-7735; Air Portugal, Av. Conselheiro de Aguiar 1472 ⓣ81/3465-8800; TAM, Praça Min. Salgado ⓣ81/3462-4466; Transbrasil, Av. Conde de Boa Vista 1546 ⓣ81/3423-2566; United Airlines, Rua Progresso 465 ⓣ81/3423-2444; Varig, Av. Conselheiro de Aguiar 456 ⓣ81/3464-4440.

Banks and exchange Most banks have ATMs. The Banco do Brasil has branches at the airport (daily 10am–9pm), at Av. Dantas Barreto 541, at Av. Rio Branco 240 (4th floor), and on Rua Sete de Setembro in Boa Vista, all charging commission. You're much better off going to a *casa de câmbio* or a travel agency: the Mônaco agency at Praça Joaquim Nabuco 159 (ⓣ81/3224-4289) in Santo Antônio will change dollars or cheques free of charge. You'll also get reasonable rates in the seafront hotels in Boa Viagem. Exchange rates tend to drop around Carnaval time, with the influx of dollars from foreign tourists, so, if you can, delay changing large amounts until afterwards. Shopping centres all have ATMs, banks and money changing facilities that stay open until 9pm Monday to Saturday. The Bradesco bank on Conde de Boa Vista has an ATM that accepts most Visa cards. Don't at any time change money with people who approach you on the street.

Car rental Avis ⓣ81/3462-5069; Budget ⓣ81/3341-2505; Hertz, at airport ⓣ81/3800-8900.

Consulates UK, Av. Eng. Domingos Ferreira 4150, Boa Viagem (Mon–Fri 8–11.30am, Tues & Thurs also 2–4.30pm; ⓣ81/3325-0247); US, Rua Gonçalves Maia 163, Boa Vista (Mon–Fri 8am–5pm; ⓣ81/3421-2441).

Health matters Albert Sabin, Rua Senador José Henrique 141, Ilha do Leite ⓣ81/3421-5411.

Music shops Oficina da Musica, Ladeira da Se, Carmo, Olinda (ⓣ81/3051-0289); Disco 7, Rua Sete de Setembro, is small, but the best record shop for Brazilian music in the Northeast (ⓣ81/3222-5932).

Internet Cybercafe Olind@.com at Kua Joâo Pessoalz, Carmo, by Praça Maxabomba, Olinda; and at Shopping Boavista and Shopping Center Recife.

Post office The main post office is the Correio building on Av. Guararapes in Santo Antônio (Mon–Fri 9am–5pm). There is also a branch on Recife island at Av. Marquês de Olinda.

Taxis Disk Taxis Recife (ⓣ81/3424-5030) and Teletaxi (ⓣ81/3429-4242) are both safe, or you can just pick up a taxi from the ranks found on many prominent street corners all over town.

Telephones Inter-city and international telephone offices are located at the Telemar office, Praça do Carmo (next to Praça Maxambomba; daily 6am–11pm) in Olinda. International calls can also be made direct with phone cards from phone kiosks throughout the city.

Travel and tour companies Among the best tour companies in and around Recife are Evatur, Av. Cons. Aguiar 1360, loja 14, Boa Viagem (ⓣ81/3465-1164) for city tours, Porto de Galihnas and other local tours and destinations; Martur, Rua Dr. Nilo Dornelas Camara 90, Loja 02, Boa Viagem (ⓣ81/3463-3636, ⓦwww.martur.com.br) from flights, cruises and trips to Fernando de Noronha; Soltur, Rua Matias de Albuquerque 233 (ⓣ81/3424-1965); Uru Tur (ⓣ81/3272-5177 ⓦwww.urutur.com); Káritas Turismo e Ecologia, Rua Ribeiro do Brito 1002 (ⓣ81/3466-5447); and, for flights and tickets, Flytour, Av. Rua Montevidéu 260, Graças (ⓣ81/3221-4265, ⓦwww.flytour.com.br).

Olinda

OLINDA is, quite simply, one of the largest and most beautiful complexes of **colonial architecture** in Brazil: a maze of cobbled streets, hills crowned with brilliant white churches, pastel-coloured houses, Baroque fountains and graceful squares. Not surprisingly, in 1982 it was designated a cultural heritage site by UNESCO. Founded in 1535, the old city is spread across several small hills looking back towards Recife, but it belongs to a different world. In many ways Olinda is the Greenwich Village of Recife; it's here that many of the larger city's artists, musicians and liberal professionals live, and it's also the centre of Recife's gay scene. Olinda is most renowned, though, for its **Carnaval**, famous throughout Brazil, which attracts visitors from all over the country, as well as sizeable contingents from Europe.

A city in its own right, Olinda is far larger than it first appears. Yet despite its size, Olinda has become effectively a neighbourhood of Recife: a high proportion of the population commutes into the city, which means that **transport links** are good, with buses leaving every few minutes. Olinda's old colonial centre is built on the hills, slightly back from the sea, but arching along the seafront and spreading inland behind the old town is a modern Brazilian city of over 300,000 people – known as Novo Olinda, it's the usual bland collection of suburbs and main commercial drags. Like Recife, Novo Olinda has a growing reputation for robberies, but the heart of colonial Olinda is safe enough. There's a calm, almost sleepy atmosphere about the

place, and wandering around at night is pretty safe. Finally, if you want to swim or enjoy a sunbathe, you'll need to head out of town, as Olinda's beach is fairly polluted and smelly.

Arrival, information and accommodation

Buses from Recife follow the seafront road; get off in the Praça do Carmo, just by Olinda's main post office, from where it's a two-minute walk up into the old city.

A reasonable town map is available from the Secretaria de Turismo in the **Biblioteca** (daily 9am–5pm) at the foot of Rua do Sao Francisco near Praça do Carmo. The **municipal tourist office** in Rua São Bento can help with information about accommodation during Carnaval, but it's not geared up for much more than this. There's also an information kiosk on Praça do Carmo, where the buses stop, but it's not particularly useful.

There are a huge number of teenagers and young men offering themselves as **guides** to the city, and you'll probably find yourself besieged as soon as you get off the bus. Those wearing yellow T-shirts with the words "Guia Mirim" written on the back and laminated ID cards are official guides, but no longer receive support from the municipality. They generally do their job pretty well and depend entirely on tips. They are mostly ex-street kids and a percentage of their earnings goes towards their ongoing work with street kids, so they are well worth supporting (the recommended tip for guides is R$12–15 an hour per person), though few speak fluent English. Others, generally wearing white T-shirts and yellow caps with the acronym AGTIO, are from the Associação de Guias Turísticas Independentes, and should also have ID cards to prove this.

For **Internet access**, try the Olind@.com cybercafé opposite the *Hotel Pousada São Francisco* on Rua do Sol, Carmo. At the Telemar **phone office** you can also make inter-city and and international calls on the Praça Maxambomba. For a reliable **taxi** driver, contact Flavio on ⓣ81/3429-0852 or ⓣ9961-9544.

Accommodation

There are dozens of **hotels** in all price ranges in Olinda. It's probably cheapest to stay in the more modern part of the city, further north down the seafront road from Recife, but you'll be seriously missing out on the old city's atmosphere if you do, and it's worth shopping around for cheaper options in the historic area. Prices vary enormously throughout the year – high-season prices are given below, but bear in mind that, if you go between March and June or between August and November, it will be cheaper. During Carnaval it's virtually impossible to get a room unless you've booked months in advance.

If you want to stay for a while and **rent a room**, look for signs outside people's houses saying "*Aluga-se*". Alternatively, you can participate in the **Cama a café scheme**, which is a network of homes taking in guests; the programme works out to be quite cheap and gives great cultural insight; either ask at one of the tourist offices in Recife or Olinda, or contact the organizer on ⓣ21/9606-0692. For something else entirely, there's a **campsite**, *Camping Olinda*, just inside the old city at Rua do Bom Sucesso 262, Amparo (ⓣ81/3429-1365), but do watch your valuables.

Costeiro Olinda Hotel Av. Ministro Marcos Freire 681, Bairro Novo ⓣ81/3429-4877. Three-star hotel in the modern part of the city; somewhat bland compared to the other places in this price range. ❻

Hostal Albergue de Olinda Rua do Sol 233, Carmo ⓣ81/3429-1592, ⓕ3439-1913, ⓦwww.alberguedeolinda.com.br. An excellent, very comfortable youth hostel with a nice hammock area and a small swimming pool; it's also close to the seafront, though right on a busy road.

Hotel Pousada dos Milagros Rua Manuel Borba 235 (ⓣ81/3439-0392). This is a very friendly *pousada* close to the seafront and beach; it has a pleasant courtyard as well as a small pool. ❹

Hotel Pousada São Francisco Rua do Sol 127, Carmo ⓣ81/3429-2109, ⓕ3429-4057, ⓦwww.pousadasaofrancisco.com.br. Located on the main road but quite close to the seafront; has a swimming pool and all mod cons. ❹

Hotel Sete Colinas Ladeira de São Francisco 307, Carmo ⓣ81/3439-6055 or 3439-0220, ⓦwww.hotel7colinasolinda.com.br. This fabulous hotel right in the centre of Olinda is set in beautiful gardens with modern sculpture and a fine swimming pool. There's a range of rooms, suites and luxury apartments, and a good restaurant too. It isn't cheap but it's still good value. ❽

Okakoaras Bungalow Hotel Av. Cláudio J. Gueiros 10927, Praia de Maria Farinha ⓣ81/3436-1754. Set on a palm-lined beach, this peaceful hotel is a half-hour bus ride from Olinda. Offers cosy, bungalow-style accommodation, a swimming pool and pleasant service. ❸

Pousada Alquimia Rua Prudente de Morais 292 ⓣ81/3429-1457. Cheap and cheerful, this well-located little *pension* has a front parlour full of paintings and nice, if basic, rooms. ❷

Pousada d'Olinda Praça João Alfredo 178 ⓣ81/3439-1163, ⓦwww.hoteldolinda.com.br. This centrally located *pousada* is excellent value and has everything from a fine swimming pool to a good restaurant, inexpensive bungalow-style rooms and a penthouse suite. ❹

Pousada do Amparo Rua do Amparo 199 ⓣ81/3439-1749. Quality place set in a colonial mansion; features excellent rooms, a restaurant, a sauna, a pool and an art gallery. ❹

Pousada dos Quatro Cantos Rua Prudente de Morais 441 ⓣ81/3429-0220, ⓕ3429-1845, ⓦwww.pousada4cantos.com.br. Beautiful, small mansion with a leafy courtyard, right in the heart of the old city. A range of rooms and suites are available; the cheapest have shared bathrooms. ❸

Pousada Peter Rua do Amparo 215 ⓣ81/3439-2171, ⓦwww.pousadapeter.com.br. Located among other art galleries, this is a comfortable gallery-cum-lodging situated in a colonial-style building. The front rooms and entry form most of the gallery, with guest rooms out back. Good value. ③

The Town

Olinda's hills are steep, and you'll be best rewarded by taking a leisurely stroll around the town. A good spot to have a drink and plan your attack is the **Alto da Sé** (the highest square in the town), not least because of the stunning view of Recife's skyscrapers shimmering in the distance, framed in the foreground by the church towers, gardens and palm trees of Olinda. There's always an arts and crafts **market** going on here during the day, peaking in the late afternoon, and while much of what's on offer is pretty good, the large numbers of tourists have driven prices up, and there's little here you can't get cheaper in Recife or the interior.

The **churches** you see are not quite as old as they look. The Dutch burnt them all down, except one, in 1630, built none of their own, and left the Portuguese to restore them during the following centuries. There are eighteen churches dating from the seventeenth and eighteenth centuries remaining today, seemingly tucked around every corner and up every street. Very few of them have set opening times, but they're usually open during weekday mornings, and even when they're closed you can try knocking on the door and asking for the *vigia*, the watchman.

If you have time to see only one church it should be the **Convento Franciscano** (Mon–Fri 8–11.30am & 2.30–5pm, Sat 8am–5.30pm), tucked away on Rua São Francisco. Built in 1585, the complex of convent, chapel and church has been stunningly restored to its former glory; particular highlights are the tiled cloister depicting the lives of Jesus and St Francis of Asissi, and the sacristy's beautiful Baroque furniture carved from jacaranda wood. In the north wing there's an elaborate two-tiered altarpiece in gold leaf and white, and behind the convent there's a grand patio with even grander panoramas across the ocean.

Among other churches, the **Igreja da Misericórdia**, built right at the top of an exhaustingly steep hill, has a fine altar and rear walls covered in blue *azulejo*, while the **Basilica e Mosteiro de Sâo Bento** (Mon–Fri 8am–noon & 2–6pm, Sat 8am–noon, Sun 10am–5pm) looks quite wonderful from the outside with palm trees swaying in the courtyard, though the interior is less striking. The **Igreja da Sé**, on the *praça* of the same name, is rather bland and austere inside – more of a museum than a living church – but is worth a look if only to see the eighteenth-century sedan chair and large wooden sculptures in the small room at the northeast wing. At the back of the church is a patio from where you'll have good views of the surrounding area.

By the Praça do Carmo, there's the rundown but quite splendid **Igreja do Carmo**, which sits majestically on a small hill looking down on the busy streets below, while up Rua do Amparo there's the fine eighteenth-century **Igreja do Amparo**, and within view of this the deserted ruins of the **Igreja de São João Batista dos Militares**, the one church that escaped the Dutch invaders' fires of 1630.

There's also a good sampling of religious art on display in the **Museu de Arte Sacra de Pernambuco** (Mon–Fri 8am–1pm), in the seventeenth-century bishop's palace by the Alto da Sé. The **Museu Regional** (Tues–Fri 9am–5pm, Sat & Sun 2–5pm), at Rua do Amparo 128, is well laid out, too, although the emphasis is too much on artefacts and too little on history.

There's more contemporary interest in the colourful **graffiti** in which the old city is swathed. The local council commissions artists to adorn certain streets and walls, which has the twin advantage of keeping local talent in work and ensuring Olinda has the highest-quality graffiti in Brazil. Some are political, urging people to vote for this or that candidate, some are more abstract – illustrated poems about Olinda being especially popular – but all are colourful and artistic and blend in uncannily well with the colonial architecture. One of the best places to see them is along the municipal cemetery walls on the Avenida Liberdade, but there's good graffiti all over the old city, especially during elections and Carnaval.

More serious modern art is to be found in the **Museu de Arte Contemporânea**, on Rua 13 de Maio next to the market (Tues–Fri 9am–noon & 2–5pm, Sat & Sun 2–5pm). This fine eighteenth-century building was once used as a jail by the Inquisition, though the exhibits themselves are a bit disappointing. Much more interesting is the **Museu do Mamulengo** (Tues–Fri 9am–5pm, Sat & Sun 2–5pm) at Rua do Amparo 59, which houses an excellent collection of traditional puppets.

Olinda's several markets and endless *artesanato* shops make it a good place for **shopping**. The Mercado da Ribeira, built in the sixteenth century, is at Rua Bernardo Vieira de Melo 160, and offers the usual range of craft goods, while a ten-minute walk down Rua 15 de Novembro from the governor's palace brings you to another bigger *artesanato* and antique market housed in the long pink building by the main road, Largo do Varadouro.

Eating, drinking and nightlife

Olinda's relaxed atmosphere draws many *recifenses* at night, when tables and chairs are set on squares and pavements, and bars that are tucked away in courtyards amid spectacular tropical foliage make the perfect escape. There is always plenty of music around and, at weekends, a lot of young Brazilians out for a good time – all in all, a good recipe for enjoying yourself. If it's just drinks and a snack you're after, try *Bodega de Veio*, Rua do Amparo 198 (opposite *Pousada Peter*), which is occasionally the scene for live music in the evenings.

Eating and drinking

The best place to go for crowds and serious eating and drinking is the **Alto da Sé**. The good, cheap **street food** here, cooked on charcoal fires, can't be recommended too highly; try *acarajé*, which you get from women sitting next to sizzling wok-like pots – bean-curd cake, fried in palm oil, cut open and filled with green salad, dried shrimps and *vatapá*, a yellow paste made with shrimps, coconut milk and fresh coriander. If you sit in the Alto da Sé for any length of time, you're bound to be approached by one of Olinda's many **repentistas** (see p.342), who will try to improvise a song about you. The results are sometimes wonderful, sometimes embarrassing, but they will expect a small payment, so if you don't want to shell out make it clear from the start that you're not interested.

Olinda also has countless **restaurants** you can sample. If you want to eat for around R$10 or less, try the *comida por kilo* places along the seafront and in the new part of town. However, for just a little bit more, you can eat far better in the old town. The moderately priced *Blues Bar*, in the garden of an old house at Rua do Bonfim 66 (Tues–Thurs 6pm–1am, Fri & Sat 6pm–3am, Sun 11am–8pm; ⓣ81/9156-6415), does excellent meat dishes and plays authentic blues music much of the time. More expensive – and air-conditioned – is *Mourisco*, at Praça Conselheiro João Alfredo 7, which specializes in seafood; a good meal with wine will cost R$30–40. *Goya Restaurant*, Rua do Amparo 157, is hard to beat for imaginative Brazilian and French cuisine, the *Restaurante Flor do Coco*, Rua do Amparo 199, has excellent regional cuisine, and the *Creperia*, Praça João Alfredo 168 (Ⓣ81/3429-2935), serves great salads as well as the crepes. Other good spots at the higher end of the price range are the *Porta D'Italia*, Rua do Bonfim, which offers well-prepared Italian food and a good wine list, and the *Oficina do Sabor*, Rua do Amparo 365, for excellent local cuisine – the shrimps in mango sauce are a highlight. If it's just good coffee you're after, try the *Café Adego*, at Rua 27 de Janeiro 70.

The streets around the Alto da Sé hold a couple of good **bars** that are well worth seeking out, including the *Cantinho da Sé*, just a few steps down the Ladeira da Sé, almost always crowded and very lively indeed at night.

Nightlife

Nightlife in Olinda can be very hectic, especially at the end of the week. At times the drums or bass lines carry so loudly across the town that you may think they're calling out to you. Places to visit, apart from the ones along the Alto da Sé, are the seafront restaurants and bars, many of which have *forró* groups on Friday and Saturday nights. The *Acoustico Pub*, for instance, at Rua do Sol 283 has a good scene. If you get bored with *forró* – and the beat does get a bit monotonous after a while – try the more samba-like rhythms of the *Z-4 Club* or the *Clube Atlântico,* both near the Praça do Carmo. Every Friday and Saturday night (starting at 11pm) it hosts the *Noites Olindenses*, dances to an eclectic variety of very loud music – *frevo*, samba, *forró*, merengue, and even non-Brazilian styles like salsa and tango – either recorded or performed live by energetic groups. You pay an entrance fee of about R$8–12, and both the music and the dancing can be quite superb. There are sometimes extras like magicians and *capoeira* displays going on between and even during acts. To find out what's happening in the local art scene, check out Ⓦwww.arte.olinda.info.

Carnaval and other festivals in Olinda

Olinda's **Carnaval**, with a massive 560 *blocos*, is generally considered to be one of the three greatest in Brazil, along with those of Rio and Salvador. It overshadows the celebrations in neighbouring Recife and attracts thousands of revellers from all over the Northeast. It's easy to see why Olinda developed into such a major Carnaval: the setting is matchless, and local traditions of art and music are very strong. Like the other two great Brazilian Carnavals, Olinda has a style and feel all its own: not quite as large and potentially intimidating as in either Rio or Salvador, the fact that much of it takes place in the winding streets and small squares of the old city makes it seem more manageable. The area of town around the *Pousada dos Quatro Cantos* is one of the liveliest during Carnaval. The music, with the local beats of *frevo* and *maracatu* predominating, the costumes and the enormous *bonecos* (papier-mâché figures of folk heroes or savage caricatures of local and national personalities), make this celebration unique.

Carnaval in Olinda actually gets going the Sunday before the official start, when the Virgens do Bairro Novo, a traditional *bloco* several hundred strong, parades down the seafront road followed by crowds that regularly top 200,000. By now the old city is covered with decorations: ribbons, streamers and coloured lanterns are hung from every nook and cranny, banners are strung across streets and coloured lighting is set up in all the squares. Olinda's Carnaval

△ Carnaval in Olinda

is not only famous for its *bonecos*, which are first paraded around on Friday night and then at intervals during the days, but also for the decorated umbrellas that aficionados use to dance the *frevo*. The tourist office has lists of the hundreds of groups, together with routes and approximate times, but there is always something going on in most places in the old city. The most famous *blocos*, with mass followings, are Pitombeira and Elefantes; also try catching the daytime performances of *travestis*, transvestite groups, which have the most imaginative costumes – ask the tourist office to mark them out on the list for you.

Inevitably, with so many visitors flocking into the city, **accommodation during Carnaval** can be a problem. It's easier to find a room in Recife, but, unless you dance the night away, transport back in the small hours can be difficult; buses start running at around 5am, and before then you have to rely on taxis. This is not always easy, as many taxi drivers stop work to enjoy Carnaval themselves. Even if you do find one, you'll have to pay an exorbitant fare, and run the risk too of **drunken taxi drivers** – dozens of people are killed on the road during Carnaval every year, and it's best to avoid travelling by road in the small hours.

In Olinda itself you might as well forget about hotels if you haven't booked a room months in advance. Many locals, though, rent out all or part of their house for Carnaval week; the municipal tourist office has a list of places and prices, which start at around R$600 for the week, going up to as much as R$5000. If all the places on the tourist office lists are full – more than likely if you arrive less than a week before Carnaval starts – or if you fancy your chances of getting a cheaper and better deal on your own, wander round the side streets looking for signs saying "*Aluga-se quartos*"; knock on the door and bargain away.

The Torneio dos Repentistas

There are plenty of festivals other than Carnaval in Olinda, as its location and cultural traditions make it a popular venue. Definitely worth catching if you happen to be visiting in late January is the **Torneio dos Repentistas**, which is centred on and around the Praça da Preguiça and lasts for three days. A *repentista* is a Northeastern singer-poet who improvises strictly metered verses accompanied only by a guitar. Olinda's *torneio* is one of the most famous events of its kind in the region, bringing in *repentistas* from all over the Northeast who pair off and embark on singing duels while surrounded by audiences; the audiences break into spontaneous applause at particularly good rhymes or well-turned stanzas. During the rest of the year, most *repentistas* make a living singing on street corners, in squares or at markets, commenting wittily – and often obscenely – on the people going by or stopping to listen, or elaborating on themes shouted out by the audience. Even if you don't understand the lyrics, a *repentista*'s act is worth catching, especially if you can find a *cantoria*, a sing-off between two or more *repentistas*, who take alternate verses until a draw is agreed or until the audience acclaims a winner.

North from Recife

North from Recife, the **BR-101 highway** runs a little way inland through low hills and sugar-cane fields, a scenic enough route but one that offers little reason to stop off anywhere, except perhaps at the small pottery centre of **Goiana**. The **coast** north of Recife is best explored along the smaller roads that branch off the highway. Nevertheless, it's as well to bear in mind that the Pernambuco coast is thickly populated by Brazilian standards. This isn't to say there aren't relatively peaceful spots, but what seems a deserted retreat during the week can fill up quickly at weekends, with *recifenses* heading for the beaches, enlivening or destroying the rural atmosphere, depending on your point of view.

Along the BR-101: Goiana and Pitimbu

At **GOIANA**, 80km north of Recife on BR-101, parts of the town are still made up of rows of nineteenth-century terraced houses, built for workers in the local cotton mill, which has been long since bankrupted. **Pottery** has taken over as the main economic activity, and Goiana is one of the most important centres of the flourishing Pernambucan ceramics industry. The town centre is dotted with workshops, their wares spilling out onto the pavements, and there are some good bargains to be had. You can watch the potters at work in many places, like Zé do Carmo in Rua Padre Batalha. Opposite here, there's a good restaurant, the *Buraco da Giá* at no. 100 (Ⓣ81/3626-0150; daily 11am–10pm), where the trained crab that offers you a drink is perhaps the real highlight of any visit to the town. To get here, take one of the six daily buses from the Recife Rodoviária.

If you want to spend some time in the area, it's better to get out of Goiana and head 30km over a country road to the coastal fishing village of **PITIMBU**, just across the border in Paraíba state. There are four buses a day from Goiana, the last around 2pm; it's a crowded and bumpy ride but Pitimbu is worth it. It has friendly inhabitants and a good, 10km beach, although the stretch closest to town can be dirty, and there's only one **hotel**, the *Pitimbu Mar* (Ⓣ83/3299-1035; ❸), which has a pool and six chalets. Camping on the beach is also possible, or you can negotiate with local bar owners for hammock space in a back room. It's a quiet, sleepy place, ideal for a couple of days of doing nothing at all, with excellent fresh seafood available in several beachside bars. It's also a good place to see *jangadas* – the small fishing rafts with huge curving triangular sails – in action. They go out at dawn and return in mid-afternoon and are quite a sight, as they rear and plunge through the surf.

Along the coast towards Itamaracá

From Olinda, **local buses** continue 11km along the coastal road to the beautiful palm-lined beaches of **Rio Doce, Janga** and **Pau Amarelo**. Until recently these were pretty much deserted, and, although weekend homes are going up now, development, so far, is less obtrusive than in many places on the coast. Being close to major population centres, however, the water quality at Rio Doce and Janga is not always the best. The area gets busy at weekends, especially in Janga, when there's music and dancing in the beachside bars at night. At Pau Amarelo you can still see one of several local star-shaped forts left behind by the Dutch in 1719.

A more popular and even more scenic route north is through the pleasantly rundown colonial villages of **Igarassu** and **Itapissuma** to the island of Itamaracá. Hourly **buses** to Igarassu, with easy connections to Itamaracá, leave from Avenida Martins de Barros, on Santo Antônio island in Recife, opposite the *Grande Hotel*. Another possibility is to go there **by boat**: every travel agency in Recife runs trips, stopping at beaches on the way, for around R$90–100.

Igarassu

Turning off the highway past Olinda's ugly industrial suburb of Paulista, the road wends its way through a rich green landscape of rolling hills and dense palm forest. The first town on the route, 25km from Olinda, is **IGARASSU**, an old colonial settlement built on a ridge rising out of a sea of palm trees: the name means "great canoe" in the language of the Tupi Indians, the cry that went up when they first saw the Portuguese galleons. The town was founded in 1535, when during a battle with the Indians the hard-pressed Portuguese commander vowed to build a church on the spot if victorious; the **Igreja de São Cosme e Damião**, one of the oldest churches in Brazil, is still there on the ridge. Down the hill the **Convento de Santo Antônio** is almost as old, built in 1588. Both are simpler and more austere than any of the churches in Recife or Olinda.

Most of the houses in Igarassu make up the rows of tied cottages that are characteristic of the old *engenhos*, or sugar estates. You can get a good idea of what a traditional *engenho* was like at the **Engenho Monjope**, an old plantation that has been tastefully converted into a **campsite** (Ⓣ81/3543-0528). The *engenho* dates from 1756; there's a decaying mansion, a chapel, water mill, cane presses and a *senzala*, the blockhouse where slaves lived. Minibuses back to Recife from Igarassu drop you at the turn-off (ask for "*o camping*"), and the estate is an easy ten-minute walk from there. The campsite is separate from the buildings, and you can ask at the entrance to look around even if you don't want to stay. Thirteen kilometres north of Igarassu, there are a couple of more upmarket places to stay at the pleasant **Praia da Gavoa**: the *Pousada Porto Canoas*, Estr. do Ramalho 230 (Ⓣ81/3424-2845; ❸), has chalets, a pool and a restaurant, and the *Hotel Gavoa Praia* (Ⓣ81/3543-7777, Ⓦwww.hotelgavoa.com.br; ❻) offers everything you could need, including a pool and sauna.

Eight kilometres further on from Praia da Gavoa at **ITAPISSUMA**, a causeway connects the mainland to the island of Itamaracá.

Itamaracá

Local legend has it that the island of Itamaracá was once the site of the Garden of Eden, and the short drive across the causeway from Itapissuma promises much, passing amongst thousands of palm trees lapped by fields of sugar cane – the rich but sickly smell just before the harvest in March is enough to make you feel queasy. So it's a shame to have to say that the town of **ITAMARACÁ** is something of a disappointment. It's very crowded and increasingly scarred by the hundreds of weekend homes springing up in ugly rashes along the beaches – alongside the humble wattle huts roofed with palm leaves where the original islanders have managed to hold on. One of the first parts of Brazil to be settled by the Portuguese, Itamaracá was so prosperous as a sugar plantation that it was also the first part of Pernambuco to be occupied by the Dutch, who built a fort here.

Itamaracá has a reputation as an idyllic rural retreat, away from the pressures of life in Recife. This might have been true fifteen years ago, but it's stretching things a little now. Nonetheless, there are a couple of places of interest. The first building you see as you arrive on the island is an enormous open prison: all the fields are cultivated by prisoners, easily recognizable in blue and grey uniforms with ID cards pinned to their chests. The prisoners also run a group of cafés and shops on the road just past the prison, selling handmade jewellery and bone carvings. These shops are built near the **Engenho São João** (Mon–Sat 10am–5pm), much better preserved than Monjope (see p.344), with most of the original machinery used for pressing cane, boiling the syrup and refining sugar still intact. A turn-off just before the town (you'll probably end up walking, as local buses exist but are very infrequent) leads 5km through tacky villas before rewarding you with the **Forte Oranje**, another star-shaped Dutch fort built in 1631 by Maurice of Nassau to protect the newly occupied sugar estates.

There's a vicious *enfilade* at the front gate, where attackers were filtered through a zigzag corridor and exposed to musket fire from slits on all sides, and there are a few old cannons lying around on the ramparts with the makers' crests still visible. The souvenir shop inside is the most overpriced in Pernambuco, but the beachside **bars** opposite are really good value and their food is excellent – a highlight is the *casquinho de carangueijo*, crab meat fried with garlic and onions, served in the shell and covered with roasted manioc flour. Downing a couple of iced beers at one of these bars while looking out across the bay should be enough to make you feel better disposed towards the island, especially if you catch somebody selling the delicious local oysters out of a bucket. You buy them by the half dozen, for around R$2.50: the seller flicks them open with a knife and supplies a lime to squeeze over them.

There are the usual beachside bars and restaurants on Itamaracá, and a few **hotels**, including the *Hotel Do Maranjo*, Rua Padre Machado 85 (Ⓣ81/3544-1157; ❷), the *Orange Praia* (Ⓣ81/3544-1194, Ⓕ3544-1176; ❹), some 8km from the town in a wonderful beachside location at the Praia do Forte Oranje and, nearby, the excellent-value *Casa da Praia* (Ⓣ81/3544-1255; ❸). **Camping** on the beach is technically illegal but people sometimes do it anyway, although it's not advisable, especially with valuables. The best of the **restaurants** is the *Sargaço*, Rua Santino de Barros 270 (Ⓣ81/3544-1180), which has fine, reasonably priced seafood and, on Friday and Saturday nights, a *ciranda* – a circular dance to lilting, rhythmic music from flutes, guitars and drums. Out at the Praia do Forte Oranje there's a superb fish restaurant, *A Peti Tosa*, but it's only open for lunch on weekdays.

The beaches

The **beaches** are very good – wide and lined with palms – and they are a popular night venue for Carnaval celebrations, which attract hundreds of visitors. Unfortunately, however, stretches around the town and along as far as the Forte Oranje have been blighted by unregulated building. There are better, deserted beaches round about, but none less than a couple of hours' walk along the shoreline in either direction.

There are *jangadas*, too, but they're a rather poignant symbol of what has happened to the town. A few years ago many families supported themselves by a combination of fishing and farming, and the *jangadas* were very much working fishing boats. A few *jangadeiros* still fish, but most of them now take weekenders and tourists out on trips; a couple of hours costs usually around R$15–20. These trips are not advisable, however, unless you're a reasonable swimmer, and even then you should be careful if the sea is at all rough; there's nothing to stop you being swept overboard, and no life jackets are provided.

South from Recife

The coast south of Recife has the best **beaches** in the state and is all too quickly realizing its tourist potential – the sleepy fishing villages are unlikely to remain so for much longer. Almost all **buses** to cities south of Recife take the BR-101 highway, which runs inland through fairly dull scenery, made worse by heavy traffic. The trick is to get a bus that goes along the much more scenic **coastal road**, the PE-60, or *via litoral*; they leave from either Avenida Dantas Barreto or the Recife Rodoviária for the string of towns down the coast from Cabo, through Ipojuca, Sirinhaém, Rio Formoso, to São José da Coroa Grande. Before São José, where the road starts to run alongside the beach, you may need to catch another local bus to get to the beachside villages themselves. In theory, you could hop from village to village down the coast on local buses, but only with time to spare. Services are infrequent – early morning is the usual departure time – and you might have to sleep on a beach or find somewhere to sling a hammock, as not all the villages have places to stay. As you move south, bays and promontories disappear, and walking along the beaches to the next village is often quicker than waiting for a bus.

Gaibú and Santo Agostinho

The first stop out of Recife is the beach at **GAIBÚ**, a sizeable resort some 40km south of Boa Viagem – catch a bus to Cabo from Avenida Dantas Barreto, and then another local one to Gaibú. Gaibú sports the familiar setup – palm trees, bars and surf – and is a good base for village-hopping, with a youth hostel and a couple of cheap **pensões**: the pleasant *Pousada Aguas Marinhas* (❸) is right on the beach, run by a Belgian-Brazilian couple who serve fine breakfasts in their beach garden and have mountain bikes for rent. They can also arrange sightseeing trips in boats with local fishermen. Gaibú gets crowded at weekends, but there's a particularly beautiful stretch of coastline nearby, close enough to explore on foot. Just before Gaibú village, a turning in the dirt road heads off to the right, leading to the cape of **São Agostinho**, a pleasant walk uphill through palms and mango trees, past the odd peasant hut in the forest. Three kilometres up is a ruined Dutch chapel, so overgrown it's almost invisible, and a path to the left leads out onto a promontory where the forest suddenly disappears and leaves you with a stunning view of the idyllic, and usually deserted, beach of **Calhetas**. You can clamber down to the beach, a ring of sand in a bay fringed with palm forest, the distant oil refinery at Suape providing the only jarring note. This beach is particularly good for surfing. If you continue on from the ruined chapel, you'll come to the sleepy hamlet of **SANTO AGOSTINHO**. During the Dutch occupation there was vicious guerrilla fighting here, and an infamous massacre took place when Dutch settlers were herded into a church that was then burnt down. A small chapel still stands on the spot and there are the pulverized remains of a fort. On the cape itself are burntout shells of Dutch buildings from the same campaign, and there's also a plaque commemorating the Spanish conquistador, Yanez Piñon, blown south by storms on his way to the Caribbean in 1500. He put in here for shelter a couple of months before Cabral "discovered" Brazil, and sailed off without knowing where he was – thus ensuring Brazil would end up speaking Portuguese rather than Spanish. The cape is crisscrossed with several walking trails, few of which are properly signposted, and a little exploring will soon bring you to the tiny village of Nazare, where there's little to keep you apart from a ruined Dutch chapel and a small bar managed by the local lighthouse-keeper.

If you find the need **to stay**, the Praia de Suape has two good options: the five-star *Blue Tree Park* beach resort and the delightful *Sitio Paraiso* (☎81/3522-6061; ❹), a cosy *pousada* set in the middle of fruit gardens (pick your own limes for cocktails). The owner is knowledgable about local activities and will help arrange boat trips to the Suape Islands through mangrove swamps.

Porto de Galinhas to Barra de Santo Antônio

The slightly curious name of Porto de Galinhas, meaning "Chicken Port", derives from a history of slave running; tax-dodging, life-dealing smugglers would arrive to shore proclaiming they had a shipment of "Angolan chickens". Today, Porto de Galinhas, on the southern coast of Pernambuco, has a number of very fine beaches, notably Muro Alto, Serrambi (some 5km long and particularly good for surfing) and Enseada dos Corais. In the high season, several of Recife's best clubs open shop here. As well as beautiful landscapes, the Porto de Galinhas area abounds with old sugar mills and churches.

Some buses for Porto de Galinhas leave from the old Recife airport or the square near it with the company Real Alagoes (ⓣ81/3452-3888). Other buses can be caught from Avenida Dantas Barreto in Recife (hourly 6.30am–7.30pm, last bus leaving Porto at 5.40pm). Another glorious Brazilian beach, **PORTO DE GALINHAS** (only 65km from Recife), is deservedly popular – if in danger of becoming overdeveloped. Outside of high season, it's quiet enough during the week but still very crowded at weekends. From here **jangadas** will take you out to the small natural coral pools just off the coast, and there is some excellent **surfing** here, too. Good fresh fish is to be had in the **beachside cafés**; fried needle fish, *agulhas fritas*, is a great snack with a cold beer as you wiggle your toes in the warm sand. If you want **to stay**, there are two campsites and numerous *pousadas*, as well as an increasing number of upmarket hotels on the seafront. Right on the main beach are the luxury *Village Porto de Galinhas* (ⓣ81/3552-1038, ⓕ3552-1277; ❺), with its own pool, and the smaller *Recanto*, Avenida Beira Mar (ⓣ81/3552-1251; ❸). The *Pousada Litoral* (❷), just three blocks from the ocean at the corner of Rua da Esperança and Beijupira, has clean simple rooms. For unbelievably tasty shrimps, lobsters and local *sobremesas*, visit the excellent *Beijupirá* **restaurant** (ⓣ81/3552-2354; daily from noon till 11pm) in the road of the same name.

The main drag, Rua da Esperança, is where you'll find the **tourist information** office (ⓣ81/3552-1480) and the **post office**; lines of dune buggies are at the sea end, looking for business (R$45–50 for 2–3hrs). If you'd rather get behind the wheel, try Buggy Tour, Rua do Colegio (ⓣ81/3461-1902 or 3552-1400).

Four or five kilometres away – easily reached by either a forty-minute walk along the beach or a R$12 dune-buggy ride – is one of the finest beaches in the area, the **Praia de Macaripe**, where there are plenty of bars and restaurants as well as good waves, reefs and *jangada* rides on offer. The *Pousada dos Coqueiros* (ⓣ81/3552-1294, ⓕ3552-1736, ⓦwww.pousadadoscoqueiros.com.br; ❷) is a good place to stay, especially if you're here to surf. Another 10km further south is the beautiful **Praia da Ponta de Serrambi**, popular with windsurfers. For total luxury, *Intermares Village*, right on the beach (ⓣ81/3527-4200, ⓕ3527-4006; ❼), has its own pool, sauna, jet skis and *jangadas*.

South again are the sleepy fishing villages of **TAMANDARÉ** and **SÃO JOSÉ DA COROA GRANDE**, where, for the time being, fishing still dominates, with *jangadas* drawn up on the beaches and men repairing nets, though even here weekend houses for city slickers are going up. In Tamandaré (served by direct bus from Recife's *rodoviária*), apart from the usual stunning beach, there are the ruins of the fort of Santo Inácio, destroyed in 1646, and a small hotel, *Marinas Tamandaré*, Loteamento Anaisabela, Lote 15A (ⓣ81/3675-1388; ❺). A little way south, in São José da Coroa Grande, where the *litoral* road finally hits the coast (also served by direct bus from Recife's *rodoviária*), there are bars, a huge beach and the overpriced *Hotel Francês*, Rua Antonia Valdemar Acioli Belo 279 (ⓣ81/3688-1169; ❹). Just offshore from here is the Ilha de Santo Aleixo, where there are a couple of good beaches.

Inland from Recife

In contrast to the gentle scenery of the coastal routes out of Recife, heading **inland** brings you abruptly into a completely different landscape, spectacular and forbidding. The people, too, look and speak differently; the typical *sertanejo* is short and wiry, with the high cheekbones and thin nose of an Indian ancestor. They speak a heavily accented Portuguese, much ridiculed elsewhere, but really one of the loveliest Brazilian inflections.

Buses inland all leave from the Recife Rodoviária, and the best place to head for is the market town of **Caruaru**, 130km from Recife and the largest town in the *agreste*. The frequent buses there take two hours and are very comfortable; buy your ticket a day in advance. Seats on the right-hand side of the bus have the best view.

The route to Caruaru: Vitória, Gravatá and Bezerros

The **BR-232** highway heads directly away from the sea into gentle hills covered with enormous fields of sugar cane; the size of the estates gives you some idea of the inequality of land distribution in the Northeast, and explains why this part of Pernambuco has been in the forefront of the struggle for agrarian reform in Brazil. It was here in the late 1950s that the Peasant Leagues started, a social movement pressing for land reform through direct action and one of the factors that frightened the military into launching their coup in 1964. Most of the cane is destined for the first town en route, **Vitória de Santo Antão**, where, on the left-hand side of the road, you'll see the factory that produces the most widely drunk rum in Brazil, Pitu – you can't miss the thirty-metre-high water tank cunningly camouflaged as an enormous bottle of the stuff.

After Vitória you begin to climb in earnest into the **Serra da Neblina**, threading into the hills of the *agreste* proper. Gradually the air becomes cooler, the heat drier, and highland plants replace the palms and sugar cane of the coastal strip. On a clear day the views are stunning, with rows of hills stretching into the distance on both sides and the coastal plain shimmering in the background. The fertile hills facing the sea get a lot of rain, cotton taking over from sugar as you climb, but deeper inland the hills are brown and parched, and farming becomes more difficult. You begin to see cattle and strange-looking fields filled with neat rows of cactus. These fields are called *palma*, and they're a foretaste of the harshness of *sertão* life: in times of drought, the cactus is chopped down and fed to cattle, thorns and all. It's a feed of last resource but, remarkably, the cactus contains enough water to keep cattle alive for a few more crucial months in the wait for rain.

Gravatá

The next town, 50km down the road, is **GRAVATÁ**, one of several *agreste* towns that has optimistically tagged itself "The Switzerland of Pernambuco" on the strength of its cool hill climate – temperatures average around 21°C. There are lots of villas and a hotel built in Swiss-chalet style, rather incongruous in a landscape that is parched brown as often as not. If you want to break your journey here, the best hotels are the chalet-style *Casa Grande*, BR-232, Km 83 (Ⓣ81/3533-0920, Ⓕ3533-0812; ❺), which has a pool and a sauna; the *Portal de Gravatá*, BR-232, Km 83 (Ⓣ81/3533-0288, Ⓕ3533-0610; ❻), with similar facilities as well as a fishing lake; and the *Grande Hotel da Serra*, BR-232, Km 83 (Ⓣ81/3533-0114; ❸), one of the cheapest hotels in the area, offering decent rooms with private showers. After Gravatá, it soon becomes obvious that you are nearing a major market from the activities at the roadside. Every few hundred yards boys and men stand as far into the road as they dare, leaping aside at the last moment, flourishing their wares at passing motorists: chickens, piglets and the delicious fruit of the interior – pomegranates, *jaboticaba* (like a cross between a plum and a sweet grape), *mangaba*, a delicious red berry that stains the mouth black, and *umbu*, which looks like a gooseberry but doesn't taste like one. *Sempre Verde Viviencias e Cavalgadas* (Ⓣ81/3533-7524) is a *fazenda* offering horse riding at 800m above sea level, a cool thing to do and just 30 minutes by car from Gravatá; they have accommodation (Ⓣ81/9958-3861, Ⓦwww.sempreverde.tur.br; ⑤) as well as offering environmental education and treks through the forest to waterfalls and natural pools.

Bezerros

BEZERROS, the last town before Caruaru, is the home of a famous artist and printer, **Jota Borges**, some of whose work you may have seen in the Casa da Cultura and the Penha craft shop (see p.328) in Recife. Borges has a roadside workshop on the left as you leave town. Inside, you can see the carved wooden plates he makes to manufacture the prints on paper and cloth; the smaller ones are for the covers of *cordel* (see p.328), a large library of which takes up one corner of the workshop. Borges himself is often at the market in Caruaru or delivering in Recife, but a family member is usually on hand to show visitors around. The absurdly inexpensive prints are simple but powerful depictions of peasant life.

Caruaru

Home of the largest market in the Northeast, **CARUARU** is also ideally placed for excursions into the *sertão*. Saturday is the main market day, but Wednesday and Friday are busy, too.

People come from all over the Northeast for the **market**, which dominates the town, with stalls filling the squares and people clogging the streets. It's a slightly less traditional affair than it used to be, with Asian electronic goods playing an increasingly important part, but the atmosphere is still worth savouring. The market is devoted to food, arts and crafts, and is famous for its songbirds and the so-called **troca-troca**, where things are swapped rather than bought. The **songbird market** is illegal but flourishing nonetheless, with dozens of species in small handmade cages. The *troca-troca*, starting early on Saturday morning and finishing by noon, is taken over by a crowd of people wandering around with whatever they want to swap: tapes and records, an old radio, used clothes, car parts – things that it would be difficult to sell for cash, which is why you don't see livestock or food being traded. It's fascinating to watch, but keep to the sidelines as locals don't appreciate wandering tourists getting in their way. It's also used by pickpockets unloading hot goods in a hurry, so if you don't want to see your own things being bartered, keep an eye on your bag. Wandering around the **food market** introduces you to some characteristic sights and smells of the interior: the blocks of hard white *sertão* cheese, delicious when eaten with fruit; piles of leaves, roots and barks used in popular medicine; brown blocks of *rapadura*, a sweet with a rich and sickly smell made from unrefined sugar; and rows of mules having their teeth examined by prospective buyers.

The **mercado de artesanato** is becoming as near to a tourist trap as the interior ever gets, and, while there is some dross, there's also a large amount of interesting work at prices far lower than in Recife. It's divided into sections – straw, leather, pottery and so forth – but most popular are the small, inexpensive clay statues for which this area is nationally famous, the **figurinhas de barro**. Caruaru is the main outlet for the renowned potters of Alto do Moura (see p.350), just up the road, and if you've seen the work of Mestre Vitalino in Recife you'll instantly recognize their vivid peasant style.

Practicalities

The **bus station** (ⓣ81/3721-3869) is 2km out of town, but buses from Recife stop in the centre, and you can also get off there. It's perfectly possible to see the market, make a trip out to Alto do Moura and get back to Recife in a day – which is what most people do. If you want to stay over, however, or intend to move on the next day further into the interior, there is no shortage of places to sleep. The best **hotels** include the three-star *Hotel do Sol* at the crossroads between the BR-104 and BR-232, 3km from the centre (ⓣ81/3721-3044, ⓕ3721-1336; ④); the central *Hotel Centenário*, Rua Sete de Setembro 84 (ⓣ81/3722-4011; ③), which has a sauna but no pool; and the excellent value *Hotel Central*, Rua Vigário Freire 71 (ⓣ81/3721-5880; ③). Among **restaurants**, *Le Cottage* at Av. Agamemnon Magalhães 752, slightly north of the centre, serves good, low-cost meals from a varied menu; the *Bar da Perua*, Rua Aliança 175 (ⓣ81/3722-3266), and the *Mestre Vitalino*, to the west of town at Rua Leão Dourado 13, both offer a wide range of local dishes at lunchtime and are reasonably priced.

Alto do Moura

To explore the tradition of *figurinhas* further, it's worth making the short journey to **ALTO DO MOURA**, 6km up the road from Caruaru: take a taxi or the marked bus (departures every 2hr) from Rua 13 de Maio, one of the roads leading out of the centre towards the *rodoviária*. It's a dirt road to a small yet busy village that seems entirely unremarkable, except that every other house on the only street, **Rua Mestre Vitalino**, is a potter's workshop, with kilns resembling large beehives in the yards behind. The first house on the left was Mestre Vitalino's, and is now a small museum, with his widow and grandchildren still living in the simple hut next door. There's a plaque on the adobe wall and, inside, the hut has been kept as Vitalino left it, with his leather hat and jacket hanging on a nail. The only sign that Vitalino was somebody special is the framed photos of him being feted in Rio de Janeiro and introduced to the president. There's a visitors' book, and one of Vitalino's grandchildren is on hand to show you around. It's free, but do leave a donation: Vitalino's widow lives in penury next door without any kind of pension, a sad memorial to a man who brought fame and fortune to the town of his birth.

All the workshops are piled with pottery and *figurinhas* for sale, and are fascinating to browse around; each potter has a unique individual style. One of the most individual, and certainly the most eccentric, is **Gaudino**, on the corner opposite the solitary café. His inspiration comes to him in dreams, and much of his work consists of fantastic clay monsters, each with a poem, describing the dream that gave birth to it, stuffed into its mouth. Apart from his talents as a potter, Gaudino is a very skilled *repentista*: he can immediately improvise a stanza of welcome, rhyming your name to the last word of every line. Of the dozens of other workshops, the best are those of the children and grandchildren of Vitalino and his contemporaries: Manuel Eudócio at no. 151, who specializes in decorative pots; Luiz Antônio at no. 285; and Vitalino's son, Severino Pereira dos Santos, at no. 281. One more essential stopping point is the Casa de Arte Zé Caboclo at no. 63, one of the workshops of the large and extraordinarily talented family of **Zé Caboclo**, who along with Vitalino was the founder of the *figurinhas* tradition. His work is larger and cruder than Vitalino's, but has a vivid energy that many of the Alto do Moura potters rate more highly. Here you can also see his granddaughter Marliete's work, most of which is not for sale. She is the best of the younger generation: her delicate miniaturized figurines, superbly painted, show how the special skills of Alto do Moura are revitalized with each generation that passes, a tribute to the strength of popular culture in the interior.

Nova Jerusalém

In Easter week, Caruara's market crowds are swollen with tourists and pilgrims heading for **NOVA JERUSALÉM**, in the heart of the *agreste*, 50km from the bustling town; the turn-off is on the right just after Caruaru, on the BR-104, marked "Campina Grande". After 24km another turn-off, to the left, the PE-145, leads to the small town of **Fazenda Nova**, just outside which is the site of Nova Jerusalém.

A granite replica of the old city of Jerusalem, it was built in the early 1970s by a local entrepreneur who cashed in on the deep religious feeling of the interior by mounting a **Passion play** based on that of Oberammergau in Germany. Over the years, this Paixão do Cristo has become a tradition of the *agreste*, attracting thousands of spectators to watch five hundred costumed actors, mostly local amateurs, recreate the Passion and Crucifixion. The "replica" of Jerusalem is in fact a third of the size of the original, and is basically a setting for the twelve stages on which the action takes place, each representing a Station of the Cross. There's an enjoyable air of tackiness about the whole production, which is very free with the tomato ketchup in the whipping and crucifixion scenes. Next to the site is a **sculpture park**, where local artists have set up several impressively large granite statues of folk heroes done in the style of the interior, the largest versions you'll see of the *figurinhas de barro*.

The Passion is performed daily from the Tuesday before Easter to Easter Sunday inclusive, taking up most of the day. The most convenient way to see it is to go on one of the day tours that many travel agents in Recife – and other Northeastern cities – run there during Holy Week. It's also easy to get there under your own steam, as there are buses to Fazenda Nova from Caruaru and a **campsite** when you get there, as well as several simple *dormitórios*. Entry to the spectacle costs about R$50.

Into the sertão

The **Pernambucan sertão** begins after Caruaru, though there's no sudden transition; the hills simply get browner and rockier, dense thorny scrub takes over from the hill plants, and there are cacti every few yards, from tiny flowering stumps to massive tangled plants as large as trees. And, above all, it is hot, with parched winds that feel as if someone is training a hairdryer on your face. The Pernambucan *sertão* is one of the harshest in the Northeast, a scorched landscape under relentless sun for most of the year. This is cattle country, home of the *vaqueiro*, the Northeastern cowboy, and has been since the very beginning of Portuguese penetration inland in the seventeenth century; it is one of the oldest frontiers in the Americas.

The main highway that runs through the hilly Pernambucan *sertão* winds through scenery unlike any you'll have seen before – an apparently endless expanse of cactus and scrub so thick in places that cowboys have to wear leather armour to protect themselves. If you travel in the rainy season here – March to June, although rain can never be relied upon in the interior – you may be lucky enough to catch it bursting with green, punctuated by the whites, reds and purples of flowering trees and cacti. Massive electrical storms are common at this time of year, and at night the horizon can flicker with sheet lightning for hours at a stretch.

Towards Petrolina

After Caruaru the highway passes through a number of anonymous farming towns. **ARCOVERDE**, 130km to the west, has a market on Saturdays and a reasonable **hotel**, the *Grande Majestic*, Av. Cel. Antônio Japiassu 326 (☎87/3821-1175; ❷), which doesn't quite live up to its name but is a cheap and handy place to break the journey. You may need to do just that, as the best *sertão* towns to make for are buried deep in the interior, some eight or ten hours by bus from Caruaru.

The last place that could really be called a town is **SERRA TALHADA**, some 200km west of Arcoverde. Here, the *Pousada da Serra*, Rua Dr Ademar Xavier 1055, Alto da Conceição (☎87/3831-1536; ❸), is reasonable. From here on, the road passes through a succession of flyblown villages, all of which would look vaguely Mediterranean – with their whitewashed churches, cafés, dusty squares and rows of tumbledown cottages – if it weren't for the startling landscape in which they are set. Eighty kilometres beyond Serra Talhada, a turning leads north to Juazeiro do Norte (see p.365), while one Petrolina bus turns south to follow an alternative route parallel to the São Francisco valley. The others continue for another 110km, across one of the most desolate semi-arid desert landscapes in the Northeast, before reaching **OURICURI**, a shady spot with a couple of hotels that's quite a pleasant place to break your journey; from here it's another 213km south along the BR-122 to Petrolina.

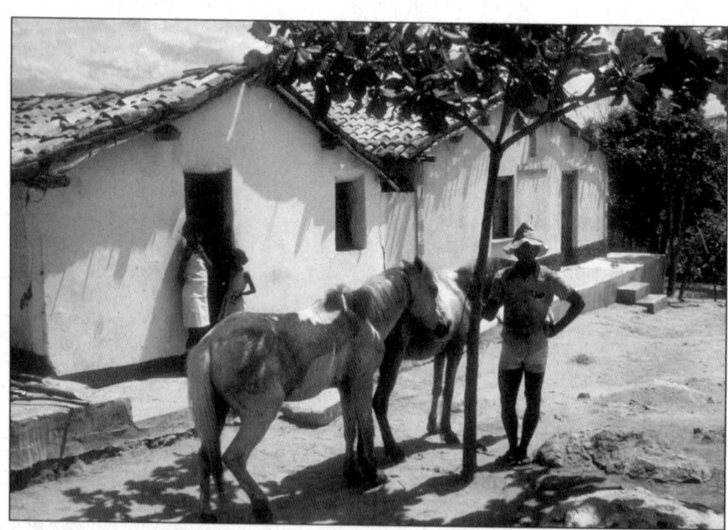

△ In the sertão

Petrolina

After the villages that have gone before, **PETROLINA** seems like a city. Certainly, by the standards of the *sertão*, it's a large, thriving and relatively prosperous town, thanks to the river trade to places downstream. On the waterfront, you can occasionally see riverboats adorned with *carrancas*, carved wooden figureheads bolted onto the prow, brightly painted and with a grotesque monster's head, meant to frighten evil spirits lurking in wait for unwary mariners. Petrolina also has an interesting **Museu do Sertão** (Mon–Fri 10am–6pm, Sat 2–6pm, Sun 8am–noon), on Praça Santos Dumont on the road to the airstrip, about ten minutes' walk from the centre of town. Small but well put together, the museum documents *sertão* life and history through assorted relics and some fascinating photographs, including a couple of the bespectacled social bandit Lampião and his gang, popular heroes who roamed the *sertão* until they were shot dead in 1938. Lastly, Petrolina has a **market** on Friday and Saturday that brings people in from the *sertão* for miles around.

The **rodoviária** (ⓣ87/3861-3512) is quite central and there are a couple of *dormitórios* close by. Better **places to stay** are the *Hotel Central*, on Praça Dom Malan, adequate for the price (❷), and the *Hotel Reis Palace*, Rua Manuel Clementino 1157 (ⓣ87/3861-2431; ❸), which has apartments plus a bar and a small pool. The *Petrolina Palace*, Av. Cardoso de Sá 845 (ⓣ87/3862-1555, ⓦwww.petrolinapalacehotel.com.br; ❹–❺), and the *Hotel do Grande Rio*, Avenida Pe. Fraga (ⓣ87/3862-3344; ❹) both have pools. Excellent regional **food** is served at *O Barranqueiro*, Rua Rio Beberibe 50 (ⓣ81/3864-2356), although it's not cheap and the restaurant is some 4km from the town centre, while *Chimarrão*, Av. Mons. Angelo Sampaio, Cohab 3, is the place for hungry carnivores. There are three **buses** daily to Petrolina from Recife, which can be picked up at Caruaru.

Juazeiro

Over the bridge, or across the river by boat, and into Bahia state lies Petrolina's poorer sister town, **JUAZEIRO**, not to be confused with Juazeiro do Norte. Many of its inhabitants had their homes flooded when dams created the enormous **Sobradinho** lake just upstream in the 1960s. Since then the area around Juazeiro has become something of a showcase for **irrigation schemes**, and all kinds of fruit – including unlikely products like grapes and asparagus – are grown here. The town has several **hotels**, a good choice being the *Grande Hotel do Juazeiro*, Rua José Petitinga (ⓣ74/3611-7710; ❺), not as grand as the name would suggest, but situated on the riverfront with a pool, bar and very good restaurant. The cheaper but spotless *Rio Sol*, Rua Cel. João Evangelista 3 (ⓣ74/3611-4481; ❷), is another good bet. There is an unusual attraction in the form of a nineteenth-century paddle steamer, the *Vaporzinho*, built in 1852 to ply the São Francisco river; it's been restored, turned into a **restaurant** and is now moored on the riverfront.

Juazeiro is the northern terminus for the **river services** of the Companhia de Navegação do São Francisco, which once ran frequent boats as far south as Minas Gerais but is now in decline. It still runs one monthly boat to Pirapora in Minas Gerais, from where there are bus connections to Brasília and Belo Horizonte, but its departure has become increasingly irregular. Times and dates are available from tourist information offices in Recife and Salvador; the journey itself takes three or four days. There are also smaller boats to towns both upstream and downstream leaving from the waterfront in Juazeiro; most of them are river traders and are quite happy to take paying passengers – although always check during negotiations when they return, as it may not be for a couple of days. It's remarkable how appealing the idea of even a short boat trip becomes after the heat and dust of the *sertão*, whose hills crowd right down to the Sobradinho lakeside. Tempting though it is, however, you should **avoid swimming** in the lake, as schistosomiasis – also known as bilharzia – is endemic here.

From Juazeiro you can continue south by bus along the BR-407 to Feira de Santana (see p.292) and Salvador (see p.260). Alternatively, if you're interested in the history of the *sertão*, you might want to make the five-hour journey southeast to Canudos (see p.293).

Fernando de Noronha

The beautiful and environmentally protected archipelago of **FERNANDO DE NORONHA**, lies in the equatorial Atlantic some 545km from Pernambuco, though it's actually nearer to Rio Grande do Norte. Access is mainly from Natal, Recife and São Luís. Boasting more than sixteen very clean and stunning beaches, it's hard to beat for **scuba diving** – its clear water stretches down to a depth of 40m in places, with a white sandy sea bottom, plenty of coral, crustacean, turtles, dolphins and a wide ranges of fish species and shoal types. The islands are also breeding territory for a number of tropical Atlantic birds.

European explorers first came here in 1503, and after a struggle between various powers, with the Dutch running the show from 1700 to 1736, the islands ended up under the control of the Portuguese in 1737. Lisbon considered the archipelago strategically important enough to build the **Forte dos Remédios**, of which only some remains can now be seen.

In recent years the archipelago has become well known as an ecotourist destination. Most of it has been protected as a **marine national park**, created in 1988 in order to maintain the ecological wonders that have been preserved by the islands' isolation from the rest of Brazil. The vegetation is fairly typical Northeastern *agreste*, but the wildlife is magnificent: birdwatchers will be amazed by the variety of **exotic birds**, including several types of pelicans, and you'll be moved by the remarkable sight of thousands of dolphins entering the bay every day between 5am and 6am, viewed from the harbour.

The main island, **Ilha de Fernando de Noronha**, shelters plenty of stunning **beaches**. The water can sometimes be turbulent and not perfectly clear, but it is a fairly constant and very comfortable 28°C. The best beaches are probably Praia da Atalaia and Cacimba do Padre, and at Mirante dos Golfinhos you can watch dolphins leaping over the waves – visitors used to be able to swim with them, but this has been banned. A number of **ecological trails** allow good birdwatching, and several companies specialize in **scuba-diving** courses and trips, including Aguas Claras (Ⓣ81/3619-1225), Atlantis (Ⓣ81/3619-1371) and Noronha Divers (Ⓣ81/3619-1112). Various companies also offer **boat trips** around the archipelago, leaving from the ports at the northeastern tip of the island and from the Bahia dos Golfinhos at the island's southern end. Boat trips from the latter leave most days (R$40 per person including transport to the harbour; Ⓣ81/3619-1295).

Practicalities

All visitors to the islands are expected to pay the TPA tax (Taxa de Preservação), which goes toward protecting the environment, but this can be done in advance online (Ⓦwww.noronha.pe.gov.br). To reach Fernando de Noronha, you can **fly** from either Recife or Natal with Nordeste airlines (Ⓣ81/3619-1144, Ⓦwww.voenordeste.com.br) or Trip (Ⓣ81/3463-4610 or 3619-1379, Ⓦwww.voetrip.com.br); tickets are available from a number of travel agents in both cities (see "Listings" on p.335 and p.376). A return flight from Natal will set you back at least R$750, one from Recife slightly more, though there are more frequent flights from the latter. Bring plenty of local currency with you as you won't be able to change money during your stay, and also bring anything else you think you may need: prices in Fernando de Noronha are high, and you should try to avoid doing much shopping while you're there. Fernando de Noronha is best visited between August and January, when the rainfall is lowest.

The few facilities that the islands have, including the **airport** (Ⓣ81/3619-1311), are all found on the main island. Here you'll find the **tourist information** office (Ⓣ81/3619-1352) in the main settlement of **VILA DOS REMÉDIOS**, a small town in the northern part of the island, and, some 10km to the south near the airport, the **Centro de Visitantes** (daily 8am–10.30pm; Ⓣ81/3619-1171).

Tours these days are the obligatory way to get to Fernando de Noronha (an attempt to limit the impact of tourism on the fragile environment) and are generally arranged by travel agencies in Recife or Natal, such as Dolphin Travel, at Av. Eng. Domingos Ferreira 4267 (Ⓣ81/3326-3815) in Boa Viagem; they usually include a return flight, accommodation, food and tours of the island. Prices start at around R$1400 for two nights, R$1600 for three nights and R$1800 for five nights. *Ambiental Expedições* (Ⓣ11/3819-4600, Ⓦwww.ambiental.tur.br) run good trips, but are a São Paulo-based company.

On the main island, **buggies**, **jeeps** and **motorbikes** can be rented from several operators, including Locbuggy (Ⓣ81/3619-1142) and Eduardo Galvao de Brito at the *Esmeralda do Atlântico Hotel* (Ⓣ81/3619-1335). Many hotels and *pousadas* rent out their own buggies, which can work out to be less expensive. You can arrange **diving trips** through your travel agent, but Atlantis Divers (Ⓣ81/3619-1371, Ⓦwww.atlantisnoronha.com.br) are probably the best dive operator on the island.

Paraíba

Most people who are travelling north from Recife head directly for Ceará and Rio Grande do Norte's beaches, missing **Paraíba state** and its capital of **João Pessoa** altogether. This is a big mistake, as João Pessoa is the most attractive of the smaller Northeastern cities, with everything you could reasonably ask for: some of the finest town beaches in the area, a beautiful setting on the mouth of the Rio Sanhauá and colonial remains, including one of Brazil's most striking churches. In addition, not enough foreign travellers make it to the city for the *pessoenses* to have become blasé about them, and you're likely to be approached by smiling kids who are anxious to practise their hard-learned English.

Out of the city, there are even nicer beaches to the north and south, while the highway inland leads to **Campina Grande**, a market town strategically placed at the entrance to the *sertão*. The main target of the interior is the fascinating pilgrim town of **Juazeiro do Norte**; while it's actually in neighbouring Ceará state (see p.380), it's covered here because it's most easily accessible from Paraíba.

João Pessoa

JOÃO PESSOA is one of the oldest and one of the poorest cities in Brazil. In the last two decades, there's been massive new development along the city's two main beaches, but an air of dilapidated elegance remains around the old part of town. Of all the Northeast's city centres, this is the one least scarred by modern developers. Just a few kilometres away, the town beaches of **Cabo Branco** and **Tambaú** are well on their way to becoming much the same as most others in the Northeast, with towering skyscrapers stretching back towards the old town. There aren't enough of them yet, though, to detract from the stunning beauty of the vast white sandy beach, and, out of season, tourists are still few and far between.

Arrival, orientation and information

The **rodoviária** (☎83/3221-9611) in João Pessoa is conveniently near the city centre. Any bus from the **local bus station**, opposite the *rodoviária*'s entrance, takes you to the city's one unmistakeable, central landmark: the circular lake of the Parque Solon de Lucena, which everybody simply calls the **Lagoa**, spectacularly bordered by tall palms imported from Portugal. All **bus routes** converge on the circular Anel Viário skirting the lake, some en route to the

beach districts, others heading further afield – to the northern beaches, the neighbouring town of Cabedelo and the village of Penha to the south of the city. Buses for the beach can also be caught directly from the *rodoviária*; look for the ones marked "Tambaú" (#510 or #513).

The Presidente Castro Pinto **airport** (Ⓣ83/3232-1200) lies just 11km west of the city centre and is connected to the *rodoviária* by regular buses; taxis into town cost around R$30.

Orientation

João Pessoa's **centre** is just to the west of the Lagoa. To the east **Avenida Getúlio Vargas** leads out of town towards the skyscrapers and beachside *bairros* of Cabo Branco and Tambaú. At the city's core is **Praça João Pessoa**, which contains the state governor's palace and the local parliament; most of the central hotels are clustered around here. The oldest part of the city is just to the north of Praça João Pessoa, where **Rua Duque de Caxias** ends in the Baroque splendour of the **Igreja de São Francisco**. The steep Ladeira de São Francisco, leading down from here to the lower city and the bus and train stations, offers a marvellous tree-framed view of the rest of the city spread out on the banks of the **Rio Sanhau**.

The two sweeping bays of **Cabo Branco** and **Tambaú** are separated by the futuristic, luxury *Hotel Tambaú* (see p.358) – more commonly known as the *Tropical Tambaú Center Hotel* – and the nearby Centro Turístico Tambaú shopping centre. This area is also where the highest concentration of nightspots can be found. The southern boundary of the city is the lighthouse on Ponta de Seixas, the cape at the far end of Cabo Branco. Locals claim it as the most easterly point of Brazil, a title disputed with the city of Natal to the north – though the *pessoenses* have geography on their side.

Information

Official **tourist information** is available from the state tourist board, PB-Tur, at the *rodoviária* (daily 8am–6pm; Ⓣ83/3222-3537), the airport (daily 9am–4pm) and in the Centro de Turismo in Tambaú, opposite the *Tropical Tambaú Center Hotel* at Av. Almirante Tamandaré 100 (daily 8am–7pm; Ⓣ83/3247-0505). You can also find a post office and a *posto telefônico* here. An additional source of information is the English-speaking **Disque Turismo** hotline (Ⓣ514).

Accommodation

The very cheapest **places to stay** are the *dormitórios* opposite the *rodoviária*. You can find good budget and medium-range hotels both in the centre and on the beaches, but five-star luxury is only available by the sea. Hotels in João Pessoa rarely seem to charge the full price displayed at the reception desk, and you can get some pretty hefty discounts if you ask.

City centre

Hotel Rio Verde Rua Duque de Caxias 263 Ⓣ83/3222-4369. Right in the middle of the old centre, this is a no-frills but clean and good-value option. ❶

J.R. Hotel Rua Rodrigues Chaves 87 Ⓣ & Ⓕ83/3241-2104. A large but good modern option, with clean rooms and friendly service. ❸

Lagoa Park Hotel Parque Solon de Lucena 19 Ⓣ83/3241-1414. Not as expensive as it looks, this hotel offers adequate rooms, some with great views over the Lagoa. ❸

Paraíba Palace Praça Vidal de Negreiros Ⓣ83/3221-3107. A good-value, centrally located option with simple, cosy rooms. ❸

Pousada Raio de Luz, Praça Venancio Neiva 44 Ⓣ83/3221-2169. An inexpensive hotel offering by far the best value in the city centre; rooms are tidy and some have private showers. ❷

The beaches

Escuna Praia Hotel Av. Cabo Branco 1574 ⓣ83/3226-5611. Well located on a nice part of the beach, the *Escuna* is clean, pleasant and even better value out of season. ④

Hotel Pouso das Aguas Av. Cabo Branco 2348 ⓣ & ⓕ83/3226-5003, ⓦwww.pousadadasaguas.com.br. Small but comfortable spot with a garden and a pool. Right on the seafront. ⑤

Hotel Praia Mar Av. Almirante Tamandaré 864 ⓣ & ⓕ83/226-2515. Yet another inexpensive but good mid-range option right on the beach. ④

Mar Azul Hotel Pousada Av. João Maurício 315 ⓣ83/3226-2660. Despite not providing breakfast, this seafront budget hotel at Tambaú offers excellent value. ③–④

Pousada Canta–Maré Rua Osório Paes 60 ⓣ83/247-1047 or 226-4809. Amongst the cheapest accommodation in Tambaú, this is a small and basic but relatively comfortable lodging. ②

Pousada Lua Cheia Mar Av. Cabo Branco 1710 ⓣ83/3247-2470. Small, clean and very friendly, this place is located at one of the best parts of the beach, between Tambaú and Cabo Branco. ③

Tropical Tambaú Av. Almirante Tamandaré 229 ⓣ83/3218-1919, ⓦwww.tropicalhotel.com.br. One of the city's landmark modernist buildings (it looks a bit like a flying saucer), this luxury beachside hotel offers a sauna, pool, games room, fitness suite and classy restaurant – though the service is not really worth the money. ⑥–⑦

Victory Business Flat Av. Almirante Tamandaré 310 ⓣ83/3247-3100, ⓕ3247-5332, ⓦwww.victoryflat.com.br. More or less opposite the *Tropical Tambaú Center Hotel*, the *Victory* offers equally luxurious rooms at less than half the price outside high season; it also has a pool and good service. ⑥

Xénius Hotel Av. Cabo Branco 1262 ⓣ83/3226-3535, ⓕ3226-5463 ⓦwww.xeniushotel.com.br. Pleasant modern hotel with a rooftop pool, a very good restaurant, a bar and the usual mod cons. ④

Camping

João Pessoa's beautiful **campsite**, on a promontory past the Ponta de Seixas, can be reached by taking the Cabo Branco bus to its terminal and then walking (for about 45min) past the lighthouse and along the road beyond it until the signposted fork to the left. Easier on the legs is taking the Penha bus from the Anel Viário or the local bus station: it passes near the campsite but only operates every couple of hours. Clean and well run, on a fine beach with a spectacular view of the city, the campsite is often full, especially from January to March, so it's advisable to book beforehand in the centre at sala 18, Rua Almeida Barreto 159 (ⓣ83/3221-4863).

The City

The centre of João Pessoa is dotted with **colonial churches**, **monasteries** and **convents**, some of which are extremely beautiful. Until 1992 they were all being allowed to fall into ruin but, not a moment too soon, the state government and the Ministry of Culture mounted a crash restoration programme, for once using historians and archeologists to return the buildings to their original glory rather than gutting them. These days, modernization has certainly taken its toll on the city, but you can still see mule carts sitting alongside BMWs at the city's traffic lights.

São Francisco

João Pessoa's most spectacular church is the **Igreja de São Francisco** (Mon 2–5pm, Tues–Sun 9am–noon & 2–5pm), which sits in splendid isolation atop the hill that bears its name, at the end of Rua Duque de Caxias, and now forms part of the **Centro Cultural de São Francisco**.

The exterior alone is impressive enough. A huge courtyard is flanked by high walls beautifully decorated with *azulejo* tiling, with pastoral scenes in a series of alcoves. These walls funnel you towards a large early eighteenth-century church that would do credit to Lisbon or Coimbra: its most remarkable feature is the tower topped with an oriental dome, a form that the Portuguese encountered in Goa and appropriated for their own purposes. Older than the church by a few decades is the stone cross opposite the courtyard, at the foot of which is a group of finely carved pelicans, once believed to selflessly tear flesh from their own chests to feed their young, and so commonly used to symbolize Christ. You reach the church through an entrance that has marvellously carved wooden panels and doors. Beyond the church are the chapels and cloister of the **Convento de Santo Antônio**, and upstairs there's an excellent **museum** of popular and sacred art.

Around São Francisco

The other places worth seeing in the centre are within a short walk of São Francisco. A little way down the steep Ladeira de São Francisco is the oldest building in town, the Casa da Pólvora, a relic of the times when the Dutch and Portuguese fought for control over this sugar-rich coastline. The squat, functional building was once the city arsenal, but is now the home of the **Museu Fotográfico Walfredo Rodriguez** (Mon–Fri 8–11.30am & 2–5pm), given over to a collection of enlarged photographs of the city taken in the early decades of this century.

If you go back up the Ladeira de São Francisco, turn right and right again, you'll end up on Rua General Osório. Here you'll find the cathedral, **Igreja de Nossa Senhora das Neves**, which boasts a well-proportioned interior that, for once, forgoes the Rococo excesses of many colonial cathedrals. Its large, rather plain facade fronts a small square with majestic views north to the wooded river valley and, to the west, green suburbs. Further down Rua General Osório, the seventeenth-century **Mosteiro de São Bento** (Tues–Sat 2–5pm) has a simple, beautifully restored interior with a lovely curved wooden ceiling. Other colonial churches are cheek by jowl on Rua Visconde de Pelotas, two blocks to the east: the **Igreja de Nossa Senhora do Carmo** here is well worth a look, both for its ornate Baroque exterior and the gold-leaf-covered altar inside.

The beaches

The beach areas of Tambaú and Cabo Branco are linked to the centre by frequent buses from the Anel Viário and the local bus station. The **Cabo Branco** seafront is especially stylish, with a mosaic pavement and thousands of well-tended palm trees to complement the sweep of the bay. This is best viewed from the **Ponta de Seixas lighthouse** at the southern end, where a plaque and a monument mark Brazil's easternmost point. From here, it's only 2200km to Senegal in Africa, less than half the distance to Rio Grande do Sul in the south of Brazil or the state of Roraima in the north. To get to the lighthouse, take the "Cabo Branco" bus to its terminal on the promontory at the end of the bay and walk up the hill. At the top, you'll find a park and a couple of tacky souvenir shops, but the main draw here is the view, which is glorious – Cabo Branco beach stretches out before you in an enormous arc, 6km long. Cabo Branco itself is one of the city's exclusive upper-class suburbs, where the rich stay hidden in their large detached houses, their high walls shutting out both the people and the view. The beach has the usual string of bars and several hotels, but they are sparser and less intrusive than on Tambaú, and during the week, there's not much more at the southern end of Cabo Branco than the rustle of wind in the palm trees to disturb you.

Tambaú is a lot more lively, dominated by its eponymous hotel, which forms one end of a small square. Nearby, on the corner of Avenida Nossa Senhora dos Navegantes and Avenida Rui Carneiro, is a modern building housing the **Mercado de Artesanato Paraíbano**. Although not up to the standards of Pernambuco, Paraíba has distinctive *artesanato* that's worth checking out: painted plates and bowls, and striking figurines made out of sacking and wood. North of the market you encounter busier and larger clusters of beachside bars and restaurants, and at weekends they and the beach get crowded. There are the usual simple cafés and vendors selling fruit and fish, and *jangadas* aplenty. Anywhere here is a good place for a *caipirinha* and a view of an invariably spectacular sunset.

Eating, drinking and nightlife

As usual in a coastal capital, the centre tends to get deserted after dark, as people looking for a night out head for the beaches, particularly Tambaú. However, there are several **restaurants and bars** in the centre worth trying out.

João Pessoa has a surprisingly rich but fluctuating **music scene** for a city of its size, concentrated at the beaches: the only nights it is difficult to catch something are Sunday and Monday. Venues open and close with bewildering frequency, so it's best to ask the tourist office for a current list of venues and suggestions, though they will direct you to the more expensive upmarket clubs unless you are persistent. Alternatively, look in the entertainment guide of the local paper, *O Norte*.

City centre

The *Casino da Lagoa* is a bar-restaurant in a small park looking out across the Anel Viário, on the right coming down from the centre: the food is no more than average but the view is excellent, especially at night. Some of the best **sertão food** in the city is served at the *Recanto do Picuí*, Rua Felicinano Dourado 198 (Ⓣ83/3224-1400); the *carne do sol* here is excellent, best accompanied by green beans and *batata doce assado*, roast sweet potatoes. *Miralha*, on Avenida Epitácio Pessoa (Ⓣ83/3226-3982), is a bar and *churrascaria* with live *forró* music on Monday evenings. For self-service lunches it's difficult to beat the quality and value offered at *Salutte*, Rua 13 de Maio 73 (open Mon–Sat). **Vegetarians** can try the reasonably priced *Natural*, Rua Rodrigues de Aquino 177, down from Praça João Pessoa – unfortunately only open for lunch.

Finally, stop by the *Bar da Pólvora*, behind the Casa da Pólvora. No more than a bar with tables set out on the patio, serving only beer, *caipirinhas* and soft drinks, it has two major advantages: one is the setting, beneath the ancient walls of the arsenal, with a stunning view out across the river; the other is the clientele – young, student-dominated and very Bohemian. The best time to go is Thursday evening, when a small fee is charged for a table and there's a show, whose basic format is a few groups/poets/singers doing spots, plus whoever else in the audience feels like doing a turn. As you might expect, some of the acts are appalling, notably the local poets reading interminable extracts from their work, but the music is sometimes excellent.

The beaches

The more expensive restaurants (R$45–80 range) in the beach areas are in **Cabo Branco**. There are a couple of particularly good places on the seafront: the *Tábua do Marinheiro*, Av. Cabo Branco 1780 (Ⓣ83/247-5804), serves pasta, seafood and a range of meat; the *Olho de Lula*, Av. Cabo Branco 2300 (Ⓣ83/3226-2328), is a popular, if slightly exclusive, seafood resturant. Further down, at no. 5100, is *Marina's*, one of the few seafront bars in Cabo Branco, which also does seafood: a local speciality is *polvo ao leite de coco*, octopus in coconut milk. Also in Cabo Branco, the *Restaurante Caçuá,* Rua Adolfo Loureiro 65 (Ⓣ83/247-3237), specializes in regional cuisine, and the *Sashami & Grill*, Av. Beira Rio 71 (daily 6–11pm), is a reasonably good sushi restaurant.

In **Tambaú**, the *Tábua de Carne*, at Av. Rui Carneiro 648 (Ⓣ83/3247-5970), one of the roads running away from the beach, is a good place for meat and *sertão* food. *Mangai*, Av. Edson Ramalho 696, boasts a wide range of dishes, with much of the produce coming fresh from the restaurant's own ranch; this is regional cooking at its best, though it's not cheap. For a decent Italian meal, *La Boca de La Verita*, Av. Olinda 193 (Ⓣ83/3247-3334; closed Tues), is easily your best option, while the *Tereré,* Av. Rui Carneiro 791 (Ⓣ83/3226-1717), is an excellent *churrascaria*. For good coffee or cake, head for the *Doce Delícia*, just inside the Centro Turístico Tambaú.

The square in front of the *Tropical Tambaú Center Hotel* is a relaxed place for a drink and some **live music**. It's surrounded by restaurants and bars, and on Friday and Saturday nights tables and chairs are put out in the square, drink starts flowing and after about 9pm things start getting very lively. Every other bar has a *forró* trio, and guitarists and accordion players stroll through the crowds. There's no shortage of good, cheap food sizzling on the charcoal grills of the street vendors if your budget doesn't stretch to a restaurant. In the streets behind there are any number of small **bars and clubs**, which close down and reopen too quickly to keep track of them, so just wander around and stop by anywhere you see lights and music, though they tend not to get going until 11pm at the earliest. There are a couple of fairly lively **gay bars**, too, in the streets behind Avenida Nossa Senhora dos Navegantes in Tambaú.

Listings

Airlines TAM Ⓣ83/3232-2002; Varig, Av. Presidente Pessoa 1251 Ⓣ83/3232-1515.

Banks and exchange There are ATMs around the city centre and the beaches, and you can change money and traveller's cheques at Câmbio Turismo, which has branches at Rua Visconde de Pelotas 54 in the city centre (Mon–Fri), and in the shopping centre on Tambaú beach (Mon–Sat).

Car rental Localiza, at Av. Epitácio Pessoa 4910 Ⓣ83/3232-1130 or at airport Ⓣ0800/992-0000.

Post office The main office is on Praça Pedro Américo, two blocks downhill from Praça João Pessoa.

Taxis Disk taxi Ⓣ0800/83-1310; Teletaxi Ⓣ0800-83-2056 or Ⓣ83/3241-5656.

Telephones Domestic and international calls are easiest with a phonecard from any of the public telephones around town, though marginally cheaper from the TELPA building, off Rua Visconde de Pelotas in the centre (daily 8am–10pm).

Travel and tour companies Roger Turismo, Av. Almirante Tamandaré 229, Tambaú (Ⓣ83/3247-1856 Ⓕ3247-1533, Ⓔroger@zaitek.com.br), offer a full range of tours and travel services. Sem Fronteiras, Av. Nossa Senhora dos Navegantes 521, Loja 208, Tambaú (Ⓣ83/3247-3311, Ⓕ3247-5352, Ⓔmtulio@netwaybbs.com.br), is an innovative eco-adventure tour company offering expeditions to a number of out-of-the-way places in their four-wheel-drive vehicles. Dune-buggy trips (see p.373) can be booked through either Oswaldo (Ⓣ83/3962-0962) or Evandro (Ⓣ83/3984-7073).

Along the coast

Like so much of Brazil, Paraíba is blessed with many wonderful **beaches** along its 140-kilometre coastline. Unlike some other parts of the Northeast, however, many of its beaches are, for the time being, largely undeveloped and many require somewhat difficult journeys by bus and then on foot or by taxi to reach them.

South to Penha and Tambaba

Just to the **south** of João Pessoa is the fishing village of **PENHA**, served by local buses from outside the *rodoviária*. Strung out along a fine beach set in the midst of dense palm forest, Penha is distinguished from other fishing villages round about by a nineteenth-century church, the **Igreja de Nossa Senhora da Penha**, which is a pilgrimage centre and focus of much popular devotion. The beach near the church is also used by followers of *candomblé*, who identify the Virgin with Iemanjá, the goddess of the sea. According to legend, over a century ago an image of the Virgin was dredged up by fishermen in their nets, and worked so many miracles that the community adopted her as their patron saint and built the simple chapel to house her icon. Along the beach there are several rustic **bars** where you can eat and also string a hammock for a nominal fee. Discreet camping on the beach is also possible.

TAMBABA is set on a volcanic outcrop and lies some 30km to the south of João Pessoa. It's the first officially recognized nudist beach in the Northeast and is well off the beaten track. Getting here involves a bus ride from the *rodoviária* to the small seaside town of **Jacumã**, followed by an eight-kilometre walk along a rough road. If you don't want to walk, it's probably better to take a taxi than risk bringing a rented car along here as the dirt-track road is more difficult than it looks. The beach is superb and there's a small if somewhat overpriced bar here. Alternatively, and a little nearer to Jacumã, is the **Praia Coqueirinho**, which is a popular spot for the local children in the surrounding villages. Again, you'll need to take a taxi here. **Camping** is possible at the beach of Tabatinga, just to the north, otherwise there are places to stay in Jacumã.

North towards Cabedelo

Penha apart, most of the readily accessible **beaches** are to the **north**, off the road that leads to Cabedelo, 18km or 45 minutes by frequent local buses from the Anel Viário in João Pessoa – they get very crowded at weekends. The road runs a little inland and there are turn-offs leading to the beaches on the way: it seems to depend more on the drivers' whim than a timetable as to whether the bus takes you right to the beach, but hop on the Cabedelo bus anyway, and get off at the relevant turn-off if need be; it'll only be a short walk to the sea.

BESSA is the generic name for the stretch of coastline immediately north of Tambaú (see p.359). Six kilometres out of town is a turn-off that leads to the yacht club and a cluster of bars, which have a rather more upmarket clientele than the next village along, **POÇO**, where there is a chapel, some weekend homes, a fine palm-fringed beach with the obligatory bars and several good fish restaurants: *Badionaldo* serves delicious crab stew (*ensopado de carangueijo*), a local speciality, while at the *Bar e Restaurante do Marcão*, four crabs for R$10 will satisfy even the greediest of appetites. From there, you could walk the 10km along the beach to Cabedelo; otherwise hourly buses to Cabedelo, or back to João Pessoa, leave during the day from the bus stop near the church.

CABEDELO itself is older than it looks. It was much fought over in the Dutch wars, and the star-shaped fort of **Santa Caterina** (Tues–Sat 8am–5pm), dating from 1585, is the major sight in the village. Unfortunately, Petrobrás have built a series of oil storage tanks right up to its ramparts, and it's difficult to get a sense of its strategic position, commanding as it does the only deep-water anchorage on this stretch of coast. Nowadays, Cabedelo's main claim to fame is as the starting point for the famous **Transamazon highway** – the Transamazônica – and there's a sign proving it over the João Pessoa road. The Transamazon was seen by its creators as the conduit along which would flow the "people without land" to the "land without people", as poor Northeasterners were funnelled towards Amazônia – a political signal to the large landowners of the Northeast that the government had no intention of tackling the region's problems by implementing agrarian reform. The only thing the poor of Paraíba got was a convenient escape route.

There's no reason to hang around in Cabedelo and plenty of reason to continue 20km to two superb and largely unspoilt beaches. For the more adventurous camper there is the **Praia do Oiteiro**, a wild and beautiful beach backed by hills covered with tropical vegetation but little in the way of modern comforts. **Campina**, just north of Oiteiro, is similarly idyllic but with the addition of a small fishing settlement. You can get to both beaches on the same bus from João Pessoa via Cabedelo, or you could try renting a boat in Cabedelo as it's only half the distance along the coast.

Inland to Campina Grande

The BR-230 highway, a good-quality asphalt road, bisects Paraíba and leads directly into the *sertão*. The green coastal strip is quickly left behind as the road climbs into the hills; two hours' driving and you arrive in the second city of Paraíba, **CAMPINA GRANDE**, linked to João Pessoa by hourly bus. It's a large town, similar in many ways to Caruaru in Pernambuco: even the slogan you see at the city limits – "Welcome to the Gateway of the *Sertão*" – is identical. Like Caruaru (see p.349), Campina Grande owes its existence to a strategic position between the *agreste* and the *sertão* proper. It's a market town and centre of light industry, where the products of the *sertão* are stockpiled and sent down to the coast, and where the people of the *sertão* come to buy what they can't make. At a large Wednesday and Saturday **market** you can see this process unfolding before your eyes.

You may also see evidence of the fierce competition between Campina Grande and João Pessoa. *Campinenses* proudly contrast their industries and commercial know-how with the decadence and stagnation of João Pessoa,

Campina Grande's festivals

In June Campina Grande hosts a month-long **festival** that uses the São João holiday – the **festas juninas** – as an excuse for a general knees-up. Streets are filled with stalls selling food and drinks and various events are scheduled. This imakes June one of the best times to visit, and the wonderfully named *forrodrómo* in the centre of town, an enormous cross between a concert hall and a *dancetaria*, is where much of the action happens.

But Campina Grande is equally well known for its out-of-season Carnaval, the **Micarande**, an event in late April that attracts some 300,000 people over a period of four days and is the largest of its kind in Brazil. The music, best described as frenetic electric, reaches fever pitch as the *trios elétricos* (Carnaval trucks), with live *frevo* bands playing on top, work their way through the crowds with their followers in train, the music lasting until dawn. Accommodation during this period is particularly scarce and expensive even for the humblest of abodes, so it's best to get in touch with one of the leading organizers, the state tourist authority, before setting out. A word of warning, however: although the event itself is very well policed, take care when making your way to it as the streets and buses are very crowded.For details on either of these parties call ⓣ83/3310-6100.

and there is concerted pressure from the people of Campina Grande to make this the new capital of Paraíba. To the traveller, though, João Pessoa's elegance is something of a contrast with Campina Grande, which even locals admit is rather ugly. Still, it's a good place to sample the distinctive culture of the *sertão*, without having to suffer its discomforts, and also to experience some unforgettable **festivals**.

The **climate** in Campina Grande is always pleasant, as its height takes the edge off the coastal heat without making it cold, though you may need a sweater at night during the rainy season.

The City

Although the city sprawls out into anonymous industrial suburbs, the **central layout** is compact and easy to get the hang of. The city's heart, and most useful landmark, is the obelisk in the **Parque do Açude Novo**. The park itself straddles the **Avenida Floriano Peixoto**, which bisects Campina Grande from west to east, and the stretch of the avenue from the obelisk to the cathedral is the centre proper, where most of the things to do and see are concentrated.

The highlight of Campina Grande is its **market**, held every Wednesday and Saturday. The market takes over the area around the cathedral and the municipal market behind it, and although not quite on the scale of Caruaru or Feira da Santana in Bahia it is the largest in the northern half of the Northeast. Saturday is busiest, but to catch it at its peak you need to either arrive on the Friday or make an early start from João Pessoa, as it starts to wind down from around noon. Most entertaining are the cries, improvised verses, chants and patters of the scores of street sellers: you may be lucky enough to come across hawkers going head to head, when two vendors set up shop next to each other and try to outdo the other in extravagant claims and original turns of phrase. Sometimes sellers of *cordel* (see p.328) recite chunks of the ballads to whet the public's appetite, and clusters of people gather around to shout comments and enjoy the story. If you miss the market, but still fancy trying to get hold of **artesanato** and **cordel**, good places are the cooperative Casa do Artesão, Rua Venâncio Neiva 85, near the Rique Palace, and Kaboclinha, nearby at Rua Vidal de Negreiros 36.

There are three museums in Campina Grande. By some way the best is the **Museu de Arte Assis Chateaubriand**, part of the complex of buildings in the Parque do Açude Novo (Mon–Fri 9am–noon & 2–10pm, Sat & Sun 2–10pm). It's a source of justifiable civic pride, boasting a good gallery of modern art, devoted entirely to Brazilian artists, with a special emphasis on work from the Northeast. Some of Brazil's greatest modern painters are represented, notably Cândido Portinari, whose large canvasses fuse social realism with modernist technique in their depiction of workers and workplaces. The most intriguing part of the museum is the *atelier livre*, where local painters, carvers and sculptors exhibit their works in progress. They are not very cheap, but for the quality and originality the price is often more than reasonable.

In contrast, the **Museu Histórico e Geográfico**, at Av. Floriano Peixote 825 (Mon–Fri 8am–6pm, Sat & Sun 8am–noon), is loaded with period furniture, weapons, maps and historical photos relating to the city's heritage. In a similar vein, the **Museu do Algodão** (Mon–Fri 8am–noon & 2–6pm), in the tourist centre inside the old train station, concentrates on the history of the cotton plantations of the area, including some fearsome chains, stocks, iron collars and whips used on the slaves.

Practicalities

The **rodoviária** (Ⓣ83/3337-3001) is on the outskirts of town at Avenida Sen. Argemiro de Figueiredo in Catolé; local buses marked "Centro" take you downtown. The **tourist office** is situated at Praça Clementino Procópio (Mon–Fri 8am–5pm; Ⓣ83/3251-7717) and you can get a useful city map here.

There's a good choice of **accommodation** in Campina Grande. The cheaper *dormitórios* are clustered around the old train station and there are plenty of mid-range places close to each other around the city centre. The centrally located *Belfran*, Av. Floriano Peixoto 258 (Ⓣ83/3341-1312; ❸), is one of the best budget choices in town, with cheerful, well-kept rooms. Also in the heart of the city are the comfortable *Majestic*, Rua Maciel Pinheiro 216 (Ⓣ83/3341-2009, Ⓕ3321-6748; ❷), and the *Ouro Branco*, Rua Cel. João Lourenço Porto 20 (Ⓣ83/3341-2929; ❹), one of Campina Grande's luxury hotels, though hardly special. Out of the centre, the comfortable *Hotel Village*, Rua Otacílio Nepomuceno 1285 (Ⓣ83/3310-8000, Ⓦwww.hoteisvillage.com.br; ❺), near the *rodoviária*, offers a pool and a sauna, plus a bar and decent restaurant. Further out, in a beautiful location near a lake, the *Lago Dourado*, Açude Boqueiro, Município de Boqueirão (Ⓣ83/226-1686; ❸–❹), is excellent value.

Two of the best **restaurants** in town, *Dona Nina*, Rua Augusto dos Anjos 183 and *Tábua de Carne* (Ⓣ83/3341-1008) at Av. Manoel Tavares 1040, both specialize in regional cuisine. A meal at *Dona Nina* will run to around R$25 a head, while *Tabua* is slightly cheaper.

Into the sertão

The BR-232 continues threading its way though the *sertão* to the town of **PATOS**: hot, flyblown, and looking like a spaghetti-western set with pick-ups instead of horses. If you need to stop, use the *Hotel JK*, Praça Getúlio Vargas (Ⓣ83/3421-6181; ❸–❹). Then it's on to **SOUSA**, an otherwise unremarkable *sertão* town five hours west of Campina Grande, with two hotels and one of the Northeast's more unusual sights, the **Vale dos Dinosauras**, "Dinosaur Valley", formed by the sedimentary basin of the Rio Peixe. At one time, difficult though it is to imagine in this searing semi-arid landscape, all was swamp and jungle here. Various prehistoric reptiles left their footprints, preserved in stone, at several sites in the area around the town. The only way to get to them is by battered taxi over the dusty road. The nearest site is called A Ilha, about 5km out of town, which will cost you around R$35 in a taxi. Here the prehistoric tracks are striking. One beast clearly lumbered along the riverbed for a while and then turned off; you can see a series of footprints the size of dinner plates, some with two claws visible at the front.

Juazeiro do Norte

The main centre of the deep *sertão* is 500km west of Campina Grande – actually in the south of Ceará state – where a series of hill ranges, higher ground blessed with regular rainfall, provides a welcome respite. Food crops can be grown here, and every available inch of land is used to grow fruit and vegetables, or graze cattle. Here there are two towns within a few kilometres of each other, Crato and **JUAZEIRO DO NORTE**, and it was in this area that one of the most famous episodes in the history of the Northeast took place (see box, p.367). It is still the site of a massive annual pilgrimage.

The pilgrim route

If you want to do what the pilgrims do, the first stop is Padre Cícero's **tomb** in the church of **Nossa Senhora do Perpétuo Socorro**, to the left of the square. A small monument sits outside, always decorated with *ex votos*, tokens brought by those praying for help. Inside the plain church you'll see a constant stream of *romeiros* praying intensely and queuing to kiss the marble slab by the altar, which you might think is the grave but isn't: that is outside to the left, an unpretentious tomb covered in flowers and ribbons. The church is surrounded by souvenir shops, which specialize in the figurines of Padre Cícero with hat and walking stick that you can find all over the Northeast.

The next destination is the **statue** of Padre Cícero on the peak of the **Serra do Horto**, the hill that looks down on the town. The soft option is to take a taxi or bus for 3km along a road that winds up the hill – a route that can be walked if you want to see the fine views of the **valley of Cariri** unfold, with the town of Crato visible to the west. The other way is to follow the **pilgrim route**, a track from the town directly up the hill: it isn't signposted but people will willingly direct you to it if you ask for *a picada dos romeiros* or *a Via Sacra*. It's a brisk hour to the top, and at several points the pilgrims have cut steps. Thousands walk the trail on July 20, "paying the promise", that is, performing penances for help received; a few hardy souls make the journey on their knees.

Once on top, the main attractions are not so much the statue – 27m high but hardly a masterpiece – as the panoramic views and the **chapel** and **museum of ex votos** next to it. Room after room is piled high with stacks of offerings from the grateful thousands for whom Padre Cícero interceded over the decades: countless artificial limbs, wooden models of body parts, photos of disasters escaped and crashes survived, even football jerseys from victorious players, including one from Brazil's winning 1970 World Cup team. As a demonstration of the hold that religion has on the daily lives of millions of *nordestinos*, only the *ex votos* at the church of Bonfim in Salvador rival it.

△ Statue of Padre Cícero

The pilgrim's route finishes up at Padre Cícero's **house**, signposted from the church where he is buried, and now a cross between a museum and a shrine. It's a simple dwelling, with large rooms, a garden and glass cases displaying everything anybody could find that was even remotely connected to the great man: his glasses, underwear, hats, typewriter, bed linen, even the bed he died in.

The last act of pilgrimage is to be **photographed** to prove to the folks back home that you've made the trip. This ensures a steady flow

Miracle at Juazeiro

In 1889 Juazeiro was no more than a tiny hamlet. There was nothing unusual about its young priest, **Padre Cícero Romão Batista**, until a woman in Juazeiro claimed the wine he gave them at Communion had turned to blood in their mouths. At first it was only people from Crato who came, and they were convinced by the woman's sanctity and the evidence of their own eyes that Padre Cícero had indeed worked a miracle. As his fame grew, the deeply religious inhabitants of the *sertão* came to hear his sermons and have him bless them. Padre Cícero came to be seen as a living saint: miraculous cures were attributed to him, things he had touched and worn were treated as relics. The Catholic Church began a formal investigation of the alleged "miracle", sent him to Rome to testify to commissions of enquiry, rejected it, sent him back to Brazil and suspended him from the priesthood – but nothing could shake the conviction of the local people that he was a saint. Juazeiro mushroomed into a large town by *sertão* standards, as people flocked to make the pilgrimage, including legendary figures like the bandit chief Lampião.

By the end of his long life, Padre Cícero had become one of the most powerful figures in the Northeast. In 1913 his heavily armed followers caught the train to the state capital, Fortaleza, and forcibly deposed the governor, replacing him with somebody more to Padre Cícero's liking. But Padre Cícero was a deeply conservative man, who restrained his followers more often than not, deferred to the Church, and remained seemingly more preoccupied with the next world than with this. When his more revolutionary followers tried to set up a religious community nearby at Caldeirão, he didn't deter the authorities from using the air force against them, in one of the first recorded uses of aerial bombs on civilians. When he finally died, in 1934, his body had to be displayed strapped to a door from the first floor of his house, before the thousands thronging the streets would believe he was dead. Ever since, pilgrims have come to Juazeiro to pay homage, especially on the anniversary of his death on July 20; an enormous white statue of the priest looks out from a hillside over the town he created.

of work for the many photographers clustered around the last church on the way to the hill, the **Igreja Matriz de Nossa Senhora das Dores**. They all have a series of props to help you pose: life-size statues of Padre Cícero, dozens of hats, toy elephants and so forth, and although the snap takes two or three hours to develop it comes ready-mounted in a mini-viewer, far more durable than a photo proper – the ideal souvenir.

Practicalities

When booking a ticket to Juazeiro make sure you specify Juazeiro do Norte, or you run the risk of ending up in Juazeiro in Bahia, several hundred kilometres south. The **rodoviária** is a couple of kilometres out of the town, which is smaller than its fame suggests. There is one central square where you'll find the best and most expensive **hotel**, the *Panorama* (Ⓣ88/3512-3100, Ⓦwww.panoramahotel.com.br; ❹–❺), but finding somewhere to stay is the least of your worries in a town geared to putting up pilgrims: there are small hotels and *dormitórios* everywhere. Among these, the *Hotel Municipal* (❷) on Praça Padre Cícero, is a good budget option.

There are two main places **to eat**: the *Restó Jardim*, in Lagoa Seca at Av. Leão Sampaio 5460 (Ⓣ88/3571-7768; closed Mon), serves a wide variety of regional and international dishes, while the pricier *Restaurante O Capote*, Rua José Barbosa dos Santos 83 (daily 11am–midnight), specializes in quality local cuisine.

Leaving town, seats fill up fast on the daily buses to João Pessoa, Recife and Fortaleza, so if you're staying overnight book a ticket when you arrive. Alternatively, it is usually possible to get a seat on one of the **pilgrim buses** parked around town; their drivers sell seats for the same price as on the regular bus, and groups come from all the major cities, so just pick a bus going your way.

Rio Grande do Norte

Until the late 1980s, the small state of **Rio Grande do Norte** and its capital, **Natal**, were sleepy, conservative backwaters rarely visited by tourists. It's still true to say that there's little of historical interest among Natal's modern hotels and office buildings, and the interior is poor and thinly populated, the only place of any size being the town of **Mossoró**. But two things have transformed Rio Grande do Norte into one of the Northeast's biggest tourist centres: **beaches** and **buggies**. The beaches were always there, but the sometimes hair-raising buggy rides for which the state is famous have taken off only in the past fifteen years.

One big difference between Rio Grande do Norte and the states to the south is in its **landscape**, for this is where the Northeastern sugar belt finally peters out, drastically changing both history and landscape. The region is not without income; it supplies petroleum oil directly to several major factories and is also a major exporter of fruit. However, **north of Natal**, the *sertão* drives down practically to the coast, and the idyllic palm-fringed beaches give way to something wilder as the coastline changes character, with massive sand dunes replacing the flat beaches and palm trees. The further north you go, the less fertile the land becomes and the flatter the *sertão*, given over largely to scrawny cattle scratching a living along with the people. The black Brazilian population shrinks with the sugar zone, and in Rio Grande do Norte dwindles to almost nothing.

Natal

NATAL is a medium-sized city of about 600,000 people, built on the banks of the Rio Potengi and founded sixty years later than planned, after the Potiguar Indians stifled the first Portuguese landing on the coast in 1538. They continued to hold the invaders off until 1598, when the Portuguese built the star-shaped fort at the mouth of the river – the city's most enduring landmark. Natal is at the heart of one of the most spectacular strings of beaches in the Northeast: in fact, given that you could rent a beach buggy in Genipabu, just north of Natal, and drive along 250km of dunes uninterrupted until Areia Branca, practically on the border with Ceará, Natal is at one end of what amounts to a single enormous beach.

Stranded at the eastern tip of the Northeast, away from the main international tourist routes, and with little industry to provide employment, Natal has lately been developing tourist facilities with the desperation of a place with few other economic options. It's become a popular destination for Brazilian

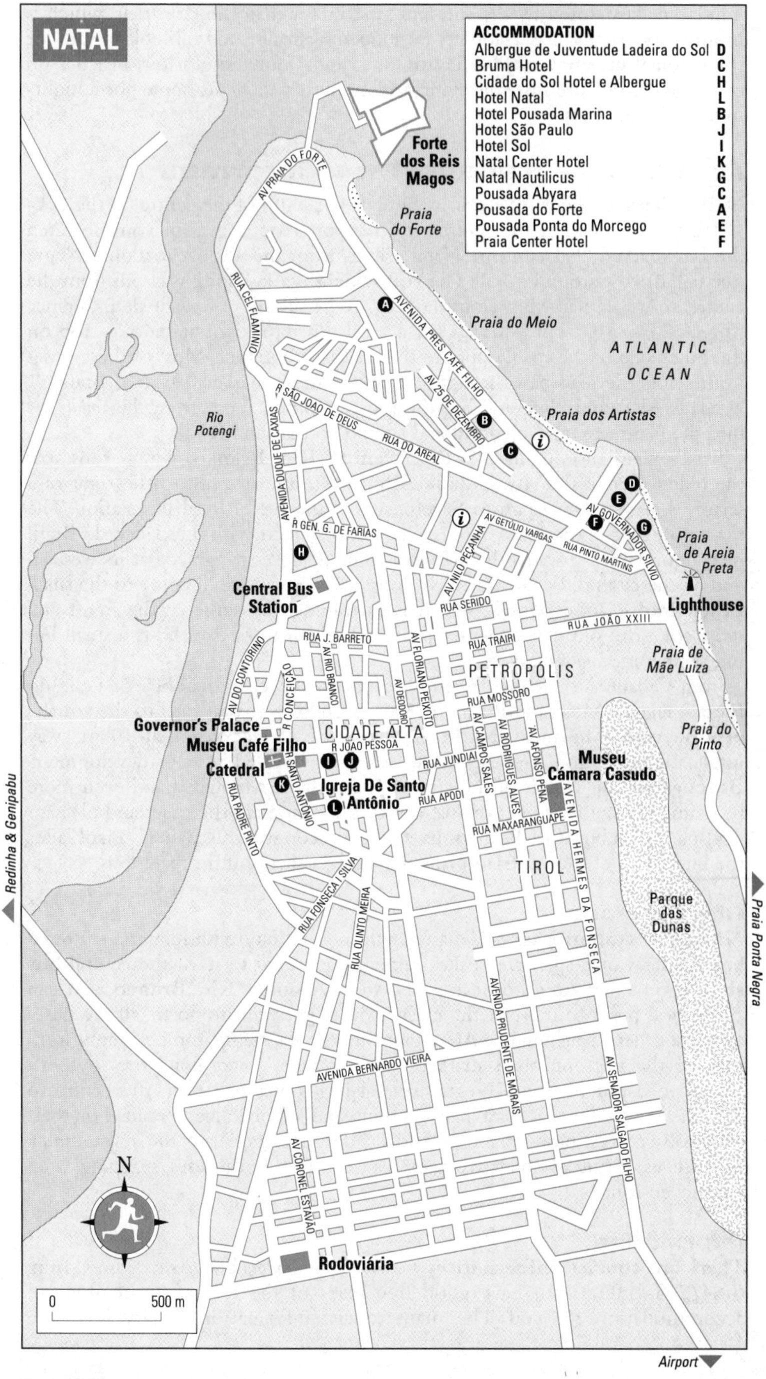

NATAL

ACCOMMODATION

Albergue de Juventude Ladeira do Sol	D
Bruma Hotel	C
Cidade do Sol Hotel e Albergue	H
Hotel Natal	L
Hotel Pousada Marina	B
Hotel São Paulo	J
Hotel Sol	I
Natal Center Hotel	K
Natal Nautilicus	G
Pousada Abyara	C
Pousada do Forte	A
Pousada Ponta do Morcego	E
Praia Center Hotel	F

Forte dos Reis Magos

Praia do Forte

Praia do Meio

ATLANTIC OCEAN

Praia dos Artistas

Praia de Areia Preta

Lighthouse

Praia de Mãe Luiza

Praia do Pinto

Parque das Dunas

Rio Potengi

Central Bus Station

Governor's Palace

Museu Café Filho

Catedral

Igreja De Santo Antônio

Museu Câmara Casudo

Rodoviária

PETROPÓLIS

CIDADE ALTA

TIROL

AV PRAIA DO FORTE

RUA CEL FLAMINIO

AVENIDA PRES CAFE FILHO

AV 25 DE DEZEMBRO

R SÃO JOAO DE DEUS

RUA DO AREAL

AVENIDA DUQUE DE CAXIAS

R GEN. G. DE FARIAS

AV GETÚLIO VARGAS

AV NILO PEÇANHA

AV GOVERNADOR SILVIO

RUA PINTO MARTINS

RUA SERIDO

RUA JOÃO XXIII

RUA J. BARRETO

RUA TRAIRI

AV DO CONTORINO

R CONCEIÇÃO

AV RIO BRANCO

AV DEODORO

AV FLORIANO PEIXOTO

RUA MOSSORO

AV CAMPOS SALES

AV RODRIGUES ALVES

AV AFONSO PENA

R JOÃO PESSOA

RUA JUNDIAI

RUA APODI

RUA MAXARANGUAPE

AVENIDA HERMES DA FONSECA

RUA PADRE PINTO

R SANTO ANTÔNIO

RUA FONSECA I SILVA

RUA OLINTO MEIRA

AVENIDA PRUDENTE DE MORAIS

AV SENADOR SALGADO FILHO

AVENIDA BERNARDO VIEIRA

AV CORONEL ESTAVÃO

N

0 500 m

Redinha & Genipabu

Praia Ponta Negra

Airport

holiday-makers, lured by the sun and sand rather than the city itself, which is mostly modern and has a sloppily developed seafront: you will look in vain for the colonial elegance of João Pessoa or Olinda. But the glorious beaches do compensate, and amid the development and hotels there are some good night-spots and *dancetarias*.

Arrival, city transport and information

Natal's **airport**, Augusto Severo, is about 15km south of the centre on the BR-101 highway; a taxi to the centre will cost you about R$25, or you can catch the bus marked "Parnamirim–Natal". Taxis from the airport to Ponta Negra (see p.376) cost around R$30. The **rodoviária** is also a long way out from the centre, at Av. Capitão Mor-Gouveia 1237 in the suburb of Cidade de Esperança (Ⓣ84/3232-7310), but you can get a local bus into town at the bus stop on the other side of the road, opposite the *rodoviária* entrance. Most of these buses from across the road pass through the centre: those marked "Av. Rio Branco", "Cidade Alta" and "Ribeira" are the most common. Taxis from the *rodoviária* into the centre are also plentiful and should cost around R$20.

Natal's main thoroughfare is the **Avenida Rio Branco**, which runs past the oldest part of the city, **Cidade Alta**, and terminates just to the right of a scruffy square, Praça Augusto Severo, site of the useful local bus station. The main post office is on block 5 of Avenida Rio Branco, with the Banco do Brasil next door. Cutting across the *avenida* is Rua João Pessoa, graced at its western end by the city's old cathedral. East along João Pessoa, you'll come to the small **Praça Padre João Maria**, which is surrounded by some of the finest and most colourful old mansions in Natal, and which most days hosts a small but interesting *artesanato* market.

From Cidade Alta, roads descend straight to the **city beaches** of Praia do Forte, Praia do Meio and Praia dos Artistas, and the coastal road to the **southern beaches**. The most important of these is Ponta Negra, at 10km away just far enough from the city centre to have survived massive development. **Beaches to the north** of the city are generally less crowded and even more beautiful, but harder to get to. Just out of the centre are the quiet and pleasant grid-pattern suburbs of **Petrópolis** and the incongruously named **Tirol**, after the birthplace of the Austrian planner who laid them out in the 1930s.

City transport

Natal's **bus system** is easy to master, and in a hot city with hills and scattered beaches it's worth spending a little time getting used to it. At the central **bus station** on Praça Augusto Severo, and from **Avenida Rio Branco**, you can catch local buses to most of the places you might want to go to: all the buses to the southern beaches, like Areia Preta and Ponta Negra, can be caught from here or the seafront; buses marked "Via Costeira" head along the southern coastal road out to Ponta Negra. Several bus routes run from the centre to the *rodoviária*, taking at least half an hour and often longer because of their circuitous routes; buses marked "Cidade de Esperança" are the most direct. **Minibuses**, acting as collective taxis, also compete with buses, stopping at all corners en route.

Information

There are **tourist information** posts at the *rodoviária* (daily 7am–11pm; Ⓣ84/205-1000); both have good free maps of the city and can organize accommodation for you. The main tourist information facility is at the

Centro de Turismo (Mon–Fri 7am–11pm; ⓣ84/3211-6149 or 3232-9061) in the old prison, perched on top of a hill at Rua Aderbal de Figueiredo 980 in Petrópolis, where there are beautiful views of the beaches and city, the lovely café *Marenosso* and scores of quality arts and crafts, with an emphasis on cotton products. On the first floor there's also an interesting Galeria de Arte Antigua e Contemporanea, filled with ceramics, weavings, paintings and antiques. There is also a tourist information booth (Mon–Sat 8am–6pm; ⓣ84/3232-2500) on Avenida Presidente Café Filho, at Praia dos Artistas, though it's not always functioning. Alternatively, you can ring the **tourist hotline** Disque Turismo for information (ⓣ84/3232-7248) where you may find someone who speaks English. For information on events and films, your best bet is the *Fim de Semana* section of Friday's *Tribuna do Norte* newspaper.

If you want to take a **tour** to Fernando de Noronha (see p.354), the Reis Magos Viagems e Turismo, at Av. Sen. Salgado Filho 1799 (ⓣ84/3206-5888, ⓕ3296-6628) has information on this amazing archipelago and organizes trips there, too. Alternatively, try Aventura Expedições, Av. Prudente de Morais 4262, Loja 3B, Lagoa Nova (ⓣ84/3206-4949).

Accommodation

Hotels are plentiful in both the city centre and the beach areas. A good alternative option, if you want to get away from traffic and urbanization, is to stay at one of the beaches outside the city, like Ponta Negra to the south (see p.376) or Redinha and Genipabu to the north (see p.378).

The city centre

Cidade do Sol Hotel e Albergue Av. Duque de Caxias 190 ⓣ84/3211-3233. This youth hostel near the central bus station has decent rooms and a nice garden at the back. ❷

Hotel Natal Av. Rio Branco 740, Cidade Alta ⓣ84/3222-2792, ⓕ222-0232. Basic but clean, with a choice of rooms with either fan or a/c. Very cheap for a central hotel. ❷

Hotel São Paulo Av. Rio Branco 697 ⓣ84/3211-4485. Refurbished budget hotel with good breakfasts. The entrance is on Rua General Osório. ❷–❸

Hotel Sol Rua Heitor Carilho 107 ⓣ84/3221-1157. Good-value hotel in the older part of the upper city, with its own restaurant and smallish but pleasant rooms with private baths. ❸

Natal Center Hotel Rua Santo Antônio 665 ⓣ84/3221-2355, ⓦwww.natalcenterhotel.com.br. One of the smartest options in the old city centre, yet surprisingly good value and welcoming. Amenities include a good restaurant, a swimming pool, a fitness suite and a sauna. ❹

The beaches

Albergue de Juventude Ladeira do Sol Rua Valentim de Almeida 8, Praia dos Artistas ⓣ84/3202-1699. A pleasant youth hostel offering private or shared rooms. R$50.

Bruma Hotel Av. Pres. Café Filho 1176, Praia dos Artistas ⓣ84/3211-4947. This hotel overlooks the beach and is worth staying in mainly for the beautifully designed building. ❹

Hotel Pousada Marina Av. Pte. Café Filho 860, Praia do Meio ⓣ84/3202-3223. Right on the seafront near the Praia das Artistas, the Hotel Pousada Marina mainly attracts downmarket Brazilian business travellers, with spartan but reasonably comfortable rooms and private baths. ❷

Hotel Vila do Mar Via Costeira 4233 ⓣ84/4009-4900, ⓦwww.viladomar.com.br. Luxury hotel close to the sea with all the facilities you'd expect, including a pool and tennis courts. ❼–❽

Pousada Abyara Av. Pte. Café Filho 1174 ⓣ84/2611-1042. This very friendly place is clean and well run, with pleasant rooms – some of which have views and most have private baths. Conveniently located by Praia dos Artistas. ❸

Pousada das Dunas Rua João XXIII 601 ⓣ84/3202-1820. A warm, family-run *pousada* just a bus ride from the Praia dos Artistas in the Mãe Luiza district; the basic rooms are spotless and comfortable. ❷

Pousada do Forte Av. Pres. Café Filho 786, Praia do Meio ⓣ84/3211-6080. Large, well-kept rooms

with all the modern conveniences, located on the beachside opposite the statue of Iemanjá. ④
Pousada Ponta do Morcego Rua Valentim de Almeida 10, Praia dos Artistas ☎84/3202-2367. An extremely inexpensive, no-frills option, right next to the youth hostel. ②

Praia Center Hotel Rua Fabrico Pedrosa 45, Petrópolis ☎84/3202-4407. A fairly nice concrete hotel, very close to the Praia das Artistas. Rooms are quite basic, but have TVs and private bathrooms; the attractive breakfast patio has views over to the ocean and the small hotel pool. ⑤

The City

For a city that was founded nearly four centuries ago there is surprisingly little of historical interest in Natal itself, apart from the distinctive, whitewashed **Forte dos Reis Magos** (daily 8am–4.45pm), which dominates the river entrance. Like most of Brazil's colonial forts it looks very vulnerable, directly overlooked by the hill behind it and with thick, surprisingly low walls. Although there is not much to see apart from a couple of token museums, the city is interesting to wander around in.

The oldest part of Natal is formed by the closely packed streets and small squares of Cidade Alta, but the street plan itself is one of the only things that remains from colonial times. Instead, the architecture that has survived the modern thrust for development is clustered around the administrative heart of the city, **Praça Sete de Setembro**, which is dominated by the **governor's palace**, built in tropical Victorian style in 1873. Also in the square is the **Espaço Cultural** (Mon–Fri 8am–6pm), with changing shows of mainly local artists, and the restored **Teatro Alberto Maranhão**, a Neoclassical structure built in 1898. In the neighbouring Praça Albuquerque, you'll find the **Instituto Histórico e Geográfico** (Mon-Fri 8am–noon & 2–5pm), a quaint nineteenth-century edifice housing period furniture and archives relating to the region's history, while the old **Catedral** next door (daily 4.30–6pm) was built in 1862 but is unexceptional for all that. Smaller, and rather more interesting, is the **Igreja de Santo Antônio** (Mon–Fri 8–11.30am & 2–5.30pm, Sat 8–11.30am) nearby at Rua Santo Antônio 683, a Baroque church known as the

△ Forte dos Reis Magos

Igreja do Galo, after the eighteenth-century bronze cock crowing on top of its Moorish tower; inside you'll find a well-respected **museum of religious art** (Mon–Sat 1–6pm).

Just off Praça Sete de Setembro is the most interesting museum in a city largely bereft of them, the **Museu Café Filho** (Mon–Fri 8am–5pm, Sat 8–10am), dedicated to the only *rio grandense* to become president of Brazil – a corrupt and incompetent paternalist, despite the attempts by the museum to present him as a statesman. But he had the good taste to live in a fine two-storey mansion, at Rua da Conceição 630, which is worth seeing – more than can be said for the yellowing papers and heavy furniture of the long-dead president. Also worth a visit is the **Museu Cámara Casudo**, at Av. Hermes da Fonseca 1398, in Tirol (Tues–Fri 8–11am & 2–5pm; US$1), which is dedicated to local ecology, history and geology. Sponsored heavily by Petrobrás, the museum contains a large flashy exhibit on oil drilling, but nevertheless, it's well thought out and presented, with dinosaur fossils, a *jangada* and a range of other interesting exhibits.

The beaches

What Natal lacks in attractions for the culturally minded, it makes up for in facilities for the beach bum. There are fine **beaches** right inside the city, beginning at the fort where arcs of sand sweep along the bay to the headland and

Beach buggies

Going to Natal without riding a **beach buggy** is a bit like going to Ireland and not drinking Guinness – you may or may not enjoy it, but you might as well try it seeing as you're there. Buggies have become a way of life in Natal, providing employment for the young drivers or *bugeiros* who race around the city and its beaches in their noisy, low-slung vehicles. After a period of explosive, unregulated growth during which unqualified cowboy *bugeiros* risked their and their passengers' necks, the buggy industry has settled down a bit, though you should still check that your driver has **accreditation** and **insurance** – most of them do.

There are two basic kinds of buggy rides. One possibility is to go on a **day**- or **half-day trip**, which involves riding either north or south down the coast, mainly along the beaches. Many firms offer a full day's outing with the *litoral norte* in the morning and the *litoral sul* in the afternoon, or vice versa. The *bugeiro* will perform a few stunts along the way, surfing the sand dunes, but it's mainly an opportunity to explore the beautiful coastline around Natal. A day-trip costs about US$100 for four people.

However, the real thrills and spills are to be found on specific beaches, especially at **Genipabu** to the north of Natal. Here you pay by the ride or by the hour for fairground-type stuff, with the *bugeiros* making full use of the spectacular sand dunes to push your heart through your mouth. These rides are not cheap, and you may find yourself paying over R$100 for an hour's entertainment.

Conditions inside the buggies are cramped. Most *bugeiros* will try and fit three or four people in on each trip, with two people sitting outside at the back hanging on to a metal bar. You'll need plenty of **sun protection** and an extremely tight-fitting hat. However, there's no doubt that it's an exhilarating business, with the wind whipping through your hair as you bounce around the sand dunes.

Most hotels have deals with buggy companies, and you'll find yourself besieged by offers of rides wherever you are in Natal. Most rides cost between R$25 and R$50 per person for a day's outing. If you want to deal with the **companies** directly, try Alfatur Passeio de Buggy (☎84/3219-5542) at Av. Ervian Franca 153, Ponta Negra; Top Buggy (☎84/3219-2820) also in Ponta Negra.

Mãe Luiza lighthouse, a useful point to take bearings from. Buses marked "Mãe Luiza" transport you from the seafront to the foot of the hill crowned by the lighthouse, which you can walk up, but you will be besieged by children offering guided tours. From the top there is a magnificent view of the **Praia do Meio**, the beach that stretches from the fort to the headland of the Ladeira do Sol, and the **Praia da Areia Preta**, curving between the headland and the lighthouse. Technically the Praia do Meio is composed of three beaches: the small Praia do Forte next to the fort, the Praia do Meio and the **Praia dos Artistas**. Here, too, you'll find dune buggies lined up looking for customers. All the beaches are lined with stalls serving the usual array of cold drinks and food, and numerous hotels and bars are strung along the inland side of the seafront, which gets lively on weekend evenings.

On the other side of the lighthouse is another enormous beach, **Praia de Mãe Luiza**, accessible along the tourist development highway known as the Via Costeira, which takes you to Ponta Negra, 10km away. Although large, the Praia de Mãe Luiza is rarely used, much of it rocky and much of the remainder taken up by brand-new concrete developments.

Keep in mind that the beaches near the centre of town should be treated with respect: the combination of a shelving beach and rollers roaring in from the Atlantic often makes the surf dangerous, and a few tourists are drowned every year.

Some 8km south of Praia Pipa, an hour from Natal by bus, the **Barra da Cunhau** beach is breathtakingly beautiful, with miles of white sands bordered by red sandstone cliffs, and usually almost completely deserted. At the centre of the beach, fresh seafood platters including swordfish and lobster are served most days by the *Solimar* restaurant. A further 10km south from here, through sugar cane plantations and really only accessible by buggy, you'll find the **Lagoa de Coca Cola**; this black lake, made acidic by the specific plantlife there, is part of a nature reserve where there are cashew trees as well as fragrant bark trees which are used to make some perfumes.

△ A sand buggy on Natal's sand dunes

Eating, drinking and nightlife

Restaurants are one of Natal's strongest points, and the regional cuisine has, if anything, been strengthened by the influx of Brazilian tourists, as many see eating Northeastern food as an important part of their holiday.

Bar do Cação on the seafront near the Forte dos Reis Magos. Choose from a selection of good oyster and shellfish dishes.

Carne de Sol Benigna Lira Rua Dr José Augusto Bezerra de Menezes 9, Praia dos Artistas ⓣ84/3202-3914. The speciality of this moderately priced restaurant is sun-dried meat, as good as you'll find anywhere in Brazil.

Casa da Mãe Rua Pedro Afonso 230, Petrópolis. Notable for the *galinha cabidela* – chicken stewed in a sauce enriched by its own blood and giblets. The giblets are sieved out before serving, and the meal is delicious and inexpensive.

Chaplin Av. Presidente Café Filho 27 ⓣ84/3211-7457. This somewhat overpriced international restaurant and bar on the Praia dos Artistas has a good atmosphere at weekends.

O Crustáceo Rua Apodi 414 ⓣ84/3222-1122. Excellent, inexpensive seafood in unpretentious surroundings, right in the city centre.

Macrobiótica Rua Princesa Isabel 528 ⓣ84/3222-6765. As the name suggests, a macrobiotic restaurant, in the centre of Natal. Mon–Sat 11am–2pm.

Restaurante Chines Rua Ulisses Caldas 144. Simple Chinese and Brazilian food at very reasonable prices and accompanied by excellent service. Close to the old city centre and Praça Sete de Setembro.

Saborosa Av. Campos Sales 609, Petrópolis ⓣ84/3222-7338. Inexpensive restaurant serving an excellent range of regional food by the kilo.

Samó Av. Eng. Roberto Freire 9035, Ponta Negra ⓣ84/3219-3669. A very appealing seafood restaurant, with delicious lobsters and some French cuisine too.

Nightlife

Most of Natal's nocturnal action takes place on or around the beaches rather than in the centre. One good spot to head for is **Praia dos Artistas**, the stretch of beach about halfway between the fort and the headland, which hosts plenty of live music at night, especially on weekends. *Chaplin Night and Shopping* presents mainly *forró* on Fridays and Saturdays, while the *Balada Club* next door plays a wider variety of sounds. A few hundred yards up the beach there's the *Casa do Pagade*, a club inside the *Bar and Restaurant Don Pedro*, and host to plenty of good *forró* and *pagode* at weekends after 9pm.

If all you want to do is sip a *caipirinha* and watch the sun set, a good place is the *Canto do Mangue* on the banks of the Rio Potengi: it's a taxi ride away near the municipal fish market in the *bairro* of **Ribeira**, where Rua Coronel Flaminio runs into Rua São João. It's also one of the best places to eat fish in the city: a speciality is fresh fish fried and served in tapioca with coconut sauce (*peixe ao molho de tapioca*). Be warned, however, that Ribeira can be a fairly rough neighbourhood, especially at night, so it's best to take a taxi there and back.

For good **live music** head for *Forró com Turista*, in the Centro de Turismo, Rua Aderbal de Figueiredo 980, Petrópolis (ⓣ84/3211-6218; Fri from 10pm). The *Kapital Eurodance*, at Praia do Meio, has a varying programme throughout the week, ending in excellent live *pagode* on Sunday nights.

Listings

Airlines TAM, Rua Seridó 746 ⓣ84/3643-1624 or 3202-3385; Varig, Rua Mossoró 598 ⓣ84/3644-1252 or 3211-4453.

Banks and exchange There's a branch of Banco do Brasil (with ATMs) at Av. Rio Branco 510, Cidade Alta.

Car hire Avis ⓣ84/3644-2500; Hertz ⓣ84/3207-3399; Localiza ⓣ84/3206-5296.

Post office The main branches are at Rua Princesa Isabel 711 and Av. Rio Branco 538, both in Centro.

Shopping The two best shopping centres are the Praia Shopping Centre, Av. Eng. Roberto Freire

8790, near Ponta Negra, and Natal Shopping, at Av. Sen. Salgado Filho 2234 in the Candelária district.
Taxis Radio Taxi ⓣ84/3221-5666 and Disk Taxi ⓣ84/3223-7388.
Telephones TELERN is at Rua Princesa Isabel 687, Centro.
Travel and tour companies Casablanca Turismo (office at airport ⓣ85/3466-6000) books mainly flight and bus tickets but can arrange upmarket tours in the region or elsewhere in Brazil; Manary Ecoturs, based at the *Manary Hotel* in Ponta Negra (ⓣ84/3219-2900, ⓦwww.manary.com.br), operate minibus trips into the *sertão* to visit local communities, archeological sites and cave paintings; La Palma Spedizione (ⓣ84/3231-6616) run tours up and down the *litoral*, and into the *sertão*; and Aventura Expedições & Turismo (ⓣ84/3206-4949, ⓦwww.aventuraturismo.com.br) specialize in tours of the coast between Natal and Fortaleza.

South of Natal

Talking of things to do and places to go around Natal boils down to talking about **beaches**. The beach *par excellence* – and the easiest southern beach to get to from Natal – is **Ponta Negra**, 10km out of town along the Via Costeira, linked by regular buses from the local bus station that you can also catch from the seafront. **Further south**, the beaches get less crowded, but access can be difficult.

Ponta Negra

Following close on the heels of Bahia's Morro de São Paulo, **Ponta Negra** is one of the finest beaches in the Northeast. Running along a sweeping bay under steep sandy cliffs, the beach is magnificent, sheltered from Atlantic rollers, though still good for surfing. It's jam-packed with places to stay and often quite crowded; bars and restaurants range from trendy beach shacks to serious seafood restaurants, and there's a constant party atmosphere.

On a relatively quiet part of the beach, just a few hundred metres from the main action, there's the *Manary Praia Hotel*, Rua Francisco Gurgel 9067 (ⓣ & ⓕ84/3219-2900, ⓦwww.digi.com.br/manary; ④), which has some **rooms** with nice hammock balconies looking over the ocean and a large beach terrace. Also right on the beach are the friendly *Blue Beach Pousada*, Av. Beira Mar 229 (ⓣ84/3641-1046, ⓦwww.bluebeach-inn.com.br; around R$50), which is actually a hostel with its own beach café and front rooms priced slightly more for their sea views; and the *Visual Praia Hotel*, Rua Francisco Gurgel 9184 (ⓣ084/3646-4646, ⓕ3646-4647, ⓦwww.visualpraiahotel.com.br; ⑤), very comfortable and large, with a pool, a big terrace and a children's play area. The *Hotel Continental Plaza* (ⓣ84/3219-3346; ④) is a reasonably priced and comfortable mid-range option right at the busy part of Ponta Negra beach, where the road comes down to the beach. One of the cheapest and most basic options, and also very busy, is the *Hotel Costa Brasil* next door at no. 36 (ⓣ84/3236-2013; ③). In town, the newly built *Pousada America do Sol*, Rua Erivan França 35 (ⓣ84/3219-2245, ⓦwww.pousadaamericadosol.com.br; ③) has very comfortable rooms and great service for the price; it runs a reliable travel agency, too, organizing buggy rides, boat trips and excursions as far afield as Fernando de Noronha. If you're on a tight budget, there's the appealing youth hostel *Albergue da Juventude Lua Cheia*, Rua Dr Manoel de Arauja 500 (ⓣ84/2336-3696, ⓕ236-4747, ⓦwww.luacheia.com.br; R$50–60), just 200m from the beach; it also has its own bar and live music Tuesday to Sunday nights from 10pm.

There are several good **places to eat**: *Don Vincenzo* serves good pasta and seafood on a pleasant verandah overlooking the beach next to the large, pink

Ingá Praia Hotel. Close by, at Rua Erivan França 36, the *Bar Rústico* is a hectic 24-hour bar and restaurant, catering mainly to the surfing crowd. Perhaps the best of the places on the beachfront is the *Bar Pirata*, towards the southern end, just past the *jangada* boats; this bar-restaurant plays good rock and reggae music most of the time and has live *pagode* on Saturday nights. The *Churrascaria Tereré*, Estrada de Pirangi 2316, Rota do Sol (Ⓣ84/3219-4081), offers excellent *gaucho*-influenced *rodizio de carne*, giving you the chance to try a wide range of beef cuts.

A ten-minute taxi ride from Ponta Negra, the *Guinza Blue*, Via Costeira 4 (Ⓣ84/3219-3765), has good **live music** and dancing most weekends. For *forró*, head for the *Forró da Quartuda*, Estrada de Ponta Negra, Super Park (Ⓣ84/3234-1000; Wed from 10pm).

South of Ponta Negra

The beaches **south of Ponta Negra** are more remote and consequently less crowded. The only problem is getting to them without a car, as there are usually only one or two buses a day to most of the villages from Natal's bus station. Check the times with the tourist office, but they usually leave early in the morning and you may not be able to get back to Natal the same day. The villages normally have a *pousada* or two, however, and it is easy to come to an arrangement about stringing up hammocks in bars and houses. An alternative way of reaching the beaches is to take a **bus** along the main BR-101 highway to Recife from the *rodoviária*, and get off at Nízia Floresta, from where there are pick-ups, trucks and a local bus service along the dirt road to the coastal fishing villages and beaches of **BÚZIOS** and **BARRA DE TABATINGA**, 20km and 25km from Natal.

More direct is to take the bus from the Natal Rodoviária to **PIRANGI DO NORTE**, 30km out of town. Apart from the beach, the village's other famous attraction is the biggest **caju tree** in the world, centuries old and with branches that have spread and put down new roots. Although Brazilians know *caju* as a fruit, its seeds, once roasted, become the familiar cashew nut. It's difficult to believe this enormous (over 7000 square metres) expanse of green leaves and boughs could be a single tree; it looks more like a forest. It still bears over a ton of fruit annually, so it's not surprising that Pirangi is known for its *caju*-flavoured rum.

To get away from people, you have to travel further south to the stunning **Praia da Pipa**, 80km away, and the **Praia Sagi**, which virtually lies on the border with Paraíba state some 120km from Natal. The latter is particularly inaccessible and can only be approached by four-wheel-drive vehicles or on foot, but the result is that it is virtually untouched. The **Praia da Pipa** ("Kite Beach"), on the other hand, is set in idyllic surroundings with dolphins regularly swimming near the beach, and sports a decent selection of facilities: an increasing number of *pousadas* are springing up all over the place and there are also well-established bars like *Yahoo!* where all the nightlife takes place. Once again access is only realistically possible by car or on foot, although there are some irregular local bus services.

North of Natal

Most of the recent hotel-building and development has been funnelled south of Natal by the building of the Via Costeira, which makes the **northern**

beaches an attractive option. The two main places to head for are Redinha and Genipabu.

REDINHA, 16km from Natal, is a small fishing village facing the city on the northern mouth of the Rio Potengi, and marks the southern end of the enormous beach that effectively makes up the state's northern coastline. The beaches are notable for their huge shifting **sand dunes**, many metres high, which cluster especially thickly to tower over Genipabu. Redinha itself (hourly buses from the local bus station in Natal) is surprisingly undeveloped for somewhere so close to the city, retaining the air of a simple fishing village, with a small chapel and beachside stalls that fry the freshly caught fish and chill the beer.

There are regular buses to **GENIPABU** leaving from Natal's local bus station, every two hours from Monday to Saturday and hourly on Sunday. Genipabu is still a fishing village, but these days depends more on tourism for its income. The massive dunes are spectacular and great fun to run down: the sand is so fine it often looks like it came from an egg-timer. A favourite local pastime is to roar up and down them in **beach buggies** (see box p.373). Good excursions along the dunes are to the mineral-water spring at Pitangui, and the lovely beach of Jacumã. There are plenty of *pousadas* in Genipabu, so accommodation is no problem. However, the beach stalls operate a cartel and are very expensive for what they offer; the restaurant, *O Pedro*, just to the side, compares very favourably for similar prices and serves a wide range of seafood.

West towards Ceará

The highway **west** to Fortaleza, capital of Ceará state, would be one of the most dramatic in the region if it followed the coast; sadly, though, the BR-304, a good-quality asphalt road, takes a more direct inland route and is pretty dull as a result. The **interior** of Rio Grande do Norte is flatter than the *sertão* of the states to the south, plains of scrubby *caatinga* and cacti only rarely broken up by hills or rocky escarpments. Even on a moving bus you can feel the heat, and you get some idea of why this is one of the poorest and most unforgiving areas in the Northeast. From Natal three daily **buses** make the five-hundred-kilometre run to Fortaleza, taking around nine hours. It's a good stretch of road to do overnight: about the right length to get some sleep, and no spectacular scenery for you to regret missing.

Mossoró

The one place you might think of stopping off at before crossing into Ceará state is **MOSSORÓ**, in many ways an archetype of the *sertão* town in which so many of the inhabitants of the Northeastern interior live. Mossoró has a population of over 200,000 and is growing fast, although you wouldn't guess it from the centre, very much that of a small market town: market, square and a couple of ornate 1930s public buildings, with white plasterwork set off against walls of bright pink, looking for all the world like wedding cakes.

The Town

It's easy to get your bearings in Mossoró, despite the lack of town maps and tourist information. The main street is **Avenida Augusto Severo**, which runs down past the municipal market and local bus station to the two linked squares that are the hub of the city, **Praça Vigário Antônio Joaquim**, where the cathedral is, and **Praça da Independência**. To the left is the road leading to the old jail and town museum; straight on takes you to the Rio Apodi, where – over the bridge – is a small *artesanato* market.

The quickest way to get a flavour of Mossoró is by wandering around the **municipal market**. It gives you an instant handle on the social and economic fabric of the *sertão*, both from the goods on sale – dried meat, medicinal herbs and barks, slabs of salt – and the wiry, straw-hatted peasants and townspeople milling around. The brightly painted trucks and buses, most of which you wouldn't see outside a museum in the developed world, are the more remote villages' only link with Mossoró and, through it, to the outside world. On the fringes of the market simple stalls sell food and rum and iced *caldo de cana* (sugar-cane juice) to the shoppers, and small vendors spread their wares out on the pavement. Look for the *funilaria*, kerosene lamps and other simple household items made with great ingenuity from old tins.

However, the main places of interest in the city are connected with Mossoró's enduring claim to fame, a glorious moment in 1924 when the townspeople fought off a full-scale attack by the legendary bandit leader **Lampião** and his band. It's an event that's still celebrated every June 13 with Masses and re-enactments. To follow the Lampião trail, first stop is the **Igreja de Santo Antônio**, near the centre. In accordance with Northeastern form there was no question of a surprise assault when Lampião mounted his attack. He had announced his intention to hold the town to ransom well in advance and had taken landowners in the surrounding countryside hostage to show he meant business – an audacious thing to do, since even then Mossoró was the second city of Rio Grande do Norte. The townspeople decided to resist him, digging trenches in the main streets and fortifying public buildings. On June 13, 1924, Lampião attacked with a band of about fifty outlaws, or *cangaçeiros*, and there was fierce fighting, concentrating on the church, where the mayor, his family and retainers had barricaded themselves in. By late afternoon the bandits were driven off with several wounded, one dead, and one famous black outlaw, Jararaca, wounded and captured. Despite being a humiliating defeat for Lampião, the battle of Mossoró became one of the most famous events in his much celebrated life. On the church there's a plaque commemorating the event, and you can still see the walls and tower pockmarked with bullet holes, carefully preserved.

The next step is to make your way to the **Museu Histórico Municipal**, Praça Antônio Gomes 514 (Tues–Fri 8am–8pm, Sun 8–11am), housed in the oldest building in town, a solid late nineteenth-century structure that was once a jail: it's signposted from Praça Vigário Antônio Joaquim. It contains a remarkable collection of photographs and newspaper articles of the attack and its aftermath, together with the guns used, clothing taken from the bandits and maps of how the action developed, amongst other things. The most fascinating pieces are the powerful and eloquent photographs of the wounded **Jararaca**, kept in a cell in the very building that houses the museum. Jararaca was in jail for a day, treated by the town doctor, interviewed by the local paper, visited by town luminaries, constantly photographed by the town photographer, and then taken out at dawn to the municipal cemetery, stabbed, thrown into a newly dug grave, and shot. Reading what he said that day, it's clear he knew his fate, but he expressed no fear or regret, only his determination to die like a man, which by all accounts he did. The final stop on the tour is a visit to his grave, in the **cemitério municipal** near the church. The grave isn't signposted, but anyone, except a priest, will point you in its direction, left of the single path as you enter. The final twist is that the outlaw got his own back in death, becoming a mythical figure and saint for the poor of the region, despite attempts by the

Church and the municipal authorities to put a stop to it. His grave is covered with flowers, candle stumps, *ex votos* and prayers written on scraps of paper, and regularly visited by supplicants. The best time to see this popular devotion in action is on December 13, when thousands flock to Mossoró from all over the interior of Rio Grande do Norte to celebrate the holy day of Santa Luzia, the city's patron saint.

Practicalities

Mossoró is 276km from Natal, about four hours' drive, and served by several buses a day. The *rodoviária* is on the edge of town, from where there are regular **local buses** into the centre; or it's about ten minutes by taxi. **Leaving**, you can get a bus to the *rodoviária* from the local bus station on the fringes of the municipal market.

The best **hotel**, the *Hotel Thermas*, Av. Lauro Monte 2001 (Ⓣ84/3318-1200, Ⓦwww.hotelthermas.com.br; ⑥), is a couple of kilometres out of town, built around some thermal pools. The others are simple and all in the centre of town: try the *Del Prata* (Ⓣ84/3321-3846; ②), or the *Hotel Imperial*, Rua Santos Dumont 237 (Ⓣ& Ⓕ84/3316-2210; ③–④). There's a pleasant **bar**, *O Sujeito*, built on the riverbank just by the *artesanato* market.

Ceará

The state of **Ceará**, covering a vast area but with less than nine million inhabitants, has long borne the brunt of the vagaries of the Northeastern climate. In the 1870s, as many as two million people may have died in a famine provoked by drought, and as recently as the early 1980s people were reduced to eating rats, while the population of Fortaleza grew by about a third as rural people fled to the coastal city to escape severe drought in the interior.

Yet for all its problems Ceará has kept a strong sense of identity, making it a distinctive and rewarding state to visit. Its capital, **Fortaleza**, is the largest, most modern and cosmopolitan city in the Northeast after Recife and Salvador; the sum of its skyscraping architecture is a futuristic cityscape. In stark contrast, the **sertão** is unforgiving to those who have to live in it, but in Ceará it rewards the traveller with some spectacular landscapes: as you travel west, the flat and rather dull plains of Rio Grande do Norte gradually give way to ranges of hills, culminating in the extreme west of the state in the highlands and lush cloud forest of the **Serra da Ibiapaba**, the only place in Brazil where you can stand in jungle and look down on desert. To the south there are the hills and fertile valleys of **Cariri**, with the pilgrim city of Juazeiro do Norte (see p.365). And the coastline boasts some of the wildest, most remote and beautiful **beaches** in Brazil.

Save for a few sheltered valleys with relatively reliable rainfall, sugar cane does not grow in Ceará and it never developed the plantation economy of other Northeastern states. Ceará was and remains **cattle** country, with the main roads and centres of population in the state following the route of the old cattle trails. As settlement by the Portuguese and serious economic development began over a century later than in the sugar-zone states, and only really got going in the last century, there are very few buildings that date back to colonial times – and, indeed, nothing colonial remains in Fortaleza.

In recent years, Ceará has developed a reputation as one of the best-governed states in Brazil. Successive governors from the **PSDB**, the Social Democratic Party of President Fernando Henrique Cardoso, have done much to reduce poverty and disease through imaginative health and education schemes. For the visitor, all this gives Ceará the feeling of an up-and-coming place where things are changing fast both economically and culturally.

Fortaleza

FORTALEZA is a sprawling city of over two million inhabitants, the centre bristling with offices and apartment blocks. It has, for well over a century, been the major commercial hub of the northern half of the Northeast. More recently it has poured resources into expanding its tourist trade, lining the fine city beaches with gleaming luxury hotels and developing the city centre. Taken together, this means that little trace remains of the Fortaleza's eventful **early history**, the clue to which is in its name: Fortaleza means "fortress". The first Portuguese settlers arrived in 1603 and were defeated initially by the Indians, who killed and ate the first bishop (a distinction the city shares with Belém), and then by the Dutch, who drove the Portuguese out of the area in 1637 and built the Forte Schoonenborch. In fact the Portuguese were restricted to precarious coastal settlements until well into the eighteenth century, when the Indians were finally overwhelmed by the determined blazing of cattle trails into the interior. Another fort – the Fortaleza de Nossa Senhora da Assunção – was built by the Portuguese in 1816 on the site of the earlier Dutch one.

It was in Fortaleza that the independence movement in northern Brazil was organized, and it was one of the few places where the Portuguese actually made a fight of it, massacring the local patriots in 1824 before being massacred themselves a few months later. The city did well in the **nineteenth century**, as the port city of a hinterland where ranching was expanding rapidly. For decades, though, one of the city's most important exports was the people of the state: shipping lines transported *flagelados* (poor people who had come here because of severe droughts in the region) from Fortaleza to the rubber zones of the Amazon and the cities of southern Brazil. These days, Fortaleza has something of the same atmosphere as Rio, especially when it comes to the good things in life like food, beaches and fun. It's not a beautiful city as such, though the coastline and weather make up for that. But it certainly has a safe, friendly and relaxed atmosphere, and the nightlife is superb.

Arrival, city transport and information

The **rodoviária** and **airport** are some way from the centre in the southern suburb of Fátima, but getting into town is easy thanks to the comfortable *frescão* service operated by the Top Bus company (R$7). The buses will stop to let you off – or can be flagged down – wherever you want along their circular route, which takes in both the airport and the *rodoviária* before winding its way through the crowded city centre to the beach areas; it's supposed to run throughout the night, but the service is less frequent then, and you should check with the tourist office if you're relying on it to catch an early-morning bus or

FORTALEZA

0 250 m

ATLANTIC OCEAN

N

Ponte dos Ingleses

Praia de Iracema

Praia do Mucuripe

Praia do Meireles

Estação Ferroviária

CENTRO

Buses to Caucaia

MEIRELES

VARJOTA

ALDEOTA

FATIMA

Buses to Aquiraz

Praça Coração de Jesus

Estação Rodoviária

Rio Cocó

Shopping Iguatemi

Rua dos Tabajaras
Av. Almirante Barroso
Av. Monsenhor Tabosa
Rua Tenente Benévolo
Av. Beira Mar
Av. Abolição
Rua Pereira Valente
Avenida Santos Dumont
Avenida Heraclito Graça
Av. Padre Antônio Tomás
Rua Antônio Sales
Avenida Pontes Vieira
Rua João Cordeiro
Avenida Barão de Studart
Av. Desembargador Moreira
Av. Senador Virgilio Távora
Av. Eng. Santana Júnior
Av. Visconde Rio Branco

see map below for detail

ACCOMMODATION
Hotel Beira-Mar A
Hotel La Maison B
Hotel Marina Praia A
Mundo Latino C

RESTAURANTS
Cemoara 1

▼ Airport

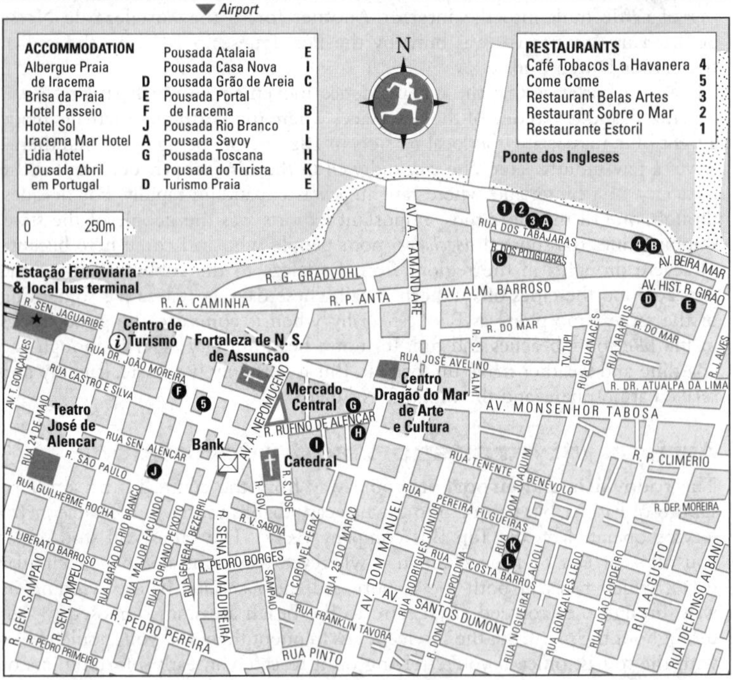

ACCOMMODATION
Albergue Praia de Iracema D
Brisa da Praia E
Hotel Passeio F
Hotel Sol J
Iracema Mar Hotel A
Lidia Hotel G
Pousada Abril em Portugal D
Pousada Atalaia E
Pousada Casa Nova I
Pousada Grão de Areia C
Pousada Portal de Iracema B
Pousada Rio Branco I
Pousada Savoy L
Pousada Toscana H
Pousada do Turista K
Turismo Praia E

RESTAURANTS
Café Tobacos La Havanera 4
Come Come 5
Restaurant Belas Artes 3
Restaurant Sobre o Mar 2
Restaurante Estoril 1

N

0 250m

Ponte dos Ingleses

Estação Ferroviaria & local bus terminal

Centro de Turismo

Fortaleza de N. S. de Assunçao

Mercado Central

Centro Dragão do Mar de Arte e Cultura

Teatro José de Alencar

Bank

Catedral

Rua dos Tabajaras
R. dos Potiguaras
Av. Beira Mar
Av. Hist. R. Girão
R. G. Gradvohl
R. A. Caminha
R. P. Anta
Av. Alm. Barroso
Av. A. Tamandaré
R. Sen. Jaguaribe
Rua Dr. João Moreira
Rua Castro e Silva
Av. A. Nepomuceno
R. Rufino de Alencar
Rua Sen. Alencar
R. São Paulo
Rua Guilherme Rocha
R. Liberato Barroso
R. do Mar
Rua José Avelino
Almi
Tv. Tupi
Rua Guanacés
Rua Ararius
R. J. Alves
R. Dr. Atualpa da Lima
Av. Monsenhor Tabosa
Rua Tenente Benévolo
R. P. Climério
R. Dep. Moreira
Rua Pereira Filgueiras
Rua Dom Joaquim
Rua Costa Barros
Av. Santos Dumont
Av. T. Gonçalves
Rua 24 de Maio
Rua Barão do Rio Branco
Rua Major Facundo
Rua Floriano Peixoto
Rua General Bezerril
R. Sena Madureira
R. Gov. Sampaio
R. S. José
R. V. Saboia
R. Pedro Borges
R. Coronel Feraz
Rua 25 do Março
Av. Dom Manuel
Rua Rodrigues Júnior
Rua Dona Leopoldina
Rua Nogueira Acioli
Rua Gonçalves Ledo
Rua João Cordeiro
Rua Algusto
Rua Idelfonso Albano
Rua Franklin Tavora
Rua Pinto
R. Pedro Pereira
R. Gen. Sampaio
R. Sen. Pompeu
R. Pedro Primeiro

plane. If there are more than two of you, it might be cheaper to take a taxi, which costs around R$20 to the airport from most places in the city.

Fortaleza also has plenty of **local buses**. Useful routes that take you out to the main beach areas and back to the city centre are those marked "Grande Circular", "Caça e Pesca", "Mucuripe" and "P. Futuro". Two buses, the "Circular 1" and "Circular 2", run services that cover the outskirts and central part of Fortaleza respectively. The local bus station is located in the old city centre, in the square in front of the old railway station. There are loads of taxis, too, which are essential for getting around late at night. You may also choose to walk around Fortaleza quite a lot: the city is heavily policed and feels much safer than many other Brazilian cities, though the usual basic precautions are still necessary.

Information and practicalities

Fortaleza is geared towards catering for visitors. The **main information office** of the state tourist office, SETUR (Mon–Sat 8am–6pm, Sun 8am–noon; ⓣ85/3488-7411), is in the Centro de Turismo in the centre, at Rua Senador Pompeu 350, and should be your first port of call; the staff know their stuff, and are especially good on the complicated bus journeys that are often necessary to get to the out-of-town beaches. The **tourist information posts** are also friendly and efficient; they give out free city maps, and if you're planning to travel in the state outside Fortaleza you should stock up on the relevant information here. There are information posts at the airport (ⓣ85/3477-1667; 24hrs) and at the *rodoviária* (daily 6am–6pm; ⓣ85/3256-4080). The best maps of Fortaleza are usually to be obtained from the municipal tourist organization, **FORTUR**, who have an information post (daily 8am–5pm; ⓣ85/3252-1444) on Praça do Ferreira in the centre.

There are ATMs in the shopping district and along the beach front, or you can **change money** at numerous places down on the beach, such as the blue kiosk in the shadow of the *Imperial Othon Palace Hotel*, and, in the city centre, at Tropical Viagens, Rua Barão do Rio Branco 1233 (Mon–Fri 9am–5pm, Sat 8am–noon).

Accommodation

The budget hotels, as ever, tend to be in the **centre**, which hums with activity during the day but empties at night, and the more expensive ones are generally out by the **beaches**, notably Iracema and Meireles. But this is not a hard-and-fast rule; there are literally hundreds of hotels of all shapes and sizes throughout the city, although very few bargains are to be had on the seafront itself. You should remember that Fortaleza can get very hot, and either air conditioning or a fan is essential. Since Fortaleza is essentially split into two parts – the downtown shopping area and the beaches, you might want to spread your stay between two different *pousadas* in different areas.

The city centre

Hotel Passeio Rua Dr João Moreira 221 ⓣ85/3226-9640, ⓕ3253-6165. Well-run hotel located opposite the pleasant Praça dos Mártires and just a block from the Centro de Turismo. A bit musty, with rooms cooled by ventilator fans or a/c. ❷

Hotel Sol Rua Barão do Rio Branco 829 ⓣ85/3211-9166, ⓕ3262-1021. Well maintained and with great service, the *Hotel Sol* has pleasant, airy rooms and a swimming pool. ❹

Lidia Hotel Rua Rufino de Alencar 300 ⓣ85/3252-4174. This friendly, very small hotel was converted from a house; rooms are simple and clean. ❷–❸

Pousada Casa Nova Rua Pedro Ángulo 56 ⓣ85/3252-4179. A family-run *pousada* right in the heart of the centre, with eighteen spotless and a/c suites. ❸

Pousada Rio Branco Rua Pedro Ángulo 46 ⓣ85/3226-5801. Next door to the *Pousada Casa*

Nova, the rooms in this converted house are small but adequate. Ring the doorbell for service. ❷

Pousada Toscana Rua Rufino de Alenar 272 Ⓣ85/3231-6378, Ⓦwww.pousadatoscana.hpg.com.br. Very close to the Mercado Central and the Centro Dragão, this very clean, well-run hostel in an attractive house has bright and airy rooms with comfortable beds. Very good value. R$50-60.

Praia da Iracema

Albergue Praia de Iracema Av. Almirante Barroso 998, Praia de Iracema Ⓣ85/3252-3267. Fortaleza's youth hostel is in an excellent location near the best nightlife. R$50.

Brisa da Praia Av. Beira Mar 982, Praia de Iracema Ⓣ85/3219-4699, Ⓕ3219-1964, Ⓦwww.bphfortal.com.br. This modern, medium-sized hotel is right on the seafront, with a small pool, a decent bar and a rooftop terrace. ❺

Pousada Abril em Portugal Av. Almirante Barroso 1006, Praia de Iracema Ⓣ85/3231-9508. A good-value budget hotel near the youth hostel. ❷

Pousada Atalaia Av. Beira Mar 814 Ⓣ85/3219-0658, Ⓦwww.pousadaatalaia.com.br. Possibly one of the best-located youth hostels in the Americas, right opposite the beach on the Praia Iracema and within shouting distance of Fortaleza's top nightlife spots. Accommodation is mostly in dormitories, though some private rooms are available too. R$60.

Pousada Grão de Areia Rua Dos Potiguaras 80 Ⓣ85/3219-1704. One of the cheapest options near the busy nightlife scene around the Ponte dos Ingleses. Though small, the *pousada* has helpful staff, plus some rooms have TV and a/c. ❸

Pousada Portal de Iracema Rua dos Ararius 2, Praia de Iracema Ⓣ85/3219-0066, Ⓕ3219-3411, Ⓔpousada@ultranet.com.br. Well-located *pousada* very close to the sea and near the centre of the nightlife district, yet surprisingly quiet. Rooms are clean and bright and have TVs and *frigobars*; additionally, good English is spoken, service is conscientious, and the breakfasts are lovely. ❸

Turismo Praia Av. Beira Mar 894, Praia de Iracema Ⓣ85/3219-6133, Ⓕ3219-1638. Small, good-value hotel with functional rooms, a tiny pool, and a modest restaurant. The location is great, opposite the beach. ❸

Praia Meireles

Hotel Beira-Mar Av. Beira Mar (Av. Presidente Kennedy) 3130, Praia de Meireles Ⓣ85/3242-5000, Ⓕ3242-5659, Ⓦwww.hotelbeiramar.com.br. Luxury hotel with a pool, right next to the Praia de Meireles. ❻

Hotel La Maison Av. Desembarador Moreira 201 Ⓣ85/3242-7017, Ⓦwww.hotellamaison.com.br. This thirteen-room *pousada* is in a tastefully converted house just a few blocks from the beach; the rooms are pleasant and have TVs, telephones and a/c. French and English is spoken and parking is available. ❹

Hotel Marina Praia Rua Paula Barros 44 Ⓣ85/3242-7734, Ⓕ3242-5275, Ⓦwww.hotelmarinapraia.com.br. A small, spick-and-span hotel, little bigger than a house and less than a block from the beach in the Nautico section of Praia Meireles. It somehow fits 25 apartments into its comfortable and colourful interior, and there's also a little patio out front. Good value. ❹

Pousada do Turista Rua Dom Joaquim 351 Ⓣ85/3231-6607. Budget hotel run by French-speakers, with pleasant, a/c rooms. Located in a peaceful area within ten minutes' walk from the city centre and the beach. ❷–❸

Pousada Savoy Rua Dom Joaquim 321 Ⓣ85/3226-8426. Basic, affordable hotel next door to the *Pousada do Turista*. ❷

The City

The only visible legacy of Fortaleza's crowded history is a **gridded street pattern** laid out in the nineteenth century by a French architect, Adolphe Herbster. Herbster was contracted by the ambitious city fathers to turn Fortaleza into "the Paris of the North" – and you can only hope that they got their money back.

The **layout of the city** is easy to grasp, despite its size. The **centre**, laid out in blocks, forms the commercial, administrative and religious heart, with markets, shops, public buildings, squares and a forbiddingly ugly concrete cathedral; it's quite possible to walk and take in most of the sights in one day, though you'd probably want to take longer. To the west of the centre, undistinguished urban sprawl finally gives way to the beaches of **Barra do Ceará**, but most of the action is to the east, where the main city beaches and the chic middle-class *bairros* of **Praia de Iracema** and **Meireles** are to be found, linked by the main seafront road, **Avenida Presidente Kennedy**, usually known as **Avenida Beira Mar**. These give way to the *favelas* and docks of the port area, **Mucuripe**, the gateway to the eastern beaches, notably **Praia do Futuro**, beyond which the city peters out.

While not the most visually attractive of Brazilian city centres, there is enough going on in the heart of Fortaleza to merit more attention than it usually gets from visitors. It certainly can't be faulted for being boring: the streets are very crowded, with shops and hawkers colonizing large areas of pavement and squares, so that much of the centre often seems like a single large market. Fortaleza is an excellent place for **shopping**, and you should stock up here if you're heading west, as you won't get comparable choice until you hit Belém, 1500km away. Clothes are plentiful and cheap, there is also good *artesanato* to be had, notably lace and leather, and Fortaleza is the largest centre for the manufacture and sale of hammocks in Brazil.

The Mercado Central and around

Set right next to the grimy, neo-Gothic cathedral on Rua Conde d'Eu, the striking new **Mercado Central**, a huge complex holding hundreds of small stores, dominates the skyline. The market, along with the nearby shops on the other side of the cathedral, is the best place to buy a hammock in the city: if you're going to use one on your travels, purchase it with care (see box, below).

Opposite the Mercado Central, the nineteenth-century **Fortaleza de Nossa Senhora da Assunção** – the city's namesake – is easily identified by its thick, plain white walls and old black cannons. It belongs to the Tenth Military Regiment of the Brazilian army, but is open to visitors on request (Mon–Fri 9am–5pm; ⓣ85/3255-1600); visits are best organized the day before.

The Centro Dragão do Mar de Arte e Cultura

The **Centro Dragão do Mar de Arte e Cultura**, a couple of blocks east of the market, makes a striking contrast to the rest of the city. Architecturally it's very modern, but its steel and glass curves blend sensitively with the attractive old terraced buildings over and around which it is built. The whole thing feels like a modern and stylish university campus and, importantly, serves as an ideal link between the beaches and the city centre, which essentially starts on the landward side of the complex on the small Praça Municipal. Within the complex, there's a small, shiny-domed planetarium, cinemas, an auditorium, a couple of museums – one dedicated to contemporary art – an information

Buying a hammock

If you're looking to buy a hammock, cloth ones are the most comfortable, but they're also heavier, bulkier and take longer to dry out if they get wet. Less comfy in the heat, but more convenient, much lighter and more durable are nylon hammocks. Aesthetically, however, nylon hammocks are no match for cloth ones, which come in all colours and patterns. You ought to be able to get a perfectly adequate cloth hammock, which will stand up to a few weeks' travelling, for around R$25 for a single and R$45 for a double; for a nylon hammock, add R$10 to the price. If you want a more elaborate one – and some handwoven hammocks are very fine – you will pay more. Easing the path to slinging hammocks once you get home are metal *armadores*, which many hammock and most hardware shops sell: these are hooks mounted on hinges and a plate with bolts for sinking into walls. When buying a hammock you are going to use, make sure it takes your body lying horizontally across it: sleeping along the curve is uncomfortably bad for your back.

hall and bookshop, toilets and a good coffee bar, the *Torre do Café*, located in the tower that supports the covered walkway between the two main sections of the Centro. On the ground level there's also a shop selling quality regional *artesanato*.

The Centro de Turismo and the Museu de Arte e Cultura Popular

Overlooking the sea at the bottom of Rua Senador Pompeu is the **Centro de Turismo**, housed in the city's old prison – a perfect place to stop and have a beer in the bar in the one-time exercise yard, shaded by mango trees. The centre is also the location of the best museum in the city, the **Museu de Arte e Cultura Popular** (Mon–Fri 8am–6pm, Sat 8am–noon). Well laid out in a single huge gallery on the first floor, this is a comprehensive collection of *cearense artesanato* of all kinds, together with a sample of the painting and sculpture produced by the best of the state's modern artists. What distinguishes the museum is the imaginative juxtaposition of more traditional popular art with modernism. Both collections are of very high quality: the modern art is often startlingly original, as in the sculptures of bolts, nuts and scrap metal of Zé Pinto, but in style and subject matter you can see how profoundly it is rooted in the tradition of popular art all around it. In the same building (and included in the entry price) is the smaller **Museu de Mineralogia** (same times), stuffed full of massive quartz crystals and a wide range of semi-precious stones.

The Passeio Público and Praça dos Mártires

Two blocks from the Centro de Turismo is another survivor of nineteenth-century Fortaleza: the old municipal boulevard, the **Passeio Público**, which sits beside the pleasant shady **Praça dos Mártires**. Both are popular with children and families – as well as prostitutes. The Passeio looks out over the waterfront, and stallholders set up chairs and tables under the trees, from where they sell cold drinks and simple food. It's a good place to go in the late afternoon or early evening, when the workers stroll around after they get out of their offices, watching the variety of street entertainers and hawkers. The municipality often lays something on: small fairs, dances – the ubiquitous *forró* pumped out by tannoy or thumped out by *trios* – or concerts. Even without entertainment, it has a relaxing feel, and is certainly the best place, away from the beaches, to watch the sunset.

Praça José de Alencar

The nerve centre of this part of the city, however, is its largest square, **Praça José de Alencar**, four blocks inland from the train station at the heart of the commercial district. In the late afternoon and early evening, the crowds here attract *capoeira* groups, street sellers of all kinds and especially *repentistas*. Fortaleza seems to specialize in these street poets, who with great skill and wit gather an audience by improvising a verse or two about those standing around watching, passing round a hat for you to show your appreciation. If you refuse, or give what they consider too little, the stream of innuendo and insults, in a variety of complicated metres, is unmistakeable, even if you don't understand a word (see p.342).

On the square you'll also find the one truly impressive building in the city, the beautiful **Teatro José de Alencar**, named after the great nineteenth-century novelist and poet who was a native of the city. Built in the first decade of the twentieth century, the theatre's fine tropical Edwardian exterior is in fact only an elegant facade, which leads into an open courtyard and the main body of the theatre. It is built in ornate and beautifully worked cast-iron sections, which were brought over complete from Scotland and reassembled in 1910. Surprisingly, for a building made out of iron, it is extremely cool and pleasant to be in, even when the sun is at its height: the ironwork is open and lets in the air without trapping heat, a masterly example of Scottish design in the least Scottish setting imaginable. In 1991 it was superbly restored and is now a key venue for theatrical performances and concerts. The best time to see it is at night, when it opens for business, a favourite venue for *cearense* music of all varieties and exhibitions in the courtyard. Friday and Saturday are the likeliest nights to find something on: the staff can let you know what's happening, or try looking under the heading *Lazer* in the local papers.

The city beaches

The main city beaches are the **Praia de Iracema** and the adjacent **Praia do Meireles**, both focal points for Fortaleza's nightlife. As beaches go, the Praia do Meireles wins hands down with its greater expanse of sand, though the water is not as clean as the beaches out of town, due to the proximity of docks both east and west; the further away from the centre, the better for swimming. That said, both beaches are good for sunset watching, the seafront boulevard is well laid out, punctuated by clumps of palm trees, and there is no shortage of watering holes. By day there are surfers on the waves and beach parties at the *barracas*, and in the early evening it seems everyone in the city turns out to stroll or rollerblade down the boulevard, which has replaced the city's squares as the favoured meeting place.

If you're a beach devotee, cleaner water, higher rollers and better seafood are to be had further out past Mucuripe at **Praia do Futuro**: take buses marked "Caça e Pesca" or "P. Futuro" from Rua Castro e Silva in the centre. The beach *barracas* here are very good: the fried fish is fresh and comes in enormous portions. The ultimate surfing beaches, however, are 6km beyond the Praia do Futuro, at **Porto das Dunas** and **Prainha**, 11km in combined length. Porto das Dunas also has an aquatic theme park called **Beach Park** (daily 9am–5pm; ⓣ85/3360-1150), the largest of its kind in Latin America.

Eating, drinking and nightlife

You'll be all right in the centre during the day if you want something to eat, as there are countless places to grab a snack. However, most of what Fortaleza has to offer your palate is to be found on the beaches, especially around **Rua dos Tabajaras** on Praia de Iracema. The pier here, known as Ponte dos Ingleses, is a lovely place to have a beer and watch the sunset. Rua dos Tabajaras itself is a joy to wander around, with its brightly coloured bars and **restaurants**, and glamorous young people out enjoying themselves. The airy *Restaurant Belas Artes* (ⓣ85/3219-0330), Rua dos Tabajaras 179, has a good range of Brazilian and international dishes and an excellent bar. Nearby, the boat-like *Restaurant Sobre o Mar*, Rua dos Tremembes 2 (ⓣ85/3219-7999), serves delicious lobster and a good range of wines; there's a R$2–3 cover charge for the frequent live music shows. *Restaurante Estoril* (ⓣ85/3219-8389) makes the best of its setting at Rua dos Tabajaras 397, serving excellent *cearense* cuisine, offering shows at weekends and comedy on Tuesday nights, but it's quite pricey. Much further south along the seafront, past Praia do Futuro at Av. Beira Mar 4566, the *Marquinhos Restaurante* (ⓣ85/3263-1204) serves excellent seafood (try the skewered lobster); it's not cheap but the service is good and the restaurant open and airy. If you happen to end up in the old city centre at lunchtime, try

Come Come, at Rua Castro e Silva, a self-service café offering a very cheap but satisfying *comida por kilo* option near the cathedral (it's cooler and larger inside than it looks). For a filling breakfast, fresh fruit juices and excellent coffee in a relaxed café setting, you'll do no better than *Café Tobacos La Havanera* on the corner of Rua dos Ararius and Avenida Beira Mar. Arguably the best restaurant in the city is *Cemoara*, Av. Abolição 3340 (℡85/3263-5001), where the service is superb and the food even better, specializing mainly in Brazilian dishes, particularly *cearense*.

Two **bars** on Avenida Beira Mar, just along from Rua dos Tabajaras, offer a wonderful combination of eating, drinking and live music: the *Pontal de Iracema* at no. 680 and the *Cais Bar* at no. 696 are extremely trendy nightspots where you have to arrive early to get a seat.

Forró: dancing and clubs

Fortaleza is justly famous for its **forró**. Nowhere is it so popular, and there is no better way to see what *cearenses* do when they want to enjoy themselves than to spend a night in a *dancetaria* here. And spending the night is literally what you need to do: although most *dancetarias* open at 10pm, people don't really start arriving until around midnight, and peak time is in the early hours of the morning.

Pirata at Rua dos Tabajaras 325 (℡85/3219-8030), one of the most easily accessible nightclubs in Fortaleza, has live music from Tuesday through Saturday, including *forró* but with other sounds as well; it's a great night out for usually less than R$10. *Subindo ao Céu*, at Av. Zezé Diogo out on Praia do Futuro, is a popular venue on Tuesday nights. On Wednesdays the scene shifts to the *Clube do Vaqueiro* (℡85/3276-2014), a taxi ride away out on the periphery of the city along the BR-116 highway leading east to Natal. As its name implies, the club has everything for the cowboy: the huge complex is sometimes used for rodeos during the day, and on Wednesday nights the cavernous interior throbs with *forró* rhythms and hundreds of dancing couples.

Other nightlife

Besides *forró*, there's plenty else in Fortaleza to keep you busy into the evenings. For **jazz**, try the *Ludvico Bar* and *Restaurante*, at Rua do Mirante 161, Mucuripe (℡85/3263-1545), on most Thursday evenings. Most weekends, the *Disco Bar Desigual*, on the seafront between the pier and *Paraiso do Praia Hotel*, pulls in a young crowd with its loud live music. One of the best venues for live **dance shows**, is *Docas Bar e Café Teatro*, beside the Centro Dragao at Rua Jose Avelino 491 (℡85/3219-8209), which showcases costumed dance styles every Wednesday from 9pm, among them *Afro* (slave), *Caboclinhos* (jungle) and *Maracatu* (colonial). On Fridays the same venue usually presents local pop bands, while on weekends the music tends to be more mixed, though with heavy doses of samba.

Listings

Airlines TAM ℡85/3477-1945; Varig ℡85/3477-1710.

Banks and exchange Banco do Noreste, Rua Major Facundo 372, offers the most services, but you're likely to get faster service at Wall Street, Av. Santos Dumont 3000, Aldeota (℡85/3486-3900) or Av. Beira Mar 2982, Loja 02.

Car hire RCA ℡85/3219-7000; RHP ℡85/3257-7533.

Internet Beira Mar Internet Café, Beira Mar 2120-A; Cachaça-Cearapontocom, Av. Beira Mar 720; Diabesso Internet Café, Av. Beira Mar 3222 (Loja 20, entrance past the restaurants up a small side street); and Interschool, Av. Abolição 3089.

Post office The main post office is at Rua Senador Alencar 38 (Mon–Fri 8am–6pm).
Taxis Radio Taxi ⓣ85/3254-5744.
Telephones There are public telephone offices for inter-urban and international calls across the city, including one near the beach at Av. Beira Mar 730 by the *Naredomus Hotel*.
Travel and tour companies Ernahitur, Av. Barao de Studart 1165, 1st floor, Conjunto 101-107, Aldeota (ⓣ85/3244-9363, ⓕ3261-6782, ⓦwww.ernanitur.com.br) and Wall Street, Av. Santos Dumont 3000, Aldeota (ⓣ85/3486-3900) or Av. Beira Mar 2982, Loja 02 (ⓣ85/3242-2235) arrange trips to Jericoacoara (R$120), Canoa Quebrada (R$30) and Lagoinha (R$25), as well as city tours (R$25). Praia Turismo (ⓣ85/9989-6685), run similar tours for slightly less and will also pick up from hotels; their sales van is parked by the beach on Beira Mar (at the Praia Iracema end) on most mornings. Trip da Areia, at Av. Beira Mar 3120, sala 03 (ⓣ85/3242-3985, ⓦwww.tripdaareia.com.br), run excellent one- to four-day expeditions from Fortaleza to the neighbouring beaches and resorts.

Around Fortaleza: the beaches

The **beaches** of Ceará are what attract most visitors, and both east and west of Fortaleza they stretch unbroken for hundreds of kilometres. They are invariably superb, a mixture of mountainous sand dunes, palm trees and Atlantic breakers, wilder than the sheltered reef beaches of the southern states of the Northeast. The area has strong and predictable winds which, combined with good surf, means it's a windsurfer's paradise. Even some of the most remote beaches have been "discovered" by tourists, but there is no need to scorn them on that account: the coastline is more than big enough to swallow large numbers of property developers and visitors without getting crowded. It's easy to bewail the passing of the simple life in the fishing villages, but talk to their inhabitants and you'll find they are still functioning communities, making money from tourists on the side. What travellers see as an idyllic, rustic existence seems more like poverty to those who live it.

Any description of the beaches becomes repetitive: they are all stunning, among the most beautiful anywhere in the world. Travelling along the coast, while often leisurely, is not difficult. To reach the beaches, as a rule, you will need to get off at a town and catch a connection to the nearby coast, and the local bus network covers most places: at the better-known beaches, shoals of pick-ups and beach buggies meet the buses from Fortaleza.

East to Aracati and Canoa Quebrada

There are two basic routes that take you **east of Fortaleza**. The first heads along a coastal road that branches off the BR-116 just south of the city to Beberibe. The first coastal village along this route is **AQUIRAZ**, where there are the beaches of **Iguape** and **Prainha**. Buses to Aquiraz are run by the São Benedito company and leave from a stop on the corner of Avenida Domingos Olímpio and Avenida Aquanambi. For anywhere east of Aquiraz, buses can be caught at the *rodoviária*. Thirty kilometres beyond Aquiraz is Cascavel, 12km inland but a starting point for two more beaches: **Caponga** and, less crowded, **Aguas Belas**. Twenty kilometres further on is **BEBERIBE** itself, the drive there a lovely one on a country road through palm forests and dunes. The irregularly shaped dunes of Beberibe's beach, **Morro Branco**, are fifteen minutes away. Five kilometres from here is the small fishing village and mineral-water spring of **PRAIA DAS FONTES**, which also boasts a luxury hotel of the same name, reasonably priced and serving excellent food (ⓣ85/3338-1179; ⑤).

A more direct route east takes you to **ARACATI**, two hours from Fortaleza, a once properous small textile town with half a dozen derelict, and a couple of functioning, eighteenth-century churches. It is also the jumping-off point for Ceará's best-known and most fashionable beach, **Canoa Quebrada**, half an hour along a dirt road from Aracati: pick-ups meet every bus from the city, so access is no problem. Canoa Quebrada is popular with foreigners and young Brazilians alike, the atmosphere is relaxed, and it's fairly lively at night. Certainly, if you want company and *movimento* it's the beach to head for, and there's good buggy riding here in the sand dunes of the surrounding environmental reserve. The road to Canoa Quebrada is flanked by dozens of boards advertising *pousadas* and restaurants and there's no shortage of either. The beach served directly by road from Aracati, **Majorlândia**, is less crowded and a lot quieter. It's certainly as good as Canoa Quebrada, there are *jangadas* on the beach and surf here as well, and it's just as easy to find places to stay. A good place to try is the *Pousada Fortaleza* (☎98/3421-7019), 200m from the beach (☎85/3242-3985, reservations at Av. Beira Mar 3120, sala 3; ④), which has air-conditioned apartments equipped with *frigobars*, TVs and hammocks, as well as a pool.

West to Jericoacoara

The choice of beaches **west of Fortaleza** is equally rich. Only 8km from Fortaleza you'll find the town of **Caucaia**, which is served by buses from Avenida Rui Barbosa (outside the *Ideal Clube*) on Praia de Meireles. From Caucaia, local buses head out to the beaches of **Icaraí** (not to be confused with another Icaraí more than 150km to the west), **Pacheo** and **Tabuba** where, even by *cearense* standards, the coastline is really something, with dunes, lagoons, palm forests and enormous expanses of sand; the road ends up in the fishing village of Cumbuco.

Frequent buses from the Fortaleza Rodoviária (tickets from Brasileiro Transporte) go to **SÃO GONÇALO DO AMARANTE**, only an hour and 57km away. From here, you can head on to the beaches of **Pecém**, 15km away, and the glorious beach of **Taíba**, 6km on. Not all buses to São Gonçalo continue to the beaches, but if they don't there are pick-ups and local buses. The beach town of **PARACURU**, 80km from Fortaleza (frequent buses from the *rodoviária*, also

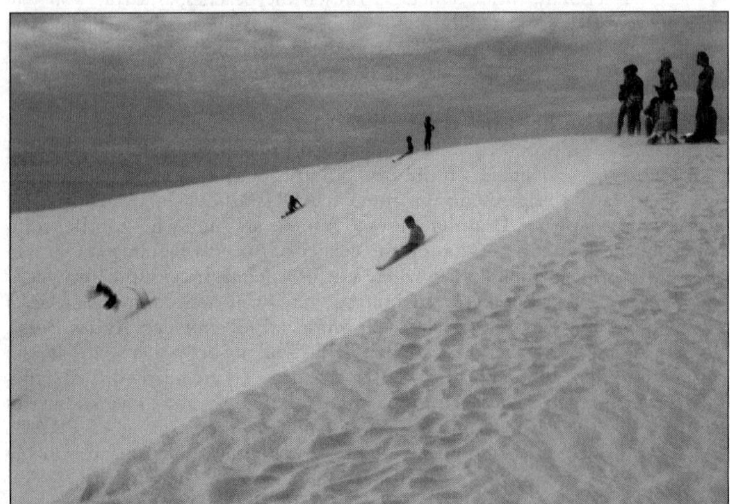

△ Jericoacoara

with Brasileiro Transporte), is being rapidly developed and gets crowded during weekends, but is less frenetic during the week.

After Paracuru, you head out of Fortaleza's influence and the further west you go, the less crowded the beaches become. A good place to head for, reasonably remote but not impossible to get to, is **TRAIRI**, 118km from Fortaleza, served by direct buses from the *rodoviária*, which take around three hours. From here it's a few kilometres to the beautiful and usually deserted beaches of **Mundaú**, protected by a 100m reef, and **Fleixeiras**, more deserted still. When the tide is out, you can walk for an hour along the beach to the fishing hamlet of **GUAJIRU**, named for the indigenous local fruit that still grows abundantly in the scrubby bushes scattered around the dunes. There is no electricity or running water, but the people are friendly and the scenery marvellous.

Ceará's most famous beach, **JERICOACOARA**, lies 320km west of Fortaleza, a remote hangout with huge dunes of fine white sand, and turquoise *lagoas*. This is one of Brazil's best beaches for wind and surf activities, and most tour agents offer packages here. For the independent traveller, two buses a day from Fortaleza cover the seven-hour journey to the village of Gijoca, where pick-up trucks and buggies will meet you for the hour-long ride over the sands to Jericoacoara. It's still a primitive place, unconnected to the main electricity grid, but there are plenty of spots to stay as well as several outfitters renting out surfboards and windsurfing equipment. Kitesurfing (call ⓣ88/3369-2359 for local information on this sport) is very popular here, particularly at Praia do Prea, a small fishing village some 10km down the beach (43km by road). For accommodation, *Wind Pousada*, Rua Forro 33 (ⓣ85/9953-9596; ❸), has attractively rustic rooms just 50m from the beach, all with TVs, *frigobars*, air conditioning and hot showers. There's also the *Pousada das Dunas*, Rua das Dunas (ⓣ88/3699-2002, or in Fortaleza at Av. Beira Mar 3120 ⓣ85/3242-3985; ❺), which offers good service and more comfort, and the *Pousada da Renata* (ⓣ88/3669-2061), close to the beach, with pleasantly decorated rooms (❸–❹). There are also tours here from Fortaleza starting at R$90 per day – see p.389 for a list of tour operators.

On to Piauí: the Serra da Ibiapaba

Apart from the beaches, there is little to detain you as you head west from Fortaleza, though it's a fine drive, with rocky hills and escarpments rising out of the *sertão* and the road snaking through occasional ranges of hills. You pass through the town of **SOBRAL**, an ugly industrial centre nestling in the middle of a spectacular landscape very typical of the interior of the Northeast: fiercely hot, cobalt-blue skies, flinty hills and *caatinga*. It would be very easy to sit back, enjoy the scenery and head directly west for Piauí and Maranhão in one go, but if you did you'd miss one of the finest sights Ceará state has to offer: the beautiful hills and cloud forest of the highlands that run down the border between Ceará and Piauí – the **Serra da Ibiapaba** – and the caves of **Ubajara**.

Serra da Ibiapaba

You reach the Serra on buses arriving from either east or west, along the BR-222 highway that links Fortaleza with Teresina, capital of the neighbouring state of Piauí. You can get off at **TIANGUÁ**, a pleasant, sleepy town on the *cearense* side of the border: from here there are frequent local connections to Ubajara, 15km away (see p.392), also served by direct buses from Fortaleza (Ipu Brasília line).

Whether you approach from Teresina or Fortaleza the effect is the same. The buses drive across a bakingly hot plain, which begins to break up the nearer you get to the state border, rearing up into scattered hills and mesas covered with scrub and enormous cacti. Then on the horizon, in view hours before you actually start to climb it, all the hills seem suddenly to merge into a solid wall that rears up 900m from the parched plain below, its slopes carpeted with thick forest: the **Serra da Ibiapaba**.

Ironically, the abundance of the highland forest is part of the explanation for the parched landscape below. The sheer slopes of the *serras* are well watered because they relieve any clouds of their surplus water before they drift over the plains. As the bus begins to climb, winding its way through gorges choked with forest, the broiling heat of the plain is left behind and the air gets fresher and more comfortable. When you reach the tableland on top, it seems another world. Everything is green and fertile: the temperature, warm but fresh with cool breezes, is an immense relief, and the contrast with the conditions only half an hour's drive away below couldn't be more marked. En route to Ubajara you'll see how *nordestinos* treasure those few parts of the interior blessed with fertile soil and regular rainfall: the highlands are intensively farmed by smallholders and supply fruit, vegetables, sugar and manioc for the whole region.

Ubajara

UBAJARA is a small, friendly town nestling in picturesque hills. There are a couple of simple but perfectly adequate **hotels** near the single church and quiet square, together with one or two **bars** and **restaurants**. It's a pleasant place to stay, but probably the best option is to head a couple of kilometres out of town, along the road leading away from Tianguá, to the comfortable *Pousada da Neblina*, Estrada do Teleférico (Ⓣ88/3634-1270, Ⓦwww.pousadaneblina.com.br; ❸). Standing in splendid isolation at the foot of a hill covered with palm forest, it has a restaurant and swimming pool, and is remarkable value; you can also camp here. Another option is *Sítio Santana* (Ⓣ88/9961-4645), known as "Sítio do Alemão" by the locals, which provides small chalets on a coffee plantation (❸). The view from the chalets is spectacular and it's only a short taxi ride away from town; alternatively, the owner will pick you up – just ask anyone in town to put you in touch with him.

Parque Nacional de Ubajara

A twenty-minute walk along the road from the *Pousada da Neblina* will bring you to the gatehouse of the **Parque Nacional de Ubajara**, which ensures that the magnificent forest remains untouched. The park, nestling attractively amidst low hills, is very small (less than six square kilometres), but tourism facilities have developed rapidly in recent years and the park now has a **visitors' centre** (daily 9am–6pm; Ⓣ88/3634-1388). There are also plenty of local guides available (Ⓣ88/3634-1219) starting at around R$45 per day) to show you round the park's ecotrails, large caves and impressive waterfalls; they are also a good source of up-to-the-minute local information.

Continuing past the gatehouse brings you to the *mirante*, a viewing platform with a small café built onto the rim of an escarpment. North and south of here the *serra* breaks into ridges covered with forest and tumbles down into the plain, which stretches as far as the eye can see. The view is punctuated by jagged hills, towns and villages connected by vein-like roads, and the whole panorama is laid out as if seen from the cockpit of an aeroplane.

From here a **cable car** swoops down 400m to the cave complex of the **Gruta de Ubajara**. It's an unforgettable ride, plunging down and skimming the top of the forest before arriving at the caves. If you feel more adventurous, there is a **path** down that can be negotiated with a guide. On no account try it on your own; though it's not dangerous, it's very easy to stray off the route. The forest wardens are always on duty at the gatehouse, and can help arrange guides. Guides prefer to start early in the morning, so you do the bulk of the walk before the heat gets up: take liquids, and wear sneakers or decent walking shoes. Going down takes a couple of hours, returning twice that, but there are streams and a small waterfall to cool off in along the way. There are also caves to explore: huge caverns with grotesque formations of stalactites and stalagmites. Technically, the wardens are meant to guide you as part of their job, but as they're extremely badly paid they appreciate some recompense for spending several hours of their time making sure you come to no harm.

Piauí

Piauí is shaped like a ham, with a narrow neck of coastline 59km long that broadens out inland. It's a very distinctive state, but unfortunately most of the reasons for this are depressing. Despite its size it has fewer than two million inhabitants and by far the lowest population density in the Northeast. Subject to drought, and with virtually no natural resources except the *carnaúba* palm, it is Brazil's poorest state.

Few travellers spend much time in Piauí. The capital, **Teresina**, is strategically placed for breaking the long bus journey between Fortaleza and São Luís, but it's a modern, rather ugly city where the heat can be oppressive. The southern half of the state merges into the remoter regions of Bahia and forms the harshest part of the Northeast. Much of it is uninhabited, largely trackless, arid badlands, in the midst of which lies, ironically, the oldest inhabited prehistoric site yet found in Brazil. Cave paintings show that this desert was once jungle. Other than the capital, there are two places worth making for: the pleasant coastal town of **Parnaíba**, which has excellent beaches, and the **Parque Nacional de Sete Cidades**, good walking country with weird and striking rock formations. Strangely, this poorest of states has an excellent **highway** system and the main roads between Teresina and Parnaíba and towards Ceará are very good: as the country is largely flat, the buses really fly.

Piauí was sparsely settled by cattle drovers moving westwards from Ceará in the second half of the eighteenth century and has a violent history. The few Indians were never really conquered and were assimilated with the newcomers rather than being defeated by them, leaving their imprint in the high cheekbones and copper skin of a strikingly handsome people. Apart from cattle, the only significant industry revolves around the **carnaúba palm**, a graceful tree with fan-shaped leaves that grows in river valleys across the northern half of the state. The palm yields a wax that was an important ingredient of shellac, from which the first phonogram records were made, and for which there is still a small export market. It's also a source of cooking oil, wood, soap, charcoal and nuts, and many livelihoods depend on it.

Teresina

People from **TERESINA** tell a joke about their city: "Why do vultures fly in circles over Teresina? Because they glide with one wing and have to fan themselves with the other!" Brazil's hottest state capital, Teresina sits far inland on the east bank of the Rio Parnaíba, where it bakes year-round in an average temperature of 40°C (which means it regularly gets hotter than that). The rains, meant to arrive in February and last for three or four months, are not to be relied upon – though, ironically, twice in the last fifteen years they have actually flooded the city. Unless you're used to such heat, you'll find it tiring to move around; rooms with at least a fan, and preferably air conditioning, are a necessity.

There's not a great deal to do or see in Teresina, but there's enough to occupy you for a day if you feel like breaking the long bus journey from Ceará. Besides having some comfortable hotels, it's the only place between Fortaleza and São Luís where you can do things like cash traveller's cheques or have money cabled out to you.

The City

Thankfully, in such a hot place, most of the things worth seeing and doing are reasonably close to each other. The best place to start is the **market** that occupies most of the main square of the city, technically called Praça da Bandeira, but universally known by its old name, **Marechal Deodoro**. It's a smaller, more urbanized version of the typical Northeastern market, with packed stalls forming narrow streets, determined shoppers, energetic sellers, noise, loud music and plenty of *caldo de cana* kiosks, where you can slurp freshly crushed sugar cane and watch the city at work. There is *artesanato* scattered around, and the hammocks from the interior are high quality; both are cheaper here than in the craft shops run by the state tourist authority PIEMTUR.

Overlooking the market, in one of the very few fine old buildings in the city, the **Museu do Piauí** at Marechal Deodoro 900 (Tues–Fri 8am–6pm, Sat & Sun 8am–noon) is definitely worth seeing. A governor's palace, built in 1859, it has been beautifully restored, with the exhibits well displayed in simple, elegant rooms, many with high arched windows and balconies perched just above the crowded market stalls. The collection is the usual eclectic mix, and pride of place must go to a collection of early radios, televisions and stereograms, a must for lovers of 1950s and 1960s kitsch. There are also fossils as well as fine examples of the two things that distinguish *artesanato* in Piauí: sculpture in straw and beautifully tooled leather.

You might also want to investigate the crafts and culture complex run by PIEMTUR, the **Centro de Comercialização Artesanal**, also known as the Mercado Central. Located in the old military barracks at Rua Paissandu 1276, overlooking Praça Dom Pedro Segundo, it's a small but pleasant place to wander around. The *artesanato* is laid out in booths and is good quality, although a little expensive; the leatherwork is especially fine. Upstairs is a nice café with restaurant attached, where the *carne do sol* is excellent.

Practicalities

The **rodoviária** (Ⓣ86/3218-1514) is on the southeast outskirts of the city and has a **tourist information post** (Mon–Fri 8am–noon & 2–6pm, Sat 8am–noon) run by PIEMTUR, where you can pick up free booklets with a city map. Frequent buses run into the centre, and there are cheap taxis, too. You will also find an information post on the corner of Magalhães Filho and Alvaro

Mendes in the centre of town five blocks from the Praça da Liberdade. It's very easy to find your way around as the streets are organized in a grid pattern.

There are a number of good **hotels** opposite the *rodoviária*. Both the *Elite* (❷), and the *São Francisco* (❷), are no-frills options. Among those in the city centre overlooking the river is the luxury *Luxor do Piauí*, Praça Mal. Deodoro 310 (ⓣ86/3221-3306, ⓕ221-5171, ⓦwww.luxorhoteis.com.br; ❺), with disabled access, a restaurant, quite smart rooms and a pool, while cheaper places are nearby around Praça Saraiva. Mid-range hotels include the cosy *Sambaiba*, Rua Gabriel Ferreira 230 (ⓣ86/3222-4911; ❸), the *Teresina Palace*, Rua Paissandu 1219 ⓣ86/3221-2770, ⓕ3221-4476 (❸), and the *Royal Palace*, Rua 13 de Maio 233 ⓣ & ⓕ86/3221-7707 (❹), where you'll want to avoid the windowless basement rooms, though all have decent air conditioning.

Restaurants in the city are not especially cheap. Good regional food is served at *Celsos*, Rua Agelica 1059 (ⓣ86/3232-2920), a short taxi ride away from the centre in the *bairro* of Fátima. You'll find excellent seafood at *Camarão de Elías*, Av. Pedro Almeida 457, in the *bairro* of São Cristóvão (ⓣ86/3232-5025; closed Sun). *Piauienses* excel at meat: a good place to try the *cabrito*, young goat, deliciously tender and served either roasted over charcoal or *ao leite de coco*, stewed in coconut milk, is *Asa Branca*, Av. Frei Serafim 2037, in the centre, with live music (Thurs–Sat). If you're after a meat feast, the *rodizio* at *Rio Poty*, Av. Mal. Castelo Branco 616, is the place to go.

The city's **nightlife** lacks the focus of the coastal capitals, but there is life here after dark. The bank of the Rio Parnaíba is the best place from which to enjoy the sunset. A kilometre or so south of the centre, along the riverfront road, is **Prainha**, a series of bars and restaurants built along the riverbank, shaded by planted trees: buses run there, but are very infrequent by late afternoon – use the taxis in Teresina, which are cheap.

Carnaúba country

Heading **west** from Ceará towards Amazônia, there are two routes you can follow. The fastest and most direct is simply to take the highway through Teresina and on to São Luís or, a day from Teresina, to Belém and Amazônia proper. But if you have the time, there is a much more interesting and scenic route **north** up the BR-343 highway, a fine drive through a plain studded with *carnaúba* palm plantations to **Parnaíba** and the coast. From Parnaíba there is a direct bus service, over country dirt roads that get seriously difficult to travel on during the rainy season, to São Luís (see p.398), capital of neighbouring Maranhão state, where the Amazon region begins.

Parnaíba

PARNAÍBA, with its attractive natural anchorage on the Rio Igaraçu, was founded over fifty years before Teresina. For the Portuguese, it was the obvious harbour from which to ship out the dried meat and *carnaúba* (a wax derived from *carnauba* palm) of the interior and, in the nineteenth century, it was a thriving little town; you can still see the chimneys of the cotton factories put up by British entrepreneurs a century ago. Then the river silted up, the port moved to Luiz Correia at the mouth of the river, and the town slipped into decline. Today, Parnaíba has a lazy feel, but is still the second largest city in the state with around 125,000 inhabitants. Located anywhere else it would be a thriving resort town; the **beaches** nearby are excellent.

There is not too much to do in Parnaíba except waste time pleasantly. The commercial area in the centre is busy, and **Praça da Graça**, with its palms and cafés, is an enjoyable place to hang about. The liveliest place in town, though, is the riverfront **Avenida Nações Unidas**, a grandiose name for a small promenade lined with cafés and restaurants. There are also boat trips to the islands at the mouth of the Rio Parnaíba, organized by the state tourist authority **PIEMTUR**, based in the Centro Cultural Porto das Barcas, beside the river at the end of Avenida Getúlio Vargas (daily 8am–1pm & 2–7pm; ⓣ86/3321-1532).

The modern **rodoviária** is on the edge of town, and buses for the short ride to the centre leave from outside. The centre is small and contains all Parnaíba's **hotels**, best of which is the *Hotel Cívico*, Av. Chagas Rodrigues 474 (ⓣ86/3322-2470, ⓕ3322-2028; ❹), which has a pool, restaurant and a reasonable bar. There's also cheap, clean accommodation at the *Pousada Rio Igaraçu*, Rua Almirante Gervásio Sampaio 390 (ⓣ86/3322-3342; ❷), and the *Casa Nova Hotel*, at Praça Lima Rebelo 1094 (ⓣ86/3322-3344; ❸). For something a little different, check out the *Pousada Ecológica Ilha do Caju* (ⓣ86/3321-3044 or ⓕ3321-1308; ❼), located in a private ecoreserve on an island accessed by boat (4hr) from Parnaíba.

The beaches

You might as well follow the locals and head off to the **beaches** if you want to relax. Not served by bus, but only a short taxi ride away, is the **Lagoa do Portinho**, a freshwater lake with palms and chalets to stay in, and a good restaurant.

There are simple hotels and *dormitórios* if you want to stay in **LUIZ CORREIA**, a fishing village 8km north of Paranaíba, with a small modern port attached. From here you can either walk or get the bus to the huge and popular **Praia de Atalaia**. At weekends practically the entire population of Parnaíba decamps here and the crowded bars reverberate to *forró* trios. A less crowded beach, **Coqueiro**, is 12km from here, but there are only a couple of buses there a day.

Hourly **local buses** to Luiz Correia and Praia de Atalaia leave from the terminus next to Praça Santo Antônio in Parnaíba, three blocks along the pedestrianized shopping street that leads down from Praça da Graça; they take about 20 minutes to arrive in Luiz Correia, and another five to hit the beach – stay on till the end of the line to be dropped at the liveliest stretch.

Parque Nacional de Sete Cidades

The **Parque Nacional de Sete Cidades** comprises thirty square kilometres of nature reserve that could hardly be more different from the forest reserve of Ubajara, a couple of hundred kilometres east. Here it's the spiky, semi-arid vegetation of the high *sertão* that is preserved – cacti and stubby trees. The really special feature of the reserve is its eroded **rock formations**, many streaked with prehistoric rock carvings. From the air they look like the ruins of seven towns, hence the name of the area, and their striking shapes have given rise to all sorts of theories about the area having been a Phoenician outpost in the New World. In fact the rock sculpting is the entirely natural result of erosion by wind and rain.

There are two ways of **getting to the park**, depending on whether you approach from Ceará state or elsewhere in Piauí. Coming **from Fortaleza**

or Ubajara, get off the bus at the town of **Piripiri**, from where a free bus or transit van leaves at 6.45am (Tues–Fri) and takes you to the national park hostel run by the IBDF, the Brazilian forestry service. If you arrive too late, or on a day when the bus isn't running, you could take a local bus from Piripiri to the turn-off to the park 15km north, and walk (3hr) from there, or alternatively take a taxi (R$40). Coming **from Teresina or Parnaíba**, get a bus to Piracuruca and take a taxi to the park – the taxi ride costs about R$50. There are perfectly adequate, cheap and clean **hotels** near the bus stations in both Piripiri and Piracuruca.

Despite its good facilities and its position near the main Teresina–Fortaleza highway, not as many people visit the park as you might expect. Consequently, it's the ideal place to get off the beaten track without actually venturing far from civilization.

Into the park

There are two **places to stay** in the park. At the entrance is the *Fazenda Sete Cidades* (Ⓣ86/3276-2222; ❺), with a restaurant, pool and regular pick-up shuttle into the park itself, which you can use whether you stay there or not. More convenient for walking, and just as comfortable, is the cheaper *Abrigo do Ibama* (Ⓣ86/3343-1342; from R$25 per person) hostel and **campsite** in the centre of the park, again with a restaurant and bathing nearby in a natural spring.

Walking in Sete Cidades is not difficult. There are a series of **trails** and several **campsites**, and the staff at both the *fazenda* and the *Abrigo do Ibama* are good at suggesting routes; there are very cursory sketch maps on sale, but don't rely on their accuracy. The walks are not especially strenuous, but take care all the same; it gets extremely hot and a stout pair of shoes, plenty of liquids and a broad-brimmed hat are essential. Start out as near sunrise as you can manage, when the park is at its most beautiful. And when you approach the rocks make some noise: rattlesnakes sometimes sun themselves on them, but they are very shy and slither away if they can hear you coming. The **rock formations** themselves make very good landmarks and their different shapes have lent them their names: the "Map of Brazil", the "Tortoise", the "Roman Soldier", the "Three Kings", the "Elephant" and so on.

Maranhaõ

Maranhão is where the separate but interlinked worlds of the Northeast and Amazônia collide. Although classed as a Northeastern state by Brazilians, its climate, landscape, history and capital of **São Luís** are all *amazônico* rather than *nordestino*. Maranhão is the only state in the Northeast to which more people migrate than emigrate from. Drought is not a problem here; the **climate** is equatorial – humid, hot and very wet indeed. The rainy season peaks from January to April, but most months it rains at least a little, and usually a lot – although only in concentrated, refreshing bouts for most of the year. Maranhão has more fertile, well-watered land than the rest of the Northeast put together. Much of it is flat, the east and north covered with palm forest, and the centre and west riddled, in typical Amazonian fashion, with large rivers and fertile riverine plains – one of the main rice-producing areas of Brazil.

Further west begins the tropical forest and savanna of Amazônia proper, as you hit the eastern boundary of the largest river basin in the world. The **coast** also changes character: the enormous beaches give way, from São Luís westwards, to a bewildering jumble of creeks, river estuaries, mangrove swamps and small islands, interspersed with some of the most remote beaches in Brazil – almost five hundred kilometres of largely roadless coastline with towns and villages accessible only from the sea.

Like most zones of geographical transition, Maranhão also marks a historical and cultural divide. The **people** are a striking contrast to the ethnic uniformity of the states immediately to the east: here blacks, Indians and Europeans form one of the richest cultural stews to be found in Brazil. Catch the great popular festival of **Bumba-meu-boi** in June and you'll get some idea of how different from the rest of the Northeast Maranhão really is.

The main population centres in the state are on and around the island of São Luís, and deep in the interior along the banks of the **Rio Tocantins**, a tributary of the Amazon but a mighty river in its own right. The contrast between the two regions could hardly be more stark. Only thirty years ago the Rio Tocantins was the boundary between Brazil and largely unknown Indian country. Today, as people flood into eastern Amazônia, **Imperatriz**, with 295,000 inhabitants, is the second city of the state, and even dozy, historic São Luís, founded in 1612, has been transformed by docks and factories linked to the huge development projects of eastern Amazônia – the subject of much international controversy.

Routes into Maranhão

There are two **routes** into Maranhão from the east: scooting along the good asphalted highway that links Teresina to São Luís, a six-hour bus ride; or lurching along country roads from Parnaíba, which is more interesting but not to be attempted in the rainy season, when the non-asphalted roads in Maranhão become quagmires. Either way, there's little to detain you before you get to São Luís, as you watch the land transforming itself into the tropics along the way. The *carnaúba* palm of Piauí gives way to the taller trunk and straight fronds of the most common tree in Maranhão, the **babaçu palm**, on which even more livelihoods depend than on *carnaúba*: it provides nuts, cooking oil, soap, charcoal, rope fibre, timber and thatch.

São Luís

Although clearly once a lovely colonial city, **SÃO LUÍS** has really been left behind by the rest of Brazil, despite President Lulas posters plastered everywhere promising change. A poor city even by Northeast standards, it's the most emphatically Third World of all the state capitals in this region. Power cuts (usually kicking in around 8pm) and electricity rationing are still routine, and many things simply don't work. Some of the historic city centre is literally falling to pieces and the infant mortality rate is comparable to those of poor African countries. It has a huge black population, a legacy of plantation development during the eighteenth and nineteenth centuries. It is also far larger than it seems from the compact city centre; about 740,000 people live here, most of them in sprawling *favelas*, with the middle classes concentrated in the beach areas of Ponta da Areia, São Francisco and Olho d'Agua, linked to the

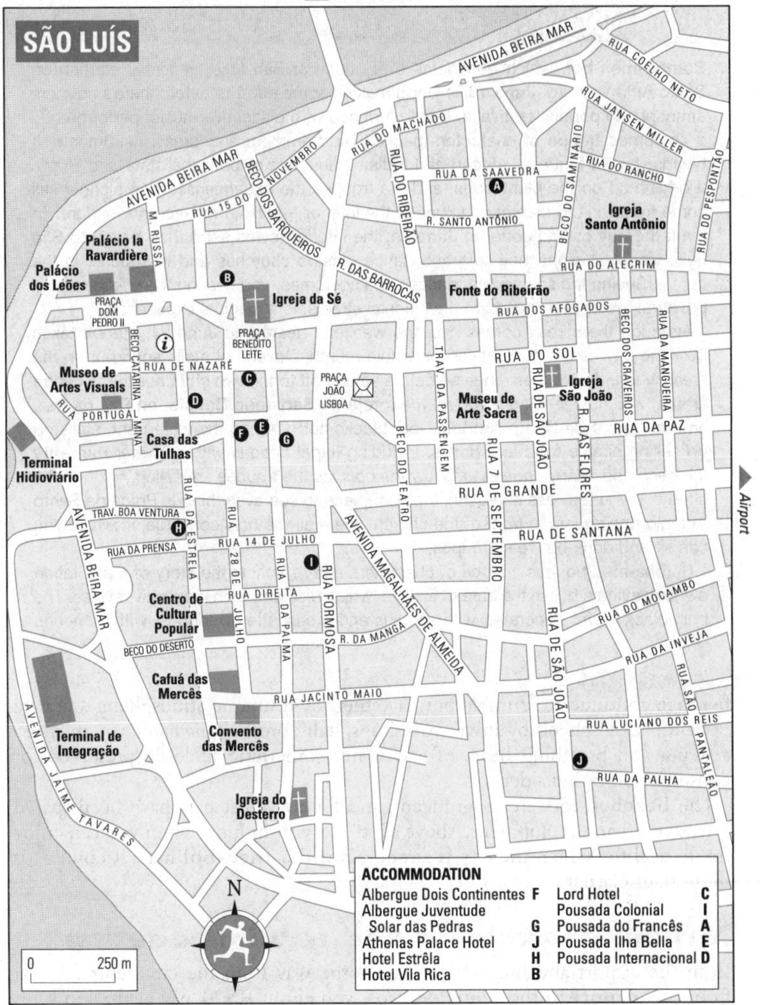

rest of the city by a ring road and the bridge built out from the centre across the Rio Anil.

But, for all its problems, São Luís is still a fascinating place, and it's famous as Brazil's capital of reggae music. Certainly, music, street theatre, food and beaches are the city and region's main pull, along with the decrepit but impressive colonial historic centre. Built across the junction of two rivers and the sea, on an island within the larger delta formed by the **Pindaré** and **Itapicuru** rivers, it has the umbilical connection with rivers that marks an Amazon city, but is also a seaport with ocean beaches. Since 1989, two hundred buildings in the historic centre, the **Zona** (or **Praia Grande**), have benefited from a large-scale restoration programme, the **Projeto Reviver**. Meanwhile, other parts of the colonial

Bumba-meu-boi

Bumba-meu-boi, which dominates every June in São Luís (generally starting on Santo Antônio's day, **June 13**) is worth making some effort to catch: there's no more atmospheric popular festival in Brazil. A dance with distinctive music, performed by a costumed troupe of characters backed by drummers and brass instruments, it blends the Portuguese, African and Indian influences of both the state and Brazil. It originated on the plantations, and the troupes the *maranhenses* rate highest still come from the old plantation towns of the interior – Axixá, Pinheiro and Pindaré. To mark the day of São João on **June 24**, the interior towns send their bands to São Luís, where at night they sing and dance outside churches and in squares in the centre. Seeing the spectacular dances and costumes, and hearing the spellbindingly powerful music echoing down the colonial streets, is a magical experience.

Although the climax comes over the weekend nearest to June 24, *bumba* takes over the city centre at night for the whole month. Dozens of stalls spring up in the areas where the troupes rehearse before setting off to the two churches in the centre around which everything revolves: the **Igreja de São João Batista**, on Rua da Paz, and the **Igreja de Santo Antônio**, four blocks north. Along the waterfront, stalls go up selling simple food and drinks, including lethal *batidas* with firewater rum – try the *genipapo*. Many choose to follow the *bois*, as the troupes are called, through the streets: if you feel less energetic, the best place to see everything is Praça de Santo Antônio, the square in front of the church where all the *bois* converge, in which you can sit and drink between troupes.

Bumba-meu-boi has a stock of characters and re-enacts the story of a plantation owner leaving a bull in the care of a slave, which dies and then magically revives. The bull, black velvet decorated with sequins and a cascade of ribbons, with someone

heritage continue to crumble but have their own unique atmosphere: there are people packed cheek by jowl, workshops, stalls, brothels, *dormitórios* – in short, a living and breathing heart of a city, not something lifelessly preserved for consumption by outsiders.

The **beaches**, too, are magnificent, and for the most part have been spared intrusive urban development. Above all, try to visit in June, when you can enjoy the festival for which the city is famous, **Bumba-meu-boi** here, it counts for more than Carnaval.

Arrival, information and accommodation

Both the airport and the *rodoviária* are some way from the city centre. A taxi from the **airport** to the centre will cost you about R$20: pay at the kiosk on the left as you come out of the luggage collection area and hand the coupon to the driver. Alternatively you can catch the bus outside marked "São Cristóvão". From the **rodoviária** a taxi to the centre costs about R$12. Buses connect the *rodoviária* with the local bus station, the **Terminal de Integração** at Praia Grande, by the waterfront in the city centre. Once there you shouldn't need to use public transport very much: the area of interest is small and most things are within walking distance.

The availability of the **tourist information** office, run by FEMTUR, at the Praça Benedito Leite (Mon–Fri 8am–7pm, Sat & Sun 9am–5pm; ⓣ98/3231-9086) is unreliable, with opening hours being more like 10am to 5pm daily. FEMTUR's so-called 24-hour information post at the airport is not always staffed. Other offices that you may find open are at the Praça Deodoro (Mon–Fri 8am–6pm, Sat & Sun 9am–noon) and the *rodoviária* (daily 8am–11pm). You can inside whirling it around, is at the centre of a circle of musicians. The songs are belted out, with lyrics declaimed first by a lead caller, backed up only by a mandolin, and then joyously roared out by everyone when the drums and brass come in. *Bumba* drums are unique: hollow, and played by strumming a metal spring inside, they give out a deep, hypnotically powerful backbeat.

The troupe is surrounded by people singing along and doing the athletic dance that goes with the rhythm. There are certain old favourites that are the climax of every performance, especially *São Luís*, the unofficial city anthem: *São Luís, cidade de azulejos, juro que nunca te deixo longe do meu coracão* – "São Luís, city of *azulejos*, I swear I'll never keep you far from my heart", it begins, and when it comes up there is a roar of recognition and hundreds of voices join in. The sound of the people of the city shouting out their song radiates from Praça de Santo Antônio across the centre, turning the narrow streets and alleys into an echo chamber.

Bumba-meu-boi starts late, the troupes not hitting the centre until 11pm at the earliest, but people start congregating, either at the waterfront or in the square, soon after dark. *Bois* don't appear every night, except during the last few days before the 24th: ask at the place where you're staying, as everyone knows when a good *boi* is on. Bumba-meu-boi troupes are organized like samba schools; towns and city *bairros* have their own, but thankfully the festival hasn't been ruined by making them compete formally against each other. Informal rivalries are intense, all the same, and *maranhenses* love comparing their merits: most would agree that Boi de Madre de Deus is the best in the city, but they are eclipsed by the troupes from the interior, Boi de Axixá and Boi de Pinheiro. The best day of all is **June 29** (St Peter's Day), when all the *bois* congregate at the Igreja de São Pedro from 10pm until dawn.

change money at the Wall Street Cambio, next to the tourist office on Praça Benedito Leite, at either the HSBC bank on Rua Joao Lisboa, by the Praça João Lisboa, or the Banco da Amazônia on Praça Dom Pedro Segundo or at the Casa 711, Av. Beira Mar 544, right next to the bridge that connects the old city with São Francisco and the other beach areas. For Internet access try the Saint Louis Internet Café at Rua da Estrela 125 or the *Antiguamente Restaurant* at Rua da Estrela 220. Radio taxis are available from Coopertaxi (Ⓣ98/3245-4404) and Crisbell (Ⓣ3244-1131); the latter also offer a minbus service.

One other thing you should bear in mind is that, as in Salvador, many streets have two names: Rua do Trapiche, for example, is also known as Rua Portugal.

Accommodation

Places to stay are divided between the beaches – where there are a few medium-range hotels but no cheap ones – and the centre. To get a flavour of the city's atmosphere there's no substitute for staying in the historic centre, but you should be aware that there are sometimes extremely loud reggae nights that may keep you awake.

Albergue Dois Continentes Rua 28 de Julho 129 Ⓣ3222-6286, Ⓦwww.alberguedoiscontinentes.hpg.com.br. In the middle of Praia Grande area, this popular youth hostel is neat and comfortable, with shared or private rooms at reasonable prices. R$50.

Albergue Juventude Solar das Pedras Rua da Palma 127 Ⓣ3232-6694. Busy and cheerful youth hostel right in the heart of the action in Praia Grande, with tidy shared rooms and double rooms only. R$55.

Athenas Palace Hotel Rua Antônio Rayol 431 Ⓣ98/3221-4163 or 3221-4225. Though quite good value, with some spacious and quite comfortable rooms with private baths, it's not ideally located for trips into the Zona. ❸

Hotel Estrêla Rua da Estrela 370 ⓣ98/3232-7172. A budget option right in the heart of the old city. It's fairly well-kept, but rooms (with fans) are stuffy ❷

Hotel Sofitel Av. Avicência ⓣ98/3216-4545, ⓕ3235-4921 ⓔsofitel@accor.com.br. Luxury hotel set above Calhau beach some 10km from the city centre. Endowed with all possible comforts, including a sauna as well as tennis, basketball, swimming and football facilities. ❻

Hotel Vila Rica Praça Dom Pedro Segundo 299 ⓣ98/3232-3535, ⓕ3232-7245, ⓦwww.hotelvilarica.com.br. Comfortable but not as luxurious as it was a few years ago, this concrete monstrosity is well located on the edge of the historic centre, close to the tourist information office. Rooms have small balconies and there's a pool. ❻

Lord Hotel Rua Joaquim Távora 258 ⓣ98/3221-4655. Set in a colonial building with a rather grand entrance and lobby, this slightly faded two-star hotel may be the ideal option if you want to stay just on the edge of the historic centre without spending too much money. Rooms come with or without both baths and a/c. ❸

Pousada Colonial Rua Afonso Pena 112 ⓣ3232-2834, ⓦwww.guiasaoluis.com.br. Finely maintained mansion offering comfort and good service in pleasant surroundings. Very good value and close to the historic centre. ❸

Pousada do Francês Rua da Saavedra 160, corner of Rua Sete de Setembro ⓣ98/3231-4844. A bit rundown (though clearly once one of the best in town), this basic *pousada* is on the edge of the Zona, in a poorly restored eighteenth-century mansion. ❹

Pousada Ilha Bella Rua da Palma 92 ⓣ98/3231-3563. One of the cleanest and least expensive of the budget hotels in the Zona. ❷

Pousada Internacional Rua da Estrela 175. Friendly hostel located in one of the city's best spots for nightlife, just around the corner from the tourist information office. R$40.

The City

The city's central **layout** is easily grasped. Built on a headland that slopes down to rivers on two sides, the city's largest square is **Praça Deodoro**, from where the narrow but crowded Rua da Paz and Rua do Sol, each only with room for one lane of traffic and perilously tight pavements, lead down to **Praça João Lisboa**, which marks the edge of the **Zona** – the nickname for the colonial core of the city. From here steep streets lead down to the river waterfront. It's on the buildings fronting Praça João Lisboa that you will first see the lovely, glazed-tile frontages, the **azulejos**, which are the city's signature. Salvador has finer individual examples of *azulejo*, but taken as a whole the *azulejos* of colonial São Luís are unmatched for the scale of their use and their abstract beauty. Most are early nineteenth-century; some, with characteristic mustard-coloured shapes in the glazing, date back to the 1750s. Remarkably, many of the oldest tiles arrived in São Luís by accident, as ballast in cargo ships.

The Zona

The **Zona** – also called the **Reviver** after the project to restore it – covers a small headland overlooking the confluence of the Rio Anil and the Atlantic Ocean, and though it may not look like much, a defensible harbour on this flat coastline was of some strategic importance. Now the waterfront is no more than a landing place for fishing boats and ferries, but slave ships once rode at anchor here, bringing in workers for the cotton and sugar plantations upriver. Then, the harbour was crowded with cargo boats, mostly from Liverpool, shipping out the exports of what – from about 1780 to 1840 – was a prosperous trading centre, for the first and last time in its history.

But the Zona predates even that colonial boom. São Luís shares with Rio the distinction of having been founded by the French, and is the only city in Brazil to have been ruled by three European countries. The French, decimated by a lethal combination of malaria and Indians, were soon dislodged by the Portuguese in 1615; then the Dutch sacked the city and held the area for three years from 1641, building the small fort that now lies in ruins on a headland between Calhau and Ponta da Areia. Over the next hundred years, the original shacks were replaced by some of the finest colonial buildings in northern Brazil.

The only way to explore the Zona is on foot. A good place to begin is the Praça Benedito Leite, a small leafy square where you'll find the tourist information office along with the **Igreja da Sé**, a cream and white cathedral completed in 1699 and given a Neoclassical facelift in 1922. Around the corner is the **Praça Dom Pedro II**, where the official buildings that line the square are splendidly proportioned survivors of the pre-Baroque colonial era. The oldest is the municipal hall, which dates from 1688: it still houses the Prefeitura and is called the **Palácio La Ravardiere**, after the French buccaneer who founded São Luís and is commemorated by a piratical bust on the pavement outside. In November 1985 the building was torched by an angry crowd, with the newly elected mayor inside, after an election acrimonious even by *maranhense* standards. Next door is the tropical Georgian elegance of the state governor's residence, the **Palácio dos Leões**, built between 1761 and 1776 and currently closed for restoration.

On the other side of the square from the Palácio dos Leões, steps lead down to the steep colonial street, **Beco Catarina Mina**, that takes you to the heart of the Zona, block after block of buildings, many restored whilst others are in an advanced state of decay. With its cobbled streets, *azulejos* and the vultures on the tile roofs, the Zona remains physically much as it was 150 years ago, although the colonial merchants and plantation owners who built it would have turned up their noses at its modern inhabitants. As economic decline bit deep, they sold up and moved on.

Beco Catarina Mina runs into the finest array of *azulejos* in the city, the tiled facades of the **Rua do Trapiche** (Rua Portugal), with the **Mercado da Praia Grande**'s gorgeous arches perfectly set off by the piercing-blue tiles and symmetrical windows and balconies. This area is the best-restored part of the Zona, given a magical feel by the brightly coloured *azulejos*, and has plenty of bars and restaurants and a lively street life at any time of day or night. The **Casa das Tulhas**, on Rua da Estrela, is an early nineteenth-century mansion now crammed with market stalls selling *artesanato*, including locally produced foods, quality cotton clothing, hammocks and tablecloths.

Many **churches** in the city have exteriors dating from the seventeenth century, and the most beautiful of these is the **Igreja do Desterro**, with its Byzantine domes, at the southern end of the Zona, though none of the church interiors has survived successive restorations. It was in these churches that the Jesuit **Padre Antônio Vieira** preached his sermons three hundred years ago, berating the plantation owners for enslaving Indians before the Jesuits had a chance to do so – sermons that are often taken to be the finest early Portuguese prose ever written.

Museums

There are two **museums** worth visiting on Rua do Trapiche. The **Salão de Bens Culturais** (daily 9am–9pm), at no. 303, houses an interesting collection of sacred and contemporary art, but the highlight is the display of brightly coloured cloth *bois*, or bulls, used in the festival of Bumba-meu-boi (see box, p.400). There's also a video of the festival permanently playing in the museum. Part of this collection is also housed in the Centro de Cultura Popular Domingos Vieira Filho, Rua do Giz 221, Praia Grande (Tues–Sat 9am–7pm). Back on Rua do Trapiche, at no. 273, is the **Museu de Artes Visuais** (daily 9am–7pm), a gallery that displays work by local artists.

Down at the other end of the Zona is the **Cafuá das Mercês**, the old slave market, which now houses the rather depleted collection of the **Museu do Negro**. Slaves who survived the journey across from West Africa were marched up here from the harbour and kept in the holding cells until they could be auctioned off in the small square outside. Nearby on Rua da Palma is the **Convento das Mercês**, an attractive spacious wooden building that houses a selection of presidential memorabilia belonging to one of Maranhão's most famous sons, the walrus-lookalike José Sarney. Despite having been a mediocre president, Sarney obviously benefits from having a sense of humour: many of the photographs and pictures on display mock him in one way or another.

One of São Luís's best museums lies outside the Zona. The **Museu de Arte Sacra**, Rua São João 500 (Tues–Fri 9am–6pm, Sat & Sun 2–6pm), houses some superb religious art from the seventeenth, eighteenth and nineteenth centuries. One of the outstanding pieces is a small wooden statue of St Paul embedded with incredibly lifelike glass eyes. There's also a statue of St John the Baptist with an incision in the neck: the space was used to hide jewels that were being smuggled out of the country.

The beaches

São Luís is blessed with a chain of excellent **beaches**, all of which can be reached by bus from the Terminal de Integração. The surf can be dangerous and people drown every month, so take care. It's also worth noting that swimming after sunset is not a good idea, as there are occasional attacks by sharks that are attracted by the kitchen waste dumped by ships offshore.

Ponta da Areia is the closest beach to the city centre, located by the ruins of the Forte São Marcos. Some 8km out of town, the dune beach of **Calhau** is larger and more scenic than Ponta da Areia: when the tide is out there is a lovely walk along the sands to Ponta da Areia, two hours' leisurely stroll west. After Calhau comes **Olho d'Agua**, equally fine, close to the dunes but a bit windy and well developed with houses and beach kiosks. Finally there's **Araçagi**, 19km out of town, the loveliest beach of all, an expansive stretch of sand that's also studded with bars and restaurants. It's served by hourly buses, but unless you rent a car you won't make it back the same day; there is a small hotel, though, the *Araçagi Praia* (Ⓣ98/3226-3299; ❹), which offers smart rooms.

Eating, drinking and nightlife

At weekends virtually the entire city moves out to the beaches, which are large enough to swallow up the masses without getting too crowded. You will quickly discover one of the delights of this coast: the **seafood**. The seas and rivers around here teem with life, most of it edible. The beach stalls do fried fish, the prawns are the size of large fingers, and whatever they don't cook you can buy fresh from a stream of vendors – juicily tender crabs, battered open with bits of wood, or freshly gathered oysters, dirt-cheap, sold by the bagful, helpfully opened for you and sprinkled with lime juice. One thing you won't find outside Maranhão is *cuxá* – a delicious dish made of crushed dried shrimp, garlic and the stewed leaves of two native plants.

Except during Bumba-meu-boi and Carnaval, São Luís is quieter than most Brazilian cities of its size. The largest concentration of nightspots is just over the bridge, in **São Francisco**, a little on the tacky side for the most part. On Wednesday nights, when the historic centre really lets its hair down, loud reggae music blasts out till dawn.

Eating out in town is rewarding, thanks to the abundant seafood. The best in São Luís is the *caldeirada de camarão* (shrimp stew) at the *Base do SENAC*, Rua de Nazare 242 (Ⓣ98/3232-6377), a piano bar located on the Praça Benedito Leite that's also a training ground for serious apprentice chefs. Good options in the Zona are *Antiguamente*, Rua da Estrela 220 (Ⓣ98/232-3964) and *La Papagaio*, more or less next door, both of which have varied menus, including local seafood dishes like *file de peixe ao molho de castanhas* (fish in a nut sauce) and pastas, too; the former also puts on decent rock music. There's also the excellent and traditional *Base do Edilson* restaurant buried deep in the *bairro* of Vila Bessa, at Rua Alencar Campos 31, but the short taxi journey from the centre is well worth the effort. Good *caldeirada* is also to be had at the *Base do Germano*, also a short taxi ride from the centre on Avenida Wenceslau Brás, in the *bairro* of Camboa. In the city centre, one of the better seafood restaurants is the *Base da Lenoca*, at Av. Dom Pedro II 181.

Along the coast

Travel in Maranhão outside São Luís is made difficult by a road system that is limited and – given the rains – often precarious. If you want to travel **along the coast** the most practical way is by boat, an option, however, that is not to be taken lightly as it's hard going: no schedules or creature comforts, and no one who speaks English. Don't do it unless you're healthy, a good sailor, not fussy about what you eat, have at least basic Portuguese and aren't too worried about time. But if you want to get completely off the beaten track, there's nothing to rival a sea journey.

The place to start is the **Estação Marítima** in São Luís, on the waterfront at the end of Praça Dom Pedro II. This is the local station for boats, which supply the nearby coastal villages and towns, take on passengers and cargo and wait for the tides. Brightly painted, these boats are built by artisans along the coast who still know how to put an ocean-going vessel together from timber.

There are sailings to the main coastal towns to the **west** about once a week. Pick a destination and ask at the booth in the Estação Marítima for the day and time: you either buy your passage there and then, or negotiate with the captain. The main coastal towns, as you head west, are Guimarães (half a day away), Turiaçu (two days) and Luis Domingues and Carutapera (three days). Take plenty of food and drink; *maranhenses* scratch limes and smell them to guard against seasickness, and it does seem to help.

If you wish to take an **organized tour** – often the simplest and fastest way to reach many of the places along this coast – it's best to go through one of the tour companies in São Luís. Simsol Turismo (Ⓣ98/3245-9655, or Ⓣ98/3349-0260 in Barreirinhas) organize two-day trips to the Parque Nacional dos Lençóis for around R$150. Rio Ave Turismo, based at Av. Dom Pedro II 221 (Ⓣ98/3221-0238) in Praia Grande offer a similar tour, as well as tours of the city both day and night, trips along the coast to Ribamar and to the historic city of Alcântra, one hour away by boat from São Luís. Labotur (Ⓣ98/3217-8346) run inexpensive ecotourism trips to the Ilha do Medo, usually leaving from the Ponta da Espera around 8am and returning around 5.30pm.

São José do Ribamar

Fortunately, not all the interesting places are difficult to get to. Easiest of all are the fishing towns on the island of São Luís: Raposa, a simple village on a beach, an hour away by bus from Praça Deodoro or Rua da Paz; and **SÃO JOSÉ DO RIBAMAR**, which you can reach on the bus marked "Ribamar" from the same stops, or from outside the *Athenas Palace Hotel*.

It's 32km to São José, about an hour's drive, a lovely route through thick palm forest and small hills. The bus deposits you in the small town centre, where straggling houses on a headland have sweeping views of a fine bay; it's easy to stay over, as there are several **pensões** in the centre. São José is an important fishing town, as well as being a centre of skilled boat-building by traditional methods – you can see the yards, with the half-finished ribs of surprisingly large boats, behind the houses running inland from the small landing quay and large beach. There's a very relaxing feel to the town. The people are friendly, the scenery splendid, and it's not difficult to while away a few days doing nothing in particular. There are some good **restaurants**, too: the *Ribamar*, serving mainly seafood, has a terrace looking out to the bay, and the rustic *barracas* on the waterfront are ideal spots to chat and watch the sunset from.

A lot of the **boats** that ply the coast both east and west drop in at São José, and it's a convenient place to begin a boat trip. Easiest places to head for, and with a fair degree of certainty that there'll be a boat back within a day or two, are Icatu, the mainland village on the other side of the bay, and Primeira Cruz on the east coast. From the latter, it's a short hop to the interior town of Humberto de Campos, where you can catch a bus back to São Luís.

Parque Nacional dos Lençóis

From Primeira Cruz, you can also continue to what is arguably one of the most beautiful sights in Brazil, the **Parque Nacional dos Lençóis**, a desert some 370km to the east of São Luís covering around 300 square kilometres. What makes it so special is that it is composed of hundreds of massive sand dunes that reach towering heights but are subject to prolonged rainfall. The result is that the dunes are sprinkled with literally hundreds of crystal-clear freshwater lagoons. To get there either continue from the small town of Primeira Cruz, or, direct from São Luís, catch the bus to Barreirinhas from the *rodoviária* (hours variable so check beforehand with MARATUR), which takes about eight hours to get there. If you wish to stay overnight here, there are some very modest *pousadas*, including the *Pousada Lins*, Av. Joaquim Sueiro de Carvalho 550 (☎98/3349-1203; ❷), which has a good restaurant; the *Pousada do Buruti*, Rua Inácio Lins (☎98/3349-1053; ❷), and the even cheaper *Pousada El Casarão*, Rua Inácio Neves 110 (☎98/3349-1078; ❷). From Barreirinhas, it's a three-hour journey down the Rio Preguiças to the dunes themselves. If you don't fancy organizing the trip for yourself then there are a couple of agencies in São Luís that will: Giltur, Rua do Giz 46, in the Zona (☎98/3232-6041), and Taguatur, Rua do Sol 141, inside the shopping centre (☎98/3231-4197 or 3232-0906), both of which organize trips by bus and boat or by plane. The overland trip takes three days and will set you back about R$225; the plane trip takes a day and costs about R$425. For further information on the *parque*, contact IBAMA, the national parks authority (☎98/3231-3010).

Across the bay: Alcântara

Set in a wonderful tropical landscape on the other side of the **bay of São Marcos** from São Luís, **ALCÂNTARA** is now no more than a poor village built around the ruins of what was once the richest town in northern Brazil.

São Luís had already eclipsed it by the end of the eighteenth century, and for the last two hundred years it has been left to moulder quietly away. The measure of its decline is that there are now no roads worthy of being called that going there; the only way is by sea from the Estação Marítima at the end of Praça Dom Pedro II in São Luís.

Alcântara is a ninety-minute chug across the bay, which can still sometimes get choppy enough to make you thankful you've arrived. The alternative is a large motorboat – the *Batevento* – which takes half the time but is twice the price R$30). The regular boat leaves at 7am, the motorboat around 9.30am. There's a fine view of ruins and the houses of the town as you arrive, strung out along a headland, the skyline dominated by imperial palms; you face a short walk uphill after you disembark. Most of the ruins you see are from the seventeenth century: Alcântara, founded in 1648, was the first capital of Maranhão and the main centre of the first stretch of coastline that the Portuguese converted to sugar plantations.

The main square, **Praça da Matriz**, gives you an idea of how grand it must have been in its heyday, surrounded on three sides by colonial mansions. In the centre of the square is a curious corroded stone post, erected in 1647, on which you can still see the carved arms of the Portuguese Crown: this is the *pelourinho*, a whipping post, set up to mark the king of Portugal's claim to the coast.

If you thought some of the buildings in the colonial zone of São Luís were in bad repair, Alcântara proves how much worse things can get, notwithstanding its more recent efforts at restoration. Very few of the oldest buildings have survived; for the most part only the facade and walls are standing, many with coats of arms still discernible. The roofs went generations ago and most have large trees growing out of them. On the main square is a small **museum**, in a restored mansion with a fine *azulejo* frontage, which has a good collection of artefacts and prints to give you an idea of what the place was once like. It doesn't keep regular visiting hours, but they will open it up for you if you ask nicely; they'll know where the key is at the *Hotel Pelourinho* (see below).

The ruins, the views, the beaches and the friendliness of the people combine to make Alcântara a very atmospheric place. Short **walks** or **canoe rides** in either direction take you to deserted **beaches** where there are rustic cafés and bars serving chilled beer. Better still are boat trips through the mangroves, where you will see *guarás*, birds resembling flamingoes except they are bright red instead of pink; against the green background they look extraordinary.

Practicalities

The last boat back to São Luís leaves daily at 4pm, so if you want to stay for more than eight hours you'll have to spend the night. The two **hotels** on Praça da Matriz are both good: *Pousada do Imperador* (❸), with spacious rooms and private baths, and the clean and comfortable *Hotel Pelourinho* (Ⓣ98/3337-1150; ❷). There's also the more expensive *Pousada do Modomo Régio*, Rua Grande 134 (Ⓣ98/3337-1197 or 3337-1575; ❹), which has a decent restaurant. The cheapest option is to string your **hammock** in a house: groups of children meet incoming boats looking for tourists for exactly that purpose, so finding somewhere is easy. The deal will include an evening meal and breakfast, simple but wholesome; just don't drink the water. The best **restaurant** in town is at *Hotel Pelourinho*, its home-brewed fruit liqueurs a speciality; try the refreshing guava (*goiaba*). Just off the main square there's a TELMA post, from where you can make **telephone calls**.

The interior

Travel in the **interior** of Maranhão is limited by the road system: there is only one highway out of São Luís, which forks east to Teresina and west to Belém (see p.421). Although asphalted, chunks of it often get washed away during the rainy season. You'll usually get through eventually – even if you have to push with the rest of the passengers – but things like timetables cease to have any meaning. The worst part of the road is the bit from São Luís to Santa Inês.

The **road to Belém** is now a lot better than it was, although the link southwest to Imperatriz can still be a bit dodgy. There's little to keep you in central Maranhão, although the journey is interesting: travel by day if you can. The area you pass through was first populated on a large scale thirty years ago and the towns, the largest en route being Bacabal and Santa Inês, are young but growing rapidly. By the time you get to Santa Inês you're in Amazônia, but don't expect to see any forest en route to Belém; most of it was cut down for cattle ranching twenty years ago.

Although there's nowhere worth getting off the bus, this final western stretch of Maranhão is fascinating. Inland, a **gold rush** has been going on since 1982. Many of the people getting on and off at the roadside villages past Santa Inês, especially at the town of Maracassumé, are *garimpeiros*, gold-miners. Just over the border with Pará you even get to see a gold camp, Cachoeira, where a village has developed around a gold strike; you can just about see the diggings from the road, but it's not advisable to get off for a closer look.

South to Imperatriz and Carolina

At Santa Inês a fork heads southwest to **IMPERATRIZ**, a mushrooming city on the Belém–Brasília highway: 280,000 people where as recently as twenty years ago there was only a small town of about 10,000. There's little reason to go to Imperatriz for its own sake. The town is teeming with people on the move, and even basic facilities have been swamped. The atmosphere here is made worse by the violent **land conflicts** in the region, and Imperatriz is where the gunmen hang out between contracts. However, it does lie en route to Brasília and, more immediately, **CAROLINA**, the only town in southern Maranhão of any conceivable interest to tourists. Situated on the banks of the Rio Tocantins, Carolina's attraction is that it lies in a region of spectacular waterfalls, the most famous being those at **Pedra Caída**, more than 30km out of town. If you're coming from São Luís, you should get the train as far as Imperatriz before changing to the bus for a four-hour ride to Carolina. There are a few **places to stay**, including the *Recanto Pedra Caída* (☎99/3731-1318; ❸), an atmospheric place right by the falls, and the *Pousada do Lajes* (☎99/3531-2348; ❸), which has a pool but no restaurant.

Travel details

Buses

Fortaleza to: João Pessoa (4 daily; 8hr); Natal (10 daily; 8hr); Salvador (1 daily; 21hr); São Luís (3 daily; 18hr).

João Pessoa to: Cabedelo (every 30min; 45min); Campina Grande (hourly; 2hr); Fortaleza (8 daily; 9hr); Juazeiro do Norte (2 daily; 10hr); Mossoró (several daily; 4hr); Penha (every 2hr; 45min).

Maceió to: Aracaju (6 daily; 5hr); Paulo Afonso (2 daily; 4hr); Penedo (6 daily; 2hr).

Natal to: Fortaleza (4 daily; 8hr); João Pessoa (10 daily; 3hr); Salvador (1 daily; 20hr).

Recife to: Amarelo (every 30min; 1hr); Aracaju (2

daily; 8hr); Belém (5 weekly; 35hr); Belo Horizonte (3 daily; 35hr); Brasília (3 daily; 48hr); Caruaru (at least hourly; 2hr); Fortaleza (6 daily; 12hr); Goiânia (6 daily; 2hr); João Pessoa (10 daily; 2hr); Maceió (20 daily; 4hr); Natal (20 daily; 4hr 30min); Petrolina (4 daily; 12hr); Porto de Galinhas (every 30min; 1hr); Rio (2 daily; 42hr); Salvador (6 daily; 13hr); São José da Coroa Grande (hourly; 1hr 30min); São Paulo (4 daily; 48hr).

Teresina to: Belém (1–2 daily; 24hr); Fortaleza (2 daily; 15hr); São Luís (several daily; 10hr).

Flights

João Pessoa, Natal, Maceió, Fortaleza and Recife are all connected by at least daily flights. Natal, Maceió, Fortaleza and Recife also have daily connections to Salvador.

5

The Amazon

VENEZUELA
GUYANA
SURINAME
FRENCH GUIANA
COLOMBIA
N
5
4
3
PERU
7
6
BOLIVIA
2
8
1
PARAGUAY
CHILE
9
ARGENTINA
0
1000 km
URUGUAY

CHAPTER 5 Highlights

* **Ver-o-Peso Market** Best visited in the early morning, Belém's traditional market is a great place to watch the local trade. See p.426
* **Borboletário Marcio Ayres** A magical hummingbird and butterfly reserve in Belém's newest park. See p.428
* **Alter do Chão** Close to Santarém, this beautiful bay boasts a Caribbean combination of white sand and turquoise water that flows from the river Tapajós See p.448
* **Teatro Amazonas** A full-blown European opera house in one of the least likely locations. See p.465
* **Amazon wildlife** Make sure to spend at least a few days in the jungle if you want to spot magnificent toucans, alligators and much more. See p.472
* **Jungle river trips** Take in the lush forest scenery, fascinating river settlements and beautiful sight of the river itself. See p.472
* **Madeira-Mamoré Museu Ferroviário** This fascinating railway museum in Porto Velho will appeal to casual visitors and railroad buffs alike. See p.495

△ Amazon wildlife

The Amazon

The Amazon is a vast forest – the largest on the planet – and a giant river system. It covers over half of Brazil and a large portion of South America. The forest extends into Brazil's neighbouring countries (Venezuela, Colombia, Peru and Bolivia), where the river itself begins life among thousands of different headwaters. In Brazil only the stretch between Manaus and Belém is actually known as the **Rio Amazonas**: above Manaus the river is called the **Rio Solimões** up to the border with Peru, where it once again becomes the Amazonas. The daily flow of the river is said to be enough to supply a city the size of New York with water for nearly ten years, and its power is such that the muddy Amazon waters stain the Atlantic a silty brown for over 200km out to sea. This was how the Spaniard Vicente Yanez Pinon, while sailing the Atlantic in search of El Dorado, first identified it: he was drawn to the mouth of the Amazon by the sweet freshness of the ocean or, as he called it, the Mar Dulce.

To many Indian tribes, the Amazon is a gigantic mythical anaconda, source of life and death. In its upper reaches, the Rio Solimões from Peru to Manaus, it is a muddy light brown, but at Manaus it meets the darker flow of the Rio Negro and the two mingle together at the famous "meeting of the waters" to form the Rio Amazonas. There are something like 80,000 square kilometres of **navigable river** in the Amazon system, and the Amazon itself can take ocean-going vessels virtually clean across South America, from the Atlantic coast to Iquitos in Peru. Even at the Óbidos narrows, the only topographical obstruction between the Andes and the Atlantic, the river is almost 2km wide and for most of its length it is far broader – by the time it reaches the ocean the river's gaping mouth stretches further apart than London and Paris.

Ecology and development

The Amazon is far more than just a river. Its catchment basin contains, at any one moment, over one-fifth of all the world's fresh water, and the **rainforest** it sustains, which is a vitally important cog in the planet's biosphere controls, covers an area of over six million square kilometres, stretching almost right across the continent. There are over a thousand tributaries (several larger than the Mississippi), whose combined energy potential is estimated at over 100,000 megawatts daily (an endlessly renewable supply equivalent to five million barrels of oil a day). Eletronorte, the region's electricity supply company, today produces around 20,000 megawatts from Amazonian hydroelectric power.

Although in 1639 Pedro Teixeira travelled 2000 miles up the Amazon and claimed all the land east of Ecuador for Portugal, the Portuguese really gained control of the Brazilian Amazon, in a political sense, through the Treaty of

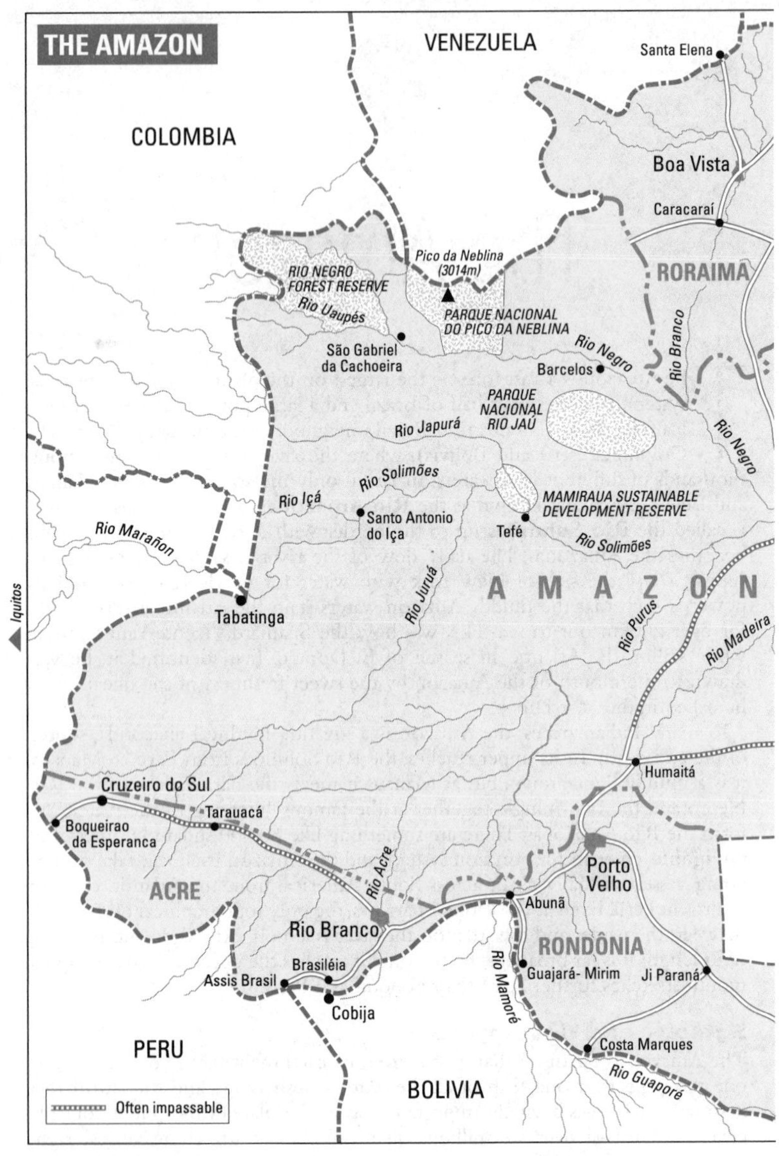

Madrid in 1750. Four years later, Governor Mendonça Furtado was appointed Boundary Commissioner and began his tour of inspection in the Amazon. He saw the prosperity of the Carmelite missions on the Rio Negro and initiated the Directorate System of controlling "official" Indian villages that were essentially labour camps; witnessing how effective the missionaries had been in manipulating native workers, the governor was determined to do the same. Some Indians,

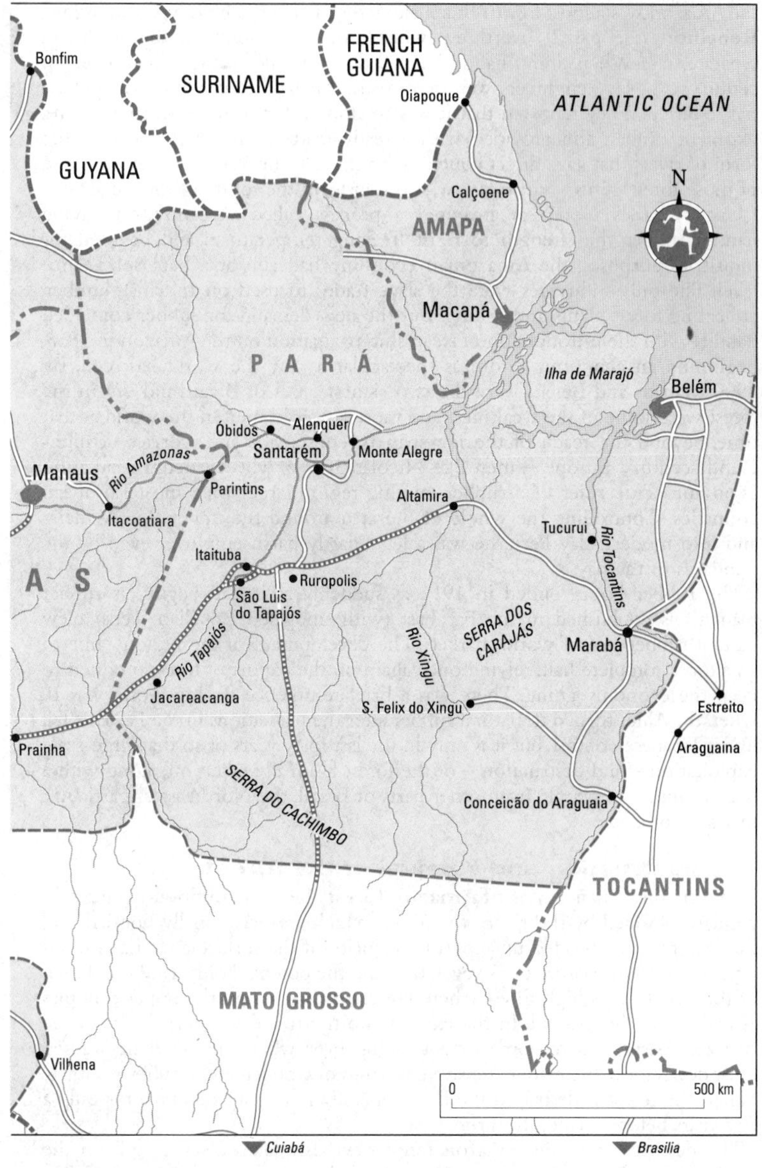

remaining free in the regions upstream on the major tributaries, tended to gather in villages at portage points such as difficult rapids where they acted as guides and muscle-power for traders. Others retreated deeper into the forest.

The region was only integrated fully into the Brazilian political scene after Independence in 1822, and even then it remained safer and quicker to sail from Rio de Janeiro to Lisbon than to Manaus. Within a few years of Independence the Amazon was almost lost to Brazil altogether when the bloody **Cabanagem Rebellion** (see p.422) overthrew white rule and attempted to establish a separate state. When things had quietened down a little, in the mid-nineteenth century, US Navy engineers were sent to the Amazon to check out its potential resources. They reported that it was wealthy in forest gums, fruits, nuts and excellent timber, and provided with a ready-made transport network in the form of rivers that gave direct contact with the Atlantic. Within a few years one of those forest gums – **rubber** – was to transform the future of the Amazon.

Until Charles Goodyear invented a process called vulcanization, giving natural rubber the strength to resist freezing temperatures and be used for industrial purposes, the Amazonian economy had run at a bare subsistence level. The only industries were the slave trade (focused on Indians), lumber, collecting forest plants and fishing. But the new demand for rubber coincided handily with the introduction of steamship navigation on the Amazon in 1858, beginning an economic boom as spectacular as any the world has seen. By 1900 Manaus and Belém were the two richest cities of Brazil, and out in the forest were some of the wealthiest and most powerful men in the world at that time, beyond the reach of the newspapers, conscience and worries of nineteenth-century Europe – men like Nicolas Suárez, who earned a reputation as an autocratic ruler of a rubber-tapping region larger than most European countries. Controlling the whole of the area around the upper Rio Madeira and into modern-day Peru, he was a legendarily harsh employer even by the standards of the day.

The rubber boom ended in 1911 as suddenly as it had begun, as rubber plantations established in the Far East (with smuggled Brazilian seeds) blew natural rubber out of world markets. The development of the region came to an almost complete halt, relying once again on the export of forest products to keep the economy going. There was a brief resurgence during World War II, when the Allies turned to natural rubber after the plantations in the Far East fell under Japanese control, but it is only in the last forty years or so that large-scale exploitation – and destruction – of the forest has really taken off, along with a massive influx of people from other parts of Brazil, the Northeast in particular, in search of land.

The destruction and survival of the forest

There are three main **types of Amazon forest**: the *várzea* or flood-plain zones, regularly flooded by the rivers; the *igapós*, which are occasionally flooded; and the *terra firme*, unflooded uplands, the majority of the surface area. Each forest type differs in the nature of its vegetation and the potential of its land use. Much of the *terra firme* is high forest where life exists as much in the upper canopies as it does on the ground. In the extreme northern and southern limits of the Amazon Basin, and to some extent taking over where mankind has caused most devastation, there are extensive coverings of wooded and scrubby savannas. When the forest is destroyed the land generally remains productive for only a few years before turning to scrub.

The destruction of the Amazon forest obviously takes a severe toll on the area's unique **flora and fauna**. There are believed to be as many as 15,000 animal species in the Amazon – thousands of which have still to be identified – and untold numbers of so far unclassified plants. Since they remain unknown, it is impossible to say quite what damage the destruction of the rainforest is doing, but there can be no doubt that many animal and plant species will be lost before anyone has had a chance to study them. The loss of this gene pool – with its potential use for medicines, foods and other unknown purposes – is serious; perhaps only the indigenous people of the forests will really know what has been lost – if they survive.

The Brazilian riposte, of course, is that the Western nations have no right to occupy any moral high ground, or to stand in the way of what they see as the essential economic development of their country. And they generally further add that the area being lost is insignificant compared to what survives. For all the damage to the ecology and the peoples of the Amazon, it is hard, however, to argue that Brazil should be denied the right to utilize its mineral and natural resources by people who have already exploited so much of the rest of the world.

The deforestation of the Amazon reached a peak in the late 1980s; large-scale ranching was mainly to blame, along with the huge volume of small-scale subsistence and cash-crop farming. In the following decade the destruction continued but at a slower pace. However, now there is once again mounting stress on the Amazon forest, this time from agribusiness companies producing beef and grains, especially soya. Ironically, the next Amazon boom will probably be biofuels – although reducing carbon emissions in general, the expansion of sugarcane into the Amazon may well drive deforestation in the future.

There are hopeful signs, however. People are increasingly discovering that in many areas cultivation – particularly cattle ranching – is not an efficient way to use the jungle, and that the productivity of the land decreases rapidly after the first few years. Scientists are just beginning to demonstrate (and developers to accept) that the environmental services provided by standing forests are in the long run more profitable than cleared land. Another good sign is the growth of interest, among tourists and Brazilians alike, in **ecotourism**. This pursuit, properly managed, brings money into the region and provides employment for its inhabitants, through an industry that conserves rather than exploits the natural environment. For more on the Amazon environment see p.810.

Getting around the Amazon

Most people who visit Brazil will, at some time or other, have dreamt about taking a **boat up the Amazon** (see box pp.418–419). This is not hard to do, though it's not as comfortable or easy going as daydreams might have made it seem. Given the food on some boats, the trip can be tough on the stomach, and you'll need meditative patience or a botanical degree to appreciate the subtle changes in the forest scene on the often-distant riverbanks. But as many boats have a bar on their top decks, most passengers, whether Zen adepts or not, make a great time of it.

The classic journey is the five or six days from **Belém**, the largest city in the Amazon and its most interesting urban destination, to **Manaus** in the heart of the jungle – and perhaps on from there on a wooden river boat to Iquitos in Peru via Tabatinga on the Brazilian frontier. But sticking only to the main channel of the Amazon is not the way to see the jungle or its wildlife: for that you'll want to take trips on smaller boats up smaller streams, an option that is particularly rewarding in the west where the rivers aren't quite so wide.

Thirty years ago river travel was virtually the only means of getting around the region, but in the 1960s the **Transamazônica** – Highway BR-230 – was constructed, cutting right across the south of Amazônia and linking the Atlantic coast (via the Belém–Brasília highway) with the Peruvian border at Brazil's western extremity. It remains an extraordinary piece of engineering, but is now increasingly bedraggled. Lack of money to pay for the stupendous amount of

River journeys

Any journey up the Rio Amazonas is a serious affair. The river is big and powerful and the boats, in general, are relatively small, top-heavy-looking wooden vessels on two or three levels. As far as **spotting wildlife** goes, there's very little chance of seeing much more than a small range of tropical forest birds – mostly vultures around the refuse tips of the ports en route – and the occasional river dolphin, although your chances increase the smaller the craft you're travelling on, as going upriver the smaller boats tend to hug the riverbanks, bringing the spectacle much closer. Going downstream, however, large and small boats alike tend to cruise with the mid-stream currents, taking advantage of the added power they provide. Whichever boat you travel with, the river is nevertheless a beautiful sight and many of the settlements you pass or moor in are fascinating.

It's important to **prepare** properly for an Amazon river trip if you want to ensure your comfort and health. The most essential item is a **hammock**, which can be bought cheaply (from about US$8) in the stores and markets of Manaus, Santarém or Belém, plus two stout pieces of rope to hang it from – hooks are not always the right interval apart for your size of hammock. Loose **clothing** is OK during daylight hours but at night you'll need some warmer garments and long sleeves against the chill and the insects. A **blanket** and some **insect repellent** are also recommended. Enough **drink** (large containers of mineral water are the best option, available in the bigger towns) and extra **food** – cookies, fruit and the odd tin – to keep you happy for the duration of the voyage may also be a good idea. Virtually all boats now provide mineral water, and the food, included in the price, has improved on most vessels, but a lot of people still get literally sick of the rice, meat and beans served on board, which is, of course, usually cooked in river water. If all else fails, you can always buy extra provisions in the small ports the boats visit. There are toilets on all boats, though even on the best they can get filthy within a few hours of leaving port. Again, there are exceptions, but it's advisable to take your own roll of **toilet paper** just in case. **Yellow fever inoculation** checks are common on boats leaving Belém to travel upriver, and for travellers unfortunate enough not to have a valid certificate of vaccination, you risk having a compulsory injection.

There are a few things to bear in mind when choosing **which boat** to travel with, the most important being the size and degree of comfort. The size affects the length of the journey: most small wooden boats take up to seven days to cover Belém to

△ Taking a boat along the Amazon

Manaus, and the larger vessels generally make the same journey in five to six days (four to five days downriver). See the "Listings" section for Belém, Santarém and Manaus for more on boat operators.

Better value, and usually more interesting in the degree of contact it affords among tourists, the crew and locals, is the option of taking a **wooden river boat** carrying both cargo and passengers. There are plenty of these along the waterfront in all the main ports, and it's simply a matter of going down there and establishing which ones are getting ready to go to wherever you are heading, or else enquiring at the ticket offices; these vessels are essentially water-borne buses and stop at most towns along the way. You'll share a deck with scores of other travellers, mostly locals or other Brazilians, which will almost certainly ensure that the journey never becomes too monotonous. The most organized of the wooden river boats are the larger **three-deck vessels**, on which the Belém–Manaus trip costs $70 for hammock space (US$50 downriver); this is negotiable if you're really stuck for cash, and will often come with a small discount if you buy your tickets two or more days before departure. The smaller **two-deck boats** are cosier, but often only cover shorter legs of the river. This is fine if you don't mind spending a day or two waiting for your next connection to load up. All of these wooden vessels tend to let passengers stay aboard a night or two before departure and after arrival, which saves on hotel costs.

There's room for debate about whether hammock space is a better bet than a **cabin** (*camarote*; currently around US$110 upriver), of which there are usually only a few. Though the cabins can be unbearably hot and stuffy during the day, they do offer security for your baggage, as well as some privacy (the cabins are shared, however, with either two or four bunks in each) and, in most cases, your own toilet (which can be a blessing, especially if you're not very well). The hammock areas get extremely crowded, so arrive early and establish your position: the best spots are near the front or the sides for the cooling breezes (it doesn't really matter which side, as the boat will alternate quite freely from one bank of the river to the other), though the bow of the boat can get rather chilly if the weather conditions turn a bit stormy. If it really gets unbearably crowded, you can always take your chances by slinging your hammock on the lower deck with the crew, though you'll also have to share your space with cargo and throbbing engine noise.

maintenance the network needed has now made much of it impassable. West of Altamira it has practically ceased to exist, apart from the Porto Velho–Rio Branco run and odd stretches where local communities find the road useful and maintain it. The same fate has met other highways like the Santarém–Cuiabá and the Porto Velho–Manaus, on which great hopes were once pinned. With the exception of the Belém–Brasília, Cuiabá–Rio Branco and the Manaus–Boa Vista highway corridors, transport in the Amazon has sensibly reverted to rivers. Access to what remains of the Transamazônica from Belém or Brasília is via Estreito, the settlement at the junction where the BR-230 turns west off the old north–south highway, the BR-153/BR-010.

One thing to bear in mind while travelling is that there are three **time zones** in the Amazon region. Belém and eastern Pará are on the same time as the rest of the coast, except from October to February when Bahia and the states of the Southeast and the South switch to summer time, leaving Belém an hour behind. At the Rio Xingu, about halfway west across Pará, the clocks go back an hour to Manaus time. Tabatinga, Rio Branco and Acre, in the extreme west of the Amazon, are another hour behind again.

Eastern Amazônia

Politically divided between the states of Pará and Amapá, the eastern Amazon is essentially a vast area of forest and savanna plains centred on the final seven hundred miles or so of the giant river's course. **Belém**, an Atlantic port near the mouth of the estuary which has undergone something of an urban renaissance in recent years, is the elegant capital of Pará and a worthwhile place to spend some time. The city overlooks the river and the vast **Ilha de Marajó**, a marshy island in the estuary given over mainly to cattle farming, but with a couple of good beaches.

Pará has always been a relatively productive region. In the late eighteenth century it was an important source of rice (allowing Portugal to be "self-sufficient" in the commodity), and it also exported cacao and, later, rubber. Sugar and cotton plantations along the coast account for the African influence you see traces of among the people and food of the eastern Amazon. Very little of the wealth, however, ever reached beyond a small elite, and falling prices of local commodities on the world markets have periodically produced severe hardship. Today, the state is booming once again, largely thanks to vast mining and hydroelectric projects in the south and west of the state. The landscape of southern Pará, below **Marabá** and the Tocantins-Araguaia rivers, is essentially a scrubby savanna known locally as *cerrado*: traditionally the home of the *Gê*-speaking Indians, it forms the major part of the central Brazilian plateau or shield. Over the last twenty years some of the most controversial developments in the Amazon have been taking place here.

Amapá, a small state on the northern bank of the Amazon opposite Belém, is a fascinating place in its own right. A poor and little-visited area, it nevertheless offers the opportunity of an adventurous overland route to French Guiana and on into Suriname, Guyana and Venezuela – or even back to Europe via a regular Air France flight between Cayenne, capital of French Guiana, and Paris.

Apart from Belém and the area around it, the most interesting section of the eastern Amazon is the western part of Pará state, where the regional centre is **Santarém** and the neighbouring beach village of **Alter do Chão** is one of the most beautiful spots in the Amazon. **Connections** in the region are pretty straightforward, in that you have very few choices. The main throughway between Belém and Manaus is still the Amazon, with stops at **Monte Alegre**, set amidst a stunning landscape of floodplains and flat-topped mesas housing some of South America's most important archeological sites, Santarém, at the junction of the Amazon with the most beautiful of its tributaries, the turquoise Tapajós river, and the less enticing **Óbidos**. As far as roads go, there are good highways south from Belém towards Brasília (the BR-010) and east into the state of Maranhão (the BR-316). Across the river on the north bank of the Amazon there is just one road from **Macapá**, the capital of Amapá state, towards the border with French Guiana. It is only asphalted for the first third of its length and is often impassable in the rainy season. The BR-010 crosses the powerful Rio Tocantins near Estreito (in Maranhão) close to the start of the **Transamazônica highway**. If you're coming from the south, connections with westbound buses and other traffic are best made at Araguaina (in Tocantins) where there's a small *rodoviária* and several hotels. The first stop on the Transamazônica within Pará is **Marabá**, some 460km (12hr) by bus from Belém. Continuing from here, the

Transamazônica reaches **Altamira**, on the navigable Rio Xingu, a small, relatively new city over 300km west of Marabá. With a population that's grown from 15,000 in 1970 to over 130,000 today, Altamira is at the centre of an area of rapidly vanishing jungle. Beyond here the Transamazônica becomes impassable. The Transamazônica highway and southern Pará are, it must be said, among the least attractive and most desperate places to visit in Brazil. The poverty and sheer ugliness of the region after four decades of deforestation are the best counter-arguments to the common Brazilian claim that clearing the forest is necessary for development. Pigs will fly before development comes to southern Pará on this evidence.

Belém

Although less well-known than Manaus, **BELÉM**, the only city in the Amazon that is truly old, has much more to offer: an unspoilt colonial centre, one of Brazil's most distinctive cuisines, a stunning collection of architectural survivals from the rubber boom and, to cap it all, an **urban revitalization** over the last decade that has seen new parks, imaginatively restored historic buildings and leisure complexes transform its centre and riverfront into easily the most attractive city for tourism in the Amazon.

Founded just a couple of decades later than the colonial cities of the Northeast coast, Belém at its heart looks very much like them, with the obligatory Portuguese fort, cathedral square and governor's palace. Strategically placed on the Amazon river estuary commanding the main channel, the city was settled by the Portuguese in 1616. Its original role was to protect the river mouth and establish the Portuguese claim to the region, but it rapidly became an Indian slaving port and a source of cacao, timber and spices gathered from the forests inland. Such was the devastation of the local population, however, that by the mid-eighteenth century a royal decree was issued in Portugal to encourage its growth: every white man who married an Indian woman would receive "one axe, two scissors, some cloth, clothes, two cows and two bushels of seed".

Despite the decree, Belém was deep in decline before the end of the century, precipitated by a shrinking labour force and, in the 1780s, the threat of attack by a large contingent of Munduruku Indians. In the nineteenth century it sank still further, as the centre of the nation's bloodiest rebellion (see box, p.422), before the town experienced an extraordinary revival as the most prosperous beneficiary of the Amazon rubber boom. By the turn of the twentieth century Belém was a very rich city, accounting for close to half of all Brazil's rubber exports. As a result of the boom, thousands moved into Belém from all over the country, and the few decades of prosperity left an indelible architectural mark on the city. Much of the proceeds were invested in houses and palaces, most of which still survive (unlike in Manaus) and make Belém one of Brazil's top cities to walk around, despite the heat. After the rubber market crashed just before World War I the city entered a long decline, but it kept afloat, just about, on the back of Brazil nuts and the timber industry until the highways and development projects from the 1960s on turned it into the city it is today.

Belém remains the economic centre of the North and the Amazon's main port. The wealth generated by the rubber boom is most evident in the downtown area, where elegant central avenues converge on two luxuriant squares: **Praça da República** and **Praça Batista Campos.** These border the old heart of the city, the harbour and colonial centre, the focus of intensive revitalization

The Cabanagem Rebellion

The **Cabanagem Rebellion** ravaged the region around Belém for sixteen months between January 1835 and May 1836, in the uncertain years following Independence and the abdication of Pedro I. What started as a power struggle among Brazil's new rulers rapidly became a revolt of the poor against racial injustice: the *cabanos* were mostly black and Indian or mixed-blood settlers who lived in relative poverty in *cabaña* huts on the flood plains and riverbanks around Belém and the lower Amazon riverbanks. Following years of unrest, the pent-up hatred of generations burst in August 1835. After days of bloody fighting, the survivors of the Belém authorities fled, leaving the *cabanos* in control. In the area around the city many sugar mills and *fazendas* were destroyed, their white owners being put to death. Bands of rebels roamed throughout the region, and in most settlements their arrival was greeted by the non-white population's spontaneously joining their ranks, looting and killing. The authorities described the rebellion as "a ghastly revolution in which barbarism seemed about to devour all existing civilization in one single gulp".

The rebellion was doomed almost from the start, however. Although the leaders attempted to form some kind of revolutionary government, they never had any real programme, nor did they succeed in controlling their own followers. A British ship became embroiled in the rebellion in October 1835, when it arrived unwittingly with a cargo of arms that had been ordered by the authorities before their hasty departure a couple of months previously. The crew were killed and their cargo was confiscated. Five months later, a British naval force arrived demanding compensation from the rebels for the killings and the lost cargo. The leader of the *cabanos*, Eduardo Angelim, met the British captain and refused any sort of compromise; British trade was now threatened, and the fleet commenced a blockade of the fledgling revolutionary state. Meanwhile, British troops from the South prepared to fight back, and in May 1836 the rebels were driven from Belém by a force of 2500 soldiers under the command of Francisco d'Andrea. Mopping-up operations continued for years, and by the time the Cabanagem Rebellion was completely over and all isolated pockets of armed resistance had been eradicated, some 30,000 people are estimated to have died – almost a third of the region's population at that time.

efforts in recent years, which have transformed the riverfront into the Amazon's most attractive and interesting urban space.

But the first thing visitors will notice is the heat and humidity. Always hot and often wet too, the **climate** takes some getting used to by day (at night, however, it's always pleasant). The rain, as you would expect, is torrential, and the **rainy season** runs from January to May. Fortunately it falls as showers rather than persistent rain, and typically the skies clear after an hour or so of even the most intense downpour. The central zone of the city is lined by **mango trees**, over a century old and proportionately massive, which provide shade and protection from the broiling sun. When strolling around, just be sure to do it slowly, and remember that mangoes ripen in October – keep half an eye and ear out for falling fruit or you're in for a lump on your head and some intensive shampooing.

Arrival, orientation and information

Belém's **rodoviária** is situated some 2km from the centre at the start of Avenida Almirante Barroso, the only road out of town – the city is hemmed in by rivers in every other direction. Any bus from the stops opposite the entrance to the *rodoviária* will take you downtown. If you want Praça da República, take one with "P.Vargas" on its route card; for the port area look for "Ver-o-Peso". There

BELÉM

Airport

1&2 ▲ 3, 4, 5, 6&7 ▲ A, Rodoviária, Bosque Rodrigo Alves, Parque Ambiental de Belém, Parque da Residencia, Icoaraçi & Mosqueiro ▲

C, 8, 9, 10, ▶ Basilica & Museu Paraense Emílio Goeldi

▶ F&11

▶ 12 & Plaça Batista Campos

▶ Iguatemi Mall & São José Liberto

▶ M, 15 & 16

NAZARÉS B

BENJAMIN CONSTANT
GEN MAGALHAES
REDUTO
28 DE SETEMBRO
SENADOR MANUEL BARATA
ARISTIDES LOBO
TIRADENTES
D
E
AV GOVERNADOR MALCHER
AV NAZARE
AVENIDA MARECHAL HERMES
AVENIDA PRESIDENTE PIEDADE
Paratur
AVENIDA ASSIS VASCONCELOS
Main Docks
PRAÇA MAESTRO WALDEMAR HENRIQUE
Boats to Manaus & Ilha do Marajó
GASPAR VIANA
Captain of the Port
Supermarket
ENASA Office
COMÉRCIO
G
13
PRAÇA DA REPUBLICA
Teatro da Paz
Companhia Docas do Pará
I
R PRESIDENTE VARGAS
H
Varig Office
J
K
SILVA SANTOS
RUFINO
Banco do Brasil
VASP
Estação das Docas
AVENIDA 15 DE NOVEMBRO
AV CASTILHOS FRANCA
SANTO ANTONIO
O. DE ALMEIDA
A. LOBO
Telephones
RIACHUELO CRUZ
GEN GURJAO
CARLOS GOMES
28 DE SETEMBRO
Igreja das Mercês
L
FRUTUOSO GUIMARAES
TAMANDARE GAMA ABREU
CAMPOS SALES
Amazon Star Turismo
Telepura
SENADOR MANUEL
TRAVESSA PADRE EUTIQUIO
PRAÇA MARINHO
SAO PEDRO
JOAO ALFREDO
Mercado Municipal
7 DE SETEMBRO
DE BRAGANCA
AV SAO FRANCISCO
JOÃO DIOGO
BARATA
13 DE MAIO
Rio Amazonas
Ver o Peso Market
DE BRAGANCA
AVENIDA PORTUGAL
Palácio Antônio Lemos
16 DE NOVEMBRO
Old Port
PEDRO RAIOL
PRAÇA DOM PEDRO
POMBAL
ANGELO CUSTODIO
Forte do Castelo
Igreja Santo Alexandre
Palácio Lauro Sodré
JOAQUIM TAVORA
R. SANTOS
P. ALBUQUERQUE
Catedral da Sé
PRAÇA DA SÉ
DOUTOR MALCHER
Casa das Onze Janelas
14
CIUADE VELHA
Largo do Carmo
Porto do Sal
Igreja Nossa Senhora do Carmo
DOUTOR ASSIS
Mangal das Garças

0 400 m

ACCOMMODATION	
Beira-Rio	M
Belém Hilton	K
Central	I
Equatorial Palace	F
Excelsior Grão-Pará	J
Ferrador	H
Machado	E
Manacá	C
Massilia	D
Regente	B
Sagres	A
Vidonho's	G
Vitória Régia	L

RESTAURANTS	
Armazém do Santo Antônio	10
Café Sol	6
Cantina Italiana	11
Cheiro Verde	9
Hikari Sushi	12
Lá em Casa	13
Palafita	14
Pomme D'Or	8
Saldosa Maloca	15
Trapiche	16
Xicara da Silva	3

BARS & CLUBS	
Cachaçaria Agua Doce	5
Casablanca	2
Iguana	1
Jungle	7
Lord Lion	4

are good facilities and services at the *rodoviária*, including a Parátur information office (not always open, even when it's meant to be).

If you're coming by scheduled airline, you'll arrive at Belém **airport**, 15km out of town. Tourist information is available here (see below) and there's the usual system of co-op taxis opposite the arrivals hall, for which you buy a ticket at the kiosk, but this is an expensive way of getting into town (R$30 for a 15min ride). Turn left coming out of arrivals to the far end of the terminal where you'll find the taxi stand for ordinary city cabs, which are half the price. Or you can take the "Marex Arsenal" bus from the airport to the *rodoviária* and continue into town from there, although this is definitely not recommended if you have luggage. **Larger riverboats** dock at the port near the town centre, from where you can walk or take a local bus up Avenida Presidente Vargas (not recommended if you have luggage or if it's late at night), or catch a taxi. **Smaller riverboats** come in at the Porto de Sal, in the old colonial area, also near the centre. (For information on boat services see p.447.) Your best option is to take a taxi to a hotel, which will be around R$10 – at night it is unsafe to do anything else.

Avenida Presidente Vargas is the modern town's main axis, running from the Praça da República and the landmark Teatro da Paz right to the riverfront. A short walk down Avenida Serzedelo Correa takes you to Praça Batista Campos, another central landmark. Buses coming into Belém's centre from the airport and *rodoviária* travel down the dock road before turning up Vargas. Most of the hotels are along Presidente Vargas, or just off it. **Tourist information** (patchy at best in Belém) is officially available from Parátur offices downtown at the Feira de Artesanato do Estado on Praça Maestro Waldemar Henrique, close to the junction of Presidente Vargas with the docks, but your best bet are the kiosks at the airport and bus station. The staff at Parátur are charming and anxious to help, but have little available other than pamphlets. City maps can be bought cheaply from the newspaper kiosks along Presidente Vargas, or in the foyer of the *Hilton* hotel, looming unmistakably opposite the Teatro do Paz.

Belém is not especially dangerous, but the usual cautions apply regarding **security**. Be careful about walking the narrow streets off Presidente Vargas around Praça da República at night, as it's been a red-light district for centuries. The *Bar do Parque* on the Praça next to the Teatro da Paz is one of the loveliest places to sit and drink a beer in the city, but it's unfortunately infested by pimps, prostitutes and various low-lifes drawn like a magnet by the hope of snaring a rich tourist from the *Hilton* across the road. The whole area around Ver-o-Peso market is an essential sight, but keep a sharp eye on your pockets and be careful about cameras and bags. The riverfront street leading down from the fort to the harbour is picturesque but to be avoided at night and treated with caution even in daylight. Though bustling during the week, the whole central area empties at weekends, when you should not stray off the main streets.

There is one confusing thing about the city that's important to understand. The main riverfront focus for nightlife is "Estação das Docas". You might want to get a boat from the docks, in which case you need to head for "as docas". The area around Avenida Souza Franco is also a likely destination, thanks to its bars and restaurants. This region is known as "Docas", without the definite article, which creates immense potential for confusion with taxi drivers.

Accommodation

There are plenty of **hotels** in Belém, many of them overpriced, but there is adequate accommodation for every budget. Most of the more expensive and mid-priced hotels are located on Avenida Presidente Vargas; more basic hotels are in the narrow streets just off Vargas.

Beira-Rio Av. Bernardo Sayão 4804 ⓣ91/3249-7111. Located in the *bairro* of Guamá and reachable by bus (Guamá or UFPA) or taxi from the centre. There are great views out across the river as well as an excellent riverside restaurant, but it's a bit remote and the neighbourhood is grim; don't walk around it. The boat across to the *Saldosa Maloca* restaurant is a big plus, however. ❹

Belém Hilton Av. Presidente Vargas 882 ⓣ91/4006-7000, ⓦwww.amazon.com.br/hilton. Belém's best and most expensive hotel, which dominates the Praça da República, offers luxurious rooms with excellent air conditioning; some have superb views across the cityscape, river and forests. Radical price reductions are occasionally available at slack times of year. ❻

Central Av. Presidente Vargas 290 ⓣ91/3241-4800. Popular with budget travellers but rundown and dangerous, as a guest was murdered in his room in 2005. If you need a cheap hotel, go for *Ferrador*, *Vitória Régia* or *Vidonho*'s instead.

Excelsior Grão-Pará Av. Presidente Vargas 718, ⓣ91/3242-9044. This is the best deal in town: R$60 gets you a basic but a/c room in an efficient, modernized hotel in a central downtown location. Highly recommended. ❸

Equatorial Palace Av. Bras de Aguiar 621 ⓣ91/3241-2000. Less expensive and with a more cosy ambience than the international-flavoured *Hilton*, this hotel, while still overpriced, has pleasant enough rooms and a small rooftop pool with a good view. ❺

Ferrador Rua Ó de Almeida 476 ⓣ91/3241-5999. Reasonable and very central hotel that caters mainly to a Brazilian business clientele; guest rooms are modern. *Ferrador* shares its building with *Hotel Vidonho's* (ⓣ91/3242-3109) also good value. ❸

Machado Rua Henrique Gurjão (next to Massilia) ⓣ91/4008 9800. A new, functional hotel just off Praça da República that's aimed at business travellers. Through the rooms are rather lacking in character, they're very efficient (featuring cable and broadband, for example), and are good value compared to others in this price range. ❺

Manacá Travessa Quintino Bocaiuva, ⓣ91/3223-3335. This pleasant, quiet, family hotel is in a downtown area that's still dominated by rubber-boom buildings. Offers all modern conveniences. ❹

Massilia Rua Henrique Gurjão 326, ⓣ91/3222-2834. Belém's best medium-price option has a quiet central location, a small pool and a restaurant that's worth eating in whether you stay here or not. The front desk will arrange tours in the French owner's boat for cheaper than what most local tour agencies charge. Excellent value. ❹

Regente Av. Gov. José Malcher 485 ⓣ91/3241-1222 or 3241-1333. Musty and overpriced, but the central location is good. ❺

Sagres Av. Gov. José Malcher 2927 ⓣ91/3266-2222. This hotel near the *rodoviária* has a decent bar, a sauna and a pool. While the restaurant isn't worth bothering with outside of breakfast, the rooms and the views from them are fine, though overpriced. ❹

Vidonho's Rua Ó de Almeida 476 ⓣ91/3242-1444, ⓕ3224-7499. Good-value, modern hotel, with a/c in all rooms and good showers. Well located, if a bit noisy, just off the Av. Presidente Vargas. ❸

Vitória Régia Rua Frutuoso Guimarães 260 ⓣ & ⓕ91/3212-3301, 3212-3628, ⓔh.v.r@uol.com.br. A cheap, clean and friendly place with a pleasant staff. R$30 gets you a room with a fan, R$40 gets you a/c; there's a 10 percent discount if you pay cash in advance. Internet access is available in the lobby, but the connection is none too reliable. ❷

The City

The **Praça da República**, an attractive cross between a square and a park with plenty of trees affording valuable shade, is the best place from which to get your bearings and start a walking tour of Belém's downtown and riverfront attractions. At its heart is the most obvious sign of Belém's rubber fortunes: the **Teatro da Paz**. In business since 1878 and recently restored, it's open for visits (Mon–Fri 9am–6pm; free). Although not as spectacular as the Manaus opera house, it is still a wonderful example of early rubber-boom architecture and is very much a working theatre, regularly used for plays, operas and recitals. A concert there is an unforgettable experience and a visit to the box office is always in order; tickets are subsidized to the hilt and very cheap. Dress codes are informal and the air conditioning is efficient; if there is an interval, head for the first-floor terrace and one of the best night-time views the city has to offer.

The markets and Estação das Docas

Heading down Presidente Vargas towards the river, an old part of town lies off to the left, full of crumbling Portuguese colonial mansions and churches. This is a pleasant area to wander during business hours, and walking parallel to the river will bring you to the old harbour – always crowded with riverboats and overlooked on one side by an unmistakably Portuguese fort and on the other by one of the most interesting traditional markets in all of South America, **Ver-o-Peso.** An essential stop, Ver-o-Peso ("see the weight") is reason enough in itself to visit Belém. There are sections devoted to fish, aromatic oils, medicinal plants and herbs and an expanding sector selling locally produced craft goods.

The market is at its most interesting from around 4am, when the boats from the interior start coming in with the two Pará products the city needs above all else: fish and *açaí,* a palm fruit from which one brews a purple mush that is a staple of Amazonian cuisine, and which no self-respecting *paraense* can get through the day without drinking straight, eating mixed with a variety of ingredients or freezing and consuming as ice cream. The fish is either sold right there on the dockside or hauled into the cast-iron market overlooking the harbour (Scots reminded of home are quite right; the sections were made in Scotland in the 1890s and then assembled here). The *açaí* comes bundled up in baskets woven from the palm leaves, and is immediately pounced on by traders and customers in a hubbub of shouting and early-morning bustle. Getting there at a more realistic hour, around 8am, there is still plenty of fish to see in the old market, and stretching beyond it are, in order, an equally fascinating medicinal herbs and spices market, all grown in backyards or fresh from the forest; the colonial customs house, now restored; and a more orthodox market under modern awnings which is a good place to buy hammocks, mosquito nets, football shirts and other necessities. A little further up on the opposite side of the road is the faded but still impressive wrought iron entrance to the **Mercado Municipal**, another rubber-boom survival that today sells an array of fascinating local products. With the iron bars above, it feels like a jail: they were added to keep the vultures away from the meat and fish the market sold when it was built.

In recent years, the once-derelict riverfront promenade both sides of Ver-o-Peso has been transformed. Where Ver-o-Peso ends, a row of old warehouses has been converted into **Estação das Docas**, a complex of restaurants, bars, stalls, exhibition spaces, shops and a cinema/theatre, where you can choose between strolling inside in the air conditioning or outside along the river (a great option at night). The designers sensibly kept everything intact and reconditioned it, rather than building anew, so you can still see the old loading cranes, now painted bright yellow. A wonderful touch is the hydraulic loading trolley, which runs beneath the warehouse roof: it has been turned into a moving stage where live music serenades the crowds every night over a poster saying "*cultura em cima de tudo*" – Culture Above All.

Estaçao das Docas is great at any time of day but comes into its own at night. You can stroll down and take your pick of a row of restaurants (*Lá Em Casa* has the best regional food), there is a microbrewery with very good locally brewed beer, the music is good, the atmosphere is lively and the river traffic is a constantly fascinating backdrop. It is also the departure point for another essential Belém activity, the **sundowner river cruise**, which leaves every day at 5pm from the end nearest Ver-o-Peso; tickets (R$25 a head) can be bought from the Valeverde Turismo office there. It may look like a cheesily tourist thing to be doing, a suspicion not exactly laid to rest by the colossally vulgar boat sporting a large fibreglass Indian figurehead, but – fear not – it's wonderful. The city is best seen close up from the river, the guides are friendly, the tourists are mainly Brazilian and, best surprise of all, the live "regional music and dancing" is in fact genuinely regional and excellent, with the boat invariably arriving two hours later back at its starting point with most of its passengers dancing. Drinks and light refreshments are served at reasonable prices, with *tacacá* soup (see box, p.434) the highlight.

Cidade Velha

Across from Ver-o-Peso in the opposite direction to Estação das Docas is the **colonial heart of Belém**, Cidade Velha. The small Neoclassical building on the water's edge is the old *necrotério*, where dead bodies from villages in the interior without a priest would be landed so they could be given proper burial in the city. Behind is the bulk of the old Portuguese fort, the **Forte do Castelo**, which is mostly mid-eighteenth century, though its earliest parts date from the 1620s. There is a small, very interesting (and air-conditioned) museum inside, open Monday to Friday 9am to 4pm (R$2). The most enjoyable thing to do, however, is walk the battlements, with views down to the harbour and across the river.

The cathedral square outside the fort, the **Praça da Sé**, looks very much as it did in the late eighteenth century; it is a wonderful place to sit at night and admire the views before moving on to the many options for eating and drinking in the neighbourhood. Next to the fort is the archbishop's palace, which houses a worthy but dull religious art museum, the **Museu de Arte Sacra** (Tues–Fri 10am–4pm, R$2); the mid-eighteenth century cathedral known universally as the Catedral da Sé dominates the other side of the square. The exterior is classically Portuguese (although in fact built by an Italian, Antônio Landi), but the interior has been gutted by successive restorations and little of interest remains.

On the other side of the square is another essential Belém sight, the **Casa das Onze Janelas**. Dating from the early eighteenth century, it was originally the town jail and then an arsenal; today it is a cultural centre, with a mediocre restaurant downstairs, an art gallery upstairs and by far the most important feature out back: **Belém's best bar**, the *Boteco das Onze Janelas*. On a terrace behind the building, linked to the fort by a walkway and with a marvellous view of the river, the excellent beer is from the local microbrewery, and waiters circulate with trays of delicious savouries: the bean soup (*caldo de feijão*) is recommended as a stomach-liner before or after if you're getting down to serious drinking. It is a great place to arrive in the late afternoon and watch the sunset over the river. To the side is the only non-colonial addition to the complex, a floodlit set of fountains.

To the left of the cathedral square as you exit the fort are the magnificent **palaces** of Lauro Sodré and Antônio Lemos – the former, along with the Teatro da Paz, being the finest building left in Belém by the rubber boom. Until recently the seat of the mayor and state governor respectively, and more than a little rundown, they have been sensitively restored. No visit to Belém would be complete without seeing them.

The **Palácio Antonio Lemos** (Mon–Fri 9am–6pm, Sat 10am–6pm), finished in the 1890s at the height of the rubber boom, has an elegant blue-and-white Neoclassical colonnaded exterior and a series of airy arched courtyards that are occasionally used as galleries for travelling exhibitions. Upstairs is the

Salão Nobre, a huge suite of reception rooms running the entire length of the frontage and featuring crystal chandeliers, beautiful inlaid wooden floors and Art Nouveau furniture; it's marred only by a few grim paintings. A separate section of the palace houses the **Museu de Arte do Belém** (Mon–Fri 9am–6pm, Sat 10am–6pm, Sun & holidays 9am–1pm), with paintings dating back to the eighteenth century, though none worth seeing.

Next door, the dazzling white **Palácio Lauro Sodré** (Tues–Fri 9am–noon & 2–6pm, Sat 9am–1pm) was built in the 1770s by Antônio Landí, a talented emigré Italian who, as an artist, sketched the first scientifically accurate drawings of Amazonian fauna. It was in this palace that the joint Portuguese–Spanish border commissions set out to agree the frontiers of Brazil in colonial times. Pará's independence from Portugal in 1822 and adhesion to the Republic in 1888 were declared from here, and it was on the main staircase that President Lobo de Souza was shot down on January 7, 1835, in the early hours of the Cabanagem Rebellion (see p.422). The palace later became the centre of days-long street fighting at the rebellion's height, which left hundreds dead. Today it houses the **Museu do Estado do Pará**, showcasing the usual dull historical pieces but worth seeing for the stunning (though small) collection of Art Nouveau furniture. It is the building itself, however, that is the real highlight. Apart from the magnificent central staircase, resurfaced with marble during the rubber boom, the ground floor and half of the first floor are still much as they were in the eighteenth century – uncluttered and elegant. The reception rooms overlooking the square were rebuilt at the turn of the twentieth century with no expense spared and, perhaps even more than the Manaus Opera House, give an idea of what an extraordinary period the rubber boom was.

Largo do Carmo, Mangal das Garças and São José Liberto

Back on the Cathedral square, head down the narrow Rua Siqueira Mendes (easily identified by the exquisite Art Nouveau Clube do Remo building on the corner): it is the city's oldest street. A few minutes brings you into the perfectly preserved and quite gorgeous **Largo do Carmo**, an eighteenth-century square dominated by the church of the same name (another Landí creation), which, as usual, has an exterior that's more interesting than the interior. A little further on, crossing the Avenida Almirante Tamandaré, with its unmistakable drainage channel, swing right at another rubber-boom jewel, the local naval headquarters on the Praça do Arsenal, and you find yourself at Belém's newest and in some ways most successful urban renewal project: the park of **Mangal das Garças** (daily 10am–6pm; the restaurant is open until midnight).

Set on the banks of the Guamá river the park is dominated by an observation tower and a large Indian-influenced wooden building with a restaurant, *Manjar das Garças*, on the upper floor that's best enjoyed at night, when it is cool enough to eat on the terrace looking out across the river. The ground floor is given over to a museum of Amazon boats and boatbuilding – a lot more interesting than it sounds. A wooden walkway leads out to a platform over the mudflats, where the combination of shade, river traffic and birdlife is hypnotic. But the highlights here are two striking pavilions: an **aviary** and a reserve for butterflies and hummingbirds, the **Borboletário Márcio Ayres.**

On entrance to the aviary, guides give visitors a laminated sheet that identifies all of the birds; you'll then spend a fascinating time marking them off, from the easy – the spectacular scarlet ibis – to ones that are less well known but equally gorgeous when seen close up, like the tanagers. Even more compelling is the nearby *borboletário*, a combined butterfly and hummingbird sanctuary named after a pioneering Amazonian conservationist who died tragically young of cancer. As with the aviary, guides give you a laminated sheet when you enter, but the first thing you notice is the wonderful coolness of the air. This comes from pipes high above spraying water droplets to create the humidity and moisture both the hummingbirds and butterflies need. The combination of fluttering butterflies and darting hummingbirds is, quite simply, magical.

Elsewhere in the park you'll find kiosks with refreshments, a bookshop, and a small artificial lake teeming with herons and scarlet ibis. Wandering around is free but to get into the aviary, museum, *borboletário* or go up the observation tower (a great view) you need to buy tickets from a kiosk at the bottom of the observation tower: a combination ticket covering everything for R$10 is your best option. The only problem with the park is the lack of shade; although trees have been planted, Mangal das Garças was only opened in 2005 and they have not yet had time to grow.

For your final stop in Cidade Velha, take a short taxi ride (R$5; taxis are always around at the Mangal entrance) to yet another historic building imaginatively converted into a cultural centre, **São José Liberto**. The square it fronts on, Praça Amazonas, used to be the city's execution grounds, and São José, when originally built in the 1730s as a Franciscan monastery, supplied the friars who accompanied felons to the gallows. After the Jesuits were expelled in 1759 following the Guaraní War, the building was converted into the city prison, which it remained until the late 1990s. This grim history has vanished without trace in an imaginative restoration and conversion: it is now a cultural complex housing exhibition space, a fascinating museum of minerals and precious stones, and a number of workshops where you can see gemcutters at work and purchase their output directly at source. Entrance is free and the complex is open Monday to Friday 9am to 5pm and Saturday and Sunday 3 to 8pm.

The entrance hall, a modern annex built onto the colonial core, has a café and an excellent ice-cream stand (part of the Cairú chain) but the highlight – apart from the air conditioning – is the several stalls selling the best of local handicrafts, notably the very distinctive Indian-influenced ceramics produced at Icoarací (see p.435). Buying here will save you a long bus ride, and it's exactly the same stuff (although rather more expensive). The space is also often used for shows and live music performances in the late afternoon and evening, especially at weekends; it's always worth asking if anything is scheduled.

The gemology museum and jewellery workshops are in the colonial part of the building; the workers ply their trade behind glass walls, for all the world like fish in an aquarium, with a number of bijou shops displaying the finished products nearby. The work is distinctive and cheap for what it is. Much more interesting than it sounds, the **gemology museum** offers a fascinating display of precious and semi-precious stones (cut and uncut) in a strongroom, but the highlight is a section of fossilized tree, against which a dinosaur might have scratched itself.

Turn right coming out of the entrance, follow the buses around the curve to the right and turn left at the light, where a four-block walk will bring you out on **Praça Batista Campos**, another gorgeous square with a cluster of rubber-boom buildings. From here, a short walk down Serzedelo Correa will take you back to Praça da República and complete the circuit.

Avenida Nazaré: the Basílica and Museu Goeldi

Two of the most important and worthwhile sights in Belém lie about fifteen minutes' walk up from the Praça da República along Avenida Nazaré. The first is the **Basílica de Nossa Senhora de Nazaré** (daily 6.30–11.30am

& 2.30–7pm) on Praça Justo Chermont. Created in 1908, and supposedly modelled on St Peter's in Rome, it rates – internally at least – with the most beautiful temples in South America. It somehow manages to be ornate and simple at the same time, its cruciform structure bearing a fine wooden ceiling and attractive Moorish designs decorating the sixteen main arches. Most importantly, however, this is home to one of the most revered images in Brazil, the small **Nossa Senhora de Nazaré** statue. There are the usual cluster of legends about the image's miraculous properties, and for *paraenses* it is something like a combination of patron saint, first port of spiritual help when trouble strikes and symbol of the city. Wherever they are, someone from Belém will do whatever they can to be back in the city in October for Brazil's most spectacular religious festival, the **Cirio de Nazaré**, when the image is paraded around in front of enormous crowds.

Cirio de Nazaré

Cirio climaxes on the second Sunday of October, but for weeks beforehand the city is preparing itself for what in Belém is by far the most important time of year, easily outstripping secular rituals like Carnaval. The centre is swept and cleaned, houses and buildings on the image's route (much of the centre of town) put up decorations, bunting and posters in the saint's yellow and white colours, and hotels fill up while anticipation builds. The first sense of what is to come is on the Friday night before the climax, when hundreds of thousands of people accompany a cortege with the image borne aloft on a flower-covered *palanque* down Avenida Nazaré from the Basilica, through Praça da República to a chapel where it spends the night. It is something to see; hundreds of thousands of people quietly and in perfect order walking along with the image, residents of buildings applauding and throwing flowers as it passes, with choirs stationed at improvised stages en route serenading it with hymns. On Saturday morning is, in some ways, the visual highlight of the entire period, the *procissão fluvial*, when the image is put onto a decorated boat and sailed around the riverfront accompanied by dozens of boats full of devotees, so that the sailors and river boats so central to the life of the city get a chance to show their devotion too. This is best seen from the battlements of the fort or the walkway next to it, but get there no later than 10am or the places will be taken. It being Brazil, the next part of the festivities is secular: around 1pm a riotous procession dominated by young people, with bands and drummers pounding away, wends its way through the Praça da Sé, down Rua Siqueira Mendes and ends up at the Largo do Carmo, where groups set up on stage and entertain the multitude with excellent regional music until the evening. Sunday morning is the climax, as the decorated *palanque* makes its way back through the centre of town and up Avenida Nazaré to the Basilica. The crowd tops a million, but is very non-intimidating: the atmosphere is saturated with devotion and everyone is very orderly – at least away from the cortege. The self-flagellating side of Catholicism is much in evidence: the image is protected on its travels by a thick anchor rope snaking around the cortege, and those with sins to pay for or favours to ask help to carry the rope, where the squeeze of bodies is intense – at the end of the day the rope is stained red by blood from the hands of devotees. The especially devout (and the mentally ill, one is tempted to think) follow the cortege on their hands and knees, with equally bloodstained results after several miles of crawling on asphalt. The image is usually back at the Basilica by noon, at which point families unite for the *paraense* equivalent of a Thanksgiving or Christmas dinner, with turkey being substituted by *pato no tucupí*, duck in *tucupí* sauce, and *maniçoba*, a fatty, smoky-tasting stew of pork and manioc leaves, which takes days to prepare. All in all, the largest and most spectacular religious festival in Brazil is worth going to some trouble to catch – but be sure to book your hotel well in advance if you go.

Two long blocks up Avenida Magalhães Barata (the continuation of Nazaré) from the basilica, you'll find the excellent **Museu Paraense Emílio Goeldi**. (Tues–Thurs 9–11.30am & 2–5pm, Fri 9–11.30am, Sat & Sun 9am–5pm, closed Mon; botanical gardens R$2, aquarium R$2). Actually more of a botanical garden and a zoo than a museum these days, it is an essential stop: the gardens are beautiful as well as educational, and any money you spend here goes not only to the upkeep of the museum and its grounds but also to a wide programme of research in everything from anthropology to zoology. This is one of only two Brazilian research institutes in the Amazon, and it plays a vital role in developing local expertise.

A small **zoo** is set in the compact but beautifully laid-out botanical gardens. Tapirs, manatees, big cats, huge alligators, terrapins, electric eels and an incredible selection of birds make this place an important site for anyone interested in the forest, and by Brazilian standards the animals are reasonably kept, too. The highlight is the Art Nouveau aquarium, with its selection of piranhas overmatched for sheer ugliness and menace by the (actually quite harmless) *matamata* turtle. The only problem is that most of the Goeldi's museum collection, including incomparable pre-Columbian funeral urns from Marajó, are in mothballs for want of exhibition space; the main exhibition hall has been closed for repairs for two years now.

Two blocks up from the museum is the **Parque da Residência**, where what used to be the official residence of the governor has been converted into a small park and cultural centre. This very pleasant spot houses one of Belém's better restaurants, the *Restô do Parque*, which does an excellent *por kilo* buffet at lunchtime. There is also a theatre, where the old governor's limo is displayed in the foyer, and, in a very *paraense* touch, an old railway wagon from the early twentieth century has been converted into an ice-cream parlour.

The Bosque Rodrigo Alves and the Parque Ambiental

One of the surprising things about Belém is that enough patches of forest survive within the city limits to give you a real sample of the jungle all around. A taste can be had in about half an hour from the centre by any of the many buses marked "Almirante Barroso" to the **Bosque Rodrigo Alves** (Tues–Sun 8am–5pm): it's on the left and unmistakable, an entire city block of trees as tall as a five-storey building. Though not as domesticated as the Goeldi botanical garden, it's well kept and actually better for seeing river life: here you'll find hundreds of turtles, a small but very imaginative aquarium and a café by the side of an artificial lake. The highlight, however, is without doubt the Amazon manatee, the *peixe-boi* (literally, fish-cow, and up close you see why – it's *big*). These mammals are increasingly rare in the wild. As this is the only chance you will have to see one in the Amazon, you should grab it with both hands: they are astonishing creatures, combining breathtaking ugliness with sheer grace as they move through the water. The enclosure at the Bosque includes a bridge built over the water – where it grazes on aquatic grasses – allowing you within a few feet.

For a real idea of the forest, head for the **Parque Ambiental de Belém** (Tues–Fri 9am–5pm), also known as the *Parque do Utinga*, after the *bairro* where it is located. Within easy reach of the centre of town, this is an area of several hundred hectares of preserved forest, protecting two lakes that provide the city's fresh water. It is astonishingly unpublicized in the city's tourist information, perhaps because officials don't understand that foreigners might actually like walking around a forest without a guide or much in the way of facilities.

The park is run by the local water company, COSANPA, and is at the very far end of Avenida 1 de Dezembro. You can get there by bus but, given that it doesn't look like a park, you are probably better off going by taxi – about R$20 from Downtown but much less if you go direct from the Bosque Rodrigues Alves, which is very close. Some preparation is necessary: you will need your passport or another photo ID to get in, and there are no facilities inside, so take sunscreen, a hat and enough water and food. You will arrive at what looks like a COSANPA water treatment plant; there is no sign and the only clue as to where you are is the forest behind. The guard will take your details and you can then just walk down the road; the forest closes in around you after about ten minutes or so. There is an extensive system of trails but, since none of them are marked and there are no maps, your best bet is probably to stay on the road, which is quite as scenic as the trails and will lead you after a couple of miles to two lakes and a visitors' centre; the centre is very basic but it's a good observation platform, with views out to the lake. There are birds all over the place, and you are likely to see monkeys, *capivara* and other wildlife. You could easily spend a day here, and getting back to Downtown is easy: turn left out of the entrance, walk down a couple of hundred yards to Avenida 1 de Dezembro, and any bus heading in the same direction you are walking will take you back to the *rodoviária*. Make sure you get the bus before dark: this isn't an area to be walking around at night, although it is perfectly safe during the day.

Eating, drinking and nightlife

Belém is a great place to eat out and get acquainted with the distinctive dishes of the Amazon region (see box p.434). Estação das Docas and the Docas area around Avenida Visconde Souza Franco are good places to start, and they are two of the city's main focuses for nightlife as well. Belém has the best ice-cream chain in Brazil, Cairú, specializing in regional flavours; half a dozen branches across the centre are strategically placed along the walking circuit. **Street food** is also good, even for those not on a budget: fantastic roast leg of pork sandwiches (*pernil*) can be had from the stall on the corner by the Cine Olimpia, on Praça da República, and for the more adventurous palate, *tacacá* and *açaí* are safe and delicious from the stalls of Dona Miloca, in front of the Goeldi museum, and Maria do Carmo, in front of the Colégio Nazaré on Avenida Nazaré, just before the Basilica. Other cheap eating options are off Presidente Vargas but cater mainly for the lunchtime office crowd. All the restaurants listed below take major credit cards unless otherwise specified.

Amazon Beer The microbrewery at Estação das Docas is worth visiting at any time but especially so during Sat lunch, when it serves the city's best *feijoada* – actually more of a *feijoada* buffet. Be sure to arrive hungry.

Armazém do Santo Antônio Travessa Quintino Bocaiúva 1696. This café attached to a bakery and deli is always a good place for snacks. It really comes into its own, however, for Sat and Sun brunch, with a buffet that includes fresh fruit, bacon, eggs and *beijú* manioc pancakes. Forget your hotel restaurant and eat breakfast here.

Café Sol Av. de Visconde Souza Franco 1122. Good coffee, savouries and light meals are offered alongside a panoramic view. Unfortunately, the place closes early, at 9pm, but there are plenty of other options around here for afterwards.

Cantina Italiana Travessa Benjamin Constant 1401. This small family restaurant, open for lunch and dinner, is the best Italian option in town. Offers excellent, moderately priced antipasto. Visa only.

Cheiro Verde Av. Bras de Aguiar, near the *Equatorial Palace Hotel* and the Basilica. Good cheap *comida por kilo* restaurant, with vegetarian options as well as meat and fish, and a great salad bar. Always packed, with live music performed after 9pm on Fri and Sat.

Hikari Sushi Av. Serzedelo Correa 220, just off Praça da República. Belém's Japanese community dates from the 1930s and this is the best of a number of good sushi places in town.

Lá em Casa Av. Gov. José Malcher 247. Very good Amazonian food is served underneath an enormous mango tree, with a retractable roof in case of rain. Regional dishes are recommended (the menu has a helpful English translation). Another very good branch is located in Estação das Docas.

Manjar das Garças Mangal das Garças park. The combination of Amazonian ingredients and a chef from southern Brazil doesn't always work, but the setting, especially at night, is fantastic, and the lunch buffet is one of the best in the city. On the expensive side, but worth it – pack plastic.

Palafita Rua Siqueira Mendes 264. Just off the cathedral square in Cidade Velha, wend your way through a colonial house to a wooden platform built over the river, where you'll enjoy excellent, moderately priced regional food. Try the *pastel de pato*, duck pasties served with *tucupí* to dip them in, and the *caldeiradas*, fish stews. Visa only.

Pomme D'Or Generalissimo Deodoro 1513. A good quality, cheap, *comida por kilo* place just off the Basilica.

Restô do Parque Parque da Residência, just up from the Goeldi museum. This *comida por kilo* restaurant, serving regional dishes and excellent salads, is much classier than the others in Belém. The macaws outside bite, so steer clear of them.

Saldosa Maloca Located on Combú island, with a fantastic view of the city, *Saldosa Maloca* is a great place to go on a weekend. The restaurant has a boat that leaves from the Beira Rio hotel and takes customers across for R$5 a head. Make sure you take the bigger of the two boats you'll see (located on the right as you look across the river), since a neighbouring restaurant has a boat that leaves from the same spot but is nothing like as good. The (surprisingly cheap) food at *Saldosa Maloca* is local cuisine; recommended dishes are the *filhote na brasa* (grilled fish) and *costela de porco* (rack of pork ribs). Behind the restaurant, an elevated wooden walkway passes through *açaí* palm forest, a *casa de farinha*, where you can watch manioc flour be made, and an *açaí* pulper, where you'll see the fruit be turned into deep purple juice and taken straight to the tables. Only open for lunch on Sat and Sun, unfortunately.

Trapiche Av. Bernardo Sayão 4906. A little further up from the Beira Rio hotel, this riverside restaurant has the usual good Amazonian food, but it also has a dance floor with fine live music (regional with a touch of *brega*). It's a slightly older crowd than at the more central clubs, but you'll see some great dancing. The music isn't so loud that it interferes with the eating, if that's what you want to focus on. Moderately priced.

Xicara da Silva Av. Visconde Souza Franco 978. Belém's best restaurant is set in a surprisingly quiet and tranquil spot on a very busy street. The moderately priced food (given the quality) features local ingredients served in imaginative new ways. Highly recommended are the duck in tamarind sauce and the *escondidinho,* jerked beef served with mashed manioc. The pizza is the best in town.

Bars and nightlife

Belém's real **nightlife** rarely begins much before 10 or 11pm, with Estação das Docas and the Docas area around Visconde de Souza Franco being the main focus in the centre. Several places cluster on Avenida Wandenkolk, one block up and parallel to Visconde de Souza Franco: *Lord Lion* at 419, *Jungle* at 800 and *Iguana* at 247. For a more intimate, romantic setting, try *Roxy Bar* at Av. Senador Lemos 230, also in Docas. If you want to dance rather than hang out, *Casablanca* is close by at Av. Senador Lemos 175; music is loud and techno, but the club is in a beautiful old house and there is a soundproofed restaurant as well. Calmer live music (with the largest *caipirinhas* you're ever likely to see) along with a gourmet selection of *cachaça* is also close by at *Cachaçaria Agua Doce,* Rua Diogo Moiá 283.

The other area for **live music** is the western *bairro* of **Condor**, on the banks of the Rio Guamá. There are numerous clubs to choose from, with the scene particularly lively on Thursday, Friday and Saturday, but you'll need to take a taxi there and back. *Lapinha*, Trav. Padre Eutiquio 390, is the best known and most enjoyable, though it doesn't get going much before midnight. It's not too glitzy, there's usually good food and a live band at weekends, and it may be the only club in the world that has three toilet categories – "Men", "Women" and "Gay". A similar popular destination is the riverside *Palácio dos Bares*, specializing in *forró* and *brega*. Lapinha and the Palácio are large, frenetic and fun, but if it's decent music you want, the best option is *Casa do Gilson*, Travessa Padre Eutiquio 3172, with *choro* on Friday nights, samba on Saturday afternoons into the early hours, and either on Sunday evenings.

Amazon cuisine

As you might expect from the richest freshwater ecosystem in the world, **fish** takes pride of place in Amazonian cooking, and you'll come across dozens of species. There are many kinds of huge, almost boneless fish, including *pirarucu*, *tambaqui* and *filhote*, which come in dense slabs sometimes more like meat, and are delicious grilled over charcoal. Smaller, bonier fish, such as *surubim*, *curimatã*, *jaraqui*, *acari* and *tucunaré*, can be just as succulent, the latter similar to a large tasty mullet. Fish in the Amazon is commonly just barbecued or fried; its freshness and flavour need little help. It's also served *no escabeche* (in a tomato sauce), *a leite de coco* (cooked in coconut milk) or stewed in *tucupí*.

The other staple food in Amazônia is **manioc**. *Farinha*, a manioc flour consumed throughout Brazil, is supplied at the table in granulated form – in texture akin to gravel – for mixing with the meat or fish juices with most meals, and is even added to coffee. Less bland and more filling, manioc is also eaten throughout Amazônia on its own or as a side dish, either boiled or fried (known as *macaxeira* in Manaus and western Amazônia or *mandioca* elsewhere). A more exciting form of manioc, **tucupí**, is produced from its fermented juices. This delicious sauce can be used to stew fish in or to make *pato no tucupí* (duck stewed in *tucupí*). Manioc juice is also used to make *beiju* (pancakes) and *doce de tapioca*, a tasty cinnamon-flavoured tapioca pudding. A gloopy, translucent manioc sauce also forms the basis of one of Amazônia's most distinctive dishes, *tacacá*, a shrimp soup gulped from a gourd bowl and sold everywhere from chichi restaurants to street corners. Other typical regional dishes include *maniçoba*, pieces of meat and sausage stewed with manioc leaves, and *vatapá*, a North Brazil version of the Bahian shrimp dish.

Finally, no stay in the Amazon would be complete without sampling the remarkable variety of **tropical fruits** the region has to offer, which form the basis for a mouthwatering array of *sucos* and ice creams. Most have no English or even Portuguese translations. Palm fruits are among the most common; you are bound to come across *açai*, a deep purple pulp mixed with water and drunk straight, with added sugar, with tapioca or thickened with *farinha* and eaten. Other palm fruits include *taperebá*, which makes a delicious *suco*, *bacuri* and *buriti*. Also good, especially as *sucos* or ice cream, are *acerola* (originally it came over with the first Japanese settlers in the 1920s, although Amazonians will swear blind it is regional), *peroba*, *graviola*, *ata* (also called *fruta de conde*) and, most exotic of all, *cupuaçú*, which looks like an elongated brown coconut and floods your palate with the tropical taste to end all tropical tastes.

For a night at the **cinema** there is only one surviving large-screen spot, the *Nazaré* on the Basilica, which shows mainstream releases. There's also a good triple-screen arthouse, *Cinema 1-2-3*, on Travessa São Pedro behind the Iguatemi mall in Batista Campos: take any bus with an "Iguatemi" card in front, get out at the mall, and walk through it onto the street behind to reach the cinema.

Listings

Airlines Varig now at the airport only; TAM, Av. Assis de Vasconcelos 265 ⓣ91/3212-2166. Belém has some international connections for the adventurous; Air Surinam three times weekly to Paramaribo via Cayenne, and connections to Georgetown, and Air Caraibe three times weekly to Cayenne and the French Antilles, with Air France connections to Paris from either Cayenne or Port-au-Prince. All are best contacted via their offices in the airport.

Banks and exchange Banco da Amazônia, Av. Presidente Vargas; HSBC Bank, Av. Presidente Vargas 670; Banco do Brasil, 2nd floor, Av. Presidente Vargas 248. Many of the larger shops, travel agents and hotels will change dollars. Banco 24 like a ranch. These packages range in price, from moderate to expensive; ızon Star and Valeverde Turismo in Belém have good deals, starting at ınd R$100 a day but including full board and all travel. Three recommended ces at the moderate end actively courting the foreign ecotourism market are racauary Ecoresort (ⓦwww.paracauary.com.br), *Hotel Fazenda Sanjo* (the only orking ranch) and *Pousada dos Guarás*. There is one luxury ecoresort, *Marajó ırk Resort* (actually on Mexiana island, just off the north coast of Marajó; ⓦwww.marajoparkresort.com.br), where prices start at around US$200 a night or a couple and include a ride in a small plane to the hotel from Belém; expensive though it may be, booking via a Belém operator will still be around twenty percent cheaper than booking it from abroad or from southern Brazil.

Soure, Salvaterra and Joanes

A quiet town with pleasant beaches where you can relax under the shade of ancient mango trees, **SOURE** is where most visitors head for at first. The *Hotel Soure*, just a few blocks from the docks in the town centre, is very basic, while the *Hotel Marajó*, Praça Inhangaiba (ⓣ91/3741-1396), and the *Hotel Ilha do Marajó*, Av. Assis de Vasconcelos 199 (ⓣ91/3224-5966, ⓦwww.dadoscon.com.br/himarajo), both offer more comfort and a pool. The best restaurant in Souré is *Delícias da Nalva*, Quarta Rua 1051, whose speciality *marajoara* banquet includes a *filé a marajoara* (buffalo meat covered with cheese), a *filhote* with crab sauce, fried shrimp and much more, all served in a beautiful, overgrown garden. In **SALVATERRA**, on the other side of the estuary and linked to Soure by a regular ferry service, is the *Beira-Mar*, on the corner of Quinta Rua with Segunda Travessa – simple, clean and starting at R$40 a night.

Both Soure and Salvaterra are occasionally noisy at night during the weekend, with partying groups over from Belém. If it's tranquillity you want, your best option is the village of **JOANES**, which has a magnificent beach, a headland with a wind turbine that supplies the town with the energy it needs and the excellent *pousada Ventania do Rio Mar* (ⓣ91-3646-2067, ⓔventaniapousada@hotmail.com); rates start at R$40. Run by a Belgian woman and much frequented by young Brazilian and foreign travellers, it has a range of accommodations (from beach chalets to guest rooms), good food and a splendidly panoramic bar.

On all beaches, take care about stingrays – they are particularly common on Marajó. Stick to places with waves and moving water, and avoid wading in rivers and streams.

Southern Pará

The southern half of Pará, whose main towns are **Marabá** and **Altamira**, has virtually nothing to recommend it to the traveller: largely denuded of forest, it is now a jumble of unproductive ranches, poor peasants and depressing towns. When it hits the headlines it is always for the wrong reasons, such as the assassination of American nun Dorothy Stang in 2005. You are much better advised to head for western Pará and the area around Santarém, which has far more to offer. Basic details on southern Pará are given here, but our recommendation is that you avoid it unless you have good reason to go. Even then, take care.

Marabá

MARABÁ, on the banks of the Rio Tocantins, almost 600km south of Belém and 400km north of Araguaina on the Belém–Brasília road, is often described

Horas cash machines in most supermarkets and many *farmácias*.

Boats See also box, pp.418–419. Boats leave Belém regularly for upstream Amazon river destinations, even as far as Porto Velho (at least one a day to Macapá, Santarém and Manaus). However, boats don't have set times of departure, as this depends on tides and river conditions, and there are a huge number of different companies, with no central place where you can get information. Any travel agent will book a ticket for you (just say when and where you want to go), or speak to the captains on the docks (try the waterfront by Armazém 3 and also 10, and the Porto do Sal terminus on Rua Siqueira Mendes in Cidade Velha). Failing that, for Santarém, Manaus and Macapá, tickets are available through the Agência Amazonas at Av. Castilho Franca 548; Amazon Star and Valeverde Turismo, below, will also book you tickets.

Car hire The usual suspects are Avis, Rua Sen. Lemos 121 ⓣ91/3257-2277, and Localiza, Av. Gov. José Malcher 1365 ⓣ91/3257-1541, both also with kiosks at the airport. But better rates can (surprisingly) be had from the local car-hire agency in the basement of the *Hilton* (see p.425).

Internet Amazon, Estação das Docas, 2nd floor; *Cybercafé*, Av. Bras de Aguiar 742; Inter-Belem, Av. Jose Malcher 189, with more opening all the time.

Laundry Lavanderia Marajo, Av. Bras de Aguiar 408; Lavanderia Tintuvana, Av. Presidente Vargas 762 (inside the arcade).

Post office The central post office (Mon–Sat 9.30am–6pm) is at Av. Presidente Vargas 498; however, as the place is frequently crowded, it's often quicker to walk to the small post office at Av. Nazaré 319, three blocks beyond the Praça da República.

Shopping Belém is one of the best places in the world to buy hammocks (essential if you are about to go upriver) – look in the street markets between Av. Presidente Vargas and Ver-o-Peso, starting in Rua Santo Antônio. For *artesanato*, head for Casa Amazônia, Av. Presidente Vargas 512; the Loja Victoria Regia, Av. Presidente Vargas 550; or the Cantô do Uirapurú, Av. Presidente Vargas 594. Orion Perfumaria, Frutuoso Guimarães 270, produces and sells a wide range of rainforest oils, scents and cosmetic products.

Travel and tour companies There are two good tour agencies in Belém for foreigners, both with a reasonably priced selection of tours around Belém: Amazon Star Turismo, Rua Henrique Gurjão 236, ⓣ91/3212-6244, 3241-8624, (ⓦwww.amazonstar.com.br), an excellent French-run agency specializing in ecotourism, and Valeverde Turismo, at Estação das Docas (ⓣ91/3212-3388) and Av. Alcindo Cacela 104 (ⓣ 91/3218-7333), ⓦwww.valeverdeturismo.com.br. Packages from these two are your best bet if you want to explore the islands around Belém or spend much time in Marajó, where transport is difficult if you don't speak Portuguese. Both offer excursions to Ilha dos Papagaios, an island near Belém where tens of thousands of parrots zoom out of the trees at dawn, an unforgettable sight and cheap at R$70 a head, including pick-up from your hotel at 4.30am and a hearty breakfast. It's worth the bleary eyes. Both are used to foreign tourists and have guides who speak good German and French, as well as English.

Around Belém

There are interesting places near Belém, although you should mostly resist the temptation to swim at the river beaches anywhere close to the city. The locals, indifferent to high fecal counts, regularly do, but it plays havoc with the unaccustomed. Easiest to reach is **ICOARAÇI**, with local buses from anywhere downtown taking about an hour. Walk towards the river from the bus terminus and you'll hit the two things that make the trip worthwhile. One is the **ceramic workshops** on the newly paved and reconditioned riverfront, which sell distinctive pottery well known in Brazil that is based on the ancient designs of the local Indians. The skill involved in shaping, engraving, painting and firing these pots is remarkable. Some of the ceramics are very large and, except to the expert eye, barely distinguishable from the relics in the Goeldi museum. They are cheap and the shops are well used to crating things up for travellers; for a little extra they will deliver to your hotel the following day. The other thing justifying the trip is one of the region's best restaurants, *Na Telha*, which serves mouthwatering fresh fish and *moquecas* in the eponymous tile; one dish easily does for two people, and try if you can to get there during the week, since you can barely move for people here at the weekend.

The closest large beaches to Belém are at **OUTEIRO**, but should be avoided like the plague: they are filthy at all times and hugely crowded at the weekend, when drunk drivers by the score, fighting youths and unbelievably crowded Kombis make the whole area a danger zone. A much better bet is **MOSQUEIRO**, some 70km east of Belém but with frequent bus service from the *rodoviária* (it's about a 2hr ride). The trip to Mosqueiro is also a good excursion in a rented car; it is difficult to get lost, as Belém has only one road out of town – go up Almirante Barroso, follow the signs to the BR-316 (right fork at the Castanheira shopping centre), and keep going, turning left at the sign to Mosqueiro about 30km later. Mosqueiro is actually an island but well connected to Belém by a good road and bridge; the ride is pleasant, and a fine opportunity to see the country beyond the city. Unfortunately, the beaches close to the town are picturesque but too dirty to swim at, and you need to take a local bus from the main square to the best option, **Praia do Paraíso,** about half an hour away. Stay on the bus until the end of the line and you find yourself at a gorgeous headland, with a hotel behind you and a clean, swimmable beach in front. The *Lafaiete* restaurant serves excellent *caldeiradas* and *isca de peixe*, mouthwatering pieces of freshly fried fish. If you come this far you might as well make a night of it; the hotel is good (comfortable and with air conditioning) but expensive (R$80). Alternatively, there are a couple of cheap *pousadas* further back along the beach road.

Just 18km east from Belém, the island haven of **Cotijuba** is replete with beautiful beaches, rainforest and access to *igarapé* creeks. It's the perfect place for birdwatching and nature walks. Trips are arranged by Amazon Star Turismo (see p.435), with accommodation in native-style bungalows.

Your best bet, however, for getting a sense of coastal, rural Pará is to head for another island, **Algodoal**. Reaching there is half the fun. The jumping-off point is the small town of **Marudá**, a four-hour bus ride from the Belém *rodoviária* via a Rápido Excelsior bus: several run a day (R$11 each way), but buy a ticket the day before and catch one that leaves early in the morning, to ensure that you don't have to stay the night in Marudá. The bus leaves you close to the port – actually no more than a wooden jetty – where a forty-minute boat crossing (R$4; buy tickets at the booth at the jetty entrance) takes you to Algodoal island. You will be met by a number of mule-pulled carts, there being no way for cars to get to the island, or roads for them to drive if they could. You can take a cart or walk to the small village, where there are a dozen cheap *pousadas*, or take a cart to the best option, *Jardim de Eden* (ⓦwww.algodoal-amazon-tourism.com.br, ⓔjardimdoeden@hotmail.com), a more isolated *pousada* on Praia do Farol owned by a Brazilian-French couple, who also speak English and Spanish and are very attentive and helpful. The *Jardim* has an idyllic location, a variety of cheap to moderately priced accommodations – from camping space and hooks to sling a hammock to chalets and a bungalow – plus the best food on the island, which includes very fresh shrimp and fish. Algodoal can get moderately crowded at weekends and holidays, but nothing compared to most places on this coast. The beaches are enormous and beautiful. If you want to relax and do nothing for a few days or longer in sleepy tranquillity, this is the place to head. But take as much cash as you'll need; electricity only arrived here in 2005, and credit cards are as yet unknown.

Further east, this entire coastline is being rapidly developed. Many people from Belém head for the mainland beaches here, **Ajuriteua** and the resort of **Salinas** especially. But the truth is facilities haven't kept up with the pace of development, and the crowds that descend on places like Salinas every weekend have long since ruined it.

Ilha do Marajó

The **Ilha do Marajó** is a vast, 40,000-square-kilometre
habited mangrove swamps and beaches in the Amazon
Belém. Roughly the size of Switzerland, it is by some w
island in the world. Created by the accretion of silt and san
years, it's a wet and marshy area: the western half is covered in
east is flat savanna, it's swampy in the wet season (Jan–June) and
in the dry season (June–Dec). Originally inhabited by the Mar
famed for their ceramics, these days the savannh is dominated by *fa*
water buffalo are ranched; some 60,000 of them roam the island, an
meat and hides to Belém is Marajó's main trade. Other animal lif
including numerous snakes, alligators and venomous insects, so b
where you walk. Among the most spectacular sights are the flocks of sc
guará, which can vary in colour from flamingo pink to blood red. Co
on Marajó but an endangered species in the rest of Brazil, they are born
– it is the red crabs they eat that turn their feathers red over time. Maraj
beautiful sandy beaches, and it's become a popular option for Brazilian sunse
ers and ecotourists alike.

Although it was settled by Jesuits in the seventeenth century, Marajó's earlie inhabitants left behind burial mounds, 1000 years old and more, in which many examples of the distinctive Marajó pottery were found. The most spectacular are large funeral urns, decorated with geometric engravings and painted designs – the best examples are in the Museu Goeldi in Belém. When the Jesuits arrived and established the first cattle ranches, the island was inhabited by Aurá Indians, who lasted no more than a few decades; later its vast expanses offered haven to runaway slaves and to refugee Indians who wanted to trade with Belém without too much direct interference into their culture from white settlers. Water buffalo, ideally suited to the marshy local conditions, were imported from India during the rubber boom – or, if you believe local legend, were part of a French cargo bound for Guiana and escaped when the ship sank. River navigation around Marajó is still a tricky business, the course of the channels constantly altered by the ebb and flow of the ocean tides.

Practicalities

For such a big island there are very few anchorages, and the only **point of entry** into Marajó from Belém is the tiny port of Foz do Camará, where buses and Kombis meet all incoming boats and ferry visitors to **Soure, Salvaterra** and **Joanes** – the main destinations – all some 25km away. Three boats leave Belém daily. A car-ferry that also takes passengers leaves from Icoaraçí at 6.30am, with an additional 4am departure on Saturday. If you're renting a car, you should seriously consider a few days pottering around Marajó as an option (just make sure you leave Belém with a full tank). The ferry terminal is just to the left of the restored part of the riverfront where the Icoaraçí ceramic sellers congregate. Without a car, the Navegação Arapari ferryboat leaves daily from gates 10 and 15 of the Belém docks at 6.30am and 2.30pm; additional departures are occasionally added on holidays and weekends.

In general, you have two options when visiting Marajó: independent travel without a car basically means a beach holiday spent checking out Soure, Salvaterra and Joannes. There are few roads in Marajó, and little public transport. Alternatively, if you want to see the interior of Marajó, your best bet is to get a package tour through an operator in Belém who will set you up at a *hotel fazenda* – a ranch geared up to receive visitors or a specialist hotel got up to

as the worst of all Amazon towns. It's the market centre for the region, and also the place where the ranchers, construction workers, truckers and gold-miners come for entertainment: it has a bad reputation for theft and violent crime, and it's not a place you should (or would want to) hang around any longer than you have to.

Marabá is a city of three parts, all of them easily reached by bus from Araguaina or from Belém and linked by bridges across the river. The earliest part of town was founded on the south side of the river on ground that was prone to flooding; later settlers created the Cidade Nova on the north side, hoping to escape the waters. In the 1970s the completion of the Transamazônica led to the foundation of Nova Marabá, back on the south side.

Buses will drop you at the *rodoviária* at Km 4 on the Transamazônica in Nova Marabá; small local buses or taxis run from here to just about every part of town. The airport (ⓣ94/3324-1383) is just 3km out of town near the Cidade Nova. The choice of **accommodation** is relatively small: in Nova Marabá there's the *Hotel Itacaiúnas*, Folha 30, Quadra 14, Lote 1 (ⓣ & ⓕ94/3322-1326; ❸–❹); and the *Hotel Vale do Tocantins*, Folha 29, Quadra Especial, Lote 1 (ⓣ94/3322-2321, ⓕ3322-1841; ❸–❹), both with pool, bar and restaurant and rates starting at R$60. Cheaper accommodation can be had in Cidade Nova at the *Hotel Vitória*, Av. Espírito Santo 130 (ⓣ94/3528-1175; ❷), and the *Hotel Keyla*, Transamazônica 2427 (ⓣ94/324-1175; ❷–❸). Nearer the *rodoviária* there's also the basic, even cheaper and somewhat noisy *Pensão Nossa Senhora do Nazaré* (❶). The town's best fish **restaurant** is *Bambu*, Travessa Pedro Carneiro 111, Cidade Nova (ⓣ91/3324-1290), and there's a good Japanese restaurant, *Kotobuki*, at Av. Tocantins 746, Novo Horizonte (closed Tues).

Amapá

The **state of Amapá**, north of the Amazon, is one of Brazil's poorest and least populated regions. Traditionally it was dependent primarily on rubber exports, but manganese was discovered in the 1950s and this, together with timber and other minerals, is now the main source of income. A standard-gauge rail line links the mining camps to the northwest with **Porto do Santana**, near the capital Macapá, crossing the dry, semi-forested plains of the region en route. Amapá doesn't have much going for it, other than as a transit route to **French Guiana**, and it suffers the most marked dry season in the Amazon, running from June to December, when it can get extremely hot. **Macapá** fights it out with Palmas in Tocantins for the title of dullest state capital in Brazil, but at least it's cheap – also, like Manaus, it's a freeport, exempt from customs duties.

Macapá

On the north bank of the Amazon and right on the equator, **MACAPÁ** is the gateway to the state of Amapá and home to three-quarters of its population. Surrounded by uninhabited forests and hills, it dominates the northern section of the Amazon estuary. If you're coming by ferry from Belém you'll actually arrive to the southwest at **Porto do Santana**, just twenty minutes by bus or an hour by boat from Macapá, though it lies on the other side of the equator. The **airport** is 4km from town on Rua Hildemar Maia (ⓣ96/3223-2323). The **rodoviária** (ⓣ96/3242-5193) faces the Polícia Técnica, 5km outside town on the BR-156; from there, local buses run to Praça Veiga Cabral in the centre.

The countryside around Macapá is, like the Ilha do Marajó in the estuary, roamed by large herds of water buffalo. In town there is not a great deal to do. The highlight is the **Fortaleza de São José do Macapá** (daily 9am–6pm, closed Mon), one of the largest colonial forts in Brazil, built in 1782 from material brought over as ballast in Portuguese ships, in response to worries that the French had designs on the north bank of the Amazon. The fort is often closed, but nobody will mind if you slip through the enormous main gates for a stroll along the battlements. There's an interesting daily artisan market nearby on Canal da Fortaleza, and you could fill some more time checking out the eighteenth-century **Igreja São José de Macapá** on the Praça Veiga Cabral and the **Museu Histórico** (Tues–Sun 8am–noon & 2–6pm) at Av. Mário Cruz 17. The **Museu do Desinvolvimento Sustenavel**, at Av. Feliciano Coehlo 1509 (Mon–Fri 8am–noon & 2.30–5.30pm, Sat 3–5.30pm, closed Sun) has a comprehensive collection of indigenous crafts from the tribes of the region. There's also a small private museum, the **Instituto de Estudos e Pesquisas de Plantas Medicinais (IEPA)** at Av. Feliciano Coelho 1509, holding the Valdemiro Gomes collection of minerals, Amazon woods and medicinal plants (Mon–Fri 9am–noon).

Practicalities

For **accommodation**, the *Hotel Tropical*, Av. Antônio Coelho de Carvalho 1399 (ⓣ96/3231-3759; ❷), is excellent value with spacious rooms. The *Hotel São Antônio* (❶) is better placed on the main *praça*, and even cheaper, but not quite as good; additionally, there's the clean and friendly *Hotel Mara* in Rua São José (ⓣ96/3222-0859; ❷–❸). Out near the airport, the *Hotel San Marino*, Av. Marcílio Dias 1395 (ⓣ96/3223-1522, ⓕ3223-5223; ❹–❺), offers more comfort and a pool, while top of the range for creature comforts is the *Ceta Hotel* on Rua do Matadoro 640, in the Fazendinha district (ⓣ96/3227-3396, ⓦwww.ecotel.com.br; ❺–❻). By far the best option, however, is the *Pousada Ekinox*, a short walk from the centre at Rua Jovino Dinoa 1693 (ⓣ96/3222-4378, ⓔjef@brasnet.online.com.br; ❹–❺). This small but lovely *pousada*, which doubles as the **French consulate**, has French-Brazilian owners, and the food is as good as that combination suggests. It's a popular place to stay, so you'll need to ring ahead and make a reservation.

As for **food**, Macapá's position as a river and sea port means that there's plenty of excellent fish to be had. The *Lennon Restaurant* downtown is a popular dining spot, but greater variety can usually be found at the *Restaurante Boscão*, Rua Hamilton Silva 997. Superb fish is served at *Martinho's Peixaria*, Av. Beira-Rio 140, and at *Cantinho Baiano*, on the same street at no. 328. The coast road in either direction from the fort has the most pleasant **bars** in town, always well ventilated by the sea breeze. For unrestrained night-time entertainment, try *Rithimus*, at Rua Odilardo Silva 1489, where the sounds of samba and reggae are regularly heard, or, further out at the *Marco Zero* **nightclub**, for a mix of samba and mainstream sounds; it's located 5km on the Fazendinha road near the equatorial monument **Marco Zero**.

For information about **boats** to the north or to Belém, the Captain of the Port, Av. FAB 427 (ⓣ96/3223-9090 or 3223-4755), can be contacted at his offices most weekdays between 8am and 5pm. Most boat companies sell tickets through the agency Sonave at Rua Sao Jose 2145 (ⓣ96/3223-9090). The main companies, all based at Porto do Santana, are ENAVI (ⓣ96/3242-2167), with irregular sailings via Belém as far as Santarém, and Silnave (ⓣ96/3223-4011) for car-carrying boats to Belém (Tues & Fri). Varig is at Rua Cândido Mendes 1039 (ⓣ96/222-7724), but TAM (ⓣ96/3223-2688) has a more extensive route network from Macapá, including direct flights to Brasília. For **car rental**, contact Localiza (☎96/3223-2799).

Into French Guiana

One reason to come to Amapá is to get to **French Guiana** (or Guyane): the key road in the state connects Macapá with the town of **OIAPOQUE**, on the river of the same name that delineates the frontier. The road isn't asphalted all the way, but even where it's dirt it's usually good going in the dry season; in the wet season, however, it can take days, and you're better off flying directly to Cayenne from Belém. If you want to make it in one run, the regular buses to Oiapoque can take as little as twelve hours in the dry season. It's unfortunately a rather boring drive, largely through savanna rather than forest, with mile after mile of scrubby pine plantations blocking any view. You could break the journey in **CALÇOENE**, eight hours by bus from Macapá. A pleasant, sleepy town built around rapids on the river of the same name, Calçoene has several cheap hotels and regular bus connections on to Oiapoque. While there you may feel tempted to visit the nearby gold-mining town of Lourenço. Don't – it's dangerous and very malarial.

A more leisurely option is to go **by boat** from Macapá to Oiapoque, a journey of two days (one night); boats depart once a week or so, but there's no regular schedule. If you're interested in this option, simply go to the docks and ask around: if a boat is leaving, seek out its captain and negotiate for hammock space, which should cost no more than US$20 in either direction. The best hammock spaces are those with open sides, preferably on the middle deck. This is the Atlantic, however, and it can get rough.

If you are not a citizen of a European Union country, the US or Canada, you will need a **visa** to enter French Guiana. There is a French consulate in Macapá at the *Pousada Ekinox* (see opposite), though it's better to try to arrange the visa before you leave home. If you're going to travel overland, buy **euros** in Belém or Macapá. You can get them in Oiapoque but the rates are worse, and you can't depend on changing either Brazilian currency or US dollars for euros in the border settlement of Saint-Georges in Guyane.

Dug-out taxis (or canoes) are the usual means of transport between Oiapoque and Saint-Georges, about ten minutes downriver. Brazilian **exit stamps** can be obtained from the Polícia Federal at the southern road entrance into Oiapoque; on the other side you have to check in with the *gendarmes* in Saint-Georges. Buses to Cayenne take some eight hours over a good quality asphalt highway.

Santarém

Around 700km west of Belém – but closer to 800 as the river flows – **SANTARÉM** is the first significant stop on the journey up the Amazon, a small city of around 130,000 people, which still makes it the fourth largest in the Brazilian Amazon. Agreeable and rather laid-back, it feels more like a large town than a city – a world away from the bustle of Belém and Manaus. Even though the area around it has lately been transformed by a soy-growing boom, and the docks are now dominated by a Cargill grain terminal, this hasn't had much impact on the town's languid feel. But don't be deceived: there are plenty of things to do here, and Santarém, positioned right in the centre of a region still largely (and inexplicably) unvisited by tourists, is the perfect base for exploring some of the most beautiful river scenery the Amazon basin has to offer.

Santarém is located at the junction of the **Tapajós river** and the Amazon; the waters mix in front of the city and the contrast between the muddy waters of the Amazon and the deep blue and turquoise of the Tapajós is as spectacular as the much better known merging of the Rio Negro and the Amazon in front of Manaus. During the dry season (June-Nov) the Tapajós drops several metres, fringing the entire river system with stunning white sand beaches. This is the time to visit **Alter do Chão,** Santarém's beach resort and certainly the most beautiful that the Amazon has to offer.

It is likely that this area once supported one of the highest populations in the Americas before Europeans arrived, with towns and villages stretching for miles along the riverbanks, living off the rich stocks of fish in the river, and farming corn on even richer alluvial soils, replenished annually when the Amazon flooded. On all the distinctive flat-topped hills around Santarém, there is evidence of **prehistoric Indian occupation**, easily identified by the *terra preta do Indio* (Indian black soil), a black compost deliberately built up over generations by Indian farmers. If you do any walking up and down these hills, especially around Belterra, keep your eyes open for ceramic shards. In recent years, thanks to the work of an American archeologist, Anna Roosevelt, it has become clear that Santarém and its surrounding area make up one of the most important archeological sites in the Americas.

The very first European accounts of the middle Amazon date from the early sixteenth century, and talk of swarms of canoes coming out to do battle and longhouses lining the riverbanks. The river asssumed its current lightly populated look in the centuries after first contact, as disease and slavery wiped out

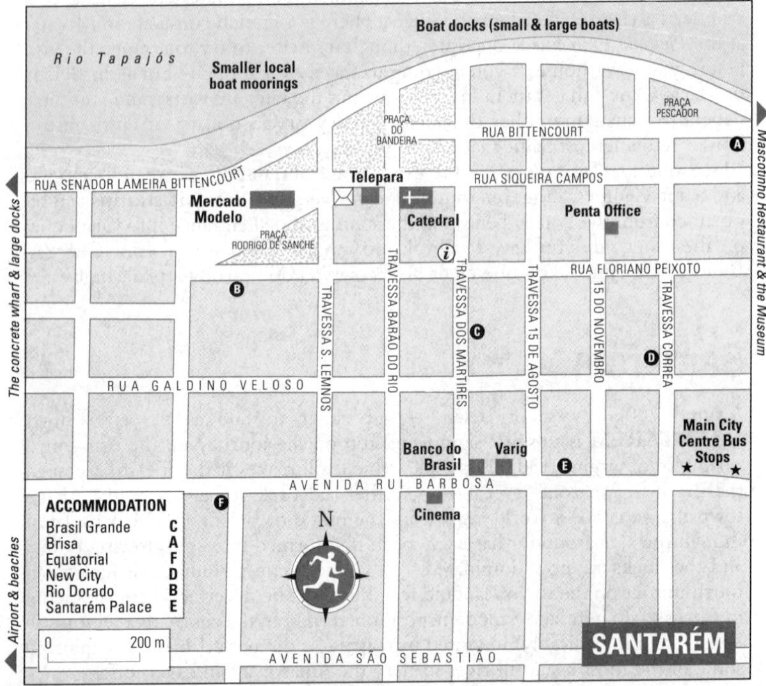

Prehistoric finds

Thirty kilometres east of Santarém, more easily accessible by river than by road, is a nineteenth-century sugar plantation called **Taperinha**. In an excavation there in 1991, American archeologist Anna Roosevelt unearthed **decorated pottery** almost 10,000 years old – twice as old as the oldest ceramics found anywhere in the Americas. This suggests that the Amazon basin was settled before the Andes, and that the Americas had been settled much earlier than previously thought. Later excavations in **Monte Alegre** confirmed that the middle Amazon played an important role in the prehistory of the Americas with cave and rock paintings dotting the surrounding hills also being dated at around 10,000 years old. About two thousand years ago, Indian culture in the region entered a particularly dynamic phase, producing some superbly decorated ceramics comparable in their sophistication with Andean pottery; there are beautiful pieces in the small museum in Santarém, and even more in the Museu Goeldi in Belém (see p.429).

the Indians or drove them way upriver; as late as 1960 some two hundred Indians were massacred by settlers on a sandbank just south of Itaituba.

Some history

Santarém in its modern form began life as a Jesuit mission in the seventeenth century. It grew only slowly during subsequent centuries, but its convenient location made it popular as a base for the several European naturalists who wrote the first travel books about the Amazon in the 1840s and 1850s. At the time Santarém was a town of five thousand people locking themselves up after dark as jaguars prowled the streets. It was the **rubber boom** that proved the making of Santarém, and the town grew into an important trading centre. The region also became a refuge for two diametrically opposed groups: escaped slaves, who founded communities along the Trombetas and Maicurú rivers on the Amazon's north bank, which were never conquered; and refugee Confederates, who made the big mistake of moving to Santarém under the misapprehension that they could grow cotton there. By the time they realized they had been misinformed, most of them had died of malaria and yellow fever; the survivors moved into sugar and prospered, although in time their descendants intermarried with locals and adopted their language and now the only trace of them is the occasional surname like Riker, Higgins or Macdonald.

Meanwhile, in 1874 an Englishman named **Henry Wickham** settled at Santarém with his wife and went on to be almost single-handedly responsible for the collapse of the Amazon rubber boom, smuggling quantities of valuable rubber seed from the heart of the Amazon (at a price of £10 for every 1000 seeds) to the Royal Botanical Gardens in London and from there to British-owned plantations in Asia that were already prepared and waiting. It took over twenty years for the first crop to mature to anywhere near peak production, but when it did the bottom fell out of the Brazilian rubber market. British plantations produced four tons of rubber in 1900, but 71,000 tons by 1914. This was not only more than Brazil was producing, but also a great deal cheaper, since the plantations were far more efficient than the labour-intensive wild rubber-tree tapping practised in the Amazon. Rubber was to feature again in local history through the development of **Belterra** and **Fordlândia** (see p.450). More recently, Santarém underwent explosive growth after the Santarém–Cuiabá highway was completed in the early 1970s, but, as the highway deteriorated and finally become impassable in the mid-1980s, and gold-mining continued to decline in the interior, the town slumped. Tourists are therefore very welcome here, and you will find prices in Santarém and the surrounding area quite low. In time this may change, as plans are afoot to asphalt the BR-163 highway and turn it into an export corridor for soybean production from the northern Pantanal and Mato Grosso. But that's a few years away yet.

Arrival, information and accommodation

Santarém is a busy port, serving river communities for over 300km around as well as operating long-distance services to Manaus and Belém. **Boats** to and from Manaus and Belém arrive and leave most days: the journey time is two to three days in either direction and the cost can vary, so it's worth shopping around. The appalling state of the roads in the region means that the **rodoviária** on the outskirts of town is largely symbolic, as there are no interstate buses to anywhere. Buses to places within an hour or two of Santarém – notably Alter do Chão, Belterra and Fordlândia – leave from the Mercado Modelo or along Avenida Rui Barbosa, not from the *rodoviária*.

Santarém does have a useful small **airport** (Ⓣ93/3522-4328) some 14km from the centre, with a bus connection to Avenida Rui Barbosa (travelling from the town centre, take the "Aeroporto" bus, not to be confused with "Aeroporto Velho", which goes nowhere near the airport). There is also a Kombi connecting the *Hotel Amazon Park* and the airport most mornings. TAM is the only national airline that flies there now, but nevertheless the airport is still a regional hub. Regional air companies Puma, Meta, Rico, Penta and Tavaj run daily flights to Belém and Manaus considerably cheaper than TAM, and have routes to Macapá and São Luís that save you at least a day by not passing through Belém. It is even possible to get as far south as Cuiabá, with connections to southern Brazil, on three weekly flights run by Cruiser.

Local buses in Santarém are sometimes useful, despite the small size of the city, to save you roasting yourself walking in the heat. Any bus heading left down the riverfront as you stand facing the river will take you to the Mercado Modelo, a hideous large concrete structure that houses a very useful market for stocking up on fruit and other essentials for a river journey.

For **tourist information**, most hotels have piles of a useful booklet, *Guia Turistíco de Santarém*, on their reception desk. There is an excellent **tourist agency** in Santarém, run by an expatriate American, Steve Alexander, called *Amazon Tours* (Travessa Turiano Meira 1084; Ⓦwww.amazonriver.com, Ⓔamazonriver@netsan.com.br). They have a private nature park, the Bosque Santa Luzia, where they run excellent tours; they are also the best option if you want to really do the archeological sites around Santarém and Monte Alegre, for which having a guide along really helps, or visit a nearby national park, the **Floresta do Tapajós**.

Accommodation

Santarém is well supplied with **hotels** to suit every pocket. Along with Manaus, this is one of the best places to take a break from a long-distance boat trip, and you could well find yourself staying a few days. Accommodation in Alter do Chão is listed separately.

Amazon Park Av. Mendonca Furtado 4120 Ⓣ93/3522-3361, Ⓔamazon@netsan.com.br. A living piece of modern Amazonian history: this massive 1970s complex was built by the military to enable the city to cope with the economic boom they confidently expected the highway to bring. But the boom never came and the hotel has been quietly declining ever since. Still impressive, however, are the glorious views out across the river, and, with rates starting at R$80, this place is a bargain. ④

Barão Center Av. Barão do Rio Branco 352, ⓣ93/3523-1050. Spanking new business hotel aimed at the soy growers and those who supply them. Has the only reliable hotel Internet connection in the city as well as a reasonable restaurant with great views across the river. ❹

Brasil Grande Trav. 15 de Agosto 213 ⓣ93/3522-5660. Fine mid-range hotel right in the centre of the commercial district, with all the usual amenities like TV, a/c and *frigobar.* ❸

Brisa Av. Senador Bittencourt 5 ⓣ93/3522-1018, ⓔbrisahotel@tap.com.br. Excellent budget option well run by a friendly family; clean rooms have either fans or a/c. ❷

Equatorial corner of Av. Rui Barbosa and Silvino Pinto ⓣ93/3522-1135. Centrally located, no-frills hotel where you're likely to meet all sorts of travellers. Rooms are clean and airy and some have a/c. ❷

New City Trav. Francisco Corréa 200 ⓣ93/3522-3764 or 3522-4719. A clean, modern and very friendly spot. The hotel organizes river tours and airport pick-ups or boat drops. ❷

Rio Dorado Praça Rodrigues dos Santos 887 ⓣ93/3522-3814. Opposite the Mercado Modelo, this recently refurbished hotel is one of the best mid-range places around. Rooms are clean if nondescript but staff are welcoming. The location is noisy during the day, however. ❷

Santarém Palace Av. Rui Barbosa 726 ⓣ93/3523-2820, ⓕ3522-1779. A good mid-range hotel with tidy modern rooms in the centre of town. Also runs reasonably priced river tours. ❸

The city and its beaches

By far the most interesting place in Santarém, at any hour of the day or night, is the **waterfront**. There are always dozens of boats tied up here, with the accompanying bustle of people and cargoes being loaded and unloaded, and constant activity in the shops and outfitters by the water. You will probably have to wander along the waterfront anyway to find boats to points elsewhere, but a sunset stroll is reason enough to venture down this way. Many of the city's restaurants and nightspots are here, but it is especially lively during the rainy season, when the beaches are under water.

The area also boasts a surprisingly good museum, the **Centro Cultural João Foua**, a fine turn-of-the-century building constructed during the rubber boom and standing in splendid isolation on Praça Santarém, just past the *Mascotinho* restaurant (see p.446). The highlight of the collection is some stunning Indian pottery, small but elaborately decorated and around 2000 years old. The building itself is also very pleasant and the shady internal courtyard is a good spot to hide from the sun on a hot day.

Piranhas and stingrays

One thing definitely worth bearing in mind if you are swimming anywhere in the Amazon is that **piranhas** and **stingrays** (*raia*) are common. Piranhas are actually much less of a problem than you would expect. Forget any films you have seen; they don't attack in shoals, prefer still water to currents and no death or serious injury from piranha attack is on record. Nevertheless, they can give you a nasty bite and are indeed attracted to blood. They frequent particular spots, which locals all know about and avoid, so ask for advice.

Stingrays are more of a problem. They love warm, shallow water and are so well camouflaged that they are practically invisible. If you tread on one, it will whip its sting into your ankle causing a deep gash and agonizing pain for at least 24 hours. However, stingrays really hate noise, crowds, waves and strong currents, and so are rarely found on regularly used beaches, such as Alter do Chão, near Santarém. But off the beaten track, they are an ever-present threat. You can minimize the danger by wearing canvas boots or trainers and by splashing and throwing sand and stones into shallow water if you intend to swim there.

Beaches

Unlike the eastern and western reaches of the Amazon, the region around Santarém has a very distinct **dry season**, stretching from June to December. During this time, Santarém and its surroundings get extremely hot, even by Brazilian standards, with a particularly enervating dry heat. Fortunately this is also the time of year, especially between July and February, when the Tapajós drops and the region's magnificent **river beaches** are exposed.

In the city itself, the beach that forms at the waterfront in the dry season is definitely not recommended, despite the number of locals you'll see swimming there: you can count the raw sewage outlets draining directly into the water as you walk along the promenade. A much better option is to take the local bus to **Maracanã** beach on the far side of town, which is clean. There are lots of small bars and restaurants here serving delicious, freshly caught fish. The very best beach near Santarém, however, is 15km away at Alter do Chão (see p.448).

Eating, drinking and nightlife

You'll find many of Santarém's **restaurants** along the waterfront, but the city's side streets are also a good hunting ground, as is the beach at Maracanã. As you'd expect, fish is the main cuisine. For delicious home-made **ice cream** using regional fruits, go to *Nido* on Mendonça Furtado between Assis Vasconcelos and 2 de Junho; try the *castanha*, the best brazil-nut ice cream you'll ever have. The ice cream at the *Panificadora Lucy*, on the Praça do Pescador, is also very good.

Amazonia Bar on the waterfront. Good bar with one of the nicest atmospheres in town; it also serves great, though not cheap, food.

Bar Mascote Praça do Pescador 10. One of the city's popular waterfront places, with regular live music at weekends. Serves a wide range of moderately priced fish and meat dishes, and a lunchtime *comida por kilo* buffet.

Bom Paladar Av. Cuiabá. Regional fish any way you want it – the *caldeirada* (fish stew) is particularly recommended. Live music on Fri and Sat nights.

Churrascaria Tapajós Av. Tapajós. Along the waterfront, by the gas station and just past the Mercado Modelo, this is the best option for carnivores tired of eating fish. Has a good range of salads as well.

Lumi Av. Cuiabá 1683. A good and moderately priced Japanese restaurant and the best option for vegetarians – the tempura is delicious.

Mascotinho Restaurant-Bar on the waterfront by the Praça Manoel de Jesus Moraes. The place to come for pizza and to enjoy a wonderful location – the restaurant is built out onto the river, right in the heart of town.

Peixaria Piracatú Av. Mendonca Furtado 174. The best fish restaurant in town. Unpretentious, with a distinctly unscenic location, this is the place to come for regional food during lunch and dinner.

Sacy Caseiro Rua Floriano Peixoto 521. Probably the best and busiest lunch-time *comida por kilo.*

Uirapirú on the waterfront opposite *Mascotinho.* The food is mediocre but the good atmosphere and great views out across the river make this a relaxing spot for a beer.

Yacht Clube The restaurant here serves excellent fish and is walkable from the *Amazon Park Hotel*; otherwise take a taxi and arrange for it to pick you up afterwards, as no buses pass this way. Despite its name, it's not at all exclusive, nor are you likely to come across any sailing types. The good-value food costs around R$40 for a meal for two, plus there are lovely views across the Tapajós.

Nightlife

There's no shortage of options when it comes to **nightlife**. On Friday and Saturday nights, the *Mascote*, *Mascotinho* and other waterfront dives have live music; people start here and then head out to the serious music places. The *Yacht Clube* usually has something going on starting at around midnight, and *Sygnus*, a nightclub at Av. Borges Leal 1227 (Ⓣ93/3522-4119) gets going around the same time – most local buses from the centre pass by. One of the coolest spots these days is *La Boum*, at Av. Cuiabá 694, Liberdade (℡93/3522-3632), with live Brazilian dance music until the early hours every Friday and Saturday night, or, if you want to make an all-nighter of it, *Denis Bar* on Mendonça Furtado is the place to go and, unlike the other clubs, it has no cover charge. Not far away on Mendonça is the *Babilônia*, a cavernous hangar with a stage, live music and wild crowds every weekend night. The *Bom Paladar* restaurant on Avenida Cuiabá becomes a nightclub on Friday and Saturday nights and there's good dancing here, but it's the sort of place where you might expect to see Popeye and Bluto trading blows in the corner – get under the table if you hear any shots.

Listings

Airlines Penta, Trav. 15 de Novembro 183 ℡93/3523-4004; Tavaj, corner of Rua Floriano Peixoto with Travessa S. Lemos ℡93/3523-1600.
Banks and exchange Changing cash is a problem in Santarém. None of the banks changes foreign currency. But there are HSBC and Banco do Brasil cash machines which take foreign plastic on Mendonça Furtado in the centre.
Boats Head for the docks nearer the large concrete wharves for river boats to Manaus and Belém, where you can ask the various captains when they're leaving and how much they'll charge. Companies running boats to Manaus and Belém include Antônio Rocha, Rua 24 de Outubro 1047 ℡93/3522-7947; Marquês Pinto Navegação, Rua do Imperador 746 ℡93/3523-2828; and Tarcisio Lopes, Rua Galdino Veloso 290-B ℡ & ⓕ93/3522-2034. Wandering along the waterfront is the best way to find boats heading to the towns between Belém and Manaus; although the larger boats stop at them as well, it's better to get one of the medium-sized boats that only ply that route, since everyone on it will be local and it will probably be less crowded. These boats usually have placards hanging from their side or set out on the concrete promenade, advertising their destinations and departure times. They are very cheap, and most serve beers and soft drinks en route, but your best bet is to take your own food.
Car rental Bill Car, Av. Constantino Nery 111 ℡93/3522-1705; Rede Brasil, Av. Mendonça Furtado 2449 ℡93/3522-2990.
Health matters Should you have health or dental problems, contact Fundação Esperança, Rua Coaracy Nunes 3344, an American-managed clinic and health centre. Santaremzinho, Starenzinho, Aeroporto Velho and Amparo/Conquista buses take you right to the door. Consultations cost R$5.
Internet Tapajós On Line, Av. Mendonça Furtado 2454, sala A (ⓔtapajosonline@tap.com.br).
Shopping For crafts, try the Loja Regional Muiraquita, Rua Bittencourt 131, or the Casa do Artesanato, Rua Bittencourt 69.

Around Santarém

The area around Santarém is richly rewarding, with a variety of day-trips possible out to **Alter do Chão**, **Belterra** or **Fordlândia** as well as boat journeys further afield. Due north, on the opposite bank of the Amazon, some six hours away by boat, is the town of **Alenquer**, the jumping-off point for the stunning waterfall of Véu da Noiva, on the Rio Maicuru. Similar journey times west along the Amazon will land you in **Óbidos**, east takes you to the beautiful town of **Monte Alegre**, and a slightly longer trip south up the Rio Tapajós, through gorgeous river scenery, will bring you to **Itaituba**, a classic gold-rush town 250km from Santarém. To head into less disturbed forest and consequently have better access to wildlife, you could take a **jungle tour** from Santarém led by Amazonas Indian Turismo (see p.476) or one of the tour operators in Alter do Chão. An excellent option is a visit to the **Floresta Nacional do Tapajós**, a national park some forty miles out of town down the Santarém-Cuiabá highway.

Alter do Chão

The municipality of Santarém, which is slightly bigger than Belgium, has just 32km of asphalted road. A good two-thirds of this is accounted for by the road that leads from Santarém to its beach resort of **ALTER DO CHÃO**, and you can't fault their transport priorities. Alter do Chão is a very beautiful bay in the Rio Tapajós overlooked by two easily climbable hills, one the shape of a church altar, giving the place its name. Most of the year the bay is fringed by **white sand beaches**, which combine with the deep blue of the Tapajós to give it a Mediterranean look. In the dry season a sandbank in the middle of the bay is accessible either by wading or by canoe, and simple stalls provide the fried fish and chilled beer essential to the full enjoyment of the scene. During the week you'll almost have the place to yourself, unless you're unlucky enough to coincide with one of the periodic invasions by hundreds of elderly tourists from a cruise ship docked at Santarém. Weekends see the tranquillity shattered, as *Santarenhos* head out en masse for the beach – be careful if you're heading back

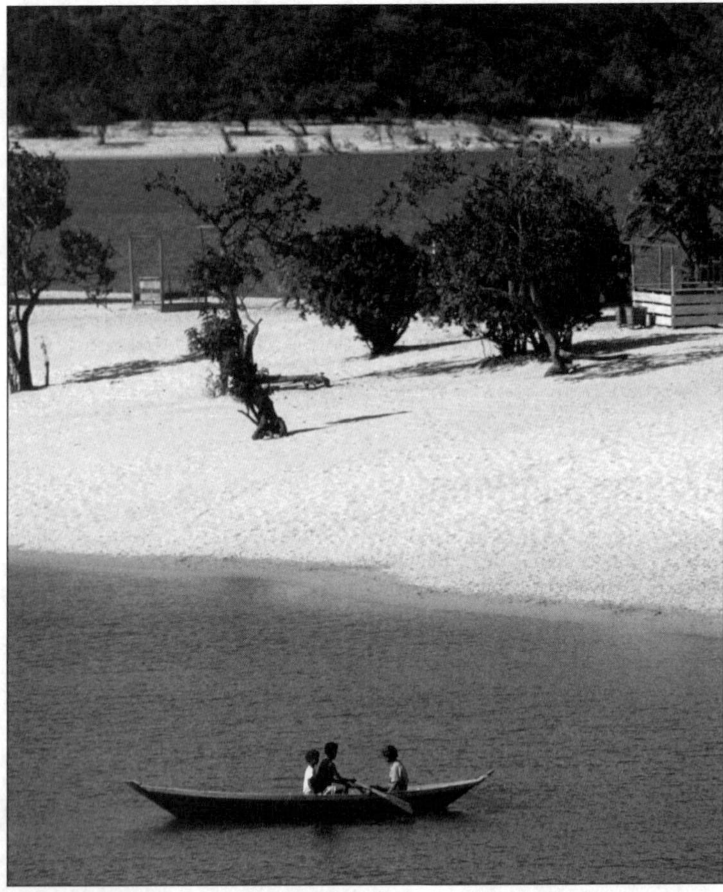

△ Alter do Chão

to Santarém on a weekend afternoon as many drivers on the road will be drunk. If the beach is too crowded, get a canoe to drop you on the other side of the bay at the entrance to the path leading up to the higher conical hill. It's a half-hour walk through the forest and finally up above it to the top to a breathtaking view of the meeting of the Tapajós, Amazon and Arapiuns rivers.

In recent years Alter do Chão has become something of a cult destination on the alternative travel circuit. A couple of **tour operators** geared to this market have opened up; *Vento em Popa* (Ⓣ93/3527-1379, Ⓔventoempopa@netsan.com.br) on the main square, Praça 7 de Setembro, and *Mãe Natureza Ecoturismo* (Ⓣ93/3527-1264, Ⓔmaenatureza@hotmail.com or Ⓔmaenatureza@uol.com.br). They both do reasonably priced forest treks, fishing expeditions and boat trips, with a day costing around R$50 per person. They will also handle renting a house in Alter do Chão, the most economic form of accommodation if you fancy staying a week or two – which many people do, once they see the place.

Practicalities

At weekends there are **buses** every hour to Alter do Chão from in front of the Mercado Modelo in Santarém, with the last one returning at 7.30pm; during the week there are only three buses a day, with two daily returning to town. If you don't feel like getting the last bus back, you might as well make a night of it and stay at one of the three **pousadas** in town, all of them cheap and clean: *Pousada Alter do Chão*, on the waterfront at Rua Lauro Sodré 74 (Ⓣ93/3527-1215; ❶), which has a good restaurant open to non-residents as well; *Pousada Tia Marilda* (❶–❷) on the street leading up from the square; and *Pousada Tupaiulandia*, at Rua Pedro Teixeira 300 (Ⓣ93/3527-1157; ❷), a block further up, which is the best of the bunch. All have ranges of accommodation, starting at around R$30. Away from the beach, the town square is surrounded by **restaurants**, which are all cheap if you stick to the fish. There is also one exceptionally good hotel, with a stunning lakeside setting and rates starting at R$110: the *Hotel Belo Alter* (Ⓣ93/3527-1230 Ⓦwww.beloalter.com.br). They will pick you up from the airport if you reserve in advance.

Half-way along the Alter do Chão road is a signposted turn-off to **Ponto das Pedras**, some 15km along a good-quality dirt road that is easily passable in the dry season and less so in the rains (though still manageable with an ordinary car). This is another of the stunning river beaches in which the Tapajós specializes, with a row of bars and simple restaurants. Depending on what time of year you get there, the rocks that give the beach its name can be either walked or swum out to. There is one basic *pousada* here but no bus services; it's only a practical option by car.

The Floresta do Tapajós

An essential day-trip if you can manage it is to one of the Amazon's few national parks within easy reach of a town or city, the **Floresta Nacional do Tapajós**. Some 30,000 hectares of preserved upland forest riddled by trails, it includes around 50km of Tapajós river frontage, where there are a number of small communities living within the reserve's boundaries. The forest is magnificent, climax primary rainforest towering over the secondary scrubland which the area around has been reduced to by waves of colonization over the last fifty years, with the soy growers being merely the latest of a succession of new arrivals.

There are two ways of visiting the Floresta. The first, by far the easiest, is as part of a package organized by a tour operator in Santarém or Alter do Chão.

You can choose one of two points of entry; the river or one of the communities, in which case you'll be hiking up from floodplain into the uplands, or direct into the upland forest via the Santarém-Cuiabá highway. Here you will drive a few kilometres along a forest road until a clearing where there are a couple of houses belonging to park rangers, from where you hike into the forest proper. The second option is to go there independently, which can be done but only if you rent a car. You will first need to get an entry permit from the park agency IBAMA on Avenida Tapajós, on the waterfront a couple of blocks past the Mercado Modelo. The IBAMA office is actually a complex of buildings; look for the office of the Floresta Nacional on the first floor of the building on the far left as you face the entrance – the guards will point you in the right direction. You must bring your passport and pay a R$6 fee; it will take them just a few minutes to type up the permit, and there is never a queue. They will also give you useful pamphlets and maps. Then just drive some 60km down the highway and the entrance is on the right, with unmissably large placards. If you do not have the permit, the guard at the entrance will not let you in. If there is no guard, unhook the chain and drive in anyway, and eventually, if you don't get pulled over on the way, you'll run into the park rangers in the clearing the road terminates in.

Fordlândia and Belterra

Fordlândia and Belterra are the fruits of an attempt by Henry Ford to revive the Amazon rubber trade in the first half of the twentieth century. Ford's intention was to establish a Brazilian plantation to challenge the growing power of the British- and Dutch-controlled rubber cartels, based in the Far East. He was sold a vast concession on the banks of the lower Rio Tapajós by a local man named Villares. What no one seemed to notice at the time was that Villares also organized the Amazon survey, which ended up visiting only his piece of land. Though it was vast – almost 25,000 square kilometres in all – the tract of land he sold had marginal potential for a plantation of any kind. It depended on seasonal rather than regular rains, it was hilly and therefore awkward to mechanize, the soil was sandy and over-leached and it was beyond the reach of ocean-going vessels for several months every year.

Nevertheless, Henry Ford went ahead with a massive investment, and the construction of **FORDLÂNDIA**, 100km south of Santarém, began in 1928. Cinemas, hospitals and shops were built to complement the processing plants, docks and neat rows of American staff homes; there was even an independent power supply, designed in Detroit. Nothing like it existed within a thousand kilometres in any direction. Unfortunately the rubber planting proceeded at a much slower rate. Difficulties were encountered in trying to clear the valuable timbers that covered the land, and even when it was cleared there was a shortage of rubber-tree seeds. After five years only about ten square kilometres a year were being cleared and planted, at which rate the process would still have been only half completed in the year 3000.

In the 1930s a new site for the plantation was established at **BELTERRA**, and high-yield rubber seeds were imported back from Asia. Belterra is a plain, around 150m above sea level and about 20km from Santarém on the east bank of the Tapajós, at a point where the river is navigable all year round. Even here, though, Ford never looked likely to recover his money, and poor labour relations combined with poor growth to ensure that he didn't. Although the plantations are still operative, they have always suffered from loss of topsoil and from South American Leaf Blight fungus, and they have never made a significant contribution to the world's rubber supply. By the late 1930s Ford himself had lost interest, and in 1945 he sold out to the Brazilian government for $250,000, having already invested well in excess of $20 million.

If you do visit, these are pretty bizarre places. They mimic small-town America exactly, with whitewashed wooden houses, immaculate gardens, fire hydrants, churches and spacious tree-lined streets. The only jarring note is the potholed roads. Belterra is built on a bluff overlooking the Tapajós, with spectacular views down to the river. Fordlândia, with its water towers and the ruined hulk of the rubber-processing factory, is actually on the river and more easily accessible by boat. All boats to Itaituba stop at Fordlândia, the journey taking six to twelve hours depending on the time of year. There's no accommodation but you can probably string your hammock up in the school; and bring your own food as there isn't a restaurant. A daily bus runs to Belterra from the Mercado Modelo, but the road is difficult during the rains. There is one bus a day back, but it's in the morning – again there's no accommodation – so it's not a practical proposition unless you have a car or you can get on an excursion organized by a travel agent in Santarém.

Alenquer

Some five or six hours away from Santarém by boat, through a maze of islands and lakes on the north bank of the Amazon, is **ALENQUER**, a typical small Amazon river town rarely visited by tourists. The town is interesting enough, but wouldn't on its own detain you for more than a couple of hours. The streets are pleasant, the waterfront occasionally bustles and has a good view of the river, and there are a couple of atmospheric public buildings from the days of the rubber boom. However, the surrounding countryside is strikingly beautiful with lakes, an abundance of wildlife and the gorgeous **waterfall** of **Véu da Noiva**, all accessible by either road or boat.

Renting a boat for the day costs about the same as hiring a taxi for a day – around R$80 – and, although the birdlife in the lakes surrounding Alenquer is not as rich as around Monte Alegre (see p.452), the creeks and islands you can explore are, if anything, more scenic. The lakes are actually quite heavily populated, by Amazonian standards, and your boatman is almost certain to take the chance to stop off and visit a relative somewhere on the way, giving you the opportunity to glimpse some rural life. *Botos* (river dolphins) are common and, with luck, you might even see a group of them leaping out of the water together. Unfortunately, piranhas are also common, so be careful about swimming. As for supplies, you will need to take food and water for you and the boatman.

Practicalities

There are two decent **hotels** in town, the *Hotel Cirio* (Ⓣ93/3526-1218; ❶), on the waterfront street to the right as you arrive at the quayside, and the *Pepita Hotel* (Ⓣ93/3526-0002). The owner of the *Cirio*, Dona Maria José, can arrange boats for exploring the lakes and taxis for visiting the waterfall. As tourists in Alenquer are still relatively rare, things are cheap and both of these trips will set you back about R$75 if you arrange them through the hotel; they're well worth it.

There are **boats** every day between Santarém and Alenquer, but you'll need to check on boats coming back before leaving Santarém if you are on a tight schedule – the crew of the departing boat will be able to tell you when the next one back will be. You will have a choice between the regular boats and the high-speed launch, Vendaval. The regular boats, which are much cheaper, take around 10 hours with stops; these leave at 6pm on Monday, Wednesday and Friday and 8pm on Tuesday, Thursday and Sunday from the Santarém waterfront. Vendaval takes only three hours and leaves from next to the *Mascotinho* restaurant at 3pm on Monday, Friday and Sunday, and noon on Saturday. There are also boat connections from Alenquer to Belém, Manaus and Monte Alegre. In the dry season there are **buses** to Óbidos, Oriximiná and Monte Alegre, but the schedule is irregular and depends on the condition of the road, which is usually bad but passable.

Véu da Noiva

The **Véu da Noiva waterfall** is on the Rio Maicuru, a couple of hours' drive from Alenquer on a dirt road that eventually leads to Monte Alegre. A taxi will take you as far as it can and you have to walk the last 3km or so – a beautiful stroll down a forested valley with occasional glimpses of river, before the path drops down right in front of the magnificent waterfall, which is over 6m high and about 45m wide. The waterfall cascades into a glade in the forest with deep pools of deliciously cool water to swim in. Below the falls you can wade with care through shallow rapids, but watch your step on the sharp-edged rocks. It's an idyllic spot and well worth the effort involved in getting here. You will need to take everything for the day with you, including lunch for yourself and your taxi driver (who will wait for you at the end of the road), some water (don't drink the river water no matter how clear it looks), and, most importantly, a note from the owner of the private land on which the waterfall is located – who happens to be a relative of Dona Maria at the hotel, hence the advantage of arranging the trip through her. Without a note, the watchman on the estate won't let you in.

Monte Alegre

If you only have time to visit one river town in the middle Amazon, it should be **MONTE ALEGRE**. Most of the town is built along the brow of a steep hill with spectacular views out across marshes and freshwater lakes, with the Amazon to the south and jagged hills to the north and west, the only pieces of high ground between Belém and Manaus. With its obvious strategic advantages, this was one of the first places on the Amazon to be colonized by Europeans; a small group of English and Irish adventurers settled here in the 1570s, almost fifty years before Belém was founded. They were soon expelled by the Portuguese, and Monte Alegre was a ranching and farming settlement, then a centre of the rubber trade before becoming the prosperous river town it is today. However, there is a much longer history of human settlement in the region. At various points the hills behind the town are covered in spectacular **Indian rock paintings** – one of the main reasons for visiting – that range from abstract geometric patterns through stylized representations of animals and human stick figures to the most compelling images of all: palm prints of the ancient painters themselves. The paintings have been dated at just over 10,000 years old, making Monte Alegre one of the most important archeological sites in South America. Some of the paintings are on rockfaces large enough to be seen from the road, but others are hidden away, requiring a steep climb to see them, so wear good shoes. Also, whatever time of year you go, it is likely to get very hot during the day: take plenty of water, a hat and sunscreen.

You will only be able to visit the paintings by **four-wheel-drive transport** and you will need a **guide**; expect to pay around R$100 a day for the two if you arrange this in Monte Alegre. Amazon Tours in Santarém (see p.444) also does packages to Monte Alegre that take in the paintings. Depending on how many people you can get together, this trip can be very reasonable as it is an all-day expedition. Nelsi Sadeck, Rua do Jaquara 320 (☎93/3533-1430 or 3533-1215), can also arrange trips. Everyone knows him and will point you in the direction of his house. Although he only speaks Portuguese, he is used to taking parties of tourists around the hills, and if he knows people want to go he can usually rustle up a few locals interested in coming along, which will bring the price of the truck rental down. Nelsi can also arrange **boat rental** for around R$75 a day. The water world around Monte Alegre is one of the richest **bird** sites in Amazônia. All along the banks of the Amazon, huge freshwater lakes are separated from the river by narrow strips of land. Depending on the time of year, the lakes either flood over the surrounding land, become marshland or even, in places, sandy cattle pasture. The whole area is thick with birdlife: huge herons, waders of all kinds and a sprinkling of hawks and fish eagles. At sunset, thousands of birds fly in to roost in the trees at the foot of the town. The stunning waterscapes set against the dramatic backdrop of hills make a boat trip really worth doing, even if you can't tell an egret from your elbow. Take everything with you for the day, including lunch for you and the boat owner.

Finally, for a spot of relaxation, head for the **hot springs** at Aguas Sulforosas, 10km inland and reached by taxi or minibus; you can relax free of charge in the springs, and there's a bar, picnic area and pool close by.

Practicalities

Monte Alegre has begun to expand facilities for the still relatively small number of tourists who pass through here. The more basic **places to stay** are on the riverfront: the *Beira Rio Hospedaria* (❷) is pleasant and clean, very friendly and serves excellent food. The better options, however, are in Cidade Alta, up the hill; best of all is the *Hotel Panorama II* (❷) on the Praça Fernando Guilhon, which has a sister hotel on Rua Arnóbio Franco; another good option is the *Hotel Acapulco* (❷) – all are good value. The main square has a fabulous view out across the Amazon and the lakes, and there's a bar here, *Bar do Mirante*, conveniently situated for you to watch the sunset. **Eating options** are simple but good; *Restaurante Panorama* on Travessa Oriental has the best view, though also recommended are *Mistura Fina* on Rua João Coelho 123, and *Pontão das Aguas* on Avenida Presidente Vargas. All the hotels above have basic restaurants as well.

Transport connections are good. Monte Alegre is one of the main stops on the Belém–Santarém–Manaus **boat** route, and there are also dedicated services from both Santarém and Belém that are usually less crowded. Boats from Prainha and Macapá also stop here. Leaving, you won't wait more than two days wherever you're headed.

Itaituba

Travelling south up the Rio Tapajós, between twelve and fourteen hours from Santarém depending on the time of year (the current is much stronger in the rainy season), you come to another face of the Amazon, the gold-rush town of **ITAITUBA**. The **boat journey** here is one of the main reasons for going – the broad mouth of the Tapajós, over 30km wide where it joins the Amazon just west of Santarém, soon narrows enough so you can appreciate the forest on either side. There is usually plenty of wildlife to be seen, including anteaters swimming across the river, dolphins and parrots galore.

Gold prospecting and **mining** began in the headwaters of the Tapajós in the 1950s with a few skilled prospectors from former British Guyana. Itaituba remained no more than a tiny village, living more from trade in rubber and animal pelts than gold until the early 1970s when the Transamazônia highway arrived and changed everything. The highway itself was only open for a few years; it was too expensive to maintain and was soon reclaimed by forest. Nevertheless, it was long enough to channel a new wave of migrants into the area, and when the price of gold started to rise after 1974 there was capital and labour available to begin exploiting the mines in a big way. The city mushroomed, and its current population of 53,000 makes it by far the biggest town on the Tapajós, even in its current depressed state (the gold has been giving out and the price has fallen since the boom years of the mid-1980s). Many mine owners are forming partnerships with big Brazilian mining companies now that the easily available gold has been mined, and Itaituba will continue to be a mining town for the foreseeable future, albeit with fewer miners and nothing like as wild a nightlife as it used to have.

The town seems unprepossessing at first, all of its buildings modern and most of them ugly, but there is a certain energy and frontier feel about the place. You'll soon start to see the gold-buying shops in the commercial area, dominating everything with their signs "*Compra-se Oura*" (we buy gold). Go inside and you can watch miners bringing in gold dust and fragments that are then burned (don't get too close; the smoke is mercury vapour), weighed and purchased with bundles of notes. Miners, despite their fearsome reputation, are quite friendly if you're polite, and are usually proud to show off their gold. Things are quieter now than they used to be but Itaituba is still the trading centre of the largest gold field in the Brazilian Amazon, supplying scores of mines (*garimpos*) scattered in the forest to the south of town and usually only accessible by air.

Practicalities

Itaituba has several **bars** and **restaurants** on the waterfront, and no shortage of **hotels**; the best is the *Juliana Park* (Ⓣ93/3518-0548; ❸), with excellent breakfasts and air conditioning – essential because it's hot here all the time. The riverfront has a couple of bars serving fish but so many non-Amazonians live here that local tastes run more to meat; there are a couple of *churrascarias* and street corners with bars cooking up *carne do sol*. It is possible to rent boats to go further upriver but you can only go about an hour or so before major rapids just past the village of São Luís do Tapajós make the river impassable. Boats back to Santarém leave every day, usually in the early evening; ask about them at the waterfront.

Óbidos

Around forty million years ago, when the Andes began to form themselves by pushing up from the earth, a vast inland sea burst through from what is now known as the main Amazon basin. The natural bursting point was more or less the site of modern-day **ÓBIDOS**. The huge sea squeezed itself through where the Guyanan shield to the north meets the Brazilian shield from the south, and cut an enormous channel through alluvial soils in its virgin route to the Atlantic. The river is some seven kilometres wide at Santarém, while at Óbidos, about 100km upstream, it has narrowed to less than two kilometres. Physically then, Óbidos is the gateway to the Amazon; there's an old fort to protect the passage, and most boats going upstream or down will stop here for an hour or two at least.

In the Cabanagem Rebellion (see box, p.422), most of the town's leading white figures were assassinated by rebels, and Óbidos was looted and left ungoverned for years. Describing this period, the English botanist Richard Spruce remarked that anti-white feeling ran so strong in Óbidos that the mob considered the wearing of a beard as a crime punishable by death.

Óbidos is now a pretty river town with a very attractive **waterfront** that's little changed since the 1920s. It makes a good stopover if you feel like breaking the journey between Manaus and Santarém or Belém. The sights won't keep you more than a morning, but it is a pleasant town to stroll around. The main thing to see is the seventeenth-century **Forte Pauxis** on the Praça Coracy Nunes, which played a crucial strategic role in Amazon history. Since that era this has been the jumping-off point for the settlement of the upper Amazon, and the cannons still in position on the ramparts command the whole width of the river. Its strategic importance meant that Óbidos was the largest town on the middle Amazon during colonial times, but the fort is the only colonial relic. Elsewhere the town has some fine buildings dating from the rubber boom and identified by metal plaques giving their history (in Portuguese only). Most of them are in the commercial area just off the waterfront, constructed by trading families as emporiums on the ground floor with living quarters above. Most are still shops, selling simple hammocks and pots and pans.

The only really interesting **museum** in town depends on the enthusiasm of a single person, Dona Maria, who lives next door, on the road leading down from the main square. Everyone knows her so just ask for her by name. If the museum isn't open, knock on her door and she will be only too pleased to let you in. The small collection is eclectic, ranging from Indian pottery to imported British household luxuries from the rubber-boom days. There are also some intriguing old photographs: you can see that the town has hardly changed since the early years of the century. Entrance is free, but leave some money for its upkeep and sign the visitors' book; Dona Maria, who likes exotic signatures, will insist.

The town's other attractions are river-based, as you might expect. Just 25km from Óbidos along the PA-254, you can go bathing in the beautiful **Igarapé de Curuçambá**, which is served by local buses. There are also organized trips to the narrowest of Amazon river straits with impressive forested river cliffs and close-up views of riverbank homesteads and jungle vegetation. Ask about trips at the port or the *Braz Bello* hotel.

If you end up **staying** try the *Braz Bello*, Rua Marios Rodrigues de Souza 86 (Ⓣ93/3547-1411), which is a reasonable mid-range hotel, while along the waterfront you'll find several decent bars and restaurants. Alternatively there's the slightly cheaper *Pousada Brasil* on Rua Correia Pinto, which offers a range of rooms. **Boats** travel in and out of Óbidos every day. If you're heading to Santarém, take the smaller boats that only ply that route rather than hopping onto one of the larger Manaus–Belém boats, which tend to be slower and more expensive.

Western Amazônia

An arbitrary border, a line on paper through the forest, divides the state of Pará from the western Amazon. Encompassing the states of **Amazonas**, **Rondônia**, **Acre** and **Roraima**, the western Amazon is dominated even more than the east by the Amazon and Solimões rivers and their tributaries. This is a remote and poorly serviced region representing the heart of the world's largest rainforest. The northern half of the forest is drained by two large rivers, the gigantic Rio Negro and its major affluent, the Rio Branco. Travelling north from Manaus, the dense rainforest phases into the wooded savannas and then the mysterious mountains of Roraima at the border with Venezuela and Guyana. To the south, the Madeira, Purús and Juruá rivers, all huge and important in their own way, meander through the forests from the prime rubber region of Acre and the recently colonized state of Rondônia.

The hub of this area is undoubtedly **Manaus**, more or less at the junction of three great rivers – the Solimões/Amazonas, the Negro and the Madeira – which, between them, support the world's greatest surviving forest. There are few other settlements of any real size. In the north, **Boa Vista**, capital of Roraima, lies on an overland route to Venezuela. South of the Rio Amazonas there's **Porto Velho**, capital of Rondônia, and, further west, **Rio Branco**, the main town in the relatively unexplored rubber-growing state of Acre – where the now famous Chico Mendes lived and died, fighting for a sustainable future for the forest.

Travel is never easy or particularly comfortable in the western Amazon. **From Manaus** it's possible to go by **bus** to Venezuela or Boa Vista, which is just twelve hours or so on the tarmacked BR-174 through the stunning tropical forest zone of the Waimiris tribe, with over fifty rickety wooden bridges en route. You can also head east to the Amazon river settlement of Itacoatiara; but the BR-317 road from the south bank close to Manaus down to Porto Velho is presently open only for adventurous four-wheel-drive vehicles, having been repossessed by the rains and vegetation for most of its length. **From Porto Velho** the Transamazônica continues into Acre and **Rio Branco**, from where the route on to Peru is slowly being paved and is really only possible in the dry season. Alternatively, from Porto Velho, the paved BR-364 offers quick access south to Cuiabá, Mato Grosso, Brasília and the rest of Brazil.

The rivers are the traditional and still very much dominant means of communication. Entering from the east, the first places beyond Óbidos are the small ports of **Parintins** and **Itacoatiara.** The former is home to the internationally known Bio Bumbá festival every June and the latter has bus connections with Manaus if you're really fed up with the boat, though the roads are often very hard-going in the rainy season (Dec–April). From Itacoatiara it's a matter of hours till Manaus appears near the confluence of the Negro and Solimões rivers. It takes another five to eight days by boat to reach the Peruvian frontier, and even here the river is several kilometres wide and still big enough for ocean-going ships.

The western Amazon normally receives a lot of rain – up to 375cm a year in the extreme west and about 175cm around Manaus. In December 2005, however, the latter region suffered the worst drought in 40 years (with 65 percent less rainfall than average for this time of year), prompting the governor to declare a state of emergency. Many fish died, stranded in pools as the rivers receded, and entire communities were cut off, with boat-dependent island settlements surrounded by drying mud and rotting fish. Forty schools were forced to close and there were fears of disease spreading through the unsanitary conditions created by the lack of water. In ordinary circumstances, the area's heaviest rains fall in January and February, with a relatively dry season from June to October. The humidity rarely falls much below eighty percent, and the temperature in the month of December can reach well above 40°C. This takes a few days to get used to: until you do it's like being stuck in a sauna with only shady trees, an occasional breeze, air conditioning or cool drinks to help you escape.

Amazon **flora and fauna**

The Amazon rainforest is the largest and most biodiverse tropical forest on earth. Its sheer abundance is overwhelming: many thousands of species of plants and nearly a thousand species of bird, not to mention numerous mammals, reptiles and unidentified animal species, call the jungle – and often nowhere else – home. Through it all runs the mighty Amazon River; while a trip on the river itself doesn't provide many wildlife-spotting opportunities, during the rainy season in particular (Dec–April), plenty of river banks and flood plains in the region are perfect for such sightings.

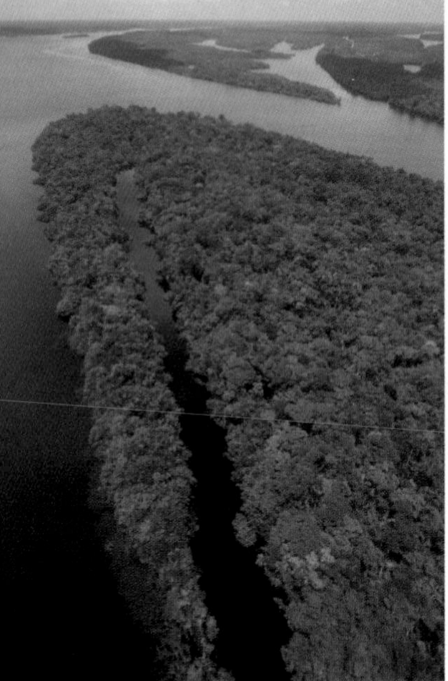

▲ Permanently flooded forest

Flora

The Amazon rainforest has enormous **structural diversity**, with layers of vegetation from the forest floor to the canopy about 30m above providing a vast number of habitats. With the rainforest being stable over longer periods of time than temperate areas (there was no Ice Age here, nor any prolonged period of drought), the **fauna** has had freedom to evolve, and to adapt to often very specialized local conditions.

Like other rainforests, the Amazon has well over two hundred tree species per hectare, most of them broad-leafed and evergreen and suited to warm and wet tropical conditions. Branches and leaves are generally shed throughout the year while flowers – many with very bright red and yellow colours – are more seasonal. Among these, the heliconia demonstrates **flora and fauna interdependency**: the bronze hummingbird's long, nectar-probing beak is perfectly designed to pollinate this brilliant Amazon plant. Bromeliads are largely specific to the Americas and there are over 1800 such species in the Amazon forest; pollination is also by hummingbirds, but sometimes by bats, moths or bees as well. Due to their speciality of collecting water in their leaves, bromeliads can be **a source of clean water** for anyone unfortunate enough to be lost and parched in the forest.

Fauna

Exotic **tropical birds** are commonplace in the Amazon. Even birds that are endangered or rarely seen in Europe, like the osprey (fish eagle), are frequently spotted here, and ibis, macaws, toucans, herons and the various kingfishers can be sighted in a day or two on the river. The harpy eagle is rare, but sometimes seen, while **reptiles**, particularly caiman, are easy to spot along the rivers' edges. Occasionally an iguana might leap from branch to ground, making a thrashing noise as he goes. Snakes are common, though rarely encountered, while ants – including the fascinating leaf-cutter – are everywhere.

▼ Piranha

Mammals are generally harder to see, though it's not unusual to come across three or more species in a three-day jungle trip. Howler monkeys, woolly monkeys, spider monkeys, dusky titis, capuchin and red-faced Ukari monkeys all make themselves visible or audible now and again. Lonesome sloths are frequently seen high up in the canopy, sleeping or munching leaves. Tapir, wild boar and

Common plants and trees

Amazon lily The night-blooming Amazon lily (*Victoria amazonica*) has nine- to twelve-inch creamy white flowers that become pink later in the day and then a purplish red the third day before dying. Its leaves – which, along with its stems, are covered in sharp spines on its undersides – are the plant's most amazing feature. More or less round and up to six feet in diameter, their ribbing gives them a tremendous strength: small children (up to 10 kilos) can sometimes sit on a leaf without it sinking.

▲ Brazil nut tree

Brazil nut tree (Bertholletia excelsa) Known in Brazil as *castanho do pará*, this tree can grow to more than 30m tall and live for hundreds of years. After reaching nut-bearing maturity, a single specimen can produce over 450kg of nuts every year during the rainy season. The nuts grow like segments of an orange inside a coconut-sized outer shell at the end of the trees' branches. Once the nuts ripen, the shells crash to the ground from high above the canopy and are collected and broken open with a machete. Brazil nuts are a large-scale yet totally sustainable export product with a ready market all over the world.

▼ Rubber tree

Rubber tree (Hevea brasilensis) The rubber tree, called *seringuera* in Brazil, is the best-known of all Amazon trees. It produces a liquid extract called latex, which is the primary source of rubber. A hundred years ago the rubber tree was the basis of an export boom that transformed the Amazon, and rubber is still a valuable export in Brazil today.

jaguar are harder to come across, but not impossible to find. **Swimming with dolphins** is an increasingly popular pastime in the Amazon – both pink and grey ones abound, often spotted looking for food where one river enters another. The Amazon is also famous for its great **fresh-water fishing** and most visitors have a go, usually quite successfully, at catching a **piranha** or two for supper.

▼ Ukari monkey

Common birds and mammals

▲ Tapir

Harpy eagle (*Harpia harpyja*) The most powerful of all birds of prey, the harpy eagle can grow up to 105cm. It has a black chest and a distinguishing bifurcated black crest on its head; its feathers have been used for millennia to adorn the headdresses of tribal chiefs across the Amazon. The harpy spends most of its time wheeling skilfully between branches in search of monkeys, snakes, sloths and birds to feed on.

Macaw (*Psittacidae*) Noisy, gregarious creatures with strong bills, the macaw mates for life (which can be as long as a hundred years), and pairs fly among larger flocks. Common macaws include the blue-and-yellow macaw (*Ara ararauna*), which grows to almost 1m and has a very long, pointed tail; the scarlet macaw (*Ara macao*); and the red-and-green macaw (*Ara cloroptera*).

Brazilian tapir (*Tapirus terrestris*) At around 2m long, the Brazilian tapir is the largest land mammal in the forest. It's brown to dark grey in colour and is noted for its large upper lip, while its tail is stumpy, its feet are three-toed and its back is noticeably convex. Largely nocturnal, the tapir browses swampy forests for fruit and grasses.

Dolphins The pink river dolphin (*Inia geoffrensis*) is about 2m long and has a noticeable dorsal fin. It feeds exclusively on fish and will swim with (or within a few metres of) people. The smaller grey dolphin, or *tucuxi* (*Sotalia fluviatilis*), achieves a maximum length of 1.5m and has a more prominent dorsal fin; it usually jumps further and is more acrobatic than the pink dolphin.

Giant otter (*Pteronura brasiliensis*) Just over 1m long, the giant otter has a thickish tail with a flattened tip. Its alarm call is a snort, and it is very aggressive when in danger. It eats fish and moves in extended family groups, with the males doing the least fishing but the most eating.

Jaguar (*Pantera onca*) Powerfully built, the jaguar is almost 2m long, with black spots on silvery to tan fur; it hunts large mammals, though it fishes too. Mainly rainforest dwellers, the jaguar is most frequently spotted sunning itself on fallen trees. If you meet one, the best way to react is to make lots of noise.

▼ Spotted jaguar

Manaus and around

MANAUS is the capital of Amazonas, a tropical forest state covering around one and a half million square kilometres. The city is also the commercial and physical hub of the entire Amazon region. Most visitors are surprised to learn that Manaus isn't actually on the Amazon at all. Rather it lies on the Rio Negro, six kilometres from the point where that river meets the Solimões to form (as far as Brazilians are concerned) the Rio Amazonas. Just a few hundred metres away from the tranquil life on the rivers, the centre of Manaus perpetually buzzes with energy: always noisy, crowded and confused. Escaping from the frenzy is not easy, but there is the occasional quiet corner, and the sights around the port, markets, Opera House and some of the museums make up for the hectic pace downtown. In the port and market areas, pigs, chickens and people selling hammocks line the streets and there's an atmosphere that seems unchanged in centuries.

For the Amazon hinterland, Manaus has long symbolized "civilization". Traditionally, this meant simply that it was the **trading centre**, where the hardships of life in the forest could be escaped temporarily and where manufactured commodities to make that life easier – metal pots, steel knives, machetes and the like – could be purchased. Virgin jungle seems further from the city these days (just how far really depends on what you want "virgin forest" to mean), but there are still waterways and channels within a short river journey of Manaus where you can find dolphins, alligators, kingfishers and the impression, at least, that humans have barely penetrated. Indeed, most visitors to Manaus rightly regard a **river trip** as an essential part of their stay; various **jungle tour and lodge** options are set out on pp.476–477 (see also box, pp.418–419 for longer river journeys, and boat details under "Listings" on p.471). Even if you can't afford the time to disappear up the Amazon for days at a stretch, however, there are a number of sites around Manaus that make worthwhile day excursions, most notably the **meeting of the waters** of the yellow Rio Solimões and the black Rio Negro, and the lily-strewn **Parque Ecólogico Janauary**. Additionally, a six-hour bus ride will take you to Novo Aírão, where it's possible to bathe in clean rivers and swim with pink dolphins at the port.

Some history

Established as a town in 1856, the name Manaus was given for the Manaós tribe, which was encountered in this region by São Luís do Maranhão while he was exploring the area in 1616. Missionaries arrived in 1657 and a small trading settlement, originally known as São José da Barra, evolved around their presence. The city you see today is primarily a product of the **rubber boom** and in particular the child of visionary state governor **Eduardo Ribeiro**, who from 1892 transformed Manaus into a major city. Under Ribeiro the Opera House was completed, and whole streets were wiped out in the process of laying down broad Parisian-style avenues, interspersed with Italian piazzas centred on splendid fountains. In 1899 Manaus was the first Brazilian city to have trolley buses and the second to have electric lights in the streets.

At the start of the twentieth century Manaus was an opulent metropolis run by elegant people, who, despite the tropical heat, dressed and housed themselves as fashionably as their counterparts in any large European city. The rich constructed palaces and grandiose mansions and time was passed at elaborate parties, dances and concerts. But this heyday lasted barely thirty years; Ribeiro committed suicide in 1900 and by 1914 the rubber market was collapsing fast. There was a second brief boost for Brazilian rubber during World War II, but

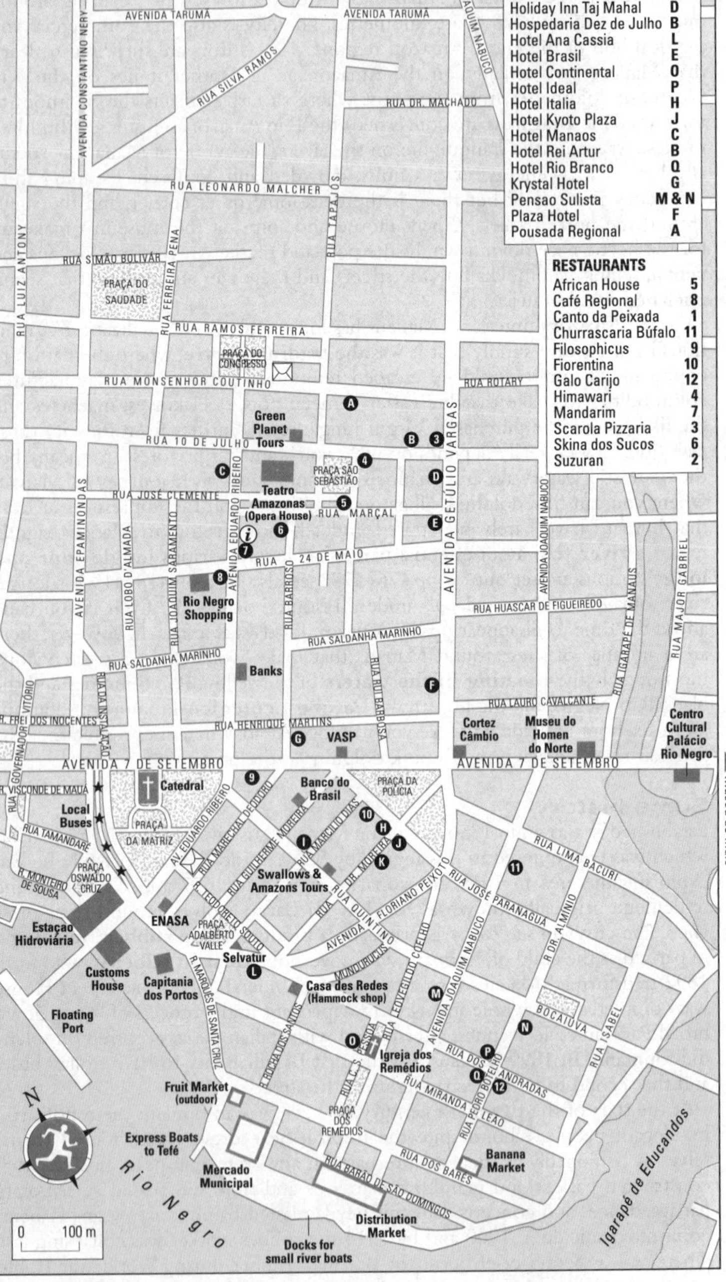

MANAUS
1 & 2
ACCOMMODATION
Best Western Hotel I
Central Hotel K
Holiday Inn Taj Mahal D
Hospedaria Dez de Julho B
Hotel Ana Cassia L
Hotel Brasil E
Hotel Continental O
Hotel Ideal P
Hotel Italia H
Hotel Kyoto Plaza J
Hotel Manaos C
Hotel Rei Artur B
Hotel Rio Branco Q
Krystal Hotel G
Pensao Sulista M & N
Plaza Hotel F
Pousada Regional A
RESTAURANTS
African House 5
Café Regional 8
Canto da Peixada 1
Churrascaria Búfalo 11
Filosophicus 9
Fiorentina 10
Galo Carijo 12
Himawari 4
Mandarim 7
Scarola Pizzaria 3
Skina dos Sucos 6
Suzuran 2
AVENIDA TARUMÃ
AVENIDA CONSTANTINO NERY
AVENIDA JOAQUIM NABUCO
RUA SILVA RAMOS
RUA DR. MACHADO
RUA LEONARDO MALCHER
RUA TAPAJÓS
RUA SIMÃO BOLIVÁR
RUA LUIZ ANTONY
RUA FERREIRA PENA
PRAÇA DO SAUDADE
RUA RAMOS FERREIRA
PRAÇA DO CONGRESSO
RUA MONSENHOR COUTINHO
RUA ROTARY
Green Planet Tours
RUA 10 DE JULHO
PRAÇA SÃO SEBASTIÃO
AVENIDA GETÚLIO VARGAS
AVENIDA EDUARDO RIBEIRO
Teatro Amazonas (Opera House)
RUA JOSÉ CLEMENTE
RUA MARÇAL
AVENIDA EPAMINONDAS
RUA LOBO D'ALMADA
RUA JOAQUIM SARAMENTO
RUA 24 DE MAIO
RUA BARROSO
Rio Negro Shopping
AVENIDA JOAQUIM NABUCO
RUA MAJOR GABRIEL
RUA HUASCAR DE FIGUEIREDO
RUA IGARAPÉ DE MANAUS
RUA SALDANHA MARINHO
Banks
RUA RUI BARBOSA
RUA DA INSTALAÇÃO
AVENIDA GOVERNADOR VITÓRIO
RUA LAURO CAVALCANTE
R. FREI DOS INOCENTES
RUA HENRIQUE MARTINS
VASP
Cortez Câmbio
Museu do Homen do Norte
Centro Cultural Palácio Rio Negro
AVENIDA 7 DE SETEMBRO
Museu do Indio
R. VISCONDE DE MAUÁ
Catedral
Banco do Brasil
PRAÇA DA POLICIA
Local Buses
PRAÇA DA MATRIZ
RUA TAMANDARÉ
AV. EDUARDO RIBEIRO
RUA MARECHAL DEODORO
RUA GUILHERME MOREIRA
RUA MARCILIO DIAS
RUA DR. MOREIRA
RUA LIMA BACURI
PRAÇA OSWALDO CRUZ
R. MONTEIRO DE SOUSA
Swallows & Amazons Tours
RUA FLORIANO PEIXOTO
RUA JOSÉ PARANAGUA
R. TEODORETO SOUTO
RUA QUINTINO
Estação Hidroviária
ENASA
PRAÇA ADALBERTO VALLE
AVENIDA
R. DR. ALMINIO
Customs House
Capitania dos Portos
Selvatur
R. MARQUES DE SANTA CRUZ
MUNDURUCUS
RUA LEOVEGILDO COELHO
Casa des Redes (Hammock shop)
Floating Port
RUA ROCHA DOS SANTOS
RUA PESSOA
BOCAIUVA
RUA ISABEL
Igreja dos Remédios
RUA DOS ANDRADAS
RUA C. S.
RUA MIRANDA LEÃO
RUA PEDRO BOTELHO
Fruit Market (outdoor)
PRAÇA DOS REMÉDIOS
N
Express Boats to Tefé
Rio Negro
RUA DOS BARÉS
Banana Market
Igarapé de Educandos
Mercado Municipal
RUA BARÃO DE SÃO DOMINGOS
Distribution Market
Docks for small river boats
0 100 m

today's prosperity is largely due to the creation of a **Free Trade Zone**, the Zona Franca, in 1966. Over the following ten years the population doubled, from 250,000 to half a million, and many new industries moved in, especially electronics companies. An impressive international airport was opened in 1976 and the floating port, supported on huge metal cylinders to cope with variations of as much as 14m in the level of the river, was modernized to accommodate the new business.

Today, with over one and a half million inhabitants, Manaus is an aggressive commercial and industrial centre for an enormous region – the Hong Kong of the Amazon. Over half of Brazil's televisions are made here and electronic goods are around a third cheaper here than in the south. It is Brazil's ninth biggest city and home to over ten percent of North Brazil's population. Cheap electronic products as much as the lure of the Amazon drives the city's buoyant domestic tourism – Manaus airport is often crowded with Brazilians going home with their arms laden with TVs, hi-fis, computers and fax machines. Landless and jobless Brazilians also flock here looking for work, particularly as there are more prospects in Manaus than in many parts of the Northeast.

Arrival, information and accommodation

Try to avoid arriving on a Sunday, when the city is very quiet and few places are open. If you arrive in Manaus by river, your **boat** will dock right in the heart of the city, either at the riverside *hidroviária* near the Mercado Municipal or more likely a short distance away in the Porto Flutuante (floating port) complex, known these days as the **Estação Hidroviária Internacional de Manaus** where you also need to go to buy boat tickets to most destinations. The Estação Hidroviária has a tourist information booth and affords good views over the port from a new indoor centre, featuring shops and cafés, which is accessed via a walkway from Avenida Marques de Santa Cruz. If you're arriving from Peru or Colombia, don't forget to have your passport stamped at the Customs House, if you haven't already done so in Tabatinga. The **rodoviária** (☎92/3642-5805)

△ Boi Bumbá festival

Boi Bumbá in Parintins

Parintins is an otherwise unremarkable small river town with a population of around 100,000 lying roughly halfway between Santarém and Manaus. In the last twenty years, however, it has become the unlikely centre of one of the largest mass events in Brazil, the Boi Bumbá celebrations, which take place in the last weekend of June every year. Highly popular, the official name is the Festival Folclórico de Parintins, but it is often called Boi Bumbá after the name for a funny and dramatized dance that is traditionally performed at the festival concerning the death and rebirth of an ox. The seeds go back at least a hundred years, when the Cid brothers from Maranhão arrived in the area bringing with them the Bumba-meu-boi musical influence from the culture-rich ex-slave plantations.

Thanks to astute marketing, what began as a local custom has now become a megabucks spectacle, attracting tens of thousands of visitors to a stadium unforgettably called the Bumbódromo and built to look like a massive stylized bull. Located in the Convention Centre of Amazonino Mendes, the stadium hosts a wild, energetic parade by something resembling an Amazonian version of Rio samba schools – and the resemblance is not coincidental, the organizers having consciously modelled themselves on Rio's Carnaval.

Boi Bumbá in Parintins revolves around two schools, Caprichoso and Garantido. Each year they vie for a championship by parading through the Bumbódromo, where according to custom supporters of one school must watch the opposing parade in complete silence. You thus have the strange spectacle of 20,000 people going wild while the other half of the stadium is as quiet as a funeral, with roles reversed a few hours later. Much like the Bumbá-meu-boi of São Luís (see p.400), Parintins' Boi Bumbá has its high point with the enactment of the death of a bull, part of the legend of the slave Ma Catirina who, during her pregnancy, developed a craving for ox tongue. To satisfy her craving, her husband, Pa Francisco, slaughtered his master's bull, but the master found out and decided to arrest Pa Francisco with the help of some Indians. As the legend would have it, however, the priest and the witch doctor managed to resuscitate the animal, thus saving Pa Francisco; with the bull alive once more, the party begins again at fever pitch, with a frenetic rhythm that pounds away well into the hot and smoke-filled night.

The parade is undeniably spectacular, and the music infectious. But don't be deceived by all the references to tradition and Indian culture: the parades have only existed on this scale since the 1990s, and have about as much to do with Indian

is on Avenida Recife some 10km north of the centre; #306 buses run every twenty minutes down Avenida Constantino Nery (two streets from the bus station), to Praça da Matriz in the heart of town, while taxis cost around R$25. The **airport** (Aeroporto de Eduardo Gomes; Ⓣ92/3652-1212) is on Avenida Santos Dumont in the Tarumã district, 17km from town in the same direction. It is also served by bus #306 (first bus 5.30am, last bus around midnight; 40min); alternatively, take a taxi for around R$35. Many tour operators offer airport pick-up if you're booked with them; and Geraldo Mesquita of Amazon Gero Tours (Ⓣ & Ⓕ92/3232-4755, mobile Ⓣ9983-6273, Ⓔgeromesquita@hotmail.com) also offers a reliable airport pick-up (approx. R$35 for up to four passengers or R$45 for five to ten people).

The most central of the **tourist offices**, the main Central de Atendimento ao Turista, operated by the state tourism company (Amazonastur Ⓦwww.visitamazonas.com.br and Ⓦwww.amazonastur.am.gov.br), is close to the Teatro Amazonas opera house, behind and downhill from the theatre building, on Av. Eduardo Ribeiro 666 (Mon–Fri 8am–6pm, Sat 8am–1pm, Sun culture as the Rio samba schools that served as a model. All the same, it is enjoyable, and is an enormous benefit to the people of the town, which has little else going for it economically. Thousands of people get through the rest of the year on the proceeds of catering for the huge influx of visitors during the festivities. If you're going to participate, remember that joining in with the Caprichoso group means you mustn't use red clothing; if you're dancing with the Garantido school, you need to avoid blue clothes as far as possible.

The number of people who descend on Parintins is considerably larger than the town's population. During the festival, forget about accommodation in any of the town's few hotels: they are booked up months in advance. Your best chance in this case is simply to stay on a boat: in all the towns and cities of the region – notably Manaus and Santarém – you will find boats and travel agencies offering all-inclusive packages for the event, with accommodation in hammocks on the boats, and this is by far the easiest way to do it. Seeing the town harbour crammed with hundreds of boats is a sight in itself. Most of the riverboat companies offer three- or four-day packages, costing between R$200 and R$700. The trips (26hr from Manaus, 20hr from Santarém) are often booked well in advance, and are advertised from March onwards on banners tied to the boats. As you might expect, there is a lot of petty thieving and pickpocketing, so take extra care of anything you bring with you.

During the rest of the year there are a couple of good places to stay: *Hotel Avenida* at Av. Amazonas 2416 (☎92/3533-1158; ❷) has clean and good-value rooms, while the *Hotel Uirapuru* at Rua Herbert de Azevedo 1486 (☎92/3533-0226; ❸), though smaller, is more comfortable and has excellent service. The best restaurant is *Aos Amigos*, at Av. das Nacoes Unidas 2883 (☎92/3533-1446), which serves typical Amazon cuisine and is open until midnight (closed Mon).

For tourist information, the Secretaria de Estado da Cultura, Turismo e Desporto (SEC), has an office at Rua Jonathas Pedrosa 247-A, in Manaus Centre (daily 8am–noon & 1–6pm, ☎92/3533-2215). It can provide details on accommodation in Parentins, as well as programme lists and entrance prices. The airport (☎92/3533-2700), on the Parananema road, is just 4km from town.

If you want to contact a Boi Bumbá band in Manaus, try Filhos da Amazonia ☎92/3635-0884; Banda Doce Magia ☎92/3238-6094; or, Guerreiros do Boi ☎92/3671-7256.

8am–2pm; ☎92/3232-1998), where the friendly staff can advise on the city's sights and entertainment and provide maps and brochures. You can also check the background of any tour operator here or lodge a complaint against one if need be. There are other tourist offices, however, at the **airport** (☎92/3652-1120, in the main arrivals hall, daily 7am–11pm); at the **Amazonas Shopping** centre, Av. Djalma Batista 482 (☎92/3648-1396, Mon–Sat 9am–10pm & Sun 3–9pm); at the **rodoviária** on Avenida Recife in the Flores district (daily 7am–11pm); and at the Estação Hidroviária (☎92/3233-8698; Mon–Fri 8am–5pm).

Accommodation

Plenty of travellers end up in Manaus, so there's a wide range of places to stay, with a number of perfectly reasonable **cheap hotels**, especially in the area around Avenida Joaquim Nabuco and Rua dos Andradas. The downtown centre is just a few blocks from here, with the docks for boats up and down the Amazon and Rio Negro also nearby. Even cheaper are the hotels along

Rua José Paranaguá, two blocks north of Rua dos Andradas, though this road is particularly unsafe at night. Some streets close to the Teatro Amazonas, particularly along Rua 10 de Julho, are increasingly popular as places to stay. Although there is still room for improvement, the area is relatively safe; many buildings have been renovated and new café-bars have opened around the Praça São Sebastião. If you want to **camp**, it may be possible to find a secure option beyond the *Tropical Hotel* at the sites around Praia Ponta Negra.

Best Western Lord Manaus Hotel Rua Marcílio Dias 217 ⓣ92/3622-2844, ⓕ3622-2576, ⓦwww.bestwestern.com.br). Relatively plush for central Manaus, with apartments and suites; this is the best value hotel in central Manaus. Some rooms have views over the city centre, but there is no pool. ❼

Central Hotel Rua Dr Moreira 202 ⓣ92/3622-2600, ⓕ3622-2609 ⓔhcentral@terra.com.br. Offers a wide choice of comfortable rooms, all with TV, *frigobar* and a/c. There's a good restaurant on-site, too, and 24-hour room service. Excellent value. ❹

Holiday Inn Taj Mahal Av. Getulio Vargas 741 ⓣ92/3627-3737, ⓦwww.grupotajmahal.com.br. Arguably Manaus's grandest modern hotel, with top-quality rooms, adequate service and a circular, rotating restaurant affording the best possible views over the Opera House. The fish dishes here are especially good. Offers an airport transfer for a small fee. ❾

Hospedaria Dez de Julho Rua Dez de Julho 679 ⓣ92/3232-6280, ⓔhtdj@vivax.com.br, ⓦwww.hoteldesdejulho.com. This family-run hotel is located near the Opera House in a pleasant part of the city. Rooms are modern and clean, with TVs and bathrooms, though some of the newer ones lack finishing and could do with additional furnishings to make them feel more homely. The rooms upstairs have more light; breakfast is included. Amazon Gero Tours operates from an office next door and Iguana Tours have an office inside. ❸

Hotel Ana Cassia Rua dos Andrades 14 ⓣ92/3622-3637, ⓔhacassia@terra.com.br. Located in a tall modern building close to the port, the hotel's top-floor restaurant is arguably the best place for breakfast, with its views over the river. Rooms are modern and well appointed with TV, shower, a/c and *frigobar*. There's a pool and the service is OK, though not brilliant. ❼

Hotel Brasil Av. Getulio Vargas 657 ⓣ92/3233-6575, ⓔhotel-brasil@internext.com.br. Modern and busy, this mid-range hotel has a small pool inside and a bar out front by the rather noisy road. Rooms are plain, but comfortable and nice enough; service is hospitable. ❹

Hotel Continental Rua Coronel Sergio Pessoa 189 ⓣ92/3233-3342. Large, clean rooms, with good showers and TVs; some overlook the Rio Negro while others face onto the Praça and Igreja dos Remédios. ❸

Hotel Ideal Rua dos Andradas 491 ⓣ92/3233-9423. Opposite the *Rio Branco*, the rooms here are much the same (clean and basic), though they tend to be darker. Choose between rooms with a fan or a/c. ❶–❷

Hotel Italia Rua Guilherme Moreira 325 ⓣ92/3635-7500, ⓔhotelitalia@globo.com ⓦwww.hotelitaliamanaus.com. Pleasant enough rooms, if small, with TV, frigobar and a/c. Service is friendly and a nice breakfast is included. ❸

Hotel Kyoto Plaza Rua Dr Moreira 232 ⓣ92/3233-6552, ⓕ3232-5439. Lower mid-range hotel offering smallish rooms with TV and a/c in a friendly atmosphere. ❸

Hotel Manaos Av. Eduardo Ribeiro 881 ⓣ92/3633-5744 ⓕ3232-444, ⓔmanaos@argo.com.br, ⓦwww.hotelmanaos.brasilcomercial.com. A modern, large, well a/c hotel very close to the Teatro Amazonas. The service is cheerful and efficient, and the ambience is unpretentious. Rooms have all the modern conveniences. ❹–❺

Hotel Rei Artur Rua Dez de Julho 681 ⓣ92/3622-5525 or 3232-6280. Located in a good area, right next to *Hotel Dez de Julho*, this place has a dark but spacious reception. The rooms are crammed off one main corridor and rather starved of air and light, but they're bearable. ❷

Hotel Rio Branco Rua dos Andradas 484 ⓣ & ⓕ92/3233-4019. A secure, family-run hotel with clean, spartan rooms (some with shared baths). Ground-floor rooms can be damp, and some others don't have windows. A basic breakfast is included. ❶–❷

Krystal Hotel Rua Barroso 54 ⓣ92/3233-7335, ⓕ3233-7882, ⓔhotelkrystal@internext.com.br. The *Krystal*, located near the cathedral, is very good value for its modern, well-kept rooms – all include TV, phone and *frigobar*. ❹

Pensão Sulista Av. Joaquim Nabuco 347 ⓣ92/3622-0038 or 3234-5814. A pleasant, old, colonial-style building with clean but small rooms equipped with fans. Along with the *Rio Branco*, this is the only cheap hotel that doesn't admit prostitutes. Their annex at Rua Pedro Botelho 162, the *Hotel Sulista* (ⓣ92/3233-4538), has better rooms and is only marginally more expensive. ❶

Plaza Hotel Av. Getúlio Vargas 215 ⓣ92/3232-7766, ⓕ3234-0647 ⓔplazahotelmanaus@uol.com.br. Next door to the similar but twice-as-expensive *Hotel Imperial*, the towering *Plaza* has comfortable, well-appointed rooms and a pool. It's good value, though at this price the service could be better. ❹

Pousada Regional Rua Monsenhor Coutinho 768 ⓣ92/3232-3505. Run by Dona Fernanda, this small, traditional place is tucked away near the Teatro Amazonas. Though there are only three rooms, they're well equipped and comfortable, and the service is very friendly; it's just like staying in someone's home. Downstairs there's a small street café where breakfast is served. ❸

Tropical Hotel Estrada da Ponta Negra 9015 ⓣ92/3658-5000, ⓕ3658-5026, ⓔreservas.thm@hotel.com.br, ⓦwww.tropicalhotel.com.br. This popular five-star resort hotel and busy convention centre lies right by the chic city beach, Praia Ponta Negra, 15km northwest of town and 8km from the airport. Facilities include a pool, tennis courts, good nightlife options, fine river beaches and even water-skiing on the Rio Negro – plus the service is excellent. The *Tropical* has its own buses from the airport; from Downtown, take the #120 bus from Praça da Matriz. ❼–❽

The City

It's not hard to get used to the slightly irregular **layout** of Manaus, and, apart from the Teatro Amazonas and many of the museums, most places of interest are relatively close to the river in the older parts of town. From the Estação Hidroviária and floating port where the big ships dock, riverboat wharves extend round past the market, from one end of Rua dos Andradas to the other. The busiest commercial streets are immediately behind, extending up to the Avenida Sete de Setembro, with the cathedral marking one end of the Downtown district, the leafy and popular Praça da Polícia the other. Beyond Avenida Sete de Setembro, towards the Teatro Amazonas, it's a bit calmer, and the square at the entrance to the famous theatre is developing into an artists' quarter with bars and trendy cafés. The busy Praça da Matriz by the cathedral is the main hub of city communications, with **buses** to local points around the city and suburbs; another good connection point for city buses and taxis is the east side of Avenida Getúlio Vargas, just north of Avenida Sete de Setembro.

The townsfolk, known as Manauanas, are attractive and friendly. There is great ethnic variety here, but the distinctive Manauana look comes from a genetic blending of local Indian, black and European stocks. Their hair tends to be black and wavy; they are usually short in stature, strongly built, with dark coppery skin. There are lots of young people in the population and the fact that they like to party, as much if not more than Brazilians everywhere, can be witnessed almost any night at the bars and clubs in and around the city.

Around the docks

Since it's the docks that have created Manaus, it seems logical to start your exploration here – though it's certainly the most atmospheric part of town. The **port** itself is an unforgettable spectacle. A constant throng of activity stretches along the riverfront, while the ships moored at the docks bob serenely up and down. Boats are getting ready to leave or, having just arrived, are busy unloading. People cook fish at stalls to sell to the hungry sailors and their passengers, or to the workers once they've finished their shift of carrying cargo from the boats to the distribution market. Hectic and impossibly complex and anarchic as it appears to the unaccustomed eye, the port of Manaus is in fact very well organized, if organically so. During the day there's no problem wandering around, and it's easy enough to find out which boats are going where just by asking. At night, however, this can be a dangerous area and is best avoided: many of the river men carry guns.

△ Docks at Manaus

From the Praça Adalberto Valle, the impressive **Alfândega** or Customs House (Mon–Fri 8am–1pm) stands between you and the floating docks. Erected in 1906, the building was shipped over from England in prefabricated blocks, and the tower once acted as a lighthouse guiding vessels in at night. The Porto Flutuante, or floating docks, here were built by a British company, at the beginning of the twentieth century. To cope with the Rio Negro rising over a 14m range, the concrete pier is supported on pontoons that rise and fall to allow even the largest ships to dock here all year round (the highest recorded level of the river so far was in 1953, when it rose some 30m above sea level). The **Estação Hidroviária Internacional** is right next to the Customs House and has been recently built, not least to impose some order on the comings and goings of the port. Downstairs at the Hidroviária you buy tickets for boats and there are a few shops and small cafés; upstairs there is a viewing area over the port, with better restaurants, smarter shops and a tourist information desk.

A couple of blocks east of the Customs House, on Rua dos Andradas, the **Praça Terreira Araña** has a clutch of stalls selling indigenous Amazon *artesanato*, leather sandals and jungle souvenirs, and there's a small café here too that's open only in the daytime.

Following Rua Marquês de Santa Cruz down towards the new docks will bring you to the covered **Mercado Municipal Adolfo Lisboa** (Mon–Sat 5am–6pm, Sun 5am–noon), whose elegant Art Nouveau roof was designed by Eiffel during the rubber boom and is a copy of the former Les Halles market in Paris. Inaugurated in 1882, the market features an assortment of tropical fruit and vegetables, jungle herbs, scores of different fresh fishes and Indian craft goods jumbled together on sale. Just to the east of this market is the **wholesale port distribution market**, where traders buy goods from incoming boats and sell them on wholesale to shops, market stalls and restaurants. There are also a substantial number of retail traders here where you too can buy the goods at prices only a little over wholesale. The distribution market is at its busiest first thing in the morning; by the afternoon most of the merchants have closed shop, and the place looks abandoned. In the early 1990s, this market was modernized – turning rat-infested wood and mayhem into concrete-based organized chaos. Much of the original charm has given way to the clinicality of the twentieth century, but the port and markets are still fascinating places to wander.

The commercial centre and the Opera House

Almost as busy by day as the docks themselves, Manaus's downtown commercial centre begins only metres inland from the waterfront and stretches up most of the way to the Opera House. Much of this area is designated a Free Trade Zone, though in reality it's little more than an electronics market. Everything from appliances to shoes can be bought here, at prices that are very cheap by Brazilian standards.

On a small hill, several blocks north away from the river and Free Trade Zone lies the city's most famous symbol, the **Teatro Amazonas** or Opera House (Mon–Sun 9.15am-8.30pm; ⓣ92/3232-1768; R$10), which seems even more extraordinary lying in the midst of this rampant commercialism. The whole incongruous, magnificent thing, designed in a pastiche of Italian Renaissance style by a Lisbon architectural firm, cost over R$6 million. After twelve years of building, with virtually all the materials – apart from the regional wood – brought from Europe, the Opera House was finally completed in 1896. Its main feature, the fantastic cupola, was created from 36,000 tiles imported from Alsace in France. The theatre's main curtain, painted in Paris by Brazilian artist Crispim do Amaral, represents the meeting of the waters and the local Indian water goddess Iara. The four painted pillars on the ceiling depict the Eiffel Tower in Paris, giving visitors the impression, as they look upwards, that they are actually underneath the tower itself. The chandeliers are of Italian crystal and French bronze, and the theatre's seven hundred seats, its main columns and the balconies are all made of English cast iron. If you include the dome, into which the original curtain is pulled up in its entirety, the stage is a vertical 75m high.

Major restorations have taken place in 1929, 1960, 1974 and, most recently, in 1990, when the outside was returned from blue to its original pink. Looking over the upstairs balcony down onto the road in front of the Opera House, you can see the black driveway made from a special blend of rubber, clay and sand, originally to dampen the noise of horses and carriages as they arrived. Yet the building is not just a relic, and it hosts regular concerts, including, in April, the **Festa da Manaus**, initiated in 1997 to celebrate thirty years of the Zona Franca. There is a resident orchestra, the Amazon Philharmonic, with a high proportion of talented Russian or Eastern European musicians. The theatre can be visited only by guided tour and never within two hours of any scheduled performances; a forty-minute tour is often given at midday.

In front of the Teatro, the wavy black-and-white mosaic designs of the **Praça São Sebastião** are home to the "Monument to the Opening of the Ports", a marble and granite creation with four ships that represent four continents – America, Europe, Africa and Asia/Australasia – and children who symbolize the people of those continents. The Praça São Sebastião is getting trendier by the year, with a growing number of interesting shops, bars and arty cafés. Also on the *praça* is the beautiful little **Igreja Largo São Sebastião** (daily 5–9am and 3–7pm), built in 1888, and, like many other churches in Brazil, with only one tower due to the nineteenth-century tax levied on those with two towers. Despite being one of the more pleasant suburbs of central Manaus, the area still has its seedy side, as evident from the male and female prostitutes working the street just yards from the church. Nearby at Avenida Eduardo Ribeiro 833, you'll find the **Palácio da Justiça** (8am–1pm Mon-Fri), opposite the Amazonastur tourist offices. Supposedly modelled on Versailles, the Neoclassical building functions as the main state court, and, contrary to the popular image, its famous statue of the Greek goddess Themis is not blindfolded.

Some three blocks further away from the river, up Rua Tapajós, you'll find the old **Central Post Office**, another imposing reminder of the glorious years of the rubber boom. On the pavement around the back there's an ornate, much-photographed antique postbox, dated 1889.

Along Avenida Sete de Setembro

Back towards the river, the **Catedral de Nossa Senhora da Conceição** (more commonly known as Igreja Matriz) on Avenida Sete de Setembro is a relatively plain building, surprisingly untouched by the orgy of adornment that struck the rest of the city – though judging by the number of people who use it, it plays a more active role in the life of the city than many more showy buildings. The original cathedral, built mainly of wood and completed in 1695 by the Carmelite missionaries, was destroyed by fire in 1850, and the present building dates from 1878, with most of its materials brought from Europe, mainly Portugal. Around the cathedral are the **Praça Osvaldo Cruz** and the **Praça da Matriz**, shady parks popular with local courting couples, hustlers and sleeping drunks.

About 500m west of the cathedral, at Av. Sete de Setembro 1385, is the **Instituto Geográfico e Histórico do Amazonas** (Mon–Fri 2–5.30pm; ⓣ92/3232-7077), Rua Bernardo Ramos 117. Founded in 1917 on one of the city's oldest streets, the building is now a heritage site and has been recently restored. The institute's small museum includes a collection of ceramics from various tribes, a range of insect displays and indigenous tools like stone axes and hunting equipment.

The **Museu do Homem do Norte** (Museum of Northern Man; Mon–Fri 8am–noon & 1–5pm; ⓣ92/3232-5373), in the opposite direction at Av. Sete de Setembro 1385, near Avenida Joaquim Nabuco, offers a quick overview of human life and ecology in the Amazon region including exhibitions on guaraná and rubber production. Also worth at least a quick visit is the **Centro Cultural Palácio Rio Negro** (Tues-Fri 10am-5pm, Sat & Sun 2-6pm; free), a gorgeous colonial-period mansion that houses the archives (manuscripts, drawings and plans) of the nineteenth-century Portuguese naturalist and scientist Alexandre Rodrigues Ferreira. The centre also hosts a wide range of exhibitions, videos, drama and events, and has a good café and bookstore; an annex is home to two small museums: the Museu Numismatica and the Museu do Imagem e do Som.

The excellent **Museu do Índio**, Rua Duque de Caxias 356 (☎92/3635-1922, Mon–Fri 8am–noon & 2–5pm, Sat 8am–noon; R$5), lies about 500m further east along Avenida Sete de Setembro. The museum is run by the Salesian Sisters, who have long-established missions along the Rio Negro, especially with the Tukano tribe. There are excellent, carefully presented displays, with exhibits ranging from sacred ritual masks and inter-village communication drums to fine ceramics, superb palm-frond weavings and even replicas of Indian dwellings. Neatly complementing this collection is the **Museu Amazônico da Universidade do Amazonas**, to the north of the centre at Rua Ramos Ferreira 1036 (☎92/3234-3242), which houses a small collection of sixteenth-century documents and engravings relating to the first explorations of the interior.

Out of the centre

The most popular and widely touted day-trip around Manaus is to the **meeting of the waters**, some 10km downstream, where the Rio Negro and the Rio Solimões meet to form the Rio Amazonas. The alkaline Solimões absorbs the much more acid Rio Negro over several kilometres. For this distance the waters of the two rivers continue to flow separately: the muddy yellow of the Solimões contrasting sharply with the black of the Rio Negro. Interestingly, the Rio Negro is almost always ten to fifteen degrees centigrade warmer than the Solimões. The lighter colour of the Solimões is mainly due to the high levels of soil suspended in the water, which has mostly come here as run-off from the Andes. The Rio Negro is particularly dark because most of its source streams have emerged in low-lying forests where rotting vegetation rather than heavier soil is absorbed into the river drainage system. It creates a strange sight, and one well worth experiencing. If you're going under your own steam, take the "Vila Burity" **bus** (#713) from Praça da Matriz to the end of the line at Porto de Ceasa, from where you can take a free half-hourly government ferry over the river, passing the meeting of the waters.

Most **tours** taking you there leave the docks at Manaus and pass by the shantytown of Educandos and the Rio Negro riverside industries before heading out into the main river course. Almost all will also stop at the **Parque Ecólogico do Janauary**, an ecological park of 9000 hectares some 7km from Manaus on one of the main local tributaries of the Rio Negro. Usually you'll be transferred to smaller motorized canoes to explore its creeks (*igarapés*), flooded forest lands (*igapós*) and abundant vegetation. In the rainy season you'll explore the creeks and flood lands by boat; during the dry season – between September and January – it's possible to walk around.

One of the highlights of the area is the abundance of *Victoria Amazonica* (previously *Victoria Regia*), the extraordinary giant floating lily for which Manaus is famous. Found mostly in shallow lakes, it flourishes above all in the rainy months. The plant, named after Queen Victoria by an English naturalist in the nineteenth century, has huge leaves – some over a metre across – with a covering of thorns on their underside as protection from the teeth of plant-eating fish. The flowers are white on the first day of their life, rose-coloured on the second, and on the third they begin to wilt: at night the blooms close, imprisoning any insects that have wandered in, and releasing them again as they open with the morning sun.

The river beach at **Praia Ponta Negra**, about 13km northwest of Manaus near the *Hotel Tropical*, is another very popular local excursion, and at weekends is packed with locals. Once the home of the Manaós Indians, today the beach is an enjoyable spot for a swim, with plenty of bars and restaurants serving freshly cooked river fish. You can also catch regular music and other events at the massive modern amphitheatre nearby. The beach is at its best between September and March, when the river is low and exposes a wide expanse of sand, but even when the rains bring higher waters and the beach almost entirely disappears, plenty of people come to eat and drink. Soltur's Ponta Negra bus (#120) leaves every half hour for the beach: catch it by the cathedral on Praça da Matriz.

The nearby military-run **CIGS Zoo** (Tues–Sun 9am–4.30pm; ⓣ3625-2044; R$2.50), Estrada Ponta Negra 750, is also an army jungle training centre, and many of the animals in it were captured, so they say, on military exercises out in the forest. The zoo has been recently redesigned to cater better for visitors, and you can expect to see alligators, monkeys, macaws and snakes among the more than 300 animals and 73 species kept here. To reach the zoo, take the #120, or the "Compensa" or "São Jorge" bus from the military college on Avenida Epaminondas.

The **Parque do Mindú**, out in the direction of the airport, is the city's largest expanse of public greenery, incorporating educational trails (on which visitors can walk along suspended walkways), an *artesanato* shop and an exhibition centre. Closer to the city centre, the **Bosque da Ciência**, Alameda Cosme Ferreira 1756, Aleixo (Tues–Sun 9am–3pm, ⓣ3643-3293), is an ecological park created by the Instituto Nacional de Pesquisas de Amazônia (National Institute for Amazon Research; INPA), home to otters, manatees, monkeys, snakes and birds. Both sites are easiest to reach by taxi, but you can also get there on buses #508, #424, #505 or #504. INPA are based at Av. A. Araújo 1756 (daily 9am–noon & 2–5pm; ⓣ92/643-3377), and run free two-hour video screenings at weekends (10am and 2pm). A taxi ride away from here, there's more wildlife at the **Museu de Ciências Naturais da Amazônia**, Colônia Cachoeira Grande, Estrada Belém, Km 15, Aleixo (ⓣ92/3644-2799, Mon–Sat 9am–5pm; R$5), including fish such as the *piraruca* – in a 37,000-gallon aquarium – butterflies, insects and a good *artesanato* shop.

The waterfalls of **Cachoeira do Tarumã**, about 20km northwest of the city, are the last of the local beauty spots within easy reach of Manaus. Though no longer unspoiled, thanks to commercialization and weekend crowds, this is still a fun trip – there's good swimming and on busy weekends you'll often find live music in the town's bars. The cascades themselves, supplied by the Rio Negro, are relatively small white-water affairs that more or less disappear in the rainy season (Apr–Aug). Soltur buses (#11) run here approximately every 20 minutes from the Praça da Matriz, taking about half an hour.

About an hour outside the town, the **Museu do Seringal Vila Paraíso** recreates the living and working conditions of the traditional rubber tappers from around one hundred years ago (Wed–Sun 8am–4pm). To get here, take the bus to Ponta Negra and then catch a dug-out taxi from the side of the

Tropical Hotel at the Marina David to Igarapé São João – an affluent of the Taruma-Mirim that empties into the left bank of the Rio Negro. Tickets for the museum can be bought in advance from the tourist information offices in Manaus.

Eating and drinking

There are very few places in Manaus where you can sit down and enjoy any peace, and even the cafés and bars are too full to give you much elbow room. One advantage of the crowds is that there's **street food** everywhere, especially around the docks, the Mercado Municipal and in busy downtown locations like the Praça da Matriz, where a plate of rice and beans with a skewer of freshly grilled meat or fish costs well under R$5. One traditional dish you should definitely try here is **tacacá** – a soup that consists essentially of yellow manioc root juice in a hot spicy dried-shrimp sauce. It's often mixed and served in traditional gourd bowls, *cuias*, and is usually sold in the late afternoons by *tacacazeiras* (street food vendors).

For your own food, there's a **supermarket** at the corner of Avenida Joaquim Nabuco and Avenida Sete de Setembro, and another towards the market on Rua Rocha dos Santos. The following **restaurants** are closed Sundays unless otherwise stated, and be warned that prices in Manaus are significantly higher than you might find in the rest of the country.

African House Praça São Sebastião. A delightful café with a vaguely Parisian feel, opening out onto the square in front of the Opera House. Choose from light meals like burgers and grilled or fried chicken, washing it down with juices mixed with vitamins or *guaraná* (a health supplement made from the seeds of an Amazonian bush).

Café Regional Rua Costa Azevedo 369 ⓣ92/3233-1028. A small café specializing in Amazon breakfasts and vegetarian lunches, just a stone's throw from the Teatro Amazonas.

Canto da Peixada Rua Emilio Moreira 1677 ⓣ92/3234-3021. Arguably Manaus's best regional and river-fish restaurant, this place is not cheap, but good value nonetheless. Try the excellent *dourado* fish steaks. Usually open until 11.30pm.

Choupana Rua Recife 790, Adrianopolis ⓣ92/3635-3878. Possibly the best regional cuisine on offer in or around Manaus and in a pleasant airy space; try the *tucupi* duck baked in manioc juice and jambu leaves with shrimps. Expensive but worth the money.

Churrascaria Búfalo Av. Joaquim Nabuco 628A ⓣ92/3633-3773. One of the best meat restaurants in downtown Manaus, with excellent *rodízio*. It's expensive, though, at around $50 a head.

Filosophicus Rua Sete de Setembro 752, 2nd floor. A large, clean and enjoyable vegetarian restaurant with good self service, one block east from the cathedral. Open Mon–Fri lunchtime.

Fiorentina Jose Paranagua 44, Praça da Polícia, Centro ⓣ92/3215-2233. Upmarket Italian restaurant right in the heart of town with good but quite expensive food. The menu ranges from local river-fish dishes to traditional pastas and steaks.

Galo Carijó Rua dos Andradas 536. Opposite the *Hotel Dona Joana*, this is a simple, inexpensive but excellent local fish restaurant and bar. Closed Sat evening.

Himawari Rua 10 de Julho 618 ⓣ92/3233-2208. A spacious Japanese restaurant with quality food and service, conveniently located on the Praça São Sebastião. Closed Mon.

Kaktus Restaurant Av. Joaquim Nabuco, at the corner of Leonardo Marcher. This pleasant restaurant has decent self-service lunches but specializes in fish dishes in the evenings. Closed Mon.

Mandarim Av. Eduardo Ribeiro 650, at the corner of Rua 24 de Maio. Excellent and reasonably priced Chinese restaurant, with a *comida por kilo* lunch and an à la carte dinner (6–10.30pm). Try one of their *chopa* (sizzling platter) dishes.

Scarola Pizzaria Rua Dez de Julho 739. Though away from the action a little, this pleasant pizzeria has a nice patio, good service and reasonable food. At lunchtime they have a decent and inexpensive self-service option.

Skina dos Sucos corner of Av. Eduardo Ribeiro with the Rio Branco Shopping Centre. Superb little café specializing almost exclusively in tropical fruit juices, served iced or pure. Service is fast.

Sorveteria Glacial corner of Rua Henrique Martins Calvante with Av. Getulio Vargas. Of the several tropical fruit ice-cream cafés around Manaus, this (and another across the road) are two of the busier ones, thanks to delicious goods and kid-friendly decor.

Suzuran Rua Teresina 155 ⓣ92/3234-1693. This very good restaurant is worth the taxi ride to the trendy Adrianopolis suburb. It's the best of the city's three Japanese dining options, but without the top-tier prices. Open daily.

Nightlife

Like most large port towns, Manaus is busiest in the early mornings and again at night, with plenty of bars, clubs and other venues that are worth exploring if you're in town for a few days; Friday editions of *Amazonas Em Tempo* carry fairly comprehensive listings of what's going on.

The rowdiest **bars** are bunched in and around the Mercado Municipal, and along the entire length of Avenida Joaquim Nabuco south of Avenida Sete de Setembro. The usual starting place, for beer, snacks and a lively atmosphere, is either the Bohemian *MacIntosh Bar* on Avenida Eduardo Ribeira, just up from the Palacio da Justicia, or the *Pizzaria Scarola* on the corner of Avenida Getulio Vargas and Dez de Julho, with a patio that makes it a popular meeting place in the early evenings. By the Praça da Policia there's the busy evening *Bar do Marqinho*. Around the port, to the west of Praça da Matriz on Rua M. Sousa, a couple of even louder places – *Holanda Bar* and *Recanto da Natureza* – stay open all night. There are also a number of inexpensive bars around the Praça Sebastião, including the *Bar do Amandó* in front of the Opera House, which frequently has locals playing guitars and singing inside. Also by the Opera House, under the Radio Rio Mar tower and building, is the *Jungle Disco*, usually the scene of Brazilian pop and samba dancing at weekends. There are several more expensive bars, some with restaurants, out at Ponta Negra. *O Laranjinha* Estrada Ponta Negra 10675 (ⓣ92/3658-6666; daily until 1am) is one of the most popular of the restaurant-bars; it has a large open space and stage where there are nightly performances, often including some Bio Bumba music and dance groups.

As for **clubs**, the most exciting are undoubtedly those along the Estrada Ponta Negra and around Praia Ponta Negra itself. Though their names change frequently, the music is always an enticing blend of old and modern sambas – it's worth coming just to see the formation dancing of the crowds. One of the best clubs at the moment is *Tucano*, near the *Tropical Hotel*. Given Manaus's prohibitive taxi fares, most of the Praia Ponta Negra clubs remain open all night, so you might as well bring a towel for a sobering early-morning dip in the river. Similarly distant is *Bora Bora*, a top club located at Av. do Turismo 121 (ⓣ92/8118-4489), about 16 km away in the Trauma district. *Talismão* at Av. Ajurocaba 800 (ⓣ92/3233-5520), slightly nearer the centre, is one of the best straight clubs, located out in the suburb of Cachoeirinha. Rustic and very vibrant at weekends, the *Pagode do Almirante*, at Rua Padre Agostinho Caballeiro Martins 287, is a gay-friendly place pumping out reggae on Sundays and dance or pagoda most other evenings in Santo Antonio suburb a few kilometres east of the centre.

More central is the touristy *Boiart's* club, Rua Jose Clemente 500 (ⓣ92/3637-6807), near the Opera House, which puts on frequent dance presentations loosely based on Amazon tribal dances (open Wed–Sat, shows start around 11pm). The *Cheik Clube*, Av. Getúlio Vargas 773, has a solid reputation for modern dance music (house and techno as well as salsa). The main cinemas, again very popular, include several screens at Amazonas Shopping (see "Listings", under "shopping" for directions).

Listings

Airlines BRA, at Av. Eduardo Ribeiro 893 ⓣ92/3652-1507 or 3631-0007 ⓦwww.voebra.com.br offer the cheapest flights from Manaus to major destinations in Southern and Central Brazil, but they only fly a few times a week; Gol, at airport ⓣ92/3652-1634; Lloyd Aereo Boliviano, Av. 7 de Setembro 993 or at the airport ⓣ92/3652-1513; Penta (covering the eastern Amazon), Rua Barroso 352 ⓣ92/3234-1046 and at the airport ⓣ92/3652-1161; Rico (covering Western Amazon region), Rua 24 de Maio, Loja 60-B, Edificio Cidade de Manaus ⓣ92/3233-1853 or ⓣ92/3652-1391 at airport; Tam, Rua João Valerio 123, Nosso Sra. das Gracas ⓣ92/3232-8833; Tavaj, at the airport ⓣ92/3652-1486; and Varig, Rua Marcílio Dias 284 ⓣ92/3083-4521 or ⓣ92/3652-1598 at airport.

Banks and exchange Câmbio e Turismo Cortez (Mon–Fri 9am–5pm, Sat 9am–12.30pm), at the corner of Av. Getúlio Vargas 88 and Av. Sete de Setembro 1188 and their office in Amazonas Shopping Centre Lote 149, Av. Djalma Batista, has good rates and fast service for both cash and traveller's cheques, unlike the Banco do Brasil, Also try Amazonia at Rua Guilherme Moreira 315. There are several banks on Av. Eduardo Ribeiro, just a block or two down the street from the SEC tourist offices.

Boats There are regular passenger boat services to: Belém, Santarém and all ports along the Rio Amazonas; along the Rio Solimões to Tabatinga; and up the Rio Madeira to Porto Velho. Less frequent services go up the Rio Negro to São Gabriel da Cachoeira and up the Rio Branco to Caracaraí. Tickets for the regular services can be bought from the ticket windows inside the Estação Hidroviária Internacional off the Praça da Matriz. The boats are moored along the riverside near the Mercado Municipal for the days leading up to their departure, so it is possible to check them out before buying a ticket. It's best to avoid paying the captain directly, however, since tickets are now sold by the officials from the *guichês* (sales windows; open daily 6am–7pm) in the Estação Hidroviária, which are operated by the Agencia Rio Amazonas (ⓣ92/3621-4310). It's sensible to buy tickets here days in advance and always get on your boat a good two hours or more before it's due to depart. Standard boats from Manaus to Belém can cost anything from R$100 to R$200 and take three to five days, often stopping off in Santarém. Smaller boats with no regular schedules, and those serving local settlements up the Rio Negro, are found to the east of the Mercado Municipal. See also the "River Journeys" box, pp.418–419. If you are interested in a luxury boat cruise, Iberostar (Rio ⓣ21/3325-0351 ⓦwww.iberostar.com) have their Grand Amazon boat with swish accommodation for over seventy passengers, including two restaurants, two bars and two pools, all on four levels plus top deck. For a faster speed boat to either Santarém (R$200, 13hrs down, 15hrs back up) or Tefe (R$180, 13hrs up, 10hrs back down) take the Expreso Barcos service from the Hidroviária near the Mercado Municipal; they leave at 6am (Tues and Fri for Santarém, Wed and Sat for Tefe.

Car rental Avis, Rua Major Gabriel 1721, 14 de Janeiro ⓣ92/3234-4440; Interlocadora, Rua Duque de Caxias 750, Centro ⓣ92/3232-1558; Localiza, Rua Major Gabriel 1558, Centro ⓣ92/3233-4141; Unidas ⓣ92/3651-2558.

Consulates Bolivia, Av. Engenio Sales 2226, Quadrant B-20 ⓣ92/3236-9988; Colombia, Rua 24 de Maio 220 ⓣ92/3234-6777; Peru, Rua A – C/19 – Conj. Aristocratico, Chapada ⓣ92/3656-3267 or 656-1015; UK, Rua Poraque 240 ⓣ92/3613-1819; US, Rua Recife 1010 – CCI – Adrianópolis ⓣ92/3633-4907; Venezuela, Rua Ferreira Pena 179 ⓣ92/3233-6004.

Health matters For tropical complaints the best spot is the Instituto de Medicina Tropical, Av. Pedro Teixeira 25 ⓣ92/3656-1441 or 3656-4573. Also, there are the Hospital Tropical at Av. Pedro Teixeira 25 ⓣ92/3656-1441, which specializes in tropical ailments, and the Hospital Aventista de Manaus at Rua Gov. Danilo de Matos Areosa 139 in the Castelo Branco district, where there is also an emergency department. The Drogueria Nossa Senhor de Nazare, Sete de Setembro 1333, is a reasonably well-stocked pharmacy. The emergency ambulance number is ⓣ192.

Internet Amazon Cybercafé, Av. Getulio Vargas 625 (opposite the bottom end of Dez de Julho), has lots of terminals, serves free coffee and is inexpensive. Alternatively, try: Cybercity Internet, next to the Sorveteria Glacial at Avenida Getulio Vargas 188; Meeting Point, Rua dos Andrades 408; Flash Internet, Rua Dez de Julho 637; and Discover Internet, Rua Marcílio Dias 320, Loja 7.

Laundry Lavalux, at both Rua Mundurucus 77 ⓣ92/3233-7672 and Rua Acre 77 ⓣ92/3622-4262; Jo Lavanderia, at Rua Luisz Antony 503A, Centro.

Police ⓣ190.

Post office The main one, with a reliable poste restante service (1st floor), is just off the Praça da Matriz on Rua Marechal Deodoro at the corner with Rua Teodoreto Souto (Mon–Fri 9am–5pm, Sat 8am–noon). There's a smaller, quieter branch just

Novo Aírão and swimming with dolphins

Novo Aírão, a small jungle town on the west bank of the Rio Negro, is some 115km (six hours by bus) from Manaus. By boat it's around 130km (eight hours). From Manaus's *rodoviária*, the bus (daily at 6am and 1pm) takes the Porto São Raimundo ferry and continues to Manacapuru before turning north and following the BR-352 to its end at the port of Novo Aírão, which sits opposite the Arquipelago Anavilhanas. It's too far a distance to travel in a day, but it makes a good overnight trip from Manaus. The main attraction at Novo Aírão is the chance to feed pink dolphins from the floating restaurant (next to the tourist information office) in the small port here. The times for seeing the dolphins are Mon–Sat 9am–midday & 3.30–5pm, Sun 9am–midday. The owner of the restaurant who has "trained" the dolphins charges R$10 for a plate of fish to feed them. For the bold, it's possible to get in the water with the dolphins, who will swim around you, splashing and bumping into you, hoping for some food. Otherwise, there's not that much else to see in town; there are a couple of *pousadas* and a few restaurants, and Internet access is available at a café at Rua Rui Barbosa 41. The best *pousada* is undoubtedly *Bela Vista*, at Av. Presidente Vargas 47 (℡92/3365-1023; ❸), which has small but pleasant rooms and serves delicious breakfasts on a patio overlooking the Rio Negro. If the *Bela Vista* is full, or if you want cheaper accommodation, try the *Pousada Rio Negro* (❷) on the central *praça*.

beyond the top of Av. Eduardo Ribeiro, on the leafy Praça do Congresso, and another in Amazonas Shopping.

Shopping The best selection of *artesanato* is at the lively Sunday morning street market, which appears out of nowhere in the broad Av. Eduardo Ribeira, behind the Teatro Amazonas. The Museu do Índio (see p.467) and several shops around the square in front of the Opera House also sell *artesanato*. Indian crafts are sold at the Mercado Municipal. Interesting *macumba* and *umbanda* items, such as incense, candles, figurines and bongos, can be found at Cabana São Jorge at Rua da Instalação 36. Duty-free electronic and all kinds of other luxury items can be bought everywhere in the centre. The modern Amazonas Shopping, at Av. Djalma Batista 482, Parque 10 de Novembro, is 4–5km from the centre by taxi or bus #306. It has hundreds of shops and cafés, plus six cinemas. A good hammock shop is Casa des Redes on Rua dos Andradas. For photographic film and developing, try Foto Nascimento, Av. Sete de Setembro 1194. For books, the Livraria Nacional, Rua Vinte e Quatro de Maio 415, has the widest selection.

Taxis Amazonas ℡92/3232-3005; Rádio Táxi ℡92/3633-3211; Tocantins ℡92/3656-1330.

Telephones National and international calls can be made with phonecards in public booths around the city; alternatively, the Telmar office (Mon–Fri 8am–6pm, Sat 8am–noon) is on Av. Getúlio Vargas 950, close to the junction with Rua Ramos Ferreira.

Travel Agents Amazon Explorers, Praça Tenreiro Aranha ℡92/3633-3319; Turismo Cortez, at the corner of Av. Getúlio Vargas 88 and Av. Sete de Setembro 1188 ℡92/3622-4222 and their office in Amazonas Shopping Centre Lote 149, Av. Djalma Batista ℡92/3642-2525; Fontur, Tropical Hotel, Ponta Negra ℡92/3658-3052. All are good for flights and city tours (Fontur will arrange free hotel pick-ups in the city centre for its city tours). Tucunare Turismo, Rua Henrique Martins 116 (℡92/3234-5071, ⓦwww.tucunareturismo.com.br), offer city tours, and trips to the meeting of the waters, fishing sites and the waterfalls of Presidente Figueiredo.

Jungle trips from Manaus

Manaus is the obvious place in the Brazilian Amazon to find a **jungle river trip** to suit most people's need. Although located in the heart of the world's biggest rainforest, you have to be prepared to travel for at least a few days out of Manaus if you are serious about spotting a wide range of wildlife. The city does, however, offer a range of organized tours bringing visitors into close contact with the world's largest tropical rainforest. Unfortunately, though, since Manaus has been a big city for a long time, the forest in the immediate vicinity is far from virgin. Over the last millennia it has been explored by Indians, missionaries, rubber gatherers, colonizing extractors, settlers, urban folk from Manaus and, more recently, quite a steady flow of eco-minded tourists.

The amount and kind of **wildlife** you get to see on a standard jungle tour depends mainly on how far away from Manaus you go and how long you can devote to the trip. Birds like macaws, humming birds, jacanas, cormorants, herons, kingfishers, hawks, chacalacas and toucans can generally be spotted, but you need luck to see hoatzins, trogons, cock-of-the-rock or blue macaws. You might see alligators, snakes, sloths, river dolphins and a few species of monkey on a three-day trip (though you can see many of these anyway at the Parque Ecólogico do Janauary; see p.467). Sightings for large mammals and cats, however, are very rare, though chances are increased on expedition-type tours of six days or more to deep forest places like the Rio Juma. On any trip, make sure that you'll get some time in the smaller channels in a canoe, as the sound of a motor is a sure way of scaring every living thing out of sight.

There are a few Brazilian **jungle terms** every visitor should be familiar with: a *regatão* is a travelling boat-cum-general store, which can provide a fascinating introduction to the interior if you can strike up an agreeable arrangement with one of their captains; an *igarapé* is a narrow river or creek flowing from the forest into one of the larger rivers (though by "narrow" around Manaus they mean less than 1km wide); an *igapó* is a patch of forest that is seasonally flooded; a *furo* is a channel joining two rivers and therefore a short cut for canoes; a *paraná*, on the other hand, is a branch of the river that leaves the main channel and returns further downstream, creating a river island. The typical deep red earth of the Western Amazon is known as *tabatinga*, like the city on the frontier with Peru and Colombia; and regenerated forest, like secondary growth, is called *capoeira*.

There are scores of different **jungle tour companies** in Manaus offering very similar services and the competition is intense, which means you're likely to get hassled by touts at the airport and all over town; the sales patter can be unrelenting. Most companies have websites that give a reasonable feel for what's being offered. If possible, book in advance through one of the more established outfits registered at the Amazonastur information offices. While you may be able to bargain the price down a bit if you turn up in Manaus without a booking (groups can always get a better deal than people travelling alone), there is a surprising range of options and prices if you shop around.

You can generally get a tour cheaper if you're prepared to hang around for the operator to find others to make up a larger group. It's always a good idea to pin your tour operator down to giving you specific details of the trip on paper, preferably in the form of a written **contract**, and you should always ask about the accommodation arrangements, what the food and drink will consist of and exactly where you are going – ask to see photos and be wary of parting with wads of cash before you know exactly what you'll be getting in return. A circular trip may sound attractive, but the scenery won't change very much, whatever the name of the *rio*. You should also check that the guide speaks English, whether the operator has an environmental policy and what insurance coverage they offer (usually nil in the case of the cheaper operators). Check at the Amazonastur information office (Mon–Fri 8am–6pm, Sat 8am–1pm, Sun 8am-2pm; Ⓣ92/3232-1998) to see if the company is registered with EMBRATUR (if they are it is much easier to make a claim against them if something goes wrong). Ask what is not included in the price, and whether you can get your money back, or part of it, if the trip turns out to be disappointing. On a more upmarket tour, you should check that binoculars and reference books are provided on the boat, if you haven't already got your own, and, on any tour, you of course have the right to expect that any promises made – regarding maximum group size, activities and so on – are kept. If not, then a promise to complain to Amazonastur may give you some leverage in obtaining redress. You can also check with Amazonastur for reports on complaints that might have been made against a particular tour operator in the past.

The most dependable and comfortable way to visit the jungle is to take a package tour that involves a number of nights in a **jungle lodge** – though for the more adventurous traveller the experience can be a little tame. The lodges invariably offer hotel-standard accommodation, full board and a range of activities including alligator spotting, piranha fishing, trips by canoe and transport to and from Manaus. Some lodge-based tours integrate the opportunity to spend a night or two camping out in the forest. The least expensive jungle tour options are those offering hammock space accommodation, perhaps combined with a night in the forest; the most expensive should see visitors in four-star comfort. You can either book a jungle lodge tour through a tour operator, or approach the lodge operators directly at their offices in Manaus (see box, pp.476–477). Some of the better tour companies run their own small riverboats for more leisurely exploration, sometimes with room for up to 20 people to sleep in comfortable, if small, cabins.

△ A squirrel monkey in the Amazon rainforest

If you want to forgo organized tours entirely and travel independently, **milk boats or regatão** trading boats are a very inexpensive way of getting about on the rivers around Manaus. These smaller vessels, rarely more than 20m long, spend their weeks serving the local riverine communities by delivering and transporting their produce. You can spend a whole day on one of these boats for as little as R$25, depending on what arrangement you make with the captain. The best place to look for milk boats is down on the wharves behind the distribution market. Approach the ones that are obviously loading early in the morning of the day you want to go, or late in the afternoon of the day before. Other commercial boats bound for the interior – some of them preparing for trips up to a month long – can be found at the port end by the Mercado Municipal. There are other small ports and ferry points around Manaus which also have boats travelling into the interior. In eastern Manaus, the **Porto São Raimundo** has a ferry over to the other side of the Rio Negro and sometimes boats go up river from here. Far west, along the Avenida Min. João Gonçalves de Araujo, there's the fruit port **Porto de Ceasa**, another ferry point. From here, it crosses the Rio Negro and enters the Solimões, passing the meeting of the waters, en route to the start of the BR-319, the overgrown, potholed and essentially unusable road to Porto Velho. Any expedition into protected areas of forest will require permission from the state agency IBAMA, whose offices in Manaus are at BR-319 137, Castelo Blanco district ⓣ92/3613-1703.

Tour itineraries

The **basic options** for jungle tours run from one-day through to three-, five- or even fifteen-day expeditions into the forest – almost all of them dominated by river travel. They usually include the services of local guides and forest experts. Some offer accommodation on boats, some in hammocks in forest clearings; others offer both in the same three-day-trip. The more expensive ones offer the added luxury of jungle lodges and comfortable riverboats with cabin accommodation.

The **one-day river trip**, usually costing around R$150 per person, generally includes inspecting the famous meeting of the waters, some 10km downriver from Manaus (see p.467). More often than not, this trip will also visit one or two fairly typical riverine settlements and take a side trip up a narrow river channel to give at least some contact with birdlife and a tantalizing taste of the forest itself. One-day river trips usually leave port around 8 or 9am, returning before 6pm, though some last barely six hours.

The other most popular jungle river trips tend to be the **three- to five-day expeditions**. If you want to sleep in the forest, either in a lodge, riverboat or, for the more adventurous (and perhaps those on a low budget), swinging in a hammock outside in a small jungle clearing, it really is worth taking as many days as you can to get as far away from Manaus as possible. The usual price for guided jungle tours, including accommodation and food, should be between R$100 and R$250 a day per person (no matter what the sales pitch), more again if you opt for an upmarket jungle lodge or a decent riverboat. You might find it worth paying a few more dollars a day to ensure that you're well looked after.

The most commonly operated tours are three-day trips combining both the **Rio Negro** and **Rio Solimões**, although some trips only cover the former, as it is more accessible from Manaus. Four-day trips should ideally also include both a good day's walk through the jungle and some exploring of the **Anavilhanas archipelago** opposite Novo Airão on the Rio Negro; the second-largest freshwater archipelago in the world, it has around four hundred isles and is a fine place to see white-sand river beaches and their associated birdlife. The Rio

Jungle tour operators and lodges in Manaus

Jungle tour operators are not difficult to find in Manaus, but it is quite hard to identify the best and most trusted operators and guides just by meeting them at the airport or in the streets of the downtown area. If you can, it's much better to book in advance, easily done on the Web or by email. Some of the companies or agents listed below have their own lodges, riverboats and houseboats, while one or two of them select and book an appropriate lodge or boat for each tour. The Fiscalizacão Federal and Amazonastur are presently implementing a significant tightening of regulations concerning the environmental impact of tourist lodges and the licensing of guides.

Tour operators

Arquipelago Anavilhanas Tours Rua Dr. Moreira 163, 1st floor, Centro Ⓣ92/3231-1067, Ⓔarquipelagotours@internext.com.br, Ⓦwww.arquipelagotours.com.br. Specializing, as the name suggests, in tours to the fantastic Anavilhanas complex of islands. This reliable and efficient operator also offers city tours, trips to the meeting of the waters and more adventurous and distant fishing or safari-type tours, including to waterfalls in the Presidente Figueiredo area.

Amazon Gero's Tour Dez de Julho 679, Centro Ⓣ92/3232-4755, mobile Ⓣ9983-6273, Ⓔgeromesquita@hotmail.com, Ⓦwww.amazonjungletour.com and Ⓦwww.amazongerotours.com. A reliable and experienced operator with guides that speak excellent English and Spanish. Geraldo (Gero) Neto Mesquita organizes tours mainly to the Mamori and Juma areas (Rio Negro on request) and he recently built a well-located lodge on Lago Arara (see opposite). Gero will also help book hotels, boats and arrange airport pick-up. Tours include boat and canoe trips, jungle hiking and visits to native people, with accommodation in hammocks, overnight in the bush, at local family houses, or in luxury lodge accommodations.

Amazonas Indian Turismo Rua dos Andradas 311 Ⓣ92/3633-5578. A basic but long-established operator, and one of the least pushy of the budget crowd. Run by Amazon Indians, they offer good jungle trekking, lots of opportunities for spotting wildlife (mainly birds – including toucans – dolphins and alligators), canoe trip exploring *igarapés*, piranha fishing and visits to local communities. Guides vary in quality (some speak only Portuguese) but they can be good value (R$120–200 a day). Tour groups tend to be smaller than most, and more personalized itineraries are possible as well. They also operate a basic but very hospitable lodge camp around 200km from Manaus.

Amazon Explorers kiosk in Praça Tenreiro Aranha, in the centre's Zona Franca shopping area (Ⓣ92/3613-1210), or the main office at Rua Nhamundá 21, Praça N.S. Auxiliadora (Ⓣ92/3633-3319, Ⓦwww.amazonexplorers.com.br.) This reputable operator runs a reservations service for upmarket jungle lodges, luxury boat hire and fishing trips, and organizes jungle tours, with boat accommodation (from around R$230 per person a day, minimum two people for two days) and a six-hour trip to the meeting of the waters and Parque Janauary. As a travel agency, it offers a ticketing service for air and boat travel.

Amazon Nut Safaris Av. Beira Mar 43, São Raimundo Ⓣ92/3234-5860 Ⓕ3622-2821, Ⓦwww.amazonnut.com. Offers upmarket ecological expeditions to the Anavilhanas archipelago and also operates a fleet of boats and a small nine-room lodge, Apurissawa, on the Rio Cuieiras (Rio Negro area), four hours by boat from Manaus. Tours include trips to the meeting of the waters, alligator- and bird-watching expeditions, and visits to local *caboclos* (traditional river-dweller) communities. They have a kiosk at the airport.

Eco Discovery Tours Rua Coelho 301 Ⓣ92/3082-4732 Ⓦwww.ecodiscovery.hpg.com.br. This company runs a range of jungle tours, mainly lodge-based and around the Lago Mamori area; they also specialize in expeditions to the Parque Nacional de Jaú.

Iguana Dez de Julho 667, Centro ⓣ92/3633-6507 ⓔiguanatour@amazonbrasil.com.br, ⓦwww.amazonbrasil.com.br. Based in the *Hotel Dez de Julho*, this company, which operates regularly in the Juma and Mamori areas, are able to organize most kinds of trips, from overnights in the forest to longer lodge- or camp-based trips.

Swallows and Amazons Rua Quintino Bocaiúva 189, 1st floor, sala 13 ⓣ & ⓕ92/3622-1246, ⓦwww.swallowsandamazonstours.com. A small company with an excellent reputation, specializing in private and small-group houseboat, riverboat, jungle lodge and rainforest adventure tours. Most trips explore the Rio Negro and the Anavilhanas archipelago, but custom tours are also possible. The company runs Over Look Lodge, 50km from Manaus on the Rio Negro. Rates R$200–350 per person per day.

Lodges and camps

Jungle lodges offer travellers the opportunity to experience the rainforest while maintaining high levels of comfort, even elegance. There are scores of lodges in and around the Manaus area, most operated by tour companies.

Acajatuba Jungle Lodge Rua Lima Bacuri 345 ⓣ92/3233-7642, ⓦwww.acajatuba.com.br. A lodge with large communal areas, spacious, clean cabins, and trips from one to four nights. *Acajatuba* is located in the Anavilhanas archipelago and has wooden elevated footbridges joining the various parts of the site. Night-time lighting is from battery-powered bulbs, so there's rarely any generator noise to drown out the sounds of the jungle.

Amazon Ecopark Lodge Praça Auxiliadora 4, grupo 103 ⓣ & ⓕ92/3656-0027, ⓔecopark@horizon.com.br, ⓦwww.amazonecopark.com or in Rio de Janeiro, Lauro Muller 360, Suite 510 ⓣ21/2275-5285. Located in a nature reserve on the west bank of the Rio Tarumã; at just over 20km from Manaus, and less than an hour by either boat or road, it is an easy day-trip. Monkeys, birds, ungulates, rodents and reptiles are presented in their natural habitats at the adjacent "Amazon Monkey Jungle". From R$150 per person for a day-trip, or R$350 for an overnight stay; if you can get there under your own steam (phone for transport options and opening times before setting off) you can stay overnight in a forest camp for R$35.

Amazon Gero's Lodge, Dez de Julho 679, Centro ⓣ92/3232-4755, mobile ⓣ9983-6273, ⓔgeromesquita@hotmail.com, ⓦwww.amazonjungletour.com and ⓦwww.amazongerotours.com. This highly recommended lodge has been recently built on Lago Arara, just off the Parana do Mamori. Well located in terms of peace and quiet and wildlife, it offers a range of prices and levels of comfort from family suites and standard rooms to hammock space in the round viewing platform above the circular restaurant.

Amazon Lodge, Rua Santa Quitéria 15, Presidente Vargas ⓣ92/3656-6033, ⓦwww.naturesafaris.com.br. Powerful motor boats take you 80km (4 hrs) via the Parana do Mamori to Lago Juma and the operator's very comfortable floating lodge with fourteen double rooms and a restaurant. Expensive at R$550 for three days and two nights.

Amazon Swiss Lodge Av. Eduardo Ribeiro 620, sala 215 ⓣ92/3633-2322. Situated on the Rio Urubu and reached by road (182km to Lindóia), then a thirty-minute boat ride. The lodge is relatively small, with sixteen wooden cabin-style rooms, collective toilets and a restaurant. Overnights in the jungle are possible. Prices are R$180 per person per night, or R$38 to camp.

Amazon Village Grand Amazon Turismo, Rua Ramos Ferreira 1189, sala 403 ⓣ92/3633-1444, ⓦwww.amazon-village.com.br. On Lago Puraquequara, 50km from Manaus. It's much larger than the Amazon Lodge (32 rooms) and has better facilities, but it's not quite as wild in terms of the surrounding forest.

Additional jungle tour operators and lodges in Manaus

Ariaú Amazon Towers Rio Amazonas Turismo, Hotel Monaco, Rua Silva Ramos 41 ⓣ92/2121-5000, ⓦwww.ariau.tur.com; also an office in the US at 905 Brickell Bay Drive, Suite 1930, Miami ⓣ305/371-7871. Only 60km up the Rio Negro from Manaus (3hr by boat) by Ariaú Lake, this is one of the largest and most developed of the jungle lodges, with a helicopter pad, swimming pool, almost 100 rooms (mostly in wooden chalets) and a 35-metre viewing tower from which you get an exceptionally close and breathtaking view of the forest canopy. It's a must if your budget isn't restricted (from R$700 per person for three days and two nights).

Dolphin Lodge operated by Maia Expeditions, Rua Dr. Odilon 16 ⓣ92/3613-4683, ⓔmaiaturismo@uol.com.br, ⓦwww.maiaexpeditionstur.com.br. A comfortable lodge with wooden double bedrooms and a pleasant circular restaurant and bar space. Based in the Parana do Mamori, there is plenty to see and do in the immediate vicinity.

Hotel Ecológico Terra Verde (Green Land Lodge), Rua Silva Ramos 20, sala 305 ⓣ92/3622-7305, ⓕ3622-4114, ⓔterraverde@internext.com.br. Located in a small ecological reserve on the Fazenda São Francisco, 50km from Manaus over the other side of the Rio Negro on Lago Acajatuba, this lodge has five relatively luxurious cabins, a floating swimming pool and horse-riding facilities. A comfortable and interesting place, but probably a bit tame for the adventurous traveller. From around R$350 per person for two days and night. Boats run daily to the lodge from the pier at the *Tropical Hotel* (8am and 2pm).

Negro region has a very distinctive beauty influenced by the geology of the Guiana Shield where the main river sources are and the consequent soil types and topography. The waters are very acidic and home to far fewer mosquitoes than you find in other regions. The Negro also tends to have less abundant wildlife than some of the lakes and channels around the Rio Solimões. You can still see much the same species in both regions, but the densities are lower on the Rio Negro and many of its tributaries. Plenty of tours combine both the Solimões and Negro rivers in their itineraries.

On the Solimões, some of the three- to five-day options include trips to Lago Mamori or Manacapuru. Although well visited and only half a day's travel by road and boat from Manaus, **Lago Mamori** offers reasonably well-preserved forest conditions in which you'll see plenty of birds, alligators and dolphins and have the chance to do some piranha fishing. Slightly further into the forest, the **Parana do Mamori** is a quieter river-like arm from Lago Mamori and a zone where numerous birds, sloths, pink dolphins, caiman and monkeys are easily spotted. **Lago Arara**, accessed by a pink dolphin feeding ground of a *furo* from the Parana do Mamori, is a beautiful and relatively well-preserved corner in this area. As well as wildlife, the Parana do Mamori allows close contact with the local riverine communities of *caboclo* people (the settlers who have been here for generations and who dedicate their time to fishing, farinha making, cattle-ranching and, some of them, tapping rubber). From the Parana Mamori there is a large *furo* connection with the quieter **Lago Juma**; from here the **Rio Juma** region is accessible; remote and malarial, but excellent for wildlife, you need a minimum of five or six days to make the travel time worthwhile. Much further south of Manaus, again, the **Igapó Açu** area is one of the best sites for wildlife and, despite its remoteness, it can also be easily reached from Manaus (by boat and road) in a five-or six-day trip; there are no lodges here, but it is possible to stay with locals and ideally your guide will have good contacts. West of Manaus, on the north bank of the Solimões, **Manacapuru**, also accessible by road and boat, is closer to large population centres and therefore offers more in the way of a visit to lakes, plant-familiarization walks, including access to Brazil-nut tree trails. It's also an area where visitors can make interesting excursions up smaller tributaries in search of birdlife, alligators and spectacular flora, such as the gigantic **samaumeira tree** with its buttress base (one of the tallest trees in the Amazon).

Further up the Solimões, the **Mamirauá Sustainable Development Reserve** is an area of relatively untouched seasonally flooded *várzea*-type vegetation offering close contact with the flora and fauna, including pink dolphins. After fifteen years of intense conservation in the immediate environment, the low-impact Uacari Floating Lodge and a fleet of boats make it possible to explore the unspoilt surroundings from a comfortable base within the reserve. Small groups of four visitors and a guide get access to forest trails, lakes and local riverine *caboclo* communities. Access to the reserve can be organized through some Manaus tour companies or direct with the Programa de Ecoturismo (Ⓣ97/3343-4160, Ⓔecoturismo@mamiraua.org.br, Ⓦwww.mamiraua.org.br) in Tefé (the nearest town), a one- to two-day journey (450km) upstream from Manaus. Tours tend to be costly, not least because most visitors choose to fly to Tefé. Uacari Floating Lodge is less than two hours by road and river boat from the airport.

Presidente Figueiredo lies 100km by road north of Manaus and sits at the heart of waterfall country. There's a tourist information kiosk (Ⓣ92/3324-1158) at the *rodoviaria* there, but you can also book tours with guides from some of the tour agents in Manaus. Two hours by bus from Manaus and ten hours south of Boa Vista, there are several hotels and restaurants in town, but the Pousada Cuca Legal Rua Manaus 1, Centro (Ⓣ92/3324-1138, Ⓦwww.pousadacucalegal.com.br; ④) offers a rural retreat with a pool and small but airy rooms and a good restaurant. The Iracema Falls are only 12km away, and, similarly, there is also Santuario (16km), Portero (19kms) and the very impressive Pedra Furada (60kms). Closer to town there's the Water Mammal Preservation Centre (Mon–Sat 8am–midday & 2–4pm. Ⓣ92/3312-1202).

Located on the west bank of the Rio Negro, just below the confluence with the Rio Branco, is Brazil's largest national park – the 23,000 square kilometre **Parque Nacional de Jaú**, which cannot be entered alone or without official permission;

△ Hiking in the jungle

Yanomami tours: a warning

Some tourists are offered trips to the Yanomami or other Indian reserves. These are difficult to obtain these days following recent outbreaks of violence between miners and the Yanomami. Such a trip is only possible with valid permission from IBAMA (BR-317 137, Castelo Branco district ⓣ92/3613-1703) and FUNAI (Rua Maceio 224, Adrianopolis ⓣ92/3233-7103), which you have to obtain yourself. If a company says they already have permission, they're probably lying, as each visit needs a new permit. In any case, permission is generally impossible to get, so that the trips offered may actually be illegal and could land you in serious trouble. Of course, the ethics of such visits are in any case clear: isolated groups of Indians have no immunity to imported diseases, and even the common cold can kill them with devastating ease.

it is always best to do this through a local tour operator (such as Eco Discovery Tours; see p.476) who has the necessary contacts with IBAMA and the national park offices. It takes time and money to visit the park, but this is exceptionally remote forest and well conserved; the tour operators should also be able to provide reliable guides, camping equipment and transport to the area.

The Rio Solimões and the journey to Peru

The stretch of river upstream from Manaus, as far as the pivotal frontier with **Peru** and **Colombia** at Tabatinga, is known to Brazilians as the **Rio Solimões**. Once into Peru it again becomes the Rio Amazonas. Although many Brazilian maps show it as the Rio Marañón on the Peru side, Peruvians don't call it this until the river forks into the Marañón and Ucayali headwaters, quite some distance beyond Iquitos.

From Manaus to Iquitos in Peru, the river remains navigable by large ocean-going boats, though few travel this way any more: since the collapse of the rubber market and the emergence of air travel, the river is left to smaller, more locally oriented riverboats. Many travellers do come this way, however; and, although some complain about the food and many get upset stomachs (especially on the Peruvian leg), it can be a quite pleasant way of moving around – lying in your hammock, reading and relaxing, or drinking at the bar. Against this, there are all the inherent dangers of travelling by boat on a large river, especially at night. Boats have been known to sink (though this is rare) and they do frequently break down, causing long delays; many captains seem to take great pleasure in overloading boats with both cargo and passengers. In spite of the discomforts, however, the river journey remains popular and is unarguably an experience that will stick in the memory.

The river journey is also, of course, by far the cheapest way of travelling between Brazil and Peru. There are reasonable facilities for visitors in the border town of **Tabatinga** and the adjacent Colombian town of **Leticia**. All boats have to stop at one of these ports, and most will terminate at the border whichever direction they've come from.

The boat trip from Manaus to Tabatinga – five to eight days upstream – costs around R$160 inclusive of food (though bring some treats, as the fare on board, though good, does get a bit monotonous). The downstream journey, which is often very crowded, takes three to four days and costs upward of R$120. If you want to break the journey, you can do so at **Tefé**, around halfway, and visit the beautiful **Mamirauá Sustainable Development Reserve** (see p.479), a wild but accessible area of rainforest upstream from the town or, if you really can't face the boat journey any longer, take one of the weekly flights from Tefé to Manaus and Tabatinga. There's also an *expresso* boat service connecting Tefé with Manaus (see Manaus Listings, p.471).

Several large boats currently ply the river upstream from Manaus on a regular basis, all pretty similar and with good facilities (toilets with paper, showers, mineral water and enough food). Smaller boats also occasionally do the trip, but more often terminate at Tefé, from where other small boats continue. On the other side of the border, the boat trip to Iquitos from Tabatinga costs around R$90–150 and takes three or four days; sometimes more, rarely less. Coming downstream from Iquitos to Tabatinga (R$60–85 gives you one and a half days on the river. It's advisable to take your own food and water – all normal supplies can be bought in Tabatinga. There are also more popular super-fast, sixteen-seater powerboats connecting Tabatinga and Leticia with Iquitos that cost upwards of R$160 and take roughly ten to twelve hours. Small planes also connect Iquitos with Santa Rosa, an insignificant Peruvian border settlement just a short boat ride over the river from Tabatinga and Leticia; there is at least one flight a week operated by the Peruvian airline TANS.

The three-way frontier

The point where Brazil meets Peru and Colombia is known as the **three-way frontier**, and it's somewhere you may end up staying for a few days sorting out red tape or waiting for a boat. Some Brazilian boats will leave you at Benjamin Constant, across the river from Tabatinga, but, if you do have to hang around, then Tabatinga, or the neighbouring Colombian town of Leticia, are the only

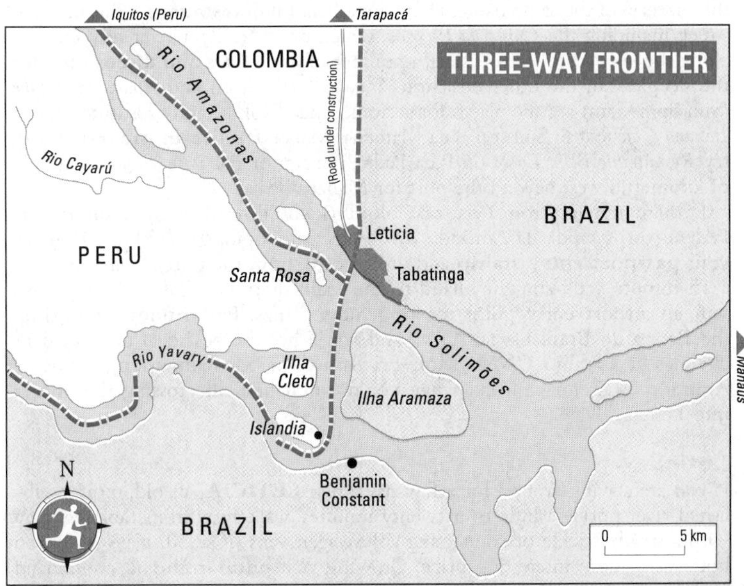

places with any real facilities. A fleet of motorboat taxis connect these places, and Islandia and Santa Rosa in Peru: Benjamin Constant to Tabatinga takes half an hour and costs around R$7; Tabatinga to Islandia or Santa Rosa takes fifteen minutes and costs R$5. When you're making plans, bear in mind that the three countries have differing time zones: make sure you know which you are operating on (Tabatinga is an hour behind Manaus).

For many centuries the three-way frontier has been home to the Tikuna Indians, once large in number, but today down to a population of around 10,000. Their excellent handicrafts – mainly string bags and hammocks – can be bought in Leticia.

Tabatinga

TABATINGA is not the most exciting of towns, and many people stuck here waiting for a boat or plane to Manaus or Iquitos prefer to hop over the border to Leticia for the duration of their stay, even if they don't plan on going any further into Colombia. Tabatinga is the place to complete Brazilian exit (or entry) formalities with the Polícia Federal (see below for details). The town also has an airport with regular flights to Manaus. Many of the boats into Peru leave from here, and if you're coming or going the other way most downstream boats start their journeys here too (south down Rua Tamandaré, then right after the Marine base), before really filling up at Benjamin Constant.

Accommodation in Tabatinga isn't that great – a good reason to stay on the boat if you can or, if you really need a night of luxury, to try out the hotels in neighbouring Leticia (see below). In Tabatinga, your choice is limited to the friendly but very basic *Hotel Pajé*, Rua Pedro Teixeira 367 (⊕97/3412-2774; ❶); the fairly pleasant *Hotel Rasgo da Lua* at the start of Rua Marechal Mallet (⊕97/3412-2571; ❷); the *Pousada do Sol*, Rua General Sampao (⊕97/3412-3355; ❸), with nice but plain rooms, a sauna and a small pool; and the *Hotel Te Contei*, on the main drag Avenida da Amizade at no. 1813 (⊕97/3412-4548; ❷), which is clean but a bit noisy and entered up the rickety spiral stairway over the pizzeria of the same name. There are a handful of **restaurants** on the same street, including the *Canto do Peixada*, which does excellent river fish. Further along the *avenida*, towards Leticia, a number of lively **bars and discos** cater for the sleepless. In the other direction, *Scandalo's* (Fri–Sun) and *Amazonas Clube* (Sun 8pm–5am) are the places for serious dance freaks – and prostitutes – as is *Banana Café* (Sat & Sun) on Rua Marechal Mallet. For **live music** (Fri & Sat), try *Restaurante Bella Epoca* on Rua Pedro Teixeira or *Bar Porto Seguro*, a couple of kilometres west beyond the port for Manaus boats.

If you're arriving from Peru or Colombia, you'll need to go to the Polícia Federal on Avenida da Amizade (Mon–Fri 8am–6pm, ⊕97/3412-2180) for your **passport entry stamp** and visitor card; from the port at Tabatinga, it's a 15-minute walk straight inland to the main drag. The Polícia Federal also staff an airport entry point meeting most planes. For **money changing**, the Banco do Brasil has an ATM, and you'll get the best deal for traveller's cheques at Câmbio CNM (Mon–Fri 8am–5pm, Sat 8am–noon), at Av. da Amizade 2017; for cash exchange you're often best off crossing the border into Leticia.

Leticia

If you are staying around for a few days then **LETICIA**, an old, more established river port – a little over twenty minutes' walk away from Tabatinga and with a steady trickle of connecting Volkswagen vans (R$2.50) if it's really too hot – is a more interesting place. Growing rich on tourism and contraband

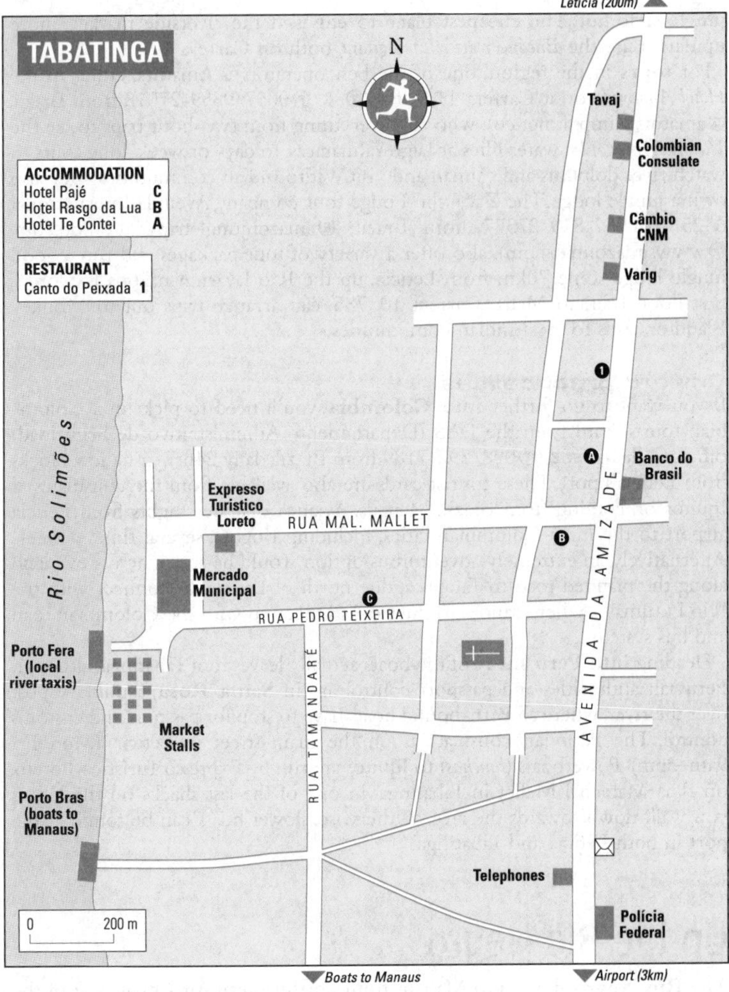

(mostly cocaine), it has more than a touch of the Wild West about it. There's no physical border at the port or between Leticia and Tabatinga, though people getting off boats sometimes have to go through a customs check and you should carry your passport at all times.

There are endless kiosks **changing dollars** into Brazilian, Colombian and Peruvian currency, mostly on the riverfront, but also on the boundary between Tabatinga and Leticia. Leticia is also a good place to buy hammocks, and if you're looking for a little pampering there are a couple of very good hotels in town, though it's quite expensive by Peruvian (and Brazilian) standards. Best of the basic **hotels** are *Residencial Monserrate* (❸) and *Residencial Leticia* (❷), but much nicer are the *Colonial*, near the port square on Carrera 10 (Ⓣ0057-919/27164 from Brazil; ❺), and the swish *Anaconda* (Ⓣ0057/9859-27891 or 9859-27119 from Brazil; ❼), which has a pool and a bar in an attractive jungle-style hut. The cheapest place to **eat** is at the riverside market; more upmarket are the *Bucaneer* and *La Taguara*, both on Carrera 10.

For **tours** in the region, one of the best operators is Amaturs, either in the *Hotel Anaconda* or at Carrera 11, 7–84 (Ⓣ & Ⓕ0057/9859-27018 from Brazil, Ⓔamaturs@impsat.net.co), who run everything from two-hour trips to see the *Victoria Amazonica* water lilies at Lago Yahuaracas, to day- or week-long tours to watch river dolphins and caiman and visit Witito Indian communities; they also own a jungle lodge. The Zacambu Lodge tour company, Avenida Internacional 6–25 (Ⓣ0057-819/27377 from Brazil, ⒺamazonjungletripsZ@yahoo.com, Ⓦwww.amazontrip.com), also offer a variety of tour packages and run a good jungle lodge some 70km from Leticia, up the Rio Javari. Amazons Explorers, first floor, Edificio Matiz, Carrera 10, 785, can arrange trips out to Monkey Island or visits to local Indian communities.

Onward practicalities

If you want to go further **into Colombia**, you'll need to pick up a Colombian tourist card from the DAS (Departamento Administrativo de Seguridad) office, Calle 9, 9–62 (Ⓣ098/592-7189 from Brazil; daily 24hr), just a few blocks from Leticia's port. These tourist cards are also available from the consulates at Iquitos or, coming from Brazil, Manaus. Avianca operates flights from Leticia airport to the main Colombian cities, including Bogotá, several times a week. Alternatively, an extremely adventurous option would be to cut across overland along the planned road to Tarapacá, due north of Leticia, to connect with the Rio Putumayo, where canoes to Puerto Asis meet up with the Colombian road and bus system.

Heading **into Peru**, many of the boats actually leave from Tabatinga, although Peruvian authorities and passport control are in **Santa Rosa**, a military post over the river, where all Peru-bound boats have to stop for passport and customs control. The Peruvian consulate is on the main street in Leticia (Mon–Fri 9am–3pm). Powerboats (*lanchas*) to Iquitos are run by Expresso Turístico Loreto, on Rua Marechal Mallet in Tabatinga, in one of the last shacks on the left as you walk down towards the river. Otherwise, slower boats can be found at the port in both Leticia and Tabatinga.

Up the Rio Negro

The **Rio Negro** flows into Manaus from northwestern Amazonas, one of the least explored regions of South America. There's virtually nothing in the way of tourist facilities in this direction, but it's possible to make your way up the Rio Negro by boat from Manaus to Barcelos, from Barcelos to São Gabriel, and from there on to the virtually uncharted borders with Colombia and Venezuela. Alternatively, there are reasonably fast boats from Manaus every Friday, run by Asabranca, which call in at Barcelos (two days; R$100–200) on their way to São Gabriel (about five days up, three downriver; R$150–220). There are also daily **flights** to São Gabriel from Manaus, stopping off en route on alternate days at either Barcelos or Tefé on the Rio Solimões. To leave Brazil via these routes requires expedition-level planning and can take up to several weeks or longer, but it's an exciting trip nonetheless.

The first part of the journey, from Manaus to **Novo Aírão**, towards the middle of the Anavilhanas archipelago, is usually reached in a day; but beyond here ice and most luxury items, including foodstuffs, are pretty well impossible to find. The best part of another day or two brings you to **Moura,** a smaller river port town with few facilities. Half a day from here the Rio Negro meets the Rio Branco and just beyond is another small town, **Carvoeiro**.

A more important settlement, **BARCELOS**, is as much as another day's boat journey up the Rio Negro from Carvoeiro. As well as the faster Asabranca boat from Manaus to Barcelos, there are ordinary boats at least twice a week ($50), taking around sixty to eighty hours; the *Irmãos Feraes* is particularly recommended, with good, fresh river food aboard. Other boats leave fairly frequently but with no predictable regularity from the docks behind the Mercado Municipal in Manaus: look for the destination signs. Alternatively, you can hire a river taxi from the floating port to help you find a boat bound for Barcelos since they also moor to the west of the main port. Fix a price with the taxi first; it should cost no more than R$15–20. In Barcelos, the Nara family offer **accommodation** and good food to visitors who are going on their **jungle tours**. Run by Tatunca Nara, a local native, the tours take you deep into the forest where there's a better chance of spotting wildlife than there is closer to Manaus. Contact Tatunca's wife, who speaks English, in advance: Dr Anita Nara, c/o Unidade Mista, Barcelos, Amazonas 69700 (ⓣ92/3721-1165).

At least two days further upriver, the town of **SÃO GABRIEL DA CACHOEIRA** is the next settlement of any size. Besides the Asabranc service, boats from Barcelos leave at irregular intervals, but generally several times a week; expect to pay between R$60 and R$100. It's a beautiful place where the jungle is punctuated by volcanic cones, one with a Christ figure standing high on its flank. Superb views can be had across the valley from the slopes around the town, and there's a good **pensão** and several **restaurants** here as well.

A little further upriver you reach the **Rio Negro Forest Reserve**, where local guides will take you camping from around R$50–70 a day. At present this park zone – a massive triangle between the headwaters of the Rio Negro and its important tributary the Rio Uaupés, both of which rise in Colombia – is crawling with military personnel. It's a sensitive zone, partly because of fears of narcotics smuggling, but also because it forms part of the national frontier: Venezuela, Brazil and Colombia meet here, and the Rio Negro itself serves as the border between Venezuela and Colombia for some way. There are also plans to put a highway through the park – the projected BR-210 or Perimetral Norte – which is destined to run from Macapá on the Atlantic coast to São Gabriel, passing south of Boa Vista on the way. From São Gabriel it should eventually make its way across the Amazon via Tabatinga to Cruzeiro do Sul, where it would link up with the westerly point of the Transamazônica, making it feasible to do an enormous circle by road around the Brazilian Amazon. Exactly when this will happen is anybody's guess (to date only 650km of road near Boa Vista has been built), and some of the regions that have been proposed for the road are incredibly remote.

You may also be able to get a guide to take you into the **Parque Nacional do Pico da Neblina**. The Pico da Neblina itself, Brazil's highest peak at 3014m, is on the far side of the park, hard against the Venezuelan border. You will need permission from IBAMA just for entering the protected area.

To proceed **beyond São Gabriel** by river is more difficult, particularly in the dry season from May to October. The river divides a few hours past São Gabriel. To the right, heading more or less north, the Rio Negro continues (another day by boat) to the community of Cucui on the Venezuelan border – there's also a very rough road from São Gabriel. It is possible to travel on from here **into Venezuela** and the Orinoco river system, through the territory of Yanomami Indians, but this involves a major expedition requiring boats, guides and considerable expense: cost aside, it is also potentially dangerous, and you should get a thorough update on the local situation before attempting this route (FUNAI and IBAMA in Manaus are the obvious points of reference, as well as jungle tour operators). In recent years the region has become the focus for the *garimpeiros*, who were effectively pushed out of the Yanomami territory in Roraima during the early 1990s and so moved further west into this region, which is clearly one of the last Amazonian frontiers.

The left fork in the river is the **Rio Uaupés**, where the **Araripirá waterfalls** lie a day or two upstream, just before the border settlement of Iaurete. The Uaupés continues, another day's journey, along the border to the Colombian town of Mitu. Again, this is a potentially hazardous area, home to Maku Indians and, more worryingly, to coca-growing areas and members of the Colombian underworld.

Roraima

In the far north of Brazil, the **state of Roraima**, butting against Guiana and Venezuela, was only created in 1991, and came to world notice in 1998 when devastating forest fires wreaked havoc on the area. It's an active frontier zone. When the grasslands here were discovered in the mid-eighteenth century they were thought to be ideal cattle country, and it was the Portuguese who first moved in on them. But the current national borders weren't finally settled until the early part of the twentieth century. During the early 1990s, there was a massive gold rush here, with an influx of as many as 50,000 *garimpeiros* (compared to a total population of around 200,000 previously). This was centred above all in the northwest, up against the Venezuelan border in the Serra Pacaraima in the territory of the **Yanomami Indians**, Amazonian tribal peoples living on both sides of the border.

In 1989 the plight of the Yanomami, whose lands were being invaded by prospectors, brought about an international outcry that forced the Brazilian government to announce that they would evacuate all settlers from Yanomami lands. But the project was abandoned almost as soon as it began: protection of the region's valuable mineral reserves was deemed to necessitate the strengthening of the country's borders and the settlement of the area. Following the successful demarcation of Yanomami lands in 1992, and the territory's official recognition by the Federal State, things have improved, and there are now fewer *garimpeiros* prospecting in Yanomami forests. However, many vested interests were thwarted when the Yanomami's land was officially demarcated, and there remain high-level moves to take some of the land back from the Yanomami. For more on this tribe, see p.819.

Up the Rio Branco

These days it's relatively easy to get from **Manaus to Boa Vista**, the capital of Roraima, by tarmacked road, usually taking twelve hours by **bus** ($35). It is also possible to take a **boat** all the way from Manaus up the Rio Negro and Rio Branco as far as the waterfalls of **Caracaraí**, from where you can join the bus to Boa Vista (some boats also go from Caracaraí to Boa Vista, but they're few and far between). It isn't an easy trip and it has been known to take over two weeks, with lots of stopping and starting and depending on local river people for hospitality and food. If you can get a boat that is going direct, all the better. Expect to pay at least $100 for the trip, more if you're boat hopping.

△ Roraima Mountain

It's sometimes easier to travel first to Barcelos from where there are occasional boats bound up the Rio Branco, but it's all very much hit and miss once you're on the rivers.

Those who do make it up the Rio Branco are generally rewarded for their steadfastness by the sight of river dolphins, alligators and plenty of birdlife. At Caracaraí there are very few tourist facilities, but there are two very basic **hotels**, the *Hotel Márcia*, Rua Dr Zanny (☎95/232-1208; ❶), and, marginally better, *Hotel Maroca*, Av. Pres. Kennedy 1140 (☎95/232-1292; ❷).

Boa Vista

BOA VISTA is a fast-growing city of 200,000 people, an unrelentingly hot, modern and concrete monument to its Brazilian planners who laid it out on a grand but charmless scale, with broad tree-lined boulevards divided by traffic islands and a vast Praça do Centro Cívico, swirling with traffic, from which streets radiate just unevenly enough to confuse the otherwise perpendicular grid. Clearly this is meant to be a fitting capital for the development of Roraima – and there are large stores full of ranching and mining equipment that reflect that growth. Busy as it is, though, Boa Vista has far to go to fulfil its ambitious designs. The huge streets seem half empty, reflecting the waning of the gold boom after the initial rush in the late 1980s and early 1990s, and many of the old hotels and gold-trading posts have closed down, or have turned into travel agencies, small-time banks and restaurants. The new layout obliterated many of the town's older buildings, which means that there's little of interest to see in the city itself. Most visitors to Boa Vista are on business or travellers passing through on the overland route from Venezuela to Manaus.

Arrival and information

Over 800km from Manaus, on the edge of the city, surrounded by timber yards and agricultural supply stores, stands the large, modern **rodoviária** (☎95/623-2233), housing several stores, a *lanchonete* and a local **tourist office** (Mon–Sat

10am–5pm; ☎95/623-1238). **Taxis**, which are relatively expensive here, line up outside; on the main road beyond them (from the same side as the terminal) you can catch a **local bus** towards the centre. This takes something of a detour past outlying areas before heading back to near the *rodoviária*, where it turns down past the prison and heads along the broad Avenida Benjamin Constant towards the central *praça*. Buses for the *rodoviária* from town, which bear the "Joquie Clube" sign on the route card, can be caught either at the urban bus terminal (the Rodoviária Urbana) on Rua Dr Silvio Botelho, or along the Avenida Ville Roy. Coming from the **airport** (☎95/623-0404) – where there's another tourist information office (Mon–Sat 8am–6pm, Sun 9am–1pm) – you'll have to take a taxi ($10) for the three-kilometre ride into town.

Arrival in Boa Vista can be awkward because, thanks to the gold rush, international interest in the plight of the Yanomami Indians and the fact that the area is increasingly used by cocaine smugglers, there are lots of military personnel about who are very suspicious of foreigners: you're likely to have your luggage taken apart and to be questioned about your motives. The best bet is probably to play the dumb tourist, and say you're heading for Venezuela or Manaus.

Tourist information is available at the Roraima Tourism Office, Rua Coronel Pinto 241 (Mon–Fri 7.30am–1.30pm & 3.30–5.30pm; ⓣ95/623-1230). Further information and regional tours can be organized through Toca Turismo, Rua Dom Pedro 82 (ⓣ95/623-8175, ⓦwww.tocaturismo.com.br).

Accommodation

Budget **accommodation** in Boa Vista, mainly along Avenida Benjamin Constant, is pretty dire, as most hotels were originally designed to meet the needs of the now ailing *garimpeiro* market, and few of them are accustomed to tourists. There are a couple of good places close to the *rodoviária*, though, while in the centre of town you'll find a handful of upmarket places, aimed at businessmen, with their own swimming pools and restaurants.

Euzébio's Hotel Rua Cecilia Brasil 1107 ⓣ95/623-0300, ⓕ623-9131. The most popular of the town's upmarket hotels, and often full, but not particularly central. It has a swimming pool and an expensive restaurant, yet much of its accommodation is in small, surprisingly dingy units. Make sure you get a room worth the money you're paying. 4

Hotel Aipana Plaza Praça do Centro Cívico 53 ⓣ95/224-4800, ⓕ224-4116, ⓔaipana@tecbet.com.br. The best hotel in Boa Vista, with a pool, bar and a good restaurant, but it's overpriced among the hotels in its price range. 4

Hotel Barrudada Rua Araújo Filho 228 ⓣ95/623-9335. Once a charming private house of a hotel, its popularity was such that it was knocked down in 1996 and replaced by a modern six-storey edifice. The staff remain helpful, however, and the rooms are still good value. 2–3

Hotel Monte Libano Av. Benjamin Constant 319 ⓣ95/224-7232. Probably has the edge over other budget hotels in the centre, as its staff are friendlier and the rooms are in slightly better condition. 1

Hotel Três Nações Av. Ville Roy 1885 ⓣ95/224-3439. Virtually opposite the *rodoviária*, this place is spick-and-span with pleasant rooms around an open courtyard. Because there aren't that many buses passing through, it's not as noisy as many hotels near bus stations elsewhere. 2

Itamaraty Palace Avenida N.S. da Consolata 1957 ⓣ95/224-9757, ⓕ623-0977, ⓦwww.hotelitamaraty.com.br. One of the best-value options among the mid-range hotels, the *Itamaraty Palace* offers a swimming pool, relatively clean and comfortable rooms, a bar, restaurant and a/c. The downside is it's located a kilometre or two from the centre. 4–5

Pousada Beija Flor Av. Nossa Senhora da Consolata ⓣ95/224-8241, ⓕ224-6536. A gem of a place run by a Brazilian–Belgian couple who are tuned in to backpackers' requirements. The accommodation is basic but clean, and Néa and Jean offer a range of reasonably priced tours around Roraima, plus a wealth of information. From the *rodoviária*, walk six blocks down Av. Ville Roy, turn right at the lights and then left onto Av. Consolata; the *pousada* is two blocks further down. 1

Uiramutum Palace Av. Cap. Ene Garcez 427 ⓣ95/624-4700. Located a few blocks from the Palacio do Governo, this place is good value with nice rooms, a pool, a/c and friendly service, though the restaurant is nothing special. 4

The City

As capital city of one of Brazil's newest states, Boa Vista makes great efforts to establish its identity. Opposite the biggest landmark in town, the huge cylindrical concrete tube pointing towards the skies from the roof of the Embratel telephone offices on the Avenida Cap. Ene Garcez, there's a semicircular **amphitheatre** with three statues – one of a *garimpeiro* holding a shovel and a gold-panning bowl; one of a *fazendeiro* wielding a lasso; and, the central one, an Indian with a bow and arrow. Just down the road, in the centre of the Praça do Centro Cívico, there's the better-known **Monument to the Garimpeiro**, which clearly speaks more to local businessmen than it does to environmentally minded foreign visitors.

On the south side of the *praça*, the modest-sized **Catedral** has an interesting curvaceous design, very airy, with a ceiling reminiscent of the hull of a huge wooden boat. On the other side of the square is the **Palácio da Cultura**

(Mon–Fri 8am–7pm, Sat 8am–1pm), with its well-stocked public library and a very smart auditorium that occasionally holds theatre and music performances. Down in the old waterfront district, connected to the *praça* by the main shopping street, Avenida Jaime Brasil, you'll find a cluster of sights, including the small Portuguese-style **Igreja Nossa Senhora do Carmo**, an open-air *anfiteatro* now used as a music venue, and the **Casa da Cultura** gallery-space – an exact replica of the city's first Prefeitura that was destroyed as part of the zealous modernization of the 1960s. Facing it is an imposing concrete **Monument to the Pioneers of Roraima**. The huge bust of a Yanomami chief dominates the sculpture, his shoulder somewhat ambiguously being trampled over by a pioneer on horseback.

The **Casa do Artesanato**, on the riverbank on Rua Floriano Peixoto 192 (Mon–Sat 8am–6pm; ⓣ95/623-1615), is also worth a visit: its selection of handicrafts is not wide but there's some interesting stuff and it's all very cheap. There are great views from the *Restaurante Panorama Macuchik* (see below) and the riverbank near the Casa do Artesanato out across the Rio Branco, towards the large-span, modern concrete bridge and the forest stretching beyond.

Eating and drinking

Lanchonetes are everywhere in Boa Vista, though more substantial **restaurants** are surprisingly scarce as well as expensive. In the centre, the *Restaurante La Gondola*, on the corner of Avenida Benjamin Constant and the Praça do Centro Cívico, is fine for *comida por kilo* and very popular. At night, the *Hotel Euzébio*'s restaurant serves good meals and, virtually next door, the lively *Pigalle* has good pizzas and fish, but neither place is exactly on the cheap side; both also function as bars. More reasonable, and with excellent views, are a growing number of restaurants along the riverfront: the *Restaurante Panorama Macuchik*, close to the Casa do Artesanato at Rua Floriano Peixoto 114 (ⓣ95/623-1346), is highly recommended, as is the fish restaurant *Ver o Rio* (closed Mon lunchtime; ⓣ95/224-6964), two buildings down on the same road. For more evening atmosphere, but without the river view, try the *Black and White Restaurant*, one road back on Rua Barreto Leite 11 (closed Mon; ⓣ95/224-5372).

As for **bars and clubs**, *Clube ABB* near the airport is the most popular nightspot (Fri & Sat only); also well worth trying is the *Zanzibar*, corner of Avenida Sebastião Diniz and Rua Coronel Pinto, which has a good atmosphere and hosts local bands on Friday and Saturday (9pm onwards; ⓣ95/224-0093). Straightforward drinking bars are surprisingly few, the best being *Meu Cantinho* opposite the *Panorama* and with equally good views (daily until midnight).

Listings

Airlines Varig have an office at Av. Getúlio Vargas 242 (ⓣ95/224-4143). To and from Manaus, planes can be solidly booked for days if not weeks ahead, especially at holiday times, though you might get lucky with the waiting list.

Air taxis Meta (ⓣ95/224-7677) is based at the airport.

Banks and exchange The best place to change money in Boa Vista is the private backroom office of Casa Pedro José, Rua Araújo Filho 287, which gives excellent rates and a fast, efficient service. Otherwise, the Banco do Brasil, on the *praça* near the Palácio Municipal, changes money between 8am and 12.30pm (arrive early).

Car rental Localiza ⓣ95/224-5222; Unidas ⓣ95/224-4080.

Consulates Venezuela, Av. Benjamin Constant 525 ⓣ95/224-2182 or 623-9285. If you hope to get a visa in a single day then arrive early: hours are officially Mon–Fri 8.30am–1pm but they may open later in the afternoon to give your completed visa back. You'll need to show your passport and have a photo and an onward ticket – though you may be able to get round the latter by having plenty of money and a good excuse. From the consulate they'll send you to a doctor for a cursory medical examination (US$10 for this privilege) and from there you go to a clinic for a blood test (free), which they claim is for malaria. Having passed these you can usually go back in the afternoon, clutching the certificates, to pick up your passport and visa.

Post office Praça do Centro Cívico (Mon–Fri 9am–5pm).
Taxis ⓣ95/224-4223 or 224-4823.
Telephones National and international calls can be made from public booths with phonecards; alternatively the Embratel office is on Rua Cel. Pinto, close to the junction with Av. Cap. Ene Garcez.

Around Boa Vista

Situated as it is on the northern edge of the Amazon forest, where it meets the savanna of Roraima, the region around Boa Vista boasts three different forms of ecosystem: tropical rainforest, grassland savanna plains and the "Lost World"-style tepius mountain, flat plateau-like rock rising out of the savanna. Still fairly undeveloped in terms of its tourism infrastructure, the area is exceptionally beautiful, with a wealth of river beaches, and has a very pleasant climate (hot with cooling breezes). As the options for ecotourism are developed, more opportunities will no doubt emerge for visitors to explore Roraima in some depth.

Your first port of call in Boa Vista should be the tourist office, which has details of new destinations, circuits and accommodation options in the state. At present, **independent travel** in the region can be problematic, with only sketchy bus services, so you might find it easier simply to hire a car (see "Listings", opposite). **Organized tours**, usually dependent on enough tourists filling spaces, are operated by Baba's Home (ⓣ95/623-7304), Iguana tours (ⓣ95/224-6576), Tocatur (ⓣ95/623-2597), and ECOTUR, Rua Barreto Leite 46 (ⓣ95/224-6010), while the agency inside *Euzébio's Hotel* deals in six-day packages for around US$450–500. Much cheaper, and virtually the only outfit in town able to arrange tours for small groups, is *Pousada Beija Flor*, who combine enthusiasm with a wealth of knowledge about the state.

Places to head for include the famous painted rock, **Pedra Pintada**, en route to Santa Elena and Venezuela; the ruined eighteenth-century **Forte São Joaquim**, two hours from Boa Vista by boat; the ecological island reserve of **Ilha do Maracá**, located on the fairly remote Rio Uraricoera; and the very pleasant **Lake Caracaranã** with its fine beaches fringed by shady cashew trees, 180km from Boa Vista in Normandia. This is currently almost the only place in the state outside Boa Vista that has adequate facilities for tourists, with fifteen chalets and ten apartments for hire, the four-bed chalets a bargain at US$50; ⓣ95/262-1254 or contact Transeme Turismo in Boa Vista, Av. Sebastião Diniz 234 (ⓣ95/224-9409 or 224-6271). Also of note are the **Igarape Agua Boa**, where there are islands, fine sandy beaches (US$10; 2–3hr), and the **Serra Grande**, where you'll find more islands and beaches plus trails in the forest to the waterfall of the same name (1hr).

Into Venezuela and Guyana

It's now relatively straightforward to go from Boa Vista to Santa Elena in **Venezuela**, and beyond to Ciudad Guyana and Ciudad Bolívar – even right on to Puerto La Cruz on the north coast if you're that anxious to escape the interior – a daily União Cascavel bus leaves Boa Vista at 7am. Santa Elena is also served by six daily Eucatur buses (3hr, plus 2hr for border formalities). The road, the BR-174, is now fully tarmacked, which means that the União Cascavel bus arrives at the border in time for lunch; it stops at a very expensive restaurant, though, so bring your own lunch if you're running short on money. The journey from Boa Vista, across a vast flat savanna that is dusty in the dry season, boggy in the wet, offers very little in the way of scenery, but there is a great deal of wildlife, especially birds: white egrets, storks and all sorts of waders in the rainy season, flycatchers and hawks; and also the chance of some fairly large animals, including giant anteaters. As the border approaches the land begins to rise slightly: to the northeast lies **Monte Roraima**, the fourth-highest peak in Brazil at 2875m, at the point where Brazil, Guyana and Venezuela meet.

Allow a couple of hours to cross the border itself (the bus waits while everyone has passports stamped and luggage checked); **SANTA ELENA DE UAIRÉN** is barely twenty minutes further. It's not necessary to spend the night here, as the União Cascavel bus continues further up into Venezuela, but if you fancy a break Santa Elena is a tiny place with the real feel of a border town in its low, corrugated-roofed houses and dusty streets. You can see the whole place in an hour's walk, but the *Hotel Frontera* also runs tours to local waterfalls and native communities. If you're staying overnight, good **hotels** include the *Frontera* (3), the simple *Hotel Marcia* (2), and the *Hotel Lucas* (4), which has a casino. There's good **food** at the *Restaurante Itália* (the spaghetti is the cheapest thing to eat in a relatively expensive town). **Money** is hard to change here: various traders will accept cash dollars or Brazilian currency – try the *Hotel Frontera* – but there's nowhere at all to change traveller's cheques. **Leaving**, there's a 5am bus to Ciudad Bolívar (12hr), as well as the União Cascavel bus late at night, and a daily flight (2hr). If you're heading for Brazil, there are at least seven buses a day. Don't forget to get your Venezuelan exit stamp from the office next to the police station on the hill behind the bus terminal. The terminal doesn't open until 8am.

Guyana is less straightforward. It's easy enough to get to **Bonfim** on the border, just over 100km away (two daily buses with Eucatur), though the road is pretty grim, but it's much less easy to continue beyond there, and strict Guyanan entry regulations on the border mean there's a fair chance you may even be refused entry. All in all, if you want to go to Guyana, it's easier to fly; there are flights from Manaus to Georgetown, but no longer any services from Boa Vista.

Rondônia and Porto Velho

A large, partially deforested region in the southwest corner of the Brazilian Amazon, the **state of Rondônia** has undergone the first phase of its environmental destruction. Roads and tracks, radiating like fine bones from the spinal highway BR-364, have dissected almost the entire state, bringing in their wake hundreds of thousands of settlers and many large companies who have moved in to gobble up the rainforest. Poor landless groups are a common sight, some the surviving representatives of once-proud Indian tribes, living under plastic sheets at the side of the road. The BR-364 cuts the state more or less in half and, from east to west, connects a handful of rapidly growing nodal towns: Vilhena, Pimenta Bueno, Ji-Paraná, Ouro Preto, Jaru, Ariquemes and Jamari. Ji-Paraná is the largest, having grown from a tiny roadside trading settlement to a significant sky-scraping town of 113,000 people in the last forty years.

The state of Rondônia was only created in 1981, having evolved from an unknown and almost entirely unsettled zone (then the Territory of Guaporé) over the previous thirty years. The new, fast-changing Rondônia was named after the famous explorer, Indian "pacifier" and telegraph network pioneer Marechal Cândido Rondon. It's not exactly one of Brazil's major tourist attractions, but it is an interesting area in its own right, and it also offers a few stopping-off places between more obvious destinations**; Porto Velho**, the main city of the region, is an important pit stop between Cuiabá and the frontier state of Acre. Rondônia also offers border crossings to Bolivia, river trips to Manaus and access to overland routes into Peru.

Given that it is such a recently settled region, the system of road **transport** is surprisingly good, and combines well with the major rivers – Madeira, Mamoré and Guaporé. The main focus of human movement these days is the fast BR-364, which caused a massive surge of development after its completion in the 1980s. Manaus and Porto Velho are well connected by a four-day boat journey, with usually at least three leaving weekly in either direction.

Porto Velho

The capital of Rondônia state, **PORTO VELHO**, overlooks the Amazon's longest tributary, the mighty Rio Madeira. With over 380,000 inhabitants, Porto Velho has evolved from a relatively small town in just twenty years. In the 1980s, settlers arrived in enormous numbers in search of land, jobs and, more specifically, the mineral wealth of the area: gold and casserite (a form of tin) are found all over Rondônia. As in most regions, the gold boom has bottomed out and the empty gold-buying stores are signs of the rapid decline. Seen from a distance across the river, Porto Velho looks rather more impressive than it does at close quarters, though even more than Ji-Paraná, its newest buildings are reaching for the sky and the younger generation ensures that their partying at weekends brings the modern Brazilian vibe through music, too. The two bell towers and Moorish dome of the cathedral stand out strikingly above the rooftops, while alongside the river three phallic water towers sit like waiting rockets beside a complex of military buildings. A little further downstream the modern port and the shiny cylindrical tanks of a petrochemical complex dominate the riverbank.

In the town itself, the main street – Avenida Sete de Setembro – boasts most of the shops and has a distinctive market atmosphere about it, with music stores blaring their sounds, traders shouting out their wares and stallholders chattering on about their predominantly cheap plastic goods. Every other lamppost seems to have a loudspeaker attached to it. The city has a more relaxed ambience down on the far side of the old railway sheds, where you'll find outdoor bars and cafés spread along the riverfront.

Arrival and accommodation

Porto Velho's **airport** (Ⓣ69/3025-7450), Belmont, is 7km out of town and served by local buses and taxis (US$5). The **rodoviária** (Ⓣ69/3222-2233), with daily connections to Guajará-Mirim and the Bolivian border, Cuiabá and Rio Branco, is also some way out on Avenida Kennedy; catch a local bus into town from here to Sete de Setembro. **Tourist information** is best from the Museu Estadual de Rondônia building on Avenida Sete de Setembro or the EMBRATUR office at Presidente Dutra 3004 (Mon-Fri 9am-5pm; Ⓦwww.rondonia.com). Regular **boats** link Manaus and Porto Velho, and the docks are located just 1km west of the main waterfront area.

There is plenty of **accommodation** to choose from in Porto Velho as it's a settlement serving a large hinterland of farmers, prospectors and businessmen, as well as a growing number of tourists.

PORTO VELHO
ACCOMMODATION
Central B
Cuiabano E
Floresta F
Hotel Vila Rica A
Samauma C
Yara D
RESTAURANTS
A Caravela do Madeira 1
Almanara 4
Emporium 2
Oriente 5
Restaurante Mirante II 3
Airport
Rodoviária
RUA CARLOS GOMES
RUA DOM PEDRO
Watertowers
Teleron
Banco do Brasil
Catedral
PRAÇA DA PREFEITURA
Prefeitura
University of Rondônia
R J. DO PATROCINO
JOSÉ BONIFACIO
RUA GONCALVES DIAS
RUA J. DE CASTILHO
RUA BARÃO DO BRANCO
CENTRAL PRAÇA
AV. FARQHUAR
Mercado Central
Sorveteria Mamoré
River boats (short tours)
Barracas
Museu da Estrada de Ferro Madeira-Mamoré
Museu Estadual
DO CUNHA
Small Street Market
AVENIDA ROGEIRO WEBER
AVENIDA PRESIDENTE DUTRA
RUA JOSÉ DE ALENCAR
Casa de Artesanato
AVENIDA 7 DE SETEMBRO
Rio Madeira
CENTRAL CERON
Museu Estadual de Rondônia
PRAÇA RONDON
RUA N. ALBUQUERQUE
PRUD. MORÃES
Buses to Airport & Rodoviária
AV OSORIO
IRMA CAPELLI
AVENIDA CAMPOS SALES
RUA T. ARANHA
AVENIDA MARECHAL DEODORO
AVENIDA JOAQUIM NABUCO
RUA EUCLIDES
Local Bus Terminal
Madeira-Mamoré Rail Line
ALMIRANTE BARROSA
N
Main port for river boats to Manaus
0
400 m

Central Rua Tenreiro Aranha 2472 ⓣ69/3224-2099 ⓕ3224-5114, ⓦwww.enter-net.com.br/central. A good mid-range place with spacious and clean rooms, most with TV, a/c and fine views across the city. ❸–❹

Cuiabano Av. Sete de Setembro 1180 ⓣ69/3221-4084. A decent budget place with rooms set around a courtyard, only some of which come with a private bathroom. Can be quite noisy during the day as it's located on the main commercial drag. ❶

Floresta Rua Almirante Barroso 502 ⓣ69/3221-5669. This popular spot has a pool and a relatively quiet location, but is within easy walking distance of the town centre. ❸

Rondon Palace Av. Gov. Jorge Teixeira 491 ⓣ69/3224-2718, ⓕ3224-6160. Close to the airport and some way from the centre, this modern, soulless hotel has a pool, a bar and a quite good restaurant. ❹

Samauma Rua Dom Pedro II 1038 ⓣ69/3224-5300. A moderately sized and fairly modern hotel with a bar and restaurant and very reasonable rates. Rooms are adequate and all have a/c. ❷–❸

Vila Rica Rua Carlos Gomes 1616 ⓣ69/3224-3433, ⓦwww.hotelvilarica.com.br. As the tallest building in the town's centre, this hotel is unmissable. The luxury-class rooms are tastefully decorated, and there's a nice pool as well. Good value and hospitable. ❺–❻

Yara Av. General Osório 255 ⓣ69/3221-2127. Bustling modern hotel with basic and small but clean rooms with private baths, TV and a/c. The central location makes it convenient but noisy. ❸

The Town

Although it's a lively town and an enjoyable place to spend some time, Porto Velho doesn't have much in the way of a developed tourist scene beyond its main attraction, the wonderful **Madeira-Mamoré Museu Ferroviário** (daily 8am–6pm, ⓣ69/3216-5131) and the neighbouring **Museu Geologico**. Run with the help of the eloquent Sr. Johnson and his colleagues, the railway museum is jam-packed with fascinating period exhibits, from photographs of important railway officials and operatives from the past (including Johnson's father), to station furniture, equipment and mechanical devices, including an entire and quite spectacular locomotive, built in Philadelphia in 1878. For railway buffs, there's also plenty of equipment and other locomotives to see around the old railway terminal adjacent to the museum. The Madeira-Mamoré (or Mad Maria) Railway was planned to provide a route for Bolivian rubber to the Atlantic and therefore the markets of Europe and the eastern US, but due to a series of setbacks during its forty-year construction it was only completed in 1912 – just in time to see the price of rubber plummet and the market dry up. Some estimates say that as many as fifty thousand men died – mostly of malaria – building the rail line, though in truth the figure was probably a tenth of that. The line was closed in 1960, and in 1972 many of the tracks were ripped up to help build a road along the same difficult route. There is also an *artesanato* and souvenir shop in the old railway ticket office building.

The other museum in town, the **Museu Estadual de Rondônia** (Mon–Fri 7.30am–6pm), on Sete de Setembro, has an ever-changing collection of historic photographs (from its archive of some 60,000) which often shows early explorers and pioneers travelling up uncharted rivers; it also has rooms with ethnographic artefacts gathered from indigenous tribes of the region as well as a paleontological display and a large exhibition of diverse crystals, fossils and minerals discovered locally. There's little else to see: the **University of Rondônia** is not a very inspiring building, and the **Catedral** is better appreciated from the far side of the river. One of the best things to do while you're here is to take a short trip on a **floating bar**. They set out at intervals during the day – there's almost always a 5pm sundowner tour and more frequent sailings at weekends – and for a few *reais* and the price of a beer or two you can spend a pleasant couple of hours travelling up and down the Madeira, sharing the two-storey floating bar with predominantly local groups. The atmosphere is invariably lively, and there's often impromptu music.

Eating, drinking and nightlife

There are some decent places to **eat and drink** in Porto Velho, though beer here is more expensive than on the coast. Food, on the other hand, tends to be a little cheaper. The Mercado Central, at the bottom end of town close to the railway museum on Avendia Farqhua, is a good place to buy your own food or get a cheap meal. For decent and very good-value *comida por kilo* lunches, the best place is *Asados & Salados*, Av. Sete de Setembro 504, which also has great juices.

It may not look like it, but Porto Velho has one of the best **restaurants** in Brazil. Tucked away down an obscure side street on the riverfront, it's impossible to find without a taxi but every taxi driver knows where it is. The wonderful *A Caravela do Madeira*, Rua José Camacho 104, Arigolandia (Ⓣ69/3221-6641; closed Sun evening & Mon), is an enormous wooden, hillside building that overlooks the Rio Madeira. River fish is the speciality here; try *costeleta de surubim* or the equally delicious *pirarucu na brasa*. A meal with a taxi to and from the centre will set you back around R$50; additionally, there's sometimes live music on Saturdays.

A number of good restaurants and bars can be found along Avenida Presidente Dutra, including the stylish *Emporium* at number 3366 (Ⓣ69/3221-2665); tables are both inside and out and it plays good Brazilian rock and serves fun cocktails. Otherwise, the best place for restaurants is the stretch of Avenida Joaquim Nabuco behind the *Hotel Vila Rica*. For genuine Chinese food, try *Oriente*, at Av. Amazonas 1280 (closed Mon), and for reasonable Arabic–Brazilian cuisine there's the *Habibe*, Av. Lauro Sodré 1190 (closed Mon), and the *Almanara*, Av. José de Alencar 2624.

Great ice cream is available at the *Sorveteria Mamoré*, overlooking the port side of the railway sheds, and there are reasonable drinks, snacks and fish meals at the very popular *barracas* that line the riverfront promenade. Close to the military complex on the hill above the town, the *Restaurante Mirante II* has a good view over the river and often has live music on Friday evenings. As the night progresses, the *Wau Wau* **bar**, in the *Hotel Vila Rica*, generally offers good entertainment, and there are also a few **nightclubs**, notably *Amazon House* at Avenida Pinheiro Machado 753 (Ⓣ69/3223-9561), *Original*, on Rua Guanabara, which plays a range of music including *forró*, samba and *pagode*, and *Bungalo*, on the same road but closer to the centre.

Listings

Airlines Varig, Av. Campos Sales 2666 Ⓣ69/3224-4224, and at the airport Ⓣ69/3224-2262; TAM, J. Castilho 530 Ⓣ69/3221-6666 or 3229-6816; Rico, Av. Pinheiro Machado 744 Ⓣ69/3224-2105; Tavaj, at Av. Gov. Jorge Teixeira 6490 and the airport (Ⓣ69/3225-2999), covers most of the western Amazon.

Banks and exchange HSBC, at Av. Jorge Teixeira 1350 (has ATM); Banco do Brasil, at the corner of José de Alencar and Dom Pedro II (*câmbio* upstairs). Traveller's cheques and cash can be exchanged at the *Ourominas* office, Rua Jose de Alencar; cash only can also be changed at the *Hotel Floresta* and the *Vila Rica*. Note that most banks only open between 8am and 2pm in the hottest months, between December and March.

Boats The main commercial port is easily located about 1km upstream from the rail yards; you'll have to go there to check out all the possibilities. For Manaus there are frequent boats offering first- and second-class passages for the four-day trip. The boats at the port generally display their destinations; otherwise it's a matter of asking the crew of each vessel and making a deal with the captain whose itinerary suits you best. Conasa (Ⓣ69/3229-4946) and Silnave (Ⓣ69/3229-3456) are among the companies operating boats up and down river from here. Boats for Santo Antonio (45mins) leave from the riverfront close to the Praça da Madeira-Mamore and railway museum.

Car hire Localiza Ⓣ69/3224-6530, Ximenes at Av. Carlos Gomes 1055, Centro Ⓣ69/3224-5766 and Avis Ⓣ69/3225-1011.

Post office The main post office is in Av. Presidente Dutra, just off Sete de Setembro (Mon–Fri 9am–5pm).

Shopping The well-stocked Casa do Artesanato, Av. Sete de Setembro 488, is a good place for *artesanato*; but there's also the excellent Casa da Artes close to the vegetable market and the Casa do Artesanato based in the railway museum. The best places for photographic film and developing are Colortec, at Rua José de Alencar 2850, at the corner with Rua Floriano Peixoto, or the nearby Casa do Fotografo, on Av. Presidente Dutra.

Taxi Cooptaxi ⓣ69/3225-1414.

Telephones There are offices where you can make international calls at both Av. Presidente Dutra 3023 and Av. Carlos Gomes 728 (daily 8am–11pm).

Around Porto Velho

Despite its location on a great river and deep in the Amazon basin, it is surprisingly difficult to experience the forest around Porto Velho, as certain infrastructure – such as lodges, guides and operators – is lacking. Rondônia is home to the Parque Nacional Pacaás Novos, featuring mountains that are rarely visited but remain the source of nearly all of the state's important rivers, which fan out from it in every direction. You'll need IBAMA permission (Av. Jorge Teixeira 3559, ⓣ69/3223-2023) to enter the park, and the terrain is very hard going.

Going north, the BR-319 en route to Manaus is presently paved for only the first 20km and passable only via a four-wheel-drive vehicle. There are plans to pave another 260km over the next few years, and, while such an improvement may open up new areas to ecotourism in the future, for now there are only a couple of places where you can get close to the forest around Porto Velho. Undoubtedly the finest spot is *Salsalito Jungle Park*, about a forty-minute drive from Porto Velho and located at Km 43 of the BR-364 towards Ariquemes (ⓣ69/3224-5300 or 3230-1307, ⓦwww.junglepark.com.br; ③–④). Here there are several nice detached bungalows for rent and a floating restaurant in a beautiful part of the river; activities include horse riding, boat safaris, fishing trips, dolphin spotting and hikes along short forest and river-edge trails. The river is spectacularly beautiful and just upstream you'll discover the big dam serving the hydroelectric plant that feeds off the massive artificial Lago da Usina, which flooded over 74,000 hectares some 20 years ago. Nearby, at Km 673 (a 35min drive from Porto Velho), the *Tres Capelas Eco Resort* (ⓣ69/3259-1010 ⓔtrescapelas@uol.com.br; ④–⑤) offers bungalow accommodation, a restaurant, a bar and a swimming pool in a pleasant but not very distinctive setting. The *Pousada Rancho Grande*, c/o Haarald Schmitz, Fazenda Rancho Grande, Lote 23, Linha C20, Cacaulandia (ⓣ69/3535-4301; ④), is a unique lodge run by a German family in the middle of rainforest and plantations. The *fazenda*, which requires advance reservations for stays, is located about 260km south of Porto Velho, about 28km off the BR-364, and is best approached from Ariquemes (if you are coming from Cuibá). They offer bird-watching, horse riding, jungle walks and a visit to the biggest tin mine in the world at Bom Futuro.

West from Porto Velho

The backbone of modern Rondônia, the **BR-364** highway links the state more or less from north to south, connecting Porto Velho with Cuiabá, Brasília and the wealthy south coast markets. The state's main towns are strung out along the BR-364, almost all of them – including Porto Velho itself, Ji-Paraná and Vilhena at the border with Mato Grosso – marking the points where the road crosses major waterways. It's a fast road, and in the final analysis there's little to stop for anywhere in this direction: you're better off heading straight through to Cuiabá.

Travelling **west from Porto Velho** is a very different matter and soon begins to feel like real pioneering. The further you go, the smaller and wilder the roads, rivers and towns become. The main attractions are Rio Branco (see opposite) and the border crossings into Peru, in the state of Acre, and **Guajará-Mirim**, where you can cross into Bolivia or undertake an adventurous visit to the Forte Príncipe da Beira. The BR-364 in this direction is asphalted, although heavy rains still have a habit of washing great sections of it away.

Most of the land beside the road between Porto Velho and Abunã has already been bought up by big companies, and much of the forest cleared. Meanwhile, many of the smaller *fazendas* have started actively producing beef cattle and other tropical cash crops. Water birds like the *garça real* (an amazing white royal heron) can frequently be spotted from the bus, fishing in the roadside streams and ditches, but the general picture is one of an alarming rate of destruction.

At **ABUNÃ** – some five hours out of Porto Velho – there are often long lines at the ferry that takes vehicles over the wide Rio Madeira into Acre. It's not a particularly pleasant town, caught at the end of a gold rush in which it expanded too fast for its own good, and the river itself is awash with wrecked gold-mining machinery half-sunk on large steel cylinders. Following the road towards Rio Branco, Bolivia lies across the Rio Abunã to your left, but if you want to cross the border the closest place to do so is Guajará-Mirim to the south. The road there turns off to the east of the ferry crossing at Abunã, following the Rio Mamoré via the small settlement of Taquaras.

Guajará-Mirim and beyond: Bolivia and the Rio Guaporé

GUAJARÁ-MIRIM is easy enough to reach by bus from Porto Velho (6 daily; 5 or 6 hours), and once you get there it's a surprisingly sophisticated place with several **hotels**, the best of which are the *Hotel Mini-Estrela*, Av. 15 de Novembro 460 (Ⓣ69/3541-2399; ③), the *Hotel Lima Palace*, on the same street at no. 1613 (Ⓣ69/3541-3421, Ⓕ3541-2122; ②), and the *Hotel Jamaica*, Av. Leopoldo de Matos 755 (Ⓣ69/3541-3721, Ⓕ3541-3722; ②). There are good restaurants here, too, including the *Oasis*, at Av. 15 de Novembro 460, which serves a varied menu at decent prices. There are, however, only two reasons you might come here – to get to Bolivia or to head up the Mamoré and Guaporé rivers on a trip to the Forte Príncipe da Beira.

The valley of the **Rio Guaporé**, around 800km in length, is an obvious destination for an adventurous break from routine town-to-town travelling. Endowed with relatively accessible rainforest, a slow-flowing river and crystal-clear creeks, it is a favourite fishing region with townspeople from Porto Velho. Likely catches include the huge *dourado*, the *tambaqui*, the *pirapitanga* and *tucunaré*. Heading towards the Guaporé, there are amazing rapids on the Rio Mamoré just south of Guajará-Mirim, close to the place where the Rio Pacaás Novas flows in.

The star-shaped **Forte Príncipe da Beira** makes a supurb destination for a prolonged river trip in this region. Built in 1773 by pioneering colonists, the fort is situated on the edge of the Rio Mamore in a remote location strategically marking the border with Bolivia. Originally this was an advanced border post designed to mark out Portuguese territory from the Spanish lands across the water in the Bolivian jungle. By river, it will take at least three days to reach the fort from Porto Velho: the first day by bus to Guajará-Mirim, then two or three more by boat 150km to the fort itself. A road connects the fort to the small river town of Costa Marques, some 25km away, where you'll find a hotel, restaurants and even a small airstrip. The road continues to Ji-Paraná for connection with the BR-364.

Another attraction in the area is the **Reserva Biologica do Guaporé**, a swampy forest home to many birds and in a zone that is probably the breeding ground for innumerable rare and common tropical birds that inhabit both the Amazon and Pantanal regions. Contact IBAMA in Porto Velho, Av. Jorge Teixeira 3477 (☎69/223-3607) for permission before setting out.

As for **Bolivia**, if all you want to do is see it, join a sightseeing tour by motor barge from Guajará-Mirim; ask at *Hotel Jamaica*, Av. Leopoldo de Matos 755 (☎69/3541-3721). These tours leave frequently, visiting the main sights and often stopping at the islands between Guajará-Mirim and Guayaramerin, on the Bolivian side. If you actually want to cross the border it's equally easy to get a boat over the Rio Mamoré to **GUAYARAMERIN**. This is something of a contrast to the Brazilian town – far more of a border outpost, with no roads, though there is a good air taxi service to La Paz, Cochabamba and Santa Cruz with TAM and Lloyd Aéreo Boliviano. If you plan on travelling into Bolivia, get your passport stamped by the Bolivian consul in Guajará-Mirim, Av. Costa Marques 495 (☎69/3541-5876), and visit the Polícia Federal, Av. Presidente Dutra 70 (☎69/541-2437), for an exit stamp before crossing the river. If you want to stay in Guayaramerin, try the *Hotel Plaza* (❸), four blocks from the port. Boats to Guayaramerin leave from the port end of Av. 15 de Novembro. The tour operator Enaro, Avenida Beira Rios (☎69/3541-2242), can be a helpful source of information, especially for travel arrangements.

Rio Branco

Crossing from Rondônia into the state of **Acre**, territory annexed from Bolivia during the rubber-boom days in the first years of the twentieth century, there's nowhere to stop before you reach the capital at **RIO BRANCO**. The state is a vast frontier forest zone, where it comes as a real surprise to find that Rio Branco is one of Brazil's funkiest cities. It's a small place with little of specific interest to point at, but it's exceptionally lively, with a strong student influence that means plenty of music and events to fill a stay of a few days. Arriving at night (as you usually do) after an eight-hour journey through the desolation of what's left of the jungle between here and Porto Velho, the brightly coloured lights and animated streets can make you wonder if you've really arrived at all, or simply drifted off to sleep. By the light of day Rio Branco doesn't have quite so much obvious charm, but it remains an interesting place full of interesting people.

Much of the reason for all this life is that Rio Branco is a federal **university town**, second only to Belém on the student research pecking order for social and biological studies associated with the rainforest and development. Consequently the place has more than its fair share of young people, and of Brazilian intellectuals. On top of this, the region's burgeoning development means that Rio Branco is also a thriving and very busy market town, pivotally sited on the new road and with an active, if tiny, river port.

Arrival, information and accommodation

Rio Branco is divided in two by the **Rio Acre**, whose old Indian name was Macarinarra, or "River of Arrows", because of the arrows that were cut from the flowering bamboo canes that were found here. The commercial zone, most of the hotels and much of the nightlife are situated north of the river. In the dry season, there is a good river **beach** on the curve in the river – just upstream from the bridges and on the *rodoviária* side of town.

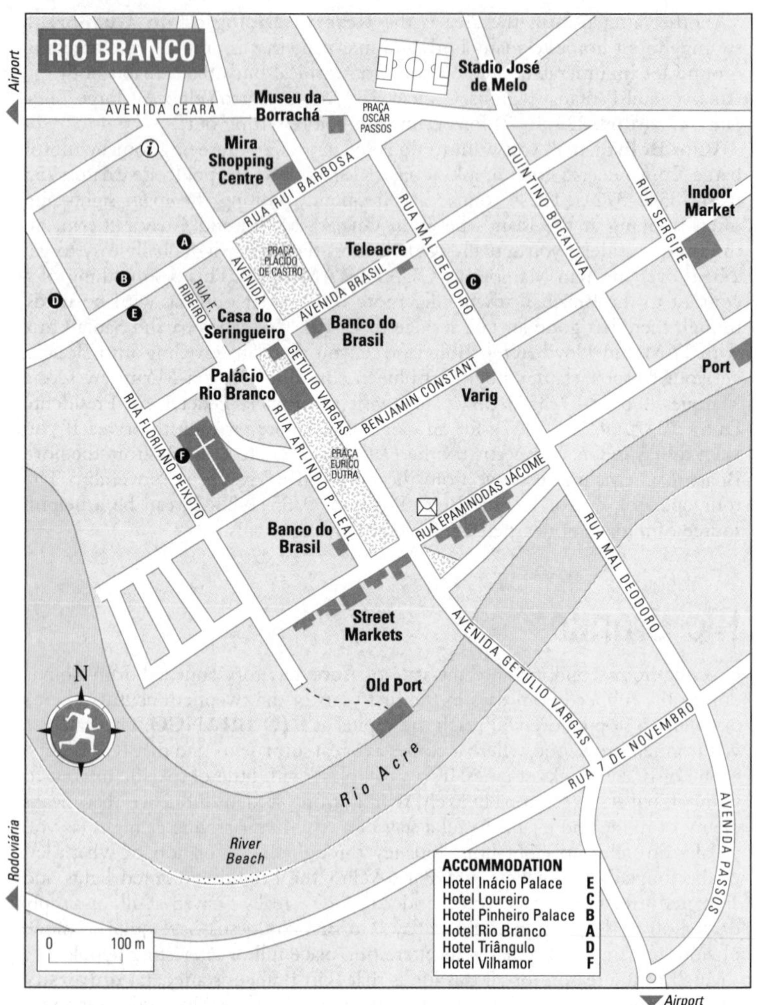

The **rodoviária** (℡68/221-4195), 3km southwest of the river in the Cidade Nova, is just about within walking distance of the centre, or you can take a taxi; note that the area between the *rodoviária* and the river is considered unsafe at night. The **airport** (℡68/211-1000) is 25km northwest of town, but is well served by the green and white ECTA airport bus that runs more or less hourly to the centre; if you're in a hurry you'll probably want to take a taxi (R$15).

The regional **tourist office**, Av. Getúlio Vargas 659 (℡68/224-3997), can supply maps of the town and information on hotels and travel in the region; Ⓦwww.amazonlink.org is another excellent source of information. If you happen to be in Rio Branco during the third week of November, don't miss the **Feira de Productos da Floresta do Acre** (Acre's Rainforest Products Fair), usually housed in the splendid SEBRAE building on Avenida Ceará (take the

Conjunto Esperança bus from the central terminal and follow the signs), and accompanied by local bands.

Accommodation

There is no shortage of **hotels** in Rio Branco, though the better ones aren't cheap. Top of the range is the *Hotel Pinheiro Palace*, Rua Rui Barbosa 450 (Ⓣ68/223-7191, Ⓕ223-6397, Ⓦwww.irmaospinheiro.com.br; ❹), with swimming pool, bar and pretty comfortable rooms with all mod cons. The *Hotel Rio Branco*, Rua Rui Barbosa 193, on the corner of Avenida Getúlio Vargas (Ⓣ68/224-1785, Ⓕ224-2681; ❸), is modern, with excellent service and TVs in all rooms, and is great value. The *Hotel Inácio Palace*, on the same street at no. 469 (Ⓣ68/223-6397, Ⓕ223-7098; ❸), is of similar standard, but the atmosphere is impersonal; guests can use the *Pinheiro*'s pool. Cheaper but still overpriced is *Hotel Triângulo*, Rua Marechal Peixoto 727 (Ⓣ68/224-4117, Ⓕ224-9265; ❸), though some rooms overlook the river. The *Hotel Vilhamor*, at Rua Floriano Peixoto 394 (Ⓣ68/223-2399; ❸), is central, modern and clean, and some rooms have views across the river valley. The *Hotel Loureiro*, Rua Marechal Deodoro 196 (Ⓣ68/224-3110 or 224-9627, Ⓕ224-6806; ❷), also has good rooms, while the cheapest (and dirtiest) in town is *Hotel Etienne*, at Rua Jacomé 2755 (Ⓣ68/225-7909; ❶), near the port. Very close to the *rodoviária*, the *Hotel Uirapuru* (❶) is clean, with fans in most rooms and its own pool table. There is also a decent *Albergue de Juventude* at Fronteira Verde, Travessa Natanael de Albuquerque (Ⓣ68/225-7128; ❶–❷).

The City

If you set out to explore Rio Branco, you'll soon find that there's not a great deal to see. Of the two main tourist attractions, the more interesting is the **Museu da Borrachá**, Av. Ceará 1177 (Mon–Fri 7am–5pm; free), essentially an ethno-historical collection focusing on archeological finds, ethnographic items such as feather crafts and basketry, and a range of exhibits dealing with the rubber boom. More relevant to recent history, perhaps, though closed at the time of writing for renovations, is the **Casa do Seringueiro**, Av. Brasil 216 (Tues–Fri 7am–1pm & 2–5pm, Sun 4–7pm), near the corner with Avenida Getúlio Vargas, which houses displays about Chico Mendes and the life and times of rubber tappers in general. Nearby is the crumbling but still used **Palácio Rio Branco**.

The real attraction of Rio Branco, however, lies in the life of the bars, restaurants, streets and markets. The main square – the large **Praça Plácido de Castro** – is a lively and popular social centre for the town, with concerts, mime and all kinds of live activities happening throughout the year. Every Sunday between 5 and 10pm, the **Feira de Artesanato** takes place in the SEBRAE building on Avenida Ceará. Here you can find a good selection of rainforest crafts produced from sustainable rainforest products, including jewellery made from *tagua*, an attractive palm nut that is dense and white like ivory. The **port** is also worth seeing – small and shabby, but still an interesting spectacle in its own right. There are no regular organized **boat trips**, but it's often possible to travel on the rivers with traders and in *fazendeiros*' river boats: ask in the *Bar dos Linguarudos*, down Rua Sergipe and onto the wooden steps behind the covered market on Rua Benjamin Constant.

Acre, and in particular Rio Branco, is a strong centre for some of Brazil's fastest-growing **religious cults**. A number of similar cult groups are based in the region, connected essentially by the fact that they use forest "power plants"

Acre and the rubber conflict

The relaxed air of Rio Branco masks many tensions, above all to do with population movement – people are still arriving here from the east – and the conflicting claims of small rubber tappers and multinational companies on the jungle. The tappers, who have lived here for a long time and who know how to manage the forests in a sustainable way, see the multinationals as newcomers who aim to turn the trees into pasture for beef cattle and short-term profit, destroying not only the forest but also many local livelihoods. When the leader of the rubber tappers' union, **Chico Mendes**, was shot dead by hired gunmen working for the cattle ranchers in 1988, the plight of the forest peoples of Acre came to the attention of the world. Today, the political situation in Acre remains uneasy, with the second- and third-generation tappers and gatherers joining forces with the native population in resisting the enormous economic and armed might of the advancing cattle-based companies.

– like the hallucinogenic vine *banisteriopsis* – to induce visionary states. Having evolved directly out of native Indian religious practice and belief, these cults are deeply involved in a kind of green nature worship that relates easily to the concept of sustainable forest management. If you want to visit a "Santo Daime" village, contact the travel agent Acretur (see opposite) for details. The groups operate in a vaguely underground way, keeping their sanctuaries secret to non-participants. Interestingly, these cults have now spread to the fashionable coastal areas of Brazil where, behind closed doors in São Paulo and Rio de Janeiro, intellectuals participate in visionary ceremonies.

Eating, drinking and nightlife

For **eating out** it is hard to beat the *Restaurante Casarão*, at Av. Brazil 110 (closed Sun lunchtime; ⓣ68/224-6479), by the bottom end of the Praça Plácido de Castro, near the Teleacre office. The *comida por kilo* food is good and, at weekends, there's live music and an excellent atmosphere. On just about any evening it's also a good place to meet people – a hangout of students, musicians and poets. Cheaper *comida por kilo* is available at the *Restaurante El Dorado*, at the corner of Rua Deodoro and Benjamin Constant. The *Hotel Triângulo* has a good *churrasco* restaurant, and *Oscar's*, Rua Franco Ribeiro 73, is also a popular meat-house, but for a broader range of regional dishes, try the *Kaxinawá*, Rua Rui Barbosa on the corner with Avenida Ceará (closed Wed and Sun) – it's also a lively night spot. The *Pizzeria Bolota*, Rua Rui Barbosa 62, is a relatively quiet spot, next to the *Hotel Inácio Palace*, with a patio out front and occasionally live music at weekends. More or less next door is the pleasant, good-value *Inácio's*. For **street food** you'll find some good, extremely cheap stalls by the outdoor market, near the old bridge at the bottom of Avenida Getúlio Vargas. For quality local and international dishes it's hard to beat the centrally located *Restaurante Anexo*, Rua Franco Ribeiro 99 (daily 11am–2.30pm & 7–11pm; ⓣ69/224-1396).

There are a couple of typical wooden-verandah **bars** overlooking the river and port area, down the alley leading into the main commercial market zone, by the Praça da Bandeira. A great place to meet people in the evening is in the small triangular Praça Oscar Passos, which is stuffed with chairs and tables served by a number of small bars under a giant mango tree; it's always very lively on weekend evenings. You might also try *Alek's Bar* on Rua Rio Grande do Sul near Rua Marechal Peixoto, which to all appearances is in someone's back garden. As to **clubs**, currently packing them in is *14 Bis*, right next to the airport (take a taxi), which has live salsa bands (Thurs to Sat, 7pm to very late). Also very popular is the *Maloca Club* out on Avenida Getúlio Vargas, open till late on Fridays and Saturdays.

Listings

Airlines Tavaj, at the airport (☎68/211-1008), covers most of the western Amazon including Cruzeiro do Sul, São Gabriel do Cachoeira and Tabatinga; Varig, Rua Marechal Deodoro 115 (☎68/229-2539), and at the airport (☎68/224-2719), has daily flights to Brasília, Campo Grande, Cuiabá, Manaus, Porto Velho, Rio and São Paulo; VASP, Rua Quintino Bocaiúva 105 (☎68/211-1133); Andino (☎68/223-3666) organizes charter flights to Peru for between US$120 and $300 (return).

Air taxis There are half a dozen air-taxi companies based at the airport, including Táxi-Aéreo Rio Branco ☎68/224-1384.

Banks and exchange The Banco do Brasil, Rua Arlindo P. Leal 85, set back from the Praça Eurico Dutra (Mon–Fri, *câmbio* between 8am and 12.30pm), will change US dollars and traveller's cheques – arrive early as it takes around two hours; you can also change dollars at the bigger hotels.

Car rental Localiza ☎69/224-7746.

Post office Rua Epaminondas Jácome (Mon–Fri 9am–5pm), by the corner with Av. Getúlio Vargas.

Shopping Aside from the Sunday-only Feira de Artesanato, by far the best place for *artesanato* is Boutique da Floresta at Av. Getúlio Vargas 1067. The street market along Av. Getúlio Vargas sells all the usual fruit and vegetables, and there's an indoor section for everything from machetes, fishing nets and medicinal herbs to umbrellas and cassette tapes.

Telephones The Teleacre office is at Av. Brasil 378, near the bottom of Praça Plácido de Castro (daily 6am–10pm); it has external street-side booths and a telephone card sales point.

Travel and tour companies Ocitur, corner of Av. Getúlio Vargas and Rua Rui Barbosa, sells mostly plane tickets; Acretur, Rua Rui Barbosa 193 (☎68/224-2404), next to the *Hotel Rio Branco*, organizes trips to Brazil-nut forest ranges and *seringais* (rubber-tapping zones), starting at about US$30 a day.

On to Peru: Brasiléia and Cruzeiro do Sul

There are really only two onward routes from Rio Branco, and both of them end up in Peru. The fastest route into Peru heads south to Brasiléia (4–6 hours by bus), which is actually on the border with Bolivia. The route continues from here to Assis Brasil for the border crossing into the Peruvian jungle region of Madre de Dios. From Assis Brasil there's a river crossing with a brand new road bridge to Iñapari in Peru. The river bridge was only completed in December 2005 and the Peruvian side road was still being paved in 2006. The new international road here will be linking the Atlantic with the Pacific, allowing overland road travel from Salvador to Lima. The opening up of this route over the next few years will make for interesting tourism, linking Cusco to the Brazilian Amazon. Cocaine smuggling does happen on this frontier and, although it's much easier to make the crossing by public transport these days, you should not undertake this route lightly. The other, slower route travels west along the BR-364 all the way to Cruzeiro do Sul. This route is being rapidly improved from Rio Branco westwards, where it is now a proper freeway in a few sections. From Cruzeiro do Sul your options are limited still to onward connections via river or air to Pucallpa in Peru.

Brasiléia and Assis Brasil

The small town of **BRASILÉIA** is 220km and six hours by bus from Rio Branco; if you're crossing the border this is where you have to visit the Polícia Federal for your exit (or entry) stamp. The office (daily 8am–5pm) is just to the right of the church as you head from the international border with Bolivia, at the bus terminal just to the left. If you have to stay the night, the *Hotel Major*, Rua Salinas 326 (❶), is cheap and cheerful. Much better rooms, and with air conditioning, are at *Pousada Las Palmeiras*, on Odilon Pratagi (ⓣ68/3546-3281; ❸) or the *Kador Hotel*, Avenida Santos Dumont, Centro (ⓣ68/3546-3206). You can change money at the Casa Castro, over the river on the road towards Assis Brasil.

It's possible to cross to Bolivia here but there seems little point. The small town of **Cobija** on the other side, once an important rubber-collecting station, has a few expensive hotels and, at present, very limited onward land transport.

ASSIS BRASIL is a further 110km beyond Brasiléia, and the rough road can be slow going by bus. If you can't get across the border the same day – which should be just about possible if you set off early enough from Rio Branco, and the buses connect – there's a reasonable hotel on the *praça* (❷), or you can camp near the river and leave your bags at the police station. It's then just a two-kilometre walk across the border to the small settlement of **Iñapari** in Peru. The *Hotel Aquino* here is basic (❶), but there's the better *Pousada Renascer*, Rua Valerio Magalhaes 443, Centro (ⓣ68/3548-1006; ❸) and the larger *Hotel Assis Palace* at Rua Eneide Maria Batista 375, Centro (ⓣ68/3548-1056; ❸); it's also possible to camp by the football pitches over the road from the hotel. From Inapari you can travel by *colectivo* (shuttle bus), or truck the 230km to **Puerto Maldonado** in Peru, a journey that used to take a few days even in the dry season, but, if the Peruvian side of the road is finished being paved, should be possible in a day by the time this book is in the shops. Cusco, in the high Andes of Peru, is only another 520km by road from here. There are also irregular flights to Maldonado from Assis: fares vary in price from R$100 to R$200 and trips can be organized at the Assis airstrip. From Puerto Maldonado there are road and regular air links with Cuzco and the rest of Peru.

Cruzeiro do Sul

Totally isolated some 770km west of Rio Branco on the western edge of the Brazilian Amazon, **CRUZEIRO DO SUL** is a town of some 50,000 inhabitants, many of whom, as in Rio Branco, are social science or biology students; many others are involved in cocaine smuggling. The only dependable links with the outside world are by air, either to Rio Branco (daily; 2hr) and from there the rest of Brazil, or to Pucallpa, a jungle city in the Peruvian Amazon. The road to Rio Branco is generally only passable between June and October and even then there is no bus service.

There is little obvious attraction to Cruzeiro, though it's possible to make **river trips** to extraordinarily isolated *seringais*: they can be booked through most **hotels** from around R$75 a day. The very good-value *Hotel Novo Acre* (❷) is both tidy and hospitable, and the *Hotel Flor de Maio* (❸), overlooking the Rio Ituí, is even more affordable. Of a better standard, *Sandra's Hotel*, Av. Celestino M. Lima 248 (ⓣ68/3322-2481; ❸), is one of the cleanest in town, and it's similar to *Savone Hotel*, Trav. M. Lobão 53 (ⓣ68/3322-2349; ❸). But the only reason people come here is to cross from Brazil to Peru or vice versa – and even then this is one of the more obscure border crossings. The quickest way to Peru once you're here is to **fly** direct to Pucallpa – about one hour in a small plane that generally leaves on Tuesdays – check with TASA, Peoreira 84 (ⓣ68/3322-3086). There is no bus link between the airport and Cruzeiro's town centre some 7km away; taxis cost R$15–25. The aggressively adventurous option, only possible in the rainy season between November and March, is to go by boat, which takes anything between one and two weeks and involves at least two or three days' walking between the Ucayali and Juruá watersheds. This involves travelling through a remote and relatively dangerous part of the Peruvian jungle, where terrorism and smuggling make tourism rather risky, and is not recommended.

If you've arrived from Peru, you can get up-to-date information about the road to Rio Branco from the land transport group Organização Geral Transportes, Av. Celestino M. Lima 79 (Ⓣ68/3322-2093). Airlines that operate **flights within Brazil** from Cruzeiro include: BRA, Rico, TAM and Varig. Varig are based at Av. Celestino M. Lima 90 (Ⓣ68/322-2359).

Travel details

Buses

Belém to: Brasília (6 daily; 36hr); Marabá (4 daily; 14hr); Salvador (1 daily; 32hr).
Boa Vista to: Bonfim (2 daily; 4hr); Manaus (6 daily; 12hr); Santa Elena (6 daily; 3hr).
Manaus to: Boa Vista (6 daily; 12hr).
Marabá to: Araguaina (several weekly; 13hr); Belém (4 daily; 14hr); Tucurui (several weekly; 6hr).
Porto Velho to: Cuiabá (4 daily; 22hr); Guajará-Mirim (5 daily; 4-6hr); Rio Branco (5 daily; 8–9hr); São Paulo (2 daily; 48hr).
Rio Branco to: Brasiléia (3 daily; 4-6hr); Porto Velho (5 daily; 8-9hr).

Boats

Belém to: Macapá (several weekly; 1–2 days); Manaus (several weekly; 4–6 days); Santarém (several weekly; 2–3 days).
Macapá to: Belém (several weekly; 1–2 days); Oiapoque (1 weekly; 2 days); Puerto La Cruz, Venezuela (1 daily; 18hr).
Manaus to: Belém (several weekly; 3–5 days); Caracaraí (irregular; 4–8 days); Humaitá (4 weekly; 3–4 days); Porto Velho (3 weekly; 4–6 days); Santarém (daily; 2 days, or 11hrs in speed boat); São Gabriel da Cachoeira (weekly; 5–7 days); Tabatinga (several weekly; 5 days plus upstream, 3–4 downstream); Tefe (daily; 2 days, or 11hrs in speed boat).
Porto Velho to: Manaus (3 weekly; 3–4 days).
Santarém to: Belém (several weekly; 2–3 days); Macapá (several weekly; 2–3 days); Manaus (1 daily; 2–3 days, or 13 hours in a speed boat).
Tabatinga to: Iquitos (several weekly; 3–4 days or 12hr by speedboat); Manaus (several weekly; 4–5 days).

Planes

Belém to: Boa Vista (1 daily; 4hr); Brasília (1 daily; 2hr); Macapá (1 daily; 1hr); Manaus (2 daily; 2hr); Porto Velho (1 daily; 5hr); and at least once daily to all other major Brazilian cities.
Manaus to: Alta Floresta (1 daily; 1hr 30min); Barcelos (3 weekly; 1hr); Belém (2 daily; 2hr); Boa Vista (2 daily; 2hr 30min); Brasília (5 daily; 3hr); Cuiabá (1 weekly; 3hr); Porto Velho (1 daily; 2hr); Rio Branco (several weekly; 2hr 40min); Rio de Janeiro (3 daily; 3hr 30min); São Gabriel da Cachoeira (1 daily; 3hr); São Paulo (several daily; 4hr); Tabatinga (1 daily; 2hr 30min); Tefé (4 weekly; 1hr).
From **Porto Velho**, **Rio Branco** and **Marabá**, there are daily services to most major Brazilian cities.

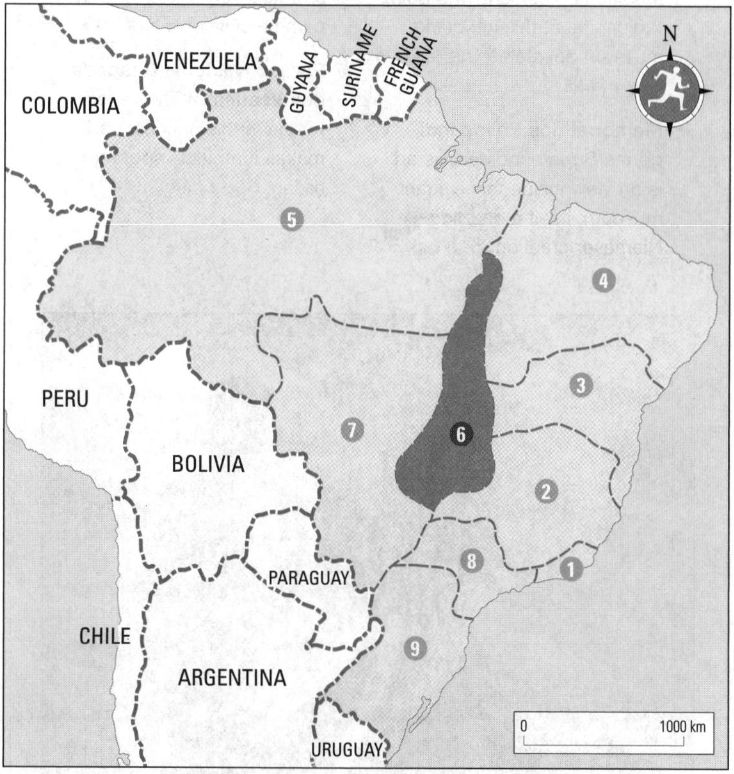

6

Brasília, Goiás and Tocantins

VENEZUELA
GUYANA
SURINAME
FRENCH GUIANA
COLOMBIA
N
5
4
3
PERU
7
6
BOLIVIA
2
8
1
PARAGUAY
CHILE
9
ARGENTINA
0
1000 km
URUGUAY

BRASÍLIA, GOIÁS AND TOCANTINS

CHAPTER 6

Highlights

* **Catedral Metropolitana** Contemplate the soaring statues of St Peter and the angels from the sunken floor of this landmark cathedral. See p.523
* **Juscelino Kubitschek Memorial** Learn about the ambitious president who built the capital at this intriguing museum devoted to his life. See p.526
* **Memorial dos Povos Indígenas** Superb indigenous art is on view inside this elegant museum, itself a dazzling Niemeyer creation. See p.526
* **Salto de Itiquira** Best known for its more than 90-metre waterfall, this delightful park near Formosa makes a worthwhile day-trip from Brasília. See p.533
* **Goiás Velho** A picturesque colonial town, well preserved and relatively untouched by commercialism. See p.543
* **Parque Nacional Chapada dos Veadeiros** The varied terrain in this national park makes it an ideal spot for hiking. See p.548

△ Catedral Metropolitana

Brasília, Goiás and Tocantins

The geographical heart of Brazil is the central highlands (Planalto Central), shared between the states of **Goiás**, **Tocantins** and parts of Mato Grosso. This rapidly developing and increasingly prosperous agricultural region was as recently as fifty years ago still largely Indian country, with a few colonial towns precariously linked by oxcart trails to the rest of the country. The founding of the national capital, **Brasília**, in the late 1950s changed all that, shifting Brazil's centre of gravity decisively from the coast to the interior and opening up an entire region of the country to settlement and development.

Love it or loathe it, Brazil's capital is like nowhere else on earth; the world's largest, most successful and in its own weird way most beautiful planned city, it remains the main reason for visiting the *planalto*. Brasília's chief attraction is its extraordinary **city architecture**, its late-Fifties vision of the future now charmingly retro, even sliding over into kitsch. While the capital is no metropolis it is much more cosmopolitan than its relatively small size suggests, heaving with restaurants and bars where much of the city's business is transacted, as befits a place where politics is the main local industry. Brasília is well connected by long but good-quality **roads** to the rest of the country – to Mato Grosso to the west, to Belém and the Northeast, to Rio, São Paulo and the South, and to the even more distant Rondônia and Acre in the western Amazon.

Although Brasília may be the region's main draw, it is by no means the only one. In recent years, the city has become the base for a significant **ecotourism** boom, still almost entirely Brazilian, and made up of middle-class punters from Brasília itself and landlocked Minas Gerais. People come for the emptiness and beauty of the landscape a few hours north of Brasília, as well as great **hiking** and more specialized outdoor pursuits like caving and rock climbing. The main centre, **Parque Nacional Chapada dos Veadeiros**, is an easy excursion from Brasília, and if time is limited, the spectacular waterfall of **Salto de Itiquira** is a rewarding day-trip. There is also a national park, the **Parque Nacional de Brasília**, with hiking trails on the city's periphery.

The *planalto* itself is still at that ideal stage of tourist development where there is enough infrastructure to make it accessible and enjoyable, but not so much that you ever feel things are too crowded or over-commercialized. The highlands were traversed in their earliest days by Portuguese expeditions, and many

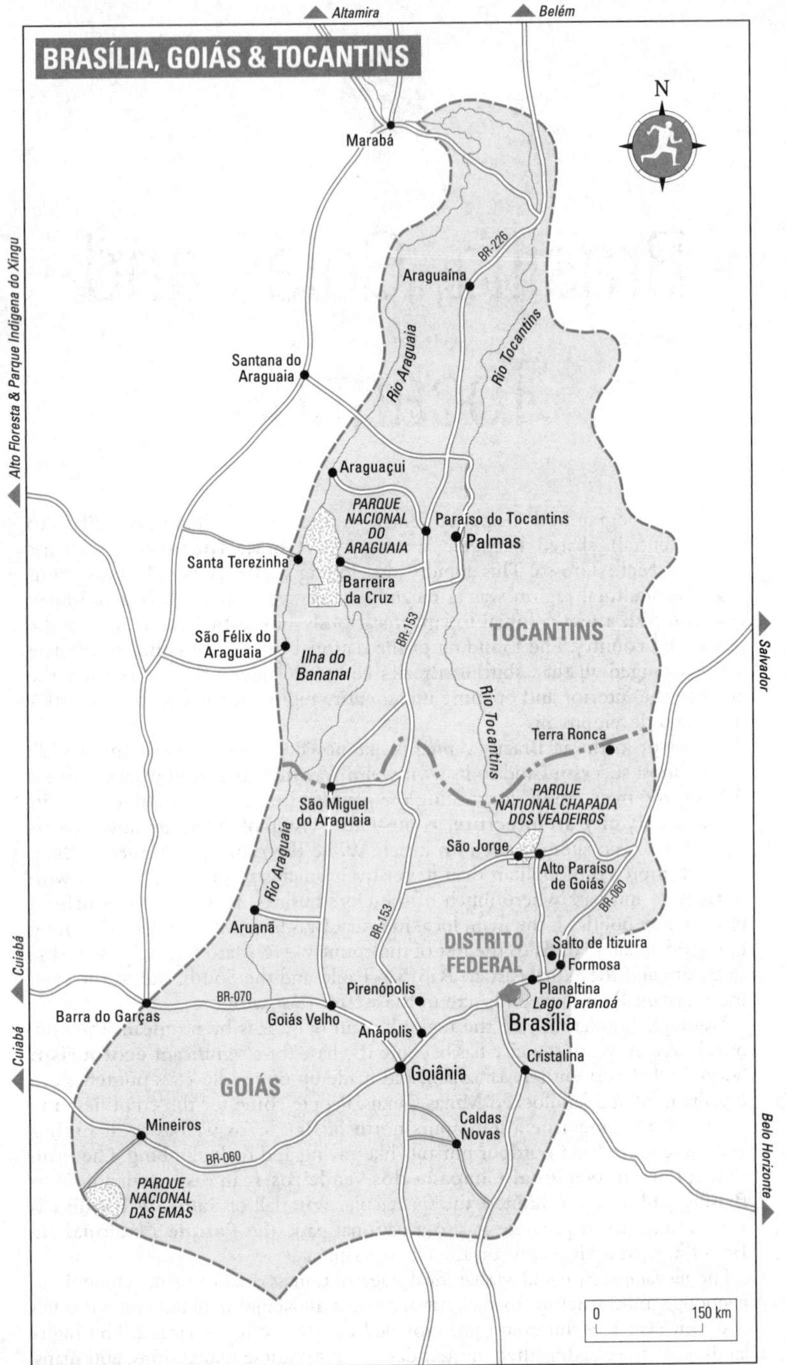

BRASÍLIA, GOIÁS & TOCANTINS
Altamira
Belém
N
Marabá
BR-226
Araguaína
Rio Araguaia
Rio Tocantins
Santana do Araguaia
Araguaçui
PARQUE NACIONAL DO ARAGUAIA
Paraíso do Tocantins
Palmas
Santa Terezinha
Barreira da Cruz
BR-153
TOCANTINS
São Félix do Araguaia
Ilha do Bananal
Rio Tocantins
Salvador
Terra Ronca
São Miguel do Araguaia
PARQUE NATIONAL CHAPADA DOS VEADEIROS
Rio Araguaia
São Jorge
Alto Paraíso de Goiás
BR-060
Aruanã
BR-153
DISTRITO FEDERAL
Salto de Itizuira
Formosa
Cuiabá
Planaltina
Lago Paranoá
BR-070
Pirenópolis
Barra do Garças
Goiás Velho
Brasília
Anápolis
Cuiabá
Cristalina
Goiânia
GOIÁS
Mineiros
Caldas Novas
Belo Horizonte
BR-060
PARQUE NACIONAL DAS EMAS
0
150 km
São Paulo & Curitiba
Alto Floresta & Parque Indígena do Xingu

a *planalto* town can trace its origins to a *paulista bandeira* looking for mines and Indian slaves. Two colonial towns in particular are worth visiting, both in Goiás: **Pirenópolis**, within easy reach of Brasília, and the old capital of Goiás state, **Goiás Velho**, a little-visited jewel that is as beautiful as any of the better known *cidades históricas* of Minas Gerais. Further north still, the **state of Tocantins** has its eastern and western frontiers defined by two of the largest tributaries of the Amazon, the **Araguaia** and **Tocantins**, but with the exception of one of the largest riverine islands in the world, the **Ilha do Bananal**, the state has little to offer the visitor and is best bypassed on the way to more interesting destinations in the North or Northeast.

Brasília

Arriving in **BRASÍLIA**, especially at its futuristic airport, is like falling into a science-fiction novel. The entire city, and especially the central area, has a startlingly space-age feel and look, albeit with a decidedly retro twist. Originally

The planalto

The topography and ecology of the **planalto** are unique, known within Brazil as the *cerrado*, only partly translated by the word "savanna". Much of it looks startlingly African: red earth, scrubby vegetation, dusty in the dry season, missing only giraffes and zebras for the illusion to be complete. What makes it spectacular is the topography, which begins to break up the highland plains into a series of hill ranges, cliffs, mesas, plateaus and moorlands almost as soon as you start heading north from Brasília. This irregular landscape is strategically situated between two enormous watersheds, the Paraná to the south and the Amazon to the north, both of which have the headwaters of major tributaries in the *planalto*. The hills and mountains are riddled with thousands of **rivers and streams**, forming spectacular waterfalls and swimholes within easy reach of Brasília.

As ecotourism in the region grows, so too do the **threats** to the *planalto*. Good soils and communications, and its proximity to the markets and capital of Minas Gerais and São Paulo mean that development here is far more intense than it ever has been in the Amazon. The ranchers who spearheaded the early wave of settlement of the *planalto* are still there, but are increasingly giving way to large-scale commercial agriculture, especially soybeans. This has underlain the development of the two largest cities in Goiás, **Goiânia,** the state capital, and **Anápolis**, modern and prosperous by Brazilian standards, but about as interesting to visit as, say, Indianapolis. In fact, much of the *planalto* looks like the US Midwest when you fly over it or drive through, with endless geometric fields and irrigation canals stretching to the horizon. Over eighty percent of the native vegetation has been converted to farmland or pasture, compared to fifteen percent of the Amazon, and the unique flora and fauna of the *cerrado* – the giant anteater and armadillo, the maned wolf, the glorious wildflowers that speckle the area with colour in the rainy season – are all increasingly endangered. If things continue at the present rate, within a generation the only islands of true *cerrado* left will be the national parks.

intended for a population of half a million by the year 2000, Brasília today has close to four million people and is the only one of Brazil's major metropolitan areas that is still growing fast. Looking at the gleaming government buildings or zooming down the city's excellent roads, it really can seem that Brasília is the modern heart of a new world superpower – an illusion that is rapidly dispelled by driving ten minutes outside Brasília in any direction, when you start hitting the miles and miles of low-income housing of the millions of people who commute from the so-called *cidades satélites*, the satellite cities, serving the needs of the government-employed elite who live in Brasília itself. As well as being the national capital, Brasília is also the capital of its own state, the **Distrito Federal**,

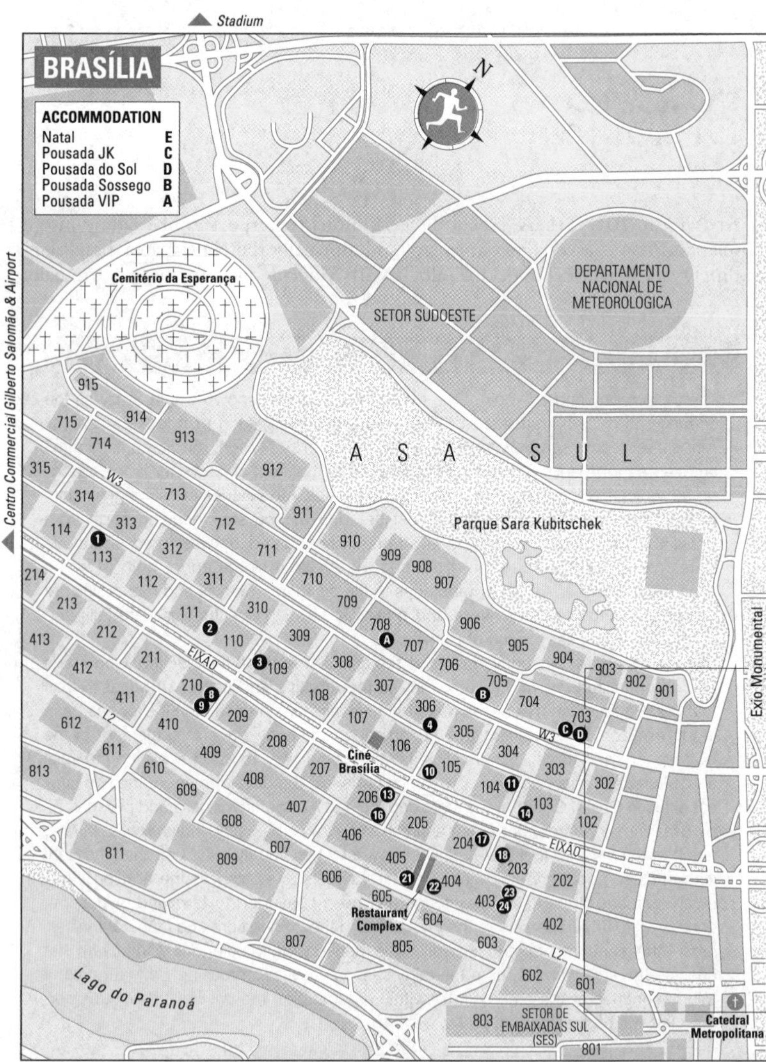

the Federal District, which also includes the satellite cities. The whole Federal District is in fact the perfect symbol of modern Brazil, though not in the way its creators intended: affluence close to but segregated from poverty, *favelas* over the horizon, and poor newcomers invading the countryside where the country's elite have their walled-off weekend retreats.

Brasília's highlights are all fairly obvious **architectural** ones. Anyone with a taste for the best of Fifties and Sixties architecture will think they have died and gone to heaven, but there are other attractions, too. Attractive parks, popular for weekend picnics, encircle the entire city, while in the downtown zone, by the central bus station, a busy mess of people and trade generates a lively

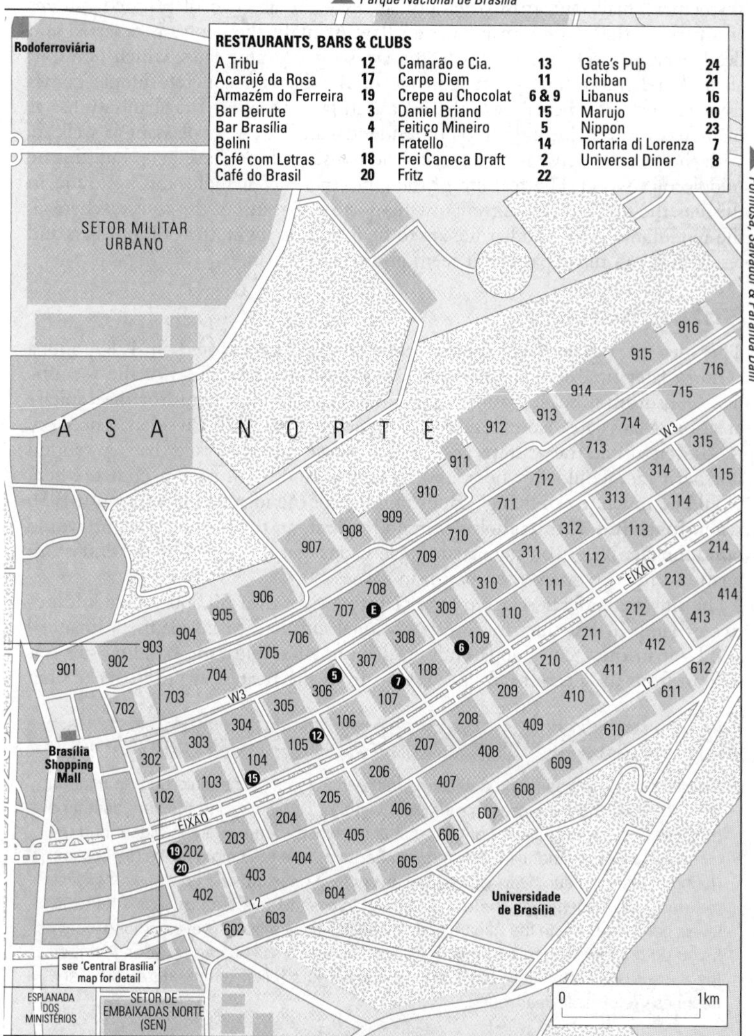

atmosphere. **Nightlife** is energetic, revolving around huge numbers of bars and restaurants that benefit from the city's marvellous nocturnal climate, fresh and pleasant all year round. **Cinema** is especially good here, patronized by a large local middle class with an appetite for foreign films, and one side-benefit of the presence of the elite is the regular appearance of top-level **performing arts**.

Brasília's design also has a **mystic** side to it. On Brazilian Republic Day (April 21), the sun rises through the concrete "H" shape of the parallel twin towers that poke out of the National Congress building, provoking images of a futuristic Stonehenge. There is a distinct New Age feel to parts of the city and environs; it has a special attraction for the wacky religious cults and UFO enthusiasts in which Brazil abounds. Some visitors find Brasília alienating, and the central part of the city can certainly seem that way, with its jumble of undistinguished skyscrapers, malls and massive empty spaces – the absence of planned gardens and parks is the centre's major design flaw. At night the centre is deserted and dead, even at weekends, thanks to the city's rigid zoning laws, which have put all its hotels there. The popular image of Brasília as a concrete jungle comes from visitors who never leave the centre; in fact, no other Brazilian city has as many trees and parks, and the older residential areas are very pleasant to walk in, with the trees so dense it often seems the housing blocks have been built in the middle of a wood. The real life of the city, especially at night, can be found in the *asas*, the residential wings that swing north and south of the centre, where all the restaurants, clubs and bar life are to be found. At night, the outdoor bars and restaurants can make parts of it seem positively Parisian.

Some history

The idea of a **Brazilian inland capital** was first mooted in 1789, and a century later (in 1891) the concept was written into Article 3 of the Republic's Constitution, setting aside some 14,400 square kilometres for the capital's creation. Many sites were considered; indeed, in 1913 US President Theodore Roosevelt visited the western edge of the *planalto* and remarked that "any sound northern race could live here; and in such a land, with such a climate, there would be much joy of living". But fulfilment of the idea had to wait until 1956 when **Juscelino Kubitschek** became president, on the promise that he would build the city if he won the election. He had to get it finished by the end of his term of office, so work soon began in earnest.

The site was quickly selected by aerial surveys of over 50,000 square kilometres of land. In less than four years a capital city had to be planned, financed and built in the face of apparently insurmountable odds: the building site was 125km from the nearest rail line, 190km from the nearest airport, over 600km

Brasília's climate

Brasília's **climate** has marked seasonal differences that you should bear in mind in timing a visit. The rainy season runs from October to March, and the very best time to come is the spring, from April through June, when the trees are in bloom and the climate is pleasant and mild. July through September is the height of the dry season: during the day the sun beats down hard, everything dries out and hot winds blow fine red dust over everything. The extraordinary dryness of this time of year – humidity levels comparable with the Sahara – often causes sinus problems even among locals. If you do come during this time of year, drink as much as you can and don't stint on the sunscreen. Fortunately, night always comes as a relief; temperatures drop and freshness returns all year round.

from the nearest paved road; the closest timber supply was 1200km distant, the nearest source of good steel even further. Still, in **Oscar Niemeyer**, the city's architect, Brasília had South America's most able student of Le Corbusier, founder of the modern planned city and a brilliant designer of buildings. Alongside Niemeyer, who was contracted to design the buildings, **Lúcio Costa** was hired for the awesome task of Brasília's urban planning.

Design and construction

Costa produced a **city plan** described variously as being in the shape of a bow and arrow, a bird in flight or an aeroplane. Certainly, on maps or from the air, Brasília appears to be soaring, wings outstretched, towards the eastern Atlantic coast. The main public buildings, government ministries, palace of justice and presidential palace line the "fuselage", an eight-kilometre-long grass mall known as the **Eixo Monumental** (Monumental Axis), with the **intercity bus and train station**, the *rodoferroviária*, at one end, and the heart of government, the Praça dos Três Poderes (Square of the Three Powers) grouping the Congress building, the Supreme Court and the presidential palace at the other. The main residential districts branch out to the north and south, in the arc of the bow, while the business districts are clustered where the wings join the fuselage.

Money for the **construction** came from all over the world in the form of grants and loans, and from the printing of money, a move that increased inflation in the short term. The whole operation was incredibly expensive, not least because everything – workers, food, cement and the like – had to be flown in, as work started long before the first access roads appeared. At the time of construction, and even after inauguration, many considered the whole scheme to be a complete waste of time and money: Rio's *Correio da Manhã* newspaper famously called it "The Limit of Insanity".

Nevertheless, exactly three years, one month and five days after the master plan was unveiled, 150,000 people arrived in Brasília for the official **inauguration**, in April 1960. (The event is celebrated today as the Festa da Cidade on April 21 each year). It must have been a hectic time. There were only 150 first-class hotel rooms completed for the five thousand visiting dignitaries, but the celebrations went ahead, topped by a spectacular 38-tonne firework display. When the smoke cleared in the morning it was apparent to everyone that, despite the finished government complexes, 94 apartment buildings, around five hundred one- and two-storey houses plus their local schools and shops, there was still years of work left to do. Road junctions were not the super-slick lane mergers that had been promised, pedestrians and apartments still had to be separated from traffic, and the accommodation units had none of their intended leafy surroundings – the flats supposedly close enough to the ground for a mother to call her child. In time, the city slowly grew to fill in the spaces left for more organic expansion, most of the residential areas were landscaped and greened, and Brasília gradually developed some of the maladies that affect the rest of urban Brazil, like rush-hour traffic-jams.

Growth and layout

As Brasília developed it became apparent that the original **city plans**, based on Le Corbusier's notions of urban progress through geometrical order and rectilinear planning, would have to be modified if Brazilians, the least rectilinear of people, were going to feel comfortable here. Partly this was accomplished by Niemeyer's brilliant and innovative buildings, full of curves and circles. Still alive and designing away in his nineties he continues to be the city architect and all Brasília's major buildings, from the angular government ministries in the Fifties to the sinuous curves of the federal prosecutor's building completed in 2003, were designed by him, giving the city a unique aesthetic unity. Partly it was accomplished by time; as the city matured, its inhabitants started to subvert its rigid zoning and building codes by adding houses and expanding leisure areas, especially in the commercial sections of the *asas*). One essential point to bear in mind is that Brasília is dominated by its **road traffic** system like no other Brazilian city; everyone, including visitors, is obliged by its enormous spaces to move around by car and bus; **walking**, like everything else in Brasília, is zoned. There are parks and residential areas specifically designed for strolling; elsewhere you should forget about walking as the city's not made for it.

The residential wings are divided into *superquadras*, complexes of apartment buildings (see box on pp.518–519 for a complete guide to Brasília's zoning system). There are sixteen in each wing, lower numbers closer to the centre, so just by looking at the address you can tell roughly how far from the centre it is. Between every *superquadra* is a **commercial area**, where local shops, bars and restaurants are found; most of Brasília's nightlife is concentrated in these, and to save confusion they are referred to here as a *comercial*, reflecting local usage; a *candango* (someone from Brasília) giving directions to a bar will say "*comercial 206 norte*", for example.

The costs: financial and environmental

On the face of it at least, Kubitschek lived up to his electoral campaign promise of fifty years' progress in five. What he hadn't made clear before, though, was just how much it would cost Brazil. When Kubitschek stood down in 1960, his successor, **Jânio Quadros**, broadcast a jaundiced message to the nation, saying "All this money, spent with so much publicity, we must now raise – bitterly, patiently, dollar by dollar, *cruzeiro* by *cruzeiro*". With outstanding foreign loans of two billion dollars, the city seemed an antisocial waste of resources to many, and it was certainly responsible for letting loose inflation, a problem that would take a generation to resolve.

As it turned out, however, Brasília paid for itself many times over, and very quickly. The rapid **development of the planalto** that followed transformed the entire region into one of the most developed agricultural areas in the country, and the taxes, jobs and production generated swiftly made the decision to build Brasília seem inspired; Kubitschek's reputation has steadily climbed since his death in 1976, and he is now usually thought of as Brazil's most visionary and successful president. The costs have proved to be more environmental than financial, with the rapid conversion of much of the *planalto* to farmland and the destruction of forest along the Belém-Brasília highway corridor. As ever, those with most cause to complain were the **indigenous peoples** of the *planalto*; groups like the warlike **Xavante** did what they could to halt the tide, but it was hopeless, and by the 1970s they were all confined to reservations a fraction the size of their previous territories.

Orientation, arrival and information

Although initially quite confusing, Brasília is laid out with geometric precision. It is neatly divided into sectors: there are residential sectors – each with its own shopping and other facilities – hotel sectors, embassy sectors and banking and commercial sectors. Roads are numbered, rather than named, with digits representing their position and distance north or south of the **Eixo Monumental**, and east or west of the other main axis, the **Eixo Rodoviário**, universally known as the Eixão. The different sectors are given acronyms, most fairly easy to work out (see box, pp. 518–519).

The central *rodoviária*, the urban bus station, is the main hub of movement within Brasília, with the Eixo Monumental passing around it and the Eixo Rodoviário crossing over the top of it. Up above the *rodoviária*, you can see at a glance the main areas of interest. Looking east, towards the main government buildings that resemble great green dominoes, is the unmistakeable Aztec form of the **Teatro Nacional**, and the conical crown of the **Catedral** a little further away to the right; both are within easy walking distance. Slightly further away, but still within a half-hour's stroll, are the striking bowls and towers of the **Congresso Nacional** complex. Immediately on either side of the *rodoviária* there are two separate, rather tacky shopping centres, the **Conjuntos de Diversões**, one to the north, another to the south. Twenty years ago these vast concrete boxes were overshadowed only by the TV Tower, but nowadays the modern towers of the nearby **Setores Hoteleiros** (hotel sectors), **Setores Comerciais** (business sectors) and **Setores das Autarquias** (government agency sectors) dominate the scene, together with the bank and government buildings on either side of the Eixo Monumental. The most distinctive is the central bank building in Setor das Autarquias Sul, black boxes hung around a central concrete framework, looking for all the world like an enormous stereo speaker.

Arrival

The **airport** (Ⓣ61/3365-1941) is 12km south of the centre, and bus #102 runs every hour from there into Brasília, dropping you at the downtown *rodoviária*. A taxi should cost you less than R$20 to the hotel sectors. Inter-city and long-distance buses use the **rodoferroviária** (Ⓣ61/3233-7200), the bus and former train station at the far western end of the Eixo Monumental. From here, the #131 bus (Platform B, stand 3) covers the 5km of the Eixo Monumental to the downtown *rodoviária*, passing the famous statue of Juscelino Kubitschek on the way. Once at the downtown *rodoviária*, go up the escalators to the second level for the shopping centres and upper roads, from where you can see most of central Brasília, and the hotel sectors are a short taxi ride. Taxis to the hotel sector from the *rodoferroviária* are about R$15.

Information

The best place for **tourist information** is the kiosk at the airport (daily 8am–8pm; Ⓣ61/3365-1024), which stocks a range of leaflets, maps and brochures, and also has a useful touch-screen computer terminal. There's also a helpful tourist office on the Praça dos Três Poderes (Mon 1.30–6pm, Tues–Sun 8am–6pm; Ⓣ61/3325-5730), and in a kiosk underneath the TV Tower, with the same hours. Apart from this, you can pick up leaflets from the main hotels. By far the most detailed and useful map of Brasília is to be found at the front of telephone directories and yellow pages, which you'll find in most hotel rooms. There is an excellent listings site for Brasília at Ⓦwww.candango.com.br, unfortunately with no toggle for English, but click on Mapas. The main newspaper, the *Correio Brasiliense*, publishes a daily listings supplement, the *Guia*, with comprehensive information on films, exhibitions, live music and opening hours; though in Portuguese, the details are pretty easy to work out.

Addresses in Brasília

Most people in Brasília live in *superquadras* – massive apartment complexes, some of which you can see coming in along the Eixão from the airport. Finding out where someone lives or works can seem impossible from the **address**, but there is a perfect internal logic to the system. For example, the address

SQS 105
Bloco A – 501
70.344-040 Brasília - DF

means *superquadra* south no. 105, building A, apartment 501, postcode 70.344-040. The three-digit *superquadra* number here (105) gives the location: the first digit represents the position east or west of the Eixo Rodoviário (or Eixão), with odd numbers to the west, evens to the east, increasing the further away from the centre you get. The last two digits represent the distance north or south of the Eixo Monumental, so that, for example, SQN 208 is five *superquadras* north from SQN 203, SQS 110 five south from SQS 105. Unfortunately, addresses are rarely written out in full: you'll have to watch out for "Q" (*quadra*, and often used for *superquadra*, too), "L", "lj" or "lt" (*loja* or *lote*, meaning "lot" or "shop", used for commercial addresses), "B" or "bl" (*bloco*) and "cj" (*conjunto* meaning "compound").

A similar logic applies to main roads. Even numbers apply east of the Eixão, odd to the west, prefaced for good measure by a letter that tells you which side of the Eixão it runs, L for east (*leste*), W for west (technically *oeste*, but the planners shrank from OE). The roads that run parallel to the Eixão on either side with exits to all the *superquadras* are the ones used by the local bus services, and are universally called the Eixinhos, the "little *eixos*", Eixinho L east of the Eixão, Eixinho W west. The main commercial street, the only one that looks anything like a normal Brazilian street in the entire city, is W3, which runs the entire length of both *asas*.

The other terms you are most likely to come across are:

Asa Norte/Asa Sul General terms for the two "wings" (*asas*) of the city, comprising the avenues Eixo Rodoviário Norte and Eixo Rodoviário Sul, and the roads running off and parallel to them (the latter lettered "W" to the west, and "L" to the east, eg W-3 Norte, L-4 Sul).

Getting around

It is not difficult to see most of Brasília's traditional sights in a day, though if you are foolish enough to walk after 10am it gets extremely tiring wandering around the open spaces of the centre in the heat. There are two or three **city bus routes**, instead, which can save you a lot of shoe-leather. Details of these are given in the text, and there are also two **circular bus routes** that are very handy for a cheap overview of the city: buses #105 and #106 leave from and return to the downtown *rodoviária*, Platform A (Ⓣ61/3223-0557) after a long outer city tour; just try to avoid these routes between 4 and 6pm on weekdays when the buses are particularly crowded. Keep an eye out for pickpockets when standing in line for the buses, though once on the bus you should be all right.

The city has a good **taxi** service. Flag a taxi down when you want one, or pick one up at the many ranks throughout the city; every *superquadra* has at least one. Most people drive their own cars, and if you want to join them see p.531 for addresses of **car rental** firms; it'll cost you from R$50 a day, less if you rent over a longer period.

CLN/CLS or **SCLN/SCLS** (Setor) Comércio Local Norte/Sul. These terms describe the shopping blocks interspersed throughout the residential *superquadras* that comprise Asa Norte and Asa Sul. Their numbering follows that of the *superquadras*, so that CLN 208 is near SQN 208.

Eixinho The smaller, marginally slower main roads with exits to every *quadra* either side of the Eixão, the main central artery.

EQN/EQS Entrequadras Norte/Sul. Literally "between *quadras*", referring to the area bordering the Eixinhos.

SBN/SBS Setor Bancário Norte/Sul. The two banking sectors either side of the Eixo Monumental.

SCN/SCS Setor Comercial Norte/Sul. The two commercial office block areas, set back from the Conjuntos de Diversões shopping centres. Often confused with CLN/CLS (see above).

SDN/SDS Setor de Diversões Norte/Sul. The two shopping centres (*conjuntos*) either side of Eixo Monumental.

SEN/SES Setor de Embaixadas Norte/Sul. The embassy sectors, east of the bank sectors.

SHIN/SHIS Setor de Habitações Individuais Norte/Sul. The two peninsulas that jut into Lago Paranoá, the northern one accessible from the end of Eixo Rodoviário Norte, the southern one, also called Lago Sul, connected by bridges from Avenida das Nações.

SHN/SHS Setor Hoteleiro Norte/Sul. The hotel sectors either side of the Eixo Monumental, west of the *rodoviária*.

SQN/SQS or **SHCN/SHCS** Superquadras Norte/Sul. The individual *superquadras* in the main residential wings, Asa Norte and Asa Sul.

Although the system takes some getting used to, it's useful in pinpointing exactly where an address is located in the city – a good defence against dishonest taxi drivers, useful when walking, and a boon if your Portuguese is too elementary for directions.

City tours

If you have limited time and want someone else to take care of things then the expensive but reliable **city tours** might be the thing for you. Most hotels in Brasília are keen to offer city tours to their guests, as they take a percentage of the fee for themselves. It's worth shopping around – the *Hotel El Pilar* can sometimes work out up to 25 percent cheaper than the *Hotel Nacional* – or you can book direct with one of the tour organizers: Power Turismo (Ⓣ61/3332-6699); AeroVan Turismo (Ⓣ61/3340-9251); or Monserat Turismo (Ⓣ61/3326-1407, Ⓔmonserrat@conectanet.com.br). Tours cost from R$25 to R$60 per person, and range from three-hour programmes covering commercial, banking and residential sectors as well as prominent buildings, to the night-time tour (R$65-100) that ends with an evening meal. While not necessarily the best time to see most of the sights, the evening tour does give you the chance to experience the city by neon. In many ways Brasília seems easier to comprehend in the light-studded darkness when the wide-open spaces melt away. If you want to hire your own personal English-speaking guide to the city, Waldeck Costa (Ⓣ61/3384-1909 or mobile 61/9964-8673) is reliable and knows his stuff.

Accommodation

Brasília has a vast range of accommodation to suit all wallets, contrary to its reputation as being an over-expensive place to stay. The **central hotel sectors** are split into three categories of hotel, distinguishable by height, all of which post prices that are actually considerably more than they really charge if you ask for a discount. The five-star skyscrapers are the closest to the centre, offering top-range beds from around R$150 a night; smaller four- and three-star hotels are to be found either side of W3 and are more than reasonable at R$50–75; while R$35 will get you perfectly adequate accommodation at the squat one- and two-star hotels.

If you're on a tight budget, R$15–30 will get you a bed at a *pousada*; these cluster on W3 Sul, starting at *quadra* 703 to around 708. Most are squalid and none too secure; the ones recommended below are the pick of the bunch, but are still below the standards of the worst of the hotels. Staying in campsites or in the satellite cities is definitely not recommended; besides being dangerous, it costs much the same as accommodation in Brasília.

Central hotel sectors

Alvorada SHS Q.4 ⓣ61/3222-7068. Cheap, central and good-value hotel, though noisy unless you get an apartment facing away from W3. ❷–❸

Aracoara SHN Q.5 ⓣ61/3328-9222. Comfortable mid-range hotel, very good value, but in a marginally inconvenient location with nothing in walking distance. The surrounding area is even deader than usual for the centre at night. ❷–❸

Aristus SHN Q.2 ⓣ61/3328-8675, ⓕ3326-5415. One of the cheapest options in this good location, offering a choice of basement rooms at rates slightly lower than their other rooms. ❶–❷

Bonaparte Hotel Résidence SHS Q.2 ⓣ61/3322-2288 or 0800/619-991, ⓦwww.bonapartehotel.com.br. A top-notch hotel, with a large convention facility and all mod cons. ❹–❺

Brasília Imperial SHS Q.3 ⓣ61/3223-7252, ⓦwww.brasiliaimperialhotel.com.br. Excellent value and location. ❶–❷

Bristol SHS Q.4 ⓣ61/3321-6162, ⓕ3321-2690. Comfortable and with a rooftop swimming pool, this is a good-value hotel without being top of the range; highly recommended. ❷–❸

Byblos SHN Q.3 ⓣ61/3326-1570, ⓕ3326-3615. Unlike most of the hotels in SHS and SHN, this one is low-rise. Clean and spartan, but its rooms aren't as nice as the *Casablanca*'s (see below) and are slightly more expensive to boot. ❶–❷

Carlton SHS Q.5 ⓣ61/3226-8109, ⓦwww.carltonhotel.com.br. Older upmarket hotel, with great 1960s decor, but slightly expensive compared to similar places. ❺–❻

Casablanca SHN Q.3 ⓣ61/3328-8586, ⓕ3328-8273. Close to the Eixo Monumental and within sight of the TV Tower, a small and friendly hotel with excellent rooms and a nice restaurant. Good value at the lower end of this price bracket. ❶–❷

El Pilar SHN Q.3 ⓣ61/3326-5353. This cheap, low-rise hotel is a little spare, but the location is good and the staff friendly. ❶–❷

Eron SHN Q.5 ⓣ61/3329-4000. Another good value mid-range hotel, with fine views from the upper floors and handy for the TV Tower but little else. ❷–❸

Hotel das Américas SHS Q.4 ⓣ61/3321-3355 or 0800/118-844, ⓦwww.hoteldasamericas.com. Comfortable and modern, with an excellent restaurant, but overpriced if you don't get a discount. ❷–❸

Kubitschek Plaza SHN Q.2 ⓣ61/3329-3333 or 0800/613-995, ⓦwww.kubitschek.com.br. Among the best of the five-star hotels, built in a strange blend of Space Age and ancient Egyptian styles. Everything you'd expect at this price – pool, gymnasium, sauna, plus free medical insurance throughout your stay. ❹–❺

Manhattan SHN Q.2 ⓣ61/3319-3060 or 0800/612-400, ⓕ3328-5683. Less extravagant than its stable-mate the *Kubitschek Plaza*, but still extremely smart, attracting a slightly younger clientele. Good Japanese restaurant attached. ❹–❺

Metropolitan SHN Q.2 ⓣ61/3424-3500. Swanky but reasonably priced for all the mod cons you get – along with the excellent views. ❹–❺

Nacional SHS Q.1, ⓣ61/3321-7575, ⓦwww.hotelnacional.com.br. The oldest of the big hotels, reflected in fine retro-1960s kitsch decor. Well run with the added advantage of having all of the major airline offices out front. ❹–❺

Planalto Bittar SHS Q.3 ⓣ61/3322-217. Just about the best of the cheaper hotels, slightly more expensive but better quality than others in this market. Good location. ❷–❸

St Paul SHS Q.2 ⓣ61/3317-8400, ⓔstpaul@tba.com.br. Large hotel with excellent service, plus a sauna, pool, good restaurant and bar. ❹–❺

Pousadas and pensões

Natal 708 Norte, Bloco B ⓣ61/3340-1984. Most comfortable of the *pousadas*; breakfast included. ❷

Pousada do Sol 703 Sul, Bloco K ⓣ61/3224-9703. Along with neighbouring *Pousada JK*, this is the best of a cluster of cheap places. ❶–❷

Pousada Sossego 705 Sul, facing W3 ⓣ61/3224-5050. Aimed at the lower end of the Brazilian business market, with clean rooms. ❶–❷

Pousada VIP 708 Sul, Bloco C ⓣ61/3340-8544. Doesn't quite live up to its name, but it's clean and includes basic breakfast. ❶–❷

The City

Brasília's overriding attraction is the unique environment produced by its stunning **architecture**. The blue sky that normally hangs over the city contrasts well with the modern buildings and the deep red earth of the *planalto*. Visitors normally head straight for the downtown sites, but it's best to put them in context first on one of the circular bus routes from the *rodoviária*.

Below, the main sights in downtown Brasília are divided into three sections, following the head, body and tail concept of the bird or aeroplane that the city resembles; the outlying areas of the city are dealt with afterwards.

The Esplanada dos Ministérios

The focus of the Brazilian government complex, known as the **Esplanada dos Ministérios**, is the unmistakable twin towers of the Congress building. All of the structures here are within a few minutes' walk of each other, entrance is free and they can be seen in half a day, though you can easily spend more time than this exploring. All were designed by Niemeyer, and are rightly regarded as among the best, if not the best, modernist buildings in the world. The combination of white marble, water pools, reflecting glass and the airy, flying buttresses on the presidential palace and Supreme Court make these buildings remarkably elegant. At night floodlighting and internal lights make them even more impressive; a slow taxi or bus ride around the Esplanada in the early evening, when people are still working and the buildings glow like Chinese lanterns, is a must. The only blemish is the enormously ugly and vulgar flagpole at the centre of the square, which sits there like a black bluebottle on a white plate, mute testimony to the crassness and bad taste of the military regime that plonked it there over Niemeyer's protests.

At the centre of the complex is the **Praça dos Três Poderes** (Square of Three Powers), representing the Congress, judiciary and the presidency. The **Congresso Nacional** is the most recognizable landmark in Brasília – in a way, everything else flows from here. If you accept the analogy of the city built as a bird, then the National Congress is its beak, something it clearly resembles with its twin 28-storey towers. The two large "bowls", one on either side of the towers, house the Senate Chamber (the smaller, inverted one) and the House of Representatives, and were designed so that the public could climb and play on them, though the only people allowed to play there now are the patrolling soldiers of the Polícia Militar. Visitors can attend debates when in session, however, something you might want to enquire about at the front entrance desk. The chambers themselves are a hoot – as Sixties as the Beatles, though they haven't aged as well. To see them, you must take one of the guided tours that leave every half hour on weekdays and hourly at weekends. Most guides speak

ACCOMMODATION

Alvorada	F	Bristol	E	El Pilar	J	Kubitschek Plaza	O	Nacional	M
Aracoara	A	Byblos	I	Eron	B	Manhattan	Q	Planalto Bittar	G
Aristus	N	Carlton	C	Hotel das Américas	D	Metropolitan	P	St Paul	L
Bonaparte Hotel Résidence	K	Casablanca	H						

some English and there is a strict dress code – long trousers, shirt and shoes for men, smart casual for women (Senate tours Mon–Fri 1.30–5.30pm, Sat & Sun 10am–2pm; ⓣ61/3311-2149 for information; House of Representatives tours Mon–Fri 1–5pm, Sat & Sun 9am–2pm; ⓣ61/3318-5092 for information).

The **Palácio da Justiça** (Mon–Fri 10am–noon and 3–5pm; same dress code as for Congress) is beside the Congress building, on the northern side of the Esplanada dos Ministerios. Created in 1960 with a concrete facade, the building was covered with fancy – and, to many, elitist – marble tiles by the military government during the dictatorship. With the return to democracy the tiles were removed, laying bare the concrete waterfalls between the pillars, but the water has been shut off for years as the pools proved to be a perfect breeding ground for the dengue mosquito. The structure is much less interesting inside than any of the other buildings, and without the waterfalls the exterior is more than a little bleak.

Much more worthwhile is the **Palácio Itamarati** (Mon–Fri 2–4.30pm, Sat & Sun 10am–3.30pm, no guided tours but visitors are restricted to certain areas, with same dress code as for congress; ⓣ61/3411-6159 for information), the vast Foreign Office structure. Combining modern and classical styles, it's built around elegant courtyards, sculptures and gardens, and inside its airiness and sense of space is breathtaking, well set off by a carefully chosen selection of modern art and wall-hangings. Outside, the marble *Meteor* sculpture by Bruno Giorgi is a stunning piece of work, its five parts representing the five continents.

Behind the Congresso Nacional, on the northern side, the **Palácio do Planalto** houses the president's office which can be visited only by guided tour (Sun 9.30am–1.30pm; same dress code as for Congress). Of all the Niemeyer buildings this is the most spectacular, both outside and in; the interior is dominated by sleek columns and a glorious, curving ramp leading up from the reception area. On weekdays, however, visitors will have to content themselves with a changing of the guard out front at 8.30am and 5.30pm daily. Nearby in Praça dos Três Poderes, the signposted **Museu Histórico de Brasília** (Mon–Sat 9am–1pm & 2–5pm) tells the tale of the transfer of the capital from Rio; the large-scale architectural model of the entire city, with lights for points of interest, is fun and useful to the newly arrived. The **Supremo Tribunal Federal** (Mon–Fri 1–5pm), interesting enough but not in the same class inside as the Itamaratí or the presidential palace, is open to the public; entrance is with formal dress only (jacket required). Outside there's a concrete monument to Justice, although one to Self-Importance would be more appropriate.

From here, you can take a **bus** to the downtown *rodoviária*, or it's a twenty-minute walk west through the esplanade of ministry buildings to the cathedral and downtown commercial centre. But to complete your tour of Niemeyer gems, it's worth taking the short taxi or bus ride from here to the president's official residence two miles away, the **Palácio da Alvorada** (bus #104, leaves from stand 13 of Platform A at the *rodoviária*), which some consider the most beautiful of Niemeyer's buildings. The residence is nestled behind an emerald-green lawn and beautifully sculpted gardens, which perfectly set off the brilliant white of its exterior – note the architect's distinctive slender buttresses – and its blue-tinted glass. Somehow the fact that you're only allowed to see it from fifty yards away adds to its delicateness and elegance.

If you go by taxi, make sure it waits for you in the car park to the right – taxis rarely pass by here. Guards will shout intimidatingly at you if you sit in the car in the left parking lot, the only one with the clear view, due to heightened security concerns, here as everywhere else.

On your way back, look out for Niemeyer's most recent building, the circular, twin mirrored-glass towers of the attorney general's headquarters, immediately behind the Praça dos Três Poderes, opened in 2003.

The cathedral and the commercial sectors

Between the ministries and the downtown *rodoviária*, and within walking distance of either, the **Catedral Metropolitana Nossa Senhora Aparecida** is one of Brasília's most striking edifices (daily 7am–6.30pm; no shorts allowed). Marking the spot where the city of Brasília was inaugurated in 1960, it is built in the form of an inverted chalice and crown of thorns; its sunken nave puts most of the interior floor below ground level. Some of the glass roof panels in the interior reflect rippling water from outside, adding to the sense of airiness in the cathedral, while the statues of St Peter and the angels suspended from the ceiling (the inspired gravity-defying creations of Brazilian sculptor Bruno Ceschiatti) help to highlight the feeling of elevation. Nevertheless, although some 40m in height and with a capacity of two thousand, the cathedral seems surprisingly small inside.

About ten minutes' walk away, on the northern side of the Eixo Monumental, is the **Teatro Nacional**. Built in the form of an Aztec temple, it's a marvellous, largely glass-covered pyramid set at an angle to let light into the lobby, where there are often good art exhibitions with futuristic and environmental themes. Inside are three halls: the Martins Pena, the Villa-Lobos (the largest, seating 1200) and the much smaller Alberto Nepomuceno. Most theatre productions are in Portuguese, but all three venues are also used for **music concerts** – Brasília has a symphony orchestra, and popular music stars often play here as well. As the main city venue for **ballet and dance**, the theatre is always worth checking out; thanks to the presence of the government and diplomatic corps, you might luck out and catch an illustrious visitor like the Bolshoi.

The main central shopping centre, the **Conjunto Nacional**, stands on the northern side of the *rodoviária*. Contained in a huge concrete block that's covered with massive product advertisements, the flashy jewellery and furniture shops combine with restaurants and fast-food outlets, and unlike the modern shopping centres in other Latin American cities the Conjunto Nacional is not just a playground for the rich; everyone seems to shop here. The busy northern *conjunto* is much more upmarket than its neighbour across the way, the **CONIC** centre, which is increasingly rundown and now actively dangerous at night, when the only people moving are the prostitutes and clientele patronizing a basement complex of fleapit sex cinemas. Stuck underground between the two giant shopping blocks, the downtown **rodoviária** bus station is also on three levels, and here you'll find more shops, toilets, snack bars and a bus information office.

A fifteen-minute walk west of here in the Setor Comercial Norte, on the far side of W3, is the glitzy **Brasília Shopping** mall, a towering glass disc half sunk in the ground, and a busy meeting place packed with shops of all kinds (the Varig office is conveniently opposite). By far the most interesting place to visit within easy walking distance of the *rodoviária* can be found in the unlikely setting of the **Central Bank building**, the unmistakable concrete and black glass skyscraper in Setor das Autarquias Sul, visible from anywhere in the centre. Tucked away by the building's rear entrance is the **Museu da Moeda**, or the

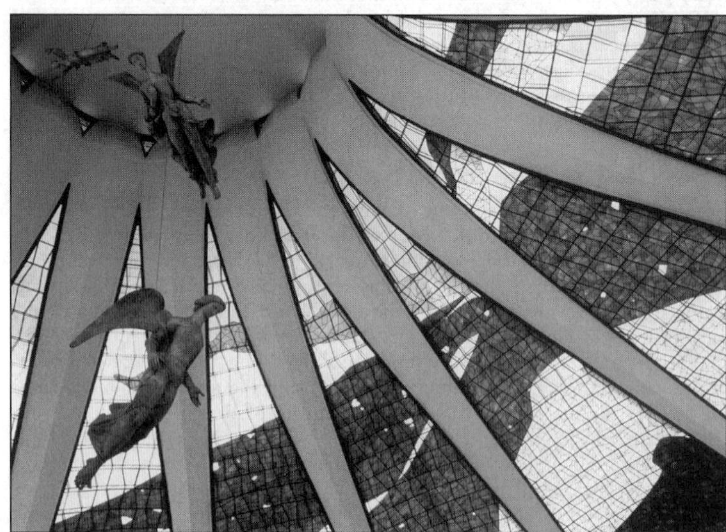

△ Catedral Metropolitana Nossa Senhora Aparecida

Oscar Niemeyer

Still working at the grand old age of 99 in 2006, Oscar Niemeyer is the greatest architect Latin America has produced. Best known for his unique contribution to Brasília, during his long and highly productive life he has left his mark on virtually all of Brazil's major cities, especially Rio and Belo Horizonte. Widely regarded as the most influential modernist architect of the twentieth century after Le Corbusier, he has also left important buildings in Europe, notably the Serpentine Gallery in London and the Le Havre Cultural Centre in France. But it is above all as the architect of Brasília that he will be remembered.

Born in Rio in 1907 he was influenced as a student by Le Corbusier's geometric ideas on urban planning and design and his first major commission, the building of the Ministry of Education in Rio in 1937, now known as the Palácio Gustavo Capanema, shows this influence clearly. But already in the 1940s Niemeyer began to show his independence and originality with a series of buildings in the Belo Horizonte suburb of Pampulha which gave a recognizably Brazilian twist to Le Corbusier, adding curves, ramps and buttresses to buildings that were decades ahead of their time. It was controversial: the São Francisco church in Pampulha was completed in 1943 but not consecrated until 1959, so reluctant was the Catholic Church to endorse such a radical departure. But the germs of Brasília are already clearly evident in his work in Pampulha a decade before Brasília was begun.

After Brasília Niemeyer became an international star and beyond criticism in his own country - which had its advantages, since he was the only militant communist never to be troubled by the military dictatorship. He built a number of other unforgettable buildings, the most spectacular being the Museum of Modern Art in Niteroi, across the bay from Rio, perched like a modernist flying saucer over the sea. With major buildings spread over eight decades as Brazil's leading architect, Niemeyer has made a major contribution not just to Brazilian culture, but to its modern history as well.

Museum of Money (Tues–Fri 10am–4.30pm, Sat 2–6pm; free, show your passport to get past reception), where you'll find a quirky but fascinating display of Brazilian currency from colonial times. It's very interesting as social history, but overshadowed by the second part of the display, an extraordinary exhibition behind armoured glass of the largest gold nuggets ever found in Brazil – most dating from the 1980s, when the Central Bank was buying nuggets from the Amazon gold rush. Behind the bank building is **Centro Cultural da Caixa**, the city's main art gallery, at any one time housing at least two travelling exhibitions, dependably high quality and free as well.

The Torre de Televisão, JK Memorial and Parque Sara Kubitschek

The **Torre de Televisão** (TV Tower) on Eixo Monumental is an obvious city landmark and easily reached on foot or by bus (#131 from the *rodoviária*). The 218-metre-high tower's viewing platform (Tues–Sun 9am–9pm) is a great place from which to put Brasília into perspective, and there is no better spot to watch the sunset, though frustratingly there is no bar to watch it from. Lower down, above its weird concrete supports, is the **Museu Nacional das Gemas** (Tues–Fri 3–8.30pm, Sat & Sun 10.30am–6.30pm; US$1), which is actually little more than a glorified and quite expensive gem shop. At the weekend the tower is also popular for its craft market, held around the base – a good place to pick up cheap clothes.

Further up the Eixo is the famous **Juscelino Kubitschek (JK) Memorial** (Tues–Sun 9am–5.45pm, US$2 entrance charge), best reached by one of the shoals of buses heading up the Eixo as it's too far to walk. Here, a rather Soviet-like statue of Brasília's founder stands inside an enormous question mark, pointing down the Eixo towards the heart of government. The museum below reverently reproduces JK's library and study, while the man himself lies upstairs in state in a black marble sarcophagus, backlit by an extraordinary combination of purple, violet and orange lights – the only thing missing is a sound system piping in "The Age of Aquarius". All around is a fascinating display of personal mementoes of JK's career and the founding and construction of the city, including photos and video clips of his funeral and the dedication of the Memorial – in turning out in their hundreds of thousands in his honour, despite the desire of the military dictatorship to keep the event low key, the population of the Distrito Federal made the first important anti-military demonstration, one of the reasons for the subsequent slow relaxing of the military's grip on power.

A short walk from Setor Hoteleiro Sul, taking up one entire side of the Eixo, is the enormous **Parque Sara Kubitschek**, named after JK's wife (bus #152 from the *rodoviária* passes by) – a massive mosaic of playgrounds, jogging tracks, bars and restaurants, picnic grounds, artificial lakes, parklands and woods. If you want to walk or jog in Brasília, this is the place to do it. The southern entrance, a block away from the hotel sector, is where many of the attractions are concentrated, including an enjoyably tacky but perfectly safe (despite appearances) **funfair** that will appeal to young children, and a place to hire *pedalôs* – adult-sized tricycles that are harder work than they look, but great fun nonetheless. The best time to visit is Sunday morning, when the locals turn out en masse, jogging, working out, sunbathing, reading the paper and the like, while dozens of kiosks and street-sellers tout everything from iced green coconuts to a shiatsu massage.

The Memorial dos Povos Indígenas

Across the road from the JK Memorial is another Niemeyer building, the white and curving **Memorial dos Povos Indígenas** (Tues–Fri 10am–4pm), which houses one of the best collections of **indigenous art** in Brazil, much of it from the *planalto* itself and produced by the indigenous groups who inhabit the headwaters of the Xingú river. Highlights are the extraordinary ceramic pots of the Warao, the Xingú's ceramic specialists, beautifully adorned with figures of birds and animals, and vivid, delicate featherwork. The rotating exhibits and regular travelling shows are uniformly fascinating, but the building alone is worth the visit; the gallery is set in a long, downward curve around a circular courtyard, the smoked glass set against Niemeyer's trademark brilliant white exterior. At the lower end is a **café**, virtually never open but where Indians up from the Xingú often leave artwork for the museum staff to sell for them; bargaining for these good-quality and reasonably priced items would be churlish.

Run by the chronically hard-up state government, the museum keeps opening hours that are theoretical rather than real. If you arrive on the weekend or on Monday, and find the main entrance at the top of the ramp shut, slip down to the large metal door at ground level, to the right of the ramp, and bang hard; either a security guard or one of the museum staff will let you in. It's definitely worth making the effort.

Indigenous craft market

One of Brasília's least-known but by far its most interesting market is the impromptu **indigenous craft market** that has grown up in the patio of the headquarters of FUNAI, the federal Indian agency, in the Setor de Rádio e Televisão Sul. The market, in its own small way, is the perfect symbol of what has changed in the relationship between Brazil's Indians and the federal government in recent years. Time was when FUNAI controlled all the marketing of indigenous art, via its own chain of craft shops, one of which you can still find inside FUNAI's entrance hall if you venture in. But too much of the revenue stayed with FUNAI rather than the producers, who have now taken matters into their own hands; every weekday, around 9am, groups of indigenous people start setting out their wares on the patio, mainly basketware and ceramics but much more besides, most of it pretty good quality and always interesting to check out. The bulk of it comes from the Xingú, far northeast of the *planalto* and the closest sizeable indigenous area to Brasília. But since Indians come to FUNAI from all over to sort out their many problems, and usually bring whatever they can stuff into a bag or two to sell and make a little money on the side, the anthropologically minded can find people and *artesanato* from all over Brazil, especially the Amazon. This is one of the rare places where the shopper often needs to pay more than asked; many sellers have only vague notions of market values and ask ridiculously low prices, US$2 or US$3 for items that are patently worth far more.

The market is a short walk from the main entrance to the Parque Sara Kubitschek, or from Setor Hoteleiro Sul along W3; go past the Pátio Brasil mall, turn right after the Assis Chateaubriand building, helpfully identified by enormous letters on its side, and the market is one block up on the other side of the road, next door to the Dom Bosco school.

Further out: the asas, Jardim Botânico and Parque Nacional de Brasília

The residential parts of Brasília are rarely thought of as a destination for visitors, but the older areas are by far the best place for a stroll during the day. The parks and gardens between the blocks are extremely well designed, and even at the hottest times of year you can walk for hundreds of yards in certain areas without leaving the shade. The oldest *superquadras* are all in Asa Sul; 108 Sul was the first to be completed in the whole city, designed as a showpiece to make the city tolerable for those bureaucrats moving here from Rio (a miserable failure in that respect at the time, but things eventually improved as the trees grew). The adjacent blocks from 107 down to 104 were all built shortly after and make for a great **urban walk** – take a bus or walk up W3 Sul, get off at the 508 block, walk two blocks down, and then start strolling towards the centre. There are plenty of *comercials* along the way if you want to make a pit stop.

For a taste of the *cerrado* before heading deeper into the *planalto*, or just a temporary break from the city, consider venturing to the Jardim Botânico, at the far end of Asa Norte, and the Parque Nacional de Brasília, across the striking JK Bridge over Lago Paranoá in Lago Sul. Both were created in the early 1960s to preserve large green spaces within easy reach of the city – it seemed superfluous then, but the pace of development has been so fast that there would be very little native *cerrado* anywhere near the ciy without them. The **Jardim Botânico**, at Setor de Mansões Dom Bosco in Lago Sul (Tues–Sun 9am–5pm; R$5, taxi around R$20 from centre; bus route #147 from *rodoviária*, stands 8 & 9 at Platform A), is a calm and well-organized retreat where you can experience the flora and fauna of the *cerrado* at first hand. There's an information centre, a large display of medicinal plants of the region, a herb garden, and over forty square kilometres of nature reserve with an extensive network of trails. It's good hiking, but make sure you bring a hat and water.

The **Parque Nacional de Brasília,** the city's very own national park (daily 8am–4pm; admission R$2), at the far end of Asa Norte, is the only area of native vegetation large enough around Brasília to support proper wildlife populations. During the week, you will have the place largely to yourself, and while the park itself is enormous, visitors are restricted to its southern corner, where the main attractions are two very large **swimming holes**, Piscina Velha and Piscina Nova, both a short, well-signposted walk from either of the two entrances, and built around a stream, preserving the natural flow of the water. When there is nobody there, this is a lovely spot – especially for a picnic. You may spot capuchin monkeys leaping acrobatically through the trees, but they have become used to scavenging picnic remains so take care not to leave food lying around, and be sure to pack plastic bags away as the monkeys regularly choke on them.

Although the pool area gets very crowded at weekends, virtually everyone sticks to the water, so if you want space and some solitude, head up the slope to a small fenced trail through a section of gallery forest – ideal for kids – and continue up the hill until you come up onto open *cerrado* savanna. Here you'll find another much longer trail, a four-mile circuit called the **Água Cristal** (crystal water trail), which lives up to its name, taking you through a number of clearwater streams before dumping you back more or less where you started. The views are beautiful, although it is frustrating that you can't hike into them.

Eating, nightlife and entertainment

One of the best things about Brasília is the wide variety of **bars and restaurants**; in fact, a combination of the government, the university and diplomats supports one of the densest concentrations of good restaurants in the country. *Candangos* eat late, hanging around in bars until at least 10pm before heading off to eat. Moreover, bars and restaurants aren't always easily distinguishable – a place that looks and feels like a bar can sometimes serve substantial meals, so the listings are somewhat arbitrary.

With some deserving exceptions, the following concentrates on the best places within easy reach of the hotel sectors. Prices are more than reasonable; unless noted, a full meal with drinks averages around R$25 per head, often less. Cheaper food can be found in the street markets and stalls scattered around

Getting to and from Parque Nacional de Brasília

The national park is a R$20 **taxi ride** from the centre, but you have to arrange a rendezvous to return, since very few unoccupied taxis pass by – the **bus** is a better bet, but not easy. Astonishingly, there is no bus stop at the park entrance: the closest you can get here is by picking up the W3 Norte Circular on W3 and asking the driver to drop you off as it reaches the end of W3 and turns – look hard and you can see the park entrance on the other side of the highway.

This is the one place where it is actually easier to get a **perueiro**, one of the illegal but ubiquitous and highly organized white minibuses that shadow the bus routes. Look for *perueiro* lines #82 and #84, with an orange stripe on the side: the easiest place to catch them is the car park above the *rodoviária*, opposite the Conjunto Nacional – they wait until they fill up and then go, but you'll have to tell the driver to let you off near the park entrance.

the *rodoviária*, Conjunto Nacional, and in the large Pátio Brasil shopping centre next to the Setor Hoteleiro Sul, dominated by *comida por kilo* places catering to lunching office workers. If you're walking, you should have no problems with safety around most places in Asa Norte and Asa Sul, but W3 and the deserted central area should be walked around with caution at night. Most restaurants close on Monday night rather than Sunday.

Restaurants

A good place to start, especially on a weekend night, is **comercial 404/405 Sul**; some *comercials* specialize and this one, known locally as *Restaurantelândia*, is lined on both sides with at least a dozen different national cuisines from four continents, and heaves with people at weekends. Although better food is to be had elsewhere, this is a good place to bar hop and then have a range of eating options to choose from. Recommended places are all in the numbered *comercial*, unless otherwise indicated.

A Tribu 105 Norte. Best vegetarian food in the city, imaginative and full of flavour. Offers a lunchtime buffet, and is open at night too. The newly opened branch in Setor dos Clubes Norte, near the JK bridge and accessible only by taxi (R$10 from centre) is even better, built in the form of an indigenous roundhouse, lit by fires at night.

Acarajé da Rosa 204 Sul. Cheap, unpretentious Bahian food, especially pleasant at night in the dry season, when you can sit outside beneath the trees.

Belini 113 Sul. Everything you need under one roof – excellent deli, good espresso bar, and classy but still reasonably priced restaurant upstairs.

Camarão e Cia. 206 Sul. Good seafood buffet at lunchtime, followed by Bahian food at night.

Carpe Diem 104 Sul. Deservedly the best-known bar/restaurant in town: great atmosphere, renowned politico hangout and very reasonably priced. Famous among locals for the best salad bar and lunch buffet in the city (you pick the salad ingredients, they whip it up for you) and the Saturday *feijoada*; food and drinks served practically 24/7, apart from a few hours in the morning.

Crepe au Chocolat 109 Norte and 210 Sul. Eat elsewhere, head here for dessert and be stretchered home – not for the faint of heart.

Don Durica 201 Norte. Serving an excellent lunch and evening buffet of traditional, quite heavy Brazilian food, such as stewed rabbit and various dishes of lamb, pork and suckling pig. If you want something lighter, try the extremely tasty soup buffet.

Espettus Setor Hoteleiro Sul. Best option if you're staying in one of the nearby hotels and don't feel like going far – good, varied *churrascaria*, infinitely preferable to any of the hotel restaurants.

Feitiço Mineiro 306 Norte. Even without the live music at weekends (see opposite), this spot is worth patronizing for the food alone; a buffet of *comida mineira* (Minas Gerais food), heavy on the pork, bean sauce and sausages, prepared the traditional way on a wood-fired stove. Open for dinner only.

Fratello 103 Sul. Best pizza in town: wood-fired kiln and original ingredients. Try the eponymous Fratello, based on sweet pickled aubergine.

Fritz 404 Sul. Brazilian waiters serve very German food – stodge heaven and cheap.

Ichiban 405 Sul. Good sushi, sashimi and whatever other Japanese food you fancy; divided into Western and Japanese seating sections, the latter can be hard on the knees if you're not used to it.

Kosui Academia de Tênis, Setor dos Clubes Norte. Arguably the best Japanese restaurant in the city and certainly the best located of any of them, next to the Academia's art-cinema complex, handy if you want to do dinner and a film. Good Italian and seafood restaurants are also part of the complex.

Nippon 403 Sul. A good, reasonably priced Japanese place, similar to Ichiban above.

Patu Anú Setor dos Mansões Lago Norte (SMLN), ML12, Conjunto 1, Casa 7I, near the Paranoá dam ⓣ1/3369-2788 or 3922-8930. The very best of Brazilian cuisine, served in a fantastic lakeside location. The menu is exclusively game – wild boar, alligator, *capivara* (the largest rodent in the world, which actually tastes great) and more, cooked with mouthwatering sauces, and regional fruits and vegetables. Dinner and drinks cost about R$80 a head, plus R$50 each way for the taxi. Get a taxi via your hotel and make sure you show this address to the driver before you set out. Reservations are a good idea (English spoken), and the restaurant will get you a cab for the return trip.

Porcão Pier 21 Shopping Centre, Asa Sul. A short taxi ride from the centre, this spot ("big pig" in Portuguese) certainly lives up to its name as the largest and most varied *churrascaria* in Brasília, and is strictly for carnivores. Drinks are overpriced, so concentrate on the food.

Sabor do Brasil 302 Sul. For those on a strict budget this place offers the best meal in town – for around US$5 a head. A soup buffet with trimmings, very traditional Brazilian fare, good vegetarian options but soups for carnivores too. Open for lunch and at night. Good place to line the stomach before heading out for a night on the town, or to sober up coming back from one.

Universal Diner 210 Sul. Take your pick: the lively, crowded and loud bar downstairs or the very good restaurant upstairs, serving Brazilian and international food.

Bars and cafés

Even discounting the hotel bars – and there are plenty of those – there's a good selection of **places to drink**, though the scene as a whole is nothing like as lively as Rio.

Armazém do Ferreira 202 Norte. Popular with politicians, this place is best late at night when it gets very crowded. The tables outside are very pleasant, huddled under trees; the similar *Café do Brasil* next door is also good.

Bar Beirute 109 Sul. Often very lively and packed at night with a young crowd, with Lebanese food that's no more than OK but cheap. There's also a playground for kids.

Bar Brasília 506 Sul. Successful recreation of an old-style Brazilian bar, complete with surly waiters; as a bar very good, but the view out across a car park leaves something to be desired.

Café com Letras 204 Sul. Pleasant café above a good bookshop, with some English titles, open into the small hours. The verandah is a good spot to watch the students and young professional crowd.

Daniel Briand 104 Norte; side of Bloco A. Highly recommended spot, especially for a late breakfast on weekends or afternoon tea any day. This French-owned patisserie and tea house serves the best quiche and cakes in town. There's nowhere better for coffee and reading; the only problem is the early and rigidly enforced closing at 10pm – both un-French and un-Brazilian.

Frei Caneca Entrequadra 110/111 Sul. Large beer hall that only really gets going late at night, with good atmosphere and live music every weekend.

Libanus 206 Sul. Perennially crowded spot serving up excellent-value, hearty Lebanese food; the playground makes it a good place for families in the afternoons, but turns into a young and humming scene at night.

Marujo 105 Sul. Constantly crowded bar, where despite the terrible food, the outdoor tables under trees make it pleasant enough as a hangout.

Tortaria di Lorenza 107 Norte, 302 Sul. Inexpensive place for gooey, tempting cakes, espresso coffee and savouries.

Live music

Brasília is a good place to catch **live music**. Although not what it was – displaced by techno and house like everywhere else – the city's rock scene was particularly lively back in the 1990s: one local band, Legião Urbana, achieved megastardom and another, Os Raimundos, were well respected. The main place to catch local and visiting bands today is *Gate's Pub* (403 Sul), much bigger than it looks from the outside, with a series of rooms and small stages – resembling in a weird way a British pub-rock venue. Thursday nights are particularly lively. Student hangout *Frei Caneca Draft*, in the Brasília Shopping mall, also often has local bands on weekend nights. *Café Cancún* in the Liberty Mall, Setor Comercial Norte, transcends its unpromising setting late on Friday and Saturday nights with live music and great DJs, Brazilian rhythms mixed with *salsa*.

You can see more traditional first-class Brazilian music live at *Feitiço Mineiro* (see above under "Restaurants"), and, especially, at the *Clube do Choro* (central strip of the Eixo Monumental, next to the convention centre – all the taxi drivers know it). Ask at your hotel or check the listings, but it's usually open at night from Thursday to Saturday, with live music on Thursdays and Fridays, turning into a *gafieira* (dance-hall), on Saturday night, with its own house band and older, intimidatingly good dancers. On Thursdays and Fridays, chairs and tables are set in front of the small stage, and the house specializes in *choro*, the oldest and arguably most beautiful of Brazilian musical genres, played here by masters young and old to an appreciative, knowledgeable audience. If you've never been in a crowd brought to its feet by a fast mandolin solo, you haven't lived. This is as good a club venue as you'll find anywhere in the country.

Visiting megastars, Brazilian and otherwise, will play either the Teatro Nacional or, more likely these days, the plush *Americel Hall* in the Clube de Tênis, Setor dos Clubes Sul.

Cinema

Brasília is an excellent place to go to the cinema, with a large and appreciative audience for good films. The **Clube de Tênis** hosts the annual international film festival in October and also houses the Academia, probably the best cinema complex between São Paulo and Mexico City, with twelve screens of exclusively arthouse films to choose from year-round, not to mention several restaurants and a large bar. If you want commercial films, head for the malls. Worthy of special mention is Cine Brasília, a splendid example of early 1960s kitsch at Entrequadra 106/107 Sul that has a huge screen. Run by the Ministry of Culture, the cinema is free to ignore commercial considerations completely and show the latest Iranian masterpiece, or classics of European and American cinema history.

Listings

Airlines Mostly found around the *Hotel Nacional* in various agents' shops. The main Brazilian companies are Nordeste, airport ⓣ61/3365-1022; TAM, SHS 1, Galeria Hotel Nacional 61 ⓣ61/3223-5168, and at the airport ⓣ61/3365-1000; Varig/Cruzeiro, ground floor of the Conjunto Empresarial Varig building opposite Brasília Shopping mall ⓣ61/3329-1169, and at the airport ⓣ61/3364-9583, 24-hour reservations, English spoken on ⓣ0800/99-7000. Cheap newcomer Gol has no agencies but has phone lines and encourages on-line bookings ⓣ300/789-2121, ⓦwww.voegol.com.br. Among overseas airlines are Air France, SHS 1, Galeria Hotel Nacional 39/40 ⓣ61/3223-4152, ⓕ3223-2299; Alitalia, SHS, Galeria Hotel Nacional, Loja 36/37 ⓣ61/3321-5266, ⓕ3223-2498; British Airways, SHS, Galeria Hotel Nacional, Loja 18 ⓣ61/3226-4164, ⓕ3321-9016; KLM, SHS 1, Galeria Hotel Nacional 51 ⓣ61/3321-3636 or 3225-5915; Lan Chile, SCS, Q8, Bloco B-60, Ed. Venâcio ⓣ61/3226-0318; Lufthansa, SHS 1, Galeria Hotel Nacional, Loja 1 ⓣ61/3223-5002 or 3233-8202.

Airport enquiries ⓣ61/3365-1941, 3365-1024, 3365-1224 or 3365-1947.

ATMs International bank cards are accepted at Banco do Brasil and HSBC at the airport; Citibank at the Setor Bancário Sul opposite the Pátio Brasil mall, with another Citibank ATM tucked away at the Blockbuster video in 506 Norte; HSBC at 502 Sul, on W3; BankBoston next door to Citibank at Setor Bancário Sul, and most central Bancos do Brasil.

Books and newspapers English-language papers, magazines and books at Sodiler, ground floor of the Conjunto Nacional and Millenium Revistas at 303 Sul; both bookshops also at the airport.

Car rental The usual suspects all line the airport road: Avis ⓣ61/3365-2991, Localiza ⓣ0800-992000, Hertz ⓣ61/365-4747, Unidas ⓣ0800/121-121. Avoid paying a hefty surcharge at the airport by heading into town by taxi and renting from there; highly recommended is Via Rent-A-Car ⓣ61/3322-3181 or 9985-4717, SHS Q6 Cj. A, Bloco F, Loja 50, or, more comprehensibly, the side of the *Hotel Melia*.

Driving Brasília, uniquely among Brazilian cities, is blanketed by speed cameras. If you're caught jumping a light or speeding in a hired car, the fine will be taken off your credit card.

Embassies For the Setor de Embaixadas Sul (SES), take a bus to Av. das Nações, or just walk. Argentina, SHIS QI 01, Cj. 01, Cs. 19 ⓣ61/3365-3000; Australia, SHIS QI 9, Cj. 16, Cs.1 ⓣ61/3248-5569; Bolivia, SHIS QL 10, Cj. 1, Cs. 6 ⓣ61/3364-3362; Canada, SES Av. das Nações 803, Lote 16, sala 130 ⓣ61/3321-2171; Colombia, SES Av. das Nações 803, Lote 10 ⓣ61/3226-8997; Ecuador, SHIS Q1 11, Cj. 09, Cs. 24 ⓣ61/3248-5560; Paraguay,

SES Av. das Nações 811, Lote 42 ⓣ61/3242-3732; Peru, SES Av. das Nações 811, Lote 43 ⓣ61/3242-9435; UK, SES Av. das Nações 801 ⓣ61/3225-2710; US, SES Av. das Nações 801, Lote 3 ⓣ61/3321-7272; Venezuela, SES Av. das Nações 803, Lote 13 ⓣ61/3223-9325.

Emergencies Medical ⓣ192; police ⓣ197; fire brigade ⓣ193.

Exchange Cash and traveller's cheques are accepted at Banco do Brasil, SBS, Edifício Sede 1, Terreo (Mon–Fri 10am–5pm). Reasonable rates with no commission apply at the *câmbio* in the *Hotel Nacional* (Mon–Fri 9am–6pm).

Health matters Dr C. Menecucci, Centro Medico, Av. W3 Sul 716, Bloco D, sala 16, speaks good English. For quick blood tests, the Clínica SOS Check-Up de Brasília, SHIS 9, Bloco E, Loja 312 ⓣ61/3248-4093, at the Centro Clínico do Lago, is efficient. Hospitals are: Da Base do Distrito Federal, SMHS 101 ⓣ61/3325-5050; and Santa Lúcia, SHLS 716, Bloco C ⓣ61/3245-3344.

Post office Brasília's main post office (Mon–Sat 9am–6pm) is the small, white building in the open grassy space behind the *Hotel Nacional*.

Shopping You can buy almost anything in the Conjuntos de Diversões or Brasília Shopping mall (see p.524). For *artesanato* and other craft goods, there's a good market underneath the TV Tower on Saturdays, Sundays and most public holidays; see p.525. A smaller market next to the cathedral sells an incredible range of dried and dyed flowers. For regional craft specialities try the Galeria dos Estados, in the subway connecting the Setor Bancário Sul with Setor Comercial Sul. Good-value gems are available from Pedras Nativas, Conjunto Venâncio 2000, Terreo. For incense, tiger balm, tie-dye wraps and the like, try the Mercado Alternativo in the Centro Cultural Le Corbusier, at Centro Comercial Gilberto Salomão.

Taxis Cidade ⓣ61/3321-8181, Coobras ⓣ61/3224-1000, Radiotaxi ⓣ61/3325-3030.

Travel and tour companies For local tours and air tickets try Buriti, CLS 402, Bloco A, Loja 27 ⓣ61/3225-2686, ⓕ3226-1814; Presmic, SHS 1, Galeria Hotel Nacional 33/34 ⓣ61/3225-5515, ⓕ3321-1191; and Power Turismo, SHS 1, Galeria Hotel Nacional 48 ⓣ61/3332-6699, ⓕ3322-5658.

Around Brasília

Although it is sometimes difficult to imagine in the concrete heart of Brasília, the city is at the centre of some spectacular natural scenery that is easily accessible as day-trips from the capital. Here we've concentrated on straight day-trips or places where an overnight stay is possible but not really worthwhile; other destinations a little further out, like **Pirenópolis** (see p.540) and **Chapada dos Veadeiros**, where you can really get to grips with the *cerrado* rather than get a taste of it, are dealt with separately.

Lago Paranoá

Covering forty square kilometres, **Lago Paranoá** is a man-made recreation area, created by the diversion of three rivers to humidify the dry climate. Despite suffering from an algae problem, it's the scene of water sports, clubhouses and the **Ermida Dom Bosco**. This small conical hermitage, sitting alone on the edge of the lake, around 20km from the downtown *rodoviária*, offers fine views over the lake towards the Palácio da Alvorada, while below the nearby Paranoá dam there are amazing waterfalls during the heavy summer rains. **Buses** from the *rodoviária* go right around the lake in a couple of hours: #123 and #125 cover the southern half, finishing up in a shanty settlement after crossing the main dam; for the northern end of the lake, take buses #136-1 or #136-2 "Clube do Congresso".

Exploring the cerrado

If you don't have the few days necessary to go deep into the heart of *cerrado* country in the national parks, you can still get a sense of the wildness further north as a day trip from Brasília. It only takes a short drive from the city to drop behind a ridge and find yourself in another world of dirt roads, small villages, hills and rivers. The countryside around Brasília is dotted with walks, waterfalls, swimholes and cave systems, and has spawned a local ecotourism industry. Most of the natural attractions are difficult to get to, however: many of the best destinations, like the spectacular **Poço Azul waterfall** or the forested gorge and cave systems of **Buraco de Araras** aren't linked by roads or public transport, and part of their attraction is that they have to be hiked to over trails. Fortunately, you have the option of using local guides, and a couple of city tour operators also run specialized day-trips aimed at the ecotourism market, a wonderful option if you want to combine the comforts of staying in town with hiking the *cerrado* during the day. Expect to pay around R$150 a day, which can work out to be cheap for groups, and includes everything except food and drink. Recommended English-speaking outfits and guides are Gilmar at Soul Hard Ecoturismo (Ⓣ61/3944-3711), Ricardo at Be Hard Tribo Esporte (Ⓣ61/3340-4816) and Leonardo at Ibiti Ecoturismo (Ⓣ61/3340-6990 and 3447-4523).

At all times of year the sun is hot and the altitude means you will burn quickly and imperceptibly, so a hat and lashings of sunscreen are essential. You will be able to cool off at least with regular dips in natural swimholes along the way, one of the joys of walking the *cerrado*. Stout sandals are the best footwear, allowing you to negotiate the rocky, uneven beds of the streams and swimholes. Be aware that flash floods are a danger in gorges during the rainy season. Even when the sun is shining, rain can be falling unseen in headwaters – another reason for making sure you go with a guide.

Cristalina, Formosa and the Itiquira waterfall

From Brasília, an easy day-trip involves taking one of the frequent buses from the *rodoferroviária* to the town of **CRISTALINA**, a two-hour ride south of Brasília into the Goiás plateau. Indeed, the journey itself is one of the main reasons to go, as you'll pass through the distinctive rolling hills of the *planalto* along the BR-040 towards Belo Horizonte. Prospectors who came here looking for gold in the early eighteenth century came across a large quantity of rock crystal; the European market opened up over a century later, and today Cristalina is an attractive, rustic town, based around the mining, cutting, polishing and marketing of semi-precious stones. Quartz crystals and Brazilian amethyst can also be bought here at very reasonable prices, mostly from enormous warehouses on the edge of town that pull in passing motorists. If you want to stay, *Hotel Attie*, Praça José Damian 34 (Ⓣ61/3612-1252; ❷), and *Hotel Goyá*, Rua da Saudade 41 (Ⓣ61/3612-1301; ❷), are both good value. The town boasts an excellent *churrasco* restaurant, *Churrascaria Rodeio*, Rua 7 de Setembro 1237, where the Sunday lunch alone is worth the trip.

If you only have time for one day-trip, though, your best bet is to take the two-hour bus ride to the town of **FORMOSA**, not so much for the place itself, pleasant though it is, as for the stunning waterfall and park of **Salto de Itiquira**, for which Formosa is the jumping-off point. The park, which is about 40 kilometres away, is well signposted if you are in a rented car, but haggling with a local taxi driver at the bus station should get you a return trip for around R$50. It's worth it: the drive is beautiful, with the spectacular 90-metre waterfall visible from miles away as a white line against the towering cliffs of the Serra Formosa. Surrounding the waterfall is a municipal park (admission R$5), well laid out with a series of swimholes that make it a great place to spend the day.

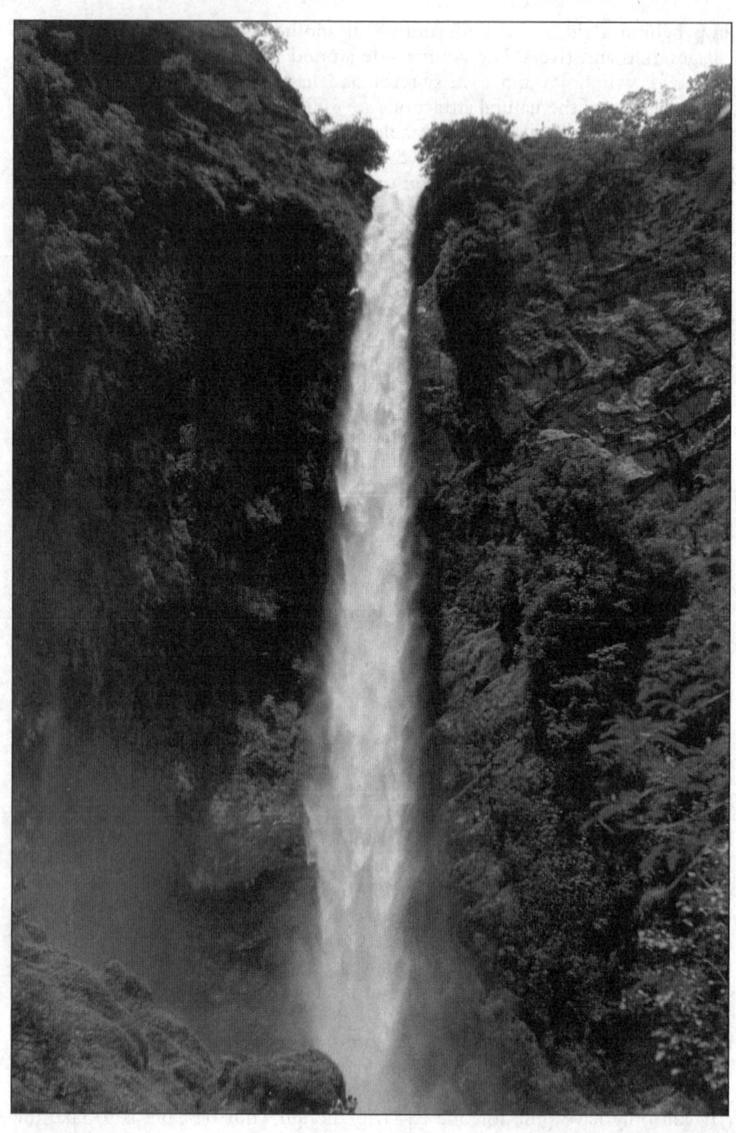

△ Salto de Itiquira

The most spectacular of all is at the very top of the only path, where the waterfall comes plunging down. Although there is a snack bar at the car park, by far the best place to eat is the *Dom Fernando* restaurant, with an excellent buffet of local food, and freshly grilled meats to order. It's located in splendid isolation at Km 6 on the road to the waterfall, but is only open weekends and holidays – otherwise there's a restaurant to the right of the park entrance. As ever, the park is at its best during the week, when you will probably have it to yourself.

The states of Goiás and Tocantins

Beyond the city and Federal District of Brasília, the hill-studded, surprisingly green *cerrado* of **Goiás state** extends towards another planned city, **Goiânia**, and the historic old towns of **Pirenópolis** and **Goiás Velho**, the latter in particular worth going out of your way for. Although gold mining started there in a small way during the seventeenth century, the first genuine settlement didn't appear until 1725. These days agriculture is the main activity: cattle, pigs, rice and maize are important but it is soya that is booming, driving the conversion of the dwindling remnants of *cerrado* into enormous farms. The small rural towns are all increasingly prosperous as a result, the state road system is excellent by Brazilian standards, and it's easy to imagine most of Goiás looking like the interior of São Paulo a generation from now. Indeed, the main cities of **Goiânia** and **Anápolis**, with their rising affluence and acres of new high-rises, already look very much like the cities of the *paulista* interior – and are about as interesting to visit, which is not very.

In the north of Goiás is the heart of the *planalto*, a jumble of cliffs, spectacular valleys and mountain ranges in and around the national park of **Chapada dos Veadeiros**, excellent for hiking and a thoroughly worthwhile excursion from Brasília, although you'll need a few days to do it justice. In the south, the thermal springs of **Caldas Novas** and **Rio Quente** bubble up into giant hotel complexes, while, over on the western border with Mato Grosso, the Parque Nacional **Emas** has less spectacular landscapes than Chapada dos Veadeiros but is wilder, a little more inaccessible (although still easily reached from Brasília), and a better place to see wildlife, in particular the large American rhea.

The mighty Rio Araguaia (which means Macaw River in the Tupi Indian language), with its many beautiful sandy beaches, forms the 1200-kilometre-long western frontier of both Goiás and Tocantins states. The latter, created for political rather than geographic or economic reasons in 1989, contains the huge river island, **Ilha do Bananal**, and its **Parque Nacional do Araguaia**. The main and central section (BR-153) of the 2000-kilometre-long highway from Goiânia and Brasília to Belém also runs through Tocantins. The only town of any significance is **Araguaína**, a flyblown settlement in the middle of a largely deforested savanna.

Goiânia

The other modern, planned city in central Brazil, **GOIÂNIA** was founded in 1933, becoming the state capital four years later. Over a million strong, cheaper than Brasília, with some good hotels and only 209km from the federal capital, the city is a good stopping-off point, since it is well connected by road to most other Brazilian cities. Goiânia earns its living as a market centre for the surrounding agricultural region, which specializes in rice and soya, and while it lacks the futuristic style of Brasília it makes up for it with a more genuine heartbeat and, with its less arid climate, a lusher, greener environment.

Arrival, information and accommodation

Both the **rodoviária** (☎62/3096-1000 and 3224-8466) and Santa Genoveva **airport** (☎62/3265-1500) lie in the northern sectors of town. The *rodoviária* is around twenty minutes by foot from Setor Central along Avenida Goiás, or a short ride by local bus. The airport is linked to the centre, 6km away, by bus (#190 or #162 "Circular Aeroporto"); a taxi to most central hotels will cost around R$20. To catch local buses in town, there are main stops on Avenida Araguaia just south of Rua 4, and along Avenida Goiás opposite *Hotel Paissandu*. There's a **tourist information** booth (daily 8am–6pm; ☎62/3281-2111) at the airport, which has free maps, though better maps (R$4) can be bought from the newsagent opposite. In the centre, the regional tourist authority, SEBRAE, has an office on Rua 30 at the Centro de Convenções (ⓣ62/3217-2055 and 3217-1100, ⓦwww.goiania.net) and should also be able to help.

The wide central streets are almost handsome in their blending of prewar Continental-style grandeur with modernist concrete and glass, skyscraping offices and homes for the rapidly growing middle-class population of the city. The main node of the concentric city plan is the Centro Cívico and Praça Dr Pedro Ludovico, at the head of the massive Avenida Goiás, whose broad and leafy pavement extends all the way down its middle between both directions of busy traffic. The city is divided into several sectors, the most important being the Setor Central, Setor Oeste and Setor Universitário, and many of the streets have numbers rather than names.

Accommodation

Goiânia has a wide range of **hotels**, wider, in fact, than Brasília. As well as giving you a greater choice of accommodation, this also means that you're more likely to be able to negotiate discounts – many of the larger hotels, as a matter of course, discount their prices out of season by twenty to forty percent.

Augustus Hotel Av. Araguaia 702, Centro ⓣ62/3216-6600, ⓦwww.augustus-hotel.com.br. Located on the Praça Antônio Lisita next to the *Araguaia*, this hotel is much flashier than its neighbour, with good rooms – though a little dark – plus a pool and sauna. ⑤

Castro's Park Hotel Av. República do Líbano 1520, Setor Oeste ⓣ62/3096-2000, ⓦwww.castrospark.com.br. Luxurious hotel with immaculate service, as well as swimming pools and a superb restaurant. Outside holiday times it's a good place to try for discounted rooms. ⑥–⑦

Hotel Araguaia Av. Araguaia 664, Centro ⓣ & ⓕ62/3212-9800, ⓦwww.araguaiahotel.com.br. Overlooking the little Praça Antônio Lisita, this hotel has an impressive lobby, which the rooms conspicuously fail to live up to. Good value nonetheless, especially if you can negotiate a discount. ③–④

Hotel Bandeirantes Av. Anhangüera 3278, Centro ⓣ & ⓕ62/3224-0066. Flashy and a/c but with no pool; it's particularly worth bargaining over room prices here. ⑥

Hotel Karajás Rua 3, #860, Centro ⓣ62/3224-9666, ⓦwww.hotelkarajas.com.br. Very comfortable twenty-storey block with good-sized rooms. Same price for singles, however. ⑤

Hotel Paissandu Av. Goiás 1290, Centro ⓣ62/3224-4925. Situated beyond the heart of the city, though within walking distance of it, this hotel is good value, if a touch basic, with TVs in all rooms, and singles considerably cheaper than doubles. ③

Hotel Papillon Av. Republica do Libano 1825, Setor Oeste ⓣ62/3219-1500, ⓦwww.papillonhotel.com.br. A luxury modern hotel with pool, sauna and bar, as well as exceptionally comfortable rooms and great breakfasts. ⑥

Pousada Ginza Av. Professor Alfredo de Castro 179, Setor Oeste ⓣ62/3223-5118, ⓕ3224-4196. A bland and fairly basic place, but it's friendly, clean and well located close to the centre, not far from Praça Tamandaré. Excellent value. ③

Príncipe Hotel Av. Anhangüera 2936, Centro ⓣ62/3224-0962, ⓕ3224-2831. Modern place with rather small rooms, where the cheaper *quartos* come with shared bathrooms. ②–③

The City

One of the first things visitors note when they arrive in Goiânia is the size of the place, its modern skyline dominating the horizon for some time before you reach the city's limits. The city ranks among Brazil's ten biggest, created to function as a regional agricultural and livestock market centre as gold has became less important in Goiás. Like several South American cities it has a spring-like climate year-round, of which it takes good advantage through its extensive network of established green spaces – mainly large *praças*, public parks and sports grounds. Pleasant enough in its own right, Goiânia lacks any sights of outstanding interest or stunning architectural gems, though the

Complexo Memorial do Cerrado Pe Pereira makes for an interesting out-of-town trip.

The Bosque dos Buritis, Parque Mutirama, Parque Botafogo and the city museums

Just two blocks due west of the Centro Cívico, the woods of the **Bosque dos Buritis** (daily 9am–6pm) spread over 140,000 square metres and contain a huge water-jet fountain as well as the free and reasonably interesting **Museu de Arte**, Rua 1, no. 605, Setor Oeste (Tues–Sun 8am–6pm), which has paintings of the city and stone sculptures on display. For a better selection of both Brazilian and international paintings with more frequently changing exhibits, try the **Museu de Arte Contemporânea**, lost in the concrete depths of the city's business heart in the Parthenon Centre, Rua 4, no. 515 (Tues–Fri 8am–6pm). Over in Praça Cívica, the **Galeria Frei Confaloni** is a small gallery displaying contemporary works by mainly local artists. Entry is free but the door is difficult to find around the back of the Centro Cultural building. Just a few metres away, the **Museu Zoroastro Artiaga**, Praça Cívica 13 (Tues–Fri 9am–5pm, Sat, Sun & holidays 9am–noon & 2–4pm), exhibits mainly artefacts, crafts and art from the region, but also houses roaming exhibitions, sometimes of ethnographic interest.

Goiânia's other museums include, in the east of the downtown area, the anthropological museum, the **Museu Antropologógico**, Praça Universitária 1166 (signposted "Instituto de Artes & Escritorio Tecnico Administrativo"; Tues–Fri 9am–5pm), home to a surprisingly wide range of traditional indigenous handicrafts and, nearby, the less interesting archeological museum, the **Museu Goiano de Pré-História e Arqueologia**, Praça Universitária 1440 (Mon–Fri 8–11am & 1–5pm); both museums can be reached on buses #167, #170, #164 or #162. If you're en route for some ecotourism and birdwatching in Goiás or Mato Grosso, the **Museu Ornitológia**, Av. Para 395, Setor Campinas (daily 8am–10pm), which displays around six thousand stuffed birds, may be of greater interest.

One of the main public parks in Goiânia, **Parque Mutirama**, in the northeast of the city at the junction of *avenidas* Araguaia and Contorno (Mon–Fri 1–6pm, Sat & Sun 9am–6pm), is very popular with local kids, who enjoy the delights of its ingenious amusement centre, skating rink and planetarium (Sun 3.30pm & 4.30pm). Opposite the park, the woods of the **Parque Botafogo** (closed Mon), with their reforested native trees, help the centre of the city to breathe; on the last Sunday of every month, there's also good live music here.

Jardim Zoológico

One of the town's main outdoor features, the **Jardim Zoológico** (Tues–Sun 8am–5pm; R$2.50), located some nine long blocks west along Avenida Anhangüera from the Teatro Goiânio, is a pleasant and well-managed public park. At its northern end around the muddy Lago das Rosas, the park is home to a number of semi-tame monkeys, while the southern corner houses a large and well-stocked zoo, which is a must for anyone interested in wildlife. You'll see *emas* (rheas), *tuiuius* (red-throated storks) and *jacarés* (alligators) closer here than you will in the wild.

The Feira Hippie, Feira da Lua and Feira do Sol

The **Feira Hippie** is a fascinating street market open every Sunday from early in the morning until mid-afternoon, dominating the stretch of Avenida Goiás from Rua 4 up to the Praça do Trabalhador. Originally a market for local crafts people, it has evolved to incorporate a wide range of more general alternative handicrafts, plus the global variety of socks, underwear, watches, electrical goods and all kinds of imported plastics. If you're around on a Saturday between 5 and 10pm, head for the **Feira da Lua**, which sells mainly *artesanato* in the tree-studded and lively Praça Tamandaré, a few blocks west of the Centro Cívico. Finally, the smaller **Feira do Sol**, on the Praça do Sol in the Setor Oeste, has around two hundred stalls selling crafts, antiques, foods, pets and fine arts every Sunday between 4 and 9pm.

The Complexo Memorial do Cerrado Pe Pereira

The **Complexo Memorial do Cerrado Pe Pereira** (daily 9am–5pm; taxi to the centre around R$30) is a large and well laid-out museum, model village and ecocentre developed on the site of an old estate some 10km south of the city on the BR-153 towards São Paulo. The museum is dedicated to the evolution of the planet, with displays on geology, indigenous cultures, and the wildlife and flora of the region's *cerrado* ecosystem, a unique form of Brazilian savanna. There are also some botanical gardens, a plant nursery with both common and endangered *cerrado* plant species, and a fascinating model of a nineteenth-century *cerrado* village, including everything from the village shop and church to the bordello – an important public service in most *cerrado* settlements, which were after all just remote cowboy pit stops.

Eating, drinking and nightlife

Legend has it that, being a remote frontier in the eighteenth and early nineteenth centuries, the state of Goiás developed an exquisite **cuisine** in order to prolong the stay of passing travellers. Even today, in Goiânia as in Goiás Velho, the people are justly proud of their cooking. Local delicacies range from rice with *pequi* fruit through pasties (*empadões*) to roast sow with fried banana (*leitão assada com banana frita*). You may find, however, that the increasing popularity of the self-service *comida por kilo* system means that it's almost impossible to track down seriously good food at lunchtime, unless you're happy dining at the most expensive restaurants. There are, however, a number of reasonable restaurants, *lanchonetes* and pizzerias around Praça Tamandaré, plus a few more *lanchonetes* around the cheaper hotels in Setor Centro. In general, the further south you go, the more expensive the restaurant.

Anhangüera Av. Anhangüera near the corner with Av. Paranaíba, Centro. Next to the Pro Brazilian supermarket, this is one of the cheapest and busiest lunchtime *comida por kilo* places.

Assoluto Av. Cel. Eugenio Jardim 300, Setor Marista ⓣ62/3092-8281. Located in the Marista sector west of the city, this is the best place for quality Italian cuisine; it has fine wines and excellent service in a pleasant roomy space.

Caterete Rua 10, Setor Oeste ⓣ62/3214-2025. Located in an outer suburb beyond the centre, this expensive restaurant is worth a taxi ride (about R$20) for its selection of the very best meat dishes including an excellent *rodizio*.

Chão Nativo Av. Rep. do Libano 1089, Setor Oeste ⓣ62/3223-5396. Located in the western sector it has one of the best self-service lunch spreads in the city and also serves a wide range of evening dishes; very popular with locals.

Ki-sabor Rua 3, no. 67, Centro. This budget-priced but very pleasant *comida por kilo* restaurant is open for lunch; get there by 1.30pm to be sure of a good choice of dishes.

Piquiras Av. República do Líbano 1758, Setor Oeste ⓣ62/3223-8168. One of the city's better all-round restaurants, with reliably good-quality food; you can eat inside or on a large terrace open to the road.

Vegetariano Rua 7, no. 475, Centro ⓣ62/3225-7290. Simple, well-presented vegetarian dishes in a small but friendly space.

Nightlife

Goiânia has quite a lively nightlife, but most of the best **clubs** change names and venues every few months as they go in and out of fashion. Prices tend to be high, with some places charging US$10 entrance as well as imposing a minimum spending limit once inside (usually also US$10). Praça Tamandaré is always a good place to start your evening, with a number of bars and cafés and, later on, nightclubs on or near the square. The best of these is currently the terminally designer *Draft Casual Bar & Diner*, south down Avenida República do Líbano on the corner of Rua 22 and Rua 23, Setor Oeste (Tues–Sun). Nearby, on República do Líbano almost on the Praça Tamandaré, the 24-hour *Big Paint American Bar* (open daily) is another more conventional but flashy option. A little further west, *Chocolate Chic*, Av. Portugal 719, is full of the tackiness that passes as style among Goiânia's monied youth, but it's still a fun night out. Also fairly reliable are the *Bavária*, Rua T-51, no. 1054, Setor Bueno, and *Boate People*, Rua 7, no. 1000, Setor Oeste. As for straight drinking **bars**, there aren't that many. Very busy is *O Ceará*, on the corner of Rua 2 and Rua 8. Try also *Chopp 10*, Avenida T-1, 2.215, Setor Bueno (daily 4pm until late), or the *Cervejaria Brasil* on Praça Antônio Lisita (closed Sun), which has a good range of bottled beers and cocktails.

Listings

Airlines Pantanal Linhas Aéreas, Rua Dona Gercina Borges 34, Setor Sul ⓣ62/3224-4286; TAM, Av. 85, no. 944, Setor Sul ⓣ62/3207-1800; Varig, Av. Goiás 285, Centro ⓣ62/3207-1743 or 0800/997-000.

Air taxis Goiás ⓣ62/3207-1616; Anhangüera ⓣ62/3207-2727.

Banks and exchange Good money-changing service on the first floor at the Banco do Brasil, Av. Goiás 980, Centro (Mon–Fri 10am–6pm); there's an ATM at the *rodoviaria*.

Car rental Hertz, Av. República do Líbano 1880, Setor Oeste ⓣ62/3223-6000; Localiza, Av. Anhangüera 3520, Setor Oeste ⓣ62/3261-7111; Unidas, Av. Caiapó, Quadra 85, Lote 123, Santa Genoveva, Setor Oeste ⓣ62/3207-1297.

Health matters Hospital Santa Helena ⓣ62/3219-9000.

Shopping The largest and flashiest shopping complex is Flambouyant Shopping, Av. Jamel Cecilio 3900, Jardim Goiás, Setor Pedro Ludovico, south of the city centre (daily 10am–10pm), followed closely by Bougainville, at Rua 9, no. 1855, Setor Oeste (Mon–Sat 10am–10pm). Crafts are available from the Feira Hippie along Avenida Goiás on Sunday mornings and the Feira da Lua on Saturdays (see p.539), or from the Handicraft Centre, Praça do Trabalhador, a producers' shop located in the old train station (daily 8am–6pm).

Taxis Araguaia ⓣ62/3285-2222; Coopertaxi ⓣ62/3212-6000; Rádio-Táxi ⓣ62/3285-1366.

Travel and tour companies SINGTUR (Sindicato dos Guias de Turismo), Alameda Progresso 511 (ⓣ62/3271-6970) is the regional tour guide syndicate, and provides accredited guides for the Parque Nacional das Emas (see p.545) and the Parque Nacional Chapada dos Veadeiros (see p.548). Turisplan Turismo, Rua 8-388, Centro ⓣ62/3224-1941 speak good English and run a range of local tours; NatureTur, Av. República do Líbano 2417, Setor Oeste (ⓣ62/3215-2000, ⓕ215-2011), are especially good for visits to Caldas Novas (see p.547); Toriua Turismo, Av. Tocantins 319, Centro (ⓣ & ⓕ62/3223-2333), can help with flights, tickets and hotel bookings.

Pirenópolis

PIRENÓPOLIS, a picturesque market town of about 21,000 people, straddles the Rio das Almas, 112km north of Goiânia in the scrubby mountains of the Serra dos Pireneus. Founded by *bandeirantes* in 1727 as a gold-mining settlement, it's a popular weekend retreat for residents of Brasília, well supplied with accommodation to suit all wallets.

The main street, **Avenida Sizenando Jayme**, is a broad, peaceful, tree-lined avenue where the old men, with their ponies and carts, and visiting *fazendeiros* hang out chatting in the shade; on Sunday mornings there's a produce market here. Just a couple of blocks down the hill is the site of the oldest church in Goiás, the **Igreja Nossa Senhora do Rosário de Meia Ponte** (1728–1732), once an attractive colonial edifice but tragically almost completely destroyed by fire in 2002 – only parts of the walls are left, a sad hulk supported by scaffolding awaiting the promised rebuilding. Opposite the church, the ruined late nineteenth-century theatre is also being rebuilt, and should, when finished, be once more the venue for plays and other distractions. The local **tourist office**, well supplied with leaflets, is just up the hill behind the Rosário ruins.

The town centre's only remaining colonial church is east along the very attractive Rua Bonfim da Serra dos Pireneus. **Igreja Nosso Senhor do Bonfim**, built in the 1750s, is famous for its image of Nosso Senhor do Bonfim, originally brought here by two hundred slaves. Also in the upper part of town, at Rua Direita 39 between the remains of Rosário and the *rodoviária*, you'll find the small **Museu das Cavalhadas** (Fri–Sun 9am–5pm), located in a family's front room (knock if it appears closed). The museum contains displays of incredible carnival costumes from the Festo do Divino Espírito Santo, a lively and largely horse-mounted religious festival that takes place in the town exactly six weeks after Easter Sunday. The festival combines dances with mock battles from the Crusades, and the costumes include ornate metal armour, demonic masks and animal heads. Another tiny museum, the **Museu da Família Pompeu**, in the family's home on the same road at no. 28 (Mon–Sat 9am–6pm), may in future become the *museu municipal*, with its odd collection of colonial and later bric-a-brac, including an old printing press, municipal newsletters and silver jewellery.

Below the Igreja N.S. do Rosário, the town has a different atmosphere. Swimming and sunbathing spots line the river by the old stone and wood bridge, which links the main settlement with the Carmo section of town on the north bank, and there's a vibrant **alternative scene** reflected in a handful of interesting bars, organic cafés and New Age stores: Homeostratum at Rua do Rosário 12 sells homeopathic products, natural foods, alternative magazines and *artesanato*, and Nataraja has a wide range of hippie-style clothes, crystals and alternative medicines. However, Pirenópolis is most famous in Brazil for its **silverwork**, mostly inset with semiprecious stones. The craft was introduced here just over twenty years ago by the hippies who came and stayed, and nowadays, with over two hundred artisans working in around a hundred workshops, you'll find jewellery for sale in dozens of shops, much of it inspired by Asian designs.

On the north side of the river, housed in the eighteenth-century Igreja Nossa Senhora do Carmo, the **Museu Sacro** (Mon–Sat 9am–6pm) displays an image of the town's patroness, which was originally brought here from Portugal.

One very worthwhile excursion into the surrounding countryside is to the **Santuário Vagafogo** (Tues–Sun 8am–5pm; R$10), a beautifully preserved patch of gallery forest with streams, swimholes, trails with walkways over the muddy patches and stairs up the steep sections, and a hammock-strung gazebo to relax in after your walks. Look hard and you can see the remains of colonial goldmining beneath the undergrowth – part of the main trail is an eighteenth-century sluice bed. At weekends and on holidays, the small restaurant at the reserve entrance serves quite superb, very reasonably priced brunches, using home-grown ingredients: the jams and pickles using *cerrado* fruits are deliciously unusual. Eat first and walk it off down the trails. Access is a problem, since it is not well signposted and lies some 6km out of town. Your best bet is to catch a *moto-taxi* at the *rodoviária*, one of the motorbike taxis that hang out in groups at a pick-up point opposite the platforms (20min; around R$15). It is a bumpy but enjoyable ride down a dirt track, with pleasant scenery. Once there, hiking back is easy, or arrange to be picked up again.

Practicalities

Pirenópolis is well connected by road to the other major towns of the region. There are three direct **buses** a day from Goiânia and four from the important junction town of Anápolis (which in turn has frequent connections with Goiânia). Brasília is just 172km east along the BR-070 (6 buses daily). The *rodoviária* (Ⓣ62/3331-1080) is on the eastern edge of town on Avenida Neco Mendonça, five minutes' walk from the centre. **Tourist information** is available from the Centro do Atendimento ao Turista, Rua Bonfim da Serra dos Pireneus (Mon–Sat 8am–8pm; Ⓣ62/3331-1299 and 3331-2729), and the council publishes an excellent annual *Guia do Turista* (free), available in most of the hotels and establishments mentioned below.

Accommodation

A popular local resort, Pirenópolis has dozens of **hotels** to choose from, many of them merely private homes with a few rooms for rent. The quality is generally well above average, and discounts are available mid-week or out of season. The most central hotel is the reasonably comfortable *Pousada das Cavalhadas*, Praça da Matriz (Ⓣ & Ⓕ62/3331-1261; ❸), opposite the Igreja N.S. do Rosário, although its singles are overpriced. On the small square to the right of the church, the *Hotel Rex*, Praça Emmanoel Lopes 15 (Ⓣ62/3331-1121; ❷), has several quaint rooms, some self-contained, along the edge of a traditional courtyard. Further up, the more basic *Lanchonete Pousada Central* (Ⓣ62/3331-1625) rents out five beds in two rooms at US$10 a person. One road away, at Rua Nova 25, is one of the town's nicest hotels, the *Pouso do Sô Vigário* (Ⓣ62/3331-1206; ❹–❺), housed in the old priest's residence, but now embellished with a pool and sauna. On the main street, at Av. Sizenando Jayme 21, is the *Pousada Imperial* (Ⓣ62/3331-1382, Ⓕ3331-1340; ❸), a friendly and well-appointed place, with great views of the Serra dos Pireneus over the river and half-price singles. On the other side of the river, the *Pousada dos Pireneus* (Ⓣ & Ⓕ62/3331-1028, Ⓦwww.pousadadospireneus.com.br; half board ❺) is the main upmarket place, with its own rambling gardens, pool, even a small water park with chutes that kids will love, and horse-riding facilities – including amusing half-hour jaunts by carriage through town for a mere R$12 for four people. The *pousada* also rents bicycles for R$10 an hour, but insists you stay within town, which is most unhelpful for visiting any of the surrounding attractions.

Eating and drinking

There are several good **restaurants** along Avenida Sizenando Jayme, including *As Flor* at no. 16, unprepossessing in appearance but one of the best at lunchtime for regional cooking, though evening fare can dip in quality. *Pamonharia*, around the corner going down to the church, is also cheap. Other, but much more expensive, restaurants can be found in the lower part of town around the river; try *Restaurante Dona Cida* (Fri–Sun only) on Rua do Carmo 22A for *galinha caipira*, small succulent chicken oven-baked with saffron, or else baked in its own blood as *galinha cabidela molho pardo*. For reasonable Italian food, the *Boca do Forno*, on Travesa Santa Cruz (Ⓣ62/3331-1790) is open daily until 11.30pm except Mondays. The *Restaurant Nena* (Ⓣ62/3331-1470), at Rua da

Aurora 4, serves good self-service *comida por kilo* lunches and local dishes. There are small **supermarkets** at Av. Sizenando Jayme 30 and by the river opposite the police station. The best **bars** are down by the river, notably the communally run *Aravinda Bar* on Rua do Rosário 25, a place where beer hogs meet patchouli oil and incense in a very relaxing and friendly way (open Thurs–Sun only; live New Age music Sat night); it also serves food, including excellent *peixa na telha* (fish baked in an earthenware dish).

Tours

A number of guides and agencies offer ecological **tours** of the surrounding region, taking in sites within the Parque Estadal da Serra dos Pirineus and the Reserva Ecologica Vargem Grande. The region boasts many great trails and a host of impressive waterfalls. Sites include the Abade, Inferno and Corumbá waterfalls. Based at Rua Emílio de Carvalho 18 (Ⓣ62/3331-1392), Dinis, who during the week drives a school bus, runs guided ecotours (R$45 for 3–4hr). So do Cerrado Ecoturismo, Rua Bonfim da Serra 46 (Ⓣ62/3331-1240), who are agents for several private wildlife sanctuaries in the region. More alternative guided tours (bicycles a speciality) are offered by Calango Expedições, Bairro do Carmo (Ⓣ62/3331-1564). For rafting try Turismo Aventura (Ⓣ62/3331-3336). Another guide worth contacting, though you'll need your own transport, is silversmith Alcides dos Santos Filho, at Rua Anduzeiro 20 (Ⓣ62/331-1416).

West of Goiânia

Renowned for its religious architecture and historic feel, the town of **Goiás Velho** is the main settlement west of Goiânia. Despite this town's attractions, however, it is shiny and mighty **Rio Araguaia** that brings most visitors to Goiás. Even though most of the river now falls within the state of Tocantins, the Goiás section has hundreds of fine **sandy beaches** suitable for camping, and some well-established resorts, very popular with the residents of Goiânia and other towns in Goiás. Rich in fish, the Araguaia is particularly busy during the dry season from May to September when the water level drops, and serious anglers come from São Paulo and Goiânia to compete. The gateway to the river is **ARUANÃ**, a small town served by only a few hotels, just over 380km northwest of Goiânia.

The **best place to stay**, and as comfortable as hotels come in this town, is the *Pousada Acauá*, Rua José Eufrasio de Lima (Ⓣ & Ⓕ62/3376-1294, Ⓦwww.pousadaacaua.com.br; ④), which has a pool, bar and reasonable restaurant. The *Recanto Sonhado Hotel*, Avenida Altamiro Caio Pacheco (Ⓣ62/3376-1230, reservations Ⓣ62/3212-3955; ④), is also very good, and has a pool, sauna and facilities for jet-skiing. At the same price but with less on offer (you should get a discount) is *Hotel Araguaia*, Praça Couto Magalhães 53 (Ⓣ62/3376-1251; ④), also with a pool. Cheaper still is the *Hotel Do Sesi* (Ⓣ62/3376-1221; ②). You can arrange boat trips to go fishing or rent your own boat in Aruanã, and it's also one of the main ports of access for the Ilha do Bananal (see p.552). In July, the busiest month, it can prove difficult even to get a room.

Goiás Velho

Some 144km northwest of Goiânia, and a six-hour bus ride from Brasília, is the historic town of **GOIÁS VELHO** – originally known as Vila Boa, and now often just called Goiás. Strung along and up a steep valley cut by the Rio

Vermelho, it is one of the most beautiful colonial towns in Brazil, without the great churches and museums of the best of the *cidades históricas* in Minas but easily the equal of any of them in the calm elegance of its cobbled streets and squares, and much their superior in lack of commercialism. Its more remote location well to the north of the country's other eighteenth-century mining zones has made it the best-preserved colonial town in the country. With the effects of a disastrous flood in 2001 now largely repaired, the town is simply gorgeous, fully deserving its recent listing as a UNESCO World Heritage Site.

Founded in 1726 as a gold-mining settlement by the *bandeirantes*, Goiás Velho remained the state capital until 1937. Nowhere else in Brazil is there a stronger sense of the colonial past, palpable in the cobbled streets and the many well-preserved eighteenth- and nineteenth-century buildings. Stone houses and quaint squares, the gaslit town centre and the occasional metallic clip-clop of mule hooves create a timeless atmosphere, one that's enhanced annually during the colourful torchlit Easter Fogareu procession.

There is more than enough here to occupy you for a few days – apart from the town itself, the surrounding countryside is worth exploring, with good hiking amid the trails, waterfalls and swimholes characteristic of the *cerrado*.

In town, you'll find the usual collection of small local museums. The **Palácio Conde dos Arcos**, built in 1755 on the main Praça Dr Tasso de Camargo, was the old governor's palace and has the usual clunky period furniture; the best feature is an attractive Portuguese-style garden (Tues–Sat 8am–5pm, Sun 8am–noon; R$5). The most interesting exhibits are actually more modern, such as a nineteenth-century photo of the great-grandfather of two-term Brazilian president Fernando Henrique Cardoso, proudly pointed out by the museum guide who accompanies you, and the original application documents for their UNESCO World Heritage listing, reverently displayed in a velvet case, though you are allowed to leaf through the supporting photos.

The **Museu das Bandeiras**, situated up the hill on the Praça Brasil Ramos Caiado (Tues–Sat 8am–noon & 1–5pm, Sun 8am–noon; R$2.50), recounts the story of the gold rush through artefacts like slave shackles and chains, but a unique feature here is the building itself, which has a combined governor's office and council chamber upstairs, and jail downstairs – an arrangement typical of early eighteenth-century Brazilian towns. The room to the right of the entrance desk was once part of the jail and has changed very little since it was built.

The town's **Museu de Arte Sacra da Boa Morte**, in the 1779 Igreja da Boa Morte on Praça Dr Tasso de Camargo (Tues–Fri 8–11.30am & 1–5pm, Sat 9am–5pm, Sun 9am–1pm), is not very good; all of the local churches have had their interiors ruined by a combination of fires and misguided "improvements" – the worst example being the slave church of **Rosário dos Pretos** across the river, levelled on its bicentenary in 1934 and replaced by an incongruous Gothic structure. The other local museum worth checking out is the house of **Cora Coralina**, a local poet who never left the town in all of her 96 years of life but used it as raw material and became nationally famous. Located on the corner of Rua Dom Cândido, a colonial street overlooking the Rio Vermelho, the museum (Tues–Sat 9am–5pm, Sun 9am–4pm; R$2) is a hodgepodge of old furniture, photos and manuscripts, giving you a glimpse into small-town life.

Exploring the countryside

If you need to cool off in the afternoon after walking the old city streets, there's a natural swimming pool out by the **Cachoeira Grande waterfalls** on the Rio Vermelho, just 7km east of town – the best (and cheapest) way to get there is on the back of one of the local motorbike taxis. The pool is pleasant when quiet, but it can get crowded at weekends. The most beautiful sight in the area is the **Cachoeira das Andorinhas** (Swallow Waterfall), 8km out of town, which makes for a wonderful day-trip. On the only road out of town, cross the Rio Vermelho, passing by the pretty church of **Igreja de Santa Bárbara**, perched on a small hill overlooking the municipal cemetery. Taking the dirt road to the left of the church (signposted *Hotel Fazenda Manduzanzan*), continue 7km through picturesque hill country until you reach a signposted trail entrance in front of the hotel (❻), which has a pool and offers horse riding. The waterfall is another kilometre from here – when in doubt, always bear left. The last few hundred yards rise steeply through a forested gorge before ending at a glorious, tree-choked swimhole with a waterfall and, true to its name, swallows darting around. A highlight is a natural rock chamber that channels part of the waterfall into a cavern – you can brace against the rock surface and have the cold water pound you into a jelly; exhilarating, especially after a hot walk.

Bear in mind that Goiás is hot year-round, and baking hot in the dry season, so the usual precautions of carrying water, sunscreen and hats apply. To save yourself some effort, consider having a motorbike taxi drop you off at the trail entrance (R$5), thereby halving the distance you need to walk. Consider heading out early for the trek, stopping afterward at the hotel for its excellent lunch (open to non-guests) and a doze in its hammocks, waiting until the sun starts to set and the heat lessens before heading back.

Practicalities

The **rodoviária** (Ⓣ62/3371-1510), which has connections to Goiânia and Anápolis, is down by the river, and most accommodation and eating spots are close by. The town has several good lodging options, including the *Villa Boa Hotel*, Avenida Dr Deusdete Ferreira de Moura (Ⓣ & Ⓕ62/3371-1000; ❻), with a decent pool and sauna; the cheaper and more central *Hotel Serrano*, on the same street, (Ⓣ62/3371-1825; ❸); and the *Araguaia* at no. 8 (Ⓣ62/371-1462; ❸), which is cheaper still. Cheapest of all, but still very pleasant, is *Pousada do Sol* at Rua Americano Brasil 17 (Ⓣ62/3371-1717; ❷). Highly recommended is the more upmarket *Pousada Ipê* (Ⓣ62/3371-2065), on the other side of the river at Rua do Fórum 22, where R$50 gets you essentials such as air conditioning and pool access. The best-value hotel in the centre is *Hotel Casa da Ponte* (Ⓣ62/3371/4467; ❺), on Rua Moretti Foggia right in the heart of town, with air conditioning and TV in all rooms.

For regional **food,** the *Restaurante Caseiro*, Rua D. Cândido 31, is an inexpensive option for lunch. You can also try two excellent local restaurants. *Flor do Ipê*, at Rua Boa Vista 32 (Ⓣ62/3372-1133), which is across the small square from the *Pousada Ipê* (see above), serves a typical regional buffet that includes salads, pork, stewed chicken, okra and regional vegetables like *piquí*, slowly cooked on a traditional wood-fired stove; the restaurant is closed on Mondays but otherwise open for lunch and dinner. For more creative dishes based on local ingredients, the equally good *Beco do Sertão* is very central at Rua 13 de Maio 17 (Ⓣ62/3371-2459) but open only in the evenings. On a clear night the tables in the courtyard are a great place to dine.

The best way to **get around,** other than your own two feet, are the local motorbike taxis; you'll see a stand of them in most squares, and they are usually plentiful around the bus station and its associated market.

Parque Nacional das Emas

Down in the southwestern corner of Goiás state, the **Parque Nacional das Emas** (8am–5pm) is a *cerrado* reserve that was once the domain of zoologists and botanists but is gradually opening up to regular tourism. Located in the central Brazilian highlands near the Mato Grosso do Sul border, the park consists of some 1300 square kilometres of fairly pristine *cerrado*, mostly open grasslands pocked by thousands of termite hills, but with occasional clumps of savanna forest. While it lacks the scenic grandeur of Chapada dos Veadeiros, thanks to its relative isolation the reserve is one of the last places where you can find *cerrado* wildlife in some abundance, supporting an enormous population of **emas** (South American rheas) and also large herds of **veado-campeiro** deer, often shadowed by the solitary **lobo guará** (the maned wolf); all are more easily spotted here than anywhere else in Brazil. The Emas park is also famous for its wide range of variously coloured and extremely large **anthills**, which are used by *coruja-do-campo* owls as lookout posts dotted across the flat plain, and are a good source of food for *bandeira* anteaters. Due to the activity of larvae living inside them, some of the anthills glow phosphorescently green and blue – an amazing sight on a dark night, though you can only catch it in October, when the conditions are right.

It's easy to get to the area by bus from Brasília, but a bit of a logistical challenge once you're here: without a car distances are long, local buses are almost non-existent, and you have to rely on your guide's contacts to get around. As there is no **accommodation** in the park itself, you'll have to base yourself in the small towns of **MINEIROS** or **CHAPADÃO DO CÉU**, though both are a considerable distance from the park; the former, geared more to visitors and with a population of around 43,000 people, is unfortunately 85km away. The latter, only 27km from the park, is more rustic, and much smaller with less than 5000 inhabitants. You'll also need to hire a local guide, who will arrange transport, and the package will set you back around R$150 a day. Within the park, as ever, you are restricted to set trails – although here they traverse most of the park – and camping is not permitted. Beware of *mucuim*, irritating tiny ticks that jump onto legs and leave clumps of fantastically itchy reddish bites; wearing long trousers is your best defence, although this will be a drag in the dry season.

Both Mineiros and Chapadão do Céu have a highly organized association of **local guides**, which should be your first port of call, as they will arrange transport, quote you a price and take care of the formalities with IBAMA, the national parks authority, such as registering entry and exit and paying the R$5 entrance fee (you also have to pay for your guide). Bear in mind that you will rarely be able to set out until the following day, as cars have to be rustled up and drivers found. Given the time it will take to reach the park itself, your best bet is to complete the formalities the day before and set off at dawn the next day. The association in Mineiros is located on Praça Marcelino Roque (Ⓣ64/661-7153, Ⓔednaldo.marelo@bol.com.br), and although the English spoken there is rudimentary, you can get by. In Chapadão do Céu, the association is at Avenida Ema, quadra 51 (Ⓣ64/634-1228); ask for Sr Rubens or Sra Elaine on Ⓣ62/634-1309. A day's hiking with guide and any transport costs is likely to cost between R$50 and R$100 per person, but at the cheaper end for larger groups.

Although there aren't many accommodation options, all are perfectly adequate and cheap. Of the **hotels in Mineiros**, the best is the *Pilões Palace* (Ⓣ64/3661-1547; ❹-❺), on Praça Assis, with its own restaurant and bar. The *Dallas* at 223 Quinta Avenida (Ⓣ64/3661-1534; ❷-❸) has quite comfortable rooms, while the *Líder* (Ⓣ64/3661-1149; ❸) on Rua Elias Machado and *Pinheiros* (❷) on Rua Oito are serviceable if basic. **Accommodation in Chapadão do Céu** is much more basic. In town, your best options are *Hotel Ipe* (Ⓣ64/3634-1722; ❸), Rua Ipe 213, *Pousada das Emas* (Ⓣ64/3634-1382; ❸) on Rua Ipê, and

Hotel Rafael (❷) on Avenida Indaia. Out of town, the *Fazenda Santa Amelia* (Ⓣ64/3634-1380; ❹) has a pool, chalets and apartments, horse-riding and a reasonable restaurant out at Km 65 of the GO-050 road; to find the place take the sign-posted turn-off from the GR-050 for 15km (the last 5km of this is dirt track). As for **dining options**, you'll be limited to a couple of *churrascarias* in each town, plus the hotel restaurants – not *haute cuisine*, but satisfying after a day's hiking. There are direct **buses** to Mineiros from both Brasília and Goiânia, and to Chapadão from Goiânia only.

Caldas Novas and Rio Quente

More easily accessible than many of Goiás's attractions, the adjacent **thermal resorts** of Caldas Novas and Rio Quente, around 185km south of Goiânia, are incredibly popular with Brazilians from beyond the state. Taken together they lay claim to being the world's largest hot-spring aquifers, a massive and very hot natural subterranean reservoir. The healing reputation and the sheer joy of relaxing in the natural spa resorts lure plenty of people from the urban sprawl of the São Paulo region.

CALDAS NOVAS sometimes gets crowded in the dry season, which lasts from May to September, but there are thousands of hotel beds and over seventy hotels (which is over half the hotels in the entire state) within this relatively small town of only around 40,000 people. The town is not very attractive by Brazilian standards, but the therapeutic properties of the waters are said to reduce blood pressure and blood viscosity, dissolve kidney stones, improve digestion, alleviate rheumatic symptoms and even, it is claimed, stimulate endocrine glands and sexual vitality, among other things. While some people do come for long expensive courses of treatment, most visitors are simply here on holiday, relaxing, sunbathing and taking the waters for a few days or a week.

Hotel reservations are best made in advance, usually from Goiânia. Among the better **hotels**, *Thermas di Roma*, Rua São Cristóvão 1110, Solar de Caldas, on the exit for Morrinhos (Ⓣ64/3455-9393, Ⓦwww.diroma.com.br; half board ❻), has a beautiful location out of town with panoramic views, over two hundred rooms, nine thermal pools and a sauna. On the whole, it's excellent value, as is *Taiyo Thermas*, in the town itself at Rua Presidente Castelo Branco 115 (Ⓣ & Ⓕ64/3455-5555, Ⓦwww.hoteltaiyo.com.br; ❺), with three pools and a sauna. Slightly less expensive, but with singles priced the same as doubles, is the smaller *Hotel Roma*, Praça Mestre Orlando 368 (Ⓣ64/3453-1335, Ⓦwww.hotelroma.com.br; ❺), which has six thermal pools. Cheaper still are *Hotel Triângulo*, Av. Orozimbo Correia Neto 157 (Ⓣ & Ⓕ64/3453-1709, Ⓦwww.hoteltriangulo.com.br; ❹), with only one pool, although the waters are no doubt just as efficacious as elsewhere, and *Hotel Santa Clara*, Rua América 226 (Ⓣ64/3453-1764; ❷), which lacks a pool, but has reasonable rooms. For **camping**, *CCB-GO-2*, 4km along the road for Ipameri (Ⓣ64/3223-6561), is in a beautiful location, and there is a designated site at Lagoa Quente (Ⓣ64/3453-1250), on the road to Pires do Rio at Km 5, around 8km from town. As for **restaurants**, the better hotels have their own, but you could also try the *Restaurante Papas* at Praça Mestre Orlando 12, which serves a wide variety of Brazilian dishes. **Tourist information** is available from the Sebrae office, on the Praça Mestre Orlando (daily 9am–6pm; Ⓣ64/3454-3524), and for banking needs, head to the Banco do Brasil at Rua Santos Dumont 55. For information on **buses**, go to the *rodoviária* or call Ⓣ64/3453-1135.

Nearby **RIO QUENTE**, quieter and more relaxing than Caldas Novas, consists of a huge hotel complex attached to a small service town of just under three thousand inhabitants. The main feature, the *Rio Quente Resorts* complex (Ⓣ62/3512-8000, reservations Ⓣ11/3888-8300, Ⓦwww.rioquenteresorts.com.br; ❼), offers superb-quality accommodation in two hotels: the four-star *Hotel Pousada* and the five-star *Hotel Turismo*. The whole complex is arranged around a natural hydrothermal spa, and in high season the minimum stay is two nights, with cheaper (but still ❼) four-day packages offered Sunday to Wednesday.

Parque Nacional Chapada dos Veadeiros

The **Parque Nacional Chapada dos Veadeiros** in the north of Goiás is the heart of the *planalto*, its stunning natural scenery among the most beautiful and distinctive in Brazil. The hundreds of square kilometres of wild and sparse vegetation, extraordinary geological formations, cave systems, waterfalls and hiking trails make this one of the best destinations for **ecotourism** in the country. A few hours north from Brasília and easily accessible by bus, the park has good local support for tourism, and apart from the occasional holidaying diplomat up from the capital, it is still remarkably unknown as a destination to foreign tourists. Note that visitors to the park must be accompanied by a guide – for details see p.540.

Alto Paraíso

The main point of arrival for visitors to the park is **ALTO PARAÍSO DE GOIÁS**, some 240km north of Brasília and connected by regular buses; see the "Travel Details" section at the end of this chapter. The town, which lives largely on the profits of ecotourism, is also overcrowded with spiritualists, clairvoyants,

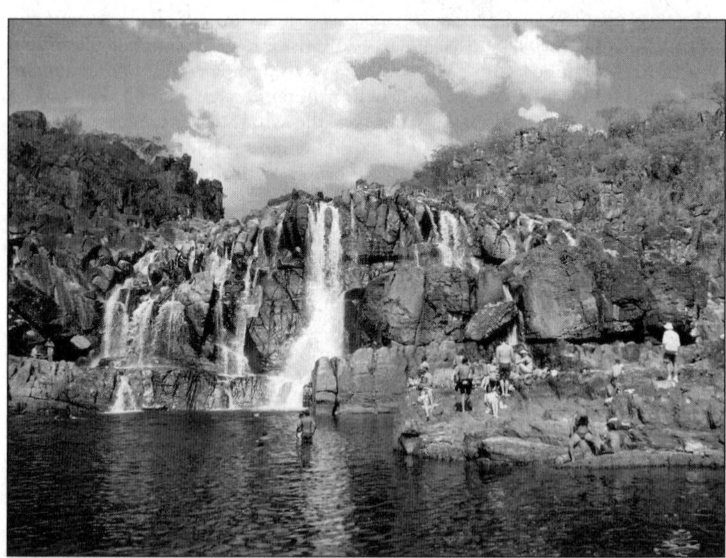

△ Parque Nacional Chapada dos Veadeiros

astrologers and UFO-seekers – fun at first but tedious for any length of time. Alto Paraíso is a base from which to explore the surrounding countryside more than a place to hang out in itself. If you really want to explore the Chapada, your best bet is to take the bus to the village of São Jorge (see p.549), which is much closer to the national park and the best hiking, but if you have only limited time the countryside around Alto Paraíso is also rewarding.

If you are on a tight schedule, you're better off having one of the local **ecotourism agencies** arrange everything for you; they offer a wide menu of day hikes into the countryside, and charge from around R$120–150 per head per day. One reliable agency is Travessia Ecoturismo at Ary Valadão 979 (Ⓣ62/3446-1595, Ⓦwww.travessiatur.com.br); others include Alpatur (Ⓣ62/3446-1820) and Alternativas Ecoturismo (Ⓣ62/3446-1000). There are many new agencies starting up, so if you're in doubt, it may be best to ask for advice at the **tourist information** office – the Centro de Atendimento ao Turista (Mon–Sat 9am–6pm; Ⓣ62/3446-1159), close to the *rodoviária* on Avenida Ari Valadao – for advice on **guides**. The contact number for the National Park office is Ⓣ61/3459-3388. You can pick up maps of the park at the tourist office as well as the worthwhile booklet *Guia da Chapada dos Veadeiros* (R$7.50), a comprehensive listing of all the hikes and accommodation options in and around the park, organized by town, and one of the few such publications with a good English translation. Also spend a few cents on the invaluable map *O Melhor da Chapada dos Veadeiros*, which is based on a satellite image and has all the region's roads and main sights marked.

If you want to **hike on your own**, your best bet is to walk 4km up the GO-118 road north of the town, and then take the signposted dirt road right another 3km to the **Cristal waterfall**. The Cristal is at the head of a beautiful valley, where a series of swimming holes and small waterfalls have been created by a cool mountain stream as it plunges into the valley.

You will be spoilt for choice for **accommodation**. Most hotels are concentrated on the central Avenida Ary Valadão; best of these are the *Hotel Central*, the *Nunes* and the *Tradição*, all very reasonably priced in the US$15–25 range, while the most kitsch is the *Camelot Inn* (GO-118 road at km 168, about 1km from town; Ⓣ62/3446-1449), a Monty Pythonesque fake medieval castle, opposite the exit to the town centre. Slightly away from the centre is the city's best hotel, the *Europa*, at Rua 1 Quadra 7, Setor Planalto, not far from the bus station (❸). Dozens of *pousadas* cater to ecotourists and weekend trippers from Brasília (all ❷–❸). Recommended are the upmarket *Pousada Alfa & Ômega*, Rua Joaquim de Almeida 15 (Ⓣ62/3446-1225, Ⓦwww.veadeiros.com.br); the New-Agey *Aquárius* (Ⓣ62/3446-1952) further up the same street at no. 326; the *Pousada Maya* (Ⓣ62/3446-1200) at Rua Coleto Paulino 732, even more New Age but very comfortable; and *Pousada do Sol* (Ⓣ62/3446-1201), Rua Gumercindo Barbosa. The *Pousada Camelot Inn* (Ⓣ62/3446-1449, Ⓦwww.pousadacamelot.com.br; ❺) offers great value, with pool, bar, sauna and very comfortable rooms. Several **campgrounds** are located on the edge of town; the tourist office will have details on these. **Restaurants** are equally thick on the ground, especially on Ary Valadão; all are very similar, but the lunchtime salad bar at the *Clube da Esquina* stands out and the Italian *Massas da Mamma*, Rua S. Jose Operario 305 (Ⓣ62/3446-1362), is pretty good for pizzas and pasta and the ambience is pleasant enough.

São Jorge

Alto Paraíso is really only an introduction to Chapada dos Veadeiros; to really get to grips with it you need to head 37km further up a good-quality dirt road to the small village of **SÃO JORGE**, which is next to the only entrance to the national park. From Alto Paraíso, there is one daily bus from the *rodoviária* (☎62/3446-1359), Empresa São Jorge, leaving daily at 4pm, and a more irregular Kombi run by a São Jorge tourist agency; ask at the Alto Paraíso tourist office for details.

From the village, you can either hike into the national park or explore the truly spectacular countryside around São Jorge, which is dotted with waterfalls, strange geological formations and natural swimholes – best are the otherworldly rock formations of the **Vale da Lua**, and the swimholes and waterfalls of **Raizama** and **Morada do Sol**, both a short drive or a two-hour hike away.

Looking around São Jorge, you can see the potential that ecotourism has to protect landscapes and generate jobs and income at the same time. Before the creation of the national park in 1980, the main industry hereabouts was the mining of rock crystals. When the practice was eventually made illegal in and around the park, the parks authority, prodded and helped by the **World Wildlife Fund**, recognized the need to create jobs linked to the park and invested heavily in training local ex-miners to be guides – the perfect guides, since no one picked over every remote nook and cranny of the landscape quite like them. So there is a good reason why IBAMA, the federal parks authority, makes it compulsory for visitors to the park to be accompanied by a guide.

Practicalities

The **tourist office** (Mon–Sat 9am–6pm ☎62/3446-1090 and 3446-1159), which provides some useful maps, is located in a modern pavilion at the village entrance, and all restaurant and accommodation options are within five minutes of the village centre, where the bus sets you down.

Despite its small size, São Jorge has no shortage of **accommodation**. The most upmarket option, the *Pousada Casa das Flores* (reservations advisable, ☎62/3455-1055, Ⓦwww.pousadadasflores.com.br; ❺), includes very high-quality breakfast and lunch in the rates, while the pool, candlelit rooms and smoochy live music in the evenings make this a great place for a romantic weekend. More reasonably priced are several very pleasant *pousadas*, including *Trilha Violeta,* Rua 12, qd. 7, Lote 5 (☎62/3455-1088; ❸), *Recanto da Paz* (☎61/646-1983; ❸) and *Pousada Palipalan* (on block 2 of Rua 2, ☎62/3455-1005; ❹; reservations required). There are also a large number of campsites and rooms from US$5 upwards. At all times of the year, if you're planning to stay in one of the *pousadas*, it's a good idea to ring ahead and make a reservation – most of them have a Brasília-based reservation service. At holiday periods, especially Carnaval and the New Year, São Jorge fills up and can be noisy. Bear in mind as well that at the height of the dry season (September), the village has been known to run out of water.

The best **food** in town can be found at *Papalua*, located on Rua 12 (block 7, Lote. 8, ☎62/3455-1085; open for dinner daily except Thurs). Its varied menu covers Brazilian and international dishes. For good cheap meals check out *Bar do Pelé*, in the centre; other central options include the *Casa das Flores* restaurant, which is open to non-guests, and a couple of pizzerias.

As for **finding a guide**, in the unlikely event that locals don't come touting for business where you're staying, let the owner know you're interested and someone should be there within a few minutes. Guides charge a daily rate of around US$12, not including the entrance fees to the national park, if you choose to hike there. If you want to go on a long hike outside the park, it's still a good idea to hire a guide to make sure you don't get lost.

Hiking in the park

Visitors to the park are restricted to two **trails** in its southern corner, both 10km long and each a day's worth of exploring. Although you'll only see a fraction of the park, this area is scenically the most spectacular, an unforgettable blend of hills and cliff-faces (mostly in the middle distance; fortunately you don't have to climb them), plunging waterfalls, swimholes and forests. You encounter the full range of *cerrado* vegetations as well: *veredas* (open moorlands lined by *buriti* palms), *floresta de galeria* (full-sized deciduous forest along watercourses) and *campo sujo* (the classic, shrubby savanna characteristic of Africa).

Of the two trails, one includes the park's main highlight – the marvellous **Salto do Rio Preto**, where two separate waterfalls plunge almost 130m into a pool 440m across. The trail's other notable sight is the **Pedreiras**, a series of natural rock pools. On the other trail, the highlight is Salto **Cariocas falls**, a series of falls with a sand beach at the top, and you will also pass **Canion 1 e 2**, two canyons cut by the Rio Preto and lined with granite cliffs.

Your guide's first stop will be the IBAMA office to register entry and pay the fee (R$5 a head); you are responsible for your guide's fee. Take plenty of water and enough food for a day (agree beforehand whether or not you will be providing your guide's food as well), and stick to the trails, taking your rubbish home with you, and, most importantly, in the dry season **do not smoke**. Fires are the worst problem the park has, and the vegetation is tinder-dry between July and October. Bringing a change of clothes and swimwear is a good idea as you'll be cooling off in swimholes between treks.

Hikes around São Jorge

Hiking options around São Jorge are less strenuous than in the national park, but still scenically spectacular. You could easily spend a week doing a series of rewarding day hikes without even entering the national park, and for those travelling with children, for whom the long hikes in the park are not realistic, these shorter hikes are a great family outing. All destinations are reached by heading along the road that passes the village, either west or east – that is, towards or away from Alto Paraíso.

The most striking hike around São Jorge leads to **Vale da Lua**, a forested valley where the river São Miguel has carved a narrow canyon through an extraordinary series of sculptured granite curves. To get there from the village, head to the main road and continue 4km east – in the direction of Alto Paraíso. On your right you come to a signposted trail into the Vale da Lua. There is a nominal entrance fee; you can either follow the trail directly to a swimhole, or else peel left, along a different route towards the swimhole, by walking down the valley, which is the best route to see the extraordinary geology of the valley. Flash floods can be a problem here in the rainy season, given the narrowness of the gorge, so exercise caution.

Back at São Jorge, heading in the opposite direction, away from Alto Paraíso, will take you, in quick succession, to **Raizama**, a beautiful gorge with a series of swimholes and waterfalls, and **Morada do Sol**, which has less spectacular waterfalls, but more spectacular views up and down the valley. Another 5km up the main road will bring you to a private estate, **Água Quente**, where the owner has channelled a natural warm spring – tepid rather than hot – into a couple of large pools, making this a wonderful place to soak and recover from the walk. All of the above destinations charge a R$2.50–5 entrance fee.

Tocantins

Created in 1989, the **state of Tocantins** is not an obvious geographical or cultural unit, merely a political and bureaucratic invention. Most visitors pass through the region rather than spend time around the state's hot and flyblown towns. Apart from the main north–south artery, the BR-153 highway, **transport** is difficult, and getting to the state's main attraction – the **Ilha do Bananal** – can be an expensive headache unless you're taking a guided tour (usually from Goiânia or Barra do Garças on the Mato Grosso border). As Brazilians catch on to the attractions of ecotourism, however, things are bound to change, and probably quite rapidly. The few options that do exist for the independent traveller are detailed below.

The Ilha do Bananal

Most travellers spending time in Tocantins come to explore the **Ilha do Bananal** and the **Parque Nacional do Araguaia** in the island's northern reaches, an emerging ecotourist destination. Bananal is the world's largest river island, over 300km long from head to tail, and is home to the intrepid, canoe-faring Karajá tribe, still renowned for their fine feather craftsmanship and clay dolls. You will need **permission** to enter the park from IBAMA, which is easiest to arrange through an association of local guides; for details see p.546.

Although designated a national park, the Ilha do Bananal has lost over fifty percent of its area to settlers and development. In 1958, the British explorer Robin Hanbury-Tenison visited the island and its communities of several thousand Indians and witnessed two shamans performing ritual dances. Yet just thirteen years later there were only eight hundred Indians left on the island, and today the few hundred survivors are far outnumbered by the many thousands of non-Indian Brazilian settlers – traditional Indian dances are rarely performed except on official state occasions. This apart, it's an easy place to immerse yourself in the wonders of the forest. **Wildlife** is varied and plentiful, and it's even possible to spot a maned wolf or otters if you've the time to spend searching during the rainy season. However, as there are no roads on the island, travel is only possible by boat, which means either renting one, with a boatman as guide, in one of the few settlements on the island fringes or in Aruanã (see p.543), or else taking an **organized tour** from Barra do Garças on the Mato Grosso border (see p.607) or from one of the big cities. Travel agents in Goiânia (see p.540) and Brasília (see p.532) can put together tours; in São Paulo, Iate Clube, Rua Maurício Jaquei 62 (Rudge Ramos), São Bernardo do Campo (Ⓣ11/3457-3277), offers fishing trips on the Rio Cristalino, a tributary of the Araguaia, including stays in their four-bed cabins in the park. The cabins on Bananal and a few *pousadas* at São Félix Do Araguaia (see opposite) are the best accommodation options.

Access to the southern part of the island is usually from **SÃO MIGUEL DO ARAGUAIA**, some 480km northwest of Goiânia, where the Rio Araguaia starts to split to form the boundaries of the island. Nearby, the picturesque fishing port of **Porto Luís Alves** functions as the starting point on the river, and has a couple of good but expensive **accommodation** options: try the *Hotel Mirante do Araguaia* (Ⓣ62/3382-1155; ❺), which has boats for hire, or the *Pousada do Pescador* (Ⓣ62/3382-3100; ❺), which has a pool, sauna and information on boat trips, especially for fishing. You should also try the boat crews themselves at the docks for possible river journeys (from R$500 per day for a boat carrying up to eight people). São Miguel is much cheaper for accommodation.

Outstanding value, with good, clean rooms, all with TVs and fridges, is *Pousada Luz do Araguaia*, Rua 12, no. 371, Setor Oeste (Ⓣ62/3382-1122; ❸); singles are especially cheap here. Another good option is the *Hotel Paraíso*, Av. José Pereira Nascimento 317 (Ⓣ62/3382-1061; ❷). There are daily overnight **buses** to São Miguel and Porto Luís Alves from Goiânia.

Further north, facing the island about halfway along its western edge, is the port of **SÃO FÉLIX DO ARAGUAIA**. The only settlement of any size around the island, São Félix is one of the few places where you can buy much from stores, and there's also a nice beach, the **Praia do Morro**, 2km north of town. The *Pousada Kuryala*, 20km away on the São Antônio road, is a good if expensive base (❼); you can make reservations at their Goiânia office on Avenida República do Líbano (Ⓣ62/3215-1313). The *Hotel Xavante*, Av. Severiano Neves 391 (Ⓣ65/3522-1305; ❷), is more central and much better value. For boat trips, ask at the port along Avenida Araguaia. Irregular **buses** link the town with Barra do Garças along the BR-158. São Félix is also served by **air taxis** from Brasília and Goiânia, which you can arrange at the airstrip itself (from around R$300).

Some 150km further north is **SANTA TEREZINHA**, the nearest point of access to the Parque Nacional do Araguaia. There are no facilities for tourists as yet, and access to the town is along a very bad dirt road or else by air. As there are no bus services, you could try hitching a lift from Santana do Araguaia (300km north), which is connected by bus to Araguaína.

Much easier to reach is the small settlement of **PARAÍSO DO TOCANTINS**, another base for visiting the northern section of Ilha do Bananal and the Parque Nacional do Araguaia. Located due west of Palmas on the BR-153, the settlement has one excellent-value hotel, *Serrano's Park*, Av. Bernardo Sayão 250 (Ⓣ63/3602-1410, Ⓕ3602-1463; ❹), with a pool and sauna. From Paraíso, a long dirt road runs to the settlement of **Araguaçui**, 200km northwest on the Rio Araguaia, from

△ Parque Nacional do Araguaia

where it should be possible to hitch a lift on a boat south along one of the two rivers flanking the Ilha do Bananal. Alternatively, another dirt road swings off west from the BR-153 some 40km south of Paraíso to connect with the even smaller settlement of **Barreira da Cruz** on the eastern side of the Ilha; here there are no facilities at all for visitors and the success of your trip will depend entirely on your skills in negotiating boat rental and guides with local *fazendeiros*.

Palmas

The capital state of **PALMAS** has held this title since only 1989. Home to almost 190,000 residents, it lies just under 1000km north of Brasília and just over 1200km south of Belém. The town itself, which has long, wide avenues and a pleasant average temperature of around 27°C, is inconveniently set back on the banks of the Rio Tocantins, some 150km by minor roads from the main Brasília–Belém highway BR-153, and there's little reason to come here. If you do get stuck in Palmas, the best **hotel** is the *Rio do Sono*, ACSUSO 10, conjunto 1, Lote 10 (Ⓣ & Ⓕ63/3219-6800, Ⓦwww.hotelriodosono.com.br; ⑤), with nice bright rooms and a pool. Slightly cheaper, but also with a pool, is *Casa Grande*, Av. Joaquim Teotônio Sugurado, ACSUSO 20, conj. 1, Lote 1 (Ⓣ & Ⓕ63/3215-1813, Ⓦwww.hotelcasagrandepalmas.cjb.net; ④).

Araguaína

Lying 400km north of Palmas, **ARAGUAÍNA** is many times larger, but no more attractive a place to stay. It dominates the road network in northern Tocantins, located as it is almost exactly halfway between the Araguaia and Tocantins rivers. If you do end up staying here, perhaps while changing from one bus to another, there are a few possible **places to stay**. The best is some 7km from town, the *Olyntho*, BR-153 Sul, Km 125, Gurupi exit (Ⓣ & Ⓕ63/3415-7600; ③–④) based on a ranch. *Araguatins*, at Av. Tocantins 250 (Ⓣ63/3415-7500; ③) is a little cheaper and beside the *rodoviária*. For **restaurants**, *Maresia's*, Rua das Mangueiras 868, has fine fish dishes; the *Estancia Gaúcha*, at Praça Pio XII 33 (Ⓣ63/3242-8731) serves good *rodizio* and specializes in meat dishes.

Travel details

Buses

Brasília to: Alto Paraíso (2 daily; 3hr); Anápolis (every 30min); Belém (2 daily; 36hr); Belo Horizonte (7 daily; 14hr); Cristalina (3 daily; 2hr); Cuiabá (6 daily; 20hr); Formosa: (8 daily; 2hr); Goiânia (every 30min; 2hr 30min); Pirenópolis (6 daily; 3hr); Recife (1 daily; 48hr); Rio (6 daily; 20hr); Salvador (1 daily; 26hr); São Paulo (7 daily; 16hr).
Goiânia to: Brasília (every 30min; 2hr 30min); Alto Paraíso: (1 daily; 6hr); Palmas (6-8 daily; 9hr); Caldas Novas (8 daily, 3hr).

Planes

Brasília is second only to Rio and São Paulo for number and frequency of flights, although they are exclusively domestic. There are direct flights to most state capitals, and the rest are reachable after one stop. Flights to Rio and São Paulo average at least one an hour throughout the day; several flights daily to the state capitals of southern and northeastern Brazil. If you are heading to the Amazon, there are four flights daily to Belém and Manaus, but other Amazonian state capitals have only one or two flights daily, leaving in the evening. TAM, Varig, and Gol all serve Brasília.

7

Mato Grosso

CHAPTER 7

Highlights

* **Piranha fishing** Fish for your supper with a simple line and hook; the peaceful town of Coxim is a good place to arrange fishing trips, though piranha can be caught easily in pools and lakes throughout the Pantanal. See p.568

* **Aquário Natural** A spectacular river pool near the sleepy town of Bonito, offering good opportunities for snorkelling among a wide range of tropical fish. This region is also great for other adventure and eco pursuits, including white water rafting, caving, trekking and horse-riding. See p.575

* **Bais do Chop** The perfect spot to enjoy an ice-cold beer, this waterfront restaurant/bar in Corumbá also plays excellent live music at weekends. See p.580

* **The Pantanal** The largest concentration of wildlife in the whole of the Americas; a terrific place to spend a few days on eco-safari to see jungle mammals, exotic birds and caiman in the wild. See p.583

* **Chapada dos Guimarães** A breathtaking plateau with a pleasant small town, lots of trails, and the geodesic centre of South America. See p.601

△ A Pantanal fisherman

7

Mato Grosso

Very Brazilian, in both its vastness and its frontier culture, the **Mato Grosso** region is essentially an enormous plain, home to the sprawling Pantanal swamp and rippled by a handful of small mountain ranges. Equally Brazilian, there's a firm political boundary, a line on a map, across the heart of the swamp (the best place in Brazil for seeing wildlife and one of the world's largest wetlands), marking the competing ambitions of two mammoth states: **Mato Grosso** and **Mato Grosso do Sul**. The latter state, the northern half of the region, is sparsely populated, with the only settlements of any size – Cuiabá, Rondonópolis and Cáceres – having a combined population of around one and a half million. The name Mato Grosso, which means "thick wood", is more appropriate to this northernmost state, where thorny scrubland passes into tropical rainforest and the land begins its incline towards the Amazon, interrupted only by the beautiful uplifted plateau of the Chapada dos Guimarães.By contrast, most of the state of Mato Grosso do Sul, which is marginally more populous, is either seasonal flood plain or open scrubland. To the west of Mato Grosso do Sul are Bolivian swamps and forest; the mighty rivers **Araguaia** and **Paraná** (one flowing north, the other south) form a natural rim to the east, while the **Rio Paraguai** and the country named after it complete the picture to the south.

The simple road network and the limited sprinkling of settlements make **getting about** within Mato Grosso fairly hard work. Distances are enormous, and, although most of the buses and trunk roads are in relatively good condition, any journey is inevitably a long one. That said, the variety of landscape alone – from swamps and forests to cattle ranches, riverine villages and Indian reservations – makes the trip a unique one and, for the adventurous traveller, it's well worth the effort given the options for exploring wilderness and wildlife.

The cities of Mato Grosso are particularly deceptive. Although surprisingly modern and developed, they've only recently received the full trappings of civilization. Portuguese colonists began to settle in the region fairly late, at the time of the great **Cuiabá** gold rush of the early eighteenth century, though Cuiabá town itself remained almost completely isolated from the rest of Brazil until its first telegraph link was installed in the 1890s. Masterminded and built by a local boy made good – a down-to-earth army officer named Rondon – the telegraph lines were Mato Grosso's first real attempt to join the outside world. Since the 1980s, with the completion of Highway BR-364, Cuiabá has again become a staging post for pioneers, this time for thousands of Brazilian peasants in search of land or work in the western Amazon states of Rondônia (named after the same local boy) and Acre.

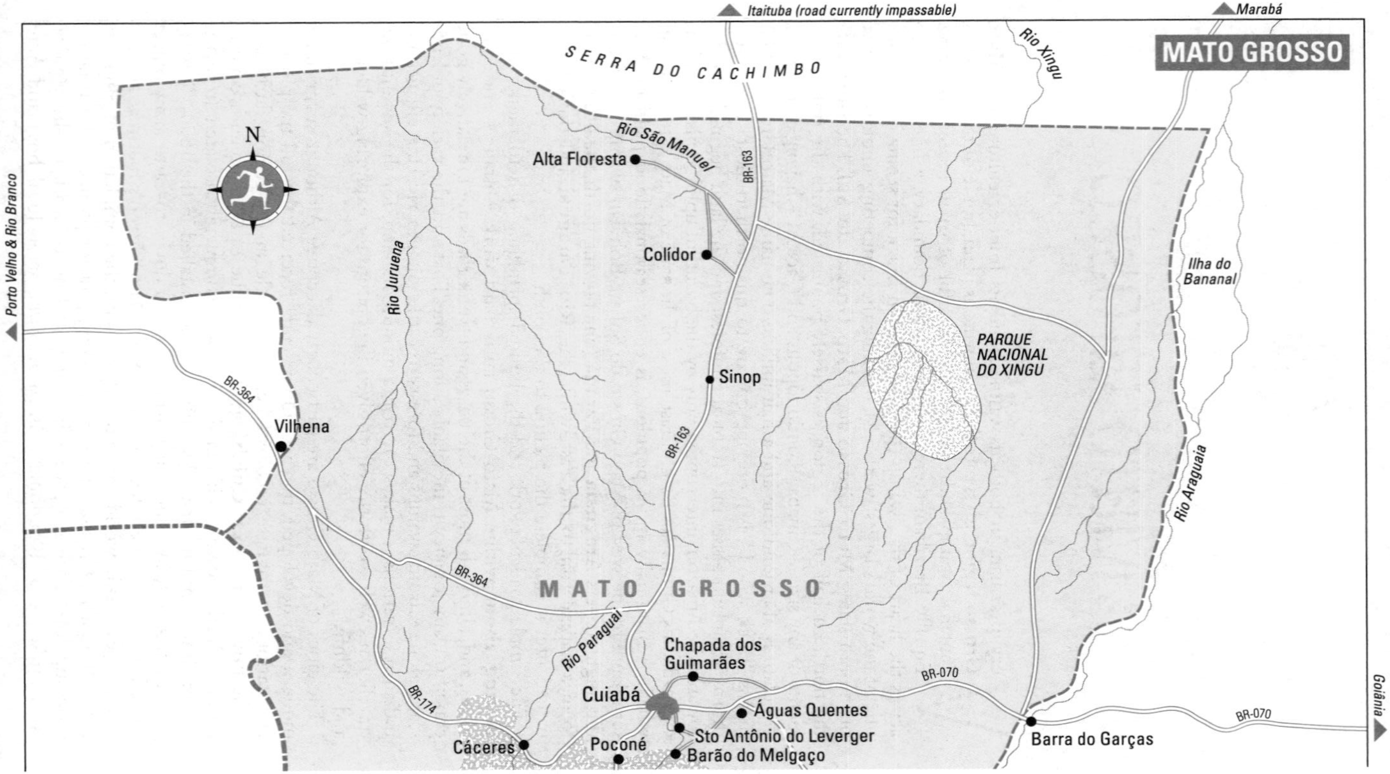

MATO GROSSO

Itaituba (road currently impassable)
Marabá
Porto Velho & Rio Branco
Goiânia
SERRA DO CACHIMBO
Rio Xingu
Rio São Manuel
Rio Juruena
Rio Paraguai
Rio Araguaia
Ilha do Bananal
PARQUE NACIONAL DO XINGU
N
Alta Floresta
Colídor
Sinop
Vilhena
MATO GROSSO
BR-163
BR-364
BR-174
BR-070
Chapada dos Guimarães
Cuiabá
Águas Quentes
Sto Antônio do Leverger
Barão do Melgaço
Poconé
Cáceres
Barra do Garças

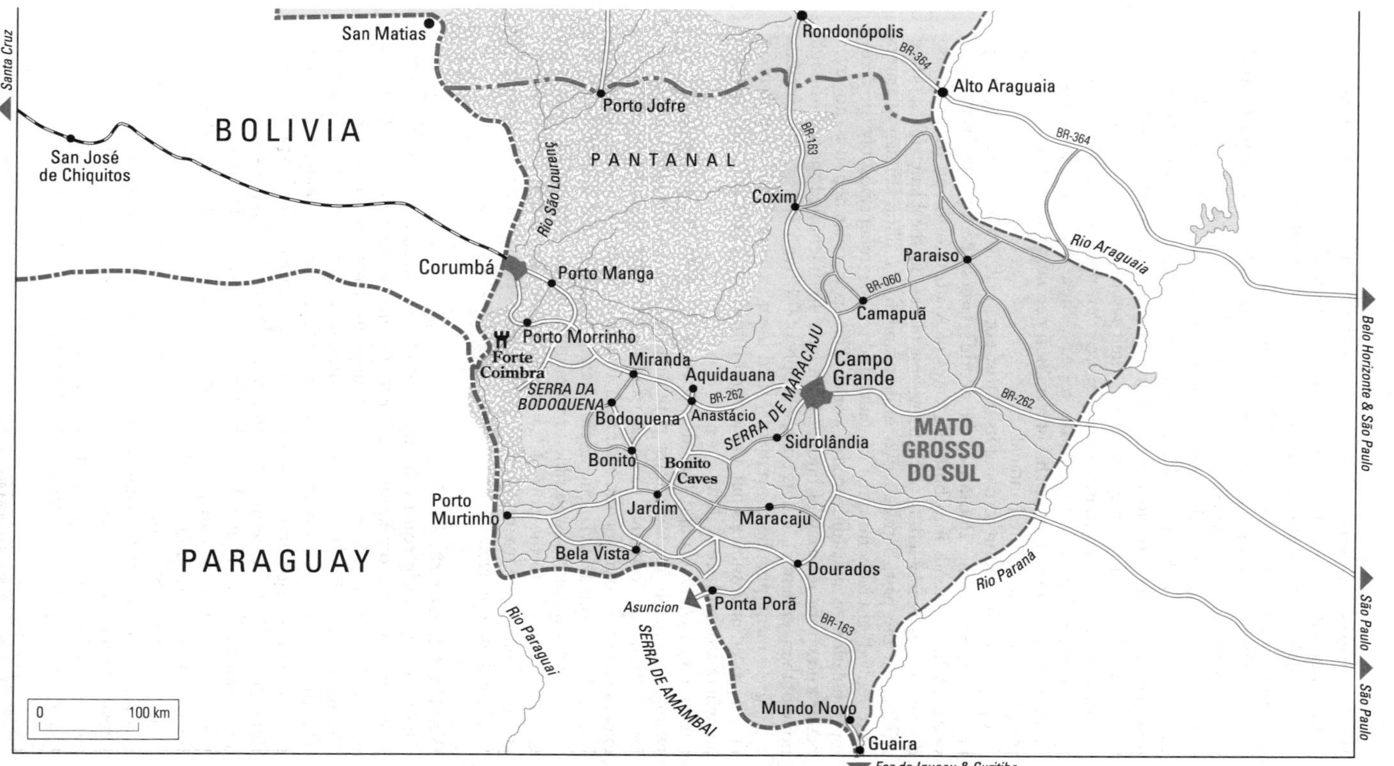
Belo Horizonte & São Paulo
São Paulo
São Paulo
Santa Cruz
Foz do Iguaçu & Curitiba
BOLIVIA
PARAGUAY
MATO GROSSO DO SUL
PANTANAL
San Matias
Rondonópolis
BR-364
Alto Araguaia
Porto Jofre
BR-163
San José de Chiquitos
Rio São Lourenç
Coxim
Rio Araguaia
Paraiso
BR-060
Camapuã
Corumbá
Porto Manga
Porto Morrinho
Forte Coimbra
Miranda
Aquidauana
Campo Grande
SERRA DE MARACAJU
SERRA DA BODOQUENA
BR-262
Anastácio
Bodoquena
Sidrolândia
Bonito
Bonito Caves
Jardim
Maracaju
Porto Murtinho
Bela Vista
Dourados
Rio Paraná
Asuncion
Ponta Porã
Rio Paraguai
SERRA DE AMAMBAI
Mundo Novo
Guaira
0
100 km

While Cuiabá can't exactly claim to be a resort town – it's highly urbanized with a high-rise city centre as well as an old colonial nucleus of streets – it is, nevertheless, a natural stepping stone for exploring either the Pantanal, or the mountainous scenery of the Chapada dos Guimarães.

Until 1979 Cuiabá was capital of the entire Mato Grosso. **Campo Grande** in the south, however, was also growing rapidly and playing an increasingly important financial and administrative role within Brazil. When the old state was sliced very roughly in half, Campo Grande became capital of the brand-new state of **Mato Grosso do Sul**. This tightening of political control over the various Mato Grosso regions reflects their rapid development and relative wealth – a complete contrast to the poorer, even more expansive and much more remote wilderness of the Amazon basin. These days Campo Grande is a bustling, very modern city of almost a million people, with most visitors stopping here en route to the Pantanal.

Topographically, and in terms of its tourist potential, Mato Grosso will always be dominated by the **Pantanal**, the world's largest contiguous wetland or swamp, which extends into both the states of Mato Grosso and Mato Grosso do Sul, and is renowned as one of the best places on the planet for spotting wildlife. In the past, between two million and five million caiman alligators were "culled" annually from the Pantanal, and today it retains possibly the densest population of alligatoids in the world. This spectacular region is, however, better known for its array of birdlife, with over 464 identified species (though none of them endemic), and its endless supply of fish, with 325 species – including a great many piranha conveniently used in an excellent local soup dish. So far it's proved impossible to put a road right through the Pantanal, and travelling anywhere around here is slow.

After Cuiabá and Campo Grande, **Corumbá**, on the western edge of the swamp, is probably the next most popular urban destination and a good base for the Pantanal. Compared to Cuiabá and the northern areas, it's usually a less expensive entry point for the swamp. A relatively small city, Corumbá is only half an hour from Bolivia, but seven or eight from Campo Grande, the nearest Brazilian outpost. It is possible to travel through the Pantanal by river from Corumbá, directly to the port of Cáceres near Cuiabá, though unless you can afford a tailor-made luxury tour this adventurous fluvial route takes at least a week, and often longer.

Getting around

There are three main **routes** through Mato Grosso. Coming from the east and south, two roads fan out around the main Pantanal swamplands in tweezer-like form and run east to west: the most heavily used road, the BR-364 through Cuiabá, and the BR-262, which runs through Campo Grande to Corumbá. The third road, the BR-163, runs from south to north, connecting Campo Grande with Cuiabá and overland routes north to Alta Floresta and beyond through much of the central Amazon and to Santarém (impassable by buses) and south to Paraguay and Asunción. Given the distances involved, anyone in possession of a Brazilian **air pass**, or simply limited by time, might well consider the occasional plane hop.

Mato Grosso do Sul is officially one hour behind the standard **time** of Brasília and the coast. In Campo Grande, however, not everybody operates on Mato Grosso do Sul time, so it's always a good idea to synchronize with the right authority when arranging bus or plane reservations. Mato Grosso and Cuiabá, to the north, operate on standard Brasília time.

Mato Grosso do Sul

A fairly new state, **Mato Grosso do Sul** is nevertheless considered to be one of Brazil's better-established economic regions. It has a distinct cowboy flavour: here, close to the border with Paraguay and just a bit further from Argentinian *gaucho* territory, it's not uncommon to end up drinking *maté* sitting on a horse under the shade of a tree by day or dancing Spanish polkas through the night in some of the region's bars. Until the eighteenth century the whole region was Indian territory and was considered an inhospitable corner of the New World. A hundred and fifty years and numerous bloody battles later, Mato Grosso do Sul might now be developed and "civilized" but – thankfully – it's still a place where you can forget about industrial ravages and wonder at nature's riches. The downside is that the Brazilian Ministry of Health recommend yellow fever innoculations for this area.

The state capital, **Campo Grande**, is a useful base from which to delve deeper into Mato Grosso do Sul or to expore one of the largest and most beautiful wetlands in the world. The road connection to Corumbá, a frontier settlement on the edge of both the swamp and Bolivia, is well served by daily buses, and some tour companies operate from here, so reaching the depths of the Pantanal is fairly easy. The swamp, however, is vast, so whilst you can also get a feel for what it's like from a variety of road-linked places closer to Campo Grande – like **Coxim**, north of the city, or **Aquidauana**, to the west – exposure to the flora and fauna is best off road.

The south of the state is favoured by the beautiful hills of the **Serra da Bodoquena** and **Serra da Maracaju** and, deep in the Bodoquena hills, you can visit the spectacular cave systems, forests and rivers of the **Bonito** area, another major destination in itself. Further south, 319km from Campo Grande, **Ponta Porã** sits square on the Paraguayan border, from where there's a two-day overland route to Asunción. There are also several daily bus services from Campo Grande via **Dourados** and **Mundo Novo** to Guaira and the amazing falls of Foz do Iguaçu in the neighbouring state of Paraná.

Campo Grande

Nicknamed the "brunette city" because of its chestnut-coloured earth, **CAMPO GRANDE** has in the last forty years been transformed from an insignificant settlement into a buzzing metropolis with a population of over 700,000. Founded in 1889, the city was only made the capital of the new state of Mato Grosso do Sul in the late 1970s, since when it has almost doubled in size, though it retains a distinctly rural flavour: its downtown area manages to combine sky-scraping banks and apartment buildings with ranchers' general stores and poky little shops selling strange forest herbs and Catholic *ex votos*. Reminiscent in parts of quiet southern US cities, it's a relatively salubrious market centre for an enormous cattle-ranching region, as well as being an important centre of South American trade routes from Paraguay, Bolivia, Argentina and the south of Brazil. A pioneering place, many of the early twentieth-century settlers here were Arabs, who have since gone mostly into business; there is also a large Japanese section of the immigrant population, which has left its mark on the local culinary trade. The city has a number of

The Campo Grande railroad

Look at any map of the region and you'll see a thin black line tracing the path of a long railroad that connects São Paulo on the Atlantic with Campo Grande, where it forks to Corumbá on the Bolivian border, and to Ponta Porã on the Paraguayan frontier. Unfortunately, the privatization of the Brazilian railways has led to the closure of all passenger lines west of Bauru, perhaps forever. This is a real shame, not least because the Corumbá line formed part of an even longer rail system, connecting with the Bolivian *Tren de los Mortes* to Santa Cruz, from where it's still possible to continue by train into Chile or via La Paz into Peru, over Lake Titicaca (by boat or around it on a bus) and on to Cuzco. There seems little chance in the immediate future of the lines being reopened (though freight trains are still running), but with ever-increasing tourist interest in the Pantanal and Mato Grosso do Sul, we can only hope that services may in the course of time resume.

splendidly planned *praças* and parks bringing large, leafy trees and wild birds from the countryside into the modern centre.

An obvious place to break a long journey between Cuiabá or Corumbá and the coast, Campo Grande tries hard to shake off the feeling that it's a city stuck in the middle of nowhere. Apart from the *gaucho* influence, the town centre is much like that of any other medium-sized city; the people are friendly and there's little manifest poverty. The generally warm evenings inspire the locals to turn out on the streets in force. People chat over a meal or sip ice-cold beers at one of the restaurants or bars around Avenida Afonso Pena, the Praça Ari Coelho or blocks 22-23 of Rua Dom Aquino, and guitars, maracas and congas are often brought out for an impromptu music session.

Arrival, information and accommodation

The **rodoviária** (Ⓣ67/3321-8797) is a ten-minute walk west of the central Praça Ari Coelho at Rua Joaquim Nabuco 200. A surprisingly large bus terminal, it also houses six hairdressers, a cinema, bookstores and several bars. The area around the *rodoviária* is fine during the day but can be a little rough at night; despite this it boasts some reasonable hotels and the city's Youth Hostel. Similarly, the district south of Avenida Afonso Pena has a slightly dodgy reputation. If in doubt, take a **taxi**: there's a rank in the bus station, or phone Rádio Táxi on Ⓣ67/3387-1414. The other point of arrival is the **airport**, Aeroporto Internacional Antônio João (Ⓣ67/3368-6000), 7km out of town on the road towards Aquidauana. Buses from the airport to the *rodoviária* cost around R$2, taxis R$20–25.

Tourist information is readily available at the airport (usually open 9am–6pm; Ⓣ67/0800-6476050 and 3318-6060) or in town at the very helpful Morada dos Bais tourist office at Av. Noroeste 5140, on the corner with Avenida Afonso Pena (Tues–Sat 8am–7pm, Sun 9am-noon; Ⓣ67/3324-5830 and 3382-9244). Here, as well as city maps and information on attractions and accommodation, you'll find a noticeboard with details on cinema, theatre and exhibition listings. The SEDEC Departmento de Turismo, Rua Bahia 470, Jardin dos Estados (Ⓣ67/3314-3580, Ⓔsedec.turismo@pmcg.ms.gov.br) is not frontline but can offer further detailed information on tourism in the area. A fun way to get to know Campo Grande, **Official City Tours** operating from the Morada dos Bais tourist office (Ⓣ67/3321-0800), visit the main sights, including the parks and museums, on an open-topped double decker bus.

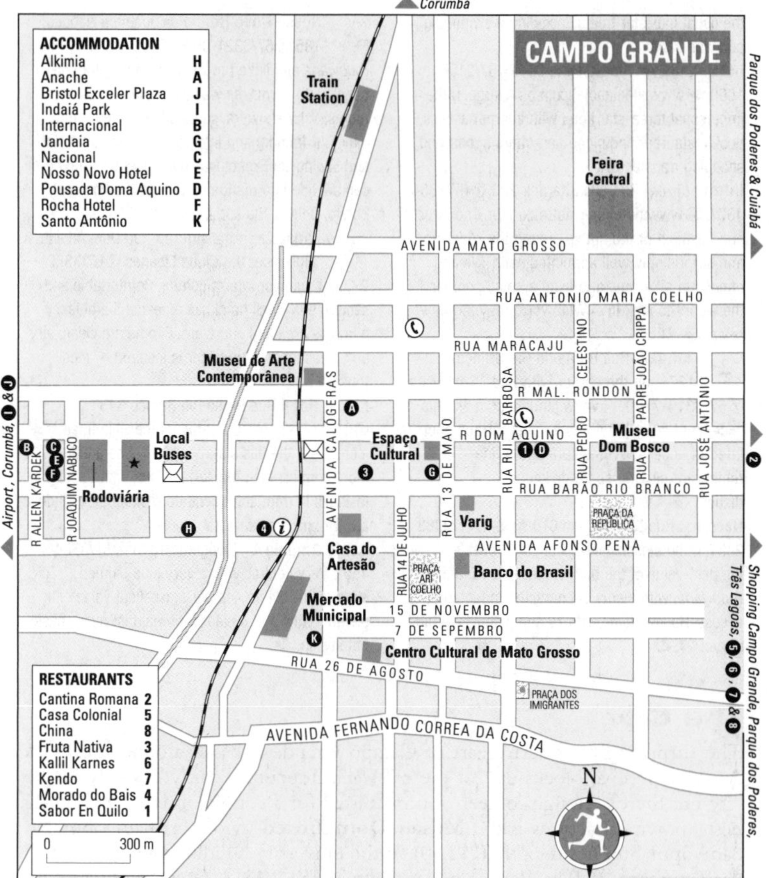

Accommodation

With the demise of passenger trains, smarter, more comfortable **hotels** have appeared around the *rodoviária* and today offer quite acceptable alternatives to both the downtown and rather defunct train station options. There are reasonable budget and mid-range choices around the junction of Rua Barão do Rio Branco and Rua Allan Kardek, one street west of the *rodoviária*, though the more central *pousadas* and hotels within a few blocks of the Praça Ari Coelho are closer to the modern city's heart. For **camping**, there's the *Estancia Vovo Dede* (☎67/3321-0077), 23km from Campo Grande, which offers walking trails, horse riding, a pool and fishing; the *Estancia* is also contactable through Asteco Turismo at Rua 13 de Maio 3192.

Alkimia Av. Afonso Pena 1413, Centro ☎67/3324-2621. A modern, medium-sized hotel between the centre and the *rodoviária*; rooms have TVs, *frigobar* and a/c. Friendly staff. ❸

Anache Rua Cândido Mariano Rondon 1396 ☎67/3383-2841. A no-frills option with shared bathrooms and fans rather than a/c, but clean and safe, and in a good central location, with friendly service. ❶

Bristol Exceler Plaza Av. Afonso Pena 444 ☎67/3321-2800, ⓦbristolhoteis.com.br. A plush hotel where you'll be coddled and swaddled in all the usual four-star treats, including a swimming pool and sauna. 5–6

Indaiá Park Av. Afonso Pena 354 ⓣ67/2106-1000, ⓦwww.indaiahotel.com.br. A large, rather impersonal three-star hotel with Internet access, pool, restaurant and piano bar; offers airport and shopping transfer. 5

Internacional Rua Allan Kardek 223 ⓣ67/3384-4677, ⓦwww.hotelintermetro.com.br. The largest and flashiest of the hotels around the *rodoviária*, and surprisingly well appointed, with TVs and phones in all rooms and even a small pool for the weary to sink into. Well worth the extra few *reais*. 3–4

Jandaia Rua Barão do Rio Branco 1271, on the corner with Rua 13 de Maio ⓣ67/3316-7700, ⓦwww.jandaia.com.br. This excellent luxury hotel has a small terrace pool, Internet access, gymnasium and a fine restaurant serving some delicious local dishes. 5–6

Nacional Rua Dom Aquino 610 ⓣ & ⓕ67/3383-2461, ⓔhotelnacional@ig.com.br. Probably the best-value of the budget places around the *rodoviária*, with plenty of character and Internet access. Rooms come with TV and a choice of fans or a/c. 3–4

Nosso Novo Hotel Rua Joaquim Nabuco 185 ⓣ67/3321-0505. Close to the *rodoviária* and linked to Youth Hostelling International, with dorms, as well as single and double rooms, solar showers, some private bathrooms, plus TVs, laundry and Internet facilities. Hotel staff and Ecological Expeditions (who operate from here) can provide information on trips to the Pantanal, Bonito, Bolivia, Rio and Iguazu. 1–2

Pousada Doma Aquino Rua Dom Aquino 1806, near the Clube Libanes ⓣ67/3382-9373, ⓔpaquino@terra.com.br. Comfortable and secure, this small hotel has a peaceful ambience, a lounge area and courtyard. Rooms are clean, airy and pleasant and the decor is inspired by local tribes. 3–4

Rocha Hotel Rua Barao Rio Branco 343 ⓣ67/3325-6874, ⓔajcampogrande@hotmail.com. Near the bus station and offering a little more comfort than the *Nosso Novo*, with parking facilities in front and adequate rooms that include a/c, TV and breakfast. 2

Santo Antônio Av. Calógeras 1813 ⓣ67/3324-4552. Very central, with a very blue painted exterior, the *Santo Antônio* is excellent value with private baths and a pleasant breakfast room; basic but stylish. 2

The City

The surprisingly modern heart of Campo Grande is based around the Praça Ari Coelho, five blocks east of the *rodoviária*. Tourism is fairly low-key in the city, but there's enough to keep you interested for a couple of days. One of the best-known attractions is the **Museu Dom Bosco** (Mon–Fri 8am–6pm, Sat 8am–5pm, Sun noon–6pm; R$2.50), in the university building facing the Praça da República, at Rua Barão do Rio Branco 1811-43. A fascinating place, it's crammed full of exhibits, ranging from superb forest Indian artefacts to over ten thousand terrifying dead insects and some astonishingly beautiful butterflies. Most impressive of all is the vast collection of stuffed birds and animals, including giant rheas (the South American version of an ostrich), anacondas and examples of the Brazilian marsupials – the gamba and the quica.

Closer to the city centre, the **Casa do Artesão** (Mon–Fri 8am–6pm, Sat & Sun 9am–noon), on the corner of Avenida Calógeras and Avenida Afonso Pena, has a large collection of crafts, reflecting this huge region's numerous indigenous cultures, including the Terena, the Kadiwéu – whose ancestors were called the Mbaya Guaicuru - and the Guato peoples. It sells mostly local works, the best pieces without a doubt being the seed jewellery and the woodcarvings, often depicting mythical symbols like fish-women and totemic figures; all are relatively inexpensive. Just down the road from here, the Centro de Informações Turisticas e Culturais (tourist and cultural information office), in the 1918 **Morada dos Bais** building at Av. Noroeste 5140 (Tues–Sat 8am–7pm, Sun 9am-noon; free), also houses a small historical museum with period furniture and photos of early Campo Grande, plus a couple of art galleries showing changing exhibitions.

Campo Grande also hosts several **markets**: the **Mercado Municipal** (Tues–Fri noon-6.30pm, Sat 6.30am-6.30pm, Sun 6.30am-noon), built in 1933, sells a good range of inexpensive souvenirs, including cow-horn trumpets, horn goblets and drinking gourds; the **Feira Indigena** (daily 6.30am-8pm), just outside the Mercado Municipal in the Praça Oshiro Takemori, devotes itself almost exclusively to market-garden produce, including lovely honey and some simple seed necklaces made from wild *mata* products; and the **Feira Central**, Esplanada da Ferrovia, Avenida Calogeras at the corner with 14 de Julho, takes place three times a week (Wed & Fri after 5pm, Sat from 10am), overnight until 6am, attracting a large number of forest Indians selling potions and bundles of bark, beads and leatherwork, as well as a few Paraguayans selling toys. The eclectic blend of peoples is further compounded by the variety of foods on offer, ranging from *churrasquinho* to Japanese *yaki soba*.

There's good-quality *artesanato* on sale, mainly handicrafts such as cotton embroidery and leatherwork, at **Feria de Artesanato de Artistas Sul Mato Grossenses**, Praça dos Imigrantes (Mon–Fri 9am–6pm, Sat 9am-2pm), where there's also a small outdoor café. For the flip side to contemporary Mato Grosso culture, head for the **cowboy shop** at Rua Barão do Rio Branco 1296, near the *Jandaia Hotel*, which sells gun belts, holsters, saddles and boots. You can see some of this gear in action at the **horse racing**, out at the Hipódromo, run by the Jóquei Clube de Campo Grande; the Hipódromo is 5km along the BR-167, beyond the exit for Dourados. Finally, there is also the old railway station, the brick Estação Ferroviaria, which was built in a distintive British style and began operating in 1914, bringing a new era of growth to the city.

Just beyond the town centre, at the eastern end of Avenida Mato Grosso, is the **Parque dos Poderes** (Mon–Fri noon–6pm). This calm ecological reserve is home to a variety of native plants and a small selection of the region's wild animals; there are a few short walking trails and the habitat is scrubby woodland. Buses for the Parque de Poderes can be caught going east along Avenida Afonso Pena from the centre. At the entrance to Poderes there's the **Parque das Nações Indígenas**, consisting of some 120 hectares of paths serviced by cafés and toilets, plus there's a small but usually colourful modern art museum, the **Museu de Arte Contemporânea de Mato Grosso do Sul (MARCO)**, Av. Maria Coelho 6000 (Tues–Fri 9am–6pm, Sat & Sun 9am–4pm; free). The MARCO houses plastic art exhibitions from local artists as well as temporary exhibits from out-of-state artists.

Just to the south of the Parque de Poderes (or east from the centre along Av. Joaquim Murtinho), you'll find the **Memorial de la Cultura Indígena**, Rua Terena in the Aldeia Indígena Urban (Urban Indigenous Village), Bairro Tiradentes (daily 8am-6pm, ⓣ67/3314-3589; groups by appointment only), where there is a craft workshop, visitor reception and many genuine Indian craft goods for sale, including ceramics and paintings. Inhabited by people of the Terena tribe, the surrounding brick urban settlement is a planned municipal project. The memorial building itself is an imposing traditional-looking hut with a palm-frond roof standing some 8m tall; it incorporates innovative construction techniques, such as bent bamboo.

Eating, drinking and nightlife

Eating out is an important part of the local lifestyle and this is reflected in the diversity of restaurants. There are scores of **lanchonetes**, especially around the *rodoviária* and east along Rua Dom Aquino, and, during the hot afternoons, the city's many **juice bars** do brisk business: you'll find them on most street corners. This is a cattle-ranching market centre, and a lot of cows get roasted daily in Campo Grande, so if you're mad for **beef** you're in for a treat; however, there are also vegetarian options and several good oriental restaurants.

Cantina Romana Rua da Paz 237 ⓣ67/3324-9777. Wonderful Italian food, good atmosphere, fine wines and a/c; very fair prices.
Casa Colonial Av. Afonso Pena 3997 ⓣ67/3383-3207 or 3042-3207. Primarily a *churrascaria,* this place serves excellent Brazilian *rodizio*, where you can eat meat till you drop. Expensive, but the decor is refined, quite spacious and pleasant.
Casa do Peixe Rua João Rosa Pires 1030 ⓣ67/3382-7121. Very popular spot for delicious regional dishes, with fish as the main speciality, and often with live music at weekends. Exceptional value and excellent service. Closed Sun evening.
China Rua Pedro Celestino 750 ⓣ67/3382-4476. One of the best Chinese restaurants in town, with very reasonable prices; the fried duck (*pato frito*) is particularly recommended.
Don Leon Av. Afonso Pena 1901 ⓣ67/3384-6520. A popular *churrascaria* and pizzeria, with scores of tables, fast friendly service and the added bonus of live music some evenings.
Fruta Nativa Rua Barão Rio Branco 1097. This busy lunchtime snack bar serves light and inexpensive meals, including chips and chicken, outside at the yellow tables. Next door there's an unnamed juice bar where you can sip on *sucos de guarana* and munch on *pastels* (cakes) and *tortas* (tarts).
Kallil Karnes Rua Rubens Gil de Camilo 142, near Shopping Campo Grande towards the eastern end of Av. Afonso Pena ⓣ67/3326-3715 (Mon–Sat 11am–2.30pm & 7–11pm, closed Sun evening). Meat house with a good reputation for excellent *rodizio*, but somewhat out of the way unless you're thinking of clubbing afterwards.
Kendo Av. Afonso Pena 4150 ⓣ67/3382-9000. The best of the town's Japanese restuarants; as well as fine fish soups, you'll also find pork and chicken soups with refined oriental spices. It's open Tues-Sun, 7pm to midnight.
Morado do Bais Av. Noroeste 5140, on the corner with Av. Afonso Pena ⓣ67/3383-1227. An often-lively courtyard restaurant near the tourist information and cultural centre, serving a range of local dishes including *sopa paraguaia* (a soup with cheese and onions). Live music occasionally at weekends. Closed Mon.
Sabor En Quilo Rua Dom Aquino 1786 ⓣ67/3352-5102. An excellent Japanese-run restaurant with good self-service lunches in a spacious, cool and clean environment; the sushi is tasty, and it also serves more traditional Brazilian *feijoada*, too.
San Marino Pizzas Av. Afonso Pena 2716 ⓣ67/3321-5084. One of several reasonable pizzerias on Afonso Pena, with delivery service.
Seriema Restaurante Av. Afonso Pena 1919 ⓣ67/3721-2475. Near *Don Leon's* (see above), this is also a lively steak house, with cheap lunchtime *rodizio*.
Viva a Vida Rua Dom Aquino 1354, 1st floor ⓣ67/3384-6524 and Av. Fernando Corréa da Costa 2177 ⓣ67/321-3208. Campo Grande's favourite vegetarian restaurant (meat also available) is self-service, and open lunchtimes only. Closed Sat.

Nightlife

Most of Campo Grande's action happens at weekends, when the *churrascarias* and other large restaurants generally serve their food to the energetic sounds of Paraguayan polkas (*Don Leon*'s has them on weekdays as well). **Nightclubs** tend to change quickly, but those currently popular are *Limit*, 200m off Avenida Afonso Pena by Shopping Campo Grande; *Stones* (ⓣ67/3326-4957), on block 21 of Avenida Ceara for rock and jazz music; and *Tango*, Rua Candido Mariano 2181, to the east of the city centre, all offering a mix of Brazilian, European, Stateside and underground sounds. There's also *Acustic Bar*, with mainly electronic Brazilian music on Rua 13 de Julho 945 (ⓣ67/3385-5500).

The Glauce Rocha **theatre**, out of town in Cidade Universitária, often hosts interesting Brazilian works – call ⓣ67/3387-3311 for details, or check the local papers *Folho do Povo* or *Correio do Estado*. *Peña Eme-Ene*, on the corner of Avenida Afonso Pena and Rua Barbosa, is a popular meeting place for artists and musicians, and has live regional music every Thursday night from 8pm – no entrance fee but you're expected to take dinner (Mon–Wed & Fri 7.30am–6pm, Thurs 7.30am–midnight, Sat noon–6pm; ⓣ67/3383-2373).

Listings

Airlines BRA, Gol, Trip, TAM, Av. Afonso Pena 1974 ⓣ67/368-6161 or at the airport ⓣ67/368-6152; Varig/Rio-Sul, Rua Barão do Rio Branco 1356 ⓣ67/3325-4070 and at the airport ⓣ67/3763-1213.

Banks and exchange There are ATMs by most banks, at the airport and at strategic points in the city, such as the corner of Rua 13 de Maio with Afonso Pena, by the main *praça* Coehlo; you can also change money in the Banco do Brasil, just off the main square at Av. Afonso Pena 133 (Mon–Fri 10am–5pm); at the HSBC bank, Rua 13 de Maio 2836; at the Cámbio, Rua 13 de Maio 2484; or at the airport bank.

Car rental Brascar, Rua Fernando Corréa da Costa 975 ⓣ67/3383-1570; Lemans, Rua 7 de Setembro 334, Centro ⓣ0800/92-5100; Unidas, Av. Afonso Pena 829 ⓣ67/3384-5626.

Consulates If you're heading into either Paraguay or Bolivia from Campo Grande, you should check on border procedures and visa requirements. The Paraguayan consul is at Rua 26 de Agosto 384 (ⓣ67/3324-4934), and the Bolivian consul at Rua João de Souza 798 (ⓣ67/3382-2190); both are open Mon–Fri 9am–5pm.

Health matters The Santa Casa hospital is at Rua Eduardo Santos Pereira 88 (ⓣ67/3322-4000).

Internet Blue Sky Net, Av. Calogeras 2069 (ⓣ67/3321-0304) has efficienct a/c; there's also the Sala Brasil CH@T Room Cyber Café, Rua Pedro Celestino 992 (ⓣ67/3383-4231) and Iris Cybercafe and bar, Av. Afonso Pena 1975.

Laundry Planet Clean, Rua Joaquim Murtinho 135, close to the Praça dos Imigrantes.

Pharmacy Rua Barbosa, on the corner of the main square by Rua 14 de Julho and Av. Afonso Pena.

Police Emergency number ⓣ190.

Post offices The branch at Av. Calógeras 2309, on the corner with Rua Dom Aquino, is open Mon–Fri 8am–5pm, Sat 8–11.30am; the one on Rua Barão do Rio Branco by the *rodoviária* stays open till 6pm Mon–Fri.

Shopping Shopping Campo Grande, Av. Afonso Pena 4909, is a large and flashy shopping centre towards the eastern end of Av. Afonso Pena, replete with multiplex cinemas and over 170 shops. The busiest shopping streets in the town centre are mostly congregated in the square formed by Av. Calógeras, Av. Afonso Pena, Rua Cândido Mariano Rondon and Rua Pedro Celestino. A street market selling plastic goods and electronics sets up daily along Rua Barão do Rio Branco between the *rodoviária* and Av. Calógeras. The Barroarte shop at Av. Afonso Oena 4329, Jardin dos Estados, has a wide range of good local ceramics, sculptures and paintings; it's some distance from the centre, but en route to Shopping Campo Grande. For precious and semi-precious stones, the Garimpo shop, Av. Afonso Pena 2882, has many interesting items.

Telephones Rua Dom Aquino 1805 (daily, 7am-10pm).

Travel and tour companies NPQ Turismo, Av. Afonso Pena 2081, on Praça Ari Coelho (ⓣ67/3725-6789), is good for flights and some bus tickets. If you're on a tight budget, Ecological Expeditions (ⓣ67/3321-0505, ⓦwww.pantanaltrekking.com) offers a range of affordable tours (see p.589 for more information). Impacto Turismo, Rua Padre João Crippa 1065, sala 106 (ⓣ67/3382-5197 or 3724-3167), also runs good Pantanal tours; Ney Gonzalves is an excellent guide. Also in Campo Grande, Lilian Borges Rodrigues is a very good English-speaking guide; contact her at Rua Octavio de Souza 464, Monte Libano (ⓣ67/3742-2204). See also the box "Upmarket Pantanal Agents and Operators" on p.588.

North to Coxim

The area of scrub forest to the east of Coxim and north of Campo Grande used to be the territory of the **Caiapó** Indian nation, who ambushed miners along the routes to Goiás and Cuiabá from São Paulo, posing a serious threat to Portuguese expansion and development in the mid-eighteenth century. In reaction to the successful use of Bororo Indian mercenaries against their main villages in the Camapua area, the Caiapó took their revenge on the growing numbers of Portuguese settlers and their farm slaves in the area. In 1751 – the same year that the governor of Brazil declared an official military campaign against them – the Caiapó went as far as attacking the town of Goiás, beyond the northern limits of their usual territory.

Today, **COXIM** is a quiet town of some 33,000 people, easily reached by bus from Campo Grande in around three to four hours (six or seven hours from Cuiabá). Situated on the eastern edges of the Pantanal, it's a fantastic **fishing** centre: the fisherman Pirambero runs excellent trips into the swamp, down the Rio Taquari, to catch piranhas (ask for him at the port). If you're really serious about angling, contact IBAMA, at Rua Floriano Peoxoto 304 (Ⓣ67/3291-2310) or the Banco do Brasil for a **temporary fishing permit** (R$25) and, for more detailed local information, try the local fishing club, the Iate Clube Rio Verde, at Rua Ferreira, Bairro Piracema (Ⓣ67/3291-1246). Besides fishing, swimming in the Rio Taquari around Campo Falls is another popular pastime, in spite of the razor-teethed fish, and, nearby on the Rio Coxim, the **Palmeiras Falls** are a good place for a picnic or to camp a while. From November through to January, the two falls are the best places to see the incredible *piracema* spectacle – thousands of fish, leaping clear of the river, on their way upstream to the river's source to lay their eggs.

For more information on Coxim's attractions, you could try the **tourist information** office at the bus station (Ⓣ67/3291-2669), though its opening hours are very unpredictable The town offers plenty of **accommodation** possibilities, including the *Hotel Neves* (Ⓣ67/3291-1273; ③) in an old brick farmhouse one block from the *rodoviária* and five minutes by bus from the town centre; the more central *Hotel Santa Ana*, Rua Miranda Reis 931 (Ⓣ67/3291-1602; ③), with a pool and bar; and the *Coxim*, 4km from town (Ⓣ67/3291-1480; ③), which also has a pool and restaurant. There are other hotels, *fazendas* and *pousadas*, mostly aimed at fishing holiday-makers, several of them 5km away in the neighbouring village of Silviolândia. When it's time to move on, it might be worth enquiring about river boats to Corumbá. The Rio Taquari has silted up considerably in recent years – the effect of land clearance for cattle grazing and agriculture, leading to huge amounts of topsoil being shifted into the river systems – and as a result, boats along the river are now rare, though there are still a few.

South to the Paraguayan border

There's no great draw – in fact, no draw at all – in the towns south of Campo Grande en route to the Paraguayan border. The only settlement of any size is **DOURADOS**, 225km from the state capital, a violent, rapidly expanding place which recently overtook Corumbá as Mato Grosso do Sul's second-largest city. Its name is a reminder of the fact that the spot was first settled by travellers en route to the Cuiabá gold mines. These days it's the region's most important agricultural centre, but there's little of interest to the tourist except bus connections to points further south and west (the daily bus to Bonito currently leaves at 3pm). Should you get stranded overnight, three reasonable **accommodation** options are *Dourados Park,* Avenida Guaicurus Km 2 (Ⓣ67/3426-1309, Ⓦwww.douradosparkhotel.com.br; ④), one of the most comfortable in town; *Hotel Alphonsus*, Av. Presidente Vargas 603 (Ⓣ67/3422-5211; ③–④) with pool; and, cheapest of all, *Turis Hotel*, Av. Marcelino Pires 5932 (Ⓣ67/3422-1909, Ⓕ3421-8827; ②).

MUNDO NOVO, about eleven hours by bus from Campo Grande, is another unattractive transport terminus. From here, buses run to the crossing point for ferries to Guaira, and to Porto Frajelli and Foz do Iguaçu. If you have to stay over, the *Hotel Marajoara*, Av. Castelo Branco 93 (Ⓣ67/3474-1692; 2), has decent rooms.

Ponta Porã

Despite the distinctly unthrilling towns that have gone before, **PONTA PORÃ** itself is an attractive little settlement, right on the Paraguayan border up in the Maracaju hills. The **Avenida Internacional** divides the settlement in two – on one side of the street you're in Brazil, on the other in the Paraguayan town of **Pedro Juan Caballero**. On the Paraguayan side you can polka the night away, gamble your money till dawn or, like most people there, just buy a load of imported goods at the duty-free shops, while the Brazilian side is a little more staid. There's a strange blend of language and character, and even a unique *mestizo* cuisine, making it an interesting place to spend a day or two. Ponta Porã also has a tradition as a distribution centre for *maté* – a herb brewed to make a tea-like drink.

There are plenty of **hotels** to choose from, with most of the budget places over the road from the train station. Better choices include the *Internacional*, Av. Internacional 2604 (ⓣ67/3431-1243; ❸), a mid-range hotel with regular hot water, while for a plusher stay it's hard to beat the *Pousada do Bosque*, just outside Ponta Porã at Av. Presidente Vargas 1151 (ⓣ67/3431-1181, ⓦhotelpousadadobosque.com.br; ❹), with its welcoming swimming pool.

Into Paraguay

Crossing the border is a simple procedure for most non-Brazilians. An exit stamp must be obtained from the Polícia Federal at Rua Mal. Floriano 1483 (ⓣ67/3431-1428) on the Brazilian side, then it's a matter of walking four or five blocks down Rua Guia Lopes to the Paraguayan customs and control. If you need a visa for Paraguay you can get this from the consulate on Avenida Internacional (ⓣ67/3431-6312) on the Brazilian side. If you're pushed for time, catch a cab from the bus station to complete exit and entry formalities; the fare is about R$20, including waiting time. Once in Paraguay, there's a reasonably good road direct to Concepción, a major source of imports and contraband for Brazilians; daily buses make the five- or six-hour trip in good weather. It's another five hours from there to Asunción; there's also a direct service (8–10hr) from the bus station in Pedro Juan Caballero. There's no problem **changing money** at decent rates on Avenida Internacional, but it's impossible to change travellers' cheques on Sundays and holidays.

Bela Vista and Porto Murtinho

The two other interesting destinations on the Paraguayan border are Bela Vista and Porto Murtinho, both to the west of Ponta Porã and harder to reach. While they don't serve as gateways to Paraguay (it's technically illegal to cross the frontier at these places), they are worth visiting for the splendour of their natural setting alone. Both towns are served by **bus** from Dourados (a good day's journey), and from Jardim (8hr), which in turn is connected daily with Anastácio (4hr).

In **BELA VISTA** you can explore the natural delights of the Piripacu and Caracol rivers, behind which are the unspoilt peaks of the Três Cerros and Cerro Margarida. There's also the extraordinary **Nhandejara bridge**, a water-eroded underground passage over 30m long. Most Brazilians, however, come here for the opportunity to buy imported goods: over the border is the Paraguayan town of Bela Vista, which has a road connection (a day's travel) to Concepción. If you need to stay, try the *Pousada da Fronteira*, Av. Teodoro Sativa 1485 (ⓣ67/439-1487; ❸).

Remote and tranquil, **PORTO MURTINHO** owes its foundation 453km south of Campo Grande to the thriving trade in the tea-type herb, *erva maté*. The town of 13,000 inhabitants sits on the banks of the Rio Paraguai, over 470km southwest of Campo Grande, near where the river finally leaves Brazilian territory. Well blessed with abundant wildlife and luxuriant vegetation, it marks the very southern limits of the Pantanal swamplands. You can take fairly cheap riverboat excursions from Porto Murtinho, though you might be expected to haggle over the price a little, since there are often several boatmen to choose from at the riverfront.

For **accommodation**, *Hotel Americano*, Rua Dr Corréa 430 (Ⓣ67/3287-1344, Ⓕ3287-1309, Ⓦwww.donipesca.com.br; ❺ full-board), has 38 large, air-conditioned rooms as well as boats for residents' use (rowing boats R$40/3hr, motorboats R$120/3hr), while 1km out of town, in the Fazenda Saladero, is the similar *Saladero Cue* (Ⓣ67/3287-1113, Ⓦwww.hotelsaladerocue.com.br; ❹), with a beautiful riverside location and boats for hire. Slightly cheaper but not as nice is the *Pousada do Pantanal*, Rua Alfredo Pinto 141 (Ⓣ67/3287-1325; ❸). Lastly, the *Americano* owns and runs *Hotel Nabileque* (❺), 120km upriver on the Rio Nabileque, and primarily a base for anglers. The hotel is actually built on the river, supported on stilts, and has boats for hire. Daily boats (3hr) from the *Americano* will get you out there.

West towards Corumbá

Several daily **buses** connect Campo Grande with Aquidauana/Anastácio (2hr) and Corumbá (7hr), the scenery becoming increasingly swamp-like the further west you travel. It may still be worth enquiring about the axed passenger train to Corumbá (see p.562) in case someone has had the good sense to restart it.

West of Campo Grande, the savanna becomes forested as the road approaches the first real range of hills since leaving the Atlantic coast. Sticking up like a gigantic iceberg in the vast southern Mato Grosso, the **Serra de Maracaju** provided sanctuary for local Terena Indians during a period of Paraguayan military occupation in the 1860s. Under their somewhat crazy and highly ambitious dictator, Solano López, the Paraguayans invaded the southern Mato Grosso in 1864, a colonial adventure that resulted in the death of over half the invasion force, mostly composed of native (Paraguayan) Guarani Indians. This was one period in Brazilian history when whites and Indians fought for the same cause, and it was in the magnificent Serra de Maracaju hills that most of the guerrilla-style resistance took place. Beyond, interesting geological formations dominate the horizon: vast towering tors, known as *torrelones*, rise magnificently out of the scrubby savanna. Further west, around the small train station of **Camisão**, is a relatively lush valley supporting tropical fruits, sugar cane and, of course, beef cattle.

Aquidauana and Anastácio

The next town, **AQUIDAUANA**, 130km from Campo Grande, is a lazy-looking place and very hot, sitting under the beating sun of the Piraputanga uplands. Since the demise of the passenger trains to Corumbá, it sweats somewhat uncomfortably some distance from the main BR-262 highway, and, though it still serves as one of several gateways into the Pantanal, it's better known for fishing and walking, with some superb views across the swamp. These days, most visitors see little more than the signpost at the crossroads where the highway bypasses the town; if you stop by here, it'll most likely be to use the highway café or toilet facilities at the junction. If you do go into town or stay over here, it's worth enquiring about two nearby but seldom visited sites: the **ruins of the Cidade de Xaraés**, founded by the Spanish in 1580 on the banks of the Rio

Aquidauana; and the **Morro do Desenho**, a series of prehistoric inscriptions on the riverbank and in the nearby hills.

The river running through the town boasts some pleasant sandy **beaches**, quite clean and safe for swimming between May and October; **fishing** championships are an integral part of the annual São João August festival here. There's a reasonable choice of **hotels**, including the quiet *Hotel Pantanal* (ⓣ67/3241-1929; ❷) at Rua Estevão Alves Correa 2611 opposite the *rodoviária*. The *Portal Pantaneiro*, Rua Pandiá Calógeras 1067 (ⓣ67/3241-4328, ⓕ3241-4327; ❸), has a pool and very comfortable rooms; and the *Hotel Tropical*, Rua Manoel Aureliano Costa 533 (ⓣ67/3241-4113; ❸), with its smart rooms and good showers, is another one of the best in town. **Aquidauana** is often the base for switching from public transport to local cars in order to reach a couple of interesting *fazendas*: the *Pousada Pantaneira* (ⓣ3245-0949, ⓦwww.pantanalpequi.com.br; ❺–❻), a comfortable mid-priced lodge with a swimming pool and restaurant that offers horse, vehicle and boat expeditions; and the expensive but rather special *Fazenda Rio Negro* (ⓦwww.fazendarionegro.com.br; ❼), run by environmental NGOs. If you don't have your own car, try calling either place first and see if they will pick you up from town. One of several decent **restaurants** is the *O Casarão,* Rua Manoel Antônio Paes de Barros 533 (ⓣ67/3241-2219), which is expensive but serves delicious, though not exclusively Brazilian, dishes.

The neighbouring town of **ANASTÁCIO** – half an hour's walk on the other side of the river – has some nice beaches of its own, but is best known for the large *jaú* fish (often weighing over 75kg) that live in its river. Anastácio is the transport hub of the region, with daily bus services to Bela Vista, Bonito, Miranda and Ponta Porã, as well as Campo Grande and Corumbá. If you're lucky enough to have your own wheels, there's an infrequently taken road that skirts the south-eastern rim of the Pantanal right up to **Rio Verde do Mato Grosso**, 200km north of Campo Grande on the way to Cuiabá, which has ample opportunities for bathing in the transparent waters and cascades that feed the Rio Verde.

Fifty kilometres south of Aquidauana on the road towards Bonito, the *Cabana do Pescador* **luxury fishing lodge** on the Rio Miranda (ⓣ67/3245-3697; ❺) is another relaxing destination and a possible base from which to go horse riding or take a tour to the Bonito caves (see p.574); buses between Aquidauna and Bonito take you past the Cabana.

Miranda

Seventy kilometres west of Anastácio, the small town of **MIRANDA** sits straddling the BR-262 at the foot of the Serra da Bodoquena by the Rio Miranda. Once the scene of historic battles, Miranda has been somewhat ignored by visitors since the demise of the old Campo Grande to Corumbá rail service, but it's a pleasant town that is known for excellent fishing and for Terena and Kadiwéu artefacts. It's also a good base for visiting Bonito (128km) or the Pantanal swamp.

If you plan on staying, there are several reasonable **hotels**, including *Pantanal Hotel*, Av. Barão do Rio Branco 609 (ⓣ & ⓕ67/3242-1608; ❹), which has a pool; the *Hotel Roma*, a good cheap option at Praça Agenor Carrillo 356 (ⓣ67/3242-1321; ❸); and *Hotel Chalé*, just up from the *rodoviária* on Rua Barão do Rio Branco (ⓣ67/3242-1216; ❸), which is similarly good value, with clean, modern rooms, all with air-conditioning. The best hotel, however, is the *Pousada Águas do Pantanal*, Av. Afonso Pena 367 (ⓣ67/3242-1242, ⓦwww.aguasdopantanal.com.br; ❹), with a pool and excellent service, which includes offering safaris into the Pantanal. The management here also runs the *Fazenda San Francisco*, 36km down the road to Bonito (ⓣ67/3242-1497; ❻), which offers lots of activities, but at a cost. The *Refúgio Ecológico Caiman* (ⓣ67/3242-1450, reservations ⓣ11/3079-6622,

The Terena Indians

West beyond Aquidauana lies the traditional territory of the **Terena people**, for whom there was little peace even after the Paraguayan occupation of the 1860s. The late nineteenth century saw an influx of Brazilian colonists into the Aquidauana and Miranda valleys as the authorities attempted to "populate" the regions between Campo Grande and Paraguay – the war with Paraguay had only made them aware of how fertile these valleys were. Pushed off the best of the land and forced, in the main, to work for new, white landowners, the Terena tribe remained vulnerable until the appearance of **Lieutenant Rondon** (after whom the Amazonian state of Rondônia was named). Essentially an engineer, he came across the Terena in 1903 after constructing a telegraph connection – poles, lines and all – through virtually impassable swamps and jungle between Cuiabá and Corumbá. With his help, the Terena managed to establish a legal claim to some of their traditional land. Considered by FUNAI (the federal agency for Indian affairs) to be one of the most successfully "integrated" Indian groups in modern Brazil, the Terena have earned a reputation for possessing the necessary drive and ability to compete successfully in the market system – a double-edged compliment in that it could be used by the authorities to undermine their rights to land as a tribal group. They live mostly between Aquidauana and Miranda, the actual focus of their territory being the town and train station of **Taunay** – an interesting little settlement with mule-drawn taxi wagons and a peaceful atmosphere. You'll find Terena handicrafts on sale in Campo Grande.

Ⓦwww.caiman.com.br; ⑨) is one of the most luxurious of all Pantanal *fazenda*-lodges, based some 40km out of town and set in 53,000 hectares of swampland. For **camping**, ask the staff at *Perqueiro Camping Lopes* around the corner from the *rodoviária* about their site 12km away. One really good **restaurant** in town is the *Cantina del Amore*, Rua Barrão do Rio Branco 515, which serves mainly standard Brazilian dishes including fresh fish.

Bonito and around

Nestling in the Bodoquena hills, over three hours by bus from Anastácio and Miranda, four from Campo Grande and Dourados, **BONITO** is a small, somewhat sleepy sprawl of a town, which comes to life during the main holiday seasons when it's invaded by hordes of young people from southern Brazilian cities. But the dirt tracks that make up most of the region's roads conceal the fact that ever since Bonito starred as an "undiscovered" ecological paradise on TV Globo in 1993, it has become one of Brazil's major **ecotourist** destinations. Needless to say, visitors have been swarming to the town ever since (especially over Christmas and Easter, and in July and August), although the mood, out of season, is surprisingly relaxed and not at all pushy. Located as it is at the southern edge of the Pantanal, a visit to Bonito can happily be combined with a trip exploring the world's biggest inland swamp. Between Bonito and the Pantanal it's possible to experience a fantastic range of wildlife and ecology. Culturally it doesn't offer loads, but in July there is a festival – Festival de Inverno (Ⓦwww.festinbonito.com.br) – with street theatre, art and music.

Arrival, information and accommodation

The **rodoviária** (Ⓣ67/3255-1606) is located up Rua Vicente Jacques, several blocks and a ten-minute walk from the main street Rua Cel. Pilad Rebuá, where many of the town's hotels and most of its tour operators are located. Here you'll find the SETUR **tourist information** office at no. 1780 (Mon–Sat 9am–5pm; ⓣ67/3255-1850, ⓦwww.bonito-ms.com.br and also ⓦwww.portalbonito.com.br). Alternatively, the English-speaking tourist service Linha Direta con a Natureza ("Direct Line to Nature"; ⓣ67/3255-1850) is a useful source of information and can make bookings for local tours.

Taxis are an easy way of getting about Bonito and its outlying areas, and there are several taxi points in town; Ponto Taxi, Rua Monte Castelo 824 (ⓣ67/3255-1760) charges R$3–5 a ride in and around town. A cheaper alternative, particularly if you're travelling alone, is taking a **mototaxi**, or motorbike taxi (75¢ a ride in town and up to R$10 a trip to sites out of town).

Daily Cruzeiro do Sul **buses** connect Bonito with Campo Grande, Corumbá, Dourados and Ponta Porã; nevertheless, you'll need to stay two nights if you want to include even one trip to the caves or rivers (organized tours generally leave around 7.30am), though there are so many possible day- and half-day trips in the area that most people stay longer.

Accommodation

There are plenty of **places to stay** in Bonito, so finding a room should be easy even in high season. Most accommodation is budget-range – there are over a dozen cheapies on Rua Cel. Pilad Rebuá, two blocks up from the *rodoviária* – but there are also a fair number of classier options.

Outside of town, a delightful place is the *Pousada Bacuri*, 7km away beside the Aquário Natural (ⓣ67/3255-1632, or reservations in Bonito at Rua 15 de Novembro 632; ④). It's a little paradise run by a charming family, with a number of basic but clean dormitories, and a gorgeous stretch of the Rio Formosinho for swimming, complete with four waterfalls and virgin forest inhabited by monkeys and macaws; camping is also allowed (R$25 per person). A little further afield, the *Projeto Vivo* (ⓣ67/3255-3803, ⓦwww.projectovivo.com.br; ⑤), some 30km away, offers good-quality *fazenda*-style accommodation in a tranquil setting by the Ilha do Padre; there's a pool, and horse riding and river rafting are also on offer, but you need to book in advance through one of the local travel agents – try Natura Tour (see "Listings", p.577). For more details on the *Projecto Vivo*, see p.576.

There are also more than ten **campsites** around the Bonito area; you can get their details from the travel agents in town or, in advance, from the tourist information office in Campo Grande (see p.562). The nearest to town are *Camping Boa Vista*, Rua Ari Machado (ⓣ67/3255-1764) on the outskirts, and *Ilha do Padre* (ⓣ67/3255-1430) about 10km further out.

Albergue de Juventude do Ecoturismo Rua Lício Borralho 716 ⓣ67/3255-1462, ⓦwww.ajbonito.com.br. Located ten blocks north of the *rodoviária* and a 15min walk into the town centre, it has pretty good facilities including pool, laundry, bar-café, kitchen and games area. They rent bikes for a couple of hours a time and will put you in touch with local tour operators. ①

Hotel Gemila Palace Rua Luis da Costa Leite 2085 ⓣ67/3255-1421, ⓕ255-1843. The best mid-range choice – a very friendly, family-run place with a/c rooms and a great buffet breakfast. ⑤

Paraíso das Aguas Rua Cel. Pilad Rebuá 1884 ⓣ67/3255-1296, ⓦwww.paguas.com.br. The rooms at this tidy, welcoming and very central hotel with pool come with a/c, TV and *frigobar*. ④–⑤

Pousada Muito Bonito Rua Cel. Pilad Rebuá 1448 ⓣ & ⓕ067/3255-1645, ⓦwww.muitobonito.com.br. One of the best backpacker options; very friendly, and with staff who speak several languages, including English. Spotless rooms, all with private bath, and a pleasant terrace for breakfast. Has its own tour agency. ②

Pousada Olho d'Agua Estrada Baia das Garças, 3km from the centre on the northwestern end of town ⓣ67/3255-1430,

Ⓦ www.pousadaolhodagua.com.br. No less luxurious than the *Zagaia Resort*, but arguably more personal and affordable, this place offers delightful bungalow accommodation in intimate wooded surroundings, with excellent service and food, and its own tour agency. ❺

Zagaia Eco-Resort 2km from the centre by the airfield Ⓣ67/3255-1280, Ⓦ www.zagaia.com.br. Top of the range, an ultramodern complex with three swimming pools, various playing fields, horse riding, numerous restaurants and even a cabaret – popular with holiday-makers from Rio. ❼

Trips from Bonito

Bonito's tour companies are unusually well tuned in to the requirements of overseas visitors, and all offer identical trips at identical – and very reasonable – prices to all the places described below, plus a wide range of other options. The municipality limits the numbers of visitors to Bonito's natural wonders and systematically enforces a whole array of regulations intended to protect this ecologically "pure" region. Many of the sites charge for entry, and for some, such as the famous Lago Azul cave, you require both authorization and a guide to visit. Such **permits** and **guides** are arranged by the tour companies or hotels. Almost all the sites require transport, which makes it virtually impossible to visit them independently. Some hotels, like *Pousada Muito Bonito*, can arrange daily **car rental** for around R$70, and someone may be happy to rent you his or her bicycle for the day, but you'll still need a guide to access the main sites.

The Gruta do Lago Azul

The **Gruta do Lago Azul** (daily 8am–2pm, 7am–4pm on holidays; no children under 5; usual guide fee R$12) is a deep, large and cathedral-like cave some 20km from Bonito, out beyond the tiny municipal airstrip. It's set in forested hills that are rich in limestone, granite and marble, and full of minerals – as well as a growing number of mercury, uranium and phosphorus mines. Even before the mines, though, these hills, which reach up to about 800m above sea level, were full of massive caves, most of them inaccessible and on private *fazenda* land.

Rediscovered in 1924 by local Terena Indians, the entrance to the cave is quite spectacular. Surrounded by some 250,000 square metres of ecological reserve woodland, it looms like a monstrous mouth inviting you into the heart of the earth. At first you climb down a narrow path through vegetation, then deeper down into dripping stalactite territory some 100m below to the mists hovering above the cave's lake. The pre-Cambrian rocks of the cave walls are striated like the skin of an old elephant and there are weird rock formations such as the easily recognized natural Buddha. Light streams in from the semicircular cave opening, but only penetrates right to the lake level in the bottom of the cave for 45 minutes on 30 days each year.

Until twenty years ago the cave was used much like a local rubbish tip, but tourism revived the local council's interest in the site and since 1989 a number of expeditions have attempted to fathom the depths of the lake, but with no success (70m is the deepest exploration to date). One of these, a joint French-Brazilian expedition, discovered the bones of prehistoric animals (including a sabre-toothed tiger) and even human remains. The blue waters of the lake extend into the mountain for at least another 300m and are exceptionally clear, with only shrimps and crustacea able to survive in the calcified water.

There is another spectacular cave in the area, **Nossa Senhora Aparecida**, 30km from Bonito, which can only be visited with a guide and special permission from the Prefeitura; contact the Conselho Municipal de Turismo (COMTUR; Ⓣ067/255-2160, Ⓔ comtur.bonito@bonitonline.com.br).

The Aquário Natural

The **Aquário Natural** complex (daily 9am–6pm; all-inclusive price for a half-day excursion is around R$60, covering guide, permit, and access to snorkelling equipment and boats) is justifiably Bonito's next most popular attraction. Located at the river's source, 7km from town, the Aquário itself is a small sanctuary with water so clear and full of fish that the experience is like looking into an aquarium – something you can take advantage of by a ride in one of the glass-bottomed boats. In fact, visitors are encouraged to put on a floating jacket, mask and snorkel, and to get into the water with the 35 or so species of fish, mainly *dourado* and 35cm *piripitanga* fishes – a tickling experience with no danger from piranhas, who never swim this far upriver. The sanctuary is accessed by a path from the reception through a swamp and *mata* nature reserve, the **Parque Ecológico Bahia Bonita**, replete with wildlife, including white-collared peccaries, agouti and the majestic *caramugeiro* snail hawk. From the Aquário, the **Bahia Bonita**, a kilometre-long stretch of river, runs down to meet the Rio Formoso, where there's a death-slide (a pulley and rope system for exciting splashdowns into the river), and trampoline-based river fun.

The Aquário Natural is only one of several snorkelling locations in the area, though it has by far the most developed infrastructure. If you're on a tight budget, the nearby *Pousada Bacuri* (R$7 admission), 500m from the Aquário Natural, has a stretch of river all of its own, with *dourado* fish, four small waterfalls and a small forest in which you're free to wander about. Tour companies also offer snorkelling trips to the **Rio Sucuri** (R$35 half day), and the **Rio da Prata** (R$45 full day). One of the best local scuba sites is the **Gruta do Mimosa** (R$250 full day); a trip here requires both a guide and permit, best obtained through either the Pousada Olho d'Agua travel agency or Ygarapé Tours (see "Listings", p.577).

Ilha do Padre

Around 12km from Bonito down the Rio Formoso, there's an interesting island, the **Ilha do Padre**, which has been turned into a public nature

△ Aquário Natural

reserve and campsite. It costs R$12 to enter (no guide or authorization is required) and R$20 per person to camp, or you can pay a little more (R$30) to use the primitive wooden chalets. **White-water rafting** down to Ilha do Padre (R$250 half day, sometimes done by moonlight) is one of the more exciting options available from tour agents in Bonito (see "Listings", p.577). The island is surrounded by 22 waterfalls of varying sizes and covers almost 50,000 square metres. Although the Formoso is an active white-water rafting river, there are also delightful natural swimming spots, lots of exotic birdlife and lush vegetation. It's not quite as beautiful as the Aquário Natural at the river's source, but still very pleasant, although come prepared for the biting flies and mosquitoes. The island is annoyingly busy at peak holiday times (such as Easter).

Fazenda da Barra Projeto Vivo

The **Fazenda da Barra Projeto Vivo**, an ecological visitors' centre 31km from Bonito at the point where the Formoso and Miranda rivers meet, provides a vivid example of how the apparently conflicting interests of ecology and business can be combined for profit, pleasure and education. The centre is one of the first of its kind in Brazil and has been very successful. Full- and half-day trips from Bonito are organized by the local travel agencies: a full day costs R$80, a half-day R$50 (children half-price), including transport to and from Bonito, a guided forest walk, river-rafting, horse riding and meals. There's a small eco-library for those who read Portuguese and, needless to say, it's an excellent place for children, with plenty of additional hands-on activities (painting, paper-recycling and the like) to keep them happy. If you really take a shine to the place, you can stay in one of their chalets sited 200m from the Rio Formoso: *Chalé das Artes* (❸) with eight beds, or *Chalé Eden* (❻) with only two. For more details, contact the *fazenda* direct (Ⓣ67/3255-3803, Ⓦwww.projectovivo.com.br), or the tour companies Hapakany or Natura Tour (see "Listings", p.577).

Eating and drinking

Although Bonito is a small town, it has a large number of **restaurants** catering for the summer tourist trade; out of season, their quality is somewhat variable. Consistently the best are the *Pousada Olho d'Agua* (see "Accommodation" p.573) and the *Restaurante Tapera*, Rua Cel. Pilad Rebuá 1961 (Ⓣ67/3255-1110), both serving excellent if pricey fish and other dishes in the evening. There are plenty of ice-cream parlours on Rua Cel. Pilad Rebuá, while for a quick lunch *Pousada Muito Bonito* has good home cooking in pleasant surroundings, and popular *Gula's Restaurante* at Rua Cel. Pilad Rebuá 1626 is especially good for pizzas and inexpensive *comida por kilo* lunches. The tasty and varied menu at nearby *Restaurante O Casarão*, on the same street at no. 1835 (Ⓣ67/3255-1850), is quite affordable, too, and equally popular with locals.

As far as **bars** go, *Bar O Pirata*, at Rua 29 de Maio, the *Taboa Bar*, Rua Cel. Pilad Rebuá 1841, and *Restaurante Tapera* (see above) are all quite lively from about 9pm, but only at weekends do they stay open much beyond midnight.

Listings

Banks and exchange Bradesco, Rua Cel. Pilad Rebuá 1942; Banco do Brasil, Rua Luis da Costa Leite 2279, by the central square; HSBC, Rua Cel. Pilad Rebuá 680.

Car rental Yes Ⓣ67/3255-1702; Translocar, Rua Cel. Pilad Rebuá 976 Ⓣ67/3255-1391; Unidas, Rua das Flores Ⓣ67/3255-1066.

Hospital Hospital Municipal Ⓣ67/3255-3455.

IBAMA ⓣ67/3255-1765.
Internet Casa do Computador, Rua Santana do Paraíso 1760 (ⓣ67/255-1463) offers reasonably cheap public access (R$5/hour), or try Caffe.com, Rua Frei Mariano 635.
Local guides The local tour guides association is AGTB (ⓣ67/3255-1837).
Pharmacy Farmácia Drogacruz, Rua Cel. Pilad Rebuá 1629.
Post office On the main street Rua Pilad Rebua 1759 (Mon–Fri 8am–noon and 1–4.30pm).
Travel and tour companies Some of the better hotels, like *Olho d'Agua* and *Muito Bonito*, have their own tour agencies, or can help you arrange a trip with one of the tour companies. Some of the better options are: Hapakany Tours, Rua Cel. Pilad Rebuá 1837 (ⓣ & ⓕ67/3255-1315, ⓦwww.hapakany.com.br); Muito Bonito Turismo, Rua Cel. Pilad Rebuá 1448 (ⓣ & ⓕ67/3255-1645, ⓦwww.muitobonito.com.br), run by the hotel of the same name; Natura Tour, Rua Cel. Pilad Rebuá 1820 (ⓣ67/3255-1544, ⓦwww.naturatour.com.br); and Ygarapé Tours, Rua Cel. Pilad Rebuá 1956 (ⓣ & ⓕ67/3255-1733, ⓦwww.ygarape.com.br), who also offer scuba diving for beginners.

Corumbá and around

Far removed from mainstream Brazil, hard by the Bolivian border and 400km west of Campo Grande, the city of **CORUMBÁ** provides a welcome stop after the long ride from either Santa Cruz (in Bolivia) or Campo Grande. As an entrance to the Pantanal, Corumbá has the edge over Cuiabá in that it is already there, stuck in the middle of a gigantic swamp, only 119m above sea level. Its name, in Tupi, means the "place of stones" and, not surprisingly, Corumbá and the Pantanal didn't start out as a great source of attraction to travellers. As early as 1543, the swamp proved an inhospitable place to an expedition of 120 large canoes on a punitive campaign against the Guaicuru tribe. Sent by the Spanish governor of Paraguay, it encountered vampire bats, stingrays, biting ants and plagues of mosquitoes. And while it doesn't seem quite so bad today, it's easy to understand why air-conditioning is such big business here. It was Corumbá's unique location on the old rail link between the Andes and the Atlantic that originally brought most travellers to the town, but, ironically, the same swamp that deterred European invaders for so long has rapidly become an attraction, at the same time as the Brazilian part of the rail link has been closed down.

Arrival, information and accommodation

As there are now only freight trains to and from Corumbá, you're likely to arrive by either bus or plane. The **rodoviária** is close to the train station on Rua Porto Carrero (ⓣ67/3231-2033) and is served by daily buses from Campo Grande, São Paulo and even further afield. From the *rodoviária*, it's a fifteen-minute walk into town, or there are buses and taxis (R$12) plying the route. The **airport** (ⓣ67/3231-3322) is a half-hour walk or a R$25 taxi ride west of the city centre.

What little **tourist information** there is can be obtained from SEMATUR, Rua Manoel Cavassa 275, down at the port (Mon 1–6pm, Tues–Fri 8.30am–noon & 1.30–6pm; ⓣ67/3231-7336 or 3231-9747), or in the Casa do Artesão, Rua Dom Aquino Corréa 405 (same hours; ⓣ67/3231-2715).

Accommodation

Hotels in Corumbá vary considerably but their sheer quantity (the following are just a selection) means you should have no trouble finding a room, even from August to October. Out of season, especially January–Easter, there are heavy discounts all round, and prices can be bargained even lower.

The most centrally located for shops and the port, and so noisiest at night, are the clutch of cheap lodgings around **Rua Delamare**, west of Praça da República; they tend to be very popular with backpackers and are good places to

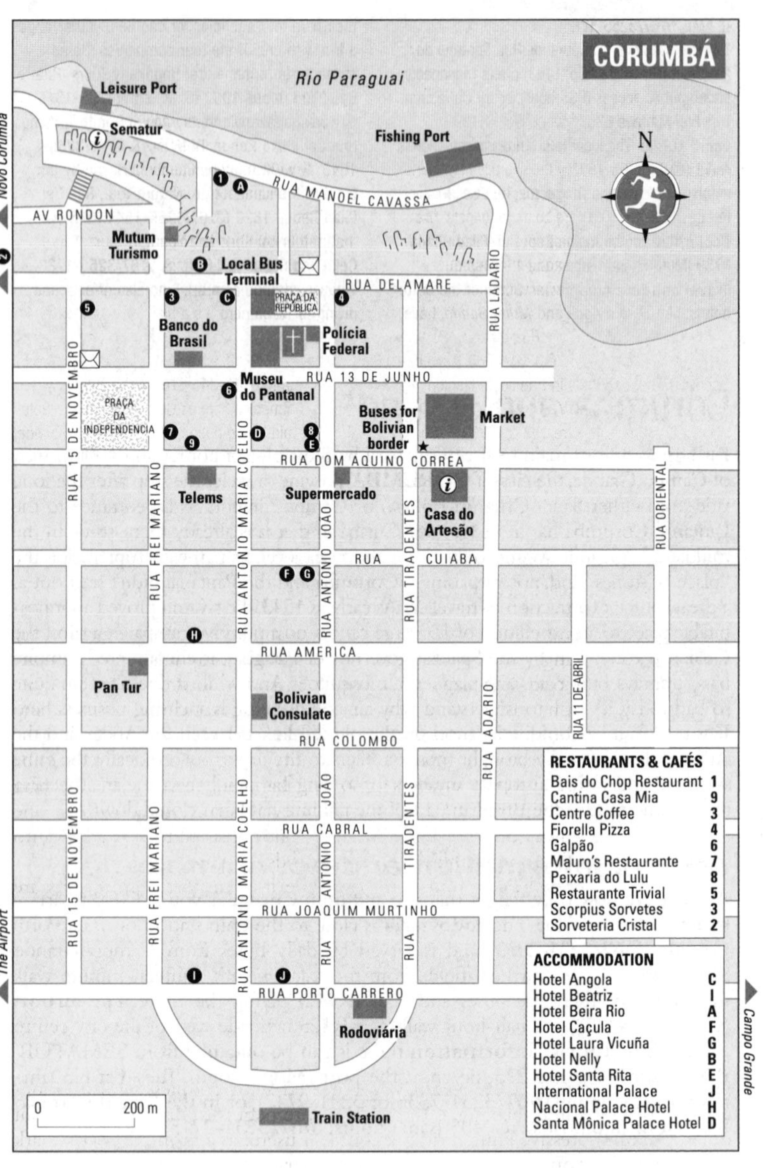

meet companions for trips into the Pantanal. For those travelling in a group, the tour agent Urcabar, by the river at Rua Manoel Cavassa 181 (☎67/231-3039), has a house to rent (nine beds in two rooms) for R$150-plus a day.

Hotel Angola Rua Antônio Maria Coelho 124 ☎67/3231-7233. Safe, perfectly reasonable and cheapest of the bunch around Rua Delamare in low season (singles from R$12). ❷–❸

Hotel Beatriz Rua Porto Carrero 896 ⓣ67/3231-7441. Facing the *rodoviária*, very cheap and pretty basic, but useful if you arrive late at night by bus and can't face the 2km hike into town. ❶

Hotel Beira Rio Rua Manoel Cavassa 109 ⓣ67/3231-2554, ⓕ3231-3313. One of the more characterful hotels right by the shore, with cheerful management. Its best rooms overlook the river and the Pantanal, and there are boats for guests' use. ❷

Hotel Caçula Rua Cuiabá 795 ⓣ67/3231-5745, ⓕ3231-1976. Next door and better value for money than the *Laura Vicuña*, with good clean rooms, each with TV. ❷

Hotel Laura Vicuña Rua Cuiabá 775 ⓣ67/3231-5874, ⓕ3231-2663. A peaceful place, very neat and tidy in traditional fashion. All rooms have phone and TV. ❸

Hotel Nelly Rua Delamare 902 ⓣ67/3231-6001, ⓕ3231-7396. Long a favourite haunt for budget travellers and kids from Rio and São Paulo, and excellent value, if a little dank. Rooms with TV cost more. ❶–❷

Hotel Santa Rita Rua Dom Aquino Corréa 860 ⓣ67/3231-5453, ⓕ3231-4834. Rooms are clean and airy at this good-value hotel – where the more expensive ones come with a/c and TV. There's also a reasonable on-site restaurant. ❷–❸

International Palace Rua Dom Aquino Corréa 1457 ⓣ67/3231-6247. Comfortable mid-range place with sauna, pool, restaurant and bar. ❹

Nacional Palace Hotel Rua América 936 ⓣ67/3234-6000, ⓔhnacion@brasinet.com.br. Pretty much top of the range in Corumbá. It's convenient and has a pool (non-residents can use it for R$25), but it's a bit flashy and over-priced. ❺

Santa Mônica Palace Hotel Rua Antônio Maria Coelho 345 ⓣ67/3231-3001, ⓦwww.hstmonica.com.br. Corumbá's largest hotel and best mid-range option, offering excellent value: rooms come with all mod cons including a/c and fridges, and the added luxury of a pool (non-residents can use it for R$12), sauna and riverboats for hire. ❺

The City

Commanding a fine view over the Rio Paraguai and across the swamp, the city is small (approaching 100,000 inhabitants), and is really only busy in the mornings – indeed it's one of Brazil's most laid-back towns south of the Amazon, basking in intense heat and overwhelming humidity. Even at the port nothing seems to disturb the slow-moving pool games taking place in the bars. Because of the heat, there's a very open-plan feel to the city and the people of Corumbá seem to be equally at home sitting at tables by bars and restaurants, or eating their dinners outside in front of their houses. In every street, there's at least one television blaring away on the pavement, and it's not unusual to be invited into someone's house for food, drinks or – at weekends – a party.

Corumbá's life revolves around its **port**, while its transport connections are at the other end of town around the *rodoviária* and airport; if you're intending to stay more than one night, the port end is your best bet. Within a few blocks of the riverfront you'll find the **Praça da Independência**, a large, shaded park with ponds, a children's playground and a few unusual installations dotted around: a streamroller, imported from England around 1921, whose first job was flattening Avenida General Rondon, and an antique water wheel, also English, which served in a sugar factory until 1932. Early in the day, the *praça* is alive with tropical birds, and by evening it's crowded with couples, family groups and gangs of children relaxing as the temperature begins to drop. The large but otherwise unimpressive church on this square is useful as a prominent landmark to help you get your bearings in this very flat, grid-patterned city.

A stone's throw away on the smaller **Praça da República** stands the stark late nineteenth-century Igreja Matriz Nossa Senhora da Candelária. Next door at Rua Delamare 939, facing the local bus terminal, is the fascinating **Museu do Pantanal** (Mon–Fri noon–5pm; free), which encompasses a collection of stuffed animals, artefacts from various indigenous tribes of the region, some archeological specimens, and changing exhibits of modern art. If you need advice or information about the local flora or fauna, contact the museum office. The only other thing to see is the **Casa do Artesão** at Rua Dom Aquino Corréa 405 (Mon–Fri 8–11am & 2–5pm, Sat 8–11am). It's housed in Corumbá's most historic edifice – the old prison, dating from 1900 – and is a great place to track down some local craft work (especially wood and leather), as well as local liquors and *Farinha da Bocaiúva*, a flour made from palm-tree nuts and reputed to be an aphrodisiac.

Eating, drinking and nightlife

For **self-catering**, there's a branch of Supermercado Ohara on the corner of Rua Dom Aquino Corréa and Rua Antônio João, and three butchers opposite. The covered market, one block east, should complete your provisions. There's only one place for really good coffee and great juices – *Centre Coffee*, at Rua Delamare 967. For ice cream try *Scorpius Sorvetes* at the corner of Rua Cuiabá and Rua Frei Mariano, and *Sorveteria Cristal* on the corner of Rua Delamare and Rua 7 de Setembro.

There's no shortage of **restaurants** in Corumbá. The best are to be found on Rua Frei Mariano and Rua 15 de Novembro, though there are plenty of cheap snack bars throughout town, especially on Rua Delamare west of the Praça da República, serving good set meals for less than R$12. Being a swamp city, fish is the main local delicacy, with *pacu* and *pintado* among the favoured species. For upmarket local cuisine try *Peixaria do Lulu*, Rua Antônio João 410 (⊕67/3232-2142), or the smart *Cantina Casa Mia*, opposite the telephone office at Rua Dom Aquino Corréa 928 (closed Mon; ⊕67/3231-1327). *Mauro's Restaurante*, facing the Praça da Independência at Rua Frei Mariano 383, is one of the classiest and most popular eateries, particularly at lunchtimes when it has a splendid selection of surprisingly good-value self-service dishes. There's a huge choice of inexpensive meat and fish in vast portions from *Galpão*, Rua 13 de Junho 797 at the corner of Rua Antônio Maria Coelho; more modest is the calm *Restaurante Trivial* at Rua 15 de Novembro 146/188, which has self-service *comida por kilo* most lunchtimes and evenings. For pizza freaks, there's *Fiorella Pizza*, on the eastern corner of Praça da República and Rua Delamare. Lastly, for those who like to **cruise** with their food, the restaurant-boat *La Barca Tur* (⊕67/3231-3106) does five-hour lunch trips in high season, including the inevitable piranha soup, for R$60.

As to **bars**, you'll find these all over town, though with few exceptions they're spit-and-sawdust joints, rough-looking and a little intimidating at first. The town is not safe at night, so you do need to take care and perhaps try to avoid walking the streets after 10pm. The more relaxed bars are those down on the riverfront – where you can usually get a game of pool with your drink. **Night-life** is best at the trendy *Bais do Chop* restaurant (⊕67/3231-1079) located on the waterfront along Rua Manoel Cavassa in a lovingly restored mansion down at the port next to the *artesanato* shops; it plays good live music at weekends.

Listings

Airlines TAM (⊕67/3231-7099) and Pantanal Linhas Aéreas (⊕67/3231-1818) fly regularly from Corumbá to Campo Grande, and from there to other destinations. Tickets for all companies can be brought from Mutum Turismo (see "Travel and tour agencies" below), or at the airport after 9.30am.

Banks and exchange You can change cash and travellers' cheques at the *casa de câmbio* at Rua 15 de Novembro 212 (Mon–Fri 8.30am–5pm). Otherwise, there's a host of banks including HSBC, some with ATMs, on Rua Delamare west of Praça da República (all Mon–Fri 10am–3pm), as well as the Banco do Brasil, Rua 13 de Junho 914 (10am–5pm). Out-of-hours exchange is sometimes possible at the desk in the *Nacional Palace Hotel*, Rua América 936, or ask other hotel or shop managers.

Boats There are plenty of boats waiting on the riverfront off Rua Manoel Cavassa that will take you into the Pantanal swamp or Bolivia; these include the Albatroz (Ⓣ67/3231-4858) which has eighteen cabins and does five-day trips and the Pira Miuna (Ⓣ67/3232-1204) which does cheaper three-day trips and has only two cabins. See box on p.588 for details of Pantanal operators, or ask around at the numerous offices on the waterfront. Small motorboats can be hired (two to four passengers) from *Hotel Beir Rio* and Urcabar, also on Rua Manoel Cavassa, for about R$150–200 a day (fuel is extra – you'll need up to 50 litres in a day). One option, a little hit or miss, is joining a cargo boat bound for Asunción. If you do find a Paraguayan trading boat, you should take care of the necessary paperwork with the Polícia Federal, Praça da República (Ⓣ67/3231-5848 or 3231-2413), and the Paraguayan consulate (see below) before leaving town, as well as with the Capitania dos Portos (Ⓣ67/3231-6444) at Rua Delamare 806, next to the post office.

Car rental Localiza is at Rua Frei Mariano 51 (Ⓣ67/3231-6379); Unidas, Rua Drei Mariano 633 (Mon–Sat 8am–6pm; Ⓣ67/3231-3124), has reliable cars that can be taken out of Brazil, but must be returned to Corumbá. Both charge R$220 a day upwards.

Consulates Bolivia, Rua Antônio Maria Coelho 852 Ⓣ67/3231-5605; Paraguay, Rua Cuiabá Ⓣ67/231-4803.

Health matters Clinica Samec Ⓣ67/3231-3308.

Laundry There's an expensive same-day laundry service at Apae, Rua 13 de Junho 1377.

Post office The main post office is at Rua Delamare 708, opposite the church on Praça da República (Mon–Fri 9am–5pm, Sat 8–11.30am). A smaller office is near Praça da Independência on Rua 15 de Novembro (same hours).

Shopping For the Casa do Artesão and for food shopping, see opposite. Two of the shops on Praça da Independência are devoted entirely to hunting, fishing and cowboy paraphernalia, like saddles and guns, and there's a shop on Rua Antônio Maria Coelho, three blocks from the river, stuffed with garish Catholic *ex votos* and plastic icons. There are numerous photographic shops throughout town; Fotocor, Rua Delamare 871, has a good reputation.

Taxis Ponto Taxi Ⓣ67/3231-4043 (taxi rank at southeast corner of Praça da Independência); Mototaxis Ⓣ67/3231-7166.

Travel and tour agencies Pantur, Rua Frei Mariano 1013 (Ⓣ67/3231-2000) is a reliable air and train ticket sales agent and can also help organise comfortable *fazenda* trips into the swamp; Corumbá Tur, Rua Antônio Maria Coelho 852 (Ⓣ & Ⓕ67/231-1532 or 1260), an upmarket operator dealing with *fazendas* and luxury angling cruises, also does half-day cruises to Puerto Suarez in Bolivia (R$40; no passport required), a good place for silverwork and tax-free goods. Green Track, Rua Antônio João 216 (Ⓣ67/3231-2258, Ⓔgreentk@terra.com.br), runs recommended packages of up to five days in the Pantanal. Mutum Turismo, Rua Frei Mariano 17 (Ⓣ67/3231-1818 or 3231-1768, Ⓕ231-3027), deals with flights and ticketing, and has a list of approved Pantanal guides. Fishing-based tours are operated by Pérola do Pantanal, Rua Manoel Cavassa 255, Porto Geral (Ⓣ67/3231-1460, Ⓦwww.msinternet.com.br/perola). Down on the riverfront there are several smaller boat tour company offices that run fishing and safari trips, incuding Urcabar, Rua Manoel Cavassa 181 (Ⓣ67/3231-3039) and La Barca Tour (Ⓣ67/3231-3016). See also the list of upmarket Pantanal operators on p.588. Budget Pantanal tours are run by all of the cheap hotels around Rua Delamare, whose touts will probably find you as soon as you get off the bus. Make sure you get authorized receipts for any money or valuables you deposit with a tour company or hotel; there have been reports of problems with this kind of practice in Corumbá.

Around Corumbá

Apart from the Pantanal itself (see p.583), there isn't a great deal to visit around Corumbá. Probably the most interesting place is the ruins of the eighteenth-century **Forte de Coimbra** (daily 8.30–11.30am & 1.30–4pm), 80km to the south. Theoretically, the fort can only be visited with previous permission from the Brigada Mista in Corumbá, Av. General Rondon 1735 (Ⓣ67/3231-2861 or 3231-9866), although visitors unaware of this fact are sometimes allowed in. On the other hand, the Brigada Mista is as good a place as any to find out about transport to the fort. The fort is accessible only by water, and is most easily reached via Porto Esperança, an hour's bus ride from Corumbá (buses leave from outside *Hotel Beatriz* several times a day). The journey there is an interesting one along the edge of the swamp, and once in Porto Esperança you should have little difficulty renting a boat, or finding a guide, to take you a couple more hours downriver to the fort (it will cost at least R$50, however). It's also possible to approach the fort in traditional fashion, by following the Rio Paraguai all the way from Corumbá in a boat (from around R$35 a person, depending on size of your group), but this takes around seven hours and involves going through a tour agency in town. One bonus of going by this route, however, is that you'll pass two little-visited natural caves, **Gruta do Inferno** and **Buraco Soturno**, sculpted with huge finger-like stalactites and stalagmites.

The Forte de Coimbra was built in 1775, three years before Corumbá's foundation, to defend this western corner of Brazilian territory and, more specifically, to protect the border against invasion from Paraguay. In 1864 it was attacked by the invading Paraguayan army, which had slipped upriver into the southern Mato Grosso. Coimbra provided the first resistance to the invaders, but it didn't last for long as the Brazilian soldiers escaped from the fort under cover of darkness, leaving the fort to the aggressors. Nearly three thousand Paraguayans continued upstream in a huge convoy of ships and, forging its way north beyond Corumbá, the armada crossed the swamps almost as far as the city of Cuiabá, which was saved only by the shallowness of its river. Nowadays the fort is a pretty dull ruin (except perhaps for military enthusiasts), and it's the journey there that's the real draw.

You may also be able to visit one of the planet's largest manganese deposits, currently being mined in the Urucum hills, just south of Corumbá off the BR-262. The hills rise more than 950m above the level of the swamp, and, although much of the area is technically out of bounds, organized visits to the **Minas do Morro do Urucum at Mineradora**, 24km from Corumbá, with their subterranean galleries (Grutas dos Belgas), can still be arranged through most tour agencies in Corumbá – or contact the company office at Av. General Rondon 1351 (☎67/3231-1661). If you decide to chance a visit unaccompanied, buses to Urucum depart from a lot next to *Hotel Beatriz* on Rua Porto Carrero.

Finally, if you're not going to have the time to get any further into the Pantanal, you can get a taste of the swamp life, without spending a lot of money,

Crossing the Bolivian border

Crossing into or out of Bolivia from Corumbá is a slightly disjointed procedure. **Leaving Brazil**, you should get an exit stamp from the Polícia Federal at Praça da República 51 in Corumbá (easiest before 11am or between 7pm and 9pm), before picking up a Bolivian visa (if you need one) from the consulate at Rua Antônio Maria Coelho 881 (☎67/3231-5605). After that, it's a matter of taking the bus (from the Praça Independência on Rua Dom Aquino Corréa) the 10km to the border, checking through Bolivian immigration and receiving your passport entry stamp. **Money** can be changed at decent rates at the border.

Train tickets for Santa Cruz should be bought at La Brasilena train station in **Quijarro**, a few minutes by *colectivo* (a type of shuttle bus; R$5) or bus from the Bolivian immigration office. First class to Santa Cruz costs R$60, second class R$35. The first-class carriages are comfortable, with videos, but everything sways and the toilets are dirty. Limited food is available on board, and also from the trackside villages during the train's frequent stops. Insect repellent and clothes that cover your flesh are essential, as the lights of the carriages attract all manner of biting insects at night. Drinking water and a torch are also useful. As timetables vary considerably, check at the station in Corumbá or Quijarro at least a couple of days in advance. It's worth going to Quijarro the day before departure to actually make your booking.

Entering Brazil from Bolivia is essentially the same procedure in reverse, although US citizens should remember to pick up visas in the Brazilian consulate in Santa Cruz before leaving.

at two settlements on the Rio Paraguai. **PORTO MORRINHO** is the easier to get to, 67km or an hour by bus from Corumbá, just west of Porto Esperança on the main road to Campo Grande, with ample birdlife and creeks to explore. The town has a few cheap hotels, such as the *Pousada do Pescador* (Ⓣ67/3287-1693; ❷–❸) and the *Hotel Tuiui* (❹), the latter some 200m by *balsa* (raft) from Porto Morrinho on the banks of the river. The *Tuiui* rents out motorboats for R$80 a day and rowing boats for R$30. About the same distance from Corumbá on the old Campo Grande road (the unsurfaced MS-184/MS-228) is **PORTO MANGA**, which is renowned as a centre for wildlife-spotting and fishing on the Rio Paraguai, particularly in September. There are a couple of hotels here, including the *Pesqueiro* (Ⓣ67/3231-1987; ❷–❸), whose clean rooms have private baths, as well as some riverboats and boatmen for hire, and various potential camping locations in and around the settlement. From Porto Manga onward it's only 70km via Passo do Lontra to rejoin the BR-262.

The Pantanal

Fed by rivers from the Andes to the west and the Brazilian central plateau to the north, **THE PANTANAL** is an open swampland larger than France that extends deep into the states of Mato Grosso and Mato Grosso do Sul. A slightly daunting region to visit, running 950km north to south and averaging around 500km from east to west, it is one of those places in Brazil where you're more likely to find wildlife than nightlife. In fact, you see so many birds and animals that you start to think you're in a well-stocked wildlife park – the wildlife is wild, but not at all shy. Capybaras, wild boar, monkeys, yellow anacondas (*sucuri amarela* in Portuguese or *Eunectes notaeus*) and over four hundred bird species, including the *tuiuiú* (giant red-necked stork) are common sights in the Pantanal, and it's probably the best place for wild mammals and exotic birds in the whole of the Americas. There are in fact 124 wild mammal species, 177 reptile species and a further 41 amphibian species in these swamps. Having said that, it's only fair to mention that you'll still see more cattle and *jacarés* (*Caiman yacare*, alligators) than any other creatures. It has been a fabulous fishing spot for thousands of years and new species of fish and vascular plants are still being regularly discovered here. One of the tastiest and most popular fish – *pacu* – has been endangered by illegal over-fishing, much serving the markets of southern Brazil.

Although having only thirty percent natural forest cover, over 4.5 percent of the trees (some 6260 square kilometres) has already been destroyed by human activity – mainly cattle ranching. The region is a stunning blend of swamp water with gallery forest, savanna and lakeside scrub forest. The region is dissected by around 175 rivers into roughly seventeen segments, each with its own distinctive landscape and micro-ecosytem. It was designated a UNESCO World Heritage Site in 2000 and became a Biosphere Reserve in the last few years; the protected areas of the Pantanal have expanded almost threefold since the late 1990s.

Taking off into the Pantanal is what most independent travellers have in mind when they arrive in Mato Grosso, but as no road or rail track crosses the swamp it's a tricky place to travel. The easiest and one of the best ways to experience

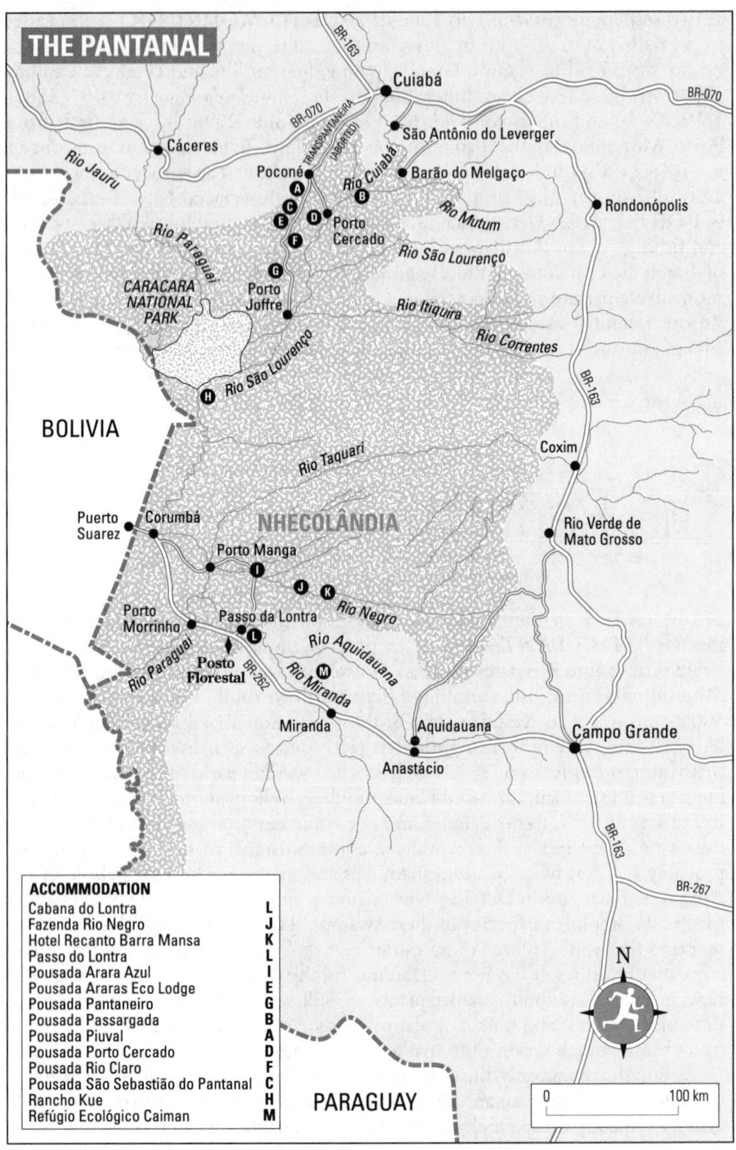

the Pantanal is by taking an **organized tour**, perhaps spending a night or two at a **fazenda-lodge** (called **pousadas** in the northern Pantanal). The *fazenda*-lodges, mostly converted ranch-houses with decent facilities, are generally reached by jeep; those that require access by boat or plane are usually deeper into the swamp, which increases your chances of spotting the more elusive wildlife. At least one night in the swamp is essential if you want to see or do anything other than sit in a bus or jeep the whole time; three- or four-day excursions will give you a couple of full days in the swamp. Without an organized trip, unless you've got bags of money or are travelling in a large group (in which case you can hire boats to get you almost anywhere), you're dependent on local **cargo boats**, which inevitably take much longer than expected. Organized tours are also more likely to go out of their way to show you the wildlife than will a captain whose boat is brimming over with livestock. **Renting a car** is also a slim possibility, though without four-wheel drive you're limited to only a few tracks on the fringes of the swamp where the wildlife makes itself scarce.

Most organized tours enter the Pantanal by road and spend a couple of days exploring in canoes, small motorboats or on horseback from a land base. The most obvious initial target is **Corumbá** in Mato Grosso do Sul. There is lots of accommodation here and no end of agencies and operators running trips into the swamp. Other routes into the swamp are from **Campo Grande** in the east or **Cuiabá**, to the north, through settlements like **Porto Jofre** and **Cáceres**. The **best time** to explore the Pantanal is probably towards the end of the rainy season, around April, when your chances of spotting wildlife are high.

Some background

There are very few places on earth where it is so easy to see so much wildlife as in the Pantanal, which occupies an arguably unique ecological niche as an unparalleled bio-genetic reservoir. It's almost unnerving spending the afternoon on the edge of a remote lagoon in the swamp, surrounded by seemingly endless streams of flying and wading birds – toucans, parrots, red and even the endangered hyacinth macaws, blue herons, and the symbol of the Pantanal, the magnificent *jabiru*, or giant red-throated storks, known locally as *tuiuiú*. Unlike in most other areas of wilderness, the birdsong and density of wildlife in the Pantanal frequently lives up to the exotic soundtrack of Hollywood jungle movies, and in the middle of the swamp it's actually possible to forget that there are other people in the world – though it's difficult to forget the **mosquitoes**. (Malaria is supposedly absent in the Pantanal, so you'll only have the insufferable itching to worry about.) The mosquitoes should be no surprise really, given that the Pantanal is the biggest inland swamp in the world, covering some 230,000 square kilometres of the upper Rio Paraguai basin.

The entire region acts as an immense sponge, seasonally absorbing the swollen waters of three large rivers – the Paraguai, Taquari and Cuiabá. During the **rainy season**, from November to March, river levels rise by up to 3m, producing a vast flooded plain with islands of scrubby forest amidst oceans of floating vegetation. Transport is necessarily dominated by the rivers, natural water channels and hundreds of well-hidden lagoons, though most of the *fazendas* are still reachable by road. The islands of vegetation created during the rains crawl with wild animals – jaguars, monkeys, tapirs, capybaras (the world's largest rodents) and wild boar living side by side with domesticated cattle. Many birds are harder to spot, nesting deeper in the forests for the breeding season; nevertheless, there are still plenty of birds and other creatures to see all year round, including hawks and kingfishers.

At other times of the year, much of the Pantanal is still very boggy though interspersed with open grassy savannas studded with small wooded islands of taller vegetation, mainly palm trees. The **dry season**, from April to October, with its peak normally around September, transforms the swamp into South America's most exciting natural wildlife reserve. This is the **best time** to see wildlife, when

△ A capybara in the swamp

much of it is attracted to the lakes and riverbanks in search of food and water: the swamp's infamous piranha and alligator populations crowd into relatively small pools and streams, while the astonishing array of aquatic birds follows suit, forming very dense colonies known here as *viveiros*. Treeless bush savanna alternates with wet swamp, while along the banks of the major rivers grow belts of rainforest populated with colonies of monkeys (including spider monkeys and noisy black gibbons). Note, however, that the previously metronomic regularity of the seasons has become most unpredictable of late, with the onset of global warming.

History and development

The Pantanal is known to have been inhabited for at least five thousand years. Ceramics were being produced by 1500 BC and strange mounds were created, possibly ritual sites, around the same era. These were occupied until 1000 AD, then re-utilized by various of the Pantanal's tribal groups: Paiaguá, Gutao, Terna and Mbayá-Guaicuru. At the time of early Portuguese explorations, and the first unsuccessful attempts at populating the region by the Spanish in the sixteenth century, the region was dominated by three main tribes. In the south lived the horse-riding **Guaicuru**, who adopted stray or stolen horses and cattle from the advancing white settlers, making the tribe an elite group amongst Indians. Wearing only jaguar skins as they rode into battle, they were feared by the neighbouring **Terena** (Guana) tribe, who lived much of their lives as servants to Guaicuru families. In many ways, the nature and degree of their economic and social interaction suggests that the two might once have been different castes within the same tribe. Another powerful people lived to the north – the **Paiaguá**, masters of the main rivers, lagoons and canals of the central Pantanal. Much to the chagrin of both Spanish and Portuguese expeditions into the swamps, the Paiaguá were superbly skilled with both their canoes and the bow and arrow.

In 1540, the Spaniard Alvar Nuñez Cabeza de Vaca explored some of the Pantanal. Having previously explored Texas and southeast USA, he was particularly impressed here with the extraordinary fishing and the healthy constitutions of the people. Some Spanish adventurers also arrived here in the late sixteenth century, bringing with them the first cattle. They were soon evicted by Brazilian Bandeirantes, but left their cattle behind to go feral. It wasn't until the **discovery of gold** in the northern Pantanal and around Cuiabá during the early eighteenth century that any genuine settlement schemes were undertaken. A rapid influx of colonists, miners and soldiers led to several bloody battles. In June 1730 hundreds of Paiaguá warriors in 83 canoes ambushed the annual flotilla, which was carrying some 900kg of gold south through the Pantanal from Cuiabá. They spared only some of the women and a few of the stronger black rowers from the flotilla: all of the gold and most of the white men were lost. Much of the gold eventually found its way out of Brazil and into Spanish Paraguay where Cautiguacu, the Paiaguá chief, lived a life of luxury in Asunción until his death 55 years later.

The decline of the gold mines during the nineteenth century brought development in the Pantanal to a standstill and the population began to fall. The twentieth century saw the establishment of unrestricted **cattle-grazing** ranches – *fazendas* – and today over twenty million head of cattle roam the swamp. Party time here is during the bull castration period, when the local delicacy becomes readily available. Droughts and diseases ravaged the Pantanal cattle industry in the late 1960s and early 1970s. Then the 1980s and 90s saw significant replacement of the traditional *gaucho* ranch worker with the introduction of mechanized vehicles and light aircraft. Thankfully, however, Brazilian cowboys still abound.

To the east, the BR-163 between Campo Grande and Cuiabá skirts around the Pantanal, and Ministry of Transport plans for a Transpantaneira road from Cuiabá to Corumbá have been shelved for the sake of the region's ecological balance. For all that, tourism has developed greatly in the region over the last few years, coinciding with a slump in the price for cattle. The papers are full of auction notices for *fazendas*, livestock and equipment, though some *fazendeiros* have been quick to realize the potential of converting their farms and land into ecological reserves.

Wildlife trade and ranching were at their peak here between the late ninetheenth century and the end of World War II, when the demand for beef in particular dropped off. The Pantanal, however, is still **under threat** from the illegal exploitation of skins, fish and rare birds, and even gold panning. The chemical fertilizers and pesticides used on the enormous *fazendas* to produce cash crops such as soya beans are also beginning to take their toll. **Ecotourism** has been heralded as a potential savior for the swamp, but this will only work if sufficient money is ploughed back into conservation. The Pantanal has its own Polícia Florestal who try to enforce the environment-friendly regulations now being strictly applied to visitors and locals alike: no disposal of non-biodegradable rubbish, no noise pollution, no fishing without a licence (it costs R$250) or between November and January during the breeding season, no fishing with nets or explosives and no removal of rocks, wildlife or plant life.

Practicalities

If you talk to locals about visiting the Pantanal they will almost certainly recommend going in by road. This is usually cheaper and quicker than renting a boat or going on one of the cruises. The main problem, though, is knowing where and how to go, and which company or lodge to choose. This section gives a rough overview of the various options, together with a box listing a selection of recommended **tour operators** (see p.588). The following sections describe some possible **routes**, from Corumbá and from Cuiabá, together with details of **accommodation** in *fazenda*-lodges and *pousadas*. The box on pp.590–591 describes the options for **boat trips** from Cáceres and Corumbá.

Upmarket Pantanal agents and operators

The following is a selection of the more upmarket Pantanal operators who deal with both complete packages and bookings for boats and/or lodges; for other agents and guides, see under "Listings" for Cuiabá, Campo Grande and Corumbá.

Aguas do Pantanal Av. Afonso Pena 367, Miranda ⓣ67/3242-1242. This company owns and runs several *pousadas* around Miranda, Passo do Lontra and Porto Morrinho on the Rio Paraguai.

Anaconda Rua Marechal Deodoro 2142, Centro, Cuiabá ⓣ65/3624-4142. Short but well organized and comfortable tours in the Pantanal and elsewhere in the Brazilian wilderness.

Corumbá Tur Rua Antônio Maria Coelho 852, Corumbá ⓣ & ⓕ067/3231-1532. Corumbá's leading upmarket agency, dealing with all the main *fazendas* and luxury boat cruises, as well as organizing its own fishing and photography tours (anywhere from R$120 per person per day). Prices for the fishing cruises (departing Sun on a variety of boats) range from R$1500 to R$3000 per person per week.

Fish World Rua Lucélia 85, Vila Castelo, Campo Grande ⓣ67/3383-3709, ⓕ3382-8152. Efficient agents for a large number of luxury boat trips, specializing in angling trips, as well as bookings for *fazenda*-lodges.

Pantanal Explorers Av. Gov. J.P. Arruda 670, Várzea Grande, Cuiabá ⓣ65/3682-2800 or 682-1260. Agents and operators for tours and boats based around Cuiabá and Cáceres.

Pan Tur Rua America 969, Corumbá ⓣ67/3231-2000. Agents for almost everything, who also run their own Pantanal tours from around R$160 a day.

Pérola do Pantanal Rua Manoel Cavassa 255, Corumbá ⓣ67/3231-1460, ⓦwww.msinternet.com.br/perola. Agents for upmarket cruises from Corumbá.

If you want to go **independently** remember that the Pantanal is a difficult and dangerous place to travel in. There are very few roads and, although hundreds of tracks sneak their way into the swamp, they are used only by *fazenda* workers who know them inside out. An inexperienced driver or hiker could easily get lost – or worse. That said, there's no better way to see the wildlife than to camp or stay on a boat deep in the swamp, away from roads, tracks or *fazenda*-lodges, but to do this you will need a local **guide**; these are generally available only at lodges or in end-of-the-track settlements like Porto Jofre. Also, it's important to take all the **equipment** you need with you if you're going it alone like this in the Pantanal – food, camping gear, a first-aid kit and lots of mosquito repellent. It's possible to take **buses** and **boats** from Cuiabá and Corumbá to places such as Cáceres, Coxim, Porto Jofre or Aquidauana, and it's then a matter of finding a boat going your way deeper into the swamp or paying a local guide or *fazendeiro* to take you on a trip. This will cost around R$60–120 per person per day, including canoe or vehicle transport and a guide/boatman/driver. Local guides and *fazendeiros* usually prefer to use the road networks to reach *fazenda*-lodges within the swamp, and explore in canoes or on horseback from there. Cheaper still, and certainly the most unusual alternative, is to buy a passage (around R$25–50 a day; hammock essential) on one of the few **trading boats** still crossing the Pantanal between Corumbá and Cáceres, and occasionally Porto Jofre (both connected by road to Cuiabá).

Most people, however, go on **organized tours**, entering the swamp in jeeps or trucks and following one of the few rough roads that now connect Corumbá, Aquidauana, Coxim and Cuiabá (via Poconé or Cáceres) with some of the larger *fazenda* settlements of the interior. The short **jeep trips**, often run by freelance operators, are relatively cheap (especially from Corumbá, where a hammock and truck tour can cost as little as R$60–70 a day per person; from Cuiabá, it's more like US$50-60), but they offer little more than a flavour of the swamp. Details of some freelance operators are given on p.600 (Cuiabá), p.567 (Campo Grande) and p.581 (Corumbá). Instead, it's better to seek out reliable and recommended companies which can offer lodge- or *fazenda*-based safaris to suit your budget. It is also possible to take **small boat trips** (around R$90–200 a day, from Corumbá, Porto Jofre or Cáceres; there are no agencies for this sort of trip, so just ask around), or a **combination of jeep and boat**, over four or five days, which would certainly give the trip a taste of adventure, and could work out cheaper if you and your companions (there's usually a minimum number of passengers needed for boats) are happy braving the mosquitoes in hammocks. Note that if you're in Campo Grande, the trips you might be offered will invariably be luxury cruises.

Swamping it in comfort is getting easier, at one of an increasing number of **fazenda-lodges** in the Pantanal, well away from towns and main roads. However, with few exceptions these cost upwards of R$150 a night per person, and R$450–500 is not uncommon. In their favour, though, is that the prices invariably include various activities, including trips by boat or jeep, horse riding, guided walks or fishing expeditions, as well as meals. Prices are generally more reasonable in the northern Pantanal (accessible from Cuiabá) than in the south (Corumbá, Miranda and Aquidauana). Also including nights in *fazenda*-lodges are **all-inclusive package tours**, though their prices vary wildly, sometimes undercutting the official lodge price, at other times almost doubling it – it's worth shopping around and bargaining (the tour operators listed in the box opposite all have a selection). As a general rule, however, you'll pay less if you deal direct with a *fazenda*-lodge owner in Porto Jofre, Cáceres, Aquidauana and even Corumbá, rather than through their agents. Most of the *fazenda*-lodges are located east and northeast of Corumbá, and also on either side of the Rio Cuiabá in the north, accessible for the most part via the aborted Transpantaneira road between Poconé and Porto Jofre. If you really have money to burn, signing up for a **luxury cruise**, or even **hiring a boat** for a week or so, is the ideal option – see the box on pp.590–591. If you want to arrange tours from home before you leave for Brazil, see the "Basics" section of this guide for operators.

Into the swamp: routes from Corumbá and Campo Grande

Corumbá is well placed for getting right into the Pantanal by bus or jeep, and has a welter of guides and agencies to choose from, as well as boats for hire. Though farther from the action, Campo Grande has better hotels and communications with the rest of Brazil, so it's as likely an entry point as Corumbá. Currently the most popular *fazenda*-lodges are those in Nhecolândia, roughly speaking the area between the *rios* Negro and Taquari east of Corumbá. These benefit from a well-established dirt access road, the MS-184/MS-228 (the old Campo Grande road), which loops off from the main BR-262 highway 300km from Campo Grande near Passo do Lontra (it's well signposted), and crosses through a large section of the swamp before rejoining the same road some 10km before Corumbá. The track also passes through Porto Manga (see p.582).

If you're coming from **Campo Grande**, one of the best budget options is to hook up with Ecological Expeditions, Rua Joaquim Nabuco 185 (Ⓣ67/3382-3504, 67/9984-0450 or 67/3321-0505, Ⓦwww.pantanaltrekking.com), who offer one of the cheapest options for going deep into the swamp area by using

Pantanal boat tours

At present, two basic types of **cargo boat** cross the swamp between Cáceres and Corumbá on a fairly regular basis – **soya** and **cattle barges**. Neither has fixed schedules or itineraries, so it's a matter of checking on departure dates when you arrive at either town. The trip usually takes about six to ten days upstream from Corumbá, three to six downstream, with plenty of time for relaxing and looking out for wildlife. The barges, though, do tend to keep to the main channel of the Rio Paraguai, which obviously doesn't give you a good chance of spotting anything particularly shy or rare. However, if you can find space on one of these boats, then it's a very inexpensive as well as unusual way of seeing some of the Pantanal. Apart from your hammock, take some extra food (tins, biscuits, bottled drinks and the like), insect repellent and a few good books. And a bottle of whisky or good *cachaça* wouldn't go amiss with the captain.

The only other problem is that travelling on the barges hasn't been strictly legal since 1985, when the son of a naval minister accidentally died while on board one of the cement barges that used to ply the same route. Passengers have consequently been "smuggled" aboard in dinghies, under cover of darkness. However, you might find it's still possible to buy a ride simply by asking the *comandante* of Portobras, one of the barge companies – they have offices on the waterfront in both Corumbá and Cáceres (☎65/3222-1728). The cattle barge between Corumbá and Cáceres run by Serviço de Navegação da Bacia da Prata also often picks up passengers from the ports at either end, but leaves at irregular intervals. Other cattle boats leaving Corumbá are willing to take passengers on return journeys within the swamp, delivering and picking up cattle from various *fazendas*.

Luxury fishing boats are the other option, prohibitively expensive for most, but an ideal way to encounter the swamp's wildlife on the end of a line and ultimately on your plate. Essentially floating hotels designed with the Brazilian passion for angling in mind, one of these for a week costs anything from R$1500 to R$5000 a head, though the price is full-board and usually includes ample drink, food and unlimited use of their small motorboat tenders for exploring further afield. Note that for **families with small children**, any river trip is inadvisable as none of the boats currently in use has guard-rails safe enough to keep a toddler from falling in.

Most of the boats are based in Corumbá, with some others in Cáceres, Barão do Melgaço and Cuiabá, and all can be booked through the upmarket agents on p.588. In high season, they tend to run pre-scheduled trips, departing and returning Sundays; routes are mentioned where they remain fixed from year to year. Out of season, they're up for rent, with a minimum number of passengers and days

camping facilities. They also run various tours including bush walking, horse riding, vehicle safaris, canoeing (in the wet season), piranha fishing, and wildlife spotting. Tour prices are also reasonable, with a three-day tour at around R$350 (four days R$400 and five days R$450).

Fazenda-lodges in the southern Pantanal

The following *fazenda*-lodges are accessible from Corumbá, Miranda or Aquidauana; they offer full-board accommodation and swamp trips, and can be booked through the addresses given below or through the upmarket Pantanal operators listed in the box on p.588.

Cabana do Lontra Passo do Lontra ☎67/3383-4532. Situated near where the MS-184 crosses the Rio Miranda, some 100km southeast of Corumbá and 7km off the main BR-262. The *Cabana*, with over twenty rooms and its own motorboats, is located in a good spot for most wildlife; excellent for fishing. ❺ invariably demanded, though bargaining is possible. You can find them tied up at their home ports.

Luxury boats from Cáceres

Botel Pantanal Explorer II ⓣ65/3682-2800. Mainly covering the Rio Paraguai, this boat is very small with only three quadruple cabins. Upwards of R$300 per person per day.

Cobra Grande ⓣ65/3223-4203. A small boat with five cabins and an adequate dining room; book well in advance. Prices run R$100–200 a day per person.

Rei do Rio and Velho do Rio Contact Moretti Serviços Fluviais, Cuiabá ⓣ65/3361-2082, ⓕ3322-6563. A couple of Louisiana-style houseboats intended primarily as bases for fishing expeditions. R$100–200 a day per person.

Luxury boats from Corumbá

Arara Tur Rua Manoel Cavassa 47, by the port, Corumbá ⓣ67/3231-4851, ⓦwww.araratur.com.br. This company runs a fine boat – the *Albatroz* – beautifully furnished with bars and cosy but very comfortable cabins. Choose from a wide range of short and longer boat tours in the Pantanal, specializing in photo safaris on the Rio Paraguai. Costs R$500 per person per day, five days minimum.

Cabexy II Pantanal Tours, Rua Manoel Cavassa 61, Corumbá ⓣ67/3231-1559, ⓦwww.pantanaltours.tur.br. Two two-tiered riverboats for rent, similar in style to the *Kalypso* (see below) but holding a maximum of eight passengers each, and rather more exclusive. Motorboats and fishing accessories provided. Five-day minimum period, R$500 per person per day. Reservations and R$7000 deposit required.

Kalypso Book direct on ⓣ67/3231-1460 or through agents Corumbá Tur, Mutum Turismo or Pan Tur. Brazil's answer to Nile cruisers, the *Kalypso* is a spacious three-tier affair with berths for 120 passengers, and looks for all the world like a pile of portacabins on a barge (which is what it once was). The interior is wood-panelled, the restaurant is self-service, and there's a pool on top in which to escape the mosquitoes and the heat. Originally designed as a base for fishing trips, it has a number of small motorboats and a giant fridge in which you can keep your catch. Prices start at R$300 per person per day, with a minimum stay of six nights.

Millenium This luxury vessel has ten cabins and can only be booked for six days at a time; bookings on ⓣ67/3231-3372 or ⓦwww.opantaneirotur.com.br. From R$180 a day per person.

Fazenda Rio Negro Rua Antônio Correa 1161, Bairro Monte Libano, Campo Grande) ⓣ67/3351-5191, ⓦwww.fazendarionegro.com.br. One of the Pantanal's oldest ranches, founded in 1895 by Cicíaco and Thomázia Rondon. Located up the Rio Negro with access from Aquidauana, this is an upmarket place with boats, horses and good guides. It's been made very famous across Brazil over recent years as the location for filming the popular soap opera "Pantanal". Two adjacent *fazenda* areas have now also been bought and are protected, creating a total conservation area around the *fazenda* of 24,000 hectares. As well as ecotourism, the *fazenda* is now a centre for research, some supported by Earthwatch and also the Ford Motor Company. A biodiversity corridor is planned to link the *Fazenda Rio Negro* with the Serra de Maracaju. Air transfer from Campo Grande or Aquidauana is R$250 return. ⑧

Hotel Recanto Barra Mansa Rio Negro (owned by Guilherme Rondon) ⓣ67/3325-6807, ⓦwww.hotelbarramansa.com.br. Further east from *Fazenda Rio Negro* (see above) on the north shore of the river, 130km from Aquidauana, with room for twelve guests. Specializes in game and fly fishing. Daily buses run here from Corumbá. ⑧

Passo do Lontra Some 8km into the Pantanal from the BR-262 between Campo Grande and Corumbá ⓣ67/3231-6569, ⓦwww.pousadadolontra.com.br. One of the rare relatively inexpensive options (with substantial reductions in low season), although a minimum of six guests may be required. They also allow camping. ❺

Pousada Arara Azul Rio Negrinho on the Estrada Parque ⓣ67/3865-5131, ⓦwww.fazendaararaazul.com.br. Close to the Rio Negro in Nhecolândia, 38km up the MS-184 past Passo do Lontra, this *pousada* offers all the comforts you could want, plus guaranteed access to virtually all the bird and mammalian wildlife apart from the rarer jaguars and wolves. Excellent for piranha fishing, night-time *jacarés* viewing and horse riding. Camping allowed, too (R$25 a night), though they may require a minimum stay of two days in the lodge. ❼

Refúgio Ecológico Caiman Rio Aquidauana. Reservation centre in São Paulo where most bookings are taken (ⓣ11/3706-1800, ⓦwww.caiman.com.br), or book with Impacto Tour in Campo Grande (ⓣ67/33251333 and 3382-5197). The luxurious Pantanal jungle lodge experience. The *Refúgio* is located some 240km west of Campo Grande, 36km north of Miranda, and covers over 530 square kilometres. There are four *pousadas*, all with good facilities and a distinctive style to match the surroundings. Main activities include horse riding, nocturnal safaris, hikes, boat trips and cattle-drives (around 70 percent of the reserve's income still derives from cattle). The *Refúgio* has its own airstrip and offers transfer services leaving from Campo Grande four times a week. Full board, all activities and bilingual guide services are included in the daily rate of R$500 per person per night in a double room.

Into the swamp: routes from Cuiabá

One of the simplest ways into the swamp is to take a **bus** (3hr) from Cuiabá south to **BARÃO DO MELGAÇO**, a small, quiet village on the banks of the Rio Cuiabá. Although not quite in the true swamp, and therefore with less in the way of wildlife, Barão is perfect if you're short on time and just want a taste of the Pantanal. There's a reasonable hotel by the river in town, the *Barão Tour Pantanal Hotel* (bookings at Rua Joaquim Murtinho 1213, Cuiabá ⓣ65/3713-1166, ⓕ3624-8743; ❸), which also has boats for hire, while the exclusive *Pousada do Rio Mutum* is just an hour away by boat, in a stunning location on the Baía de Siá Mariana bay near the Rio Mutum (ⓣ65/3331-1223 or book through Eldorado Exec. Centre, Av. Rubens de Mendonça 917, sala 301, Cuiabá ⓣ & ⓕ65/3321-7995; ❻). Although Barão is no longer served by regular boats from Corumbá, it might still be worth asking around should a shallow-draught vessel be covering the journey – an unforgettable experience right through the centre of the swamp.

Poconé and Porto Jofre

The most exploited option from Cuiabá is to follow the route south to Poconé and Porto Jofre. There are daily **buses** from Cuiabá's *rodoviária* as far as **POCONÉ** along a paved and fairly smooth hundred-kilometre stretch of road. Like Barão do Melgaço, Poconé is not real Pantanal country, but it's a start and there are plenty of **hotels in town** if you need to stay over. On the main square, Praça Rondon, the *Hotel Skala* at no. 64 (ⓣ65/3721-1407; ❸), and a couple of restaurants take most of the trade. At the southern end of town at the start of the road to Porto Jofre, the cheaper *Hotel Santa Cruz* (ⓣ65/3721-1439; ❸) is recommended for relatively clean and comfortable lodging. Cheaper still, but slightly grubby, is *Dormitório Poconé* (❶), near the *rodoviária*.

The swamp proper begins as you leave the town going south, along the aborted Transpantaneira road. In fact it's just a bumpy track, often impassable during the rains, but you'll see plenty of wildlife from it, as well as signs marking the entrances to a number of *fazenda*-lodges and *pousadas* set back from the road around various tributaries of the Rio Cuiabá, notably the Pixaim and Rio Claro. Although pricey, they're cheaper than their counterparts in the southern

Pantanal, and all have restaurants and facilities for taking wildlife day-trips into the swamp by boat, on horseback or on foot. Another track from Poconé, in an even worse state, trails off southeast to Porto Cercado on the banks of the Rio Cuiabá itself, and also has a few *pousadas*.

After 145km, having crossed around a hundred wooden bridges in varying stages of dilapidation, the track eventually arrives at **PORTO JOFRE**. After Cuiabá, Porto Jofre appears as little more than a small fishing hamlet, literally the end of the road. This is as far as the Transpantaneira route has got, or ever looks like getting, thanks to technical problems and the sound advice of ecological pressure groups. As far as **accommodation in town** goes, the quite adequate *Hotel Porto Jofre* (closed Nov–Feb; ⓣ65/322-6322; ❻) has a monopoly. If you have a hammock or a tent, it's usually all right to sleep outside somewhere, but check with someone in authority first (ask at the port) and don't leave your valuables unattended. There are no other options unless you can get someone to invite you to their house.

From Porto Jofre, there are irregular cargo **boats** to Corumbá (about twice a month), normally carrying soya or cattle from Cáceres; the journey takes between two and five days, depending on whether the boats sail through the night. It's also possible to arrange a day or two's excursion up the Piquiri and Cuiabá rivers from Porto Jofre.

Pousadas around Poconé and Porto Jofre

All of the following can be booked through the addresses given below or through tour or travel agents in Cuiabá; some lodges insist on advance reservations and won't let you in unannounced, but others might relent if you just drop by. All the lodges below offer full-board accommodation, with swamp trips included in the price; they're listed in loose geographical order, from northeast to southwest.

Pousada Araras Eco Lodge office at Cuiabá airport, or Av. Ponce de Arruda 670, Várzea Grande ⓣ65/3682-2800, ⓦwww.ararаslodge.com.br. At Km 29 of the Transpantaneira, this long-established *pousada* is an old brick ranch building, more atmospheric than most of the more modern *pousadas*, with a pool, as well as boats and horses, but its fourteen rooms are likely to be full in high season. ❺

Pousada Pantaneiro (bookings through Cuiabá's travel agents). Approximately 100km south of Poconé, a small place (five rooms) and one of the more reasonably priced *pousadas* which, although not on a river itself, offers swamp trips on horseback. It should be OK to camp here, too, and they also have tents for hire. ❸–❹

Pousada Passargada (bookings through Cuiabá's travel agents, or in Rio ⓣ021/3235-2840 or São Paulo ⓣ011/3284-5434). Linked in the dry season by the Porto Cercado track, most of the year it's more easily reached by boat (1hr 30min) from Barão do Melgaço. A good place directly on the Rio Pixaim. ❻

Pousada Piuval Rodovia Transpantaneira, Km 10, Poconé ⓣ65/3345-1338, ⓦwww.pousadapiuval.com.br. A comfortable spread 110km from Cuiabá with a fine pool and small but pleasant rooms. Well equipped with horses, open truck and boats for exploring deeper. ❺–❻

Pousada Porto Cercado Around 40km along the Poconé to Porto Cercado road ⓣ67/3688-2021, ⓦwww.sesc.com.br. Very large with over a hundred apartments, a pool, sports facilities, horse riding, boating and fishing all available. ❻–❼

Pousada Rio Claro ⓣ67/3345-1054, ⓦwww.pousadarioclaro.com.br. Located at Km 41 of the Transpantaneira, it is quite large, comfortable and with a pool. ❻

Pousada São Sebastião do Pantanal ⓣ65/3322-0178, ⓕ3321-0710. Situated 34km from Poconé at Km 27 of the aborted Transpantaneira road, and usually reachable even in bad weather. A first-class establishment (with pool) located close to the river in pleasant wooded surroundings, offering horse and boat safaris. Good for families. ❻

Rancho Kue ⓣ67/3241-1875. This is one of the best-located *fazendas*, right in the centre of the swamp and close to the confluence of the big *rios* Paraguai and São Lourenço. Access by plane. ❼

Cáceres

Although less frequented than the Porto Jofre route, **CÁCERES** is another good target from Cuiabá, 233km west of the city. It's a very pleasant, laid-back place, and given the prices of accommodation along the Transpantaneira, definitely deserves consideration as a base for visiting the Pantanal. It's a three- to four-hour journey by bus, several of which leave daily from the *rodoviária* in Cuiabá. On the upper reaches of the Rio Paraguai, which is still quite broad even this far upstream, Cáceres is a relatively new town, made up largely of wooden shacks, bars and pool rooms. There are lots of cheap **hotels**, the best of which is the *Santa Terezinha*, Rua Tiradentes 485 (ⓣ65/3223-4621; ❷), which is clean and hospitable. More upmarket, the *Hotel Ipanema* at Rua Gen. Osorio 540 (ⓣ65/3223-1177; ❹) has a pool and also has air-conditioning and TV in all rooms. The *Hotel Comodoro*, Praça Duque de Caxias 561 (ⓣ65/3223-2078; ❹), has **motorboats** for hire, as do the *Barco Hotel Santa Maria*, Rua Marechal Deodoro 73 (ⓣ65/3223-5455; ❸), and the small but well-equipped Lancha Gaiva tour boat company (ⓣ65/3223-4956) whose office is at the Praça Duque de Caxias 206; the typical cost for boat hire is around R$50 an hour. The **travel agency** Natureza, at Rua Coronel José Dulce 304 (ⓣ65/3223-1997), can arrange *pousada* accommodation and a number of good-value tours.

About 60km south of Cáceres on the confluence of the *rios* Paraguai and Jauru the touristy, Japanese-owned *Hotel Fazenda Barranquinho* (ⓣ65/3624-5755 or 65/3223-1081; ❼) can be reached by track or boat in around three hours from Cáceres. It's a beautiful spot, but is still not far enough into the swamp for the best chance of spotting wildlife. Best bet for this is to take one of the **cargo boats** to Corumbá from Cáceres – see the box on pp.590–591, which also gives details of luxury fishing boats. Several boats operate from here, including the Babilonia (ⓣ67/3223-9777, ⓦwww.barcobabilonia.com.br), which has six cabins and usually goes out for seven days, and the Talisma (ⓣ67/3223-4128) which has four cabins and also goes out for a week at a time.

The only road to go further into the Pantanal is the track that leads on to the **Bolivian border** settlement of San Matias; from here you can fly to Santa Cruz (best to sort out exit stamp and entry visas, respectively, with the Brazilian Federal Police in Cáceres or Cuiabá and the Bolivian Consul in Cuiabá).

Mato Grosso state

The state of Mato Grosso is dominated completely by **Cuiabá**, a city of over half a million people, in spite of the fact that this city is located in the very south of the political region. Roads radiating from this commercial and administrative centre appear on a map like the tentacles of a gigantic octopus extending hungrily over the plains in every direction. The city is over 1000km from Brasília, almost 1500km from Porto Velho and more than 1700km from São Paulo: an opportune place to break a long overland haul. Beyond its strategic importance, though, Cuiabá's friendly personality and interesting city centre, combined with the breathtaking scenery of the nearby Chapada dos Guimarães, can easily lure you into staying longer than planned.

Cuiabá is as good a springboard for a trip into or through the **Pantanal** as Campo Grande or Corumbá. Furthermore, it offers longhaul but simple access by bus west into the remoter Amazon region, east towards Goaiania and Brasília, and north, for the more adventurous, towards Santarem and Manaus. No longer a true frontier zone, it's an established cattle-ranching and soya-producing region where cows and beans are much bigger business than tourism. The use of GM seed stocks in agriculture is a major issue here.

Apart from the mysterious and stunning **Chapada dos Guimarães**, there is relatively little tourism infrastructure outside Cuiabá and the Pantanal. The reality for most travellers will be a flight or an intrepid journey by bus (and perhaps river) to some other distant city. The most arduous of the options used to be the awful **Highway BR-163** from Cuiabá to Santarém, which, in theory, connects at Itaituba with the BR-230 Transamazônica Highway for Altamira, Marabá and Belém. However, around 400km of road has been reclaimed by jungle along the Rio Jamanxim in southern Pará, making it impassable to anything other than four-wheel-drive vehicles for the foreseeable future: the furthest north you can drive is the Serra do Cachimbo on the fringes of Pará state. The fastest road is **Highway BR-364** (known as the BR-070 in Mato Grosso) through Cuiabá, which ultimately links São Paulo with Rio Branco and Cruzeiro do Sul.

Cuiabá

The southern gateway into the Amazon, **CUIABÁ** has always been firmly on the edge of Brazil's wilderness. Following the discovery of a gold field here in 1719 (one version of the town's name means the "river of stars"), the town mushroomed as an administrative and service centre in the middle of Indian territory, thousands of very slow, overland miles from any other Portuguese settlement. To the south lay the Pantanal and the dreaded Paiaguá people who frequently ambushed convoys of boats transporting Cuiabá gold by river to São Paulo. The fierce Bororo tribe, who dominated Mato Grosso east of Cuiabá, also regularly attacked many of the mining settlements. Northwest along a high hilly ridge – the Chapada dos Parecis, which now carries BR-364 to Porto Velho – lived the peaceful Parecis people, farmers in the watershed between the Amazon and the Pantanal. By the 1780s, however, most Indians within these groups had been either eliminated or transformed into allies: the Parecis were needed as slave labour for the mines; the Bororo either retreated into the forest or joined the Portuguese as mercenaries and Indian hunters; while the Paiaguá fared worst of all, almost completely wiped out by cannon and musket during a succession of punitive expeditions from Cuiabá.

The most important development came during the 1890s, when a young Brazilian army officer, Lieutenant **Cândido Rondon**, built a telegraph system from Goiás to Cuiabá through treacherous Bororo territory – assisted no doubt by the fact that he had some Bororo blood in his veins. By 1903 he had extended the telegraph from Cuiabá south to Corumbá, and in 1907 he began work to reach the Rio Madeira, to the northwest in the Amazon basin. The latter expedition earned Rondon a reputation as an important explorer and brought him into contact with the Nambikwara Indians. Since then, Cuiabá has been pushing forward the frontier of development and the city is still a stepping stone and crossroads for pioneers, with a population approaching one million. Every year, thousands of hopeful settlers stream through Cuiabá on their way to a new life in the western Amazon.

The established farmlands around the city now produce abundant crops – maize, fruits, rice and soya. But the city itself thrives on the much larger surrounding **cattle-ranching region**, which contains almost a quarter of a million inhabitants. Future prosperity is assured, too: a large lead ore deposit is being worked close to the town, and oil has been discovered at Várzea Grande; but it is more sustainable industries, like rubber, palm nuts and, of course, ecotourism, that will provide income in years to come. The good facilities offered in Cuiabá - in terms of hotels, restaurants and tour companies – means that ecotourism is developing rapidly and is being increasingly seen by the younger *fazenda* owners as the way forward.

Arrival, information and accommodation

Both the **BR-163** and the **BR-364** run to Cuiabá. Whether you're coming from São Paulo, Rio, Brasília or the Northeast, you'll want to take the BR-364 for travelling overland into the western Amazon.

The **rodoviária** (☎65/3621-1040) on Avenida Marechal Rondon is an ultra-modern complex, 3km north of the city centre: from here it's a fifteen-minute ride into Cuiabá on buses #202, #304 or #309, or ten minutes by taxi (R$25). The **airport** (☎65/3614-2510), 8km south in Várzea Grande, is connected to the centre by buses marked "Tuiuiu" and taxis (about R$25).

You'll be able to get **tourist information** from SEDTUR's new office in the centre of town on Rua Voluntarios da Patria close to the corner with Rua Ricardo Franco (daily 8am–6pm; ☎65/3613-9300 and 65/3624-9060).

Accommodation

With the *rodoviária* relatively close, most people prefer to stay in or near the busy city centre, where there's a good range of places. There are also numerous two- and three-star hotels around the airport and on the way into town.

Amazon Plaza Av. Getúlio Vargas 600 ⓣ65/2121-2000, ⓦwww.hotelamazon.com.br. Recently renovated, this is one of the smarter and most comfortable downtown options. Rooms are large with TV and a/c, there's a small pool and garden patio-bar. Breakfasts are fantastic and the service is good. ❻–❼

Central Rua Galdino Pimentel ⓣ65/3321-8309. A budget option in the heart of the old town, with very basic rooms, very poorly maintained and a little dodgy at night. Its neighbour *São Marcos*, on the same street (ⓣ65/624-2300), offers much the same. ❶

Colorado Palace Av. Jules Rimet 32 ⓣ65/3621-3763. One of a dozen three-star hotels along the main road from the *rodoviária* into town, this one's right opposite the bus station. The rooms are predictably noisy and not particularly good value, but convenient if you're leaving by bus early the next day. ❹

Deville Av. Isaac Póvoas 1000 ⓣ65/3319-3000, ⓦwww.hoteiseldorado.com.br. A five-star hotel, at the top of its range, with 182 rooms, arctic-strength a/c, pool, and decent restaurant. ❻

Ecoverde Rua Pedro Celestino 391, Centro ⓣ65/3624-1386, ⓦwww.ecoverdestours.com. This lovely *pousada* is based in a modest but attractive and safe colonial house with extensive gardens right at the heart of the old city centre. It has six rooms, all with fans; bathrooms are shared, but there are four of them. There's also a good reference library, a rest area with shade and hammocks, laundry and cooking facilities, as well as links to one of the best Pantanal tour operators. Breakfasts are stupendous and very fresh. ❷

Hostel Pantanal Av. Isaac Póvoas 655 ⓣ65/3624-8999, ⓦwww.portaldopantanal.com.br. Linked to Youth Hostelling International, this friendly place has all the usual facilities, plus Internet access, kitchen and surprisingly comfortable beds. ❷

Mato Grosso Rua Comandante Costa 2522 ⓣ65/3614-7777, ⓕ614-7053. Within three blocks of Praça da República, this place has decent breakfasts and offers excellent-value rooms with private showers. ❷

Mato Grosso Palace Rua Joaquim Murtinho 170 ⓣ65/3614-7000, ⓦwww.hotelmatogrosso.com.br. Part of the Best Western chain. Situated in a grand building behind the Fundação Cultural, with excellent service and pleasant enough rooms, some with good views. No pool. ❻

Samara Rua Joaquim Murtinho 270 ⓣ65/3322-6001. A simple but clean and friendly hotel that's a good option if other budget places are full. ❶

The City

Perhaps because of its busy feel, Cuiabá is an exciting place to spend a few days. There's certainly a lot to see and do in the city's relatively self-contained centre, where modern skyscrapers long ago won the battle for attention with the now hidden ornate facades of crumbling, pastel-shaded colonial villas, churches and shops.

The central **Praça da República** is a hive of activity from daybreak onwards. It's the city's main meeting spot, and the cathedral, post office, the cultural foundation and university all face onto the square, while under the shade of its large trees, hippies from the Brazilian coast sell crafted jewellery and leather work. The most interesting old mansion in town, the **Paláçio da Instrução**, is on the square at no. 151. Now the **Fundação Cultural de Mato Grosso** (Mon–Fri 8.30am–4.30pm; free), it houses three excellent **museums** of history, natural history and anthropology, with exhibits spanning prehistoric to colonial times. There are some fascinating old photos of Cuiabá, along with rooms full of stuffed creatures from the once forested region and, best of all, a superb array of Indian artefacts such as feather headdresses, gourd maracas and woven fibre utentsils. The **Catedral do Bom Jesus**, next door, was built in the 1960s to replace the old cathedral, a beautiful Baroque affair that was then thought old-fashioned. Constructed of pinkish concrete with a square, vaguely Moorish facade, the new cathedral has a predictably vast, rectangular interior; its main altar is overshadowed by a mural reaching from floor to ceiling that depicts a sparkling Christ floating in the air above the city of Cuiabá and the cathedral.

The only other church of any real interest in Cuiabá is the early twentieth-century **Igreja de Nossa Senhora do Bom Despacho**, though both it and its splendid religious art collection are currently closed to visitors. Sitting on the hill to the south, across the Avenida Tenente Coronel Duarte from the cathedral side of town, Bom Despacho used to dominate the cityscape before office buildings and towering hotels sprang up to dwarf it in the latter half of the twentieth century.

Just to the northeast of Praça da República, a few narrow central lanes – Pedro Celestino, Galdino Pimentel, Ricardo Franco and Rua 7 de Setembro – form a crowded pedestrian shopping area. It's here that you'll find the city's oldest church, the simple but rundown **Igreja Nossa Serhora do Rosário e Capela de São Benedicto**, completed in 1722, and the unusual **Museu de Pedras**, Rua Galdino Pimentel 195 (Mon–Fri 7–11am & 1–4pm; R$5). Packed tightly into just two rooms, the museum contains the marvellously eccentric collection of local man Ramis Bucair, comprising gemstones, crystals, fossils, Stone Age artefacts, stuffed animals, birds and snakes. The exhibits are a hotchpotch of genuinely fascinating pieces – rocks containing liquid and loose diamonds, and a dried catfish tongue, once used as a rasp for grating *guaraná* (a tropical berry) – mixed with some outrageous fakes, such as the inch-high carved stone purported to be a shrunken human skull from some remote Indian tribe, and a display case containing a large fossilized bone, discovered locally and boldly claimed to be that of a *Tyrannosaurus rex*. An equally dubious claim is made in Praça Moreira Cabral, along Rua Barão de Melgaço by the state assembly buildings: a small post enclosed by a tall thin pyramid marks what was considered to be, until the advent of satellite topography, the geographical centre of the South American continent. The actual place, for what it's worth, is 67km away in the Chapada dos Guimarães.

△ Praça da República

Having exhausted the central possibilities, there are a couple of other museums in Cuiabá, which are worth an hour or so of your time if you have any interest at all in the indigenous culture. The **ethnographic collection** belonging to the offices of FUNAI, the Foundation for Indian Affairs (☎65/3644-1850), includes feather handicraft, basketry and wooden carved objects; additionally, the foundation has a shop around the corner from the tourist office, at Pedro Celestino 301 (☎65/3623-1675), en route to and on the same side as Pousada Ecoverde. Easier to find is the smaller university-run **Museu do Índio Marechal Rondon**, on Avenida Fernando Corréa da Costa (Mon–Fri 7.30–11.30am & 1.30–5.30pm, Sat & Sun 7.30–11am; free), which also focuses on local Indian culture and features more feather, fibre, ceramic and wooden objects representing the material culture of several local tribes, including the Bororo and Nambikwara. The museum is beside the university pool, 5km east of town off BR-364, in the sector known as Cidade Universitária; buses #133, #505, #513, #514 and others from Avenida Tenente Coronel Duarte will take you there. Also in the Cidade Universitária is a small **zoological garden** (daily 7.30-11.30am and 1.30–5.20pm, closed Mon; ☎65/3615-8007; free) where you'll find swamp creatures including caimans, tapirs and capybaras, a small consolation if you don't have time for a Pantanal tour.

Finally, focusing mainly on work by early Republican and modern Brazilian artists, there are two **art galleries** in Cuiabá – one in the Casa da Cultura, Rua Barão de Melgaço, the other, Laila Zharan, at Av. Marechal Deodoro 504. Both are small and quiet but worth a visit for insight into local perspectives on the region's landscapes, history and other relevant issues.

Eating, drinking and nightlife

Cuiabá has a surprising range of cuisine and some excellent **restaurants**, although you'll find almost everything closed on Sundays. Avenida Getúlio Vargas hosts an array of very swish and expensive modern Italian restaurants, such as *Adriano* at no. 985 and *Tavola Piena* at no. 676; *Getúlio's* at no. 1147 offers decently priced drinks and cocktails, if you want to watch the cream of Cuiabá cruise by in their dream wagons in the evenings. For **cheaper eating** and *lanches* there are plenty of places in the area around Praça Alencastro, at the north end of Travessa João Dias near Rua Comandante Costa, and in the shopping zone between Rua Pedro Celestino and Rua Galdino Pimentel. **Ice-cream parlours** are an essential ingredient of any city with temperatures often over 40°C. The best in Cuiabá are *Alaska*, Rua Pedro Celestino 215, *Patotinha*, Av. Generoso Ponce 761, and *Flocky's* on Avenida Isaac Póvoas. For your own supplies, the busy **Mercado Municipal** is on Avenida Generoso Ponce (Mon–Sat 7.30am–6pm, Sun 7.30am–noon).

Restaurants

Barranco Bar Rua Pedro Celestino. Inexpensive food and drinks and live Brazilian music, in a modest but inviting place – as good as any to meet the local people. One of the few inexpensive spots open Sun.

Choppão Praça 8 de Abril, Goiabeiras ☎65/3623-9101. Probably the best and most traditional restuarant-bar in the city centre. Very lively in the evening, with lots of tables in a big corner space, some outside where there is occasionally street entertainment. They serve traditional *escaldo* (egg- and fish-based soup) along with the beer and have some fascinating historical photos on the walls.

Haus Bier Av. Mato Grosso 764 ☎65/3621-1020. Five blocks down from Avenida Getúlio Vargas, one of Cuiabá's trendiest restaurant-bars and the evening focus for brash young Cuiabanos, with excellent but expensive food featuring a wide range of Brazilian and international dishes – everything form pizza to Amazon swamp fish as well as very potent cocktails. Daily 4pm–3am.

Le Bam Rua Comandante Costa. Around the corner from *Hotel Presidente*, a gem of a *lanchonete*: cheap and delicious food with exceptionally friendly owners. Closed Sun.

Meridiano 56 Av. Isaac Póvoas 1039 ☎65/3322-4321. Reasonably priced, fairly central and well-regarded fish restaurant. Tues–Sat evenings, Sun mornings.

Mistura Cuiabana Rua Pedro Celestino 8. Refreshingly cool interior of an airy colonial mansion at the heart of the city, this is a lunchtime restaurant serving excellent self-service *comida por kilo*. Mon–Fri 11am–3pm.

Presto Pizzas Av. Getúlio Vargas 1371 ⓣ65/3624-4600. Good popular pizza restaurant with fast service; also operates a delivery service. Closed Sun.

O Regionalíssimo Rua 13 de Junho ⓣ65/3322-4523. Excellent, moderately priced regional dishes. On Wed they serve a speciality of beef with green bananas, and there's sometimes live music at weekends. Closed Mon.

Restaurante e Peixaria La Barca Located by the Ponte Nova, this floating fish restaurant gives a wonderful perspective on the city at lunchtime or at night; try a fish *rodizio* (as much as you can eat).

Tio Ari Natural Restaurante Rua Comandante Costa 770. Excellent, largely vegetarian food near the Caixa Economica bank, all at very low prices. Mon–Sat 9am–5pm.

7

MATO GROSSO | Cuiabá

Bars and nightlife

Although beer is twice as expensive here as it is on the coast, you'll find that **nightlife** in Cuiabá revolves mainly around the bars and restaurants in the town centre, especially along Rua Isaac Póvoas. *Haus Bier* (see "Restaurants" above) has a good atmosphere, while beyond the downtown area, along the large Avenida CPA, there are several more bars and clubs. One of the most popular is *Deck Aveinda* at number 635; *Terraço*, close by, offers live music at weekends; and *Tucano*, also on Avenida CPA, offers a diverse mix of dance music. The *Veneza Palace Hotel*, Av. Cel. Escolastico 738 in Bandeirantes (ⓣ65/3661-1480 or 321-4847), has occasional big-name bands from Rio playing live, while the main gay venue, though not exactly a scream, is the bar under the decrepid *Hotel Presidente*.

Listings

Airlines TAM, Av. Isaac Póvoas 586 ⓣ65/3682-1702; Varig, Av. 15 de Novembro 230 ⓣ65/682-1140; Cruiser ⓣ65/3682-7000 (flies all over Mato Grosso and to Santarem); Trip ⓣ65/3682-2555 (to Sinop and Alta Floresta); Gol ⓣ65/3682-1666.

Banks and exchange Cuiabá is the only place in the region where you're likely to be able to change travellers' cheques. Visa card cash advances can be obtained and cheques and notes exchanged in the Banco do Brasil, Av. Getulio Vargas (Mon–Fri

Tour operators and guides in Cuiabá

All of Cuiabá's travel agents offer trips into the Pantanal or to the closer sites, like Chapada dos Guimarães, although their primary occupation is selling flights within Brazil. For more personal service, however, you'd do better to contact one of the local **tour operators**, which tend to be smaller and offer specialist knowledge. Highly recommended is Ecoverde Tours run by the wildlife ecologist Joel Souza, a very reliable operator who speaks excellent English and German, among other languages; he often has a presence at the airport, but also has an office at Av. Getúlio Vargas 155-A as well as a base at the Poudasa Ecoverde, Rua Pedro Celestino 391, Centro (ⓣ65/3624-1386, ⓦwww.ecoverdestours.com). Also recommended are Natureco, Rua Barão de Melgaço 2015 (ⓣ & ⓕ65/3624-5116) and Ecological Pantanal Tours, Rua Joaquim Mutinho 1134, Centro (ⓣ65/3623-4607 and 9954-8955, ⓔecotours@terra.com.br). Tours within the region tend to cost upwards of R$180 a day per person including transport, accommodation in *pousadas*, good food, horse riding and photo-safari outings. In low season it may be worth bargaining, particularly if there are four or more of you travelling together. Note that in low season you may also have to wait a few days for enough tourists to make up your group, unless you're happy paying more. Individual independent **guides** and the operators mentioned above tend to approach arriving passengers at the airport.

10am–3pm). HSBC, also on Getulia Vargas, has an ATM; dollars cash can be exchanged at good rates at the Ouro Minas office, Rua Mariano Candido 401, or in some of the larger hotels.

Buses All buses run from the *rodoviária*; the two most useful are probably Expresso Rubi ☎65/3621-1764 (for Porto Velho) and Cascavel ☎65/3621-2551 (for most major destinations).

Car rental Localiza, Av. Dom Bosco 965 ☎65/3624-7979; Unidas, Praça do Aeroporto ☎65/3682-4052.

Post office At Praça da República (Mon–Fri 9am–6pm, Sat 9am–noon).

Shopping Explore the streets between the Praça da República and the Igreja do Rosário or try the Casa do Artesão, corner of Rua 13 de Junho and Rua Senador Metello, or FUNAI's ArtIndia shop, Rua Pedro Celestino (close to the Tourist Information office) for local handicrafts. There's another good *artesanato* shop at Joaquim Murtinho 170 in the centre. For hats (essential wear for the hot Pantanal sun) the best in town is Casa do Ginete, Av. Ten. Cel. Duarte 256, in the centre. *Guaraná* drinks, seeds and tubes can be bought in the interesting shop at 27 de Dezembro 30. Homeopathic remedies can be found at Fraternidade, Rua Galdino Pimental 162. More curious is the magic shop on Av. Tenente Coronel Duarte, near the corner with Av. Generoso Ponce – its shelves are stacked with ceremonial swords, North American Indian ceramic figurines, incense, pots decorated with gods and demons, strings of jungle beads and seed pods. Also worth a visit is the shop Guaraná Maués, Av. Isaac Póvoas 611, which specializes in *guaraná*, grown locally in Mato Grosso state. There are two decent photographic shops on Rua Joaquim Murtinho: Cuiabá Color at no. 789, and the friendly Artcolor next door.

Telephones The Telemat office is at Rua Barão de Melgaço (Mon–Sat 7.30am–5.30pm).

Travel Agents Ametur, Rua Joaquim Murtinho 242 (☎65/624-1000) sell tickets and can arrange day-trips by boat to Barão de Melgaço; another choice is Anaconda, Av. Isaac Povoas 606 (☎65/3624-4142). See also the list of upmarket operators on p.588.

Around Cuiabá

Although it's a major staging post for the Pantanal, there isn't a lot in terms of organized tourism in the immediate region **around Cuiabá**, and what there is is mostly aimed at local people. Nevertheless, the scenery and air of mystery around **Chapada dos Guimarães** makes for a rewarding side-trip from the city – much more of a draw than either the hot springs of **Aguas Quentes** or the beach at **São Antônio do Leverger**.

Chapada dos Guimarães

A paved road winds its way up to the scenic and increasingly popular mountain village of **CHAPADA DOS GUIMARÃES**, set on the plateau of the same name just 64km from Cuiabá. Located bang on one of the oldest tectonic plates on the planet, it also sits close to the geodesic centre of South America (the equidistant point between the Atlantic and Pacific Oceans). Nine daily **buses** run by Expreso Rubi make the one-hour journey from Cuiabá's *rodoviária*.

It is here on this plateau that the true geodesic centre of South America was pinpointed by satellite, much to the chagrin of the Cuiabanos who stick resolutely to their old 1909 mark; the actual spot, the **Mirante da Geodésia**, is located on the southern continuation of Rua Clariano Curvo from Praça Dom Wunibaldo, 8km away. Parochial disputes aside, Chapada is an interesting settlement in its own right, containing Mato Grosso's oldest church, the **Igreja de Nossa Senhora de Santana do Sacramento**, a fairly plain colonial temple built in 1779, which dominates the top end of the town's leafy Praça Dom Wunibaldo. These days, with a population nearing sixteen thousand, the town has something of a reputation as a centre for the Brazilian "New Age" movement, with crystal shops, health food stores and hippy communities springing up over the last years. If you're here in July, you're in for a treat, with the staging of the **Festival de Inverno** – a mix of drama, exhibitions and music, the latter ranging from traditional, sacred and Indian music to funk and rap.

Most of the year, however, it's not the town itself that brings most people out to Chapada. The stunning countryside, of which over three hundred square kilometres is protected as the **Parque Nacional da Chapada dos Guimarães**, consists of a grassy plateau – at 800m, the highest land in Mato Grosso – scattered with low trees, a marvellous backdrop for photographing the local flora and birdlife. Within walking distance, there are waterfalls, fantastic rock formations and precipitous canyons, as well as some interesting, partially excavated archeological sites. The most spectacular of all the sights around the village is the **Véu de Noiva waterfall**, which drops over a sheer rock face for over 60m, pounding into the forested basin below. You can take a tour there with most of the operators listed below (from around R$20 a person a day, depending on how big the group is). Alternatively, you can get there by walking or perhaps hitching from the village of Buruti, on the road from Cuiabá, about 12km before Chapada dos Guimarães; Buruti is accessible by bus and only about 6km or an hour and a half's walk from the falls. Alternatively, the falls lie within a couple of kilometres of the road if you jump off the bus some 6km beyond Salgadeira (ask the driver to show you the track).

Other highlights in the park include, about 25km to the north of town, the impressive and weird rock formations of **Cidade da Pedra**, some of them up to 300m tall, the spectacular waterfalls of **Cachoeira da Martinha**, 30km further north, and a couple of interesting cave systems – the **Casa de Pedra**, not far from Véu da Noiva and, further afield, the **Caverna Aroe Jari**, the latter with cave paintings. Good views of the Cidade da Pedra can be had from **Porto do Inferno**, a viewing point some 16km from the village on the road into the Chapada from Cuiabá.

Practicalities

There's a good range of **places to stay**, both in the village and in the surrounding countryside. The cheapest option, and perfectly reasonable, is the *Quincó* (Ⓣ65/3301-1284; ❷) on the Praça Dom Wunibaldo. Also on the square, at no. 641, the *Pousada Bom Jardim* (Ⓣ65/3301-2668 and 65/3301-1244; ❸–❹) is central, clean and very friendly, with OK breakfasts; some rooms are nicer than others. The *Hotel Turismo* at Rua Fernando Corréa 1065 (Ⓣ65/3301-1176, Ⓦwww.hotelturismo.com.br; ❹–❺) has exceptionally comfortable beds, good showers and can sometimes change dollars cash, while close by, the *Pousada Rios* at Rua Tiradentes 333 (Ⓣ65/3301-1126; ❸) is one of the best basic places with TV and air-conditioning in most rooms. The *Solar do Ingles* at Rua Cipriano Curvo 142, close to the main square (Ⓣ65/3301-1389, Ⓔsolardoingles@vsp.com.br; ❺) offers quaint and comfortable accommodation. Just outside town at Km 63 on Rodoviária. Emanuel Pinheiro, the *Chapada Holistica* (Ⓣ65/3301-1171, Ⓔchapadaholistica@terra.com; ❺) offers an interesting mix of spacious rooms, pool, sauna and alternative therapies.

There are also a number of good *pousadas* dotted about the Chapada, many with superb views: *Pousada Penhasco*, on the southern precipice side of town, beyond the outskirts of the village (Ⓣ65/3301-1555, Ⓦwww.penhasco.com.br; ❺), is a large, quite plush place with apartments, pool and sports facilities; similarly comfortable but smaller and more cosy is the *Fazenda Santa Tereza* (Ⓣ65/3624-9197, Ⓔjvalberici@hotmail.com; ❻) deeper into the plateau, which also offers horse riding. Similar in style, the *Pousada Chapada Aventura* (Ⓣ65/3301-2153; ❺), close to the southern edge of town, has three chalets beside lovely woodlands and enough room for up to thirteen visitors. One of the best spots for **camping**

△ Véu de Noiva waterfall

is the *Vale da Boçátina Camping Ecológico* (Ⓣ65/3301-1393, 3301-2074 or 3301-1154), 10km from the village on a beautiful site near waterfalls and streams; if you contact them in advance they'll arrange transport out there.

Most of Chapada dos Guimarães' best **restaurants** can be found, not surprisingly, around the Praça Dom Wunibaldo: *Felipe's*, Rua Cipriano Curvo 598 (Ⓣ65/3301-1793), is one of the most popular restaurant-bars with *comida por kilo* at lunchtime; next door, the *Trapiche* has an airy terrace and good self-service lunches; while the *Casa do Artesão* in Rua Quinco Caldas serves excellent local dishes at very reasonable prices. A busy spot in the evenings is the *Maloca* restaurant-bar a few blocks from the *praça* at Rua Fernando Correa 1020 (Ⓣ65/3301-3405), where you will find a range of meat dishes served in an open-sided corner space with roof cover.

Tourist information – incuding details of bus times, information on campsites, contact lists for local guides and maps of the Chapada – is available from the helpful Centro de Apoio Ao Turismo on the corner of Rua Dr. P. Gomez with Rua 7 Perimetral, just a few blocks from Praça Dom Wunibaldo (Mon–Sat 9am–6pm; Ⓣ65/3301-1690). Information can also be obtained from the national park office (daily 8.30am–5pm; Ⓣ65/3301-1133), while the website (Ⓦwww.chapadadosguimaraes.com.br), run by Ecoturs, offers photos, hotel information, etc, though all in Portuguese. There are also a couple of good **tour agents** in town. Eco Turismo Cultural, Praça Dom Wunibaldo 464 (Ⓣ65/3301-1393, Ⓦwww.chapadadosguimaraes.com), organize good-value and reliable tours of the region and have an English-speaking guide; their prices depend on numbers but range from around R$50 per person a day, upwards. Atma, Rua Cipriano Curvo 655 (Ⓣ65/3301-3391, Ⓦwww.chapadaatma.com.br), specialize in adventure tours, mainly trekking and caving, and cascading, but also offer trips to the main sites in the area. Joel Souza, who operates the tour company Ecoverde from Cuiabá (see p.600), is also worth contacting for guide services. For **changing money**, the Banco do Brasil is on the Praça Dom Wunibaldo. The Chapada is a good place to find **artesanato shops**; these are mainly around the central square but the best is Arte Indigrna at Rua Quinco Caldas 550. Artes das Tribus, Rua Cipriano Curvo 343, is another good one. There's a very professional **alternative therapy centre** in town, Cosmus at Rua Turadentes 45 (Ⓣ65/3301-1846), which offers acupuncture, reiki and massage among other treatments.

Águas Quentes and São Antônio

The hot baths of **ÁGUAS QUENTES**, 86km east of Cuiabá in the Serra de São Vicente, just off the BR-364 towards Rondonópolis, function as a weekend and honeymoon resort for locals. Apart from the baths, though, there is little of interest. The water, said to be mildly radioactive, comes in four different pools, the hottest at around 42°C, and is regarded as a cure for rheumatism, liver complaints and even conjunctivitis. There are daily **buses** to the town (1-2 hours) from the *rodoviária* in Cuiabá, but be warned that the resort has only one **hotel**, the expensive hydrotherapy centre of *Hotel Águas Quentes* (ⓣ65/3614-7500, ⓦwww.hotelmatogrosso.com.br; ❻-❼).

The closest **beach** to Cuiabá is at **SÃO ANTÔNIO DO LEVERGER**, 35km south of the city on the Rio Cuiabá. It's as much fun as most of the beaches on the coast, even if it seems a little incongruous given the jungle backdrop, but the waters are now far from clean, carrying with them much of Cuiabá's effluent. The dry and relatively cool month of July is designated a beach festival. Again, there are **buses** every day from the *rodoviária* in Cuiabá.

On from Cuiabá

Cuiabá is a central point for all sorts of long-distance trips within Brazil and a launching pad for onward travel into neighbouring countries. The two main regional highways, the **BR-163** and the **BR-364**, are accessible from the city: the BR-364 is particularly important as a link between the Amazon and almost all other regions, although parts of its westernmost sections are impassable for much of the year.

West to Rondônia and Porto Velho

Heading **west from Cuiabá**, Porto Velho and Rio Branco are both possible destinations in their own right, or could serve as relaxing stops on the way to Manaus, Peru or Bolivia. Following Rondônia's telegraph link to Manaus in the early twentieth century, **Highway BR-364** to northern Mato Grosso and south-western Amazon was the next development to open up the region. Paving the BR-364 cost around US$600 million – partly financed by the World Bank – but construction was held up for a while when anthropologists realized that it was planned to cut straight through **Nambikwara** tribal lands. The road was eventually completed by making a large detour around these Indians, who still live in small, widely scattered groups that have very little contact with each other.

Leaving the industrial fringes of Cuiabá, the road soon enters the well-established pastoral farmlands to the west. At **Cáceres** (see p.594), three hours out of Cuiabá, the highway starts to leave the Pantanal watershed and climbs gradually towards the inhospitable but beautiful ridges of the **Chapada dos Parecis** and the state frontier with Rondônia. Here, at Vilhena, everyone sometimes has to pass through the **yellow fever checkpoint**: busloads of people spend half an hour either getting inoculated or showing their vaccination certificates. The Nambikwara and Sararé Indians live to the south of the Chapada escarpment, while to the north there are settlements of Parecis and various other groups. The process of occupation in this region is so recent and intense that the Indians have suffered greatly. Most of their demarcated lands have been invaded already and the situation is worsening all the time; local newspapers are full of reports concerning police operations aimed at removing the illegal *garimpeiros* from the reserves. The Indians don't generally come out to the highway, though sometimes you'll see a family or two selling crafted goods – bows and arrows, beads or carvings – beside the road at small pit stops.

The road from Cuiabá to Porto Velho passes through the humanized remains of tropical rainforest. There's the occasional tall tree left standing, but more usually it's acres of cattle ranches, and the occasional burgeoning frontier town, crowded with people busy in mechanics' workshops, construction, trading or passing the time playing pool. This is **Rondônia** (see p.492), a relatively recently established jungle state, which has already, even by official reckoning, lost over fifteen percent of its original forest. **JI PARANÁ** is one of the main towns and nodal points along the BR-364, with a population that's grown from nine thousand in 1970 to over 110,000 in 2006. Now Rondônia's second-largest city, its main drag is dominated by a massive Ford showroom, while thousands of gigantic tree trunks sit in enormous piles by the roadside. Even from the bus you can hear the grating noise of circular saws, slicing the forest into manageable and marketable chunks. And on the outskirts of town, hundreds of small, new wooden huts are springing up every month. It's another five hours, through decimated jungle scenery, before you reach the jungle frontier town of Porto Velho (see p.493), capital of Rondônia state.

Alta Floresta and Serra do Cachimbo

Turning west off the BR-163 some 150km before the Serra do Cachimbo, a dirt road leads to **ALTA FLORESTA**, a rapidly growing frontier town of around 43,000 people. Located almost 800km north of Cuiabá, it's a remote but thriving agricultural settlement with regular bus and plane connections to Cuiabá and elsewhere. There's little of immediate interest unless end-of-road towns are your thing, but the town has in recent years opened its doors to **ecotourism** in the form of a four-star **hotel**, the *Floresta Amazonica*, Av. Perimetral Oeste 2001 (Ⓣ66/3512-7100, Ⓦwww.fah.com.br; ❺), a tastefully developed place with expansive jungle grounds that serves as a base for the associated *Cristalino Jungle Lodge* (❻). Deeper in the forest on a tributary of the Rio Teles Pires, which ultimately flows into the Amazon, the lodge offers a wide choice of trips and activities (around R$190–350 per person per day), including visits to an *escola rural productiva* where you can buy paintings and other artefacts from local Kayaby Indians. The forest around here is particularly rich in **birdlife**, and there are several set birding trails where you can also see alligators and capuchin, spider and howler monkeys. A similar but even more remote development, accessible only by air taxi, lies 140km northwest of Alta Floresta on the Rio São Benedito, on the Pará state border: *Pousada Salto Thaimaçu* (Ⓣ66/3521-3587, Ⓦwww.thaimacu.com.br; ❼) offers fishing and boat trips, and very pleasant chalet accommodation. You can book all of these places through Floresta Tour (Ⓣ66/3521-1396, Ⓦwww.florestatour.com.br), who organize a range of forest- and lodge-based trips. If you are trying to get to **Xingu** (one of the most important indigenous Indian reserves in Brazil, located deep in the eastern forests of the northern Mato Grosso), the staging post is the town of Sinop, but you can get there with, as well as stay at, the costly *Xingu Refugio Amazonico* (Ⓦwww.xingurefuge.com).

Back in town, the *Grande Hotel Coroados*, Rua F-1, 118 (Ⓣ66/3521-3111; ❷), is exceptionally good value, with cosy rooms, an excellent pool and even a sauna. Difficult to find (there are few street signs in Alta Floresta), the hotel is one street back from Avenida Ludovico da Riva Nato in "Bloco F" at the end of a cul-de-sac. *Lisboa Palace Hotel*, at Av. Jaime Verissimo 251 (Ⓣ66/3521-2876, Ⓕ3531-3500; ❸), has larger rooms but no pool. A good budget option is the

Hotel e Restaurante Luz Divina, opposite the *rodoviária* on Avenida Ludovico da Riva Nato (☎66/3521-2742 or 3521-4080; ❶), offering a wide choice of clean, modern rooms.

Flying is the only easy and sure option **northwards from Alta Floresta**, except if you're travelling to Serra do Cachimbo, for which there are regular buses. The **airport**, 2km northwest of Alta Floresta on the Avenida Ariosto da Riva (☎66/3521-3360; R$25 by taxi), has daily flights north to Itaituba, Santarém and Belém, and south to Cuiabá and São Paulo.

Crossing the hills to the north of Cuiabá, the BR-163 heads up towards **Serra do Cachimbo**; the 2000-kilometre continuation to the Amazon and Santarém – a bold but untenable attempt to cross what is still essentially a vast wilderness – is currently impassable. As the road climbs towards the rim of the Amazon basin, the forest becomes thicker and the climate muggier, and the road surface soon deteriorates. This transitional zone is one of the best areas south of Boa Vista for large-scale ranching, and there are plenty of open grasslands, dry enough in the dry season for ranchers to burn off the old pastures to make way for fresh shoots with the first rains. Interspersed among the grasses and tangled bamboo and creeper thickets are large expanses of cane, grown as fodder for the cows after the pasture has been burnt. It's still very much a frontier land, with small settlements of loggers and brick-firers springing up along the roads as the forest is cleared away forever.

Colonel P.H. Fawcett, the famous British explorer, vanished somewhere in this region in 1925, on what turned out to be his last attempt to locate a lost jungle city and civilization. He'd been searching for it, on and off, for twenty years, the story entertainingly told in his edited diaries and letters, *Exploration Fawcett* (see "Books", p.834). This last expedition was made in the company of his eldest son, Jack, and a schoolfriend of Jack's, and following their disappearance various theories were put forward as to their fate, including being kept as prisoners of a remote tribe or, more fancifully, adopted chiefs. Possibly, they were murdered out in the wilds, as were dozens of other explorers, although Fawcett had travelled for years among the Indians without coming to any harm. More likely, they merely succumbed to one of the dozens of tropical diseases that were by far the biggest killer at the time. But the fate of the colonel still remains a mystery: in 1985, the same team who had identified the body of the Nazi Josef Mengele announced that they had identified bones found in a shallow grave as those of the colonel; but in 1996 another expedition, Expedição Autan, dissatisfied with the Mengele team's proofs, set off to try to make a DNA match, but found no trace of either the colonel or his companions.

Rondonôpolis and Jatai

For those who have arrived in Cuiabá from the Amazon, the city acts as a gateway to the rest of Brazil. From the earliest times, São Paulo was the main source of settlers arriving in Mato Grosso, though until the twentieth century the route followed the river systems. These days, the **BR-364** runs all the way (over 1700km) from Cuiabá to São Paulo, with several daily buses taking around 24 hours minimum.

On the headwaters of the Pantanal's Rio São Lourenço, two to three hours from Cuiabá, the large industrial town of **RONDONÔPOLIS** with over 160,000 inhabitants, also serves as a base for visiting the local **Bororo Indians**. In the present political climate, visits to Indian reservations are not always permitted – and you might consider the ethics of such visits before you decide to go. In any case, permission must be obtained first from FUNAI (see opposite), and they'll decide if, when and where you can go. Meanwhile, if you decide to stay here, there's a range of **hotels**, including the cheap but clean *Turis Hotel* on Rua Alagoas 61 (Ⓣ66/3421-7487; ❷). Good mid-range hotels include the *Hotel Nacional*, right by the *rodoviária* at Av. Fernando Corréa da Costa 978 (Ⓣ66/3423-3245; ❹) and the *Guatujá* at Av. Fernando Corréa da Costa 624 (Ⓣ66/3423-2111; ❹). The more luxurious *Novotel* is at Rua Floriano Peixoto 711 (Ⓣ66/3314-1000, Ⓦwww.acornhotels.com.br; ❼) with pool and restaurant; and the Vila Verde, Av. Pres. Medici 4406 (Ⓣ66/3423-2605; ❹) offers some comfort, air conditioning and good value.

The small town of **JATAI** is almost halfway to São Paulo, about ten hours from Cuiabá in the state of Goiás. This is where many passengers will be getting off and on the bus, changing to one of the other routes which emanate from here – to Brasília, Goiânia, Belo Horizonte, Rio de Janeiro, the Northeast and Belém.

Barra do Garças

An alternative route from Cuiabá to Goiás Velho, Goiânia and Brasília runs east via the **BR-070**. Over 500km from Cuiabá, on the frontier between Mato Grosso and Goiás states, **BARRA DO GARÇAS** is a useful and interesting point at which to break a long bus journey. This small and isolated, but still fast-growing town of some 70,000 people sits astride the Rio das Garças, one of the main headwaters of the Araguaia, underneath low-lying wooded hills. It's a surprisingly good base for a variety of nature-based hikes or relaxing in hot-water springs, and the nearest beach, the **Praia de Aragarças**, is barely 1km away. In the mountainous terrain that stretches from Barra do Garças up to the Serra do Cachimbo, the most impressive feature is the highly eroded red-rock cliff of the 700-metre **Serra do Roncador**, 150km due north of the town. Waterfalls and caves abound in the region; close to the limits of the town there are fourteen waterfalls in the Serra Azul alone, a range that rises to over 800m.

Much nearer, just 6km northeast of town, there are more fine river beaches and the popular natural hot baths of the **Parque Balneário das Águas Quentes** (daily 6am–9.30pm). Besides curing all the usual complaints, the waters are proudly proclaimed by the town's tourist office to have the capacity to augment one's *vitalidade sexual* – you have been warned! Nearby, too, there are the reserves of the Xavante and Bororo Indians. For information and to find out about written authorization to enter one of the reserves, contact FUNAI at Rua Muniz Mariano 3, Setor Dermat (Ⓣ66/3861-2020).

Practicalities

The swishest **place to stay** is the *Serra Azul Plaza*, at Praça dos Garimpeiros 572 (Ⓣ66/3401-6663; ❺), followed closely by *Toriuá Parque*, with a beautiful pool some 4km beyond Barra do Garças on Avenida Min. João Alberto (BR-158), Chácara Rio Araguaia (Ⓣ & Ⓕ66/3638-1811; ❹). In the centre, the *Hotel Presidente*, Av. João Alberto 55 (Ⓣ66/3861-2108; ❸) has the most comfortable rooms. There are also two **campsites**, one at the Porto Bae on the banks of the Rio Araguaia (access from Avenida Marechal Rondon), and the other at the Parque das Águas Quentes, 6km from town.

There's not a huge choice of **restaurants** in Barra do Garças, but the food is reasonably good and not particularly expensive. The *Restaurante Encontro das Aguas* Ⓣ66/3401-3536), at the riverside on Avenida Min. Joao Alberto, is great for fish and is open for lunch and dinner every day. The *Rock Café*, Av. Rio das Garças 4 (opposite *Aquarius Pizzeria*), is a trendy place to be seen eating and drinking in the evenings, with a wide range of snacks and light Brazilian meals.

There is a municipal **tourist office**, FUNDATUR, on Praça Tiradentes (Mon–Sat 9am–6pm; ⓣ66/3861-2227 or 3861-2344), and there are also three **environmental organizations** in town who may be able to help with information on the region and ecotours, as well as possibilities for **rock climbing**, **pot-holing** and **canyoning**: CELVA, Centro Etno-Ecológico do Vale do Araguaia (ⓣ66/3861-2018); União Eco-Cultura do Vale do Araguaia, Av. João Alberto 100; and the Fundação Cultura Ambiental do Centro Oeste (Caixa Postal 246). Barra do Garças also serves as a possible starting point for visits to the world's largest river island, the Ilha do Bananal, in Tocantins state (see p.552).

You can **change money** at the Banco do Brasil on Praça Tiradentes, or nearby at HSBC, Av. Min. João Alberto 528. The central **post office** is at Rua 1 de Maio 19, and **car hire** is available from Localiza (ⓣ66/3861-2140). Bus connections from the **rodoviária** on Rua Bororós (ⓣ66/3401-1217) along the BR-070 between Cuiabá and Brasília are good, and there is also an **airport**, Julio Campos, 15km out of town (ⓣ66/3401-2218), which is served by the local air taxi service BRC (ⓣ66/3861-2140) and operates flights to Brasília, Cuiabá, Goiânia and Rondonôpolis.

Travel details

Buses

Except on the Campo Grande-Corumbá route, which is monopolized by Andorinha, there are scores of different bus companies competing for the same routes as well as opening up new ones. Each company advertises destinations and departure times at its ticket office windows, making it relatively easy to choose a route and buy a ticket. Note that going north from Cuiabá, buses only go as far as Alta Floresta, or to Rio Branco via Porto Velho. Manaus, Itaituba, Santarém and Belém are all advertised by the bus companies, but are reachable only by enormous detours taking several days via Goiânia. Cruzeiro do Sul has no reliable road access.

Anastácio to: Bonito (1 daily; 4hr); Campo Grande (8 daily; 2hr); Corumbá (8 daily; 5hr); Ponta Porã (2 daily; 4–6hr).

Bonito to: Anastácio (1 daily; 4hr); Campo Grande (1 daily; 5hr); Corumbá (Mon–Sat 1 daily; 8hr); Dourados (1 daily; 5hr); Miranda (Mon–Sat 1 daily; 4hr); Ponta Porã (1 daily; 7hr).

Campo Grande to almost everywhere in Brazil, including: Alta Floresta (3 daily; 22hr); Anastácio/Aquidauana (8 daily; 2hr); Belo Horizonte (1 daily; 23hr); Bonito (1 daily; 5hr); Brasília (1 daily; 24hr); Corumbá (11 daily; 7hr); Coxim (4 daily; 3–4hr); Cuiabá (5 daily; 11hr); Dourados (5 daily; 4hr); Foz do Iguaçu (10 daily; 15hr); Miranda (11 daily; 3hr); Ponta Porã (4 daily; 5–6hr); Rio de Janeiro (4 daily; 22hr); São Paulo (6 daily; 14hr). There is also a weekly service to Asunción in Paraguay, leaving Sunday mornings (Amambay company).

Corumbá to: Campo Grande, via Anastácio/Aquidauana and Miranda (11 daily; 7hr; change in Campo Grande for most onward destinations); Rio de Janeiro (4 daily; 32hr); São Paulo (4 daily; 26hr).

Cuiabá to: Alta Floresta (4 daily; 12hr); Brasília (6 daily; 20hr); Campo Grande (6 daily; 11hr); Chapada dos Guimarães (9 daily; 1hr); Coxim (6 daily; 6–7hr); Goiânia (6 daily; 14hr); Porto Velho (4 daily; 23hr); Rio Branco (4 daily; 32hr); Rio de Janeiro (1 daily; 31hr); Rondonópolis (10 daily; 3hr); São Paulo (1 daily; 24hr-plus).

Planes

Campo Grande Several daily flights (Varig, TAM, Pantanal Linhas Aéreas) to Brazil's main cities; also to Vilhena (halfway between Cuiabá and Porto Velho).

Corumbá Daily flights (TAM and Pantanal Linhas Aéreas) to Campo Grande, Rio de Janeiro and São Paulo; and to Santa Cruz in Bolivia (Aerosul, Lloyd Aereo Boliviano or air-taxi service). Note that for Corumbá flights the Varig air pass is not valid.

Cuiabá Varig and TAM cover the main cities.

São Paulo

VENEZUELA
COLOMBIA
GUYANA
SURINAME
FRENCH GUIANA
N
5
4
3
PERU
7
6
BOLIVIA
2
8
1
PARAGUAY
CHILE
9
ARGENTINA
0
1000 km
URUGUAY

CHAPTER 8

Highlights

* **Memorial do Imigrante museum** Explore this fascinating museum, which was once a hostel that tens of thousands of immigrants passed through upon arriving in Brazil. See p.629

* **Mercado Municipal** Look out for the lovely stained-glass windows depicting scenes of Brazilian agricultural production. See p.629

* **Avenida Paulista** A showcase for modern São Paulo, this avenue also features lavish mansions from bygone eras. See p.634

* **Paranapiacaba town** This remarkable late nineteenth-century British railway village is a popular base for hikes in the surrounding Mata Atlântica. See p.656

* **Fazenda Pinhal** An intriguing relic of the state's nineteenth-century coffee boom, this is one of the oldest surviving and best-preserved rural estates in the state of São Paulo. See p.661

* **Ilhabela** Protected as a state park, this island – the most beautiful spot on São Paulo's coast – remains unravaged by tourism. See p.668

△ Sailing off the coast of Ilhabela

8

São Paulo

In many ways **São Paulo**, the country's most populous state and home to by far its biggest city, is atypical of Brazil, thanks to its status as an economic powerhouse. Home to nearly half the country's industrial output, it is also an agricultural sector that produces, among other things, more orange juice than any single nation worldwide. Its eponymous city boasts a dizzying variety of cultural centres and art galleries, and the noise from its vibrant fashion and music scenes is heard around the globe. Although most people come to the state in order to visit the city (usually for business or study), São Paulo has numerous attractions other than the concrete jungle at its heart. The beaches north of the important port of Santos – especially on **Ilhabela** and around **Ubatuba** – rival Rio's best; those to the south, near **Iguape** and **Cananéia**, remain relatively unspoiled. Inland, the state is dominated by agribusiness, with seemingly endless fields of cattle pasture, sugar cane, oranges and soya interspersed with anonymous towns where the agricultural produce is processed; additionally, some impressive **fazenda houses** remain as legacies of the days when São Paulo's economy was pretty well synonymous with coffee production. To escape scorching summer temperatures, or for the novelty in tropical Brazil of a winter chill, you can head to **Campos do Jordão**, one of the country's highest settlements and a kitsch Alpine-style resort seen through a peculiarly Brazilian lens.

São Paulo state's economic pre-eminence is a relatively recent phenomenon. In 1507, São Vicente was founded on the coast near present-day **Santos**, the second-oldest Portuguese settlement in Brazil, but for over three hundred years the area comprising today's São Paulo state remained a backwater. The inhabitants were a hardy people, of mixed Portuguese and indigenous origin, from whom, in the seventeenth and eighteenth centuries, emerged the **bandeirantes** – frontiersmen who roamed far into the South American interior to secure the borders of the Portuguese Empire against Spanish encroachment, capturing natives as slaves and seeking out precious metals and gems as they went.

It wasn't until the mid-nineteenth century that São Paulo became rich. Cotton production received a boost with the arrival of Confederate refugees from the American South in the late 1860s, who settled between **Americana** and **Santa Bárbara d'Oeste**, about 140km from the then small town of **São Paulo** itself. But after disappointing results with cotton, most of these plantation owners switched their attention to coffee and, by the end of the century, the state had become firmly established as the world's foremost producer of the crop. During the same period, Brazil abolished slavery and the plantation owners recruited European and Japanese immigrants to expand production. Riding the wave of the coffee boom, British and other foreign companies took the opportunity to

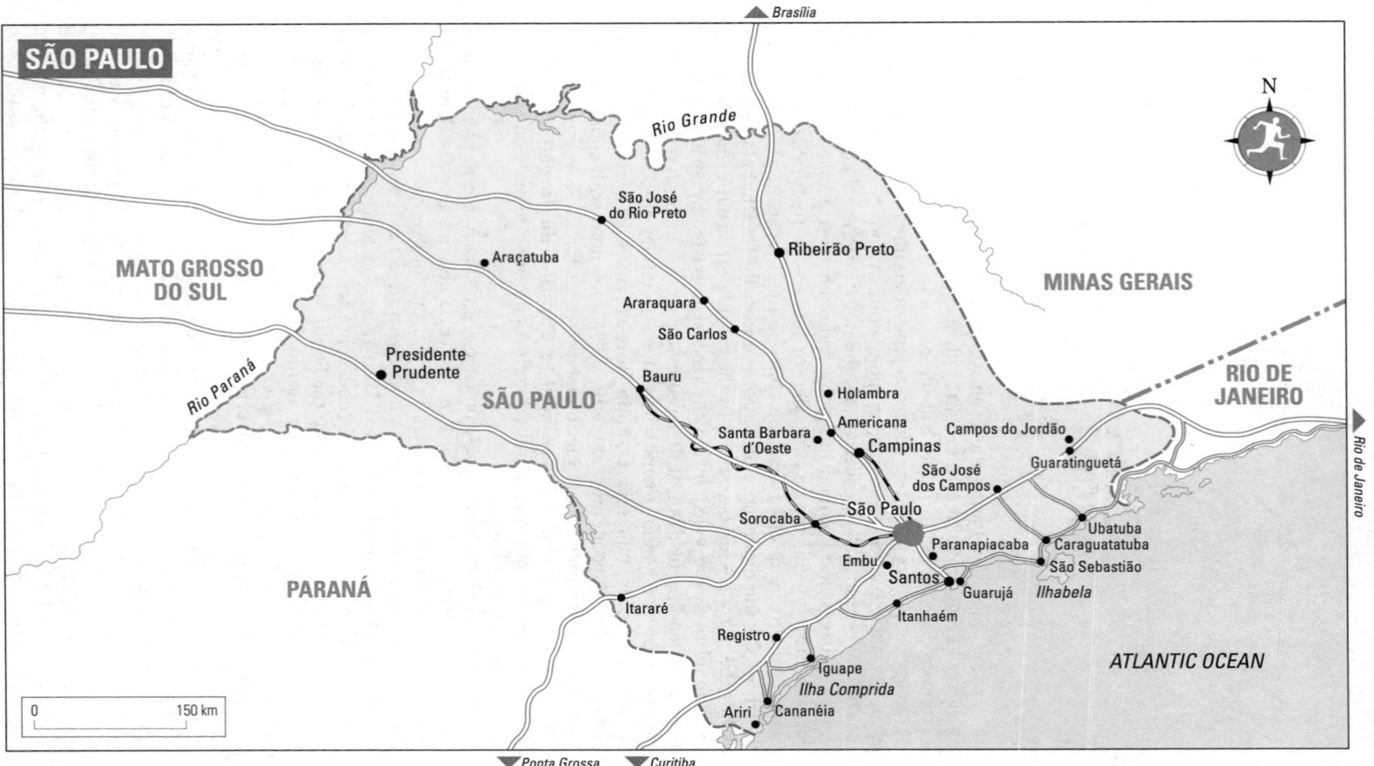
SÃO PAULO
Brasília
Campo Grande
Campo Grande
Rio Grande
São José do Rio Preto
Ribeirão Preto
Araçatuba
MATO GROSSO DO SUL
MINAS GERAIS
Araraquara
São Carlos
Presidente Prudente
Rio Paraná
SÃO PAULO
Bauru
Holambra
RIO DE JANEIRO
Americana
Santa Barbara d'Oeste
Campinas
Campos do Jordão
Guaratinguetá
Rio de Janeiro
São José dos Campos
São Paulo
Sorocaba
Ubatuba
Paranapiacaba
Caraguatatuba
Embu
São Sebastião
Santos
Guarujá
Ilhabela
PARANÁ
Itararé
Itanhaém
Registro
ATLANTIC OCEAN
Iguape
Ilha Comprida
0
150 km
Ariri
Cananéia
Ponta Grossa
Curitiba
N

invest in port facilities, rail lines and power and water supplies, while textile and other new industries emerged, too. Within a few decades, the town of São Paulo became one of Latin America's greatest commercial and cultural centres, sliding from a small town into a vast metropolitan sprawl. Although the coffee bubble eventually burst, the state had the resources in place to diversify into other produce and São Paulo's prominence in Brazil's economy was assured.

São Paulo city

Rio is a beauty. But São Paulo – São Paulo is a city.

Marlene Dietrich

Nicknamed "Sampa" – the title of a well-known Caetano Veloso song about the city, in which he admits that, "when I arrived here I didn't understand the hard concrete poetry of your streets and the discreet casual beauty of your girls" – São Paulo does not have an immediately appealing aesthetic. It's a place most people come for business; residents of the city, *paulistanos*, boast frequently of their work ethic, supposedly superior to what dominates the rest of Brazil, and speak contemptuously of the idleness of *cariocas* (in reply, *cariocas* joke sourly that *paulistanos* are simply incapable of enjoying anything – sex in particular).

Increasingly, though, visitors are also coming to São Paulo to play. Often described, not inaccurately, as "the New York of the tropics", the city lays claim to having long surpassed Rio as Brazil's **cultural** centre, with a lively and varied programme of exhibitions and shows; its **food** is often excellent, in part thanks to immigrants from so many areas of the world and a new wave of imaginative cooks; its wide range of stores make it Latin America's best place to **shop**; and its vibrant **nightlife** has put it firmly on the international clubbing map. With over 70 museums, 120 theatres, 50 parks, 30 cinemas, and not forgetting 15,000 bars, you certainly have no excuse for being bored in São Paulo.

Some history

In 1554, the Jesuit priests José de Anchieta and Manuel da Nóbrega established a mission station on the banks of the Rio Tietê in an attempt to bring Christianity to the Tupi-Guarani Indians. São Paulo dos Campos de Piratininga, as the site was called, was situated 70km inland and 730m up, in the sheer, forest-covered inclines of the Serra do Mar, above the port of São Vicente. The gently undulating plateau and the proximity to the Paraná and Plata rivers facilitated traffic into the interior and, with São Paulo as their base, roaming gangs of *bandeirantes* set out in search of loot. Around the mission school, a few adobe huts were erected and the settlement soon developed into a trading post and a centre from which to secure mineral wealth. In 1681, São Paulo became a seat of regional government and, in 1711, it was made a municipality by the king of Portugal, the cool, healthy climate helping to attract settlers from the coast.

With the expansion of **coffee** plantations westwards from Rio de Janeiro, along the Paraibá Valley, in the mid-nineteenth century São Paulo's fortunes looked up. The region's rich red soil – *terra roxa* – was ideally suited to coffee cultivation, and from about 1870 plantation owners took up residence in the city, which was undergoing a rapid transformation into a bustling regional centre. British, French and German merchants and hoteliers opened local operations, British-owned rail lines radiated in all directions from São Paulo, and foreign water, gas, telephone and electricity companies moved in to service the city. In the 1890s, enterprising "coffee barons" began to place some of their

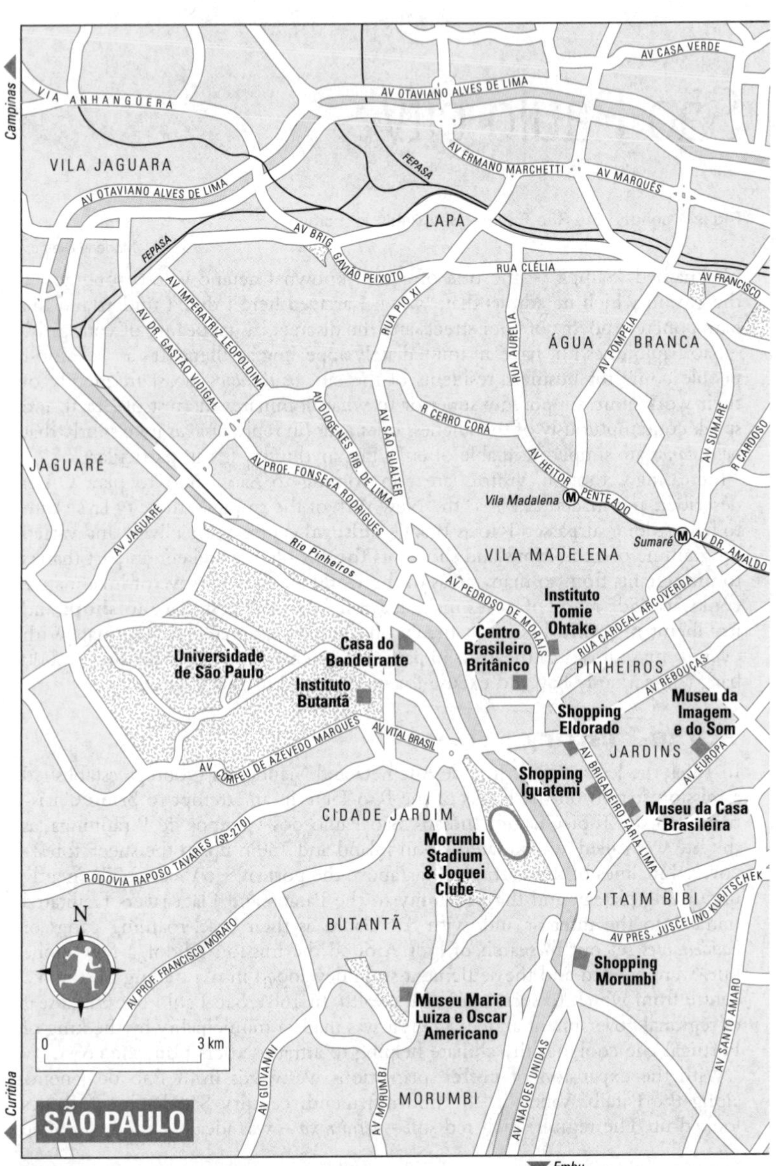

profits into local industry, hedging their bets against a possible fall in the price of coffee, with textile factories being a favourite area for investment.

As the local population could not meet the ever-increasing demands of plantation owners, factories looked to **immigrants** for their workforce (see box, p.633). As a result, São Paulo's **population** soared, almost tripling to 69,000 by 1890 and, by the end of the next decade, increasing to 239,000. By 1950, when

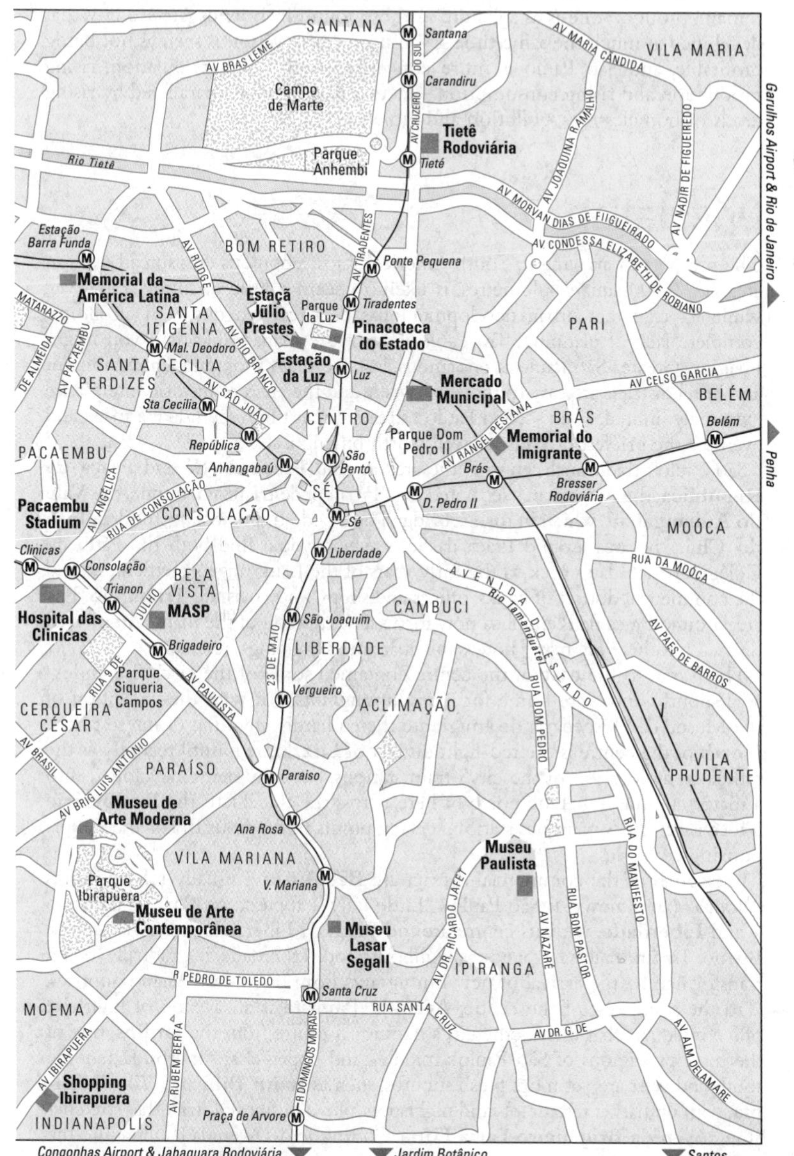

it had reached 2.2 million, São Paulo had clearly established its dominant role in Brazil's urbanization. Today, with a population of over twenty million, including its sprawling suburbs, São Paulo is the fifth largest city in the world.

To keep pace with the growth of industry, trade and the population, buildings were erected with little time to consider their aesthetics and, in any case, often became cramped as soon as they were built, or had to be demolished to make way for a new avenue. Some grand **public buildings** were built in the late nineteenth and early twentieth centuries, however, and a few still remain, though none is as splendid as those found in Buenos Aires, a city that developed at much the same time. Even now, conservation is seen as not being profitable, and São Paulo is more concerned with rising population, rising production and rising consumption – factors that today are paralleled by rising levels of homelessness, pollution and violence.

Orientation

The prospect of arriving in South America's most populous city, spread over an area of 30,000 square kilometres, is likely to seem a little daunting. However, while it's true that urban development has been carried out with an almost complete lack of planning, São Paulo is far more manageable than you might imagine. Greater São Paulo is enormous, but the main shopping, entertainment and hotel districts are easy to move between, and the areas of historic interest are extremely limited. Even so, São Paulo's streets can at times seem like a maze and even for the briefest of visits it's well worth buying a street guide.

São Paulo's traditional centre is the area around **Praça da Sé** and **Praça da República**, the two squares separated by a broad pedestrianized avenue, the **Vale do Anhangabaú**, which in turn is bridged by a pedestrian crossing, the **Viaduto do Chá**. The area around Praça da Sé is where you'll find both the Pátio do Colégio, which dates back to the early years of the Jesuit mission settlement, and the commercial district of banks, offices and shops, known as the **Triângulo**. The area around Praça da República now forms an extension of the main commercial district, but there are many hotels and apartment buildings here, too.

The *bairros* to the **east** of the centre contained some of the city's first industrial suburbs and were home for many immigrants, but with the exception of the Museu da Hospedaria do Imigrante there's hardly anything of interest here. **North** of the centre is the red-light district of **Luz**, known until recently as the rather seedy location of the city's train stations, but now being developed into a major cultural hub. Due north of here, across the Rio Tietê, the **Rodoviária Tietê** is the city's main bus station, serving points throughout Brazil and neighbouring countries.

Just **south** of the commercial district are **Bela Vista** – usually referred to as "Bixiga" (and known as São Paulo's "Little Italy"), focused on Rua 13 de Maio – and **Liberdade**, with its centre around Praça da Liberdade and Rua Galvão Bueno. Traditionally a Japanese neighbourhood, Liberdade is gradually being transformed by the arrival of new immigrants from other east-Asian countries.

To the southwest of the centre, **Avenida Paulista** is an avenue of high-rise office buildings that divides the city's traditional centre from the **Jardins**, one of the most prestigious of São Paulo's middle- and upper-class suburbs. Extending south and west are yet more plush suburbs, such as **Itaim Bibi** and **Vila Olímpia**, with upmarket restaurants and nightspots, plus a business district that stretches along **Avenida Brigadeiro Faria Lima**. Cutting across Avenida Paulista into the

Avoiding trouble in São Paulo

Assaults and robberies are favourite topics of conversation amongst *paulistanos*, with the city's crime statistics consistently higher than those of Rio. Nevertheless, by using a little common sense you're unlikely to encounter any real problems. With such a mixture of people in São Paulo, you're far less likely to be assumed to be a foreigner than in most parts of Brazil, and therefore won't make such an obvious target for pickpockets and other **petty thieves**.

At night, pay particular attention around the central red-light district of **Luz**, location of the city's main train stations and – though not as bad – around **Praça da República**. Also take special care late at night in **Bixiga** (also known as Bela Vista), or if you venture into **Praça Roosevelt**. Always carry at least some money in an immediately accessible place so that, if you are accosted by a **mugger**, you can quickly hand something over before he starts getting angry or panicky. If in any doubt at all about visiting an area you don't know, don't hesitate to take a taxi.

Jardins is **Rua Augusta**, which begins in the centre at Praça Franklin Roosevelt; many of São Paulo's best restaurants and shopping streets are located around here. **Vila Madalena** is west of the Jardins, and **Pinheiros** southwest ofVila Madalena – both are mainly residential neighbourhoods that are amongst the city's most fashionable nightspots. Just across the Rio Pinheiros lies the vast campus of the **Universidade de São Paulo** and the Instituto Butantan, while to the southeast lies the **Parque Ibirapuera**, one of the city's great parks.

Greater São Paulo includes huge, sprawling, industrial suburbs where people are housed in a mixture of grim-looking high-rise tenements, small houses and, on just about every patch of wasteland, *favelas* – the slum homes for some two million of the city's inhabitants. The most important **industrial areas** are the so-called "A B C D" *municípios* of Santo André, São Bernardo, São Caetano and Diadema, the traditional centre of Brazil's motor vehicle industry and of the city's militantly left-wing political tradition. In the 1940s, Santo André elected Brazil's first Communist Party mayor, while from the Metal Workers' Union and the autoworkers' strikes of the late 1970s emerged Lula, the leader of the PT (the Workers' Party), who was inaugurated as Brazil's president in January 2003.

Arrival, information and tours

With trains being limited to suburban services, virtually all arrivals to São Paulo are by plane or bus. Watch your belongings at all times, as thieves thrive in the confusion of airports and stations.

By air

São Paulo is served by two airports. Most domestic flights and all international flights use the modern **Guarulhos** (sometimes called "Cumbica") airport (ⓣ11/6445-2945), 30km from the city. Just to the south of the centre, the always congested **Congonhas** (ⓣ11/5090-9000 or 5090-9032) handles services within the state of São Paulo, but also operates the shuttle service (the Ponte Aérea) to Rio, as well as some of the flights to other destinations, including Curitiba and Belo Horizonte. In addition, bad weather frequently leads to the diversion of planes from Guarulhos to Congonhas.

On arrival at either airport, you will find desks that change cash or travellers' cheques, or you can use the airport ATMs. The city **tourist information** department has desks at terminals one and two in Guarulhos, which can provide maps and transport details (6am–10pm). **Taxis** are readily available at both airports: the fare to the centre is around R$60 from Guarulhos and R$35 from Congonhas. At both airports there are taxi desks in the arrivals halls and you pay a fixed price depending on the distance of your destination.

If you're travelling alone, it's more economical, at R$24 per person, to go for the express, air-conditioned, 24-hour airport **bus service** (ⓣ11/6221-0244, ⓦwww.airportbusservice.com.br). This connects Congonhas and Guarulhos at roughly half-hourly intervals, less frequently at night. The buses also link Guarulhos with the western side of Praça da República and the Rodoviária Tietê, leaving at least once an hour during the day, less frequently at night; going back from the Praça da República to Guarulhos, there are no buses between 11.40pm and 5.40am. Finally, during the day (6am–11pm) there's a service from Guarulhos to the top hotels around Avenida Paulista – if you are staying at a hotel in Itaim Bibi or elsewhere to the southwest of Jardins, your best bet is to take this bus and disembark at the *Hotel Renaissance*, from where you can take a taxi onwards.

Even cheaper, but only really practical if you have little luggage, is to take a bus to the Bresser *metrô* station (5am–11pm; R$2), from where you can catch a train into the city centre.

By bus

Inter-city bus services arrive at one of four *rodoviárias*, all connected to the *metrô* system. Serving all state capitals as well as destinations in neighbouring countries, the major terminal is **Tietê** in the north of the city, the second largest bus terminal in the world (after one in New York City). Don't be daunted – the exits, ticket offices, etc, are well sign-posted and there's a helpful information desk (*Informações*). To the south of the centre, **Jabaquara** is for buses to and from the Santos region and São Paulo's south shore as far as Peruíbe. **Barra Funda**, near the Memorial da América Latina, serves destinations in southern São Paulo and Paraná. Finally, **Bresser** is for buses to Minas Gerais. For times and fares, there is a central information line (ⓣ11/3235-0322), while ⓦwww.socicam.com.br has the phone numbers and destinations of the individual bus companies. Bus tickets to most destinations can be bought in advance at many of the city's travel agents.

Information

Anhembi Turismo, the city's tourism department (ⓣ11/6224-0615; ⓦwww.cityofsaopaulo.com), maintains several **information booths** throughout the city, with English-speaking staff who are especially helpful for general directions or for local transport details. The ephemeral nature of the booths – their locations are forever changing – is frustrating, but good bets are the ones in Galería Olido at Av. São João 465, at Avenida Paulista (across from MASP), and at Iguatemi shopping centre (see p.653); all are open daily 9am–6pm. The state **tourist office**, at Av. São Joao 465 (Mon–Sat 8am–8pm), can provide you with colourful leaflets and answer your queries on travel within the state.

For up-to-date **listings** of what's going on in the city, the São Paulo edition of the weekly magazine *Veja* contains an excellent entertainment guide, and the daily newspaper *Folha de São Paulo* lists cultural and sporting events and, on Friday, contains an essential entertainment guide, the *Guia da Folha*. On the **Web,** the Guia Internet São Paulo (ⓦwww.guiasp.com.br) is a good source of up-to-the-moment information on São Paulo's culture and nightlife in Portuguese, while ⓦwww.gringoes.com provides English-language information on living in Brazil for expats, with a particular focus on São Paulo (where most live), and featuring a weekly newsletter and lively forums.

Finding a good **map** of a city as spread out as São Paulo is not easy. The Insight Fleximap, available outside Brazil, is clear and easy to fold, but omits Vila Madalena and much of the Jardins area. The free tourist office maps vary in quality, with their Downtown maps generally better than the citywide ones. If you're planning on staying more than a day or two in the city, it's well worth investing R$30 in the *Guia Quatro Rodas* Ruas São Paulo, an (inevitably thick) indexed street atlas, available at newsstands and book stores.

City transport

São Paulo's **public transport** network is extensive, but traffic congestion and a seemingly perpetual rush hour can make travelling by bus or taxis frustratingly slow going. Matters are made even worse when it rains: São Paulo's drainage system cannot cope with the summer rains and, as many roads are transformed into rivers, the city grinds to a halt – just take cover in a bar or *lanchonete* and sit it out. São Paulo's *metrô* network, by contrast, is fast, clean and efficient, though limited in extent. As a **safety precaution**, when using public transport always make sure you have some small notes at hand, so as not to attract attention to yourself by fumbling through your wallet or bag for change.

The main difficulties of driving your own car in São Paulo are the volume of traffic and finding a parking space – you're therefore better off sticking with public transport. Roads are, however, well signposted and it's surprisingly easy to get out of the city. For a list of **car rental firms**, see p.654.

Buses

Traffic congestion rarely allows São Paulo's **buses** to be driven at the same terrifying speeds as in Rio, though drivers do their best to compete. Despite everything, the network is remarkably efficient and includes trolley buses as well as ordinary buses, for which there is a flat fare of R$2.

On the downside, **bus routes** often snake confusingly through the city, and working out which bus to take can be difficult. The number of the bus is clearly marked at the front, and cards posted at the front and the entrance (towards the back) indicate the route. At **bus stops** (usually wooden posts) you'll have to flag down the buses you want: be attentive or they'll speed by. Buses run between 4am and midnight, but avoid travelling during the height of the evening rush hour (around 5–7pm) when they are overflowing with passengers.

The metrô

Quiet, comfortable and fast, São Paulo's **metrô** would be by far the easiest way to move around the city were it not limited – for the moment – to just three

Some useful bus routes

From Praça da República to Avenida Brigadeiro Faria Lima (via Rua Augusta): #702P.

From Praça da República to Butantã (via Rua Augusta and Avenida Brigadeiro Faria Lima): #107P.

From Avenida Ipiranga to Butantã and Universidade de São Paulo: #702P.

From *metrô* Ana Rosa along Avenida Paulista: #875P.

From Rodoviária Tietê to Rodoviária Jabaquara via Largo de São Bento and Avenida Liberdade: #501M (midnight–5am only).

lines. The north–south **Linha Azul** (blue line) has terminals at Tucuruvi in the far north of the city and Jabaquara *rodoviária* and also serves the Tietê *rodoviária* and Luz train station. The **Linha Vermelha** (red line) extends east–west with terminals at Corinthians–Itaquera and Barra Funda, intersecting with the Linha Azul at Praça da Sé. There's also the **Linha Verde** (green line), a shorter east–west line that runs underneath Avenida Paulista from Ana Rosa to Vila Madalena, stopping at the Museu de Arte de São Paulo (Trianon–MASP station).

Work is well underway on extending the network – by 2008, the Linha Verde will reach further east to Oratório, and by 2012 a new, much anticipated Linha Amarelo (yellow line), connecting Luz to Praça República, Higienópolis, Avenida Paulista, Oscar Freire, Faria Lima, Pinheiros, Butantâ, Morumbi and out to Taboão da Serra, should be operational.

The *metrô* runs every day from 5am until midnight, although the ticket booths close at 10pm. **Tickets** cost R$2.10 for a one-way journey and come either as singles (*ida*), doubles (*duplo*), or valid for ten journeys (*bilhete com dez unidades*), costing R$20. You can also buy integrated bus and *metrô* tickets; many buses stop at the *metrô* stations, with the names of their destinations well marked.

Taxis

São Paulo is very much a car-orientated city. Walking around it is hard work, and sooner or later you will find yourself in need of a **taxi**. Luckily, they are reliable and abundant but, given the volume of traffic and the often considerable distances involved in navigating the city, fares quickly mount. With irregular – or no – bus services at night, taxis are also really the only means of transport after midnight. There are two main types: the yellow *comuns* and the *rádiotáxis*.

The **comuns**, generally small cars that carry up to three passengers, are the cheapest and are found at taxi ranks or hailed from the street. **Rádiotáxis** are larger and more expensive, and are ordered by phone: try Coopertax (Ⓣ11/6195-6000) or Ligue Táxi (Ⓣ11/3866-3030). Both types of taxi have meters with two fare rates, and a flag, or *bandeira*, is displayed on the meter to indicate which fare is in operation: fare "1" is charged from 6am to 9pm Monday to Saturday; fare "2" is charged after 9pm and on Sunday and public holidays, costing twenty percent more.

Accommodation

Finding somewhere to stay in São Paulo is rarely a problem and, as there are several areas where hotels are concentrated, you should get settled in quickly. The

Helicopters over São Paulo

One of São Paulo's trademark sights in recent years has been the helicopter, swooping over the skyscrapers at rush hour, allowing hard-working *paulistanos* to flit from meeting to meeting without getting snarled up in the city's notorious gridlock (and avoid the perceived risk of carjacking and kidnap). Helipads are everywhere, and some top hotels even have private top-floor receptions, so the high-flying executives don't even have to descend to the ground to check in. Many of the choppers are privately owned, although there are dozens of air-taxi firms as well. If you fancy an aerial spin around the city, helicopter tours are also available, costing around R$100 for a 60-minute trip – try Spin Receptive (Ⓣ11/3486-8715, Ⓦwww.spinreceptive.com) or Helimarte (Ⓣ11/6221-3200, Ⓦwww.helimarte.com.br).

prices of hotels vary enormously throughout the year, with hefty **discounts** offered during the quieter summer months of December, January and February. Weekend discounts of fifty percent or even more are usually given, especially at the better hotels that otherwise cater largely to business executives.

Although prices have risen notably in the last couple of years, rooms at the top hotels still cost less than comparative spots in European or North American cities; these places tend to be found in the affluent southwest of the city With some exceptions, budget and mid-priced places are located around Downtown, in parts of the city where visitors, especially women, may feel distinctly uncomfortable walking alone at night. The dangers, however, are often more imaginary than real and, by simply being alert and taking taxis late at night, you should have no problems.

Downtown

Lots of inexpensive and mid-priced hotels are in the traditional centre of São Paulo, around Praça da República and Avenida São Luís. Even cheaper accommodation can be found towards Estação da Luz in the Santa Ifigénia district, but most of these are aimed at either long-staying guests or couples checking in for an hour or two; further, at night the area has a distinctly dangerous edge to it. The Praça da República area has a much more comfortable feel and there are a number of fine hotels here that would command far higher rates if in the Jardins. Nevertheless, at night, when there are a lot of suspicious-looking individuals milling around the *praça*, you're best off relying on taxis to come and go. Budget around R$20 for a taxi each way to the restaurants and bars of Vila Madalena and surrounding neighbourhoods.

Bourbon Av. Viera de Carvalho 99 ⓣ11/3337-2000, ⓦwww.bourbon.com.br. One of the smartest hotels in the Praça da República area, the *Bourbon*, which is aimed at business travellers, has comfortable a/c rooms and extras such as a sauna and business centre. ❺

Cambridge Av. 9 de Julho 216 ⓣ11/3101-8826. If it wasn't for its location on an ugly, multi-lane inner-city avenue, this hotel would command far higher rates. Rooms are well equipped, if rather tatty, and the communal areas – in particular the busy bar, which hosts popular themed nights – have a cosy old-fashioned feel. Located near the central banking and business district and on the edge of the city's lively "Little Italy". ❸

Eldorado Boulevard Av. São Luís 234 ⓣ11/3214-1833. A good mid-range hotel popular among budget-oriented Brazilian and foreign executives for its comfortable if small rooms and larger suites. The 24-hour coffee shop attracts theatre-goers, journalists and other late-nighters. ❺

Gávea Palace Rua Conselheiro Nébias 445 ⓣ11/3331-7921. While not exactly a palace, this hotel on a side street full of motorbike repair shops is clean and comfortable, and, not surprisingly, popular with bikers. Near Praça da República ❷

Marian Palace Av. Cáspar Libero 65 ⓣ11/3228-8433, ⓦwww.marian.com.br. Though updated over the years, this Art Deco gem retains many of its original features in its guest rooms and public areas. A nice pool and garden terrace help compensate for the neighbourhood, which can be dodgy at night. ❹

Municipal Av. São João 354 ⓣ11/3228-7833. This friendly hotel, located in a part of the centre that, while busy, feels safe day and night, is a protected historic monument; the functional 1940s architecture is practically antique in a city with such a rapid rate of change. Though its simple rooms have hardly been updated since it opened, they remain perfectly adequate. ❷

Normandie Design Hotel Av. Ipiranga 1187 ⓣ11/3311-9855, ⓦwww.normandiedesign.com.br. You'll either love or hate the general look here – everything white, black and chrome. The staff are enthusiastic, the bedrooms are comfortable (if on the small side) and the price is very reasonable. ❹

República Park Av. Vieira de Carvalho 32 ⓣ11/3331-5595, ⓦwww.republicaparkhotel.com.br. The chandeliers, velvet furnishings and marble bathrooms have clearly seen better days, but the hotel is comfortable and great value. Ask for a room on an upper floor with a balcony overlooking the Praça da República. ❸

São Paulo Hostel Rua Barão de Campinas 94 ⓣ11/3333-0844, ⓦwww.hostel.com.br. This city centre hostel offers dormitory beds (R$27) and individual rooms (from R$39)

– the large size and relative comfort of the latter making them a better deal than at most hotels. With laundry facilities and its own bar, the hostel's only drawback is its rather uninspiring and dodgy-feeling neighbourhood. A sister hostel at Rua Pageú 266 (ⓣ11/5071-5148, ⓦwww.sphostel.com.br), in a quiet residential area near Praça da Árvore, is popular with longer-term visitors.

São Sebastião Rua Sete de Abril 364 ⓣ11/3257-4988. Quiet but with dark and rather musty rooms (all with shower), the *São Sebastião* has a 24-hour secure reception and is located just minutes from the entrance to the Praça da República *metrô* station. A popular choice with European backpackers. ❷

Liberdade

Like Downtown, São Paulo's Japanese *bairro*, **Liberdade**, has mostly low- and mid-priced hotels. These are well worth considering if you're on a budget – not least because the area is one of the safest parts of central São Paulo (but avoid wandering far from the *metrô* station at night). Although the overwhelming majority of people staying here are either Japanese-Brazilians or visiting Asian businessmen, other guests are made to feel just as welcome.

Akasaka Praça da Liberdade 149 ⓣ11/3207-1311. While not recognizably Japanese, this newly reopened hotel remains a good budget choice for those wanting to be in the heart of Liberdade. Rooms (including some singles) are spacious, with the brightest overlooking the *praça*, although bathrooms are shared. ❸

Barão Lu Rua Barão de Iguape 80 ⓣ11/3341-4000, ⓦwww.hotelbaraolu.com.br. Chinese owned and managed, this mid-range hotel features spacious rooms and a decent on-site restaurant serving Shanghai food. ❺

Nikkey Palace Rua Galvão Bueno 425 ⓣ11/3207-8511, ⓦwww.nikkeyhotel.com.br. This comfortable hotel markets itself to Japanese businessmen and is well known for its health club, which guests can use for free. Choose between standard rooms or larger, minimalist-style ones and either a continental or Japanese buffet breakfast. ❻

Rua Augusta and around

This area offers old-fashioned five-star comfort, as well as some more affordable options along and just off Rua Augusta in the direction of Downtown. The hotels here are convenient for the city centre, the international banks of Avenida Paulista and the fashionable Jardins. While the area is quite safe, walking along Rua Augusta late at night can be unpleasant, as you're likely to be accosted by men touting on behalf of sleazy nightclubs.

Augusta Palace Rua Augusta 467 ⓣ11/3256-1277. Part of the Best Western chain, the four-star *Augusta Palace* is an unremarkable but comfortable business-orientated hotel located nearer to Rua da Consolação than Av. Paulista, which makes it handy for the Praça da República area. It's worth calling in advance for weekend discounts. ❺

Augusta Park Rua Augusta 922 ⓣ11/3124-4400, ⓦwww.augustapark.com.br. Rooms are small but well equipped at this medium-sized hotel, and the staff are helpful with local information. ❹

Cá d'Oro Rua Augusta 129 ⓣ11/3236-4300, ⓦwww.cadoro.com.br. An easy stroll from Av. Paulista, this excellent hotel offers five-star standards in a less ostentatious environment than is often the case with São Paulo's luxury hotels. The large and simply furnished rooms are extremely comfortable and also excellent value. ❼

L'Hotel Alameda Campinas 266 ⓣ11/2183-0500, ⓦwww.lhotel.com.br. Upmarket place that sets itself apart from its rivals with old-fashioned furnishings, antiques sprinkled throughout the lobby and halls and attentive customer service. ❾

Maksoud Plaza Alameda Campinas 150 ⓣ11/3145-8000, ⓦwww.maksoud.com.br. For many years São Paulo's most distinguished hotel, the *Maksoud Plaza* and its luxurious rooms now seem positively mundane compared to the extravagance of new places like the *Unique* or *Renaissance*. Nonetheless, the staff are efficient and welcoming and there's a pool and several decent on-site restaurants. Hardly cheap, but a comparative bargain. ❼

Pergamon Rua Frei Caneca 80 ⓣ11/3123-2021, ⓦwww.pergamon.com.br A mid-range hotel that goes for a chic, contemporary look, with artfully placed lighting and black leather furniture. Ask for a room on one of the upper floors for a great view of Downtown. ❺

Pousada dos Franceses Rua dos Franceses 100 ⓣ11/3262-4026, ⓦwww.pousadadosfranceses.com.br. This small property in a quiet location, just behind the *Maksoud Plaza* and a couple of blocks from both Bixiga and Av. Paulista, has been converted into a simple but very friendly *pousada*. Guests have use of the kitchen, but be prepared to pay for any extras, including breakfast. Rates start at R$25 per person per night in a dorm, although single and double rooms are also available. ❸

Jardins

The south side of Avenida Paulista marks the beginnings of Jardins, a wealthy residential neighbourhood that houses some of the city's most fashionable (and expensive) shops and restaurants. It makes an excellent base: relatively safe by day and night, and with some excellent accommodation options.

Emiliano Rua Oscar Freire 384 ⓣ11/3069-4369, ⓦwww.emiliano.com.br. With just 57 rooms, São Paulo's trendiest – and most expensive – hotel is small compared to its other luxury spots, but the *Emiliano* prides itself on offering individual attention and lots of nice touches like free wine and massage. The light, airy rooms feature soft beds dressed in Italian linen, en-suite marble bathrooms, home cinema systems and hi-tech a/c. For an extra charge you can arrange to be transferred to and from Guarulhos airport by helicopter. ❾

Formule 1 São Paulo Paraiso Rua Vergueiro 1571 ⓣ11/5085-5699, ⓦwww.accorhotels.com.br. This small and extremely simple French-owned hotel (one of several Formule 1's in the city) offers a double bed (with a single bunk bed above), a sink and TV (but no telephone) in all rooms. A good location by the Paraiso *metrô* station and rates that are the same whether single, double or triple occupancy make this a very popular choice; reservations are always highly recommended. ❸

Paulista Center Rua Consolação 2567 ⓣ11/3852-0733, ⓦwww.paulistacenterhotel.com.br. Almost at the intersection with Av. Paulista at the edge of Jardins, this plain hotel – one of the cheapest hereabouts – is just a couple of blocks from fine restaurants and bars. All the rooms are decently sized, but in summer it's worth paying an extra R$10 for a "Master" room with a/c. ❹

Pousada Dona Ziláh Alameda Franca 1621 ⓣ11/3061-5413, ⓦwww.zilah.com. This pretty former home (now Jardin's only *pousada*) is one of the cheapest places to stay in the neighbourhood – although the rather small singles are still a bit overpriced. The atmosphere is friendly but unobtrusive, and there's always someone on hand to offer local advice. ❹

Regent Park Rua Oscar Freire 533 ⓣ11/3064-3666. A very good apartment-hotel, mainly with one-bedroom units, but also a couple of two- and three-bedroom ones; all include a living room and a small but fully equipped kitchen. There's also a rooftop pool with panoramic views of the city. ❼

Renaissance Alameda Santos 2233 ⓣ11/3069-2233, ⓦwww.marriottbrasil.com/saobr. Designed by renowned Brazilian architect Ruy Ohtake (see p.637), the burgundy-striped twin towers of *Renaissance* are not as daring as most of his other work. Part of the *Marriott* chain, the hotel boasts a high-tech business centre, a helipad, large, colourful and well-appointed guest rooms, a pool and a health club – though it offers little that isn't available at the similarly luxurious *Maksoud Plaza* for a quarter of the price. ❾

Transamerica Flats International Plaza Alameda Santos 981 ⓣ11/3146-5961, ⓦwww.transamericaflats.com.br. Self-catering one- or two-bedroom flats have kitchenettes and more space than the average hotel room. There are a dozen or so *Transamerica*s throughout the city, but this one is close to the MASP and has a top-floor bar with excellent views. ❺

Unique Av. Brigadeiro Luía Antônio 4700 ⓣ11/3055-4700, ⓦwww.hotelunique.com.br. Nothing if not unique, São Paulo's newest and most fashionable Ruy Ohtake-designed hotel looks rather like a cruise ship that's been experimented upon by extraterrestrials. It's so hip there's no sign outside, nor any reception, and your cash gets you plenty of funky perks, such as a red-lit swimming pool (where you can hear the DJ's tunes perfectly underwater) and sliding hatches in rooms that allow you to watch a plasma TV from your digitally-controlled hydro-bath. The rooftop bar is open to non-guests if you want to see what all the fuss is about. ❾

Itaim Bibi and Pinheiros

The stretch along Avenida Brigadeiro Faria Lima that links Itaim Bibi with Pinheiros is a rapidly expanding business district. While the number of hotels here are increasing, they're mostly bland (but well-equipped) franchises of international chains. At night these areas offer plenty of street life, thanks to the many excellent restaurants and clubs, and walking around feels quite secure.

Hotel de la Rose Praça dos Omáguas 106, Pinheiros ⓣ11/3812-9097, ⓦwww.hoteldelarose.com.br. This charming and unpretentious rose-coloured hotel offers small and simple rooms, all with private bathrooms and a/c. ❸

Radisson Faria Lima Av. Cidade Jardim 625, Itaim Bibi ⓣ11/2133-5960, ⓦwww.atlanticahotels.com.br. The most luxurious hotel in the area, located in the heart of the Faria Lima business district. The standard rooms are well-equipped and have large TVs, but on the Royal Floor you can also enjoy DVDs and breakfast in bed. In addition, the *Radisson* offers a business centre and meeting rooms, plus a sauna, fitness centre and attractive pool. ❽

Tryp Iguatemi Rua Iguatemi 150, Itaim Bibi ⓣ11/3065-2450, ⓦwww.solmelia.com. Although a typically characterless example of the Spanish Meliá chain – which is all over São Paulo – this hotel has comfortable rooms, a fine buffet breakfast, a small rooftop pool and a pleasant staff who provide helpful and efficient service. ❹

The City

For visitors and locals alike, the fact that São Paulo's history extends back over four centuries, well beyond the late nineteenth-century coffee boom, usually goes completely unnoticed. Catapulted virtually overnight from being a sleepy, provincial market town into one of the western hemisphere's great cities, there are few places in the world that have as comprehensively turned their backs on the past as São Paulo has done. In the nineteenth century, most of colonial São Paulo was levelled and replaced by a disorganized patchwork of wide avenues and large buildings, the process repeating itself ever since; today, not only has the city's colonial architectural heritage all but vanished, but there's little physical evidence of the coffee boom decades either.

Nevertheless, a few relics have, somehow, escaped demolition and offer hints of São Paulo's bygone eras. What remains is hidden away discreetly in corners, scattered throughout the city, often difficult to find but all the more thrilling when you do. There is no shortage of **museums**, but with a few significant exceptions they are disappointing for a city of São Paulo's stature. Collections have frequently been allowed to deteriorate and exhibits are generally poorly displayed. Fortunately, museum **charges** are negligible, around R$5, and are only given in the text below where they are above this figure.

There are several sights associated with the vast influx of immigrants to the city (see box, p.633), and it's worth visiting some of the individual *bairros*, detailed in the text, where the immigrants and their descendants have established communities: the food, as you'd expect, is just one reason to do this.

Around Praça da Sé

Praça da Sé is the most convenient starting point for the very brief hunt for **colonial São Paulo**. The square itself is a large expanse of concrete and fountains, dominated by the **Catedral Metropolitana** (Mon–Sat 8am–noon, Sun 8am–1pm & 3–6pm), a huge neo-Gothic structure with a crypt and a capacity of 8000; although mostly unremarkable, the doorway has distinctly tropical details such as coffee beans and crocodiles alongside the more usual apostles and saints. Completed in 1954, it replaced São Paulo's eighteenth-century cathedral, which was demolished in 1920. During the day the square outside bustles with activity, always crowded with hawkers and people heading towards the commercial district on its western fringes. Look out for the sundial just outside the cathedral, taken as the very centre of the city from which all roads are measured; the inscription indicates the direction of other Brazilian states. At night the square is transformed into a campsite for homeless children, who survive as best they can by shining shoes, selling chewing gum or begging. Be very careful in the surrounding roads (day and night), which are notorious for frequent muggings.

Along Rua Boa Vista, on the opposite side of the square from the cathedral, you'll find the site of the city's origins. The whitewashed Portuguese Baroque **Pátio do Colégio** is a replica of the college and chapel that formed the centre of the Jesuit mission founded here by the priests José de Anchieta and Manoel da Nóbrega in 1554 (on January 25th, an anniversary celebrated as a citywide holiday every year). Although built in 1896 (the other buildings forming the Pátio were constructed in the twentieth century), the chapel (Mon–Fri 8am–5pm) is an accurate reproduction, but it's in the **Museu Padre Anchieta** (Tues–Sun 9am–5pm), part of the Pátio, that the most interesting sixteenth- and early seventeenth-century relics – mostly old documents, maps and watercolours – are held. The complex also has a pretty outdoor café and a craft shop, whose proceeds go to a local charity. Outside, on the left as you enter the Pátio, look out for the Marco da Paz peace bell (Ⓦwww.marcodapaz.org.br), the first "Peace Landmark" (others are planned); feel free to go ahead and ring it.

Virtually around the corner from the Pátio do Colégio at Rua Roberto Simonsen 136 is the **Museu da Cidade** (Tues–Sun 9am–5pm). More interesting than the museum's small collection chronicling the development of São Paulo is the building that it's housed in, the **Solar da Marquesa de Santos** – an eighteenth-century manor house that represents the sole remaining residential building in the city from this period. A couple of hundred metres from here, at Av. Rangel Pestana 230, the well-preserved **Igreja do Carmo** (Mon–Fri 8am–noon & 1–5pm, Sat & Sun 7–11am) was built in 1632 and still retains many of its seventeenth-century features, including a fine Baroque high altar.

It is in these streets, particularly around Rua 25 de Março, that São Paulo's **Lebanese and Syrian community** has traditionally concentrated. Although less in evidence than they once were, you'll find stores selling Middle Eastern souvenirs and excellent Arab food. The community is fairly evenly divided between Muslims and Christians, and you'll find a beautiful **Orthodox church** hidden away at Rua Cavalheiro Basilio Jafet 15.

Over on the other side of the Praça da Sé (a two-minute walk down Rua Senado Feijó to the Largo de São Francisco), the **Igreja de São Francisco de Assis** (Mon–Fri 7am–7.30pm, Sat & Sun 7am-6pm) is one of the best-preserved colonial buildings in the city. Built between 1647 and 1790, it is a typical Portuguese Baroque church of the period, featuring intricately carved ornaments and an elaborate high altar. While here, step inside the adjoining courtyard of the Faculdade de Direito de São Paulo – the country's best and most exclusive law school, and one of its first higher education institutions, founded in 1824 – and take a look at the huge 1930s stained-glass window depicting the Largo de São Francisco in the early nineteenth century. Before leaving this area, it's worth visiting the **Igreja de Santo Antônio**, at Praça do Patriarca, by the Viaduto do Chá (a pedestrian bridge linking the two parts of the commercial centre). Built in 1717, its yellow and white facade has been beautifully restored; the interior, meanwhile, has been stripped of most of its eighteenth-century accoutrements, though its simple, painted, wooden ceiling deserves a glance.

North of Praça da Sé

The coffee boom that led to the dismantling of São Paulo's colonial buildings provided little in terms of lasting replacements. In the city's first industrial

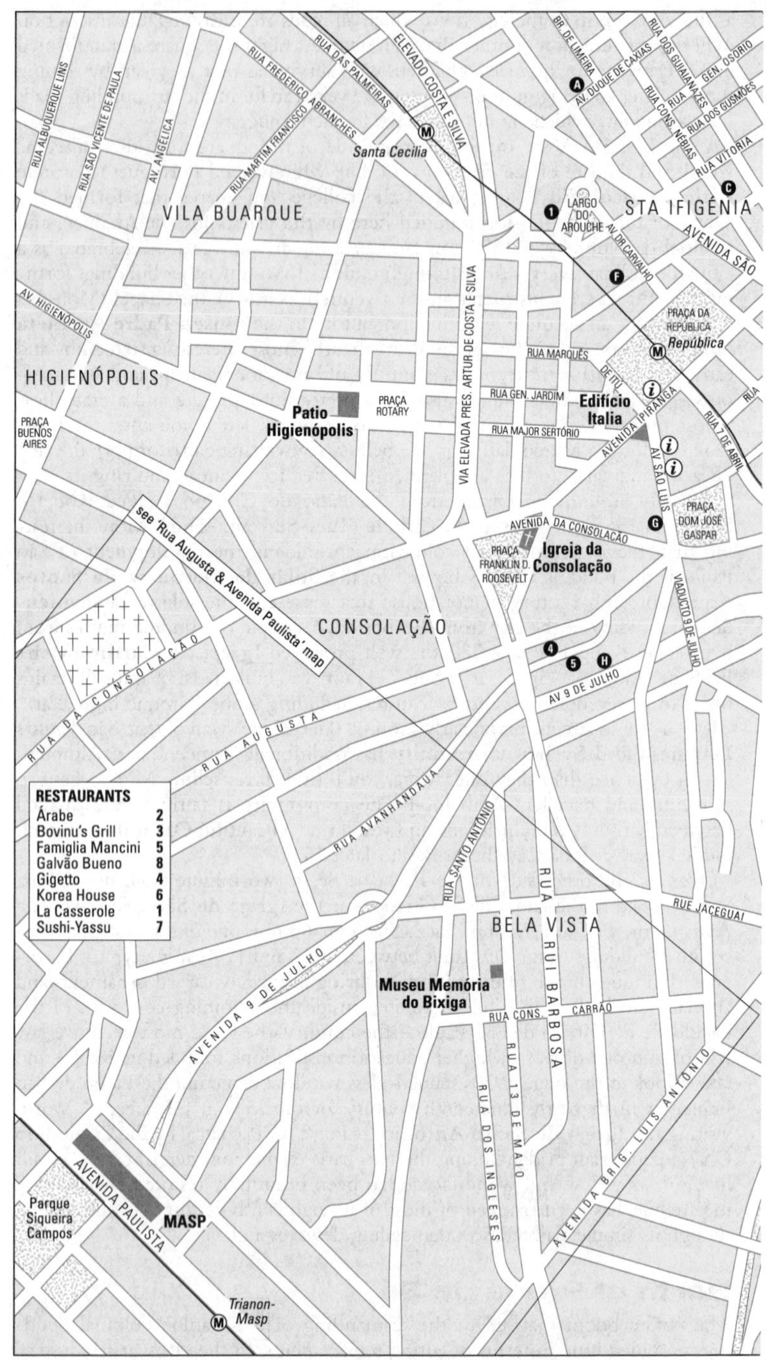

VILA BUARQUE
STA IFIGÊNIA
HIGIENÓPOLIS
CONSOLAÇÃO
BELA VISTA
Santa Cecilia
República
Trianon-Masp
Patio Higienópolis
Edifício Italia
Igreja da Consolação
Museu Memória do Bixiga
MASP
PRAÇA ROTARY
PRAÇA BUENOS AIRES
PRAÇA DA REPÚBLICA
PRAÇA DOM JOSÉ GASPAR
PRAÇA FRANKLIN D. ROOSEVELT
LARGO DO AROUCHE
Parque Siqueira Campos
see 'Rua Augusta & Avenida Paulista' map
RESTAURANTS
Árabe 2
Bovinu's Grill 3
Famiglia Mancini 5
Galvão Bueno 8
Gigetto 4
Korea House 6
La Casserole 1
Sushi-Yassu 7

8 SÃO PAULO

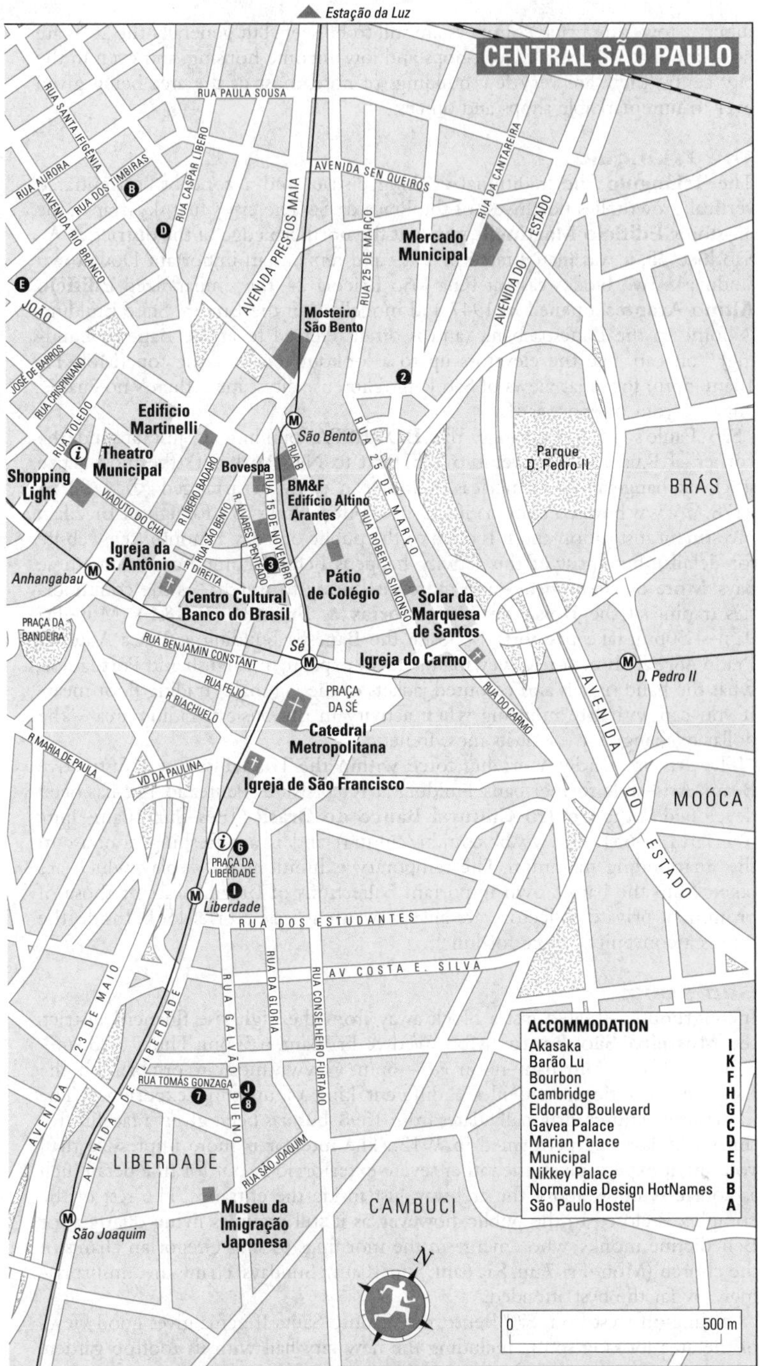
CENTRAL SÃO PAULO
Estação da Luz
Mercado Municipal
Mosteiro São Bento
Edifício Martinelli
Theatro Municipal
Shopping Light
Bovespa
BM&F Edifício Altino Arantes
Igreja da S. Antônio
Pátio de Colégio
Solar da Marquesa de Santos
Centro Cultural Banco do Brasil
Igreja do Carmo
Catedral Metropolitana
Igreja de São Francisco
Parque D. Pedro II
BRÁS
MOÓCA
LIBERDADE
CAMBUCI
Museu da Imigração Japonesa
São Bento
Anhangabau
Sé
D. Pedro II
Liberdade
São Joaquim
PRAÇA DA SÉ
PRAÇA DA BANDEIRA
PRAÇA DA LIBERDADE
ACCOMMODATION
Akasaka I
Barão Lu K
Bourbon F
Cambridge H
Eldorado Boulevard G
Gavea Palace C
Marian Palace D
Municipal E
Nikkey Palace J
Normandie Design HotNames B
São Paulo Hostel A
0 500 m
N

suburbs, towering brick chimneys are still to be seen, but generally the areas are now dominated by small workshops and low-income housing, and even in the city centre there are very few buildings of note, most of the area being given over to unremarkable shops and offices.

The Triângulo

The **Triângulo**, the traditional banking district and a zone of concentrated vertical growth, lies northwest of the Praça da Sé. The city's first skyscraper, the 35-storey **Edifício Martinelli**, stands at the northern edge of the district, at Av. São João 35; it was inaugurated in 1929 and remains an important Downtown landmark. Two blocks east, at Rua João Brícola 24, the similar-sized **Edifício Altino Arantes**, opened in 1947 and modelled on the Empire State Building, is home to the Banespa bank (and is often referred to as the Banespa building). You can take the elevators up to a lookout tower at the top (Mon–Fri 10am–5pm) for great views of São Paulo's intense cityscape – there's no charge, but take your passport as ID.

São Paulo's stock exchange, the **BOVESPA** building, is just around the corner, at Rua 15 de Novembro 275: next to New York's, it's the most active stock exchange in the Americas. A tour can easily be arranged (Ⓣ11/3233-2178, Ⓦwww.bovespa.com.br) if you have official links to a foreign or Brazilian investment institution and it is open to the public one day a month (see website for details), but most of the activity happens behind computer screens these days. More old-fashioned – and more interesting to watch – is the commodities trading at the **Bolsa de Mercadorias & Futuros (BM&F)** (Mon–Fri 9am–4.30pm; take passport), opposite the Banespa building at Praça Antonio Prado 48. Panels next to a viewing platform explain, in English and Portuguese, what the hand signals and coloured jackets of the (all male) trading floor mean. If you can, visit late morning when activity in the busiest trading area – the dollar exchange pit – is at its most frenetic.

The arts are hardly a driving force within the Triângulo, but a distinctive Beaux Arts–style former bank building at Rua Álvares Penteado 112 has been developed as the **Centro Cultural Banco do Brasil** (Tues–Sun 10am–9pm; Ⓣ11/3113-3651, Ⓦwww.bb.com.br/cultura) and is a refreshing contrast to the surrounding mammon. The temporary exhibitions on display, which are taken from the bank's own important collections of Brazilian art or those of prominent private collectors, are always worth at least a brief look. Inside, the café is a convenient place for lunch.

São Bento

Incongruously situated just a block away from the high-rise financial district, the **Mosteiro São Bento** (Mon–Wed & Fri 6am–6.30pm, Thurs 11.30am–6.30pm, Sat & Sun 6am–noon & 4–6pm; Ⓦwww.mosteiro.org.br), on the Largo de São Bento, provides a different kind of uplifting experience. The monastery's church originally dates from 1598, but has been given a facelift five times (the last one performed in 1912). The interior is more impressive than you might expect, given the rather severe exterior; look out for fine detail such as zodiac symbols above the archway, just inside the entrance. The rest of the complex is closed to the public, however, as it still provides living quarters for Benedictine monks, who emerge in the mornings to sing Gregorian chants in the church (Mon–Fri 7am, Sat 6am, Sun 10am); Sundays' chants are, unsurprisingly, by far the best attended.

Leading off west from São Bento, the Viaduto Santa Ifigênia gives good views of the area looking south, including the new city hall with its rooftop garden.

The attractive green area immediately below, the **Vale do Anhangabaú** (or Demon's Valley), stretches between this viaduct and the Viaduto do Chá; recently smartened up with palm fronds and fountains, it's a popular place with skateboarders and young couples, and is much safer to wander than it once was – in the day time, at least.

Mercado Municipal

About 1km to the northeast of São Bento, at Rua da Cantareira 306, you'll find the **Mercado Municipal**, an imposing, vaguely German neo-Gothic hall, completed in 1933. Apart from the phenomenal display of Brazilian and imported fruit, vegetables, cheese and other produce, the market (Mon–Sat 7am–6pm, Sun 7am–4pm) is most noted for its enormous stained-glass windows depicting scenes of cattle raising, market gardening and coffee and banana plantations. Traditionally, Brazilians eat *pastel de bacalhau* – a salt fish and potato pie – here. If that doesn't sound very appetizing, then head up to the new mezzanine, where a range of patio **restaurants** make up a food court that is considerably more colourful and authentic than the kind you find in shopping malls.

Memorial do Imigrante

East of the Mercado Municipal, the rundown neighbourhood of Brás would have little to offer if it wasn't for the superb **Memorial do Imigrante** at Rua Visconde de Paraíba 1316 (Tues–Sun 10am–5pm; Ⓦ www.memorialdoimigrante.sp.gov.br). The hostel buildings house an immigration research centre, a basic café and one of the best museums in São Paulo.

The museum has a permanent collection of period furniture, documents and photographs, and regularly hosts temporary exhibits relating to individual nationalities or particular aspects of immigration history. The main building itself is the most interesting feature of the complex, however, with vast dormitories and its own rail siding and platform that were used for unloading immigrants and their baggage. Near the entrance, a separate building contained the rooms where new arrivals met their prospective employers – the government

△ Memorial do Imigrante

providing interpreters to help the immigrants make sense of work contracts. Designed to hold 4000 people, the hostel housed as many as 10,000 at times, with immigrants being treated little better than cattle. In its early years, the place was a virtual prison: the exit ticket was securing a contract of employment, and control was considered necessary, since few people actually wanted to work in the plantations and there was a large labour leakage to the city of São Paulo itself. The last immigrants were processed here in 1978.

Although the museum is only a five-minute walk from Brás and Bresser *metrô* stations, it is next door to a hostel for homeless men and you may feel uncomfortable walking in the area – however, taxis can easily be found at the stations, and the museum staff will be happy to call one for your return journey (about R$5 each way). On weekends and holidays you have more interesting transport options: either a wonderful nineteenth-century train that connects the complex with Brás and Moóca stations or a tram that runs between the front entrance and Bresser *metrô* station (both R$4).

Luz

Further north, the once affluent and still leafy *bairro* of Luz is home to São Paulo's two main train stations and, for many years, has been one of the city's seediest red-light districts. Recently, though, Luz has been undergoing a remarkable renaissance, with massive city and state government investment aimed at transforming the area into a top-rank cultural centre. While there is a substantial and very visible police presence here, normal care should be taken in the *bairro*, especially when alone and at night.

At the intersection of Rua Duque de Caxias and Rua Mauá is the **Estação Júlio Prestes**, built between 1926 and 1937 and drawing on late nineteenth-century French and Italian architectural forms. The building's most beautiful features are its large stained-glass windows, which depict the role of the railway in the expansion of the Brazilian economy in the early twentieth century. Although part of the building still serves as a train station for suburban lines, its Great Hall was transformed in the late 1990s into the Sala São Paulo, home of the Orquestra Sinfônica do Estado de São Paulo, and centrepiece of the **Complexo Cultural Júlio Prestes** (ⓣ11/3337-5414). Guided tours are offered Mon–Fri at 12.30pm & 4.30pm.

Nearby, along Rua Mauá at Largo General Osório 66, there are signs of further changes to the area. The infamous Edificio DOPS, a large, anonymous-looking building that was once the headquarters of the Departamento de Ordem Política e Social, and one of the two main torture centres in São Paulo during the 1960s–1980s military dictatorships, is known today as the **Memorial da Liberdade** (Tues–Sun 10am–6pm). It serves as an exhibition centre, which commemorates its ugly past with displays charting Brazil's history of repression, from the rise of Getulio Vargas in the 1930s to the more recent struggle for democracy. Temporary art exhibitions on related themes are also held here.

Further along Rua Mauá, towards Avenida Tiradentes, the **Estação da Luz** is part of the British-owned rail network that did much to stimulate São Paulo's explosive growth in the late nineteenth century. The station was built in 1901, and everything was imported from Britain for its construction – from the design of the project to the smallest of screws. Although the refined decoration of its chambers was destroyed by fire in 1946, interior details (iron balconies, passageways and grilles) bear witness to the majestic structure's original elegance. Also worth a look is the **Vila Inglesa** at Rua Mauá 836, a group of 28 distinctively English-style houses built in 1924 for British railway engineers and their families but which have long since been used as shops and offices.

The **Parque da Luz** (Tues–Sun 9am–6pm) is one block north on Avenida Tiradentes. Dating back to 1800, the park was São Paulo's first public garden, and its intricate wrought-iron fencing, Victorian bandstands, ponds and rich foliage attest to its prominent past. Until recently, the park was considered off limits, but security is now excellent and, as one of the few centrally located patches of greenery in the city, it is popular with local residents and visitors to the surrounding cultural centres. The space includes large display panels (in English and Portuguese) on the history of the Luz district and has been developed as a sculpture park.

Adjoining the park, at Av. Tiradentes 141, is the **Pinacoteca do Estado** (Tues–Sun 10am–6pm), the gallery of São Paulo state. Housed in an imposing Neoclassical building constructed in 1905 and thoroughly renovated in 1998, this is one of the most professionally maintained galleries in Brazil, and one of the most interesting, with an excellent and well-displayed permanent collection of Brazilian paintings. Pride of place in the nineteenth-century galleries goes to images of rural São Paulo by Almeida Júnior (of which the Pinacoteca boasts some major pieces), but the work of other Brazilian landscape, portrait and historical artists of the period is also represented. The twentieth-century galleries include Cubist-influenced engravings; important paintings by the German expressionist turned Brazilian modernist Larsar Segall; and works by other painters, such as Emiliano Di Cavalcanti, noted for his choice of Afro-Brazilian and urban themes, Cândido Portinari, whose work contained clear social and historical references, and the vibrant paintings of Tarsilla do Amaral. There is also a very pleasant café with a large terrace opening onto the Parque da Luz.

One of the city's few surviving colonial churches, the **Igreja do Convento da Luz** (daily 6.30–11am & 2–5pm), is a short walk north of the Pinacoteca, by the Tiradentes *metrô* station at Av. Tiradentes 676. This rambling structure of uncharacteristic grandeur was built on the site of a sixteenth-century chapel; the former Franciscan monastery and church date back to 1774, but they've been much altered over the years. Today the site houses the **Museu de Arte Sacra** (Tues–Sun 11am–7pm), whose fine collection includes Brazilian seventeenth- and eighteenth-century wooden and terracotta religious art and liturgical pieces.

To the north, the adjoining *bairro* of **Bom Retiro** is known for its shops selling cheap clothes and fabric. At the turn of the twentieth century the neighbourhood was predominantly Italian, with successive waves of Jewish, Greek, Korean and Bolivian immigrants becoming the most prominent ethnic groups as the century progressed. It is mostly a quiet, residential area, and the main reason for visiting would be to sample the food at a neighbourhood café; the most noteworthy are the Jewish delis (see p.646).

Around Praça da República

Praça da República is now largely an area of office buildings, hotels and shops, but it was once the site of the lavish **mansions** of the coffee-plantation owners who began to take up residence in the city from about 1870. However, no sooner had the mansions been built – constructed from British iron, Italian marble, Latvian pine, Portuguese tiles and Belgian stained glass – than they were abandoned: the city centre took on a brash and commercial character, and the coffee barons moved to new homes in the Higienópolis district, a short distance to the west, and so called because it was supposedly more hygienic than the spit 'n' sawdust Praça da República. The central mansions were all knocked down, though a few remain in Higienópolis; completed in 1902, the Art Nouveau-influenced

Vila Penteado, on Rua Maranhão, is a fine example and was one of the last to be built in the area. The Praça da República itself – once home to a bullring - has a green area with a small lake where turtles sunbathe and rows of fortune tellers throw shells and cards to part the gullible from their *reais*.

Two blocks to the east, in the direction of Praça da Sé, the **Theatro Municipal** (Ⓣ11/3334-0001) is São Paulo's most distinguished public building, an eclectic mixture of Art Nouveau and Italian Renaissance styles. Work began on the building in 1903, when the coffee boom was at its peak and São Paulo at its most confident. The theatre is still the city's main venue for classical music, and the auditorium, lavishly decorated and furnished with Italian marble, velvet, gold leaf and mirrors, can be viewed by attending a performance, or by contacting the theatre to arrange a free guided tour (Tues–Thurs). Outside, just down the steps leading into the Vale do Anhangabaú (see p.616), a dramatic sculpture fountain represents the characters from Carlos Gomes' opera *O Guarani*, based on the book by José de Alencar. (The opera, a story set among the Guaraní, premiered at La Scala in 1870 and was one of the first works by a New World composer to achieve success in Europe.) There's also a small theatre museum here, but, at time of writing, it was closed for renovation, and is expected to be operational again by 2007. If you need a break from pavement pounding, **Shopping Light**, an imposing mid-1920s building across from the theatre, is a good place to escape: one of São Paulo's newest shopping centres, it is also the only upmarket collection of shops downtown.

On Avenida São Luís, the street leading south from the Praça da República, is the 46-storey **Edifício Itália**, built in 1965 to dwarf the Edifício Martinelli, and for many years Latin America's tallest building. On cloud- and smog-free days, the *Terraço Itália* restaurant on the 41st and 42nd floors is a good vantage point from which to view the city; unfortunately, you will either have to pay R$15 for the privilege, or else buy an expensive and poor quality meal. (You can get a similar view from the Edifício Altino Arantes – see p.628 – free of charge.) In the 1940s and 1950s, **Avenida São Luís** was São Paulo's version of New York's Fifth Avenue, lined with high-class apartment buildings and offices, and, though no longer fashionable, it still retains a certain degree of elegance. Admirers of the Brazilian architect Oscar Niemeyer will immediately recognize the serpentine curves of the 1950 **Edifício Copan**, by far the largest of the apartment and office buildings on the avenue. It's regarded as something of a social experiment in this otherwise sharply divided city, with its residents paying a wide variety of prices for the 1160 apartments that range in size from 26 to 350 square metres.

The Memorial da América Latina

The strikingly ugly **Memorial da América Latina** (Tues–Sun 9am–6pm; Ⓣ11/3823-4600, Ⓦwww.memorial.org.br) lies northwest of Praça da República along the Avenida São João, close to the Barra Funda *metrô* station. Designed by Oscar Niemeyer in 1989, this is a building that even the most avid fans of the architect find it hard to say anything good about, looking as it does more like a nuclear weapons site than a showcase for Latin American culture. Apart from a permanent display of Latin American folkloric art, the Memorial hosts occasional exhibitions, concerts and conferences.

Bela Vista and Liberdade

Since the early twentieth century, the *bairro* of **Bela Vista**, lying just southwest of Downtown, has been known as "Little Italy" (it's also commonly called Bixiga). Calabrian stonemasons built their own modest houses here with

Immigration and São Paulo

São Paulo is a city built on **immigrants**: largely due to new arrivals, São Paulo's population grew a hundred-fold in 75 years to make it the country's second-largest city by 1950. Besides sheer numbers, the mass influx of people had a tremendous impact on the character of the city, breaking up the existing social stratification and removing economic and political power from the traditional elite groups at a much earlier stage than in other Brazilian cities.

Although there had been attempts at introducing Prussian share-croppers in the 1840s, mass immigration didn't begin until the late 1870s. Initially, conditions were appalling upon arrival: many immigrants succumbed to malaria or yellow fever while waiting in Santos to be transferred inland to the coffee plantations, where they were to work. In response to criticisms, the government opened the Hospedaria dos Imigrantes in 1887, a hostel in the eastern suburb of Brás, now converted to a museum (see p.629).

Immigration to São Paulo is most closely associated with the **Italians**, who constituted 46 percent of all arrivals between 1887 and 1930. In general, soon after arriving in Brazil they would be transported to a plantation, but most slipped away within a year to seek employment in the city or to continue on south to Argentina. The rapidly expanding factories in the districts of Brás, Moóca and Belém, east of the city centre, were desperately short of labour, and well into the twentieth century the population of these *bairros* was largely Italian. But it is **Bela Vista** (or, in popular parlance, Bixiga) where the Italian influence has been most enduring, as catalogued in the **Museu Memória do Bixiga** (see p.634). Originally home to freed slaves, Bela Vista had by the early 1900s established itself as São Paulo's "Little Italy". As immigration from Italy began to slow in the late 1890s, arrivals from other countries increased. From 1901 to 1930 **Spaniards** (especially Galicians) made up 22 percent, and **Portuguese** 23 percent, of immigrants, but their language allowed them to assimilate very quickly. Only Tatuapé developed into a largely Portuguese *bairro*.

The first 830 **Japanese** immigrants arrived in 1908 in Santos, from where they were sent on to the coffee plantations. By the mid-1950s a quarter of a million Japanese had emigrated to Brazil, most of them settling in São Paulo state. Unlike other nationalities, the rate of return migration among them has always been small: many chose to remain in agriculture, often as market gardeners, at the end of their contract. The city's large Japanese community is centred on **Liberdade**, a *bairro* just south of the Praça da Sé and home to the excellent **Museu da Imigração Japonesa** (see p.634).

São Paulo's **Arab** community is also substantial. Arabs started arriving in the early twentieth century from Syria and Lebanon and, because they originally travelled on Turkish passports, are still commonly referred to as *turcos*. Typically starting out as itinerant traders, the community was soon associated with small shops, and many Arabs become extremely successful in business. Numerous boutiques in the city's wealthy *bairros* are Arab-owned, but it's in the streets around **Rua 25 de Março**, north of Praça da Sé, that the community is concentrated (see p.625).

The **Jewish** community has prospered in São Paulo, too. Mainly of East European origin, many of the city's Jews started out as roaming pedlars before settling in **Bom Retiro**, a *bairro* near Luz train station (see p.631). As they became richer, they moved to the suburbs to the south of the city, but some of the businesses in the streets around Rua Correia de Melo are still Jewish-owned and there's a synagogue in the area. As the Jews moved out, **Greeks** started moving in during the 1960s, followed in larger numbers by **Koreans**. The area has long been known as a centre of the rag trade and in the Korean-owned sweatshops the latest immigrant arrivals – **Bolivians** – are employed, often illegally and amid appalling work conditions.

leftover materials from the building sites where they worked, and the neighborhood's narrow streets are still lined with these homes today. In an otherwise ordinary house at Rua dos Ingleses 118, the **Museu Memória do Bixiga** (Wed–Sun 2–5pm) enthusiastically documents the history of the *bairro*, and has a small collection of photographs and household items. Italian **restaurants** exist throughout the city, but the greatest concentration (if not the greatest quality) can be found in Bixiga. This normally quiet neighbourhood springs to life in the evening when people throng to the central Rua 13 de Maio, and the streets running off it, which are lined with *cantinas*, pizzerias, bars and small theatres. During the day on Sunday there's a lively flea market, Antiguidades e Artesanato do Bixiga, at Praça Dom Orione (see p.654).

Just east of Bixiga, the *bairro* of **Liberdade** is the traditional home of the city's large Japanese community, though in recent years a number of Vietnamese, Chinese and especially Koreans have settled here. Rua Galvão Bueno and intersecting streets are devoted mostly to Japanese and other east Asian restaurants as well as shops selling semiprecious stones, Japanese food and clothes. The **Museu da Imigração Japonesa**, Rua São Joaquim 381 (7th, 8th and 9th floors; Tues–Sun 1.30–5.30pm), has a Japanese-style rooftop garden and excellent displays honouring the Japanese community in Brazil, from their arrival in 1908 to work on the coffee plantations to their transition to farming and their varied contributions to modern Brazil. On the same road, alongside drab-looking office and apartment buildings is the instantly recognizable **Templo Busshinji** at no. 285 (daily 9am–7pm), a Japanese Buddhist temple built in 1995; visitors are welcome to look around the wooden building and attend ceremonies.

Along Avenida Paulista

By 1900, the coffee barons had moved on from Higienópolis to flaunt their wealth through new mansions set in spacious gardens stretching along the three-kilometre-long **Avenida Paulista** – then a tree-lined avenue set along a ridge 3km southwest of the city centre. (Look out for old photos – sold as postcards – showing

△ Avenida Paulista

the startlingly different avenue a century ago.) In the late 1960s, and throughout the 1970s, Avenida Paulista resembled a giant construction site, with banks and other companies competing to erect ever-taller buildings. There was little time for creativity, and along the entire length of the avenue it would be difficult to single out more than one example of decent modern architecture. There are, however, about a dozen Art Nouveau and Art Deco mansions along Avenida Paulista, afforded official protection from the developers' bulldozers. Some lie empty, the subjects of legal wrangles over inheritance rights, while others have been turned into branches of *McDonald's* or prestigious headquarters for banks.

One mansion well worth visiting is the French-style **Casa das Rosas**, Av. Paulista 37 (Tues–Sun 10am–6pm; ⓣ11/3258-6986, ⓦwww.casadasrosas.sp.gov.br), near Brigadeiro *mêtro* station at the easterly end of the *avenida*. Set in a rose garden with a beautiful Art Nouveau stained-glass window, and constructed in 1935 as a private residence, it contrasts stunningly with the mirrored-glass and steel office building behind it. The Casa das Rosas is now a cultural centre owned by the state of São Paulo, where poetry-related exhibitions are often held. A block from here at Av. Paulista 149, the **Instituto Itaú Cultural** (Tues–Fri 10am–9pm, Sat & Sun 10am–7pm; ⓣ11/2168-1776, ⓦwww.itaucultural.org.br) features temporary exhibitions of contemporary Brazilian art.

Museu de Arte de São Paulo (MASP)

One of the few interesting modern buildings along Avenida Paulista is the **Museu de Arte de São Paulo** at no. 1578 (Tues–Sun 11am–6pm; R$10; ⓣ11/3251-5644, ⓦwww.masp.art.br). Designed in 1957 by the Italian-born, naturalized-Brazilian architect Lina Bo Bardi and opened in 1968, the monumental concrete structure appears to float above the ground, supported only by remarkably delicate pillars. MASP is the pride of São Paulo's art lovers, and it is considered to have the most important collection of Western art in Latin America, featuring the work of great European artists from the last five hundred years on its top floor. For most North American and European visitors, notable though some of the individual works of Bosch, Rembrandt and Degas may be, the highlights of the collection are often the seventeenth- to nineteenth-century landscapes of Brazil by European artists – none more important than the small but detailed paintings by Frans Post, a painter of the Dutch Baroque school whose rich Brazil-inspired works were used as tapestry designs by the French Gobelins factory, some of which are also displayed in the museum. MASP is one of Brazil's few museums that regularly hosts international visiting exhibitions and there's also a regular Pirelli exhibition, showcasing superb Brazilian contemporary photography. The museum's very reasonably priced lunchtime restaurant makes for an excellent escape from the crowds, exhaust fumes and heat of Avenida Paulista outside.

Parque Siqueira Campos

Almost directly across Avenida Paulista from MASP is one of São Paulo's smallest but most delightful parks, the **Parque Siqueira Campos** (daily 6am–6pm). Created in 1912 when building in the area began, the park was planned by the French landscape artist Paul Villon and based around local vegetation with some introduced trees and bushes; in 1968 it underwent a thorough renovation, directed by the great designer Roberto Burle Marx. The park consists of 45,000 square metres of almost pure Atlantic forest with a wealth of different trees, and there's a network of trails as well as shaded benches for escaping the intense summer heat. While the park is well patrolled by wardens, a degree of alertness is still called for – don't doze off.

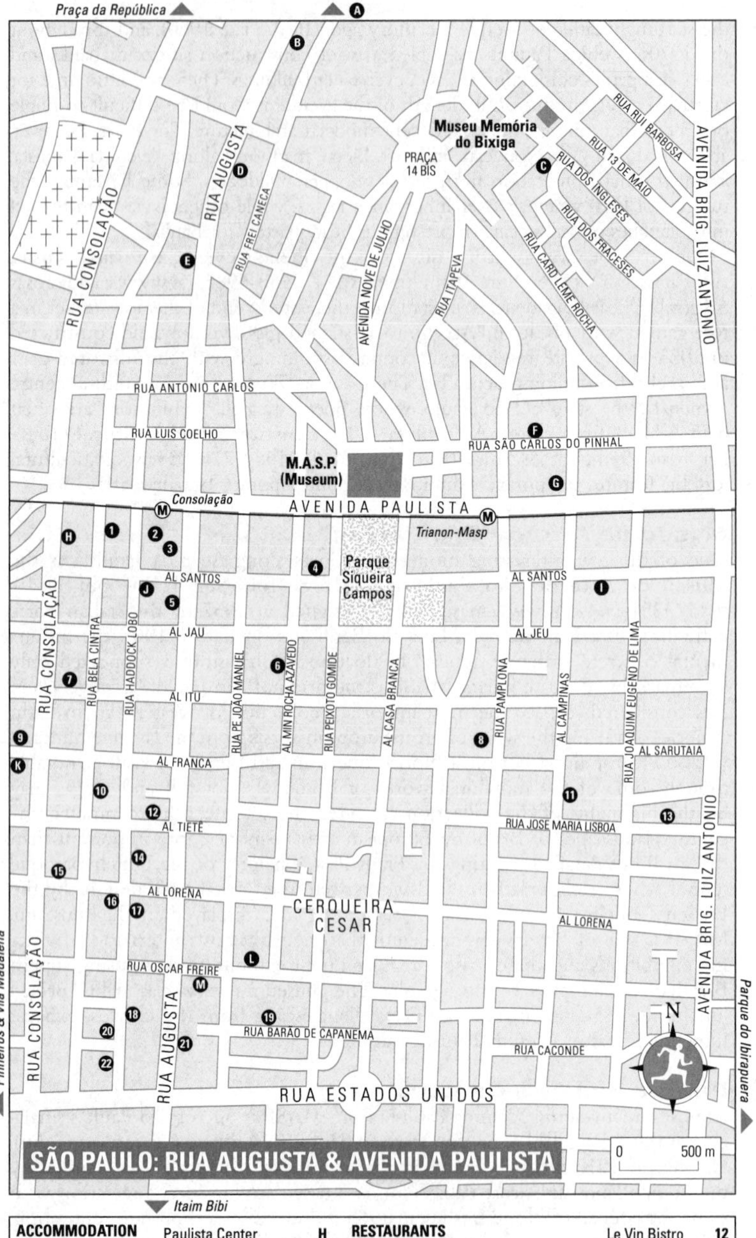

ACCOMMODATION

Augusta Palace	D
Augusta Park Residence	E
Cá d'Oro	B
Emiliano	L
L'Hotel	G
Maksoud Plaza	F
Paulista Center	H
Pergamon	A
Pousada Dona Ziláh	K
Pousada dos Franceses	C
Regent Park	M
Renaissance	J
Transamerica Internaional Plaza	I

RESTAURANTS

Antiquarius	15
Arábia	17
Asia House	5
Camelo	8
D.O.M.	21
Deloonix	10
Dona Lucinha	18
East	6
Emporio Siriuba	9
Esplanada Grill	22
Fasano	20
Folha de Uva	1
Habibs	3
Jun Sakamoto	13
Le Vin Bistro	12
Margherita	14
Massimo	4
Pasta e Vino	19
Sativa	7
Subito	2
Templo da Bahia	11
Z-Deli	16

The Jardins, Itaim Bibi and Pinheiros

Avenida Paulista marks the southwestern boundary of Downtown São Paulo, and beyond that are Jardim Paulista, Jardim America and Jardim Europa – the **Jardins** – which were laid out in 1915 and styled after the British idea of the garden suburb. These exclusive residential neighbourhoods have long since taken over from the city centre as the site of most of São Paulo's best restaurants and shopping streets, and many residents never stray from their luxurious ghettos – protected from Third World realities by complex alarm systems, guards and fierce dogs.

At the northeastern edge of the Jardins, the neighbourhood of **Jardim Paulista** lies within the wider district of Cerqueira César, which straddles both sides of Avenida Paulista. Just a few blocks into the Jardins from Avenida Paulista is a mixed bag of hotels, offices and apartment buildings interspersed with shops, restaurants and bars geared towards the city's upper middle class. Wander along Rua Oscar Freire and the intersecting *ruas* Haddock Lobo, Bela Cintra and da Consolação for some of the neighbourhood's most exclusive boutiques and excellent restaurants.

Rua Augusta, lined with shops of all sorts, bisects Jardim Paulista and then turns into Rua Colômbia and Avenida Europa in the adjoining **Jardim America** and then **Jardim Europa**. Unfortunately, the winding tree-lined roads of these largely residential neighbourhoods afford only occasional glimpses of the Victorian or Neoclassical houses that are all but hidden behind their gardens' high walls. In Jardim Europa, it's worth stopping off at Av. Europa 158, near the intersection with Rua Groenândia, to see what's on at the **Museu da Imagen e do Som** (Tues–Fri 12.30–8.30pm, Sat & Sun 11am–8pm; ⓦwww.mis.sp.gov.br), which draws on its vast film and photography archive to host often fascinating exhibitions of contemporary and historic Brazilian photography and a varied international film programme. Continuing along Avenida Europa you'll reach Avenida Brigadeiro Faria Lima, where, at no. 2705, the **Museu da Casa Brasileira** (Tues–Sun 10am–6pm; ⓣ11/3032-3727, ⓦwww.mcb.sp.gov.br) boasts a varied collection of seventeenth- to twentieth-century Brazilian furniture and decorative items. The building itself – an imposing ochre-coloured Palladian villa built in the 1940s – is typical of Jardim Europa's mansions. In the villa's kitchen, and extending into the garden, there's an excellent lunchtime restaurant, the *Quinta do Museu* (see p.645).

The traffic-choked Avenida Brigadeiro Faria Lima, with the mixed residential and commercial neighbourhoods of **Itaim Bibi** towards its southern end, and popular after-dark destination **Pinheiros** to the north, is the main artery of São Paulo's newest business expanse. Although the latest buildings around here have generally been constructed at a break-neck speed, leaving little time for architectural reflection, Pinheiros is not without its attractions, although you'll have to go some distance from the main concentration of office development to find them. One construction that you won't fail to notice is the striking purple-and-blue office building at Av. Brigadeiro Faria Lima 201 designed by **Ruy Ohtake**, one of Brazil's most important contemporary architects (see also his hotels *Renaissance* and *Unique*, p.623). Opened in 2002, the building is notable for its curved lines and use of colour, both characteristic of Ohtake's work and a deliberate move away from the modernist tradition that has been so dominant in Brazilian architecture.

Housed on the lower floors of the building, and with its entrance on Rua Coropés, the **Instituto Tomie Ohtake** (Tues–Sun 11am–8pm; ⓣ11/2245-1900,

Ⓦwww.institutotomieohtake.org.br) honours the Japanese-Brazilian artist Tomie Ohtake – the architect's mother. The artist's early Brazilian work (notably landscapes) is most closely informed by her Japanese background, but this is even apparent after her shift to abstraction, in which the restrained brushstroke remains the key element. Although only a small portion of the exhibition space features her work, in rotating displays that highlight particular periods or themes, this section is always well worth a look. Otherwise the galleries are devoted to temporary exhibits of contemporary Brazilian artists or influential twentieth-century Brazilian constructivists. There's also a good gift-shop focusing on modern Brazilian art and design, as well as a restaurant (see p.642).

Four blocks west of Avenida Brigadeiro Faria Lima, at Rua Ferreira de Araújo 741, the **Centro Brasileiro Britânico** houses the British Consulate, the BBC, the British Council and various other British cultural and community organizations. Opened in 2000, the building is almost boastfully modern, its steel, plate-glass and concrete construction managing to appear both imposing and inviting. The occasional unremarkable art exhibition is held here, but most people come for the bar and restaurant, *Drake's Bar & Deck* (see p.647).

The Parque do Ibirapuera and around

The **Parque do Ibirapuera** (daily 5am–midnight), southeast of the Jardins, is the most famous of São Paulo's parks and the main sports centre for the city. It's a ten-minute bus ride from the bus stops on Avenida Brigadeiro Luís Antônio. Officially opened in 1954, the park was created to mark the 400th anniversary of the founding of the city of São Paulo. Most of the buildings were designed by Oscar Niemeyer and impressive designs for landscaping were produced by Roberto Burle Marx.

At the park's main north entrance, in Praça Armando Salles de Oliveira, look out for the **Monumento às Bandeiras**, by Victor Brecheret. One of the city's most popular postcard sights, the 1953 sculpture shows a *bandeirante* expedition setting off, led by a Portuguese and a native on horseback. Inside the park, attractions include the peaceful and unusual **Bosque de Leitura** (reading woods) – where on Sundays (10am–4pm) you can borrow books from a small outdoor library and sit amongst the trees reading them – and several of the city's museums. The **Museu de Arte Contemporânea** (Tues–Sun 10am–7pm; Ⓣ11/3091-3039, Ⓦwww.macvirtual.usp.br), located in the Pavilhão da Bienal in the park – and also on a larger site at Rua da Reitoria 160 (Tues–Fri 10am–7pm, Sat & Sun 10am–4pm) in the Universidade de São Paulo complex – regularly alters its displays, drawing upon its huge stored collection. Although the collection includes work by important European artists like Picasso, Modigliani, Léger and Chagall and Brazilians such as Tarsilla do Amaral, Di Cavalcanti and Portinari, the pieces that are selected for exhibition can be disappointing. Next door to the Pavilhão da Bienal in the Marquise do Parque do Ibirapuera, the **Museu de Arte Moderna**, or MAM (Tues–Thurs, Sat & Sun 10am–6pm, Fri 10am–10pm; Ⓣ11/5549-9688, Ⓦwww.mam.org.br), is a much smaller gallery that mainly hosts temporary exhibits of the work of Brazilian artists. There's an excellent café here serving light meals and snacks, and a good bookshop. The new **Museu Afro-Brasil** (10am–5pm, closed Tues; Ⓦwww.museuafrobrasil.prodam.sp.gov.br), which opened in 2004 at the Pavilhão Manoel da Nóbrega in the northern part of the park near the lake, has temporary exhibitions of photos and artwork relating to African Brazilians, whose experience has been a neglected subject in this part of the country. The museum has yet to fully find its feet, with rather dry and poorly labelled exhibits that don't quite live up to the large, airy

The São Paulo Bienal

The **São Paulo Bienal** has been held in the Parque do Ibirapuera every two years since 1951. It's widely considered to be the most important exhibition of contemporary visual art in Latin America and is only rivalled in the world by the similar event held in Venice. Each country sponsors work by its most influential contemporary artists, while a select few artists (living or dead) are also chosen by the Bienal's curators. At best, the Bienal can be an exhilarating venue to see important retrospectives and experience a wealth of innovative art, but at worst it can be little more than an embarrassing – or amusing – showing of fourth-rate global art. The Bienal is now held in October and November in even-numbered years. For advance information contact the cultural attaché of any Brazilian embassy, check http://bienalsaopaulo.globo.com or write directly to São Paulo Bienal, Parque do Ibirapuera, Portal 3, 04090-900 São Paulo – SP (Ⓣ11/5574-5922).

space or the potential of the subject matter. Right across, it's hard to miss the UFO-shaped **Planetarium**, reopening in 2007 after extensive refurbishments.

If you're on the art-gallery trail, a couple of other nearby museums are well worth seeking out. The *bairro* due east of the Parque do Ibirapuera, Vila Mariana, contains the wonderful **Museu Lasar Segall** at Rua Berta 111 (Tues–Sat 2–7pm, Sun 2–6pm, Ⓦwww.museusegall.org.br). As most of Lasar Segall's work is contained in this museum (which served as his home and studio from 1932 until his death in 1957), the Latvian-born, naturalized-Brazilian painter is relatively little known outside Brazil. Originally a part of the German Expressionist movement at the beginning of the twentieth century, Segall settled in Brazil in 1923 and became increasingly influenced by the exuberant colours of his adopted homeland. Look out especially for the vibrant jungle green of *Boy with gecko* and the inter-racial *Encounter*, an early and sensitive treatment of a complex Brazilian theme. East of here in the *bairro* of Ipiranga, the **Museu do Ipiranga** – also known as the Museu Paulista – (Tues–Sun 9am–4.45pm; Ⓣ11/6165-8000, Ⓦwww.mp.usp.br), at the intersection of *avenidas* Nazareth and Dom Pedro in the Parque da Independência, is worthwhile if you have a passing interest in Brazilian history: the museum is especially strong on the nineteenth century, featuring many paintings, furniture and other items that belonged to the Brazilian royal family. The park is also significant as the site where, in 1822, Brazilian independence was declared; in the centre of the park, at the end of Rua dos Sorocabanos, is a monument celebrating the event – a replica of the Casa do Grito, the simple house where Dom Pedro I slept – and the chapel where he and his wife were later buried.

Butantã and Morumbi

If you've got the time, it's worth making the trek out to the *bairros* of Butantã and Morumbi, in southwest São Paulo. No houses from the colonial era remain standing in the city centre, but out here in the suburbs a few simple, whitewashed adobe **homesteads** from the time of the *bandeirantes* have been preserved. The **Casa do Bandeirante** (Wed–Sun 9am–5pm), near the huge Universidade de São Paulo campus at Praça Monteiro Lobato, Butantã, is the only one open to the public. It's a typical early eighteenth-century *paulista* dwelling containing period furniture and farm implements. This part of Butantã, where many of the university teaching staff live, is extremely pleasant to wander around – tasteful hammock-slung little houses are set amid lush foliage noisy with birdsong and cicadas.

One of the city's more popular attractions is also situated in the *bairro* of Butantã, on the university campus itself. Founded in 1901, the **Instituto Butantan**, Av.

Vital Brasil 1500 (Wed–Sun 9am–4.30pm; ⓣ11/3726-7222, ⓦwww.butantan.gov.br), was one of the world's foremost research centres for the study of venomous snakes and insects and the development of anti-venom serums. Despite financial cuts, it still produces over 80 percent of the country's serums and important vaccines, its most recent development being a new rabies vaccine. The highlight for visitors is the **Museu Biológico**, which showcases snakes from around Brazil – including anacondas, rattlesnakes and iridescent Amazon boas – as well as iguanas, a bizarre monkey frog and the innocuous-looking brown spider, whose painless but fatal bite makes it the country's most dangerous. Outside, there are huge snake pits with the odd, sleepy inhabitant (in the past used for venom extraction shows, now stopped for animal welfare reasons), a new museum of microbiology, a gift shop and a simple café. The campus also houses a number of other small, special-interest museums in faculties such as archeology and geoscience.

The nearest train station is Cidade Universitária, connected to Vila Madalena *metrô* station via a free bus service, the Ponte Orca. From the station, it is better to take a taxi than to try and find your way on foot around the extensive and poorly signposted campus.

Fundação Maria Luiza e Oscar Americano

Situated in the elegant suburb of Morumbi, the **Fundação Maria Luiza e Oscar Americano**, Av. Morumbi 4077 (Tues–Fri 11am–5pm, Sat & Sun 10am–5pm; R$8; ⓣ11/3742-0077; ⓦwww.fundacaooscaramericano.org.br), is a sprawling modernist house full of eighteenth-century furniture, tapestries, religious sculptures and collections of silver, china, coins and tapestry. Amongst the most valuable works are Brazilian landscapes by the seventeenth-century Dutch artist Frans Post, and drawings and important paintings by Cândido Portinari and Emiliano di Cavalcanti. The hilltop house, designed by Oswaldo Arthur Bratke, is clearly influenced by the work of the American architect Frank Lloyd Wright, and the beautiful wooded estate, which mainly features flora native to Brazil, helps make this spot an excellent escape from the city. A superb tearoom serves English-style high teas until 6pm daily, and classical

△ Zoológico de São Paulo

music concerts are held some Sunday mornings. Courses on music, art and architecture are offered during the week at an on-site auditorium.

Parque do Estado and Zoo

South of the city centre, near Congonhas airport, is the largest expanse of greenery within the city: the **Parque do Estado**. The park features an extent of Mata Atlântica (the Atlantic Rainforest), with trails and picnic areas, but by far the biggest draw is the **Zoológico de São Paulo** (Tues–Sun 9am–5pm; R$10; ⓣ11/5073-0811, ⓦwww.zoologico.com.br); one of the largest zoos in the world, it houses an estimated 3200 animals from around the globe – predominantly Brazilian and African species. The reptile and monkey houses have especially important collections of the latter, while the natural habitat of the park draws several thousand migratory birds annually. The other big attraction of the park is the **Jardim Botânico** (Wed–Sun 9am–5pm), next to the zoo, featuring both native and exotic flora; its "garden of the senses" comprises plants with unusual textures or heavy scents. Guided visits (in Portuguese) are available at 9am & 2pm Wed–Sun (R$6). The easiest way to get to the park is by *metrô* to Jabaquara station, followed by a short taxi ride.

Eating

Eating out is a major pastime for middle- and upper-class *paulistanos*, who take great pride in the vast number of restaurants in the city. By Latin American standards, the variety of options is certainly impressive, but by international standards the quality and taste can be disappointing, even at the more expensive end of the scale. Fortunately, though, chefs are becoming more creative with traditional Brazilian dishes, as well as adapting European and Asian ones to suit Brazilian tastes and make use of local ingredients.

Fast food and cafés

Paulistanos are reputed to be always in a hurry, and on just about every block there's someplace serving **fast food**. *Lanchonetes* do snacks and cheap, light meals and – in direct competition – so too do the likes of *McDonald's* and *Pizza Hut*. The *Ponto Chic*, at Largo do Paissandu 27, Centro, claims to have invented the traditional *bauru* sandwich (made with roast beef, salad and melted cheese), while **sandwich bars** popular with a younger crowd include the *Frevo*, Rua Oscar Freire 603; the 1950s diner-style *Rockets,* serving up burgers and shakes at Alameda Lorena 2096; and *Pops,* Bela Cintra 1541, a funky café-bar that does delicious filled bagels. (All are in Jardim Paulista.) For Italian-style ice cream and fruit sorbets at their absolute best, try *Gelatería d'Arte* at Alameda Lorena 1784.

Oddly, for a city built on immigrants and coffee, São Paulo has no **café** tradition. **Coffee** is drunk endlessly in the form of the small, gooey and not very appealing *cafézinhos*. It's not usually lingered over, but if you want to take your time with something more drinkable there are an ever-increasing number of places with an espresso machine. Among several branches of *Fran's Café* in Downtown São Paulo, the most popular is on the ground floor of the Edifício Itália. Open 24 hours a day, it serves delicious *canelinha* – espresso with milk and cinnamon. The R$2 espressos at *Santa Grau* at Rua Oscar Freire 413 in Jardim Paulista also have an enthusiastic following, and its pleasant patio is a great place to people watch.

São Paulo has a few good **tearooms,** too, such as the elegant *Tatou,* at the corner of Rua Oscar Freire and Rua Haddock Lobo, serving good-quality tea and cakes in Jardim Paulista. For a novel experience, try *As Noviças,* Av. Cotovia 611, Moema (closed Mon), where waitresses dressed as nuns serve teas against a background of religious music. If you have time, escape the crowds and fumes of the hectic business districts and head out to the Fundação Maria Luiza e Oscar Americano (see p.640), where superb English-style high teas are served, at R$35 a head.

Restaurants

São Paulo's restaurants are concentrated where the money is, in the city centre and especially in the middle- and upper-class suburbs like **the Jardins**, **Itaim Bibi**, **Pinheiros** and **Vila Madalena**. You can get away with paying R$5 or even less for a standard dish of rice, beans and meat at a small, side-street restaurant, and even at the most elegant places in the wealthiest neighbourhoods you'll be very hard-pressed to pay more than R$100 per person unless you opt for expensive imported wines. There is, of course, a huge array of options between these price extremes, so you won't have any trouble finding places to suit your tastes and budget. Many moderately priced restaurants run around R$30–40 a head.

Asian

As home to the largest Japanese community outside Japan, it's no surprise that São Paulo has many excellent Japanese restaurants, though you won't find anything resembling the new wave, fusion, Japanese food found in the US, for example. Make for **Liberdade**, traditionally considered São Paulo's "Japanese quarter", where restaurants and sushi bars are everywhere. Restaurants with menus from elsewhere in Asia tend to be disappointing, but there are exceptions, with some Chinese and Korean spots in particular offering decent, and usually low-priced, fare.

Asia House Rua Augusta 1918, Jardins and Rua da Glória 86, Liberdade. The excellent-value Japanese *comida por kilo* buffet here is particularly suitable if you want to make a foray into Japanese cuisine but find the thought of a Japanese-Portuguese sushi menu a little daunting.

China Massas Caseiras Rua Mourato Coelho 140, Pinheiros. Huge quantities of extremely cheap, unsophisticated Cantonese-style food are served in a more downmarket part of Pinheiros. The main draws are the restaurant's lively atmosphere and super-low prices.

East Alameda Jaú 1303, Cerqueira César. At this highly regarded Asian restaurant, dishes from China, Thailand, Vietnam, Korea, India and Japan are served with a distinctly Brazilian flair, such as beef with wasabi and manioc, or steamed *robalo* fish with Chinese greens. Expect to pay around R$60 for a three-course meal.

Galvão Bueno Rua Galvão Bueno 451, Liberdade. A Korean barbecue is cooked on a small grill at your table at this good-value, all-you-can-eat place; Japanese items are on the menu as well. Around R$20 per person.

Govinda Rua Princesa Isabel 379, Brooklin Paulista. Dishes at this place – the oldest Indian restaurant in the city – are tempered to suit Brazilian tastebuds, and may seem distinctly lacking in spice for those accustomed to the cuisine. The highlight is the plate of chutney served as an entree. Govinda is not cheap, and is really worthwhile more for the lavish decoration than the food. Closed Sun evening.

Instituto Tomie Ohtake Av. Brigadeiro Faria Lima 201 (entrance on Rua Coropés), Pinheiros. Even if the art in the cultural centre (see p.638) leaves you cold, the restaurant is well worth a visit. This is a rare – and generally successful – attempt at fusing Brazilian dishes with pan-Asian (especially Japanese and Thai) flavours; the menu changes every three months. Tues–Sat noon–3pm, with brunch served on Sundays noon-4pm.

Jun Sakamoto Rua José Maria Lisboa 55, Jardim Paulista ⓣ11/3088-6019. This expensive restaurant – expect to pay at least R$70 for a meal – stands out amongst São Paulo's many Japanese eateries, with its attractive steel and wood setting and a daring chef who adds modern twists to otherwise classic dishes. The sushi is creatively presented, and the tempura, in a light batter with sesame seeds, is excellent. Reservations are recommended on weekends, when the restaurant is very popular. Evenings only, closed Sun.

Kabuki Mask Rua Girassol 384, Vila Madalena. Good Japanese food and live Brazilian music in the evening draw a trendy crowd. Open daily for dinner and also lunch Sat & Sun.

Korea House Rua Galvão Bueno 43, Liberdade. Despite the city's sizeable Korean community, this is one of only a few Korean restaurants in São Paulo. Many dishes are prepared at the table, and the inexpensive, often spicy meals are very different from Chinese or Japanese ones.

Sushi-Yassu Rua Tomás Gonzaga 98A, Liberdade. Excellent, traditionally presented sushi, sashimi, noodle and other Japanese dishes are offered here – though not cheaply (about R$70 a person). Unusual for Brazil, eel (sautéed with soy sauce and sake) is regularly served, and sea urchins are frequently on the menu.

Middle Eastern

In general, Middle Eastern restaurants in São Paulo are extremely reliable and excellent value. Almost all serve Lebanese or Syrian food – typically a large variety of small dishes of stuffed vegetables, salads, pastries, pulses, minced meat, spicy sausages and chicken.

Agadir Rua Fradique Coutinho 950, Vila Madalena. This quite simple but pleasant restaurant features moderately priced Moroccan food – in this case entirely based on couscous and served with a choice of chicken, lamb, beef or vegetable stews or tagines. Tues–Sat dinner, Sun lunch only.

Arabe Rua Com. Abdo Schahin 126, Centro. Though crowded at lunchtime with Lebanese diners, for the rest of the day this inexpensive restaurant mainly sees elderly local men spending hours dawdling over their coffees or mint tea.

Arábia Rua Haddock Lobo 1397, Cerqueira César. Excellent and moderately priced Middle Eastern fare, with an emphasis on Lebanese cuisine, is served in very pleasant and spacious surroundings. The *mezze* is a good way to sample a mixture of dishes, or look for *kibe* stuffed with pine nuts and *coalhada,* a sort of sweetened yoghurt.

Folha de Uva Rua Bela Cintra 1435, Cerqueira César. A combination of Brazilian fast food and a buffet of Middle Eastern snacks that's popular with the lunchtime crowds. Also open Tues–Sat evening.

Habibs Rua Augusta 1894, Cerqueira César. Cheap, 24-hour Arab-style fast food joint just off Av. Paulista. The menu includes tabbouleh and shish kebabs alongside the more usual burgers and fries fast food favourites.

Traditional Brazilian

Apart from *lanchonetes* and *churrascarías,* "typical" regional Brazilian food, such as *feijoadas* or *moquecas* (see p.49), are surprisingly hard to come by in São Paulo – perhaps because of the immigrant origins of so many of the city's inhabitants. However, traditional Brazilian cooking does exist, with *bahian* and *mineiro* cuisine being the most commonly found.

Andrade Rua Artur de Azevedo 874, Pinheiros. Northeastern food is the speciality here, with dishes like *carne do sol* (sun-dried beef) served with pumpkin, sweet potato and mandioca. Portions are moderately priced and easily serve two people. Live *forró* music is performed during Sun lunch.

Bargaço Rua Oscar Freire 1189, Cerquiera César. In Salvador, Bargaço is considered by many to be the best *bahian* restaurant; it's more debatable whether this is the best *bahian* food in São Paulo, but it's certainly very good. The menu, while varied, concentrates on seafood, with *mocequas* (coconut fish stews) inevitably the biggest draw, and it's upmarket yet reasonably priced. Closed Mon lunch.

Bolinha Av. Cidade Jardim 53, Jardim Europa. Traditionally, *feijoada* (a black bean, pork and sausage stew) is served in Brazil only on Wed and Sat, but here it's the house staple every day, served as a *rodizio* along with *farofa* (toasted manioc), rice, sliced oranges and other trimmings. Choose either the traditional *feijoada* – complete with ear, nose, trotter and bacon – or the leaner "*feijoa* lite". Moderate.

Capim Santo Rua Arapiraca 152, Vila Madalena. Excellent and moderately priced food is served in an attractive patio setting, landscaped with palms and jungle fronds. The lunch buffet is a great way to experience the highlights of *bahian* food, and in the evening the à la carte offerings provide a similarly wide choice of dishes; try the shrimp cooked with *banana da terra*, a variety of plantain. Tues–Sat lunch and dinner, Sun lunch only.

Consulado Mineiro Praça Benedito Calixto 74, Pinheiros. Authentically hearty *mineiro* food makes this a popular spot, but it's particularly bustling on weekends when Praça Benedito Calixto hosts an antiques and crafts market. Dishes are mostly meat served with all the trimmings (*farofa,* sweet potato, etc); each costs around R$35 but is easily enough for two. Closed Mon.

Deli & Cia Rua Tabapua 716, Itaim Bibi. Although this friendly, busy restaurant has a wide-ranging à la carte menu, you're best off going with the buffet for both variety and value (salads, meat, fish, pasta dishes); the *feijoada* buffet on Sat is not to be missed. Mon–Sat lunch only.

Dona Lucinha Av. Chibarás 399, Moema. The best *mineiro* food that you're likely to taste in São Paulo is served at this place, the only other branch of Belo Horizonte's highly regarded *Dona Lucinha* (see p.189). Begin with one of the many *cachaças* before sampling a huge range of typical, and more unusual, vegetable and meat dishes and desserts that make up the excellent-value R$25 buffet. Tues–Sat lunch and dinner, Sun lunch only.

Espírito Capixaba Rua Francisco Leitão 57, Pinheiros. Unique in the city, this quiet side street restaurant specializes in food from the overlooked state of Espírito Santo. Lots of seafood dishes are on offer – most notably distinctive *moquecas* (fish stews) cooked in tomato sauce rather than coconut milk, as in Bahia.

O Novo Templo da Bahia Alameda Campinas 720, Jardim Paulista. This *bahian* restaurant is known for its beautifully presented – and extremely tasty – dishes. If you're new to *bahian* food, choose one of the many *moquecas* or try a platter of *acarajé* (fried bean cakes) and *bolinhos de bacalhau* (small cod pastries). Moderately priced.

O Profeta Alameda dos Aicás 40, Indianópolis. Authentic and fairly inexpensive food from Minas Gerais. The extensive buffet includes over thirty different dishes.

Churrasco

Grass-fed beef in a bewildering variety of cuts is at the centre of the **churrasco** (barbecue), and locals and expats alike agree that it's in the *churrascarías* that São Paulo really comes into its own. Tasty lamb, chicken, pork and fish are served as well, along with huge salads.

Baby Beef Rubaiyat Av. Brigadeiro Faria Lima 2954, Itaim Bibi ☏11/3078-9488. Airy, modern surroundings and meat of the highest quality have helped make this top-of-the range *churrascaría* a firm favourite among locals. The menu is bewildering, but if in doubt choose the house speciality – the exceptionally tender Baby Beef Brangus, sourced from the restaurant's own ranch. An excellent *feijoada* featuring baby boar is served on Wed and Sat, when it's advisable to reserve a table. A two-course meal with drinks is likely to set you back at least R$70.

Bovinu's Grill Rua 15 de Novembro 250, Centro. Just off Praça da República, this excellent-value *churrascaría* and *por kilo* restaurant is always packed with local office workers. There's a huge selection of salads, Brazilian stews and other dishes, and, of course, lots of meat – various cuts of beef as well as pork, chicken and fish. Expect to spend around R$15 per person. Mon–Fri lunch only. Other branches include one at Alameda Santos 2100, Jardim Paulista, which is open in the evening and costs R$20 for all you can eat.

Dinho's Alameda Santos 45, Paraíso, ☏11/3016-5333. One of the city's oldest *churrascarías*, *Dinho's* stands out for its famously high quality Wed and Sat *feijoada* buffets. Fairly expensive but consistently high quality.

Esplanada Grill Rua Haddock Lobo 1682, Jardim Paulista. This elegant and expensive (at least R$60) place is particularly recommended for its outstanding thinly sliced *picanha* (rump) steak.

Av. Moreira Guimarães 964, Moema. A bit of a trek, but this authentic *gaúcho*-style *churrascaría* – a branch of a Porto Alegre-based chain – is rated by many *paulistanos* to have the best meat in São Paulo; this is straightforward food, without bells and whistles, that relies on the sheer quality of the ingredients. Expect to pay around R$60 per person for a full meal.

Galeto's Alameda Santos 2211, Jardim Paulista. Since the 1970s, this inexpensive restaurant has specialized in barbecued chicken, served with salad and polenta, although beef and vegetable dishes are also sold. This site is the original, but there are a number of branches, including in most of the shopping centres

Grill da Villa Rua Inácio Pereira da Rocha 422, Vila Madalena. Quality meat is served in this moderately priced restaurant, located in one of São Paulo's most fashionable neighbourhoods for nightlife.

Paulista Grill Rua João Moura 251, Jardim Paulista. What this large and rather characterless *rodizio* on the corner of Av. Reboucas lacks in atmosphere it makes up for with good quality beef and other meat at a very reasonable set price: R$25 includes free rein on the extensive salad bar.

Contemporary Brazilian

A more modern, lighter cuisine has emerged on São Paulo's restaurant scene in recent years, as chefs have started to combine the enormous wealth of exotic Brazilian flavours with traditional Italian, French and Asian styles of cooking. Although a welcome addition to the city's menus, the places that specialize in this kind of thing tend to be expensive and can be as popular for seeing and being seen as for the actual food.

Cantaloup Rua Manoel Guedes, Itaim Bibi ⓣ11/3078-3445. Known for placing ingredients from the tropics alongside French and Italian ones, always with mouthwatering results. The seafood dishes are particularly good – try *namorado* fish with almond croquante and palm heart risotto. Lush foliage and friendly, efficient service create an intimate atmosphere in this converted warehouse. Fairly expensive but excellent.

Carlota Rua Sergipe 753, Higienópolis. Thanks to careful selection and precise matching of ingredients, this elegant spot is one of the most successful East Asian/Italian/Brazilian fusions you'll find in São Paulo. Reservations aren't taken, so expect a long wait if you arrive after 9pm. Closed Mon lunch and Sun evening.

Deloonix Bela Cintra 1709, Jardim Paulista. *Deloonix* claims to be the only place in Brazil that offers "raw" cuisine (although it also does cooked) and is particularly good for vegetarians; the Brazilian, Asian and Mediterranean dishes served here have a strong emphasis on healthy and organic products. Cheaper than most contemporary places, at around R$25-30 for a main course, but still very good.

D.O.M. Rua Br. De Capanema 549, Jardim Paulista ⓣ11/3088-0761. Chef Alex Atala is considered one of the best in Brazil, and the faultless fusion cooking at *D.O.M.* is as good as you'd expect (and as expensive – expect to pay around R$70 for the main dish alone). Try the local *robalo* fish with tapioca and cassava, or the lamb with mashed *cará,* a kind of wild potato.

Quinta do Museu Av. Brigadeiro Faria Lima 2705, Jardim Europa. Located in the old kitchen and gardens of a 1940s villa that now houses the Museu da Casa Brasileira (see p.637), this is a wonderful place for an al fresco lunch or afternoon tea. The moderately priced cuisine is a successful blend of Brazilian and Italian that's much lighter than the standard Italo-Brazilian fare – the sole with basil and roast tomato is particularly recommended. Lunch only, closed Mon.

Santa Gula Rua Fidalga 340, Vila Madalena ⓣ11/3812-7815. This restaurant, in the back garden of an old house, is surely one of the most beautiful in São Paulo – its sunny patios with their earthy colours, tiled floors and antique mismatched chairs evoking a rustic Mediterranean ambience. The menu, a blend of Italian and Brazilian cuisines, includes *carne seca* and pumpkin ravioli, creative risottos, grilled meats and delicious mousses made from unusual Brazilian fruit. Fairly expensive (about R$50 a head), and reservations are essential. Closed Sun evening and Mon lunch.

Tribeca Rua Jerônimo da Veiga 163, Itaim Bibi. Choose from a small but carefully thought-out menu that's strong on fish and vegetables, with Asian dishes such as Thai prawns mingling with more Brazilian ingredients (for example, fish is served with *mandioca* rather than potato puree). The appealing dining room has a light and airy feel.

French

French restaurants include some well-established places that have been serving traditional, rich French cuisine to *paulistanos* for years. The food is often excellent but always expensive – expect to pay at least R$80 a head.

La Casserole Largo do Arouche 346, Centro ⓣ11/3331-6283. An old favourite for a romantic evening out, with ever-reliable, classic French food. The *bouillabaisse* is particularly good. Closed Sat lunch and Mon.

Le Coq Hardy Rua Jerônimo da Veiga 461, Itaim Bibi ⓣ11/3079-3344. Arguably São Paulo's best traditional French restaurant, and almost certainly its most expensive. The food is well prepared and rich in a very old fashioned way – as far removed from *nouvelle cuisine* as you can get. Choices include *penne* pasta with duck ragu, or chateaubriand in Dijon sauce; leave room for the profiteroles. On weekdays there's a comparatively good-value lunch menu. Closed Sun.

Le Vin Bistro Alameda Tietê 184, Jardim Paulista. Simple but attractively presented food, particularly good as a light lunch. Well-known for its oysters, though the salmon is recommended too. Around R$50 a head.

Italian

With so many immigrants from Italy, it's hardly surprising that São Paulo has a huge number of Italian restaurants, ranging from family-run *cantinas* and pizzerias to elegant, expensive establishments. For the most part, the city's Italian restaurateurs are the children or grandchildren of immigrants, and they've adapted mainly northern recipes to suit Brazilian tastes as well as the availability of ingredients. São Paulo's "Little Italy", Bixiga, is good for a fun night out, with countless inexpensive eateries, but the food there is nothing special, and you'll find better fare in other neighbourhoods.

Braz Rua Vupabussu 271, Pinheiros. Quite possibly the best pizzas in São Paulo (and even, some say, the world) busy *Braz* strives to live up to expectations. The secret lies in the generosity of their toppings – hunks of mozzarella, roast vegetables and meat, drizzled with olive oil.

Camelo Rua Pamplona 1873, Jardim Paulista. This long-running establishment offers the heavy, thick variety of pizza that is typical in Brazil.

Castelões Rua Jairo Góis 126, Brás. Although it's a bit out of the way, Castelões is one of the most traditional pizza houses in the city and, while perhaps not worth making a special trip for, should certainly be tried if you're in the area, which is otherwise under-represented for good places to eat.

Famiglia Mancini Rua Avanhandava 81, Centro. The fun atmosphere is especially active late at night, when the restaurant is crowded with young people. Long queues for a table are common (reservations aren't accepted), though the food is mediocre apart from the fabulous *por kilo* antipasto buffet. Inexpensive.

Fasano Rua Taiarana 78, Cerqueira César ⓣ11/3062-4000. Serving without a doubt the best Italian food in São Paulo, this elegant hotel restaurant is a good choice for celebrating special occasions. Renowned for its top quality ingredients and unusual vinegar marinades, the chef adds his own twist to dishes from different Italian regions, with creations such as risotto with Tuscan ham, white beans and wine or polenta with gorgonzola. The atmosphere of the marble dining room is understated formality, and the price tag over R$90 per person.

Gero Rua Haddock Lobo 1629, Cerqueira César ⓣ11/3064-0005. This relaxed bistro-style restaurant with the same owners as *Fasano* has a smaller but still very good menu. The food is more moderately priced than other places like it (though it's hardly cheap), and the diners are rather trendy. Expect a wait for a table.

Gigetto Rua Avanhandava 63, Centro. Brazilian families crowd into this restaurant just off Rua Augusta, on a road lined with several other Italian restaurants. The food's excellent – the *cappelletti a romanesca* (alfredo, or creamy sauce with ham and peas) is a good choice - and very inexpensive.

Jardim de Napoli Rua Dr Martinico Prado 463, Higienópolis. A simple *cantina* where some of São Paulo's best Italian food is served at moderate prices. Justifiably famous for its giant meatballs (*polpettone*), it also does excellent pasta.

Margherita Alameda Tietê 255, Cerqueira César. Fairly authentic thin and crispy Italian pizzas are served at this popular pizzeria.

Massimo Alameda Santos 1826, Cerqueira César ⓣ11/3284-0311. Reliable pasta and polenta dishes as well as excellent main courses – such as roast lamb or suckling pig – are served at this venerable spot. Fairly expensive, but the atmosphere is relaxed.

Pasta e Vino Rua Barão de Capanema 206, Cerqueira César. The pasta and other Italian dishes served here are adequate, but what makes this moderately priced restaurant really useful is that it's open 24 hours.

Subito Av. Paulista 2073. Popular with nearby office workers at lunchtime, this place offers good-value risotto, pasta and salads in a small mall on Av. Paulista. Note there's no table service – you simply order, pay and pick up your plate at the counter.

Jewish

São Paulo's substantial Jewish population is reflected in a handful of authentic, and very good restaurants, located in the traditional Jewish *bairros* of Higienópolis and Bom Retiro. The delis are particularly good for lunch or for stocking up for a picnic.

Cecília Rua Tinhorão 122, Higienópolis. Authentic, moderately priced Polish Jewish dishes are served here, and on weekends you can try a Central European version of *feijoada* made with white beans, beef and potatoes. Closed Mon.

Shoshi Delishop Rua Correia de Melo 206, Bom Retiro. Stop in for Eastern European Jewish food (such as *gefilte* fish and ox-tongue accompanied by buckwheat) and dishes incorporating contemporary Italian-Brazilian touches (like salmon risotto). Lunch only.

Z-Deli Alameda Lorena 1689, Cerqueira César. People who live or work in this trendy neighbourhood come to this small Jewish deli for *gefilte* fish, falafel, cheesecake and more. Another branch with the same hours is at Alameda Gabriel Monteiro da Silva 1350, Jardim Paulista. Mon–Fri 8am–6.30pm, Sat 8am–4pm, closed Sun.

Portuguese

Considering the size and overall importance of the Portuguese community in São Paulo, there are surprisingly few Portuguese restaurants, and you get what you pay for: if it's cheap, it tends not to be very good.

Antiquarius Alameda Lorena 1884, Jardim Paulista ☎11/3064-8686. Excellent – but very expensive – Portuguese food and wine is served here. The seafood is especially good, and the desserts are fabulous, but the rustic nature of many Portuguese dishes sits uncomfortably with the formal, not to say gaudy, surroundings. Closed Mon lunch & Sun evening.

Presidente Rua Visconde de Parnaíba 2438, Brás. Long-running establishment offering very good food, including top-notch *bacalhau* (salted cod) and *dourada* fish, simply cooked and presented. About R$50 a head. Closes daily at 9pm; Sat & Sun lunch only.

Rei do Bacalhau Rua Bianchi Bertoldi 36, Pinheiros. Old-fashioned, family-style place serving traditional Portuguese dishes, many of which incorporate *bacalhau*. Good, although a little overpriced (at least R$60 a head). Closed Mon.

Other cuisines

The cooking on offer in São Paulo increasingly includes the flavours of other **Latin American** countries, especially Mexico and Argentina. Most **European** cuisines also have at least one representative in the city. German restaurants, in particular, are popular places to go for a few drinks and some hearty if rather unimaginative food. **Seafood** tends to be incorporated on various menus rather than sold at exclusively fish restaurants, but there is a sprinkling of (mostly expensive) seafood places around town.

Acrópoles Rua da Graça 364, Bom Retiro. Traditional Greek food, including moussaka, is served in this long-established, popular and moderately priced restaurant.

Amadeus Rua Haddock Lobo 807, Cerqueira César ☎11/3061-2859. Offers the best and probably the most expensive seafood in the city. The oysters are especially good, but all the prawn and fish dishes can be relied on. Expect to pay over R$80 per person.

Bierquelle Av. Aratus 801, Moema. A cosy place serving German and Swiss dishes – try the delicious fried, grated potato with apple sauce. Moderately priced.

Don Curro Rua Alves Guimarães 230, Pinheiros. This large and longstanding Spanish seafood restaurant features excellent *paellas* (serving two or three people) as well as octopus, lobster and squid. Expensive.

Drake's Rua Ferreira de Araújo 741, Pinheiros (in the Centro Brasileiro Britânico). There's no new-wave British cooking here to match the centre's forward-looking design (see p.638); instead you'll find traditional English dishes such as shepherd's pie, alongside American-style burgers and bar food.

Dr Tche Parrilla Rua Franca Pinta 489, Vila Mariana. Even Brazilians admit that Argentine beef is the best there is. If you won't be heading south, then dine at this authentic *parrilla* (barbecue), where you can try cuts that are hard to find outside South America, such as *vacio* (flank), served with tangy *chimichurri* condiment. Moderately priced and good value for money.

Juca Alemão Rua Min. José Galotti 134, Brooklin Paulista. Serves plain, cheap German food – heavy on sausages and potato salad – that's strangely popular amongst Brazilians. Young people are drawn here more by the beer than the food.

Lone Star Alameda Min. Rocha de Azevedo 1096, Jardim Paulista. Quesadillas and enchiladas fight it out with burgers and chilli fries at this Tex-Mex bar-restaurant.

Oba Rua Melo Alves 205, Jardim Paulista. Authentic Mexican dishes – rare in a city where Tex-Mex is the rule – are washed down with excellent and imaginative *caipirinhas*; try the mango, ginger and lime one. There's also a sprinkling of delicately flavoured Brazilian and Thai dishes, although this isn't fusion cooking. About R$40 a head.

Vegetarian

There's nowhere in Brazil where it's easier to be a vegetarian than in São Paulo: barring *churrascarías*, many restaurants offer some kind of non-meat dish, although it can still be hard work to find options at the cheaper end of the market. Fortunately, there are also a surprising number of specifically vegetarian restaurants, which have varied (and usually inexpensive) menus.

Apfel Rua Barão de Itapetinga 207 (1st floor), Centro. An excellent vegetarian buffet features both hot and cold dishes at around R$15 per person. Mon–Fri lunch only; another branch is in Jardim Paulista at Bela Cintra 1343.

Cheiro Verde Rua Peixoto Gomide 1413, Jardim Paulista. Fairly sophisticated, this vegetarian restaurant serves excellent and inexpensive fare. The simple menu changes with the seasons.

Emporio Siriuba Alameda Franca 1590, Jardim Paulista. This healthfood store has its own lunchtime café at the rear, situated on an attractive outdoor patio. Slightly more upmarket and imaginative than many healthfood places, with the chance to try vegetarian versions of dishes such as the *bahian moqueca* (here, a shitake and coconut stew). Expect to pay R$15-R$20.

Grao do Soja Rua Girassol 602, Vila Madalena. Soya is at the heart of most dishes at this vegetarian place; there's even a soya *feijoada*. Located on a hippyish street in Vila Madalena, with suitably Bohemian decor.

Lótus Rua Brigadeiro Tobias 420, Luz. This inexpensive vegetarian *por kilo* restaurant has a mainly Chinese menu. It's well located for the nearby cultural centres. Lunchtimes only, closed Sun.

Sativa Alameda Itu 1564, Jardim Paulista. In an otherwise expensive area, during the week this pleasant little restaurant serves an excellent-value lunchtime *prato del dia* (dish of the day), with freshly squeezed juice, for just R$9. In the evening there is a similarly inexpensive á la carte menu.

Bars, nightlife and entertainment

Whether you're after "high culture", a thumping club or just a bar to hang out in, you won't encounter much of a problem in São Paulo. The city has four main centres for nightlife: **Bela Vista**, with mixed crowds and live music; **Vila Madalena** and adjoining **Pinheiros**, which host the lion's share of trendy bars, including some with a slightly Bohemian feel; **Jardins**, offering both quieter, upmarket bars, popular with an older crowd, and gay bars; and **Itaim Bibi** and **Vila Olímpia**, together best known for their flashy *baladas* (clubs). For the trendy bars and clubs, be aware that Wednesday and Thursday nights are as popular, and in many ways considered more hip, than weekend nights, particularly in the summer when those who have the means tend to escape the city.

Places come and go in São Paulo continually, so on-the-spot advice is vital. Some suggestions are detailed below, but for the full picture of what's going on, consult the weekly *Veja* magazine, the daily *Folha de São Paulo* newspaper (especially its Friday supplement) and the website Ⓦwww.guiasp.com; additionally, the funky Ⓦwww.obaoba.com.br has all the essential club listings. Many places in fact have their own websites featuring their upcoming programmes; where these exist, they are mentioned in the listing.

São Paulo has a large **gay** population but, with some exceptions, clubs and bars tend to be mixed rather than specifically gay, with the scene mainly

Brazilian food and drink

With food and drink in Brazil reflecting the country's remarkable geographic and cultural diversity, it's hardly surprising that no true national cuisine has emerged. While it's easy to identify indigenous Indian, African and Portuguese influences, as well as Italian, German, Arab and Japanese ones, the pleasure of dining in Brazil has to do with the predominance of regional cuisines – all enhanced by the county's abundance of fruit, vegetables and spices, which you can see for yourself while walking through any local food market.

▲ Fruit stand

Regional fare

There are five main regional cuisines in Brazil, and sampling them is one of the best parts of visiting the country. **Comida baiana**, from the coast around Salvador in the state of Bahia, is seemingly the most exotic. With solid West African roots, *comida baiana* uses palm oil, coconut milk, fresh fish, shellfish, coriander and chilli peppers to remarkable effect – both in its visual impact and its taste. Although *comida baiana* is at its best in its region of origin, *baiana* restaurants are found in cities and beach resorts throughout the country.

Comida mineiro can also be enjoyed outside of its home state, with restaurants specializing in the food of Minas Gerais being widely popular. Virtually every *comida mineiro* recipe – even ones based on beans and fresh vegetables – include pork or bacon and have a tendency to be heavy. Desserts, in particular cheeses and rich, fruit-based preserves, are also a specialty of *comida mineira*, and no meal is complete without at least two shots of *cachaça* – one at the start and one at the end.

In the grasslands of the South, **comida gaúcha** emerged as one of Brazil's most carnivorous cuisines. When Brazilians think of *comida gaúcha*, what usually comes to mind are *churrascarias* – restaurants specializing in barbecue beef and other meats – which have become standard features of even small-town dining. But there's much more to *comida gaúcha* than grilled meat. Rice cooked with *charque* (jerked beef) and thick mutton stews, manioc, pumpkin and squash dishes are standard fare in the *pampas* and highland ranching country of Rio Grande do Sul.

A comparative rarity outside of its home region is **comida amazônica**, based on river fish, manioc, yam, palm products and fruit that are almost entirely unknown in the rest of Brazil. Far less varied, but similarly difficult to find elsewhere in the country, is **comida do sertão**, the cuisine of the parched interior of the Brazilian Northeast. Food here is based on dehydrated *carne de sol*, beans, manioc and other tubers – ingredients that reflect the agriculturally precarious conditions of the region.

Feijoada

The one dish that's typically associated with Brazil is **feijoada**, a rich, liquid stew usually based on *feijão preto*. Once thought to have been created by African slaves, prepared with a mix of their normal staples and leftovers, it's far more likely that *feijoada* evolved from the bean-and-pork dishes of Portuguese immigrants in **Rio de Janeiro**.

▼ Feijoada

Apart from **beans**, *feijoada* includes various **meat products** such as salted pork trimmings (ears, tail, trotters), bacon, smoked pork ribs, sausage and *charque* (jerked beef). The dish is traditionally prepared in a thick clay cooking pot over a slow fire and its strong taste is fairly salty but not at all spicy. The dish is always served with rice and accompanied by chopped sautéed *couvé* (kale), *farofa* (lightly roasted manioc flour) and a peeled orange. Other common

Beans

Regardless of region, there's no more key ingredient in Brazilian cooking than beans – indeed, to many people a meal is not a meal without them. Beans are prepared in a variety of ways, served almost soup-like or refried with onion. Dried beans come in numerous sizes and colours, with subtle differences in texture and flavour. *Carioquinha* (brown beans) are by far the most widely consumed, but they're a comparatively recent introduction to the Brazilian diet. *Feijão preto* (small black beans) are the standard fare in both Rio de Janeiro and Rio Grande do Sul; other regional varieties include *fradinho* beans (black-eyed peas) – used in the traditional Bahian recipe for *acarajé* – white beans (consumed in Santa Catarina) and a red kidney bean variation (popular in Pará).

side dishes are boiled or fried manioc, fried plantain, *torresmos* (fried pig skin) and preserved chilli peppers. The meal is often washed down with a *caipirinha* or two.

Since it is such a heavy dish that takes several hours to cook, *feijoada* is consumed in Brazil only occasionally, and generally at lunch. Restaurants rarely offer it more than once or twice a week, usually on Saturdays or sometimes on Wednesdays or Sundays.

Drinks

Whereas there's no truly national cuisine, there are a number of **drinks** that are popular throughout the country. Brazil is the world's largest producer of **coffee** – though most of the best is exported, and what's usually served up can be virtually undrinkable without lashings of sugar. That said, quality coffee is increasingly making an appearance at espresso bars and fine restaurants, many of which make great efforts to source their beans from the country's premier coffee plantations, concentrated in Minas Gerais.

▼ Caipirinha

Guaraná, a sweet, fizzy drink based on an Amazonian berry that offers a caffeine-like kick, is consumed just about everywhere, including the most sophisticated restaurants. A far more refreshing beverage is **maté gelado**, something that's typically associated with relaxing on the beach. The main ingredient of this ice tea-like treat is *erva maté*, the toasted leaf of a holly-like bush that in Rio Grande do Sul is enjoyed as **chimarrão**, sipped hot through a silver straw from a gourd.

Thanks to the amazing variety of fruit that is always available, one's spoilt for choice when it comes to **sucos** (juices). Specialist *casas de sucos* are found in most town centres, but even the most humble *lanchonete*, or snack bar, offers a range of choices that would put to shame most European or North American juice bars.

Alcohol

When it comes to alcohol, **beer** is very much the Brazilian drink of choice. Typically, Brazilian beer is a light, Pilsner-type brew that's rather flavourless and always demanded ice cold. Although just one company dominates the market – owning all four (very similar tasting) leading brands – there are a few smaller producers: Cerpa, brewed in Belém, is pretty good and widely available, while genuinely excellent is Eisenbahn, from Blumenau, a part of Brazil largely settled by German immigrants.

A uniquely Brazilian drink, however, is **cachaça**, a spirit that's made by distilling fermented sugarcane juice. The largest producers are in the states of Ceará and São Paulo, but there are also thousands of artisanal mills all over the country, with the best being in Minas Gerais. Many of these mills use traditional methods of production and age the *cachaça* in barrels made from a variety of native or exotic woods.

Cachaça can be enjoyed neat from a small shot glass, but it's often used as the basis of a **batida** (a cocktail). The **caipirinha** – made from lime, sugar, ice and *cachaça* – is as intrinsic to Brazil as samba and football. The drink's simplicity, sweetness and tangy flavour have made it popular not only in Brazil but throughout the world. Extreme care should be taken when enjoying the cocktail, however: it's as painless to drink as lemonade, and therefore all too easy to forget about the alcoholic content until the following morning, when you're hit by a giant, thumping headache.

▼ Cachaça

in the Jardins area. In May or June, the city hosts a huge Gay Pride along Avenida Paulista. For more information, see the local gay and lesbian website Ⓦ www.comunidadeglbt.com.br.

Bars

The liveliest bars in the city are found around Rua 13 de Maio in Bela Vista (often with live music) or in fashionable Vila Madalena and Pinheiros. A cover charge is levied in most places, making a bar crawl an expensive prospect. The amount you pay varies according to the day, the time and your sex (men usually pay double the amount women do), but count on an average of about R$15.

All Black Irish Pub Rua Oscar Freire 163, Jardim Paulista Ⓦ www.allblack.com.br. A swish and successful theme pub serving expensive Irish and European beers (plus affordable Brazilian lagers), a range of Irish whiskeys and bar food that extends from Irish to Thai. The pub hosts live rock and blues bands many evenings.

Astor Rua Delfina 163, Vila Madalena. This well-established bar is one of the neighbourhood's trendiest meeting points. Excellent beer and *petiscos* (snacks) make this a good place to start or end a night out in Vila Madalena.

Bar Brahma Av. São João 677 (at the corner with Av. Ipiranga), Centro. Opened in 1948, this is one of the city's oldest bars. Once a haunt for musicians, intellectuals and politicians, today it draws a post-theatre crowd to the bar and insomniacs to its 24-hour café.

Bar do Sacha Rua Original 45, Pinheiros. Located on a hill with a pleasant garden, this is a nice place to come for a drink on a sunny day. Opens at noon daily.

Barnaldo Lucrecia Rua Abilio Soares 207, Paraíso Ⓦ www.barnaldolucrecia.com.br. A young crowd is drawn to this bar, located in an easy to spot yellow house. There is live music most evenings, but it's especially festive on Fri.

Cachaçaria Paulista Rua Mourato Coelho 593, Pinheiros. This is a great place for sampling *cachaça*: there are over 200 kinds here, and it's open from 6pm until the last customer leaves.

Café do Bixiga Rua 13 de Maio 76, Bela Vista. Excellent *chopp* and a carefully nurtured Bohemian atmosphere are the main attractions here. A good place to stop for a post-theatre drink.

Charles Edward Av. Pres. Juscelino Kubitschek 1426, Itaim Bibi. Known as something of a meat market, this bar is popular with people in their 30s and 40s. Live music and dancing are frequently on offer.

Dado Bier Av. Juscelino Kubitschek 1203, Itaim Bibi. Arrive for an early evening drink (the club boasts one of the city's few micro-breweries), stay for dinner (pizza or sushi), check out the art gallery, and then dance to techno, ska and rock music until dawn. Tues–Sun 7pm–late, happy hour 7.30–8.30pm.

Drake's Centro Brasileiro Britânico, Rua Ferreira de Araújo 741, Pinheiros Ⓦ www.drakesbar.com. Popular with a middle-aged British expat crowd, *Drake's* has an attractive outdoor decking area and is trying hard to attract younger patrons and locals with live music at the weekends.

Empanadas Rua Wisard 489, Vila Madalena. The simple but effective selling point of this busy bar is that, in addition to beer, it serves *empanadas* (savoury pastries popular throughout South America but usually referred to as *empadas* in Brazil). And very good ones too – especially at 3am.

Favela Rua Prof Atilio Innocenti 419, Vila Olímpia. This rather tastelessly named but attractive patio bar is always buzzing with activity. It's one of the few sit-down bars in Vila Olímpia, which is better known for its hip late-night clubs.

Fidalga 33 Rua Fidalga 32, Vila Madalena Ⓦ www.fidalga33.com.br. In addition to offering live jazz and Brazilian music during the week, this cosy bar also has its own small bookstore.

Kia Ora Dr Eduardo de Souza Aranha 377, Itaim Bibi. With the same Kiwi owners as *All Black*, *Kia Ora* has raced into the lead as the number one favourite pub for both young expats and *paulistanos*. It's absolutely packed to the rafters some nights – don't be surprised if there's a long wait just to get in.

O'Malley's Alameda Itú 1529, Jardins Ⓦ www.gomalleys.com. An Irish-theme bar that bills itself (in English) as a "home away from home" and is mostly frequented by an over-40 expat crowd. There's a wide range of beer and pub grub, and it often features jazz and other live music.

Posto 6 Rua Aspicuelta 644, Vila Madalena. This lively corner bar, in one of the few areas of the city where bars cluster together, is a popular place for friends to meet up at the beginning (or even end) of a night.

Pirajá Av. Brigadeiro Faria Lima 64, Pinheiros. This attractive, mahogany bar serves tasty Spanish-style tapas and is well-known for its excellent *chopp*. Packed from 8pm onwards.

Rey Castro Rua Min. Jesuino Cardoso 181, Vila Conceicão. It's debatable what Castro would make of this Cuban-themed bar (with its R$45 entrance fee), but its mojitos, cigars and waiters dressed as guerrillas – not to mention the live salsa music – go down well with *paulistanos*.

Ritz Alameda Franca 1088, Cerqueira César. During the day this spot is a quiet restaurant serving hamburgers and sandwiches, but at night it's a lively bar popular with the gay crowd.

Live music

São Paulo has quite an imaginative **jazz** tradition, as well as plenty of **Brazilian music**, of course. Check the entertainment listings in local newspapers for touring artists or, if you're feeling slightly adventurous, visit a **gafieira** – a dance hall where working-class and Bohemian chic meet. Be warned that *gafieiras* tend to be out of the centre and in poor neighbourhoods. Very much community spots, they can seem rather alien and disconcerting places if you've only just arrived in Brazil; in no time, however, you'll be made to feel welcome. Cover charges are similar to those of bars, occasionally a little more.

A Lanterna Rua Fidalga 531, Vila Madalena. A fun place to drop by that's popular with the under-25s. The house band plays music from the 1960s to the 1980s. Open 6pm–2am; closed Mon.

All of Jazz Rua João Cachoeira 1366, Vila Madalena ⓦwww.allofjazz.com.br. Intimate, laid-back place with excellent live jazz.

Avenida Club Av. Pedroso de Morães, Pinheiros ⓣ11/3814-7383. The best-known place in São Paulo for formal dancing; it features everything from ballroom to samba, *forró* and merengue.

Bourbon Street Music Club Rua dos Chanés 127, Moema ⓦwww.bourbonstreet.com.br. This consistently good, though very expensive (R$35 upwards), jazz club hosts visiting international artists and frequent festivals.

Café Piu-Piu Rua 13 de Maio 134, Bela Vista ⓦwww.cafepiupiu.com.br. Although this bar has a nice neighbourhood feel to it, the wide range of Brazilian music – including live samba and MPB – draws a mixed crowd into the early hours of the morning. A lively venue for some very good jazz and *choro*.

Carioca Club Rua Cardeal Arcoverde 2899, Pinheiros. Live samba, *pagode* and MPB bands are interspersed with a house DJ playing a range of Brazilian disco beats. Attracts a good mix of the over-20s.

Centro Cultural de São Paulo Rua Vergueiro 1000 (by the Vergueiro *metrô* station) ⓦsampa3.prodam.sp.gov.br/ccsp. Regular performances feature Brazilian folk, popular and New Wave music.

Clube do Choro Rua João Moura, between Rua Artur Azevedo and Rua Teodoro Sampaio, Jardim America. On Sat and Sun evenings the street is closed off, a stage is erected and tables and chairs are put out so that you can sit and listen to some excellent music. There's a small cover charge and food and drink are available, too.

Grazie a Dio! Rua Girassol 67, Vila Madalena ⓦwww.grazieadio.com.br. This popular live music venue showcases mainly samba-rock bands. Serves good Mediterranean food as well.

Pedro Sertanejo Rua Catumbi 183, Brás. A *gafieira* that's always packed to the rafters with migrants from the Northeast dancing to *forró*. Sat & Sun only.

Samba Rua Fidalga 308, Vila Madalena. As the name suggests, this is the place to head for if you want to listen to Brazil's most famous musical export. It's open daily but the best time to go is for the *roda de samba* (Tues–Fri at 9pm), when the audience joins in with the musicians.

Clubs

The international **clubbing** scene has got wise to São Paulo's lively clubbing and musical tradition. Top DJs from around the globe regularly head the bill at the city's coolest hangouts, but there's plenty of homegrown talent around too, with São Paulo particularly noted for its **drum 'n' bass** DJs like DJ Marky and XRS, considered among the best in the world. However, the scene is fairly underground and you'll have to keep your eyes and ears open to hit the right spots (a good starting place is *Lov.E* on Thurs– see below). **Brazilian funk** has now come out of the *favela* and crossed over to the club scene; more traditional Brazilian music like samba and the at times execrable MPB is also often thrown into the mix. Look out also for Skolbeats, Latin America's biggest **dance festival**, which has been taking place in São Paulo each April/May since 2000. Note that clubs playing electronic music are considered very much the preserve of the young upper classes; they are therefore also places where English tends to be widely spoken. Cover charges again vary wildly; expect to pay normally between R$15 and R$40, sometimes with a drink or two thrown in, although if a big name is DJing at a top club you could be looking at anything up to R$100.

A Loca Rua Frei Caneca 916, Bixiga Ⓦwww.aloca.com.br. Though well-known on the gay scene, this determinedly "underground" club attracts a very diverse crowd. On Fri and Sat it hosts nosebleed techno nights, while Thurs and Sun see more eclectic disco and pop tunes.

Blen Blen Brasil Rua Inácio Pereira da Rocha 520, Vila Madalena Ⓦwww.blenblen.com.br. Besides being a nice place for a drink and some jazz, this fashionable yet not overly trendy club has several dance floors with a constantly changing mix of everything from techno to *forró* to MPB.

D-Edge Alameda Olga 70, Barra Funda Ⓦwww.d-edge.com.br. DJs spin everything from drum'n'bass and hip hop to punk and heavy metal at this very eclectic and cool underground club.

Ipsis Club Rua Padre Garcia Velho 63, Pinheiros. This large modern club has some great DJs and occasional live music, and it's one of the most popular gay and lesbian hangouts in the city. Thurs–Sat 11pm–5am; Sun 7pm–3am. Closed Mon–Wed.

Lotus Av. Naçôes Unidas 12551 Ⓦwww.lotussp.com.br. Located on the second floor of the *Hotel Gran Meliá*, this ultra-sophisticated lounge club is the sister club to *Lotus New York*. It plays house and hip hop Thurs–Sat and its cover charge is around R$60.

Lov.E Club Rua Pequetita 189, Vila Olímpia Ⓦwww.loveclub.com.br. *The* club of the moment, featuring funk and breakbeats on Wed; drum'n'bass on Thurs; techno on Fri and Sat; and R&B on Sun. Opens at midnight and serves breakfast at 5am.

Manga Rosa Guarapes 1754, Brooklin Novo Ⓦwww.clubmangarosa.com.br. A great, well-established club for trance and progressive house. Open Wed–Sat.

Matrix Rua Aspicuelta 459, Vila Madalena Ⓦwww.matrixbar.com.br. Popular with students, São Paulo's main "alternative" club plays indie, gothic, rock, etc. A bit watered down, but definitely a different vibe from most places.

Show Bar Lounge Rua Cardeal Arcoverde 1393, Pinheiros Ⓦwww.showbarlounge.com.br. Though lively and fun, *Show Bar* is more down-to-earth than most Sampa clubs. It's best known for its Fri night fire-breathing shows, but in general the music is a mix of MPB, samba, house and hip hop.

Ultralounge Rua da Consolação 3031, Jardim Paulista. Swanky gay club, with all-day chilled-out music on Sun.

Vermont Itaim Rua Pedroso Alvarenga 1192, Itaim Bibi Ⓦwww.vermontitaim.com.br. This classy gay-and-lesbian club plays samba, MPB and Brazilian funk, plus there's an on-site restaurant.

Cinema, theatre and classical music

In general, **films** arrive in São Paulo simultaneously with their release in North America and Europe and are subtitled rather than dubbed. Most cinemas, which charge around R$15, are on Avenida Paulista, but there are also several downtown on Avenida São Luís. All the shopping centres (see p.653) have cinema complexes and show the latest blockbusters. Keep a special eye out for what's on at CineSesc, Rua Augusta 2075; Espaço Unibanco de Cinema, Rua Augusta 1470 (both Cerqueira César); and the Centro Cultural de São Paulo, Rua Vergueiro 1000 (Ⓦwww.centrocultural.sp.gov.br), by the Vergueiro *metrô* station – all of which are devoted to Brazilian and foreign art-house films. Art-house films are also shown at the Belas-Artes at Rua da Consolação 2423, on the corner of Avenida Paulista.

Carnaval

Although São Paulo's **carnaval** is not as spectacular or glamorous as its *carioca* sister, neither is it low-key. São Paulo has its own enthusiastically supported samba schools, which spend all year preparing for the festival and collectively form the union of *paulistano* samba schools, UESP (Ⓣ11/3171-3713; Ⓦwww.uesp.com.br). As in Rio, the samba competition takes the form of a massive parade, held in the Oscar Niemeyer-designed *sambódromo*, a 530m-long stadium that can accommodate around 26,000 and is part of the huge Parque Anhembi leisure complex, near the Tietê bus terminal north of the city centre. Ticket prices are cheaper than their Rio counterparts, starting at around R$15 for a bench seat up in the gods – where you'll get a flavour of the event but won't see very much – and rising to around R$1000 for a seat in a VIP box. In general, the closer you are to the ground, the better the view and the more you pay. Many local travel agents sell tickets (see p.655); alternatively, try Ticketmaster (Ⓦwww.ticketmaster.com.br) or the city tourist office in Anhembi (Ⓣ11/6226-0400). In the weeks leading up to carnaval, you can sometimes attend rehearsals at the city's samba schools – one of the best to visit is Rosas de Ouro in Barra Funda (Ⓣ11/3931-4555).

As Brazil's theatrical centre, São Paulo boasts a busy season of classical and avant-garde productions; a visit to the **theatre** is worthwhile even without a knowledge of Portuguese. Seats are extremely cheap, starting at around R$10, and available via **ticket offices** that have details of all current productions: try the FNAC (see "Shopping", p.654), or Ticketmaster (Ⓣ11/6846-6000, Ⓦwww.ticketmaster.com.br). The Brasileiro de Comédia, Rua Major Diorgo 311, and the Teatro Sérgio Cardoso, Rua Rui Barbosa, both in Bixiga, have particularly good reputations for putting on high quality performances.

The traditional focal point for São Paulo's vibrant **opera** and **classical music** season is the Theatro Municipal (Ⓣ11/3334-0001; Ⓦportal.prefeitura.sp.gov.br/secretarias/cultura/theatromunicipal; see also p.632), on Praça Ramos de Azevado in the city centre, where, in the 1920s, Villa-Lobos himself performed. São Paulo has always been less important than Rio when it comes to the operatic and classical music world, but now Brazilian and foreign performers divide their time between the two cities. The beautifully renovated Estação Júlio Prestes in the *bairro* of Luz is home to the world-class Orquestra Sinfônica do Estado de São Paulo and has a new 1500-seat concert hall, the Sala São Paulo (Ⓣ11/3337-5414; Ⓦwww.salasaopaulo.art.br; see also p.630). Concerts usually take place Fridays at 9pm, Saturdays at 4.30pm and Sundays at 5pm; seats cost between R$25 and R$80.

Shopping

São Paulo's **shopping** possibilities are as varied as the city's restaurants. In the wealthy southwestern Jardins suburb, shops are far more impressive than those in just about any other South American city, and the quality way above par. For visitors, there are no obvious **souvenirs** of São Paulo, as such, but the city is a good place to find the things Brazil generally does well – from *cachaça* and samba records to bikinis and flip-flops. Even if you're not intent on a spree, the shopping centres and stores are worth a tour to experience the opulent surroundings, while at the other end of the spectrum the fine selection of **markets** provides exposure to both local colour and good food.

The main **shopping streets** in the centre of the city are near Praça da República, especially the roads running off Avenida Ipiranga: Rua Barão de Itapetinga, Rua 24 de Maio, and Rua do Arouche. South of the Mercado Municipal, Rua 25 de Março is another busy street, lined with hawkers selling everything from pirate CDs to carnaval costumes. Most of the stores downtown are of the cheap 'n' cheerful variety – they sell clothes, but you'll rarely find the latest fashions.

South of Avenida Paulista is where the money is – and where all the best stores are. You'll find lots of boutiques selling clothes and accessories from Brazilian, European and US designers, especially in the streets running parallel to and crossing Rua Augusta (most notably Rua Oscar Freire, Alameda Lorena, Rua Haddock Lobo, Rua Bela Cintra and Rua Dr Melo Alves). Although expensive, prices often compare well to Europe and the US. São Paulo's **shopping malls** – air-conditioned temples to hedonism – are hugely popular amongst the city's middle class as places to escape to and feel utterly insulated from their less fortunate fellow citizens. Each centre tries to outdo the other, with mirrored walls and ostentatious fountains – you won't feel closer to North America than this during your stay in Brazil. Shopping centres are usually open Monday–Saturday 10am–10pm, and Sunday after lunch to around 7pm.

Shopping malls

Daslu Av. Chedid Jafet 131, Vila Olímpia. Not a shopping centre as you know it, Daslu is created to look less like a mall and more like a country mansion, complete with chandeliers, marble staircases and chaise lounges. In trying to be exclusive, it manages to be the most tasteless and vulgar paean to obscene wealth you're ever likely to come across. Go for the experience, and certainly not to pick up a bargain. Open Mon & Wed–Sat 10am–8pm, Tues 10am–10pm.

Eldorado Av. Rebouças 3970, Pinheiros. Though rather downmarket, Eldorado is nevertheless vast and features one of the largest ranges of shops in the city. Its crèche and play area make it popular with families.

Ibirapuera Av. Ibirapuera 3103, Moema. This plush shopping centre in an upmarket residential area is strong on Brazilian fashion design.

Iguatemi Av. Brigadeiro Faria Lima 1191, Jardim Europa. The oldest of the city's many shopping centres – and constantly being remodelled and relaunched. Well located for the Jardins area, with a mix of mid-range and boutique clothing stores.

Patio Higienópolis Av. Higienópolis 615. The most exclusive of the city's shopping centres until Daslu came along, this glass and wrought-iron building features lots of top-end boutiques and an above-average food hall.

Shopping Light Corner of Rua Xavier de Toledo and the Viaduto do Chá, Centro. While quite small, this centre is the only place downtown to find the more stylish kind of clothing store, including those of local designers. You'll also find accessories, music and luxury goods.

Arts and crafts

Espaco Brasil Alameda Franca 1173, Jardim Paulista. Three floors showcase handicrafts, including much from Bahia, such as naïf ornaments and *berimbaus,* as well as items from elsewhere in Brazil that are, on the whole, reasonably priced.

Galeria Arte Brasileira Alameda Lorena 2163, Jardim Paulista. A mix of tacky souvenirs and well-chosen artisan products from throughout Brazil, especially the Amazon and the Northeast, are on sale here.

Galeria Brasiliana Rua Artur de Azevedo 520, Jardim America. Popular Brazilian paintings and other artwork – not cheap, but of excellent quality, with the pieces made by top craftspeople.

Books and music

Casa Amadeus Av. Ipiranga 1129, Centro. Near the Praça da República, this place has a good selection of Brazilian sheet music, percussion and stringed instruments.

Cultura Conjunto Nacional building, Av. Paulista 2073. One of the best bookshops in São Paulo, spread over three different rooms within the same building (one specializes in travel and language, one in art, and the other – the largest – in everything else). Mon–Sat 10am–7pm.

FNAC Centro Cultural Av. Pedroso de Moraes 858, Pinheiros. Good range of CDs and books, including a nice array of English-language titles and high-quality Brazilian art and other coffee-table books. The area around is clustered with independent music and book shops, too. There's a smaller branch at Av. Paulista 901. Daily 10am–10pm.

Galeria do Rock Rua 24 de Maio 62, Centro. The place to go to buy Brazilian music, both past and present, CD and vinyl. Located just behind the Theatro Municipal.

Markets

Antiguidades do MASP Museu de Arte de São Paulo (MASP), Av. Paulista 1578 (Sun 10am–5pm). Comprising mostly medals, old letters, ceramics, etc, this is a fun place to browse, but don't expect to find much worth buying.

Antiguidades e Artes Praça Benedito Calixto, Pinheiros (Sat 9am–7pm). Cheaper, livelier and with a larger collection of bric-a-brac than the similar market beneath MASP (see above), you may in fact pick up the odd bargain here. Some good restaurants are located around the square and food stalls are in the market itself.

Antiguidades e Artesanato do Bixiga Praça Dom Orione, Bela Vista (Sun 9am–6pm). This flea market has little worth purchasing, but lots of local atmosphere.

Casa Santa Luzia Alameda Lorena 1471, Jardim Paulista. An amazing gourmet supermarket, this is the perfect place to stock up if you're staying in an apartment hotel in the area. Otherwise, check out the luxury Brazilian food items that include preserves, wines and liquors. Open until late daily.

Feira Oriental Praça da Liberdade, Liberdade (Sun 10am–7pm). Japanese horticulturalists sell house plants here and some stalls sell good Japanese meals and snacks – usually prepared and sold by kimono-clad Afro-Brazilians.

Mercado de Flores Largo de Arouche, Centro. A dazzling daily display of flowers (8am–4pm).

Mercado Municipal Rua da Cantareira 306, Centro (Mon–Sat 4am–4pm; see also p.629). About the most fantastic array of fruit, vegetables, herbs, meat, fish and dairy produce that you're likely to find anywhere in Brazil. Excellent meals and snacks are also available.

Feira das Artes Praça da República and Av. Veira de Carvalho, Centro (Sun 9am–5pm). Amongst the tack in this vast tented street market, there are some interesting handicrafts, vintage records and semiprecious gems.

Listings

Airlines Aerolíneas Argentinas ⓣ11/3214-4233 & 6445-3806; Air Canada ⓣ11/3254-6630 & 6445-2462; Air France ⓣ11/3049-0900 & 6445-2887; Alitalia ⓣ11/2171-7600 & 6445-5053; American Airlines ⓣ11/4502-2100 & 6445-3234; British Airways ⓣ11/3145-9700 & 6445-2142; Continental ⓣ11/2122-7500; Delta ⓣ11/4003-2121 and 11/6445-3926; GOL ⓣ0300/789-2121 & ⓣ11/5090-9349; Iberia ⓣ11/3257-6711 & 6445-2726; Japan Airlines (JAL) ⓣ11/3175-2270 & 11/6445-2040; KLM ⓣ0800/880-1818; Lan Chile ⓣ11/2121-9000 & 6445-3757; Lloyd Aéreo Boliviano ⓣ11/3258-8111 & 6445-2425; Lufthansa ⓣ11/3048-5800 & 6445-2220; Pluna ⓣ11/3231-2822 & 6445-2130; South African Airways ⓣ11/3065-5115 & 6445-4151; Swissair ⓣ11/3016-4747 & 6445-2535; TAM ⓣ0300/123-100 & 11/4002-5700; TAP ⓣ0800/070-7787 & 6445-2400; United Airlines ⓣ11/3145-4200 & 11/6445-3039; Varig ⓣ11/5091-7000 & 6445-3117; VASP ⓣ0300/789-1010.

Airports Flight information: Congonhas ⓣ11/5090-9000 & 5090-9191; Guarulhos ⓣ11/6445-2945.

Banks and exchange Branches are scattered throughout the city, but are concentrated along Av. Paulista, Av. Brigadeiro Faria Lima and Rua 15 de Novembro. Between 10pm and 6am the access door to many ATMs is locked. The best exchange rates for cash can be found along Av. Sao Luis in the centre; at weekends, ask your hotel or try the souvenir shops and jewellers in Liberdade, the Japanese *bairro*.

Car rental Avis, Rua da Consolação 382, Centro ⓣ11/3259-6868; Hertz, Rua da Consolação 431, Centro ⓣ11/3258-9384; Localiza, Rua da Consolação 419, Centro ⓣ11/3231-3055.

Consulates Argentina, Av. Paulista 2313 Cerqueira César ⓣ11/3897-9522; Australia, Alameda Ministro Rocha Azevedo 456 Jardim Paulista ⓣ11/3085-6247; Bolivia, Rua Oscar Freire 379 13th floor, Jardim Paulista ⓣ11/3081-1688; Canada, Av. das Nações Unidas 12901, 16th floor, Itaim Bibi ⓣ11/5509-4321; Chile, Av. Paulista 1009, 10th floor, Cerqueira César ⓣ11/3284-2044; Colombia, Rua Tenente Negrão 140 Itaim Bibi ⓣ11/3078-0322; Ireland, Av. Paulista 2006, 5th floor, Cerqueira César ⓣ11/3287-6362; New Zealand, Al. Campinas 579, 15th floor, Cerqueira César ⓣ11/3148-0616; Paraguay, Rua Bandeira Paulista 600, 15th floor, Itaim Bibi ⓣ11/3167-0455; Peru, Rua Venezuela 36, Jardim Paulista ⓣ11/3063-5989; South Africa, Av. Paulista 1754, 12th floor, Cerqueira César ⓣ11/3285-0433; UK, Rua Ferreira de Araújo 741, Pinheros ⓣ11/3094-2700; Uruguay, Rua Estados Unidos 1284, Jardim Paulista ⓣ11/3085-5941; USA, Rua Henri Dunant 500, Campo Belo ⓣ11/5186-7000; Venezuela, Rua Veneza 878, Jardim Europa ⓣ11/3887-2318.
Cultural institutes São Paulo has a vast number of privately and publicly supported cultural centres and institutes, with exhibition spaces, cinemas and theatres often boasting first-rate programmes. Many of these are discussed in the Guide, but in addition the activities of the following overseas-based institutes may be of interest: Alliance Française, ⓣ0800/55-0000; Cultura Inglesa, Rua Ferreira de Araújo 741, Pinheiros ⓣ11/3222-3866; Goethe Institut, Rua Lisboa 974, Pinheiros ⓣ11/3088-4288; Instituto Italiano de Cultura, Rua Frei Caneca 1071, Bela Vista ⓣ11/3285-6933; União Cultural Brasil–Estados Unidos, Rua Cel. Oscar Porto 208, Paraíso ⓣ11/2148-2900.
Dress Business travellers in particular will notice a very different dress code in São Paulo than in Brazilian cities to the north. For men, suits and ties are pretty much the order of the day, though jackets tend to be carried rather than worn. Evenings are as informal as anywhere else in Brazil and even in top restaurants people lean firmly towards the casual. Nightlife, too, follows the Brazilian pattern of casual dress – even the trendiest clubs don't base entry on this.
Football There are two major First Division teams based in São Paulo: Corinthians, who usually play at either Parque São Jorge, Rua São Jorge 777 (*metrô* Bresser and bus #278A) or the Pacaembu, Praça Charles Miller, Consolacão, near the end of Av. Paulista; and São Paulo, who play at Morumbi Stadium (bus #775P from Av. Paulista). Matches are generally held on Wed and Sat – Corinthians' fixture list can be found at ⓦwww.corinthiansfutebol.com.br/pt-br/futebol/progsemanal.asp and São Paulo's is at ⓦwww.saopaulofc.net.
Health matters The private Albert Einstein Clinic, Av. Albert Einstein 627, Morumbi (ⓣ11/3747-1233) is considered to be the best hospital in Brazil. For dentistry, Dental Office Augusta, Rua Augusta 878, Cerqueira César (ⓣ11/256-3104), or Consultorio Dentario (open 24 hours), Av. 9 de Julho 3446, Jardins (ⓣ11/3062-0904), are both expensive but have good reputations.
Internet Almost all hotels offer Internet access to their guests and/or can advise on where to find the nearest Internet café. If all else fails, FNAC Centro Cultural (the city's best book and music store) at Av. Pedroso de Moraes 858, Pinheiros, has terminals and is open 10am–10pm.
Laundry It is expensive to have your hotel wash your clothes, and while there are very few self-service laundries in São Paulo, conveniently located spots are at Alameda Tietê 96, near the intersection with Rua Augusta, Cerqueira César, and at Alameda Joaquim Eugenio Lima 1696, Cerqueira César.
Newspapers and magazines Most newspaper kiosks downtown and in Jardins sell English-language newspapers: the *Financial Times*, *Miami Herald* and *International Herald Tribune* are the most widely available. Haddock Lobo Books and Magazines, Rua Haddock Lobo 1503, Cerqueira César (open until midnight), has a particularly good selection of European magazines and newspapers, as do Jardim Europa, corner of Av. Europa and Rua Groenlândia (open 24hr) and FNAC Centro Cultural at Av. Pedroso de Moraes 858, Pinheiros, open 10am–10pm.
Police Emergencies ⓣ190. DEATUR, a special police unit for tourists (ⓣ11/3214-0209), is located at Av. São Luís 91, one block from Praça da República.
Post office The main post office is downtown at Praça Correio, at the corner of Av. São João, and is open Mon–Fri 8am–10pm. Yellow-coloured postal kiosks are scattered throughout the city, including several along Av. Paulista.
Public holidays In addition to the normal Brazilian public holidays (see p.65), most things close in São Paulo on January 25 (Founding of the City) and on Ash Wednesday.
Telephones TELESP (the state telephone company) has an office on Rua Sete de Abril 295, just off Praça da República (Mon–Fri 8am–8pm, Sat & Sun 8am–6pm).
Travel agents Travel agents tend to cater towards locals trying to escape São Paulo, with city tours few and far between – though there are exceptions. Odyssey South America, Largo do Arouche 63, Centro (ⓣ11/3331-0278, ⓦwww.odysseysouthamerica.com.br) do interesting

walking tours of the city centre (R$20) and can make the arrangements if you want to see a football match (R$60, minimum 4 people), as well as offering longer trips to *fazendas* (ex-coffee plantations). Graffit (☎11/5549-0528, Ⓦwww.graffit.com.br) offers a variety of themed tours, such as art, nightlife or religion, in and around São Paulo, while Terra Nobre, Rua Tagipuru 235, Perdizes (☎11/3662-1505, Ⓦwww.terranobre.com.br) also has city tours, including an all-day one.

Visas To extend your visa, visit the Polícia Federal, Av. Prestes Maia 700, Luz (Mon–Fri 8am–3pm; ☎11/3315-2211).

Around São Paulo

What only a few years ago were clearly identifiable small towns or villages are today part of Greater São Paulo. Despite the traffic, however, escaping from the city centre is surprisingly easy, and there are even some points on the coast that can make for good excursions (see p.663).

Embu

Founded in 1554, **EMBU** was a mere village before São Paulo's explosive growth in the twentieth century. Located just 27km west of the city, Embu has now effectively merged with its massive neighbour, and yet, surprisingly, it has managed to retain its colonial feel. Quaint buildings predominate in the town's compact centre, which is traffic-free on weekends.

In the 1970s, Embu was a popular retreat for writers and artists from São Paulo, many of whom eventually set up home here. Today, the **handicraft market** (Sun 9am–6pm) in Largo dos Jesuitas, the main square, makes the town a favourite with *paulistano* day-trippers. The shops around the main square stock a similar selection to what's on offer in the market – pseudo-antiques, rustic furniture, ceramics, leather items, jewellery and homemade jams – but they are also open during the week (although many close on Mondays).

Largo dos Jesuitas holds an eighteenth-century church called **Igreja Matriz Nossa Senhora do Rosário**. While its exterior is typical colonial Baroque, its interior retains almost no original features. Attached to the church is the **Museu de Arte Sacra dos Jesuítas** (Tues–Sun 9am-5pm), which houses an interesting collection of eighteenth-century religious artefacts. Otherwise, you might as well sit down and eat at one of several **restaurants** on Largo 21 de Abril and along the adjoining streets: *Patacão* at Rua Joaquim Santana 90 is a particularly good place to sample traditional regional cooking – rare in the city of São Paulo itself – or try *Orixás* at Rua Nossa Senhora do Rosário 60 for excellent Afro-Brazilian food.

For general orientation, there's a well-organized **tourist information** office on Largo 21 de Abril (9am–6pm; ☎11/4704-6565). To get here from São Paulo, catch the "Embu Cultural" **bus** (every 30min) from outside the Tietê Rodoviária; the ride takes less than an hour.

Paranapiacaba

For most of its history, communications from São Paulo to the outside world were slow and difficult. In 1856 the British-owned São Paulo Railway Company was awarded the concession to operate a rail line between Santos and Jundaí, 70km north of São Paulo city, in what was then a developing coffee-growing region. The 139-kilometre line was completed in 1867, remaining under British control until 1947. Overcoming the near-vertical incline of the Serra do Mar that separates the interior of the state from the coast, the line was an engineering miracle and is slowly being restored today.

Paranapiacaba, 40km southeast of São Paulo and the last station befo rack railway plunges down the coastal escarpment, was the administrativ engineering centre for the rail line and at one time home to four thou workers, many of them British. Neatly laid out in the 1890s in a grid pattern, the village has remained largely unchanged over the years. All that remains of the original train station is the clock tower, said to be a replica of London's Big Ben, but the workers' cottages, locomotive sheds (which house old British-built carriages and steam engines) and funicular cable station are in an excellent state of preservation; some are even open to the public. On a hilltop overlooking the village you'll find the wooden Victorian-style Castelinho: once the residence of the chief engineer, today the building houses the **Centro Preservação da História de Paranapiacaba** (Tues–Sun 9am–4pm), which displays old maps and photographs of the rail line's early years.

You don't have to be a railway buff to appreciate Paranapiacaba, however. The village is set amidst one of the best preserved areas of Mata Atlântica in the

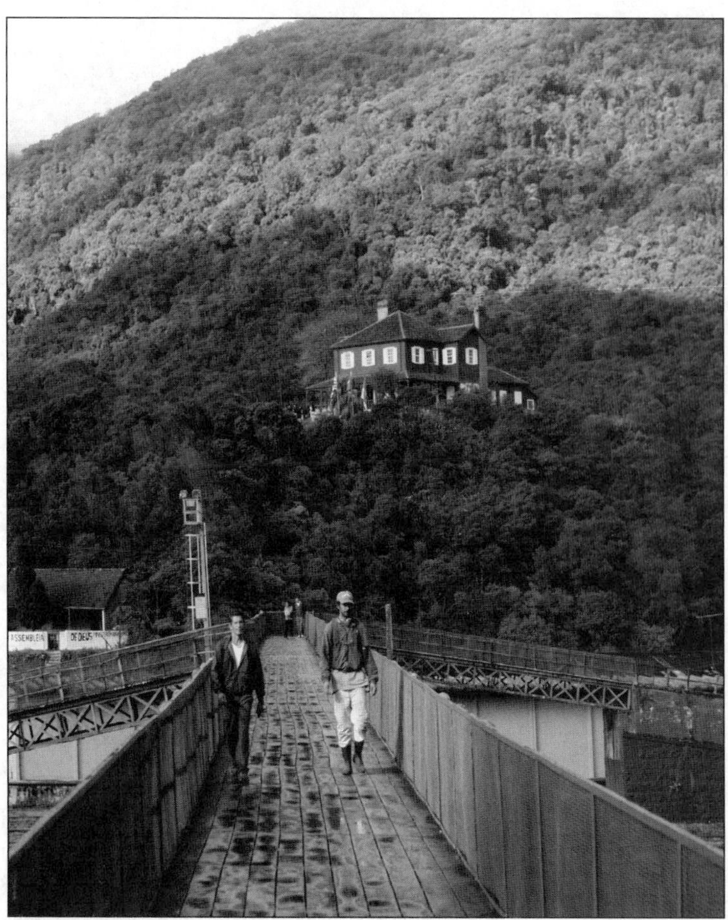

△ Paranapiacaba

country and most visitors use it as a starting place for fairly serious hikes into the thickly forested **Parque Estadual da Serra do Mar**, notable for its amazing orchids and bromeliads. Employing a guide is strongly advised as trails are unmarked, often very narrow and generally hard going, and poisonous snakes are common. There's an office of the association of licensed guides as you enter the settlement from the station; expect to pay around R$60 for a day and bring food, drink and sturdy footwear. The weather in this region is particularly unreliable but, as a general rule, if it's cloudy in São Paulo you can count on there being rain in Paranapiacaba.

Getting to Paranapiacaba is easy. Take a train from São Paulo's Luz station to Rio Grande da Serra (every 15min; 45min; R$2), where, if you're lucky, there'll be a connecting service continuing the two stops to Paranapiacaba. If there's no train, take a bus from outside the station (R$2), or a taxi (about R$15). Most visitors return to São Paulo the same day, but guides can point you towards villagers who charge around R$25 per person for simple **bed-and-breakfast** accommodation.

São Paulo state

Away from the city, the state's main attraction is its coastline. **Santos**, Brazil's leading port, retains many links with the past, and a number of the **beaches** stretching north and south from the city are stunning, particularly around **Ubatuba**. The towns and cities of the state's **interior** are not so great an attraction – the rolling countryside is largely devoted to vast orange groves and fields of soya and sugar. Fortunately, good-quality roads run through this region, including major routes to the Mato Grosso and Brasília.

The interior

Although there's not much to hold your interest inland from São Paulo, **Americana** and **Santa Bárbara d'Oeste** do have traces of Confederate history, while more recent Dutch immigrant arrivals have had a far greater impact on nearby **Holambra**. Further into the interior is coffee country, where it's possible to visit some old *fazenda* houses. To escape the summer heat, the resort of **Campos do Jordão**, northeast of the city, offers some attractive hill scenery and hiking possibilities.

Campinas

Around 100km northwest of São Paulo, **CAMPINAS** has been in relative decline compared to its neighbour since the nineteenth century, when it was by far the more important of the two cities. It started life as a sugar plantation centre, produced coffee from 1870 and later made its money as a hub for agricultural processing and, more recently, high-tech industry and education. An attractive city, with a reasonably compact centre, it doesn't offer many reasons for visiting, though it's interesting enough to take a tour around Largo do

Rosário, with its **Catedral** that was inaugurated in 1883. About 13km from the city centre you'll find **Unicamp**, the Universidade Estadual de São Paulo. Founded in 1969 on land belonging to Colonel Zeferino Vaz, during the worst years of military terror the university became – thanks to the protection afforded by Vaz – a refuge for left-wing teachers who would otherwise have been imprisoned or forced into exile. Unicamp rapidly acquired an international reputation and today is widely considered to be Brazil's best university, though you're only likely to visit on academic business as the campus is architecturally unremarkable. With a student population of 100,000, Campinas has a reasonably lively cultural life, centred on the **Centro de Convivência Cultural**, at Praça Imprensa Fluminense in the centre. In addition to a theatre and art galleries, the centre is home to the fine Orquestra Sinfonia.

If you have a car, one of the most interesting places to visit near Campinas is the **Fazenda Monte d'Este**, 12km from town, just off the SP-340 (the road leading to Holambra). Built during the nineteenth-century coffee boom, the beautiful *fazenda* house is open to the public and contains a small museum outlining the development of the area's former coffee-based economy. A tour of the place, which lasts 2hrs, costs R$45, or R$60 including an excellent lunch (bookings essential on Ⓣ19/3257-1236, minimum 5 people).

Practicalities

Campinas is a major transport hub, and there are **buses** from the city to most places in the state and many beyond. The highway to São Paulo itself is one of Brazil's best, and the hourly buses from Barra Funda take an hour and a quarter. The **rodoviária** in Campinas is at Rua Barão de Itapura, a twenty-minute walk from the city centre down Rua Saldanha Marinho.

With São Paulo so close you won't necessarily need to stay in Campinas, but there is plenty of centrally located **accommodation**: the *Royal Palm Tower* at Praça Carlos Gomes (Ⓣ19/3731-5900, Ⓦwww.royalpalmhoteis.com.br; ❼) is a very comfortable, newly built business hotel, while the *Ermitage* at Av. Francisco Gilcério 1444 (Ⓣ19/3234-7688, Ⓦwww.ermitage.com.br; ❺) and the *Opala Barão* at Rua Barão de Jaguara 1136 (Ⓣ19/3232-4999, Ⓦwww.hoteisopala.com.br; ❹) are cheaper but perfectly decent. There is no shortage of **places to eat** in Campinas either. The three branches of *Giovanetti* in Praça Carlos Gomes and Largo do Rosário are popular student hangouts selling drinks and excellent sandwiches. The *Steiner Bar do Alemão* at Av. Benjamim Constant 1969 offers reasonable German food and cold beer amidst a sometimes raucous atmosphere, while the *Red Angus Beef* at Rua Gen. Osório 2310 is the best *churrascaria*. Finally, excellent Japanese food is served at the *Restaurante Taka* in the *Hotel Vitória* at Av. José de Souza Campos 425.

Americana

Although there are perhaps as many as 100,000 Brazilians of Confederate descent (see box, p.660), there are few obvious signs of this in the two towns most associated with them. **AMERICANA**, an hour beyond Campinas, is a bustling city of about 180,000 people, but there are only 25 English-speaking families. On the main square, Praça Comendador Muller, you'll find the simple but adequate **hotel** *Cacique* (Ⓣ19/3461-0734; ❷), and for a bit more comfort there's the *Nacional* at Rua Washington Luís 399 (Ⓣ19/3461-8210, Ⓦwww.hotelnacionalamericana.com.br; ❹). For **food** there are plenty of *lanchonetes*, as well as a very good *churrascaria*, the *Cristal*, at Av. Fortunato Faraoni 613. But apart from the odd Confederate emblem, don't expect much to do with the American South.

Santa Bárbara d'Oeste

Some 13km west of Americana, **SANTA BÁRBARA D'OESTE**, much the smaller of the two cities, is home to about 30 families of Confederate origin, most of whom still speak English with more than a touch of Dixie in their voice. Near the main square, a short walk from the *rodoviária*, the excellent **Museu da Imigração** (Tues–Sat 10am–10pm, Sun 10am–10pm) has displays relating to the history of the Confederates in the area, and that of other nationalities, chiefly Italian.

About 10km from town, the **Cemitério do Campo** is a cool and shaded cemetery on a hill overlooking endless fields of sugar cane. It dates back to 1910 and all the tombstones, as well as the monument commemorating the Confederate immigrants, bear English inscriptions. There's a small chapel here, too, and a picnic area where, four times a year (the second Sunday of January, April, July and October) around 250 members of the Fraternidade Descendência Americana arrive from throughout Brazil to renew old ties. The cemetery is very isolated and can only be reached by car: a taxi will charge around R$50 to take you there, and will wait for you while you look around. However, as not all taxi drivers know exactly where the cemetery is, ask the museum attendant to order a taxi for you and give your driver precise directions.

As for **accommodation** in Santa Bárbara, there are a handful of modest hotels: try *Nosso* on Av. de Cillo 445 (19/3455-1106; ❷), or *Casablanca* on Rua General Osório 407 (19/3455-7419; ❷), both in the town centre.

Holambra

Some 40km northeast of Americana is the small town of **Holambra**, established in the nineteenth century by settlers from the Netherlands and retaining to this day a great deal of its Dutch character. Twentieth-century arrivals to Holambra (its name is a contraction of Holândia, América and Brasil) from Holland specialized in the cultivation of flowers, and today's residents like to boast that their prosperity is based on the work ethic that the immigrants brought with them. Despite the arrival of non-Dutch migrants attracted by the town's growing prosperity, the

Confederates in Sao Paulo

In the face of humiliation, military defeat and economic devastation, thousands of former **Confederates** from the American South resolved to "reconstruct" themselves in often distant parts of the world, forcing a wave of emigration without precedent in the history of the United States. Brazil rapidly established itself as one of the main destinations, offering cheap land, a climate suited to familiar crops, political and economic stability, religious freedom and – more sinisterly – the possibility of continued slave ownership. Just how many Confederates came is unclear: suggested numbers vary between 2000 and 20,000, and they settled all over Brazil, though it was in São Paulo that they had the greatest impact. While Iguape, on the state's southern stretch of coast, had a large Confederate population, the most concentrated area of settlement was the Santa Bárbara colony, in the area around present-day **Americana** and **Santa Bárbara d'Oeste**.

The region's climate and soil were ideally suited to the growing of **cotton** and the Confederates' expertise soon made Santa Bárbara one of Brazil's biggest producers of the crop. As demand for Brazilian cotton gradually declined, many of the immigrants switched to **sugar cane**, which remains the area's staple crop, though others, unable to adapt, moved into São Paulo city or returned to the United States.

Dutch origins are played up, and the urban centre can best be described as Dutch kitsch. Most people get around by bicycle, many of the buildings have Dutch-style facades, and gardens are neatly tended and filled with flowers, while the public telephone stands are in the ludicrous shape of a giant wooden clog. The highlight of the year here is **Expoflora**, the annual spring flower festival, which takes place on most weekends throughout September; the event attracts not only commercial buyers but also ordinary individuals drawn by the colourful displays, Dutch folk dancing, musical shows and food.

There are hourly bus services to Holambra from Campinas and several buses a day from São Paulo. One of the main reasons to visit is the **restaurants**. The excellent *Confeitaria Martin Holandesa*, Rua Doria Vasconcelos 15, serves up tea and cakes, while for meals that are more traditionally Dutch try *Casa Bela* at Rua Dória Vasconcelos 81 or *Old Dutch* (closed all Mon and Sun evening), 1.5km from the centre of town at *Fazenda Ribeirão*. Both places combine the sausages and potatoes familiar from German cooking with the more exotic paprika sauces and fruits that its ex-colony Indonesia contributed to Dutch cuisine. There are a handful of simple but good **hotels**, the best being *Parque Hotel das Flores* (T 19/3902-4006, W www.phf.com.br; 3) at Rua das Dálias 100 in Jardim Holanda; at no. 57 on the appropriately named Avenida das Tulipas is the more central *Hotel Shellter* (T 19/3820-1329, W www.shellterhotel.com.br; 3).

Fazenda Pinhal

During the late-nineteenth-century coffee boom, the interior of São Paulo state was synonymous with coffee, and the area around **São Carlos**, now a bustling university city 150km northwest of Americana, was particularly productive. Today the farms around the city are largely given over to sugar cane and oranges, and little evidence remains of the area's coffee-producing past. However, the **Fazenda Pinhal**, one of the oldest surviving and best-preserved rural estates in the state of São Paulo, is well worth a visit. The *casa grande*, the main house, was built in 1831 and, typical of the period, modelled after the large, comfortable Portuguese city dwellings of the eighteenth century; it still retains its original furnishings. There are numerous outbuildings and it's possible to stay the night in tasteful, country-style rooms on the estate (T 16/3375-7142; W www.fazendapinhal.com.br 8). The *fazenda* is an easy day-trip from either Americana or Campinas – and, at a stretch, São Paulo – but you'll need your own transport. Located off the SP-310 highway, at Km 227 take the exit for Riberão Bonito and then turn immediately onto the much smaller Estrada da Broa. After about 4km you'll see a sign marking the *fazenda*'s entrance. It's essential to call in advance; the entrance charge is R$15, plus R$40 for an excellent two-hour tour – a fixed fee for either a large group or an individual.

There's another *fazenda* 47km to the northwest at SP-310 km 274, just outside Araraquara, which has been developed into a superb luxury hotel, the *Fazenda Salto Grande* (W www.hotelfazendasaltogrande.com.br; 6 full board). Constructed to serve as a coffee plantation in the late nineteenth century, today the estate offers two swimming pools, horse riding, very comfortable guest rooms and excellent country cooking.

Campos do Jordão

When temperatures plunge to 15°C, São Paulo's citizens generally shiver and reach for their mothballed woollens. But to experience something approaching genuine cold weather they have to head into the highlands. East of the city, in the direction of Rio, the **Serra da Mantiqueira** boasts the lively winter resort of **CAMPOS DO JORDÃO**, 1628m above sea level. Founded by the British in the late nineteenth century, the town lies on the floor of a valley, littered with countless hotels and private houses resembling English country houses and Swiss chalets, and divided into three sections: **Abernéssia**, the older, commercial, less touristy centre and location of the *rodoviária*; and, a fifteen-minute bus ride away, **Juaguaribe** and **Capivari**, where most of the boutiques, restaurants and hotels are concentrated.

The novelty of donning sweaters and legwarmers draws the crowds in the southern winter, who spend their days filling in the hours before nightfall when they can light their fires. Day-time temperatures at this time of year are typically very pleasant, the sky is clear and the trails dry. In the summer the altitude offers relief from the searing heat of the coast – but avoid going after heavy rains, which can make walking unpleasant.

There's not much in the way of entertainment in the town itself, unless you have a thing for pastiche alpine, but in the surrounding area there are some good walks, with well signposted trails. The **Parque Estadual Campos do Jordão** is 12km outside the town and its vegetation, including graceful *araucária* (*Paraná* pine) trees, provides a striking counterpoint to the lower altitude Mata Atlântica. Its most accessible part, the Horto Florestal (daily 8am–7pm), can be reached by hourly buses from opposite the tourist office and has a number of short trails, the nicest being the *Cachoeira* trail, which leads to a waterfall. A tougher option is to climb the nearby 1950m **Pedra do Baú** peak, for which you must hire a guide (R$80) – call the guides' association at ⓣ12/3663-4122, or ask at the tourist office (see below). For a less strenuous view over Campos do Jordão and the surrounding Paraíba valley, take the ski lift, the *teleforico* (daily 10am–5pm; R$8), from near the small boating lake in the centre of Capivari: it whisks you up to the **Morro do Elefante**, where you can hire horses. Other **horse treks** in the area are possible as well, lasting between 30 minutes and four hours (R$37 per hour) and taking in hilltop viewpoints and pine forests; your hotel or the tourist office will be able to provide details. There are also a number of **tourist trains** (ⓣ12/3644-7400, ⓦwww.efcj.com.br; R$10–35) that traverse the local area. Most are short trips of about 40 minutes, such as the one to the tiny village of Pindamonhangaba, surrounded by cattle and rice plantations. Finally, **bikes** can be hired from Av. Frei Orestes Girardi 175 in Abernéssia – these are a popular choice, and useful for getting around the spread-out town, although you probably wouldn't want to take them on the rather bumpy trails.

Practicalities

A very helpful tourist information office (daily 8am–6pm), located by the town gate on the main road (SP-123) leading into Campos do Jordão, has maps of the resort and outlying areas and can advise you on room availability and other local interests. Despite there being dozens of **hotels**, finding a room – especially during the winter months of June and July – is difficult, and landing an affordable one can be impossible. During this high season, many places demand a minimum stay of three or even seven nights.

One of the more reasonably priced places is the small and pleasant *Pousada Recanto do Sossego*, Praça Benedito Albino Rodrigues (ⓣ12/3662-4224; ④), in Abernéssia, which offers simple rooms. Also in Abernéssia, the *Campos do Jordão Hostel,* at Rua Pereira Barreto 22 (ⓣ12/3662-2341, ⓦwww.camposdojordaohostel.com.br; ④), charges R$28 for a dorm bed and resembles a slightly tatty B&B more than it does a traditional youth hostel; however, the staff go out of their way to be of help and the price is one of the cheapest in town. Otherwise, you're best off walking along the tree-lined Avenida Macedo Soares (in Capivari), where many of the cheaper, but more comfortable, hotels are located, including the *Casa São José* at no. 827 (ⓣ12/3663-3353; ❺) and the *Nevada* at no. 27 (ⓣ12/3663-1611; ⓦwww.hotelnevada.com.br; ❼). One of Campos do Jordão's more appealing hotels, the *Recanto Duas Quedos*, Rua Manoel Ribeiro de Toledo 255, Vila Britânia (ⓣ12/262-2492; ❸), has basic rooms but is noteworthy for its location in a beautiful park with waterfalls nearby; the hotel also rents simple chalets that sleep six to eight people for around R$70 per chalet. For more luxury, the *Pousada Villa Capivary*, Av. Victor Godinho 131 (ⓣ12/3663-1736, ⓦwww.capivari.com.br; ❾ full board), is a very comfortable Swiss chalet-style hotel in Capivari.

Although many people eat in their hotels, there are still plenty of pseudo-Swiss fondue **restaurants**, mostly in Capivari, to keep you going: try *Só Queijo*, Av. Macedo Soares 642, or the *Matterhorn*, Rua Djalma Forjaz 10. The *Bia Kaffee*, Rua Professora Isola Orsi 33, is a very good and reasonably priced German restaurant serving full meals, teas and coffee. *Choc Araucaria* at Soares 135 is a must for chocoholics, though the goods may not be quite up to Swiss standards. The best food, though, is found just out of town at *Harry Pisek,* Av. Pedro Paulo 857, which specializes in sausages, and lots of them – Harry studied sausage making in Germany.

The **bar** *Baden Baden* at Djalma Forjaz 93 in Capivari is one of the town's most visited attractions, popular with the shades and cellphone set; expect a fight for a table at busy times. As well as crafting its own reasonable Baden Brew – you can visit the brewery at the town entrance (Mon–Fri 9am–noon & 1–5pm, Sat 10am–5pm, Sun 11am–2pm) – it also does very good schnitzels and potato dishes. After dark, people congregate around the terrifyingly kitsch "medieval" shopping arcade in Capivari, drinking hot mulled wine at the top of the arcade's tower or, for a really big evening out, watching the electronic thermometer.

The coast

Despite its proximity to the city, most of the 400km of São Paulo's **coast** have, until recently, been overlooked by sun and beach fiends in favour of more glamorous Rio. But don't listen to *paulistanos* who sniff that the state's beaches aren't up to par; by European or North American standards, they're still pretty fabulous. Nevertheless, foreign visitors are relatively rare, and most services are aimed at Brazilians. To the northeast, following the coast up to the border with Rio state, the area is developing all too rapidly, but this part of the coast still offers great contrasts, ranging from long, wide stretches of sand at the edge of a coastal plain to idyllic-looking coves beneath a mountainous backdrop. Having the use of a car is an advantage for exploring the more isolated, less spoilt, beaches (see p.654 for car rental info); however, if it's a lively beach resort you're after, public transport can take you there from São Paulo in less than half a day. Southwest of Santos, tourism has still to take hold, in part because the roads aren't as good, but also because the beaches simply aren't as beautiful.

Santos

SANTOS, one of Portugal's first New World settlements, was founded in 1535, a few kilometres east of São Vicente. Today it is home to Latin America's largest and arguably most important port, through which a large proportion of the world's coffee, sugar and oranges pass. The city stands partly on São Vicente island, its docking facilities and old town facing landwards, with ships approaching by a narrow, but deep, channel. In a dilapidated kind of way, the compact centre retains a certain charm that has not yet been extinguished by the development of the enormous port complex. It's massively popular with local tourists, and, although you may want to skip the rather murky beaches, there is a good deal of historical and maritime interest around the city.

Arriving in Santos and getting oriented couldn't be easier. The **rodoviária**, at Praça dos Andradas, is within walking distance of the Centro, on the north side of the island: from it, walk across the square to Rua XV de Novembro, one of the main commercial streets. One block on, turn left at **Rua do Comércio**, along which you'll find the ruins of some of Santos' most distinguished buildings. Although only the facades remain of some of the nineteenth-century former **merchants' houses** that line the street, they are gradually being restored, the elaborate tiling and wrought-iron balconies offering a hint of the old town's lost grandeur. At the end of Rua do Comércio you'll find the **train station**, built between 1860 and 1867, and, while the city's claim that the station is an exact replica of London's Victoria is a bit difficult to swallow, it is true that the building wouldn't look too out of place in a British town. Next to the station in Largo Marquês de Monte Alegre, the **Igreja de Santo Antônio do Valongo** (Tues-Sat 8am-6pm, Sun 8am-7pm) was built in 1641 in colonial Baroque style, but with its interior greatly altered over the following centuries; few of its original features remain. Back on Rua XV de Novembro, at no. 95, is the former **Bolsa de Café** (Tues–Sat 9am–5pm, Sun 10am–5pm), where coffee prices were fixed and the quality of the beans assessed; the building retains its original fixtures but is now an exhibition centre charting the history of the coffee trade. At the end of the street is another Baroque building, the **Convento do Carmo** (Mon–Fri 7am–7pm, Sat 4–6pm, Sun 10–12am & 5–7pm), which is, again, seventeenth century in facade only. Running right through the historical centre, the new **tourist tram** (Tues–Sun, 11am–5pm; R$3) is a slightly twee but popular way to see the sights. The restored tram (*bonde*), originally brought over from Scotland in 1910, departs regularly from Praça Mauá by Rua do Comércio and takes 15 minutes to do the 1.7-kilometre trip. To get a great view over the whole of Santos, head three blocks south to Praça Correia de Mello 33, where a funicular railway (daily 8am–8pm; R$10) pulls you 150m up **Monte Serrat**; alternatively, you can save cash and climb the steps.

The city is also home to **Santos Football Club**, best known as the club for whom the great Pelé played for most of his professional life (from 1956 to 1974). The stadium, the Vila Belmiro at Rua Princesa Isabel 77, is open to the public when there's no game on (Mon 1–7pm, Tues–Sun 9am–7pm; ⓣ13/3225-7989, ⓦwww.santosfc.com.br). In addition to honoring Pelé at the club's small museum, you can take an hour-long guided tour and snoop around the players' dressing rooms (R$7).

Santos' **beaches** are across town from Centro on the south side of the island, twenty minutes by bus from Praça Mauá or R$12 by taxi. The beaches are huge, stretching around the Atlantic-facing Baía de Santos, and popular in summer, but they're also fairly scruffy. Alongside the beach, facing the Baía de Santos, **Gonzaga**, a *bairro* of apartment buildings, restaurants and bars, is the main tourist area. To the east, the huge **port area** is a fascinating place, with its giant elevators pouring grain into ships, and warehouses piled to the roof with sugar, but its sheer size means that you really need transport to get around it.

Practicalities

Coming from São Paulo, be sure to remember that buses to Santos leave from the Jabaquara Rodoviária and not from Tietê. In Santos, there are **tourist offices** (8am–8pm) at the *rodoviária* in Centro, and at the corner of Avenida Ana

Costa and the seafront Avenida Presidente Wilson in Gonzaga, in a converted tram car. From outside the latter, the local tourist board runs an excellent **city tour** (R$15), departing once an hour between 10am and 6pm and lasting about an hour and a half. It takes in all of Santos' main sights, including the port area, and at weekends it stops at the various attractions, giving you the option of getting off and on again as many times as you like.

Hotels in Santos are concentrated in Gonzaga. For such a tatty town, they're surprisingly dear; one of the cheapest places is the basic *Pousada do Marquês*, Av. Floriano Peixoto 202 (Ⓣ13/3237-1951; ❸), which provides an old but functioning bed and shower, while *Mendes Panorama* at Rua Euclides da Cunha 15 (Ⓣ13/3289-2627, Ⓦwww.grupomendes.com.br; ❺) is the best-value mid-range place around, although it often fills with conference attendees and tour groups. Alternatively, try the once grand, but now slightly rundown, *Avenida Palace* (Ⓣ13/3289-3555, Ⓦwww.avenidapalace.com.br; ❺) at Av. Presidente Wilson 10. The *Ritz*, set back at Av. Marechal Deodoro 24 (Ⓣ13/3284-1171; ❺) is hardly, well, the Ritz, being rather worn at the edges, but it's friendly and large, and is worth trying if you've drawn a blank elsewhere. For a bit more comfort try the *Parque Balneário* (Ⓣ13/3289-5700, Ⓦwww.parquebalneario.com.br; ❼) at Av. Ana Costa 555, a luxurious high-rise hotel with a pool. For dining, there are some reasonable seafood **restaurants** in Centro: try *Café Paulista* at Praça Rui Barbosa 8, or *Rocky* at Praça dos Andradas 5. Otherwise most eateries are in Gonzaga: for reliable Japanese food, there's *Tika* at Rua Bahia 93 (Fri & Sat evening & Sun lunch only), or for good Portuguese food check out *Último Gole* at Rua Carlos Afonseca 214.

Guarujá, Boiçucanga and Maresias

The very commercialized and usually crowded **GUARUJÁ** is São Paulo's most popular beach resort. Getting there is easy: there are half-hourly buses from the city's Jabaquara Rodoviária that take little more than an hour to travel the 85km to the resort. From Santos, take a bus from Gonzaga east along the beach avenue to Ponta da Praia, from where a ferry makes the ten-minute crossing of the Santos channel, and then it's a fifteen-minute bus ride on to Guarujá itself.

The resort features a set of large apartment buildings alongside lengthy, rather monotonous beaches, as well as the slightly dubious attraction of South America's biggest **aquarium**, Acqua Mundo, at Av. Miguel Stéfano 2001, Praia da Enseada (Tues–Fri & Sun 10am–6pm, Sat 10am-10pm; Ⓣ13/3351-8867; R$20), with over 30 inadequately sized tanks of unfortunate sharks, turtles, penguins and fish from around the world. In the summer, finding space on the main beach, **Pitangueiras**, can be difficult, and the beaches within walking distance, or a short bus ride away, to the northeast are little better. In fact, without a car and considerable local knowledge, Guarujá is best avoided; in any case, finding a reasonably priced **hotel** in the summer can be almost impossible. Your best bet around Praia das Pitangueiras is the small and friendly *Hotel Rio Guarujá* at Rua Rio de Janeiro 131 (Ⓣ13/3355-9281, Ⓦwww.hotelrio.com.br; ❺), just a block from the sea, or at the adjoining Praia Guarujá, the *Guarujá Praia*, Praça Brigadeiro Franco Faria Lima 137 (Ⓣ13/3386-1901; ❹). For a local map, detailed instructions on outlying beaches and hotel information, contact the helpful **tourist office** at Rua Quintino Bocaiúva 248 (Mon–Fri 9am–6pm; Ⓣ13/3387-7199).

From Guarujá's *rodoviária*, buses run east as far as Ubatuba (see p.671), stopping off at points along the way. For much of the first 90km the road passes inland, but approaching **BOIÇUCANGA** it again skirts the coastline, and the landscape grows increasingly mountainous as the forested Serra do Mar sweeps down towards the sea. Set on a large bay fringed by a fine beach, the once quiet resort has fallen victim to the worst excesses of uncontrolled development, and you'll find hastily built holiday homes, *pousadas* and shopping galleries occupying every square metre of land. If you need to stay overnight you won't have any problem finding a room but, as elsewhere along the coast, summer availability is limited. Two *pousadas* worth trying are the *Casarão* at Rua Apiacás 44 (Ⓣ12/3865-1690; ④) and the *Marambaia* at Rua Itaberaba 534 (Ⓣ12/3865-2372, Ⓦwww.pousadamarambaia.com.br; ⑤); both are small and simple but have pools. West of the resort, there are more accommodation options on quieter beaches: one of the best of the state's **hostels** is the *Camburi Hostel* at Rua Tijucas 2300 (Ⓣ12/3865-4160, Ⓦwww.ajcamburi.com.br; ④) on Camburi beach, 5km to the west of Boiçucanga and popular with surfers. With dorm beds costing at least R$30, it's more expensive than most hostels, but the forest setting, hammocks, and pool make it worthwhile. Further up the scale, the lovely *Pousada da Foca* (Ⓣ12/3863-6880, Ⓦwww.pousadadafoca.com.br; ⑦) offers comfortable rooms near the best beach, **Barra do Sahy**, a further 6km west. Otherwise, the **tourist office** at Praça Pôr do Sol (daily 10am–8pm) should be able to point you towards *pousadas* with available rooms. Another good beach near Boiçucanga is Praia Brava – reachable only by walking along a two-kilometre trail, it's fairly undeveloped but often crowded nonetheless.

From Boiçucanga the road rises steeply inland through the Serra do Mar, from which you'll catch the occasional glimpse of the distant ocean through the trees. The road eventually descends into the neighbouring resort of **MARESIAS**, a draw for surfers and clubbers; if you want to beach it until sunset and then party until dawn, this is where to head. Accommodation here is plentiful and expensive: the *Pousada Brig a Barlavento*, set just fifty metres from the beach at Av. Francisco Loup 1158 (Ⓣ12/3865-6527, Ⓦwww.brig.com.br; ⑥), is a very attractive option with a nicely landscaped garden, a good pool and rooms of varying standards; 2km from the beach, the *Pousada Pé da Mata*, at Rua Nova Iguaçu 1992 (Ⓣ12/3865-5019, Ⓦwww.pedamata.com; ⑤), also has a nice pool as well as a pretty forest setting. Alternatively, try the youth hostel, the *Pousada San Sebastian,* at Rua Sebastião Romão César 406 (Ⓣ12/3865-6612, Ⓦwww.maresiashostel.com.br; R$26 per person for a dorm bed, or R$65 for a double), though at summer weekends it's often full. The reason many partygoers flock to Maresias is the fabled *Sirena* **nightclub** at Rua Sebastião Romão César 418 (Ⓣ12/3865-6681, Ⓦwww.sirena.com.br), which attracts enthusiastic clubbers from all over the state and beyond; as well as the best Brazilian DJs, it has played host to top international names like Paul Oakenfold and Fatboy Slim. Other places, such as *Lao Bar,* opposite *Sirena,* have popped up around it to catch the overflow.

Some 10km or so further on from Maresias you'll find the much quieter and less developed **Praia Toque-Toque Pequeno** and **Praia Toque-Toque Grande**, which are probably the prettiest beaches in the area and good for snorkelling. They are armed with nothing more than a few shops and restaurants, and make a good day trip from Maresias, although unless you're prepared to walk it you'll need your own transport.

São Sebastião

The bustling little town of **SÃO SEBASTIÃO** is a further 27km northeast, on the mainland, directly opposite the island of Ilhabela (see p.668). Founded in the first years of the seventeenth century, São Sebastião relied on its sugar cane and coffee farms until the eighteenth century, when the town entered a period of decline. Emerging from this stagnation only in the last few decades with the growth of the fishing industry and the development of a large oil refinery, São Sebastião has retained many of its colonial and nineteenth-century buildings.

Unlike in similar towns, these have not been taken over by wealthy city-dwellers, since São Sebastião's beaches, in both directions from the centre, are poor and completely cut off from the open sea by the much more beautiful Ilhabela.

The narrow roads that make up the historic centre allow for pleasant wanderings among the pastel-coloured Portuguese colonial-style facades. Praça Major João Fernandes is the heart of São Sebastião and home to a slew of one-storey snack bars and stores, all dominated by the quietly impressive **Igreja Matriz**, built in 1636 and almost as old as the town (although its interior is twentieth-century plaster). The simple white construction, topped with a red-roofed bell tower, is typical of Franciscan-built churches of the period. On summer evenings, the waterfront becomes the site of a fair selling all manner of clothes and bric-a-brac, in addition to hosting free outdoor concerts. The waterfront also faces São Sebastião's visitor centre complex, which contains fascinating displays of old photographs and scale models that chart the town's development, as well as handicrafts by Tupí-Guaraní people who live in outlying parts of the *município*. The centre also houses the **tourist office** (daily 10am–8pm; ⓣ12/3892-1808) where you can find information on both the town and the surrounding villages and countryside (although not Ilhabela, which is in a separate *município*); stop by to pick up free maps and get specifics on trails and hotel room availability.

Accommodation

Due to its proximity to Ilhabela, São Sebastião has a fair selection of simple **hotels** and **pousadas**, considerably cheaper than those on the island and, in some cases, just as nice. Transport connections to Ilhabela are good – see p.668 – though be prepared for some early starts if you're going to be touring the island.

Hotel Porto Grande Av. Guarda Mór Lobo Viana 1440 ⓣ12/3892-1101, ⓦwww.pelotastur.com.br/porto1. This pretty, whitewashed, colonial-style hotel with a pool is just a ten-minute walk from town and set in park-like gardens that stretch down to the beach. Rooms are spacious and well equipped, but there's ample road noise from the adjacent coastal highway. ❸

Hotel Roma Praça Major João Fernandes ⓣ12/3892-1441. A good range of rooms (sleeping 1 to 4 people either with or without a private bathroom) is offered at this rather rundown but visually imposing and welcoming 100-year-old hotel set on the city's main square. The rooms are surrounded by an attractive garden. ❸

Pousada da Ana Doce Rua Expedecionário Brasileiro 196 ⓣ12/3892-1615, ⓦwww.pousadaanadoce.com.br. *Ana Doce* is the prettiest, and one of the friendliest, places to stay in the town's historic centre. The small but perfectly adequate rooms, each with a thatched verandah, are set around a delightful courtyard garden. ❺

Pousada da Sesmaria Rua São Gonçalo 190 ⓣ12/3892-2347, ⓦwww.pousadadasesmaria.com.br). Rooms are small but comfortable at this charming, centrally located *pousada* with colonial-style furnishings. An excellent breakfast is included . ❺

Santa Rosa Tres Bandeirantes 167, no phone. Though a bit dingy and basic, the *Santa Rosa* is by far the cheapest place to stay. Bathrooms are shared. ❷

Eating and drinking

Most of the town's dining options focus on snacks and ice cream, but along the waterfront Rua da Praia (more formally called Av. Dr Altino Arantes) there's a small cluster of places doing more substantial meals. Unsurprisingly, they primarily serve seafood; the most popular of these – and deservedly so – is *Canoa*, at no. 234, which offers particularly good dishes featuring *pejerrey*, a white fish, and shrimp. *Bombordo* at no. 68 also prepares seafood, and sometimes puts on live bands in the evenings – the cocktails are truly dreadful, though, so stick to the beers. To the north of Rua da Praia, on Praça Antonio Cândido, *Casa Grande*, housed in an attractive lemon-coloured colonial-style building, affords the chance to eat Italian-style pizza while enjoying a view over the harbour.

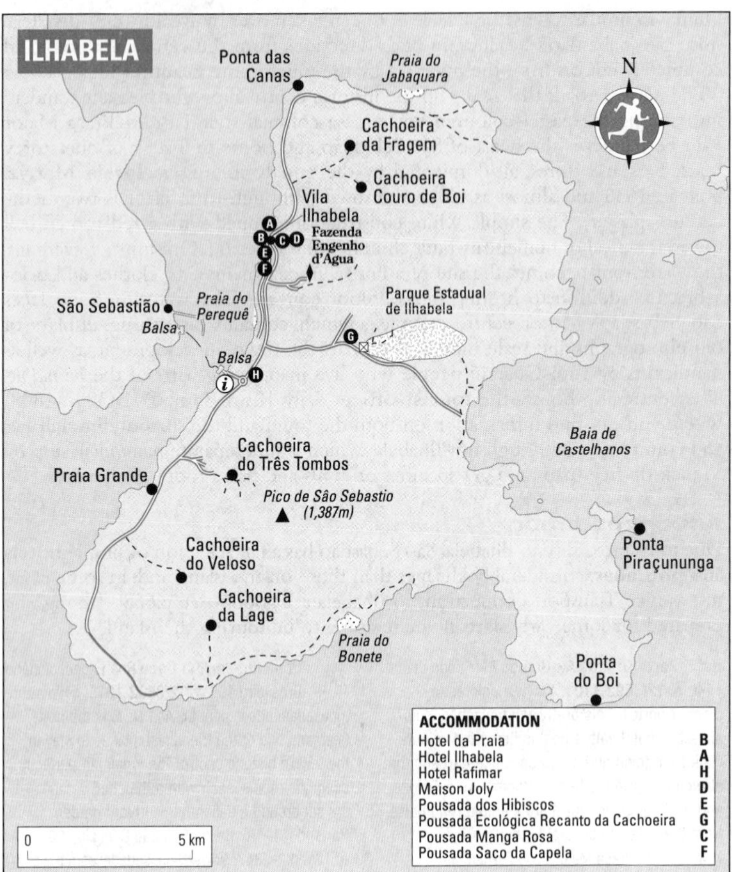

Ilhabela

Without a shadow of a doubt, **Ilhabela** is one of the most beautiful spots on the coast between Santos and Rio, though it's developing fast and can get rather crowded in late December and early January. Of volcanic origin, the island's startling mountainous scenery rises to 1370m and is covered in dense, tropical foliage. With much of the island protected within the boundaries of the **Parque Estadual de Ilhabela**, the dozens of waterfalls, beautiful beaches and azure seas have contributed to the island's popularity; old or new, most of the buildings are in simple Portuguese colonial styles, as far removed from brash Guarujá as you can get. The island is a haunt of São Paulo's rich who maintain large and discreetly located homes on the coast, many with mooring facilities for luxury yachts or with helicopter landing pads.

Ferries (24 hr; pedestrians free, cars R$16) depart from São Sebastião's waterfront every half hour and the crossing to the island's ferry terminal at Perequê takes about twenty minutes. If you're driving, be prepared for a long queue for the ferry during the summer unless you book in advance (☎0800-704-5510).

On the island, buses (R$1.70) depart regularly from outside the Perequê terminal to **Vila Ilhabela**.

There are also **launches** (R$4) that cross from São Sebastião direct to Vila Ilhabela and back again about once an hour during the day – ask at the tourist office (see p.667) for the current timetable.

Vila Ilhabela

Almost all of the island's 20,000 inhabitants live along the sheltered western shore, with the small village of **VILA ILHABELA** (often referred to as "Centro") serving as the main population centre. After about twenty minutes, drive from the ferry landing, look out on the right-hand side of the road for the grand eighteenth-century main house of the **Fazenda Engenho d'Agua**, which is located a few kilometres outside the village. This was one of the largest sugar plantations on the island, famous for its high-quality *cachaça*. Today there's virtually no agricultural production on Ilhabela, its economy completely geared to tourism. On the waterfront at Rua do Meio, a **tourist office** (daily 9am–10pm; ⓣ12/3896-2440, ⓦwww.ilhabela.sp.gov.br) offers a map of the island and can advise on transport and tours; a smaller office with similar hours can also be found at the ferry port.

Vila Ilhabela, which has a few pretty colonial buildings, is dominated by the **Igreja Matriz**, a little church completed in 1806. Situated on a hill, the white and blue wedding-cake building has a Spanish marble floor and provides both a cool retreat from the sun and a good view over the area. Additionally, there are banks, restaurants and stores selling overpriced beach gear. In the evenings, people congregate on the pier, catching swordfish with remarkable ease, or take a leisurely drink at one of the town's few, laidback bars.

The rest of the island

Getting around the island can be a problem, as the only bus route is along Ilhabela's western shore north as far as the lighthouse at Ponta das Canas and south to Porto do Frade – the limits in both directions of good-quality roads. Following the coastal road south along this mainland-facing shore from Vila Ilhabela, the beaches are small, but pleasant enough, the calm waters are popular with windsurfers and bars and restaurants dot the roadside as far as **Perequê**, the island's second biggest town, about halfway south along the island and the location of the ferry port.

There are more attractive beaches on the further-flung coasts of the island, most of which can be reached by schooner and/or jeep. Pretty beaches in coves along the northern coast, such as the **Praia do Jabaquara**, can only be reached by boat or by clambering down steep trails hidden from view from the road. It's along this stretch of coast that some of the island's most exclusive villas are located, and their owners have an interest in making sure the road remains in bad condition and that the beaches are difficult to reach. The road is also poor along the southern shore, where some of the best beaches are located: after the road ends at Borifos, it's a two-hour walk along an inland trail to the tiny fishing hamlet at **Praia do Bonete**, just beyond which lie a couple of other fine beaches. Along the way you'll pass an impressive waterfall, the **Cachoeira do Late**, beneath which a natural pool has formed.

The entire eastern half of the island falls within the **Parque Estadual da Ilhabela** and, as such, is protected from commercial tourist development. The east coast beaches of the **Baia de Castelhanos**, 25km across the island via a steep mountain road often washed out by heavy rain, have the most surf and are considered by many to be the island's most beautiful. As Castelhanos is in the park, you'll need both a permit and a jeep to visit; the easiest way round this is

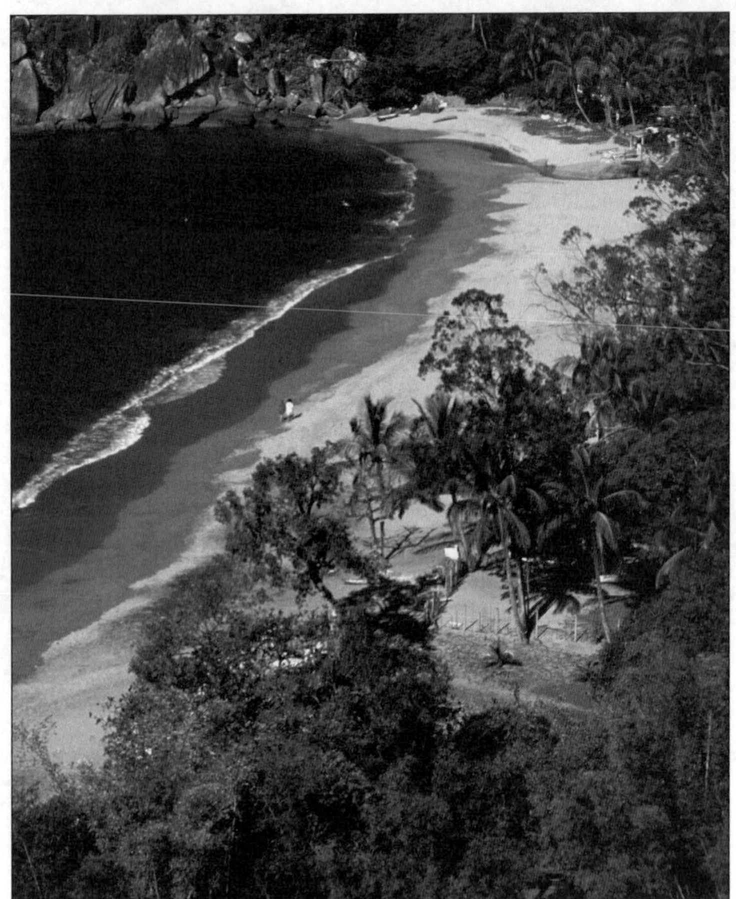

△ Ilhabela

to book an all-day tour, costing around R$50 per person. Travel agencies that run various boat and jeep combos exploring the island include Portal Ilhabela at Rua do Meio 38, Vila Ilhabela (Ⓣ12/3896-3086, Ⓦwww.portalilhabela.com.br), and Lokal Adventure, Av. Princesa Isabel 171, Perequê (Ⓣ12/3896-5777, Ⓦwww.lokaladventure.com.br). If you want to move around under your own steam, Lokal also rents out cars, jeeps, scooters, bicycles, horses and canoes.

Accommodation

Throughout the year Ilhabela is the most expensive spot on São Paulo's coast, and in the summer it can be difficult to find a place to stay (reservations are essential). The island has several **campsites**, including *Canto Grande* at Praia Grande (Ⓣ12/3894-9423, Ⓦwww.cantogrande.com.br) and *Pedras do Sino,* 4km north of Vila Ilhabela (Ⓣ12/3896-1266); in general, camping on beaches is strictly forbidden, but no one cares if you set up your tent on the virtually uninhabited eastern side of the island.

Hotel da Praia Av. Pedro Paulo de Moraes 578 ⓣ12/3896-1218, ⓦwww.hoteldapraiadeilhabela.com.br. Comfortable rooms sleep 2 to 4 people and a large, pleasant garden leads down to the beach on the southern outskirts of Vila Ilhabela village. ❺

Hotel Ilhabela Av. Pedro Paulo de Moraes 151 ⓣ12/3896-1083, ⓦwww.hotelilhabela.com.br. Somewhat devoid of character, but rooms are large and there's a good-sized pool. ❼

Hotel Rafimar Av. Faria Lima 71 ⓣ12/3896-1539, ⓦwww.rafimar.com.br. While it's not in the prettiest part of the island, this simple hotel is the area's cheapest and it has a pool. The nearby ferry landing at Perequê is convenient for reaching the mainland. ❺

Maison Joly Rua Antônio Lisboa Alves 278 ⓣ12/3896-1201, ⓦwww.maisonjoly.com.br. Located on a hill above the village, this is the place to go for a serious splurge. All of the hotel's luxurious but tastefully furnished rooms have private terraces with spectacular ocean views, plus it has a pool and the island's best restaurant, which is strong on seafood dishes in a mix of Brazilian and French styles. ❾

Pousada dos Hibiscos Av. Pedro Paulo de Moraes 720 ⓣ12/3896-1375, ⓦwww.pousadadoshibiscos.com.br. A reception and courtyard brimming with flowers make this one of the prettiest *pousadas* to stay in; it also has a pool. The rooms feature cool white linen, tiled floors, and wooden furniture – the hotel's website allows you a bird's-eye view of them all in advance. ❺

Pousada Ecológica Recanto da Cachoeira Rua Benedito Garcêz 180 ⓣ12/3896-3098, ⓦwww.ecoilha.com.br. This attractive inland option is on the edge of the Parque Estadual, just off the road leading to the Baia de Castelhanos. The rooms are basic but comfortable and the property is entirely surrounded by tropical forest – making a good supply of insect repellent essential. ❺

Pousada Manga Rosa Rua Francisco Gomes da Silva Prado 34 ⓣ12/3896-1118, ⓦwww.ilhabela.com.br/pousadamangarosa. Three blocks from the centre of Vila Ilhabela, this new *pousada* is conveniently located and offers simple, clean rooms connected by a series of wooden walkways. ❺

Pousada Saco da Capela Rua Itapema 167 ⓣ12/3896-8020, ⓦwww.pousadasacodacapela.com.br. This recently renovated *pousada* at Saco da Capela, just south of Vila Ilhabela, has beautiful rooms with verandahs, lush tropical gardens and a pool. ❼

Eating and drinking

Eating, like everything else on Ilhabela, is quite expensive. Apart from the excellent and rather elegant seafood restaurant in the *Maison Joly* (see above), the other notable restaurant on the island is *Viana*, just north of the village at Av. Leonardo Reale 1560 (closed Mon–Thurs Apr–June & Aug–Nov), which also specializes in seafood. Cheaper options line the beach road between Vila Ilhabela and Perequê, such as the *comida pro kilo* joint *Resto do Cura* at Av. Princesa Isabel 337, or, on a sideroad, *Paulinho* at Rua Pedro de Freitas 201. Live jazz and blues can be heard during the summer at *Jamba!*, Av. Pedro Paula de Moraes 1006.

Ubatuba and beyond

From São Sebastião, the highway continues along the coast, passing close to isolated and deserted coves of dazzling beauty, with occasional detours through forested areas inland. Buses stop in Caraguatatuba, an extremely ugly sprawling town with a long, gently curving beach alongside the main road, but you're better off carrying on towards **UBATUBA**. The real draw here is not the rather ordinary town but the local beaches, 72 in all, on islands and curling around inlets, and reckoned by some to be among the state's best.

Ubatuba is centred on Praça 13 de Maio, a couple of blocks from the *rodoviária* on Rua Conceição. On the seafront at the end of Thomaz Gallardo there's a very helpful **tourist office** (daily 8am–6pm; ⓣ12/3833-7300), which supplies maps of the coast and whose staff will make hotel reservations for you. Also worth a visit is the local branch of the environmental organization Projeto Tamar, Rua Antônio Athanásio 273 (daily 10am–8pm summer; 10am-6pm rest of year), which has display panels (in English and Portuguese) on their work protecting **sea turtles** (mainly loggerheads) that graze offshore, and live turtles on view in pools, too. Otherwise Ubatuba's main urban area has little going for it apart from hotels, rather uninspired bars and restaurants, banks and other services.

Accommodation

While not exactly a bargain, the hotels in and around Ubatuba tend to be better value for money than elsewhere along São Paulo's north coast. The town itself makes a good base if you plan to explore the surrounding beaches - accommodation here is mostly concentrated in the area around Rua Conceição. Alternatively, there are plenty of other places to stay in outlying parts. For travellers on tighter budgets, the only alternative is to head for a campsite – the nearest to town is the Sítio Usina Velha (Ⓣ12/3832-3629), some 3km north on the road to Parati, where you can pitch a tent or rent a small cabin (❷).

Itamambuca Eco Resort Rodovia Rio-Santos Km 36, Praia de Itamambuca Ⓣ12/3834-3000, Ⓦwww.itamambuca.com.br. Set back amongst the trees near Itamambuca, one of the area's best beaches, this resort (about 15km north of Ubatuba) has attractive cabins of varying degrees of luxury, with its own on-site restaurants and activities for children. ❼

Parque Atlântico Rua Conceição 185 Ⓣ12/3832-1336, Ⓦwww.parqueatlantico.com.br. Comfortable, well-kept hotel with light, airy rooms. A substantial discount on single rooms makes this place particularly good value for solo travellers. ❹

Pousada da Ana Doce Praia do Lázaro Ⓣ12/3842-0102, Ⓦwww.pousadaanadoce.com.br. Linked to the *pousada* in São Sebastião (see p.667), this is almost as charming, plus it has a pool. Located at Praia do Lazaro, about 20km south of Ubatuba. ❺

Pousada da Praia Praia do Félix Ⓣ12/3845-1196, Ⓦwww.praiadofelix.com.br. Simple bungalow apartments, each with a verandah, are situated near one of the area's prettiest beaches. ❺

Pousada das Artes Praia das Toninhas Ⓣ21/3842-0954, Ⓦwww.pousadadasartes.com.br. Arty and slightly pretentious, this is nevertheless a comfy place to stay south of town. Themed guest rooms are based on different cultures, including Arabian, Japanese, and Brazilian itself. ❺

Pousada Todas as Luas Praia Itamambuca Ⓣ12/3845-3129, Ⓦwww.todasasluas.com.br. This basic *pousada* is to the north of town, near the lovely Itamambuca beach, and surrounded by lush forest. ❺

São Nicolau Rua Conceição 213 Ⓣ12/3832-5007. Book ahead at this popular place, next door to the Parque Atlântico, that's been offering good-value accommodation to beach-goers since the 1960s. Rooms are pleasant and inexpensive, with TVs and fans. ❹

Eating and drinking

Most **restaurants** are on Avenida Iperoig, which curves alongside the town's beach, the Praia de Iperoig, and you'll find a good variety of seafood, Italian and other types to choose from. For outstanding seafood at low prices, head for *Peixe com Banana* on Ubatuba's seafront at Rua Guarani 255, which specializes in the local dish, *azul-marinho* (essentially fish stewed with green banana). Close by at no. 377, *Como se bom* is in a similar sort of vein, while *Pequim* at no. 385 offers tasty Italian food.

Around Ubatuba

Although there's nothing wrong with the town's **Praia de Iperoig**, Ubatuba is best used as a base from which to visit some of the numerous other beaches accessible by bus or private boat. The least developed – and the most attractive – are to the **northeast** of town, with the furthest, Camburi, 46km away on the border with Rio state. To get to these beaches, take the **local bus** marked "Prumirim" from the *rodoviária* and ask the driver to stop at whichever stretch takes your fancy. One possible point to make for is the Bairro do Picinguaba, a fishing village with a couple of bars and simple restaurants that's set alongside a very pretty beach and is connected to the main road by a three-kilometre-long narrow winding road.

The more popular beaches are to the south of Ubatuba and also easily reached by bus from the town centre, although almost all of them are fringed with hastily built condominiums as well as shopping and entertainment complexes. **Enseada**, 9km from Ubatuba, is lined with expensive beachfront hotels; nestled in a bay protected from the lively surf, its beach is popular with families, and in the summer it's always uncomfortably crowded.

Across the bay are a series of beautiful isolated beaches that draw fewer people. Walk out of Enseada on the main road for about 2km until you reach Ribeira, a yachting centre and colourful fishing port. From here, there are trips on sailing boats to the **Ilha Anchieta**, a state park on an island where only a few fisherfolk live. These will cost between R$17 and R$35, depending on the itinerary: enquire at Mykonos, Rua Flamenguinho 17, Saco da Ribeira (Ⓣ12/3842-0329, Ⓦwww.mykonos.com.br). Beyond Ribeira are sandy coves that you can reach by clambering down from the trail on the cliff above the sea.

It's also easy to arrange hikes inland, in the Parque Estadual Serra do Mar, from Ubatuba; try the tour agency Belmar, at Rua Conceição 200 (Ⓣ12/3833-7422, Ⓦwww.ubatubasurfcam.com.br/belmar), which will provide transport and a guide for R$60–R$150, depending on the trail length.

Incidentally, if you're touring the state, you can travel between Ubatuba and Campos do Jordão by picking up a (frequent) connection in Taubaté.

Southwest of Santos

The coastal escarpment **southwest of Santos** begins its incline 20–30km inland from the sea. Lacking the immediate mountain backdrop, and with large stretches of the coast dominated by mangrove swamp, this region was for years left more or less untouched by tourism. However, holiday development companies have been moving in recently, aiming at *paulistanos* who can't afford places further north.

Heading south from Santos, the road follows the coast as far as Peruíbe, then moves inland onto higher, firmer terrain before heading back to the coast down the Serra do Mar. The road is slow but, passing through small fishing villages, banana and sugar plantations and cattle-grazing land, you're reminded that there's more to Brazil than just beaches. Bear in mind that from São Paulo, rather than travelling via Santos, it's faster to take a direct bus to Iguape and Cananéia.

Iguape

IGUAPE, roughly 180km from Santos, was founded in 1538 by the Portuguese to guard against the possibility of Spanish encroachment on the southern fringes of the empire. Its poor strategic location at the tip of an estuarine island, however, means that it has forever remained a backwater –with the effect that many of its colonial buildings survive today in good condition. The greatest concentration of these are found around **Largo da Basílica**, Iguape's main square, which is rimmed by whitewashed and brightly coloured buildings built in colonial, nineteenth-century and even Art Deco styles.

During the summer, Iguape is popular with *paulistas* seeking a beach vacation away from the sophistication, crowds and expense of resorts further north. The nearest good beach on the mainland is **Barra do Ribeira**, frequented by surfers; it's a 15-minute boat ride to get there from Iguape, or a twenty-kilometre car ride over rough track. Facing Iguape is another island, the **Ilha Comprida**, 86km long but just 3km wide, with an interior of light forest; an uninterrupted beach stretches the entire Atlantic-facing length of the island. In the summer it gets very crowded near the access road that crosses the island, where the beginnings of urban development, including some basic hotels and snackbars, is increasing apace; if you want to be alone, just walk south for a few kilometres. Alternatively, the island can be reached from Cananéia (see below). A bridge links Iguape to the mainland, and frequent buses head inland from both the centre of the island and the **rodoviária**, located a good twenty minutes' walk (or short taxi ride) from the town centre.

Iguape has a good selection of **accommodation**, with the *Pousada Solar Colonial* at Praça da Basílica 30 (Ⓣ13/3841-1591, Ⓦwww.guiadeiguape.com.br/sites/solar; ④) the nicest by far. The comfortable rooms in this refurbished nineteenth-century mansion are tremendous value, with the best ones overlooking the main square. A few blocks away are the *Pousada Casa Grande* at Rua Major Rebelo 768 (Ⓣ13/3841-1920; ③) and the *Itamiaru* at Rua Princesa Isabel 731 (Ⓣ13/3841-1428; ③), both less characterful, but pleasant nonetheless. For **food**, you'll find very good fish entrees at the *Panela Velha* at Rua 15 de Novembro 190 and at the *Itacurumins* at Rua Porto do Rosário 2.

The helpful **tourist information office** is located at Largo da Basílica 272 (Ⓣ13/3841-1209; 8am–5.30pm).

Cananéia and around

More appealing than Iguape, **CANANÉIA**, 50km further south and also on an island, lies between the mainland to which it's linked by a short bridge and the Ilha Comprida. Frequent **ferries** run between the town centre and the Ilha Comprida, from where you can either take a bus (every hour) or follow the road for 3km straight ahead by foot or bicycle to the beach (bikes are available for around R$20 per day from Silva Rent a Bike, at Av. Independência 840). Where the road hits the beach, there are a couple of very simple *pousadas* and bars. In the height of summer it gets almost crowded here, but for the rest of the year, both the town and beaches are extremely quiet.

In the old centre of Cananéia, in particular along *ruas* Tristão Lobo, Bandeirantes and Dom João II, you'll find many ochre-coloured and whitewashed colonial and nineteenth-century buildings. Except for a few, such as the well preserved, seventeenth-century **Igreja São João Batista** (Wed–Sun 9am–noon & 2–6pm), on Praça Martim Afonso de Souza, they're in very poor condition and for some only the facade remains. The **Museu Municipal** (Mon–Fri 9am–6pm, Sat & Sun 9.30am–6.30pm), also on the *praça,* is worth a brief look, with pride of place among its exhibits going to a preserved shark that weighed 3500kg.

To the south of Cananéia, another island, the **Ilha Cardoso**, is a protected **nature reserve**, with isolated beaches, fishing villages and some wonderful trails. Karl Beitler, a long-term German resident in Cananéia who runs the ecotourism agency Lagamar at Rua Silvino de Araújo 166 (Ⓣ13/3851-1613, Ⓦwww.cananet.com.br/lagamar), knows the area well and leads tours to the island and elsewhere. Schooner trips to Cardoso, departing from the wharf at Beira Mar, last five or six hours (daily Dec–Feb; R$15 per person), including a stop at a long beach – deserted except for a small café and rangers' post – and the chance to go for undemanding treks through the reserve. The waters are home to around 3000 Tucuxi dolphins, which can easily be seen from the boat and come in amazingly close to shore. If you want longer treks in the reserve, call the guide association on Ⓣ13/3851-1995, or visit their office next to the *Golfinho Plaza* hotel (see below).

Practicalities

The most comfortable **hotel** in the area is the new ★ *Sol a Sol* at Av. Luis Wilson Barbosa 573 (Ⓣ13/3851-1851, Ⓦwww.hotelsolasol.cananeia.net; ④), located in Retiro, about 500m from the town centre; it has large, comfortable rooms – the best of which are on the top floor, with sea views – and a sizeable pool. Otherwise, Cananéia's best accommodation options are located on Av. Independência, the main road leading into town. The ⚑ *Golfinho Plaza* (Ⓣ13/3851-1655, Ⓦwww.golfinhoplazahotel.com.br; ❸), at no. 885, is the choice of these, and the only other place locally with a pool, while the *Pousada Bom Abrigo* at no. 374 (Ⓣ13/3851-1546; ❸) offers good-value basic accommodation. Other hotels can be found along or near the waterfront in the same vicinity: these include the bungalow-style *Beira-Mar*, at Av. Beira Mar 219 (Ⓣ13/3851-1115; ❸) and the bright orange *Recanto do Sol*, at Rua Pedro Lobo 271 (Ⓣ13/3851-1162, Ⓦwww.cananet.com.br/recantodosol; ❸).

You can **eat** quite well in Cananéia, where, apart from pizza, the mainstays are fish, mussels, octopus and, the town's speciality, oysters. Restaurants are mainly found on Av. Independência, and straightforward but good choices include the *Posto do Camaroe*, at no. 655 and *Bacharel*, at no. 835, both of which are strong on seafood. In Retiro, the *Naguissa do Silêncio* at Av. Luís Wilson Barbosa 401 is a slightly more upmarket restaurant specializing in seafood as well.

Nightlife is low-key here, even in summer, but several bars are located on the waterfront, alongside the *praça*, while a block away at Av. Beira Mar 71 there's the appealing ⚑ *Kurt Kaffee* – a bar, restaurant and antique shop that stays open until late at night and attracts an eclectic crowd.

At low tide, cars are permitted to **drive** along the beach between Iguape and Cananéia, a journey that can be completed in less than an hour; check and double check tidal times and drive carefully, neither too near the water's edge nor too high up the beach or you risk getting stuck in the sand. Otherwise, **buses** have to take a circuitous route inland, an 80km trip that takes about two hours, with departures several times a day between the towns.

On from Iguape and Cananéia

If travelling south to Paraná, you'll have to change buses in **Registro**, a bustling and rather ugly town an hour inland from both Iguape and Cananéia in the heart of Brazil's main tea-growing region. Registro's once overwhelmingly Japanese character has been greatly diluted in recent years with the arrival of migrants from other parts of the state and with a gradual exodus of young people of Japanese descent drawn to greater opportunities elsewhere. If you're unlucky with connections and need to **stay**, the most comfortable place in town is the *Lito Palace* (Ⓣ13/3821-1055, Ⓦwww.litopalacehotel.com.br; ❸), at Av. Jonas Banks Leite 615.

It's also possible to reach Paraná by **boat**: three days a week there are launches from Cananéia (Mon 1pm; Wed & Thurs 8am; Ⓣ13/3851-1268; R$45) that travel via a tranquil, inland waterway to Ariri (see p.704), a small fishing community just within the state of Paraná. Although the journey there takes only three hours, there is a small risk of no connecting launch if you're planning to visit Guaraqueçaba or Paranaguá. If you find yourself stuck for a night, there are a couple of rustic *pousadas* (❷–❸) in the fishing village of Marujá, a couple of kilometres away, which also has a great beach and wonderful forest trails.

Travel details

Buses

Campinas to: Curitiba (5 daily; 6hr); São Paulo (hourly; 1hr 15min).
Cananéia to: Registro (6 daily; 1hr); Santos (1 daily; 5hr); São Paulo (2 daily; 4hr 30min).
Iguape to: Registro (13 daily; 1hr); Santos (3 daily; 4hr); São Paulo (4 daily; 4hr).
Santos to: Cananéia (1 daily; 5hr); São Paulo (every 15min; 1hr).
São Paulo to: Americana (14 daily; 2hr); Bauru (7 daily; 4hr 30min); Belo Horizonte (hourly; 12hr); Campinas (hourly; 1hr 15min); Campo Grande (8 daily; 16hr); Cananéia (2 daily; 4hr 30min); Corumbá (4 daily; 26hr); Curitiba (hourly; 6hr); Embu (every 30min; 1hr); Florianópolis (8 daily; 12hr); Guarujá (every 30min; 1hr); Holambra (6 daily; 2hr); Iguape (4 daily; 4hr); Recife (4 daily; 40hr); Rio (every 30min; 6hr); Salvador (4 daily; 30hr); Santa Bárbara d'Oeste (8 daily; 2hr); Santos (every 15min; 1hr); São Sebastião (6 daily; 3hr); Ubatuba (6 daily; 3hr 30min).
Ubatuba to: Parati (3 daily; 1hr 30min); Rio (2 daily; 5hr); São Paulo (6 daily; 3hr 30min).

Trains

São Paulo to: Bauru (4 daily; 5hr 30min); Rio Grande da Serra (for Paranapiacaba; every 15min; 45min).

Boats

Cananéia to: Ariri (3 weekly; 3hrs); Ilha Comprida (frequent; 20 mins).
Santos to: Guarujá (frequent; 10 mins)
São Sebastião to: Ilhabela (every 30 mins; 20 mins).

The South

COLOMBIA
VENEZUELA
GUYANA
SURINAME
FRENCH GUIANA
N
PERU
BOLIVIA
PARAGUAY
CHILE
ARGENTINA
URUGUAY
0 1000 km

CHAPTER 9

Highlights

* **Ilha do Mel** One of Brazil's most relaxing islands, blessed with little development and no cars. See p.700

* **Iguaçu Falls** No trip to the South is complete without a visit to these breathtaking falls. See p.708

* **Florianópolis beaches** Known as one of Brazil's surfing hot spots, Florianópolis offers plenty of calm swimming beaches as well. See p.722

* **Old-world settlements** Head to the rural south for enduring influences of European pioneer settlers such as Germans in Pomerode, Italians in the Vale dos Vinhedos and Ukrainians in Serra do Tigre. See p.740, p.769 & p.708

* **Churrascarias** Choose from a staggering selection of cuts at these popular barbecue houses – two outstanding options are Na Brasa and Galpão Crioulo in Porto Alegre. See p.759 & 758

* **Rio Grande do Sul's cattle country** For a taste of *gaúcho* life, attend a **rodeio** in Vacaria, go horse riding in the highlands around Cambará do Sul or stay on a working cattle *estância* near Bagé or at an historic *charqueada* outside Pelotas. See p.769, p.765, p.783 & p.772

* **São Miguel** The fine Jesuit ruins of São Miguel are dramatically sited in the sparsely inhabited interior of Rio Grande do Sul. See p.777

△ Curitiba

9

The South

The states forming the **South** of Brazil – **Paraná**, **Santa Catarina** and **Rio Grande do Sul** – are generally considered to be the most developed parts of the country. The smallest of Brazil's regions, the South maintains an economic influence completely out of proportion to its size. This is largely the result of two factors: the first is an agrarian structure that, to a great extent, is based on highly efficient small and medium-sized units; and the second is the economically active population that produces a per capita output considerably higher than the national average. Without widespread poverty on the scale found elsewhere in the country, the South tends to be dismissed by Brazilians as being a region that has more in common with Europe or the United States than with South America.

Superficially, at least, this view has much going for it. The inhabitants are largely of European origin, anyway, and live in well-ordered cities where there's little of the obvious squalor prevalent elsewhere. Beneath the tranquil setting, however, there are tensions: due to land shortages, people are constantly forced to move vast distances – as far away as Acre in the western Amazon – to avoid being turned into mere day-labourers, and *favelas* are an increasingly common sight in Curitiba, Porto Alegre and the other large cities of the South. From time to time these tensions explode as landless peasants invade the huge, under-used *latifúndios* in the west and south of the region, and it is no coincidence that it was here that the Landless Movement (Movimento dos Sem Tera) first emerged.

For the tourist, though, the region offers much that's attractive. The **coast** has a subtropical climate that in the summer months (November to March) draws people who want to avoid the oppressive heat of the northern resorts, and a vegetation and atmosphere that feel more Mediterranean than Brazilian. Much of the Paraná's coast is still unspoilt by the ravages of mass tourism, and building development is essentially forbidden on the beautiful islands of **Paranaguá Bay**. By way of contrast, tourists have encroached along Santa Catarina's coast, but only a few places, such as **Balneário Camburiú**, have been allowed to develop into a concrete jungle. Otherwise, resorts such as most of those on the **Ilha de Santa Catarina** around **Florianópolis** remain small and do not seriously detract from the region's natural beauty.

The **interior** is less frequently visited. Much of it is mountainous, the home of people whose way of life seems to have altered little since the arrival of the European pioneers in the nineteenth and early twentieth centuries. Cities in the interior that were founded by Germans (such as **Blumenau** in Santa Catarina), Italians (**Caxias do Sul** in Rio Grande do Sul) and Ukrainians (**Prudentópolis** in Paraná) have lost much of their former ethnic character, but only short

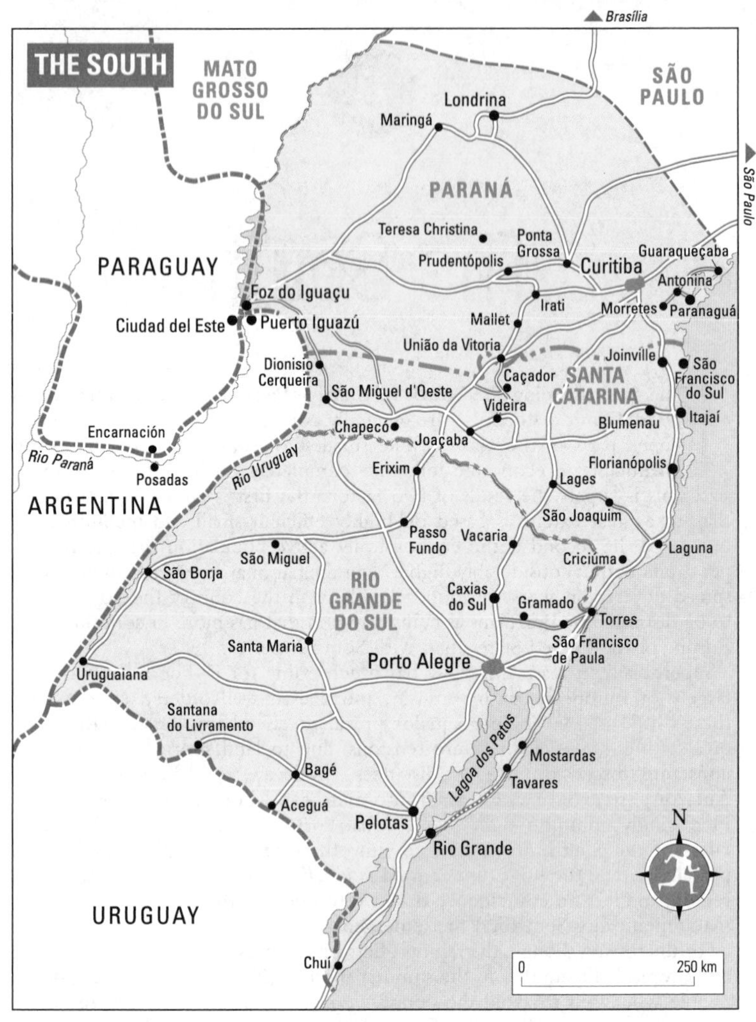

distances from them are villages and hamlets where time appears to have stood still. The highland areas between **Lages** and **Vacaria**, and the grasslands of southern and western Rio Grande do Sul, are largely given over to vast cattle ranches, where the modern *gaúchos* (see box p.782) keep alive many of the skills of their forebears. The region also boasts some spectacular natural features, the best known being the **Iguaçu waterfalls** on the Brazilian–Argentine frontier and the incredible canyons of the **Aparados da Serra**.

Travelling around the South is generally easy, and there's a fine **road** network. Most north–south **buses** stick to the road running near the coast, but it's easy to devise routes passing through the interior, perhaps taking in the Jesuit ruins of **São Miguel**.

Paraná

Paraná is the northernmost of Brazil's southern states and one of the wealthiest in all Brazil. Its agricultural economy is based on a mix of efficient family farms and highly capitalized larger land holdings, while its modern industries, unlike those of neighbouring São Paulo, have been subject to at least limited planning and environmental controls. Although the state's population is ethnically extremely diverse, it is comprised largely of the descendants of immigrants. All of this combines to give Paraná something of the feel of an American Midwestern state transplanted to the subtropics.

For several decades after breaking away from São Paulo in 1853, Paraná's economy remained based on pig-raising, timber extraction and *erva maté* (a South American bush, the leaves of which are used to make a tea-like beverage), and in its early years the province was linked to the rest of Brazil only by a network of trails along which cattle and mules passed between Rio Grande do Sul's grasslands and the mines and plantations of the northern provinces. Paraná was sparsely populated by Indians, Portuguese and mixed-race *caboclos*, who worked on the *latifúndios*, scratched a living as semi-nomadic subsistence farmers or, on the coast, fished.

Then, the provincial government turned to **immigration** as a means to expand Paraná's economy and open up land for settlement. The first immigrant colonies of British, Volga-Germans, French, Swiss and Icelanders were utter failures, but from the 1880s onwards, others met with some success. As mixed farmers, coffee or soya producers, Germans moved northwards from Rio Grande do Sul and Santa Catarina; Poles and Italians settled near the capital, Curitiba; Ukrainians centred themselves in the south, especially on Prudentópolis (see box, p.706); Japanese spread south from São Paulo, settling around Londrina and Maringá; and a host of smaller groups, including Dutch, Mennonites, Koreans, Russian "Old Believers" and Danube-Swabians established colonies elsewhere with varying success rates. Thanks to their isolation, the immigrants' descendants have retained many of the cultural traditions of their forebears, traditions that are gradually being eroded by the influences of television and radio, the education system and economic pressures that force migration to the cities or to new land in distant parts of Brazil. Nevertheless, this multi-ethnic blend still lends Paraná its distinct character and a special fascination.

Unless you're heading straight for the **Iguaçu** waterfalls, **Curitiba** makes a good base. Transport services fan out in all directions from the state capital and there's plenty to keep you occupied in the city between excursions. **Paranaguá Bay** can be visited as a day-trip from Curitiba, but its islands and colonial towns could also easily take up a week or more of your time. Inland, the strange geological formations of **Vila Velha** are usually visited from Curitiba – by changing buses in Ponta Grossa, you can stop off here before heading west to the Ukrainian-dominated region around the towns of **Prudentópolis** and **Irati**, and from there head yet further west to Foz do Iguaçu.

Curitiba

Founded in 1693 as a gold-mining camp, **CURITIBA** was of little importance until 1853 when it was made capital of Paraná. Since then, the city's population has steadily risen from a few thousand, reaching 140,000 in 1940 and some 1.7 million today. It's said that Curitiba is barely a Brazilian city at all, a view that has some basis. The inhabitants are descendants of Polish, German, Italian and other immigrants who settled in Curitiba and in surrounding villages that have since been engulfed by the expanding metropolis. On average, *curitibanos* enjoy Brazil's highest standard of living: the city boasts health, education and public

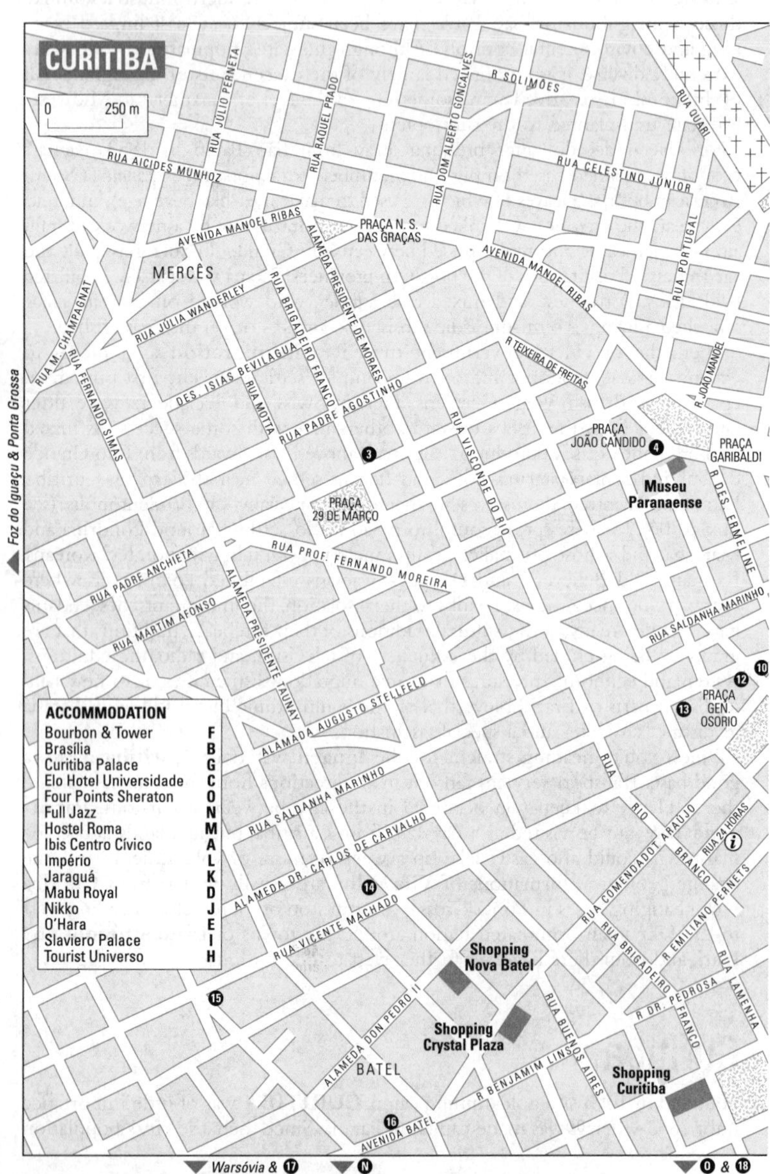

transport facilities that are the envy of other parts of the country. There are *favelas*, but they're well hidden and, because of the cool, damp winters, sturdier than those in cities to the north. The wooden houses of Curitiba's lower and middle classes often resemble those of frontier homesteads and frequently betray their inhabitants' Central or Eastern European origins, with half-hip roofs, carved window frames and elaborate trelliswork. As elsewhere in Brazil, the rich live in

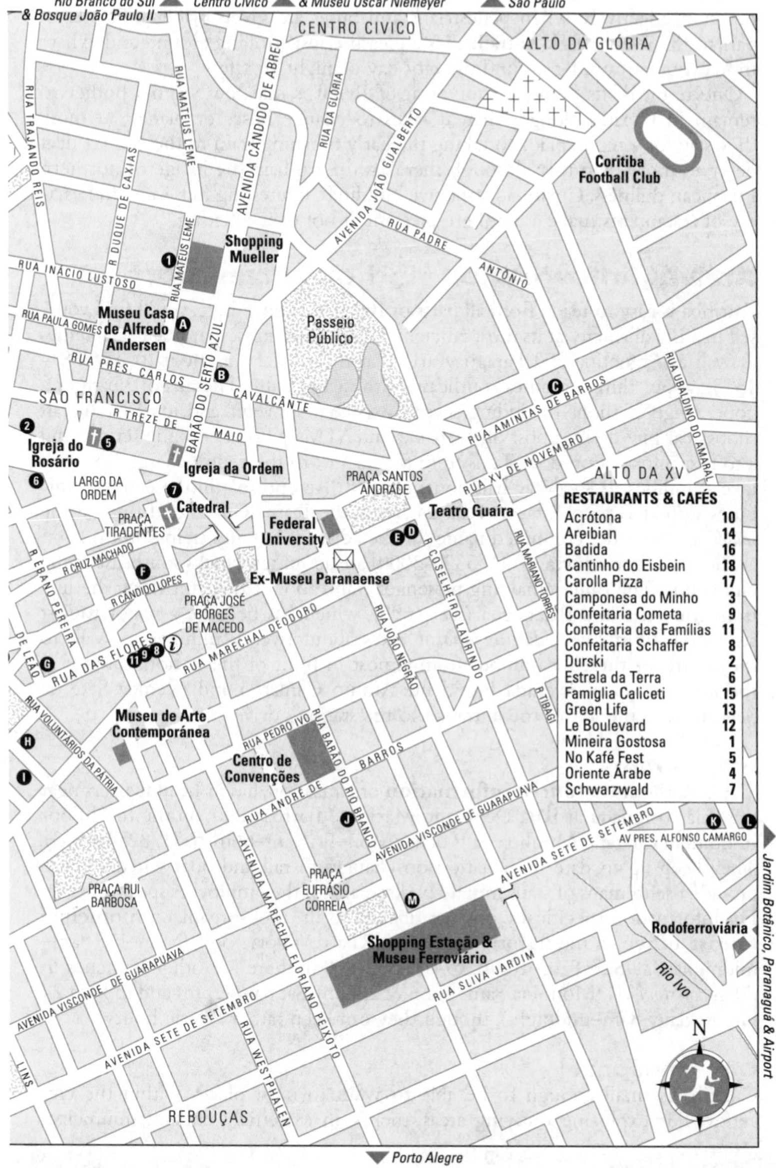

mansions and luxury condominiums, but even these are a little less ostentatious, and need fewer security precautions, than usual.

Many nineteenth- and early twentieth-century buildings have been saved from the developers who, since the 1960s, have ravaged most Brazilian cities, and there's a clearly defined **historic quarter** where colonial and nineteenth-century buildings have been preserved. Much of the centre is closed to traffic and, in a country where the car has become a symbol of development, planners from all over Brazil and beyond descend on Curitiba to discover how a city can function effectively when pedestrians and buses are given priority. Thanks in part to the relative lack of traffic, it's a pleasure just strolling around and, what's more, you can wander around the city, day or night, in safety.

One result of its being so untypical of Brazil is that few visitors bother to remain in Curitiba longer than it takes to change buses or planes. At most, they stay for a night, prior to taking the early morning train to the coast. But it deserves more than this: although there's some truth in the image of northern European dullness, Curitiba's attractive buildings, interesting museums and variety of restaurants make a stay here pleasant, if not over-exciting.

Arrival, information and city transport

Curitiba is easy to reach from all parts of Brazil and, once here, you'll find yourself in a Brazilian city at its most efficient. Flights from most major Brazilian cities as well as Argentina and Paraguay arrive at the modern **airport** (Ⓣ41/3381-1515), about thirty minutes southeast of the city centre. The airport features a good range of shops (including several excellent souvenir and local handicraft shops), car hire desks, a post office, banks and ATMs, a hotel booking service and a tourist information desk. Taxis from the airport to the centre charge R$50, or take a minibus (R$6, every half hour) marked "Aeroporto" (in the centre, minibuses stop at Espaço Estação, Rua 24 horas, the Teatro Guaíra and outside the *rodoferroviária* – the combined name for the adjacent bus and train stations).

The **rodoferroviária** (Ⓣ41/3320-3000) are about ten blocks southeast of the city centre. The only remaining passenger trains to Curitiba run along the line from Morretes and Paranaguá (see p.699), which has become a major tourist attraction. From the *rodoferroviária*, it takes about twenty minutes to walk to the centre, or there's a minibus from almost in front of the station: catch it at the intersection of Avenida Presidente Afonso Camargo and Avenida Sete de Setembro, to the left of the entrance to the station's drive.

Information

SETUR, the **state tourist information** organization, has its headquarters near the Palácio Iguaçu at Rua Deputado Mário de Barros 1290, on the third floor of Edifício Caetano Munhoz da Rocha (Mon–Fri 9am–6pm; Ⓣ41/3254-6933). They keep up-to-date information on changes to rail and boat schedules and provide useful maps of trails in state parks; many of the employees speak English. For information specifically on Curitiba, go to the well-organized **municipal tourist office** in the historic centre on Rua da Glória 362 (Mon–Fri 8am–midnight, Sat–Sun 8am–10pm; Ⓣ41/3352-8000); there are other branches in the *rodoferroviária* (Mon–Fri 8am–noon & 2–6pm, Sat 8am–2pm) and in Rua 24 Horas (daily 8am–midnight), though they can keep rather erratic hours.

City transport

Curitiba is small enough to be able to **walk** to most places within the city centre. For exploring outlying areas, there's an extremely efficient municipal

Linha Turismo

If you have limited time in Curitiba, an excellent way to view the city's main attractions is to take a **bus tour**. Buses of the *Linha Turismo* depart from Praça Tiradentes every half-hour year-round (Tues–Sun; first bus leaves 9am, last bus 5.30pm; R$15) and stop at twenty-five attractions around the city centre and suburbs. The bus takes just over two hours to complete the itinerary, but tickets allow passengers to get off at five of the stops and rejoin the tour on a later bus.

bus network that's considered the envy of all other Brazilian cities. In the city centre, the two main bus terminals are at Praça Tiradentes and Praça Rui Barbosa, from where buses (R$1.80) head out into the suburbs as well as to neighbouring *municípios*. **Taxis** are easy to come by and, as distances are generally small, they're not too expensive.

Accommodation

If your sole reason for being in Curitiba is to catch the dawn train to the coast, you're best off staying at the youth hostel or at one of the numerous cheap and mid-range **hotels** within a few minutes' walk of the *rodoferroviária*. Otherwise, places in the centre are widely scattered but within walking distance of most downtown attractions and are generally remarkable value. It's worth phoning around to compare prices, as many of the better hotels offer substantial discounts at weekends and at other times when occupancy by business executives is low.

Bourbon & Tower Rua Cândido Lopes 102 ⓣ41/3321-4600, ⓦwww.bourbon.com.br. Widely considered the best hotel in the city, with an atmosphere of traditional elegance combined with every modern facility, including a pool, business centre and very good restaurants. ❼

Brasília Rua Presidente Carlos Cavalcanti 518 (ⓣ41/3221-6811). A good option if you're seeking inexpensive accommodation near the historic centre. Rooms are clean but, being located by a busy intersection, there's a lot of traffic noise. ❷

Curitiba Palace Rua Ermelino de Leão 45 ⓣ41/3322-8081, ⓦwww.curitibapalace.com.br. Centrally located, long-established mid-range choice; rooms – all of which have a balcony – are spacious and have recently been refurbished. ❹

Elo Hotel Universidade Rua Amintas de Barros 383 ⓣ41/3028-9400, ⓦwww.hoteiselo.com.br. Modern, rather characterless hotel with a pool, situated next to the university's main administrative building. The rooms are clean and comfortable and the staff are very helpful: excellent value and highly recommended. ❸–❹

Four Points Sheraton Av. 7 de Setembro 4211 ⓣ3340-4000, ⓦwww.starwood.com. Located in the upmarket residential and commercial inner-city *bairro* of Batel, this is Curitiba's latest luxury hotel aimed primarily at business travellers. Offers all that you'd expect from a new *Sheraton*, including a pool, business centre and multilingual staff. Rooms are all large and bright with sitting area, large-screen TV and wireless Internet access. ❼

Full Jazz Rua Silveira Peixoto 1297 ⓣ41/3312-7000, ⓦwww.hotelslaviero.com.br. As its name suggests, the hotel is themed around jazz, with a programme of live performances, a restaurant inspired by the flavours of New Orleans and a jazz DVD and CD library. Rooms have modern furnishings and the location, in fashionable Batel, is convenient for some of Curitiba's best restaurants. ❺

Hostel Roma Rua Barão do Rio Branco 805 ⓣ41/3224-1212, ⓦwww.hostelroma.com.br. Curitiba's new HI-affiliated youth hostel, located alongside the Shopping Estação, just four blocks west of the *rodoferroviária*. As well as dorms (R$25 per person), there are rooms with private bathrooms that sleep two to four people (❷).

Ibis Centro Cívico Rua Mateus Leme 358 ⓣ41/3324-0469, ⓦwww.ibis-brasil.com.br. The hotel's reception and dining area is in an attractive, German-style house, and small but well-appointed guest rooms are in an interlinked tower block behind. Excellent value and a central location near the historic centre and Shopping Mueller make reservations essential. ❸

Império Av. Presidente Afonso Camargo 367 ⓣ41/3264-3373. One of several cheap, but perfectly respectable, hotels located virtually opposite the *rodoferroviária*, useful if you have an early morning train or bus to catch. Offers good, but small, rooms and a nice atmosphere. ❷

Jaraguá Av. Presidente Afonso Camargo 279 ⓣ41/3362-2022. Directly opposite the *rodoferroviária*, and with slightly better facilities than the other hotels in the vicinity. The rooms (some of which accommodate three people) are larger than most, the service is efficient and breakfast is available for guests departing early. ❸

Mabu Royal Praça Santos Andrade 830 ⓣ41/3219-6000, ⓦwww.hoteismabu.com.br. Good location and attentive service but, although the facilities are good, its small rooms are overpriced. ❻–❼

Nikko Rua Barão do Rio Branco 546 ⓣ0800/709-1808, ⓦwww.hotelnikko.com.br. Modern Japanese-style hotel set behind a pretty nineteenth-century facade. The small rooms are simply and attractively furnished, with mineral water supplying the bath and shower. There's a small Japanese-style garden, a tiny swimming pool and a sushi bar as well. ❺

O'Hara Praça Santos Andrade 770 ⓣ41/232-6044. Well located on the continuation of Rua XV de Novembro, just ten minutes' walk from the *rodoferroviária*. Its central location and rates mean that it's very popular, though rooms are small, dark, musty and rather overpriced. ❸

Slaviero Palace Rua Senador Alencar Guimarães 830 ⓣ0800/704-3311, ⓦwww.hotelslaviero.com.br. Situated a couple of blocks from Rua das Flores, this well-established hotel is popular with business travellers. The rooms are pleasant and large and there's an excellent restaurant. ❺

Tourist Universo Praça Osório 63 ⓣ41/322-0099, ⓕ223-5420. Attractively situated with the nicest rooms overlooking the tree-lined *praça*. There's a friendly atmosphere and, although the rooms are overdue for refurbishment, they're good value and have the standard minibar, TV and a/c. ❸

The City

Being comparatively compact, much of Curitiba is best explored on foot and, apart from the museums – many of which are located in the central commercial district – most interest is concentrated in the historic centre, around the Largo da Ordem. The main commercial district, with Rua das Flores (part of Avenida XV de Novembro) at its heart, is only a couple of blocks south of the historic quarter.

△ Curitiba

The commercial district: Rua das Flores and around

The **Rua das Flores** – a pedestrianized precinct section of the Rua XV de Novembro lined with graceful, and carefully restored, pastel-coloured early twentieth-century buildings – is the centre's main late afternoon and early evening meeting point, its bars, tearooms and coffee shops crammed with customers. Few of the surrounding streets are especially attractive, but the **former city hall**, at Praça José Borges across from the flower market, is definitely worth a look. Built in 1916, the magnificent Art Nouveau construction was later converted for use as the Museu Paranaense. In 2003, however, the museum was transferred to a new site (see p.688) and the building has since stood empty, its future still undecided. Just off Praça General Osório, at the far end of Rua das Flores, there's a small shopping arcade, the **Rua 24 Horas**, an attempt by city planners to keep the centre of Curitiba alive outside of office hours. As its name suggests, businesses here are open around the clock, useful if you have a 4am urge to buy a T-shirt, have a snack or get a haircut.

There are a number of other museums within the commercial centre (the tourist office has a complete list), but only two are really worth going out of your way for. Of obvious interest to rail buffs, the **Museu Ferroviário**, at Praça Eufrásio Correia (daily 12.30–8.30pm), contains relics from Paraná's railway era. The building housing the museum was the original terminus of the Curitiba–Paranaguá line, and now forms the centrepiece of the **Estação Shopping**, which encompasses over a hundred shops, ten cinema screens and plenty of places to eat. **The Museu de Arte Contemporânea**, at Rua Westphalen 16 (Tues–Sat 10am–7pm; Ⓦwww.pr.gov.br/mac), concentrates on local artists in its permanent and temporary exhibits. A brief look round the museum's diminutive collection will be enough to recognize that Paraná has not established itself as a trendsetter in the Brazilian contemporary art scene.

A couple of blocks north from Rua das Flores is Praça Tiradentes, where the **Catedral Metropolitana** is located. Inaugurated in 1893, and supposedly inspired by Barcelona's cathedral, it's a totally unremarkable neo-Gothic construction. If you feel the need for a break from the city crowds, head east for a few blocks to the **Passeio Público**, Curitiba's oldest park. Opened in 1886, it has two large boating ponds at its centre and a network of paths to wander along, shaded by tall trees. Of particular interest here are the aviaries housing local species of brightly feathered birds.

The historic quarter

Near the cathedral, a pedestrian tunnel leads to Curitiba's **historic quarter**, centred on Largo da Ordem and the adjoining Praça Garibaldi, an area of impeccably preserved eighteenth- and nineteenth-century buildings. With few exceptions, the whitewashed buildings of the old town are of a style that would not be out of place in a small village in Portugal. Today the buildings all have state preservation orders on them and do duty as bars, restaurants, art and craft galleries and cultural centres. On Sundays (9am–2pm) in the Largo da Ordem and Praça Garibaldi, the **Feira de Artesanato** has a range of local handicrafts and cuisine representing the state's diverse ethnic traditions.

Two of Curitiba's oldest churches physically dominate the historic quarter. Dating from 1737, with the bell tower added in the late nineteenth century, the **Igreja da Ordem Terceira de São Francisco das Chagas**, on Largo da Ordem, is the city's oldest surviving building and one of the best examples of Portuguese ecclesiastical architecture in southern Brazil. Plain outside, the church is also simple within, its only decoration being typically Portuguese blue and white tiling and late Baroque altars. The church contains the **Museu de**

Arte Sacra (Tues–Fri 9am–noon & 1–6pm, Sat & Sun 9am–2pm), with relics gathered from Curitiba's Roman Catholic churches. Opposite the church is the mid-eighteenth-century **Casa Romário Martins** (Tues–Fri 9am–noon & 1–6pm, Sat–Sun 9am–2pm), Curitiba's oldest surviving house, now the site of a cultural foundation and exhibition centre for artists from Paraná. A short distance uphill from here, on the same road, the church of **Nossa Senhora do Rosário** dates back to 1737, built by and for Curitiba's slave population. However, after falling into total disrepair, the church was completely reconstructed in the 1930s and remains colonial in style only.

Further up the hill is the newly opened **Museu Paranaense**, on the corner of Rua Kellers and Praça João Cândido (Tues–Fri 9.30am–5.30pm, Sat–Sun 11am–3pm; Ⓦwww.pr.gov.br/museupr; R$2), in a beautifully renovated Neoclassical-style building that once served as the state governor's residence. One of Curitiba's more interesting museums, it is an attractively displayed collection of artefacts, paintings, maps and photographs that chart in detail the history of Paraná from pre-colonial conquest into the twenty-first century. There's a tea room here and a shop selling a good selection of local books and handicrafts.

Back down the hill, at Rua Mateus Leme 336, off the Largo da Ordem, is a much smaller art museum that's worth a visit. The well-organized **Museu Alfredo Andersen** (Mon–Fri 9am–6.30pm, Sat–Sun 10am–4pm; Ⓦwww.pr.gov.br/maa) is dedicated to the work of the eponymous Norwegian-born artist and is located in his former home and studio. Although a gifted painter, Andersen is hardly known in his native country, in part because the majority of his artistic output is in Brazil and because his subject matter – late nineteenth- and early twentieth-century landscapes and rural people – solely concerned Paraná. The museum's gift shop, selling books and souvenirs relating to Andersen, opens at 1pm.

The outskirts

In the suburbs that ring the historic and commercial centre of Curitiba are several sights that are well worth visiting; although mostly some distance from one another, they're linked by the Linha Turismo bus (see p.685). About 3km to the north of Curitiba's old town is the **Centro Civico**, the sprawling complex of state government buildings with park-like surrounds that was created in the 1980s. The Centro Cívico itself has little architectural merit, but alongside it is the stunningly beautiful **Museu Oscar Niemeyer** (Tues–Sun 10am–8pm; Ⓣ41/3350-4400, Ⓦwww.museuoscarniemeyer.org.br; R$4), by far Curitiba's best art museum. Designed by Niemeyer and opened in 2003, the building has won over even the architect's most bitter critics. Like all Niemeyer buildings, the structure is visually imposing – in this case dominated by a feature that resembles a giant eye – but it also works well as an exhibition space, something that isn't the case with Niteroi's Museu de Arte Contemporânea (see p.142). The museum is now home to the **Museu de Arte do Paraná** collection, but the consistently good exhibitions – based either on the museum's own catalogue or visiting exhibitions of Brazilian or other Latin American art – are all temporary.

Adjoining the grounds behind the Museu Oscar Niemeyer is the **Bosque Papa João Paulo II** (Mon 1–6pm, Tues–Sun 9am–7.30pm), a park created to commemorate the papal visit to Curitiba in 1980. In the heart of the park, the **Museu da Imigração Polonesa** (same hours) celebrates Polish immigration to Paraná. It's made up of several log cabins, built by Polish immigrants in the 1880s and relocated here from the Colônia Thomaz Coelho (near Araucária – see p.693). The cabins contain displays of typical objects used by pioneer families, and one building has been turned into a shrine to the "Black Madonna of Czestochowa". There's a **shop** attached to the museum selling Polish handicrafts, books, vodka, and souvenirs marking the papal visit. On the side road as you enter the park, there's a tearoom, *Kawiarnia Krakowiak* (daily 10am–9pm), where you can get delicious home-made Polish-Brazilian cakes, light meals and superb locally produced vodkas.

To get to both the Bosque Papa João Paulo II and Museu Oscar Niemeyer, take the *Linha do Turismo* or a yellow bus going to Abranches (a suburb with a high concentration of Poles) from Praça Tiradentes and get off at the **Portal Polaco**, a huge concrete structure extending over the road leading north out of town. Alternatively, take any bus that goes to the Centro Cívico.

A short distance north of the park is the **Universidade Livre do Meio Ambiente** (Ⓦwww.unilivre.org.br), not a university in the traditional sense but more a park and exhibition centre promoting environmental awareness. Established in 1992 as one of the centrepieces of Curitiba's self-proclaimed status as the "environmental capital of Brazil", the grounds – a former quarry – are certainly an attractive place for a stroll. The central building (daily 7am–6pm) is visually striking – it forms an arch and aims at evoking the four elements of fire, earth, wind and water – and hosts stimulating exhibitions on themes such as the regeneration of the Atlantic forest, recycling and alternative forms of energy, as well as courses for adults and children relating to environmental studies. The easiest way to get there is with the *Linha Turismo* bus; alternatively catch a yellow bus marked "Bosque Zaninelli" or "Jardim Kosmos" from Praça Tiradentes. Just west of here in the Parque Tingüi, the **Memorial da Imigração Ucraniana** (Tues–Sun 10am–6pm) is a Ukrainian-style onion-domed replica church modelled on the much larger one in Serra do Tigre (see p.708) and small historical museum that celebrates Paraná's Ukrainian heritage, with a shop selling Ukrainian-Brazilian handicrafts (Tues–Sun 2.30–6pm); take the *Linha Turismo* bus to the Parque Tingüi or catch a yellow bus marked "Raposo Tavares" from Praça Tiradentes.

On the other side of town is the **Jardim Botânico** (daily 7am–8pm; R$3), another high-profile project promoting the city's green image. Created in 1991, in the formal style of a French garden, the Jardim Botânico is still in its infancy, its limited attraction being its flowerbeds and the small Museu Botânico (Mon–Fri 8am–5pm). The Linha Turismo includes the gardens as a stop, or take a red express bus from Praça Tiradentes marked "Capáo da Imbuia/Centenário".

Eating, drinking and nightlife

Given Curitiba's prosperity and its inhabitants' diverse ethnic origins, it's not surprising that there's a huge range of **restaurants** here. There are also numerous **cafés**, and a fair amount of evening **entertainment**, too, based around the usual bars, cinemas and theatres. There's an excellent selection of produce available at the Mercado Municipal at Av. Sete de Setembro 1865.

Restaurants

Acrótona Rua Cruz Machado 408. A cheap restaurant where the speciality is unusual Brazilian, Portuguese, Ukrainian and other soups. Evenings only.

Areibian Rua Presidente Taunay 435, Batel. Relatively sophisticated Lebanese dishes at very reasonable prices. The buffet offers an assortment of thirty dishes, many of them suitable for vegetarians. Closed Sun evening.

Badida Av. Batel 1486, Batel. A slightly upmarket *churrascaria* with a menu extending beyond beef to include other meats and salads. Good lunch specials. Closed Sun evening.

Camponesa do Minho Rua Padre Anchieta 978, Mercês. A long-established and remarkably good-value Portuguese restaurant. The menu's pride of place goes to dishes (most of which are easily large enough for two people) based on imported dried cod (*bacalhau*). Closed Sun evening & Mon.

Cantinho do Eisbein Av. Dos Estados 863, Água Verde. German restaurant with excellent duck and pork dishes that easily feed two people. Good value. Closed Sun evening & Mon.

Carolla Pizza Alameda Dom Pedro II 24, Batel. The wood-fired ovens turn out the best pizzas in Curitiba, made with buffalo mozzarella and other fine ingredients, and there's also a fine selection of pasta dishes and salads. Moderately priced. Evenings only (from 7pm).

Durski Rua Jaime Reis 254. Curitiba's only Ukrainian restaurant, located in a renovated house in the heart of the historic centre looking onto Largo da Ordem. The food (including some Polish, Russian and Brazilian dishes) is attractively presented and very tasty. Closed Sun evening.

Estrela da Terra Rua Jaime Reis 176. An excellent and moderately priced restaurant in the historic centre, providing *paranense* cooking at its most varied. There's an excellent *por kilo* buffet or choose from the menu that includes *barreado* (see p.698) and *charque* (dried salted beef), as well as dishes representing the Italian, Dutch, Ukrainian and Polish immigrant traditions. Lunch only.

Famiglia Caliceti (Bologna) Rua Carlos de Carvalho 1367. Most of Curitiba's Italian restaurants are concentrated in Santa Felicidade (see p.692); this is one of the few very good ones close to the downtown area. The moderate-to-expensive menu includes *carpaccio de carne* using beef of the highest quality, and there's an outstanding choice available of tortelloni and other filled pasta. Closed Sun evening & Tues.

Green Life Rua Carlos de Carvalho 271. A large, varied and inexpensive all-you-can-eat buffet drawing on produce from the restaurant's own organic farm located near Curitiba. Attached is a natural food store. Lunchtime only.

Kawiarnia Kwakowiak Travessa Woellinto de Vianna 40. This small and very authentic Polish restaurant is located at the main entrance to the Bosque João Paulo II (see p.688). A meal featuring borscht *bigos* and *pierogi* costs R$15, but it's the large assortment of delicious cakes that's the particular attraction. Open daily 10am to 9pm.

Le Boulevard Rua Voluntarios da Pátria 539 (Ⓣ41/224-8244). One of the best restaurants in Curitiba, featuring (expensive) French meals with Italian twists, all aimed at Brazilian tastes. The beef is superb. Closed Sat lunch & Sun.

Mineira Gostosa Rua Mateus Leme 491. An inexpensive self-service restaurant with a full range of typical Minas Gerais dishes. Closed Sun evening.

No Kafé Fest Rua Duque de Caxias 4. Located along an alley next to the Igreja do Rosário in the historic centre. An excellent and reasonably priced *por kilo* buffet of hot and cold dishes is served at lunch, and a German-style high tea is offered in the afternoon, in a building shared with an art gallery.

Oriente Árabe Rua Kellers 95. A good Lebanese restaurant overlooking Praça João Cândido in the historic centre. At R$16 per person, the *rodizio* is excellent value; you may also wish to try the Brazilian creation of *feijoada árabe* – *feijoada* made with lamb instead of pork. Closed Sun evening.

Schwarzwald (Bar do Alemão) Rua Claudino dos Santos 63. Located in the historic centre's Largo da Ordem, this always-crowded bar and restaurant is as popular for the range and quality of its beers as it is for its German food. Sausages and other pork dishes are the mainstays, but the roast duck is also excellent. Daily 5pm to late.

Warsóvia Av. Batel 2059. Offers moderately priced traditional Polish dishes – in many ways as "typical" a Curitiba meal as you're likely to find. Situated south of the centre in Batel, it's reachable either via a short taxi ride or a bus from Praça Tiradentes. Closed Sun evening & Mon.

Cafés and tearooms

Modern Paraná was founded on coffee and European immigrants, and one result in Curitiba has been a profusion of old-world-style **cafés** and **tearooms**, most concentrated on the Rua das Flores. Virtually unchanged in style and clientele since opening in the 1920s (elderly ladies and gentlemen in ill-fitting grey suits predominate) are the *Confeitaria Schaffer* (at no. 424), the *Confeitaria das Famílias* (no. 372) and the *Confeitaria Cometa* (no. 410), at all of which the coffee's good, the tea's bad and the cakes are sticky. In the historic centre, a very good high tea is served in attractive surroundings at *No Kafe Fest* (see above). For superb cakes, it's well worth making the trek out to the Bosque João Paulo II where there's an excellent Polish tearoom, the *Kawiarnia Krakowiak* (see above). For a pre-dawn coffee or snack, you can always join the crowds at Rua 24 Horas (see p.686).

Bars

During the late afternoon and early evening locals congregate in the pavement cafés at the Praça Osório end of Rua das Flores, but as the evening progresses the historic centre comes to life, its **bars** and restaurants attracting a mainly young and well-heeled crowd. On Praça Garibaldi, and the streets extending off it, there are numerous bars, many with **live music** – typically Brazilian rock music, jazz and what seem to be parodies of country and western. Also in the historic centre, several small bars popular with students dot Rua Mateus, just off the Largo da Ordem.

Cinema and theatre

Films reach Curitiba fast, and details of the latest releases are found in *Bom Programa*, a weekly events leaflet distributed by the municipal tourist office and most hotels. There are two good arts cinemas showing non-Hollywood productions: the Cine Groff in the Galleria Schaffer, Rua das Flores 424, and the Cine Ritz on the same street.

During the winter, the Teatro Guaira at Praça Santos Andrade, across from the Federal University, has a varied schedule of **theatre**, **ballet** and **classical music**. With three excellent auditoriums, the Guaira is justified in its claim to be one of the finest theatres in Latin America and is often host to companies from the rest of Brazil, and even international tours.

Listings

Airlines Aerolíneas Argentinas ⓣ41/3232-9012; Gol ⓣ41/3381-1744; Rio-Sul ⓣ41/3381-1644; TAM ⓣ41/3323-5201; Varig 41/3381-1588.

Banks and exchange Main offices of banks are concentrated at the Praça Osório end of Rua das Flores. ATMs are found throughout the city.

Books The best bookshop in Curitiba – and probably the best anywhere south of São Paulo – is the Livraria do Chain at Rua General Carneiro 441 (near the intersection with Rua Amintas de Barros).

Car rental Avis ⓣ41/3381-1381; Hertz ⓣ41/3269-8000; Localiza ⓣ41/3253-0330; Unidas ⓣ41/3332-1080.

Consulates Argentina, Rua Benjamin Constant 67, 15th floor ⓣ41/3222-9589; UK, Rua Presidente Faria 51, 2nd floor ⓣ41/3322-1202.

Health matters In emergencies use the Pronto-Socorro Municipal hospital at Av. São José 738 (ⓣ41/3262-1121). Otherwise, go to Nossa Senhora das Graças hospital at Rua Alcides Munhoz 433 (ⓣ41/3222-6422).

Laundry There's a self-service laundry on the corner of Trajano Reis and Treze de Maio, near Praça João Cândido in the historic quarter.

Post office The main office is at Rua XV de Novembro 700, by Praça Santos Andrade.

Shopping On Sundays (9am–2pm) the Feira de Artesanato takes over the Largo da Ordem and Praça Garibaldi, with stalls selling handicrafts produced in Curitiba and elsewhere in Paraná. For Polish and Ukrainian items, including simple embroideries and intricately painted eggs, try the shops at the Memorial da Imigração Ucraniana and in the Bosque João Paulo II (both on p.688). There's a surprisingly good selection of handicrafts, T-shirts and other souvenirs available at the airport. Shopping centres include Shopping Mueller, Av. Cândido de Abreu 127, with over two hundred shops; Shopping Curitiba, Rua Brigadeiro Franco 2300; the upscale Crystal Plaza Shopping, Rua Comendador Araújo 731, Batel, which has dozens of shops as well as a cinema; the small and exclusive Shopping Novo Batel, Alameda Dom Pedro II 5259, Batel, which specializes in women's clothing and accessories; and the enormous Shopping Estação, behind the old railway station, which has over 130 shops, numerous restaurants, ten cinema screens and a huge bowling alley.

Telephones The telephone office is next to the main post office on Praça Santos Andrade and there are small kiosks along Rua das Flores.

Around Curitiba

Apart from heading down to the coast (see "Paranaguá Bay", p.694), there are several places easily reachable by bus that are well worth seeing on day-trips from Curitiba. On the city's outskirts, **Santa Felicidade** is near enough to visit for an evening, to eat at one of the many Italian restaurants there, while **Lapa**, a small colonial country town 80km southwest is a pleasant place to go for a typical *paranaense* Sunday lunch. The agricultural processing town of **Araucária** offers interesting insights into Polish pioneer life, while just under 100km west of Curitiba is **Vila Velha**, home of a strange rock formation that's the basis of a state park.

Santa Felicidade

An outer suburb of Curitiba, about 8km northwest of the city, **SANTA FELICIDADE** was founded as a farming colony in 1878 by Italians transferred from failed coastal settlements and by newly arrived immigrants from northern Italy. Only the oldest inhabitants still speak the Veneto dialect of their immigrant forebears and Santa Felicidade now has little Italian feel to it; the European legacy is essentially that of grape and wine production, culinary traditions and periodic music and folk-dancing festivals (the highlights of which are the annual grape harvest festival in February and the wine festival in late June and early July). Across the road from the church there's an interesting **cemetery**, dating from 1886, but the only real reason to visit Santa Felicidade is for the **restaurants** that line the main road, Avenida Manoel Ribas, alongside shops selling plants, wooden furniture, wicker items, wine and other produce of the local smallholders.

The restaurants compete fiercely for customers, each vying to surpass the next in brashness. Many of the restaurants are enormous – with some seating over two thousand diners – and are favourites of visiting tour groups and Curitiba families alike. As far as the food goes, in theory most varieties of Italian regional cooking can be found, but it's best to avoid those claiming to specialize in Sicilian or Neapolitan dishes and instead try those with no particular regional claim. These places generally offer the northern Italian food in which the local cooking is rooted, with chicken and polenta being the centrepieces of any meal – the *Veneza* (closed Mon), at Av. Manoel Ribas 6860, is especially worth seeking out. Don't expect the same style of food (not to mention wine, made from locally grown American grapes) that you may have tasted in Italy. Dishes have been adapted according to the availability of ingredients and the results are, at best, an interesting blend of local Brazilian and Italian influences – rustic dishes as eaten by the *colonos* themselves. At worst, they're simply poor imitations of Italian cooking. Whether in a restaurant decked out to look like a pseudo-Italian palazzo, a medieval castle or somewhere less pretentious, charges remain much the same: about R$20 per person for the *rodizio di pasta*, a continuous round of pasta, salad and meat dishes.

Yellow **buses** to Santa Felicidade can be caught on Travessa Nestor de Castro, at the intersection of Rua do Rosário, just below Curitiba's historic quarter; the journey out along Avenida Manoel Ribas takes about 45 minutes. The Linha Turismo (see p.685) also includes Santa Felicidade on its route.

Lapa

Also worth visiting for culinary reasons, if for little else, is **LAPA**, a sleepy provincial town founded in 1731 on the trail linking Rio Grande do Sul to the once important cattle market in Sorocaba. It's only because Lapa is one of the very few towns in Paraná's interior that has made any efforts to preserve its late eighteenth- and early nineteenth-century buildings – typical rustic Portuguese-style colonial structures – that the town has become a favourite place for Sunday excursions from Curitiba.

Four blocks behind the *rodoviária*, Lapa's main church, the **Igreja Matriz de Santo Antônio** (Tues–Sun 9–11.30am & 1–5pm) dominates the principal square, Praça General Carneiro. Built between 1769 and 1784, the church is a charmingly simple Portuguese colonial structure, but its interior displays – all too typically – no original features. There are several small museums of mild interest nearby, most notably the **Museu de Epoca** (Tues–Sun 1.30–5pm), an early nineteenth-century house furnished in period style, on Rua XV de Novembro 67, opposite the Panteon dos Herois. The **Museu de Armas** (Sat & Sun 9–11.30am & 1–5pm), on the corner of Rua Barão do Rio Branco and Rua Henrique Dias, in a house of the same period, contains a poor collection of nineteenth-century weaponry.

It's the chance to sample **paranaense cooking**, rare in Curitiba itself, that makes Lapa really worth a visit; the inexpensive and excellent *Lipski Restaurante* (41/3622-1202; closed Sun & Mon evenings) is just a few metres uphill from the *rodoviária* at Av. Manoel Pedro 1855. *Lapeana* cooking is rooted in the early nineteenth century and the food carried by the cattlemen who passed through the town en route from Rio Grande do Sul to São Paulo. In particular, no meal is complete without a plate of *arroz de carreteiro* – *charque* (jerked beef) cooked with rice, onion and tomato. There are ten **buses** a day between Curitiba and Lapa covering the 80km in less than an hour; if you want to **stay** over, modest but perfectly comfortable **accommodation** is available at the *Pousada da Lapa*, Av. Manoel Pedro 2069 (41/3822-1422; 2).

Araucária

The ethnic group most often associated with Paraná are the Poles who settled in tightly knit farming communities around Curitiba in the late nineteenth and early twentieth centuries. Poles came to Brazil in three main waves: the smallest number between 1869 and 1889, the largest during the period of so-called "Brazil fever" that swept Poland and the Ukraine between about 1890 and 1898, and the next-largest contribution in the years just before World War I. Most of the Poles settling in the vicinity of Curitiba arrived in the 1880s with subsequent immigrants settling further afield in south-central Paraná.

Well into the twentieth century, the Polish community was culturally isolated, but as Curitiba expanded, absorbing many of the Polish settlements, assimilation accelerated and today the lives of most *paranaenses* of Polish origin are indistinguishable from those of their non-Polish neighbours. In recent years, however, there has been a tremendous revival of interest in people's Polish heritage, and, wherever there are large concentrations of Poles, children are encouraged to join Polish language classes, and folk dance and music groups are being established to preserve folk traditions.

One small town within easy reach of Curitiba that is making a strong effort to promote and preserve elements of the Polish immigrant heritage is **ARAUCÁRIA**, situated some 25km south of the state capital. In most respects a thoroughly unremarkable agricultural processing town, Araucária has made particular efforts to record its history. Within walking distance of the town centre is the **Parque Cachoeira**, a large recreational area with a small lake, dotted with distinctive *araucária* (Paraná pine) trees that once characterized the region's landscape. The park is the location of the **Museu da Mata e Imigração Polonesa** (Tues–Sun 10am–5pm), an outdoor museum that serves as a tribute to the area's first Polish settlers who arrived in 1886. Resembling a small village, the museum is similar to the one in Curitiba's Bosque João Paulo II, but larger. Abandoned buildings from outlying parts of this largely rural *município* have been transported to the park and renovated and, so far, the village consists of early pioneer log cabins, a granary, chapel and school, as well as a pig pen, beehive and various agricultural implements. There's an excellent book and gift store, and traditional Polish food is available.

Buses leave Curitiba's Praça Rui Barbosa hourly for the fifty-minute journey to Araucária. Once there, you'll find **tourist information** and details of special cultural events in and around Araucária at the Secretaria Municipal de Cultura e Turismo, Praça Dr Vicente Machado 25 (Mon–Fri 9am–noon & 2–6pm; ⓣ41/3843-1300).

Parque Estadual de Vila Velha

Just short of 100km west of Curitiba, in the midst of the Campos Gerais, Paraná's rugged central plateau, is **Vila Velha**, the site of 23 rock pillars carved by time and nature from glacial sandstone deposits, and looking from a distance like monumental, abstract sculptures. The formation is a result of sand deposited between 300 and 400 million years ago during the Carboniferous period, when the region was covered by a massive ice sheet. As the glaciers moved, the soil was affected by erosion and the ice brought with it tons of rock fragments. When the ice thawed, this material remained and, as natural erosion took its course and rivers rose, these deposits were gradually worked into their current formations.

The **Parque Estadual de Vila Velha** (8.30am–5.30pm, closed Tues; ⓣ42/3228-1539; R$7) is an hour and a half by **bus**, from Curitiba; from the city's *rodoviária*, take a *semi-direito* bus (roughly every hour) to Ponta Grossa and ask to be let off at the park's entrance, a twenty-minute walk from the rock formations. If you're lucky, the driver may enter the park itself, leaving you only a few metres from the beginning of the area where you can wander between and above the fantastically shaped stones, around the lakes and springs and in the wooded section behind.

Facilities in the park are excellent due to a complete redevelopment of infrastructure in 2002 and include a couple of modest **restaurants**. You can also stay in considerable comfort just outside the park at the *Fazenda Capão Grande* (ⓣ42/3228-1198; reservations essential; ❻ half-board), which offers horse riding on trails around the *fazenda*. If you decide not to stay the night, there are good late-afternoon bus services back to Curitiba, so there's no chance of being left stranded. If you're travelling on to Iguaçu, there's no need to return to Curitiba: instead, take a bus to Ponta Grossa, 20km northwest, from where you can catch an overnight bus to Foz do Iguaçu. If you don't make the connection in Ponta Grossa, the *Hotel Casimiro*, next to the *rodoviária* at Rua Fernandes Pinheiro 49 (ⓣ42/3224-0205; ❷) is a decent place to stay.

Paranaguá Bay

Sweeping down from the plateau upon which Curitiba lies, the dramatic mountain range known as the **Serra do Mar** has long been a formidable barrier separating the coast of Paraná from the interior. Until 1885 only a narrow cobblestone road connected Curitiba to the coast and **Paranaguá Bay**, and it took two days for mules and carts to cover the 75km from what was, at the time, the main port, **Antonina**. In 1880, work began on the construction of a **rail line** between Curitiba and **Paranaguá**, a port capable of taking much larger vessels than Antonina could. Completed in 1885, this remains a marvel of late nineteenth-century engineering and the source of much local pride, as it is one of the country's few significant rail lines developed with Brazilian finance and technology. Sufferers from vertigo be warned: the line grips narrow mountain ridges, traverses 67 bridges and viaducts and passes through fourteen tunnels as the trains gradually wind their way down to sea level (see below for details of schedules). Passing through the **Parque Estadual de Marumbi** (see p.697), on a clear day the views are absolutely spectacular, and the towering Paraná pines at the higher altitudes and the subtropical foliage at lower levels are unforgettable. If you want to explore the surrounding area, the charming colonial town of **Morretes**, near the foot of the mountain range, is a good base.

If the fight to save the Amazon rainforest is now on, that for the **Mata Atlântica** (the Brazilian Atlantic forest), today covering barely three percent of its original area, has been all but lost. The forbidding terrain of Paraná's Serra do Mar, however, has provided limited natural protection from exploitation by farming and lumbering interests and, since 1986, legal protection for a wider area has been granted by the state government. In theory, the region's future development must serve the needs of local communities, though the regulations are being blatantly flouted, most persistently by ranchers and plantation owners in remote regions such as on the road between Antonina and **Guaraqueçaba**, the only town on the north shore of Paranaguá Bay.

It remains to be seen to what extent the Paraná's coastal zone will remain unspoilt, but at least the future of the islands seems reasonably secure. Although beautiful beaches and coastal trails attract large numbers of visitors to the **Ilha do Mel**, strict building codes limit the possibility of anything but low-key tourist development. Other islands – most notably **Superagüi** – remain even less touched by tourism, their sole inhabitants being fisherfolk and a few people running very basic *pousadas*.

Passenger **trains** (*trem convencional*) depart from Curitiba's *rodoferroviária* to the coast at 8.15am every day, arriving at Morretes at 11.15am and (weekends only) at Paranaguá at 12.15pm; the return train departs from Paranaguá at 2pm (weekends only) and Morretes at 3pm, arriving in Curitiba at 6pm. It's advisable to buy tickets in advance from the *rodoferroviária* (to Morretes/Paranaguá R$45 second class, R$70 first class; to Curitiba R$30 second class, R$43 first class). There's also an air-conditioned tourist train, the *Litorina*, which operates at weekends and holidays, stopping at scenic points along the way. It departs from Curitiba at 9.15am and arrives in Morretes at 12.15pm; on the return leg it leaves Morretes at 2.30pm to arrive in Curitiba at 5.30pm. Tickets for the *Litorina* (to Morretes R$105; to Curitiba R$77) must be purchased several days before, either from a travel agent, or direct from the operating company, Serra Verde Express (Ⓣ41/3323-4007, Ⓦwww.serraverdeexpress.com.br) at the *rodoferroviária*. Note that only hand luggage can be carried. For the best views, sit on the left-hand side going down to the coast and on the right when returning. Avoid being persuaded on the train to buy the video of the route as it's really terrible.

If timing doesn't allow you to travel by train to the coast, take a **bus** from Curitiba that follows the **Estrada da Graciosa** (2 daily), a dramatic twenty-eight-kilometre route with 149 hairpin bends that's almost as beautiful as the rail line's. There are also hourly buses between Curitiba and Morretes, Antonina and Paranaguá by the new highway (journey time approximately 1hr 30min); many people return by bus rather than on the train. Buses between Guaraqueçaba and Curitiba take six hours (2 daily), and between Guaraqueçaba and Paranaguá four hours (2 daily), both services going via Antonina. If travelling to or from Santa Catarina, Curitiba can be avoided by taking a bus between Paranaguá and Guaratuba (15 daily, most via Pontal do Sul for access to the Ilha do Mel), and another between Guaratuba and Joinville.

Morretes

MORRETES, a small colonial town founded in 1721, lies 16km inland from Antonina at the headwater where the Rio Nhundiaquara meets the tidal

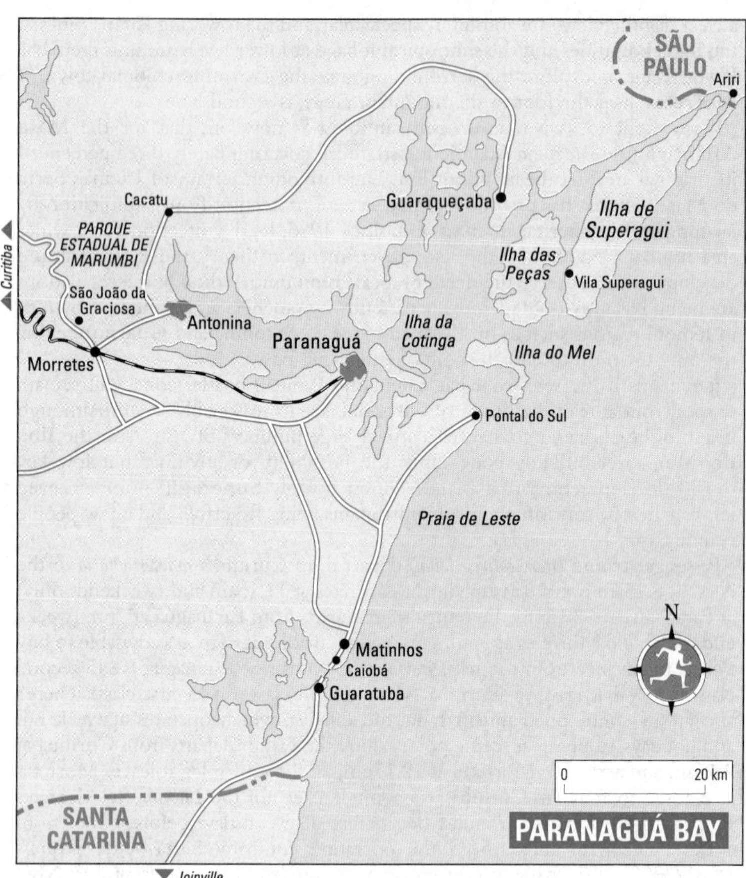

waters of Paranaguá Bay. Buses constantly pass Morretes on their way between Curitiba and Antonina, and Antonina and Paranaguá, but it remains a sleepy little town noted mainly for its production of *cachaça*, for its *balas de banana* (chewy sweets typical of the region) and for *fandango*, a local dance introduced into the area during Spanish colonial times. Most people only stay long enough for lunch, but the cobbled streets and pretty colonial-era houses and small-town atmosphere make this spot an attractive base.

Morretes is extremely compact and you just have to stroll a few hundred metres to get out of town. For a pleasant walk, the Porto Morretes *cachaça* distillery is a particularly attractive destination. Located 4.5km from town along the beautiful Estrada Marumbi, an unpaved road that winds its way through lush countryside following the course of a fast-flowing river, the distillery (daily 9am–5pm; Ⓦwww.portomorretes.com.br) produces *cachaça* that rivals some of Brazil's best, thanks to the high quality of the local sugar cane and water). Continue another 3km along the road and you'll reach a grouping of eighteenth-century sugar *fazenda* buildings, including a beautifully preserved *casa grande*, water-powered mill and distillery. Although the buildings are not open to the public, you can walk freely around the sloping grounds that feature well-tended lawns studded with imperial palms, gorgeous flowering trees and bushes. There's a simple restaurant here, the *Panorâmico Ponte Velha* (March–Nov Tues–Wed & Fri–Sun 11am–4.30pm, Dec–Feb daily 11am–4.30pm), serving delicious regional farmhouse food.

Morretes can also be used as a base for visiting the Parque Estadual de Marumbi (see p.697), and Antonina is just a short bus ride away. You can get park and local information from the very helpful **tourist office** in the Casa Rocha Pombo, Largo José Pereira 43 (daily, 8am–6pm; Ⓣ41/3462-1024).

There are several basic **hotels** in Morretes; the best is the *Nhundiaquara Hotel*, Rua Carneiro 13 (Ⓣ41/3462-1228; ③), picturesquely positioned on the river in the town centre. With less character, but more expensive and with air conditioning, is the *Porto Real Palace*, Rua Visconde do Rio Branco 85 (Ⓣ41/3462-1612; ③). The cheapest option, 500m from the *rodoviária* at Rua 15 de Novembro 1000, is the well-kept *Pousada Vista do Marumbi* (Ⓣ41/3462-1573; ②). As well as sampling the excellent local *cachaças*, you can eat well in the town's **restaurants**, mostly specializing in seafood and the regional dish *barreado* (see p.698). For the best *barreado*, head for the the *Armazém Romanus*, at Rua Visconde do Rio Branco 141 (closed Sun & Mon evening), though the restaurant at the *Nhundiaquara Hotel* also serves good food.

Parque Estadual de Marumbi

Occupying one of the largest and least-spoilt stretches of Mata Atlântica in the country, the **Parque Estadual de Marumbi** features a wealth of flora and fauna and a fine network of trails that, on all too rare clear days, provide stunning views across Paranaguá Bay. Among them is the original **Graciosa trail** (Caminho Colonial da Graciosa), constructed between 1646 and 1653 to link Curitiba with the coast, sections of which are slowly being reclaimed from the forest. If you're travelling by car, the Estrada da Graciosa takes you through the park, with rest areas at especially scenic spots.

From Morretes, there's a **bus** to the village of **São João de Graciosa**, a two-kilometre walk from the park's entrance; if you're coming directly from Curitiba, get off the train at the Marumbi stop, which lies within the park. At the entrance there's a **park office** (Ⓣ41/3432-2072), where you can pick up a trail map and information about the very basic **camping sites**; the only site hereabouts that's equipped with any kind of facilities is in São João. In any case, it's not the best spot to camp because of the heavy rainfall and mosquitoes that are characteristic of the entire region. If you're not camping, you'll find **accommodation** either in Morretes or one of the several *pousadas* located around the small village of Porto de Cima, just off the road between Morretes and São João. Especially attractive is the *Ilha do Rio*, Estrada da Graciosa Km 7.5 (Ⓣ41/3462-1400, Ⓦwww.pousadailhadorio.com.br; ⑤ half-board) with a rustic main building and cabins set within a beautiful garden with a pool. Slightly larger is the *Santuário Nhundiaquara*, Caminho do Itupava Km 2 (Ⓣ41/3462-1938, Ⓦwww.nhundiaquara.com.br; ⑤–⑥), set in park-like grounds from where you can reach forest trails, both easy ones and others that require a bit more stamina. In the park itself there are no places to eat, but São João sports numerous small **restaurants** and bars.

Antonina

An important port until the mid-1940s, **ANTONINA** has all the atmosphere of a town that has long since become an irrelevance. As ships grew larger and access to Antonina's harbour was restricted by silt, the town abandoned its role as Paraná's main port and entered a long period of stagnation. Due to its decline, many of Antonina's eighteenth- and nineteenth-century buildings have largely been saved from the developers, leaving the town with a certain dilapidated, backwater charm. With neither masterpieces of colonial architecture, nor beaches immediately accessible, the town attracts few other than Sunday visitors from Curitiba. Nonetheless, along with its much smaller neighbour, Morretes, Antonina is the most pleasant of Paraná's coastal towns, and is a considerably better place to stay than Paranaguá, only a 45-minute bus ride away. It also has an important Carnaval.

The **rodoviária** is located right in the town centre. Turn right onto Rua XV de Novembro, the main commercial thoroughfare, and walk two blocks, past some rather elegant nineteenth-century merchants' houses, then one block along Rua Vale Porto to reach Antonina's very pretty main square and evening meeting point, **Praça Coronel Macedo**. This is where you'll find the town's principal church, **Nossa Senhora do Pilar**; imposing rather than interesting, it dates back to 1714 and is built in typical Portuguese colonial style. Its interior has sadly been completely remodelled and preserves no original features. Across from the church at no. 214 is Antonina's oldest house, which is of late seventeenth-century origin.

The **tourist office** is at the railway station (Mon–Fri 9am–5pm, Sat–Sun 10am–5pm; ⓣ41/3432-4134), a couple of minutes' walk from the town centre. Boats serve the otherwise inacessible fishing hamlets across the bay from Antonina – the tourist office can provide details of departure times and destinations.

Of the places to **stay**, the *Hotel Capela* (ⓣ41/3432-3267; ❸–❹) is the most distinctive, built amid the ruins of an eighteenth-century Jesuit mission right on the main square, and has the added attraction of a pool. Also on Praça Coronel Macedo is the *Pousada Atlante* (ⓣ41/3432-1256; ❹), with very comfortable rooms, some overlooking the *praça*, and a small pool, as well as the *Monte Castelo* (ⓣ41/3432-1163; ❷), which offers basic and much cheaper accommodation.

As for **meals**, avoid the *Regency Capela*'s mediocre "international" restaurant and go instead to one serving seafood or the regional speciality, **barreado**, a dish typical of the Paraná coast and most easily found in Antonina. An especially good *barreado* (as well as fine seafood) can be found at the *Restaurante Albatroz*, Travessa Marquês do Herval 14, just off the main *praça*. For lunch try the excellent food stalls in the municipal market by the *rodoviária*, serving fresh seafood at low prices; for Dutch specialities and seafood there's the *Buganvills*, at Av. Conde Matarzzo 721.

Barreado

In Paraná's coastal towns (in particular Morretes, Antonina and Paranaguá) **barreado**, the region's equivalent of *feijoada*, appears on most restaurants' menus. This speciality, a convenience dish that can provide food for several days and requires little attention while cooking used only to be eaten by the poor during Carnaval, but is now enjoyed throughout the year. Traditionally, *barreado* is made of beef, bacon, tomatoes, onion, cumin and other spices, placed in successive layers in a large clay urn, covered and then "*barreada*" (sealed) with a paste of ash and *farinha* (manioc flour), and then slowly cooked in a wood-fired oven for twelve to fifteen hours. Today pressure cookers are sometimes used (though not by the better restaurants), and gas or electric ovens almost always substitute for wood-fired ones. *Barreado* is served with *farinha,* which you spread on a plate; place some meat and gravy on top and eat with banana and orange slices. Though tasty enough, *barreado* is very heavy and a rather more appropriate dish for a chilly winter evening than for summer and Carnaval, as originally intended.

△ Paranaguá Bay

Paranaguá

Propelled into the position of Brazil's third most important port for exports within a couple of decades, **PARANAGUÁ** has now lost most of its former character. It was founded in 1585, and is one of Brazil's oldest cities, but only recently have measures been undertaken to preserve its colonial buildings. While both Antonina and Morretes boast less of interest than Paranaguá, they have at least remained largely intact and retain instantly accessible charm. Paranaguá doesn't, though what is worth seeing is conveniently concentrated in quite a small area, allowing you the possibility of spending a few diverting hours between boats, trains or buses.

The **train station** is three blocks from the waterfront on Avenida Arthur de Abreu, with services limited to the weekend Litorina tourist train to and from Curitiba (see p.681). Inside the building is a very helpful **tourist office** (Ⓣ41/3422-6882), which has useful maps of the city, hotel lists and boat, bus and train information. The **rodoviária** (Ⓣ41/3423-1215) is on the waterfront, a few hundred metres beyond the Jesuit college. Both bus and train stations are only a few blocks from Paranaguá's historic centre, and in walking from one to the other you'll pass most of what's worth seeing of the city. Turning left out of the train station, it's three blocks or so to Rua XV de Novembro. Here, on the corner, is the **Teatro da Ordem**, housed in the very pretty former **Igreja São Francisco das Chagras**, a small and simple church built in 1741 and still containing its eighteenth-century Baroque altars. Further along is the **Mercado Municipal do Café**, a turn-of-the-century building that used to serve as the city's coffee market. Today the Art Nouveau structure contains handicraft stalls and simple restaurants serving excellent and very cheap seafood.

Just beyond the market, Paranaguá's most imposing building, the fortress-like **Colégio dos Jesuítas** (the old Jesuit college) overlooks the waterfront. Construction of the college began in 1698, sixteen years after the Jesuits were invited by Paranaguá's citizens to establish a school for their sons. Because it lacked a royal permit, however, the authorities promptly halted work on the college until 1738, when one was at last granted and building recommenced. In 1755 the college finally opened, only to close four years later with the Jesuits' expulsion from Brazil. The building was then used as the headquarters of the local militia, then as a customs house, and today is home to the **Museu de Arqueologia e Etnología** (Tues–Fri 9am–noon & 1–6pm, Sat–Sun noon–6pm). The stone-built college has three floors and is divided into 28 rooms and a yard where the chapel stood, until it was destroyed by a fire in 1896. None of the museum's exhibits relates to the Jesuits, concentrating instead on prehistoric archeology, Indian culture and popular art. The displays of local artefacts are of greatest interest, and there are some fine examples of early agricultural implements and of the basketry, lace-making and fishing skills of the Tupi-Guaraní Indians, early settlers and *caboclos*.

Away from the waterfront, in the area above the Jesuit college, the remaining colonial buildings are concentrated on Largo Monsenhor Celso and the roads running off it. The square is dominated by a cathedral that dates from 1575 but which has since suffered innumerable alterations. On nearby Rua Conselheiro Sinimbu is the charming little **Igreja São Benedito**, a church built in 1784 for the use of the town's slaves, and one that is unusual for not having been renovated. Beyond the church is the **Fonte Velha** or **Fontinha**, a mid-seventeenth-century fountain, and Paranaguá's oldest monument.

Practicalities

In the end, Paranaguá remains basically a place to pass through – it's worth getting details about leaving immediately you get here, and only later setting out to explore the city. If you find you have no alternative but to spend a night, there are several inexpensive and centrally located **hotels**, including the excellent-value *Pousada Itiberê*, just a few blocks back from the waterfront at Rua Princesa Isabel 24 (ⓣ41/3423-2485; ❷), and the more comfortable *Monte Líbano*, nearby at Rua Júlia da Costa 152 (ⓣ41/3422-2933; ❸). There are numerous **restaurants** specializing in seafood and *barreado*, the best of which is the *Casa do Barreado* at Rua Antonio da Cruz 9 (open only Sat, Sun & holidays), which offers an excellent buffet of regional dishes at a remarkably low price. Alternatively, the *Danúbio Azul*, right on the waterfront at Rua XV de Novembro 95, is reliable, or for lunch only try the excellent and inexpensive seafood restaurants in the Mercado Municipal do Café.

Paranaguá is a departure point for **scheduled boat services** to Ilha do Mel, Ilha de Superagüi and Guaraqueçaba. Boats make the ninety-minute crossing to Ilha de Superagüi every Saturday (10am) and Sunday (1.30pm) and charge R$18. The three-hour crossing to Guaraqueçaba stops off at the Ilha das Peças (departures Mon–Sat 9.30am & noon and Sun 9.30am; R$7). To Ilha do Mel there are daily boats at 9.30am and 3pm (1hr 45min; R$10). Additional boat services for Ilha do Mel leave from Pontal do Sul. Keep a careful eye on the weather as storms blow up quickly (especially in September and October, the months of heaviest rainfall), making crossings uncomfortable and potentially dangerous – if travelling in a privately owned boat check that life jackets are carried.

The Ilha do Mel and the southeast coast

To the east of Paranaguá are Paraná's main **beach resorts**, principally attracting visitors from Curitiba seeking open sea and all the familiar comforts of home. The surrounding countryside is relentlessly flat and the beaches can't really compare with those of Santa Catarina or, for that matter, most other parts of Brazil. There is, however, one notable exception, the **Ilha do Mel**, which, despite being Paraná's most beautiful island, has been protected from tourism's worst effects by being classified as an ecological protection zone – the number of visitors to the island is limited to 5000 per day, building is strictly regulated and the sale of land to outsiders is carefully controlled.

The Ilha do Mel

Of the islands in Paranaguá Bay, **ILHA DO MEL** has the most varied landscape, the best beaches and most developed (though hardly sophisticated) tourist infrastructure. With barely nine hundred permanent residents – visitors greatly outnumber locals during the peak summer months – it still has by far the largest population of any of the islands.

ENCANTADAS is the smaller of the island's two settlements but the one that attracts most of the day-trippers. Apart from fishermen's clapboard houses, all there is to Encantada is some **bars**, three or four **pousadas** offering basic but good-value accommodation (❸), a few simple restaurants, a campsite (Ⓣ41/9959-6132; R$10 per person) and a police post. In a sheltered position facing the mainland, it can feel rather claustrophobic due to the mountains all around, but only a few minutes' walk behind the village on the east side of the island is the **Praia de Fora**, where powerful waves roll in from Africa.

Livelier than Encantadas, but lacking the intimate fishing-village atmosphere, is **NOVA BRASÍLIA**, where the bulk of the island's 1200 inhabitants are concentrated. Stretched between two gently curving, sheltered bays on a narrow strip of land linking the flat western section of the island to the rugged, smaller, eastern portion, this is where most tourist facilities (such as they are) are located. Close to the jetty where the passenger boats land, there's a **campsite**, the ecological station, a police, medical and telephone post, and beyond this an immense beach along which are several *pousadas*, as well as **restaurants** and **bars** that are crowded with young people in the evenings. These are not always immediately visible, as many are hidden along paths leading from the beach. For a pleasant and undemanding fifty-minute stroll, wander along the beach towards the ruins of **Fortaleza**, the Portuguese fort (built in 1769 to guard the entrance of Paranaguá Bay), in the opposite direction from the lighthouse that overlooks Nova Brasília.

The most beautiful part of the island is the series of **beaches** along its mountainous southeast side, between Encantadas' Praia de Fora and the Praia do Farol, near Nova Brasília – an area of quiet coves, rocky promontories and small waterfalls. It takes about three hours to walk between the two settlements but, because of the need to clamber over rocks separating the beaches, the journey should only be undertaken at low tide. As the tide comes in, be extremely careful on the rocks: it's easy to slip or get pulled into the ocean by a wave. Let someone where you're staying know where you're going, and carry a bottle of water (there's a clean mountain stream about halfway for a refill) and enough money to be able to return by boat if need be. If you're carrying too much luggage to walk between Encantada and Nova Brasília, it's usually easier and cheaper to return to the mainland and pick up another boat from there rather than wait for a boat going directly between the two settlements.

Practicalities

The island is reached by direct boat services from Paranaguá (see p.699) or, more frequently, hourly **buses** from Paranaguá or Guaratuba to Pontal do Sul (where you'll find the *Hotel Jhonny*, at the bus stop, if you're stuck); the last bus stop is the beach, where small boats depart for the island. If travelling by car, there are private parking areas where you can safely park for a charge of R$12 per day. The

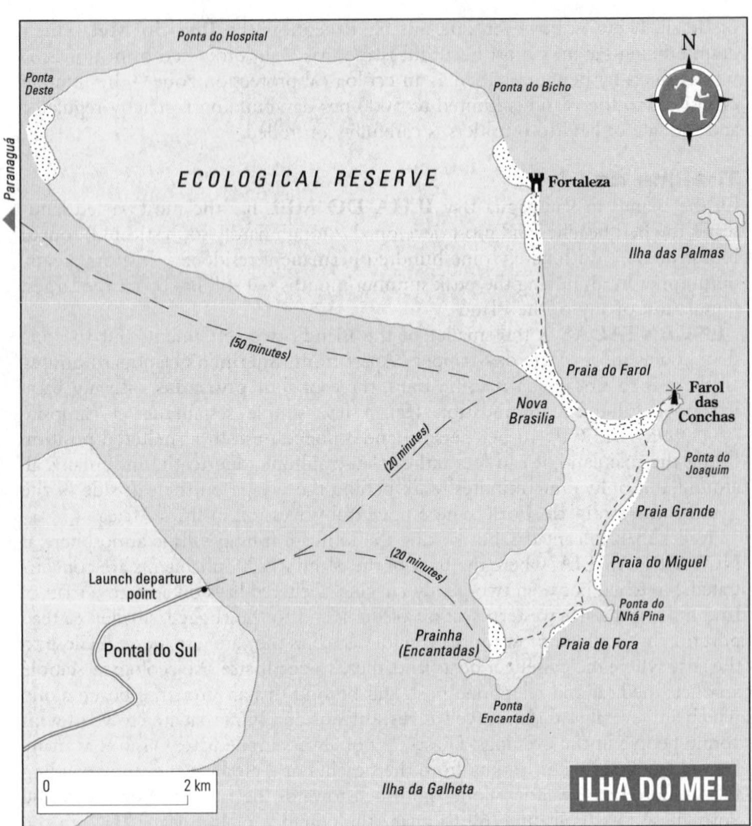

boat crossing to Encantadas (also referred to as Prainha) or Nova Brasília, the only villages on the island, takes between twenty and forty minutes, with boats departing hourly from 8am to 6pm (R$7). If you miss the last boat, it's easy to find a small launch to take you to the island at a charge of R$20–30 for the ten-minute crossing. These boats can take up to four passengers and there are usually people around to share the costs with. As there are no shops on the island, it's worth coming supplied with a flashlight and candles (electric current is available for only a few hours a day), mosquito coils, fruit and fruit juices.

If you plan to visit in the height of summer, it's best to arrive during the week and as early as possible in the morning as **accommodation** is scarce. The island is always filled to capacity over New Year and Carnaval when reservations are essential and are accepted only for minimum stays of four or five nights. There's only one genuine **hotel**, the rather ugly *Park Hotel Ilha do Mel* ⓣ41/3426-8075, ⓦwww.parquehotelilhadomel.com; ⑤ including dinner), a 45-minute walk out towards Fortaleza – they will meet you in Nova Brasília and carry your luggage. Following the trail leading from the jetty in Nova Brasília, one of the first **pousadas** is the justly popular *Pousadinha* (ⓣ41/3426-8026, ⓦwww.pousadinha.com.br; ③). The young, multilingual employees are friendly, and rooms (with or without a bathroom) are simple but comfortable. A little further along the trail, the more intimate *Pousada das Meninas* (T 41/3426-8023, W www.pousadadasmeninas.com.br; 3), is largely built from driftwood, local stone and recycled materials. The owner, Suzy, speaks some English and, if you gather together a small group, her husband will take you to outlying islands on his motorboat. There's also the extremely pretty *Pousada Praia do Farol* (T 41/3426-8014, W www.praiadofarol; 3–4 including dinner), on a beautiful stretch of beach, with fourteen rooms (half of which have private bathrooms) and a shady garden. In Encantadas try the *Ephira Pousada* (T 41/3426-9056, W www.ephira.cjb.net; 3), where the well-appointed rooms (all with private bathroom) sleep up to five people. A similarly attractive option is the *Pousada Estrela do Mar* (T 41/3426-9013, W www.pousadaestreladomar.com.br; 3).

The southern coast of Paraná

In contrast to the Ilha do Mel it's hard to find anything positive to say about the rest of the **southern coast of Paraná**, except that it's easy to get to it from Curitiba, making it a popular location for second homes for the city's inhabitants. Twenty kilometres south of Pontal do Sul is the first such resort, **PRAIA DE LESTE**, attracting families and campers. **MATINHOS**, 20km further down the coast, is Paraná's surfing capital and, during the summer months, **hotels** here are fairly expensive – though, in any case, they tend to be fully booked. If you're stuck, however, the *Casarão* and the *Beira-Mar*, both on Rua Reinoldo Schaffer, and the *Praia e Sol* on Rua União (all 3–4), are the cheapest hotels in town and worth a try.

Ten kilometres further south down the coastal road, and a ten-minute ferry ride from Caiobá, across the entrance of Guaratuba Bay, is **GUARATUBA** itself, Paraná's most upmarket resort. The best beaches are only accessible by car or private boat, so unless you enjoy being surrounded by luxury hotels and multistorey apartment buildings, Guaratuba offers little but the buses going to and from Santa Catarina.

Guaraqueçaba and its islands

North of Paranaguá, directly across the bay, lies Guaraqueçaba, Paraná's poorest and fifth-largest *município*. With 55 isolated settlements, a few poor roads and a widely scattered population of only 8000 (including a few surviving Tupi-Guarani Indians, sometimes seen by roadsides selling basketware), Guaraqueçaba's mountainous interior, coastal plain and low-lying islands give the authorities huge administrative headaches. The sole town, also called **GUARAQUEÇABA**, is really only visited by the most dedicated of fishing enthusiasts and people interested in the conservation zone which, in theory at least, encompasses ninety percent of the *município*. Guaraqueçaba is marked by a tremendous feeling of isolation, connected as it is to the outside world only by sea and an unpaved and severely potholed road, which winds about the interior for the convenience of the *latifúndios*. The owners – usually São Paulo-based corporations – are illegally cutting down the forest, most of which falls within the Guaraqueçaba conservation zone, for development as buffalo pasture or banana and *palmito* plantations. Isolation apart, the town's lack of beaches, and rain that seems to pause only long enough to enable mosquitoes to breed, do little to encourage visitors. The town is, however, useful as a starting point for visiting nearby islands, and is reached by a very bumpy three and a half-hour bus ride from Antonina (3 daily) or a three-hour boat crossing from Paranaguá. Once in Guaraqueçaba, you'll find three **places to stay** with rooms that sleep up to six people: the air-conditioned *Hotel Eduardo I* on the waterfront at Rua Paula Miranda 165 (T 41/3482-1225; 2–3), the comparatively luxurious *Hotel Guarakessaba* at Rua 15 de Novembro (T 41/3482-1217,

Ⓦwww.hotelguarakessaba.com.br; ❸) and the basic *Pousada Chauá* nearby on Rua Ferreira Lopes (Ⓣ41/3482-1265; ❶–❷). There are several **restaurants** serving home-style dishes, usually some sort of fish option. In town try *Guaricana* and *Thaíco*, both located in town on the waterfront.

None of Guaraqueçaba's buildings bear witness to the fact that, in the seventeenth century, the town was a more important port than Paranaguá. Nor, apart from the former banana producers' cooperative building at Rua Dr Ramos Figueira 3 (now the local headquarters for IBAMA, the national environmental protection body), do more than a few buildings remain from its heyday between 1880 and 1930 when ships sailed from here to Europe and the River Plate laden with bananas and timber. Today, a shadow of its former self, the port is used only by local fishermen and by boats belonging to the ecological station and municipal authorities, which are used to visit otherwise inaccessible parts of the *município*. In the IBAMA building, there's a visitors' information centre and fascinating small **museum** (Wed–Sun 9am–9pm; Ⓣ41/3482-1262) depicting the history of the *município*; reproductions of the paintings of William Michaud, a settler from Switzerland, provide vivid images of the area in the nineteenth century. Some interesting **handicrafts** are produced in and around Guaraqueçaba, with the best outlet being the non-profit Casa do Artesanato on Rua 15 de Novembro (7–10pm), which sells sculptures and basketwork produced by Guaraní Indians and ceramics, violas and other musical instruments crafted by local artisans.

Boats and islands

From Guaraqueçaba, there are scheduled **boat services** to Paranaguá (Mon–Sat 5am & 3.30pm, Sun 3.30pm; 90min; R$7). Alternatively, it's easy, but quite expensive, to charter a boat – you may find people to share one with. Though rare, good weather is highly desirable for exploring this, one of the more inaccessible and least spoilt parts of Brazil's coastline, but what is absolutely essential is plenty of time, patience, mosquito repellent and anti-mosquito coils for overnight stays. You may get stuck somewhere for days if there are storms.

Boats to Paranaguá stop off at the **Ilha das Peças**, which forms part of the Parque Nacional de Superagüi and is noted for its marine and Atlantic forest birds. You can be let off on the island and collected again later in the day on the boat's return journey (though confirm that the boat will in fact collect you).

The other regular service is a fortnightly boat to **ARIRI** (first and third Thurs of the month, returning the next day), a small fishing village just within Paraná on the border with São Paulo. On this extremely rewarding trip, the boat stops off at **VILA FATIMA**, a tiny settlement on the northwest coast of the island of Superagüi (see below), before passing through the **Canal da Varadouro**, a long, narrow mangrove-fringed channel. Ariri is only a very short boat trip from **ARARAPIRA**, a village just inside the state of São Paulo, from where another boat leaves the following day (though schedules are extremely fluid) for Cananéia and Iguape.

An occasional boat service also links Guaraqueçaba with the island of **Superagüi** and its village, **VILA SUPERAGÜI**, but as departures depend on the islanders' medical needs the village is more easily reached from Paranaguá either by a fishing boat or, in the summer, with a passenger boat (leaving Paranaguá Sat 10am, returning from Superagüi Sun 3pm; R$20 one way); a crossing from either Guaraqueçaba or Paranaguá takes about three hours. There are just a few basic *pousadas*: the *Sobre as Ondas* (Ⓣ41/3482-7118, Ⓦwww.superagui.net; ❷); the *Bella Ilha* (Ⓣ41/9978-3893, Ⓦwww.lol.com.br/~bellailha; ❷); *Crepúsculo* (Ⓣ41/3482-7135; ❷); and *Centauro* (Ⓣ41/9959-8427; ❷). All have boats that can collect you in Paranaguá and they also arrange boat trips to outlying beaches and islands. On the east side of the island, a short walk or boat ride from the village, is **Praia Deserta**, a beach stretching 34km. Here you'll see marine birds such as cormorants and frigates, and in March and April these are joined by thousands of migratory birds from North America. There are many trails on the island but only researchers working with IBAMA are allowed to venture out of the immediate area of the village or Praia Deserta.

South-central Paraná

The hilly – and in places almost mountainous – region of **south-central Paraná** makes a good stopover between Curitiba and the Iguaçu Falls for anyone interested in European, especially **Ukrainian**, immigration. As none of the towns in the region is especially distinctive, it's better to use them more as bases from which to visit nearby villages and hamlets where the pioneering spirit of the inhabitants' immigrant forebears remains. The houses, made of wood and sometimes featuring intricately carved details, are typically painted in bright colours and are usually surrounded by flower-filled gardens. Because of the ethnic mix, even small villages contain **churches** of several denominations; most hamlets have at least a chapel with someone on hand to open it up to the rare visitor.

Prudentópolis and around

The administrative centre of a *município* where 75 percent of the inhabitants are of Ukrainian origin, **PRUDENTÓPOLIS** is heralded as the capital city of Ukrainian Brazil. However, in common with the other regional urban centres, there's little in the city of Prudentópolis to indicate the ethnic background of most of its citizens. Blond heads and pink noses do predominate, but if you're expecting plump, Tolstoyesque peasants wearing elaborately embroidered smocks and chatting to one another in Ukrainian, you'll be extremely disappointed.

At a glance, Prudentópolis is much like a thousand other nondescript small towns in the interior of southern Brazil. At the heart of the city is a large Roman (not Ukrainian) Catholic church set in a park-like square totally disproportionate in size to the town. The surrounding buildings are the usual mix of anonymous breeze-block and concrete-slab municipal buildings, houses, *lanchonetes* and small stores. Still, committed Ukrainophiles should not despair. A closer look around town will reveal some traces of the Ukraine: many of the older houses bear a resemblance to peasant cottages of Eastern Europe, in particular in the style of the window frames and roofs. As throughout the region, the Ukrainian Catholic Church displays a strong presence, most visibly in the form of the **seminary**, a large mustard-coloured building next to the Ukrainian Catholic cathedral of São Josafat (masses held in Ukrainian Mon–Sat 6am & 7pm, Sun 6am, 8am, 10am & 5pm). Across the road from the seminary is the church's printing press where Ukrainian-language propaganda is churned out on machinery that has remained unchanged since soon after the first Ukrainians arrived in Brazil. A block from here in Praça Ucrânia, the excellent **Museu do Milênio** (Mon–Sat 8–11.30am & 1.30–6pm) traces the history of Ukrainian settlement in Brazil. Amidst the photographs, documents and old farming equipment are some wonderful examples of embroidery, the most interesting being those that combine traditional Ukrainian designs with representations of Brazilian birds and flowers. A women's **handicrafts** cooperative is based at the museum with a shop selling intricately painted eggs and embroidery. The work, produced mainly in outlying parts of the *município*,

Ukrainians in Paraná

In the late nineteenth and early twentieth centuries, European and North American companies were contracted to construct a rail line linking the state of São Paulo to Rio Grande do Sul. As part payment, large tracts of land were given to the companies and, as in the United States and the Canadian West, they subdivided their new properties for sale to land-hungry immigrants who, it was hoped, would generate traffic for the rail line. Some of the largest land grants were in southern central Paraná, which the companies quickly cleared of the valuable Paraná pine trees that dominated the territory. Settlers came from many parts of Europe, but the companies were especially successful in recruiting **Ukrainians**, and between 1895 and 1898, and 1908 and 1914, over 35,000 immigrants arrived in the Ukraine's "other America". Today, there are some 300,000 Brazilians of Ukrainian extraction, of whom eighty percent live in Paraná, largely concentrated in the southern centre of the state.

As most of the immigrants came from the western Ukraine, it's the Ukrainian Catholic rather than the Orthodox Church that dominates – and dominate it certainly does. Throughout the areas where Ukrainians and their descendants are gathered, onion-domed churches and chapels abound. While the Roman Catholic hierarchy, in general, is gradually becoming sensitive to the need to concentrate resources on social projects rather than in the building of more churches, new Ukrainian Catholic churches are proliferating in ever more lavish proportions, sometimes even replacing beautiful wooden churches built by the early immigrants. In Brazil, the **Ukrainian Catholic Church** is extremely wealthy, and its massive landholdings contrast greatly with the tiny properties from which the vast majority of the poverty-stricken local population eke out a living. Priests are often accused of attempting to block measures that will improve conditions: they are said to fear that educational attainment, modernization and increased prosperity will lessen the populace's dependence on the Church for material and spiritual comfort, so reducing their own influence.

The Ukrainians' neighbours (*caboclos*, Poles, Germans and a few Italians and Dutch) frequently accuse them and their priests of maintaining an exclusiveness that is downright racist in character. While inter-communal tensions certainly exist, the few non-Brazilian visitors to this part of Paraná are treated with the utmost civility, and if your Portuguese (or Ukrainian – the language is still universally spoken, in rural areas at least, by people of all ages) is up to it, you should have no problem finding people in the region's towns and hamlets who will be happy to talk about their traditions and way of life.

is technically accomplished, but sadly most pieces are mere copies of items found in books and on the Internet rather than inspired by Brazil.

There are two modest **places to stay** in town, both a couple of blocks from the main square. The best of these is the *Hotel Mayná*, Rua Osório Guimarães 935 (Ⓣ42/3446-2091, Ⓦwww.hotelmayna.com.br; ❸) with simple, clean rooms and very helpful staff. If that's full, try the *Hotel Lopes*, Av. São João 2595 (Ⓣ42/3446-1476; ❷), which is somewhat gloomy but adequate. Close by is the *Churrascaria do Penteado*, at Rua Domingos Luiz de Oliveira 1378, which, if you don't feel like grilled meat and can provide a few hours' notice, offers a hearty Ukrainian-style meal that includes a vast assortment of traditional dishes such as cabbage rolls, *bigos*, *borscht*, *pirogi* and *krakóvia*.

It's a fairly simple matter to reach Prudentópolis, well served by **bus** from Curitiba (4 daily), Foz do Iguaçu (3 daily) and most nearby centres. However, as one of Paraná's largest and most sparsely populated *municípios*, travelling far beyond the city without a car is difficult. To see some of the rural environs, though, you could always take a **local bus** (2 daily) about 10km northwest of town to the villages of **NOVA GALICIA**, sporting a beautiful old domed wooden church, and **ESPERANÇA**, where there's a school staffed by Ukrainian nuns. If you're really keen, you could then turn off the road and head north for 6km to **BARRA BONITA**, another poor and overwhelmingly Ukrainian settlement. Without a guide, however, these and other villages are awkward and time-consuming to reach. Maynátur (Ⓣ42/3446-2446, Ⓦwww.maynatur.com.br), a local agency based at the *Hotel Mayná* in Prudentópolis, supplies drivers (expect to pay about R$100 for a day) and guides (R$50 a day) who know the back roads and outlying communities well. A particularly noteworthy stop is the impressive **waterfalls** hidden amidst virtually untouched forest, which require a guide to lead you along the approach trails.

Bairro dos Binos

While descendants of Ukrainian immigrants form the great majority of Prudentópolis' population, immigrants have arrived from elsewhere as well. Perhaps the strangest, as well as earliest, arrivals were the **French** of **BAIRRO DOS BINOS**. In 1858, 87 French families arrived in Brazil to form a farming community in what was then – and still is – an extremely isolated part of Paraná. After a few years the colony all but disintegrated, with only a few families remaining. Disappointingly, but not surprisingly given the the remoteness, there remain only the faintest traces of Bairro dos Binos' French origins – the odd family carrying French surnames, and some uncharacteristic stone houses of the pioneer settlers.

Getting to Bairro dos Binos is very time consuming: take a **bus** from Prudentópolis to **Teresa Cristina** (140km north), from where it's a ten-kilometre walk west. Still, the journey to Teresa Cristina is fascinating, with the road passing through isolated communities and mountainous terrain, and Bairro dos Binos itself is quite pretty. Aim to return to Prudentópolis on the same day, but if you get stuck ask the priest at Teresa Cristina's church if he can help find a bed for the night.

Irati, Mallet and around

Smaller, and with a greater ethnic diversity than Prudentópolis to the north, **IRATI** and **MALLET** are not especially interesting in themselves, but both are useful jumping-off points for visiting the Ukrainian villages and hamlets nearby. The two towns are very similar in character, both straddling the rail line to which they owed their existence and growth during the first decades of the twentieth century. Mallet – smaller and generally less developed – is marginally the more attractive of the two, and its small Ukrainian Catholic church is worth a visit, as is the train station that dates back to 1903.

Regular **buses** link Irati and Mallet with each other, as well as with União da Vitória, useful if you're travelling to or from Santa Catarina; there are also three buses a day to and from Prudentópolis, and two to and from Curitiba. On weekdays, finding **accommodation** in Irati can be a problem, but if the business-traveller-oriented *Hotel Colonial Palace*, across from the bus station (Ⓣ42/3423-1144; ❸) is full, try the somewhat spartan *Hotel Luz*, Rua 15 de Julho 522: walk downhill to the end of the road, turn left and take the second right (Ⓣ42/3422-1015; ❷). In Mallet, there's always room at the basic *Hotel Brasil* (❷), next to the bus station. **Food** here means meat, with *churrascarias* located near the bus stations of both towns.

Gonçalves Júnior

About 12km west of Irati, the small village of **GONÇALVES JÚNIOR** is well worth a visit if you want to get an idea of local rural traditions. Of the village's four

churches (Lutheran, Roman Catholic, Ukrainian Catholic and Ukrainian Orthodox) the only one that deserves much attention is the Orthodox, which serves 24 local families. The small church, built in 1934, has an extremely beautiful interior featuring Orthodox icons, and a ceiling and walls bearing intricately painted traditional frescoes. From Gonçalves Júnior, take the Linha "B" road, along which there's a pretty chapel cared for by Ukrainian Catholic nuns. If you're walking to the chapel (allow at least an hour), you will no doubt come across plenty of *colonos*, Ukrainian-, Polish-, German-, Italian- and Dutch-speaking peasant farmers who live in the colourful wooden houses that front the dirt road, who will be happy to chat to you about their lives and those of their parents and grandparents.

Serra do Tigre

Without any doubt, the most interesting and most eye-catching Ukrainian church hereabouts is in **SERRA DO TIGRE**, a small settlement south of Mallet that still retains much of its Ukrainian character. Built in 1904, the church, spectacularly positioned high upon a mountain top near the heart of the village, is the oldest Ukrainian Catholic church in Paraná. In traditional fashion, the church was constructed totally of wood – including, even, the roof tiles – and both the exterior and the elaborately painted interior frescoes are carefully maintained as a state monument.

Without your own transport, getting to Serra do Tigre is not terribly easy. Immediately on arrival in Mallet, go to the Prefeitura and ask for a lift to Serra do Tigre on the school bus, which departs very early in the morning and then again at about noon. Alternatively, take a bus from Mallet to the village of **DORIZON**, 10km south, from where it takes about an hour to walk up the very steep hill to Serra do Tigre. The *Hotel Dorizzon* is a spa resort with reasonable food and a natural swimming pool (Ⓣ42/3542-1272, Ⓦwww.dorizzon.com.br; ❺ full board).

The Iguaçu Falls and around

The **Iguaçu Falls** are, unquestionably, one of the world's great natural phenomena. To describe their beauty and power is a tall order, but for starters cast out any ideas that Iguaçu is some kind of Niagara Falls transplanted south of the equator – compared to Iguaçu, with its total of 275 falls that cascade over a precipice 3km wide, Niagara is a ripple. But it's not the falls alone that make Iguaçu so special: the vast surrounding subtropical **nature reserve** – in Brazil the Parque Nacional do Iguaçu (Ⓦwww.cataratasdoiguacu.com.br), in Argentina the Parque Nacional Iguazú (Ⓦwww.iguazuargentina.com) – is a timeless haunt that even the hordes of tourists fail to destroy.

The Iguaçu Falls are a short distance from the towns of **Foz do Iguaçu** in Brazil, **Puerto Iguazú** in Argentina and **Ciudad del Este** in Paraguay – which makes the practical details of getting in and out that bit trickier. Foz do Iguaçu and Puerto Iguazú are both about 20km northwest of the entrances to the Brazilian Parque Nacional do Iguaçu and the Argentine Parque Nacional Iguazú, while Ciudad del Este is 7km northwest of Foz do Iguaçu. Most tourists choose to stay in Foz do Iguaçu, much the largest of the three towns, though many visitors prefer the relative tranquillity and frontier atmosphere of Puerto Iguazú.

Foz do Iguaçu

The **airport** (Ⓣ45/3521-4200) at **FOZ DO IGUAÇU** is served by flights from Curitiba, São Paulo, Rio de Janeiro, Brasília, Salvador and Belém. From

here, regular buses (5am–midnight, Mon–Sat every 15min, Sun every 50min; R$1.85) head to the **local bus terminal** in the centre of town on Avenida Juscelino Kubitschek. If you want to go straight to Argentina, get off the bus at the *Hotel Bourbon* and then cross the road for a bus to Puerto Iguazú (R$2.30). By taxi, the fixed fare into Foz is R$30, or R$45 to Puerto Iguazú (see p.712). Arriving by bus, Foz do Iguaçu's **rodoviária** (☎45/3522-3633) is located on the northern outskirts of town by the road to Curitiba and is served by buses from throughout southern Brazil, and from as far north as Rio and Mato Grosso do Sul, as well as Asunción and Buenos Aires. Buses #01, #02 and #03 link the *rodoviária* with the local bus terminal in town; taxis cost around R$15.

There are **tourist offices** at the airport (daily 9am–11pm), at the *rodoviária* (daily 6am–6pm), and on the Brazilian side of the Ponte Tancredo Neves (daily 8am–6pm). In town, there are offices at the local bus terminal (daily 9am–6pm), on Rua Barão do Rio Branco (daily 7am–10pm), and at Rua Almirante Barroso 1300 (Mon–Fri 9am–5pm). For information by phone, call the Foz tourist office, Teletur on ☎800-45-1516.

Accommodation

Finding **somewhere to stay** in Foz do Iguaçu is usually easy, and outside the peak tourist months of January, February and July, and over Easter, you are likely to be offered a knock-down rate at all but the top-end establishments. Many of

△ The Iguaçu Falls

the **hotels**, including some of the best, are located some distance from town on the road leading to the falls, and most of the cheaper ones in town cater largely to shoppers bound for Paraguay. During the summer months, the town is very hot, but all mid-range hotels have air conditioning and most have a pool.

Albergue da Juventude Paudimar Av. das Cataratas, Km 12.5 ⓣ45/3529-6061, ⓦwww.paudimar.com.br. An excellent HI-affiliated complex with superb facilities, including a large pool and an on-site travel agency offering a range of excursions. Cabins (with a private bathroom) sleep five to eight people and there are also double rooms. Lunch is available for R$5 and dinner is R$7. Although near the airport, it's a half-hour walk from the main road but regular buses pass the hostel. From the main road it's easy to flag down a bus going to Foz, the Brazilian *parque nacional* or Puerto Iguazú. R$21 per person or ③

Continental Inn Av. Paraná 1089 ⓣ45/2102-5000, ⓦwww.continentalinn.com.br. Excellent value for a high-quality – if somewhat anonymous – downtown hotel. The well-equipped rooms are spacious, breakfasts are ample, the staff are efficient and there's a good pool. ⑤

Dany Palace Hotel Av. Brasil 509 ⓣ45/3523-1530. No frills, but prides itself on cleanliness. Rooms at this centrally located spot are a/c, and some sleep three people. ③

Hotel Internacional Foz Rua Almirante Barroso 2006 ⓣ45/3521-4100, ⓦwww.internacionalfoz.com.br. The most upmarket hotel in town, with luxury facilities including a large pool, a gift shop and a nightclub. ⑧

Hotel Rafain Centro Rua Marechal Deodoro 984 ⓣ45/3521-3500, ⓦwww.rafaincentro.com.br. The rooms are large here, with balconies, and the service is friendly. Ask for a room overlooking the pool at the rear of the building. ⑤

Pousada Evelina Navarrete Rua Kalichewski 171 ⓣ45/3574-3817, ⓔpousada.evelina@foznet.com.br. An extremely friendly family-run place in the city centre that mainly attracts foreign backpackers. Rooms, all of which have en-suite bathrooms, are simple but spotless; breakfasts are adequate, there's Internet access and multilingual Evelina goes out of her way to be helpful. Well located for buses to the falls. ③

Pousada da Laura Rua Naipi 629 ⓣ45/3574-3628. This friendly, small B&B-style *pousada* has become a firm favourite for budget-conscious backpackers. Although the house is located in a central, pleasant residential section, care should be taken as young men from the neighbouring *favela* have been known to rob tourists. R$20 per person.

San Martín Rod. das Cataratas, Km 17 ⓣ45/3529-8088, ⓦwww.hotelsanmartin.com.br. Located just a few steps from both the

Parque das Aves and the entrance of the Parque Nacional. Although the spacious rooms are perfectly comfortable, the garden is the hotel's best feature, offering both landscaped areas (with an attractive pool) and natural forest with nature trails. 6

Tropical das Cataratas Eco Resort Parque Nacional do Iguaçu ⓣ45/3521-7000, ⓦwww.tropicalhotel.com.br. The only hotel within the Brazilian national park, located just out of sight from the falls. Rooms are surprisingly basic and the hotel's general feel is institutional rather than luxurious. Although the location is perfect for an early-morning view of the falls, it's inconvenient for visiting the Argentine park. The restaurant is open to non-guests and offers an excellent buffet lunch. 9

Eating and drinking

Foz do Iguaçu is certainly no gastronomic paradise, but it's possible to **eat** well without paying too much. If you're on a tight budget, try one of the numerous buffet-style *por kilo* restaurants on Rua Marechal Deodoro.

As Portugalios Av. das Cataratas 569 ⓣ45/572-3927. Friendly and attractive establishment serving excellent Portuguese food at reasonable prices. Evenings only.

Bier Kastell Av. Jorge Schimmelpfeng 362. A lively beer garden where you can enjoy ice-cold *chopp* and German-style sausage and other light meals.

Búfalo Branco Rua Rebouças 530. Upmarket *churrascaria* with the all-you-can-eat *rodizio* system and an excellent salad bar. Around R$40 per person.

Café Libano Av. Jorge Schimmelpfeng 648. Excellent-value Lebanese restaurant, equally good for just a cold drink and a bowl of humous and pitta bread as for a full meal.

Clube Maringá Porto Meira ⓣ45/3527-3472. Justly popular among locals for its superb *rodizio de peixe* lunch and stunning views of the Iguaçu river. As well as a selection of local freshwater fish, there's an excellent salad bar and you can pay a little extra for fresh sashimi. Expect to pay R$30 per person. Take the "Porto Meira" bus

and ask for directions, or take a taxi (R$10). Closed Sun evening.

Recanto Gaúcho Av. Cataratas, Km 15, near the turnoff to the airport ☎45/3572-2358. A favourite Sun outing for locals: the atmosphere's lively, the meat's excellent and cheap (R$15 per person for all you can eat) and the owner (who always dresses in full *gaúcho* regalia) is a real character. Turn up soon after 11am; food is served until 3pm. It's advisable to phone ahead. Closed Dec and Jan.

Sushi Hokkai Av. Jorge Schimmelpfeng. A fairly upscale Japanese restaurant in downtown Foz that offers reliable food and an escape from the city's bustle and often stifling heat. A varied mixed plate of sushi costs R$38; a meal of assorted tempura is R$25.

Trigo & Cia Rua Almirante Barroso 1750. Adjoining the *Hotel Internacional Foz*, this busy café serves tasty savoury snacks, good coffee and the best cakes in Foz. Open until 11pm.

Tropical das Cataratas Eco Resort Parque Nacional do Iguaçu. The only hotel restaurant worth going out of your way to try. It offers an excellent buffet lunch of typical Brazilian dishes for R$45 as well as a separate barbecue area at the *gaúcho*-themed outdoor grill.

Zaragoza Rua Quintino Bocaiúva 882. Decent Spanish restaurant specializing in fish though, being so far from the coast, you'd do well to opt for the freshwater options like *surubí* or, if available, *dourado*. A meal will cost around R$40 per person.

Listings

Airlines TAM ☎45/3523-8500; Varig/Rio-Sul ☎45/3529-6601.

Banks and exchange Dollars (cash or traveller's cheques) can be easily changed in travel agencies and banks along Av. Brasil; the latter also have ATMs.

Car rental Avis (☎45/3529-6160), Localiza (☎45/3529-6300), and Yes (☎45/3522-2956) are all represented at the airport and will deliver a car to your hotel. Note that if you are just travelling between Foz do Iguaçu and Puerto Iguazú or the two national parks, then no special car documentation is required to cross the Brazilian/Argentine border. If, however, you intend taking your rental car to the Paraguayan or Argentine Jesuit missions (see p.780) or anywhere else south of Puerto Iguazú, only Yes will issue the necessary documents (an extra R$15 per day is charged), or you will be turned back by customs officers.

Consulates Argentina, Rua Dom Pedro II 28 ☎45/3574-2969; Paraguay, Rua Bartolomeu de Gusmão 777 ☎45/5323-2898.

Horse riding You can hire horses at the *Recanto Gaúcho* (see above). Reservations are essential and the cost is R$30 per person for a two-hour ride accompanied by a guide through forested and open country trails.

Post office Praça Getúlio Vargas near Rua Barão do Rio Branco.

Puerto Iguazú

In complete contrast to neighbouring Foz, **PUERTO IGUAZÚ** is sleepy, safe and small (its population is just 30,000, compared to Foz do Iguaçu's 300,000). If you want to avoid the crowds, the town makes a better place to spend time when not visiting the park than Foz do Iguaçu, especially if you're on a tight budget, as simple hotels are more pleasant on the Argentine side of the border.

Although Puerto Iguazú is basically a relaxed place to spend an evening or two between visits to the falls, there are a few attractions besides. The **Museo Mbororé**, at the intersection of Avenida Misiones and Brasil (irregular hours, usually open in the afternoon), is worth a brief look, for its small exhibition relating to the indigenous Guaraní Indians. For a spectacular view towards Paraguay, across the Paraná River, and Brazil, across the Iguazú River, walk to the end of Avenida Victoria Aguirre (about 30min), or catch a bus, where you'll find the Marca de las Tres Fronteras, a monument proclaiming friendship between the three countries.

Accommodation

There's a good range of budget and medium-priced **places to stay** in Puerto Iguazú, as well as a number of more upmarket options. Unless otherwise indicated,

Fishing on the Rio Paraná

The upper reaches of the Rio Paraná are home to one of the world's greatest freshwater game fish, the **dourado**, a beautiful silver and gold fish with deep orange marking on its fins and tail. Known as the "golden salmon", these immensely powerful fish have long been popular with South American and European anglers alike. Similar in character to the better-known East African tiger fish, the migrating *dourado* is found as far north in Brazil as the Pantanal, but it's in the fast-flowing stretch of the Rio Paraná between Argentina and Paraguay around Iguaçu that the largest fish can be caught. *Dourado* are caught from boats positioned side-on and allowed to drift with the current, and they weigh between 13 and 18kg. The *dourado* season is from October to March, with the best time to fish being November, December and January.

Macuco Safari (Ⓣ45/3523-6475, Ⓦwww.macucosafari.com.br), organizes well-equipped fishing trips in large, safe aluminium launches. For half a day (4 hours) on the river, including collection from your hotel and all fishing equipment and bait, the rate is US$60 per person for a minimum of two people. A full day costs US$100 and includes lunch.

the following places are concentrated within a couple of blocks of the bus station. If you want to **camp**, use the good site at Puerto Canoas on the Argentine side of the national park (see p.717).

Corre Caminos Rua Paulino Amarante 48 Ⓣ3757/420-967, Ⓦwww.correcaminos.com.ar. A short walk from the bus station, this is the most popular youth hostel in town. Rooms are hot and cramped but the front yard is a relaxing place to mix with other travellers. Double room with a private bathroom for A$50 (❷) or A$20 in a dorm.

Hostel-Inn Ruta 12, Km 5 Ⓣ3757/421-823, Ⓦwww.hostel-inn.com. Buses between the town and the park stop outside this flagship hostel, which is on the main road to the park. Formerly a hotel, it offers a range of rooms that sleep two to four people, an inexpensive restaurant, free Internet, laundry facilities and a good-sized swimming pool. Although not quite as lively as the youth hostel across the border in Brazil, this is more comfortable and much more convenient for the parks. Double room with a private bathroom for A$120 (❹) or A$25 in a dorm.

Hostel Park Calle Paulino Amarante 111 Ⓣ0357/424-342, Ⓦwww.hostelparkiguazu.com.ar A block beyond the more popular Corre Caminos, the rooms in this friendly hostel are more spacious and there's an added bonus of a pool. A$20 in a dorm or A$45 for a double room.

Hosteria La Cabaña Av. Tres Fronteras 434 Ⓣ0357/420-564. Opened in the early 1950s, this is the oldest guesthouse in town, the original Bavarian-style log cabin blending well with the surrounding forest. The hosteria is quietly located a fifteen-minute walk from the town centre and the garden (which has a pool) has spectacular views down towards the Paraná River. Rooms (which sleep between two and five people) are quite basic, but all have en-suite bathrooms. The owner speaks excellent English and German. ❷–❸

Hostería Los Helechos Calle Paulino Amarante 76 Ⓣ3757/420-338. A simple hotel with a small pool that offers superb-value rooms for one to four people. ❷–❸

Hotel Saint George Av. Córdoba 148 Ⓣ3757/420-633, Ⓦwww.hotelsaintgeorge.com. A few metres from the bus station, this is largest and most expensive place to stay in town. Rooms are on the small side, smell of damp and are altogether rather gloomy, but there's a very nice pool and garden and the staff are efficient. ❺

Orquídeas Palace Hotel Ruta 12, Km 5 Ⓣ03757/420-472, Ⓦwww.orquideashotel.com. By far the most attractive and friendliest of the numerous hotels on the road between the town and the park. The rooms are perfectly comfortable, while the pool and five hectares of grounds are delightful. ❹–❺

Residencia Paquita Av. Córdoba 731 Ⓣ3757/420-434. Very basic accommodation directly across the road from the bus station. ❷

Residencial King Av. Victoria Aguirre 916 Ⓣ3757/420-360. Very competitively priced for larger-than-normal rooms, all with en-suite bathrooms. There's a very attractive garden with well cared for lawns, flowering bushes and a small pool. ❸

Sheraton Internacional Iguazú Resort Parque Nacional Iguazú ⓣ3757/491-800. ⓦwww.starwoodhotels.com. Located within the Parque Nacional, this rather hideous-looking concrete structure offers spacious rooms with balconies and outstanding views of the forest or, for a bit more, the falls. 9

Eating and drinking

What nightlife there is in Puerto Iguazú takes place in the "downtown" **bars** on Avenida Victoria Aguirre, where the town's two Internet cafés are also located. This being Argentina, **food** means beef (although most restaurants also serve *surubí*, the local fish, and pasta) accompanied by decent wine. The best *parrillas* (grills) in town are *Charo* and, slightly more elegant and expensive, *La Rueda*, both near the bus terminal on Avenida Córdoba. For a lighter meal, an attractive option is the *Café Jaroba* in the small, shady Plaza Pueblo on Avenida Victoria Aguirre. The cakes, drinks and *empanadas* here are all excellent, but what's really unusual is that the menu includes some indigenous Guaraní-influenced options.

Practicalities

Puerto Iguazú has daily direct **flights** to and from Buenos Aires, Cordoba and Mendoza; buses (A$8) to town meet arriving flights and taxis are available (A$40 to Puerto Iguazú or A$70 to Foz do Iguaçu). The car rental companies Avis and Hertz are both represented at the airport. Aerolíneas Argentinas' office is on Avenida Victoria Aguirre (ⓣ3757/420-168). Puerto Iguazú's combined local and long-distance **bus terminal** is in the town centre, with several daily departures to Buenos Aires and Posadas, near the Jesuit ruins of San Ignacio Miní (see p.780). There's a **tourist office** at Av. Victoria Aguirre 396 (daily 8am–8pm; ⓣ3757/420-800), but only the most basic of information concerning Puerto Iguazú and the wider area is supplied.

Ciudad del Este and around

Located on the west bank of the Paraná River and connected by bridge to Foz do Iguaçu, the Paraguayan city of **CIUDAD DEL ESTE** must rank as one of South America's more unpleasant urban areas. When it rains, the city is awash with mud and it can be dangerous to cross a road for fear of vanishing into one of the many potholes. In dry weather, the place is coated with a thick layer of red dust. In former years, Ciudad del Este's tax-free status made it a magnet for Brazilian shoppers, but the lowering of Brazilian duty-free allowances has resulted in a decline in cross-border trade. In response, the city is attempting to redefine its economy, stressing the financial services sector and, curiously, higher education – its two universities attract significant numbers of Brazilian students in fields as diverse as medicine and philosophy. But unless you're in

Estancia Las Mercedes

If you have your own transport, a wonderful hotel that's well worth considering as a base for both the Iguazú falls and the Jesuit missions (see p.777) is the *Estancia Las Mercedes* (ⓣ03751/431-511, ⓦwww.estancialasmercedes.com.ar; US$80 per person full board), 95km south of Puerto Iguazú (an easy 90min drive) near the bustling little town of Eldorado. The *estancia* was established as an *erva maté* plantation by immigrants from New Zealand in 1923, who built the main house and outbuildings in a style akin to that of a sheep station in their home country. Today the grandchildren of the founder run *Las Mercedes* as a cattle ranch and country hotel. There's a pool in the attractive grounds, and horse riding and canoeing are included in the rates.

desperate need of buying a cheap camera or bottle of whiskey or are heading into Paraguay, Ciudad del Este is a place to avoid.

The **bus terminal** is just south of the centre, to which it is linked by local buses. If you arrive from Asunción or Encarnación (see p.781) after dark it makes sense to cross into Brazil the next morning. The frequent buses between Ciudad del Este and Foz do Iguaçu (daily 7am–8.50pm) stop on the main street, Avenida Monseñor Rodríguez, and the parallel Avenida Adrián Jara. Depending on traffic, it can take between fifteen minutes and two hours to go from city centre to centre – it's often faster to walk across the international bridge and pick up a bus heading into Foz do Iguaçu. Day and night there are taxis available for around R$15. If you're just crossing for a day you need only wave your passport at the immigration officials, but otherwise remember to be stamped in or out of the respective countries. The Brazilian **consulate** is at Tenente Coronel Pampliega 337 (Ⓣ61/31-2309).

Ciudad del Este's **tourist office** is at the Paraguayan immigration post but you can expect only the most basic of assistance. Dollars, *pesos* and *reais* are all accepted in town, but if you're travelling further into Paraguay you'll need Paraguayan **guaranies**, available at similar rates in *casas de câmbio* in Foz do Iguaçu, Puerto Iguazú and, in Ciudad del Este, on Avenida Monseñor Rodríguez. The **post office** is opposite the bus station at Alejo García and Oscar Rivas Ortellado.

If you need **accommodation**, there are two good hotels sitting opposite one another on Avenida Adrián Jara, near the intersection with Alejo García. The *Mi Abuelo* (Ⓣ61/62373; ❷) is friendly, quiet and has an attractive courtyard, and the *Convair* (Ⓣ61/62349; ❹) is more impersonal but with air-conditioning, TVs and minibars. German speakers may be attracted to the friendly *Hotel Vienna* (Ⓣ61/68614; ❷), in Calle Emiliano Fernández, between Calle Miranda and Calle Morgelos. Restaurants are generally poor although there are a few reasonable, but very simple, Lebanese Chinese, Japanese and Korean places, oriented to Ciudad del Este's substantial Asian and Arab communities. Most are on Avenida Adrián Jara and the side roads, such as Calle Abay. For more traditional Paraguayan offerings, try *Mi Ranchito*, an outdoor *parrilla* at the corner of Calle Curupayty and Avenida Adrián Jara.

Puerto Bertoni

Definitely worth the effort is a visit to **Puerto Bertoni**, 26km south of Ciudad del Este on the banks of the Paraná River. This remote spot was the home of the Swiss naturalist and ethnologist Moises Bertoni, who settled in the area in 1890, remaining until his death in 1929. Surrounded by a small jungle reserve, Bertoni's house and outbuildings are now a museum (Ⓦwww.mbertoni.org.py), housing a small botanical collection and excellent panels (in English and Spanish) describing Bertoni's life and work. A few hundred metres from the buildings is a small village inhabited by some seventy Guaraní Indians who survive by subsistence farming and the sale of simple handicrafts to visitors. Trips to Puerto Bertoni, departing twice a day (9am & 2pm), are organized by the tour operator Macuco Safari (Ⓣ45/3527-1444, Ⓦwww.macucosafari.com.br) in Foz do Iguaçu; they last about four hours and cost R$75. From the meeting point at the restaurant of the Clube Maringá (see p.711) in Porto Meira, you'll be led to the old Brazilian ferry landing and then taken by launch 8km downriver to the Puerto Bertoni landing. From here it's a steep fifteen-minute walk up the river embankment along a jungle trail to the Bertoni's house and the Guaraní village beyond.

The falls

The **Iguaçu Falls** are formed by the Rio Iguaçu, which has its source near Curitiba. Starting at an altitude of 1300m, the river snakes westward, picking up tributaries and increasing in size and power during its 1200-kilometre journey. About 15km before joining the Rio Paraná, the Iguaçu broadens out, then plunges precipitously over an eighty-metre-high cliff, the central of the 275 interlinking cataracts that extend nearly 3km across the river. There is no "best time" to visit since the falls are impressive and spectacularly beautiful whatever the season. That said, the rainy season is during the winter months of April to July, and at this time the volume of water is at its greatest – but then the sky is usually overcast and the air, especially near the falls themselves, is quite chilly. By the end of the summer dry season, around March, the volume of water crashing over the cliffs is reduced by a third (only once, in 1977, did the falls dry up altogether), but even then there's no reduction in impact, with the added attraction of the rainbow effects from the splashing of falling water and the deep-blue sky. The one time to avoid at all costs is Easter, when the area attracts vast throngs of Argentine and Brazilian tourists.

Although many people arrive at Iguaçu in the morning and depart the same evening, the falls should really be viewed from both the Brazilian and the Argentine sides of the river: at least two days are needed to do them justice and you could easily spend longer. Crossing the **frontier** to see both sides is easy, and if you're of a nationality that normally requires a visa to visit either Argentina or Brazil you won't need one just for a day-trip. If, however, you're not returning to Foz do Iguaçu or Puerto Iguazú the same day, you'll have to go through normal **immigration** formalities on either side of the **Ponte Presidente Tancredo Neves**, the bridge that crosses the Rio Iguaçu between the two towns. There are good bus services between the two cities and onwards to the falls, but consider renting a car if your time is limited; see "Listings" p.712 for car rental details.

The Brazilian side

The finest overall view of the falls is obtained from the Brazilian side, best in the morning when the light is much better for photography. You'll only need about half a day here (longer if you're also visiting the Parque das Aves), since, although the view is magnificent and it's from here that you get the clearest idea as to the size of the falls, the area from which to view them is fairly limited.

From the local bus terminal in central Foz do Iguaçu, there are **buses** every half hour (daily 8am–7pm) to the "Parque Nacional", which cost around R$1.85 and take about 45 minutes. Buses stop at the Visitors' Centre at the park entrance where, after paying the R$20 entrance fee, you are encouraged to vist the exhibition on the ecology and history of the park before transfering onto an electric-powered open-top double decker bus that takes you to the falls. Buses stop on the road beneath the renowned hotel the *Tropical das Cataratas* (see p.712), where you're only a couple of minutes' walk from the first views of the falls.

From the bus stop, there's a stairway that leads down to a 1.5-kilometre cliffside **path** near the rim of the falls. At the beginning of the path there are trails leading to a tree walk course – a series of ropes and ladders above the forest canopy (R$80) – and to a 55-metre cliff face that you can abseil down (R$70). From spots all along the main path there are excellent views, at first across the lower river at a point where it has narrowed to channel width. At the bottom of the path, where the river widens again, there's a walkway leading out towards the falls themselves. Depending on the force of the river, the spray can be quite heavy, so if you have a camera be sure to carry a plastic bag. From here, you can either walk back up the path or take the elevator to the top of the cliff and the road leading to the hotel.

Every fifteen minutes or so you'll hear the buzzing from a **helicopter** flying overhead. It takes off just outside the park's entrance, across from the *Parque das Aves*, and offers ten-minute flights over the falls for US$60, or a 35-minute flight over the falls and Itaipu for US$150. In recent years the helicopter has been the cause of a minor rift between Brazil and Argentina: the Argentines refuse to allow it to fly over their side of the falls as they claim that it disturbs the wildlife. Whether this is in fact true is a matter of fierce debate, but certainly the view from above is spectacular and the ride exhilarating.

The Argentine side

For more detailed views, and greater opportunities to experience the local flora and fauna at close range, Argentina offers by far the best vantage points. The falls on the Argentine side are much more numerous and the viewing area more extensive and this, combined with the fact that many people only visit the Brazilian side, means that you'll rarely be overpowered by fellow tourists. With a good eye, toucans and other exotic birds can be spotted, and brilliantly coloured butterflies are seen all about in the summer months. In warm weather, be sure to bring your bathing gear as there are some idyllic spots to cool off in the river.

Getting to the Argentine side of the falls from Foz do Iguaçu is straightforward enough, but if your time is very limited it makes sense to join an **excursion**, which most travel agencies and the better hotels organize (from around R$80). Otherwise, from Foz do Iguaçu's local bus terminal take a **bus to Puerto Iguazú** (R$1.80) – there are departures every 40 minutes (7am–6.45pm; 30min); if you miss the last bus in either direction a taxi will cost around R$30. From Puerto Iguazú's bus terminal, there are then buses every hour (6.30am–7.30pm, returning 8am–8pm; A$2.80) that take thirty minutes to reach the national park's new visitors' complex where you pay an entrance fee of A$30 (or A$15 for children between 6 and 12 years old), and where you'll be given a very useful map. Bear in mind that Argentine time is one hour behind the Brazilian; Brazilian *reaís*, US currency and Argentine *pesos* are all accepted for the bus fare between Puerto Iguazú and the falls, snacks and drinks, and the Argentine park entrance charges.

At the visitors' complex you'll find a large car park, souvenir shops, a café and a restaurant as well as an impressive **Centro de Interpretación de la Naturaleza** (7am–8pm). This makes a good first stop with its **museum** focusing on the region's natural history. It's here that you'll see the extremely shy, and mainly nocturnal, forest animals – though they're all stuffed. From the centre transfer to the grandly named **Tren de la Selva**, a miniature railway that winds its way through the forest between the park's entrance and the falls. The first stop is the Estación Cataratas for the *Sheraton Hotel* and the Circuito Inferior trail; the second is the Estación Garganta del Diablo.

The **Circuito Inferior** involves an easy walk that, with a few interruptions to admire the scenery, is likely to take a couple of hours – wheelchairs are available at the Centro de Interpretación. Despite not being as dramatic as the falls upriver, few parts of the park are more beautiful and the path passes by gentler waterfalls and dense vegetation. At the river shore, **boats** (9am–4pm; free) cross to the **Isla San Martín**, whose beaches are unfortunately marred by the streams of sand flies and mosquitoes present. One of the many enchanting spots on the island is **La Ventana**, a rock formation that's framed, as its name suggests, like a window. From here you can continue around the marked circuit, but, if you are at all agile, haul yourself instead across the rocks in front and behind La Ventana where, hidden from view, is a deep natural **pool** fed by a small waterfall, allowing some relaxing swimming.

The Argentine falls embrace a huge area, and the most spectacular spot is probably the **Garganta del Diablo** (Devil's Throat) at **PUERTO CANOAS**. The Garganta del Diablo marks a point where fourteen separate falls combine to form the world's most powerful single waterfall in terms of the volume of water flow per second. Catwalks lead into the middle of the river to a central viewing platform, from where it's easy to feel that you will be swallowed by the tumbling waters: be prepared to get drenched by the spray, mist and rain. From Puerto Canoas the train will take you back to the park's entrance complex from where there are frequent buses that link directly with Puerto Iguazú.

The forest

One of the remarkable aspects of the park is that visitors can gain access to a **semi-deciduous tropical rainforest** without any difficulty and without posing a threat to people or nature. Even by keeping to the main paths around the falls, it's easy to get a taste of the jungle, in particular in the Argentine park. The forest is home to over two thousand plant varieties, four hundred bird species, dozens of types of mammals and innumerable insects and reptiles. It's essentially made up of four levels of vegetation: a nearly closed canopy reaching over 35m; a layer of trees between 3 and 10m in height; a lower layer of shrubs; and a herbaceous ground level. In reality the levels are not so pronounced, as epiphytes and other plants intertwine, at times creating a mass of matted vegetation.

Within the forest lives a rich diversity of **wildlife** species, but they are spread out over a wide area, are often nocturnal and are usually extremely timid. However, if you get up early, walk quietly away from other people and look up into the trees as well as towards the ground, you have a chance of seeing something. Jaguars and mountain lions have been seen in Iguaçu, but they keep so well hidden and so few remain that realistically your chances of observing them are minimal. Around the water's edge, you may occasionally see **tapirs**, large animals shaped rather like a pig with a long snout. Smaller, but also with a pig-like appearance is the **peccary**, dangerous when cornered, but shy of humans.

Far more common is the **coatimundi**, the size of a domestic cat but related to the racoon. Even on the main paths on the crowded Brazilian side of the falls, you often come face to face with coatimundi, hoping to scrounge food from tourists although feeding the animals is strictly forbidden. The *caí*, or **capuchin monkey**, is also often seen and is recognizable by its long legs and tail, small size and black skullcap mark that gives it its name. These monkeys travel the forest canopy in large groups and emit strange bird-like cries. Far bigger and with a deep voice is the **howler monkey**. You may not see any, but you're likely to hear their powerful voices emanating from the jungle. Insects, however, are always to be seen, with butterflies one of the forest's most memorable sights, especially in the summer.

The forest is also home to a rich variety of **birdlife**, and with a good eye you should be able to see toucans, parakeets and hummingbirds even without straying from the main paths. Again, their most active hours are soon after dawn when it's cooler. For a more reliable view of local birdlife, a visit to the **Parque das Aves** (daily 8.30am–6.30pm; US$8 or the equivalent in Brazilian reais) is highly recommended, although serious bird watchers are likely to be scornful of a place that allows such effortless viewing. Located just 100m from the Visitors' Centre of the national park on the Brazilian side of the falls, the bird park maintains both small breeding aviaries and enormous walk-through aviaries, still surrounded by dense forest. There's also a large walk-through butterfly cage – butterflies are bred throughout the year and released when mature. All the butterflies and eighty percent of the birds are Brazilian, most of them endemic to the Atlantic forests, the main exception being those in the Pantanal aviary.

Trips into the forest are organized in the Argentine park, and tickets are available at the offices of Iguazú Jungle Explorer (ⓣ3757/421-600, ⓦwww.iguazujungleexplorer.com) located at the Circuito Inferior. A typical trip lasts around two hours (A$80), and involves being driven in the back of a truck along a rough road through the forest, a walk down a narrow trail to the river, and a wild boat ride down some rapids towards the Garganta del Diablo. Don't expect to see any wildlife (much of which is nocturnal), but guides may point out some of the flora. You stand a better chance of seeing some animals – or at least hearing them – at night; escorted moonlit walks take place on two or three nights a month around the time of the full moon (8–10pm; A$15). Sign up at the Visitors Centre (Centro de Visitantes).

It's also possible to rent **mountain bikes** from Iguazú Jungle Explorer; you will be given a map with which you can explore some of the trails.

Yacutinga

About 50km east of the Parque Nacional Iguazú in Argentina, the smaller **Refugio de Vida Silvestre Yacutinga** (Ⓦwww.yacutinga.com) is in many ways a more appealing experience for visitors. The reserve is located on the Yacutinga peninsula, on the south bank of the Iguaçu River, and covers 570 hectares, almost all of it Mata Atlântica. As well as conducting environmental research projects, the privately run reserve works with neighbouring farming communities to encourage environmental awareness and sustainable agriculture. Expert English-speaking **guides** take you along trails within the refuge, with walks typically lasting an hour or two, while float trips on the Iguaçu River and tributaries are also offered most days. What you see, of course, varies enormously, but capuchin monkeys, deer, otters, caimans and other lizards are common sights, and there are ample birdwatching opportunities to satisfy both casual and serious birdwatchers alike. Although the longer trails require a guide, there is one short and clearly signposted trail that you can take unaccompanied, and you'll also find walkways strung between trees from where you can look out for birds or animals or just take in the serenity of the rainforest.

Visits to Yacutinga must be arranged in advance through a **travel agent**; contact the reserve by email for an agent in your locality. The cost for two nights and three days at the *Yacutinga Lodge*, with full board and the services of the local guides, is about US$350 per person. The price includes transfer by truck and river to the lodge – the road is atrocious, the three-hour drive is bone shattering, but the scenery is fascinating , at first passing through the Parque Nacional before entering a zone of smallholdings, mainly farmed by families of German descent. Accommodation is in rustic but extremely comfortable cabins, all of which have a private bathroom and a wood stove (essential for the chilly winter nights). The main lodge, which is built largely from local stone and wood from naturally fallen trees and blends remarkably unobtrusively into its forest setting, has a lounge, bar and restaurant, while outside there's a swimming pool and an open-air bar. Meals are superb, with an emphasis on varieties of locally sourced squash, beans and other vegetables.

Itaipu

While there's complete agreement that Iguaçu is one of the great natural wonders of Brazil, there's bitter debate as to what **Itaipu** – the world's largest hydroelectricity scheme – represents. Work on the dam, 10km north of Foz do Iguaçu, began in the early 1970s at a cost of US$25 billion, and its eighteen 700,000 kilowatt generators became fully operational in 1991. Proponents of the project argue that the rapidly growing industries of southeastern Brazil needed nothing less than Itaipu's huge electrical capacity, and that without it Brazilian development would be greatly impeded. However, critics claim that Brazil neither needs nor can afford such a massive hydroelectric scheme and that the country would have been much better served by smaller and less prestigious schemes nearer to the centres of consumption. In addition, they point to the social and environmental upheavals that have been caused by the damming of the Rio Paraná and the creation of a 1350-square-kilometre reservoir: forty thousand families have been forced off their land; a microclimate with as yet unknown consequences has developed; and – critics say – the much publicized animal rescue operations and financial assistance for displaced farmers barely address the complex problems.

Visiting Itaipu is easy, with hourly **buses** from Foz do Iguaçu's local bus terminal. You're dropped at the **Visitors' Centre** where a film about the project, in English and other languages, is shown, and from where **guided tours** of the complex depart (Mon–Sat 8 daily; 2hr; R$30; Ⓦwww.itaipu.gov.br). The film is extremely slick and, until you stand on the dam and look across the massive reservoir stretching into the horizon, it's easy to be convinced by Itaipu's PR machine that the project was, at worst, no more than a slight local inconvenience.

Santa Catarina

Santa Catarina shares a similar pattern of settlement with other parts of southern Brazil, the indigenous Indians rapidly being displaced by outsiders. In the eighteenth century the state received immigrants from the Azores who settled along the coast; cattle herders from Rio Grande do Sul spread into the higher reaches of the mountainous interior around **Lages** and **São Joaquim**; and European immigrants and their descendants made new homes for themselves in the fertile river valleys. Even today, small communities on the **island of Santa Catarina**, and elsewhere on the coast, continue a way of life that has not changed markedly over the generations. Incidentally, to prevent confusion with the name of the state (though barely succeeding at times), most people call the island of Santa Catarina **Florianópolis**, which is actually the name of the state capital – also situated on the island. Elsewhere, cities such as **Blumenau** and **Joinville**, established by German immigrants, have become totally Brazilianized, but in the surrounding villages and farms many people still speak the language of their forebears in preference to Portuguese.

On the coast, tourism has become very important and facilities are excellent, though the considerable natural beauty is in danger of being eroded by the uncontrolled development that has been taking place in recent years. Inland, though, visitors rarely venture, despite the good roads and widely available hotels. Here, with the minimum of discomfort, it's possible to get a sense of the pioneering spirit that brought immigrants into the interior in the first place – and keeps their descendants there.

The island of Santa Catarina

The **island of Santa Catarina** is noted throughout Brazil for its Mediterranean-like scenery, attractive fishing villages and the city of Florianópolis, the state's

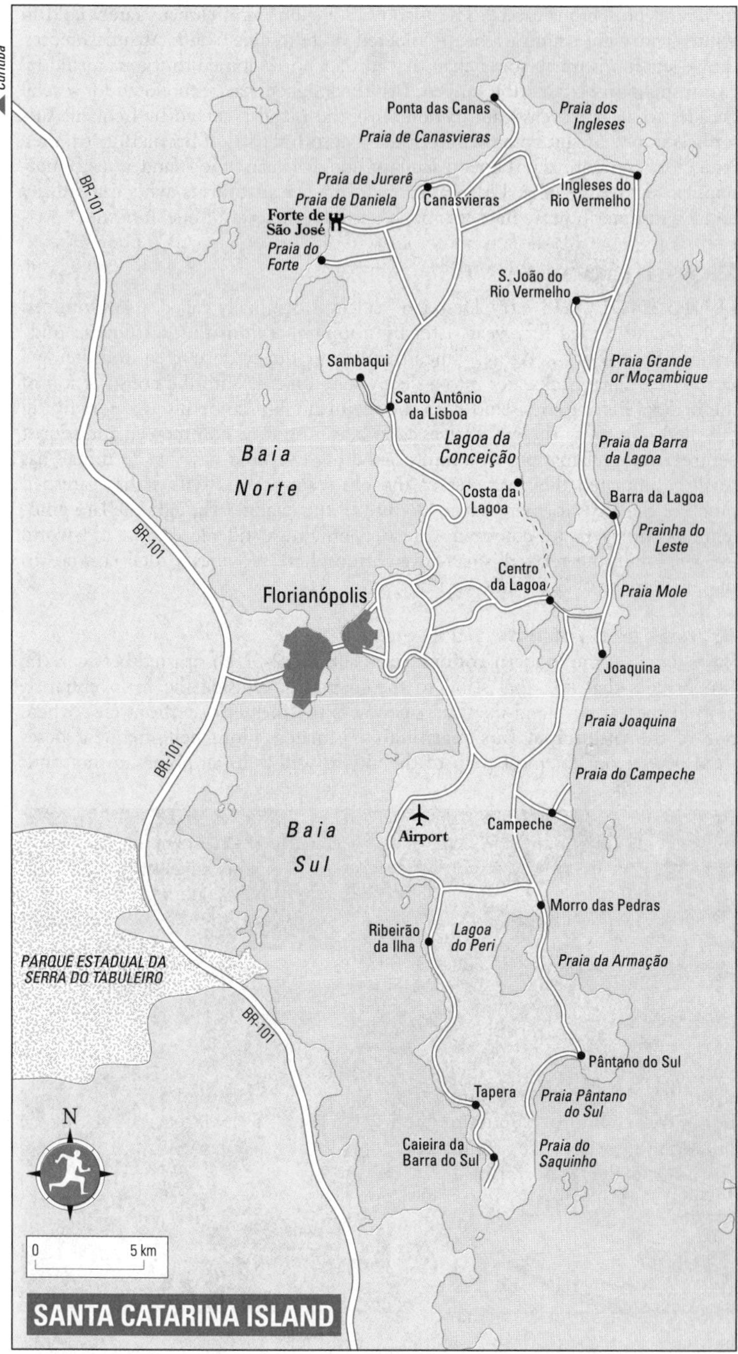
Curitiba
Ponta das Canas
Praia dos Ingleses
Praia de Canasvieras
Praia de Jurerê
Canasvieras
Ingleses do Rio Vermelho
Praia de Daniela
Forte de São José
Praia do Forte
S. João do Rio Vermelho
BR-101
Sambaqui
Praia Grande or Moçambique
Santo Antônio da Lisboa
Lagoa da Conceição
Praia da Barra da Lagoa
Baia Norte
Costa da Lagoa
Barra da Lagoa
Prainha do Leste
Centro da Lagoa
Florianópolis
Praia Mole
Joaquina
Praia Joaquina
Praia do Campeche
Baia Sul
Airport
Campeche
Morro das Pedras
Ribeirão da Ilha
Lagoa do Peri
Praia da Armação
PARQUE ESTADUAL DA SERRA DO TABULEIRO
Pântano do Sul
Tapera
Praia Pântano do Sul
Caieira da Barra do Sul
Praia do Saquinho
N
0
5 km
SANTA CATARINA ISLAND
Porto Alegre

small and prosperous capital. The island has a subtropical climate, rarely cold in winter and with a summer heat tempered by refreshing South Atlantic breezes; the vegetation is much softer than that further north. Joined to the mainland by two suspension bridges (the longest, British-designed, has been closed for several decades to all but cyclists and pedestrians), the island is served by frequent **bus** services connecting it with the rest of the state, other parts of Brazil, Buenos Aires, Asunción and Santiago. During January and February the island is extremely popular with Argentine, Uruguayan and Paraguayan tourists who can usually enjoy a summer holiday here for much less than the cost of one at home.

Florianópolis

FLORIANÓPOLIS – or "Desterro" as it was originally called – was founded in 1700 and settled fifty years later by immigrants from the Portuguese mid-Atlantic islands of the Azores. Since then, it's gradually developed from being a sleepy provincial backwater into a sleepy state capital. With the construction of the bridges linking the island with the mainland, Florianópolis as a port has all but died, and today the city thrives as an administrative, commercial and tourist centre. Land reclamation for a multi-laned highway and new bus terminals has totally eliminated the character of the old seafront, and with it has vanished much of the city's former charm. Despite all the changes, though, the late nineteenth-century pastel-coloured, stuccoed buildings still recall faint old-world images, while the relaxed, small-town atmosphere provides a total contrast to the excitement of São Paulo or Rio.

Arrival and information

Buses arrive at the modern **rodoviária** (Ⓣ48/3212-3100) situated between the two bridges that link the island to the mainland. Outside the main entrance, beyond the car park and dual carriageway, is the former waterfront area where one of the **municipal bus terminals** is situated. From here, frequent buses (R$1.90) set out for most parts of the city as well as to all points in the south

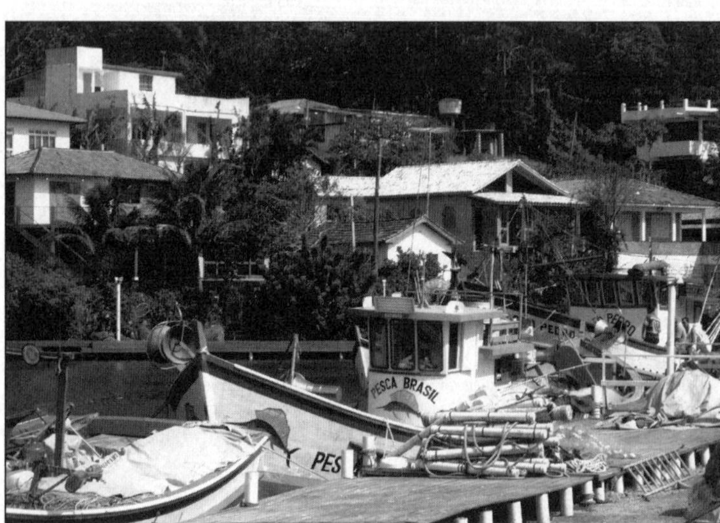

△ Florianópolis

of the island. Otherwise, buses to the northern and eastern beach resorts depart from the corner of Rua José da Costa Moelmann and Avenida Mauro Ramos, a fifteen-minute walk around the hillside. These buses run to a surprisingly accurate timetable (check times at the information booths) and are cheap, though generally crowded. Alternatively, from both terminals there are faster, more comfortable and more expensive *executivo* minibuses ($1) to most of the beaches.

The **airport** (ⓣ48/3331-4000) serves São Paulo, Curitiba, Porto Alegre and Brasília as well as destinations in the western Santa Catarina and Argentina. Located 12km south of the city centre, the airport is served by taxis (R$32 to the city centre or R$40 to Lagoa) and "Aeroporto" buses (R$1.90), which take about forty minutes to get to the centre.

In the city centre's Mercado Público**, there's a tourist information kiosk** (Dec–March Mon–Sat 7am–10pm, Sun 7am–7pm; April–Nov Mon–Sat 8am–6pm; ⓣ48/3212-3127), where very good, free maps of the island and city are available; there are also branches at the *rodoviária* (daily 8am–7pm) and at the airport (daily 8am–7pm). Listings of events in Florianópolis and elsewhere in Santa Catarina can be found in the daily newspaper *Diário Catarinense*.

Accommodation

Most tourists choose to stay at the beaches and resorts around the island (see "The rest of the island" pp. 726–731), but staying in the city centre has the benefit of a concentration of reasonably priced hotels, and direct bus services to all parts of the island. Try to arrive early in the day as **accommodation** is snapped up quickly during the peak holiday periods, and it's especially difficult to get a bed at the well-cared-for **youth hostel** at Rua Duarte Schutell 227 (open year-round; ⓣ48/3225-3781; R$25 per person). Many of the cheapest **hotels** are located on, or just off, Rua Felipe Schmidt, only a few minutes from both Praça XV de Novembro and the bus terminals.

Baía Norte Palace Av. Beira Mar Norte ⓣ48/3229-3144, ⓦwww.baianorte.com.br. Pleasant rooms, but be sure to ask for one facing the ocean. Although just a short walk from good bars and restaurants, it's a longer trek into the commercial centre itself. ❺

Colonial Rua Conselheiro Mafra 399 ⓣ48/3222-2302. Simple, good-sized rooms, often none too clean, but the service is friendly. ❷

Faial Rua Felipe Schmidt 603 ⓣ48/3225-2766, ⓦwww.hotelfail.com.br. Large, modern hotel with spacious, if bland, rooms, and helpful staff. Good value. ❺

Felipe Rua João Pinto 26, at the intersection with Rua Antônio Luz ⓣ48/3222-4122. The rooms here are neat and small, with ten percent discounts offered to youth hostel association card-holders. ❷

Florianópolis Palace Rua Artista Bittencourt 14 ⓣ48/2106-9633, ⓦwww.floph.com.br. The nearest there is to a luxury hotel in the city centre, with good facilities and a certain fading elegance. ❻

Ibis Av. Rio Branco 37 ⓣ48/3216-0000, ⓦwww.accorhotels.com.br. A typical Ibis value-for-money package featuring small, well-laid-out rooms and friendly, efficient service. Always popular and reservations are highly recommended. ❹

Oscar Palace Av. Hercílio Luz 760 ⓣ48/3222-0099, ⓦwww.oscarhotel.com.br. Favoured by Argentine tourists and business travellers, this hotel offers comfortable rooms and friendly service. ❹

Sumaré Rua Felipe Schmidt 423 ⓣ48/3222-5359. Long-established, very basic budget hotel, good for the price and location in the heart of the city centre. The best rooms overlook the pedestrianized street and all have a private bathroom. ❸

Valerim Plaza Rua Felipe Schmidt 705 ⓣ48/2106-0200, ⓦwww.hotelvalerim.com.br. A good budget hotel with rooms (some sleeping up to six) that are air-conditioned and equipped with TV and *frigobar*. ❹

The City

With the notable exception of Carnaval – rated among the country's most elaborate, and certainly the liveliest south of Rio – few tourists visit the island for the limited charm and attractions of Florianópolis itself. However, being so centrally located, the city does make a good base for exploring the rest of the island, as most points are easily reached within an hour by bus. Take time, though, for at least a stroll around Florianópolis before heading out to the beaches.

On the former waterfront, you'll find two late nineteenth-century Neoclassical ochre-coloured buildings, the **Mercado Público** (Mon–Fri 7am–7pm, Sat 7am–1.30pm), which contain some excellent bars and small restaurants, and the **Alfândega** (Mon–Fri 9am–6.30pm, Sat 8am–noon), the former customs house that has been converted for use as the Casa das Açores crafts market. From here, there's a steep walk up Rua Deodoro, past the early nineteenth-century Igreja São Francisco, to the **Rua Felipe Schmidt**, the commercial artery of the Praia de Fora, the "new town". At the end of the pedestrianized section of Rua Felipe Schmidt is the main, tree-filled square, **Praça XV de Novembro**, very much the heart of the new town. On one side of the square is the **Palácio Cruz e Souza**, an imposing pink building built between 1770 and 1780 as the seat of provincial government. It's now open to the public as the **Museu Histórico de Santa Catarina** (daily 10am–4pm; R$4) and it's worth taking a brisk walk around the building to admire the ornate nineteenth-century interior decoration, rather than to examine the unexciting collection of guns, swords and official scrolls. On the other side of the *praça* is Florianópolis' main post office and, just behind it at Rua Victor Meirelles 59, the **Museu Victor Meirelles** (Tues–Fri 1–6pm; Ⓦwww.museuvictormeirelles.org.br). Meirelles was born in this building in 1832 and went on to become famous for his historically themed paintings. The museum is surprisingly interesting: sixteen of Meirelles' paintings are displayed on the first floor (most notable being the *Battle of Guararapes*, which celebrates Portugal's acquisition of Northeastern Brazil from the Dutch in 1649), while the first floor is used for visiting exhibits of other Brazilian artists.

Overlooking the square from the highest point is the utterly unremarkable **Catedral Metropolitana**; it was originally constructed between 1753 and 1773, but was enlarged and totally remodelled in 1922, so you'd be hard-pressed to identify any original features. The only church in the city centre dating back to the colonial era is the simple but charming mid-eighteenth-century **Igreja de Nossa Senhora do Rosário**, higher up from the cathedral and best approached by a flight of steep steps from Rua Marechal Guilherme.

On the campus of the Federal University (UFSC), twenty minutes by bus from the city centre, the **Museu de Antropologia** (Mon–Fri 9am–noon & 1–5pm) has a small collection of artefacts belonging to Santa Catarina's decimated Kaingang and Xokleng forest Indians and objects relating to early Azorean immigrants that's worth an hour or so on a rainy day. The **Museu de Arte de Santa Catarina** (Mon–Fri 9am–noon & 3–9pm, Sat & Sun 5–10pm), in the Centro Integrado de Cultura (reached by buses marked "Agronomica"), hosts permanent and temporary exhibitions by local and national artists of often dubious talent. The centre itself also boasts an arts cinema; a detailed programme is published in the *Diário Catarinense*.

Eating, drinking and nightlife

In **the centre**, on the roads that run off the main square in all directions, are numerous cheap, but largely uninspiring **restaurants**. One of the more distinctive is *Kaffa*, on Rua Victor Meirellas behind the main post office, which offers huge portions of satisfying and very reasonably priced Lebanese food. Good vegetarian meals are available in the centre at *Vida*, Rua Visconde de Ouro Preto 62 (Mon–Sat lunch only), as well as at the *Sol da Terra*, Rua Nereu Ramos 13, *Natural Familia Doll*, Rua Vidal Ramos 43a (both close at 5pm), and out near the federal university (UFSC) at *Soul Salada* in Trinidade Shopping, Rua Lauro

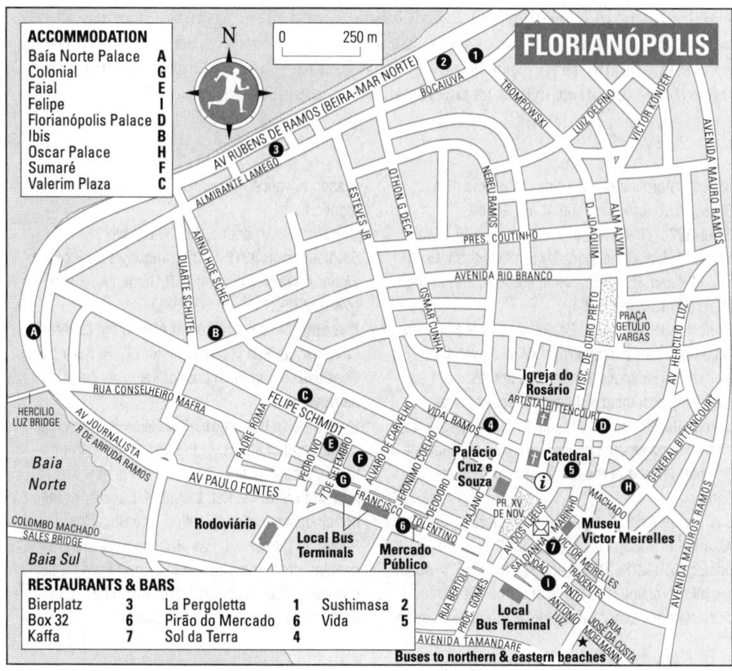

Linhares (Mon–Sat to early evening). There are several excellent bars and simple restaurants in the Mercado Público, serving cold beer, light meals and tasty snacks: *Box 32* (closed Sat evening and Sun) is especially good and is known as a meeting point for local politicians and artists, while *Pirão do Mercado* (Mon–Sat lunch only) specializes in local dishes of Azorean origin.

Come evening, there's very little life in the commercial centre around Praça XV de Novembro. Instead, people head for the **bars and restaurants** that spread out along the **Beira Mar Norte** (or Avenida Rubens de Arruda Ramos as it is officially called), a dual carriageway that skirts the north of the city along reclaimed land starting at the Hercílio Luz bridge, or head for much more fashionable Lagoa (see p. 727). Places move in and out of popularity rapidly and in summer you'll find that the bars – the first two of which are situated virtually under the bridge itself – are either packed solid with wealthy young people or, for no apparent reason, totally empty. Unfortunately the restaurants here aren't particularly good either and are generally expensive, but there is at least a fair choice, which is more than can be said for the commercial centre. Towards the far end of Beira Mar Norte (take any bus that reads "via Beira Mar Norte") there are several worth noting: at no. 1990 on the avenue itself, *Sushimasa* (closed Tues–Fri lunch & Mon) is a competent Japanese restaurant, and nearby are some pretty good Italian places, the best being *La Pergoletta* (open Tues–Sat evening and Sun) at Travessa Carreirão 62. Cold beer and hearty German dishes are available until late into the night at the *Bierplatz*, Beira Mar Norte 210. Further north, in the Beira Mar Norte Shopping Center (Mon–Sat 10am–10pm), there are a dozen fast-food outlets including the usual hamburgers as well as seafood and a decent vegetarian restaurant. The best Japanese food on the island is at *Miyoshi*, located yet further north, at Km 3.5 of the SC-

401 highway, in the suburb of Saco Grande; a taxi there from the centre will cost around R$20. The best times to go are Tuesday and Friday evenings when there's a very reasonably priced *por kilo* buffet that includes an excellent sushi and sashimi selection – on other evenings the restaurant is much more expensive.

Listings

Airlines Aerolíneas Argentinas, Rua Tenente Silveira 200, 8th floor, and at the airport ⓣ48/3224-7835; Gol, at the airport ⓣ48/3331-4127; TAM, at the airport ⓣ48/3331-4085; Varig/RioSul/Pluna, Rua Felipe Schmidt 228, and at the airport ⓣ48/3331-4154.
Banks and exchange Banks are located on Rua Felipe Schmidt and by Praça XV de Novembro.
Books Florianópolis' bookshops are poor, but you may find something of local interest at Livros e Livros, Rua Deodoro 191, sala 2; Lunardelli, Rua Victor Meirellas 28; Livraria Catarinense, Rua Felipe Schmidt 60 and in the Beira Mar Norte Shopping Center.
Car rental Avis (ⓣ48/236-1426), Hertz (ⓣ48/236-9955), Localiza (ⓣ48/236-1244), Unidas (ⓣ48/236-0607) and Yes (ⓣ48/284-4656) are all represented at the airport and can arrange delivery in the city centre. During the peak summer season advance reservations are strongly recommended.
Consulates Argentina, Av. Rio Branco 387, 5th floor ⓣ48/3216-8903; Uruguay, Rua Prof. Walter de Bona Castelan 559, Jardim Anchieta ⓣ48/3222-3718.
Internet There's an Internet café in the Livraria Catarinense, Rua Felipe Schmidt 60 (R$5 per hour).
Post office The main post office is on Praça XV de Novembro.
Shopping In the centre, Rua Felipe Schmidt has a full range of shops. At the former waterfront, the Alfândega building (see p.724) is now an arts and crafts market, though the quality of the merchandise is disappointing. The Beira Mar Norte Shopping Center is on Av. Rubens de Arruda Ramos heading north from the centre. Apart from numerous surf-oriented shops, it contains all the usual Brazilian fashion brand-name shops.

The rest of the island

Most people arriving in Florianópolis head straight for the **beaches**, undoubtedly the best of which are found on the **north** and **west** coasts. With 42 beaches around the island to choose from, even the most crowded are rarely unbearably so, and they're all suited to a few days' winding down. Despite the existence of a good **bus network**, this is one place where **renting a car** (see "Listings" above) should be seriously considered, especially if you have limited time and want to see as much of the island as possible: the roads are all excellent, though crowded in summer, and the drivers fairly civilized.

The north coast

The island's increasingly built-up **north coast** offers safe swimming in calm, warm seas and, as such, is particularly popular with families. The long, gently curving bay of **CANASVIERAS** is the most crowded of the northern resorts, largely geared towards Paulista, Argentine and Uruguayan families who own or rent houses near to the beach. Most of the bars along the beach cater to the tourists, playing Argentine and North American pop music, and serving Argentine snacks accompanied by Brazilian beer. By walking away from the concentration of bars at the centre of the beach, towards the east and Ponta das Canas, it's usually possible to find a relatively quiet spot. Unless you're renting a house for a week or more (agencies abound), finding **accommodation** is difficult, as the unappealing hotels are usually booked solid throughout the summer months. However, if you're set on staying here, by asking in the souvenir shops and restaurants you'll eventually be directed to someone with a spare **room to rent**. The local **restaurants** mostly offer the same menu of prawn dishes, pizza and hamburgers, with only the *Restaurante Tropical*, on the road that runs parallel to the beach, and its *bahian* dishes standing out as different.

Heading westwards you'll reach **JURERÊ**, another long beach that almost exclusively attracts families, and is separated from Canasvieras by a rocky promontory. Still further west, a series of coves fringed by luxuriant vegetation – reached by clambering down from the road skirting the coast, or by climbing over the rocks that separate one cove from another – link Jurerê to **DANIELA**, a smaller and less developed beach. Though it amounts to nothing special, the turquoise waters of the nearby coves are well worth the small effort needed to reach them, and basic **rooms** (❷–❸) are available next to the *Lancheria Palheiro*. Roughly midway between Jurerê and Daniela, stunning views of the coast and across to the mainland can be appreciated from the ruins of the **Forte de São José** (usually referred to as Forte Jurerê), built in 1742 to guard the northern approaches to Desterro. Next to the fort there's a small eighteenth-century chapel.

To the east of Canasvieras, at the extreme northern tip of the island, is the almost two-kilometre-long **Praia da Lagoinha**, the prettiest beach hereabouts and with the island's warmest water. The beach has a wooded backdrop and, compared to the rest of the north coast, what development has taken place is remarkably tasteful. Located just metres from the shore is one of the most exclusive places to stay in Florianópolis, the *Pousada da Vigia*, Rua Conêgo Walmor Castro 291 (Ⓣ48/3284-1789, Ⓦwww.pousadadavigia.com.br; ❼). Once the private residence of a former state governor, the property has been turned into a *pousada* of understated luxury.

The east coast

If you find the north coast too crowded and developed, head for the **east coast**, where Atlantic rollers scare away most of the families. Take extreme care yourself, though, as the undercurrents here make for dangerous swimming. There are a couple of places to avoid: **PRAIA BRAVA** (the most northerly of the east coast beaches) is dominated by huge condominium complexes that have resulted in this beautiful stretch of coast becoming the island's ugliest corner. There's been similar uncontrolled development at **INGLESES**, a little further south. Instead you're better off returning to Florianópolis and crossing the island to the Lagoa da Conceição, a large saltwater lagoon in the centre of the island.

Lagoa da Conceição

The **Lagoa da Conceição** is very popular amongst families and others who want to swim, canoe or windsurf. **CENTRO DA LAGOA** (usually simply referred to as Lagoa), a bustling little town at the southern end of the lagoon, is a very pleasant place to stay: there are good bus services from here into Florianópolis and to the east coast beaches, a post office, a branch of Banco do Brasil (with an ATM), grocery stores and numerous restaurants and bars on the main road. This is one of the most lively nightspots on the island during the summer and at weekends throughout the year, with restaurants always crowded and people overflowing into the street from the bars until the small hours of the morning. **Accommodation** is scarce, however: try the rather spartan *Pousada Águia Pequena*, a couple of minutes' walk from the bridge that crosses the lagoon, at Rua Rita Lourenço da Silveira 114 (Ⓣ48/3232-2339; ❹), or the very similar *Pousada do Grego* at Rua Antônio da Silveira 58 (Ⓣ48/3232-0734; ❸). If they're fully booked, try the large, rather institutional *Hotel Samuka*, Travessa Pedro Manuel Fernandes 96, at the intersection with Avenida Das Rendeiras (Ⓣ48/3232-5024; ❹). An alternative option is the *Pousada Ilha da Magia* (Ⓣ48/3232-5038, Ⓦwww.pousadailhamagia.com.br; ❹) chalets set alongside the Lagoa da Conceição, 1km east of town on the road leading to Joaquina and Mole beaches.

Lagoa's beaches are close to the centre of town; cross the small bridge on the road leaving Centro da Lagoa and it's a ten-minute walk. There are also some attractive beaches on the isolated northwest shore of the lagoon – one of the most beautiful parts of the island – around **COSTA DA LAGOA**, a charming fishing village barely touched by tourism. The area is impossible to reach by road and involves either a three-hour walk along a trail skirting the lagoon, or an hour's boat ride; boats leave every hour (7.30am–6pm; R$2) from beneath the bridge in Centro da Lagoa, stopping off at isolated houses and tiny fishing hamlets on the way. Once at Costa da Lagoa, a ten-minute walk along a rough trail will take you to a nearby waterfall, where you can take a refreshing dip in the natural pool. Back in the village there are swimming beaches and a couple of restaurants, but you'd do better taking the trail that hugs the shore of the lagoon back south towards Centro da Lagoa; a twenty-minute walk will bring you to a much more attractive beach, which has an excellent seafood **restaurant** and bar. If you're tempted to stay, **rooms** are available above the restaurant here (❷), but otherwise you can either continue back along the trail to Centro da Lagoa, or wait at the pier for the hourly boat.

BARRA DA LAGOA, the village at the entrance to the Lagoa da Conceição, has succeeded fairly well in allowing tourism to develop alongside the inhabitants' traditional main activity – fishing. There are beautiful cliffside walks from here, the best reached by crossing the Ponte Pêncil, a rickety suspended footbridge that leads to the very pretty **PRAINHA DO LESTE**, a small cove flanked by forbidding rock formations where beach parties are often held in summer. Barra da Lagoa has several **restaurants**, a **campsite** and plenty of **rooms** and cabins to rent. There are also several **pousadas** in Prainha, including the *Gaivota* (Ⓣ48/3232-3253; ❸), which offers no-frills bed and breakfast accommodation, and the rather more comfortable *Vipaz* (Ⓣ48/3232-3193; ❸–❹), across the Ponte Pêncil, with spacious rooms sleeping two to four people, and cooking facilities as well. You may, however, have better luck finding a room at the much larger *Recanto dos Pinhais* (Ⓣ48/3232-3662, Ⓦwww.recantodospinhais.odi.com.br; ❹–❺), located amidst pleasant park-like gardens just outside Barra, alongside the Reserva Florestal do Rio Vermelho (see below).

North of Lagoa da Conceição

Stretching north for kilometres, Barra da Lagoa's beach merges into **PRAIA DA MOÇAMBIQUE** (also known as Praia Grande). This is the longest beach on the island, over 12km, and also one of the least developed, thanks to the **Reserva Florestal do Rio Vermelho**, a huge expanse of pine trees that takes up most of its hinterland. Inland from here on the Estrada Geral do Rio Vermelho – the road that leads to the village of Rio Vermelho – is one of the most outstanding, and surprising, **restaurants** on the island, well worth going out of your way for. *Chez Altamiro* (Ⓣ48/3269-7727; reservations strongly advised) is run by an islander who, despite having never set foot in France, cooks extremely good traditional French food for around R$60 a head. The restaurant is in the middle of nowhere, but is easily recognized by the tricolor that adorns the outside of the wooden building.

South of Lagoa da Conceição

South of Barra da Lagoa, the road climbs steeply, passing mountain-sized sand dunes to the secluded **PRAIA GALHETA**, the only nudist beach on the island, and **PRAIA MOLE**, whose beautiful beach is slightly hidden beyond the sand dunes and beneath low-lying cliffs. Mole is extremely popular with young people but, rather surprisingly, commercial activity has remained low-key, probably because there's a deep drop-off right at the water's edge.

Approached by a road passing between gigantic dunes, the next beach is at **JOAQUINA**, very popular with surfers, particularly so during the Brazilian national surf championships, held annually in the last week of January. The water's cold, however, and the sea rough, only really suitable for strong swimmers. If you have the energy, climb to the top of the dunes where you'll be rewarded with the most spectacular views in all directions. The dunes are a popular location for paragliding (see box below) and sandboarding – no skill is required if you sit, rather than stand, on a board as you hurtle down a dune (board rentals at the roadside for R$6 an hour). Accommodation by the beach is limited to two **hotels**, the *Joaquina Beach* (Ⓣ48/3232-5059, Ⓦwww.joaquinabeachhotel.com.br; ④), usually booked solid in the summer, and the *Cris Hotel* (Ⓣ48/3232-5104, Ⓦwww.crishotel.com; ⑤) which is slightly newer and has better views along the coast. Alternatively, there's the smaller and friendlier *Pousada Bizkaia* (Ⓣ48/3232-5273, Ⓦwww.bizkaia.com.br; ④), 1.5km from the beach on the road to Lagoa.

Joaquina beach stretches 3.5km to the south, blending into **PRAIA DO CAMPECHE**, so by walking for fifteen minutes or so you can escape Joaquina's crowds and be almost alone. Campeche, which itself merges into Morro das Pedras and Armação (see below), is considered by many to be the most beautiful stretch of the island's coast, but due to the strong current and often ferocious surf fewer people are attracted here than to the beaches to the north. Consequently, there's been comparatively little building work, and only slowly are houses, bars and the like appearing, concentrated around the southern portion of the beach. One rather beautiful **hotel** complex is the *São Sebastião da Praia* at Av. Cameche 1373 (Ⓣ48/3338-2020, Ⓦwww.hotelsaosebastiao.com.br; ⑥). Accommodation is set within lush, landscaped grounds with a mix of lawns, orginal trees and flowering bushes.

Continuing south, you reach the fishing village of **ARMAÇÃO**, whose lovely hilly backdrop gives it a stunning location. There's an attractive beach – though, here too, the waves and currents are unforgiving – and well-marked trails leading both inland and to more protected coves. There are some very good **places**

△ Joaquina

to stay here. The *Pousada Alemdomar* (Ⓣ48/3237-5600, Ⓦwww.alemdomar.com.br; ⑤), some 250m south of the village near the Lagoa do Peri, has brightly-coloured rooms (all of which have either a terrace or a balcony, some with sea views) and an extremely relaxing atmosphere, while on the beach is the more exclusive *Pousada Pénaria* (Ⓣ48/3338-1616, Ⓦwww.pousadapenareia.com.br; ⑤). The best budget option is the well-equipped youth hostel, the *Albergue Armação* (Ⓣ48/3389-5542, Ⓔalbergue@brturbo.com; R$20 per person), but beds fill up fast; in summer reservations are essential. Armação is also the nearest point to the **Ilha do Campeche**, where the pristine white sand beach is protected from any form of development – only four hundred visitors are permitted at any one time, along with a few people selling refreshments. Boats from Armação take about 30 minutes to complete the three-kilometre crossing (R$15 return).

Beyond here, practically at the end of the road, is **PÂNTANO DO SUL**, a rather larger fishing village at the end of a well-protected bay with a mountainous backdrop. The village itself is not at all attractive, but the water is calmer here than elsewhere on the east coast, the views of the small, uninhabited islands offshore are pleasant, and you can eat well. There are several **restaurants** right on the beach, including the *Bar do Arante*, known for serving some of the best seafood on the island, and a couple of **pousadas**, the very pleasant *Sol de Costa* (Ⓣ48/3222-5071; ③), and the *Pescador* (Ⓣ48/3237-7122; ④). Tourism has had only a minimal impact on the inhabitants' lives and Azorean traditions have remained strong, most visibly during Carnaval when brass bands wind their way through the streets and along the beach, the rhythms very different from the familiar beat of samba drums.

The west coast

The principal places of interest on the **west coast** are **SAMBAQUI** and **SANTO ANTÔNIO DE LISBOA** to the north of Florianópolis, and **RIBEIRÃO DA ILHA** to the south. As the island's oldest, most attractive and least-spoilt settlements, the houses in these places are almost all painted white and have dark blue sash windows – in typical Azorean style – and each village has a simple colonial church. As was the case with most of the island's settlements, these villages were founded by immigrants from the Azores, and their present-day inhabitants – who still refer to themselves as being Azorean – retain many traditions of the islands from which their forefathers came. Fishing, rather than catering to the needs of tourists, remains the principal activity of the three

Paragliding on Santa Catarina

The state of Santa Catarina has some good paragliding locations, in particular in the east of the island of Santa Catarina and on the mainland in Santo Amaro da Imperatriz (see opposite) and Pomerode (see p.740). Established in 1991, Parapente Sul, based at Rua João Antônio da Silveira 201, Centro da Lagoa (Ⓣ48/3232-0791, Ⓦwww.parapentesul.com.br) is one of the pioneers of paragliding on the island and has acquired a strong and well-deserved reputation. Courses cost about US$250 with as many lessons given as needed (usually about fifteen) at the Joaquina sand dunes on the island before you graduate with a jump off the cliff and flight over Praia Mole.

If you want to simply get a taste of paragliding, you can take a tandem flight (*vôo doplo*) over Praia Mole with an experienced instructor for R$80. There are two jump-off points – one at the north end of the beach and the other at the southern end – depending upon the wind direction, and the instructors are extremely responsible, always erring on the side of caution. Generally speaking the conditions are very forgiving and the thought of a cool drink and beautiful beach at the end of the flight makes the experience even more pleasurable.

villages, and the waters offshore from Santo Antônio and Ribeirão da Ilha are used to farm mussels and oysters, considered the best anywhere in the island. Azorean immigrants brought their lace-making skills to Santa Catarina, too, and intricately fashioned lace tablecloths, mats and other items are displayed for sale outside some of the houses in Ribeirão da Ilha – or you can buy them at the Casa Açoriana, Rua Cônego Serpa, in Santo Antônio. Local handicrafts are also on display, along with exhibits on the Azorean settlement of the island, at the **Ecomuseu** (Tues–Fri 9am–noon & 1.30–5pm, Sat, Sun & holidays noon–6pm; R$3) in Ribeirão da Ilha. Because the beaches are small and face the mainland, tourism has remained low-key, and the few visitors who are about are usually on day-trips from resorts elsewhere on the island. They stay just long enough for a meal: especially recommended are the oyster dishes served at *Ostradamus*, on the waterfront in Riberão da Ilha and the shellfish and grilled fish at the charming *Restinga Recanto*, overlooking the beach outside of Sambaqui towards Santo Antônio. In the village of Santo Antônio itself there's a bar on the beach directly in front of the church that serves fried fish and the freshest of oysters, while next to the church is the *Restaurante Açores* offering inexpensive meals.

South of Ribeirão da Ilha, hugging the steep hillside as it passes tiny, deserted coves, the dreadfully potholed road leading to Barra do Sul runs through some of the most stunning scenery on the island. The rainfall here is extremely heavy, nurturing a profusion of rich foliage, most noticeably flamboyants and bougainvillaea.

If you choose **to stay** in one of the west coast villages, finding a room can be quite a problem, but if successful you'll be rewarded by complete tranquillity of a kind lost to most of the rest of the island over the course of the last couple of decades. Your best chance is in Santo Antônio: the *Pousada Caminho dos Açores* (T48/3235-1363; 4) is set in a lovely garden and has an attractive pool, or there's the *Pousada Mar de Dentro* (T48/3235-1521; 5), very similar, with a tiny pool, but right on the beach. Across from the beach is the very friendly *Quintal da Sol* (T48/325-2334, Wwww.quintaldasol.com.br; 3), which, although simple, has cabins sleeping two to seven people, all with kitchenettes and a separate living room. In Ribeirão da Ilha try the modest *Pousada do Museu* (T48/3237-8148, Wwww.pousadadomuseu.com.br; 4), which fronts onto the beach by the Ecomuseu.

Around Florianópolis: the mainland

On the mainland, 30km inland and southwest of Florianópolis, lies the small resort of **SANTO AMARO DA IMPERATRIZ**, served by four buses daily from Praça da Bandeira. In the late nineteenth century, Imperatriz (the name commemorating the visit in 1845 of Brazil's emperor, Dom Pedro II and his wife, the Empress Teresa Cristina) was quite a fashionable spa town. The *Hotel Caldas da Imperatriz* (T48/3245-7088, Wwww.hotelcaldas.com.br; 5 full board) was opened to celebrate the imperial visit, and for years afterwards succeeded in mimicking the European idea of the Grand Hotel, attracting wealthy Brazilians from as far away as Rio. Today most of the hotel's visitors are elderly *catarinenses* and *gaúchos*, especially chronic sufferers of rheumatism and those with digestive or nervous disorders, though the baths are also open to non-guests on payment of a small fee.

A few kilometres up the narrow, tree-filled valley is another spa, the more recently developed **ÁGUAS MORNAS** and its luxury *Palace Hotel* (T48/3245-7015, Wwww.aguasmornaspalacehotel.com.br; 7 half board), favoured by the seriously rich. The spa itself is not particularly attractive, but the approach road and general setting are delightful.

Parque Estadual da Serra do Tabuleiro

For anyone with even a vague interest in the fauna of Santa Catarina, a visit to the nature reserve of the **Serra do Tabuleiro** (daily 8am–5pm; ⓣ48/3286-2624) is a must. Animals and birds from throughout the state live in as near to natural conditions as is possible, and endangered species are bred in the hope that they will eventually be returned to the wild. You'll see alligators, tortoises, twenty species of birds (including rheas, emus and flamingoes – and even the odd lost penguin from Patagonia), anteaters and deer and, best of all, get no feeling that you're in, essentially, a zoo.

To get to the reserve from Florianópolis, take a **bus** (Empresa Paulo Lopez line, or any bus heading south along the main coastal highway, the BR-101) and ask to be let off at the entrance to the "Parque da Serra". From the park's entrance, it takes about half an hour to walk to the reserve. As the journey time there is about two hours, you'd do best to take the 7am or, at the latest, the 10.30am bus from Florianópolis; count on returning on the 2pm or 4.30pm bus. It's a tiring excursion, but well worth it.

The north coast: to São Francisco do Sul

If you're going to travel by bus on Santa Catarina's coastal highway (the BR-101) **north of Florianópolis** in the Brazilian summer you're best off keeping your eyes firmly closed. The bumper-to-bumper traffic moves at terrifying speeds, with cars, trucks and buses constantly leapfrogging one another for no apparent advantage; the wrecked cars that litter the highway are enough to make you get out of the bus and walk to your destination – something that, at times, might be faster anyway. But worse, if you don't have a car of your own, is that much of the BR-101 passes alongside absolutely stunning beaches, some of which have remained totally devoid of buildings and people. If you're on the bus, there's no hope of stopping for a refreshing dip, and you'll just have to make do with the idyllic images out of the window.

Porto Belo

Although the stretch immediately north of Florianópolis is probably the most beautiful part of the Santa Catarina coast, during the peak summer season it is completely overrun by Argentine and *paulista* tourists. Less than two hours from Florianópolis, the peninsula and city of **PORTO BELO** is easily reached by bus, and although the local authority's claim that there are 32 beaches around Porto Belo is highly suspect, the beaches there certainly are numerous and large enough to cope with the visitors – at least outside of the peak months of January and February.

The "city" of Porto Belo is, in reality, just an overgrown village containing a tourist office (ⓣ47/3369-5638), post office, and a few bars and restaurants, but from here frequent local buses fan out to **beaches** around the peninsula, stopping along the road to pick up passengers. The most attractive beaches are **Bombas** and **Bombinhas**, 5km and 8km east of Porto Belo respectively and separated from one another by a rocky promontory. The bay in which they're found is very pretty, with rich vegetation behind, and the waves here are suitable for inexperienced surfers. South of Bombinhas, if you're looking for open sea and more powerful waves, the east-facing **Praia do Mariscal** is better, but should be braved by only the most expert of surfers. In complete contrast, the nearby **Praia do Canto** is ideal for anyone merely seeking a gentle swim.

Hotels in Porto Belo are generally small and fairly expensive – you're unlikely to find a room for less than R$100 a night, and you may have to pay considerably more. The best hope of finding somewhere to stay is in Bombinhas: try the Spanish colonial-style *Pousada Águas* (Ⓣ47/3340-5799; ④) or, with panoramic views and a small pool, the *Pousada das Palmeiras* (Ⓣ47/3369-2222; ④). Quite expensive, but worth every *real* is the *Pousada do Arvoredo* (Ⓣ47/3369-2355, Ⓦwww.pousadadoarvoredo.com.br; ⑤), which has attractive chalets or rooms with balconies overlooking the gardens and the ocean, and a pool. Back in Porto Belo itself, there's the *Pousada Enseada das Garoupas* (Ⓣ47/3369-4383; ⑤) or the more basic *Pousada das Vieras* (Ⓣ47/3369-4468; ④). The only inexpensive place around, at R$20 per head, is the **youth hostel** (Ⓣ47/3369-4483; open Nov–April, summer reservations essential), about ten minutes' walk from the bus terminal, on Rua José Amancio 246.

Balneário Camboriú

Just 20km north of Porto Belo lies **BALNEÁRIO CAMBORIÚ**, Brazil's answer to the worst wall-to-wall concrete high-rise Spanish resort. It's got the lot, though you probably won't want any of it: huge hotels, a towel-sized patch of beach per person, and nightclubs that celebrate "Carnaval" all summer, with dance troupes imported from the tropical, more "exotic" Brazil to the north.

Stretching for 5km along the Avenida Atlântica, Camboriú is only a few streets deep. With the mountains behind the resort plunging almost straight into the sea, it's just about possible to imagine how beautiful it once was before the developers moved in, back in the 1930s. Today, there's precious little natural beauty still in evidence but, if you do want to stick around, there's rarely a problem finding a room, although many hotels are block-booked by Argentine tour operators; the cheapest **hotels** are centrally located, near the *rodoviária* (from where buses leave for just about every city in South America south of Rio; Ⓣ47/3367-2901), and on the streets set back from the beach. The **tourist office** (Dec–March daily 8am–8pm, April–Nov Mon–Fri 8am–noon & 2–6pm; Ⓣ47/3367-8122), with branches at Praça Papa João Paulo I 320 and Praça Tamandaré, provides helpful information on hotel availability, a list of the phenomenal number of **restaurants**, most of which only open between December and March, and the latest information on the constantly changing nightclub and disco scene.

Itajaí

Santa Catarina's most important port, **ITAJAÍ** is located at the mouth of the Rio Itajaí-Açu, 10km north of Balneário Camboriú. Although it was founded in the early eighteenth century, Itajaí looks fairly new, with few buildings dating back to before 1950 – and with nothing of any tourist interest. However, it's an important transport centre, and it may not be possible to avoid the city altogether. Fortunately, most buses pass straight by it, with only a minority actually stopping to pick up and put down passengers in the city. And as there's a constant flow of buses to Blumenau, Joinville and Florianópolis, as well as further afield in all directions, there are few reasons actually to stay in Itajaí. One reason might be to catch an early morning plane from nearby Navegantes **airport** (Ⓣ47/3342-9200), from where you can fly to Florianópolis, Porto Alegre and São Paulo. To get to the airport, take the ferry from Avenida Argentina across the river, and then a taxi at around R$20; for slightly more, taxis will take you direct from Itajaí, via the ferry, to the airport. Should you need a **hotel**, a convenient option clearly visible from the *rodoviária* is the *Itajaí Tur* at Rua Alberto Werner 133 (Ⓣ47/3348-4600, Ⓦwww.itajaitur.com.br; ③), with rooms of varying levels of comfort and price. Downtown at Rua Felipe Schmidt 198, the *Grande Hotel* (Ⓣ47/3348-2179, Ⓦwww.grandehotelitajai.com.br; ④) is a comfortable, executive-style place.

If for some reason you really can't get out of Itajaí, and have some time to spare, the city's **beaches** aren't bad. From the local bus terminal in the city centre, near the intersection of Rua Joinville and Avenida Victor Konder, buses take about twenty minutes to reach the nearest beaches, **Atalaia** and **Geremias**, or a little longer to get to the cleaner **Praia Cabecudas**.

The Ilha de São Francisco

North of Itajaí, the highway gradually turns inland towards Joinville (see p.735), but 45km east of Joinville is the **Ilha de São Francisco**, a low-lying island separated from the mainland by a narrow strait that is spanned by a causeway. As Joinville's port and the site of a major Petrobras oil refinery, São Francisco may seem like a place to avoid, but this isn't the case. Both the port and refinery keep a discreet distance from the main town, São Francisco do Sul, and the beaches, while the surprisingly few sailors who are around blend perfectly with the slightly dilapidated colonial setting.

São Francisco do Sul

The island was first visited by European sailors as early as 1504, though not until the middle of the following century was the town of **SÃO FRANCISCO DO SUL** established. It's one of the oldest settlements in the state and also one of the very few places in Santa Catarina where colonial and nineteenth-century buildings survive concentrated together. During most of its first two hundred years, São Francisco do Sul was little more than a naval outpost, its simple local economy based on fishing and sugar-cane production. In the nineteenth century, with the opening of nearby areas to immigrants from Germany, the town grew in importance as a transfer point for people and produce. Merchants established themselves in the town, building grand houses and dockside warehouses, many of which remain today – protected from demolition and gradually undergoing restoration. Dominating the city's skyline is the **Igreja Matriz**, the main church, originally built in 1665 by Indian slaves; completely reconstructed in 1884, the church has lost all of its original features. You might want to visit the **Museu Histórico** (Tues–Fri 9am–6pm, Sat & Sun 11am–6pm) on Rua Coronel Carvalho, housed in São Francisco's nineteenth-century prison building (which, incidentally, stayed in use until 1968). The former cells have been converted into small exhibition halls; the most interesting exhibits are nineteenth-century photographs of the town. The **Museu Nacional do Mar** on Rua Manoel Lourenço de Andrade (Tues–Fri 10am–6pm, Sat & Sun 10am–7pm; R$5) has a collection devoted to the technology of ocean travel and the people who make their living from the sea, with an emphasis on southern Brazil.

Most of the island's visitors bypass the town altogether and head straight for the beaches to the east, so, even in midsummer, there's rarely any difficulty in finding a **hotel** with room. Quite comfortable, and with sea views, is the *Hotel Kontiki* (Ⓣ47/3444-2232; ③) at Rua Camacho 33, near the market or, if you want a pool, there's the relatively luxurious *Hotel Zibamba* (Ⓣ47/3444-2020; ⑤) at Rua Fernandes Dias 27. Eating out holds no great excitement, with the *Hotel Zibamba*'s seafood restaurant the best of a generally poor bunch.

From the market in the town centre, there are **buses** to the *rodoviária* (Ⓣ47/3444-8086) beyond the town's limits, from where there are hourly connections to Joinville as well as daily services to São Paulo and Curitiba.

The island's beaches

The prettiest beaches, **Paulos** and **Ingleses**, are also the nearest to town, just a couple of kilometres to the east. Both are small, and have trees to provide shade, and surprisingly few people take advantage of the protected sea, ideal for weak swimmers. On the east coast, **Praia de Ubatuba** and the adjoining **Praia de Enseada**, about 15km from town, are the island's most popular beaches, with enough surf to have fun in but not enough to be dangerous. At Enseada there are a couple of **campsites** and an overpriced hotel, while Ubatuba caters mainly for families who rent or own houses that front the beach. By way of contrast, a ten-minute walk across the peninsula from the eastern end of Enseada leads to **Praia da Saúde** (also referred to as Prainha), where the waves are suitable for only the most macho surfers.

Frequent **buses** to Enseada and Ubatuba leave from the market in the town centre, with the last buses in both directions departing at about 9.30pm.

Northeast Santa Catarina

Although the northeast of Santa Catarina is populated by people of many ethnic origins, it's an area most associated with **Germans**, who so obviously dominate both culturally and economically. **Joinville** and **Blumenau** vie with each other to be not only the economic powerhouse of the region, but also the cultural capital. However, both cities lose out in terms of tourist interest to the small towns and villages of the interior, where old dialects continue to be spoken. One such community is **Pomerode**, which is set in a picturesque area and does much to promote its German heritage.

Joinville and around

An hour from São Francisco, the land on which **JOINVILLE** was settled was originally given as a dowry by Emperor Dom Pedro to his sister, who had married the Prince of Joinville, the son of Louis-Philippe of France. A deal with Hamburg timber merchants meant that, in 1851, 191 Germans, Swiss and Norwegians arrived in Santa Catarina, to exploit the fifty square kilometres of virgin forest, stake out homesteads and establish the "Colônia Dona Francisca" – later known as Joinville. As more Germans were dispatched from Hamburg, Joinville grew and prospered, developing from an agricultural backwater into the state's foremost industrial city. This economic success has diluted much of Joinville's once solidly German character, but evidence of its ethnic origins remains: the largely Germanic architecture and the impeccably clean streets produce the atmosphere of a rather dull small town in Germany.

The Town

Shops and services are concentrated along Rua Princesa Isabel, while Rua XV de Novembro and Rua IX de Março run parallel to each other, terminating at the river. However, the points of interest associated with Joinville's German heritage are more widely scattered but still easily reached on foot. The first place to head for is the **Museu Nacional de Imigração e Colonização** at Rua Rio Branco 229, near Praça da Bandeira (Tues–Fri 9am–5pm, Sat & Sun 11am–5pm; ⓣ47/3433-3736, ⓦwww.museunacional.com.br), an excellent introduction to the history of German immigrants in Santa Catarina in general and Joinville in particular. In the main building, formerly the Prince of Joinville's palace, built in 1870, there are some late nineteenth- and early

German Santa Catarina

In the nineteenth century, as it became more difficult to enter the United States, land-hungry European immigrants sought new destinations, many choosing Brazil as their alternative America. Thousands made their way into the forested wilderness of Santa Catarina, attempting to become independent farmers, and of all of them, it was the **Germans** who most successfully fended off assimilationist pressures. Concentrated in areas where few non-Germans lived, there was little reason for them to learn Portuguese, and, as merchants, teachers, Catholic priests and Protestant pastors arrived with the immigrants, complete communities evolved, with flourishing German cultural organizations and a varied German-language press. After Brazil's entry into World War II, restrictions on the use of German were introduced and many German organizations were proscribed, accused of being Nazi fronts. Certainly, "National Socialism" found some of its most enthusiastic followers among overseas Germans and, though the extent of **Nazi activity** in Santa Catarina is a matter of debate, for years after the collapse of the Third Reich ex-Nazis attracted sympathy in even the most isolated forest homesteads.

Later, due to the compulsory use of Portuguese in schools, the influence of radio and television and an influx of migrants from other parts of the state to work in the region's rapidly expanding industries, the German language appeared to be dying in Santa Catarina. As a result, in **Joinville** and **Blumenau** – the region's largest cities – German is now rarely heard. However, in outlying villages and farming communities such as **Pomerode**, near Blumenau, German remains very much alive, spoken everywhere but in government offices. Recently, too, the German language and Teuto-Brazilian culture have undergone a renaissance and the German government has provided financial support. Property developers are encouraged to heed supposedly traditional **German architectural styles**, resulting in a plethora of buildings that may be appropriate for alpine conditions, but look plain silly in the Brazilian subtropics. A more positive development has been the move to protect and restore the houses of the early settlers, especially those built in the most characteristic local building style, that of **enxaimel** ("Fachwerk" in German) – exposed bricks within an exposed timber frame. These houses are seen throughout the region, concentrated most heavily in the area around Pomerode. Keen to reap benefits from the new ethnic awareness, local authorities have also initiated pseudo-German **festivals**, such as Blumenau's Munich-inspired "Oktoberfest" (see p.739) and Pomerode's more authentic "Festa Pomerana" (see p.740), both of which have rapidly become major tourist draws.

twentieth-century photographs, though the museum's most interesting features are an old barn containing farm equipment used by early *colonos*, and a typical nineteenth-century *enxaimel* farmhouse with period furnishings. If you've more than a passing interest in Joinville's history, also visit the superbly organized **Arquivo Histórico** (Mon–Fri 8am–4pm), Av. Hermann August Lepper 650, where temporary, mainly photographic, exhibitions are held.

As throughout the region, Joinville's municipal authorities are making efforts to preserve the surviving **enxaimel houses**. Although scattered throughout the city, they can be seen in some concentration along the former main approach road, the cobbled **Rua XV de Novembro**. On the same road, about twenty minutes' walk from the centre, is the **Cemitério dos Imigrantes**, the final resting place of many of Joinville's pioneer settlers. Covering a hillside from where there are fine views of the city, the cemetery has been preserved as a national monument, the tombs and headstones serving as testimony to Joinville's ethnic origins. If you have some time on the way to the cemetery, take a brief look around the **Museu de Arte**, Rua XV de Novembro 1400 (Tues–Fri 9am–9pm, Sat & Sun 11am–6pm). The museum, housed in a small

German-style mansion built in 1864, has a small collection of works by mainly local artists and also hosts visiting exhibitions. There's a **cinema** featuring non-commercial, often German, films as well.

It's also worth popping into the **Mercado Público Municipal** (Mon–Fri 7am–7pm, Sat 7am–1pm) near the local bus terminal in the centre, which sells food and some handicrafts produced by local German *colonos*. On the second Saturday of each month a **handicraft market** is held in the nearby Praça Nereu Ramos.

Practicalities

The **rodoviária** (ⓣ47/3433-2991) is 2km from the city centre, reached in five minutes by bus or in half an hour on foot by walking down Rua Ministro Calógeras and then left along Avenida Kubitschek. Bus services to neighbouring cities are excellent. The terminal for **city buses** and those to Dona Francisca (see p.738) is in the centre, at the end of Rua IX de Março. There's an **airport** (ⓣ47/3467-1000), 13km north of the city, with flights to Florianópolis, Porto Alegre and São Paulo.

Opened in 1910, Joinville's **train station** – an imposing construction with a German half-hipped roof – is the oldest one still functioning in Santa Catarina. Today, the only passenger trains are laid on for tourists in the summer months, going east to São Francisco do Sul; enquire at the **tourist information** office at Rua XV de Novembro 4305 (daily 8am–8pm; ⓣ47/3453-0177).

Finding a comfortable, spotlessly clean and reasonably priced **hotel** is usually easy, though Joinville has become a popular place for conferences, during which accommodation is scarce. In the city centre, on Rua Jerônimo Coelho near the local bus terminal, try the *Ideal* (ⓣ47/3422-3660; ❷) at no. 98, or, if you prefer a private bathroom, the *Príncipe* (ⓣ47/3422-8555; ❸) at no. 27. Nearby is one of Joinville's priciest places to stay, the *Tannenhof* (ⓣ47/3433-8011, ⓦwww.tannenhof.com.br; ❺) at Rua Visconde de Taunay 340, with all the features you'd expect of a large, luxury hotel. Smaller but with much more character and better value is the *Anthurium Parque Hotel*, Rua São José 226 (ⓣ47/3433-6299, ⓦwww.anthurium.com.br; ❹), a curious building supposedly of "Norwegian–German" style, set in pretty grounds near the cathedral. Around the corner from here at Rua Ministro Calógeras 612 is the *Germânia* (ⓣ47/3433-9886, ⓦwww.hotelgermania.com.br; ❹), which to all appearances is just another modern tower block, but which has extremely comfortable rooms, helpful staff and very friendly owners.

Not surprisingly, **German restaurants** abound, but most are of the sausage, pig's knuckle, potato and sauerkraut level of sophistication. The *Bierkeller*, conveniently located at Rua XV de Novembro 497 (closed Mon), is typical, or try one of the many self-service restaurants in the Shopping Müeller, a large shopping centre next to the *Hotel Tannenhof*. If you're desperate for a decent meal, you'll have to go out to the suburbs (a R$8 taxi ride) to the *Sopp* (evenings only, closed Sun) at Rua Marechal Deodoro 640, the best restaurant in Joinville. The menu, based on German cooking, is varied enough for most tastes and there's an unusually good choice of beers. For **afternoon tea**, you'll get good cakes at the *Delicatesse Viktoria* at Rua Felipe Schmidt 400, near to the Shopping Müeller; alternatively, all the upmarket hotels serve a good high tea (*café colonial*).

There's a cultural institute in Joinville, the Instituto Cultural Brasil-Alemanha on Rua Princesa Isabel, near Rua Sergipe, and students congregate in the nearby **bars** in the evenings after classes. Since 1937, the **Festa das Flores** has been held for ten days during the second half of November, the height of the orchid season – flower shows, German folk dancing, music and food are the main attractions. Pride of place in the cultural calendar goes to the annual **Festival Internacional de Dança** (ⓣ47/3423-1010, ⓦwww.festivaldedanca.com.br), the largest event of its kind in Latin America. For twelve days in late July, dance companies from around the world descend on Joinville, attracting an audience from throughout Brazil. So strong is Joinville's association with dance that in 1999 it was chosen by the Bolshoi as the location of its first ballet school outside Russia (Ⓦwww.escolabolshoi.com.br).

Around Joinville: Estrada Bonita and Estrada Dona Francisca

Although Joinville itself has developed increasingly into a rather anonymous big city, its rural, German-speaking hinterland to the west has changed little over the past few decades. There are two distinct areas to head for: the **Estrada Bonita**, with its well-organized small farms selling home-made jams, *cachaça* and biscuits, and the **Estrada Dona Francisca**, where you'll find some of the oldest and best-cared-for *enxaimel* houses in Santa Catarina. In both areas, visitors are warmly received. For Estrada Bonita's *colonos*, tourism enables them to sustain a reasonable standard of living and keep young people from moving to Joinville, while in the Dona Francisca area local awareness of the historic importance of the old buildings is high, and people are happy to show their homes to visitors. The landscape is also beautiful in this region: flat, rich farmland set against a dramatic forested mountain backdrop.

Joinville's tourist office distributes a useful free **brochure** and **map** covering the Estrada Bonita area, as well as details of the *colonos* who are members of the Turismo Rural project and therefore happy to open their farms to visitors. The homesteads are widely scattered, however, and a car is pretty essential; alternatively, the tourist office runs a weekly bus **tour** of the area, departing from the tourist office at 9.30am on Saturdays (R$20 including lunch). In the Dona Francisca area, the most interesting houses are dispersed over a large area and often hidden in forest, and you're best off accompanied by someone who knows the area well; ask at the tourist office for the name of a taxi driver who's familiar with the area, and negotiate a price (about R$50 for a couple of hours). If you want to stay over, you'll find a couple of simple but comfortable *pousadas* along the Estrada Bonita: the *Grün Wald* at the intersection with the BR-101 highway (Ⓣ47/3464-1271, Ⓦwww.grunwald.com.br; ❸) and the *Vale Verde* at Km 2.5 (Ⓣ47/3464-1377, Ⓦwww.pvaleverde.com.br; ❹).

Blumenau

Despite Joinville's challenge, **BLUMENAU** has succeeded in promoting itself as the "capital" of German Santa Catarina. Picturesquely located on the banks of the Rio Itajaí, Blumenau was founded in 1850 by Dr Hermann Blumenau, who served as director of the colony until his return to Germany in 1880. Blumenau always had a large Italian minority, but it was mainly settled by Germans and, as late as the 1920s, two-thirds of the population spoke German as their first language. In the surrounding rural communities an even larger proportion of the population were German speakers, many of them finding it completely unnecessary to learn Portuguese. Well into the twentieth century Blumenau was isolated, with only poor river transport connections with the rest of Brazil beyond the Itajaí valley – circumstances that enabled its German character to be retained for longer than was the case in Joinville.

Today, Blumenau's municipal authority never misses an opportunity to remind the world of the city's German origins, the European links helping tourism and attracting outside investors. And, superficially at least, Blumenau certainly looks, if not feels, German. The streets are sparkling clean, parking tickets are issued by wardens dressed in a uniform that Heidi would have been comfortable in, most buildings are in German architectural styles and geranium-filled window boxes are the norm. But since German is almost never heard, and the buildings (such as the half-timbered Saxon-inspired department store and the Swiss chalet-like Prefeitura) are absurd caricatures of those found in German cities, the result is a sort of "Disneyland" interpretation of Germany.

It's easy to sneer, but tourists from São Paulo are impressed by Blumenau's old-world atmosphere and visit in large numbers, especially during the annual **Oktoberfest** (Ⓣ47/3326-6901, Ⓦwww.oktoberfestblumenau.com.br). Held, since 1984, over eighteen days in October, the festival is basically an advertising gimmick thought up by Hering, the Blumenau-based textile and agro-industrial giant. Besides vast quantities of beer and German food, the main festival attractions are the local and visiting German bands and German folk-dance troupes. Performances take place at PROEB, Blumenau's exhibition centre, located on the city's outskirts (frequent buses run during the festival period), as well as in the downtown streets and the central Biergarten. So successful has the Oktoberfest been in drawing visitors to Blumenau – a million people attended the festivities during its peak year in 1992 – that the city's authorities came to realize that the event's local flavour had been swamped by outsiders and have now successfully halved attendance.

The rest of the year, local German bands perform every evening from 5pm in the **Biergarten**, the city's main meeting point, in the tree-filled Praça Hercílio Luz. In the oldest part of Blumenau, across a small bridge on the continuation of the main street, Rua XV de Novembro, the Biergarten is only a short walk from the **Museu da Família Colonial**, one of the city's few museums, at Alameda Duque de Caxias 78 (Tues–Fri 9am–5pm, Sat 9am–noon & 2–4.30pm, Sun 9am–noon). The museum's buildings, constructed in 1858 and 1864 for the families of Dr Blumenau's nephew and secretary-librarian, are two of the oldest surviving *enxaimel* houses in Blumenau. Exhibits include nineteenth-century furniture and household equipment, documents relating to the foundation of the city, photographs of life in the settlement during its early years, and artefacts of the Kaingangs and Xoklengs – the indigenous population displaced by the German settlers. But it's in the beautiful forest-like garden that you'll find the most curious feature: a cemetery, the final resting place for the much-loved cats of a former occupant of one of the houses.

A good half-hour walk from Praça Hercílio Luz, on the river at Rua Itajaí 2195, is the **Museu de Ecologia Fritz Müller** (Mon–Fri 8am–6pm, Sat–Sun 8–11.30am & 2–5pm), built in 1867 and the former home of the eponymous German-born naturalist. Born in 1822, Müller lived in Santa Catarina between 1852 and 1897, and was a close collaborator of British naturalist Charles Darwin; the small museum is dedicated to the work of the lesser-known scientist.

Practicalities

The **rodoviária** (Ⓣ47/3323-0690) is 7km from the city centre in the suburb of Itoupava Norte (the "Cidade Jardim" bus runs into the centre). There are hourly services to Florianópolis, Joinville and Itajaí, and frequent services to western Santa Catarina, Curitiba and São Paulo. Buses to Pomerode leave roughly hourly from Rua Paulo Zimmermann, located near the Prefeitura and Praça Victor Konder; if in doubt, ask for the bus stop of the Volkmann company.

Tourist information offices are found at Rua XV de Novembro 420, at the corner of Rua Nereu Ramos (daily 9am–9pm; Ⓣ47/3326-6931), at the *rodoviária* (daily 9am–6pm), and in the Prefeitura (Mon–Fri 9am–5pm) at Praça Victor Konder. There's a **German consulate** at Rua Caetano Deeke 20 on the eleventh floor.

Centrally located **hotels** are plentiful, so accommodation shouldn't pose a problem, except during the Oktoberfest. At the lower end of the price range, look no further than the wonderful *Hotel Hermann* (Ⓣ47/3322-4370; ❷–❸), an early twentieth-century *enxaimel* building in the heart of the city at Rua Floriano Peixoto 213, by the intersection with Rua Sete de Setembro. More expensive, but also German in style, is the *Hotel Steinhausen Colonial*, Rua Buenos Aires 275 (Ⓣ47/3322-5276, Ⓦwww.hotelsteinhausen.com.br; ❹–❺) with comfortable guest rooms, landscaped gardens and a pool. Blumenau's most expensive hotel is the *Plaza Blumenau*, Rua Sete de Setembro 818 (Ⓣ47/3231-7000, Ⓦwww.plazahoteis.com.br; ❻), but there are several other medium-priced hotels on the same road, including the *Glória* at no. 954 (Ⓣ47/3326-1988, Ⓦwww.hotelgloria.com.br; ❸). There's also an excellent HI-affiliated **youth hostel**, the centrally located *Pousada Grün Garten*, Rua São Paulo 2457 (Ⓣ47/3323-4332, Ⓦwww.grungarten.com.br; R$25 per person or ❸). In a well-preserved German-style house built in the 1920s, the hostel offers a range of dorms, single, double and family rooms.

In general, food in Blumenau is poor and largely takes the form of **snacks** to accompany beer. An excellent **café colonial**, or high tea, however, can be found at the *Cafehaus* (daily 3–8pm) in the *Hotel Glória* which serves the best cakes in Blumenau.

There are several **German restaurants**, by far the most pleasant-looking being the *Frohsinn* (closed Sun). The food here is not particularly special (it's fairly expensive and the service is slow), but the location – on a beautiful, cool, pine-clad hill with excellent views over the city – makes the journey worthwhile. It's a bit of an effort to get there: from Praça Hercílio Luz, walk for about fifteen minutes along Rua Itajaí and turn right on Rua Gertrud Sierich – the restaurant is at the top of this very steep road. Nearer to the centre, huge portions of passable German food are served at the *Cavalinho Branco*, Alameda Rio Branco 165, but it's accompanied by loud Teutonic music. If you're sick of pork, cross the bridge to the *Restaurante Moinho do Vale* at Rua Paraguai 66, which serves more typically Brazilian and international food. It's rather expensive but worth it for the beautiful setting overlooking the river.

Pomerode

Thirty kilometres to the north of Blumenau, **POMERODE** probably has the best claim to be the most German "city" in Brazil. Not only are ninety percent of its 24,000 widely dispersed inhabitants descended from German immigrants, but eighty percent of the *município*'s population continue to speak the language. Unlike Blumenau, in Pomerode German continues to thrive and is spoken just about everywhere, although in schools it takes second place to Portuguese. There are several reasons for this: almost all the immigrants – who arrived in the 1860s – came from Pomerania, and therefore did not face the problem of mixing with other immigrants speaking often mutually unintelligible dialects; as ninety percent of the population are Lutheran, German was retained for the act of worship; and, until recently, Pomerode was isolated by poor roads and communication links. This isolation has all but ended, though. The road to Blumenau is now excellent, buses are frequent, car ownership is common and televisions are universal. However, despite the changes, German looks more entrenched than ever. The language has been reintroduced into the local school curriculum, cultural groups thrive and, where the government has exerted pressure, it has been to encourage the language's survival.

Pomerode is renowned for its **festivals**, the chief of which is the **Festa Pomerana**, a celebration of local industry and culture held annually for ten days, usually from around January 7. Most of the events take place on the outskirts of town, on Rua XV de Novembro, about 1km from the tourist office, and during the day thousands of people from neighbouring cities descend on Pomerode to sample the local food, attend the song and dance performances and visit the commercial fair. By late afternoon, though, the day-trippers leave and the Festa Pomerana comes alive as the *colonos* from the surrounding areas transform the festivities into a truly popular event. Local and visiting bands play German and Brazilian music, and dancing continues long into the night. In July, Pomerode organizes the smaller, though similar, **Winterfest**.

There are more regular festivities too, as every Saturday the local hunting clubs take turns to host **dances**. Visitors are always made to feel welcome, and details of the week's venue are displayed on posters around town, or ask at the tourist office. As many of the clubs are located in the *município*'s outlying reaches, a bus is laid on, leaving from outside the post office on Rua XV de Novembro.

The main activity for visitors, other than attending the town's famous festivals and dances, is **walking**. Pomerode has Santa Catarina's greatest concentration of nineteenth and early twentieth century **enxaimel farm buildings**, most proudly preserved, the largest number found in the município's Wunderwald district: to reach them, cross the bridge near the Lutheran church, turn left and continue walking along the road for about twenty minutes, then turn right just before a bridge across a small stream. If you're feeling energetic, return to the main road and cross the bridge, walk on another hundred metres or so and turn left along the Testo Alto road; about 3km up the steep valley, you'll arrive at the **Cascata Cristalina**, where you'll be able to cool off under the tiny waterfall or use the swimming pool (Oct to mid-Dec & mid-Jan to March Sat, Sun & holidays 8am–7pm, mid-Dec to mid-Jan daily 8am–7pm; R$5). The views are marvellous and you may well be tempted to stay at the basic *pousada* here (❸). An alternative way of getting around is by **bike**: the tourist office rents them out at about R$3 for two hours, along with a useful map.

Practicalities

Buses to and from Blumenau stop outside the *Hotel Schroeder* and the Lutheran church on Rua XV de Novembro, the main street, which sprawls alongside the banks of the Rio do Testo. At no. 818 the very helpful **tourist office** (Mon–Fri 7.30am–6pm, Sat & Sun 10am–4pm; ⓣ47/3387-2627) provides a good map and details of forthcoming events, and has a small selection of local wooden and ceramic handicrafts for sale.

Accommodation is always easy to find, even during the Festa Pomerana. The largest hotel in town is the rather soulless *Hotel Bergblick* (ⓣ47/3387-0952, ⓦwww.bergblick.com.br; ❹), on the outskirts at Rua George Zepelin 120. Just as comfortable, much more central and cheaper is the long-established *Hotel Schroeder*, Rua XV de Novembro 514 (ⓣ47/3387-0933; ❸). Much prettier, but a half-hour walk from the centre of town, is the *Pousada Mundo Antigo*, Rua Ribeirão Herdt, Km 5 (ⓣ47/3387-3143, ⓦwww.mundoantigo.com.br; ❺), housed in several early twentieth-century *enxaimel* farm buildings in a beautiful rural setting. If these are full or too expensive, the tourist office will find you a **room** with a local family.

You can **eat** well in Pomerode. There's no attempt to reproduce old-world cooking, but instead simple local dishes are prepared. Pork is, of course, ever present, but it's *marreco* (wild duck) that's considered the local speciality. The *Wunderwald* (closed Sun evening & Mon) is, without doubt, Pomerode's best restaurant, serving typical regional food at bargain prices in a perfectly preserved early twentieth-century *enxaimel* farmhouse. To get to the restaurant from the centre, cross over the bridge near the church and turn left; the *Wunderwald* is at Rua Ricardo Bahr 200, a small road to the left immediately after the hospital. Nearby, on the same street, the restaurant of the *Pousada Mundo Antigo* serves a very similar range of local dishes. For a reasonable **café colonial** try the *Torten Paradies* at Rua XV de Novembro 211.

There are almost hourly **buses** to and from Blumenau, but as the last goes to Blumenau at 6pm and returns at 10.10pm, going into the city for an evening out is only just about possible. There are also four buses each day direct to Curitiba.

The south coast to Laguna and Criciúma

Unlike the northern stretch of coast, heading south from Florianópolis doesn't offer as many temptations to leap off the bus and into the sea. Most of this part of the BR-101 highway is too far inland to catch even a glimpse of the sea but, in any case, south of Laguna, the beaches are less attractive and more exposed. Many of the coastal settlements were founded by Azorean immigrants in the late seventeenth century and early eighteenth century, and they've retained the fishing and lace-making traditions of their ancestors. Inland, settlement is much more recent and the inhabitants are a blend of Germans, Italians and Poles, whose forebears were drawn in the late nineteenth century by promises of fertile land and offers of work in the region's coal mines. However, apart from a handful of farms and villages where Portuguese-influenced Italian dialects are spoken, only surnames and scattered wooden and stone houses of the early settlers remain of the immigrant heritage.

Garopaba and Imbituba

The first accessible spot worth stopping at is **GAROPABA**, a fishing village inhabited by people of Azorean origin, which, despite attracting more and more people every summer, has not yet been totally overwhelmed by tourism. In the 1970s, Garopaba was "discovered" by hippies from Porto Alegre, attracted to the area by the peaceful atmosphere and beautiful beaches. During the 1980s, surfers from throughout Brazil and beyond descended on the village, which fast developed a reputation for having some of the best surfing in the country.

The **beaches** are excellent, but are located a short distance from the village. The main village beach is fine, and large enough to take the summer crowds, but try to make it to the outlying beaches. Ten kilometres to the north is **Praia Siriú**, backed by huge dunes, while 6km further on, **Praia da Gambora** is a good beach for swimming, with a beautiful mountain backdrop. The best beaches for surfing are to the south, the most challenging being **Praia do Silveira** (3km from Garopaba) and **Praia do Rosa** (18km). Most visitors arrive in the summer, but between mid-June and mid-November, Garopaba is the most popular place on the Brazilian coast for **whale watching**. With luck you should be able to spot humpback whales swimming just thirty metres from the beach, but for near-certain viewing of both adult whales and their calves it's best to take a boat excursion: the *Pousada Vida, Sol e Mar* (R$100; see below) is the most experienced operator, with boats especially designed for whale watching.

Facilities in Garopaba are mainly geared to campers and the very few **restaurants** are mainly simple places serving fried fish. There's a good, and in the summer usually full, **youth hostel**, the *Hostel Praia do Ferrugem* (Ⓣ48/3254-0035, Ⓦwww.hostelferrugem.hpg.com.br; ❷) at Estrada Geral do Capão, Praia da Ferrugem, opposite the Paulotur bus terminal. Of Garopaba's dozen or so **hotels**, amongst the cheapest is the very pretty *Pousada Casa Grande e Senzala* at Rua Dr Elmo Kiseki 444 (Ⓣ48/3254-3177; ❸), but being small, it's often full in summer. However, by asking around you can nearly always find a room in a private house. There are also plenty of places to stay around Praia do Rosa, 18km to the south, the most picturesque and least developed beach hereabouts, with several attractive *pousadas* (all ❻ and with pools) hidden amidst the hills behind the beach: try *Quinta do Bucanero* (Ⓣ48/3355-6056, Ⓦwww.bucanero.com.br), *Morada dos Bougainvilles* (Ⓣ48/3355-6100, Ⓦwww.pousadabougainville.com.br) or the largest, the *Vida, Sol e Mar* (Ⓣ48/3355-6111, Ⓦwww.vidasolemar.com.br). Despite Garopaba's size, **bus** services are good, with buses to Florianópolis leaving from Rua Marquês Guimarães, and those destined for points south as far as Porto Alegre leaving from Praça Silveira. There are also frequent local services plying the route between Garopaba and Praia da Rosa.

Thirty kilometres south of Garopaba, **IMBITUBA**, once one of the most attractive points along the coast, should be approached with caution. Imbituba's main function is that of a port serving the nearby coalfields; from here coal is sent north to the steel mills of Volta Redonda for coking. The town's beaches are polluted and so too is the air, thanks to the carbo-chemical plant.

Laguna and around

LAGUNA, 125km from Florianópolis and the closest Santa Catarina gets to having a near-complete colonial town, is an excellent place to break your journey. Sitting at the end of a narrow peninsula, at the entrance to the Lagoa Santo Antônio, Laguna feels like two distinct towns. Facing west onto the sheltered lagoon is the old port (long surpassed by Imbituba) and Laguna's historic centre, protected as a national monument. Two kilometres away, on the far side of a granite outcrop of mountainous proportions that separates the city's two parts, is the new town, facing east onto the Atlantic Ocean.

The Town

As a beach resort, Laguna's attraction is limited. The city's importance lies in its **old town**, which, even during the height of the summer tourist season, attracts few people – which is just as well, as it's quite small and could easily be overwhelmed. The one time of year that Laguna gets unbearably crowded is during Carnaval as the town is rated as having one of the best celebrations south of Rio.

Laguna was significant as early as 1494, being the southern point of the line dividing the Americas between Spain and Portugal (the northern point was at Belém), 370 leagues west of the Cape Verde Islands. A **monument** near the *rodoviária*, a few minutes' walk from the centre, marks the exact spot. However, a permanent settlement wasn't established until 1676, but it rapidly became the pre-eminent port of the southern fringes of the Portuguese empire, and a base for the exploration and colonization of what is now Rio Grande do Sul.

Although by no means does all of Laguna's old town date from the eighteenth century, its general aspect is that of a Portuguese colonial town. The oldest streets are those extending off **Praça Vidal Ramos**, the square that holds the **Igreja Santo Antônio dos Anjos**. Built in 1694, the church retains its late eighteenth-century Baroque altars and, though rather modest, is considered the most important surviving colonial church in Santa Catarina.

On the same square as the church is the **Casa de Anita** (daily 8am–6pm), a small museum housed in a modest house built in 1711 and dedicated to Anita Garibaldi, the Brazilian wife of Giuseppe Garibaldi, maverick military leader of the Italian unification movement. Garibaldi was employed as a mercenary in the Guerra dos Farrapos, between republicans and monarchists, and it was in Laguna that a short-lived republic was declared in 1839. There are some fine photographs of nineteenth-century Laguna on display, but – oddly perhaps – there's little on Anita's life and republican activities; scissors and hairbrushes that once belonged to her are typical of the exhibits. In Praça República Juliana in the former town hall and jail, built in 1747, is the **Museu Anita Garibaldi** (daily 8am–6pm), housing a rather dreary collection of local Indian artefacts and items relating to the Guerra dos Farrapos. Close by, on Praça Lauro Muller, the **Fonte da Carioca** is the oldest surviving fountain in Laguna, dating back to 1863, covered in blue and white Portuguese tiles.

Practicalities

The **rodoviária** (Ⓣ48/3644-2441) is at Rua Arcângelo Bianchini, a couple of minutes' walk from the waterfront and the old town. Located at the official entrance to town, 3km from central Laguna, on Avenida Calistralo Muller Salles is the **tourist office** (Mon–Sat 8am–6pm, Sun 8am–1pm; Ⓣ48/3644-2441), which provides excellent maps of Laguna and the surrounding area.

Most of Laguna's hotels and restaurants are in the **new town**, alongside and parallel to the **Praia do Mar Grosso**, the city's main beach. **Hotels** here tend to be large and fairly expensive, but moderately priced exceptions are the *Mar Grosso*, Av. Senador Galotti 644 (Ⓣ48/3644-0298; ❸), the *Hammerse*, Av. João Pinho 492 (Ⓣ48/3647-0598, Ⓦwww.hammers.com.br; ❸), and the *Monte Líbano*, Av. João Pinho 198 (Ⓣ48/3647-0671; ❸). There's also a youth hostel at Rua Aurélio Rótolo 497; reservations during the summer months and July are essential (Ⓣ48/3647-0675, Ⓔ lagunahostel@terra.com.br; ❷). The clutch of seafood **restaurants**, in the middle of Avenida Senador Galotti, are good, though there's little to distinguish one from another.

Apart from during Carnaval, **rooms in the old town** are easy to find. The *Hotel Farol Palace* (Ⓣ48/3644-0596; ❸), on the waterfront opposite the market, is a good choice. There are also a couple of extremely cheap *dormitórios* behind the hotel. **Restaurants** in this part of town are uninspiring, the best being two pizzerias on Praça Juliana.

Around Laguna: the Farol Santa Marta

About 19km out of town to the south is the **Farol Santa Marta**, a lighthouse that was transported piece by piece from Scotland in 1891. The third-tallest lighthouse in the Americas, it's surrounded by bleak but beautiful scenery offering wild seas (suicidal for even the strongest of swimmers) and protected beaches. Between June and September this stretch of shore is a popular spot from which to watch the migrating **humpback whales**, which are clearly visible from shore with binoculars. There are no buses here, but if you have your own transport (most of the road is unpaved, so drive especially carefully after heavy rain) or are prepared to hitch a lift you'll discover a comfortable **hotel**, *Farol de Santa Marta* (Ⓣ48/9986-1257; ❹), complete with a heated pool, as well as the *Jurikão* (Ⓣ48/691-8000; ❸), a basic hotel, and a couple of **restaurants**.

South to Criciúma

The **coastline** between Laguna and the Rio Grande do Sul border is effectively one long beach – though it's of no great beauty and can be passed without much regret. The coastal plain, which stretches inland some 30km, provides little in the way of natural attractions, and the region's two largest towns, Tubarão and Criciúma, were founded as coal-mining centres; the area remains one of Brazil's very few producers of the mineral. Should you need to stay, **CRICIÚMA** is marginally the more pleasant and less polluted of the two.

The **rodoviária** is centrally located on Avenida Centenário, the main artery that bisects the town, and as there are frequent buses to all points in Santa Catarina it's unlikely that you'll have to stay the night. However, if you arrive late, there are two very good **hotels**, virtually alongside the *rodoviária* – the very comfortable *Crisul* (Ⓣ48/3437-4000, Ⓦwww.crisulhotel.com.br; ④) and the somewhat basic *Turis Center* (Ⓣ48/3633-8722; ③). You'll find the **tourist office** at Praça Nereu Ramos, a five-minute walk from the back of the *rodoviária*.

Killing time in Criciúma is fairly easy. The **Museu da Colonização**, Rua Cecília Daros Casagrande (Mon–Fri 9am–6pm; take the "Bairro Comerciario" bus), with its exhibits relating to Italian and German immigrants, is worth a look, but, if you've only got a couple of hours to spare, a visit to the **coal mine** (daily 8–11.30am & 1–6pm; R$4), Criciúma's prime tourist attraction, is really the best idea. It's 3km from the city centre: take the "Mina Modelo" bus from the local bus terminal, which is next to the *rodoviária*. Coal seams were discovered around Criciúma in 1913, and this mine entered production in 1930, ceasing production in the late 1950s. Visitors are taken through the coal mine by retired workers from other local mines, who grind out, in exhausting detail, information about the local geological structure and mining techniques. The deepest the mine goes is just 42 metres, but the squeamish should note that it is home to huge numbers of – quite harmless – fruit bats.

Central and western Santa Catarina

Until the road-building programme of the 1970s, mountainous **central and western Santa Catarina** was pretty much isolated from the rest of the state. Largely settled by migrants from neighbouring states, this territory has inhabitants of diverse origins including Germans and Italians in the extreme west, Austrians, Italians and Ukrainians in the central Rio do Peixe Valley, and *gaúchos* – and even Japanese – in the highlands of the Serra Geral. In the more isolated areas, dominated by a single ethnic group, traditions and languages have been preserved but, as elsewhere in southern Brazil, they are under threat.

Any route taken to reach the **Serra Geral** is spectacular, but if you enter the region directly from the coast the contrasts of landscape, vegetation and climate unfold most dramatically. From the subtropical lowlands, roads have been cut into the steep escarpment and, as the roads slowly wind their way up into the *serra*, dense foliage emerges – protected from human destruction by its ability to cling to the most precipitous of slopes. Waterfalls can be seen in every direction until suddenly you reach the *planalto*. The graceful Paraná pine trees are fewer in number on the plateau but are much larger, their branches fanning upwards in a determined attempt to re-form the canopy that existed before the arrival of cattle and lumber interests.

For tourists, towns in the *serra* are generally places to travel towards rather than destinations in their own right. Even if it means going a considerable distance out of the way, most **bus** services from the coast to the highland town of **Lages** travel via the BR-470 – Santa Catarina's main east–west highway – before turning onto the BR-116, which cuts north–south through the state. To and from Florianópolis, for example, it's usually much faster and more comfortable for buses to travel via Blumenau; however the twice-daily services from Florianópolis direct to Lages via Alfredo Wagner are far more picturesque. From the southern coast of Santa Catarina, the *serra* can be approached by bus from Criciúma on the even more spectacular road leading up via São Joaquim to Lages.

Urussanga and Orleans

The route into the Serra Geral from Criciúma at first passes through a gently undulating landscape, inhabited largely by the descendants of northern Italian immigrants who settled in the region in the 1880s, before climbing the steep escarpment into the highlands. If possible choose a clear day to make the trip as the views east towards the coast are absolutely spectacular.

Some 20km from Criciúma the road passes through **URUSSANGA**, a small agricultural processing town. Urussanga and the surrounding countryside is noted for its stone farm buildings dating from the arrival of the first Italian settlers and, with federal government support, the authorities have been making tremendous efforts to restore them. A handful are located in the town itself, but to see those in outlying areas you'll need to get detailed directions from the Prefeitura. If you need somewhere **to stay**, make for the *Pousada da Vinícola Mazon* (☎48/3465-1500; ❸), some 6km from town towards the village of São Pedro. The *pousada* is set in pretty countryside, the hillsides covered in grape vine, and you can eat here too – the meals are superb examples of local Italian country cooking.

A further 20km along the road is the small town of **ORLEANS**, lying on a fairly busy crossroads, from where it's easy to pick up buses to São Joaquim, Criciúma or Laguna. If you decide to stop over, there are a couple of modest **hotels**: the *São Francisco* (☎48/3666-0282; ❸), at Rua Aristiliano Ramos 120, and the *Brasil* (❷), at Rua Getúlio Vargas 9. An unremarkable little town in most ways, Orleans does boast the excellent outdoor **Museu do Imigrante** (Mon–Fri 9am–noon & 1.30–5.30pm, Sat–Sun 9am–5.30pm; R$5), which records early immigrant life and industry and features a water-powered sawmill and other buildings moved here from the surrounding area.

São Joaquim

Formerly just a small highland ranching centre, **SÃO JOAQUIM**, ninety steep kilometres beyond Orleans, has only really been on the Brazilian map since the mid-1970s when apple orchards were introduced here. Within twenty years, Brazil changed from importing nearly all the apples consumed in the country to becoming a major exporter of the fruit. At an altitude of 1360m (making this the highest town in Brazil), apple trees are in their element in São Joaquim, benefiting from the very pronounced seasonal temperature variations. Temperatures in the winter regularly dip to -15°C and, as this is one of the few parts of Brazil that sees regular snowfalls, there is a surprising amount of tourism in the winter, with camping being especially popular amongst Brazilians as a way of truly experiencing the cold. Anyone with a specific interest in apples can visit the **Estação Experimental de São Joaquim**, a research centre and orchard on the outskirts of town. On Sundays there's a handicrafts market on the town's main square, Praça João Ribeiro, with stalls selling local food produce too, including apples.

The **rodoviária** (☎49/3233-0400), a couple of minutes' walk from the city centre, has good connections to Lages, Criciúma and Florianópolis. For accommodation, there's a reasonable **hotel**, the *Nevada*, on Rua Manoel Joaquim Pinto (☎49/3233-0259; ❷–❸) as well as the newer, and more comfortable, *São Joaquim Park* at Praça João Ribeiro 58 (☎49/3233-1444, Ⓦwww.saojoaquimparkhotel.com.br; ❹). Despite the presence of some fifty Japanese apple-growing families, the only **restaurants** are a pizzeria, the *Agua na Boca* on Rua Marcos Batista

907, and the *Casa de Pedra* on Rua Manuel Joaquim Pinto 360, which offers a buffet of varied hot and cold dishes and a *rodizio de carnes*.

Lages

Although founded in 1766, nothing remains in **LAGES**, 76km northwest of São Joaquim, from the days when it was an important resting place for cowhands herding cattle and mules on the route northwards to the market in Sorocaba. Nowadays, it's a collection of anonymous post-1950s buildings, and only the presence in town of visiting ranchers and cowhands, dressed in the characteristic baggy pantaloons, sash and poncho, reminds you of its position at the northern edge of *gaúcho* country. Because so many knife-carrying men come into town at the weekend for supplies and a good time, Lages is reputed to be the most violent town in the state. However, the general atmosphere is dull rather than menacing, and tourists are unlikely to get caught up in any trouble.

The reason to visits Lages is for a taste of life in the *gaúcho* high country. The tourist office promotes the **Turismo Rural** project, which provides opportunities for people to visit typical cattle *fazendas* and catch a glimpse of life in outlying parts of the *serra* – otherwise extremely difficult for tourists to see. For day-trips, only groups are catered for, so ask at the tourist office whether you can join one that has already been formed. Alternatively, several *fazendas* accept guests, who are encouraged to participate in the everyday activities of the cattle ranches. Otherwise, the best way to get a feel for the region is to attend one of the periodic **rodeios**; again, the tourist office can provide information.

Practicalities

The **rodoviária** (Ⓣ49/3222-6710) is a half-hour walk southeast of the centre, or you can take a bus marked "Dom Pedro". The **tourist office** (Mon–Fri 8am–noon & 2–6pm; Ⓣ49/3223-6206) is in the centre of town at Rua Hercílio Luz 573, and distributes a good map of Lages.

Reasonable, modestly priced **hotels** are easy to come by. The *Hotel Presidente*, Av. Presidente Vargas 106 (Ⓣ49/3224-0014; ❷), is quite good and only a few minutes' walk from the cathedral and main square, Praça Waldo da Costa Avila. If you want a bit more luxury, try the *Grande Hotel Lages*, Rua João de Castro 23 (Ⓣ49/3222-3522; ❸) or the newer, but otherwise similar, *Le Canard* at Av. Presidente Varga 255 (Ⓣ49/3224-5566, Ⓦwww.lecanard.com.br; ❸–❹). However, to really experience *serra* life you should arrange to stay on a **cattle fazenda**, all located some distance from town. A full list and advice is available from the tourist office and if you don't have your own transport you can arrange with the *fazenda* to be picked up in town. Especially recommended are the rustic *Seriema* (Ⓣ49/9986-0051; ❹ full board); *Nossa Senhora de Lourdes* (Ⓣ49/3222-0798 or 9983-0809; ❺ full board), a mid-nineteenth-century *fazenda* house with period furnishings and a pool (no children accepted); and the more hotel-like *Barreiro* (Ⓣ49/3222-3031, Ⓦwww.fazendadobarreiro.com.br; ❺–❻ full board), which traces its origins to the late eighteenth century, though its buildings are all of recent contruction. Reservations are essential for all three. While the landscape of the *serra* is extremely rugged and the life of the highland *gaúcho* is often harsh, the *fazendas* provide comfortable accommodation, and excellent food and facilities.

Back in town, **restaurants** are, of course, largely meat-oriented, the best being the *Laghões*, at Rua João de Castro 27. There are also a number of vaguely Italian restaurants: *Cantina d'Italia*, at Rua Francisco Furtado Ramos 122, is worth a try.

Rio do Peixe valley

Immigrants were introduced to the **Peixe valley** in around 1910 by the American-owned Brazil Railway Company. For completing the São Paulo–Rio Grande rail line, the company received land from which they could extract valuable timber and which they could divide for sale to homesteaders. Due to the region's isolation, war in Europe, anti-immigration legislation and the discovery that the soil was not as fertile as had been believed, fewer people than hoped moved into the area. Of those who did come, most were from neighbouring states, mainly Slavs from Paraná, and Germans and Italians from Rio Grande do Sul.

Joaçaba

The region's most important town is **JOAÇABA**, 462km west of Florianópolis, on the Peixe's west bank, directly across the river from the smaller town of Herval d'Oeste. Perhaps due to the narrowness of the valley, whose slopes rise precipitously along one entire side of town, Joaçaba has an oppressive, almost menacing, atmosphere. Although the population is dominated by descendants of Italian immigrants, no obvious Italian influences remain, and, as Joaçaba developed into an important centre of light industry and agribusiness, it lost any frontier charm that might have once existed. However, if you're visiting the Rio do Peixe area, Joaçaba is difficult to avoid altogether. Buses from here serve all surrounding districts and towns to the west, and there are regular departures to Blumenau, Florianópolis, São Paulo and Foz do Iguaçu.

With the **rodoviária** located just a few minutes' walk from the town centre, arriving in Joaçaba couldn't be easier. On leaving the *rodoviária*, turn right onto Avenida XV de Novembro, the road that runs alongside the river through town; turn right again on Rua Sete de Setembro and you'll find an inexpensive **hotel**, the *Comércio* (Ⓣ49/3522-2211; ❷). A few doors away is the modern luxury *Hotel Jaraguá* (Ⓣ49/3522-4255, Ⓦwww.hoteljaraguareal.com.br; ❹), which has a pool and a reasonable restaurant. Also on Avenida XV de Novembro are a couple of *churrascarias* and pizzerias.

Treze Tílias

Of the region's ethnic groups, it is one of the smallest – the Austrians – who have been most stubborn in resisting cultural assimilation. The claim of the *município* of **TREZE TÍLIAS** to be the "Brazilian Tyrol" is by no means a baseless one. In 1933, 82 Tyroleans led by Andreas Thaler, a former Austrian minister of agriculture, arrived in what is now Treze Tílias. As the dense forest around the settlement was gradually cleared more settlers joined the colony, but after Germany's annexation of Austria in 1938 immigration came to an end – as did funds to help support the pioneers during the difficult first years. With the onset of war, communications with Austria ceased altogether and, with no country to return to, abandoning the colony was not an option. During the immediate postwar years, contacts with Europe were minimal, but as Austria grew more prosperous Treze Tílias began to receive assistance. The area eventually came to specialize in dairy farming and today its milk products are sold in supermarkets throughout Santa Catarina.

Treze Tílias is only an hour north of Joaçaba and west of Videira and it's perfectly practical to use it as a base for getting to know the wider region. All buses stop right in the centre of the village outside the *Hotel Áustria* (Ⓣ49/3537-0132; ❷–❸), the oldest, most basic and one of the friendliest of Treze Tílias' numerous **hotels**. Also in the centre, the *Hotel Tirol* (Ⓣ49/3537-0125, Ⓦwww.hoteltirol.com.br; ❹), a typical Tyrolean-style chalet, complete with geraniums hanging from every balcony, has very comfortable rooms and a pool. You'll get similar floral comforts and style at the nearby *Hotel Dreizehnlinden*

(Ⓣ49/3537-0297, Ⓦwww.hotel13linden.com.br; ❸) and at the more intimate *Hotel Schneider* (Ⓣ49/3537-0184, Ⓦwww.hotelschneider.com.br; ❸). All of these hotels have good restaurants serving standard Austrian dishes at lunch, and *café colonial* in the late afternoon and evening. If you want to **eat** somewhere with more local character, make for the *Berenkamp*, right behind the Prefeitura. The food here is good, cheap and abundant, and the atmosphere is about as close as you're likely to come outside Austria to an ordinary Tyrolean pub. The best time is early evening, when elderly locals drop by to eat and chat – German speakers will be intrigued by the local Tyrolean-Brazilian dialect that has developed in Treze Tílias over the past seventy years. Other reliable options in town for Austrian food are the *Kandlerhof*, Rua Videira 80 (closed Sun) and the *Edelweiss*, Rua Dr Gaspar Coutinho 439 (evenings only, closed Mon).

But for the absence of snow-capped mountain peaks, the general appearance of Treze Tílias is not dissimilar to that of a small alpine village. **Walking** in any direction, you'll pass through peaceful pastoral landscapes. The gentle seven-kilometre walk to the chapel in the hamlet of **Babenberg** is particularly rewarding. If you decide to visit the local **waterfalls** a few kilometres outside town, get very detailed directions before setting out.

In Treze Tílias itself, try to visit some of the **woodcarvers**, several of whom have shops in the centre of the village where items, large and small, are for sale. The best woodcarvers learned their craft in Europe, and their work is in demand by churches throughout Brazil. On the main street, the **Museu do Imigrante** (Mon–Sat 9.30am–noon & 2–6pm, Sun 10am–noon & 2–5pm) features a small collection of photographs and paintings of the area in the 1930s and 1940s, as well as items brought with the immigrants from Austria. The **Tirolerfest** during the first two weeks of October is a lively display of Austrian folk traditions including singing and dancing.

Videira

On the eastern fringes of Treze Tílias, along the Linha Pinhal road leading to the neighbouring town of **VIDEIRA**, the population is mainly of Italian origin, descended from migrants who came from Rio Grande do Sul in the 1940s, their brightly painted wooden houses instantly distinguishable from the Austrians' chalets. Vines dominate the landscape, and if you visit a *colônia* you'll probably be invited to taste their home-produced salami, *cachaça* or the wine – it's only polite to buy a bottle before leaving. In Videira itself the small, but well-organized **Museu do Vinho** (Mon–Fri 9–11.30am & 1.30–5.30pm, Sat 9am–noon) next to the main church, is worth half an hour or so. The displays relate to the local wine-making techniques in the early years of settlement.

Videira itself doesn't justify more than the briefest of pauses between buses, which are, unfortunately, far less frequent than those from Joaçaba. If you need a **hotel**, and there's no time to go to Treze Tílias, walk down the hill on Avenida Dom Pedro II from the *rodoviária* and turn right at the Shell station onto Rua Brasil (the main commercial street); the inexpensive *Savanna Hotel* (❷) and **restaurant** is the first building on the left. Alternatively, by crossing the river over the bridge at the bottom of Rua Brasil, next to the local bus terminal, you'll come to Videira's luxury *Hotel Verde Vale Palace* (Ⓣ49/3566-1622, Ⓦwww.hotelverdevale.com.br; ❸–❹), whose reasonably priced restaurant serves the town's best food – a mix of standard Brazilian and Italian dishes.

Caçador

The next town on the Rio do Peixe, 35km north of Videira, **CAÇADOR** is very different in character from the largely agricultural settlements to the south, with a workaday atmosphere and a landscape dominated by pine plantations. The one reason to stop is to visit the small **Museu do Contestado** (Tues–Sun 8.30–11.30am & 1.30–5.30pm), housed in the old railway station. The museum commemorates the brutal war that took place in the Rio do Peixe valley from 1912 to 1916 between the Brazilian government, which was protecting the interests of the American-owned railway company that had been awarded huge land grants in the region, and the displaced native and *caboclo* population. The war eventually led to the deaths of 20,000 people, and well-presented exhibits in the museum commemorate the lives of the local Indians and *caboclos* who fought in the conflict. Outside the station is a perfectly preserved 1907 Baldwin locomotive and passenger carriage.

There are several **hotels** within minutes of the museum if you need to stay over, the best being the modern *Le Canard* (Ⓣ49/3563-1000, Ⓦwww.lecanard.com.br; ❸–❹). Otherwise there are good bus services to Florianópolis, União da Vitória and Curitiba from the **rodoviária** (Ⓣ49/3563-0225) across from the museum. If you're travelling north towards Paraná by car there are two possible routes; the paved SC-451 road connecting to the BR-153 is the fastest, but much more interesting is to take the road to Calmon, a village on the banks of the Rio do Peixe and continue on north to União da Vitória. The road is absolutely appalling but the landscape is starkly dramatic, dominated by huge plantations of imported pine trees and the occasional patch of original Paraná pine.

The extreme west

Until the 1950s, most of the population of the extreme west of Santa Catarina were Kaingang Indians and semi-nomadic *caboclos* who harvested the *erva maté* grown in the region. As land became increasingly unavailable in Rio Grande do Sul, peasant farmers moved north into Santa Catarina and the area has since become the state's foremost producer of pigs and chickens.

Chapecó and around

Unless you have an interest in agriculture, **CHAPECÓ** – or indeed any other town in the region – is unlikely to hold your attention for longer than the time it takes to change buses. Fortunately, Chapecó is well served with **buses** to points throughout Santa Catarina and Rio Grande do Sul, to Dionísio Cerqueira (for Argentina), Curitiba and Cascavel (for connections to Foz do Iguaçu) in Paraná. If you have to stick around for a while, frequent buses connect the *rodoviária*, on the city's outskirts, with the local bus terminal, which is located virtually on the main square. There are a couple of **places to stay** near the bus terminal – including the comfortable *Hotel Eston* (Ⓣ49/3323-1044, Ⓦwww.estonhotel.com.br; ❸) – and two more on the main street, Avenida Getúlio Vargas.

Chapecó's self-proclaimed status as regional capital simply means that its slaughterhouses are larger than those in the surrounding towns. If you happen to be in town during the month of August, you'll coincide with the **Festa Nacional do Frango e do Peru**, an absurdly contrived affair celebrating chicken and turkey production – almost as ridiculous as the town's **Wurstfest**, an annual jamboree in November in celebration of the sausage. Otherwise there's not much to delay you, though if you're stuck browse around Bolicho do Gauderio, on the main square – a general outfitters aiming at fashion-conscious young *gaúchos* and a good place to pick up souvenirs. On a sadder note, souvenirs can also be purchased from forlorn-looking Kaingang Indians, who wander around town attempting to sell their brightly coloured basketwork and bows and arrows. One possible excursion, however, is to the **Museu**

Entomológico Fritz Plaumann (Mon–Thurs & Sat 8am–noon & 1–5pm; ⓣ49/3452-1191, ⓦwww.museufritzplaumann.ufsc.br) in **Nova Teutônia**, an overwhelmingly German community some 45km east of Chapecó near the town of **Seara** (any bus between the two towns will drop you off there). Housed in a large 1940s wooden house typical of the region, the museum boasts what is quite possibly the most important collection of insects in Latin America. Plaumann (1902–94) arrived in Nova Teutônia from Germany in 1924 and went on to dedicate his life to entomological studies, collecting 80,000 specimens, representing 17,000 species, including 1500 that had previously been unknown. Pride of place goes to the displays of butterflies at every stage of development, but what's truly impressive is that the entire collection is supported by detailed notebooks, correspondence and other documentation representing seventy years of Plaumann's professional and personal life.

Abelardo Luz

Ninety kilometres north of Chapecó is **ABELARDO LUZ**, a small town near Paraná's border. In the mid-1980s Abelardo Luz briefly hit the headlines in Brazil, when thousands of landless peasants from neighbouring areas moved onto the huge estates of absentee landowners in this, one of the poorest and most sparsely populated parts of Santa Catarina.

The unrest – one of the first land invasions organized by the Movimento dos Sem Terra – has long since subsided and the reporters from throughout Brazil who descended on this little town are now just an exciting distant memory for this otherwise sleepy place. However, small numbers of tourists do stop off in Abelardo Luz, on their way between eastern Santa Catarina, Rio Grande do Sul and Foz do Iguaçu, to see the beautiful waterfalls, **Quedas do Rio Chapecó**, a 45-minute walk from town. To reach the falls, walk up Abelardo Luz's main street and, at the top, turn left and walk until you reach an asphalted highway where you turn right. Walk along the road past the horseshoe-shaped entrance to the park, cross a bridge and continue until you come to signs for the "*quedas*", indicating a road to the left. You'll be charged a small entrance fee, but facilities are good; there's a **campsite**, a **restaurant** and snack bar. There's also a spa **hotel**, the *Quedas* (ⓣ49/3445-4811, ⓦwww.hotelquedas.com.br; ❸) with an indoor pool. The falls themselves extend across the river and take the form of eight steps varying in breadth and width. Walkways cross parts of the waterfalls and there are numerous small natural pools by the side of the tourist complex. But to swim properly, you need to go 3km upriver to **Prainha**, a beach where there's also a campsite.

Apart from at the falls themselves, the only **place to stay** is a very grim, but cheap, hotel (❷) on the main street in town. **Buses** leave from virtually outside the hotel and there's an hourly service to **Xanxerê**, a dull agro-processing town an hour south of Abelardo Luz, from where there are frequent connections to points within Santa Catarina and Rio Grande do Sul. If you're travelling to or from Foz do Iguaçu, take a bus to Cascavel (Paraná) or Dionísio Cerqueira and change there.

Dionísio Cerqueira

Situated in the extreme northwest corner of Santa Catarina, **DIONÍSIO CERQUEIRA** virtually merges with the smaller town of **Barracão** in Paraná and, just across the Argentine border, **Bernardo de Irigoyen**. Dionísio Cerqueira has become a busy shopping centre, attracting cross-border shoppers from Argentina, but it's an unremarkable town and you're unlikely to want to stay longer than is needed to catch a bus out. Fortunately each of the border towns is well served by **bus** companies. Dionísio Cerqueira's *rodoviária*, a few blocks back from the border, has frequent departures to all main towns in Santa Catarina, Rio Grande do Sul and Posadas in Argentina. The nearby Barracão Rodoviária serves Paraná, including Curitiba and Foz do Iguaçu. From Bernardo de Irigoyen's bus station, there are services throughout the Argentine province of Misiones, including Posadas (for the nearby Jesuit ruins, or for connections further south or west into Argentina) and Puerto Iguazú.

If you do need to stop over, it's easy to find a **hotel**. The best place to stay (and eat) is the very reliable *Motel ACA* (Ⓣ751/92218; ❸) near the bus station in Bernardo de Irigoyen. In Dionísio Cerqueira there's the very basic *Hotel Iguaçu* (Ⓣ49/3844-1029; ❷), at Rua Mário Cláudio Turra 260 and only one real **restaurant**, the *Medieval* at Av. Santa Catarina 190, which serves standard Brazilian fare. For those who prefer to stay in Barracão, the *Província* (Ⓣ49/3844-1261, Ⓦwww.provincia.com.br; ❷–❸) at Rua São Paulo 411 is a perfectly comfortable hotel with a restaurant.

The **border crossing** is very relaxed and is open between 7am and 7pm. Argentine passport control is located right on the border, whereas the Brazilian Polícia Federal is two blocks back from the border on Dionísio Cerqueira's main road, at Rua República Argentina 259.

Rio Grande do Sul

For many people the state of **Rio Grande do Sul**, bordering Argentina and Uruguay, is their first or last experience of Brazil. More than most parts of the country, it has an extremely strong regional identity – to the extent that it's the only state where the possibility of independence is discussed. Today, the Santa Cruz do Sul-based **Movimento Pro-Pampa** campaigns for the separation of Brazil's three southernmost states to create the República Federal da Pampa Gaúcha. Central government's authority over Brazil's southernmost state has often been weak: in the colonial era, the territory was virtually a no-man's land separating the Spanish and Portuguese empires. Out of this emerged a strongly independent people, mostly pioneer farmers and the descendants of European immigrants, isolated fishing communities and, best known, the *gaúchos* (see p.782), the cowboys of southern South America whose name is now used for all inhabitants of the state, whatever their origins.

The **road and bus network** is excellent and it's easy to zip through the state without stopping if need be. However, Rio Grande do Sul is as Brazilian as Bahia or Rio and it would be a shame to ignore the place. The capital, **Porto Alegre**, is southern Brazil's most important cultural and commercial centre but, like all the other cities in Rio Grande do Sul, has little to detain tourists. However, it's also the state's transportation axis and at some point you're likely to pass through the city. For a truer flavour of Rio Grande do Sul, visit the principal region of Italian and German settlement, around the towns of **Caxias do Sul**, **Bento Gonçalves** and **Nova Petrópolis**, a couple of hours north of Porto Alegre. And for the classic image, head for the cattle country of the *serra* and *campanha* where old *gaúcho* traditions still linger.

Porto Alegre

The capital of Rio Grande do Sul, **PORTO ALEGRE**, lies on the eastern bank of the Rio Guaiba, at the point where five rivers converge to form the **Lagoa dos Patos**, a giant freshwater lagoon navigable by even the largest of ships. Founded in 1755 as a Portuguese garrison, to guard against Spanish encroachment into this part of the empire, it wasn't until Porto Alegre became the port for the export of beef that it developed into Brazil's leading commercial centre south of São Paulo.

With a rather uninteresting feel to it, like a cross between a southern European and a North American city, most people will be tempted to move straight on from Porto Alegre, unless they're waiting to make a transport connection. Fortunately the city has considerable life, if not much visible history, and you'll find many ways to occupy yourself, particularly if your visit coincides with one of the main festivals: Semana Farroupilha (Sept 13–20) features traditional local folk dancing and singing, while the highlight of Festa de Nossa Senhora dos Navegantes (Feb 2) is a procession of fishing boats.

Arrival, information and accommodation

There's hardly an airport in southern Brazil that doesn't serve Porto Alegre, and there are international services to Buenos Aires, Montevideo and Santiago, too. The **airport** (Ⓣ51/3358-2000) is linked by *metrô* to the Mercado Público, in the city centre just 6km away, or take the L.05 bus, which links the airport with Praça Parobe (next to the Mercado Público). Taxis into the city cost about R$20.

Buses from throughout Brazil and neighbouring countries stop at Porto Alegre's **rodoviária** (Ⓣ51/3210-0101), which is within walking distance of the centre; however, because the *rodoviária* is virtually ringed by a mesh of highways and overpasses, it's far less confusing, and safer, to use the *metrô* from here. Porto Alegre used to be a major **rail** hub but only suburban passenger routes still run, otherwise services are limited to hauling freight. Trains depart from the **ferroviária**, just outside the city centre in the direction of the airport, also accessible by *metrô*.

The **metrô** (daily 5am–11.20pm; R$1.40) has its city centre terminal at the Mercado Público, but as the system is very limited in extent it's only really of use when you arrive and leave Porto Alegre.

The city's **tourist office** (Ⓣ0800-51-7686) has very helpful branches at the airport (7am–midnight), at the *rodoviária* (7am–10pm), the Centro Cultural Usina do Gasômetro (Tues–Sun 10am–6pm) and at the Mercado Público (Mon–Sat 9am–6pm). SETUR, the state tourist office (Ⓣ51/3228-7377, Ⓦwww.turismo.rs.gov.br), has kiosks at the *rodoviária* (daily 7am–7pm) and the airport (same hours), but is of more limited assistance. Both agencies hand out excellent free maps of Porto Alegre. For up-to-date **listings**, consult the monthly *Programa*, produced by the tourist office, or the events listings in the newspaper *Zero Hora*.

Accommodation

There's a good range of **hotels** scattered around the city centre, and as distances are small it's possible to walk to most places, although great care should be taken at night when the area tends to be eerily quiet. There are a couple of upscale options in the residential and business suburb of Moinhos de Vento, a good spot to stay in that allows for evening walks and offers a choice of bars and restaurants. Hotels are geared towards business travellers and as a consequence most offer substantial discounts at weekends. Porto Alegre can get quite cold in the winter and very hot and humid in the summer, but fortunately most hotels have central heating and air conditioning.

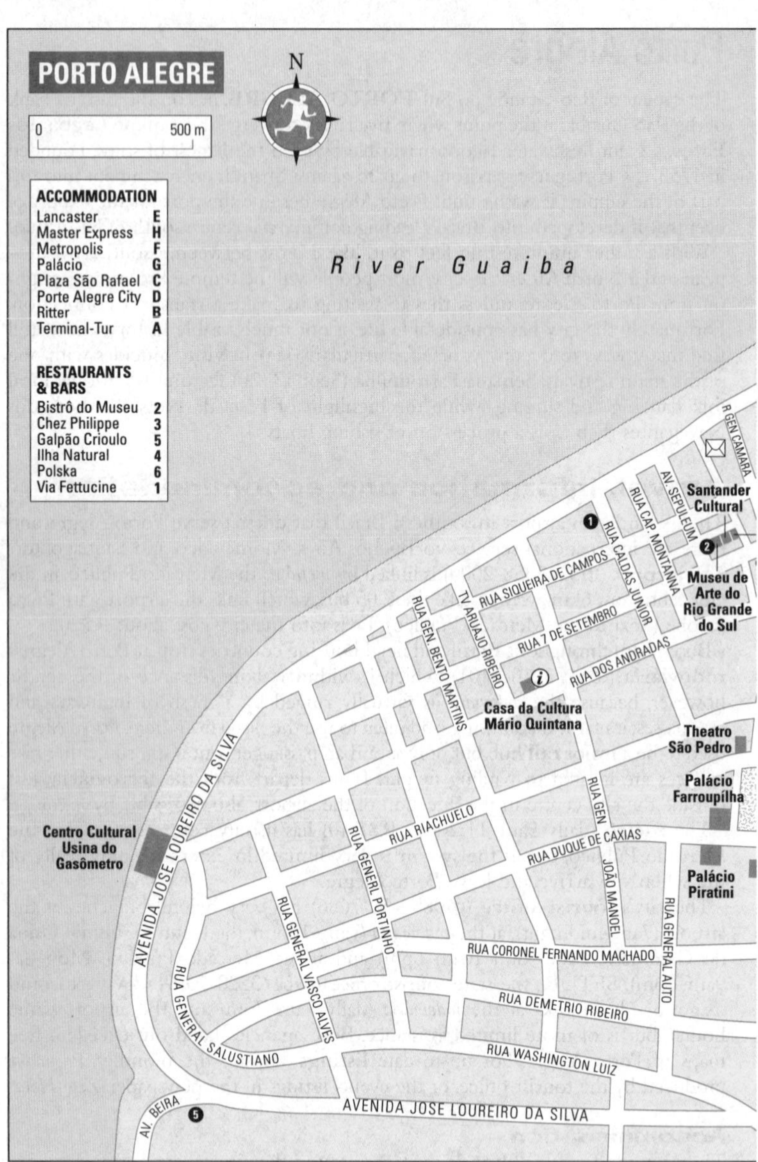

Blue Tree Towers Av. Coronel Lucas de Oliveira 995 ⓣ51/3019-8000, ⓦwww.bluetree.com.br. Excellent value for a luxury hotel in the pleasant residential district of Bela Vista. The guest rooms are tastefully furnished and the hotel has its own sushi bar. ❺–❻

Hostel Hotel Elevado Av. Farropos 63 ⓣ51/3224-5250, ⓦwww.hotelelevado.com.br. This HI-affiliated hostel near the *rodoviária* offers secure accommodation and a friendly atmosphere. Single, double and triple rooms are offered with or without private bathrooms. ❷

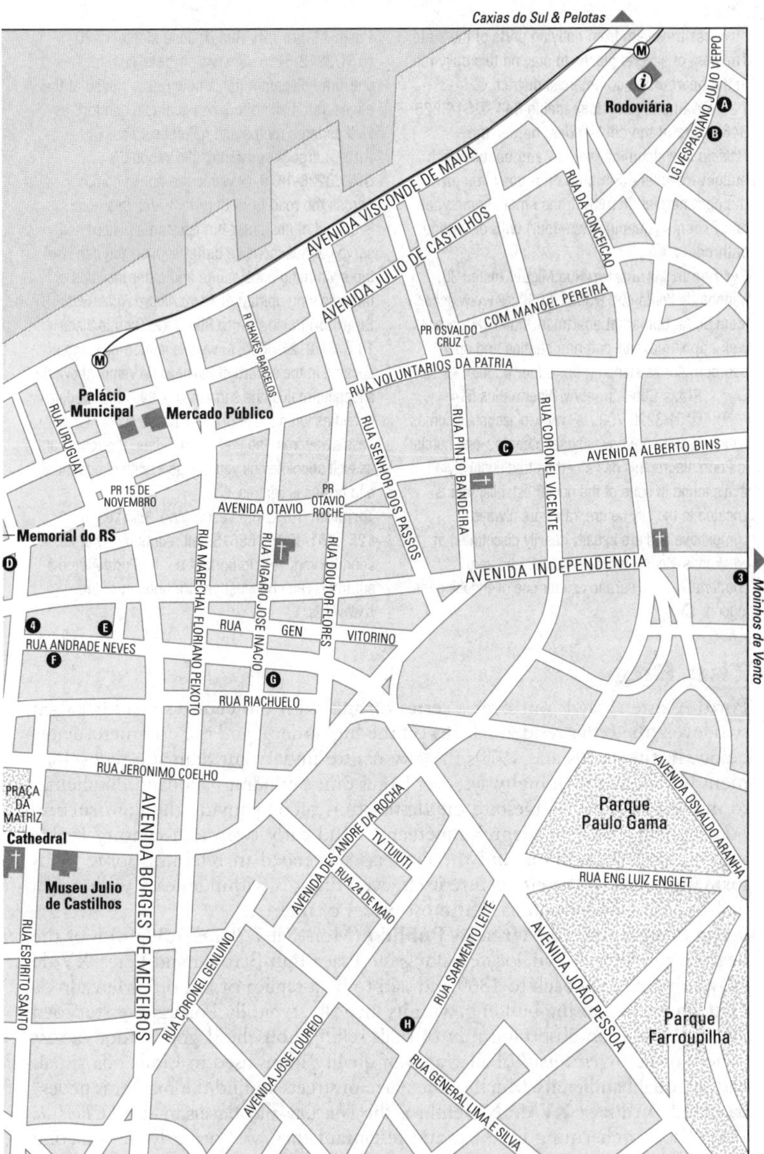

Lancaster Travessa Acelino de Carvalho 67 ⓣ51/3224-4737, ⓦwww.hotel-lancaster-poa.com.br. Located in one of the liveliest commercial areas downtown, this modern hotel is set behind an imposing 1940s facade. Rooms are small but well equipped, and excellent value for money. ❸–❹

Master Express Rua Sarmento Leite 865 ⓣ51/3018-3636, ⓦwww.master-hoteis.com.br. Efficient but rather sterile hotel in a good location, with low rates and helpful staff. ❸

Metropolis Rua Andrade Neves 59 ⓣ51/3226-1800. Basic but neatly kept rooms, popular with business travellers from outlying parts of the state. The best of several places to stay on this busy road in the heart of the commercial district. ❸

Palácio Rua Vigário José Inácio 644 ⓣ51/3225-3467. One of the city's oldest hotels, the *Palácio* is welcoming, secure and popular with budget travellers. Situated on a busy lane in the commercial district, it has small, somewhat noisy rooms (sleeping two–four) with or without bathrooms. ❸

Parthenon Manhattan Rua Miguel Tostes 30, Minhos de Vento ⓣ51/3024-3030, ⓦwww.accor.com.br. An upmarket apartment-hotel with a pool, well-appointed, self-catering studios and one-bedroom suites sleeping up to four people. ❺–❻

Plaza São Rafael Av. Alberto Bins 514 ⓣ51/3220-7000, ⓦwww.plazahoteis.com.br. Although there are now several other top-end hotels in Porto Alegre, this has a certain traditional style that's found in none of the newer establishments. Located in the city centre, rates are always competitive and are usually heavily discounted at weekends. Rooms are all spacious and very comfortable – be sure to ask for one overlooking the lagoon. ❺

Porto Alegre City Rua Dr José Montaury 20 ⓣ51/3212-5488, ⓦwww.cityhotel.com.br. This one-time elegant hotel is now rather frayed at the edges, but it still offers considerable comfort, as well as large rooms and helpful service. ❹

Ritter Largo Vespasiano Júlio Veppo 55 ⓣ51/3228-1610, ⓦwww.ritterhoteis.com.br. Across the road from the *rodoviária*, this hotel is devoid of character but is clean, efficient and serves an inexpensive buffet supper. You can use the swimming pool, sauna and other facilities of the adjoining upmarket *Porto Alegre Ritter Hotel*. ❹

Sheraton Porto Alegre Rua Olavo Barreto Viana 18 ⓣ51/2121-6000, ⓦwww.sheraton-poa.com.br. Located in the suburb of Moinhos de Vento, above the shopping mall of the same name, this ultra-modern hotel has lured much of the expense account business away from the Plaza São Rafael. The rooms are as well appointed as you'd expect, with good fitness and business centres. ❽

Terminal-Tur Largo Vespasiano Júlio Veppo 125 ⓣ51/3227-1656. Small rooms but with air conditioning, very important during Porto Alegre's summer. The cheapest secure hotel near the *rodoviária*. ❸

The City

Porto Alegre sprawls out over a series of hills with the centre spread between two levels, the older residential area on the higher level and the commercial area below. In the 1960s and 1970s the city centre underwent dramatic redevelopment with new urban highways, ever larger office buildings and landfill schemes to improve the docks. Despite the destruction accompanying the construction boom, many of Porto Alegre's nineteenth- and early twentieth-century buildings escaped demolition, and the city has succeeded in retaining some of its former dignity. In the city centre itself, everything is within an easy walk, and a half-day or so is enough to visit most places of interest.

The ochre-coloured **Mercado Público** (Mon–Sat 7.30am–7.30pm) is at the heart of the lower town, located alongside Praça Rui Barbosa and Praça XV de Novembro. Dating back to 1869 and said to be a replica of Lisbon's Mercado da Figueira, this imposing building, with its intricate, typically Portuguese, stuccoed detail, contains an absorbing mix of stalls selling household goods, food, a vast variety of herbs, *erva maté* of all grades of quality, items used in Umbanda rituals and regional handicrafts. Much of the maze of streets around the market is pedestrianized; on Praça XV de Novembro, the century-old Bavarian-style *Chalé da Praça XV* – a charming little bar and restaurant that was formerly the meeting place of the city's artists and intellectuals – is an especially good spot from which to watch the world go by. To the left of the market is the **Palácio Municipal**, the old *prefeitura*, built in Neoclassical style between 1898 and 1901, its impressive proportions an indication of civic pride and self-confidence during the period when Porto Alegre was developing from being a mere southern outpost into an important city. Between about 1880 and 1930, Porto Alegre attracted large numbers of southern and eastern European immigrants and in front of the palace is the **Talavera de la Reina**, a fountain, given to the city in 1935 from its once considerable Spanish community.

△ Mercado Público, Porto Alegre

The streets along the steep slope rising from the low-lying parts of the centre (Rua dos Andradas, Rua General Vitorino and Rua Andrade Neves, which becomes Avenida Senador Salgado Filho) mark Porto Alegre's main **commercial district** of clothing stores, travel agents and banks. Further up the hill are Praça da Matriz (officially called Praça Marechal Deodoro) and Largo João Amorim do Albuquerque, where the former legislative assembly and some of Porto Alegre's oldest buildings are concentrated. Despite the buildings in this part of the city having late eighteenth- to mid-nineteenth-century origins, they have undergone so many renovations and additions over the past couple of centuries that only vaguely, if at all, do they bear any resemblance to their colonial predecessors. Though the foundations of the **Catedral Metropolitana** are built over those of a church that dates back to 1772, the present Italianate structure was only begun in 1921, and wasn't completed until 1986. Work on the former legislative assembly also started in 1772 but, likewise, it has undergone innumerable renovations over the years. The **Palácio Piratini** (the state governor's residence; Mon–Fri 9–11am & 2–5pm; Ⓦwww.palaciopiratini.rs.gov.br) dates from only 1909, while across from it the **Teatro São Pedro** (Tues–Fri noon–7pm, Sat & Sun 3–9pm; Ⓣ54/3227-5100, Ⓦwww.teatrosaopaulo.rs.gov.br) was inaugurated in 1858. Surprisingly, the Neoclassical building and Portuguese Baroque-style interior has remained largely unmolested, and the theatre is an important venue for local and visiting companies. Also around the Praça da Matriz are several impressive nineteenth-century mansions, including the former **Consulado Italiano** (Italian consulate) at no. 134, whose prominent position reflects the important role Italians played in Porto Alegre and elsewhere in Rio Grande do Sul. Nearby is the **Museu Júlio de Castilhos**, Rua Duque de Caxias 1231 (Tues–Fri 10am–7pm, Sat & Sun 2–5pm; R$4), which presents a patchy and poor history of the state.

Porto Alegre's other **museums and cultural centres** are generally a poor bunch, which is somewhat surprising for a city that has long been prosperous and is the most important cultural centre south of São Paulo. One that does stand out is the **Casa de Cultura Mário Quintana**, Rua dos Andradas 736 (Tues–Fri 9am–9pm, Sat & Sun noon–9pm; Ⓦwww.ccmq.rs.gov.br), one of the city's largest cultural centres. Designed in Neoclassical style by the German architect Theo Wiederspahn in 1923, the extremely elegant rose-coloured building was a hotel until 1980 and as such was once a popular meeting point for local artists, intellectuals and politicians, including presidents Vargas and Goulart. The poet Mário Quintana was a long-time resident (hence the name), and his room is assiduosly maintained as it was while he lived there. In addition to numerous exhibition galleries, the Casa de Cultura houses a library, a bookshop, a cinema, a decent restaurant and a café. Nearby, on Praça da Alfândega, are three other exhibition centres housed in imposing French-style Neoclassical buildings that are always at least worth a peek. Although the **Museu de Arte do Rio Grande do Sul** (Tues–Sun 10am–7pm; Ⓦwww.margs.org.br), has been devastated by thefts, it still has a small collection of work by *gaúcho* artists, among which the nineteenth-century landscapes deserve particular attention; it also hosts occasional special exhibitions. Alongside, the **Santander Cultural** (Mon noon–8pm, Tues–Sat 10am–8pm, Sun 10am–6pm; Ⓦwww.santandercultural.com.br) puts on temporary exhibitions of Brazilian art, often important collections first displayed in São Paulo. The building itself, a converted 1920s bank, features some remarkable stained-glass windows depicting positivist themes. Next door, the city's very grand, Neoclassical-style, former main post office building is now the **Memorial do Rio Grande do Sul** (Tues–Sat 10am–6pm; Ⓦwww.memorial.rs.gov.br). Housed here are the state archives, along with an oral history centre and various other collections preserving the history of Rio Grande do Sul. Pride of place goes to the large permanent display explaining the origins and mission of the **World Social Forum**, the anti-globalization coalition that first came together in Porto Alegre in 2001 and returned to the city in 2002, 2003 and 2005.

Eating, drinking and nightlife

As you'd expect, meat dominates menus here and *churrascarias* abound. However, the city centre has only a limited selection of **restaurants** of any sort, with the best located in the suburbs – which, fortunately, are rarely more than a R$12 taxi fare away.

Although during the daytime you can walk around most places in the city in safety, take care after dark, as Porto Alegre is developing a reputation for street crime to rival the worst of Brazilian cities. Nevertheless, it's a lively place with plenty going on until late into the evening.

Restaurants

Al Dente Rua Mata Bacelar 210, Auxiliadora Ⓣ51/3343-1841. The best of several very good Italian restaurants in the suburb of Auxiliadora, 3km northeast of the centre. Fairly expensive northern Italian food served in attractive surroundings. Reservations advised at weekends. Evenings only, closed Sun.

Bistô do Museu Praça da Alfândega, Centro. In the Museu de Arte do Rio Grande do Sul and with tables on the *praça* itself, this is one of the few restaurants in the area. Food is simple – pastas, steak, salads and the like – but good. Closed Mon.

Café do Porto Rua Padre Chagas 293, Moinhos do Vento. Excellent light meals, sandwiches, cakes and wine are served in this very laid-back café on a fashionable side street filled with similar places.

Chez Philippe Av Independência 1005, Independência Ⓣ51/3312-5333. Housed in a beautiful early twentieth-century residence, this is arguably Porto Alegre's best restaurant and certainly its best French restaurant. The French chef is imaginative, and not afraid of combining local ingredients with traditional recipes. Although expensive, the five-course menu at R$100 per person is good value. Evenings only. Reservations advised.

Galpão Crioulo Parque da Harmonia, Centro. A huge and always reliable *churrascaria* in the city centre near the Centro Cultural Usina do Gasômetro, with a bewildering selection of meats in its *rodizio* and good range of salad and vegetable offerings. In the evenings there's *gaúcho* music and traditional dance performances.

I Puritani Rua Hilário Ribeiro 208, Moinhos de Vento. A plush bistro serving a mix of French-, Italian- and Brazilian-influenced dishes, such as artichoke risotto, wild boar in an apricot sauce and passionfruit mousse served with a *jabuticaba* sauce.

Ilha Natural Rua Andrade Neves 42, 1st floor, Centro. One of Porto Alegre's rare vegetarian restaurants, but the food is fairly unimaginative. Inexpensive. Mon–Fri lunch only.

Koh Pee Pee Rua Schiller 83, Rio Branco ⓣ51/3333-5150. A brave and very successful attempt to introduce Thai food to Porto Alegre, offering authentic dishes served in appealing surroundings. Expensive. Mon–Sat evenings only.

Na Brasa Av. Ramiro Barcelos 389, Floresta ⓣ51/3225-2205. In the opinion of many locals, this is Porto Alegre's best *churrascaria* – quite something in a city where people appreciate meat. Located between downtown and Moinhos de Vento, this unpretentious-looking restaurant boasts *rodizio* offerings of the highest quality and a high quality and tremendously varied salad bar. Around R$50 per person.

O Galo Av. Aureliano Figueiredo Pinto 904, Cidade Baixa ⓣ51/3228-7148. Very reasonably priced, this is the best traditional Portuguese restaurant in the city centre. Specializing in seafood, the shellfish and *bacalhau* (salted cod) dishes are particularly good. Closed Mon.

Polska Rua João Guimarães 377, São Geraldo ⓣ51/3333-2589. Extremely well-presented and fairly expensive Polish cooking that tastes delicious on a cold Porto Alegre winter's day. Closed Mon.

Sanduíche Voador Praça Mauricio Cardoso 23, Moinhos de Vento. Delicious sandwiches, salads and desserts in the heart of one of Porto Alegre's most fashionable suburbs. Equally good for a light meal, afternoon tea or a cold beer on the terrace. Closed Sun.

Stübel Rua Quintino Bocaiúva 940, Moinhos de Vento. Hearty German food and an unusually good choice of beer are the attractions of this popular local restaurant. Pork features most prominently on the menu, but roast duck is cooked to perfection. Moderate. Evenings only, closed Sun.

Via Fettuccine Largo Visconde de Cairú 17, 7th floor, Centro. An excellent-value buffet of hot and cold Brazilian and international dishes draws business diners to this anonymous downtown office block. But what's really special is the stunning view out towards the lagoon and beyond. Mon–Fri lunch only.

Nightlife and entertainment

Bars, some with live music and most with a predominantly young and arty clientele, are spread out along, and just off, Avenida Osvaldo Aranha, alongside the Parque Farroupilha and near the Federal University. Favourites change constantly, but the *Ocidente*, on Avenida Osvaldo Aranha itself, is usually lively and good for dancing as well. Also try the upscale suburb of Moinhos do Vento, especially along Rua Padre Chagas and Rua Fernando Gomes, near the Moinhos do Vento shopping mall. On Rua Fernando Gomes, there's excellent beer at *Dado Pub* and good music at the *Jazz Café*. Be warned, though, that things don't get going until around 11pm. If you want to meet locals keen to speak English, head for the Dutch-owned *Start Talking Café* (Tues–Sat 4–11pm) at Rua Mariland in the suburb of Auxiliador. The entire environment is in English and people of all ages are attracted to the bar/café to practice their language skills. On Thursday evenings there's live music – local bands singing, unfortunately, in English.

Porto Alegre boasts a good popular **music scene** and a considerable **theatrical** tradition. Foreign performers of all kinds usually include Porto Alegre on any Brazilian or wider South American tour. The *Sala Jazz Tom Jobim* at Rua Santo Antônio 421 (ⓣ51/3225-1229) features the city's best **jazz**, and there are live afternoon jazz sessions at the *Café Concerto* within the Casa de Cultura (see p.757). These days *the* place to go **dancing** is the huge *Dado Bier* complex in the eastern suburb of Chácara das Pedras (take a taxi). Inauspiciously located in the Bourbon Country shopping mall, the club features top bands from all over Rio Grande do Sul.

There's a good **art-house cinema** in the Casa de Cultura, and three more screens at Espaço Unibanco, Rua dos Andradas 736 (ⓣ51/3221-7147), another place for art-house films. The Centro Cultural Usina do Gasômetro, a converted 1920s power station on the banks of the river just west of the centre is well worth a visit; there's always something going on in its cinema, theatre and galleries, and it also has a café and a good bookshop. Finally, throughout the year, Porto Alegre's numerous Centros de Tradição Gaúcha organize traditional meals, and also music and dance performances that are hugely popular with locals; for full details, contact the Movimento Tradicionalisto Gaúcho, Rua Guilherme Schell 60 (☎51/3223-5194).

Listings

Airlines Aerolíneas Argentinas ☎51/3221-3300; Gol ☎51/3358-2028; TAP ☎51/3226-1211; Varig/Rio-Sul ☎51/3358-2595.

Banks and exchange There are numerous banks and *casas de câmbio* along Rua dos Andradas and Avenida Senador Salgado Filho near Praça da Alfândega, and ATMs throughout the city. The *casa de câmbio* at the *rodoviária* changes traveller's cheques and dollars cash.

Boats One-hour excursions on the Rio Guaiba leave from the Centro Cultural Usina do Gasômetro (see p.759) Mon–Fri 3pm, Sat 3.30pm & 5.15pm, Sun 11.30am, 2pm, 3.30pm & 5.15pm (R$7).

Consulates Argentina, Rua Coronel Bordini 1033 ☎51/3321-1360; Uruguay, Av. Cristóvão Colombo 2999 ☎51/3325-6200; UK, Rua Antenor Lemos 57, Conj 303, Memino Deus ☎51/3232-1414.

Health matters Pronto-Socorro Municipal hospital is on Av. Osvaldo Aranha at the intersection with Venâncio Aires (☎51/3231-5900).

Shopping Handicrafts from throughout the state are available at Artesanato Rio Grande do Sul, Av. Senador Salgado Filho 366, and the Feira do Artesanato on Praça da Alfândega (between *ruas* da Praia and Sete de Setembro) is worth a look, too. Casa do Peão, Av. Alberto Bins 393, has a fine stock of *bombachas*, lassoes and other *gaúcho* paraphernalia. The Sunday Redenção Bric-a-Brac in the Parque Farroupilha is well worth a visit for regional handicrafts; there's a lively atmosphere, with street performers and thronging bars and restaurants.

The Serra Gaúcha

North of Porto Alegre is the **Serra Gaúcha**, a range of hills and mountains populated mainly by the descendants of German and Italian immigrants. The Germans, who settled in Rio Grande do Sul between 1824 and 1859, spread out on fairly low-lying land, establishing small farming communities, of which **Nova Petrópolis** is just one that still retains strong elements of its ethnic origins. The Italians, who arrived between 1875 and 1915, settled on more hilly land further north and, being mainly from the hills and mountains of Veneto and Trento, they adapted well and very quickly specialized in **wine production**. **Caxias do Sul** has developed into the region's most important administrative and industrial centre, but it is in and around smaller towns, such as **Bento Gonçalves** and **Garibaldi**, that the region's – and, in fact, Brazil's – wine production is centred.

To the **east**, and at much higher altitudes, are the resort towns of **Gramado** and **Canela**, where unspoilt landscapes, mountain trails, refreshing temperatures, luxurious hotels and the *café colonial* – a vast selection of cakes, jams, cheeses, meats, wine and other drinks produced by the region's *colonos* – attract visitors from cities throughout Brazil. Beyond here lies some even more rugged terrain, this highland area largely given over to cattle ranching. What little population there is you'll find concentrated in the small towns of **São Francisco de Paula** and **Cambará do Sul**. Although both centres remain first and foremost ranching communities, they've become important jumping-off points for visiting the majestic canyons of **Parque Nacional dos Aparados da Serra**, one of southern Brazil's most impressive geological sites.

Nova Petrópolis and around

The main road north from Porto Alegre passes **São Leopoldo** and **Nova Hamburgo** (Rio Grande do Sul's first two German settlements but now mere industrial satellites of the city) before entering more hilly terrain inhabited by peasant farmers. In most of the family farms, German-based dialects are still spoken, but in the majority of towns and villages Portuguese is the dominant language. However, in architecture and culture, the ethnic origins of the townsfolk are quite obvious, and considerable pride is taken in the German heritage.

Thoroughly unremarkable in most respects, **NOVA PETRÓPOLIS**, 100km north of Porto Alegre, makes the greatest effort in promoting its German character although here too, the language – specifically the Hunsrück dialect of the Rhineland – only really survives in outlying farming communities despite (or even because of) persistent attempts to teach High German in local schools. The municipal authorities encourage new building to be in "traditional" German architectural styles (which is why there's a plethora of alpine chalet-like structures around), and **festivals** take on a distinct German flavour. Principal amongst these are the *Festa de Verão* (weekends during Jan & Feb), the *Festa do Folklore* (weekends in July) and the *Oktoberfest* (October weekends), all held in the **Parque do Imigrante**. But while clearly German-inspired, the events have little in common with the popular culture of the region's *colonos*. Indeed, of rather more interest is the Parque do Imigrante itself, where a village much like many in the region during the late nineteenth century has been created (daily 8am–6pm; R$2). The black-and-white half-timbered buildings, dating from between 1870 and 1910, were brought to the park from outlying parts of the *município* and include a Protestant chapel and cemetery, a general store with a dance hall, a credit agency (*Bauernkasse*), a school house and a smithy.

Disappointingly, given its picturesque setting, Nova Petrópolis is not a place for walks as there are no trails leading out from town. Instead, take a bus to the nearby hamlet of **Linha Imperial** and walk from there into the surrounding countryside. The scenery is hilly and pastoral and it's a good area to view rural life close up. There are a couple of hotels here, the *Veraneio Schoeler* (①54/3298-1052; ②) and the *Vila Verde* (①54/3298-1161; ③), which are remarkably comfortable for such a backwater.

Practicalities

The **rodoviária** is centrally located just off Avenida XV de Novembro, with good connections to Porto Alegre, Gramado and Caxias do Sul, as well as local buses to Linha Imperial and other outlying parts of the município. You'll find the helpful **tourist office** (daily 8am–6pm; ①54/281-1398) at the entrance to the Parque do Imigrante.

As you might expect of somewhere so German-influenced, the **hotels** here are always impeccably clean. The most pleasant by far is the *Recanto Suiço*, Av. XV de Novembro 2195 (①54/3281-1229, Ⓦwww.recantosuico.com.br; ③–④), on the principal road running through town. The main building of the hotel feels like a diminutive Swiss inn, and in the extensive tree-filled gardens there's a small pool and chalets. The friendly owner speaks excellent English and, of course, German. With less character but just as friendly and cheaper is the *Hospedaria Austríaca* (①54/3298-8066; ③) at Rua da Lagoa 64, a block from the main street from where it's well signposted. The elderly Austrian owner also speaks English and German. There are several other hotels on the main road or just off it, all providing similar facilities at around the same price. Typical of the rather characterless alternatives is the *Hotel Petrópolis*, near the *rodoviária* at Rua Coronel Alfredo Steglich 81 (①54/3281-1091, Ⓦwww.hotelpetropolis.com.br; ④), in a modern chalet-style building with an attractive garden, pool and beautiful mountain views.

Eating options in town are remarkably limited. The *Hotel Recanto Suiço* has an excellent and inexpensive restaurant featuring standard German dishes. If you want to have supper there, advance notice is required. At lunchtime, *Colina Verde*, 3km from Nova Petrópolis heading towards Porto Alegre (closed Mon), serves superb local German, Italian and highland *gaúcho* dishes in a pretty country setting. *Opa's Kaffeehaus* at Rua João Leão 96 (R$20 per person; Tues–Fri 2–8pm) offers a wonderful *café colonial* in a spot with spectacular views. On the main street, *Café e Cia* serves very good soups and cakes.

Gramado

Thirty-six kilometres due east of Nova Petrópolis, along a beautiful winding road, is **GRAMADO**, Brazil's best-known mountain resort. At 825m you're unlikely to suffer from altitude sickness, but Gramado is high enough to be refreshingly cool in summer and positively chilly in winter. Architecturally, Gramado and the neighbouring resort of Canela try hard to appear Swiss, with alpine chalets and flower-filled window boxes the norm. It's a mere affectation, though, since hardly any of the inhabitants are of Swiss origin – and only a small minority are of German extraction. The most pleasant time to visit the area is during the spring (Oct & Nov) when the parks, gardens and roadsides are covered in flowers, though the hydrangeas remain in bloom well into January. For a week in mid-August, the resort is overrun by the prestigious **Festival de Cinema**, (Ⓣ54/3286-1475, Ⓦwww.festivaldegramado.net), which since 1973 has developed into the most important event of its kind in Brazil. In winter the festival **Natal Luz** (mid-Nov to early Jan) stirs things up with concerts, an ersatz German Christmas market, topped by Carnaval-style parades in December that end in an (artificial) snow storm, but unless the kitchness of it all appeals to you, the entire event is something to avoid.

At other times there isn't much to do in town, but a stroll around the large and flower-filled **Parque Knorr** (daily 9am–6pm) and the secluded **Lago Negro**, surrounded by attractive woodland, can fill the hours between meals. The surrounding region is magnificent, but difficult to explore properly without a car, though tours taking in the back roads are available (see below). Just 6km from town is the beautiful **Vale do Quilombo**, where much of the original forest cover has survived intact. It's a difficult trek, though, and you'll need a local map (available from the tourist office), to identify the incredibly steep, unpaved approach road, Linha 28. For **guided tours** along the forest trails, contact the **Refúgio Família Sperry** (Ⓣ54/3504-1649, Ⓦwww.refugiosperry.com.br) an organic farm where an amazing diversity of primary forest remains. The English-speaking owner is extremely knowledgeable about the local flora and fauna and takes individuals or small groups through the forest and past dramatic waterfalls. A neighbouring family-owned vineyard, the *Quinta dos Conte*, offers tours of its small-scale wine and liquor production facilities, as well as the family's home, which was built by the original German owners. Arrangements to visit both properties should be made in advance and together by calling the *Refúgio Família Sperry*.

Practicalities

Gramado can easily be reached by **bus** from Porto Alegre and Caxias do Sul, and in the summer from Torres. The **rodoviária** (Ⓣ54/3286-1302) is on the main street, Avenida Borges de Medeiros, a couple of minutes' walk from the town centre. The **tourist office** (Mon–Thurs 9am–6pm and Fri–Sun 9am–8pm; Ⓣ54/3286-1475) at no. 1674 is extremely well organized and provides reasonable maps and comprehensive lists of local hotels and restaurants.

Most hotels offer steep discounts outside the peak summer and winter months, especially during the week, though accommodation is hard to find during the Festival de Cinema. There's an excellent **youth hostel** (Ⓣ54/3295-1020,

ⓦwww.gramadohostel.com) 1.5km from the centre at Avenida das Hortências 3880, towards Canela, with small dorms (R$20 per person) and some double rooms (❷–❸). The lowest-priced **hotels** are the *Planalto* across from the *rodoviária*, at Av. Borges de Medeiros 554 (ⓣ54/286-1210; ❷), and, also in the centre, the *Dinda*, Rua Augusto Zatti 160, at the corner with Av. Borges de Medeiros (ⓣ54/286-2810; ❷). There's no lack of more expensive places to stay: the *Casa da Montanha* at Av. Borges de Medeiros 3166 (ⓣ54/3286-2544, ⓦwww.casadamontanha.com.br; ❼–❽) has rustic-style but extremely comfortable rooms and an indoor heated pool, while smaller, but rather more luxurious, is the *Estalagem St Hubertus*, at Rua da Carriere 974, overlooking Lago Negro (ⓣ54/3286-1273, ⓦwww.sthubertus.com; ❼), set in attractive grounds with a heated pool. Similar in style, but less expensive, is the long-established *Hotel das Hortênsias* at Rua Bela Vista 83 (ⓣ54/3286-1057, ⓦwww.hoteldashortensias.com.br; ❺). A good mid-range option near the centre for families is *Pousada Sonnenhof* at Rua Nações Unidas 191 (ⓣ54/3286-7788, ⓦwww.sonnenhof.com.br; ❺), with small, well-appointed rooms and friendly service.

Gramado has some reasonably good **restaurants**. Both *Belle du Valais* at Av. das Hortênsias 1432 and *Chez Pierre* at Av. Borges de Medeiros 3022 (closed Sun), in the centre, serve tasty *fondue bourguigonne* (meat fondue); though very popular, their house specialities, the cheese fondues, are disappointingly bland. For fairly authentic and reasonably priced northern Italian dishes, there's *Tarantino Ristorante*, also in the centre at Av. das Hortênsias 1522, by Praça Major Nicoleti. More intriguing are the game dishes at *La Caceria* (evenings only, closed Mon–Wed) in the *Hotel Casa da Montanha* (see above), which combine wild boar, venison, partridge, duck and capybara with unusual tropical fruit sauces. Rather formal and expensive, the restaurant includes some excellent and very unusual Brazilian wines on its extensive wine list.

For **getting around the backroads**, most of which are unpaved and treacherous following heavy rain, Casa da Montanha Adventures (ⓣ54/3286-2544) is especially recommended. The English-speaking drivers know the region well and will take you in Land Rovers to places near Gramado and further afield, such as the Parque Nacional dos Aparados da Serra (see p.764). Prices vary according to distance and whether you can join an existing group: speak to one of the drivers at their desk at the *Hotel Casa da Montanha* (see above).

Canela

The resort town of **CANELA**, 8km further east, down a road bordered on both sides by hydrangeas, is slightly lower, smaller and not as brashly commercialized as Gramado, though it strives to be like its neighbour. Canela offers little of particular beauty within its small urban area, but it is better situated for the **Parque Estadual do Caracol** (daily 8.30am–5.30pm; R$8), 8km to the north. You can reach the park by bus – marked "Caracol Circular" (4 daily) – which leaves from Canela's *rodoviára*; get off at the restaurant-tourist complex in the park. From here, a path leads 927 steps down to the foot of a **131-metre waterfall** from where visitors can best appreciate its power. From there you will find other small falls and the surrounding forest. A further 5km along the Caracol road is the **Parque da Ferradra** (daily 9am–5.30pm; R$6), a forest reserve offering panoramic views into the deep Arroio Caçador canyon and waterfall and onto a **horseshoe-shaped** section of the Rio Caí.

Canela's **rodoviária** (ⓣ54/3282-1375) is just behind the central main street, with regular buses from Porto Alegre and Caxias do Sul and services at least every hour to Gramado. The **tourist office**, at Largo da Fama 227 (Mon–Sat 8am–6pm,

Sun 8am–1pm; ⓣ54/3282-2200), is staffed by enthusiastic students from the local tourism colleges, for which Canela has become renowned in Brazil.

There's a good **youth hostel** across the road from the *rodoviária* at Rua Ernesta Urbani 132 (ⓣ54/3282-2017; R$20 per person), but over winter weekends it can be difficult to find a bed. The cheapest **hotels** are *Bela Vista* at Av. Osvaldo Aranha 160 (ⓣ54/3282-2136; ❸) and the very similar *Turis* at Rua Oswaldo Aranha 223 (ⓣ54/3282-8436, ⓦwww.turishotel.tur.br; ❸), both centrally located but pretty basic, while there are a number of mid-range *pousadas* just outside the centre providing accommodation in comfortable but modest cabins: try the *Alpes Verdes*, Rua Gilda Tanello Bolognese 1001 (ⓣ54/3282-1162; ❹) and the *Vila Verde*, Rua Boaventura Garcia 292 (ⓣ54/3282-4133, ⓦwww.hotelvilaverde.com.br; ❹), both of which are set in park-like gardens with a pool. For more luxury, the thirteen-room *Quinta dos Marques*, Rua Gravataí 200 (ⓣ54/3282-9813, ⓦwww.quintadosmarques.com.br; ❻), is the most distinctive choice available, the imposing 1930s wooden building – in typical highland style – beautifully renovated to offer rustic-chic accommodation.

Most visitors dine at their hotels, but if you'd rather **eat out**, your best bet is the *Coelho* at Av. Danton Corrêa 251, near the intersection of the main avenue, Osvaldo Aranha, which has an inexpensive *rodizio* of decent local-style Italian dishes. The town's **bars**, clustered along Avenida Osvaldo Aranha, tend to be livelier than those in Gramado, with students spilling into the street well into the night at weekends.

Templo Budista Chagdud Khadro Ling

Just 30km south but a world away from both Canela and Gramado, is the **Templo Budista Chagdud Khadro Ling** (ⓣ51/3546-8200, ⓦwww.chagdud.org), the only Tibetan Buddhist temple complex in Latin America, attracting devotees from all over Brazil and the United States. Situated on a hilltop outside the largely German village of **Três Coroas**, the temple was founded by **Chagdud Tulku Rinpoche** (1930–2002), a high lama who left Tibet for Nepal following the Chinese invasion in 1959, settling in Brazil in 1995. On a clear day you can see the buildings – red in colour, adorned with yellow details and colourful symbols that sparkle like jewels – from far into the distance. Seen close up, the remarkable site includes a huge statue of Buddha, eight large *stupas* (holy structures representing the enlightened mind), the **temple** itself with remarkable murals depicting Buddha's life, and various other buildings erected by devotees, and artists and craftsmen from Nepal. The temple is open to the public (Mon–Fri 9am–noon & 1–5pm, Sat–Sun 9am–5pm), but it's a good idea to phone ahead to make sure your visit is convenient. Getting to Khadro Ling is straightforward. From Porto Alegre there are several **buses** a day to Três Caroas, while from Gramado buses to Taquara stop off in Três Caroas, where you can get a **taxi** (R$10) up to the temple. Apart from during retreats, it's not possible to stay at Khadro Ling, but there's the basic *Pousada das Águas* (ⓣ51/3501-1218; ❷) in **Três Coroas** if you don't care to stay in Gramado.

Parque Nacional dos Aparados da Serra

The dominant physical feature of south central Brazil is a **highland plateau**, the result of layer upon layer of ocean sediment piling up and the consequent rock formations being lifted to form the Brazilian Shield. Around 150 million years ago, lava slowly poured onto the surface of the shield, developing into a thick layer of basalt rock. At the edge of the plateau, cracks puncture the basalt and it is around the largest of these that the **Parque Nacional dos Aparados da Serra** (Wed–Sun 9am–5pm; R$6) was created.

The park lies 100km east of Canela. Approaching it from any direction, you pass through rugged cattle and sheep pasture, occasionally interrupted by the distinctive umbrella-like Paraná pine trees and solitary farm buildings. As the dirt road enters the park itself, forest patches appear, suddenly and dramatically interrupted by a canyon of breathtaking proportions, **Itaimbezinho**. Some 5800m in length, between 600m and 2000m wide and 720m deep, Itaimbezinho is a dizzying sight. The canyon and the area immediately surrounding it have two distinct climates and support very different types of vegetation. On the higher levels, with relatively little rainfall, but with fog banks moving in from the nearby Atlantic Ocean, vegetation is typical of a cloud forest, while on the canyon's floor a mass of subtropical plants flourishes. The park has abundant birdlife and is home to over 150 different species.

In the park, there's a **visitors' centre** (Ⓣ54/3251-5289 or 3251-1277) with an exhibition explaining the park's history and geological structure and a snack bar. From here, you can hire a guide to lead you down the steep trail (including a five-metre vertical incline that you must negotiate by rope) to the canyon floor. You'll need to be physically fit, have good hiking boots and be prepared for flash floods. Most visitors, however, follow the well-marked paths keeping to the top of Itaimbezinho, enjoying views either into the canyon (a 2hr 30min walk from the visitors' centre) or out towards the sea (a 45min walk).

Visiting the park

The Parque Nacional dos Aparados da Serra can be visited throughout the year, but spring (Oct & Nov) is the best time to see flowers. In the winter, June through August, it can get very cold, though visibility tends to be clearest. Summers are warm, but heavy rainfall sometimes makes the roads and trails impassable, and fog and low-lying clouds can completely obscure the spectacular views. Avoid April, May and September, the months with the most sustained rain. As only 1000 visitors are permitted to enter the park each day, it's advisable to phone the visitors' centre in advance to reserve a place. Bring with you strong footwear and mosquito repellant.

Unless you have your own transport, **getting to the park** is quite difficult. To reach it by public transport, take a bus from Porto Alegre, Gramado or Canela to **São Francisco de Paula**, 69km from the park's entrance. From São Francisco, you need to take another bus northeast to **Cambará do Sul** and ask to be let off at the entrance to the park. From here it's a further 15km to Itaimbezinho. Buses occasionally run between São Francisco or Cambará and **Praia Grande** (which has a couple of basic hotels, one on the main square and the other at the *rodoviária*), on the Santa Catarina side of the state line. These will drop you just 3km from Itaimbezinho. In São Francisco, you may be able to join a tour group headed for the park – check with a local hotel or ask at the tourist office (see below). Coming from Cambará, the park entrance is only 3km away and you should be able to get a taxi to take you. A very reliable tour operator based in Cambará is Canyon Turismo at Av. Getúlio Vargas 812 (Ⓣ54/3251-1027, Ⓦwww.canyonturismo.cjb.net) that arranges transfers to and from the park as well as trekking in the park and the surrounding area. Visiting the park as a day-trip from Canela or Gramado is also feasible: Casa da Montanha Adventures (see p.763) escort individuals or groups for around R$120 per person, which includes a delicious lunch.

São Francisco de Paula and Cambará do Sul

The cattle communities of São Francisco and Cambará are both good places to use as a base for visiting the park. In **SÃO FRANCISCO DE PAULA**, the larger of the two towns, you'll pass the **tourist office** on the way into town (daily 8am–7pm; Ⓣ51/244-1602), where you may be able to get advice on getting to the park. There's a wide choice of places **to stay** in and around São Francisco, much the larger though the less attractive of the two towns. Two good places to try, both a couple of kilometres from town and well signposted are the *Pousada Pomar Cisne Branco* (ⓣ51/244-1204; ❸ including dinner) and the *Hotel Cavalinho Branco* (ⓣ51/244-1263; ❷). The best place **to eat** is the *Pomar Cisne Branco*, which serves superb, inexpensive home-style meals.

In **CAMBARÁ DO SUL**, the **tourist office** is situated in the Centro Cultural (daily 8am–6pm; ⓣ54/3251-4320), an old bright-yellow wooden building typical of the region. There are several simple but very pleasant **pousadas** in the village, including the *Favo de Mel* (ⓣ54/3251-1706; ❸), the *Paraíso* (ⓣ54/3251-1352; ❸) and the *Pindorama* (ⓣ54/3251-1225; ❸). If you want to experience highland *gaúcho* life, the *Paradouro da Fortaleza* (ⓣ54/3504-5183, ⓦwww.paradourodafortaleza.com.br; ❸) is a good option, especially if you're keen on horse riding. By far the most comfortable hotel in the area, however, is the *Parador Casa da Montanha* (ⓣ54/3504-5302 and 9973-9320, ⓦwww.paradorcasadamontanha.com.br; ❼ half board), situated at the beginning of the road that leads to the Parque Nacional dos Aparados da Serra. Accommodation is in thermal tents, but they're secure even in the strongest of winds and have every comfort of a good hotel room. In the lodge, there's a sitting and dining area, and a terrace with views out towards a sheep-rearing *fazenda*. The food here is superb – based on local beef, mutton, squash and bean dishes, and the restaurant is open to non-guests. In Cambará itself, your **eating** options are entirely meat-based, with the *Restaurante Galpão Costaneira* especially recommended for its inexpensive, authentic local dishes served in a rustic, but attractive, setting.

Caxias do Sul

Around 70km west of Gramado and 37km north of Nova Petrópolis is **CAXIAS DO SUL**, Rio Grande do Sul's third-largest city. Italian immigrants arrived in Caxias (as the city is known) in 1875, but the only obvious indication of the city's ethnic origins is its *adegas*, now huge companies or cooperatives that produce some of the state's poorest wine. Caxias' most important wine producer is the Château Lacave but, located 9km from town, it's not worth the effort involved in getting there. A better bet is the *cantina* (wine producer) **tours** offered by several wine producers in the city centre that end with free tastings: Riograndense, Rua Os 18 do Forte 2346, are especially used to receiving visitors. If you're interested in the history of the region, the **Museu Casa de Pedra** (Tues–Sun 8.30am–5.30pm) at Rua Matteo Gianella 531 is well worth a look. Housed in a late nineteenth-century stone farmhouse, it contains agricultural implements, old photographs and other artefacts relating to the first Italian immigrants. The most important festival in Caxias is the **Festa Nacional da Uva**, a two-week celebration of Italian traditions and local industry – most importantly wine production. The event is held in February and March (in even-numbered years) at the Parque Exposições Centenário, on the outskirts of the city.

You'll find the **tourist office** (Mon–Fri 9am–5pm; ⓣ54/3222-1875) on the main square, Praça Rui Barbosa, along with several inexpensive **hotels** including the *Alfred*, Rua Sinimbu 2266 (ⓣ54/3221-8655, ⓦwww.alfredhoteis.com.br; ❸), which is particularly good value. There are plenty of more expensive options, the best being the *Reynolds International*, Rua Dr Montaury 1441 (ⓣ54/3223-5844, ⓦwww.reynolds.com.br; ❺), a small luxury hotel.

For authentic – and inexpensive – northern Italian **food**, try *Zanottoo*, Rua Visconde de Pelotas (closed Sun evening) and, in particular, *La Vindima*, Av. Júlio de Castilhos 962 (closed Sun and all Jan), both good for country-style chicken and polenta dishes.

Caxias is a major transport centre and **buses** run to towns throughout Rio Grande do Sul, and to states to the north, from the **rodoviária** (Ⓣ54/3218-3000), seven blocks east of Praça Rui Barbosa. There's also an **airport** (Ⓣ54/3213-2566), 4km south of the city centre, with flights to Porto Alegre and São Paulo.

Flores da Cunha and around

Virtually all the towns and villages in the area to the north and west of Caixas do Sul were founded by northern Italian immigrants and, set amidst the mountainous landscape, **FLORES DA CUNHA** is considered to be the most Italian of Brazilian *municípios*, retaining thriving Italian folk traditions. The town itself is quite unremarkable in appearance, but the **Museu Histórico** (Mon–Fri 8–11.30am & 1–5.45pm, Sat 1–4.45pm), in the old town hall on Rua 25 de Julho, provides a good overview of the region's history, with displays of old photographs, documents and tools relating to the settlers. The **tourist office** (Mon–Fri 9am–5pm) is located in the same building. There are just two **hotels**: the very plain but clean *Fiório* (Ⓣ54/3292-2900, Ⓦwww.hotelfiorio.com.br; ③) on the way into town at Av. 25 de Julho 5500 (the RS-122 road), and the slightly more comfortable *Villa Borghese Albergo* (Ⓣ54/3292-2355; ③, includes dinner), also on the outskirts of town at Rua John F. Kennedy 1031. The best **restaurant** in town is *L'Osteria del Gallo* at Rua Heitor Curra 2354 (closed Mon evenings), which serves reasonably priced local-style Italian food. The town is a good base from which to explore the surrounding countryside and stop off at some of the *colônias* selling their home-made cheeses, salamis, liqueurs and wine. Both in town and in the region around, there are innumerable *cantinas*, that welcome visitors for tasting.

For a stronger taste of the local Italian heritage, head out to the neighbouring villages – a particularly attractive option is **OTÁVIO ROCHA**, 13km south-west of town (two buses daily). The people here are almost all of Veneto origin and still maintain their pioneer forebears' dialect and customs. The village comes alive in the last two weeks of July when the **Festo do Colono** takes place, but throughout the year the hamlet is delightful. Vines are planted on just about every patch of land, extending down to the main street itself, and the smell of fermenting grapes is remarkable. If you want to stay over in Otávio Rocha, there's a good **hotel,** the *Dona Adélia* (Ⓣ54/3292-1519; ③) and a couple of restaurants serving authentic *colono* food – huge meals at less than R$15 per person. A further 7km west, the village of **NOVA PÁDUA** is another good place to head for: the *Albergue Belvedere Sonda* Travessa Mutzel (Ⓣ54/3296-1200; reservations essential; ④ full board) is a modern guesthouse a few kilometres from the village in the direction of Nova Roma, with spectacular views of the Rio das Antas, and serving excellent local dishes.

Thirty-four kilometres north of Flores da Cunha, **ANTÔNIO PRADO** was founded in 1886 by another group of northern Italian immigrants. The **Museu Municipal** in Praça Garibaldi (Tues–Fri 8.30–11.30am & 1.30–5pm, Sat, Sun & public holidays 1–5pm) tells the usual story of the first pioneers, but it's Antônio Prado's wealth of well-preserved **wood and stone houses** and farm buildings that makes it particularly interesting. Until about 1940 the village and its hinterland prospered, but over the following decades the local economy stagnated and *colonos* moved as far away as the western Amazon. The town was left with dozens of disused late nineteenth- and early twentieth-century buildings, and 47 of them now have preservation orders on them – especially worth visiting are the **Casa da Neni** at Rua Luíza Bocchese 34, where local handicrafts, preserves and liquors are sold (9am–noon & 1.30–6pm), and the **Farmácia Palombini** at Av. Valdomiro Bocchese 439, whose interior remains unchanged since it opened in the 1930s. For a local map, and information on the farm buildings scattered along the *município*'s back roads, ask at the helpful **tourist office** in the Prefeitura at Praça Garibaldi 57 (Mon–Fri 8.30–11.30am & 1.30–5pm; ⓣ54/3293-1500) or at the museum. Many of the best-preserved houses, built from a combination of wood and stone, are found along Linha 21 de Abril (off the RS-122 road, 6km in the direction of Flores da Cunha). The decrepit, but functional, *Hotel Piemonte* (ⓣ54/3293-1280; ❷), across from Praça Garibaldi, is the only place **to stay** in Antônio Prado itself. Much nicer is the *Pousada Colonial de Rossi* (ⓣ54/3293-1771, ⓦwww.pousadaderossi.com.br; ❹ full board), 6km from town on Linha Silva Tavares, off the RS-448 road in the direction of Nova Roma. **Places to eat** in town are disappointing, limited to a few *lanchonetes*. Instead you're best off driving or taking a taxi to the *Pousada Colonial de Rossi* which serves excellent and inexpensive local food, or to *Nostra Cantina*, a few kilometres from town on the RS-122 road towards Flores da Cunha.

Bento Gonçalves and around

Approach **BENTO GONÇALVES**, 40km west of Caxias, from any direction and there's no doubting that this is the heartland of Brazil's wine-producing region. On virtually every patch of land, no matter the gradient, vines are planted. Wine production entered a new era in the late 1970s as huge cooperatives developed, local *cantinas* expanded and foreign companies set up local operations. The results have been somewhat mixed. In the past, the locals relied almost exclusively on North American grape varieties and produced their own distinctive wines. Gradually, though, they were encouraged to join a cooperative or agree to sell their grapes exclusively for one company. New European and, more recently, Californian vines enabled companies to produce "finer" wines of a type until then imported. All this means that the *colonos* now rarely produce more than their own family's requirements, and high-tech stainless steel vats and rigidly monitored quality control have rapidly replaced the old oaken barrel tradition; with few exceptions, the resulting wines are, at best, mediocre.

Bento Gonçalves itself is an undistinguished-looking town whose economy, of course, totally revolves around grape and wine production. There are numerous **cantinas** in the centre of town offering free tours and tastings and a **Museu Casa do Imigrante**, at Rua Erny Hugo Dreher 127 (Tues–Fri 8–11.15am & 1.30–5.15pm, Sat 1–5pm, Sun 9am–noon), documenting the history of Italian immigration and life in the area. There's a **youth hostel**, the *Pousada Casa Mia* at Traversa Niterói 71 (ⓣ54/3451-1215, ⓦwww.pousadacasamia.co.br; R$20 per person), while **hotels**, of which there is no shortage, are mainly found in the streets around the very helpful **tourist office**, Rua Marechal Deodoro 70 (Mon–Fri 8–11.45am & 1–7pm, Sat 9am–5pm; ⓣ54/3451-1088). The newest and most luxurious hotel in town is the *Dall'Onder Vittoria* at Rua 13 de Maio 800 (ⓣ54/3455-3000, ⓦwww.dallondervitoria.com.br; ❻), while the *Vinocap* at Rua Barão do Rio Branco 245 (ⓣ54/3451-1566, ⓦwww.vinocap.com.br; ❸–❹) offers almost as plush rooms at a much cheaper price.

The surrounding area

It's worth visiting the surrounding countryside and villages, where, on the surface at least, the way of life has changed little over the years. The calendar revolves around the grape, with weeding, planting, pruning – and the maintenance of the characteristic stone walls – the main activities during the year, leading up to the harvest between January and late March. An excellent way to admire the beautiful countryside is to take the tourist **steam train** (year round Wed & Sat 9am & 2pm from Bento; tickets, R$45 return, from Giordani Turismo, Rua Erny Hugo Dreher 197; ⓣ54/3452-6042, ⓦwww.mfumaca.com.br) into the vine-dominated landscape. Along its 48-kilometre route (formerly part of a line extending south to Porto Alegre), the train stops at some of the more scenic spots, of which the most spectacular is the view over the **Vale do Rio das Antas** where the river's path takes the form of a horseshoe. The train continues to **Garibaldi**, a small town mainly notable for its production of some remarkably good Champagne-style sparkling wines; if you want to stay over here, the place to head for is the *Casacurta* (Ⓣ54/3462-2166, Ⓦwww.hotelcasacurta.com.br; ④), a stylish early 1950s hotel that is excellent value.

Over recent years the quality of Brazilian wine has been improving greatly, with some of the most inovative producers located to the southwest of Bento Gonçalves in the very beautiful area that has become known as the **Vale dos Vinhedos**. Even more than other wine-producing areas in this part of the state, the economy and way of life here is dominated by wine, with grapes growing on every patch of farmland. The best approach is from Bento Gonçalves along the main BR-470 highway, turning off onto the RS-444, a county road also called Linha Oito da Graciema (any southbound bus from Bento Gonçalves will drop you off at the intersection). Here you'll find an excellent **information centre** (daily 9am–6pm; Ⓣ54/3451-9601, Ⓦwww.valedosvinhedos.com.br) where you can pick up a map that indicates wineries and other local business that are open to visitors. Basically the circuit includes Linha Oito da Graciema and Linha Leopoldina and a few well-signposted side roads. The **wineries** vary enormously in character and it's wise to settle on just a few to stop off for tastings. Miolo, probably the best of Brazil's large-scale producers, and Casa Valduga, the first producer to introduce modern wine-making techniques and European vines, are certainly worth visiting, but some of the smaller wineries are much more distinctive. Villaggio Laurentis is an up-and-coming producer of what pass locally as "fine wines" while Pizzato is still very much a family concern. Although not producing wine but instead excellent grape juice, the Famiglia Tasca should not be missed: located on a side road in the extreme west of the Vale dos Vinhedos, the well-maintained **wood and stone farm buildings** are some of the oldest in the area and the views across the neighbouring Aurora valley are breathtaking.

The best time to visit is January through March when the grapes are harvested, but visitors are welcomed throughout the year for tastings. There are some extremely comfortable – and quite expensive – **places to stay** including the *Pousada Casa Valduga,* Linha Leopoldina Km 6 (Ⓣ54/3453-1154, Ⓦwww.casavalduga.com.br; reservations essential; ⑤), the *Pousada Borghetto Sant'Anna* Linha Leopoldina Km 8 (Ⓣ54/3453-2355, Ⓦwww.borgettosantanna.com.br; ⑤) and the *Hotel Villa Michelon* Linha Oito da Graciema Km 18.9 (Ⓣ54/3459-1800, Ⓦwww.villamichelon.com.br; ⑤). Even if you don't stay at the *Villa Michelon*, it's worth a brief visit as it houses the **Memorial do Vinho**, an exhibition that charts the history of wine production in the area. Eating possibilities are surprisingly limited but the *Casa Valduga* serves good, and reasonably priced, local-style Italian food.

To the immediate west of the Vale dos Vinhedos is the hilltop village of **MONTE BELO**, which wouldn't look out of place in Italy. From here there are fine views in all directions and with a basic, but cheap **hotel** (②) whose **restaurant** serves authentic *colono* food – a complete meal costs just R$10 – Monte Belo is a fine base from which to wander along pathways and tracks between the vineyards.

Vacaria

On the northeastern plateau, 955m above sea level, **VACARIA** is a quiet administrative and commercial centre for the surrounding cattle country. The road to Vacaria from Caxias do Sul, 100km to the south, is extremely beautiful, rising sharply from vine-clad hill slopes before reaching the near treeless *planalto* cattle country. Normally there would be absolutely nothing to detain you in town, but Vacaria comes to life when people from throughout southern Brazil and beyond come to participate in the **Rodeio Crioulo Internacional**, one of the country's most important *rodeios*, held in the first weekend of February (in even-numbered years).

All the **events** that you'd expect are included, like lasso-throwing, horse-breaking and steer-riding competitions, in addition to the real purpose behind a *rodeio*, the accompanying cattle and horse shows, and song and dance events. While nattily dressed urban *gaúchos* show up in impeccably tailored *bombachas* and distinguished-looking capes, Vacaria's *rodeio* is first and foremost a popular event, attended by ordinary people of the *campanha* and cattle-ranching *serra*.

Huge **tents** are erected at the *rodeio* grounds on the outskirts of town (reached by constant buses from Vacaria's main square), in which most of the spectators and competitors stay, despite the often bitterly cold midsummer temperatures. Several simple **hotels** are on, and just off, the main square: there's usually space, even during *rodeio* week. The best equipped are the *Pampa*, Rua Júlio de Castilhos 1560 (ⓣ54/3232-1333; ❷–❸), the *Real*, Rua Ramiro Barcelos (❷) and the *Querencia*, Rua Mal. Floriano (❷). A more fitting place to stay is the *Fazenda Capão do Índio* (ⓣ54/3324-0980; ❹ full board), 5km from town off the BR-285 in the direction of Lago Vermelho; accommodation is comfortably rustic and horse riding is available, too. You can also participate in the day-to-day work on the ranch, which is dedicated to raising horses. At the *rodeio*, **food** means meat – and only meat – and at the *rodeio* ground's restaurants you're expected to come equipped with your own sharp knife. However, in the town centre, just off the main square, there's a pizzeria where you can retreat.

The coast: the Litoral Gaúcho

The **coast** of Rio Grande do Sul is a virtually unbroken 500-kilometre-long beach, dotted with a series of resorts popular with Argentines, Uruguayans and visitors from Porto Alegre and elsewhere in the state. In winter the beaches are deserted and most of the hotels closed, but between mid-November and March it's easy to believe that the state's entire population has migrated to the resorts. The attraction of this area, the **Litoral Gaúcho**, is essentially one of convenience: from Porto Alegre many of the resorts can be reached within two or three hours, making even day-trips possible. But for anyone travelling to or from points north, the beaches here can be safely ignored. Those resorts that are accessible are crowded, while – due to the influence of the powerful Rio Plate – the water is usually murky; and, even in summer, Antarctic currents often make for chilly bathing.

Torres

The northernmost point on the Litoral Gaúcho, 197km from Porto Alegre, **TORRES** is the state's one beach resort that is actually worth going out of your way for. It's considered Rio Grande do Sul's most sophisticated coastal resort, and the beaches behind which the town huddles, **Praia Grande** and **Prainha**, are packed solid in the summer with *gaúcho* and Uruguayan holiday-makers. However, by walking across the Morro do Farol (a hill, identifiable by its lighthouse) and along the almost equally crowded Praia da Cal, you come to the **Parque da Guarita** (always open; ⓦwww.parquedaguarita.com.br) one of the most beautiful stretches of the southern Brazilian coast. The development of the park was supervised by the landscaper Roberto Burle Marx together with Brazil's foremost environmentalist, José Lutzenberger.

The state park is centred on a huge basalt outcrop, with 35-metre-high cliffs rising straight up from the sea, from where there are superb views up and down the coast. At several points, steps lead down from the clifftop to basalt pillars and cavern-like formations, beaten out of the cliff face over the years. Although there are areas where it's both possible, and safe, to dive from the rocks, generally the sea is inaccessible and ferocious. Continue along the clifftop, and you'll eventually reach the **Praia da Guarita**, a fairly small beach that is never as crowded as those nearer town. Just beyond a further, much smaller outcrop, there's another beach, this one stretching with hardly an interruption all the way to the border with Uruguay.

Practicalities

From the **rodoviária** (ⓣ51/3664-1787), served by buses from Porto Alegre, Florianópolis, São Paulo, Curitiba, Buenos Aires and Montevideo, walk down Avenida José Bonifácio to Avenida Barão do Rio Branco. Here, turn right for the centre and the beach (six blocks) or left (one block) for the **tourist office** (Dec–April 8am–10pm and May–Nov 8am–6pm; ⓣ51/3626-1937). Torres has countless **hotels**, with many of the cheaper ones located on Barão do Rio Branco and the two streets running parallel to it. Even so, in midsummer accommodation is predictably difficult to track down, so try to arrive early in the day. Hotels and *pousadas* here are an undistinguished lot and you can expect to pay at least R$90 for a double room. Worth trying are the *Vitória Praia*, Praça 15 de Novembro 16 (ⓣ51/3664-2692; ④), the *Bauer*, Rua Ballino de Freitas 260 (ⓣ51/664-1290; ④) and the *Pousada la Barca*, Av. Beira-Mar 1020 (ⓣ51/3664-2925, ⓦwwwpousadalabarca.com.br; ⑤), all of which are good value.

All the best **restaurants** are by the river, twenty to thirty minutes' walk from the centre. Either walk along Praia Grande in the opposite direction from the lighthouse or, quicker, along Rua Sete de Setembro, a couple of streets back from the beach. Especially recommended are *Gaviota* and *Anzol*, for their wide selection of seafood. In the centre, there are plenty of beachside **bars**, some serving light meals, while at Rua José Luís de Freitas 800, the *Galeto Régis* serves excellent chicken dishes (closed April–Nov).

Capão da Canoa and Tramandaí

Typical of resorts popular with day-trippers and weekend visitors from Porto Alegre are **CAPÃO DA CANOA** and **TRAMANDAÍ**, respectively 140km and 120km northeast of Porto Alegre. Unless you're spending time in Porto Alegre and want to get away briefly from the often intense summer heat, neither resort has much to recommend it. Tramandaí is the larger of the two, with more hotels, more restaurants and even more people. Both share an identical lack of character, based on wide, open beaches with little in the way of vegetation, and plenty in the way of beachside bars.

The most reasonably priced **hotels** in Tramandaí are the *Amaral Praia*, Rua Amâncio Amaral 1127 (ⓣ51/3661-2479; ②), and the huge *Beira-Mar*, Av. Emancipação 521 (ⓣ51/3661-1234; ③). In the centre of Capão da Canoa try the *Maquine* at Rua Andira 320 (ⓣ51/3665-2323; ③), or the *Kolman* at Rua Sepé 1800 (ⓣ51/3625-2022; ③).

Parque Nacional da Lagoa do Peixe

If you're travelling south along the coast from Torres down to the Uruguayan border at Chuí, it's normally necessary to go inland via Porto Alegre. But if time's no problem, it is possible to take buses from village to village along the RS-101 road and the narrow peninsula that protects the Lagoa dos Patos from the sea. The road is unpaved and often in the most appalling state, while the landscape is barren and windswept, but the remote fishing communities along the way have consequently been protected from the ravages of tourism. The inhabitants, largely of Azorean stock but also descendants of shipwreck survivors and renegades fleeing other parts of Rio Grande do Sul, make a living by fishing, growing onions, raising chickens and sheep, and increasingly through tourism.

At the midpoint of the peninsula is the **Parque Nacional da Lagoa do Peixe**, centred on an area surrounding a long and narrow lagoon – so shallow that trucks can drive across it. The park is one of the most important **bird sanctuaries** in South America. Migrating birds stop here, attracted by the clean, brackish water rich in algae, plankton, crustacea and fish. The **best time to visit** is between September and March, when the lagoon shelters birds from the northern hemisphere winter, and then birds landing on their way north from the Patagonian winter. However, birdwatching opportunities are generally good year round, and even those with a passing interest in birds won't fail to be impressed by the pink flamingoes. The area also provides a rich habitat for reptiles and mammals; in the winter months, sea lions share the sands with Malalhães penguins, and you might spot whales in the distance offshore, returning from their mating and feeding grounds.

There is no infrastructure for receiving visitors, so you'll need to track down someone with considerable local knowledge if you want to see anything of the park. It's best to head for **MOSTARDAS**, an attractive village dominated by simple Azorean-style buildings along its narrow streets. Basic **accommodation** is available at the *Hotel Mostardense,* Rua Bento Gonçalves 1020 (ⓣ51/3673-1368; ❷), the *Hotel Municipal,* Rua Independente 761 (ⓣ51/3673-1500; ❷) and the *Hotel Scheffer*, Rua Almirante Tamandaré (ⓣ51/3673-1277; ❷).

On Praça Prefeito Luiz Martins, the main square, is the **Casa da Cultura** (daily 8–11.30am and 1–4.30pm), worthwhile for its display of photographs and books documenting the area; you'll also be able to pick up information on local events, such as dances, too. To find a **guide**, go to the local office of IBAMA, which administers the national parks (Mon–Fri 8am–noon and 2–5pm; ⓣ51/3673-1464,), also located on the main *praça.* You might be able to latch onto a prearranged group; otherwise a private guide isn't likely to charge more than R$60 for an early-morning or late-afternoon excursion to Barra da Lagoa do Peixe, where the greatest concentration of migratory birds is to be found. You'll need to count on plenty of time to enjoy the area, not only because of difficulties in gaining access to the park but because of the appalling state of the RS-101 – the so-called *Estrada do Inferno*, or Road of Hell – often washed out by flash floods, and because of poor bus services between the peninsula's small settlements; before heading south of Mostardas, ask at IBAMA about the current state of the road. You may find it much easier to head down the peninsula on the Atlantic beach, as the sand is hard enough to take the weight of a car, although you will have to negotiate the few streams that cut across the beach and also watch out for sudden tidal surges. Also bear in mind that the climate differs widely during the year – in the winter it can be bitterly cold, while summers are warm and perfect for mosquitoes.

Pelotas

Rio Grande do Sul's second-largest city, **PELOTAS**, 270km to the south of Porto Alegre, is situated on the left bank of the Canal de São Gonçalo, which connects the Lagoa dos Patos with the Lagoa Mirim. Founded in 1812 as a port for the *charque* (jerked beef) producers of the surrounding region, Pelotas rapidly emerged as the wealthiest city in Rio Grande do Sul, becoming a by-word for conspicuous consumption.

The first **charqueada** was established in the Pelotas area in 1780 and by the late 1820s there were two dozen producers of *charque*. Cattle were herded from *estancias* from as far away as Bagé (see p.783) to be slaughtered, the meat salted and sundried. The *charqueadas* consisted of a long strip of land bordering the Arroio Pelotas along which *charque* was transferred to the port of Pelotas for shipment elsewhere in Brazil. Production was a brutal affair, relying almost wholly on slave labour, and when cattle were being slaughtered the river was stained bright red from the blood and waste. Evidence still remains of the *charqueadas* with several ruins on the banks of the Arroio Pelotas as well as two fine houses built by *charqueadores* that are open to visitors. The oldest, the **Charqueada São João** (Sun 2–5pm and by arrangement; Ⓣ53/3228-2425, Ⓦwww.charqueadasaojoao.com.br; R$10) was established in 1810 and the house contains period furniture as well as tools. Almost alongside is the **Charqueada Santa Rita** (Ⓣ53/3228-2024, Ⓦwww.charqueadasantarita.com.br), the colonial-style house built in 1826. Santa Rita now serves as a *pousada* (see below) but its small **Museu do Charque** is open to the public (R$8). The *charqueadas* are located about 5km northeast of the centre of Pelotas. A taxi will cost around R$15 or take any bus to "Laranjal" and get off just before the bridge that crosses the Arroio Pelotas.

With the introduction of refrigeration in the late nineteenth century, demand for beef increased, and with it Pelotas' importance as a port and commercial centre. However, by the turn of the century, Rio Grande's port, able to take larger ships, had superseded it and the local economy entered a long period of decline.

While a slowdown in investment might have been bad for the city's economy, it saved Pelotas' Neoclassical centre from the developers. **Praça Coronel Pedro Osório**, the main square, is the city's heart, and most of the very elegant, stuccoed buildings with wrought-iron balconies overlooking the square date from the nineteenth or early twentieth centuries. Buildings here to look out for include the Prefeitura (completed in 1881), the Biblioteca Pública (1875), the former Grand Hotel (1928, now the city's Casa da Cultura) and the Teatro 7 de Abril (1834). Adjoining the *praça*, to the south, is the **Mercado Público** (Mon–Fri 7am–7pm, Sat 7am–1pm), a distinguished-looking building constructed in 1849, with a mix of stalls selling food and general goods.

As a railhead, port and an important commercial centre, late nineteenth-century Pelotas was home to a considerable British and American community. Bearing witness to this is an Anglican church, the **Igreja Episcopal do Redentor**, a block from the Mercado Público on Rua XV de Novembro. Built in 1909, the ivy-covered church would go unnoticed in any English town, but in Brazil it looks completely alien. In fact, in Rio Grande do Sul such churches have become a part of the urban landscape, with some fifty others dotted around the state, although hardly any of the members of their congregations are of British origin.

Six blocks to the north of Praça Osório, on Praça José Bonifácio, is the grand **Catedral de São Francisco de Paula** (Mon–Fri 10am–noon & 1.30–7pm, Sat 2–7pm, Sun 8am–noon & 7–8pm). While its interior has undergone some alteration over the years, the exterior, crowned with a majestic dome, has not been fundamentally altered since it was built in 1853.

Scattered around the city are numerous mansions that once housed the *pelotense* aristocracy. Many of these are in a state of disrepair, but a fine example survives as the **Museu da Baronesa** (Tues–Fri 1.30–6pm, Sat–Sun 2–5.30pm; R$3) at Av. Domingos de Almeida 1490 in the suburb of Areal, about 1km northeast of the cathedral (take a bus marked "Laranjal"). The pink and white stuccoed building was built in 1863 as a wedding present to the son and daughter-in-law of a banking family, its grandeur symbolic of the wealth that was generated during the *charque* era. The museum includes a mix of family mementoes and period furniture and offers a glimpse into the lifestyle of nineteenth-century high society.

Practicalities

The **rodoviária** (☎53/3284-6700) is way out of town, with buses running into the centre every ten minutes. There are long-distance services from Rio Grande and Porto Alegre, and less frequently from Bagé, Santo Ângelo, Santa Maria, Uruguaiana and Montevideo. For tourist information, head for the **tourist office** (Mon–Fri 9am–6pm; ☎53/3225-3733) at Praça Coronel Pedro Osório 6. On the same square you'll find several cheap **hotels**, of which the best is the very basic *Rex* (☎53/3222-1163; ❷). For more comfort, try the *Curi Palace* at Rua General Osório 719 (☎53/3227-7377, Ⓦwww.curipalacehotel.com.br; ❸–❹) or, at the top end, the *Jacques Georges* at Rua Gonçalves Chaves 512 (☎53/3284-9000, Ⓦwww.jghotel.com.br; ❺). By far the most distinct and pleasant place to stay is the *Charqueada Santa Rita* (☎53/3228-2024, Ⓦwww.charqueadasantarita.com.br; ❺), located on the outskirts of the city on the Estrada da Costa. A former *charqueada* (see above), the *pousada* offers unpretentious but high levels of comfort and the setting couldn't be more relaxing. There's a pool and the very helpful Anglo-Brazilian owner offers boat trips on the very pretty Arroio Pelotas that backs onto the property.

For a city of this size and importance, the **restaurants** are generally poor, but there are a few that are well worth seeking out. Meat – here meaning beef – is the local staple, and the quality is especially good at the moderately priced *El Paisano*, Rua Deodoro 1093 (Tues–Sat from 7pm and Sun 11am–2pm & from 7pm), a cosy Uruguayan *parrilla* (grill). For more sophisticated surroundings and similarly good Uruguayan-style cooking, try *Grelhados Batuva*, Rua General Osório 454 (Mon–Sat from 8pm, Sun noon–2.30pm). The best place for reasonably priced Portuguese food is the *Vila do Conde*, Rua Andrade Neves 1321 (closed all Mon and Sun evening) while *Lobão Galeteria*, Rua Dr Amarante, at the corner of Rua Gonçalves Chaves, offers good, inexpensive, Italian-style meals based on chicken, polenta and salad. Pelotas is famous for its intense Portuguese-style **sweets and cakes**, and the best place to try them is the *Doçaria Pelotense* at the corner of Rua Sete de Setembro and 15 de Novembro.

The city has developed a reputation as a good place to buy **antiques**, with curios and furniture items being sold by old *pelotense* families. Rua Anchieta, in the centre of town, is where the antique shops are concentrated, with *Inês* (at no. 2373) and *Lalique* (at no. 2208) being especially reliable.

Rio Grande and around

RIO GRANDE was founded on the entrance to the Lagoa dos Patos in 1737, at the very southern fringe of the Portuguese empire. With the growth of the *charque* and chilled beef economy, Rio Grande's port took on an increasing importance from the mid-nineteenth century. Rather more spread out than Pelotas, it does not share that city's instant charm. However, you'll find some distinguished-looking colonial and late nineteenth-century buildings in the area around Rua Floriano Peixoto and **Praça Tamandaré** (the main square), which is almost next to Largo Dr Pio and the much-renovated eighteenth-century **Catedral**. On Rua General Osório, by the corner of Rua General Neto, is the **Biblioteca Rio-grandense** (Mon–Fri 8am–noon & 2–6pm, Sat 8am–noon), dating from 1846, the oldest and still the most important library in the state. The library is especially significant for its nineteenth-century collection, which features many rare volumes. Among the city's museums, you'll want to visit the **Museu Oceanográfico** at Rua Reito Perdigão 10 (daily 9–11am & 1.30–5.30pm), perhaps the most important of its kind in Latin America and stuffed with fossils and preserved sea creatures. Also worthwhile is the **Museu Histórico da Cidade do Rio Grande** on Rua Riachuelo (Tues–Sun 9–11.30am & 2–5.30 pm), whose photographic archive and objects trace the city's history. The museum is housed in the old customs house (*alfândega*), a Neoclassical building built in 1879.

Just a stone's throw from the cathedral, the **waterfront** is always busy with ocean-going ships, fishing vessels and smaller boats. From here boats cross the mouth of the Lago dos Patos to the small village of **São José do Norte**, one of the oldest settlements in the state, where there's a simple church, **Nossa Senhora dos Navegantes**, built in 1795.

As far as **beaches** are concerned, though, you'll need to go to **Cassino**, a resort facing the Atlantic that's very popular with Uruguayans, 25km south of Rio Grande and served by buses from Praça Tamandaré. Like most of the rest of the Litoral Gaúcho, the beaches here are long, low and straight and only merit a visit if you have time between buses.

Practicalities

A few blocks from Praça Tamandaré is Rio Grande's **rodoviária** (Ⓣ53/3232-8444), served by buses from most cities in Rio Grande do Sul, and from cities as far north as Rio de Janeiro. Though rarely open, the **tourist office** is at Rua Riachuelo 355, in front of the Câmara de Comércio, by the waterfront.

Built in 1826, the *Paris Hotel*, on the waterfront at Rua Marechal Floriano 112 (Ⓣ53/3231-3866, Ⓦwww.hotelvillamoura.com.br; ❸), was once the place **to stay** in Rio Grande and, after decades of neglect, much of its former "Grand Hotel" feel and fabric have been restored, making it an important sight in its own right. There's a wood-panelled breakfast room and an extremely pretty courtyard with a central fountain, and while most of the bedrooms are fairly basic, some have period furnishings and offer amazing value. If the *Paris* is full, there's the *Taufik*, near the cathedral at Rua General Neto 20 (Ⓣ53/3231-3755; ❸), though it has no character. For **eating**, try the *Pescal*, Rua Aarechl Andrea 269 (closed Sun), which specializes in fish; the *Angola*, Rua Benjamin Constant 163 (closed Mon), for Portuguese specialities; or *Pimenta Americana* at Rua General Câmara 443 (Thurs–Sat lunch and dinner, Sun–Wed lunch only), which has an excellent all-you-can-eat buffet (R$12) of hot and cold home-style Brazilian dishes. For emergencies, contact the British Honorary Consulate at Rua Riachuelo 201 (Ⓣ53/3233-7700).

The Uruguayan border: Chuí

Unless you're shopping for cheap Scotch whiskey or visiting the casino, there's absolutely nothing in **CHUÍ** (or "Chuy" on the Uruguayan side of the frontier) to stick around for. **Buses** entering and leaving Brazil stop at an immigration office a short distance from town for passports to be stamped. The Brazilian **rodoviária** (Ⓣ53/3265-1498; frequent services from Porto Alegre, Pelotas and Rio Grande), on Rua Venezuela, is just a couple of blocks from Avenida Brasil, which divides the Brazilian and Uruguayan sides of town; you can cross back and forth quite freely. Onda, one of Uruguay's main bus companies, stops on the Uruguayan side of Avenida Brasil and has frequent departures for Punta del Este and Montevideo. If you are travelling to or from western Uruguay and Treinta y Tres, you will have to walk 3km down Calle General Artigas (follow the signs to Montevideo) to the Uruguayan immigration post for an entry or exit stamp in your passport. If you need a **visa** to enter Brazil, there's a Brazilian consulate on the Uruguayan side of town at Calle Fernández 147, while in Brazil the Uruguayan consulate is at Rua Venezuela 311.

Changing money is easy: either use a Uruguayan *casa de cambio* or bank before travelling on into Brazil where you'll receive the equivalent of the best rates available in Brazilian cities, or wait until you cross into Chuí where there are ATMs. If you can, try to avoid **staying** in Chuí as hotels are overpriced and unpleasant; as a rule, those on the Brazilian side of the common avenue are cheaper, those on the Uruguayan side cleaner and more comfortable. **Restaurants**, even the most simple ones, are better on the Uruguayan side of the avenue – *Jesus* and *Los Leños* are both good *parillas* (*churascarrias*).

Santa Maria and around

In the centre of Rio Grande do Sul, just at the point where the *campanha* hits the escarpment leading up into the *serra*, is **SANTA MARIA**, a city of some 250,000 inhabitants. A farming, administrative and educational centre and rail junction, Santa Maria is the most important city west of Porto Alegre. And, with a pleasant, lively atmosphere (owing to the presence of three universities), it makes a good stopping-off point on the way into or out of Brazil.

Founded in 1797, it wasn't until the late nineteenth century, with the rise of the cattle economy and the arrival of the rail line, that Santa Maria became of significance. However, while there are a number of interesting buildings dating back to about 1900, nothing much remains from earlier times. On the main square in the heart of the city is the **Catedral**, Baroque in style, but built at the beginning of the twentieth century. On the same square there's another church, Anglican and – like many of the others in the state – built in 1907 for the employees of the once important British rail line and meat-exporting interests. On Rua Daudt, a few blocks from Praça Saldanha Marinho, is another typically English building, from the same period but of otherwise uncertain origin – a curious ivy-clad house set in a beautiful garden. Many of the rail engineers at the beginning of the twentieth century were from Belgium, and they were housed in the **Vila Belga**, a row of 84 very pretty but somewhat dilapidated cottages built in 1903 on Rua Ernesto Beck, Rua Dr Valtier, Rua Manoel Ribas and Rua André Marques near the train station.

Practicalities

Buses from all points in Rio Grande do Sul, Curitiba, São Paulo and Montevideo arrive at Santa Maria's new **rodoviária** (Ⓣ55/3222-4747) on the outskirts of the city from where there are buses to the city centre. There's a **tourist office** (Mon–Fri 9am–5.45pm, Sat 9am–3pm) at the *rodoviária*.

Several cheap **hotels** are gathered near the old *ferroviária*, but a much safer inexpensive option (though a little more expensive) is the *Morotin*, Rua Ângelo Uglione 1629 (Ⓣ55/3222-4453, Ⓦwww.morotin.com.br; ❷–❸). The best place to stay in town is the *Itaimbé Palace Hotel* at Rua Venâncio Aires 2741 (Ⓣ55/222-1144, Ⓦwww.hotelitaimbe.com.br; ❸–❹), which is large, efficient, comfortable and excellent value. There are plenty of **restaurants** about, but few that are especially good. The *Vera Cruz* at Av. Nossa Senhora Medianeira 1600 and *Augusto* at Rua Floriano Peixoto 1354 both serve Italian-inspired chicken dishes, flavoured with bacon and herbs, that are distinctive to Santa Maria.

Around Santa Maria: Vale Veneto and Mata

The immediate area around Santa Maria is now mainly given over to cattle and soya. Italians from northeastern Rio Grande do Sul have had some considerable success farming the very picturesque **Vale Veneto** (take a bus to Nova Palma), about 45 minutes from Santa Maria, but Bessarabian Jews were not so fortunate. In 1904, eighty Jewish families arrived in Santa Maria with the intention of establishing a farming colony. They were given land 15km north of the city, but it slowly became apparent that the soil would only be of use for cattle. Over a forty-year period, settlers drifted from the **Colônia Philippson** – as it was known – into Santa Maria, where there survives a small Jewish community who still maintain a synagogue (at Rua Otavio Binato 49, Santa Maria). Virtually in the middle of nowhere, on a hill surrounded by cattle pasture, is the colony's small cemetery, located within what is now the Fazenda Philippson: to get there, take any bus heading north on the BR-158 and, on the left, a few kilometres past the Oásis swimming centre (at Km 311 – 14km from Santa Maria), is the *fazenda*'s clearly marked entrance (45min from town). From there, ask for directions to the cemetery.

With even just a faint interest in geology you should find a visit to **MATA**, an hour by bus from Santa Maria, worthwhile. Scattered everywhere in the small town are massive petrified tree trunks. The **Museu Guido Borgomanero** (Mon–Fri 8am–6pm and Sat–Sun 9–11.30am & 1.30–5.30pm) has a well-catalogued collection of fossils of all kinds, and the steps leading to the local Catholic church – itself unremarkable – are made entirely of fossilized wood. If you need a **hotel** in Mata, there's the very simple *Paleon* (ⓣ55/3259-1165; ❷) by the Catholic church, and a basic **restaurant**, too.

The Jesuit missions and Iraí

For much of the seventeenth and eighteenth centuries, the **Guaraní Indians** of what is now northeastern Argentina, southeastern Paraguay and northwestern Rio Grande do Sul were only nominally within the domain of the Spanish and Portuguese empires, and instead were ruled – or protected – by the Society of Jesus, the **Jesuits**. The first **redução** – a self-governing Indian settlement based around a Jesuit mission – was established in 1610 and, within a hundred years, thirty such places were in existence. With a total population of 150,000, these mini-cities became centres of some importance, with *erva maté* and cattle the mainstay of economic activity, though spinning, weaving and metallurgical cottage industries were also pursued. As the seventeenth century progressed, Spain and Portugal grew increasingly concerned over the Jesuits' power, and Rome feared that the religious order was becoming too independent of papal authority. Finally, in 1756, Spanish and Portuguese forces attacked the missions, the Jesuits were expelled and many Indians killed. The missions themselves were dissolved, either razed to the ground or abandoned to nature, surviving only as ruins.

São Miguel and around

Of the thirty former Guaraní mission towns, sixteen were in present-day Argentina, seven in Paraguay and seven were situated in what is now Brazil, and almost all were completely levelled. The one exception in Brazil is **SÃO MIGUEL** (daily 9am–noon & 2–6pm; R$5), not to be compared in extent and significance to San Ignacio Miní in neighbouring Argentina, but still of considerable visual interest, particularly for its dramatic location on a treeless fertile plain. Despite

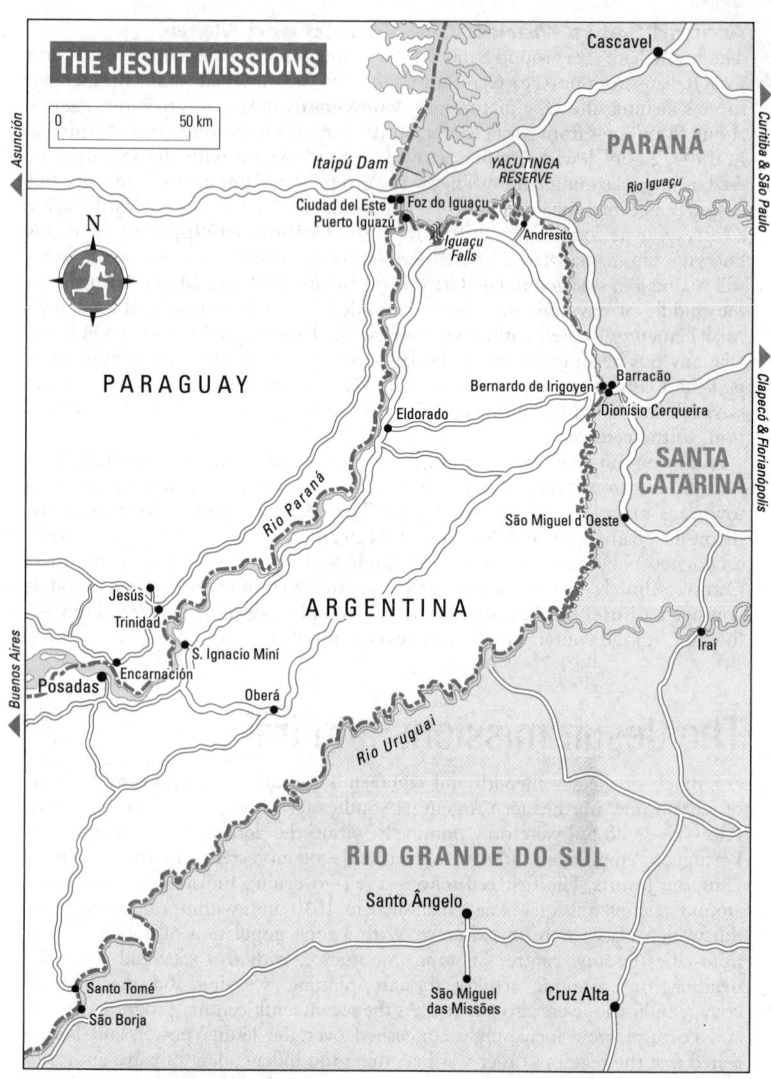

vandalism and centuries of neglect, São Miguel's ruins offer ample evidence of the sophistication of Guaraní Baroque architecture, and of *redução* life generally. Founded in 1632, to the west of the Rio Uruguai, São Miguel moved only a few years later to escape Paulista slavers, and then a few years after that it was destroyed by a violent windstorm. After being rebuilt, its population increased rapidly and in 1687 it was relocated across the river to its present site.

The initial priority was to provide housing, so not until 1700 did work begin on the **church**, designed by the Milanese Jesuit architect Giovanni Baptista Prímoli, the ruins of which still stand. The facade is a handsome example of colonial architecture. One of the church's two towers is missing, but otherwise its stone structure is reasonably complete, the lack of a vault or dome explained by the fact that these would have been finished with wood. Other aspects of the ruins are of less interest, but the outline of the *redução*'s **walls** provides a guide to the former extent of São Miguel which, at its peak, was home to over 4000 people. The **museum** (daily 9am–6pm) has an excellent collection of stone and wood sculptures, which are beautifully displayed in Jesuit-influenced but stylistically modernist buildings designed by Lúcio Costa, the urban planner of Brasília. Every evening (8pm in winter, 9.15pm in summer; R$5) there's a **sound and light show**, which, even if you don't understand the Portuguese narrative, is well worth staying for. You can actually **stay** in the quiet village here, which will give you an ideal opportunity to wander round the ruins early in the day before most of the other tourists arrive. In any case, if you're attending the sound and light show, there are no late buses returning to Santo Ângelo. Right next to the ruins, there's the excellent *Pousada das Missões* (ⓣ55/3381-1202, ⓦwww.albuergues.com.br/saomiguel; ❸) and the *Wilson Park* (ⓣ55/3381-2000, ⓦwww.wilsonparkhotel; ❸–❹), a comfortable, modern hotel with a pool. There are a couple of basic **restaurants** next to the ruins, or you can eat at the *Wilson Park*.

Santo Ângelo

São Miguel is 55km from **SANTO ÂNGELO**, a town in a farming region inhabited predominantly by people of German origin. There's not much to see in the town itself, although the **Catedral** (daily 8.30am–5pm), on the main square, Praça Pinheiro Machado, is worth a look as it's a fair replica of São Miguel's church. Santo Ângelo is served by buses from throughout Rio Grande do Sul as well as from Curitiba, São Paulo and Rio. If you're planning on visiting the Jesuit ruins in Argentina and Paraguay, there's a daily **bus** to Posadas, or take a bus to the border town of São Borja and change there. The **rodoviária** is within a few

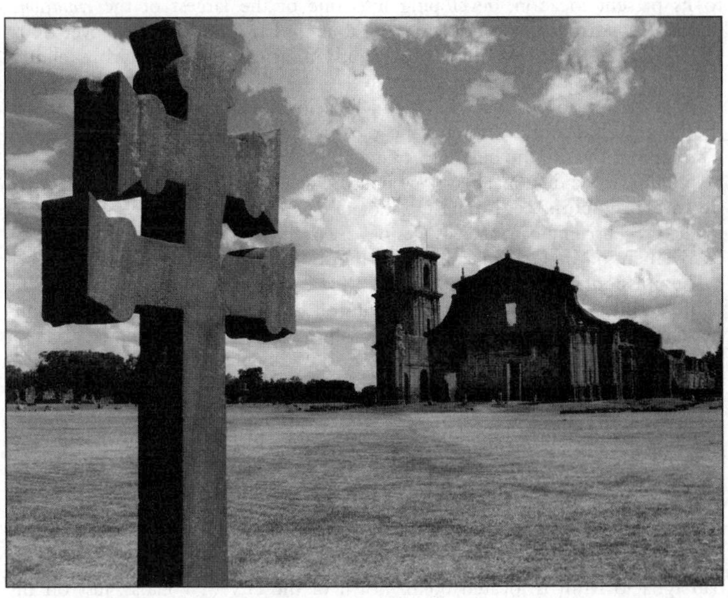

△ São Miguel

blocks of Praça Pinheiro Machado; there are four buses a day to and from São Miguel, with the last going to the ruins at 5pm and returning at 7pm. A few kilometres out of town is the **airport**, with several flights a day from Porto Alegre.

The best cheap **hotel** in Santo Ângelo is the *Santo Ângelo Turis* (Ⓣ55/3312-4055; ❷), just off the main square at Rua Antônio Manoel 726, or for more comfort try the *Maerkil* at Av. Brasil 1000 (Ⓣ55/3313-2127; ❹). The best **restaurant** in town is a *churrascaria*, the *Chico*, at Rua Antônio Manoel 1421.

The Argentine and Paraguayan missions

Argentina and Paraguay each have one fine ruin of a Jesuit mission and, without too much difficulty, it's possible to get to them in combination with a visit to São Miguel. There are direct bus services every day between Santo Ângelo, which serves the **São Miguel** site in Brazil, and Posadas in Argentina, crossing the border at São Borja (see p.786). Posadas is a short distance from Argentina's **San Ignacio Miní** ruins and Paraguay's **Trinidad**. Alternatively, these latter two missions are an easy side-trip from the Iguaçu falls; the lovely country hotel *Estancia Las Mercedes* (see p.714), roughly midway between the two areas near Eldorado, makes a convenient base.

San Ignacio Miní

Like many of the missions, **SAN IGNACIO MINÍ** was initially established on another site and later relocated for safety. Consecrated in 1609 as San Ignacio-guazú across the Rio Paraná in present-day Paraguay, the mission was moved to the Rio Yabebiry in 1632 due to constant attacks by slave-hunting *bandeirantes*. This site proved unsuitable and in 1695 the mission was moved a short distance to its present location, developing into one of the largest of the *reducciones* (*redução* in Portuguese) with, at its peak, an Indian population of over 4000. Following the Jesuits' expulsion from South America, San Ignacio Miní fell into decline, its ruins not discovered until 1897.

Of all the mission ruins, those of San Ignacio Miní (daily 7am–7pm; A$5) are the largest in area and feature some of the most interesting museum displays. Throughout the site the buildings, trees and bushes are labelled in Spanish, so it's helpful to carry a dictionary. As you enter the site, be sure not to miss the **Centro de Interpretación Regional**, its elaborate stage-prop-style displays depicting an idyllic pre-Hispanic past, the voyages of "discovery", the clash of cultures and the enslavement of the Guaraní, and finally the rise and fall of the Jesuit *reducciones*.

The mission is centred around the **Plaza de Armas**, dominated by the church. Visitors can wander into the ruins of the red sandstone buildings flanking the plaza: these served as workshops, schools, cloisters and living quarters for the Indians and missionaries. Completed in 1724, and designed by the Italian architect Giovanni Brazanelli, the huge Baroque church was, and still is, the focal point of the mission, although only part of the facade and a few other parts of the structure remain standing. The church, like many of the other buildings, is decorated with delicate, mainly floral designs, bas-relief sculptures by Guaraní artisans. Near the exit from the ruins is a small **museum** where sculptures excavated over the years are displayed.

Practicalities

San Ignacio Miní is located 60km north of the city of Posadas, just off the main highway to Puerto Iguazú. There's a constant flow of buses between

Puerto Iguazú (see p.712) and Posadas, most of which stop off at the sleepy little village of **SAN IGNACIO** (3hr 30min from Puerto Iguazú, 1hr from Posadas), adjoining the ruins, a pleasant place to spend a night. If travelling from São Miguel, the best option is a bus from Santo Ângelo to São Borja from where you can catch a bus to Posadas and another to San Ignacio. There are two good **accommodation** options in San Ignacio. On the village's central plaza is the comfortable, air-conditioned *Hotel San Ignacio* (⊕752/470047; ❸), while near the ruins' entrance is the friendly and very clean *Hospedaje Los Alemanes* (⊕752/470362; ❷). Nearby are numerous **restaurants**, with little to choose between them, except that *La Carpa Azul* has a swimming pool, wonderful on a hot summer afternoon. Argentine *pesos* are available from an **ATM** located next to the church.

Trinidad and Jesús

Of the three best-preserved Jesuit mission ruins, those of **TRINIDAD** (Mon–Sat 7.30–11.30am & 1.30–5.30pm, Sun 1.30–5.30pm; US$1) in Paraguay are the least visited. Founded in 1706, Trinidad was one of the last *reducciones*, but it grew quickly and by 1728 it had a Guaraní population of over 4000. The mission was designed by the Milanese architect Giovanni Baptista Prímoli, and the work wasn't completed until 1760, just a few years before the Jesuits' expulsion from South America. Trinidad prospered, developing *maté* plantations, cattle *estancias* and a sugar plantation and mill, and its Guaraní artisans became famous for the manufacture of organs, harps and other musical instruments, bells and statues, exported throughout the Rio Plate region and beyond. One of the most grandiose of the missions, Trinidad is thought to have been the regional centre for Jesuit activity in Paraguay. Following the departure of the Jesuits, the community fell into rapid and terminal decline, the final blow coming in 1816 when Paraguay's dictator, José Gaspar Rodríguez de Francia, ordered the destruction of all Indian villages as part of his infamous scorched earth policy.

Trinidad is Paraguay's best-restored Jesuit ruin and there is intense local pride in its status as a UNESCO World Heritage Site. Occupying a hilltop position surrounded by soya fields and cattle pasture, the site is not as extensive and the church not as large nor as complete as at San Ignacio Miní and São Miguel. Even so, much of the **church** remains in remarkable condition, including the elaborate pulpit and some of the most beautiful and intricate of **Guaraní Baroque frescoes**. Especially charming is the procession of little angels carved in sandstone that has somehow survived the centuries. Behind the ruins of the church is a small chapel: ask the guard to let you in as it contains yet more stunning wood and stone statues of angels. For an excellent view of the entire mission site and across the surrounding countryside climb the church's bell tower.

Ten kilometres to the north lies the Jesuit mission of **JESÚS**. Not strictly speaking ruins, Jesús (same hours and fees as Trinidad), founded in 1685 but only settled in 1763, is really an unfinished construction site, the large **church** half built when the Jesuits were ordered out of South America. What exists of the church has been restored, its beautiful arched portals resembling shamrocks, and it has an enormous half-erected guardian tower. Lacking the wealth of other missions, Jesús was not such a target of treasure seekers and remained relatively intact.

Practicalities

Trinidad is located 28km (45min) northeast of Paraguay's third-largest city, Encarnación. There aren't many facilities in Trinidad (and there are even fewer in Jesús) and most visitors stay in Encarnación or in Posadas. There are frequent buses between the two cities and also good bus services from Ciudad del Este

(4hr; see p.714) for Iguaçu. Inexpensive and comfortable **hotels** are easy to find in **Encarnación**. An excellent budget choice is the *Viena* (ⓣ71/3486; ❷), a couple of blocks behind the bus terminal at Calle P.J. Caballero 568. Near Plaza Artigas is the modern *Paraná*, at Av. Estigarribia 1414 (ⓣ71/4480; ❸), while the *Cristal* at no. 1157 (ⓣ71/2371; ❹) is the best hotel in town.

There are some good **parrillas** (grills): on Avenida Mariscal Estigarribia near Plaza Artigas is the excellent *Rancho Grande*, while the *Cuarajhyon*, actually on Plaza Artigas, is also reasonable. Meat, of course, dominates menus, but vegetarians can enjoy huge salads and should try *sopa paraguaya*, a national staple that is not, as its name suggests, soup but corn bread made with onion and cheese.

The border towns: gaúcho country

Apart from Chuí (see p.775), the most commonly used **border crossing** into **Uruguay** is at **Santana do Livramento**. While most buses cross into **Argentina** via **Uruguaiana**, you may find **São Borja** quicker if you're travelling

Gaúchos

During the colonial era and well into the nineteenth century, Rio Grande do Sul's southern and western frontiers were ill-defined, with Portugal and Spain, and then independent Brazil, Argentina and Uruguay, maintaining garrisons to assert their claims to the region. Frontier clashes were frequent, with central government presence weak or non-existent. If anyone could maintain some measure of control over these border territories it was the **gaúchos**, the fabled horsemen of southern South America. The product of miscegenation between Spanish, Portuguese, Indians and escaped slaves, the *gaúchos* wandered the region on horseback, either individually or in small bands, making a living by hunting wild cattle for their hides. Alliances were formed in support of local *caudilhos* (chiefs), who fought for control of the territory on behalf of the flag of one or other competing power. With a reputation for being tough and fearless, the *gaúcho* was also said to be supremely callous – displaying the same indifference in slitting a human or a bullock's throat.

As the nineteenth century ended, so too did the *gaúcho*'s traditional way of life. International boundaries became accepted, and landowners were better able to exert control over their properties. Finally, as fencing was introduced and rail lines arrived, cattle turned into an industry, with the animals raised rather than hunted. Gradually *gaúchos* were made redundant, reduced to the status of mere *peões* or cattle hands.

Still, more in Rio Grande do Sul than in Argentina, some *gaúcho* traditions persist, though for a visitor to get much of a picture of the present-day way of life is difficult. In general, the cities and towns of the state's interior are fairly characterless, though travelling between towns still brings echoes of former times, especially if you get off the beaten track. Here, in the small villages, horses are not only a tool used to herd cattle, but remain an essential means of transport. While women are no differently dressed than in the rest of Brazil, men appear in much the same way as their *gaúcho* predecessors: in *bombachas* (baggy trousers), linen shirt, kerchief, poncho and felt-rimmed hat, shod in pleated boots and fancy spurs. Also associated with the interior of Rio Grande do Sul is *chimarrão* (sugarless *maté* tea), which is sipped through a *bomba* (a silver straw) from a *cuia* (a gourd). In the towns themselves, cattlemen are always to be seen, purchasing supplies or just around for a good time. But undoubtedly your best chance of getting a feel of the interior is to attend a **rodeio**, held regularly in towns and villages throughout *gaúcho* country, and most notably at Vacaria (see p.769). Branches of the state tourist office, CRTur, will have information about when and where *rodeios* are due to take place.

between Jesuit mission sites or making your way north to the Iguaçu Falls. Alternatively, use a smaller border crossing point, like **Aceguá**, near **Bagé**, where at least your first impressions of Uruguay or Brazil will be of cattle and ranch hands rather than duty-free shops and casinos. Rarely do people remain in the border towns longer than it takes to go through immigration formalities, but, if you're trying to get a taste of *gaúcho* life, check to see if there's a *rodeio* about to be held somewhere around or, to witness the everyday working life of the pampas close up, you could arrange to stay at an *estância* – a cattle ranch.

Bagé and Aceguá

Of all the towns on or very near Rio Grande do Sul's border with Argentina and Uruguay, **BAGÉ** is the only one with genuine charm, full of stately late nineteenth- and early twentieth-century buildings and a place that remains first and foremost a cattle and commercial centre, rather than a transit point. Like all towns in the *campanha*, Bagé has its own lively events, which attract people from the surrounding *estâncias*. The most important **festival**, held in January in odd-numbered years, is the **Semana Crioula Internacional**, but the *Semana de Bagé* (a folklore festival held annually from July 10 to 17), or even the *Exposição* (first half of Oct), will give you a taste of the *campanha*. For details of these and other events ask at the **tourist office** at Praça Silveira Martins (Mon–Fri 8am–6pm, Sat 9am–7pm). For an understanding of the region's history, a visit to the **Museu Dom Diogo de Souza**, Av. Emílio Guilayn 759 (Tues–Fri 8–11.30am & 1.30–6pm, Sat & Sun 1.30–5.30pm), is a must. Also worth visiting is the **Museu da Gravura Brasileira** at Rua Coronel Azambuja 18 (Mon 1.30–5.30pm, Tues–Fri 1.30–7.30pm), which has an important collection of ceramics, photography and, especially, engravings: Rio Grande do Sul has a long tradition of this art form and some of the most important artists worked in Bagé.

Hotels in Bagé are plentiful, with the clean and friendly *Mini*, on Avenida Sete de Setembro, near Praça General Osório (❷), the centre's cheapest, while for just a few more *reais* you could stay in much greater comfort at the *City Hotel* (Ⓣ53/3242-8455, Ⓦwww.bagecityhotel.com.br; ❸), nearby at Av. Sete de Setembro 1052. With much more character, however, there's the *Pousada do Sobrado* (Ⓣ53/3242-2713, Ⓦwww.pousadadosobrado; ❺), 5km from the town centre along the Rua São João. The *pousada* is based on a beautiful *estância* house built in 1820, and has a large pool in the grounds. There are just three guest rooms (all with period furniture) and reservations are advisable.

Ideally, though, you should **stay at a working estância** in the surrounding pampas. The owners of the *Estância Retiro* (Ⓣ53/3242-8002, Ⓦwww.estanciaretiro.com.br; R$150 per person, full board) have opened their 1300-hectare property, 25km from town, to paying guests and delight in receiving visitors. Built in 1834, the main house is one of the oldest around and guests stay either in one of its very comfortable bedrooms or a converted barn. On arrival at the *estância*, you first have to show whether you can handle a horse. If you can't, you're quickly coached to develop some basic equestrian skills. You can spend your time joining the owner and his workers on horseback in their day-to-day duties minding the thousand head of cattle on the property or learn about the very distinctive local cooking. There's a swimming pool and streams for cooling off in on hot summer days, while the open fires are essential features for the often bitterly cold winter evenings. Reservations are essential and you can arrange to be collected from town.

ACEGUÁ, 60km south and the actual frontier crossing point, is very much a back door into Brazil and Uruguay, with only a Uruguayan immigration post (remember to be stamped in or out of the country) and a few houses and stores

Arriving and departing

Arriving in Bagé from the Uruguayan border (Melo is the nearest Uruguayan town), ask to be let off at the **Polícia Federal** at Rua Barão do Trunfo 1572, a few blocks from the main square, Praça General Osório. It's here, not at Aceguá (see below), that you'll need to have your passport stamped. Arriving in Bagé from elsewhere, take a "Santa Tecla" bus into the centre from the main road next to the **rodoviária** (Ⓣ53/3242-7433; buses from Santa Maria and Porto Alegre, Santo Ângelo and, via Curitiba, São Paulo). If you're leaving Brazil, have your passport stamped; failing to report to the Polícia Federal here will mean that you're likely to have difficulties entering or leaving Brazil later on.

– certainly not a place to spend a night. However, as the four buses a day in each direction between Bagé and Aceguá connect with others to and from Melo (Uruguay), this shouldn't be a problem – but check bus times carefully before setting out.

Changing money is best done at a *casa de câmbio* in Melo, but in Aceguá there are always plenty of men milling about offering reasonable rates for dollar bills. In Bagé, if you can't wait for the border, you can change dollars at Bradesco and many of the other banks in town are equipped with an ATM.

Santana do Livramento and around

Few people stay in **SANTANA DO LIVRAMENTO** long, apart from Brazilians attracted to the casino and the duty-free shopping in **Rivera**, the Uruguayan border town into which Livramento (as it's usually known) merges. Unless you're in pursuit of *gaúchos* and intent upon taking local buses to outlying villages, the only time when Livramento is actually worth visiting in its own right is when there's a livestock exhibition, *rodeio* or cultural event on. The most important such **events** are the *Charqueada da Poesia Crioula* (last two weeks in April), the *Exposição Internacional do Corriedale* (March 5–12) and the *Exposição Agropecuária* (last two weeks in Sept), but check with the **tourist office** at Rua Tamandaré (Mon–Sat 7am–1pm & 3–6pm, Sun 3–8pm) to see if there are any other smaller events due, in or around the town. Livramento is also a very good place to purchase **gaúcho clothing and accessories**, with Correaria Gaúcha, Rua Rivadávia Correia 184, and Correaria Nova Esperança, Rua Duque de Caxias and Rua 24 de Maio, having good selections.

Otherwise, the only possible reason not to move straight on would be a visit to the surrounding *campanha*, the rolling countryside traditionally given over to raising cattle and, to a lesser extent, sheep. For a more authentic *gaúcho* experience, visit the *Fazenda Palomas* (Ⓣ55/3242-2551, Ⓦwww.fazendapalomas.com), located 20km from Livramento with the access road at Km 480 of BR-158 in the direction of Porto Alegre. Founded in 1897, the 1000-hectare *fazenda* receives visitors during the daytime for horse riding or to participate in cattle round-ups and other daily activities (around R$40 per person). It's possible to stay the night in one of the three comfortable guest rooms (❺–❻ full board). For another nearby excursion head to **Vila Palomas**, a village 15km from Livramento, the centre of the new and increasingly important wine industry. Of all Brazil's large **wineries**, Almadén is one of the best, and their *cantina* is open to visitors (Ⓣ55/3242-5151; 9am–6pm).

Practicalities

Livramento's **rodoviária** (Ⓣ55/3242-5322), at Rua Sen. Salgado Filho 335, serves most points in Rio Grande do Sul while **from Rivera**, there are several departures a day for Montevideo from the bus terminal.

If you need to stay, **hotels** are cheapest in Livramento. The *Laçador* (❶) near the park, at Rua Uruguai 1227, is basic, or try the *Livramento*, opposite the *rodoviária* (Ⓣ55/3242-5444; ❷). For more comfort, a good option is the *Jandaia* at Rua Uruguai 1452 (Ⓣ55/3242-2288, Ⓦwww.jandaiah.com.br; ❸–❹). There's a **youth hostel** at Rua Manduca Rodrigues 615 (Ⓣ55/3242-3340; R$20 per person), about five blocks from the *rodoviária*, while across in Rivera there's another hostel at Uruguay 735. **Restaurants** are better in Rivera: the best is the *Dan Servanda*, Calle Carambula 1132, around the corner from the immigration office, or for excellent Uruguayan snacks and *dulces*, head for *Confeitaria City* on Avenida Sarandí.

Before **leaving** Livramento and Rivera, you'll need a Brazilian exit (or entry) passport stamp from the Polícia Federal, Rua Uruguai 1177, near the central park, and a stamp from Uruguay's Dirección Nacional de Migración, Calle Suarez 516 (three blocks from Plaza General José Artigas, Rivera's main square). If you have problems, Brazil's **consulate** in Rivera is at Calle Caballos 1159 (Ⓣ622/244-3278), and Uruguay's is in Livramento at Av. Tamandaré 2110 (Ⓣ55/3242-1416). **Change money** at a *casa de câmbio* or bank in Rivera, where exchange rates are as good as you'll find in Brazil and the process much faster, or use a Brazilian ATM.

Uruguaiana

The busiest crossing point on Rio Grande do Sul's border with Argentina, **URUGUAIANA** is also one of the state's most important cattle centres. However, unless you're around while there's a livestock show or folklore festival, there's little incentive to remain here: ask about festival dates at the **tourist office** (Mon–Sat 8.30am–6pm) in the Prefeitura, Praça Barão do Rio Branco. The most important annual events are the *Campeira Internacional* (a festival of regional folklore) held in the first half of March, *Semana Farroupilha* (another folklore festival) held September 13–20, and a huge livestock show, the *Expofeira Agropecuária*, held in the first half of November. Otherwise, the **Museu Crioulo, Histórico e Artístico** (Mon–Fri 8.30am–noon & 2–5.30pm), in the cultural centre on the corner of *ruas* Santana and Duque de Caxias (by the main square), is worth a look for its interesting collection of *gaúcho*-related items.

Uruguaiana is connected to Argentina and the town of **Paso de los Libres** by a 1400-metre-long bridge spanning the Rio Uruguai. Frequent **local buses** connect the train and bus stations, and the centres of each city, and **immigration** formalities take place on either side of the bridge. If you have problems entering Argentina, the **consulate** in Uruguaiana is at Rua Santana 2496 (Ⓣ55/3412-1925). The Brazilian consulate in Paso de los Libres is at Calle Mitre 918. You're best off **changing money** in Paso de los Libres, but failing this there are plenty of banks with ATMs in Uruguaiana. If you need **accommodation**, the fairly modest hotels in Uruguaiana include the *Wamosy* (Ⓣ55/3412-1326; ❷) and *Mazza Tur* (Ⓣ55/3412-3404; ❸), at Rua Sete de Setembro, nos. 1973 and 1088 respectively. For a little more luxury try the new *Elyt* at Av. Presidente Vargas 3718 (Ⓣ55/3411-8800; ❸). If you're stuck in Paso de los Libres, make for the *Las Vegas* (Ⓣ3772/423490; ❸), a pleasant mid-range hotel one block from the main square, Plaza Independencia, at Sarmiento 554. **Restaurants** (for carnivores only) are better over the border in Argentina; however, in Uruguaiana, the *Casa d'Itália* at Rua Dr Maia 3112 has a varied menu to choose from.

Bus services from Uruguaiana are excellent, and you can get to or from most of the important centres, from Rio southwards. From Paso de los Libres, there are equally good services to points within Argentina, including Buenos Aires, Posadas and Puerto Iguazú. Finally, there are daily **air services** from Uruguaiana to Porto Alegre and from Paso de los Libres to Buenos Aires.

São Borja

Today a fairly major border crossing point and regional trading centre, **SÃO BORJA** is best known in the rest of Brazil as the birthplace of two of the country's most controversial presidents: **Getúlio Vargas** and **João Goulart**. In São Borja, if nowhere else in Brazil, the populist Vargas remains a venerated figure, and his former home, at Av. Presidente Vargas 1772, is now open to the public as the **Museu Getúlio Vargas** (Mon–Sat 8am–5pm), containing his library and personal objects and furniture. Goulart, whose incompetent presidency led to the military's seizure of power in 1964 followed by 25 years of often ruthless rule, is someone that São Borja tries to forget.

As a **border crossing**, São Borja is most useful when travelling between the Brazilian Jesuit mission of São Miguel and those in Argentina and Paraguay. São Borja has good **bus** connections with Santo Ângelo (for São Miguel), most other important towns in Rio Grande do Sul, Curitiba, São Paulo and, across the bridge that links Brazil with Argentina, the Argentine town of Santo Tomé. From Santo Tomé there are several bus services a day to Posadas, Puerto Iguazú, Buenos Aires and other towns in Argentina.

If you need to stay over in São Borja, the cheapest **hotel** is the *Itaipu* at Rua Aparício Mariense 1167 (Ⓣ55/3431-1577; ❷), while the *Executivo* at Av. Presidente Vargas 2515 (Ⓣ55/3431-3741; ❸) offers slightly greater comfort. In Santo Tomé, the *Residencial Paris*, at Calle Mitre 890 on the corner of Calle Beltrán (❷), is a fall-back for budget travellers, while the best place in town is the *Hotel Santo Tomé* (Ⓣ756/20161; ❸).

Travel details

Buses

Antonina to: Curitiba (9 daily; 2hr); Guaraqueçaba (3 daily; 3hr 30min); Morretes (hourly; 30min); Paranaguá (hourly; 45min).
Blumenau to: Florianópolis (6 daily; 3hr); Itajaí (hourly; 2hr); Joinville (hourly; 2hr); Pomerode (hourly; 45min).
Curitiba to: Antonina (9 daily; 2hr); Blumenau (10 daily; 4hr); Buenos Aires (2 daily; 37hr); Florianópolis (14 daily; 5hr); Foz do Iguaçu (14 daily; 12hr); Guaraqueçaba (2 daily; 6hr); Joinville (hourly; 2hr 30min); Paranaguá (hourly; 2hr); Pomerode (4 daily; 3hr); Porto Alegre (10 daily; 11hr); Prudentópolis (4 daily; 3hr 30min); Rio (9 daily; 11hr); São Paulo (hourly; 6hr).
Florianópolis to: Blumenau (6 daily; 3hr); Buenos Aires (2 daily; 30hr); Curitiba (14 daily; 5hr); Foz do Iguaçu (2 daily; 16hr); Joinville (hourly; 3hr); Porto Alegre (10 daily; 7hr); Rio (8 daily; 18hr); Santo Amaro da Imperatriz (4 daily; 1hr); São Paulo (10 daily; 12hr).
Foz do Iguaçu to: Curitiba (14 daily; 12hr); Florianópolis (2 daily; 16hr); Itaipu (hourly; 1hr); Prudentópolis (3 daily; 7hr); Rio (4 daily; 22hr); São Paulo (7 daily; 18hr).
Joinville to: Blumenau (hourly; 2hr); Curitiba (hourly; 2hr 30min); Florianópolis (hourly; 3hr); Porto Alegre (2 daily; 10hr); Rio (1 daily; 15hr); São Francisco do Sul (hourly; 1hr); São Paulo (7 daily; 9hr); Vila Dona Francesca (hourly; 45min).
Pelotas to: Porto Alegre (hourly; 3hr); Montevideo (2 daily; 8hr); Rio Grande (hourly; 1hr).
Pomerode to: Blumenau (hourly; 45min); Curitiba (4 daily; 3hr).
Porto Alegre to: Buenos Aires (2 daily; 22hr); Curitiba (10 daily; 11hr); Florianópolis (10 daily; 7hr); Livramento (4 daily; 7hr); Montevideo (3 daily; 12hr); Pelotas (hourly; 3hr); Rio (6 daily; 26hr); Rio Grande (hourly; 1hr); Santo Ângelo (6 daily; 6hr 30min); São Paulo (8 daily; 18hr).
Prudentópolis to: Curitiba (4 daily; 3hr 30min); Foz do Iguaçu (3 daily; 8hr); São Paulo (3 daily; 10hr).

Train

Curitiba to: Morretes (1–2 daily; 3hr); Paranaguá (2 weekly; 4hr).

Boats

Guaraqueçaba to: Ariri (2 weekly; 10hr); Paranaguá (2 weekly; 3hr).

Contexts

Contexts

The historical framework 789–809

Amazon ecology and Indian rights 810–821

Race in Brazilian society... 822-823

Music 824–832

Books.. 833–848

Brazilian cinema... 849–852

The historical framework

Brazil's recorded history begins with the arrival of the Portuguese in 1500, although it had been discovered and settled by Indians many centuries before. The importation of millions of African slaves over the next four centuries completed the rich blend of European, Indian and African influences that formed modern Brazil and its people. Achieving independence from Portugal in 1822, Brazil's enormous wealth in land and natural resources underpinned a boom-and-bust cycle of economic development that continues to the present day. The eternal "Land of the Future" is still a prisoner of its past, as industrialization turned Brazil into the economic giant of South America, but sharpened social divisions. After a twenty-year interlude of military rule, the civilian "New Republic" has struggled, with some success, against deep-rooted economic crisis and has managed to consolidate democracy. Although social divisions remain, the current economic and political outlook is the best it has been for a generation.

Early history

Very little is known about the thousands of years that Brazil was inhabited exclusively by **Indians**. The first chroniclers who arrived with the Portuguese – Pedro Vaz da Caminha in 1500 and Gaspar Carvajal in 1540 – saw large villages, but nothing resembling the huge Aztec and Inca cities that the Spanish encountered. The fragile material traces left by Brazil's earliest inhabitants have for the most part not survived. The few exceptions – like the exquisitely worked glazed ceramic jars unearthed on Marajó island in the Amazon – come from cultures that have vanished so completely that not even a name records their passing.

The Indians fascinated the Portuguese, and many of the first Europeans to visit Brazil sent lengthy reports back home. The most vivid account was penned by a German mercenary, **Hans Staden**, who spent three nervous years among the cannibal **Tupi** after being captured in 1552. He tells how they tied his legs together, ". . . and I was forced to hop through the huts, at which they made merry, saying 'Here comes our food hopping towards us.'" Understandably, his memoirs were one of the first bestsellers in European history, and contained much accurate description of an Indian culture still largely untouched by the colonists. The work of Staden and the first explorers and missionaries offers a brief snapshot of Indian Brazil in the sixteenth century, a blurred photograph of a way of life soon to be horribly transformed.

It was unfortunate that the Portuguese first landed in the only part of Brazil where ritualized cannibalism was practised on a large scale; away from the Tupi areas it was rare. Nowhere was stone used for building. There was no use of metal or the wheel, and no centralized, state-like civilizations on the scale of Spanish America. There are arguments about how large the Indian population was: Carvajal described taking several days to pass through the large towns of the Omagua tribe on the Amazon in 1542 but, away from the abundant food sources on the coast and the banks of large rivers, **population** densities were much lower. The total number of Indians was probably around five million. Today there are around 350,000 in Brazil.

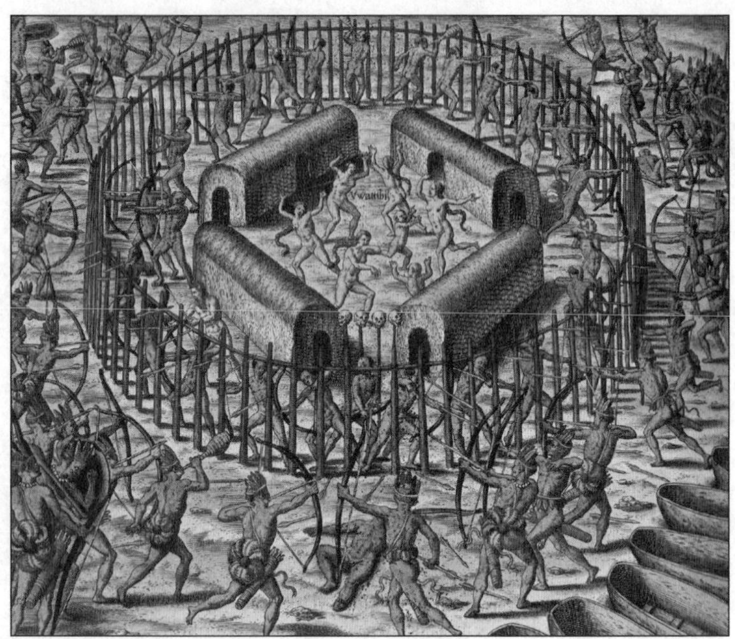

△ Sixteenth-century woodcut of an Indian attack

Conquest

The Portuguese discovery of Brazil, when **Pedro Alvares Cabral** landed in southern Bahia on April 23, 1500, was an accident, an episode in Portugal's thrust to found a seaborne empire in the East Indies during the sixteenth century. Cabral was blown off course as he steered far to the west to avoid the African doldrums on his way to Calcutta: after a cursory week exploring the coast he continued to India, where he drowned in a shipwreck a few months later. King Manuel I sent **Amerigo Vespucci** to explore further in 1501. Reserving the name of the continent for himself, he spent several months sailing along the coast, calendar in hand, baptizing places after the names of saints' days: entering Guanabara Bay on New Year's Day 1502, he called it Rio de Janeiro. The land was called Terra do Brasil, after a tropical redwood that was its first export; the scarlet dye it yielded was called *brasa*, "a glowing coal".

Portugal, preoccupied with Africa and the lucrative Far East spice trade, neglected this new addition to its empire for the first few decades. Apart from a few lumber camps and scattered stockades, the Portuguese made no attempt at settlement. Consequently, other European countries were not slow to move in, with French and English privateers using the coast as a base to raid the spice ships. Finally, in 1532, King João III was provoked into action. He divided up the coastline into **sesmarias**, captaincies fifty leagues wide and extending indefinitely inland, distributing them to aristocrats and courtiers in return for undertakings to found settlements. It was hardly a roaring success: Pernambuco, where sugar took hold, and São Vicente, gateway to the Jesuit mission station of São Paulo, were the only securely held areas.

Irritated by the lack of progress, King João repossessed the captaincies in 1548 and brought Brazil under direct royal control, sending out the first governor-general, **Tomé da Sousa**, to the newly designated **capital** at Salvador in 1549. The first few governors successfully rooted out the European privateers, and – where sugar could grow – wiped out Indian resistance. By the closing decades of the century increasing numbers of Portuguese settlers were flowing in. Slaves began to be imported from the Portuguese outposts on the African coast, as **sugar plantations** sprang up around Salvador and Olinda. Brazil, no longer seen merely as a possible staging point on the way to the Far East, became an increasingly important piece of the far-flung Portuguese Empire. When Europe's taste for sugar took off in the early seventeenth century, the Northeast of Brazil quickly became very valuable real estate – and a tempting target for the expanding maritime powers of northern Europe, jealous of the Iberian monopoly in the New World.

War with the Dutch

The **Dutch**, with naval bases in the Caribbean and a powerful fleet, were the best placed to move against Brazil. A mixture of greed and political self-interest lay behind the Dutch decision. From 1580 to 1640 Portugal was united with Spain, against whom the Dutch had fought a bitter war of independence, and they were still menaced by the Spanish presence in Flanders. Anything that distracted Spain from further designs on the fledgling United Provinces seemed like a good idea at the time. As it turned out, neither the Spanish nor the Portuguese crowns played much of a role in the war: it was fought out between the Dutch, in the mercantile shape of the Dutch West India Company, and the Portuguese settlers already in Brazil, with Indian and *mameluco* (mixed race) backing. Although the Dutch occupied much of the Northeast for thirty years, they were finally overcome by one of South America's first guerrilla campaigns, in a war made vicious by the Catholic–Protestant divide that underlay it: few prisoners were taken and both sides massacred civilians.

In 1624 a Dutch fleet appeared off Salvador, taking the governor completely by surprise, and the city by storm. After burning down the Jesuit college and killing as many priests as they could find (like the good Calvinists they were), they were pinned down by enraged settlers for nine months and finally expelled in 1625 by a hastily assembled combined Spanish and Portuguese fleet – the only direct intervention made by either country in the conflict. When a Dutch force was once more repulsed from Salvador in 1627, they shifted their attention further north and found the going much easier: Olinda was taken in 1630, the rich sugar zones of Pernambuco were occupied, and Dutch control extended up to the mouth of the Amazon by 1641. With settlers moving in, a strong military presence and a fleet more powerful than Portugal's, Dutch control of the Northeast looked as if it would become permanent.

Maurice of Nassau was sent out as governor of the new Dutch possessions in Brazil in 1630, as the Dutch founded a new capital in Pernambuco: Mauritzstaadt, now Recife. His enlightened policies of allowing the Portuguese freedom to practise their religion, and including them in the colonial government, would probably have resulted in a Dutch Brazil had it not been for the stupidity of the Dutch West India Company. They insisted on Calvinism and heavy taxes, and when Maurice resigned in disgust and returned to Holland in 1644 the settlers rose. After five years of ambushes, plantation burnings and massacres, the Brazilians pushed the Dutch back into an enclave around Recife. The Dutch poured in reinforcements by sea, but their fate was decided by two climactic battles in 1648 and 1649 at **Guararapes**, just outside Recife, where the Dutch were routed and their military power broken. Although they held on to Recife until 1654, the dream of a Dutch empire in the Americas was over, and Portuguese control was not to be threatened again until the nineteenth century.

The bandeirantes: gold and God

The expulsion of the Dutch demonstrated the toughness of the early Brazilians, which was also well to the fore in the penetration and settling of **the interior** during the seventeenth and eighteenth centuries. Every few months expeditions set out to explore the interior, following rumours of gold and looking for Indians to enslave. They carried an identifying banner, a *bandeira*, which gave the name **bandeirantes** to the adventurers; they became the Brazilian version of the Spanish *conquistadores*. São Paulo, thanks to its position on the Rio Tietê, one of the few natural highways that flowed east–west into the deep interior, became the main *bandeirante* centre.

The average *bandeira* would be made up of a mixed crew of people, reflecting the many – and often conflicting – motives underlying the expedition. None travelled without a priest or two (*bandeirantes* may have been cut-throats, but they were devout Catholic cut-throats), and many *bandeiras* were backed by the Jesuits and Franciscans in their drive to found missions and baptize the heathen. The majority combined exploration with plundering and could last for years, with occasional stops to plant and harvest crops, before returning to São Paulo – if they ever did: many towns on the Planalto Central or Mato Grosso have their origins in the remnants of a *bandeira*. The *bandeirantes* had to fight Indians, occasionally the Spanish, and also themselves: they were riven by tension between native-born Brazilians and Portuguese, which regularly erupted into fighting.

The journeys *bandeiras* made were often epic in scale, covering immense distances and overcoming natural obstacles as formidable as the many hostile Indian tribes they encountered, who were defeated more by diseases to which they had no resistance, than by force of arms. It was the *bandeirantes* who pushed the borders of Brazil way inland, practically to the foothills of the Andes, and also supplied the geographical knowledge that now began to fill in the blanks on the maps. They explored the Amazon, Paraná and Uruguai river systems, but the most important way they shaped the future of Brazil was in locating the Holy Grail of the New World: gold.

Gold was first found by *bandeirantes* in 1695, at the spot that is now Sabará, in Minas Gerais. As towns sprang up around further gold strikes in Minas, gold was also discovered around Cuiabá, in Mato Grosso, in 1719, adding fresh impetus to the opening-up of the interior. The 3500-kilometre journey to Cuiabá, down five separate river systems, took six months at the best of times; from São Paulo it was easier to travel to Europe. Along the way the *bandeirantes* had to fight off the Paiaguá Indians, who attacked in canoes and swam like fish, and then the Guaicuru, who had taken to the horse with the same enthusiasm the Plains Indians of North America were later to show. They annihilated entire *bandeiras*; others following observed "rotting belongings and dead bodies on the riverbanks, and hammocks slung with their owners in them, dead. Not a single person reached Cuiabá that year."

But the *paulista* hunger for riches was equal even to these appalling difficulties. By the mid-eighteenth century, the flow of gold from Brazil was keeping the Portuguese Crown afloat, temporarily halting its long slide down the league table of European powers. In Brazil, the rush of migrants to the gold areas changed the regional balance, as the new interior communities drew population away from the Northeast. The gateways to the interior, Rio de Janeiro and São Paulo, grew rapidly. The shift was recognized in 1763, when the capital was transferred from Salvador to Rio, and that filthy, disease-ridden port began its transformation into one of the great cities of the world.

The Jesuits

Apart from the *bandeirantes*, the most important agents of the colonization of the interior were the **Jesuits**. The first Jesuit missionaries arrived in Brazil in 1549 and, thanks to the influence they held over successive Portuguese kings, they acquired power in Brazil second only to that of the Crown itself. In Salvador they built the largest Jesuit college outside Rome, and set in motion a crusade to convert the Indian population. The usual method was to congregate the Indians in **missions**, where they worked under the supervision of Jesuit fathers. From 1600 onwards, dozens of missions were founded in the interior, especially in the Amazon and in the grasslands of the Southeast.

The role the Jesuits played in the conversion of the Indians was ambiguous. Mission Indians were often released by Jesuits to work for settlers, where they died like flies; and the missionaries' intrepid penetration of remote areas resulted in the spread of diseases that wiped out entire tribes. On the other hand, many Jesuits distinguished themselves in protecting Indians against the settlers, a theological as well as a secular struggle, for many Portuguese argued that the native population had no souls and could therefore be treated like animals.

The most remarkable defender of the Indians was **Antônio Vieira**, who abandoned his position as chief adviser to the king in Lisbon to become a missionary in Brazil in 1653. Basing himself in São Luís, he struggled to implement the more enlightened Indian laws that his influence over King João IV had secured, to the disgust of settlers clamouring for slaves. Vieira denied them for years, preaching a series of sermons along the way that became famous throughout Europe, as well as Brazil: "An Indian will be your slave for the few days he lives, but your soul will be enslaved for as long as God is God. All of you are in mortal sin, all of you live in a state of condemnation, and all of you are going directly to Hell!" he thundered from the pulpit in 1654, to the fury of settlers in the congregation. So high did feelings run that, in 1661, settlers forced Vieira onto a ship bound for Portugal, standing in the surf and shouting "Out! Out!"

But Vieira returned, with renewed support from the Crown, and Jesuit power in Brazil grew. It reached a peak in the remarkable theocracy of the **Guaraní missions**, where Spanish and Portuguese Jesuits founded over a dozen missions on the pampas along the Uruguayan border. Left alone for the first fifty years, they effectively became a Jesuit state, until the Treaty of Madrid in 1752 divided up the land between Spain and Portugal; the treaty ordered the missions abandoned, so that settlers could move in. The Guaraní rebelled immediately and, while the Jesuit hierarchy made half-hearted efforts to get them to move, most of the priests stayed with their Guaraní flocks. Resistance was heroic but hopeless: the superior fire power of a joint Spanish–Portuguese military expedition decimated both Guaraní and Jesuits in 1756.

Jesuit involvement in the Guaraní war lent added force to the long-standing settler demands to expel them from the colony. This time, they were helped by the rise to power of the **Marquis de Pombal**, who became the power behind the Portuguese throne for much of the eighteenth century. Seeing the Jesuits as a threat to Crown control, he seized upon the Guaraní wars as an excuse to expel the Order from Brazil in 1760. The Jesuits may have been imperfect protectors, but from this time on the Indians were denied even that.

Independence

Brazil, uniquely among South American countries, achieved a peaceful transition to independence. The odds seemed against it at one point. Brazilian resentment at their exclusion from government, and at the Portuguese monopoly of foreign trade, grew steadily during the eighteenth century. It culminated, in 1789, in the **Inconfidência Mineira**, a plot hatched by twelve prominent citizens of Ouro Preto to proclaim Brazilian independence. The rebels, however, were betrayed almost before they started – their leader, **Tiradentes**, was executed and the rest exiled. Then, just as the tension seemed to be becoming dangerous, events in Europe once again took a hand in shaping Brazil's future.

In 1807, **Napoleon** invaded Portugal. With the French army poised to take Lisbon, the British navy hurriedly evacuated **King João VI** to Rio, which was declared the temporary capital of the Portuguese Empire and seat of the government-in-exile. While **Wellington** set about driving the French from Portugal, the British were able to force the opening-up of Brazil's ports to non-Portuguese shipping, and the economic growth that followed reinforced Brazil's increasing self-confidence. João was entranced by his tropical kingdom, unable to pull himself away even after Napoleon's defeat. Finally, in 1821, he was faced with a liberal revolt in Portugal that threatened to topple the monarchy, and he was unable to delay his return any longer. In April 1822 he appointed his son, **Dom Pedro**, as prince regent and governor of Brazil; when he sailed home, his last words to his son were "Get your hands on this kingdom, before some adventurer does."

Pedro, young and arrogant, grew increasingly irritated by the strident demands of the Côrtes, the Portuguese assembly, that he return home to his father and allow Brazil to be ruled from Portugal once again. On September 7, 1822, Pedro was out riding on the plain of Ypiranga, near São Paulo. Buttoning himself up after an attack of diarrhoea, he was surprised by a messenger with a bundle of letters from Lisbon. Reading the usual demands for him to return, his patience snapped, and he declared Brazil independent with the cry "Independence or death!" With overwhelming popular support for the idea, he had himself crowned **Dom Pedro I**, Emperor of Brazil, on December 1, 1822. The Portuguese, preoccupied by political crises at home and demoralized by Pedro's defection, put up little resistance. Apart from an ugly massacre of Brazilian patriots in Fortaleza, and some fighting in Bahia and Belém, the Portuguese withdrawal was peaceful and by the end of 1823 no Portuguese forces remained.

Early empire: revolt in the regions

Although independence had been easily achieved, the early decades of empire proved much more difficult. The first problem was Dom Pedro himself: headstrong and autocratic, he became increasingly estranged from his subjects, devoting more attention to scandalous romances than affairs of state. In April 1831 he abdicated, in a fit of petulance, in favour of the heir apparent, **Dom Pedro II**, and returned to Portugal. Pedro II would later prove an enlightened ruler, but as he was only five at the time there were limits to his capacity to influence events. With a power vacuum at the centre of the political system, long-standing tensions in the outlying provinces erupted into revolt.

There were common threads in all the **rebellions** in the provinces: slaves rebelling against masters, Indian and mixed-race resentment of white domination, Brazilians settling scores with Portuguese, and the poor rising against the rich. The first, and most serious, conflagration was the **Cabanagem Rebellion** in Pará, where a mass revolt of the dispossessed began in 1835. The rebels took Belém, where, in a great moment of retribution, the Indian Domingues Onça killed the governor of Pará. The uprising spread through the Amazon like wildfire and took a decade to put down. A parallel revolt, the **Balaiada**, began in Maranhão in 1838. Here the rebels took Caxias, the second city of the state, and held out for three years against the army. Similar risings in Pernambuco, Bahia and Rio Grande do Sul punctuated the 1830s and 1840s; the disruption was immense, with large areas ravaged by fighting that threatened to tear the country apart.

The crisis led to Dom Pedro II being declared emperor four years early, in 1840, when he was only fourteen. Precociously talented, he was a sensible, scholarly man, completely unlike his father. His instincts were conservative, but he regularly appointed liberal governments and was respected even by republicans. With government authority restored, the provincial rebellions had by 1850 either blown themselves out or been put down. And with **coffee** beginning to be planted on a large scale in Rio, São Paulo and Minas, and the flow of European immigrants rising from a trickle to a flood, the economy of southern Brazil began to take off in earnest.

The War of the Triple Alliance

With the rebellions in the provinces, the **army** became increasingly important in Brazilian political life. Pedro insisted they stay out of domestic politics, but his policy of diverting the generals by allowing them to control foreign policy ultimately led to the disaster of the war with Paraguay (1864–70). Although Brazil emerged victorious, it was at a dreadful cost. The **War of the Triple Alliance** is one of history's forgotten conflicts, but it was the bloodiest war in South American history, with a casualty list almost as long as that of the American Civil War: Brazil alone suffered over 100,000 casualties.

It pitted, in an unequal struggle, the landlocked republic of Paraguay, under the dictator **Francisco Lopez**, against the combined forces of Brazil, Argentina and Uruguay. Although the Paraguayans started the war, by invading Uruguay and parts of Mato Grosso in 1864, they had been sorely provoked by Brazilian meddling in Uruguay. The generals in Rio, with no more rebels to fight within Brazil, wanted to incorporate Uruguay into the empire; Paraguay saw Brazil blocking its access to the sea and invaded to pre-empt a Brazilian takeover, dragging Argentina reluctantly into the conflict through a mutual defence pact with Brazil.

The Brazilian army and navy were confident of victory as the Paraguayans were heavily outnumbered and outgunned. Yet the Paraguayans, for the first time, demonstrated the military prowess that would mark their history. United under the able leadership of Lopez, the Paraguayan army proved disciplined and fanatically brave, always defeated by numbers but terribly mauling the opposition. It turned into a war of extermination and six terrible years were only ended by the killing of Lopez in 1870, by which time the male adult population of Paraguay is said to have been reduced (by disease and starvation as well as war) to under twenty thousand, from over a million in 1864.

The end of slavery

From the seventeenth to the nineteenth century around ten million Africans were transported to Brazil as **slaves** – ten times as many as were shipped to the United States – yet the death rate in Brazil was so great that in 1860 Brazil's black population was half the size of that in the US. Slavery was always contested: slaves fled from the cities and plantations to form refugee communities called *quilombos*; the largest, **Palmares**, in the interior of the northeastern state of Alagoas, was several thousand strong and stayed independent for almost a century.

But it was not until the nineteenth century that slavery was seriously challenged. The initial impetus came from Britain, where the abolitionist movement became influential just when Portugal was most dependent on British capital and British naval protection. Abolition was regarded with horror by the large landowners in Brazil, and a combination of racism and fear of economic dislocation led to a determined rearguard action to preserve slavery. A complicated diplomatic waltz began between Britain and Brazil, as slavery laws were tinkered with *para inglês ver* – "for the English to see" – a phrase that survives in the language to this day, meaning to do something merely for show. The object was to make the British believe slavery would be abolished, while ensuring that the letter of the law kept it legal.

British abolitionists were not deceived, and from 1832 to 1854 the Royal Navy maintained a squadron off Brazil, intercepting and confiscating slave ships, and occasionally entering Brazilian ports to seize slavers and burn their ships – one of history's more positive examples of gunboat diplomacy. The slave trade was finally **abolished** in 1854 but, to the disgust of the abolitionists, slavery itself remained legal. British power had its limits and ultimately it was a passionate campaign within Brazil itself, led by the fiery lawyer **Joaquim Nabuco**, that finished slavery off. The growing liberal movement, increasingly republican and anti-monarchist, squared off against the landowners, with Dom Pedro hovering indecisively somewhere in between. Slavery became the dominant issue in Brazilian politics for twenty years. By the time full **emancipation** came, in the "Golden Law" of May 13, 1888, Brazil had achieved the shameful distinction of being the last country in the Americas to abolish slavery.

From empire to republic

The end of slavery was also the death knell of the monarchy. Since the 1870s the intelligentsia, deeply influenced by French liberalism, had turned against the emperor and agitated for a republic. By the 1880s they had been joined by the officer corps, who blamed Dom Pedro for lack of backing during the Paraguayan war. When the large landowners withdrew their support, furious that the emperor had not prevented emancipation, the **monarchy collapsed** very suddenly in 1889.

Once again, Brazil managed a bloodless transition. The push came from the army, detachments led by **Marechal Deodoro da Fonseca** meeting no resistance when they occupied Rio on November 15, 1889. They invited the royal family to remain, but Dom Pedro insisted on exile, boarding a ship to France, where he died in penury two years later in a shabby Parisian hotel. Deodoro, meanwhile, began a Brazilian tradition of hamfisted military autocracy. Ignoring the clamour for a liberal republic, he declared himself dictator in 1891, but was forced to resign three weeks later when even the army refused to support him. His deputy, **Marechal Floriano de Peixoto**, took over, but proved even more incompetent; Rio was actually shelled in 1893 by rebellious warships demanding Peixoto's resignation. Finally, in 1894, popular pressure led to Peixoto stepping down in favour of the first elected civilian president, **Prudente de Morais**.

Coffee with milk – and sugar

The years from 1890 to 1930 were politically undistinguished, but saw Brazil rapidly transformed economically and socially by large-scale **immigration** from Europe and Japan; they were decades of swift growth and swelling cities, which saw a very Brazilian combination of a boom-bust-boom economy and corrupt pork-barrel politics.

The boom was led by **coffee** and **rubber**, which – at opposite ends of the country – had entirely different labour forces. Millions of *nordestinos* moved into the Amazon to tap rubber, but the coffee workers swarming into São Paulo in their hundreds of thousands came chiefly from Italy. Between 1890 and 1930 over four million migrants arrived from Europe and another two hundred thousand from Japan. Most went to work on the coffee estates of southern Brazil, but enough remained to turn São Paulo into the fastest-growing city in the Americas. Urban industrialization appeared in Brazil for the first time, taking root in São Paulo to supply the voracious markets of the young cities springing up in the *paulista* interior. By 1930, São Paulo had displaced Rio as the leading industrial centre.

More improbable was the transformation of **Manaus** into the largest city of the Amazon. Rubber turned Manaus from a muddy village into a rich trading city within a couple of decades. The peak of the **rubber boom**, from the 1870s to the outbreak of World War I, financed its metamorphosis into a tropical *belle époque* outpost, complete with opera house. Rubber exports were second only to coffee, but proved much more vulnerable to competition. Seeds smuggled out of Amazônia by Victorian adventurer Henry Wickham in 1876 ended up in Ceylon and Malaya, where – by 1914 – plantation rubber pushed wild Amazon rubber out of the world markets. The region returned to an isolation it maintained until the late 1960s.

Economic growth was not accompanied by political development. Although not all the early presidents were incompetent – **Rodrigues Alves** (1902–6), for example, rebuilt Rio complete with a public health system, finally eradicating the epidemics that had stunted its growth – the majority were corrupt political bosses, relying on a network of patron–client relationships, whose main ambition was to bleed the public coffers dry. Power was concentrated in the two most populous states of São Paulo and Minas Gerais, which struck a convenient deal to alternate the presidency between them.

This way of ensuring that both sets of snouts could slurp away in the trough uninterrupted was called "**café com leite**" by its opponents: coffee from São Paulo and milk from the *mineiro* dairy herds. In fact, it was coffee with milk and sugar: the developing national habit of the sweet *cafezinho* in the burgeoning cities of the South provided a new domestic market for sugar, which ensured support from the plantation oligarchs of the Northeast. In a pattern that would repeat itself in more modern times, the economy forged ahead while politics went backwards. The saying "Brazil grows in the dark, while politicians sleep" made its first appearance around this time.

The revolution of 1930

The revolution of 1930 that brought the populist **Getúlio Vargas** to power was a critical event. Vargas dominated Brazilian politics for the next quarter-century, and the Vargas years were a time of radical change, marking a decisive break with

△ Getúlio Vargas with Franklin D. Roosevelt

the past. Vargas had much in common with his Argentinian contemporary, Juan Perón: both were charismatic, but also cunning and ruthless, and created new power bases in their countries rooted in the urban working class.

It was the **working class**, combined with disillusion in the junior ranks of the military, that swept Vargas to power. Younger officers, accustomed to seeing the armed forces as the guardian of the national conscience, were disgusted by the corruption of the military hierarchy. When the **Great Depression** hit, the government spent millions protecting coffee growers by buying crops at a guaranteed price; the coffee was then burnt, as the export market had collapsed. Workers in the cities and countryside were appalled, seeing themselves frozen out while vast sums were spent on landowners, and as the economic outlook worsened the pressure started building up from other states to end the São Paulo and Minas grip on power. This time, the transition was violent.

In 1926, **Washington Luis** was made president without an election, as the elite contrived an unopposed nomination. When Luis appeared set to do the same thing in 1930, an unstoppable **mass revolution** developed, first in Vargas's home state of Rio Grande do Sul, then in Rio, then in the Northeast. There was some resistance in São Paulo, but the worst fighting was in the Northeast, where street battles left scores dead. The shock troops of the revolution were the young army officers who led their units against the *ancien régime* in Minas and Rio, and the *gaúcho* cavalry who accompanied Vargas on his triumphant procession to Rio. Although São Paulo rose briefly against Vargas in 1932, the revolt was swiftly crushed and Getúlio, as Brazilians affectionately knew him, embarked on the longest and most spectacular political career in modern Brazilian history.

Vargas and the Estado Novo

It was not just Vargas who took power in 1930, but a new generation of young, energetic administrators, who set about transforming the economy and the political system. Vargas played the nationalist card with great success, nationalizing the oil, electricity and steel industries, and setting up a health and social welfare system that earned him unwavering working-class support that continued even after his death.

Reforms this fundamental could not be carried out under the old constitutional framework. Vargas simplified things by declaring himself **dictator** in 1937 and imprisoning political opponents – most of whom were in the trade union movement, the Communist Party or the *Integralistas*, the Brazilian Fascists. He called his regime the "New State", the **Estado Novo**, and certainly its reforming energy was something new. Although he cracked down hard on dissent, Vargas was never a totalitarian dictator. He was massively popular and his great political talents enabled him to outflank most opponents.

The result was both political and economic success. The ruinous coffee subsidy was abolished, industry encouraged and agriculture diversified: by 1945 São Paulo had become the largest industrial centre in South America. With the federal government increasing its powers at the expense of state rights, regional government power was wrested out of the hands of the oligarchs for the first time.

It took **World War II** to bring Vargas down. At first Brazil stayed neutral, reaping the benefits of increased exports, but when the United States offered massive aid in return for bases and Brazilian entry into the war, Vargas joined the Allies. Outraged by German submarine attacks on Brazilian shipping,

Brazil was the only country in South America to play an active part in the war. A **Brazilian Expeditionary Force**, 5000-strong, fought in Italy from 1944 until the end of the war. When they returned the military High Command was able to exploit the renewed prestige of the army, forcing Vargas to stand down. They argued that the armed forces could hardly fight for democracy abroad and return home to a dictatorship, and, in any case, after fifteen years a leadership change was overdue. In the election that followed in 1945 Vargas grudgingly endorsed the army general **Eurico Dutra**, who duly won – but Getúlio, brooding on his ranch, was not yet finished with the presidency.

The death of Vargas

Dutra proved a colourless figure, and when Vargas ran for the presidency in 1950 he won a crushing victory, the old dictator "returning on the arm of the people", as he wrote later. But he had powerful enemies, in the armed forces and on the right, and his second stint in power was turbulent. Dutra had allowed inflation to climb, and Vargas proposed to raise the minimum wage and increase taxation of the middle classes. In the charged climate of the Cold War this was denounced by the right as veering towards communism, and vitriolic attacks on Vargas and his government were made in the press, notably by a slippery, ambitious journalist named **Carlos Lacerda**.

Vargas's supporters reacted angrily and argument turned into crisis in 1954, when shots were fired at Lacerda, missing their target but killing an air force officer guarding him. The attempt was traced to one of Vargas's bodyguards, but Vargas himself was not implicated. Even so, the press campaign rose to a crescendo, and finally, on August 25, 1954, the military High Command demanded his resignation. Vargas received the news calmly, went into his bedroom in the Palácio de Catete in Rio and shot himself through the heart.

He left an emotional suicide note to the Brazilian people: "I choose this means to be with you always . . . I gave you my life; now I offer my death. Nothing remains. Serenely I take the first step on the road to eternity, as I leave life and enter history". The initial stunned popular reaction gave way to fury, as Vargas's supporters turned on the forces that had hounded him to death, burning the newspaper offices and forcing Lacerda to flee the country. Eighteen months of tension followed, as an interim government marked time until the next election.

JK and Brasília

Juscelino Kubitschek, "JK" to Brazilians, president from 1956 to 1961, proved just the man to fix Brazil's attention on the future rather than the past. He combined energy and imagination with integrity and great political skill, acquired in the hard school of the politics of Minas Gerais, one of the main nurseries of political talent in Brazil. Although the tensions in the political system were still there – constitutionalists in the armed forces had to stage a pre-emptive coup to allow him to take office – Kubitschek was able to serve out his full term, still the only elected civilian president to do so in modern times. And he left a permanent reminder of the most successful post-war presidency in the form of the country's new capital, Brasília, deep in the Planalto Central.

"Fifty years in five!" was his election slogan, and his economic programme lived up to its ambitious billing. His term saw a spurt in growth rates that was the platform for the "economic miracle" of the next decade; the economic boom led to wider prosperity and renewed national confidence. Kubitschek drew on both in the flight of inspired imagination that led to **the building of Brasília**.

It could so easily have been an expensive disaster, a purpose-built capital miles from anywhere, the personal brainchild of a president anxious to make his mark. But Kubitschek implanted the idea in the national imagination by portraying it as a renewed statement of faith in the interior, a symbol of national integration and a better future for all Brazilians, not just those in the South. He brought it off with great panache, bringing in the extravagantly talented **Oscar Niemeyer**, whose brief was to come up with a revolutionary city layout and the architecture to go with it. Kubitschek spent almost every weekend on the

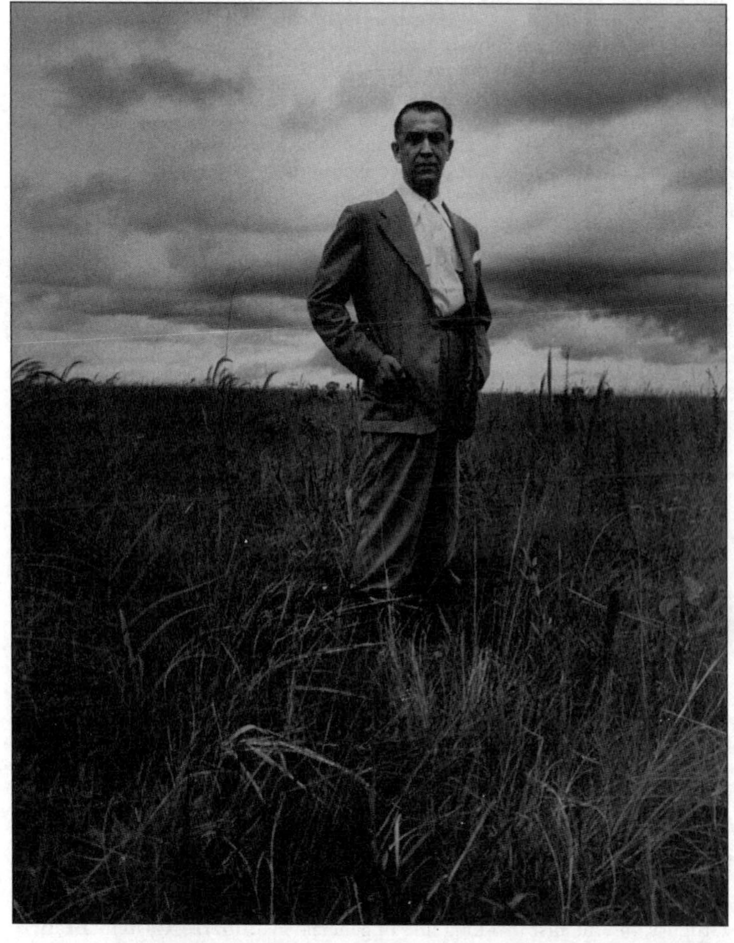

△ Juscelino Kubitschek

huge building site that became the city, consulted on the smallest details and had the satisfaction of handing over to his successor, **Jânio Quadros**, in the newly inaugurated capital.

1964: the road to military rule

At the time, the **military coup of 1964** was considered a temporary hiccup in Brazil's post-war democracy, but it lasted 21 years and left a very bitter taste. The first period of military rule saw the famous economic miracle, when the economy grew at an astonishing average annual rate of ten percent for a decade, only to come to a juddering halt after 1974, when oil price rises and the increasing burden of debt repayment pushed it off the rails. But most depressing was the effective end of democracy for over a decade, and a time – from 1969 to 1974 – when terror was used against opponents by military hardliners. Brazil, where the *desaparecidos* numbered a few hundred rather than the tens of thousands butchered in Argentina and Chile, was not the worst military regime on the continent. But it is difficult to overestimate the shock even limited repression caused. It was the first time Brazilians experienced systematic brutality by a government, and even in the years of economic success the military governments were loathed across the political spectrum.

The coup of 1964 was years in the brewing. It had two root causes: a constitutional crisis and the deepening divides in Brazilian society. In the developed South, relations between trade unions and employers went from bad to worse, as workers struggled to protect their wages against rising inflation. But it was in the Northeast that tension was greatest, as a result of the **Peasant Leagues** movement. Despite industrial modernization, the rural Northeast was still stuck in a time-warped land tenure system, moulded in the colonial period and in many ways unchanged since then. Peasants, under the charismatic leadership of **Francisco Julião** and the governor of Pernambuco, **Miguel Arrães**, began forming cooperatives and occupying estates to press their claim for agrarian reform; the estate owners cried communism and openly agitated for a military coup.

The crisis might still have been avoided by a more skilful president, but Kubitschek's immediate successors were not of his calibre. Quadros resigned after only six months, in August 1961, on the anniversary of Vargas's suicide. He apparently wanted popular reaction to sweep him back into office, but shrank from suicide and ended up shooting himself in the foot rather than the heart. The masses stayed home, and the vice-president, **João Goulart**, took over.

Goulart's accession was viewed with horror by the right. He had a reputation as a leftist firebrand, having been a minister of labour under Vargas, and his position was weakened by the fact that he had not succeeded by direct popular vote. As political infighting began to get out of control, with the country polarizing between left and right, Goulart decided to throw himself behind the trade unions and the Peasant Leagues; his nationalist rhetoric rang alarm bells in Washington, and the army began to plot his downfall, with tacit American backing.

The coup, in the tradition of Brazilian coups, was swift and bloodless. On March 31, 1964, troops from Minas Gerais moved on Rio; when the military commanders there refused to oppose them, the game was up for Goulart. After futile efforts to rally resistance in Rio Grande do Sul, he fled into exile in Uruguay, and the first in a long line of generals, **Humberto Castelo Branco**, became president.

Military rule

The military moved swiftly to dismantle democracy. Congress was dissolved, those representatives not to military taste being removed. It then reconvened with only two parties, an official government and an official opposition ("The difference," ran a joke at the time, "is that one says Yes, and the other, Yes Sir!"). All other parties were banned. The Peasant Leagues and trade unions were repressed, with many of their leaders tortured and imprisoned, and even prominent national politicians like Arrães were thrown into jail. The ferocity of the military took aback even those on the right who had agitated for a coup. Ironically, many of them were hoist with their own petard when they voiced criticism, and found themselves gagged by the same measures they had urged against the left.

The political climate worsened steadily during the 1960s. An **urban guerrilla campaign** took off in the cities – its most spectacular success was the kidnapping of the American ambassador in 1969, released unharmed in return for over a hundred political detainees – but it only served as an excuse for the hardliners to crack down even further. General **Emílio Garrastazú Médici**, leader of the hardliners, took over the presidency in 1969 and the worst period of military rule began. Torture became routine, censorship was strict and thousands were driven into exile: this dark chapter in Brazilian history lasted for five agonizing years, until Médici gave way to **Ernesto Geisel** in 1974. The scars Médici left behind him, literally and metaphorically, have still not completely healed.

The economic miracle

Despite the cold winds blowing on the political front, the Brazilian economy forged ahead from the mid-1960s to 1974, the years of the **economic miracle** – and the combination of high growth and low inflation indeed seemed miraculous to later governments. The military welcomed foreign investment, and the large pool of cheap but skilled labour was irresistible. Investment poured in, both from Brazil and abroad, and the boom was the longest and largest in Brazilian history. Cities swelled, industry grew, and by the mid-1970s Brazil was the economic giant of South America, São Paulo state alone having a GNP higher than any South American country.

The problem, though, was uneven development. Even miraculous growth rates could not provide enough jobs for the hordes migrating to the cities, and the squalid **favelas** expanded even faster than the economy. The problem was worst in the Northeast and the Amazon, where industry was less developed, and drought combined with land conflict to push the people of the interior into the cities. It was also the miracle years that saw the origins of the **debt crisis**, a millstone around the neck of the Brazilian economy in the 1980s and 1990s.

After 1974, a lot of petrodollars were sloshing around the world banking system, thanks to oil price rises. Anxious to set this new capital to work, international banks and South American military regimes fell over themselves in their eagerness to organize deals. Brazil had a good credit rating: its wealth of natural resources and jailed labour leaders saw to that. The military needed money for a series of huge development projects that were central to its trickle-down economic policy, like the **Itaipú dam**, the **Carajás** mining projects in eastern Amazônia, and a **nuclear power programme**. By the end of the 1970s the debt was at $50 billion; by 1990 it had risen to $120 billion, and the interest payments were crippling the economy.

Opening up the Amazon

The first step towards opening up the vast interior of the **Amazon** was taken by Kubitschek, who built a dirt highway linking Brasília to Belém. But things really got going in 1970, when Médici realized that the Amazon could be used as a huge safety valve, releasing the pressure for agrarian reform in the Northeast. "Land without people for people without land!" became the slogan, and an ambitious programme of highway construction began that was to transform Amazônia. The main links were the **Transamazônica**, running west to the Peruvian border, the **Cuiabá–Santarém** highway into central Amazônia, and the **Cuiabá–Porto Velho/Rio Branco** highway, opening access to western Amazônia.

For the military, the Amazon was empty space, overdue for filling, and a national resource to be developed. They set up an elaborate network of tax breaks and incentives to encourage Brazilian and multinational firms to invest in the region, who also saw it as empty space and proceeded either to speculate with land or cut down forest to graze cattle. The one group that didn't perceive the Amazon as empty space was, naturally enough, the millions of people who already lived there. The immediate result was a spiralling land conflict, as ranchers, rubber tappers, Brazil-nut harvesters, gold-miners, smallholders, Indians, multinationals and Brazilian companies all tried to press their claims. The result was – and remains today – chaos.

By the 1980s the situation in the Amazon was becoming an international controversy, with heated claims about the uncontrolled destruction of forest in huge annual burnings, and the invasion of Indian lands. Less internationally known was the **land crisis**, although a hundred people or more were dying in land conflicts in Amazônia every year. It took the assassination in 1988 of **Chico Mendes**, leader of the rubber tappers' union and eloquent defender of the forest, to bring it home. Media attention, as usual, has shed as much heat as light, but there are grounds for hope. For all the destruction, Amazônia is very large – there is still time for more sensible development to protect what remains. (See also "Amazon Ecology and Indian Rights", p.810.)

The abertura

Growing popular resentment of the military could not be contained indefinitely, especially when the economy turned sour. By the late 1970s debt, rising inflation and unemployment were turning the economy from a success story into a joke, and the military were further embarrassed by an unsavoury chain of corruption scandals. Geisel was the first military president to plan for a return to civilian rule, in a slow relaxing of the military grip called *abertura*, the "opening-up". Yet again, Brazil managed a bloodless – albeit fiendishly complicated – transition. Slow though the process was, the return to democracy would have been delayed even longer had it not been for two events along the way: the **metalworkers' strikes** in São Paulo in 1977 and the mass **campaign for direct elections** in 1983–84.

The São Paulo strikes began in the car industry and soon spread throughout the industrial belt of São Paulo, in a movement bearing many parallels with Solidarity in Poland. Led by unions that were still illegal, and the charismatic young factory worker **Lula (Luís Inácio da Silva)**, there was a tense stand-off between army and strikers, until the military realized that having São Paulo on strike would be worse for the economy than conceding the right to free trade unions. This dramatic re-emergence of organized labour was a sign that the military could not control the situation for much longer.

Reforms in the early 1980s lifted censorship, brought the exiles home and allowed normal political life to resume. But the military came up with an ingenious attempt to determine the succession: their control of Congress allowed them to pass a resolution that the president due to take office in 1985 would be elected not by direct vote, but by an electoral college made up of congressmen and senators, where the military party had the advantage.

The democratic opposition responded with a counter-amendment proposing a direct election. It needed a two-thirds majority in Congress to be passed, and a campaign began for **diretas-já**, "direct elections now". Even the opposition was surprised by the response, as the Brazilian people, thoroughly sick of the generals, took to the streets in their millions. The campaign culminated in huge rallies of over a million people in Rio and São Paulo, and opinion polls showed over ninety percent in favour; but when the vote came in March 1984 the amendment just failed. The military still nominated a third of Senate seats, and this proved decisive.

It looked like defeat; in fact it turned into victory. The moment found the man in **Tancredo Neves**, ex-minister of justice under Vargas, ex-prime minister, and a wise old *mineiro* fox respected across the political spectrum, who put himself forward as opposition candidate in the electoral college. By now it was clear what the public wanted, and Tancredo's unrivalled political skills enabled him to stitch together an alliance that included dissidents from the military's own party. In January 1985 he romped home in the electoral college, to great national rejoicing, and military rule came to an end. Tancredo proclaimed the civilian **Nova República** – the "New Republic".

The New Republic: crisis and corruption

Tragically, the New Republic was orphaned at birth. The night before his inauguration, Tancredo was rushed to hospital for an emergency operation on a bleeding stomach tumour: it proved benign, but in hospital he picked up an infection and six weeks later died of septicaemia. His funeral was the largest mass event in Brazilian history; a crowd of two million followed his coffin from the hospital where he had died in São Paulo to Guarulhos airport. The vice-president, **José Sarney**, a second-league politician from Maranhão, who had been fobbed off with a ceremonial post, suddenly found himself serving a full presidential term.

His administration was disastrous, though not all of it was his own fault: he was saddled with a ministerial team he had not chosen, and a newly powerful Congress that would have given any president a rough ride. But Sarney made matters worse by a lack of decisiveness, and wasn't helped by the sleaze that hung like a fog around his government, with **corruption** institutionalized on a massive scale. No progress was made on the economic front either. By 1990 inflation accelerated into **hyperinflation** proper, and, despite spending almost $40 billion repaying interest on the foreign debt, the principal had swollen to

$120 billion. Popular disgust was so great that on every occasion Sarney found himself near a crowd of real people, he was greeted with a shower of bricks and curses. The high hopes of 1985 had evaporated: Sarney had brought the whole notion of civilian politics into disrepute, and achieved the near-impossible of making the military look good.

Collor and Franco: marking time

Despite everything, Brazil still managed to begin the next decade on a hopeful note, with the inauguration in 1990 of **Fernando Collor de Melo**, the first properly elected president for thirty years, after a heated but peaceful campaign had managed to consolidate democracy at a difficult economic moment. In the last months of his administration, Sarney had presided over the take-off into hyperinflation, and it was clear the new president would have to come up with fast economic answers if he was to survive.

The campaign had passed the torch to a new generation of Brazilians, as the young Collor, playboy scion of one of Brazil's oldest and richest families, had squared off against **Lula**, who had come a long way since the São Paulo strikes. Now a respected – and feared – national politician, head of the Workers' Party that the strike movement had evolved into, Lula took most of the cities, but Collor's conservative rural support was enough to secure a narrow victory.

Collor's presidency began promisingly enough, as he pushed for a long-overdue opening-up of the economy and implemented the most draconian currency stabilization plan yet, the infamous **Plano Collor**, hated by the middle classes because it temporarily froze their bank accounts. The economy resisted all attempts at surgery, and inflation began to climb again. Collor became even more unstable than the economy; he was increasingly erratic in public, and rumours grew about dark goings-on behind the scenes. Thanks to fine journalism and a denunciation by Collor's own brother, apparently angry that Fernando had made a pass at his wife, it became clear that a web of **corrupt dealings** masterminded by Collor's campaign treasurer, **P. C. Farias**, had set up what was effectively a parallel government. Billions of dollars had been skimmed from the government's coffers, in a scam breathtaking even by Brazilian standards.

Impeachment proceedings were begun in Congress: few politicians expected them to get anywhere. But then demonstrations began to take off in the big cities, led initially by students but soon spreading to the rest of the population and numbering hundreds of thousands of angry but peaceful citizens. It rapidly became clear that if Congress did not vote impeachment through, there would be hell to pay. In September 1992 Collor was duly impeached and replaced by his vice-president, **Itamar Franco**. Farias was jailed, later to die in mysterious circumstances: he was allegedly murdered by a girlfriend who then committed suicide, but it is likely the full story of his death will never be known. His master, Collor, who may know more than most about the murder, lives in gilded semi-exile in Miami, to the fury of most Brazilians. Specimen corruption charges failed, and his continued liberty is testimony to the weakness of the Brazilian legal system.

Franco, like Sarney before him, proved a buffoon left minding the shop. The real power in his government was the finance minister, **Fernando Henrique Cardoso**, who staked his claim to the succession by implementing the **Plano Real** in 1994. This finally tamed inflation and stabilized the economy, for the first time in twenty years. A grateful public duly gave him an overwhelming first-round victory in the presidential election later that year, when he trounced Lula in every state bar Brasília and the Distrito Federal.

Cardoso: stability and reform

Uniquely among modern Brazilian presidents, Cardoso, a donnish ex-academic from São Paulo universally known after his initials FHC, proved able and effective. Ironically, before he became a politician he was one of the world's most respected left-wing theorists of economic development. His political career, however, moved along a different track, as his government opened up the Brazilian economy and pushed through important political reforms.

Cardoso entered office with a clear vision of Brazil's economic and political problems, and how to cure them. On the economic front he built on the Plano Real by pushing through a privatization programme in the teeth of fierce nationalist opposition, cutting tariff barriers, opening up the economy to competition and making Brazil the dominant member of **Mercosul**, a regional trade organization that also includes Argentina, Uruguay and Paraguay. During his first term the result was healthy growth, falling unemployment and low inflation, an achievement without precedent in modern Brazilian history. Politically, he steered a skilful middle course between dinosaurs of right and left, corrupt *caudilhos* and their patron–client politics on the one hand, and time-warped nationalists still clinging to protectionism and suspicious of the outside world on the other. In a steady if unspectacular process, a series of constitutional amendments were passed reducing the role of the state and reforming the political system.

The stabilization of the economy that Cardoso achieved through the Plano Real was not forgotten by the poor, who were the most affected by hyperinflation; Cardoso was **re-elected** in 1998, providing a much-needed period of stability at the top. His second term proved more difficult, however. The Asian financial collapse of 1998 brought down much of Latin America with it, including Brazil; there was a sharp recession for a year, and GDP growth during FHC's second term ran at an anaemic annual average of just under two percent, barely staying ahead of population growth. But despite devaluations of the *real* foreign investment kept coming and inflation remained low, an important break with the economic patterns of the 1980s and 1990s, and a sign that at least some of Cardoso's reforms were working. Certain sectors of the economy, notably aerospace, telecommunications and agriculture, grew to become internationally competitive, and imaginative administration in health and education led to significant improvements in social indicators like life expectancy, literacy and child mortality.

Cardoso's legacy was not all positive, however. Corruption, social inequality and regional imbalances still plagued Brazil, although growing public impatience was reflected in a newly aggressive and powerful federal prosecutors system, which started to take on powerful vested interests and eventually ended the careers of a number of notoriously corrupt but very powerful national politicians. Cardoso's reliance on a broad centrist coalition limited his ability to deal with rural inequalities or really get to grips with environmental issues, and the public finances remained perennially in deficit because of a bloated public sector pensions system that is extraordinarily resistant to reform, not least because among those who benefit from it most directly are members of Congress and the judiciary. The judicial system, equally resistant to reform, is a joke, which is much more of a problem than it seems. It underlies the frightening level of violence in Brazilian society, since those using it know they will almost certainly not be brought to book, and it also encourages corruption, for the same reason.

Lula: left turn?

Historic is an over-used word, but there is no question it is the only one to describe the **2002 election** of Lula to the presidency of Brazil, at the fourth attempt. The outcome represented the final consolidation and maturing of Brazilian democracy, as the generation that had been tear-gassed by the military and opted for armed struggle suited up and became ministers (there were four ex-guerrilla ministers in the Lula government, and its dominant figure, **José Dirceu**, had plastic surgery in Cuba and lived underground for five years). **Lula** himself is a truly historic figure whatever the fate of his government: he is the first Brazilian president not to be a member of the country's elite, and the story of his life is extraordinary. Born in desperate poverty in the Pernambuco *sertão*, like millions of Northeasterners he made the journey as a child to São Paulo on the back of a truck. He worked as a shoeshine boy before becoming a factory worker at a car plant, eventually rising to leadership of the strike movement in the early 1980s and founding the PT (Partido dos Trabalhadores, or Workers' Party), which allied the union movement to the liberal middle class and evolved into what is now the largest political party in Brazil. With FHC's retirement no other Brazilian politician was able to match Lula's charisma, and the PT did what it had to do, learning from defeat and moderating its policies to bring it closer to the centre, where Brazilian elections are won.

Lula proved adept at keeping his party happy with tubthumping rhetoric and playing up his image as a reformist on the international conference circuit, but in fact his government bore a distinct resemblance to that of his predecessor. **Antonio Palocci**, a quiet but competent finance minister, kept the economy open and inflation down – which was just as well, since politically the government rapidly ran into deep trouble.

Corruption again

Lula had been elected in large part because the Brazilian electorate believed his PT, the Workers' Party, was, uniquely among Brazilian political parties, largely untouched by corruption. They were rapidly disabused. From late 2004 Brazilian journalism yet again proved itself the healthiest part of the body politic by revealing a series of large-scale scams and rackets commanded by Lula's political enforcer, **José Dirceu**. Although it was clear Lula was at least aware of what was happening, he managed to avoid impeachment by firing Dirceu and convincing the opposition, by now fancying its chances in the 2006 election, that the national interest would be best served by having the government finish its term.

Brazilians moved into the election year more cynical than ever about their politicians. Lula may well be re-elected, as the left has nowhere to go, but the enthusiasm and self-confidence of Lula's early years has gone. There is little difference between the economic policies of Lula and **José Serra**, his centrist opponent, and neither will command a majority in Congress, which means further deal-making and continuing corruption, since it is the oil in an increasingly dysfunctional political and judicial system. As in all countries with serious corruption problems, this means it is difficult ever to know where real power lies. The saving grace is that a succession of competent presidents and finance ministers has managed to insulate the economy from the worst effects of political mismanagement, but this may not continue forever and Brazil is still vulnerable to external shocks.

Brazil's increasingly dysfunctional politics and incompetent political class stands in sharp contrast to the dynamism and self-confidence of Brazilian culture and parts of its economy. Few developing countries are better placed to benefit from globalization. Brazil often gets bad press abroad, but burning rainforests and urban drug wars are only part of the country's story. Now a stable and consolidated democracy, Brazil has grown and matured as many of its neighbours have gone backwards, limping from crisis to crisis.

All the same, a national report card would read, "Could do much better". Brazil is best compared with other large, populous developing countries like India and China, but its growth rates are mediocre in comparison, despite Brazil having much greater natural resources than either and becoming self-sufficient in oil in 2006. While poverty is slowly falling and life expectancy increasing, inequality continues to be shamefully high as corruption and the lack of a legal system hold Brazil back. Economic success, and therefore being able to reduce inequality, depends upon ending the **culture of impunity** that has allowed Brazilian politicians to get away with so much for so long. But at least in the short term there is no prospect of the serious political and legal reforms that would entail.

Amazon ecology and Indian rights

The Amazon rainforest is not just an icon for the environmental movement, but the largest and most biodiverse tropical forest on Earth. It is culturally diverse too; the Brazilian Amazon is home to over 300,000 Indians, some still uncontacted, speaking over two hundred languages. The two issues that predominate in the environmental debate – the destruction of the rainforest and the plight of the indigenous Indian population – are in many cases inextricably linked. Brazilians typically react with outrage at being lectured on the preservation of their environment and the protection of native peoples by North Americans and Europeans. Justifiable as Brazilian accusations of hypocrisy may be, they cannot hide the fact that there is a real environmental crisis in Brazil. It has increasingly high visibility as an issue inside Brazil as well as abroad, and there is a real momentum for reform.

Amazon ecology

The Amazon is larger than life. It contains one fifth of the world's fresh water, sustaining the world's largest rainforest – over six million square kilometres – which in turn supports thousands upon thousands of animal and plant species, many of them still unknown. At the heart of the forest, the Amazon river is a staggering 6500km from source to mouth. But perhaps the most worrying statistic is that about fourteen percent of the Brazilian Amazon has been deforested, mostly in the last thirty years, and at least as much again has been affected by selective cutting of trees and other environmental stresses, like over-hunting. With global warming promising to increase drought and hence susceptibility to fire, over the course of this century, there is real long-term danger to the integrity of this extraordinary complex of ecosystems.

Terrain

The Amazon is generally thought of as flat, steamy, equatorial forest. This is misleading – it has mountains, parts of it suffer droughts, and by no means all of it is jungle. To begin with, chunks of the Amazon are not forested at all, for the simple reason that around 25 percent of the Amazon is actually savanna, known in Brazil as **cerrado**, and concentrated in a vertical band through the central Amazon from Roraima to southern Mato Grosso, where soil and rain conditions are markedly dry. Between five and ten percent of the Amazon, depending on time of year, is **várzea** (flood plain), a zone of marshes, lakes, wetlands and annually flooded forest (*igapó*) that is the most varied and among the most biodiverse of the Amazon's ecosystems, but also one of the most threatened, since for historical reasons all of the Amazon's larger cities and most of its human population are concentrated on the flood plain. The Amazon also has a long **coastline**, where mangroves alternate with sand dunes, and the largest and most ecologically complex river estuary in the world.

Amazonian rivers are equally varied. There are three main river types, classified by the nature of the area they drain. The Amazon itself is a deep brown river, the sediments scoured from the Andes giving it the colour of milky tea or coffee; other rivers of this type include the Madeira, Juruá and Purus. **Blackwater** rivers drain granite uplands with few sediments, and are stained black by chemicals released by decomposing vegetation: they are much poorer in nutrients and have much less aquatic biodiversity as a result, but have the side-benefit of being blessedly free of mosquitoes, and insects in general. Rivers of this type in the Amazon include, as the name suggests, the Rio Negro, but many other smaller rivers, like the Arapiuns near Santarém. The third type of river drains areas between these two extremes and is the most beautiful of all, with a blueish-green colour; the Tapajós is the largest river of this type.

Flora and fauna

The most distinctive attribute of the Amazon basin is the overwhelming abundance of plant and animal species. Over six thousand species of plant have been reported from one square kilometre tract of forest, and there are close to a thousand species of birds (the Amazon contains one in five of all the birds in the world) spread about the forest. The rainforest has enormous structural diversity, with layers of vegetation from the forest floor to the canopy 30m above providing a vast number of habitats. With the rainforest being stable over longer periods of time than temperate areas (there was no Ice Age here, nor any prolonged period of drought), the fauna has also had freedom to evolve, and to adapt to often very specialized local conditions. South America has been separated from the other continents for more than 100 million years – and was separate from North America until just a few million years ago – long enough to evolve its unique flora and fauna.

Most of the **trees** found in the Amazon rainforest are tropical palms, scattered between which are the various species of larger, emergent trees. Those plants which are found growing on the forest floor are mostly tree **saplings**, **herbs** (frequently with medicinal applications) and **woody shrubs**. The best-known of all Amazon trees is the **rubber tree** (*Hevea brasiliensis*), known as *seringuera* in Brazil. Still a valuable export in Brazil today, a hundred years ago the rubber tree was the basis of an export boom that transformed the Amazon. Also familiar is the **Brazil nut tree** (*Bertholletia excelsa*), which grows to 30m and takes over ten years to reach nut-bearing maturity; once this is reached, a single specimen can produce over 450kg of nuts every year.

The big **Inga tree** (*Inga edulis*) belongs to the mimosa family, and can grow to 36m. It has colourful patchy bark, large leaves and white hair-like flowers, similar to the mimosa, but its most distinctive feature is its bean pods, sometimes over half a metre long. The pods contain sweet white pulp and large seeds that some Indian groups use to treat dysentery, others for cleaning their teeth. The **turtle-ladder vine** (*Leguminosae casalpinioideae*), known as *escada-de-jabuti* in Brazil, is an unusual-looking liana that spirals high up from the earth to blossom in the canopy of primary forests. Often these lianas are older than the trees on which they can be seen growing.

There are a vast number of different **spiky-rooted palm trees** found throughout the forest. The main trunk starts some two or three metres off the ground, with its exposed roots protected from foraging animals by spikes; in this way the trunk is kept away from flood waters and the exposed roots are able to absorb nitrogen from the atmosphere rather than the soil. One example of this type of tree is the **walking palm** (*Socratea exercisia*), the wood of which is often used for parquet flooring. Tradition has it that it developed spikes to protect itself against the now extinct giant sloth, which used to push it over. The related **stilt palm** (*Socratea exorrhiza*) also grows abundantly in the Amazon, reaching heights of up to 15m. It has a thin trunk, very thorny stilt roots that grow like a tepee above the ground, and long thin leaves that are used by some indigenous groups as a treatment for hepatitis. The most utilized part, however, is the very hard bark, which can be taken off and unwrapped in one piece for use as floor or wall slats.

Good areas for spotting **wildlife** in the Amazon are the richly diverse river banks and flood plains: here you are likely to see **caimans**, **macaws** and **toucans**, and you should catch sight, too, of one of a variety of **hawks**. With luck and observation you may spot a **river dolphin**, **capybara** or maybe even one of the **jungle cats**. In the jungle proper you're more likely to find mammals such as the **peccary** (wild pig), **tapir**, **tamanduá** (anteater) **tree sloth** and, very rarely, the second-largest cat in the world, the powerful **spotted jaguar**. In general though, the open spaces of the Pantanal (see p.583) are better for spotting wildlife than the Amazon, where movement through the rainforest is limited to narrow trails and rivers, and the vegetation usually makes it difficult to see more than a few yards.

The endangered forest

Advances in satellite imagery over the last twenty years have radically improved our knowledge of what is actually happening in the Amazon, how far it has gone and what the trends are over time. So far, about sixteen percent of the Brazilian Amazon has been deforested. About the same amount again has suffered some fragmentation of forest cover. The amount that is deforested varies from year to year because of a number of factors, especially climate. In El Niño years, such as 1998, the Amazon is much drier than usual, fires start more easily, and deforestation is higher. In interpreting the data, what matters is not a deforestation spike in one year or another, but general trends over time. These show that deforestation climbed alarmingly in the 1970s and 1980s, fell back in the 1990s, and then rose again in the early twenty-first century. Furthermore, much deforested land is abandoned and re-grows over time; although it usually does not return to the level of ecological complexity it had, deforested land can re-acquire some of its biodiversity value.

In other words, all is not lost; the bulk of the Amazon is intact, and even the damaged areas need not be written off. The other thing to remember is that the frontier period of Amazonian development is largely over. The Amazon's population is stable, and rapidly urbanizing; almost seventy percent of the Amazon's population lives in cities. There are no longer waves of migrants flooding to the region, or a growing rural population putting pressure on the forest. Policymakers and Amazonians themselves are realizing it makes more sense to concentrate development efforts into degraded areas, where there are already roads and people living, intensifying development instead of extending it. This is unfortunate for the environmental integrity of the 25 percent or so of the Amazon in this position, but it offers the real prospect that pressure on the remaining 75 percent will diminish.

Forest clearance generally follows **road building**. When a road reached into new territories in the glory days of highway building into the Amazon in the 1970s and 1980s, it brought with it the financial backing and interests of big agricultural and industrial companies, plus an onslaught of land-seeking settlers. Historically, the great villain in the deforestation piece has been **ranching** – the latest research suggests around eighty percent of forest cleared was turned into pasture, dwarfing the deforestation caused by smallholders, commercial agriculture and logging.

Although much has been written recently about **soy farming** as a cause of deforestation, most soy planting takes place on land that has already been cleared, and it remains a very minor cause of deforestation. Forest **fires** are a major threat, generally caused by colonizing farmers and ranchers, often exacerbated by the process of selective **logging**, which opens up the forest canopy and leaves debris ripe for lighting. Alongside the logging, cattle ranching and smaller-scale farming, **hydroelectric dams** also caused serious damage to the Amazonian environment: north of Manaus, for example, the Balbina hydroelectric dam inundated an area of over 2000 square kilometres of forest, and there are plans for new dams on the Xingú river, in the central Amazon. As well as the obvious environmental impact of the flooding of this vast region, further previously unforeseen problems are now being faced. The water in the reservoir above dams is often turned acidic by the decomposing vegetation trapped underneath the surface, causing turbines to corrode.

Until the Amazon was opened up by roads, many areas were inhabited and exploited only by **Indian tribal peoples**, who had long since retreated from the main rivers. When the Spanish and Portuguese first explored the Amazon they noted that a well-established, highly organized, apparently agriculturally based Indian society thrived along the banks of the main rivers. Within two hundred years this relatively sophisticated Indian culture had vanished. Although many had died from the initial effects of new diseases (flu, smallpox, measles, etc), a large proportion had escaped into more remote areas of the forest.

The rainforest is still seen by many in Brazil as a resource to be exploited until it no longer exists, much like fossil fuels and mineral deposits. The indigenous Indians and many of the modern forest-dwellers – including rubber tappers, nut collectors and, increasingly, even peasant settlers – view the forest differently, as something which, like an ocean, can be harvested regularly if it is not overtaxed.

Chico Mendes, the Brazilian rubber tappers' union leader who was shot dead in 1988, was the best-known voice on the side of the established Amazon-dwellers: "the forest is our mother, our source of life", he argued. He was killed by hired gunmen outside his house in the state of Acre in the southwest Amazon. Acre however became the showpiece state of the Brazilian environmental movement from 1998, when a PT government, led by **Jorge Viana** and dominated by old friends and colleagues of Chico Mendes, implemented a radical environmental programme, including a rubber subsidy to help rubber tappers remain in the forest, and a series of innovative initiatives for marketing forest products. In fifteen years, the environmental movement in Acre has moved to the centre of Brazilian political life: Viana was triumphantly re-elected in 2002, and a close friend, **Marina da Silva**, an ex-rubber tapper from Acre who had been a colleague of Chico Mendes in the rubber tapper union movement, was sworn in as national minister of the environment in January 2003, in the incoming Lula government.

Deforestation: the regional and global consequences

In regional terms, the most serious effects of the destruction of the Amazon rainforest are twofold:

• **Local climate change**. There is now hard scientific evidence from the deforested highway corridors that removing forest reduces rainfall, creates dry seasons where there were none, and extends them where they already existed. This has obvious implications for crops, soils, flora and fauna.

• **Loss of the forest itself**. This may sound a circular argument, but the fact is that as the forest goes, so does an endless potential supply of rubber and other valuable gums, medicines, nuts, fruits, fish, game, skins and the like. Only a small proportion of the plants that exist in the Amazon have been studied, and there is a real danger of losing a genetic pool of vital importance.

Deforestation also has important global implications:

• **Global climate change**. All modelling of future climate change is controversial when you descend to specifics, but it is clear that continuing large-scale deforestation would change weather patterns in the rest of the hemisphere (ironically, given responsibilities for global warming, the agricultural areas of the US Midwest look likeliest to be affected). The destruction of the forest has two effects on the earth's atmosphere. The smoke from the vast forest clearances makes a significant direct contribution to the **greenhouse effect**; tropical deforestation as a whole accounts for around twenty percent of global carbon emissions. The exact percentage contributed by Amazonian deforestation is controversial. Few experts accept a figure of less than five percent of global emissions, but this is fiercely contested by the Brazilian government. Less immediately, the fewer trees there are to absorb carbon dioxide, the faster the greenhouse effect is likely to build.

• **Loss of resources**. This is a world problem almost as much as it is a regional one. A growing proportion of the chemicals or medicines found in a high-street chemist originate from rainforest products, and there can be little doubt that there are many more medical breakthroughs waiting to be discovered.

Forces driving deforestation

The blame for deforestation is often wrongly attributed. The following are some popular, but mistaken, explanations:

• **Population and land pressures**. Perhaps the most popular theory of all, certainly in Brazil, is that an unstoppable tide of humanity is swamping the forest. While there was something to this between the 1960s and the early 1990s, the rural Amazon has been losing population for a decade, and the region as a whole has a stable population with, according to the 2001 census, a small net migration to other parts of Brazil.

• **Debt**. Brazil's external debt is another popular scapegoat, but this is even less convincing. The bulk of the capital that Brazil borrowed to create the debt was invested in southern Brazil. The need to make interest payments has not been a driver of economic policy in Brazil since the debt was restructured in the early 1990s. Most of the borrowed capital that was invested in the Amazon went into the mineral sector and into building dams, neither of which were significant causes of deforestation compared to ranching and agriculture.

• **The logging industry**. Virtually no deforestation can be directly attributed to logging. The biodiversity of the Amazon means that economically useful trees are jumbled together with valueless ones. As a result, clearcutting-removing forest tracts for timber, is almost unknown. Logging is more selective, resulting in the fragmentation of forest cover – degradation rather than deforestation. One often hears that logging trails open up areas into which deforesters later move, but the reverse is actually the case. Since logs have to be cut and transported from a point not too far from where they are felled, it is usually the loggers who head down the trails made by others.

• **"Big business"**. It is certainly true that most of the deforestation in the grim decades of the 1970s and 1980s was driven directly by big business, specifically the tax breaks that attracted large companies to the region, and the ignorance and arrogance that led them to think that megalomaniac development projects in the jungle would make money. But when the tax breaks were withdrawn in the early 1990s, most of the large companies left. The big companies that remain in the Amazon – mainly in mining and commercial agriculture - work in areas degraded long ago, and are not drivers of much new deforestation.

A number of reasons are put forward for the continuing destruction of the rainforest. A complete answer would include the following four major factors:

• **The Brazilian economy**. Save for minerals and soya, the vast bulk of what the Amazon produces is consumed within the Amazon, or goes elsewhere in Brazil. For every cubic metre of tropical hardwood that is exported, for example, two cubic metres are consumed in Brazil, largely by the furniture and construction industry. The export of Amazonian timber is highly regulated; educated consumers in the US and EU demand proof that Amazon timber in products they buy has been sustainably produced – non-certified Amazon timber is barred from the EU, for example. There is no such demand among the vast majority of Brazilian consumers and, until there is, the domestic economy will be the single biggest driver of deforestation.

• **Soya**. While not a significant driver of deforestation at the moment, this is what keeps Brazilian environmentalists awake at night. Chunks of the central and eastern Amazon are potentially suitable for soya production. Brazil is already the world's largest soya producer, and has lower labour and land costs than the US, its main competitor. Soya has already been successfully produced on a large scale in the southern Amazon, in Mato Grosso. Once the Santarém–Cuiabá highway is asphalted, as is inevitable, a soya boom up the highway corridor is the most immediate large-scale threat the Amazon faces.

• **Government policy**. Regional development policy is one of the most unreconstructed areas of the federal government, run by old-fashioned developmentalists whatever the political complexion of the government. Corruption, in the form of loosely monitored federal contracts and regional development funds that operate as slush funds for politicians of every ideological complexion, hangs like a fog over everything the government does in the Amazon, as elsewhere in the country.

• **Amazonian states**. With a couple of exceptions, most notably Acre, Amazonian states tend to be run by old-style oligarchs, ignorant, provincial, and deeply hostile to an environmental agenda they feel is threatening to "development". As far as they can – which fortunately is not very far, given their limited resources – they tend to back policies harmful to the forest. Egregious recent examples include the partially successful attempt by the Rondônia state government to sell off chunks of the state park system between 1998 and 2002, and the attempt by the Roraima state government to block the declaration of indigenous reserves in the state.

Possible solutions

Deforestation happens, in the final analysis, because it makes economic sense for the person cutting the tree down. It follows that the key to preserving the forest is to make sure it makes more economic sense to keep it standing. A perfect example of the latter is the case of Belém; the largest city in the Amazon is surrounded by extensive areas of intact flood plain forest. This is because there is massive demand for *açaí*, a palm fruit central to Amazonian cuisine, and palm-heart. Both are locally consumed in large quantities, but also preserved, packed and exported to the rest of Brazil and the world. Both products come from flood-plain palm forests and, as a result, without subsidies or development projects, vast areas of flood-plain forest are preserved. Because gathering these forest products can never be mechanized, tens of thousands of livelihoods are assured, and the industry is sustainable. Overharvesting does not happen because everyone knows the level of production the ecosystem can sustain, and that they would shortly be out of a job if they went beyond it.

But this is only half the story. Gathering palm products is a living, but there is not much money in it. Or wasn't. A few years ago, DaimlerBenz was looking for a way to reassure its German shareholders of its environmental responsibility. The R&D department discovered that compressed fibres from Amazon palms could be used to stuff upholstery and also to make a material from which sunshields could be manufactured. They hooked up with the local university in Belém, which brokered a series of contracts with cooperatives in Marajó to supply and process palm fibre, creating what by local standards are scores of well-paid jobs. Everybody won: the local people, the local university (which gets a cut of each contract), the foreign corporation, the Brazilian consumer in southern Brazil driving the car, and, most of all, the environment. The Marajó villagers are now going to the university for help in reforesting deforested areas – because it makes economic sense.

So far these are isolated success stories, but they are part of a trend. Other companies looking to the Amazon to source products include Pirelli, which is producing tyres in southern Brazil with Acrean rubber; and Hermès, the French luxury goods firm, which is using *couro vegetal*, a form of latex treated to look and feel like leather, to make handbags and briefcases. A number of venture capital firms have sprung up in São Paulo, looking to finance environmentally sound but also profitable projects in the Amazon such as ecotourism, organic agriculture, sustainable production of certified timber, furniture-making and fruit-pulp processing. Even big companies investing in the Amazon, like Cargill and Alcoa, are looking to minimize potential damage to their reputation by setting up compensation funds and managing their supply chain to reduce environmental impacts.

The principles underlying this sea-change are clear. First, long-term success usually lies in satisfying local and regional demand, not the export market. Brazilian ecotourism grew in the aftermath of the terrorist attacks of September 11, 2001, for example, because the growing number of Brazilian ecotourists compensated for the drop in international, especially American, travellers. Second, interventions are often necessary; partly the removal of subsidies that reward destruction, now largely accomplished, but also incentives to encourage more environmentally friendly land use. A recent example is the national credit programme for family farms, PRONAF, which established a credit line for small Amazonian farmers who want to do agro-forestry, rather than straight farming, with subsidized rates of repayment. Thousands have so far taken it up. If this can be increased to tens or hundreds of thousands, it could transform the scene in the rural Amazon.

The other principles are more controversial, and are still not widely accepted by the international environmental movement, which lags way behind Brazilian environmentalism in its understanding of what needs to be done. First, it is always going to make economic sense for certain parts of the Amazon to be

dedicated to production, not conservation. No country refuses to develop rich mineral deposits, or blocks investments in commercial agriculture with high rates of return. The choice is not whether or not to develop, but where development takes place and whether the environmental movement has any influence in channelling and controlling it. Looking at the broader picture, it makes better political and economic sense to accept the more controllable form of development – capitalism – in areas already degraded, and thus ensure the frontier fills out rather than moves on to new areas where the damage would be much greater.

Finally, it needs to be recognized that many parts of the Amazon, because of their remoteness or lack of marketable resources, are never going to be able to generate income or jobs. These areas do however provide valuable **environmental services**; their forests remove carbon from the atmosphere, reducing global warming, and keeping forests intact also protects watersheds and soil quality beyond the areas themselves. As things stand neither the Brazilian government nor the inhabitants of these areas receive any compensation for these environmental services, although perhaps in the future new markets in areas like carbon sequestration will fill some of the gap. In the meantime they should be protected, and the international community should be willing to pay most of the costs toward this, which to an extent is already happening: the Global Environment Fund is paying more than $350 million dollars over ten years from 2002 to extend and consolidate the system of federal protected areas in the Amazon. But much more needs to be done, especially for indigenous areas.

The future

It is actually possible to feel optimistic about the future of the Amazon, especially when comparing the situation now to that of twenty years ago. Deforestation, while still a problem to be watched closely, is at a manageable level. Crucial players, like the Brazilian president, the ministry of the environment, the World Bank and the scientific community inside and outside Brazil, are stressing environmental safeguards and the importance of reconciling conservation with development, the opposite of their positions a generation ago. Increasing areas of the Amazon are being put under strict or partial protection, and, astonishingly, 22 percent of it has been demarcated and ratified as indigenous reserves. Perhaps most encouraging, a state government – Acre – running on an explicitly environmentalist platform has been wildly successful in attracting investment and resources to a remote part of the western Amazon. In Brasília, people who had been persecuted union leaders or dissident academics a decade or two ago are now running government departments or representing Brazil at international conferences. What had been a dangerous set of opinions, for which people like Chico Mendes and many others had died, is becoming, in the jargon of the bureaucrats, "mainstreamed".

All the same, there is some way to go. The **murder of American missionary Dorothy Stang** in February 2005 was a salutary reminder that going up against ranchers and illegal loggers in much of the Amazon is still potentially lethal. Sister Dorothy was killed because she was trying to protect local smallholders from ranchers by forming them into an association and pressing for the creation of a sustainable development reserve. The international outcry at her murder forced the Brazilian government to act, and her murderers, unprecedentedly, were tried and convicted a few months later, although, typically, only the gunmen were caught, with the people who ordered her murder left untouched.

It is still too early to say whether all this will be enough in the long term. Even if Brazil gets its act together, the fate of the Amazon is not only determined within Brazil. Global climate change is already having an impact in the Amazon. Even without further ill-judged development the area of dry forest vulnerable to fire will expand whatever Brazil, and Amazonians, do on their own. But if things come as far in the next twenty years as they have in the last twenty, and if the pressure is kept up, the satellite images may in the future be showing recovery, as well as loss.

Indian rights

Today, there are around 330,000 Indians in Brazil, spread between more than two hundred tribes speaking a hundred and eighty languages or dialects. When the Portuguese first arrived in the sixteenth century, there were probably over five million indigenous inhabitants.

The **Tupi** tribe was the first Brazilian "Indian nation" to come into serious conflict with the outside world. Twelve colonies had been established in Brazil by the Portuguese king, João III, to exploit trade in wood and sugar, but slavery and death were the only things that the Tupi got out of the exchange – a pattern that was to continue for the next five hundred years in Brazil. Perhaps even more devastating than murder or slavery was the spread of white man's **disease**: dysentery and influenza hit within the first two years; smallpox and the plague followed. When the Jesuit missionaries attempted to gather the natives into "reduction" missions, epidemics killed hundreds of thousands of Indians in just a few decades.

The first century and a half of contact was funded by the need for cheap labour and new resources. Spreading steadily into the savanna of the Gê-speaking peoples, and the forests of Pará and the Amazon, the colonists established cattle ranches, plantations, lumber extraction regions and mining settlements – all of which were met by considerable native resistance. Later, the development of vulcanization in the 1870s led to an international demand for **rubber**. Prices rose rapidly and, during the boom which lasted for almost fifty years, Indians were killed, moved around and enslaved by the rubber barons.

By the second half of the twentieth century, most surviving Indian groups had taken refuge in the deep interior. The opening up of first the Centre-West region in the 1950s with the construction of Brasília, and then the Amazon from the 1960s, was an unmitigated disaster for Brazil's indigenous peoples. They were dispossessed of their lands, and one of the consequences of the chaotic settlement of new frontiers was the spread of diseases, which brought many groups to the verge of extinction. The military regime regarded Indians with open racism: the Indian Code, which the military drew up in 1973 (and is still technically in force today, although widely ignored), explicitly said it was a transitional set of legal regulations to be enforced until Indians were assimilated, and indistinguishable from other Brazilians. In the Amazon especially, many non-indigenous people in the areas around indigenous reserves are still openly racist, a sad legacy of their forebears who migrated there a generation ago.

Within Brazil indigenous peoples have always had defenders, notably in the Catholic church, in the universities, and even in more liberal circles in the Brazilian military and FUNAI (the federal Indian agency), where some individuals were able to make a difference. The best examples were the brothers

Claudio and Orlando Vilas-Boas, who were able to create a reserve area in southern Mato Grosso in the 1960s, which turned out to be crucial in assuring the eventual survival of many indigenous groups of the southern Amazon. But these were isolated actions in the midst of what would best be described as accidental genocide.

The beginnings of change came in the darkest days of military repression and unrestrained road building in the late 1960s and early 1970s, when a combination of embarrassing international media coverage, foreign pressure and lobbying by the Catholic church forced the military to curb the worst excesses of development in indigenous areas, and provide emergency medical assistance – too late in many cases. With the fall of the military regime, the situation gradually improved: the **1988 Constitution** guaranteed indigenous land rights and protection of indigenous languages and culture, and although enforcing it has been problematic, it at least provided a legal basis for enforcement, which became more and more important as a strategy during the 1990s.

The situation now is incomparably better than it was a generation ago. The presidencies of Fernando Collor and Fernando Henrique Cardoso, whatever their other shortcomings, were quite sound on indigenous issues. **Ruth Cardoso**, Fernando Henrique's wife, was an anthropology professor and very effective advocate for indigenous peoples behind the scenes. During the 1990s most of the outstanding issues to do with the demarcation and full legalization of indigenous areas were resolved. A remarkable 22 percent of the Brazilian Amazon is now officially indigenous land – an area more than twice the size of France. While there are still occasional invasions of indigenous lands, the combination of a free press, more responsive policing and political will at the highest levels of the Brazilian government means that invasions are much less of a problem than they once were.

Perhaps the greatest grounds for hope in the future is the strength of the **indigenous movement**. Born out of the patient organizational and educational work of the Catholic church from the 1960s, the movement rapidly outgrew its religious roots to become an important secular force, founding local associations and regional confederations, and learning from their non-indigenous colleagues in the rural union and rubber tapper movements. Prominent national leaders like **Mário Juruna**, elected federal deputy for Rio in the 1980s despite being from Mato Grosso, were important in getting the movement off the ground. Juruna died in 2002, but an able new generation of younger indigenous leaders – **Daví Yanomami**, **Jorge Terena**, **Gerson Baniwa**, **Escrawen Sompre** and others – have taken up the torch. An especially encouraging sign in recent years has been the central government's willingness to take important responsibilities like **education and health care** out of the hands of FUNAI – still plagued by corruption and inefficiency – and transfer them to the indigenous movement itself, with support and financing from government ministries. While this has not worked well everywhere, in many areas it has resulted not only in better education and health care for indigenous peoples, but in much greater autonomy and self-confidence, a by-product of the training programmes which emphasized that as much teaching and health care as possible should be provided by indigenous people themselves.

Case study: the Yanomami

Straddling the hilly area of rainforest on the border between Brazil and Venezuela live the **Yanomami** tribe. One of the largest Amazon Indian groups still surviving today, there are around 10,000 living on the Brazilian side of the frontier, and around another 20,000 in Venezuela. Traditionally inhabiting circular villages of up to two hundred people, the Yanomami led a way of life that was very much in balance with the natural environment, depending on a combination of hunting, gathering and gardening.

However, in 1987, coming in the wake of local military-built airstrips and the announcement that the Yanomami were soon to be given "official" rights to their traditional land, a trickle of **gold-miners** began to invade their territory. Sufficient gold was found in the Indians' hills to bring more and more miners, or *garimpeiros*, into the Yanomami Reserve, and by 1990 there were some 45,000 *garimpeiros* in the region – far outnumbering the Yanomami. The intensified contact introduced deadly strains of disease into the tribe, with malaria epidemics especially devastating to children and old people. What made this case different from many similar episodes elsewhere in the 1980s was that it came after a presidential campaign whose winner, Fernando Collor, had made public pledges to protect Indians and the environment, which in turn attracted crowds of foreign media to cover the Yanomami story. It rapidly became a huge international embarrassment for the Brazilian government.

Demarcation of the Yanomami reserves finally happened in 1992. Nevertheless, around eleven thousand *garimpeiros* reinvaded Yanomami land in 1993, encouraged to do so by local politicians and miners' unions in the state of Roraima. Malaria, TB and other diseases tightened their grip on the tribe once again and the inevitable friction between *garimpeiros* and Indian communities exploded into **violence**. In August 1993, around ten (the full number will never be known) Yanomami of the Hashimu community were shot by gold-miners and their bodies burnt – most of the dead were women and children. This finally pushed the federal authorities to expel the miners – the deposits were already giving out – dynamiting their airstrips to ensure they stayed out. Although small crews of miners are still occasionally found, the main environmental issue for the reserve now is the rehabilitation of the areas degraded by the invasions.

The invasion emergency prompted a group of concerned Brazilians, mainly anthropologists, to found a non-governmental organization called CCPY (Comissão para a Criação do Parque Yanomami – Commission for the Creation of a Yanomami Park), which lobbied hard for Yanomami rights and set up a number of effective health and education projects in Yanomami territory. After the reserve was finally demarcated and ratified by the federal government, CCPY switched focus to lobby for effective health care and education for the Yanomami. When these were taken out of FUNAI's hands in the late 1990s, CCPY together with the Yanomami set up an independent NGO, Urihi, based in the state capital of Boa Vista, to provide health care in the Yanomami reserve but with funding from the federal ministry of health. Urihi is now the largest private sector employer in Roraima, and has set up a chain of health posts throughout the reserve as well as a very active training programme for Yanomami paramedics with training material in all the Yanomami dialects, as well as Portuguese. The results have been remarkable. In 2002, for the first time ever, there were no recorded cases of malaria in the reserve, and many Yanomami from the Venezuela side were moving across the frontier to take advantage of the better health care on the Brazilian side. Despite such advances, potential threats remain, chief among them the army, whose presence in this remote region (to guard the borders with Venezuela) has resulted in at least a dozen soldiers fathering children with Yanomami women, as well as incidences of venereal disease and social disruption.

For further information contact:

Survival, 6 Charterhouse Buildings, London EC1M 7ET, UK ⓣ020/7687-8700, ⓕ020/7687-8701, ⓦwww.survival-international.org
World Wildlife Fund in Brazil ⓦwww.wwf.org.br

Also check out ⓦwww.socioambiental.org and the Brazil & Amazon Resources and Links site at ⓦwww.geocities.com/RainForest/Canopy/1316 for information and news on the Amazon, environmental issues, NGOs working in the region, maps and other more general travel and political links.

Case study: the Makuxí

The struggle continues in Roraima. In March 1994, the **Makuxí**, Ingariko, Wapixana and Taurepang Indian groups set up roadblocks to protest at invasions of their lands by settlers, miners and road builders in a large reserve called Raposa-Serra do Sol, a stunning complex of savanna, forests, rivers and mountains that includes the Brazilian side of Mount Roraima. Although the reserve had been demarcated in the late 1980s, ratification was challenged by the state government and snarled up in the courts for years. It was a transparent manoeuvre on the part of local non-indigenous interests to stall the creation of the reserve long enough for their invasions to become permanent. Although up to five hundred Indians operated the blockades, they were violently attacked. But as each barrier was bulldozed, new blockades appeared.

In 1992, Roraima's state electricity company obtained permission to study the Raposa/Serra do Sol region with a view to building a dam. This is in the traditional territory of the Makuxí Indians, of whom nearly fifteen thousand live in Brazil and some seven thousand over the border in Guyana. The proposed dam threatened to flood around forty square kilometres of Makuxí land. After years of legal battles, and much lobbying by the Makuxí and NGOs in Brazil, the dam project was finally shelved. But this did not prevent the driving of a road deep into the reserve, nor the (illegal) creation of a municipality, Uiramutã, in the heart of the reserve. An army post in Uiramutã (presumably originally placed there to deter the powerful Guyanan army from swarming southwards) could have prevented the invasions – every one of the five hundred people living in the village is there illegally – but instead harasses the local indigenous villages with low-flying helicopters.

But the Makuxí are justly famous for their political skills. With support from the Catholic church, Oxfam, Rainforest Foundation, the Nature Conservancy and others, several years ago they founded a multi-ethnic indigenous association, CIR (Conselho Indígena de Roraima – the Indigenous Council of Roraima). CIR has evolved into one of the most effective regional indigenous organizations in the Amazon, and helped by other Brazilian NGOs it took the state government to court. After a series of court cases, the reserve was finally ratified in 2005, a great victory for the Brazilian indigenous movement, settling the most important demarcation case in the Amazon. But anyone thinking that would be the end of the story was rapidly disabused. In September 2005 a mob invaded the Surumú mission inside the reserve, a training centre and vocational school run for Indians by the Catholic church, and burnt it down. The fight, in every sense, goes on.

Race in Brazilian society

The significance of race in Brazilian society has long been a controversial topic in Brazil. Until recently, despite the country's ethnic and racial diversity, official thinking refused to acknowledge the existence of minority groups, promoting the concept of the Brazilian "racial democracy" and denying absolutely the existence of racism or racial discrimination. If, in a country where blacks and mulattoes form at least half of the population, there are few dark-skinned people at the upper levels of society – so the theory runs – this simply reflects past disadvantages, in particular poverty and lack of education.

Myth . . .

No one contributed more to the consolidation of this myth of racial brotherhood than the anthropologist **Gilberto Freyre**. In the early 1930s he advanced the view that somehow the Portuguese colonizers were immune to racial prejudice, that they intermingled freely with Indians and blacks. If **Brazilian slavery** was a not entirely benevolent patriarchy, as some people liked to believe, the mulatto offspring of the sexual contact between master and slave was the personification of this ideal. The **mulatto** was the archetypal social climber, transcending class boundaries, and was upheld as a symbol of Brazil and the integration of the nation's cultures and ethnic roots. "Every Brazilian, even the light-skinned and fair-haired one," wrote Freyre in his seminal work, *Casa Grande e Senzala*, "carries about him in his soul, when not in soul and body alike, the shadow or even birthmark, of the aborigine or negro. The influence of the African, either direct or remote, is everything that is a sincere reflection of our lives. We, almost all of us, bear the mark of that influence." The myth has endured, even in the minds of those who are also prepared to admit its flaws: "I believe in our illusion of racial harmony", said the (white) singer Caetano Velosa, in an interview in early 2000.

Accepted with, if anything, even less questioning outside Brazil than within, the concept of a racial paradise in South America was eagerly grasped. For those outside Brazil struggling against the Nazis or segregation and racial violence in the US, it was a belief too good to pass up. "Whereas our old world is more than ever ruled by the insane attempt to breed people racially pure, like race horses or dogs", wrote the Austrian writer Stefan Zweig in exile in Brazil, "the Brazilian nation for centuries has been built upon the principle of a free and unsuppressed miscegenation, the complete equalization of black and white, brown and yellow" (*Brazil – Land of the Future*, 1942). Brazil was awarded an international stamp of approval – and its **international image** is still very much that of the happy, unprejudiced melting pot.

Anomalies were easily explained away. A romanticized image of the self-sufficient **Indian** could be incorporated into Brazilian nationalism as, deep in the forested interior and numbering only a quarter of a million, they posed no threat. Picturesque Indian names – Yara and Iraçema for girls, Tibiriça and Caramuru for boys – were given to children, their white parents seeing them as representing Brazil in its purest form. Afro-Brazilian religion, folklore and art became safe areas of interest. **Candomblé**, practised primarily in the northeastern state of

Bahia and perhaps the purest of African rituals, could be seen as a quaint remnant from the past, while syncretist cults, most notably **umbanda**, combining elements of Indian, African and European religion and which have attracted mass followings in Rio, São Paulo and the South, have been taken to demonstrate the happy fusion of cultures.

. . . and reality

Many visitors to Brazil still arrive believing in the melting pot, and for that matter many leave without questioning it. It is undeniable that Brazil has remarkably little in the way of obvious **racial tension**; that there are no legal forms of racial discrimination – indeed *anti*-discrimination is enshrined in the constitution; and that on the beach the races do seem to mix freely. But it is equally undeniable that race is a key factor in determining social position. Institutional racism, born of prejudice and stereotyping, affects access to education, employment opportunities and the treatment of black people within the criminal justice system, manifested most notably in day-to-day harassment and violence from the police.

To say this in Brazil, even now, is to risk being attacked as "un-Brazilian". Nevertheless, the idea that race has had no significant effect on social mobility and that socio-economic differentials of a century ago explain current differences between races is increasingly discredited. It is true that Brazil is a rigidly stratified society within which upward mobility is difficult for anyone. But the lighter your skin, the easier it appears to be. Clear evidence has been produced that, although in general blacks and mulattoes (because of the continuing cycle of poverty) have lower education levels than whites, even when they do have equal levels of education and experience whites still enjoy substantial economic benefits. The **average income** for white Brazilians is twice that for black, and while there is a growing black Brazilian middle class, it is concentrated in the arts, music and sports – black people are still hugely under-represented in the middle and upper ranks of politics, business and industry.

Perhaps the most surprising realization is that, except amongst politically developed intellectuals and progressive sectors of the Church, there seems little awareness or resentment of the link between colour and class. The black consciousness movement has made slow progress in Brazil – although grassroots community groups and national coalitions of organizations representing black people have emerged over the past decade or two – and most people continue to acquiesce before the national myth that this is the New World's fortunate land, where there's no need to organize for improved status.

Music

Brazil's talent for music is so great it amounts to a national genius. Out of a rich stew of African, European and Indian influences it has produced one of the strongest and most diverse musical cultures in the world.

Most people have heard of samba and bossa nova, or of Heitor Villa-Lobos, who introduced the rhythms of Brazilian popular music to a classical audience, but they are only the tip of a very large iceberg of genres, styles and individual talents. Music – heard in bars, on the streets, car radios, concert halls and clubs – is a constant backdrop to social life in Brazil, and Brazilians are a very musical people. Instruments help but they aren't essential: matchboxes shaken to a syncopated beat, forks tapped on glasses and hands slapped on tabletops are all that is required. And to go with the music is some of the most stunning dancing you are ever likely to see. In Brazil, no one looks twice at a couple who would clear any European and most American dance floors. You don't need to be an expert, or even understand the words, to enjoy Brazilian popular music, but you may appreciate it better – and find it easier to ask for the type of record you want – if you know a little about its history.

The roots: regional Brazilian music

The bedrock of Brazilian music is the apparently inexhaustible fund of "traditional" **popular music**. There are dozens of genres, most of them associated with a specific region of the country, which you can find in raw uncut form played on local radio stations, at popular festivals – Carnaval is merely the best known – impromptu recitals in squares and on street corners, and in bars and *dancetarias*, the dance halls that Brazilians flock to at the weekend. The two main centres are Rio and Salvador. There's little argument that the best Brazilian music comes from Rio, the Northeast and parts of Amazônia, with São Paulo and southern Brazil lagging a little behind. Samba, and later bossa nova, became internationally famous, but only because they both happened to get off the ground in Rio, with its high international profile and exotic image. There are, though, less famous but equally vital musical styles elsewhere in Brazil, and it's difficult to see why they remain largely unknown to audiences outside the country – especially given Western music's current obsession with the Third World.

Each local musical genre is part of a **regional identity**, of which people are very proud, and there's a distinct link between geographical rivalry and the development of Brazilian music. *Nordestinos*, in particular, all seem to know their way around the scores of Northeastern musical genres and vigorously defend their musical integrity against the influences of Rio and São Paulo, which dominate TV and national radio. A lot of people regret *carioca* and *paulista* domination of the airwaves, fearing that it's making Brazilian music homogeneous, but if anything it has the opposite effect. People react against the Southeast music by turning to their local brands – which often develop some new enriching influences, picked up along the way.

Samba

The best-known genre, samba, began in the early years of the twentieth century, in the poorer quarters of Rio, as Carnaval music, and over the decades it has developed several variations. The deafening **samba de enredo** is the set piece of Carnaval, with one or two singers declaiming a verse joined by hundreds, even thousands, of voices and drums for the chorus, as the *bloco*, the full samba school, backs up the lead singers. A *bloco* in action during Carnaval is the loudest music you're ever likely to come across, and it's all done without the aid of amplifiers: if you stand up close, the massed noise of the drums vibrates every part of your body. No recording technology yet devised comes close to conveying the sound, and recorded songs and music often seem repetitive. Still, every year the main Rio samba schools make a compilation record of the music selected for the parade, and any record with the words *Samba de Enredo* or *Escola de Samba* will contain this mass Carnaval music.

On a more intimate scale, and musically more inventive, is **samba-canção**, which is produced by one singer and a small back-up band, who play around with basic samba rhythms to produce anything from a (relatively) quiet love song to frenetic dance numbers. This style transfers more effectively in recordings than *samba de enredo*, and in Brazil its more laid-back sounds make it especially popular with the middle-aged. Reliable, high-quality records of *samba-canção* are anything by **Beth Carvalho**, acknowledged queen of the genre, **Alcione**, **Clara Nunes**, and the great **Paulinho da Viola**, who always puts at least a couple of excellent sambas on every record he makes. You can get a taste of the older samba styles that dominated Rio in the 1940s and 1950s in the records of acknowledged old-school greats like **Cartola**, **Bezerra da Silva** and **Velha Guarda de Manueira**.

Since the early 1990s, a refreshing trend in samba has been the revival of **samba-pagode**, a back-to-the-roots reaction against the increasing commercialization of samba in the 1980s. *Pagode* means a simple dance hall, and *samba de pagode* is not a different style of samba so much as a good-time samba, played by a small group, for dancing and general enjoyment in a bar or *dancetaria*. This has always flourished year-round in Rio, but since the 1970s, Carnaval and glitzy versions of *samba-canção* had increasingly become the public face of samba, dominating recording output and being heavily marketed to outsiders. Many of the musicians on whom samba depended for its continuing vitality were sidelined, reduced to making a precarious living doing live shows in the lower-income parts of Rio. Fortunately, people are now returning to *samba-pagode* in a big way, with established *sambistas* like **Agepê** and **Martinho da Vila** following their audience and switching to *pagode* on their records. A number of *pagode* groups have become major national stars, including **Zeca Pagodinho**, **Raça Negra**, **Ginga Pura** and **Banda Brasil**.

Choro

Much less known, **choro** (literally "crying") appeared in Rio around the time of World War I, and by the 1930s had evolved into one of the most intricate and enjoyable of all Brazilian forms of music. Unlike samba, which developed variations, *choro* has remained remarkably constant over the decades. It's one of the few Brazilian genres that owes anything to Spanish-speaking America, as it is clearly related to the Argentinian tango (the real River Plate versions, that is, rather than the sequined ballroom distortions that get passed off as tango outside South America). *Choro* is mainly instrumental, played by a small group: the backbone of the combo is a guitar, picked quickly and jazzily, with notes sliding all over the place, which is played off against a flute, or occasionally a clarinet or recorder, with drums and/or maracas as an optional extra. It is as quiet and intimate as samba is loud and public, and of all Brazilian popular music is probably the most delicate. You often find it being played as background music in bars and cafés; local papers advertise such places. The loveliest *choros* on record are by **Paulinho da Viola**, especially on the album *Chorando*. After years of neglect during the post-war decades *choro* is now undergoing something of a revival, and it shouldn't be too difficult to catch a *choro conjunto* in Rio or São Paulo.

Other genres

A full list of other "traditional" musical genres would have hundreds of entries and could be elaborated on indefinitely. Some of the best-known are **forró**, **maracatú**, **repentismo** and **frevo**, described at greater length in the "Northeast" chapter (starting on p.305): you'll find them all over the Northeast but especially around Recife. **Baião** is a Bahian style that bears a striking resemblance to the hard acoustic blues of the American Deep South, with hoarse vocals over a guitar singing of things like drought and migration; **axé**, a percussion musical style from Bahia that's related to samba; **carimbó** is an enjoyable, lilting rhythm and dance found all over northern Brazil but especially around Belém (a souped-up and heavily commercialized version of *carimbó* enjoyed a brief international vogue as **lambada** in the 1990s); and **bumba-meu-boi**, one of the strangest and most powerful of all styles, the haunting music of Maranhão state.

A good start, if you're interested, is one of the dozens of records by the late **Luiz Gonzaga**, also known as **Gonzagão**, which have extremely tacky covers but are musically very good. They have authentic renderings of at least two or three Northeastern genres per record. His version of a beautiful song called *Asa Branca* is one of the best loved of all Brazilian tunes, a national standard, and was played at his funeral in 1989.

The golden age: 1930–60 and the radio stars

It was the growth of radio during the 1930s that created the popular music industry in Brazil, with home-grown stars idolized by millions. The best-known was **Carmen Miranda**, spotted by a Hollywood producer singing in the famous Urca casino in Rio and whisked off to film stardom in the 1940s. Although her hats made her immortal, she deserves to be remembered more as the fine singer she was. She was one of a number of singers and groups loved by older Brazilians, like **Francisco Alves**, **Ismael Silva**, **Mário Reis**, **Ataulfo Alves**, **Trio de Ouro** and **Joel e Gaúcho**. Two great songwriters, **Ary Barroso** and **Pixinguinha**, provided the raw material.

Brazilians call these early decades *a época de ouro*, and that it really was a golden age is proved by the surviving music on record. It is slower and jazzier than modern Brazilian music, but with the same rhythms and beautiful, crooning vocals. Even in Brazil it used to be difficult to get hold of **records** of this era but after years of neglect there is now a widely available series of reissues called *Revivendo*. They send catalogues abroad, if you can't make it to Brazil to buy the records: write to Revivendo Músicas Comércio de Discos Ltda, Rua Barão do Rio Branco 28/36 – 1. andar, Caixa Postal 122, Curitiba, Paraná, Brazil.

International success – the bossa nova

With this wealth of music to work with, it was only a matter of time before Brazilian music burst its national boundaries, something that duly happened in the late 1950s with the phenomenon of **bossa nova**. Several factors led to its development. The classically trained **Tom Jobim**, equally in love with Brazilian popular music and American jazz, met up with fine Bahian guitarist **João Gilberto** and his wife **Astrud Gilberto**. The growth in the Brazilian record and communications industries allowed bossa nova to sweep Brazil and come to the attention of people like Stan Getz in the United States; and, above all, there developed a massive market for a sophisticated urban sound among the newly burgeoning middle class in Rio, who found Jobim and Gilberto's slowing down and breaking up of what was still basically a samba rhythm an exciting departure. It rapidly became an international craze, and Astrud Gilberto's quavering version of one of the earliest Jobim numbers, *A Garota de Ipanema*, became the most famous of all Brazilian songs, *The Girl from Ipanema* – although the English lyric is considerably less suggestive than the Brazilian original.

Over the next few years the craze eventually peaked and fell away, though not before leaving most people with the entirely wrong impression that bossa nova is a mediocre brand of muzak well suited to lifts and airports. In North America it eventually sank under the massed strings of studio producers, but in Brazil it never lost its much more delicate touch, usually with a single guitar and a crooner holding sway. Early bossa nova still stands as one of the crowning glories of Brazilian music, and all the classics – you may not know the names of tunes like *Corcovado*, *Isaura*, *Chega de Saudade* and *Desafinado* but you'll recognize the melodies – are on the easily available double-album compilations called *A Arte de Tom Jobim* and *A Arte de João Gilberto*; Jobim's is the better of the two.

The great Brazilian guitarist **Luiz Bonfá** also made some fine bossa nova records: the ones where he accompanies Stan Getz are superb. The bossa nova records of **Stan Getz** and **Charlie Byrd** are one of the happiest examples of inter-American cooperation, and as they're easy to find in European and American shops they make a fine introduction to Brazilian music. They had the sense to surround themselves with Brazilian musicians, notably Jobim, the Gilbertos and Bonfá, and the interplay between their jazz and the equally skilful Brazilian response is often brilliant. **Live bossa nova** is rare these days, restricted to the odd bar or hotel lobby, unless you're lucky enough to catch one of the great names in concert – although Tom Jobim, sadly, died in 1995. But then bossa nova always lent itself more to recordings than live performance.

Tropicalismo

The military coup in 1964 was a crucial event in Brazil. Just as the shock waves of the cultural upheavals of the 1960s were reaching Brazilian youth, the lid went on in a big way: censorship was introduced for all song lyrics; radio and television were put under military control; and some songwriters and musicians were tortured and imprisoned for speaking and singing out – although fame was at least some insurance against being killed. The result was the opposite of what the generals had intended. A movement known as **tropicalismo** developed, calling itself cultural but in fact almost exclusively a musical movement, led by a young and extravagantly talented group of musicians. Prominent amongst them were **Caetano Veloso** and **Gilberto Gil** from Bahia and **Chico Buarque** from Rio. They used traditional popular music as a base, picking and mixing genres in a way no one had thought of doing before – stirring in a few outside influences like the Beatles and occasional electric instruments, and topping it all off with lyrics that often stood alone as poetry – and delighted in teasing the censors. Oblique images and comments were ostensibly about one thing, but everyone knew what they really meant. Chico Buarque's great song, *Tanto Mar*, for example, is apparently about the end of a party, but everyone except the censor recognized it was a salute to the Portuguese revolution, the "Revolution of the Carnations", as it's known.

It was a fine party
I had a great time
I've kept an old carnation as a memento
And even though the party's been shut down
They're bound to have forgotten a few seeds in some corner of the garden

Caetano, Gil and Chico – all of Brazil is on first-name terms with them – spent a few years in exile in the late 1960s and early 1970s, Caetano and Gil in London (both still speak fluent English with immaculate BBC accents) and Chico in Rome, before returning in triumph as the military regime wound down. They have made dozens of records between them: the best way to get to grips with their work quickly is through the compilation albums, *A Arte de. . .* , *O Talento de. . .* , or *A Personalidade de. . .* , collections of their back catalogues with all their most famous songs up to the mid-1970s. They are still the leading figures of Brazilian music, despite being in their late fifties. Gilberto Gil, after a long period in the doldrums where he experimented unsuccessfully with rock-based formats, has recently returned to form, apparently inspired by a new wave of Bahian musicians. His stint as **Minister of Culture** in Lula's government, while thin on political achievements, at least meant Brazil could boast unquestionably the coolest government minister on the planet. Chico Buarque's dense lyrics and hauntingly beautiful melodies are still flowing, although he produces recordings more rarely now, devoting more of his time to novel-writing and theatre. Pride of place, however, has to go to Caetano Veloso. Good though he was in the 1960s and 1970s, he is improving with age, and his records over the last fifteen years have been his best: mature, innovative, lyrical and original as ever. Highlights of his most recent work include a stunning live album *Circulado Vivo*, *Fina Estampa*, a beautiful tribute album to Spanish Latin American music, and *Livro*, an intoxicating mix of tradition and the avant-garde. His continuing originality has kept him at the leading edge of Brazilian popular music, acknowledged everywhere from the *favelas* of Rio to New York's Carnegie Hall as the greatest modern Brazilian musician.

△ Gilberto Gil

Female singers

Brazilian music has a strong tradition of producing excellent women singers. The best of all time was undoubtedly the great **Elis Regina**, from Rio Grande do Sul, whose magnificent voice was tragically stilled in 1984, when she was at the peak of her career, by a drug overdose. She interpreted everything, and whatever Brazilian genre she touched she invariably cut the definitive version. Two of her songs in particular became classics, *Aguas de Marҫo* and *Carinhoso*, the latter being arguably the most beautiful Brazilian song of all. Again, the *A Arte de Elis Regina* double album is the best bet, although there is also a superb record of Elis with Tom Jobim, called *Elis e Tom*. After her death the mantle fell on **Gal Costa**, a very fine singer although without the extraordinary depth of emotion Elis could project, whose version of *Aquarela do Brasil* inspired Terry Gilliam to the idea for the film "Brazil", and whose LP, named after the song, is highly recommended, along with the *A Arte de Gal Costa* compilation. And then there's **Maria Bethania**, Caetano's commercially more successful sister, who, after forty years of performing and recording, still succeeds in producing original material.

A new generation of women singers has carried the tradition forward. The most prominent amongst those who have come into their own in recent years has been Rio's **Marisa Monte**; the classic *Cor de Rosa e Carvão* is the best introduction to her enormous talent. Other up-and-coming women singers include **Silvia Torres**, **Belô Veloso** (a niece of Caetano), and the latest sensation, **Virginia Rodrigues**; it took a couple of CDs for her remarkable voice to find the right producer, but with *Nós* in 2003 she gave a hint of her potential. A figure from São Paulo to emerge more recently is **Fernanda Porto**, who also has a great voice and whose musical style is a fusion of samba and drum 'n' bass.

The Bahian sound

Although Rio is the traditional capital of Brazilian music, for some years now it has been overtaken, in vitality and originality, by **Salvador**, the capital of Bahia. Bahia in general, and Salvador in particular, have always produced a disproportionate number of Brazil's leading musicians including Caetano Veloso, Maria Bethabia, Gilberto Gil, Gal Costa, the Caymmi family and João Gilberto, but in recent years their status has progressed from important to dominant. The main reason is the extraordinary musical blend provided by deep African roots, Caribbean and Hispanic influences coming in through the city's port, and a local record industry that quickly realized the money-making potential of Bahian music. They didn't invent *lambada*, for example, but it was Salvador record producers who transformed it into a global hit. Tellingly, all over Brazil (except in Rio, naturally), it is now more common to hear the Salvador's *axé* Carnaval hits than samba during Carnaval.

The new Bahian sound, an exhilarating blend of Brazilian and Caribbean rhythms, is exemplified by groups like **Reflexus**, and singers like **Luis Caldas**, **Margareth Menezes** and **Daniela Mercury**. Its guiding light is the percussionist and producer **Carlinhos Brown**; a great performer and songwriter in his own right, he is also the *éminence grise* behind the rise of other prominent artists like Marisa Monte with whom he joined forces, together with the experimental poet, singer and sculptor Arnaldo Antunes to create the **Tribalistas**, whose one-off CD was an amazing hit in 2002–03, described as "neo-hippy" and a blend of Brazilian sounds at their most melodic.

Contemporary singers and musicians

The number of high-quality singers and musicians in Brazilian music besides these leading figures is enormous. **Milton Nascimento** has a talent that can only be compared with the founders of *tropicalismo*, a remarkable soaring voice, a genius for composing stirring anthems and a passion for charting and celebrating the experience of blacks in Brazil. Since his emergence from Minas Gerais in the 1960s, he has become a prominent spokesperson of black Brazilians. **Fagner** and **Alceu Valença** are modern interpreters of Northeastern music, and strikingly original singers. The latter is the creator of what has been termed "*forró rock*". **Elba Ramalho** is a Northeastern woman with an excellent voice, which she too often wastes on banal rock rather than the more

A selected discography

Apart from the *A Arte de. . .*, *O Talento de. . .*, *A Personalidade de. . .* and *Revivendo* series mentioned on pp.827–828, recommended recordings easily available in Brazil include the following (artists in bold, listed – as in Brazilian music stores – according to the first name of the artist):

Alceu Valença
Mágica (Barclay 1984)
Araketu
Ara Ketu (Continental 1987)
Belô Veloso
Belô Veloso (Velas 1997)
Bezerra da Silva
Se não fosse o samba (RCA Victor 1989)
Caetano Veloso
Velo (Philips 1984)
Estrangeiro (Philips 1991)
Circulado Vivo (Philips 1993)
Fina Estampa (Polygram do Brasil 1994)
Livro (Polygram do Brasil 1998)
Cartola
Cartola (Discos Marco Pereira 1990)
Chico Buarque
Ópera do Malandro (Philips 1979)
Vida (Philips 1980)
Para Todos (Philips 1994)
Uma Palavra (Ariola 1995)
Daniela Mercury
Daniela (Polygram do Brasil 1992)
Canto da Cidade (Polygram do Brasil 1993)
Dorival Caymmi
A música de Caymmi (Continental 1981)
Elis Regina and Tom Jobim
Elis e Tom (Philips 1974)
Fernanda Porto
Fernanda Porto (Trama, 2002)
Gal Costa
Aquarela do Brasil (Philips 1980)
Gilberto Gil
Parabolicamera (Philips 1991)
Gilberto Gil and Caetano Veloso
Tropicalia 2 (Philips 1994)
Jorge Ben Jor
Acústico (Universal 2002)
Maria Bethania
Ambar (EMI 1996)
Marisa Monte
M (EMI 1994)

traditional material she excels at. **Renato Borghetti**, from Rio Grande do Sul, has done much to popularize *gaúcho*-influenced music through his skill on the accordion and his adaptations of traditional tunes. **Ney Matogrosso** has a striking falsetto voice that sounds female, but he is a man – although sometimes self-indulgent, he can be very good. **Jorge Ben** is a fine Rio singer, responsible for many modern classics of Brazilian song, including the definitive Rio verse in his *País Tropical*:

I live in a tropical country
Blessed by God with natural beauty
In February there's Carnaval
I own a guitar and drive a Beetle
I support Flamengo and have a black girlfriend called Tereza.

Vinícius de Morães and **Toquinho** are (or were, in the case of Vinícius) a good singer and guitarist team, and **Dorival Caymmi** at over 70 is the doyen of Bahian musicians. Whilst all these figures have been going strongly for decades now, an artist to look out for is **Zeca Baleiro** from Maranhão who, with his *bumba-meu-boi*- and reggae-influenced style, is one of the most innovative

Cor de Rosa e Carvão (EMI 1995)
Barulhinho Bom (EMI 1998)
Memórias, Crônicas e Declarações de Amor (EMI 2000)

Milton Nascimento
Clube da esquina (Polygram do Brasil 1981)
Ao vivo (Polygram do Brasil 1983)

Olodum
Egito-Madagáscar (Continental 1987)

Paulinho da Viola
Cantando (RCA Victor 1982)
Chorando (RCA Victor 1982)
Eu canto samba (RCA Victor 1989)
Bebadosamba (BMG 1996)

Reflexús
Reflexús da mãe Africa (EMI 1987)

Renato Borghetti
Renato Borghetti (RCA Victor 1987)

Seu Jorge
Cru (Favela Chic/Beleza/Naïve 2005)

Silvia Torres
Silvia Torres (Melodie 1999)

Tribalistas
Tribalistas (EMI 2002)

Velha Guarda da Mangueira
E Convidados (Nikita 1999)

Vinícius de Morães
with Marilia Medalha and Toquinho
Como dizia o poeta. . . – música nova (RGE 1971)

Virginia Rodrigues
Sol Negro (Hannibal 1997)
Nós (Hannibal 1999)

Zeca Baleiro
Por onde andará Stephen Fry? (MZA, 1997)
Vô imbolá? (MZA, 1999)
Líricas (MZA, 2000)

As for Brazilian **CDs available abroad**, only the jazz/bossa nova records of Getz and his Brazilian collaborators are easily available. However, recent interest in Brazilian music has spawned a few compilation albums: notably *Brazil Classics: Volume 1* (a sort of Brazilian greatest hits) and *Volume 2* (a samba collection), both on EMI and the excellent *Forró: Music for Maids and Taxi Drivers* (Globestyle Records). One of the best international mail-order suppliers is Globestyle Records (48–50 Steele Rd, London NW10 7AS) .

performers to have emerged in Brazil in the 1990s. More recently still, in no small part thanks to his acting role in the acclaimed film *Cidade de Dios* ("City of God"), the singer **Seu Jorge** and his samba-driven style has deservedly taken his place on the international stage. Born Jorge Mário da Silva and raised in a *favela* outside of Rio, Seu Jorge is often considered one of Brazil's most inspirational singer-songwriters.

But too many musicians these days waste their time attempting to fuse Brazilian genres with rock-based formats. It's not that it can't be done – *tropicalismo* pulled it off several times in the 1960s – but the type of Brazilian rock music currently most popular in the country, appalling heavy metal and stadium rock, is completely incompatible with the subtle, versatile musical imagination of Brazilians. National radio and the dominant São Paulo radio stations pump out the worst kind of British and US FM blandness, and this has spawned a host of Brazilian imitations, almost all of them embarrassingly bad. Only a relatively few – such as **Lulu Santos** and **Charlie Brown Junior** – have succeeded in developing an enduring national following.

The other possible criticism of Brazilian music is that, while its popular roots are healthier than ever, nobody of similar stature has come up to succeed the towering figures of the 1960s and 1970s. Elis is dead, Gil, Caetano, Chico and Milton are still producing but are no longer young, and, while younger talent abounds, there's nothing at the moment that could be called genius – a lot to demand of anyone, but it's a tribute to Brazilian music that its pedigree allows us to judge it by the highest standards.

Live music and recordings

If you want to see or hear **live music**, look for suggestions in this book, buy local papers with weekend listings headed *Lazer*, which should have a list of bars with music, concerts and *dancetarias*, or ask a tourist office for advice.

Local radio is often worth listening to – you won't regret taking a transistor along and whirling the dial – and there are also local TV stations that often have **MPB** (Música Popular Brasileira) programmes; the TVE, Televisão Educativa network, funded by the Catholic Church and the Ministry of Culture, is worth checking – if you see the initials FUNARTE, it might well be a music programme.

Finally, a word about **buying CDs**. The price varies according to how well known the recording artist is. Recordings even by leading artists are less expensive than in the US or Europe, and those by more obscure artists and regional music are cheaper still. At the upper end of the scale, but dependably high quality, are the *A Arte de. . .* , *O Talento de. . .* or *A Personalidade de. . .* series, often double albums, which are basically "Greatest Hits" compilations of the best-known singers and musicians. The best place to buy any music, no matter how regional, is São Paulo, then Rio, with cities like Recife, Salvador, Belo Horizonte and Porto Alegre a long way behind. Outside Rio and São Paulo there are good music shops, but they're few and far between: look in local papers to see if there are adverts for *Loja de Disco* (record shop), with MPB or *discos nacionais* mentioned in the advert. You will see pirated CDs being sold on street corners and stalls everywhere – while the rip-offs of major artists will be terrible quality, this is a good way of buying local music, since many local musicians use streetsellers to make extra money even if they have a record contract. Vendors are happy to play you sample tracks.

Books

The flood of books on the Amazon masks the fact that Brazil is not well covered by books in English. With some exceptions, good books on Brazil tend to be either fairly expensive or are out of print. Easily available paperbacks are given here, together with a selection of others that a good bookshop or library will have in stock or will be able to order. Apart from the novels of Jorge Amado, for example, the riches of Brazilian literature lie largely untranslated. There is still no widely available translation of Graciliano's *Barren Lives*, the best modern Brazilian novel. Where separate editions exist in the UK and US, publishers are separated by a semicolon in the listings below, with the UK company given first. University Press is abbreviated to UP, out of print to o/p.

Brazil itself has been publishing a growing number of beautifully produced coffee-table books on its architectural and artistic heritage and natural history, often with parallel English-language text. These make great souvenirs, but you'll need to snap them up as print runs tend to be small and you may not find the same book later.

The best introductions

Elizabeth Bishop *One Art* (Farrar, Straus and Giroux). One of the best American poets of the twentieth century spent much of her adult life in Brazil, living in the hills behind Petrópolis from 1951 to 1969 but travelling widely. This selection from her letters and diaries is an intimate, sharp-eyed chronicle of Brazil in those years, and much else.

Annette Haddad and Scott Doggett (eds) *Travelers' Tales: Brazil* (Travelers' Tales). A superb anthology of extracts from books and magazine articles by journalists, anthropologists, historians and other travellers to Brazil, which will make you want to search out the publications they're drawn from. Although a great read, it's a pity that more wasn't done to include the work of Brazilian authors.

D. Hess and R. DaMatta *The Brazilian Puzzle* (Columbia UP). A rare and useful collection of Brazilian perspectives on Brazilian culture; sociologists and anthropologists contribute essays on a variety of topics – race, gender, politics, the courts, sex – of variable quality, but a valuable chance to see Brazil through Brazilian eyes, for a change.

Ruth Landes *The City of Women* (New Mexico UP). New edition of a classic first published in 1947: an American woman anthropologist remembers her time in Bahia studying *candomblé* and Afro-Brazilian culture. Written for the general reader, and over fifty years on still the best introduction there is to both the Northeast and racial issues in Brazil.

Claude Lévi-Strauss *Tristes Tropiques* (Picador, o/p; Penguin). The great French anthropologist describes his four years spent in 1930s Brazil – arguably the best book ever written about the country by a foreigner. There are famous descriptions of sojourns with Nambikwara and Tupi-Kawahib Indians, epic journeys and a remarkable eyewitness account of São Paulo exploding into a metropolis. Essential reading. *Saudades do Brasil: A Photographic Memoir* (Washington UP) is a beautifully produced collection that makes a wonderful companion to *Tristes Tropiques*, featuring some of the thousands of photographs Lévi-Strauss took, few of which were ever published.

Robert M. Levine and John J. Crocitti (eds) *The Brazil Reader: History, Culture, Politics* (Latin America Bureau; Duke UP). The breadth of subject matter in this thoughtful anthology is impressive, covering Brazil from colonial times to the present, using book and article extracts, original documents and historical photographs. If it wasn't for the volume's sheer weight, the book would be the perfect travel companion.

Hugh Raffles *In Amazonia: A Natural History* (Princeton UP). Superbly written mixture of history, anthropology and geography, exploring the gap between the way outsiders and Amazonians think about the region and its landscapes, and periodically very moving in its interweaving of personal memory with wider concerns.

Thomas E. Skidmore *Brazil: Five Centuries of Change* (Oxford UP). Readable account of the emergence of Brazilian national identity, from the first European contact to the present day. The author, a renowned US "Brazilianist", made important contributions to the discussion of racial ideology and the analysis of twentieth-century Brazilian political development, and this book is an excellent synthesis of his work and that of other Brazilian and foreign scholars.

Travel

The Amazon

Alan Campbell *Getting to Know Waiwai: An Amazonian Ethnography* (Routledge). Superbly written and wrenching book. A Scottish anthropologist writes of two years among the Wayapí of Amapá, as they try to come to terms with Brazilian society.

Colonel P. H. Fawcett *Exploration Fawcett* (o/p). Fawcett carries his stiff upper lip in and out of some of the most disease-infested, dangerous and downright frightening parts of interior Brazil. It's a rattling good read, compiled by his son from Fawcett's diaries and letters after his disappearance. Readily available in secondhand bookshops. For more on Fawcett, see p.606.

Stephen Nugent *Big Mouth: The Amazon Speaks* (Fourth Estate, o/p; Brown Trout Publications). Essential

Useful addresses

Anglo-Brazilian Society 32 Green St, London W1Y 3FD ⓣ020/7493-8493. Organizes events based on the culture and history of Brazil.

Brazilian Contemporary Arts Palingswick House, 241 King St, London W6 9LP ⓣ020/8741-9579, ⓦwww.brazilian.org.uk. Promotes Brazilian cultural events and festivals, and offers language classes as well.

Canning House Library 2 Belgrave Square, London SW1X 8PH ⓣ020/7235-2303, ⓦwww.canninghouse.com. An excellent source of old and new books on Brazil in English.

Latin America Bureau 1 Amwell St, London EC1R 1UL ⓣ020/7278-2829, ⓦwww.latinamericabureau.org. Publishers. A number of their titles appear in this book list.

and hilarious reading, not least as an antidote to the gooey rainforest literature. Jaundiced anthropologist returns to old haunts in Belém and Santarém, debunking as he goes. There is no better guide to the complexities of modern Amazônia; convincing and depressing at the same time.

Anthony Smith *Explorers of the Amazon* (Chicago UP). A chapter devoted to each of the main explorers of the Amazon from the sixteenth to the nineteenth centuries, written for the general reader and showing that truth can be stranger than fiction; those who remember Klaus Kinski's demented portrayal of Aguirre in the film *Aguirre, Wrath of God* will be shocked to realize he actually played down the extent of the conquistador's madness.

Nigel Smith *The Amazon River Forest: A Natural History of Plants, Animals and People* (Oxford UP) An expert with the rare knack of writing clearly and interestingly for the general public tells you all you need to know about the flood plain from the year dot to the present. A great book for a long river journey, and many fine photos too.

Mato Grosso and Brasília

Richard Gott *Land Without Evil: Utopian Journeys Across the South American Watershed* (Verso). Although the subject matter is centred on eastern Bolivia, this is an important look at the swampland between the River Plate and the River Amazon, exploring the region through the adventures of missionaries and explorers and through the travels of the author himself.

Alex Shoumatoff *The Capital of Hope: Brasília and its People* (Vintage). The author talked with government officials and settlers – rich and poor – to weave a very readable account of the first 25 years of the Brazilian capital.

Minas Gerais

Glenn Alan Cheney *Journey on the Estrada Real: Encounters in the Mountains of Brazil* (Academy Chicago, US). A beautiful account of a walk tracing the northern section of the *Estrada Real* (the Royal Road, also known as the *Caminho do Ouro*) from Mariana to Diamantina. Cheney offers descriptions of hamlets and villages way off the beaten track – where, for better or worse, life appears to have stood still for generations – and meditations on how communities such as these can survive "devlopment" and the impact of globalization.

Rio de Janeiro

Ruy Castro *Rio de Janeiro (*Bloomsbury*)*. Ruy Castro, a renowned journalist, offers an historical and cultural overview of Rio and, far more importantly, captures his fellow *cariocas'* soul. Leaving Castro's sometimes irritating generalizations, this book provides an alluring entry into Rio life.

The South

Alexander Leonard *The Valley of the Latin Bear* (o/p). A delightful account of everyday life in an isolated German village in Santa Catarina. Although written some forty years ago, the account remains very recognizable and it's still well worth seeking out.

Guy Walmisley-Dresser *Brazilian Paradise* (o/p). Romantic reminiscences of growing up on a cattle ranch in Rio Grande do Sul in the late nineteenth century. The anecdotes are both amusing and full of insight and tell of a part of Brazil that, although distinctive in character, is all but ignored by travel writers.

The Northeast

Peter Robb *A Death in Brazil* (Bloomsbury UK; John Macrae Books, USA). Sporadically vivid travel writing focused mainly on Recife and Alagoas, interspersed with analysis of the Collor years. Those coming to this from Robb's brilliant *Midnight in Sicily* will be disappointed with his much more superficial knowledge of Brazil. But the quality of his writing makes this a good introduction to the Northeast all the same.

History

Euclides da Cunha *Rebellion in the Backlands* (Picador; Chicago UP). Also known by its Portuguese title *Os Sertões*, this remains perhaps Brazil's greatest historical account. An epic tale of Antônio Conselheiro's short-lived holy city, the Canudos Rebellion and its brutal suppression that left some 15,000 dead, the book is also a powerful meditation on Brazilian civilization.

R.B. Cunningham Graham *A Vanished Arcadia* (o/p). Cunningham Graham's passionate and rather romanticized account of the rise and fall of the Jesuit missions in South America was first published in 1901 and has become a classic on the subject.

Cyrus and James Dawsey (eds) *The Confederados: Old South Immigrants in Brazil* (Alabama UP). An extremely readable collection of essays by US and Brazilian scholars looking at different aspects of the experience of immigrants from the former Confederacy and their descendants. Contributions discuss the history of the agricultural settlements as well as the cultural (in particular religious) influence of the immigrants on the wider society and linguistic change.

Warren Dean *With Brandaxe and Firestorm* (California UP). Brilliant and very readable environmental history that tells the story of the almost complete destruction of the Mata Atlântica, the coastal rainforest of southern Brazil, from colonial times to the twentieth century.

Todd Diacon *Millennarian Vision, Capitalist Reality: Brazil's Contestado Rebellion 1912–1916* (Duke UP). An analysis of the motivation behind the men and women caught up in the Contestado Rebellion, exploring both the millennarian aspects and the response to the seizure of territory by European immigrants. The rebels attacked train stations, sawmills and immigrant colonies in Santa Catarina and Paraná but were ultimately outnumbered and outgunned. An important ground-up look at the last dramatic attempts at survival on the part of a subsistence-based economy.

Boris Fausto *A Concise History of Brazil* (Cambridge UP). The best single-volume introductory history of Brazil, written by an eminent historian from São Paulo. The author successfully demonstrates how Brazil has changed, both politically and socio-economically, despite being so often characterized by apparent historical inertia.

John Hemming *Red Gold: The Conquest of the Brazilian Indians* (o/p). The definitive history of the topic, well written and thoroughly researched. Both passionate and scholarly, it's a basic book for anyone interested in the Indian question in Brazil. Companion volumes, *Amazon Frontier: The Defeat of the Brazilian Indian* (Pan) and *Die if You Must: The Brazilian Indians in the Twentieth Century* (Pan), bring the depressing story up to date.

Thomas H. Holloway *Coffee and Society in São Paulo, 1886–1934* (North Carolina UP, US, o/p). A detailed look at the labour system that evolved on the coffee plantations of São Paulo, and the experiences of two million immigrants who worked them.

Billy Jaynes Chandler *The Bandit King: Lampião of Brazil* (Texas UP, US). Compulsive reading that seems like fiction but is well-documented fact. Based on original sources and interviews with participants and witnesses, an American historian with a talent for snappy writing reconstructs the action-packed (and myth-encrusted) life of the famous social bandit, complete with fascinating photographs.

Robert M. Levine *Vale of Tears: Revisiting the Canudos Massacre in Northeastern Brazil 1893–1897* (California UP). A vivid portrait of backland life and a detailed examination of the myths behind the community, arguing that the Canudos threatened the labour supply of local landowners, causing the state government to begin its campaign against the settlement by portraying the inhabitants as degenerate fanatics. Shocking but utterly compelling reading.

Stephen Lone *The Japanese Community in Brazil, 1908–1940* (Palgrave). This is a welcome introduction to the history of Brazil's important Japanese community, drawing largely from Japanese sources. The author argues against the uniqueness of the Japanese community, suggesting that they were not particularly the subject of racism or hostility and that the hardships that were overcome were no greater – and sometimes less – than those of other immigrant groups.

Frederick C. Luebke *Germans in Brazil: A Comparative History of Cultural Conflict During World War I* (Louisiana State UP). One of the very few studies in English on Germans in Brazil. Despite the title, this social history covers the period 1818–1918, though the focus is World War I, when Brazilians of German origin began to accept that they could not remain foreigners in their own country.

Oliver Marshall *English, Irish and Irish-American Pioneer Settlers in Nineteenth-Century Brazil* (Centre for Brazilian Studies, University of Oxford). In the 1860s and 1870s several thousand people were recruited in England and New York for agricultural settlements in southern Brazil. This book discusses what motivated the organizers of this venture and vividly describes the grim fate of the immigrants.

Katia M. de Queiros Mattoso *To be a Slave in Brazil, 1550–1888* (Rutgers UP, US). A history of slavery in Brazil, unusually written from the perspective of the slave. Writing for the general reader, the author divides her excellent study into three themes: the process of enslavement, life in slavery and the escape from slavery.

Colin McEwan, Cristiana Barreto and Eduardo Neves (eds.) *Unknown Amazon: Culture in Nature in Ancient Brazil* (British Museum). Fantastically illustrated and photographed companion volume to a 2001 exhibition at the British Museum, revealing revolutionary discoveries on the scale and complexity of late prehistoric indigenous cultures in the Amazon.

Joseph A. Page *The Brazilians* (Addison-Wesley). A cultural history of Brazil in a clear if eclectic style, drawing on sources ranging from economics and political psychology to film and literature. The author is a professor of law at Georgetown University.

João José Reis *Slave Rebellion in Brazil: The Muslim Uprising of 1835 in Bahia* (Johns Hopkins UP). The last major slave rebellion in Brazil began on January 24, 1835, confronting soldiers and civilians. This is a unique portrait of urban slavery and an absorbing account of the most important urban slave rebellion in the Americas and the only one where Islam played a major role, detailing the background of the conspiracy and the brutal repression and punishment of Africans that followed.

Peter Rivière *Absent-Minded Imperialism: Britain and the Expansion of Empire in Nineteenth-Century Brazil* (Tauris). Hilarious, dryly written account of how the border between Brazil and French Guiana came to be drawn, an extraordinary and forgotten story of fanatical missionaries, mutual misunderstanding between British and Brazilian officials, and bewildered Indians stuck in the middle unaware of the diplomatic problems they were causing. A minor classic.

Eduardo Silva *Prince of the People: The Life and Times of a Brazilian Free Man of Colour* (Verso). Was Dom Obá II d'Africa a genuine prince, or was he merely an unbalanced son of slaves with delusions? Whatever the truth, Dom Obá was revered by the poor around him, and his story also sheds light on the life of slaves and people of colour in Rio, and on popular thought during the final decades of slavery.

Stanley Stein *Vassouras: A Brazilian Coffee County, 1850–1900* (Princeton UP). Re-edition of a 1940s classic that improves with age. On the surface, a straightforward reconstruction of the rise and fall of the coffee plantation system in a town in the interior of Rio. Look closer and you see a devastating indictment of slavery, based on archive work but also, uniquely, on the memories of the last generation to have been born as slaves. Also includes a fascinating selection of photos.

Patrick Wilcken *Empire Adrift: The Portuguese Court in Rio de Janeiro 1808–1821* (Bloomsbury). In 1807 the Portuguese royal family, accompanied by 10,000 aristocrats, servants, government officials and priests, fled Lisbon in advance of Napoleon's invading army, which was sweeping across the Iberian Peninsula. In this wonderfully lively account, the author brings to life the incredible atmosphere in Lisbon and Rio during this key episode in Brazilian history.

Politics and society

Sue Branford and Bernardo Kucinski *Politics Transformed: Lula and the Workers' Party in Brazil* (Latin America Bureau). An impassioned if rather starry-eyed look at the rise of the PT, the most powerful socialist party in the Americas, charting its development from trade union resistance to the military regime in São Paulo to the election of its leader – Lula – as president of Brazil in 2002.

Sue Branford and Jan Rocha *Cutting the Wire: The Story of the Landless Movement in Brazil* (Latin America Bureau). Written by journalists with long experience of Brazil, this book tells the story of one of the most remarkable popular movements of modern times, the MST (or Landless Workers Movement). This much-needed book discusses the historical background as well as the movement's links with wider anti-globalization struggles, deforestation and rural violence.

Gilberto Dimenstein *Brazil: War on Children* (Latin America Bureau; Monthly Review, o/p). A grim but compelling picture of life for the street children of São Paulo, but true also for most Brazilian cities. The children, living in constant fear of death squads made up of off-duty police and other vigilantes, survive as best they can as petty criminals, beggars and prostitutes, supporting one another in small gangs.

Tobias Hecht *At Home in the Street* (Cambridge UP). Excellent study of street children and those who deal with them, from death squads to social workers. Based on work in Recife, but equally applicable to any large Brazilian city.

Dan Linger *Nobody Home: Brazilian Selves Remade in Brazil* (Stanford UP). Brazil has the largest Japanese population outside Japan and many Brazilians, Japanese and not, move back and forth between the two countries doing the work the Japanese prefer to leave to others. This is a sensitive, accessible study of their lives, problems and dreams.

Maxine L. Margolis *Little Brazil: An Ethnography of Brazilian Immigrants in New York City* (Princeton UP). Since the early 1980s, there's been considerable migration from Brazil, especially to Europe and the US. The greatest concentration of expatriate Brazilians – especially educated middle classes from Minas Gerais – is in the New York City area, with most living in Long Island, Manhattan and Astoria. The community's heart is Little Brazil, a one-block stretch of Manhattan's West 46th Street, and this is a thoroughly readable exploration into community life.

Roberto da Matta *Carnival, Rogues and Heroes* (Notre Dame UP, o/p). A collection of essays by one of Brazil's leading anthropologists, who also teaches in the US. They include some very stimulating – and entertaining – dissections of Carnaval.

Ruben Oliven *Tradition Matters: Modern Gaúcho Identity* (Columbia UP). This is not about the life of "cowboys" in southern Brazil, but rather an examination of the predominantly urban, middle-class social movement that prizes an idealized rural lifestyle of which it has no real experience. Oliven points up the apparent paradox in Brazil (as elsewhere) of ever-increasing cultural globalization and the strengthening of regional identity. An important study illuminating a part of Brazil largely ignored by outsiders – Brazilian as well as foreign.

Thomas Skidmore *Politics in Brazil 1930–1964; The Politics of Military Rule in Brazil 1964–85* (Oxford UP). The former is the standard work on Brazilian politics from the rise of Vargas until the 1964 military takeover. The latter continues the story to the resumption of Brazil's shaky democracy.

Gender issues

Caipora Women's Group *Women in Brazil* (Latin America Bureau). Articles, poems and interviews about life for women on farms, in fishing communities and in *favelas*. The issues repeat themselves: racism, machismo, legal rights, religious and feminist beliefs. A welcome relief from published doctoral dissertations, this is both important and highly readable, both depressing and uplifting.

Herbert Daniel and Richard Parker *Sexuality, Politics and AIDS in Brazil* (Falmer Press, US). Excellent, clearly written history of AIDS in Brazil, covering the way the epidemic has developed in relation to popular culture at one end, and government policy at the other. There are bright spots – Brazilian TV health education slots on AIDS may be the best in the world, completely frank, and often screamingly funny, but this book will help you understand how this can coexist with a scandalous lack of supervision of blood banks.

Richard Parker *Bodies, Pleasures and Passions* (Beacon Press, US). A provocative analysis of the erotic in Brazilian history and popular culture, written by an American anthropologist resident in Brazil. Tremendous subject matter and some fascinating insights into sexual behaviour, combining insider and outsider perspectives.

Daphne Patai *Brazilian Women Speak: Contemporary Life Stories* (Rutgers UP, US). Oral testimony forms the core of this very readable work that lets ordinary women from the Northeast and Rio speak for themselves to describe the struggles, constraints and hopes of their lives.

Nancy Scheper Hughes *Death Without Weeping: The Violence of Everyday Life in Brazil* (California UP). An often shocking, ultimately depressing anthropological study of *favela* women, and in particular of childbirth, motherhood and infant death. Although over-long – judicious skipping is in order – it is very accessible to the general reader, interesting, and often moving.

João Trevisan *Perverts in Paradise* (GMP, US, o/p). This is a fascinating survey of Brazilian gay life ranging from the papal inquisition to pop idols, transvestite *macumba* priests and guerrilla idols.

Race

Darién J. Davis *Afro-Brazilians: Time for Recognition* (Minority Rights Group, UK). A valuable introduction to the role of black people in Brazilian society, focusing on Afro-Brazilians in national culture and the human rights struggle. Produced for a respected British-based NGO, the report is scholarly, impassioned and essential reading for anyone wanting to understand the often contradictory nature of Brazilian racial ideology and politics.

Gilberto Freyre *The Masters and the Slaves* (California UP, US, o/p). Classic history of plantation life in the Northeast, with a wealth of detail (includes index headings like "Smutty Stories and Expressions" and "Priests, Bastards of"). Very readable, even if Freyre's somewhat simplistic theories are now out of fashion or discredited. His *The Mansion and the Shanties* (Greenwood) deals with the early growth of urban Brazil.

George Reid Andrews *Blacks and Whites in São Paulo 1888–1988* (Wisconsin UP). Why is the notion of a racial democracy still so widely accepted while at the same time people are fully aware that for all practical purposes it's a complete myth? For large proportions of Brazilians, racism is a fact of life and this is an interesting examination of how the state has long encouraged myths of black inferiority and perpetuates racial stereotypes.

Thomas E. Skidmore *Black into White: Race and Nationality in Brazilian Thought* (Duke UP). First published in 1974, this 1993 edition has a new preface to bring the book up to date. A landmark in the intellectual history of Brazilian racial ideology, examining scientific racism and the Brazilian intellectual elite's supposed belief in assimilation and the ideal of whitening.

Frances W. Twine *Racism in a Racial Democracy* (Rutgers UP). Fascinating ethnography of racism in a small Brazilian town, by a black American sociologist interested in the differences between Brazilian and American racial politics.

The Amazon

David Cleary *Anatomy of the Amazon Gold Rush* (Macmillan, o/p; Iowa UP). Clearly written introduction to an important topic, with some spectacular photographs.

Warren Dean *Brazil and the Struggle for Rubber* (Cambridge UP). Good environmental history of the rubber boom and subsequent failed attempts to set up rubber plantations in the Amazon.

Peter A. Furley (ed) *The Forest Frontier: Settlement and Change in Brazilian Roraima* (Routledge, UK). An interesting and rare look at the state of Roraima, one of Brazil's last regions to be settled by outsiders. Dry academic geography in style but a wealth of up-to-date detail on Indian life and the history of colonization, land use, environmental change and the effects of deforestation.

Susanna Hecht and Alexander Cockburn *The Fate of the Forest* (Penguin; Verso). Head and shoulders above other studies of the crisis in the Amazon. Excellently written and researched – check out the footnotes – this is as good an introduction to the problem as you will find. Very strong on Amazonian history, too – essential to understanding what's going on, but often ignored by Amazon commentators.

Gordon Macmillan *At the End of the Rainbow* (Earthscan; Columbia UP). Very interesting dissection of the issues behind the headlines about the Yanomami Indians and the invasion of their reserves by gold-miners.

Chico Mendes and Tony Gross *Fight for the Forest: Chico Mendes in His Own Words* (Latin America Bureau; Inland Book Co). Long, moving passages from a series of interviews the rubber tappers' union leader gave shortly before his assassination in 1988. Well translated and with useful notes giving background to the issues raised. Direct from the sharp end of the Amazon land crisis.

Marianne Schmink and Charles Wood *Contested Frontiers in Amazonia* (Columbia UP). The best of the more recent academic books on modern Amazônia that examines a town and region in southern Pará before, during and after the construction of the highway network. Clearly written and very interesting, especially in its description of how the Kayapo Indians adapted to a gold rush.

Candace Slater *Dance of the Dolphins* (Chicago UP). Interesting compendium of the many legends and folk tales centring on river dolphins, beautifully translated. There is a clumsy academic subtext linking the stories with environmental destruction in the Amazon, but you can skip those bits. There is no better book for giving you a feel for the popular imagination in the small towns you pass through on a river trip.

Charles Wagley *Amazon Town* (o/p). Classic anthropological study of an interior Amazon town during the 1940s that inspired generations of students. Written with incisive style and complete command of the material.

Flora and fauna

Henry Bates *The Naturalist on the River Amazon* (o/p). A Victorian botanist describes his years spent collecting in the Amazon, in an obscure but wonderful book. Bates's boyish scientific excitement illuminates every page – a fascinated, and very English, eye cast over the Amazon and its people.

Balthasar Dubs *Birds of Southwestern Brazil* (Beltrona, Switzerland). Essential reading if you're heading for the Pantanal. The main body of the book is a comprehensive annotated and illustrated list of species in the region.

Margaret Mee *In Search of the Flowers of the Amazon Forest* (Nonesuch, UK). The best of the natural history books by some way. Mee was a British botanist who dedicated her life to travelling the Amazon and painting its plant life. She died in a car crash in 1988, and this beautiful book is a fitting tribute to her. It includes descriptions of her many journeys, good photographs, and lavish reproductions of her wonderful drawings and paintings.

David L. Pearson and Les Beletsky *Brazil: Amazon and Pantanal – The Ecotravellers' Wildlife Guide* (Academic Press). The main body of this book examines the regions' ecosystems and the threats they face before moving on to chapters discussing insects, amphibians, reptiles, birds, mammals and fish. Richly illustrated and clearly written, the book will enrich any visit to the Amazon or Pantanal.

Philips Guides (Horizonte Geografico). An excellent Brazilian series of English language guides aimed at the ecotourist. So far, titles include the *Amazon*, *Pantanal*, *National Parks of Brazil*, *Northeast* and *South*, and all are full of practical information and photos, and especially useful for hikers, nature-lovers and beach bums. In Brazil, good bookshops in large cities should stock them. Also check ⓦwww.horizontegeografico.com.br for details on ordering them from abroad.

Helmut Sick *Birds in Brazil* (Princeton UP). An English translation of an encyclopedic Brazilian work. The illustrations are superb, but it's too hefty to travel with. More portable guides include Hilty and Brown's *A Guide to the Birds of Colombia* (Princeton UP), and Schaunsee's *Birds of Venezuela* (Princeton UP), which both have considerable overlap for Brazil's western and northern Amazônia, while Narosky and Yzuriea's *Birds of Argentina and Uruguay: A Field Guide* (Vazques Mazzini) is valuable for southern Brazil.

Deotado Souza *All the Birds of Brazil: An Identification Guide* (DALL, Brazil). This handbook clearly describes birds that are found in Brazil, and includes location maps and fairly good colour illustrations. Although published in Brazil, don't expect to stumble across a copy there; instead purchase one from a specialist bookseller before leaving home. An essential companion for any remotely serious Brazil-bound birdwatcher.

Arts and leisure

Architecture

Lauro Cavalcanti *When Brazil Was Modern: Guide to Architecture, 1928–1960* (Princeton Architectural Press, US). This valuable guide to Brazil's unique contribution to modernist architecture discusses the work of over thirty architects, with sections on specific sites such as Brasília, Pampulha (Belo Horizonte) and the Ministry of Health and Education building in Rio. Compact, but well illustrated, the book makes a perfect travel companion for modernist junkies.

Deutsches Architektur Museum (ed) *Oscar Niemeyer: A Legend of Modernism* (Birkhäuser). This sumptuously produced book is a concise survey of Niemeyer's work from his first commissions in Rio in the early 1930s, through Pampulha and Brasília in the 1940s to 1960s, to Niterói's Museu de Arte Contemporânia of the late 1990s. Included are essays by architectural critics which, although at times overly fawning, help illuminate Niemeyer's architectural legacy.

Marta Iris Montero *Burle Marx: The Lyrical Landscape* (Thames & Hudson; California UP). A beautifully illustrated book celebrating the life and work of one of the twentieth century's foremost landscape architects, who designed many of Brazil's prominent parks, gardens and other urban spaces (the most famous of which are probably the flowing mosaics alongside Copacabana and Flamengo beaches).

Fernando Tasso Fracaso Pires *Fazenda: The Great Houses and Plantations of Brazil* (Abbeville Press). A lavish coffee-table book, richly illustrated with photographs of coffee, sugar and cattle *fazenda* houses. There's a useful historical introduction discussing the importance of the *casa grande* in Brazilian society, followed by a look at individual houses, mainly in rural Rio de Janeiro and São Paulo, but also Minas Gerais, Pernambuco, Bahia and Rio Grande do Sul.

Fine art and photography

Gilberto Ferrez *Photography in Brazil 1840–1900* (New Mexico UP, US, o/p). One of the little-known facts about Brazil is that the first-ever non-portrait photograph was taken of the Paço da Cidade in Rio in 1840, by a Frenchman hot off a ship with the new-fangled Daguerrotype. This is a fascinating compendium of the pioneering work of early photographers in Brazil, including material from all over the country, although the stunning panoramas of Rio from the 1860s onward are arguably the highlight.

Daniel Levine (ed) *The Brazilian Photographs of Genevieve Naylor, 1940–1942* (Duke UP). Recently uncovered photographs by a young American photographer, mainly of Rio, Salvador and the small towns of the interior. They are a revelation: Naylor was a great photographer, interested in people and street scenes, not landscapes, and this is a unique visual record of Brazil and its people during the Vargas years.

Edward Lucie-Smith *Latin American Art of the Twentieth Century* (Thames & Hudson). It's a pity there aren't volumes on other periods in Latin American art in this excellent and easy-to-obtain series. Still, this is valuable as a look at the Brazilian scene in the context of Latin American art in general.

Edward J. Sullivan (ed) *Brazil Body & Soul* (Guggenheim Museum, US). Remarkably, there is still no thorough overview of Brazilian art history, but this lavishly illustrated catalogue to the 2001/2002 New York and Bilbao exhibition is a pretty good starting point. The catalogue offers glimpses of the art of indigenous cultures and the paintings of Frans Post and Albert Eckhout, two seventeenth-century Dutch visitors, before moving on to discuss in greater detail Baroque art and architecture, Afro-Brazilian art, and twentieth-century artistic movements including Brazil's important contributions to modernist and concrete art.

Alberto Taliani *Brazil* (Tiger Books International; Smithmark). A coffee-table book with around one hundred moody and eye-catching photos depicting Brazil as a diverse nation, including some striking juxtapositions of race, culture and wealth (or lack of it). From wildlife to beach life, and from Indians to modern architecture, the book stands as much on the thematic eye of the photographer as it does on the good-quality images themselves.

Music, dance and capoeira

Bira Almeida *Capoeira – a Brazilian Art Form* (North Atlantic Books). A *capoeira mestre* (master) explains the history and philosophy behind this African–Brazilian martial art/dance form. The book offers valuable background information for those who practise *capoeira* and for those who are merely interested.

Ruy Castro *Bossa Nova – The Story of the Brazilian Music That Seduced the World* (A Capella). A welcome translation of an excellent book by a Brazilian journalist and biographer. This is basically an oral history of bossa nova, packed with incidental detail on Rio nightlife and city culture of the 1950s and early 1960s. A very good read.

Alma Guillermoprieto *Samba* (Bloomsbury, o/p; Vintage). The author, a trained dancer and a well-known journalist, describes a year that she spent with Rio's Mangueira samba school, introducing us to other participants who dedicate their lives to preparing for the four days of Carnaval.

Chris McGowan and Ricardo Pessanha *The Brazilian Sound: Samba, Bossa Nova and the Popular Music of Brazil* (Temple UP). An easy-to-flick-through and well-written basic manual on modern Brazilian music and musicians. Good to carry with you if you're planning on doing some serious music buying. There's also a useful bibliography and a good discography.

Claus Schreiner *Musica Brasileira* (Marion Boyars, US). Detailed coverage of all aspects of Brazilian music from colonial times through to the present within the broader context of the country's culture and history. One for the specialist.

Caetano Veloso *Tropical Truth: A Story of Music and Revolution in Brazil* (Bloomsbury; Knopf). The maestro's account of *tropicalismo* and his early career, including exile, from the 1960s to the early 1970s. Veloso is as good a writer as you would expect, a little over-anxious to show off his learning sometimes, but this is a fascinating despatch from the culture wars of the 1960s.

Cooking

Michael Bateman *Street Café Brazil* (Conran Octopus; Contemporary Books). The title is rather deceptive, as you're unlikely to come across many of these recipes on Brazilian street stalls, but the recipes are authentic, and the lavish pictures are enough to inspire you to attempt to reproduce them at home.

Christopher Idone *Brazil: A Cook's Tour* (Pavilion; Clarkson Potter). A region-by-region look at Brazilian cooking, its origins and influences, with a few recipes thrown in as well. The colour photos of ingredients, markets and dishes are mouthwatering and the text lively and informative. It's good to see São Paulo and the Amazon being discussed separately and at length (when it comes to cookbooks usually only Rio and Bahia get a look in), but why is the South completely ignored?

Joan and David Peterson *Eat Smart in Brazil: How to Decipher the Menu, Know the Market Foods & Embark on a Tasting Adventure* (Ginkgo Press). The title says it all: a guide for selecting food, both in shops and markets and off a menu, in Brazil. The book is divided into three main sections: a region-by-region account of food ingredients and cooking styles, with some recipes and listings of Brazilian ingredients and dishes. A must for any foodie who needs to know the difference between *pimenta malagueta*, *pimenta-do-cheiro* and *pimenta-do-reino*.

Football

Alex Bellos *Futebol: The Brazilian Way of Life* (Bloomsbury). Long overdue, accessible, literate and engaging analysis of Brazilian football, from its early history to the present day and its compulsive mixture of world-class players on the pitch and equally world-class levels of corruption. Written by a journalist with an eye for original stories such as homesick Brazilians playing in the Faroe Islands, tactics for transvestites, and much more. Essential reading.

Josh Lacey *God is Brazilian: Charles Miller, the Man Who Brought Football to Brazil* (Tempus, UK). A well-researched and entertaining account of the life and times of Charles Miller, the Anglo-Brazilian who is credited with introducing modern football to Brazil. Football apart, the book offers fascinating observations regarding late Victorian and Edwardian British society both in England and São Paulo.

Pelé *Pelé – The Autobiography* (Simon & Schuster, UK). Published to coincide with the 2006 World Cup, the long-awaited autobiography of the world's most famous Brazilian should appeal not just to those obsessed by football. The book is sure to please anyone interested in Pelé's remarkable life, from his childhood in Bauru to years playing football in Brazil and the US to his involvement in national and international politics.

Chris Taylor *The Beautiful Game: A Journey Through Latin American Football* (Latin America Bureau; Perennial). Pinching Pelé's catch phrase for the title, this clever paperback is a journalistic report on the football subculture in Brazil and other Latin American countries, often linked to both big business and drug trafficking.

Fiction

Works by Brazilian authors

Jorge Amado *Gabriela, Clove and Cinnamon*; *Tereza Batista* (both Abacus, o/p; Avon); *Dona Flor and Her Two Husbands* (Serpent's Tail; Avon); *The Violent Lands* (Collins; Avon). Amado is the proverbial rollicking good read, a fine choice for the beach or on long bus journeys. He's by far the best-known Brazilian writer abroad – there is even a French wine named after him. Purists might quibble that the local colour is laid on with a trowel, but Amado's blend of the erotic and exotic has him laughing all the way to the bank.

Mário de Andrade *Macunaíma* (Quartet Books, UK). First published in 1928, *Macunaíma* is considered one of the greatest works of Brazilian literature. In this comic tale of the adventures of a popular hero, Macunaíma, a figure from the jungle interior, Andrade presents his typical wealth of exotic images, myths and legends.

Machado de Assis *Posthumous Memoirs of Brás Cubas* (Oxford UP). The most important work by the finest novelist Brazil has yet produced. Told by one of the most remarkable characters in fiction, this is an often-hilarious tale of absurd schemes to cure the world of melancholy and half-hearted political ambitions unleashed from beyond the grave. For good translations of Machado's great short stories, *The Devil's Church and Other Stories* (Texas UP, US, o/p) and *Helena* (California UP) are worth going to some trouble to get hold of. His cool, ferociously ironic style veers between black comedy and sardonic analysis of the human condition.

Patrícia Galvão (Pagu) *Industrial Park: A Proletarian Novel* (Nebraska UP). An avant-garde novel first published in 1933. Set in the rapidly changing São Paulo factory district of Brás, this remarkable novel captures the sense of time and place, reproducing the voice of a city in the midst of rapid change.

Luiz Afredo Garcia-Roza *The Silence of the Rain* (Picador; Henry Holt). A police procedural thriller by one of Brazil's bestselling writers. Inspector Espinosa is the unorthodox detective who solves a complex web of crime – murder, robbery and fraud – against the backdrop of the sometimes seedy, sometimes exotic, setting of Rio. The inspector returns in the equally compulsive mysteries *December Heat* and *Pursuit*.

Milton Hatoum *The Brothers* (Bloomsbury). Set in late nineteenth-century Manaus, this is a family saga based on Lebanese twin brothers and their relationship with their mother. Filled with local colour, this is one of the best Brazilian novels in translation to emerge in recent years.

Paulo Lins *City of God* (Bloomsbury; Grove Press). The author, who went on to become a photo journalist, was brought up in Rio's *Cidade de Deus* housing project and uses his knowledge of drug trafficking and gang warfare as the basis of this remarkable novel, the book behind the internationally acclaimed film.

Clarice Lispector *The Hour of the Star* (New Direction, US). The most instantly approachable translation of this work by the important Ukrainian-born writer. Her short stories are carefully constructed but, as an author to whom the existence of plot doesn't seem to matter, her books can be difficult. Other translated titles include *Family Ties* (Carcanet, o/p; Texas UP) and *The Foreign Legion* (New Direction, US).

Patrícia Melo *Inferno* (Bloomsbury, UK). A thriller set in a *favela* in Rio, this is a powerful story of an 11 year-old boy who becomes a local gang leader. Though his story's often grim, the central character is a complex figure in terms of his relationships with other gang members and his family.

Antônio Olinto *The Water House* (Carroll & Graf, US). A wonderful story about an African matriarch and her progeny over a seventy-year period, and the story of her return to West Africa from Bahia after the abolition of slavery. The family saga continues in the *King of Ketu* (R. Collings, US).

Graciliano Ramos *Childhood* (o/p); *São Bernardo* (o/p). Works by the Northeastern novelist who introduced social realism into modern Brazilian fiction. Neither is as good as his masterpiece *Barren Lives* (Texas UP, US), or his prison memoir, *Memórias do Cárcere* (Memories of Jail).

Darlene J. Sadlier (ed) *One Hundred Years After Tomorrow* (Indiana UP). An excellent anthology of short stories introducing the work of twenty twentieth-century Brazilian women, some famous and others less well known.

Moacyr Scliar *The Collected Stories of Moacyr Scliar* (New Mexico UP). Scliar, who hails from Porto Alegre, is Brazil's most distinguished Jewish writer. This anthology includes haunting, comic and bleak stories that proclaim Sciar as a master of the short story.

Márcio Souza *Mad Maria* (Avon, US, o/p). A comic drama set against the backdrop of the absurdity of rail construction in nineteenth-century Amazônia. Souza's excellent *The Emperor of the Amazon* (Abacus, o/p; Avon, o/p) is another humorous and powerful description of the decadence that characterized late nineteenth-century Amazonian society.

Antônio Torres *The Land* (Readers International). Set in a decaying town in the parched interior of the Northeast, this is a grim tale of people trapped and people trying to get away. In *Blues for a Lost Childhood* (Readers International), Torres continues with the same theme, but this time focusing on a journalist who makes it to Rio but finds life there to be a living nightmare.

João Ubaldo Ribeiro *An Invincible Memory* (Faber; HarperCollins, o/p). A family saga spanning a 400-year period from the arrival of the Portuguese in Brazil to the present day, featuring anecdotes, history and myths narrated through the experiences of two Bahian families, one aristocratic, the other enslaved. The book was wildly popular when published in Brazil and is considered a national epic.

Works set in Brazil

Jean-Christophe Rufin *Brazil Red* (Picador; W.W. Norton). The winner of France's prestigious Goncourt literary award, this action-packed historical novel is set against France's ill-fated attempt to conquer Brazil in the sixteenth century as well as questions about the nature of civilization and culture, religion and freedom.

Mario Vargas Llosa *The War of the End of the World* (Faber; Penguin). Goes well with da Cunha. The Peruvian writer produced this haunting novel, based on the events of Canudos, in the 1970s. The translation is good and the book is easy to obtain.

Karen Tei Yamashita *Brazil-Maru* (Coffee House Press, US). The story of Brazil's Japanese immigrant population is told through a multi-generational saga involving conflicts between family members seeking individual freedom in their adopted country and those striving to maintain community cohesion.

Children's literature set in Brazil

Josua Doder *Grk and the Pelotti Gang* (Andersen Press). Along with his dog Grk, Tim, a brave (and fool-hardy) British child finds himself in the mean streets of Rio in search of the notorious Pelotti gang. Fast-paced and funny and with lots of local colour, Tim and Grk survive being kidnapped and being held in a Rio *favela* as well as jungle adventures. Suitable for 8 to 12 year olds.

Eva Ibbotson *Journey to the River Sea* (Macmillan; Puffin). Set at the turn of the twentieth century in Manaus amidst the Amazon rubber boom, this old-fashioned adventure story unfolds in an environment that its host of amusing characters either cherishes or feels nothing but contempt for. Suitable for 9 to 13 year olds.

Brazilian cinema

Brazil and Mexico are the only Latin American countries with strong national cinemas, and the best Brazilian directors, like the best Mexican ones, now work outside Brazil on international productions (Walter Salles on *Motorcycle Diaries* and Francisco Meirelles on *The Constant Gardener*, for example). Brazil has produced excellent films since the 1950s, many of them widely available abroad, and a few nights in front of the DVD player before departure is a good investment in getting the most out of your trip.

Two-way traffic

Brazil, for understandable reasons, has long attracted foreign filmmakers looking for exotic scenery – from James Bond fight sequences on the Pão de Açúcar cable car to *Blame It on Rio*, the lowest moment of Michael Caine's distinguished career. Fred Astaire and Ginger Rogers danced together for the first time in *Flying Down to Rio*, in which 1930s Copacabana, complete with a half-built *Copacabana Palace Hotel*, can be glimpsed below the legs of the dancing girls on the top wing of the biplane in the climactic dance sequence – all of which took place on a Hollywood film set, needless to say.

But other foreigners made a more serious cultural contribution. **Orson Welles** spent many months filming in Brazil immediately after *Citizen Kane* had made him a star. Although he was, characteristically, never able to finish the project, the footage was later put together into a documentary film called *It's All True*, an invaluable record of Rio and Carnaval in the early 1940s. Two decades later, French director Marcel Camus filmed *Orfeu Negro* ("Black Orpheus") in Rio with a largely amateur cast, resetting the Orpheus myth during the Rio Carnaval and putting it to an unforgettable soundtrack by Tom Jobim. *Pixote*, a searing 1982 film about street children in Rio that also used amateurs was directed by Hector Babenco, an Argentinian.

More recently, Brazilians have been moving the other way. Sônia Braga traded in success in Brazilian films in the 1970s for a career in US independent cinema from the 1980s on, but the country's most distinguished cinematic exports have been directors, most notably **Walter Salles**, who caught international attention with *Central Station* in 1998 and the underestimated, beautifully filmed biopic of Che Guavara's early life, *Motorcycle Diaries*, and **Fernando Meirelles**, whose brilliant *City of God* in 2003 led to his being offered *The Constant Gardener* (2005), the first international Hollywood hit to be directed by a Brazilian. Meirelles's filming in the Nairobi slums, conditioned by his experiences of doing the same in Rio, together with his cool, outsider perspective on the British in Africa and at home, was a revelation. His success outside Brazil, with four Oscar nominations so far, is an indication of how Brazilian talent can be a shot in the arm for international cinema.

But Brazilian cinema's recent international success was built on decades of hard work, establishing a national cinema industry and somehow keeping it going in the face of intense competition from television on the one hand and Hollywood on the other. Along the way Brazil has created a national cinema like no other South American country, returning again and again to its history for inspiration.

The early years: chanchadas and cinema novo

The history of Brazilian cinema goes right back to the earliest years of the medium: the first cinematograph arrived in Brazil in 1897 and there were already 22 cinemas registered in Rio by 1910. But the first decades of cinema in Brazil were dominated by American and European silent films, and it was not until the early years of sound that the first Brazilian features, primitive as they were, were made. The first Brazilian film studio, Cinedia, based in Rio, was making Carnaval films and slapstick comedies, nicknamed *chanchadas*, from the early 1930s – Carmen Miranda was the major star of the period, making her film debut in *A Voz do Carnaval* ("The Voice of Carnaval") in 1932. But in an indication of the low quality of the Brazilian film industry in those years it was not her films that led to her discovery by Hollywood, but the fact that a Hollywood producer saw her sing and dance in the legendary Urca casino in the late 1930s and took her home for a screen-test, with the rest, as they say, being history.

Serious cinema in Brazil really began in the early 1950s when Assis Chateaubriand, a larger than life press baron and early media entrepreneur, put up the money to create Vera Cruz Studios and hired director **Lima Barreto** to make *O Cangaçeiro* ("The Outlaw"). Very loosely based on the true life story of Lampião in the northeastern *sertão*, it was by far the most expensive Brazilian film made up to that point. It was shot on location in the Northeast, and Barreto, heavily influenced by John Ford, made what was basically a Brazilian western, with the landscape just as much a character as any of the actors – which was just as well, since the acting was pretty dire. But the film, shot in luminous black and white, looked fabulous, and was a minor sensation in Europe, winning Brazilian cinema's first international award for best adventure film at Cannes in 1952.

O Cangaçeiro was a forerunner of what by the late 1950s was being called *cinema novo*: heavily influenced by the Italian neo-realism of masters like Vitorio da Sica, young Brazilian directors took a hard look at the trials and tribulations of daily life in Brazil. The Northeast loomed large in *cinema novo*; the two classics of the genre, *Vidas Secas* ("Barren Lives"), directed by Nelson Pereira dos Santos in 1963, and *O Pagador de Promessas* ("The Promise Keeper"), directed by Anselmo Duarte in 1963, are both set in the region and were both banned by the military after the 1964 coup for their unflinching portrayal of poverty and rural desperation.

Cinema under dictatorship

The military had a paradoxical effect on Brazilian cinema. On the surface they were every bit as repressive as one would expect: films and scripts were subject to rigid censorship and regularly banned, and anything that could be considered unpatriotic – such as the portrayal of poverty or social problems – was put off limits. Italian neo-realism, for example, was definitely out. On the other hand, the military did believe that a flourishing national film industry was a form of building national prestige, and in 1969 set up a state film production and financing company, **Embrafilme**, still going today and without which the modern Brazilian film industry would not exist. As a channel for (modest) government subsidy towards the film industry, it allowed a generation of Brazilian filmmakers to hone their talents without having to spend all their time chasing commercial work, and with expanding television networks supplying increasing numbers of professional actors to the film industry, the 1960s and 1970s saw a sharp rise in the number of films produced in Brazil.

In cinema, as in other forms of popular culture, especially music, this was a time of great inventiveness in Brazil. Filmmakers reacted to military censorship in a number of ways. One was diverting political comment into genres that the authorities usually didn't bother to monitor, such as erotic films, where the usual scenes of rumpy-pumpy would be interrupted by political soliloquies as the characters smoked cigarettes in bed together afterwards. Another was to make dramas that faithfully portrayed episodes of Brazilian history, but in a way pregnant with meaning for the present. This was a style that one of the masters of *cinema novo*, the director **Nelson Pereira dos Santos**, made his own with two superb films during the dictatorship. *Como Era Gostoso o Meu Francês* ("How Delicious Was My Frenchman"), released in 1971, went so far as to be shot largely in Tupi and French instead of Portuguese. It was a faithful historical reconstruction of the earliest days of Brazil but also a hilarious political allegory. *Memórias do Cárcere* ("Memories of Jail"), produced in 1984, was based on Graciliano Ramos's prison diaries during his various incarcerations by Getulio Vargas in the 1930s and 1940s. Another example of the genre was **Joaquim Pedro de Andrade**'s *Os Inconfidentes* ("The Conspirators"), released in 1974 at the peak of the dictatorship. An uncensorable reconstruction of the national hero Tiradentes's eighteenth century conspiracy against the Portuguese crown, so well researched that much of the dialogue is taken from court transcripts of the period, its portrayal of the brutal repression of dissent by the colonial authorities was a brilliantly subversive use of a national myth to make contemporary political points.

The other response was to make films so elliptical and packed with symbolism that nobody outside film schools could understand them. The influence of 1960s French filmmakers, especially Goddard, was overwhelming in the main exponent of this genre, **Glauber Rocha**. Still widely admired by the Brazilian intelligentsia, his films created a minor stir on the European art-house circuit of their time, but his best-known works, *Terra em Transe* "Land In Trance"; 1967) and *Antônio das Mortes* (1969), are unwatchable today, save for their historical interest, even though the latter won Rocha the Best Director award at Cannes in 1969.

Modern Brazilian Cinema

As the military dictatorship wound down, realism returned to Brazilian cinema, notably with Leon Hirszman's portrayal of the São Paulo car factory strikes in *Eles Não Usam Black Tie* ("They Don't Wear Black Ties"; 1981) and Cacá Diegues's excellent *Bye Bye Brazil* (1979), which followed a tawdry group of circus perfomers through the country's hinterland against a marvellous soundtrack by Chico Buarque. Hector Babenco's *Pixote* (1982) became the best-known film abroad from this period, but *Bye Bye Brazil* is the real classic.

It was not until the consolidation of democracy in the 1990s that Brazilian filmmakers could relax, put politics in its proper place as part of life rather than the crux of everything and start producing the kind of films that could catch the attention of international audiences in a way that Brazilian cinema in previous decades – often fascinating but ultimately a little parochial – was never quite capable of doing.

There were indications of new directorial talent well before the hits came. Female directors emerged for the first time, with **Carla Camaruti** producing a highly entertaining take on early Brazilian history in *Carlota Joaquina* (1994), and **Helen Solberg**'s intelligent and thought-provoking exploration of Carmen Miranda's life and myth in the drama-documentary *Carmen Miranda*

– *Bananas Is My Business* (1994). Young directors also emerged: **Andrushka Waddington** was all of 30 when he directed *Eu Tu Eles* ("Me You Them") in 2002, a reworking of the old *cinema novo* theme of life in the Northeastern *sertão*, but this time with the central character a woman choosing from a variety of husbands rather than the other way around, and with yet another superb soundtrack, this time by Gilberto Gil.

But three films in particular catapulted Brazilian cinema to international attention. *O Que É Isso Companheiro* (literally "What's Up Comrade", but sensibly renamed "Four Days in September" for English-speaking audiences), released in 1997, is a taut, beautifully done thriller directed by Bruno Barreto, recreating very accurately the kidnapping of the American ambassador in 1969 and featuring Alan Arkin in a cameo role as the ambassador. It was a hit internationally, but not as big a hit as two later films by the young and extravagantly talented directors **Walter Salles** and **Fernando Meirelles**.

Salles's *Estação Central* ("Central Station"), released in 1998, tells the story of the developing relationship between a young boy and an old woman thrown together by chance, as they travel by bus from Rio into, inevitably, the interior of the Northeast, where all Brazilian filmmakers seem to head when they need a metaphor for the national condition. The plot, which could easily have turned sentimental and mawkish in less assured hands, is excellently acted and directed and becomes almost unbearably moving at the end.

Cidade de Deus ("City of God"), Fernando Meirelles's stunning directorial debut released in 2003, tells the story of a real Rio *favela* from its early days in the 1960s to the mid-1980s. It is a remarkable film. The cast is largely amateur, drawn from Cidade de Deus itself, with a few professional actors thrown in (including the mesmerizing Matheus Nachtergaele as a gunrunning gangster, also to be seen in an almost equally memorable performance as a cold-blooded terrorist in *Four Days in September*). Meirelles came to cinema from shooting mainly commercials and music videos for television, and it shows, with his jumpy editing and distinctive, stylish use of colour and sound. The novel on which it is based is – it should be stressed – a novel rather than a memoir, but in its unflinching portrayal of the descent into urban hell that drug wars have produced in many of Rio's *favelas*, there is more truth in the film than in most documentaries.

In their different ways – *Estação Central*'s quiet building of character and atmosphere, *Cidade de Deus*'s pyrotechnic brilliance – Salles and Meirelles are examples of the heights to which Brazilian cinema can now reach. But as they would be the first to admit, they stand on the shoulders of predecessors who for over fifty years struggled to create what is now the liveliest and most innovative national cinema in South America. With the best of Brazilian cinema now easily available on DVD everywhere, investing a little time in your living room is a quick, painless and above all entertaining way to get to know Brazil, wherever and whenever you go.

Language

Language

Pronunciation 855

Brazilian Portuguese words and phrases 858

A Brazilian menu reader 860

A glossary of Brazilian terms and acronyms 864

Language

Learning some Portuguese before you go to Brazil is an extremely good idea. Although many well-educated Brazilians speak English, and it's now the main second language taught in schools, this hasn't filtered through to most of the population. If you know Spanish you're halfway there: there are obvious similarities in the grammar and vocabulary, so you should be able to make yourself understood if you speak slowly, and reading won't present you with too many problems. However, Portuguese pronunciation is utterly different and much less straightforward than Spanish, so unless you take the trouble to learn a bit about it you won't have a clue what Brazilians are talking about.

Unfortunately, far too many people – especially Spanish-speakers – are put off going to Brazil precisely by the language, but in reality this should be one of your main reasons for going. Brazilian Portuguese is a colourful, sensual language full of wonderfully rude and exotic vowel sounds, swooping intonation and hilarious idiomatic expressions. You'll also find that Brazilians will greatly appreciate even your most rudimentary efforts, and every small improvement in your Portuguese will make your stay in Brazil ten times more enjoyable.

People who have learned their Portuguese **in Portugal or in Lusophone Africa** won't have any real problems with the language in Brazil, but there are some quite big differences. There are many variations in vocabulary, and Brazilians take more liberties with the language, but the most notable differences are in pronunciation: Brazilian Portuguese is spoken more slowly and clearly; the neutral vowels so characteristic of European Portuguese tend to be sounded in full; in much of Brazil outside Rio the slushy "sh" sound doesn't exist; and the "de" and "te" endings of words like *cidade* and *diferente* are palatalized so they end up sounding like "sidadgee" and "djiferentchee".

The best **dictionary** currently available is the *Collins Portuguese Dictionary*. There is a pocket edition, but you might consider taking the fuller, larger version, which concentrates on the way the language is spoken today and gives plenty of specifically Brazilian vocabulary. For a **phrasebook**, look no further than *The Rough Guide to Portuguese*, with useful two-way glossaries, basic grammar and more.

Pronunciation

The rules of **pronunciation** are complicated, but the secret is to throw yourself wholeheartedly into this explosive linguistic Jacuzzi.

Non-nasal vowels

A shouldn't present you with too many problems. It's usually somewhere between the "**a**" sound of "b**a**t" and that of "f**a**ther".

E has three possible pronunciations. When it occurs at the beginning or in the middle of a word, it will usually sound either a bit like the "**e**" in "b**e**t"– eg ferro (iron) and miséria (poverty) – or like the "**ay**" in "h**ay**"– eg mesa (table) and pêlo (hair). However, the difference can be quite subtle and it's not something you should worry about too much at the start. The third pronunciation is radically different from the other two: at the end of a word, "**e**" sounds like "**y**" in "happ**y**", eg fome ("fommy", hunger) and se (if), which actually sounds like the Spanish "si".

I is straightforward. It's always an "**ee**" sound like the "**i**" in "pol**i**ce", eg *isto* (this).

O is another letter with three possible pronunciations. At the beginning or in the middle of a word, it normally sounds either the way it does in "d**o**g" – eg *loja* (shop) and *pó* (powder) – or the way it does in "go"– eg *homem* (man) and *pôquer* (poker). At the end of a word "**o**" sounds like the "**oo**" in "b**oo**t", so *obrigado* (thank you) is pronounced "obri-GA-doo". And the definite article "**o**" as in *o homem* (the man) is pronounced "**oo**".

U is always pronounced like "**oo**" in "b**oo**t", eg *cruz* (cross).

There are also a variety of vowel combinations or diphthongs that sound pretty much the way you would expect them to. They are **ai** (pronounced like "i" in "r**i**de"); **au** (pronounced as in "sh**ou**t"); **ei** (pronounced as in "h**ay**"); and **oi** (pronounced as in "b**oy**"). The only one that has an unexpected pronunciation is **ou**, which sounds like "o" in "r**o**se".

Nasal vowels

The fun really starts when you get into the **nasal vowel sounds**. Generally speaking, each "normal" vowel has its nasal equivalent. The trick in pronouncing these is to be completely uninhibited. To take one example, the word **pão** (bread). First of all, just say "pow" to yourself. Then say it again, but this time half close your mouth and shove the vowel really hard through your nose. Try it again, even more vigorously. It should sound something like "powng", but much more nasal and without really sounding the final "g".

There are two main ways in which Portuguese indicates a nasal vowel. One is through the use of the **tilde**, as in *pão*. The other is the use of the letters **m** or **n** after the vowel. As a general rule, whenever you see a vowel followed by "m" or "n" and then another consonant, the vowel will be nasal – eg *gente*. The same thing applies when the vowel is followed by "m" at the end of a word, eg *tem*, *bom* – in these cases, the "m" is not pronounced, it just nasalizes the vowel.

Below are some of the main nasal vowels and examples of words that use them. However, it must be emphasized that the phonetic versions of the nasal sounds we've given are only approximate.

Ã, and **-am** or **-an followed by a consonant** indicate nasal "**a**" – eg *macã* (apple), *campo* (field), *samba*.

-ão or **-am at the end of a word** indicate the "**owng**" sound, as explained above in *pão*. Other examples are in *estação* (station), *mão* (hand), *falam* ("FA-lowng"; they talk).

-em or **-en followed by a consonant** indicate a nasalized "**e**" sound – eg *tempo* (weather), *entre* (between), *gente* (people).

-em or **-ens at the end of a word** indicate an "**eyng**" sound – eg *tem* ("teyng"; you have or there is), *viagens* ("vee-A-zheyngs"; journeys).

-im or **-in at the end of a word** or followed by a consonant are simply a nasal "**ee**" sound, so *capim* (grass) sounds a bit like "ca-PEENG".

-om or **-on at the end of a word** or followed by a consonant indicate nasal "**o**". An obvious example is *bom* (good), which sounds pretty similar to "bon" in French.

-um or **-un at the end of a word** or followed by a consonant indicate nasal "**u**"– eg *um* (one).

-ãe sounds a bit like "**eyeing**" said quickly and explosively – eg *mãe* (mother).

-õe sounds like "**oing**". Most words ending in "-ão" make their plural like this, with an "s" (which is pronounced) at the end – eg *estação* (station) becomes *estações* (stations).

Consonants

Brazilian **consonants** are more straightforward than the vowels, but there are a few little oddities you'll need to learn. We've only listed the consonants where they differ from their English counterparts.

C is generally pronounced hard, as in "**c**at" (eg *campo*). However, when followed by "i" or "e", it's pronounced softly, as in "**c**eiling"(eg *cidade*, city). It's also pronounced softly whenever it's written with a cedilla (eg *estação*).

CH is pronounced like English "**sh**", so *chá* (tea) is said "sha".

D is generally pronounced as in English. However, in most parts of Brazil it's palatalized to sound like "**dj**"whenever it comes before an "i" or final "e". So *difícil* (difficult) is pronounced "djee-FEE-siw", and the ubiquitous preposition *de* (of) sounds like "djee".

G is generally pronounced hard as in English "**g**od" (eg *gosto*, I like). But before "e" or "i" it's pronounced like the "**s**" in English "vi**s**ion" or "mea**s**ure" – eg *geral* (general) and *gíria* (slang).

H is always silent (eg *hora*, hour).

J is pronounced like the "**s**" in English "vi**s**ion" or "mea**s**ure"– eg *jogo* (game) and *janeiro* (January).

L is usually pronounced as in English. But at the end of a word, it takes on a peculiar, almost Cockney pronunciation, becoming a bit like a "**w**". So Brasil is pronounced "bra-ZEEW". When followed by "h", it's pronounced "**ly**" as in "million"; so *ilha* (island) comes out as "EE-lya".

N is normally pronounced as in English, but when it's followed by "h" it becomes "**ny**". So *sonho* (dream) sounds like "SON-yoo".

Q always comes before "u" and is pronounced either "**k**" or, more usually, "**kw**". So *cinquenta* (fifty) is pronounced "sin-KWEN-ta", but *quero* (I want) is pronounced "KE-roo".

R is usually as in English. However, at the beginning of a word it's pronounced like an English "**h**". So "Rio" is actually pronounced "HEE-oo", and *rádio* (radio) is pronounced "HA-djee-oo".

RR is always pronounced like an English "**h**". So *ferro* is pronounced "FE-hoo".

S is normally pronounced like an English "**s**", and in São Paulo and the South this never changes. But in Rio and many places to the north, "**s**" sounds like English "**sh**" when it comes before a consonant and at the end of a word (*estação*, "esh-ta-SOWNG").

T is normally pronounced as in English but, like "d", it changes before "i" and final "e". So *sorte* (luck) is pronounced "SOR-chee", and the great hero of Brazilian history, Tiradentes, is pronounced "chee-ra-DEN-chees".

X is pronounced like an English "**sh**" at the beginning of a word, and elsewhere like an English "**x**" or "**z**". So *xadrez* (chess) is pronounced "sha-DREYZ", while *exército* (army) is pronounced "e-ZER-si-too".

Stress

Any word that has an accent of any kind, including a tilde, is stressed on that syllable, so *miséria* (poverty) is pronounced "mi-ZE-ree-a". If there is no accent, the following rules generally apply (the syllables to be stressed are in capitals):

• Words that end with the vowels a, e and o are stressed on the penultimate syllable. So *entre* (between) sounds like "EN-tree", and *compro* (I buy) "KOM-proo". This also applies when these vowels are followed by -m, -s or -ns: *falam* is stressed "FA-lowng".

• Words that end with the vowels i and u are stressed on the final syllable: *abacaxi* (pineapple) is pronounced "a-ba-ka-ZEE". This also applies when i and u are followed by -m, -s or -ns, so *capim* is pronounced "ka-PEENG".

• Words ending in consonants are usually stressed on the final syllable, eg *rapaz* (boy), stressed "ha-PAZ".

Some useful examples:

Rio de Janeiro HEE-oo djee zha-NEY-roo
Belo Horizonte BE-loo o-ri-ZON-chee
Rio Grande do Sul HEE-oo GRAN-djee doo Soow
Recife he-SEE-fee
rodoviária ho-do-vee-A-ree-a
onde (where) ON-djee
não entende (he doesn't understand) now en-TEN-djee
sim (yes) SEENG (but hardly sound the final "g")
ruim (bad) hoo-WEENG (again hardly sound the "g")
vinte (twenty) VEEN-chee
correio (post office) co-HAY-oo

Brazilian Portuguese words and phrases

Basic expressions

sim, não	Yes, No
por favor	Please
obrigado (men)/ obrigada (women)	Thank you
onde, quando	Where, When
que, quanto	What, How much
este, esse, aquele	This, That
agora, mais tarde	Now, Later
aberto/a, fechado/a	Open, Closed
entrada, saída	Entrance, Exit
puxe, empurre	Pull, Push
com, sem	With, Without
para	For
bom, ruim	Good, Bad
grande, pequeno	Big, Small
um pouco, muito	A little, A lot
mais, menos	More, Less
outro/a	Another
hoje, amanhã	Today, Tomorrow
ontem	Yesterday
mas (pronounced like "mice")	But
e (pronounced like "ee" in seek	And
alguma coisa, nada	Something, Nothing
ás vezes	Sometimes

Greetings and responses

oi, tchau (like the Italian "ciao")	Hello, Goodbye
bom dia	Good morning
boa tarde/boa noite	Good afternoon/ night
desculpa	Sorry
com licença	Excuse me
como vai?	How are you?
bem	Fine
parabéns	Congratulations
saúde	Cheers

Useful phrases and colloquial expressions

você fala inglês?	Do you speak English?
não entendo	I don't understand
não falo português	I don't speak Portuguese
como se diz em português?	What's the Portuguese for this?
o que você disse?	What did you say?
meu nome é...	My name is…

como se chama?	What's your name?
sou inglês/americano	I am English/ American
você tem...?	Do you have...?
as horas?	the time?
tudo bem	Everything's fine
tá bom	OK
estou com fome	I'm hungry
estou com sede	I'm thirsty
me sinto mal	I feel ill
quero ver um medico	I want to see a doctor
qual é o problema?	What's the matter?
há...(?)	There is (is there?)
quero...	I want, I'd like...
posso...	I can...
não posso...	I can't...
não sei	I don't know
está quente	It's hot
está frio	It's cold
está legal	It's great
é chato	It's boring
estou chateado	I'm bored, annoyed
estou de saco cheio	I've had it up to here
não tem jeito	There's no way
louco/a, maluco/ a	Crazy
cansado/a	Tired

Asking directions, getting around

Onde fica...?	Where is...?
a rodoviária	the bus station
a parada de ônibus	the bus stop
o hotel mais próximo	the nearest hotel
o banheiro/ sanitário	the toilet
esquerda, direita, direto	Left, right, straight on
vai direto e dobra à esquerda	Go straight on and turn left
de onde sai o ônibus	Where does the bus
para...?	to...leave?
é esse o ônibus para Rio?	Is this the bus to Rio?
você vai para...?	Do you go to...?
quero uma pasagem	I'd like a (return)
(ida e volta) para...	ticket to...
Que horas sai	What time does it
(chega)	leave (arrive)?
longe, perto	Far, Near
devagar, rápido	Slowly, Quickly

Accommodation

você tem um quarto?	Do you have a room?
com duas camas/ cama de casal	with two beds/ double bed
é para uma pessoa/	It's for one person/
duas pessoas	two people
Está bom, quanto é?	It's fine, how much is it?
é caro demais	It's too expensive
tem algo mais	Do you have anything
barato?	cheaper?
Tem um hotel/ camping por aqui?	Is there a hotel/ campsite nearby?

Numbers

um, uma	1
dois, duas	2
três	3
quatro	4
cinco	5
seis	6
sete	7
oito	8
nove	9
dez	10
onze	11
doze	12
treze	13
quatorze	14
quinze	15
dezesseis	16
dezessete	17
dezoito	18
dezenove	19
vinte	20
vinte e um	21
trinta	30
quarenta	40
cinquenta	50
sesenta	60
setenta	70
oitenta	80
noventa	90
cem	100
duzentos	200
trezentos	300
quinhentos	500
mil	1000
dois mil	2000
cinco mil	5000

Days and months

segunda-feira (or segunda)	Monday
terça-feira (or terça)	Tuesday
quarta-feira (or quarta)	Wednesday
quinta-feira (or quinta)	Thursday
sexta-feira (or sexta)	Friday
sábado	Saturday
domingo	Sunday
janeiro	January
fevereiro	February
março	March
abril	April
maio	May
junho	June
julho	July
agosto	August
setembro	September
outubro	October
novembro	November
dezembro	December

A Brazilian menu reader

Basics

açúcar	sugar
alho e óleo	garlic and olive oil sauce
almoço	lunch
arroz	rice
azeite	olive oil
café colonial	high tea
café de manhã	breakfast
cardápio	menu
carne	meat
colher	spoon
conta/nota	bill
copo	glass
entrada	hors d'oeuvre

faca	knife	**peixe**	fish
farinha	dried manioc flour	**pimenta**	pepper
garçom	waiter	**prato**	plate
garfo	fork	**queijo**	cheese
garrafa	bottle	**sal**	salt
jantar	dinner, to have dinner	**sobremesa**	dessert
legumes/verduras	vegetables	**sopa/caldo**	soup
manteiga	butter	**sorvete**	ice cream
mariscos	seafood	**taxa de serviço**	service charge
molho	sauce	**tucupi**	fermented manioc and chicory sauce used in Amazonian cuisine
ovos	eggs		
pão	bread		

Cooking terms

assado	roasted	**mal passado/ bem passado**	rare/well done (meat)
bem gelado	well chilled	**médio**	medium-grilled
churrasco	barbecue	**milanesa**	breaded
cozido	boiled, steamed	**na chapa/na brasa**	charcoal-grilled
cozinhar	to cook		
grelhado	grilled		

Seafood (frutos do mar)

acarajé	fried bean cake stuffed with *vatapá* (see below)	**pescada**	seafood stew, or hake
agulha	needle fish	**pirarucu**	Amazon river fish
atum	tuna	**pitu**	crayfish
camarão	prawn, shrimp	**polvo**	octopus
caranguejo	large crab	**siri**	small crab
filhote	Amazon river fish	**sururu**	a type of mussel
lagosta	lobster	**vatapá**	Bahian shrimp dish, cooked with palm oil, skinned tomato and coconut milk, served with fresh coriander and hot peppers
lula	squid		
mariscos	shellfish		
moqueca	seafood stewed in palm oil and coconut sauce		
ostra	oyster		

Meat and poultry (carne e aves)

bife	steak	**frango**	chicken
bife a cavalo	steak with egg and *farinha*	**leitão**	sucking pig
cabrito	kid	**lingüiça**	sausage
carne de porco	pork	**pato**	duck
carneiro	lamb	**peru**	turkey
costela	ribs	**peito**	breast
costeleta	chop	**perna**	leg
feijoada	black bean, pork and sausage stew	**picadinha**	stew
fígado	liver	**salsicha**	hot dog
		veado	venison
		vitela	veal

Fruit (*frutas*)

L LANGUAGE

abacate	avocado	**limão**	lime
abacaxi	pineapple	**maçã**	apple
ameixa	plum, prune	**mamão**	papaya
caju	cashew fruit	**manga**	mango
carambola	star fruit	**maracujá**	passion fruit
cerejas	cherries	**melancia**	watermelon
côco	coconut	**melão**	melon
fruta do conde	custard apple (also *ata*)	**morango**	strawberry
goiaba	guava	**pera**	pear
graviola	cherimoya	**pêssego**	peach
laranja	orange	**uvas**	grapes

Vegetables and spices (legumes e temperos)

alface	lettuce	**ervilhas**	peas
alho	garlic	**espinafre**	spinach
arroz e feijão	rice and beans	**macaxeira**	roasted manioc
azeitonas	olives	**malagueta**	very hot pepper, looks like red or yellow cherry
batatas	potatoes	**mandioca**	manioc/cassava/ yuca
canela	cinnamon	**milho**	corn
cebola	onion	**palmito**	palm heart
cenoura	carrot	**pepinho**	cucumber
cheiro verde	fresh coriander	**repolho**	cabbage
coentro	parsley	**tomate**	tomato
cravo	clove		
dendê	palm oil		

Drinks

água mineral	mineral water
batida	fresh fruit juice with *cachaça*
cachaça	sugar-cane rum
café com leite	coffee with hot milk
cafézinho	small black coffee
caipirinha	rum and lime cocktail
cerveja	bottled beer
chopp	draught beer
com gás/sem gás	sparkling/still
suco	fruit juice
vinho	wine
vitamina	fruit juice made with milk

A glossary of Brazilian terms and acronyms

Agreste In the Northeast, the intermediate zone between the coast and the *sertão*

Aldeia Originally a mission where Indians were converted, now any isolated hamlet

Alfândega Customs

Amazônia The Amazon region

Artesanato Craft goods

Azulejo Decorative glazed tiling

Bairro Neighbourhood within town or city

Bandeirante Member of a group that marched under a *bandeira* (banner or flag) in early missions to open up the interior; Brazilian conquistador

Barraca Beach hut

Batucada Literally, a drumming session – music-making in general, especially impromptu

Bloco Large Carnaval group

Bosque Wood

Caatinga Scrub vegetation of the interior of the Northeast

Caboclo Backwoodsman/woman, often of mixed race

Candomblé African-Brazilian religion

Cangaceiro Outlaws from the interior of the Northeast who flourished in the early twentieth century; the most famous was Lampião

Capoeira African-Brazilian martial art/dance form

Carimbó Music and dance style from the north

Carioca Someone or something from Rio de Janeiro

Carnaval Carnival

Cerrado Scrubland

Choro Musical style, largely instrumental

Convento Convent

Correio Postal service/post office

CUT/CGT Brazilian trades union organizations

Dancetaria Nightspot where the emphasis is on dancing

Engenho Sugar mill or plantation

Estado Novo The period when Getúlio Vargas was effectively dictator, from the mid-1930s to 1945

EUA USA

Ex voto Thanks-offering to saint for intercession

Favela Shantytown, slum

Fazenda Country estate, ranch house

Feira Country market

Ferroviária Train station

Forró Dance and type of music from the Northeast

Frescão Air-conditioned bus

Frevo Frenetic musical style and dance from Recife

FUNAI Government organization intended to protect the interests of Brazilian Indians; seriously underfunded and with a history of corruption

Garimpeiro Prospector or miner

Gaúcho Person or thing from Rio Grande do Sul; also southern cowboy

Gringo/a Foreigner, Westerner (not derogatory)

Ibama Government organization for preservation of the environment; runs national parks and nature reserves

Iemanjá Goddess of the sea in candomblé

Igreja Church

Largo Small square

Latifúndios Large agricultural estates

Leito Luxury express bus

Literatura de cordel Literally "string literature" – printed ballads, most common in the Northeast but also found elsewhere, named after the string they are suspended from in country markets

Litoral Coast, coastal zone

Louro/a Fair-haired/blonde – Westerners in general

Maconha Marijuana

Macumba African-Brazilian religion, usually thought of as more authentically "African" than candomblé; most common in the North

Marginal Petty thief, outlaw

Mata Jungle, remote interior (Mata Atlântica - jungle covering the coastal parts of southern Brazil)

Mercado Market

Mineiro Person or thing from Minas Gerais

Mirante Viewing point

Mosteiro Monastery

Movimentado Lively, where the action is

MPB Música Popular Brasileira, common shorthand for Brazilian music

Nordeste Northeastern Brazil

Nordestino/a Inhabitant thereof

Nova República The New Republic – the period since the return to civilian democracy in 1985

Paulista Person or thing from São Paulo state

Paulistano Inhabitant of the city of São Paulo

Pelourinho Pillory or whipping-post, common in colonial town squares

Planalto Central Vast interior tablelands of central Brazil

Posto Highway service station, often with basic accommodation popular with truckers

Praça Square

Praia Beach

Prefeitura Town hall, and by extension city governments in general

PT Partido dos Trabalhadores or Workers' Party, the largest left-wing party in Brazil, led by Lula

Quebrado Out of order

Rodovia Highway

Rodoviária Bus station

Samba Type of music most associated with Carnaval in Rio

Selva Jungle

Senzala Slave quarters

Sertanejo Inhabitant of *sertão*

Sertão Arid, drought-ridden interior of the Northeast

Sesmaria Royal Portuguese land grant to early settlers

Sobrado Two-storey colonial mansion

Terreiro House where *candomblé* or *umbanda* rituals and ceremonies take place

Umbanda African-Brazilian religion especially common in urban areas of the South and Southeast

Vaqueiro Cowboy in the North

Visto Visa

Travel store

ROUGH GUIDES Complete Listing

UK & Ireland
Britain
Devon & Cornwall
Dublin **D**
Edinburgh **D**
England
Ireland
The Lake District
London
London **D**
London Mini Guide
Scotland
Scottish Highlands & Islands
Wales

Europe
Algarve **D**
Amsterdam
Amsterdam **D**
Andalucía
Athens **D**
Austria
The Baltic States
Barcelona
Barcelona **D**
Belgium & Luxembourg
Berlin
Brittany & Normandy
Bruges **D**
Brussels
Budapest
Bulgaria
Copenhagen
Corfu
Corsica
Costa Brava **D**
Crete
Croatia
Cyprus
Czech & Slovak Republics
Dodecanese & East Aegean
Dordogne & The Lot
Europe
Florence & Siena
Florence **D**
France
Germany
Gran Canaria **D**
Greece
Greek Islands
Hungary
Ibiza & Formentera **D**
Iceland
Ionian Islands
Italy
The Italian Lakes
Languedoc & Roussillon
Lanzarote **D**
Lisbon **D**
The Loire
Madeira **D**
Madrid **D**
Mallorca **D**
Mallorca & Menorca
Malta & Gozo **D**
Menorca
Moscow
The Netherlands
Norway
Paris
Paris **D**
Paris Mini Guide
Poland
Portugal
Prague
Prague **D**
Provence & the Côte D'Azur
Pyrenees
Romania
Rome
Rome **D**
Sardinia
Scandinavia
Sicily
Slovenia
Spain
St Petersburg
Sweden
Switzerland
Tenerife & La Gomera **D**
Turkey
Tuscany & Umbria
Venice & The Veneto
Venice **D**
Vienna

Asia
Bali & Lombok
Bangkok
Beijing
Cambodia
China
Goa
Hong Kong & Macau
India
Indonesia
Japan
Laos
Malaysia, Singapore & Brunei
Nepal
The Philippines
Singapore
South India
Southeast Asia
Sri Lanka
Thailand
Thailand's Beaches & Islands
Tokyo
Vietnam

Australasia
Australia
Melbourne
New Zealand
Sydney

North America
Alaska
Baja California
Boston
California
Canada
Chicago
Colorado
Florida
The Grand Canyon
Hawaii
Las Vegas **D**
Los Angeles
Maui **D**
Miami & South Florida
Montréal
New England
New Orleans **D**
New York City
New York City **D**
New York City Mini Guide
Orlando & Walt Disney World® **D**
Pacific Northwest
San Francisco
San Francisco **D**
Seattle
Southwest USA
Toronto
USA
Vancouver
Washington DC
Washington DC **D**
Yosemite

Caribbean & Latin America
Antigua & Barbuda **D**
Argentina
Bahamas
Barbados **D**
Belize
Bolivia
Brazil
Cancùn & Cozumel **D**
Caribbean
Central America
Chile
Costa Rica
Cuba
Dominican Republic
Dominican Republic **D**
Ecuador
Guatemala
Jamaica
Mexico
Peru
St Lucia **D**
South America
Trinidad & Tobago
Yúcatan

Africa & Middle East
Cape Town & the Garden Route
Egypt
The Gambia
Jordan
Kenya
Marrakesh **D**
Morocco
South Africa, Lesotho & Swaziland
Syria
Tanzania
Tunisia
West Africa
Zanzibar

D: Rough Guide **DIRECTIONS** for short breaks

Available from all good bookstores

ROUGH GUIDES Complete Listing

Travel Specials
First-Time Around the World
First-Time Asia
First-Time Europe
First-Time Latin America
Travel Online
Travel Health
Travel Survival
Walks in London & SE England
Women Travel

Maps
Algarve
Amsterdam
Andalucia & Costa del Sol
Argentina
Athens
Australia
Barcelona
Berlin
Boston
Brittany
Brussels
California
Chicago
Corsica
Costa Rica & Panama
Crete
Croatia
Cuba
Cyprus
Czech Republic
Dominican Republic
Dubai & UAE
Dublin
Egypt
Florence & Siena
Florida
France
Frankfurt
Germany
Greece
Guatemala & Belize
Hong Kong
Iceland
Ireland
Kenya & Northern Tanzania
Lisbon
London
Los Angeles
Madrid
Mallorca
Malaysia
Marrakesh
Mexico
Miami & Key West
Morocco
New England
New York City
New Zealand
Northern Spain
Paris
Peru
Portugal
Prague
The Pyrenees
Rome
San Francisco
Sicily
South Africa
South India
Spain & Portugal
Sri Lanka
Tenerife
Thailand
Toronto
Trinidad & Tobago
Tuscany
Venice
Vietnam, Laos & Cambodia
Washington DC
Yucatán Peninsula

Dictionary Phrasebooks
Croatian
Czech
Dutch
Egyptian Arabic
French
German
Greek
Hindi & Urdu
Italian
Japanese
Latin American Spanish
Mandarin Chinese
Mexican Spanish
Polish
Portuguese
Russian
Spanish
Swahili
Thai
Turkish
Vietnamese

Computers
Blogging
iPods, iTunes & music online
The Internet
Macs & OS X
PCs and Windows
PlayStation Portable
Website Directory

Film & TV
American Independent Film
British Cult Comedy
Chick Flicks
Comedy Movies
Cult Movies
Gangster Movies
Horror Movies
Kids' Movies
Sci-Fi Movies
Westerns

Lifestyle
Babies
eBay
Ethical Shopping
Pregnancy & Birth

Music Guides
The Beatles
Bob Dylan
Classical Music
Elvis
Frank Sinatra
Heavy Metal
Hip-Hop
Jazz
Book of Playlists
Opera
Pink Floyd
Punk
Reggae
Rock
The Rolling Stones
Soul and R&B
World Music (2 vols)

Popular Culture
Books for Teenagers
Children's Books, 5-11
Conspiracy Theories
Cult Fiction
The Da Vinci Code
Lord of the Rings
Shakespeare
Superheroes
Unexplained Phenomena

Sport
Arsenal 11s
Celtic 11s
Chelsea 11s
Liverpool 11s
Man United 11s
Newcastle 11s
Rangers 11s
Tottenham 11s
Poker

Science
Climate Change
The Universe
Weather

Small print and Index

A Rough Guide to Rough Guides

Published in 1982, the first Rough Guide – to Greece – was a student scheme that became a publishing phenomenon. Mark Ellingham, a recent graduate in English from Bristol University, had been travelling in Greece the previous summer and couldn't find the right guidebook. With a small group of friends he wrote his own guide, combining a highly contemporary, journalistic style with a thoroughly practical approach to travellers' needs.

The immediate success of the book spawned a series that rapidly covered dozens of destinations. And, in addition to impecunious backpackers, Rough Guides soon acquired a much broader and older readership that relished the guides' wit and inquisitiveness as much as their enthusiastic, critical approach and value-for-money ethos.

These days, Rough Guides include recommendations from shoestring to luxury and cover more than 200 destinations around the globe, including almost every country in the Americas and Europe, more than half of Africa and most of Asia and Australasia. Our ever-growing team of authors and photographers is spread all over the world, particularly in Europe, the USA and Australia.

In the early 1990s, Rough Guides branched out of travel, with the publication of Rough Guides to World Music, Classical Music and the Internet. All three have become benchmark titles in their fields, spearheading the publication of a wide range of books under the Rough Guide name.

Including the travel series, Rough Guides now number more than 350 titles, covering: phrasebooks, waterproof maps, music guides from Opera to Heavy Metal, reference works as diverse as Conspiracy Theories and Shakespeare, and popular culture books from iPods to Poker. Rough Guides also produce a series of more than 120 World Music CDs in partnership with World Music Network.

Visit www.roughguides.com to see our latest publications.

Rough Guide travel images are available for commercial licensing at www.roughguidespictures.com

Rough Guide credits

Text editor: Amy Hegarty
Layout: Ankur Guha, Pradeep Thapliyal
Cartography: Katie Lloyd-Jones, Karobi Gogoi, Alakananda Bhattacharya
Picture editor: Sarah Smithies
Production: Aimee Hampson
Proofreader: Helen Castell
Photographer: Alex Robinson
Cover design: Chloë Roberts
Editorial: **London** Kate Berens, Claire Saunders, Geoff Howard, Ruth Blackmore, Polly Thomas, Richard Lim, Alison Murchie, Karoline Densley, Andy Turner, Keith Drew, Edward Aves, Nikki Birrell, Helen Marsden, Alice Park, Sarah Eno, Joe Staines, Duncan Clark, Peter Buckley, Matthew Milton, Tracy Hopkins, David Paul, Lucy White, Ruth Tidball; **New York** Andrew Rosenberg, Steven Horak, April Isaacs, AnneLise Sorensen, Sean Mahoney, Ella Steim
Design & Pictures: **London** Simon Bracken, Dan May, Diana Jarvis, Mark Thomas, Jj Luck, Harriet Mills; **Delhi** Madhulita Mohapatra, Umesh Aggarwal, Ajay Verma, Jessica Subramanian, Sachin Tanwar, Anita Singh
Production: Sophie Hewat, Katherine Owers
Cartography: **London** Maxine Repath, Ed Wright; **Delhi** Rajesh Chhibber, Jai Prakash Mishra, Ashutosh Bharti, Rajesh Mishra, Animesh Pathak, Jasbir Sandhu, Amod Singh
Online: **New York** Jennifer Gold, Kristin Mingrone; **Delhi** Manik Chauhan, Narender Kumar, Shekhar Jha, Rakesh Kumar, Amit Verma, Amit Kumar, Rahul Kumar
Marketing & Publicity: **London** Richard Trillo, Niki Hanmer, Louise Maher, Jess Carter; **New York** Geoff Colquitt, Megan Kennedy, Katy Ball; **Delhi** Reem Khokhar
Custom publishing and foreign rights: Philippa Hopkins
Manager India: Punita Singh
Series editor: Mark Ellingham
Reference Director: Andrew Lockett
PA to Managing and Publishing Directors: Megan McIntyre
Publishing Director: Martin Dunford

Publishing information

This sixth edition published November 2006 by
Rough Guides Ltd,
80 Strand, London WC2R 0RL
345 Hudson St, 4th Floor,
New York, NY 10014, USA
14 Local Shopping Centre, Panchsheel Park,
New Delhi 110017, India
Distributed by the Penguin Group
Penguin Books Ltd,
80 Strand, London WC2R 0RL
Penguin Putnam, Inc.
375 Hudson Street, NY 10014, USA
Penguin Group (Australia)
250 Camberwell Road, Camberwell,
Victoria 3124, Australia
Penguin Books Canada Ltd,
10 Alcorn Avenue, Toronto, Ontario,
Canada M4V 1E4
Penguin Group (NZ)
67 Apollo Drive, Mairangi Bay, Auckland 1310,
New Zealand
Cover concept by Peter Dyer.

Typeset in Bembo and Helvetica to an original design by Henry Iles.

Printed in Italy by LegoPrint S.p.A

888pp includes index

A catalogue record for this book is available from the British Library

ISBN 10: 1-84353-659-5

ISBN 13: 9-78184-353-659-8

1 3 5 7 9 8 6 4 2

Help us update

We've gone to a lot of effort to ensure that the sixth edition of **The Rough Guide to Brazil** is accurate and up to date. However, things change – places get "discovered", opening hours are notoriously fickle, restaurants and rooms raise prices or lower standards. If you feel we've got it wrong or left something out, we'd like to know, and if you can remember the address, the price, the time, the phone number, so much the better.

We'll credit all contributions, and send a copy of the next edition (or any other Rough Guide if you prefer) for the best letters. Everyone who writes to us and isn't already a subscriber will receive a copy of our full-colour thrice-yearly newsletter. Please mark letters: "**Rough Guide Brazil Update**" and send to: Rough Guides, 80 Strand, London WC2R 0RL, or Rough Guides, 4th Floor, 345 Hudson St, New York, NY 10014. Or send an email to **mail@roughguides.com**

Have your questions answered and tell others about your trip at
www.roughguides.atinfopop.com

Acknowledgements

Oliver Marshall Thanks are due to Amy Hegarty for her editorial attention and also to Richard Koss and Melissa Graham for their additional editorial inputs. I'm grateful to the assistance provided by Embratur and its London representative, Silvana Nascimento, and to the many municipal tourist offices and CVBs in Brazil that provided help, in particular the Iguaçu CVB and its director Maurício do Amaral Lupion and the Rio CVB and its New York representative, João Rodriques. I'm immensely grateful to Eduardo Silva, Graça Salgado and Isaura for their welcome in Rio as well as to Ben and Neto for their hospitality in Paraty and Suzete and Roderick Clark in Pelotas. Meroslawa Krevei, the director of Prudentópolis' Museu do Milênio, offered fascinating insights into the Ukrainian communities that we toured, while Claudio Neves of Grand Tour Ouro Preto was similarly helpful in Minas Gerais. George Mészarós provided valuable advice on Florianópolis, while Duncan Crossley and Karin Hanta offered useful tips on Rio. Finally, in London, thanks to Margaret and Anneliese for all their support.

Dilwyn Jenkins thanks Joel Souza (Ecoverde, Cuiaba), Geraldo Mesquita (Gero's Tours, Manaus) and Cecilia McCallum.

Rosalba O'Brien would like to thank Paloma Lisboa, Luciana Mota, *São Paulo Hostel*'s Aussie barmen, Bruna & Ilan, Ilha Cardoso rangers, Esteban Fernandez Balbis and Arwen.

The editor would like to thank the authors, Ankur Guha, Pradeep Thapliyal, Umesh Aggarwal, Katie Lloyd-Jones, Karobi Gogoi, Alakananda Bhattacharya, Punita Singh, Sarah Smithies, Alex Robinson, Melissa Graham, Aimee Hampson, David Paul, Helen Castell, Chlöe Roberts, Steven Horak, AnneLise Sorensen and Andrew Rosenberg.

Readers' letters

Thanks to all the readers who have taken the time to write in with comments and suggestions (and apologies if we've inadvertently omitted or misspelt anyone's name):

Ruth Baldwin, Kim Bryan, Carol Buchman, C.R. Caldas-Coulthard, Peter Castro, Mark Danter, Sarah Deakin, Peter Elford, Jimena Elias, Sara and Yonatan Eyal, Alan Foster, Adriana Gallo, Jennifer Grossman, Peter Hewitt, Steev Hise, Barnaby Hodgson, Peter Ito, James Larragy, Albert Vila Mallarach, Giles Mason, Sharlene Matsuhara, Dominik Matter, Claire McGuire, Ethan Munson, Pedro Novak, Alberto Poli, Billy Rawcliffe, Kate Rayner, Mark Rickards, Karen Serres, Alice W. Smith, Kevin Spencer, David Steinberg, Marika Linda Stone, Roy Tamboli, Patrick Towell, Sander van Hulsenbeek, Sandra and Terry Wall, Eveline Welschen, Gill Whitelegg, Richard Williams, Roland Wirth

Photo credits

All photos © Rough Guides except the following:

Title page
Morro de São Paulo, Tinharé Island, Bahia © Bertrand Gardel/Hemispheres Images/Alamy

Full page
Paraty © Peter Adams Photography/Alamy

Introduction
Carnaval drums in Salvador © Sylvain Safra/Hemispheres Images/Alamy
Igreja do Bonfim, Salvador © Werner Otto/Alamy
Carnival in Olinda © Peter Adams/Photolibrary.com/Jon Arnold Images
Start to a boat trip on the Rio Negro © Guenter Fischer/imagebroker/Alamy
Teatro Amazonas, Manaus © Michael Dunning/Getty Images

Things not to miss
01 Beija Flor Samba School during Carnaval in Rio de Janeiro © Marion Morrison/South American Pictures
02 Iguaçu Falls © Oliver Marshall
03 Teatro Amazonas, Manaus © Paul Edmondson
04 Reggae band Olodum performs in Salvador's Pelourinho Square © Ricardo Azoury/Corbis
05 Christ the Redeemer statue on the Corcovado, Rio de Janeiro © Angelo Cavalli/Getty Images
06 Ruins of the Jesuit mission church of São Miguel © Bojan Brecelj/Corbis
07 Ouro Preto, Minas Gerais © Peter M. Wilson/Axiom
08 Parque Nacional da Tijuca, Rio de Janeiro © Dave G. Houser/Post-Houserstock/Corbis
09 Riverboat captain awaits passengers on the Amazon River © David Muenker/Alamy
11 Tourists in Caverna Lapa Doce Chapada Diamantina © StockBrazil/Alamy
12 *Last Supper*, from *The Passion*, by Aleijadinho © Tony Morrison/South American Pictures
14 Sand dunes at Jericoacoara beach © Cristiano Burmester/Alamy
15 Ilhabela coastline © Cristiano Burmester/Getty Images
16 Caiman crocodile, the Pantanal © Jeffrey Rich/Jupiterimages/ImageState
17 Pedra Azul, Espírito Santo © Ricardo Siqueira/BrazilPhotos/Alamy
20 Carioquinhas waterfall in Parque Nacional Chapada dos Veadeiros © Pedro Luz Cunha/Alamy
22 Olinda © Peter Adams/Jon Arnold Images/Photolibrary.com
24 Fazenda Pinhal © Francesco Venturi/Corbis
26 Jurerê beach, Florianópolis © Fabio Pili/Alamy
28 Igreja das Dores, Paraty © Oliver Marshall
31 Participants circle a priestess during a religious ceremony © Bill Leimbach/South American Pictures
32 Freshwater plants and curimbatá in the Aquário Natural, Bonito © Andre Seale/Alamy

Colour section: Brazilian food and drink
Brazilian *feijoada* © Clicio/Getty Images
Stew of beans and manioc © mediacolor's/Alamy
Cachaça © Oliver Marshall

Colour section: Amazon flora and fauna
Giant water lily pads (*Victoria Amazonica*) © Theo Allofs/Getty Images
Anavilhanas archipelago in the Rio Negro © Solvin Zankl/Nature Picture Library
Piranha © FLPA/SA TEAM/FOTO NATURA
Brazil nut tree in the Amazon rainforest © Edward Parker/Alamy
Rubber tapping © Peter Oxford/Nature Picture Library
Red-faced Ukari monkey in the Amazon rainforest © Pete Oxford/Nature Picture Library
Tapir in the Brazilian Amazon © Nick Gordon/Nature Picture Library
Spotted jaguar © Tony Morrison/South American Pictures

Black and whites
p.70 Christ the Redeemer, the Corcovado © Andy Caulfield/Getty Images
p.90 Centenary fig tree on Praça XV de Novembro © Fabio Pili/Alamy
p.100 Tram in Santa Teresa © travelstock44/Alamy
p.110 Igreja da Nossa Senhora da Glória do Outeiro, with the Corcovado in the background © Tony Morrison/South American Pictures
p.120 Parque Nacional da Tijuca © Galen Rowell/Corbis
p.131 A busy street bar in the Lapa district of Rio © Mimi Mollica/Corbis
p.143 Museu de Arte Contemporânea, Niteroi © Sergio Moraes/Reuters/Corbis
p.159 Paraty © Tony Morrison/South American Pictures
p.172 Igreja São Francisco de Assis, Ouro Preto © Jtb Photo/Photolibrary.com
p.177 Belo Horizonte train station © Oliver Marshall
p.185 Edificio Niemeyer © Oliver Marshall
p.202 Ouro Preto © David Davis/Photolibrary.com
p.213 *Prophet Ezekiel* by Aleijadinho, Basilica do Senhor Bom Jesus de Matosinhos © Tony Morrison/South American Pictures
p.222 Uninhabited colonial housing in Diamantina © Tony Morrison/South American Pictures
p.227 Woman making cotton thread © Lena Trindade/BrazilPhotos/Alamy

p.245 Convento da Penha, Vila Velha © Andre Seale/Alamy
p.251 Parque Estadual da Pedra Azul © Ricardo Siqueira/BrazilPhotos /Alamy
p.258 Igreja da Nossa Senhora dos Pretos © Mauritius Die Bildagentur Gmbh/ Photolibrary.com
p.268 Palacio do Rio Branco, Salvador © Jtb Photo/Photolibrary.com
p.272 Igreja da Nossa Senhora dos Pretos © Tony Morrison/South American Pictures
p.278 Dancing in Pelourinho © Corbis
p.298 Cacti growing in the Chapada Diamantina © Jacques Jangoux/Alamy
p.303 Parque Nacional Marinho dos Abrolhos © Andre Seale/Alamy
p.306 Beach in Recife © Sue Cunningham Photographic/Alamy
p.327 Renovated old city of Recife © Tony Morrison/South American Pictures
p.341 Carnaval street scene in Olinda © Tony Morrison/South American Pictures
p.352 A farmer in the sertão © Tony Morrison/ South American Pictures
p.366 Statue of Padre Cicero, Juazeiro do Norte © Diego Lezama Orezzoli/Corbis
p.372 Forte dos Reis Magos, Natal © Sue Cunningham Photographic/Alamy
p.374 Tall white dunes and beach buggies, Natal © Sergio Pitamitz/Corbis
p.390 Local children sandboarding down the main dune at Jericoacoara © Jon Crwys-Williams/Alamy
p.412 Rare Ukari monkey in Brazil's Amazon © Edward Parker/Alamy
p.418 Fisherman in a canoe along the Amazon River © Nick Gordon/Nature Picture Library
p.448 Boys in a canoe at Alter do Chão © Sue Cunningham/Worldwide Picture Library/Alamy
p.459 Dancer at the Boi Bumbá festival © Alex Maddox/Alamy
p.464 River boats docked at Manaus © Neil Hepworth/Alamy
p.474 Squirrel monkey in the rainforests of the Amazon © Mason Fischer/Peter Arnold, Inc/Alamy
p.478 Trekking in the Brazilian jungle © Alex Segre/Alamy
p.487 Vegetation on the summit of Roraima Mountain © Luiz Claudio Marigo/Nature Picture Library
p.508 Statues outside of Catedral Metropolitana © Tony Morrison/South American Pictures
p.524 Stained-glass interior of Cathedral Metropolitana © Peter M. Wilson/Alamy
p.534 Salto de Itiquira © Pedro Luz Cunha/Alamy
p.548 Waterfall in Parque Nacional Chapada dos Veadeiros © Pedro Luz Cunha/Alamy
p.553 Hoatzin (*Opisthocomus hoazin*) © Genevieve Vallee/Alamy
p.556 Pantanal fisherman in a canoe in the early morning © Tony Morrison/South American Pictures
p.575 Snorkeller in the Aquário Natural, Bonito © Andre Seale/Alamy
p.586 Capybara © Anna Bailetti/South American Pictures
p.598 Praça da República, Cuiabá © Tony Morrison/South American Pictures
p.603 Véu de Noiva waterfall © Tony Morrison/ South American Pictures
p.610 Sailing, Ilhabela © Cristiano Burmester/ Alamy
p.670 Pria do Jabaquara, Ihabela © Cristiano Burmester/Alamy
p.678 Polish Park in South Curitiba © Oliver Marshall
p.686 Museu Paranaense, Curitiba © Tony Morrison/South American Pictures
p.699 Paranaguav Bay © Sue Cunningham Photographic/Alamy
p.710 Iguaçu Falls © Oliver Marshall
p.722 Barra da Lagoa Florianópolis © Oliver Marshall
p.729 Joaquina beach, Florianópolis © Fabio Pili/Alamy
p.779 The Jesuit mission of São Miguel © Tony Morrison/South American Pictures
p.757 Mercado Público, Porto Alegre © Oliver Marshall
p.790 *How the Tuppin Ikins Came As I Had Predicted* by Theodor de Bry © Archivo Iconografico, S.A./Corbis
p.798 President Roosevelt meets with President Getulio Vargas of Brazil aboard a U.S. Navy destroyer, 1943 © Bettmann/Corbis
p.801 President of Brazil Juscelino Kubitschek, 1957 © Dmitri Kessel/Getty Images
p.828 Brazilian singer Gilberto Gil performs during a concert © Tom Maelsa/dpa/Corbis

Index

Map entries are in colour.

A

Abelardo Luz 751
Abunã 498
academic visits...............63
accommodation...... 47–49
Aceguá 783
Águas Mornas..............731
Águas Quentes.............604
air passes 41
airlines 33
Alcântara 406
Aleijadinho......18, 196, 212
Alenquer 451
Alta Floresta 605
Alter do Chão 448
Alto do Caparaó 235
Alto do Moura 350
Alto Paraíso de Goiás...548
Amapá 439–441
Amazon, the........ 411–506
Amazon, the........ 414–415
books on 840
cuisine of..........................434
deforestation of.........813–816
destruction of........... 416, 813
ecology of 413, 810–818
flora and fauna of..... 416, 811 & *Amazon flora and fauna* colour section
health in 40
jungle lodges.................... 477
organized tours of.....472–480
river journeys through...10, 17, 418, 475
Americana 659
Anastácio......................571
Anchieta 247
Angra dos Reis.............152
Antonina 697
Antônio Prado 767
Aquário Natural 24, 575
Aquidauana 570
Aquiraz 389
Aracaju 318
Aracati 389
Araçuai 226
Araguaína 554
Ararapira.......................704
Araruama......................145
Araucária 693
Arcoverde 352
Arembepe.....................282
Argentina, crossing to 717, 752, 780
Ariri 704
Arraial d'Ajuda.............301
Arraial do Cabo 146
Aruanã 543
Assis Brasil...................504
Atalaia Nova 319
Atalaia Velha................319

B

Bagé 783
Bahia 257–304
Bahia 259
Bahian serão....... 291–298
Bairro dos Binos...........707
Balaiada Revolt 795
Balneário Camboriú 733
banks 64
Barão de Melgaço........592
Barcelos 485
Barra Bonita 707
Barra de Santo Antônio 314
Barra de Tabatinga.......377
Barra do Garças...........607
barreado 698
Basilica do Bom Jesus de Matosinhos...............212
Beberibe 389
Bela Vista 569
BELÉM................ 421–435
Belém 423
BELO HORIZONTE 176–193
Belo Horizonte..... 178–179
Belterra........................450
Bento Gonçalves..........768
Bessa...........................362
Bezerros 349
Blumenau 738–740
Boa Vista 487–491
Boa Vista.....................488
boats 46
Boi Bumba 460
Boiçucanga 665
Bolivia, crossing to 582, 594
Bonfim 492
Bonito 572–577
books 833–848
Brasiléia.......................503
BRASÍLIA............ 511–532
Brasília 512–513
accommodation 520
addresses........................ 518
airlines 531
airport............................. 517
arrival 517
bars 530
bus routes 518
bus station 517
car rental 531
cash machines 531
Catedral Metropolitana Nossa Senhora Aparecida 523
Central Bank building 524
Central Brasília................ 522
Centro Cultural da Caixa........................... 488
cinema 531
city tours 519
city transport................... 418
climate............................ 514
Congresso Nacional 521
CONIC center 524
Conjunto Nacional 524
consulates....................... 531
currency exchange 532
drinking 530
driving 531
eating 528
Eixo Monumental..... 515, 517
Esplanada dos Ministérios 521
history 514-516
indigenous craft market... 526
information 517
Jardim Botânico.............. 527
Juscelino Kubitschek (JK) Memorial....................... 526
live music 530
Memorial dos Povos Indígenas 526
Museu da Moeda............ 524
Museu Histórico de Brasília 523
Museu Nacional das Gemas 525
newspapers..................... 531
Niemeyer, Oscar 525
Palácio da Alvorada......... 523
Palácio da Justiça............ 522
Palácio do Planalto.......... 523
Palácio Itamarati 522
Parque Nacional de Brasília 528
Parque Sara Kubitschek... 526
post office 532

INDEX

Praça dos Três Poderes... 521
shopping ... 532
Supremo Tribunal Federal ... 523
taxis ... 518, 532
Teatro Nacional ... 523
Torre de Televisão ... 525
tour companies ... 532
train station ... 515
Bumba–meu–boi ... 400
Burle Marx, Roberto ... 187
buses ... 43
Búzios (Rio de Janeiro) ... 147–150
Búzios (Rio Grande do Norte) ... 376

C

Cabanagem Rebellion ... 422, 795
Cabedelo ... 362
Cabo Frio ... 145
Caboclo, Zé ... 329
Caçador ... 749
Cáceres ... 594
Cachoeira ... 286–288
Cachoeira do Tarumã ... 468
Calçoene ... 441
Caldas Novas ... 547
Cambará do Sul ... 765
Cambuquira ... 230
Campina Grande ... 363–365
Campinas ... 658
camping ... 48
Campo Grande ... 561–567
Campo Grande ... 563
Campos ... 150
Campos do Jordão ... 662
Cananéia ... 674
Candéias ... 285
candomblé ... 24, 269, 279, 287
Canela ... 763
Canudos ... 293
Capão da Canoa ... 771
capoeira ... 21, 270
car rental ... 45
Caraíva ... 302
Caravelas ... 302
Carnaval ... 14, 54
in Olinda ... 340
in Recife ... 334
in Rio de Janeiro ... 134–138
in Salvador ... 280
Carolina ... 408
cars ... 43
Caruaru ... 349
Caxambu ... 230
Caxias do Sul ... 766
Ceará ... 380–393
Central Vitória ... 242
Chapada Diamantina ... 18, 294
Chapada dos Guimarães ... 601
Chapadão do Ceu ... 546
Chapecó ... 750
Chuí ... 775
cidades históricas ... 195–229
cinema ... 848–851
Ciudad del Este ... 714
climate change ... 31
coffee ... 795, 797
Colombia, crossing to ... 484
Conceição da Barra ... 248
Congonhas ... 211–214
Conselheiro, Antônio ... 293
consulates ... 61
Copacabana ... 114
Corumbá ... 577–581
Corumbá ... 578
Costa do Sol ... 144–150
Costa Verde ... 150–162
costs ... 57
Cotijuba ... 436
Coxim ... 568
credit cards ... 64
Criciúma ... 745
crime ... 58
Cristalina ... 533
Cruzeiro do Sul ... 504
Cuiabá ... 595–601
Cuiabá ... 596
Curitiba ... 681–691
Curitiba ... 682–683
currency ... 64

D

Da Silva, Luis Ignacio ... 805, 806, 808
Diamantina ... 221–226
Dionísio Cerqueira ... 751
disabled travellers ... 60
Distrito Federal ... 510
dolphins ... 472
Domingos Martins ... 249
Dorizon ... 708
Dourados ... 568
drinks ... 51, 52
& *Brazilian food and drink* colour section
driving ... 45
drugs ... 59

E

ecology ... 810–818
electricity ... 60
email ... 63
embassies ... 61
Embratur ... 66
Embu ... 656
Encantada ... 701
Encarnación, Paraguay ... 782
Enseada ... 673
Esperança ... 707
Espírito Santo ... 237–255
Espírito Santo ... 175
Estrada Dona Francisca ... 738
exchange rates ... 65

F

favelas ... 118–119, 803
Fazenda da Barra Projeto Vivo ... 576
Fazenda Pinhal ... 22, 661
Fernando de Noronha ... 354
festivals ... 54
film ... 848–851
flights
from Australia and New Zealand ... 30
from South Africa ... 31
from the UK and Ireland ... 28
from the US and Canada ... 27, 28
in Brazil ... 41–42
Flores da Cunha ... 767
Floresta Nacional do Tapajós ... 449
Florianópolis ... 23, 722–726
Florianópolis ... 725
food ... 49–52
& *Brazilian food and drink* colour section
food, vegetarian ... 51
menu terms ... 860–863
football ... 11, 62
Fordlândia ... 450
Formosa ... 533
Fortaleza ... 381–389
Fortaleza ... 382
Foz do Iguaçu ... 708–712

Foz do Iguaçu..............711
Francisco Lisboa,
Antônio..............196, 212

G

Gaibu...........................346
Garopaba......................742
gaúchos........................782
gay Brazil........................62
Genipabu......................378
glossary........................864
Goiana..........................343
Goiânia................535–540
Goiânia.........................536
Goiás....................535–551
Goiás...........................510
Goiás Velho.................543
Gonçalves Júnior.........707
Gramado......................762
Gravatá........................348
Gruta do Lago Azul......574
Gruta Rei do Mato........193
Guajará-Mirim..............498
Guajiru.........................391
Guarapari.....................246
Guaraqueçaba.............703
Guaratuba....................703
Guarujá........................665
Guayaramerin..............499
Guyana, crossing to.....492

H

health.......................36–40
history of Brazil...789–809
Holambra......................660
holidays..........................65
hostels......................48, 49
hotels.............................47

I

Icoaraçi........................435
Igarassu.......................343
Iguaçu Falls...15, 708–719
Iguaçu Falls................709
Iguape..........................673
Ilha Anchieta................673
Ilha Cardoso................674
Ilha Comprida..............673
Ilha das Peças.............704
Ilha de Boipeba............290
Ilha de Paquetá............141
Ilha de São Francisco...734
Ilha de Tinharé.............289
Ilha do Bananal............552
Ilha do Marajó.............437
Ilha do Mel.................701
Ilha do Mel..................702
Ilha do Padre................575
Ilha Grande..................153
Ilhabela..........20, 668–671
Ilhabela.......................668
Ilhéus..........................298
Imbituba.......................743
Imperatriz....................408
Inapari (Peru)...............504
Inconfidência Mineira...204
Indian rights........818–823
insurance........................35
Internet..........................63
Irati..............................707
Iriri..............................247
Itacaré.........................299
Itacimirim.....................282
Itacuruçá......................151
Itaipu...........................719
Itaituba........................453
Itajaí............................733
Itamaracá.....................344
Itaparica......................282
Itapissuma...................344
Itatiaia.........................131

J

Jacobina......................292
Jararaca......................379
Jatai............................607
Jequitinhonha Valley...226
Jericoacoara...........19, 391
Jesuit missions...........16,
777–782, 793
Jesuit missions...........778
Jesús (Paraguay)..........781
Ji Paraná.....................605
Joaçaba.......................748
João Pessoa.......356–361
João Pessoa................356
Joinville................735–738
Juazeiro do Norte.........365
Juazerio......................353

K

Kubitkschek, Juscelino....
224, 514, 526, 800–802

L

Lages...........................747
Lago Paranoá...............532
Laguna.........................743
Lambari........................232
Lampião.......................313
language.............855–866
Lapa (Rio de Janeiro)...692
Laranjeiras..................319
laundry..........................63
Lençóis.......................294
Lençóis.......................295
Leticia.........................482
Litoral Gaúcho....770–778
living in Brazil.................63
Luiz Correia.................396
Lula *see* da Silva, Luís
Inácio

M

Macaé..........................150
Macapá........................439
Maceió................310–316
Maceió................310–311
magazines......................53
mail...............................63
Mallet..........................707
MANAUS.............457–486
Manaus.......................458
accommodation..............461
airport..........................460
boat, arrival by...............459
bus station....................459
consulates.....................471
eating and drinking.........469
history..........................457
jungle trips...............472-480
meeting of the waters......467
Museu do Homem do
Norte...........................466
port..............................463
Teatro Amazonas.......14, 465
tour operators.................442
Mangaratiba................152
Manhumirim.................235
maps.............................64
Marabá........................438
Maragogi.....................314
Maranhão............397–409
Marechal Deodoro........316
Maresias......................666
Mariana................208–211
Maricá.........................144
Mata............................776
Matinhos......................703
Mato Grosso.......594–608

Mato Grosso........558–559
Mato Grosso do Sul.....................561–583
Mato Grosso do Sul.....................558–559
media..............................53
Mem de Sá..................269
Mendes, Chico.....502, 804
Milho Verde.................228
Mina da Passagem.......210
Minas Gerais.......173–237
Minas Gerais...............175
Mineiros.......................546
Miranda........................571
money...........................64
Monte Alegre...............452
Monte Belo..................769
Morretes......................695
Morro de São Paulo.....289
Mosqueiro....................436
Mossoró.............378–380
Mostardas....................772
Mundo Novo................568
Museu de Arte Contemporânea, Niterói............................21, 142
music..................824–832

N

Natal....................368–376
Natal...........................369
newspapers...................53
Niemeyer, Oscar..........142, 187, 525, 632, 801
Niterói.........................142
Northeast, the.....305–410
Northeast, the.............308
Nova Brasília................701
Nova Friburgo...............169
Nova Galiciá.................707
Nova Jerusalém...........351
Nova Pádua..................767
Nova Petrópolis............761
Novo Ariao...................472

O

Obidas.........................454
Oiapoque.....................441
Olinda...........22, 335–342
Olinda..........................336
Olivença.......................299
opening hours................65
Orleans........................746
Otávio Rocha...............767
Ouricuri........................352
Ouro Preto.....17, 199–208
Ouro Preto..................200
Outeiro.........................436

P

package tours...............34
Padre Cícero Romão Batista.......................367
Palmas.........................554
Pantanal, the................20, 583–594
Pantanal, the...............584
boat trips in......588, 590–591
ecology..........................585
tours of..........................588
Paracuru......................390
Paraguay, crossing to.......................569, 780
Paraíba................355–368
Paraíso do Tocantins....553
Paraná................681–720
Paranaguá....................699
Paranaguá Bay...694–705
Paranaguá Bay...........696
Paranapiacaba............657
Paraty...........23, 155–161
Paraty..........................156
Parintins......................460
Parnaíba......................395
Parque do Caraça........194
Parque Ecólogico Janauary...........457, 467
Parque Estadual da Guarita......................770
Parque Estadual da Serra do Tabuleiro..............732
Parque Estadual de Marumbi...................697
Parque Estadual de Vila Velha.........................694
Parque Nacional Chapada dos Veadeiros......21, 548
Parque Nacional da Chapada Diamantina................295
Parque Nacional da Lagoa do Peixe....................771
Parque Nacional das Emas.........................545
Parque Nacional de Brasília.......................528
Parque Nacional de Sete Cidades....................396
Parque Nacional de Ubajara.......................392
Parque Nacional do Araguaia...................552
Parque Nacional do Caparaó....................235
Parque Nacional do Itatiaia........................163
Parque Nacional do Pico da Neblina.................485
Parque Nacional dos Aparados da Serra....764
Parque Nacional dos Lençóis......................406
Parque Nacional Marinho dos Abrolhos.............304
Patos...........................365
Paulo Afonso...............317
Pedra Azul..............20, 247
Pedro Alvares Cabral...............300, 790
Pedro Juan Caballero...569
Peixe Valley.........748–750
Pelé........................11, 230
Pelotas.........................772
Penedo........................318
Penedo (Rio de Janeiro)....................163
Penha..........................362
pensões.........................48
Pernambuco........320–355
Peru, crossing to..........484
Petrolina......................353
Petrópolis............166–168
Petrópolis...................165
pharmacies....................36
phones..........................65
Piauí....................393–397
Pico da Bandeira..........236
Pirangi do Norte...........377
piranhas.......................445
Pirenópolis..........540–543
Pitimbu........................343
Plano Collor.................806
Poço............................362
Poconé........................592
Poços de Caldas..........232
police............................59
Pomerode....................740
Ponta Negra................376
Ponta Porã..................569
Pontal do Sul...............701
Ponte Branca...............161
Porto Alegre........753–760
Porto Alegre.........754–755
Porto Belo...................732
Porto de Galinhas........347
Porto Jofre..................593
Porto Luís Alves...........552
Porto Manga................583
Porto Morrinho............583

Porto Murtinho 569
Porto Seguro 300
Porto Velho.......... 493–497
Porto Velho 494
Posadas, Argentina 780
post 63
postos.............................48
pousadas.........................48
Praia das Fontes 389
Praia de Leste 703
Praia do Forte...............282
Praia Ponta Negra........468
Prudentópolis 705
public holidays 65
Puerto Bertoni 715
Puerto Canoas 717
Puerto Iguazú 712–714
Puerto Maldonado........504

R

race issues 822–823
radio 53
RECIFE 321–335
accommodation 322
airlines............................ 334
airport.............................. 321
banks 334
Boa Viagem............. 326, 331
bus station 322
Capela Dourada 327
car rental 335
Carnaval.......................... 334
Casa da Cultura de Pernambuco 328
Castle Museum 330
Central Recife 324–325
city transport................... 322
currency exchange 335
drinking 333
eating 331
Horto Zoobotânico........... 330
information 321
Instituto Ricardo Brennand 330
Internet............................ 335
Mercado de São José 328
Museo do Trem 328
Museu da Cidade 328
Museu de Arte Moderna Aloisio Magalhães 329
Museu de Arte Popular de Recife........................... 327
Museu do Estado............. 330
Museu do Homem do Nordeste 329
Museu Militar 329
nightlife............................ 332
post office 335
Praça da República 326
Santo Antônio do Convento de São Francisco 326
São Pedro 327
taxis.................................. 322
tour companies 335
Recôncavo, the... 284–288
Recôncavo, the 285
Redinha 378
Regência 247
reggae bands 15, 399
Registro 675
Reserva Natural da Vale do Rio Doce....................247
restaurants......................50
Rio Branco ...486, 499–503
Rio Branco 500
RIO DE JANEIRO...73–141
Rio de Janeiro 74
accommodation 82–87
airlines 140
airports 77, 140
Alfandega Antiga............... 93
Arco de Teles 91
Arcos da Lapa........... 97, 101
arrival 77–79
Arpoador 115
arrival 71
Avenida Presidente Vargas 92
Avenida Atlantica 115
Avenida Nossa Senhora da Copacabana 115
banks 140
Barra de Tijuca................. 120
beach activities 18, 108–109
Biblioteca Nacional 98
Bom Retiro 122
Botafogo 112
bus stations 78, 80
buses 78, 80–81
Campo de Santana............ 95
Capela do Mairynik.......... 122
car rental 140
Carnaval...................134–138
Catete 110
Catete 111
Cemitério dos Ingleses 96
Centro Cultural Banco do Brasil...................... 92, 133
cinema 133
city centre 75–99
city centre 88–89
city transport................79–82
classical music................. 133
consulates....................... 140
Convento de Santa Teresa 101
Convento do Carmo 90
Copacabana.................... 114
Copacabana.................... 114
Corcovado 16, 102
crafts 139
currency exchange 140
dancing 132
dentists 140
discos.............................. 130
Dom Pedro II station (Central Station)............. 96
drinking 122–129
driving 82
eating 122–129
email............................... 130
entertainment...........129–134
Espaço Cultural da Marinha.......................... 91
favelas......................118–119
Feira Hippie..................... 116
Feira Nordestina.............. 104
ferries 81
film 133
Flamengo 111
Flamengo 111
forró................................ 133
gafieras 132
Gávea.............................. 117
gay Rio 129
Glória............................... 109
Glória............................... 111
hang–gliding.................... 117
health 140
history 73–75
hydrofoils 81
Igreja da Santa Rita 93
Igreja da Nossa Senhora da Glória do Outeiro 22, 109
Igreja de Nossa Senhora de Bonsucesso 99
Igreja de Nossa Senhora de Candelária 92
Igreja de Nossa Senhora do Carmo da Antigá Sé....... 91
Igreja de Santa Luzia 98
Igreja de São Francisco de Paula............................. 94
Igreja e Mosterio de São Bento 93
Igreja y Convento de Santo Antônio 94
Ilha Fiscal 91
Instituto Moreira Salles 118
Internet............................ 140
Ipanema 115
Jardim Botânico............... 117
Jardim Zoólogico 104
jazz clubs 131
Jockey Club 117
Lagoa 116
Lapa 22, 98
Largo da Carioca 94
Largo de São Francisco de Paula............................. 94
Largo do Boticário 103
Largo Santa Rita 93
Laundry 140
Leblon 115
Leme 114
Leme 114
live music 131–132
Maracanã Stadium........... 105
markets 90, 104, 116
media 140
metrô................................. 79

INDEX

Monumento Nacional aos Mortos na Segunda Guerra Mundial ... 98
Morro da Urca ... 113
Museu Carmen Miranda ... 112
Museu Casa de Rui Barbosa ... 112
Museu Chácara do Céu ... 101
Museu da Fauna ... 104
Museu da Imperial Irmandade de Nossa Senhora da Glória ... 109
Museu da República ... 101
Museu de Arte Moderna ... 98
Museu de Folclore Edison Cruz ... 110
Museu do Bonde ... 101
Museu do Imagem e Som ... 99
Museu do Índio ... 113
Museu Histórico da Cidade ... 118
Museu Histórico de Exército ... 115
Museu Histórico e Diplomático do Itamaraty ... 96
Museu Histórico Nacional ... 99
Museu Nacional ... 104
Museu Nacional das Belas Artes ... 97
Museu Nacional de Arte Naïf ... 103
Museu Naval e Oceanográfico ... 91
Museu Villa-Lobos ... 112
newspapers ... 140
nightlife ... 22, 129–134
Nova Catedral Metropolitana ... 96
orientation ... 75–77
Orquestra Sinfonica Brasileira ... 133
Paço Imperial ... 90
Palácio do Itamaraty ... 96
Pão de Açúcar ... 113
Parque da Catacumba ... 116
Parque da Cidade ... 118
Parque das Ruínas ... 102
Parque do Catete ... 110
Parque João Furtado ... 95
Parque Nacional de Tijuca ... 17, 121
Passeio Público ... 98
pharmacies ... 140
police ... 140
post offices ... 141
Praça da República ... 95
Praça Floriano ... 97
Praça Tiradentes ... 95
Praça XV de Novembro ... 89
Praia de Copacabana ... 115
public holidays ... 141
Quinta da Boa Vista ... 103
Real Gabinete Português de Leitura ... 94
Riotur ... 79
TurisRio ... 79
Saara ... 93
safety ... 76, 109
samba ... 130
samba schools ... 96, 114, 135
Sambódromo ... 136
Santa Casa de Misericórdia ... 99
Santa Cruz dos Militares ... 92
Santa Teresa ... 101–103
shopping ... 138
Sitio Burle Marx ... 120
Sugar Loaf ... 113
taxis ... 80
Teatro João Caetano ... 95
Theatro Municipal ... 19, 97
tourist agencies ... 79
tours ... 80
trams ... 82
Urca ... 113
visas ... 141
Zona Norte ... 95–97
Zona Sul ... 105–129
Zona Sul ... 106–107
Rio de Janeiro state ... 141–170
Rio de Janeiro state ... 72
Rio Grande ... 774
Rio Grande do Norte ... 368–380
Rio Grande do Sul ... 752–786
Rio Negro ... 484
Rio Negro Forest Reserve ... 485
Rio Quente ... 548
Rio Solimões ... 480
Rondônia ... 492–499
Rondonopolis ... 606
Roraima ... 486–492
round-the-world flights ... 31
rubber boom ... 797

S

Sabará ... 196–199
SALVADOR ... 260–282
Salvador ... 261
accommodation ... 264
airport ... 262
banks ... 281
Câmara Municipal ... 268
candomblé ... 279
capoeira ... 270
car rental ... 281
Carnaval ... 280
Casa de Jorge Amado ... 271
Cidade Alta ... 267
Cidade Baixa ... 274
Cidade Baixa ... 266–267
city transport ... 263
comida Baiana ... 276
consulates ... 281
Convento da Ordem Primeira do Carmo ... 272
currency exchange ... 281
eating and drinking ... 275
festivals ... 278
football ... 281
Igreja da Nossa Senhora dos Pretos ... 271
Igreja da Ordem Terceira de São Francisco ... 271
Igreja da Ordem Terdeira de Nossa Senhora do Carmo ... 272
Igreja de Nossa Senhor do Bonfim ... 274
Igreja de São Francisco ... 271
information ... 262
Internet ... 281
Magalhâes, Antonio Carlos ... 273
Mem de Sá's tomb ... 269
Memorial dos Governadores ... 268
Mercado Modelo ... 274
Museu Abelardo Rodrigues ... 271
Museu Afro-Brasiliero ... 269
Museu da Cidade ... 271
Museu de Arte Sacra ... 273
Museu dos Ex-Votos do Senhor do Bonfim ... 275
Museu Nautico da Bahia ... 275
nightlife ... 277
Palácio do Rio Branco ... 268
post office ... 281
Praça de Sé ... 269
Praça Municipal ... 268
safety ... 263
Santo Antônio Além do Carmo ... 273
shopping ... 281
Terreiro de Jesus ... 269
tour companies ... 282
San Ignacio ... 781
San Ignacio Miní (Argentina) ... 780
Santa Bárbara d'Oeste ... 660
Santa Catarina ... 720–751
Santa Catarina ... 680
Santa Catarina, Island of ... 720–731
Santa Catarina, Island of ... 721
Santa Elena de Uairén ... 492
Santa Felicidade ... 692
Santa Leopoldina ... 254
Santa Maria ... 254, 776
Santa Rosa ... 484
Santa Teresa ... 252
Santa Terezinha ... 553
Santana do Livramento ... 784

Santarém 441–447
Santarém 442
Santo Agostinho 346
Santo Amaro 285
Santo Amaro da
Imperatriz 731
Santo Ângelo 779
Santos 663
Santuário do Caraça 194
Santuário Nacional Padre
Ancieta 247
São Antônio do
Leverger 604
São Borja 786
São Carlos 661
São Cristóvão 320
São Felix do Araguaia ... 553
São Francisco de
Paula 765
São Francisco do Sul ... 734
São Gabriel da
Cachoeira 485
São Gonçalo do
Amarante 390
São Gonçalo do Rio das
Pedras 228
**São João del
Rei** 214–218
São João del Rei 215
São Joaquim 746
São Jorge 549
São José da Coroa
Grande 347
São José do Ribamar ... 406
São Lourenço 231
São Luis 398–405
São Luis 399
São Miguel 777
São Miguel do
Araguaia 552
SÃO PAULO 611–656
São Paulo 614–615
accommodation 620–624
airlines 654
airports 617, 654
arrival 617
Avenida Paulista 23, 634
Avenida Paulista 636
Avenida São Luis 632
banks 654
bars 649
Bela Vista 632
Bixiga 634
Bolsa de Mercadorias &
Futuros (BM&F) 628
Bom Retiro 631
Bosque de Leitura 638
BOVESPA building 628
buses 618, 619
car rental 654
Carnaval 652
Casa das Rosas 635
Casa do Bandeirante 639
Casa do Grito 639
Catedral Metropolitana 624
Central São Paulo 626–627
Centro Brasiliero
Britânico 638
Centro Cultural Banco de
Brasil 628
cinema 651
city transport 619
classical music 652
Confederates in 660
consulates 655
crime 617
drinking 649
eating 641–648
Edificio Copan 632
Edificio DOPS 630
Edificio Itália 632
Edificio Martinelli 628
Estação da Luz 630
Estação Júlio Prestes 630
exchange 654
football 655
Fundaço Maria Luiza e
Oscar Americano 640
health 655
helicopters 620
history 613
Igreja de Santo Antônio ... 625
Igreja de São Francisco de
Assis 625
Igreja do Carmo 625
Igreja do Convento
da Luz 631
immigration 633
information 618
Instituto Butantan 640
Instituto Itaú Cultural 635
Instituto Tomie Ohtake 638
Internet 655
Itaim Bibi 637
Japanese
community 633, 634
Jardim America 637
Jardim Botanico 641
Jardim Europa 637
Jardim Paulista 637
Jardins 637
laundry 655
Liberdade 634
Luz 630
markets 654
media 655
Memorial da América
Latina 632
Memorial da Liberdade 630
Memorial do Imigrante 629
Mercado Municipal 24, 629
Mosteiro São Bento 628
Museu Afro-Brasil 638
Museu Biologico 640
Museu da Casa
Brasiliera 637
Museu da Cidade 625
Museu da Imagen e do
Som 637
Museu da Imigraçao
Japonesa 634
Museu de Arte
Contemporânea 638
Museu de Arte de São Paulo
(MASP) 635
Museu de Arte Moderna ... 638
Museu de Arte Sacra 631
Museu do Ipiranga 639
Museu Lasar Segall 639
Museu Memória do
Bixiga 634
Museu Padre Anchieta 625
Museu Paulista 639
music, live 650
newspapers 655
nightlife 648, 650–651
Ohtake, Ray 637
orientation 616
Parque da Luz 631
Parque do Estado 640
Parque do Ibirapuera 638
Parque Siquiera
Campos 635
Pátio do Colégio 625
Pinacoteca do Estado 631
Pinheiros 637
police 655
post office 655
Praça da República 631
Praça da Sé 624
public holidays 655
Rua Augusta 636
safety 617
São Paulo Bienal 639
shopping 652–654
Solar de Marquesa de
Santos 625
taxis 620
Teatro Municipal 632
telephones 655
Templo Busshinji 634
tours 655
travel agents 655
Triângulo, the 628
Vila Penteado 632
Vila Inglesa 630
visas 655
Zoológico de São Paulo 641
São Paulo state ... 658–676
São Paulo state 612
São Pedro da Aldeia 145
São Sebastião 666
Saquerema 144
Serra da Ibiapaba 391
Serra do Cachimbo 606
Serra do Mar 153
Serra do Tigre 708
Serra dos Órgãos 168
Serra Gaúcha 760–770
Serra Talhada 352
Serro 228
sexual harassment 57
ships from Britain 31
Sobral 391

INDEX

soccer *see* football
Souré ... 438
Sousa ... 365
South, the ... 677–786
South, the ... 680
study programmes ... 63

T

Tabatinga ... 482
Tabatinga ... 483
Tamandaré ... 347
Tambaba ... 362
Tarituba ... 155
taxis ... 46
telephones ... 65
television ... 53
Templo Budhsta Chagdad Khadro Ling ... 764
Terena Indians ... 572
Teresina ... 394
Teresópolis ... 168
three-way frontier ... 481–484
three-way frontier ... 481
Tianguá ... 391
time zones ... 66
tipping ... 62
Tiradentes ... 218
Tocantins ... 552–554
Tocantins ... 510
Torres ... 770
tour operators ... 33
tourist information ... 66
trains ... 42
Trairi ... 391
Tramandi ... 771
Trancoso ... 302
travel agents ... 33
travellers' cheques ... 64
Três Corações ... 230
Treze Tilias ... 74
Trinidad (Paraguay) ... 781

U

Ubajara ... 392
Ubatiba ... 144
Ubatuba ... 671
Uruguaiana ... 785
Uruguay, crossing to ... 775
Urussanga ... 746

V

Vacaria ... 769
Vale dos Dinosauras ... 365
Valença (Bahia) ... 288–289
Valença (Rio de Janeiro) ... 164
Vargas, Getúlio ... 97, 798–800
Vassouras ... 164
vegetarian food ... 51
Venda Nova do Imigrante ... 250
Venezuela, crossing to ... 485, 491
Véu da Noiva ... 452
Videira ... 749
Vila do Abraão ... 153
Vila dos Remédios ... 355
Vila Fatima ... 704
Vila Ilhabela ... 669
Vila Superagüi ... 704
visas ... 60
Vitória ... 238–246
Vitória ... 239
Volta Redonda ... 162

W

water ... 37
women travellers ... 57
work programmes... ... 63

X

Xingu ... 605

Y

Yacutinga ... 719
Yanomami tribe ... 480
youth hostels ... 48, 49

Map symbols

maps are listed in the full index using coloured text

International border
State border
Chapter division boundary
Major road
Minor road
Steps
Path
Railway
Metro station & line
Ferry route
Waterway
Funicular
Cable car
Bridge/tunnel
Mountain peak
Cave
Marsh
Waterfall
Cliffs
Hill shading
Point of interest
Viewpoint
Lighthouse
Fort
Airport
Bus stop
Tourist office
Post office
Telephone office
Accommodation
Statue/memorial
Church (regional)
Church (town)
Building
Market
Stadium
Cemetery
Park, national park or reserve
Beach
Swamp

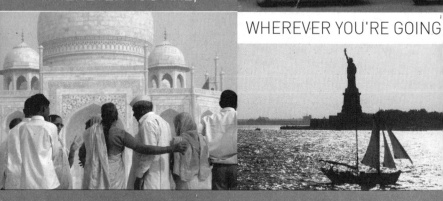